INTERNATIONAL ENCYCLOPEDIA OF ADULT EDUCATION AND TRAINING

SECOND EDITION

Resources in Education

This is a new series of Pergamon one-volume Encyclopedias drawing upon articles in the acclaimed *International Encyclopedia of Education, Second Edition*, with revisions as well as new articles. Each volume in the series is thematically organized and aims to provide complete and up-to-date coverage on its subject. These Encyclopedias will serve as an invaluable reference source for researchers, faculty members, teacher educators, government officials, educational administrators, and policymakers.

The *International Encyclopedia of Adult Education and Training, Second Edition,* contains 161 articles on adult education and training. This Encyclopedia deals with the financing and organization of adult education and continuing vocational training throughout the world. The volume provides extensive coverage of lifespan development, cognition, adult learning, and theories and methods for the teaching of adults both now and in the future. Adult education and continuing vocational training are no longer considered as two separate fields and their merger has provoked increased attention on theories and practice, with particular focus on human resource development. A complete bibliography and further reading at the end of each article provides references for further research. An extensive subject and author index are also included.

Other titles in the series include:

POSTLETHWAITE (ed.)
International Encyclopedia of National Systems of Education, Second Edition

CARNOY (ed.)
International Encyclopedia of Economics of Education, Second Edition

ANDERSON (ed.)
International Encyclopedia of Teaching and Teacher Education, Second Edition

PLOMP & ELY (eds)
International Encyclopedia of Educational Technology, Second Edition

DeCORTE & WEINERT (eds)
International Encyclopedia of Developmental and Instructional Psychology

KEEVES (ed.)
International Encyclopedia of Educational Research, Methodololgy, and Measurement, Second Edition

INTERNATIONAL ENCYCLOPEDIA OF ADULT EDUCATION AND TRAINING

SECOND EDITION

Edited by

ALBERT C. TUIJNMAN

Organisation for Economic Co-operation and Development (OECD)
Paris, France

PERGAMON

UK   Elsevier Science Ltd, The Boulevard, Langford Lane,
            Kidlington, Oxford OX5 1GB, UK

USA   Elsevier Science Inc, 660 White Plains Road, Tarrytown, New
            York 10591-5153, USA

JAPAN   Elsevier Science Japan, Tsunashima Building Annex, 3-20-12
            Yushima, Bunkyo-ku, Tokyo 113, Japan

Second edition 1996

Library of Congress Cataloging in Publication Data
International encyclopedia of adult education and training /
edited by Albert C. Tuijnman. — 2nd ed.
    p.   cm.
  Rev. ed. of: Lifelong education for adults / edited by
Colin J. Titmus. 1st ed. 1989.
  Draws upon articles in International encyclopedia of
education, 2nd ed., rev. and updated.
   Includes bibliographical references and index.
    1. Adult education—Handbooks, manuals, etc.
2. Continuing education—Handbooks, manuals, etc.
I. Tuijnman, Albert.   II. Lifelong education for adults.
III. International encyclopedia of education (2nd ed.).
LC5215.I586   1996
374'.0202—dc20   95-53922

British Library Cataloguing in Publication Data
A catalogue record for this book is available from the
British Library.

ISBN 0–08–042305–1

⊗™   The paper used in this publication meets the minimum requirements of the
American National Standard for Information Sciences—Permanence of Paper for Printed
Library Materials, ANSI Z39.48–1984.

Printed and bound in Great Britain by BPC Wheatons Ltd, Exeter.

Contents

Contents

Contents

Contents

Contents

Preface

The International Encyclopedia of Adult Education and Training represents a systematic attempt to present an up-to-date, wide-ranging and international overview of scholarship and knowledge of adult education and training problems, theories, policies, practices, and institutions. It is designed to provide answers to questions such as: What is the state of the art of the theoretical and empirical knowledge base of adult education and training? How does this knowledge base relate to educational policy-making? What further research may be needed in the various domains of the field?

The knowledge base of adult education and training is heuristic and multidisiplinary. It is not a field of scholarly studies unified by a single disciplinary tradition. Instead, there are many established academic disciplines which contribute important knowledge elements and insights to the common core. Because of this eclectic orientation, there are no straightforward answers to the question as to what constitutes this core, and how and why. The knowledge base of adult education is diffuse and incomplete. Any attempt to structure the body of knowledge relevant to adult education meets with immense, if not unsurpassable difficulties, because many elements are either still missing or have not been recognized yet. *The International Encyclopedia of Adult Education and Training* is the first of its kind, in that it purports to organize knowledge and insights relevant to the whole, but highly diverse field commonly subsumed under the labels "adult education," "training," and "lifelong learning." Hopefully it will be seen as making a contribution. By taking a broad definition as its point of departure, by emphasizing the multiplicity of the sources of the knowledge that constitute the field, by exposing the nature of the epistemological conflicts that underlie it, and by contrasting the associated academic disciplines and their preferred research methodologies, the *Encyclopedia* seeks to draw attention to the unfinished but promising character of adult education. This volume is unique in that it brings together a vast body of scholarship that is international rather than national or regional in perspective. All major areas deemed important to adult education are covered, albeit with varying depth, and the material has been organized by taking into account the various research paradigms and the practices of adult education in different political, cultural, and socioeconomic contexts.

1. Stages in Preparing the Encyclopedia

The 161 entries presented in this Encyclopedia were written by leading scholars, drawn from over 35 countries, who represent all regions of the world. Most of the entries were originally commissioned for inclusion in *The International Encyclopedia of Education*, 2nd Edition, which was published by Pergamon Press in April 1994. The work on this 12-volume parent Encyclopedia began in earnest in 1990 when Professor Emeritus Torsten Husén and Professor T. Neville Postlethwaite, the Editors-in-Chief, appointed an Editorial board and invited the members to prepare, for assigned Sections, lists of recommended entry topics complete with abstracts and suggested contributors and back-up authors. The undersigned, who in 1990 had been appointed Editor of the Section on Adult Education, originally submitted a proposal listing 95 separate entries. The topics and the number of words to be allocated to each entry were identified mainly on the basis of syntheses of scholarship and current overviews of research studies. The proposed contributors were selected on the strength of their reputation and their capacity to write on a given topic from an international perspective. The original proposal was somewhat modified and expanded to 118 entries at a meeting of the Editorial Board and representatives of the Publisher in February 1991. A final list was prepared following that meeting, and soon after the process of commissioning authors and reviewing and editing their manuscripts commenced. In 1994, once the parent *Encyclopedia* had been launched successfully, a decision was taken

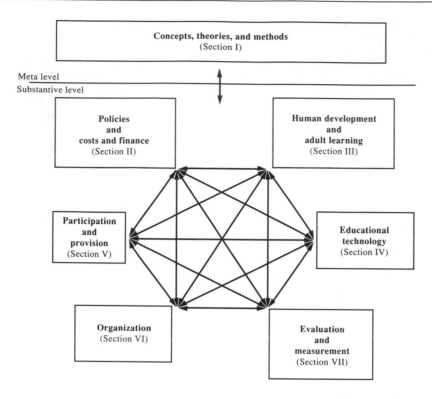

Figure 1
Schematic representation of the Encyclopedia

to prepare *The International Encyclopedia of Adult Education and Training*. One consideration was that scholarship in the field of adult education had expanded and advanced to the point where the publication of a separate *Encyclopedia* summarizing the research on topics of relevance would be warranted. Another argument was that such a reference volume could be useful to the many scholars and practitioners for whom access to the parent *Encyclopedia* might be difficult. *The International Encyclopedia of Adult Education and Training* thus includes revised and updated versions of the entries originally written for the parent *Encyclopedia*, although new entries have also been added. These additional entries were required because the conceptual framework that has guided the selection of topics for this volume is more elaborate than the one employed for the parent *Encyclopedia*.

2. Conceptual Framework of the Encyclopedia

The term adult education is used to denote both a process and the structures and institutions which have been created to promote it. A widely accepted definition of adult education is the one adopted by the General Conference of UNESCO in 1976 (see *Introduction to Section I*). According to this definition, adult education denotes all organized educational processes, whether formal or otherwise, whereby persons regarded as adult by the society to which they belong engage in systematic and sustained learning activities. This definition is very wide; it includes adult education for leisure and adult education for investment, vocational education for out-of-school youth and adults, on-the-job training, and continuing vocational training. The conceptual framework of this *Encyclopedia* is based on UNESCO's definition of the field. Hence it is a defining characteristic of this *Encyclopedia* that adult education and continuing vocational training are not considered as separate fields. Many entries have an inclusive orientation and address both domains. Where clarity is best served by drawing attention to specific issues, entries dealing with aspects of liberal adult education appear side by side with entries addressing aspects of continuing vocational training.

The conceptual framework of the *Encyclopedia* is depicted in Fig. 1. The organizing scheme shows that the entries have been grouped under seven sections. Under each of these sections, entries are listed under two or more sub-sections that draw attention to substantive areas of specificity. Figure 1 also illustrates the assumption that there are two main levels of knowledge about adult education and training. The first carries the label "meta-knowledge," and the second "substantive knowledge."

"Meta-knowledge" refers to knowledge of the main epistemological positions and methodological paradigms that exist in the natural and social sciences. In addition, meta-knowledge also refers to knowledge of the main conceptual and theoretical positions that exist in the field of adult education. It follows that the knowledge base of adult education is diverse; it includes knowledge of the epistemological underpinnings of empiricist and rationalist ways of knowing; knowledge of the principles that underscore the "quantitative" and "qualitative" research paradigms; and knowledge of the meaning of the important concepts, theories, and themes. Figure 1 indicates that the entries making up the first section of this *Encyclopedia* present the meta-knowledge of adult education. This first section is divided into four subsections: concepts; themes and theories; disciplinary orientations; and epistemology and research methodology. These four subsections are assumed to be interrelated.

"Substantive knowledge" refers to information about the goals, means and ends of adult education. It includes information about the following aspects of adult education: policies and practices; the organization of adult education as a component of socioeconomic and educational systems; institutions and their clientèles; adult learning processes; instruction and methods for facilitating adult learning; and the theory and practice of field-specific evaluation and measurement. Figure 1 shows that substantive information is presented in six relatively distinct yet interrelated areas of knowledge of adult education, which correspond to the following sections of the *Encyclopedia:* Policies and Costs and Finance (Section II); Human Development and Adult Learning (Section III); Educational Technology (Section IV); Participation and Provision (Section V); Organization (Section VI); and Evaluation and Measurement (Section VII).

It is recognized that the above classification is arbitrary to an extent, given that certain entries which are included in one section might also have found an appropriate place in another section. Where this occurs the reader is alerted in the introductions to the separate sections and also by the cross-references that are placed at the end of the entries. Although the entries are presented in alphabetical order within each section, their ordering is nevertheless consistent with the framework.

3. Contents of the Encyclopedia

The 161 entries that comprise the contents of this volume are organized on the basis of the conceptual framework presented in Fig. 1. They offer summaries of current knowledge about all major topics in the field of adult education, gathered from worldwide sources.

The 34 entries included in Section I offer highly varied perspectives on the conceptual delineations, themes and theories, disciplinary orientations, and the research methodologies applicable to the field of adult education. Definitions of adult education, lifelong learning, continuing education, and vocational education and training are given in the first subsection. The delineation of the field is broadened in the second subsection, in which an overview is given of the main themes and theories of adult education. The perspectives include literacy, community education, and popular education, as well as critical approaches to adult education theory. The notion of adult education for social change and reform carries much currency in many parts of the world. Normative theories are therefore given explicit attention in this *Encyclopedia*. The third subsection deals with the question of whether adult education might be considered as a scientific discipline in its own right, or whether it can be identified more appropriately under the general banner of education. The position taken in this *Encyclopedia* is that adult education should not be considered as a separate science. Educational practice, as carried out by teachers and learners, whether they may be children or adults, is influenced by an amalgamation of previous experience and theoretical insights. These insights are gained from a wide range of behavioral, social science and humanities disciplines that, collectively, constitute the "foundations" of the body of knowledge in education. The study of adult education attracts scholars with different backgrounds in research training, substantive interests, and focuses and ideas, and this diversity not only characterizes the field but also constitutes its strength. This position is underscored by the inclusion, in this subsection of the *Encyclopedia*, of separate entries devoted to anthropology, economics, philosophy, political science and policy analysis, psychology, and sociology. This selection of disciplinary orientations reflects a choice constrained by the limitation of available space. The fourth and last subsection draws attention to the fact that the field of adult education is divided along epistemological and methodological lines. The purpose is not to offer exhaustive descriptions of the various perspectives and related research methods that may be employed in the field. Instead, the goal is to show that the different views on the nature and scope of adult education which are offered in this *Encyclopedia* derive from fundamental differences in the way scholars position themselves vis-à-vis epistemological questions about the nature and uses of knowledge.

Section II comprises 20 entries dealing with many aspects of adult education policy, including cost analysis and finance. The rationale for grouping the entries in two subsections, namely Adult Education Policy, and Costs and Finance, is that this approach contrasts the different value premises and beliefs about how the theoretical positions elaborated in Section I should be translated into agendas for policy-making and intervention. The common theme concerns the question whether, and to what extent, national governments should be seen as carrying the main responsibility for ensuring a sufficient supply of relevant learning opportunities for adults. The entries included in this Section offer views ranging from the endorsement of state responsibility for adult education provision to the opposite position, that governments should not interfere at all in the markets for educational services and adult learning. Eight entries address many questions concerning the costs and financing of adult education. An explanation is called for because some readers will no doubt find this emphasis on finance excessive. The point is that the grand schemes of recurrent education and lifelong learning, which were proposed several decades ago, have remained utopia in large part because of an unwillingness to address the financial implications. It is therefore imperative that careful thought be devoted to costs and finance, especially now that adult education has once again become a rising star on the policy agenda of many governments.

Section III is divided into two subsections. The first includes seven entries that offer a perspective on theory and research on human development. The second subsection comprises 14 entries that deal with the theory and practice of adult learning. The research field associated with the study of phenomena, mechanisms, and determinants of human development is vast and comparatively well-developed. The seven entries offer an adequate introduction to this field, in that they describe the central theories, controversies, and perspectives that have currency in social psychology, cognitive psychology, and lifespan developmental psychology. The entries in the second subsection are devoted to adult learning. The basic premise is that learning is at the heart of all adult education. Collectively, the entries show that there is a large and still growing body of information about how to facilitate adult learning, and which factors improve the effectiveness of learning.

Section IV is comprised of 15 entries devoted to many aspects of educational technology—that is, to the design, implementation, and evaluation of environments, processes, and resources for adult learning. The choice of the label, educational technology, may come as a surprise to some readers. The advantage of this term is that it calls attention to the purposefulness of adult learning and teaching, as well as to the requirement that many organized learning encounters, whether they depend on instruction in classrooms or learning at a distance, need to be systematically designed, implemented, and also evaluated. In adult education these concepts are not self-evident. With the attention of many adult educators focussed on the goal of fostering open, experiential, and self-directed learning, terms such as teaching and instruction have become less applicable than before. The label "educational technology" is used in the heading of Section IV in order to draw attention to the possibility that open and self-directed learning, especially learning by means of new multimedia systems, may well require that more, not less, thought must be devoted to the design of appropriate resources for adult learning.

Section V includes 23 entries which are grouped into two subsections concerned with the demand for and the supply of learning opportunities for adults. This *Encyclopedia* departs from the approach commonly taken in previous handbooks in that—with the important exception of women and part-time students in higher education—it does not devote separate entries to the many different audiences and target groups for adult education. The clientèle of adult education is described in one synthetic entry, Clientèles and Special Populations, thus making room for new topics that deal less with input and more with process. The entries in the subsection devoted to participation address topics such as the antecedents of participation, the role of motivation, counseling, dropout and outreach initiatives, and student support systems in adult education. The second subsection is devoted entirely to descriptions of the different institutional arrangements for adult learning. Three entries describe the institutional providers that offer formal curricula and qualifications equivalent to the levels of education defined in the International Standard Classification of Education (ISCED). The other entries deal with specific institutional providers of adult education, such as the Nordic folk high schools and study circles, the North American community colleges, and the more universal libraries, universities, and institutions for distance education.

Section VI of the *Encyclopedia* is focussed on the international, regional, and in the cases of China and Japan, the national organization of adult education. The section is divided into two subsections. The first addresses issues in the international organisation of adult education. Included are entries dealing with comparative and international studies in adult education and continuing vocational training. The history, aims, and program of work of the International Council for Adult Education is described, as are those of two key UN organizations, the United Nations Educational and Scientific Organization and the International Labour Office. The second subsection offers overviews of the organization, institutional arrangements, and practices of adult education, literacy, and continuing vocational training in all major regions of the world.

Section VII, finally, offers perspectives on the evaluation and measurement of adult education and continuing vocational training. The entries included in this section relate closely to several entries presented in Section I, particularly those dealing with epistemology and research methodology. Whereas the entries belonging to Section I address the meta-knowledge of research paradigms and associated methods, those included in Section VII deal with the specific and substantive aspects of evaluation and measurement in adult education. The entries in the first subsection offer perspectives on the nature, scope, design, implementation, and uses of evaluation in adult education. Separate entries address the evaluation of adult education, distance education, and public training programs. The entries included in the second subsection focus on measurement and statistics. These topics are given relatively broad coverage in this *Encyclopedia*, partly because their importance has been underplayed in the past, and also because the demand for valid and reliable data has increased. Decisions about adult education policy and the priorities for further research need to be informed by a comprehensive set of information of a qualitative as well as quantitative nature. Compared with the available statistical information about the inputs, processes, and outcomes of mainstream schooling, the databases involving adult education, literacy, and continuing vocational training are underdeveloped in many countries. The purpose of this subsection is to draw the attention of readers to the need to strengthen the research expertise and the capacity for data collection in the field of adult education.

Despite the vastness of the ground covered in this *Encyclopedia*, it is highly likely that some omissions have occurred. New concepts, theories, and methods, new research studies, and new policy issues appear frequently in the expanding literature on adult education, literacy, and continuing vocational training. It is to be hoped that any such omissions are few, and that the inclusions will prove durable and useful for years to come.

4. Scope and Constraints

Although *The International Encyclopedia of Adult Education and Training* should be relevant to different audiences in many countries, and even though much effort has been spent to ensure that the information it offers is accurate, up-to-date, comprehensive, and international in scope, there are some factors that constrain its breadth and diversity of reference.

First, some limitations had to be placed on the size, and therefore the scope, of this volume. For example, the specific audiences of adult education, such as young and older adults, rural and urban women, workers in agriculture, industry, and other formal and informal sectors of the labor market, the long-term unemployed, the disabled, and the socially isolated are covered synthetically and not in separate entries, as has often been the case in previous handbooks. For the same reason there are no regional and national overviews of research and studies in adult education. Information about the state of the research field is conveyed in entries that deal with substantive topics. Second, in terms of content coverage, the volume is somewhat oriented towards the industrialized countries in North America and Europe. This bias necessarily reflects the state of a field in which most scholarly activity is carried out in the countries of the North. Language is another limiting factor. The *Encyclopedia* is published in English because this has the benefit of making it available to a very wide audience. Yet the use of English has imposed certain constraints on the selection of the authors. Scholars from countries where the language of academic discourse is other than English may have been handicapped by the requirement that all manuscripts be submitted in this language. The language factor is reflected both in the selection of the authors themselves and in these authors' choices of references to interesting country examples, case studies, and published scholarly work. A further limiting factor, closely related to the previous one, concerns the persistent confusion over definitions and the meaning of important terms. Major concepts of adult education and training are used differently in different countries and over time. Although internationally agreed definitions do exist in many cases, the concepts are nevertheless used in many different ways. Although the ambition at the outset was to ensure that the usage of terms and their associated meanings would be as internationally consistent as possible, the variations in the authors' interpretations of important concepts and terms were too large and important for consistency to be imposed by the Editor.

5. How to Use the Encyclopedia

This *Encyclopedia* is designed to be of interest to all people who are engaged in and concerned by the education and training of adults. Readers can use the *Encyclopedia* as a means of obtaining comprehensive and systematic knowledge either of the whole field of adult education or of important, large areas that form parts of the whole. They may begin their search with examining the sections of this Preface concerned with the conceptual framework of the *Encyclopedia* and its content. In a further step the Table of Contents might be consulted in order to see the titles of the individual entries and where they fit into the general framework. The Table of Contents provides a useful, schematic overview of the titles of all entries included in the seven sections comprising the volume. Subsequently, the reader may wish to turn to the Introductions to each of the sections. These introductions offer summaries of the content of the entries making up each section. They also indicate associations between the individual entries and others, both in the same section and in other sections.

The reader can also look for individual entries that offer authoritative statements about specific topics in adult education. An efficient method to locate specific information is to examine the comprehensive, multilevel Subject Index. This index was designed to assist readers in locating individual topics suited to their interests. The authors were asked to identify key words or phrases in their manuscripts which constitute cornerstones in the structure of the information they wished to convey. These key words formed the basis of the Subject Index. The Author Index also provides a useful entry point, since it directs readers to the bibliographies given at the end of each entry. These bibliographies list both specific references and more general suggestions for further reading about the topic. Many entries also offer cross-references to other, related entries. Finally a List of Contributors is placed at the end of the volume. This index lists the names and affiliations of the authors and shows the titles of their contributions.

6. Acknowledgments

The preparation of this *Encyclopedia* has required an enormous amount of work. A special debt of gratitude is due to several persons. First, I am grateful to Torsten Husén and Neville Postlethwaite, the Editors-in-Chief of the parent *Encyclopedia*, who invited me to edit the section on adult education, and who have been a reliable and constant source of support. Second, I would like to thank Barbara Barrett, Editorial Director at Pergamon, who supported the decision to publish this *Encyclopedia*. Third, I am indebted to Colin Titmus, who served as the editor of the previous volume, *Lifelong Education for Adults: An International Handbook*, which in many ways has influenced the design and content of this *Encyclopedia*. Further, I am grateful to the 169 authors who contributed substantive articles, often written under severe time constraints. At Pergamon, I would like to express my deep gratitude to Angela Greenwell, the Editorial Manager, who with friendship, zeal, and a high level of professional skill facilitated the publication process in all its stages. My sincere thanks are also due to Michèle Wheaton, Debbie Wilton and many others at Pergamon who contributed importantly.

Finally, I am greatly indebted to my dear family, Hendrika, Teodor, and Lovisa, for their patience and encouragement throughout the years it took to complete this task. This voluntary assignment, which has come on top of my regular duties at the OECD* and elsewhere, has taken a heavy toll on family leisure. This *Encyclopedia* is therefore rightly dedicated to them.

March 1996

ALBERT C. TUIJNMAN
Paris, France

* The opinions expressed in this *Encyclopedia* by the Editor are his own and do not necessarily reflect the views of the Organisation of Economic Co-operation and Development.

SECTION I

Concepts, Theories, and Methods

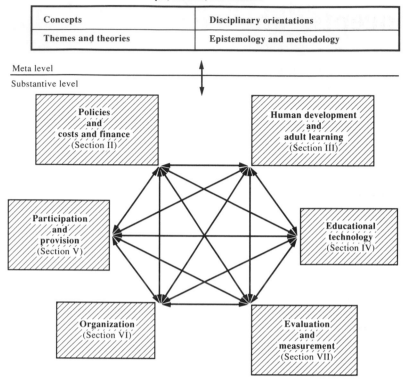

Concepts, theories, and methods

Concepts	Disciplinary orientations
Themes and theories	Epistemology and methodology

Meta level

Substantive level

**Policies
and
costs and finance**
(Section II)

**Human development
and
adult learning**
(Section III)

**Participation
and
provision**
(Section V)

**Educational
technology**
(Section IV)

Organization
(Section VI)

**Evaluation
and
measurement**
(Section VII)

Figure 1
Schematic representation of Section I in relation to the other Sections

SECTION I

Concepts, Theories, and Methods

Introduction

A. C. Tuijnman

What is adult education, and what is training? What conceptual and theoretical frameworks are employed, and to what extent are these specific to the field? Is adult education an art, an education discipline, or might it be better considered as a science in its own right? Have researchers working on problems in adult education and training developed their own methodological toolbox, or do they tend to employ the same research paradigms and methods as those used in other fields of disciplined inquiry? These questions are representative of the issues addressed in Section I of *The International Encyclopedia of Adult Education and Training*.

The 34 entries included in Section I offer insights that belong to the meta-knowledge of adult education and training. They offer many perspectives on the development, purpose, content, and specificity of the field. The section is divided into four subsections. Definitions of adult education, lifelong learning, literacy, vocational education, and continuing vocational training are given in the first subsection. The delineation of the field is broadened in the second subsection, in which an overview is given of the main themes and theories of adult education and training. Whereas the third subsection offers a choice of disciplinary perspectives on the field, the fourth deals with basic epistemological and methodological issues in educational research.

1. Concepts

As Titmus notes in the opening entry of this first subsection, adult education is commonly understood to refer to both a process of learning and the supporting arrangements, which call attention to specific features, such as the voluntariness of learning, the commitment to personal growth and development, and the deliberate structuring of learning activities. Adult education can be defined as the work of institutions; as a distinctive relationship, for example between pedagogy and andragogy; as a profession or field of study; as stemming from an identification with social movements; and as being distinguished from other kinds of education by its main goals and functions (cf. Courtney 1991). Darkenwald and Merriam (1982) offer the following definition: "Adult education is a process whereby persons whose major social roles are characteristic of adult status undertake systematic and sustained learning activities for the purpose of bringing about changes in knowledge, attitudes, values or skills" (p. 9).

The above definition calls attention to the meaning of the term "adult" as opposed to notions such as "child" and "youth." It also raises the question as to where one can draw the line between schooling and tertiary education, on the one hand, and adult education and continuing vocational training, on the other. The term "adult" normally refers to a person who has reached a certain degree of physical and emotional maturity. The latter concept implies that a stage of "readiness" has been reached. In contrast, "youth" can be taken to imply "not mature, not yet finished." It is evident that both childhood and adulthood are subjective constructs, since their meaning is obviously culturally and historically relative. Darkenwald and Merriam (1982) choose to define an adult not in biological, psychological, or legal terms, but as a person whose major roles are characteristic of adult status. The emphasis on roles, socioculturally defined, leads Darkenwald (1992) to define an adult as ". . . a person who has terminated continuous formal education and has assumed the roles characteristic of adult status in society." This approach leads to the exclusion from the definition of adult education of all full-time education catering for children and young adults. Included would be part-time education and training for out-of-school youth, workers, and unemployed people. Concepts such as continuing education and further education and training in a similar way draw a line between initial and postinitial learning trajectories.

A widely accepted definition of adult education appears in the *Recommendation on the Development of Adult Education* (UNESCO 1976 p. 2), which was adopted on 26 November 1976 by the General Conference

3

of UNESCO at its nineteenth session in Nairobi. The entire definition is reproduced below. Many standard texts on adult education leave out the second, very significant part, which calls attention to the role of adult education in a context of lifelong education and learning:

> ... the term "adult education" denotes the entire body of organized educational processes, whatever the content, level and method, whether formal or otherwise, whether they prolong or replace initial education in schools, colleges and universities as well as in apprenticeship, whereby persons regarded as adult by the society to which they belong develop their abilities, enrich their knowledge, improve their technical or professional qualifications or turn them in a new direction and bring about changes in their attitudes or behavior in the two fold perspective of full personal development and participation in balanced and independent social, economic and cultural development;
>
> adult education, however, must not be considered as an entity in itself, it is a sub-division, and an integral part of, a global scheme for lifelong education and learning;
>
> the term "life-long education and learning," for its part, denotes an overall scheme aimed both at restructuring the existing education system and at developing the entire educational potential outside the education system; in such a scheme men and women are the agents of their own education, through continual interaction between their thoughts and actions;
>
> education and learning, far from being limited to the period of attendance at school, should extend throughout life, include all skills and branches of knowledge, use all possible means, and give the opportunity to all people for full development of the personality;
>
> the educational and learning processes in which children, young people and adults of all ages are involved in the course of their lives, in whatever form, should be considered as a whole. (UNESCO 1976)

The World Declaration on Education for All, adopted in March 1990 in Jomtien, Thailand, articulates a framework for action designed to meet the basic learning needs of children, adolescents, and adults of all nations. The declaration affirms the concept and principles of lifelong learning, as set out in the UNESCO definition above, as learning that goes on not just in school and other educational institutions, but also at home and in the workplace, at all ages, in all cultures, and in all languages. The principles of lifelong learning, which are explained more fully in the entry by Hasan, challenge the adequacy of using an age criterion in describing the processes and structures of adult education and training.

UNESCO's definition of adult education draws attention to the distinction between formal, nonformal, and informal education. Whereas formal education refers to any organized and systematic education provided by schools and other educational institutions, nonformal education is defined as any organized and systematic educational activity that is carried on outside the formal system. In contrast, informal education refers to a lifelong process of experiential learning—a process of informally acquiring certain values, attitudes, skills, and knowledge from experience, from learning resources available in the environment, and through independent, self-directed learning. In his entry, Colletta observes that the distinction between formal, nonformal, and informal education is equally applicable in the case of youth and adults. In fact, in many developing countries, the term nonformal education has carried more currency than those of adult education or training. In Southeast and East Asia, the Arab countries, and in Africa and Latin America, nonformal education denotes a range of educational activities comprising literacy and postliteracy programs, part-time general as well as vocational education and training for youth and adults, and community education and community development. The role of nonformal education in a strategy for attaining the goal of education for all, as set out in the Jomtien Declaration mentioned previously, continues to receive widespread attention in both developing and developed countries.

Another observation is that both UNESCO's definition of adult education and the Jomtien declaration on basic literacy and lifelong learning do not draw a sharp distinction between adult education and continuing vocational training. In fact, continuing vocational training is considered an integral element of adult education in the perspective of lifelong learning. In their entry on the convergence between education an training, de Moura Castro and de Oliveira explain why it has become increasingly difficult to make conceptual and practical distinction between education and training. This point is elaborated by King, who offers a broad overview of the institutional arrangements for vocational education and training in school, postschool, and workplace locations. An entry by Bowman concerned with the theory and economics of on-the-job training completes this first subsection devoted to the meta-knowledge relevant to adult education and training.

In conclusion, in *The International Encyclopedia of Adult Education and Training*, the term adult education is used as a generic term that refers to formal, nonformal, and informal education, as well as to vocational education and continuing vocational training for out-of-school youth and adults. It denotes both a concept, a field of study, and an area of educational practice.

2. Themes and Theories

Over the years a number of specific themes and theories have emerged. With one or two exceptions they were not intended as a blueprint for a coherent theory of adult education, but offered new ideas and insights pointing to a particular problem and a way to address it in practice. The notable exception is the idea that education should not be confined to the early part of the lifespan, but should be a process that continues throughout life. Sutton, in the previous subsection, argues that this idea has had a stupendous impact on the development of educational thought and, albeit to a lesser extent, on the perception of the aims, organization, and functioning of initial schooling and adult education and training in a scheme for lifelong learning. The principles of lifelong learning have given rise to specific policies intended to integrate various learning environments—for example, the home, the school, and the workplace—and to create real possibilities for learning across the lifespan, by expanding the provision of adult education, widening access to conventional educational programs, and opening new channels of delivery targeted to people at home and in the workplace.

Many writers consider that the central goal of adult education is not to assist the individual learner to gain access to continuing vocational training, or to achieve promotion to an occupational and social position with a higher level of pay and prestige. Neither is its mission considered to be one of serving as a vehicle for investment in the skills and competencies that are widely seen as principal factors in labor market adjustment and macro-economic growth. At a more fundamental level, adult education is viewed as a social conscience and grassroots movement, and as a way of uniting communities with the common goal of creating a "better" society. In many countries, popular education, which forms part of a political process aimed at liberation and the building of democratic institutions, has been a principal factor in social and cultural development. For many theorists and practitioners, the phrase "adult education for social change" carries real meaning; it denotes the belief that adult education is something apart from, compensating for, and even oppositional to the formal education system which, through processes of socialization and reproduction, sustains a discriminatory and undemocratic social order. These and other normative theories of adult education are introduced in the entry by Westwood. They are given much coverage also by other contributors to the *Encyclopedia*.

The issues and the related questions for policy are addressed in several entries relevant to an understanding of adult education theory and practice. Cunningham describes the notions of community education and community development. She also describes forms of grassroots endeavors seeking social transformation by means of popular education, participatory research, and education provided by social movements. The theme of popular education and its role in conscientization is elaborated in an entry by Evans. The ideas and methods of action research and participatory research, which are rooted strongly in adult education practice in Central and Latin America, are explained by Hall in the next subsection. Additional perspectives on adult education for social change are offered by Davies, who writes about population

education, and Wulf, who deals with the important subject of peace education.

The International Encyclopedia of Adult Education and Training contains a number of entries dealing with the theory and practice of adult literacy. In the first of these entries, Olson offers a general perspective on the meanings, contexts, and functions of literacy, in particular as regards writing and decoding skills. Baker and Street develop this theme further by considering both mainstream and alternative, or cultural, models of literacy and numeracy. Benton adds to this the perspective of postliteracy. In Benton's entry, the notion of postliteracy is discussed in relation to the changing skill requirements of the labor forces in industrialized societies. Methodologies and issues in the conceptualization and measurement of postliteracy are also addressed in other sections of the *Encyclopedia*. Examples are the subsequent entries contributed by Lind and Johnston, Kamper, Marsiske and Smith, Kutner, Lowerie, Napitupulu, and Wagner.

In their entry on family life education, Vandemeulebroecke and Crombrugge offer a perspective on adult education that is both different from and complementary to Cunningham's views about the role of adult education in community development. Family life education refers to the variety of educative actions that aim at strengthening and enriching individual and family well-being. The discussion is focussed on learning processes in the areas of human development and sexuality, interpersonal relationships, family resource management, education about parenthood, ethics, and family and society.

Two complementary entries complete this subsection. The first, by Niemi, explains the concept of human resource development. Tuijnman, in the second entry, describes the concepts and principles of recurrent education and alternation education as originally proposed in the late 1960s. Some of the problems associated with the theory of recurrent education are discussed, and reasons for the decline of interest in the policy concept noted. Recurrent education called for a large role of public intervention in the funding and provision of adult education. In contrast, a human resource development strategy does not to a similar extent depend on government initiative. Because the focus of human resource development is on structured on-the-job training and informal learning in the workplace, the concept emphasises "adult learning" instead of "adult education."

3. Disciplinary Orientations

Both scholars and practitioners have long argued the case that adult education differs in fundamental respects from formal schooling. It is recognized that there are some major differences between the general aims, means, and ends of adult education and those of the school. Yet the main distinctive characteristic of adult education, it is argued, lies not so much in its instrumentalism as in its epistemological orientation, which refers to both humanist and critical notions of knowledge, and which involves concepts such as self-directedness, facilitation, and emancipation. This line of reasoning has led some influential writers to claim that adult education, or andragogy, cannot and should not be subsumed under the general flag of education, or pedagogy (cf. Knowles 1988).

The above claim has been and remains popular among many writers in the field of adult education. Its popularity derives, at least in part, from the need to justify the establishment and subsequent development of adult education as a specialist field of study in a competitive academic world. Over the years, the recognition of the specificity of adult education has no doubt been a major factor in the growth of adult education, as evidenced by the establishment of a large number of specialized institutions and research centers in many countries of the world. However, there has also been another, less fortunate outcome. The emphasis on specificity has fostered a largely artificial separateness among related fields, by creating a tendency to disregard as suspect theories and research methods developed in mainstream education and in other behavioral, social science, and humanities disciplines. The fear was, and among some writers still is, that the influx of ideas from other fields—notably cognitive and developmental psychology, sociology, economics, and even pedagogy, didactics, and instructional psychology—would undermine the effort and prospect of developing an independent theorical basis that eventually would establish "a science of helping adults learn" (Knowles 1988).

There are also some authors who call into doubt the feasibility—and even the desirability—of establishing a separate science of adult education. In the preface to the first edition of *The International Encyclopedia of Education*, Husén and Postlethwaite (1985 p. xiii) note that "education as a field of scholarly endeavor is located at the crossroads of several academic disciplines. Education, as such, is not a scientific discipline of well-structured concepts, theories, and facts in the same sense as are physics and mathematics." A similar argument is advanced by de Landsheere (1988 p. 16), who concludes his survey of the history of educational research with the statement that "like medicine, education is an art. That is why advances in education do not produce a science of education, in the positivist meaning of the term, but yield increasingly powerful foundations for practice and decision-making." Educational practice, as carried out by teachers and learners, and regardless of whether it involves children or adults, is influenced by an amalgamation of previous experience and theoretical insights. These insights are gained from a wide range of behavioral, social science, and humanities disciplines that, collectively, constitute the "foundations" of the body of knowledge in education (cf. Husén and Postlethwaite 1994 p. xii).

If the systematic study of education, and the art of teaching and learning denoted with the label pedagogy, can claim little in the way of separate scientific status, then adult education should likewise not be considered as a separate science. The study of problems and issues in adult education and training attracts scholars with differences in research training, substantive interests, focuses and ideas, and this diversity not only characterizes the field of adult education and training but also constitutes its strength. As a field of study it draws from—but also contributes to—a multidisciplinary body of knowledge. Adult education may be said to benefit from this widening of theoretical perspectives, as it can draw from a broad theoretical and practical framework. For the same reasons as the attempt to establish the basic principles of a "science of education" has been largely unsuccessful, the effort to define a "science of adult education" has likewise been unfruitful.

Both the study and practice of adult education are shaped by the social, ideological, and political contexts within which it has evolved. Changes in demography and political economy, and shifts in cultural trends are factors that impact on the orientation of adult education and training. In turn, adult education also aims at producing and facilitating change at both the societal and the personal level. This dialectic relationship typifies practice, and explains why multidisciplinarity, as is the case in education more generally, is a fundamental characteristic of adult education. While it would seem justified to assert that "the theory of adult education cannot find an adequate place as a sub-theory of pedagogy" (Pöggeler 1992 p. 164), this does not imply that the future of adult education is best served by continuing its separate existence. The situation in the United States is not atypical: the annual conventions of the American Educational Research Association (AERA) attract thousands of researchers, writers, and practitioners; yet very few of them are professionally concerned with adult education or training, or would consider themselves as adult educators. In parallel, the American Association of Adult and Continuing Education (AAACE) also holds its annual, well-attended meetings. The two groups appear to live a separate life; they do not mix, and even tend to regard each another with a dose of suspicion. Whereas a respect for specificity may be advantageous, an emphasis on separateness is counter-productive for the development and unity of the field concerned with the theory and practice of lifelong learning—a field to which research on formal schooling and research on adult education both contribute.

Thus, in *The International Encyclopedia of Adult Education and Training*, the field is perceived to comprise not only the practices of formal, nonformal, and informal education and training for out-of-school youths and adults, but also the knowledge derived from a number of scholarly disciplines associated with education. This position is reflected in the decision to include in the *Encyclopedia* a selection of entries concerned with the disciplinary orientations of adult education and training. Although the *Encyclopedia* devotes separate entries to anthropology, economics of adult education and nonformal education, philosophy and ethics, political science and policy analysis, psychology, and sociology, the picture of the disciplinary allegiances of adult education it offers is incomplete. The contributions made by other disciplines, for example medicine and neurology, should also be considered.

In the first entry of the subsection, Rubenson offers a useful overview of the disciplinary allegiances of adult education research. The author notes that it is impossible to offer a representative picture of the disciplinary orientations of the field in a single entry. Rubenson makes it very clear that the question of the scientific status of adult education is still the subject of debate. Support for an exclusive perspective is offered in the entry by Van Gent, who explains the concept and theory of andragogy. The author observes that andragogy denotes not only a specific approach to the teaching of adults, but also a preoccupation with social work and community development.

Most anthropological studies in education have dealt with schooling. However, the overview presented by Lancy shows that cultural and educational anthropologists have also devoted much work to literacy and numeracy. Economics is the subject of two related entries. In the first of these, Tuijnman introduces the main theories and topics considered in the economics of adult education and training. In the second entry, Ahmed deals with the substantive issues in the economics of nonformal education. Ahmed concludes that nonformal education programs expand the range of choices in analysis and action in respect of critical economic concerns, such as reducing the wastage of resources, improving efficiency and cost-effectiveness, and mobilizing additional resources for investment in education.

The next entry by Pöggeler deals with the history of adult education. This entry does not deal with the methods of historiographic study, but is written from the perspective of an author whose disciplinary footing and allegiance are squarely in the field of adult education. The next two entries deal with philosophy, ethics, political science, and policy analysis in adult education. Lawson exposes the reader to the questions philosophers ask, and Griffin introduces the theoretical frameworks employed by political scientists. The last two entries in this subsection deal with the application of psychological and sociological theories to adult education. Pieters introduces the psychology of adult education from two broad angles, paying attention to both disciplinary and applied perspectives on adult education. In the entry on the sociology of adult education, Jarvis examines the relationship between society and social change, on the one hand, and the formal, informal, and nonformal structures of adult education, on the other. Jarvis concludes that the forms and structures of adult education and training correspond closely to the structures and levels of development of entire societies.

4. Epistemology and Research Methodology

The fourth subsection deals with epistemology and research methodology. The first entry, by Rubenson, offers a review of the research field. It addresses the assumptions and perceptions of the territory to be covered by such research, examines the main traditions and paradigms, reviews the criteria for assessing it as a field of study, and proposes questions for research studies still to be undertaken. It will be clear both from what has been said above and from Rubenson's discussion of research traditions in adult education that the field is divided along epistemological and methodological lines. The purpose of this cluster of entries is not to offer an exhaustive description of the different research methods employed in the field. Rather, the aim is to show that the opposed views on the nature and methods of adult education and training, which were highlighted in the previous subsections, derive from fundamental differences in why and how researchers position themselves vis-à-vis epistemological questions about the nature and uses of knowledge. These perceptions are influenced by ideology, and are in no way specific to the field of adult education and training.

Phillips takes up the question of the meanings and relationships between positivism, antipositivism, and empiricism. Much attention is paid to the challenges to empiricism and positivism, although the difficulties of antipositivist positions in educational research are also mentioned. Epistemology, which refers to the study of the nature, scope, and applicability of knowledge, is the subject of the next entry by Walker and Evers. This entry does not focus on adult education research per se, but deals with various epistemological issues in educational research more generally. Yet the issues raised are highly relevant also for the field of adult education. Following a thought-provoking discussion of the paradigm controversy in educational research, Walker and Evers conclude that a holistic perspective on theory and method underscores the epistemological unity of research into education, regardless of whether the focus of that research is on children or adults. In a subsequent entry, Entwistle returns to the discourse in adult education, by discussing different ideologies with reference to the content, the style, and the clientele of adult education and training.

Three entries with a focus on research methodology conclude this subsection. It should be noted that the choice of the methods dealt with is somewhat arbitrary, given that other, frequently used methods and techniques are not covered. However, upon reading the three entries the reader will note that the authors do not deal with methodology in a narrow sense, since underpinning the choice of method are questions about the purposes of the research study, and hence about the nature of the knowledge thus generated. The entries thus complement the previous ones that dealt with ideology, epistemology, and research paradigms in education.

Hall describes the notion and principles of participatory and action research in adult education. The issues raised by Hall connect closely with those discussed previously by Westwood, in that participatory research is defined as a social process that is biased in favor of dominated, exploited, poor, or otherwise excluded people. Participatory research sees no contradiction between the goals of collective empowerment and the deepening of knowledge. A quite different perspective is offered in the following entry by von Eye and Spiel, who describe the methods used in research on human development and adult learning. The authors discuss various research designs, including the cross-sectional, longitudinal, and time-lag designs. Methods depending on intervention and experimentation are also presented. A third entry deals with the principles of scientific research. Kaplan advocates that the principles of scientific research are uniformly applicable, regardless of the specific questions that may be addressed. The entry has an important place in this *Encyclopedia* because it exposes a number of assumptions that underpin much current practice in adult education research.

References

Courtney S 1991 Defining Adult and Continuing Education. In: Merriam S B, Cunningham P M (eds.) 1991 *Handbook of Adult and Continuing Education.* Jossey-Bass, San Francisco, California

Darkenwald G G 1992 Adult Education. In: Alkin M C (ed.) 1992 *Encyclopedia of Educational Research*, 6th edn. Macmillan, New York

Darkenwald G G, Merriam S B 1982 *Adult Education: Foundations of Practice.* Harper and Row, New York

de Landsheere G 1988 History of Educational Research. In: Keeves J P (ed.) 1988 *Educational Research, Methodology, and Measurement: An International Handbook.* Pergamon, Oxford

Husén T, Postlethwaite T N 1985 Preface. *International Encyclopedia of Education*, 1st edn. Pergamon, Oxford

Husén T, Postlethwaite T N 1994 Preface. *International Encyclopedia of Education*, 2nd edn. Pergamon, Oxford

Knowles M 1988 *The Adult Learner: A Neglected Species*, 3rd edn. Gulf Publishing, Houston, Texas

Pöggeler F 1992 Germany. In: Jarvis P (ed.) *Perspectives on Adult Education and Training in Europe.* National Institute of Adult Continuing Education, Leicester

UNESCO 1976 *Recommendation on the Development of Adult Education.* UNESCO, Paris

(a) Concepts

Adult Education: Concepts and Principles

C. J. Titmus

This entry examines the evolution of the concepts, purposes, and principles which are associated with the term "adult education." It attempts to describe them in relation to current practice. It examines the difficulties of formulating a definition of adult education as it is now practiced, and relates its inconsistencies and contradictions to its origins in Europe and North America, its spread worldwide, and the extension of its field to cover the whole range of organized educational processes for those people recognized as adult, undertaken either for individual development or the collective good. It discusses the importance of international communication in the field and the difficulties of terminology that arise. Finally it raises the question of the future of "adult education" as an umbrella concept on a global scale.

1. Growth of the Concept

Although its origins can be found in the eighteenth century, the development of the education of adults as a distinctive sector of education is essentially a product of the nineteenth and twentieth centuries and of Europe, in particular Northwest Europe, and North America. In the United Kingdom, where the term "adult education" appears to have been first used, it did not enter into common use until the second half of the nineteenth century and its use to denote a peculiar, coherent body of knowledge and practice certainly belongs to the twentieth century. In the United States the term does not even appear to have been in regular use until well into the twentieth century (see Grattan 1959 p. 328). In the languages of a number of other countries, where provision of education for adults spread later than in the United Kingdom, a literal translation of the term entered even more slowly into general use, if it did so at all.

However the term was understood, the inspiration of early initiatives in adult education was neither specifically nor primarily a concern for adults as adults, it was wider. Much of the terminology involved in the field reveals the influence of the Enlightenment

and movements for the education of the people. Indeed, some of the expressions which are still in current use in a number of languages as the equivalents of the English language term "adult education" reflect these influences. The Czech language still has *osvĕta* (enlightenment) and in French there is *éducation populaire* (popular education). In German *Volksbildung* (popular education) embraced both the ideas of the common people and, principally, that of the *Volk*, the German people or nation. In Danish *folkeoplysning* (popular enlightenment) refers both to the target population and the philosophical movement so important in its inspiration. These expressions did not denote a concept of education aimed exclusively at adults, but embraced all ages. In France, for example, the original emphasis of the movement for *éducation populaire* lay primarily on the achievement of universal schooling. The position was similar in Germany, where, moreover, the nationalist overtones conveyed the message that *Volksbildung* was not intended to be confined to the lower orders of society. While terminological variations reflected differences in the characteristics and situations of individual countries, on the other hand, the similarities suggest ideas and purposes that cross national and linguistic frontiers (see Grattan 1955, Titmus 1981).

As the nineteenth century progressed, the separation of education for grown persons from that for children increased. With the achievement of universal childhood education the emphasis of movements for popular education or enlightenment shifted and concentrated more on the needs of adults. Because it was linked with the professionalization of school teaching, education as a field of study grew, but, by stressing the specificity of the learning stages of childhood, its theories became increasingly inapplicable to the context of the education of adults. There has been too little study of the history of the relationship between the development of concepts of child and adult education for any firm conclusions to be drawn about this. Histories of the latter stress associations, policies, purposes, and forms of organization rather than pedagogical or andragogical theory (see *Andragogy*). It can be said only that the creation of specialized departments of education (meaning schooling) in institutions of higher education was followed, after a substantial time-lag, by others devoted to the training of adult educators and the study of adult education. As members of these departments sought to create a profession of adult education, they felt it necessary, in order to gain recognition for their claims, not only to establish a code of conduct, but, like other professions, to build up a body of theory specific to it too. It is probably no exaggeration to say that such departments, in the United States, and later in other countries, have been largely responsible for constructing the corpus of theory and practice that formed the basis for the evolution of the contemporary concept of adult education, influential worldwide (see *Professional Associations*).

2. Historical Limitations of the Concept

The break with the ideas of the regular education system was only partial. In their concept of what constituted education adult educators followed it. Their principal purpose was to develop and improve the whole person, to give a general or liberal education. The needs of industrialization may have constituted a major stimulus of educational initiatives for adults, but, during the nineteenth century, it was perceived as a lower level of activity. In the United Kingdom and the other English-speaking countries that shared its traditions, vocational training was not considered to be adult education. Likewise, in Norway and Sweden, the voluntary associations, which, from the beginning of the twentieth century built up a monopoly of *voksenopplæring* and *vuxenundervisning* (both meaning adult education), did not initially include occupational training among their functions. In Germany it was not until *Volksbildung* was replaced as the umbrella expression by *Erwachsenenbildung* (adult education), after the Second World War, that occupational education became established as one of its activities. Even in the United States, where vocational provision became dominant, the "classic emphasis" among theorists of adult education, if not practitioners, was on ". . . the improvement of men in terms of secular knowledge, morals, or spiritual understanding, and only incidentally, or by implication, in terms of earning power" (Grattan 1959, p. 10).

The range of educational opportunities for adults included under the rubric "adult education" was limited in other ways. For example, according to their public pronouncements most adult education professionals were primarily concerned with the educationally disadvantaged, who were, almost by definition, the lower socioeconomic classes. The idea that education should be a lifelong process, and that all persons, whatever their previous education or their social status, needed therefore, to continue it in adult life, was not unknown in the nineteenth century, but only in the second half of the twentieth has it spread to achieve almost universal acceptance.

3. Worldwide Expansion

The real growth of adult education, in which it has become a worldwide phenomenon, only gained impetus after 1945. The first UNESCO World Conference, in 1949, only attracted 79 people, nearly all from Europe and the United States. By the time the fourth was held, in Paris in 1985, the attendance had risen to over 800 persons, and 120 states were represented. The first meeting, although "essentially a Western European regional conference" (Kidd 1972), established what, for UNESCO, adult education was to mean and that Euro-American stamp has prevailed ever since, in spite of slow accommodations to the special conditions of other member states (see *UNESCO and Adult Education*).

Democratization of education, the replacement of material resources by knowledge as the basis of economic prosperity and rapid obsolescence of skills brought about by the pace of technical advance have all contributed to transform adult education from a minor activity on the periphery of the educational world to a sector of central importance to society.

4. Formulation of the Concept and its Difficulties

Under such pressures, and compounded by theories derived from the study of the ways in which adults learn, a much wider concept of adult education's nature and range came to challenge more traditional ones. In 1976 at the General Conference of UNESCO, representatives of 142 countries unanimously approved a General Recommendation on the Development of Adult Education, which included the following definition:

> The term, "adult education," denotes the entire body of organized educational processes, whatever the content, level, and method, whether formal or otherwise, or whether they prolong or replace initial education in schools, colleges, and universities, as well as an apprenticeship, whereby persons regarded as adult by the society to which they belong develop their abilities, enrich their knowledge, improve their technical or professional qualifications, or turn them in a new direction and bring about changes in their attitudes or behaviour in the two-fold perspective of full personal development and participation in balanced and independent social, economic, and cultural development. (UNESCO 1976)

This is probably the most widely accepted statement of the phenomenon, but it is only partial, since "adult education" may specify the areas of human activity in which the processes occur, or the institutions and procedures by which adults are enabled to experience the processes in a particular society (Titmus 1980 p. 135). The latter is the case, for instance, when one speaks of "Chinese Adult Education" (see *China, People's Republic*). Taken at its widest it comprehends all three aspects. As a definition of process it has its weaknesses and omissions, that largely spring from the nature of adult education itself.

5. What is Meant by "Adult"?

"Persons regarded as adult by the society to which they belong" is an attempt to deal with the enduring problem of what is meant by "adult," recognizing that the concept differs from society to society. For organizational purposes, in order to determine the target population, the almost universal criterion is one of age. Only people above a certain minimum age may attend courses offered under the banner of adult education. Where compulsory school attendance is almost universal, the age may coincide with that for the termination of obligatory schooling: in the United Kingdom it is 16. Not all those persons who study beyond that age are considered, however, to be participating in adult education since according to most operational definitions, it can only begin after the completion of all available years of full-time initial education. As the average age of university graduation in Germany, for example, is 27 and an individual may carry on full-time to graduate study after that, many persons participating in study, who are considered for all other purposes to be well into adulthood, are not in adult education, nor are the establishments in which they learn part of its institutional structure.

As a field of practice, adult education's concern is perceived to be the meeting of all the educational needs of a category of persons called adults that are required to be met in order that they may function as adults. Seen from this point of view, adulthood is identified with the fulfillment of a collection of roles, with a number of situations, individual and collective, which may be broadly classified under the headings of earning a living, marriage or sexual partnership, parenthood, citizenship, social and cultural activities in leisure time, and retirement. According to this view, these are the functions that distinguish adults from children and adolescents, not a particular age, although they are, for the most part, broadly age related. It is the specific purpose of enabling people to carry them out, entailing as it does its own peculiar organization, methods, and curriculum, which distinguishes adult education from any other field of education.

While accepting that these considerations should be taken into account, adult educationists have been much influenced in their thinking by the concept that "adult" denotes a distinctive stage or distinctive stages of physiological and psychological development, extending, for example, Piaget's stages of childhood development. It signifies a cognitively and affectively mature human being, who, because of this maturity, learns differently and has different educational needs from those of a person at earlier stages of development.

The process of adult education, is widely understood as the educating of such people, and because of this requires its own organization, methods, and curriculum, irrespective of the social roles that an adult may have to fulfill.

Neither the UNESCO definition, nor, it appears, any other, manages to reconcile these different senses of "adult" in the term "adult education." Not all persons who, according to chronological and administrative criteria, are engaged in adult education, are adults in terms of social function or developmental maturity. Some of those who are, are not considered to be participating in adult education. Some people who, for instance, are to be treated as adults because of their role as wage-earners or parents, are not at an adult level of cognitive or affective maturity.

6. The Sense of "Education"

By not specifying what is meant by "organized educational processes," the UNESCO definition leaves unclarified the dimensions and nature of "education" in adult education. It certainly removes the distinction between "education" and "training." It is not, however, clear that it would embrace self-directed learning (see *Self-directed Learning*). Some societies would still require that for education to take place there must be transmission of knowledge and/or skills from an educator, whether viewed as a teacher or facilitator, to the learners. Most educators would require that the knowledge in question should be "worthwhile" (Paterson 1979 p. 85), or at least not specifically harmful, even though that criterion boils down to a nebulous value judgment and leaves room for much disagreement. There are, for example, hierarchies of worthwhileness. In a number of countries the allocation of state funding to adult education is made according to a judgment of the comparative value of the knowledge or skills being taught. Increasingly, knowledge that does not have an occupational application is considered less deserving of support than that which has (Department of Education and Science 1991).

Some learning may be considered positively evil. Adult education to provoke action intended to bring about radical social or political change has a respectable pedigree (see *Critical Approaches to Adult Education*). Nevertheless, in many states any knowledge likely to challenge the dominant ideology or promote such action, however peaceably, will not be considered worthwhile, and indeed advocacy, or even discussion of this theme will be forbidden. Paolo Freire was forced to leave both Brazil and Chile on these grounds.

7. Questions of Structure

The UNESCO definition begs the question of exactly how structured the processes have to be. Other categories, primary, secondary, tertiary, initial and higher education, for example, are conceived as operating within a well-defined, permanent institutional framework. In order to retain the capacity for flexible response to whatever temporary or permanent adult needs arise, adult education has traditionally avoided identification with institutionalization and the rigid constraints that have been held to be inseparable from it. Although this principle is observed less and less and has never been given much attention in some of those activities which have only been claimed by it, adult education in the second half of the twentieth century is still perceived as less institution-bound than other sectors. It is widely believed that the widest possible interpretation of "organized educational processes" should be permitted in duration, degree of permanence, and the extent to which courses are structured.

8. Purposes of Adult Education

It is a matter of some debate whether in order for activities to be educational they have to be aimed principally at education, or whether education can be incidental to other purposes. For the most part, it is held that learning should be intentional. A session which had as its explicit purpose coaching in the skills of soccer would be recognized as education, but playing in a soccer match, even though one might learn from it, would hardly qualify. Whose intention should determine the purpose of the activity, that of the educators, learners, or sponsors of the activity, raises further problems.

8.1 Limiting Factors

The motivating forces behind adult education have been diverse, even from the early days. Nevertheless, the purposes of adult education were subjected to limiting factors, for example, the concentration of emphasis on the needs of certain socioeconomic groups and the exclusion of vocational training in some countries. While the broadening of the field in the second half of the twentieth century, which the UNESCO definition reflects, has, in theory, vastly extended its potential, so that it includes any organized cognitive, psychomotor, or affective learning by adults that is socially acceptable in the society in which it occurs, in practice, it has narrowed the range.

8.2 Who Determines Purposes?

In determining the purpose of any adult education activity three categories of person or organization have a direct interest: sponsors, who commission and generally pay for it, at least in large part; educators, whose function is to teach or to facilitate the learning for which the activity is undertaken; and participants, who engage in the activity in order to learn. Society, and the state as its representative, is perceived to have a direct interest in adult education as a whole, while the recognition of its social importance has engendered a

further, indirect interest in it, hence the requirement of social acceptability. Membership of any one of the interested parties does not exclude membership of any other, even in the same activity: in a mutual assistance group or a study circle, participants may be both sponsors and educators. The state may play the role of sponsor and, through its educational institutions, of educator too.

8.3 Regulatory Powers of the State

Through its legislative powers one unique and increasingly influential role falls to the state, that of regulator (European Bureau of Adult Education 1985). Throughout the modern period the power to make laws has enabled governments to prevent provision of the adult education of which they did not approve.

The power of the state to make laws is, however, of limited positive effect in the majority of areas, unless it ensures that resources are made available to facilitate their implementation. Ultimately, the power to give or withhold money is as important, if not more so, than legislation alone. Those who pay are the most influential in determining what adult education provision should be made. Increasingly, the principal paymasters are employers and public authorities, at national, regional, or local levels. Their support is not, however, indiscriminate. By selective allocation of funds they influence the learning opportunities offered so that priority is given to the populations and purposes they favor, notably the undereducated and continuing vocational training respectively.

8.4 Limitations on State Power

The domination of the state apparatus in determining the purposes and extent of adult education varies from society to society. It is absolute under state socialist regimes, as in the People's Republic of China and Cuba, but is mitigated to varying extents under other regimes (e.g., those of Western Europe, North America, Japan, and India), where power or principle ensures that countervailing influences are maintained. There are important private sponsors, notably employers and professional associations, but also political, religious, and social agencies, which use their own funds to obtain the kind of education that will serve their interests. In many countries, it has become an important, legally established principle, that private agencies should be guaranteed a major role in adult education provision.

8.5 Identity and Conflict of Purpose

In so far as many sponsors are also providers of the education they sponsor, there is identity between those who pay and those who educate. Many educational organizations, that have their own purposes and initiate their own programs to achieve them rely, however, on outside sponsorship or subsidy to finance their programs. They may also provide programs commissioned to the order of sponsors. Even public educational establishments do this to the order of employers. In such cases it cannot be assumed that identity of purpose between sponsor and provider always exists.

8.6 Purposes of Learners

Actual and potential learners have their own purposes, cognitive, affective and social, which may be different from those of sponsors and educators. Since they are not under any legal compulsion to participate (although there may be coercion), some attention must be paid to these if the educational experience is to have any success. It is a limiting factor on sponsors and providers, in that they avoid offering programs that adults are unwilling to accept. With this proviso, programs are determined by the purposes of sponsors and, to a lesser extent those of providers. Only to the degree that the two coincide are the purposes of students met. Some ways of overcoming the constraint on student purpose do exist: mutual assistance groups and other forms of individual or collective self-directed learning, for instance, as long as the participants meet their own costs.

In many countries adults circumvent the difficulty by turning to private agencies, which offer programs in order to make a profit. In a number of countries these agencies are subject to no regulation at all and where rules exist they do so only to ensure quality and fair treatment for the customer, not to affect the nature of the curriculum. Since, for the most part, the agencies exist by meeting the demands of the customer who pays the full cost of study, the influence of the latter, whether an individual learner or corporate body (many employers use such providers to meet their training needs), is considerable (see March and Wilson 1989).

8.7 Other Factors Influencing Purpose

A feature of educational experiences designed for adults is their great variety of forms, which sets them apart from schooling. For example, the duration of a single experience may range from a few hours to several years. It may be offered full-time or part-time, in working hours or outside them, in the daytime, evening, or at weekends, and running continuously or in recurrent blocks of study. It is tempting to assume that the form is determined by the purposes and content of the experience; in fact, the cause and effect relationship is more complex. There is a strong element of interaction between form and purpose. The latter may have to be adapted to the constraints of practical considerations, of money and time in particular.

9. Typology of Purpose

The purposes of any adult study experience are not confined to those advertised. Those of sponsors, providers, and students may be different. The hidden agenda of the sponsor of civic education may be conformism, religious education, or social peace. An adult may attend a recreational class in a foreign language perceiving it as an aid to job advancement. This acknowledged, this entry will take into consideration only the ostensible, publicized purposes, on the assumption that it is in these that sponsors, providers and participants come closest together. A number of attempts have been made to reduce the manifold purposes of adult education to a typology. The following is based on one which has been recognized as applicable to Europe and appears to fit North America to a large degree (Titmus 1976). It groups purpose under the five broad headings: second-chance education, vocational education, social role education, social welfare education, and individual self-development.

9.1 Second-chance Education

This, it may be argued, is only an appropriate term in those societies which have a system of universal initial education. It denotes the offer of opportunities for learning normally available in the course of initial education to persons who have terminated it and missed out on these opportunities when they were at that stage. In less developed societies the term "compensatory education" is more accurate, including as it does the offer to adults of learning experiences normally available in initial education in advanced societies, but not in their own. Worldwide, the most common purpose of second-chance education is to provide literacy and basic education (see *Literacy; Literacy and Numeracy Models; Adult Basic Education*), but more highly developed societies also offer compensatory secondary and higher education programs (see *Postliteracy; Adult Secondary Education; Adult Tertiary Education; University Adult Education*).

9.2 Vocational Education

Vocational education, and such education as literacy and numeracy teaching, which is intended to prepare the student for specific vocational training, ranges from the acquisition of occupational skills by those who entered the job market with none, to further education for senior executives and highly qualified professionals. It may embrace revising and updating existing knowledge and skills, as well as the acquisition of new ones. Unsurprisingly this area of adult education purpose is the most dominated by state and employer interests, attracts the most promotional legislation and resources, and is the greatest motivator of participants (see *Market Concepts in Provision; Market Failure in Adult Education and Training*). From the nineteenth century, adult educationists have bemoaned the excessive emphasis placed on education as a means of earning a living to the detriment of the role of education for the development of the whole person (see Grattan 1959, p. 116).

9.3 Social Role Education

As used here, the term "social role education" denotes education intended to make adults better able to perform the roles they may be called upon to play in their family and societal life, except for occupational ones. It ranges from those that every individual may be expected to undertake as a citizen and participant in the political process, through those of spouse, parent, and retired person, to those filled by only a limited number —for example, committee member, trade unionist, elected representative in local, regional, or national legislatures, and voluntary social or welfare worker. Education for this purpose goes back to the ancient world and can be found in tribal societies. Changes in society and the rapid obsolescence of knowledge relating to social relations and mental and physical health have greatly reduced the traditional reliance of younger generations on the wisdom of older ones, and this, plus the proliferation of recognized social roles, has greatly increased the importance of social role education as a function of contemporary adult education.

9.4 Social Welfare Education

There are kinds of educational provision, that do not fit comfortably under the headings already listed, nor do they aim primarily at individual improvement. Their purpose is preventive or curative in that they seek to protect society against major social ills, by bringing it to become aware of and to understand them and then to address the means of overcoming them. Examples under the general title of "health education" are campaigns directed against AIDS and drug abuse and the major efforts made in the Third World to teach the importance of using clean water. Also to be included in the category of social welfare are peace education and population education. Probably, on grounds of their intention, so are educational movements designed to promote particular social or political ideologies such as Marxism or nationalism.

9.5 Individual Self-development

Individual self-development comprises education with the primary purpose of the growth and enrichment of the individual as a person, irrespective of any occupational or social role. When providers offer programs with this intention they commonly include arts and crafts, history, philosophy, and others that are usually advertised as general, cultural, leisure time, or recreational (see *Time, Leisure and Adult Education*). The issue of intention is specially important to defining this category, in which activities not included under the other purposes tend to be grouped. It is argued that any learning contributes to self-enrichment, whatever its prime intention. However, many educators complain, particularly about vocational education, that the general enrichment of the participant is treated as an incidental, rather than the intentional outcome that it should be, even in programs with more specific objectives.

10. Individual and Collective Purpose

In some societies, particularly in the United States, prevailing opinion among those who identify themselves as adult educators would make individual self-development the primary goal of all adult education. In other societies, in contrast, more importance is attached, either by the currently prevailing ideology or by tradition (China is under the influence of both), to collective interests. In some of these societies the concept of individual self-identity has no place (Pratt 1989); in others individualization is recognized, but it is emphasized that full self-realization is inseparable from the collective good. The UNESCO definition, in its requirement of ". . . the two-fold perspective of full personal development and participation in balanced and independent social, economic, and cultural development," expresses the dominant view of those who see themselves as adult educators: that all their activities should have a dual goal, of which individual self-enrichment should always be one part.

11. Principles of Adult Education

The competing claims of society and the individual are only one of the issues of principle in adult education ("principles" here meaning those ideas guiding practice that derive their legitimacy from beliefs and values about human beings, society, and education, rather than empirical evidence, although they may find some support in the latter).

Fundamentally, the spread of adult education worldwide has been inspired by the belief that all adults can learn, that all persons need education periodically throughout life, that it is their right, and that it is the duty of society to make lifelong education possible for everyone. Behind these principles lies the faith that, because human beings are by nature learning animals, they are naturally inclined to undertake organized, intentional learning, if the appropriate opportunity is offered in the right circumstances. On the assumption that adults are mature, free, responsible citizens, however, it is believed that it is also their right to decide whether or not to participate in education in adulthood. Moreover, many educators believe, as a matter of principle, that grown persons know best what they should study, when, where and how. Those who have accepted Malcolm Knowles's theory of andragogy would make it a criterion of full maturity that adults should wish to take charge of their own learning (see Knowles 1980).

It is doubtful whether adult education would have spread so fast if had been perceived as having value only to the individual participant. From the beginning of its modern development, in the nineteenth century, sponsors and providers have been motivated by some concern for individuals and a large belief that it should serve a collective good, to themselves, to certain other interest groups, or society as a whole. It is undoubtedly contemporary assessment of the community's economic need, as much as any support for individual rights or benefit, which has impelled states and companies to promote the education of adults to an increasing degree (see *Economics of Adult Education and Training; Economics of Nonformal Education; Technological Change and Education*).

11.1 Conflicts of Principle

Not all principles are universally accepted and some are mutually incompatible. Unfettered individual development may conflict with the public good. The belief of some that adult education should be free of charge, as initial education is, and the less extreme and more widely held belief that nobody should be prevented from participation by financial considerations conflict with the claim of others that, as a matter both of principle and practicality, those who benefit from it should pay for it.

The interests of sponsors and participants do not always conform to the beliefs of educators. Employers frequently do not accept any responsibility for the personal development of their personnel, only for the inculcation of knowledge and skills specific to the needs of the enterprise. They certainly do not share the view that learners should decide the content, manner, and purpose of their learning, unless they pay for it. Surveys of participants in vocational courses tend to demonstrate that not merely the prime, but the only interest of the majority lies in acquiring an occupational skill as quickly as possible, and that they have no interest in using the course to further any wider self-development. Practical considerations of cost in money and time frequently focus purpose more narrowly than principle would require. There is little strategic planning, and learning experiences are often very fragmentary. Increasingly, as in the case of mature-student courses in higher education, adults have the opportunity for lengthy study, but, for the majority, each course or program is brief and tends to be perceived in isolation, as it is perceived also by its sponsors and providers. In such cases, courses are organized and undertaken for narrowly defined, immediate needs. This applies not merely to vocational programs, but to many social role and social welfare ones too.

12. Erosion, Diversification, and Confusion of Ideas

Even within that body of activities calling itself "adult education" uniformity of concept, purpose, or principle is lacking. The view of it as a specific sector of education, the peculiar characteristics of which are conferred upon it by its concern only for persons called "adult," however that term is defined, is only the product of a specific geographical area sharing a largely common culture and fundamental concepts and values, and it is not universally current even there. The bringing of a considerably extended range of activities within the organizational field of adult education has contributed to its diversity and fragmentation. The belief has grown that, because of their life experience and the stage or stages of their physiological and psychological development, adults engaged in any kind of organized study require specific treatment on the part of educators and, frequently, special curricula. Therefore, as a field of study, adult education is extending into other sectors, notably vocational and higher education. The concepts and organization of education for adults have penetrated to some extent into these sectors, and it is claimed that teachers in them should see themselves as adult educators, in addition to their other functions.

The stretching of the territory of itself erodes the specificity of the term "adult education" and all that goes with it. Much that belongs to it, according to the concept and principles discussed in this article, is not seen either by sponsors, providers, or participants to do so. Or, while they recognize what is being discussed, they would describe in terms other than "adult" their perception of what they are engaged in, holding a more accurate description, for instance, to be "higher education," "workers' education," and "popular education." This may suggest that, while in certain contexts the adulthood of the learners is the chief influence on learning, in others their socioeconomic situation, the level and purpose of the learning experience play a more important role (see *University Adult Education; Worker Education and Labor Education*).

Within some of the activities in which they now engage, concepts and principles dear to adult educators cannot be reasonably accommodated. Indeed, the conflicting definitions of "adult"—recognition that there is no sharp cut-off between childhood, adolescence, and adulthood, strong doubts over whether adulthood constitutes a single, coherent stage of development, and failure to arrive at an agreed psychology of adult learning applicable to all situations—is raising doubts about the utility of the term "adult education" even as an umbrella designation for a largely unrelated collection of educational activities. It is not without significance that "continuing education" is either replacing or being used alongside "adult education." In France, the translation of the former, *formation continue*, is preferred to "adult education." In Germany *Weiterbildung* (continuing education) is used alongside *Erwachsenenbildung*, although usually of vocational adult education, as "continuing education" is in the United Kingdom (see *Lifelong and Continuing Education; Recurrent Education*).

13. Worldwide Expansion

With all its culturally specific characteristics, its complications and confusions, it is not surprising, however, that adult education has spread round the world. In the first place, those who evolved the concept believed that in its essentials it was universally applicable. Among them colonial powers, particularly the United Kingdom, had for years the power to impose it. The economic influence of the United States, the aid programs of the World Bank, UNESCO, and countries such as Canada and Germany have exerted great pressure. To a large extent, adult education promised to fill a gap that existed in the educational provision of most developing countries. These countries tended also to believe that imitation of advanced countries' education was essential to becoming as rich as they were, so adult education did not have to be imposed, it was embraced.

In the process, however, the Euro-American principles of adult education have had to be adapted to the realities of the economic, political, social, and cultural circumstances in which they are to be applied. In societies where the right to any education at all is not guaranteed, education cannot be offered to every adult. People may use their right not to study, but if they do have the chance of adult education, there is less choice of what to study than in the developed countries. The Western concept of adult education is pervaded by the principles of liberal education, with its free, critical approach to knowledge and its emphasis on individual development. Many developing societies perceive these ideas as luxuries they cannot afford. Their priorities are overwhelmingly social—to achieve basic education as a necessary instrument for establishing a national identity, for economic growth, health, and population education. In countries where only a minority may have obtained formal education the problems posed by the distinctiveness of adults as learners is of marginal importance. Experience with learners brought up in other cultures—those with oral traditions, for example—calls into question the validity of applying ideas about adult learning derived from European and North American practice in other societies.

Numerous efforts are being made to root education of all levels in local traditions that are more appropriate to the culture. In many developing societies attempts are being made, as in the *Sarvodaya Shramadana* Movement in Sri Lanka and *Khit-Pen* in Thailand (see Titmus 1989, pp. 547 and 549), to reassert their strongly religious base, Muslim, Hindu, Buddhist, for instance, against the Western concept which, in spite of its origins, is now an essentially secular one. However, many promising adult educators of the Third World are still being sent to study in the graduate schools of Europe and North America, so that Western ideas are perpetuated, irrespective of their relevance to the situation particular to their own countries.

14. Problems of Communication

There have always been interlingual problems of communication in the field of educational provision for adults, as has already been seen. The expansion of its purpose to cover a much larger territory and the diversity of forms, functions, and concepts has compounded these difficulties. "Recurrent education," "alternation education," "community education," "permanent education," "lifelong education" and its variants, are some of the terms which educators need to understand. There are others that do not include "education," but denote activities that involve a large element of "postinitial education," such as "community development" and "human resource development" (see *Community Education and Community Development; Lifelong and Continuing Education; Human Resource Development; Recurrent Education*). Worldwide expansion has compelled educators to understand expressions devised to denote initiatives undertaken in consideration of the special conditions of the Third World, such as "integrated rural development," or "formal education," "informal education," and "nonformal education" (see *Formal, Nonformal, and Informal Education*).

As the difficulties have increased, so has the recognition of the importance of communication. Whatever the variations, and even contradictions, there is growing awareness that many of the problems of postinitial and compensatory education are shared by societies across the world, and that international cooperation may offer the only way to overcome them. The need for accurate understanding of what all those concerned mean has been highlighted by the UNESCO World Conferences. A number of attempts have been made to overcome the terminological problem, notably by the UNESCO *Terminology of Adult Education* (Titmus et al. 1979), which, although it originally offered only English, French, and Spanish, has also inspired versions in other languages, for example, in Chinese, Japanese, and Slovenian. Unfortunately, the nature of adult education is such that terminologies risk being out-of-date before they are published. As the editors of the UNESCO *Terminology* wrote, "Adult education is a field of activity characterized by diversity and instability. New goals, new forms of action continually appear and modify the content covered by these . . . terms" (Titmus et al. 1979 p. 28). It is also true that adult education is more remarkable for its richness than its precision, either of thought or action. Not only is the sense of existing terms eroded, but new terms and concepts proliferate.

15. Issues and Trends

The principal theoretical issue of adult education ought, perhaps, to be whether a concept, evolved in restricted regions of the northern hemisphere over a long period of time, springing from circumstances peculiar to that area, covering only limited educational activities, and targeting only part of the population in its age range can accommodate expansion to cover any organized educational processes after or in compensation for initial education. Whether it can do this throughout the world, at a time and in circumstances so very different from those out of which it has evolved, without undergoing such fundamental modifications as to threaten its nature and its effectiveness as a guide to principle and practice has to be a question of prime importance. The increasing role of the state is imposing greater uniformity in organization, but, on the other hand, the growing specialization and fragmentation of purposes and target audiences calls into question whether a comprehensive concept can be devised which has any practical utility. Is its distinctiveness to be built around the concept of adulthood, given the uncertainties and anomalies of that term? If some other criteria are to be used, then which ones? All those so far suggested, "continuing education" and "postinitial education," for example, have their weaknesses, particularly when applied to societies where there is not much initial education to continue. The growth of lifelong education from theoretical to practical acceptance may resolve the problem, by making the present two-part division into initial and whatever continues or replaces initial education no longer either conceptually or practically of importance (see *Demand, Supply, and Finance of Adult Education*).

There are no problems as yet which have attracted great attention. There exists, however, considerable concern about the increasing concentration on vocational education at the expense of general education. Various practices, such as "human resource development," are being developed to restore the balance between them, mainly by attempting to integrate the development of the whole person into programs of vocational education. The chief difficulty in the way of their success is that the trend toward vocational emphasis appears to respond to the wishes of the majority of sponsors, especially the state, and of participants too. It is only seriously challenged by educators, some of whom fear the complete marginalization of liberal or general adult education and thereby the undermining of what are regarded as key principles of adult education.

References

Department of Education and Science 1991 *Education and Training for the 21st Century*. HMSO, London
European Bureau of Adult Education 1985 *A Survey of Adult Education Legislation*. European Bureau of Adult Education, Amersfoort
Grattan C H 1955 *In Quest of Knowledge: A Historical Perspective on Adult Education*. Association Press, New York
Grattan C H (ed.) 1959 *American Ideas about Adult Education 1710–1951*. Teachers College, Columbia University, New York
Kidd J R 1972 The multitude of the wise; the welfare of the world. 1972 World conference on adult education. *Convergence* 5(1):10–16
Knowles M S 1980 *The Modern Practice of Adult Education: From Pedagogy to Andragogy*. Association Press, New York
March L, Wilson I 1989 Adult education for profit. In: Titmus C J (ed.) *Lifelong Education for Adults: An International Handbook*. Pergamon Press, Oxford
Paterson R W K 1979 *Values, Education and the Adult*. Routledge and Kegan Paul, London
Pratt D D 1989 Andragogy and China: Cross-cultural considerations: In: Charters A, Cassara B (eds.) *Papers on Comparative Adult Education from Sessions Organized by the Committee for the Study and Research in Comparative Adult Education at the 7th World Congress on Comparative Education, Montreal, Canada, June 26–30*. Coalition of Adult Education Organizations, Washington, DC
Titmus C J 1976 Proposed theoretical model for the comparative study of national adult education systems in Europe. *Society and Leisure* 8(2)
Titmus C J, Buttedahl P, Ironside D, Lengrand P 1979 *Terminology of Adult Education*. UNESCO, Paris
Titmus C J 1980 Local decision making, private provision and the role of the state in adult education. In: Knoll J H (ed.) 1980 *Internationales Jahrbuch der Erwachsenenbildung*. Böhlan, Cologne
Titmus C J 1981 *Strategies for Adult Education: Practices in Western Europe*. Open University Press, Milton Keynes
Titmus C J (ed.) 1989 *Lifelong Education for Adults: An International Handbook*. Pergamon Press, Oxford
UNESCO 1976 *General Conference, Nairobi. 19th Session Report*. UNESCO, Paris

Further Reading

Bhola H S 1989 *World Trends and Issues in Adult Education*. UNESCO, Paris
Jensen G E, Liveright A A, Hallenbeck W (eds.) 1964 *Adult Education: Outlines of an Emerging Field of University Study*. Adult Education Association of the United States, Washington, DC
Kelly T 1970 *A History of Adult Education in Great Britain*, 2nd edn. Liverpool University Press, Liverpool
Lowe J 1982 *The Education of Adults: A World Perspective*, 2nd edn. UNESCO, Paris and Ontario Institute for Studies in Education, Toronto
Titmus C J 1991 Adult Education as Concept and Structure: An Agenda for Research. *International Journal of University Adult Education* 30(3):1–11
UNESCO 1985 Fourth International Conference on Adult Education. *Prospects* 15(3):427–42

Convergence between Education and Training

C. de Moura Castro and J. B. A. de Oliveira

Education and training have often been considered as polar extremes, the former being the development of the mind and the latter the mastery mainly of manual endeavors. However, good training can include serious conceptual development, and education becomes more meaningful when it is contextualized in practical activities.

There are definitional problems concerning education and training which may lead to a misunderstanding of these concepts and to misguided policies. There is a need for a clear understanding of the overlaps and contrasts between the two concepts. While this lack of definition has been detrimental to policy for a long time, changes in the workplace make this even more serious. Developments in labor organization are making the former distinctions between forms of training and education increasingly obsolete.

1. Theoretical and Territorial Disputes

There is a long-standing controversy in the literature concerning education and training. Quintilian claimed that oratory was more useful than philosophy, thereby stating the superiority of training over education, but for many centuries education was closer to philosophy than to applied endeavors. "One is educated to become an archaeologist, historian or lawyer whereas one is trained to take up the profession of nursing or of electronics engineering. . . . There is a military connotation of the word training" (Adamson-Macedo 1991).

Some educators use the word "training" in a derogatory way, as if to suggest that such learning is intellectually shallow, or that it goes with attempts to educate the poor. In contrast, some trainers refer to education as vacuous, imprecise, and rambling learning that is good only for wasting the time of students. As a result of this unfortunate and misplaced competition, there has been a tendency to confuse administrative mandates of learning institutions and agencies with the meanings of education and training. Thus, what is offered at academic schools is automatically defined as education and what is offered at training centers as training. The borderlines between education and training are thereby defined but at the cost of conceptual clarity and narrow-minded policies. This is an unfortunate situation in which vocabulary drives action in the wrong directions.

2. Overlap Between Education and Training

This section seeks to demonstrate that instead of competing, the two fields of occupational training and conceptual development help each other in the process of learning.

When dealing with students who have hitherto not received a large amount of schooling, vocational subjects can be used to motivate and to create a familiar environment. Good training may function as a conduit for the best possible education for students less ready for abstraction. By using practical situations as starting and end points, abstract concepts can be introduced and mastered by students who would otherwise be low achievers in academic schools. The environment created by good vocational schools can give students a sense of involvement in a concrete job. This can in turn generate a degree of motivation and sense of self-efficacy conducive to the mastery of abstract concepts that would fail to be communicated to students taught at academic schools. Such schools have difficulties in creating environments that motivate low-achieving students.

Good vocational training makes use of the context of the practical subjects to teach mathematics, writing, reading, and science. Students are asked to read the instructions of what they are doing and write down the procedures they will execute. Concrete workshop situations are conceived, for instance, to make students convert inches to centimeters, Fahrenheit to Celsius, and so on. Consequently, proportion will be learned as a by-product of solving workshop problems and mathematics is incorporated into the practicalities of shop work (de Moura Castro 1988). Good training institutions have different versions of mathematics—one for machinists, another for electricians, and so on.

As research in the psychology of learning suggests, the mastery of subjects increases when the contexts in which phenomena are examined become fully familiar to the students (Raizen 1991). Experiments have shown that a physical principle is better understood when the students are given the broad context in which it applies. For instance, it has been shown that students acquired a better grasp of the concept of density when they were shown a clip from the film "Raiders of The Lost Ark" in which the hero, Indiana Jones, has to replace the golden skull sitting on a platform by his bag filled with rocks of the same weight. Students were asked to estimate the weight of the golden skull by measuring the approximate volume of a human skull and multiplying it by the relative density of gold (Vanderbilt Group 1991). Such concrete problems based on concrete needs arising in the practical tasks to be performed are presented in the workshop.

However, training merely offers the possibility to tap this potential; there is nothing automatic about it. Training can fail to use these opportunities. Training by itself is bad training or incapable of going beyond the transmission of a low degree of dexterity. How to put out a fire or unblock a pipe is useful knowledge in its own right and needs to be taught, but it is different from longer training programs which contain more conceptual and theoretical structures (de Moura Castro 1988).

The "basic skills" movement consists of improving the knowledge of the fundamental literacy and numeracy skills of workers who are learning a trade or have already mastered the more practical and manual aspects of their occupations. However, the essence of successful strategies is to use the same workplace operations as a scaffold on which to build the conceptual or cognitive skills that are missing. The worker learns how to read by reading the manual that has to be read to perform the job correctly.

Vocational contents can be an ideal context in which to plant cognitive development of a higher order. Thinking skills and good reading and writing habits can be developed while doing practical tasks that lead to marketable skills. Similarly, academic education may resort to practical endeavors in order to carry the more general message. Laboratory classes try to do this and the "Indiana Jones" example illustrates another deliberate attempt to bring context to learning. Arguably, theory is generalization and conceptualization about real world observations. Formulas written on the blackboard merely display a packaged and sanitized version of the intense intellectual effort that was required to arrive at them. The idea of having the students "rediscover" physical principles is analogous.

3. Differences Between Education and Training

When examining how education and training are defined, the assumption is that the borderline may be arbitrary and that in many cases it does not make much sense. For example, the usual distinction is based on the institution that is offering the instruction. If in the course of training one learns how to read, is it training or education? Is "basic skills" education or training? Some claim it must be training since it is often attached to ministries of labor and not education. When students improve their writing skills by preparing reports on what they did in the workshop or filling work sheets, is that education or training? If one learns French in school it is supposed to be education; when an organization teaches French to its officers who are going abroad is it then training? What if the teacher is the same and so is the book? When German apprentices learn the German language in the day they spend in the training center, this is supposedly training. When their *Realschule* colleagues take the same course, it is said to be education. This entry tries to demonstrate that in most cases this distinction is too sharp.

The explanation is sometimes given that in training, the instructor starts with the intention of offering useful skills and in education, the teacher is more concerned with the "fundamentals." Perhaps the students do not even appreciate what the original intentions were, or perhaps they do not concern themselves with the division between education and training. Students learn what is taught, or something else, not necessarily what authorities write in the syllabus. When vocational "learning" institutions are moved by law from a ministry of labor to a ministry of education, does training technically become education? When studying the motion of parts within a motor it is training. But when the motion of bodies in the universe is taught, it is education.

There are modes of education that are of little use in the labor market (e.g., Latin, music, history), but the converse is not true. It is difficult to imagine a good training program that is not also good education, in the sense that considerable conceptual and symbolic learning is also taking place. However, bad training inevitably abounds, and this example merely illustrates the fact that reputable training institutions are adept at offering training that has a very high educational content.

4. New Technologies and the Distinction Between Education and Training

This reasoning implies that the differences between education and training have always been exaggerated and that most reputable training programs are education as much as training. Recent developments in technology and work organization seem to be blurring even further the distinction between education and training (Carnevale et al. 1990, Elan 1989, Eliasson 1988). In industrialized countries a significant share of manufacturing activities has changed considerably and incorporates new technologies, particularly those based on microprocessors and the variety of automation techniques that result from them. This is also the case in some successful industrializing countries. However, manufacturing in most developing countries has moved at a much slower pace, though in limited but critical areas, technologies that also incorporate different forms of automation are chosen.

New production technologies seem to require flatter organizational structures, broader occupational definitions for workers, and greater responsibilities for those at a lower level of the hierarchy. In practice, it requires more reading, writing, applied mathematics, and science (de Moura Castro and Oliveira 1991). In the past, all these cognitive skills were, at best, a means to master these trades (e.g., one needs to know how to read to take the machinist course because some of the instruction is written in books or handouts), but are presently becoming part and parcel of the occupational profile. For example, if reading is directly useful for the performance of the core tasks of the occupation, can it then be said that reading and mathematics are vocational subjects? Centuries ago reading and writing were vocational subjects, as people learned them in order to become writers of letters or public documents. After the spread of literacy, reading became part of general culture, but something that people with simple occupations rarely needed in their jobs. However, new technologies and the contemporary forms of work organizations are classifying reading once again as a vocational skill in simple occupations. Even employees on the shop floor of modern organizations have to read and write quite often (US Department of Labor 1990).

At more sophisticated levels, workers need a much deeper and broader mastery of the contents of conventional education. They need to evaluate concrete problems and make decisions. In order to do that, an understanding of the functioning of the machines is essential. In that respect, the simplest electric or electronic circuitry requires a vast amount of skills that are eminently school "theory." An understanding of Ohm's Law is required to calculate how many amps a fuse should have, and this elementary electronic principle requires an understanding of electricity, voltage, resistance, and so on. The increasing complexity of machines mean, that the idea of learning everything about their functioning and maintenance cannot be accomplished merely by their disassembly and learning the part names. Memory and manipulative abilities are still required but since the machine is constantly increasing in complexity, the underlying theoretical principles of its operation need additional studies of a more theoretical nature.

5. The Potential and Limitations of Learning by Doing

Abstract concepts detached from everyday life are less conducive to learning. Celestial mechanics is less motivating to adolescents than auto mechanics. This simple and true principle has been often used to justify hands-on activities in the learning process. This seems to remain a sound pedagogical principle. If the ultimate goal is preparation for the labor market, the school should look and operate like a factory as far as possible. In other words, this ideal vocational school would reproduce factory conditions to the highest possible degree. Indeed, many schools go to great lengths to operate like a factory.

It is indeed true that people learn in factories: this is how most workers acquired their skills throughout the Industrial Revolution. In the workplace people learn about the organizational culture of factories, values, discipline, and dealing with authority. The advantages of learning by doing are accompanied by limits and shortcomings (de Moura Castro and de Andrade 1990). It is a mistake to reintroduce these shortcomings into schools just to make school activities closer to factory activities. Students clocking in and out may add an

extra touch of realism to training, but when it comes to hands-on activities, the limitations of factory-based learning become obvious.

The core of the shortcomings of factory routines in the learning place is that they are optimized for production and not for learning. The ideal factory machine is one that never breaks, never needs serious overhauls, and works continuously at the same optimal pace. A machine that never breaks, in a factory that seldom changes products and that operates without troubles or the requirement of delicate adjustments, teaches very little, however. The ideal "learning machine" would drive the factory bankrupt, requiring frequent adjustments, changing products all the time, being frequently upgraded and modified, and challenging the troubleshooters during down time. The learning that takes place during routine operations can be done quickly in most cases and, from then on, the repetition adds little to the mastery of the occupation. By contrast to teaching workshops or labs, the factory machines are not built to be understood by beginners but rather to maximize production and minimize breakdowns.

The above arguments constitute the most serious critique that can be levied against the training-cum-production schemes that are so common in socialist and former socialist countries. Under the training-cum-production model, schools operated miniature factories inside their walls, selling conventional products in the market. Students were put to work on the production lines, just like regular workers in a real factory. There are great merits to these schemes that cannot be examined here. They create the atmosphere of factories with the inherent discipline and routines of managing production. However, from the strict point of view of learning, they are usually as poor as a factory line of production. There is no experimentation and the logic is that of producing more. Furthermore, in a school that depends on the revenues of the sale of goods and services, the incentives to experiment with different products and different production processes are severely reduced.

In summary, abstract subjects that are removed from the everyday life of students offer arid ground for learning. Latin declensions, French irregular verbs, underground geological layers, the successions of kings of France, and the capitals of African states are not the subjects that fascinate the average student. Hence, they are not the ideal place to graft the broad basic skills that constitute an education for a modern society. Vocational schools can avoid these motivational difficulties by bringing in the world of the factory, with its practicalities and the inherent motivation of learning some skills that have immediate market value. Nevertheless, not everything that happens in the factory is ideal for the process of learning. In particular, the factory routines teach mostly how to deal with repetitive activities. This is a worthy objective of short training courses and for the preparation of workers who lack the prerequisites for further development. This may be justified in many cases but it is not what is considered the optimal environment for broad learning.

6. Implications for Policy

The implications of this lack of definition between education and training need further exploration. It is doubtful whether the usual way of distinguishing the two is worth retaining. Societies need new ways of looking at the differences between what takes place in this continuum of institutions that span the range of knowledge from the most abstract to the most concrete. Practical knowledge and abstract concepts get intertwined in multiple ways.

A basic principle in this field is that the presence of training contents that may be applicable in the workplace does not vary inversely with the presence of fundamental concepts and abstraction. Both poetry and solid-state physics are rich in abstraction; the former has little direct applicability at the work place while the latter has ample utilization. Basket weaving has hardly any abstraction or conceptualization and finds little demand in modern societies. Cutting hair offers little in abstract thinking but there are ample economic applications for this skill.

It is necessary to stress that theory and practice are not the extremes of the same continuum but are independent concepts that admit all possible combinations of highs and lows as exemplified above. Fortunately, one does not have to forego learning the practicalities of life and work to have the high theoretical and conceptual content that educates and sharpens the mind. Both vocational training and general education involve theory and practice. The main hypothesis of this entry is that the occupational training that fetches a good market is comparable with any other environment in educating the mind in the fundamental concepts that are usually found in good education.

Training should not be considered poor in theory and conceptualization. Education should not be considered helplessly impractical; it may or may not be directly applicable. There are no good reasons to be overconcerned with the differences between education and training. Instead learning opportunities should be offered that have both.

See also: Technical and Vocational Education and Training; Recurrent Education; Government Role in Adult Education and Training; Technological Change and Education; Statistics of Employee Training

References

Adamson-Macedo C 1991 Training for new technology. Background paper prepared for the Tripartite European Meeting on the Impact of Technological Change on Work and Training, Geneva

Carnevale A, Gainer L, Meltzer A 1990 *Workplace Basics: The Essential Skills Employers Want*. Jossey Bass, San Francisco, California

Cognition and Technology Group at Vanderbilt 1990 Anchored instruction and its relationship to situated cognition. *Educ. Researcher* 19(6): 2–10

de Moura Castro C 1988 The right courses for the wrong jobs? Or vice versa? In: Haq K, Kirdar U (eds.) 1988 *Managing Human Development*. North South Round Table, Islamabad

de Moura Castro C, de Andrade A C 1990 Supply and demand mismatches in training: Can anything be done? *Int. Lab. Rev.* 129(3): 349–69

de Moura Castro C, Oliveira J B A 1991 Education for all and the roles of training. Regional UNESCO Conference on Educational For All, Cairo

Elan M 1989 *A Critical Introduction to the Post-Fordist Debate: Technology, Markets and Institutions*. Working Paper No. 45, Linkoping University, Department of Technology and Social Change, Linkoping

Eliasson G 1988 *The Knowledge Base of an Industrial Economy*. Industrial Institute for Economic and Social Research, Stockholm

Raizen S 1991 Learning and work: The research base. Paper presented at the United States/OECD Seminar on Linkages in Vocational-Technical Education and Training: Challenges, Responses, Actors. Phoenix, Arizona

United States Department of Labor 1990 *The Bottom Line: Basic Skills in the Workplace*. Washington, DC

Further Reading

Berryman S, Bailey T 1992 *The Double Helix of Education and the Economy*. Institute on Education and the Economy, New York

Campinos-Dubernet M 1991 Training and automation in production activities: A logic of profiles or of levels? Paper presented at the Switzerland/OECD Seminar on Technological Innovation and Economic Change: Pedagogical and Organizational Implications for Vocational and Technical Education and Training, Sainte-Croix

Eliasson G 1995 *The Market for Learning and Competence*. OECD, Paris

Dougherty C 1990 Education and skill development: Planning issues. Paper presented at the Asian Development Bank/World Bank Regional Seminar on Technical and Vocational Education and Training, Bangkok

ILO 1991 The impact of technological change on work and training. Paper prepared for the Tripartite European Meeting on the Impact of Technological Change on Work and Training, Geneva

ILO 1992 *Report of the Tripartite European Meeting on the Impact of Technological Change on Work and Training*. ILO, Geneva

Kaplinsky M 1988 Restructuring the capitalist labour process: Some lessons from the car industry. *Cambridge Journal of Economics* 12(4): 451–70

Oliveira J B A 1994 *The Business of Learning*. ILO, Geneva

Paracone C, Uberto F 1988 *Le Nuove Frontiere della Produttività: La Flessibilità Totale*. Editore SIPI, Rome

Scribner S, Sachs P 1991 *Knowledge Acquisition at Work*.

Teachers College, Columbia University, New York

Simon H 1980 Problem solving and education. In: Tuma D T, Reif F (eds.) 1980 *Problem Solving and Education: Issues in Teaching and Research.* Lawrence Erlbaum Associates, Hillsdale, New Jersey

United States Department of Labor 1991 *What Work Re-quires of School—A SCANS Report for America 2000.* Washington, DC

World Bank 1991 *Vocational and Technical Education and Training.* Washington, DC

Zuboff S 1988 *The Age of the Smart Machine. The Future of Work and Power.* Heinemann, Oxford

Formal, Nonformal, and Informal Education

N. J. Colletta

This entry clarifies the terms and definition of formal, informal, and nonformal education. It then proceeds to review the historical rise of nonformal education following the world educational crisis highlighted by Philip Coombs in 1968. The entry places nonformal education within the broader context of human resource development and meeting basic needs, examining the many issues from economic, political, and sociocultural perspectives. It concludes with an examination of the steps necessary to plan nonformal education as well as a research agenda.

1. The Rise of Nonformal Education

Since the early 1970s the term "nonformal education" has not only gained popular currency, but accumulated a relatively thick mantle of general bibliographies, case studies, and readers, as well as a number of more specific writings on alternative forms of educational delivery, on the development of appropriate materials and the design of training programs, on planning and coordination, and on political, economic, and sociocultural implications.

Nonformal education is not an entirely new concept. Variants of this approach have appeared before under such terms as "out-of-school education," the "shadow school system," the "educational complex," "learning networks," and "non-conventional" education. In most instances these formulations have reflected concern at the inability of a school-based educational system to meet adequately the diverse learning needs of a society in change. Nonformal education emerged as a result of the realization that universal compulsory schooling, with its high costs and labor intensive characteristics, is not necessarily the most appropriate technology for meeting the diverse learning needs of a developing society. Nonformal education theory questions the adequacy of learning that is rigidly organized within limited time periods and circumscribed space, the dogmatism of entrenched subject matter, the structured inequality inherent in social mobility patterns that neglect the needs of the poor, the illiterate, and the unemployed, and the alienation and wastage of youth reflected in high dropout rates (Colletta and Radcliff 1980).

2. Concepts and Definitions

After Philip Coombs coined the term "nonformal education" in his incisive delineation of an impending world educational crisis (Coombs 1968), a vast amount of time, energy, and resources was expended simply in trying to define the term. Nonformal education was described by some as all systematic communication of skill, knowledge, and attitude provided outside the limits of the formal school, or as all education outside the conventional "academic" stream. Others attempted to define it more positively by specific context. Amid this barrage of definition (generally by negation), of distinctions between education, schooling, and training, and admitting the sociological contradiction of a "non-systemized system," there did emerge a useful distinction between three basic modes of transmission: "formal," "nonformal," and "informal."

By "formal education" is meant the deliberated and systematic transmission of knowledge, skills, and attitudes (with the stress on knowledge) within an explicit, defined, and structured format for space, time, and material, with set qualifications for teacher and learner, such as is typified in the technology of schooling. "Informal education" is the incidental transmission of attitudes, knowledge, and skills (with the stress on attitudes) with highly diverse and culturally relative patterns for the organization of time, space, and material, and also for personal roles and relationships, such as are implicit in varying configurations of the family, household, and community. "Nonformal education" is like formal education in the deliberate and systematic transmission of knowledge, attitudes, and skills, but here the stress is on skills. In terms of process it avoids the technology of formal schooling, permitting a more diverse and flexible deployment of space, time, and material, and accepting a relaxation of personal qualifications, in response to

Table 1
Basic nonformal education transmission model

Needs Assessment and Evaluation		
Development agent (Learning content)	(Delivery System 1) (Delivery System 2) (Learning need/demand	Client/Beneficiary Population (Delivery System 3)

Individual Delivery System Components: 1. Development content, 2. Materials design, 3 Methodology

the structure of the workplace. Thus the subsidiary distinguishing definitions of these three modes of educational transmission pertain to four areas: the degree of deliberation; the varied deployment of structural elements of space, time, material, and people; the relative emphasis on the functional principles of knowledge, skill, and attitude generation; and the degree to which formal certification is given.

This search for defining characteristics revealed that nonformal education was a process with which social anthropologists and educational psychologists have been working for decades. Such notions as "cultural transmission," "indigenous education," "human ecology," "enculturation," and "learning theory" took on renewed meaning. Unfortunately, an integrated and multidisciplinary effort at clarification have been hampered by rigid lines of academic separation, fortified by specialized jargon. Only since the mid-1980s have the concepts of socialization, conditioning, communication, enculturation, and learning begun to fuse into an integrated concept of nonformal education.

3. Transmission

One prominent notion that nonformal education draws from earlier social science transmission theory is the view that the process of interchange between teacher and student is dynamic, real, experience-based, and oriented to *meeting basic human needs* in a specific sociocultural context. In effect, the transmission is immediate, and is the critical link between man and the environment in the struggle for survival. Learning and productivity become one, as the waste of scarce natural resources or human energies in the storing of competencies as abstract symbols for unguaranteed use at some later time is minimized. Literacy and numeracy, in the Western sense of these terms, are not prerequisites for participation, nor are they equated or confused with the concept of intelligence. The transmission is highly task oriented, and competence is measured by functional ability to meet basic needs for survival, rather than certification of abstracted achievement. Moreover, the space and time dimensions of the process are relatively open-ended (Coombs et al. 1973) (see *Literacy; Literacy and Numeracy Models*).

Learning or transmission adjusts itself to accord with the changing demands of the life-cycle and the environment. Each transaction can be viewed as a complete unit, not necessarily as a step toward a second- or third-level transaction. Learning needs (as survival skills) are met wherever and whenever they arise, by the most immediately appropriate methods. The human dynamics of this process are multidirectional. Peer learning plays as significant a role as intergenerational transmission. Frequently work, learning, and play blend into the same activity. Lines of transmission often run along natural networks of exchange, distribution, and consumption.

Thus, the contemporary characterization of education in such terms as modular instruction, open education, competency-based education, field-centered learning, lifelong education, and total learning systems, and the analytical breakdown of nonformal education in terms of structure, content, methods, sponsorship, and so on have a theoretical basis in the history of humanity's attempts to come to terms with its environment to acquire basic knowledge and skills to maximize survival.

4. Human Resource Development Model

Placing nonformal education within the broader parameters of human resource development, we can now examine the process by which a given development agent seeks to transmit knowledge, skill, or attitude to a given client population through a delivery system (see Table 1). Such a system would consist of the subcomponents of content, materials design, and methodology (see *Human Resource Development*). Methodology, in turn, comprises the organized deployment of time, space, materials, and people. "Delivery system" in this case is synonymous with the concept of "technology," and it is particularly productive if the relation is made in terms of appropriate technology. Again, the feedback (assessment and evaluation) channel can include predelivery, concurrent, or postdelivery elements, or a mixture of these.

In application, the crucial factor in the overall transmission process is the effective use of feedback between the development agent and the client population. It is through this feedback linkage that the technology of the delivery system can be finely tuned and appropriated to the development content and strategy which is selected. Malcolm Knowles (1970) makes a useful distinction between possible development strategies in his definition of pedagogical as contrasted with androgogical approaches to human resource development, and Brembeck and Grandstaff (1973) have developed a similar distinction in their discussion of imposed as compared with emergent designs for nonformal education. In a *pedagogical* strategy the teaching–learning process is mechanistic, with the subject as a passive or, at best, reactive recipient; content is transmitted from source to receiver, with no prior recognition of client needs. *Androgogical* strategy views the object as developing and active and the process as organic; the model emphasizes consciousness-awakening knowledge acquired by experience, dialogue, and dynamic interaction between agent and client. Thus feedback from the target population to the development agent is a necessary first step and part of the continuing development process. Whereas a pedagogical strategy is learner and teacher and content centered, an androgogical strategy is process oriented (see *Andragogy*).

5. The Economics and Political Dimensions of Nonformal Education

Political motivations blend into economic concerns as the central issue becomes how to use learning networks to link people's needs to systems of production and consumption in the most efficient and effective manner. The problem is to bridge the gap between training and employment, learning and productivity, so that wastage of human energies and natural resources is minimized while the equitable distribution of goods and services is maximized. In short, the challenge becomes one of how to make capital intensive educational activities more socially productive; how to match human resource development with a changing opportunity structure, related to market demands, through an efficient and effective transmission network. This has been a fundamental concern of development organizations since they have recognized the need to absorb trained persons into a fluctuating labor market in a harmonious fashion, thus providing technical skills to support a growing economy, while at the same time providing stability through the generation of employment opportunities.

While it is true that the universal extension of formal education is still a remote aspiration, it is also valid that school-based education has extended far beyond the present opportunity to use it in most countries. There is little need to call further attention to Foster's (1965) point that emphasizing vocational schooling is a shortsighted solution. Clearly learning has to move as close as possible to the point of utilization and productivity. Callaway's (1964) stress on apprenticeship is one firm step in this direction. Owens and Shaw's (1972) suggestion of a "knowledge–communication–production-system" emphasizing horizontal rather than vertical relationships as central to reconsidering development is another step in meeting the problem. Further lessons can be gained from examination of the experience of Tanzania, Cuba, and China in the modification of schools into production units and of farms into education units, or reviewing the experience of the Botswana Youth Brigade movement which combined training and productivity in and out of school settings (Paulston 1974, Hoppers 1985, Gustafsson 1987). Governments could consider the subsidization of educational components in the private sector as one strategy for moving learning closer to the workplace. Here the division of nonformal education financing into public and private sectors becomes an additional issue. In terms of cost-effective analysis, there is much work still to be done on such experimental linkages between learning and productive activities. An emergent area for nonformal education applications is in the micro enterprise or informal sector of many rapidly urbanizing Third World countries. Here informal apprenticeship arrangements are becoming fertile cost effective means for human capital formation.

Turning to a discussion of cost-effectiveness as compared with cost-efficiency the overlap between the politics and the economics of nonformal education becomes increasingly evident. Cost-effectiveness is not a matter of dollars and cents, a quantitative assessment of the human values expressed in ideological tenets and political structures. It is not sufficient to be concerned only with the image of an affluent society, but the needs of a human society must be recognized as well. What is at issue goes beyond the traditional emphasis on economic growth to its concomitant political relationship with equity and distribution. One cannot separate the economic issues of production and the political issues of allocation from the intervening forces of educational transmission. However, unfortunate though it may be, the paucity of cost-effectiveness analysis of nonformal education remains a major challenge for researchers and evaluators.

One further question is whether or not nonformal education is a new answer to the problem of providing adequate employment for the presently schooled unemployed, thus displacing the earlier manifest objective of providing training and employment opportunities for the nonschooled. Thus formal and nonformal educational strategies might collude to form a huge welfare bureaucracy for the more effective placement of the politically volatile schooled but unemployed elites, while perpetuating a convenient system of mass exploitation, with increasing inefficiency and ineffectiveness. To decipher the political economy of nonformal education, transmission and opportunity structures must be examined as a symbiotic whole in the process of development.

6. *The Sociocultural Dimensions of Nonformal Education*

Concentration on problems of transmission in relation to political and economic structures cannot exclude consideration of, and respect for, the existing cultural environment. Recent studies have paid increasing attention to the contribution of traditional values to the development process (see, e.g., Carron and Carr-Hill 1991). The crux of the culture-development dilemma is to discover the most efficient means of introducing skills, knowledge, and attitudes within existing cultural patterns, institutions, values, and human resources so that economic development is optimized and sociocultural change occurs in a meaningful, harmonious fashion. The entire theme of "institution building" in development theory often implicitly assumes that there are no viable institutions existing within the client population. This attitude ignores reality, is ethnocentric and discriminatory, and thus in consequence limits impact. Changing opportunities can most readily be grasped when they present themselves within the context of being additive rather than substitutional, for then it is possible to effect a smoother transition to a new cultural world view.

Human resource development cannot, therefore, expect success founded upon the false premise that external forces operate in a vacuum. It should not assume that natural networks of leadership, organization, and transmission are lacking, nor that the projected "needs" for change imposed by external agents will have greater legitimacy and acceptance in the community than the logic of real needs as established by traditional indigenous processes. Peasants are often more rational than most development agents are capable of seeing or willing to admit, for their perceptions are based on the communal accumulation of experience. Development agents can greatly improve their relationship with client communities, and thus enhance their contribution, by taking better account of formal and informal processes of indigenous decision-making, and by recognizing the validity of indigenous sanctioning and transmission channels as practical education networks for novel messages. This requires understanding and respect for indigenous values, reward systems, learning styles, mental processes, human interaction patterns, and other culturally specific variables, as both constraints on and inputs to a human resource development program. The fact that development agents and local communities may be operating under different definitions of reality rooted in variant world views, must be recognized and worked within the process of maintaining cultural continuity in the face of adaptive change. Indeed, this is the point which holds the greatest potential from a development perspective. Between formal schooling (the agent usually of a wider universe of knowledge but often transmitted as an alien imposition), and informal education as the bearer of cultural continuity and community values, nonformal education can play a harmonizing role. The application of this principle could possibly be one of the greatest strengths, and challenges, of the nonformal education movement.

7. *Planning Nonformal Education: From Theory, through Art, to Practice*

Given the preceding political, economic, and cultural factors as both constraining and enabling forces, how should the planning of nonformal education proceed? Although elaborate multivariate research designs and computer simulation models have given educational planning an aura of scientific legitimacy, the basis of planning remains the "art" of asking the right questions. In order for planning to be consistent with the overriding character approach to human resource development, it must be a holistic attempt to unite the interrelated areas of learning needs, educational objectives, learning environments (physical and cultural), transmission modalities, and opportunity structures. It must seek the fine balance between growth and equity, quantity and quality, content and process, management and participation, stability and change. It cannot operate in a cultural or material vacuum, but must be sensitive, problem and learner centered, and relevant. In the end, it must be as diverse and flexible as the vast heterogeneity of physical and cultural environments it chooses to work in, and the human needs which it seeks to serve.

Several key steps have been suggested in a contextually designed nonformal education planning process:

(a) a careful diagnosis of a given ecological setting noting existing human and natural resources as both potential constraints and inputs into a successful intervention strategy;

(b) the identification of specific problems in the context of learning needs, learning audience, and learning objectives;

(c) the mapping of all existing and alternative transmission modalities both within and without the given context as possible intervention strategies or parts thereof;

(d) the matching and pilot testing of various transmission modalities with specific learning needs as experimental intervention strategies for solving problems within particular contexts;

(e) the continuous monitoring, evaluating, and adapting of intervention strategies in line with clearly stated performance objectives;

(f) the diffusion of the most successful strategies

within the same ecological setting or to other similar settings;

(g) the linking of any one localized strategy to larger strategies and objectives at the regional and national levels (going to scale).

8. Nonformal Education: Research Agenda

This entry began with an investigation into the maze of formal, informal, and nonformal education with a look at the origin, its definition, and character, seeking to construct a tentative model of transmission in the broader framework of human resource development. This was followed by a discussion of some of the key operational issues in nonformal education, and finally concluded with a planning approach in hand. The pieces of the map are like propositions in a general theory. The ability to exit from the maze depends upon the ability to integrate each piece into the total map. The task is to test these pieces as propositions of a broader theory of learning. What might some of these propositions be?

(a) Formal, informal, and nonformal education are structurally unique; the components of each may be distinguished in terms of content, medium, and methodology. While they share the critical structural elements of space, time, material, and people, they are uniquely differentiated by their techniques (methodology) for organizing these elements.

(b) The unique structural arrangements in a given methodology integrate the components of content and medium into the "gestalt" of a distinctive mode of transmission. It is this gestalt that enables a particular mode to perform certain educational functions better than others.

(c) Formal transmission is more effective when the educational function is cognitive, abstract, and valuative . . . as best represented in the technology of schooling.

Informal transmission is more effective when the educational function is affective, related to values and beliefs . . . as best illustrated in the sociocultural techniques of family, peer, group, and community.

Nonformal transmission is more effective when the educational function is psychomotor, concrete, and skill oriented . . . as best exemplified in the technologies of the workplace.

(d) Formal transmission is best at storing knowledge in the form of thought; informal transmission is best at storing emotion in the form of sentiment; and nonformal is useful in welding thought and sentiment into useful action (praxis).

Nonformal methods are best at meeting real needs arising from concrete objectives of physical survival, whereas formal and informal methods are better equipped to attend to felt needs and abstract goals in relation to sociopsychological adaptation.

(e) Although different in structure and priority of educational function, the formal, informal, and nonformal modes are not found in isolation or serving only a single educational function. If transmission is recognized as a life process, then formal, informal, and nonformal may wave in and out of one another, taking priority according to changing individual and social developmental strategies of the life-cycle: informal—childhood, family; formal—adolescence, school; nonformal—adulthood, work. Thus formal, informal, and nonformal education interface in such a way that each can support the other.

(f) All three educational modalities are capable of being exploited for political purposes both in terms of resource allocation and in terms of political socialization. All three can narrow or broaden the gap between class, ethnic, and geographical divisions, as a function of the manipulation of differential payoff attached to each. Nonformal education, however, has the potential of greater cost-efficiency, due to its ability to move the cost along with the transmission process closer to the point of use and productivity. This ability can be strategically linked to progressive egalitarianism and integration.

See also: Human Resource Development; Popular Education and Conscientization; Anthropological Study of Literacy and Numeracy; Economics of Nonformal Education; Adult Literacy in the Third World; Development Through Nonformal Education; Statistics of Employee Training

References

Brembeck C S, Grandstaff M 1973 *Non-Formal Education as an Alternative to Schooling.* Program of Studies in Non-Formal Education. Discussion Papers No. 4. Institute for International Studies in Education, Michigan State University, East Lansing, Michigan

Callaway A 1964 Nigeria's indigenous education: The apprentice system. *Journal of African Studies* 17: 62–69

Carron G, Carr-Hill R A 1991 *Non-formal education: Information and Planning Issues.* Research Report No. 90. International Institute for Educational Planning, UNESCO, Paris

Coletta N J, Radcliff D 1980 Non-formal education: An educological approach. *Canadian and International Education* 9(2): 1–27

Coombs P H 1968 *The World Educational Crisis: A Systems Analysis.* Oxford University Press, New York

Coombs P H, Prosser R C, Ahmed M 1973 *New Paths to Learning for Rural Children and Youth: Non-formal*

Education for Rural Development. International Council for Educational Development (ICED), Essex, Connecticut

Foster P 1965 The vocational school fallacy in development planning. In: Anderson C A, Bowman M J (eds.) 1965 *Education and Economic Development*. Aldine, Chicago, Illinois

Gustafsson I 1987 *Schools and the Transformation of Work: A Comparative Study of Four Productive Work Programmes in Southern Africa*. Studies in Comparative and International Education No. 10. Institute of International Education, University of Stockholm, Stockholm

Hoppers W 1985 *From School to Work: Youth, Nonformal Training and Employment in Lusaka*. Center for the Study of Education in Developing Countries (CESO), The Hague

Knowles M S 1970 *The Modern Practice of Adult Education: Andragogy versus Pedagogy*. Association Press, New York

Owens E, Shaw R 1972 *Development Reconsidered: Bridging the Gap between Government and People*. Lexington Books, Lexington, Massachusetts

Paulston R G 1974 Cuban rural education: A strategy for revolutionary development. In: Foster P J, Sheffield J R (eds.) 1974 *The World Yearbook of Education 1974: Education and Rural Development*. Evans, London

Further Reading

Ahmed M 1975 *The Economics of Nonformal Education: Resources, Costs, and Benefits*. Praeger, New York

Bhola H S 1989 *World Trends and Issues in Adult Education*. UNESCO, Paris

Bock J C, Papagiannis G J 1976 *The Demystification of Nonformal Education*. Center for International Education, Amherst, Massachusetts

Coombs P H 1985 Suggestions for a realistic adult education policy. *Prospects* 15(1): 27–38

Coombs P H, Ahmed M 1974 *Attacking Rural Poverty: How Non-formal Education can Help*. Johns Hopkins University Press, Baltimore, Maryland

Colletta N J 1971 *Bibliographies in Non-formal Education*, 3 vols. Institute for International Studies in Education, Michigan State University, East Lansing, Michigan

Colletta N J, Todd T A 1982 The limits of nonformal education and village development: Lessons from the Sarvodaya Shramadana movement. In: Bock J C, Papagiannis G J (eds.) 1982 *Nonformal Education and National Development*. Praeger, New York

Evans D R 1981 *The Planning of Non-formal Education*. Fundamentals of Educational Planning No. 30. International Institute for Educational Planning, UNESCO, Paris

Hamadache A 1991 Non-formal education. A definition of the concept and some examples. *Prospects* 21(1): 111–24

La Belle T J 1976 *Non-formal Education and Social Change in Latin America*. Latin American Studies, Vol. 35. UCLA Latin American Center, University of California, Los Angeles, California

La Belle T J 1981 An introduction to the non-formal education of children and youth. *Comp. Educ. Rev.* 25: 313–29

La Belle T J 1982 Formal, non-formal and informal education: A holistic perspective on lifelong learning. *Int. Rev. Educ.* 28(2): 159–75

World Conference on Education for All 1990 *Meeting Basic Learning Needs: A Vision for the 1990s* (Background document). World Bank, Washington, DC

Lifelong and Continuing Education

P. J. Sutton

The concept of "lifelong learning" implies more than the observation that learning takes place accidentally and incidentally throughout life, and that it is not confined to childhood and adolescence, or to educational institutions. The term achieved general currency in the 1970s, and signifies the organizational and didactic structures and strategies which will permit learning to take place from infancy throughout adulthood. Lifelong learning, as a policy concept and a strategy for the development of industrialized countries undergoing rapid structural adjustment, has made a strong comeback in the mid-1990s, partly as a consequence of policy development in the OECD (see *Lifelong Learning*).

"Continuing education," a concept in use over a longer period, refers properly to that part of education which takes place after the conclusion of initial or basic (elementary) education. The term is more particularly applied to courses other than full-time further or higher education, and it need not be certificated; hence, part-time further education, much adult education, and vocational and recurrent professional training are all commonly provided for under the label of "continuing education." Increasing demands for such courses have been made since the 1970s in the light of labor-market changes, technological innovations, and the general perception that initial education can no longer equip young adults for all life's requirements.

While numerous, frequently disconnected, continuing education courses have been devised to meet the vocational and leisure (nonvocational) needs of younger and older adults, and their needs in basic literacy, lifelong education remains an overarching concept with many adherents. An attempt is made here to address the considerable overlap and confusion between terms. In doing so, use is made of entries on lifelong education in the first edition of the *Encyclopedia* (Cropley 1985a, 1985b, Gelpi 1985b, Lengrand 1985).

1. Definitions of Related Terms

Jourdan (1981 p. 16) attempts to clarify some terminological distinctions:

> The envisaged function of "permanent education" is that of refreshing, keeping pace and keeping abreast, so that the individual is and remains in top form and up-to-date. The envisaged function of "continuing education" is that of rounding off the individual's education, of providing further education or of retraining, so that, for example, the individual can always meet increased or new professional demands.
>
> The term "lifelong learning" is used in a more general sense, referring to the utilization of all the educational programmes offered by different institutions and agencies, including the education sponsored by industry, the churches, political parties, and trade unions, as well as by other institutions of further education.
>
> "Recurrent education" is a lifelong process consisting of a discontinuous, periodic participation in educational programmes aimed at gradually dissolving the blocks of compulsory education and working life (see *Recurrent Education*).

The Council of Europe (1971 pp. 1–2) elaborates several of the usual features of an ideal "permanent education": a system of flexible study units; a range of general, vocational, cultural, social, and civic studies; continuous educational guidance; encouragement of creative and critical faculties; and self-education using modern communication techniques. It is admitted that this vision might be thought futuristic and utopian, but the Council insists that permanent education begins with preprimary education and demands adequate paid time for adults to study.

It should be remarked that some confusion is caused by translation between English and French. "Permanent education" is still sometimes used by analogy with the original French *éducation permanente*, of which the more usual rendering is now "lifelong education": hence the Council of Europe description could equally be applied to this term. French may also use *éducation permanente* where English has "continuing education" and "recurrent education," although *éducation continue* and *éducation récurrente* are also used. (There are similar difficulties over the French equivalents of "basic education" and "literacy.") The interference between these translations is important, given that major international organizations promote the concepts in both languages.

"Lifelong education" does not appear in Jourdan's list, although the terms "lifelong learning" and "lifelong education" have sometimes been used interchangeably. What he says of lifelong learning applies to lifelong education, within a broader perception that is outlined below.

The term "continuous education" is also sometimes encountered. This is an alternative to permanent or lifelong education, but is now not commonly used.

2. Development of the Concept of Lifelong Education

The term "lifelong education" appeared in English-language literature in the 1920s, while in Germany the debate on the humanistic reform of education launched before the First World War already contained a commitment to adult education, exemplified by those associated in the 1920s with the *Hohenrodter Bund*. The tradition of adult education of the Nordic countries, dating from the mid-1800s, has also influenced the concept (see *History of Adult Education*). The International Conference on Adult Education held by UNESCO in Montreal in 1960 sought to situate adult education within the global context of education, and a document subsequently prepared for a follow-up conference in 1965 formulated a series of proposals for the implementation of *éducation permanente* (Lengrand 1965). Jarvis (1983) points out that it was adult education which gave rise to the concept of lifelong education, and many of the ideas present in the literature of the 1970s are found in English-language literature immediately after the Second World War.

The concept was initially expressed in English as "permanent education," but the term was superseded by "lifelong" or "recurrent" education. The latter term has been traced to a speech made in 1969 by the then Swedish Minister of Education, Olof Palme (Houghton 1974 p. 6), but it has been pointed out that both "*ständig*" (permanent) and "*livslång utbildning*" (lifelong education) were terms already being discussed in Sweden (Jourdan 1981 p. 16).

It was largely through the promotional efforts of UNESCO in publications and conferences (e.g., Asian Institute of Educational Planning and Administration 1970) that the term "lifelong education" began to be used internationally in the early 1970s. Widespread interest in the concept was aroused by the publication of the report *Learning to Be*, commissioned by UNESCO (Faure et al. 1972). As a starting point for criticism of contemporary education, the report briefly considers alternative models of education drawn from societies widely separated by time or geographical distance from the Western norm. It also refers to social and technological trends, sets out the need for universal schooling, and draws attention to the inadequacy and irrelevance of elements of the conventional curriculum. It enumerates possibilities for opening access to education through shift systems, the use of semitrained assistant teachers, and other practical measures, but it also lays great emphasis on the potential for development of the human intellect through scientific humanism in a world context of solidarity between peoples. It therefore lies within the tradition of the notion of the perfectibility of man.

Besides lifelong education, the term "lifelong learning" also came to be used. This did not mean the spontaneous learning of everyday life, but what Tough (1971) calls "deliberate" learning. In consequence interest was created in the administrative arrangements and curricular adjustments which could bring this about (Cropley 1980).

What is meant by "lifelong education" depends to a degree on the political and philosophical perceptions of the individual author or agency, as the concept is open to selective interpretation. There is, nonetheless, a core of common elements. These concern the desire for universal access to education, which includes children and adults currently lacking opportunities of education; recognition of the role of settings of education outside formal institutions; diversity of learning materials; and, most importantly, the promotion in learners of the personal characteristics required for subsequent lifelong learning, including the motivation, cultural values, and ability necessary for independent self-learning (Dave 1973). These elements have been made explicit in the discussion of the means of creating a "learning society," a term which has also achieved some currency (Husén 1974, 1986). Some authors have sought antecedents for the concept in Plato, Comenius, Condorcet, and Dewey.

The learning presupposed in "lifelong learning" will allow each individual to continue to develop his or her physical, emotional, and intellectual potential, and will reveal the interrelatedness and the relativity of areas of knowledge and of human endeavors and perceptions (Lengrand 1985). The limits to the possibility of self-learning among those with previously low educational attainment have been pointed out (Joblin 1988).

3. The Concepts of Continuing and Recurrent Education

The term "continuing education" implies a continuation of elementary or basic education, and it has been used—sometimes through mistranslation— in the broad sense of all adult recurrent, permanent, or lifelong education. A symposium on continuing education held at Oxford University Department of Extramural Studies in 1967 (Jessup 1969) included papers on the roles of museums and libraries, of the mass media, and of voluntary associations. These are means of nonformal or informal education more usually associated with lifelong education (see *Formal, Nonformal, and Informal Education*). The explanation lies in the fact that the inspiration for the meeting was the 1965 session of the UNESCO International Committee for the Advancement of Adult Education, at which the seminal paper by

Lengrand (1965) on "*éducation permanente*" was read.

"Continuing education" is, nonetheless, the usual terminology of university extension provision for mature (adult) students: the Center for Continuing Education of the University of Michigan, for instance, was opened as long ago as 1951. But it has also acquired a vocational, functional emphasis, in contrast to lifelong education: Levin and Slavet (1970) include in the concept not only vocational, literacy, citizenship, and nonvocational adult education, but also "agency training and staff development and agency citizen–client education" (p. 1). However, the term is more commonly used to refer specifically to occasional retraining.

The relationship between the terms "continuing" and "adult" education was extremely close in the 1960s and 1970s, at a time when it became apparent that initial vocational and professional training would need updating or replacing as patterns of work changed. This is exemplified in the incorporation of "continuing" into the titles of professional associations of adult educators—the American Association for Adult Continuing Education (AAACE) and the National Institute of Adult Continuing Education (NIACE). Especially in the United States, community colleges began to offer courses to adult students under the rubric of continuing education, and this development has been reflected in the practices of the vocational and professional training establishments of other countries (see *Community Colleges*). The more traditional nonvocational range of adult education was thereby considerably extended.

Implicit in the term "recurrent education" is a cyclical aspect, which is in turn underlaid by the assumption that initial basic education is commonly available, and that the majority of the units of education taken up in later life can therefore be related to occupational or cultural activities. There are thus close links between recurrent education and the looser term, "continuing education." Recurrent education is self-evidently continuing, but it presupposes a systematized access to education throughout life which, while less all-embracing than lifelong education, goes further than piecemeal postinitial courses (Tuijnman 1991). It can be seen as a practical strategy of lifelong education, for postchildhood phases of life (cf. OECD 1973). The Organisation for Economic Co-operation and Development has retained the overall concept of lifelong education, which is set out in recent documents as the context for OECD programs in the 1990s.

Houghton (1974) is unusual in considering recurrent education yet more radical than lifelong education, because the former poses a direct challenge to the practices of educational systems, while the latter only acknowledges the influence of agencies previously ignored by educationists (for another view, see Ryba and Holmes 1973).

4. Lifelong and Continuing Education as Criticism of Conventional Education

The most fundamental aspect of the lifelong education approach is the realization that each educational experience is one of a lifelong sequence of learning events (i.e., vertical articulation), and that it is situated in a context of other events determined by the surrounding society. These other events (i.e., horizontal articulation) may have no formal relation to education but nonetheless influence its effects.

The primary, secondary, and tertiary education systems of the 1960s and 1970s were criticized for following the "front-end model," believing that they could adequately load pupils with all they would need for adult life, in accordance with the traditional belief that it is possible to divide life into distinct parts. Subsequent changes in employment demands, and the need for the continuing education of adults lacking skills required by technological innovations, have vindicated this element of the criticism.

It has also been argued forcefully that education is dominated internationally by Western indigenous values. The feeling is that the West is parading as universal and humanistic, while in fact deriving its policies from a narrowly ethnocentric view of the world. Similarly, it has been said that conventional formal education prepares the masses for a life of subservience to the economic needs of the ruling class, thereby reinforcing social selection for the pre-existing social order (Gelpi 1985a, 1985b, Pineau 1977). Lifelong education has been advanced as an alternative concept which would overcome the insufficiencies of traditional education in these respects. It would re-emphasize the individuality and creative abilities of learners, leading to an improvement in their ability to express their feelings, to understand and maintain their health, and to see beneath the superficial social and economic arrangement of society.

Many curricular issues arise out of this wider interpretation of lifelong education. New attention to arts, physical health, and technology has been called for (Lengrand 1985), and it has been pointed out that the hierarchical methods traditionally used to teach children can have no place in the lifelong education available to adults. The intention is not to extend traditional schooling throughout adult life, but there have been suggestions that school education could benefit from the influence of adult education methods, as well as from other, outside social actors, even leading to a "deschooling" of society (Ohliger 1971; cf. Illich 1971).

5. The Place of Adult Education in the Implementation of Lifelong and Continuing Education

The vertical integration presupposed in lifelong and recurrent education has seldom been realized in any planned way, still less the horizontal articulation. This is not to say, though, that nothing has been done to make education more generally accessible, or to vary types of provision and to tailor them to the situations of learners. Varied programs, some for specific target groups, have been launched under the rubric of "adult education." The number of bibliographic references to lifelong and continuing education dropped during the 1980s, while the use of the term "adult education" has continued without marked change in frequency.

Adult education provision in Denmark, for instance, has been described as offering the following range, which might be thought to go some way toward lifelong provision: nonvocational weekly courses; general education through day folk high schools for the unemployed, and through residential folk high schools; primary and secondary examination courses; open university courses; job-specific courses for unskilled workers; continuing education for public employees; and management training in enterprises (Danish Research and Development Center for Adult Education 1991 p. 6) (see *Europe, Nordic Countries*). This list covers the vast majority of the adult population, and is presented in the context of a holistic approach to individual development which points out how difficult it is to differentiate between vocational and nonvocational skills (see *Convergence between Education and Training*).

It is widely seen that what in the 1970s was considered to be a revolutionary change in perception has now passed into the general assumptions of adult education. Long (1983), while emphasizing continuing education in the early 1980s, sees it only as a kind of education for adults in the context of corporate and vocational training in a later publication (Long 1987). Knowles and Klevins (1982) make little distinction between adult, continuing, and lifelong education, and attempt a further synthesis by insisting that education is necessarily continuous. Knox (1987) offers practical guidance on helping adults to learn in various settings, including museums, adult basic education, continuing professional education, and adult religious education, without resort to the term "lifelong education."

In addition, distance education and open learning at both university level (see *Open University*) and at lower levels have spread, not only in industrialized countries but also in developing countries (e.g., through the incipient Open University of Southern Africa or the well-established Open School in New Delhi).

6. New Priorities: Literacy, Basic Education for All, and Community Development

"Education for all" was demanded initially as an element of lifelong education. The term has become particularly associated with the World Conference on Education for All, jointly held in Jomtien, Thailand, in March 1990 by UNDP, UNICEF, UNESCO, and the World

Bank, and with the subsequent effort to attain universal basic education by the year 2000. While UNESCO has continued to organize international conferences on adult and distance education, the major commitment of the organization has shifted from the promotion of the totality of lifelong education to that of universality and quality of initial or basic education for children and hitherto illiterate or undereducated adults.

This shift is fueled by grave doubts as to whether those who engage in the various forms of lifelong and continuing education are in fact those who need them most. It has been seen that the level of initial formal education is still the principal factor in the decision to participate in continuing education (e.g., Tuijnman 1990), and it is felt by some that lifelong education is less revolutionary than it claims, as it is structurally tied to a socially conservative paradigm (Collins 1984). There has also been criticism that alternative forms of education for adults with low levels of formal schooling, or for young people who were never enrolled, have remained—or are perceived as remaining—inferior channels of second chance education.

It is now acknowledged that it is wildly unrealistic to demand the fulfillment of each person's human potential through a network of lifelong educational provision while the most elementary provision is in places lacking or inadequate. Even in industrialized countries, a social rather than an individual approach to educational development has been adopted, for example, through the Council of Europe (1986) project on Adult Education and Social Change (the French title is notably different: *développement communautaire*), which led up to a conference in Strasbourg on Adult Education and Social Integration in 1992.

Those targeted by adult education providers are frequently affected by unemployment and low previous levels of schooling. The Council for Cultural Co-operation of the Council of Europe, the body promulgating permanent education in the 1970s, also mounted a project in the late 1980s and early 1990s on adult education that was especially for the long-term unemployed, as well as for older adults. The former group has been the target of numerous training programs organized by national governments in industrialized countries, and of support projects conducted by the Commission of the European Communities (EC) (see *European Union: Continuing Vocational Training*).

7. Lifelong and Continuing Education: Present Status and Future Development

In the 1970s and 1980s, of the major international organizations first in the field, the OECD gave its attention mostly to recurrent education (*éducation récurrente*), while UNESCO and the Council of Europe spoke of lifelong education (*éducation permanente*).

The OECD again refers to lifelong learning as a means of facilitating skill formation at the beginning of the 1990s. Despite overlaps between concepts and confusion in terminology, there are real differences in emphasis among the programs of national and international agencies, and in the commentaries of individual authors. These can be seen as forming a spectrum.

At one end is lifelong education. This is a vision of the learning society, in which education is freely accessible to all, and relevant to the interests and cultural values of learners. It takes place in formal institutions, through nonformal provision (such as part-time evening courses with or without certification) and even in informal settings not usually thought of as educational. It meets the needs of the learner at his or her actual stage of knowledge and awareness, be that illiteracy, semi-literacy, or high qualifications honed by professional experience. Ideally, learning throughout life should contribute to the intellectual and artistic development of the learner.

Progressing through the spectrum, lifelong learning principles include the development of the capacity for self-learning, so that all members of society can continue to develop their potential even if not enrolled in formal or nonformal education. Meanwhile, recurrent education, while accepting the overall vision of lifelong education, considers more clearly the means of creating opportunities for lifelong learning, starting from the constraints of existing formal and nonformal institutions, structures, and disposable finance. At the further end of the spectrum, continuing education refers to post-initial courses, paid for by government, employers, and learners, but does not necessarily see these as part of a comprehensive lifelong system or societal vision.

Adult education has been reinvigorated by the perceptions of the foregoing concepts and sometimes subsumes these, leaving the formal education of children and young people relatively untouched by them.

The widest claims of lifelong education, with their immense implications for the structure and funding of education, were, in the late 1980s, temporarily put aside in favor of concentration on the universalization of basic education and the social advancement of disadvantaged groups, including women and girls. At the same time, the ethos of lifelong education has had a significant influence on thinking about the aims of education, the needs for retraining, and alternative methods of delivery. Especially in developing countries, nonformal provision had been adumbrated, with the insistence that this can be of equal or superior value to traditional formal education, because it has the flexibility to respond directly to the perceived needs and occupations of learners. As yet, however, it is not seen as an equal partner in the provision of initial education.

As pointed out by Cropley (1985b), traditional research studies of lifelong education are extremely difficult to conduct. One is dealing with a guiding principle or statement of belief, rather than a precise planning proposal, and in the nature of the approach a multitude of horizontal factors should be taken into account. It is therefore not surprising that early development of the concept was restricted to discussions between experts, and an eventual decline in activity, but what may yet be attempted is an assessment of how far existing provision in a given society goes in meeting the target of lifelong accessibility and articulation between sectors.

It is certain that much research relevant to lifelong and continuing education will in the future, as in the past, be indexed under adult education, further education, distance education, vocational retraining, and other descriptors, as well as under the portmanteau terms discussed above.

See also: Adult Education: Concepts and Principles; Recurrent Education; Adult Education for Development; Market Concepts in Provision; Time, Leisure and Adult Education; Time Policies for Lifelong Learning; Financing Lifelong Learning; Development of Learning Across the Lifespan; Learning to Learn

References

Asian Institute of Educational Planning and Administration 1970 *Lifelong Education: Report of the Meeting of Experts Held at New Delhi 10–18 August 1970.* AIEPA, New Delhi

Collins C B 1984 The limitations of lifelong education: A critique of predominant paradigms. *Convergence* 17 (1): 28–37

Council of Europe, Council for Cultural Co-operation 1971 *Permanent Education: Fundamentals for an Integrated Education Policy.* Studies on Permanent Education 21. Council of Europe, Strasbourg

Council of Europe, Council for Cultural Co-operation 1986 *Adult Education and Social Change.* Conference Report Document CC-GP-G (86) 6. Council of Europe, Strasbourg

Cropley A J (ed.) 1980 *Towards a System of Lifelong Education.* Pergamon Press, Oxford

Cropley A J 1985a Lifelong education: Interaction with adult education. In: Husén T, Postlethwaite T N (eds.) 1985 *The International Encyclopedia of Education*, 1st edn., Vol. 5. Pergamon Press, Oxford

Cropley A J 1985b Lifelong education: Research strategies. In: Husén T, Postlethwaite T N (ed.) 1985 *The International Encyclopedia of Education*, 1st edn., Vol. 5. Pergamon Press, Oxford

Danish Research and Development Center for Adult Education (DRDCAE) 1991 *Qualifications in the Year 2001.* DRDCAE, Copenhagen

Dave R H 1973 *Lifelong Education and School Curriculum.* UNESCO Institute for Education, Hamburg

Faure E et al. 1972 *Learning to Be.* UNESCO, Paris

Gelpi E 1985a *Lifelong Education and International Relations.* Croom Helm, London

Gelpi E 1985b Lifelong education: Issues and trends. In: Husén T, Postlethwaite T N (eds.) 1985 *The International Encyclopedia of Education*, 1st edn., Vol. 5. Pergamon, Oxford

Houghton V 1974 Recurrent education. In: Houghton V, Richardson K (eds.) 1974 *Recurrent Education.* Ward Lock Educational/Association for Recurrent Education, London

Husén T 1974 *The Learning Society.* Methuen, London

Husén T 1986 *The Learning Society Revisited.* Pergamon Press, Oxford

Illich I 1971 *Deschooling Society.* Harper & Row, New York

Jarvis P 1983 *Adult and Continuing Education.* Croom Helm, Beckenham, New York

Jessup F W (ed.) 1969 *Lifelong Learning: A Symposium on Continuing Education.* Pergamon Press, Oxford

Joblin D 1988 Self-direction in adult education: An analysis, defence, refutation and assessment of the notion that adults are more self-directed than children and youth. *Int. J. Lifelong Educ.* 7 (2): 115–25

Jourdan M (ed.) 1981 *Recurrent Education in Western Europe.* NFER-Nelson, Windsor

Knowles M S, Klevins C S 1982 Philosophical and Historical Perspectives. In: Klevins C S (ed.) 1982 *Materials and Methods in Adult and Continuing Education.* Klevens, Los Angeles, California

Knox A B 1987 *Helping Adults Learn.* Jossey-Bass, San Francisco, California

Lengrand P 1965 *Education permanente.* UNESCO, Paris

Lengrand P 1985 Lifelong education: Growth of the concept. In: Husén T, Postlethwaite T N (eds.) 1985 *The International Encyclopedia of Education*, 1st edn., Vol. 5. Pergamon Press, Oxford

Levin M R, Slavet J S 1970 *Continuing Education.* D C Heath, Lexington, Massachusetts

Long H B 1983 *Adult and Continuing Education.* Teachers College Press, New York

Long H B 1987 *New Perspectives on the Education of Adults in the United States.* Croom Helm, London

Organisation for Economic Co-operation and Development (OECD)/Centre for Educational Research and Innovation (CERI) 1973 *Recurrent Education: A Strategy for Lifelong Education.* OECD, Paris

Ohliger J 1971 *Lifelong Learning and Lifelong Schooling.* Syracuse University Publications in Continuing Education/ERIC Clearinghouse on Adult Education, Syracuse, New York

Pineau G (ed.) 1977 *Education ou aliénation permanente: Repères mythiques et politiques.* Organisation et sciences humaines, Montreal

Ryba R, Holmes B (eds.) 1973 *Recurrent Education—Concepts and Policies for Lifelong Education.* The Comparative Education Society in Europe, London

Tough A 1971 *The Adult's Learning Projects: A Fresh Approach to Theory and Practice in Adult Learning.* Research in Education Series No. 1. Ontario Institute for Studies in Education, Toronto

Tuijnman A 1990 Adult education and the quality of life. *Int. Rev. Educ.* 36 (3): 283–98

Tuijnman A 1991 Emerging systems of recurrent education. *Prospects* 21 (1): 17–24

Further Reading

Botkin J W, Elmandjra M, Mircea M 1979 *No Limits to Learning: Bridging the Human Gap.* A Report to the Club of Rome. Pergamon, Oxford

Coombs P H 1985 *The World Crisis in Education: The View from the Eighties*. Oxford University Press, Oxford

Dave R H (ed.) 1976 *Foundations of Lifelong Education*. Advances in Lifelong Education. Pergamon Press, Oxford

Davies J H, Thomas J E (eds.) 1988 *A Select Bibliography of Adult and Continuing Education in Great Britain*, 5th edn. NIACE, Leicester

Jarvis P 1990 *An International Dictionary of Adult and Continuing Education*. Routledge, London

Lengrand P 1975 *An Introduction to Lifelong Education*. UNESCO, Paris

Lengrand P 1986 *Areas of Learning Basic to Lifelong Education*. Pergamon Press/UNESCO Institute for Education, Oxford/Hamburg

Marsick V J 1987 *Learning in the Workplace*. Croom Helm, London

Merriam S B, Cunningham P M (eds.) 1989 *A Handbook of Adult and Continuing Education*. Jossey-Bass, San Francisco, California

Schwartz B 1988 Education permanente et formation des adultes: Evolution des pratiques, évolution des concepts. *Educ. permanente* 92: 7–21

Solinger J W (ed.) 1990 *Museums and Universities: New Paths for Continuing Education*. National University Continuing Education Association/Macmillan, New York

Titmus C J (ed.) 1989 *Lifelong Education for Adults: An International Handbook*. Pergamon Press, Oxford

UNESCO Principal Regional Office for Asia and the Pacific 1987 *Continuing Education in Asia and the Pacific*. Bulletin 28 of PROAP. PROAP, Bangkok

Wain K 1987 *Philosophy of Lifelong Education*. Croom Helm, London

Lifelong Learning

A. Hasan

1. Lifelong Learning: Origins of the Concept

The concept of "lifelong learning" is rapidly gaining wide acceptance as a basis for reforming education and training systems. Its origins lie in related terms such as "lifelong education," "recurrent education," "continuing education," and in the French *"éducation continue," "éducation permanente,"* and *"éducation recurrente"* (see Kallen 1979 for definitions and distinctions between the terms). The term "lifelong education" itself first appeared in English in the 1920s, linked to the tradition of adult education in the Nordic countries, dating from the mid-1800s (Sutton 1994). Despite the long history, the concept was discussed widely only after the Second World War and assumed policy significance in the 1960s. Since then, the meaning of the term "lifelong learning" has evolved gradually and changes are ongoing. The increasing political importance of the concept can be inferred from the title of the January 1996 meeting of Education Ministers of the OECD countries, "Making Lifelong Learning a Reality for All" (OECD in press). This can also be seen in the use of "learning throughout life" as the key concept for the 1996 UNESCO report by the International Commission on Education for the Twenty-first Century, and in the designation by the European Union of 1996 as the year for lifelong learning. Simultaneously, lifelong learning has become a pivotal framework for educational reforms in a large number of countries, both industrialized and developing (OECD 1992, 1994, 1995a, UNESCO 1995).

2. Lifelong Learning and Recurrent Education

In the 1960s, the first usage of the term "lifelong education" was in the context of adult education (Jarvis 1983). The International Conference on Adult Education held by UNESCO in Montreal in 1960 sought to integrate adult education in the wider educational system and a document prepared for the follow-up conference in 1965 formulated proposals for the implementation of *éducation permanente* (Lengrand 1965). The Ottesen Committee in Norway put forward a programme of postwork education in 1967 with the emphasis on the updating of knowledge and counteracting obsolete qualifications. However, as a distinct concept, "recurrent education" was first launched in a speech by the Swedish Minister of Education, Olof Palme, in 1969 at the Versailles Conference of European Ministers of Education (Houghton 1974, Schuller and Megarry 1979). In the early 1970s the concept became popular internationally through the efforts of UNESCO (Faure et al. 1972), OECD (1973, 1975, 1977–81, 1991, 1992), and the Council of Europe (Council of Europe 1978) (see *Lifelong and Continuing Education*).

Recurrent education has been called "the first new idea in education this century" (Houghton 1974). Its basic principle was that postschool education should be provided on a recurring basis, involving alternation between work and study, and opportunities for this should be effectively available to all individuals throughout their active life. The idea was developed in a "Clarifying Report," prepared by the OECD and presented to the 1973 Conference of European Ministers of Education, held in Berne, Switzerland. Recurrent education was defined as "a comprehensive educational strategy for all postcompulsory or postbasic education, the essential characteristic of which is the distribution of education over the total lifespan of the individual in a recurring way, i.e. in alternation with other activities, principally with work, but also with

33

leisure and retirement" (OECD 1973) (see *Recurrent Education*).

The term can be interpreted in a narrow or broad sense. In the narrower meaning, "recurrent education" envisages a discontinuous, periodic participation in educational programs by adults who missed out on opportunities to initial schooling in early phases of their lives. In this sense it is *an alternative* to the ever-lengthening period of continuing education for youth (OECD 1973). In its broader manifestation the term involves a gradual blurring of distinctions between the blocks of compulsory education and working life (Jourdan 1981). In this formulation, the concept of recurrent education proposed a concrete framework —which differed from the Council of Europe's concept of "permanent education" that emphasized the sociocultural aspects—in implicitly advocating the principle of alternation between education and other activities. It encompassed not only education after schooling but also within it and implied major changes in sociopolitical and economic institutions (Kallen 1979, Bengtsson 1985).

The focus was on two main points. Firstly, the insistence on the necessity of a comprehensive policy for all precompulsory education and for adaptation of compulsory schooling to the recurrent education policy. This involved providing all young people with the basic knowledge, attitudes, and skills that would allow them to profit fully from the possibilities for educational, professional, and personal development offered to them on leaving compulsory schooling. In operational terms it was proposed to modify the upper secondary curriculum so that the final grades of secondary schooling offer the students a real choice between further study and work and to abolish "terminal stages" in the formal education system so that all programs lead on to other programs. Secondly, the insistence on the necessity to change the world of work, to achieve not only a better match between education and the labor market but to emancipate the individual from socioeconomic constraints. It involved increasing the participation of adults in tertiary education; by recognising the value of work experience; "opening up" the universities to extend the provision of formal adult education to a wider audience; and making provision for alternating work and education careers in an intermittent way, with such measures as paid study leave, maternity leave, and general income maintenance during periods of "significant nonwork."

Several factors encouraged the development of the broader concept of recurrent education. Firstly, educational expansion of the 1960s and 1970s failed to meet the demand for social equality that arose out of sustained postwar economic development in the industrialized world. Secondly, some form of continuing or permanent education was essential to meet the changing occupational requirements of economies that were undergoing rapid change. Thirdly, the separation of formal education from learning experience was becoming more and more untenable and made some form of "deschooling" a necessity (OECD 1973). Finally, there was an argument for intergenerational equity, to reduce the gap between the educational opportunities provided to the young and those from which the other generations benefited. Although all of these factors were at play, the overriding concern was the persistence of social inequities which the education system failed to overcome. There was frustration with the fact that neither the strategies for compensation at the preschool and primary levels, nor the comprehensive schools at the secondary level and the diversification of postsecondary structures, proved capable of overcoming socially-determined inequities (Papadopoulos 1994). Similarly, a deschooling strategy, which was one response to these frustrations, and which aimed at liberating individuals of the constraints of institutionalized schools, was not viewed as a credible alternative as it would not necessarily improve the educational chances of the weak in unequal socioeconomic systems and might indeed make them worse.

In spite of considerable growth in adult education since 1960 and repeated formal declarations by governments and other bodies of importance, the sector remained isolated and financially weak. Increased government support was channelled primarily to boosting the occupational preparation of the workforce and, in many respects, adult education continued to be a community-based and financed activity rather than a vital sector of public policy. However, even though no country managed to apply recurrent education as a consistent strategy, some of the changes advocated did become part of educational policy and practices (Papadopoulos 1994). These included the development of more flexible postcompulsory education structures, the growth of modular courses and new admission procedures in higher education, new combinations of work and study programs and the educational recognition of work experience, to name but a few. The broader conclusion remains, however, that much of the progress was of a piecemeal nature and that adult education continued to remain a discrete and financially weak sector.

3. Lifelong Learning: The Concept Today

The term "lifelong learning" came to be used in the early 1970s, and is closely linked to recurrent education. This can be seen in the titles of publications of this period such as *Recurrent Education: A Strategy for Lifelong Learning* (OECD 1973) and *Recurrent Education and Lifelong Learning* (Schuller and Megarry 1979). However, the concept has evolved in distinctive ways from that of recurrent education, and has also evolved from UNESCO's view of the early 1970s (Faure et al. 1972).

Many of the same forces lay behind the advocacy of recurrent education but they had further intensified during the 1990s and posed new imperatives for the systems of education and training. The importance of the "human factor" as being fundamental to economic activity, competitiveness, and social advance was rediscovered. Lifelong learning is seen as offering an appropriate framework for addressing the new imperatives. The new idea underpinning lifelong learning goes beyond providing a second or third chance for adults and embraces individual and social development of all kinds and in all settings—formally, in schools, vocational, tertiary, and adult education institutions, and nonformally, at home, at work, and in the community. The approach is system-wide and it focuses on the standards of knowledge and skills needed by all, regardless of age. It emphasizes the need to prepare and motivate all children at an early age for learning over a lifetime, and directs effort to ensure that all adults, employed and unemployed, who need to retrain or upgrade their skills, are provided with opportunities to do so. As such, it is geared to serve several objectives: to foster personal development, including the use of time outside of work; to strengthen democratic values; to cultivate community life; to maintain social cohesion; and to promote innovation, productivity, and economic growth.

The meaning of the term "lifelong learning" is still evolving and it is open to different interpretations. Yet there exists a core of common elements in most interpretations (see Sutton 1994, Titmus 1994, Tuijnman 1994). These include, firstly, a strong belief in the intrinsic as opposed to instrumental value of education and learning. Secondly, there is a common desire for universal access to learning opportunities, regardless of age, sex, or employment status. A third common denominator is the recognition of the importance of nonformal learning in diverse settings: people learn not only in classrooms, but informally at work, by talking to others, by watching television and playing games, and through virtually every other form of human activity. Similarly, lifelong learning differs from more conventional approaches in the recognition it gives to the diversity in means and methods of teaching. It emphasizes "learning to learn" and promotes in learners personal characteristics required for subsequent learning, including the motivation and capacity to engage in self-managed, independent learning. Finally, the lifelong learning concept is advanced as a critique of and an alternative to conventional, "front-end" educational philosophies.

Some of these characteristics are shared with the concept of recurrent education, but there are important differences as well. Firstly, recurrent education emphasizes the correspondence between formal education and work and implies instances of interruption in the lifelong process of education. While it proposes that educational opportunities should be spread out over the entire lifespan, the proposal is an *alternative* strategy to the lengthening of formal schooling. In contrast, today's concept of lifelong learning is one of continuity—a "seamless" view of learning, combining the nonformal and informal in a variety of settings—at home, at work, and in the community. This stress on the integration of the formal and nonformal forms of learning goes further than do strategies of recurrent education, which were largely conceived as giving a second chance to adults.

Secondly, full retention in broad-based secondary education until at least 17 or 18, and even the expansion of tertiary education, which was considered problematic by strategies of recurrent education are no longer called into doubt in many countries. Achieving a full cycle of secondary education for all has become one of the corner-stones of strategies for realizing lifelong learning for all.

Thirdly, the concept of "social demand," central in the recurrent education philosophy, appears to have been replaced with "individual demand" as key to the provision of adult education, training, and learning more generally. Increased reliance on the responsibilities of employers and individual learners is also reflected in the reluctance of many countries to legislate and implement arrangements for paid study leave. Concomitantly with the rising emphasis on accountability, choice, and even in certain OECD countries "markets for learning" (see Miller 1993), financing mechanisms are being reviewed (see *Lifelong Education: Financing Mechanisms*).

Finally, a major difference concerns the role of government. Partly because it emphasized formal education, the recurrent education strategy assigned a large role for government in organizing, managing, and financing the system. The past years have seen a partial retreat from this principle, and partnership and shared responsibility have been emphasized. The shifting view is reflected in recent policies to strengthen the development of continuing vocational training, especially on-the-job training, rather than expanding formal adult education in institutions fully or partly financed from the public budget. The notion that work ought to be alternated on a sporadic basis with formal education has been replaced by strategies to promote learning while working and working while learning.

4. The Rationale for Lifelong Learning

The evolution of the concept of lifelong learning can be best understood in the context of the ongoing broader national and global trends. Beginning with the oil crisis of the mid-1970s, the advanced industrial economies experienced major structural change which also had repercussions for the global economy. The opening up of international markets added further stimulus to the need for restructuring. The information revolution, which was gathering momentum since the early 1970s, put a premium on "learning societies" and the knowledge base became an ever more important determinant of social and economic progress. Products and skills became obsolete more rapidly as the pace of introduction of new products and services quickened. The ageing of populations in industrialized countries and improvements in health and leisure time worldwide made it possible to prolong working life even as the period of initial education was extended in early life. Finally, a variety of factors contributed to raising individual demand for learning.

The contextual developments and ongoing trends globally help to explain the rationale behind the emerging new view of lifelong learning. They give rise to four sets of arguments in favor of the lifelong learning approach. Firstly, there is the economic argument based on the needs of an increasingly knowledge-based economic system both nationally and internationally. Advanced industrialized societies in particular, and others in general, are experiencing a growing dependence on the creation and manipulation of knowledge, information, and ideas. The defining features of the knowledge and information-intensive society affect everyone; mature adults are just as much part of it as are children and youth. Countries and regions that do not foster learning societies, and those individuals who do not participate in them, are increasingly disadvantaged and likely to be left behind, not only nationally but also in the international context.

Secondly, given the importance of the learning foundations and of continued learning in knowledge-intensive societies characterized by rapid change, those who miss out—either initially or later on—suffer effective exclusion. An increase in inequalities of income has occurred in many countries over the last two decades, markedly so in some cases (OECD 1994b), which endangers social cohesion. There is evidence of close and cumulative links between successful learning in childhood and youth, and the motivation and capacity to continue to learn throughout life. Social cohesion is undermined by the failure to put firmly in place these virtuous circles of successful learning. Learning is the most necessary insurance against exclusion and marginality. Educational activity represents a particularly important source of involvement and participation in light of the many pressures now putting social cohesion at risk.

Thirdly, there is the broader need for enhancing the adaptive capacity of societies. Although quantitative evidence to support the idea is difficult to gather, it is widely believed that the "speed" of technological change is accelerating and is unlikely to slow down. There is the need not only for the constant renewal of knowledge and skills to keep up with change but also for securing human capacity for flexibility and coping with change, and maintaining cultural coherence and quality in the face of knowledge and information "overload."

A fourth rationale is linked to the ageing society phenomenon and is based on "life-cycle redistribution" considerations. Economic and labor market activity is increasingly being compressed into the middle period of life, between a prolonged education at the beginning and an extended retirement period at the other end. There is a growing expenditure burden on the "shrinking middle." There is an important economic and social case for combining productive work and learning so that economically productive periods are not curtailed unduly.

5. Lifelong Learning: Implementation Strategies

The all-embracing view of lifelong learning described above cannot be appropriately addressed in a piecemeal fashion but requires system-wide reforms. Strategies to implement the concept must recognise that building an inclusive learning society is a long-term goal and achieving it will take sustained efforts over many years. There is no single, unified, and hierarchically structured "system" of lifelong learning that suits all countries. Rather it will need to reflect specific national and cultural heritages and particular conditions and needs. The very nature of lifelong learning—diverse, pluralistic, and undertaken over a lifetime—depends on a great variety of initiatives taken by different actors in many spheres of life and work. It cannot be imposed, but rather calls for cooperation and coordination among many policy sectors. Taking these factors into account, implementation strategies for lifelong learning need to identify at least four elements: the goals and standards; priority areas of action; the instruments to be used for carrying out the strategies; and the roles and responsibilities of different actors.

Goals and standards. Given the overall objectives of lifelong learning strategies, policymakers must consider whether the goals, standards, and methods of evaluation pertaining to specific aspects of provision meet the requirements for lifelong learning. Reviewing and redefining goals for education systems in the light of the requirements of lifelong learning is a necessary step for establishing operational standards for educational inputs, processes, and outcomes. A final step in the process is to implement the methods and procedures required for the monitoring of progress toward attaining the overarching goals and objectives.

Priority action areas. Lifelong learning can be viewed as a chain of provision and participation. The weakest links in the chain in most countries appear to be deficiencies in the *foundations* for lifelong learning, difficulties of *transitions* between the worlds of education and work, and insufficient *learning opportunities* for adults, especially those over the age of 45.

Strengthening the foundations. Early schooling leaves much to be desired as providing an early start for lifelong learning. Since the foundations of lifelong learning are laid down from birth, priority needs to be given to the extension and strengthening of early childhood education, especially for 3 and 4 year olds. Completed upper secondary education is still not universal, even in the more advanced industrialized societies. Approximately 15 to 20 percent of the students in the relevant age group leave school without the adequate foundation of qualifications or skills that would equip them for lifelong learning. The provision of solid foundations is not only a matter for the young: a large percentage of adult population, even in the more advanced societies, have rudimentary literacy and numeracy skills (OECD and Statistics Canada 1995).

Education as providing the foundations for lifelong learning has to be rethought. It must aim to foster an interest, motivation, and capacity for learning in all. In order for the school to be a place where all learners *like* to be—regardless of age—and feel motivated not only to perform optimally given their conditions and interests but also to continue learning beyond school, learning environments need to be "positive"—stimulating, challenging, and rich in content and opportunity. Long-established traditions about the organization of the school will need to be reviewed to provide appropriate flexibility in practices currently characterized by detailed and standardized curricula, classrooms organised by age or grade divisions and ability tracking, fixed and narrow timetables, authoritarian teaching and assessment styles, and rote learning. Subject-based theoretical knowledge must be better linked to its practical applications, and young people should have sufficient opportunities to develop such critical "cross-curriculum" competencies as interpersonal and social relations, communication skills, problem-solving, and "learning to learn." Assessment for selection should be linked to assessment which fosters the individual's capacity and motivation to learn. New approaches to assessment and certification would be needed, as many of the skills and areas of knowledge that are vital in establishing sound foundations for lifelong learning cannot be assessed using conventional methods.

Advances in pedagogy, the wider use of new information technologies and the pervasive impact of the mass media need to be harnessed to define what the school of tomorrow would look like. The notion of "value-added learning," which supposes individualized instruction, personal development plans, and evaluation of personal growth targets in learning will be the basis of the "school of the future," which also carries with it multiple implications for educational buildings, their architecture and interior design, workspaces, science laboratories, group rooms, libraries, and outdoor and recreational facilities.

5.1 Linking Education and Work and Promoting Adult Education

A second area of major weakness in the chain of provision for lifelong learning are the links between the worlds of work and education and training. As the diversity of provision multiplies, participation increases across a wide range, and the application of information technology widens, the education and work pathways followed by individuals are becoming more varied. Transitions—particularly from school to work—are becoming more critical. But articulations and links between the various pathways in education and learning, and between them and the worlds of work and community life are insufficiently developed, rigid, and without sufficient bridges to encourage efficient mobility. The provision of lifelong learning for adults carries significant risks of incoherence unless the aim of fostering flexible and interconnected pathways is made a high priority.

A strengthening of work-based learning in upper-secondary and tertiary education can be an important step in facilitating transitions. A review and overhaul of current approaches to certification and qualification is required. Learning achievements must be recognized and valued regardless of where they have been acquired. Skill accreditation, the assessment of prior learning and, especially, a credit transfer system must be introduced. Educational institutions at all levels need to be encouraged to forge closer links with local enterprises and their surrounding communities, not only through "learning with production," partnerships with employers and other sponsors, and the presence of returning adults, but also by opening their doors to the voluntary assistance of adults with teaching and other functions, to teaching assistants, to workers who can demonstrate aspects of their professionalism, and to cultural civic organizations. Individual adult learners, as well as those who provide the opportunities, require adequate information on the various options that are available or in demand, their costs and quality, and their effectiveness in delivering qualifications. This implies an extension of the educational and career guidance and counseling functions, not only of those connected with schools, but also those in workplaces and communities.

5.2 Instruments for Implementing Lifelong Learning Strategies

Three instruments deserve close attention: financial resources, human resources and infrastructure, and policy support mechanisms including education R&D.

Financing. The cost of implementing strategies for life-long learning may well be high. Viewed in the long-run, there may be, however, some scope for reducing costs by reallocating funds and increasing effectiveness. If efficiently implemented, investment in lifelong learning should contribute to economic and productivity growth and thereby help to increase the resource base. Costs of remedial education and training that are currently incurred may be lowered in a regime of lifelong learning. Extensive use of new technologies and distance learning may reduce the unit cost of provision. Economies may also be gained through better policy coordination, for example, with expenditures incurred on training programs run by different ministries, such as the active labor market programs. Despite these potential savings, lifelong learning, if applied to all, would require more resources, even considerably more resources (OECD in press). In order to make it affordable, cost-effectiveness must be improved and better coordination achieved between public and private efforts. Even so, incentives would need to be introduced to mobilise new investment.

Financing models that allow genuine choices by individual learners and the different partners will need to be considered. Market-oriented approaches have an important role to play, especially in the postschool sectors. A useful scheme is the individual entitlements/parafiscal approach, combined with income-contingent loans and, possibly, supplemented by a training levy. Increased contributions from the private sector would not mean that governments can reduce their commitments. They will continue to be responsible for the fair distribution of funds for foundation learning and have a responsibility to ensure that there is a fair opportunity for all to participate in adult education and training.

Human resources and other support systems. The goal of improved quality in teaching and learning must engage those most centrally involved: teachers and facilitators, and the learners themselves. The human capital that is invested in the knowledge and experience of teachers and other personnel is the most important resource for promoting lifelong learning. The professional development of teachers and trainers must be a prime objective of policy. Initial teacher training should be the first stage of a continuing staff development program that gives teachers not only professional support in the classroom but also access to research results and new developments in subject matter, teaching methods, and assessment techniques. The retraining effort should take place both outside and within the schools, through the allocation of time for team reflection and internal development and planning. Teachers must be encouraged, with appropriate incentives, to work in teams, not for the sole purpose of teaching specific subjects, but for the benefit of ensuring mutual professional support and good working conditions in the face of challenging tasks.

Education R&D. There is underinvestment in educational R&D and its revitalization must be an important object of strategic policy (OECD 1995c). Education authorities need to establish comprehensive and accessible information bases, not only for their own use but for access by institutions and suppliers of learning opportunities, communities and the general public, enterprises, and the individual learners themselves. Educational research needs to be sustained at a critical level for producing policy advice of direct relevance to decision-makers. The bulk of the financial resources for educational R&D have come from governments while the private sector contributes only a tiny fraction. A system of incentives will need to be developed so that all partners are willing to contribute to the revitalization of educational R&D. The development of an appropriate knowledge base should take into account not only the need of the individual or of national governments but also the increasing importance on the one hand of devolution of decision-making at the national level and, on the other hand, globalization at the international level. Autonomy of local institutions requires a parallel devolution of knowledge. On their part, governments need to start working towards a shared knowledge base at the international level.

5.3 Redefining the Role of Partners

Lifelong learning takes place through a complex variety of environments and forms of provision. It involves many participants, partners, and stakeholders of which government is only one. In view of this diversity of actors and stakeholders there is a need to redefine their roles and responsibilities. Governments themselves will need to choose between a wide range of alternative policy orientations—direct management, control, and regulation; steering and framework setting; establishing and intervening in training markets. What role markets should play is particularly important for clarification and for the identification of legislative and incentives schemes that can foster flexibility and responsiveness in the markets. Such clarification and a redefinition of roles would require close consultation with other partners.

In education as much as elsewhere, there is a broad trend towards the devolution of management responsibilities to levels other than the center, with implications for the roles of government and the nature of policy-making and governance. It is important to identify those aspects of the lifelong learning network where the public education authorities should contribute only as one among a number of partners or in a secondary capacity. With devolved forms of governance and partnership approaches, the functioning of intermediate bodies—including those engaged in curriculum development, teacher training, and monitoring and evaluation—would require strengthening through training, support, and explicit guidelines. The conditions for successful partnership need to be clarified, including the distribution of powers and resources consistent with the new lines of responsibility. These need to recognize the close interaction between the organization of learning, governance, and the use of resources.

Within government the responsibility for lifelong learning is shared across different policy areas, and the success of many educational policies is bound up with the policies for employment, social development, health care, and taxation. The special responsibilities of the education authorities would need to be clarified and strengthened. Education and training policies should be coordinated with other economic and social policies, especially those for taxation, employment, social insurance, and pensions, in the light of the need to secure sufficient investment in human capital. In many countries the pressure resulting from reduced numbers in mid-adulthood supporting growing numbers at each end of the age spectrum is growing rapidly.

6. Barriers to the Implementation of Lifelong Learning Strategies

A number of major barriers to adult learning have been identified in the research literature and in OECD's work on adult learning and recurrent education (OECD 1975, OECD 1977-81, Levin and Schütze 1983, Schütze and Istance 1987, Kawanobe et al. 1993). Based especially on the framework devised by Cross (1981), the distinction can be drawn between barriers that operate at the structural/contextual level, those at the institutional level, and individual/dispositional barriers to learning. In practice, lack of participation cannot be attributed exclusively to the presence of just one of these barriers; rather they arise from combinations of all of them (see *Participation: Antecedent Factors*).

Structural/contextual barriers refer to the socioeconomic, labor market, financial, and political conditions which influence participation in learning. The nature of people's living conditions, communities, and sense of security and other structural/contextual factors influence both the "supply" side of provision, programs and opportunities and the "demand" side of individual expectations and motivations. Dealing with this set of factors will often not be within the direct province of the education authorities, since a large number of actors, partners, and policy jurisdictions are involved, including at various levels of government. Indeed, these factors may indeed operate at the most general level of the values, belief systems, habits, and traditions that constitute the very fabric of societies.

Institutional barriers: the "supply" of learning opportunities that individuals and groups perceive as relevant to their lives is shaped by the programs available; their timing and accessibility; the quality and ethos of teachers, trainers, and support staff; the location of institutions; the environment for nonformal and informal learning to flourish; and so forth. Examples of institutional barriers include the factors that prevent students from progressing along their routes or that limit access. Inadequate use of new technologies and insufficient and ineffective guidance and counseling services that assist people in creating individually relevant pathways for lifelong learning are other limiting factors. Or, most simply, suitable programs and pathways may just not be in place.

Individual dispositional barriers comprise the dispositions, values, and attitudes of individuals to education and learning more generally. They are, of course, closely shaped by the structural institutional factors outlined above—factors which are both more directly shaped by and further removed from the influence of education systems and their authorities. These individual factors, in their turn, shape the play of those structural and institutional forces. While this dimension becomes manifest in the dispositions and attitudes of individuals, it does not follow that it reflects the purely personal and hence lies outside the realm of legitimate policy intervention. Personal attitudes are very closely shaped by broad cultural contexts. Attitudes to learning are especially sensitive to the general culture, the respect that this gives to the improvement of knowledge, and skills, and the extent to which this improvement is regarded as rightfully "for all," or only for certain sections of society (see *Participation: Role of Motivation*).

7. Addressing the Bottlenecks to a Systemic Culture of Lifelong Learning

The barriers outlined above manifest themselves in different forms among different participating and stakeholder groups. These are only examples, not meant to typify all individuals, teachers, employers, and politicians. Among individuals, there is often a lack of insight into what is possible, as well as an innate conservatism about venturing into new fields of learning in order to create a valuable and relevant foundation of knowledge and skills. Among teachers, protection of professional self-interest can stand in the way of the structural, organizational, and pedagogical changes—at the system, institutional and individual levels—that the realization of lifelong learning entails. Within many of the discrete sectors of education and training systems, as well as the separate government departments, are the territorialism and viewpoints that prevent the emergence of the larger, holistic visions implied by lifelong learning. Among employers in many countries, there is often a marked inconsistency between the demands made for the creation of a high-level knowledge and skills base on the one hand, and willingness to match such demands with corresponding support on the other. Among politicians and decision-makers there is too often only a superficial espousal of the grand principles and no real willingness to confront the consequences for action stemming from that espousal. Among parents, there are—depending on the system in question—examples of efforts to maximize the comparative advantage of their own children's education might endanger much-needed reforms for the general good. In some communities, including those most in need of educational and cultural investment, the attitude may prevail that learning is something for the specialist education and training bodies with little connection with those in the community.

The existence of these barriers helps to explain why, despite receiving political support in industrialized countries, the concept of recurrent education was only partially translated into effective policy. There were principally three reasons for this. Firstly, the application of recurrent education would have required a major transformation of the formal education system for which the sector was not ready. Secondly, effective implementation of the recurrent education policy required coordinated approaches with other policies—labor, employment, social welfare, and income transfer policies—and there were not sufficient political imperatives to push for major changes in social and political organization to achieve the required coordination. Finally, the financial implications of the strategy, including how the burden might be shared, were not adequately worked out. The slowing down of the economy and the rise in unemployment that set in around the mid-1970s dampened further the possibilities of its realization.

In reviewing the changing educational policy contexts in OECD countries since the 1960s, Papadopoulos (1994) refers to the "double challenge" posed by recurrent education: vertically, to the established patterns of progress through education, and horizontally, to education's place in broader social policy. He concludes: "Few governments, even if they were willing to accept this double challenge, had the machinery to confront it effectively. Yet it must not be assumed that the effort had been wasted. Many of the efforts of the recurrent education strategy in fact gradually found their way into national education policies and practices. Above all, the long debate around recurrent education helped to bring about greater awareness among educationists as well as other stakeholders of the inter-relatedness of their concerns and the need for concerted action." The experience of the 1980s and the 1990s has, however, invested new urgency in the concept of lifelong learning and there is evidence of wider support emerging. It remains to be seen whether the political support for the concept will crystalize into effective implementation.

References

Bengtsson J 1985 Recurrent education. In: Husén T, Postlethwaite T N (eds.) 1985 *International Encyclopedia of Education, 1st edn*. Pergamon Press, Oxford

Council of Europe 1978 *Permanent Education: Final Report*. Council of Europe, Strasbourg

Cross K P 1981 *Adults as Learners*. Jossey-Bass, San Francisco, California

Faure E et al. 1972 *Learning To Be: The World of Education Today and Tomorrow*. UNESCO, Paris

Houghton V 1974 *Recurrent Education—An Alternative Future?* The Open Univesity Press, Milton Keynes

Jarvis P 1983 *Adult and Continuing Education*, Croom Helm, New York

Jourdan M 1981 *Recurrent Education in Western Europe*. NFER, Windsor

Kawanobe S et al. 1993 *A Study of Lifelong Education in Selected Industrialized Countries*. National Institute for Educational Research, Tokyo

Kallen D 1979 Recurrent education and lifelong learning: Definitions and distinctions. In: Schuller T, Megarry J (eds.) 1979

Lengrand P 1965 *Éducation Permanente*, UNESCO, Paris

Levin H M, Schütze H G (eds.) 1983 *Financing Recurrent Education: Strategies for Increasing Employment, Job Opportunities, and Productivity*. Sage Publications, London

Miller R 1993 Investment knowledge and knowledge investment: The need to rethink human capital information and decision-making systems. Document DEELSA/ELSA/ED (93) 16 OECD, Paris

Organisation for Economic Co-operation and Development (OECD) 1973 *Recurrent Education. A Strategy for Lifelong Learning*. OECD, Paris

Organisation for Economic Co-operation and Development (OECD) 1975 *Recurrent Education. Trends and Issues*. OECD, Paris

Organisation for Economic Co-operation and Development (OECD) 1977-81 *Learning Opportunities for Adults*, Vols. 1-5 OECD, Paris

Organisation for Economic Co-operation and Development (OECD) 1991 *The lifelong learner in the 1990s*. Document CERI/CD(91)16 OECD, Paris

Organisation for Economic Co-operation and Development (OECD) 1992 *High Quality Education and Training for All*. OECD, Paris

Organisation for Economic Co-operation and Development (OECD) 1994a *The OECD Jobs Study*, Vols. I-II. OECD, Paris

Organisation for Economic Co-operation and Development (OECD) 1994b Lifelong learning: From ideal to reality. Presented at the International Conference on Learning Beyond Schooling, Paris, 7-8 December

Organisation for Economic Co-operation and Development (OECD) 1995a Meeting of the OECD Council at ministerial level: Communique Document SG/PRESS (95) 41. OECD, Paris

Organisation for Economic Co-operation and Development (OECD) 1995b *The OECD Jobs Study: Implementing the Strategy*. OECD, Paris

Organisation for Economic Co-operation and Development (OECD) 1995c *Educational Research and Development: Trends, Issues, Challenges*. OECD, Paris

Organisation for Economic Co-operation and Development (OECD)/Statistics Canada 1995 *Literacy, Economy and Society: Results of the First International Adult Literacy Survey*. OECD, Paris/Statistics Canada, Ottawa

Organisation for Economic Co-operation and Development (OECD) in press. Making lifelong learning a reality for all. Background Report for the Meeting of the Education Committee at Ministerial Level. OECD, Paris

Papadopoulos G 1994 *Education 1960-1990: The OECD Perspective*. OECD, Paris

Schuller T, Megarry J (eds.) 1979 *Recurrent Education and Lifelong Learning*. World Yearbook of Education, Kogan Page, London

Schütze H G, Istance D 1987 *Recurrent Education Revisited* Almqvist and Wiksell, Stockholm

Sutton P 1994 Lifelong and Continuing Education. In: Husén T, Postlethwaite T N (eds.) 1994 *International Encyclopedia of Education*, 2nd edn. Pergamon Press, Oxford

Titmus C J 1994 Concepts, principles and purposes of adult education. In: Husén T, Postlethwaite T N (eds.) 1994 *International Encyclopedia of Education*, 2nd edn. Pergamon Press, Oxford

Tuijnman A C 1994 Adult education: Overview. In: Husén

T, Postlethwaite T N (eds.) 1994 *International Encyclopedia of Education*, 2nd edn. Pergamon Press, Oxford.

UNESCO 1995 Preliminary Synthesis. Report of the Commission, International Commission on Education for the Twenty-first Century UNESCO, Paris

Technical and Vocational Education and Training

K. King

Technical and vocational education and training (TVET) is a title that encompasses a great deal. Its emphasis both on education and on training means that there is a considerable variety of locations in which TVET is pursued. This institutional diversity provides one of the commonest sources of debate about the character of TVET and what can be expected of its outcomes. Intimately connected with the different institutional sites for TVET is a series of issues concerning the clienteles or participants in TVET programs. In this respect there are not only major contrasts across countries and regions, reflecting different historical and cultural traditions, but within countries over time it is possible to identify many more dramatic shifts in the clienteles of TVET than of other curriculum areas. A rich variety of provision would also be characteristic of the TVET curriculum itself, reflecting as it does the range of eventual work and employment positions for which TVET is regarded, in different societies, as an orientation or a preparation. A final thread that runs through much discussion of TVET is the issue of control, and in particular the extent to which the state, the private sector, and other nongovernmental agencies should have responsibility for providing, financing, and overseeing the domain of technical and vocational education and training for youths and adults.

1. The Multiple Locations of TVET

In any country, TVET can generally be said to be located in one or more of at least three distinct institutional settings: formal schools; postschool adult education and training institutions; or enterprises, whether large or small, industrial or commercial. In most countries there is a predominant modality, as well as examples of TVET in alternative institutional settings. In examining the significance of this diversity, it is not the intention to suggest that there is a preferred site for TVET, but rather to note what some of the trends are within and among these different locations.

1.1 School-based TVET

Even within the school setting, there is no single modality. In some situations, principally in the developing world where primary schooling may be effectively terminal for the majority of pupils, governments have encouraged varieties of exposure to practical subjects, manual activities, and even elementary business awareness within the primary school cycle (see King 1991). At the secondary level, however, there are three broad distinctions: (a) Within the general secondary or high school, it is possible to select a variety of courses which may be termed vocational; thus in the United States a wide range of high school graduates pick up as much as 20 percent of their total credits from vocational subjects; (b) In other comprehensive high school traditions, the single upper secondary school, for example in Sweden, provides 13 broad vocational lines, in addition to general education lines, and a technician line. This is a much more structured presentation of vocational options than in the United States or United Kingdom; (c) There is then the tradition of quite separate vocational and technical schools running alongside the general secondary school. Increasingly within those Western European countries that have this provision, the separate types of school divide at the end of 9 years of general education. Even here there are exceptions, with the Netherlands having a lower secondary technical school starting after primary, at the same point as the general secondary.

This third type—of separate vocational and technical schools—is not restricted to Western Europe. Across the former Soviet Union, for example, it was commonplace to have in addition to the general secondary school a secondary vocational school, providing matriculation as well as a vocational qualification, and a lower vocational school that offered just a skilled worker qualification. Understandably, much of Eastern Europe was similar in structure, as was China prior to the Cultural Revolution. In the developing world, the tradition of the separate vocational school has remained important—for example, in much of Latin America, parts of Southeast Asia, and the Middle East. In francophone Africa, there has been influence from the French practice of having a technical stream and a vocational stream running alongside the academic upper secondary. Meanwhile in anglophone Africa, the absence of a distinctive school-based TVET stream in the United Kingdom during the colonial period, is still partly reflected in the now independent states of the continent.

It is important to emphasize that there is a large number of different school-based versions of vocational and technical education in operation around the world, many of which account for a considerable proportion of the relevant age cohort. Thus when China decided shortly after the Cultural Revolution to restore the proportion of pupils entering vocational upper secondary education to 50:50 with general secondary, it was not dramatically out of line with several other countries. By contrast, it is well-known that the World Bank, which in the 1960s and 1970s had supported a great deal of "diversified" secondary education (through agricultural, technical, commercial, and home economics options in regular secondary schools) had by the mid-1980s decided that this style of school-based vocationalization was not effective: "These 'diversified' programmes are no more effective than academic secondary education in enabling graduates to enter wage or self-employment" (World Bank 1991 p. 9).

So widely have the Bank's criticisms of diversification been disseminated that it is worth underlining the fact that it was commenting on only one of the three modalities of school-based vocational education —what could be termed the least structured version of secondary vocational education. Although the World Bank has phased out its financing for this type, and also reduced its funding of separate vocational schools, it should be noted that in many parts of Western Europe it is precisely the upper vocational and technical school streams that have been expanding faster than the general streams in the late 1980s and early 1990s.

This expansion of upper secondary technical education is in these OECD countries clearly linked to the need for larger numbers of technicians to operate in the rapidly changing structures of work. Even at the level of reform proposals for the upper secondary school, the suggestion in the report of the committee reviewing Scottish education in 1992 was for no less than 70 percent of the cohort to follow a vocational track (SOED 1992).

1.2 Postschool TVET Programs

The term "postschool" is used for what is a very wide range of provision. In the industrialized countries what is referred to is effectively postsecondary, or at least postcompulsory. It is important to distinguish what may be termed regular programs from special provision. The regular programs refer to the opportunities in, for example, the community colleges and technical institutes of the United States or in the further education colleges of the United Kingdom. Special programs refer to what was commonplace in many OECD countries at times when youth employment had become politically sensitive. These were institutional programs intended to help in the transition from

school to work. There was a bewildering variety of such initiatives in the United Kingdom, but by far the largest of them was the Youth Training Scheme, which at its peak covered almost half a million young people, in a two-year exposure to both on- and off-the-job training. The problem, however, with these special, emergency training initiatives was that they had a tendency, most evident in the United Kingdom, to weaken the traditional training arrangements and make training increasingly dependent on state financing (see *Postliteracy; Adult Secondary Education*).

In the developing countries, the role of postschool training is in many ways structurally different. The equivalents of what were termed the regular programs in the OECD countries have often been very small in number and coverage and have been predominantly oriented to the formal sector of the economy. This has been particularly true of Africa, where in addition to being few in number such postschool vocational training centers were often originally externally funded and have sometimes continued to be in part dependent on donor resources. In Latin America, by contrast, the postschool vocational training institutes are organized under the aegis of the different national training agencies, serve very wide constituencies, and their funding is generally secured through payroll levies on industrial and/or commercial enterprises.

The nearest parallel in the developing world to the special programs of the OECD countries are a host of usually small-scale initiatives that have often been associated with nongovernmental organizations (NGOs). In situations where, outside the newly industrializing countries, there is seldom anything approaching universal secondary education provision, postschool will generally mean postprimary school training. At this level, therefore, there are significant numbers of quite small NGO programs targeting rural and urban youth. Unlike the regular provision which is linked to the formal industrial sector, their goal will generally be to help young people develop skills for income generation in the informal or micro-enterprise sectors, so few are the opportunities of getting employed in the modern sector of the economy (see *Nongovernmental Organisations*).

This is not to say that the state is not involved at all in special training programs in developing countries. In some cases, the government has actually taken over and expanded a successful NGO training initiative, for example the original village (now youth) polytechnic movement in Kenya, or the Botswana Brigades. In other cases, especially in Latin America, NGO programs that were developed with external assistance during the long periods of authoritarian rule now find themselves being jointly funded by NGOs and the new democratic regimes (see *Latin America: Adult Education; Latin America: National Training Agencies*).

In many developing countries in the 1990s, the state faces a major dilemma in postschool vocational training. On the one hand, it is under pressure to expand publicly funded vocational training since local industry and the trainees themselves are often unwilling or unable to bear the costs. On the other, the state is itself unable to ensure the quality of even the small provision for which it is responsible, let alone anything approaching universal entitlement to vocational training. For many developing countries, therefore, the distinction between regular and special provision of vocational training is academic, since even the "regular" support of TVET is minute in scope. The notion that the state could also launch a special program to aid transition to employment is doubly unrealistic, since there is no capacity to afford it, and no further employment opportunities in the formal sector toward which such an expanded provision could be oriented.

A version of this dilemma is now beginning to affect the countries of Eastern Europe and the former Soviet Union. From a position where the majority of young people had been sure to find a job, linked to the particular vocation to which they had been assigned, the macro-economic shifts now imply the end of these older certainties. The transition of the states themselves toward a market economy means that the old transition from vocational school to its linked enterprise has been broken. The new category of official unemployment is now widely acknowledged, and with it a recognition for the first time that special initiatives may be necessary if a new relationship to the emerging labor market is to be developed by young people leaving the many vocational schools. As in a number of the developing countries, however, the financial resources to support a large-scale special program are not readily available.

1.3 Work-based TVET

Historically work itself was the site of training, and apprenticeships, whether as silversmiths or trainee lawyers, took place entirely on the job. Although in the twentieth century a great variety of school-based and postschool training arrangements has been evident, there have been a number of developments in the late 1980s and early 1990s that have rekindled interest in the potential of work-based vocational training. One of these has been the recognition of the crucial role of the employers in the very different vocational training systems of Japan and Germany (see *Europe: Western and Southern; Japan: Vocational Education and Training*). Parallel to these in the developing world would be the acknowledged dynamism of the national training agencies in much of Latin America where again there has historically been a strong involvement of employers.

A second, more general tendency that has encouraged an interest in the role of enterprise-based training has been the search to reduce dependency on the state and the public sector, and to encourage more of a market approach, even in the provision of social services. This trend has been evident in many OECD countries.

It has been dramatically obvious also in the political and economic shifts in Eastern Europe and the former Soviet Union. In the developing world, meanwhile, the criticism of the state and the case for reducing its role have been closely associated with the World Bank and the International Monetary Fund; one of their principal concerns has been to restructure developing economies in ways that give greater salience to free market principles.

There have been several consequences for TVET of this widespread desire to involve the private sector more substantially in the economy, while reducing the role of government. One is that there has been considerable interest in schemes such as work experience or work placement that give trainees direct experience of the working environment, even if their training is not entirely based in industry. More generally, there has been a search for mechanisms which make TVET more responsive and accountable to private sector employers. These range from initiatives like performance contracting in California—which made the payment of private training contractors depend on their successfully placing trainees in employment—to a variety of partnerships, compacts, and joint ventures between enterprises and training institutions. Within the United Kingdom, this trend has led to the government transferring the control of state TVET activities to publicly funded companies and councils which are controlled by private sector employers.

Within the developing world the interest in strengthening the role of the private sector in TVET has been greatly assisted by the advocacy of the World Bank, and in particular by the publication and dissemination of its policy paper on vocational and technical education and training (World Bank 1991). Although this document argued also for more effective and efficient public sector training, it was widely held to have made a powerful case for the private sector in TVET: "Training in the private sector—by private employers and in private training institutions—can be the most effective and efficient way to develop the skills of the work force" (World Bank 1991 p. 7).

On the other side of the debate about work-based TVET there have been concerns that training on the job will, on its own, prove to have serious limitations. These shortcomings are perhaps most obvious in the majority of small and micro-enterprise firms which generally do not have their own in-house training department. In the widespread local apprenticeship systems of West Africa, for example, young people learn entirely on the job, and in these artisanal and craft modes of production, a great deal of skill can be acquired within the firm itself. What may be lacking in this completely firm-based training is any exposure to new technologies of production or to product diversification. In the much more automated production lines of modern manufacturing, it is much less obvious that the work site alone provides an adequate environment for technical and vocational skills development. By themselves the routines of an efficient factory do not offer a rich vein of training through production.

The example of Japan suggests that the excellence of their work-based TVET depends on the pedagogical skills of the supervisors and more experienced workers, on the strong employer encouragement to workers to engage in self-development, and in mechanisms such as job rotation and quality control circles that are a source of informal skill development. Similarly in Germany, and in the other countries that maintain a dynamic, modern apprenticeship, it is the combination of work-based TVET with the exposure to further skills in the linked institutional training of these "dual" systems that gives this form of apprenticeship an advantage over training that is merely on the job. In addition, the quality of this apprenticeship is crucially associated with the interest of the employers and their organizations in financing it, setting its standards and certification, and actively seeking its development.

Confirmation of the importance of systematic on-the-job training with further training organized off the job comes from a comparison of matched factories in Germany and the United Kingdom. A significant element in the productivity difference between the two sets of factories derives from the much higher proportions of formally trained workers and supervisors in the German samples. By contrast, a much larger number of workers and supervisors in the United Kingdom had been promoted on the basis of experience on the job alone.

It is clear that there is no evidence for a single preferred site for training. Nor is there robust evidence for what might be termed a "stages of growth" approach to TVET, whereby governments have to intervene to provide training (in vocational schools or postschool centres) in the early stages of industrialization when the private sector is too small or too little diversified to provide it; but that in mature economies the government role can be expected to change from direct provision to more of a standard-setting and monitoring role, while private employers take on more of a broad-based involvement. This evolutionary approach to TVET can be identified in the World Bank's analysis as well as in the early thinking of German agencies concerned with aid to vocational education in the developing world).

In Latin America a trend has been noted in which some training responsibilities are being transferred from the institutes of the national training agencies to the enterprises themselves (see *Latin America: National Training Agencies*). It could also be argued that the role of the state in TVET has shifted in the United Kingdom, so that it is principally concerned in the early 1990s with some special unemployment-related programs, and with standard setting and monitoring of provision. Elsewhere it is difficult to point to any marked diminution in state provision and financing of vocational secondary education or postschool centers, except for reasons of economic crisis.

2. Patterns of Participation in TVET

Another of the central debates about TVET is concerned with participation. The question of whether vocational and technical education streams and schools are for those who fail to be selected for academic schools has had a long history. In a number of Western societies trade schools of various types did traditionally provide short courses for those (including working-class children) who were not expected to proceed through the academic lines. In many of the colonial dependencies also, it was evident that low-level manual or industrial education and training were thought by the ruling powers to be particularly appropriate to subject peoples (King 1971). These early associations of vocational education with courses thought particularly relevant to colonial peoples and certain socioeconomic classes ensured that for a time there was a negative reaction to this kind of provision. Thus at Independence in many anglophone African countries, manual or industrial education was dropped from the syllabus of basic education.

However, the situation is in many ways fundamentally different in the early 1990s. It may be appropriate, therefore, to re-examine the discussions about differentiation, selectivity, and participation from a contemporary perspective.

2.1 A Trend Toward Vocational Education for All

One tendency may be noted in a number of school systems that are not sharply differentiated into different vocational, technical, and general streams. This is the incorporation of a common vocational element to be taken by all pupils. It may not necessarily be termed "vocational" or "technical," but it is usually justified on the grounds that the vocational impulse should really be part of general education. Thus design and technology is one of the foundation subjects in the national curriculum of England and Wales, and there are elements derived from the Technical Vocational Education Initiative, such as work experience, which are common to all pupils across the United Kingdom (King and Layton 1992).

Many developing Commonwealth countries, after the initial rejection of this field at Independence, have reintroduced vocationally oriented subjects for all children, sometimes at primary school level, and sometimes at secondary (Commonwealth Secretariat 1988). The justification for this is frequently for both general educational and labor market reasons. The latter, labor market rationale for prevocational education is often elaborated in terms of preparing young people for entering self-employment. In this respect, these vocational-education-for-all policies appear to run counter to the well-known argument of Foster: that "the vocational aspirations of children . . . are almost exclusively determined by factors which lie outside schools" and "that no amount of formal technical, vocational or agricultural instruction alone is going to . . . reduce the volume of unemployment" (Foster 1963 p. 153). Since Foster elaborated his "vocational school fallacy," a great deal has changed in the external environment of schools, and not least in the traditional distinctions between a modern sector job and self-employed work. Whether these changes in the opportunity structure are sufficient to make vocationally oriented schemes successful it is too early to say.

2.2 Differentiation in Vocational Education

Running counter to the inclusion of vocational education as an ordinary part of general education there is a strong trend also to stream and track pupils into quite separate sections or separate schools. Some of these different divisions have been outlined above. Many educational systems do track into different versions of general academic school (e.g., Germany) or of academic, vocational and technical schools. It is frequently the case that the vocational school recruits at an allegedly lower level of ability than the technical, and both the vocational and technical at lower levels than the academic or general secondary schools. This tendency was traditionally reinforced by there being no possibility of continuing with further tertiary level education from the vocational school. The same was true of skilled worker schools in Eastern Europe and the former Soviet Union.

There is no reason why vocational or technical education should have no scope for progression. In other vocational and technical traditions (e.g., Latin America) there are varieties of both terminal and nonterminal vocational and technical education. Indeed, it has been argued that the majority of technical schools in Latin America are not terminal; rather they have a dual purpose of training technicians and preparing students for further studies in higher education (see *Latin America: National Training Agencies*). Nor is it impossible that a vocational or technical school should be a center of academic excellence. In Brazil, for example, there are highly prestigious federal technical schools, as well as elite technical schools run by the national training agency (SENAI).

What seems increasingly likely to alter once lowly status of vocational and technical schools, especially in the OECD countries, are the rapid changes in the organization of work. The old stratification of work in terms of skill and semiskill has become increasingly obsolete, and the requirement now is for much more flexible workers, versed in technical, scientific and information skills. These radical changes in manufacturing and commerce are in part what have produced the remarkable expansion of upper secondary technical education in many of the Western European countries, including a tendency in France for high school graduates with a technological baccalaureate to continue their studies at a postsecondary technical level.

What these developments point to in the more industrialized countries is an important realignment in the classical contrast between vocational training and academic education. It is a contrast that was possibly always somewhat exaggerated, but the revolutions in new technology in particular have blurred the distinctions even further. There is accordingly a substantial convergence identifiable between the domains of education and training, but one that is much more evident in OECD than in the developing countries (see *Convergence between Education and Training; Technological Change and Education; Demand, Supply, and Finance of Adult Education*).

2.3 Vocational Education and Disadvantage

Despite the pointers to significant changes in work organization and their implications for education and training, vocational education does continue to provide opportunities for disadvantaged youth in many different types of program. In the United States, for example, federal vocational education policy has over the course of the twentieth century moved from an encouragement to the states to provide separate instruction in specific vocational trades (that would prepare public school children in general for useful employment) to a situation in the 1990s where federal vocational education was primarily a program of support for disadvantaged and other special students. In other words, the target constituency for federal policy had narrowed to focus particularly on improving the access to good quality vocational education of many different disadvantaged groups, including handicapped people.

This did not mean that vocational education in the regular school system was being restricted to such students. Rather, it may suggest that for many categories of less motivated or less linguistically competent students, vocational subjects can act as an alternative route to the mastery of some of the same abstract concepts that are acquired in the so-called academic subjects.

In the developing world the flexible use of vocational education and training to meet the needs of disadvantaged young people is perhaps most evident in Latin America. There the national training agencies have tried to adjust their traditional, formal provision to reach workers in the informal and microenterprise sector. It is the NGOs which have developed a whole strategy for reaching disadvantaged groups via vocational education and training. Typically, such methods will involve local craft workers, as part-time instructors, and will make links with community development programs rather than insisting that trainees come to fixed training premises.

There is, however, an ongoing debate about NGO strategies for encouraging income generation through vocational and entrepreneurial skills development. A strong tendency in many NGOs is critical of individualistic business success, and their target is often "the poorest of the poor" rather than potential entrepreneurs. By contrast, the World Bank is perhaps much more inclined to target the upper end of the informal sector. The International Labour Organisation can probably be situated in between these two poles, in its own programs that seek to improve training opportunities for women, unemployed youth, refugees, and other vulnerable groups (see *International Labour Organisation*).

3. The Content of the Vocational Curriculum

A number of important aspects of the vocational curriculum have already been touched upon above, but there are several further significant themes which perhaps serve to provide some linkage between the variety of sites of vocational training and the variety of participants.

3.1 Restructuring Vocational Content and Delivery

There are at least two complementary developments going on in the framing and delivery of vocational education. The first relates to the shift toward what is termed "competency-based training," a move that emphasizes the specification of particular knowledge and skills and their application to standards of performance required in the workplace. This approach is frequently associated with the modularization of the vocational curriculum. In combination, these initiatives have tended to stress individualized, self-directed learning. Equally important, the specification of learning objectives in a modular structure makes it possible for learning to take place according to common standards in any of the three locations discussed in this entry: the school, postschool training, or the workplace. Common learning outcomes also make it possible for trainees to follow modules through distance or open learning, as well as through full- or part-time modes (see *Modularization in Adult Education and Training*).

A parallel curricular development concerns the regrouping of vocational specializations. In many parts of Eastern Europe and the former Soviet Union, the lower vocational schools have been characterized by considerable specialization, with preparation for some 250 different occupations, and even more at the upper secondary level. In Western Europe, where similar overspecialization occurred, moves have been made progressively to regroup and reformulate qualifications so that a significant decrease in specialisms has been obtained.

The reforms in France and the United Kingdom are driven by a desire to prevent too early specialization by young people, but at the same time to ensure that the qualification system captures the changes in work organization in the enterprises.

It should be stressed that even within the European Community, these kinds of curricular developments have not thus far led to anything remotely like a single European vocational curriculum. Indeed, it is acknowledged that there is, even within this small group of nations, considerable diversity in terms of the duration, content, objectives, and organization of vocational education. Nevertheless, with the onset of the Single European Market in 1993, and the implications for mobility of labor, an impetus has certainly been given to the work on assessing the comparability and equivalency of vocational qualifications (see *European Union: Continuing Vocational Training*).

3.2 Vocational Education and Enterprise

A curriculum innovation that has spread rapidly, particularly in the developing world, is the notion that, given the grave shortage of employment, trainees in vocational education and training should be exposed not just to a particular craft or technical skill but also to business and enterprise development. In the national training agencies of Latin America, this focus on business management and organization has become increasingly salient. In Africa, Kenya is not alone in arguing, in its 1992 Sessional Paper on small enterprise, that all universities and training institutions should introduce entrepreneurship education in their regular programs (Kenya Government 1992).

As far as the relevance of business training for self-employed craft workers is concerned, opinion is divided. One view suggests that training can be an important complement to other essential elements such as credit in an integrated package of support to small enterprise (World Bank 1991). Another argues that the integrated approach is too costly and ultimately unsustainable; instead, a so-called "minimalist" approach urges the identification and treatment of whatever the single main obstruction may be for entrepreneurs.

In this discussion about the importance of adding business education to practical skills training, it is possible to detect combinations in all three locations of vocational education and training. In Kenya, for example, business education is offered as early as the sixth year of primary education, along with several prevocational subjects. It is provided also in all postschool training institutes; and finally there are opportunities for business training offered to working micro-entrepreneurs through many different schemes. There is no agreement about the single best site for entrepreneurial training.

4. The Role of the State in TVET

A final short section considers the role of the state in TVET policies. Again, several aspects of this have already been mentioned in other contexts, but there are a number of major issues that still need to be underlined (see *Government Role in Adult Education and Training*).

4.1 TVET in Relation to the Macro-economic Context

In the early 1990s, and especially since the World Bank's TVET policy paper (1991), some discussion has centered on the extent to which the character and provision of TVET is actually affected by the broad economic policy of the state. It is argued that in export-oriented trade regimes there will be greater incentives for enterprises to undertake training than in inward-looking economies where policies may seek to protect firms from global competition. More specifically, it is suggested by the Bank that particular policies such as minimum wages, guarantees of employment, or narrow differentials between trainee and skilled worker wages (all of which may have a social justification) can also have a direct bearing on whether firms or individuals invest in training. It is still too early to be sure precisely what kind of knock-on effect these wage policies and trade policies may have on TVET, but there is certainly a case for further research.

On the other side of the argument, there perhaps needs to be caution about the conditions under which a more free-market approach to the economy generally, and a greater privatization of training, will necessarily produce successful skills development. The United Kingdom provides one example of where it is unclear that the historic problem of low employer commitment to TVET has really been addressed by the succession of initiatives that promoted privatization and reduced the role of the state in TVET. Elsewhere, some of the most admired training systems, such as Germany's, illustrate a complex negotiation about the roles of the state, the employers, and the unions. The dual system is far from being a private sector training system. Indeed, it has been argued that the relative strength of the apprenticeship training system in Germany derives in part from very deliberate government policies, including in the field of educational differentiation and in the restriction of full-time vocational schools.

There is no easy formula for establishing the preferred role for the government and the private sector in training. All countries will already have developed a tradition of how vocational training is handled, and radical reforms of the existing training arrangements will generally prove difficult to contemplate except where, as in the case of the former Soviet Union and Eastern Europe, there is massive change being considered in the wider economy. Ultimately the rationales for government intervention in the financing and delivery of training must take account of the circumstances of each individual country, but it may prove useful to consider the role for government after examining the performance of its markets, the capacity of its private sector to train, and its own concerns about social equity.

In this regard, there is a particular responsibility for external agencies—whether bilateral or multilateral donors—to play a sensitive role vis-à-vis governments that desperately require financial support. This is the situation now for a very large number of developing countries, as well as many states in Eastern Europe and the former Soviet Union. It is fashionable in the development assistance community to think that the focus of grants or loans should not be a few selected items like instructor training but should first be ensuring an effective national policy framework for TVET (see *International Labour Organisation*). There is clearly no single, widely accepted version of best practice in TVET. Hence external agencies will need to guard against proposing universal prescriptions when the more appropriate course may be to build upon the culture of TVET that has already been long established in a particular country (see King 1991).

See also: Adult Education: Concepts and Principles; Convergence between Education and Training; Training on the Job; Economics of Adult Education and Training; Recognition and Certification of Skill; Technological Change and Education; Women and Access to Vocational Training; Polytechnical Education; Comparative Studies: Vocational Education and Training; Evaluation of Industry Training: Cost-Effectiveness; Evaluation of Public Training: Cost-Effectivenesss

References

Commonwealth Secretariat 1988 *Survey of Vocationally-oriented Education in the Commonwealth*. Commonwealth Secretariat, London

Foster P J 1965 The vocational school fallacy in development planning. In: Anderson C A, Bowman M J (eds.) 1965 *Education and Economic Development*. Aldine Press, Chicago, Illinois

Kenya Government 1992 Small enterprise and jua kali development in Kenya, sessional paper no. 2. Nairobi

King K J 1971 *Panafricanism and Education*. Clarendon Press, Oxford

King K J 1991 *Aid and Education in the Developing World*. Longman, Harlow

King K J, Layton D (eds.) 1992 Education in science and technology: Innovations and implications for the developing world. *Science, Technology and Development* 10(2): whole issue

Scottish Office Education Department 1992 *Upper Secondary Education in Scotland*. HMSO, Edinburgh

World Bank 1991 Vocational and technical education and training: A World Bank policy paper. Washington, DC

Training on the Job

M. J. Bowman

The term "on-the-job training" is used in several overlapping ways, all of which are usually focused on postschool learning. The first part of this entry discusses briefly the scope of and variations in on-the-job training as discussed in the descriptive and nontechnical literature. The second and third parts deal with the meanings and treatments of on-the-job training in human capital investment theory and its applications. Attention is then turned in the fourth part to a well-known view of institutional adaptations associated with on-the-job training in a dynamic context, characterizing some of the work on what have come to be labeled "internal labor markets" (internal, that is, to particular firms or agencies). Finally, the largely unseen informal economy is noted along with the training and learning activities that go on in its many crannies.

1. On-the-job Training in Nontechnical Usage

At one extreme the term on-the-job training is used quite literally to refer to organized instruction in the workplace. Somewhat less narrowly (and more often) it covers job-related training sponsored by an employer or required as a condition of promotion even when conducted on other premises and irrespective of whether direct outlays are covered by the individual or by the employer.

Remarkably little attention is given in most discussions that use the term in this way, to the many variants of apprenticeship and modifications over time with changes in economic structures. Nevertheless, apprenticeship training in great variety and with all degrees of formalization has remained of critical importance in both the less and the more developed countries. It is important not only for the more traditional manual skills but for other skills as well; indeed, recipients of doctorates have absorbed large amounts of apprentice training in the process of acquiring competence in research. Apprenticeship clearly constitutes a form (or set of forms) of on-the-job training even in a relatively narrow definition of that term. This is normally recognized where apprenticeship programs are developed as part of an organized government policy, but it is often ignored when apprenticeship arrangements evolve spontaneously and their structure remains relatively informal. These biases in what comes to be included have had counterparts in analyses of labor market and of human resource development. Fortunately, this fact is coming to be more adequately recognized in some of the less developed countries (LDCs).

Meanwhile, increasing alertness has emerged among both planners and researchers to the fact that time in school and time in the labor force need not be, and often are not, separated by a sharp divide. The long-established German system of extended part-time vocational education for young people in their first jobs is a striking example. If the vocational training is related to the jobs held and promotions in them, this is unambiguously a variant of on-the-job training. A quite different but equally interesting type of arrangement is exemplified by the *Servicio Nacional de Aprendizaje* (SENA) in Colombia and the complex of related programs in Brazil, in which some students are individually sponsored by firms that will employ them later or may be employing them at intervals during the training program. In the United Kingdom the university-level polytechnics provided "sandwich courses" which interspersed academic training with periods at work, an approach since adopted by some other countries. The list is easily extended.

Yet another step toward generalization about what is counted as on-the-job training is the inclusion of much of the wide range of activities encompassed in what has sometimes been called "nonformal education" (public or private) and in the vogue for "recurrent education," which was pioneered in Sweden and evoked varying responses elsewhere from about 1970 onward. Much of this type of training is indistinguishable in practice from activities commonly labeled as on-the-job training though often it might be more accurately termed "out-of-a-job training in hope of a job."

The common element that brings together a diverse array of activities under the broadly defined umbrella term on-the-job training is not, in fact, whether the training is received by an individual virtually as part of the job (whether in the workplace or elsewhere). Rather, what seems to be common to all cases is the training of active members of the labor force with the purpose of improving career prospects. There are costs involved in such training, however those costs may be shared. On-the-job training entails investments in the human capital of men and women who have already joined the labor force. These investments are oriented toward their futures in paid or (less often) in independent employment.

2. Opportunity Costs and On-the-job Training

Studies of schooling as an investment constitute only one element in human capital theory. A seminal contribution to that theory came with Becker's incorporation of investments in human beings on through the postschool years into a theory about investments in schooling (Becker 1962, 1983). There were two essential elements in Becker's formulation. The first was the application of an old and powerful concept that lies at the heart of economic theory, the concept of opportunity cost, to the costs of spending time in school or training—commonly referred to in the literature on human capital as forgone earnings. The second element was the analytical distinction made between general and specific training of human capital. While opportunity costs are entailed in both sorts of human capital formation, the most direct applications in empirical work on earning streams deal only with the general (portable) components of learning and earning in the school years and in later years. Though presented initially in terms of time diverted from earning to learning, analysis was subsequently expressed in "time-equivalent units" and emphasis shifted to the importance of experience as an indicator of potentials for on-the-job training. Earnings are forgone when a person takes a job on which he or she will receive lower immediate pay but a compensating increase in the value of his (or less often her) portable investment in acquisition of that human capital. It does not matter, at this level of analysis, whether the accumulation of human capital occurs through formal instructional programs or in the most informal ways through cumulative experience on a job in which a person learns by doing. There may very well be a mixture of both elements of learning, as there has always been in apprenticeship for the skilled crafts and as there is, in fact, in much white-collar employment. In any case, estimates of the extent of investment through forgone earnings were designated on-the-job training in the first empirical forays by Mincer (1962), a designation that has been carried over into much subsequent work.

The initial formulations, along with most of the theoretical and empirical models that followed in the later 1960s and the 1970s, viewed the investments individuals make in themselves as outcomes of a sequence of decisions made implicitly at frequent intervals. Along with the further simplifying assumption that marginal rates of return to schooling and to postschool investments were equal, this way of formulating the process allowed researchers to estimate the time path of investments and returns over a man's life. (Analysis for women, incorporating periods out of the labor force, came later.) Experiments have been conducted that dispense with the assumptions of the equality of marginal rates of return to schooling and to postschool investments, and skill obsolescence has been brought into the picture. This initial and simplest model remains at the core of these refinements, however, and it must suffice here.

Using the Mincerian approach in its initial form, it is possible to separate out the schooling and on-the-job training components of earning streams (Mincer 1962, 1974, Bowman 1968, 1974). Suppose that two male populations have been matched as far as socioeconomic background, health, innate ability, and so

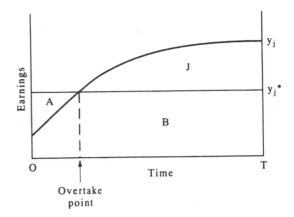

Figure 1
Earnings paths

forth are concerned, but that one of these populations has completed the ith level of schooling whereas the other has completed schooling $i + m$. The focus of comparison is formed by the schooling and on-the-job training components that account for the differences in the average earning streams of these two populations. In analyzing this problem, two highly simplified models may be devised.

2.1 Model 1

Earnings differentials match differences in productivity; they are determined solely by differences in schooling; those earning differentials are realized immediately; and productive capacity is maintained intact until its complete demise. Designating the cost of schooling increment m as Cm and the rate of return on that investment as Rm, the incremental earning path will be unchanging at the value $RmCm$. Starting from an earning path for no schooling and adding to those earnings incrementally for each increment of schooling would give the earning path for a person with schooling $i + m$. Taking $(i + m) = j$ gives the line labeled Yj^* in Fig. 1 for earnings over the period from $t=0$ to $t=T$, when earnings cease.

2.2 Model 2

The potential productivity differentials determined by schooling are the same as in Model 1, taking effect immediately and being sustained intact throughout working life. In addition, however, there are opportunity-cost investments in on-the-job learning, which account for the concavity of observed earning streams. The internal rate of return to an increment of schooling m and rates of return to associated postschool investments are equal. The curve Yj which includes effects of investments in the postschool accumulation of human capital, intersects Yj^* from below because of the forgone earnings in the early years. The point of intersection is known in economics following Mincer (1974) as the "overtake point," at which observed earnings (which are net of opportunity-cost investments in oneself) come to match and then to surpass the return to investments of the individual in on-the-job training. If the assumptions of Model 2 are retained, which are Mincer's assumptions (Mincer 1962, 1974), the area $(J - A)$ is the undiscounted aggregate net return to investments of the individual in on-the-job learning or training. The area $(A + B)$ is the undiscounted gross return to the investment in schooling, and the net contribution of schooling is $(A + B - C)$. The undiscounted total net contribution of investments in schooling and on-the-job training is thus $(B + J - C)$ and the postschool proportion of this total is $(J - A) (B + J - C)$ (see Fig. 1).

Model 2 is a powerful simplification and the ratio $(J - A) (B + J)$ with or without a correction for C can be a useful descriptive statistic even when the assumptions of the model are challenged. In any case, challenges must arise in any careful consideration of empirical findings using age cross-section data. Other problems of specification aside, each observation of people of a given age at a given calendar date is an observation referring to members of a particular and hence necessarily unique cohort.

3. "General" Training and the Individual as Investor

The models laid out thus far refer only to that part of on-the-job training that is implicitly financed and returns on which are received by the individual. The share of investment costs borne and the returns received by a firm or employing agency will not show up in the individual's earning stream. In the terminology of human-capital theory, only "general" human capital is picked up in the above formulation. "Firm-specific" human capital is not.

There are two main overlapping concepts of general training or learning. The first of these, which may be designated here for convenience as general I training, refers to the acquisition of capabilities or traits that have value over a wide range of uses and activities. The most general of all training is in literacy and numeracy, usually acquired in elementary schools. Most fundamental in general training is learning to learn. Persons with a foundation in the most general capabilities will be more readily trainable in many more specialized skills. By the same token, such training is the foundation of capabilities to communicate effectively, to seek out and interpret information, and to adjust to changing situations and opportunities. What is often regarded as specialized training may be classified as general I, however, in that it may be useful in a wide range of uses and diverse settings; carpentry and clerical skills are examples. Indeed, such skills may be far more general in their applications than the

supposedly "general" education popularly associated with graduates of Oxford or Cambridge universities who were recruited by the British Foreign Office.

What might be designated here as general II training is the concept associated with human capital theory. General human capital (in contrast to specific human capital) is portable. In other words, the general human capital embodied in a person can be applied in agencies other than the one in which the capabilities were acquired. General I training is necessarily also portable, but portability does not necessarily imply general I training or capabilities. A doctor may have been trained in a highly specialized skill, such as open heart surgery; this is hardly a general I type of skill, but the heart surgeon is not limited to practice in the hospital in which he or she received his or her training. The skills embodied in the heart surgeon are portable, and hence in this sense general. So are the skills of a cook or a barber (as are, in most industrialized economies, those of semiskilled operatives in textile factories), however specialized these skills may be.

General skills defined in terms of portability have a central place in the treatment of learning in school and at work as parts of an integrated theory of human capital. This was first refined by Becker (1962) and has been applied empirically by Mincer (1958, 1962, 1974), in the interpretation of the concave shapes of earning paths over a man's (and to a lesser degree a woman's) life. Taking as a first example the employer providing the training, the following situation may be hypothesized. If this employer paid the trainee full-time wages without regard to the time spent on learning and the direct costs of the instruction, but the trainee then went to another employer, carrying the full value of the newly acquired human capital, the first employer would get no return on his or her investment in training. Indeed, the employer would not make that investment unless he or she could shift the costs onto the trainee. What happens in the extreme case of completely general formation of human capital is then a shift of the investment cost to the trainee in the form of partially forgone earnings. In effect, the employer sells and the employee buys the increments to the individual's portable human capital.

An essential element in this theoretical construct is the concept of opportunity costs, or "forgone earnings," whether in attending school or later on. Thus the individual may take a job that yields only small earnings at first if by doing so he or she can build up general human capital from which greater returns can be expected later on. The difference between current earnings in this job and what could be earned initially in a dead-end job is the opportunity cost incurred as an investment by the individual in the acquisition of human capital. (Forgone earnings when attending school is simply a special case of opportunity-cost investments in oneself.) Readiness to bear the full opportunity costs of earnings forgone in school or at work depends on the extent to which the individual can carry the compensating accumulation of human capital elsewhere—that is, on the portability of the skills acquired. It follows from this view of labor markets that the steeper the gradient of earnings and the lower the associated initial earnings, the greater must be the postschool investments that people are making in themselves. At least, this is the case so long as the human capital is fully portable.

To the extent to which the accumulation of human capital in an employee is specific to the firm (nonportable) the situation is changed. While earning paths may still provide rough clues to the costs borne by individuals and the returns on those investments, they cannot capture that part of the costs of on-the-job training that is ultimately borne by the employer, or the employer's share in the rewards.

4. Firm-specific Training and the Sharing of Costs and Returns

The term "specific training," as it has been used in human capital theory since Becker's seminal work (1962, 1983), carries the precise meaning of nonportability. This is not the same thing as specialized training, which may or may not be portable. Rarely does anyone acquire specific human capital without at the same time acquiring at least some additions to his or her general human capital. A secretary, for example, may be of greater value as he or she comes to know the informal communication networks in which the boss participates. More generally, productivity in an enterprise depends not only on the aggregate of capabilities of individuals taken separately, but also on the development of effective interaction patterns and team work; an individual who has become integrated into joint activities and ways of doing things has acquired specific human capital that makes him or her more valuable than a new recruit to the enterprise, but that human capital cannot be carried elsewhere.

Both the firm and the individual have a stake in the accumulation of specific human capital, and the result spelled out in human capital theory is a sharing of the costs of and returns to the formation of such capabilities. Other things being equal, a large admixture of firm-specific relative to general (portable) human capital would be reflected in flatter life-earnings paths than where the proportion of portable human capital is higher. Other things are rarely equal, however.

5. Firm-specific Human Capital and Labor Market Structures

It is not enough to look at on-the-job training from the perspective of either individuals or firms as investors in some given institutional context, for institutions themselves both affect and are affected by the processes of human resource development. Multiple endogenous variables are at issue here. For one thing, there is usually a much greater investment in the firm-specific skills of men than of women; flatter age–earning curves will be observed in enterprises that hire a relatively large number of women, even though these enterprises are likely also to be characterized by little firm-specific human capital. Even considering men only, arrangements that foster the development of firm-specific human capital are often in turn fostered by the enlargement of such capital as a substantial component in the assets of both the firm and its individual personnel. Such arrangements include management practices and personnel policies that discourage turnover of a firm's labor force through resignations and layoffs alike. Both the costs of and the returns to investments in human resource formation at work are shared by employers and employees, since both have an interest in stabilizing the association. As Oi showed many years ago (1962), labor then becomes a "quasi-fixed factor of production."

The relative importance of firm-specific human capital (and hence of the formal or informal training through which such capital is acquired) depends in part on the size of an economy. In a small country in which there is only one textile mill, for example, skills learned by operators in that mill may be specific to it so long as there are substantial barriers (formal, cultural, or linguistic) to international migration. However, this also illustrates the fact that what makes a skill specific may often depend as much on institutional constraints on mobility as on the nature of a skill (Bowman 1965). The development of customs that have constrained mobility between firms in Japan are frequently cited in discussions of specific human capital. The degree of uniqueness of the Japanese situation and of its limitations on interfirm mobility are often exaggerated, however, even when analogous situations elsewhere are ignored. Moreover, substantial investments in firm-specific human capital do not mean a lack of flexibility in the development and allocation of human resources where internal labor markets are large and well-developed.

Stability in attachments between firms and their employees and the formation of firm-specific human capital are mutually supportive features of labor markets, both "external" and "internal," but most obviously and directly of internal labor markets. This means, among other things, an extension of time horizons in the formal or implicit terms of contracts between employer and employee. The longer those horizons, the greater the scope for variations in trade-offs over time. Investments in and returns to on-the-job training can come to be confounded in earnings data by arrangements that constitute in part an internal capital as well as an internal labor market, the internal capital market performing a hidden function of lending and borrowing between firm and employee that is adapted in part to the economic life cycles of

51

consumption and earnings. This phenomenon is especially important for interpretations of the workings of Japanese internal labor markets as agencies of human resource development. Those markets often differ substantially from internal provisions but with quite different management–labor relations and sources of seniority arrangements. Nobody who is at all familiar with management and personnel policies in Japan would question the importance of on-the-job training in its firms.

In sum, when human capital theory is applied to analysis of the rational behavior of firms as well as of individuals in a world in which training and human capital are a mixture of the general and the specific, the importance of association between on-the-job training and long-term commitments is underlined. Rough measurement by methods applicable to general training may still have its uses, but some of the elegant optimal control models run into severe problems. One direction that further work has taken has been a shift toward greater emphasis on the new economics of information and the "matching" of firms and employers in search processes. This has reduced somewhat the attention given to investments by either individuals or firms in on-the-job training, but without challenging the earlier work. Meanwhile research on life-cycle earnings and learning at work has been enriched by studies of the participation in the labor force by women and of the effects of interruptions in the continuity of their employment on subsequent life-earning prospects.

6. On-the-job Training and Institutional Adaptation to Change

The term "internal labor market" is entirely appropriate to analysis of adjustments by firm and individual in human capital theory. That term is more often used in other contexts, however, and it has spread rapidly since about 1970. In so doing, it has taken on at least as many variants as on-the-job training, especially in the sociological literature, as is amply demonstrated in Berg (1981). Of greatest interest here, however, must be the line of thought stimulated by Doeringer and Piore (1966). The focus in this and in related subsequent work is on how economic institutions adapt to provide education and training for adults in skills that come into being and are increasingly demanded by innovative change in a dynamic economy. In some respects the work by Doeringer and Piore stands at the opposite extreme from the optimal control models stimulated by human capital theory. It gives far more explicit attention to economic change and far less to life-cycle experiences. It provides good descriptive analyses of some of the institutional options in adjustment to and furtherance of innovative change.

It is often supposed that this line of work runs counter to human capital theories. Perhaps, however, this is instead a case of potential complementarity of

endeavor, but with insufficient communication among economists who have started from different initial perspectives. After the investigation of internal labor markets that he and Doeringer had conducted for the United States Department of Labor, Piore wrote:

> the training process yields one explanation for the rigidity of internal wage structure and the use of seniority to govern promotion and lay off. Without the protection which these provide, experienced workers would be reluctant to cooperate in training, for fear that the competition of newly trained workers would undermine income and job security. (Piore 1968 p.439)

This conclusion points to relationships ignored in most of the human capital literature. At the same time, it bypasses completely the whole question of the part managements and personnel policies may play in the creation and modification of incentive structures in the work force, along with related questions about the nature of labor unions and contrasts in their histories and modes of operation in different countries (and even within a single country). It also bypasses, perhaps for the same reasons, the question of what may be the incentives to workers and to employers to invest in the formation of human capital. One result has been a failure in most of the literature on internal labor markets to probe more deeply into the ways in which costs of labor turnover (resignations as well as layoffs) and investments in on-the-job training may be affected by, and may themselves affect, other aspects of institutional structures and behavior. To the extent that economists have approached these questions, they have worked primarily from a combination of human capital theory and search theory.

7. On-the-job Training in the Invisible Economy

It is undoubtedly the case that on-the-job training, however defined, is of crucial importance not only for economic growth but for the sustained viability of an economy in the modern world. What, if anything, governments could or should do about it is a matter of hot debate in both industrially advanced countries and LDCs. Meanwhile, consideration of the training and learning that takes place in the less visible sectors of the economy is what has most often been neglected. This neglect characterizes even the research on Japan, despite the proliferation of painstaking studies of labor efficiency in larger firms in that country. Most serious, however, has been a propensity to ignore the importance of learning systems that have evolved informally in many of the LDCs when public policy has given scope for the exercise of ingenuity in the unseen eddies of economic life. Such training and learning tends to elude conventional quantitative counts. It is an integral factor in determining age–earning streams, but no analysis at the level of aggregation that has characterized empirical estimates in the human capital tradition will illuminate these facets of the life of a people. A few sallies into this large but largely unexplored territory have shown that it may be much richer than commonly has been supposed. Work by King (1977) on Kenya is an illuminating example, but the Kenyan government has not penalized initiative in the informal sectors of the economy as some of the LDCs have. It is not known how much on-the-job training goes on in the less developed countries, or to what extent such activities are inadvertently discouraged (or encouraged) by public policies.

See also: Economics of Adult Education and Training; Market Failure in Adult Education and Training; Demand, Supply, and Finance of Adult Education; Costs of Adult Education and Training; Learning in the Workplace; Job and Task Analysis; Evaluation of Public Training: Cost-Effectiveness; Measurement of Industry Training; Measurement of Training Costs

References

Becker G S 1962 Investment in human capital: A theoretical analysis. *J. Pol. Econ.* 70(5, Part 2): 9–49
Becker G S 1983 *Human Capital: A Theoretical and Empirical Analysis with Special Reference to Education*, 2nd edn. University of Chicago Press, Chicago, Illinois
Berg I E (ed.) 1981 *Sociological Perspectives on Labor Markets*. Academic Press, New York
Bowman M J 1965 From guilds to infant training industries. In: Anderson C A, Bowman M J (eds.) 1965 *Education and Economic Development*. Aldine, Chicago, Illinois
Bowman M J 1968 The assessment of human investments as growth strategy. In: Joint Economic Committee, 90th Session of the US Congress 1968 *Federal Programs for the Development of Human Resources*. US Government Printing Office, Washington, DC
Bowman M J 1974 Learning and earning in the postschool years. In: Kerlinger F N, Carroll J B (eds.) 1974 *Review of Research in Education*, Vol. 2. Peacock, Itasca, Illinois
Doeringer P B, Piore M J 1966 *Internal Labor Markets, Technological Change, and Labor Force Adjustment*. Report submitted to the Office of Manpower Policy, Evaluation, and Research, US Department of Labor, Cambridge, Massachusetts
King K 1977 *The African Artisan: Education and the Informal Sector in Kenya*. Heineman, London
Mincer J 1958 Investment in human capital and personal income distribution. *J. Pol. Econ.* 66(4): 281–302
Mincer J 1962 On-the-job training: Costs, returns and some implications. *J. Pol. Econ.* 70(5 Pt. 2): 50–79
Mincer J 1974 *Schooling, Experience, and Earnings*. Columbia University Press, New York
Oi W Y 1962 Labor as a quasi-fixed factor. *J. Pol. Econ.* 70(6): 538–55
Piore M J 1968 On-the-job training and adjustment to technological change. *J. Hum. Resources* 3(4): 435–49

Further Reading

Barron J, Black D, Loewenstein M 1989 Job matching and on-the-job training. *J. Labor Econ.* 7: 1–19
Bishop J 1990 Job performance, turnover, and wage growth. *J. Labor Econ.* 8: 363–86
Gill I 1989 Technological change, education, and obsolescence of human capital. Ph.D. dissertation. University of Chicago, Chicago, Illinois
Jorgenson D W, Fraumeni B M 1989 The accumulation of human and nonhuman capital, 1948–84. In: Lipsey R E, Tice H S (eds.) *The Measurement of Saving, Investment, and Wealth*. University of Chicago Press, Chicago, Illinois
Lillard L, Tan H 1986 *Private sector training: Who gets it and what are its effects?* Report R-3331-DOL/RC. The RAND Corporation, Santa Monica, California
Lynch L (ed.) 1994 *Training in the Private Sector: International Comparisons*. University of Chicago Press, Chicago, Illinois
Mincer J 1987 *Job Training, Wage Growth, and Labor Turnover*. National Bureau of Economic Research Working Paper No. 2680. Department of Economics, Columbia University, New York
Mincer J 1989 Human capital and the labor market. *Educ. Researcher* 18: 27–34
Mincer J 1993 *Investment in U.S. Education and Training*. National Bureau of Economic Research Discussion Paper No. 671. Department of Economics, Columbia University, New York

(b)   Themes and Theories

Community Education and Community Development

P. M. Cunningham

This entry is about community education and community development and its many faces. Included are programs known as "community schools," "community education," and "community development." Also described are forms of grassroots endeavors seeking social transformation by means of popular education, participatory research, and education provided by social movements. Finally, the role of popular theater and popular culture in the education of adults is discussed.

Education is not a neutral activity. Hence the discussion of the various manifestations of community education must be placed in a social and political context. Accordingly, the "functionalist–development"

and "conflict–change" sociological concepts are utilized to interpret the varying ideologies that drive educational practice.

1. The Conceptual Framework

In adult education there has been continued debate regarding the extent to which the main purpose of schooling is to reproduce the power relationships existing in a society, or whether the school and adult education serve as the sorting mechanisms by which complex modern societies assign, through an egalitarian process, particular roles to their citizens

Table 1
Functionalist/development and conflict/change theories of community education and community development

Theory	Functionalist/development	Conflict/change
Characteristics	consensus–integration reformation	conflict–transformation
Definition of community	geographical communities	geographical; racial/ethnic, gender, social class communities; social issue (environment, peace) groups
Forms	centered in formal; use of nonformal	centered in nonformal; use of formal
Educational program	community education community development community college	community-based education popular education social movement learning
Knowledge production	logical positivistic research	participatory research; transformative research
Culture	"High Culture"—e.g., museums and libraries	"Popular Culture"—e.g., popular theater and popular art
Historical roots	Henry Morris—England Frank Manley—USA	Father Coady—Canada Paulo Freire—Brazil Rajesh Tandon—India Myles Horton—USA Julius Nyerere—Tanzania

based on meritocratic achievement (Rubenson 1989). The first interpretation, in which power is the key concept, leads to a conflict model in which variables such as race, class, and gender are powerful means for explaining education for domestication. The concept of domestication is central in analyses of class struggle and resistance (Giroux 1983). Key concepts in the second, functionalist interpretation are modernization and evolutionary change through development in which consensus and integration are emphasized. Schools prepare citizens, both cognitively and through socialization, to take their social and economic roles based on their achievement in a competitive system.

Table 1 describes aspects of community education and community development from both analytical perspectives. To illustrate the categories in Table 1, one can contrast community education and community-based education in the United States.

1.1 Community Education

Community education developed from the Mott-funded community school movement in Flint, Michigan. Defined as "an educational and community development process for the development of human potential and participation in the local decision making process" (Kerensky 1989 p. 63), it is in practice associated with the functionalist paradigm. The process assumes equality regardless of race, class, or gender. It also assumes equality in the democratic decision-making process. The ubiquitous nature of the public primary school and a desire for its efficient use is the rationale for making the school a community resource, intended to increase participation of the community by providing for financial, educational, recreational, and avocational needs. The idea is that, with citizen participation in education, other community problems may be identified and addressed. Formal societal structures are not seen as the problem; the problem is the involvement of citizens in a community. Accordingly, some theorists in the United States promote the use of community education organized around the local school as one way of solving problems such as schools failing to prepare competitive workers, the perceived failure of the family, and the apparent disintegration of moral values in the society. The emphasis is on making the community function as it should (Kerensky 1989).

1.2 Community-based Education

In contrast, Community-based Education (CBE) assumes a more radical stance. The Association for Community Based Education defines the concept as responding to underserved populations by carrying out a range of activities that include economic development, housing rehabilitation, health services, job training, adult literacy, and continuing education programs. The premise is that education cannot be separated from the culture and community in which it occurs—it is linked to community development and the empowerment of communities. In this definition the commitment is to bring about development and empowerment in poor communities. In practice CBE's may be organized around special populations such as women, or an environmental concern as well as a geographic community. Rarely would a community-based organization be located in a public school. The definition of the problem is poverty and power relationships, not citizen participation.

To make the language even more complex the term "community education" in the United Kingdom may encompass both types described above. There are community education programs based on what is termed a "liberal" philosophy, while others operate with a "liberating" philosophy (Fletcher 1980 p. 10). These types parallel the functionalist and conflict models indicated in Table 1.

2. Definitions of Community

The complexity of the term, "community" is captured by the editors of the two volumes of *Harvard Educational Review* issued in 1989 and 1990 dedicated to community-based education:

> Community is the configuration of people we live next to, as well as of people with whom we share deep common bonds: work, love, an ideology, artistic talent, a religion, a culture, a sexual preference, a struggle, a movement, a history, and so on. Community can be difficult to define uniformly in terms of where people live; for within the same geographical area there can exist different communities, and it is not uncommon for their interests to clash. Such is the case with Palestinian communities within Israeli communities, Black South Africans under apartheid; communities of women within patriarchal culture; Asian, African American, Latinos and Native Americans in racist cities and rural areas in the United States; poor and working class people struggling against homelessness while right next door affluent communities prosper; and gay and lesbian communities within a larger homophobic society. (Munoz and Garcia-Blanco 1989 p. 5)

Not only is the definition of the word "community" complex but "one of its central features is that it is used to avoid the discomfort of being understood exactly" (Jackson 1980 p. 39). Jackson notes there is a significant "difference between being part of a pleasant, cozy, residential neighborhood where one can be certain that everyone will be socially acceptable and being in a community organized by professional social workers. Again the idea of community obscures the most important social and economic relationships involved. Local social relationships are important to people but the nature and strength of those relationships are determined by factors beyond the locality" (p. 42). Accordingly, Jackson (1980) challenges the definition of community as a local neighborhood. Such a definition plays an important ideological function since it promotes the ideal that "local factors determine the nature of social and personal problems while diverting attention from criticism of fundamental, political and economic institutions or dominant social belief" (p 43).

In community education or community development, one's definition of community and assumptions about the forces that define the community will in turn define one's educational ideology and the goals that one subsequently formulates. The following anecdote is illustrative: A folk school teacher in the United States was approached for help by a community group called "Not in My Back Yard," which was fighting toxic waste being deposited in their community. The teacher asked, in whose back yard should it be deposited? By asking that question the problem was redefined and communities joined together to educate and organize around the newly framed problem, "Not in Any of Our Back Yards." The problem was not toxic waste dumping in a community, but a society which allows industrial plants to pollute any local community which cannot protect itself.

3. Community Education

In the affluent countries of the northern hemisphere, "community education" is usually defined as a participative educational process based within a local public school or occasionally a community college or other adult education institution. The school, formerly limited to children, is opened up to the entire community for both academic and social education, recreation, and avocational pursuits.

One of the major issues in community education is whether it is a process or a program. This fundamental distinction has encouraged elaborations on process as the one proposed by Warden (1979):

(a) process as procedure where process is used to involve people in achieving a specified goal by a specified time;

(b) process as community problem-solving where problems are identified and solutions attempted;

(c) process as community power where the community organizer assists the mobilization of power against a particular adversary;

(d) process as psychological and social development in which persons through their activity grow and become self-actualized.

Only (c) utilizes a conflict orientation. Thus, the program–process argument is not always ideological, but rather one of procedure.

Martin (1987 p. 24), reflecting the United Kingdom experience, divides community education into universal, reformist, and radical models. In the universal model, professional leadership operates out of a formal setting; the reformist model targets low-income communities and through partnership aims for positive discrimination; the radical model involves issue-oriented, "class"-based approaches to change community structure.

Thorpe (1985), with a similar analysis and speaking from the Australian context, assumes community education is about change. She defines three models of social change: consensus (based on cooperation and participation); pluralist (recognizes inequality and negotiates social planning); and structuralist (feminist, socialist, Marxist, or anarchist analysis supporting consciousness raising and direct action).

All of the above authors attempt to specify the differences one finds in philosophy, goals, and method in analyzing practice; what is clear is the diversity of community education.

Community education programs which are consensual in nature are characterized by educational offerings for all ages, recreational programs which make full use of the resources available, and avocational training. Intergrated approaches to education such as family education and age-mixed events are planned to overcome the separateness of modern age groupings. Administration of the community school tends to be lean, and the director may report directly to an advisory council; teachers and facilitators are usually hired part-time or volunteers are utilized. Financing can be mixed with public funds, private or philanthropic funding, and, in some cases, tuition fees from participants.

Community education which is more process-oriented goes beyond programming activities to solving problems. The process-oriented community education administrator would help mobilize persons or resources to work on a solution. Community education which is conflict-oriented would operate more as popular education does and is discussed below.

A National Center for Community Education has been developed in Flint, Michigan in the United States. It is dedicated to leadership development and community education training. There are over 100 community education centers located in universities or state departments of education providing training (Brown 1990). In the United Kingdom, a Community Education Development Center (CEDC) was built in Coventry for promoting the concept and providing consultative services to local communities (Watts 1990). There are national community education associations in each country, as well as advanced degree programs in community education. Organized in 1978 and based at Coventry in the CEDC, an International Community Education Association has as its purpose the extension of the community education model worldwide.

4. Popular Education and Community-based Education

Popular education (known as community-based education in North America) is based on the conceptual work of Paulo Freire (1970). It is defined as a social behavior situated within a framework broader than that dealing with education. It aims at making persons self-aware political subjects. Popular education is characterized by horizontal relationships between facilitators and participants, popular participation in the planning of training and action, and the assumption that problems and solutions must emanate from the community.

Popular education is about understanding and interrogating one's own oppression. It utilizes the means of problem posing, develops a collective response, acts on the response, and then critically reflects on the quality of the response as parts of the process. However, there is no one methodology. This is because popular education is always contextualized and action must be organically related to the context. The final result is the development of the capacity to transform reality and the ability to challenge oppressive power relationships. Put simply, the end result of popular education is the ability to read one's world. Cadena (1984) states that the results should be an increasing ability of people to: (a) consciously appropriate their own reality; (b) influence and control the processes in their own lives, including equalization of the distribution of goods and services; (c) defend their own interests and the kind of society that would serve them best; and (d) make the society less hegemonic and more responsive to them.

Conceptually, popular education proceeds from the understanding that knowledge is socially produced, that there are intellectuals in all social classes, and that collectively, seemingly powerless groups can mount strong counterhegemonic forces through producing their own knowledge and challenging the official knowledge of the dominant group. Popular education is also driven by the dialectical concepts of the base (economic production) and the superstructure (cultural reproduction). Accordingly, popular education recognizes the importance of culture as well as economic power (see *Popular Education and Conscientization*).

4.1 Popular Culture

Those popular educators who make their analysis through a conflict model recognize that culture is a place to make war on hegemony. Hegemony (defined as the making common to all social classes the cultural and social formations of the dominant, high culture in order to impose control through consent) can only be opposed by countering cultural imposition. High culture is found in museums, libraries, galleries, and concert halls; pop or mass culture is the culture of fashion, celebrity, and popularity spread, for example, through television. Traditional popular culture comes from the grass roots: folk art, folk songs, folk dance, folk tales, and folk medicine (see *Providers of Adult Education: An Overview; Libraries as Learning Resources*).

Popular theater is an important part of popular culture because participants can creatively enact the dilemmas, induced by hegemony, which they face in society. This is a cultural expression for those who produce it; it is equally an educative event for the spectators. Popular theater can, according to Lambert (1982), be divided into agitprop (produced by professionals around local themes), participatory (produced by and for people with spectators), or conscientization (produced by and for people without spectators). Boal (1979 p. 122), a primary interpreter of popular theater, states: "I believe that all the truly revolutionary theatrical groups should transfer to the people the means of production in the theater, so that people themselves may use them. The theater is a weapon, and it is the people who should wield it."

4.2 Participatory Research

One object of participatory research is the creation of popular knowledge. Participatory research is an important part of popular education because those who learn to read their world are able to participate in the production of knowledge.

Participatory action research has a rich history with origins in Latin America, Asia, and Africa (Fals-Borda and Rahman 1991). It is based on the existential concept of experience proposed by José Ortega y Gasset: "through actual experiencing we intuitively apprehend its essence—thereby place our own being in a wider more fulfilling context" (quoted in Fals-Borda and Rahman 1991 p. 4). This concept of *experience* along with the idea of *authentic commitment* allows those external or internal to the exploited class to recognize that knowledge is the basis for social transformation, thus allowing them to work together in a subject–subject relationship (see *Participatory Research*).

4.3 Popular Education Programs

Popular education, like community education, is also manifested in many different ways. Popular education as used in Latin America is best described in the words of the local people who practice it. Archer and Costello (1990), for example, collected 10 case studies of popular education projects in Latin American countries. They conclude that Freirean approaches to literacy education cannot "be simply grafted on; they must be relevant to the concrete reality of the situation. Thus television, radio, and video may be more relevant when communication is less dependent on the written word" (pp. 200–01). A second conclusion is that appropriate organizational structures to give learner's demands a collective voice are needed.

In contrast, Melo and Benavente (1978) present their own analysis of the popular education movement in Portugal following the fall of the dictatorship. They carefully contextualized the rise of hundreds of local popular groups which helped to define adult education in modern Portugal and whose work helped to bring significant changes in the new Constitution. Worthy of note is the study by Chené and Chervin (1991), who provide an excellent description of popular education in Québec.

4.4 Folk High Schools

Folk high schools, which originated in Denmark in the nineteenth century, continue to respond to community needs and popular social movements (see *Folk High Schools*).

In Tanzania, with the help of the Swedish Government, folk development colleges were established in 52 districts with mixed success. Local funds to support the colleges and student enrollment were not always forthcoming from the villages. Few of the colleges were able to raise funds through self-reliance efforts (Mosha 1983).

In Chile, a network of folk schools has been developed for the purpose of training local leaders in appropriate technology techniques, literacy, ecology, and women's programming. *El Canelo*, a major resource center, receives "monitors" from a feeder system of community centers to do short-term (2–4 weeks) residential training. This Center is successful in engaging the poor. Grass root leaders studying at the Center may never have previously been away from their district.

4.5 Study Circles

Study circles have spread from the Nordic countries to many parts of the world. They have become an integral part of the idea of "circles of culture" advocated by Freire (see *Study Circles*).

With the assistance of the Kettering Foundation and the National Issues Forum, the publishing of a book on study circles by Oliver (1987), and the establishment of a Study Circles Resource Center, the study circle has taken root in North America. The goal of study circles is to advance deliberative democracy and improve the quality of public life and to promote small-group democratic, participatory discussions on social and political issues. Sometimes study circles may be utilized by community education, as in the state of Minnesota where 420 of the 432 school districts have publically supported community education.

Through a similar program, *La Mesa*, study circles are being used by popular educators in Chile and Brazil. Study circles played an important part in the mobilization of literally hundreds of thousands of mothers in Sao Paulo, who took action because of the difficulties they faced in feeding their families in a high inflation economy. Eventually, the popular mothers' groups in Brazil delivered over 1 million signatures to the president to demonstrate the depths of their dilemma.

4.6 Social Movements

Communities of special interest such as peace, environment, and women's rights, provide natural contexts for the development of popular education within a social movement. Community here is defined as a group assembled around a common interest. For example, learning for environmental action is one of four major concerns of the International Council for Adult Education. With an international office in Sao Paulo and networks organized in each of its six regions throughout the world, there is an effort to link local environmental groups into an international coalition to bring pressure to bear on environmental concerns (see *International Council for Adult Education*).

5. Community Development

"Community development" also has many definitions; it can be a process, a method, a program, or a movement. By definition, the value positions on what constitutes development are normative. Much of so-called "community development" has been used by dominant groups to exploit weaker sectors of the society. Such development is top down, benefits either internal or external elites, and may do cultural violence to existing community members. The imposition of Western institutions on indigenous persons in the name of development has been well-documented. Accordingly, the defining characteristics of liberating community development must be participatory, broadly educative, and in harmony with community values. International examples to illustrate this view of community development are examined below.

5.1 Khit-Pen

The term *"Khit-Pen,"* coined by Kowit Varapipatana in 1974, signified a new approach to community development by Thai adult educators and a rejection of Western economic and technocratic definitions of development. Based on a mixture of Buddhism and Western humanistic thought, *Khit-Pen* works along three axes: information on methods of Buddhist introspection, information on society and environment as defined by sociopsychological and ecological fields, and technical information or book knowledge. By emphasizing problem posing, the ultimate goal is to transform the Thai adult into a critical thinking person. This objective connects *Khit-Pen* to Freire's conscientization movement (Nopakun 1985). *Khit-Pen* has been translated into a national strategy for adult education aimed at the transformation of Thai rural villagers into more independent persons.

5.2 Saemaul Education

Faced with the need to develop rural villages in Korea, a national economic strategy called *"Saemaul Undong"* was initiated to promote community development. The idea was to use seasonally unemployed workers in productive work. Almost immediately the need for education of leaders emerged. *Saemaul* education was established to train village leaders in good thinking, leading to good action, leading to national development. Values taught were diligence, self-reliance, and cooperation. *Saemaul* training is done nonformally, through both residential and distance education, with an emphasis on experiential learning from successful case studies. This integrated plan of nation-building based on village-building has reportedly been successful. Benefits include the will toward development and cooperation, an active role for women, adoption of a work ethic, and a sense of village community (Cheong 1987 p. 11).

5.3 A European Cooperative Plan

The Council of Europe, through its Council for Cultural Cooperation, initiated in 1975 a cooperative program to investigate how education through community development could contribute to economic, social, and cultural innovation. Three priority groups were considered: women, the elderly, and the illiterate. Three areas were identified for study: (a) participation of women and men in decisions affecting their daily lives, (b) responses to unemployment and economic restructuring, and (c) evolution of the social and cultural roles of men and women. A number of projects were identified as exemplary and were monitored for 2 years. The monitors reported the results, and in 1987 recommendations were made to all member countries through a "Declaration" on practical strategies to solve problems arising in community development (Council of Europe 1987).

5.4 Tribal Colleges

Worthy of note are the 27 tribal colleges which have emerged since 1969 in the United States when the first—the Navajo Community College—was founded. Organized and administered by Native Americans, they now enroll over 5,000 full-time students. Though their work includes a formal college curriculum, the tribal college has a strong outreach into the entire community process. Almost all are located on reservations. Boyer (1989 p. 53) states: "Tribal Colleges are in the vanguard of cultural renaissance in all of their communities. On the Senta Gleska College Campus, the Lakota studies department offers classes in Sioux history, oral literature, Lakota thought and a series of Lakota language courses."

In Canada, the Gabriel Dumont Institute of Native Studies and Applied Research in Saskatchewan organizes both formal and nonformal educational programs and native teacher education programs, and promotes both cultural and historical research on the activities of native peoples. Community development is defined as "taking back" the village and reservation schools, encouraging indigenous language and cultural expression, and diffusing information throughout the sparsely populated region using indigenous language broadcast by radio stations controlled by the community.

The Saskatchewan Indian Federated College (SIFC) is the only North American Indian-controlled university offering graduate as well as undergraduate studies. Elders from the five Indian tribal groups in the province are employed as staff to counsel and advise faculty and students. While the College seeks to strengthen local community leadership, it also has a program to link the indigenous people of Canada to indigenous peoples worldwide.

These tribal community colleges in North America parallel the community colleges in Australia and the South Pacific that likewise are controlled by indigenous people. The agenda is for colleges and their communities to recapture lost history, songs, dances, language, tales, medicines, and the healing arts. These are then utilized to contextualize and understand modern day experience, which is markedly alienating to indigenous communities.

5.5 Development and Social Justice

In India, an experiment in micro action by grass roots groups was initiated in 1980 because of the ineffectiveness of established, large organizations in improving the lot of the poor (Bhatt 1989). The large and comprehensive community development programs of the 1950s and 1960s had not made a difference in alleviating poverty.

Instead, in many communities poverty had become even more acute. In the 1970s a new, concentrated effort was made through separate, exclusively targeted programs such as the Tribal Development Plans, Integrated Rural Development, and the Child Health and Nutritious Schemes. Again there was documented failure, as economic exploitation continued.

It is in this context that different grass root organizations developed and began to redefine politics to include health, rights over forests and community reserves, education, and ecological and cultural issues. Working with advocates of poor people in the voluntary sector these spontaneous groups provided critiques and alternatives to strategies of development masterminded by governmental and nongovernmental organizations (NGOs). Bhatt (1989) studied 38 of these spontaneous groups in two districts in India. He found that with modest small grants from Oxfam, an international NGO, these grass root groups (with leaders as young as 21) accomplished an extraordinary amount of work which directly affected the quality of community life. His recommendation is that more funds should be allocated directly to grass root groups, with minimal or no external intervention, to bring about change organized and directed by the poor themselves.

5.6 North American Community Development

Community-based development organized around economics received its impetus in the late 1960s when readiness was high to bring about social change. It was in this context that the Community Development Corporation (CDC) was set up in North America by young community activists. The Corporation is defined as "a coalition organization of neighborhood residents to carry out their own comprehensive program of local renewal activities, especially including business development" (Perry 1987 p. 8). The success of local organizations of poor people bringing economic vitality to their community has kept alive federal funding through community development grants given directly to poor communities. These funds have allowed the development of community-based education programs as well as economic development schemes. Gaventa et al. (1990) documented efforts by rural community-based researchers to facilitate poor communities in learning about the reasons for their economic plight. Working with Appalachian and southern communities they reported on studies examining attempts to strengthen the informal sectors of the economy by means of community-based education. These case studies demonstrate how participatory research can be linked to social, cultural, and economic development.

See also: Formal, Nonformal, and Informal Education; Critical Approaches to Adult Education; Popular Education and Conscientization; Sociology of Adult Education; Ideologies in Adult Education; Participatory Research; Adult Education for Development; Community Colleges; Nongovernmental Organizations

References

Archer D, Costello P 1990 *Literacy and Power: The Latin American Battleground*. Earthscan, London

Bhatt A 1989 *Development and Social Justice: Micro Action by Weaker Sections*. Sage, New Delhi

Boal A 1979 *Theater of the Oppressed*. Urizen Books, New York

Boyer E L 1989 *Tribal Colleges: Shaping the Future of Native America*. Princeton University Press, Princeton, New Jersey

Brown D 1990 USA: The National Center for Community Education. In: Poster C, Krüger A (eds.) 1990 *Community Education in the Western World*. Routledge, London

Cadena F 1984 Popular education and peasants movements for change. *Convergence* 17(3): 31–36

Chené A, Chervin M 1991 *Un(e) Air(e) Populaire: L'education populaire authonome au Quebec* (Popular Education in Quebec: Strengthening Social Movements) (In both French and English). American Association for Adult and Continuing Education, Washington, DC

Cheong J W (ed.) 1987 *Promising Education for Community Development*. National University Press, Seoul

Council of Europe 1987 *Adult Education and Community Development*. Council for Cultural Cooperation, Council of Europe, Strasbourg

Fals-Borda O, Rahman M A (eds.) 1991 *Action and Knowledge. Breaking the Monopoly with Participatory Action-Research*. Apex Press, New York

Fletcher C 1980 Developments in community education: A current account. In: Fletcher C, Thompson N (eds.) 1980 *Issues in Community Education*. Falmer Press, Lewes

Freire P 1970 *The Pedagogy of the Oppressed*. Herder and Herder, New York

Gaventa J, Smith B E, Wellingham A (eds.) 1990 *Communities in Economic Crises: Appalachia and the South*. Temple University Press, Philadelphia, Pennsylvania

Giroux H 1983 *Theory and Resistance in Education*. Bergin and Garvey, South Hadley, Massachusetts

Jackson K 1980 Some fallacies in community education and their consequences in working class areas. In: Fletcher C, Thompson N (eds.) 1980 *Issues in Community Education*. Falmer Press, Lewes

Kerensky V M 1989 *The Sovereign New Perspectives on People, Power and Public Education*. Kendall/Hunt, Dubuque, Iowa

Lambert P 1982 Popular theatre: One road to self determined development action. *Comm. Dev. J.* 17(3): 242–49

Martin I 1987 Community education: Towards a theoretical analysis. In: Allen G, Bastani J, Martin I, Richard K (eds.) 1987 *Community Education: An Agenda for Educational Reform*. Open University Press, Milton Keynes

Melo A, Benavente A 1978 *Experiments in Popular Education in Portugal*, No. 29. UNESCO, Paris

Mosha H F 1983 United Republic of Tanzania: Folk development colleges. *Prospects* 13(1): 95–103

Munoz B, Garcia-Blanco A M 1989 *Harvard Educational Review* 59(4) (Special issue on Community Based Education, Part I)

Nopakun O 1985 *Thai Concept of Khit-pen for Adult and Non-Formal Education*. Chulaongkorn University, Bangkok

Oliver L 1987 *Study Circles*. Seven Locks Press, Washington, DC

Perry S 1987 *Communities on the Way*. State University of New York Press, Albany, New York

Rubenson K 1989 The sociology of adult education. In: Merriam S, Cunningham P (eds.) 1989 *Handbook of Adult and Continuing Education*. Jossey-Bass, San Francisco, California

Thorpe R 1985 Community work and ideology: An Australian perspective. In: Thorpe R, Petruchenia J (eds.) 1985 *Community Work or Social Change*. Routledge and Kegan Paul, London

Watts J 1990 UK: Community Education Development Centre. In: Poster C, Krüger A (eds.) 1990 *Community Education in the Western World*. Routledge, London

Warden J 1979 *Process Perspectives: Community Education as Process*. Mid-Atlantic Community Education Consortium, Charlottesville, Virginia

Further Reading

Bookman A, Morgen S 1988 *Women and the Politics of Empowerment*. Temple University Press, Philadelphia, Pennsylvania

Christie P 1985 *The Right to Learn: The Struggle for Education in South Africa*. Ravan Press, Johannesburg

Epskamp K 1989 *Theater is Search for Social Change*. CESO, The Hague

Hinzer H 1991 *Adult Education and Development* 37: September (Special issue on Environment)

Lovett T 1988 *Radical Approaches to Adult Education: A Reader*. Routledge, London

Mangione J 1985 *A Passion For Sicilians: (The) World Around Danilo Dolci*. Transaction Books, Oxford

Maguire P 1987 *Doing Participatory Research: A Feminist Approach*. Center for International Education, University of Massachusetts, Amherst, Massachusetts

Matwana M, Walters S, Groever Z 1989 *The Struggle for

Democracy: A Study of Community Organizations in Greater Capetown from the 1960's to 1988. Centre for Adult and Continuing Education, University of the Western Cape, Capetown

Munoz B, Garcia-Blanco A M 1990 *Harvard Educational Review* 60(1) (Special issue on Community Based Education, Part II)

Osteria T, Okamura J (eds.) 1986 *Participatory Approaches to Development Experiences in the Philippines.* De La Salle University, Manila

Reed D 1984 *Evaluating Community Organizing in the Philippines.* La Ignacia Centre Printing Press, Manila

Welton M 1987 *Knowledge for the People: Adult Life, Learning and Social Change in Canada.* OISE Press, Toronto

Critical Approaches to Adult Education

S. Westwood

Adult education is a field marked by conflict in which diverse ideologies have sought to define the terrain and the agendas for action. The strands which form this contested terrain of theory and practice have long histories and are not necessarily easily separable. Generally, critical approaches to adult education have been informed by the radicalism of the times, but the meanings of radicalism have shifted, not least in the 1980s across Europe and in North America where "Right Radicalism" has challenged the forged identity of radical with "Left" politics. This notion has developed historically, as a result of the identification of critical approaches in adult education with the politics of the labor movement and socialist ideals.

The purpose of this entry is to review some part of this history and the ways in which it bears upon radical approaches in adult education. The following themes are addressed: (a) adult education in early socialist ideas; (b) state, class conflict, and adult education; (c) Marxism and adult education; (d) the "community" approach; and (e) adult education and the new social movements. This entry neither addresses mainstream adult education policy and practice nor the institutional base of adult education.

1. Adult Education in Early Socialist Ideas

The late eighteenth century was marked by the French Revolution with its call for equality, fraternity, and liberty. This reverberated throughout Europe and influenced early attempts to create a radical adult education. In France, Germany, and the United Kingdom the early years of the nineteenth century were marked by political activism generating both the proto-socialism of Charles Fourier in France and the Owenite communities and the 1840s Chartists in the United Kingdom with their call for the vote—initially for women and men and subsequently for men alone. Within all these movements the importance of education was underlined, but it was to be an education for the people and in the interests of the people. These early forms of adult education were not specifically tied to adults, but brought adults and children together in an educational experience. These forms of learning were to be integrated with other areas of life, including work. Knowledge and learning were seen as crucial to the exercise of power.

Thus, education was not considered to be a neutral, technical attribute, but one aspect of a developing politics that was tied to "class."

The Owenites were consistently critical of "schooling" and all forms of rote learning, competition, and disciplinary modes, offering instead an emancipatory vision of learning that emphasized cooperation and a collective educational experience designed to empower the individual. The Chartists also emphasized the enabling power of education and its links with everyday life, especially through the popular press as it developed. Both the Owenites and the Chartists were deeply suspicious of the developing role of the state and of all forms of paternalism and philanthropy. This set the scene for a view of popular education which was independent of state and philanthropy, and which endures to this day. The Chartists were also concerned with citizenship and the rights of working people to a place in the nation and the polity. Their concern with citizenship and the educational forms that promote it remains a key issue for adult education across the world. The Chartist leader Ernest Jones said: "A People's education is safe only in a people's hands." This vision of an independent "peoples" education is still a powerful one in adult education (see *History of Adult Education*).

2. State, Class Conflict, and Adult Education

The state became more interventionist during the nineteenth century and it became difficult to maintain a position of popular independence in adult education. The contradictions erupted in the twentieth century in the United Kingdom in the struggles over the Central Labour College. During the 1850s, philanthropy initiated the working men's colleges and fueled the university extension movement, which took Oxford and Cambridge "dons" to "the people." Those in favor of this promoted the ideals of the nation-state and consensus building through a shared literary and scientific culture into which the working classes would be inducted. This vision of nationhood and consensus building through education was located with White "English" men, and the extension of patronage to one specific section of the working class—the respectable, skilled, and organized fraction. It was a constituent part of the development of the Danish folk high schools.

The critique of patronage was a key *motif* in the ideas developed by working people, for example, the ideas that formed the background to the development of the Workers' Educational Association in Canada, Australia, and the United Kingdom. These movements were fueled by a liberal view of adult education that saw individual advance and self-development as key elements. This was an adult education that was constructed as a public enterprise concerned with men —yet women were already involved in large numbers and had, through organizations such as the Cooperative Women's Guild in the United Kingdom, already rekindled an earlier collective radicalism which sought to place women's concerns on the agenda, both publicly and privately. Similar collective and cooperative concerns were developed in Canada through the Antigonish Movement, which brought different popular movements driving concepts such as university extension, Christian ethics, and social and economic change, together.

By the turn of the century the bifurcated vision of adult education, especially in the United Kingdom, Canada, and Australia—one radical and the other liberal—had clearly developed, but what both shared was a conception of the working class as a single unitary group. Such a view belied the ways in which the working class was simultaneously fractured by skill, region, gender, ethnicities, and the ways in which these came together in specific cultures. The radical vision was tied to socialist ideals of collective goals and mobilization for emancipation through working-class institutions. In contrast, the liberal view was wedded to notions of gradual, individual advance through education.

These two views came into sharp conflict following the events at Ruskin College, a philanthropic venture in Oxford, which sought to bring working-class people into Oxford. Founded in 1899, it brought trades union and socialist activists into full-time study programs. This group soon came into conflict with the Oxford education authorities over the curriculum and other issues of control. A strike by the students was supported by the major trade unions, which proceeded to set up their own institution, the Central Labour College, in 1909. Its journal, *The plebs*, became a major vehicle for the debate on independent working-class education. The main enemies of the working class were

identified not only among the bourgeoisie, but also within the Workers' Educational Association (WEA), which received government support and was committed to liberal education. The issue was not simply one of funding, but a struggle for hegemony in relation to working-class education. The dispute between the WEA and the Labour College Movement was played out around the key themes of the role of the state, the importance of Marxism, and the relationship between education and the working-class movement; themes such as feminism and racism were conspicuously absent from the debates at that time.

The debates between the Labour College Movement and the WEA serve well as an illustration of the contested terrain of adult education as it developed in the period preceding and immediately following the First World War. Briefly, the first of these debates concerned the importance of independent working-class education, where independence meant separation from the state. State involvement was seen as contrary to the goal of emancipation of the working class. This meant, of course, that there was no space within this account for a strategic engagement with the state. All encounters with the state were seen by radicalists as a dilution of the socialist agenda. This was, of course, in a time prior to welfarism and struggles around the state which have marked the politics of adult education during the 1970s and 1980s (see *Political Science and Policy Analysis in Adult Education*).

The second crucial area of debate concerned the curriculum and the relationship between knowledge and power. The Labour College Movement accused the WEA of promulgating "bourgeois social science" tied to the university discourses of learning which could not, by definition, be liberatory. Instead, the Labour College Movement proposed Marxism as a route to political action. While the WEA taught Marshall and Marx, the Labour College Movement taught Marx on economics, Engels on anthropology, and Dietzgen on philosophy. The issues with which both parties struggled in the early years of the twentieth century were based on a "Manifesto Marxism" which was economistic and did not have the value of Gramscian insights on hegemonic relations that would have assisted in the development of a counter-hegemonic working-class education (see *Worker Education and Labor Education*).

3. Marxism and Adult Education

The discourses surrounding the debates on the role of Marxism in radical adult education have changed over time with the development of Marxism and the incorporation of different strands from the original "Manifesto Marxism," which inspired the Labour College Movement and the radical workers movements that developed in France, Italy, Germany, Canada, Australia, and the United States. In the latter country, the IWW (Industrial Workers of the World) created and sustained the Work People's College (1903–41). It envisaged an economistic Marxism tied to the power of waged labor in the capitalist system. In Russia, a politics of adult education developed around the notion of "*Proletcult*," through socialist realism in art and film, and an attention within education to the development of the new woman and man of socialism. Within this frame the working class was treated as homogenous. The developing communist parties across Europe sought to educate their members and workers through the major trade unions which often, as in France, were allied with the Communist party. Alongside economism there was a commitment to the creation of a "vanguard"—the "advanced" section of the working class that was to be educated in Marxism in order to further the struggle against capitalism.

However, since its development from Marx's original writings Marxism has been, like adult education, constested terrain. A powerful critique of "Manifesto Marxism" and economism was developed by Antonio Gramsci in Italy during the 1920s (Hoare and Nowell Smith 1971). Gramsci sought to highlight the importance of ideologies and cultural forms in relation to the political project of the Party. His own involvement with the radical workers councils in Turin was a powerful example of collective struggle and adult education side by side in the development of both a critique of the capitalist labor process and worker-controlled alternatives. Gramsci's work emphasized the importance of ideological struggles in the revolutionary process because he believed that domination was as much a product of "consensus" as coercion. From this came his conception of ideological hegemony. Hegemony, however, implies the possibility of counterhegemonic work. Thus, radical educators in adult education have used this insight to generate counterhegemonic practices, not least in Turin. Gramsci's work has had an increasing influence on critical theorists, for example on Paolo Freire, the celebrated Brazilian educator. Much of the work of popular education in Latin America can be traced to Gramscian premises. This is reflected in the search for an understanding of hegemony, the role of the state, and the importance of civil society.

In France, in the 1970s, Louis Althusser used Gramscian insights and structuralism to develop an alternative account of Marxism. This was an attempt to break with economism and to emphasize the role of ideologies and politics offering these spheres a "relative autonomy." In his now famous essay "Ideology and Ideological State Apparatuses" Althusser drew attention to the role of the state in reproducing ideology and consensus especially through the education system which, under capitalism, not only produced workers technically skilled for their place in the capitalist division of labor, but also ideologically schooled for their place in the system (Althusser 1971).

Althusser's work emphasized "struggle in the ideological sphere." With this he drew attention to the processes and curriculum of adult education. His analysis is useful in examining the power of the state and offers one way in which to understand adult education as part of a state strategy—for example, the "Americanization" process in the United States which sought to produce "Americans" from the diverse ethnicities that were part of the migration into the United States.

4. The "Community" Approach

Adult education and workers' education, across Europe, became part of the post-1944 welfare state and was organized around a liberal rather than a class-based model. Radicalism resurfaced through the community education movement of the 1970s. This reintroduced the issues of knowledge and power, state intervention, and the autonomy of the adult learner—now not in relation to the state but to that of locale and the politics of community. In the same way that class had been constructed as the unitary site around which to organize, similarly "community" came to occupy this space with too little attention to the diversity of communities and the stratification of groups by class, gender, and race (see *Community Education and Community Development*).

The experiments with community intervention in the United Kingdom, the Netherlands, and the United States in the 1970s were tied to the regeneration of working-class neighborhoods through education and community development. Thus, Saul Alinsky in Chicago and Midwinter and Lovett in Liverpool worked through schools and institutions pioneering forms of informal education in pubs and clubs with working-class women and men. But, although women figured strongly in Lovett's (1975) account of his community education work, there was no specific attempt to activate the role of adult education in women's lives. An alternative, and more politicized account of community education appears in the work of Ashcroft and Jackson (1974), who used the vehicle of the mass meeting as an educative forum for raising local political agendas. This was a form of experiential learning in which participants, through direct action, learned how capitalism and the local state worked.

Throughout the 1970s, many urban areas moved into community education, based on the adult education model. In the United Kingdom, these initiatives reflected a homogenizing notion of community located with a White Englishness that ignored the ethnic, racial, class, and gender diversities of the United Kingdom's urban areas. In addition, "community" became allied with consumption and with forms of familialism which further emphasized consensus building and the pursuance of common interests rather than the power relations of community or family life. Yet some authors and community workers recognized that the issues raised around power and knowledge and the debate on a "relevant" curriculum were important. It was, in fact, Paolo Freire who gave a new impetus to community education and literacy work through his reiteration of the view that education was either for domestication or liberation (Freire 1972).

5. Adult Education and the New Social Movements

The work of Freire had a major impact on adult education worldwide during the 1980s. Here was a vision of literacy work as popular education which was not functional but made the politics of language and symbols central. Freire's work incorporated notions of cultural struggles found in the writings of Mao Tse-tung, Che Guevera, and Antonio Gramsci, as part of a general emancipatory politics. Freirian discourse was an eclectic and heady mix incorporating Marxism within liberation ideology. Freire's radical humanism was in conflict with a productionist Marxist account. Therefore, it connected with the growing appeal of emerging social movements, such as those for women's emancipation, racial justice, gay liberation, and peace and green issues. These are issues with which community-based strategies could also connect, because they were related to struggles over public resources, collective consumption, and areas of representation and language.

Thus, in the 1980s, critical approaches to adult education became more diffuse and more clearly allied with the new social movements. This led to a feminist critique of adult education in the United Kingdom, Germany, Canada, and the United States and the promotion of a women's studies agenda, while issues of social class re-emerged in much of the work with the unemployed and the unwaged more generally. Feminism has a long history, emerging in Europe with the French Revolution and the women's clubs that sought to put women's rights on the agenda and raised again in relation to the struggles around enslavement in the United States. Mary Wollstonecraft published *A Vindication of the Rights of Woman* in 1792. Across Europe, North America, and Australia, women organized in unions, guilds, and clubs throughout the nineteenth century and gave a special role to the power of education in their lives. These struggles continued into the twentieth century, foregrounding citizenship rights and access to education, training, and the professions; and a new wave of feminism arrived in the post-1968 era in Europe, Canada, Australia, and the United States where it was greatly influenced by the civil rights and Black Power movements (see *Women and Adult Education*).

Feminism, like Marxism, has never been unitary and debates between radical feminists, Marxist feminists, and "Black" feminists are ongoing. In relation to adult education, radical feminism generated a womanist perspective challenging the knowledge base of traditional subjects in relation to the patriarchal power implied.

This generated a quest for women's knowledge and the development of women's studies which is now part of adult education. Marxist-feminists brought class and gender together and intervened in relation to workers' education, generating simultaneously a critique of patriarchal and capitalist relations. Both these feminisms were criticized by "Black" feminists for the ethnocentrism of their accounts of the world, and from this developed both Black feminist studies and Black studies as part of the African diaspora.

The issue of racism, however, so crucial to the 1990s, has received much less attention than feminism, and still needs to be centrally placed within the adult education agenda (Westwood 1991). The civil rights and Black Power movements of the 1960s and 1970s in the United States raised once again issues like: the relationship between citizenship and the state; and the importance of education in relation to cultural and ideological struggles (reproduced in the United Kingdom in the politics of education and in the ways in which African-Caribbean and South Asian diasporic communities sought to unite around a political identity as Black people, in the struggle against racism). Alongside these developments has been the growth in access work which seeks to provide opportunities for adults to move into higher education. Within this sphere, the issue of racism has been highlighted and some courses have provided a specific space for African-Caribbean and Asian people to move into higher education. But there is concern that this will be seen as the "ultimate" answer to the question of racism and equal opportunities.

Peace studies, too, have become part of the agenda of adult education and the International Council of Adult Education now includes a peace education network (see *Peace Education*). Similarly, ecological issues are well represented in the popular education movement in Latin America, and across Europe with the "Green University" in Italy. The issues raised provide an important focus for global concerns and new discourses within which to understand imperialism and underdevelopment, the relationships between the "North" and the "South," and fundamental questions on the world's resources.

In so far as much that has been named as "radical" in adult education has been located with the labor movement and the socialist agenda, these are contradictory times for critical approaches because the socialist project itself, following the events in Eastern Europe and the Soviet Union, is undergoing a profound period of reappraisal. The banners declaring the importance of citizenship against the designation "comrade" speak volumes for the failures of an economistically based account of the future tied to the command economy which has shown itself less effective than capitalism in delivering certain consumption goods. However, the demise of the Soviet bloc is no triumph for the West and the forms of capitalism that continue to lurch from crisis to crisis with poverty, unemployment, and despair in its train. The current profound restructuring of capitalism globally with the new forms of work relations have also meant the diminished effectiveness of trades union power and collective strength of working people. There is some suggestion that the new forms of the labor process will allow those with jobs the opportunity for a more democratic life at the workplace. If this is to be the case, then adult education is well placed to connect with these new forms and to bring the past and the present together around the notions of citizenship and workers' control, which have been so important throughout the history of adult education.

There is also another task related to the unemployed and to those whose work is increasingly casualized. This peripheral workforce is both feminized and racialized, and thus the issues brought to the fore by the women's and anti-racist movements need to be set firmly at the center of the adult education agenda.

This relates to the problem of nationalism and ethnic identities in Europe and globally, where a politics of difference is unfolding in very contradictory ways generating both a new sense of histories submerged, but also new racism and nationalisms which are located with a dangerous exclusivity. This calls for profound changes in the ways in which adult education curricula view the world. It is no accident that the work of Paolo Freire has had such an impact on adult educators of the North. Part of this impact has been a re-examination of the power/knowledge complex and the ways in which adult education discourses construct adult learners and their relationship to knowledge and thereby to empowerment. It is here that the work of Michel Foucault with his emphasis upon micropolitics and the diffuse nature of power has important insights for critical adult education.

6. Conclusion

Adult education faces an increasingly fractured world in which some of the old certainties have disappeared. The states in various countries seek to harness adult learning in relation to a human capital agenda and adult educators struggle for greater resources in a critical engagement with the state. A new politics for adult education across the old divide between radical and liberal, vocational and nonvocational, can also be noted. Adult education has consistently worked at the interface of economics, politics, and cultures, and in the spaces opened up by these interfaces. It may well continue to do so in the 1990s and beyond in relation to the new social movements, emancipatory views of learning, citizenship, and democracy.

See also: Community Education and Community Development; Literacy and Numeracy Models; Popular Education and Conscientization; History of Adult Education; Political Science and Policy Analysis in Adult Education; Ideologies in Adult Education; Adult Education for Development; Women and Adult Education; Worker Education and Labor Education; Nongovernmental Organizations

References

Ashcroft B, Jackson K 1974 Adult education and social action. In: Jones D, Mayo M (eds.) 1974 *Community Work One*. Routledge, London

Althusser L 1971 Ideology and ideological state apparatuses: Notes towards an investigation. In: Althusser L (ed.) 1971 *Lenin and Philosophy and Other Essays*. New Left Books, London

Freire P 1972 *Pedagogy of the Oppressed*. Penguin, Harmondsworth

Hoare Q, Nowell Smith G (eds.) 1971 *Selection from the Prison Notebooks of Antonio Gramsci*. Lawrence and Wishart, London

Lovett T 1975 *Adult Education, Community Development and the Working Class*. Ward Lock, London

Westwood S 1991 Constructing the "Other": Minorities, the state and adult education in Europe. In: Westwood S, Thomas E J (eds.) 1991 *Radical Agendas? The Politics of Adult Education*. National Institute of Adult Continuing Education, Leicester

Further Reading

Alinsky S 1969 *Reveille For Radicals*. Vintage, New York

Brown G 1980 Independence and incorporation: The Labour College movement and the Workers' Educational Association before the Second World War. In: Thompson J (ed.) 1980 *Adult Education For A Change*. Hutchinson, London

Fieldhouse R 1977 *The Workers' Educational Association. Aims and Achievements 1903–1977*. Syracuse University, Syracuse, New York

Freire P 1985 *The Politics of Education: Culture, Power and Liberation*. Macmillan, London

Gordon C 1980 *Power/Knowledge: Selected Interviews and other Writings 1972–77 by Michel Foucault*. Pantheon Books, New York

Hall S, Jacques M 1989 *New Times: The Changing Face of Politics in the 1990's*. Lawrence and Wishart, London

Hooks B 1984 *Feminist Theory: From Margin to Center*. SouthEnd Press, Boston, Massachusetts

Johnson R 1988 "Really useful knowledge" 1790–1850: Memories for education in the 1980's. In: Lovett T (ed.) 1988 *Radical Approaches to Education: A Reader*. Routledge, London

Rattansi A 1982 *Marx and the Division of Labour*. Macmillan, London

Simon B 1990 The struggle for hegemony, 1920–1926. In: Simon B (ed.) 1990 *The Search For Enlightenment*. Lawrence and Wishart, London

Thomas J E 1982 *Radical Adult Education: Theory and Practice*. University of Nottingham, Nottingham

Thompson E P 1963 *The Making of the English Working Class*. Gollancz, London

Family Life Education

L. Vandemeulebroecke and H. Van Crombrugge

Family life education is the variety of educative actions that aim at strengthening and enriching individual and family well-being, by organizing learning processes in the field of human development and sexuality; interpersonal relationships; family interaction; family resource management; education about parenthood, ethics, and family and society. However, the interpretation of terms as "individual well-being" and "quality of family life" is constantly evolving and differs according to the historical and societal circumstances. Because of this, family life education varies depending on place and time. It can be organized in formal educational activities as well as in nonformal contexts. Further, its general aim can be realized in different ways: either deficiency-oriented (curative and preventive programs) or growth-oriented (enrichment programs). Family life education programs can also be distinguished by their underlying paradigm, the predominant paradigm being the instrumental/technical one versus the interpretative and the critical/emancipatory paradigm. As well as the differences that refer to the historical and societal situations, one can distinguish programs with reference to the target group, the content, or the working method.

1. Definitional Questions

There are various different definitions of family life education. The reason for this is that a definition is often formulated with reference to a particular historical or social situation, which is not recognized as such by other forms of family life education. This situation then leads to still other definitions. Darling's critical appraisal of different definitions leads to the following general definition: "an interdisciplinary field of study concerned with preserving and improving the quality of human life by the study of individuals as they interact with the resources in their multifaceted environments" (Darling 1987 p.818).

Three critiques can be formulated with respect to this definition. In the first place, family life education is not so much a study but an educative action directed at change. Next, this action is more specific than the stimulation of the quality of human life. After conceptual analysis, it appears that "the most appropriate statement of general purpose was: to strengthen and enrich individual and family well-being" (Thomas and Arcus 1992). Finally, the definition does not give any indication about the content of family life education. After careful research, Arcus (1987) distinguishes the following most important areas of family life education: (a) human development and sexuality,

(b) interpersonal relationships, (c) family interaction, (d) family resource management, (e) education about parenthood, (f) ethics, and (g) family and society. Thus, family life education can best be defined in these terms.

The problem of such a definition is that it refers to family life education as it exists in the industrialized countries. However, the priorities in less industrialized countries and in developing countries are of a completely different kind. Hence, the improvement of the quality of family life requires different approaches, according to concrete circumstances and motives, and in respect of constant evolution. A brief historical description will make this clear.

2. Historical Background

Interest in the subject of family life education dates from early history: it can be regarded as a function of the modernization of societies. The Industrial Revolution led to many changes in social life in general and private life in particular, so that the organization of family life had to be changed. Combined with the typical Enlightenment conviction that by means of education and instruction humankind can be elevated to a better, happier, and more reasonable existence, this led to the idea that the quality of family life can be improved by means of education.

This education differed according to one's position in this societal evolution. In Western Europe and North America, the middle classes felt obliged to educate the lower social classes to accept a healthier family life. On the one hand matters of hygiene were emphasized, particularly with regard to pregnancy and the cure of new-born infants; on the other hand matters of sexual morality were considered (warning against premarital sex and sexually transferable diseases, and urging young men to act responsibly).

A similar orientation toward family life education is emerging in newly industrialized Third World countries. The situation of family life education in many Latin-American countries, for example, is comparable to family life education in nineteenth-century Western Europe (Sepulveda Lagos 1991). In Africa, family life education is predominantly concerned with family planning and birth control.

In Western countries the (again growing) interest in family life education is the result of two tendencies. First, family life education is organized as an answer to the psychological and cultural consequences of a "postmodern" society. Second, part of family life education is directed at groups that are the structural victims of rapid modernization. In this case, attention is especially directed toward the relational aspects of family life.

There is a distinction between developments that enhance the need with regard to family relations, and the circumstances that make it difficult for families to solve these needs themselves. Among the factors that cause problems in family relations (e.g., the loss of a normative model of family life in general and of child rearing in particular) a distinction can be made between interactive, cultural, and social factors.

The interactive factors include: changing role-patterns; the increasing variation in forms of non-traditional families; problems of attunement between different educational settings; the influence of the media; the reduction of family size, which leads to more intense family relations but also to fewer chances to learn how to deal with children; the increasing mobility of families; and the dismantling of wider supportive networks.

Among the cultural factors are: the disappearance of generalizing social norms; professionalization, and the discussion of traditional norms that goes with it; planned parenthood; the scientization of parenthood; individual self-realization; negotiative housekeeping and gender equality in education; the multicultural society; and changing attitudes relating to deviating and acceptable life-styles.

Social factors include the problems of housing in an aging society; the financial and material problems of many households (e.g., one parent families); the economic crisis; the impact of work and life situations; and family policies.

However, only under certain circumstances do these developments lead to an actual inability of parents and families to educate and to live together in a family relationship. Risk factors can be: the socioeconomic inferiority of certain groups (low income, little schooling, unemployment, bad working conditions); living conditions that lead to isolation (old neighborhoods, inadequate housing, single parents, immigrants); or the transition to new situations (new parenthood, divorce, moving, changing cultural background, foster parenthood). The real impact of these risk factors is connected with the way the families involved cope with difficult situations, the degree to which parents are prepared for child rearing, and the presence of a supporting social network.

It has already become clear that there are significant differences in family life education, according to the social situation of specific countries. There are differences in content, teaching methods, the concrete aims, the place and manner of organization, the justifications, and the basic theoretical frameworks. Furthermore, differences on one level will go with differences on other levels: for example, there is a relationship between the actual economic circumstances, the theoretical framework that is chosen, and the aims

and working methods of a program for family life education.

3. Forms of Family Life Education

The existing forms of family life education can be examined on the basis of a number of such differences. These are represented as possible alternatives: formal versus nonformal; deficiency- versus growth-oriented; technical, interpretative, or emancipatory paradigm; general versus specific target group; individual, in groups, or mass media; and comprehensive versus specific content. Within these alternatives, still other distinctions are made.

3.1 Organization: Formal and Nonformal

Family life education is organized in formal as well as nonformal educational activities (see *Formal, Nonformal, and Informal Education*). In formal education, it can be found at various educational levels. In the 1980s, in the United States and in Great Britain, heated debates were held, especially about the position of family life education as a compulsory subject in secondary schools. These debates related partly to didactic matters, concerning the possibility of family life education, considering for example the needs of pupils, teacher preparations, and the problems of evaluating such a subject. The debates also related to the aim that had to be pursued, against the background of the lack of a social consensus on the position and meaning of the family in society, and the role education plays in this. Some hold the view that education at school has to pass on traditional family values to children in order to strengthen the nation. Liberals, however, state that the aim of the organization of family life education in schools has to be to foster tolerance among pupils toward a variety of life-styles (Macklin 1985). Others state that this discussion neglects the real issues, that is, the socioeconomic problems of certain categories of families (e.g., the feminization of poverty).

Although the problems of formal family life education are to some extent also the problems of nonformal family life education, there are some notable differences. This has to do with the fact that formal education is directed to children and youth and their future family life, whereas nonformal family life education is mostly directed to people who already have a family, or intend to have one. The didactic problem is different. The needs of nonformal education are much clearer: they can be expressed by the parents themselves or they can be concretely indicated by third parties with respect to the families, for example by social workers. Furthermore, the ideological discussion is not of a general kind, as the "pupils" have already opted for a specific form of cohabitation, and because the aims that are connected with the signalled needs can be concretely formulated. Moreover, nonformal family education, as opposed to formal family education, is often organized by private organizations that already represent an ideological point of view (e.g., family movements, women's movements, etc.).

3.2 Aim: Deficiency- versus Growth-oriented

The general aim of family life education—the improvement of the quality of family life—can be realized in two fundamentally different ways. Either one takes the problems as a starting point and defines family life education as the prevention or solution of these problems, or one does not start from problems but from the needs and possibilities of families to improve the quality of life.

In the adult education terminology that was developed by Boshier in the context of research on educational needs (Boshier 1977), it is possible to speak of family life education that is deficiency-oriented and that is restricted to the safeguarding of life chances, versus family life education that is growth-oriented and that aims at enlarging the life space itself.

The first kind of family life education includes all preventive and curative programs. Preventive programs aim at preventing problems, curative programs aim at solving them. Examples of preventive programs can be found in the context of the preparation of families for the situation after divorce. There are programs for parents (e.g., Buehler et al. 1992) and programs for children. A typical problem in preventive programs concerns the best moment to intervene, and to whom and what to direct oneself in the first place. Postdivorce prevention programs for children appear to be most effective when affective, cognitive, and behavioral issues are addressed (Pedro-Carroll and Cowen 1985), and this in a very structured way. However, parents' programs are most effective when parenting skills and the parent–child relationships are addressed; for this group discussion seems to be particularly effective, the best period for which is the first year after the divorce. Preventive programs also include programs for future mothers that aim especially at providing them the necessary caring skills and insights with regard to the early development of the child (for a survey of such programs, see Joy et al. 1980).

As mentioned before, curative programs aim at solving problems. Examples of such family life education programs can be found in the context of multiproblem families. These families are instructed individually and collectively about all kinds of skills that are necessary for survival: beside parental skills, budget management and other economic topics are an important issue (for a survey and Belgian example see Ghesquiere and Hellinckx 1989). Here, the boundaries between family therapy, social work, and education become very faint. Hence, the term "family support," which has education as a central element, is coming to be preferred.

This last evolution also brings deficiency-oriented family life education closer to growth-oriented family life education. In the Anglo-Saxon literature, the latter can be found predominantly under the term "family enrichment" (see Mace 1984). In the European continental language areas, this enrichment is implied when using equivalents of "education." In German, for example, the terms *Bildung* (education), *Elternbildung* (parent education) and *Familienbildung* (family life education) are used (Strunk 1985). In spite of the multitude of forms that this enrichment can take, the most essential one is the aim of allowing families to grow, to enrich themselves. Therefore, the contents are not defined as starting from a certain problem, but from an ideal view of the functioning of the family.

There is a distinction between two forms of enrichment, according to the way in which ideal family functioning is defined. Either this is done in a prescriptive way, or the participants themselves try to formulate an ideal and a corresponding objective. When ideal family functioning is defined prescriptively, still another distinction can be made. Either the ideal has its roots in religious and ideological frameworks, or it is derived from scientific research concerning the functioning of healthy families. Numerous examples of religiously motivated family life education can be found in Roman Catholic programs as they are conceived in, for example, Latin America; these programs are grounded in a Christian anthropology (e.g., see Beens 1991 for the case of Panama). Another working method is to derive the aims of enrichment from scientific research concerning healthy and strong families. The dimensions of healthy family functioning are identified via empirical research, and attempts are made to relate these dimensions to education that will improve the quality of family life.

Quite different are the programs in which directions are determined by starting from the participants themselves. One of the best examples of this approach is "family clusters" (Sawin 1986). The educator does not start from a preconceived curriculum, but first makes up an inventory of the issues that all members of all families want to work on in the coming year. Starting from these interviews, he or she works out a proposal and asks for approval. When the participants arrive at a consensus about the content, the program can start. It is, however, possible for the content to be frequently re-examined. This approach is also the basic principle of family activities in sociocultural work as it exists in Germany and Belgium. Similar approaches can also be found in the context of social work, for example in the training of experienced foster parents (for survey and examples see Van Crombrugge and Vandemeulebroecke 1994), and also in working with minimally educated parents. The differences between the prescriptive and the more inductive method of determining the contents of family life education, also relate to differences in underlying paradigms, from which one starts when planning family life education.

3.3 Paradigms: Technical, Interpretative, Emancipating

The different family life education programs can be considered with respect to their underlying paradigm. By paradigm is meant the basic presumptions concerning relationships among human interests, needs, knowledge, and human actions, which are shared by groups of people in general and members of a scientific community in particular. In connection with modern sociophilosophical insights, three paradigms have been distinguished for the field of family life education: an instrumental/technical paradigm, an interpretive paradigm, and a critical/emancipatory paradigm (Morgaine 1992).

The predominant paradigm in family life education is the instrumental/technical one. Basic assumptions are that there is a single reality of life which is independent of human uniqueness; the laws of human behavior are able to be discovered through research; human needs can be satisfied by predicting cause and effect relationships and controlling human actions. The basic element of the paradigm is that it suffices to provide people with scientific insights and technical skills in order to prevent and/or solve problems. The typical examples of programs that start from such principles are Parent Effectiveness Training and also the parent training programs inspired by behavior modification, such as Systematic Training for Effective Parenting. In this example, a number of formal skills are learned, that apply to every situation.

As a reaction to programs that reduce and formalize family life to a matter of skills, insights, and methods, programs have been developed that start from an interpretative paradigm. The hypotheses of this paradigm are contradictory to those of the former paradigm. The basic assumption is that the experiences of people are unique and that actions have to be understood and approached from these experiences, if they are to change. Because of this approach, the accent in these programs is put upon the exploration and teaching of family members in how to voice their own experiences, and also on the confrontation with the interpretations and voices of other participants, in order to come to a more adequate self-understanding. The already mentioned family clusters are an example of this paradigm. Another example is: "How to talk so kids will listen and listen so kids will talk."

Critical/emancipatory family life education goes one step further than the interpretative paradigm. The explored experiences are interpreted from critical theories that indicate how experiences and actions are determined by social structures and prevailing ideologies. Morgaine (1992) refers to his own program "Process Parenting" as an example of such programs. In continental Europe a great number of family life

education courses, organized by women's organizations, that can be thought of as enrichment programs, are emancipatory in this sense.

3.4 Target Group: General, Specific

As well as the differences that result from the varying historical and societal situations, the concrete organizational context, and the underlying paradigm, one can also distinguish among programs for family life education with reference to the people they are intended for. A first important distinction is among courses that, on the one hand, aim at all parents without distinction and, on the other hand, the programs that are directed at specific groups. In the last group, a distinction can be made between family life education for specific families and family life education for professionals. The last one includes social workers and trainees, and those preparing for teaching family life skills to families, parents, and so on (Allen and Crosbie–Burnett 1992).

In describing the programs aimed at specific groups of parents, pre-, peri- and postbirth programs, programs for foster parents, for multiproblem families, and for postdivorce families have already been mentioned. One can also add family life education for family day care providers (e.g., see Pettinger 1990 for the German pilot project), or for dual-earner couples (Hawkins and Roberts 1992).

3.5 Content: Comprehensive, Specific

In discussing the definition, the different main areas of family life education were mentioned. It has however become clear that, according to the extension of the target group, the contents of the courses can also differ. It has already been indicated how in the less industrialized countries the emphasis is different, that is, more on hygiene and birth control. There are also different ways to determine the content of programs, and because of this, the content will vary.

3.6 Working Method: Mass Media, Group, Individual

Most of the programs that have been mentioned work with groups of families and/or family members. There are, however, other possibilities, especially in the media. In Spain and Latin America, family life education is often taught by means of the radio (Espinada Cepeda 1982), often in combination with learning groups. Television is also an effective instrument for family life education. The United Kingdom's BBC, for example, regularly broadcasts programs on family life education, which are very popular. Another medium that cannot be underestimated is the enormous quantity of books (Clarke-Stewart 1974), which in recent years has been followed and supplemented by videocassettes. In Flanders (Belgium), for example, the government provides a videocassette to all mothers who have recently given birth, giving information on the care and education of their children. Very specific and much read also are the brochures which parents receive individually during the growth period of their child (Lüscher et al. 1984). Furthermore, some programs combine different media. The combination of radio and group work has already been mentioned. Programs on television are often accompanied by a manual or a magazine. Another combination, for example, is groupwork based on articles on education and family in popular magazines; the objective is that the participants themselves compose a kind of manual. This method is used in the Walloon part of Belgium.

4. Evaluation of Family Life Education

People who are directly involved (participants, assistants, organizing institutions) often evaluate family life education on mere subjective grounds: are the participants (assistants, organizers) satisfied? Does something appear to have been learned, or something been changed?

A more systematic objective or scientific evaluation deals with methodological and ethical difficulties; for example, which standards have to be used to evaluate effects? Does one interfere too much with the private life of the participants when looking for transfer effects? Is it possible to work with control groups? Is each group so unique that one cannot generalize the results for other situations? In case of observed effects, what are the determinant factors, and so on.

From the 1970s onward, more and more systematic research has been conducted concerning the effectiveness of family life education programs. Giblin et al. collected 85 studies on effects of premarital, marital, and family enrichment programs, carried out between 1970 and 1982, that include a control group. They conducted a meta-analysis on these studies and observed that the enrichment programs had an average effect size of 0.44, which means that "the average participant in enrichment programs is better off following intervention than 67 percent of those who do not" (Giblin et al. 1985). From their study, they conclude that the effectiveness of enrichment programs may be accepted. However, the size of the stated effects appeared to be strongly connected with the chosen measure (behavioral versus self-report indexes) used to investigate the changes, and in a lesser degree to the chosen research design. The connection between effects and program features such as content, structure, leadership, and participant group varied from poorly defined to slight.

Guerney and Maxson later commented on the research of Giblin et al. in the light of more recent studies (Guerney and Maxson 1990). They also conclude that enrichment programs generally have positive effects, and therefore find these programs completely legitimate. They also recommend investigating factors which can further improve the programs, rather than continuing effectiveness research.

5. Conclusion

Family life education is a multilayered and multifaceted reality, related to social evolution and responding to changing questions and needs. It is a field of study where many disciplines can meet and can work in an action-directed way. Finally, it is a field of work that can have an important significance for the emancipation of individuals and groups and for the democratization of societies.

See also: Population Education; Time, Leisure and Adult Education; Time Policies for Lifelong Learning; Lifespan Development; Environments for Learning

References

Allen K R, Crosbie-Burnett M (eds.) 1992 Innovative ways and controversial issues in teaching about families. A special collection of family pedagogy. *Fam. Relat.* 41(1): 9–73
Arcus M 1987 A framework for life-span family life education. *Fam. Relat.* 36(1): 5–10
Beens F 1991 La familia urbana y sub-urbana de Panamá desde una antropologia cristiana. In: Laboa J M (ed.) 1991 *Políticas de la familia.* Publicaciones Universidad P. Comillas, Madrid
Boshier R 1977 Motivational orientations re-visited: Lifespace motives and the education participation scale. *Adult Educ.* 27(2): 89–115
Buehler C, Betz P, Ryan C M, Legg B H, Trotter B B 1992 Description and evaluation of the orientation for divorcing parents: Implications for postdivorce prevention programs. *Fam. Relat.* 41(2): 154–62
Clarke-Stewart K A 1974 Popular primers for parents. *Am. Psychol.* 29: 359–69
Darling C A 1987 Family life education. In: Sussman M B, Steinmetz S K (eds.) 1987 *Handbook of Marriage and the Family.* Plenum, New York
Espinada Cepeda L 1982 Radio ECCA, Canary Islands. In: Kaye A, Harry K (eds.) 1982 *Using the Media for Adult Basic Education.* Croom Helm, London
Ghesquiere P, Hellinckx W 1989 A home-based parenting program for abusive multiproblem families. Paper presented at the 2nd European conference on child abuse and neglect, Brussels, April 1989
Giblin P, Sprenkle D H, Sheehan R 1985 Enrichment outcome research: A meta-analysis of premarital, marital and Family interventions. *Journal of Marital and Family Therapy* 11: 257–71
Guerney B, Maxson P 1990 Marital and family enrichment research: A decade review and look ahead. *J. Marriage and Fam.* 52(4): 1127–35
Hawkins A J, Roberts T A 1992 Designing a primary intervention to help dual-earner couples share housework and childcare. *Fam. Relat.* 41(2): 169–77
Joy L A, Davidson S, Williams T M, Painter S L 1980 Parent education in the perinatal period: a critical review of the literature. In Taylor P M (ed.) 1989 *Parent–Infant Relationships.* Grune and Stratton, London
Lüscher K, Köbbel I, Fisch R 1984 *Elternbildung durch Elternbriefe. Möglichkeiten und Grenzen einer aktuellen*

familicnpolitischen Massnahme. Universitätsverlag, Konstanz

Mace D R (ed.) 1984 *Prevention in Family Services. Approaches to Family Wellness*. Sage, London

Macklin E D 1985 Education for choice: Implications of alternatives in lifestyles for family life education. In: Gutknecht D B, Butler E W (eds.) 1985 *Family, Self and Society. Emerging issues, Alternatives and Interventions*. University Press of America, London, Maryland

Morgaine C A 1992 Alternative paradigms for helping families change themselves. *Fam. Relat.* 41(1): 9–11

Pedro-Carroll J A, Cowen E L 1985 The children of divorce intervention program: An investigation of the efficacy of a school-based prevention program. *J. Consult. Clin. Psychol.* 53(5): 603–11

Pettinger R 1990 The pilot project: Tagesmütter. In: Peeters J, Braam J, Van den Heede R (eds.) 1990 *Family Day Care. Family Day Care Provider: Teacher or Substitute Mother?* Kind & Gezin – VBJK, Brussels

Sawin M M 1986 The family cluster approach to family enrichment. In: Denton W (ed.) 1986 *Marriage and Family Enrichment*. Haworth, London

Sepulveda Lagos J 1991 La educacion familiar y sexual en Latinoamerica. In: Laboa J M (ed.) 1991 *Politicas de la familia*. Publicationes Universidad P. Commillas, Madrid

Strunk G 1985 Familienleben, Familienerziehung und Familienbildung. In: Raapke H D, Schulenberg W (eds.) 1985 *Didaktik der Erwachsenenbildung*. Klett-Cotta, Stuttgart

Thomas J, Arcus M 1992 Family life education: An analysis of the concept. *Fam. Relat.* 41(1): 3–8

Van Crombrugge H, Vandemeulebroecke L 1994 Improving the quality of foster care through foster parent education. In: McKenzie B (ed.) 1994 *Current Perspectives on Foster Family Care*.

Further Reading

David M 1986 Teaching family matters. *Br. J. Sociol. educ.* 7(1): 35–57

Dinkmeyer D, McKay G 1983 *Systematic Training for Effective Parenting*. American Guidance Service Circle Pines, Minnesota

Family support movement 1989 Special section of *Am. J. Orthopsychiatry* 59: 6–58

Pourtois J P 1984 *Eduquer les parents. Ou comment stimuler la compétence en éducation*. Labor, Brussels

Pugh G, De'Ath E 1984 *The needs of Parents. Practice and Policy in Parent Education*. MacMillan, Basingstoke

Stolberg A L 1988 Prevention programs for divorcing families. In: Bond L A, Wagner B M (eds.) 1988 *Families in Transition. Primary Prevention Programs that Work*. Sage, London

Human Resource Development

J. A. Niemi

The concept of human resource development (HRD) is assuming greater importance within organizations as they continue to search for excellence and grapple with environmental turbulence caused by the accelerating rate of technological change, expansion of the global economy, fluctuating world politics, and the changing nature of the workforce. In order to cope with these conditions, organizations must recognize the importance of HRD as an integral part of their mission and goals, and begin transforming themselves into learning organizations.

1. Basic Concepts

1.1 Human Resource Development

The narrow concept of "training" was incorporated by Nadler and Nadler (1989) into the broader concept of "human resource development" that also included the concepts of "education" and "development." Nadler viewed training as the acquisition of knowledge and skills for the present job, so that workers could undertake immediate assignments more efficiently and effectively. The subcategory of education was described by him as a more long-range process aimed at preparing workers for future positions. The concept of development encompassed long-range personal growth not necessarily tied to a position. Gilley and Eggland (1989) collapsed these two concepts into the concept of "career development" that undergirds such HRD activities as mentoring, career counseling, and career pathing. Career pathing includes the sequencing of different job assignments that provide varied experiences in a particular area of work. Rothwell (1985) defined HRD as:

> . . . any planned training, educational, or developmental activity sponsored by a work organization . . . It connotes the humanistic philosophy aimed at integrating the goals and mission of an organization and the personal need and career aspirations of each individual in that organization for the purposes of increasing work productivity and improving job satisfaction. (p.15)

1.2 Organization Development

The concept of "organization development" (OD) alludes to planned change within an organization. Often it relies on HRD as a way to foster the knowledge and skills required to overcome problems through systematic learning activities that produce change in an organization. Such OD may be initiated by employing the services of an external consultant, or it could be initiated through an internal practitioner who may also fill the HRD role. The OD process includes identification of a problem, action research aimed at diagnosing its elements, suggestions for its solution, implementation of the required intervention, and a process for formative and summative evaluation. Training programs in HRD are typically conducted at the intervention stage.

2. Distinction Between HRD and Vocational–Technical Education

The distinction between HRD and vocational–technical education resides chiefly in the manner in which learning activities are initiated, funded, and conducted. A primary goal of vocational–technical education is the preparation of workers for entry level jobs through pre-employment education and/or apprenticeship training. However, vocational–technical schools throughout the world bear responsibility (under government funding) for training that upgrades workers both in and out of the workforce. For business, industry, and government, vocational–technical education schools may be more effective than in-house activities designed to meet the learning needs of a particular segment of the workforce. Advisory committees made up of representatives from business, industry, and government contribute to this effectiveness by assisting vocational–technical schools to fulfill the personnel needs of employers in a community (see *Technical and Vocational Education and Training*).

3. Distinction Between HRD and Continuing Professional Education

As indicated in the foregoing discussion, HRD is a function of the organization that impels it to become more efficient or productive. On the other hand, continuing professional education (CPE) places the responsibility for keeping abreast of new developments in their fields squarely upon individual professionals. Such professionals often seek educational opportunities from four types of providers: institutions of higher education, professional associations, independent (proprietary) agencies, and agencies that employ these professionals. However, the distinction between HRD and CPE becomes blurred when professionals seek education from agencies that employ them, instead of assuming personal responsibility for their own education. As Cervero (1988) pointed out, CPE becomes subservient to the organization's goals. Under this constraint, CPE is forced to adopt a more limited vision of the educational strategies that exist within the corporate culture (see *Lifelong and Continuing Education; Polytechnic Education; Professional Associations*).

4. HRD in the United States

A major HRD goal is improving the organization's growth by training new workers and enhancing the performance of present workers through specific learning activities. Both cases require workers to be equipped with the knowledge and skills needed to fill current positions, or make lateral or upward moves within the organization (career development). Needs assessments discern gaps between ideal and actual performance as either deficiencies that characterize past or present performance, or opportunities that impel future job changes.

On the basis of these expressed needs, different modes may be applied to curriculum design. A highly structured, content-centered design that is primarily the responsibility of the HRD practitioner may best meet those needs. On the other hand, a collaborative mode, in which the learner and the HRD practitioner jointly determine a curriculum focusing on problem-centered or learner-centered learning, might be more appropriate. A modified version of the content-centered mode is the Critical Events Model (CEM) created by Nadler (1982). The uniqueness of this model lies in the process that continuously provides managers and supervisors with opportunities for evaluation and feedback, from the needs assessment stage to the design and conduct of training. Such involvement of managers and supervisors could impel them to utilize all four of Kirkpatrick's (1987) evaluation steps. These are:

(a) reaction of trainees to a particular training program;

(b) learning (principal facts learned or attitudes changed);

(c) behavior (changes in job behavior as a result of the program);

(d) results (tangible benefits of the program to the organization).

Preparation of practitioners to serve HRD programs is a major objective of universities and professional organizations. However, as Nadler (1984) pointed out, three categories of personnel conduct the HRD function: the HRD practitioner who views this activity as a commitment to the field, a generalist manager with a temporary assignment who has no special commitment to HRD and no intention of pursuing it as a career, and line supervisors and managers who perform the HRD role as a collateral duty. The weakness of the last two categories resides in the absence of a specific commitment to HRD.

According to Gilley and Eggland (1989), the development of a professional HRD field is of paramount importance. They reported on nine major studies that have helped to shape this field. *Models for Excellence* (McLagan 1983), a study published by the American Society for Training and Development (ASTD), presented a competency-based research study that examined the human resource developer's role in the field. This purpose was addressed through analysis of 15 roles, accompanied by a supporting body of knowledge that included 31 competencies (knowledge/skill areas). One example is the program designer's role. For this specialist role, the following competencies are listed: computer competence, organization behavior understanding, writing skills, intellectual versatility, adult learning understanding, competency identification skills, objectives, preparation skills, training and development techniques understanding, and model-building skills. This competency-based approach has both benefits and drawbacks for graduate HRD programs and the HRD field. The benefits are that: (a) institutions of higher education have a field-based model from which to develop academic programs for preparing HRD practitioners; (b) a comprehensive model provides employers with criteria for job design and for the identification of qualified applicants; and (c) experienced HRD staff in an organization have a tool for self-assessment that assists them in planning their own learning.

A major drawback of the competency-based approach is its excessive reductionism, whereby human behavior is interpreted in mechanistic terms. This approach is considered by some to be confining, because it fails to encompass the wide range of human behavior. On the whole, HRD graduate programs housed in adult education faculties demonstrate a more humanistic orientation, based on the principles of adult learning and development.

4.1 Recent Developments

In the past, HRD has been viewed as a staff activity that held learning subordinate to organizational purposes. In other words, training and education were seen as the means for an organization to perform its mission and goals. These HRD programs were commonly used to improve internal operations, so that workers could efficiently produce an organization's goods and services. The HRD operation was one based on the organization's past performance with a view either to correct deficiencies or provide learning to handle new technologies. At that period, certain assumptions prevailed, chiefly that the future would be much like the past.

The concept of "strategic HRD" relates to ways in which organizations are developing strategic training plans that link training to business objectives. According to Rothwell and Kazanas (1989):

> strategic HRD integrates long-term, intermediate term, and short-term learning plans designed to cultivate needed talent. It helps meet needs created by Strategic Business Plans . . . [by] a comprehensive, general instructional plan . . . that integrates such HRD functions as organization, development, employee education, and employee training. (p. 153)

Another new concept is "learning organization," described by Senge (1990) as:

> an organization that is continuously expanding its capacity to create its future. For such an organization, it is not enough merely to survive. "Survival learning," or what is more often termed "adaptive learning," is important—indeed, it is necessary. But, for a learning organization, "adaptive learning" must be joined by "generative learning," learning that enhances our capacity to create. (p. 14)

Woolner (1991) emphasized the importance of creating a learning organization by broadening the concept of the workplace, viewing it as an environment for learning. In this environment, each time a task is performed by workers, a learning experience occurs that will enable future tasks to be performed more effectively. In other words, the process is cumulative. In the following discussion, Japan and Finland have been selected as countries that display versions of the learning organization, although that term is not used in those countries. Bengtsson (1991) offers further analyses of the notion of the learning organization in an international perspective.

5. HRD in Japan

Human resource development in Japan is intricately entwined with the culture of the country, with emphasis on egalitarianism, groupism, and lifetime employment. The concept of egalitarianism provides a framework for a broad scope of training that produces a multiskilled workforce. Thus, workers have equal opportunities to advance in a job. Moreover, through a system of participatory management, workers share the power of decision-making in what are termed "quality circles." Lindbergh (1991) reported that such power motivates workers to utilize their full potential. Through such participation, workers acquire experience that will help them to perform the next task more effectively. Groupism gives to workers a sense of identity and allegiance to the group and to the company. This collective allegiance is sometimes criticized as a closed system. The concept of lifetime employment offers job security that is reinforced by long-term career development. Such lifetime employment prepares workers as generalists through job rotation, in which they learn a variety of skills. The inherent drawback of lifetime employment is that it permits only a limited influx of new workers.

In Japan, then, there are few formal training programs, aside from orientation for new workers. Instead, the corporate culture provides training through a system of worker development made possible through job rotation, participatory decision making, and learning in a collective.

6. HRD in Finland

Human resource development in Finland did not become an integral part of educational policy until the 1970s, when several workforce concerns became apparent: the need for workers to stay abreast of new knowledge while on the job, the need for retraining of workers because of structural changes in the organization, and the need for additional training of workers in different age groups.

Prior to 1977, formal university preparation of HRD practitioners did not exist. Since then, the University of Helsinki has conducted a program to prepare HRD practitioners for the workforce. The theoretical basis of this program is the work of cognitive psychologists and "activity" theorists of the former Soviet Union. Tenets espoused by Engestrom (1987) illustrate a blending of these two approaches. His "learning by expanding" theory embraces three pairs of concepts. The first pair—learning motivation and contradiction—involves recognizing and resolving contradictions between previous thinking about a task and new responsibilities and subject matter required by the new task. The second pair of concepts—mental structures and orientation basis—entails comprehending the subject matter as a whole in which everything is related. The third pair of concepts refers to the total learning process, which incorporates and utilizes the knowledge gained, and evaluates its potential (Pulkkis et al. 1987). As in Japan, the quality of working life is a major concern, with workers assuming a long-term commitment to the organization, which, in turn, offers them lifetime employment after a probationary period.

7. Emerging Issues in HRD

The first issue emerges from the changing nature of the workforce. Demographic data reveal that a large percentage of new personnel will be women, as well as immigrants and other minorities. The implications for organizations are that they must deal with people possessing different expectations and voicing different demands. Moreover, these new workers must be accepted by and integrated into the existing workforce.

Demographic data also reveal the graying of the workforce. Japan has responded to this challenge by raising the male retirement age from 50 to 55, so as to retain skilled, experienced workers. In the United States, there is concern that older workers, especially those with limited education, may not be able to cope with new learning. It is important for HRD practitioners to comprehend the anxieties that beset these workers in unfamiliar situations. The situation is compounded, in some cases, by physiological changes wrought by the aging process, such as sensory deterioration and loss of energy.

A second issue relates to workforce literacy, which involves equipping workers with minimum basic skills required for the pursuit of further training. This issue is specially pertinent in urban centers in the United States, where the school dropout rate is extremely high. Characteristically, the people in question exhibit low self-esteem and shun learning, which they associate with unsympathetic teachers, low grades, and punishments. The issue of workplace literacy is extremely complex, woven into a social fabric of poverty and despair, that demands joint action by government agencies, community-based organizations, service organizations, educational institutions, and industry itself. This issue is not confined to the United States, but finds expression in the Third World as well, where workers must go beyond the vernacular to learn the language of commerce.

A third issue is the impact of technology in the workplace. Whereas some workers adapt easily to this fast-growing, ever-changing phenomenon, others (especially older workers) fear it. While training their workers in the use of computers and other technologies for new learning, the organization must not overlook the value of other delivery systems. Equally important is learning that occurs through the group process and through such individual interaction as internships and mentoring.

A fourth issue relates to the international scene. In a global world in which joint ventures are becoming commonplace, there is a need for learning to take place at two levels. Countries that provide expertise and funding must not only understand other cultures and languages, but draw upon their strengths. For example, in order to assist with the creation of a market economy, the development of HRD in the former Soviet Union should be modified to include the philosophy of the collective, with its emphasis on working for the common good.

8. HRD Research Needs

A primary research need pertains to the adequacy of current programs that prepare practitioners. Roles of such individuals are changing from that of a remote staff resource to an integral component of the management team. The main research questions that have evolved from these shifting roles are:

(a) What management skills do HRD practitioners require in their new expanded role?

(b) How can they assist management to understand the value of an HRD strategic plan for addressing issues of productivity, quality, and change?

A second research need pertains to workers as learners in the learning organization.

(a) What specific knowledge and skills do they require to further their own learning?

(b) How can workers be motivated to assume responsibility for learning in the workplace?

(c) How can immigrants, other minorities, and women obtain the learning necessary to take their places as happy and productive workers in the organization?

(d) How can workplace literacy programs be designed to meet both workers' needs and the organization's needs?

A third research need pertains to the use of technology in the workplace.

(a) How might HRD practitioners use technology creatively to enhance individual and group learning?

(b) What steps could an organization take to allay workers' anxieties about using technology?

(c) What impact would the development of workers' technological competency have on the organization's productivity?

A fourth research need pertains to the international scene.

(a) How can an organization best prepare their HRD practitioners for international assignments?

(b) What specific HRD competencies are needed for joint ventures?

(c) How can international collaboration be fostered now that HRD is rapidly becoming a worldwide phenomenon?

See also: Technical and Vocational Education and Training; Recurrent Education; Economics of Adult Education and Training; Technological Change and Education; Program Design: Effectiveness; Evaluation of Public Training: Cost-Effectiveness

References

Bengtsson J 1991 Human resource development. *Futures* December 1991: 1085–1106

Cervero R 1988 *Effective Continuing Education for Professionals.* Jossey-Bass, San Francisco, California

Engestrom Y 1987 *Learning By Expanding.* OrientaKonsultit Oy, Helsinki

Gilley J W, Eggland S 1989 *Principles of Human Resource Development.* Addison-Wesley, Reading, Massachusetts

Kirkpatrick D 1987 Evaluation. In: Craig R (ed.) 1987 *Training and Development Handbook*, 3rd edn. McGraw-Hill, New York

Lindberg K J 1991 The intricacies of training and development in Japan. *Hum. Resource Dev.* 2(2): 101–14

McLagan P A 1983 *Models for Excellence.* American Society for Training and Development, Washington, DC

Nadler L 1982 *Designing Training Programs: The Critical Events Model.* Addison-Wesley, Reading, Massachusetts

Nadler L (ed.) 1984 *Handbook of Human Resource Development.* John Wiley and Sons Inc., New York

Nadler L, Nadler Z 1989 *Developing Human Resources*, 3rd edn. Jossey-Bass, San Francisco, California

Pulkkis A, Teikari V, Vartiainen T 1987 The role of training in changing a work organization. *Adult Education in Finland* 24(1–2): 50–53

Rothwell W 1985 Management training in support of organization strategic planning in twelve Illinois organizations. Doctoral Dissertation, University of Illinois

Rothwell W J, Kazanas H C 1989 *Strategic Human Resource Development.* Prentice-Hall, Englewood Cliffs, New Jersey

Senge P M 1990 *The Fifth Discipline: The Art and Practice of the Learning Organization.* Doubleday, New York

Woolner P 1991 Integrating work and learning: A developmental model of the learning organization. Speech 1991 Annual Conference of the Commission of Professors, Montreal

Literacy

D. R. Olson

This entry is concerned with the uses of writing systems or scripts, specifically who uses them and what they are used for. Literacy may be defined as competence in the use of a script for a particular purpose or range of purposes. Different scripts are based on different principles and involve different competencies. Logographic scripts, such as the one invented by the Chinese almost four millennia ago, employ distinctive characters to represent different morphemes or meaning units. Syllabaries such as those used by the Cree Indians of North America use signs to represent syllables. Alphabets use distinctive signs to represent the phonemes of the language. The choice of unit determines the number of signs required. Logographic scripts may employ thousands of distinctive characters and consequently require a long period of learning. Syllabaries may employ perhaps a hundred signs, alphabets between 20 and 30 signs (Sampson 1985). Although scriptal differences influence the ease or difficulty of becoming literate, cultural attitudes to literacy and the availability of schooling tend greatly to outweigh such differences (Stevenson et al. 1982).

General familiarity with the nature and function of a script is referred to as basic literacy; familiarity with the use of a script for a specified set of functions is referred to as functional literacy. Competence with the formation and interpretation of specialized texts in a domain of expertise is sometimes referred to as elite literacy. As scripts have evolved and as the functions a script serves have changed culturally and historically, literacy as a form of human competence has also acquired a history. The forms this competence takes is a second concern of this entry.

1. Literacy and History

Havelock, a foremost scholar of the implications of literacy, has claimed: "Literacy, though dependent on the technology deployed in inscriptions, is not to be defined in terms of that technology. It is a social condition which can be defined only in terms of readership" (Havelock 1976 p.19). An important dimension of the development of literacy is the invention of scripts which were readily learned and which could be exploited for a broad range of functions. Although all currently functioning scripts or writing systems or orthographies are thought to be adequate to all of the functions they are designed to serve, two properties of scripts are important in understanding the growth of literacy, namely, learnability and expressive power. Learnability refers to the ease with which the script can be acquired. Expressive power refers to the script's ability to express unambiguously the full range of meanings available in the oral language. These two factors are inversely related to each other. Simple, restricted codes or scripts are readily learned but express a limited range of meanings. Pictographic signs such as those used in "environmental writing," including brands, crests, hallmarks, and logos are readily learned even by the youngest children. Full scripts, whether logographic scripts such as those used by the Chinese or alphabetic scripts familiar in the West or mixed scripts such as those used by the Japanese, are more difficult to acquire but once acquired can serve a much broader range of functions.

Alphabets are sometimes claimed to be ideal scripts but more recently this has been shown to be a form of ethnocentrism. Needham (1954–59), an authority on Chinese science, has concluded that the Chinese script was not a significant factor in the failure of the Chinese to develop modern science nor is it an inhibiting factor in modern Chinese scientific work. High levels of literate competence, therefore, have more to do with such factors as the availability of reading materials, availability of instruction in reading and writing, and the perceived relevance of literacy to social and cultural life (Harris 1989). Even in so-called literate societies, most readers learn to read only a select range of written materials; specialized materials, such as those pertaining to religion, science, and government, tend to remain the domain of an elite whose members require several years of education.

Changes in literacy are related to cultural changes but whether literacy produces social change or accompanies social change remains controversial (see *Adult Literacy in the Third World*). Historically, the rise of cities coincided with the development of a script suitable for serving bureaucratic purposes. Later, the scientific and philosophical tradition that originated in classical Greece and which has prevailed in the West until this day, developed along with the alphabet. Many writers, including Havelock, maintain that the alphabet was a decisive factor (Gelb 1963, Diringer 1968). McLuhan (1962) and Ong (1982) have claimed that the rise of literacy and the decline of "orality" in the later Middle Ages were fundamental to the Renaissance.

Writers such as Harris (1986) and Gaur (1984) have pointed out that no writing system completely represents speech. Stress and intonation as well as tone of voice convey important aspects of meaning which scripts capture only with difficulty, if ever. For example, how is a script to represent a sneering intonation? The fact that writing systems capture primarily lexical and syntactic properties of speech has the consequence that problems of interpretation are markedly more severe in reading a text than in listening to speech.

There is wide agreement with the more limited claim that literacy has an important effect on consciousness of speech. People familiar with an alphabet perceive speech to be composed of segmentable phonemes; those familiar with a syllabary perceive it as composed of syllables; those familiar with a logography perceive it as composed of morphemes. Consciousness of the language in terms of the properties of the script also induces a certain blindness; namely, the belief that what is written is a complete representation of what the writer meant or intended. Aspects of language and meaning not explicitly represented in a script (i.e., how the writer intended the utterance to be taken —whether seriously, facetiously, ironically, literally, metaphorically—clues to which are often carried by intonation in speech) have been the most difficult to infer in reading and have, historically, provided the most serious obstacles to interpretation. Medieval theologians, for example, debated whether Jesus spoke literally or metaphorically when, taking a piece of bread, he said "This is my body." This has led some writers to suggest that the history of Western thought can be explained in part in terms of the history of reading and interpreting texts (Olson and Torrance 1991, Olson 1994).

2. Functions of Literacy

As writing serves many functions, literacy takes many forms. One of literacy's most important functions in Western culture is that associated with the uses of writing to develop an accumulative research tradition

(Eisenstein 1979). Writing permits the accumulation of information collected by many hands over many lifetimes so that "what is known" is no longer identifiable with what anyone knows. But the form of literate competence required to exploit and contribute to that archival form has become highly specialized. It depends not only on literacy skills themselves but on a deeper understanding of the domains represented by those texts. Consequently, literacy trails off into forms of specialized knowledge; at higher levels of competence, literacy and specialized knowledge have become indistinguishable. The popular assumption that literacy training will compensate for this specialized knowledge is misguided. On the other hand, the attempt to use writing for these specialized purposes has contributed to the development of particular literate artifacts such as lists, tables, recipes, indexes, pattern books, dictionaries, thesauri, as well as diagrams, maps, and charts, each of which calls for particular literate competencies. Similarly, the invention of certain literary forms, such as the novel, depended on the existence of a broad-based reading public.

Although social functions such as religion, government, administration as well as the applied arts of agriculture, navigation, and the like exist both in cultures with and without writing, and therefore, with or without literacy, literacy does seem to give these activities a distinctive set of properties. During the Middle Ages, as European societies became more literate, writing came to be used for functions that had earlier been carried out by oral language and ritual. Clanchy (1992) and Stock (1983) have shown how the indenture of servants, deeding of property, evidence at trials, and the preservation of accounts of the lives of the saints, all came to rely increasingly on the use of written texts. As literacy became the dominant means of communication in bureaucratic societies, oral language came to be seen as "loose and unruly" and lacking in authority. People who could not read or write came to be regarded as rude, ignorant, and "illiterate." Street (1984) questions whether the increased reliance on writing was in the service of justice, suggesting rather that it was a means of consolidating power and authority (see *Literacy and Numeracy Models*).

Rising levels of literacy were closely related to the great social transformations, the Protestant Reformation and the rise of modern science. The ability to read the Bible for oneself and to discover its meaning was a fundamental basis of Protestantism and the private study, criticism, and updating of objective accounts on the basis of observation were important to the rise of modern science. Both of these functions were enormously facilitated by the rise of printing with movable type in the fifteenth and sixteenth centuries and the translation of important books from scholarly Latin into ordinary vernacular languages. With more material available to be read and with writing playing a prominent role in official business, writing came to take on increased authority and significance. Knowledge came to be identified with the content of books. In the eighteenth and nineteenth centuries in Western Europe and America, even before the establishment of public schooling, more than half of the population had some level of literate competence. Compulsory schooling at the end of the nineteenth century made this level of competence more or less universal.

3. Literacy and Illiteracy

Because of the close association between schooling and literacy, literacy levels are often defined exclusively in terms of length of attendance at school. Three levels of literacy are frequently distinguished: no schooling whatever ("illiteracy"); elementary schooling lasting some four to six years ("basic literacy"); and completion of high school ("high" or "functional literacy"). Such categories are useful for demographic reports that require an indication of the educational levels in particular countries or their regions, but they have little scientific value. Indeed, the appeal to notions of literacy in such contexts is inappropriate and misleading. Arbitrarily identifying "functional literacy" with the completion of secondary school, as was done by the Adult Education Act passed by the United States Congress in 1966, has allowed some writers to claim that "somewhere between 54 and 64 million" Americans, that is, some 25 percent of American adults, are functionally illiterate (Hunter and Harman 1979). Some see in such figures a social problem of great significance and insist on programs of educational reform that would result in higher levels of literacy. However, most scholars criticize both such figures and the resulting claims about "illiteracy" (see *Literacy Research and Measurement; Literacy Testing and Assessment*).

First, such figures reflect experience with a single institution, the school, rather than with the relevant contexts of application. A person could be highly literate, say in Bible reading or in reading automotive-parts manuals, even if opportunities for schooling were limited. Secondly, the appellation "illiterate" has pejorative connotations implying serious human failing when in fact it merely means the inability to read. It is extremely rare to encounter an individual in a predominantly literate society who cannot read anything and the ability to read in a predominantly "oral" culture may have extremely limited utility.

As an alternative to simply identifying levels of literacy with years of schooling, some scholars have distinguished levels of literacy in another way. Environmental or lay literacy is thought of as the form of unspecified competence involved in dealing generally with a literate environment. Such literacy need never be taught. It is the type of literacy that is acquired through living in an environment organized by written signs, labels, sports scores, and trademarks and in which literate experts aid people in dealing with complex written documents. Almost everyone in a literate society is literate in this sense. Everyone knows the nature, uses, and functions of writing even if they do not personally practice literate skills.

Functional literacy is the degree of literate competence required for dealing with the variety of literate forms encountered in daily life. Employers frequently cite the lack of literate skills of workers as causes of loss of productivity. Closer inspection, however, has indicated that when reading failures occur they are more often a matter of failing to understand the workings of a system than the ability to read. The bottleneck in "reading" is now understood to be a problem of comprehension. That in turn is a function of the depth of knowledge that the reader brings to a text being read rather than a simple familiarity with words and letters. While some attempts have been made to design a test of functional literacy by selecting items that measure the ability to interpret an invoice or to interpret an advertisement correctly, such tests are bedeviled by the fact that no particular literate activities are functional for everyone. To be literate in Reformation Germany in the sixteenth century meant to possess the ability to read the Bible; to be literate in nineteenth-century Boston meant being able to read Henry Thoreau and Oliver Wendell Holmes; to be literate on a twentieth-century building site means having the ability to read blueprints and materials catalogs. No single skill is functional for everyone.

A literate society is also dependent on the development of elite literacy, a high level of literate competence in specialized domains such as law, science, or theology. Such high levels of literate competence involve learning not only to read and write but also to acquire the specialized vocabulary and the basic principles fundamental to the domain in question. It is estimated that ordinarily literate people have a "reading" vocabulary based on the words they encounter only in reading and writing. This is more than double the size of their speaking and listening vocabulary. In becoming "scientifically literate," for example, a person must acquire not only the concepts specific to a particular scientific domain, concepts such as molecule or gene, but also epistemological concepts, such as assumption, hypothesis, inference and conclusion. In addition the person must learn specialized grammatical forms appropriate to the form of argument, such as setting out claims relative to the evidence for the claims, and learn to distinguish specialized genres such as the descriptions, explanations, arguments, and narratives appropriate to particular literary undertakings. These specialized skills, dependent on high levels of literate competence, require years of formal schooling often accompanied by appropriate apprenticeships.

Part of the significance of literacy comes from the fact that once particular literary forms have been mastered they can be employed equally well in speech as in writing. Consequently, literacy cannot simply be identified with reading and writing. One can write in an essentially oral style or one can speak in a manner characteristic of a book. Literacy makes it possible to speak a written language. In this way literacy has been associated with the evolution of a particular form of thought. As Goody has written: "The advent of a simpler writing system and a larger reading public were clearly factors of great social and intellectual importance in the Mediterranean world and it is not accidental that at the present day so much stress is laid on literacy in programmes of social development" (Goody 1975).

See also: Literacy and Numeracy Models; Postliteracy; Anthropological Study of Literacy and Numeracy; Economics of Nonformal Education; Adult Literacy in the Third World; Adult Basic Education; UNESCO and Adult Education; Asia, Southeast: Literacy; Literacy Research and Measurement

References

Clanchy M T 1992 *From Memory to Written Record: England 1066–1307*, 2nd edn. Blackwell, Oxford

Diringer D 1968 *The Alphabet: A Key to the History of Mankind*, 3rd edn. Funk and Wagnalls, New York

Eisenstein E 1979 *The Printing Press as an Agent of Change: Communication and Cultural Transformations in Early Modern Europe*, Vols. 1–2. Cambridge University Press, New York

Gaur A 1984 *A History of Writing*. British Museum, London

Gelb I J 1963 *A Study of Writing*. University of Chicago Press, Chicago, Illinois

Goody J 1975 *Literacy in Traditional Societies*. Cambridge University Press, Cambridge

Harris R 1986 *The Origin of Writing*. Duckworth, London

Harris W V 1989 *Ancient Literacy*. Harvard University Press, Cambridge, Massachusetts

Havelock E 1976 *Origins of Western Literacy*, Four lectures delivered at the Ontario Institute for Studies in Education, March 1974. Monograph Series 14. OISE Press, Toronto (Reprinted in: Havelock E 1982 *The Literate Revolution*. Princeton University Press, Princeton, New Jersey)

Hunter C St J, Harman D 1979 *Adult Illiteracy in the United States*. McGraw-Hill, New York

McLuhan M 1962 *The Gutenberg Galaxy: The Making of Modern Man*. University of Toronto Press, Toronto

Needham J 1954–59 *Science and Civilization in China*, 3 Vols. Cambridge University Press, Cambridge

Olson D R 1994 *The World on Paper*. Cambridge University Press, Cambridge

Olson D R, Torrance N (eds.) 1991 *Literacy and Orality*. Cambridge University Press, Cambridge

Ong W 1982 *Orality and Literacy: The Technologizing of the Word*. Methuen, London

Sampson G 1985 *Writing Systems: A Linguistic Introduction.* Hutchinson, London

Stevenson H W et al. 1982 Reading disabilities: The case of Chinese, Japanese, and English. *Child Dev.* 53: 1164–81

Stock B 1983 *The Implications of Literacy: Written Language and Models of Interpretation in the Eleventh and Twelfth Centuries.* Princeton University Press, Princeton, New Jersey

Street B 1984 *Literacy in Theory and Practice.* Cambridge University Press, Cambridge

Further Reading

Coulmas F 1989 *The Writing Systems of the World.* Blackwell, Oxford

de Francis J 1989 *Visible Speech: The Diverse Oneness of Writing Systems.* University of Hawaii Press, Honolulu, Hawaii

Tuijnman A C, Kirsch I, Wagner D A (eds.) 1995 *Adult Basic Skills: Advances in Measurement and Policy Analysis.* Hampton Press, New York

Literacy and Numeracy Models

D. Baker and B. Street

This entry examines debates in the respective fields of literacy and numeracy, using as a framework a distinction between "autonomous" and "cultural" models. An "autonomous" model of literacy or numeracy assumes that the skills of reading, writing, enumerating, and "doing maths" are independent of social context, have "autonomous" characteristics that are universal across time and space, and generate consequences—for cognition, social progress and individual achievement—that are general rather than culture specific. The "cultural" model sees reading, writing, enumerating, and "doing maths" as social practices, learnt in specific cultural contexts and imbued with epistemological significance. In this model the uses and meanings of literacy and numeracy cannot easily be generalized across cultures but have to be understood in their context. Some exponents of this latter view also argue that such practices and concepts are always implicated in power relations and contests over meanings and resources. Since the "autonomous" model of literacy and numeracy is the dominant view in both policy and educational contexts, comparatively more space is devoted to explicating the newer and less widespread "cultural" view.

1. Literacy

1.1 Definitions

In the post-Second World war era, definitions of literacy developed by UNESCO have been influential. In 1956, Gray stated: "A person is functionally literate when he has acquired the knowledge and skills in reading and writing which enable him to engage effectively in all those activities in which literacy is normally assumed in his culture and group" (cited in Oxenham 1980 p. 86). Some years later, a group of international experts expanded this definition and concluded: "A person is literate when he has acquired the essential knowledge and skills which enable him to engage in all those activities in which literacy is required for effective functioning in his group and community, and whose attainments in reading, writing and arithmetic make it possible for him to continue to use these skills towards his own and the community's development" (Oxenham 1980 p. 87). In practice, this apparently relativistic and functional definition of literacy has been associated with narrowly defined programs with work-related objectives concerned with improvements in labor productivity, such as the now discredited Experimental World Literacy Programme (EWLP) (UNESCO 1976). Ideologically, objectives tend to be disguised behind a supposedly neutral model of literacy as simply technical skills. In contrast, Paulo Freire, a Brazilian educator whose work has been influential both among development workers and, more recently, in literacy programs in industrialized countries, has developed a more explicitly political definition of literacy. For him literacy is about "reading the world" rather than just reading the "word" (Freire and Macedo 1987). Literacy programs should help people to critically challenge dominant assumptions and expose unequal power relations: literacy is not a neutral skill.

Some writers, historians and anthropologists, as well as educationalists have attempted to formulate less prescriptive definitions of literacy. An historian, for instance, in a critical survey of criteria used to measure literacy rates, such as census measurements, school completion levels and formal tests, points out "the meanings and uses of literacy are more complex and diverse than these typical questions and tests allow" (Graff 1979 p. 5). Graff calls for a broader definition: "Literacy requirements, we now understand, vary among different social and economic groups, regions and communities . . . Thus measures of literacy must be comparative" (p. 5). Heath (1982) has coined the phrase "literacy events" to refer to "any occasion in which a piece of writing is integral to the nature of participants' interactions and their interpretive processes," whilst Scribner and Cole (1981) proposed a "social practice" view of literacy: "we approach literacy as a set of socially organised practices which make use of a symbol system and a technology for producing and disseminating it" (p. 236). Street (1993) has extended the concept of "literacy practices" further to refer to "both behaviour and conceptualisations related to the uses of reading and/or writing. 'Literacy practices' incorporate not only 'literacy events' as concrete occasions to which literacy is integral, but also folk models of those events and the ideological preconceptions that underpin them" (p. 13). He uses the term "literacy" "as a shorthand for the social practices and conceptions of reading and writing" (Street 1984 p. 1). Many researchers maintain that there are "multiple literacies" rather than a single one.

1.2 Alternative Visions of Literacy

The field of literacy studies has expanded considerably in recent years. Until the early 1980s the literature was relatively sparse. One reason for this increase has been the importance placed on acquiring literacy in both development campaigns in the poorer countries and national political programs in more industrialized societies, where the fears associated with a "literacy crisis" have been high on the political agenda (Bloom 1987). There has also been a challenge to dominant assumptions about the nature and consequences of literacy.

1.3 The Autonomous Model of Literacy

The dominant view of literacy has been what Street (1984) calls the "autonomous" model. In this model, emphasis is placed upon the cognitive consequences of literacy acquisition, on the implications of literacy for social and economic development, and on individual problems in acquiring the written code. Much of the research on these issues was conducted by means of experimental methods. An emphasis on cognitive consequences of literacy is prominent, for instance, in the work of Goody (1977), Olson (1977), and Ong (1982), all of whom in different ways asserted the importance of literacy acquisition for cognitive skills, such as explicitness, memory, detachment, logical thought, use of syllogisms, and "scientific thinking." In similar vein, Hirsch (1987) and Bloom (1987) in the United States have argued that standards of literacy were falling as a result of "progressive" schooling methods and that a "return to basics" was necessary to re-establish national confidence in the economy. Teaching methods have become a focus of intense political confrontation in the United Kingdom, Australia, and Canada, in all of which an association has been made between "basics"—learning to decode letters; learning to read and write through rigorous, disciplined procedures including phonics; curriculum-centered programs, and so on—and the achievement of social and economic development (Lawlor 1988).

Likewise in the development field, many literacy campaigns of the postwar years had assumed that if people were taught decoding skills they would then be "literate," with significant consequences for individual cognitive enhancement and for social and economic development (Bhola 1984). Anderson (1966) estimated that for a developing country to reach economic "take off" 40 percent of the population needed to be literate. This notion of a "literacy threshold" lay below the target of many campaigns and much expenditure. It was on these theoretical bases that many of the UNESCO literacy programs were founded (see *UNESCO and Adult Education*).

1.4 The Cultural Model of Literacy

While the view cited above still dominates much of the research and policy literature, there has been a major shift toward a more socially oriented view of literacy and an associated shift in teaching methods from "basics" toward more student-centered and culturally sensitive methods (Willinsky 1990). The key questions from this perspective concern the different meanings and uses of literacy in different cultural contexts, the problems of literacy transfer across cultures and in particular the need to avoid imposing the literacy conventions of one culture on members of another culture, and the significance of literacy practices for relations of power. The methods for researching these issues have also shifted, toward more qualitative enquiry using ethnographic approaches and focusing upon the meanings of literacy practices for the actors themselves.

The research of Scribner and Cole (1981) has been influential. They worked for eight years on a project in Liberia among the Vai people to test for the effects of different literacies. The Vai, like many peoples (Probst 1989), have their own invented writing system, which is mostly used for sending letters and is learnt on a one-to-one basis from elders. They also use Arabic script for religious purposes, learning memorization, and some decoding skills in Koramic schools; and some Vai use English written in Roman script for purposes of bureaucracy and for modern schooling. Scribner and Cole (1981) tested for the effects of both literacy and schooling—which they wanted to separate as distinct variables. They gave cognitive tasks, such as serial memory recall, explicitness, and ability to recognize semantic units, to various groups. The major finding was that literacy in itself did not significantly affect major cognitive skills, but that specific practices did promote specific skills. Those who learnt English were better at some school-related tasks because they were attending English-based schools, not because of literacy per se; those who attended Koranic schools were better at some memory tasks, associated with the learning techniques used there; and those literate in Vai were particularly good at making statements explicit, a technique that is conventional in Vai letter writing. These findings demonstrate the need for more information on literacy variation in different cultures and the importance of not attributing to the literacy of other cultures features specific to ones own culture or to schooling.

The period since the early 1980s has seen a great deal of ethnographic research on literacy, in which the researcher investigates the uses and meanings of reading and writing in specific cultural contexts through talking with people in their own language and observing literacy practices and literacy events closely over extended periods. Heath (1983) used ethnographic methods among communities in the Piedmont Carolinas in the United States and found that the literacies associated with each community varied considerably and had far-reaching implications for children's performance in school. She documents closely the uses of reading matter, posters, and so forth that surround children from birth, as well as the assumptions their parents make about how language and literacy are to be learnt and what their own role is in their children's literacy acquisition. A Black working-class community, for instance, focused strongly on oral skills, on imaginative play with language, and on storytelling, while parents assumed children simply picked up language as they went along. Thus, there was no need for explicit intervention. Among White working-class parents, the moral values associated with strong Christian tradition put a premium on "truth" rather than storytelling, and on children being taught the labels and names attached to things in the world. These would be pointed out when picture books with written captions were read to them. The children from these different backgrounds thus arrived at school with different linguistic skills and different conceptions about learning and about literacy. Heath argues that this affected their response to teachers, who employed different assumptions, again having mostly come from another background: less religious and more middle class. Heath and her team tried to help teachers modify their curriculum and teaching methods to be more sensitive to the underlying epistemologies and language conceptions of their pupils and her notion of "teacher as ethnographer" has become the basis for much practice in contemporary teaching.

Similar insights are beginning to be applied to the field of development education, where mainly Western assumptions about the meanings and uses of literacy have dominated both research and teaching practice. UNESCO and the World Bank are now showing more concern for the cultural implications of literacy. The World Conference on Education for All at Jomtien, held in connection with the International Literacy Year in 1990, pointed out the "human, cultural and institutional dimensions of education," and within the framework of the "World Decade for Cultural Development" literacy projects are being set up to promote and sustain local as well as national cultural knowledge and educational agendas (UNESCO 1992).

1.5 Implications for Curriculum and Teaching

In the development field, some of these changes of perspective have been linked with the work of Paulo Freire, who as noted above, has challenged the "top-down" view of education and inspired grassroots literacy programs (Freire 1985). Rejecting what he called a "banking" theory of education that assumed students to be simply empty deposits into which knowledge and literacy would be invested, he argued that literacy acquisition is associated with power relations and with ideological assumptions. A literacy program should challenge the dominant assumptions, especially where the receivers are poor people, peasants, inhabitants of shanty towns, and so on. The job of the literacy campaign is "conscientization"—to bring them to awareness of the causes of their oppression and poverty. Freire's work has been criticized (Verhelst 1990) on the ground that animators and program designers frequently continue to impose their own "key concepts" behind the guise of democratic, "bottom-up" teaching methods. The debate itself indicates that the agenda has shifted from the days when it was believed that a literacy program was a simple matter of teaching decoding skills and cognitive enhancement.

A similar debate is taking place in the industrialized world, where the 1980s revealed large pockets of adult illiteracy, particularly among poor and disadvantaged groups (Barton and Hamilton 1990). While educators and program planners are learning some of the lessons of Third World literacy campaigns (Kirkwood and Kirkwood 1989), researchers are discovering the variety and complexity of literacy practices in different parts of the world (Street 1993), among urban adolescents (Shuman 1986), and in the family (Taylor 1983). Some of the differences between literacy at home and at school are now seen not as problems needing remediation but as evidence of the richness and variety of "community literacies" (Barton and Ivanic 1991). The problem lies with the traditional approaches and their narrow cultural assumptions about what constitutes literacy (Varenne and McDermott 1986).

Some of these shifts in the emphases of researchers and developers are matched by the experiences of many classroom teachers (Meek 1991). A movement has grown up that sees learning literacy in the classroom as a more child-centered process, requiring self-consciousness about the cultural meanings being introduced into the school, and arguing the importance of children learning a wide repertoire of writing and reading practices (Britton 1970, Barnes 1991). Hall (1987), among others, has drawn attention to "emergent literacy"—the early stages of the entry into writing language and how this can be built into literacy teaching. The "writing process" approach, often associated with language across the curriculum (Goddard 1974) and employing new interactive aspects of writing development (Czerniewska 1992), such as journals, logs, and diaries, has been documented in Willinsky's book *The New Literacy* (1990). These approaches, he argues, reflect a new educational philosophy: they are not just "add ons" to be employed as novel techniques. These new developments, meanwhile, have themselves been challenged by those advocating a "back-to-basics" approach (Lawlor 1988, Bloom 1987).

2. Numeracy

2.1 Definitions

One of the most dramatic developments in the field of mathematics since the early 1980s has been the application of some of the insights outlined above with regard to literacy to the field of numeracy. Indeed, historically the term "numeracy" was first used by Crowther (1959) in the United Kingdom as the "mirror image of literacy." His report implied a view of numeracy that included fairly broad mathematical ideas, linking it to scientific reasoning and the appreciation of statistical concepts. In 1977 the Education Department of Western Australia published a policy on literacy and numeracy that, with some slight modifications, extended Crowther's view and complements the UNESCO definition of literacy mentioned above. It stated that: "The term numeracy is understood to mean mathematical literacy . . . A person is considered to be literate and numerate when he has acquired the skills and concepts to function effectively in his group and community, and when his attainment in reading, writing and mathematics makes it possible for him to use these skills to further his own and his community's development" (cited in Willis 1990 p. 4). However, the pressure of the "back-to-basics" movement, particularly in the United States, subsequently resulted in a more limited use of the word numeracy. Thus, the Cockcroft Report (1982) in the UK, reported that the "words numeracy and numerate had changed their meaning considerably in the last twenty years" and had become much more narrow, often applying only to basic arithmetic calculations. The report instead proposed that the word numeracy should remain broad and have two particular attributes. The first related to "an at-homeness with numbers and an ability to make use of mathematical skills which enable an individual to cope with practical mathematical demands of his everyday life" (p. 11). The second "is an ability to have some appreciation and understanding of information which is presented in mathematical terms, for instance, graphs." A numerate person should therefore "be expected to be able to appreciate and understand some of the ways that mathematics can be used as a means of communication." The dichotomy between the view of numeracy as limited to arithmetic calculations and broader visions of it as mathematics and ways of thinking mathematically—perhaps of "numeracy practices"

—continues to this day in many countries and in the early 1990s provides the main background against which a present-day account of "numeracy" has to be seen.

2.2 Alternative Visions of Numeracy

The vision of numeracy as the performance of basic arithmetic operations is often labeled as part of "back-to-basics." The pressure for such a restriction of numeracy has come from two directions. The first, as exemplified in England by the Centre for Policy Studies, is the concern that "too many pupils leave school innumerate without a knowledge of even basic arithmetic" and "the emphasis at the start should be —as it has traditionally been—on arithmetic and on pupils becoming numerate" (Lawlor 1988 p. 30). The argument is, on the one hand, that the broader approach to mathematics is not taxing the children adequately and, on the other, that it introduces mathematical concepts that are too complicated for children. The Beazley Committee of Inquiry into Education in Western Australia (Beazley 1984) similarly recommended a narrowing down of the mathematics curriculum. The second direction is from groups who perceive basic arithmetical skills as an essential prerequisite for gaining employment. For example COSATU (Confederation of South African Trade Unions) has recently stressed the importance of "basic" literacy and numeracy skills as a priority for their members to gain access to employment. The role of mathematics as a gatekeeper for qualifications and entry to employment is a part of society's pressure that affects the use and meaning of the word numeracy and is similar to that evident in the field of literacy.

The broader vision of numeracy that has emerged since the 1970s sees mathematics as more than a body of knowledge of facts, skills, and concepts. It also includes ways of "thinking mathematically." The essence of this is the development of problem-solving techniques or heuristics. General processes of mathematical thinking that have been identified by Mason et al. (1985) are conjecturing, specializing, generalizing, and convincing. These processes, plus explaining and describing (which involve written symbolization and recording) and written, oral, and physical explanations can be described metaphorically as mathematical literacy. These are all part of the image of mathematics, as a "means of communication which is powerful, concise, and unambiguous" as presented by the Cockcroft Report (1982 p. 11). These processes are seen to be as essential to solving mathematical problems as the restricted features of "basic arithmetic" put forward in the "back-to-basics" movement.

2.3 An Autonomous Model of Numeracy

In applying the notion of the "autonomous" model of literacy to numeracy, we find that similar assumptions have been made regarding the universal, neutral, and culture-free nature of mathematics. In the autonomous model, numeracy like literacy is seen as the embodiment of rationality and reason. Bishop (1988 p. 62) has questioned the belief that rationalism "is at the heart of Mathematics . . . with its focus on deductive reasoning as the only true way of achieving explanation and conclusions, challenged and eventually superseded trial and error pragmatism, traditional wisdom, inductive reasoning and analogistic reasoning." In this rationalist view, mathematics is concerned with the internal logic, consistency, and completeness of argument, and it attaches qualities of elegance and aesthetics to the most concise, rational, and coherent arguments. In looking for logical and unambiguous forms, mathematics, therefore, becomes the construction and presentation of abstract reasoning.

The model of mathematics as pure, value-free, and abstract has been dominant in many civilizations. Mathematics was often accorded mystical qualities, and in ancient Greece the Pythagoreans formed themselves into secret societies. Similarly, Shan and Bailey (1991 p.3) state that in "ancient Hindu society, mathematics was regarded as sacrosanct, awesome and the purest of all disciplines." In all of these cases, the tension between claims for neutrality and universality on the one hand, and actual cultural and political partiality on the other is evident. The Greek model, for instance, can be described as an "autonomous" model of numeracy in the same sense as contemporary academic models: the notion purveyed in both cases is one of mathematics as a system of pure, culture-free abstraction. Facts like 2+2=4, the properties of triangles, and the techniques of the calculus are in this model taken to be true anywhere and everywhere.

2.4 The Cultural Model of Numeracy

The alternative to the autonomous model is the "cultural" one. Here it is argued that mathematics is both the product of cultural history and the basis of a given society's commerce, science, technology, and other everyday transactions. It therefore cannot be free of political or social influences and tends to be culture-bound. Some scholars argue that the propositions of the Pythagoreans and other such mathematical societies are dependent on shared cultural conventions, not on some universal truth. The same is evident, it is argued, in contemporary academic mathematics in universities and schools which claim to be founded upon universal truths and techniques, but in fact privilege particular subsectors of society, often to the disadvantage of cultural minorities (Bishop 1988, Street 1984, Mellin-Olsen 1987).

Bishop (1988) discusses research done by Gay and Cole in 1967 on the mathematical skills of Kpelle children in Liberia. From their research it was suggested that the Kpelle live in a society largely unaffected by mathematics. Yet on closer scrutiny it was clear that the Kpelle had taboos associated with numbers and

some numbers had magical and mysterious attributes. For the Kpelle it is not safe to count certain things. For instance, it is not proper to count chickens or other domestic animals aloud, for it is believed that some harm will befall them. The development of number and number systems in their society is therefore different to other societies. It is interesting to note that "sophisticated" societies also attribute mystical properties to numbers. In many Western countries, 13 is said to be an unlucky number, so that many high buildings skip the 13th floor. Bishop (1988) cites a study by Lewis in 1976 of the Australian aborigines' ability to locate themselves on a seemingly featureless landscape, an ability that seemed extraordinary to people from Western society: "There was no doubt that the people Lewis studied carried an internalised compass in their heads . . . They could talk about this system of location and their use of it—its relation to the sun, and to the temperature of the wind—and their language reflected this ability" (Lewis cited in Bishop 1988 p. 30). Their mathematics, unusual and specific to their social and geographical needs, was therefore culturally affected. Similarly, navigators in the South Pacific use locally developed systems of reference, time, and space to locate themselves and chart their lengthy sea journeys.

The cultural model of numeracy also focuses on the social and political aspects associated with the new technologies and their effect on mathematics. First, there is social pressure to keep up with developments in technology which have increased the status of mathematics and enhanced the position of those that have acquired the new skills. Second, the increased availability in some societies of calculators and computers has meant the reconsideration of what numeracy is and how it ought to be taught. In response to the advent of calculators and changes to systems of measurement, the National Curriculum for England and Wales (1989) has proposed a numeracy curriculum where fractions have become a very limited area of content for children up to age 11. Papert (1980) argues more strongly that children having access to computers changes the relationship between the learner and the teacher. The child would be in control of more aspects of learning situations and the teacher would become more of a resource. This shift of control or power within a classroom's numeracy practices could be analyzed in terms of an "ideological" model of numeracy. Melin-Olsen (1987 p. 15), for instance, defines "folk mathematics" as mathematical "knowledge biased by culture (or social class)." He goes on to say: "To what extent folk mathematics is recognised as important knowledge is a political question and thus a question about power." One aspect of numeracy as a political matter, also raised above, is the use many societies make of numeracy as a gatekeeper for entrance to employment groups. In many parts of the world, qualifications in mathematics are deemed necessary for entry into teacher education.

2.5 Implications for Curriculum and Teaching

Approaches to the teaching of numeracy, based on the autonomous model, tend to be along traditional lines. In these traditional approaches, the teacher selects the content or body of knowledge to be taught. The selection is made from the curriculum which is seen as fixed and is devised by the education system in the particular society. Learners are introduced to the concepts involved, they then practice these skills, and finally use them to tackle problems chosen by the teacher. In this model the teacher is the holder of the knowledge and the learner is the receiver. The teacher takes full responsibility for deciding what will be taught and how it will be taught. The learners are engaged in activities that may or may not be meaningful or relevant to them. There are close similarities between this and what Freire calls the "banking" model of education previously associated mainly with literacy education.

An alternative approach to teaching numeracy based on the cultural model is referred to as the "whole maths" position. Tried in Australia and England (Baker et al. 1990) and related to existing language work in literacy, it begins with contexts chosen by the learner and the content is derived from these contexts. The learners engage in problems within their own selected contexts and together with other learners and the teacher identify skills and knowledge need to solve the problem. The teacher sets up a "teaching clinic" where the particular skills are to be taught. The learner and the teacher take joint responsibility for the content and how it is taught. The learner is responsible for providing meaningful situations for the work. These are therefore selected from within the learners' culture and are linked to the cultural model of numeracy knowledge. Both the teacher and the learner are seen as holders of knowledge and experience.

Out of these academic arguments have emerged teaching and curriculum models and programs that put quite a new slant on mathematics. A special edition of the *World Studies Journal* entitled "Global Pie" places mathematics within human experience through discussions of ways in which mathematics can be a "vehicle for better global understanding" (Swetz 1985). This is complemented by sources like Shan and Bailey (1991), Bishop (1988), and the Equals Project at Berkeley, California. These developments are similar to those in the field of literacy, probably best known through the work of Paolo Freire, though also evident in much adult literacy work in the Third World and in industrialized societies (Barton and Hamilton 1990).

3. Conclusion

Debates in the fields of numeracy and literacy are, then, in many ways parallel, and similar shifts in emphasis and agenda can be observed. The claims and assertions of the "cultural" models of literacy and numeracy challenge the dominating "autonomous" model. Within this climate, the implications of these newer approaches will be tested against both classroom experience and crosscultural research. The existence of an increased body of knowledge and concepts that are more culturally sensitive will make it harder for narrow culture-based assumptions being treated as universals. One may expect the defining and analysis of both literacy and numeracy skills and processes and the approaches to teaching and learning to be refined in response to this debate.

See also: Critical Approaches to Adult Education; Popular Education and Conscientization; Anthropological Study of Literacy and Numeracy; Adult Literacy in the Third World; Literacy Research and Measurement

References

Anderson C A 1966 Literacy and schooling on the development threshold: Some historical cases. In: Anderson C A, Bowman M (eds.) 1966 *Education and Economic Development*. Frank Cass, London

Baker D A, Semple C, Stead T 1990 *How Big is the Moon? Whole Maths in Action*. Oxford University Press, Melbourne

Barnes D 1991 *Writing in School: Learning the Groundrules*. Open University Press, Milton Keynes

Barton D, Hamilton M 1990 *Researching Literacy in Industrialised Countries: Trends and Prospects*. UIE, UNESCO, Hamburg

Barton D, Ivanic R (eds.) 1991 *Writing in the Community*. Sage, Newbury Park, California

Beazley K 1984 *Education in Australia: Report of the Committee of Inquiry into Education in Western Australia*. Education Department of Western Australia, Perth

Bhola H 1984 *Campaigning for Literacy*. UNESCO, Paris

Bishop A 1988 *Mathematical Enculturation*. Kluwer Academic, Dordrecht

Bloom A 1987 *The Closing of the American Mind*. Simon and Schuster, New York

Britton J 1970 *Language and Learning*. Allen Lane, London

Cockcroft W H 1982 *Mathematics Counts*. HMSO, London

Crowther G 1959 *A Report of the Central Advisory Council for Education*. HMSO, London

Czerniewska P 1992 *Learning About Writing: The Early Years*. Blackwell, Oxford

Freire P 1985 *The Politics of Education: Culture, Power and Liberation*. Macmillan, London

Freire P, Macedo D 1987 *Literacy: Reading the Word and the World*. Bergin and Garvey, South Hadley, Massachusetts

Goddard N 1974 *Literacy: Language-Experience Approaches*. Macmillan, London

Goody J 1977 *The Domestication of the Savage Mind*. Cambridge University Press, Cambridge

Graff H 1979 *The Literacy Myth: Literacy and Social Structure in the 19th Century City*. Academic Press, London

Hall N 1987 *Emergent Literacy*. Edward Arnold, London

Heath S B 1982 What no bedtime story means: Narrative skills at home and at school. *Lang. Soc.* 11(1): 49–76

Heath S B 1983 *Ways with Words: Language, Life and Work*

in Communities and Classrooms. Cambridge University Press, Cambridge

Hirsch E D Jr 1987 *Cultural Literacy: What Every American Needs to Know.* Houghton Mifflin, Boston, Massachusetts

Kirkwood G, Kirkwood C 1989 *Living Adult Education. Freire in Scotland.* Open University Press, Milton Keynes

Lawlor S 1988 *Correct Core. Simple Curricula for English, Maths and Science.* Centre for Policy Studies, London

Mason J, Burton L, Stacey K 1985 *Thinking Mathematically.* Addison Wesley, London

Meek M 1991 *On Being Literate.* Bodley Head, London

Mellin-Olsen S 1987 *The Politics of Mathematics Education.* Reidel, Dordrecht

National Curriculum 1989 *Mathematics in the National Curriculum (England and Wales).* HMSO, London

Olson D 1977 From utterance to text: The bias of language in speech and writing. *Harv. Educ. Rev.* 47(3): 257–81

Ong W 1982 *Orality and Literacy: The Technologising of the Word.* Methuen, London

Oxenham J 1980 *Literacy: Writing, Reading and Social Organisation.* Routledge and Kegan Paul, London

Papert S 1980 *Mindstorms. Children and Computers and Powerful Ideas.* Basic Books, New York

Probst P 1989 The letter and the spirit: Literacy and religious authority in the history of the Aladura movement in W Nigeria. *Africa* 59(4): 471–95

Scribner S, Cole M 1981 *The Psychology of Literacy.* Harvard University Press, Cambridge, Massachusetts

Shan S-J, Bailey P 1991 *Multiple Factors: Classroom Mathematics for Equality and Justice.* Trentham Books, Stoke-on-Trent

Shuman A 1986 *Storytelling Rights: The Uses of Oral and Written Texts by Urban Adolescents.* Cambridge University Press, Cambridge

Street B 1984 *Literacy in Theory and Practice.* Cambridge University Press, Cambridge

Street B 1993 The new literacy studies. In: Street B (ed.) 1993 *Cross-Cultural Approaches to Literacy.* Cambridge University Press, Cambridge

Swetz F 1985 Mathematics—a vehicle for better global understanding. *Math. Teach.* 78(3): 207–15

Taylor D 1983 *Family Literacy: Young Children Learning to Read and Write.* Heinemann, London

UNESCO 1976 *The Experimental World Literacy Programme: A Critical Assessment.* UNESCO, Paris

UNESCO 1992 *Education for All: An Expanded Vision.* Roundtable Themes II, World Conference on Education for All. UNESCO, Paris

Varenne H, McDermott R 1986 "Why" Sheila can read: Structure and indeterminacy in the reproduction of familial literacy. In: Schieffelin B, Gilmore P (eds.) 1986 *The Acquisition of Literacy: Ethnographic Perspectives.* Ablex, Norwood, New Jersey

Verhelst T 1990 *No Life Without Roots: Culture and Development.* Zed Press, London

Willinsky J 1990 *The New Literacy: Redefining Reading and Writing in the Schools.* Routledge, London

Willis S 1990 *Being Numerate: What Counts?* Australian Council for Educational Research, Hawthorne, Victoria

Peace Education

C. Wulf

Adequate education is not possible without reference to notions of a more just and more peaceful society. Among other things, education teaches the individual to cast a critical eye over existing conditions and to take seriously the responsibility of preparing future generations to improve them. Education organized according to these ideas must also make reference to "peace" as an objective of social and individual development: therefore it may at the same time be regarded as education for peace, in the sense of instilling peace as an ideal. Seen in this way, "peace" must be a dimension of every form of education, whether for children or adults.

1. Premises

In the 1990s it appears most meaningful to speak of education for peace in a narrow sense. Despite the end of the Cold War, the menace that war and violence pose to the human race has rarely been so threatening. Peace has become the overriding precondition for continued human existence. The life of individuals, generations, and nations, indeed the survival of the human race as a whole, now depends on preserving or bringing about peace. It is thus essential that education also addresses the conditions that engender war, violence, and material need, and that it seeks ways to help mitigate or even overcome these conditions. Education for peace represents education's contribution to their elimination. Of course, it should be clearly understood that many of these conditions are systemic problems caused by macrostructures, only some of which can be mitigated with the help of education. A premise of education for peace is that coming to grips with the major issues confronting humanity today will require a systematic and sustained learning effort that is part of a lifelong learning process beginning in childhood.

2. The Context and International Character of Education for Peace

In the 1990s, education for peace is part of the curriculum in school and adult education in the United States; Japan; Western, Central, and Eastern Europe; as well as in many countries of the Third World. Naturally, the way in which it is taught in the various regions of the world differs considerably. In most countries of the Third World, education for peace is an attempt to promote economic, social, national, and, in some cases, regional development. In the former socialist countries of Eastern Europe, all education was regarded in principle as education for peace because peace was considered as the objective of the historical development of socialist society. However, in the mid-1990s peace was not a key concept of education in those countries. Nevertheless, many educational responsibilities arise in the transition from the old social structures to new ones, and many among them fall directly into the category of education for peace. In the United States and Western Europe, education for peace teaches people to adopt a discerning perspective on their own society and its role in international affairs. Since the early 1980s, a link has thus been established between the international environmental movement and the peace movement. Education for peace overlaps with approaches that pursue related goals, though under different names, and with changes of emphasis. They include education for international understanding, international education, survival education, global education, and education for world citizenship.

3. Peace Studies and Education for Peace

Education for peace is usually understood as part of political socialization, but earlier education in this sphere had a quite different basis. In the 1960s the goal was to cultivate understanding between the peoples of the world and to instill thinking in terms of peace. The earlier approaches were based on the assumption that the human being in principle had a peaceable nature, that this nature was threatened merely by aggression, and that peace was primarily a question of moral behavior. In recognition of the human being's aggressive urges, earlier efforts were geared to developing a sense of responsibility, teaching nonviolent behavior, and emphasizing the notion that a personal desire for peace and the actions taken by individuals to foster peace might lead to peace in the real political sphere. The idea that war began in the minds of people and had to be combatted there was characteristic of this position. According to this view, the chief aim was to change human consciousness in order to create the social conditions for a higher degree of justice. If the way to peace were through people's minds, then education for peace would logically acquire extraordinary significance.

In the early 1970s, however, peace studies acknowledged that peace cannot be brought about by changes in human consciousness alone. The experience of the peace movement since then has confirmed this insight.

Belligerence and violence are so deeply anchored in social structures that they cannot be overcome solely by people's will to bring about peace. Concerted political action that counteracts the violence rooted in the structures of society and in international affairs is also necessary. Terms such as "organized belligerence" (Senghaas 1972) and "structural violence" (Galtung 1969) indicate that peace is a problem of effecting change in social structures. Education can only make a limited, albeit important, contribution to solving this problem.

In the 1990s, too, education for peace should rely on key concepts such as "organized belligerence," "structural violence," and "social justice." They make the social character of peace clear and guard against both the delusion of omnipotence and naive, simplistic interpretations of the problem. According to Galtung's key differentiation, peace should not be understood merely as the absence of war and direct violence (the negative concept of peace). Education for peace is seen instead as aiming to establish conditions under which the individual and society suffer the least possible amount of structural violence and hence enjoy a high degree of social justice (the positive concept of peace). As a result of this conception of peace, education focuses not only on war or direct violence between nations and in international affairs, but also on intrasocial conditions engendering violence, including elements of violence in family upbringing and formal schooling.

4. Goals, Content, and Forms

Education for peace is not a sphere that can be clearly delineated and defined. However, a few major themes of peace education in the early 1990s can be identified:

(a) the problems stemming from the postwar East–West conflict, with the nuclear threat that still confronts the human race;

(b) the North–South conflict, with the southern hemisphere's deepening impoverishment due partially to the international division of labor;

(c) the problems posed by the pollution and destruction of the environment;

(d) the scarcity of natural resources and food;

(e) the population explosion;

(f) the obstacles to more extensive human rights and social justice.

Unless education explicitly addresses these problems it will fail in its responsibility to prepare young people for the future, and to help adults bring about and cope with change.

Education for peace does not live up to expectations if it is confined merely to passing on information about the themes cited above. Important as such knowledge is, it is necessary to do more than simply convey information when treating these issues. An informed debate is needed that raises the level of concern and leads the individual to dispel prejudices and hostility. In treating these issues, it is thus necessary to ask how hostility and prejudice are produced and what function they have in perpetuating structures of violence. Education for peace must therefore also discuss attitudes and offer ways of examining them. It must encourage people to look at their patterns of life and give them the opportunity to review their self-images in confronting peace issues. They might thereby be enabled, if necessary, to develop a modified self-concept that could help them to a more profound understanding of the world and society.

To achieve peace-oriented learning that might prompt a corresponding willingness to take action, apathy and helplessness must be overcome, for they prevent empathy and involvement in such learning processes. One learning strategy that can help overcome feelings of impotence is to see one's own lack of experience as a necessary by-product of global problems. The insight that a person's life is determined, indeed even threatened, by certain macrostructural forms of conflict instills the motivation to champion the cause of peace. Education can thereby succeed in doing more than merely transmit knowledge—it can lead to changes in attitudes and to political involvement intended to bring about an altered kind of political action.

Education for peace, however, has a structural problem associated with it. As education, it can effect lasting change in the ideas and attitudes of those individuals and groups of individuals to whom it is directed, but that does not necessarily mean that these changes will lead directly to potentially less violent social structures. Stamina and persistence are thus important aids for the task of educating people for peace. It is essential to complement education with practical policies and action pertaining to peace.

Education for peace requires certain modes of communication. It should promote nonviolent learning processes when possible, so it must develop primarily those kinds of learning that involve participative and self-initiated learning (see *Popular Education and Conscientization; Experiential and Open Learning; Self-directed Learning*). In these learning processes, a major part of the initiative and responsibility lies with the people at whom education for peace is aimed. They are encouraged to work out for themselves the various forms conflict may take and, in doing so, to use their imagination to speculate on peaceful outcomes. Development of a historical sense of the origins of situations of conflict and their fundamental mutability plays a key role in this regard, for it helps the learners design scenarios of change that are Utopian yet also tempered by everyday experience. It also ensures an awareness of the future in the consideration of peace issues.

5. Education for Peace as a Social Learning Process

Education for peace must be understood as a social learning process in the course of which various problems and conflicts can be addressed. It also involves the development of individual skills without which peace-oriented action is unlikely to succeed:

(a) *Recognition of one's own self*. Sensitivity in perceiving and dealing with one's own and others' feelings and attitudes.

(b) *Recognition of one's own dependencies and those of society*. Sensitivity in the perception of sociostructural dependencies; awareness of one's own situation in life; analysis of patterns of social relations in which the individual is integrated.

(c) *Role distance*. The ability to gain critical distance from social roles previously played and to express one's distance when acting out a role or to question closely and, if appropriate, to modify the normative demands it entails.

(d) *Empathy*. The ability to project oneself into the expectations of one's social opposite and to show understanding for them.

(e) *Tolerance of ambiguity*. The ability to perceive and bear with others' equivocal situations and contradictory expectations, even if one's own needs are likely to go largely unmet.

(f) *Competence in communication*. The ability to articulate one's own needs and interests in an appropriate way, that is, neither living entirely for nor completely ignoring the expectations of others, but rather establishing one's own balance between various standpoints through a process of communication.

These abilities of the individual, which can be acquired through social learning in school and adult education, are prerequisites and elements of autonomous social action oriented toward peace. The last four categories in particular describe relatively general competencies whose full import for peace education becomes clear only in interaction with the substantive questions and problems discussed above. Not until education for peace is understood and practiced as social learning can a social competence for overcoming feelings of political impotence and apathy and for creating the inclination toward peace-oriented action be developed.

6. Target Groups

Education for peace can take place in many social institutions. It may begin in the family, where the parents can model this type of learning for their children by giving attention in their daily lives to the problems of furthering the cause of peace. It can be made a subject of discussion in schools, adult education centers, and universities. Basically, there are two ways in which this can be achieved. First, education for peace can take place by including the dimension of preserving and promoting peace in a variety of topics. Peace education in this form becomes an instructional principle. Second, units of instruction on peace-related issues can be developed, tested, and taught. Such units have their place, for example, in classes on civics, literature, and religion.

Education for peace can also be undertaken through the mass media—television, newspapers, magazines, and films. The possibilities vary largely according to the nature of the specific medium.

Finally, education for peace can be enacted in churches, political parties, unions, and grassroots groups. The people who learn and become involved in these institutions are usually adults who have recognized that helping improve the conditions for peace is an obligation to the next generation. On the whole, the success of efforts on behalf of peace will depend primarily on the interaction between education, relevant scholarly research, and practical policies.

7. Conclusions

There are several irreconcilable polarities inherent in education for peace.

(a) *The relation between the macrolevel and microlevel.* In education for peace, the polarity of these two levels must be accepted and understood as a constitutive element. Work for peace must not be confined to the microlevel; moreover, given the complexity of structures of violence at the macrolevel, neither should the importance of small advances at the microlevel be underestimated. The absorbing task of education for peace is to mediate between the two levels.

(b) *The relation between reflection and action.* One aim of education for peace is to offer information and enlightenment about important subjects that influence the life of the human race. An objective in this regard is to increase knowledge and, consequently, the power of judgment. At the same time, education for peace is designed to change attitudes and build up the willingness to act for the sake of peace. It is even aimed at prompting appropriate action itself. Conflicts obviously arise between the two objectives.

(c) *The relation between analysis and change.* Education for peace is an attempt to penetrate

structures of violence with the insights of the critical mind. However, it cannot ignore the question of what a less violent world would look like. Education for peace must be prepared to design conditionally Utopian scenarios for a more peaceful world and to appraise reality accordingly.

(d) *The relation between feeling and rationality.* Education for peace aims to engender concern and involvement, even partiality. Without them, the aspiration of preparing for political action cannot be met. Nevertheless, education for peace is subject to the norms of rationality, which require that one appreciate the pros and cons of one's own position and eliminate the uncertainties that this exercise gives rise to.

(e) *The relation between form and content.* Can learning processes relevant to peace occur under conditions of structural violence? Are closed institutions with highly prestructured forms of learning more suitable than others to the learning of matters relevant to peace? Or do such structures corrupt that which is learned, so turning it also into a channel for violence? If so, one would have to question the value of school-related learning about peace and consider transferring peace education to the extracurricular sphere. Or does precisely an institution such as school offer the test opportunities for learning about peace, particularly since relatively young people are subject to the learning process in this forum? The answer to these questions remains open.

Education for peace can be understood as a sphere of educational work in which the links to pedagogy, peace studies and conflict research, the peace movement, and peace policies are essential, but not so central that it loses its separate identity.

See also: Community Education and Community Development; Popular Education and Conscientization; Population Education; International Adult Education; Nongovernmental Organizations

References

Galtung J 1969 Violence, peace and peace research. *Journal of Peace Research* 6: 167–91
Senghaas D 1972 *Abschreckung und Frieden. Studien zur Kritik organisierter Friedenslosigkeit.* Suhrkamp, Frankfurt

Further Reading

Barash D P 1991 *Introduction to Peace Studies.* Wadsworth, Belmont, California
Bjerstedt A 1991 Peace education: A selective bibliography. Peace Education Reports 3, School of Education, Malmö
Bose A 1991 *Peace and Conflict Resolution in the World Community.* Advent, New York
Buddrus V, Schaitmann G W (eds.) 1991 *Friedenspädagogik*

im Paradigmenwechsel. Deutscher Studienbuch Verlag, Weinheim

Curle A 1973 *Education for Liberaliens.* Tavistock Publications, London

Haavelsrod M (ed.) 1976 *Education for peace: Reflections and Action.* IPC Science and Technology Press, Guildford

Heck G, Schurig M (eds.) 1991 *Friedenspädagogik.* Wissenschaftliche Buchgesellschaft, Darmstadt

Jares X R 1991 *Education para la paz: Su teoria y su practica.* Editorial Popular, Madrid

Jontiez P L, Harris D (eds.) 1991 *International Schools and International Education. The World Year-book of Education.* Nichols, Brunswick, New Jersey

Smoker P, Davies R, Munske B (eds.) 1990 *A Reader in Peace Studies.* Pergamon Press, Oxford

The Union of International Associations (eds.) 1991 *Encyclopedia of World Problems and Human Potential*, 3rd edn. K G Saur, New Providence, New Jersey

Wulf C (ed.) 1973 *Kritische Friedenserziehung.* Suhrkamp, Frankfurt

Wulf C (ed.) 1974 *Handbook on Peace Education.* International Peace Association, Frankfurt

Popular Education and Conscientization

D. R. Evans

The experience of educators, concerned clergy, and community workers in Latin America produced the realization that traditional approaches to education for adults were largely irrelevant for those who lived in poverty and misery, and, even worse, served to further entrench the structures and power relationships that were the causes of the problems. An alternative form of education was needed, one which allowed the learner to see the situation differently, understand the larger causes, and take personal responsibility to create changes. While many have been involved in the evolution of these ideas, they were crystallized by the thought and writing of Paulo Freire, a Brazilian educator, in his seminal work *Pedagogy of the Oppressed*, which introduced the concept of "conscientization." This and later writings proved enormously influential in the following decades, spreading slowly from Latin America to North America, and were then echoed by the work of others in Asia and Africa (see *Critical Approaches to Adult Education*).

Application of the insights of Freire and others to adult education took many forms, encapsulated by terms such as "conscientization," "nonformal education," "popular education," and "education for social mobilization." The use of these terms is varied and frequently overlapping, although distinctions are often argued fiercely on the basis of the ideological beliefs of proponents.

1. Conscientization

Although the concept of "conscientization" was known and used by other radical Catholics in Brazil before Paulo Freire, the term has come to be synonymous with him and his explication of it as an idea and a process. Mackie (1981) describes Freire's philosophy as an eclectic mixture which was not built up systematically, but which emerged and continues to be shaped through praxis—the continuing cycle of action and reflection. Freire drew upon a variety of European philosophers and from the many radical Catholics writing in the context of Latin America, yet his philosophy originated in his experiences with poor adults in the Third World and was addressed explicitly to the oppressed of the Third World. His pedagogy for adults is grounded in the social reality of the poor and the need to address their reality as the first priority in any approach to adult education.

1.1 Adult Literacy—Learning to Read the World and the Word

Initially, Freire's approach to adult education arose from his experiences with poor adults in Recife, Brazil in his role as municipal coordinator for adult literacy. There he developed "culture circles" as alternative learning environments for adults where active, critical dialogue could take place. Work with the culture circles evolved into a more fully developed literacy method which can be briefly summarized in a few lines. Working with community members, Freire and his colleagues chose generative themes which reflected the social and political realities of the learners' lives—themes which engaged workers in problematizing their situation. These themes were then captured in a series of generative words which had the emotional impact needed to stimulate discussion and which contained the core phonemes of Portuguese. Typically they chose words with two or three syllables, beginning with words containing simple syllables common to the language such as *"tijolo"* (brick) or *"favela"* (slum). Each of the syllables could then be used to explore the family of syllables so that the *"ti"* in *tijolo* expands into the syllables *"ta te ti to tu."* From these syllables new words can be formed. A total of about 16 or 17 words was sufficient to cover the basic sounds for syllabic languages like Portuguese or Spanish (for a sample list of words, see Freire 1973 pp. 82–84). In Latin America, this approach is known as the "psychosocial method."

The first step, though, was to use a picture or drawing of the concept contained in the word to discuss its meaning in the local context. The picture of a brick provokes discussion of building with bricks, housing as a community problem, and the obstacles to better housing. The word itself was presented only after this discussion took place. He explicitly rejected primers which use an external message rather than the words and thoughts of the learners because he believed that they lead to domesticating rather than liberating education by encouraging uncritical acceptance.

Freire's approach to literacy has stimulated the development of literally hundreds of adaptations to a wide variety of literacy and adult education situations throughout the world. Srinivasan (1977) reports another approach, the Apperception–Interaction Method (AIM), that was used in functional literacy programs in the United States, Thailand, the Philippines, and Turkey. This method uses problem themes from the daily lives of learners, starting with a provocative photograph or drawing complemented by a short drama or narrative to stimulate discussion. A word or phrase is then introduced based on the theme. The Nicaraguan Literacy Crusade of the early 1980s also provides a good example. Miller (1985) describes the evolution of the methodology which used pictures, dialogue, and a series of 23 keywords beginning with the word "*la revolución*."

In many cases, there is tension between the desire to create primers which contain content viewed as essential, particularly in immediate postrevolutionary situations like Nicaragua, and Freire's pedagogy which argues that the themes and the conclusions must come from the learner if they are to be truly liberational. Srinivasan (1977 p. 91) feels similarly that materials must be truly open to local concerns rather than constraining the learners to react to content chosen by the curriculum designers. Most programs confront this tension when they move beyond pilot activities to larger scale implementation.

1.2 Conscientization—Overcoming the Psychology of Oppression

To interpret Freire's theory of conscientization as solely, or even primarily, a method for achieving adult literacy would seriously underestimate his importance. Following in the footsteps of Fromm, Fanon, and Memmi, Freire's theory is a description of the psychology of the oppressed, an analysis of how the oppressed and the oppressor behave, and a pedagogy for freeing both from the structures of oppression.

Conscientization is the humanization of people, transforming them from objects to subjects, from dehumanized individuals trapped in oppressive structures to more fully human beings (see Freire 1970 pp. 27–56). Since both oppressed and oppressor are trapped in the same structure, both are dehumanized and both need to be liberated. Liberation comes about through a painful process of rebirth in dialogue between humans, and between humans and the world. Critical and liberating dialogue must be part of a dialectical process between action and reflection, which Freire calls "praxis." Neither reflection nor action alone is sufficient.

The central point of Freire's philosophy is mirrored in the title of his book—*Pedagogy of the Oppressed* (1970). Oppression cannot be overcome by well-intentioned actions on the part of individual oppressors. Only the oppressed can initiate the process of praxis which has the power to free both themselves and their oppressors. The oppressed must move from seeing themselves as objects to people engaged in the vocation of becoming more fully human. In the process, they will come to understand that the oppressors are also trapped in the same dehumanizing structure. Only the oppressed can free themselves through a process of reflection and action to transform the dehumanizing situation. Conscientization is the process by which the oppressed liberate themselves and their oppressors.

Freire articulates three levels of consciousness which characterize individuals in the struggle to overcome oppression: magical, naive, and critical. In each stage, individuals name (problematize), reflect, and act in characteristic ways which reflect their stage of consciousness (see discussion in Smith 1976). These levels are characterized as follows:

(a) The magical state—conforming—is characterized by problem denial or avoidance, simplistic causality which focuses on things like lack of money or poor health, and inaction justified by fatalism or passively playing "host to the oppressor."

(b) The naive state—reforming—names the problem as individual oppressors who are bad, accepts the oppressor's ideology and explanations for what is essentially a good system, and actively plays "host to the oppressor" by defending them and blaming the oppressed for acting inappropriately.

(c) The critical state—transforming—names the problem as the whole dehumanizing structure, affirms the goodness of the oppressed and their values, and understands the contradictions that trap both the oppressors and the oppressed. The critical individual is self-actualizing, seeking to transform the system through acting as a subject, having faith in one's peers, and working to change the structure.

Conscientization is the process of growth through these stages, although the process is uneven, with individuals often regressing or being in different states simultaneously in different contexts.

Freire's lifetime of writing, speaking, and doing, the veritable library of references and writings which it has inspired, and the legion of followers who have been energized by his insights have all combined to have a significant effect on adult education efforts around the world. Anywhere there is a group which feels oppressed, one is almost certain to find an educational effort informed in part by Freire's analysis of oppression and his vision of a pedagogy which can liberate. These efforts are as much present in the First World—gays and lesbians, racial or ethnic groups, women's groups, native peoples—as they are in the Latin American setting in which Freire first worked.

2. Popular Education

La Belle (1986) documents a conceptual split between consciousness raising, as exemplified by Freire and others, and popular education for structural change. Torres (1990 p. 18) traces popular education back to at least the socialist education process in Mexico during the 1930s. Popular education, then and now, is characterized as being oriented toward political development, is highly participative and mobilizing with an emphasis on social change, and is sensitive to the structure of power in society. Freirean approaches became so well-known in the 1970s that they tended to be co-opted into official, government adult education programs which kept the rhetoric without being liberatory in nature. Partly in response to the perceived failure of consciousness raising and the nonformal education programs which sometimes incorporated it, popular education has gained new prominence, emphasizing social class, participatory organizations, and strategies for the transformation of society.

Current popular education is heavily influenced by the Marxist perspective of Antonio Gramsci, particularly his vision of cross-class coalitions to support change movements rooted in the lower classes and his concept of organic intellectuals—peasants and workers who serve as linkages between concrete knowledge and general knowledge, local and national issues, and social formation and the mode of production (Fals-Borda 1981). Gramsci argued for the organization of workers to counteract the hegemony of the state and its support for the interests of the dominant classes. The focus of popular education is therefore on preparing the lower classes to take advantage of opportunities to exercise power in an organized manner that will alter the balance of power in capitalist societies. This emphasis is in contrast to the more individualistic psychological and intellectual awareness produced by consciousness raising efforts. Popular education recognizes that consciousness raising is an important component of social change, but that it is inadequate on its own. Current popular education activities often begin with some form of participatory investigation by the community (referred to also as "action research," "participatory action research," or "participatory education"). Using a dependency perspective, Fals-Borda, for example, says that knowledge is produced by and

reflects the class interests of the dominant groups. He promotes four techniques: collective research by the group to gather information, a critical recovery of local history from the perspective of the people, valuing and using popular culture to support social mobilization of the people, and production and diffusion of new knowledge generated by these methods. The organizations and the awareness created by participatory research constitutes the foundation for ongoing education and action for social change.

A typical example of a popular education activity is provided by the Learning Workshops Program in Chile which has been in operation since 1977 and has served over 10,000 children (Vaccarro 1990). The Learning Workshops are alternative learning centers for poor children who have dropped out of school. The workshops are run by community adults who serve as monitors and coordinators. They are trained with a participatory process which leads them to problematize the reality which has created the poverty and the children who are unable to learn in school. The workshop becomes an activity which is "appropriated" by the community as one way in which they can begin to transform their reality. The process of appropriation begins immediately, when the initial proposal offered by an external agent is subject to discussion and modification by the participants and grows throughout the process until they become independent.

La Belle (1986 pp. 210–14) uses three goals to assess the outcomes of popular education: development of local participatory organizations, forging of linkages across and within social classes to generate power for the poor, and designing strategies to shift concentrations of power to the poor. He concludes that the evidence to date of success with popular education is limited: not being noticeably more successful than earlier community development approaches in building nondependent, participatory organizations, making some gains in forging within class alliances, and having little impact on power concentrations. However, the support for popular education approaches remains strong, partly because it provides a means for the oppressed to participate effectively in local development.

3. Conclusion

Conscientization and popular education are unique as development approaches because they originated in the Third World and speak from the realities of that setting, not from those of the First World. The rich ferment generated by peasants, workers, local leaders, intellectuals, and scholars, initially in Latin America but now increasingly throughout the world, has forced the development industry to recognize the social and human costs of dominant approaches to development. Yet within conscientization and popular education tensions continue to emerge between local generation of knowledge and the use of these techniques as a means for mobilizing a society in support of new national ideologies. The role of conscientization and social mobilization will continue striving to build effective linkages between micro-level and macro-level development, trying to balance national economic power with the rights and needs of people. For many knowledgeable and concerned educators, these approaches offer the only hopeful alternatives.

See also: Formal, Nonformal, and Informal Education; Community Education and Community Development; Critical Approaches to Adult Education; Ideologies in Adult Education; Participatory Research; Adult Education for Development; International Council for Adult Education; Adult Literacy in the Third World

References

Fals-Borda O 1981 The challenge of action research. *Development* 23(1): 55–61

Freire P 1970 *Pedagogy of the Oppressed*. Herder and Herder, New York

Freire P 1973 *Education for Critical Consciousness*. Seabury Press, New York

La Belle T J 1986 *Nonformal Education in Latin America and the Caribbean: Stability, Reform or Revolution?* Praeger, New York

Mackie R 1981 Contributions to the thought of Paulo Freire. In: Mackie R (ed.) 1981 *Literacy and Revolution: The Pedagogy of Paulo Freire*. Continuum, New York

Miller V 1985 *Between Struggle and Hope: The Nicaraguan Literacy Crusade*. Westview Press, Boulder, Colorado

Smith W A 1976 *The Meaning of Conscientizacao: The Goal of Paulo Freire's Pedagogy*. The Center for International Education, University of Massachusetts, Amherst, Massachusetts

Srinivasan L 1977 *Perspectives on Nonformal Adult Learn-
ing: Functional Education for Individual, Community, and National Development*. World Education, New York

Torres C A 1990 *The Politics of Nonformal Education in Latin America*. Praeger, New York

Vaccaro L 1990 Transference and appropriation in popular education interventions: A framework for analysis. *Harv. Educ. Rev.* 60(1): 62–78

Further Reading

Arnold A et al. 1991 *Educating for a Change. A Handbook for Community Educators*. Between the Lines/Doris Marshall Institute for Education and Action, Toronto

Barndt D 1989 *Naming the Moment: Political Analysis for Action: A Manual for Community Groups*. The Jesuit Centre, Toronto

de Kadt E 1970 *Catholic Radicals in Brazil*. Oxford University Press, Oxford

Fals-Borda O, Rahman M A (eds.) 1991 *Action and Knowledge: Breaking the Monopoly with Participatory Action-Research*. Apex Press, New York and Intermediate Technology Publications, London

Freire P 1972 *Cultural Action for Freedom*. Penguin, Harmondsworth

Freire P 1978 *Pedagogy in Process: The Letters to Guinea-Bissau*. Seabury Press, New York and Writers and Readers Publishing Cooperative, London

La Belle T J 1987 From consciousness raising to popular education in Latin America and the Caribbean. *Comp. Educ. Rev.* 31(2): 201–17

Magendzo S 1990 Popular education in nongovernmental organizations: Education for social mobilization. *Harv. Educ. Rev.* 60(1): 49–61

Zachariah M 1986 *Revolution through Reform: A Comparison of Sarvodaya and Conscientization*. Praeger Greenwood, New York

Population Education

C. T. Davies

This entry explains the purpose and history of population education. It also discusses the disciplinary orientations of the subject, in particular its relations with other areas of educational activity, such as environmental education, peace education, and education for development.

1. Purpose

Population education aims to allow people to acquire the knowledge, abilities, attitudes, and values necessary for the understanding and evaluation of population situations, the dynamic forces that have shaped them, and the effects they will have on the present and future quality of life. Additionally, those who receive such education should be able to make informed and responsible decisions, based on their own assessments, and to participate in collective decisions which will help to promote social and economic development. Population education requires the most objective teaching–learning situation possible in which the "teacher" assists the "learner" in acquiring a set of facts and values that will allow him or her to evaluate the whole range of options on a given issue leading to desirable behavioral change.

Population education is essentially an educational response to demographic problems. It emerged from a growing awareness of the importance of such worldwide population phenomena as slow and rapid population growth rates, migration, urbanization, and deterioration of the environment. For example, a rapidly growing population may exhaust certain resources or make it difficult to meet such basic needs as employment, education, and healthcare, resulting in a threat to the quality of people's lives. A declining population or an aging population may be seen in some cases as a threat to a country's economy or vitality. Migration from rural to urban areas may deplete rural areas of human resources while placing a strain on urban social services.

2. History

Historically, the development of population education goes back to the 1940s, when there was concern about population decline, particularly in the United States and Sweden. However, in other parts of the world in the 1950s and 1960s the main concern was that of high birthrates and growing populations. As a result, many family planning programs were established. These programs, especially in the developing world, were not highly successful. They seemed to have concentrated on adults who had to overcome deeply entrenched traditional learning. Through the late 1960s and early 1970s, educational programs were developed for children and youth whose reproductive years were still ahead of them and during this period the term "population education" was almost synonymous with school population education programs. During the 1970s, however, the educational settings of population education began to include a whole range of educational institutions, both formal and nonformal. Furthermore, the content of population education was broadened beyond the topics of fertility and growth to include a much wider range of population processes and characteristics related to various aspects of development and, since the 1980s, to the AIDS pandemic.

3. Orientation

It is commonly argued that population education is not an attempt to develop a new discipline but that facts, theories, and concepts are borrowed from a broad spectrum of academic disciplines and professional fields in order to assist individuals and societies in understanding fully population interactions and the effect of population factors on the quality of individual and collective lives. The sum of all these knowledge bases is referred to as population studies. Thus, population education embraces the field of population studies which comprises the body of knowledge, concepts, and theories that describe and attempt to explain the dynamics of human populations and their relationships with the social, cultural, economic, political, and biological environments. It involves examining a wide range of population issues and is, therefore, much broader than family planning or demography. Essentially, it is people-centered. The people themselves set the agenda through the articulation of their own population-related problems. Any curriculum in population education, therefore, requires a situational definition.

4. Related Areas

Because of the nature of population education a number of other educational activities inevitably share some of the content associated with it. The greatest confusion that arises concerns population education's relation to family-life education, sex education, environmental education, and development education. Family-life education and sex education do indeed share certain concerns with population education, such as human reproduction and life-cycle decision-making, but they concentrate on interpersonal relations and in general have not thus far concerned themselves with the consequences of population decision-making for the wider society.

In rather different ways, environmental education and development education also make use of content drawn from population studies, especially that which describes and analyzes how population processes operate in order to understand better the nature of social and economic development or the interaction of humans and the biosphere. However, differences in goals and objectives give population education a separate identity at its present stage of development.

Nevertheless, there is no systematically organized body of knowledge and no single textbook which can be referred to on population education. The problem stems from the fact that population phenomena affect so many aspects of life at so many different levels—political relations, resources, the environment, health, social services, education, employment, and human rights—that nations, regions, and individuals have differing viewpoints about population questions. These viewpoints range along a continuum from those which regard population growth as a crisis, to those which seek to encourage population growth in order to help solve social problems.

5. Importance

There is a diversity of views on the importance of population education. Some contend that population is a false issue, fostered by wealthy industrialized nations to divert attention from problems faced by developing nations. The real problem, according to this view, is not population growth, but the unequal distribution of wealth and resources, the lack of integrated economic development, overconsumption, and the affluent lifestyle of many industrialized nations, all of which pose a more direct threat to the preservation of the environment and resources than the higher population growth rates of the developing nations.

The various viewpoints will, of course, be given different emphases in the different population education programs being conducted in various parts of the world. Population education in the formal system takes a number of forms, moving from the introduction of population concepts at the elementary and secondary school levels to more advanced work in universities and specialized training colleges. Large-scale projects are being carried out in all parts of the world.

6. Conclusion

In both developing and industrialized countries there exists a great diversity of population education programs. These programs are promoted by international organizations, governments, and nongovernmental associations, and they are offered in both formal, informal and nonformal settings. Poverty reduction by reducing population growth is a primary objective of population education. Women form the principal target of population education, given that the more educated a woman, the lower is her fertility and mortality, and the healthier is the child.

See also: Adult Education for Development; Women and Adult Education; UNESCO and Adult Education

Bibliography

Cleland J, Wilson D 1987 Demand Theories of the Fertility Transition: An Iconoclastic View. *Population Studies* 41: 5–30

Elo I 1992 Utilization of Maternal Health-care Services in Peru: The Role of Women's Education. *The Health Transition Review* 2(1)

Johnston T 1990 *The Population IEC Operation in Eastern and Southern Africa.* UNFPA/CIDA, Nairobi

King E, Hill M A 1991 *Women's Education in Developing Countries: Barriers, Benefits and Policy.* Background Paper Series # 91/40. The World Bank, Washington, DC

Oni G A Effects of Women's Education on Postpartum Practices and Fertility in Urban Nigeria. *Studies in Family Planning* 16(6)

Udo R K (ed.) 1979 *Population Education Source Book for Sub-Saharan Africa.* Heinemann, Nairobi

UNESCO 1978 *Population Education: A Contemporary Concern.* Education Studies and Documents No. 28, UNESCO, Paris

UNESCO 1980 *Study of the Contribution of Population Education to Educational Renewal and Innovation in El Salvador, the Republic of Korea, Philippines and Tunisia.* UNESCO, Paris

United Nations 1986 *Education and Fertility: Selected Findings from the World Fertility Survey Data.* United Nations Population Division Working Paper ESA/P/WP/96. United Nations, New York

World Bank 1994 *Enchancing Women's Participation in Economic Development.* The World Bank, Washington, DC

Postliteracy

L. Benton

Low and insufficient literacy is a problem not just in developing nations, but also in OECD countries. A significant proportion of adults lack adequate skills in reading, writing, and numeracy, as various national assessment studies show. The problem has grave economic implications, particularly because economic restructuring since the mid-1970s has also altered jobs and increased skill requirements for some workers. Reforms aimed at addressing the problem in new ways include more participation by both labor unions and learners in program design, greater integration of literacy and work training, and efforts to build learning into job structures. Constraints on policy effectiveness are evident in the fragmented structure of various national literacy campaigns. "Postliteracy," if taken to mean achievement of universal basic literacy levels, still lies in the future.

In this entry, the concept of postliteracy is discussed in relation to changes affecting the skill requirements of the labor force. Methodologies and issues in the measurement of literacy are presented, and postliteracy programs in different industrialized countries are described. Attention is also given to emerging trends and opportunities for the formation of a broad coalition to support the expansion of literacy training.

1. The Meaning of Postliteracy

The term "postliteracy" can be problematic if it is taken to imply the universal attainment of basic levels of literacy. Serious illiteracy problems persist even in the most advanced countries, and these problems affect not just populations that are perceived as "marginal" (e.g., immigrants, the unemployed, or school dropouts) but also significant, and perhaps growing, numbers of adult workers. One can therefore understand "literacy" to mean not a limited set of skills but a learned ability to interpret complex messages and codes of all kinds. "Postliteracy" is better defined, then, as the condition of countries where very basic abilities in reading and writing are indeed widely held, but where many cannot perform the literacy-related tasks needed to function fully at home, at work, and in civic life. This condition is shared by most economically advanced countries and by some developing countries. Particularly in the former, overcoming the problem of adult illiteracy is increasingly tied to the goal of enhancing international economic competitiveness.

This shift in the understanding of literacy is forcing policymakers to confront a series of new issues. One problem is how to assess the phenomenon of insufficient literacy skills in a meaningful way. Earlier measures of literacy, as discussed below, are at best crude indicators of the ability to complete various literacy-related tasks. New, more sophisticated methods of measurement have been developed, but they have not yet been widely used (see *Literacy Research and Measurement*).

The new approaches to measuring illiteracy inevitably call attention to other problems that have been poorly perceived in the past. Levels of literacy that are actually required for individuals to function effectively in different contexts have rarely been systematically studied. Of particular importance is understanding the literacy requirements of jobs, including entirely new categories of jobs. This problem ties literacy research to broader investigations into the nature of economic change since the mid-1970s, when the advanced economies began the shift to a "post-Fordist" economy characterized by unstable markets, large-scale sectoral restructuring, and firm shake-ups. This process has involved the reorganization of many jobs and important shifts in the skill requirements for workers.

Related to both these issues is the question of how to alter government policies and programs. Surveying the efforts of national and local governments in some of the industrialized countries reveals a broad movement toward merging literacy concerns with economic goals. Although it is possible to point toward some particularly compelling experiments, no single strategy has gained a solid reputation for effectiveness. Even where government efforts share some similar features and are guided by similar concerns, differences in local and national politics tend to lead literacy policies across nations toward different outcomes.

2. Measuring Literacy

The current situation contrasts with that of the early 1980s, when literacy was typically defined in terms of grade attainment. One advantage of this method was that data on grade completion were widely available, and it was thus possible to compare literacy rates defined by grade attainment internationally and also over time within individual countries. The drawback, of course, is that there was little evidence that grade attainment was an accurate indicator of literacy skills.

Rather than seeking to identify levels of basic literacy (the ability to write and/or decipher simple messages), most researchers now recognize the need to measure a more complex social construction, "functional literacy," or the ability to perform a complex range of tasks. The dimensions of the problem of functional illiteracy are just becoming known. Several national efforts to arrive at a more precise measure of the problem deserve mention.

A methodological approach developed in the 1975 Adult Performance Level (APL) survey in the United States was influential because it used performance tasks as indicators of literacy competency. A more complex method based on this approach was pioneered in the 1985 United States Department of Education survey of young adults (aged 21 to 25)—the National Assessment of Educational Progress (NAEP) (Kirsch and Jungeblut 1986). This survey assessed respondents' performance in three categories—prose literacy, document literacy, and quantitative literacy—and reported results by placing respondents' abilities along three scales corresponding to the differnt types of competencies. The authors of the study intended to shift the emphasis away from reporting flat rates of "illiteracy" or "functional illiteracy" and toward a more nuanced understanding of the problem.

The NAEP study showed that patterns of economic inequality paralleled the distribution of literacy skills. Poor minority groups performed at levels significantly lower than those of young White adults. The study also confirmed that classically defined illiteracy—the inability to read—was indeed a relatively small problem (affecting only about 2% of the sample), while a significant proportion of young adults were unable to complete many of the literacy-related tasks and only 10 to 40 percent could reliably complete the most complex, multistep tasks (Kirsch and Jungeblut 1986). The results of the NAEP survey encouraged the Department of Education to conduct a national adult literacy assessment for individuals aged 16 to 64 in 1992 (Kirsh et al. 1993). In 1989, the Department of Labor also commissioned literacy assessments of three special populations of adults who were unemployed or in training.

Other attempts to assess the literacy problem nationally have been influenced by these efforts. A very comprehensive project is a 1989 study in Canada called the Survey of Literacy Skills Used in Daily Activities (LSUDA). This study surveyed 9,455 individuals between the ages of 16 and 69 with the goal of producing a separate test score for each respondent in reading, writing, and numeracy. The results confirmed that functional illiteracy is a significant problem, even though the majority of Canadian adults can read and would be classified as literate by standard proxy measures (Neice et al. 1992).

The study permitted a division of respondents into various categories of skill attainment and found that while relatively small proportions of respondents had no appreciable skills in reading, writing, and numeracy, significant proportions had skill levels that limited their abilities to complete daily functions. For example, 62 percent of Canadians were classified as reading at "level 4" (i.e., with skills that enabled them to complete most tasks and also gain further knowledge from printed materials); 22 percent of adult Canadians were classified as being able "to carry out simple reading tasks within familiar contexts with materials that are clearly laid out (level 3)"; and 16 percent of adults were found to have skills so limited that they could not understand most written material they would be likely to encounter in everyday life (Statistics Canada 1991). The study also found that reading, writing, and numeracy skills were closely linked to levels of schooling, to age, to region, and, for immigrants, to year of arrival in Canada.

Other countries have moved toward producing similar national assessments of literacy. France also revised the definition of functional illiteracy to include "individuals with difficulties in mastering basic skills" (*personnes en difficulté de maîtrise des savoirs de base*). A large-scale assessment of key skills was conducted in 1990 and was administered to a sample of 1,500 long-term unemployed individuals in five major cities: Paris, Marseilles, Lyon, Lille, and Toulouse. The skill areas analyzed were more extensive and were differently defined than in the studies in the United States and Canada. This survey, and other studies underway in France, promise to provide a much clearer profile of the functionally illiterate population in France than has been available to policymakers in the past.

An important finding shared across these studies is that although disadvantaged populations—migrants, young adults, minorities—may suffer disproportionately from literacy problems, they are likely to be outnumbered among the ranks of functional illiterates by apparently "mainstream" individuals, especially older, adult workers. This fact in turn suggests necessary revisions in the assessment of the effects of literacy on the economy and in the response to the problem through educational programs.

3. Literacy and Work

It has become commonplace to observe that workforce education problems in the advanced economies are related to the fact that such groups as women, young people, migrants, and minorities are growing quickly as a proportion of the workforce; because these groups have had a difficult time gaining equal access to education, the argument goes, they are less well-prepared for jobs. In fact, the sources of problems related to workforce preparedness are far more complex. Firm restructuring in response to widespread market instability has resulted in the reorganization of many jobs to entail a larger number and wider variety of tasks; it has also prompted the need to restructure the relationship of those tasks to others more frequently.

These shifts have been documented most clearly in manufacturing. So-called "Fordist" strategies of production for mass markets entailed the breakdown of jobs into easily performed tasks to which unskilled workers could be—at least in theory—indiscriminately assigned. Since the massive restructuring of those markets after the global crisis of the mid-1970s, firms have had to switch to strategies that emphasize production of short series, quick response to market shifts, and variability within product lines. One result has been a restructuring of jobs to allow for greater flexibility. Many unskilled jobs are disappearing, while skilled jobs tend to entail the performance of more varied tasks and a conceptual rather than a routine mastery of those tasks (Piore and Sabel 1984, Bailey 1989, Benton et al. 1991).

A similar transformation has also taken place in the services, where job creation in the advanced economies is the fastest. Although a rapid increase in the demand for low-level service workers is a feature shared by many of the advanced economies, this trend is part of a more complex story. Similar pressures as in manufacturing—to diversify product lines, to respond more quickly to market shifts, and to pursue specialized market niches—have led to a flattening of organizational structures. A larger percentage of the service workforce must have the communications skills necessary to participate directly in sales and customer/client service. As service firms work to distinguish themselves in the marketplace by developing proprietary technology and firm-specific procedures, workers must also learn to apply broad guidelines of action to specific cases and, moreover, to prepare to learn new guidelines as market positioning shifts again (Noyelle 1990, Benton et al. 1991).

These and other, related changes have meant that workers are being called on not only to arrive at work with a higher level of skills but also to be prepared to *learn at work*. Jobs for workers with very low literacy skills are disappearing. There is a noticeable trend within business toward providing in-house training to larger proportions of workers. This trend, in turn, feeds into a wider, growing movement in support of context-related instruction. Business interests, educators, and policymakers seem to be converging in support of a type of literacy training that promotes mastery of broad sets of skills by teaching their application to specific work-related tasks. This strategy contrasts with the more traditional approach of teaching basic skills as a step preparatory to, or at least separate from, job training.

4. Program Reforms

Several trends in program development appear to be shared across a range of more advanced countries. They are union participation in instruction, curriculum reform, the restructuring of work as a training strategy, and learner-centered instruction (see Benton and Noyelle 1992). Taken together, these trends share an emphasis on context-specific (especially work-centered) instruction for adults already in the workforce.

Although many firms and business leaders remain opposed to union participation in designing training, numerous ongoing experiments suggest that unions may be uniquely positioned to interpret training needs and encourage worker participation. In at least one country, Sweden, union participation in literacy training has been sweeping. The unions already had a strong tradition of participation in adult education, and they run high schools and other programs that target working adults. Union pressure prompted a 1985 policy requiring firms to set aside a portion of profits for a renewal fund partially dedicated to training. Although many firms have resisted using the funds to improve the skills of poorly educated workers, unions have pushed for such use. They have thus been important actors in creating and promoting programs that link basic skills and job skills training (Tuijnman 1989).

In the United States, union participation has been less consistently important, although a few cases suggest the promise of joint union–management training efforts. In the automobile industry, the United Auto Workers (UAW) has reached agreements with the three big automobile makers to co-manage training centers, accessible to workers at all education levels, that are richly funded through a "tax" on employee earnings. An example of even more direct union involvement is an innovative program in Ontario, Canada, run by the Ontario Federation of Labor. The Basic Education for Skills Training Program (BEST) is run entirely by unions and structured to emphasize the linkage between learning and workplace experience. The program is worker-run and worker-designed, and its success depends on the ability of the union to recruit and retain learners.

Curriculum trends in work-based, union-run programs are also apparent in other types of training. In many countries, traditional remedial adult training consists of standard high school equivalency training or basic skills instruction that varies little depending on the backgrounds or occupations of learners. But a trend toward developing *customized* curricula is clearly in place. In both North America and Western Europe, various programs can be identified that use materials borrowed directly from work or community settings. Some publishers have also begun developing printed curricula customized for particular sectors or populations (see *Curriculum in Adult Education; Modularization in Adult Education and Training*).

Such organizational and curricular changes are being complemented in a number of cases by strategies to restructure jobs themselves in ways that will encourage on-the-job learning. This trend is itself often simply an outcome of a more general strategy of firm competitiveness through increased flexibility and quick response to market shifts. In some places, though, the enhanced promise of learning on the job has become an explicit goal as well as an unintended outcome. Classic examples of such concerted efforts to increase worker participation as a means of enhancing competitiveness are manufacturing firms in the so-called "Third Italy," where employers encourage flexible production through flexible job assignments (Capecchi 1989).

Related to this trend toward structured learning on the job is a tendency to develop literacy programs that are "learner-centered." Community activists have been particularly outspoken in arguing that learners must play an active role in designing curricula and in devising methods of instruction. The BEST program described above, for example, works entirely with instructional materials provided by learners. In a community-based program run in Washington, DC, to take another example, learners identify practical, attainable goals (such as obtaining a driver's license) and gear learning specifically toward those goals. Such learner involvement is clearly tied to the other three trends of union participation, contextually structured curricula, and opportunities for learning at work.

5. Policy Responses

Whether or not these and other efforts will be effective appears to depend much on the larger institutional framework in which they operate. The national commitment to literacy training has varied over time and across countries. Patterns of government authority can also constrain literacy efforts in important ways. Consider the very different problems posed by the political contexts in the following cases.

In the United States, responsibility for literacy programs rests mainly at the state level. Although the federal government has recently publicized the problem of functional illiteracy, its support for actual programs remains limited. At the same time, the pressure on states to improve literacy training is increasing. With the decline of traditional manufacturing in many states, local and state governments seek to draw services and high-tech industry with the claim that they can provide highly trained workforces. Yet state policymakers have discovered that efforts to increase and improve literacy and basic skills training are complicated by a highly fragmented funding and administrative structure that distributes responsibility for adult literacy training among a handful of programs (the two most important of these are the Job and Training Partnership Act, or JTPA, and Adult Basic Education, or ABE). Funding is also inadequate, with a total of US$1–$2 billion being spent each year by the federal government in all states (Chisman 1989).

In Canada, which has no Department of Education at the federal level, there is little federal involvement in literacy programs (Thomas 1983). This has been both a strength and a weakness for the country's literacy movement. One problem has been the unevenness of resources for literacy instruction. A few provinces have provided services to low-literate learners for decades and have backed scores of community groups involved in training, while others have left the task to traditional providers and have committed few resources. Yet lack of federal oversight has also given ambitious communities more room for experimenting with diverse providers and curricula. Thus providers in British Columbia can target loggers in need of retraining, while in Quebec funds can be used to help level educational opportunities for French and English speakers. In Canada, as in the United States, there remains a clear need for systems of evaluation of programs, as well as for administrative structures that can serve to replicate successful local programs reliably over a wider area.

In most European countries—with the possible exception of France and the United Kingdom—the perception until the late 1980s was that a major literacy problem did not exist. Yet recent evidence from the Netherlands and Sweden suggests that the need for some literacy and basic skills training extends beyond the immigrant population (Fransson and Larsson 1989). Perhaps better than any other national system among the developed countries, the Swedish system of adult education should be able to respond to this challenge using institutional arrangements already in place. The country has a well-established, multifaceted adult education system, with both national and local support (Abrahamsson 1988). Still, the system has tended in the past to benefit mostly those workers who already have average or above-average preparation, together with specially targeted populations such as immigrants or learning disabled students.

In France, the problem of illiteracy also used to be most closely associated with immigrants, but recent studies have signaled a much wider problem. Because illiteracy was thought of as a problem limited to special populations, programs have been separated from the rest of the education system. The result has been that literacy training programs of various kinds have remained fragmented. Some recent efforts promise to help. A national system of "individualized training credits" (*crédit-formation individualisé*) will allow school dropouts and others with low levels of schooling to qualify easily for remedial training (see *Recognition and Certification of Skill*).

These examples draw attention to some underlying constraints for expanding and improving literacy training. One constraint is the relationship of literacy initiatives to schooling in general. Where literacy training is considered an integral part of a system that serves citizens throughout their lives, as in Sweden, the necessary adjustments may be far easier to make. A second constraint is the relationship between national and local or regional politics. Local programs may be very innovative, but national support seems crucial to replicate successful strategies.

6. Conclusion

A valuable opportunity has emerged for the formation of a broad coalition to support the expansion of literacy training. Employers now recognize illiteracy as a problem they have to address directly, and many educators who once resisted emphasizing economic interests in the quest for universal literacy recognize that the best instructional methods often focus on skills needed by adults in the workplace. Local policy leaders also perceive that promoting literacy in the local workforce may be crucial to economic viability, given the new requirements of many firms. And learners, too, are becoming more active participants in planning the contents and goals of literacy and postliteracy programs. Whether or not effective action will result from this peculiar convergence of interests depends upon local and national political conditions and constraints. The opportunity, at least, clearly exists for building truly literate societies.

See also: Human Resource Development; Literacy; Literacy and Numeracy Models; Market Concepts in Provision; Technological Change and Education; The Development of Competence: Toward a Taxonomy; Adult Basic Education; Adult Secondary Education; Literacy Research and Measurement; Measurement of Adult Education; Statistics of Employee Training

References

Abrahamsson K 1988 *Adult Literacy, Technology and Culture—Policies, Programs and Problems in Sweden.* Swedish National Board of Education, Stockholm

Bailey T 1989 *Changes in the Nature and Structure of Work. Implications for Employer-Sponsored Training.* Columbia University, New York

Benton L, Bailey T, Noyelle T, Stanback T 1991 *Employee Training and US Competitiveness: Lessons for the 1990s.* Westview Press, Boulder, Colorado

Benton L, Noyelle T (eds.) 1992 *Adult Illiteracy and Economic Performance.* Organisation for Economic Co-operation and Development, Paris

Capecchi V 1989 The informal economy and the development of flexible specialization in Emilia Romagna. In: Portes et al. 1989 *The Informal Economy: Studies in Advanced and Less Developed Countries.* Johns Hopkins University Press, Baltimore, Maryland

Chisman F 1989 *Jump Start: The Federal Role in Adult Literacy*. Final Report of the Project on Adult Literacy. Southport Institute for Policy Analysis, Washington, DC

Fransson A, Larsson S 1989 *Who Takes a Second Chance? Implementing Education Equality in Adult Basic Education in a Swedish Context*. Report No. 1989–02. Department of Education and Educational Research, Gothenburg University, Gothenburg

Kirsch I, Jungeblut A 1986 *Literacy: Profiles of America's Young Adults*. Final Report. National Assessment of Educational Progress. Educational Testing Services, Princeton, New Jersey

Kirsch I, Jungeblut A, Jenkins L, Kolstad A 1993 *Adult Literacy in America: A First Look at the Results of the National Adult Literacy Survey*. National Center for Education Statistics, United States Department of Education, Washington, DC

Neice D, Adsett M, Rodney W 1992 Direct versus proxy measures of adult functional illiteracy: A preliminary re-examination. In: Benton L, Noyelle T (eds.) 1992

Noyelle T 1990 *Skills, Wages, and Productivity in the Service Sector*. Westview Press, Boulder, Colorado

Piore M, Sabel C 1984 *The Second Industrial Divide: Possibilities for Prosperity*. Basic Books, New York

Statistics Canada 1991 *Adult Literacy in Canada: Results of a National Study*. Minister of Industry, Science, and Technology, Ontario

Thomas A 1983 *Adult Illiteracy in Canada: A Challenge*. Occasional paper No. 42, Canadian Commission for UNESCO, Ottawa

Tuijnman A C 1989 *Further Education and Training in Swedish Working Life: A Discussion of Trends and Issues*. OECD, Paris

Further Reading

Fuchs-Brüninghoff E, Kreft W, Kropp U 1986 *Functional Illiteracy and Literacy Provision in Developed Countries: The Case of the Federal Republic of Germany*. UNESCO Institute for Education, Hamburg

Levine K 1986 *The Social Context of Literacy*. Routledge and Kegan Paul, London

Limage L 1987 Adult literacy policy in industrialized countries. In: Arnove R, Graff H (eds.) 1987 *National Literacy Campaigns*. Plenum, New York

Skagen A 1986 *Workplace Literacy*. American Management Association, New York

OECD/statistics Canada 1995 *Literacy, Economy and Society: Results of the First International Adult Literacy Survey*. OECD/Statistics Canada, Paris/Ottawa

Tuijnman A C, Kirsch I S, Wagner D A (eds.) 1995 *Adult Basic Skills: Advances in Measurement and Policy Analysis*. Hampton Press, New York

Recurrent Education

A. C. Tuijnman

This entry describes the concept and principles of recurrent education as proposed in the late 1960s. Two special features of recurrent education—postponement policy and alternation policy—are also discussed. Some of the main criticisms leveled against the concept are summarized, and reasons are given for the apparent failure of recurrent education to catch on in practice in the 1970s. The entry also describes how the strategy of recurrent education has changed in subsequent years in response to emerging concerns and demands. Finally, some trends that may have an impact on the relevance of recurrent education in guiding future policy development are presented.

1. Definition of the Concept

The concept of recurrent education, which emerged in the late 1960s and early 1970s, can be defined as:

> ... a comprehensive educational strategy for all post-compulsory or post-basic education, the essential characteristic of which is the distribution of education over the total life-span of the individual in a recurring way, i.e. in alternation with other activities, principally with work, but also with leisure and retirement. (CERI 1973 p. 16)

2. Development of the Concept

The development of the idea of recurrent education was influenced by serious doubts regarding the capacity of formal education to achieve many of the goals sought by policymakers. Mr Olof Palme, then a minister of education in Sweden, launched the concept at a meeting convened by the Organisation for Economic Co-operation and Development (OECD) in Versailles in 1968. In his keynote, Palme envisaged recurrent education primarily as a means to promote social democracy and guarantee individual freedom of choice. The idea was also taken up by the Swedish Education Commission of 1968 (1969). Although the Commission emphasized the objective of promoting equality of opportunity, it also interpreted recurrent education as a means of solving certain acute problems besetting the system of education at a critical stage in its development.

The concept was subsequently worked out in detail by the OECD and its Centre for Educational Research and Innovation (CERI 1973). The parties involved in this work took the view that the organizing principle for all education should be "lifelong" rather than "front-loaded." The objective of recurrent education was the modification of the educational system so that learning opportunities and access to organized and systematic education would be made available throughout the lifetime of each individual (see *Lifelong and Continuing Education; Lifelong Learning*).

3. Principles of Recurrent Education

The principles and goals of recurrent education as originally advocated by the Organisation of Economic Co-operation and Development (CERI 1975; Bengtsson 1985; Tuijnman 1991) can be described as follows:

(a) Promoting complementarity between learning taking place in schools and learning occurring in other life situations. This implies that degrees and certificates should not be looked upon as an "end result" of an educational career but rather as steps in a process of lifelong education and personal development across the lifespan.

(b) Reviewing the structure and curriculum of compulsory schooling. The view of many proponents of recurrent education was that the final grades of secondary schooling should provide a curriculum giving students a real choice between further study and work. Curricula and teaching methods should moreover be worked out in cooperation with the different parties involved, for example, students, teachers, and school administrators, and be adapted to the interests and needs of different groups.

(c) Coordinating educational policy with public policy generally and with labor market policy in particular.

(d) Introducing compensatory education at the primary, secondary, and upper-secondary school level.

(e) Increasing the participation of adults in higher education by "opening up" adults' opportunities for learning in traditional educational institutions, including universities.

(f) Extending the provision of planned adult education to a wider audience. The distribution of facilities should be so as to make education available to all individuals, as far as possible wherever and whenever they need it.

(g) Acknowledging the value of credits gained through nontraditional educational routes. It was considered that work and other relevant experience should be seen as conferring instrumental qualifications in their own right and hence should form part of admission requirements.

(h) Abolishing "terminal stages" in the system of formal education, so that all tracks will lead into other programs. This refers to the principle that access to postcompulsory education should be guaranteed to each individual at appropriate moments in life.

(i) Alternating education and work at the level of upper-secondary school as well as university and the workplace. The principle was stressed that it should be possible to pursue any career in an intermittent way, alternating work, study, leisure, and other personal projects such as childrearing. Thus, on completion of compulsory schooling, each individual should be given the right to maternity and study leave, which also implied that the necessary provisions for maintaining both job and social security should be set up.

4. Recurrent and Lifelong Education

Recurrent education had much in common with the concept of *education permanente* advanced by the Council of Europe (Schwartz and De Blignières 1978) and lifelong education proposed by UNESCO in a seminal report entitled *Learning to Be* (Faure et al. 1972). These notions were accepted as representing policy objectives rather than concrete educational policies. They paid tribute to the conviction that access to educational opportunities should not be confined to the individual's early years but be available over the whole lifespan. Despite this basic similarity there were also important differences (see *Lifelong and Continuing Education*).

The concept of recurrent education, as envisaged by the OECD in the 1970s, was in a sense more limited in scope and more utilitarian than lifelong education. It emphasized the correspondence between education and work, and the interdependence of educational policy, labor market policy, social policy, and economic policy. Recurrent education moreover implied instances of interruption in the lifelong process of education, as it advocated the idea that education should be spaced cyclically and in alternation with other activities. Whereas lifelong education and *education permanente* emphasized holistic and humanistic ideals, recurrent education seemed to offer more scope for actual implementation, mainly because it was expected that governments, employers, and other responsible parties would be more easily persuaded to finance the more limited provision of educational opportunities. It is important to mention that recurrent education was from the outset regarded as a planning strategy for the introduction of lifelong education. Thus the proponents of recurrent education did not advance the concept as being fundamentally distinct from or opposed to lifelong education. There was a difference in focus, however, in that the former was interpreted as being concerned mainly with postsecondary education, whereas lifelong education was considered to comprise the entire system from preprimary to adult education. This distinction was impractical, however, and differences in the vocational and skill orientation of the two approaches were later targeted as the main classification principle (Ryba and Holmes 1973).

Models of lifelong education have tended to emphasize the extension of educational provision into adult life as a basic human right, whereas models of recurrent education have paid more attention to the degree of correspondence among the goals and functions of education and work. The notion of recurrent education is based on the view that educational opportunities should be spread out over people's life careers, alternating principally with work, and as an alternative to the lengthening of the period of schooling early in life. In contrast, lifelong education has implied neither a delay or shortening of some part of initial education, nor made the alternation principle central to the definition (Tuijnman 1991).

5. Recurrent Education as a Planning Strategy

Recurrent education was originally seen as an instrument of macroeconomic policy. The concept carried the hallmark of functionalist thinking concerning the consequences of modernization for the relationship between labor markets and educational systems. Recurrent education presented an attractive means of strengthening the degree of correspondence between education and work, managing trade-offs between equity and efficiency, and solving either actual or anticipated problems obstructing progress in rapidly developing economies. Important among these were the expected explosion of enrollment in uppersecondary and higher education and perceived imbalances between labor supply and demand. Educational planners anticipated a shortage of professionals and skilled middle-level technicians and an oversupply of young adults whose schooling was believed to be deficient in vocational training (Coombs 1968). Hence recurrent education was looked upon as a means of checking the pressure of numbers in university-type higher education, expanding vocational programs, and above all, of supplying labor markets with the skilled workforce required to sustain economic growth and, in the Swedish context, full employment.

It was recognized at the outset that the realization of recurrent education would depend on the implementation of supportive policies outside the traditional area of formal education. Rehn (1974, 1983) proposed a comprehensive model for influencing the allocation of time for work and nonwork that could be integrated into labor market policies, especially policy for matching labor supply and demand, alleviating the unemployment–inflation dilemma, enhancing labor quality, and promoting labor productivity. In a

system of drawing rights, every citizen would have a personal account—as in the case of a retirement pension insurance system—registering year by year how many funds are credited. Whereas in a pension scheme these funds have very limited applicability, in a drawing rights system the individual would be able to exercise a right to draw money on one's account for personal income maintenance during periods of voluntary or age-determined nonwork, for example, for the financing of youth education, adult studies, vacation, temporary or old-age retirement, and other nonwork pursuits for which income maintenance is a requirement.

Paid educational leave was another strategy, dependent on supportive policies, that drew attention to the principle of alternating education and work (see *Financing Lifelong Learning; Paid Educational Leave and Collective Bargaining; Payroll Levies*). Even though ideas such as the drawing rights proposal and paid educational leave were politically controversial, recurrent education did not necessarily imply a radical break with the past. This aspect is brought clearly into the open in the seminal study, *Recurrent Education: A Strategy for Lifelong Education*, as follows:

> Yet, however strong the case for recurrent education may be, it would be naive to seek or expect a major reversal of educational policy. Education is too sensitive and complex a system to respond to surgery. Recurrent education is to be looked upon as a framework for a major but gradual reorientation of policy towards new objectives rather than as an immediate, radical change. (CERI 1973 pp. 5–6)

In line with the above is the conviction that there is hardly a point at which one can firmly state that a given system has turned into a system of recurrent education. Although many of the changes that have been introduced in educational systems in recent years carry characteristics of recurrent education, they nevertheless have to be seen as sequential developments. Even if the adoption of recurrent education as a principle for planning can be made at a single determinable moment, its implementation consists of a series of measures whose cumulative effect will give the appearance of a recurrent education system only over an extended period of time.

Many policymakers and others with an interest in the implementation of recurrent education in the 1970s were aware of the fact that pervading reforms could not be realized overnight. The OECD publication on recurrent education (CERI 1973) already recognized this. It made a distinction between short-term priorities for the general development of educational systems and long-term policy for the implementation of recurrent education. It was thus acknowledged at the outset that the development of recurrent education, since it involved thorough changes not only in education but also in other areas of public policy, would be a slow and time-consuming process (see *Demand, Supply, and Finance of Adult Education; Market Concepts in Provision*).

6. Obstacles to Implementation

Recurrent education was advocated at a time when much of the optimism about the possibility of "front-loaded" education achieving a fair and equitable society had begun to erode. In several OECD countries the emphasis had gradually shifted from formal schooling to vocational education and adult learning. This orientation implied that organized and systematic procedures for the facilitation of learning in adult life needed to be established. However, whereas several countries had expressed an interest in recurrent education in the 1970s, very few members of the OECD group had ventured to any significant extent into the policy domains which were implicated (Blaug 1985). The gap between verbal adherence and the lack of policy action can be explained in several ways.

The gap can of course be seen as a result of the long-term character of a recurrent education strategy. Another position is that national diversity in conceptions and approaches resulted in a more piecemeal and ad hoc approach than the unified and demanding one suggested by the initial formulation of the strategy. The following factors may also have played a role:

(a) the inadequacy of conventional mechanisms for the financing of adult education in general and student aid in particular (see *Financing Lifelong Learning*);

(b) the skepticism of some political parties toward further rises in public expenditure on education (see *Costs of Adult Education and Training*);

(c) high unemployment especially among young adults (see *Overeducation; Market Failure in Adult Education and Training*);

(d) limited access opportunities to programs of study offered in universities and other institutions of higher education (see *Adult Tertiary Education; University Adult Education*);

(e) insufficient legislation, particularly with respect to the rules regulating the right to educational leave and income maintenance during a period of study (see *Legislation in Adult Education*);

(f) structural obstacles to policy coordination arising from diversification and diffusion of responsibility in the postcompulsory sector of education (see *Market Concepts in Provision*).

It can be concluded that the implementation of recurrent education depends on a variety of factors. As a strategy for redistributing educational opportunities and resources over the whole lifespan of individuals, recurrent education is directly dependent on the social and economic factors that determine the functioning of labor markets, the conditions of work, and the time that people can allocate to family, leisure activities, and education (see *Time, Leisure and Adult Education*). Moreover, recurrent education cannot be solely interpreted in terms of educational policy. It extends into areas of social and economic policy, and its main objectives mirror this breadth in purpose.

7. Criticisms of Recurrent Education

It may be concluded that the failure to implement recurrent education in the 1970s was to an extent caused by a situation in which important prerequisites for a thorough change in education could not be met. In response to economic conditions of austerity, demographic change, and new political priorities, the usefulness of recurrent education was increasingly called into doubt. In spite of appealing arguments favoring recurrent education, several major criticisms were raised against it.

At the core of the first criticism was the idea that recurrent education could well have negative repercussions on efforts to achieve social equality. These negatives effects could occur if selection procedures discriminated against the participation in recurrent education of certain groups in society, for example, immigrants or unskilled workers. In this case recurrent education could lead to a widening of the gap between the initially well-educated and poorly educated people in a society. The closeness of the link between recurrent education and policies for labor market intervention and adjustment may put recurrent education policy in danger of (unintentionally) endorsing ascription in the allocation of individuals to positions in the social, economic, and political "space" of a society (see *Economics of Adult Education and Training*).

Although recurrent education implied a break with the "quasi-monopoly" of education exercised by the school (Ryba and Holmes 1973), it did not originate in the radical, widespread criticisms of the school as a social and educational institution, which were advocated in the early 1970s (Goodman 1971). From the "deschooling" perspective recurrent education was criticized not only for its alleged neglect of a perspective on individual development, but also because it was interpreted as a strategy for steering gradual, organizational change in education without questioning the basic functions of schooling in a society. Hence it was feared in some quarters that recurrent education would provide legitimacy for conventional practices of education and, by limiting the scope of reform to minor innovations in the prevailing system, would endorse the critical role of early formal education in the perpetuation of social and economic inequality among individuals and groups.

A third criticism of recurrent education did not challenge the rationale for redistributing learning opportunities across the lifespan, but instead questioned the timing of labor market entrance, the nature and frequency of alternation between education and work, and, particularly, the feasibility and adequacy of postponement policy.

8. The Postponement Principle

Central to the original idea of recurrent education was the delay of one or several components of upper-secondary and higher education until a certain mature age was reached, so that educational careers would be motivated by actual experience of work, realistic self-assessment, and informed occupational choices. The postponement of a part of initial formal education was considered essential in a strategy which aimed to enhance the efficiency and flexibility of the connection between education and work, and safeguard free choice. However, it also provided a means, implicitly at least, to control overeducation while increasing the supply of middle-level workers. As a strategy of diversion (Murray 1988), conceived to contain and redirect excessive individual demand for higher education, postponement policy was advantageous, not least for educational planners, budget controllers, and politicians.

Postponement policy was also criticized because the benefits, especially the private benefits, were in doubt. As a result, postponement policies were not matched by the appropriate incentives for individuals to forego conventional patterns of education for those of recurrent education (Levin and Schütze 1983). Instead of explicitly pursuing a policy of postponement, which would be seen by many young people as a deliberate attempt to thwart their aspirations for higher education, policymakers generally opted for less drastic ways of reducing public demand for continuing formal education. Thus, for ideological as well as more practical reasons, the postponement aspect of recurrent education has gradually lost some its policy relevance. This development was reinforced by falling school enrollments as a consequence of a declining birthrate, renewed emphasis on human capital as a crucial factor in the production of goods and services, and, in some countries, a reduced or otherwise modest transition rate of young students to university-type higher education. Instead of delaying a part of formal education until a mature age, policymakers have stressed the importance of developing alternation education and apprenticeships.

9. The Alternation Principle

In documents published by the OECD, the term "alternation education" has been used to denote the systematic inclusion in the educational program of periods of work outside the institution. The principal aim of alternation education is to improve the transition from school to work by bringing both upper-secondary and higher education into a functional relationship with the labor market, for example, by introducing vocational elements in the syllabuses and by including periods of practical work outside the educational institution. It follows that alternation education can be regarded as a partial strategy within the wider context of recurrent education.

Many school leavers were seen as being inadequately prepared for the labor market, and the first jobs young people got no longer formed part of an established career path. The interest in recurrent or alternation education for the 16- to 19-year olds has to be considered in this context. Interest in alternation education, for example, in the form of trainee apprenticeships, derives from a certain skepticism vis-à-vis the measures against youth unemployment that were implemented in various countries since the mid-1970s.

The educational strategies for helping young people who face problems in finding jobs and who have rejected the option of staying on in school have been insufficient and unclear. They have been mainly of three kinds. The first involved the offering of guidance and counseling services for students. A second response has been to strengthen the vocational component of upper-secondary schooling. Offering vocational preparation may not suffice, however, because many young people are tired of school. They may also consider it risky to choose a vocational course because of the danger of being tied to a particular occupation too early in life. The third approach was to encourage young adults to stay on at school. However, a policy of using the educational system as a mechanism for keeping young people out of squeezed labor markets may be indefensible in a long-term perspective.

Alternation education forms an important complement to the measures mentioned above. The main thrust of the proposal was the principle of alternating and combining education and work. Such a flexible approach would be beneficial to youth aged 16 to 19 years, who opt for some form of upper-secondary education, but who for some reason prefer a less rigid and traditional form of education at this level, for example, a study program that would make it possible to accept work on a part-time basis in alternation with schooling. Another target group for alternation education would comprise youth who left school when it was no longer compulsory, but who after some years of varied labor market experience, often including spells of unemployment, would be willing to return to school or to undertake adult education or training.

Whereas postponement policy was regarded by many critics as contrary to the need of society and the individual, the value of the alternation aspect of recurrent education was not called into doubt. The belief in the usefulness of this strategy in facilitating new relationships between school and work is based on a number of assumptions. For example, the inclusion in the syllabuses of periods of work outside the educational institution is thought to have desirable effects on the students' attitudes toward both education and work. Second, it is argued that the youth who have had some work experience tend to be more realistic about their educational and occupational expectations compared with those who left the educational system without such experience. Thus it is assumed that alternation education increases the internal and external efficiency of school systems, since the content of provision can be aligned with the preferences of students and especially of local employers. Because alternation education relies heavily on local conditions with respect to the supply of trainee places and apprenticeships, it has the advantage of increasing the flow of information from students to employers and vice versa and, accordingly, improving job matching (see *Economics of Adult Education and Training*).

In summing up this section it can be concluded that the principle of alternation education has had some impact in certain countries. In Germany and the Netherlands, for example, alternation education is now accepted as a matter of course. Yet in the majority of OECD countries the impact has mostly been limited. The reasons for this are manifold, ranging from a traditional social demand for education which reinforces, rightly or wrongly, the view that the best guarantee of success in life career is to stay in education as long as possible; to the concrete problem of how to organize alternation education, in particular, how to find trainee places for youth. Another factor may be that, in some countries, the central authorities themselves have been reluctant to develop alternation education because it would limit the scope of their involvement in education.

10. The Impact of Recurrent Education

The relevance of recurrent education for educating and training the 16- to 19-year olds is emphasized above. But recurrent education is not just concerned with these early years. It emphasizes the interaction of education and work across the whole lifespan. In this perspective change toward recurrent education has been less marked. Yet whereas recurrent education may be considered to have failed with respect to policies such as the postponement of a certain component of formal education until a time late in an individual's life career, the central idea of recurrent education, namely, the development of organized procedures for the facilitation of systematic learning in adult life, has had an impact on educational systems in many industrialized countries.

Though reality may appear bleak compared with the grand visions painted in some of the plans originally formulated, stocktaking by the early 1990s showed that progress toward recurrent education has nevertheless occurred. Noteworthy developments are, first, that the demand for adult education has markedly increased and, second, that public commitment to recurrent education and especially training has increased. Third, both public and private provision have expanded in innovative ways in response to increased demand and commitment, although the increase in total expenditure on adult education during the 1980s was mainly accounted for by private investment. In conclusion, the statistics collected in some industrialized countries bear witness to an increased commitment to recurrent education of a vocational type (see *Evaluation of Industry Training: Cost-Effectiveness; Evaluation of Public Training: Cost-Effectiveness; Statistics of Employee Training*). The rapid advance in the participation of workers in employer-sponsored training has a parallel in the growth of liberal adult education in countries such as Japan and Canada. As a result, many women and men are now being exposed to systematic learning experience in the years following their exit from the system of initial education. Despite the relative lack of support from public authorities, adult education has both broadened and expanded and, as a result, is no longer serving a small minority but a large portion of national populations.

11. Scenarios for Educational Development

A publication in the mid-1970s envisaged four possible futures for recurrent education, that took the form of a guide to policy development (CERI 1977):

(a) to let it evolve, as in the past, in a spontaneous and sporadic fashion without reference to any explicit public intervention;

(b) to strengthen and coordinate the existing range of activities but not to perceive it as an active instrument of public policy in the social and economic arenas;

(c) to strengthen and coordinate the existing range of activities while simultaneously pursuing a positive policy of support for specific activities judged to be national priorities, for example, secondary education equivalency programs designed to promote equality;

(d) to create a comprehensive service of adult education as an integral element of broadly conceived educational systems and to relate its functions to the social, economic, and cultural objectives of the nation.

The OECD report also noted that most industrialized countries were pursuing (c), with only a few countries moving in the direction of (d). It is therefore not surprising that, fifteen years later, Lowe (1992) observed that little progress has been made toward realizing objective (d). In fact, some regression had occurred, and the priorities of countries were shifting to the development of a new strategy involving private provision and a diminished role of governments, defined as one of selectively stimulating development as well as monitoring relevant trends (see *Market Concepts in Provision*).

In retrospect it can be noted that many industrialized countries have pursued a policy of encouraging employers and individuals to share the costs of vocationally oriented recurrent education, while at the same time localizing responsibility for the supply of formal adult education of a liberal type. Another conclusion is that, although many policymakers seem to agree that initial and postinitial education cannot be completely separated, the policy originally implied by the strategy of recurrent education, namely, that adult education and continuing vocational training should be integrated with the system offering formal education, has so far had only a modest impact on practice.

12. Trends Relevant to Recurrent Education

As indicated above, policymakers around the world have generally accepted recurrent education as a principle for the guidance of educational development—yet in most countries implementation has so far been of a piecemeal character. It is therefore not unduly cynical to pose the question as to what would be the relevance of recurrent education in the context of current needs and challenges in the making. Since recurrent education is best seen as a long-term strategy, and one in its formative stage, it is important to examine macroeconomic and social trends, anticipate how they might influence the evolution of educational development, and speculate about the ways in which education and training can contribute. Bengtsson and Wurzburg (1992) and Tuijnman (1992) discuss several "cardinal issues" with "major implications" for recurrent education. Among these are demographic trends, new technology, international trade competition, and the emergence of market models relying on private initiative to match provision to demand.

In comparing the situation of the 1990s with that characterizing the developed countries at the time when recurrent education was first formulated as a major policy strategy in the late 1960s, one is struck by both stability and change. Perhaps the most remarkable aspect of stability is that the traditional education–work–retirement pattern is still dominant. Yet there is also change, for example, with respect to the increased, and still rising, numbers of women who work or seek paid work, the aging of the population, and the fact that people live longer, thus prolonging the period of retirement. Also other demographic trends call for the extension of learning opportunities in adult life. Since new entrants typically make up only a very small percentage of the labor force in Western industrialized countries, adults will have to feature prominently in a strategy for skill formation. These trends raise the question as to how work and nonwork

time may be efficiently and agreeably distributed over the lifespan of individuals. Education is only one among several institutitions that will have to respond in a creative way to the implied challenge.

A second aspect is that many governments have become very concerned with the question whether front-end educational systems are adequately equipped to meet increasing international trade competition and the challenges posed by technological development (see *Technological Change and Education*). This concern was fueled in the 1980s by the apparent paradox that economies were growing fast without a markedly reduced level of unemployment. The fact that new technology, especially microelectronics, has had only a relatively small impact on productivity and employment growth is explained by some economists as a result of the failure to match new technology with the necessary innovation at the workplace and increase the skills required of the labor force. It is moreover stressed that the economic potential of technology cannot be fully realized without concomitant, even anticipatory, social and institutional changes, of which those bearing on recurrent education are particularly crucial.

Third, there is evidence indicating that the economic value of recurrent education has vastly increased. Even if recurrent education had real inherent economic value during the 1970s, its perceived economic value grew enormously in the 1980s. The idea that recurrent education represented not only a consumptive good but also an investment yielding economic value over time, which had been persistently argued by advocates of the strategy in the early 1970s, was finally acknowledged. The circle of stakeholders in recurrent education has broadened beyond the usual providers and consumers of adult education, and includes employers and workers, trade unions, and national governments and international bodies with portfolios ranging from education to labor market, industrial, trade, and general economic policy. Thus the idea advanced since the early days of recurrent education, that it should be seen as a strategy involving a broad array of policies, is now beginning to take hold.

Finally, concomitantly with its increased economic significance during the 1980s, recurrent education is also becoming a crucial determinant of employment, life career, and lifetime earnings. Hence questions of provision and equal access, and of the social distribution of costs and benefits, are gaining in importance. As a consequence, there is a lot of interest in the workplace as an environment for learning (see *Learning in the Workplace*).

The conclusion is that recurrent education—and varieties going under labels such as continuing education and further education and training—has assumed vastly greater visibility and importance in industrialized countries during the 1980s, mainly on the strength of a new appreciation of its potential economic consequences. Yet, though its importance as an educational and economic activity is recognized in the early 1990s, recurrent education remains structurally weak. An important reason for this is the mixture of public authority, voluntary organization, and private provision, as well as the heterogeneous learning needs to which provision is responding. This raises some interesting questions concerning the scenarios for change and development in the 1990s and beyond.

13. Conclusion

The difficulty of implementing a sweeping change in education in a context of stagnating government revenues and increasing competition for funds among the sectors of public policy led to some disillusionment with recurrent education in the late 1970s and early 1980s. However, since then, some progress has been made. Given that the trends mentioned above have stupendous implications for the relationship between education and work, it can be hypothesized that in future an increasing number of countries will follow the examples of Sweden and Norway and, more recently, Japan and Canada, and search for ways to increase coherence in lifelong education, and to create a comprehensive service by imposing some structure on the variety of often ad hoc approaches existing at present. Recurrent education as constituting a strategy for long-term planning and development may therefore be relevant in the 1990s and beyond.

References

Bengtsson J 1985 Recurrent education. In: Husén T, Postlethwaite T N (eds.) 1985 *The International Encyclopedia of Education*, 1st edn. Pergamon Press, Oxford

Bengtsson J, Wurzburg G 1992 Effectiveness research: Merely interesting, or actually relevant? *Int. J. Educ. Res.* 17(6): 527–35

Blaug M 1985 Where are we now in the economics of education? *Econ. Educ. Rev.* 4(1): 17–28

Centre for Educational Research and Innovation (CERI) 1973 *Recurrent Education: A Strategy for Lifelong Learning.* OECD, Paris

Centre for Educational Research and Innovation (CERI) 1975 *Recurrent Education: Trends and Issues.* OECD, Paris

Centre for Educational Research and Innovation (CERI) 1977 *Comprehensive Policies for Adult Education.* OECD, Paris

Coombs P H 1968 *The World Educational Crisis: A Systems Analysis.* Oxford University Press, New York

Faure E et al. 1972 *Learning to Be: The World of Education Today and Tomorrow.* UNESCO, Paris

Goodman P 1971 *Compulsory Miseducation.* Penguin, Harmondsworth

Levin H M, Schütze H G (eds.) 1983 *Financing Recurrent Education: Strategies for Improving Employment, Job Opportunities and Productivity.* Sage Publications, London

Lowe J 1992 Public intervention in adult education. In: Tuijnman A C, van der Kamp M (eds.) 1992 *Learning Across the Lifespan: Theories, Research, Policies.* Pergamon Press, Oxford

Murray M 1988 *Utbildningsexpansion, jämlikhet och avläankning.* Göteborg Studies in Educational Sciences 66, University of Göteborg, Göteborg

Rehn G 1974 Towards flexibility in working life. In: Mushkin S J (ed.) 1974 *Recurrent Education.* National Institute of Education, US Department of Health, Education and Welfare, Washington, DC

Rehn G 1983 Individual drawing rights. In: Levin H M, Schütze H G (eds.) 1983

Ryba R, Holmes B (eds.) 1973 *Recurrent Education—Concepts and Policies for Lifelong Education.* The Comparative Education Society in Europe, London

Schwartz B, De Blignières A 1978 *Final Report of the Steering Group on Permanent Education.* Council for Cultural Cooperation, Council of Europe, Strasbourg

Tuijnman A 1991 Emerging systems of recurrent education. *Prospects* 21(77): 17–24

Tuijnman A 1992 The expansion of adult education and training in Europe: Trends and issues. *Int. Rev. Educ.* 38(6): 673–92

Further Reading

Blaug M, Mace J 1977 Recurrent education—The new Jerusalem? *Higher Educ.* 6(3): 277–99

Centre for Educational Research and Innovation (CERI) 1978 *Alternation Between Work and Education: A Study of Educational Leave of Absence at Enterprise Level.* OECD, Paris

Kallen D 1979 Recurrent education and lifelong learning: Definitions and distinctions. In: Schuller T, Mcgarry J (eds.) 1979 *World Yearbook of Education: Recurrent Education and Lifelong Learning.* Kogan Page, London

OECD 1992 *Adult Illiteracy and Economic Performance.* OECD, Paris

OECD 1993 *Industry Training in Australia, Sweden, and the United States.* OECD, Paris

(c) Disciplinary Orientations

Adult Education: Disciplinary Orientations

K. Rubenson

To give a representative picture of the disciplinary orientations of adult education in the entire world in a brief entry is impossible. Thus the presentation will be limited to some broad observations on the status of adult education theory and research in the various regions of the world.

The first issue to be addressed concerns the discourse on whether or not adult education possesses an authorized and unique map of the territory. The different positions on this issue are related to the historical development of the field of study. The present direction and state of the field of study in the early 1990s are also discussed. Finally, some future directions of adult education research are explored.

1. The Debate over the Disciplinary Nature of Adult Education

Houle (1964) observed:

> There is probably almost as much discussion and disagreement about adult education as a discipline as about its right to be called a profession. If we accept the definition of a discipline in Webster's New Collegiate Dictionary as "a branch of knowledge involving research," adult education would seem to qualify as a discipline. (p. 89)

Houle's standpoint, while representative of North America, is less accepted in some areas of the world. The international literature reflects various and strong views on if and how a unique body of knowledge can be developed in adult education.

Using Premfors' (1987 p. 147) conceptualization of the discussion related to higher education as a field of study, there are three main positions with respect to the role of disciplines:

(a) Disciplines pursue their research in an isolated fashion, utilizing adult education as but one among many imaginable empirical applications. Knowledge cumulates as bits and pieces from the efforts of traditional disciplines.

(b) Disciplinary perspectives are integrated in a way which justifies the characterization of the study of adult education and research as a new discipline. Knowledge cumulates largely through efforts within this new discipline.

(c) Processes (a) and (b) occur—although to a limited extent—simultaneously. A "core" of integrated and interdisciplinary efforts is surrounded by a larger "periphery" of single-discipline contributions. Knowledge grows through both types of process—but also through the interaction between "core" and "periphery". In particular, one would expect traffic from the latter into the former.

Advocates for the first position can hardly be found in adult education circles, but it is often voiced by critics outside the field. However, until recently, there has been an almost total lack of interest from the core disciplines in issues pertaining to adult education. In fact, one can detect a certain lack of scientific curiosity.

The main discussion in adult education has centered around positions (b) and (c). Thus a fundamental discourse within the field is the location of adult education in relation to other disciplines. According to Kranjc (1987 p. 75), adult education research has been organized along three different assumptions of the field: (a) research on and theory of adult education remaining within the boundaries of pedagogy; (b) research into adult education as a meeting point of related disciplines; and (c) formation of a distinct science—andragogy.

Kranjc gives the following description of the three categories. The first model is found in countries where pedagogy has been expanding horizontally. The focus is on adult education as a liaison of the formal system and less attention goes to nonformal and informal adult education as the practice of adult education follows the line established for regular school education. This umbrella model tends to neutralize the political and societal realities and implications of adult education (Mader 1988).

According to Kranjc (1987) the "interdisciplinary" approach (the second category) can give no more than a mosaic of individual details—a mosaic composed of sociological, psychological, or biological problems. Therefore, she contends that: "Comprehensiveness in the study of adult education cannot be achieved in an inter-disciplinary way" (p. 75). Mader (1992a p. 145), analyzing the situation in the former Federal Republic of Germany, concludes that normally the relationship between a science of adult education and other disciplines has been of the import–export type. Within this tradition, the adult education researchers see themselves primarily as representing an established academic discipline (e.g., psychology) and adult education is to them a field of application, and not a guiding paradigm for their research.

Kranjc's third category (the formation of a separate scientific discipline often called "andragogy") stems predominantly from the former Yugoslavia and Poland, but also has followers in the United States, Germany, and the Netherlands (see *Andragogy*).

The argument for andragogy, as it is presented in North America, stems mainly from a micro perspective and rests on assumptions about the characteristics of the learner. The critique against this position within the North American context is that education is a single fundamental human process and that the learning activities of men and women are not essentially different from those of boys and girls (Houle 1972 p. 221). The advocates for a discipline of adult education in Germany, or andragogy in the former Yugoslavia and Poland, or what is called "andragology" in the Netherlands, refer more extensively to the social role of adult education (Hake 1992, Kranjc 1987, Mader 1988).

From a macro perspective, others argue that one cannot separate the process of cultural and social transmission into two separate fields of study. Instead they insist that the two fields are closely related. The process includes not only the transmissions of a tradition from one generation to the next, but also the transmission of knowledge or cultural and social patterns from anyone who "knows" to anyone who does not.

An often debated issue closely related to the second and third category in Kranjc's taxonomy is whether or not to borrow theories, concepts, and results from other fields of study. Jensen (1964), discussing the situation of the United States, suggested that adult education could develop a unique body of knowledge suited to its purposes through two methods: (a) experiences from practice could be used to formulate principles or generalizations, and (b) knowledge which has been developed in other fields of study could be borrowed and reformulated for use in adult education.

In view of Jensen's suggestion it is of interest to note that to an increasing extent, researchers in adult education who publish in the leading United States scholarly journal have come to rely on adult education literature. In 1968, only 20 percent of citations appearing referred to adult education sources. By 1977 this figure had increased to almost 60 percent (Boshier and Pickard 1979). Behind this development is the view that not only is borrowing of little value for adult education, but it is also harmful.

In redefining the discipline of adult education, Boyd and Apps (1980) argue that it would be an error to seek assistance from recognized disciplines before the field of adult education itself is clearly understood. At the heart of the matter seems to be a fear that by borrowing concepts from other disciplines, those disciplines will come to define adult education.

The attitude toward borrowing from other disciplines is linked to the institutional setting. In countries where there are sufficient "social demand" and resources for a significant number of specialized adult education departments, as in North America, there is a stronger emphasis on (a) increasing their professional status, and (b) legitimating their existence within the university community.

Developments in the former Federal Republic of Germany have partly followed the directions suggested by Jensen. In the 1970s, scholars from different disciplines—psychology, sociology, economics, political science, history, philosophy, and education—who were experienced in various practice fields of education were brought together (e.g., at the University of Bremen). By integrating the various disciplines, the aim was to begin to weave a paradigm (in Kuhn's sense) of adult education research (Mader 1988). As a recent review of German scholarly approaches in adult education shows, it is questionable how far one has come in weaving a new and exclusive paradigm (Mader 1992b).

In the Nordic countries, as in several other countries where the specialization has not gone as far as the United States or Yugoslavia, efforts to "discipline" adult education as a separate field of study are seen as unrealistic and undesirable.

In conclusion, there are strong disagreements among scholars in adult education as to whether adult education is, or rather ought to be, seen as a separate discipline. This controversy is a partial reflection of the historical development of adult education research.

2. Forces Behind the Development of the Disciplinary Orientation of Adult Education

There exists a vast literature on the process of specialization whereby new disciplines and/or fields of studies emerge. Elzinga (1987 p. 19) suggests three main types of innovation through which a new field gets established:

(a) A new discipline develops by virtue of research being focused on a new area (territory) of reality.

(b) A new discipline emerges when an earlier field of research and its territory is seen in a new light (perspective shift).

(c) A new discipline emerges when new types of knowledge and skills need to be developed.

Elzinga's points (a) and (b) are related to the process of differentiation whereby new disciplines and specialties emerge and are established. Internally, this may be seen as the result of new disciplines splitting off from older ones. Point (c) relates to the consequences of socioeconomic demands or political decisions or a combination of these.

Looking at the development of adult education research around the globe, one can detect various patterns of development according to Elzinga's schema. To do a proper comparative study on these developments and how they have come to influence research would be most valuable, but cannot be achieved within the framework of this entry. What follows is therefore limited to some possible interpretations of the development of adult education research and the consequences thereof.

In general, adult education as a specific area has developed as a response to broad socioeconomic demands (see point (c) in Elzinga's schema). In the United States, where universities have had a long tradition of training professionals, graduate programs in adult education were already started in the 1930s. The first was established at the Teachers College of Columbia University in 1930 and the first doctorate awarded in 1935. This program grew out of Edwin L Thorndike's research on adult development and learning, and was set up to respond to the growing need for training of leaders in adult education. Thus, the interesting point is that one can detect the process of differentiation behind the start of the first program, as well as the impact of social forces on research. Soon after, programs were established at other universities. The major growth, however, came in the late 1950s and early 1960s. With the exception of the first program at Columbia, there does not seem to have been any link to the discovery and development of knowledge in related areas of research. Instead, the training of professionals has been the driving force (see *Training of Adult Educators*).

Western Europe shows a mixed pattern. Compared to the United States, research in adult education is a rather recent phenomenon in Western Europe. This can be mainly explained by two circumstances. First, European universities have traditionally been less responsive to social pressure and therefore paid less attention to the training of professionals than their United States counterparts. Second, the providers of adult education, often connected to a popular movement, have been suspicious of the universities and the elitist ethos that they portray. In order to preserve the nature of a social movement, they have rebelled against the professionalization of adult education (Titmus 1985).

The situation changed in the late 1960s and since then there has been a growing involvement in research. The underlying pressure, although in some instances expressed differently than in the United States, has been the need for knowledge to train the practitioner. In the former Federal Republic of Germany, where the first formal degree program in adult education was established in 1969, the typical popular educator by calling or as a hobby vanished and was replaced by a professionalized full-time adult educator (Peters 1992). This process was closely linked to the policy of the welfare state which made adult education an essential part of its intervention area (Thomssen in Mader 1992b). There are some exceptions to this general trend that are worth noting as the differences affected the direction of research. For example, the initation in Finland of a research chair in 1946 was established as an outgrowth of the social sciences. That process, using Elzinga's schema, was one where the new discipline was established by virtue of research being focused on a new area. This direction has, by and large, been maintained in Finland. University-based research has, in comparison with the situation in other countries, focused to a large extent on theory formation and to a lesser degree on the applied issues (see Sect. 3 below).

Sweden is also of interest because the development of research, which is a recent phenomenon, is so visibly linked to adult education becoming a major issue in creating public policy. The underlying processes in Sweden are, as in most countries, external societal forces. However, it was not professionalization, but the need for knowledge connected to broad social policies that led to an explosion in the amount of adult education research being supported.

Despite some fundamental differences between Eastern and Western Europe, there are several similarities in the involvement of adult education as an area of scholarship. Prior to the 1960s, whatever serious writing and publishing were done in adult education were primarily in the areas of theory building and conceptualization based in Marxist–Leninist social theories. These articles had strong elements of ideological arguments (Kulich 1984 p. 127). In Elzinga's terms, this development reflects how major social changes, such as those that occur while building a new morality, affect the direction of research. In the 1960s, there was a rapid expansion. As in Western Europe, research had primarily an instrumental function and was mainly related to problems of vocational education, particularly of supervisors and managers (Kulich 1984, Livećka 1985). It is not clear how the momentous changes in Central and Eastern Europe of the late 1980s will affect the disciplinary orientations of adult education; however, there are no doubts that the changes will be dramatic. The quality and direction of the existing university programs are being seriously questioned and many programs will be closed down or totally altered (Kulich 1994).

The instrumental aspect of adult education research is even more apparent in the developing world where the impetus for research has come from the need to build an infrastructure of adult education.

The degree to which adult education research is a consequence of social demand, rather than a development within a specific discipline, is also reflected in the important role that international and national organizations have played in research. Commonly, research is primarily associated with universities and research institutes. In adult education, the situation is somewhat different. National and international organizations, whose primary roles are to promote the practice of adult education, have played an important role in knowledge creation. Intergovernmental organizations like UNESCO, OECD, and the Council of Europe have indirectly and directly had a profound impact on the systematic scrutiny of the field (see *Comparative Studies: Adult Education; International Adult Education; UNESCO and Adult Education*).

Another international body that has had great importance, especially for comparative research, is the now closed European Centre for Leisure and Education. In addition, nongovernmental bodies have been involved in the study of adult education. Among these are the International Council of Adult Education, the European Bureau of Adult Education, and national umbrella organizations like the Folk High School Association in Germany and the *Institute Nationale d'Education Populaire* in France (see *Nongovernmental Organizations; International Council for Adult Education*).

In summary, the process by which adult education has become a specialized field of study has, with a few exceptions, been linked to the professionalization of adult education. What has occurred is a "scientification" of traditional practitioner vocations which have until recently, managed quite well without a research connection or "basis" in science (Elzinga 1987 p. 7). In some countries, the other major societal force has been the demand for policy-oriented research. This process through which the field has been established has come to direct the drawing of the map.

3. Areas of Research

From the previous description of the development of adult education research, two things are evident. First, the accumulation of knowledge has been based almost solely on efforts to improve the practice of adult education, and second, intradisciplinary concerns have been rare. Jensen (1964 p. 106) reflects the pervasive conception of the territory when he argues that adult education is a practical discipline. Its ultimate goal is to give to adult education practitioners better control

over factors associated with the problems they face. This view, to a large extent, has determined which questions have been regarded as legitimate within the discipline. Knox (1985), reviewing the situation in the United States 20 years after Jensen's commentary, reflects the same ethos when he states: "One major reason for adult education research is to produce findings the practitioner can use to improve practice" (p. 183). Consequently, changes in the practices of adult education can be expected to have consequences for the disciplinary orientation of adult education. This process is very evident in the shift among adult education scholars since the late 1980s toward work-related issues (see Hake 1992, Klasson et al. 1992, Mader 1992b). The emergence of an information economy, where international competitiveness and employability are increasingly being seen as linked to an effective utilization of competencies, learning, and knowledge, has altered the domain of adult education and consequently also the disciplinary orientation. It is interesting to note that the 1992 Nordic Research Conference on Adult Education was totally devoted to the world of work. Although the response differs from country to country, one can find the same stress on practicability and the needs of the field.

Long and Agyekum's (1974) analysis of content of articles from 1964 to 1973 in the United States journal *Adult Education* indicates that the three most frequent areas for research were program planning and administration, instructional materials and methods, and adult learning. Together they represented 55 percent of the articles published in *Adult Education*. Another finding from this study was that these areas of research became more predominant between 1964 and 1973. The continuation of this trend is further established by Lee (1979) and Long (1991). Despite a growing interest in critical theory during the late 1980s, practical matters continue to dominate.

In Canada, the most frequent areas of research were foundations of adult education, adult learning, and administration (Garrison and Baskett 1989). Pantzar (1985), comparing the content of adult education research in the Nordic countries and the Federal Republic of Germany, found a similar pattern (see Table 1).

Table 1 shows that research in the countries investigated was largely concentrated on the teaching–learning process and its results. Pantzar (1985) concluded that what is being researched in adult education has more to do with which institution performs the research project than the country in which the research is done. With the exception of Sweden, the overwhelming proportion of research done within adult education institutes had to do with the teaching activity. To the extent that these were projects on the ideological and theoretical basis of research, they were done mainly within a university setting. However, it should be noted that university-based research, in all countries except Finland, devoted substantially less attention to this element of research than to the two categories more directly related to the practice of adult education.

The fact that a large amount of the research in Sweden and Norway falls within the category of "functional" planning of adult education relates to the tradition in these countries of basing educational reforms on prior official inquiry. The large reforms in adult education in the 1970s gave rise to policy-oriented research focusing on the role of adult education in social change.

Unfortunately, similar studies which cover other parts of the world are not generally available. However, surveys of adult education in other Western European countries (Titmus 1985) and Eastern Europe (Kulich 1994, Livečka 1985) show the same general trends. Without reporting the absolute amount of research in various areas, these studies reveal that there is a continuous concern, often in connection with vocational education, with the methods and techniques of education of adults.

Although there have been underlying themes common to adult education research in nearly all the former socialist European countries, each country has its own national interest (Kulich 1994, Livecka 1985). For example, the overall theme in the former German Democratic Republic has been the development of workers' personal lives, while Hungary paid special attention to adult teaching and learning. In the early 1980s, research into adult education in the former Soviet Union was concentrated in historical, sociological, didactic, economic, and organizational methodological questions. Most of these topics could also be found in the former Yugoslavia, although under the heading of "andragogy." Polish researchers have paid particular attention to nonformal education and self-directed learning (see *Baltic Countries; Europe, Central and Eastern*).

Despite the fact that research in North America and Western Europe is equally instrumental in nature, there are rather obvious epistemological differences. Most obvious is the stronger emphasis on psychologically oriented theories in North America and, in relative terms, the greater preoccupation with social theory in Europe. This difference should be understood in the larger context of social and cultural traditions and the impact of these on research traditions (Popkewitz 1984 p. 6). United States society, with its decentralized political and economic system and individual emphasis on social mobility, promotes a research focus on the individual. The strong emphasis on psychologically oriented theories by North American adult education researchers is in accordance with the dominant tradition in educational research in general. To use Kuhn's concept of paradigm at the metalevel, the tradition within adult education research is part of the dominant *Weltanschauung*. The same is of course true of European research, the only difference being in the *Weltanschauung* that governs the research tradition. However, the Europeans also, to a large extent, include the broader policy level.

The defining of adult education as a practical discipline and the consequences this has had on the

Table 1

The contents of research projects on the basic elements of adult education research, classified by countries, in percentages

Basic elements of adult education research	Country									
	Federal Republic of Germany		Finland		Sweden		Norway		Denmark	
	Univ	Total	Univ	Total	Univ	Total	Univ	Total	Univ	Total
Ideological and theoretical basis of adult education	13	10	41	18	24	13	12	4	13	7
Functional prerequisites and planning of adult education	29	28	12	31	32	44	50	40	48	35
Teaching activity	58	62	47	51	44	43	38	56	39	58
Total percent	100	100	100	100	100	100	100	100	100	100
Number of projects	185	271	12	61	34	86	24	71	31	71

Source: Pantzar 1985 p. 32

direction of research has created an ongoing debate on the quality of the research and the criteria for judging that quality.

4. Quality–Maturity

To judge the quality–maturity of adult education as a field of study is a subjective undertaking and the conclusion depends on the criteria that are used. There are different views of what these ought to be within the adult education community.

One camp promotes the use of traditional scholarly criteria for which the focal point is the contribution to the development of the discipline. The advocates for this position constantly point out that not only does adult education lack theories, but there is also a resistance within large parts of the university community to traditional disciplinary development (Bright 1989, Hake 1992, Mader 1992b).

The general mood among departments of adult education has moved from guarded optimism and growth during the 1970s to increased self-criticism and decline in the late 1980s.

Dickinson and Rusnell (1971) stated that the gradual emergence of a discipline (between 1950 and 1970) of adult education was indicated by, among other things, an increasing number of articles in *Adult Education* classified as empirical research (8 to 44%), interpretive literature reviews (3 to 12%), and historical studies (1 to 8%). Further, they observed a growing sophistication in research methodology. The experimental studies rose from zero to 35 percent and the surveys became less descriptive in character. Long and Agyekum (1974) also pointed to the growing emphasis on research between 1964 and 1973. While the quantity and proportion of descriptive research articles were rather constant, the reviewers found that the quality of the descriptive research had increased from rather loose case-reports and status surveys to more analytical, multivariate, descriptive studies. Together they claim that the quality of descriptive studies has been enhanced by the development of more powerful statistical tests and that more studies have been formulated within a theoretical framework. Thus, the early claim for growing intradisciplinary importance of adult education research was mainly made on the basis of growing empiricism and the use of more advanced statistical methods. The primary focus in these and similar reviews has not been on the conceptualization of essential problems regarding the territory—that is, the development of theories that could give answers to vital questions—but rather has been on the use of more sophisticated methodology. Cross (1981), commenting primarily from a United States perspective, found that although recent articles showed considerably more research emphasis, articles dealing with theory were still rare in adult education.

In the early 1990s, departments of adult education are threatened in several countries. In North America, some programs of adult education have disappeared while others have been amalgamated with other programs. In the Netherlands, the new discipline of andragology, which enjoyed a period of vigorous growth during the 1970s, lost its status as an independent discipline in 1987 (Hake 1992). After 20 years of work establishing a science of adult education within the former Federal Republic of Germany there are serious doubts as to whether or not it has grown out of fragmentation (Mader 1992b). A review of the epistemological debate in adult education among scholars from the United Kingdom showed a consensus of opinion concerning adult education's lack of rigor relative to the views adopted by the conventional disciplines (Bright 1989). However, there were different opinions regarding the relevance of traditional criteria of scholarship for adult education.

As Thomas (1987 p. 57) points out, the creation of departments of adult education, usually at the graduate level, has resulted in an uneasy mixture of technical and "academic" courses, and in a division of faculty members between those preoccupied with conventional scholarship and those concentrating on building a profession. Further, there has been a tension between the dominant university values of scholarship and the direction of the adult education departments. Those within adult education research that promote the traditional scholarly values often have their backgrounds in other disciplines and have entered into adult education through the research of a specific adult education phenomenon. However, a large segment of the faculty members in university departments of adult education have been recruited on grounds of considerable experience within the field. This group questions the narrow definition of traditional scholarship. Their view is that adult education programs ought to be seen as professional schools with a knowledge base different from that which can be found in disciplinary departments. Given the dominant perspective in adult education, one important question becomes the extent to which research done within adult education informs practice.

There is a constant debate on whether or not adult education research is useful. Knox (1985 p. 183) notes that it is frustrating that few research and evaluation reports are read and that many practitioners are unaware of relevant research available to them. Probably the situation is quite similar in other parts of the world. It is interesting to note that a Swedish Royal Committee on educational research found that the research findings were known and used at the policy level, while instructors and administrators were skeptical as to their usefulness (SOU 1980). As mentioned before, it is these latter groups that are seen as the primary receivers of research information in North America. One of the main reasons for the tension between practitioner and the research community could be that many of the problems faced by the former are not research problems.

The dilemma facing adult education is that despite strong emphasis on adult education as a "practical discipline," there are criticisms from two directions. The graduate programs, especially in North America but also in Europe, are threatened by the academic establishment for lack of scholarly sophistication, while at the same time the practitioners are somewhat doubtful of the usefulness of the research.

5. Conclusion

Responding to the double dilemma—criticism from practitioners as well as from the academic community—is a challenge for adult education research. Criticism from practitioners about the lack of relevance has partly to do with false or misleading expectations of what can be achieved through research, that is, the link between research and practice. The basis of the problem lies in the "scientification" of traditional practitioner vocations which, as mentioned above, managed quite well for so long without a research connection. A suggested solution is that more of the responsibility for adult educational development should be given to the various institutions and persons involved in the direct delivery of adult education. These developmental activities ought to take as a point of departure everyday problems facing the practitioner and become an integrated part of the institution's activity (SOU 1980).

The criticism of lack of traditional scholarship poses a threat for specialized centers of adult education (see, e.g., Thomas 1987). Premfors (1987), discussing the situation within higher education, argues against turning the study of higher education into a new integrated discipline on the grounds that the best research in this field is not performed within such permanent or semipermanent settings. Instead he maintains it emanates from reseachers or research groups linked with research environments of a broader kind—traditional departments or institutes encompassing more than the study of higher education and research. The same may very well be true for adult education, with the only differences being that the traditional disciplines have so far paid less attention to adult education than higher education.

The dilemma for the specialized departments of adult education is that, with some exceptions, they are created for the dissemination of knowledge, not the generation of knowledge. Accepting the necessity for professional programs and recognizing the limited attention to intradisciplinary concerns, one solution could be to consciously develop adult education as an interdisciplinary area of study. As Kranjc (1987) has pointed out, this could not be achieved simply by a multidisciplinary approach as this would give no more than a mosaic composed of various disciplines. Instead, true interdisciplinary efforts are needed. Adult education could be described as a "core" of interdisciplinary efforts surrounded by a periphery of single discipline contributions. A chief aim of this strategy is to try to marry the two traditions—adult education as a practical discipline and adult education as a traditional scientific area of inquiry.

See also: Adult Education: Concepts and Principles; Andragogy; Economics of Adult Education and Training; History of Adult Education; Philosophy and Ethics in Adult Education; Political Science and Policy Analysis in Adult Education; Psychology of Adult Education; Sociology of Adult Education; Adult Education Research; Ideologies in Adult Education

References

Boshier R, Pickard L 1979 Citation patterns of articles published in adult education 1968–1977. *Adult Educ.* 30(1): 34–51

Boyd R D, Apps J W (eds.) 1980 *Redefining the Discipline of Adult Education.* Jossey-Bass, San Francisco, California

Bright B P (ed.) 1989 *Theory and Practice in the Study of Adult Education: The Epistemological Debate.* Routledge, London

Cross K P 1981 *Adults as Learners.* Jossey-Bass, San Francisco, California

Dickinson G, Rusnell D 1971 A content analysis of adult education. *Adult Educ.* 21(3): 177–85

Elzinga A 1987 Internal and external regulatives in research and higher educational systems. In: Premfors R (ed.) 1987

Garrison D R, Baskett H K 1989 A survey of adult education research in Canada. *Can. J. Study of Adult Educ.* 3(2): 32–46

Hake B J 1992 Remaking the study of adult education. The relevance of recent developments in the Netherlands to the search for disciplinary identity. *Adult Educ. Q.* 42(2): 63–78

Houle C 1964 The emergence of graduate study in adult education. In: Jensen G, Liveright A A, Hallenbeck W (eds.) 1964 *Adult Education—Outlines of an Emerging Field of University Study.* AEA, Washington, DC

Houle C 1972 *The Design of Education.* Jossey-Bass, San Francisco, California

Jensen G 1964 How adult education borrows and reformulates knowledge of other disciplines. In: Jensen G, Liveright A A, Hallenbeck W (eds.) 1964 *Adult Education—Outlines of an Emerging Field of University Study.* AEA, Washington, DC

Klasson M, Tuomisto J, Wahlgren B (eds.) 1992 *Social Change and Adult Education Research—Adult Education Research in the Nordic Countries 1990/91.* Linköping Studies in Education and Psychology, Linköping

Knox A 1985 Adult education research: United States. In: Husén T, Postlethwaite T N (eds.) 1985 *The International Encyclopedia of Education*, 1st edn. Pergamon Press, Oxford

Kranjc A 1987 Research in adult education: Major areas of theory and inquiry. In: Duke C (ed.) 1987 *Adult Education: International Perspectives from China.* Croom Helm, London

Kulich J 1984 Approaches to theory-building and research in adult education in Eastern Europe. *Int. J. Lifelong Educ.* 3 (2): 127–36

Kulich J 1994 *The Role of Adult Education in the Post-Communist Era. Reconstruction and Restructuring in the Countries of Central and Eastern Europe*

Lee J A 1979 The contribution of graduate research to the body of knowledge in adult education. Paper presented to Graduate Student Section of the AEA (USA) Conference, Boston, Massachusetts, November 5–9

Livećka E 1985 Adult education research: Eastern Europe. In: Husén T, Postlethwaite T N (eds.) 1985 *The International Encyclopedia of Education,* 1st edn. Pergamon Press, Oxford

Long H B, Agyekum S 1974 Adult education 1964–1973: Reflections of a changing discipline. *Adult Educ.* 24(2): 99–120

Long H B 1991 Evolution of a formal knowledge base. In: Peters J M, Jarvis P (eds.) *Adult Education.* Jossey-Bass, San Francisco, California

Mader W M 1988 Adult education within the network of scientific disciplines: A roundabout way toward a paradigm of adult education. *Can. J. Study of Adult Educ.* 2(1): 43–52

Mader W M 1992a Psychology and adult education. In: Mader W M (ed.) 1992b

Mader W M (ed.) 1992b *Adult Education in the Federal Republic of Germany.* Centre for Continuing Education, University of British Columbia, Vancouver

Pantzar E 1985 The contents of adult education research in five countries. *Adult Education in Finland* 22(3): 25–36

Peters R 1992 Adult education as a vocation—lay job or profession? In: Mader W M (ed.) 1992b

Popkewitz T S 1984 *Paradigm & Ideology in Educational Research.* Falmer Press, London

Premfors R 1987 Are some disciplines more relevant than others? In: Premfors R (ed.) 1987 *Disciplinary Perspectives on Higher Education and Research.* Department of Political Science, Report 37. Stockholm University, Stockholm

SOU 1980 *Skolforskning och Skolutveckling,* Vol. 2. Norstedt, Stockholm

Thomas A 1987 Academic adult education. *Can. J. Study of Adult Educ.* 1(1): 51–58

Titmus C J 1985 Adult education research: Western Europe. In: Husén T, Postlethwaite T N (eds.) 1985 *The International Encyclopedia of Education,* 1st edn. Pergamon Press, Oxford

Andragogy

B. Van Gent

The term "andragogy" is used in a variety of ways. To some it is another word for the education of adults, just as "pedagogy" may stand for the education of children. To others the word "andragogy" denotes a specific approach to the teaching of adults that is considered to be essentially different from the teaching of children. To still others the concept of andragogy includes not only adult education but also social work, personnel management, and community organization.

1. Origins of Andragogy

Pedagogy stems from the Greek word *paidagôgia,* a compound of the noun *pais,* genitive case *paidos* (child), and the verb *agein* (to lead or educate). A *paidagôgos* is a leader or educator of children. The German word *Pädagogik* is said to be derived from "*paidagôgikè technè*" (the art of leading or educating children), but this term has not been found in ancient Greek. Theoretically, however, such a term was not impossible, since a construction like "*rhètorikè technè*" (the art of eloquence) was used.

The noun *anèr,* genitive case *andros,* means man or adult, but the ancient Greeks did not use terms like "*andragôgia*" or "*andragôgos.*" The term "*Andragogik*" was probably coined by the German high school teacher Kapp who, in 1833, published a book on the educational views of the Greek philosopher Plato.

Eleven years later, a German pedagogue by the name of Mager used the term "*Sozialpädagogik*" for what was presumably the first time. This latter concept was to play a major role in the Dutch discussion about andragogy.

According to Kapp, Plato's *Pädagogik* was meant to educate the minds of the young through science, their bodies through gymnastics, and their souls through art. *Andragogik* has different goals. Education in science and art is no longer necessary for adults: attention should be given to the improvement of self-knowledge and character formation. The major part of this "education at the mature age," however, should consist of vocational training through philosophical methods and rhetoric (Van Enckevort 1972 p. 20). The ideas of Kapp did not gain wide acceptance. On the contrary, they were heavily critized by his compatriot Herbart, an influential pedagogue, who opposed the education of adults. His opinion was that a child should be educated to become an autonomous personality; once an adult, a human being can only engage in self-education. For Herbart, the entry of andragogues would lead to general dependence and tutelage.

After this attack, the term "*Andragogik*" virtually disappeared from the stage, although some vestiges can be found in, for example, Russia around 1885 (Savicevic 1991). It also saw a modest revival in the first decades of the twentieth century, mainly in Germany. In 1926, the sociologist and adult educator Rosenstock-Huessy made a distinction between *Pädagogik, Andragogik,* and *Demagogik* (Van Enckevort 1972 p. 28). From 1920 till 1922, Rosenstock-Huessy was in charge of the Akademie der Arbeit (Academy of Labour) in Frankfurt-am-Main, a cadre training institute for the German workers' movement. In *Education through Experience* Lindeman, professor at the New York School of Social Work, described, together with Martha Anderson, the activities of the Academy (Anderson and Lindeman 1927). In their report they declared: "Pedagogy is the method by which children are taught. Demagogy is the path by which adults are intellectually betrayed. Andragogy is the true method of adult learning" (Brookfield 1987 p. 27).

In 1951, the Swiss remedial educationalist Hanselmann published his *Andragogik: Wesen, Möglichkeiten, Grenzen der Erwachsenenbildung* (Andragogy: Essence, Possibilities, Limits of Adult Education). In line with his profession, Hanselmann considered andragogy as "in the first place, an allround support of the adult in his pursuit of self-education . . . and in the second place the resuscitation of this pursuit when it has been led astray" (Hanselmann 1951 p. 59). This book was followed in 1957 by Pöggeler's *Einführung in die Andragogik: Grundfragen der Erwachsenenbildung* (Introduction to Andragogy: Basic Questions of Adult Education). Unfortunately, Pöggeler used the term "*Andragogik*" in three different ways. It not only stood for the science and practice of adult education, but also for a specific doctrine in this field (Pöggeler 1957 pp. 7, 14, and 179).

Soon afterwards, words like *andragogie* and *andragogija* were employed in the Netherlands and former Yugoslavia respectively. These examples were followed by many other European countries. The term "andragogy" became popular in the United States after 1970, when Knowles published *The Modern Practice of Adult Education: Andragogy versus Pedagogy.*

2. Varieties of Andragogy

In countries where "pedagogy" has the status of an established expression, "andragogy" is often used to denote the education of adults. In this way, one can avoid the terminological embarrassment of, for instance, "adult pedagogy." The word *agogy,* then, serves as a common denominator for pedagogy and andragogy (Van Gent 1991). Where a more neutral word such as "education" is customary, there seems to be no direct need for another generic term to replace "adult education." Often, however, the term "andragogy" is applied to indicate either a comprehensive field of activities of which adult education only forms a part, or, in sharp contrast, a specific approach to adult education. The first use is the case in the Netherlands, whereas examples of the second application can be found in Germany, the United States, and the United Kingdom.

2.1 Andragogy as a Comprehensive Concept

Dutch educators played a pioneering role as far as the professional training for social and educational work is concerned. A School for Social Work was founded in Amsterdam as early as 1899. Contrary to the use of the term in the Netherlands at present, the notion of "social work" at first not only meant public assistance, but also popular education. The professionals in the emerging fields of social work and adult education sought to establish a science of their own. This was found in "social pedagogy," a developing field in Germany at that time. In the Netherlands itself, social pedagogy was barely subjected to theoretical scrutiny before 1940. Its theoretical basis developed to a large extent after the Second World War, with the advent of the welfare state.

In 1950, Ten Have was appointed to the chair of social pedagogy at the University of Amsterdam. The reintroduction of *Andragogik* by Hanselmann enhanced Ten Have's objections to the use of the term "social pedagogy" when applied to adults. Later, Ten Have proposed three different terms:

(a) *Andragogie* (andragogy) denotes the practice of social and educational work with adults.

(b) *Andragogiek* (andragogic) refers to a normative theory on behalf of the art of social work and adult education. In such a prescriptive theory which is meant to serve as a guideline for practitioners, specific assumptions or statements on the nature of adults, the preferred educational goals, and the best didactic methods should be combined in a systematic manner. In this way, one can distinguish several andragogics for social work or adult education, each based on different normative choices. In the field of social work, for example, social casework can be seen as such an andragogic. Likewise, Pöggeler (1957 p.179) propounded a Roman Catholic *Andragogik* in the field of adult education.

(c) *Andragologie* (andragology) denotes the science (in Greek—*logos*) of adult education (cf. psychology or sociology).

It may be noted that, since these terms are not generally known outside the Netherlands and Germany, the term "andragogy" will, by want of clarification, still have to be used as a generic concept subsuming the specific distinctions discussed.

In 1970, a royal decree authorized the admission of andragogy to the roster of every university in the Netherlands. In the explanatory memorandum, the connection was drawn between andragogy and the fields of social work, personnel management, community organization, and adult education. Soon afterwards, however, the edifice of the Dutch welfare state began to show many fissures. To an increasing extent, professionals working in social work and adult education went their separate ways. Each sought shelter in safer areas that were less threatened by financial cuts. Social work went looking for help from the stronghold of medicine. Adult education moved in the direction of formal primary, secondary, and higher education or vocational training, where the quest for diplomas and certificates is predominant. A new royal decree, issued in 1985 and effective in 1988, deprived andragogy of its status as an autonomous discipline (Van Gent 1991).

2.2 Andragogy as a Specific Approach

In his influential book *The Modern Practice of Adult Education: Andragogy versus Pedagogy*, Knowles (1970) defined andragogy as "the art and science of helping adults learn." This can be considered as an unfortunate use of the term "andragogy" for two reasons. First, the term "andragogy" refers, strictly speaking, not to the art or the science of helping adults learn, but to the practice of teaching adults. Secondly, by using only one term, Knowles, like Pöggeler before, obscures the difference between a normative art and the science of adult education.

The main theme of his book, summarized in the polemic subtitle, caused many controversies, known as the Andragogy–Pedagogy Debate. For Knowles, andragogy was at first premised on a set of four assumptions about adult learning that were in his view very different from the assumptions about child learning on which pedagogy is based. As a person matures:

(a) his or her self-concept moves from a dependent human being towards a self-directing personality;

(b) his or her growing reservoir of experience becomes an increasing resource for learning;

(c) his or her readiness to learn becomes more oriented to the developmental tasks of his or her social roles;

(d) his or her orientation towards learning shifts from subject-centeredness to problem-centeredness (Knowles 1970 p. 39).

Later, Knowles conceded that andragogy and pedagogy were not antithetical models, one for adults and the other one for children. In many circumstances, the andragogical model could be applied to children and vice versa. Nevertheless, he still described pedagogy as a content model, which is associated with traditional learning, based on the teacher's direction, transmission techniques, and prescribed subject matter, whereas he considers andragogy to be a new approach, in which the teacher is primarily a facilitator of the learning process. Confusingly enough, the pedagogical model remains for Knowles an ideological model which excludes the andragogical assumptions, while the andragogical model is not considered to be an ideology, but "a system of assumptions which includes the pedagogical assumptions" (Knowles 1990 p. 64). In many ways, however, Knowles himself pays tribute to the normative positions of the humanistic psychology of Maslow and Rogers, in which the social context is conspiciously absent. His conception of andragogy is, in fact, a good example of a prescriptive and humanistic andragogic in the Dutch sense of the word. In the same way, Mezirow's "Charter for Andragogy" can be considered as a critical andragogic based, as it is, on the "critical theory" of the Frankfurt School and the more recent publications of Habermas (Mezirow 1983), just as the Nottingham Andragogy Group in the United Kingdom developed a dialectic andragogic that was inspired by the theories of Riegel and Freire (Allman 1983).

3. Phases of Andragogy

Several schemes have been developed for the art of teaching adults. The so-called "andragogical cycle," which was developed during the 1950s and 1960s in many European countries, consists of five different phases:

(a) the assessment of educational needs;

(b) the definition of goals;

(c) the planning of content and of didactic methods;

(d) the implementation of the program;

(e) the evaluation of the process and the outcomes (Krajnc 1989, Van Gent 1991).

A single adult educator or several specialists may carry out these different tasks. In both cases, this can be done with or without the active involvement of the learner in each of the various stages. The andragogical model proposed by Knowles is an example of the latter version and involves seven elements:

(a) establishing a climate conducive to learning;

(b) creating a mechanism for mutual planning;

(c) diagnosing the needs for learning;

(d) formulating program objectives;

(e) designing a pattern of learning experiences;

(f) conducting these experiences with suitable techniques and materials;

(g) evaluating the learning outcomes and rediagnosing learning needs (Knowles 1990).

These cycles are, of course, not characteristic for andragogy only. They can all be seen as more or less directive and nondirective variations on the basic scheme of rational planning: diagnosis, goal setting, strategy plotting, implementation, and evaluation (Van Gent 1991).

4. Future of Andragogy

The rise of andragogy has to be considered in the context of a process of professionalization within the field of adult education. A profession can be distinguished from other occupations by several features. Its members belong to an association that sets standards for their occupational competence and tries to protect their field of expertise against invasion by other professions. The know-how required is complex and can only be mastered after thorough training. In addition, the professional activities must be guided by a code of ethics. Fundamental, then, to the process of professionalization is the creation of a body of scientific and ethical knowledge fit to serve as material for research and study at an institute for higher education.

Professionalization cannot derive only from the sheer ambition of practitioners and academics, who for many reasons seek a territory of their own and the improvement of their standing. It should always be seen within the specific historical, cultural, economic, and political context of a particular society.

The Dutch interpretation of the word "andragogy" as a concept that covers a wide range of activities was apparently not successful. During a period of economic hardship, the dividing lines between social work and adult education became all too clear. Andragogy as it was propagated by Knowles in the form of a specific doctrine to guide practitioners, suffers from the fact that social conditions and cultural trends are subject to rapid change. The rise of critical theory as a new paradigm for adult education, first in Europe and later in the United States, makes this clear.

If the word "andragogy" has any future, it can only be in the form of a generic term for adult education and as a complement to pedagogy. A distinction between pedagogy and andragogy should not be derived from an identification of the first with tradition and content, and of the second with progress and process. A division of labor between pedagogy and andragogy is primarily connected with "the nature of child and adult and their respective positions in society" (Ten Have 1972 p. 60). A child is on its way to adulthood. The relationships of authority between parents or teachers and children are different from those between educators and adults. In this respect, the contrast between compulsory and voluntary education has also to be taken into account.

The concept of andragogy as a synonym for adult education, however, is not without complication. In a great many countries, the term "adult education" itself covers a wide range of divergent activities such as personal development, formal education, and vocational training.

See also: Adult Education: Concepts and Principles; Adult Education: Disciplinary Orientations; History of Adult Education; Adult Education Research

References

Allman P 1983 The nature and process of adult development. In: Tight M (ed.) 1983 *Education for Adults: Adult Learning and Education*, Vol. 1. Croom Helm, Kent

Anderson M L, Lindeman E C 1927 *Education through Experience*. Workers' Education Bureau, New York

Brookfield S (ed.) 1987 *Learning Democracy: Eduard Lindeman on Adult Education and Social Change*. Croom Helm, London

Hanselmann H 1951 *Andragogik: Wesen, Möglichkeiten, Grenzen der Erwachsenenbildung*. Rotapfel Verlag, Zürich

Knowles M S 1970 *The Modern Practice of Adult Education: Andragogy versus Pedagogy*. Association Press, New York

Knowles M S 1990 *The Adult Learner: A Neglected Species*. Gulf Publishing Company, Houston, Texas

Krajnc A 1989 Andragogy. In: Titmus C J (ed.) 1989 *Lifelong Education for Adults: An International Handbook*. Pergamon Press, Oxford

Mezirow J 1983 A critical theory of adult learning and education. In: Tight M (ed.) 1983 *Education for Adults: Adult Learning and Education*, Vol. 1. Croom Helm, Kent

Pöggeler F 1957 *Einführung in die Andragogik: Grundfragen der Erwachsenenbildung*. Henn Verlag, Rattingen

Savicevic D M 1991 Modern conceptions of andragogy: A European framework. *Stud. Educ. Adults* 23 (2): 179–201

Ten Have T T 1972 Pedagogie en Andragogie in Onderlinge Verhouding. In: Bolleman Th G (ed.) 1972 *Pedagogiek in Ontwikkeling*. Zwijsen, Tilburg

Van Enckevort G 1972 De Lotgevallen van de Term "Andragogie(k)". In: Van Gent B, Ten Have T T (eds.) 1972 *Andragologie*. Samsom, Alphen aan den Rijn

Van Gent B 1991 *Basisboek Andragologie; een Inleiding tot de Studie van het Sociaal en Educatief Werk met Volwassenen*. Boom, Amsterdam

Further Reading

Brookfield S D 1986 *Understanding and Facilitating Adult Learning*. Open University Press, Milton Keynes

Davenport J, Davenport J A 1985 A chronology and analysis of the andragogy debate. *Adult Educ. Q.* 35(3): 152–59

Jarvis P 1983 *Adult and Continuing Education: Theory and Practice*. Routledge, London

Yonge G D 1985 Andragogy and pedagogy: Two ways of accompaniment. *Adult Educ. Q.* 35(3) 160–67

Anthropological Study of Literacy and Numeracy

D. F. Lancy

Anthropology of education describes theories, methodologies, substantive issues, and approaches of diverse fields of study, including anthropology, ethnomethodology, sociolinguistics, and symbolic interaction. The anthropology of education has both action and academic dimensions; some scholars regard education as a subject of basic academic research, whereas others are more committed to bringing about change and improvement through applied research.

Anthropology of education is a relatively new field. Although some textbooks had been prepared (Spindler 1963, Kneller 1965) in the 1960s, educational anthropology hardly existed as an academic subfield prior to 1970 (Roberts 1976, Ogbu 1994). Until that time educational anthropologists were largely reacting to problems of methods and theories in education raised by other social and behavioral scientists, and analytical frameworks were confined to the application of ethnographic concepts and methods to the study of educational processes and institutions (Spindler 1974). The field grew remarkably during the 1970s and 1980s, however, as new theories and analytical frameworks, such as transactional, ecological and communicative models of the educational world, were developed and applied. New, substantive areas of study also emerged. Whereas early studies had focused on continuities and discontinuities in the evolution of education, the sociocultural milieu of schools, and the structure and function of educational institutions, later studies concentrated on cognition, language, and communication as key concepts in the study of the role of education in social and cultural change (Wertsch 1985, Stigler et al. 1991).

Anthropologists have studied many aspects of formal, informal and nonformal education in both developing and industrialized countries, although the focus has been mainly on the education of children (Hansen 1979, Briscoe and Ross 1991). This entry deals with one aspect in particular, namely the anthropological study of literacy and numeracy. This is an area of inquiry that should be of substantive interest to both researchers and practitioners in the field of adult education. Yet, unfortunately, anthropologists have, until recently, contributed little to the growing and very rich body of literature on the *practice* of literacy and numeracy. As Basso (1974) notes: ". . . contemporary anthropologists . . . are of the opinion that the study of writing, though certainly not without intrinsic value, has little relevance to broader problems in [their] field" (p. 426), and the anthropological study of mathematics has been ". . . pursued only to a very limited—and we might say—timid extent" (D'Ambrosio 1985 p. 44). It has been left to cognitive psychologists, linguists, social historians, and others to probe the relationships between culture and literacy/numeracy and this accounts for the use of research techniques, assumptions, and questions which would not be a normal part of the anthropologist's stock-in-trade.

The first section of this entry focuses primarily on literacy at the *societal* level. Next literacy in the *home* as it varies across class and ethnic boundaries is considered. Research on the literacy and numeracy used by people in their everyday lives is then reviewed. Finally, the implications of this research for intervention—in new programs for parents and in classrooms—are examined.

1. Literacy and Numeracy in Culture

Scholars have, for centuries, been drawn to study the origins of writing and mathematics and to theorize about the impact these inventions had on society. Havelock's analysis of the impact of alphabetic literacy on Greek society is one example. Olson (1984), in reviewing this work, argues: "It is now generally agreed that literacy is associated with both a distinctive form of social organization, a *literate society*, and with a distinctive form of thought and talk, a *literate mind* . . ." (p. 185). More specifically, Goody (1987) discusses the vastly expanded information store that writing and numbers make available to people. In fact, postulation on the transformative effects of literacy on individuals and societies has been the inspiration for national literacy campaigns in the Third World (see *Adult Literacy in the Third World*).

However, research suggests that these claims may be overstated. Stock (1983) shows the profound effect that print had on European society as, for example, in the church—issues like sainthood and heresy were increasingly examined in the light of written documents rather than torture, and scapulamancy (a form of divination). But this process took several centuries. Similarly, Reder and Green (1983), in their study of the Seal Bay Eskimo Community, show how conservative society is with respect to the adoption of literacy. While public school instruction in English has been available locally for at least 50 years, levels of academic literacy remain low, because, in this fishing/hunting community, it is of little value. With the growth of a social service bureaucracy, the lure of paid employment provides sufficient incentive to induce some community members to become literate.

Historians have also documented how few individuals could actually read and write in so-called "literate" societies. In a landmark study in Liberia, Scribner and Cole (1981) showed how the cognitive effects of literacy can more appropriately be credited to prolonged exposure to formal education. In a society with an indigenous script but no tradition of school-based literacy, literacy is used to a very limited extent and, consequently, its practice does not confer the sort of general abilities associated with the term "literate mind." Also, Heath (1983), in a comparative study of three distinct, but neighboring, communities in North Carolina, finds that literacy seems to have few of the effects claimed for it.

The sharp distinction between literate and oral cultures is better seen as a gradation from communities where literacy plays a valuable but very limited role to those which are saturated with literacy, where literacy functions not only as a tool but where reading and writing become ends in themselves. This is certainly the case with Heath's (1983) communities and she shows how literacy in culture also includes a complex of beliefs and routines about how adults and children should interact vis-à-vis literacy and connects these patterns to the varied experiences that children and adults from these communities face when they encounter academic literacy.

Heath's three communities of Maintown (middle-class White), Roadville (working-class White), and Tracton, an impoverished (to outsiders, not to the residents themselves) Black neighborhood reflect three points along this gradation. Literacy is present in all three communities but, as she says of the seven uses of literacy in Tracton: "It is significant that these types do not include those uses—critical, esthetic, organizational, and recreational . . . usually highlighted in school-oriented discussions of literacy uses" (Heath 1986 p. 22). A fourth possibility, that of a community in which literacy is absent, is identified in Purcell-Gates's (1994) research. A parallel gradation has been noted in Morocco (Wagner et al. 1986), where the elite are literate in French and send their children to schools where the language of instruction is French, through communities where scribes (*fquih, adil*) are available, for a fee, in the marketplace to perform any and all literacy services for their illiterate clients. In Morocco, there is also a widespread form of literacy primarily for ". . . communication to or about God . . . [which] . . . was a restricted literacy" (Goody 1987 p. 139). That is, individuals laboriously *memorize* lengthy passages in order to "read" the Koran.

2. Literacy in the Home

Taylor (1983) documented literacy practices in six stereotypical "all-American" families: the fathers are all professionals; the mothers are well-educated but working at home; and there are two to three children.

Their lives are permeated by literacy. One passage, in which a mother and her two daughters spend an evening reading and discussing the French edition of *Peter Rabbit* (pp. 82–83), shows the critical role that literacy and literature play in bonding family members. Heath also describes, in Maintown, adult–child interaction pivoting around books or "book-talk." She notes the large libraries of picture books, of bedroom furnishings patterned with literary characters and themes, and the complexity of the bedtime story ritual.

Parent–child interaction in reading has attracted a great deal of attention from scholars. In observing mothers reading to infants, it has been shown that far more than just reading is involved. The mother labels and talks about the pictures, asks her nonverbal child questions about the book *and* she supplies the answer. In middle-class homes, storybook reading is an occasion for knowledge acquisition and for learning about a myriad of language conventions, a process Lancy and his colleagues (Lancy et al. 1989) refer to as an "expansionist" strategy. With somewhat older children, parents ask questions about the text and these have a different structure than those asked about the illustrations (Altwerger et al. 1985).

2.1 Families Where Literacy is More Restricted

Outside the middle-class mainstream the picture is less clear. There is a "restricted" role for literacy in these communities and considerable variation among families within the same community (Goody 1987). Among the Amish, parents stress the importance of becoming literate and do a variety of things to promote early literacy but the goals are different from the cultural mainstream (Hostetler and Huntingon 1972). The family is annoyed if children bring work home from school and they strongly discourage their children from continuing beyond the eighth grade. A wide variety of printed material is in regular use, however, much of it being unique to the Amish. Contariwise, many works—such as paperback novels—found in most homes, are absent. The parents ". . . attempt to carefully control the reading material that enters their home" (Fishman 1990 p. 31). Similar restrictions extend to writing at home and in school. Creative writing, for example, is nonexistent: "not only do community constraints limit the number of appropriate topics and forms an Amish writer may use, but original approaches to or applications of these topics and forms is explicitly discouraged . . ." (p. 37). Similarly, in Roadville, Heath's working-class community, there is much print material in the home but it is used to only a very limited degree.

Newly migrant Mexican–American families also utilize literacy to a limited extent although some do read to their children. Many also tell stories, specifically to enlighten and entertain children. Parent book reading outside the mainstream does not have an "expansionist" quality, they merely read the book

(Allexsaht-Snider 1991) or, at best, engage the child in picture-labeling.

Scholars have also provided a glimpse of homes in which literacy is extremely limited, as in Snow et al.'s (1991) study of working-class families near Boston. Purcell-Gates (1994) describes how even environmental print is invisible in an illiterate Appalachian migrant neighborhood in Cincinnati. When members of this community ask over the phone for directions they request visual cues that do not require reading signs. Familiar with trademarks and logos from television advertisements, they are able to grocery shop without reading labels. There may be books in the home that adults have somehow acquired, but they remain unread.

Communities where literacy is limited and where parents do not introduce children to books tend to be poor, but are not associated with any particular ethnic group nor are they exclusively composed of single-parent households (Teale 1986). Just as certain specific patterns of adult–child verbal interaction are found in societies where literacy is central, contrasting patterns are found where literacy is peripheral. In Tracton, children are not encouraged to ask questions and adults do not "scaffold" children's language acquisition by expanding holophrases; asking known answer questions; and simplifying speech directed to them. This same pattern has been observed widely in non-Western societies without print literacy.

3. The Transition to Reading in School

A large part of the motivation to study the home as a literacy environment comes from research that links aspects of this environment to the classroom. Studies concern ". . . how families participate in reproducing their own literacy, and through this, the literacy of the whole society" (Varenne and McDermott 1986 p. 204). The mainstream preoccupation with providing a rich early literacy experience for children is not recent. As far back as 1800 in Sweden, books were published for parents advising them on the value of such experience. In this Lutheran country in which literacy was a precondition for church participation (indeed one could not marry without first demonstrating literacy), teaching members to read was a family responsibility.

There is ample evidence of a connection between home and school literacy. For example, ". . . children who have been read to during their preschool years possess lexical and syntactic knowledge of sentence-level features typical of written narrative before they begin formal literacy instruction" (Purcell-Gates 1988 p. 129) and ". . . there is a strong . . . relation . . . between children's knowledge of nursery rhymes and the development of their phonological skills . . . [which] children acquire . . . a long time before learning to read . . ." (Maclean et al. 1987 p. 278).

4. Mathematics in Public

While literacy is used to some degree in most families, mathematics is relatively rare even in mainstream homes. No ethnographic study is available, but a survey of middle-and working-class mothers (Saxe et al. 1987) suggests that children are exposed to activities involving number, but less often than literacy-related activities; there is nothing parallel to the "bedtime story"; activities involving number are primarily initiated and structured by children themselves rather than by the parent; and there are social-class differences in the degree and complexity of number activities paralleling the differences in literacy activities between Roadville and Maintown. The paucity of mathematics in the home may account for the fact that scholars who are interested in mathematics have gone into public areas, especially those that involve sales.

Gay and Cole (1967) took as their point of departure for the study of Kpelle (Liberia) mathematics the failure of children to understand the arithmetic they were taught in public school. They noted that the Kpelle have no general system of measurement, no sense of geometry, and little use of number. Arithmetic in the school was not only new to the children, they could see no application of it in the village. However, as Bishop (1988) notes, the Kpelle, as people everywhere, do make use of mathematical *principles*. Men, in particular, accustomed to buying and selling rice, are very good at estimating the number of cups in a bag of rice—the two principal units by which rice is measured. Bishop argues that people invent or borrow mathematical tools as the need arises. The abacus and Incan *quipu* are two fascinating examples. Lancy (1983) found that counting systems varied enormously in complexity and utility in Papua New Guinea as a function of people's need to count and keep track of things, but as money became available and goods and services to spend it on, indigenous systems that were something other than base 10 disappeared from use and were replaced by "more efficient" base 10 counting in English/Pisin.

Practical, everyday mathematics can be contrasted with formal mathematics which is founded on an assumption of "universal" truths. This "Mathematics with a capital M" is also multicultural, drawing on ideas initiated in many different societies (Bishop 1988). It is the rare mathematical tool or system that cannot be accommodated within this all-encompassing mathematics that is also, not coincidentally, the mathematics of science, engineering, commerce, and . . . the public schools. But it is the contrast between everyday practice and the lessons taught in school that have motivated those who study mathematics in culture.

Scribner studied the mathematics imbedded in the role assignments of dairy workers, finding evidence of unique invented strategies for solving problems involving quantity (Scribner and Cole 1981). However, the predominant theme in this literature is that, in everyday practice, people tend to avoid information processing when they can and this includes calculating. Quinn (1978) studied fish sellers in Ghana: "Biriwa sellers probably do not utilize all supply and demand information and do not combine such information to arrive at an overall assessment of market condition because, like all other decision-makers, they avoid complex calculations" (p. 274).

Mathematics avoidance is not just characteristic of unschooled individuals. Lave (1988) and her students followed middle-class adults around a supermarket as they shopped for their families. Only 16 percent of purchases involved calculations of some kind. Indeed people used mathematics only in situations of high confidence. On those occasions when shoppers entered an unknown territory, mathematically speaking, they would ". . . stop part way through the process and use some means other than math to resolve a quantitative dilemma (e.g., postponing a purchase or 'taking the big one' . . .)" (p. 58). However, there is considerable evidence to suggest that people may avoid calculating because other non-quantitative variables need to be taken into account such as personal preference, shelf-life, and storage space at home. The practical nature of everyday mathematics is also borne home by the findings that the shoppers were very good at estimating the total cost of their groceries (critical information) and very poor at estimating the total number of items purchased (trivial information).

Nine participants in "Weight Watchers" were also studied by the Lave group. This is a fee-based diet plan which, among hundreds of competing plans, has the unique feature that all foods are to be carefully measured prior to preparation and/or consumption. Despite this bedrock premise, the dieters actually go to great lengths to avoid calculations. Over time they tend to substitute local household containers to obviate the need for measuring. However, the Weight Watchers fell into two distinct groups, one of which had bought into the Weight Watcher philosophy and continued to measure ". . . 61% of the food items they recorded in their food diaries . . ." (pp. 129–30) whereas another group shared the philosophy that ". . . so long as you feel hungry, you must be losing weight" (p. 129) and this group ". . . measured only 26% of the time" (p. 130). Lave (1988) does not speculate on why these people would continue to pay for a diet plan and then violate its basic premise. One might suggest that while mathematics avoidance is characteristic of mainstream society—people practice a restricted numeracy—mathematics and science are invested with great, almost magical power. In other words, the potency of a "precision" diet plan may be so great that you do not even have to follow it too closely to have it work for you.

Street sales represent another arena where mathematics is used in public. Several studies (Stigler and Baranes 1988) have been done in Brazil, where the exploding population and weak economy have forced even very young children to become self-sufficient through direct selling. Saxe (1990), for example, studied the relationship between in-school and out-of-school mathematics. Strategies learned in school do transfer to nonschool contexts, in many cases, but the reverse is not true. That is, sellers (and bookies in one study) are unable to apply calculation algorithms learned on the street to analogous "textbook" problems. However, young children or those with little schooling can be quite successful entrepreneurs by soliciting help from numerate store clerks or inventing procedures to calculate price and profit. Interestingly, despite the claim that practical mathematics is "socially constructed" (Lave 1988), there is little evidence from these studies that invented solutions to mathematics problems are *shared* within the group (Millroy 1991).

5. Implications for Policy Initiatives

On the CBS television (USA) evening news on September 30, 1991, the president of Motorola claimed that "Less than 50% of job applicants can function at the 7th grade level or higher in mathematics and their literacy skills are even less developed." The company, as a consequence, has had to greatly expand its training programs to include adult basic education. This kind of story is quite common in the United States and, indeed, worldwide. As governments move to address this "crisis," research will increasingly be needed. A catalog of some typical government-sponsored initiatives and their effects includes:

(a) One response has been to exhort parents to read to their children. Such is certainly the case with "Running Start," a much-touted program funded by the Chrysler Corporation. However, this research suggests that reading with children is a form of cultural capital that is not widely available outside the mainstream. Heath's work with Charlene Thomas, a teenaged mother of three who had dropped out of school in the 9th grade, indicates that some parents may need rather extensive coaching in order to bring them to a point where they can replicate the adult–child literacy patterns found in mainstream homes. Purcell-Gates (1994) did provide such extensive coaching, working with an illiterate mother and her son and was, over a two-year period, successful with both. Other examples are reports on a successful intervention program with Hispanic families in Los Angeles. However, Delgado-Gaitan (1990) reports from a similar program that was also successful with some parents, that: ". . . parents with minimal Spanish and English literacy experienced feelings of constraint in their ability to do literacy activities with their children . . ." (p. 108). Another problem with programs that attempt to mobilize parents in communities where literacy is restricted is that they believe they have acquired little value out of schooling and have tended to withhold any investment in their children's education or school readiness (cf. Ogbu 1988). The informants in Taylor and Dorsey-Gaines's (1988) study of literacy in inner-city Black families frequently express this view.

(b) Similarly, studies in Papua New Guinea and Africa convey the sense that campaigns to promote literacy via "universal" basic education may be misguided. Literacy is associated in people's minds with having a white-collar job in town and when these employment opportunities are not available, children and adults alike lack incentives to learn.

(c) There are a variety of programs such as "Head Start" which, in the United States, go under the heading of "compensatory" education. Lubeck's (1984) comparative analysis of a nursery school serving White suburban children and a Head Start class for Black inner-city children reveals that adult–child language and literacy practices are imported from the community. That is, Black Head Start teachers treated the students as Tracton parents treat their children and White nursery school teachers behaved just like Maintown mothers. These programs appear then to *reproduce* existing literacy patterns in society and do not function in a compensatory manner.

(d) A frequently voiced argument is that the curriculum in school and adult education should be adapted to the learner's culture. Gerdes's (1988) solution to the problem of the ". . . educational failure of many children from third world countries and from ethnic minority communities in industrialized countries . . . [would be] to *(multi)culturalise* the curriculum . . . mathematics . . . has to be "imbedded" into the cultural environment of the learners" (p. 35). To illustrate, he suggests that the pythagorean theorem be taught to Salish Indians using their traditional basketry designs. Gerdes seems to imply that the basketry construction in general, and the "star" pattern in particular, are part of the cultural repertoire of Indian people in coastal British Columbia. This being the case, teachers should build on this pre-existing knowledge in introducing the pythagorean theorem. However, he never tests this assumption. In fact the two works which he cites on Indian basketry are dated 1900 and 1908. It is quite likely that Salish children are no more familiar with basketry patterns than children from Toledo, Ohio. Also, it has been shown that young weavers do not generalize the patterns they weave to more abstract geometry problems.

In conclusion, calls to imbed the curriculum of adult education in the local culture ignore the findings reported here—that literacy may be used to only a limited extent and that mathematics is avoided. When calculation cannot be avoided, imprecise and inefficient routines may be used. But, just as clearly, the "worksheet, textbook, skill, and drill" curriculum also teaches and reinforces a restricted and individually limiting culture of literacy and numeracy. The research reviewed here strongly reinforces the view that curriculum must be imbedded in "Culture with a capital C"; it must be "anchored" in a rich micro-world of characters, places, and storyline. This Culture must reflect the diversity inherent in the society at large, it must be multi-Cultural. But to draw only, or even primarily, on the local culture to create a curriculum ". . . would lead to segregation on an unimaginable scale. It could also promote rigid teaching based on a stereotyped and romanticized vision of minority culture" (Weisner et al. 1988 p. 345).

See also: Literacy; Literacy and Numeracy Models; Postliteracy; Epistemological Issues in Educational Research; Adult Literacy in the Third World; Adult Learning: An Overview; Environments for Learning; Literacy Research and Measurement

References

Allexsaht-Snider M 1991 Family literacy in a Spanish-speaking context: Joint construction of meaning. *Quarterly Newsletter for the Laboratory of Comparative Human Cognition* 13(1): 15–21
Altwerger B, Diehl-Faxson J, Dockstader-Anderson K 1985 Read-aloud events as meaning construction. *Language Arts* 62(5): 476–84
Basso K H 1974 The ethnography of writing. In: Bauman R, Sherzer J (eds.) 1974 *Explorations in the Ethnography of Speaking*. Cambridge University Press, New York
Bishop A J 1988 *Mathematical Enculturation: A Cultural Perspective on Mathematics Education*. Kluwer Academic, London
Briscoe D B, Ross J M 1991 Racial and Ethnic Minorities in Adult Education. In: Merriam S B, Cunningham P M (eds.) 1991 *Handbook of Adult and Continuing Education*. Jossey-Bass, San Fransisco, California
D'Ambrosio U 1985 Ethnomathematics and its place in the history and pedagogy of mathematics. *For the Learning of Mathematics* 5(1): 44–48
Delgado-Gaitan C 1990 *Literacy for Empowerment*. Falmer Press, New York
Fishman A R 1990 Becoming literate: A lesson from the Amish. In Lunsford A A, Moglen H, Slevin J (eds.) 1990 *The Right to Literacy*. Modern Language Association, New York
Gay J, Cole M 1967 *The New Mathematics and an Old Culture*. Holt, Rinehart, & Winston, New York

Gerdes P 1988 A widespread decorative motif and the pythagorean theorem. *For the Learning of Mathematics* 8(1): 35–39

Goody J 1987 *The Interface Between the Written and the Oral: Studies in Literacy, Family, Culture and the State.* Cambridge University Press, Cambridge

Hansen J F 1979 *Sociocultural Perspectives on Human Learning: An Introduction to Educational Anthropology.* Prentice-Hall, Englewood Cliffs, New Jersey

Heath S B 1983 *Ways with Words: Language, Life and Work in Communities and Classrooms.* Cambridge University Press, Cambridge

Heath S B 1986 The functions and uses of literacy. In: deCastell S, Luke A, Egan K (eds.) 1986 *Literacy, Society and Schooling.* Cambridge University Press, Cambridge

Hostetler J A, Huntingon G E 1972 *Children in Amish Society: Socialization and Community Education.* Holt, Rinehart and Winston, New York

Kneller G F 1965 *Educational Anthropology: An Introduction.* Wiley, New York

Lancy D F 1983 *Cross-cultural Studies in Cognition and Mathematics.* Academic Press, New York

Lancy D F, Draper K D, Boyce G 1989 Parental influence on children's acquisition of reading. *Contemporary Issues in Reading* 4(1): 83–93

Lave J 1988 *Cognition in Practice: Mind, Mathematics and Culture in Everyday Life.* Cambridge University Press, New York

Lubeck S 1984 Kinship and classrooms: An ethnographic perspective on education as cultural transmission. *Sociol. Educ.* 57(4): 219–32

Maclean M, Bryant P, Bradley L 1987 Rhymes, nursery rhymes and reading in early childhood. *Merrill-Palmer Q.* 33(3): 255–81

Millroy W L 1991 An ethnographic study of the mathematical ideas of a group of carpenters. *Learning and Individual Differences* 3(1): 1–25

Ogbu J U 1988 Literacy and schooling in subordinate cultures: The case of Black Americans. In: Kintgen E R, Kroll B M, Rose M (eds.) 1988 *Perspectives on Literacy.* SIU Press, Carbondale, Illinois

Ogbu J U 1994 Anthropology of Education: History and Overview. In: Husén T, Postlethwaite T N (eds.) 1994 *International Encyclopedia of Education*, 2nd edn. Pergamon Press, Oxford

Olson D R 1984 See! Jumping! Some oral language antecedents of literacy. In: Goelman H, Oberg A A, Smith F (eds.) 1984 *Awakening to Literacy.* Heinemann, Portsmouth, New Hampshire

Purcell-Gates V 1988 Lexical and syntactic knowledge of written narrative held by well-read-to kindergarteners and second graders. *Research in the Teaching of English* 22(2): 128–60

Purcell-Gates V 1994 Non-literate homes and emergent literacy in a non-literate home. In: Lancy D F (ed.) 1994 *Children's Emergent Literacy: From Research to Practice.* Praeger, Westport, Connecticut

Quinn N 1978 Do Mfantse fish sellers estimate probability in their heads? *American Ethnologist* 5: 206–26

Reder S, Green K R 1983 Contrasting patterns of literacy in an Alaskan fishing village. *Int. J. Sociology of Language* 42: 9–39

Roberts J I 1976 Introduction. In: Roberts J I, Akinsanya S (eds.) 1976 *Educational Patterns and Cultural Configurations: The Anthropological of Education.* David McKay, New York

Saxe G B, Guberman S R, Gearhart M 1987 Social processes in early number development. *Monogr. Soc. Res. Child Dev.* 52(2), serial number 216

Saxe G B 1990 *Culture and Cognitive Development: Studies in Mathematical Understanding.* Erlbaum, Hillsdale, New Jersey

Scribner S, Cole M 1981 *The Psychology of Literacy.* Harvard University Press, Cambridge, Massachusetts

Snow C E, Barnes W S, Chandler J, Goodman I F, Hemphill L 1991 *Unfulfilled Expectations: Home and School Influences on Literacy.* Harvard University Press, Cambridge, Massachusetts

Spindler G D (ed.) 1963 *Education and Culture: Anthropological Approaches.* Holt, Rinehart and Winston, New York

Spindler G D 1974 *The Transmission of Culture.* In: Spindler G D (ed.) 1974 *Education and the Cultural Process: Towards an Anthropology of Education.* Holt, Rinehart and Winston, New York

Stigler J W, Baranes R 1988 Culture and mathematics learning. In: Rothkopf E Z (ed.) 1988 *Review of Research in Education*, No. 15. AERA, Washington, DC

Stigler J W, Shweder R A, Herdt G (eds.) 1991 *Cultural Psychology. Essays on Comparative Human Development.* Cambridge University Press, Cambridge

Stock B 1983 *The Implications of Literacy: Written Language and Models of Interpretation in the Eleventh and Twelfth Centuries.* Princeton University Press, Princeton, New Jersey

Taylor D 1983 *Family Literacy: Young Children Learning to Read and Write*, Heinemann, Portsmouth, New Hampshire

Taylor D, Dorsey-Gaines C 1988 *Growing up Literate: Learning from Inner City Families.* Heinemann, Portsmouth, New Hampshire

Teale W H 1986 Home background and young children's literacy development. In: Teale W H, Sulzby E (eds.) 1986 *Emergent Literacy: Writing and Reading.* Ablex, Norwood, New Jersey

Varenne H, McDermott R P 1986 "Why" Sheila can read: Structure and determinancy in the reproduction of familial literacy. In: Schiefflin B B, Gilmore P (eds.) 1986 *The Acquisition of Literacy: Ethnographic Perspectives.* Ablex, Norwood, New Jersey

Wagner D A, Messick B M, Spratt J 1986 Studying literacy in Morocco. In: Schiefflin B B, Gilmore P (eds.) 1986 *The Acquisition of Literacy: Ethnographic Perspectives.* Ablex, Norwood, New Jersey

Weisner T S, Gallimore R, Jordan C 1988 Unpackaging cultural effects on classroom learning: Native Hawaiian peer assistance and child-generated activity. *Anthropol. Educ. Q.* 19(4): 327–53

Wertsch J V (ed.) 1985 *Culture, Communication and Cognition.* Cambridge University Press, Cambridge

Economics of Adult Education and Training

A. C. Tuijnman

The purpose of this entry is to offer an overview of major issues and questions for which answers may be sought within the domain of the economics of adult education. Although economists contribute many useful insights, adequate answers to the questions raised can be obtained only in a multidisciplinary framework, which requires the cooperation of educationists, psychologists, sociologists, and others. Topics addressed include costs and finance, educational production, labor markets and adult education, manpower requirements, employment and unemployment, productivity and economic competitiveness, and the private and social rates of return to investment in adult education and industry training. Some of these topics are elaborated in additional entries presented in subsequent sections of this volume.

1. Concepts and Definitions

Economics is a broad-ranging social science discipline concerned with the study of how scarce resources are used in production to create value added, and how the benefits are distributed to satisfy the demand of individuals and groups in a society. The discipline of economics is aimed at creating knowledge and insights that help in understanding and predicting the behavior of people and economic systems. Like anthropology, psychology, and sociology, economics is a field of social and behavioral study. The key concepts in economics are scarcity of resources, choice and desirability, production, and distribution.

The field of education may be defined as the area of study concerned with the deliberate production and distribution of knowledge and competence that influence the behavior of people, whether children or adults, and whether the production takes place in schools, institutions of adult education, or other institutions in a society, such as churches, libraries, or the military. From an economic viewpoint, the key notions are the same as those characterizing the wider discipline of economics.

The economics of education, which is a relatively recent branch of economics, thus deals with the production and distribution of knowledge and competence. Knowledge is not the same as competence, since the latter implies a capacity of organizing knowledge and applying it efficiently and effectively for some demanding purpose. Competence is a scarce and valuable resource. It is both a product of and an input into a complex production process. The field of the economics of education is concerned with how scarce resources, such as money and time, are allocated in producing competence, how competence is distributed among individuals and social groups, how that competence is allocated and used in further production processes, and how the resulting benefits are distributed among the individuals and groups in a society.

The research and policy questions that apply to the economics of school education are in principle the same as those asked in the economics of adult education. In both cases the key issue is the allocation of scarce financial, human, and physical resources to a process of education and learning that is designed to produce beneficial outcomes. Economists then ask the following questions: Is the investment optimal, given that there is a choice of alternative resources that may be used? Is the learning process efficient, given that there are different teaching methods and approaches that can yield the same outcomes at a lower cost? Is the product cost-effective, given the costs, the intended uses, and the benefits thus generated? And are these benefits then distributed equitably among the individuals and groups in a society, given the needs and desires of people and the applied method of financing the learning process?

Although the broad questions for research and policy are similar, there are of course some differences between school education and adult education that influence the specific questions that are asked and the approach taken in answering them. The principle of voluntariness is important in this respect, because it has consequences for the characteristics of the people who engage in adult education. Differences in maturity, motivation, learning style, and choice may interact with differences in the organization of the learning process. These differences may also have an impact on the costs, the method of financing, and the eventual distribution of the benefits accruing to the learning process.

Because of its voluntary nature and the application of free choice principles, adult education is offered by a broad range of providers catering to highly heterogeneous audiences. This diversity introduces a number of variables that must be taken into account in economic studies of adult education. It requires that attention be paid to the various orientations of adult education programs, which may range from public basic education provided in the formal system of education to informal learning in the work place and the continuing education of highly skilled professionals.

A distinction is sometimes made between adult education for consumption and adult education for investment (Tuijnman 1994). Consumption education is directed mainly to personal goals, often in connection with the development of leisure. In contrast, investment education is usually aimed at the formation of competence and skills for work. Measures of the public and private costs of adult education and training can be used to determine the orientation of a program. A second method is to consider whether upon successful completion a program affords a qualification or credential that carries information value in the labor market. A third method is to look at the goals or objectives of the participants. Education aimed at personal development or the enrichment of leisure is properly studied using other conceptual frameworks and variables than would be used in an analysis of the effectiveness of public or firm-based training programs. Although the distinction between adult education for consumption and investment is essential, the practical usefulness of the dichotomy is limited. Problems arise because an educational program is seldomly undertaken only for consumption or only for investment. Yet despite this difficulty, the distinction offers a theoretical means of conceptualizing the field with which the economics of adult education is primarily concerned.

2. Costs and Financing of Adult Education

A wide variety of institutions operate in the markets for adult education and training, which are also referred to as "markets for competence" (Eliasson 1995). This diversity makes it nearly impossible to obtain accurate and consistent information about the costs of alternative adult education and training programs. The absence of adequate cost data renders decision-making intransparent and risky, because the performance of one program cannot be assessed against the costs and benefits associated with alternative policy options. The markets for competence are therefore both imperfect and inefficient.

The OECD recently launched two programs to improve the availability and transparency of statistical information about the costs and finance of adult education. The first was taken in connection with the OECD-led project on the development of Indicators of National Education Systems (INES). In the INES project steps were taken to develop indicators of participation in adult education and training, and steps were subsequently set to identify public expenditures for adult education separately from expenditure for other public provisions. The second OECD initiative concerns the development of a conceptual framework and instruments for the collection of training statistics. The preliminary version of the *Manual for Training Statistics* (OECD 1995) distinguishes 30 cost components which ideally should be reflected in statistics of industry training. Crucial cost components are the labor costs of the trainers, the value of the trainees' marginal revenue products foregone, the labor costs of the trainees' replacements, the rental of physical facilities hired for training purposes, the financial cost of enterprise-owned physical facilities, the cost of training levies, and the fees or payments to external institutions for purchased training. This list, which can easily be extended, serves to illustrate the difficulty of ensuring that the cost estimates are derived in a way that is both transparent and consistent across firms, labor market sectors, and also countries. Current practices for calculating the costs of adult education and training are far from uniform. Despite the urgency of the need for such information, it will take much time and effort before reliable and valid data on the costs of adult education and industry training become available at the national and international levels (see *Costs of Adult Education and Training*).

Information on the main sources of financing is also scarce, even in the OECD countries. In most countries finance for adult education is provided from both public and private sources. The funds are raised through general taxation or, in some countries, through earmarked taxes on luxury goods, property taxes, or lotteries organized to raise money for education. Some countries, such as Australia, France and Sweden, use special payroll taxes for the financing of adult education and training. Apart from some public subsidies, adult education and training programs are to a large extent privately financed. The main responsibility lies usually with the individual, who pays tuition fees and purchases books, equipment, and other materials, and the employer, who may subsidize the tuition fee for adult education and who often provides workers with time off from work for learning. A third category of finance is made up of private funds expended by trade unions, religious, cultural and other voluntary associations, and international donor agencies. However, little is known about the balance of the shares in total spending of the central and local government authorities, firms, and individuals. Although estimates of public and private expenditure on institutional adult education are available in many countries, this information is mostly incomplete and unreliable, given the lack of a proper distinction between spending before and after government transfers.

Policy-making is a hazardous task in the absence of reliable and comprehensive information about the costs and finance of programs of adult education and training. The controversy over possible under- or over-investment in adult education and training is a result of insufficient data about who pays and who benefits (see *Market Failure in Adult Education and Training; Overeducation*).

3. Production of Adult Education

The production of knowledge and competence through learning occurs in all life settings: the family, the school, the community library, the museum, and the workplace. There are two main approaches to the economics of educational production.

In the traditional approach it is assumed that schools

and adult education institutions function much like private, profit-making firms, with the institution as the producing unit, the learners as workers, and the teacher as the supervisor of production. The objective of management in private firms is to maximize profit. There are several keys to achieving this goal. Among these are cost control and efficient production. Efficiency and cost-effectiveness are also two important concerns in the adult education sector. Cost control is an important element of public policy for adult education. In contrast, private sector training has relied more on ways to improve the efficiency of educational production. In contrast, schools and institutions of adult education are considered as "public sector" organizations in the alternative approach to the economics of educational production. Not profit maximization but political and institutional goals rank foremost in this perspective, in which less importance is attached to criteria of cost and efficiency and more to issues such as allocation, control over content, and distribution (Carnoy 1994). The emphasis in this second perspective is on reproduction instead of production, and the preferred techniques are derived from a critical rather than a systems analytical perspective.

The process of adult education involves the allocation of scarce resources to a learning process that yields certain outputs. This process can be represented in an educational production function. An educational production function is, in principle, no different from any other production function. It is a mathematical expression that relates inputs to outputs. Many factors can be included in such a function. The input factors usually include financial, human and physical capital items, such as money, teachers, students, and buildings. An important issue concerns the distinction between manipulable and nonmanipulable factors. Decision-makers seeking ways of improving efficiency can usually do little about the socioeconomic position or the capacity to learn of the adult population, but they can allocate more or less funds, and increase or decrease the supply of learning opportunities. Many different output variables can be specified as well, for example, knowledge, different skills, values and attitudes. Whereas production functions purport to describe how inputs are transformed into outputs, the variables that explain how that transformation process actually occurs are not modeled explicitly but inferred from the evidence of the relationships among the other variables included in the function. Of the many criticisms leveled against the modeling of educational production, the lack of attention to process has been a main argument.

4. Labor Markets and Adult Education

Three theories are relevant to a discussion of adult education and the labor market: human capital theory; screening or filtering theory; and job matching theory. Screening and job matching theories are closely

related. Both question the simple idea of a linear relationship between an investment in adult education and worker productivity, since such an investment may also lead to overschooling, which tends to lower worker productivity. Although the individual tends to derive a positive return on overschooling, the costs may outweigh this return. This problem of overschooling is not sufficiently addressed in the economics of adult education.

The individual benefits of education are emphasized in the human capital approach, using personal income as the criterion. The relationship between adult education and productivity is considered to be straightforward: adult education results in a higher wage because it confers competence which increases the capacity of workers to perform their jobs efficiently. Two relationships are hypothesized: an effect of adult education on worker productivity, and an effect of productivity on individual income. Studies conducted in this perspective focus on the relationship between education and personal income; the relevance of education for productivity is usually taken for granted.

Compared with human capital theory, the screening or filtering perspective hypothesizes a different connection between adult education and individual earnings. It holds that people invest in adult education because the qualifications which are acquired can be used to inform potential employers that they possess certain scarce skills and other personality traits, such as motivation and perseverance, which are likely to make them more productive in a given job than the competitors who lack these specific characteristics. Adult education thus presents a means to identify and select workers with a high expected marginal productivity. In this perspective, it is not productivity but self-selection that forms the basis for the relationship between adult education and individual earnings. Hence adult education is not necessarily seen as a strategic investment; it may also be given as a reward.

Information is a central variable in both screening and job matching theory. The two approaches are therefore closely related. In screening theory the emphasis is on the comparative advantage of the individual, who holds vital information vis-à-vis the employer, who lacks such information. In job matching theory it is considered that both workers and employers can derive useful information from the fact that workers participate in adult education. This information can be used by both parties to improve the match between the skills possessed by workers and the competence demanded by the job. The central hypothesis is that adult education has a positive effect on productivity not only because it raises performance-relevant competence but also because it offers a signal for allocating the right people to the right jobs. Productivity increases are only forthcoming if the signals help to improve the job match of an employee, and the new competence is actually used on the job. But if adult education widens the discrepancy between workers' competence and the skills demanded at work then the effect on productivity may be nil or negative.

5. *Manpower Requirements, Employment, and Unemployment*

Manpower analysis and planning has been a major concern of economists over the decades. Although the traditional approach to manpower requirements modeling and forecasting has been totally discredited, work in the area continues to be carried out, possibly because of a demand for such forecasting studies by policymakers.

The manpower requirements approach defines a method of projecting the demand for labor by various educational and occupational categories under various assumptions. Adult education has become part of the picture because of the so-called "two percent argument." The argument is that the annual influx from external to internal labor markets—mainly school leavers and graduates entering the labor market for the first time—is about two percent per year. A labor shortage may occur if exits from the labor force as a consequence of retirement or for other reasons exceed two percent. Forecasts show that this may soon be happening in many industrialized countries. If such countries seek to upgrade the educational qualifications of their work forces then they should invest heavily in adult education in addition to schooling, given that new entrants will only comprise 10 percent of the work force after five years. If a country were to invest much more in schooling than adult education, then it might take 25 years to upgrade the skills of only half the workforce—by which time the skills of those who entered the labor market 10 or 15 years before may already to an extent have become obsolete due to technological advances and economic restructuring.

There have been many criticisms of the manpower requirements approach in educational planning and forecasting. The main point is that such forecasts have tended to be mostly inaccurate, reflecting the use of untenable assumptions, poor data availability, weaknesses in applied methodology, and the inpredictability of the future (Dougherty 1983). As a result of the devastating criticisms levelled against the traditional methods for manpower planning, economists have attempted to develop new approaches and techniques. In essence the outcome has been a thrust to understand better the organization and functioning of labor markets in relation to educational production. This has required an understanding of what it is that schools and adult education "produce," and how these "products" find their ways into the labor market, whether in formal or informal sectors. Adult education has received much attention also in this "new" approach.

There is much support for the hypothesis that adult education and industry training carry significance in explaining the differences in labor market status between workers with similar levels of schooling and work experience, even if other variables such as cognitive ability, achievement motivation and personal work histories are held constant. Findings from Swedish research indicate that the direct effect of initial education on occupational status reaches a maximum at around age 30 and then gradually decreases in strength. In contrast, the effect of adult education increases cumulatively from early to late career (Tuijnman 1989). As workers get older, the effect of schooling becomes increasingly mediated by adult education and by personal work histories. For workers over 50 years the effect of adult education on occupational status exceeds that of initial schooling. Bishop (1991) also finds that job-relevant adult education of a formal type results in greater occupational mobility than on-the-job training and informal learning at the work place. The explanation seems to be that competence acquired in formal education is easier to certify than skills acquired informally on the job.

Important is the question of the relationship between adult education, employment security, and occupational mobility in and across internal labor markets. Adult education is often seen as an instrument for enhancing employment security and facilitating mobility. However, there is some evidence that these two goals are at odds. Theory predicts that firm-specific training improves employment security. This is so because workers who have acquired skills that are central to the operations of the firm run less risk of being laid off at times of economic hardship than workers with a general training. However, customized education also limits the free flow and turnover of labor. In contrast, adult education of a general type reduces employment stability but facilitates mobility. The pay-off from adult education to the firm depends on how long workers remain in the service of the employer after having received training. Firms are therefore likely to invest more in workers who are likely to stay. The evidence bears this out. Trainees who receive firm-based education are on the average less mobile prior to receiving the education than other workers, and their mobility is further reduced by that education (Mincer 1989). Employment security apparently promotes investment in skill formation, and such investment in turn promotes employment stability, since both employers and employees will try to maximize their returns.

The incidence of unemployment is generally lower the higher the level of initial education (OECD 1994). There is evidence that this also applies to adult education. Compared with untrained workers, those who receive adult education show a lower incidence of unemployment. Mincer (1987) observes that workers with less than 12 years of schooling are 170 percent more likely to suffer unemployment, and they experience spells of unemployment 30 percent longer than workers with 16 or more years of schooling. Educated workers are moreover likely to search for a new job while still employed, thus reducing search costs; educated workers acquire and process information more efficiently than less educated workers; and employers and workers both search more intensively to fill more skilled slots (Berryman 1995). Because such education influences employment status independent of initial schooling, it also helps to consolidate or strengthen the labor market attachment of workers. Adult education thus increases employability and decreases both the likelihood of becoming unemployed and the chance to remain unemployed for a long time once laid off. The problem of insufficient information leading to a poor job match, which lowers the efficiency and productivity of schooling, is less pronounced in adult education. This implies that adult education can, at least potentially, be effective in reducing unemployment pressure in information-poor labor markets.

6. Adult Education and Productivity

Productivity can be assessed in terms of the aggregate output of an economy, the output of a branch of industry or a specific work place, and the output of an individual worker. All three criteria are considered below.

Neoclassical theory is at the heart of most studies of the relationship between education and macroeconomic growth. These studies have often used simple production functions, which hold that the output of an economy depends on the amount of capital and labor employed and on the flow of new technology. Increases in capital and labor typically account for nearly half of the growth in output. The residual variance is attributed to technology. Education is usually not entered explicitly but it is assumed to influence both labor quality and technological progress. Hence the finding that studies estimating simple production functions with aggregate data support the view that education and macroeconomic growth are related.

A new theory of growth is gaining in importance since the mid-1980s. Extended production functions take not only capital and labor but also knowledge into account. Knowledge, which is usually measured in terms of the educational attainment of a population, is considered a primary rather than a secondary production factor. Studies comparing growth rates in different countries found that lack of human capital and education, not lack of labor or investment in physical capital, is what prevents economic growth in poor countries. Since there is ample evidence that adult education adds to the stock of human capital in a population, it may be concluded that not only initial schooling but also adult education and industry training contribute to the growth of aggregate output in an economy.

The effects of adult education on the productivity of firms are investigated in several studies. In this case possible indicators are the turnover of the firm multiplied by the average percentage share of value-added in the turnover of the relevant branch; the annual growth of turnover by worker; the growth of production volume minus the growth of labor volume; profitability; and the change in market share over time.

Studies of the relationship between adult education and the productivity of firms have usually emphasized the role of firm-specific training. Blakemore and Hoffman (1989) and Bishop (1990), among others, report a positive correlation between training investment and output. Yet the direction of this relationship is often unclear. Profitable companies, high-technology enterprises, and large firms with low turnover tend to invest more in training than low-technology and smaller firms. But studies unequivocally showing that this investment also raises the output of firms are scarce. Exceptions are Bishop (1987), Barron et al. (1989), and Mendes et al. (1989). These authors show in well designed studies that continuing education has a significant effect on labor productivity in firms. Barron et al. (1989) find that a 10 percent increase in training investment leads to a growth of three percent in labor productivity. Bartel (1991) estimated that an increase in training expenditure yielded a 16 percent return in productivity after a certain period of time. For manufacturing firms in the United States, Lynch (1995) found that a 10 percent increase in the proportion of workers trained led to a 1.4 percent increase in total sales within three years.

It is often assumed that the positive relationship between adult education and personal income is indicative of differences in productivity between workers according to the acquired level of education. However, it is found in studies of firms that income, although predicted by the level of education, does not equal the real value of the marginal product (Brown 1989, Bishop 1991). The theory of implicit wage contracts explains this in terms of the distribution of risk taking between workers and employers. Another explanation is that employers who carry most of the costs of specific training will offer incomes lower than the value of the marginal product. The extent to which adult education is an investment in general human capital is seen as an important determinant of the distribution of the costs and benefits of adult education. Since the value-added of specific training falls in large measure to the employer, the return on adult education in terms of increased productivity is therefore likely to be greater than the return suggested by wage growth.

7. Benefits of Adult Education

The possible economic benefits of adult education can be measured in different ways and at different levels. Microscopic studies are focused on variables that carry meaning for individuals, for example whether a qualification was obtained or whether improvements in life satisfaction, employment opportunities or income were recorded. By contrast, macroscopic studies are concerned with the effects of adult education on labor supply and demand, the functioning of internal labor markets, productivity, and aggregate economic growth.

Economic theory predicts that the microscopic or private returns and the macroscopic or social returns to an investment in adult education and training are interrelated. That is, if the return—the balance between costs and benefits—is positive for individuals and firms, then there may well be a gain also for the nation. This postulate explains the interest of policymakers in adult education and training.

7.1 Private Returns

Studies of average age-earning profiles in industrialized countries show, according to Blaug (1976) and Psacharopoulos (1987), that the relationship between formal education and earned income increases in strength up to a point between 40 and 45 years of age, and then levels off. The age at which this peak is manifested tends to be higher the higher the level of initial education. This can be interpreted as a sign of decreasing marginal productivity, where depreciation sets in earlier for the poorly educated than well educated workers. The later in life the effects of formal education on earnings are estimated, the more likely it is that these are mediated by other variables, notably by previous labor market experience. There is evidence that adult education is also implicated: the turning point in earnings power arrives at a later age for workers with additional training compared with workers who lack training (Mincer 1991). The cumulative effects of adult education on earnings seem to increase with age (Brown 1989, Tuijnman 1989).

Estimates of the private rate of return on formal education show a great deal of cross-national consistency (Psacharopoulos 1985). Rates of return to primary and secondary education appear to be higher than those of higher education (Psacharopoulos 1993), especially the social returns. Most industrial countries show returns on higher education similar to those in the United States, where the private return varied from six percent in the 1970s to between seven and 11 percent in the mid-1980s (Cohn and Geske 1990). But private rates of return to higher education appear to have increased since 1985 in many OECD countries (Alsalam and Conley 1995, Addison and Cohn 1995). Studies conducted in both developed and developing countries find that the return on training for young workers is at least as high as that on higher education (Lillard and Tan 1986, Brown 1989, Bishop 1991, Psacharopoulos and Velez 1992).

Mincer (1991) reanalyzed data collected in the United States in the 1970s and 1980s. Using an eight-year timespan for depreciation, he finds a return on one-year with adult education and training of 23.5 percent for all male workers, 26.5 percent for new hires and 37.5 percent for older cohorts. If the training investment is written off over a 25 year period, then the corresponding estimates are 12.8 percent for all workers, 16 percent for new hires and 26 percent for older cohorts. Thus the private rate of return on adult education is higher than the return on both schooling and higher education. Mincer (1991) concludes:

> The range of estimates of *worker* returns to training based on several data sets seems to exceed the magnitude of rates of return usually observed for schooling investments. Given the data on worker's firm tenure, it appears also that training remains profitable to *firms*, even in the face of average worker mobility. The rates of return here calculated may be large enough to suggest underinvestment in training relative to that in schooling.

The direct effect of adult education on individual earnings is not significant statistically once job level is held constant in the equation (Tuijnman 1989), although the indirect effect mediated by job level is significant and positive. Job matching theory offers a possible explanation for this finding. The theory holds that adult education only increases earnings if it improves worker productivity. Hence the pay-off to the individual depends on whether a qualification or other means of sending a signal to employers is obtained, whether the person can make effective use of the new skills on the job, and whether the productivity gain is noticed and warrants higher pay. Support for this interpretation of the relationship between adult education and earnings is offered by sociological studies of internal labor market organization.

7.2. Social Returns

Screening theory predicts that the private returns from education will exceed the social returns, and that this imbalance will be more pronounced in adult education than in primary and secondary education. The assumption is that the larger the distance to compulsory education, the more the social rate of return diminishes relative to the private rate of return. Because workers sacrifice little or no pay to get adult education, and since both firms and society subsidize a major part of the direct costs of this education, the individual return is likely to be higher than the social return. Unfortunately there is little evidence to support or reject this hypothesis (OECD in press).

There is some indication that adult education and industry training influence aggregate productivity in an economy, since they influence the efficiency of employing other relevant factors of production, such as capital and technology. This insight is behind the rapidly increasing interest in the economics of skill formation since the mid-1980s (Mankiw et al. 1992).

The huge investment in new technology since the 1970s should have raised productivity and growth, but in the industrialized countries the gains were generally disappointing. This apparent contradiction gave rise to the formulation of a new theory of economic growth.

Some economists have postulated that misallocated and insufficient skills explain, at least partly, why the cumulative input of capital, labor and technology has produced below-expected economic growth in some Western economies. This argument focuses attention on the role of interaction effects among technology and intangible variables such as the knowledge and skills of workers, information, and social capital in influencing the marginal productivity of other factors of production. Adult education has moved to frontstage because it is believed to confer scale economies to capital, labor, and technology inputs. Economic growth thus depends not only on the amounts of tangible input factors but especially on their optimal allocation, given the strongly diminishing returns to investment in intangible capital. Because intangible capital is associated with people and organizations, productivity growth cannot be separated from worker skills and the quality of interpersonal relationships that occur as micro phenomena in the workplace. With the human factor assuming such prominence, questions about the possible consequences of under- or overinvestment and the effects of the inequitable distribution of learning opportunities on the efficiency of educational production have come to the foreground of the debate.

8. Conclusion

There was until recently little interest in the economics of adult education. Studies of adult education finance, cost-benefit analyses, and studies of the effects of adult education on employment and unemployment, and the productivity of individuals and firms have typically not been carried out by adult educators, who have tended to be skeptical of such research, but by researchers with a footing in educational sociology and the economics of education. Adult educators have had a different perception of the relevant questions for research. Hence the available empirical work on the economics of adult education has come mainly from research workers with a loose connection with the adult education field. This has advantages, since the interaction enriches the field in many ways, but also disadvantages. A problem arises because the questions economists ask inevitably put an emphasis on education for investment. Consequently there is little evidence about the possible benefits of general or liberal adult education. Because decisions about the worthwhileness of an adult education program should not be based solely on economic cost-benefit criteria, there is a need for adult education researchers to contribute other theories and criteria of effectiveness that may help to broaden the perspective.

See also: Economics of Nonformal Education; Government Role in Adult Education and Training; Market Concepts in Provision; Demand, Supply, and Finance of Adult Education; Costs of Adult Education and Training

References

Addison J, Cohn E 1995 *The Economic Returns to Lifelong Learning* (mimeo). OECD, Paris

Alsalam N, Conley R 1995 The rate of return to education: A proposal for a new indicator. In: OECD 1995 *Education and Employment.* OECD, Paris

Barron J M, Black D A, Loewenstein M A 1989 Job matching and on the job training. *J. Labor Econ.* 7(1): 1–19

Bartel A 1991 Employee training programs in US business. In: Stern D, Ritzen J M M (eds.) *Market Failure in Training: New Economic Analysis and Evidence on the Training of Adult Employees.* Springer-Verlag, Berlin

Berryman S E 1995 The contribution of literacy to the wealth of individuals and nations. In: Tuijnman A C, Kirsch I, Wagner D A (eds.) 1995 *Adult Basic Skills: Advances in Measurement and Policy Analysis.* Hampton Press, New York.

Bishop J 1987 The recognition and reward of employee performance. *J. Labor Econ.* 5: S36-S56

Bishop J 1990 Job performance, turnover and wage growth. *J. Labor Econ.* 8(3): 363–86

Bishop J 1991 On the job training of new hires. In: Stern D, Ritzen J M M (eds.) 1991 *Market Failure in Training? New Economic Analyses and Evidence on the Training of Adult Employees.* Springer-Verlag, Berlin

Blakemore A, Hoffman D 1989 Seniority rules and productivity: An empirical test. Econometrica 56: 359–71

Blaug M 1976 *Introduction to the Economics of Education.* Penguin, Harmondsworth

Brown J 1989 Why do wages increase with tenure? On the job training and life cycle wage growth observed within firms. *Am. Econ. Rev.* 79(4): 971–91

Carnoy M 1994 Political economy of education production. In: Husén T, Postlethwaite T N (eds.) 1994 *International Encyclopedia of Education*, 2nd edn. Pergamon Press, Oxford

Cohn E, Geske T G 1990 *The Economics of Education, 3rd edn.* Pergamon Press, Oxford

Dougherty C 1983 Manpower development from three points of view: Country technical assistance agency, and lending agency. In Psacharopoulos G, Hinchliffe K, Dougherty C, Hollister R 1983 *Manpower Issues in Educational Investment: A Consideration of Planning Processes and Techniques.* World Bank, Washington, DC

Eliasson G 1995 *The Markets for Competence and Educational Services: Microeconomic Explanations of Macroeconomic Growth.* OECD/CERI, Paris

Lillard L A, Tan H W 1986 *Training: Who Gets it and What are its Effects?* RAND Corporation, Santa Monica, California

Mankiw G, Romer D, Weil D 1992 A contribution to the structure of economic growth. *Q. J. Econ.* 106: 407–37

Mendes de Oliviera M E, Cohn E, Kiker B 1989 Tenure, earnings, and productivity. *Oxford B. Econ. Statis.* 51: 1–14

Mincer J 1987 *Job Training, Wage Growth, and Labor Turnover.* National Bureau of Economic Research Working Paper 2680. Department of Economics, Columbia University, New York

Mincer J 1989 Human capital and the labor market. A review of current research. *Educ. Researcher* 18: 27–34

Mincer J 1991 Job training: Costs, returns, and wage profiles.

In Stern D, Ritzen J M M (eds.) *Market Failure in Training? New Economic Analysis and Evidence on Training of Adult Employees.* Springer-Verlag, Berlin

OECD 1994 *The Jobs Study*, Vols. I–II. OECD, Paris

OECD 1995 *Manual for Training Statistics* (restricted, draft version). OECD, Paris

OECD in press How to pay for lifelong learning for all? In: *Background Report, Making Lifelong Learning a Reality for All.* Meeting of the Education Committee at Ministerial Level, January 16-17, 1996. OECD, Paris

Psacharopoulos G 1985 Returns to education: A further international update and implications. *J. Hum. Resources* 20: 583–604

Psacharopoulos G 1987 Earnings functions. In: Psacharopoulos G (ed.) 1987 *Economics of Education: Research and Studies.* Pergamon Press, Oxford

Psacharopoulos G, Velez E 1992 Does training pay independent of education? Some evidence from Columbia. *Int. J. Educ. Res.* 16: 581–591

Psacharopoulos G 1993 *Returns to Investment in Education: A Global Update.* World Bank, Washington, DC

Tuijnman A C 1989 *Recurrent Education, Earnings, and Well-being: A 50-year Longitudinal Study of a Cohort of Swedish Men.* Acta Universitatis Stockholmiensis, Almqvist and Wiksell, Stockholm

Economics of Nonformal Education

M. Ahmed

Major practical economic issues relating to the planning and management of education are how to maximize the efficiency of resource allocation and utilization, and how to ensure adequate financing for the educational needs of society. Nonformal education, by expanding the range of options for educational programs and processes, also expands the range of choices for dealing with economic efficiency and financing issues in educational programs.

1. Significance of Nonformal Education

The basic principles, methods, and purposes of economic analysis in nonformal education are not different from those in other modes of education. It is now generally recognized that the significance of nonformal education lies in the flexibility and choices it opens up in educational programs rather than it being a discrete and self-sufficient category of education serving learning objectives and learning groups which differ from those of formal education (see *Formal, Nonformal, and Informal Education*).

While in administrative and organizational terms, certain programs may be labeled as nonformal—and since the 1970s many countries have established separate directorates, departments, and programs of nonformal education—the spread of the concept of nonformal education has also led to methodological and organizational flexibilities in established formal programs.

From the point of view of economic analysis, the significance of nonformal education is that it opens the possibility for altering the "production function"—the combination of different educational inputs, such as the pupils' and instructors' time, physical facilities, and learning materials, which produce an educational output. The production function is relatively stable in formal education. Note, for instance, the preponderance of teaching personnel costs in education budgets, the narrow variation in teacher–pupil ratios, and duration of courses in multiples of a year and uniform for all learners. Nonformal approaches have shown that the conventional input combination can be substantially varied (by using, e.g., mass media-based distance learning techniques, self-instructional materials, skill modules, apprenticeship training, self-supporting educational programs, or peer-teaching), thus affecting costs, finances, and outputs of education (Ahmed 1975 p. 12).

The economic questions about education have to be asked within a framework of accepted notions of what is to be achieved in education. There has to be a general agreement on answers to a number of questions before the economic aspects of an educational program can be meaningfully examined. These questions may be:

(a) How widely should educational opportunities be dispersed?

(b) How equitably should educational opportunities be made available, taking into account regional disparities, urban–rural differences, gender disparities, and socioeconomic stratification?

(c) What would be acceptable as to the content, quality, and purposes of the educational program?

(d) How should the burden of the costs of educational services be shared and distributed?

(e) What patterns and flows of skills would be needed by a projected course of socioeconomic development and how would these be provided?

(f) What should be the time frame for achieving the accepted goals and how should the process be phased?

All these questions predicate economic questions regarding the availability and constraints of resources and how the resources can be put to optimal use. Widely accepted answers to these questions also indicate the need for exploiting the possibilities of re-arranging the production function of all educational programs, for instance, by introducing nonformal features in schools and by incorporating certain organizational disciplines of the institutional approach in nonformal programs (Ahmed 1975 pp. 13–15).

2. Enhancing Efficiency

Enhancing efficiency of resources in education calls for the examination of the costs of programs and their benefits leading to the consideration of ways of having maximum benefits at the least cost. As nonformal education programs do not exist on a large scale as a discrete category, the practical approach to examining costs is to look at the cost patterns in the mainstream educational programs and explore ways of improving cost-efficiency by incorporating nonformal features in the programs.

2.1 Cost Patterns

A set of generalizations drawn from a series of 27 case studies of educational costs shows a pattern and indicates the potential that may exist for greater efficiency:

(a) Personnel costs dominate educational budgets. The labor-intensive nature of education combined with the organizational features of formal education create this effect. Personnel costs in primary education are typically over 90 percent in developing countries.

(b) There is a trend of continuous rise in the cost per student. As economic conditions improve and wages rise, the salaries of teachers also rise. As long as educational technology requires a heavy input of paid labor, unit costs will continue to rise (see *Evaluation of Distance Education: Cost-Effectiveness*). The pressure for improvement in the quality of instruction and the diversification of content of learning also contributes to rising personnel costs. On the other hand, in recent years, economic recession and the burden of external debt have forced many developing countries to cut back on educational budgets, retrenching the teachers' roll and limiting or even reversing salary increases for teachers. High price inflation also has significantly eroded the real income of teachers in many countries. However, this situation is generally not seen as a desirable development and an aberration in the trend of rising unit costs.

(c) The *structure* of educational costs, despite the trend of rising costs, is remarkably stable. The high share of personnel costs serves as a ballast and keeps the composition of educational cost elements relatively unchanged, even though total and unit costs continue to rise.

(d) Unit costs are higher at higher levels of education. In formal education, unit costs rise with each successive level of education, regardless of whether it is general or technical and vocational education.

(e) The academic calendar of formal education imposes a cost burden. Typically, classes are held for five or six hours a day, during which time only a part of the total facilities—laboratories, libraries, playgrounds, sport facilities, or classrooms—are used. Long vacations, holidays, and weekends take up almost one-half of the calendar year. All of these add up in total costs. The more expensive the facilities, such as those in technical and higher education, the higher the cost of wastage.

(f) Economies of scale are available to a limited degree in formal education. It has been observed in many countries that consolidation of primary and secondary schools has resulted in a reduction of unit costs, while at the same time, the variety and scope of the school programs and their quality have improved. The same phenomenon can be observed in respect to technical education and universities. There is, however, a limit to this: economies disappear when the overheads of administration, management, and central services begin to be spread too thinly, and too large a concentration of people and activities adversely affects the social and psychological environment. A trade-off point is reached where the cost advantages are more than offset by the deterioration in the quality of learning (Coombs and Hallak 1972 Chap. 6).

2.2 Reducing Costs

To what extent can the features of nonformal education be incorporated into the mainstream educational programs to achieve cost reduction without sacrificing results? The answer depends largely on the willingness of mainstream educational establishments and policymakers to re-examine the goals and process of the educational program and adopt the potential flexibilities (see Stromquist 1982 pp. 69–94).

Lowering capital costs. In many nonformal programs there is little or no capital cost involved specifically with the educational activity. Other programs can make use of existing physical facilities during off-hours. Still others have physical facilities that are low cost because they are adapted to local needs and conditions, built largely with local materials, labor, and techniques, and in some cases with contributions in cash and kind from the community.

Although expensive facilities are not needed at the field level in most nonformal programs, any program that reaches a large audience and expects to have a significant impact must be supported by backstopping facilities, although the per learner capital costs may not be high even in these cases. Examples of such well-developed central facilities are the Cooperative Education Center and Wings in Tanzania, the Mobral Central facilities in Brazil, and the central facilities of open universities.

In the primary education system in developing countries, capital cost constitutes a significant new investment just to keep up with the growth of the primary school entrants. Variations in the total length of the school cycle and the annual and daily calendar, the entrance age for the cycle, and multiple shifts are nonformal features which can lead to savings in capital costs. Increasing interest in primary education by international development finance institutions such as the World Bank and the Regional Development Banks and their offers of assistance largely concentrated on capital investments have heightened the concern about high-cost and high-technology physical facilities which are inappropriate for local conditions, difficult to maintain, and fail to promote community involvement.

Efficiency in personnel costs. Since personnel costs are recurrent, any increase or saving in personnel costs has a permanent effect on the cost of the program. Opportunity for savings in personnel costs arise from the use of part-time instructors for a proportionate or less than proportionate part-time wage, volunteers who serve as instructors or instructional help at no charge or a small charge, and local people with special experience or expertise who offer their services. Use of these approaches requires the relaxation of the professional training and qualification requirements in formal programs.

Although a program can make use of local low-cost personnel, this does not negate the role of the competent and well-qualified staff. The flexibility of nonformal educational approaches makes it possible, however, to use highly qualified personnel at supervisory, planning, and evaluation tasks for supporting and guiding the field-level activities, thus using relatively scarce talents to maximum advantages, multiplying the impact of professional personnel for a larger population, and reducing operational costs.

Self-financing. A number of nonformal programs have been able to reduce their net operating cost burden by generating some income or in-kind contribution from program activities. The practical and production-oriented bias, particularly of the occupational training programs, makes it possible to produce commodities and services in the programs that can be sold outside or used to supplement the programs' resources. Other types of programs that depend mainly on local resources and support can also be largely self-supporting in the sense that they need not rely on large outside subvention—the necessary materials being generated locally or provided by the learners themselves.

Marginality of nonformal education costs. Educational programs minimize net costs when they are able to use existing resources and facilities without diverting these resources from other uses or when they require the investment of a relatively small amount of additional resources. A school-equivalence program that uses existing school facilities during the evening (when the school building is unused,) and also engages school teachers as instructors on a part-time salary (without incurring the pre-service and inservice teacher-training costs or the full costs of producing textbooks and instructional materials) can be run at a fraction of the cost of a regular school—such as the school equivalency program in Thailand and nonformal educational programs for adults in other countries.

Educational programs that rely on part-time and volunteer personnel and facilities are enjoying the advantages of cost-marginality because they are using resources that have already been developed at some cost to society but have not been utilized to the fullest extent. The distance education programs that use the existing communication infrastructure have to pay only a fraction of the real costs of establishing and maintaining communication facilities, such as the radio and television network, the newspaper (when special newspaper supplements or columns are used for an educational program), and the postal system (in the case of a correspondence course).

Any educational activity that is part of a broader development program, such as an educational program for youth and women within a rural extension program, enjoys the benefits of cost-marginality. The larger program provides the organizational structure; many of the physical facilities, equipment, and instructional and administrative personnel who are already there; and, above all, a receptive audience.

3. Cost-effectiveness

It is not very helpful, in the planning and management of education, to examine costs without looking at the outcome of the learning process. It makes little sense to talk about high or low costs without relating costs of an educational activity to the results achieved. Economic analysis of educational programs, therefore, leads inevitably to the juxtaposition of the costs incurred and the benefits derived (see Ahmed 1975 Chap. 5).

3.1 Internal Efficiency

The relationship between cost inputs and the direct learning outputs (such as knowledge, skills, and so on) embodied in the learner is known as the internal efficiency of the educational program. The relationship between the benefits derived from an educational program and the cost inputs is referred to as the external productivity of the educational program which also can be expressed in numerical terms as the benefit–cost ratio.

Although the internal efficiency and external productivity of a program are related, the relationship may not be linear. High internal efficiency does not guarantee high external productivity, though generally a high benefit–cost ratio implies a high measure of internal efficiency. In fact, a program can have high internal efficiency and low or negative external productivity— for example, when a program uses resources efficiently to teach the wrong things in terms of the real needs of the learners or the usability of what is taught.

Evaluation of educational programs often focus on the internal efficiency of the program: the didactic processes, the direct learning achievements, the number of learners who complete the course, and the corresponding cost inputs. Internal efficiency measures are sometimes equated to cost-effectiveness measures, implying that the effectiveness of a program is judged by the immediate learning outputs. Assessment of the cost–benefit relationships requires the examination of internal efficiency; but the results of such an examination alone will not answer the significant cost–benefit questions. One method of cost–benefit analysis, the rate-of-return study, has been particularly appealing to some economists, because it purports to demonstrate the economic return to the investment in the educational program and to provide a basis for making educational investment decisions. It has now become widely recognized that although a useful analytical tool in some situations, the rate-of-return study is an inadequate basis for educational decisions and can even be misleading if only because it takes into account an incomplete view of both costs and benefits. (For an early critique of this technique, see Bowles 1969.) A host of factors extraneous to the educational program itself determines how effectively the educational output is used for individual and social benefits.

The categories of factors affecting the cost–benefit relationship include the general ecological endowment of a geographical area which imposes basic constraints on the socioeconomic development of the area served by the educational program; economic dynamic and prospects of the area affecting economic employment and opportunities; provisions for supplies such as agricultural inputs, raw materials and equipment for rural industry, and medical and family planning supplies; physical infrastructure such as roads, irrigation systems, and communication facilities; institutional infrastructure including local organizations, financial institutions, land tenure systems, and so on. Overall national and local educational policies and strategies place the individual program in a broader context and define its links with other programs, enhancing the effectiveness of the individual program as well as of the learning system. Cost–benefit analysis is more of a notional concept, because the full range of benefits from a program cannot be fully quantified or estimated with precision.

3.2 Pragmatic Compromise

The practical necessities of educational planning and management can be served by a pragmatic compromise between the narrow internal efficiency approach and the impossible task of a total cost–benefit analysis. Judging a programs' value, deciding whether it is achieving its main objectives at a reasonable cost, and improving its performance—such efforts can be enormously helped by attempts to juxtapose the known cost inputs against the evidence that can be gathered of the achievement of the main stated and predetermined objectives and the intended benefits of the program. This modest but feasible effort can be a firmer basis for forming a realistic cost-effectiveness judgment about a program than the misleading "precision" of internal efficiency measures, the benefit–cost ratio, or the rate of return. It is certainly more useful for planners and managers of education to view cost-effectiveness as the relationship between costs and the stated objectives of a program or whatever proxy measures or indication of their attainment are available than to equate it to the relationship between costs and the immediate process outputs, which, by themselves, are unimportant.

4. Mobilizing Resources

A major obstacle to achieving the educational goals of developing countries such as those advocated by the World Conference on Education for All is scarcity of resources. In the last two decades, two successive world recessions in the mid-1970s and the early 1980s followed by the international debt crisis have caused a decline in real terms in public budgets for education in the majority of developing countries.

Moreover, in many developing countries, especially in sub-Saharan Africa and Latin America, the large proportions of government budgets already devoted to education leave limited scope for further increases in public spending. (Haddad et al. 1990 p. 34, also UNESCO 1991 pp 38–39). A very important way of stretching resources, of course, is to reduce the costs and make the existing resources more productive, as noted above. But, however much the efficiency of resources is improved, the fact is that in most developing countries significantly more resources will be needed to meet their educational goals.

Taking only the needs of primary education, leaving aside other elements of basic education for youth and adults, and assuming that effective universalization of primary education is the goal for the decade of the 1990s, it is estimated that China and India need to increase their primary education resources by four to six times the current absolute amounts in ten years. Such an order of increase will mean at least doubling the present share of gross national product (GNP) devoted to primary education (Ahmed et al. 1991 pp. 150–51).

A major increase in educational finance does not necessarily mean that all or most of the increase has to come from public revenues, especially central revenue. Depending on the specific circumstances of the country, various sources have to be tapped, including different levels of government, the noneducation sectors, communities, public and private employers and the direct beneficiaries (see Bray and Lillis 1988). The rigid structure of nonformal education allows limited opportunities for use of unconventional resources. In contrast, the expansion of nonformal education or the "deformalizing" of formal education can spur greater contributions of various kinds from nonmarket and nonbudgetary resources.

Decentralized local management of educational programs and community involvement (features that are more compatible with nonformal approaches) facilitate mobilization of nonmarket and nonbudgetary resources. By planning and operating educational activities suitable for local conditions and relevant to local development goals, the support and contribution of local people can be harnessed.

5. Conclusion

In summary, nonformal education approaches for youth and adults, by widening organizational and methodological options in educational programs, widens the possibilities of combining economic analysis with key educational considerations such as equity, relevance of content, and quality of learning, thus contributing to improved decision-making in education. Nonformal education programs, or the adoption of nonformal features in educational programs—the label attached to a program is inconsequential—also expand the range of choices in analysis and action in respect of critical economic concerns such as reduc-ing wastage of resources, improving efficiency and cost-effectiveness, and mobilizing larger amounts of resources.

See also: Formal, Nonformal, and Informal Education; Economics of Adult Education and Training; Demand, Supply, and Finance of Adult Education; Evaluation of Distance Education: Cost-Effectiveness; Evaluation of Industry Training: Cost-Effectiveness; Evaluation of Public Training: Cost-Effectiveness

References

Ahmed M 1975 *The Economics of Nonformal Education: Resources, Costs and Benefits.* Praeger, New York

Ahmed M, Cheng Kai Ming, Jalaluddin A K, Ramachandran K 1991 *Basic Education and National Development: Lessons from China and India.* United Nations Children's Fund, New York

Bowles S 1969 *Planning Educational Systems for Economic Growth.* Oxford University Press, New York

Bray M, Lillis K (eds.) 1987 *Community Financing of Education: Issues and Policy Implications in Less Developed Countries.* Pergamon Press, Oxford

Coombs P H, Hallak J 1972 *Managing Educational Costs.* Oxford University Press, New York

Haddad W D, Carnoy M, Regel O, Rinaldi R 1990 *Education and Development: Evidence for New Priorities.* World Bank Discussion Paper No. 95, World Bank, Washington, DC

Stromquist N 1982 A review of educational innovations to reduce costs. In: International Development Research Center 1982 *Financing Educational Development.* Proceedings of an International Seminar. International Development Research Center, Ottawa

United Nations Educational Scientific and Cultural Organization 1991 *World Education Report.* UNESCO, Paris

Further Reading

Fullan M G, Stiegelbauer S 1991 *The New Meaning of Educational Change.* Cassell Educational, London

Caillods F 1989 *The Prospects for Educational Planning.* International Institute for Educational Planning, UNESCO, Paris

History of Adult Education

F. Pöggeler

The historiography of adult education has mainly been devoted to adult education in just one state, people, or nation. However, it must also be grasped as regional, continental, and world history with comparative aspects (Leirman and Pöggeler 1979). In the history of adult education, the interdependence between education, politics, economy, and social life must be considered. The history of adult education is also the history of institutions, organizations, people and their motives for lifelong learning. The influence of creative personalities as founders of new institutions and as stimulators was always greater than in school systems for children and young people. One reason is that participation in adult education was normally voluntary, while school education was compulsory. As an organized system, adult education has existed since the nineteenth century. Hence it is much younger than the school system. It is a late product of the history of education, a child of the Enlightenment movement.

1. Political Factors

The Enlightenment movement of the eighteenth century was the political origin of people's education as the precursor of adult education. If all people tend to equal intellectual perfectibility, they must have the same human rights. They must also have the same education in order to be able to participate in political responsibility (Condorcet 1847–49). In this sense "people" are no longer identical with the lower classes but the totality of citizens. In fact, the political aims of the Enlightenment were not realized until the nineteenth century. As proletariats came into existence in the industrial countries, workers established their own educational associations especially in the United Kingdom, and in Germany after 1840, where the principle "Knowledge is power and power is knowledge" (Liebknecht 1920) was adopted. Consequently the workers' educational associations developed into labor unions and socialist political parties. Adult education thus became an instrument of political change and did much toward opening parliamentary and governmental participation to members of the working classes (see *Worker Education and Labor Education*).

As with workers' education, a new style of farmers' education in the nineteenth century also caused a reform of the structure of state. In Denmark, N F S Grundtvig founded the folk high school in 1844 with the intention of strengthening the ethnic, cultural, and political identity of the Danish people after a long period of dependence on Germany. By participating in "higher" adult education the farmers, as the largest group of citizens, would learn to participate in political discussions and decisions at least on a local and regional level.

The pioneers of adult education in industrialized countries of the nineteenth and early twentieth century also believed that a reform of the state can be realized by a reform of adult education. For instance, in Germany the "intensive–creative people's education" inspired by theorists such as Rosenstock-Huessy after the First World War attempted to create a new national and ethnic unity of the people by education in group work (*Arbeitsgemeinschaften*). Their slogan was: "People's education is the making of a new unity of a nation" (*Volksbildung ist Volk-Bildung*). However, this aim was too high and utopian, and adult education could not avoid the rise of fascism and Hitler.

Similar attempts and experiences at political reform through adult education were made in the "re-education" of the German and Japanese people. Deeply ingrained political attitudes cannot be altered quickly and the influence of education on politics is limited by traditional habits and economic circumstances. It is also true that it is easier to reform education by the state than the state by education. In any case, the political power of adult education is more efficient in democracies than in totalitarian states, which fear enlightened and self-responsible citizens and do not support the liberal education of adults, because by such education the citizens become more critical and aware of political manipulation. The history of the former Soviet Union and other communist states has shown that adult education there was not a favored part of the educational system (compared with the education of children and young people), and that adult education was more or less controlled as a system for professional and ideological qualifications (Siebert 1970). Also national socialism and fascism did not allow liberal education. Instead they closed the adult education institutions of the independent agencies and social movements.

New states in particular invest much hope in adult education, because they know that the success of a state depends upon the educational level of the adult citizens. An important example since 1948 is the new state of Israel. New immigrants, who came from different parts of the world were given a fundamental education in the *Ulpanim*. Not only were they taught Modern Hebrew, but also political convictions that were essential for the new state (Schachar 1976). So far Israel is an "educational society," in which all inhabitants are accustomed to lifelong learning according to Jewish faith.

Democratic states limited their activities in adult education to: (a) sponsoring the initiatives of independent bodies in establishing institutions for adult education; (b) establishing a legal basis for adult education; (c) encouraging cooperation between different organizers and institutions of adult education; and (d) connecting the system of adult education with other parts of the educational system.

Special laws for adult education came into existence in 1945 after long periods of experimentation, especially with regulations for finance, administration, and personnel. The fact that laws were passed rather late (much later than school laws) marks the full integration of adult education with educational systems at large. For example, in the United Kingdom official reports on the situation and future of adult education (Stock 1979) seem to have had more influence on its development and innovation than laws.

2. Organizations

From its very beginning, organized adult education included a great number of institutional types. The variety has its origin in the initiatives of many nongovernmental and independent bodies, and of individuals who founded institutions or movements on their own, which was not always welcomed by the ruling political powers.

Before adult education was institutionalized (about the middle of the nineteenth century), people's education took place in scientific reading associations and circles. Here new books on science and literature were read and discussed by members of the middle and upper classes. In particular for women, who could not attend university lectures at that time, the educational associations were the only opportunity to get acquainted with scientific knowledge. Since the time of the Enlightenment, the popularization of science became one of the most notable goals of adult education. Workers' educational organizations followed, and did much for the political and intellectual emancipation of the lower classes. In the United Kingdom and Austria after 1871 the universities arranged lectures and courses for nonacademic people in cooperation with the workers' educational associations. The opening of the universities had two directions: nonacademic citizens came into the university, and the university started extramural studies or university extension courses in the regions around them. Also, some university professors began to give lectures in new institutions of scientific adult education, for example, the "Urania Houses" in Austria and Germany and new people's academies.

Educational associations usually started and developed through a cooperation between workers' unions, cooperative movements, scientific academies, and universities. While in Germany these educational associations lost their importance and influence after 1900 (in consequence of the establishment of folk high schools and similar institutes), in many other countries the work continued, with many participants and gaining a high prestige. Before the First World War some of the educational associations had more than one million members and published a great quantity of popular scientific literature. The end of many of these associations was caused by a crisis of the popularization of new goals for people's education, which argued for other than scientific content for people's education. Adult education should no longer be a simplified form of the university education, but a new "thinking people" should be established (Mann 1948, Flitner 1921, Wartenweiler 1949). Instead of passively listening to scientific lectures in mass audiences, people should learn solutions for their life problems in small working groups with members of all classes of the population.

The educational associations gained some inspiration from great social movements that used adult education for disseminating their aims: for example, the women's, the peace, the cooperative, and the socialist movements. Education became a means for establishing or stressing the political and intellectual identity of the movements. They tried to achieve stability by organizing their structures. But as they did so they lost their enthusiasm, and came up against the conflict of "initiative versus establishment." After 1970 the ecological movement in the industrial countries of Europe and North America favored an unstructured and nonformal education without the straitjacket of institutions (von Werder 1981).

In the nineteenth and twentieth centuries adult education was not only promoted by special educational associations, but also by political, vocational, and religious organizations, which had and have an interest in educating their members or in winning new ones. The engagement of churches, political parties and labor unions in people's and adult education often raised the question, if there must be a difference between a "free" and open style of adult education and "bound" education; adult education should always be open and available for all interested people and not only for members of the groups mentioned (Becker 1957, 1975).

In Europe and in North America top councils of the big organizations of adult education became national bases informing the organizations about common political trends and events of common importance and to find a common strategy for adult education politics. National associations were created in many countries, with the aim of making their adult education "speak with one voice."

As a result of political and economic development, there seems to have evolved a North–South divide in the continents of Europe and North America as well as in the world as a whole. The northern countries were more or less industrialized, the southern countries scarcely or not at all. Northern nations like the Scandinavian countries, the United Kingdom, Germany, or Austria were the "mother countries" of adult education, while the number of institutions for organized people's education in parts of Southern Europe was scarce. The same situation characterized Asia. Since 1900 adult education was established in countries with comparatively industrialized regions like India, Korea, and Japan (see Ambroise 1990, Ki Un Hahn 1979, Luhmer 1979). In Africa, institutions for adult education were established mostly in urban areas, sometimes under the influence of colonialization (Mock 1978, Khalifa 1979).

3. Institutions

While the schools for children and young people were formed by states, churches, and similar organizations, the institutions of adult education were mostly created by individuals and were stamped by the ideas of these founders, for example, the folk high school by Grundtvig (in 1844), the beginning of the university extension by James Stuart (in 1873), the people's library by Preusker (in 1847), or the hostels for journeyman workers (*Gesellenhaus*) by Kolping (in 1849). Adult education covers a great variety of institutions, most of them developed since the beginning of the twentieth century. One can differentiate between the first period of institutions from the middle of the eighteenth to the end of the nineteenth century, characterized by the educational associations and the second period of institutions, which were founded in the nineteenth century with the people's library, the folk high school, and the hostels for journeyman workers. Many new types of adult education started after the First and Second World Wars, often specialized for certain fields of education: parents', women's, farmers', and political, economic, religious, or vocational education. Such fields gave the framework for classification of the many different institutions.

Institutions of adult education have not been so much bound to one nation or state as have schools. Many of them migrated from one country to another and were assimilated into the ethnic and cultural peculiarities of the nations. It is important for the history of adult education, that there has been an intensive exchange of ideas and experiences between the nations and cooperation between the leaders of the various movements.

The great influence of certain individuals and nongovernmental bodies on forming the institutions has resulted in governments and other official bodies refraining from defining the characteristic of the institutions. Consequently the extent of bureaucracy could often be limited to a necessary minimum, so that the institutions could work as living bodies with the chance of change and renewal. In the course of the educational reforms in Latin America and Africa, some experts, such as Illich and Freire proposed a far-reaching "deschooling of society" with a moving of the center of education from the instruction of young people to the education of autonomous adults.

4. Content of Adult Education

People's education in the era of the Enlightenment opened fields of science and knowledge to all groups of the population by "translating" them into the mentality of nonacademic people. This was a "revolution of education" indeed, because up to that time many fields of knowledge were closed to the uneducated and only accessible to academic people. Then in the epoch of Romanticism, people's education aimed at reviving interest in old traditions, folksongs, legends, customs, fairy tales, proverbs, and so on. Also, the underlying ethical and religious beliefs of the people became topics of their education. In the nineteenth century the educational associations for workers and craftspeople favored "practical" knowledge for professional and social life, including politics. This practical knowledge should not be taken from books, but from life. Grundtvig called the "book school" a "school of death," that is, a useless institution. Instead, he advocated "people's knowledge" as a means for becoming aware of the political vitality of a nation that loves its own values. Lectures should be the opening for free dialogues. Learning should be the inspiration for humanization, and therefore the methods of learning gained an anthropological dimension. Methods of learning became identified with methods of living.

Nevertheless, a great part of adult education during the second half of the nineteenth century was dominated by popularized academic lectures with large audiences. Recycling of academic knowledge was the main task; a critic called that method a "gathering of crumbs that fall down from the high desk of science to the ground." After the First World War, when a new campaign of adult education began in many countries, knowledge for "the people" was still limited in some institutions. For instance, in the people's libraries the readers could not obtain all kinds of scientific books, and instead of the "free-hand principle" the "counter principle" was usual; the librarian decided on the "right" book for the reader.

As participation in adult education is voluntary in democracies, the adult must decide about the content of learning, and the institutions can only offer and recommend. According to a new anthropology of mental maturity and autonomy after the Second World War, those responsible for educational planning were encouraged to take the view that fields of knowledge like history, economy, science, and politics can better be understood by adults than by youngsters and that it is better to teach and learn these objects in adult education (Livingstone 1959, Pöggeler 1964). The interest in knowledge changes from one stage of life to the next, so that every subject must be taught or learned again newly at all stages, and not only once in childhood or youth, as happened in the past. Adult education became most continuing and recurrent education, not only as liberal and general education but also as vocational education. Knowledge quickly becomes out of date and irrelevant. Since the 1960s the vocational parts of adult education have gained importance in many countries (see *Economics of Adult Education and Training*).

5. Teaching and Learning

While the methods of adult teaching and learning during the period of the Enlightenment were the same as in schools and universities, special methods for adult education came into circulation during the nineteenth century. For example, in the Romantic period there were new methods of talking and reading, and Grundtvig's approach to people's education presented new methods of rhetoric. The teacher should be a narrator, who presents knowledge by story-telling and singing. Informal methods were preferred, and the result of teaching and learning was not only gaining new knowledge, but also new enthusiasm for values and for models of life. A certain dualism between scientific and popular traditional methods of academic teaching and learning were also reactivated, when universities started to take an interest in people's education in the last third of the nineteenth century. In evening schools for adults, academies of "Urania" or in educational associations, the teachers were proud if "the people" (of the lower or the middle classes) filled the lecture rooms.

In the course of the twentieth century methods of "mass education" lost their attractiveness, and methods of group and course learning came to the fore. In small groups people should not be the objects, but the subjects of their further education, and teaching should animate the self-learning of the group or class. In the Scandinavian "evening study circles," which during the twentieth century became the biggest category of adult education, the choice of methods was no longer the privilege of the teacher. All participants were given the opportunity of choosing the most suitable method (Husén 1958). So adult learning and teaching changed, and methods of traditional school learning were no longer accepted. Adult teaching and learning came to be regarded as social processes, as a change of attitudes, and as communication. Adult teaching and learning became an important element in social and political reform. In Latin America, Africa, and Asia even alphabetization was no longer practiced as a "technical" task but as a new method of political enlightenment of underprivileged people (Freire 1970). Learners took the role of teachers according to the slogan: "Each one teach one!" In this light, the history of adult learning and teaching must be interpreted as a history of emancipation.

See also: Adult Education: Concepts and Principles; Critical Approaches to Adult Education; Popular Education and Conscientization; Sociology of Adult Education

References

Ambroise J 1990 Adult education in the context of South Asia with special focus on Indian society. In: Pöggeler F (ed.) 1990 *The State and Adult Education*. Peter Lang, Frankfurt

Becker H 1957 *Bildung zwischen Plan und Freiheit*. Klett Verlag, Stuttgart

Becker H 1975 *Weiterbildung. Aufklärung, Praxis, Theorie 1956–1974*. Klett Verlag, Stuttgart

Condorcet M J A N 1847–49 *Oeuvres publiées par A.Condorcet*, 12 vols. O'Connor A C, Hrago M F (eds.) 1847–49. Paris

Flitner W 1921 *Laienbildung*. Diederichs, Jena

Freire P 1970 *Pädagogik der Unterdrückten*. Klett Verlag, Stuttgart

Grundtvig N F S 1927 *Schriften zur Volkserziehung und Volkheit*. Tiedge J (ed.) 1927. Diederichs, Jena

Husén T 1958 *Vuxna lär*. Ehlins, Stockholm

Khalifa M 1979 Ägypten. In: Leirman W, Pöggeler F (eds.) 1979

Ki Un Hahn 1979 Süd Korea. In: Leirman W, Pöggeler F (eds.) 1979

Leirman W, Pöggeler F (eds.) 1979 *Erwachsenenbildung in fünf Kontinenten*. W. Kohlhammer, Stuttgart

Liebknecht W 1920 *Wissen ist Macht—Macht ist Wissen*. Festrede von 1872. Berlin

Livingstone, Sir R 1959 *Zukunft der Erziehung*. Dümmler Verlag, Bonn

Luhmer K 1979 Erwachsenenbildung. In: Leirman W, Pöggeler F (eds.) 1979

Mann A 1948 *Denkendes Volk—Volkhaftes Denken*, 2nd edn. Franz Mockrauer

Mock E 1978 *Afrikanische Pädagogik*. Jugenddienstverlag P Hammer, Wuppertal

Pöggeler F 1964 *Der Mensch in Mündigkeit und Reife*. Schöningh

Schachar 1976 *Social Changes in Adult Education in Israel*. Hebrew Tarbuth Vehinkh, Tel Aviv

Siebert H 1970 *Erwachsenenbildung in der Erziehungs gesellschaft der* DDR. Bertelsmann University, Düsseldorf

Stock H 1979 Grossbritannien. In: Leirman W, Pöggeler F (eds.) 1979

von Werder L 1981 Erwachsenenbildung und Bildungspolitik. In: Pöggeler F, Wolterhoff B (eds.) 1981 *Neue Theorien der Erwachsenenbildung*. W. Kohlhammer, Stuttgart

Wartenweiler F 1949 *Erwachsenenbildung gestern, heute und morgen*. Rotapfel, Erlenbach

Philosophy and Ethics in Adult Education

K. H. Lawson

Although it may be assumed that adult education is conducted according to some set of principles and values embodied in a working philosophy, it is not always easy to establish direct connections with more general philosophical ideas. The relationships tend to be implicit and unrecognised as part of a common cultural and political background, which is itself shaped in part by particular philosophical traditions.

In various ways therefore, philosophical ideas do underpin adult education practice and provide some of its ethical values, but variations make it impossible to give a concise and complete description. There are, for example, such considerable differences between Western and Eastern philosophies and cultures—as well as within them—that it might be questioned whether a common conception of adult education can exist. This entry will, therefore, be highly selective and illustrative rather than comprehensive in attempting an account of the influences of philosophy upon adult education.

1. Unity or Diversity?

Despite efforts to produce a unified concept of "adult education," its continuing fragmentation in terms of theory and practice is well charted (Schroeder 1970, Plecas and Sork 1986). Philosophical issues have also been discussed (Kallan 1962, White 1970, Elias and Merriam 1980, Paterson 1979, Lawson 1975, Wain 1987). Despite this attention, however, it is still possible to echo Knowles' assertion that "Adult education has often been criticised for having no foundational and unifying philosophy" (in Preface to Elias and Merriam 1979).

The absence of such a philosophy raises the question whether the idea of a single foundational philosophy is viable. There is at present a strongly held view among Western philosophers—led by such thinkers as Rorty (1980)—that the idea of foundational philosophy in the tradition of Descartes and Kant is unattainable, since there can be no philosophical finality.

Other arguments support this view in relation to adult education and training:

(a) Its cultural specificity is reflected in the diversity of adult education thought and practice on a global scale.

(b) The term "adult education" is language specific and rooted in educational traditions derived in part from Classical Greece, which makes translation into other languages difficult without change of meaning (see *Andragogy*).

(c) In common usage, the term "education" is highly normative—it presupposes a particular kind of curriculum based on a concept of individual development that is, somehow, differentiated from "learning" and "training."

(d) The narrow interpretation of the term "education" has led to the development of new concepts as replacements for "adult education," such as "recurrent," "lifelong" and "continuing" education, and these are not linguistic equivalents. They imply distinctive philosophical positions which either weaken or dispense with the idea of adult education as an age-related sector of educational provision.

(e) Finally, it has been pointed out that this age-related concept is excluded by the French *education populaire* and the Italian *scuola populare* (Titmus 1981).

2. The Ethos of Adult Education—A Humanistic Perspective

It should now be apparent that a total global survey is impossible and the examples discussed will be selections. They are chosen for their significance in relation to the point about unity and diversity.

A useful starting point is an article by Burstow (1984) who, writing from Canada states "When I hear the terms that have become our hallmark—terms like 'self-directed learning' and 'ongoing learning' I am aware that these imply some sort of image of the learner that is libertarian and emergent." This image is a recurring one which suggests a philosophy already immanent in the practices of adult education and, because it makes points which have an ethical dimension, there are the beginnings of a normative view of adult education. But, Burstow continues, the image is "not rooted in ontology . . . it is not rooted in an understanding of what is fundamental to existence generally and human existence in particular." She clearly is not satisfied with the status of the prevailing ethos and feels that it is in need of further justification. Her next move is interesting. She casts around for an independent foundational philosophy to validate what is already implicit in adult education, and her choice is French "existentialism" as expounded by Sartre. This philosophical standpoint, she believes, provides the understanding of authentic human existence. It fits a preconceived perception of what adult education requires and this is a good example of one way in which philosophy is used by adult educators.

No historical connection is demonstrated between existentialism and adult education. The relationship is contingent but there is logical compatibility. Existentialism is not a necessary foundation but it is sufficient. Other philosophies might equally be valid, therefore there is a foundation in what might be called a weak sense only. It is one possible choice.

Existentialism is also an example of a "humanistic" philosophy, a characteristic of which is a belief that it is based on human nature. In that sense, they are naturalistic but they may also be regarded as normative. They represent views of how human beings ought to be and this is an example of an ethical stance.

For Sartre, our humanity lies in the ability to behave intentionally in defining ourselves as the kind of person that we want to be. This in turn presupposes the freedom to choose as well as the ability to do so. From an adult education point of view its purpose is to foster and encourage the development of self-defining individuals, but the extent to which this is possible depends upon the kind of society within which they live. A very open culture and political circumstances which permit freedom are both essential, and these aspects are not fully taken into account within the existential ethic. Burstow, in making her original assumptions about the libertarian ethos of adult education, can only do so because she already works within a liberal democratic framework which has to be taken into account when theorising begins.

3. Humanism and Andragogy

Other humanistic philosophies have influenced adult education. The concept of andragogy, developed and popularized by Knowles (1970, 1980), is a prime example. Both historically and logically, this concept helped to create the ethos to which Burstow responded, but again it must be stressed that sociopolitical circumstances were conducive to the development of Knowles' theories.

Although associated mainly with Knowles in the United States, there are also European variants described by Van Enkévort (1971) and discussed briefly by Long (1991). The argument here is confined to the American version, which is in fact rooted in what might be called "philosophical psychology" and social science rather than pure philosophy. Rank, Rogers and Sedlin together with Maslow, Erikson and Lindeman are cited by Knowles as his sources (Knowles, 1972).

Andragogy may be described as "humanistic" because it refers to a system of adult education based upon allegedly human characteristics. The word "allegedly" is used advisedly because an element of value judgement is involved. The characteristics referred to are "desirable" in the eyes of the theorists, and a central example is the ideal of a "self-actuating person." This is linked to "self direction" in the choice of learning goals and the idea of the teacher as a "facilitator." The curriculum of adult education is regarded as being open ended and linked to individual perceptions of learning needs and developmental tasks related to stages in life. Andragogy thus becomes a system which is contrasted with pedagogy and it is based upon a conception of "adulthood" which is contrasted with "childhood."

Despite its different mode of argument, the andragogical concept has affinities with the existential view already discussed. It can be noted once again that different premises and philosophical stances might variously be used to provide a theoretical foundation for otherwise similar practices. Each philosophy can be regarded as foundational, but none has a greater intrinsic claim other than its cogency and tightness of argument.

4. Analytical Philosophy and Liberal Adult Education

Throughout the 1960s in Australia, the United Kingdom, and the United States, a new approach to the philosophy of education developed that eventually also came to embrace adult education.

Known as "analytical philosophy of education" or APE, the new movement reflected developments in what has come to be called "Anglo-Saxon, analytic philosophy." Its origins are various and they are to be found in the Vienna Circle, Wittgenstein, Frege, and Russell together with Austin and others at Oxford. The distinctive feature of this approach was its emphasis upon language and the analysis of meaning as the key to philosophical understanding. It concentrated on techniques rather than on doctrines and to some extent the inspiration came from the physical sciences and from studies on logic. Language and logic were the philosophers' equivalent to the scientists' empirical data.

APE first concerned itself with the analysis of language used in the discourse of education and, later, the specific discourse of adult education.

The argument advocated by Peters (1979) was that the term "education" was more evaluative than descriptive. It was a normative concept which conferred status on certain forms of learning, and "education" was contrasted with "training," "socialisation," and "indoctrination". Criteria which qualified for the appellation "education" were derived mainly from the "classical" tradition which had its roots in classical Greece. In identifying these criteria, APE philosophers were in fact covertly prescriptive under the guise of analysis.

Writers such as Paterson (1979) and Lawson (1975) applied analytical techniques to concepts such as "adult" as a qualifier of the concept of "education" thus establishing the credentials of a distinctive "adult" form of education. Comparison may be made here with what is said about andragogy, in relation to the beginnings of a unifying theory which would help to identify the field of adult education "properly understood" within the terms of the analysis.

"Adulthood" was also explained in terms of "status" rather than in terms of adult psychology and an ethical–political dimension may be added in the form of "rights" and "responsibilities." There is therefore a considerable divergence from the androgogical model despite superficial similarities. Nevertheless, both modes presuppose the same kind of open, liberal structure within which adult education is conceptualised.

It is now obvious that what APE analysts were engaged in, was the analysis of a particular tradition in adult education. They were covertly prescriptive under the guise of analysis and phrases such as "a *correct* understanding" are typical. Despite the criticism, however, a valuable contribution has been made to the study of adult education. The arguments used are precise, painstakingly detailed and fine logical distinctions are made, thus we find Paterson (1979) saying ". . . the concept of the intended result may or may not form part of the activity in question . . . the concept of the result is logically quite distinct from the concept of activity."

The method is reminiscent of painstaking investigation within science except that it is language which is being studied. The whole analysis, however, depends upon an assumption that "meaning" is analytically (in the logical sense) contained within meaning. "Education," in common with terms such as "democracy" have connotations which *must* be understood in order for a word to be used and interpreted correctly. It is a very regimented view of language which in some ways reflects the precision demanded by Latin scholars. As Elias and Merriam (1980) have pointed out, however, analysis "may arrive at a false precision which then leads to unwelcome consequences (such as) a devaluing of certain forms of adult education." This is a valid criticism of what in the end is a highly context and tradition specific philosophy of adult education. Whether or not it could be otherwise is still an open question.

5. Liberal Adult Education and Liberal Philosophy

It is impossible to give a rounded account of the liberal approach to adult education as discussed in the previous section without making some reference to the political philosophy which also informs it. It is the philosophy implicit in and providing theoretical support for liberal democracy and it is a very old tradition with roots in Platonic thought and in Roman, Judaic, and Christian scholarship. In its more recent manifestation, a convenient starting point is the 17th century with the philosophy of Locke (1690). His starting point was the idea that individuals are logically prior to and conceptually independent of the state, which is only a device for providing mutual support and protection. The relationship between individuals and the state is contractual and the contract embodies rights for the protection of individuals. It is this set of ideas which puts the individual firmly at the centre of liberal adult education. Individual development is the prime purpose of liberal adult education but such development is not only personal. It is also development of the citizen.

More recently, liberalism has been updated by writers such as Rawls (1972) and Nozick (1974) and one of their central principles is that no human being can, or has the right to say what is good for another human being. Each is free, in the sense of having a right to choose. This is the ethical and judicial strand in their philosophy. There is also an ontological element derived in part from Descartes (1637) and from Kant (1781), namely that human beings are autonomous centers of consciousness. They are moral agents and ends in themselves and they are also the source of knowledge based upon their combined observational and rational faculties. Each individual human being is the Cartesian "I" which thinks and in this group of related ideas is the origin of the liberal adult education student.

As Paterson (1979) puts it, (liberal) adult education is an education that ". . . directly touches us in our personal being, tending our identity at its roots and ministering directly to our condition as conscious selves aspiring in all our undertakings to a greater fullness and completeness of being." The affinities with existentialism may be noted here and although the style of argument is different in the two examples they both home in on the "liberation ethos" already discussed.

It should be stressed, however, that liberal theory also rests on an epistemology which is rational–empirical and formulated in "forms of knowledge" (see Hirst 1974) which roughly equate with conventional categories of academic knowledge. These provide the liberal adult education curriculum taught not *ex cathedra* but as knowledge which may be questioned, assessed, and revised. All knowledge claims are provisional and the development of ability to criticise and assess knowledge claims is one of the goals of a liberal curriculum.

From a different perspective, this theme will reappear in the next section.

6. Radical Adult Education and Hermeneutic Philosophy

This is another loosely defined category and one of the best known names associated with it is Paulo Freire, who is usually said to draw upon a mixture of Marxist and Christian ideas. Although originated in Brazil, his views and methodology have been taken up in other parts of the world. Freire is, however, only one member of a developing tradition which has intellectual roots in theoretical sociology as well as in philosophy —if indeed such a distinction is acceptable to radicals. Names to be found in the literature include Althuser, Bowles and Gintis, Basil Burnstein, Bourdieu and Gramsci, not all of whom would regard themselves as radicals.

Two aspects of the radical tradition as here defined, will be discussed: (a) its methodological and practical implications; and (b) its theoretical antecedents and assumptions.

From a practical point of view, the chief characteristic of radical adult education is a concern for social criticism and social change rather than the transmission of academic knowledge and existing social values. Adult education does not simply reflect political ideas, it is itself a part of the political process (see *Critical Approaches to Adult Education*).

It might be argued that in its early manifestations, liberal adult education had similar goals and ideas, but it was concerned mainly with extending and strengthening liberal–democratic frameworks, not with radically changing them. In contrast, as one writer has put it, there is a need for ". . . a more general will to restructure the curriculum, to challenge conventional definitions and distribution of knowledge and to regard education as an important part of the struggle for socialism . . ." (Thompson 1980). A similar point of view is expressed by Freire (1972) when he claims that "No pedagogy which is truly liberating can remain distant from the oppressed by treating them as unfortunate and by presenting for their emulation models from among the oppressors."

Within radical frames of reference individuals are not the universal abstractions of liberalism as described by writers such as Rawls (1972) and Nozick (1974). Instead they are members of social groups sharing common political viewpoints, and the adult educators' task is to help them to identify and analyse their oppressed state. Adult education is therefore seen as overtly political, and it is aimed at particular groups. It is not intended to be universal provision.

It is not only the individuals who are regarded as being socially and historically situated. Knowledge also is defined in relation to historical and social contexts. Such knowledge is not simply "knowledge of the way the world is." It does not have a universal and objective quality. It has significance specific to those who formulate it, and in this respect the argument moves closer to pragmatism. There is a rejection of the idea of knowledge as foundational and underpinning thought and action. Rather, it expresses intention and determines action, an ideal exemplified in the term "praxis" or the uniting together of knowledge and action or practice and theory in a single concept. Knowledge is not merely related to understanding which need not lead to action. Knowledge is formulated with action already in mind and the goal is "liberation."

At a deeper level, the radical conception of adult education and its associated conception of knowledge, seems to have a close affinity with developments in the field of general philosophy where the idea of objective and universal or unhistorical knowledge is under attack. Here radicalism can be united with a new orthodoxy which makes use of the idea of subjectivity and the contextualization of knowledge. Here lies the relationship with the field of "hermeneutics" or philosophy as interpretation, which begins from the stand point of particular individuals in concrete situations. The concern is not with overt social and political action but the neutrality and universality of knowledge is rejected.

One of the best known exponents of these views is Rorty (1980) but there are intellectual links with such writers as Heidegger, Habermas, Feuerbach, Gadamer, Pierce, Dewey and Recouer as well as with Hegel and Marx. A good exposition of the hermeneutic tradition is given by Richard Burnstein (1982).

This is a complex field, but a link with radicalism may be made with the idea that knowledge is not "discovered" in an objective way using approved methodologies as in say, the empirical sciences, or by getting back to some foundational principle in the Cartesian tradition or in transcendentalism. The hermeneutic view is that analysis originates with a particular viewpoint and a history of community and personal experience which influence the interpretation of subsequent experience. This interpretation is what is regarded as "hermeneutic knowledge."

As Taylor (1979) expresses it, a hermeneutical science of man ". . . would not be founded on brute data; its most primitive data would be readings of meanings . . . which are partially constituted by self-definitions and which can thus be re-expressed by a science of politics . . . the subject may be a society or community . . ." There is "a vision of the agent and his society." The emphasis then moves away from

"knowledge" towards meanings and significance, and the idea of "intentionality" also emerges. This is not totally at variance with the empirical sciences which already contain a pragmatic element. Typically a scientist begins with a problem and data collection is determined by the perception of that problem, the solution of which is a "live option." The search for solutions is not totally disinterested.

Modern philosophy including the philosophy of science under the influence of writers such as Kuhn (1970), Rorty (1980) and others, increasingly recognises a weakening of the idea of definitive or absolute conceptions of knowledge. In what is called the "Post Modern" phase (see, for example, Lyotard 1979), there is emphasis on ideas such as "dialogue," "discussion," "exploration" and "socially constructed" rather than "discovered" knowledge. Such developments may be seen as consistent with the various conceptions of adult education discussed above—and to that extent there are the beginnings of a unifying philosophy —although it has many dimensions and no single philosophic thinker provides a foundation. Indeed the whole idea of adult education and "liberating" process requires that there be no firm foundation because that would represent an unacceptable constraint. Nevertheless, there is still a firm commitment to the ethical notion of "freedom" as a fundamental human right and an implicit set of political, ethical, and legal concepts appears to be accepted paradoxically as a foundational constraint. It may be concluded, therefore, by repeating a point already made, that adult education reflects its parent culture and cannot be universally defined or justified. Its foundations are in particular traditions and normative values which are justified or supported by philosophy which is also consonant with the same tradition.

7. African and Asian Philosophical Considerations

Despite what has been said about the context-relatedness of adult education there is considerable evidence of Western cultural hegemony. This hegemony is not without problems, and it is not always welcome. For example, Urevebu (1985) pointed out that Nigeria which already has many subcultures, has had to absorb "completely different cultures into an already complex system." "Westernisation" has therefore "resulted in numerous problems." This point has been made more strongly in Japan, where Mochida (1983) has described the Western educational heritage as "a yoke."

7.1 Japanese Buddhism

It might be expected therefore that local practices would be based on indigenous philosophies and ideologies. Yet modern examples appear to be rare. Mochida (1983), however, has sketched a Buddhist alternative to imported Western individualism.

Buddhist philosophy, which has its roots in the eighth century AD also has many branches and like Western philosophy it cannot be neatly encapsulated. What follows therefore is based upon Mochida's already attenuated version. His starting point is that there is "no absolute God," and that all mankind is capable of attaining "Buddhahood," a state of freedom and equality. In contrast to Western individualism, "man is not conceived of as an individual atom." He is a member of a community "related with others by 'karma' (fate, destiny) and dependent upon others."

Against this background, human development is not fettered by fixed doctrines because "all phenomena are transitory and in constant motion." Knowledge is not objective, it is a subjective relationship, "in unity with man" and the Japanese word translates into "wisdom." The relationship between educator and learner is one in which personal faith or belief "edifies" others. Teaching is not conceived as the giving of instruction but as a mutual search for truth in the daily practices of mankind living together in society. There are no standardized educational outcomes or standardized ways of life and the "Buddhist" ideal of education is both humanistic and anarchistic despite the emphasis on community and cooperation.

7.2 Neo-Confucianism and Dewey

An interesting blend of indigenous philosophy and Western philosophy may be seen in China in the first half of this century. Tao Xingzhi (1985) is said to have absorbed the Neo-Confucianism of the 15th century Wang Yang-ming for whom men's own nature provided moral criteria for action (or "practical reasoning" in Kantian terms).

On to this view, Tao Xingzhi grafted Dewey's educational theories which placed education in a pragmatic way, at the heart of living. Learning was influenced by perceptions of what was needed at particular times in order to solve perceived problems, which in China in the 1920s and 1930s included mass literacy programs and the training of schoolchildren to teach workers' classes. Knowledge therefore was not academic but practical. It was knowledge related to action and in this principle, the two systems of thought were linked.

7.3 An Indian Example

Given the complexity of Indian philosophy and the sharing of similar ideas between various forms of Hinduism and Buddhism, Rabindranath Tagore (1928) provides a rather eclectic example. As a Bengali he had experience of an Anglicised educational system in India but his own adult education philosophy was a blend of Indian traditions.

For Tagore education was concerned with the growth and freedom of the human spirit or soul and in "The Summary of a Lecture" (Tagore 1928) he stresses the way ". . . which in the Western races have to deal with Nature as the antagonist," thus emphasising ". . . the dualist aspect of truth (as) the eternal conflict between good and evil".

In contrast the Aryan immigrants in India found shelter and nourishment in the forests where they ". . . realised the spirit of harmony with the universe and emphasised in their minds the monistic aspect of Truth. They sought the realisation of their souls through union with all."

These ideas were embodied in an "Ashramic" education carried out between teacher and pupil in an "Abode of Peace" or "Shantinikitan" where the aim was the development of personality. Nevertheless, he still regarded the "alien movement" from Europe as being extremely important as "the very contradiction it offers to (India's) mental traditions" (Tagore 1928).

Tagore's last point is of considerable significance for non-Western cultures based upon an ethic of "unity" and "harmony" between man and man, and man and nature. The tensions and contradictions between cultures may be seen as creative as well as destructive. For practical purposes. Western epistemologies are used in connection with science and industry while "personal development" may be defined more in terms of traditional philosophies which draw fewer distinctions between religion and philosophy.

Such blending of traditions is not new and it has already been suggested that "no definition of what is typically Hindu philosophy is possible" and that "early Islamic philosophy is characterised by a profound tendency towards syncretism" or the "blending of inharmonious elements" (Speake 1984).

8. Conclusion

Summarizing the diversity of philosophical positions and traditions is virtually impossible but the indications point in one direction. Adult education can be justified from many points of view. There is no single unifying philosophy on a world-wide scale, and adult educators seeking a basis for action, make use of particular philosophies or implicitly reflect them in their diverse practices. Surveys of the literature on adult education moreover suggest that philosophy plays a minor role and there is relatively little explicit exposition of adult education philosophy. The field is eclectic and pragmatic.

See also: Adult Education: Concepts and Principles; Convergence between Education and Training; Adult Education: Disciplinary Orientations; Andragogy; Empiricism, Positivism and Anti-Positivism; Epistemological Issues in Educational Research; Ideologies in Adult Education

References

Burstow B 1984 Adult education: A Sartrean based perspective. *Int. J. Lifelong Educ.* 3 (3): 193–202

Burnstein R J 1983 *Beyond Objectivity and Relativism.* Basil Blackwell, Oxford

Descartes R 1637 *Discours de la Méthode* (Discourse on Method). In: Haldane E S, Ross G T R (eds.) 1955 *The Philosophical Works of Descartes*, 2 Vols. (In English) Cambridge University Press, Cambridge

Elias J L, Merriam S 1980 *Philosophical Foundations of Adult Education*. Robert Kreiger Publishing Co., New York

Freire P 1970 *Pedagogy of the Oppressed*. Herder & Herder, New York

Hirst P H 1974 *Knowledge and the Curriculum*. Routledge Chapman & Hall, New York

Kallen H 1962 *Philosophical Issues in Adult Education*. Charles C Thomas, Springfield, Illinois

Kant I 1781 *Kritik de reinen Verurft. Critique of Pure Reason*. Trans. Smith N K 1929 Macmillan, London

Knowles M S 1970 *The Modern Practice of Adult Education: Andragogy versus Pedagogy*. Association Press, Chicago, Illinois

Knowles M S 1972 The relevance of research for the adult education teacher trainer. *Adult Lead.*

Knowles M S 1980 *The Modern Practice of Adult Education: From Pedagogy to Andragogy*. Chicago Association Press, Chicago, Illinois

Kuhn T S 1970 *The Structure of Scientific Revolution*, 2nd edn. University of Chicago Press, Chicago, Illinois

Lawson K H 1975 *Philosophical Concepts and Values in Adult Education*. Open University Press, Milton Keynes

Locke J 1690 Second Treatise on Civil Government. In: Barker E (ed.) 1956 *Social Contract*. Oxford University Press, Oxford

Lyotard J F 1979 *La Condition postmoderne: rapport sur le savoir*. Les Editions de Minuit. *The Postmodern Condition: A Report on Knowledge*. Trans. Bennington G, Massumi B 1992 Manchester University Press, Manchester

Mochida E 1983 A critique of modern education with special reference to the East. In: *International Journal of Lifelong Education*, Vol. 2, No. 1 Taylor and Francis Ltd, London

Nozick R 1974 *Anarchy, State and Utopia*. Blackwell, Oxford

Paterson R W K 1979 *Values, Education and the Adult*. Routledge and Kegan Paul, Boston, Massachusetts

Peters R S 1979 (ed.) *The Concepts of Education*. Routledge & Kegan Paul, Boston, Massachusetts

Plecas D B, Sork T J 1986 Curing the ills of an undisciplined discipline. *Adult Educ. Q.* 37 (1): 48–62

Rawls J A 1972 *Theory of Justice*. Oxford University Press, Oxford

Rorty R 1980 *Philosophy and the Mirror of Nature*. Oxford University Press, Oxford

Schroeder W L 1970 Adult education defined and described. In: Smith R M, Aker G F, Kidd J R, (eds.) 1970 *Handbook of Adult Education*. Macmillan, London

Speake J (ed.) 1984 *A Dictionary of Philosophy*. Pan Books Ltd

Tagore R 1928 *Letters to a Friend*. George Allen and Unwin Ltd.

Tao Xingzhi 1985 Entry In: Thomas J E, Elsey R (eds.) 1985 *International Biography of Adult Education*. Department of Adult Education, University of Nottingham, Nottingham

Taylor C 1979 *The Ethic of Authenticity*. Harvard University Press, Cambridge, Massachusetts

Thompson J L (ed.) 1980 *Adult Education for a Change*. Hutchinson, London

Titmus C 1981 *Strategies for Adult Education*. Open University Press, Milton Keynes

Urevebu A 1985 Integrating science and technology into a policy of lifelong education. *Int. J. Lifelong Educ.* 4 (4)

Wain K 1987 *Philosophy of Lifelong Education*. Croom Helm, London

White T J 1970 Philosophical Considerations. In: Smith R M, Aker G F, Kidd J R (eds.) 1970 *Handbook of Adult Education*. Macmillan London

Further Reading

Bagnall R 1990 The intrinsic nature of educational goals: A critique. *Int. J. Lifelong Educ. 9 (1)*

Davidson D 1984 *Enquiries into Truth and Interpretation*. Clarendon Press, Oxford

Frankena W K 1973 The concept of education today. In: Doyle J E (ed.) 1973 *Educational Judgements*. Routledge and Kegan Paul, London

Houghton V, Richardson K (eds.) 1974 *Recurrent Education*. Word Lock Educational, London

Langford G, O'Connor D J (eds.) 1973 *New Essays in the Philosophy of Education*. Routledge and Kegan Paul, London

Lawson K H 1982 *Analysis and Ideology: Conceptual Essays in the Education of Adults*. Department of Adult Education, University of Nottingham, Nottingham

Lawson K H 1995 From citizen to self: Political and ethical foundations of adult education. In: Wallis J (ed.) 1996 *Liberal Adult Education: End of an Era?* Department of Adult Education, University of Nottingham, Nottingham

Putnam H 1981 *Reason, Truth and History*. Cambridge University Press, Cambridge

Political Science and Policy Analysis

C. M. Griffin

Adult education worldwide is increasingly conceptualized as a system of human resource development (Nordhaug 1991) and has for some time been seen as a major factor of social and economic development (Rogers 1992). In the case of industrial and post-industrial society too, adult education has been perceived instrumentally, for example in terms of its capacity to address issues such as unemployment (Senior and Naylor 1989) or worker education (Burton 1992). In all such cases as these, the formulation of adult education as social policy has increasingly become apparent in the literature (Pöggeler 1990), Griffin (1987).

This entry will review the current position of adult education as an object of political science and policy analysis. To begin with, however, it is necessary to locate these disciplines in the wider context of the social sciences, since, as the literature of adult education suggests, they have been applied very selectively.

1. Political Discourses

Several academic disciplines have politics as their object, of which political science is only one, and it is important to distinguish amongst them. This is particularly necessary in relation to adult education. As the name implies, political science comprises the systematic and empirical study of political systems, and especially of the state and the machinery of government. This would also include, for example, the study of political parties, elections, and voting behavior. Related to this, but distinctive as an academic discipline, is political sociology, the concern of which is with politics as a function of social organization: for example, the correlation of social divisions of class, race, or gender with political behavior and participation.

It is important to distinguish between political science and political sociology, on the one hand, and political theory and political philosophy on the other. The latter disciplines are not so much concerned with political behavior and institutions as with concepts, theories, and normative issues of politics. It is therefore possible to speak of several discourses of politics, which may be scientific, empirical, conceptual, or normative.

2. Political Discourse of Adult Education

The discourse of adult education itself has traditionally been more normative than scientific (see *Adult Education Research*). Its focus has been rather strongly in the West upon individual adult learners and the principles of "good" adult education practice. There is also a strong normative focus upon the profession of adult education itself (Collins 1991).

Jarvis (1993) recently explored the idea of adult education as an object of state policy, but having its roots in civil society. Such distinctions as that between the state and civil society characterize a conceptual and normative discourse of politics. Thus, in reviewing theories of the state in relation to adult education, Jarvis is concerned with such matters as

justice, citizenship, rights, the civilized society, and utopian thought.

It is difficult to draw clear lines of division between the various discourses of politics, and many writers on the politics of adult education in fact shift imperceptibly from a scientific and empirical towards a normative and conceptual analysis. They shift, in other words, from a social science towards a theoretical and philosophical analysis, and often, it has to be said, towards utopianism (see *Philosophy and Ethics in Adult Education*).

In the light of this, it would be more accurate to speak of a mixed political discourse of adult education. There is a considerable literature on politics and adult education, but very little of it could be said to constitute a political science analysis as such.

3. A Comparative Model

It was said at the outset that increasing state intervention in adult education, as a function of economic planning and human resource development, is taking place worldwide. It is thus from a comparative perspective that a model for expressing the relations between the state and adult education can most likely be derived. Such a model has been proposed by Bown (Corner 1990), who constructs a typology of what she calls "state character" along dimensions of intervention, policies, infrastructure, and action. Bown's typology is shown in Fig. 1.

Like Jarvis (1993), Bown (quoted in Corner 1990) suggests that if adult education is to move from its historic marginality to a more central role in social and economic development, then its relations with the state must be confronted. A politics of adult education in a

	State character Nature of Intervention Policies: Supportive or constraining Political infrastructure Action
1. *Laissez-faire* 2. Colonial 3. Post-colonial or Post-imperial	
a. Mobilizing b. Post-mobilizing c. Welfare d. Other	

Figure 1
A model for examination of relations between adult education and the state
Source: Bown, in Corner 1990, p. 20

scientific sense is most likely to become possible in a comparative perspective, where the policy interventions of the state may be historically and empirically investigated:

"The problem lends itself to comparative treatment, taking cases from differing political environments; and for those of us in Britain there is certainly merit in looking at what has happened in some African countries, where the State's impact has been more direct and where on occasion there has evolved some theory on the roles of State and adult education in relation to each other." (Bown, quoted in Corner, 1990 p. 21)

What such a model suggests is that a political science of adult education could develop together with the increasing role of the state in promoting or controlling it, and that comparative policy analysis could prove a major factor in this development. At present, models of state intervention in a comparative framework remain to be worked out, and other political perspectives on adult education, which have been much more developed, need to be reviewed (see *Comparative Studies: Adult Education*).

4. Radical Politics of Adult Education

There has long been a literature of radical politics of adult education, which it is important not to confuse with political science and its focus upon the state and political behavior and organization (see *Critical Approaches to Adult Education; History of Adult Education*).

The meaning of the word politics is inevitably tied to power and its distribution in society. But there exist a broader and a narrower view of politics: political science focuses more narrowly upon the formal organization of power in political systems. A broader view of politics, usually the one taken by political sociologists, sees all social relations as expressing the distribution of power, so that it becomes possible to speak of a politics of the family, of the classroom, and of the workplace. Above all, perhaps, a politics of class or ethnic or gender divisions. On these broader political themes, there are major traditions in the literature of adult education (see *Women and Adult Education*).

The integral relation of adult education to the state has been expressed in terms not of policy but of political struggle or liberation. In this tradition the thought of Paulo Freire (Taylor 1993) is undoubtedly the best known, and has achieved worldwide recognition as a universal model of radical pedagogy. This has been regarded as relevant not only to the South American context where it was generated, but to any situation of cultural, social, or political oppression. It could not be said that Freire's work lies within any traditional category of political science, but it remains for many one of the most authoritative statements of the essentially political nature of adult learning. In terms of

the role of the state, there is some Marxist analysis (Youngman 1986) but predictably this is concerned with the capitalist state rather than with the state as such. The changing nature of the state in relation to international economic relations is also an issue raised by the work of Gelpi (1985) on the idea of lifelong education.

The radical politics of adult education, perhaps like the radical politics of anything, tends to fragment into a politics of radical movements (Westwood and Thomas 1991, Leirman and Kulich 1987), rather than the politics of class which were once more prominent in the literature (Cowburn 1986, Ward and Taylor 1986). Nevertheless, environmental and community issues, together with an ongoing politics of equal opportunity, continue to be an important tradition of adult education (Cassara 1990).

The influence of the critical theory movement has propelled adult education theory more in this direction than in that of traditional political science with its focus on system and state: possibly the philosophical divide between the hermeneutic and positivist traditions of enquiry has influenced trends in theory. The work of Habermas has been particularly significant in this process, since it has seemed to many to resonate with precisely those principles of liberating and transforming adult learning which practitioners have often embraced (Mezirow 1990).

The radical politics of adult education has taken diverse forms, as might be expected of diverse political cultures in the United Kingdom, Brazil, or the United States, where educational projects such as Antigonish or Highlander reflect the community learning philosophies of the Danish Folk High Schools, rooted in quite different traditions.

Radical politics is therefore a relative term, and adult education theory has sometimes been divided between those who see it in political terms and those who do not; there is an ongoing tension between those who would like to see it repoliticised towards social concerns and those who take a more technical or individualistic view. There remains a divide between the Freireans and the more pragmatic liberals. A recent trend has been towards a vocational stress upon critical practice and the need for adult educators to promote critical thinking amongst adult learners (Brookfield 1987). This movement has drawn upon the diverse political discourses of Freire and Habermas, and left adult education with unresolved political agendas (see *Postscript*).

It is not always obvious, therefore, what the 'politicizing' and 'depoliticizing' trends amount to, but there does remain considerable resistance to the incorporation of adult education into state systems and policies.

The perception of the adult educator's role as a political vocation remains strong: "A critical practice of adult education provides a context where shared commitments towards a socially more free, just and rational society will coalesce" (Collins 1991 p.119). On the other hand, it has been argued (Evans 1987) that adult educators have been unwise to adopt radical stances too far removed from the mainstream forms of political life.

From a perspective of political science, much adult education provision may be conceptualized and researched as the politics of interest groups, concerned with the advocacy and assertion of the rights of the disadvantaged in society. In the United Kingdom, for example, the leading professional body has embraced such a conception of the role of adult education strongly over the last few years.

So politics and adult education are linked at many points: the nation, the state, social classes and divisions, and interest groups. In so far as some versions of perspective transformation and critical thinking are concerned, the individual as such is the unit of politics: the personal is the political. Clearly, this is not a concept that traditional political science perspectives could accommodate: according to such perspectives, we are only political actors in a limited sense in our lives, that is, when we vote or take part in formal political activities. This means, in effect, that the distinction between the political and the nonpolitical is clearly maintained for purposes of theory and research. As has been suggested, the largely normative discourse of adult education renders such a distinction meaningless, and in this sense a political *science* of adult education is ruled out. However, as has been seen, a political *theory* of adult education is not, and it is relatively easy to locate its function in political structures and struggles.

It has often been observed (e.g., Keddie 1980) that adult education reflects a liberal–humanist individualism, and that its discourse is therefore relatively narrow. And yet current controversies are generated sometimes by the increasing tendency of the state to interfere with and manipulate provision in accord with social and economic priorities such as employment training or community development. It is the instrumentalism inherent in such policies of incorporation (often assimilating adult learning into the education system as such through funding and accreditation) that has stimulated a defence of traditional, more voluntaristic or local adult education, alongside its social purpose or more overtly political traditions.

5. Development Education

Lalage Bown's typology (see Fig.1) for expressing the relations between the state and adult education incorporates the dimension of intervention and its nature, and one of the most obvious instances of intervention is constituted by development education.

In political terms, this entails analytic categories of market and command economies, not simply of developed or developing countries. Broadly, development education refers to the educational aspects of economic and human resource development: agricultural extension in the United States, or national development strategies for combatting poverty or promoting economic growth (Duke 1985, Rogers 1992). There are case studies of health education, literacy, rural development, the role of women etc. from around the world (McGivney and Murray 1991). What development education demonstrates generally is that the world economy needs to be seen in global terms, and that age categories of education are rapidly becoming obsolete in the face of the need for lifelong education (Gelpi 1985). The global division of power and control is the focus of these kinds of studies, which invoke the role of colonialism and international corporations in the political systems of different countries.

Development education may be broadly categorized as a feature of state intervention in a wide range of social, political, cultural, and economic affairs, and comparative studies show how it may take different forms, reflecting the ideologies and politico-economic systems which exist in the world: literacy programmes, rural development schemes, population control measures, together with human resource development in industrial and postindustrial societies. All these are examples of adult or lifelong education sponsored by the state or international agencies all exercising a degree of local influence. They also reinforce the need for comparative policy research and analysis (Postlethwaite 1988, Fägerlind and Saha 1989), although it has to be said that comparative policy research is still a relatively new discipline.

Political science is concerned with the distribution of power in political systems, and some examples of adult education in relation to politics have now been reviewed. It has been seen that such examples have stimulated a normative or theoretical discourse of politics rather than an empirical investigation of the political system of adult education itself. Case study research of development education has suggested that the best way forward is likely to be that of comparative policy analysis, which is a well-established academic discipline.

6. Policy Analysis

Academic disciplines exist in a political context, and this is most obviously true in the case of policy analysis, since ultimately social policy is a function of the political organization of society. Adult education has become an object of policy research and analysis as a result of the increasing concern of states to promote social, economic, and cultural goals. Policy analysis entails categories of policy (social, economic, political) and typologies of political systems. The significance of policy reflects the democratic or undemocratic distribution of power in society. For this reason, perhaps, policy analysis has been a discipline of sociology rather than political science. This is despite the fact that distinct categories of economic, social, and political policy are difficult to establish, and that adult education policies are often better termed as human resource policies (see *Human Resource Development*).

In Britain, for example, social policy analysis has been historically linked with the concept of social welfare, and the welfare state has provided the social conditions which made the discipline possible. The history of the welfare state in the United Kingdom during the twentieth century has therefore been the subject of considerable research, and an associated body of theory, concepts, and models of policy has been established for some time. Alternative welfare policy models (residual, redistributive, and resource development) have suggested some analytic frameworks for the study of adult education itself (Griffin 1987).

Nevertheless, the study of early compulsory childhood education or schooling continues to be the primary focus of policy analysis, as can be seen from the content of such journals as *Educational Policy* or the *Journal of Education Policy*. This can be expected to continue while the initial education system remains so significant in material and ideological terms. Adult education is only now beginning to move into the mainstream of policy and away from the margins of political debate and economic significance. Historically, its policy profile has been utopian or futurological rather than analytic (Leirman and Kulich 1987).

As a result of all this, policy analysis of adult education remains largely an extrapolation from policy analysis of schooling. Apart from the focus of educational policy journals, policy studies of particular issues, such as the curriculum, remain largely directed towards school and childhood education (Moore and Ozga 1991). Similarly, the policy debate about the National Curriculum and the Education Reform Acts in the United Kingdom has produced many analytic studies (Bash and Coulby 1989, 1991, Flude and Hammer 1990). These studies are primarily concerned with school education, as are most major sources of policy analysis in education generally (Ball 1990, Dale 1989, Granheim 1990, Hargreaves and Reynolds 1989, Howell and Brown 1983, Kogan 1975, McNay and Ozga 1985, Silver 1990). Even the philosophical and normative dimensions of policy analysis have tended to focus upon initial education (Strike and Egan 1978).

These conceptual and empirical studies of education policy all provide a range of concepts, models and methodology for analyzing adult education. The degree to which they may be suggestive or actually useful in an adult context does, however, depend upon normative and ideological factors of adult education itself, the study of which has been traditionally dominated by adult learning theory and the evolution of professional practice. The history of educational policy analysis, and indeed that of policy analysis itself, suggests that the field is functionally related to the political profile and significance of its subject. If it is indeed the case that adult education, perhaps in some form of lifelong learning, is achieving a higher political profile worldwide, then there already exists a range of framework concepts and methodologies to build a discipline of policy analysis for the field.

7. Conclusion

There is a long and traditional connection between adult education and politics in some form or other. Its historical origins can often be traced to social and political struggles, to colonialization, to exploitation. It has other traditions too, though, which focus more upon individual fulfilment and development in a spirit of liberal learning. The balance between such traditions continues to shift, and the "politicizing" and "depoliticizing" tendencies continue to be represented, their relative strengths reflecting perhaps the political conditions of society itself (Westwood and Thomas 1991). Within the political tradition too, there are radical and liberal ideologies.

However, as this entry has suggested, the political nature of adult education has not necessarily rendered it available for political analysis. As its social and economic profile becomes stronger, however, adult education has become much more available for social policy analysis. There are various ways forward, which have been introduced here and which may equally prove fruitful:

(a) As human resource development, which assimilates adult education to production, employment, and training models. Such an approach would focus, for example, upon the re-siting of adult learning in community, workplace or other socio-economic settings for lifelong education.

(b) As a framework of public provision, in the tradition of social welfare policy analysis models which have been generated in liberal or social democratic Western societies. This approach would reflect the residual, redistributive, and resource development alternatives available in such societies, and focus, for example, upon the influence of professional adult educators upon the policy community (see Quigley 1993).

(c) As an aspect of development education, in a worldwide comparative policy analysis framework. Comparative policy analysis is still relatively in its infancy as a discipline, even in a school education context. However, this approach would permit a global perspective and incorporate political science categories of system, intervention, policies, infrastructure, and action, which Bown's model incorporates.

With the incorporation of adult education into a range of social, economic, and political policies by states at different stages of development, and having different systems of government or ideology, a combination of these three perspectives seems the most likely future for policy analysis.

See also: Adult Education: Concepts and Principles; Community Education and Community Development; Critical Approaches to Adult Education; Adult Education: Disciplinary Orientation; Adult Education Research; Epistemological Issues in Educational Research; Adult Education for Development; Development through Nonformal Education; Comparative Studies: Adult Education

References

Ball S J 1990 *Politics and Policy Making in Education.* Routledge, London

Bash L, Coulby D (eds.) 1989 *The Education Reform Act.* Cassell Educational, London

Bash L, Coulby D (eds.) 1991 *Contradiction and Conflict: the 1988 Act in action.* Cassell Educational, London

Brookfield S 1987 *Developing Critical Thinkers.* Open University Press, Milton Keynes

Burton L E (ed.) 1992 *Developing Resourceful Humans.* Routledge, London

Cassara B (ed.) 1990 *Adult Education in a Multicultural Society.* Routledge, London

Collins M 1991 *Adult Education as Vocation.* Routledge, London

Corner T E (ed.) 1990 *Learning Opportunities for Adults.* Routledge, London

Cowburn W 1986 *Class Ideology and Community Education.* Croom Helm, London

Dale R 1989 *The State and Education Policy.* Open University Press, Milton Keynes

Duke C (ed.) 1985 *Combatting Poverty Through Adult Education.* Croom Helm, London

Evans B 1987 *Radical Adult Education.* Croom Helm, London

Fagerlind I, Saha L 1989 *Education and National Development*, 2nd edn. Pergamon Press, Oxford

Flude M, Hammer M (eds.) 1990 *The Education Reform Act.* Falmer Press, Basingstoke

Gelpi E 1985 *Lifelong Education and International Relations.* Croom Helm, London

Granheim M et al. (eds.) 1990 *Evaluation as Policymaking.* Jessica Kingsley, London

Griffin C 1987 *Adult Education as Social Policy.* Croom Helm, London

Hargreaves A, Reynolds D (eds.) 1989 *Education Policies.* Falmer Press, Lewes

Howell D, Brown R 1983 *Educational Policy Making.* Hutchinson Educational, London

Jarvis P 1993 *Adult Education and the State.* Routledge, London

Keddie N 1980 Adult education: An ideology of individualism. In: Thompson J (ed.) 1980 *Adult Education for a Change.* Hutchinson, London

Kogan M 1975 *Educational Policy Making.* Allen and Unwin, London

Leirman W, Kulich J (eds.) 1987 *Adult Education and the Challenges of the 1990s.* Croom Helm, London

McGivney V, Murray F 1991 *Adult Education in Development.* NIACE, Leicester

McNay I, Ozga J (eds.) 1985 *Policy-Making in Education.* Pergamon Press, Oxford

Mezirow J et al. 1990 *Fostering Critical Reflection in Adulthood.* Jossey-Bass, San Francisco, California

Moore R, Ozga J (eds.) 1991 *Curriculum Policy.* Pergamon Press, Oxford

Nordhaug O 1991 *The Shadow Educational System.* Norwegian University Press, London

Pöggeler F (ed.) 1990 *The State and Adult Education.* Verlag Peter Lang, Frankfurt am Main

Postlethwaite T (ed.) 1988 *The Encyclopedia of Comparative Education and National Systems of Education.* Pergamon Press, Oxford

Quigley B 1993 To shape the future. *Int. J. Lifelong Educ.* 12 (2) 117–127

Rogers A 1992 *Adults Learning for Development.* Cassell, London

Senior B, Naylor J (eds.) 1987 *Educational Responses to Adult Unemployment.* Croom Helm, London

Silver H 1990 *Education, Change and the Policy Process.* Falmer Press, Lewes

Strike K, Egan K (eds.) 1978 *Ethics and Educational Policy.* Routledge and Kegan Paul, London

Taylor P 1993 *The Texts of Paulo Freire.* Open University Press, Milton Keynes

Ward K, Taylor R (eds.) 1986 *Adult Education and the Working Class.* Croom Helm, London

Westwood S, Thomas J (eds.) 1991 *The Politics of Adult Education.* NIACE, Leicester

Youngman F 1986 *Adult Education and Socialist Pedagogy.* Croom Helm, London

Psychology of Adult Education

J. M. Pieters

The psychology of adult education can be approached in at least two ways. On the one hand, the subject can be dealt with from a disciplinary perspective, paying attention to, for example, developmental psychology, social psychology, personality, and experimental psychology. On the other hand, adult education can be approached from the applied areas of psychology, such as educational psychology, human performance, clinical psychology, cultural psychology, and psychogerontology. In this entry, both approaches will be followed.

The psychology of adult education will be treated

as Baltes (1987) described lifespan development: "Lifespan developmental psychology involves the study of constancy and change in behaviour throughout the life (ontogenesis), from conception to death." The scope of lifespan development will be restricted to adulthood. Thus, the goal of this entry is to describe knowledge related to the psychology of adult education. It examines general principles of adult development, characteristics of adult learning and cognition, biological differences, motivation, and personality, as well as the application of all these factors in education.

1. Adult Development

"Adult development" refers to orderly and sequential changes in cognitive characteristics and attitudes that adults experience over time. It tends to be concentrated especially around periods of change in cognitive processes, physical condition, personality, and in the social setting (i.e., family, work, and community).

Two kinds of models are pertinent in the study of adult development: stage models and process models. These two models are dealt with in this section, as well as lifespan development and biological differences.

1.1 Stage and Process Models

Stage models are focused on changes that are periodic, appearing at specified times in the course of a typical adult life. Emphasis is on age-related changes that elicit seemingly new versions of a person. Major characteristics of stage models are: descriptive, age-related, and interindividual. Stage models are based on the fact that the social setting encourages adults to move through their lives in similar sequential ways. Fales (1985) adopted the developmental or psychosocial tasks orientation. In this view, each period is characterized by specific tasks to be fulfilled. For instance, tasks are related to self-supporting, family independence, and forming attachments with peers for people in their twenties (separating from family orientation). During their thirties (thirties stabilization), people's tasks include self-direction and attachment to family matters (see *Lifespan Development: Phases*).

Whereas stage models combine processes that underlie changes in biological maturation, socialization to new roles, and psychological adaptations, process models consider inner growth that fosters delineation of stages.

Major characteristics of process models are: investigative, no strict age-related development, and intraindividual. Adult changes are seen as individually differing processes that proceed at varying rates over the lifespan and are either basically biological, social, psychological, or a combination of these. A major concern of process models, as opposed to stage models, is contextualism. Stages seem to be unaffected by environmental pressures and context. However, research

studies show that both positions may be valid (Fischer and Silvern 1985). Whereas psychological differences between widely different age groups highlight stage-like aspects of development, consistent differences in the development of individuals over long periods and the relation of those differences to personal and societal history accentuate the importance of individual diversity.

A major question in the debate about stage and process models concerns developmental plasticity ("maturation" as it used to be called): development varies in response to environmental variation. The origins of developmental plasticity come from behavioral biology, ethology, and embryology. Members of the same species developing in different contexts may vary dramatically not only in social-related developmental aspects, but also in gross morphology and physiology.

1.2 Lifespan Development

Contemporary studies in adult development have been dominated by the lifespan development perspective. Lifespan developmental psychology involves the study of constancy and change in behavior from conception to death (Baltes 1987). The goal is to obtain knowledge about general principles of lifelong development and interindividual differences and similarities in development, as well as the degree and conditions of individual plasticity or modifiability of development.

Lifespan developmental psychology has its roots in developmental or child psychology. Observations from literature, history, sociology, and anthropology suggest that lifespan development is not identified with one single theory. In addition, efforts have been made to examine whether lifespan research suggests a particular metatheoretical worldview of the nature of development.

According to Baltes (1987) the major beliefs shared by workers in the field of lifespan development are: "Lifespan development is a lifelong process, multidirectionality of changes in development, development as gain (growth)/loss (decline), intraindividual plasticity related to life conditions and experiences, historical embeddedness in social–cultural conditions during the lifetime, contextualism as paradigm, and field of development as multidisciplinary (various disciplines as anthropology, biology, psychology, and sociology)."

1.3 Biological Differences

Various changes occur when people grow older. Apart from changes due to accidents, traumas, and so forth, there are considerable changes in physical condition, in neurophysiological behavior, in the central nervous system, and in the visual and auditive system. Some changes are influenced by heredity, others by (mal)nutrition and other contextual factors.

In a physical sense, old age is a relative concept.

Physical deterioration may begin in young adulthood. Regular exercise and proper nutrition will keep oneself healthy and fit. Exercise can improve the strength and circulatory capacity of cardiac muscles and reduce the severity of arteriosclerotic lesions. Exercise of the leg muscles appears to facilitate the flow of blood to the heart and thus indirectly to maintain bodily functioning in all areas, including the brain.

The body reaches its maximum physical strength between the ages of 19 and 26, at least as far as the muscles and internal organs are concerned. There is about a 10 percent loss in muscle strength between the ages of 30 and 60. Reaction time, which improves from childhood until age 19 or 20 and remains constant until approximately age 26, gradually declines thereafter. Life expectancy in European and North American countries is about 7 years longer for women than for men: almost 75 compared with less than 68. There are considerable differences between countries and regions due to nutrition, health conditions, and accident proneness. Recent studies reveal that, at least in Western countries, there is a stabilization in long lifetime due to work-related stress, insufficient sleep, and overeating, even though medical conditions are often optimal.

There are several trends during adulthood in the functioning of the central nervous system (CNS) that appear to be related to a progressive slowing of reaction time and reduction in coordination. The general effect of these trends is a reduction in the efficiency of signal transmission, which progressively impairs signal strength, and an increase in random background activity within the nervous system, which constitutes neural noise. The aging trend is toward impairment of the signal–noise ratio, which reflects various combinations of reduced signal strength and increased neural noise. Some major aging trends in the CNS are the following (adapted from Knox 1977): (a) cell reduction—a gradual reduction in the number of nondividing neurons over the years; (b) increased random activity—an increase in random cell activity and subsequent neural noise; (c) increased after-effects—for older adults, stimulation of the motor cortex tends to continue much longer after the stimulus stops; and (d) altered arousal—for older adults, signals need to be more intense in order to be detected.

The visual, as well as the auditive system, may be affected by age changes both peripherally (lens in the eye, or organ of corti in the ear) and centrally, leading to phenomena of far-sightedness and high tone deafness with normal loudness perception. The following age trends are some of those which can be listed for the visual system (from Knox 1977): (a) pupil size—the average diameter of the pupil gradually declines with age; (b) adaptation rate—the amount of time required for the eye to become fully dark adapted increases with age; (c) lens accommodation—between the ages of 20 and 50 there is typically a loss of accommodation power and elasticity of the lens, after which the

decline is more gradual; and (d) color vision—due to yellowing of the lens with old age, less blue and violet light is transmitted, leading to a lessened ability in discriminating blues and greens.

Hearing loss and hearing problems are less drastic than problems of the visual system. Two such hearing problems are worth mentioning: those affecting discernment of pitch and loudness. The ability to hear very soft sounds and very high-frequency sounds starts to decline by adolescence. Between the ages of 20 and 50 a gradual decline is observed, but after the age of 50 the rate of impairments increases rapidly.

2. Learning and Cognitive Processes

Whereas in personality and social developmental studies a number of stage models have been proposed, in cognitive development studies no explicit model of phases has been published. The only model that is referred to is the model of cognitive development of Jean Piaget. However, this model comprises mainly the first 15 years of one's life.

In this section, four approaches to adult learning and development (adopted from Rybash et al. 1986) will be discussed: the psychometric approach, the genetic–epistemological approach, the information-processing approach, and the cognitive approach.

2.1 Intelligence: The Psychometric Approach

In almost all studies of adult learning, the measurement of cognitive ability is determined as a dependent variable by intelligence test scores. Studies by Horn and Cattell (summarized by Sternberg 1985, Sternberg and Wagner 1986) reveal that when primary mental abilities are further analyzed, two factors emerge: fluid intelligence and crystallized intelligence. These follow different trends during adulthood, providing a useful basis for understanding shifts in the ability to learn various types of tasks. The basic premise is that cohesion in intelligence is produced by two contrasting but interacting influences: neurophysiology and acculturation.

"Fluid intelligence" is a representation of neurophysiologically based mental abilities to perceive complex relations, engage in short-term memory, form concepts, and engage in abstract reasoning. Fluid intelligence is relatively formless and independent of experience and education.

"Crystallized intelligence" is considered to be the culturally based ability to perceive relations and to engage in formal reasoning or abstractions based on a familiarity with knowledge of a society's intellectual and cultural heritage.

Together, these two kinds of intelligence cover many of the learning tasks that adults confront and constitute the global capacity to learn, reason, and solve problems that most refer to as "intelligence." They are complementary in that some learning may take place mainly by exercising either fluid or crystallized intelligence.

Fluid intelligence, along with crystallized intelligence, increases during childhood and on into adolescence. However, with the slowing of the maturation process, fluid intelligence tends to peak during adolescence and young adulthood and declines gradually thereafter. Crystallized intelligence continues to increase gradually throughout adulthood. The distinction between fluid and crystallized intelligence can be attributed to the difference in the product and the process types of cognition (Salthouse 1989). The first hypothesis suggests there is indeed an increase in acquired cognitive products, but with some of them lost over time resulting in a stable net performance or even a slight decrease for high age groups. The second hypothesis states that intelligence tests measure general abilities, whereas the acquisition of knowledge and skills leads to a specialization over years. This implies that although one's abilities increase with age, one's performance on intelligence tests will decrease due to an insensitivity of these tests for the acquired specialized knowledge and skills.

Considerable evidence supports the decrease of the process performance of cognition with age. Salthouse (1989) introduces three hypotheses for this decrease; the speed hypothesis—age-related decline in test performance due to reductions in the speed of peripheral sensory or motor processes; the disuse hypothesis—performance on several subtests declines because of the nature of the required cognitive activity, and the fact that intelligence tests were originally designed for young children's school performance assessment and contain tasks that have hardly been practiced by older adults since their childhood; and the changing environment hypothesis—changing circumstances contributed to physical differences between young people now and a century ago. There is positive and negative evidence to support these three hypotheses, but they can still be used to provide at least a partial explanation of changing cognitive performance in old age. Salthouse (1989) mentions research activities more directed toward decomposing cognitive activities and studying the differential effects of resulting contributing components to cognitive performance in older adults.

Studies on cognitive development deal with changes in thinking strategies, in creativity, in problem-solving capacity, in critical thinking, and in wisdom (Baltes and Smith 1990). Experience expressed by crystallized intelligence is analyzed in contextual perspective: the process of intellectual development does not occur in social isolation. Both personality and contextual factors contribute to the development of intellectual capabilities over the lifespan. Studies by Berg (1986) and Sternberg (1985) reveal that "intelligence" can best be defined as the mental abilities that are necessary to produce an optimal fit between individuals and their environment. The contextual perspective of intellectual development posits that the demands and presses of the environment interact with an adult's mental functioning. This implies that there can be no fixed point where development ends. The concept of developmental tasks, essential for creating a personal identity, is relevant in this respect. Adult life is assumed to be an ongoing adaptation to the accomplishments of life, initially social and later personal. Developmental tasks vary over time. In early adulthood, tasks become socially oriented, involved with establishing new social roles (e.g., selecting a mate, starting a family, rearing children, and getting started in an occupation). In middle age and later life, tasks involve adjustment and adaptation to social and biological losses (e.g., assisting teenagers to become responsible, happy adults; relating to spouse as a person; adjusting to aging parents; adjusting to decreasing physical strength; adjusting to death of spouse; and establishing satisfactory living arrangements). The process of adaptation and adjustment is essential in cognitive development. It may be defined as the way in which one fits oneself to one's environment. "Environment" is used as a generic term for the external psychological, biological, physical, sociocultural, and historical circumstances of humankind.

Berg (1986) considers three strategies in adapting to environmental demands: adapting, selecting, and shaping. The adapting strategy aims at the adjustment to environmental requirements. The selecting strategy aims at an optimal fit between one's competencies and the environment. The shaping strategy adjusts the environments to meet one's competencies. According to Berg (1986) four social competence components are used in adapting: prosocial skills (psychological and social empathy), instrumental skills (skill in achieving goals), social ease (social responsiveness), and self-efficacy (social effectiveness).

2.2 Postformal Thinking: The Genetic–Epistemological Approach

The point of departure of the genetic–epistemological approach is Piagetian theory (Piaget 1972). Piaget was specifically interested in the way the individual acquires a scientific understanding of the environment. In his view, knowledge of the environment evolves through the formation of logical–mathematical thought structures. Knowledge reflects the continuous relationship between the mind's attempt to structure its environment and the environment's attempt to structure the mind. Based upon these ideas, Piaget proposed a theory of cognitive development, the stages of which are: (a) sensori-motor, (b) preoperations, (c) concrete operations, and (d) formal operations. According to Rybash et al. (1986), formal operational thinking is a powerful but limited basis from which to understand the physical and social environment. Its disadvantages are that it is assumed that there is one concrete solution to a problem that can be deduced through logical reasoning. An overemphasis is placed on logical abstractions and absolutes, and on problems that are of a physical or scientific nature. Problems are considered to be from a closed system (i.e., there is a finite number of knowable variables which produce a specific and reliable outcome). These variables are assumed to be separable and independent so that they can be analyzed independently from each other. Real-life problems that are open, and in which the variables are often interdependent and inseparable, are not considered within formal operational thinking. Formal operations, therefore, do not allow a thinker to understand the contextual nature of knowledge and reality. Nor does it allow for metacognition—that is, the formal thinker does not understand the structure of his or her thought in any conscious or self-reflective manner.

To overcome these discrepancies, a new stage of thought has been developed in genetic–epistemological theory, called "postformal operations." Three basic characteristics of postformal thinking have been identified: (a) possessing an understanding of the relative, nonabsolute nature of knowledge; (b) recognizing contradiction as being a basic element of reality; and (c) instead of viewing a contradictory situation as requiring a choice between alternatives, the postformal thinker sees it as requiring an integration of alternatives. This mode of thinking is sometimes called "dialectic thinking." The postformal thinker necessarily sees reality as an open system and his or her thinking is grounded in contextualism.

2.3 Memory Functioning: The Information-processing Approach

Not only do physical capabilities decrease when a person gets older, but the cognitive abilities measured by memory functioning also deteriorate. Results from different studies on memory functioning have to be carefully assessed because of differences assigned to memory loss, normal aging, and senile dementia.

"Dementia" is a kind of dysfunctioning related to a process of physiological degeneration in the brain. A special characteristic of this type of disorder is a severe degree of anterograde amnesia and disorders in a later phase, like aphasia or apraxia. Symptoms of dementia are like the ones of the amnesic syndrome: general loss of acquisition of new information, but without a corresponding loss of memory for facts acquired many years ago when dementia started. This disorder is also characterized by its irreversibility, although it is not certain whether this disorder can be effectively treated by medication. Dementia is difficult to discern from "pseudo-dementia." The latter generally occurs after a psychological or physical trauma (e.g., anaesthesia or a state of confusion in depressive patients). Dementia is different from "normal aging," which is characterized by general forgetfulness, in particular for names and data.

Results from studies on normal aging are often difficult to interpret due to methodological problems. The difference between two samples differing in age can be explained by aging, but also by differences in education. Some researchers propose using a combination of cross-sectional and longitudinal research: generation effects and age effects can thus be studied apart from each other.

Aging affects long-term memory functioning, rather than short-term memory capacity. A loss in functioning of long-term memory can be caused by a decrease in acquisition, as well as a decrease in the capability to retrieve information from memory. A traditional means to investigate this difference is to compare recognition and recall performance. It is assumed that retrieval processes are active with recall, but inactive with recognition. A classical study by Schonfield and Robertson (1966) revealed that recognition performance remains at a high level irrespective of age, whereas recall performance decreases. This result could mean that retrieval processes are disturbed in aged persons. Retrieval is also strongly related to acquisition. The way in which information is acquired is decisive for the effectiveness of the retrieval process. Studies reveal that the use of contextual information and the activation of semantically related material function less well in older adults. Young adults have no problems processing contextual information and its storing happens automatically. However, in older adults it takes cognitive effort to store contextual information. Activation of semantically related information is also dependent upon the difference between automatic and nonautomatic activation. If activation and, consequently, acquisition and retrieval of recent information are disturbed, it does not mean that the retrieval of facts and events that happened many years previously is not affected. There still are, however, equivocal results from several studies.

2.4 Knowledge Construction: The Cognitive Science Approach

Individuals are rarely expert in more than a couple of domains. This is due to the kinds of abilities and the large amount of domain-specific knowledge required to be an expert in any field. Although there is a deterioration of generalized cognitive ability with age, there is a stability and sometimes an increase of cognitive ability within areas of specialization and expertise.

Most theory and research is concerned with general abilities which are assumed to cut across different domains of specialization. Therefore, a shift in focus point is necessary in order to solve this paradox. This shift has been made by cognitive scientists. There are several research directions which attempt to explain this paradox. One has shown the beneficial effects of mnemonic training on generalized measures of intelligence. A second is concerned with explaining the multidimensionality of adult intelligence. As mentioned above, research has revealed that fluid intelligence declines with age, whereas crystallized intelligence remains stable or possibly even increases with age. Some authors warn that these results should be handled with care, as fluid and crystallized intelligence provide inaccurate measures, due to contextualism and domain-related factors. A third approach is represented by the cognitive science approach. Cognitive scientists claim that general mental processes play a minor role in problem-solving, but that problems are solved using domain-specific knowledge or task-specific heuristics.

Within cognitive science, there are several descriptions of the nature of knowledge (Alexander et al. 1991). An important one is the distinction made by Anderson (1983) between declarative and procedural knowledge. The former consists of factual information, the latter a set of rules that explain how and when declarative knowledge is to be applied. These forms are sometimes referred to as "heuristics." Declarative and procedural forms of knowledge may be viewed as categories, prototypes, or schemes. Knowledge schemes are presumed to assist in the organization and acquisition of knowledge. Functionally, individuals impose organization on incoming information by combining it with knowledge already in the memory. Therefore, knowledge manifests itself in certain forms, and has a developmental history. Anderson (1983) suggests that development of knowledge proceeds through the stages encoding, proceduralization, composition, and automatization. Another description is that knowledge becomes increasingly expert during the adult years. In fact, there is a "novice–expert" shift. These terms are used intuitively, as there is no general consensus as to the characteristics and definition of expertise (Chi et al. 1987). A typical difference between experts and novices is that experts are not conscious of the knowledge processes and rules that enable them to act competently (Rybash et al. 1986).

Even though there are age-related declines in the acquisition and processing of new information, most adults continue to use acquired knowledge in an effective and proficient manner throughout their later years (i.e., expertise compensates for decrements in fluid abilities and physical powers). Although older adults become less skilled at general problem-solving, they become more skilled within more specialized areas. It may also be the case that older adulthood is characterized by the development of personal knowledge: the understanding of both inter- and intrapersonal relations.

3. Motivation

Motivating people to participate in education has two phases: a phase in which people are invited to enter education and a phase in which people are motivated to remain students.

Some adults, especially those with higher levels of formal education, continually engage in educational activities and are more successful than lower educated people. The former read books and magazines, consult experts, and engage in part-time educational activities related to work, family, and leisure time. The new ideas and competencies they acquire enable them to adapt, grow, change, solve problems, and grasp the opportunities that confront them. Educational activities are an essential and central ingredient in their self-regulated and evolving lifestyle.

On the other hand, some adults seldom engage in any activity for the main purpose of expanding what they know and are able to do. Of course, they continue to learn and change in incidental ways but this is a by-product of experience and not part of deliberate efforts to choose, plan, and guide educational experiences.

Reasons for participation in continuing education (Cross 1981) also vary with the level of occupational prestige. At lower socioeconomic levels, the emphasis is on coping with daily concerns. Blue-collar workers participate mainly for vocational reasons, especially preparation for a new job. A small proportion of white-collar adults participate for occupational reasons, mostly for advancement of their present job (see *Participation: Role of Motivation*).

Self-initiated learning is probably not the means to encourage participation of those who belong to the hard core of unemployment. Several studies express the necessity to integrate educational activities with realistic expectations for jobs. What motivates people most is the expectation that goals to be achieved are important to them and that there is a fair chance of success for their endeavors (Weiner 1980). People cannot be concerned about higher human needs—in Maslowian terms, "recognition," "achievement," and "self-realization"—until the lower fundamental needs —survival, safety, and belonging—have been met. This would suggest that poorly educated people will be interested primarily in education that meets survival needs (e.g., job training and adult basic education).

To describe adult motivation, Cross (1981) used a model based on several theories and ideas about participation of adults in learning activities. The model assumes adult participation to be the result of a chain of responses related to the position of an adult in an environment: self-evaluation, attitudes about education, importance of goals and expectation that participation will meet goals, life transitions, opportunities and barriers, information, and participation itself. Each of these responses can be rated positively or negatively, from which the total net result can be beyond or below some threshold, indicating yes or no toward participation (see *Participation: Role of Motivation*).

Remaining motivated during education and instruction is the second phase in the process of participation. Keller (1983) proposes a model for the design of instruction, based on motivational theories. His theory of motivation, performance, and instructional influence is a macro theory that incorporates cognitive and environmental variables in relation to effort, performance, and consequences. The model also includes three types of influence of instructional design: motivational design, learning design, and reinforcement–contingency design. The model is based on the assumption that any instructional event will have these three influences, and that the task of the instructional designer is to understand and control them. In order to produce instruction that is interesting, meaningful, appealing, and appropriately challenging, the instructional designer must respond to four categories of motivational conditions: Attention, Relevance, Confidence, and Satisfaction (abbreviated to the ARCS model). Attention refers to triggering curiosity and arousal. Relevance is related to personal needs. Sustained motivation requires the participant to perceive that important personal needs are being met by the learning situation. Confidence refers to the belief that the participant's attitudes toward success or failures can be attributed to actual events. Satisfaction includes several factors that influence the perception of goal accomplishment and the motivation to continue pursuing similar goals.

4. Personality

Adult education psychology was long dominated by personal growth theorists such as Allport and Maslow; and by ego-psychologists such as Jung, Bühler, and Erikson. Subsequent researchers such as Gould, Levinson, Neugarten, Loevinger, and Havighurst combined growth theory and ego-psychology about personality and social life. They may be considered stage theorists, although they do not ignore the developmental process. Erikson, Gould, and Levinson base their theories of development on their own perceptions of the complex interaction of biological, social, and psychosocial processes. Erikson describes development as a psychosocial process, and as part of epigenesis. Gould describes development as a psychological process that involves both the social experiences of leaving home, working, and marrying, and the biological experience of maturational push. Levinson describes the evolution of the life structure as combined inner psychological processes and outer social processes, within the framework of life's seasons, all of which are biological.

4.1 Ego-psychology

Erik Erikson was of great influence in adult developmental theories. Most people working in the field of adult development and adult education are familiar with his "eight stages of man" model. He formulated each stage as a time of creative tension between two opposing forces within a person. Each stage is marked by a crisis. "Crisis" is not meant to denote impending disaster; rather it is meant positively, as a turning point, a crucial moment in the lifespan. Development can be seen as an accumulated outcome of crises in the adjacent stages. The first crisis in human life is related

to trust. A child in the younger years experiences moments of trust and mistrust, and it is the result of competing forces of trust and mistrust that defines the growing and psychological well-being of the child. The second crisis in a child's younger years is related to autonomy on the one hand, and shame and doubt on the other. The third crisis, between the ages of 5 and 10, is characterized by initiative and guilt. The fourth, during late childhood and early adolescence is characterized by industry and inferiority, and the fifth, during late adolescence and early young adulthood, by identity and identity diffusion. The identity crisis is considered to be the crucial crisis. It is also the first stage during which personal preferences and societal opportunities will compete. The three developmental stages that Erikson describes as occurring during adulthood entail developing a sense of intimacy, generativity, and integrity.

4.2 Attitudes and Adaptation

A personality is a pattern of cognitions, beliefs, and behavior, resulting in reacting in the same ways to similar situations. Psychologists believe that personality is shaped by interpersonal interactions, but that its psychological basis, consisting of goals, beliefs, and cognitive schemata regulates these interpersonal relationships. Thus personality has interpersonal and intrapersonal sources. The goals, beliefs, and schemata become tuned by these interpersonal interactions, resulting in assimilation and accommodation toward an image of a personality delivered by the outer environments. Some people adapt passively, others actively, both consciously or unconsciously to a self-concept determined by these interpersonal relationships.

"Attitudes," a combination of cognitions and beliefs with a behavioral counterpart, and the process by which the shaping and tuning of the personality will take place, called "adaptation," are of great importance in psychological research on adult development. Attitudes, being cognitions and beliefs shaping the perception of society, are the residues of past experiences and predispose one in the choice of activities, companions, and environments.

A major concern within studies on the role of attitudes in adult development is whether attitudes change across the lifespan. There are at least four hypotheses for possible variations: lifelong openness, lifecycle view, the impressionable years' viewpoint, and persistence. New studies have concentrated on the components of attitudes and the changes they may undergo during one's lifetime (Costa and McCrae 1989).

The process by which a personality is shaped according to societal rules, and rules set by the narrow social context, is called "adaptation." Scholars have described the fascinating process of social participation and its related adaptation. Strongly related to the concept of participation and adaptation is the occurrence of change events. A "change event" can be defined as an event in a person's life that affects their cognitive representation of themselves and others. The set of goals, cognitions, and behaviors that was adequate in interacting with the environment has to be changed and tuned to a new developmental task. Lifespan development is a continuous adaptation to new events and related tasks. The quality of the solution to new life-problems is decisive for the quality of adaptation. Of particular interest are the changes that a person's goals, cognitions, and behavior undergo. Recent studies on the process of adaptation, affected by the cognitive orientation, reveal the change in cognitive representations that accompanies a change event. Also, the process of adaptation can be explained by its constituent stages of adapting to a new task: prestructure, anticipation, actual change event, disorganization, and poststructure.

5. Future Research on the Adult Learner

Several researchers have noted the importance of the social context in which intelligence occurs and have observed that, with growing age, adults tend to conceptualize intelligence within the concept of personal intelligence. The individual capability to cope and adapt to everyday life, especially in the sphere of inter- and intrapersonal relationships, is considered to be the measure of intelligence. By encapsulating basic cognitive processes, adults adapt to real-life social and personal problems; with advancing age, adults apply postformal styles of thinking to their accumulated knowledge in the personal domain in order to cope and adapt. The encapsulation model, advocated by Rybash et al. (1986), conceptualizes cognition as consisting of three interrelated dimensions that must be addressed and unified in any comprehensive theory of adult cognitive development: processing, knowing, and thinking.

Processing has been explored by researchers from the psychometric and information-processing disciplines, knowing by the cognitive science framework, and thinking by the genetic epistemologists. Up to the early 1990s, each discipline has studied one of these aspects to the exclusion of the others. The encapsulation model attempts to integrate all three, and is therefore worth studying. Future research has to pay attention to the operationalization of certain components of the encapsulation theory, such as how knowledge encapsulation and expertise occur.

See also: Human Development; Lifespan Development; Adult Learning: An Overview; The Implication for Educators

References

Alexander P A, Schallert D L, Hare V C 1991 Coming to terms: How researchers in learning and literacy talk about knowledge. *Rev. Educ. Res.* 61(3): 315–43
Anderson J R 1983 *The Architecture of Cognition.* Harvard University Press, Cambridge, Massachusetts
Baltes P B 1987 Theoretical propositions of life-span developmental psychology: On the dynamics between growth and decline. *Dev. Psychol.* 23: 611–26
Baltes P B, Smith J 1990 Toward a psychology of wisdom and its ontogenesis. In: Sternberg R J (ed.) 1990
Berg C A 1986 The role of social competence in contextual theories of adult intellectual development. *Educational Gerontology* 12(4): 313–25
Chi M T H, Glaser R, Farr M J (eds.) 1988 *The Nature of Expertise.* Erlbaum, Hillsdale, New Jersey
Costa P T Jr., McCrae R R 1989 Personality continuity and the changes of adult life. In: Storandt M, VandenBos G R (eds.) 1989 *The Adult Years: Continuity and Change.* American Psychological Association, Washington, DC
Cross K P 1981 *Adults as Learners.* Jossey-Bass, San Francisco, California
Fales A W 1985 Learning development over the life span. In: Husén T, Postlethwaite T N (eds.) 1985 *The International Encyclopedia of Education*, 1st edn. Pergamon Press, Oxford
Fischer K W, Silvern L 1985 Stages and individual differences in cognitive development. *Annu. Rev. Psychol.* 36:613–48
Keller J M 1983 Motivational design of instruction. In: Reigeluth C M (ed.) 1983 *Instructional Design Theories and Models.* Erlbaum, Hillsdale, New Jersey
Knox A B 1977 *Adult Development and Learning.* Jossey-Bass, San Francisco, California
Piaget J 1972 Intellectual evolution from adolescence to adulthood. *Hum. Dev.* 15(1):1–12
Rybash J M, Hoyer W J, Roodin P A 1986 *Adult Cognition and Aging: Developmental Changes in Processing, Knowing, and Thinking.* Pergamon Press, New York
Salthouse T A 1989 Age-related changes in basic cognitive processes. In: Storandt M, VandenBos G R (eds.) 1989 *The Adult Years: Continuity and Change.* American Psychological Association, Washington, DC
Schonfield D, Robertson B A 1966 Memory storage and aging. *Can. J. Psychol.* 20(2):228–36
Sternberg R J 1985 *Beyond IQ: A Triarchic Theory of Human Intelligence.* Cambridge University Press, Cambridge
Sternberg R J, Wagner R K (eds.) 1986 *Practical Intelligence: Nature and Origins of Competence in the Everyday World.* Cambridge University Press, Cambridge
Weiner B 1980 *Human Motivation.* Holt, Rinehart and Winston, New York

Further Reading

Abeles R P (ed.) 1987 *Life-span Perspectives and Social Psychology.* Erlbaum, Hillsdale, New Jersey
Alexander C, Langer E (eds.) 1990 *Higher Stages of Human Development: Perspective on Human Growth.* Oxford University Press, New York
Baltes M M, Baltes P B (eds.) 1986 *The Psychology of Control and Aging.* Erlbaum, Hillsdale, New Jersey
Baltes P B, Baltes M M (eds.) 1990 *Successful Aging: Perspectives from the Behavioral Sciences.* Cambridge University Press, Cambridge
Birren J E, Schaie K W (eds.) 1990 *Handbook of the Psychology of Aging*, 3rd edn. Academic Press, San Diego, California

Commons M L, Sinnott J D, Richards F A, Armon C (eds.) 1989 *Adult Development. Vol. 1: Comparisons and Applications of Developmental Models.* Praeger, New York

Holliday S G, Chandler M J (eds.) 1986 *Wisdom: Explorations in Adult Competence.* Contributions to Human Development 17. Karger, Basel

Hunter S, Sundel M (eds.) 1989 *Midlife Myths: Issues, Findings and Practice Implications.* Sage, Newbury Park, California

Labouvie-Vief G, Blanchard-Fields F 1982 Cognitive aging and psychological growth. *Aging and Society* 2(2):182–209

Lerner R M 1990 Plasticity, person-context relations, and cognitive training in the aged years: A developmental contextual perspective. *Dev. Psychol.* 26(6):911–15

Lovelace E A (eds.) 1990 *Aging and Cognition: Mental Processes, Self-awareness and Intention.* North-Holland, Amsterdam

Poon L W, Rubin D C, Wilson B A (eds.) 1989 *Everyday Cognition in Adulthood and Late Life.* Cambridge University Press, Cambridge

Salthouse T A 1982 *Adult Cognition: An Experimental Psychology of Human Aging.* Springer-Verlag, New York

Salthouse T A 1985 *A Theory of Cognitive Aging.* North-Holland, Amsterdam

Sternberg R J (ed.) 1990 *Wisdom: Its Nature, Origins, and Development.* Cambridge University Press, Cambridge

Schooler C, Schaie K W (eds.) 1987 *Cognitive Functioning and Social Structure Over the Life Course.* Ablex, Norwood, New Jersey

Sociology of Adult Education

P. Jarvis

Whereas the sociology of school education is a well-established field of specialization, sociological studies of adult education are more infrequent. This entry seeks to demonstrate the complexities of the concept of adult education and, thereafter, to examine ways by which it might be analyzed using conceptual frameworks derived from sociology. In the process reference will be made to some seminal, sociological studies of children's and adults' education.

1. The Concept of Adult Education

There are many ways in which adult education differs from school education, but perhaps the most obvious sociological difference is that whereas school education occurs almost entirely in that sector of society called "education," this is not the case for adult education: adults are educated in college, in their work, in their leisure, at home, in and by a variety of different organizations, and so on. Educators of children are schoolteachers, but educators of adults might be adult educators, university teachers, human resource developers, vocational educators, trainers, or even political activists seeking to educate the general public about specific concerns. Hence, it may be seen that there are many fields of practice in which the teaching and learning process occurs among adults, but many of them are not within the education sector of society.

Adult education is operationally defined as the institutionalized processes of teaching and learning that exist for those individuals who are regarded as adults, irrespective of the sector of society in which it occurs. Such a broad and imprecise definition suggests that the boundaries of the concept are blurred, which reflects the social reality. Indeed, as societies have become more complex through the growth in technological knowledge, the division of labor, and the subsequent creation of pluralism, so the education of adults has expanded to perform educative functions in each of the different social institutions (see *Providers of Adult Education: An Overview*).

Following Coombs and Ahmed (1974) (see also LaBelle 1982), the education of adults may be broadly divided into three categories: (a) formal, where the education occurs in educational institutions, for example, schools, vocational schools, colleges, and universities; (b) nonformal, where the education takes place outside of such organizations, for example, in the community, or popular education; and (c) informal, where the education occurs through personal interaction or participation (see *Formal, Nonformal, and Informal Education*). While this distinction does not adequately categorize adult education, it does provide a framework for the first three sections of the following discussion, although it is recognized that some forms may be located in more than one division, for example, adult basic education, or study circles. In Sect. 5 the emergence of distance education is taken as an example of a form of education for adults which reflects late modernity. In Sect. 6 some of the dominant theoretical areas of study that have been addressed by adult education scholars will be discussed, and in the final section the professionalization of adult education will be examined.

2. Formal Adult Education

Formal education for adults is conducted within an organizational context, with there being a variety of providers. Obviously the state is a major provider of formal adult education, which may be either vocational or nonvocational, but there are others, such as employers, professional organizations, labor unions, private and voluntary educational agencies, and voluntary agencies such as the churches. By definition, educational providers organize and run educational programs for adults, although they do not necessarily have to be the funding agency—often the providers act as agents of the state, although others are independent, financially and otherwise.

While it is possible to find similarities between the sociological analyses of formal adult education and school education, it would be simplistic to suggest that the two were the same, as the following example demonstrates. Governments with right-wing political ideologies have influenced the curriculum of schools so that they include a greater emphasis on science and technology, but this change in curriculum has not had a great effect upon the structures of schooling. However, in some instances the implementation of the same policies in the education of adults has resulted in continuing professional education and liberal adult education being almost totally separated from each other and regarded as different forms of education, with the former being treated as important and centrally funded, while the latter is regarded as a leisure-time pursuit to be followed at the learners' own expense in their own free time. Such a division is rather artificial: all forms of education can assist learners to develop self-confidence which may have effects on both work and leisure, and some people may learn a subject, such as a foreign language, as a leisure-time pursuit, but then use it in the course of employment. However, the fact that this separation has occurred illustrates that formal education funded by the state, whether it be for children or adults, is controlled and functions to produce the outcomes desired by government. Such conclusions allow for Marxist analyses of adult education, of which there have been a limited number (e.g., Youngman 1986).

It could be argued that all technological societies need a highly skilled and knowledgeable work force and that one of the functions of formal adult education is to produce this. By contrast, it would be possible to argue, following Althusser (1971), that the elite ruling capitalist class controls the apparatus of state and that it uses the formal education of adults to ensure that there is a highly skilled work force that will perpetuate the capitalist system. Hence the emphasis on vocational education to this end, rather than the liberal adult education which might produce articulate adults who might question the whole system.

All organizations operate systems of control, so that the education provided by the churches, and some other similar organizations, is designed either to initiate or socialize the participants into the culture and beliefs of the organization, or else to prepare the workers in the organization to be more efficient in what they do. This form of education is thus an agency of cultural, or subcultural, hegemony in the sense Gramsci used the concept, since it does not involve physical coercion (Entwistle 1979 p. 12). This interpretation is applicable to a great deal of adult educational activity. Consequently, it can be argued that formal education for adults serves as a mechanism of cultural reproduction (Bourdieu and Passeron 1977), whether it occurs at the level of the state or the organization.

In the United Kingdom there are only a few voluntary organizations, such as the Workers' Educational Association and the Women's Institute, which seek to offer education for personal and social development, much of which is a leisure-time pursuit, and it is significant that the right-wing government of the 1980s restricted the funding of both liberal adult education and the Workers' Educational Association, and their future was immediately placed in jeopardy (see *Worker Education and Labor Education*).

Personal and social development is also the theme of much adult education for women (Thompson 1983) and ethnic minorities (Cassara 1990). In these instances, adult education can be viewed as an instrument of empowerment, providing a sense of identity and purpose for those who are underprivileged and oppressed.

Some forms of education may, therefore, be viewed as dysfunctional, and in these instances those who exercise power seek to control or to curtail these activities. It may thus be concluded that the formal education of adults is recognized by those who exercise power as a potentially significant political phenomenon, which is precisely the argument put forward by Freire (1972), who claimed that education could be both oppressive and liberating. There are two distinct sociological paradigms, the functionalist and the conflict, which have been used by scholars analyzing formal adult education, and when contrasted in this way it is easy to place value judgments upon it, from whatever ideological persuasion it is analyzed.

One of the common criticisms of functionalism is that it implies an unchanging society, whereas conflict is trying to generate change. However, it is also possible to argue that, although there is a tendency to inertia in bureaucratic organizations, including the state, one of the aims of the formal education of adults is to produce change and through the implementation of the government policy of supporting vocational education, this is being achieved. Adult educators, who tend to adopt a more individualistic and psychological approach to education, often claim that education produces change agents, but clearly the education of adults is being used by government as an agent of social change (moreover in accord with its own ideological predispositions) rather than individual change. There are similar examples, such as the use of formal adult education to acculturate immigrants to their new country, for example, in the United States, where Carlson (1987) called it "Americanization education" (see also Thomas 1991). Therefore, the education of adults in its formal sense is often an instrument in governmental policy. Griffin (1987) has provided the most complete analysis of adult education and social policy.

Since formal adult education is organizational it is hardly surprising that a great number of studies have been conducted about enrollment and participation. Many of these have tended to adopt a psychological approach because this has been the dominant perspective in United States adult education. Even so, there has been a general acceptance that adult education tends to be a middle-class pursuit, since it is middle-class people who have sufficient cultural capital to benefit from it (Bourdieu 1973). Courtney (1992), however, began to analyze participation in sociological terms and noted that some of the functions of participation included social mobility and the reinforcement of the cultural values acquired during the mobility process. In Sweden, in a continuation of the Malmö longitudinal study which was commenced in 1938, Tuijnman (1989) has shown that male attendance at adult education classes throughout the life span influences career prospects, job satisfaction, well-being, and, indirectly, earnings.

A great deal of the formal education of adults which has been discussed in this section may also be categorized as "education from above" (Jarvis 1985a); the same could not be claimed for the nonformal education of adults, which is much more a form of "education of equals."

3. Nonformal Education of Adults

Nonformal education for adults occurs outside of the formal educational institution and may be discovered in a variety of different forms, such as adult literacy, study circles, personal development training, health education, community development, and even social action campaigns. They are not all regarded as educational, but all have an educative function which may be intended or unintended. Many of these activities are fully institutionalized, even to the extent of there being departments and units of government for nonformal education in some countries, and in most societies in the world adult literacy is at least partially government funded. Nonformal education, therefore, is a recognized type of education occurring outside of the formal structures of the educational system. It need not take place in a classroom or even in a building, and it often involves a teacher and a small group of students.

Each of these types of nonformal education for adults is different and has varying social functions, some of which are discussed here. While the individual benefits of literacy may be self-evident, the social functions are less obvious. Its social significance, for instance, is acknowledged by the term "functional literacy," which tends to mean that individuals should acquire the necessary literacy skills to play their part in society, including its occupational and economic

life. At this level, literacy programs can help individuals play a full part in society, but such programs serve other functions, for example, the modern state is bureaucratic and its language is writing, so it is important for the smooth operations of the state that its citizens can read and write. Indeed, illiterate citizens cannot read instructions, census returns, or even their tax returns, so that surveillance cannot be effective nor can these matters be recorded or controlled easily. Thus literacy education has a number of less frequently acknowledged functions. Perhaps the term "computer literacy" indicates how the concept is relative and changing as society becomes increasingly technological. This is more fully discussed by Levine (1986).

In certain democracies in the world, the state also provides financial support for nonformal liberal adult education in the form of study circles. The support of the state for such activities demonstrates something of the democratic nature of society, although the control of the funding indicates that there are limits placed on the democratic process. Where the support is enshrined within a legal framework, as it is for the study circles in Scandinavia, then liberal adult education may serve a democratic political function in society.

Nonformal adult education also occurs through the educative function of certain movements and pressure groups. The fact that these groups, however radical, see themselves as having an educative function indicates that they have not moved to a revolutionary position—for education is a prerevolutionary activity and, in this sense, while appearing to be radical, it acts as a focus for discontent and dissatisfaction within society. Hence the twofold nature of this educative exercise: (a) to focus and manage discontent, and (b) to perform a democratic function of educating people to be more active in changing their society. Many of these movements and groups are discussed in the adult education literature under the rubric of radical adult education (Lovett 1988). Occasionally, however, there is the recognition that community education must spill over into social, even revolutionary, action (Freire 1972). There are many similar nonformal radical adult education groups performing the same functions and having aims in society, however, working primarily and peacefully for community development. These are generally classified as forms of community education (see Fletcher and Thompson 1980).

Additionally, nonformal education has been institutionalized in some professions through the use of trained mentors or teacher–practitioners whose work function is to train new recruits to occupations and professions in the workplace. In these instances, skilled practitioners receive some training in teaching techniques so that they can mentor new recruits. Naturally, this serves to ensure that practical knowledge and skills are transmitted to new recruits, but it also has a socializing function—new recruits are socialized into the current practices of the workplace without disrupting the work situation and so cultural reproduction is facilitated.

4. Informal Education

Some scholars might question the extent to which informal education is actually education, since it is individualistic, noninstitutionalized, and experiential. In this sense they seek to distinguish clearly between education and learning in a way that some adult education literature fails to do. However, there are institutionalized processes of teaching and learning that are more informal. For instance, there have been a number of studies of learning in the workplace (Marsick 1987), where the institutionalized supervisory role is educative.

The growth of the affective adult education movement, often regarding itself as experiential education and going under a number of names from encounter groups to human potential development, is certainly one major development in informal education, although it might also legitimately be categorized as nonformal education. This movement combines both educational and therapeutic functions of group dynamics. One of its major exponents has been Rogers (1983), and this movement has provided therapy, a sense of belonging, and even a sense of religious purpose to its participants. In this context, it is a form of sedative, and yet it also helps prevent the growth of alienation, which is a feature of contemporary society.

LaBelle (1982 p. 162) actually suggests that peer group participation and daily experience provide informal education situations. Certainly they provide the basis of informal learning, but the extent to which this is education is debatable. Certainly it is sometimes claimed that the mass media provide another form of ideological control and so there have been a number of papers advocating that critical reflection is an important part of the learning process (Jarvis 1985b, Brookfield 1987).

However, this does also indicate that as society has become more individuated there has been a corresponding emphasis upon individual and experiential learning. Indeed, there have been sociological studies of adult learning (Jarvis 1987) in which it has been recognized that learning is itself a social phenomenon. One of the major influences underlying this approach is the work of Mead (Strauss 1964). However, one other factor which has played a significant part in this emphasis on learning has been the work on reflection by Freire (1972) and Habermas (1972), among others. Habermas, for instance, was instrumental in Mezirow's (1981) discussion of levels of reflective learning. This approach to adult learning has become central to much discussion and thinking about adult learning, and it also mirrors Giddens's (1979) emphasis on reflexivity as a crucial element in understanding human action in contemporary society. While some adult educators tend to relate their thinking about reflective learning and individual criticality to critical theory, it would be true to claim that there have been very few studies of adult education from this perspective, the exceptions being Collins (1991) and Hart (1992).

5. Distance Education: An Educational Structure for Late Modernity

Distance education has its beginnings at the end of the nineteenth century but it was in the mid twentieth century that this approach to education really developed. Although distance education has been utilized in school education, its expansion has taken place in the field of adult education. It may be regarded as a production of industrial capitalism. Peters (1988) has argued for many years that distance education is rationalistic, entrepreneurial, and involves the division of labor and the technological production and transmission of teaching materials. This argument can be extended to demonstrate that the teaching materials are now an educational commodity and sold in a market-place which is becoming increasingly international. Since the law of the market is operating, there is a danger that the weak will suffer—hence the possibility exists that a new form of cultural imperialism could reassert itself.

However, it is not only the production of teaching materials and the market-place that is significant about the distance-teaching universities for adults: they manifest the structural symbols of modernity. Giddens (1990) has suggested that late modernity is characterized by three elements: the separation of time and space; the development of disembedding mechanisms; and the reflexive appropriation of knowledge. It is suggested here that distance education epitomizes all three of these symbols: there is space–time distancing in teaching and learning, a disembedded structure, and reflective learning (see *Distance Education*).

6. Dominant Theoretical Perspectives

Having analyzed four specific forms of adult education, this section is designed to examine from a sociological perspective some of the major adult educational theories that have arisen in literature, such as andragogy, self-directed learning, empowerment, and liberation.

Theoretical perspectives on adult education were emerging in the earlier part of the twentieth century —the first doctorate in the study of adult education being given by the University of London in the early 1920s on a topic, "Adult Education and Spiritual Values," which reflects many of its origins. However, it was not until graduate programs were commenced in the United States that theoretical perspectives really developed and since this was at Teachers College, University of Columbia, it is hardly surprising that Dewey's influence can be detected. The dominant theories of the later part of the century have also been influenced by the culture of the time when they emerged—the 1960s— which embraced the values of humanism, individualism, and self-achievement.

Two American scholars, Cyril Houle and Malcolm Knowles, have been the key figures in this development. Houle (1961) wrote a small book which stimulated a great deal of research on self-directed learning (see *Self-directed Learning*). Malcolm Knowles, a doctoral student of Houle, introduced the concept of andragogy to United States adult education in a number of books and articles (see *Andragogy*). In a sense, self-directed learning reflects the American culture of individualism and self-achievement, so that research in this area has become central to much United States thinking. Knowles learned the term "andragogy" from a Yugoslav adult educator, as andragogy has been prominent there for many years. Unfortunately Knowles did not use the term in the same way as the Yugoslavian adult educators, but it is the United States version which has become well-known in the English-speaking world. Knowles (1970, 1980) originally postulated four assumptions about andragogy: (a) adult learners are self-directed, (b) they have experience which is a reservoir for future learning, (c) they are ready to learn, and (d) they will learn more readily the things relevant to their lives. Immediately it may be seen that Knowles was reflecting some of the same aspects of the 1960s United States culture as Houle, but he also emphasized the humanistic element. There is a sense in which the term "andragogy" itself was as important as its content. United States adult education was growing in the 1960s, many new university departments were being established, and adult education needed an identity which made it distinct from school education; the term "andragogy" provided it. Andragogy, as a concept, emerged when the time was ripe for it, and while Knowles has changed and developed his ideas and heavily criticized the concept itself (Jarvis 1984), andragogy provided adult education with an identity, and its content reflected the culture of the time during the growth period of adult education in the United States.

Radical adult educators, working with the underprivileged and with oppressed groups, have adopted the dominant theme of empowerment to describe a great deal of their work. Clearly, adult education does act to change people, helping them to see themselves as more significant in society (see *Critical Approaches to Adult Education*).

7. Professionalization of Adult Education

There have been attempts by the Commission of Professors of Adult Education in the United States to professionalize adult education, but such a move is fraught with difficulties because of the nature of the occupation. Unlike more traditional occupations, adult education has neither a single structure nor a controlling body. As was pointed out at the beginning of this entry, adult education occurs in many different sectors of society, each sector being able to control its own educators. Hence, nursing education, for instance, can recruit, train, and license its own educators without reference to any other branch of adult education. Indeed, in the higher status professions the educators are much more likely to identify with their profession than they are with a lower status occupation like adult education. Thus the education of adults might be conceptualized as a functional occupation or profession which will not professionalize along any of the paths that students of the professions have, at various times, suggested (e.g., Wilensky 1964). Different sectors may professionalize within their own profession, but this will not directly affect any other branch of adult education.

8. Conclusion

As the population ages, so adult education assumes new forms, but performs similar functions with different age groups. For instance, as people leave their work on retirement and enter what will be for many a prolonged period of leisure, many employers are introducing preretirement education to prepare their workers for the future. Indeed, educational gerontology is a rapidly developing field of adult education, with its own journals and research interests, as it is performing a leisure-time function for the elderly (see, e.g., Glendenning and Percy 1990).

It may be seen, therefore, that the forms and structures of adult education are related to the structures and the levels of development of the societies in which they occur. This leads one to wonder about the insights a science of comparative adult education could contribute (see Lichtner 1989). At the same time, the functions that it performs are similar throughout but, naturally, there is a greater concentration upon leisure-time pursuits among the elderly, compared with those who are still in employment.

See also: Adult Education: Concepts and Principles; Critical Approaches to Adult Education; Adult Education: Disciplinary Orientations; Women and Adult Education; Comparative Studies: Adult Education; Comparative Studies: Vocational Education and Training; Professional Associations

References

Althusser L 1971 (trans. Brewster B) *Lenin and Philosophy and Other Essays*. New Left Books, London

Bourdieu P 1973 Cultural reproduction and social reproduction. In: Brown R (ed.) 1973 *Knowledge, Education, and Cultural Change.* Tavistock, London

Bourdieu P, Passeron J-C 1977 (trans. Nice R) *Reproduction in Education, Society and Culture.* Sage Publications, London

Brookfield S D 1987 *Developing Critical Thinkers.* Jossey-Bass, San Francisco, California

Carlson R A 1987 *The Americanization Syndrome: A Quest for Conformity*, rev. edn. Croom Helm, London

Cassara B (ed.) 1990 *Adult Education in a Multicultural Society.* Routledge, London

Collins M 1991 *Adult Education as Vocation.* Routledge, London

Coombs P H, Ahmed M 1974 *Attacking Rural Poverty: How Non-Formal Education Can Help.* Johns Hopkins University Press, Baltimore, Maryland

Courtney S 1992 *Why Adults Learn: Towards a Theory of Participation in Adult Education.* Routledge, London

Entwistle H 1979 *Antonio Gramsci: Conservative Schooling for Radical Politics.* Routledge and Kegan Paul, London

Fletcher C, Thompson N (eds.) 1980 *Issues in Community Education.* Falmer Press, Lewes

Freire P 1972 (trans. Ramos B) *Pedagogy of the Oppressed.* Penguin, Harmondsworth

Giddens A 1979 *Central Problems in Social Theory: Action, Structure and Contradiction in Social Analysis.* Macmillan, London

Giddens A 1990 *The Consequences of Modernity.* Polity Press, Cambridge

Glendenning F, Percy K (eds.) 1990 *Ageing, Education and Society.* Association for Educational Gerontology, University of Keele, Keele

Griffin C 1987 *Adult Education as Social Policy.* Croom Helm, London

Habermas J 1972 (trans. Shapiro J J) *Knowledge and Human Interests.* Heinemann Educational, London

Hart M U 1992 *Working and Educating for Life.* Routledge, London

Houle C O 1961 *The Inquiring Mind.* University of Wisconsin Press, Madison, Wisconsin

Jarvis P 1984 Andragogy—a sign of the times. *Studies in the Education of Adults* 16: 32–38

Jarvis P 1985a *The Sociology of Adult and Continuing Education.* Croom Helm, London

Jarvis P 1985b Thinking critically in an information society: A sociological analysis. *Lifelong Learning: An Omnibus of Practice and Research* 8(6): 11–14

Jarvis P 1987 *Adult Learning in the Social Context.* Croom Helm, London

Knowles M S 1970 *The Modern Practice of Adult Education: Andragogy versus Pedagogy.* Association Press, Chicago, Illinois

Knowles M S 1980 *The Modern Practice of Adult Education: From Pedagogy to Andragogy*, rev. edn. Follett, Chicago, Illinois

LaBelle T J 1982 Formal, non-formal and informal education: A holistic perspective on lifelong learning. *Int. Rev. Educ.* 28(2): 159–75

Levine K 1986 *The Social Context of Literacy.* Routledge and Kegan Paul, London

Lichtner M (ed.) 1989 *Comparative Research in Adult Education.* Centro Europeo dell'Educazione, Frascati

Lovett T (ed.) 1988 *Radical Approaches to Adult Education: A Reader.* Routledge, London

Marsick V J (ed.) 1987 *Learning in the Workplace.* Croom Helm, London

Mezirow J A 1981 Critical Theory of Adult Learning and Education. *Adult Educ.* 32(1): 3–24

Peters O 1988 Distance teaching and industrial production: A comparative interpretation in outline. In Sewart D, Keegan D, Holmberg B (eds.) *Distance Education: International Perspectives*, 2nd edn. Routledge, London

Rogers C 1983 *Freedom to Learn for the 80's.* Merrill, Columbus, Ohio

Strauss A (ed.) 1964 *George Herbert Mead on Social Psychology.* University of Chicago Press, Chicago, Illinois

Thomas A M 1991 *Beyond Education: A New Perspective on Society's Management of Learning.* Jossey-Bass, San Francisco, California

Thompson J L 1983 *Learning Liberation: Women's Response to Men's Education.* Croom Helm, London

Tuijnman A 1989 *Recurrent Education, Earnings and Well-being.* Almqvist and Wiksell International, Stockholm

Wilensky H A L 1964 The professionalization of everyone? *Am. J. Sociol.* 70: 137–58

Youngman F 1986 *Adult Education and Socialist Pedagogy.* Croom Helm, London

(d) Epistemology and Research Methodology

Adult Education Research

K. Rubenson

The continuously growing interest in adult education research in developed as well as in developing countries is a very recent phenomenon. During the rapid expansion of the social sciences, especially of education in the 1950s and 1960s, very little attention was paid to adult education. The lack of interest in conducting research in adult education could be explained by the marginality of the adult education enterprise or, as in the Scandinavian countries, for example, by the independent standing adult education has had in relation to government and the public school system. In addition to considering the fact of marginality and independence, another reason for the lack of research in adult education may have been the strong influence of the need for practicability in programs and training of instructors.

During the 1970s, adult education shed its marginal role and came to the forefront of public interest. It is now increasingly being regarded as an integrated part of the education sector—especially in some of the Third World countries and in the Nordic countries. Another sign of this phenomenon has been the development of concepts such as lifelong education, *education permanente*, and recurrent education (see *Lifelong and Continuing Education; Lifelong Learning; Recurrent Education*). The new role for adult education in society has created an interest for research corresponding to the one which emerged during the period of enormous growth of public expenditures on schools and universities in the 1860s.

The response to the demand for research has varied between countries depending on governmental policy and the institutional context of research. In the Nordic countries, improvement in the status of adult education in the 1970s was followed by a sharp rise in the resources for research and development in this area. Norway has established a special institute for research and development in adult education outside the university structure. In Sweden the adult education share of the National Board of Education's research and development grants increased from 1 percent in 1969 to 20 percent in 1980–81. Further, the Swedish parliament

has decided to create a chair in adult education. This is remarkable as it is the first time that the authorities have allowed a specialization and differentiation in the discipline of education.

Looking at Continental Europe, it is possible to observe the beginning of an institutionalization of adult education in the universities as indicated by the creation of special chairs. After a decade of exciting developments in adult education research, there is a need to scrutinize the state of this field of study.

Törnebohm (1974) states that any scientific discipline might, on an epistemological level, be described in terms of its territory. He further assumes that research is concerned with a part of the real world and that knowledge produced in a field may then be described as an authorized map of the territory. Departing from Törnebohm's epistemological perspective, this article is intended to analyze what governs the drawing of the map (the knowledge production) in adult education. This will be done by trying to answer the following two questions:

(a) Which assumptions and perceptions of the territory govern the efforts to accumulate knowledge within adult education, that is, which questions are regarded as legitimate within the field?

(b) Which research traditions, that is, scientific ideals and perspectives, govern the research efforts in adult education?

The choice of material to be analyzed will, of course, determine the answer to the questions posed.

Up until the late 1960s, with some exceptions, there existed little systematic research in the area of adult education outside the United States. Therefore, it is understandable that it is research done in the United States that has come to set the boundaries of the field. Due to the rapid expansion of research in other parts of the world, this is less true today than it was in the early 1970s, despite the overwhelming number of studies produced in North America. One problem in trying to give a balanced picture is the lack of material describing and analyzing research outside the Anglo-Saxon countries.

1. Assumption and Perceptions of the Territory

The question on which assumptions and perceptions of the territory have governed the research will be answered by looking at the following three aspects: (a) adult education as a field of practice versus (b) adult education as a field of scholarly inquiry borrowing from various disciplines, and (c) conceptualizations of research questions.

1.1 Field of Practice Versus Scientific Discipline

One of the classic debates is whether adult education is only a field of social practice or if it also should be considered a science. With the institutionalization of adult education in the universities and the resultant growing body of research, this question has lost most of its relevance. The task today is rather to look at which direction the research is going with regard to practice.

In order to understand knowledge production in adult education people should be made aware that it grew as a field of study out of the movement toward professionalization and institutionalization marked by an expansion of programs in adult education. Consequently, there has been a stress on practicability and the needs of the field have come to determine which problems have been selected as "legitimate."

With reference to the somewhat hazy concept of research and development, adult education research has mostly been of the "development kind." Practice-oriented research aimed at solving an immediate problem is not intrinsically negative. The heart of the matter is the lack of balance between practice-oriented research and discipline-oriented research, where the purpose is to develop and test theories and lay the necessary foundations for applied research. Due to a lack of intradisciplinary orientation, practice-oriented research has tended to be almost atheoretical. Thus, there are two interrelated problems facing adult education— the balance between practice—and discipline-oriented research, and the atheoretical approach of applied research.

Adult education is often characterized as a normative study in which the purpose of the research is to evolve programs which have the most likelihood of promoting such learning situations in which behavior changes may best be brought about. As a consequence of the "normative" view, research has mostly come to deal with the development of programs and/or instructional methods while critical analysis of the prerequisites for developing adult education in a certain desired way has been neglected.

Since the 1970s there has been somewhat more interest in discipline-oriented questions. However, this kind of research has met sharp criticism from the field. In fact, one common characteristic among adult educators around the world seems to be a negative attitude towards research. The view is that the research carried out has been of little if any use to those concerned with the practicalities of education. Moreover, this attitude can also be found inside the universities. Many of those occupying positions of leadership in the universities have reached their positions not by doing research in adult education but by serving the field. The stress on practicalities is further nourished by graduate students in adult education. They tend to be older than the general graduate student, come from jobs which they expect to return to, and embark on research which applies directly to their own situation.

1.2 Borrowing from Other Fields of Study

Jensen (1964), discussing the situation in the United States, suggested that adult education could develop a unique body of knowledge suited to its purposes through two methods: (a) experiences from practice could be used to formulate principles or generalizations, and (b) knowledge which has been developed in other fields of study could be borrowed and reformulated for use in adult education.

With reference to the second point, adult education researchers in North America apart from some common psychological theories, failed to follow the route set by Jensen. Seldom is any serious effort made to build on or integrate findings or theories of a more general nature. In fact, Boshier and Pickard (1979) show that, to an increasing extent, researchers who publish in *Adult Education* rely primarily on adult education literature. Only 20 percent of citations appearing in Volume 19 (1968) of *Adult Education* referred to primary sources. By 1977 (Volume 27), this figure had increased to nearly 60 percent.

Among advocates for a discipline of adult education, there is a strong belief that not only is borrowing of little value for adult education, but it is also damaging. In *Redefining the Discipline of Adult Education*, Boyd and Apps (1980) argue that it would be an error to seek assistance from recognized disciplines before the field of adult education itself is clearly understood. This line of reasoning has been criticized by several scholars who argue that it is in the effort to understand the structure, the function, and the problems of adult education that help from a number of disciplines is needed. (Blunt 1994, Hake 1992, Nordhaug 1991, Rubenson 1980).

The attitude toward borrowing is linked to the institutional setting. In Sweden, adult education research has been carried out in unified departments of education research or in sociology and psychology departments. The research is judged in comparison to scholarly activities in the social sciences in general and not to adult education as a specific field of study. The same is true, but less marked, elsewhere in Europe. The situation is different in North America where almost all research in the area occurs within special units of adult education and the scholastic activities are judged within a specific field of study, adult education.

1.3 Conceptualization of Research Questions

There is a difference between North America and Europe with regard to the conceptualization of research questions in adult education. To simplify somewhat, it could be argued that the North American premise appears to be that of "people-over-society" while the European is that of "people-in-society."

A very obvious observation that can be made from reviewing research in adult education in North America is the dominant influence of psychology whether to be in program planning, instruction, or participation. The problem of instruction simply becomes a question of learning. Departing from one of the learning theories, the researcher tries to arrange, or describe, the external conditions in accordance with the theory in order to study the relationship between instruction (process) variables and student learning (product) variables.

The popularity of the psychologically oriented process-product research is easy to understand in the light of the myth that instruction derives in a linear fashion from research. The appeal of this research tradition then is that it promises results that may be directly translated into prescriptions for practice.

The individualistic perspective is also evident in research on participation, a major area of adult education research in North America. Many scholars seem to assume that motivation is the sole determinant of participation by adults in education (see *Participation: Role of Motivation*). Further, the concept of motivation has often been formulated in terms of psychological constructs that deal with people *in abstracto* (e.g., the general nature of motives and needs) and do not consider specific psychological processes as related to concrete situations.

It is especially in the area of participation research that the difference between North America and Europe becomes apparent. The North Americans have had the individual person in the focus while the Europeans have given relatively more attention to participation from a social perspective. As a consequence the latter have been less interested in motivation orientations and attitudes per se and given more attention to how the objective world influences the perception of reality. Further, Western Europeans have gone from a preoccupation with comparing participants with nonparticipants to analyzing the phenomenon in relation to broad social movements. This development should partly be understood in the political context. In those western European countries where adult education became an integrated part of the social and economic policy, the governments supported

"decision-oriented" research which greatly influenced the direction and conceptualization of participation research. The United States, and Canada to a lesser extent, with their decentralized political and economic systems and individual emphasis on social mobility, promote a research focus on the individual. The call against psychological reductionism and for integrating societal aspects into theoretical frameworks and studies has, judging from Long's (1991) review of the formal knowledge base had limited effect. This is not to deny the developments that have occurred in connection with the introduction of critical theory into North American adult education (see e.g., Deshler & Hagan 1989, Merriam 1991).

Reviewing the western European research it is possible to detect some tendencies to a situation in adult education research in which North American reductionism is replaced by "sociological deductionism" with a concomitant restriction on the development of the field of study. An understanding of problems of the complexity that adult education addresses requires not a single theory but a conjunction of a variety of theories. Thus it is difficult to perceive a single comprehensive theory on participation. Instead it has been argued that in order to understand participation, theoretical models in at least three areas are necessary; adult education as a societal process, the individual's psychological conceptual apparatus, and, in addition, the links between these levels (Rubenson1980). Recently there have been attempts to take this holistic approach in adult education research, for example, in the long-range research agenda developed by the Norwegian Institute of Adult Education.

In summary, the analysis of the first question: "Which assumptions and perceptions of the territory govern the efforts to accumulate knowledge," shows that the stress on practicability has limited the map that has been developed. Further, it reveals that the territory has been defined mainly from assumptions about the characteristics of the learner but that there is a reorientation—mainly in Europe—to a more sociological approach.

2. Governing Research Traditions in Adult Education

The question of which research traditions have governed knowledge production will be answered through looking at the criteria that have been used in review of adult education research and by looking at the latest developments in this field of research.

2.1 Criteria for Assessing Adult Education as a Field of Study

Over the years there have been attempts to examine the production of knowledge relating to adult education in North America in order to study the emergence of adult education as a field of study. Based on advances in research methodology there was a general agreement during the 1970s that the research has been of intradisciplinary importance and contributed to the development of a discipline of adult education.

Dickinson and Rusnell (1971) stated that the gradual emergence of a discipline (between 1959 and 1970) of adult education was indicated by, among other things, an increase in the number of articles classified as empirical research (from 8 to 44%, interpretive literature reviews from 3 to 12%, and historical studies (from 1 to 8%. Further they observed a growing sophistication in research methodology. The experimental studies rose from zero to 35 percent and the surveys became less descriptive in character. Long and Agyekum (1974) also pointed to the growing stress research between 1964 and 1973. While the quantity and proportion of descriptive research articles was constant, the reviewers found that the quality of the descriptive research had increased from rather loose case reports and status surveys to more analytical and multivariate studies. The same observation is made by Copeland and Grabowski (1971), with regard to adult education research in the United States in general. They claim that the quality of descriptive studies has been enhanced by the development of more powerful statistical tools and that more studies have been formulated within a theoretical framework. Boshier and Pickard (1979) stated: "It is ironic and reflective of the state of adult education research that Johnstone and Rivera's monumental survey which produced numerous bivariate contingency tables was cited twenty times, yet Miller's multivariate analysis, which portrayed participation as a function of complex multivariate interactions between psychological, social and institutional variables was cited less than six times in the ten year period" (p. 76).

The conclusion here is that the claim for the growing intradisciplinary importance of adult education research has, to quite a large extent, been made on the basis of a growing empiricism and the use of more advanced statistical methods.

The claim of intradisciplinary advancement can be criticized. If the positivistic research ideal and its set of methodological "do's and don'ts" are accepted, it is true, as the reviewers have pointed out, that there was an increase in the use of sophisticated statistical methods during the 1970s. Despite the improvements pointed out, it is possible to be skeptical as regards the viewer's positive assessment, since the methodological standard of the research seldom has been of such quality that any major development could be talked about. In fact, the technical standard of the research was never really scrutinized in the above-mentioned reviews. The low technical quality of mainstream empirical adult education research remains as a major problem (Blunt 1994). The move towards qualitative oriented research methods has not done much to improve the sophistication of adult education research (Hake 1992, Mader 1992).

The emphasis on empiricism and research methodology in order to build a field of study of adult education in North America is easy to understand as this is consistent with the prevailing tradition in education research as such.

It is not only in North America that the maturity and quality of adult education research is being questioned. Mader (1992) states that after 20 years of work establishing a science of adult education in Germany there are serious doubts as to whether or not it has grown out of fragmentation. The same is true for the United Kingdom and the Nordic countries. Looking at research done within special departments for adult education it is quite obvious that North American research is more sophisticated than that done in most parts of the world. At the same time it is also true to say that studies in the area of adult education undertaken in departments of psychology, sociology, and education tend to be of a higher quality with regard to design and methodology than research in departments of adult education.

2.2 Alternative Research Traditions

There has been growing support for alternative research traditions among adult educators. This is quite in line with the general developments in the social sciences, where the positivistic research tradition with its roots in technical rationality and male dominance has come under heavy fire. One trend is a revival of critical theory coupled with a focus on conflict, power, control, and the effect of structural factors on the educational process. The problem with much of the so-called critical literature, however, is that it is confined to introducing social theorists to an adult education audience, or that the analyses are purely theoretical, addressing issues related to various positions of leading social theorists. Valuable as it might be, it does little to inform the empirical research and, more problematic, the knowledge production is hampered by lack of a fruitful interplay between empirical research and theory development. Without this interplay, the scholarly literature in our field continues to mainly put forward normative positions without an interest in or capability to study under what conditions the ideas could be realized.

Another approach more popular in the firmament of adult educational research is the interpretative paradigm. The "interpretativists" are heavily influenced by symbolic interactionism phenomenology and ethnomethodology. These approaches, through undeniably "research," are fundamentally different from traditional positivistic research. The concern is the problem of subjective meaning as basic for an understanding of the social world.

The "interpretative school" is of special interest as its choice of research tradition is in harmony with some of the alternative views that are put forward in adult education. It is easy to understand the enthusiasm among adult educators for phenomenological-oriented approaches and the postmodern position as they seemingly fit well with the general individualistic orientation of adult education.

Finally, the Glaser and Strauss work, *The Discovery of Grounded Theory*, has had great influence on research in adult education both in North America and Europe. The strategy of grounded theory is central to adult education as it is believed that adult education partly can develop a unique body of knowledge suited to its purposes through formulating principles or generalizations from experiences in practice. In reality, however, there has been more lip-service paid than serious attempts made to generate theories from data systematically obtained from adult education research. The inductive phase, whereby the event is "translated" into concepts and the relationships between the concepts are spelled out with the purpose of forming a theory, has received little attention. The criticism is not against the way it has been used by adult education researchers to legitimate an atheoretical approach.

3. Concluding Remarks

This article has tried to outline the assumptions and perceptions that have governed the development of adult education as a field of study. The largest stumbling block in this process has been and still is the overwhelming preoccupation with practicality; and a negative and sometimes anti-intellectual attitude toward research among adult educators. A major obstacle for a theoretical development within adult education as well as the production of "real useful knowledge" is the often sharp separation that exists between theory development and empirical (qualitative as well as quantitative) research. Developing research of the proposed nature will depend on the availability of funding for this kind of activity and the ability of adult education researchers to compete for the general research funding. However, it will also require a willingness to partly change the way we do research in adult education. There would be a need for more long-term research programs, integration of empirical studies and theory development, and a willingness and capability to attack "real problems."

One positive development over the last ten years is the increased internationalization of adult education research. The previous isolationism has been replaced with a stronger effort to include research from various parts of the world. This is particularly true of the growing exchange between Europe and North America as partly evident in *Adult Education. Evolution and Achievements in a Developing Field of Study* (Peters and Jarvis 1991). The recent development of a learned society in Europe, the European Society for Research

on the Education of Adults (ESREA), provides an alternative and challenge to the North American domination in adult education research. Whether it will be possible to find a fruitful synthesis between the more sociological-directed research in Europe and other parts of the world and the more psychological-oriented research in North America is an open question.

References

Blunt A 1994 The future of adult education research. In: Garrison D R (ed.) 1994 *Research Perspectives in Adult Education. Krieger Publishing Company, Florida*

Boshier R, Pickard L 1979 Citation patterns of articles published in Adult Education 1968–1977. *Adult Educ.* 30: 34–51

Boyd R D, Apps J W 1980 A conceptual model for adult education. In: Boyd R D, Apps J W (eds.) 1980 *Redefining the Discipline of Adult Education*. Jossey-Bass, San Francisco, California

Copeland H G, Grabowski S M 1971 Research and investigation in the United States. *Convergence* 4(4): 23–32

Deshler D, Hagan N 1989 Adult education research: Issues and directions. In: Merriam S B, Cunningham P M (eds.) 1989 *Handbook of Adult and Continuing Education*. Jossey-Bass, San Francisco, California

Dickinson G, Rusnell D 1971 A content analysis of Adult Education. *Adult Educ.* 21: 177–85

Glaser B G, Strauss A L 1968 *The Discovery of Grounded Theory: Strategies for Qualitative Research*. Weidenfeld and Nicolson, London

Hake B J 1992 Remaking the study of adult education: The relevance of recent developments in the Netherlands to the search for a disciplinary identity. *Adult Educ. Q.* 42 (2): 63–78

Jensen G E 1964 How adult education borrows and reformulates knowledge of other disciplines. In: Jensen G E, Liveright A A, Hallenbeck W (eds.) 1964 *Adult Education: Outlines of an Emerging Field of University Study*. Adult Education Association of the United States, Washington, DC

Long H B, Agyekum S 1974 Adult education 1964–1973: Reflections of a changing discipline. *Adult Educ.* 24: 99–120

Mader W M (ed.) 1992 *Adult Education in the Federal Republic of Germany*. Centre for Continuing Education, University of British Columbia, Vancouver

Merriam S B 1991 In: Peters J M, Jarvis P 1991 (eds.)

Nordhaug O 1991 *The Shadow Educational System*. Norweigan University Press, Oslo

Peters J M, Jarvis P 1991 (eds.) *Adult education. Evolution and Achievements in a Developing Field of Study*. Jossey-Bass, San Francisco, California

Rubenson K 1980 Background and theoretical context. In: Hoghielm R, Rubenson K (eds.) 1980 *Adult Education for Social Change: Research on the Swedish Allocation Policy: Studies in Education and Psychology*, Vol. 9. Liberlaromedel, Stockholm

Törnebohm H 1974 *Scientific Knowledge Formation*. Department of Theory Science, University of Goteborg, Goteborg

Empiricism, Positivism, and Antipositivism

D. C. Phillips

During the closing decades of the twentieth century, members of the education research community have displayed a growing interest in the philosophical underpinnings of their work—especially of the methodological aspects. One line of evidence for this is readily available in the pages of the *Educational Researcher*, the "house journal" of the American Educational Research Association, where since the mid-1970s a large number of articles on philosophical and methodological matters have appeared, many written by nonphilosophers; another indication is the special issue of the *International Journal of Educational Research*, which, in 1991, was given over entirely to philosophical issues in research (Lakomski 1991). Special symposia have even been held to allow researchers to discuss these matters (see Guba 1990). Amongst the topics most frequently referred to has been the "demise of positivism" (see, for example, Phillips 1983, Miller and Fredericks 1991, Schrag 1992); in much of this literature, however, there has been confusion about the relationships between positivism, logical positivism, and empiricism. This entry will explore the meanings of these concepts and their relationships.

1. Empiricism

Empiricism is one of the two major, classic positions in epistemology—the other being rationalism, which, crudely put, holds that the main underpinning of human knowledge is the "light of reason." (Descartes is a quintessential figure in the history of rationalism; as is well-known, he searched through his ideas to find one which was clear and distinct to the light of reason, and which could not be doubted. Thus he arrived at his famous "cogito ergo sum," which became the ultimate foundation for his knowledge.) Both classic positions are complex, in the sense that within each there are many subschools of thought.

Empiricism, according to one authority, may be characterized as "Any of a variety of views to the effect that either our concepts or our knowledge are, wholly or partly, based on experience through the senses and introspection. The basing may refer to psychological origin or, more usually, philosophical justification" (Lacey 1976 p. 55).

Thus, one form of empiricism holds that human knowledge originates from sense experience; a representative figure here is the British philosopher of the seventeenth century, John Locke, who held that at birth the mind of the individual was a "tabula rasa" (blank tablet)—and that the origin of every simple idea could be traced to sense experience or to introspection (inner experience). Locke had a view that later followers came to call "mental chemistry," for he envisioned simple ideas being combined in various ways to form more and more complex ideas; but there was no idea whose genealogy could not be traced back down the descending path from complex to simple to eventual origin in sense experience. A person who had never experienced the color lilac could not have the idea of lilac (although the person might know the word "lilac" from having heard or read it).

Thus, for Locke, the sequence of knowledge-growth was as follows: a newborn baby, devoid of ideas but with a cognitive mechanism that was potentially able to manipulate and work with ideas (a crucial point), might experience coldness, loudness, redness, and roundness (from the surrounding environment, a toy hanging over the crib, and so forth), and these would give rise to the corresponding simple ideas; gradually complex ideas like "red ball" would be built up—but only if the requisite simple ideas had been formed. Introspection, or reflection, or inner experience, would similarly produce simple ideas like "pain" or "anger." As should be evident, Locke was a strong opponent of the view that there could be innate ideas.

As the quotation from Lacey indicates, however, there are other forms of empiricism. A person might be more interested in the question of justification than of origin. Consider the claim that unadulterated water, at normal pressure, boils at 100°C. A narrow Lockean might want to emphasize the fact that the concepts here—"water," "boils," "pressure," and so on—must all have had their ultimate origin in sense experience; but others (and, for that matter, a Lockean as well) might want to know what justifies or warrants this particular claim—why is pure water believed to boil at 100°C rather than at 90°C? Empiricists would want to say that this claim is justified by experience, or by the empirical evidence that is available.

At first sight, this justificatory version of empiricism has a lot going for it—for it is hard to see how any philosopher could advocate a position that did not in some way allow for the fact that knowledge of the world must be constrained in some fashion by the way the world is, or appears to be. (Even so strong a contemporary critic of simplistic empiricism as Paul Feyerabend admits that he is prepared to march in company with empiricism at least this far; see Feyerabend 1980.) In the second half of the twentieth century, however, some severe problems have come to the fore, especially as philosophers have pursued issues of justification with respect to the theoretical knowledge of the advanced sciences.

2. Challenges to Empiricism

Perhaps the most important challenge to empiricism has been the realization that the items constituting knowledge—theories, hypotheses, and so on—are always underdetermined by the evidence that is available. In other words, knowledge always goes beyond the evidence; or, to turn the point around, the evidence at hand at hand is always compatible with a variety of theories or hypotheses. So it cannot be claimed that the belief in theory T1 is justified by a particular body of empirical evidence, because theories T2, T3, and so on, are also justified or warranted by this same evidence. To take an oversimple example, one might claim to know that there is a golf ball lying on the table, and by way of justification one offers the fact that one experiences seeing the ball there. However, another person may claim that it is not a golf ball, but a hologram; and another might offer the opinion that it is one of those light plastic replicas that are sometimes used to play practical jokes on golfers. The point is, the evidence that warrants one's own claim can also be used to warrant the other people's. If new evidence is collected, these alternative theories may be ruled out, but others might be dreamt up that are still compatible with the finite body of evidence that is available. These rival theories might be ruled out on the grounds that they are unreasonable or improbable, given the situation in which the observations are being made, but then it is evident that the knowledge that this is indeed a golf ball is based on more than the empirical evidence that is available—for some additional principle or principles have also been drawn on (in this example, concerning what is reasonable or probable under the circumstances). (For an important discussion of the limitations of the argument concerning underdetermination, see Laudan 1990.)

Another problem concerns the status of theoretical entities; such things as quarks, or subnuclear forces, are not directly observable, and to claim that they are "indirectly" observable is also to oversimplify the chains of reasoning involved. How, then, can it be claimed that knowledge of these things "originates" in experience, or is "justified" by experience? Locke's successor Hume (1711–76) raised a similar issue about knowledge of causation in nature: Causes are not actually observed at work, rather what is seen is mere "constant conjunction" (event A seems always to be followed by event B). As a consequence of all this, there is an antirealist tendency within empiricism for it to lead to the view that the only realities are the empirically observable phenomena, and that the entities postulated within theoretical physics are "convenient fictions." (Empiricists differ over this, and other, matters.)

A further difficulty for empiricisms of both types outlined above is the fact that observation, or the gathering of empirical evidence, is not the pristine process that is presupposed by such philosophies. The varieties of empiricism discussed above make the assumption that sense experience is unadulterated, in that it is completely uncontaminated by theory; after all, experience can hardly be the origin of knowledge, or the justificatory "court" to which one appeals when one is asked to warrant knowledge claims, if prior beliefs or theories or knowledge can be shown to have influenced it. This is precisely what has been shown (by Wittgenstein, Popper, Hanson, Kuhn, and others; see Phillips 1987 for further discussion)—observation is theory-laden, and is not theory-neutral. What is seen (or felt or heard or tasted or smelled), and how it is seen (or felt . . .), is influenced by knowledge the experiencer already possesses.

Finally, given the centrality of the notion of "experience," it has been crucial for empiricists to grapple with the issue of what is actually experienced during experience. Different answers have been forthcoming: only sense data are experienced (such things as "red patch here now," although the precise formulation is a matter of learned debate); actual objects are directly experienced; objects and the relations between them are experienced.

As a result of these and other problems (see Morick 1980), an epistemological position known as nonfoundationalism or nonjustificationism has been developed (by Popper and others), according to which knowledge is not to be regarded as being based upon some indubitable and neutral foundation such as experience or the light of reason; rather, those theories or hypotheses that have been adequately tested are tentatively accepted as knowledge—with the caveat that no knowledge is ever absolutely established. Knowledge, in short, is inherently hypothetical (which is not to say that people do not usually have substantial reasons for believing the things that they do) (see *Epistemological Issues in Educational Research*).

3. Positivism

Positivism—itself a complex of several subpositions —is merely one form of empiricism, despite the fact that critics of positivism in educational research tend to identify it as being coextensive with empiricism. In other words, while all forms of positivism are forms of empiricism, it is a mistake to infer back that all empiricisms are forms of positivism. As a consequence, not all problems facing positivism necessarily face other forms of empiricism.

The term "positivist" is used very loosely in the contemporary educational research literature to which reference was made at the outset: it has become a more or less generalized and vague term of abuse. A positivist is likely to be identified, inter alia, as

170

someone who is an empiricist, a realist, a believer in the value of objectivity in research, a believer that truth is a sustainable ideal for research, an adherent of the experimental method, a supporter of quantitative/statistical methods, and a skeptic about qualitative methodologies. That such identifications are fantasies, and in some cases are directly the opposite of the true state of affairs, generally escapes notice. Certainly positivists believe a few of the things here attributed to them, but so do many others— so once again it is invalid to argue backwards and infer that anyone who holds one of these particular positions must be a positivist. Furthermore it is hard to follow the logic that leads to the conclusion that a positivist must be a lover of statistical methods and an opponent of qualitative/observational studies.

Classic positivism can be traced back to the writings of the Frenchman Comte (1798–1857), who in a multivolume work developed a position with three important prongs. First, that human knowledge has developed through three stages marked in each case by the distinctive way knowledge was established—the theological or fictitious stage, the metaphysical or abstract stage, and the scientific or positive stage (Comte 1970 p. 1). Clearly, in Comte's view, the third stage is the one which is epistemologically most adequate.

Second, that the "positive sciences" can be classified in a manner which displays their mutual dependence (and which also relates to the order in which they have been developed)—mathematics, astronomy, physics, chemistry, physiology, and social physics (sociology) (Comte 1970 pp. 46–52).

Third, that scientific knowledge "gives up the search after the origin and hidden causes of the universe and a knowledge of the final causes of phenomena" (Comte 1970 p. 2). Instead, science focuses upon observation, and what can be gleaned by reasoning about observed phenomena. (This was his "positive" method.) Here it is clear that Comte was trying—unsuccessfully—to avoid the problem of classic empiricism concerning the status of inferred theoretical entities; by eschewing the search for hidden causes in nature, he worked himself into the same corner as Locke and Hume. Comte may have allowed scientists to reason, but he did not encourage their thoughts to wander too far from the realm of the observable. (For further discussion, see Phillips 1992 Chap. 7.)

Comte's work had a marked impact on late-nineteenth- and early-twentieth-century thought about the nature of the sciences (and especially about the social sciences).

4. Logical Positivism

It is clear that Comte's ideas were strongly empiricist, and that they had an antimetaphysical thrust— as indicated by his refusal to condone the search for "hidden causes" or "final causes." These interrelated elements were taken even further by an interdisciplinary group that formed in the 1920s around Mortiz Schlick in Vienna—a group that became known as the Vienna Circle. Schlick came from physics, Carnap and Waissman from mathematics and philosophy, Neurath from sociology, Godel and Hahn from mathematics, Kraft from history, and Frank from physics. Later Reichenbach, Hempel, and Ayer, among others, became associated with the group; Karl Popper was resident in Vienna then, but was a strong critic of their ideas (this is significant, for antipositivists in the educational literature sometimes include Popper among the logical positivists). The early work of Wittgenstein was a great stimulus to the group, especially his "picture theory" of language, according to which the logical structure of meaningful statements must be directly isomorphic with the elements in reality (Wittgenstein 1961).

The group flourished into the 1930s, when the rise of Hitler and the murder of Schlick by a deranged student (who was not prosecuted by the authorities) led to its disbandment; many members took refuge in the English-speaking world. Their ideas became very influential, especially in North America where they shaped the image of the nature of science for several decades: the young Skinner met logical positivism (or logical empiricism, as it was sometimes called) while a graduate student, and his behaviorism clearly bears its stamp (Skinner 1953). The physicist Bridgman (1927) also succumbed, and developed his operationism; as a result of his work, the need for researchers to clarify their concepts by means of operational definitions (i.e., by precise specification of the procedures to be used in measuring them) became an item of faith.

Like Comte before them, the logical positivists were strongly antimetaphysical; and to expunge all traces of metaphysical from science they hit upon the strategem of defining metaphysical claims as being meaningless—literally, "non-sensical." To this end they devised the well-known logical positivist verifiability criterion of meaning. This criterion started out being quite simple, but over the years it was complexified as various problems with it were recognized. Its pristine version was as follows: "A statement is held to be literally meaningful if and only if it is either analytic or empirically verifiable" (Ayer 1960 p. 9). Colloquially this can be stated even more directly: "If it can't be seen or measured, it is not meaningful to talk about." The impact of this doctrine was colorfully described by Scriven:

> The Vienna Circle or *Wiener Kreis* was a band of cut-throats that went after the fact burghers of Continental metaphysics who had become intolerably inbred and pompously verbose. The *Kris* is a Malaysian knife, and the *Wiener Kreis* employed a kind of Occam's razor called the verifiability principle. It performed a tracheotomy that made it possible for philosophy to breathe again. (Scriven 1969 p. 195)

As already mentioned, behaviorism and operationism are related forms of this "cutthroat" doctrine in educational research.

Finally, the logical positivists, and fellow travelers such as operationists, needed to give an account of what an acceptable "verification or measurement procedure" was; and although there was much debate over details, the agreed-upon theme—reminiscent of classic Lockeanism—was that verification must be via reduction to basic "sense data."

5. Difficulties of Logical Positivism, and Antipositivism

It should be evident that the logical positivists faced the same kinds of problems that confronted all classic empiricists, only they faced these in particularly virulent forms. One additional issue concerns the status of the "verifiability criterion of meaning" itself, for it cannot be shown to be meaningful in the way that it prescribes itself; furthermore, the notion of meaningfulness embodied in this principle seems a truncated and unnecessarily narrow one. Clearly the chief embarrassment for the logical positivists was that their philosophy—which was devised to strengthen science, and to make scientific method more rigorous—actually threatened the existence of key elements of theoretical science. Laws of nature, for example, cannot be verified in terms of sense experience, for such experience can show at best only that a regularity holds in specific observed cases—experience cannot show that the purported laws hold at all times and in all places (for all times and all places can never be observed). A parallel problem exists with respect to theoretical entities: the sciences have developed theories about realms that are unobservable (the realms of quarks, the conditions inside black holes, the events in the microseconds following the big bang, and so on). It is one thing to say that one does not accept some of these theories as true; but it seems shocking to say that one regards such speculation or theorizing as literally meaningless.

To overcome such problems, many logical positivists were led in antirealist directions; they argued that such theoretical entities as subatomic particles and subnuclear fundamental forces are not to be thought of as real—they have the status of "logical constructions," or "instruments" for making calculations or predictions. Thus, for many positivists, truth and reality were restricted to the domain of the phenomenal, to the realm of sense-experience. And yet the erroneous belief persists among many educational researchers that logical positivists are, quintessentially, realists who believe in "Truth." To cite one example, a well-known contributor to the *Educational Researcher* wrote (in a passage that displays several common misapprehensions): "Philosophers of the positivist school, Carl Hempel and Karl Popper particularly, have posited that propositional statements of lawful relationship are the closest approximations of Truth—whether we are talking about physical matter or human" (Stake 1978 p. 6). (For further examples drawn from the educational literature, see Phillips 1983, and Phillips 1987 Chaps. 4, 8.)

Indeed, it can be argued that many vocal antipositivists are closer than they realize to the spirit of the logical positivists (although, of course, there are significant differences as well)—what unites them is their mutual antirealism.

See also: Adult Education: Disciplinary Orientations; Epistemological Issues in Educational Research

References

Ayer A J 1966 *Language, Truth and Logic*. Gollancz, London

Bridgman P W 1927 *The Logic of Modern Physics*. Macmillan, New York

Comte A 1970 (ed. Ferre F) *Introduction to Positive Philosophy*. Bobbs-Merrill, Indianapolis, Indiana

Feyerabend P 1969 How to be a good empiricist. In: Morick H (ed.) 1980

Guba E (ed.) 1990 *The Paradigm Dialog: Options for Inquiry in the Social Sciences*. Sage, London

Lacey A R 1976 *A Dictionary of Philosophy*. Routledge & Kegan Paul, London

Lakomski G 1991 (ed.) *Int. J. Educ. Res.* 15(6): whole issue

Laudan L 1990 Demystifying underdetermination. In: Savage C W (ed.) 1990 *Scientific Theories*, Minnesota Studies in the Philosophy of Science, XIV. University of Minnesota Press, Minneapolis, Minnesota

Miller S, Fredericks M 1991 Postpositivistic assumptions and educational research: Another view. *Educ. Researcher* 20(4): 2–8

Morick H (ed.) 1980 *Challenges to Empiricism*. Hackett, Indianapolis, Indiana

Phillips D C 1983 After the wake: Postpositivistic educational thought. *Educ. Researcher* 12(5): 4–12

Phillips D C 1987 *Philosophy, Science, and Social Inquiry*. Pergamon Press, Oxford

Phillips D C 1992 *The Social Scientist's Bestiary*. Pergamon Press, Oxford

Schrag F 1992 In defense of positivist research paradigms. *Educ. Researcher* 21(5): 5–8

Scriven M 1969 Logical positivism and the behavioral sciences. In: Achinstein P, Barker F (eds.) 1969

Skinner B F 1953 *Science and Human Behavior*. Free Press, New York

Stake R 1978 The case study method in social inquiry. *Educ. Researcher* 7(2): 5–8

Wittgenstein L 1961 *Tractatus Logico-Philosophicus*. Routledge and Kegan Paul, London

Epistemological Issues in Educational Research

J. C. Walker and C. W. Evers

Questions about the nature, scope, and applicability of knowledge in and of adult education abound. This entry addresses such questions, and explores the unity thesis in educational research.

1. Epistemology and Education

Epistemology is the study of the nature, scope, and applicability of knowledge. Educational research, in being concerned with the conduct of educational inquiry and the development and evaluation of its methods and findings, embodies a commitment to epistemological assumptions—at least it does if its findings are expected to command attention, serve as a sound basis for action, or constitute legitimate knowledge claims. These matters are the subject of epistemological theories which deal more systematically with such general corresponding issues as justification, truth, and the accessibility of reality in the search for knowledge.

In educational research, obviously, there are different methods of inquiry, ranging from controlled laboratory experiments through participant observation to action research, from historical studies to logical analysis. These have been organized in different research traditions, such as "quantitative" and "qualitative," or associated with different theoretical positions, such as behaviorism and critical theory. In practice, the categories of method, tradition, and theoretical position cut across each other to some extent.

The major epistemological question here is whether these distinctions are associated with different ways of knowing or forms of knowledge, which partition educational research so that research traditions, for example, turn out to be radically distinct epistemologically, each having its own theories and rules of justification, meaning, and truth. If so, the next question is whether findings produced by the different traditions can be rationally integrated, rendered coherent, or even compared. For this to be possible, for traditions to be commensurable, there will have to be some shared concepts and standards of justification, meaning, and truth: some epistemological touchstone. If, however, the traditions are so fundamentally disparate that any choice between them in educational research is arbitrary or the result of nonrational commitment—an act of faith—there is no touchstone. The research traditions are incommensurable.

There has long been controversy over these issues, in educational research and the social sciences generally, as advocates of research traditions variously described as "scientific," "humanistic," "quantitative," "qualitative," "positivist," and "interpretative" have tried to sort out the respective epistemological merits of these approaches and the methodological, practical, and even political relations between them.

There are three major views available, which have emerged in educational research in more or less the following historical order. First, it can be asserted that there are epistemologically different paradigms, which are incommensurable in that neither educational research nor any other form of inquiry can provide a rational method for judging between them. Moreover, they are mutually incompatible, competitive ways of researching the same territory. This may be called the "oppositional diversity thesis." Second, it could be decided that there are epistemologically distinct paradigms, but that though incommensurable they are complementary, not competitive: equally appropriate ways of approaching different, overlapping, or perhaps even the same research problems. This may be called the "complementary diversity thesis." The first and second views agree that there is a fundamental epistemological diversity in educational research. The third alternative, the unity thesis, denies this. It disagrees with the view that different research methods can be grouped under incommensurable paradigms, and asserts that the very idea of such paradigms is mistaken, even incoherent. It claims there is touchstone for judging the respective merits of different research traditions and bringing them into a productive relationship with one another. It asserts a fundamental epistemological unity of educational research, derived from the practical problems addressed.

This entry argues for the unity thesis. After a discussion of the term "paradigm," and of the oppositional and complementary diversity theses, it is shown that the theory that there are research paradigms—call it the "P-theory"—is largely responsible for both forms of diversity thesis. Some reasons are offered for believing that P-theory is incoherent, and it is argued that a coherentist epistemology sustains the thesis of the epistemological unity of educational research. A feature of this epistemology is its account of touchstone in educational research.

2. Epistemology and Paradigms

Numerous educational researchers have been drawn to the view that research traditions are best regarded as different paradigms. Indeed, as Shulman (1986 p. 3) observes, in writing about the different research programs of communities of scholars engaged in the study of teaching, "the term most frequently employed to describe such research communities, and the conceptions of problem and method they share is *paradigm*."

As the quantitative/qualitative debate shows, many writers in education distinguish two fundamental paradigms of research: the "scientific" which is often erroneously identified with positivism, and the "interpretative" or "humanistic." Husén associates the distinction with divergent forms of explanation and understanding:

> The twentieth century has seen the conflict between two main paradigms employed in researching educational problems. The one is modeled on the natural sciences with an emphasis on empirical quantifiable observations which lend themselves to analyses by means of mathematical tools. The task of research is to establish causal relationships, to explain (*Erklären*). The other paradigm is derived from the humanities with an emphasis on holistic and qualitative information and to interpretive approaches (*Verstehen*). (Husén 1988 p. 17)

In offering a broader, three-way taxonomy of research to account for diversity in inquiry, Popkewitz (1984 p. 35) says: "the concept of paradigm provides a way to consider this divergence in vision, custom and tradition. It enables us to consider science as having different sets of assumptions, commitments, procedures and theories of social affairs." He assumes that "in educational sciences, three paradigms have emerged to give definition and structure to the practice of research." After the fashion of "critical theory" (Habermas 1972), he identifies the paradigms as "empirical-analytic" (roughly equivalent to quantitative science), "symbolic" (qualitative and interpretative or hermeneutical inquiry), and "critical" (where political criteria relating to human betterment are applied in research).

Noting the influence of positivism on the formation of research traditions and the paradigms debate, Lincoln and Guba (1984 p. 15) mention another common three-way distinction, which they apply to "paradigm eras," "periods in which certain sets of basic beliefs have guided inquiry in quite different ways," rather than directly to paradigms as such. They identify these paradigm eras as "prepositivist," "positivist," and "postpositivist." Now the term "positivist" also has a history of varied usage (Phillips 1983) but, because of the practice common among educational researchers of defining their perspectives in relation to one or more of the varieties of positivism, it is important to note some of the issues involved in the transition to postpositivism.

In philosophy of science, views of the nature of science commonly described as positivist have characterized science as value-free, basing its theories and findings on logically simple and epistemically secure observation reports, and using empirical concepts themselves deriving directly from observation (Hooker 1975). Positivism in this sense, as a form of empiricism, involves a foundational epistemology. Knowledge claims are justified when they are shown to be based on secure foundations, which for positivist empiricism are the sense data acquired through empirical observation. Some positivists—the logical positivists—maintained that only the sentences of science thus conceived, and the "conceptual truths" of logic and mathematics, were objectively meaningful, and that therefore here were to be drawn the limits of genuine knowledge, not simply scientific knowledge. Thus delimited, the domain of knowledge excluded morals, politics, and indeed any field where value judgments were made, which would include much educational research. The movement to postpositivist philosophy of science has occurred because of the undermining of all such doctrines (House 1991).

This use of "positivist" needs to be clearly distinguished from use of the term to describe any view that science (and perhaps conceptual truths of logic and mathematics) is the only way to knowledge, and that the task of philosophy—which is not sharply distinguished from but continuous with empirical science—is to find general principles common to all sciences and even to extend the use of such principles to the regulation of human conduct and the organization of society. The move to a postpositivist (in the first sense) philosophy of science is quite compatible with such a view of the nature of science and its role in human affairs.

Unfortunately, this distinction is not always clearly observed in epistemological discussions of educational research. It is one thing to say, with Lincoln and Guba (1984), that since it has been recognized that science is more complex than building on theory-free and value-free observations, qualitative inquiry may be recognized as a legitimate approach; that the latest paradigm era sanctions more than one paradigm. It is another thing to identify science with positivism (in the first sense) and on the basis of this identification to attack all views suggesting an epistemological continuity between the natural and the social sciences including educational research. Ironically, many writers, while they claim to reject positivism (in both senses), retain a positivist (in the first sense) view of natural science (e.g., Habermas 1972). In this entry "positivist" is used in the first sense, to refer to positivistic empiricism, including logical positivism.

In summary, the move from a positivist to a postpositivist philosophy of science has been paralleled by a move from a view of educational research dominated by the quantitative tradition to a more pluralistic view. The advent of the postpositivist era has been characterized by an acceptance of epistemological diversity which, however, insofar as it is formulated in terms of P-theory, leaves educational research epistemologically divided. The question, then, if there are such divisions as have been noted, is whether the diversity must be oppositional, or can it be harmonious?

3. The Oppositional Diversity Thesis

Quantitative researchers have often seen qualitative research as lacking in objectivity, rigor, and scientific controls (Kerlinger 1973 p.401). Lacking the resources of quantification, qualitative research cannot produce the requisite generalizations to build up a set of laws of human behavior, nor can it apply adequate tests for validity and reliability. Moreover, the positivist fact/value distinction is often employed to discredit the claims of qualitative inquiry to produce knowledge, since knowledge is value-free whereas qualitative research is irreducibly value-laden and subjective. In short, qualitative research falls short of the high standards of objectivity and the tight criteria for truth of the quantitative, or "scientific," paradigm. Given the prestige of science, and a positivist view of science, it is easy to see why quantitative researchers have sometimes even seen qualitative research as opposed to sound scientific method.

In reply, many qualitative researchers, invoking the explanation/understanding distinction, claim that the genuinely and distinctively human dimension of education cannot be captured by statistical generalizations and causal laws. Knowledge of human affairs is irreducibly subjective. It must grasp the meanings of actions, the uniqueness of events, and the individuality of persons. From this perspective, it is easy to see the quantitative tradition as an intrusive, even alien and antihuman, approach to the study of education. "Science" may be appropriate to the study of nature, but it distorts the study of human affairs. It is easy to see why, given a perceived *de facto* domination of educational research by the quantitative tradition, qualitative researchers have sometimes seen it in oppositional, even antagonistic, terms.

Thus the debate over whether so-called quantitative research methodology is in conflict with qualitative research methodology does not revolve simply around the use of numbers, of mathematical and statistical procedures. Rather, it concerns the relation of quantification to more basic questions about objectivity, validity, reliability, and criteria for truth. For example, according to Smith and Heshusius (1986 p.9), who have reasserted the oppositional diversity thesis against the increasing popularity of the other two: "For quantitative inquiry, a logic of justification that is epistemologically foundational leads to the position that certain sets of techniques are epistemologically privileged in that their correct application is necessary to achieve validity or to discover how things really are out there." They also state: "From the perspective of qualitative inquiry, this line of reasoning is unacceptable. The assumptions or logic of justification in this case are not foundationalist and, by extension, do not allow that certain sets of procedures are epistemologically privileged." There are two key epistemological distinctions here. First, "logic of justification" (grounds for making claims) is distinguished

from research procedures (techniques used to gather, analyze, and interpret data). Second, foundational epistemologies, which provide a logic or justification basing knowledge claims on supposedly secure or certain foundations (such as empirical observations), are distinguished from nonfoundational epistemologies whose logic of justification involves no foundations. Later in this entry the assumption that quantitative inquiry must be foundationalist is queried.

The key epistemological dilemma posed by Smith and Heshusius is that for the quantitative researcher there exists a mind-independent reality "out there" that is to some extent knowable. Disciplined observation of it provides epistemic foundations. Qualitative researchers, they assert, are committed to denying this. By following certain practices of inquiry that enjoy a cluster of related theoretical advantages—the advantages of internal and external validity, reliability, and objectivity—the quantitative researcher increases the likelihood of discovering something important about that reality. Its properties and the causal structures governing the orderly behavior of its interrelated parts constitute typical goals of quantitative inquiry. What makes these goals possible, and indeed holds together the theoretical features of such inquiry, is a belief that people can know when a correspondence obtains between the sentences of a theory and the world "out there." It is this correspondence that makes knowledge claims true.

It is precisely this belief that is most often questioned by qualitative researchers. Reality, or at least social reality, they frequently maintain, is something constructed with the mind as a product of theorizing. Theorizing shapes reality, rather than the other way around. There is simply no mind-independent or theory-independent reality to match up with or correspond to sentences, to serve as a check on their acceptability. Under this assumption, the theoretical apparatus employed to characterize epistemically virtuous inquiry will apparently have little use for familiar quantitative notions. Instead, distinctly alternative networks of theoretical requirements for qualitative research will need to be devised, tied to procedures for getting at subjective, or intersubjective, symbols, meanings, and understandings.

Critical theorists go one step further in this philosophical opposition to the "intrusion" of the quantitative tradition into the search for knowledge of the "genuinely human." In addition to being unable to capture the necessary relation between the human mind and social reality, critical theorists maintain that the quantitative (or empirical-analytic) tradition cannot capture the essential role of values in that kind of knowledge needed to improve the human condition. Thus Bates (1980) argues that epistemically adequate educational research must be research that makes for "human betterment." The "praxis" tradition in epistemology, well-exemplified in the theoretical writings of Freire (1972), and more particularly in the action research tradition (Carr and Kemmis 1983), provides a rich theoretical context for elaborating further nonquantitative criteria to replace quantitative notions of validity, reliability, and objectivity. In contrast to the usual lines drawn in the quantitative/qualitative debate, the elimination of social injustice, for example, is not merely a matter of constructing alternative realities, or alternative theories. Nor is validity simply a matter of establishing a correspondence between theory and the world, when the goal is social improvement. Rather, what counts as valid inquiry, as epistemically progressive, is limited to what the surrounding epistemology counts as promoting human well-being.

4. The Complementary Diversity Thesis

Within the epistemologically softer climate of the postpositivist era, many educational researchers believe that the various research traditions, even if incommensurable, are equally legitimate and in no necessary conflict. The "scientific" and "humanistic" approaches, "are not exclusive, but complementary to each other" (Husén 1988 p.20). Indeed Shulman (1986 p.4) goes so far as to suggest that "the danger for any field of social science or educational research lies in its potential corruption . . . by a single paradigmatic view." Against what they have regarded as the unwarranted "positivist," quantitative domination of educational research, proponents of the qualitative/interpretative paradigm have succeeded in convincing a number of scholars whose work has been within the quantitative tradition (e.g., Campbell and Overman 1988, Cronbach 1975) that the qualitative approach has its own merits.

Some writers have suggested that complementarity must be recognized in view of various distinct desiderata in educational research, not all of which can be met by any one single paradigm. For example, there are pressing educational and social problems requiring policy and practical responses. The information necessary for policy formulation might not be available for controlled laboratory experiments of limited generalizability (or external validity), but might be provided by "quasi-experiments" (Cook and Campbell 1979) or qualitative research. Moreover, given the rate of social change, or the constant interactive effects of educational treatments and student aptitudes, generalizations yielded by a quantitative approach might become rapidly out of date. The project of developing a stable set of scientific educational laws may not be viable (Cronbach 1975).

For other writers espousing complementary diversity, the multifactorial complexity of educational problems supports epistemological pluralism. Keeves acknowledges that some approaches are more holistic, embracing greater complexity than others:

The techniques employed in educational research must be capable of examining many variables at the same time,

but not necessarily through the use of complex statistical procedures . . . although these have their place. Anthropologists have evolved procedures for analyzing and presenting information from a situation which involves many factors that are very different from those used by psychologists, and different again from those that might be employed by economists and sociologists. (Keeves 1986 p. 390)

Nevertheless, according to Campbell and Overman (1988), P-theoretical differences are still unavoidable because there remains a need for the kind of research produced by the tools of descriptive science and formal logic, which cannot embrace the value judgments characteristic of much nonquantitative educational inquiry. For other writers, fundamental epistemological differences between explanation and interpretation, of course, remain.

In educational research acceptance of the epistemological integrity of a nonquantitative paradigm has largely been the result of efforts by qualitative researchers to spell out alternative networks of theoretical requirements for qualitative research. These have tended to run parallel to elements in the received epistemological scheme of quantitative research (validity, reliability, etc.). One influential example, elaborated by Lincoln and Guba (1984), employs the notions of credibility, applicability (or transferability), consistency, and neutrality, as analogies respectively for internal validity, external validity, reliability, and objectivity.

The point here, however, is not so much that there is some loose analogical connection between corresponding terms in these sets. Rather, despite détente, the point to note is the persisting apparent epistemological distinctiveness of these theoretically interanimated clusters and their respective embeddings in different epistemologies. Some complementary diversity theorists might think that they can have fundamental epistemological diversity without subscribing to something as strong as the P-theory and its incommensurability doctrine. Here, perhaps, epistemological diversity is being confused with methodological diversity, a diversity of techniques of inquiry. Of course the latter is possible but, in the opinion of the authors, is best underwritten by a "touchstone" account of epistemic justification, not several incommensurable epistemologies. Such an account does not have to be fixed and absolute; it can change. The point is that at any given time it embraces those epistemological commitments that are shared by researchers. This is the unity thesis. If complementary diversity theorists wish to eschew such epistemological touchstone, then they remain committed to P-theory.

It should be noted that many advocates of equal rights for qualitative research have wished to play down the epistemological differences (Lincoln and Guba 1984, Miles and Huberman 1984). It may be that exponents of the complementary diversity thesis who persist with the term "paradigm" do not embrace P-theory's doctrine of incommensurability, although this is rarely made explicit. If they disavow incommensurability, their position would seem to collapse into the unity thesis, with revisionary consequences for the way they draw the distinctions between paradigms. These may be more drastic than at first appears. In the case of the explanation/understanding distinction, for instance, Keeves (1988), in arguing for complementarity, has adopted Giddens's (1984) reworking of this distinction. Not all complementarists have recognized the seriousness of the problem, however. As Smith and Heshusius (1986 p. 7) put it, there has been a tendency to "de-epistemologize" the debate or even ignore paradigmatic differences. Given that paradigms exist, Smith and Heshusius may well be right—but do paradigms exist?

5. Criticisms of the Paradigms Theory

It is apparent that there is some confusion over both the term "paradigm" and the problem of unambiguously identifying paradigms of educational research. Some of the confusion comes from the ambiguity of the term "paradigm" itself. On the one hand, as Husén (1988 p. 17) points out, there would be wide agreement that the most influential use of "paradigm" stems from the work of Kuhn (1970). However, Masterman (1970) identified some 21 different uses of the term in Kuhn's book; Kuhn subsequently published revisions, some substantial, to his original theory (e.g., Kuhn 1974); and finally, not all methodologists embrace Kuhn's ideas uncritically.

Kuhn has also put the principal argument for regarding paradigms as incommensurable, as incapable of being compared or measured against some touchstone standard:

> In learning a paradigm the scientist acquires theory, methods, and standards together, usually in an inextricable mixture. Therefore when paradigms change, there are usually significant shifts in the criteria determining the legitimacy both of problems and of proposed solutions.
>
> That observation . . . provides our first explicit indication of why the choice between competing paradigms regularly raises questions that cannot be resolved by the criteria of normal science . . . [scientists] will inevitably talk through each other when debating the relative merits of their respective paradigms. In the partially circular arguments that regularly result, each paradigm will be shown to satisfy more or less the criteria that it dictates for itself and to fall short of a few of those dictated by its opponent. (Kuhn 1970 pp. 109–10)

The key claim being made here is that paradigms include both substantive theories and the standards and criteria for evaluating those theories, or paradigm-specific epistemologies. As such, it is also claimed, there is no privileged epistemic vantage point from

which different paradigms can be assessed; there are only the rival epistemic standards built into each paradigm.

Kuhn's early comments on the task of adjudicating the merits of competing paradigms are instructive: "the proponents of competing paradigms practise their trades in different worlds" (Kuhn 1970 p. 150); "the transfer of allegiance from paradigm to paradigm is a conversion experience that cannot be forced" (Kuhn 1970 p. 151); such a transition occurs relatively suddenly, like a gestalt switch "just because it is a transition between incommensurables" (Kuhn 1970 p. 150).

Moreover, the belief that some research traditions are incommensurable can be made to look initially plausible by noting the kind of tradition-specific vocabularies that are used to characterize matters epistemological. As has been seen, methodological reflection on quantitative research commonly trades in such terminology as "scientific," "positivist," "foundational," "correspondence-truth," "objective," "realist," "validity," "reliability," "reductionist," and "empiricist." The qualitative network of such terms includes "nonpositivist," "antifoundational," "interpretation," "understanding," "subjective," "idealist," "relativist," and "antireductionist." The fact that key terms of epistemic conduct in one cluster are formed by negating terms in the other cluster readily suggests no common basis for the conduct and assessment of inquiry, and hence the incommensurability of these traditions.

Clearly, for a defense of the epistemological unity of educational research, the most important obstacle is this P-theoretical analysis of research traditions. So the first point to make in a defense of the unity thesis is that in philosophy, and philosophy of science in particular, P-theory is widely regarded as false. In a major review of the literature following a 1969 symposium on the structure of scientific theories, Suppe (1977 p. 647) remarks: "Since the symposium Kuhn's views have undergone a sharply declining influence on contemporary work in philosophy of science." He goes on to claim that contemporary work in philosophy of science, that is, postpositivist philosophy in science, "increasingly subscribes to the position that it is a central aim of science to come to know how the world *really is*" (Suppe 1977 p. 649). In social and educational research, however, especially among qualitative researchers and critical theorists, antirealist belief in paradigms remains strong. In the authors' opinion, the apparent ubiquity of "paradigms" in educational research occurs because the epistemological assumptions of the P-theory itself, or its P-epistemology, are largely responsible for structuring differences among research traditions into putative paradigms.

Of course epistemologists in general agree that inquiry structures knowledge of the objects of inquiry; this is part of what is involved in maintaining that all experience is theory-laden. Contrary to Smith and Heshusius (1986), it is not a feature peculiar to qualitative inquiry. The interesting question is whether there is any reason to believe that different research traditions partition into paradigms the way P-theory requires. However, it is rarely noted that whether it is even appropriate to give reasons, to marshal evidence, to analyze research practices and inquiry contexts in order to justify such a belief, will depend on whether P-theory is, by its own lights, a paradigm (or part of a paradigm), or not. If it is, then the relevant standards of reasoning, evidence, and analysis will be peculiar to P-theory (or its encompassing paradigm) and so will have rational epistemic purchase on none but the already committed. To the unbeliever, P-theory would literally have nothing to say for itself. For one to believe that educational research comes in paradigms would require an act of faith: to come to believe it after believing the contrary would require a conversion experience.

There are interesting problems with this view. For example, what happens if one is converted to it? Does one then say that it is true that educational research divides into paradigms? Unfortunately the term "true" is P-theoretical and so one needs to determine first whether, for example, the sentences of P-theory correspond to a world of real educational researchers really engaged in incommensurable research practices. If so, then P-theory is not after all a paradigm distinct from those that employ correspondence-truth. If not, then there is a genuine equivocation over the term "true" which will permit the following claims to be made without contradiction: (a) it is correspondence-true that the different research traditions are not epistemologically distinct; and (b) it is P-true that the different research traditions are epistemologically distinct.

In conceding the equal legitimacy of incommensurable rivals (whether oppositional or complementary), however, particularly a correspondence-truth rival, the P-theorist seems to be surrendering the capacity to say anything about actual educational research practices and the historical and theoretical context of current research traditions. Worse still, in eschewing any schema for determining the ontological commitments of P-theory, there seems to be no way of knowing what the P-theorist is talking about. As such, P-theory hardly provides a challenge to a realist view of the unity of educational research.

To avoid the dilemma that threatens when P-theory becomes self-referential, several options are available. Two are considered here. First, a less parsimonious attitude to rival epistemologies can be adopted by maintaining that correspondence-true theories, which caused all the trouble, are false, wrong, or, as hard-hitting relativists are fond of saying, inadequate. Indeed, getting rid of correspondence-truth may be a condition for meaningful P-theoretical claims about theorists' living in different worlds; after all, talk of

a real world tends to make other worlds pale into nonexistence. A second, opposite, strategy is to say that P-theory is not a distinct paradigm at all, but rather a set of carefully argued, evidentially supported, correspondence-true claims about the existence of paradigmatic divisions among the major research traditions. It is instructive to note that some methodologists run both these strategies simultaneously (e.g., Lincoln and Guba 1984, Eisner 1979). (For damaging criticism of Eisner's running the two strategies together, see Phillips 1983.)

Arguments for the first option are by now familiar enough. Correspondence-truth is assumed to be located in a network of terms usually associated with the quantitative research tradition. Valid and reliable knowledge about the world is said to be that which is, in some way, derivable from some epistemically secure (or even certain) foundation; in positivistic empiricism usually observations or first person sensory reports. Objectivity consists in intersubjectively agreed matchings between statements and experience. And, of course, these objectively known statements are correspondence-true just in case the required matching occurs (although often the only reality admitted was sense data).

There are many objections to foundational empiricist epistemologies (e.g., Hesse 1974, Churchland 1979), but a version of the earlier argument from self-reference will suffice to illustrate the problems. Although this is not widely recognized in positivistic empiricism, epistemology is a task that requires (as Kant saw) a theory of the powers of the mind. What one can know will depend, to some extent, on what sort of creature one is and, in particular, on what sort of perceptual and cognitive capacities one has. A theory of the mind, however, is something one has to get to know. In the case of empiricist foundationalism, it is necessary to know that one's own sensory experiences will provide one with epistemically secure foundations. Unfortunately for the foundationalist, the theory of mind required to underwrite this claim is not itself an item of sensory experience, nor an observation report. This means that knowledge of how the class of epistemically privileged items is known is not itself epistemically privileged. Indeed, the sophisticated neurophysiological models of brain functioning now typical of accounts of perception and cognition are quite ill-suited to serving the regress pattern of foundational justification. For they so far outrun the purported resources of any proposed foundation that the whole point of foundational justification here collapses. More generally, knowledge of perceptual powers, or possible foundations, like knowledge of everything, is theory-laden. The result is that there is no epistemically privileged, theory-free, way of viewing the world. There is thus no reality that can be seen independent of competing theoretical perspectives. This applies as much to the empirical sciences (and the quantitative tradition in educational research) as to other areas (see Walker and Evers 1982, Walker and Evers 1986).

From the fact that all experience is theory-laden, however, that what one believes exists depends on what theory one adopts, it does not follow that all theories are evidentially equivalent, or equally reasonable. There is more to evidence than observation, or as Churchland (1985 p. 35) argues: "observational excellence or 'empirical adequacy' is only one epistemic virtue among others of equal or comparable importance." The point is that some theories organize their interpretations of experience better than others. A humdrum example employing subjectivist scruples on evidence will illustrate this point. A theory which says that I can leave what I interpret to be my office by walking through what I interpret to be the wall will cohere less well with my interpreted desire to leave my office than a theory which counsels departure via what I take to be the door. It is all interpretative, of course, but some organized sets of interpretations, or theories, are better than others. The theory that enables a person to experience the desired success of departing the perceived enclosure of an office enjoys certain epistemic advantages over one that does not. With all experience interpreted, though, the correct conclusion to draw is not that there is no adequate objective standard of reality, but that objectivity involves more than empirical adequacy. Theoretically motivated success in getting in and out of rooms is about as basic as objectivity ever gets. There are superempirical, theoretical tests which can be couched in a "coherence epistemology." One advocate of coherence epistemology, the postpositivist philosopher Quine, sums up this standard of reality:

> Having noted that man has no evidence for the existence of bodies beyond the fact that their assumption helps him organize experience, we should have done well, instead of disclaiming evidence for the existence of bodies, to conclude: such, then, at bottom, is what evidence is both for ordinary bodies and molecules. (Quine 1960a p. 251)

Quine's point here foreshadows a significant epistemological consequence of this attack on foundationalism. According to Quine, and many coherence theorists, we need to distinguish sharply between the theory of evidence and the theory of truth (Quine 1960a, 1960b, 1969, 1974, Williams 1980). Theory of evidence is concerned with the global excellence of theory, and involves both empirical adequacy, inasmuch as this can be achieved and the superempirical virtues of simplicity, consistency, comprehensiveness, fecundity, familiarity or principle, and explanatory power. Once the best theory according to these coherence criteria has been established, it is the resulting theory itself that is used to state what exists and how the theory's sentences match up with that posited reality. What corresponds to true sentences is therefore something that is determined after the theory of evidence has done its work. It is not something that figures *a priori*, or in

some privileged foundational way in the determination of the best theory.

The evidence suggests that P-theory critiques of foundationalism draw too radical a conclusion. In terms of the quantitative/qualitative debate, for example, the coherence epistemology sanctioned by the most powerful criticisms of empiricist foundationalism cuts across this familiar methodological (putatively paradigmatic) bifurcation. In acknowledging the theory-ladenness of all experience it is nonpositivist and nonfoundational. It agrees that people's window on the world is mind-dependent and subject to the interpretations of theorists. On the other hand, it can be realist, scientific, objective, reductionist, and embrace correspondence-truth. This possibility raises serious doubts about P-theorists' claims concerning the diversity of educational research, whether oppositional or complementary.

A more systematic objection to P-theory can be raised, however, by examining the epistemological warrant for incommensurability. The belief that research methodologies comprising incommensurable networks of theoretical terms are epistemically autonomous is sustained in large measure by a particular theory of meaning, notably that terms gain what meaning they possess in virtue of their role in some network or conceptual scheme. Where conceptual schemes or theories are said to be systematically different, no basis exists for matching the terms of one theory with those of another. So expressions such as "validity" or "truth," which appear as orthographically equivalent across different schemes, are really equivocal, with systematic differences emerging as differences in conceptual role.

Both Kuhn and Feyerabend maintain versions of the conceptual role theory of meaning. The trouble, however, is that they maintain implausibly strong versions of it, for if meaning is determined entirely by conceptual role then incommensurable theories become unlearnable. This all turns on the modest empirical fact that finite learners people need some point of entry into an elaborate systematically interconnected vocabulary like a theory. In order to learn some small part of the theory, say a handful of expressions, however, P-epistemology requires mastery of the whole theory in order to appreciate the conceptual role played by these expressions. It is at this point that the theory of meaning begins to outrun its own epistemological resources: it posits learned antecedents of learning that cannot themselves be learned. The parts cannot be understood without mastery of the whole, and resources are lacking to master the whole without first scaling the parts. An implicit feature of the epistemology driving P-theory's account of meaning as conceptual role is thus an implausibly strong theory of the powers of the mind. (A P-theoretical attack on correspondence-truth appears to depend on a correspondence-true theory of mind.)

Once again P-theory may be observed getting into difficulty over self-reference. In this case an epistemology should come out knowable on its own account of knowledge. The chief advantage of arguments from self-reference is that they focus directly on the superempirical virtues or weaknesses of a theory.

Inasmuch as one is impressed by such theoretical shortcomings as inconsistency, lack of explanatory power in relation to rivals, use of ad hoc hypotheses, and so on, one is allowing these criteria to function as touchstone in the evaluation of epistemologies and research methodologies. Of course one can ignore these vices in theory-construction: they are not extratheoretical privileged foundations by which all theorizing can be assessed. Methodologists in the main research traditions, however, who expect their inquiries to command attention, serve as a sound basis for action, or constitute a particular or definite set of knowledge claims, have been unwilling to play fast and loose with such virtues as consistency (usually on the formal ground that a contradiction will sanction any conclusion whatever) or simplicity and comprehensiveness (on the ground that ad hoc or arbitrary addition of hypotheses can be used to explain anything whatsoever, and hence nothing at all). Indeed a theory cannot be empirically significant unless it is consistent. With P-theory's theory of meaning exhibiting the superempirical weakness of lack of explanatory power in relation to what it sets itself to explain, and with that weakness being traceable to a theory of mind, it should be observed that whether epistemologies or methodologies are incommensurable turns on such things as empirical theories of mind or brain functioning, or theories of learning and cognition. Epistemology itself is therefore continuous with, and relies upon, empirical science. In Quine's words (1969), epistemology is "naturalized." One consequence is that interpretative theorists, for example, must rely partly on the "scientific" paradigm in order to show the incommensurability of their own paradigm with the "scientific."

6. The Unity Thesis

Although the paradigms perspective is seriously flawed, some account of the kind of unity educational research actually enjoys still needs to be given. In arguing against P-theory, coherence epistemology has already been considered. To conclude this discussion a brief outline will be given of a particular version of coherentism, or epistemological holism, which has achieved considerable prominence in postpositivist philosophy (Quine 1974), has been applied to educational philosophy (Walker and Evers 1982), and systematically to educational administration (Evers and Lakomski 1990) and research methodology (Lakomski 1991).

A more positive epistemological agenda for educational research can be provided by responding to the second strategy a P-theorist can adopt in defending diversity. This strategy involved denying P-theory was a distinct paradigm, conceding correspondence-truth, but arguing that fundamental epistemological diversity still occurred in educational research. In replying to this claim it can be noted that the strategy will need to employ superempirical epistemic virtues to be persuasive. To be effective against a wide range of theoretical perspectives these virtues (consistency, simplicity, fecundity, etc.) will need to be recognized as such by rival epistemologies and hence function as touchstone. As a result the P-theorist's strategy is already compromised. To complete the job, however, a coherence epistemology is needed that yields a touchstone-coherent account of itself and its own epistemic virtues, that is unproblematically self-referential in scope, and that can account for the touchstone-recognized successes of alternative epistemologies and their research extensions.

In the view of the authors, the epistemology that best accounts for knowledge, its growth, and evaluation is a form of holistic scientific naturalism (in Quine's "epistemology naturalized" sense of "naturalism")— a theory that makes ready use of the best or most coherent theories of perception and cognition. According to this view, people are acquiring their theory of the world from infancy onward. Indeed, as Quine (1960b) has shown, theory precedes all learning and hence commences with the innate complement of dispositions to respond selectively to the environment. What one can know is dependent on the kind of creature one is and, as human beings, everyone is one kind of creature. Everyone shares genetically derived, though culturally expressed, refined and modified touchstone standards and procedures. Added to these is further culturally produced touchstone that people acquire as social beings sharing material problems in concrete social contexts. Knowledge is made up of theories, whose existence is to be explained causally, as problem-solving devices. There are numerous philosophical accounts (e.g., Laudan 1977) of how theories can be analyzed as problem-solving devices. In the case of epistemological theories, the problems arise from theoretical practice, including empirical (e.g., educational) research. Clearly, there are certain issues concerning whether a theory is addressing the right problems, and a theory is needed of how to distinguish between real problems and pseudoproblems, and between better and worse formulations of problems. Here the epistemology would lean on a theory of evidence and experiment, on the pragmatic relations between "theory" and "practice" (Walker 1985a).

One real problem, shared by all educational researchers, is how best to conduct inquiry into human learning itself. Without this problem there could be no debate about whether educational research is epistemologically diverse. For there to be an issue at all presupposes at least some sharing of language, including general epistemological terminology such as "truth," "meaning," "adequacy," "interpretation," "paradigm," and so on.

Competition remains, of course, but competition between theories, including theories of educational research methodology, not paradigms. Competition arises because, in addition to touchstone, there are unshared (which is not to say incommensurable) concepts, hypotheses, and rules of method. Indeed, this is part and parcel of being able to distinguish one theory from another in a competitive situation. There can be genuine competition between theories, however, only when they have an issue over which to compete, some shared problem(s). Theory A is in competition with theory B when one or more of its sentences is contrary to sentences in theory B. For this situation to obtain, theories A and B must be attempts at solving at least one common problem. To identify a shared problem involves some conceptual common ground and, if only implicitly at first, some shared method; the concepts have to be deployed. Thus one begins to discover and negotiate touchstone theory which, unlike the privileged epistemic units of foundational epistemologies, is merely the shifting historically explicable amount of theory that is shared by rival theories and theorists. Beginning with identification of common problems, one can proceed to identify further touchstone and elaborate the touchstone frameworks within which theories compete.

Having identified common ground between theories, their differences are next rigorously set out and tested against that touchstone by empirical research and theoretical analysis, seeking to identify the strengths and weaknesses of each, and reach a decision on the theory which is strongest under present circumstances (Walker 1985b), taking into account past achievements and likely future problems (Churchland 1979).

Other features of this epistemology include its capacity to survive its own test of self-reference (Quine 1969), its unified account of validity and reliability (Evers 1991), its denial that all science consists of sets of laws, and of any fundamental epistemological distinction between explanation and understanding (Walker 1985c) or between fact and value judgments (Evers and Lakomski 1990).

Finally, although in this entry it has been maintained that such a coherentist naturalistic epistemology is a sound way of underwriting the epistemological unity of educational research, achieved through touchstone analysis, it should be stressed that it is as much a competing theory as any other, and subject to theory testing (Walker 1985a). Granted that it shares touchstone with other epistemologies, arguments can of course be mounted against it; to engage in such arguments, however, all participations would be implicitly conceding the epistemological unity of research.

See also: Adult Education Research; Ideologies in Adult Education

References

Bates R J 1980 New developments in the new sociology of education. *Br. J. Sociol. Educ.* 1(1): 67–79

Campbell D T, Overman S E 1988 *Methodology and Epistemology for Social Science: Selected Papers*. Chicago University Press, Chicago, Illinois

Carr W, Kemmis S 1983 *Becoming Critical. Knowing Through Action Research*. Deakin University Press, Geelong

Churchland P M 1979 *Scientific Realism and the Plasticity of Mind*. Cambridge University Press, Cambridge

Churchland P M 1985 The ontological status of observables. In: Churchland P M, Hooker C A (eds.) 1985 *Images of Science: Essays on Realism and Empiricism*. University of Chicago Press, Chicago, Illinois

Cook T H, Campbell D T 1979 *Quasi-Experimentation. Design and Analysis Issues for Field Settings*. Rand McNally, Chicago, Illinois

Cronbach L J 1975 Beyond the two disciplines of scientific psychology. *Am. Psychol.* 30(2): 116–27

Eisner E 1979 *The Educational Imagination*. Macmillan, New York

Evers C W 1991 Towards a coherentist theory of validity. *Int. J. Educ. Res.* 15(6): 521–35

Evers C W, Lakomski G 1990 *Knowing Educational Administration*. Pergamon Press, Oxford

Freire P 1972 *Cultural Action for Freedom*. Penguin, Harmondsworth

Giddens A 1984 *The Constitution of Society: Outline of the Theory of Structuration*. Polity Press, Cambridge

Habermas J 1972 (trans. Shapiro J) *Knowledge and Human Interests*. Heinemann, London

Hesse M 1974 *The Structure of Scientific Inference*. Macmillan, London

Hooker C A 1975 Philosophy and meta-philosophy of science. Empiricism, Popperianism and realism. *Synthèse* 32: 177–231

House E R 1991 Realism in research. *Educ. Researcher* 20(6): 2–9

Husén T 1988 Research paradigms in education. In: Keeves J P (ed.) 1988 *Educational Research, Methodology, and Measurement: An International Handbook*. Pergamon Press, Oxford

Keeves J P 1986 Theory, politics and experiment in educational research methodology. A response. *Int. Rev. Educ.* 32(4): 388–92

Keeves J P 1988 Social theory and educational research. In: Keeves J P (ed.) 1988 *Educational Research, Methodology, and Measurement: An International Handbook*. Pergamon Press, Oxford

Kerlinger F N 1973 *Foundations of Behavioral Research. Educational and Psychological Inquiry*, 2nd edn. Holt, Rinehart and Winston, New York

Kuhn T S 1970 *The Structure of Scientific Revolutions*, 2nd edn. University of Chicago Press, Chicago, Illinois

Kuhn T S 1974 Second thoughts about paradigms. In: Suppe F (ed.) 1977

Lakomski G (ed.) 1991 Beyond paradigms: Coherentism and holism in educational research. *Int. J. Educ. Res.* 15(6): 449–97

Laudan L 1977 *Progress and its Problems. Towards a Theory of Scientific Growth*. Routledge and Kegan Paul, London

Lincoln Y S, Guba E G 1984 *Naturalistic Inquiry*. Sage, Beverly Hills, California

Masterman M 1970 The nature of a paradigm. In: Lakatos I, Musgrave A (eds.) 1970 *Criticism and the Growth of Knowledge*. Cambridge University Press, London

Miles M, Huberman M 1984 Drawing valid meaning from qualitative data. Towards a shared craft. *Educ. Researcher* 13(5): 20–30

Phillips D C 1983 After the wake: Postpositivistic educational thought: The social functions of the intellectual. *Educ. Researcher* 12(5): 4–12

Popkewitz T 1984 *Paradigm and Ideology in Educational Research*. Falmer Press, London

Quine W V 1960a Posits and reality. In: Uyeda S (ed.) 1960 *Bases of Contemporary Philosophy*, Vol. 5. Waseda University Press, Tokyo.

Quine W V 1960b *Word and Object*. MIT Press, Cambridge, Massachusetts

Quine W V 1969 Epistemology naturalized. In: Quine W V 1969 *Ontological Relativity and Other Essays*. Columbia University Press, New York

Quine W V 1974 The nature of natural knowledge. In: Guttenplan S (ed.) 1975 *Mind and Language*. Clarendon Press, Oxford

Shulman L 1986 Paradigms and research programs in the study of teaching. A contemporary perspective. In: Wittrock M C (ed.) 1986 *Handbook of Research on Teaching*, 3rd edn. Macmillan, New York

Smith J K, Heshusius L 1986 Closing down the conversation. The end of the qualitative/quantitative debate among educational inquirers. *Educ. Researcher* 15(1): 4–12

Suppe F (ed.) 1977 *The Structure of Scientific Theories*, 2nd edn. University of Illinois Press, Chicago, Illinois

Walker J C 1985a The philosopher's touchstone. Towards pragmatic unity in educational studies. *J. Philos. Educ.* 19(2): 181–98

Walker J C 1985b Philosophy and the study of education. A critique of the commonsense consensus. *Aust. J. Educ.* 29(2): 101–14

Walker J C 1985c Materialist pragmatism and sociology of education. *Br. J. Sociol. Educ.* 6(1): 55–74

Walker J C, Evers C W 1982 Epistemology and justifying the curriculum of educational studies. *Br. J. Educ. Stud.* 30(2): 213–29

Walker J C, Evers C W 1986 Theory, politics, and experiment in educational research methodology. *Int. Rev. Educ.* 32(4): 373–87

Williams M 1980 Coherence justification and truth. *Rev. Metaphys.* 34(2): 243–72

Further Reading

Chalmers A 1990 *Science and its Fabrication*. Open University Press, Buckingham

Keeves J P (ed.) 1988 *Educational Research, Methodology, and Measurement: An International Handbook*. Pergamon Press, Oxford

Miller S I, Fredericks M 1991 Postpositivistic assumptions and educational research: Another view. *Educ. Researcher* 20(4): 2–8

Phillips D C 1987 *Philosophy, Science and Social Inquiry*. Pergamon Press, Oxford

Salomon G 1991 Transcending the qualitative-quantitative debate: The analytic and systemic approaches to educational research. *Educ. Researcher* 20(6): 10–18

Ideologies in Adult Education

H. Entwistle

Two different meanings have become associated with the word "ideology," especially in educational discourse. The first is the more common usage, where ideology refers to a coherent, interdependent collection of values, beliefs, and objectives which are held to justify educational provision of a particular kind: such an ideology might be rooted in religious or political beliefs, or it may stem from a particular view of human nature or society. The second use of ideology is associated with Marxism and refers, pejoratively, to educational ideas, beliefs, and practices which serve only the interests of the ruling class: for example, some Marxists have tended to dismiss the historical school curriculum as ideological in consisting of a partial, distorted, or false account of reality which, they allege, fortifies ruling-class hegemony over the subaltern classes, strengthening the social control of the former over the latter. In this entry, though the focus is upon the first of these senses of "ideology," occasional reference will also be made to the second. Differing ideologies are discussed with reference to the content, the pedagogy (or andragogy), and the clientele of adult education.

1. Content

With reference to the content of adult education, the major ideological divide is between those believing that the knowledge and skills acquired should serve particular, extrinsic, utilitarian ends and those committed to the view that liberal, general, cultural knowledge should be transmitted which has relevance for the quality of life in all its various dimensions. The classical conception of adult education in Europe and North America has derived from the latter ideology.

A network of institutions, developed over more than a century, has brought the intellectual traditions of Western culture, to interested adults who, as children, had not received a secondary or higher education. Much of this adult, liberal education was conducted by academics (traditional intellectuals, in Gramsci's (1971) sense) and located either in university extension programs or in voluntary organizations, of which the Workers' Educational Association (WEA) is a good example (see *Worker Education and Labor Education*). In England, for example, early advocates and practitioners of adult education embraced the nonutilitarian ideology. R H Tawney, the foremost exemplar of the liberal educational tradition, argued in 1914: "To these miners and weavers and engineers who pursue education with the passion born of difficulties, knowledge can never be a means, but only an end; for what have they to gain from it but knowledge itself" (Tawney 1914 pp. 80–81). A parliamentary advocate of adult education agreed: "We say educate a man not simply because he has got political powers . . . but educate him because he is a man" (Thomas Burt, MP, quoted in Simon 1960 p. 367).

Throughout the twentieth century, there has been recurrent criticism of this liberal view of adult education, especially from those who believe that the education of adults must have clear and immediate instrumental values. The writing on adult education is replete with advocacy of education aimed at the resolution of particular social, economic, and political problems: education for literacy, especially as a necessary preliminary to the conquest of poverty; education for peace; and education for the liberation of women (see *Women and Adult Education*).

Much of the criticism of the liberal tradition comes from political radicals, especially those concerned with the replacement of capitalism by progressive political systems such as socialism. The tradition represented by Tawney and the Workers' Educational Association has not always struck workers and their mentors as being in the best interests of the working class. Especially from some Marxist perspectives, this essentially liberal, humanistic tradition has sometimes been dismissed as ideological in the pejorative sense: the notion that they are "men" before they are workers or political actors is believed to be blind to the dilemmas of the socially and economically disadvantaged. This kind of challenge to the liberal tradition has existed throughout the twentieth century, its most recent manifestations being well-documented in a collection of essays titled *Adult Education for a Change* (Thompson 1980).

Modern advocates of a more radical solution to current social problems have tended to criticize liberal provision of adult education on two counts. First, it is dismissed as being an instrument of social control, thus likely to dampen radical political activity and leave economic and social deprivation much as it found them. As an imposition by academic educators,

it is claimed that it has singularly failed to identify the predicaments and dilemmas facing disadvantaged adults. And, by applying the methods used in formal educational institutions (as in university extension programs, for example), it has merely offered disadvantaged adults more of the kind of learning experience which they suffered disenchantment with when in elementary and secondary schools (see *Teacher Roles and Teaching Styles*). Keddie (1980) has suggested that it is this continuity with traditional schooling, at which so many working-class adults have failed, which also makes adult education attractive to a middle-class clientele. Further, it is argued, those workers who do acquire a taste for the traditional fare of adult classes experience not a radical questioning of the status quo, but a curriculum embodying "high status knowledge." At best, such a curriculum is thought to be irrelevant to the educational needs of the working class; at worst, it beguiles workers with "high culture," diminishing their radical discontents. It is feared that working-class participants in liberal adult classes will become status-dissenting members of the working class: far from learning to question the status quo, they will develop, and come to defend, middle-class tastes and values, using education as a mean of mobility out of their community.

Keddie (1980) argues that through its orientation to middle-class values adult education has manifested that same "ideology of individualism" which characterizes the education of children. Hence, the traditional liberal curriculum is seen as neglecting the skills and knowledge essential to fuel radical social change. As such, it speaks to the condition of the satisfied and often relatively affluent citizen, rather than to a conception of radical citizenship rooted in the desire for revolutionary social change. Deeply dissatisfied adults, the critics argue, decline to participate in adult education, not because of apathy or hostility toward education, but because they deem provision to be indifferent to their needs.

This points to a second criticism of the liberal tradition in adult education. This tradition had developed essentially within the labor movements of Europe and North America (Lovatt 1989), but to an extent lost its historical clientele of manual workers, as middle-class students, already well-educated and often college graduates, increasingly filled the void left by the educationally disadvantaged working-class adult. Evidence of this middle-class takeover, especially in the United Kingdom and North America, multiplies with almost every fresh analysis of the clientele of adult classes. A study from the Republic of Ireland, for example, confirms this phenomenon in a university extramural program aimed at "citizen development" (O'Sullivan 1988). An underrepresentation of students having completed only primary schooling is reported, whereas secondary or tertiary education graduates are overrepresented. In occupational terms, farmers and manual workers are underrepresented and white-collar occupations overrepresented. It is often concluded that only an adult educational program having practical and immediate relevance to the problems of everyday life will restore adult education to its traditional clientele, the socially and educationally disadvantaged.

Not only the radical critics of liberal adult education, but also some of its staunchest advocates have been committed socialists of one kind or another (Entwistle 1981). The response against radical instrumentalist criticism of the liberal tradition amounts to the claim that radical social change is only possible through the agency of men and women who are educated in the traditional, disinterested sense. The "high culture" of the traditional curriculum has served to confer status, privilege, wealth, and power upon the ruling class. So why should the underprivileged and exploited believe that they can replace the existing hegemony without such knowledge? The superiority of traditional "high culture" over instrumental alternatives is seen as lying in its political utility. Academic knowledge can be politically powerful precisely because it offers more logical, coherent, systematic, and complete accounts of the sociopolitical system than does knowledge acquired piecemeal and pragmatically for the solution of immediate local problems.

When instrumentally oriented programs are implemented, they do not always have the anticipated results. For example, Lovett (1975) describes an experimental program in Liverpool aimed at bringing educational resources to bear on urgent problems of community development. But the demand from lower-class students was for courses related to personal development and leisure. To the extent that local residents did become active in community affairs, this tended to be a by-product of their participation in personally oriented educational activities. In a later account of the Liverpool initiative, Lovatt (1989) suggests that it is "a model which reaffirms certain aspects of the liberal tradition (requiring) hard sustained intellectual study . . . at a university level" (see *Community Education and Community Development*).

This example serves as a reminder that the ideology of liberal adult education was often subscribed to by political radicals in the belief that the most potent preparation for radical political commitment was the disinterested study of liberal culture. On this view, knowledge directed toward particular social problems quickly becomes redundant and is usually acquired too late. Antonio Gramsci (1971), a founder of the Italian Communist Party who was among the greatest of twentieth-century adult educationists, took precisely this view. He considered that piecemeal learning and teaching directed at specific problems was inferior to the liberal education of workers through immersion in the mainstream humanistic culture. He believed that the Italian working class had been ill-served, educationally, by their own political and cultural associations, and attributed this to the lack in Italy of the kind of liberal educational institutions for adults which existed elsewhere, such as the WEA. For Gramsci, replacement of the ruling-class hegemony depended upon the creation of intellectuals organic to the subaltern classes, and this required the disinterested, humanistic education which gave traditional intellectuals, the servants of the ruling class, their power.

Other examples of the radical and practical consequences of a noninstrumental and general education for adults can be given. One such is the Danish Folk High School (see *Folk High Schools; Europe, Nordic Countries*). Founded in the nineteenth century under the influence of the Lutheran cleric, Bishop Grundtvig, folk high schools were residential colleges for young men and women who spent the six winter months living and learning together. The judgment of history is that the graduates of the folk high schools revolutionized Danish agriculture, although the curriculum of the schools included neither the study of agriculture, nor of cooperative marketing, which was a significant correlate of the agricultural revival. What it did provide was a liberal education consisting mainly of the study of Danish literature, history, and what would now be called sociology. It was assumed, correctly on the evidence of history, that this liberal curriculum would inspire self-confidence and the capacity to overcome both the technical and commercial challenges facing Danish agriculture. Subsequently, though with modifications, the folk high schools became established throughout the other Nordic countries. In the twentieth century they have become a source of inspiration for adult educationists in the Third World. From these examples, it is arguable that perhaps the best preparation for problem-solving, either on a personal or cooperative level, is a liberal, general education which embraces as much as possible of human knowledge about the physical and social world, and inculcates a grasp of principles in relation to the natural and human sciences. Such principled education, transcending the parochial imperatives of the present time and place, does not have the potential for obsolescence which characterizes an education focused upon particular, temporal problems. The well-educated in a liberal sense may be best equipped to address the problems likely to confront them and their societies throughout a lifetime.

However, it is also true that the undoubted practical payoffs of a liberal education lie in the future and are unpredictable. In terms of its eventual practical outcomes, liberal education is inevitably an activity of casting one's bread upon the water: it requires a capacity for deferred gratification. The difficulty is that for those individuals and societies facing chronic "bread and butter" problems, taking such a long-term view is almost impossible. This is true of the socially and economically deprived in any society, however affluent, but it is especially true in those Third World countries where widespread chronic poverty is a fact of everyday life. There, especially, educationists are on the horns of a dilemma: while it may be a fact that higher levels of general education are the guaranteed avenues to development, it is also true that the pressures to provide instrumental knowledge which is immediately applicable are near irresistible. What is required is a pedagogy which provides an interface between liberal and instrumental knowledge and skills.(see *Adult Education for Development*)

2. Pedagogy and Andragogy

Historically, adult education (whether liberally or instrumentally conceived) has often employed a pedagogy where language, discussion, and a democratic approach to curriculum making have been central. An example of this has been Freire's (1970) *Pedagogy of the Oppressed*. His approach to literacy has been based upon the identification of a culturally realistic vocabulary aimed at "the problem of teaching adults how to read in relation to the awakening of their consciousness." The words which are basic to their literacy are *their* words, already familiar from oral articulation of their own dilemmas and predicaments. For Freire, a liberating pedagogy is a dialogue, a reciprocal relationship between teacher and learner. In the spirit of Marx's Thirteenth Thesis on Feuerbach, the educator as well as the student needs to be educated. Freire's adult educational ideology has been especially influential upon literacy programs in Africa and Latin America.

Although Freire's (1974) work has also been seminal for many educationists working in advanced industrial societies, it really embraces principles and procedures which have been commonplace in the historical traditions of adult education. Among these, for example, was the pedagogy of the Nordic folk high school built upon Grundtvig's belief in the educational potency of "the living word." Discussion, as much informally after class as in the classroom itself, was also central to Tawney's approach to his working-class students. He quoted Albert Mansbridge (founder of the WEA) to the effect that the proper vehicle for adult education "was to be found not in lectures . . . to large and miscellaneous audiences, but in a group or class sufficiently small for intimate relations to develop between its members and between them and the tutor" (Tawney 1914 pp. 80–81, 85). Another historian-practitioner of adult education, E P Thompson (1968), has claimed that dialogue in adult classes, as well as being pedagogically potent, also has an academic "payoff." He concluded that in his own field of social history, the dialectic between teacher and adult student (what he calls "the abrasion of different worlds of experience in which ideas are brought to the test of life") has led to the scholarly exploration of areas often neglected in university schools of history. And, arguably, the correlate of this fact that academic knowledge is enriched by juxtaposition with commonsense experience is that adult students' everyday perceptions of social reality are probably similarly transformed.

With reference to the above claims about the seminal possibilities of dialogue in adult education, it is noteworthy that some adult educationists, especially with reference to the Third World, have insisted upon the importance of participatory research. This, "based upon the assumption that man is a social animal, offers a process that is more consistent with adult educational principles, more directly linked to action, and more scientific because it produces a more complex and thereby more accurate picture of reality" (Swantz 1975). Participatory research is based on the assumption that research can itself be an educative experience for both researchers and their subjects (see *Participatory Research; Experiential and Open Learning*).

3. The Clientele of Adult Education

Finally, there is an ideological divide between those who argue that adult education is a universal right and need, and those who consider that it benefits relatively few people, usually those destined to be leaders. Historically, as Hoggart (1958) has suggested, active participants in adult education have been relatively few. It has failed to touch large numbers of working-class adults, appealing only to "an earnest minority," utterly untypical of the underprivileged as a whole. But in practical terms, it has not on that account been a failure. Vast social, political, and economic gains over two centuries have been achieved in some parts of the world by the underprivileged through the leadership of those of their members who availed themselves of adult education. In another phrase of Hoggart's (1958) the minority is also "a saving remnant," with the implication that the earnest minority can, under certain circumstances, lead the masses forward. Gramsci (1971) took a similar view. For him, adult education should educate what he called "organic intellectuals" as leaders of the working class and peasantry. But these were necessarily a few, even an elite: "A human mass does not 'distinguish' itself . . . innovation cannot come from the mass, at least at the beginning, except through the mediation of an elite" (pp. 5–44, 234–35). Goulet (1974) claims that Freire, "who is undoubtedly ideologically committed to equality" is, nevertheless, similarly committed to "elitist forms of leadership wherein special qualifications may be exercised, but are not perpetuated." Hence, the conception that success of an educational enterprise is to be measured by external criteria concerning social and economic change does not require the counting of heads, the implication being that adult education is not necessarily judged a failure if it lacks widespread appeal.

The viability of universal adult education has also been questioned on economic grounds. It has been customary to judge the success of education for literacy, both historically in industrialized nations and more recently in the Third World, in terms of how close results come to 100 percent literacy: the success of education for literacy in Tanzania, for example, is lauded for bringing the literacy rate from only 31 percent to just over 90 percent in 20 years. But it has recently been argued that literacy is a mixed blessing, since 40 percent illiteracy may be necessary for economic viability in some developing societies. Indeed, one observer of literacy programs apparently takes comfort from the fact that about one-third of the world's population "manages to survive" without literacy (Enzensberger 1987). This questioning of the need for universal literacy is in the spirit of: "Who will be hewers of wood and drawers of water when everyone is educated?" Realistically, of course, the best impetus to improved education of any kind will be technological innovation which makes hewers of wood and drawers of water redundant, and which motivates adult learning in response to increasing demand for "knowledge workers". Technologically, this is already a reality, but its concomitant may be massive structural unemployment, especially in traditional societies.

However, among those who are ideologically egalitarian the notion dies hard that even if an elite of intellectuals is crucial to giving direction to mass political activity, both equity (the opportunity for everyone so gifted to learn to lead) and prudence require universal access to political education. The history of labor movements, no less than histories of the ruling class, may point to an "iron law of oligarchy" but eternal vigilance is necessary if the arrogance, corruption, and decay to which elites are prone are to be avoided. If there must be adult education for political leadership, this requires that there must be political education for those who are followers—the "ordinary" citizens to whom politics is not a major interest or preoccupation. The conclusion is that political education ought to include everyone in a democracy (there is a long citizenship tradition in adult education; see Entwistle 1989).

4. Conclusion

This discussion of the ideologies of adult education has focused upon a debate ongoing since the late nineteenth century about the aims, methods, and clientele of adult education, a debate conducted largely with reference to social class. Even if the modern version of this debate is not always posed in terms of class conflict, it is often concerned with the failure of adult education to engage the interests of the underprivileged—disaffected, often unemployed youth, ethnic and racial minorities, and the poor. Historically, the ideological debate has been mainly concerned with adult education in what are now highly industrialized, affluent societies. But there may be reasonable doubt whether this ideological divide has any relevance to adult education in developing societies, where the claims of educational instrumentalism appear conclusive. For one thing, it is evident that a liberal, academically oriented education requires participants to be literate. There is no doubt that, historically, adult education has

been a remedial activity, but remedial largely in that it has provided the equivalent of a secondary or tertiary education for those having experienced only primary education. But for an estimated 850 million illiterate adults worldwide, the need is for an equivalent of primary education, even when this is provided according to a progressive model like that proposed by Freire.

However, when considering how far the historical experience of now affluent societies has anything to offer the Third World, it is well to remember that those same societies were themselves politically, socially, and economically underdeveloped two centuries ago, at the time of their own early, tentative ventures into the education of adults. And it is arguable that successful adult educational initiatives in the Third World are in the traditional mainstream of adult educational ideologies and processes (Entwistle 1981). Perhaps to ignore this mainstream tradition is to be condemned to inherit its failures, no less than to forego the gains which have accrued from the undoubted successes of adult educational institutions in the past.

See also: Adult Education: Concepts and Principles; History of Adult Education; Adult Education Research; Epistemological Issues in Educational Research

References

Entwistle H 1981 The political education of adults. In: Heater D, Gillespie J A (eds.) 1981 *Political Education in Flux*. Sage Publications, London

Entwistle H 1989 The citizenship tradition in adult education. In: O'Sullivan D (ed.) 1989 *Social Commitment and Adult Education*. Cork University Press, Cork

Enzensberger H M 1987 In praise of the illiterate. *Adult Educ. Dev.* 28: 96–105

Freire P 1970 *Pedagogy of the Oppressed*. Herder and Herder, New York

Freire P 1974 *Education for Critical Consciousness*. Sheed and Ward, London

Goulet D 1974 Editor's introduction. In: Freire P (ed.) 1974

Gramsci A 1971 *Selections from the Prison Notebooks of Antonio Gramsci*. Lawrence and Wishart, London

Hoggart R 1958 *The Uses of Literacy*. Penguin Books, Harmondsworth

Keddie N 1980 Adult education: An ideology of individualism. In: Thompson J L (ed.) 1980

Lovett T 1975 *Adult Education, Community Development and the Working Class*. Ward Lock, London

Lovatt T 1989 Adult education and the working class. In: O'Sullivan D (ed.) 1989 *Social Commitment and Adult Education*. Cork University Press, Cork

O'Sullivan D 1988 An Irish extra-mural program: Clientele, student adaptation and class participation. *Int. J. Univ. Adults Educ.* 27: 28–40

Simon B 1960 *Studies in the History of English Education*, Vol. 1. Lawrence and Wishart, London

Swantz M L 1975 Research as an educational tool for development. *Convergence* 8 (2): 44–53

Vol. 1. Lawrence and Wishart, London

Swantz M L 1975 Research as an educational tool for development. *Convergence* 8 (2): 44–53

Tawney R H 1914 *The Radical Tradition. Twelve Essays on Politics, Education and Literature.* Minerva Press, London

Thompson E P 1968 *Education and Experience.* Leeds University Press, Leeds

Thompson J L (ed.) 1980 *Adult Education for a Change.* Hutchinson, London

Further Reading

Elias J L, Merriam S (eds.) 1980 *Philosophical Founda-*

tions of Adult Education. Krieger, Huntington, New York

Lawson K H 1982 *Analysis and Ideology: Conceptual Essays on the Education of Adults.* Nottingham Studies in the Theory and Practice of the Education of Adults. University of Nottingham, Nottingham

Patterson R K W 1979 *Values, Education and the Adult.* Routledge and Kegan Paul, London

Plamenatz J V 1970 *Ideology.* Pall Mall Press, London

Participatory Research

B. L. Hall

Participatory research has been described most generally as a process that combines three activities: research, education, and action (Hall 1981). Participatory research is a social action process that is biased in favor of dominated, exploited, poor, or otherwise left-out people. It sees no contradiction between goals of collective empowerment and the deepening of social knowledge. The concern with power and democracy and their interactions are central to participatory research. Attention to gender, race, ethnicity, sexual orientation, physical and mental abilities, and other social factors are critical.

With the early support of the International Council for Adult Education, which initiated a global network in participatory research in 1977, and widespread interest over the years, the concept has been elaborated and developed much further (see *International Council for Adult Education*). Fals Borda initially referred to a similar process in which he and his colleagues were engaged in Colombia and elsewhere in Latin America in the mid-1970s as "action research" (Fals Borda and Rahman 1991). When Vio Grossi, now of Chile but earlier working in Venezuela, organized a vigorous and dynamic Latin American network under the label "participatory research," Fals Borda joined forces and modified his label to "participatory action research." Both the "participatory action research" of Fals Borda and "participatory research" refer to the same general process. Fals Borda, Rahman of Bangladesh, and scores of other colleagues have been and continue to be central figures in the international participatory research community.

Authors have characterized the nature of participatory research in the following terms:

Participatory research attempts to present people as researchers themselves in pursuit of answers to the questions of their daily struggle and survival. (Tandon 1988 p. 7)

Participatory Research is a way for researchers and oppressed people to join in solidarity to take collective action, both short and long term, for radical social change.

Locally determined and controlled action is a planned consequence of inquiry. (Maguire 1987 p. 29)

The final aims of this combination of liberating knowledge and political power within a continuous process of life and work are: (1) to enable the oppressed groups and classes to acquire sufficient creative and transforming leverage as expressed in specific projects, acts and struggles; and (2) to produce and develop socio-political thought processes with which popular bases can identify. (Fals Borda and Rahman 1991 p. 4)

Participatory research attempts to break down the distinction between the researchers and the researched, the subjects and objects of knowledge production by the participation of the people-for-themselves in the process of gaining and creating knowledge. In the process, research is seen not only as a process of creating knowledge, but simultaneously, as education and development of consciousness, and of mobilization for action. (Gaventa 1988 p. 19)

Participatory research is collaborative, endogenous, heuristic and experiential. Transculturally, this implies an ability to accept the idea of native science and a sensitivity to the process-oriented, communally-based indigenous methodology. Through joint research projects between equal partners, participatory research can act as a flow-through mechanism for scientific findings from both worlds. (Colorado 1988 p. 63)

An immediate objective . . . is to return to the people the legitimacy of the knowledge they are capable of producing through their own verification systems, as fully scientific, and the right to use this knowledge, but not be dictated by it—as a guide in their own action. (Fals Borda and Rahman 1991 p. 15).

1. Origins of Participatory Research

It is important to recognize that, while the term "participatory research" may be new, the concerns being expressed have a history and continuity in social science. Many of the ideas that are finding new opportunities for expression can be traced as far back as the early fieldwork of Frederick Engels, who investigated conditions in the early factories of Manchester in the United Kingdom in the mid-nineteenth century. Marx's use of the structured interview—*L'Enquête ouvrière*—with French factory workers is another sometimes forgotten antecedent. In later times aspects of the work of John Dewey, George Herbert Mead, and the Tavistock Institute in London have outlined methods of social investigation that are based on other than a positivistic epistemology.

By the late 1950s and early 1960s, the dominant international research paradigm was a version of the North American and European model based on empiricism and positivism and characterized by an attention to instrument construction and rigor defined by statistical precision and replicability. Through the elaborate mechanisms of colonial and postcolonial relations, international scholarships, cultural exchanges, and training of researchers in Europe and North America, this dominant paradigm was extended to the dependent and poorer nations. Research methods, through an illusion of objectivity and scientific credibility, became one more manifestation of cultural dependency.

The reaction of the Third World—beginning in Latin America—has taken many forms. Dependency theorists, such as Dos Santos, Frank, Amin, and Leys outlined some of the mechanisms of economic and cultural dependency. Hence, in the field of research methods, Third World perspectives have grown in part out of a reaction to approaches developed in North America and Europe; approaches that have not only been created in different cultural settings but which contribute to already existing class distinctions. The Third World's contribution to social science research methods represents an attempt to find ways of uncovering knowledge that can be applied in societies where interpretation of reality must take second place to the changing of that reality.

Practical experience in what was becoming known as participatory research occurred in the work of the Tanzanian Bureau of Research Allocation and Land Use Planning. Here, Marja-Liisa Swantz and teams of students and village workers were involved in the questions of youth and employment in the coast region and later in studies of socioeconomic causes of malnutrition in Central Kilimanjaro. A visit by Paulo Freire to Tanzania in 1971 was a stimulus to many social scientists who might not otherwise have been as impressed by the existing experience of many adult educators or community development workers.

What happened in Tanzania in a small way had already begun in Latin America in the early 1960s. Stimulated in part by the success of the Cuban revolution, Latin American social scientists began exploring more committed forms of research. One of the most useful roles of Paulo Freire has been to bring some of the current ideas of Latin American social scientists to the attention of persons in other parts of the world. His work on thematic investigation, first in Brazil and later in Chile, was an expression of this search. Others, such as Beltran and Gerace Larufa, have explored alternatives through concepts of horizontal communication (Beltran 1976, Gerace Larufa 1973). Fals Borda (1980) and others in Colombia have been engaged in *investigación y acción*, while the D'arcy de Oliveiras have made people aware of the value of militant observation (D'arcy de Oliveira and D'arcy de Oliveira 1975).

2. Not the Third World Alone

While the specific term "participatory research" developed in the South, consciousness was growing in Europe and North America. Critiques of positivistic research paradigms began to surface in the 1970s. The Frankfurt School was rediscovered through the work of Jürgen Habermas and Theodor Adorno. The International Sociological Association, with encouragement from Peter Park of the United States and Ulf Himmelstrand of Sweden, began to place action-oriented sociology on the agenda of many academic meetings. In Switzerland, researchers in curriculum development adapted methodologies from political research to their needs. In Canada, Stinson developed methods of evaluation along action research lines for community development (Stinson 1979). In the Netherlands, de Vries explored research alternatives as an adult educator. Brown, of the United States, brought participatory research to the world of organizational development (Brown and Kaplan 1981). The National Institute for Adult Education in the United Kingdom pioneered participatory research through its evaluation of the United Kingdom adult literacy campaign (Holmes 1976). In Italy, Paulo Orefice and colleagues at the University of Naples applied the methodology in the context of growing political decentralization (Orefice 1981). In the United States, the Highlander Center in Tennessee has used participatory research for many years to deal with issues of land ownership and use (Horton 1981) and environmental deterioration. In Canada, the Toronto-based Participatory Research Group worked with a wide variety of groups, including First Nations peoples (Jackson 1980, Jackson et al. 1982), adult educators (Cassara 1985), immigrant women (Barndt 1981), and health workers (Hall 1981). The 1991 bibliography on participatory research by the Center for Community Education and Action provides the best perspective on the use and geographic spread of the approach (Center for Community Education and Action 1991). One of the newest books on participatory research reviews the North American experiences during the 1980s (Park et al. 1993).

3. Question of Methods

The literature on participatory research has always been vague on the question of methods. This is so because for participatory research, the most important factors are the origins of the issues, the roles those concerned with the issues play in the process, the emersion of the process in the context of the moment, the potential for mobilizing and for collective learning, the links to action, the understanding of how power relationships work, and the potential for communications with others experiencing similar discrimination, oppression, or violence. In addition, participatory research is based on the epistemological assumption that knowledge is constructed socially and therefore that approaches that allow for social, group, or collective analysis of life experiences of power and knowledge are most appropriate.

This means that for participatory research there are no methodological orthodoxies, no cookbook approaches to follow. The principle is that both issues and ways of working should flow from those involved and their context. In practice a creative and very wide variety of approaches have been used. All approaches have been selected because of their potential for drawing out knowledge and analysis in a social or collective way (Participatory Research Network 1982). They include: community meetings, video documentaries, community drama, camps for the landless in India, use of drawings and murals, photonovels, sharing of oral histories, community surveys, story-telling, shared testimonies, and many more. Even questionnaires have been used at times as a first step in a group-controlled process of reflection. Barndt and the Jesuit Centre for Faith and Social Justice in Canada have developed an approach to social movement research called "Naming the Moment" which offers a method for determining the political space available to them for action (Barndt 1989). Participatory Research in Asia (PRIA) reviewed the methods and results used by 10 different grassroots groups in India (PRIA 1985). The Society for the Promotion of Education and Research (SPEAR) of Belize, Central America, produced a participatory research training guide (SPEAR 1990). Fals Borda, discussed many methodological issues on a videotape produced by the University of Calgary in 1990.

4. Issues and Debates

4.1 The Feminist Advance

Feminist critiques of research have contributed to the understanding and practice of participatory research. Both feminist approaches and participatory research are concerned with knowledge creation in ways that empower those engaged rather than maintaining the status quo. Both feminist research and participatory research seek to shift the center from which knowledge is generated. Spender (1978 pp. 1–2) has described the field of women's studies as follows:

> Its multi-disciplinary nature challenges the arrangements of knowledge into academic disciplines; its methodology breaks down many of the traditional distinctions between

theoretical and empirical and between objective and subjective. It is in the process of redefining knowledge, knowledge gathering and making . . .

In addition, Callaway has demonstrated that women have been largely excluded from producing the dominant forms of knowledge and that the social sciences have been not only a science of male society but also a male science of society (Callaway 1981). Spender urged women "to learn to create our own knowledge." It is crucially important, she states:

> that women begin to create our own means of producing and validating knowledge which is consistent with our own personal experience. We need to formulate our own yardsticks, for we are doomed to deviancy if we persist in measuring ourselves against the male standard. This is our area of learning, with learning used in a widely encompassing, highly charged, political and revolutionary sense. (Spender 1978 pp. 1–2)

Maguire has bridged feminist research approaches and participatory research in her 1987 book which points out what she has called the "Androcentric filter" in participatory research writing (Maguire 1987). Maguire has pointed out the distinct silence around gender and women in the participatory research discourse. She noted that women's ways of seeing were not mentioned until 1981 and that in the general discourse women have been excluded.

Maguire put forward a number of specific guidelines for feminist participatory research:

> (1) the critique is both of positivist and androcentric research paradigms;
> (2) gender needs to be a central piece of the issues agenda;
> (3) integrative feminism which recognizes diversity should be central to theoretical discussions on participatory research;
> (4) the role of gender needs to be taken into account in all phases of participatory research;
> (5) feminist participatory research would give explicit attention to how women and men as groups benefit from a project;
> (6) attention to gender language use is critical;
> (7) gender, culture, race and class all figure in questions about the research team;
> (8) gender should be a factor in considering evaluation;
> (9) patriarchy is a system to be dismantled along with other systems of domination and oppression. (Maguire 1987 pp. 105–08)

Smith has suggested that feminist sociology, like participatory research, must "begin where we are" with real, concrete people with actual lives if it is to do more than reproduce patriarchal patterns of relations (Smith 1979). Oral history as a particular approach to feminist research has been used in participatory research as well (Anderson et al. 1990).

4.2 Question of Voice

Participatory research fundamentally is about who has the right to speak, to analyze, and to act. It is about rural Black women in southern cooperatives in the United States speaking for themselves in obtaining loans for planting. It is about shantytown mothers in Bombay speaking for themselves. It is about citizens of Turkish descent in Germany looking at and articulating their own needs in the face of neo-Nazi revival. It is about women in Thailand's hill country protecting forests. It is about indigenous people of the First Nations of North America researching land rights. It is about people who do not read and write taking control of literacy programs. It is a process that supports the voices from the margins in speaking, analyzing, building alliances, and taking action. As Lourde's (1984) poem "Litany for Survival" says:

> and when we speak we are afraid
> our words will not be heard
> nor welcomed
> but when we are silent
> we are still afraid
> So it is better to speak
> remembering
> we were never meant to survive

According to hooks, critical theorist and Afro-American woman, "It is our responsibility collectively and individually to distinguish between mere speaking that is about self-aggrandizement, exploitation of the exotic "other", and that coming to voice which is a gesture of resistance, an affirmation of struggle" (hooks 1988).

Participatory research argues for the articulation of points of view by the dominated or subordinated, whether from gender, race, ethnicity, or other structures of subordination. Participatory research posits that an individual's position in structures of subordination shapes the ability to see the whole. hooks reflected thus on growing up Black in the United States:

> Living as we did—on the edge—we developed a particular way of seeing reality. We looked both from the outside in and from the inside out. We focused our attention on the center as well as on the margin. We understood both. This mode of seeing reminded us of the existence of a whole universe, a main body made up of both margin and center. Our survival depended on an ongoing private acknowledgment that we were a necessary, vital part of that whole. This sense of wholeness, impressed upon our consciousness by the structure of our daily lives, provided us an oppositional world view—a mode of seeing unknown to most of our oppressors, that sustained us, sided us in our struggle to transcend poverty and despair, strengthened our sense of self and our solidarity (hooks 1984 p. 9)

5. Participatory Research as Counterhegemonic Practice

Disturbed by the fact that dissatisfaction of the working class in Italy produced fascism instead of a socialist transformation as happened in the Soviet Union in 1917, Antonio Gramsci undertook a lengthy study, though this was partly brought about by his imprisonment. The translation of his work into English in the early 1970s allowed greater access to his complex and fascinating ideas (Hoare and Nowell-Smith

1971). Hegemony is one of the major concepts that helps individuals to understand participatory research. According to Gramsci, humans are controlled by both coercion and consent. Laws exist that limit actions that can be taken in redressing structural imbalances, but in fact demand most often "consent" to structures of domination or hegemony. Dominated classes, genders, races, sexual orientations, or different-ability groups internalize the views of what is "acceptable" resistance, "realistic" strategy, their own fault or the natural order of things and thereby participate in the maintenance of hegemony.

But unlike orthodox Marxism, Gramsci saw a more dialectical relationship between consciousness and reality. While not accepting the idealist position that consciousness determines reality, Gramsci allowed that human agency does have a role and that the construction of counterhegemonic patterns was what was needed. In the construction of counterhegemonic ideas there is a role for intellectuals, but new kinds of intellectuals, what he called "organic intellectuals," who are deeply rooted to and part of the class- or other dominated structures from which they come. The knowledge produced in participatory research processes can be seen as part of the counterhegemonic process.

6. Restoration of Ancient Knowledge

The growing awareness globally about environmental and ecological deterioration has reinforced many of the claims and aspirations for participatory research. Shiva of India, for example, has noted that the scientific revolution of Isaac Newton and Francis Bacon was a male, Eurocentric, white science that by its invention immediately created nonscience or ignorance among people or in places that did not share in this particular way of knowing. Western science rendered invisible ancient, feminine, proearth ways of knowing (Shiva 1989).

There is widespread interest in the recovery of ancient ways of knowing that seem more fully integrated into the world and nature as opposed to those ways that view nature as separate and needing to be conquered for human beings to prosper. There is a role for participatory research with people and by people who still have links to ancient knowledge. In this case can participatory research be part of such a recovery or restoration process (Colorado 1988)?

7. Co-optation and the Role of the University

What is the role of the academy in participatory research? What has the academy done with participatory research? What is the status of the knowledge generated in a participatory research process? Participatory research originated as a challenge to positivist research paradigms as carried out largely by university-based researchers. The position has been that the center of knowledge generation needed to be in what dominant society described as the margins: in communities, with women, with people of color, and so forth. Experience has shown that it is very difficult to achieve this kind of process from a university base; hence the need for alternative structures such as community-based networks or centers. But how can this be reconciled with the fact that so many of those who publish are university based?

If the research process is genuinely and organically situated in a community, workplace, or group that is experiencing domination, there is no need to be afraid that the knowledge being generated will be used for purposes that the community or group does not need or wish for. The difficulty arises because there are different uses of knowledge in the academy from those in community or workplace situations. According to the discourse of participatory research, knowledge generated, whether of localized application or larger theoretical value, is linked in some ways with shifts of power or structural changes. But intentions do not always produce desired results, and those who have been working along these lines for a number of years share these assumptions. It is necessary to hope for a fuller understanding of the context and conditions of both work and life.

Knowledge within the academy serves a variety of purposes. It is a commodity by which academics do far more than exchange ideas; it is the very means of exchange for the academic political economy. Tenure, promotion, peer recognition, research grants, and countless smaller codes of privilege are accorded through the adding up of articles, books, papers in "refereed" journals and conferences. Academics in the marketplace of knowledge know that they must identify or become identified with streams of ideas that offer the possibility of publishing and dialogue within appropriate and recognized settings. Collaborative research or at least collaborative publishing is informally discouraged because of the difficulty in attributing authorship. Collaborative research with persons who are not academics by the standards of the academy is uncommon. While academics in fact gain financially through accumulated publications of appropriate knowledge, community collaborators seldom benefit from such collaboration in financial terms. As can be seen, academics are under economic, job survival, or advancement pressures to produce in appropriate ways. It is this structural pressure that plays havoc with academic engagement in the participatory research process. Is it not possible that in spite of personal history, ideological commitment, and deep personal links with social movements or transformative processes that the structural location of the academy as the preferred location for the organizing of knowledge will distort a participatory research process?

Does this mean that there is no role for university-based people to be engaged in participatory research processes? Arguments exist on both sides of this question. Universities or similarly accredited researchers are clearly not *required* to animate a participatory research process. Participatory research is a tool which social movements, activists, trade unionists, women on welfare, the homeless, or any similar groups use as part of a variety of strategies and methods for the conduct of their work. If they wish to invite a university-based group to become involved they need to set up the conditions at the start and maintain control of the process if they wish to benefit as much as possible. Countless groups make use of processes that resemble participatory research without naming it or certainly without asking for outside validation of the knowledge produced.

Participatory research deserves to be taught in universities, and is increasingly being taught. The academic community deserves to discuss and challenge and be challenged by these and other ideas which raise questions of the role of knowledge and power. Adult educators, community workers, social workers, primary healthcare personnel, solidarity cooperators, cooperative movement workers, multicultural workers, teachers, and countless others who begin working after a university education deserve to study, read, and experience the ideas that make up participatory research.

Academics also do not cease to be members of the community by going to work in a university. There are countless community issues, whether related to toxic dumping, homelessness, high drop-out levels in local schools, or unfair taxation policies, that engage us all as citizens. Academics have some skills that can contribute to community action along with the skills of others in the community.

The concern with co-optation is not limited to the academy, but runs through the professional circles of those involved in international development. Rahnema, a former senior Iranian official turned advisor on nongovernmental activities for the United Nations Development Program (UNDP) and visiting university professor, has criticized participatory action research as "The Last Temptation of Saint Development" (Rahnema 1990). He says that in its most generalized form, the call for participation is naı[um]ve and by now accepted by all international agencies. He suggests that participatory research can at best only change external factors affecting people's lives and not touch the deeper conditioning that causes people to do what they do; "It serves no one to make a new fetish out of participation, only because nonparticipatory development has failed in every way" (Rahnema 1990).

8. Historical Materialism, Critical Theory, and Other Philosophical Support

Vio Grossi wrote in 1981 that:

some . . . understood that participatory research was implicitly rejecting . . . historical materialism. We were accused of integration and reformism. Participatory research is not, and has never intended to be, a new ideological and scientific holistic system, an alternative to historical materialism. On the contrary, it attempts to start the research from the concrete and specific reality, incorporating the people's viewpoints, in order to contribute to a type of social transformation that eliminates poverty, dependence and exploitation. This assertion requires a further analysis of its components. Historical materialism has been stated as a method for investigating reality with the intent of revealing the main tendencies of changes in order to orient action. (Vio Grossi 1981)

As Gramsci has said:

The starting-point of critical elaboration is the consciousness of what one really is, and in "knowing thyself" as a product of the historical process to date which has deposited in you an infinity of traces, without leaving an inventory. (Hoare and Nowell-Smith 1971 p. 326)

Early efforts to place the evolving practice of participatory research within appropriate or supportive theoretical frameworks focused on debates between pragmatic or historical materialist epistemological frameworks (Kassam and Mustapha 1982). The majority of participatory research writers found themselves agreeing that class, power, ideology, and other social structural elements were critical to understanding change and hence drew upon historical materialist sources. In the mid-1980s, and particularly in North America, contributions linked participatory research to the critical theory streams of Horkheimer, Adorno, and Habermas (Comstock and Fox 1993, Park 1993). Additional linkages were made between the concepts of "critical pedagogy," particularly as both Giroux of the United States and Simon of Canada began to move the focus of their work beyond schooling and into cultural politics and the notions of "border" pedagogies.

It is necessary to stress that the basis for a critical pedagogy cannot be developed merely around the inclusion of particular forms of knowledge that have been suppressed or ignored by the dominant culture, nor can it only center on providing students with more empowering interpretations of the social and material world. Such a pedagogy must be attentive to ways in which students make both affective and semantic investments as part of their attempts to regulate and give meaning to their lives (Giroux and Simon 1992).

9. Local Autonomy and Broader Struggles

Additional debates exist in the field. For example, there is tension between the requirement of local autonomy for a given participatory process and the demand for coordinated social action at the national or regional levels. A national action must be more than an aggregate of local experiences. At certain critical moments, will a local-level participatory research process

hinder the progress of broader social movements by overemphasizing the localized nature of the problem? There is a need to understand the relationships of different kinds of knowledge and information generating from different levels and aspects of society.

10. Question of Power

Emerging from the discussions, debates, and activities of participatory research is the central question of power. Participatory research is intended to contribute to processes of shifting power or democratizing a variety of contexts. Power can be expressed in several ways: A exercises power over B when A affects B in a manner contrary to B's interests; in other words A gets B to do what he or she does not want to do. But A also exercises power by influencing, shaping, or determining B's very wants, by controlling the agenda through a complex interplay of social control (Gaventa 1979).

How, then, can participatory research be useful in shifting power? Practitioners have suggested at least three possibilities.

10.1 Unmasking the Myths

Vio Grossi (1981) has written of participatory research as initiating a process of disindoctrination that allows people to detach themselves from the myths imposed on them by the power structure and which have prevented them from seeing their own oppression or from seeing possibilities for breaking free. Transformative action can be seen as the strategic goal to be reached in the medium or long term. A participatory research process carried out in conjunction with popular groups (and under their control) is designed to facilitate the analysis of stages toward that goal.

10.2 Creation of Popular Knowledge

Fals Borda has contributed to the discussion of popular knowledge in his paper on "Science and the Common People" (Fals Borda 1980). He says the creation of knowledge that comes from the people contributes to the realization of a people's science which serves and is understood by the people, and no longer perpetuates the status quo. The process of this new paradigm involves: (a) returning information to the people in the language and cultural form in which it originated, (b) establishing control of the work by the popular and base movements, (c) popularizing research techniques, (d) integrating the information as the base of the organic intellectual, (e) maintaining a conscious effort in the action/reflection rhythm of work, (f) recognizing science as part of the everyday lives of all people, and (g) learning to listen.

In Gaventa's terms popular knowledge can be seen as a contribution toward limiting the ability of those in power to determine the wants of others, thus in effect transferring power to those groups engaged in the production of popular knowledge (Gaventa 1979).

10.3 Contributing to Organizing

Participatory research is conceived to be an integral process of investigation, education, and action. When the question of power is addressed, it is clearer than ever that the first two aspects are empty without the third. But action must be explained still further. From several years of sharing information and results it has become clear that the most common action and the critical necessity is that of organizing, in its various phases. It has meant building alliances and strengthening links within various progressive sectors.

It would be an error to assume that naï[um]ve or uncontrolled use of participatory research results in strengthening the power of the powerless at the base of society. Where control over the participatory research process is missing, experience has shown that power can easily accrue to those already in control. There has been ambiguity in some earlier writings on participatory research which has resulted in misunderstanding and manipulation.

See also: Adult Education Research; Critical Approaches to Adult Education; Ideologies in Adult Education

References

Anderson K, Armitage S, Jack D, Wittner J 1990 Beginning where we are: Feminist methodology in oral history. In: Nielson J M (ed.) 1990 *Feminist Research Methods*. Westview, Boulder, Colorado

Barndt D 1981 *Just Getting There: Creating Visual Tools for Collective Analysis in Freirean Education Programmes for Migrant Women in Canada*. Par Res Group, Toronto

Barndt D 1989 *Naming the Moment: Political Analysis for Action—A Manual for Community Groups*. Moment Project, Toronto

Beltran L R 1976 Alien premises: Objects and methods in Latin American communication research. *Commun. Res.* 3(2): 107–34

Brown L D, Kaplan R E 1981 Participatory research in a factory. In: Reason P, Rowan J (eds.) 1981 *Human Inquiry: A Sourcebook of New Paradigm Research*. Wiley, London

Callaway H 1981 Women's perspectives: Research as re-vision. In: Reason P, Rowan J (eds.) 1981 *Human Inquiry: A Sourcebook of New Paradigm Research*. Wiley, London

Cassara B 1985 *Participatory Research: Group Self-directed Learning for Social Transformation*. Adult Education, University of Georgia, Athens, Georgia

Center for Community Education and Action 1991 *Participatory Research: An Annotated Bibliography*. CCEA and Center for International Education, Amherst, Massachusetts

Colorado P 1988 Bridging native and western science. *Convergence* 21(3/4)

Comstock D, Fox R 1993 Citizen's action at North Bonnevile Dam. In: Park P, Brydon-Miller M, Hall B, Jackson T (eds.) 1993

D'arcy de Oliveira R, D'arcy de Oliveira M 1975 *The Militant Observer: A Sociological Alternative*. Institut d'Action Culturelle, Geneva

Fals Borda O 1980 *Science and the Common People*. International Forum on Participatory Research

Fals Borda O, Rahman M A 1991 *Action and Knowledge: Breaking the Monopoly with Participatory Action-Research*. Apex, New York

Gaventa J 1979 *Power and Powerlessness: Quiescence and Rebellion in an Appalachian Valley*. University of Illinois Press, Urbana, Illinois

Gaventa J 1988 Participatory research in North America. *Convergence* 21(2/3): 19–48

Gerace Larufa F 1973 *Comunicación Horizontal*. Librería Studium, Lima

Giroux H, Simon R 1992 Popular culture as a pedagogy of pleasure and meaning: Decolonizing the body. In: Giroux H (ed.) 1992 *Border Crossings: Cultural Workers and the Politics of Education*. Routledge, New York

Hall B 1981 Participatory research, popular knowledge and power. *Convergence* 14(3)

Hoare Q, Nowell-Smith G (eds. and trans.) 1971 *Selections from the Prison Notebooks of Antonio Gramsci*. Lawrence and Wishart, London

Holmes J 1976 Thoughts on research methodology. *Stud. Adult Educ.* 8(2): 149–63

hooks b 1984 *Feminist Theory: From Margin to Center*. South End, Boston, Massachusetts

hooks b 1988 *Talking Back: Thinking Feminist Thinking Black*. South End, Boston, Massachusetts

Horton B D 1981 On the potential of participatory research: An evaluation of a regional experiment. Paper prepared for annual meeting of the Society for Study of Social Problems, Toronto, Canada

Jackson T 1980 Environmental assessment in big trout lake, Canada. Paper for International Forum on participatory research

Jackson T, McCaskill D, Hall B 1982 Learning for self-determination: Community-based options for native training and research. *Canadian Journal of Native Studies* 2(1) (special issue)

Kassam Y, Mustapha K 1982 *Participatory Research: An Emerging Alternative Methodology in Social Science Research*. ICAE, Toronto

Lourde A 1984 *Sister Outsider: Essays and Speeches*. Crossing Press, Trumansburg, New York

Maguire P 1987 *Doing Participatory Research: A Feminist Approach*. Center for International Education, University of Massachusetts, Amherst, Massachusetts

Orefice P 1981 Cultural self-awareness of local community: An experience in the south of Italy. *Convergence* 14: 56–64

Park P 1993 What is participatory research? In: Park P, Brydon-Miller M, Hall B, Jackson T (eds.) 1993

Park P, Brydon-Miller M, Hall B, Jackson T (eds.) 1993 *Voices of Change: Participatory Research in the United States and Canada*. Greenwood, Westport, Connecticut

Participatory Research Network 1982 *An Introduction to Participatory Research*. ICAE, New Delhi

PRIA 1985 *Knowledge and Social Change: An Inquiry into Participatory Research in India*. PRIA, New Delhi

Rahnema M 1990 Participatory action research: The "last temptation" of saint development. *Alternatives* 15: 199–226

Shiva V 1989 *Staying Alive: Women, Ecology and Development*. Zed Books, London

Smith D 1979 A sociology for women. In: Sherman J, Bock E (eds.) 1979 *The Prism of Sex: Essays in the Sociology of Knowledge*. University of Wisconsin Press, Madison, Wisconsin

SPEAR 1990 *You Better Belize It! A Participatory Research Training Guide on a Training Workshop in Belize*. SPEAR and PRG, Toronto

Spender D 1978 Editorial. *Womens Studies International Q.* 1: 1–2

Stinson A (ed.) 1979 *Canadians Participate: Annotated Bibliography of Case Studies*. Centre for Social Welfare Studies, Ottawa

Tandon R 1988 Social transformation and participatory research. *Convergence* 21(2/3): 5–18

Vio Grossi F 1981 The socio-political implications of participatory research. Yugoslavia. *Convergence* 14(3): 34–51

Further Reading

Hall B 1979 Knowledge as a commodity and participatory research. *Prospects* 9(4): 393–408

Hall B, Gillette A, Tandon R 1982 *Creating Knowledge: A Monopoly?* PRIA, New Delhi

Park P, Hall B, Jackson T, and Brydon-Miller M 1993 *Voices for Change: Participatory Research in Canada and the United States*. OISE Press, Toronto

Research Methodology: Human Development

A. von Eye and C. Spiel

Developmental research investigates constancy and change in behavior and learning across the human life course. This entry discusses the methods used to arrive at clear-cut statements concerning human development and adult learning, specifically, methods for data collection, data analysis, and interpretation. Examples are drawn from educational and psychological research of relevance to adult education.

1. Fundamental Methodological Paradigms

1.1 The Univariate Developmental Paradigm

One of the simplest methodological paradigms in social science research (Baltes et al. 1977) involves the mechanistic or deterministic assumption that observed behavior depends on or can be predicted from causal or independent variables. In brief, this assumption is that $D = f(I)$ where D denotes the dependent variable, for example, adults' progress in learning, and I denotes the independent variable, for example, social climate in the study groups.

From a developmental perspective the prediction of constancy and change is important. Dynamic variants of the univariate developmental paradigm predict a variable, observed at later points in time, from the same variable, observed at earlier points in time. For example, a typical question is whether high achievement motivation at the start of an adult class allows one to predict high achievement motivation in later classes. Developmental changes are inferred if prediction equations, for example, regression equations, involve parameters that indicate change, for example, average increases.

Other variants of this paradigm predict changes in behavior from variables other than the dependent ones.

For example, changes in behavior in menopause are predicted from changes in hormone levels (Paikoff et al. 1992). To be able to depict changes in behavior within individuals, at least two observations of the dependent variable are required.

1.2 The Multivariate Developmental Paradigm

In a most general sense, multivariate research involves two or more variables on the dependent variable side and two or more variables on the independent variable side (Baltes et al. 1977). In developmental research, one observes two or more variables and predicts constancy or change in these variables from earlier observations of the same variables (dynamic modeling) and/or from other variables.

There has been an intense debate as to what design for data collection is the most suitable. The following sections present the basic research designs, give an overview of this discussion, and summarize the conclusions with relevance for adult education research.

2. Designs for Human Development Research

There are three basic designs for developmental research: the cross-sectional, the longitudinal, and the time-lag designs. The advantages and drawbacks of each of these will be discussed. The basic assumption that underlies each of these designs is that individuals who participate in investigations are not systematically different from the population under study.

2.1 The Cross-sectional Research Design

In cross-sectional designs, researchers observe one or more variables at one point in time and in two or more groups of individuals differing in age. The use of cross-sectional designs is by far the most popular research strategy in developmental psychology, for the following reasons: most importantly, only one observation point is necessary, so that studies using cross-sectional observations take little time compared to studies using repeated observations. In addition, financial costs are typically relatively low. There are also benefits on the interpretational side. Because observations are made at only one point in time, sample fluctuations are, by definition, not a problem. Researchers can assume that samples are constant. Many adult education surveys employ this cross-sectional design.

However, cross-sectional research also has a number of specific deficiencies, most of which result from using only one observation point. Specifically, for conclusions from cross-sectional research to be valid one has to accept a number of assumptions. Some of these assumptions are strong, that is, they are difficult to satisfy, for the following reasons: (a) age samples ("cohorts") are drawn from the same parental population at birth. If this is not the case there is no way to discriminate between developmental processes and cohort differences; (b) differences in behavior that are related to age, that is, differences between individuals from different age groups, are stable over historical time. Again, if this is not the case there is no way to discriminate between changes in development that are caused by secular, historical changes, or by cohort differences; (c) differences between individuals from different age cohorts can be interpreted as indicating developmental changes that would occur within individuals as they move from one age group to the other.

If these assumptions do not hold, there is no reasonable way to assign developmental changes to such causes as age, adult learning, or historical time in a clear-cut way. Indeed, there is an abundance of literature showing that cohorts are different from each other (see Baltes et al. 1978). For example, researchers have suggested that the phenomenon of mid-life crisis may be less prevalent in the cohorts born around 1950 than in cohorts born in the time around the Great Depression (see Rybash et al. 1991). Thus, the development of a mid-life crisis may be viewed as a secular phenomenon rather than a ubiquitous developmental phenomenon.

Selection of methods for statistical data analysis depends on the type and distribution of data. Classical statistical methods for analysis of quantitative cross-sectional data include analysis of variance, multivariate analysis of variance, and discriminant function analysis. For qualitative data chi-square decomposition, log-linear analysis, prediction analysis, and configural frequency analysis are often recommended (see von Eye 1990a, 1990b, Rovine and von Eye 1991).

2.2 The Longitudinal Research Design

In longitudinal designs, researchers observe one or more variables at two or more points in time and in one cohort. Variation over time occurs when individuals grow older during the course of the investigation.

Longitudinal studies have a number of advantages over cross-sectional studies (Schaie 1983, Baltes et al. 1977, de Ribaupierre 1989). One of the most important advantages is that only longitudinal investigations allow one to describe intra-individual development, that is constancy and change within the individual across time. In cross-sectional research intra-individual development must be inferred under strong assumptions. However, results from cognitive studies suggest that growth curves derived from cross-sectional data do not necessarily have the same shape as curves derived from longitudinal data (Salthouse 1991).

In addition, interindividual differences in intra-individual development, that is, differences between individuals' developmental patterns, can be depicted only by observing the same individuals more than once. A typical research question is whether adult learners from disadvantaged social backgrounds derive greater benefit from attempts to teach learning strategies than students from other social backgrounds. The description of such differences is important for a researcher interested in homogeneity of development. Homogeneity of development can be investigated at the variable level; for instance, by asking whether certain cognitive abilities decline in adulthood more rapidly than others. Homogeneity can also be investigated at the differential level; for example, by asking whether (and why) individuals display different developmental trajectories.

Another major advantage of longitudinal studies is that the constancy and change in relationships among variables can be investigated. For example, one could ask whether the relationship between adult learning and cognitive capacity changes over the adult life course. One of the most important preconditions for age, cohort, and time comparisons is what has been termed "dimensional identity" (Schmidt 1977). A set of variables is considered to show dimensional identity if the interrelations among variables remain unchanged over all observation points. When variable interrelations change in cross-sectional studies, it is impossible to determine whether these changes are due to age or group differences. When variable interrelations change in longitudinal studies they reflect developmental processes. However, in both cases changes in variable interrelations render comparisons of results from different age groups or cohorts difficult.

A last advantage of longitudinally collected data concerns the investigation of causes for constancy and change. A general assumption is that causes occur prior to effects. Thus, causes for development must be observed before developmental changes occur. This observation is obviously possible only in longitudinal research. Causal analysis is of concern in adult education, because of interaction among the factors that influence participation. For example, it has been found in longitudinal studies that schooling predicts first-time participation in adult education, but that this effect diminishes with time, so that experience of adult education becomes an increasingly powerful predictor of participation at a subsequent point in the life course (Tuijnman 1991).

The desirable properties of longitudinal research are offset by a number of shortcomings. The first of these is that the wrong choice of the number and spacing of observations may prevent researchers from adequately assessing underlying processes of change. Thus, researchers may miss critical periods or events, may fail to depict validly the dynamics of change, or may even completely misrepresent the shape of a growth curve.

A second shortcoming concerns serial effects of repeated measurements, such as "testing effects." For example, when individuals score higher in a particular test (e.g., an adult literacy test) in a second measurement, one cannot be sure that the increase in performance reflects an increase in ability rather than an increase due to remembering test items or familiarization with the test situation.

Similar to cross-sectional designs, sample selection may play a critical role in longitudinal studies. There may be specific selection effects, because longitudinal studies require more effort from participants than cross-sectional studies. In addition, longitudinal studies may suffer from attrition; that is, loss of participants due to moving, loss of interest, illness, or, in particular in studies including older adults, death. Each of these problems can lead to invalid description of developmental processes.

Another important shortcoming of longitudinal research is that the costs are higher than in cross-sectional research. In addition, there are interpretational problems. Most important is that of generalizability over samples. Because of cohort differences, growth curves may not be the same for samples from different cohorts (see Baltes et al. 1977). The same applies if selection effects are taken into account.

Selection of statistical methods for analyzing longitudinal data must consider data quality, distributional characteristics, and sample size. Latent class models and structural equation models that allow the explanation of patterns of relationships among variables in nonexperimental environments are becoming increasingly popular (see Bartholomew 1987, Rovine and von Eye 1991). These methods can also be useful for estimating development and change in continuous or categorical data. (For a more detailed overview of statistical methods for analysis of longitudinal data see von Eye 1990a, 1990b.)

2.3 The Time-lag Design

In time-lag designs, researchers observe one or more variables at two or more points in time and in two or more groups of individuals that belong to different cohorts but are of the same age. Variation over time results from the spacing between observation points. Although time-lag designs are far less popular than cross-sectional and longitudinal designs, they are useful in many respects. For example, the finding that there has been a considerable variation in Standard Achievement Test performance in the United States over the last 50 years could only come from a time-lag investigation.

Time-lag investigations are selected when researchers are interested in comparing cohorts. However, time of measurement and historical time are confounded. Therefore, generalizations to other cohorts, other historical times, or even other age groups are problematic. As far as costs are concerned, time-lag designs exhibit the same problems as longitudinal designs. As far as sampling is concerned, there are similarities with cross-sectional studies. As far as interpretability is concerned, there are strong constraints resulting from the focus on only one age group. For these reasons, time-lag designs have been the least popular in research on human development and adult learning.

2.4 The Age × Time of Measurement × Cohort Design

This is the only developmental research design that varies the three aspects of time: age (A), time of measurement (T), and year of birth (cohort— C). However, there is no way to vary these three aspects independently, which would be necessary to separate their effects. The reason is that the three time variables are linearly dependent on each other. Each can be expressed as a linear combination of the other two, as is shown in the following formulas. (For the following formulas, T and C are expressed in calendar years, e.g., 1951, A is expressed in years, e.g., 40.)

(a) $A = T - C$

(b) $C = T - A$

(c) $T = C + A$

Therefore, research designs have been developed that vary only two of the three variables, A, C, and T. The following designs result: $A \times C$, $A \times T$, and $C \times T$. (For a more detailed description see Baltes et al. 1977, Schaie 1983.)

With regard to $A \times C$, researchers observe two or more cohorts over three or more observation points. At the beginning of the observation of each cohort, the cohorts are of the same age. Thus observations of the younger cohorts begin when they reach the age the older cohorts were when they were first observed. To carry out a study a minimum of three observation points and two cohorts are necessary. At least two age levels must be covered. Schaie and Baltes (1975) argue that the $A \times C$ arrangement is the most useful for ontogenetic research, because this design allows one to depict constancy and change with age; that is, intra-individual change. In addition, it allows one to depict interindividual differences in intra-individual change. However, the authors also claim that using any of the two-dimensional designs is defensible, depending on the purpose of research.

The main problem with treating A, C, and T as explanations for development is that one has to make strong assumptions when one applies the two-dimensional designs. Specifically, when applying the A × C design one must assume that the effects of T are negligible; for A × T one must assume that the effects of C are negligible; and for C × T one must assume that the effects of A are negligible.

3. Special Methods

This section covers a selection of special methods, including intervention studies, microdevelopmental studies, single case studies, and training studies.

3.1 Intervention Studies

The designs discussed above are typically applied to observe natural behavior. Intervention does not take place. In contrast, research on specific kinds of intervention, for example through adult education, and its effects is often done using randomized experiments. For example, experiments examine the effects of systematic variations in teaching behavior on learner achievement. For studying intervention effects, researchers observe one or more variables in two or more groups of students, who are randomly assigned to treatments, at one or more points in time. Whenever they can be realized, randomized experiments are the preferred designs because causal inferences can be drawn from the results. Methods for statistical analysis of data from randomized experiments most often include analysis of variance.

Examples of designs for intervention studies include reversal designs and multiple baseline designs (see Baltes et al. 1977). In reversal designs researchers first establish the rate of spontaneous behavior; that is, the baseline. Then they introduce some treatment (experimental condition) that constitutes the first reversal, and assess the rate of behavior again. The second reversal occurs at the end of the treatment, and so forth. All later assessments are compared with the first, the baseline.

Reversal designs typically are applied in learning studies. One of the basic assumptions of such studies is that it is, in principle, possible that behavior rates return to the baseline after the treatment. If behavior changes are irreversible, as is often assumed of developmental changes, reversal designs become less useful.

3.2 Single Case Studies

Single case studies, also referred to as "single subject studies," involve the detailed investigation of one individual. The primary goals pursued with single case studies include the detailed description of specific processes (e.g., language development) in individuals, the development of skills in individuals with specific deficits, and treatment of behavior disorders. For analysis of single case studies time series analysis, trend analysis, or spectral analysis are most often applied.

3.3 Training Studies

In training studies researchers often combine reversal with multiple baseline designs. Multiple behaviors are trained, assessments occur before and after training periods, but there is no assumption that training affects only one type of behavior. Goals pursued with training studies include the development of skills (e.g., learning skills), the compensation of losses (e.g., memory in old age), and the reversal of decline (e.g., achievement motivation in midlife). A large number of training studies have been concerned with intellectual development (Willis and Schaie 1986, Baltes et al. 1988). Researchers were able to show that intellectual decline in adulthood can typically be compensated by appropriate training (for a detailed discussion see Salthouse 1991).

Statistical analysis of data from training studies typically involves analysis of variance with repeated observations.

3.4 Microdevelopmental Studies

Typically, longitudinal and sequential studies span several years. For instance, Schaie's Seattle Longitudinal Study observes individuals in a 7-year rhythm. However, development also takes place in shorter time frames. Relatively short-term development is termed "microdevelopment." Studies investigating microdevelopment typically are longitudinal in nature and involve a relatively large number of observation points that are spaced in short intervals so that points in time where changes occur will not be missed (see Siegler and Crowley 1991).

An example of a microdevelopmental study is reported by Fischer and Lamborn (1989) who investigated the development of honesty and kindness in adolescents. They reported a sequence of stages. Development that carries individuals from one stage to the next is termed "macrodevelopment." Progress within stages is termed "microdevelopment." The authors specified transformation rules that describe development at the microdevelopmental level.

Statistical methods for analysis of microdevelopment include trend analysis, time series analysis, and structural equation modeling.

See also: Research Methodology: Scientific Methods; Human Development; Lifespan Development; Development of

Learning Across the Lifespan; The Development of Competence: Toward a Taxonomy

References

Baltes P B, Cornelius S W, Nesselroade J R 1978 Cohort effects in behavioral development: Theoretical orientation and methodological perspectives. In: Collins W A (ed.) 1978 *Minnesota Symposium on Child Psychology*, Vol. 11. Erlbaum, Hillsdale, New Jersey

Baltes P B, Kliegl R, Dittmann-Kohli F 1988 On the locus of training gains in research on the plasticity of fluid intelligence in old age. *J. Educ. Psychol.* 80: 392–400

Baltes P B, Reese H W, Nesselroade J R 1977 *Life-span Developmental Psychology: Introduction to Research Methods*. Brooks/Cole, Monterey, California

Bartholomew D J 1987 *Latent Variable Models and Factor Analysis*. Oxford University Press, Oxford

de Ribaupierre A 1989 Epilogue: On the use of longitudinal research in developmental psychology. In: de Ribaupierre A (ed.) 1989 *Transition Mechanisms in Child Development: The Longitudinal Perspective*. Cambridge University Press, Cambridge

Fischer K W, Lamborn S D 1989 Mechanisms of variation in developmental levels: Cognitive and emotional transitions during adolescence. In: de Ribaupierre A (ed.) 1989 *Transition Mechanisms in Child Development: The Longitudinal Perspective*. Cambridge University Press, Cambridge

Paikoff R L, Buchanan C M, Brooks-Gunn J 1992 Methodological issues in the study of hormone–behavior links at puberty. In: Lerner R M, Petersen A C, Brooks-Gunn J (eds.) 1992 *Encyclopedia of Adolescence*, Vol 2.

Garland, New York

Rovine M J, von Eye A 1991 *Applied Computational Statistics in Longitudinal Research*. Academic Press, Boston, Massachusetts

Rybash J W, Roodin P A, Santrock J W 1991 *Adult Development and Aging*, 2nd edn. Brown and Benchmark, Dubuque, Iowa

Salthouse T A 1991 *Theoretical Perspectives on Cognitive Aging*. Erlbaum, Hillsdale, New Jersey

Schaie K W 1983 What can we learn from the longitudinal study of adult psychological development? In: Schaie K W (ed.) 1983 *Longitudinal Studies of Adult Psychological Development*. Guilford, New York

Schaie K W, Baltes P B 1975 On sequential strategies in developmental research: Description or explanation. *Hum. Dev.* 18(5): 384–90

Schmidt H D 1977 Methodologische Probleme der entwicklungspsychologischen Forschung. *Probleme und Ergebnisse der Psychologie* 62: 5–27

Siegler R, Crowley K 1991 The microgenetic method: A direct means for studying cognitive development. *Am. Psychol.* 46(6): 606–20

Tuijnman A C 1991 Lifelong education: A test of the accumulation hypothesis. *Int. J. Lifelong Educ.* 10(4) 275–85

von Eye A (ed.) 1990b *Statistical Methods in Longitudinal Research. Vol. 1: Principles and Structuring Change*. Academic Press, Boston, Massachusetts

von Eye A (ed.) 1990a *Statistical Methods in Longitudinal Research, Vol. 2: Time Series and Categorical Longitudinal Data*. Academic Press, Boston, Massachusetts

Willis S L, Schaie K W 1986 Training the elderly on the ability factors of spatial orientation and inductive reasoning. *Psychology and Aging* 1(3): 239–47

Research Methodology: Scientific Methods

A. Kaplan

Methodology as a discipline lies between two poles. On the one hand is technics, the study of specific techniques of research––interpreting a Rorschach protocol, conducting a public opinion survey, or calculating a correlation coefficient. On the other hand is philosophy of science, the logical analysis of concepts presupposed in the scientific enterprise as a whole —evidence, objectivity, truth, or inductive inference. Technics has an immediate practical bearing, but only on the use of specific techniques. Philosophy of science, though quite general in application, has only remote and indirect practical bearings. Though philosophy is much exercised about the problem of induction, for instance, educational researchers and behavioral scientists would be quite content to arrive at conclusions acceptable with the same confidence as the proposition that the sun will rise tomorrow.

Methodology is a generalization of technics and a concretization of philosophy. It deals with the resources and limitations of general research methods —such as observation, experiment, measurement, and model building—with reference to concrete contexts of inquiry. No sharp lines divide methodology from technics or from philosophy; particular discussions are likely to involve elements of all three.

The concern with methodology has lessened: more and more the researchers do their work rather than working on how they should do it. There has been a corresponding lessening of belief in the myth of methodology, the notion that if only the student of adult education could find "the right way" to go about research, the findings would be undeniably "scientific."

Anxious defensiveness heightened vulnerability to the pressure of scientific fashions. Scientism is an exaggerated regard for techniques which have succeeded elsewhere, in contrast to the scientific temper, which is open to whatever techniques hold promise for the particular inquiry at hand. Computers, mathematical models, and brass instruments are not limited to one subject matter or another; neither is their use necessary for scientific respectability.

Methodology does not dictate that the educational disciplines be hardened or abandoned. Neither does methodology exclude human behavior from scientific treatment. The task is to do as well as is made possible by the nature of the problem and the given state of knowledge and technology.

Fashions in science are not intrinsically objectionable, any more than fashions in dress, nor are they intrinsically praiseworthy. What is fashionable is only one particular way of doing things; that it is in the mode neither guarantees nor precludes effectiveness. Cognitive style is a characteristic way of attaining knowledge; it varies with persons, periods, cultures, schools of thought, and entire disciplines. Many different styles are identifiable in the scientific enterprise; at different times and places some styles are more fashionable than others. Successful scientists include analysts and synthesizers; experimenters and theoreticians; model builders and data collectors; technicians and interpreters. Problems are often formulated to suit a style imposed either by fashion or by personal predilection, and are investigated in predetermined ways. Scientism is marked by the drunkard's search— the drunkard hunts for the dropped house key, not at the door, but under the corner streetlamp, "because it's lighter there." Widespread throughout the sciences is the law of the instrument: give a small child a hammer and it turns out that everything the child sees needs pounding. It is not unreasonable to do what is possible with given instruments; what is unreasonable is to view them as infallible and all-powerful.

1. Scientific Terms

Closely associated with the myth of methodology is the semantic myth—that all would be well in (adult) educational research if only their terms were defined with clarity and precision. The myth does not make clear precisely how this is to be done. Scientists agree that scientific terms must bear some relation to observations. There is no consensus on exactly what relation, nor even on whether a useful scientific purpose would be served by a general formulation of a criterion of cognitive meaning. In particular cases the issue is not whether a term has meaning but just what its meaning might be.

For some decades education was dominated by operationism, which held that terms have meaning only if definite operations can be performed to decide whether the terms apply in any given case, and that the meaning of the terms is determined by these operations. "Intelligence" is what is measured by an intelligence test; "public opinion" is what is disclosed in a survey.

Which details are essential to the operation called for and which are irrelevant presupposes some notion of what concept the operations are meant to delimit. The same presupposition underlies attempts to improve adult literacy tests and measures. A more serious objection is that the validation of scientific findings relies heavily on the circumstances that widely different measuring operations yield substantially the same results. It is hard to avoid the conclusion that they are measuring the same magnitude. Most operations relate terms to observations only by way of other terms; once "symbolic operations" are countenanced, the semantic problems which operationism was meant to solve are reinstated.

Ambiguities abound in the behavioral sciences, as in the field of education. The behavioral scientist is involved with the subject matter in distinctive ways, justifiably so. The involvement makes for widespread normative ambiguity, the same term being used both normatively and descriptively—"abnormal" behavior, for example, may be pathological or merely deviant. Also wide spread is functional ambiguity, the same term having both a descriptive sense and an explanatory sense—the Freudian "unconscious" may be topographical or dynamic. Ambiguity is a species of openness of meaning, perhaps the most objectionable. Vagueness is another species. All terms are more or less vague, allowing for borderline cases to which it is uncertain whether the term applies—not because what is known about the case is insufficient, but because the meaning of the term is not sufficiently determinate. All terms have some degree of internal vagueness, uncertainties of application, not at the borderline but squarely within the designation; some instances are better specimens of what the term designates than others (closer to the "ideal type"), and how good a specimen is meant is not wholly determinate. Most terms have also a systemic vagueness: meanings come not singly but in more or less orderly battalions, and the term itself does not identify with what system of meanings (notably, a theory) it is to be interpreted. Significant terms are also likely to exhibit dynamic openness, changing their meanings as contexts of application multiply and knowledge grows.

As dangerous as openness is the premature closure of meanings. The progressive improvement of meanings—the semantic approximation—is interwoven with the growth of knowledge—the epistemic approximation. The advance of science does not consist only of arriving at more warranted judgments but also of arriving at more appropriate concepts. The interdependence of the two constitutes the paradox of conceptualization: formulating sound theories depends on having suitable concepts, but suitable concepts are not to be had without sound theoretical understanding. The circle is not vicious; it is broken by successive approximations, now semantic and now epistemic.

Meanings are made more determinate by a process of specification of meaning. This is sometimes loosely called "definition"; in a strict sense definition is only one way of specifying meanings—providing a combination of terms, whose meaning is presumed to be already known, which in that combination have a meaning equivalent to that of the given term. Definitions are useful for formal disciplines, like mathematics; for empirical disciplines, their usefulness varies inversely with the importance of the term.

In simple cases, meanings can be specified by ostension: making what is meant available to direct experience. Empiricism regards ostensions as the fundamental anchorage for theoretical abstractions. Meanings in the educational and behavioral sciences are often specified by description of the thing meant, especially when this is included in or is close to everyday experience. Most scientific terms have a meaning specified by indication: a set of indices, concrete or abstract, often the outcomes of specified tests and measures, which constitute, not *the* meaning of the term, but some of the conditions which provide ground for applying the term. Each index carries its own weight; each case exhibits a profile, whose weight is not necessarily the sum of the weights of the constituent indices. As contexts of application change as well as what knowledge is available, so do the indications and their weight, and thereby also the meaning specified. Premature closure of meaning by definition is likely to provide false precision, groundless or unusable.

Which type of specification is appropriate depends on the scientific purposes the term is meant to serve. Observables, terms denoting what can be experienced more or less directly, invite ostension. Indirect observables lend themselves to description of what would be observed if our senses or other circumstances were different from what they are: such terms are sometimes known as "intervening variables." Constructs have meanings built up from structures of other terms, and so are subject to definition. Theoretical terms have a core of systemic meaning which can be specified only by an open and ever-changing set of indications. Many terms have sufficient functional ambiguity to exhibit characteristics of several or all of these types of terms; they call for various types of specification of meaning. "Lifelong learning" is a good example of such an ambiguous, all-encompassing concept.

2. Classes

Empirical terms determine classes; because of openness of meaning these classes are only approximations to well-defined sets in the sense of mathematical logic, where everything in the universe of discourse definitely belongs to or is excluded from the class. The approximation to a set can be made closer (the term made more precise) by restricting its meaning to what is specifiable by easily observable and measurable indices. The danger is that such classes

are only artificial, delimiting a domain which contributes to science little more than knowledge of the characteristics by which it is delimited. Natural classes correspond to an articulation of the subject matter which figures in theories, laws, or at least in empirical generalizations inviting and guiding further research. Artificial and natural classes lie at two poles of a continuum. A classification closer to being artificial is a descriptive taxonomy; one closer to being natural is an explanatory typology. Growth of concepts as science progresses is a movement from taxonomies to typologies—Linnaeus to Darwin, Mendeleef to the modern periodic table, humors to Freudian characterology.

3. Propositions

Knowledge of a subject matter is implicit in how it is conceptualized; knowledge is explicit in propositions. Propositions perform a number of different functions in science.

First are identifications, specifying the field with which a given discipline deals, and identifying the unit elements of the field. In the behavioral sciences "idiographic" disciplines have been distinguished from "nomothetic," the former dealing with individuals, the latter with general relationships among individuals (history and sociology, for instance, or clinical and dynamic psychology). Both equally involve generalizations, because both demand identifications—the same "state" with a new government, or different personalities of the same "person": sameness and difference can be specified only by way of generalizations. Which units are to be selected is the locus problem; political science, for instance, can be pursued as the study of governments, of power, or of political behavior. What is to be the starting point of any given inquiry cannot be prejudged by other disciplines, certainly not by methodology. It is determinable only in the course of the inquiry itself—the principle of the autonomy of the conceptual base.

Other propositions serve as presuppositions of a given inquiry—what is taken for granted about the conceptual and empirical framework of the inquiry. Nothing is intrinsically indubitable but in each context there is always something undoubted. Assumptions are not taken for granted but are taken as starting points of the inquiry or as special conditions in the problem being dealt with. Assumptions are often known to be false, but are made nevertheless because of their heuristic usefulness. Hypotheses are the propositions being investigated.

4. Generalizations

Conclusions of an inquiry, if they are to be applicable to more than the particular context of the inquiry, are stated as generalizations. According to the logical reconstruction prevailing in philosophy of science for some decades (but recently coming under increasing criticism), generalizations have the form: "For all x, if x has the property f, then it has the property g." The content of the generalization can be specified only in terms of its place in a more comprehensive system of propositions.

A simple generalization moves from a set of propositions about a number of individual cases to all cases of that class. An extensional generalization moves from a narrower class to a broader one. Both these types are likely to be only descriptive. An intermediate generalization moves from propositions affirming relations of either of the preceding types to one affirming a relation of both relata to some intermediate term. It begins to be explanatory, invoking the intermediate term to account for the linkage recorded in its premises. A theoretical generalization is fully explanatory, putting the original relata and their intermediates into a meaningful structure. The conclusion of a successful inquiry may produce any of these types of generalization, not only the last.

All empirical findings, whether appearing as premises or as conclusions, are provisional, subject to rejection in the light of later findings. Philosophy of science divides propositions into *a priori* and *a posteriori*; for methodology it is more useful to replace the dichotomy by degrees of priority, the weight of evidence required before a finding is likely to be rejected. In increasing order of priority are conjectures, hypotheses, and scientific laws. A law strongly supported by theory as well as by the empirical evidence may have a very high degree of priority, often marked by calling the law a principle. In a logical reconstruction of the discipline in which it appears it may be incorporated in definitions, and so become *a priori* in the strict sense.

5. Observations and Data

Unless a proposition is a definition or a logical consequence of definition, it must be validated by reference, sooner or later, to observations. Reports of observation—data—must themselves be validated; what was reported might not in fact have been observed. A magician's performance can never be explained from a description of the effect, for the effect is an illusion; a correct description would not call for an explanation.

Errors of observation are virtually inevitable, especially in observations of human behavior; in the fashionable idiom, there is noise in every channel through which nature tells us something. In some contexts, observation can be insulated, to a degree, from error—it might be made, for instance, through a one-way mirror, so that data would not be contaminated by the intrusiveness of the observer. Error can sometimes be cancelled—reports from a large number of observers are likely to cancel out personal bias or idiosyncrasy.

In special cases error can be discounted: its magnitude, or at least its direction, can be taken into account in drawing conclusions from the data—memories are likely to be distorted in predictable ways.

There is a mistaken notion that the validity of data would be guaranteed if interpretations were scrupulously excluded from reports of what is actually seen. This mistake has been called "the dogma of immaculate perception." Observation is inseparable from a grasp of meanings; interpretation is intrinsic to perception, not an afterthought. It has been well said that there is more to observation than meets the eye.

Two levels of interpretation can be discriminated (in the abstract) in behavioral science. First is the interpretation of bodily movements as the performance of certain acts—the grasp of an act meaning. Raised hands may be interpreted as voting behavior rather than as involuntary muscular contractions (such contractions may be act meanings for a physiologist). A second level of interpretation sees observed acts in the light of some theory of their causes or functions—the grasp of an action meaning. Dress and hairstyle may be seen as adolescent rebelliousness.

Both levels of interpretation are hypothetical in the literal sense—they rest on hypotheses as to what is going on. Such hypotheses in turn rest on previous observations. This is the paradox of data: hypotheses are necessary to arrive at meaningful data, but valid hypotheses can be arrived at only on the basis of the data. As with the paradox of conceptualization, the circle is broken by successive approximation.

Because observation is interwoven with interpretation, what is observed depends on the concepts and theories through which the world is being seen. Whatever does not fit into the interpretive frame remains unseen—invisible data, like pre-Freudian male hysteria and infantile sexuality. The data may be noted but be dismissed as meaningless—cryptic data, like dreams and slips of the tongue. Observation also depends on what instruments of observation are available. Techniques like mazes, projective tests, and opinion surveys have had enormous impact on research.

6. Experiments

Creating circumstances especially conducive to observation is an experiment. Not all experiments are probative, meant to establish a given hypothesis or to select between alternative hypotheses (crucial experiment). Some may be methodological, like pilot studies or the secondary experiments performed to determine factors restricting the interpretation of the primary experiment. Heuristic experiments may be fact finding or exploratory. Other experiments are illustrative, used for pedagogy or to generate ideas, a common function of simulations.

The significance of experiments sometimes appears

only long after they were performed. Experiments have meaning only in a conceptual frame. Scientific advance may provide a new frame in which the old experiment has a new and more important meaning. The secondary analysis of an experiment already performed may be more valuable than a new experiment.

Experiments in education and the behavioral sciences have often been criticized on the basis of an unfounded distinction between the laboratory and "life." There are important differences between the laboratory and other life situations—for instance, significant differences in scale. Only moderate stresses are produced—subjects may be given, say, only a small amount of money with which to play an experimental game, whose outcome may therefore have only questionable bearings on decisions about marriage, surgery, or war. Secondary experiments may be useful to assess the effect of the differences in scale. All observations, whether in the laboratory or not, are of particular circumstances; applying the findings to other circumstances always needs validation.

Not all experiments are manipulative; in some, the manipulation is only of verbal stimuli—administering a questionnaire can be regarded as an experiment. Events especially conducive to observation even though they were not brought about for that purpose are sometimes called nature's experiments—disaster situations or identical twins separated at birth. The relocation of workers or refugees, school bussing, and changes in the penal code are instances of social experiments. Experimentation and fieldwork shade off into one another.

7. Measurement

The more exact the observations, the greater their possible usefulness (possible, but not necessary). Widespread is a mystique of quality—the notion that quantitative description is inappropriate to the study of human behavior. True, quantitative description "leaves something out"—precision demands a sharp focus. But what *is* being described is more fully described by a quantitative description. Income leaves out of account many important components of a standard of living, but a quantitative description says more about income than "high" or "low."

There is a complementary mystique of quantity—the notion that nothing is known till it has been weighed and measured. Precision may be greater than is usable in the context or even be altogether irrelevant. Because quantitative data are more easily processed, they may be taken more seriously than the actually more important imponderables. The precision may be spurious, accurate in itself but combined with impressionistic data. Fashion in the behavioral sciences may invite the use of quantitative idioms even if no measurements are available to determine the implied quantities.

Measurement is the mapping of numbers to a set of elements in such a way that certain operations on the numbers yield results which consistently correspond to certain relations among the elements. The conditions specifying the mapping define a scale; applications of the scale produce measures which correspond to magnitudes. Just what logical operations on the numbers can be performed to yield empirical correspondence depends on the scale.

Numbers may be used only as names—a nominal scale—in which case nothing can be inferred about the elements save that they are the same or different if their names are such. The numbers may be used so as to take into account relations of greater and less—an ordinal scale—allowing the corresponding elements to be put into a definite order. An interval scale defines a relation of greater and less among differences in the order. Operations may be defined allowing measures to be combined arithmetically, by which magnitudes can be compared quantitatively—a ratio or additive scale. Scales can be freely constructed, but there is no freedom to choose what they logically entail. Equally restrictive are the empirical constraints imposed by the operations coordinating measures and magnitudes.

One measuring operation or instrument is more sensitive than another if it can deal with smaller differences in the magnitudes. One is more reliable than another if repetitions of the measures it yields are closer to one another. Accuracy combines both sensitivity and reliability. An accurate measure is without significance if it does not allow for any inferences about the magnitudes save that they result from just such and such operations. The usefulness of the measure for other inferences, especially those presupposed or hypothesized in the given inquiry, is its validity.

8. Statistics and Probability

No measures are wholly accurate. Observations are multiple, both because data are manifold and because findings, to be scientific, must be capable of replication by other observers. Inevitably, not all the findings are exactly alike. Inferences drawn from any measure are correspondingly inconclusive. Statistics are the set of mathematical techniques developed to cope with these difficulties.

A problematic situation is one inviting inquiry. The situation itself does not predetermine how the problem is to be formulated; the investigator must formulate it. A problem well-formulated is half solved; badly formulated, it may be quite insoluble. The indeterminacy of a situation, from the point of view of statistics, is its uncertainty. When a specific problem has been formulated, the situation is transformed to one of risk. A card game involves risk; playing with strangers, uncertainty. Moving from uncertainty to risk is the structuring problem; it may be more important than computing and coping with risk once that has been defined. How to compute risk is the subject matter of the theory of probability; how to cope with it, the theory of games, and more generally, decision theory.

The calculation of probabilities rests on three different foundations; alternatively, three different conceptions of probability may be invoked. Mathematical probability is expressed as the ratio of "favorable" cases (those being calculated) to the total number of (equally likely) cases. Statistical probability is the (long-run) frequency of favorable cases in the sequence of observations. Personal probability is an expression of judgments of likelihood (or degree of confidence) made in accord with certain rules to guarantee consistency. For different problems different approaches are appropriate. Mendelian genetics or the study of kinship systems makes use of mathematical probability. Studies of traffic accidents or suicides call for statistical probabilities. Prediction of the outcome of a particular war or labor dispute is a matter of personal probability.

Statistics begin where assignment of probabilities leaves off. A multiplicity of data are given. The first task is that of statistical description: how to reduce the multiplicity to a managable unity with minimal distortion. This is usually done by giving some measure of the central tendency of the data, and specifying in one way or another the dispersion of the data around that central measure (like the mean and the standard deviation). Inferences drawn from the data are statable as statistical hypotheses, whose weight is estimated from the relation between the data and the population about which inferences are being made (sampling theory). Depending on the nature of the sample and of its dispersion, statistical tests assign a measure of the likelihood of the hypothesis in question. Explanatory statistics address themselves to the use of statistical descriptions and hypotheses in formulating explanations (for instance, by way of correlations).

9. Theories and Models

Once a problematic situation has been structured and the data measured and counted, a set of hypotheses may be formulated as possible solutions to the problem. Generalized, the hypotheses are said to constitute a theory. Alternatively, it is possible to begin with a set of hypotheses formulated in the abstract, then interpret them as applying to one or another problematic situation. Such a set is called a model.

Often the result of structuring the problematic situation is called a model. Structure is the essential feature of a model. In an interpretation of the model, a correspondence is specified between the elements of the model and those of some situation, and between certain relations holding within each set of elements, so that when two elements of the model are in a certain relation the corresponding elements stand in the corresponding relation, and vice versa. A set of elements related in certain ways is a system; a structure is what is shared by corresponding systems (or it may be identified with the set of all possible systems corresponding to a given one and thus to each other).

A model can be a physical system (like an airplane model in a wind tunnel), in which case it is an analog. An analog computer is a device which allows such systems to be easily constructed—systems consisting, for instance, of electrical networks with certain voltages, resistances, and current flow. Operations on the analog which preserve its structure show what would happen in any other system having the same structure. If the model is a system of symbols it may be called a map. Behavioral science models are maps of human systems.

When the correspondences are only suggested rather than being explicitly defined, the symbolic system is an extended metaphor; intermediate between a metaphor and a model is an analogy, in which correspondences are explicit but inexact. All three have roles in the actual conduct of inquiry; the view that only models have a place in science makes both terms honorific.

In another honorific usage "model" is a synonym for "theory" or even " hypothesis." The term is useful only when the symbolic system it refers to is significant as a structure—a system which allows for exact deductions and explicit correspondences. The value of a model lies in part in its abstractness, so that it can be given many interpretations, which thereby reveal unexpected similarities. The value lies also in the deductive fertility of the model, so that unexpected consequences can be predicted and then tested by observation and experiment. Here digital computers have already shown themselves to be important, and promise to become invaluable.

Two dangers in the use of models are to be noted. One is map reading, attaching significance to features of the model which do not belong to its structure but only to the particular symbolization of the structure (countries are not colored like their maps; psychoanalytic models do not describe hydrodynamic processes of a psychic fluid: "psychic energy" is not equal to mc^2).

The other danger is, not that something is read into the map which does not belong to the structure, but that something is omitted from the map which does. This error is called oversimplification. All models simplify, or they would not have the abstractness which makes them models. The model is oversimplified when it is not known by how much nor even in what direction to correct the outcomes of the model so that they apply to the situation modeled. In an economic model, ignoring differences in the worth of money to the rich and to the poor is likely to be an oversimplification; ignoring what exactly the money is spent on may not be.

Theories need not be models; they may present a significant content even though lacking an exactly specified structure—as was done by the theory of evolution, the germ theory of disease, and the psychoanalytic theory of the neuroses. A theory is a concatenation of hypotheses so bound up with one another that the proof or disproof of any of them affects that of all the others. The terms in which the hypotheses are couched are likely to have systemic meaning, specifiable only by reference to the entire theory. Knowledge may grow by extension—applying a theory to wider domains. It may also grow by intension—deepening the theory, specifying more exactly details previously only sketched in or even glossed over.

Theory is not usefully counterposed to practice; if it is sound, a theory is of practice, though the theoretical problems may be so simplified that the theory provides only an approximate solution to the problems of practice, and then only under certain conditions. A theory, it has been said, is a policy, not a creed. It does not purport to provide a picture of the world but only a map. It guides decisions on how best to deal with the world, including decisions on how to continue fruitful inquiry. It raises as many questions as it answers; the answers themselves are proposed directives for action rather than assertions for belief.

10. Explanation, Interpretation, and Validation

Validation of a theory is a matter, first, of coherence with knowledge already established. A new theory may raise difficulties of its own, but it must at least do justice to the facts the older theory accounted for. Validation means, second, a certain correspondence with the world as revealed in the continually growing body of data—it must successfully map its domain. Validation, finally, lies in the continued usefulness of the theory in practice, especially in the conduct of further inquiry.

A valid theory provides an explanation of the data, not merely a shorthand description of them. The latter, even if comprehensive, is only an empirical generalization; a theory gives grounds for expecting the generalization to be indefinitely extendable to data of the same kind. A dynamic tendency is quite different from a statistical trend. The theory may allow the prediction of data not yet observed, though it may be valid without successful prediction if this is precluded by the intervention of factors outside the theory, or by cumulation of the inexactness to be found in all theories when applied to empirical findings. Conversely, an empirical generalization may suggest successful predictions even though it is unable to say why the predictions should succeed.

Deductive explanation deduces predictions from the premises postulated by the theory (together with the initial conditions of the particular situation). This type of explanation is characteristic of models. Pattern explanation makes the data intelligible by fitting them into a meaningful whole (predictions might then be made of what would fit the gaps). This is characteristic of disciplines concerned with action meanings.

Behavioral interpretation is grasping such meanings, as distinguished from model interpretation, which is setting up correspondences that give content to an abstract structure. In behavioral interpretation actions are understood as purposive, goal directed. Goals need not be conscious, deliberate, intentional—in short, motivational; they may be purely functional, as are the telic mechanisms of cybernetic systems. Interpretation in the behavioral sciences often suffers from mistaking functions for motives, then introducing abstract agents to have the putative motives—neuroses are said to defend themselves, ruling classes to perpetuate a social order, economies to seek to expand.

All explanations, at best, leave something to be desired. They are partial, dealing with only a limited class of situations. They are conditional, depending on special circumstances in those situations. They are approximate—no explanation is wholly precise. They are indeterminate, having only a statistical validity —there are always apparent exceptions. They are inconclusive, never validated beyond any possibility of replacement or correction. They are intermediate, pointing always to something which needs to be explained in turn. They are limited, serving in each instance only some of the purposes for which explanations might be sought—a psychologist's explanation of a death (as, say, a suicide) is very different from a pathologist's explanation (as, say, a poisoning). Both explanations may be equally valid. All this openness of theory corresponds in the epistemic approximation to the openness of meaning in the semantic approximation.

11. Values and Bias

Inquiry itself is purposive behavior and so is subject to behavioral interpretation. The interpretation consists in part in specifying the values implicated in specific processes of conceptualization, observation, measurement, and theory construction. That values play a part in these processes does not in itself make the outcomes of these processes pejoratively subjective, nor otherwise invalidate them. A value which interferes with inquiry is a bias. Not all values are biases; on the contrary, inquiry is impossible without values.

A distinction between facts and values remains; the distinction is functional and contextual, not intrinsic to any given content. Descriptions may be used normatively. They are also shaped by norms which guide not only what is worth describing but also what form the description should take—for instance, the degree of precision which is worthwhile, the size of sample which is worth taking, the confidence level to be demanded, and the like. Values play a part not only in choosing problems but also in choosing patterns of inquiry into them. The behavioral sciences have rightly become concerned with the ethics of the profession, as bearing, for instance, on experimentation with human beings.

A myth of neutralism supposes that scientific status requires rigorous exclusion of values from the scientific enterprise. Even if this exclusion were desirable (a value!), it is impossible. The exclusion of bias, on the other hand, *is* an operative ideal. Bias is only hidden by the pretense of neutrality; it is effectively minimized only by making values explicit and subjecting them in turn to careful inquiry.

The danger that values become biases is especially great when values enter into the assessment of the results of inquiry as distinct from what is being inquired into and how. A truth may be unpleasant, even downright objectionable, yet remain true for all that. Science must be granted autonomy from the dictates of political, religious, and other extra scientific institutions. The content of the pursuit of truth is accountable to nothing and no one not a part of that pursuit.

All inquiries are carried out in specific contexts. Validation of the results of any particular inquiry by reference to the outcomes of other inquiries is important. How important varies with the distance between their respective subject matters, concepts, data, and other components of the process of inquiry. The behavioral sciences have become increasingly willing to affirm their autonomy with respect to the physical and biological sciences. Science suffers not only from the attempts of church, state, and society to control its findings but also from the repressiveness of the scientific establishment itself. In the end, each scientist must walk alone, not in defiance but with the independence demanded by intellectual integrity. That is what it means to have a scientific temper of mind.

See also: Empiricism, Positivism, and Antipositivism; Epistemological Issues in Educational Research; Participatory Research; Research Methodology: Human Development and Adult Learning

Bibliography

Bailey K D 1978 *Methods of Social Research*. Free Press, New York

Black J A, Champion D J 1976 *Methods and Issues in Social Research*. Wiley, New York

Braithwaite R B 1953 *Scientific Explanation: A Study of the Function of Theory Probability and Law in Science*. Cambridge University Press, Cambridge

Campbell N R 1928 *Measurement and Calculation*. Longman, New York

Durkheim E 1950 *The Rules of Sociological Method*, 8th edn. Free Press, New York

Ellingstad V S, Heimstra N W 1974 *Methods in the Study of Human Behavior*. Brooks Cole, Monterey, California

Gellner E 1973 *Cause and Meaning in the Social Sciences*. Routledge and Kegan Paul, London

Hanson N R 1972 *Observation and Explanation: A Guide to Philosophy of Science*. Harper and Row, New York

Hempel C G 1965 *Aspects of Scientific Explanation, and Other Essays in the Philosophy of Science*. Free Press, New York

Kaplan A 1964 *The Conduct of Inquiry: Methodology for Behavioral Science*. Chandler, New York

Kuhn T S 1970 *The Structure of Scientific Revolutions*. University of Chicago Press, Chicago, Illinois

Lachenmeyer C W 1973 *Essence of Social Research: A Copernican Revolution*. Free Press, New York

Myrdal G 1969 *Objectivity in Social Research*. Pantheon, Westminster, Maryland

Nachmias D, Nachmias C 1976 *Research Methods in the Social Sciences*. St. Martin's Press, New York

Nagel E 1961 *The Structure of Science: Problems in the Logic of Scientific Explanation*. Harcourt Brace, and World, New York

Neale J M, Liebert R M 1973 *Science and Behavior: An Introduction to Methods of Research*. Prentice-Hall, Englewood Cliffs, New Jersey

Popper K R 1959 *The Logic of Scientific Discovery*. Basic Books, New York

Popper K R, Eccles J C 1983 *The Self and its Brain*. Routledge and Kegan Paul, London

Quyine W V, Ullian J S 1978 *The Web of Belief*, 2nd edn. Random House, New York

Runkel P J, McGrath J E 1972 *Research on Human Behavior: A Systematic Guide to Method*. Holt, Rinehart and Winston, New York

Weber M 1949 *Methodology in the Social Sciences*. Free Press, New York

SECTION II

Policies and Costs and Finance

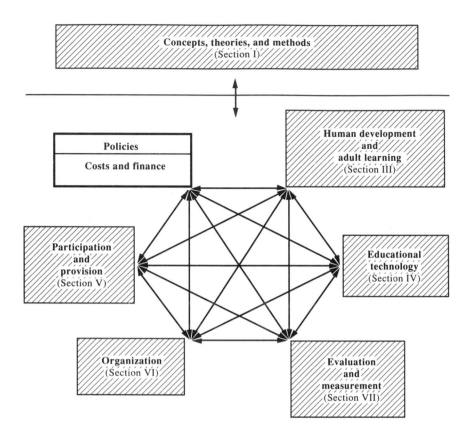

Figure 1
Schematic representation of Section II in relation to the other Sections

Policies and Costs and Finance

Introduction

A. C. Tuijnman

The 20 entries in Section II deal mostly with two broad themes: adult education policy, and costs and finance. The attentive reader will note that the distinction between these themes is sometimes blurred. Decisions about the financing of adult education and continuing vocational training obviously involve fundamental policy decisions, and sound policy decisions cannot be made without consideration of the costs and benefits to individuals, employers, and the society as a whole. It should therefore be noted that the issues of policy-making and finance are not dealt with exclusively in Section II. Many crucial policy issues are raised also in the other sections. The main reason for grouping the entries into two subsections, devoted to Adult Education Policies, and Costs and Finance, is that this approach highlights the different beliefs about what the purpose, goals, and agendas of adult education and training should be, as well as different assumptions about who should foot the bill for the financing of provision. Although the entries have certain denominators in common—for example, policy development, and costs and finance—they address different issues in the organization and implementation of adult education and continuing vocational training, extending from ideas about literacy campaigns, nonformal education, and adult education for development organized by social movements and nongovernmental organizations, to questions about the possible roles of public authorities vis-à-vis the other stakeholders in adult education and training, such as employers and labor unions, to views most appropriately described in terms of free markets for adult learning and competence development.

1. Adult Education Policy

Adult education for development is among the dearest themes in the field. One of the challenging aspects is the multidisciplinary and international orientation of the studies conducted in this area, which generally require that close attention be paid to the interplay of economic, social, cultural, and political factors in promoting development. Another interesting feature of those studies is that they tend to emphasize the linkages between theory, policy, and practice. The first entry by Torres offers an excellent introduction to these issues. The important concepts and theories of national development are summarized and classified into two major but ideologically opposed camps, labeled "clinical models" and "adult education as cultural politics." In an extension of the previous entries by Cunningham, Evans, and Westwood, the challenges faced by social movements receive particular attention.

Adult literacy undoubtedly plays an important role in the economic, social, and democratic development of nations in all parts of the world. Widespread illiteracy is therefore considered as a major impediment to balanced and sustained development. The fight against illiteracy in the Third World is the subject of the second entry, written by Lind and Johnston. The thesis advanced in this entry is that literacy is a human right and a prerequisite not only for economic growth but especially for the promotion of equality, social justice, and democracy. This theme is taken further by La Belle and Ward, who describe the role of nonformal education in national development. A main issue concerns the extent to which the poor should be involved in determining the orientation of nonformal education programs. La Belle and Ward note that the interest in nonformal education has declined since the 1970s, possibly because most consciousness-raising efforts promoted through nonformal and popular education have not achieved the desired economic and social-change objectives. This may offer an explanation for the emergence of a competing perspective in adult education policy, which is associated with the notion of free markets for adult learning and competence development.

The dogma of free markets for learning has been given close attention by policymakers in many countries, especially since the mid-1980s. The main reasons are, first, that markets are believed to facilitate the efficient organization of educational production, and second, that policymakers have generally sought to control the burgeoning costs of educational provision. Despite the common rhetoric about the importance of adult education and training in strategies for promoting growth and development, public authorities have generally been unwilling to increase expenditures on adult education and training, although, in some countries, there has been a modest increase in spending on certain programs earmarked for special audiences. Rather than considering the supply of adult education and training as a major area of public responsibility, which is regarded as an expensive option, many countries have instead relied on the initiatives of nongovernmental and voluntary associations, employers, and especially on the individual adult learner.

There has been a longstanding debate about the proper place of initial vocational education and continuing vocational training in the field labeled "adult education." Many writers distinguish between the "general" or "liberal" education of adults, on the one hand, and "education for investment," on the other. Liberal education and literacy training have long been seen as constituting the heart of adult education. In contrast, continuing vocational training and informal learning in the workplace have only relatively recently found their place in the field of adult education. UNESCO's definition of adult education, which is quoted in the *Introduction to Section I*, does not mark vocational education and training as being separate from adult education. Organization is a key element in UNESCO's definition. In order to classify as adult education the learning activity needs to involve adults or out-of-school youths, and be planned or structured in some way. This definition increasingly offers a rationale for reassessing the area of practice defined as adult education. As was noted by de Moura Castro and de Oliveira in Section I, the result of this reassessment has been that the boundaries between, first, adult education and the formal education system and, second, between adult education and continuing vocational training, are dissolving.

In the same way as an age-bound delineation of the term "adult education" is frought with pitfalls, an artificial division between adult education and training is also unworkable, if not in theory then at least in practice. Some writers are highly critical of this position, however, and they will no doubt continue to resist the merging of the two areas into a new framework for lifelong learning. One of the reasons cited for this position is fear that the emphasis on training will result in diminished autonomy for the "traditional" institutions of adult education. A second reason is that it is feared that the emancipatory function of adult education is in jeopardy as a consequence of the increased emphasis of policymakers on accountability and cost-effectiveness. These doubts notwithstanding, in many countries a new reality has emerged in public policy for adult education. More attention is being paid to the economic and labor market functions of adult education, and less to its social and cultural functions. The roles of the central government and, more generally, of public institutions, in the funding and provision of both initial schooling and adult education and training are discussed in the entry by Ziderman. A major conclusion is that the effective role for governments varies between countries and within countries over time. Hence it is recommended that governments should adopt a flexible role, reflecting the changing education and training needs of countries, which in turn will differ according to their level of economic, social, and institutional development. Ziderman's entry on the role of the public authorities in finance and the organization of provision is followed by a discussion of the role of legislation in adult education. Lowe traces the historical context before reviewing the legislation about adult education and training that has been adopted by the national or regional governments of countries in different parts of the world.

The alignment of "liberal" and "vocational" adult education can be seen not only in the patterns of public funding; clear messages also come from the private sector. This observation is advanced in several entries, notably those by Stacey and Le-To, Stern, and Bishop. The increased stake of the employment sector in adult education, which, as Carnoy notes, coincides with a concern about the consequences of technological change and a new appreciation of the role of technology in economic growth, has triggered several theoretical and practical developments in adult education. For example, more attention is now being paid to the cognitive aspects of adult learning. Accreditation has also come to the foreground, a point noted by Colardyn in her entry concerning the recognition and certification of competence. The view that continuing vocational training forms part of the delivery system for adult education, as is the case with occupational training for the long-term unemployed, is generally accepted in France, the Netherlands, the Nordic countries, and parts of North America; however, in Germany, Japan, the United Kingdom, and many countries in Latin America, the "territorial struggle" continues, albeit less vehemently than before, possibly because the case against an inclusive perspective on adult education has been undercut by recent developments in policy and practice.

The notion of the adult education market can be used to summarize the main tenets of a new approach to policy. The belief that there was overinvestment in formal education, particularly at the university level, which was popular during the mid-1970s, gave way in the 1980s to a concern with the consequences of perceived underinvestment in adult education and especially in continuing vocational training. In a policy climate in which public budgets were generally constrained to zero growth, and in which there was widespread faith in the capacity of markets to adjust to structural change and find efficient solutions, some of the ideas about how a recurrent education system could be financed and organized, which had been proposed during the late 1960s and early 1970s, and that had relied heavily on public intervention, were replaced by a theory of the adult education market. As mentioned above, the dogma of the market sets forth quite different principles for the financing and organization of adult education. However, because there is a realization that markets are inherently imperfect, that misallocations occur, and that the people who are less competitive or even absent from those markets are underserved, the governments of most countries have not altogether abandoned the idea that public intervention on behalf of certain groups is a necessity of policy. This case is argued by several authors, for example, Stern, and Bishop, who deal with the issues of market failure and overeducation.

The two entries that conclude this subsection both deal with the time dimension in the provision of adult education and training. Lowe examines the relationship between adult education and leisure, and their connections with paid work. A major issue concerns the amount of leisure and time for learning that is actually available to adult learners. Lowe concludes that despite the developments that in the wealthy countries appear to have led to an increase in the amount of time off from work, the time adults actually can spend on their own learning projects has not increased as much as is generally believed. Abrahamsson deals with time policies for lifelong learning. The entry positions adult education policy in a broader array of public policies regulating working time, retirement conditions, and leave of absence from work for holidays, sickness, childcare, and education in a truly lifelong perspective. Policies for the promotion of lifelong learning are seen as a crucial challenge for the advanced industrialized societies. But even in the rich countries such policies will have major cost implications, and hence will require that answers are sought to the question of how lifelong learning can be financed. This is the subject addressed by the entries in the second subsection of Section II.

2. Costs and Finance

The first entry, *Demand, Supply, and Finance of Adult Education*, introduces the main issues addressed in this subsection. Wurzburg first considers the forces behind the qualitative and quantitive changes in the demand for and supply of adult education and training. Insofar as the entry deals with demand and supply relationships in adult education, it serves also as a general introduction to a cluster of entries grouped in Section V. As Stacey and Le-To, Stern, and Bishop did before him, Wurzburg also investigates the notion of markets for competence development, especially in relation to the need for flexibility in the allocation of labor and in the operation of social insurance systems. Wurzburg

seems to consider such markets useful, mainly because they are efficient in allocating scarce resources and distributing the benefits.

The grand schemes of lifelong education and recurrent education, which were advocated during the late 1960s and early 1970s, were not implemented, mainly because insufficient thought was devoted to the problem of how expanded provision could be financed. Yet this failure has apparently not discouraged a host of politicians and national and international agencies from promoting lifelong learning as a panacea for solving all kinds of social and economic problems. On the contrary. The concept of lifelong learning was more popular in the mid-1990s than ever before. This situation begs the question whether the lifelong learning society is destined to remain utopia, or whether it can actually be made to happen. Lifelong learning may well remain a dream, unless societies can mobilize sufficient political and economic resources to bring about radical changes in many areas of policy. Because it seems unlikely that this will happen anytime soon, a step-by-step approach to the development of the lifelong learning society might offer a workable alternative to radical reform. Such a strategy would not focus on adult education policies per se, because it is difficult to bring about pervading change from within the system. Instead, the two areas on which to focus would be economic policy and social insurance policy, because lifelong learning must be financed in novel ways, and also because adequate learning opportunities cannot be created unless adult learning is covered by a comprehensive social insurance system. The eight entries grouped in this subsection do not offer all the answers; all they can do is paint in broad strokes a picture of the complex issues associated with the financing of adult education and training in a lifelong perspective.

The costs of adult education and training are related to questions about the scope, amount, and profitability of the investment, the cost-effectiveness and financial feasibility of alternative programs, and the planning and administration of provision. These issues are dealt with by Mun Tsang, who also examines ways of calculating the costs of adult education and training provision. Although Tsang uses examples drawn mainly from the experience of the industrialized countries, the issues are clearly relevant also for the developing countries. Tilak, in an entry on the measurement of training costs that is included in Section VII, elaborates on the implications for costing and accounting. In the concluding part of his entry, Tsang addresses the crucial question as to how the substantial costs of adult education and continuing vocational training can be financed. This question is taken up also by Timmermann, who first discusses a number of criteria for evaluating different financing policies. Timmermann then discusses six financing models that have been proposed in the literature. Additional perspectives are offered in the entries that follow. Schütze looks at one approach in particular, namely the model involving paid educational leave and collective bargaining. Schütze defines the concepts and describes the main developments in collective bargaining since the mid-1970s. In the next entry, Hirsch offers an overview of developments in another area relevant to the financing of adult education and training, namely that of public–private partnerships. Payroll levies for the financing of educational leave are discussed by Ziderman, who makes a distinction between revenue-raising schemes and the more recent approach that involves a combination of levies and grants.

Wilms and Hardcastle's entry on performance contracting in adult education and training does not deal with costs or finance per se, but since performance contracting is proposed as a strategy for increasing the efficiency and effectiveness of adult learning, while reducing the costs to employers and individuals, it does fit in with the overall themes addressed in this cluster of entries. Wilms and Hardcastle examine what is currently known about performance contracting in adult education and training. The authors then present conclusions about the feasibility of this approach in mainly the industrialized countries. A highly contrasting perspective is given in the next and last entry of this subsection. Biervliet deals with the policy and practices of training with production, with a clear focus on the developing countries. The notion of training with production refers to the general principle of combining adult learning with the production of goods or services that have an economic market value. The entry reviews issues and practices of training with production in different economic systems and in different regions of the world.

(a)   Adult Education Policy

Adult Education for Development

C. A. Torres

This entry discusses adult education for development. While a range of relevant research studies are reviewed, no specific reference is made to integrated rural development implementation strategies, nor is a systematic assessment of community education offered. The first part introduces the reader to adult education concepts, purposes, and principles. The following two parts discuss adult education and theories of national development, economic growth and modernization theories, as well as theories of adult education for development, mobilization, participation, and empowerment with a particular focus on popular education models. In the conclusion, the mainstream models of adult education labeled as "clinical models" are discussed and confronted with an alternative model of "adult education as cultural politics." In this conclusion, the challenges of social movements to adult education for development are noted.

1. Concepts and Principles

"Adult education" and "nonformal education" are sometimes used as interchangeable terms. Nonformal education is defined as "any organized, systematic educational activity carried out outside the framework of the formal system to provide selected types of learning to particular subgroups of the population" (La Belle 1986 p. 2). Concepts, purposes, and principles of adult education are related to adult education origins, functions, and the interaction between specific fields of practices and theoretical discourses which constitute adult education as an educational interdisciplinary hybrid.

Competing discourses clash over the definition of adult education itself. In historical terms, modern adult education relates to the postwar consensus trying to create a more educated and enlightened citizenship, avoiding the pitfalls in the socialization of citizens and the nurturing of a political culture which led to fascism and totalitarianism in Europe. As a result, mainstream programs of adult education share basic principles with liberalism, and contribute to social welfare

politics. However, particularly in Latin America and Africa, adult education's origins also relate to the evangelical zeal of missionaries trying to convert native Latin Americans and Africans to Christianity. In the nineteenth and twentieth centuries, there were also clear expressions of adult education for national development linked to community activism and resistance to capitalist social relations.

At the most abstract level, a number of functions of adult education can be identified. Critical perspectives argue that a principal function of adult education is the maintenance of the social system and reproduction of existing social relations. According to this perspective, the manifest and latent functions of adult education tend to increase the socialization of individuals to adapt to the world of work in a knowledge-based society with growing diversification and specialization. A second approach emphasizes that adult education has a conservative function, contributing to the transmission of knowledge and the reproduction of culture. However, the culture that is transmitted and reproduced is the dominant culture, the canon of cultural literacy rather than the competing expressions or literacies of a society segmented by race, class, gender, religion, and diverse cultural narratives. In adult education, can one justifyably define what knowledge is worthwhile without asking who determines what is valid, worthwhile, relevant, pertinent, and needed knowledge?

Technocratic perspectives consider adult education to be part of a social mechanism to guarantee individual advancement and selection. Adult education thus becomes a vehicle toward upward mobility of the labor force—through contest mobility rather than sponsored mobility—and plays an important role in the moral and technical socialization of people. One of the most prominent early advocates of nonformal education as a key for national development is Philips Coombs. In his widely read contribution, Coombs (1968) indicates a number of educational problems that plague education at the international level, including the increasing demand for education, rapidly rising educational costs, inefficient management and teaching methods, the unsuitability of the output, and the scarcity of resources available for educational expansion. As solutions, Coombs suggests the introduction of capital intensive technologies, improved teacher training, increased foreign aid, and the promotion of rapid expansion of education through nonformal education.

Coombs's contribution reflects the optimism of the time and the faith that education will decisively contribute to development. It also reflects a certain mode of analysis, according to which persons and educational systems are held accountable for school failure, rather than the broader social structures. Thus, problems such as social inequality and regressive patterns of income distribution are a consequence of individual psychological deficit rather than inequalities in power, wealth, and influence. Coombs should be credited, however, with being one of the most articulate scholars distinguishing schooling and nonformal education as two sharply distinct teaching and learning systems (see *Formal, Nonformal, and Informal Education*).

Considering the sweeping changes brought about in industrial societies by new technologies and the reorganization of the division of labor with a growing service sector, many argue that a fundamental role of adult education relates to the pursuit of leisure time activities and institutional expansion. With more advanced technologies, there is more free time for individuals, particularly the middle classes which take advantage of this increase in free time, enrolling in adult education programs in the pursuit of aesthetic or artistic knowledge (i.e., courses in painting and art appreciation, and floral arrangements) or practical activities (e.g., courses in specialized cuisine, wine appreciation, carpentry, etc.). Hence, a growing relationship between adult education programs and gerontology has resulted from the increasing number of senior citizens who are free from the demands of work and seek fulfillment in continuing education programs.

Criticisms of the overly psychologized mode of analyses are well reflected in the political economy of adult education (Bock and Papagiannis 1983, Carnoy and Samoff 1990, Torres 1990, 1991). These authors emphasized the centrality of power and knowledge as a social construct, and therefore the basic questions they asked are not how nonformal education could contribute to social change but rather: (a) Who benefits from investing in nonformal education? (b) What is the nature of the complex relationship between schooling and nonformal education? (c) How does each differentially serve those social functions that education has always served—socialization, mobility management, and transmission of cognitive and noncognitive skills? (d) How do adult education and schooling systems differ in their patterns of recruitment, in their internal structural characteristics, and in their relationship to the occupational structure and the world of work?

In studies exploring the relationships between adult education and social change, it is argued that adult education plays a fundamental role in compensatory legitimation. More often than not, adult education systems constitute a second chance to improve academic performance and credentials, particularly with many adult education courses oriented to women entering the labor force after establishing a family, with the purposes of upgrading their skills, knowledge, and abilities. Viewed as compensatory legitimation, the uses of adult education in the production of a hegemonic culture legitimates inequalities (Torres 1990 pp. 171–74).

Finally, many practitioners and scholars argue that adult and continuing education for development should be understood as liberating education (Youngman 1986, Torres 1990, Freire and Macedo 1987, La Belle 1986). For liberation pedagogues, learning is related to critical understanding, contributing to the maturity and self-realization of individuals and communities. Liberation appears as an individual as well as a social goal. Adult education therefore constitutes an essential part in the practice of social transformation, and is not reduced to critical reflection or critical teaching.

Antecedents of adult education as community resistance or revival or social movements can also be found in Europe, Canada, and the United States. In this mode adult education refers to the strengthening of workers' education, community education, and nonformal education which is not to be controlled, legislated, regulated, or financed by the state, but by individual citizens, community members, and students. North American examples are the Antigonish Movement in the Canadian Maritime Eastern Provinces, and the Highlander Institute in the Appalachians. Similar examples can be traced back to workers' education in Argentina, Brazil, and Mexico, or to anarcosyndicalism propaganda and journalism oriented to enlighten workers and serving as a tool for mobilization and organization (Welton 1987, Horton and Freire 1990).

In spite of the richness and diversity of these and many other experiences, the most articulate expression of theories of adult education for national development relates to theories of economic growth, modernization, and human capital.

2. Adult Education and Theories of National Development: Economic Growth and Modernization Theories

Human Capital Theory works in the framework of a theory of modernization. The modernization approach considers education as a variable intimately linked to the processes of socioeconomic development. Development, in its turn, is conceived as growth of the social product, following the model of advanced Western societies. The underdevelopment of the Third World is explained in terms of individual personality traits. Individuals in industrial advanced capitalism cultivate the attitude of achievement, an universalistic perspective, and a specialized and functional division of labor, while traditional individuals in underdeveloped societies struggle helplessly with an orientation toward ascribed statuses, a particularistic perspective on the world, and a nonspecialized division of labor.

The human capital approach thus points to the necessity of identifying the mechanisms through which the passage from economic backwardness to economic development can be realized in different contexts. Literacy and basic education count among the privileged mechanisms for increasing contacts with modern societies (and their products), disorganizing traditional cultures (often of oral origin) which are considered an element of backwardness, and facilitating the development of social heterogeneity in the adoption of innovations.

Mark Blaug and others have noted that literacy and the basic education of adults in general contribute to economic development in diverse forms by: (a) increasing the productivity of the newly literate; (b) increasing the productivity of those who work with the newly literate; (c) expanding the diffusion of the general knowledge of individuals (training in health and infant nutrition) and generally reducing the cost of transmitting practical information; (d) stimulating the demand for technical training and vocational education; (e) acting as an instrument for selection of the most valuable elements of the population and enhancing their occupational mobility; and (f) strengthening economic incentives (i.e., the tendency of people to respond positively to an increment of compensation for their efforts) (Blaug 1966). In these terms, literacy is seen as one of the most important elements in the process of modernization and the development of nations undergoing industrialization.

Diverse investigations have indicated there is a significant correlation between the percentage of illiterates and income per capita (0.84), as well as between illiteracy and industrialization (0.87). Further, the coefficient of multiple correlation for 54 countries between literacy, urbanization, recognition of the value of information, and political participation was 0.91. Psacharopoulos (1988) argues that:

> ... economists have established the link between increases in the educational level of the labor force and economic growth. Similarly, they have documented a direct link between increases in the level of schooling in the population and distributional equity. Sociologists have established the relationship between education and upward social mobility. Historians have documented the link between early rises in literacy and the economic take-off of nations. And a variety of other disciplines have established the relationship between education and further developmental outcomes like health, sanitation and fertility. (p. 1)

Along these lines regarding basic education, Marin and Psacharopoulos (1976) argue that giving primary education in Mexico to 10 percent of those who

lack it, would reduce a measure of income inequality by 10 percent. Regarding the contributions of adult education to political development, Huntington (1968) claims that one of the most relevant aspects in the process of political modernization is the change in attitudes, values, and expectations—changes that are a direct consequence of literacy, education, increases in communications, the exposure to mass media, and urbanization.

In summary, the range of aims and goals of adult education for development as seen by human capital theorists vary from developing positive attitudes toward cooperation, work, community and national development, and further learning to the teaching of functional literacy and numeracy; from providing a scientific outlook toward health, agriculture, and the like to incorporating functional knowledge and skills; from preparing individuals to enter into the labor market or strengthening their current occupational position to making available functional knowledge and skills necessary for civic participation. These assumptions are overtly present in the documents of the Inter-Agency Commission, particularly in the background document of the important conference on Education for All held in Thailand in 1990 (IDRC 1991, UNESCO 1991, 1992a, 1992b).

There are many criticisms of human capital theory and its application to adult education. The contribution of basic education to growth may well be smaller than the early human capital theorists and development economists anticipated. The correlation between earnings and education picks up many other influences on earnings that are also correlated with schooling and training, but should not be attributed to them. Available evidence suggests that the wage structure to an extent depends upon variables exogenous to individual productivity. These variables include gender, race, the nature of a firm's market of goods, maintenance of class structure in the face of meritocratic rules, degree of monopoly power in the market, and/or social class background (Carnoy et al. 1979). Thus, differential rates of return to education are not primarily the result of inequality in the distribution of schooling, but refer instead to the basic unequal structures of capitalist societies. In addition, the role of the state in education and income policy is a crucial variable in determining income distribution. In this sense, taxation, wage fixing, price control, inflation, and employment policies are the means by which the state exercises this power —policies that are out of reach of adult education programs (Torres 1990).

A decisive standpoint from which to study the relationships between adult education, income distribution, and capital accumulation is the theory of labor market segmentation. According to this theory, labor market conditions can be understood as outcomes of four segmentation processes: (a) segmentation into primary and secondary markets, (b) segmentation within the primary sector, (c) segmentation by race, and (d) segmentation by gender. The primary and secondary segments are differentiated as follows:

> Primary jobs require and develop stable working habits; skills are often acquired on the job; wages are relatively high; and job ladders exist. Secondary jobs do not require and often discourage stable working habits; wages are low; turnover is high; and job ladders are few. Secondary jobs are mainly (though not exclusively) filled by minority workers, women and youth. (Reich et al. 1975 p. 1)

Although the theory of segmented labor markets has a particular relevance to advanced industrial societies, it does help to understand that (adult) basic education in developing societies simply prepares people for improving their chances to enter the secondary labor markets. The notion of labor market segmentation duly cautions against assuming that education and training lead automatically to higher income distribution through increasing per capita productivity which leads, in turn, to higher earnings. Adult education does not train manual labor for all labor markets, but instead is oriented, in reality, toward the secondary work market, where the job stability is less, income low and fragmented, social benefits scarce or nonexistent, and the supply of barely qualified labor abundant. In this context, adult education could simply be preparing manual labor that will continue to function within capitalist modes of production, or it simply prepares people to assume a level of economic life marginalized from the mainstream economic lifeworld.

A major drawback of adult education programs underscored by human capital and modernization theories is that, by placing a strong emphasis on formal markets, they have virtually neglected informal labor markets, thus ignoring the actual and potential contribution of adult education planned in such markets. Hence, a discussion of informal labor markets is very relevant to adult education for development (see *Economics of Adult Education and Training; Market Concepts in Provision*).

3. Informal Labor Markets and Adult Education

Informal labor markets refer to the informal economic activities undertaken by poor workers which not only generate income, but also promote efficient economic growth. Some of the characteristics of this specific labor force and market are: its units function with low capital investments and operating capital per worker; the workforce does not require high training levels, nor formal educational inputs; and their technical demands are minimal because their technology is simple or artisanal and the tools they use are either self-made or second-hand and obsolete (Sáenz 1989).

The existence of informal (urban) sectors poses a variety of complications for governments. These economies and labor sectors are difficult to tax, regulate, assess, or measure statistically. Indeed, even in Western European societies, informal labor (considered to be "social labor") can be characterized by "freedom of entry and exit, by considerable autonomy in the programming of activity as well as by non-discriminatory and legally guaranteed rights to income" (Offe 1985 p. 79).

In synthesis, the theoretical rationale of the human capital approach has been challenged by a political economy of adult education. From this perspective a number of questions emerge: Does adult education and literacy contribute to increase output or does it allocate people to jobs with higher training requirements, productivity, and earning potential? Does adult education legitimize an unequal social structure and thereby contribute to higher output and acceptance of unequal work roles? Or, instead, does adult education reduce output through legitimizing a profit-making pattern of capital accumulation that is less than optimal for a particular society? Critical approaches will consider the role of adult education for development using analytical approaches which depart from classical human capital and modernization perspectives.

With very few exceptions, the success of adult education as rural education or education to broaden productive capacities and the distribution of goods and services in rural communities have been quite limited. At a more general and empirical level, the perception of the economic benefits of literacy and adult basic education in developing countries does not seem to be widely documented by empirical studies, with very few exceptions—Tanzania could be one of them. There do not seem to be studies that reflect these economic advantages of the investment in adult education (Bhola 1984).

Another critical objection to human capital theory is the perspective of the diploma disease (Oxenham 1984), that is, the inflation of educational credentials such that employers are constantly creating newer and greater criteria of selection where employability is defined by educational characteristics. But even if after finishing primary school individuals were given the possibility of reaching better functional positions in an organization where they were already employed, or permitted to satisfy admission requirements to some occupation, there is no guarantee that in the immediate future that credential would not lose value as the education threshold of occupations rose (see *Overeducation*).

This is a substantive problem confronting all postsecondary education programs, aggravated in the case of adult education for two reasons. First, because adult education often deals with the lowest levels of educational and occupational strata, and their educational credentials have low market value. Second, because at times adult education does not function in agreement with the criteria of supplying individuals with basic education credentials, but instead postulates the acquisition of skills and specific knowledge where credentials are not relevant.

Training of the labor force is a complex process. On occasion, once finished with their training and having achieved higher levels of technical ability, the workers remain outside the market of goods and services for which they were supposedly prepared in the first place. This occurs when the cost of employing a highly trained workforce exceeds the level of demand in relation to value and cost within the system (La Belle 1986). At times, the educational supply of highly trained manual labor greatly exceeds its demand in a market that does not create work positions with the same speed, intensity, and diversity as the supply of education.

In conclusion, the economic advantages of adult education are at the very least debatable. The disparities between the mechanisms of employment and the qualification levels that adult education provide would seem to be growing. The issue is not only whether Human Capital Theory works or not in the context of developing countries—though there is enough evidence that it does not work as efficiently and smoothly as some of its proponents may suggest (La Belle 1986). The question is why adopt a single rationale or theory when many other theories or rationales for policy planning may also prove successful for development, mobilization, participation, and empowerment of individuals, families, and communities through adult education.

4. Adult Education for Development: Mobilization, Participation, and Empowerment

Arnove and Graff (1987) report that there are clearly neglected populations regarding literacy training in industrialized societies. Looking at several campaigns in a historical and comparative perspective, they have concluded that rural populations, the working class, ethnic and racial minorities, and women have been the last to receive literacy instruction and to gain access to advanced levels of schooling. Among all these groups, women have been the most disadvantaged group. Thomas (1983) pointed to the existence of large numbers of undereducated Canadians whose low levels of literacy might place serious limitations on their participating fully in the rights, responsibilities, and privileges of citizenship. Indeed, illiteracy becomes a political as well as a cultural problem in multiethnic and multicultural societies such as Canada, where special consideration needs to be given to indigenous populations (Indians and Inuit) and immigrant populations for whom English or French are not first languages (Thomas 1983 p. 13). Consequently, the provision of ESL (English as a Second Language) literacy in large reception centers is a matter of concern for specialists (Thomas 1983 p. 101).

Stromquist (1991) explores the manner in which women are either neglected or manipulated for nondemocratic ends in many national programs of adult education and literacy training. Stromquist attributes this situation to technical problems in the design and implementation of literacy training campaigns and adult education programs, and to patriarchal structures, well-reflected in a patriarchal state which regulates, controls, and manipulates the life of women in the Third World and industrialized societies.

Adult education may serve as a springboard for social organization, organized resistance, and the development of social movements. Zachariah (1987) has demonstrated how, drawing from the contributions of Gandhi and Freire, adult education becomes an important component of the Sarvodaya and Conscientization movements, both in India and Latin America, and how adult education plays a prominent role in the Popular Science Movement in India, particularly in the province of Kerala, India, and in Sri Lanka (Zachariah 1987). Adult education as workers' education is prominent in the many attempts to construct adult education for socialism in experiences as diverse as those in northwest China, Portugal, and Kenya (Youngman 1986), and in the consolidation of the most intriguing and successful example of workers and cooperative education in the experiences of the Mondragon Cooperatives in the Basque region of Spain.

4.1 Cultural Imperialism and Dependency Theories

Canadian adult educator Welton (1987) suggests that:

> Adult learning is more central to societal reproduction, resistance and transformation than that of the children. Resistance to and transformation of societal structures emerges from the adult population, and is premised upon men and women's ability to learn new ways of seeing the world and acting within it (p. 7).

Thus, adult education may contribute to social reproduction, resistance, and transformation in many ways. Carnoy (1974) has used theories of dependency to study the role of education in development. Emphasizing the structural asymmetry of power between nations and social classes, Carnoy has challenged the perceptions about the inherent good of educational investment in the Third World, linking education with power and the construction of knowledge. Carnoy and Samoff (1990) offer concrete cases of using education for social transformation, particularly nonformal education, in China, Mozambique, Tanzania, Cuba, and Nicaragua.

Revolutionary societies or societies in the process of social transition trying to change the basic principles of social reproduction of national capitalist societies have used nonformal education, and particularly literacy training (Arnove and Graff 1987, Torres 1991) as a means of social mobilization, trying at the same time to unleash social creativity, mass participation, and critical consciousness. However, planning and implementation of adult education programs require resources which are usually unavailable to governments in many developing countries. Thus, external aid and the contribution of nongovernmental organizations (NGOs) is paramount to adult education for development (see *Nongovernmental Organisations*).

4.2 Development Aid in Adult Education

Donor and lending agencies have mobilized resources for adult and basic education for many years. In fact, some adult education policies and programs of adult education could not have been implemented without the substantial and steady flow of external assistance from international, multinational, and bilateral agencies. The role of UNESCO in advocating and supporting literacy training worldwide is widely acknowledged (see *UNESCO and Adult Education*).

However, official international assistance seems to be diminishing quite rapidly (Morales-Gómez and Torres 1992) because the focus is shifting toward the problems of poverty, homelessness, and unemployment that many of the industrial countries face. In addition, there are changing priorities for international assistance brought about by the end of the Cold War, the demise of communism, and the realignment of hegemonic countries in the world. Even private, nongovernment organizations may be retracting their budgets and programs overseas, as a reflection of the changing priorities of international philanthropy and foreign aid policies.

There are reasons to believe that external assistance to adult education policies and programs in the last decade of the twentieth century will be less relevant for the development of the programs. Its demise as an effective player in the context of growing poverty and reduced state intervention in the Third World may result in smaller budgets for adult education, and consequently in the disenfranchisement of particular clientele from programs and policies, especially the poorest of the poor in developing countries. This trend toward deinvestment on the part of the state as well as that of bilateral and multilateral donor and lending agencies in adult education may have serious consequences in the long run. For instance, official development assistance from OECD countries does not exceed 0.36 percent of their combined gross national product (GNP), and the United States (the largest donor country in the world) contributes only 0.2 percent of its GNP. Bilateral aid in education dropped from 16.5 percent in 1979 to 10.7 percent in 1989 (Morales-Gómez and Torres in 1992).

Although it is difficult to estimate how much of that aid goes to adult education for development, it is conceivable that the policy preference of many international agencies toward mainly funding primary schooling, capacity building, and system management may hurt the chances of literacy, adult education, and training programs to receive sufficient funding. The option for adult education for development may rest on a multiplicity of initiatives undertaken by NGOs and community organizations, drawing from diverse epistemological, political, and socioeconomic perspectives. Many such initiatives are usually labeled as "popular education" (see *Popular Education and Conscientization*).

5. Conscientization and Popular Education

For popular educators, adult education is a field crossed by many ideologies, theories, and discursive narratives, and it has been placed (or thought of) at the service of diverse political and pedagogical projects for national development. Popular education is an educational paradigm critical of mainstream nonformal education, seeking to empower the marginalized and poor people (La Belle 1986, Gadotti 1990, Torres 1990, 1991). This perspective sees knowledge as a social construct and a process, and not merely as a product. Freire and many practitioners of popular education propose a nonauthoritarian but directivist pedagogy for liberation. The teacher is at the same time a student; the student is at the same time a teacher. The nature of their knowledge may differ, however, but as long as education is the act of knowing and not merely transmitting facts, students and teachers share a similar status and are linked together through a pedagogical dialogue characterized by horizontal relationships. The educational agenda will not necessarily be carried out in a classroom but in a "culture circle." Emphasis is placed on *sharing* and *reflecting* critically upon learner's experience and knowledge, both as a source or rough material for analyzing the "existential themes" of critical pedagogy, and as an attempt to demystify existing forms of false consciousness.

A main characteristic of liberation pedagogues has been their resistance to be organically linked to the apparatus of the capitalist state until a political regime exists which is sympathetic to the interests and demands of the popular sectors. Important differences exist between radical pedagogues and bureaucrats, decision-makers, and teachers located within these rather large educational bureaucratic structures, pursuing knowledge-guiding interests circumscribed by instrumental rationality (Mezirow 1985).

More than 20 years of implementation show that popular education will seek to design nonformal- and NGO-sponsored educational ventures rather than working within schools and other state-sponsored institutions. It is only since the mid-1980s that the intervention in school settings, with the notion of "public popular schooling" has been advanced by Freirean pedagogues (Gadotti 1990) in the context of Brazilian debates of school autonomy. Not surprisingly, many of the representatives of this pedagogy have worked, politically and professionally, within political parties, universities, and research centers as well as with organizations which have originated in or are linked to churches.

Some of the common features of popular education projects are summarized as follows:

First, they arise from a political and social analysis of the living conditions of the poor and their outstanding problems (such as unemployment, malnourishment, poor health) and attempt to engage the poor in individual and collective awareness of those conditions. Second, they base their educational practice on collective and individual previous experiences (as previous knowledge), and they work in groups rather than on an individual basis. Third, the notion of education provided by these projects is related to the concrete skills or abilities that they try to instill in the poor . . . and these projects strive to arouse self-reliance among the participants. Finally, these projects can be originated by governments, as in Colombia and Dominician Republic or, as in Nicaragua, with the collectives of popular education, and they may be directed toward adults as well as children. (Torres 1990 pp. 9–10)

Popular education projects are not restricted to Latin America. Projects such as the 150 hours of paid educational leave designed by the Italian workers around 1971–73; the struggle of the feminist movement in Geneva (Switzerland) in the early 1970s; the experience of education practice of the PAIGC (African Party for the Independence of Guinea and Cape Verde) liberation movement in Guinea-Bissau between 1973 and 1976 (Freire et al. 1980); or the *Kerala Sastra Sahitya Parishat* (Kerala Science Literature Society) are all considered experiences of popular education (Zachariah 1987).

There are epistemological, philosophical, and methodological problems associated with the notion of popular education (La Belle 1986, Torres 1990). In spite of these problems, popular education has helped to define, in its sharpest terms, one of the main roles attributed to adult education for development: how adult education can evolve into a form of cultural politics in the constitution of the citizenship. In this aspect, popular education models are in sharp contrast with mainstream adult education models.

6. Conclusion: Challenges for Development

The key features of mainstream adult education models are their liberal–pluralist ideological foundations, their technocratic rationale, and their premises of operating programs that deal with individual deficits in the learners—a set of pathologies that should be treated by experts through a complex system of referrals and treatment. They are based on observation, and the analysis of institutional events, with a focus on the relationship between teachers and learners. The basic approach is behaviorism, and in the North American tradition, it could be related to the clinical approach to supervision developed in the 1960s. These models can be labeled "clinical models of adult education."

For clinical models, individuals are mainly organized according to the requirements of production. The whole model depends on a conceptual repertoire organized by experts (adult education teachers, managers, planners) exerting exclusive authority in naming, diagnosing, assessing a treatment, suggesting a therapy, and predicting who in this process will improve and who will not. The paradigm uses a process–product approach, based on empirical measures, a strong emphasis on the psychological functions of the educational system, and the personalized power of teachers over learners. Clinical models of adult education are challenged by notions of adult education as cultural politics, and particularly for the attempts to implement adult education as part of broader social movements.

Adult education as cultural politics opposes these clinical models. In the well-established tradition of adult education for social change, it is argued that learning new ways of seeing and acting implies the development of new forms of cultural politics. For instance, literacy training programs should not only provide reading, writing, and numeracy, but should also be considered ". . . a set of practices that functions to either empower or disempower people" (Freire and Macedo 1987 p. viii). Adult education as cultural politics challenges the paternalistic mode of adult education discourse that seems dominant in the adult education field, because emancipatory adult education ". . . becomes a vehicle by which the oppressed are equipped with the necessary tools to reappropriate their history, culture, and language practices" (Freire and Macedo 1987 p. 159). This approach is in sharp contrast to mainstream adult education models.

In this context, adult education for development should result in the constitution of a social movement. Different state agencies—many of them associated with rural or extension education—have postulated that their adult education programs try: (a) to put education and knowledge at the service of the most impoverished sectors of society; (b) to use this education as a means of liberation to people and as a mechanism of social participation; (c) to use this education as an integrating part and as the initial stimulus of a broader social movement that challenges some of the functional irregularities of capitalism, such as imbalances in income distribution, imbalances between labor market sectors and dissenting actors, problems of providing the required services, and so on; (d) to contribute to the development of a just social space, where the limitation of state authoritarianism would be a desirable consequence; and (e) to promote national development, strengthening not only the identity of social actors but also reinforcing nationalist perspectives. These objectives for adult education relate to theories of social resistance or oppositional pedagogies.

Clinical models and adult-education-as-cultural-politics models both face the challenge of established and emerging social movements. The feminist challenge should be considered, allowing women learners to express their voices openly in the constitution and operation of the programs, considering the issues of power and relevance of adult education in the life of women, and making explicit that as the personal is political, the challenge of feminism should imply a drastic revision of the epistemological foundations of adult education as well as its social and pedagogical principles. The ecological challenge will help to review the connections of adult education with the world of work, and the notion of productivity at the expense of the environment and a social organization of labor that is alienating, hierarchical, undemocratic, and wasteful of resources. The challenge of human rights movements will help to promote basic notions of equality and egalitarian goals in the context of a basic respect for life and a tolerance for diversity and even citizenship opposition. The challenge of neighborhood associations and (religious) base communities will help adult education rediscover its community roots, emphasizing cooperation and joining efforts to reintegrate and reinvigorate communities, many of them deeply affected by the dynamics of capital accumulation at global scale. Hence, adult education for development may be linked with models of moral philosophy and moral education, so easily overlooked or dismissed as irrelevant when decisions in education are only seen as simply a matter of investment, expenditures, or political control.

Only by taking up these challenges can adult education programs emerge as part of a democratic social movement, and make a meaningful and lasting contribution to the development of individuals, families, communities, and nations in the world system.

See also: Community Education and Community Development; Popular Education and Conscientization; Economics of Adult Education and Training; Economics of Nonformal Education; Ideologies in Adult Education; Adult Literacy in the Third World; Women and Adult Education; International Adult Education; Nongovernmental Organizations

References

Arnove R F, Graff H J (eds.) 1987 *National Literacy Campaigns: Historical and Comparative Perspectives* Plenum, New York.

Bhola H S (ed.) 1984 *Campaigning for Literacy.* UNESCO, Paris

Blaug M 1966 Literacy and economic development. *The School Review* 74(4): 393–415

Bock J, Papagiannis G (eds.) 1983 *Nonformal Education and National Development.* Praeger, New York

Carnoy M 1974 *Education as Cultural Imperialism.* McKay, New York

Carnoy M et al. 1979 *Can Educational Policy Equalize Income Distribution in Latin America.* Saxon House, London

Carnoy M, Samoff J (eds.) 1990 *Education and Social Transformation in the Third World.* Princeton University Press, Princeton, New Jersey

Coombs P 1968 *The World Educational Crisis: A System Analysis.* Oxford University Press, New York

Freire P, Macedo D 1987 *Literacy: Reading the Word and the World.* Routledge and Kegan Paul, London

Freire P et al. 1980 *Vivendo e aprendendo. Experiencias do Idacen educação popular.* Brasilense, São Paulo

Gadotti M 1990 *Uma só escola para todos. Caminhos da autonomia escolar.* Vozes, Petrópolis

Horton M, Freire P 1990 *We Make the Road by Walking: Conversations on Education and Social Change.* Temple University, Philadelphia, Pennsylvania

Huntington S 1968 *Political Order in Changing Societies.* Yale University Press, New Haven, Connecticut

International Development Research Centre (IDRC) 1991 *Perspectives on Education for All.* IDRC, Ottawa.

La Belle T J 1986 *Nonformal Education in Latin American and the Caribbean: Stability, Reform or Revolution?* Praeger, New York

Marin A, Psacharopoulos G 1976 Schooling and income Distribution. *Rev. Econ. and Stat.* (58): 332–38

Mezirow J 1985 Critical transformation theory and the self-directed learner. In: Brookfield S (ed.) 1985 *Self-Directed Learning: From Theory to Practice.* Jossey-Bass, San Francisco, California

Morales-Gómez D, Torres C A 1992 Introduction: Education and development in Latin America. In: Morales-Gómez D, Torres C A (eds.) 1992 *Education, Policy and Social Change. Experiences from Latin America.* Praeger, Westport, Connecticut

Offe C 1985 *Disorganized Capitalism.* Polity Press, Cambridge

Oxenham J (ed.) 1984 *Education Versus Qualifications? A Study of Relationships Between Education, Selection for Employment and the Productivity of Labor.* George Allen and Unwin, London

Psacharopoulos G 1988 Critical issues in education and development: A world agenda. *Int. J. Educ. Dev.* 8(1): 1–7

Reich M et al. 1975 A theory of labor market segmentation. In: Carnoy M (ed.) 1975 *Schooling in a Corporate Society.* McKay, New York

Sáenz A 1989 Informal labor markets and education. Department of Educational Foundations, University of Alberta, Edmonton (mimeo.)

Stromquist N 1991 *Women and Education in Latin America: Knowledge, Power and Change.* Lynne Rienner, Boulder, Colorado

Thomas A 1983 Adult illiteracy in Canada—A challenge (Occasional paper No. 42.) Canadian Commission for UNESCO, Ottawa

Torres C A 1990 *The Politics of Nonformal Education in Latin America.* Praeger, New York

UNESCO 1991 *Education for All: Purpose and Context.* UNESCO, Paris

UNESCO 1992a *Education for All: An Expanded Vision.* UNESCO, Paris

UNESCO 1992b *Education for All: The Requirements.* UNESCO, Paris

Torres C A 1991 The state, nonformal education, and socialism in Cuba, Nicaragua, and Grenada. *Comp. Educ. Rev.* 35(1): 110–30

Welton M (ed.) 1987 *Knowledge for the People: The Struggle for Adult Learning in English-Speaking Canada 1828–*

1973. OISE Press, Toronto
Youngman F 1986 *Adult Education and Socialist Pedagogy.* Croom Helm, London
Zachariah M 1987 New indigenous models of mass educa-

tion and action: Lessons from the Kerala Sastra Sahitya Parishat (KSSP) of India. Paper presented at the World Congress of Comparative Education Societies, Rio de Janeiro, July 6–10

Adult Literacy in the Third World

A. Lind and A. Johnston

Illiteracy is still one of the world's greatest social problems. In spite of progress in the independent nations of Africa, Asia, and Latin America (hereinafter called the Third World), in expanding primary schooling and literacy programs for adults, there are nearly one billion adult illiterates in the world, more than one adult in four. In 1990—the International Literacy Year (ILY)—the number of illiterates declined for the first time to an estimated 948 million; 2 million less than in 1985 (UNESCO 1991). However, the international goals of basic education for all (WCEFA 1990) and the drastic reduction of illiteracy by the year 2000 remain elusive because of the more than 100 million children not attending school in Third World countries. The vast majority of adult illiterates is found in the least-developed countries and 60 percent of them are women. The gap between men and women is, moreover, steadily increasing. Out of a total increase of 154 million illiterates between 1960 and 1985, 133 million (86%) were women (UNESCO 1987).

This entry is confined to adult literacy issues in Third World countries. The basic value assumption is that literacy is a human right and a prerequisite for the promotion of equality, social justice, and democracy.

1. Conditions Affecting Literacy

The socioeconomic, cultural, and political environment in which literacy programs are implemented is often the principal determinant of the success or failure of such programs. This is because these overall contextual conditions strongly influence the motivation of the potential adult literacy students. The marginalized and impoverished illiterate peasants or urban dwellers will use time for literacy classes only when literacy is perceived as contributing to a better life.

Economic development has helped to promote literacy, especially through universal primary education (UPE). Even countries with less-developed economies have made significant achievements in attaining widespread literacy through committed national efforts to combine UPE with literacy activities directed at adults (e.g., the former Soviet Union, Cuba, Tanzania, Ethiopia, Ecuador, and India). These and other histori-

cal examples, such as the Swedish and Finnish reading campaigns run by the Protestant Church in the seventeenth and eighteenth centuries, show that significant efforts to provide literacy have been tied neither to the level of wealth in a society nor to a particular type of political regime. "Instead they have been more closely related to efforts of government authorities to establish a moral or political consensus, and, over the past two hundred years, to nation-state building" (Arnove and Graff 1987 p. 1).

There is strong reason to doubt that primary education alone will do away with illiteracy in the Third World, in the way it has in most industrialized countries. The promotion of literacy and further education for out-of-school youths and adults is a necessary complement to quantitatively and qualitatively deficient primary schooling. A strategy for universal literacy and basic education for all requires a combined effort to improve and expand formal and nonformal basic education for children, youth, and adults (WCEFA 1990; UNESCO 1992).

Parallel efforts to introduce UPE are not the only necessary conditions in order for adult literacy programs to be meaningful. The development of conditions favorable to the promotion and maintenance of literacy is also essential, such as the existence of a widely shared written language, an accessible press, and an overall process of development toward a literacy-sustaining society.

Literacy achievements are fostered by motivation and support at all levels for the literacy process. This includes active political and economic support by the international community and the individual states, and the participation and mobilization of all state sectors, trade unions, the mass media, and voluntary organizations.

With the decolonization of the Third World, the issue of literacy was moved high up on the national and international agendas. Literacy came to be seen as a tool in economic growth, then as an ingredient in social justice, and then as an instrument of liberation. In 1990, two relatively forceful international initiatives took place advocating concerted action to universalize literacy and basic education, (i.e., the UN-declared International Literacy Year [ILY] and the World Conference on Education for All [WCEFA] sponsored by four UN agencies, including the World Bank). Both ILY and the WCEFA stressed the complementarity between primary schooling and adult literacy. The WCEFA based its arguments not only on human rights but above all on a number of utilitarian grounds. The World Bank, which has become the most powerful international actor in the field of education in Third World countries, is expected to increase by threefold its loans to primary education. Behind this lies the belief in research findings that investments in improving primary education for children (not adult literacy) render economic returns in productivity and economic growth. But most participants of the WCEFA agreed that addressing the problems of illiteracy and deficient primary education by confining attention and resources to the formal school system alone is most likely to fail since so many nonschool factors are involved. The family conditions of the pupils have a heavy impact on their attendance and learning, not only as regards poor nutrition and housing, but above all as regards their parents' low level of education.

The literacy education initiatives of 1990 did seem to contribute to a growing consciousness that adult literacy is an important step in the process of enabling greater and more equitable participation in society. There are many individual testimonies by adult students as to the benefits brought about by learning literacy and numeracy (see, e.g., Kassam 1979). They show that literacy opens up avenues of communication that would otherwise remain closed; it expands personal choice and control over one's environment, and it is necessary for the acquisition of other skills.

The ILY and WCEFA took place in the context of economic crisis, increasing debt burdens, and ensuing remedial "structural adjustment programs," particularly in the least-developed countries. This has resulted in significant budget cuts in the social sectors and a serious deterioration in general living standards. Consequently, little priority is being given to adult literacy by governments or individuals in these countries, despite the rhetoric attesting to the contrary.

2. Objectives and Strategies

Adult literacy has been the subject of intense debate for several decades. The issues debated have ranged from whether it is at all worthwhile for the state to become involved in promoting adult literacy, and to what objectives, strategies, and designs of literacy programs should be chosen. Different contexts and divergent philosophies of development and education influence different positions.

2.1 Objectives for Launching Literacy Programs

In general, the state constitutes the driving force behind the launching of large-scale literacy programs or campaigns. Although most states declare a mixture of objectives (sometimes conflicting) when they formulate national literacy aims, three principal objectives can be distinguished: (a) sociopolitical objectives (such as nation-state formation or participation in ongoing transformations), which have often been the driving force behind mass literacy campaigns; (b) economic objectives (the promoting of gradual improvement in living standards), which can either result in selective work-oriented programs within specific development projects or in a more general program as one of several inputs to building economic growth; and (c) general socioeconomic or developmental objectives (often in the context of a relatively low priority being given to literacy), where provision is made through state services in response to public and/or international demand.

Literacy programs run by nongovernmental organizations (NGOs) (i.e., community organizations, women's clubs, churches, and private companies) may fit into concerted literacy efforts by the state and society. Nevertheless, NGO objectives for literacy differ widely depending on the organization's character, ideology, or religion, and on the context. Where the state is repressive and dictatorial, literacy programs are often organized by community organizations, trade unions, or political movements as part of a liberation struggle against the structures of oppression. This has been typical for literacy work in South Africa, for example. Within popular education movements, particularly in Latin America, "empowering" literacy work often forms part of the activities. Literacy is seen as a democratic right which can enable people to fully participate in political institutions and civil society (see *Community Education and Community Development*).

2.2 Strategies for Organizing Adult Literacy

Four different strategies for organizing literacy programs will be reviewed: (a) the "one-off" mass literacy campaign of short duration, (b) the rather longer campaign series, (c) large-scale general literacy programs, and (d) small-scale selective programs. Strategies have varied and depend on the objectives of the literacy program, its scale and form of implementation, and who organizes it.

2.2.1 "One-off" mass campaigns. There are only a few examples of short, intensive and relatively successful national mass literacy campaigns: Cuba in 1961 (illiteracy reduced from 24 to 4%), Nicaragua in 1979–80 (a reduction from 50 to 13% illiteracy), South Vietnam in 1976–78 (a reduction from 25 to 14% illiteracy), Somalia in 1974–75, and most recently Ecuador in 1989. In all of these cases (apart from Ecuador), the states launched their literacy campaigns soon after revolutionary movements had acceded to power and while popular enthusiasm was at its height.

Some common important factors that made these mass campaigns successful were: the governments had a strong commitment to social justice; not more than half the adult population was illiterate; and the countries had only one principal majority language.

In countries which experienced rapid change under a socialist-inspired movement, literacy campaigns were attributed high priority as part of the strategy for promoting participation in transforming the society. They were organized in a quasi-military form, based on centralized coordination and decentralized execution involving thousands of volunteer literacy workers. The curriculum content in the campaigns largely focused around the new state's history, origins, and policies for the future.

In Ecuador, each lesson in the reader dealt with a human right such as education, health, freedom of speech, and so on. Ecuador's recent literacy campaign experience (Torres 1990) showed that it was possible to mobilize youth to engage in teaching literacy on a volunteer basis, in a nonrevolutionary situation. School teachers, parents, and NGOs were also involved in supporting the campaign activities. An important side effect of the campaign was a debate on the function and approach of the established education system. Its organization was similar to that of other "one-off campaigns," for example, it was introduced by short training courses for the literacy tutors, followed by regular inservice support. Classes were relatively small, and often taught by a team of young volunteers who also spent their time working together with and learning from their adult students. Central and local literacy committees were organized with the involvement of high-ranking officials.

The objectives in all cases were oriented toward rapid literacy teaching, so numeracy was not included in the regular campaign program. The methodological approaches varied from rather traditional "magisterial" and formal pedagogy in, for instance, Cuba and Vietnam to conscientization-oriented approaches in Nicaragua and Ecuador. As in other strategies, the problem of regression to illiteracy was strongly posed.

2.2.2 A series of campaigns. Many countries have decided to tackle the problem of adult illiteracy by organizing a series of campaigns. These campaigns were run one after the other as part of a plan to wipe out illiteracy over a number of years. The first example of a literacy campaign series is that of the Soviet Union (1919–39) where illiteracy was reduced from 70 to 13 percent. Vietnam and China followed. The 1970s saw a large rise in the use of a "campaign series" strategy (e.g., in Tanzania, Burma, Ethiopia, Mozambique, and Angola). In the 1980s, India undertook to organize campaigns in selected districts and states.

Most of the countries which have run campaign series have targeted particular groups for teaching with the hope of eventually reaching all the different sectors of the population. Governments chose this strategy due to the high levels of illiteracy, scarce human and financial resources, and multiple languages

in the country. One big problem with campaign series has been that literacy students and teachers, as well as the authorities involved, lose interest after a while because the end never comes in sight. Since the end of the 1980s, India's experience of campaigning for literacy district by district in a few states has avoided this problem by concentrating on one area at a time. In Ethiopia, the Peasant Associations served as the local cornerstones maintaining literacy classes and allowing for considerable literacy success in the early 1980s. The educational approach has varied from country to country. In Tanzania the approach was functional in that different primers were adapted to the dominant agricultural production of each region. In general, the campaign series strategy has largely resembled the one-off campaigns.

2.2.3 Large-scale general literacy programs. In some countries, governments have initiated large-scale literacy programs without the broad mobilization characteristic of mass literacy campaigns. Literacy has not been considered a must for political and economic reasons. Illiteracy has been highest among rural populations, mainly female, and the unemployed. Literacy has instead been offered mainly as a welfare service and has been formally structured. Programs of this kind have been implemented, among others, by the governments of Botswana, Kenya, Zimbabwe, Brazil, Mexico, and India. Nongovernmental organizations (NGOs) are often active partners in the program, but coordination is often weak and efforts and resources become dispersed. This has been the case of Zimbabwe (Lind et al. 1986). Each NGO involved in literacy carried on with its own agenda and the government program rapidly dropped in size and impetus, partly due to low overall government priority and partly due to the massive dropout of literacy tutors who were expected to work without being paid. High initial enrollment, followed by irregular participation and a very large dropout, is a more accentuated trait in the context of this strategy than in the campaign strategies where there is social pressure operating to uphold participation.

These literacy programs make use of a general curriculum oriented around subjects of interest to adults with which the state feels comfortable: health care, agriculture, and so forth. Often the mixture of objectives of the program combined with the efforts to make the curriculum interesting and useful to adults result in overloaded programs. Too many goals are expected to be reached by one literacy course.

2.2.4 Selective small-scale programs. Most literacy activities going on in the world are small-scale and limited to certain target groups. They can serve particular purposes not readily attainable by larger activities. The functional approach within the framework of the Experimental World Literacy Programme (EWLP— see Sect. 2.3(b) below) was selective and small-scale.

A target group working within a specific economic activity in a specific region was selected for the experiment. The EWLP projects were also intensive, in that they were limited in duration and utilized considerable resources. Selective small-scale programs are often promoted by NGOs or local communities. Some states also engage in selective programs by, for example, implementing the literacy activities in one region at a time. In most cases, however, state-promoted adult literacy ends up to be small-scale with no purpose of being selective due to lack of mobilization, resources, and priority for literacy and/or irrelevant education approaches.

Small-scale or selective literacy projects have some potential advantages compared to larger scale programs. Existing resources can be more concentrated, project organizers can be closer to the training and literacy classes, the teachers can more easily be given inservice training, and the learners' needs can more easily be identified and met. This can permit more flexibility, less bureaucracy, and more capacity to respond adequately and in time. It is thus also possible to achieve better results. However, these benefits are not an automatic outcome of limited scale. The social context, the degree of motivation, and the human and material resources for the project remain determinant.

2.3 Approaches to Teaching Literacy

There are different educational approaches to adult literacy, as well as different strategies for organizing it. However, the variety of experiences in the twentieth century clearly shows that there is no single global methodological or organizational model for adult literacy programs. The particular political, socioeconomic, and cultural circumstances to a large extent determine the design of a literacy activity and must be taken into account.

The principal approaches to teaching literacy can be identified as:

(a) *The formal education approach* which is often used in night schools for adults. Some proponents of this approach see adult literacy as a belated opportunity to provide basic education that people never had as children. The syllabus is often the same as in primary school. Examinations and certification at various points are part of the approach. The advantage of this is that people tend to like the implied social recognition and sense of achievement. The main problems with this approach are that adults are often taught as if they were children, the contents are irrelevant to the adults' lives, and there is seldom any concern for teaching people to be critical. However, formal education systems are often adapted specially for adults: levels and certificates are recognized as equivalent to the schooling system, but contents

and teaching methods are fitted to the needs of adults.

(b) *The functional approach* which has meant linking literacy instruction to practical skills training. The concept was launched in the context of the EWLP, supported by UNESCO and UNDP from 1967 to 1972. Literacy was then seen as an entry point to the improvement of productive skills and economic growth. However, this was found to be too narrow and even counterproductive when adopted as a standard approach (UNESCO/UNDP 1976). The functional approach to basic adult literacy involves combining literacy classes with teaching skills related to the participants' own living and working situations. In Tanzania, where literacy in the 1970s was integrated into a national development plan, this kind of functional approach was used with some success. Thus, for example, learners in rural areas would learn about possible ways of improving their health and increasing a specific kind of agricultural production, at the same time as learning literacy and numeracy. The advantage is, obviously, that the lesson content is meant to be directly relevant. However, several problems have been observed: it is expensive since many different course books need to be prepared to cater for all different areas of work, it complicates the training of teachers, and above all the programs become overloaded. Some studies demonstrate that people who enroll in literacy classes are, in the first instance, interested in learning how to read, write and calculate so that they do not have to rely on other people to do this for them (Lind 1988, Carron et al. 1989). In 1992, making literacy functional implied placing the adult participants at the center of their environment and providing means whereby they could develop into active participants in community life. The concept of functionality has to be adapted to the living conditions of the learners and the specific goals which they are pursuing. Nevertheless, if the means needed to apply something learnt in literacy classes are not available, it is not very meaningful.

(c) *The conscientization approach*, inspired by the Brazilian adult educator Paulo Freire, whereby literacy is seen as contributing to social transformation and giving people the skills to participate actively in a democratic society. The goal of literacy education, according to Freire, is to overcome oppression through action based upon a critical analysis of reality. This approach has been used primarily by voluntary organizations working with marginalized populations and by a few governments, for example, in Nicaragua after the overthrow of the Somoza dictatorship. Like the "functional" literacy approach, the conscientization approach is difficult to apply on a large scale. The approach has also been criticized for putting too much emphasis on discussion without imparting the reading, writing, and numeracy skills which people expected when they enrolled. The lessons are introduced by discussing a theme related to a picture and generative words identified through investigations on the learner's culture, living conditions, language, and so on. After this dialogue, a key word is presented, which should stimulate the learners into creating new words or even sentences by recombining its syllables. In this way the role of the educator becomes one of offering the literacy students instruments with which they can teach themselves to read and write. Freire has provided an important source for critical reflection and inspiration for literacy practitioners, through his criticism of domesticating and elitist approaches to literacy and his insistence on the alternative role of the educator as someone who shares experiences with the learners, teaching and at the same time learning from them. This approach has the potential to build democratic attitudes and behavior (see *Popular Education and Conscientization*). In the words of a literacy learner in South Africa:

In my learning group we are all equal people. Even the teacher is our equal. We do things and decide things together, nothing is forced on us. I think I am now beginning to understand this word democracy. (Steinberg and Suttner 1991 p. 16)

3. Individual Motivation for Literacy

Many studies show that the response among adult illiterates to literacy programs is rather positive when specific efforts have been made to stimulate motivation. Once the target population has been convinced to enroll, the problem is frequently high dropout and low attendance rates. "People would indeed like to be literate. However, the strength of their desire and its ability to carry them through to completion are still the uncertain factors" (Oxenham 1975 p. 4).

The conditions of poverty in rural areas, lack of self-confidence, disillusion regarding the benefits of literacy, discouraging teaching methods, and the lack of easy and useful reading material are factors that explain high dropout rates (see, e.g., Lind 1988, FREOP 1979, ICAE/IDRC 1979, Lind and Johnston 1990)

In many African countries far more women than men register for literacy classes, but the generally oppressed situation of women prevents them from attending classes regularly, which often leads to poor achievement compared to men. This has recently been confirmed in an in-depth study on the functioning and effects of the Tanzanian literacy program (Carr-Hill et al. 1991). The common constraints on women's participation in literacy classes, such as overwork, childbirth and child care, cultivation of fields, and so forth, as well as male resistance, are not easily overcome without determined efforts by the community and by important political or cultural leaders. Downing (1987) contends that "valorization" of literacy can be induced through persuasion, where it is not socially valorized through tradition. For instance, "In Indonesia learning groups in a literacy campaign were valorized through the support of cultural leaders. Learning groups grew fast in villages where the village chiefs were aware of the need for literacy, and very slowly otherwise" (Downing 1987 p. 32).

When there is a strongly felt need for literacy, the methods of delivering literacy do not seem very important. Where the learner's will to read "does not exist, clever pedagogy, elaborate equipment and fancy buildings are likely to prove of no avail" (Ryan 1980 p. 60).

4. Issues in the Design and Implementation of Literacy Programs

Most of the conclusions, such as those above, from studies and experiences of implementation indicate that adult literacy is a political rather than a technical issue. Nevertheless, a number of issues concerning the methodology, content, and material, as well as the resources and time available, are important for the outcome of literacy efforts, particularly when motivation is high.

4.1 The Time Factor

Compared with primary school, adult literacy classes take place under difficult conditions. The learners are not obliged to attend the classes. They have duties and obligations which often conflict with regular attendance. The scheduled number of hours for adult literacy instruction is usually low compared to the primary school schedule devoted to literacy and numeracy acquisition. Irregular attendance reduces the already limited time available for learning literacy. This results in a paradox:

Many adults require more time to achieve literacy than classes provide. On the other hand, increasing the duration of courses by dividing them into stages has usually had the effect of increasing drop-out. (Ryan 1980 p. 63)

In the Mozambican case (Lind 1988), the objectives were set too high, the stages were made too long, and many learners ended up repeating the stages they did not pass. Thus, finishing and gaining a certificate receded into the far distance. It is probably most effective for learners to attend relatively short courses and take tests at a rather low skill level with success, as this can motivate them to commit themselves to continue into a follow-up stage. The time factor has to be considered carefully in designing the curriculum and deciding the language of instruction.

4.2 Language of Instruction

The existence of a widely shared language has obviously been a favorable factor in most countries that have carried out successful literacy campaigns and programs, but it is not a sufficient condition nor is its absence fatal. The literacy campaigns carried out in Ethiopia showed that it was possible to instruct literacy in many languages in a highly multilingual country.

Given that the mother tongue, or a language that the learners are fluent in, is the most appropriate for learning, it is still not worthwhile to teach literacy in this language if there is no written material in it, or if there is no program for teaching the transition from this language to another language widely used for reading and writing. The multiplicity of languages and the scarce resources in many developing nations present enormous obstacles to the teaching of mother tongue literacy. Again, the crucial factor which needs careful consideration is what language people are motivated to learn in. For economic, cultural, or language status reasons, people in certain circumstances display resistance to learning in their home language, and in others, to learning in a second language. Consequently, the choice of language policy depends on the particular national or local conjuncture at a given time.

4.3 Literacy Teachers

Literacy teachers are often recruited from among people with a relatively low level of education. They are usually paid a small allowance or nothing at all. The maintenance of an atmosphere of priority is often crucial to sustaining the commitment of voluntary literacy teachers. If it is decided to pay literacy teachers effectively, then it is worthwhile investing in the costs of a longer and more solid pre-service training. Otherwise, it is better to choose a short and mobilizing training. In both cases, but especially the latter, it is necessary to follow up the initial training with a network of pedagogical and organizational support services and regular inservice training.

4.4 Postliteracy

The knowledge and skills acquired in the literacy class easily fade away if they are not followed up properly. In the long run, the solution has to be the development of a literate and literacy sustaining society, which involves thorough changes in the kind of information needs that people have and how they communicate. However, literacy planners and organizers must first of all ensure that there are opportunities for further learning through postliteracy programs and links with formal education. Also, there must be daily opportunities for applying recently acquired skills. In addition, it is very important to promote the use of the written word in less-privileged communities by introducing simple libraries and newsletters/papers. Several literacy specialists have recommended the introduction of easy-to-read materials before starting the literacy program (see, e.g., Laubach 1947, Gray 1969).

The neglect of literacy follow-up has been a major constraint on the lasting impact of many literacy programs. Evaluation studies of literacy rarely deal with the impact of programs, probably because such studies are hard to implement. Studies that have dealt with literacy program effects have shown that many of the learners who have maintained their skills after finishing literacy classes had attended primary school before joining adult literacy classes (Carron et al. 1989, Carr-Hill et al. 1991) (see *Postliteracy; Adult Secondary Education*).

5. Women and Literacy

Women often manifest strong motivation to learn literacy and numeracy. They frequently express a desire to be able to help their children study and to gain more self-confidence and control over their personal life. In spite of this, the multiple roles of women prevent them from regular attendance and efficient learning. Apart from their reproductive role that imposes heavy domestic duties, lack of self-confidence and relative isolation from more literate environments also work against full participation or success in literacy classes.

Even when female learners in favorable contexts have managed to acquire elementary literacy skills, the sustaining of literacy skills is often more difficult for them than for men. Available reading material is often not designed for women's interests and needs. Women often have less access to reading material and less time to read it. For example, a study on the effects of literacy in Kenya (Carron et al. 1989) found that women tend to use their newly acquired skills less frequently than men.

Surprisingly little has been reported or studied concerning adult literacy for women. However, existing studies indicate that a process of social change, including community involvement and social pressure in favor of women's participation in literacy classes, is needed to sustain attendance and overcome male resistance. A common problem is that literacy programs, often integrated with other practical activities, seldom adapt to the real learning conditions of women. Not enough time and attention is given to the literacy component and provisions for facilitating women's full participation are seldom provided. The successful examples that do exist demonstrate the importance of participation and awareness-raising, and of creative organizational and mobilizational approaches. They also show that literacy is a potential tool for empowering women (Stromquist 1987, Lind and Johnston 1990).

6. Evaluation

Systematic evaluation of literacy programs is not common. Most programs, however, have some kind of monitoring and/or evaluation system. The reports of meetings between organizers and teachers, the attendance records, or the achievement test results, when any of these methods have been implemented, are, nonetheless, very seldom analyzed.

The largest attempt to evaluate the effects of literacy was undertaken in the context of EWLP. The basic aim of the EWLP evaluation was to test the relationship between literacy and economic development. From the EWLP projects, 229 reports from 11 countries were produced. Nonetheless, UNESCO's own critical assessment of the EWLP (UNESCO/UNDP 1976) found that figures available on learning results were limited, incomplete, and of doubtful reliability. One of the identified problems was that clearly defined program objectives had never been specified for the EWLP programs.

The frequent gap between very broadly formulated objectives and quite vaguely defined operational goals poses a serious problem for the evaluation of literacy programs. Whatever the broader political, socioeconomic, or technical purposes are, achievement tests are commonly confined to measuring reading, writing, and numeracy skills. Some issues need particular attention before implementing an evaluation: whether the conditions for literacy learning were minimally sufficient for the realistic attainment of the intended goals and whether unintended effects, processes, or achievement have occurred. The feasibility of proposed test criteria amd process-oriented variables can only be confirmed through consultations and pretests among the implementors and participants of the program. The collection and use of "data generated during implementation" constitute the most important form of literacy evaluation, as the process can be formative, that is, provide a base for introducing program improvements (Bhola 1979). Any kind of literacy evaluation requires staff training at various levels of the literacy administration and training network.

7. Perspectives

Recent developments affecting the Third World present contradictory prospects for the adult literacy progress in the near future. The growing process of introducing parliamentary democracy and extending human rights would seem to be a compelling reason to take serious initiatives to reduce illiteracy among adults. In a democratic society, people need access to information on which to base their choices as well as confidence to participate in decision-making. It is obviously not easy to democratize society if large sections of the population are illiterate. However, economic crisis and the increasing debt burdens of many countries with high rates of illiteracy are likely to have a forceful negative impact on the course of adult literacy action in most Third World countries. Only a very few new large-scale national literacy programs or campaigns can be expected in this perspective. Recently independent (1990) Namibia is, in 1992, embarking on a national adult literacy program, and a future democratic South Africa can be expected to take a significant adult literacy initiative. In these cases, the experiences of Ecuador and India could provide some promising lessons. In both cases, the state has been the initiator and has relied heavily on NGOs and other partners. Otherwise, the perspective is that Third World states will be decreasing their commitment and allocation of resources to adult literacy, while the NGO sector will be increasing its involvement in adult literacy provision. International cooperation among NGOs was given a strong impetus by ILY initiatives and more agency assistance than ever before is being directed toward NGO programs.

See also: Literacy; Literacy and Numeracy Models; Postliteracy; Anthropological Study of Literacy and Numeracy; Participatory Research; Adult Education for Development; Development through Nonformal Education; Literacy Research and Measurement

References

Arnove R F, Graff H J (eds.) 1987 *National Literacy Campaigns in Historical and Comparative Perspective.* Plenum Press, New York
Bhola H S 1979 *Evaluating Functional Literacy.* International Institute for Adult Literacy Methods, Teheran
Carr-Hill R A, Kweka A N, Rusimbi M, Chengelele R 1991 *The Functioning and Effects of the Tanzanian Literacy Programme.* IIEP, Paris
Carron G, Mwirial J, Righa K 1989 *The Functioning and Effects of the Kenyan Literacy Programme.* UNESCO/IIEP, Paris
Downing J 1987 Comparative perspectives on world literacy. In: Wagner D (ed.) 1987 *The Future of Literacy in a Changing World,* Vol. 1. Pergamon Press, Oxford
FREDP 1979 *Adult Literacy Motivation. A Survey on Adult Education in Bangladesh.* FREDP, Dhaka
Gray W S 1969 *The Teaching of Reading and Writing,* 2nd edn. UNESCO, Paris (First published in 1956)
ICAE (International Council of Adult Education)/IDRC (International Development Research Center) 1979 *The World of Literacy—Policy, Research and Action.* IDRC, Ottawa
Kassam Y 1979 *Illiterate No More: The Voices of New Literates from Tanzania.* Tanzania Publishing House, Dar es Salaam
Laubach F C 1947 *Teaching the World to Read: A Handbook for Literacy Compaigns.* Friendship Press, New York
Lind A 1988 *Adult Literacy Lessons and Promises: Mozambican Literacy Campaigns 1978–1982.* Institute

of International Education, University of Stockholm, Stockholm

Lind A, Gleditsch M, Henson T 1986 Literacy and income-generating activities in Zimbabwe. NORAD consultancy report, February 1986. NORAD, Oslo

Lind A, Johnston A 1990 *Adult Literacy in the Third World—A Review of Objectives and Strategies.* SIDA, Stockholm

Oxenham J 1975 *Non-Formal Approaches to Teaching Literacy.* Program of Studies in Non-Formal Education, Supplementary Paper No 20. Michigan State University, East Lansing, Michigan

Ryan J W 1980 Linguistic factors in adult literacy. In: Kavanagh J F, Venezky R L (eds.) *Orthography, Reading and Dyslexia.* University Park Press, Baltimore, Maryland

Steinberg C, Suttner M 1991 *Never Too Old to Learn!—Towards Formulating Policy for Adult Basic Education in a Post-Apartheid South Africa.* Learn and Teach, ELP/LACOM publications, Johannesburg

Stromquist N P 1987 The state and the education of women: Towards a theoretical understanding. Paper at the CIES Annual Meeting, Washington, DC

Torres C A 1990 *The Politics of Nonformal Education in Latin America.* Praeger, New York

UNESCO 1987 *The Current Literacy Situation in the World.* UNESCO, Paris

UNESCO 1991 Press release for International Literacy Day, September 8, 1991

UNESCO 1992 *Education for All: The Requirements. Roundtables Themes III.* World Conference on Education for All, Jomtien, Thailand. UNESCO, Paris

UNESCO/UNDP 1976 *The Experimental World Literacy Programme: A Critical Assessment.* UNESCO/UNDP, Paris

WCEFA 1990 *The World Declaration on Education for All.* WCEFA Secretariat, Jomtien

Further Reading

Bataille L (ed.) 1976 *A Turning Point for Literacy.* Pergamon Press, Oxford

Bhola H S 1984 *Campaigning for Literacy: Eight National Experiences of the Twentieth Century with a Memorandum to Decision-makers.* UNESCO, Paris

Carron G, Bordia A (eds.) 1985 *Issues in Planning and Implementing Literacy Programmes.* UNESCO/IIEP, Paris

Freire P 1985 *The Politics of Education.* Bergin and Garvin, South Hadley, Massachusetts

Gorman T P (ed.) 1977 *Language and Literacy: Current Issues and Research.* International Institute for Adult Literacy Methods, Teheran

Hamadache A, Martin D 1986 *Theory and Practice of Literacy Work: Policies, Strategies and Examples.* UNESCO/Code, Paris

Ryan J W 1985 Literacy and numeracy: Policies. In: Husén T, Postlethwaite T N 1985 *The International Encyclopedia of Education*, 1st edn. Pergamon Press, Oxford

Development through Nonformal Education

T. J. La Belle and C. R. Ward

Nonformal education (NFE) is any organized, systematic educational activity carried on outside the formal system. Nonformal education policy issues in developing countries include its sponsorship and control, relations to formal schooling, and contribution to mobility and change. The methods and strategies of NFE vary. For several reasons, interest in NFE has lessened.

1. Background

1.1 Definition

The most widely accepted definition of nonformal education comes from its relation to two related forms of learning—formal and informal education. Coombs and Ahmed (1974) define these three types of education as follows:

(a) Informal education is "the lifelong process by which every person acquires and accumulates knowledge, skills, attitudes, and insights from daily experiences and exposure to the environment."

(b) Nonformal education is "any organized, systematic, educational activity carried on outside the framework of the formal system to provide selected types of learning to particular subgroups in the population, adults as well as children."

(c) Formal education is the "institutionalized, chronologically graded, and hierarchically structured educational system, spanning lower primary school and the upper reaches of the university." (p. 8)

A major difference between the first two processes is the deliberate instructional and programmatic emphases in nonformal education which are absent in informal education (see *Formal, Nonformal, and Informal Education*).

Divisions between nonformal and formal education are typical in most societies. Even in preliterate societies, both nonformal and formal education can usually be found. Initiation rituals, for example, constitute a type of systematic educational effort in these societies. Such rituals are characterized by systematic organization, an identified setting, specially designated teachers, definitive timing, a fixed curriculum, and other practices not unlike school systems in industrialized societies. Nonformal instruction in preliterate societies includes older playmates and nonkin adults passing on the society's history, music, and dance as well as stories and folklore.

1.2 History

The term "nonformal education" (NFE) was introduced in the late 1960s to signal a need for creating out-of-school responses to new and differing demands for education. Although there has long been some attention placed on out-of-school education and on the importance of community resources for teaching and learning, the new term helped to legitimize this attention.

In the early 1970s, international development agencies announced a concerted effort to address the plight of the "poorest of the poor" in less developed countries. Along with large national and international programs, the effort emphasized local-level activity through agricultural extension, literacy, health and family planning, rural–urban community action, and technical–vocational training programs. These agencies chose the term nonformal education to refer to local-level programs for the adult poor.

1.3 The Nonformal Education Term

The popularity of nonformal education as a reference to community-level programs is due to at least two factors. First, it provides a term to link numerous efforts, from consciousness raising to vocational training and community development. Second, several of the development agencies that embraced the term in the 1970s popularized it through support for research and the implementation of NFE programs.

The nonformal education term countered the tradition in local-level development programs of personnel from each government ministry or agency working in isolation in fields such as agriculture, family planning, and literacy. This reduced the resources needed to carry out programs, enabled an integrated response to multifaceted community activity, helped connect local efforts to regional or national planning goals, and broadened traditional "adult education."

The second major reason for the term's popularity was the legitimacy and funding offered by international development agencies. The work done by Coombs (1968), Coombs and Ahmed (1974), and Coombs et al. (1973), supported principally by the Ford Foundation and the World Bank, was one visible result of this support. In addition, universities in the United States, primarily funded by the United States Agency for International Development, contributed to the popularization of the NFE label.

1.4 Problems with the NFE Term

Some persons in UNESCO and in the Third World, and most of those associated with the adult education establishment, have never completely endorsed the nonformal education label. Those in the Third World often have not liked the term because it appears to be a North American invention whose use implies Third World dependency in the borrowing of educational theory and practice.

It is partly for this reason that UNESCO has not used NFE widely, and partly because it duplicates concepts and terms UNESCO was already using, such as "lifelong learning" and "functional literacy." Adult educators have not used the term, apparently because most of those who were writing on nonformal education were from fields other than adult education. Also, many specialists associated with fields like agriculture and health have avoided the NFE term, seeing it as reflecting more process than content. Bock and Papagiannis (1983) caution that the term does not reflect a new educational phenomenon, but a change in the viewpoint of educators, politicians, and academics.

Perhaps the greatest dissatisfaction with the term relates to the difficulty individuals have in differentiating nonformal education from other educational modes. Many (e.g., Sheffield and Diejomaoh 1972, Paulston 1972, Brembeck 1974, Wood 1974, La Belle 1976, Simkins 1977, Dejene 1980) have attempted to elaborate, extend, modify, and clarify Coombs and Ahmed's (1974) three-part framework. However, those who use it generally feel that the framework functions well; those who do not tend to think that teaching and learning cannot be carved up so neatly.

Two aspects of the nonformal education definition given by Coombs and Ahmed (1974 p. 8) address some of the problems with the concept. One specifies that the teaching–learning process must be an "organized, systematic educational activity" and the other that it must be "outside the framework of the formal system." The first means that casual conversation, entertainment via the media, or reading for relaxation should be considered informal rather than nonformal education. Nevertheless, when these activities become systematic attempts to change behavior they take on a nonformal thrust. Thus, when conversation becomes a means for one individual to instruct another, the activity can be considered nonformal education. When nonformal education becomes more structured, however, it still has considerable potential for flexibility in curricula, in who gets selected to teach and learn, and in determining the goals and assessing outcomes.

Second, the definitions typically accepted suggest that nonformal activity should exclude those programs that provide alternative means to deliver schooling, meaning state-sanctioned curricula associated with credits, grades, certificates, and diplomas. For example, the courses offered through a university extension office which carry credit toward a degree are part of the formal school framework. The distinction is quite important in the analysis of nonformal education. Schools, even when they operate under private sponsorship, are typically a vehicle of the state. The curricula, teacher certification, graduation requirements, and so on associated with formal education reflect the interests of those who dominate the government's decision-making structure.

The difficulties with the term "nonformal education" are not to be taken lightly as they reflect a host of conceptual, political, cultural, and linguistic issues of importance when working cross-nationally. The term cannot be invoked neutrally given its history and diffusion.

2. Main Issues

A number of policy issues related to NFE have emerged in developing countries. These include sponsorship and control, NFE and schooling, contribution to mobility and change, and strategies and methods. Each of these areas is described below.

2.1 Sponsorship and Control

Some nations restrict local groups in their sponsorship of nonformal education programs unless the programs serve to maintain or enhance the state's goals. This has been common in many centralized communist countries, such as the former Soviet Union and Cuba, as well as in authoritarian states like Chile under Augusto Pinochet. Since such control is so dominant in this type of society, schools and nonformal education programs tend to complement one another. Even when the state does not monopolize nonformal education, it may be a major sponsor, thereby extending the government's influence beyond formal education.

In societies where the state is not a primary nonformal education sponsor, the community, family, religious organization, private business, or other special interest groups may sponsor such activities. These include a wide range of ethnoreligious and political socialization activities, youth clubs, and sports and recreation programs. These may extend the influence of the parents rather than of the state. The ethnoreligious programs are typically weekend and after-school instructional activities, often tied to particular ethnolinguistic populations that transcend national boundaries. Political socialization activities among nonformal programs are also typical in many countries of the world.

The continued existence of these nonformal education programs requires sufficient political freedom and openness that is not found in all countries: Chile, China, South Africa, or Romania during much of the 1980s, for example. Even with sufficient freedom,

other conditions must exist. A society must support systematic out-of-school instruction and learning and access to programs must be realistic and feasible for differing population groups. For example, race, ethnicity, social class, and gender are important variables in determining participation rates.

2.2 Nonformal Education and Schooling

During the 1960s and 1970s, policymakers in many developing countries and international donor agencies believed that education could promote development. However, they also saw the limits of formal education systems which were often based on colonial models, seriously underfinanced, and available only to those in a limited age range. Nonformal education offered an alternative delivery system that, according to this view, was better able to match a society's developmental needs, including those for job training, with education (UNESCO 1982).

When experience began to show that NFE did not perform as well as expected in comparison to formal education, an opposing perspective developed. From this perspective, nonformal education typically provides occupational access only to the lowest-level jobs because it does not have the legitimacy to bestow school-based diplomas and credentials necessary to gain access to white-collar and professional jobs (La Belle and Verhine 1975). Furthermore, nonformal education tends to lower the aspirations of those from subordinate groups and works to their detriment, whereas those who go to schools are likely to fare better (Bock and Papagiannis 1983).

For lower class and poor adults who may have been underserved or poorly served by schools, as well as for some independent entrepreneurs, nonformal education may function differently, perhaps by linking with formal schools to gain credentials or directly with the opportunity structure to guarantee jobs.

2.3 Contributions to Mobility and Change

Nonformal education functions differently depending on the background and aspirations of participants. For the dominant group, nonformal education tends to complement and solidify power as the rich learn to share a lifestyle with others of similar status and wealth. Members of the middle and lower-middle classes, especially youths, may also engage in programs to facilitate in-group solidarity, but these individuals more often tend to seek nonformal education as a path to white-collar and professional jobs. Nevertheless, relative to schooling, nonformal education may not be a sound investment for job seekers because it cannot provide the officially sanctioned diplomas and recognition. Where nonformal education does not have to compete head on with formal schooling, it may work somewhat better. For example, farmers or small business people may find that nonformal education delivers skills and knowledge that are directly useful in daily activity. The research on NFE's effects on such outcomes as agricultural productivity, however, are mixed (Lockheed et al. 1980).

In some countries, nonformal education may help facilitate social change through highly structured participatory or grass roots efforts at the local level. One such example, referred to as *animation rurale* and used over the 1970s and 1980s in Senegal and Niger (Moulton 1983) creates bottom-up institutions that evolve from village-level development projects into national organizations, thereby allowing the peasant population economic and political self-direction. The program is based on the assumption that local village representatives, known as *animateurs*, can train fellow villagers in farming, marketing, health care, and sanitation.

Bock and Papagiannis (1983) argue that the principal mission of nonformal education is one of information diffusion from the dominant group to subordinates. Nonformal education, they contend, has not been effective in promoting upward mobility for the poor and, in fact, may be less effective in doing so than is formal education.

Included in the nonformal education and social change category are a wide variety of literacy, consciousness raising, and community development activities, typically dealt with from both an individual and group perspective. At the individual level, a common strategy is to develop pedagogical methods and instructional products to enhance the learner's skills and knowledge. Experiments with photographic novels, games, theater, critical discussion, reflections on one's position in society, comic books, radio, television, and many other forms of electronic and print media have been used to achieve psychological goals. A classic use of such materials occurred among rural peasants in Ecuador in the mid-1970s to develop an awareness of individual participants' reality, self-worth, and literacy and numeracy skills appropriate to the rural dweller's needs and interests (Evans 1975).

It is not surprising that the predominant strategy employed in nonformal education programs intended to create social change has been tied to a set of psychologically oriented assumptions about the change process. This appears to be the result of the considerable faith placed in individual human beings not only to change themselves but to change the world around them. Unfortunately, in fulfilling such optimism many program planners have learned that individuals cannot promote such change without a great deal of assistance from a supportive biophysical environment, a fluid and open social structure, and an appropriate body of knowledge, skills, and technology. A more sociologically based set of assumptions regarding nonformal education and the change process has often, therefore, been relied on. This approach seeks to achieve a coordinated and reinforcing strategy of specially designed learner experiences, follow-up and evaluation, the initiation and strengthening of local institutions, and the provision of appropriate services and support.

In such an approach there is an emphasis on the linkages among individuals, institutions, and the biophysical environment rather than the internal psychological state or skills of the individual. The most radical of these programs seek to create revolutionary political and economic change, often through guerrilla movements. Found throughout the world, this kind of conflict-oriented action usually accompanies a preparation program involving a particular ideological doctrine, literacy and basic skills, and military preparation, all of which are carried out through nonformal programs.

When Castro came to power in Cuba in the late 1950s, for example, he established a vanguard group in the rural area and began recruiting and training the peasantry. The revolution used nonformal education in military training to foster ideological commitments and worked through mass media to keep the urban population apprised of the revolution's activities and status.

While many people aspire to use nonformal education to achieve greater equality and access for the poor and disenfranchised, the outcomes of such efforts are typically less dependent on the methods and strategies adopted and more on the history and experiences of a community, nation, and region; on the problems and issues to be resolved; and on the kind of future that individuals wish to create. Further, powerful economic and political interests are likely to shape, if not determine, the outcomes of such programs.

3. Strategies and Methods of Nonformal Education

Perhaps the major issue regarding strategy is the extent to which the poor should be involved in nonformal programs as participants in determining their own destiny. The thrust of the argument is that nonformal education programs should not serve to socialize learners to accepting permanent inferior status in the social and economic system (Evans 1983). The other side of this issue concerns the ability of the poor to accomplish much on their own through teaching, learning, and organizing, when it is the rich and powerful who must also change if the poor are to receive a greater share of resources and gain more access to opportunities. In other words, providing skills and information to the poor through nonformal education so that such individuals act in their own interests politically and economically might only result in conflict and frustration, as it is power, not participation, that is the foundation of equality and justice.

Consciousness raising is an innovative nonformal education method widely used with the oppressed in Latin America. It is a group pedagogy in which participants discuss their concrete historical experiences to learn about social reality. By confronting problems and generating their own formulations of reality and community activity, participants are expected to achieve heightened, or transformed, consciousness. Sometimes it has been joined with skills transmission (La Belle 1987).

Consciousness raising typically has no fixed curriculum and does not aim to integrate the individual into the existing society. Instead, it is geared to democratic participation and the juxtaposition of a utopian future against the contradictions of the present. It assumes that the oppressed have their own ideas that come from their daily struggle for survival.

Paolo Freire is the individual most often associated with consciousness raising in Latin America. He has drawn on Marxism, phenomenology, and existentialism, as well as on other social science and philosophical tracts, as the basis for formulating his now-famous method. Freire is most often cited for his rejection of mass education, which he feels imposes silence and passivity, stifles criticism, and makes participants objects rather than subjects of reality (Freire 1970).

While many programs that use the term "consciousness raising" use only Freire's terminology and bias toward greater participation by learners in the instructional process, Freire has nevertheless provoked many to consider education from the learner's point of view and to utilize various instructional materials and methods to foster reflection on self and reality. These include games, literature, theater, and electronic media.

Most consciousness-raising efforts have not achieved social change objectives, leading to a growing disenchantment with such efforts. Some have argued that consciousness raising should not be judged for its economic and political effects, but should be viewed as a means for understanding the mechanisms of oppression and for exploring alternatives to make society more just (La Belle 1986).

4. Decline of Interest in Nonformal Education

In the 1970s, expectations for nonformal education were high. Despite successes of individual projects, these expectations have often not been met. The reasons are both local and more global.

Locally, NFE projects have often had difficulty reaching particular audiences, especially the poor; have had to compete for local power and resources, while being generally underfinanced; and have not produced the promised upward mobility that they sought. Government-sponsored NFE has generally been located in ministries of education with the resulting tendency to bureaucratize and infuse NFE with formal education values and processes, thus muting its distinctiveness (Reed 1984).

On a more global level, NFE has suffered from a general decline in the belief in education as integral to economic development and as a promoter of change. International agencies, once funders of NFE projects and research, have turned their attention elsewhere.

Much of the earlier interest in NFE and radical social change, both in practice and by theorists, came during an era of ferment and conflict in the Third World. The political changes in Eastern Europe and the Soviet Union and the decrease in the influence of revolutionary change models in Latin America and elsewhere by the early 1990s dampened this interest.

Nevertheless, NFE programs continue, and NFE policy and theory are debated, with the questions focused largely on whether NFE efforts in developing countries should teach skills, create social solidarity, or promote change. In a contribution to this debate, Torres (1990) argues that in Latin America the public policy choice for nonformal education comes down to compensatory adult education versus popular education which attempts to alter the social order.

See also: Formal, Nonformal, and Informal Education; Popular Education and Conscientization; Economics of Adult Education and Training; Economics of Nonformal Education; Adult Education for Development

References

Bock J C, Papagiannis G J (eds.) 1983 *Nonformal Education and National Development.* Praeger, New York

Brembeck C S 1974 *Nonformal Education as an Alternative to Schooling.* Institute for International Studies in Education, Michigan State University, East Lansing, Michigan

Coombs P H 1968 *The World Educational Crisis: A Systems Analysis.* Oxford University Press, London

Coombs P H, Ahmed M 1974 *Attacking Rural Poverty: How Nonformal Education Can Help.* Johns Hopkins University Press, Baltimore, Maryland

Coombs P H, Presser R C, Ahmed M 1973 *New Paths to Learning for Rural Children and Youth.* International Council for Educational Development (ICED), New York

Dejene A 1980 *Nonformal Education as a Strategy in Development: Comparative Analysis of Rural Development Projects.* University Press of America, Lanham, Maryland

Evans D R 1975 An approach to nonschool rural education in Ecuador. In: La Belle T J (ed.) 1975 *Educational Alternatives in Latin America: Social Change and Social Stratification.* UCLA Latin American Education Center, Los Angeles, California

Evans D R 1983 Participation in nonformal education at the local level. In: Bock J C, Papagiannis G J (eds.) 1983

Freire P 1970 Adult literacy process as cultural action for freedom. *Harv. Educ. Rev.* 40: 205–25

La Belle T J 1976 *Nonformal Education and Social Change in Latin America,* Vol. 35. UCLA Latin American Education Center, Los Angeles, California

La Belle T J 1986 *Nonformal Education and the Poor in Latin America and the Caribbean: Stability, Reform, or Revolution?* Praeger, New York

La Belle T J 1987 From consciousness raising to popular education in Latin America and the Caribbean. *Comp. Educ. Rev.* 31: 201–17

La Belle T J, Verhine R E 1975 Nonformal education and occupational stratification: Implications for Latin America. *Harv. Educ. Rev.* 45: 160–90

Lockheed M E, Jamison D T, Lau L J 1980 Farmer education

and farm efficiency: A survey. *Econ. Dev. Cult. Change* 29: 37–76

Moulton J 1983 Development through training: Animation rurale. In: Bock J, Papagiannis G J (eds.) 1983

Paulston R G 1972 *Non-formal Education: An Annotated International Bibliography*. Praeger, New York

Reed H 1984 Nonformal education. In: Reed H, Loughran E L (eds.) 1984 *Beyond Schools: Education for Economic, Social and Political Development*. Citizen Involvement Training Program, Community Education Resource Center, School of Education, University of Massachusetts. Amherst, Massachusetts

Sheffield J R, Diejomaoh V P 1972 *Nonformal Education in African Development*. Report of a Survey. African–American Institute, New York

Simkins T 1977 *Nonformal Education and Development*. University of Manchester, Manchester

Torres C A 1990 *The Politics of Nonformal Education in Latin America*. Praeger, New York

UNESCO 1982 *Non-formal Education in Asia and the Pacific*. UNESCO Regional Office for Education in Asia and the Pacific, Bangkok

Wood A W 1974 *Informal Education and Development in Africa*. Mouton, The Hague

Further Reading

Brembeck C S, Thompson T J (eds.) 1973 *New Strategies for Educational Development: The Cross-Cultural Search for Non-formal Alternatives*. Heath, Lexington, Massachusetts

Freire P 1970 Cultural action and conscientization. *Harv. Educ. Rev.* 40(3): 452–77

La Belle T J 1982 Formal, nonformal, and informal education: A holistic perspective on lifelong learning. *Int. Rev. Educ.* 28: 159–75

Government Role in Adult Education and Training

A. Ziderman

Governments in virtually all countries have assumed an active role in skills development. This entry discusses the rationales that underlie this central role, with particular emphasis on developing countries. The effective role for government in the finance and delivery of adult education and training is expected to vary from country to country and within countries over time. The governmental role should be an adaptive one, reflecting a country's changing training needs, which in turn will differ with its level of economic and institutional development. The understanding of this role in every country will require careful analysis focusing on the presence, or absence, of market failures and imperfections, private training capacity, and a concern for social equity.

1. Private Markets for Training

Historically (and this remains largely true in the 1990s for the traditional sector in many developing countries), the government's role in training has been a very limited one; private training markets were far more important. It was the small enterprise that assumed the dominant role in skill creation, particularly in general training in transferable skills. Informal apprenticeships in craft trades were the primary training venue, but small enterprises also offered training at other skilled levels, including internships in accountancy and law.

In the financing of training, however, the role of the enterprise was minimal. Typically, trainees paid for their training, usually by receiving a lowered wage during training (the difference between the wage of a skilled worker and the trainee wage represents the implicit fee for training); alternatively, or in combination, the trainee paid the employer a lump sum fee at the outset. In return for their investment in training, trainees expected enhanced earnings, reflecting their augmented productivity. The small enterprise, be it the master craft worker or a legal practice, assumed a dual role; in addition to serving its customers, it also sold training services to its employees.

In most countries, traditional private training markets have proved too limited to meet the broader skill needs associated with industrial development and technological change. Government has entered as a leading actor in the market for training in most countries in the world (although in the informal sectors of many developing countries, its role remains limited). It has become a major provider of training courses (in vocational schools and specialized training institutions). Moreover, it finances a significant share of training programs (see *Demand, Supply, and Finance of Adult Education*).

2. Three Roles for Government

Government's active role in adult education, training, and labor skills development is displayed in three broad, but fairly distinct, activities: providing supportive services, providing training itself, and providing financing for training.

The umbrella role of providing supportive services is relevant at all stages of national development, although coverage may vary. Among the wide range of supportive services the government may offer are measures to create a climate of opinion conducive to training, encouraging tripartite collaboration among employers, workers, and government, and enhancing the appeal of industrial careers and training (Castley and Alfthan 1986). The state (or a specialized agency) may also play a regulatory function through services that enhance the quality of training, such as testing and certification, research, and curriculum development; it may promote enterprise training by providing training assistance, know-how, and advisory services.

The main thrust of government intervention in pre-employment training has been in training provision and finance. The government may provide training directly through public-sector training institutions and state vocational schools. Alternatively it may finance, wholly or in part, a wide range of training activities, either by providing its own training courses at little or no cost or by heavily subsidizing training courses provided by nongovernmental institutions, such as private vocational schools, proprietary training institutions, or enterprise-based training (see *Demand, Supply, and Finance of Adult Education*).

Although formally distinct, the provision and financing of training are closely interconnected, a fact accounting for some lack of clarity in discussions concerning the appropriate role of government in the finance of training. This is an important issue because the rationale for government intervention differs in the two cases: a strong case for the government to finance training does not necessarily imply that the government should also provide training (and vice versa). It has to be asked whether the active role that most governments assume in providing and financing training can be justified in efficiency terms, and what the case is for state intervention in training markets (see *Market Concepts in Provision; Markt Failure in Adult Education and Training*).

3. Rationales for Government Intervention

In this part, it will be argued that sound institutional and efficiency reasons may justify a public sector role in providing adult education and training. Even where these reasons do not (or no longer) apply, government training provision may still be acceptable as long as it is effective and efficient in relation to other or potential suppliers of training services. This is particularly true where the objective of shifting the weight of the training effort more in the direction of greater enterprise-based training remains as yet unfeasible. Although some factors may militate against efficient government provision, there is no opinion per se that the state should not train.

This is not the case with public financing of training.

The benefit principle would appear to indicate that workers, not government, should finance the full costs of their training; because of their greater value in the labor market following training, workers could expect to receive enhanced earnings, sufficient to cover initial training costs. Whether workers capture the full benefits of their training is questionable. And there may be additional reasons that justify state financing. Indeed, a wide range of arguments have been adduced to support a financing role for government in training. These are discussed under four headings: external benefits, market imperfections, weak private training capacity, and equity.

3.1 External Benefits

Individuals who decide to invest in adult education and training are motivated by expected higher earnings and other, mainly job-related, benefits; they will not capture, and therefore do not take into account, any broader benefits that may accrue to society as a whole from a better-trained workforce. From a societal point of view, individuals on their own account may not invest enough in training and therefore may acquire insufficient skills. Too few resources would then flow into training and skills acquisition. The positive benefits to society from ensuring an adequate supply of skills (external benefits or "externalities") are frequently cited to justify public financing of training. Indeed, the traditional justification for government financing of education in general is couched in terms of externalities. Positive externalities derived from general education include lower fertility, the facilitation of political and economic transactions, and intangible benefits stemming from more enlightened parents and citizens. In the absence of government subsidy, too little education would be demanded—and supplied; the education system would underprovide.

Although relevant for training, the externality argument is likely to be less strong than it is for general education. Occupational education and training are much more narrowly focused on providing skills that are relevant to a specific occupation or job and are therefore unlikely to provide the full range of externality benefits that are associated with general adult education. The more narrowly vocational that training becomes, the fewer the wider societal benefits it will provide and the weaker the case for public subsidy, as the training investor (usually the worker) captures a greater proportion of the total benefits of training.

Nonetheless, there are certain externality benefits of vocational education and training that are less strongly associated with general education. The absence of government training subsidies to encourage individuals to train more would prevent the socially optimal level of training from being attained. The availability of a skilled labor force may make a contribution to the attainment of macroeconomic goals of society: these will be over and above the direct benefits of enhanced productivity stemming from (and mainly captured by) the trained workers themselves.

Occupational education and training develop a broad skilled and technical labor base that is able to meet the needs of rapidly changing industrial organization and technology as well as to engineer this process of growth and industrial change. Yet firms may not always be willing or farsighted enough to ensure that a sufficient number of people are being trained in transferable skills vital to the economy, that is, to meet national long-term needs rather than their own particular requirements over the medium term.

Some proponents of publically subsidized training contend that it can help avoid shortages of workers with key skills in new or growing industries— shortages that could act as a brake on economic development. An additional macroeconomic argument suggests that the provision of a skilled workforce can strengthen export-related industries and thus help to mitigate balance of payments problems, earn scarce foreign exchange, and promote self-sufficiency objectives.

Overall, however, only a partial case for government intervention can be made on the basis of externalities. The main case is to be made in terms of market imperfections and weak enterprise training capacity, although equity considerations may also play a role.

3.2 Market Imperfections

If training markets work imperfectly, underinvestment in human capital will ensue, and the training system will fail to provide the economy with the supplies of skilled labor necessary for development. A major cause of such market imperfections is often said to lie in the prevalent tendency among enterprises to recruit (or "poach") trained workers from other firms. However, this line of reasoning is flawed. Since recruitment of trained labor is widely viewed as a cause of market imperfections, some attention will be given to explaining the nature of this "poaching illusion" (Lees and Chiplin 1970) (see *Market Failure in Adult Education and Training*).

The poaching argument runs along these lines: to meet their skilled labor needs, firms can choose to train directly, recruit workers from outside, or opt for a combination of both. Firms that poach inflict costs on firms that train because of the loss of newly trained workers to the poaching firms. Training firms will react by cutting down on their training effort, resulting in a general underprovision of skilled workers.

This argument, however, fails to take account of the important distinction to be drawn between general and firm-specific types of training (Becker 1964). Since firms have no interest in recruiting workers with skills specific to other firms, the poaching phenomenon is confined to generally trained workers. Poaching generally trained workers does not impose costs on the training firm since it is the trainee, not the firm, who finances training in general skills. Thus, subsidies or grants made for training in transferable skills represent a reimbursement for training costs that are not in fact incurred by the firm (see *On-the-job Training*).

Other sources of market imperfections, however, do merit remedial treatment by government (see *Overeducation*). Government policies relating to aggregate economic activity and the operation of individual markets shape a country's economic environment and affect the incentives to produce and acquire skills. Broad social policies may unintentionally distort training markets by altering the benefits and costs of training for individuals and enterprises. In such cases, second-best solutions, involving other government interventions, may be necessary to balance the resulting distortion of incentives in adult education and training.

These arguments are particularly relevant to government labor market policies that adversely affect the efficiency of enterprise-based training. Workers are willing to finance enterprise training in transferable skills (Becker 1964). Minimum-wage legislation may thwart trainee-financed general training, by preventing the training wage from falling sufficiently to pay for general training; this is particularly true if workers do not possess savings or other assets to finance the training, and recourse to loan markets is limited. A minimum wage can thus lead to a shortfall of generally trained workers. A parallel argument applies when strong union pressures prevent the wages of trainees from falling to cover training costs.

Administered wage systems and unduly narrow skilled wage differentials for skilled workers discourage worker investment in general training, because workers cannot fully recoup their training costs through higher earnings after training: private returns will fall short of social returns and the system will not train enough workers. In both cases, corrective training grants to workers (which may be administered by firms) are justified.

Where generally trained workers are not freely mobile, firms are willing to take on at least part of the financing of general skill development. Such financing counters the effects of policies discouraging worker-financed training and reduces the need for state financing or subsidy. One important barrier to the mobility of generally trained workers is that outside firms are not aware of the value of training that workers have received: this reduced potential mobility of generally trained workers will make it feasible for enterprises to assume a sizeable part of the burden of financing general training, with a consequent reduced need for government financial intervention (Katz and Ziderman 1990). Governments, however, in an attempt to achieve greater overall labor market efficiency, frequently pursue policies that encourage worker mobility. One such policy is the development of national training qualifications and certificates of training attainment (such as training "passports" in Kenya). Yet such certification has a clear, and negative, effect on training: by facilitating worker mobility among firms, it reduces the incentive for firms to finance training.

Capital market imperfections and the deleterious effect of risk and uncertainty on worker-financed training also make a case for remedial action by the government. There is a limit on how much workers are willing to have their wages reduced during the training period, in return for enterprise-based training. The larger the training cost and the shorter the period of training, the greater will be the required wage reduction during training. Workers may not find it possible to sustain this loss in wage income during training, particularly if they are lacking in financial assets. Moreover, poorly functioning capital markets in developing economies deny to many workers the possibility of financing training through loans. Indeed, even in economies with better developed financial markets, loans to finance human capital investments may not be forthcoming. Unlike other investments that can constitute the collateral for the loans that finance them, human capital investments, embodied as they are in the trained workers themselves, are not readily accepted as security by financial institutions. In these situations, workers may be forced to forgo training investments, even though they are intrinsically profitable.

Even where funding is available, workers are likely to underinvest in general training. Workers pay for training in anticipation of enhanced earnings that accrue over time. They therefore face a risk that these returns will not be forthcoming. These risks will be considerably greater for the individual than for society, which can pool and diversify risk. Workers are likely to display greater risk-averse attitudes than does society as a whole, and worker-financed training is therefore likely to fall short of the societal optimum.

3.3 Weak Enterprise Training Capacity

Enterprises may prove unable or reluctant to discharge adequately their training role, thus justifying government intervention. Certainly, in those countries where the modern sector is underdeveloped, enterprises are small, and trade associations are poorly developed, the enterprise base in a particular sector may not have the capacity to provide the necessary structured on-the-job training, particularly apprenticeship training, to meet the needs of that sector. Small firms may lack the managerial competencies and foresight to organize in-house training. They may also lack relevant personnel management capacity and, because they are unable to benefit from scale economies in training, costs may be high. These firms may not be able to afford external training providers or, in a small workforce, to release workers for outside training.

This lacuna would seem to provide a clear opening for the private sector to develop specialized training institutions or for industry to devise joint off-the-job training programs. Lack of knowledge, a suitable organizational framework, or capital may stifle such initiatives, particularly in low-income countries. There are exceptions, notably in middle-income countries: Brazil's national training institution (SENAI) was set up on the initiative of industry and financed by a levy on enterprise payrolls. Apart from providing training in public institutions, other intervention measures may include the establishment of group or industry training schemes and the provision of technical assistance to promote company training.

The weak training capacity of enterprises may justify government intervention, but the case here is for providing services, not for financing them. While courses at state training centers are usually free or highly subsidized, this cannot be justified in terms of the weak training capacity of enterprises.

In countries at all income levels, there are indications that nonprofit-maximizing behavior by firms may lead them to undertrain their workers. Low levels of company training, however, do not necessarily indicate that firms are undertraining. In practice, small firms with simple technologies and low worker mobility may have minimal needs for formal training. Even in larger firms, the lack of extensive formal training courses may be veiling a broad network of nonstructured training activities (see Ziderman and Horn 1995, for some evidence on training maps in Colombia). Governments have used training subsidies and incentives (perhaps in combination with such activities as training promotion and exhortation) when firms have not provided adequate levels of training. However, if weak or inefficient management was the underlying cause of low levels of training in the first place, the positive response to these government interventions may be small.

3.4 Equity Arguments

Vocational education and training is frequently viewed as playing an important social role in meeting the needs of disadvantaged and unemployed individuals and of serving the academically less able. Thus it is argued that an expanded, open, and highly subsidized training system could make an important contribution to improving the life chances of a significant section of the population. The question at issue, however, is whether these objectives are attainable. The record has not been encouraging. The lack of employment growth in the modern sector in many developing countries makes the attainment of such objectives all but impossible. An overexpanded, overly subsidized training system that is not accompanied by increased opportunities for employment or enhanced wages will not improve welfare and is a needless waste of scarce resources. Economic growth and job creation are prerequisites for improving the living standards of the economically disadvantaged; a major contribution to equity would be the reform of distortionary economic policies that discourage employment growth and skills development.

A somewhat different equity argument is rather more persuasive. The large public subsidies for secondary and higher education in many countries are a major cause of inequity, in that they benefit those individuals who, because of their ability or social background, have the best prospects for steady employment and job income. The equity argument for extending subsidies to individuals enrolled in training courses is quite strong, particularly when pre-employment training is directed more toward less privileged students of lower ability.

There are, however, two caveats to this equity (or more correctly, parity) argument. First, in many countries the high subsidies for secondary education are not justified in efficiency terms, and greater cost recovery measures, particularly tuition fees, are warranted; in this sense, the equity argument may be very much second best. Second, the argument that extending subsidies to individuals undergoing training will improve equity is persuasive only to the extent that the overall secondary school enrollment ratio is high, so that trainees tend to be drawn from the underprivileged sections of society. This is generally the case in high-income countries, but in low-income countries with low secondary school enrollment, the students enrolled in vocational courses often come from high-income families. In those situations, training subsidies add privileges to an already advantaged group, at the expense of those lacking a basic education; attempts to improve equity are thus undermined.

4. Designing Appropriate Policies

There is no blanket case for government financial intervention or training provision. Rather, the type and extent of required government intervention in training varies from case to case, depending on a wide range of factors such as those relating to a given country's economic development, the quality of existing training institutions (on- and off-the-job), and distortions in the economic environment that may militate against training development. The case for government intervention may indicate a need for government provision but not the finance of training (and vice versa). Table 1 lays out in schematic form the main policy conclusions regarding the role of government in adult education and training that emerge from the foregoing discussion.

Of the arguments for a public role in adult education and training, the government response is clearest in the case of externalities. When private training markets do not provide enough training (in the sense that the benefits from training accruing to society exceed private benefits), government subsidies can correct the undersupply of skills. The subsidies, financed through general taxation, are justified on the ground that society as a whole benefits (via its externality effects) from the extra training thus generated. Externalities do not justify direct government provision of training.

This traditional externality argument justifying subsidies presents two practical problems. First, the elusive nature of many of these externality benefits and the notorious difficulties associated with their measurement make it difficult to determine the appropriate size of the required subsidy. The danger of costly oversubsidization and overprovision of training is ever present. Second, these externality effects, particularly those in the macroeconomic context, should not be taken as a datum: they may be available only if appropriate training policies are pursued. Providing workers with the necessary skills for economic growth and technological change is contingent both on identifying the skills needed and taking the appropriate steps to ensure that the training occurs sufficiently far in advance to make the effort worthwhile. Strengthening

Table 1
Policy options for public intervention

Reason:	Finance training	Provide training	Complementary policies[a]
	Kind of intervention:		
External benefits	P	N	None
Market imperfections	A	N	P: deal with source of market imperfections
Weak private training capacity	N	A or P	P: build firm training capacity
Equity	A	N	P: reduce subsidies to trainees' peer groups; introduce selective scholarships

Key: P = Preferred policy approach; A = Acceptable (next best) approach; N = Policy not justified
a Policies may not be feasible

the economy's export sector requires that workers in the appropriate locations be trained in the appropriate skills. These examples point to the need to link subsidies for such programs to priority economic development strategies as well as to assessments of institutional efficiency in providing the services needed.

Government economic and social policies may lead to distortions in incentives for individual and employer investment in training. To the extent that distortions cannot be eased by modifying the policies in question, government finance may be justified as a second-best solution. For example, minimum-wage legislation is widely seen as an essential measure for protecting low-paid workers. Although it is unlikely that minimum-wage laws would be repealed simply because they discourage individuals from investing in general training, some legislative compromises may be possible. The granting of a special legal status to apprentices that would exempt their wages from the effects of minimum-wage legislation is one possibility. In the absence of such arrangements, it might be appropriate to subsidize apprenticeship wages.

If for equity reasons wages are uncoupled from productivity and the wage-skill profile is compressed, individuals will underinvest in skills development. A second-best solution involves compensating for the distortion of economic benefits to individuals by reducing their costs for skills development. This can be done by the use of individual training grants or by subsidizing enterprise training.

While the development of government-backed training loan schemes would be the appropriate response to imperfectly functioning financial markets, they may not be feasible because of the lack of a sufficiently developed administrative framework in many economies, and the unwillingness of trainees to risk borrowing against future earnings. Again, in these circumstances, trainee wage subsidization may be appropriate.

It has been argued that finance intervention (though not provision) in the training market may be justified in terms of both externalities and market imperfections. However, the two cases differ in one important regard: whereas subsidies constitute the correct treatment for externalities whether in training or other markets, in the case of market imperfections it is only where more direct measures to deal with the sources of market imperfections are ruled out (usually on administrative or political grounds) that government finance is justified, as a next best solution.

In many countries the government's financing role has become more pervasive than can be justified on efficiency grounds alone. Here, efficiency considerations call for a greater use of student fees in the financing of training off-the-job, such as in vocational training centers. Governments, particularly in low-income countries, may nonetheless be reluctant to employ substantial user fees. User fees may be impractical where incomes (and savings) are low and posttraining employment prospects uncertain; in such circumstances, heavy reliance on student charges may have a discouraging effect on the very people toward whom the training courses are targeted. User charges would also lead to serious disparities with trainees' counterparts in the highly subsidized schooling system.

The appropriate policy response to correct a shortfall in enterprise training due to weak training capacity of enterprises, and consequent insufficient training (particularly on the part of small firms), is less definite. Governments may be guided by the principle that it is preferable to deal with the source of training underprovision than to offer palliatives. If the cause of institutional failure is nonprofit-maximizing behavior of firms, stemming from inefficient or weak management, then the appropriate response is a corrective, educative one. Training advisory services would have a role to play here. Yet a positive response to such policies may not be forthcoming, precisely because management is ineffective. In this case, public sector provision of training is indicated, supported by the complementary promotional policies which may achieve some degree of success over the longer term.

In practice, many countries have chosen to use financial incentives to encourage enterprises to train, employing a wide range of measures including training subsidies, grants, and writing off training expenses against tax obligations. While the available evidence is not extensive, many of these measures have not been very effective: they needlessly subsidize well-run firms that already train, while weakly managed firms either do not respond or may do so by establishing training programs designed more to maximize financial entitlement under the scheme than to contribute to relevant skill creation in the firm (Middleton et al. 1993).

The main equity case for subsidizing training costs is really one relating to parity with peers receiving excessively subsidized education within the school system, rather than equity as such, since both groups are privileged in relation to other individuals of school age, particularly where school enrollment ratios are low. While a training subsidy may be acceptable, the preferred policy approach is one that is directed toward countering the privilege in the formal school system by reducing general subsidies both in training and general secondary schooling. Given an appropriate size of the training system in relation to skills demand, selective scholarship assistance for able, but disadvantaged, youngsters is an appropriate complementary measure.

The policy matrix in Table 1 may be regarded as a checklist that can be useful for probing the justification for interventionist training policies in any given country situation. Each country may check its public sector interventions in training by carefully examining the performance of its markets, the capacity of its private sector to deliver skills training, and its own preferences for social equity. The conditions for government intervention are present in virtually all countries, developed and industrialized. However, a transition toward a stronger role for the private sector, as circumstances permit, should be encouraged to exploit the complementarities of the two sectors.

See also: Training: on the Job; Economics of Adult Education and Training; Market Concepts in Provision; Market Failure in Adult Education and Training; Overeducation; Technological Change and Education; Demand, Supply, and Finance of Adult Education; Costs of Adult Education and Training; Evaluation of Industry Training: Cost-Effectiveness; Evaluation of Public Training: Cost-Effectiveness; Statistics of Employee Training

References

Becker G 1964 *Human Capital: A Theoretical and Empirical Analysis with Special Reference to Education.* National Bureau of Economic Research, New York
Castley R, Alfthan T 1986 Training for industrial development: How governments can help. *Int. Lab. Rev.* 125(3): 545–60
Katz E, Ziderman A 1990 Investment in general training: The role of information and labor mobility. *Economic Journal* 100(4): 1147–58
Lees D, Chiplin B 1970 The economics of industrial training. *Lloyds Bank Review* 96: 29–41
Middleton J, Ziderman A, Adams A V 1993 *Skills for Productivity: Vocational Education and Training in Developing Countries.* Oxford University Press, New York
Ziderman A, Horn R 1995 Many paths to skilled employment: A reverse tracer study of seven occupations in Colombia. *Education Economics* 3(1): 61–79

Further Reading

Dougherty C, Tan J-P 1991 *Financing Training: Issues and Options*, PRE Working Paper WPS 716. World Bank, Washington, DC
Freeman R 1993 Labor market institutions and policies: Help or hindrance to economic development? In: World Bank 1993 *Proceedings of the World Bank Annual Conference on Economic Development 1992.* World Bank, Washington, DC
World Bank 1991 *Vocational and Technical Education and Training: A World Bank Policy Paper.* World Bank, Washington, DC
Ziderman A 1987 Initial vs recurrent training for skilled trades in Israel—Results of a 7-year follow-up study. *Economics of Education Review* 6(2): 91–98

Legislation in Adult Education

J. Lowe

Legislation affecting the education of adults has existed since the early 1960s, though in an attenuated form and in a minority of countries. It is only since about 1960 that the demand for legislation has become a recurrent theme in debates on adult education, and that the very phrase "legislation in adult education" has become part of the professional lexicon.

In this entry, the historical context of this development is described prior to a comparative analysis of the forms of legislation that have been adopted by national or regional authorities. The aims and actual impact of legislation are then examined in the light of the different political philosophies and constitutional traditions that prevail from one country to another. Among the key issues, two are singled out for special attention: first, the tension between the demands of adult educators for comprehensive enabling legislation and statutory networks, on the one hand, and what national authorities are prepared to concede on the other; second, the critical relationship between legislation and financing. Finally, probable trends are identified.

1. Definition and Scope

"Legislation" refers to the action of making or giving laws within sovereign states by duly elected assemblies at national or provincial level, or by a specific constitutional authority such as a monarch or president. A law may take several forms:

i) the statute or enactment of the legislature . . .;
ii) clauses in the Constitution;
iii) presidential or royal decrees or analogous instruments;
iv) regulations made under statute which require parliamentary approval;
v) regulations made under statute by Executive discretion (Jennings 1990 p. 411).

The coercive force of legislation varies considerably. On the one hand, it may be mandatory, requiring national or local government or employers or other groups to discharge a specific obligation or set of obligations. On the other hand, it may be discretionary, in that it recommends desirable actions on the part of government or other institutions but does not inflict penalties for failure to comply. Legislation may also be couched in general and often vague terms or go into detail about the modes of its implementation. These differences reflect the way states perceive and treat adult education in practice rather than theory, and explain why in some countries it has achieved a manifest legal status while in others it has not. They also reflect historic attitudes toward legislation in general. Whereas some countries are accustomed to codifying laws and regulations, often in an elaborate fashion, the Francophone countries, for instance, others prefer to keep codification to the minimum so that even the body of law affecting the education of the young is restricted.

An "adult" for educational purposes is legally defined elsewhere (see *Adult Education: Concepts and Principles*). A major difficulty in many countries, however, is that the meaning of adult education is obscure or at least open to several interpretations which may even be conflicting. This leads some authorities to define "adult education" for statutory purposes in a restricted sense, very far from the comprehensive definition provided, for example, by UNESCO (see *UNESCO and Adult Education*), and thereby to leave many organizations automatically outside the scope of legislation. A further complication is that, in federal countries, the provinces, states, or *Länder* may not only exercise their own jurisdictional authority in significantly diverse ways, but also interpret federal laws according to their own preferences and priorities (see *North America*).

2. A "Recent" Phenomenon

It is only since the 1960s that the concept of "legislation" has been readily associated with the education of adults, and that some laws have been enacted specifically citing "adult education" as distinct from "education." Even in the mid-1990s, the idea of specific law-making in favor of adult education is mainly espoused by interest groups seeking to influence the policies of national and other authorities, by international organizations, and by groups of activist adult educators joined together to foster the regional or worldwide development of the field as a whole.

The popular assumption, which is held implicitly rather than explicitly, is that adult education is a private or individual rather than a public or community good. Most adult educators do not even think about legislation as a phenomenon impinging on their work any more than primary or secondary school teachers. For their part, most governments tend not to perceive adult education as a free-standing sector requiring the underpinning of laws analogous to those that apply to the initial education of the young. At the same time, governments are influenced by equity and access arguments and the ideal of "learning societies," and laws are increasingly passed that apply to discrete sectors,

including, conspicuously, adult basic education and occupational training, or that apply to the education of adults only incidentally (see *Adult Basic Education; Lifelong and Continuing Education*).

3. An International Impulse

The pressures in favor of enacting laws in support of adult education are weak in all but a few countries. This is not only because the field itself is not perceived as a priority by governments and politicians, but also because those who advocate comprehensive policies for adult education backed by strong laws have not been sufficiently skillful and influential in cultivating legislative assemblies, public administrators, and political parties. Legislation may be initiated within the governmental apparatus or on the advice of commissions of inquiry as, for example, in Canada, or by means of public consultations, or by all these procedures. Denmark has undertaken a nationwide public consultation. After enactment, legislation is usually implemented by means of executive decisions and administrative regulations. Powerful interest groups seek to bring influence to bear on governments to introduce desired legislation and thereafter on the processes of enactment and implementation. When laws are couched in unspecific terms, as they often are, the executive decisions can be all important. In most countries, the field of adult education is too fragmented and remote from the center of power to permit the dynamic coalition of interests that might influence the three stages of initiating, enacting, and implementing legislation, and the programs of political parties, not least their election manifestos.

The case for legislation has received a much stronger impetus from international organizations—intergovernmental and nongovernmental—and movements than from pressures inside countries. This is explained by the fact that the former are convinced of the need to treat adult education as an independent and not a subsidiary public service, especially within less-developed countries, and within the context of national policies and plans for economic and social development. To that end, it appears essential for elected assemblies to enact laws and regulations promulgating national goals for adult education, allocating statutory responsibilities, and specifying minimum standards of provision, since mere exhortations and discretionary laws carry little weight with ministers of education, local authorities, and employers.

UNESCO has been the leading advocate of the case for legislation ever since the Second International Conference on Adult Education (1960) when delegates recognized that, in less-developed countries without universal primary education, it was vital to provide basic education for adults so that they might be able to live effectively both as economic producers and conscientious citizens. Such education could only be guaranteed, however, if it were legally sanctioned as a public obligation. By the time of the Third International Conference (1972), the necessity for legislation had been taken up by many leading adult educators in advanced industrialized (EBAE 1974) and less-developed countries alike, and was highlighted in the Conference deliberations.

In 1974, the General Conference of the International Labour Organisation adopted the well-known "Paid Educational Leave (PEL) Convention" that has undoubtedly inspired much subsequent national legislation on adult training. Paid educational leave is leave granted to a worker for educational purposes for a specific period during working hours, with adequate financial entitlements. Article 5 states: "The means by which provision is made for the granting of paid educational leave may include *laws and regulations*, collective agreements, arbitration awards, and such other means as may be consistent with national practice."

In 1976, as a follow-up to the Third International Conference, the General Conference of UNESCO adopted a "Recommendation on the Development of Adult Education," which had the purpose of enhancing the status of adult education in all member states by guaranteeing minimum standards of provision and encouraging governments to devise and implement appropriate sustaining laws (UNESCO 1977).

Subsequently, the Fourth International Conference on Adult Education (1985) recommended that a survey of legislative and administrative measures in member countries should be undertaken by UNESCO. The results of this survey, based on replies to a detailed questionnaire from 28 countries, provide an authoritative source for the condition of legislation on the world scale (UNESCO 1988, Federighi 1989).

4. Individual and Collective Rights and State Obligations

The most obvious difference between the initial education of the young and the education of adults is that the former is almost universally governed by statute while the latter is not. Children have the right to schooling, and the state is legally obliged to provide it. As a rule, there is a national act or law prescribing a fixed period of compulsory schooling for all children or giving every child the right to at least some years of schooling. That legislation usually specifies how schooling shall be provided, with what resources, and under what conditions. In advanced industrialized countries, initial education is compulsory for 8 to 10 years and, increasingly, young people are required to remain in one form or another of education and training up to the age of at least 18 in order to be eligible for social security payments. Beyond that age those who complete the entire secondary cycle usually have the right to proceed to a postsecondary institution, often

with the guarantee of financial support from public funds to a greater or lesser extent.

By contrast, in the great majority of countries, adult education is not an individual or collective right and the state is under no obligation to provide it even if, *de facto*, adults may be admitted to certain educational institutions (such as the universities in many socialist countries and in Sweden) and to certain programs under favorable terms (such as literacy classes). There are also a few countries (including Iraq, Syria, and Thailand) in which education is compulsory for all adults for specific purposes or as a precondition of employment in the public sector. As long ago as 1943, a law in Thailand required illiterate adults between the ages of 20 and 45 to pay a fee until they could demonstrate that they had become literate. In several countries, participation is seen as a duty. In some countries, what is commonly called "mandatory recertification" applies to such professions as medicine and law.

"Adult education" is rarely mentioned in legislation, at least explicitly, which is not surprising given that it is not usually regarded as a discrete part of education systems. In Germany, for example, "No common clauses for the promotion of adult education are to be found in the constitutions of the individual states. In Baden-Württemberg, Bavaria, Bremen, North-Rhine-Westphalia, Rhineland-Palatinate, and Schleswig-Holstein, the clauses on the promotion of adult education have only an advisory character and do not mention the form or extent of this support" (Knoll 1980 p. 17). The last two qualifications equally apply to many other countries. In terms of its impact, legislation is often as significant for what it does not say as for what it does say.

Legislation specifically citing adult education is enacted frequently in less-developed countries, which are more disposed than advanced industrialized countries to perceive it as a collective necessity. Mexico has a national law on adult education. Laws have been passed for the creation of statutory boards or councils of adult education as in India, Kenya, and Nigeria, among other countries, or for the financing of national literacy campaigns, as in Brazil and Tanzania, or for public health education, as in China, or the education of women, as in Zambia.

Among advanced industrialized countries, the outstanding exception is Norway, where Parliament passed the *Act No.35 of May 28, 1977 concerning Adult Education*. Previously, Parliament had established two principles: that is, "adult education should be on an equal footing with basic general education for children and young people, and the definition of adult education comprised vocational as well as liberal/general education" (Norwegian Association of Adult Education Associations 1985 p. 3). The Act is explicit about the relative duties of the state, counties, and municipalities, and contains detailed regulations for financing nongovernmental agencies, as well as covering a wide range of provision, classified under eight types of programs. In Sweden, the Adult Education Act of 1984 contained regulations for direct provision by the municipal authorities:

Adult basic education at the 6th grade level in the compulsory school system is guaranteed by laws. All immigrants are entitled to special programmes in Swedish as a second language. Furthermore, special measures are drawn up for functionally disabled adults. A current policy issue is if this level will be elevated to up to nine years of formal schooling or even some general subjects at upper secondary level (Abrahamsson 1990 p.9) (see *Europe: Nordic Countries*)

Although not explicitly mentioning adult education, laws frequently refer to, or make specific provision for, aspects of it under the aegis of a variety of ministries, notably Agriculture, Health, and Labor, and miscellaneous government agencies. In Italy:

. . . a survey of the entire legislative output of Parliament between 1970 and 1985 revealed that approximately 1,000 laws were enacted containing provisions relating in one way or another to adult education. This suggests that the scope of adult education legislation is much more extensive than previously thought. (Federighi 1989 p.301)

5. *Importance of Impact*

However, scope is not to be confounded with impact. In the United States: "While hundreds of federal and state enactments provide financial support for adult education [usually through narrowly targeted programs] only a few have had a broad impact nationally" (Darkenwald and Merriam 1982 p.178). It seems that the organized provision of facilities for adult education will only occur if legislation lays precise obligations on education and other statutory authorities, requires minimum levels of funding, and prescribes rights of access to individuals. In Denmark, for example, the law requires that public institutions such as schools and libraries shall provide accommodation for adult classes when they are not serving their primary purpose and that any group of 12 adults may participate in classes subsidized by the state by up to 80 percent of the cost.

It is equally evident that legislation as such may have little effect if it does not prescribe ways and means of attaining desired objectives by the use of decrees, directives, regulations, and administrative decisions. In fact, this seldom happens. In Germany, for example: "Their [the laws'] legally-binding character is still vague. The phrase which has been used in most cases is 'Adult Education has to be promoted.' The interpretation is undecided whether this prescription includes an obligatory funding for adult education or not" (Knoll 1989 p. 467).

An experience in the United States is a classic illustration. The Lifelong Learning Act, passed in October 1976, contained an extraordinarily far-ranging set of objectives for making education available to all adults, especially the underprivileged outside the mainstream economy. The Act gave an undoubted stimulus to professional workers in adult education but, according to the penetrating appraisal of Richardson, its practical impact was limited because it lacked the requirements

of a good policy (that it be directive, suggesting a course or method of selection selected from among alternatives and, in light of conditions, to guide and determine present and future decisions, that it be understandable, that it provide for conflict resolution and that it incorporate provision of systematic review and evaluation of policies, guidelines and procedures in the policy itself). So no money was ever appropriated for the Act. (Richardson 1989 p. 54)

Other commentators have also pointed out that the Act appeared not as an amendment to the Elementary and Secondary Education Act, but to the Higher Education Act. In other words, adult education was not connected to the strongly entrenched school sector but to a sector in which its status was notoriously marginal.

By contrast with the Lifelong Learning Act, the United States Adult Education Act of 1966 is generally considered to have made a considerable impact. The purpose of this Act was to initiate a nationwide program designed to help those "whose inability to speak, read, or write the English language constitutes a substantial impairment of their ability to get or retain employment commensurate with their real ability." According to Darkenwald and Merriam (1982 p. 178), "Its importance comes not so much from the size of the program in dollars or enrollment terms as from the impetus it provided for growing federal and state involvement in policy making, co-ordination, and professional leadership for an expanding segment of the field."

Does it follow from the United States experience that, as many interest groups argue, legislation should recognize adult education as the fourth estate of education having equal status with the primary, secondary, and postsecondary sectors? Should not teachers, administrators, and all those employed in adult education have the same rights as the workforce in the national education system? At the very least, should legislation not require the state to provide, directly or indirectly, learning opportunities for the underprivileged groups in society? The responses to these questions vary from country to country. In practice, legislation reflects the degree of each state's commitment according to the following categories of actual or potential intervention in the education of adults (Lowe 1992).

6. *Direct Commitment of the State*

In "socialist" countries and countries controlled by a single political party, virtually all adult education may be provided by the state or parastatal bodies, and legislated for accordingly in greater or lesser detail. The People's Republic of China offers an outstanding example of comprehensive legislation sustaining intensive adult education programs across the country. In the former Socialist Republic of Romania, the education of adults was intended to be uniform in town and country under the Law of Education and the Law on the Improvement of Vocational Training. Among the provisions of the legislation was compulsory retraining of every worker at least every five years (Nicolae 1981 p. 63).

In parliamentary democracies, the extent of direct public provision depends on national values, political traditions, and current political and economic priorities. In nearly all countries, however, it is clear that adult education policies, and any legislation designed to implement them, tend to be reactive rather than proactive and that the priorities are nearly always the same: (a) to enable adults to acquire basic knowledge and skills, which may mean becoming literate, reaching the equivalent of the end of compulsory schooling, or completing the secondary (high) school cycle, depending on a country's stage of development and level of resources; (b) to make every adult employable and productive. Through legislation, the state may address the first priority exclusively by public provision at the national, regional, or local level or by a mixture of public and nonpublic provision. Legislation to implement the second priority usually mandates public provision, notably for the training of the unemployed, and requires employers to provide direct training for their employees or pay a levy toward training to be undertaken by the public authorities or other agencies, or sometimes to do both.

7. The State as Enabler and Stimulator

In a number of countries, the state is overwhelmingly the main provider of adult education either for ideological reasons or because nongovernmental agencies and institutions have not taken root on a significant scale. In other countries, the state shares the task of provision with other agencies to a greater or lesser extent according to historic practice. Discussion on legislation then centers on what the state should do to assist agencies to deliver or service adult education programs. This is not only a question of funding, but of facilitating coordination, helping disseminate information, promoting research, and regulating the suitability and quality of the provision, particularly that which is in receipt of public financing.

In many countries, the nongovernmental and nonformal sectors provide more adult education programs than the public sector. This creates a tension that can be either constructive or unhealthy according to the cultural context. The nongovernmental sector wishes to have the maximum amount of public financing and access to public support services but with the minimum number of conditions, rules, and regulations. Thus, it will advocate the need for legislation in its favor while not welcoming the extension of direct public provision or the enactment of comprehensive regulations that might detract from its own independence.

The state may choose to support individuals directly as well as, or theoretically instead of, institutions and agencies. Grants to adult students to take up or to resume university studies offer a good example of direct provision (see *University Adult Education*). If, up to the early 1990s, the great bulk of legislation has concerned provision by public or nonpublic institutions and agencies, the issue of legislation to promote individual rights and choices is likely to become increasingly prominent.

7.1 The State as Regulator

This aspect of legislation is seldom mentioned. It mainly concerns the duty of the state to account for the proper expenditure of public funds. By and large, national, regional, and local authorities are content to attach conditions to subsidies which they expect to be obeyed but as a rule do not monitor. The programs of institutions and agencies may be occasionally inspected in accordance with the rules generally applying to the use of public financing. Governments may also monitor the integrity of programs. Thus, the Netherlands Parliament passed the Correspondence Education Act 1972 in order to ensure that adequate standards would be maintained by agencies offering correspondence courses.

7.2 The State and Support Services

Apart from directly providing programs or financing programs in the nonpublic sector, the state may legislate for the promotion of adult education in several ways including: (a) creating and subsidizing national statutory boards or councils, as in New Zealand and Singapore, or regional committees, as in Spain where the coordinating role of the public education service is made explicit under the terms of the *Regulations of May 8, 1989 concerning Public Institutions of Continuing Adult Education* issued by the Ministry of Education and Science; (b) collecting and disseminating relevant data; (c) financing research and development activities; (d) subsidizing or wholly financing the initial or inservice training of adult educators; (e) subsidizing *crèches* for parents participating in programs.

8. The Financing Connection

The key determinant of whether legislation is necessary or not and, if so, how comprehensive, depends on who is expected to pay—the state or the individual or both—and how much. Legislation and financing are inextricably intertwined. Laws promoting adult education are worthless unless they require provision of the necessary resources. Adult educators commonly believe that a lack of money to pay fees is the main deterrent to many adults to participate in programs and that a lack of mandatory support grants exposes governmental and nongovernmental providers to the fluctuations of the economic cycle. In other words, the demand is permanently kept down and the supply is regularly choked off.

In some countries, most institutions are only partially subsidized. Thus, participants must pay fees sufficient to cover all or part of the real cost. Paradoxically, those who cannot pay fees typically belong to the underprivileged in societies—low-income earners and groups which are the declared targets of national or regional policies. It is mainly for this reason that interest groups ask that the law should treat adult education as an individual *and* a collective right alongside the right to initial education, and that programs for the underprivileged should be eligible for mandatory financing. Some interest groups have further proposed that the law should require states to allocate a fixed percentage of their education budgets to adult education or include a special vote in the annual estimates of national assemblies.

Even if a state resolves that all adults shall have the right of access to educational opportunities, neither existing nor reallocated nor additional public resources can possibly meet all demands. This implies that the state must select priorities among the many forms of adult education whether explicitly or implicitly. On the one hand, it cannot fund all programs. On the other, it expects to see public funds put to the best public use. The implication is that no state is likely to risk enacting legislation that makes an open-ended commitment to financial expenditure either to institutions and agencies or to individuals. For instance, any government is bound to hesitate before enacting a law that guarantees all adults a basic entitlement in the form of an "education check" or drawing rights to so much education during their lifetime. The same constraint applies to making an irrevocable commitment to support adult education as an integral sector of the general system of education. A state may acknowledge the ideal of creating and maintaining a comprehensive public adult education service and may adopt practical measures for advancing it, but it is likely to refrain from legislation that would tie its hands in perpetuity, preferring to stick to a discretionary allocation of funds.

In practice, states can finance adult education principally in four ways: (a) by making direct provision; (b) by funding nongovernmental agencies; (c) by funding individuals or, sometimes, groups of individuals; (d) by funding such auxiliary agencies as libraries, museums, and cultural centers. These are usually governed by separate laws enacted piecemeal rather than by comprehensive legislation. In some

countries, the principles governing funding are transparent, as in Austria with the Federal Funding of Adult Education and Public Libraries Act of 1973.

8.1 Paid Educational Leave

One way in which governments can, and increasingly do, encourage the education of adults is by compelling employers to allow their employees time off for study on paid leave, which, as pointed out earlier, the International Labour Conference, Convention 140 conceived as leave granted to a worker for educational purposes for a specified period during working hours, with adequate financial entitlements. This formula ensures that workers are able to take advantage of whatever provision is available. Laws on paid educational leave now exist in many countries throughout the world.

The 1971 Vocational Training Act in France was particularly significant in its scope and concreteness. It enshrined the right of individuals to training, even for their own benefit rather than that of their employers; placed obligations on employers to provide adequate training for their employees; specified a levy on payrolls to finance programs; and interpreted "training" in a broad sense to incorporate social and cultural as well as economic needs.

As to occupational training, the role and financial contribution of the public authorities vary according to national policies and traditional practices. In the Nordic countries, with their active labor force training policies, both are of a substantial order. Many less-developed countries have passed laws in favor of work-oriented and functional literacy, some, like Turkey, requiring employers to make a financial contribution (see *Demand, Supply, and Finance of Adult Education; Paid Educational Leave and Collective Bargaining*).

9. Research Agenda

There is no serious lack of information about the scope and type of legislation that exists throughout the world, especially in Europe and North America. References to legislation or laws in adult education have multiplied in bibliographies since the early 1960s. There is an imbalance, however, between the amount of information available in Western countries and that available in other countries, particularly those in the Third World. More significantly, there has been almost no research into the processes of legislation in adult education. Such fundamental questions need to be addressed as: How do laws come into force? What has been the influence of special interest groups? How competent are they vis-à-vis such groups in other sectors? How are laws administered? What has been the impact of legislation on programs and practice?

10. Conclusion

In the broad international perspective, one can expect an overall increase in the amount of legislation in the years ahead as more countries make a formal commitment to promote lifelong learning and others strengthen their existing commitment. A commitment to recurrent education will particularly require legislation. Some branches of adult education will be favored, such as basic education, which has been viewed as a necessity of life in less-developed countries since the World Conference on Education for All, held in Jomtiem, Thailand in 1990, and occupational or career training, which many countries treat as an economic priority. However, the extent and character of legislation will continue to depend on the political philosophies and constitutional traditions that prevail within countries and whether societies see the education of adults as an important public as well as private good. Most countries will remain wary about enacting laws that entail a permanent obligation, especially the open-ended provision of public funds. Piecemeal enactments are probable rather than comprehensive laws. For their part, special interest groups will always press for binding rather than permissive legislation, especially those that seek the same legal status for adult education as for the education of the young, or those that insist upon a basic entitlement to lifelong or continuing education for all adults.

See also: Adult Education: Concept and Principles; Demand, Supply and Finance of Adult Education; Technological Change and Education; Government Role in Adult Education and Training

References

Abrahamsson K 1990 Learning rights for the next century: Improving learning options by a new deal between the public and private interests in adult learning (Discussion paper). Swedish National Board of Education, Stockholm
Darkenwald G G, Merriam S B 1982 *Adult Education: Foundations of Practice.* Harper Collins, New York
European Bureau of Adult Education (EBAE) 1974 *Adult Education Legislation in Ten Countries of Europe: A Report Commissioned by the Council of Europe.* EBAE, Amersfoort
Federighi P 1989 Adult education: Legislative and administrative measures. In: UNESCO 1989 *Adult Education: Legislative and Administrative Measures.* UNESCO, Athens (Doc. code ED 89/WS/75)
Jennings B 1990 Legislation. In: Titmus C *et al.* (eds.) 1990 *International Handbook of Adult Education,* Vol. 3. European Centre for Leisure and Education, Prague
Knoll J H 1980 *Adult Education in Europe: Federal Republic of Germany.* Studies and Documents No. 8. European Centre for Leisure and Education, Prague
Knoll J H 1989 Adult education and legislation. In: UNESCO 1989 *Adult Education: Legislative and Administrative Measures.* UNESCO, Athens
Lowe J 1992 Public intervention in adult education. In: Tuijnman A C, van der Kamp M (eds.) 1992 *Learning Across the Lifespan: Theories, Research, Policies.* Pergamon Press, Oxford
Nicolae V 1981 Education of adults in the Socialist Republic of Romania. *Convergence* 14(2): 63–69
Norwegian Association of Adult Education Associations 1985 *Adult Education in Norway.* Norwegian Association of Adult Education Associations, Oslo
Richardson P 1989 Personal versus national priorities in adult education: The adult educator's role in resolving the conflict. In: Swinburn E, Wellings J (eds.) 1989 *Government Roles in Adult Education: International Perspectives.* Grade 88 Inc., Sydney
UNESCO 1977 *Recommendation on the Development of Adult Education.* Adopted at 19th Session, Nairobi. UNESCO, Paris
UNESCO 1988 *Questionnaire on New Trends in Legislation on Adult Education: Descriptions of National Cases.* UNESCO, Paris

Further Reading

European Bureau of Adult Education (EBAE) 1985 *Survey of Adult Education Legislation.* EBAE, Amersfoort
Norwegian Institute of Adult Education 1980 *The Norwegian Adult Education Act.* Norwegian Institute of Adult Education, Trondheim
Thomas A M 1987 Policy development for adult education: The law. In: Rivera W M (ed.) 1987 *Planning Adult Learning: Issues, Practices and Directions.* Croom Helm, London
United States Congress 1976 *The Lifelong Learning Act.* US Government Printing Office, Washington, DC

Market Concepts in Provision

N. Stacey and D. le To

Adult education is reborn. Not only is the number of participants and providers growing, but also the courses and programs are changing. The purpose of this entry is to observe major trends in the market of adult education and training. The entry starts with a definition of adult education, followed by the observation of changes in the markets, based on data collected mostly from the United States.

1. Definition

Since there is no consensus of what adult education covers in the literature, an operational definition of adult education is necessary before further discussion. The following definition by Liveright (1968) has been selected for the purpose of this entry:

> Adult education is a process through which persons no longer attending school in a regular, full-time basis undertake activities with the conscious intention of bringing about changes in information, knowledge, understanding, skills, appreciation, and attitudes; or to identify and solve personal or community problems. (p. 3)

This definition differentiates between the consumers of adult education and students who pursue education in a linear (continuous) mode, and enables one to focus less on remedial education by broadening the scope of such programs. The definition also emphasizes the intention of bringing about changes in information and solving personal and community problems. This suggests that adult education is not only a learning process, but also the exchange of knowledge to solve personal problems, including acquiring job skills. Therefore, with this broad definition, the distinction between education and training is not necessary. Training consists simply of job-related education activities received by adult workers. With its emphasis on the exchange of knowledge, this definition also supports the view that adult education is a commodity that people trade in a marketplace. The following sections contain discussions of important adult education issues such as who participates and who provides it.

2. Participants

According to the 1990-91 National Household Education Survey (NHES), conducted by the United States Department of Education, approximately 57,391,000 adults in the United States participated, on a part-time basis, in adult education and training programs. These adults constitute about 32 percent of the total population aged 17 years or over (Korb et al. 1991 Table 2). (For the rest of this entry, this percentage will be referred to as the "participation rate.")

The participation rate in adult education activities in 1991 was much higher than those found a decade previously. (The 1983 Current Population Survey (CPS) shows that the participation rate was only 14%). However, it is believed that about one-third of the estimated increase is attributed to the different methods used to conduct the two different surveys. A summary of comparisons between the CPS estimates and the NHES estimates was presented in a recent report (see National Center for Education Statistics 1991 Appendix A). Data from the CPS, however, indicate that the participation rate of American adults in education and

training increased steadily from 1969 to 1983 (see Table 1).

To obtain further information on how adult workers get their training, the CPS also posed a supplemental series of questions in its January 1983 and January 1991 surveys. The supplement centered on two questions: "Did you need specific skills or training to obtain your current job?" and "Since you obtained your present job, did you take any training to improve your skills?" The comparison of responses to these questions between 1983 and 1991 reveals two important trends in the United States labor market. First, workers are more likely to indicate that they need specific skills or training to qualify for the current jobs (57 percent of workers indicated such need in 1991 in comparison with 55 percent in 1983). Second, once they have obtained the job, they are also more likely to take additional training to improve their skills. The CPS data indicate that 41 percent of the workers in 1991 took skill-improvement training; in 1983, only 35 percent of them received this kind of training (see Table 1).

The increasing need for adult education and training is not unique to the United States; it is a global phenomenon. Adults from other countries also seem to be interested in postschool education. For example, about one-fourth of Canadian workers participated in adult education, a rate similar to that in the United States (Office of Technology Assessment 1990 p. 18). A survey of adults in the United Kingdom indicates that most individuals are interested in acquiring training even though they have no expectation of taking any course. According to the survey, only 9 percent of the workforce in the United Kingdom are willing to describe themselves as not particularly interested in education and training. Furthermore, even though more than 40 percent of adult respondents do not see themselves acquiring training in the future, only 14 percent agree with the proposition that training will make little difference to their work progress.

The overwhelming interest in training shown in the United Kingdom survey is, however, not reflected by the participation rates. Only one fourth of the labor force in the United Kingdom reports that it has received employer-sponsored training in the past three years (Ryan 1991). It is unclear why adults who are interested in training do not actually participate. The following comparisons of participation rates among different demographic groups explain the issues further.

2.1 Who Participates in Adult Education and Training

Standard human capital theories predict that education and training investments decline with age. It is believed that individuals and their employers have less incentive to invest in education and training as the individuals get older because, as they get older, the remaining time for them to benefit from the investment becomes shorter and the internal rate of return lower. However, an empirical examination of the training statistics of member countries of the Organisation for Economic Co-operation and Development (OECD) does not seem to support these theories. It indicates that training participation by age shows two broad patterns. First, in some countries (especially those with strong apprenticeship systems, such as Germany, France, Ireland, Spain, and the United Kingdom), young people are much more likely to receive training and the incidence (participation rate) declines steadily with age. Second, in other countries (such as the United States), training incidence tends to increase with age, reaching a peak within the 30-44 age group and then falling off (OECD 1991 Tables 5.1a and 5.1b).

The United States data collected for the 1990-91 National Household Education Survey show an inverted U-shaped distribution of adult education participation rates by age groups, peaking at the 35-44 age group. The participation rate for the 17-24 age group was about the same as that of the 45-54 age group and smaller than any other age groups except for persons aged 55 and over (see Table 2). Similar participation patterns were also found in job training. The youngest age group (16–19) was the least likely to obtain jobs that required qualification training and also had the lowest participation rate in skill-improvment training.

Obviously, some important factors have been left out in the standard human capital theories. Indeed, the differences in participation patterns reflect, to some extent, the institutional features of the labor market in different countries. For France and Germany, the observed pattern is strongly related to apprentices, virtually all of whom are under the age of 25. Since apprentices, in general, receive more training than nonapprentices, it is not surprising that those under the age of 25 in these countries have a higher incidence of training than people at other ages. On the other hand, the relatively low participation rate of 17-24 years olds in the United States is partly reflected by the lack of employer support for the training of inexperienced workers.

Education and training participation patterns by age may change in response to the changes in technology and labor market conditions. Many human capital theorists believe that education and skills acquired at different times are associated with different technologies and, therefore not homogeneous (Johnson 1980). In general, younger workers, who acquired their skills more recently than their older peers need less training to work with new technology. As technical progress accelerates, retraining will focus on older workers, whose skills are more likely to be outdated. The CPS data in Table 1 seem to support the theory: skill-improvement training increased more rapidly between 1983 and 1991 for workers aged 35 and over than for younger workers. This difference may reflect increased mid-career retraining in response to either changing skill requirements for given jobs or more frequent job changes and reassignments.

Educational attainment also affects participation in subsequent education and training. Data collected for the CPS and the NHES in the United States since the early 1960s consistently show that the participation rate in adult education and training increases with educational attainment (see Tables 1 and 2). The same findings are also evident in almost all countries: better educated workers are more likely to receive additional education and training compared with less educated workers. The only minor exception is that German workers in apprenticeship programs and French workers who are enrolled in what are classified as "vocational-oriented programs," are more likely to receive training in comparison with other groups (OECD 1991 Table 5.3).

Educational attainment becomes even more important for obtaining better jobs and subsequent training today than a decade ago. The CPS data indicate that workers with only four-year high school education or less were less likely to report that their current jobs needed qualification training in 1991 than they did in 1983, while the opposite was reported by those with higher education (see Table 1). Furthermore, only 18 percent of the workers with less than four-year high school education received skill-improvement training in 1991—that is one-percentage point increase from 1983. On the other hand, 61 percent of the workers with four-year college education or more received such training; a 7 percentage-point increase in the same period.

2.2 The Gender Gap

Previous empirical research has shown that American Black men's and Black and White women's earnings do not increase with their experience as rapidly as the earning of White men (Mincer and Polachek 1974). One of the speculations for the causes of the flat earnings profile is that women and Black workers are less likely to get training than their counterparts. However, a recent study based on labor force survey data collected in nine OECD countries does not reveal substantial differences in the incidence of training between women and men (OECD 1991 Table 5.1a). Spain is the only country out of the nine in the sample that reveals a large gender disparity, but the incidence of training of Spanish women is larger than that of the men. Data collected in the United States also show no difference in the participation rates of adult education between men and women (see Table 2). The CPS data in Table 1 indicate that the participation rate of women in adult education in the United States was slightly lower than men's before 1975, but increased faster than that of their male counterparts from 1969 to 1984. Consequently, during the 1980s, more women participated in adult education than men. Similar patterns were also found in job training.

Table 1
Rates of participation in adult education and training, and percentage distributions of adult education courses, and occurrences of training, United States 1969–91

	Adult Education			Qualification Training		Skill Improvement Training	
	1969	1975	1983	1983	1991	1983	1991
Total adults (in thousands)	130215	146602	172583	—g	—g	—g	—g
Participants (in thousands)a	13041	17059	23303	53890	65276	33901	46814
Participation rate (%)b	10	12	14	55	57	35	41
Age:c							
17–34	14	16	16	—g	—g	—g	—g
35–54	11	13	17	—g	—g	—g	—g
55 and over	3	4	6	—g	—g	—g	—g
16–19	—g	—g	—g	25	26	18	18
20–24	—g	—g	—g	47	46	28	31
25–34	—g	—g	—g	62	60	39	41
35–44	—g	—g	—g	62	63	41	48
45–54	—g	—g	—g	57	60	37	46
55–64	—g	—g	—g	52	53	31	37
65 or over	—g	—g	—g	41	44	19	25
Gender/raced							
Male	11	12	13	56	57	35	40
Female	9	12	14	54	56	34	41
White	10	12	14	57	58	36	42
Black	8	7	7	44	47	28	34
Hispanic	—g	—g	—g	43	41	23	28
Years of school completede							
Less than 4-year high school	4	3	4	29	27	17	18
4-year high school	11	12	11	48	45	32	35
1 to 3 year college	17	18	19	62	63	41	46
4 or more years college	27	28	29	84	84	54	61
Percentage of adult education courses/training provided by:							
School	61	58	53	40	39	29	26
Elementary-secondary schools	13	6	4	6	5	1	1
2-year college	13	18	17	6	9	9	10
4-year college	27	22	17	22	23	15	12
Vocational/trade school	9	6	10	5	3	4	3
Other school	—g	3	3	—g	—g	—g	—g
Nonschool	39	42	47	60	61	71	74
Business and industry	14	12	17	51	48	61	61
Formal company training	—g	—g	—g	13	15	27	31
Informal OJT training	—g	—g	—g	38	33	34	30
Labor/professional organization	—g	5	6	—g	—g	—g	—g
Government agency	—g	6	8	—g	—g	—g	—g
Armed forces	—g	—g	—g	3	3	—g	—g
Community organization	9	8	9	—g	—g	—g	—g
Other/did not report	16	11	8	6	10	11	14

Sources: Stacey and To 1993 Table 1, US Department of Labor 1992 Tables 1, 5, 14, 38, 42 and 49, Stacey and To 1990 Tables 7.1 and 7.2

a Full-time students of colleges and elementary-secondary schools are not counted as participants in adult education. The 1969 survey did not ask those who were 35 years old or over whether they were full-time students. Therefore, some persons in this age bracket were counted as participants.   b Defined as percentage of participants in total adult population.   c For 1983, the numbers are aggregated from the age brackets: 17–24, 25–34, 35–44, 45–54, and 65 and over.   d For 1969 and 1975, numbers were not reported seperately for Hispanic.   e Numbers on training for 4-year high school and less were taken from Bower and Swaim, 1994 Table 1.   f Percent of training provided by a specific provider is obtained by dividing the number of occurrences of the specific training by the sum of all occurrences of training in the sample.   g Not available.

Table 2
Rate of participation in adult education and percentage of participants by type of employer involvement, participation objectives, and other selected characteristics: civilian adults 17 years and older, United States, 1991

| | Participation rate | | | Percentage of participants | | | | | | | | | |
| | | | | Type of employer involvement | | | | | | Objective of participation | | | |
Characteristics	Participated in the past year	Participated in the past 3 years	Ever participated	Any type	Given at workplace	Paid by employer	Provided by employer	Required by employer	Provided time off	Diploma or degree	License or certificate	Basic skills	Career-related
All adults	32	38	54	64	32	51	38	30	48	31	21	8	73
Age													
17–24 years	33	40	43	54	28	39	36	26	39	48	16	20	62
25–34 years	37	48	58	68	31	55	40	36	50	37	26	8	79
35–44 years	44	51	65	70	35	56	40	30	53	30	22	6	79
45–54 years	32	37	58	71	39	59	44	32	55	22	20	5	80
55–64 years	23	26	51	64	30	48	36	27	45	18	18	4	70
65 years and over	10	13	38	18	8	12	9	9	12	8	13	3	26
Gender/race													
Male	32	36	51	73	35	58	42	34	56	31	24	7	80
Female	32	40	55	57	29	46	35	27	41	31	19	8	68
White, non-Hispanic	33	40	56	65	32	53	39	30	49	30	22	6	74
Black, non-Hispanic	23	28	41	59	36	48	41	38	44	38	21	17	71
Household income													
$10,000 or less	14	21	39	39	18	25	24	23	29	34	13	17	62
$10,001 to $15,000	21	29	45	52	27	37	24	27	37	36	24	10	66
$15,001 to $20,000	21	26	39	57	28	42	35	29	39	33	20	11	67
$20,001 to $25,000	25	33	48	67	34	46	37	34	48	30	22	8	73
$25,001 to $30,000	30	37	52	58	30	48	38	29	39	34	21	10	69
$30,001 to $40,000	35	39	57	68	35	57	43	35	50	35	26	8	76
$40,001 to $50,000	44	49	62	67	34	55	42	33	50	33	22	6	74
$50,0001 to $75,000	46	53	68	72	35	61	43	32	58	29	18	6	79
More than $75,000	48	55	69	68	30	54	37	24	53	22	23	4	77
Years of school completed													
Up to 8th grade	7	8	17	25	18	13	16	13	15	20	9	25	32
9th to 11th grade	14	18	31	38	18	23	21	23	20	42	19	19	52
12th grade	22	29	46	62	28	50	34	30	43	30	21	10	71
Vocational school after HS	32	34	56	70	42	55	43	49	54	25	20	5	75
Some college	39	48	64	60	32	49	37	29	45	39	20	10	70
Associate degree	49	63	78	76	47	66	51	39	63	35	26	7	84
Bachelor's degree or higher	52	59	73	71	34	57	44	30	56	26	23	3	81

Source: National Center for Education Statistics 1991, Tables 1, 3, 5, and 8

While there is little difference between men and women in receiving education and training, further examination of data on types of training for several countries suggests that women are less likely to receive formal, employer-sponsored training. According to a study based on enterprise-based data collected in four OECD countries, women are less likely to receive training in all but one country, Norway. The data collected from Norway shows no difference in the incidence of training between men and women (OECD 1991 Table 5.1b).

In the United States, female workers seem to receive less education and training support from their employers than men. Only 57 percent of the women who participated in adult education and training had some form of employer involvement in these activities. This percentage is much lower than that for men (see Table 2). Another study based on CPS data also indicates that women are less likely to get formal, employer-sponsored training though they may get the same or even more qualification-training from other sources (Stacey and To 1990). However, receiving education and training from other sources, but not from the employers may put women at a disadvantaged position when seeking promotion. As shown in some studies, getting formal company (or more structured) training is important for career development and wage growth (Lynch 1994). It is also interesting to note that, while women in the United States are as likely as men to take courses for basic skills, diplomas, and degrees, they are less likely to take courses for licenses and career development (see Table 2).

A racial gap, similar to that found in the chances of receiving postschool education and training between women and men discussed above, is also a major concern in some multicultural societies such as the United States and Australia. The United States data shown in both Tables 1 and 2 consistently indicate that White adults are more likely to participate in adult education than Black adults. Unlike the gender gap indicated earlier, the difference in participation rates between White and Black adults has not narrowed, but widened during the period from 1969 to 1991 (see Tables 1 and 2). In general, the extent of employer's involvement in Black workers' education and training is also lower. As shown in Table 2, the percentages of Black and White adult education participants who had any form of employer's involvement in the activities are 59 and 65 respectively.

Some researchers believe that women and Black workers receive less employer-sponsored training because they are mostly working in dead-end jobs where training opportunities are few. This is possible because fewer women and Black adults are in managerial and professional occupations, and managerial and professional workers are more likely to participate in education and training than others (Korb et al. 1991). Black workers are also less likely to have high-level nonmanual jobs as compared to White workers. An OECD study (1991 Table 5.4) indicates that nonmanual workers seem generally more likely to receive training, especially company training, as compared to manual workers. In Australia and the United States, nonmanual workers are also much more likely to receive additional school-based or external training courses. Among nonmanuals, higher level workers seem to have a greater incidence of training than lower level workers. The manual occupations, on the other hand, exhibit no clear pattern.

In summary, adults who participate in adult education programs appear to be in occupations that either require them to take further education and training in order to remain employed or have monetary rewards closely tied to the participation. There are three implications that are worth noting. First, the participation of adults in postschool education and training could be substantially affected by the management and training practices of firms. If employers require more postschool education and training, and offer more monetary rewards for participation in such activities, the participation rate increases. Second, whether a worker gets better education and training opportunities depends on his or her occupation. Low-level manual jobs pay less and provide fewer training opportunities. However, workers with lower educational attainment are less likely to get jobs that provide better training opportunities. This creates a vicious circle for less educated and poor workers, who need training the most to improve their income and social status but are the least likely to get it. Third, a worker's occupation affects not only the amount, but also the type and frequency of training that he would receive. The 1990-91 NHES data indicate that most of the training that blue-collar workers received were technical skills and job safety, which are specific to their current jobs. Very few of them received computer-related training. For example, only 6 percent of the craft workers took computer courses as compared to 14 percent of the technical and administrative support workers. Furthermore, while managers and professionals continue to get training at age 55 and after, those in craft occupations have fewer chances to get training after 40 (Kopka and Peng 1994, Tables 4 and 5). The relatively short time and narrow focus of training for blue-collars could seriously limit their ability to adjust to rapid changes of technology.

3. Providers

Traditionally, most adults receive their education and training at schools and in the workplace. However, since the early 1970s, adult education and training markets have become more diversified and now involve providers who offer programs to adult learners in many different ways. This section discusses different types of providers and examines trends in providing adult education and training, mainly in the United States, since the early 1970s.

Providers of education and training are clustered into two groups based upon where the education takes place. They are: school-based and nonschool-based providers. School-based providers include institutions ranging from adult basic and secondary education programs to two-and four-year colleges and universities. Also included in this category are technical and proprietary schools. Nonschool-based providers include public and private employers, trade unions, professional associations, consulting firms, private instructors, churches, homes, and other community organizations.

3.1 School-based Providers

In the early 1970s, approximately 60 percent of the adult education courses were offered by schools: one-fourth were taken at four-year colleges and universities; and one-fourth were taken at elementary-secondary schools and two-year institutions. Vocational and trade schools provided about 10 percent of the courses. However, there has been a significant change in the provider's market share.

By 1983, the percentage of courses offered by schools and colleges fell from 61 percent to 53 percent, while those of nonschool-based providers—business, industry, government, and labor or professional organizations—increased from 39 percent to 47 percent. Noticeably, business and industry provided about 17 percent of the adult education courses and 8 percent were offered by federal, state, or local governments. The market shares of vocational/trade schools and two-year colleges, however, remained the same (see Table 1).

Similar changes were also found in the market of skill-improvement training in the 1980s. Between 1983 and 1991, the percentage of skill-improvement training offered by schools fell from 29 percent to 26 percent, while those of nonschool providers increased from 71 percent to 74 percent. Despite the loss in skill-improvement training market, school providers remained strong in training workers to qualify for new jobs. Their total share of qualification training only declined slightly from 40 percent to 39 percent, but there had been a notable shift in market share from vocational and technical schools to two- and four-year colleges and universities. The shift may reflect the growing concerns about the narrowness and inflexibility of traditional vocational education. Many researchers believe that adult workers today need strong basic academic skills and broader knowledge to adapt to the rapidly changing technology.

The decline in market share of school-based providers may not be as common in other countries are it is in the United States. In some countries, school-based providers still play an important role in training workers. For example, since the early 1970s, three-year vocational high schools and one-year training institutes, established under government auspices, have

helped South Korea train 2.4 million workers, about half of its workforce. By integrating vocational education and training programs into the national five-year economic development plans, the Korean government keeps these institutions attuned to the needs of the labor market. Furthermore, the government also makes vocational education programs closely related to professional certification and requires public firms and agencies to preferentially hire workers with such credentials (Lee et al. 1990).

3.2 Nonschool-based Providers

As indicated earlier; nonschool-based providers are becoming more important in providing adult education and training than was formerly the case. The increasing involvement of employers, private vendors, and governments is evident in many industrial countries. Most of the education and training provided by nonschool-based providers is job-oriented, usually in the form of apprenticeships and company training.

Germany best illustrates the apprenticeship approach. According to a research report, about 60 percent of the German workforce have completed an apprenticeship, which on average lasts for 3 years. The German apprenticeships are well-structured, combining on-the-job training with classroom instruction for at least 1 day per week. The German government works closely with trade associations and unions to define uniform national curricula and examinations for apprentices in more than 400 occupations (Office of Technology Assessment 1990 pp. 87–89). Apprentices are expected to get professional certification, which requires both passage of written tests and demonstration of practical skills.

Completing an apprenticeship is important for young German adults. According to the same report, more than 40 percent of the German certified crafts-workers in the 1980s found themselves in occupations other than those for which they apprenticed, but they were, nevertheless, much less likely to experience unemployment than unskilled workers. Many German employers, when job screening, consider completion of an apprenticeship an indication of the worker's motivation and ability to learn. Despite the fact that a substantial percentage of apprentices leave the firms in which they train, nearly 80 percent of German firms with at least 20 employees participate in apprenticeship programs.

Some countries do not put as much emphasis on apprenticeship as Germany does. For example, the total number of apprentices in the United States has remained the same (about 300,000) since the early 1980s, while the workforce has grown by 20 percent. Only 0.16 percent of the civilian workforce in the United States currently participates in apprenticeship programs. In addition, apprenticeship is concentrated in a few occupations; more than half of those in registered apprenticeship programs work in the highly unionized construction industry. Indeed, one possible explanation for the small size of the apprenticeship programs in the United States is the presence of a relatively weaker union movement (40% of the German workforce is unionized, compared to 16% of the US workforce).

While vocational schools and apprenticeship play an important role in preparing adults for entering a profession, the upgrading of their skills primarily comes from their employers. According to the 1991 Current Population Survey, employer-provided training (formal company training programs and informal on-the-job training combined) accounts for 48 percent of the occurrences of job qualification training and 61 percent of skill improvement training in the United States (see Table 1). For blue-collar, semiskilled workers, the shares of employer-provided training in total occurrences of training are even larger (Stacey and To 1990 Table 7.1). In the United Kingdom, employers provide about 75 percent of adult education and training, though it is available to only a minority of workers. Only one-fourth of the United Kingdom labor force has received employer-sponsored training during a three-year period and only 1 in 11 workers sponsor their own training (Ryan 1991).

Employer-sponsored training varies not only in intensity and strategies, but also in modes of delivery. In fact, it does not have to be delivered at the workplace. In Norway, for example, a substantial portion of employer-sponsored training for new employees was delivered at schools and other educational institutions (Lynch 1994), while in Japan most of the training was taught in-house. A 1987 Japanese Ministry of Labor survey of the training practices of 2,035 firms employing 30 or more workers shows the firms' predominant reliance on in-house training courses. Among workers who received training, 88 percent of new entrants and 75 percent of experienced blue-collar workers got training by taking in-house training courses; only 20 percent of new entrants and 30 percent of experienced blue-collar workers took training courses from private training agencies. For managers, supervisors, and clerical workers, the percentages of getting training from in-house courses all exceed 65 much larger than those of private training agencies.

Since the early 1970s, many Japanese firms have also expanded in-house training programs. The responsibility of in-house training has shifted from small groups and designated individuals to departments and sections. In 1970, approximately 61 percent of the firms assigned small groups or individuals to carry out in-house training. In 1985, only 26 percent of them still allowed small groups and individuals to do so. Instead, 19 percent of the firms had a training department and 55 percent had a training section (Cairncross and Dore 1990).

Although Japanese company training relies heavily on in-house training, many firms supplement this with outside training, mostly correspondence courses

and training for skill tests. About one-fourth of the firms in the Ministry of Labor's survey said that they encouraged (or required) their employees to take correspondence courses, and the percentage of employees who took such courses was almost as high for blue-collar workers as for technicians and managers. Since the 1980s, the University of the Air has begun to offer a wide range of courses via television and radio. By 1989, 17 Japanese universities and junior colleges agreed to give transfer credit for courses completed through the University of the Air (see *Japan: Social and Adult Education*).

Unlike Japan, many firms in the United States rely on private consultants to design and carry out their training programs. Annual sales of outside services and off-the-shelf training programs and materials grew from US$1.5 billion in 1984 to US$3 billion in 1989. As a result, the number of private training vendors increased tremendously. Recent industry sources estimate there are at least 3,500 companies supplying training programs and seminars (Office of Technology Assessment 1990 p. 139). Two advantages of using private training agencies are often mentioned. First, private training agencies are often mentioned. First, private training firms, it is believed, often respond to emerging training needs faster than public educational institutions. Second, by using outside training vendors, firms do not need to maintain their own training centers and staff.

Benefits and cost-effectiveness of training are always the major consideration for firms to make their decisions on training. Employers only provide training that they believe is critical to their organizations and more effectively taught in the workplace than in schools. In a survey of employer-provided training conducted by the United States Department of Labor (1994), most establishments said that they provided formal job skill training in 1993 because they believed the training was necessary to provide skills specific to their organizations (75%) or to keep up with the changes in technology (53%); very few of them said they did it because they were unable to hire employees with adequate skills (13%) or the training was required by collective bargaining agreement (1%). The three kinds of job skills that were most commonly taught through formal training were sales and customer relations, management skills, and computer skills. Despite their complaints on the generally poor basic reading, writing, and arithmetic skills on entry-level workers, fewer than 3 percent of all establishments in the survey provided formal training for these skills. Most employers believed these were skills better acquired at educational institutions.

Company training could also be either formal or informal depending on the type of jobs. Some job skills are more easily taught formally, rather than informally. The CPS data in Table 1 reveals a remarkable shift in the share of training occurrences from informal on-the-job training (OJT) to formal company training between 1983 and 1991. This shift may reflect the falling demand for more specific or manual jobs skills, which are better suited for informal on-the-job learning. The change was also consistent to the findings of Bowers and Swaim (1994) that formal company training had a larger effect on wages than did OJT and the wage premium of OJT declined in the 1980s. Table 1 also indicates that the total share of (formal and informal), company training did not increase during the 1980s; the real increase in the nonschool market share was caused by the increase in the unclassified category "others," which include training provided by computer and equipment vendors and tutoring services delivered by computer software and networks.

Indeed, parent companies and equipment vendors play important roles in training for adult workers. For example, in manufacturing many small firms are subsidiaries, subcontractors, and parts-makers for large corporations. The parent companies, being concerned about the quality of the products and staff of their subsidiaries, usually provide training in two ways: (a) sending their technicians (trainers) to the subsidiaries to help upgrade their skills, and (b) accepting some of the subsidiaries' technical operatives as trainees at the parent's training centers.

The role of equipment vendors in providing training to workers is becoming more important. In many cases, especially where new technologies are involved, only the vendor may have the expertise to train workers to use and maintain new equipment. The Japanese Ministry of Labor's survey indicates 18 percent of the blue-collar workers are trained by equipment vendors (Cairncross and Dore 1990). However, training provided by equipment vendors is limited for several reasons. First, equipment vendors are not specialized in providing training. In many cases, they design courses to highlight a product's features rather than to prepare trainees for trouble-shooting. Second, vendor training only reaches a few workers who use the new machines.

4. Emerging Issues and Trends

Adult education has always been a basic part of life in the United States. However, it is no longer primarily related to rehabilitation and remedial education. The observation of adult education activities in the preceding sections, however, suggests a much broader definition. Indeed, there have been substantial changes in adult education since the 1960s. It may be true that providing basic skills is still the primary mission of adult education, but what is called "basic skills" is not limited to remedial education at grade schools. Instead, basic skills include all essential skills that adults need for earning and enjoying a living. These skills are not necessarily acquired at the elementary and secondary schools. They are also developed through programs provided by colleges, workplaces, churches, and many other places.

The term "basic skills" is, however, not well-defined in many studies and surveys. How much these skills differ from what was traditionally taught in remedial education and adult literacy classes is usually unclear. Some researchers think it is useful to distinguish between workforce basic skills and workplace basic skills. To them, the workforce as a whole includes all people, employed or unemployed, who are in the labor market. So, "workforce basic skills" are the knowledge that a worker should possess in order to be competitive in the market. Remedial education is usually designed to provide workforce basic skills. On the other hand, "workplace basic skills" programs are intended to reflect the context of the workplace, and in some cases, may be customized to meet specific workplace needs.

Adult education was primarily a private affair in the early twentieth century. Federal and local governments were not seriously involved until the 1930s. Most government programs have been focused on the unemployed, minorities, and the economically disadvantaged. As a result, more women and minority workers are participating in adult education and training, and the gender training gaps have been narrowed. Moreover, the governments have become more involved in encouraging and forcing firms to provide education and training to workers. Many countries, including some developing countries, have either adopted or been considering a national training tax (or levy) system that requires employers to provide training to workers. Under the system, firms have two options: provide training themselves or pay the tax, which will go into a training fund (Lee et al. 1990, Luttringer 1991, OECD 1991).

There are five major trends in the education and training markets that are worth mentioning. First, regardless of the original intent of adult education and training programs which were targeted to special populations, more adults from all backgrounds will participate in such programs. Even if public support diminishes due to economic constraints, growing numbers of adults will continue to further their education in order to get ahead or better enjoy their lives. Second, employers, affected by global transactions, will continue to put more emphasis on occupational training as part of conditions of continuous employment. Third, the creation of a large number of institutions that provide education and training to adults will continue to create its own demand. Whether it is the libraries, the museums, or the zoos, a larger number of community-based organizations will provide education and training to adults. This indeed will serve the communities as well as the adults, since in the process of learning, adults will inevitably use their community resources and may even take on the role of being their advocates. Fourth, the application of technology will intensify and become more accessible and user-friendly to adult learners. And, finally, adult education and training programs will provide a milieu for millions of adults to socialize in order to alleviate their difficulties as they immigrate into new cultures or feel disfranchised in their own culture.

See also: Adult Education: Concepts and Principles; Recurrent Education; Market Failure in Adult Education and Training; North America

References

Bowers N, Swaim P 1994 Recent trends in job training. *Contemporary Economic Policy* (January)

Cairncross D, Dore R 1990 *Employer Training in Japan*. Report submitted to the Industrial. Technology, and Employment Program. Office of Technology Assessment, US Congress, Washington, DC

Johnson W R 1980 Vintage effect in the earnings of White American men. *Rev. Econ. Stat.* (August)

Kopka T L, Peng S S 1994 *Adult Education: Employment-Related Training*. National Center for Education Statistics, Washington, DC

Korb R, Chandler K, West J 1991 *Adult Education Profile for 1990–91*. National Center for Education Statistics, USDepartment of Education, Washington, DC

Lee J W, Lee Y, Whang K 1990 *Training of Private Sector Employees in South Korea*. Report submitted to the Industrial, Technology, and Employment Program Office of technology Assessment, US Congress, Washington, DC

Liveright A A 1968 *A Study of Adult Education in the United States*. Center for the Study of Liberal Education for Adults, Boston University, Boston, Massachusetts

Luttringer J M 1991 Worker access to vocational training —a legal approach. Paper presented at the NCAL/OECD-CERI Roundtable, "Adult Learning and Work: A Focus on Incentives", Philadelphia, Pennsylvania, 4-5 November

Lynch L M1994 Payoffs to alternative training strategies at work. In: Freeman R B (ed.) 1994

Mincer J, Polachek S 1974 Family investment in human capital: Earnings of women, *J. Pol. Econ.* 82 (2 pt.II): S76-S108

National Center for Education Statistic 1991 *Adult Education NHES: 91*. US Department of education, Washington, DC

Organisation for Economic Co-operation and Development (OECD) 1991 *Employment Outlook*, OECD, Paris

Office of Technology Assessment 1990 *Worker Training: Competing in the New International Economy*, US Congress, Washington, DC

Ryan P 1991 Adult Learning and work: finance, incentives, and certification. Paper presented at the NCAL/OECD-CERI Roundtable, "Adult Learning and Work: A Focus on Incentives", Philadelphia, Pennsylvania, 4-5 November

Stacey N, To D 1990 Adult education and training markets. In: Noyelle T (ed.) 1990 *Skill, Wages and Productivity in the Service Sector*. Westview Press, Boulder, Colorado.

Stacey N, To D 1993 Adult Education and training markets. In: Husén T, Postlethwaite T N (eds.) 1993 *International Encyclopedia of Education*, 2nd edn. Pergamon Press, Oxford

US Department of Labor 1994 BLS reports on employer-provided formal training. Bureau of Labor Statistics News. USDL 94-432 Washington, DC

US Department of Labor Bureau of Labour Statistics 1992 *How Workers Get Their Training: A 1991 Update*. Bulletin 2407, Government Printing Office, Washington, DC

Further Reading

Becker G S 1975 *Human Capital: A Theoretical and Empirical Analysis, with Special Reference to Education*, 2nd edn. National Bureau of Economic Research, New York

Boyd R et al. 1980 *Redefining the Discipline of Adult Education*. Jossey-Bass, San Francisco, California

Cappelli P 1994 *Training and Development in Public and Private Policy*. The International Library of Management, Dartmouth Publishing Company, Vermont

Collins M 1987 *Competence in Adult Education: A New Perspective*. University Press of America, Lanham, Maryland

Commission on Workforce Quality and Market Efficiency 1989 *Investing in People: A Strategy to Address America's Workforce Crisis, Background Papers*, Vols. 1 and 2 US Department of Labor, Washington, DC

Elias L J, Sharan M 1980 *Philosophical Foundations of Adult Education*. Robert E Krieger, Huntington, New York

Eurich P N 1990 *The Learning Industry: Education for Adult Workers*. The Carnegie Foundation for the Advancement of Teaching, Princeton, New Jersey

Freeman R B (ed.) 1994 *Working under Different Rules*. Russell Sage Foundation, New York

Gerver E 1984 *Computers and Adult Learning*. Open University Press, Milton Keynes

Higuchi Y 1987 *A Comparative Study of Japanese Plants operating in the US and American Plants: Recruitment, Job Training, Wage Structure and Job Separation*. Working paper 13 Center on Japanese Economy and Business, Graduate School of Business, Columbia University, New York

Hilton M 1991 Shared training: Learning from Germany. *Month. Lab. Rev.* (March): 31-37

Knowles A S 1977 Adult Education. In: Knowles A S (ed.) 1977 *The International Encyclopedia of Higher Education*. 1st edn. Jossey-Bass, San Francisco, California

Lowe J 1982 *The Education of Adults: A World Perspective*: UNESCO-OISE Press, Paris

Middleton J, Demsky T 1989 *Vocational Education and Training: A Review of World Bank Investment. Discussion paper 51*. The World Bank, Washington, DC

Mikulecky L 1991 Workplace literacy programs: organization and incentives. Paper presented at the NCAL/OECD-CERI Roundtable, "Adult Learning and Work: A Focus on Incentives," Philadelphia, Pennsylvania, 4-5 November

National University Continuing Education Association 1990 *Lifelong Learning Trends: A Profile of Continuing Higher Education*. National University Continuing Education Association, Washington, DC

Organisation for Economic Co-operation and Development (OECD) 1977 *Learning Opportunities for Adults*. Vol. 1 OECD, Paris

Tan H 1989 *Private Sector Training in the United States: Who Gets It and Why*. The Institute on Education and Economy, Teachers College, Columbia University, New York

Tan H, Chapman B, Paterson C, Booth A 1990 *Youth*

Training in the US, Great Britain, and Australia. National Center of Education and Employment/The Rand Corporation, Santa Monica, California

US General Accounting Office 1990 *Training Strategies: Preparing Noncollege Youth for Employment in the US*

and Foreign Countries. Report HRD-90-99 US General Accounting Office, Washington

Veum J R 1993 Training among young adults: who, what kind, and for how long? *Month. Lab. Rev.* (August): 27-32

Market Failure in Adult Education and Training

D. Stern

Most adult education and training occurs in schools or workplaces. The economic theory of markets for educational services and learning holds that socially efficient amounts of education and training will be provided if learners are free to buy as much as they are willing to pay for, and providers charge fees equal to marginal cost (the incremental cost of instructing the last student). An important exception to this principle is recognized if benefits accrue to people other than the adult learners themselves, in which case some subsidy is warranted. Society may also subsidize some individuals' education for reasons of fairness. Payments by government for education provided by schools is based on these considerations of fairness or external benefits, considerations which may apply to both children and adults.

In workplace education or training, an additional reason for market failure is the fact that employers control how much will be provided. Most employers in nonsocialist economies are profit-seeking firms which can be expected to provide education or training only if they can profit from the investment. If a company pays for education or training, and if the employee subsequently leaves the firm, then the company will have lost its investment. Economists have given considerable thought to how employers and employees deal with this risk. This entry summarizes the economic theory and evidence on market failure in adult education and training, and briefly discusses remedies.

1. How the Market is Supposed to Work: Becker's Hypotheses

Contemporary economic analysis of training markets begins with Gary S Becker's *Human Capital* (1964; 2nd edn. 1975). Becker originated the distinction between general training, which is "useful in many firms besides those providing it" (p. 19), and specific training, which "increases productivity more in firms providing it" (p. 26).

Becker hypothesized that "employees pay for general on-the-job training by receiving wages below

what they could receive elsewhere" (p. 21). His argument was that "perfectly general training would be equally useful in many firms and marginal products [the trained employee's productivity] would rise by the same extent in all of them. Consequently, wage rates would rise by exactly the same amount as the marginal product and the firms providing such training could not capture the return" (p. 20). If they tried to appropriate some of the return, the trained employee would quit and go to work for another firm.

"Why, then, would rational firms in competitive labor markets provide general training if it did not bring them any return? The answer is that firms would provide general training only if they did not have to pay any of the costs. Persons receiving general training would be willing to pay these costs since training raises their future wages. Hence it is the trainees, not the firms, who would bear the cost of general training and profit from the returns" (p. 20). In effect, employees buy general training from their employers. They prefer to buy it at work rather than going to school if complementarity between work and training makes learning at work more efficient than at a school.

A second hypothesis follows from the first. "Training has an important effect on the relation between earnings and age . . . Trained persons would receive lower earnings during the training period because training is paid for at that time, and higher earnings at later ages because the return is collected then. The combined effect of paying for and collecting the return from training in this way would be to make the age-earnings curve of trained persons . . . steeper than that of untrained persons, the difference being greater the greater the . . . investment" (p. 23).

Mincer (1974) applied these ideas to estimating the rate of return to on-the-job training (see *On-the-job Training*).

1.1 Is there Really a Payoff from Training?

Economists have questioned whether training is responsible for the fact that earnings increase with age. Following critiques of the human capital theory of schooling (e.g., Arrow 1973, Spence 1973), which suggested that the economic payoff from schooling may be attributable to ability screening rather than to any effect of schooling on productivity, others began to apply similar thinking to workplace training. In theory, even if individuals do not grow any more productive over time, earnings may still increase with seniority if such a wage structure discourages unproductive workers from joining the firm (Salop and Salop 1976, Nickell 1976) or deters them from "shirking" (Lazear 1981). Older workers may also earn more because they have had more time to find the jobs where they are most productive (Jovanovic 1979). Several studies (Topel 1986, Altonji and Shakotko 1987, Abraham and Farber 1987) found that seniority in a given firm appears to be less strongly associated with rising wages than is total experience in the labor market—which could be consistent with the idea that job matching rather than training is what causes earnings to increase with age.

However, these critiques are not based on direct evidence about workplace training. They are either purely conceptual models or else based on indirect inferences from data on earnings, seniority, and job mobility. In contrast, a number of studies have found positive correlations between measures of workplace training and subsequent wages. Using the Panel Study of Income Dynamics, Duncan and Hoffman (1979) and Brown (1989), among others, have found a positive association between workplace training, adult education, and subsequent earnings. Lillard and Tan (1986) found similar results using data from the 1983 Current Population Survey and the cohort of young men from the National Longitudinal Survey of Labor Market Experience (NLS). Lynch (1988) also corroborated the positive relationship between training and earnings in the NLS cohort of male and female youth. Tuijnman (1989) found adult education, including training, was positively associated with later earnings in the 50-year longitudinal study of men from Malmo, Sweden. And the Employment Opportunities Pilot Project (EOPP), which provided detailed measures of on-the-job training, also revealed a positive link between the amount of training and subsequent earnings among newly hired workers (Barron et al. 1989, Bishop 1991).

These latter studies leave little doubt that training leads to higher earnings, although they do not indicate exactly how much of the average rise in earnings with age results from training as opposed to job matching or implicit long-term wage bargains.

1.2 Do Employees Really Pay for Their Own General Training?

Although direct evidence on training and earnings supports the hypothesis that training increases subsequent wages, the evidence does not seem to support Becker's other hypothesis, that employees pay for their own general training. Barron et al. (1989) found in the EOPP data that employees who received more

training in their first three months on the job did not receive significantly lower wages. Yet most of the EOPP employers said they thought the training they gave would be useful in other firms. The absence of wage reduction during training therefore appears inconsistent with Becker's hypothesis. Likewise, Parsons (1985) found in the NLS data that young workers earned higher wages on jobs where they were acquiring skills which "would be useful in getting a better job."

The EOPP survey also estimated the increase in workers' productivity during their first two years. Barron et al. (1989) found that a given increase in the amount of training led to a productivity gain that was twice as big as the worker's wage increase. Bishop (1991), analyzing the same data, found an even bigger difference. Apparently employers are capturing a large share of the return from training. Since EOPP employers indicated that most of their training was general, these patterns are again inconsistent with Becker's hypothesis that employers cannot capture the return from general training.

Similarly, Feuer et al. (1987) discovered that scientists and engineers who had received formal education financed by their employers did not earn lower salaries than those who had paid for their own education. Since formal education is general training, this result also contradicts Becker. The authors consider it evidence in support of an alternative theory, that employers finance general training in order to encourage employees to invest in specific training (Glick and Feuer 1984).

Bishop (1991) suggests that employers may pay for training which is ostensibly useful in other firms because the other firms will fail to give an employee full credit for general skills acquired through adult education and workplace training. One reason is that different firms require different kinds of general skills, and in different proportions. The particular package of general skills obtained in one firm therefore may be less useful in another firm.

Another reason why other firms may undervalue general skills and knowledge acquired through training is simply that it is difficult for other employers to find out about it. Katz and Ziderman (1990) point out that other firms would find it particularly difficult to discover the range of adaptive abilities a worker has acquired but which are not being displayed in the present job—what they call the "options value" of general training. Bishop (1991) found that, even though formal and informal learning have approximately equal effects on a new worker's subsequent productivity, formal training—which is more visible to other employers—leads to larger wage increases than informal training.

In sum, direct evidence on training and wages indicates that employees do not pay for most, if any, of their own general training, yet they do obtain higher earnings after they receive it. This implies a very high rate of return to general training for employees, higher than the rate of return for employers, who control the amount of training provided. In spite of that, employees are evidently reluctant to pay for general training because they fear that its value may not be fully recognized if they move to a different firm. This implies that markets will provide less than the optimal amount.

1.3 Other Possible Reasons for Market Failure

There would be other possible reasons for market failure in training even if employees did pay for their own general training as Becker hypothesized (Ritzen and Stern 1991). Uncertainty is one reason. An individual considering a possible course of training will often have only a vague idea of the benefits that are likely to ensue. Individuals who are averse to risk will invest less than if they were certain of the benefit. The risk is greater if general skills and knowledge acquired through training are more useful when combined with specific training—then separation from the current employer decreases some of the value of the general, in addition to the specific, training. Ritzen (1991) has demonstrated that, in theory, protecting individuals against risk would lead to more investment in training. In addition, liquidity constraints, and inability to borrow for the purpose of financing training, could prevent workers from paying for their own general training. Minimum wage laws may also prevent some workers from accepting wages low enough to finance their training.

Even if all bargains between individual employees and employers were efficient in the existing labor market, a different macroeconomic and institutional configuration might call for a different level of investment in adult education and training. Soskice (1989) and Streeck (1989) argue that cooperation among firms, possibly including the use of governmental power, can provide greater incentive for each firm to provide a socially efficient amount of adult education and training. One important piece of this cooperative bargain is a low aggregate rate of unemployment. When unemployment is low, firms have greater difficulty replacing workers they have laid off during temporary business downturns, so if business is slack they are more likely to retain workers and use the extra time for training. The expectation of stable employment also encourages both employees and firms to invest more in adult education and training. Full employment is conducive to more skill-intensive forms of production and management practices such as quality circles, systematic job rotation, and skill-based pay (National Center on Education and the Economy 1990, Stern and Benson 1991).

In contrast, when the overall rate of unemployment increases, workers become separated from firms where they have been trained, which immediately destroys the value of their firm-specific training. The loss of valuable firm-specific knowledge and skill due to recessions is a major market failure.

2. Remedies for Market Failure

When markets fail, collective action may provide a remedy. Among the possible public policies to remedy failure in the market for adult learning through training are maintenance of full employment, imposition of a training obligation on firms, articulation of training standards to facilitate recognition of general training, and public subsidies.

A low aggregate rate of unemployment encourages investment in adult education and training. Governments in most industrialized countries list full employment as one of their goals. A few, including Sweden and Japan, have been notable in maintaining low unemployment in recent decades.

A more direct strategy for encouraging adult education and training is to require all employers to spend at least a certain minimum percentage of their payroll on providing it. France pioneered this policy in 1971 with a law initially requiring all firms employing 10 or more people to allocate at least 0.8 percent of their annual payroll to continued training; as of 1991 the required percentage had been raised to 1.2. In 1990 Australia enacted a similar law, requiring every enterprise with a payroll of A\$200,000 or more to spend at least 1 percent on training, rising to 1.5 percent in 1992 (Australian Taxation Office 1990).

Defining standards for certifying worker competence can facilitate adult education and training by making it easier for firms to recognize the results of each other's training. This is a hallmark of apprenticeship systems as in Germany. Many countries are currently extending this idea to adult education and training (e.g., National Training Board 1991). Japan awards National Trade Certificates for skilled workers in 133 occupations (Koike and Inoki 1990).

Finally, governments may directly subsidize adult education and training. Such subsidies may be targeted to smaller firms, which tend to spend less on adult education and training, or to training certain types of employees who tend to receive less adult education and training, such as workers older than 50, and those with fewer years of initial schooling (OECD 1991).

See also: Training on the Job; Economics of Adult Education and Training; Market Concepts in Provision; Government Role in Adult Education and Training; Overeducation; Demand, Supply, and Finance of Adult Education; Evaluation of Industry Training: Cost-Effectiveness; Evaluation of Public Training: Cost-Effectiveness

References

Abraham K G, Farber H S 1987 Job duration, seniority, and earnings. *Am. Econ. Rev.* 77(3): 278–97

Altonji J G, Shakotko R A 1987 Do wages rise with job seniority? *Rev. Econ. Studs.* 54(3): 437–59

Arrow K J 1973 Higher education as a filter. *J. Pol. Econ.* 2: 193–216

Australian Taxation Office 1990 *The Training Guarantee—Your Questions Answered.* Australian Taxation Office, Canberra

Barron J M, Black D A, Loewenstein M A 1989 Job matching and on-the-job training. *J. Labor Econ.* 7(1): 1–19

Becker G S 1964 *Human Capital: A Theoretical and Empirical Analysis with Special Reference to Education.* Columbia University Press, New York

Bishop J H 1991 On-the-job training of new hires. In: Stern D, Ritzen J M M (eds.) 1991 *Market Failure in Training? New Economic Analysis and Evidence on Training of Adult Employees.* Springer-Verlag, Berlin

Brown J N 1989 Why do wages increase with tenure? On-the-job training and life-cycle wage growth observed within firms. *Am. Econ. Rev.* 79(5): 971–91

Duncan G J, Hoffman S 1979 On-the-job training and earnings differences by race and sex. *Rev. Econ. Stat.* 61(4): 593–603

Feuer M, Glick H, Desai A 1987 Is firm-sponsored education viable? *J Econ. Behav. Org.* 8(1): 121–44

Glick H A, Feuer M J 1984 Employer-sponsored training and the governance of specific human capital investments. *Quart. Rev. Econ. and Business* 24(2): 91–103

Jovanovic B 1979 Job matching and the theory of turnover. *J. Pol. Econ.* 87(5): 972–90

Katz E, Ziderman A 1990 Investment in general training. The role of information and labour mobility. *The Econ. J.* 100: 1147–58

Koike K, Inoki I (eds.) 1990 *Skill Formation in Japan and Southeast Asia.* University of Tokyo Press, Tokyo

Lazear E P 1981 Agency, earnings profiles, productivity, and hours restrictions. *Am. Econ. Rev.* 71(4): 606–20

Lillard L A, Tan H W 1986 *Private Sector Training. Who Gets it and What Are its Effects?* The Rand Corporation, Santa Monica, California

Lynch L M 1988 *Private Sector Training and its Impact on the Earnings of Young Workers.* (Working paper SSWP) Sloan School of Management, Massachusetts Institute of Technology, Cambridge, Massachusetts

Mincer J 1974 *Schooling, Experience, and Earnings.* National Bureau of Economic Research, New York

National Center on Education and the Economy 1990 *America's Choice: High Skills or Low Wages!* Report of the Commission on the Skills of the American Workforce. National Center on Education and the Economy, Rochester, New York

National Training Board 1991 *National Competency Standards. Policy and Guidelines.* National Training Board Ltd., Canberra

Nickell S J 1976 Wage structures and quit rates. *Int. Econ. Rev.* 17(1): 191–203

Organisation for Economic Co-operation and Development (OECD) 1991 *Employment Outlook 1991*, Chap. 5: *Enterprise Training.* OECD, Paris

Parsons D 1985 Wage determination in the post training period. In: Parsons D 1985 *Pathways to the Future*, Center for Human Resource Research, Ohio State University, Columbus, Ohio

Ritzen J M M 1991 Market failure for general training, and remedies. In: Stern D, Ritzen J M M (eds.) 1991 *Market Failure in Training? New Economic Analysis and Evidence on Training of Adult Employees.* Springer-Verlag, Berlin

Ritzen J M M, Stern D 1991 Introduction and overview. In: Stern D, Ritzen J M M (eds.) 1991 *Market Failure in Training? New Economic Analysis and Evidence on Training of Adult Employees.* Springer-Verlag, Berlin

Salop S C, Salop J 1976 Self-selection and turnover in the labor market. *Q. J. Econ.* 90(4): 619–28

Soskice D 1989 Reinterpreting corporatism and explaining unemployment: Coordinated and non-coordinated market economies. In: Brunetta R, dell'Aringa C (eds.) 1990 *Markets, Institutions and Cooperation. Labour Relations and Economic Performance.* Macmillan, London

Spence M 1973 Job market signaling. *Q. J. Econ.* 87(3): 355–74

Stern D, Benson C S 1991 Firms' propensity to train. In: Stern D, Ritzen J M M (eds.) 1991 *Market Failure in Training? New Economic Analysis and Evidence on Training of Adult Employees.* Springer-Verlag, Berlin

Streeck W 1989 Skills and the limits of neo-liberalism. The enterprise of the future as a place of learning. *Work, Employment & Society* 3: 89–104

Topel R 1986 Job mobility, search, and earnings growth. A reinterpretation of human capital earnings functions. *Res. Lab. Econ.* 8(A): 199–233

Tuijnman A 1989 *Recurrent Education, Earnings, and Well-Being: A Fifty-year Longitudinal Study of a Cohort of Swedish Men.* Almqvist and Wiksell International, Stockholm

Overeducation

J. H. Bishop

"Overeducation" is a term which implies a judgment that a society (or an individual) has more education than is *required* or desirable. It is not a new idea, but can be found in *Ecclesiastes* (1:18): "He that increaseth knowledge, increaseth sorrow," and in the vernacular, "he knows more than is good for him." "Undereducation" implies the opposite judgment. This view is also not new; a Chinese proverb says "The schools of the country are its future in miniature." Whether a society is "undereducated," "overeducated," or neither of the above depends, of course, on the standard used to define required or desirable. Not surprisingly, analysts operating in the two main research traditions analyzing the economic role of education—manpower requirements and human capital—have different ways of defining overeducation and undereducation.

1. Manpower Requirements Perspective

In the manpower requirements paradigm, jobs and occupations have specific schooling requirements and the occupational skill demands of the economy are driven by forces external to the education sector such as consumer demand and technology. Training for skilled occupations takes many years so supplies of skilled workers cannot quickly adjust to current economic needs. Shifts in relative wage rates are not sufficient to equilibrate supply and demand for educated labor. An oversupply results in many workers having more schooling than is required by their job. This is presumed to cause job dissatisfaction, job turnover, lower productivity, and political discontent. An undersupply of skilled workers, "undereducation," creates bottlenecks which constrain economic growth. Two research programs unique to the manpower requirements paradigm employ this concept of overeducation:

(a) Estimates of the aggregate number of overeducated workers are made by counting mismatches between reported occupation and reported schooling.

(b) The impacts of overeducation on wages, productivity, job satisfaction, turnover, political alienation, and activism are studied.

1.1 Counting Aggregate Overeducation

Most studies define overeducation objectively as a mismatch between occupation and schooling in which the individual's reported schooling exceeds the amount that is presumed to be required by that job. This approach, however, suffers from two very serious measurement problems.

The reporting and coding of occupation and schooling is quite unreliable, so counts of mismatches significantly overstate their true frequency. United States Census Bureau studies have found that between 18.3 and 27.3 percent of individuals recorded as professionals, technicians, or managers in one interview, are recorded in a lower occupational category in a later interview. Furthermore, between 5.5 and 9 percent of respondents who are recorded as having 16 years of schooling or more in one interview are recorded as having fewer than 16 years of schooling in a later interview. These measurement problems mean that counts of mismatches between occupation and schooling derived from household survey data can produce truly incredible estimates. Tabulations of United States labor force surveys indicate, for example, that between 5.4 and 6.5 percent of the people who claim to be lawyers, physicians, and elementary/secondary

school teachers also claim not to have completed 16 years of schooling (Bishop and Carter 1991). Given the laws regulating entry into these professions, these estimates of undereducation are clearly not credible. Neither are the corresponding estimates of overeducation. In United States labor force surveys conducted during the 1980s about 17 percent of those reporting 16+ years of schooling also said they worked in a retail sales, clerical, service, or manual job. Mismatches of this type occur frequently, but they are less common than the 17 percent figure suggests.

The second problem with interpreting mismatches as indicators of overeducation is that they might just as easily be the result of the poor quality of the education received by some college graduates. Seventeen percent of young American college graduates read at a level below the typical 11th grader (Bishop and Carter 1991). Isn't a college educated secretary with an 11th grade reading level undereducated rather than overeducated?

Countries outside North America also have quality control problems in higher education and difficulties measuring schooling and occupation, so educational leaders throughout the world need to be skeptical of national estimates of aggregate undereducation or overeducation based on counts of occupation–schooling mismatches.

1.2 Effects of Being Overeducated

A number of studies have been conducted of the effects of being overeducated on attitudes and wage rates. When you compare people in the same occupation, those with substantially above average schooling (those who are overeducated for the job) are paid more but not as much more as someone with the same level of schooling who has obtained a job that conventionally employs people with greater schooling. This is neither a new nor a surprising finding. Essentially the point is that, when people with the same amount of schooling are compared, those who are less successful in gaining access to high status occupations are paid less. This has been a common-place of the status attainment literature for two decades.

It has also been hypothesized that "overeducation" causes political alienation, job dissatisfaction and lower productivity. Burris (1983) examined many of these hypotheses and found that while modest levels of overeducation had no effects, the highly overeducated (the 3.6% of his American sample in which schooling exceeded the norm by at least 3 years) were less satisfied with their job and less likely to affirm an achievement ideology. There was, however, no tendency for highly overeducated workers to be more liberal, to vote Democratic or to be more politically alienated, and they were substantially more likely to identify themselves as middle class and to oppose welfare spending.

Tsang et al. (1991) report finding a tendency for

highly overeducated males (but not females) to be more dissatisfied with their job and more likely to plan to leave it for another. They also tested for an effect of overeducation on drinking at work, energy level, and health, but found none. They appear to believe these results have great significance because they conclude: "This study suggests that such action may be ineffective at best and counterproductive at worst" (p. 228). This statement is completely unjustified. Job satisfaction and plans to quit are not measures of worker productivity and are only weakly correlated with direct measures of productivity. There have been thousands of studies of the relationship between direct measures of productivity such as supervisory ratings and work samples and schooling or key outcomes of schooling such as reading and mathematics test scores. Meta analyses of these studies have established that schooling and test scores are both positively correlated with direct measures of productivity. Indeed in most jobs, measures of the quality and output of schooling —reading, vocabulary, and mathematical achievement test scores—are better predictors of job performance than interviews, references, ratings of training and experience, personality tests, and comprehensive background questionnaires (Hunter and Hunter 1984).

This literature further demonstrates that a core assumption of the manpower requirements framework— that specific jobs require particular minimum levels of basic reading and mathematical skills and that once those thresholds are reached, further improvements in basic skills yield sharply diminishing productivity benefits—is invalid. The hypothesis of diminishing returns to basic skills has been tested many times and about 95 percent of the time, it has been rejected. A recent test of this hypothesis in data on 31,000 workers found significant diminishing returns only for sales clerk jobs (Bishop 1996).

These results imply that the economic case for upgrading the basic skills of the general population does not rest solely on the pace at which high skill jobs replace low skill jobs or the extent to which "high performance" work systems replace conventional Tayloristic work systems. The fact that employment in high skill occupations grows much faster than employment in low skill occupations and high performance work sites are replacing Tayloristic work sites just strengthens the case for improving the quality of elementary and secondary education (see *Technological Change and Education*).

2. Human Capital Perspective

Most research on the economic role of education employs a human capital framework. Human capital theory tends to be more optimistic about the ability of the economy to put additional skill to good use if the price employers must pay for it declines. It focuses instead on what determines the supply of skilled labor. It starts with the premise that investments of the student's time, energy, and money in learning yield benefits over many years that are both pecuniary and nonpecuniary. Expected benefits influence the decisions of some students about whether to attend, what to study, and how hard to study. When the demand for graduates in a particular field exceeds supply at current wage rates, relative wage rates rise stimulating employers to hire fewer workers trained in the field and attracting students into it and inducing them to accelerate their course of study. These student responses increase future supply and an equilibrium is established with a larger wage premium for the skill. Hence, if students are free to choose their field of study, there will be a tendency for the relative supplies of workers with different kinds of educational credentials to produce wage differentials which translate into rates of return comparable to those on alternative investments.

Rates of return will tend to be low if schools are free and easily accessible. If tuition is high, loans unavailable and admission requirements difficult to meet, high rates of return and substantial wage differentials will be necessary to attract enough students into university to supply future needs for college graduate workers. Deviations from this standard occur when large shifts in demand for or supply of graduates push the market into temporary disequilibrium, when barriers to entry (e.g., limits on the number of university places) or market failures prevent enrollment decisions from equalizing rates of return and when nonpecuniary benefits are particularly large or small.

Within the human capital paradigm terms like overeducation, oversupply, undereducation, and shortage have two quite different meanings. In the first usage these terms are descriptions of the general level of rates of return to schooling relative to historical patterns. The theme of Richard Freeman's 1976 book, *The Overeducated American*, was that rates of return to university education had fallen below previous levels. The human capital model predicts that periods of oversupply or undersupply will be temporary. There are two reasons for this. First, the circumstances that cause these disequilibria (the baby boom and the Vietnam War in the case of the 1970s oversupply of college graduates in the US) are themselves generally temporary. Second, very low (or high) rates of return set in motion a supply response (e.g., male college attendance rates in the US fell during the late 1970s) which, with a lag, tends to bring supply and demand back into balance.

Three research programs (which with modifications are shared by manpower requirements analysts) are implied by this concern for disequilibria in the balance between the supply and demand for skill:

(a) Assessments are made of the supply–demand balance for specific fields of study or occupations. (Manpower requirements analysts do this by

Table 1
Wage premiums and underemployment of university graduates by field of study in the US and the UK

	United States						United Kingdom		
	1986/90 BA Recipients								
	Unemployment rate	Full-time employment in non professional technical–management	BA Full-time starting salary premium over high school graduates working full-time with 1–5 years of experience			Earnings premium BAs over high school graduates	Premium of university graduates' salaries 5 years after graduation over average earnings of all workers		
	1987/91	1987/91	1991 Fem.	1987 M&F	1976 M&F	1984/87	1986	1976	1966
University Major	%	%	%	%	%	%	%	%	%
Engineering	4/3	6/7	165	130	89	180	49	41	102
Physical science and mathematics	4/5	12/10	124	95	8	120	48	30	91
Health	2/2	4/4	172	96	33	45	36	40	64
Business management and accounting	4/5	20/28	105	83	57	155	54	57	—
Law (7-yr degree in US)	—	—	—	—	—	(313)	62	27	124
Social science	8/5	28/31	76	76	3	72	26	25	—
economics						184	65	44	108
Biological science	7/4	26/16	79	42	0	81	28	23	74
Psychology	6/6	29/28	66	50	—	81	22	14	53
Humanities	8/6	32/33	61	40	−10	34	25	23	56
Education	3/2	13/11	63	37	−3	24	6	13	37

Sources: Column 1–5 were calculated from National Center for Educational Statistics 1993 Tables 371, 372, and 375. Column 1 is the percent of those in the labor force who were unemployed. Column 2 is the share of graduates with fulltime jobs who were employed outside of professional, technical, and managerial occupations and who report they did not need a college degree to get their job. Columns 3, 4, and 5 are the percentage by which the salary of bachelors degree recipients one year after graduation exceeded that of high school graduates with 1–5 years of work experience. Column 6 is derived from Kominski (1990), Table A and B. Columns 7–9 are from Table 1 of Dalton (1992)

counting the number of graduates in a field who are overeducated for their current job. Researchers operating in the human capital tradition focus on levels and rates of change of wage premiums for skill and rates of return to training.)

(b) Historical trends in the supply–demand balance for skilled workers are analyzed.

(c) Planners forecast future skill needs and advise policymakers on how to adjust the supply of training slots to these forecasts.

Each of these research programs will be discussed in turn. Then the second usage of the terms "undereducation" and "overeducation" will be examined.

2.1 Supply–Demand Balance for Specific Fields of Study

Graduates from different university fields of study are not close substitutes for one another in the labor market. Consequently, there is not one labor market for college graduates, there are hundreds. At any given point in time some of these markets are likely to be oversupplied and others undersupplied.

The best indicators of whether a field is in oversupply or undersupply are the level and rate of change of the relative wages of people trained in that field. Unemployment rates and proportions of graduates from a program who take jobs that do not appear to require a college degree also provide useful information. Table 1 presents US and UK data on these indicators of the supply–demand balance by field of study. In both the United States and the United Kingdom, graduates in engineering, physical science, mathematics, business, and economics fare the best. Unemployment was lower; proportions taking nonprofessional, nontechnical, and nonmanagerial (non-PTM) jobs were lower; and earnings premiums were higher than for other fields. These areas of study have two things in common: a substantial mathematics content and employment destinations primarily in the private sector.

Graduates in education and health fields have relatively low earnings but they apparently had little difficulty finding work in their field. Rates of unemployment and of taking non-PTM jobs were very low in these fields.

Graduates in humanities, social sciences other than economics, psychology, and biological sciences fared least well. Recent graduates experienced higher unemployment, higher rates of employment in non-PTM jobs, and lower monetary returns to a college degree. Humanities graduates, for example, were clearly in disequilibrium surplus during the 1970s. In 1976 starting pay was 10 percent below the wage of recent high school graduates. As a result, the share of American BAs awarded in English and foreign languages fell from 9 percent in 1971 to 3.7 percent in 1984. Since then, however, the share of BAs awarded in these two fields has risen and in 1990 it was 4.7 percent. This suggests that the nonpecuniary benefits of studying English and foreign languages (and the 34–40% wage premium over high school graduates that prevailed since 1984) may be sufficient to induce 4 to 5 percent of American college students to major in the field even though a third of young humanities graduates are likely to be forced into non-PTM jobs, and earnings over their career are likely to be only one half of those of graduates in engineering, business, and economics.

What are the policy implications of these numbers? A manpower requirements economist would probably say there are still too many humanities majors. She would doubt that most students making this choice are aware that they have less than a one-third chance of getting a job "closely related" to their field of study. The number of jobs which use the writing and language skills developed by majors in these fields is limited, she would argue, so fewer graduates would mean fewer disappointed graduates and no change in the number finding related jobs.

From human capital economists would come a proposal to inform students of the job prospects of different fields of study. Many would also support scholarships for students in shortage fields such as engineering which aid competitiveness and technological progress. Most, however, would oppose placing caps on the number of humanities majors. They would be more inclined to think that students are aware of the economic consequences of majoring in English or a foreign language and are entering the field largely for nonpecuniary reasons. Poor as the job prospects may be for humanities BAs, high school graduates have it worse, they would argue. Recent high school graduates had 19 percent unemployment rates in 1987 and almost no chance of getting a job in a humanities field such as writing. To the point that the marginal humanities major will end up in a clerical job rather than a humanities job, they would respond that

even if that is the true, job performance will improve somewhat as a result of the college experience.

2.2 Trends in the Supply–Demand Balance for Highly Educated Labor

The supply of college educated workers has been increasing rapidly all over the world. During the 1970s and 1980s the university graduate share of the population of working age grew at an annual rate of 3.34 percent in the United States, 3.55 percent in Japan, 2.75 percent in Germany, 5.6–5.8 percent in Sweden and Norway, 3.07 percent in Belgium, and 3.97 percent in Canada (OECD 1989).

Demand has also been growing rapidly. Occupations at the top of the skill continuum such as professionals, technicians, and managers (PT & M) jobs have been growing much more rapidly than manual (service, craft, operative, laborer, and farm occupations) jobs. In the United States the growth rate differential between PTM and manual jobs was 1.6 percent per year during the first half of the twentieth century, 1.9 percent per year between 1950 and 1970, 2.8 percent per year between 1970 and 1981, and 2.46 percent per year during the 1980s. The growth rate advantage of PTM jobs is even more striking in Europe and Japan. Japan's rate was 4.27 percent per year in the 1970s and 3.26 percent per year in the 1980s. Germany's rate was 3.67 percent per year in the 1970s and 2.53 percent per year in the 1980s (Bishop 1992).

Demand for highly educated workers also grows when employers decide that new hires should have greater amounts of previous training either because (a) the job has become more complex; (b) quality and job performance targets have increased; or (c) workers with school provided training have become less costly. Looking over a 70-year period, one can clearly see that most occupations—management, medicine, teaching, engineering, construction, social services, military, financial services, and manufacturing—have become more complicated. Only a few occupations—laborers, retail sales clerks, photographers, musicians, and truck drivers—have apparently not increased in complexity.

As sales, transactions, and output per worker grow, so do the costs of making mistakes and the benefits of higher quality. This has meant that it pays to strive for higher standards of performance and quality even when tasks remain unchanged. For many years there was controversy about the effect of technological progress on skill demands of specific occupations. Now, however, the predominant view is that complexity, responsibility, abstractness, and interdependence have risen in most occupations (Hirschorn 1986).

The third source of increased demand for educated workers is the transfer to schools of training tasks formerly the province of apprenticeships and employer training. The switch of training functions to schools is a natural part of the life cycle of a technology and its associated skills. As a technology matures and its use grows, the technology and its associated skills become standardized (i.e., general rather than firm specific), the demand for formal training grows, and schools enter the market as training providers. Once skills become standardized, schools have natural advantages as competitors in this market: (a) they offer students flexibility in scheduling and the choice of courses, (b) hourly costs of training are lower because teaching staff are specialized and economies result from spreading the cost of developing courses over many students, (c) school certification of skills makes them more portable, and (d) schools and students have access to public subsidies not available when training takes place at a firm. When schools become major training providers, barriers to entry into the occupation and the industry fall, the supply of skilled workers grows, the costs of employing people with the skill fall, and expanded use of the technology is facilitated. Almost every medium and high level occupation (e.g., typists, computer programmers, lawyers, and plumbers) has been through this evolution (Flynn 1988).

In most countries and most historical periods, percentage growth rates of highly educated workers have been higher than the percentage growth rates of high level occupations. Some researchers have attempted to measure other sources of increased demand for highly educated workers and then, comparing their measure of increased demand to the growth of supply, have claimed to have evidence of secular increases in "overeducation" (Rumberger 1981). This exercise is futile, however. There is no way of measuring independently how employer hiring standards are influenced by technical progress and the entry of schools into new training markets. The only way to know what has happened to the supply–demand balance for highly educated workers is to infer it from changes in the rate of return to schooling, relative unemployment rates, and proportions of graduates reporting their job does not make use of the skills developed in college. The wage premium for university graduates declined in most European countries during the 1960s and 1970s but has tended to stabilize or rise during the 1980s. At the end of the 1980s the average of the male and female earnings premiums for 45- to 64-year old university graduates was 42 percent in Denmark, 52 percent in Sweden, 66 percent in the United Kingdom, 70–72 percent in Australia and Canada, and 81–82 percent in Finland, the Netherlands, and the United States (OECD 1992).

2.3 Forecasting the Supply–Demand Balance for Highly Educated Workers

It is extremely difficult to make accurate forecasts of the supply–demand balance for highly educated labor. Small errors in forecasting rates of change of either demand or supply translate into big errors in projections of the gap between supply and demand.

An accurate forecast requires not only accurate predictions of the growth rates of hundreds of occupations, it requires accurate predictions of changes in the hiring standards for these occupations. Innovations such as high performance microcomputers, fiber optic telecommunications, global sourcing of parts and high performance work systems are bound to influence skill demands in the year 2005. But who knows how big the effects will be?

It should come as no surprise, therefore, that published forecasts of the balance between supply and demand for highly educated workers based on the manpower requirements paradigm have almost always been far off the mark. Seymour Harris's forecast of the United States labor market for college graduates was one of the first. He predicted in 1949 that:

> a large proportion of the potential college students within the next twenty years are doomed to disappointment after graduation, as the number of coveted openings will be substantially less than the numbers seeking them. (Harris 1949 p. 64)

As predicted the number of college educated workers grew dramatically, but the predicted oversupply failed to materialize because professional–technical share of the workforce grew dramatically as well, from 8.4 percent in 1950 to 13.7 percent in 1970. In fact, demand for college graduates must have grown faster than supply because the wage premium of college graduates with 1–10 years of work experience over high school graduates with similar levels of experience rose from 45 percent to 76 percent.

The US Bureau of Labor Statistics projections of the supply–demand balance for college graduates have been similarly flawed. In 1970 they predicted demand and supply would be in balance during the 1970s; a surplus ensued and college wage premiums fell. In 1980 they predicted a surplus for the 1980s; a shortage ensued and the wage premium for college graduates rose dramatically (Bishop and Carter 1991).

Richard Freeman, an economist whose work reflects the human capital perspective, has a much better forecasting record. He correctly predicted in 1976 that the college wage differential would continue to decline during the 1970s and then turn up during the 1980s (Freeman 1976).

3. Chronic Undereducation

In the second usage of terms like "undereducation" and "overeducation," a claim is being made that there is a *chronic* tendency for individuals to underinvest or overinvest in education relative to some social standard. Student decisions are motivated by the expectation of benefits that will accrue to themselves and their families, not by benefits that may accrue to others. Yet we all benefit when those we interact with have real expertise. Not only do such individuals pay more taxes and receive fewer government transfer benefits, they are more likely to make discoveries or innovations which benefit others, more likely to fix the car correctly the first time, and less likely to make mistakes which injure co-workers, customers, or the public. Economists call social benefits such as these "spillovers" or "externalities." Private decisions will lead to an insufficient quantity and quality of education and training and insufficient achievement by students, unless public agencies subsidize costs or add to the rewards. The optimal amount and character of public intervention in the education market depends on the size and character of these spillover benefits.

3.1 Years Spent in School Margin

By compelling attendance, subsidizing instructional costs, building schools in convenient locations, and providing financial aid, society induces students to choose more years of schooling than they would choose on their own. In the absence of such interventions, we would clearly live in a world of chronic underschooling. Is the current level of government support for schooling the correct level? That is much more difficult to say. Some of the spillover benefits of schooling—the tax and social insurance effects— are measurable, but most are not. Economists have tackled this issue by calculating a *lower bound* on the social rate of return to schooling. Lower bound social rates of return are calculated by comparing the impact of schooling on before tax earnings (substracting that component of the earnings differential actually due to ability and family background advantages) to the total costs (both instructional costs and student time costs) of schooling. Since the benefits of schooling accrue over many years, they must be discounted to the present before they can be compared to costs. The lower bound social rate of return to schooling is the interest rate which exactly equates discounted measurable social benefits and social costs. If this lower bound social rate of return is equal to or above the social rate of return on physical capital, a society might be said to be underschooled. If, on the other hand, the lower bound social rate of return is below the social rate of return on physical capital, we are left uncertain about whether the society is underschooled or overschooled. The answer depends on the importance of the unmeasured spillover benefits of schooling—the discoveries and innovations; greater political, racial, and religious tolerance; and so on.

3.2 Achievement Margin

Spending too few years in school is only one of the ways students may underinvest in education. How much is learnt and how expert a student becomes depends as much on individual study effort, as on the number of years spent in school. Society tries to encourage students to study harder by recruiting inspiring teachers, by conditioning access to higher levels of schooling and well-paid fields of study on performance in school, by awarding credentials only to those who achieve a minimum level of competency in their field, and by providing references for graduates who are entering the labor market. Expertise is notoriously difficult to measure, however, and the credentials that schools award do a poor job of signaling it (particularly the kinds of expertise that employers are seeking). Credentials are well rewarded by the labor market. Holding credentials constant, however, greater expertise is under-rewarded. The incentives facing students are thus to put sufficient effort into their studies to get the credential, but to do little more. This is the outcome in the United States where the high school diploma signals time spent in school and not educational achievement. Such an outcome can be legitimately characterized as chronic undereducation.

When educational systems provide finely graded certifications of academic accomplishment but ignore accomplishments relevant to employment such as computer literacy, teamwork, and occupational skills, the likely result is chronic miseducation—students studying subjects which schools think are important but the labor market does not. Japan, the United Kingdom and many developing countries suffer from this kind of problem. The German dual-system and the new French *baccalauréat* (with its technical Bacs) should be less subject to these problems. However, it is very difficult to keep instruction and credentialing up to date and in line with a nation's economic and social needs, so miseducation and undereducation along some important dimensions can never be banished from an educational system.

The question "What should our youth learn?" inevitably sparks controversy. What is miseducation or overeducation to one individual is "proper regard for our cultural heritage" to another. Those who claim that overeducation is chronic use a "Does your job require that you know it?" standard to judge what should be taught. Even if one were to accept their analysis of economic demand for learning and skills, this would be a very limiting conception of the nature of education. Surely better jobs are not the only reason for getting an education. What about desires to appreciate literature better or to make a discovery that will improve the lives of others?

The analysis just completed implies that overeducation can occur only when government gets too aggressive in promoting and subsidizing it. In the absence of such subsidies a society will be both underschooled and undereducated. Surely it is possible for governments to make mistakes. But how else is a society to make collective value judgements regarding the importance of spillovers such as discoveries, innovations and political, religious, and racial tolerance —other than through democratic political institutions? Those who want to prove that chronic overeducation exists would be well advised, therefore, to focus their efforts on a political theory showing why democratic political systems should have a systematic tendency to overinvest in education. The job requirements theory that has been used in the past appears to be a dead end.

See also: Economics of Adult Education and Training; Market Failure in Adult Education and Training; Technological Change and Education; Demand, Supply, and Finance of Adult Education

References

Bishop J H 1992 Schooling, learning and worker productivity. In: Asplund R (ed.) *Human Capital and Scandinavian Labor Markets*. Elinkeinoelaman Tutkimuslaitos Näringslivets Forskningsinstitut (ETLA), Helsinki
Bishop J H 1996 Is the college graduate labor market headed for a bust?—a critique of job requirements projections. *New England Economic Review*
Bishop J H, Carter S 1991 The worsening shortage of college graduate workers. *Educational Evaluation and Policy Analysis* 13(3): 221–55
Burris V 1983 The social and political consequences of overeducation. *American Sociological Review* 48(4): 454–67
Dalton P 1992 The market for qualified manpower in the UK. *Oxford Review of Economic Policy* 8(2): 103–29
Flynn P 1988 *Facilitating Technological Change: The Human Resource Challenge*. Ballinger, Cambridge, Massachusetts
Freeman R 1976 *The Overeducated American*. Academic Press, New York
Harris S 1949 *The Market for College Graduates and Related Aspects of Education and Income*: Harvard University Press, Cambridge, Massachusetts
Hirschorn L 1986 *Beyond Mechanization* MIT Press, Cambridge, Massachusetts
Hunter J, Hunter R F 1984 Validity and utility of alternative predictors of job performance *Psycho. Bull.* 96(1): 72–98
Kominski R 1990 *What's it Worth? Educational Background and Economic Status: Spring 1987*. US Bureau of the Census, Current Population Reports, P–70, No. 21
National Center for Educational Statistics 1993 *Digest of Education Statistics: 1993*. Department of Education, Washington, DC.
Organisation of Economic Co-operation and Development (OECD) 1989 OECD *Employment Outlook July 1989*. OECD, Paris
Organisation of Economic Co-operation and Development (OECD) 1992 *Education at a Glance: OECD Indicators*. OECD, Paris
Rumberger R 1981 The changing skill requirements of jobs in the US economy. *Industrial and Labor Relations Review* 34(4): 578–90
Tsang Mun, Rumberger R, Levin H 1991 The impact of surplus schooling on worker productivity. *Industrial Relations* 30(2): 209–28

Recognition and Certification of Skills

D. Colardyn

Certification refers to the process by which knowledge, skills, and competencies are measured and recognized. There is a demonstrated need in adult education and training for clarifying differences between concepts such as certification and validation as well as between individual-based approaches and program-based approaches to these issues. Drawing on experiences in different countries, this entry offers a discussion of major trends and issues concerning the certification and validation of skills and competencies acquired by means of adult education, experiential learning, and firm-based training. Although the focus is mainly on the industrialized countries, the problems dealt with have general applicability.

1. Challenges to Conventional Approaches to Certification

Since the 1970s several changes have occurred that justify a rethinking of certification procedures in education. One important aspect is the emergence of a global economy, which in many countries has led to a debate concerning the competitiveness of labor markets. The concomitant restructuring of labor markets and the transformation of social policies have, in the industrialized countries, given rise to a new appreciation of the social and economic imperative of developing lifelong education, including not only skills training but also "second chance" education and recurrent education for leisure and personal development (OECD 1975, 1977, 1991a). Certification has assumed vastly greater significance as a result.

The expansion of formal education is a second factor that has influenced the debate concerning certification. In a context of spreading education to the masses, diversification in funding, and rapid growth of upper secondary and higher education, the meaning and function of certification is changing. For example, in many countries, school diplomas and university degrees no longer have a common and unique meaning. This often leads to a discussion concerning the social and professional value of different qualifications. Conventional certification practices in formal education are increasingly challenged by these developments (OECD 1995).

A third factor concerns the development of "parallel" educational structures (Figeat 1984, Tanguy 1986). During the 1980s and early 1990s, many countries pursued a policy of simultaneously encouraging the development of public training schemes for the unemployed and strengthening private initiatives in adult education and continuing vocational training. Opportunities for adult learning have both increased and become more diverse as a result. Many adults are now in a position to acquire knowledge and skills by means of adult recurrent education, industrial training, and self-directed learning activities. The emergence and growth of the training market has considerably modified the certification issue (Cervero and Azzaretto 1988, Gehin 1989, Carnevale et al. 1990, Eurich 1990).

The need to recognize skills and competencies not acquired in a traditional school setting has given rise to alternative assessment and certification practices. A distinction can be made between, firstly, certification as a formal qualification and, secondly, other means for recognizing and validating skills and competencies (OECD 1990, Colardyn 1996).

2. Validation and Certification

Certification usually relates to "officially" endorsed diplomas and degrees. Recognition is typically provided by public authorities, boards in charge of educational institutions, professional bodies, or through collective bargaining. Certification is thus a concern mainly identified with formal education. It does not normally take into account the full range of an individual's personal and professional competencies, even where recognition results from a collective bargaining agreement. However, as adult education and continuing vocational training have expanded and assumed increased economic importance, the call for another approach to certification has become stronger and more urgent. The emphasis on the development of a more broadly based approach to validation has to be examined in this context (Colardyn 1996).

As opposed to formal certification, validation refers to the process of assessing and recognizing a wide range of skills and competencies which people develop throughout their lives and in different contexts, for example, through education, work, and leisure activities. These skills and competencies are "acquired" in the sense that they are tested under everyday conditions. Such acquired abilities have of course always existed; for example, they are implicit in systems of promotion by seniority. Whereas the expansion of formal education called established certification procedures into doubt, the demand for new approaches to validation resulted from technological change, the transformation of work, and the emergence of training markets (see *Market Concepts in Provision*). Validation has become very complex since the set of acquired abilities that may have to be taken into account has grown very large.

In meritocratic societies, in order to be valuable for individuals and firms, the acquired skills and competencies need to be identified, assessed, and given both professional and social professional recognition. The validation process thus confers a currency value to assessed abilities (Liétard 1991.) Validation is often focused on those abilities that are transferable from one work situation to another, from a life situation to a work situation, or from a life situation to a training situation. Indeed, facilitating transfer is one of the aims of validation. Portability may not prove valuable to the individual unless the skills and competencies previously acquired are "officially" recognized. Validation thus involves an assessment of the equivalency of recognized skills and competencies in relation to a defined standard of achievement, for example, those accepted by institutions of formal education.

3. Individual-based Approaches to Validation

Skills assessment has a long history. In the United States, for example, such assessment began on a large scale with the GI Bill passed after the Second World War, which made it possible for veterans to enroll in educational institutions in order to undertake studies interrupted or delayed by the war (see *Experiential and Open Learning*). Similar procedures were also used in Canada, especially in Quebec. Following on the Continuing Education Act that came into effect in 1971, France introduced a system of credits in short-cycle secondary education. The main purpose was to make this education accessible to adults facing redundancy (Elie 1969, Schwartz 1969). Nevertheless, in France, a need for fuller recognition of work-related skills emerged. This led, in 1986, to the creation of the assessment centers.

These centers are based on the idea that, pending full certification, some validation of acquired skills and competencies should occur (Colardyn and Parlier 1986). The assessment centers can recognize both formally taught and experiential learning, as well as skills and competencies acquired outside the educational system. The aim is to provide individuals with a permanent record of recognized skills and competencies acquired through courses or by other means. A second aim is to encourage individuals to make use of these records in negotiations concerning employment and/or further training. A third aim is to instill in individuals an awareness of the importance of their human "capital" for professional, educational, social, and cultural life (Liétard 1991).

In future, the recognition given by the assessment centers or similar institutions could be taken into account in decisions concerning formal certification, for example, in the form of credit units leading to a diploma. Such an integrated validation system would articulate knowledge-based teaching in educational institutions with competence-based learning at the workplace. Moreover, linkages with the various collective bargaining mechanisms (OECD 1994) exist or are to be envisaged to fully recognise the visibility and portability of skills and competences on the labour market.

4. Program-based Approaches to Validation

There is at present a search for linkages between formal certification and the experiential learning of workers at different occupational levels. Examples of linkages between knowledge-based certification and competence-based recognition can be found in the United Kingdom (Vaughan and Squires 1991). These projects are limited, however, in that they mostly concern the validation of skills and competencies acquired by well-educated employees, for example, engineers and managers. Examples are programs such as CATS, which is promoted by the Council for National Academic Awards and, on a smaller scale, CONTACT (Drake 1991). Similar schemes have now been extensively developed in Australia.

Adult education is characterized by a wide variety of provision, ranging from formal courses provided in schools, universities, and other institutions, to nonformal education offered by nonprofit associations, to training and retraining managed by public institutions and private, profit-making firms. The sources for funding and the quality and quantity of provision vary accordingly. This condition of diversity, which to an extent has been intentionally created through policies aimed at establishing "flexible pathways" for adult learning (OECD 1991b, 1995), raises many questions concerning the assessment and validation of skills and competencies acquired outside the system of formal education. The apparent contradiction between diversified provision and a lack of flexibility in certification can be studied by examining practices in the three sectors of the training market (OECD 1995):

(a) The *formal sector* confers recognized qualifications such as diplomas, degrees, and certificates at the secondary and tertiary levels of the educational system. These formal qualifications are essentially knowledge-based, even in the case of vocational education. Demands for employable skills are usually not determinate, in part because many employers underline the value of a broad education, which they see as providing a useful basis for further education and training.

(b) The *nonformal sector* comprises the most active partners in continuing vocational education: firms, professional associations, and trade unions. The content of the training is usually competence based. Certification can vary from a simple attendance testimony—the most frequent case—to a certificate that can be integrated with a formal qualification. These attempts at integration reflect the search for broadly based approaches to validation.

(c) The *commercial sector* takes advantage of a generally "overloaded" educational system. It is made up of profit-making training firms and schools, often privately financed, that are flexible in adjusting to changes in market demands. Here too the attendance certificate is the rule. Partly for this reason, the value of commercial adult education has been called into doubt in some countries.

The previously mentioned Council of National Academic Awards (CNAA) in the United Kingdom presents an example of a program that has, with some success, developed linkages between formal qualifications and the certificates awarded by providers of further education or training in the three sectors. The CNAA began its work in the mid-1970s by approving certificates awarded by polytechnics and colleges for continuing education which, unlike the universities, could not set up their own degrees and had to refer to the CNAA Accreditation Commission (see *Polytechnical Education*). The various parties having a stake in the proposed educational program (e.g., public authorities, employers, and trade unions) each had a representative on this commission. Based on experience gained with this initiative, the Credit Accumulation and Transfer Scheme (CNAA 1989) was a natural next step. In contrast to the approach taken in France with the assessment centers, recognition is not awarded to an individual but to a specific education or training program. The criteria for approval are duration of study in relation to orientation and program quality, and recognition may be given regardless of the sector—formal, nonformal and, commercial—in which the provider operates.

5. Integrated Approaches to Certification

The Accreditation Commission in the United Kingdom presents an interesting example of an attempt to improve coherence by linking provision to certification and validation issues. Several countries have now established similar types of boards, commissions or partnerships to tackle these issues (Australia, Canada, France, Nouvelle-Zélande, Portugal, United Kingdom, United States). In future, this could be even further enlarged as norms and standards need to be better defined. For example, one could define the equivalency of certificates awarded in the formal sector of provision with those given in other sectors, and combine these into a new qualification. This would make it possible to integrate formal education with experiential learning and firm-based training, for example, by establishing a system of credit units that collectively form a full and certified course. Such an integrated credit unit or module approach may facilitate the design of systems for continuous vertical upgrading. These systems would take the qualifications (diplomas, apprenticeship certificates, etc.) that are conferred by second-level educational institutions as their point of departure. The purpose of integrating knowledge-based certification with competence-based recognition would be to facilitate upward mobility while allowing for lateral movement across educational tracks that otherwise might lead to occupational "dead ends."

Integrated approaches to certification have several advantages. First, the relationship between initial and postinitial education and training would become more defined, flexible and permeable (Colardyn and Durand-Drouhin 1995). Second, from a labor market viewpoint, such practices would help in making the various learning options open to individuals clearer and, hence, in influencing the way individuals and firms devise their learning strategies. An additional advantage is that an integrated approach to certification may offer incentives for investment in further education and training. Such incentives could act without destroying the structure of labor markets and industrial relations systems specific to countries. Third, an integrated approach to accreditation has implications for financing. Public funding could be more easily earmarked for investment in initial education and training, whereas private resources would be particularly needed for continuing vocational education and training. The dilemma of balancing efficiency and social equity would no longer rest mainly or only with public authority but lie in the hands of all constituencies of society.

See also: Recurrent Education; Government Role in Adult Education and Training; Legislation in Adult Education; Market Failure in Adult Education and Training; Technological Change and Education; Demand, Supply, and Finance of Adult Education; Learning by Contract; Providers of Adult Education: An Overview; Measurement of Adult Education; Measurement of Industry Training

References

Carnevale A P, Gainer L J, Villet J 1990 *Training in America. The Organization and Strategic Role of Training.* Jossey-Bass, San Francisco, California

Council of National Academic Awards (CNAA) 1989 *Background Papers on the Credit Accumulation and Transfer Scheme.* CNNA, London

Cervero R M, Azzaretto J F 1988 *Visions for the Future of Continuing Professional Education.* Research report. University of Georgia, Atlanta, Georgia

Colardyn D, Parlier M 1986 *Bilan des compétences personnelles et professionnelles. Approche historique des pratiques indispensables et diversifiées.* Centre INFFO, Paris

Colardyn D 1996 *La question des compétences. Perspectives internationales. Collection Pédagogie d'aujourd'hui.* Presses Universitaires de France (PUF), Paris.

Colardyn D, Durand-Drouhin M 1995 Recognising skills and qualifications. *The OECD Observer:* 12–15 May. OECD, Paris

Drake K 1991 Recent developments of continuing professional education. United Kingdom's National Report to OECD. In: OECD 1991 *Higher Education and Employment.* OECD, Paris

Elie A 1969 Action de formation dans le bassin ferrifère. *Educ. Permanente* 1(3): 87–102

Eurich N P 1990 *The Learning Industry: Education for Adult Workers.* The Carnegie Foundation for the Advancement of Teaching, New Jersey

Figeat M 1984 *Politiques de formation de la main-d'oeuvre en France.* Collection Rapports de Recherches, INRP, Paris

Gehin J-P 1989 L'évolution de la formation continue dans les secteur d'activité. *Formation emploi* 25: 19–35

Liétard F 1991 *Institutionalisation d'une pratique: les bilans. Point de vue d'un acteur.* Education Permanente à paraître, Paris

Organisation for Economic Co-operation and Development (OECD) 1975 *Recurrent Education.* OECD, Paris

Organisation for Economic Co-operation and Development (OECD) 1977 *Learning Opportunities for Adults,* Vol. 1. OECD, Paris

Organisation for Economic Co-operation and Development (OECD) 1990 *Assessment and Recognition of Skills and Competencies: Developments in France.* OECD, Paris

Organisation for Economic Co-operation and Development (OECD) 1991a *Alternatives to Universities.* OECD, Paris

Organisation for Economic Co-operation and Development (OECD) 1991b Enterprise-related training. In: OECD *Employment Outlook* (July): 135–75

Organisation for Economic Co-operation and Development (OECD) 1994 Collective bargaining: Levels and coverage. *Employment Outlook*/OECD, Paris

Organisation for Economic Co-operation and Development (OECD) 1995 Continuing Professional Education of Highly-Qualilfied Personnel. OECD, Paris

Schwartz B 1969 Pour une education permanente. *Educ. Permanente* 1: 63–86

Tanguy L 1986 *L'introuvable relation formation-emploi. Un état des recherches en France.* La Documentation Française, Paris

Vaughan P, Squires G 1991 *Maintaining Professional Competence.* A survey of the Role of Professional Bodies in the Development of Credit-Bearing CDP courses. The University of Hull, Hull

Further Reading

Aamodt P O 1990 A new deal for Norwegian higher education? *Eur. J. Educ.* 25(2): 171–85

Blanchard S, Francequin-Chartier G, Stassinet G, Vrignaud P 1989 *Outils et procédures de bilan pour la définition d'un projet de formation personnalisée.* Institut National d'Etude du Travail et d'Orientation Professionelle, Paris

de Larminat P 1991 Historique des travaux français de

prospective emploi-formation. In: *Pour une prospective des métiers et des qualifications.* La Documentation Française Paris

Madigan K 1990 *Further Education and Training and Collective Bargaining: The Experience of Five Countries.* OECD, Paris

Organisation for Economic Co-operation and Development (OECD) 1977 *Selection and Certification in Education and Employment.* OECD, Paris

Organisation for Economic Co-operation and Development (OECD) 1987 *Adults in Higher Education.* OECD, Paris

Organisation for Economic Co-operation and Development (OECD) 1992 *Adult Illiteracy and Economic Performance.* OECD, Paris

Organisation for Economic Co-operation and Development (OECD) 1995 Assessment and Recognition of Skills and Competences. DEELSA/ED (95)11. OECD, Paris

Parry G, Wake C 1990 *Access and Alternative Futures for Higher Education.* Hodder and Stoughton, London

TAFE (Training and Further Education) 1990 *Assessment and Standards in Vocational Education and Training.* Conference Report. TAFE, Leabrook

Technological Change and Education

M. Carnoy

Technological change has profound implications for production processes, the division of labor, and labor skills. This entry assesses the extent of available knowledge about the spread of technology, its impact on skills, its consequences for educational policy at different stages of technological diffusion, and conversely, the effect of education on both the use and development of new technology. For the sake of presentation, the discussion focuses on the new information technology, since it is this that represents the most modern wave of worldwide change in production processes.

1. Technological Diffusion

The new microelectronic technologies are diffused in three major forms: (a) through their consumption (electronic consumer goods, such as radios, calculators, television sets, videocassette recorders, and video games, and through telephone availability); (b) through the use of information and telecommunications technologies in the production of traditional goods and services; and (c) through the development and production of high technology products and processes themselves.

1.1 Consumer Electronics

Although the consumption of electronic goods is not usually regarded as technology diffusion, it does have an important impact on diffusion in three ways. First, there is a logical progression from the use of electronic and telecommunication products—even when imported—to their repair locally, and then to their local production. Second, there is a logical progression from the manufacture of simple electronic consumer goods to the manufacture of more complex computer and telecommunications systems, particularly when produced for export; both require similar quality control and production processes. Finally, and most important, certain electronic goods such as telephones also serve as the underlying infrastructure for a larger information–communication network.

The greater availability of telephones and improved worldwide communications have significant implications for the way developing economies can hook into the world economy. It is difficult to say precisely what "threshold" level of telecommunications access is needed for "high technification," but it appears to be approximately four to five telephone lines per 100 inhabitants.

1.2 Applications in Production of Traditional Goods and Services

The diffusion of computers and telecommunications as investment goods employed in the production of goods and services represents a different level of technological use from consumer electronics and consumer telephone use. New technology brought into the production process enhances productivity and quality control and creates the possibility of producing new goods and services associated with the collection, treatment, and dissemination of information: new goods and services which in turn can increase productivity in existing industry.

The process of the technology diffusion through such applications is undoubtedly complex (Rosenberg 1976, Rogers 1983, Dosi 1988). Enterprises in different countries adopt new technologies at different rates depending on a number of factors, including the sector in which they are situated (Pavitt 1984). Economic and social variation at the national level (e.g., the position of labor unions, state macroeconomic policies, the role of exports in the economy) also play a significant role in technology diffusion, in addition to conditions in firms themselves (Edquist 1985, Edquist and Jacobsson 1988).

But for true technology transfer to occur, "learning

by using" (Rosenberg 1982) has to result in the adaptation and production of applications domestically as a result of importing technology. This may begin with the development and production of software applications or adapting quality control processes, but may eventually spread to the import-substitution of hardware. It is the first of these activities (software applications using imported hardware) which turns out to be far more important in terms of productivity, and far more indicative of technology diffusion than hardware production (Bhalla and James 1984). Research in the People's Republic of China (Bianchi et al. 1988) and Mexico (Miller 1986) suggests that the importation of new technology, both in the form of hardware and software without accompanying training in the use of the technology and the management of associated production processes (including quality control), creates minimal technology transfer and minimal higher productivity linkages to other firms.

1.3 The Production of High-tech Products

The last link in the technological diffusion process is the domestic production of high-tech goods and services. Such production sometimes refers to both consumer microelectronics and microelectronics for business applications. However, the two types of production require very different levels of quality control and research and development spending (hence management and labor skills), and should therefore be separated.

The development of both consumer electronic production and, even more so, microelectronics production for business purposes, depends on the presence of one or more of several key factors: (a) the availability of the management and labor skills associated with the production of high-tech goods and services; (b) supply conditions which attract transnational corporations to locate part of their production in that country for export to the world market; (c) the existence of a domestic market for such goods and services, which may be in large part the result of previous technology use; alternatively, development may depend initially on consumption by the state as part of modernizing the state sector (where the state is itself a producer of goods and services), or on the need of traditional industries to compete internationally in the sale of their products by improving their production technology; and (d) a structure of economic incentives that make it worthwhile for producers of final products to source high-tech inputs domestically, and worthwhile for local suppliers to invest in the production of such inputs.

There are several different national models in the Third World which have attempted to capture the rents associated with domestic production of business microelectronics. The Brazilian and Indian models attempt to develop autarkic production in order to satisfy domestic demand and to export to other, less developed countries (Evans 1986, Agarwal 1985). Although

their high-tech products are not competitive with the products of developed countries in terms of quality, they assure the development of a domestic industry and assure that these countries can move up the "learning curve" most rapidly by actually producing the new technology.

In the South Korean model, which applies to Hong Kong, Singapore, and Taiwan (and, to a lesser extent, Malaysia), the first phase of development was represented by foreign companies assembling goods in the country for export to their domestic markets (see Kim 1986, Amsden 1989, Henderson 1988, Henderson and Castells 1987, Salih and Young 1989). Then, due to considerable investment by the South Korean government in education and research and development, Korea first began to produce consumer electronics and other consumer goods of its own using high-technology production processes, and then moved into the production of computers, all for export. This was simultaneously accompanied by domestic consumption of these products.

A third model is found in Mexico (and, on the periphery of Europe, Spain). Mexico is in a special situation, since it borders on the world's largest economic market and also as it is historically a major recipient of United States foreign investment. In this model, foreign firms assemble high-tech products in Mexico for the Mexican market and for export to the United States and other Latin American countries. These firms are committed to hiring Mexican engineers and technicians ("learning by doing"), who, it is hoped, will eventually develop their own firms producing high-tech goods and services (Miller 1986, Montoya 1988, Warman and Miller 1988).

A fourth and final model is that of the People's Republic of China. Here, a huge potential domestic market for electronic and communications equipment is used to attract foreign firms into joint ventures to transfer technology, much as in the Mexican model. The difference between Mexico and China seems to be, however, that China is not attractive as an export platform for these foreign firms, although the Chinese would like it to be. And, unlike the Indians and Brazilians, China imports most of its new information technology for industrial applications in order to modernize manufacturing as rapidly as possible (Bianchi et al. 1988).

The data suggest that although diffusion has been limited, many developing countries in Asia and some in Latin America are already involved in the production and export of electronic goods and components. Many countries are importing new technologies. It is highly likely that production of new technologies in the developing world will increase, even though the research and development base for evolving and designing such products will remain concentrated in the Organisation for Economic Co-operation and Development (OECD) countries. This division of labor may change with the increasing importance of the software industry, which requires a much higher percentage of highly skilled labor.

2. Skill Effects

There is a long history of discussion among economists about the deskilling or reskilling effects of technology on labor. This discussion revolves around the issue of whether new technology decreases or increases the skills required in the workplace, hence lowering or raising the training and education needed by workers to do their jobs effectively. Without describing this literature in detail it is worthwhile summarizing its conclusions before going on to assess the wider relation between education and technology.

Spenner's review (1985) of results in the United States and Europe concludes that:

> There is no evidence that jobs, taken as a group, are experiencing dramatic upgrading and downgrading in terms of their skill requirements. This does not mean an absence of upgrading and downgrading changes but rather an approximate balancing in the direction and quantity of changes of an approximate conservation of total skill . . . It is intriguing that there are more hints of downgrading in studies of skill as autonomy-control and more hints of upgrading in studies of skill as substantive complexity, suggesting the possibility of divergent aggregate trends in the two dimensions of skill. (Spenner 1985 p. 141)

Spenner argues that, "the impacts of technology on skill levels are not simple, not necessarily direct, not constant across settings, and cannot be considered in isolation" (p. 146). The same innovation in different firms can alter skill requirements in different ways.

No research on developing countries is as detailed as Spenner's. However, a recent set of case studies in Asian countries (International Labour Organisation 1988) of automation in the banking, engineering, electrical appliance, and printing industries confirm Spenner's conclusions that it is difficult to identify deskilling or reskilling with automation. It seems that the new jobs being created do not require higher skills, only different skills. It also appears that the most likely workers to be made redundant when automation is introduced are unskilled workers, although this varies according to country and labor legislation. In some cases, such as in South Korea, new unskilled jobs for women were created by automation.

Intuitively, it would seem likely that, as manufacturing and services adopt more complex forms of production, more complex skills would be required. Yet Spenner's review suggests that this may not be the case. Even as new jobs are created that do require higher level skills, just as many jobs (in absolute terms) may be created that require lower level or unchanged skills (Rumberger and Levin 1984).

The changes are made even more complicated by shifts in the gender of those employed in the new manufacturing industries and services. Labor in high-tech industries—where they have an important research and development or software component—tends to be more highly educated but also more gender-stratified than either that in traditional manufacturing or the labor force as a whole. This has important implications for technological job displacement in traditional industries combined with expansion of production of new technologies. Although the production jobs involved may require similar levels of skill, microelectronics production employs a female production labor force. Males are hired into technical jobs—relatively highly educated managers, engineers, sales personnel, and technicians—demanding a different set of skills to those displaced from traditional manufacturing. Therefore, in countries where new technologies applied in traditional industries and services "release" workers, and the production of new technologies employs workers, there is very little absorption of the first by the second.

3. Implications for Education and Training Policies

3.1 The Complementarity of Schooling, Training, and New Technology

Education and training policies are key elements in the process of change occurring in the world economy, but these policies should be different at different levels of development. What is the basis for formulating such policies?

The traditional tools for analyzing public educational investment have been labor force planning and rates of return. Labor force planning attempts to use input–output analysis to predict educational "needs," given projected industry growth, fixed education–skill ratios, skill–job ratios, and job–industry ratios. The method was flawed from the start because none of these ratios was in reality fixed. Spenner's (1985) discussion makes clear that education and skill demand are not necessarily the same. Rumberger's (1981) study argues that education in the United States is increasing much more rapidly than skill requirements. Yet there have been few if any measures of changing skill requirements in other economies; hence most analysts use average education as a proxy for the "capacity to produce," or skill "availability" in the labor force.

Rate-of-return analysis also has its problems, especially when social rates of return are used to predict which levels and what kind of education and training should be subsidized by the state in order to maximize economic growth. Rapid technological change may make social rates of return in the 1990s obsolete in terms of where countries want to be or will be one or two decades hence. The future direction of an economy may well depend on the kind of educational investments made before the payoffs to that education are realized. As economies shift from agricultural to manufacturing and services and the educational system expands, the social rate of return to higher levels of education is seen to rise relative to lower levels (Carnoy 1972, Carnoy and Marenbach 1975, Ryoo et al. 1993, Knight and Sabot 1990).

The association of education with "capacity to produce" is inherently correct, particularly in terms of five variables: literacy, numeracy, socialization to "competence," (Inkeles and Smith 1974), the self-confidence to learn new skills, and the ability to adjust to change (Schultz 1989). In addition, high-level science, medical, mathematical, and management skills needed for certain kinds of production of goods and services can be associated with university education. Societies whose population has these capabilities seem to be more able and willing to learn a wide range of skills related to working with "new" technologies (i.e., new to them). A better "educated" population is more trainable into new jobs. And it is more likely to adopt new technologies and increase their own productivity by using them (Welch 1970). Schultz calls this the "adjustment to disequilibrium" (Schultz 1989).

This complementarity between new methods of production and the capacity to produce that is implied in what schools are supposed to teach is the most powerful argument for more education. As Cohen and Tyson (1989) contend, a better educated labor force will create the conditions for investing in new kinds of production and new organizations of production. This argument probably holds even in relatively low-income countries undergoing severe adjustments to the changing world economy.

Complementarity between education and new technology would contribute both to the diffusion of new growth-promoting technologies and to the employment-creation effect of technological change. A more literate, numerate, and socialized labor force would raise the rate of return to investing in new technology because it would be cheaper to train it to apply the new processes and to work in new kinds of work organizations. Moreover, in the case where labor is involved in making decisions on the use of new technology, it is more likely to use new technology and reap its benefits. An educated labor force would also represent one of the institutional conditions (in addition to a well-developed credit system, for example) required for the effects of technological change in particular firms and industries (lower prices or more employment and income) to spread to other firms and industries.

3.2 The Special Role of the University

Higher education plays a crucial role in technology transfer at two levels. First, it has the capability to develop the management skills required to utilize and organize the new technology; therefore, in terms of the analysis presented here, higher education is the key to the technology transfer process in those industries that use and produce information technology. Second, with the spread of science-based industries, the university is the site that can combine the basic research needed for the advance of such industries with the training of researchers and appliers of research for industry.

The rising rates of return in the larger, and higher educated, nonindustrialized countries (NICs) in part reflect this increasingly important economic role that the university plays in the labor force formation process. This role will increase in the future, especially in the NICs and the industrializing economies, and the more rapid the rate of growth and information-technology-orientation of the economy, the more important the university's role.

However, most universities in developing countries are not organized to combine research and training of undergraduates and graduates in the way required by the new technology and new organization of production. In Brazil, for example, the federal universities are expensive and inefficient, and produce relatively few research–training connections. Much of the teaching is not oriented toward problem-solving. In addition, space is not sufficiently utilized, keeping many qualified students out of the university system. Universities in Argentina and Mexico are much cheaper and much more crowded, but are similar in their lack of research and research–training connections. China's universities are almost purely training institutions, with research delegated to research centers that offer little training. Most developing countries' universities will have to undergo serious reforms if they are to enter into the information age.

Most countries also need to expand greatly their research program in both the universities and industry. Brazil, Argentina, and to some extent Mexico, have engaged in basic scientific research in universities and particularly research institutes. However, this effort has been small compared to the industrialized countries (Castells 1991).

The most telling variable is the degree of cross-activity between training and research on the one hand, and practical industrial applications, on the other, in the three institutions that conduct research and training in most societies: (a) universities, (b) research institutes, and (c) private and public businesses. The greater the presence of both research and training, and application activities in each of these institutions, and the greater the interaction between institutions, the greater the return to research and higher education.

3.3 The New Technology and Training

Training is also a complementary investment to new technology. Yet it must be viewed as complementary both to capital (and the technology associated with capital) and education (and the "technology" associated with education). Training can be divided into: (a) in-school training, or vocational education; (b) on-the-job training, both general and specific, designed for a particular type of production process; and (c) learning by doing, a form of on-the-job training directly connected to the production process itself.

In-school training/vocational education is most distant from the production process. It is designed to provide general skills directly applicable to the production of goods and services, and therefore falls somewhere between schooling and training. From the educators' point of view it has the distinct advantage of "taking care of" students who need preparation for the world of work but who do not perform especially well in abstract academic education. The emphasis centers more on deciding which kind of schooling and training best produces complementarity with new kinds of technology and production processes. Is vocational education more complementary to new methods of production than academic? And is vocational education more complementary than on-the-job training or learning by doing?

Grubb (1987) argues that the new information technologies' impact on skill demand should push the educational system away from vocational concerns into more general preparation of the population to think critically. In theory, this would make workers able to deal with a variety of higher quality jobs that require thought and decision-making rather than the repetitive work that characterizes Fordist technology. This approach would argue for investing in higher quality academic education rather than specific vocational, even if the two could be produced at same cost. In general, long-course vocational education is as expensive (or more so) than even relatively high-cost academic schooling.

A recent World Bank monograph (Middleton et al. 1990) makes the case that in-school vocational education, both because of its cost and its use of obsolete equipment, is not as complementary to changing technologies as in-firm training. This suggests that a more effective way to provide training is through direct subsidies to firms rather than through indirect subsidies via vocational education.

Nevertheless, there is still a case for vocational education in certain situations: (a) in countries characterized by high economic growth, especially where private enterprises are willing to bear part of its cost, or in vocations for high-growth industries (Chung 1990); (b) in situations where enterprises send workers who are already employed to be trained partially at the company's expense (examples are SENA in Colombia and SENAI in Brazil, but it should be remembered that the analyses of these programs were done in relatively high economic growth periods); (c) in countries characterized by low growth and increasing or high unemployment, short-course, self-employment-oriented training designed for new occupations in agriculture or the informal labor market may yield high returns provided that they focus on broader, "business" skills such as marketing and sales in addition to traditional production or service skills.

What is the complementarity of in-plant training to new technologies? It is commonly agreed that training programs are an important feature of successful firms producing high-technology products and those that use high-technology intensive capital (see, e.g., Shaiken and Herzenberg 1987). Less clear is the relationship of training programs to employee education and to work organization. Recent research in Mexico found that plants providing in-plant training generally geared it to certain "target" levels of education, and those targets were used in labor force hiring (Carnoy 1989). This held for production workers, as well as for management trainees and industrial engineers. There appears to be a significant relationship between the technology embodied in capital and work organization, the "optimum" level of education required of different kinds of employees who work with that capital or in that organization, and the in-plant training programs provided, although that optimum level may vary historically as the formal educational system expands. This suggests that "trainability" is as much a function of what is actually learned in various levels of schooling (the mathematics, science, and language arts curricula) as of graduates' sense of self-worth and capability. The first is an absolute consideration; employers producing particular products and using particular technology have a clear image of the minimum literacy and numeracy skills required for in-plant training in certain jobs. The availability of those school skills might be a condition of initial investment in such production. The second is relative: that is, how graduates are measured and how they measure themselves compared to others who are the same age and who are also seeking work at that point in time. A graduate with nine years of schooling in Mexico may well have a greater sense of capability than a high-school graduate in the United States. This relative notion of education is generally called its "screening" feature. The simpler the technology and the more hierarchical the organization, the less the complementarity between in-school education, in-plant training, and physical capital.

Learning by doing, unlike in-plant training, can be complemented by capital and especially by work organization. Once again, many questions arise: what is the complementarity of in-school education to learning by doing? Do more highly schooled workers learn more by doing with given capital (and therefore become more productive) than less schooled workers? Is in-plant formal training complementary to learning by doing, or are they relatively independent learning processes? Are certain types of work organization more complementary to learning by doing, given the schooling of workers and managers, than others (see Levin 1987)? Are there minimum levels of previous learning by doing which are required with certain kinds of technology or in certain industries and not in others?

The last wave of new technologies, new organizations of production, changing employment conditions, and the development of new sectors of production suggest that the complementarity of general, formal schooling, in-plant training, and learning by doing to capital investment are increasing over time and that general schooling plus on-the-job training is more complementary to new technologies than vocational schooling. The former combination is more likely to equip workers with the flexibility they require in such changing conditions. The analysis across types of sectors outlined above also suggests that different levels and conditions of development necessitate different decisions regarding schooling and training, and that many countries face the threat of being excluded from the new information revolution unless they restructure their economies and expand education and training programs with a focus on general and high-quality skill formation. The larger NICs could also fall far behind unless they, too, focus on university reform and greatly increased research and research-oriented training in higher education.

See also: Sociology of Adult Education; Economics of Adult Education and Training; Adult Education for Development; Government Role in Adult Education and Training; Demand, Supply, and Finance of Adult Education; International Labour Organisation; Latin America: National Training Agencies

References

Agarwal S M 1985 Electronics in India: Past strategies and future possibilities. *World Dev.* 13 (3): 273–92

Amsden A 1989 *Asia's Next Giant: South Korea and Late Industrialization*. Oxford University Press, New York

Bhalla A S, James J 1984 New technology revolution: Myth or reality for developing countries? *Greek Econ. Rev.* 6 (3): 387–423

Bianchi P, Carnoy M, Castells M 1988 *Economic Modernization and Technology Transfer in the People's Republic of China*. Report No. 88–26. Center for Educational Research at Stanford, Stanford University, Stanford, California

Carnoy M 1972 The political economy of education. In: La Belle T (ed.) 1972 *Education and Development in Latin America and the Caribbean*. Latin American Center, UCLA, Los Angeles, California

Carnoy M 1989 *Opening the Door: Education and Productivity*. Film produced by the International Labour Organisation, Geneva (VHS videotape, distributed by ILO, Geneva), 17 min

Carnoy M, Marenbach D 1975 The return to schooling in the United States, 1939–1969. *J. Hum. Resources* 10 (3): 312–31

Castells M 1991 The university system: Engine of development in the new world economy. Paper prepared for the World Bank Seminar on Higher Education and Development, Kuala Lumpur (mimeo)

Chung Y-P 1990 The economic returns to vocational and technical education in a fast growing economy: A case study of Hong Kong. Unpublished doctoral dissertation, Stanford University, Stanford, California

Cohen S, Tyson L 1989 Technological change, competitiveness and the challenges confronting the American educational system. Berkeley Roundtable for International Economics, University of California, Berkeley, California (mimeo)

Dosi G 1988 Sources, procedures, and microeconomic effects of innovation. *J. Econ. Lit.* 26: (3) 1120–71

Edquist C 1985 *Capitalism, Socialism and Technology: A Comparative Study of Cuba and Jamaica*. Zed Books, London

Edquist C, Jacobsson S 1988 *Flexible Automation: The Global Diffusion of New Technology in the Engineering Industry*. Basil Blackwell, Oxford

Evans P 1986 State, capital, and the transformation of dependence: The Brazilian computer case. *World Dev.* 14 (7): 791–808

Grubb N 1987 Responding to the constancy of change: New technologies and future demands on US education. In: Burke G, Rumberger R (eds.) 1987

Henderson J 1988 High technology production in Hong Kong and the making of a regional 'core'. Paper presented at the International Symposium of Technology Policy in the Americas, Stanford University, California

Henderson J, Castells M 1987 *Global Restructuring and Territorial Development*. Sage, Beverly Hills, California

Inkeles A, Smith D 1974 *Becoming Modern: Individual Change in Six Developing Countries*. Harvard University Press, Cambridge, Massachusetts

International Labour Organisation 1988 *Technological Change, Work Organization and Pay: Lessons from Asia*. Labor-Management Relations Series, No. 68. ILO, Geneva

Kim L 1986 New technologies and their economic effects: A feasibility study in Korea. Paper prepared for the United Nations University, New Technologies Centre Feasibility Study, Maastricht

Knight J B, Sabot R 1990 *Education, Productivity, and Inequality: The East African Natural Experiment*. World Bank/Oxford University Press, New York

Levin H 1987 Improving productivity through education and technology. In: Burke G, Rumberger R (eds.) 1987

Middleton J, Ziderman A, Van Adams A 1990 *Vocational Education and Training in Developing Countries*. World Bank, Washington, DC

Miller M 1986 High technology transfer: A case study of the Mexican computer electronics industry. Unpublished undergraduate honors thesis, Stanford University, California

Montoya A 1988 Telematics, knowledge and power in Mexican society: The policies of the Mexican State, 1970–1983. Unpublished PhD dissertation, Stanford University, California (mimeo)

Pavitt K 1984 Patterns of technical change: Towards a taxonomy and a theory. *Res. Policy* 13 (6): 343–73

Rogers E 1983 *Diffusion of Innovations*, 3rd edn. Free Press, New York

Rosenberg N 1976 *Perspectives on Technology*. Cambridge University Press, Cambridge

Rosenberg N 1982 *Inside the Black Box: Technology and Economics*. Cambridge University Press, Cambridge

Rumberger R 1981 *Overeducation in the US Labor Market*. Praeger, New York

Rumberger R, Levin H 1984 Forecasting the impact of new technologies on the future job market. *Technological Forecasting and Social Change* 27: 399–417

Ryoo J, Nam Y S, Carnoy M 1993 Rates of return to education in the Korea. *Econ. Educ. Rev.*

Salih K, Young M L 1989 Changing conditions of labour in the semiconductor industry in Malaysia. *Lab. Soc.* 14: 59–80 (special issue devoted to High Tech and Labor in Asia)

Schultz T 1989 Human capital in restoring equilibrium. Paper presented at the Conference on Human Capital and Economic Growth, Institute for the Study of Free Enterprise Systems, SUNY, Buffalo, New York

Shaiken H, Herzenberg S 1987 *Automation and Global Production. Automobile Engine Production in Mexico, the United States, and Canada.* University of California, Center for US–Mexican Studies, San Diego, California

Spenner K 1985 The upgrading and downgrading of occupations: Issues, evidence, and implications for education. *Rev. Educ. Res.* 55 (2): 125–54

Warman J, Miller M 1989 *Competividad de la Industria Electrónica Mexicana: Estudios de caso.* Friedrich Ebert Foundation, Mexico City

Welch F 1970 Education in production. *J. Pol. Econ.* 78(1): 35–59

Further Reading

Burke G, Rumberger R (eds.) 1987 *The Future Impact of Technology on Work and Education.* Falmer Press, London

Castells M 1985 New technologies, world development, and structural transformation: The trends and the debate. Department of City and Regional Planning, University of California, Berkeley, California (mimeo)

Rumberger R, Levin H M 1989 Schooling for the modern workplace. Background paper No.2 prepared for the Commission on Workforce Quality and Labor Market Efficiency, US Department of Labor, Washington, DC

Time, Leisure, and Adult Education

J. Lowe

The aim of this entry is to examine the relationship between adult education and leisure and their connection with paid work. A fundamental issue concerns the amount of leisure actually available in the modern world and the ways in which adults make use of it in practice. Where does organized learning rank in people's priorities? What are the barriers that inhibit participation in adult education programs? Above all, what are the implications for policymakers and providing agencies of the research findings on the uses of leisure, especially in view of the competing claims on people's time and interests?

1. Key Assumptions

In the late twentieth century, leisure is commonly treated as though it were indissociable from the idea of free or spare time and the quality of life. However, that simple understanding hides complexity, for there exists no precise and authoritative definition to which everyone can defer. Leisure is an elusive concept.

The concept of adult education is also open to different interpretations according to the context in which it is applied. Any consideration of the relationship between the two concepts must begin therefore by stating what assumptions are being made about their respective connotations. Here there are two assumptions. The first is that the education of adults, unlike that of young people, takes place mainly outside the standard hours of gainful employment, and that it is very largely a part-time activity. The second is that for pragmatic reasons, the term "adult education" should be equated with those who provide it, namely, agencies and their programs, and that the term "leisure" should be equated with the ways in which people use their free time according to the findings of objective inquiries and not popular impressions, which are often misconceived. This implies restricting the meaning of adult education as interpreted by those who specialize in its study (see *Adult Education: Concepts and Principles*).

2. Leisure as Residual Time

The notion of leisure as a discrete phenomenon is, in historical terms, relatively new, and even in the 1990s it relates more appropriately to advanced industrialized countries than to less developed countries. Its modern usage dates from the advent of large-scale industrialization in Europe in the nineteenth century, when the organization of paid employment into obligatory hours of long duration marked a distinction between the time spent at work and the time spent in other activities at home or elsewhere. In 1936, France created a short-lived "Ministry of Leisure." In the 1990s, leisure is perceived as a desirable good in most societies.

There has been little authoritative inquiry into the nature of leisure. Definitions tend to be couched in general terms, with a cultural bias towards conditions in advanced industrialized countries, especially in parliamentary democracies, and neglect of any gender implications. They also tend to be normative, stating how leisure ought to be used in an ideal world rather than specifying how people make use of it in practice. The most constructive approach has been to examine systematically the way individuals organize their everyday lives. This has led to the identification of four categories of allotted time: necessary, contracted, committed, and residual. Necessary time is that devoted to the physiological demands of human existence such as sleeping, eating, and personal hygiene. Contracted time denotes employment rewarded in cash or kind. Committed time is that taken up with family, social, civic, and other duties. Residual time is all that remains over and above the combination of the other three (OECD 1982 pp. 82–85). Leisure activities, subject to situational constraints, take place in residual time, though it must be borne in mind that:

> What constitutes leisure and leisure time activities is dependent on the view from the inside: that is, what the individual considers to be an expressive activity. An activity that an individual feels forced to do for different reasons does not qualify as leisure. (OECD 1982 p. 95)

What adults seek in their leisure time may be rest, entertainment, or physical exercise. They may also seek opportunities to learn in an organized fashion either for a nonvocational or vocational purpose. It is with the learning option that adult education is concerned.

3. Learning as a Leisure Pursuit

The following two definitions of leisure, which are strikingly similar, not only assume the pursuit of learning to be one of its main components but also that, for adults, learning is a leisure-time pursuit. The second definition goes so far as to specify that the pursuit is disinterested:

> Leisure is a set of activities exercised by man of his free choice, either for rest, entertainment, or *improving his knowledge or creative abilities*, after he has freed himself from work and obligations towards family and society. (UNESCO 1966 p. 27)

> Leisure consists of a number of occupations in which an individual may indulge of his own free will either to rest, amuse himself, *to add to his knowledge and improve his skills disinterestedly* and to increase his voluntary participation in the life of the community after discharging his professional, family and social duties. (Appleton 1974 p. xi)

This perception derives from the Western tradition of equating adult learning with liberal studies, "liberal" being "the *mot juste* with its suggestion of freedom from constraints and man choosing to spend his nonlucrative time in the pursuit of intellectual improvement" (Lowe 1974 p. 144). Significantly, social reformers in Europe in the late nineteenth and early twentieth centuries saw long working hours and the absence of free time as the main obstacles to mass participation in educational programs. In the United Kingdom, the trade union movement adopted the slogan: "Eight hours work, eight hours instruction, eight hours repose." The inference was that if only adults had ample leisure, they would devote a substantial part of it to learning.

The providers of adult education have taken it as axiomatic that their programs should be offered outside standard working hours. This explains why, at least until comparatively recently, organized adult learning remained overwhelmingly an evening and, occasionally, weekend or vacation activity divorced from working life.

The juxtaposition of liberal education and leisure is elitist. The majority of adults have less free time than is commonly supposed and leisure is conducive to purposeful learning only when individuals are suitably motivated and have already reached a certain level of initial education. If a significant number of adults in any society are to take advantage of learning opportunities, it is evident that those responsible for policies and programs should be fully aware of exactly which adults have free time and in what quantity. They should also actively stimulate the unmotivated to learn, and recognize the interdependence of work and leisure.

4. How Much Leisure Time?

The widespread belief in the 1990s that adults in general, especially those living in advanced industrialized countries, have abundant leisure arises from two apparently incontrovertible assumptions. The first is that there has been a rapid evolution from a social condition of "all work and no play" to one in which, thanks to a shorter working week, longer holidays, and earlier retirement, there is, for the majority of the working population, nearly as much or more leisure as time spent at work. A French report (European Communities Economic and Social Committee 1989) points out that the time spent at work represented only 11 percent of an average lifetime. People spend the equivalent of 24 years sleeping, *20 years of leisure*, 6 years commuting, 8 years in education, 8 years of work, 3 years of personal hygiene, and 2 years of medical care. In advanced industrialized countries, in general, the contrast with the nineteenth century is striking. In approximate figures, the working day has been reduced from 12 to 8 hours, the working week from 70 to 40 hours, and the working year from 3,600 to 1,900 hours. At the same time, people live much longer, experiencing on average 10 years of retirement.

The second assumption, reinforcing the first, is that nonwork and free time are synonymous. The truth is that, whereas some adults, including many of the retired whose numbers are rapidly increasing in the advanced industrialized countries, certainly have considerable leisure time, a surprisingly large number must organize their lives in a disciplined fashion in order to be able to devote significant time to the specific activity of organized learning.

The amount of completely free time that is actually disposable varies greatly from one individual to another. Social customs can dictate the duration of meals. Contracted time may extend from a few hours to 12 or more a day. Many workers regularly do overtime. Japanese workers frequently decline to take all the holidays to which they are entitled. A subsistence farmer may toil in the fields through all the daylight hours and still have tasks to perform after dark. In large conurbations many people are obliged to travel considerable distances in commuting to their workplace. For numerous men and women such commitments together with household and social duties may well absorb so much committed time that no residual time is left over. The amount of free time available to an individual also varies according to the different stages of the life-cycle.

Household and family duties continue to make heavy demands on women in most societies throughout the world. In less developed countries it is notorious that nearly all women lead arduous lives. In numerous advanced industrialized countries sociological surveys show that, despite the efforts of the feminist movement, the overwhelming majority of women dispose of much less residual time than men. Even in those households where at least some duties are shared between couples, working women remain disadvantaged. The increasing incidence of single-parent families, the great majority of which are headed by mothers, has exacerbated this gender imbalance, for the care of such families consumes exceptional time and energy and confines many mothers to the home all day or, if they are gainfully employed full-time or part-time, during the whole or greater part of their committed and, if any, residual time.

In advanced industrialized countries, and to a lesser extent in less developed countries, adults usually distinguish between the regular working week and weekends and annual holidays. During holidays the amount of committed time often increases but much residual time still remains. In other words, it is essential for providers to take account of the way individuals allocate their time on an annual and weekend as well as a working week basis.

Furthermore, it is a question not only of an individual having adequate residual time but a realistic range of learning activities from which to make a voluntary choice. In practice, the choice for many people is restricted by the absence of appropriate programs and by such personal constraints as limited spending power, low level of initial education, old age, lack of mobility, and undeveloped capacity for self-realization. The jobs of some workers are so physically exhausting and dehumanizing as to stifle the very taste for learning.

It is obvious that the choices before a peasant farmer in Bangladesh or Guinea Bissau are of a totally different order from those before a wealthy person in Paris or Rio de Janeiro. By the same token, the latter enjoys many more options than a functionally illiterate, single-parent or migrant worker living in the same metropolis. Choice is also circumscribed in many countries by social or political forces. In Czechoslovakia, in 1950: "The use of one's leisure time in nonproductive or nonpolitical group activity was to be strongly discouraged" (Andel 1977 p. 53). The leisure time options of individuals can be fully appraised only when all the surrounding circumstances of their lives have been taken into account.

5. Stimulating Participation

Not only is the amount of leisure available to many adults much less than is commonly supposed, but only a minority of those with considerable leisure, in all but a few countries, actively seeks organized learning opportunities. Although the pursuit of learning features prominently in the two definitions of leisure previously cited, many seek primarily rest and entertainment. Some engage in *do it yourself* activities, which may, incidentally, entail informal learning. Personal intellectual improvement, the central goal of traditional adult education programs, has little popular appeal. An illustration of this is the behavior of the elderly in many economically prosperous countries. They usually have much more residual time than other adults, but even in good health and with adequate financial resources, they do not participate in educational programs in significant numbers. Quite simply, they are not motivated. Motivation is undoubtedly conditioned by the dominant cultural values in a given society. Thus, in the Nordic countries, where a powerful adult learning tradition prevails, a large number of elderly people are to be found in classes and programs.

Research evidence shows that those adults who have both the financial and other means and the time to participate in programs usually have a wide range of interests, including reading and informal learning, that compete for the use of their leisure. An inquiry in the United States discovered that:

> Essentially, people with broad and diverse leisure activities are more likely than others to participate in adult education. This finding conflicts with a prevailing view that adult education competes with other leisure pursuits for the interest and attention of a potential audience (London and Wenkert 1969 p. 22)

In short, the demand for adult education programs is disproportionately low compared with the size of populations (see *Demand, Supply, and Finance of Adult Education*). Providers are far from catering for a captive clientele. To increase participation implies arousing public interest in learning on a prominent scale. In order even to think of becoming a student, any adult needs to know exactly where, when, and under what circumstances opportunities are available that respond to his or her aspirations and abilities. By the same token, experience shows that providers must choose with care the location, timing, and, above all, content of their programs. As in Sweden, stimulating interest also needs to become a national and regional, as well as a local government concern. In practice, the received perception of leisure as spare time in which individual choices should predominate often seems to rule out the need for government intervention. It is no accident that adult education flourishes most in those countries where its value is recognized at all levels of government, in industry and commerce, and in all walks of life, and where there is a significant level of public and private investment in programs and facilities. Stimulation at the local level is always the critical factor, however, for it is only there that the learning needs of the great majority of the population can be accurately identified, assessed, and serviced.

Two categories of adults cannot or do not take up learning opportunities that are located in institutions. The first, which has long been familiar to professional adult educators, includes those living in isolated areas, those with exacting domestic duties—overloaded committed time—those who work irregular hours, and those who are physically disabled. The second category, whose numbers were greatly underestimated until recently, consists of those who prefer to study independently, at least for a portion of the time they devote to learning. Research findings, which have multiplied since the pioneering Canadian study (Tough 1979), show that "independent learners" are to be found everywhere. Many ordinary people doing ordinary jobs plan, manage, and monitor their own learning activities and many people with an advanced initial education are continuously and deliberately extending and enriching their own knowledge and skills. Reading is a predominant interest, especially for older people. It may well be that the greatest potential for expansion of adult education lies in serving the needs of independent learners.

6. Interdependence of Work, Leisure, and Learning

Acquiring knowledge, consciously improving skills, and developing creative abilities are three pursuits that are by no means confined only to free time. They also take place during working hours at an ever-increasing rate. Furthermore, much of the education in free time is undertaken for work-related needs or interests. The reality is that for many adults a part—even a large part—of free time is dominated by concerns related to their present employment or career

ambitions. The complementarity of work and leisure assessed in a report commissioned by UNESCO in the early 1960s remains an authoritative reference:

Leisure is not an isolated social phenomenon. Both objectively and subjectively, it is intrinsically linked with work. The two time spheres are so interrelated that the one can be understood only on the basis of the other. However, work will always remain the more important factor for the social determination of human life. It is and will continue to be the most substantial sphere of human activity, so that the tendencies and possibilities of leisure are basically determined by the sphere of work. (UNESCO 1966 p. 26)

To divorce work from leisure is to perpetuate the old error of sharply distinguishing vocational, that is work-related education, from nonvocational, that is nonwork-related education. Adults' motives are often mixed or ambiguous. On the one hand, many who undergo training at work do so because it is obligatory or a welcome break from routine rather than because they have a positive desire to become more efficient or to improve their career prospects. On the other hand, many who attend courses in their free time that seem to have no connection with their paid employment and that may even be explicitly defined as nonvocational in advertised programs are in reality anxious to improve themselves in order to obtain a better job elsewhere or promotion in their present jobs. It is the individual who determines whether his or her learning is vocational or nonvocational.

There is also the question of the learning needs of the short-term and long-term unemployed whose numbers have increased in advanced industrialized countries since the mid-1970s. National authorities now acknowledge that it is on grounds not only of social justice but also of economic expedience that the unemployed should be given the opportunity to participate in education and training programs designed to equip them for a job. Such programs can scarcely be described as education for leisure, since much of the free time of the unemployed is enforced and involuntary.

The educational needs of adults can only be partially satisfied by a judicious use of their leisure time. Some subjects and some skills can best be acquired through concentrated study over an intensive period which does not entail competing with the burden and stress of regular employment. Thus, the concept of time for learning has to embrace more than leisure. Time off from employment is often required as well.

7. The Research Agenda

Research into the aims, content, and methods of adult education and the characteristics of participants in programs has multiplied in recent years. The very topic of adult education and leisure has been subjected to a systematic, comprehensive, and long-term analysis by the European Centre for Leisure and Education located in Prague, which has published an imposing series of monographs (ECLE 1969–76, 1977–86). However, whereas in the parlance of economists the research evidence is strong at the macro level and on the supply side, it is weak on the dynamics of demand, on identifying, for example, the influences that lead individuals to choose this rather than that leisure activity. It is unlikely, therefore, that future macro studies will add substantially to the existing pool of information available to practitioners. As pointed out above, the key to stimulating demand is to be found at grass-roots level in local communities. At that level it is not theorizing and inquiring into the characteristics of participants that are called for, but positive and sustained strategies of action research.

Most practitioners are well aware of how people allocate their leisure in general terms and what obstacles prevent many adults from participating in education and training programs. Providers can attract more participants only by undertaking intensive community surveys of learning needs and then designing appropriate programs. What is required then is the systematic exchange of information about successes and failures, and the replication of good practice wherever possible.

8. Facing up to Competition

The world has yet to experience a golden age of leisure and learning. The great majority of adults, even those in easy circumstances, have less free time than is commonly supposed. A significant number, especially among the poor in advanced industrialized and less developed countries alike, have very few choices in the use of free time. Nevertheless, the aggregate amount of leisure time available in societies as a whole is substantial and, to judge from present trends, it will continue to increase in the years ahead. Moreover, many people enjoy a wide range of choices.

Five factors militate, however, against education automatically having a primary option on the attention of adults. The first is the propensity of most adults to stick to passive activities like viewing television. The second is the pronounced trend in advanced industrialized countries to make the home the centre of leisure interests, the cocooning syndrome, as it has been called. The third is the ability of the leisure industry, supported by expensive and alluring mass advertising, to capture people's time by offering, for example, package holidays that remove the very need for making choices. The fourth is the inclination of many adults not to seek more leisure but to work longer hours in order to secure additional goods. The

fifth is the sheer lack of interest in organized learning of a large majority of adults in most countries. Those who wish to promote the education of adults have thus no recourse but to acknowledge the power of the competing claims on the uses of leisure and to counter it actively. As for adult education agencies, they must adopt dynamic strategies for stimulating a greater social and individual demand for learning opportunities.

See also: Adult Education: Concepts and Principles; Time Policies for Lifelong Learning; Demand, Supply, and Finance of Adult Education; Legislation in Adult Education; Participation: Antecedent Factors; Participation: Role of Motivation

References

Andel J J 1977 Leisure education in Czechoslovakia. Official attitudes and their theoretical background. *Stud. Adult Educ.* 9(1): 49–57

Appleton I (ed.) 1974 *Leisure Research and Policy*. Scottish Academic Press, Edinburgh

European Centre for Leisure and Education (ECLE) 1969–76 *Society and Leisure*, Vols. 1–8 UNESCO, Prague

European Centre for Leisure and Education (ECLE) 1977–86 *Adult Education in Europe: Studies and Documents*, Vols. 1–23 UNESCO, Prague

European Communities Economic and Social Committee 1989 *Bulletin*, No. 6. EC, Brussels

London J, Wenkert R 1969 Leisure styles and adult education. *Adult Educ. J.* 20(1): 3–22

Lowe J 1974 The Interdependence of adult education and leisure. In: Appleton I (ed.) 1974

Organisation for Economic Co-operation and Development (OECD) 1982 *Measuring the Use of Time*. OECD Social Indicator Development Programme. OECD, Paris

Tough A 1979 *The Adult's Learning Projects*, 2nd edn. Ontario Institute for Studies in Education. UNESCO, Paris

UNESCO 1966 *Adult Education and Leisure in Contemporary Europe*. Orbis, Prague

Further Reading

Dumazedier J 1974, *Sociologie empirique du loisir. Critique et contre-critique de la civilisation du loisir.* Seuil, Paris

Eide K 1981 Changing realities of work, leisure, education. In: Himmelstrup P, Robinson J, Fielden J (eds.) 1981 *Strategies for Lifelong Learning: A symposium of views from Europe and the USA*, Vol. 1. University of South Jutland, Esjberg

Sargant N 1991 *Learning and Leisure: A study of adult participation in learning and its policy implications.* National Institute of Adult Continuing Education, Lancaster

World Leisure and Recreation Association (WLRA) 1958–91 *World Leisure and Education*, Vols. 1–33. Periodical Literature. WLRA, Ottawa

Time Policies for Lifelong Learning

K. Abrahamsson

This entry presents an analysis of the notion of time policies for lifelong learning. Special reference is made to the societal, organizational, and educational conditions for the allocation of time for education across the lifespan as developed in the Swedish model of recurrent education. In this respect, the issues discussed form part of a broader array of public policies regulating working time and retirement conditions, as well as different examples of leave of absence for vacation, sickness, childcare, and education (see *Recurrent Education*).

Time policies for lifelong learning have an impact both on the temporization of education and learning over the lifespan and on the individual's time budget for learning in a daily or weekly perspective. The first aspect focuses on general characteristics of systems of education such as the age at which school starts, the duration of compulsory education, access to postcompulsory and adult education, as well as provisions for learning projects in old age.

The second dimension relates to the individual's study intensity and educational participation, including self-directed learning, over the lifespan. This aspect involves questions such as the balance between full-time or part-time studies, as well as between formal instruction and self-directed learning. It may be noted here that in most industrialized countries, the increasing number of older citizens will have strong repercussions on the demand for adult education and learning during the 1990s and beyond (see Glendenning and Percy 1990, Young and Schuller 1991).

In both dimensions, it is necessary to consider the "time policy impact" of the interplay between education, labor market, and social policies. All public policies that facilitate or limit the options for lifelong learning can play an important role in this respect. This raises a number of important questions, for example:

(a) How do different countries allocate time for education and learning across the lifespan?

(b) Which principles and institutional models can be used to guide the allocation of time for education across the lifespan, and what are the implications for the balance between youth and adult education?

(c) How can the interplay between formal and nonformal education, as well as between self-directed or incidental learning across the lifespan be managed?

(d) To what extent can the participation of adults in education be facilitated or hindered by public policies other than those of an educative nature?

(e) Is there an upper ceiling for the supply of education in a lifetime perspective in a so-called "postindustrial" society?

(f) How can access to education in a lifetime perspective be supported by legislation and/or collective bargaining agreements struck in the labor market?

1. The Social Construction of Lifelong Learning

Learning and social adjustment are inherent components of all cultures and historical periods. The social and economic transformations of a society are examples of major learning projects. In most countries, formal education has taken a significant step into its second century, while formal adult education is a product of a more recent period. The traditional model, in which school education was considered a knowledge cure with a lifelong value, has been replaced by the metaphor of a learning society (see Cross 1981, 1989).

The passages of learning from childhood to retirement depend on various historical, cultural, and social conditions. Traditional metaphors have stressed the culturally bound stages of life transition with its typical "rites of passage." Birth, infancy, childhood, youth, maturity, and marriage, work, and family, as well as retirement, old age, and death are the usual life stations symbolized in these metaphors, most of which were created long before the institutionalization of formal schooling. Relatively modern perspectives are presented by Baltes and Schaie (1973), Erikson (1950), and Havighurst (1951).

The expansion of formal education and the development of new options for adult and higher education have significantly changed the traditional model of life transition. The need for a reconceptualization of such models of lifespan development is evident for a number of reasons:

(a) The number of "life-changes" has increased.

(b) The increase in the labor force participation rate of women not only calls for educational measures, but also for a new division of responsibilities in households and families.

(c) The use of technology at work and at home has changed the demand for adult education.

(d) The development of the information economy,

which results in an ongoing structural transformation of the labor market, is followed by a need for new knowledge and skills in the workplace.

(e) The so-called "third-age" phenomenon, which is characterized by high life expectancy and a large proportion of citizens above 65 years of age, will have a significant impact on the demand for post-initial learning.

The need for lifelong education can also be analyzed with the metaphor "long-life learning" and the extended active life period. The changes in modern societies call for new ways of describing the expansion of learning over the lifespan. The conventional connotation of education comprises any form of organized learning taking place within school buildings and supported by teachers, teaching aids, and predetermined time schedules. Education is not, however, a synonym for learning. Looking at time policies and lifelong education, one has to make a distinction between time in (or years in) education and time for learning. Education is not always a necessary, or even a sufficient, condition for learning.

2. Comparative Aspects of Educational Timing Across the Lifespan

Each society can be characterized by the total amount of time allotted to education over the whole population. This so-called "educational time pool" has increased considerably since the start of public schooling in the nineteenth century. Since the 1950s, the percentage of the population enrolled in education has increased in most countries. For example, in Sweden, one out of every five individuals was registered in education in the late 1980s compared with one out of every ten in the 1930s. The main determinant of this development is the prolongation of youth education (Bottani et al. 1992).

Sweden is an example of a learning society characterized by a situation where:

(a) most young people are in school for at least 11–12 years;

(b) almost one in four students continues on to higher education;

(c) almost every second higher education student is over 25 years of age;

(d) one in two adults takes part in organized adult education;

(e) almost 80 percent of the adults—both men and women—are employed;

(f) one in four employees participates in employer-sponsored training.

Characteristic of Sweden is a high level of adult participation in organized education, but a relatively low level of transition of young students to higher education. An explanation might be the limited intake capacity of higher education.

3. Life Expectancy, Years of Schooling, and Learning Hours

Demographic data from Sweden show that the average lifespan is 75 years for men and 81 for women. This adds up to more than 650,000 hours that can be spent on learning, work, and leisure. The level of employment has increased significantly since the early 1970s, especially for women. The proportion of women in employment has increased from 58 percent in 1970 to 80 percent in 1988, while the employment rate for men was 85 percent in that year (see Statistics Sweden 1989). The employment rate has, however, decreased with around 5 percent during the unexpected Swedish unemployment crises in the early nineties.

Children and young adults spend a considerable part of their life in formal education. Compulsory schooling in Sweden adds up to 11,000 hours—over 15,000 hours if upper-secondary education is included. Adults, by contrast, attend education only a few days per year on average. Learning outside the formal system tends to be of increasing importance in a learning society. This is especially true with respect to the workplace as a center of learning and competence development.

The average number of annual working hours has, however, been reduced in many countries. Part-time work patterns are rather rare among men, but quite common among women. More than 90 percent of employed men work 35 hours a week or more, whereas the comparable share for women is 57 percent. In most cultures, the family obligations of women still take a significant part of the working week, even though a number of initiatives have been taken in order to stimulate fathers to take more responsibility for family duties and childcare.

In a lifespan perspective, the amount of working hours add up to an average of 67,500 hours. This is more than five times the time-share in youth education. But it is still not more than 10 percent of total life time-hours. These figures illustrate the scope for different combinations of formal, nonformal, and experiental learning across the lifespan.

Time policies have recently attracted much attention. In many countries, citizens and employees have the right to leave of absence for parental duties, sick-leave, vacation, and even study leave. Excluding vacation, the number of employees absent from work has increased in many industrialized countries. This figure was 10 percent in Sweden in 1988, with women being absent twice as often as men. If one looks at parents with children under 7 years of age, this difference is even more apparent: 27.1 percent for working mothers and only 6.9 percent for working fathers. It has to be underlined, however, that the high level of absenteeism for women incorporates parental leave for infants and should not be mixed up with short-time leave for sick children (Statistics Sweden 1989).

The impact of time policies has also to be considered. The most important application is, of course, the distribution of working hours over the lifespan, as well as the allocation of time for work over the year and working week. The options for more flexible life schedules have been studied by Best and Stern (1976) and Best (1991).

4. A Look at the Individual's Time Budget for Learning

There is a marked difference between the individual's time budget for learning in youth education and learning and adult education. In youth education, there are striking differences between countries in the number of school days per demographic year. The figures vary from 160 in some countries to more than 220 in Japan. Moreover, the time used for homework per week ranges from less than 2.5 hours to more than 8 hours. Furthermore, research studies show that the communication patterns within the classroom are still very teacher-centered and generally require only a minimum of group work or self-initiated activity from the students.

For adults the situation is quite different because relatively few adults enroll in full-time studies. In the early 1990s, statistics from Sweden show that more than 50 percent of adults take part in some kind of organized adult education, mostly in study circles and employer-sponsored programs. If the total amount of participation is transformed into full-time equivalents, the number of people involved is reduced from 2.5 million to less than 200,000.

Considering this, it is obvious that a crucial aspect of time policies for adult education concerns the option of dividing long-term study projects into sequences in combination with work and other responsibilities. Swedish statistics show small differences in the participation level of adults from different backgrounds. Women between 25 and 44 years of age with preschool-aged children have a participation rate of 41.2 percent, compared to 51.8 percent for the same age group having children from 7 to 18 years of age (Statistics Sweden 1991). The options of combining family responsibilities and educational interests depend on the social and economic circumstances of parents in different countries.

One in five adult students in Sweden utilize the right to educational leave of absence from work. This figure is somewhat higher for women (6.3%) than for men (4.6%). These estimates illustrate the problems of time-sharing between work, family, and leisure in a weekly perspective. To fit the working week together with family life is a social jigsaw puzzle for many parents with preschool or school-aged children.

5. Institutional Patterns Facilitating Learning Across the Lifespan

The goal of improving the balance between youth education and adult education is reflected in various institutional responses. One development in the early 1990s is to incorporate preschooling in formal education by organizing an early school start. Another idea is to create access courses, remedial programs, or preparatory classes to bridge the transition between the different stages of the formal school system (i.e., between compulsory and upper-secondary school, and between the latter and higher education). Work-study programs as well as the recognition of life and work experience are other examples of institutional responses. Different policies and institutional patterns aimed at meeting the rapidly increasing demand for adult education and training can be identified:

(a) *The prolongation of youth education.* In many OECD countries, the duration of compulsory education varies from 8 to 9 years up to 12 years, as is the case in the high school model of North America. In Sweden, compulsory education lasts for 9 years. Upper-secondary education is, however, compulsory in practice although not in principle. The duration, structure, and quality of youth education have significant repercussions on access to higher education as well as on patterns of lifelong learning. This first category also comprises different efforts of integration between preschooling and formal education.

(b) *Linking youth education with adult education.* A common policy is to create links between compulsory schooling and upper-secondary or higher education. Compensatory programs, remedial efforts as well as preparatory courses, are tools used to increase access for young students and adults with learning difficulties. Another example is work-study programs designed to motivate students to undertake learning projects. In Sweden, there is a municipal follow-up responsibility for all students who leave the compulsory school but who do not have work or continue their education elsewhere. This category also comprises access courses preparing students for higher education.

(c) *The expansion of adult education.* Another approach to problems and challenges of time policies is to expand the "second chance" opportunities through a broadened provision of adult education. This model comprises a number of institutional patterns with more or less stress on general and/or vocational adult education. Special attention is also paid to barriers to adult learning, recruitment strategies as well as various forms of study assistance and social support. Vocationally oriented adult education and labor market training programs illustrate this category.

(d) *Recurrent education and educational leave of absence.* Recurrent education can be seen as a comprehensive policy aimed at an integration of the alternation between education, work, and leisure over the total lifespan. The idea of recurrent education comprises a planning strategy which, at least in its ideal model, incorporates youth education as well as other fields of public policy. The idea is not only to support the public sector of adult education, but also to guarantee the individual's rights and access to learning across the lifespan, for example, by offering educational leave of absence.

(e) *Corporate classrooms and inservice training.* This element focuses on the development of corporate classrooms and inservice training programs. It is shared by some of the larger multinational corporations. The strategy is linked with the Japanese system of lifetime employment and is characterized by a strong focus on learning at the workplace.

(f) *Learning enterprises.* Another alternative concerns the notion of learning enterprises, in which skill formation is seen as an integral part of industrial development. This policy aims at an increase of job-inherent learning time and developing cohesive teamwork. Its focus is more on human resource development than on the participation of employees in formal education.

(g) *Individually based "competence insurance" or voucher systems.* During the early 1990s, a political and professional debate had taken place concerning a system of individually based competence insurance. The aim had been to design a system of study finance for lifelong learning based on the individual's own choice and motivated by personal and occupational incentives. The individual could draw upon certain learning benefits in periods of intensive life transition, for example, unemployment, parental duties, or civic obligations. So far, there has not been any further practical elaboration of the model. It has some similarities with the current debate on vouchers in public service provision.

(h) *Collective knowledge for a civil society.* Finally, it can be mentioned that the notion of a study circle democracy represents an alternative form of a time policy for learning. In this model, the focus is mainly oriented toward the development of collective citizen knowledge to be used for the development of a democratic society. The political preferences in this model aim to publicly support study circles, folk high schools, and popular movements, as well as trade unions and other interest groups.

6. Learning Associated Environments

There are various approaches to discussing ideas and models of allocating time for learning over the lifespan as well as over the working week. Inherent in these is the problem of conceptually distinguishing between learning as an inherent process of life and work, on the one hand, and learning in a more or less organized educational setting on the other. This distinction points to the difference between education, learning, and everyday experiences. In examining the notion of adult learning, it is necessary to identify the interplay between tacit or silent knowledge and skills, theoretical knowledge built upon a certain conceptual framework, as well as practical skills or operational knowledge (Schön 1987). The notion of competence is increasingly used in discussions of time policies for learning, particularly with respect to the need for a renewed work organization.

A shift has occurred in attitudes concerning education and learning at the workplace. Possibilities for creating a learning-associated work environment and organization are being discussed, and consequently a gradual change in emphasis from time off from work for studies to time for learning as an inherent part of a job or vocation is taking place. Thus, there is a significant difference between a model for recurrent education with an emphasis on leave of absence for education and the model of increasing the work-related learning time and other forms of on-the-job training. Research evidence shows, however, that an individual's level of initial education influences the time spent on self-directed learning (see Borgström 1988).

7. Redistributing Learning Across the Lifespan— A Future Challenge

In most societies, education and learning is mainly a youth business, and the education participation rate decreases with increasing age. In order to better cope with future challenges, however, it is necessary to increase the opportunities for learning across the lifespan. The development of comprehensive time policies supporting a flexible lifetime learning schedule is important. New options for learning at the workplace represent only one way to promote this objective. Another way would be to increase the access to adult learning in society at large. Multiskilling models as well as the search for a generic notion of citizen competence may point to ways of realizing the learning society.

Adult education and learning are not as noticeable a circumstance in society as is education for children and young people. School buildings, curricula, and fixed class hours are not as prevalent. Discussions involving adult education often depend on conditions applicable only to compulsory school. From an adult education perspective—which includes making use of life and work experience, as well as participatory and problem-oriented learning—formal youth education offers a poor starting-point for such a discussion. Instead, a policy of redistributing learning opportunities across the lifespan has to consider the need for broad access. Furthermore, it should aim at a better balance between liberal education, civic knowledge, and the humanities, on the one hand, and formal competence and vocational upgrading on the other.

The ongoing structural adjustment of labor markets and the development of a civil society, as well as the aging of the population in many highly industrialized countries, are arguments for increasing adult access to learning opportunities. Thus, in order to promote the notion of a learning society, more attention has to be paid to how educational policies are integrated with labor market policies and social policies.

See also: Recurrent Education; Economics of Adult Education and Training; Legislation in Adult Education; Time, Leisure, and Adult Education; Demand, Supply, and Finance of Adult Education; Lifelong Learning

References

Baltes P B, Schaie K W (eds.) 1973 *Life-Span Developmental Psychology. Personality and Socialization.* Academic Press, New York

Best F 1991 *Flexible Life Scheduling: Is There a Future to the Idea?* Adult Institute for Research and Planning, Sacramento, California

Best F, Stern B 1976 *Lifetime Distribution of Education, Work and Leisure.* Institute for Educational Leadership, Washington, DC

Borgström L 1988 *Vuxnas kunskapssökande. En studie av självstyrt lärande.* Stockholm Institute of Education, University of Stockholm, Stockholm

Bottani N, Duchêne C, Tuijnman A C 1992 *Education at a Glance: OECD Indicators.* OECD, Paris

Cross K P 1981 *Adults as Learners.* Jossey-Bass, San Francisco, California

Cross K P 1989 The changing role of higher education in the United States. In: Abrahamsson K, Rubenson K, Slowey M (eds.) 1989 *Adults in the Academy: International Trends in Adult and Higher Education.* (Report No. 1988: 38) Swedish National Board of Education, Stockholm

Erikson E H 1950 *Childhood and Society.* Norton, New York

Glendenning F, Percy K 1990 *Ageing, Education and Society: Readings in Educational Gerontology.* Association for Educational Gerontology, Keele

Havighurst R 1952 *Developmental Tasks and Education.* David McKay, New York

Schön D A 1987 *Educating the Reflective Practitioner: Toward a New Design for Teaching and Learning in the Professions.* Jossey-Bass, San Francisco, California

Statistics Sweden 1989 *The Labor Market in Figures, 1970–1988.* Statistics Sweden, Stockholm

Statistics Sweden 1991 *Living Conditions. Adult Education 1975–1989*, (Report No. 67). Statistics Sweden, Stockholm

Young M, Schuller T 1991 *Life After Work: The Arrival of the Ageless Society.* HarperCollins, London

Further Reading

Abrahamsson K 1985 Prior life experience in higher education. In: Husén T, Postlethwaite T N (eds.) 1985 *International Encyclopedia of Education*, 1st edn. Pergamon Press, Oxford

Abrahamsson K, Hultinger E-S, Svenningsson L 1990 *The Expanding Learning Enterprise in Sweden: A Study of the Education and Training of the Swedish Labour Force.* (Report No. 1990: 10), Swedish National Board of Education, Stockholm

Abrahamsson K, Fägerlind I, Husén T, Ringborg E 1995 *Europaskolan. Svensk utbildning och det nya Europa.* Publica, Stockholm

Organisation for Economic Co-operation and Development (OECD) 1973 *Recurrent Education: A Strategy for Lifelong Learning.* OECD/CERI, Paris

Organisation for Economic Co-operation and Development (OECD) 1975 *Recurrent Education: Trends and Issues.* OECD/CERI, Paris

Tuijnman A 1989 *Recurrent Education, Earnings and Wellbeing. A Fifty-Year Longitudinal Study of a Cohort of Swedish Men.* Stockholm Studies in Educational Psychology, No. 24. Almqvist and Wiksell International, Stockholm

(b)   Costs and Finance

Demand, Supply, and Finance of Adult Education

G. K. Wurzburg

"Adult," "further," and "postinitial" education and training are just three of the (sometimes) awkward labels for activities by which adults continue to learn and build on the early experience of school education (see *Adult Education: Concepts and Principles; Technical and Vocational Education and Training; Recurrent Education*). The awkwardness stems from recent developments involving the antecedents to adult education and training, and the nature of changes in purpose of and institutional arrangements for such education and training. The discussion below examines the socioeconomic context in which these changes have occurred, places the supply of and demand for adult education and training in the larger context of interest in "lifelong" and "lifewide" learning, and then examines evidence on supply and demand for adult education and training. This entry also considers the operation of adult education and training markets, and examines the implications for the finance of adult education and training. In covering these themes, the entry serves as an overview of all related entries in the Encyclopedia that deal with the economics of, and policies for, adult and continuing education.

1. Adult Education and Training: A Concept in Transition

The transition in the concept of adult education and training is probably best captured in terms of changes in the external environment of adult education and their institutional implications.

There is nothing new about the idea of adult participation in education, training, and learning activities. In the 1970s and 1980s there was extensive work on developing further the concepts of recurrent education and lifelong learning as an alternative to the traditional "front-end" model of uninterrupted full-time schooling (Kallen and OECD 1973, OECD 1993 p. 7) (see *Lifelong and Continuing Education; Recurrent Education*). Adult education is well established in many countries, and is anchored today in institutions such as the folk high schools in Denmark, study circles in Sweden, the University of the Air in Japan, the Open University in the United Kingdom, and community colleges in the United States (see *Folk High Schools; Open University; Japan: Social and Adult Education*). Importantly, though, the impetus behind these variations on "recurrent education" has been heavily oriented towards cultural and social goals. Although policy work on the subject envisioned that participation could be widespread—even universal in cultures with much leisure activity—in the event, participation (and the institutional arrangements for provision) in most countries has proven to be limited. Only in Sweden, where in any given year nearly half the adult population participates in some form of adult education or training (overwhelmingly study circles), has participation been broad. Usually adult education is limited in numbers and confined through a process of self-selection to adults with high levels of initial educational attainment. For individuals, the objectives and incentives might not have been persuasive. At least as importantly, there has been little support for implementing radical changes in the structure of the conventional educational system and the objectives it pursues (Kallen and OECD 1973 p. 51, OECD 1993 p. 77).

By the mid- and late 1980s support emerged for a more narrowly defined concept of adult education and training undertaken for more purely economic reasons. The earlier interest in various forms of recurrent education as a consumption good was overshadowed by the more broadly based interest in education and training for adults as an investment good (see *Time, Leisure, and Adult Education*). Employers, trade unions, and individuals alike have increasingly come to see it as being a key to short- and medium-term productivity growth and corporate competitiveness, and as the basis for adequate labor supply in the long term. The importance of the latter factor is accentuated in countries in which the climate of change and uncertainty in qualification requirements is compounded by reduced flows of young graduates entering the labor market. Together these developments force greater reliance on a continuous, lifelong process by which work-related skills are upgraded and updated.

2. Demand for and Supply of Adult Education and Training

The demand for and supply of adult education and training is best understood with reference to the changes in the concepts previously mentioned. The discussion below considers the forces behind and the nature of these qualitative changes in supply and demand.

2.1 Qualitative Shifts in Demand

The narrow, but potent, arguments today favoring adult education and training are rooted in factors that are essentially economic. Increasing internationalization of product and factor markets has intensified the pressures on enterprises and national economies to search for strategies for achieving and sustaining competitiveness, however it is defined. The pace and application of technological innovation has intensified even further the pressures to remain competitive, and underlined the importance of adaptability and speed in that process.

Human resource management strategies, as adjuncts to investment and general business strategies, are proving to be powerful determinants of the competitiveness of firms, labor market sectors, and therefore national economies (Dore et al. 1989, Porter 1990). But these developments have tended to undermine everything from traditional human resource practices within enterprises (Bertrand and Noyelle 1988) to the importance of tangible relative to "intangible" investment, including human resource development (Deiaco et al. 1990), to the foundations of theories to explain economic growth. Through it all, the reputation— if not the proven effectiveness of adult education and training—has risen considerably, raising expectations about its value and importance, sometimes unrealistically and sometimes to the exclusion of other important factors (Bengtsson and Wurzburg 1992).

Changes in perceptions about the importance and application of adult education and training are broadening their constituencies while transforming the demand for them in different ways. As the economic consequences of participation and the economic costs of nonparticipation, have increased, so too has the importance of the distribution and accessibility of opportunities grown as an issue of public concern. In political terms, this has greatly enlarged the constituency interested in the outcomes of adult education and training (BIAC/TUAC 1991). In contrast to the narrower appeal of recurrent education to particular educationalists in relatively few countries, such as Germany, Norway, Sweden, and the United States, continuing vocational training is commanding increasingly the interest of employers, trade unions, and individuals in a broad cross-section of industrialized countries (OECD 1989, 1993, 1994).

Yet the economic impetus behind this broader constituency has narrowed the focus of interest, at least for a period of time. Broadly conceived, recurrent education has tended to emphasize individual social and cultural development in addition to the development of job-related qualifications; this was an ideal rarely achieved except for small numbers of persons. By contrast, the notion of adult continuing education and training of the labor force has centered on updating and upgrading qualifications required for particular jobs and, more generally, in connection with employment.

Beyond transforming qualitatively the demand for continuing education and training, the broad, economically driven constituency interested in improving labor force qualifications appears to have led to a substantial demand for (work-related) adult education and training (see Table 1).

There is only sketchy statistical evidence on the volume of all forms of continuing education and training, and breakdowns between work-related training and broader-purpose recurrent education (see *Measurement of Adult Education; Measurement of Industry Training*). However, the evidence consistently indicates that the volume of continuing voational training is considerably greater than that of recurrent education for leisure, and is growing quickly. In fact, it is growing so quickly, some would argue, as to require fundamental institutional change:

Table 1
Summary statistics on training expenditures[a] (expressed as a percentage of labor costs, or wages and salaries across industries)

Australia	Denmark	France	Germany	Italy	Japan	Netherlands	UK
2.2	2.1	1.6	1.8	0.3	0.4[b]	1.5	1.3

Source: OECD 1991 *Employment Outlook*, p. 156.
a For sources and further details on coverage and definitions of training expenditures see OECD 1991c p. 156 and pp. 165–72   b Does not include wages

... Public providers have a large, if not dominant share of FET markets ... but because the organisation, methods, and strategies of so many public providers are rooted in the provision of initial education, there may be a need for nothing less than a major restructuring, like that in other industries overtaken by structural change. (OECD 1991a)

It is important to note that the economic necessity behind the amplified demand for continuing vocational training is in one sense less elastic than that for general adult education, and in another sense more elastic. It is less elastic in that the upgrading and updating of the qualifications of workers is indispensable to the successful introduction of advanced technologies and the larger process of enterprise and economic restructuring. Without new skills and competences, workers are not able to perform effectively in the long run, and without effective performance, gains in productivity, efficiency, and eventually competitiveness are more difficult to achieve. But it is precisely this economic exigency that is an important source of greater elasticity over the medium and longer term, because of the intense pressure it creates on finding acceptable alternatives where none exist.

A second aspect of this intensifying demand for adult education and training is its heterogeneity. The demand for *initial* education and training is in many respects homogeneous, conditioned by broadly accepted patterns of provision, which in turn are subject to practically and politically constraining institutional arrangements and customs. Choice is defined in terms of general systems of elementary, secondary, vocational/technical, and higher education, and outcomes are defined in terms of diplomas, degrees. and certificates. By comparison, the demand for continuing vocational training is defined much more in terms of the particular requirements of consumers. These vary according to the prior qualifications and personal plans of individuals, as well as firm- and sector-specific characteristics of the jobs (influencing most immediately the organization of work and associated technology) in which individuals are employed or expected to be employed (see *Participation: Antecedent Factors*). The resulting skills and qualifications requirements, in tandem with individual preferences, and enterprise production schedules dictate a highly differentiated demand for continuing vocational training. Qualitatively it varies with respect to content, venue, scheduling, pace, and methods. Quantitatively it varies with respect to desired outcomes and numbers and distribution of workers to be trained, as well as according to what might be called the "investment demand" for continuing vocational training.

The latter can be seen as the demand for training that is conditioned by the economic payoff from continuing vocational training. This is turn is affected by at least two factors. One is the presence of externally imposed "parafiscal" mechanisms (such as those found in France and Australia) requiring firms to spend a certain amount on training or pay the shortfall as a tax. This kind of mechanism relaxes the test of an economic payoff for continuing vocational training by imposing a negative return on low or no training provision, thus increasing the "investment demand" for training (see *Financing Lifelong Learning*). The other factor affecting the investment demand for training is the manner and extent to which continuing vocational training contributes to worker productivity and competitiveness (from the firm point of view), and increased wages (from the individual point of view). Inflexible forms of work organization, faulty business strategies, or uncertain portability of qualifications acquired in continuing vocational training, for example, can all reduce its actual or anticipated value (see *Economics of Adult Education and Training*).

The highly differentiated and, at times, volatile demand for continuing vocational training places particular pressures on the current and would-be providers of initial education and training.

2.2 Supply-side Responses

Countries that are as diverse in their institutional arrangements, industrial structure, and business strategies as Australia and Japan show similar tendencies to carry out large shares, if not the bulk of their further education and training, within the enterprises (Human Resource Development Bureau 1989, Australian Bureau of Statistics 1990). Yet there are sound reasons for questioning the long-term adequacy of customs, practice, and policy that are heavily dependent on enterprises providing training. The uneven distribution of continuing vocational training opportunities among workers within enterprises, the growth of unstable forms of employment in which opportunities for continuing vocational training are limited, substantial need for continuing vocational training for persons who are not even in the labor force, and the increasingly generalized need for lifelong and "lifewide" learning imply a deeper, more broadly based transformation in institutional arrangements (OECD 1991a).

Whether the expected increase in the demand for further education and training can be met effectively depends on at least three factors: the adaptability of existing institutions to provide continuing vocational training, the ability of new providers to fill gaps, and the ability of all providers to ensure that continuing vocational training and more broadly conceived forms of skill formation are cost-effective. Each factor is discussed below.

The requirements of continuing vocational training consumers are qualitatively and quantitatively different from those of initial education and training, being first and foremost more heterogeneous. The experience of institutions engaged in initial education and training to broaden their mission is mixed. In the case of the United Kingdom, for example, the PICKUP (Professional, Industrial, and Commercial Updating) program to help universities and polytechnics develop and manage industry-related courses, together with regulatory changes allowing such institutions to retain earnings from fee-for-service courses, have provided the incentives for institutional change (Stirner 1991). These and other initiatives, some in cooperation with the European Community, have raised the proportion of higher education institutions engaged in continuing vocational training from a very low base (see *European Union: Continuing Vocational Training*). But this expansion may be inadequate in relation to the needs of industry and of individual professionals. Even in the presence of concerted government policies to encourage institutional flexibility, changes can be slow. As a group, the Technical and Further Education (TAFE) colleges in Australia have proven to be particularly resistant to outside demand for more vocationally oriented initial education and training, and more recently continuing vocational training to support an ambitious program for industrial restructuring. Despite isolated cases of institutional innovation (OECD 1991b, OECD 1993), the system as a whole has fared badly. In a period when demand for upper-secondary and postsecondary education is exploding, overall enrollments in TAFE have remained flat, while participation rates for working age adults have declined (Employment and Skills Formation Council 1991).

It is difficult to gauge the ease with which more specialized alternative providers can respond to the demand that is unmet due in part to "mainstream" institutions that are unwilling or unable to change. Alternative providers may face barriers in the form of accreditation practices that are geared to more traditional courses of study, or difficult access to capital markets because of the relatively recent demand for continuing vocational training, for example. But the bigger barrier to alternative providers is the implicit or explicit subsidy that allows mainstream institutions to charge artificially low fees. Even where publicly supported institutions are required to charge fees for industry training on a full-cost recovery basis, undercharging frequently occurs because of the inexperience of such institutions in determining indirect and capital costs, for example, that are over and above the more easily measured direct costs (Stirner 1991, Foster 1988). In the years immediately following the privatization of the labor market training services in Sweden, the new agency's difficulties in working out a fee structure that reflected costs were compounded by the fact that they were frequently competing with municipally supported adult education and training schools. In the United States, publicly supported community colleges are sometimes encouraged to charge less than full cost for industry training as part of state government strategies for attracting firms (OECD 1993 pp. 88–89) (see *Market Concepts in Provision*).

A last important consideration in evaluating the supply-side response to changes in the demand for continuing vocational training is the ability of providers to ensure that it produces an economic payoff sufficient to justify its cost. Despite the fact that interest in continuing vocational training is driven mostly by its presumed economic importance as an investment good, surprisingly little is understood about the prerequisites to, or mechanics of, the economic payoff to continuing vocational training (see *Economics of Adult Education and Training*). At an aggregate, sectoral, and even enterprise level there is overwhelming evidence, for example, that continuing vocational training and other forms of "intangible investment" are essential before the full economic payoff of investment in advanced technologies can be appreciated. In short, "smart machines need smart workers" as well as changes in the organization of work (OECD 1992a pp. 113–34). But the precise consequences of the introduction of advanced technologies, as well as large-scale efforts to upgrade and update worker qualifications for the structure of tasks and management of human resources, is at best only partially explored. Thus there is no unified picture of the process by which more skilled workers become more productive, and by which more productive workers make an enterprise more competitive (for some of the few examples of this more unified approach, see Prais 1990). As long as the demand for continuing vocational training is largely expenditure driven, as it is in France, for example (see OECD 1992b), the country with the longest record of government measures to encourage continuing vocational training, there is little pressure on providers to justify continuing vocational training on the basis of hard evidence for improved worker performance.

However, as pressure intensifies on improving the cost effectiveness of continuing vocational training, the providers of continuing vocational training will be under pressure to improve the efficiency of the training process itself, and ensure that the economic benefits of continuing vocational training actually materialize. The first depends on more aggressive strategies for assessing the learning needs of participants in continuing vocational training, and adopting appropriate teaching and learning techniques (including different configurations of teaching and learning technologies). The second requires a two-pronged approach of understanding more fully how the work organization might be changed to improve adult learning, and how the relationship between formally provided continuing vocational training and less structured forms of workbased learning might be made more mutually reinforcing.

3. Markets for Continuing Vocational Training

The existence and usefulness of markets for further education and training are broadly accepted because the efficient allocation of resources for continuing vocational training depends heavily on market forces. Alternative mechanisms for the allocation of resources are less practical than in the case of initial education and training, for example, because of the highly differentiated nature of demand for continuing vocational training, and the increasingly heterogeneous nature of supply. The heterogeneous nature of supply is further complicated by the fact that continuing vocational training is provided by a mixture of public and private institutions (see *Providers of Adult Education: An Overview*). The high level of differentiation on the demand side is further complicated by the influence of changes in relative factor prices (changes in the cost of labor relative to other inputs to production, as well as changes in the relative cost of workers with certain qualifications), relative product prices, and other forces influencing the business strategies of enterprises (see OECD 1993 pp. 97–100, 1991a).

However, the operation of markets for learning is far from perfect. The market structure and other distortions in prices impinge on the efficient allocation of resources for continuing vocational training. Furthermore, market outcomes have social implications, some of which may be politically unacceptable. In view of these imperfections, there are grounds for intervention by public authorities in order to improve the efficiency and effectiveness of learning markets. The discussion below examines these imperfections and measures for correcting them.

3.1 Provisions for Continuing Vocational Training

The structure of continuing vocational training markets in many countries (such as Australia and Sweden) can be characterized best as monopolistic or oligopolistic. Provision, apart from that by enterprises for their own employees, is dominated by public institutions (OECD 1993 p. 25, 1994). Even in countries such as the United States, where for-profit proprietary institutions outnumber higher education institutions (only some of which are public) by 8,000 to 3,000 (OECD 1992c p. 4), the private share of total enrollments does not appear to be high. Though the usual effect of this kind of market structure is to keep prices artificially high, it is not necessarily proving so. Public support for initial education frequently spills over to cover indirect and capital costs of continuing vocational training that, in principle, is provided on a fee-for-service basis. Over the longer term, however, continuing vocational training prices may be pushed up by the fact that artificially low prices may discourage the entry into continuing vocational training markets of private providers dedicated entirely to continuing vocational training.

The most widespread strategy for diversifying continuing vocational training market structure is to change the "ground rules" under which publicly supported institutions operate, so as to force them to behave as if they were private providers (though the principal purpose of the strategy is frequently to relax the pressure on public funding). Aside from requiring providers to charge fees for service (which, as indicated above, may not cover full costs), these changes also entail administrative changes such as separating public consumers of training—for example, labor market authorities—from the public providers of training. The general purpose of these strategies is to give continuing vocational training consumers more choice, and in so doing, increase competition by reducing prices.

3.2 Other Sources of Price and Cost Distortion

The structure of continuing vocational training markets risks one kind of distortion in the price (and cost to consumers) of continuing vocational training because of reduced competition. But there are other sources of distortion in the price and cost of continuing vocational training that also can have adverse effects on the allocation of continuing vocational training resources. One is the risk of "externalities" in which there is a breakdown in the symmetry between the cost of continuing vocational training and its benefits (a precondition to the efficient allocation of resources). The demand of employers for continuing vocational training, for example, may be reduced if they expect trained workers to leave, or if otherwise they have no way of being indemnified for the loss of workers they have trained. Workers may be less inclined to pay the costs of continuing vocational training if the payoff in the form of increased wages or enhanced employability is low or uncertain (see *Costs of Adult Education and Training*).

Another source of distortion is the lack of information in training markets. This includes imprecise or scarce information on the nature, quality, utility, and cost of continuing vocational training on offer. In the absence of such information, competition in markets hinges less on criteria of efficiency and effectiveness, thus increasing the risk of ineffective providers remaining in learning markets, while reducing the incentive for more effective providers to enter the market. From the point of view of consumers, this in turn increases the risk of misallocation of training resources towards activities that are not cost-effective. As in other markets, and in particular as in initial education, remedies depend on the establishment of some minimal framework of standards by which, for example, costs and effectiveness might be measured, as well as the establishment of some form of clearinghouse function through which information is collected from providers and made available to consumers (see *Costs of Adult Education and Training*).

The lack of information in training markets extends to the absence of reliable and valid measures of the skills and competences acquired in continuing vocational training, and mechanisms for their recognition (see *Recognition and Certification of Skill*). In a sense, this means that the immediate outcome of continuing vocational training is poorly or undefined. As a result, consumers of continuing vocational training (be they employers or employees) do not have a clear idea of what, in functional terms, the benefits of continuing vocational training may be. This complicates the development of human resource management strategies by which workers who are more qualified by virtue of participation in continuing vocational training can be made more productive through changes in work organization, other investment strategies, and business strategies. Ultimately, the lack of mechanisms for the assessment and recognition of skills and competences risks a direct misallocation of resources for continuing vocational training by putting a low or uncertain value on the outcome of continuing vocational training, and an indirect misallocation of resources by not allowing more transparent assessment of labor force qualifications acquired by workers through continuing vocational training. Remedies depend in part on establishing frameworks within which skills and competences can be described, measured, and recognized (see *Market Failure in Adult Education and Training; Overeducation*).

3.3 Social Outcomes of Training Markets

Even if markets operate smoothly in reflecting costs and prices and allocating resources for continuing vocational training, the outcomes may not contribute sufficiently to an allocation of resources and opportunities that is acceptable to society at large. The reasons revolve around the relative strength of different actors in training markets, and the accessibility of markets.

There are "virtuous" and "vicious" circles to patterns of participation in and access to continuing vocational training: higher levels of initial qualifications, and/or employment in better jobs, lead to more continuing vocational training, which leads to better jobs, higher earnings, and more continuing vocational training; low levels of initial qualifications lead to worse jobs with less access (OECD 1993 pp. 55–56, 1991c pp. 149–50, 1994). These patterns are exacerbated by certain trends in employment patterns and labor force qualification requirements:

> There is a risk that many firms rely more on nonstandard forms of employment—fixed-term and part-time employment contracts . . . [thus] reducing for many workers the opportunity for and benefits of training . . . At the same time, the threshold of minimum skills and competences required for stable and secure employment [is rising]. (OECD 1991a p.3)

As a result, in the absence of intervention, the prevailing patterns of provision of and participation in continuing vocational training tend to widen the gulf between those who are presently adequately qualified and in good jobs, and those who are not. Remedies, besides requiring measures to narrow disparities in initial qualifications, depend on ensuring that access to

suitable continuing vocational training does not hinge entirely on that provided by employers or otherwise accessible only through employment.

4. Financing of Adult Education and Training

In view of the evident economic efficiency considerations behind the demand for continuing vocational training and the social dimension of the outcomes of markets, the question of how continuing vocational training is financed is crucial. Although it is probably helpful to start by treating the efficiency considerations and social dimensions separately, the extent to which the two in fact are either mutually exclusive or converge depends in large part on the approach to finance that is adopted (see *Financing Lifelong Learning*).

4.1 Business Investment as the Basis for Finance

The character and "roots" of continuing vocational training, distinct from those of more broadly defined adult education, argue in favor of treating it as an investment rather than a consumption good. It is undertaken not for its own sake (as with a consumption good), but for ulterior motives that are directly or indirectly economic. From the point of view of enterprises, the principal purpose is to improve productivity and competitiveness, be it through raising the general qualifications and flexibility of workers, or, for example, through more effective operation of newly acquired advanced technologies. For individuals, it is to improve earnings, employability, and general conditions of work. Though there may be some collateral purposes to continuing vocational training, such as training arrangements in some industrial relations agreements that take the form of something approaching nonwage compensation (OECD 1994), its investment character is essential. In short, continuing vocational training is undertaken with an expectation that it will produce a flow of benefits in the future (see *Economics of Adult Education and Training*).

When viewed in this context, the central question concerning the finance of continuing vocational training is one of how to achieve better symmetry between the burden of costs of continuing vocational training and the enjoyment of benefits from it. Alternatively, the question might be posed as: how can one better ensure that whoever pays for continuing vocational training benefits from it? The answer depends upon smooth functioning of markets for continuing vocational training, so that costs can be properly evaluated, and prices are reliable signals of those costs. This entails, for example, a better correlation between qualifications (acquired through continuing vocational training) and wages, as well as mechanisms that allow flexibility in the allocation of costs (to employees when skills are portable, for example). Beyond that, there is a need for minimizing the barriers that slow or otherwise hinder the process by which skills and competences acquired in continuing vocational training translate into improved productivity and competitiveness. Finally, the appropriate finance of continuing vocational training as an investment depends on treating the skills and competences acquired in continuing vocational training as assets. From the point of view of individuals, this can be accomplished when wages and salaries take account of the qualifications acquired in continuing vocational training. But from the point of view of enterprises, this requires financial accounting and reporting practices that allow "depreciation" in the values of acquired skills and competences, so as to allow spreading the cost of continuing vocational training over the time during which the benefits are realized. This also entails mechanisms for at least reflecting, if not indemnifying, enterprises for the costs of trained workers who leave.

4.2 Social Investment as the Basis for Finance

For reasons mentioned above in section 3.3, smoothly functioning training markets do not necessarily lead to an allocation of resources that is socially acceptable. In the context of the issue of finance, this could be described as a "social demand" for continuing vocational training, the finance for which cannot be met through treatment of continuing vocational training as a business or economic investment.

Finance of this "social demand" for continuing vocational training needs to be approached differently because of a breakdown in the conditions of symmetry. Business-driven investment in continuing vocational training is essentially self-financing. It produces what are largely private returns in the form of profits for enterprises and wages for individuals. But for those who for whatever reason—unemployment or employment in unstable jobs, for example—do not have access to continuing vocational training, it is not self-financing. For individuals, there are risks; the payoff to self-financed continuing vocational training in wages or improved employment prospects is less certain and possibly more remote. Moreover, the lack of access to continuing vocational training entails clear social costs in the form of increased social dependency, for example. These "external" or societal costs related to the lack of access to continuing vocational training, and the societal benefits where it is provided, imply a public role in the finance of continuing vocational training for fulfilling at least some of the unmet social demand. Some share of continuing vocational training can also be seen as a social investment to the extent that the time horizon over which it yields (more broadly distributed social) benefits may be relatively distant. This reflects not just possible differences between private and public actors in their opportunity costs, but the fact that it is easier for society at large

to capture benefits of continuing vocational training, than it is for a particular employer if a trained worker leaves.

See also: Technical and Vocational Education and Training; Training on the Job; Recurrent Education; Economics of Adult Education and Training; Market Concepts in Provision; Market Failure in Adult Education and Training; Overeducation; Costs of Adult Education and Training; Financing Lifelong Learning; Evaluation of Industry Training: Cost-Effectiveness; Evaluation of Public Training: Cost-Effectiveness; Measurement of Industry Training; Statistics of Employee Training

References

Australian Bureau of Statistics 1990 *How Workers Get Their Training.* Australian Bureau of Statistics, Canberra

Bengtsson J, Wurzburg G K 1992 Effectiveness research: Merely interesting, or actually relevant? *Int. J. Educ. Res.* 17(6): 527–35

Bertrand O, Noyelle T CERI 1988 *Human Resources and Corporate Strategy: Technological Change in Banks and Insurance Companies.* OECD, Paris

Business and Industry Advisory Committee (BIAC)/Trades Union Advisory Committee (TUAC) 1991 *Education and Training: A Joint Statement by BIAC and TUAC.* BIAC/TUAC, Paris

Deiaco E, Hornell E, Vickery G 1990 *Technology and Investment: Crucial Issues for the 1990s.* Pinter Publishers, London

Dore R, Bounine-Cabalé J, Tapiola K 1989 *Japan at Work: Markets, Management and Flexibility.* OECD, Paris

Employment and Skills Formation Council 1991 *TAFE in the 1990s: Developing Australia's Skills.* Australian Government Publishing Service, Canberra

Foster R A 1988 *Commercialisation of Government Services: A Search for Efficiency.* Discussion Paper. Common Services Section Service and ACT Branch, Commonwealth Government, Canberra

Human Resource Development Bureau 1989 *Survey of Vocational Training in Private Enterprise.* Ministry of Labour, Tokyo

Kallen D, OECD 1973 *Recurrent Education: A Strategy for Lifelong Learning.* OECD, Paris

Organisation for Economic Co-operation and Development (OECD) 1989 *Education and the Economy in a Changing Society.* OECD, Paris

Organisation for Economic Co-operation and Development (OECD) 1991a *Intergovernmental Conference on Further Education and Training of the Labour Force: Conclusions of the Chair.* Note to Editors. OECD Press Division, Paris

Organisation for Economic Co-operation and Development (OECD) 1991b *Recent Development in Continuing Professional Education: Country Report–United Kingdom.* General Distribution Document, OECD, Paris

Organisation for Economic Co-operation and Development (OECD) 1991c OECD *Employment Outlook 1991.* OECD, Paris

Organisation for Economic Co-operation and Development (OECD) 1992a *Technology and the Economy: The Key Relationships.* OECD, Paris

Organisation for Economic Co-operation and Development (OECD) 1992b *Recent Developments in Continuing Professional Education: Country Report–United States.* General Distribution Document, OECD, Paris

Organisation for Economic Co-operation and Development (OECD) 1992c *OECD Economic Surveys: France.* OECD, Paris

Organisation for Economic Co-operation and Development (OECD) 1993 *Comparative Analysis of Industry Training Strategies: Australia, Sweden, and the United States.* OECD, Paris

Organisation for Economic Co-operation and Development (OECD) 1994 *Further Education and Training of the Labour Force in OECD Countries: Evidence and Issues.* OECD, Paris

Porter M E 1990 *The Competitive Advantage of Nations.* The Free Press, New York

Prais S J (ed.) 1990 *Productivity, Education and Training: Britain and Other Countries Compared.* (Reprints of studies published in the National Institute Economic Review). National Institute of Economic and Social Research, London

Stirner P 1991 Counting the cost. *PICKUP in Progress.* Department of Education and Science. Bulletin, Autumn 25: 25–26

Costs of Adult Education and Training

M. C. Tsang

The costs of adult education and training (AET) are related to important issues in AET, such as the scope, amount, and profitability of investment in AET, the cost-effectiveness and financial feasibility of alternative AET programs, and the planning and management of AET programs. Despite substantial resources devoted to AET in many countries, cost analysis still remains a neglected area in these countries; the number of cost studies is small and cost data are lacking. By drawing upon studies in both industrialized and developing countries, this entry discusses several aspects of the costs of AET: definition and classification, expenditures and determinants of costs; applications of cost analysis, and emerging cost issues.

1. Definition and Classification

The costs of AET refer to the economic value of the various inputs used in the production of AET. The economic value or cost of an input to AET is measured in terms of opportunity cost, that is, the value of the input in its best alternative use. The total cost of an AET program is the sum of the costs of the inputs to the program. This implies that the costs of AET include not only the actual expenditures on inputs, but also the opportunity costs associated with inputs such as participants' time, donated equipment or materials, or "free" facilities.

There are some common distinctions among cost categories, such as the distinction between social costs and private costs, between direct private costs and indirect private costs, between direct institutional costs and indirect institutional costs, between recurrent costs and capital costs, between personnel costs and nonpersonnel costs, and so on. Yet, there is no one standard system of classification of the costs of AET across countries. This is not surprising because of the great variety of AET programs in terms of objectives, method of financing, sponsorship, mode of training, and method of delivery (OECD 1977). Presumably costs may be classified according to one or more of these aspects of AET. Costs may also be further broken down according to the type/category of inputs, or the function of the inputs in the education and training process. Thus a variety of schemes for cost classification is possible and different techniques are available for measuring these costs (Eicher et al. 1982, Jones 1986, Tsang 1989).

For most applications, three cost classification schemes can be considered. The first one is a classification by input categories only. This scheme provides basic information for the costing and planning of AET. The second scheme is a cost matrix which classifies costs by both input categories and sources of finance. It provides additional information which is useful for the financial management of AET. The third scheme is a cost matrix which classifies costs by both input categories and function of inputs. This scheme provides additional information which is useful for program evaluation (see *Measurement of Training Costs; Evaluation of Industry Training: Cost-Effectiveness*).

2. Problems in Estimating Training Costs

Studies of AET in both industrialized and developing countries have pointed out the lack of information on costs (OECD 1977, 1979, Anderson and Kasl 1982, Carnevale and Gainer 1988, Xiao and Tsang 1994). Lack of relevant information is certainly a barrier to a precise estimation of costs. The nature of AET also makes the estimation of national resources devoted to AET more difficult than that for formal or initial education (i.e., elementary, secondary, and regular tertiary education). First, the tremendous diversity of

Table 1
National expenditure on adult education and training

Country	Year	Amount (national currency)	Percentage of national expenditure on youth education
Canada	1970–71	CDN$683 million	14
France	1970–71	F6,280 million	24
Japan	1970	Y325 billion	14
Sweden	1970–71	SKr1,116 million	10
United Kingdom	1970–71	£1,300 million	46
United States	1984	US$218 billion	90
West Germany	1970–71	DM8,371 million	46

Sources: For Canada, France, Sweden, United Kingdom, and West Germany, see OECD 1977; for Japan, see Noda and Watanabe 1977; and for United States see Carnevale 1986

public and private AET programs make the tasks of properly identifying relevant programs and collecting cost information almost impossible. Second, many AET programs are run by government agencies or institutions for which AET is a secondary service or of peripheral concern. There is no provision to separate the cost of AET programs from the overall budget of these agencies or institutions. In other nongovernmental organizations (such as labor unions, community organizations, or professional organizations), AET programs are administered by staff members with other responsibilities. It is very rare for these organizations to record the portion of the salaries and benefits of these staff members which is related to AET. Similarly, many enterprises (especially smaller ones) do not have a separate budget for training. Third, the costs of some employer-based occupational training (such as formal or informal on-the-job training) are rather difficult to measure. Fourth, there is a danger of double counting expenditures on AET as the government may often provide substantial education and training grants to nongovernmental organizations, and that there are intergovernmental grants from higher levels of government to lower levels of government.

3. Magnitude of Training Costs and Expenditures

The following presents the findings of studies on the costs of AET in a number of industrialized and developing countries. Given the limitations in cost information described above, most of the figures indicated here are meant to provide order-of-magnitude estimates of the costs of AET. Also, because of differences in methodology, coverage of AET programs, and quality of data employed by these studies, cross-national comparison has to be undertaken with extreme caution.

Most of the studies on the magnitude of national resources devoted to AET are based on expenditures by the government, the private sector, and individuals; though some studies did include estimates of the opportunity cost of participants' time.

Consider first, total national expenditure on AET. Table 1 shows the magnitude of national expenditure on AET in a number of industrialized countries as well as how such expenditure compares with that on youth education in these countries. Although these figures are rough estimates and are increasingly out-of-date, they nevertheless indicate that significant amounts of national resources have been devoted to AET in industrialized countries. In the United States, in particular, national expenditure on AET was about 90 percent of national expenditure on youth education.

Next consider government expenditure on AET. For the United States, Christoffel (1978) estimated that, in 1976, the various federal departments and agencies provided a total funding of US$14 billion for AET programs serving various lifelong learning needs and population groups. Carnevale (1986) estimated that total spending on adult training at all levels of government amounted to five billion dollars in 1984. The large difference between the two figures may be due partly to a difference in the coverage of government AET programs and to the reduced federal spending on education and training in the early 1980s. For general (nonvocational) adult education in Sweden, the government spent SKr475 million in 1970 (OECD 1977 p. 62).

The employer is a large contributor to AET, especially in terms of formal and informal occupational training. Consider three measures of employer expenditure on training: total expenditure, expenditure per employee, and total expenditure as a percentage of total payroll cost.

For the United States, in 1984, employers spent an estimated US$12–US$30 billion in direct costs on formal training that they either provided themselves or purchased from outside suppliers of training (Brown 1989). According to an annual survey of employer-sponsored training in the United States, the budget for formal training in firms with 100 or more employees was US$40 billion in 1988, US$44 billion in 1989, US$46 billion in 1990, US$43 billion in 1991, US$45 billion in 1992, US$48 billion in 1993, and US$51

Table 2
Employer expenditure on training as a percentage of payroll cost

Income level (GNP per capita 1985)	Country	Year	Training expenditure as a percentage of payroll
Low income economies (US$400 and less)	Haiti	1990	1.0
	Kenya	1990	1.0
	Togo	1990	1.0
	Zaire	1990	1.0
	(Average)		(1.0)
Lower-middle income economies (US$401–1635)	Colombia	1990	2.0
	Costa Rica	1990	1.0
	Dominican Republic	1990	1.0
	Ecuador	1990	0.05
	Guatemala	1990	0.5–1.0
	Honduras	1990	0.5–1.0
	Ivory Coast	1990	1.5
	Jamaica	1990	3.0
	Morocco	1990	1.6
	Nigeria	1990	1.0
	Paraguay	1990	1.0
	Peru	1990	1.5
	Tunisia	1990	2.0
	Zimbabwe	1990	1.0
	(Average)		(1.3)
Upper-middle income economies (US$1636–4300)	Argentina	1990	1.0
	Barbados	1990	0.5
	Brazil	1990	1.0–1.2
	Fiji	1990	1.0
	Malaysia	1994	0.5–1.0
	Singapore	1990	1.0
	Taiwan	1990	1.5
	Venezuela	1990	2.0
	(Average)		(1.1)
Industrialized market economies (US$4290+)	Australia	1989–90	1.7
	Denmark	1984	2.1
	France	1987–89	2.5
	Germany	1984	1.8
	Italy	1984	0.3
	Japan	1988–89	0.4–0.7
	Netherlands	1986	1.5
	United States	1984–85	1.0
	(Average)		(1.4)
All	(Average)		(1.2)

Sources: For low, lower-middle, and upper-middle income countries see Whalley and Ziderman 1990 (figures for Malaysia was based on personal communication); for United States see Carnevale and Gainer 1988; and for industrialized countries except the United States see OECD 1991

billion in 1994 (Training 1994 p. 37). The total cost of informal training is even greater; a rough estimation puts it at US$180 billion in 1984 (Carnevale 1986). These figures on employer expenditure indicate that, in the United States, the employer is a much bigger contributor to AET than the government.

From a survey of personnel executives of 159 firms in the United States, the Bureau of National Affairs (1985) found that, the median expenditure on in-house training was US$122 per trainee in 1983 and US$250 per trainee in 1984. But such figures were based on a response rate of less than 16 percent. According to Japan's Ministry of Labor, employers spent an average of about Y30,000 (about US$150) per employee in 1983 (Weber 1984). In Canada, the average expenditure per employee was CDN$160 in 1986–87 (OECD 1991 p. 156).

Table 2 shows training expenditure by employers

Table 3
Training expenditure by industry in the United States (1984)

Industry	Total expenditure (million US dollars)	Expenditure per employee (US dollars per employee)
Agriculture production and services	90	54
Construction	720	127
Durable goods	4,710	314
Finance, insurance, and real estate	3,480	529
Manufacturing	6,450	258
Mining	720	566
Nondurable goods	1,740	260
Public administration	3,960	645
Services	8,700	283
Trade	2,910	136
Transportation and public utilities	2,610	351

Source: Carnavale 1986 p. 20

as a percentage of payroll cost (or labor cost) in 34 countries. These countries fall into four income groups according to the classification by the World Bank in 1987. It shows that although there is some variation among countries, training expenditure was between one and two percent of payroll cost in most of these countries; the average for the 34 countries was 1.2 percent.

Finally, individuals also contribute a significant amount of resources to AET. In the United States, surveys of participation in adult education conducted by the Bureau of Census show that for the year ending May 1981, 21 million participants in adult education took over 37 million courses. Forty-eight percent of these participants paid for the courses themselves or had the costs met by their family, with a total private expenditure of US$2.2 billion. The average cost was US$120 per course. During the year ending May 1984, 23 million participants in adult education took over 43 million courses. Forty-seven percent of these participants paid for the courses themselves or had the costs met by their family, with a total private expenditure of US$3 billion. The average cost was US$152 per course (National Center for Educational Statistics 1986).

In a study of Shenzhen (an economically fast-growing area in China) in 1990, Xiao and Tsang (1994 p. 58) found that trainees spent an average of 58RMB yuan per month on training which was equivalent to 15 percent of their average monthly income. The amount of monthly expenditure varied with the type of training centers which trainees attended. "Employee-oriented" centers run by enterprises required relatively little direct private costs since employers were the primary financing source. But trainees attending "community-oriented" centers (not operated by employers) had to pay training fees and other direct private costs of training; trainees were the major financing source for some of these centers.

Employees and other individuals had a strong demand for skill training because of favorable employment opportunities in this area of China.

4. Variation in Training Costs in Industry

There are large variations among industries and firms in their expenditure on occupational training. According to the American Society for Training and Development, total expenditure on training by industry in the United States in 1984 ranged from a low of US$90 million for the agricultural production and services industry, to a high of US$8.7 billion for the service sector (see Table 3). Total expenditure per industry obviously depends on the number of employees per industry, the percentage of employees receiving training, and the cost of training per employee.

The percentage of employees receiving training in an industry is related to the occupational structure of firms in an industry. For example, employer-based formal training is disproportionately concentrated in industries with large numbers of professionals, managers, and technicians (Carnevale and Gainer 1988).

The cost of training per employee (CPE) also varies significantly among industries. For industries in the United States in 1984, it ranged from a low of US$54 per employee for agricultural production and services, to a high of US$645 per employee for public administration (see Table 3). The Edding Commission on apprenticeship training in the former West Germany found that, in the early 1970s, the gross expenditure per trainee per year ranged from DM86 in the health industry to DM8,912 for large firms belonging to the Chambers of Industry and Commerce (OECD 1979 p. 56). For the United Kingdom, Jones (1986) found that, in 1984, the net cost (gross cost minus trainee output) of apprentice training was £8,900 per trainee for engineering firms, and £11,800 per trainee for nonengineering firms.

CPE also exhibits substantial variations among firms and industries in Asia. In a study of apprentice training in Malaysia, Cohen (1985 p. 339) found that, in 1982, the per employee total cost of training to the employer in the nonelectrical trade was RM3,175, RM5,670, and RM9,180 respectively for three different companies; and the per employee total cost of training to the employer in the metallic trade was RM2,730 for a fourth company. Based on a survey of 11 in-plant training centers in the Republic of Korea in 1984, Lee (1985 Annex 10) found that the per employee recurrent cost of training in the pipe-fitting trade was W1.45 million in the shipping industry and W1.08 million in the construction industry; and that the peremployee recurrent cost of training in the electric welding trade was W1.53 million in the shipping industry and W1.19 million in the construction industry.

5. Determinants of Training Costs

CPE is influenced by a variety of factors. One way to understand the determinants of CPE is by relating CPE to the amount of training per employee (in terms of hours per employee) and the unit cost of training (in terms of cost per training hour).

5.1 Amount of Training per Employee

The amount of training per employee has been found to depend on the nature of jobs, the characteristics of a firm, and the background characteristics of employees.

Nature of Job. Different jobs require different amounts of training. A survey of firms in the United States with 100 workers or more in 1994 found that the number of hours of training ranged from 19 hours per administrative/office worker and 30 hours per production worker, to 35 hours per professional worker and 38 hours per salesperson (*Training*, 1994, p 46). The projected distribution of the total training time (estimated to be 1.4 billion hours for all such firms) by occupation was: 2.0 percent for executives, 19.7 percent for professionals, 3.0 percent for senior managers, 7.3 percent for middle managers, 8.6 percent for first-line supervisors, 26.1 percent for production workers, 11.3 percent for salespersons, 15.2 percent for customer-service workers, and 6.8 percent for administrative employees (computed from *Training* 1994 p. 46).

Characteristics of Firms. In general, larger firms in industrialized countries provide more training to employees than smaller firms (OECD 1991 Chap. 5). But Bishop (1982) found that, in the United States, the smallest firms (less than 10 employees) did not provide the least amount of training per employee. In other words, the relationship between amount of training and firm size is a U-shape curve. Also, he found that firms with higher rates of employment growth provided more training than firms with lower rates.

Based on a survey of 5,619 firms in different industries in Taiwan in 1985, San (1990) first computed the proportion of firms in each industry that provided job-related training (with a training period of at least one month) to their employees in that year. Firms in the utility industry were found to have the highest proportion at 76.9 percent; they were followed by firms in manufacturing (24.2%), firms in mining (20.4%), firms in transportation and communication (8.8%), and firms in construction (7.9%). San pointed out that the utility industry was a highly monopolized industry and firms in this industry had a high propensity to conduct training. In contrast, construction firms were mostly small contractors with a high labor turnover rate; such firms did not find employee training a profitable investment. The author then went on to examine the factors that affected the training effort of firms in the manufacturing industry. Regressional analysis showed that firms employing a higher level of technology and firms in more concentrated industries had a higher propensity to provide training to their employees than firms with a lower level of technology and firms in less concentrated industries, respectively.

Firm size is a factor in other developing countries (Middleton et al. 1993 Chap. 6). Small firms, such as those in Indonesia, Hong Kong, and in small countries in West Africa, have a lower propensity to provide formal training to their employees than their larger counterparts. When small firms do provide training, they are more likely to use on-the-job training than more formal methods. Also, the quality and intensity of training provided by smaller firms tends to be lower than that by larger firms. However, the formation of enterprise training associations can strengthen training in small and medium-size firms. Good examples of enterprise training associations do exist, such as those found in Brazil and other Latin American countries.

Characteristics of Workers. In the United States, White workers receive disproportionately more training than minority workers. In general, workers with more formal education receive more training than workers with less formal education; though it is not clear whether a worker with a doctoral degree or professional degree receives more training than workers with a masters degree. Part-time workers receive less training than full-time workers. Though there are some inconsistencies among the findings of different studies, work experience generally enhances the training opportunities for a worker. However, there is no consensus among studies on whether male workers receive more training than female workers, and whether union workers receive more training than nonunion workers (Brown 1989).

A recent study of OECD countries has several findings regarding access to training (OECD 1991 p. 161). First, there are two broad patterns regarding training access by age. In some countries (especially those with strong apprenticeship systems, like Germany), incidence of training decreases with increasing age. In other countries, incidence of training increases with age, reaches a maximum for the 30–44 age group, and then declines afterwards. Second, there is little difference between men and women. Third, more educated workers have more access to training than less educated workers. And fourth, in general, higher level nonmanual and skilled manual workers have more access to training than lower level and less skilled workers.

Education was found to be related to training opportunities in the workplace in some developing countries (Middleton et al. 1993 p. 160). In Peru, the probability of receiving training was 25 percent higher for male workers with some secondary schooling than for workers with no secondary schooling, 52 percent higher for those who completed secondary schooling, and 63 percent higher for those with some postsecondary schooling. In Thailand, the level of formal schooling was positively related to the probability of promotion to higher-level positions which were associated with more training opportunities.

5.2 Unit Cost of Training

The cost per training hour depends on the technology of training and the prices of inputs to training (Tsang 1989).

Technology of Training. The technology of training refers to how training is provided; it concerns such matters as the curriculum, pedagogy, class size, organization, and the mode of delivery.

Anderson and Kasl (1982) found large differences in unit costs of AET among different sponsors in the United States; the cost per training hour was US$2 for public school systems, US$5 for colleges and universities, US$8 for community organizations, and US$15 for professional organizations. One reason for the low unit cost of public school systems is its above average class size.

Also, when a training organization can increase its output without increasing inputs proportionately (known as economies of scale), unit cost will be smaller. In their study of adult training centers in Shenzhen, China, Xiao and Tsang (1994 p. 60) found that both the recurrent cost per training hour and the capital cost per training hour decreased with increasing program size as measured by the number of training hours, after controlling for program quality and the type of training center.

AET programs through the new educational media (such as TV, radio and satellite) draws attention to the importance of achieving economies of scale. Since AET programs through new educational media demand heavy capital investment in their initial development, such programs require a large enrollment and a relatively long period of operation (Eicher et al. 1982).

Unit costs are related to the mode and duration of training. Enterprise-based training generally has lower unit costs than institutional-based training. Studies on Asian countries indicate that the unit costs of enterprise-based training average about 45 percent of those of institutional-based training; but this percentage shows large variations among countries. Also, longer programs have higher pertrainee costs than shorter programs (Tsang 1989, p. 30).

Prices of Inputs. For most AET programs, the payment to personnel is the key determinant of unit cost. Part-time instructors are often paid less than full-time instructors, on an hourly basis (Xiao and Tsang 1994 p. 57). The use of volunteers can reduce the direct cost of training.

Different providers of AET appear to differ significantly in how costs are distributed among different inputs to training (Anderson and Kasl 1982). For example, as a proportion of total expenditure (excluding private costs of participants), instructor costs amount to 60 percent for public school systems, 44 percent for colleges and universities, 35 percent for community organizations, and only 17 percent for professional organizations. Such variation may be due to a combination of differences in the technology of training and in the type (and thus price) of inputs employed.

6. Applications of Cost Analysis

Analyses of the costs of AET are important for decision making, planning, and management in AET. The applications of cost analysis in AET are briefly discussed in the following.

6.1 Cost–Benefit Analysis and Investment in Adult Education and Training

A key application of cost analysis in AET is economic evaluation of the profitability of investment in AET. The technique of benefit–cost analysis (or rate-of-return analysis) as applied to AET is most relevant here. It can be applied to the evaluation of AET programs for which the benefits can be quantified in monetary terms, such as higher earnings or productivity.

Obviously, there are many cost–benefit analyses that can be undertaken, for example, with respect to the sponsor, the mode of training, the type of industry and trades within an industry, the objective or kind of AET program (occupational, basic literacy, civic/political competence, etc.), and others. The literature on cost–benefit analysis in AET is much smaller than that on youth education. The available cost–benefit studies on AET are mostly dated, and other economic studies on AET tend to focus on the earnings or productivity effects of AET. Previous studies on occupational training indicate that the rates of return were either near to or much above the benchmark of 10 percent (Mangum 1989). More current estimates are needed to inform public and private investment decisions.

6.2 Cost-effectiveness Analysis

Decision-makers in AET are often faced with the task to choose among alternative programs or methods with a common objective (better verbal skill) which cannot be measured in monetary terms. An analysis of the effectiveness and costs of the alternatives can be conducted to assist decision-makers in selecting the most cost-effective alternative (see *Evaluation of Public Training: Cost-Effectiveness; Evaluation of Industry Training: Cost-Effectiveness*). For example, when two programs yield similar training effects, the less costly program should be selected, other things being equal. By incorporating cost-effectiveness analysis in the decision-making process, AET organizations can make more efficient use of their scarce resources.

6.3 Cost Functions in Training

Cost functions relate the total cost of production to the output of production. Cost functions can be estimated for different modes of (or approaches to) training. They are useful in two ways. First, given a mode of training, an estimated training cost function shows how the unit cost of training varies with the amount of training provided under that mode. Second, cost functions for different modes of training provide cost information necessary for investment decisions regarding the choice of training modes for human resource development. Cost functions have been estimated for new educational media as a training mode for AET (Eicher et al. 1982); but little work has been done on other training modes (Xiao and Tsang 1994).

6.4 Cost Information in Planning and Management

Information on costs is necessary to monitor and improve the utilization of existing resources in an AET organization. By more fully utilizing existing resources, an organization can raise its output without increasing costs, thus increasing the "internal" efficiency of the organization. The key to increased internal efficiency is to identify "slack" in the organization, such as underutilized personnel, facilities, or equipment (Tsang 1989).

Cost analysis is an integral part of the planning and management of an AET program. A careful estimation of the total cost of an AET program is necessary for several reasons. First, it simply shows how much a program costs, for accounting or budgetary purposes. Second, if some important indirect or hidden costs are not included in the proposal or contract for a program, there will likely be financial difficulties when the program is implemented. Third, the total cost estimate is needed in assessing the financial feasibility of a program.

Cost data are needed for planning future developments in AET. Historical data on unit costs (such as cost per trainee or cost per training hour) provide a basis for projecting the costs of programs in the future.

Information on cost is also indispensable for controlling or reducing the costs of AET programs. In general, there are three strategies for cost reduction. First, given a program or method of delivery, cost can be reduced by employing lower cost inputs. Thus, instead of using a qualified full-time instructor, a part-time instructor or an instructor with a lower qualification may be employed. In some situations, volunteers may fill certain personnel needs of the program and thus the direct cost of the program to the sponsor will be reduced. It should be noted that there is often a tradeoff between the cost of an input and its quality. Second, given a program or a set of programs run by an AET organization, unit costs can be reduced by more fully utilizing the existing resources for the program or the organization. When there is organization slack, cost can be reduced without affecting the level of output. Third, given a training objective, alternative technology of production of training, or training programs can be evaluated to determine their costs and effectiveness. Thus, other things being equal, an alternative with a lower cost should be preferred to another with a higher cost.

Finally, there is a long-standing observation by analysts and practitioners alike about the lack of information on the costs of AET programs. To improve the planning and management of AET programs, cost information should be regularly collected and analyzed. For large organizations which provide AET programs on a regular basis, a model for analyzing and estimating cost can be industrialized.

7. Emerging Cost-related Issues

In many countries, there is an emerging need to reassess investment activities in AET for both the government and the employer because of rapid production changes and intensifying economic competition among countries. Investment in human capital is often seen as a key strategy to deal with these changes. This raises at least four questions regarding investment in AET: Is the current level of investment in AET adequate? What kind of adult education and training should be provided? How can access to AET for disadvantaged members of society be expanded? And how should AET programs be financed? The first question concerns the changing level of demand for education and training and thus whether or not there is underinvestment in AET. The second question concerns the changing nature of the demand for education and training. The third question draws attention to the fact that the access to education and training is much more limited to certain groups of the population (such as minorities, the less educated, and the poor) and these disadvantaged groups are increasing in size and in proportion. Underinvestment in the education and training of these groups will have severe economic and social consequences. The last question points out the need to reassess the role of government, the employer, and the individual in financing AET in the near future. Further research and public discussion are needed to address these questions.

Because of the current economic difficulties in many countries, decision-makers or managers of AET programs in both the public and private sectors have to face increasing scrutiny of their demand for resources. There is a more urgent need for running efficient programs, cutting unnecessary costs, and improving the planning and management of AET programs.

See also: On-the-job Training; Economics of Adult Education and Training; Government Role in Adult Education and Training; Market Failure in Adult Education and Training; Demand, Supply, and Finance of Adult Education; Evaluation of Distance Education: Cost-Effectiveness; Evaluation of Industry Training: Cost-Effectiveness; Evaluation of Public Training: Cost-Effectiveness; Measurement of Training Costs

References

Anderson R, Kasl E 1982 *The Costs and Financing of Adult Education and Training.* D C Heath–Lexington Books, Lexington, Massachusetts
Bishop J 1982 *The Social Payoff for Occupationally Specific Training: The Employers' Point of View.* National Center for Research on Vocational Education, Columbus, Ohio
Brown C 1989 Empirical evidence on private training. In: Commission on Workforce Quality and Labor Market Efficiency 1989 *Investing in People.* US Department of Labor, Washington, DC
Bureau of National Affairs 1985 *Training and Development Programs.* Bureau of National Affairs, Washington, DC
Carnevale A 1986 The learning enterprise. *Train. Dev. J.* (January): 18–26
Carnevale A, Gainer L 1988 *The Learning Enterprise.* American Society for Training and Development, Alexandra, Virginia
Christoffel P 1978 Current federal programs for lifelong learning: A US$14 billion effort. *Sch. Rev.* (May): 348–59
Cohen S 1985 A cost-benefit analysis of industrial training. *Econ. Educ. Rev.* 4(4): 327–39
Eicher J, Hawkridge D, McAnany E, Orivel F (eds.) 1982 *The Economics of New Educational Media, Vol. 3. Cost and Effectiveness: Overview and Synthesis.* UNESCO, Paris
Jones I 1986 Apprentice training costs in British manufacturing establishments: Some new evidence. *British Journal of Industrial Relations* 24(3): 333–62
Lee C 1985 *Financing Technical Education in LDCs: Economic Implications for a Survey of Training Modes in the Replublic of Korea.* Report No. EDT6, Education and Training Department, The World Bank, Washington, DC
Mangum S 1989 Evidence on private sector training. In: Commission on Workforce Quality and Labor Market Efficiency 1989 *Investing in People.* US Department of Labor, Washington, DC
Middleton J, Ziderman A, Van Adams A 1993 *Skills for Productivity: Vocational Education and Training in Developing Countries.* Oxford University Press, Oxford
National Center for Educational Statistics 1986 *OERI Bulletin.* Department of Education, Washington, DC
Noda T, Watanabe T 1977 Educational expenditure in Japan. In: Levy-Garboua L et al. (eds.) 1977 *Educational Expenditure in France, Japan, and the United Kingdom.* OECD, Paris
Organisation for Economic Co-operation and Development (OECD) 1977 *Learning Opportunities for Adults*, Vol. 1. OECD, Paris
Organisation for Economic Co-operation and Development (OECD) 1979 *Policies for Apprenticeship.* OECD, Paris
Organisation for Economic Co-operation and Development (OECD) 1991 *Employment Outlook.* OECD Paris
San G 1990 Enterprise training in Taiwan: Results from the Vocational Training Needs Survey. *Econ. Educ. Rev.* 9(4): 411–18. *Training* 1994 Industry Report. (October): 29–74
Tsang M 1989 *The Costs of Vocational Training.* Population and Human Resources Department, The World Bank, Washington, DC
Weber D 1984 An eye to the East: Training in Japan. *Train. Dev. J.* (October): 32–3
Whalley J, Ziderman A 1990 Financing training in developing countries: The role of payroll taxes. *Econ. Educ. Rev.* 9(4): 377–87
Xiao J, Tsang M 1994 Costs and financing of adult education: A case study of Shenzhen, China. *Int. J. Educ. Dev.* 14(1): 51–64

Further Reading

Borkowski A, van der Heiden M, Tuijnman A C 1995 Continuing education and training in adults. In: Bucht B, Härnqvist K (eds.) 1995 *Education and Labour Market Destinations: OECD Indicators.* Centre for Educational Research and Innovation, OECD, Paris
Levin H 1983 *Cost Effectiveness: A Primer.* Sage, Beverly Hills, California
Lillard L, Tan H 1986 *Private Sector Training: Who Gets It and What are Its Effects?* Rand Corporation, Santa Monica, California
Lusterman S 1985 *Trends in Corporate Education and Training.* The Conference Board, New York
Organisation for Economic Co-operation and Development (OECD) 1993 *Industry Training in Australia, Sweden, and the United States.* OECD, Paris
Ryan P 1980 The costs of job training for a transferable skill. *British Journal of Industrial Relations* 18(3): 334–52
Ziderman A 1975 Costs and benefits of manpower training programmes in Great Britain. *British Journal of Industrial Relations* 13(2): 223–44
Zymelman M 1976 *Economic Evaluation of Vocational Training Programs.* Johns Hopkins University Press, Baltimore, Maryland

Financing Lifelong Learning

D. Timmermann

Education and training activities for youth and adults result from various decisions in the course of time. Seldom do these decisions reflect comprehensive concepts of education evolution. An international comparison (ARV Management Service 1979) demonstrated the diversity of education structures and financing schemes between and within countries. The ideas of lifelong learning and recurrent education are an intellectual attempt to carry the diverse education arrangements and financing schemes into a comprehensive system. The financing issue raises the question as to how a comprehensive system of lifelong learning could or should be financed. In this entry, alternative mechanisms for financing lifelong learning and recurrent education are discussed.

1. Criteria for Evaluating Financing Schemes

The number and type of goals for lifelong learning have been widened beyond the commonly used performance indicators: personal development, economic efficiency, and social equity (Schütze 1982 pp. 56–59, Timmermann 1983 pp. 99–105, CERI 1986 pp. 132–45). Encouraging lifelong learning in a recurrent way aims at replacing traditional schooling with a flexible and recurrent alternation of education, work, leisure, vacation, and sabbaticals. Increasing efficiency internally and externally refers to improving the allocation of resources within and between educational organizations, and to a better matching of education and work (see *Recurrent Education; Economics of Adult Education and Training*). Encouraging innovations in education comprises the improvement of general knowledge as well as of marketable and nonmarketable, but societally valuable innovations. As the systemic approach of lifelong learning requires the integration of segregated segments of general education and vocational training, encouraging integration is the fourth criterion for evaluating financing schemes. Considering the widespread belief that in most countries bureaucratic and hierarchic decision structures still characterize educational organizations, lifelong learning and recurrent education are aimed at encouraging individual choice and personal development. Under the given arrangements of education and training, participation in postcompulsory activities differs considerably between societal groups as to sex, age, social background, ethnical background, level of initial schooling, and continuing vocational training. Therefore, overcoming these participation patterns, promoting equality of educational opportunity, and encouraging demand for lifelong learning are further

goals. As inequality of educational opportunity is seen to help to (re)produce social and economic inequity, decreasing the degree of social and economic inequity is a complementary goal. Increasing the democratic potential of education, work, and the society as a whole, and preserving and enforcing social cohesion (so that societies can survive as cultural entities) are goals to which lifelong learning should also strive. What kind of financing modes could enable lifelong learning to develop in accordance with these goals, and what effects may be expected to emanate from each alternative to the goals? As there is also concern with regard to the impact of lifelong learning on the total costs of education as well as on the public budget, these effects will also be considered (see *Lifelong Learning*).

2. Alternative Financing Mechanisms

Six basic financing models have been discussed in the context of lifelong learning (Timmermann 1983).

2.1 The Self-financing Model

The self-financing model assumes that individuals pay for recurrent education out of savings, current income, or future earnings. The assumption states that under the basis of the "pay-as-you-use" principle, the participants in lifelong learning schemes have to bear the costs. Suppliers could be public institutions or private firms; in either case prices could be market prices. In the case of state supply, prices might be reduced to the cost-covering level.

The model does not reveal an optimistic impact perspective. For rate-of-return reasons, postponement of education activities by individuals from when they are young into their adult life is not beneficial (Stoikov 1975). Hence a recurrent mode of lifelong learning would not develop. While internal efficiency of education production and the speed of innovations are likely to increase under this model (although nonmarketable educational products and innovations might be neglected), external efficiency would probably suffer from cobweb cycles in the education and qualification markets. The integration of general and vocational education might be pushed, although the latter would tend to dominate the former (see *Convergence between Education and Training*). While individual choice and buyer sovereignty would widen, "education-distant" groups would be discouraged, and the (inequal) distribution of income would reflect the (unequal) distribution of demand for lifelong education. The equity issue would moreover remain at stake; democratization of the decision structure within education would not be expected.

2.2 The Drawing Rights Model

The drawing rights model stresses "the right to utilize one's assets in a broadened social insurance system for income maintenance during nonwork periods with a greater degree of self-determination" (Rehn 1983 p. 67), and recommends a single comprehensive system for financing all periods of nonwork by extending the social insurance system to a comprehensive personal account system which would integrate the given diverse income transfer schemes into a single one. Financial means would come from account holders and employers who would have to contribute to the account on the basis of their income or through a certain payroll levy. The self-employed would be included in the system, and the state would have to finance the contributions for those unable to cover their education expense.

The model asks for a general and compulsory membership for all citizens, who would gain the right to draw on their account up to the limits of their actual or expected assets of credits. The account holders would be allowed to overdraw in early periods but would have to balance the account over the course of a longer life-phase. Beyond a certain level of credits devoted to one's retirement pension, the individual should be free to decide how to use the drawing rights.

The model primarily aims at making the sequences of work and nonwork periods in the life of individuals more flexible. It also intends, although to a limited extent, to strengthen the free choice of individuals with regard to the allocation of time for various activities during their lives. While the model provides for income for individuals during nonwork periods, it does not solve problems associated with education supply. The self-financing and the drawing rights model differ as follows: while accumulating funds for lifelong education is voluntary in the former, individuals are obliged to save for nonwork periods in the latter. While individuals are free to use their savings for any purpose in the self-financing model, only a proportion of accumulated funds are given free for any use under the drawing rights scheme due to the necessity for withholding funds for retirement pensions or similar purposes. Also under the drawing rights scheme, the "automatic" emergence of a comprehensive recurrent system of lifelong education cannot be expected without any collective agreements or legislative actions. Moreover, as education would compete with other nonwork activities for the funds, underinvestment in lifelong education would be likely. Finally, as the drawing rights model would start at the given unequal distribution of income, the opportunities to save for and participate in lifelong education would quite directly reflect this income inequity and foster the spiral between income, investment in education, and returns.

2.3 Individual Entitlements

Financing lifelong education through individual entitlements (Levin 1977, 1983) starts from the observation that in most countries large parts of education and training are being financed by the state, the financing streams going directly from the state to the education institutions. This system is said to reproduce internal as well as external inefficiency, and also inequity of education and social rewards. The entitlement approach suggests directly supporting individuals through entitlements. Institutions would gain their returns from fees.

An entitlement would provide a guaranteed sum of money for each individual after compulsory schooling, and this could be used for attending education programs that satisfied the criteria established by the government. According to different concepts, entitlements could take the form of loans or grants, and their size as well as composition could depend on family income or the background characteristics of recipients or on the type of education chosen. Individuals would be eligible for using the entitlement over a long time span, both prior to the start of their working lives and during their working career. As the entitlement account would accumulate interest in times of nonuse, the individual would be encouraged to choose carefully between the diverse opportunities of lifelong education both at one point in time as well as over time. In order to become effective, such an entitlement scheme would require a comprehensive regulatory and information system (see Levin 1977).

The individual entitlement model also stresses the issue of individual choice in lifelong education. The main effect, however, might be the impact on improving equality. This impact would depend on the size of the entitlements, the composition of grants and loans, their stimulus with regard to demand particularly from disadvantaged groups, and the tax incidence. Under this scheme, total costs of lifelong education and the educational burden on the public budget would increase.

2.4 Single-employer Financing

Financing lifelong education by single employers would be an extension of on-the-job training, apprenticeship, and continuing vocational training systems. This model would require all employers to pay for lifelong education activities demanded by their employees and which they would be willing to support. With regard to the interests of employers (who would try to shift the burden onto the buyers), the scheme would run the danger of reducing lifelong education to firm-specific postcompulsory training so that employers were sure to internalize the returns (see *On-the-job Training; Demand, Supply, and Finance of Adult Education*). However, restriction of employee mobility might conflict with macroeconomic needs for mobility. Hence, single-employer financing might restrict the external efficieny of lifelong education, even though internal efficiency for single employers may be high. Inflexibility of those trained, cobweb cycles in the markets for lifelong education activities, overinvestment in lifelong education in one set of branches and underinvestment in others, a general tendency toward underinvestment, and competition biases are likely to produce misallocations between education and employment. The single-employer financing model would suffer from further shortcomings: the unemployed would be excluded from lifelong education, training-specific innovations would be likely to dominate general education, and individual choices would be influenced substantially by employers. Finally, one would not expect equality of educational opportunity nor social equity to improve.

2.5 Parafiscal Funds

Competitional biases and underinvestment in education might be avoided by financing lifelong education through parafiscal funds (Clement 1983). These are autonomous (centralized or decentralized) corporations intermediate between state bodies and private organizations, and constituted by deliberate or compulsory membership of employers. The main feature is their autonomy in raising and distributing funds for the purpose of lifelong education, and determining and monitoring the standards which guide the levy and distribution of the money. Some countries have applied the idea of collective parafiscal financing to initial vocational training and to retraining. Examples are the Industrial Training Boards in the United Kingdom, the Federal Employment Office in Germany, and collective training corporations in Latin American countries (SENAI [Brazil], SENA [Columbia], INTECAP [Guatemala] (see *Latin America: National Training Agencies*). The levy would be taken from (private and public) enterprises in relation to the wage-sum, profits, or value-added. A levy on value-added seems the most tenable, because wage and profit levies could discriminate against labor- or profit-intensive firms. The fund would be guided by the idea of democratic participation in that it would be governed by boards being constituted of the representatives of diverse government bodies as well as of employers, trade unions, independent experts, and educators. The boards would decide upon the levy formula and the quality standards of the education activities, and would monitor these standards. Opposed to entitlements and drawing rights, "the extent of an individual's rights to education and training and the degree of individual choice is not predetermined" (CERI 1986 p. 130).

Commonly, the model restricts itself to institutional funding. It might be worthwhile to examine the potential of an entitlement solution implanted into it.

While parafiscal funds are likely to create favorable characteristics with respect to recurrence, integration, innovation, and internal efficiency, the impact on external efficiency seems ambivalent (Timmermann 1983 p. 117), and the unemployed would again be excluded from lifelong education. Moreover, the ability of parafiscal funds to encourage demand for and to diminish the inequality of participation in lifelong education and social equity is questionable.

2.6 The State Financing Model

The state financing model would require the state to raise and spend the financial means (like the entitlement approach) for lifelong education, as well as to provide it through public programs (unlike the entitlement scheme). This approach extends the education monopoly of the state to lifelong education (see Timmermann 1982). As lifelong education is under political responsibility, encouragement of recurrence, integration, participation, realization of high and equal quality standards, equality of opportunity, and social cohesion all seem feasible. However, the ability to improve efficiency (internally and externally) may be questioned, and a uniformity of programs, instead of variety, might restrict individual choice. Moreover, particular state interests could dominate the democratic participation of learners. Finally, the assumption of the rationality of state agencies may be fundamentally questioned. Arguments of public choice theory (Gwartney 1977 pp. 60–67, 376–91) lead one to assume "state failure" as a consequence of the rational voter ignorance effect, the special interest and shortsightedness effect, the lack of stimuli to act efficiently, of political lags in decision processes, and of informational and financial as well as legitimation restrictions (see *Market Failure in Adult Education and Training; Partnerships: Initial and Adult Education*).

3. Conclusion

The discussion of alternative financing mechanisms for recurrent education and lifelong learning suggests that much theoretical and empirical work still has to be done. Empirical evidence on financing lifelong learning is meager, and theoretical reasoning is close to intelligent speculation on the basis of background theories. There is no "best" financing solution. While this conclusion seems valid, nevertheless, deeper scrutiny of each model seems necessary with respect to their regulation, information, decision, stimuli, production, and supply mechanisms. While much controversy between advocates of the models is due to the "who pays" versus "who should pay" issue, these disputes might lose power if they were concentrated more on the issue of "who bears the burden" versus "who should bear the burden" of financing lifelong learning. Here again, much empirical work has to be done to approach the answer reliably. Moreover, while —from theoretical reasoning—it seems clear that participants, employers, the state, and society benefit from lifelong learning, there is hardly any knowledge about the size and the distribution of these benefits. Nevertheless, the attempt to develop a (recurrent) system of lifelong learning could rest on a comprehensive financing scheme which would take contributions from all beneficiaries according to their ability to pay.

See also: Lifelong and Continuing Education; Recurrent Education; Economics of Adult Education and Training; Economics of Nonformal Education; Government Role in Adult Education and Training; Market Failure in Adult Education and Training; Overeducation; Time Policies for Lifelong Learning; Demand, Supply, and Finance of Adult Education; Lifelong Learning

References

ABV Management Service 1979 *Bildungswesen im Vergleich. Berufliche und nichtberufliche Weiterbildung in ausgewählten Ländern, 2 vols.* Bundesminister für Bildung und Wissenschaft, Bonn

Center for Educational Research and Innovation (CERI) 1986 *Recurrent Education Revisited.* Almqvist and Wiksell, Stockholm

Clement W 1983 Intermediate ("parafiscal") financing schemes. In: Levin H M, Schütze H G (eds.) 1983

Gwartney J D 1977 *Macroeconomics. Private and Public Choice.* Academic Press, New York

Levin H M 1977 Post-secondary entitlements: An exploration. In: Kurland D (ed.) 1977 *Entitlement Studies*, NIE Papers in Education and Work 4. US Department of Health, Education, and Welfare, Washington, DC

Levin H M 1983 Individual entitlements. In: Levin H M, Schütze H G (eds.) 1983

Rehn G 1983 Individual drawing rights. In: Levin H M, Schütze H G (eds.) 1983

Schütze H G 1982 Das OECD-Konzept "Recurrent Education" und Kriterien für die Finanzierung lebenslangen Lernens. In: Kuhlenkamp D, Schütze H G (eds.) 1982 *Kosten und Finanzierung der beruflichen und nichtberuflichen Weiterbildung.* Diesterweg Verlag, Frankfurt

Stoikov V 1975 *The Economics of Recurrent Education and Training*, International Labour Office, Geneva

Timmermann D 1982 Das Staatsfinanzierungsmodell als Finanzierungsalternative für "Recurrent Education." In: Kuhlenkamp D, Schütze H G (eds.) 1982 *Kosten und Finanzierung der beruflichen und nichtberuflichen Weiterbildung.* Diesterweg Verlag, Frankfurt

Timmermann D 1983 *Financing Mechanisms: Their Impact on Postcompulsory Education. In:* Levin H M, Schütze H G (eds.) 1983

Further Reading

Center for Educational Research and Innovation (CERI) 1987 *Adults in Higher Education.* OECD, Paris

Levin H M, Schütze H G (eds.) 1983 *Financing Recurrent Education.* Sage, Beverly Hills, California

Mincer J 1991 Job training: Costs, returns, and wage profiles. In: Stern D, Ritzen J J M (eds.) 1991 *Market Failure in Training? New Economic Analyses and Evidence on Training of Adult Employees.* Spinger-Verlag, Berlin

Mushkin S J (ed.) 1974 *Recurrent Education.* National Institute of Education, US Department of Health, Education, and Welfare, Washington, DC

Tuijnman A 1989 *Recurrent Education, Earnings and Wellbeing. A Fifty-year Longitudinal Study of a Cohort of Swedish Men.* Almqvist and Wiksell International, Stockholm

Paid Educational Leave through Legislation and Collective Bargaining

H. G. Schütze

Paid educational leave was seen in the 1970s as a way of enhancing the recurrent education of adults, especially employees. This entry describes the concept and gives an overview of the development of paid educational leave since the 1974 landmark Convention by the International Labor Organization (ILO) (see *International Labour Organisation*). (Leave as a part of apprenticeship programs or public labor market training is not covered in this entry.)

1. Definition and Scope

According to the 1974 Convention and Recommendations on Paid Educational Leave adopted by the International Labor Organization (ILO), paid educational leave is defined as "leave granted to a worker for educational purposes for a specified period during working hours, with adequate financial entitlements." Countries adopting the convention commit themselves "to formulate and apply a policy designed to promote, by methods appropriate to national conditions and practice and by stages as necessary, the granting of paid educational leave for the purpose of training at any level, general, social and civic education, trade union education" (ILO 1991 pp. 175–78).

Although as of 1992, 23 countries have ratified the Convention, there are important country-specific differences in definition as well as actual policies for implementation. Thus, while enterprise-provided continuing education and training of the workforce is considered as educational leave in the United Kingdom, this does not qualify as "leave" in Germany or France. (All three are signatories of the ILO Convention.) Another divergence occurs with respect to "adequate financial entitlements." In several European countries provisions for educational leave are automatically linked to financial support, while in other countries they are provided only for specific groups or for certain kinds of educational activities (Schütze and Istance 1987).

1.1 Developments in the 1970s

Following the discussions leading to the ILO Convention, another international organization took up the issue. The Organisation for Economic Co-operation and Development (OECD) saw educational leave as an instrument for implementing its concept of recurrent education (OECD 1976, 1978), which refers to a strategy to organize education and training in alternation with employment by spreading educational opportunities over a person's entire life rather than confining it to his or her youth years (see *Recurrent Education*).

While the concept of educational leave was embraced in many European countries, it did not have the same impact in North America. This was probably due to the lack of pressure by labor unions in the United States, which had been a principal reason for initial success in Europe (von Moltke and Schneevoigt 1977). In Canada, the main obstacle to promoting paid educational leave is the federal structure, since the responsibility for education, labor market, and labor relations rests with the Provinces. Yet such a federal structure has not been a barrier in the Federal Republic of Germany.

1.2 Categories of Educational Leave

In order to understand the variety of activities to which the label of educational leave has been attached, it is useful to classify them according to a few basic categories. Examples are the general leave provisions stipulated by law, legal provisions for specific groups, and provisions for educational leave in collective bargaining agreements.

Two established leave schemes are not included in this overview as they cannot be correctly subsumed under these categories. The first, the dual system of initial vocational training, exists in a number of European countries, notably in Austria, Germany, the Netherlands, and Switzerland. In these countries, an employer who provides apprenticeship training is obliged by law to release apprentices for vocational school attendance, either one to two days per week or in the form of block release. Although this scheme seems to represent an example of educational leave, it does not really qualify as such, given the laws requiring part-time attendance of vocational school, usually up to the age of 18. Apprenticeships in these countries must be considered as part of compulsory schooling,

because attendance under this scheme is seen not as an individual right but as a duty.

Public labor market training is also excluded. Educational leave, defined as the individual right of an employed person to take leave for educational purposes, is commonly understood as having two principal components: (a) paid time off work for learning and (b) job security. Under this definition, public labor market training and retraining for unemployed adults or those facing a risk of redundancy does not qualify. While most industrialized countries provide full-time or part-time training for the unemployed with the objective of helping trainees to find stable employment, the element of job security—in the sense of a guarantee to return to the job previously held—is lacking. The same applies to those participants who, under labor market training programs, retrain either for completely different jobs or train for positions that require higher qualifications. In all of these cases, security in a specific job and even employment are normally not guaranteed at the end of the training program. Thus, labor market training, although in many respects closely related to educational leave, is not dealt with in this entry.

2. Legislation on Paid Educational Leave

There are several Western European countries with general education leave legislation; that is, legal provision for leave that is not limited to specific populations, groups, or categories of employees holding specific functions in their firms. While general legislation on paid educational leave is not limited to the three countries mentioned below but exists in a number of others, France, Germany, and Sweden represent central examples both with respect to the number of people covered and the particular approach chosen.

2.1 France

Educational leave in France is based on a law of 1971 entitled "The Organization of Continuing Vocational Training within the Framework of Permanent Education." As the name indicates, this is not just a law on educational leave but a provision for the organization of further vocational training in general, including educational leave (see *Legislation in Adult Education*). The stated objective is to enable workers to adapt to changes in the techniques and conditions of work, to encourage social mobility, and to encourage workers' own contributions to cultural, economic, and social development. The law, which has been amended several times, for example in 1991, obliges employers to spend a certain percentage of their pay roll on further vocational training (as of 1993, 1.5% for firms with more than 10 employees, and 0.5% for firms with less than 10 employees). Twenty percent of this sum is devoted to individual training leave (*congé individuel de formation).* The law also regulates the ways in which employers can discharge this financial obligation, and determines the respective roles of the state, the training institutions, and the employers in the provision, financing, and governance of continuing education and training (see *Payroll Levies; Europe, Western and Southern; European Union: Continuing Vocational Training).*

Paid educational leave (i.e., leave for the purpose of training undertaken off the employers' premises proper and taken on the employee's rather than the employer's initiative) plays a minor role in comparison with employer-provided or other employer-sponsored training. However, the right to such leave does exist, provided that certain conditions for eligibility are met. For example, an employee must have worked for at least 24 months (at least 12 of them with his or her present firm) before he or she is eligible for individual training leave. The length of such leave must not exceed one year in the case of continuous full-time training, or 1,200 hours if the training consists of periodic or part-time courses. The purpose of training leave is defined by the law, namely "to acquire a wider cultural and social outlook." There are certain ceilings fixed by the law such that the employer can refuse a request for leave, for example, if more than 2 percent of a firm's personnel would be on training leave at any time or, more generally, when the employer claims —and the enterprise council agrees—that the absence of an employee will endanger the efficient running of the firm.

Despite these legal provisions, educational leave in France has remained marginal in importance. One of the reasons is that the right to leave is not directly connected to the right to remuneration. This question, which is crucial for the effective utilization of the right to leave, was governed by a complicated set of regulations, depending on the accreditation of the training program, its duration, and the occupational status of the trainee. If the various preconditions are met, the costs for wage maintenance are normally shared between the employers and the state, the exact formula again depending on a number of variables such as the size of the firm and the description and type of the course. It is largely because of these complex regulations concerning remuneration during the leave period and the complicated procedures regulating the leave that participation has been unimpressive (Caspar 1992).

The 1991 amendment of the law has opened up an additional and new type of short-term leave for the purpose of an assessment of individual competencies (*congé de bilan de compétences*). Under this new provision, a worker with a minimum seniority of five years is entitled to three days' leave (an entitlement that can be utilized in a block or in installments), during which the worker can have his or her skills and competencies as well abilities and motivation analyzed. The objective of this analysis is for the worker

to have a basis for the decision to undergo further training. As is the case with the regular training leave, a worker cannot be required by his or her employer to take such leave, and the results of the analysis are strictly confidential between the worker and the institution doing the analysis (see *Recognition and Certification of Skill).*

2.2 Federal Republic of Germany

The 16 federal states (*Länder*) have the power to regulate educational matters autonomously, while the federal government has only very limited jurisdiction in this area. However, since the constitution vests the power to legislate on economic and labor market matters in the federal government, it would be entitled to pass legislation on educational leave. In the absence of such federal legislation, the states are free to regulate the provision of educational leave and, indeed, since the federal government has so far refrained from introducing such legislation, general educational leave laws have been passed by eight states.

These state laws are not uniform but have differing features concerning eligibility, the contents of accreditable educational activities, and procedures for accreditation. The basic provision, however, is identical in eight states in that the laws give the beneficiaries the right to leave for one working week per year or cumulatively for two working weeks for two consecutive years, during which period the salary or wage is maintained in full by the employer.

In the laws of three states, accreditable courses are limited to continuing vocational training and civic education. In the laws of two other states, the provision also includes continuing general education in the range of accreditable activities.

According to the ILO Convention on Paid Educational Leave, it is one of the objectives of such leave to promote "the competent and active participation of workers and their representatives in the life of the undertaking and of the community" . In Germany the concept of civic education echoes these goals. Although the wording of the definition of civic education in the state laws is slightly different, they present essentially the same objective; that is, to help workers to understand their function, role, obligations, and rights, and to enable them to participate actively in social and public life. Under this definition, trade union education is not separate from, but part of, civic education. In fact, it is estimated that about 50 percent of the training programs offered under the rubric of civic education are sponsored by the trade unions and those voluntary organizations that have strong links with the unions. Most programs and courses of continuing education and training, on the other hand, are offered by adult education institutions sponsored by local government (*Volkshochschulen*), while other voluntary organizations account for the remainder (see *Folk High Schools).*

While the concept of *vocational* education is generally well-understood (i.e., to maintain, improve, or expand vocational qualifications and occupational flexibility), the meaning of *general* adult education is unclear. Even in the laws of the two states that specifically mandate general education, the term is not defined. This uncertainty occasionally leads to difficulties when employers refuse to grant educational leave to their employees for general education courses such as language programs unrelated to job requirements.

This is, however, not the only problem employers are having with paid educational leave. Generally, they are opposed to paid educational leave legislation, arguing that it violates their rights. Some have even taken that argument to the courts. In the final instance the Federal Constitutional Court, the highest legal authority, ruled that the state laws were not violating employers' rights. As to the inclusion of civic and labor education into the legal entitlement, the Court said:

> The impact of technical and social change is not confined to the spheres of work or professional life. It affects also the sphere of the family, of society and political life and creates multiple interlinkages between these spheres. Necessarily, this results in links between vocational and civic education. It is therefore in the public interest—not only to increase workers' functional skills and knowledge requisite for the exercise of their jobs but also to enhance the understanding for societal, social and political issues and their interrelationships in order to promote active participation, co-determination and the assumption of responsibilities in matters concerning the state, society, and working life, all elements of a democratic society.

The Court also underscored the necessity of lifelong learning:

> Under the conditions of permanent and accelerating change both technical and social, lifelong learning becomes a pre-requisite for individual "self-realization" and adaptability. Continuing education helps the individual to cope better with and master change both in working and in social life. At the same time it enhances the flexibility of both the economy and society as a whole to adapt to change.

Despite the fact that by 1992 around two-thirds of the German population was covered by provincial legislation and the courts had provided strong endorsement, participation in paid educational leave is generally low (between 1% and 5%). Thus, even taking into account a slight upward trend over the years, participation in these schemes has neither lived up to the aspirations of the trade unions—who were the driving force behind the legislation—nor warranted the fears of the employers who resisted it, in their concern over the costs and the possible loss of productivity.

It is difficult, if not impossible, to analyze with any degree of accuracy the underlying reasons for this low participation rate. The trade unions emphasize that continuing resistance on the part of employers,

and the resultant fear among workers of negative sanctions, are the most important obstacles to higher levels of participation. Employers deny that there are such sanctions. They point out instead that accredited courses and programs very often do not respond to the real needs which, according to them, are primarily for upgrading occupational skills and knowledge. In particular, employers have strong reservations against what they see as trade union education in the guise of civic education, on the one hand, and leisure activities in the guise of general education on the other.

The political discussion about paid education leave continues. Thus, in a 1990 report by an inquiry commission of the federal parliament, the two opposition parties recommended that federal legislation should make paid education leave a universal right throughout Germany, that each person's leave entitlement should be increased to 10 working days per annum, and that each person should be able to accumulate annual entitlements for up to five years. In order to distribute the financial burden more equitably, the commission advocated a collective fund to be financed by a special contribution by employers to unemployment insurance. While this reform of present provisions would probably remove some of the main elements of underutilization, it would not, of course, be seen favorably by employers who argue that any increase in the cost of labor would decrease the international competitiveness of industry in Germany.

In summary, the German experience with paid educational leave suggests that this instrument is underutilized. Nevertheless, most of the employees who utilize the opportunity have traditionally been underrepresented in continuing education and training. It is fair to say that they probably would not have participated without educational leave.

2.3 Sweden

In the mid-1970s, when it became clear that talks between the Swedish Employers' Confederation (SAF) and the two main trade unions (Confederation of Trade Unions or LO, and the Central Organization of Salaried Employees or TCO) would not lead to a general consensus upon which a collective bargaining agreement could be based, a law on educational leave was passed in Sweden (a signatory of the ILO Convention). This law secures the right of all employees, in both the public and private sector, to take leave for educational purposes during working hours.

This law is remarkable for a number of reasons. First, the right to educational leave covers all types of education; that is, general education, vocational training, as well as trade union education. Second, the duration of educational leave is dependent on the length of the course or program chosen. In other words, the law does not set forth a maximum length of leave. But while the law is thus very generous with respect to the contents of the educational activities for which the leave is granted and on the duration of the leave, it is silent about the financial arrangements. Thus, in contrast to the legal provisions in Germany, the 1975 law provides for educational leave but not for *paid* educational leave, deflecting the question of financial support to other laws.

Financial assistance to those taking advantage of their right to educational leave can be sought under different schemes: public labor market training grants (AMS), study assistance, and adult study assistance. The first provides for financial assistance for those trainees undergoing labor market training; that is, unemployed persons or those threatened by unemployment—thus in most cases it does not apply to genuine educational leave of absence as defined above. Study assistance is a mixed system of grants and loans for upper-secondary and postsecondary students. There is a minimum age requirement which stipulates that upper-secondary students must be 20 years of age or older in order to be eligible. There is also an age ceiling which excludes students over 45 years of age from this scheme except in special cases. The loan portion of the scheme is considerable: around 70 percent of the student support (which amounts to about two-thirds of what the average industrial worker earns per month after taxes) is repayable. In addition to a means test, support under this scheme is also dependent on study success, as the loans must be repaid in installments following a six-month period after completion of the studies—and there is an interest rate, which is linked to the prime rate.

The Adult Study Assistance Scheme, introduced in 1976, consists of several subschemes targeted at undereducated adults who wish to pursue full-time or part-time education in order to obtain formal educational qualifications corresponding to those conferred by youth education. The various subschemes can be broken down into three basic forms of financial assistance for adults. First, there is a special adult study allowance that is available for prolonged periods of study, both full-time and part-time. It is primarily awarded for adult basic and secondary education. At the postsecondary school level, it can only be awarded to students enrolled in postsecondary vocational education. The main eligibility criterion is four years of previous employment or comparable social activities (i.e., child-rearing), and there is an age ceiling of 50 years, though this is not strictly applied. In 1992 19,000 full-time grants were awarded under this program. Second, under the Adult Study Assistance Scheme there is an hourly study allowance payable to persons who participate in study circles and incur loss of earnings as a result. However, hourly assistance is available only for certain kinds of courses, in particular those that correspond to the main fields of an elementary school curriculum, trade union education courses, and special courses for handicapped persons. Third, there is a daily study allowance which makes it possible to combine study circle courses with short-term subject studies at folk high schools and "popular academies."

In summary, the Swedish system, while granting opportunities for educational leave to a wide population, targets funding almost exclusively to those with a short initial formal education. It also operates a special program to make sure that the target group is actually reached. Thus considerable funds are devoted to an outreach program at the workplace, and union officials have been given the right to spend time on providing information, counseling, and promoting education during working hours, thus acting in the capacity of education brokers (see *Worker Education and Labor Education; Student Counseling; Student Outreach; Student Support Systems*).

3. Legal Provision for Educational Leave for Specific Groups

While legislation for general education leave is limited to only a few countries, many industrialized countries have some legal provision for educational leave for specific populations, groups, or employees with particular functions or responsibilities. The most important among these in terms of numbers affected are union officials and elected members of enterprise councils who have the right to take time off during working hours for courses that prepare them for tasks relating to these functions. Such a legal right, which is often granted without full pay, exists in several Western European countries, such as Germany (where such leave is paid), France, and Sweden (where it is unpaid). It is also often contained in collective bargaining agreements (Windmuller et al. 1987). Comparable rights do exist in some countries for health and security officers in enterprises. Other examples include the representatives of handicapped employees (in Germany) and immigrants who may be eligible for paid educational leave in order to learn the country's language (as in Sweden). Many countries have leave provisions for employees in public service, most often for teachers, but also for judges or others. Still, for these groups, participation in continuing education during work time is often a privilege and not an individual right in the sense that it could be successfully claimed or enforced in court if the employer refused to grant it (Levin and Schütze 1983).

4. Educational Leave in Collective Bargaining Agreements

While there are thus a number of countries with legal provision for educational leave, the majority of countries have left this field to employers and unions to be dealt with by collective bargaining. This is even true in some countries such as France where legislation has only taken up agreements reached by their social partners in order to rubber stamp them and make the accords reached between employer and unions generally applicable.

4.1 Italy

Most prominent among the OECD countries is the Italian "150 hours" scheme. Although there is no national legislation for general paid educational leave in Italy (which has not signed the ILO Convention), there is a law of 1970 which must be considered as the forerunner of an educational leave scheme by having provided some of the framework for collective bargaining agreements. The law stipulates the right of workers to time off during working hours to enroll in recognized courses in primary, secondary, and technical schools, thus allowing them to take courses and sit examinations. Nothing, however, is said in the law about remuneration during such leave so that this question is left to the bargaining process. A collective agreement between employers and the metalworkers' union, struck in 1973, has become a model for agreements since adopted by other sectors of industry. The two salient, distinguishing features of this agreement are the following.

First the right to leave is conceived as a collective rather than an individual right, because time off during working hours is granted to the workers of a firm as a group. Paid time off for study purposes is thus allotted in a block to the total personnel in form of a fund of available leave hours, the amount of which is calculated as a function of the number of workers employed in the firm. The formula according to which the fund of hours for study leave is calculated is $H = 10 \times 3 \times N$ (where H is the amount of hours, and N the number of workers). Of this total amount of paid time off for study, the individual worker can use a maximum of 150 hours over a three-year period—hence the name of the scheme. The leave is granted on the condition that the worker devotes a number of nonwork hours to study which must be equal to the hours of paid educational leave received from the collective fund. The decision as to who among the workers will profit from the collectively allotted paid time off for studies (i.e., the distribution of available leave time) lies with the enterprise council rather than with the employer.

The second interesting feature of the scheme, which makes it distinct from the others discussed above, is that the primary utilization of the 150 hours scheme occurs in the area of general education among those workers who are underprivileged with respect to previous educational attainment. Compulsory school attendance in Italy was raised from five years to eight years only in 1963, leaving most of the older workers (the trade unions' estimate at the time was 70%) without a secondary school-leaving diploma. Thus, priority is given to compensatory rather than to civic or vocational education, and the main beneficiaries of

the scheme have been older workers trying to pass their *licencia media* (i.e., the lower secondary school diploma). This *licencia media* is of particular importance, since it has come to be the prerequisite not only for job opportunities in the public sector but also for participation in most of the qualified vocational training programs. One of the major problems with the utilization of the 150 scheme for this purpose is that the courses leading to a *licencia media* require 350 to 400 hours of course work; consequently, workers must use some 250 hours or so of their own time—just for attending the course, not counting the time required for individual study and preparation for examinations. Nevertheless, participation in these courses has been significant, amounting to 90,000–100,000 participants per year in the 1970s and early 1980s and 62,000 in 1990.

4.2 United Kingdom

There are a number of other European countries in which leave schemes can be found in collective bargaining agreements, although their impact has been relatively small. The United Kingdom can be mentioned here since a number of collective agreements at the level of the individual enterprise contain leave clauses. On the whole, the granting of educational leave is mostly at the discretion of the employer and there is no obligation on the part of the firm to maintain wages during attendance on a course or to pay for the costs of the course. There was a growth in firm-based initiatives during the 1980s, however, which gave employees an entitlement to education and training. This entitlement concerns mostly financial assistance but not time off work, and thus does not qualify as paid leave as defined in this entry. The United Kingdom under a Conservative government has moved away from a previous system of statutory levies on the payroll as a means of promoting training either by the enterprises themselves or by industrial training boards toward one of leaving the decision whether to provide training for the workforce to the private sector. In a nutshell, it is fair to say that paid educational leave legislation is not an important issue in the United Kingdom, although there have been some significant developments at company level.

4.3 Federal Republic of Germany

Germany can be mentioned again since some 220 collective bargaining agreements have included the right to educational leave, though not all such leave is paid and the majority of schemes are limited to enterprise council members. Eligibility under these schemes overlaps to a considerable extent with the legal provisions for paid educational leave in the states where such legislation exists (see above). Although the former and the latter are not mutually exclusive in principle, they are usually in practice.

5. Conclusion

The situation concerning educational leave of absence varies considerably from country to country. Hence to attempt a general assessment of the success or failure of the concept of educational leave is impossible. However, a few conclusions can be drawn.

The most obvious is that, while some countries have some kind of provision for educational leave, the map still reveals some important blank spots. Thus, it is evident that there has been no universal and sweeping movement in favor of educational leave. This should not lead, however, to the assessment that the original drive has lost its momentum. Rather, it could be claimed that progress continues to be made, although in a piecemeal manner and by trial and error rather than by comprehensive blueprint or master plan (ILO 1991). Thus, while in Germany and France legislation has been extended in favor of educational leave, in other countries—such as Italy and Belgium—governments have started to look into a thorough reform of existing schemes in order to bring them into line with newer developments in employment and in the workplace. In other jurisdictions, notably the United States and the United Kingdom, there is no government involvement, and the whole field is left to the process of collective bargaining or to action by individual employers.

To assess the actual impact of educational leave in the industrialized countries is very difficult and depends largely on the author's viewpoint. As an instrument of influencing the supply of qualified labor —an important consideration in times of high unemployment—educational leave has so far had only a marginal effect, or none at all. The reasons are many: low overall participation figures, short average leave duration with no possibility of accumulating leave over several years, and the provisions contained in most laws or agreements designed to avoid a situation where too many workers of the same firm use their leave entitlement simultaneously, thus obliging the enterprise to hire additional staff (Degen and Nuissl 1984, Mace and Yarnit 1987, Schütze and Istance 1987).

On the whole, however, paid educational leave has been an instrument for opening up education and training opportunities to workers who, without such an entitlement, would most probably not have had the chance. The fact that the entitlement has been utilized only to a marginal extent is due to a number of factors: far-reaching changes in the economic situation; higher levels of unemployment and underemployment; and lack of sufficient financial support, suitable courses, and outreach programs for the target groups—variables that tend to operate against educational leave and its efficient utilization.

On the other hand, it is undeniable that there is increasing demand for educational opportunities. Lifelong learning is increasingly accepted not only as an individual right but as a necessity as technological and social change accelerate, transforming the world in a way that makes continuing learning and training a prerequisite for growth and individual success. It is recognition of this development that keeps paid educational leave on the agenda of trade unions in many countries. Trade unions have been and remain the major driving force behind demands for educational leave, as part of collective agreements and legislation, and the implementation of leave provisions.

Employers, on the other hand, while recognizing the need for increased continuing education and training of their workers and expanding, often massively, their own provision of training, find paid educational leave too rigid and insufficiently geared to enterprises' needs, since in most cases they or their associations cannot themselves provide, or substantially influence, the programs under the leave entitlement. To the extent that employers step up their own efforts to provide continuing education and training for their workers, either on their own premises or by financially supporting participation in courses by external providers, and that unions or enterprise councils have a say in what kind of education or training is provided and to whom, paid educational leave will probably lose its importance. However, where this is not the case, paid educational leave will remain an important instrument for enhancing workers' participation in further education and training in order to promote individual development and social mobility.

See also: Demand, Supply, and Finance of Adult Education; Legislation in Adult Education; Time Policies for Lifelong Learning; Payroll Levies; Worker Education and Labor Education; International Labour Organisation; European Union: Continuing Vocational Training

References

Caspar P 1992 France. In: Jarvis P (ed.) 1992 *Perspectives on Adult Education and Training in Europe.* National Institute of Adult and Continuing Education, Leicester

Degen G, Nuissl E 1984 *Educational Leave and the Labor Market in Europe.* European Centre for the Development of Vocational Training, Berlin

International Labour Organisation (ILO) 1991 *Human Resources Development: Vocational Guidance and Training, Paid Educational Leave.* International Labour Organisation, Geneva

Levin H, Schütze H G (eds.) 1983 *Financing Recurrent Education: Strategies for Improving Employment, Job Opportunities, and Productivity.* Sage, Beverly Hills, California

Mace J, Yarnit M 1987 *Time Off to Learn: Paid Educational Leave and Low-paid Workers.* Methuen, London

Organisation for Economic Co-operation and Development (OECD) 1976 *Developments in Educational Leave of Absence.* OECD, Paris

Organisation for Economic Co-operation and Development (OECD) 1978 *Alternation Between Work and Education: A Study of Educational Leave of Absence at Enterprise*

Level. OECD, Paris

Schütze H, Istance D 1987 *Recurrent Education Revisited: Modes of Participation and Financing.* Almqvist and Wicksell International, Stockholm

von Moltke K, Schneevoigt N 1977 *Educational Leave for Employees: European Experience for American Consideration.* Jossey-Bass, San Francisco, California

Windmuller J P et al. 1987 *Collective Bargaining in Industrialized Market Economies: A Reappraisal.* International Labour Organisation, Geneva

Further Reading

Adler P S (ed.) 1992 *Technology and the Future of Work.*
Oxford University Press, Oxford

Blanchflower D G, Freeman R B 1992 Unionism in the United States and other advanced OECD countries. *Industrial Relations* 31: 56–77

Cordova E 1990 Collective Bargaining. In Blanpain R et al. (eds.) *Comparative Labour Law and Industrial Relations in Industrialized Market Economies,* Vol. 2, Kluwer, Deventer

Katz H 1993 Decentralization of collective bargaining: A literature review and comparative analysis. *Industrial and Labor Relations Review* 47(1): 3–22

Soskice D 1990 Wage determination: The changing role of institutions in advanced industrialized countries. *Oxford Review of Economic Policy* Winter: 36–61

Traxler F 1994 Collective bargaining: Level and coverage in OECD countries. *Employment Outlook* July: 167–194

Partnerships: Initial and Adult Education

D. Hirsch

During the 1980s, there was a growing tendency in most industrialized countries for public education systems to strengthen links with "outsiders," and particularly with private business. This was stimulated by two perceptions: that education was failing to provide the economy with workers with the right kinds of skill, and that education systems were failing in their own terms (e.g., by creating dropouts) in ways that could be alleviated by making them into less closed systems. By the early 1990s, it appeared that the trend toward partnership had become a permanent shift rather than an incidental fashion, in that private sector involvement had been built into the institutional and, in some cases financial, structures governing education. This entry gives an overview of that shift in four sectors: nonvocational secondary education, initial vocational education, higher education, and adult education and training. It concentrates on public–private partnerships, but public–community partnerships are also referred to.

1. Nonvocational Secondary Education

Direct links between individual businesses and secondary schools are generally based on the idea that a school curriculum needs to become more relevant to the future of the pupil in the workplace, even before the start of any directly "vocational" education program. This view has become particularly pronounced in Anglo-Saxon countries such as the United States and the United Kingdom, where there has been less reliance on vocational schooling than in Continental Europe, for example. Loud complaints by employers

in these countries about inadequate skills held by school leavers have led in part to attempts to improve vocational options, but also to a reassessment of the secondary school curriculum.

A first response was to create more liaison between businesses and schools, for example, through school visits by company staff and by work experience placements for students. However, a more sophisticated level of contact has involved a measure of curriculum reform planned in collaboration with business, and the involvement of business leaders in running schools on governing bodies. An important idea behind such change is that under a "traditional" school curriculum with a didactic teaching style, children are not learning the important generic skills such as effective teamwork, good communication, problem-solving, and decision-taking that are most needed in advanced modern enterprises. Businesses have contributed both in terms of policy-making and practical assistance to a more project-oriented style of learning, where teachers become "facilitators" rather than lecturers, and there is a strong stress on cultivating initiative-taking skills.

One of the leading programs to promote this type of partnership has been the Technical and Vocational Education Initiative (TVEI) in the United Kingdom. This initiative was originated in 1983 by the Manpower Services Commission, an agency dependent on the Department of Employment, but implemented by local education authorities. The combination of centrally initiated principles and local implementation in this scheme has not always been duplicated in other systems. North America has many individual links between businesses and schools, but weak methods of using such partnerships to implement general curriculum change. Many centralized European countries have the tools for curriculum reform, but find it hard to stimulate initiative at the local level.

2. Initial Vocational Education

Countries with strong upper-secondary vocational schooling tend to have a longstanding partnership between business and education, but in some cases this partnership does not appear to have performed well in terms of ensuring sensitivity of this system to local labor market needs. The biggest problem is that the curriculum of vocational schools is often devised at a peak level, in consultation with trade organizations but not in close cooperation with individual businesses.

The system that has most clearly avoided this problem is the "dual" system dominant in Germany, Austria, and Switzerland. Apprentices recruited and paid by employers spend one or two days a week in vocational schools, and the remainder with the firm learning a trade. This system is widely recognized as producing high quality and highly relevant vocational education and training, through a well-developed partnership involving the federal government, vocational schools, chambers of commerce, individual employers, and trade unions. The chambers of commerce play a crucial role, coordinating provision and running the final examinations.

Countries such as Sweden, France, and the Netherlands, which have vocational systems governed and supervised from the school side, have felt the need to improve their links with the labor market through partnerships similar to those described above under general secondary education. In particular, they have attempted to increase the amount of work experience involved, through the principle of "alternance" between classroom and workplace, without moving over to a full apprenticeship system where the trainee is based at and paid by a particular firm (see *Recurrent Education*).

Nevertheless, there is much debate in these countries, as in ones with weak vocational systems, about the merits of switching to a dual system. There are two factors which have tended to prevent this from happening, both crucial in the operation of partnerships. The first is the relationship between educational priorities and the interests of a particular firm. In countries where there is not a long tradition of cooperation between public and private sectors in initial training, there is a fear that the long-term interests of young people will not be best served by basing them with a single employer. The second is the dependence of a dual system on long-established institutional strengths, in particular companies' ability to provide high quality training and their willingness to cooperate to create a powerful local institution in the chamber of commerce. In countries where these traditions do not already exist, they are hard to replicate.

3. Higher Education

Universities and other higher education institutions have a stronger tradition of collaboration with private businesses and other outside institutions than do schools. However, within public higher education systems, such links have not been universally strong, and many institutions have been accused of having inadequate links with research and the labor market. New partnerships between higher education and outsiders have taken broadly three forms.

First, they have sought to strengthen the transfer of knowledge and technologies from universities to outside organizations, and in particular to private industry. This has been particularly true in the sciences, and the emergence of science parks has been a practical attempt to apply the principle of bringing university research and industrial research closer together. However, this kind of partnership has created some fundamental dilemmas. One is how to distribute ultimately scarce intellectual resources within academic institutions between basic research and commercial applications. Another is how to establish comfortable working relationships between institutions committed to pursuing knowledge for the public good and those who have an interest in using it for their own private gain, in particular through the use of patents.

Second, partnerships are being used to change the nature of higher education teaching. As with schools, the aim here is to make institutions more sensitive to the needs of the labor market. So far, the main way that they have become so is by introducing a variety of new courses in addition to the university degree, oriented in particular to continuing professional development. Progress here has varied immensely from one country to another: in North America, higher education institutions supply over one-fourth of the adult training market; in most European countries, the market share is well under 10 percent. Another potential change, which has so far progressed little, is reform of the way subjects are taught at degree level. There seems to be a particularly strong need for this in humanities subjects, whose graduates have a weaker position on the labor market than they did in the past. However, relatively weak links between business and universities in this sector has made any progress in reforming teaching methods slow.

Finally, public–private links are creating new financial relationships within higher education. Even in countries without private universities, private funding of university research has tended to increase, albeit from a low base. Furthermore, the European model of higher education institutions funded fully by the central government block grant is beginning to be undermined, and the concept of demand-driven funding—depending on student flows—has opened up the possibility of private resources on the teaching as well as the research side of higher education.

4. Adult Education and Training

In the case of adult education and training, new partnerships have involved not just those between existing educational institutions and others, but in many cases a new philosophy on how provision should be made. Advocates of adult education traditionally stressed the principle of giving adults equal access to educational resources, with the result that low-cost public provision became the dominant model. The broader notion of "lifelong learning"—for leisure, general intellectual, and work purposes—implies a greater range of providers, and in many cases provision based on partnerships.

In the case of learning for work, it has become widely accepted that where learning is "situated" in the context of the workplace in which it needs to be applied, it can potentially be more effective than when it is divorced in the context of educational institutions. This can apply not just to technical skills related to particular jobs but, for example, to basic skills such as literacy and numeracy. Yet the professional expertise in teaching such skills resides in colleges; hence the need for collaboration between education and industry to create a system capable of teaching general as well as technical skills in a relevant context. A good example of a country attempting to confront this problem is Australia. There, the system of Technical and Further Education (TAFE) colleges has traditionally been relatively detached from the workplace. However, the restructuring of industrial awards in the late 1980s in the attempt to link pay and rank to certified competence in particular areas made it necessary for TAFE to work more closely with industry, if only to define at a national level the competence standards that were to be recognized.

In the case of learning not connected to work, there has been a trend in some countries away from institutional and toward community-based provision. Often the biggest cause of this has been resource constraints, in particular as some countries attempt to concentrate subsidies for adult learning on vocationally relevant activity. However, there has also been a positive desire, both on the community and the vocational side, to site learning closer to where it will be applied. In some cases, this has led to the concept of the "learning community," for example, in the case of Japanese cities attempting to use "lifelong learning" as an instrument of community development. In these cases, as many actors as possible are brought into the learning enterprise (see *Japan: Social and Adult Education*).

5. Conclusion: A New Educational Compact

Partnerships imply new understandings between public and private actors on the division of responsibility between them for the management and financing of education and training. However, the picture is different at the various levels described in this entry. In the case of initial secondary education, despite increased private sector participation in management, financing responsibility remains firmly with the central level of public authority. In both initial vocational and higher education, the trend is toward a sharing of both management and financing responsibility. In the case of adult education and training, the vast majority of new resources are expected to come from the private sector, but in many cases, for strategic reasons, the state wants some say in their management.

Thus, education is becoming more of a shared enterprise, but at each part of the system the share in financing and decision-making is different. There is perhaps an implicit new social contract between the main partners in education, in which partners are willing to share responsibilities in different parts of the system, even in cases where financial burdens are skewed. Moreover, many partnerships require the involvement of private partners who do not gain directly from the specific project in which they take part, even though the whole economy may gain from the collection of all projects. Partnerships then involve a degree of semi-altruistic behavior by actors who rely on others to act in the same way in order that everyone may benefit.

See also: Recurrent Education; Government Role in Adult Education and Training; Market Concepts in Provision

Bibliography

Organisation for Economic Co-Operation and Development (OECD) 1984 *Industry and University—New Forms of Co-operation and Communication*. OECD, Centre for Educational Research and Innovation, Paris

Organisation for Economic Co-Operation and Development (OECD) 1992 *Schools and Business—A New Partnership*. OECD, Centre for Educational Research and Innovation, Paris

Tuijnman A C, Van Der Kamp M (eds.) 1992 *Learning Across the Lifespan: Theories, Research, Policies*. Pergamon Press, Oxford

Payroll Levies

A. Ziderman

This entry summarizes international experience in over 30 countries where levies on the payroll of enterprises have become a principal source of financing skills training. A distinction is drawn between the more traditional revenue-raising schemes (the Latin American model) and the newer levy-grant schemes. It presents an economic rationale for their growing use and considers some practical implementation issues.

1. Securing Stable Funding for Training

In most countries, governments have assumed a significant role in both the provision and finance of skills training (see *Government Role in Adult Education and Training*). Yet government budgets may not provide a secure source of finance. This is particularly so in developing countries where tax base, relying heavily on indirect (commodity) taxation, may be very narrow and where severe budgetary constraints and instability are typical.

How then may stable funding be secured for vocational training and skills development? A number of countries have earmarked the proceeds from particular taxes to finance training: for example, in Ecuador there is a 0.2 percent import tax on industrial machinery, and a levy of 0.25 percent of the value of large construction projects has been imposed in Hong Kong, where there is also a 0.03 percent levy on the value of clothing exports.

While these schemes are ad hoc, a more comprehensive system operates in Kenya. Under the 1973 Industry Training Act, training committees established in each of the 12 main sectors are empowered to impose their own form of training levy, as appears appropriate to the sector in question. Thus, the training committee for building and construction imposes a levy on all large construction projects; the levy for timber is based on quarterly turnover and for sugar on tonnage of sugar produced.

While these schemes have succeeded in generating funds for training in the industries concerned, they do not seem to have been regarded as an appropriate device for adoption elsewhere. However, in some 30 countries, levies on the payroll of enterprises have become a principal source for financing skills training, both in specialized training institutions (usually under the aegis of a national training authority) and in enterprises. The attraction of these levies is that they form a sheltered source of resources for training, as well as more generally offering a means of mobilizing funds otherwise inaccessible to the public sector.

These schemes are not free of criticism as they do raise some fundamental issues in public finance. Yet while there is a general predisposition to regard earmarked taxes as unnecessarily constraining on governments, such taxes can act as an insulator against economic uncertainty and budgetary parsimony, in situations where it is societally desirable to take a longer term view. The provision of skills to facilitate and meet the needs of economic growth and technological change may constitute a case in point. Be that as it may, this method of training finance has emerged as the most widely adopted alternative to government budgetary allocations.

2. Alternative Payroll Levy Schemes

With some variation, there are basically two major types of payroll tax schemes, reflecting rather different objectives. The traditional scheme—termed "The Latin American model" after its origin in the region—is concerned essentially with generating revenues to finance training provided by the public sector. The newer levy-grant (or rebate) scheme aims at encouraging in-plant provision of training by firms themselves through financial incentives; in these cases, payroll tax rebates are offered to enterprises to set up, or broaden, established programs of inservice training.

Any particular scheme may entail additional, complementary objectives. For example, the payroll tax-training scheme in Singapore was, at the outset, part of a broad-based economic restructuring program, aimed at skill upgrading for the whole labor force and, ultimately, a more capital-intensive, mechanized economy. However, such broader policy objectives have been largely absent in motivating the establishment or design of payroll levy schemes in developing countries.

2.1 Revenue-raising Schemes

Under this group of tax-financed training schemes, revenues are earmarked to finance training provided by the state or a national training authority. Such schemes are typically found in Latin American and Caribbean countries.

First introduced in Brazil in the early 1940s, payroll levies of this type are in place in a dozen countries in the region. Revenues from these levies have been employed to build up national training systems, usually run by a quasi-autonomous national training authority which, at its own training centers, provides a wide range of pre-employment and inservice training courses for manual workers, office workers, and managers.

In revenue-raising schemes, payroll levies are the dominant, but may not be the sole, source of finance of the national training authority. Kugler and Reyes (1978) and Ducci (1991) provide additional details on these schemes.

The emphasis in these schemes is on public sector training provision, rather than on the encouragement of firms to undertake training themselves. A variant of the scheme (operating in Brazil, Venezuela and more recently in Honduras) allows for at least partial exemption from the levy payment for those firms that provide an acceptable in-company training program. As well as raising revenue for public sector provision of training, this option also offers financial incentives to employers to set up their own in-plant training programs.

2.2 Levy-grant Schemes

In rebate, or levy-grant schemes the payroll levy is linked to a disbursement scheme, in which firms receive grants related to their level of provision of designated forms of training. Rather than using the payroll tax proceeds to establish public sector industrial training centers, the disbursement scheme creates incentives for firms to set up, broaden, or raise the quality of, programs of inservice training, thus qualifying for a rebate (usually up to a specified percentage of the tax paid). However, the efficacy of training grants and, indeed, of training subsidy schemes more generally, in leading to more or better enterprise training, remains an open question (see *Market Concepts in Provision*).

In addition to the dual aims of raising the quality and quantity of enterprise training, some levy-grant schemes have emphasized the objective of countering interfirm poaching of trained workers, via training cost redistribution. The levy-grant scheme introduced in the United Kingdom under the 1964 Industrial Training Act, the most comprehensive levy-grant scheme ever to be implemented, was based largely on the view that the poaching of trained workers was both prevalent and discouraged firms from training, thus leading to an undersupply of skilled workers.

Some 30 industrial training boards were established, each with statutory powers to exact a levy (in most cases based on a percentage of payroll) from firms within its jurisdiction. The bulk of these funds were distributed to firms in relation to their training efforts; firms that did little or no training would contribute to the costs of firms that trained in substantial numbers.

However the poaching rationale for a levy-grant system can be faulted on economic grounds. As argued by Becker (1964) the cost of general training (i.e., skills transferable between firms) is largely passed on to the workers during the training period; thus grants made to firms for training that is general represents a reimbursement for training costs not in fact borne by the training firm. Firm-specific training is largely financed by training firms but is not transferable; grants

for training that is specific subsidize training needlessly. Lees and Chiplin (1970) offer a good account of the "poaching illusion." Where market conditions are conducive to employer finance of general training, interfirm poaching is unlikely to be important (Katz and Ziderman 1990).

The United Kingdom levy-grant system, overambitious and unwieldy, was dismantled within two decades; Ziderman (1978) and Dougherty and Tan (1991) provide critical reviews of the workings of the Act.

2.3 Geographical Distribution

Table 1 shows the geographical distribution of payroll tax schemes across developing countries by broad

Table 1
Earmarked payroll taxes used to finance training in developing countries, by region[a]

Region	Revenue-raising scheme	Rebate scheme
Africa	Mauritania[b]	Benin[b]
	Zaire	Botswana[c]
		Ivory Coast
		Mauritius
		Nigeria
		Togo
		Zimbabwe
Asia		Fiji
		Malaysia
		Singapore
		Taiwan[e]
		Korea[d]
Latin America and the Caribbean	Argentina[e]	
	Barbados	
	Brazil[e]	
	Chile[e]	
	Colombia	
	Costa Rica	
	Dominican Republic	
	Ecuador	
	Guatemala	
	Haiti[b]	
	Honduras	
	Jamaica	
	Paraguay	
	Peru	
	Venezuela	
North Africa and the Middle east	Morocco	Jordan[c]
	Turkey	Tunisia

Source: Whalley and Ziderman (1990)
a El Salvador, Pakistan, and Senegal have all considered and rejected proposals for a payroll tax   b Revenues in practice not earmarked for training   c Planned, not yet implemented   d Not, strictly speaking, a payroll tax scheme (see text)   e Not in operation since 1974 Taiwan; 1976 Chile; 1981 Argentina

region and type of scheme. Revenue-raising schemes have not spread widely in the developing world beyond Latin America; the only other examples of pure revenue-raising payroll taxes seem to be those in Zaire and Morocco, where a similar payroll tax system is in force, and Turkey, where one is planned. While rebate schemes are absent in the Latin American countries, this seems to be the preferred form of payroll levy scheme in other continents.

Such schemes are typically found in lower-middle level income countries (as defined by the World Bank, countries with GNP per capita in the range US\$580 to US\$2,335 in 1989); nearly half of all such countries have introduced payroll taxes of this type.

Levy-grant schemes are to be found in some OECD countries, the most comprehensive in the Republic of Ireland; a more limited scheme, relating to three sectors only, is in place in New Zealand. The French apprenticeship tax, too, is based on a percentage of payroll. In Germany, the recommendation of the Edding Commission in 1974 to introduce a national payroll levy to finance a central apprenticeship fund was never implemented; however, such a fund is to be found in the construction industry, financed by a 3 percent payroll tax in that sector. However, these schemes are somewhat exceptional; industrial countries generally have eschewed the use of payroll taxation for training (see *Demand, Supply, and Finance of Adult Education; Paid Educational Leave and Collective Bargaining*).

The division between countries with revenue- raising schemes and those operating rebate schemes is analytically useful; yet, as with all institutional generalizations, the distinction should not be pressed too far. Countries may seek dual objectives from payroll levy schemes which, in practice, may incorporate elements of both approaches.

Thus in 1979, the Industrial Training Fund in Nigeria (the national training authority financed by the training levy), opened its first vocational training center (with direct, state-provided training). This supplemented its major activity of encouraging enterprises to train through the offer of financial incentives. In discussions in Tanzania for the introduction of a new payroll levy, earmarked for training, the proceeds would largely replace government finance of labor ministry vocational training centers; however, they would also finance an incentive scheme of grants to encourage apprenticeship and other designated forms of enterprise training. Similarly, in a number of Latin American countries, national training authorities (which are financed by payroll levies), have broadened their traditional role as leading training institutions, to become outward-oriented, encompassing the promotion and guidance of training activities in outside enterprises (Ducci 1991). Colombia, Peru, and Paraguay provide examples of this dual, complementary approach (see *Latin America: National Training Agencies*).

2.4 Coverage of Schemes

Most rates of tax vary from 0.5 to 2 percent. Tax rates have tended to be stable over time, although there are some exceptions. In Singapore, rates were set initially at 2 percent and raised some months later to 4 percent of the payroll of low-paid workers only; the rate subsequently fell and is now 1 percent. In Nigeria the rate, which stood at 3 percent at the outset, fell quickly to 1 percent, while in Morocco the rate has been raised from 1 to 1.6 percent.

Countries also differ in the sectors covered by the tax. In some cases agriculture and, more frequently, the public sector, is excluded. Generally, there are uniform tax rates across sectors, but in some countries (such as Colombia and Honduras) the government sector is taxed at a lower rate. In some countries, larger firms pay a higher tax (in both Colombia and Brazil, there is a surtax of 0.2 percent on firms with more than 500 employees), while in others small firms are exempt. Such exemptions are usually based on the number of employees (fewer than five workers in Honduras, Peru and Venezuela, fewer than 10 in Colombia, fewer than 25 in Nigeria), while in Costa Rica and Honduras exemption may be claimed, alternatively, on the basis of size of capital assets. In South Africa, 27 industrial training boards are currently in operation; most collect a training levy, either based on payroll or a flat rate per employee.

3. Economic Rationale

Why are earmarked payroll taxes so widely used, particularly in the developing world? Payroll taxes for financing training are formally levied on enterprises and are widely believed to be borne by these same enterprises, making these taxes appear to be "fair," but on whom does the ultimate burden of these levies fall? Do firms themselves indeed bear these taxes or are they passed on, either to the consumer in the form of higher prices (and thus indirectly to labor) or directly to labor in terms of lower net-of-tax wages?

While these issues have not been examined empirically for developing countries in relation to training levies, there is a sizeable literature relating to the economic effects of payroll taxes in general in industrialized countries. This literature strongly suggests that the incidence of payroll levies falls largely on labor in the form of lower real wages; see Levin (1983) for a reiteration of this view. The authoritative source of this empirical evidence is the study by Brittain (1972) of the payroll tax as a financing vehicle for the wider social security system in the United States. A recent study for Chile is provided in Gruber (1995). If it is accepted that workers bear the burden of payroll taxes, then their use to finance vocational training involves taxing employees rather than firms. This issue is treated more fully in Whalley and Ziderman (1990).

The finding that the worker bears the burden of payroll levies may provide a rationale for their use to finance training programs, in terms of a reverse social security argument. Viewed in this way, workers receive the benefits of training while they are young, and subsequently pay the taxes through the rest of their working life to cover the training costs of workers who follow them (unlike national social security schemes, where payment of contributions precedes receipt of benefits, over the life cycle). Thus, transfers take place to younger workers from older ones through the tax financing training, but over the worker life-cycle individual benefits approximate taxes paid.

Payroll taxation to finance training may thus be regarded as a form of benefit taxation, but how closely do individual tax payments in fact match the training benefits received? The nature of training programs is such that costs will differ markedly by sector; workers in the financial sector, for instance, clearly need to undergo very different training programs from workers in heavy manufacturing. These differing training programs are likely to involve substantially different training expenditures. The desirability of achieving benefit-related taxation would suggest the introduction of appropriate differentiation in tax rates across industry to reflect these variations in training costs. While developing countries usually have uniform payroll levies by sector, in some countries, though notably developed economies, the levy rates varies across different industries or is applied in some but not in others. For example, in New Zealand it is in force in the clothing, textile, and engineering industries, while in the United Kingdom scheme the individual industry boards were free to set their own levy rate. Within sectors, the larger absolute tax payments made by higher earning workers (given that payroll taxes are proportional, with no ceilings in operation), is consistent with the positive relationship between the level of a worker's formal education (and therefore earnings) and the amount of training received on-the-job (Mincer 1974).

If workers ultimately bear much of the cost of payroll levies, how equitably are training opportunities spread among workers? This may be very much influenced by the main purpose that the payroll tax serves (whether to raise revenues for public sector training provision or to encourage on-the-job training by firms), as well as by the particular set of training programs that are financed by the tax. For payroll tax schemes without rebates, which finance public sector training centers, the question at issue is: are training opportunities well spread across the various sections of the labor force, by age (thus offsetting the start up problem), by skill and occupational category, and by education level? Presumably, workers from levy-exempt firms are entitled to attend public sector training courses financed by the payroll tax,

thereby reaping the benefits of the scheme without contributing to its costs. How far this constitutes a serious problem will depend on the number of firms and workers involved.

Finally, the reverse social security argument requires that the funds raised by payroll taxation indeed be earmarked for training. Unfortunately this is not always the case. For example, in both Brazil and Singapore, revenues have been subject to diversion to other uses, and there remains the risk that funds will not be spent but amassed as surpluses, as has occurred in some Latin American countries, Kenya, Nigeria, and Singapore. Again, in practice, the training levies in Benin, Haiti, and Mauritania, for differing reasons, have not been earmarked for training but rather enter public revenues. For example, in Haiti payroll taxes are not now earmarked for training, as all taxes (and other revenues including university student fees) have been agglomerated and pass to the Treasury.

4. Practical Considerations

Enterprise payroll levies have provided stable and adequate funding for the finance of training in a number of developing countries. These taxes have probably mobilized additional funding to the public sector and have in most cases been relatively easy to administer. They have proved to be a particularly useful device for training institution building, especially in the development and strengthening of national training agencies. On the other hand these levies and, where this is the case, the national training institutions that they support, have been subject to criticism on a number of counts.

Payroll levies, being a tax on labor, tend to raise the price of labor relative to capital. By encouraging, on the margin, a move towards more capital-intensive techniques of production, they may inhibit employment growth, a disadvantage less relevant to alternative taxes, such as value-added or sales taxation. Such effects are unlikely to be pronounced, however, given the moderate tax rate levels and the possibility of passing the burden of the taxes onto workers or consumers.

Payroll levies may constitute an oversheltered source of funding, leading to unspent surpluses. The levy rate may be set at the outset at a level which generates more revenues than the administration can spend and is adjusted downwards subsequently (as in Nigeria). More usually, a rate that may have been appropriate at one time is not revised downwards as financing needs change. There is the danger that surpluses may lead to inefficiencies and top-heavy, bureaucratic administrations; alternatively, surpluses may lead to the utilization of payroll levy funds for nontraining purposes, thus considerably weakening the benefit rationale. Thus the Colombian national training authority, SENA, financed by a 2 percent payroll levy established in 1957, has built up surpluses, encouraging the gradual expansion into other areas such as agriculture, construction, and self-employment training, only loosely tied to the firms that pay the levy. The process has been accelerated by Law 55 which has moved SENA into broader areas of education even further removed from its original remit.

This example highlights the basic dilemma: how to accommodate the need for flexibility in levy yield to reflect changing expenditure requirements (and avoid surpluses) without forgoing the benefit of stable funding. This might be achieved by subjecting the levy rate to review, say, every five years, but guaranteeing a constant rate within the quinquennium. This would leave the training authority free to plan over the medium term but not allow revenues to move out of line with needs over the longer run.

While payroll levy financing on training can be broadly justified in benefit principle terms—a view endorsed by Bird (1984)—in practice many schemes have permitted a considerable departure from this principle, thus undermining the economic rationale for the levy. The following list suggests a number of general points that should guide the operation of payroll levy schemes, with the aim of maintaining the benefit relation between levy payers and training beneficiaries:

(a) Levies should be subject to periodic review to obviate the accumulation of surpluses.

(b) Levies should, where possible, vary across sector and industry to reflect differing skill composition of the labor force and training needs.

(c) Training authorities should not venture into extraneous activities.

(d) The range of training services and courses provided should be very broadly based, reflecting the range of the industry's need.

(e) Levies should be designed to promote training by enterprises.

5. Emerging Trends

The desirability of using payroll taxes to finance training, compared to the other alternatives available to developing country governments, is likely to be contingent upon the stage of a country's development. Low-income developing countries may have only limited access to such broadly based taxes as value-added taxes and tend to rely instead on trade taxes and specific excises such as on drink, tobacco, and gasoline. Where the financing options of governments are limited, as in lower income countries, payroll taxes remain attractive. However, they may not be administratively feasible; mechanisms for tax collection may

not be in place, and enterprises may resist imposition of the levy, as was the case in El Salvador. It has been noted that very few lower income countries resort to payroll levies to finance training.

For countries in the lower-middle income range, and where more broadly based financing alternatives are available, genuine issues of choice come to the fore. The reverse social security rationale for the use of payroll taxes to finance training programs, and the ability to target payroll taxes by using differential tax rates by sector, all suggest that the payroll tax approach may be more attractive than alternative broadly based taxes such as value added taxes. Most of the countries utilizing payroll taxes to finance training are situated in the lower-middle income range.

Payroll levies are a useful device for developing national training institutions, in situations where other sources of revenue may be limited; they may also offer a stable and effective way of financing programs to develop employer training. However, with a few notable exceptions, they have played a somewhat peripheral role in more developed countries. Indeed, payroll levies are to be viewed more as a transitional mechanism than a permanent solution to the problem of training finance, which will be dismantled over the longer term as economies develop and alternative sources of training finance (including direct finance by trainees and firms) are strengthened.

See also: Government Role in Adult Education and Training; Legislation in Adult Education; Demand, Supply, and Finance of Adult Education; Costs of Adult Education and Training; Paid Educational Leave and Collective Bargaining; European Union: Continuing Vocational Training; Japan: Vocational Education and Training; Latin America: National Training Agencies; Evaluation of Industry Training: Cost-Effectiveness

References

Becker G 1964 *Human Capital: A Theoretical and Empirical Analysis with Special Reference to Education.* National Bureau of Economic Research, New York
Bird R M 1984 *Intergovernmental Finance in Colombia: Final Report of the Mission on Intergovernmental Finance*, Harvard Law School International Tax Program, Cambridge, Massachusetts
Brittain J 1972 *The Payroll Tax for Social Security.* Brookings Institution, Washington, DC
Dougherty C, Tan J-P 1991 *Financing Training: Issues and Options*, PRE Working Paper WPS 716. World Bank, Washington, DC
Ducci M A 1991 *Financing of Vocational Training in Latin America*, Discussion Paper No. 71. Training Policies Branch, ILO, Geneva
Gruber J 1995 *The Incidence of Payroll Taxation: Evidence from Chile*, Working Paper No. 5053. National Bureau of Economic Research, New York
Katz E, Ziderman A 1990 Investment in general training: The role of information and labor mobility. *Econ. J.* 100(403): 1147–58

Kugler B, Reyes A 1978 Financing of technical and vocational training in Latin America. In: IADB 1978 *Seminar on the Financing of Education in Latin America*. Inter-American Development Bank and the Government of Mexico, Mexico City

Lees D, Chiplin B 1970 The economics of industrial training. *Lloyds Bank Rev.* 96: 29–41

Levin H M 1983 Individual entitlement. In: Levin H M, Schutze H G (eds.) 1983 *Financing Recurrent Education*. Sage, Beverley Hills, California

Mincer J 1974 *Schooling Experience and Earnings*. National Bureau of Economic Research, New York

Whalley J, Ziderman A 1990 Financing training in developing countries: The role of payroll taxes. *Econ. Educ. Rev.* 9(4):377–87

Ziderman A 1978 *Manpower Training: Theory and Policy*. Macmillan, London

Further Reading

CINTERFOR/ILO 1991 *Vocational Training on the Threshold of the 1990s*, 2 Vols. PHREE Background Paper 91/35. World Bank, Washington, DC

Hegelheimer A 1986 *Financing of Vocational Training*. German Foundation for International Development, Mannheim

King K 1990 *In-service Training in Zimbabwe*, PHREE Background Paper 90/278. World Bank, Washington, DC

Organisation for Economic Co-operation and Development 1995 *How to Pay for Lifelong Learning for All?* DEELSA/ED/MIN(gb)2/ANN8. OECD, Paris

World Bank 1991 *Vocational and Technical Education and Training: A World Bank Policy Paper*. Word Bank, Washington, DC

Performance Contracting

W. W. Wilms and A. J. Hardcastle

Educational performance contracting has tantalized Western policymakers for more than a century, but so far its application in the United Kingdom and the United States has been a dismal failure. Because it ties payments to learner achievement, performance contracting holds the potential for increasing student learning while reducing costs. However, for a variety of reasons, performance contracting for education has failed to live up to its potential (Stucker and Hall 1971).

Such may not be the case when this method is applied to adult education and job training, however. Spurred by shrinking resources and growing public demands for efficiency and accountability, policymakers in the United States have renewed their interest in performance contracting—but this time for job training. Although a number of states including Illinois, New York, and California have each instituted policies designed to hold training providers accountable for results, until around 1990 virtually no empirical studies had been conducted to measure the results. One exception is the state of California, which leads other states and countries around the world in a bold experiment aimed at using performance contracting to match the supply of job training efficiently with economic demand.

This entry examines what is known about the history of performance contracting in education and training. It also analyzes California's experiences with performance contracting in training and draws some tentative conclusions about the value of the approach. The entry concludes with a discussion of some of the pitfalls of and limits to performance contracting in California and settings outside of the United States.

1. The Historical Context in Education

First known as "payment-by-results," performance contracting was tried unsystematically in early-eighteenth-century independent, voluntary schools in England. Teachers were paid on the basis of how well their students learned to read, write, and do bookkeeping, with the purpose of encouraging more poor children to stay in school where they would also learn Christian values (Adamson 1905). A century or so later, in 1862, payment-by-results was advanced as a policy and dominated the way in which schools were financed for nearly 30 years (Selleck 1968). Created in part to force the schools to teach children from poor families and to reduce educational costs, payment-by-results was firmly established in the Revised Education Code of 1862 (Armytage 1970). It worked in the following way: schools could earn 4 shillings for each student who attended 200 morning or afternoon sessions. Successful schools could qualify for a second type of reward, the "result" grant. Each student who passed in reading, writing, and arithmetic earned 8 shillings for the school. However, a certain amount of risk was inherent in the system as grants could be reduced for students' failure as well. Incentive grants could be earned by students for a "good pass," meaning that 75 percent of the class did well at the examinations.

Historical accounts judge the payment-by-results system harshly. Instead of promoting educational reform, tying school payments to student performance distorted the educational process. Schools' curricula were narrowed to focus on the measurable "Three Rs," pushing out other subjects so that school gardens, drawing, science, and singing simply disappeared. One historian observed: "The Revised Code came near to the point of stupefying children between 1862 and 1890. . . . The child was literally sacrificed to the system" (Simon 1965). Serious questions were raised about how much children actually learned. One account tells of children reading flawlessly for Her Majesty's Inspectors while holding their books upside down (Coltham 1972). A former Chief Inspector of Schools remembered:

Child after child stands up, reads a minute or so, and then sits down, remaining idle and inert (except when an occasional question is addressed to him) for the rest of the time occupied by the so-called lesson. . . . Arithmetic was taught in such a way as to make the child an inefficient calculating machine, which, even when working, is too often inaccurate and clumsy, and which the slightest change of environment throws at once and completely out of gear (Simon 1965 p. 116).

Thus, in 1890, because of the inherent weaknesses of payment-by-results, the policy was dropped and was replaced by a more conventional financial arrangement which rewarded the educational process rather than its result.

Meanwhile, payment-by-results found its way to Canada in 1876, where it was credited with causing teachers and students to work harder to avoid failure. The Canadian experience showed that test scores could be increased quickly, so long as the subject matter could be narrowed and measured, but the system had the pernicious effect of narrowing the curriculum and focusing efforts on only those students who showed promise of passing the examinations (Phillips 1957). Because of widespread public protest that children's education was being sacrificed to the goal of efficiency, the experiment ended in 1883.

Almost a century passed before the idea emerged again, this time in the United States under the label of "performance contracting." By 1969 confidence in the public schools had been seriously eroded. Financial bond proposals to support schools were voted down more frequently than they were passed. Members of President Richard Nixon's administration, many of whom had been recruited from the private sector, quickly became exasperated with the slow rate of change in public education. Despite technological advances that promised new ways to individualize instruction, the basic structure of classrooms proved impervious to innovation. Finding ways to make the schools responsive and "accountable" to the public for educational results became a top priority for Nixon and his domestic advisors. In an educational policy address, Nixon laid down the gauntlet:

The outcome of schooling—what children learn—is profoundly different for different groups of children. . . . School administrators and school teachers alike are responsible for their performance, and it is in their interest as well as in the interests of their pupils that they be held accountable. . . . the avoidance of accountability is the single most serious threat to a continued, and even more pluralistic educational system (Nixon 1970).

The first federally financed performance contract began quietly in 1969 with funding from the United States Office of Education and the Office of Housing and Urban Development's Model Cities program. Located in Texarkana, Arkansas, this model project aimed to increase reading and mathematics scores for 300 high school and junior high school students (Carpenter et al. 1971). Texarkana was small enough quickly to underwrite an experimental project like this one, but it was also large enough to represent the problems of big city school districts. The district was under great pressure from the Department of Health, Education, and Welfare to desegregate its schools. Data on the district's students publicized a huge gap in academic performance between Texarkana's Black and White students. Dropout rates were high and climbing. Federal intervention came in the form of financial incentives to experiment with performance contracting.

On its surface, the Texarkana experiment appeared bound for success. An early evaluation indicated that, at least in its early stages, performance contracting had scored great gains. Students averaged more than two grade levels in reading and one in mathematics after only 48 hours of instruction. Polls showed growing public support for performance contracting because it touched popular sentiments that the return on investment was greater under private industry's approach to schooling (Mecklenburger 1972), and that the money-back guarantee was uniquely American (Hechinger 1972). However, dissenting voices from both national teacher organizations—the American Federation of Teachers and the National Education Association—opposed the idea out of fears that it would spell the loss of teacher control and demean the profession (Elmore and McLaughlin 1988).

Nevertheless, a flurry of new contracts was announced by federal authorities by the summer of 1970. The biggest announcement of all came from the Office of Economic Opportunity (OEO) of plans to commit nearly US\$6 million to an experiment to examine "scientifically" the value of performance contracting. However, the wind quickly shifted when accusations appeared in the national press that one of the major contractors had been caught teaching to the test. The revelations sent shock waves through performance contracting's supporters.

Despite the shadow caused by the scandal, in 1971 OEO's experiment went forward in 18 cities, with contractors teaching reading and mathematics under a variety of incentive schemes. However, the project seemed plagued from the beginning. Contractors were late in hiring teachers, while others failed to get cooperation from local school officials. Furthermore, despite OEO's belief that student achievement could be accurately predicted as the basis for pricing contracts, few companies were willing to commit themselves to a guarantee. Also, OEO assumed that the contractors would provide a variety of classroom approaches. While most of the companies used teaching machines and all relied on incentives, in many other respects they were similar to comparable public school classrooms. Finally, officials at OEO assumed that standardized tests would provide a reliable and valid measure of student gains; however, there proved to be substantial disagreement about the use of standardized tests for such a specific purpose. An evaluation of performance contracting showed that while some students did better in reading and mathematics than they would have done in "normal" classrooms, the results varied greatly. In some areas not covered by the contract, students actually did worse and had poorer attendance records. It was concluded that none of the contractors did well enough to justify the costs (Gramlich and Koshel 1975). Before the year was out, Nixon had vetoed OEO's appropriation bill and the experiment was declared a failure.

Looking back over the English, Canadian, and United States experiences, a number of parallels are striking. First, in each case, performance contracting limited the educational focus to only those subjects that could be measured—the three Rs—ignoring other important aspects of children's education. The narrow conception of education that evolved, particularly in England and Canada, ultimately proved unacceptable to parents and educators. Second, there is little evidence that payment-by-results or performance contracting in any way enriched classroom learning. While the United States contractors used educational technology, the basic structure of what went on in classrooms remained largely unaffected. Teachers continued to lecture to students who listened. Third, powerful incentives were created for contractors to maximize their profits by shaving costs from the educational product by taking shortcuts and cheating by teaching to the test. Finally, suits against the federal government over standards dampened federal policymakers' interests in pushing ahead with the already doomed experiment.

In conclusion, most accounts of the English, Canadian, and United States experiences with "payment-by-results" agree that performance contracting may be inappropriate for education because its many goals are comprehensive and often elude measurement. Also, it is clear that many parents and educators become ultimately disenchanted with the way performance contracting inevitably narrows education. In any case, the concept has been rejected in each of three independent contexts.

2. Applying Performance Contracting to Job Training

It is difficult to say whether the failure of educational performance contracting stems from some defect inherent in the concept, or whether it derives more from an inappropriate application to education. Job training offers a useful and interesting case to test whether or not the concept has merit beyond education. Unlike education, with its broad public mandate, job training is by definition narrow. Its purpose is the preparation of individuals to perform specific tasks in work settings. Those tasks range from simple ones, such as typing or doing simple arithmetic functions on a calculator, to more complex operations such as fixing computers. Second, job training is not bound by schoolrooms and traditional interaction between students and teachers. Rather, training is carried on in a variety of settings which are frequently determined by the demands of the workplace. Learning is reinforced by on-the-job reality where superior performance as well as mistakes usually have real consequences. Finally, widespread agreement exists as to some of the important outcomes of training—such as increased productivity, less unemployment, and higher earnings —which are more easily observed and measured than schooling (Creticos and Sheets 1992).

2.1 Performance Contracting and the California Experiment

California was led into performance contracting partly because of rapid changes in the state's economy. Despite two recessions in the early and mid-1970s, by the end of the 1970s the Californian economy was booming. It was, however, also changing. Mass primary manufacturing industries (steel, oil, automobiles) were shrinking, while new, high-technology electronics were beginning to blossom. As a result, the state experienced a seeming paradox of relatively high levels of unemployment that ranged between 7 and 8 percent accompanied by a glut of new entry-level and high-paying jobs (Munger 1978). The paradox appeared to stem from three factors. First, the number of people in the workforce was growing faster than jobs could be created. Second, while many entry-level jobs went unfilled, a large number of high-paying, high-skilled jobs were being filled by workers recruited outside the state. Third, the apparent mismatch between available jobs and skilled individuals seemed to result from vocational education and training programs that were out of tune with labor market needs. Further, employers frequently complained that public schools provided only general skill training (often at the expense of the "basics") which many found to be of marginal value (Wilms 1984). These forces, combined with rapid economic changes that led to a rash of plant closures, caused the California legislature to place a high priority on retraining experienced workers who were losing their jobs in record numbers.

Consequently, in 1982 the legislature created the Employment Training Panel, a hybrid public training agency with private sector characteristics. Its businesslike design promised to improve the reputation of training with business and labor by avoiding the image of training as a swindle. Senator Bill Greene, a black legislator from one of Los Angeles' poorest districts, was a primary architect of the Panel's legislation. Greene maintained that training without a job at the end made no sense, especially for public expenditure. On more than one occasion he charged that "swindling the public" in the name of training was an insult to the taxpayer (personal communication April 14 1982).

The Panel, whose seven members and executive director were appointed by the governor and legislature, was financed by a small surtax on the state's Unemployment Insurance Fund. It has operated as a broker between the state and organizations that train men and women for jobs—community colleges, community-based organizations, private vocational schools, labor unions, and employers themselves. Since its inception in 1982, the Panel has financed training for nearly 150,000 workers at a cost of US$336 million. Trainees qualify for training by being unemployed, collecting or having exhausted unemployment benefits, or by being in imminent danger of being laid off. What sets the Panel apart from other training efforts is its stringent measure of accountability prescribed by law. Contracts are done on an "all-or-nothing" basis, meaning that training organizations are paid only for successes. Trainees must not only complete their training, but remain on private sector jobs that use their new skills at agreed-upon wage rates for at least 90 days. No payments are made for failures.

2.2 Research Findings

As was noted earlier, virtually no empirical evidence exists as to the value of tying payments to results for education *or* training. The two studies summarized in the following text represent what is probably the first evidence about the value of performance contracting for training. The first study assesses the value of training for the nearly 4,000 men and women who completed programs under California's performance-driven system. The second study asks whether certain kinds of organization are better suited than others to take risks by providing training under such stringent conditions of accountability.

2.2.1 The impact of performance contracting on training. A study conducted in 1988 followed up the careers of 3,913 men and women who were trained under California Panel's sponsorship between 1 January 1983 and 30 December 1985 (Moore et al. 1988). Demographic and outcome data taken from official state records were analyzed to determine trainees' success in finding work and increasing their earnings after training.

The findings revealed that training was provided by a remarkably wide variety of sources, including employers, labor unions, community colleges, community-based organizations, and private vocational schools. About 60 percent of the men and women who enrolled were trained for new jobs (called "new hires"), while the other trainees (40 %) were already employed and were being retrained for new jobs. They were called "retrainers." Most trainees who enrolled in programs sponsored by the Employment Training Panel were younger and more educationally advantaged than those who enrolled in federal Job Training Partnership Act programs. Nearly two-thirds of the trainees completed their programs, and most of them were subsequently employed in related jobs for at least 90 days at an agreed-upon salary level. Nearly 36 percent of all trainees dropped out—a tendency that was more pronounced among new hires—revealing a pattern similar to trainees in traditional training programs.

Overall, completion rates were higher than in other publicly supported training programs, which typically run to 30–40 percent. Not surprisingly, those who completed training were far more likely to find employment. For instance, studies by Wilms (1975) and Wilms and Hansell (1982) compared outcomes of private and public postsecondary vocational training. They found that 40 percent of all students who enrolled for community college vocational training successfully completed their program and most found employment fairly quickly. An analysis of job training under the Comprehensive Employment Training Act reported that about a third of all trainees successfully completed their training and found some kind of work after their programs (US Department of Labor 1979).

Findings from this study also revealed substantially higher earnings for completers than did other studies of publicly supported training. For instance, those who enrolled for training as new hires and completed their programs increased their earnings by an average of US$3,745 annually, a gain of US$5,096 over those who dropped out. Retrainers showed a similar, but less dramatic pattern, increasing their annual earnings by an average of US$1,664, or a gain of US$2,531 over retrainers who dropped out. Findings from a follow-up study of trainees between 1985 and 1990 indicated even greater earnings gains to completers, particularly for new trainees whose income increased by nearly US$7,000 in the first year after training (Moore and Blake 1992). The most plausible explanation for the superior earnings of these trainees stems from incentives created by the program itself. Trainees were somewhat more advantaged than were those who enroll in traditional training programs. Finding evidence of this "creaming" effect is not surprising because, as history shows, incentives are created for schools to concentrate on those who are most likely to succeed. Similarly, this study found that training agencies tended to select trainees who had a reasonably good chance of completing their training and staying on-the-job for 90 days. Paradoxically, while such selectivity often screens out disadvantaged individuals who stand to benefit from training, such selection tends to improve the match between trainees, their training, and their ultimate employers. Good matching results in fewer dropouts, higher wages, and greater individual and social efficiency. Further, in this study there was no evidence that training agencies screened trainees on the basis of ethnicity. In fact, ethnic minorities comprised half of all trainees who enrolled under Panel programs.

2.2.2 Performance contracting and institutional type. Under performance contracting, training organizations are induced to expose themselves to risk in exchange for financial reward—an arrangement that most public institutions seldom experience. To succeed under conditions of performance contracting, training organizations must insure that trainees complete their programs and hold jobs for at least 90 days at a preagreed rate, or pay the costs of failures. Thus, agencies' survival depends on their ability to manage their programs and guarantee results.

A second study done for the California Employment Training Panel sought to answer whether certain types of organizations were naturally more suited than others to the market conditions imposed by performance contracting (Wilms 1988). For instance, since corporations and private vocational schools are naturally attuned to the demands of the marketplace, they may succeed more frequently under performance contracting than do public schools and community colleges, which are more insulated from market forces.

Data were taken from state files on all contracts written in a four-year period between 1983 and 1987. Correlations were generated between training program characteristics and trainees' success, and then each of the 524 training providers was given an expected score based on the information at hand. The top 25 percent (those that actually did better than predicted) were labeled "high-performers" while the bottom 25 percent (those that failed to achieve their predicted results) were labeled "low-performers." From this group, a stratified sample of 66 training organizations was selected for more intensive study.

Interestingly, no single type of training agency appeared to have any inherent advantage over another. Public community colleges, which are purposely insulated from market forces, were as likely to succeed in training and placement as were private corporations. However, successful programs were more often than not characterized by employing an "entrepreneur"— a capable staff member who was willing to take the risks inherent in the new training policies. Not surprisingly, the ways these individuals found to offset risks to their organizations frequently resulted in more effective training programs. For instance, one community college administrator established a network of employers he could trust to hire his graduates. In turn, the employers came to learn to trust the quality of referrals from the community college—

a type of two-way relationship few school administrators are ever able to establish. The extra revenue such success generated allowed the administrator to improve his program by providing summer salaries for teachers and buying equipment he could not otherwise obtain through the college. This example is also interesting because it shows how public institutions can become "market oriented" when they must. This finding takes on special significance in light of the growing interest by business leaders and lawmakers in promoting "privatization" policies—policies that assume that because of their market orientation, private organizations can perform social tasks more efficiently than public institutions, and that public institutions should be induced to adopt these market-driven policies.

The findings also revealed how incentives created by performance contracting hold advantages for private employers. More than two-thirds of the high-performing organizations reported that private employers perceived an immediate economic threat which drove them to seek public assistance in retraining their workers. Most often they said their workers needed training in new technologies to meet growing competition. If they were unable to retrain their workers, most employers said they would have to lay them off and rehire more highly trained workers.

For instance, one international electronics manufacturer found itself unable to compete with a flood of high-quality, low-cost Japanese products. To survive, the company installed new equipment and obtained state funding to retrain 74 workers in statistical process control to help boost quality and lower costs. The company's vice-president for quality assurance found that the new equipment and training helped improve product quality and worker efficiency to the point that the excess capacity allowed the company to hire 20 new workers and to increase output. This vice-president also reported that improved productivity and quality convinced top management about the importance of retraining, which has subsequently become a high corporate priority.

This company's experience closely followed that of other successful companies that did their own training under conditions of performance contracting. In addition to facing an immediate competitive threat, the study revealed that high-performers were significantly more likely than low-performers to report their graduates were more productive after training than before, and that the training improved the company's competitiveness and workers' job security.

In the final analysis, performance contracting appears to have a positive effect on most training organizations whether or not they are high- or low-performers. In fact, more than three-quarters of all training agencies surveyed indicated they would repeat their experience with the Employment Training Panel if they had the choice to make over again.

The evidence on job training points to a variety of benefits associated with performance contracting. Though not conclusive, the evidence suggests that performance contracting results in reasonably high completion and job placement rates. Also, substantial economic efficiencies are achieved, since under performance contracting training agencies shoulder the risk of failures and the state pays only for successes.

Training agencies tend to select trainees who have a reasonably good chance of completing their training and staying on-the-job for 90 days, though this should come as no surprise. Past experience with performance contracting reveals how incentives are created for contractors to concentrate on those who are most likely to succeed. While such selectivity does not advance equity, it does appear to improve efficiency by improving the match between trainees, their training, and their ultimate employers. Good matching also results in fewer dropouts and lower training costs. However, there was no evidence that training agencies screen trainees on the basis of ethnicity.

Despite the intuitively appealing idea that organizations that are naturally connected to the marketplace would have a higher success rate, the results showed that community colleges and union apprenticeship programs, which are not directly connected to the marketplace, succeed just as often as did private corporations and private vocational schools.

In most cases, Employment Training Panel funding appears to have the effect of motivating companies and unions to invest in training that carries long-run benefits. High-performing contractors are most likely to realize the need for training when faced with an immediate economic threat, most frequently from in-state competition. Most often, companies and unions respond by introducing new technology and training with the expectation of reducing costs and improving quality, thus gaining a larger market share. According to reports from these successful companies, unions, and schools, training makes workers more productive, which in turn makes the employing firms more competitive. As a result, employers and trainers say that workers have greater job security after training than they enjoyed prior to training. Most employers and trainers concur with the view that the experience with performance-driven training substantially raises the visibility and priority of training within the company or union, and most would repeat the choice if they had to make it again.

3. The Negative Side of Performance Contracting

Incentives set up by performance contracting appeal to the universal human drives to acquire wealth and avoid risk. Within socially acceptable bounds these motives drive the system in productive ways, but in the extreme they are harmful. For instance, in a state-wide study of the Job Training Partnership Act, a quarter of the training agencies interviewed admitted falsifying state-required reports to insure that they met performance standards (State Job Training Coordinating Council 1988). The Employment Training Panel has also been subject to abuses by training agencies, although the number of cases has been small. The most visible case of abuse was that of a San Diego project that specialized in training ex-convicts. It was forced into bankruptcy after an audit revealed that enrollment and performance reports had been falsified by the training contractor to increase profits.

Contractors do not have to operate outside the law to maximize income and minimize risk. For instance, since the Panel's first year of operation, there has been a gradual but dramatic shift away from training "new hires" in favor of training those who are already employed. Naturally, new hires represent a greater risk to training agencies because of their unemployed status than do those already employed. The President of the California Manufacturers Association explained: "New-hire programs are a problem for many of our members because of good times, which mean a shrinking pool of unemployed. It's harder and harder for companies to find clients who qualify." Additionally, however, interviews with individuals responsible for training programs make it clear that the shift is also due to risk avoidance. One corporate trainer reported that because of their work experience and employment history with the company, they would much rather retrain their own workers than hire and train new employees. In response to this shift, the Panel has established a policy earmarking a larger proportion of future funding for retraining programs.

Also, as was noted earlier, contractors frequently select trainees in ways that help to assure their income while minimizing their risk. Selecting trainees who are most likely to succeed also produces a positive economic effect. As described earlier, new economic conditions that have caused public resources to shrink have at the same time created a political demand for policies that reward efficiency and accountability. Careful selection reduces training costs and helps to assure that the training will be put to good use on the job because of the higher likelihood that trainees will complete their programs and get jobs. However, on the negative side, such selectivity does not advance the competing goal of social equity because training slots are not distributed on an equitable basis—more advantaged individuals win. For instance, many trainees are turned away from these programs because they lack the "basics"—reading, writing, and arithmetic—or because they have not yet been socialized to the real demands of the workplace. However, there is no reason that would preclude extending the advantages offered by performance contracting. For example, by increasing the price of training higher-risk individuals, programs to teach basics needed on the job could be designed and priced specifically for this clientele and provided through similar models of performance contracting—a direction the Panel is beginning to explore.

In yet another way of maximizing income while minimizing risks, some contractors have substituted Panel funds for their own. Though these cases are in the distinct minority, a nonetheless significant proportion of the contractors interviewed (19 %), admitted that they would have used their own funds to underwrite training even if the Panel had not existed. Clearly, in these cases, risk to the trainers was minimal as they would cover any losses out of their own pockets (which was cheaper than paying for all of the training). Thus, the promise of public funding was pure gain.

Finally, legislation serves as yet another way for special interests to pursue a greater share of the public wealth and reduce risk. An analysis of one year's legislation reveals repeated pressure by special interests to influence the way in which the Panel funds are spent or to relax the performance requirements.

4. Conclusions About Performance Contracting

The evidence presented here leads to the conclusion that, on balance, performance contracting for job training has seemed like a good public investment in the California environment. It has not been, however, without its problems. What stands out is that performance contracting can be part of a dynamic system serving many interests. Properly tuned, the system can achieve efficiencies for the state. Because of its nature, a performance contracting system is under relentless pressure to respond and adjust to new and changing conditions. As noted earlier, it seems axiomatic that contractors will, over time, seek to increase their own gain while reducing their risk. This can translate into contractors reducing quality and cost, thereby increasing their profit, inflating prices by adding hours of training that are not really needed, substituting state funds for their own, or simply altering how figures are reported. Because of this ever-present incentive, contractors are continually tempted to develop increasingly sophisticated means of subverting a system that uses performance contracting.

It is likely that the Employment Training Panel has suffered a minimum of scandal because of its enforcement system, in which reported placements and earnings are systematically checked against official state files. Though this kind of enforcement is expensive, particularly when done on a large scale, it is a key to insuring the integrity of performance contracting.

5. Relevance of Performance Contracting to Other Environments

The California experiment provides some important clues about the potential of performance contracting for other nations—particularly newly industrializing nations such as Brazil and South Korea, which are on the leading edge of economic and social change. When the transition of nations from "less developed" to "newly industrializing" status is analyzed, a number of parallels are striking. At the less developed stages, local authorities are frequently influenced by colonial traditions and aid-giving patterns that seem inevitably to lead to the investment of scarce resources for training in secondary vocational schools. Such a strategy makes sense as a first step, because in many cases the secondary schools are the only available infrastructure through which to implement forward-looking policies. Frequently, however, steps to develop the supply of human resources runs in advance of demand for skilled labor from newly developing economies. Further, economic demand for human resources is frequently controlled by foreign investors, thus making it even more difficult for local policymakers to forge an effective link between supply and demand. Finally, the small economies of most developing countries tend to be supported by traditional agricultural labor markets and self-employment. This suggests that developing nations' modern sectors may simply lack the capacity to absorb new entrants into the labor force, no matter how well-educated and trained. Not surprisingly, attempts to link artificially supply and demand through guaranteed employment have failed to meet changing labor market demands and are being abandoned by most developing nations.

Developing nations are thus faced with pressures to anticipate and respond to changing labor market demands for education and training, but at the same time are hobbled by antiquated and expensive training programs which are most frequently lodged in public secondary schools. As King (1988) noted, parental pressures to expand secondary education to advance their children's opportunities in turn increase competition for scarce modern-sector jobs. An increasing number of countries have begun to promote training for self-employment as a way of relieving these pressures while increasing children's productive capacities.

As less developed nations make the transition to newly industrializing status these tensions become more obvious because of the need to move training away from traditional school control and closer to the labor market. Successful examples can be seen most notably in Latin America (Ducci 1988) where differentiated programs have emerged to meet industrial demand for skilled workers through enterprise-based training and specialized training agencies financed by payroll taxes or tax credits. Training for the "disadvantaged," according to Ducci, is increasingly being absorbed by the public schools.

It seems that it is in this transitional context that performance contracting has the most to offer. Clearly, the concept has little value in developing nations, where training represents a scarce resource to be distributed widely as a message of hope to the unemployed. However, in the face of clearly articulated and rapidly changing industrial demand for skilled workers, it seems like a reasonable and efficient way to achieve necessary efficiencies and public accountability.

See also: Market Concepts in Provision; Demand, Supply, and Finance of Adult Education; Learning in the Workplace; Modularization in Adult Education and Training; Evaluation of Adult Education; Evaluation of Industry Training: Cost-Effectiveness; Measurement of Industry Training

References

Adamson J W 1905 *Pioneers of Modern Education*: 1600–1700. Cambridge University Press, Cambridge
Armytage W H G 1970 *Four Hundred Years of English Education*, 2nd edn. Cambridge University Press, London
Carpenter P, Chalfant A, Hall G 1971 *Case Studies in Educational Performance Contracting*, Vol. 3. Rand Corporation, Santa Monica, California
Coltham J 1972 Educational accountability: An English experiment and its outcome. *University of Chicago School Review*. 81(1): 15–34
Creticos P A, Sheets R 1992 *Evaluating State-financed, Workplace-based Retraining Programs: Case Studies of Retraining Projects*. National Commission for Employment Policy, National Governors' Association, Washington, DC
Ducci M A 1988 Equity and productivity of vocational training—the Latin American experience. *Int. J. Educ. Dev.* 8(3): 175–87
Elmore R F, McLaughlin M W 1988 *Steady Work: Policy, Practice, and the Reform of American Education*. Rand Corporation, Santa Monica, California
Gramlich E, Koshel P 1975 *Educational Performance Contracting: An Evaluation of an Experiment*. Brookings Institution, Washington, DC
Hechinger F 1972 Contracts: Negative verdict on a teaching program. *New York Times* February 6, p. 9
King K 1988 The new politics of job training and work training in Africa. *Int. J. Educ. Dev.* 8(3): 153–61
Mecklenburger J 1972 *Performance Contracting in Schools*. National School Public Relations Association, Arlington, Virginia
Moore R, Blake D 1992 *Does ETP Training Work?* California State University, Northridge, California
Moore R, Wilms W, Bolus R 1988 *Training for Change: An Analysis of Outcomes of the Employment Training Panel Programs*. Training Research Corporation, Santa Monica, California
Munger B 1978 *Background Report on SB 132 (Greene): The California Worksite and Training Act*. California Legislature, Sacramento, California
Nixon R 1970 *Education for the 1970s: Renewal and Reform*. US Government Printing Office, Washington, DC
Phillips C E 1957 *The Development of Education in Canada*. Gage, Toronto
Selleck R J W 1968 *The New Education*. 1870–1914 Pitman, London
Simon B 1965 *Education and the Labor Movement, 1870–1920*. Lawrence and Wishart, London
State Job Training Coordinating Council 1988 *Final Report on a Coordination Study of the SJTCC and JTPA*. Arthur Young and Training Research Corporation, Santa Monica, California
Stucker J, Hall G 1971 *The Performance Contracting Concept in Education*. Rand Corporation, Santa Monica, California
US Department of Labor 1979 *Employment and Training Report of the President*. US Department of Labor, Washington, DC
Wilms W 1975 *Public and Proprietary Vocational Training: A Study of Effectiveness*. Lexington Books, Lexington, Massachusetts
Wilms W 1984 Vocational education and job success: The employers' view. *Phi Del. Kap.* 65(15): 347–50
Wilms W 1988 *Predicting Success in Performance Contracting*. Training Research Corporation, Santa Monica, California
Wilms W, Hansell S 1982 The dubious promise of postsecondary vocational training. *Int. J. Educ. Dev.* 2(1): 43–59

Training with Production

W. E. Biervliet

Training with production relates to the general principle of combining training and working, mostly by building a component of production of salable products or services into a technical or vocational training program. This production may take place either within the training institution itself or be physically separated from the institution. In the latter case it could be undertaken in an existing work environment or in an enterprise specially established for the purpose.

Production refers to the manufacturing of goods or provision of services that are marketed externally or used within the institution or firm. In each case it must have an economic value that is accounted for. Production is therefore more narrowly defined than "productive work," which is here regarded as any work activity geared to satisfy personal and social needs. Such activity does not necessarily have an economic value.

This entry presents an outline and conceptual framework for training with production as well as a review of trends and developments in policies and practices related to training with production in different parts of the world, in the South, the North, and Eastern Europe, and in different types of systems

—planned, market, and mixed economies (Biervliet 1994). It also considers various constraints and issues faced in implementing training with production programs.

1. Outline and Scope

Training with production is broader in scope and more generally applied than many assume. It also covers alternating periods of learning in a training institution matched with practical work in a work environment. It incorporates the widely applied phenomenon of "work experience," which is usually initiated by a training institution and corresponds to the following definition by the Department of Education and Science in the United Kingdom: "An arrangement in which the pupil carries out particular jobs, more or less as a regular employee would, though with emphasis on educational aspects" (Income Date Services 1990).

Training with production equally deals with mechanisms for strengthening the liaison between universities and industries in countries belonging to the Organisation for Economic Co-operation and Development (OECD) in the framework of industrial placements; for example, arranging the participation of students in the research and development work of enterprises at science parks connected to a university, in sandwich course programs initiated by training institutions with a practical component in industry, and in project work for industry with student involvement (see *Partnerships: Initial and Adult Education*).

In the work carried out in East Africa by an international network of researchers on education with production, attempts were made to put the African experiences in a much wider, global context (Komba and Hoppers 1994). The group came to differentiate between several main types of combining learning and working. Applying this to training with production, the following categories may be distinguished.

(a) Production-based training: in such programs training is closely related to and based on production. The fundamental principle is learning by doing. The curriculum is based on an analysis of work processes; students should pass through all tasks including related theoretical components in order to meet training objectives. Training follows the production sequence, and production targets and standards are seen as strengthening the training. Theoretical components are directly linked to practical applications of production either in work stations or through limited periods of classroom instructions. Unlike on-the-job-training, production-based training is basically a training mode applied in a training environment organized as a production environment to enhance the achievement of training objectives and post-training employability.

(b) Production as learning practice: here production is an important part of the learning program, and theory components are interspersed with periods for practical application, many of which are devoted to actual production. Such work tends to take place within the training institution and the pedagogical aim tends to dominate.

(c) Production as learning projects: in this case, production is kept somewhat separate from the training curriculum and tends to be seen as an opportunity for advanced practice in a real or simulated work environment. It occurs parallel to the training or alternates with it, and takes place within the training institution (production unit) or outside (in enterprises). In such situations the pedagogical and economic purposes tend to be more balanced.

(d) Production as a distinct economic activity: here production is run on a full commercial basis and kept quite separate from the training program. It may take place in a separate unit attached to the training institution or in outside enterprises. Its main aims tend to be the generation of income for the institution and the improved capacity utilization of available workshops, facilities, and personnel. There is no explicit pedagogical linkage between production and the training program.

Combinations of training and production vary from complete absorption of production within training, through the coexistence of independent components of training and of production, to a situation of complete absorption of training within ongoing production. In this classification the physical location of the training or production components is of less importance than the degree to which the activities interrelate. Production may still be closely related to the training even if the trainees go out for attachment in a nearby enterprise, which may be the case in sandwich programs and dual approaches. Production as a distinct economic activity is increasingly applied by training centers in developing countries as an alternative cost-recovery scheme. Even though it may provide both trainees and instructors with exposure to the "world of work," it lacks the systematic interaction between training and production, and hence does not fit within the realm of training with production.

2. Traditions and Foundations

Training and production, now often separated, used to be much more integrated. In traditional societies, identity from youth through adulthood was based on productive work, which determined status in life. The competencies required for being a productive community member were based on observing other community members at work, followed by a trial and error approach. Indeed, training and production are still integrated in traditional apprenticeship schemes.

2.1 Rationales

Bringing the components together tends to stem from a variety of motivations, which are mainly of a pedagogical, social, or economic nature. The involvement of learners in production is widely regarded as a way to bridge the gap between theory and practice. People develop knowledge and skills by participating in a production process, so that they can apply what has first been learned in theory, or so that they can learn directly from the experience itself. In vocational training, production offers students a chance to be engaged in what looks like or is almost the "real thing," thereby becoming not only cognitively but also psychologically more prepared for the world of work.

Socially and economically, an important dimension of education and training with production is the bridging of the distance between institutions of learning and the local environment. It is often thought that learners should not be exempted from "normal" work activities, and even where they end up in intellectual positions they should understand and respect manual labor. In pure economic terms training with production is seen as a way to enhance the value of training as a preparation for the world of work. Where production takes place within the institution it also has the advantage of generating revenues for the institution and thus reducing the costs of education or training. In this regard production offers possibilities of providing incentives for staff and students to earn extra income.

The interest in training with production is not a Western phenomenon, nor is it exclusively associated with one particular ideological tradition. The idea that learning and working should be linked—as being essentially two facets of the same process—has found recognition in many cultures in different periods of their development. These include indigenous cultures in such countries as China and India, and also in many African countries. In India, training with production is deeply rooted in Gandhian tradition with its emphasis on manual labor as a component of education and training as a basis to revitalize the village economy (Zachariah and Hoffman 1985).

Particularly in the case of work-related skills, it is a fairly recent, Western-inspired development to separate skill development from the work activity itself. The weight of the arguments in favor of linking training and production varies from country to country, and across different cultures and ideologies. The pedagogical principle is also differently interpreted within major philosophical traditions.

3. Training and Production in the 1960s and 1970s

In capitalist societies a pragmatic approach to training and production tends to have dominated in the 1960s and 1970s, focusing on the role of production in strengthening the training or the transition of young people from school to working life. The production or work experience component was seen as an effective orientation to the shop floor as well as to prospective employers. Socialist systems, based on their conception of polytechnic education (Pfeifer and Wald 1987), used to pay much attention to work as a source of learning (e.g., specific attitudes and values) or as a way to achieve greater insight into the science and technology of production.

3.1 Socialist Experiences

In many planned economies school-run farms and enterprises or workshops have been an integral part of schools and colleges, so that general education or technical training could be directly linked to the production process. In Eastern Europe and Cuba, training with production was an integral part of a centrally planned economy, with combined training and production target-setting for well-defined occupations, unified curricula and syllabuses, and compulsory production practice periods financed by enterprises. Criticism has referred to such production practices as providing cheap labor for enterprises and schools wanting to raise income. They have also been criticized for inadequate integration of theory and practice in the overall curriculum.

In China, training with production was founded on long indigenous traditions and further enhanced by Mao Tse Tung's views on the integration of theory and practice as a means to create a socialist type of citizen. This led to a concentration on practice at the expense of theory during the Cultural Revolution of 1966–69.

In Ethiopia, too, after the 1974 revolution, a polytechnic type of education was introduced based on socialist principles. In 1976 some 70 schools were turned into experimental schools, combining education with newly developed workshops on the school premises for the production component of the curriculum. However, well before the 1990 change of government, the experimental schools for polytechnic education were evaluated and subsequently the experiment was discontinued because it was too expensive and unsuitable for nation-wide implementation. In Benin, in the 1975 education reform, involvement in and exposure to production were introduced at all education levels and a "new school" (*école nouvelle*) was created corresponding to a production unit with a cooperative as a basic core. A similar development took place in Guinea, where Revolutionary Education Centers were created to promote science, technology, and production units in all types of education provision. In Tanzania, education and training with production appealed strongly to social and ideological considerations. Here, at an early stage after independence, the integration of production in institutions of learning was promoted as a move toward a new type of education and training which would help prevent the alienation of youth from their own heritage and enable them to relate more closely to the realities of life. Training with production strongly fitted into the philosophy of education for self-reliance.

3.2 Other Traditions, North and South

In the development of education and training with production, countries with a mixed economy, in particular, have absorbed influences from different sources, including their own indigenous traditions. Social objectives have, for example, been strong in the educational systems of India. In many developing countries the combination of learning and working became attractive as a new principle for organizing education and training, one that linked up with local traditions and provided an apparent break with imposed metropolitan patterns of separating academic and manual work.

However, until the 1980s training with production in developing countries, especially as far as formal training institutions were concerned, remained largely in the realm of advocacy. In East and Southern Africa technical secondary schools have generally not developed strong training with production components. Both internal production, through institution-based production units, and external production, through effective links with industry, have been weak or nonexistent. Extensive experience in training with production is found in the array of training arrangements outside government control and run by a host of smaller and larger nongovernmental organizations, and by community associations on a nonprofit basis. Some programs, such as the Village (later Youth) Polytechnics in Kenya and the Brigades in Botswana, included a wide variety of production activities.

A general overview of education and training with production in Latin America and the Caribbean referred to Brazil as the only pure market economy in the region, with a broad action program on education and training with production, even though this was directed primarily to the rural poor and deprivileged groups (Cabral de Andrade 1987). In the Caribbean a number of training with production programs were noted, both formal and nonformal. These included programs in Jamaica such as the Human Employment and Resource Training program (HEART) and the College of Arts, Science, and Technology (CAST) where an engineering department was running an industrial training scheme involving students doing practice work at various work stations for a period of up to three months (Jennings-Wray 1983).

In South and Southeast Asia, nongovernmental organizations (NGOs) accumulated extensive experience in training with production born from the need to recover recurrent costs of training. Vocational schools run by Salesian fathers are among those well-known for quality training combined with production schemes using student participation. However, training with production in public sector provision in Southeast Asia was banned by legislation preventing production in training institutions as well as the sale of products.

In the North a pragmatic approach has tended to dominate. Systems with strong institution-linked apprenticeship and dual approaches, such as those of Germany and Switzerland, have a built-in training with production component, while Scandinavian countries also have a strong socially oriented approach toward work experience in training (Schwartz 1986). In the 1970s and early 1980s growing concern about the high unemployment rate of school leavers in Europe enhanced both national and supranational programs by focusing on the role of production and work experience in training as one of the measures to improve the transition of young people from school to work and adult life (Mehaut 1987, Schwartz 1981).

While experiences in training with production for regular training of able-bodied persons are often of an ad hoc character, vocational training and employment for the handicapped have often been conceived in an integrated way, combining training with production in a workshop and the prospect of employment in that workshop or supportive measures to enhance self-employment (OECD 1983).

4. Training and Production in the 1980s and 1990s

In the North training with production is increasingly being applied as one of the strategies to improve competitiveness and the rate of return on investments in training; in the South it is increasingly becoming a strategy for survival, to enable training systems to cope with the rising cost spiral of training provision.

4.1 Impact of Economic and Political Restructuring

In the 1980s significant worldwide restructuring processes in society occurred which had an impact on trends related to training with production. First, there was a changing role for the state in catering for the needs of citizens and a subsequent move toward decentralization and privatization. This has involved a gradual reduction in the centrality of the public sector in general and in particular a reduction in the state's combined role as financier, administrator, and provider of training (Kanawaty and de Moura Castro 1990, World Bank 1991). Second, a process of structural adjustment began. It had a tremendous impact on public sector employment as well as battering the vulnerable economies of lower income countries (King 1990). Quality and relevance also came under pressure because, in the midst of rapidly changing social and economic environments, institutionalized public sector training faced great difficulties in responding to new demands for skill acquisition. The quality and relevance problem was often exacerbated by the financial squeeze on the budgets of training systems.

Together, these structural problems resulted in institutional training facing very strong challenges from alternative forms of skills acquisition, notably those that largely take place within the work environment.

Third, there was a transition sometimes abrupt, sometimes gradual—from planned to market economies. This happened in almost all planned economies. In Eastern European and Central Asian republics, issues faced in the transition phase included: first experience of mass unemployment; privatization of state-owned enterprises without a set of market-economy-oriented mechanisms, strategies, and incentives; a deterioration of training practice periods; and increased abuse of apprentices as a source of cheap labor (Uthman 1991, Grootings 1991). Even China began to move toward a mixed economy through the introduction of components of a competitive market economy. Full central control became matched by decentralization and devolution of decision-making, allowing for regional and local authorities to attain centrally established targets—including control over resource allocation and utilization (Noah and Middleton 1988).

The need to strengthen the liaison between training and enterprises and the possibilities for combining technical and vocational training with productive work have received new attention. Although for a long time there has been a fascination with strategies to break down what have often been regarded as unnatural barriers between training and work, this has received a new impetus as a result of the crisis situation in many training systems.

4.2 Training with Production in the South: New Developments

In the South in general, the notion of production as a source of income for an institution has become a prominent feature, especially in NGO-run training institutions, but to an increasing degree also for government-run vocational training centers. Where resources were scarce and education or training appeared to remain the exclusive domain of an elite, production seemed a very promising way of increasing access to organized learning for larger numbers of disadvantaged youth, giving them a chance to prepare for jobs in the modern sector of the economy. Thus many schools and training centers were opened with a significant production component, based especially on the expectation that production would make the training affordable.

In several countries the legislative framework has become more supportive of income-generating activities run by training institutions, including training with production. Policies have been formulated to foster diversification of funding of training institutions and to enhance a stronger liaison between training institutions and private enterprises. This has been encouraged by the new emphasis in donor policies of support to technical and vocational education and training. The focus is on demand-orientation, diversification of funding, capacity building, private sector involvement, and sustainability. Even though the World Bank policy paper on vocational technical education and training only marginally refers to training with production, especially with regard to its income-generation capacity, it still reopened the possibility of dialogues between governments in developing countries and aid agencies with regard to the provision of support for training with production (World Bank 1991).

Some donor agencies, such as BMZ (Germany), SDC (Switzerland), and DANIDA (Denmark), have given long-term support to training with production programs in the South. DANIDA gave support to the Dodoma National Vocational Training Center in Tanzania for the establishment of a self-reliance unit. It provides trainees within the in-plant component with an opportunity to obtain production experience. DANIDA has also supported training-with-production schemes at production training centers in Indonesia and in India (DANIDA 1990). The German experience with the dual system has been applied in German-supported technical assistance projects in Sri Lanka and India. A somewhat different type of German support is directed to the German-Singapore Institute. This has the character of a technology transfer center or teaching factory within which the organization, structure, rules, and regulations of enterprises have been adopted to a large extent (Greinert and Wiemann 1993). The Asian Development Bank earmarked part of a technical education loan to Indonesia to provide funds for the establishment of income-generating units related to a number of senior secondary technical schools.

With regard to the potential for training with production, there are strong discrepancies between countries with high growth rates and significant modern sectors (e.g., Southeast Asia) and economies with low growth rates and a marginal modern sector in the poorer countries in sub-Saharan Africa. In East and Southern Africa formal training institutions started considering training with production in order to generate additional funds to cover recurrent costs for training and to provide more hands-on experience as a contribution to preparation for self-employment. In Southeast Asia, training with production has focused more on the strengthening of the infrastructure for industrial development, concentrating on industrial trades and preparing for both self-employment and employment in the modern sector.

4.3 Training with Production in the North: New Developments

In the North, from the mid-1980s, training-with-production programs have tended to focus on the liaison between education and industry within the framework of programs aiming at enhancing competitiveness and the capability to face technological restructuring and innovations. This shift in emphasis was partly due to decreasing birthrates which required a mobilization of human resources to meet technological requirements. Universities, however, faced with contracting public sector funding, especially for research and development, have had to focus on other sources of funds. Examples of European Community programs providing a training with production component include the Community Programme for Education and Training to Technology (COMETT), which focuses on university-industry liaison with periods of practical work experience, and the Programme on Education and Training (PETRA), which aims to improve the quality of initial training of young people, including possibilities for work placements abroad (COMETT 1990). In the 1980s European Community Action Programs on transition from school to adult and working life were launched. These programs included pilot projects catering for a combination of school-based and out-of-school learning in which the pupil performs activities varying from observation and enquiry of working life to direct productive work in order to achieve educational objectives (see *European Union: Continuing Vocational Training*).

Based on a survey in 14 countries, the OECD conducted a study on new forms of cooperation and collaboration between industry and universities. The report referred to "incubator factories," designed by some universities to assist infant industries, and to the placement of graduate students in an industrial environment and their involvement in industrial problem-solving. The report suggested that "governments can facilitate and encourage these new forms of co-operation by adjustment of legal and regulatory constraints and by provision of adequate incentives to all parties" (OECD 1994).

5. Implementing Training with Production

In the training domain the economic rationale for the inclusion of production has become much stronger than it is in the domain of general education, where, if anything, much more attention is given to pedagogical considerations. This is understandable in the light of the greater costs of training, since large sums are normally spent on nonsalary recurrent costs, such as training materials and tools. Production is often meant to help cover those costs. There has also been a much greater concern for interaction with the world of work. Participation in real production is seen as an important way of reducing the artificiality of the training environment and at the same time providing trainees with a better introduction to their future work environment.

Little attention has been given, however, to the practicalities of planning and implementing such production programs and to factors that lead to success and failure. While the possibilities for linking production components to training seem greater, experiences with production schemes related to general education have been more frequently reported upon than ones related to training. This can probably be explained by the relatively low research coverage of vocational education and training as a whole compared with research on formal general education. The restricted coverage is reflected in bibliographies, which reveal few studies concentrating on implementation issues in general and on the integration of the training and production component in particular (Haket and Hoppers 1986, Cabral de Andrade 1987, Biervliet and Haket 1994).

5.1 Scale of Implementation

In China training with production has been implemented system-wide, anchored to a set of specific policies and legislation related to fiscal resources, taxation on revenues, remuneration of teachers, equipment and material supply. However, schools have adopted different ways of implementing programs of training with production. Some have set up production and work-practice facilities at their own premises, through school-run factories and workshops. Other schools have availed themselves of production practice opportunities in external work units. Yet others have accepted production tasks on a subcontracting basis from working units and have linked these with their teaching activities (Zhou Tianxing 1988).

In many of the Eastern European and Central Asian republics, training with production continued on a system-wide basis after the breakdown of the centrally planned economies. With the consequent transition to market-oriented economies, it then faced a struggle for survival in the market economy. Competition developed for scarce practice places in enterprises. Schools had to pay for raw materials at market rates. In some of these countries legal frameworks were adopted to enable schools to obtain cooperative status with the right to market goods and services.

In Southeast Asian countries, such as Indonesia and the Philippines, policies and legislation now enable training institutions to adopt alternative cost-recovery schemes, including training with production. Pilot schemes are being tested out as a basis for system-wide implementation. In general, however, training with production has been implemented system-wide in only a few countries. In many instances, training with production is restricted to nonformal training provision through NGOs. Implementation in the formal training system is often on an ad hoc or experimental basis, sometimes supported by donor funding.

5.2 Relations between Training and Production

Where production is performed in or adjacent to a training institution, it can correspond to both the category of production-based training and production as learning practice or learning project. There are still few examples of production-based training and production as learning practice in both the North and the South. The most common mode is production as a learning project, where production is separated from the training curriculum. In the South, the production component often covers agriculture, horticulture, and animal husbandry. Where this is based on farm schools or agricultural colleges, it can be classified as production as learning practice. However, there is little evidence on the degree of integration of these field activities with the classroom curriculum; such production work is often essentially extracurricular in nature. Increasingly, production units are being established in the South under management separate from that of the training institution. Such units aim at income generation and improved capacity utilization of the training institution. This mode can, however, be seen not as training with production but as production within a training environment.

In the South, with the notable exception of sub-Saharan Africa, and in the North there are several examples of training alternating with practice periods in industry. Illustrations of this approach include the German dual system and "alternance" types of arrangement in secondary and higher vocational education in several other countries.

In all categories of training with production, the problem of curricular integration of training and production components ranks first. How should the training and production components in a curriculum be balanced so as to allow both broad-based training and the achievement of corresponding learning objectives and also the mastery of production-specific skills? Training and production components are sometimes integrated by means of comprehensive courses. In other cases they are compartmentalized in subjects such as fundamentals of production. A lack of integration is sometimes reflected in examination requirements and formal certification that do not acknowledge the production component of training. In dual schemes, this is overcome through trade-testing, even though it is not formally linked with the training-with-production programs.

Other problems relate to the different competencies required for training and production. Often training-with-production schemes lack a production and marketing strategy. Sustainability of those programs can be endangered by productivity problems leading to long delivery times, undercalculation because of poor time estimates, poor capacity utilization, and poor production coordination. As a consequence, production has sometimes generated losses rather than profits. Productivity and efficiency can be improved by recruiting management with experience in the private sector, the introduction of a production planning system, the improvement product development and marketing, and the development of a strategy for the utilization of trainees in the production department.

Possible varieties of liaison can be illustrated from DANIDA's support of production training centers. Several organizational models that combine or integrate training with production have been adopted. They range from an independent production unit model, where training and production are separate entities under separate management (in Tanzania) to a mixed model, where training is developed first and production is gradually integrated. This happened at an already established tool- and die-making training infrastructure in India. The Indonesian concept of production training centers can also be mentioned. In this, production and training are fully integrated in the sense that production is a prerequisite for training (DANIDA 1990).

5.3 Access to Training with Production

Formal training institutions that provide training with production programs tend to have high entry requirements. Hence they tend not to reach the underprivileged. Programs run by NGOs are more successful in reaching poorer youths with lower qualifications. Corvalán–Vásquez (1991) described an example of an approach to training with production specifically aiming at disadvantaged youth in the urban informal sector in Chile. It utilized ad hoc training centers in local community premises and the skills of local craftsmen. The training was directed toward the needs or microenterprises in the urban informal sector and was followed by assistance, including loans for those graduates willing to form cooperatives to establish a workshop or microenterprise. Nearly a quarter of the program's budget was derived from the production by trainees of a variety of marketable products.

6. Conclusion

The various aspects of training with production raise many questions for policymakers and practitioners who have to assess suitable modes for enhancing the quality and cost-effectiveness of training and, in the South, their capacity for income generation. An important common agenda item is the development of feasible strategies and approaches to strengthen mutual cooperation between enterprises and training institutions (Kanawaty and de Moura Castro 1990). While training with production seems to be an area of growing interest in both North and South, very little has yet been accomplished in the methodological and curriculum development area to facilitate integration of training with production.

See also: Economics of Adult Education and Training; Technological Change and Education; Demand, Supply, and Finance of Adult Education; Performance Contracting; Technical and Vocational Education and Training; Training on the Job

References

Biervliet W E 1994 *Training cum Production: Combining Separate Realities*. CESO, The Hague

Biervliet W E, Haket L 1994 *Training cum Production: An Annotated Bibliography*. CESO, The Hague

Cabral de Andrade A 1987 *Problemas y perspectivas de los Programas de Educación-Producción: Algunas Reflexiones*. CINTERFOR/ILO, Montevideo

COMETT 1990 *COMETT 1990 Compendium*. Commission of the European Communities, Brussels

Corvalán–Vásquez 1991 Training for socially disadvantaged youth and women in shanty town areas of Chile: The local dimension of CIDE's program. In: Buchert L (ed.) 1991 *Education and Training in the Third World: The Local Dimension*. CESO/CDR, The Hague

DANIDA 1990 Proceedings from a DANIDA workshop on income generating activities at vocational training centres in developing countries. DENCONSULT, Aalborg DANIDA, Copenhagen

Greinert W D, Wiemann 1992 *Produktionsschulprinzip und Berufsbildungshilfe*. Nomos Verlagsgesellschaft, Baden-Baden

Grootings P 1991 Modernisation of vocational education and training in Poland. *Eur. J. Educ.* (1): 29–40

Haket L, Hoopers W 1986 *Education with Production in East and Southern Africa; a Bibliography: Research Programme on Education and Production in Theory and Action (EPTA)*. Centre for the Study of Education in Developing Countries, The Hague

Income Data Services 1990 *IDS Study 456: Industry Links with Schools*. Income Data Service, London

Jennings-Wray Z D 1983 *Education and Productive Work in Jamaica*. CARNEID/UNESCO, Bridgetown.

Kanawaty G, de Moura Castro C 1990 New directions for training: An agenda for action. *Int. Lab. Rev.* 129(6): 751–71

King K 1990 *The Impact of Structural Adjustment on Technical and Vocational Education and Training Systems*. Training discussion paper No. 64. International Labour Office, Geneva

Komba D, Hoppers W 1994 *Productive Work in Education and Training: A State of the Art Review in Eastern Africa*. CESO, The Hague

Mehaut P 1987 *La Transition professionnelle: les jeunes de 16 à 18 ans*. Harmattan, Paris

Noah H, Middleton J 1988 *China's Vocational and Technical Training*. Policy, planning, and research working paper, education and employment No. 18. World Bank, Washington, DC

Organisation for Economic Co-operation and Development (OECD) 1983 *The Education of the Handicapped Adolescent: The Transition from School to Working Life*. OECD, Paris

Organisation for Economic Co-operation and Development (OECD) 1994 *Industry and University: New Forms of Co-operation and Communication*. OECD, Paris

Pfeifer R, Wald H 1987 *Polytechnical Education: Issues and Trends*. International Bureau of Education, Geneva

Schwartz A 1986 *The Dual Vocational Training System in the Federal Republic of Germany*. Discussion paper, education and training series, No. EDT 36. World Bank, Washington, DC

Schwartz B 1981 *L'insertion professionnelle et sociale des jeunes: rapport au Premier Ministre*. La Documentation Française, Paris

Uthmann K J 1991 Vocational education and training in Germany after unification. *Eur. J. Educ.* 26 (1): 5–12

World Bank 1991 *Vocational and Technical Education and Training*. The World Bank, Washington, DC

Zachariah M, Hoffman A 1985. Gandhi and Mao on manual labour in the school: A retrospective analysis. *Int. Rev. Educ.* 31(3): 265–82

Zhou Tianxing 1988 The development of vocational education in China. *Int. J. Educ. Dev.* 8(3): 237–38

Further Reading

Industrial Research and Development Advisory Committee 1991 *School and Industry: IRDAC Opinion*. Commission of the European Communities, Brussels

Industrial Research and Development Advisory Committee 1992 *Skills Shortages in Europe: IRDAC Opinion*. Commission of the European Communities, Brussels

Pain A 1978 Education and productive work. *Educational Documentation and Information: Bulletin of the International Bureau of Education* 52 (207) whole issue

Stern D, Raby M, Dayton C 1992 *Career Academies: Partnerships for Reconstructing American High Schools*. Jossey-Bass, San Francisco, California

Stern D, Stone J R, Hopkins C, McMillan M, Crain R 1994 *School-based Enterprise: Productive Learning in American High Schools*. Jossey-Bass, San Francisco, California

SECTION III

Human Development and Adult Learning

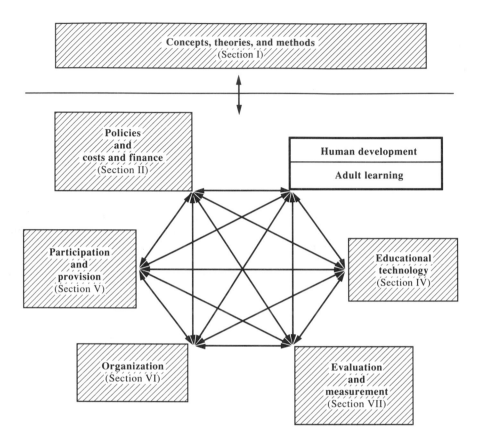

Figure 1
Schematic representation of Section III in relation to the other Sections

SECTION III

Human Development and Adult Learning

Introduction

A. Tuijnman

Learning is at the center of all adult education and training. Careful attention therefore has to be devoted to questions such as how human beings develop over the lifespan, how such development is influenced by learning, and how adults learn, and why. Two sets of entries in Section III address these substantive questions.

1. Human Development

Theories of human development center on the notion of change, as opposed to stability, across the lifespan. The different perspectives and theories have in common that the idea that "adulthood" somehow implies "being grown up and ready" has been discarded in favor of an interpretation that sees adulthood as fundamentally characterized by cognitive, psychological, and biological changes. Much research in psychology and adult education has focussed on the role of cognitive factors in motivation and engagement in organized or self-directed learning. Whereas in lifespan developmental psychology a number of general stage and process models have been proposed, in studies on cognitive development no generic models have so far been presented—the model of cognitive development in children and young adults proposed by Jean Piaget forms no exception.

Weinert presents an overview of the research field associated with the notion of human development. The focus of this entry is not on human development in general, but on psychological studies of the phenomena, mechanisms, and determinants of human development. This explains why much attention is paid to psychological studies of school learning as an antecedent of adult learning. The central theoretical orientations, controversies, and perspectives in developmental psychology are reviewed, in particular insofar these have a bearing on modern views about cognitive development and personality development in a social context. Weinert also reviews three theoretical positions concerning the relation between human development and education. The first sees human

development as an outcome of eduction, the second regards human development as a prerequisite of education, and the third considers human development as the goal of education. Weinert concludes that these three views are not exclusive, but that the different facets of human development require different concepts of education and learning.

The next entry by Schaie describes the major themes addressed in psychological studies of human development from young adulthood to old age. Age-related changes in cognition are given particular attention. There is evidence that some aspects of cognitive functioning decline with increasing age, but research studies also show that intelligence is not an obstacle to learning at an old age, thus confirming that most people have an ability to learn throughout life. The findings reviewed by Schaie lend some support to the various theories of multiple intelligences proposed by cognitive psychologists. These theories have far-reaching implications for both research and practice in adult education. Examples are the propositions that intelligence and capacity to learn at all ages are in significant measure a product of education and experience, and that adults continue to develop the abilities they use in daily life. Some of the implications for educators are explored in the entry contributed by Mackeracher and Tuijnman.

Heckhausen describes the development of the field from child psychology to lifespan development, and reviews the basic concepts of lifespan developmental psychology. An important tenet is that human development is viewed as a process involving both growth and decline, thus yielding a multidirectional perspective on human development in which growth and decline are not merely age- and period-specific, but occur concurrently along several dimensions, so that losses due to knowledge depreciation and other factors can be offset by learning gains made in another dimension. The issue of the multidimensionality of human cognition and learning is also taken up by Sternberg and McGrane. These authors review several approaches to the study of intellectual development across the lifespan, such as the traditional psychometric approach, the Piagetian approach, the information-processing approach, and the so-called contextual approach to cognition and adult learning. Sternberg and McGrance consider the contributions each approach offers to an understanding of how intelligence develops and changes over the lifespan, and how educators can best appreciate the cognitive abilities of learners. As Weinert before them, the authors conclude that each of the approaches offers important insights for educators. Although each approach captures certain important aspects of intellectual development across the lifespan, none capture its entirety. Memory development, a theme of special interest to adult educators, is the subject of an entry by Schneider. The author discusses the role of basic capacities, the effects of memory strategies, the role of metacognitive knowledge, and the impact of domain knowledge. Because these concepts apply to memory processes in both adults and children, the author approaches memory development from a lifespan perspective, dealing with recall and comprehension in both children and adults. He concludes that the decreases in memory functions observable in old adults point to neurobiological and neurophysiological contraints resulting from a lifetime of experience and cognitive activity.

Lifespan learning development is the subject of an entry contributed by Fales. This entry discusses the two major approaches that have been used to characterize learning across the lifespan. The first involves distinct life phases, and the second a series of hierarchical, sequential, and qualitative changes in psychological structures. The implications for adult education of ego-development levels for three life phases receive special attention. In the last entry of this cluster, Montada relates problems and crises in human development to incompatibilities in goal and coping strategies. It is clear that developmental problems and crises affect a person's life plans and actions. Coping with changes in developmental tasks, normative life crises, and critical life events implies flexibility and adaptation, and this will often require a new learning project.

1.2 Adult Learning

Adult learning involves a complex and dynamic interaction among a variety of physiological, personal, and environmental factors. These factors influence not only participation motivation, but also why and how adults learn. In a seminal study, Cyril O. Houle proposed that adult learners could be grouped into three categories: goal-oriented learners, the activity-oriented, and the learning-oriented. This hypothesis has been investigated in a number of studies informed by disciplines ranging from physiology and neurology, to psychology and education. This multidisciplinary body of knowledge, while being far from complete, provides useful insights into questions such as why

and how adults learn, and how learning can be facilitated. Despite the advances in knowledge, a coherent and empirically tested theory on adult learning does not exist and, because of the diversity of theoretical orientations that characterize the field, perhaps never will. A pluralistic and multidisciplinary approach to adult learning is therefore advocated in this subsection. The range and variants of adult learning seem to have increased in many countries since the mid-1980s. It has become evident—not only in theory but also in practice—that much adult learning does not occur in educational institutions and, more fundamentally, that self-directed learning at home, in cultural institutions, or informally at the workplace, in some cases may be more effective and rewarding than institutionally-based adult education. Adult learning is also an intensely personal endeavor, regardless of the institutional arrangements and contexts in which it occurs.

In the first entry Brookfield reviews four major areas of research on adult learning: self-directed learning, critical reflection, experiential learning, and learning to learn. Brookfield not only rejects the idea that these areas represent a unique and exclusive adult learning process, he also dismisses the proposal that adult learning should be considered as an entirely discrete domain, having little connection to learning in childhood or adolescence. The author concludes that it would be a grave error to attempt to construct an exclusive theory of adult learning, and that a more fruitful approach would focus on the role and specificity of adult learning in the context of lifespan development and lifelong learning. For this reason, in this *Encyclopedia*, no attempt is made to single out adult learning and treat it as being entirely separate from learning in childhood or adolescence. Although most entries are clearly focused on the adult learner, many references are made also to the theory and practice of school learning. Biggs, in the second entry, focuses on learning styles and the approaches to learning, employing four distinct theoretical frameworks, namely personal-styles theories, information-processing theories, phenomenographic studies, and systems theories. Again, these theories are seen as being not specific to adult education, but rather as forming part of a larger framework informed by many disciplines and theoretical perspectives. In the case of the learning style theory proposed by Kolb, which has received much attention during the 1980s, the author notes the lack of sufficient empirical support.

In the next entry, Howe claims—contrary to a widely held belief—there are no sharply defined "critical periods" in the lifespan during which particular skills or abilities have to be acquired. The kinds of variables that do affect learning and that account for improvements in learning across the lifespan are increases in knowledge, changes in the use of skills and strategies, and a range of influential habits and attributes that are broadly related to motivation and personality. Howe also reviews the influences of these three groups of variables on the development of lifespan learning. Collins, Greeno, and Resnick explain how new theories and the evidence gleaned from studies conducted with school children have shifted the research and policy agenda from a preoccupation with establishing effective teaching environments to one focusing on the creation of stimulating learning environments. The authors note that in the shift from the traditional environments for instruction to constructivist environments for learning, there has been a parallel shift to incorporate some of the characteristics of work environments, notably shared cognition and cooperative learning, tool manipulation, and contextualized reasoning. This development has contributed to the blurring of the boundaries between adult education and continuing vocational training, which was noted in the Introductions to Sections I and II.

Experiential and open learning are the subjects dealt with by Paul, who notes at the outset that the previously strong distinctions between "on" and "off" site learning are becoming blurred as adults increasingly engage in learning projects in informal—as opposed to formally structured—learning environments. Since education has become a lifelong activity, flexible and open learning environments become the essential means of responding to the learning needs of adults. The principles and applications of open and experiential learning, and their implications for the further development and reform of education systems, are also discussed by Paul. The author mentions seven major deterrents to participation in adult education and claims that open learning can be effective in overcoming these barriers. The next two entries deal with individual and group learning. Darkenwald notes that an understanding of theories of group behavior is essential because nearly all organized adult learning occurs in groups. Darkenwald focusses on the dynamics of learning in groups, especially voluntary discussion groups and study circles. Whereas Darkenwald concentrates on the role of the discussion leader as a facilitator of the learning process, Snow, in the next entry, focuses on the more traditional role of the educator faced with large differences between the learners in a group. This entry examines the state of knowledge about individual differences among children and adult learners, emphasizing constructs such as cognitive ability and prior knowledge, learning strategies and styles, achievement-related motivation, volition and interest, substantive understanding, and the management of the learning encounter. Snow reviews a very broad range of research on individual differences, and he contributes many insights that may be helpful in improving the conditions of instruction as well as the facilitation of adult learning more generally.

Contract learning (Rose) and learning in the workplace (Lowyck) are the subjects of the next two entries. Learning contracts are increasingly used to stimulate effective and purposeful learning, and to ensure that the acquired skills and competences are recognized. This recognition is a factor in learning transfer, a concept described by Perkins and Salomon in a subsequent entry. Informal learning in the workplace is another concept that has gained in importance in the field of adult education. Some of the factors that explain the new interest in informal learning in the workplace are reviewed in the first part of the entry. The same concerns that have produced the shift from adult education to adult learning are also behind the shift from structured occupational training, both on and off site, to learning as an integral, albeit informal component of all workplace activities. Informal learning in the workplace can thus be seen as a strategy for invigorating training policy in industry, but also as a means of upgrading and modernizing vocational education.

Smith deals with learning to learn in adult education, a subject that has received much attention of late. The entry reviews some of the existing knowledge concerning the concept of learning to learn, which is described as a complex and lifelong process through which people acquire and modify their skills and capacities for knowledge acquisition, problem-solving, and the extraction of meaning from experience. Hence the concept refers to learning about learning itself. Smith concludes that people learn to learn effectively through educational experiences and training that result in flexibility and awareness, as well as through the development of learning styles and strategies appropriate for various learning contexts. The effective learner is described as active and self-aware, in possession of a variety of learning strategies, knowledgeable about the available resources for learning, and capable of accurate self-monitoring and reflection on learning experience. Smith also notes that many of the facilitative strategies and resources for enhancing learning effectiveness are proving suitable for children as well as young and older adults. Learning to learn draws attention to the transfer of learning from one context or experience to another. In their entry, Perkins and Salomon observe that transfer is a key concept because most formal education aspires to the transfer of learning experience from one context to another. Consequently, the ends of education are not achieved unless transfer occurs. Perkins and Salomon first define transfer and then review the prospects, conditions, and mechanisms of transfer.

Self-directed learning is another key concept in adult education. Brookfield, in the first entry of this subsection, already noted that the concept focuses on the processes by which adults take control of their own learning, in particular how they set their own learning goals, locate appropriate resources, decide on which learning methods and strategies to use, and evaluate their progress. Hiemstra elaborates this description. Seven perspectives on the concept of self-directed learning are offered before its history is described. Hiemstra also synthesizes the relevant research studies and proposes the elements of a general theory of self-directed learning. Critical reflections on self-directed learning are also reviewed. Self-directed learning is very close to the notion of independent study, which is the subject of the broad review contributed by Entwistle in the next entry. Entwistle concentrates on the study and learning strategies of both young and older adults—particularly the students in institutions for higher and continuing education. This review of study skills and learning strategies pays less attention to traditional study skills training and concentrates, instead, on more recent insights about the various training methods and means of intervention which can be used to improve the effectiveness of the study strategies used by adult learners. As Howe did before him, Entwistle also reviews a number of study strategy inventories, paying special attention to the characteristics of successful learners.

Finally, Mackeracher and Tuijnman, in the last entry in Section III, provide a summary of some of the important theories and perspectives offered in the previous entries, especially insofar as these inform the practice of adult education. The focus of the entry is on the implications for adult educators, facilitators, and others involved in adult education and training, such as administrators, counselors, and program designers. The overview shows that there exists a growing body of information about how to facilitate adult learning and which factors improve the effectiveness of the learning process. Mackeracher and Tuijnman conclude that the development of powerful learning environments for adults needs to be based in adequate theories, methods, and materials of instruction. New insights about how people organize and execute their own personal learning projects are also required.

(a) *Human Development*

Human Development

F. E. Weinert

The focus of this entry is not on human development in general, but on psychological studies of the phenomena, mechanisms, and determinants of human development.

In the traditional knowledge base of all cultures and in the works of many philosophers, educators and physicians spanning different historical periods, there are observations, speculations, and considerable areas of knowledge about human development; developmental psychology as a scientific discipline, however, began only after the last third of the nineteenth century. Between 1890 and 1914 more than 20 journals and 25 research institutes devoted to child psychology were founded (Bühler and Hetzer 1929), although a few also dealt with the psychology of adult development and adult learning. Since then, scientific work on human development has expanded enormously and in the 1990s, developmental concerns are among the most prolific questions in the field of psychology. An overview of developmental theories and empirical research can therefore be only very selective and condensed.

This entry will begin with a description of some of the historical roots of scientific thinking about human development. This will be followed by a brief outline of some of the most central theoretical orientations, controversies, and perspectives in modern developmental psychology. This overview will serve as the basis for a consideration of cognitive development and personality development in a social context. The entry will end with a discussion of relations among the study of human development and the study of education.

1. Historical Roots of Modern Developmental Psychology

The roots of developmental psychology can be traced to the application of evolutionary theory to scientific psychology at the end of the nineteenth century. At that time, ideas about evolution influenced not only biology, but also philosophy and science in general. It was generally accepted that every living system developed " . . . from an indefinite, incoherent homogeneity to a definite, coherent heterogeneity" (Spencer 1881 p. 189).

Developmental psychology was accordingly understood to include not just child psychology, but also the psychology of animals, cultures, and mankind. The task set by this broad-based approach was to compare developmental variations systematically across different systems and to formulate general developmental laws of biological and mental life (Werner 1940). However, even then one of the founders of modern psychology, Wilhelm Wundt, had no doubt that, in contrast to his own theoretical position, "at least nine-tenths" of all psychologists would equate developmental psychology with child psychology (Wundt 1916 p. 196). This concern was soon evident in research activities, as childhood and adolescence became the primary subject matter of developmental psychology. However, some important elements of evolutionary theory remained central to the study of human development, even to the end of the twentieth century, by which time adult development had become an integral part of the field.

The concept of "biogenic law," which stemmed entirely from the philosophical spirit of the nineteenth century, strongly influenced the thinking of many developmental psychologists. This "law" refers to the doctrine that ontogeny recapitulates phylogeny. Briefly, development within an individual is postulated to follow a sequence of stages that correspond to the evolutionary history of the species.

The extent to which the theory of evolution and its metaphorical extensions contributed to this doctrine is well illustrated by W. Stern's characterization of human development:

In the first months of life, dominated by the lower senses and the dark and musty pull of drives and reflexes, the human infant is at the mammalian stage; in the second half year, with the acquisition of grasping and complex imitation, the infant reaches the highest mammalian level, that of the apes; the essential evolution into mankind occurs during the second year, with the acquisition of upright locomotion and speech. In the next 5 years of play and fantasy, the child is at the level of primitive natives. After this follows entry into school, a tighter integration into a social field with strict duties, and a sharp division between work and leisure—this is the ontogenetic parallel of man's entry into a civilized culture with its state and economic organizations. In the first years of school the simple behaviors of classical antiquity and Old Testament times are more suited to the child's mind; the middle years bring the visionary characteristics of the Christian culture; a mental differentiation appropriate to the culture of the present times is achieved only around the time of puberty. Certainly, puberty is described often enough as the Enlightenment of the individual (Stern 1906 p. 299).

Despite considerable fascination among North American and European turn-of-the century developmental psychologists with this idea of a condensed recapitulation of phylogeny in ontogeny, the superficial parallels did not withstand empirical scrutiny and theoretical critique. Nonetheless, some of the basic ideas underlying this philosophical and scientific tradition have remained, and are evident in modern versions of evolutionary theory, in sociobiology, in human ethology, and in cultural anthropology (see *Lifespan Development: Phases*).

The roots of developmental psychology in the ideas of evolution are expressed even more strongly in the basic theories and methodological paradigms that have dominated the field since its beginnings. For example, a typical assumption is "that cognitive changes during childhood have a specific set of formal 'morphogenetic' properties that presumably stem from the biological-maturational growth process underlying these changes. Thus, childhood cognitive modifications are largely inevitable, momentous, directional, uniform and irreversible" (Flavell 1970 p. 247).

The biological perspective in psychological theories of childhood development is complemented by similar explanations for typical changes in old age. The "maturation-degeneration-hypothesis" (patterns of decline in old age are the mirror image of growth processes in childhood) in animal and human development is one example. Thus, developmental psychologists are primarily interested in the age at which basic cognitive dispositions or behavioral competencies first appear, the cognitive prerequisites for these behaviors, how they change ("grow") over the course of time, when a mature form is achieved, and when these dispositions or competencies decrease in quantity or quality as a function of aging.

This theoretical orientation has been supported by the most common methodology used to empirically study developmental phenomena: cross-sectional studies. In these studies, behavior or performance is measured in samples of subjects of different ages, and observed age-group differences are used to infer how individuals develop over time. In addition, data are generally aggregated within age groups; thus, mean differences in the performance of different age groups are used as indicators of universal developmental patterns, and intraindividual and interindividual variations from mean age group performance are rarely attended to. There are only a very few longitudinal studies in which development is assessed by repeated measurements of the same individuals at different ages (see *Research Methodology: Human Development and Adult Learning*).

This one-sided methodological approach has meant that most theories of development are universal (they are held to be valid for all humans) and naturalistic–descriptive (they promise to describe those developmental processes that cannot be produced by environmental factors, although they may be modified by them). With such an orientation it is clear why the study of the origins of individual differences and the study of the contents of developing cognitive competencies have generally been ignored historically.

An interesting attempt to relate universal models of development to observed individual differences was undertaken by Binet and Simon (1905), who constructed the first developmental test to measure intelligence. They interpreted variations in the rate at which children's intelligence increased as an indication of stable individual differences in intellectual abilities, and thus founded the psychometric approach for describing cognitive development.

The impact of experimental psychology, which also began to establish itself as a science at the end of the nineteenth century, was much smaller than the enormous influence of evolutionary theory on subsequent developmental research. Although developmental psychologists adopted the same formal criteria for methodological and theoretical rigor as those used in experimental psychology, the function of experimental designs varied: in developmental psychology, they provided standardized conditions for observing "natural behavior" at different ages, rather than conditions for studying behavior (or its acquisition) as a function of stimulus variation.

Radical behaviorism provided an exception to this generalization. In this research tradition, individual behavioral development was seen primarily as a function of learning under appropriate environmental conditions, although species-specific inherited characteristics and maturational processes were not denied. An example (never empirically supported) of this position is Watson's famous statement: "Give me a dozen healthy infants, well-formed, and my own specified world to bring them up in and I'll guarantee to take any one at random and train him to become any type of specialist I might select—doctor, lawyer, artist, merchant-chief and, yes, even beggar-man and thief, regardless of his talents, penchants, tendencies, abilities, vocations, and race of his ancestors" (Watson 1970 p. 104).

This utopian expectation of infinite, arbitrary human malleability was contradicted even by Skinner (1966) because of the demonstrable effects of inherited characteristics on ontogenesis. Nonetheless, the importance of learning for the development of animal and human behavior was consistently and emphatically stressed in behavioristic theories.

The precise conceptual relationship between development and learning has always been somewhat controversial. However, there is no debate that the environment and individual experiences play important roles in the inception and shaping of human behavior. This view is in principle also accepted by those developmental psychologists who ascribe an important role to species-specific genetic factors, biological maturation, and the spontaneous unfolding of cognitive abilities (Chomsky 1959, Piaget 1947).

A stronger learning-centered perspective on human development appears in a variety of the different developmental theories described below.

In Freud's (1917) psychoanalytic interpretation of development, a sequence of natural stages in the development of psychosexual drives in childhood (oral, anal, phallic, and genital phases) was assumed. However, he also gave a decisive role to the social environment and argued that the individual personality characteristics were shaped by specific destiny of innate drives. This theoretical perspective became an essential principle underlying socialization research (Zigler and Child 1969).

Sociological interpretations of development (Goslin 1969) focus on the role of culture, the family milieu, socioeconomic status and interpersonal relations in development. These aspects, that is the totality of informal and institutional social learning opportunities (as well as constraints), are taken as the significant conditions that shape human development in child- and adulthood.

The cognitive approach to human development concentrates primarily on diverse changes in information processing. One result of work from this perspective has been to recognize the acquisition of domain specific knowledge as important for the development of competent thinking and acting. Learning, practice, and instruction are given a key role in cognitive development (Ericsson and Crutcher 1990).

The contrastive pairs, development and socialization, maturation and learning, universal developmental stages and individual developmental patterns represent different theoretical traditions that have existed since the beginning of developmental psychology. The contrast expressed by these pairs refers to a scientific task that is still not solved: "It is precisely the convergence of those two theoretical developments which constitutes a major challenge and promise for the future of research in developmental psychology" (Bronfenbrenner 1963 p. 538).

2. Theoretical Orientations, Controversies, and Perspectives in Modern Developmental Psychology

It is difficult to make general statements about significant research directions and scientific progress when one considers the state of developmental psychology in the 1990s. The phenomena and age ranges that are studied are diverse, and the empirical questions, methodological paradigms, and underlying theoretical models are highly varied. This gives the impression that developmental psychology is not at all a unitary research tradition that addresses some comprehensive and common questions spanning heterogeneous issues, topics, and tasks. It seems to be more a collection of many different and separate research directions that have in common only the fact that they are somehow concerned with the description or explanation of age-related differences or changes over the course of the human lifespan. The time of overarching theories and theoretical controversies in developmental psychology has ended, and has been replaced by an inflation of micromodels and some theories of medium breadth. Scientific discourse about general issues has shifted to the level of metamodels. These metamodels concern systems of relatively general assumptions about what changes and how change occurs in the development of human behavior.

2.1 Mechanistic and Organismic Models of Development

A dichotomous classification of developmental models as mechanistic or organismic that was suggested by Reese and Overton (1970, see also Overton and Reese 1973) is not concerned with psychological theories in the narrow sense, but rather with the basic philosophical and anthropological world views that underlie psychological models in general (see *Epistemological Issues in Educational Research*).

The mechanistic metamodel of development treats behavioral change as the complex outcome of more elementary, mechanistically functioning, quantifiable processes. Prototypical for these models are behavioristic learning explanations of developmental change. Not only do they explain the acquisition of motor skills, factual knowledge, or emotional reactions as the cumulative result of stimulus–response connections, they also claim that elementary learning processes and combinations of their effects can explain such complex developmental events as language development, the acquisition of creativity and the genesis of a reflexive self concept. The units of scientific analysis are elementary learning processes and their conditions (e.g., contiguity between stimulus and response, practice, reinforcement).

All in all, the importance of mechanistic models has not been very large in the history of developmental psychology; presently, they play a completely subsidiary role as metatheories, although mechanistic

341

explanations are used in many areas of developmental research.

In contrast to mechanistic models, organismic metamodels adopt a holistic world view; that is, the organism is portrayed as an integrated and internally differentiated whole. The development of this dynamic organism is characterized by qualitative, discontinuous, and stage-like changes that give rise to "novel" properties. A frequent metaphor for this process is the developmental sequence from egg to larva to butterfly.

An organismic metamodel characteristically underlies universalistic theories that treat individual development as an epiphenomenon of species-specific inherited qualities that can be influenced, but not directed by environmental conditions. Piaget's (1947) stage theory of cognitive development and Erikson's (1959) stage model of personality development are two familiar examples of this approach. The many variants of organismic metamodels have traditionally had an important role in developmental psychology (see *Lifespan Development: Phases*).

The theoretical restrictions related to the organismic model, that psychological development seems simply "a prisoner of age and stage" (Dannefer 1988 p. 7) led theorists to extend Reese and Overton's (1970) classification to further metamodels in the 1970s and 1980s. Two metamodels especially stimulated subsequent theoretical discussion and empirical research.

The first was a contextual metamodel. The emphasis in this model is on a lifelong

> ... reciprocal, or dynamic, influence of biological and psychological (or organism) processes and environmental (or contextual) conditions. In these conceptions, the reciprocal relation between the interrelated features of the person and his or her context are held to not merely 'interact' in the linear sense used in analysis of variance. Instead, person and context transact ... or 'dynamically interact'. ... By virtue of their reciprocal relation, each of the features is transformed by the other (Ford and Lerner 1992 p. 11).

As a metamodel, contextualism, in connection with systems theory and probabalistic explanatory models, has provided an important and varied framework for research in developmental psychology.

A second additional variant of the organismic world view is the attempt to formulate a metamodel to characterize specifically human attributes of development. This variant is deeply rooted in the philosophical spirit of the Enlightenment and in phenomenological and existential philosophical traditions. The anthropological roots of such a humanistic model of development can be described as follows: "As self-aware entities, human beings are intentional creatures. That means that they place meanings on things" (Kenyon 1988 p. 7). This model addresses development in a human organism that is seen as active from birth on, productively structuring its own information processing activities, and becoming increasingly more skillful in the self-organization of behavior and in self-reflective thinking.

Although the humanistic model is very important for understanding certain aspects of human development, it is not suited to the description or explanation of many other aspects of behavioral change.

2.2 Variable-centered Approach and Person-centered Approach

If one studies developmental psychology textbooks, it is possible to learn a great deal about the origins and changes of motor behavior, perception, memory, intelligence, anxiety, achievement motives, the self concept, or social behavior; however, little mention (and in many cases no mention!) is made of the developing person.

The variable-centered approach is dominant in developmental research, as it is in psychological research in general. This approach dictates the preferred theoretical constructs and methodological units used in the collection, analysis, and interpretation of empirical data. At this subpersonal level, it is typical for psychological variables to be analyzed separately and related functionally. In large, this is because of an assumption that lawful, domain-specific regularities concerning the "behavior of variables" (Wohlwill 1973 p. 359) are valid independent of the behaving person. Although this assumption has been supported in many, but not all cases, it does not allow statements about thinking, action, or development of the individual. Psychological functions and traits (e.g., motives, memory, intelligence, or temperament) are themselves neither conscious, intentional, nor self-reflective, despite what their descriptions in textbooks sometimes suggest. These qualities are properties only of individuals, not of processes or traits. Thus, it seems necessary and would be productive to complement (not replace!) the variable-centered approach with a person-centered approach.

In this case, the person is the unit of analysis in empirical research and related theoretical interpretations. Sufficient numbers of appropriate theoretical, methodological and statistical models are currently available to carry out this task.

> "The issue about person versus variable approaches is reflected in the debate over ideographic versus nomothetic, typological versus dimensional, and clinical versus statistical approaches to empirical psychological research. Most of the time, the two approaches have been regarded as contradictory. ... (We have) argued that they are compatible, and that what superficially seems to be contradictory in methodology and empirical results is often the result of inadequacies in theoretical distinctions and in methodological sophistication" (Magnusson 1988 p. 23).

2.3 Unidirectional Up-and-down Models and Multidirectional, Pluralistic Models of Development

As mentioned above, models in developmental psychology are dominated by a theoretical orientation toward the biological concepts of growth (in child-hood) and decline (in old age). A typical example was expressed by Denney, who wrote:

> The data ... clearly indicate that there is an increase in cognitive ability during childhood until a peak is reached in late adolescence or early adulthood; after that age there appears to be a decline in cognitive ability. . . . Although there are not enough data on structural change to draw any strong conclusion, these data suggest that older adults may be similar to younger children not only in their level of performance . . . but also in the structure of their abilities. This evidence suggests again that development during the latter part of the life span may mirror development during childhood (Denney 1982 p. 818).

In contrast to this restrictive growth–decline concept of development, lifespan models offer a considerably more open, liberal, and pluralistic picture of development. In these models, human development is perceived as a lifelong process. This process is polymorphic; that is, it is always composed of many, diverse changes in behavior that are combined or separate, continuous or discontinuous, and that can vary considerably in direction. There are developmental gains at all age levels (even in old age) and developmental losses at all age levels (even in childhood). This perspective assumes a large degree of plasticity in psychological development. Developmental processes are determined by biological factors (genetics, maturation, degenerative processes), historical–cultural life conditions, individual life histories, social contexts and nonnormative life events.

The lifespan approach is closely related to the contextualistic world view (Baltes 1987, Baltes et al. 1980). Although a monolithic growth model is predominant in child research, pluralistic lifespan models increase in influence on studies of other age populations.

2.4 Nature and Nurture as Determinants of Development

An especially controversial scientific issue is the relative influence of inherited factors (nature) and environmental conditions (nurture) in human development and in the development of individual differences in psychological characteristics. In discussions of this issue, the fact that two different questions are actually meant is often ignored.

One question concerns species-specific inheritance characteristics of all normal humans, that is, the genetic information that allows physical and psychological development to occur. For this type of inheritance to be expressed, some particular conditions must be met in a person's social–cultural environment (see *Environments for Learning*). According to Scarr (1992), the relation between internal and external developmental conditions is expressed in the following ways:

(a) Preadaptation: children are preadapted to react appropriately to a certain range of environmental conditions, to adapt, to process relevant information, and to acquire knowledge on the basis of their species-specific genetic inheritance.

(b) Variation: there are large variations in the stimulation and caretaking conditions within genetically specified areas in the natural environment that support normal development. These very different patterns of stimulation are "functionally equivalent opportunities for people to construct their own experiences" (Scarr 1992 p. 5).

(c) Limits: environments that fall outside the range of appropriate species-specific variations do not support normal development. "Thus, normal development does occur in a wide variety of human environments, but not in those lacking 'average expectable' conditions under which the species has evolved" (Scarr 1992 p. 5).

The second question in the nature–nurture discussion concerns the relative weight given to individual inheritance and environmental conditions in the development of interindividual differences in cognitive competencies and personality traits. The largest problem for research addressed to inherited factors is that it has not yet been possible to determine the genotype at the molecular level. Thus, genetic influences on development must be indirectly estimated. This is typically achieved by the comparison of related and nonrelated children (monozygotic twins, siblings, adopted children) that are raised together or apart. This method allows an estimation of the relative weight of genetic factors and environmental conditions that operate in a particular population in a particular historical period on variation in the development of psychological characteristics. However, it is not possible to make general statements about the importance of genetic influences for single individuals or for the species in any possible environment. This restriction is often ignored or misunderstood.

When one strictly acknowledges the methodological possibilities and constraints of estimates of heritability, the empirical results, despite public controversies, are relatively uniform and consistent. Whereas about half of the variance in the development of cognitive competencies in industrialized nations is determined by genetic differences, the genetic component in personality characteristics seems somewhat lower (Plomin 1990).

However, it is important to recognize that the influences of genetic and environmental factors are not independent of each other. There is a covariation between genetic and environmental influences that increases over the lifespan. This occurs because the environment that parents provide for their children corresponds to the parents' genetic makeup and older children and adolescents actively seek out those environments that correspond to their own genotype. It is also important to note that genetic factors do not influence the development of psychological differences directly, but through genetically determined learning processes.

Whether or not early childhood learning experiences have long term effects that are highly resistant to change, as many socialization theories suppose, is a controversial issue not resolved by the available empirical data. This controversy arises in personality development with respect to the effects of excessive gratification or frustration of early needs, or loss of an attachment figure, and in cognitive development with respect to the consequences of sensory or intellectual deprivation.

3. Cognitive Development

Everyday observations provide direct and convincing testimony of the extent to which children's understanding of physical, psychological and social phenomena, memory for new information, and complex problem solving improves over the first 15 years of life.

There is no doubt that Jean Piaget made the largest contribution to the scientific understanding of such cognitive changes. In his monumental scientific work, Piaget assumed that human intelligence allows the highest forms of both stable and flexible adaptation between an organism and its environment. Every healthy child is naturally equipped to acquire the necessary adaptive cognitive structures through a process of interaction with the environment and active processing of environmental information. This acquisition follows a universal sequence of qualitative changes in the structural base of logical thinking. According to Piaget, there are four major stages: sensory-motor, preoperational, concrete-operational, and formal-operational.

This universal and general sequence of stages of cognitive development is the result of the complex processes of assimilation (adjustment of external information to fit internally available cognitive schemes) and accommodation (adjustment of internally available cognitive schemes to fit increasingly complex external information) that serve to keep the entire cognitive system in a dynamic state of balance (equilibrium).

Piaget's scientific work has become universally known and respected. However, the structural-genetic theory has been criticized and its empirical support has been questioned. What is at issue is not so much the epistemological value of the theory, but rather its psychological implications. Piaget has been especially criticized by scientists from an information processing approach (Siegler 1991).

In this approach, it is assumed that cognitive development can be described as improvement in more or less domain specific information processing skills. These changes are explained both as age-related growth in working memory capacity and as the cumulative acquisition of declarative and procedural knowledge. In addition, processes of empirical and reflective abstraction are postulated to lead to the construction of metacognitive knowledge and skills that allow considerable improvement in the self-control of thinking and acting.

Arguments made for the importance of knowledge in the development of thinking are at times quite radical and in strict contradiction of Piagetian theory. For example, Carey (1984) wrote: "Children differ from adults only in the accumulation of knowledge (p. 37). . . . Children know less than adults; children are novices in almost every domain in which adults are experts" (p. 64).

This extreme knowledge-based explanation of cognitive development has led in part to a large degree of educational optimism (Ericsson and Crutcher 1990); however, it cannot be empirically supported in its radical version. What is not considered in this approach, and what is not considered in the Piagetian approach, are stable individual differences in intelligence and cognitive development that are partially genetically determined. The available empirical data suggest not only that all humans of all ages possess large intraindividual plasticity and untapped reserves for cognitive learning and performance, but also that interindividual differences in cognitive abilities are relatively stable. For example, when one provides children or adults with the same optimal learning opportunities, all persons in the group improve their performance considerably, but the interindividual differences remain or increase.

Results from research on mastery learning provide a good example. Mastery learning approaches attempt to have the majority of students (80–95%) reach demanding learning goals (90–95% correct answers) by giving extra optimal instructional time. The empirical results are, however, rather disappointing.

> Mastery theorists suggest an equilibrium of high and equal achievement accompanied by low and equal learning time. But equality of learning time and of achievement appear to be mutually exclusive. If equal learning time is desired, as in many current forms of schooling, the inequalities of achievement outcome appear to be an inevitable concomitant. If equality of achievement outcome is chosen as an end, as in mastery learning, the inequality of time seems necessary as a means (Arlin 1984 p. 82f).

4. Personality Development in Social Context

Cognitive development and personality development have frequently been treated as two separate research domains in psychology. Their conceptual and thematic separation makes it more difficult to perceive that there are many basic relations between changes in cognitive functioning and the development of personality traits (Thomae 1970).

Examples are the areas of motivational and moral development. Complex information from personal experiences, achievement demands, and social expectancies must be processed to set realistic behavioral goals and levels of aspiration, to specify causes for success and failure, and to construct a concept of the self. A sufficiently advanced cognitive developmental level is usually assumed to be a prerequisite condition for accomplishing these tasks.

That causal attributions for action outcomes, realistic self concepts and personal standards are closely related to the acquisition of judgment, evaluation, and decision skills during childhood, is an assumption made by theorists such as Piaget (1932), Kohlberg (1981/1984) and many others who postulate strong parallels between cognitive and moral development, and who claim that moral judgments play a key role in moral behavior.

A similar pattern was noted by Heckhausen (1982) for achievement motivation where theories

> have been based largely on the study of adult achievement behavior. Here we have attempted to extract developmental characteristics for these findings and to search for scattered empirical evidence to support a developmental theory. A logical structure of cognitive developmental steps has become visible that outlines the unfolding of achievement-oriented behavior between the ages 3 and 13 (Heckhausen 1982 p. 661).

Similar conclusions can be made concerning theories and data for the acquisition of other motivational systems governing the self concept and social behavior.

Although the demonstration of cognitive prerequisites is very convincing, a pressing question is whether these cognitive prerequisites are necessary and sufficient conditions for the acquisition of personality features or not, that is, whether "preferences need no inferences" (Zajonc 1980). It is very difficult to answer this question, because the differential development of behavioral dispositions is often lost in the scientifically inaccessible early childhood. Nonetheless, there is some evidence: for example, studies show that some even quite young children show behavioral reactions characteristic of learned helplessness after they have had clear experiences of failure (Dweck 1991). Such vulnerability in motivational states is apparently possible even when children do not have the cognitive skills to process an elaborated relation between failure and their own abilities.

Do early, endogenous temperament differences, early personal experiences, or experienced reactions from the social environment lead to such a dispositional asymmetry between positive and depressive attributional styles for success and failure? It is not yet clear either theoretically or empirically why a relatively large group of people from early childhood on

> "should disparage their own effectiveness, abilities, and competence in their own eyes and in the eyes of others, even when there is no compelling reason—when the same achievement outcomes could have been attributed so that subjects can retain a much higher sense of self-esteem without diminishing attributional plausibility. The question then is, whether such persons have acquired a negative self-image in which they intend to adhere, even after having had more positive experiences. . . . Recent findings are surprising, they show the degree to which individuals will hold to a preconceived notion even though it has been disproved by the facts . . ." (Heckhausen 1987 p. 146).

This citation raises the central question in personality research. This question concerns stability, variability and change in personality characteristics—regardless of whether they are plausible or implausible, functional or dysfunctional, helpful or hurtful to the individual. Of course, in many psychological theories personality is defined as what does not change over the life course, especially when one would expect changes.

In this definition, two types of stability are meant: the similarity of behavior across different situations (situational consistency) and the similarity of behavior across longer time spans (temporal persistency). When temporal stability is at issue, it does not imply that individual behavior always remains identical, but instead that interindividual differences in a psychological characteristic remain constant over time, that is, that the relative position of an individual in his or her reference group remains constant over time.

The dominant model used to describe human personality and the temporal stability of individual differences is the Five-Factor model ("Big Five"). The single dimensions in this model are characterized as follows: Factor I, extraversion versus introversion (surgency); Factor II, friendly compliance versus hostile noncompliance (agreeableness); Factor III, conscientiousness (will); Factor IV, neuroticism versus emotional stability; Factor V, openness to experience (intellect, culture) (Digman 1990).

The Five-Factor model (primarily assessed with questionnaires) has been demonstrated to be very useful for describing personality with both self ratings and other ratings (e.g., from teachers). By combining values on the five dimensions, it is possible to characterize individual personality, to describe individual differences, and to predict behavior, even for school age children (Halverson et al. 1993). From adolescence on, the stability of the five personality dimensions appears relatively high, and is quite high in longitudinal studies of adults (e.g., correlations of 0.8 over a six year span (see Costa and McCrae 1988)). On the other hand, it is difficult to evaluate the individual stability of personality characteristics in childhood because there are enormous differences between the temperamental factors measured in early childhood and the dimensions measured by the Five-Factor model. Whether these discrepancies are related to instability in personality characteristics in early childhood, to the different measures used, or to developmental transformations in personality characteristics is presently an open question.

What underlies the high stability of personality characteristics in later childhood and adulthood? At first glance, they seem to support "the conclusion most of us make with surprise upon seeing a good friend after many years of separation: He is just the same as he always was" (Digman 1990 p. 434).

However, beyond some stability in general personality characteristics, it often also seems that individuals show substantial changes in personal opinions, beliefs, problems, and patterns of reactions to developmental tasks. An important question is whether individual reactions to critical life events (e.g., unemployment, death of a close person, severe illness) are really predictable from the "Big Five." It appears that this is not the case. Rather, what seems to determine these reactions is much more a person's subjective interpretation of the event, the style of coping, and the degree to which social support is available (Montada et al. 1992).

Thus, to understand the relation between stability and change, an ecological model of personality development (Bronfenbrenner 1989) may be very productive and necessary. This sort of model is not concerned so much with change in single psychological variables, but with an interaction between the individual (an idiosyncratic pattern of variables) and his or her social environment.

It is without a doubt scientifically important that significant effects from genetic factors, family background, peer relations, the school experiences, social reference groups, work life, and critical life events are assessed in longitudinal studies. However, there is as yet no theoretical model that would allow assessment of the cumulative, compensatory and/or trade-off effects of these multiple factors on the development of personality. This problem is presently an issue in the many studies on the origins of sex and gender differences (Hyde and Lynn 1986) as well as in studies on the identification of individuals at risk (Kohlberg et al. 1972). Given the current state of knowledge in the field, a comprehensive model based on behavior genetics and social cognitive learning theory would seem to be the most appropriate for describing and explaining personality development in a sophisticated way.

5. Conclusion: Development and Education

Psychological development without education is an abstract fiction that does not occur in reality. The human is biologically incomplete at birth and needs intensive care, social interaction, and learning. Thus, the question for the social sciences is not whether education is necessary, but rather which different social conditions and educational interventions affect personality development and how they do so.

When education is discussed in this connection, it is generally not conscious teaching and intentional instruction that is meant, but rather the incidental learning that arises from living experiences and interactions in a sociocultural community, the many forms of learning from observation and imitation of others, as well as the countless behavioral directions, suggestions, supports, and corrections provided by adults and peers. Over the course of development, a good deal must be learned that cannot be explicitly taught (see *Formal, Nonformal, and Informal Education*).

If one defines psychological development as those changes in individual patterns of behavior that occur over the life course, then the concept of "education" refers both to those sociocultural conditions and interventions that are explicitly directed to foster desired behavior and inhibit or correct undesired behavior (intentional education) as well as to those behaviors and events in the environment that have the effect of strengthening or inhibiting behavior, but that are not planned or intentionally presented (functional education). The boundaries between unplanned socialization and planned educational interventions are fluid and cannot be sharply distinguished.

There are three different theoretical positions concerning the relation between development and education. First, development as the result of education. Proponents of this perspective (Watson 1970, Skinner 1966) assume that except for some sensory and motor abilities present at birth and some biologically preprogrammed maturational processes in the first years, all human behavior must be learned. What is meant by psychological development from this perspective is the complex outcome of many single, related and embedded processes of learning. Unplanned and planned behavioral shaping by environmental factors are relevant educational mechanisms (Langer 1969).

Second, development as a prerequisite of education. In contrast to a learning explanation of human development, advocates of this position assume that spontaneous age-typical cognitive and behavioral dispositions develop as a consequence of endogenous processes (e.g., maturationally directed increases in working memory capacity). This improvement in learning capacity that cannot itself be explained from a learning theory perspective, allows and requires concrete learning opportunities in the person's environment. According to this view, the person is reliably able to take advantage of such learning opportunities, because humans are naturally outfitted with mechanisms for active information search and processing that are appropriate for the systematic construction of cognitive structures. Under this perspective, education has only a supporting role. Spontaneous psychological development is in any case a necessary prerequisite for an explicit acquisition of cultural knowledge (Gesell and Ilg 1943).

Third, development as the goal of education. According to this view, more advanced cognitive structures cannot be directly taught; however, the processes of spontaneous development need support and facilitation from the social environment, so that they do not remain at a relatively immature stage (concrete operations) or regress to an earlier stage. Kohlberg and Mayer (1972) explicitly promote the "ideology" that it is especially important for the individual to attain the most advanced stage of cognitive development possible because personal autonomy, self responsibility, and moral action are stage-dependent. They criticize both behaviorists and advocates of an antiauthoritarian movement because in their opinion "it is better for the child to be a happy pig than an unhappy Socrates" (Kohlberg and Mayer 1972 p. 472).

The most important task of education according to this view is thus not to shape behavior or to transmit specific knowledge, but to provide optimal stimulation to foster cognitive development, that is, stage transformation. But how, for example, can education for development proceed?

The task of the teacher is to facilitate the process of change. In summary: To be effective, the teacher must have a knowledge of the learner's level of thought; match the learner's level by communicating at the level directly above; focus on reasoning; and help the learner experience the type of cognitive conflict that leads to awareness of the greater adequacy of the next stage (Kohlberg no date p. 42f).

These three different views of the relation between development and education are not currently advocated in their most radical forms, but only in more liberal interpretations. Many empirical studies have shown that different facets of human development require different concepts of education. This conclusion is not a simple eclectic compromise, but rather the pragmatic outcome of the current state-of-the-art of theory in developmental psychology.

See also: Research Methodology: Human Development and Adult Learning; Lifespan Development; Lifespan Development: Phases; Development of Learning Across the Lifespan; Individual Differences, Learning, and Instruction; Instructional Design: Guidelines and Theories; The Development of Competence: Toward a Taxonomy

References

Arlin M 1984 Time, equality, and mastery learning. *Rev. Educ. Res.* 54(1): 65–86

Baltes P B 1987 Theoretical propositions of lifespan developmental psychology: On the dynamics between growth and decline. *Dev. Psychol.* 23(5): 611–26

Baltes P B, Reese H W, Lipsitt L P 1980 Life-span developmental psychology. *Annu. Rev. Psychol.* 31: 65–110

Binet A, Simon T 1905 Application des méthodes nouvelles au diagnostic du niveau intellectuelle chez des enfants normaux et anormaux d'hospice et d'école primaire. *Annee Psychol.* 11: 245–336

Bronfenbrenner U 1963 Developmental theory in transition. *Child Psychology. The Sixty-second Yearbook of the National Society for the Study of Education. Part 1.* Chicago Press, Chicago, Illinois

Bronfenbrenner U 1989 Ecological systems theory. *Annals of Child Development* 6: 187–249

Bühler Ch, Hetzer H 1929 Zur Geschichte der Kinderpsychologie. In: Brunswik E et al. (ed.) 1929 *Beiträge zur Problemgeschichte der Psychologie.* Verlag von Günter Fischer, Jena

Carey S 1984 Cognitive development. The descriptive problem. In: Gazzaniga M S (ed.) 1984 *Handbook of Cognitive Neuroscience.* Plenum Press, New York

Chomsky N 1959 Review of Skinner's verbal behavior. *Language* 35: 26–58

Costa P T Jr, McCrae R R 1988 Personality in adulthood: A six year longitudinal study of self-reports and spouse ratings on the NEO personality inventory. *J. Pers. Soc. Psychol.* 54(5): 853–63

Dannefer D 1988 What's in a name: An account of the neglect of variability in the study of aging. In: Birren J E, Bengtson V L (eds.) 1988 *Emergent Theories of Aging.* Springer, New York

Denney N W 1982 Aging and cognitive changes. In: Wolman B B (ed.) 1982 *Handbook of Developmental Psychology.* Prentice Hall, Englewood Cliffs, New Jersey

Digman J M 1990 Personality structure: Emergence of the five-factor model. *Annu. Rev. Psychol.* 41: 417–40

Dweck C S 1991 Self theories and goals: Their role in motivation, personality, and development. In: Dienstbier R A (ed.) 1991 *Nebraska symposium on motivation*, Vol. 36. University of Nebraska Press, Lincoln, Nebraska

Ericsson K A, Crutcher R J 1990 The nature of exceptional performance. In: Baltes P B, Featherman D L, Lerner R M (eds.) 1990 *Life-span Development and Behavior*, Vol. 10. Erlbaum, Hillsdale, New Jersey

Erikson E H 1959 Identity and the life cycle. *Psychol. Iss.* 1(1): 18–164

Flavell J 1970 Cognitive change in adulthood. In: Goulet R, Baltes P B (eds.) 1970 *Life-span Developmental Psychology: Research and Theory.* Academic Press, New York

Ford D H, Lerner R M 1992 *Developmental Systems Theory: An Integrative Approach.* Sage, Newbury Park, California

Freud S 1917 *Vorlesungen zur Einführung in die Psychoanalyse.* Heller Verlag, Leipzig

Gesell A, Ilg F L 1943 *Infant and Child in the Culture of Today.* Harper & Row, New York

Goslin D A 1969 *Handbook of Socialization, Theory and Research.* Rand McNally, Chicago, Illinois

Halverson C F, Kohnstamm G A, Martin R P 1993 *The Five Factor Model and its Roots in Childhood.* Erlbaum, Hillsdale, New Jersey

Heckhausen H 1982 The development of achievement motivation. In: Hartup W H (ed.) 1982 *Review of Child Development Research*, Vol. 6. The University of Chicago Press, Chicago, Illinois

Heckhausen H 1987 Causal attribution patterns for achievement outcomes: Individual differences, possible types and their origins. In: Weinert F E, Kluwe R H (eds.) 1987 *Metacognition, Motivation, and Understanding.* Erlbaum, Hillsdale, New Jersey

Hyde J S, Linn M C (eds.) 1986 *The Psychology of Gender.* The Johns Hopkins University Press, Baltimore, Maryland

Kenyon G M 1988 Basic assumptions in theories of human aging. In: Birren J E, Bengtson V L (eds.) 1988 *Emergent Theories of Aging.* Springer, New York

Kohlberg L 1981/1984 *Essay on Moral Development*, Vols. 1–2. Harper and Row, San Francisco, California

Kohlberg L no date The concepts of developmental psychology as the central guide to education. In: *Proceedings of the Conference in Psychology and the Process of Schooling in the Next Decade: Alternative Conceptions.* University of Minnesota, Minneapolis, Minnesota

Kohlberg L, LaCrosse I, Ricks D 1972 The predictability of adult mental health from childhood behavior. In: Wolman B B (ed.) 1972 *Manual of Child Psychopathology.* McGraw-Hill, New York

Kohlberg L, Mayer R 1972 Development as the aim of education. *Harv. Educ. Rev.* 42(4): 449–96

Langer J 1969 *Theories of development.* Holt, Rinehart & Winston, New York

Magnusson D 1988 *Individual Development from an Interactional Perspective: A Longitudinal Study.* Erlbaum, Hillsdale, New Jersey

Montada L, Filipp S H, Lerner M J (eds.) 1992 *Life Crisis and Experiences of Loss in Adulthood.* Erlbaum, Hillsdale, New Jersey

Overton W F, Reese H W 1973 Models of development: Methodological implications. In: Nesselroade J R, Reese H W (eds.) 1973 *Life-span Developmental Psychology: Methodological Issues.* Academic Press, New York

Piaget J 1932 *The Moral Judgement of the Child.* Penguin Books, Harmondsworth

Piaget J 1947 *La Psychologie de l'Intelligence.* Colin, Paris

Plomin R 1990 *Nature and Nurture.* Brooks/Cole Publishing Comp, Pacific Grove, California

Reese H W, Overton W F 1970 Models of development and theories of development. In: Goulet L R, Baltes P B (eds.) 1970 *Life-span Developmental Psychology: Research and Theory.* Academic Press, New York

Scarr S 1992 Developmental theories for the 1990s: Development and individual difference. *Child Dev.* 63(1): 1–19

Siegler R S 1991 *Children's Thinking.* Prentice Hall, Englewood Cliffs, New Jersey

Skinner B F 1966 The phylogeny and ontogeny of behavior. *Science.* 153: 1205–13

Spencer H 1881 *The Principles of Psychology*, Vol. I, 3rd edn. Williams & Norgate, London

Stern W 1906 *Person und Sache. System der philosophischen Weltanschauung. I. Ableitung und Grundlehre.* Barth, Leipzig

Thomae H 1907 Theory of aging and cognitive theory of personality research. *Hum. Dev.* 12: 1–16

Watson J B 1970 (orig. 1925). *Behaviorism.* Kegan Paul, Trench, Trubner, London

Werner H 1940 *Comparative Psychology of Mental Development*, 3rd edn. Int. Universities Press, New York

Wohlwill J F 1973 *The Study of Behavioral Development.* Academic Press, New York

Wundt W 1916 *Völkerpsychologie und Entwicklungspsychologie. Psychologische Studien* 10: 189–239

Zajonc R B 1980 Feeling and thinking: Preferences need no inferences. *Am. Psychol.* 35(2): 151–75

Zigler E, Child I L 1969 Socialization. In: Lindzey G, Aronson E (eds.) 1969 *The Handbook of Social Psychology*, 2nd. edn., Vol. 3. Addison-Wesley, Reading, Massachusetts

Human Development: Aging

K. W. Schaie

The marked prolongation of the human lifespan in the twentieth century has led to an increased interest in the educational needs of adults and aging individuals. This entry discusses some of the demographic issues arising from greater aging within industrialized societies, describes major themes of psychological development from young adulthood to old age, and considers the resulting educational implications.

1. Historical Overview

The study of human aging is of relatively recent vintage within the developmental sciences. Although James McKeen Cattell published his treatise *Senescence* in 1922, very little serious work in adult development appeared prior to the 1950s. Many developmental researchers were primarily interested in discovering how individual behavior is acquired early in life. Only slowly did interest in behavioral growth advance from childhood into adolescence; there remains some reluctance to tackle the complexities of behavioral maintenance, change, and decline in adulthood. It was common to suppose that age-related changes in adulthood would be few. Personality was thought to be firmly set as maturity was reached. For, as long as divorce and mid-life career changes were rare phenomena, family and career decisions were made early in life and then maintained. Intellectual abilities were believed to peak early and decline with age; sexual prowess was thought to wane. Yet until the twentieth century few people survived into old age, so these matters could not be examined in depth.

Advances in sanitation, nutrition, and medical knowledge have changed life expectancy dramatically throughout the world. In the industrialized countries, a child born in 1900 could not have expected to reach the age of 50; now average life expectancy in the same countries is approaching 80 years. While at the beginning of the twentieth century fewer than 5 percent of the population attained the age of 65 (often considered as the threshold of old age), comparable figures now range from 12 to 20 percent. These population shifts are not simply due to improvement in medical care and life-styles but also to substantial declines in fertility rates. These rates have not only been affected markedly by the introduction of reliable methods of family planning but also by periods of war, economic expansion, and economic declines. Thus "baby boom" generations are often followed by "baby bust" generations, causing alterations in many behavioral patterns. For example, saving practices in Japan in the 1980s may well have been a function of a "baby boom" generation at its highest earning potential; this may be followed by increased consumption as these baby boomers age. The succession of a baby bust generation following the baby boomers in the United States is likewise thought to threaten the viability of the social insurance system.

The acceleration of technological change has made it quite likely that most persons will experience many job and career changes during their working lives. The rise in both the proportion and the absolute number of older persons in the population will engender a number of structural changes in society. These individuals will have to be better integrated into the social fabric so that more of them can continue to participate actively. Better health and higher levels of education will increase pressures for greater availability of educational opportunities throughout the adult lifespan (Schaie 1982).

2. Adult Cognitive Development

Most cognitive skills reach a peak by early or middle adulthood, maintain a plateau until the late fifties or early sixties, and then begin to show decline. The decline is slow at first but accelerates as the late seventies are reached. Some individuals, however, retain their behavioral competence well into advanced old age, while others show early decline (Cunningham 1987, Labouvie-Vief 1985, Schaie 1996, Willis 1985). Although the applicability of laboratory and academic tests to everyday problems has been questioned, strong relationships between these measures and competence on everyday tasks have been demonstrated (Willis and Schaie 1986).

Five major questions can be asked about the course of adult cognitive development for which well-supported answers can be provided. These questions are as follows: (a) Do cognitive skills change uniformly through adulthood or are there different life-course ability patterns? (b) At what age is there a reliably detectable age decrement in ability, and what is the magnitude of that decrement? (c) What are the patterns of generational differences, and what is their magnitude? (d) What accounts for individual differences in age-related change in adulthood? (e) Can cognitive

decline in old age be reversed? Each of these questions has educational implications which will also be considered.

2.1 Differential Patterns of Change

Age-related changes are not uniform across all cognitive skills: studies of overall IQ or of particular aspects of memory have therefore been found insufficient to monitor age changes and age differences over the adult life course for either individuals or groups. Verbal abilities continue to increase into late mid-life and are maintained well into old age, while novel tasks of an abstract nature (sometimes called "fluid" abilities) show at an early stage age differences favoring younger adults (Horn 1982, Schaie 1996, Siegler 1983). Patterns differ, however, by gender and specific cognitive skill. For example, fluid abilities begin to decline earlier, but verbal abilities appear to show steeper decrement once the late 70s are reached (Schaie 1996). Older learners are consistently better at recognition of information than at its recall. Well-established knowledge structures often tend to compensate for the disadvantages incurred by the perceptual and motor slowing that gradually affect the performance of most individuals past mid-life.

2.2. Age Level and Magnitude of Age-related Cognitive Decline

Cross-sectional studies with the Wechsler Adult Intelligence Scale (WAIS) suggest that significant age differences favoring young adults can be found by the thirties for performance tests and by the sixties for verbal tests (Matarazzo 1972). By contrast, longitudinal studies rarely find reliable age decrement prior to age 60, but observe average decline for all cognitive skills at least by age 74 (Schaie 1996). Analyses of individual differences in intellectual change, however, demonstrate that even at age 81 less than half of all observed individuals showed reliable decremental change over the preceding seven years (Schaie 1984).

Average age-related decrement until age 60 amounts to less than 20 percent of a population standard deviation (a relatively trivial amount), but by age 81 average decrement amounts to at least 1 standard deviation for most intellectual abilities (i.e., all but a small number of persons of this age perform at a level below the average of young adults).

2.3 Generational Differences

The existence of generational (cohort) differences in intellectual abilities has been conclusively demonstrated (Flynn 1984, Willis 1989). Almost linear positive cohort-shifts have been observed for inductive reasoning, with more spasmodic positive shifts for verbal ability and spatial orientation. A curvilinear cohort pattern has been found for number skills, which in the studies reported by Willis (1989) reached a peak for birth cohorts born in the 1920s and then followed a largely negative slope. A similar curvilinear cohort pattern has also been observed for word fluency (Schaie 1996). As a consequence, cross-sectional studies of intellectual aging tend to underestimate age changes prior to age 60 for abilities with negative generational trends and to overestimate age changes for abilities with positive generational trends.

2.4 Individual Differences in Age-related Change in Adulthood

Individual differences in cognitive skills are, of course, large at all ages, such that substantial overlap among different age groups can be found from young adulthood into the mid–70s (Schaie 1988). Very few individuals decline on all or most abilities. Indeed, maintenance of functioning on one or more abilities is characteristic for most individuals well into advanced old age (Schaie 1989a).

A number of factors have been identified that account for individual differences in age-related change, some of which have been shown to be amenable to experimental intervention. Variables found to be predictive of favorable cognitive aging include: (a) absence of cardiovascular and other chronic disease; (b) favorable environment as indicated by high socioeconomic status (SES); (c) involvement in a complex and intellectually stimulating environment; (d) flexible personality style at mid-life; (e) high cognitive status of spouse; and (f) maintenance of level of perceptual processing speed.

2.5 Reversibility of Cognitive Decline

Unless neurological pathology is present, cognitive interventions may serve to remediate known intellectual decline, and reduce generational differences in those individuals who have remained stable in their own performance over time but who have become disadvantaged when compared to younger persons. The effectiveness of educational interventions has been demonstrated in various laboratory studies (Schaie and Willis 1986, Willis 1987). Cognitive decline in many older people may well be due to disuse of specific skills and can be reversed by appropriate training regimens. In one of the studies by Schaie and Willis, five hours of cognitive strategy training resulted in significant improvement for two-thirds of experimental subjects over age 65, and about 40 percent of those who had declined significantly over 14 years were returned to their predecline level (Schaie and Willis 1986). Further studies are needed to assess whether educational intervention would be most effective by teaching cognitive strategies on basic ability skills or by training on specific everyday tasks. Cognitive training has been shown to be ability-specific. Because most everyday tasks involve components of basic abilities, training on multiple abilities might therefore be required. On the other hand, it is unlikely that training on specific everyday tasks would generalize to substantively different tasks (see Willis 1987, 1992 for further discussion).

3. Personality Development in Adulthood

In contrast to the age changes observed in cognitive skills across the lifespan, the evidence on personality development is one of remarkable stability. With few exceptions, observed age differences in personality traits turn out to be primarily differences between generations. In other words, societal shifts in early socialization and childrearing practices tend to contribute more to observed personality differences between young and old adults than do normative experiences encountered in adulthood.

There are several reasons why personality remains stable throughout adulthood for most persons. Traits, habits, modes of thinking, and the ways by which people cope and interact are all patterned in a unique fashion for each individual. Like any organized system, the adult personality resists change, since change in one aspect would require realignment in other interrelated parts. However, broad societal changes will also impact personality styles (Schmitz-Scherzer and Thomae 1983).

Once formed, adult personality is unlikely to change radically, even when stressful circumstances such as divorce, retirement, or impending death are encountered. Instead, personality traits established early in life determine how persons will respond to adult life stresses. For example, different reactions to retirement reflect earlier adjustment patterns. Individuals with well-integrated personalities experience little difficulty in what they see as the final stage of a series of successful life transitions. On the other hand, those with poorly integrated personalities may encounter the same event with despair and hostility; turning "sour" in the last stages of their life (Erikson 1982).

3.1 Personality Traits

Questionnaire-based studies of personality traits have been based primarily on cross-sectional studies; hence the age differences reported for them probably reflect primarily generational differences. Studies with the Minnesota Multiphasic Personality Inventory (MMPI) suggest that older age cohorts are more introverted. Both older men and women described themselves as more "masculine" than young adults. Young adults described themselves as more energetic, with attitudes that are more unusual and unconventional (Culligan et al. 1983). Questionnaire studies with other instruments, such as the California Personality Inventory (CPI), the Sixteen Personality Factor Questionnaire (16PF), the Guilford–Zimmerman Temperament Survey (GZTS), and the NEO (Neuroticism, Extraversion, and Openness) Personality Inventory show similar findings; traits tend to remain quite stable across adulthood. Most age differences represent generational shifts; and only few traits such as excitability and sociability increase with age (Gough 1969, McCrae and Costa 1987, Siegler et al. 1979, Schaie and Parham 1976). The limited observable change seems to occur largely in young adulthood, during the shift from student to employed status, and not during middle or old age (Kogan 1990).

3.2 The Self-concept

Although personality trait structure remains stable across adulthood, there have been reports of subtle changes in the self-concept. These changes involve the relative importance attributed to various life domains, in the elaboration of possible selves, and the strategies employed to preserve stability (Markus and Herzog 1992).

Traditional sex differences in self-concept are less evident as people get older. Young adult males describe themselves as more aggressive than older males, but older males were higher in cooperation and nurture. Younger women scored higher than younger men in cooperativeness, docility, and dependence. However, these differences disappeared with age; older men were only slightly more dominant than older women (Ryff 1984).

As people age, they tend to change the timing and methods of attaining a goal, they lower their expectations, and they are more ready to abandon an unattainable goal (Brim 1988). Assimilative strategies that involve active adjustment to current circumstances may be chosen in aversive situations in order to avoid depression and disappointment. Alternatively, accommodative strategies are selected in which the individual modifies desired outcomes to match current circumstances. These strategies are increasingly adopted by older adults and represent flexible adjustment to the realistic losses of old age (Brandstädter and Renner 1990).

Most would expect that body image—how a person feels about his or her physical sense—would shift across adulthood as persons age. Contrary to popular opinion, research findings suggest remarkable stability of body image, and the stereotype that older people consider themselves unattractive appears to be inaccurate (Crockett and Hummert 1987, Montepare and Lachman 1989).

Related to changes in self-concept is the maintenance of a sense of psychological well-being. This includes a sense of continued development over the life course, the capacity to maintain goals and a sense of purpose, as well as to maintain high-quality relationships with others. Empirical research on well-being in the later period of life suggest both gains and losses. There is an increase in self-acceptance and self-esteem, but a decline in the sense of personal growth

and purpose in life. However, the latter may be offset by many by their capacity to accept change and by possessing a sense of humor (Ryff and Essex 1992).

3.3 Locus of Control

Considerable attention has been devoted to this construct since the 1980s because many mental and physical outcome variables have been identified that depend largely on the extent to which the individuals actually are and—even more importantly—perceive themselves to be in control of their lives and of the resources needed to make meaningful decisions about their life circumstances (Rodin et al. 1990). It has been argued that as adults age they experience an increasing number of life events over which they have little or no control. As a consequence, one might expect a decline with age in the belief in the possibility of control with a corresponding increase in the attribution of control to external factors. Lachman (1989) found changes in control beliefs to be quite domain-specific. Higher levels of belief in external control were found with respect to health and intelligence but not for generalized measures of control. This difference is important, since low internal control beliefs have been related to a depressive outlook in personality, and unfavorable appraisal of personal development and the attainment development of developmental goals (Brandstädter et al. 1987). Changes in control belief with age may also be implicated in age-related changes in coping strategies. Older adults have been found to use more passive and emotion-focused coping strategies in contrast to young adults, who use more active and problem-focused strategies. However, it is possible that the nature of stresses changes with age rather than the coping strategies used. In fact, situationally appropriate reduction in the number of coping strategies used by older persons seems to result in greater coping effectiveness (Meeks et al. 1989).

4. The Adult Learner

In a society marked by rapid technological change, education must continue throughout life for professional updating, inevitable career changes, and the maintenance of competence to deal with a changing society (Willis and Dubin 1990). The forms of postsecondary and adult education change over time, but some of the principles that distinguish the mature and older learner from the traditional young student clearly emerge from the psychological literature (Willis 1985).

First, it is most likely that older learners have had quantitatively less education than contemporary young adults (Willis 1989). Qualitative changes in methods of instruction may also place the re-entrant into formal education at some disadvantage. Second, cumulative physiological injuries to the central nervous system will result in slower response speed (Schaie 1989b), requiring greater redundancy in the exposure to educational materials and in the acquisition of new skills. Third, older learners often do not spontaneously use encoding strategies to process new information. Fourth, accumulated knowledge structures can often be used by older learners to compensate for age-related deficits, particularly when information is to be applied to everyday circumstances with which the older learner may have greater familiarity.

Educators can greatly enhance formal and informal learning in older individuals by understanding these principles and applying them to their practice. For example, although older learners hesitate to employ encoding strategies spontaneously, they are quite capable of using such strategies. Instructors can provide mnemonics to assist the recall of technical terms. Rehearsal may be used when the goal is to retain information in short-term memory, and organization strategies may be useful for encoding into long-term memory. It is particularly important that reading materials be well-organized for older learners. Research on text recall shows that older learners remember the gist of a well-organized text as well as younger people, but that age differences increase when key points in text are hard to identify (Hultsch and Dixon 1990). The increased use of examples in instructional material has also been found to be helpful. In assessing what has been learned, older persons are likely to be at less disadvantage when tests are based on recognition rather than recall.

Cognitive training studies of older persons (Schaie and Willis 1986, Willis 1987) have found that specific ability training (such as on the ability domains of inductive reasoning or spatial orientation) may enhance basic skills in those who have not declined but who are at a disadvantage when compared to younger learners because of the lesser educational experience they received in youth (cohort differences), as well as in those who have declined from previous levels due to disuse or lack of relevant intellectual stimulation. Cognitive training efforts are now being expanded to specific domains of everyday tasks or what is sometimes termed "practical intelligence" (Willis 1992).

Of course, older learners may be anxious about undertaking new learning, in part because of stereotypes that suggest older persons have poor memories and are poorer learners. Pretraining involving anxiety reduction may therefore be helpful for accelerated learning (Yesavage et al. 1989). Finally, gradual sensory losses in vision and hearing need to be compensated for by use of materials in larger print, by improving the acoustic environment, and by reduction in the speed of presentation, to compensate for slower rates of information processing.

Adulthood and old age represent three-fourths of the life span, a period to which educators have not devoted as much attention as it deserves. The increase in average lifespan as well as educational levels among the elderly, have created great opportunities for educational interventions throughout the course of life. These opportunities can be maximized by adapting the educational process to the changing needs and attributes of the mature and older learner.

See also: Lifespan Development; Lifespan Development: Intelligence; Adult Learning: An Overview; Development of Learning Across the Lifespan

References

Brandstädter J R, Krampen G, Grewe W 1987 Personal control over development: Effects on the perception and emotional evaluation of personal development in adulthood. *International Journal of Behavioral Development.* 10(1): 99–120

Brandstädter J R, Renner G 1990 Tenacious goal pursuit and flexible goal adjustment: Explication and age-related analyses of assimilative and accommodative strategies of coping. *Psychology and Aging* 5(1): 58–67

Brim O G 1988 Losing and winning. *Psychol. Today* 34: 48–51

Crockett W H, Hummert M L 1987 Perceptions of aging and the elderly. In: Schaie K W (ed.) 1987

Culligan R C, Osborne D, Swenson W M, Offord K P 1983 *The MMPI: A Contemporary Normative Study.* Praeger, New York

Cunningham W R 1987 Intellectual abilities and age. In: Schaie K W (ed.) 1987

Erikson E H 1982 *The Life Cycle Completed: A Review.* Norton, New York

Flynn J R 1984 The mean IQ of Americans: Massive gains 1932–1978. *Psych. Bull.* 95(1): 29–51

Gough H G 1969 *Manual for the California Psychological Inventory.* Consulting Psychologists Press, Palo Alto, California

Horn J L 1982 The theory of fluid and crystallized intelligence in relation to concepts of cognitive psychology and aging in adulthood. In: Craik F I M, Trehub S (eds.) 1982 *Aging and Cognitive Processes.* Plenum Press, New York

Hultsch D F, Dixon R 1990 Learning and memory in aging. In: Birren J E, Schaie K W (eds.) 1996

Kogan N 1990 Personality and aging. In: Birren J E, Schaie K W (eds.) 1996 *Handbook of the Psychology of Aging*, 3rd edn. Academic Press, New York

Labouvie-Vief G 1985 Intelligence and cognition. In: Birren J E, Schaie K W (eds.) 1985

Lachman M F 1989 Personality and aging at the crossroads: Beyond stability vs. change. In: Schaie K W, Schooler C (eds.) 1989 *Social Structure and Aging: Psychological Processes.* Erlbaum, Hillsdale, New Jersey

Markus R L, Herzog A R 1992 The role of the self-concept in aging. In: Schaie K W (ed.) 1992

Matarazzo J D 1972 *Wechsler's Measurement and Appraisal of Adult Intelligence*, 5th edn. Williams and Wilkins, Baltimore, Maryland

McCrae R R, Costa P T Jr 1987 Validation of the five-factor model of personality across instruments and observers. *J. Pers. Soc. Psychol.* 52(1): 81–90

Meeks S, Carstensen L L, Tamsky B F, Wright T L, Pellegrini D 1989 Age differences in coping: Does less mean worse? *International Journal of Aging and Human Development.* 28(2): 127–40

Montepare J M, Lachman M E 1989 "You're only as old as you feel": Self-perceptions of age, fears of aging, and life satisfaction from adolescence to old age. *Psychology and Aging* 4(1): 173–78

Rodin J, Schooler C, Schaie K W (eds.) 1990 *Self-directedness: Cause and Effects Throughout the Life Course*. Erlbaum, Hillsdale, New Jersey

Ryff C D 1984 Personality development from the inside: The subjective experience of change in adulthood and aging. In: Baltes P B, Brim O G Jr (eds.) 1984 *Life-span Development and Behavior*, Vol. 6. Academic Press, New York

Ryff C D, Essex M J 1992 Psychological well-being in adulthood and old age: Descriptive markers and explanatory processes. In: Schaie K W (ed.) 1992

Schaie K W 1982 The aging in the coming decade. In: Schaie K W, Geiwitz J (eds.) 1982 *Reading in Adult Development and Aging*. Little, Brown & Co., Boston, Massachusetts

Schaie K W 1984 Midlife influences upon intellectual functioning in old age, *International Journal of Behavioral Development* 7(4): 463–78

Schaie K W 1988 Variability in cognitive function in the elderly: Implication for social participation. In: Woodhead M, Bender M, Leonard R (eds.) 1988 *Phenotylic Variation in Populations: Relevance to Risk Assessment*. Plenum Press, New York

Schaie K W 1989a The hazards of cognitive aging. *Gerontologist* 29(4): 484–93

Schaie K W 1989b Perceptual speed in adulthood: Cross-sectional and longitudinal studies. *Psychology and Aging* 5(2): 171

Schaie K W 1996 Intellectual development in adulthood. In: Birren J E, Schaie K W (eds.) 1996 *Handbook of the Psychology of Aging*, 4th edn. Academic Press, San Diego, California

Schaie K W, Parham I A 1976 Stability of adult personality traits: Fact or fable? *J.Pers. Soc. Psychol.* 34(1): 146–58

Schaie K W, Willis S L 1986 Can decline in adult intellectual functioning be reversed? *Dev. Psychol.* 22(2): 223–32

Schmitz-Scherzer R, Thomae H 1983 Constancy and change of behavior in old age: Findings from the Bonn longitudinal study. In: Schaie K W (ed.) 1983 *Longitudinal Studies of Adult Psychological Development*. Guilford Press, New York

Siegler I C 1983 Psychological aspects of the Duke Longitudinal Studies. In: Schaie K W (ed.) 1983 *Longitudinal Studies of Adult Psychological Development*. Guilford Press, New York

Siegler I C, George L K, Okun M A 1979 Cross-sequential analysis of adult personality. *Dev. Psychol.* 15(3): 350–61

Willis S L 1985 Towards an educational psychology of the older adult learner: Intellectual and cognitive bases. In: Birren J E, Schaie K W (eds.) 1985

Willis S L 1987 Cognitive training and everyday competence. In: Schaie K W (ed.) 1987

Willis S L 1989 Cohort differences in cognitive aging: A sample case. In: Schaie K W, Schooler C (eds.) 1989 *Social Structure and Aging: Psychological Processes*. Erlbaum, Hillsdale, New Jersey

Willis S L 1992 Cognition and everyday competence. In: Schaie K W (ed.) 1992

Willis S L, Dubin S S (eds.) 1990 *Maintaining Professional Competence*. Jossey-Bass, San Francisco, California

Willis S L, Schaie K W 1986 Practical intelligence in later adulthood. In: Sternberg R J, Wagner R K (eds.) 1986 *Practical Intelligence: Origins of Competence in the Everyday World*. Cambridge University Press, Cambridge

Yesavage J A, Lapp D, Sheick J A 1989 Mnemonics as modified for use by the elderly. In: Poon L W, Rubin D, Wilson B (eds.) 1989 *Everyday Cognition in Adulthood and Late Life*. Cambridge University Press, New York

Further Reading

Birren J E, Schaie K W (eds.) 1990 *Handbook of the Psychology of Aging*, 3rd edn. Academic Press, San Diego, California

Birren J E, Schaie K W (eds.) 1996 *Handbook of the Psychology of Aging*, 4th edn. Academic Press, San Diego, California

McCrae R R, Costa P T Jr 1984 *Emerging Lives, Enduring Dispositions: Personality in Adulthood*. Little, Brown & Co., Boston, Massachusetts

Oswald W D (ed.) 1991 *Handbuch der Gerontologie*, 2nd edn. Kohlhammer, Stuttgart

Schaie K W (ed.) 1987 *Annual Review of Gerontology and Geriatrics*, Vol. 7. Springer-Verlag, New York

Schaie K W (ed.) 1992 *Annual Review of Gerontology and Geriatrics*, Vol. 11. Springer-Verlag, New York

Schaie K W, Willis S L 1996 *Adult Development and Aging*, 4th edn. Harper Collins, New York

Lifespan Development

J. Heckhausen

The scope and potential of ontogenetic change in humans is larger than in any other species. During childhood and adolescence, but also throughout adulthood and old age, humans show impressive capacity for adaptation to new life ecologies and challenges (see, e.g., Brim and Kagan 1980). It is the unique human adaptive capacity that enables children as well as adults to learn from their parents, teachers, mentors, and other socialization agents. Only by way of human capacity for ontogenetic change can knowledge and skills be transferred from generation to generation. Lifespan developmental potential, thus, is the foundation of human culture and civilization.

1. From Child Psychology to Lifespan Psychology

Traditional and everyday conceptions view development as a unidirectional process toward improvement or growth, which produces long-term and not easily reversible outcomes. Such unidirectional growth conceptions of development stem from a preoccupation of developmental research with infancy and childhood, which has been typical of scientific research and commonsense conceptions. However, pioneers of a view encompassing lifespan development existed even in the eighteenth and nineteenth centuries (see review in Baltes et al. 1980) and early in the twentieth century (e.g., Bühler 1933, Jung 1933).

More recently, a number of research streams in different social sciences disciplines have converged to generate a new and interdisciplinary field of scientific inquiry: lifespan development (see Sørensen et al. 1986). Pioneers of a lifespan developmental perspective in the early and mid-twentieth century included both European and United States scholars, but their impact was limited until multiple institutions and disciplines joined forces. Institutional support came from a number of research centers (e.g., the universities at Bonn, Chicago, Pennsylvania State, Southern California, Syracuse, West Virginia, Wayne State) that devoted programs to lifespan development, which led to a series of conferences, conference proceedings, and annual series, such as *Life-span Development and Behavior* (see overview in Baltes et al. 1980). An important impetus was provided by a number of longitudinal studies, which had begun with large samples of children before the Second World War, and were able to target these populations in their adult years by the 1960s and 1970s (see review in Honzik 1984).

Another influential factor in the evolution of a lifespan developmental approach was the shift in population demographics toward an increasing proportion of old and very old individuals. This shift gave rise to gerontology as a new field of scientific inquiry (e.g., Birren 1964). Although gerontology took a stance against negative stereotype views of aging, the empirical evidence conveys a different message. In contrast to child-developmental research, gerontological research predominantly demonstrated age-related processes of decline in psychological functioning (e.g., Salthouse 1985).

Converging movements in other social sciences fields were particularly salient in sociology and social history (see historical review in Featherman 1983). First, the age stratification model (Riley 1987) in sociology interrelates dynamics on two levels: individual life-course processes and societal changes. The interface of typically asynchronic processes of individual aging and social change bring about new patterns of aging and change in social structure. Age stratification is conveyed by societal institutions (e.g., state-regulated entry age for school, seniority-based promotion rules) and age-normative conceptions internalized by the members of a given society (Hagestad and Neugarten 1985, Neugarten and Datan 1973).

Second, research on family history emerged from an interface of social demography and social history traditions. Such research made use of archive data to identify links between historical changes, birth cohorts, individuals' age at the time of a historical shift, and subsequent life courses, personality, and family structure (e.g., Elder 1980). In addition, long-term societal changes in life-course and family patterns were identified.

Third, socialization is a joint research arena for sociology and developmental psychology. Socialization refers to the processes involved in individuals' acquisition and modification of those values, beliefs and behavior regarded as appropriate by a given community or society. During the mid-1960s socialization research was extended beyond childhood to encompass adolescence and the adult lifespan (Brim and Wheeler 1966). Moreover, differences in social class were accounted for by class-differential successions of roles and role sequences (Clausen 1972), and differential impacts of work environments and activities on personality change (Kohn and Schooler 1983).

2. Basic Concepts of Lifespan Psychology

In contrast to unidirectional models of development, lifespan developmental psychology views development as a process involving both growth and decline (see also Bühler 1933, Erikson 1959, Levinson et al. 1978), thus yielding a multidirectional conception of development (Baltes 1987). According to the lifespan perspective, developmental growth and decline are not merely age-period-specific phenomena of change (e.g., growth in childhood, decline in old age), but instead occur concurrently (Baltes 1987). Decline on one dimension might be accompanied by growth on another dimension (gain–loss dynamic).

Advances in lifespan developmental theory have taken the notion of gain–loss dynamic one step further, in proposing that even a single event of developmental change typically involves aspects of growth as well as decline (Baltes 1987). In language acquisition, for instance, articulation skills in a given language are acquired at the expense of losing the ability to utter sounds that are not part of the language learned (Levelt 1989). This example illustrates selectivity as a fundamental causal mechanism in developmental gain–loss dynamics. Precisely because the scope of human behavior and development is extensive, developmental processes have to be selective in fostering growth in some, but not other, domains of functioning.

Growth can occur only if resources are selectively invested at the expense of options that are not chosen. Therefore, gains in one aspect will always imply losses in others. The fundamental characteristic of lifespan development can, therefore, be captured in the concept of "selective optimization" (Baltes and Baltes 1990).

Processes of selective optimization can be identified not only as active choices on the part of the individual, but also operate on the societal level. Society provides age-graded and age-sequential structures of opportunities and constraints, which channel individuals along certain life-course patterns (Hagestad and Ncugarten 1985, Kohli and Meyer 1986, Mayer and Huinink 1990). Age-normative challenges in development are captured by Havighurst's (1952) concept of "developmental task."

Along with biological processes of maturation and aging these societal influences comprise the set of *age-graded* conditions of development (Baltes 1987). Age-graded conditions also depend on cultural and historical factors, and are thus subject to *history-graded* influences. Finally, *nonnormative* events, which are irregular in their occurrence and timing represent a third class of important influences on individual development.

3. Lifespan Development and Lifespan Education

The process of aging brings about a continuous decrease in reserve capacity. While the chances for growth decrease with age, the risks for decline increase. This shifting ratio between gains and losses is also reflected in laypersons' conceptions about development in adulthood (Heckhausen et al. 1989). Figure 1 displays the expectations of young, middle-aged, and old adults about desirable and undesirable changes at various age levels. While mostly developmental gains are expected during early adulthood, increasing risks for losses are anticipated in old age.

With increasing age, the individual has to compensate actively to maintain previous levels of functioning in the face of aging-related decline. Compensation can be achieved in two ways. First, the individual can sharpen the selectivity of resource investment by focusing more exclusively on a certain domain. In this way, more resources can be invested and thus the level of functioning may be maintained. Second, the individual can rcsort to specific compensatory means, such as technical aids or other people's help. Baltes and Baltes (1990) have captured the fundamental strategies of selection and compensation in their model of "selective optimization with compensation."

The concept of "developmental reserve capacity" (Baltes 1987, Kliegl et al. 1989) plays a key role in the interface between models of lifespan development and lifespan education. Developmental reserve capacity determines the range of plasticity in performance, and thus demarcates the potential of instructional interventions. Cognitive training research with older adults has shown that, although there are important interindividual differences (Weinert et al. 1988), and although older individuals can improve their performance substantially, there are clear limits of functioning (Kliegl et al. 1989). In fluid intelligence tasks old adults never attained the level of performance achieved by young adults, especially under conditions of severe time constraints. Similar "testing-the-limits" approaches may be used to gauge the developmental potential in children (Brown and French 1979), and thus help to design appropriate curricula, age-related timetables, and strategies for instruction in formal (e.g., school) as well as more informal (e.g., family) contexts.

See also: Human Development; Lifespan Development: Phases; Development of Learning Across the Lifespan; Research Methodology: Human Development and Adult Learning

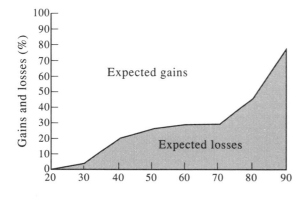

Figure 1
Age-related shifts in expected gains (increase in desirable attitudes) and losses (increase in undesirable attitudes) across the adult lifespan
Source: Heckhausen et al. 1989

References

Baltes P B 1987 Theoretical propositions of life-span developmental psychology: On the dynamics between growth and decline. *Dev. Psychol.* 23(5): 611–26
Baltes P B, Baltes M M 1990 Psychological perspectives on successful aging: The model of selective optimization with compensation. In: Baltes P B, Baltes M M (eds.) 1990 *Successful Aging: Perspectives from the Behavioral Sciences.* Cambridge University Press, New York
Baltes P B, Reese H W, Lipsitt L P 1980 Life-span developmental psychology. *Annu. Rev. Psychol.* 31: 65–110

Birren J E 1964 *The Psychology of Aging*. Prentice-Hall, Englewood Cliffs, New Jersey

Brim O G Jr., Kagan J (eds.) 1980 *Constancy and Change in Human Development*. Harvard University Press, Cambridge, Massachusetts

Brim O G Jr., Wheeler S (eds.) 1966 *Socialization After Childhood: Two Essays*. Wiley, New York

Brown A L, French L A 1979 The zone of potential development: Implications for intelligence testing in the year 2000. *Intelligence* 3(3): 255–77

Bühler C 1933 *Der menschliche Lebenslauf als psychologisches Problem*. Psychologische Monographien 4. Hirzel, Leipzig

Clausen J 1972 The life course of individuals. In: Riley M W, Johnson M, Foner A (eds.) 1972 *Aging and Society. Vol. 3: A Sociology of Age Stratification*. Russell Sage Foundation, New York

Elder G H Jr. 1980 History and the life course. In: Bertaux D (ed.) 1980 *Biography and Society: The Life History Approach in the Social Sciences*. Sage, Beverly Hills, California

Erikson E H 1959 Identity and the life cycle. *Psychol. Iss.* 1(1): 167–71

Featherman D L 1983 Life-span perspectives in social sciences research. In: Baltes P B, Brim O G Jr. (eds.) 1983 *Life-span Development and Behavior*, Vol. 5. Academic Press, New York

Hagestad G O, Neugarten B L 1985 Age and the life course. In: Binstock R H, Shanas E (eds.) 1985 *Handbook of Aging and the Social Sciences*. Van Nostrand Reinhold, New York

Havighurst R J 1952 *Developmental Tasks and Education*. Mckay, New York

Heckhausen J, Dixon R A, Baltes P B 1989 Gains and losses in development throughout adulthood as perceived by different adult age groups. *Dev. Psychol.* 25(1): 109–21

Honzik M P 1984 Life-span development. *Annu. Rev. Psychol.* 35: 309–31

Jung C G 1933 *Modern Man in Search of a Soul*. Harcourt, Brace & World, New York

Kliegl R, Smith J, Baltes P B 1989 Testing-the-limits and the study of adult age differences in cognitive plasticity of a mnemonic skill. *Dev. Psychol.* 25(2): 247–56

Kohli M, Meyer J W (eds.) 1986 Social structure and social construction of life stages. *Hum. Dev.* 29(3): 145–80

Kohn M L, Schooler C 1983 *Work and Personality: An Inquiry into the Impact of Social Stratification*. Ablex, Norwood, New Jersey

Levelt W J M 1989 *Speaking: From Intention to Articulation*. MIT Press, Cambridge, Massachusetts

Levinson D J et al. 1978 *The Seasons of a Man's Life*. Knopf, New York

Mayer K-U, Huinink J 1990 Age, period, and cohort in the study of the life course: A comparison of classical APC analysis with event history analysis or farewell to lexis. In: Magnusson D (ed.) 1990 *Data Quality*. Cambridge University Press, Cambridge

Neugarten B L, Datan N 1973 Sociological perspectives on the life cycle. In: Baltes P B, Schaie K W (eds.) 1973 *Life-span Developmental Psychology: Personality and Socialization*. Academic Press, New York

Riley M W 1987 On the significance of age in sociology. *Am. Sociol. Rev.* 52: 1–14

Salthouse T A 1985 *A Theory of Cognitive Aging* Advances in Psychology Vol. 28. North-Holland, Amsterdam

Sørensen A B, Weinert F E, Sherrod L R (eds.) 1986 *Human Development and the Life Course*. Erlbaum, Hillsdale, New Jersey

Weinert F E, Schneider W, Knopf M 1988 Individual differences in memory development across the life span. In: Baltes P B, Featherman D L, Lerner R M (eds.) 1988 *Life-span Development and Behavior*, Vol. 9. Erlbaum, Hillsdale, New Jersey

Lifespan Development: Intelligence

R. J. Sternberg and P. A. McGrane

Several approaches to the study of intellectual development across the lifespan have been developed: the traditional psychometric approach, the Piagetian approach, the information-processing approach, the learning approach, and the contextual approach. Although researchers in all of these traditions try to describe and explain the improvement in intellectual performance as children age and the apparent decline in intellectual functioning among the elderly, there is little agreement about how intelligence is best defined and studied or about what actually develops over the lifespan. This entry summarizes the major issues in the field of intellectual development and discusses each of these approaches in turn before drawing some general conclusions.

1. Major Issues in the Field of Intellectual Development

While most people think of intelligence as whatever can be measured by IQ tests, there is little agreement among researchers on how intelligence is best conceptualized and studied. It is unclear whether intelligence is best characterized as some underlying ability or group of abilities, as a combination of efficient processes and strategies, as expertise in specific areas, or whether it is merely behaviors that are valued in specific cultures. It is equally unclear how intelligence develops and changes over the lifespan and whether it even means the same thing to call a person intelligent at different points in the lifespan. For example, is it referring to the same quality when an infant and a 30-year old adult are both described as intelligent?

Additionally, there is little agreement on how intelligence changes with age and whether the same theories can accurately characterize changes in both childhood and old age. Some argue that intellectual development occurs through increases in one's knowledge base, while others believe that it is due to the automatization of processes and the acquisition of new strategies. Still others argue that intellectual development occurs through some increase in mental capacity with age, or with some decrease in mental capacity in aging. Such different understandings have very different implications for what children and adults of different ages are capable of learning and how they best acquire new information.

Finally, it is unclear how best to conceptualize individual differences in intelligence. Do individuals differ in some generalized ability or mental capacity or do they differ in specific abilities which may vary with the context of the task? Understanding such differences is essential for educators to understand why some individuals excel at tasks while others fail. In the discussion of each of the approaches that follows, it will become apparent that each approach captures part of the overall picture and offers a different understanding of intelligence and intellectual development. The implications of each of these approaches for education will be discussed in the final section.

2. Psychometric Approach

The psychometric approach was one of the earliest approaches to studying intelligence, and modern psychometric researchers have been influenced by three traditions. In the late nineteenth century, researchers such as Sir Francis Galton and James McKeen Cattell studied individual differences on a variety of physical–sensory tests, measuring reaction time, visual acuity, and sensitivity to stimuli, and tried to determine whether performance on these tasks was related to success in school and other areas of life. Generally, little relationship was found. This led researchers such as Alfred Binet to take a second approach, arguing that tests of mental ability should look at higher mental processes, such as memory, attention, and comprehension. In 1905, Binet and Théodore Simon developed a set of mental tests to identify retarded children for placement in special classes. A modern version of this test, the Stanford–Binet Intelligence Scale, is still widely used today. Finally, at about the same time, Charles Spearman tried to determine whether performance on intellectual tasks was determined by one underlying intellectual ability or multiple abilities. He developed a factor-based theory of development that looked at the relationships between performance on a variety of tests, and he found that two types of factors underlay intellectual

performance: a general ability "g" which determined performance on all types of intellectual tasks, and test-specific abilities.

Researchers today continue to use a similar technique. They give individuals a variety of ability tests and then use statistical procedures, such as factor analysis, to summarize individual differences and to look at the underlying structure of performance on these tests. By looking at how performance on different tests is related, they try to discover whether the same underlying ability determines performance on different tests. An underlying assumption of such research is that when performances on two tests rise and fall together, they share some common underlying structure, or factor. Therefore, if individuals who perform well on mathematics tests also perform well on verbal tests, researchers assume that there is only one underlying ability or factor, rather than two or more.

There has always been considerable debate as to the underlying structure of intelligence. While Spearman argued that one factor underlies performance on all tasks, others have disagreed. Unfortunately, depending on the type of factor analysis used, different underlying structures are found. For example, Louis Thurstone did not believe in a general factor, but instead proposed seven primary mental abilities: verbal comprehension, number, memory, perceptual speed, space, verbal fluency, and inductive reasoning. J P Guilford went even further, arguing for over 120 mental abilities. P E Vernon offered a hierarchical model of intelligence, which included a general factor at the top level, a verbal-educational and a spatial-practical-mechanical factor at the second level, minor factors at the third level, and test-specific factors at the fourth level. Finally, J Horn and R B Cattell have emphasized two major factors: fluid intelligence and crystallized intelligence. Fluid intelligence is believed to be biologically determined and is best measured by tests that require mental manipulation of abstract symbols. In contrast, crystallized intelligence is affected by education level and is best measured by tests that require cultural knowledge, such as vocabulary, and general information tests. Even today, there is no real agreement on the underlying structure of intelligence and little likelihood that consensus will be achieved in the near future.

Researchers in the psychometric tradition have not traditionally focused on the question of how intelligence develops, but Sternberg and Powell (1983) have noted four ways in which intelligence, from a psychometric viewpoint, has been argued to change during the lifespan.

First, the number of underlying factors or abilities may change with age. There is considerable evidence to suggest that intellectual abilities become more differentiated as children mature, and the decline in correlations between performances on different cognitive tasks as children age seems to support this idea. Some researchers have also suggested that a decrease in differentiation is found with old age, but the evidence is inconclusive.

Second, it has been suggested that the relevance of different factors may change over time. That is, what makes one infant more intelligent than another may be different from what makes one 8-year old more intelligent than another, because different abilities are more or less important at different ages. Hofstaetter (1954) found that up until the age of 20 months, sensorimotor alertness accounted for most of the differences between individuals. Between the ages of 20 and 40 months, persistence was most important, and when children were over 4 years old, symbol manipulation and abstract behavior were most important. Hence, infants' performance on intelligence tests has been found to be only minimally predictive of later intelligence levels. In later childhood, a variety of higher-order mental abilities, including verbal and mathematical skills, abstract and visual reasoning, and components of memory seem to characterize intelligence.

Third, it has been suggested that there may be a change in the content of the factors with age. Researchers in this tradition are generally trying to identify the one or more abilities that capture most of the differences between individuals at a given time. McCall et al. (1977) found that at the age of 6 months, the nature of the primary factor was manipulative exploration of objects; at 12 months, imitation of simple fine motor and elementary verbal behavior; at 18 months, verbal labeling and comprehension; and at 24 months, verbal fluency and grammar.

Finally, researchers have suggested that the amount of each factor or ability may change over time. For example, fluid intelligence seems to decrease after the age of 20 while crystallized intelligence continues to increase throughout adulthood (see *Psychology of Adult Education*).

In summary, then, psychometric researchers describe differences in intelligence with aging as changes in the underlying structure or context of abilities. They offer no explanations of the mechanisms of development, and they are particularly interested in characterizing the nature of individual differences.

3. Piagetian Approach

The Piagetian approach will be discussed only briefly here. Unlike researchers in the psychometric tradition, Jean Piaget was not interested in individual differences in intellectual development but instead tried to characterize the universal changes in the logical structures underlying thought that take place from infancy to adolescence. He believed that all children pass through four distinct stages of intellectual development. From birth to the age of 2 children are in a sensorimotor stage where they are aware of the world through their senses and are able to act physically on their environment. They begin to understand that people and objects

continue to exist when they cannot be seen, and as they become able to represent and act on objects in their minds, they enter a preoperational stage (ages 2 to 7). During the preoperational stage, children shift from a perceptual to a conceptual orientation and from an empirical to a logical orientation. They become able to focus on more than one dimension at a time and begin to understand that transformations of objects can be reversed. Children then enter a concrete operational stage (ages 7 to 12), and finally a formal operational stage. By the time they enter the formal operational stage, children can reason logically and think about hypothetical and abstract issues and problems (see *Human Development*).

How does this developmental change occur? Piaget argued that the major function of intelligence is to help the child to adapt to the environment. Children construct their own logical structures through interaction with the environment and move from one stage to another through the process of equilibration. In other words, children experience disequilibrium when they confront aspects of the environment that cannot be resolved using their currently available schemes. In order to relieve this disequilibrium, they develop new schemes by either assimilating the environment to their current logical structures or by accommodating their structures to new aspects of the environment. Assimilation and accommodation lead to a more sophisticated stage of thought and restore the child to equilibrium. Hence, each new stage is reached through the extension and reorganization of logical structures in previous stages.

Piaget's theory has come under attack for a variety of reasons. It does not appear to apply cross-culturally, and even within one culture, performance on tasks seems to be determined by a variety of influences, including familiarity with the materials used. Children also show different levels of performance on tasks in different domains that are logically equivalent, contrary to Piaget's predictions. Neo-Piagetians have altered and extended Piaget's approach in a variety of ways (see Sincoff and Sternberg 1989 for a review). For example, neo-Piagetians have added and altered stages, incorporated information-processing and skill-learning approaches, have used computer simulations, and have focused on the role of domain-specific knowledge.

Neo-Piagetians have also extended and altered Piaget's approach to include adult development, in two ways. First, they have studied decrements in performance on Piagetian tasks found in aging adults. Some studies have found that the elderly seem to regress to earlier stages of cognitive development, as they perform like young children on some Piagetian tasks. However, educational attainment and life experience seem to affect how the elderly perform on these tasks, and it is unclear that older subjects understand these tasks as experimenters intend them to. Other researchers have tried to extend Piaget's theory by proposing further stages of development that might be reached in adulthood; for example, the emergence of a dialectical mode of thinking in adulthood. Thinkers that reach this stage understand the limitations of logic, and know how to see issues in context, to formulate problems of their own, to deal with seemingly illogical paradoxes, and to resolve contradictions (see *Lifespan Development: Phases*).

Hence, although aspects of Piaget's theory have been discredited, many important ideas and aspects of this approach are widely used today by neo- Piagetian researchers studying development in childhood and throughout the lifespan.

4. *Information-processing Approach*

Researchers in the information-processing tradition have been dissatisfied with the psychometric and Piagetian approaches and have attempted to characterize the mental processes and representations by which an individual performs intellectually. They have tried to discover what occurs between the input of information and the output of specific intellectual responses and how mental processes and representations might change across the lifespan. In order to study such mental processes, researchers present people with a variety of tasks and look at how changing the task affects reaction times, error rates, number of words recalled, or problem-solving strategies, hoping to discover the underlying mental processes. They tend to focus on internal causes of development rather than studying environmental influences. Changes in intelligence are seen as being due to changes in mental processes, representations and levels of knowledge, access to knowledge, strategies, executive processes, memory, and attention.

Some researchers have suggested that the most important change with maturation is an increase in mental capacity. Case (1985) suggested that children show an increase in working memory with age and are, therefore, able to keep more facts in mind at the same time as they mature. Others argue that increases in speed of processing with age are due to use of more effective rules and strategies. Still others emphasize the greater automatization of skills with age due to increased practice.

Children also show increased knowledge of the appropriate ways of approaching tasks with age. For example, young children's poor performance on memory tasks appears to be due in part to the fact that they do not know the appropriate strategies to use in order to remember information. As they mature, they begin to learn and practice strategies such as rehearsal and elaboration of information, and their performance improves. They also learn to monitor their own thinking and to realize when they do not understand or remember something.

Children also seem to develop more effective representational abilities over time. Keil and Batterman (1984) have found that young children's representation of categories is tied to the surface features of members, and only later do they begin to develop a definitional understanding of the category. For example, young children are more likely to believe that a person with the characteristic features of a robber but not the defining feature (e.g, a smelly, mean old man with a gun who borrowed something *with* permission) is a robber than someone without the characteristic features but with the defining feature (e.g., a friendly and cheerful woman who takes something *without* permission). As children grow older, they begin to rely more on defining features to label a person.

In healthy elderly adults, there is little evidence for age-related differences in the organization, quantity, or quality of long-term knowledge representations, but researchers have found declines in the effectiveness and efficiency of many processing components and suggest that the elderly may have fewer processing resources. There is also some evidence to suggest that older adults are less able to retrieve information from memory. The research on differences in strategy use is mixed, with some researchers finding differences and others not. More research is needed in this area.

Although there do appear to be clear declines in cognition with age, the evidence suggests that the elderly are able to compensate for decreases in some cognitive skills, due to years of expertise and knowledge in certain areas (see Charness and Bosman 1990, or Salthouse 1991 for reviews). For example, elderly women are able to type as quickly as younger women because they read farther ahead on the page, giving them more time to prepare keystrokes. Similarly, older chess players examine fewer possible moves before selecting one than younger chess players, yet still seem to be able to make moves of comparable quality, possibly due to knowledge of which moves it is important to consider. Hence, although there do appear to be declines in some cognitive processes with age, on many tasks the elderly seem able to use their years of expertise and knowledge to develop alternative strategies to compensate for these declines (see *Human Development: Aging*).

5. *Learning Approach*

In the modern learning approach, researchers are less likely to see maturation and qualitative changes with age as important, emphasizing instead the day-to-day accumulation of skills and knowledge. Rather than focusing on the processes used, they focus on the amount and organization of knowledge, studying how people accumulate knowledge and how it is restructured over time. Differences between younger and older children seem to be due to differences in the amounts and kinds of knowledge that children possess about a variety of concepts, which in turn affect the efficiency of cognitive processes. These researchers argue that children are unable to perform like adults because they are "universal novices" (Brown and DeLoache 1978) and suggest that if a child and adult possess equal knowledge and expertise in an area, the child is likely to be able to perform equally well. For example, although young children typically do worse than adults on almost any memory task, Chi (1978) found that when children with extensive expertise at chess were compared with adult novices the children showed superior memory for chess positions. Similarly, Schneider et al. (1989) studied German schoolchildren who were either experts or novices about soccer, and found that level of expertise determined recall for details about soccer games much more than did grade level or performance on IQ tests. Inherent in this approach is the idea that because intellectual performance in one area is due to the amount of expertise in that area, the same individual will not perform as well in other domains where he or she has less expertise. Hence, intelligence is not a general ability; rather, intellectual performance is domain-specific. Children who are believed to have high ability may simply be those who know more about many different domains (see *Individual Differences, Learning, and Instruction*).

In adulthood, learning researchers try to explain why adults with presumably large knowledge bases show decrements in performance by considering possible disadvantages to having a large knowledge base. Charness and Bieman-Copland (1992) suggested that having a large amount of knowledge may cause three problems. First, the more related knowledge one possesses, the slower the access will be to any particular piece of information. Hence, older adults should expend more time and effort in remembering any one piece of information. Second, the more one knows, the more likely it is that one's attention will be distracted by surrounding events that automatically trigger memories. Third, the more one knows, the slower one is to learn new things, because old information interferes with the learning of new information. Hence, having a large amount of expertise may prove to have negative effects for cognitive performance that in some cases may outweigh the benefits.

6. Contextual Approaches

Contextual approaches to intellectual development grew out of a concern that previous theories of intellectual development were overly normative in trying to identify a universal pathway of development. Researchers in this tradition argue that rather than trying to find universals that may not exist, researchers should study how trajectories and endpoints of intellectual development may vary in different contexts. There is considerable variety in the positions taken by different contextual theorists. Some argue that indigenous theories of intelligent behavior are the only appropriate basis for assessing intelligence. Similarly,

researchers at the Laboratory for Comparative Human Cognition (1982 p. 710) argued that "no universal notion of a single, general ability, called intelligence, can be abstracted from the behavior of people whose experiences in the world have systematically been different from birth in response to different life predicaments handed down to them in their ecocultural niche."

Other researchers try to take context into account while still seeking universal aspects of intellectual development. Sternberg's triarchic theory takes context into account by looking at how individuals use their intelligence to adapt to different environments, either by altering the context, adapting to the context, or selecting a different context. Ceci's bio-ecological approach also incorporates context, arguing that "the role of context, broadly defined to include motivational forces, social and physical aspects of a setting or task, values inculcated through various types of parenting, and the elaborateness of the knowledge domain in which the task is embedded, are important not just in the initial period of development of the cognitive potentials, but also in their later evocation during testing" (Ceci 1990 p. 100).

Researchers using the contextual approach typically try to identify how context alters and shapes intellectual performance. For example, researchers in the tradition of L S Vygotsky believe that intellectual functioning has its origins in intellectual interactions with other people, so they typically study parent-child and child-child interactions to learn how cooperative interactions lead to independent intellectual functioning. Other researchers try to determine the broad effects of culture, schooling, and early interaction on intellectual development, and have found, for example, that schooling seems to play an important role in determining performance on IQ tests. Other researchers are interested in how performance varies in different domains and how changes in task situations can alter performance. Ceci (1990) cited a variety of research findings suggesting that performance on IQ tests may reveal little about how individuals will perform on everyday tasks, such as selecting goods with the lowest prices in a grocery store or betting on a horse race. Similarly, he discussed evidence indicating that, by slightly changing aspects of a task (e.g., making a task more like a video game), differences in intellectual performance emerge.

Contextual researchers interested in aging argue that the intellectual performance of adults must be understood in the context of the relationship between changing intellectual abilities and changing contextual demands present in the adults' environments. They are interested in individual differences in the overall trajectory of performance over time and are concerned with the role of practice and previous experience on determining individual differences in performance (see *Environments for Learning; Individual Differences, Learning, and Instruction*).

Several of these researchers have argued that most intelligence tests use academic problems, whereas most cognitive activities that older adults face are not oriented to formal educational demands. Hence, the older adults have less practice with this type of problem-solving. There is some evidence (e.g., Cornelius and Caspi 1987) to suggest that although performance on academic problem-solving tasks decreases with age, performance on everyday problem-solving tasks may increase. Others, such as Willis and Schaie (1986), have developed and administered practical tests of intelligence, looking at performance on everyday tasks, such as reading labels on bottles and understanding documents and editorials.

Some researchers have also noted the importance of environment on determining intellectual performance, pointing out that not all elderly people show the expected decline in intelligence with age, and that environmental factors such as education, socio-economic status, and occupation may play important roles. Others, such as Kliegl et al. (1990), have argued for the plasticity of intelligence, arguing that much of the decline in intellectual performance is reversible, given the appropriate training and practice. They have found that by giving older adults training and practice in academic problems, the performance of the older adults increases, implying that the deficit is not due to a lack of ability or capacity. There is, however, little evidence that such training transfers to other academic tasks.

Finally, researchers in this tradition also emphasize that not all aspects of intellectual performance decrease at the same rate, and experience and continued practice with some aspect may slow the decline. Because only certain aspects of intelligence decline, older adults may use other aspects to compensate for this decline, either by channeling their efforts into certain domains or by developing substitutable mechanisms, playing on their strengths. Research on compensation mechanisms was discussed earlier, but there is also evidence that older adults may use external aids, for example, in order to compensate for cognitive decline. Older adults appear to be much more successful on cognitive tasks when working with collaborators.

7. Conclusion

Because intellectual development is an important goal of schooling, each of the approaches discussed above provides important insights for educators. It is essential, however, to pay attention to research findings and theories from all of these approaches, because although each approach captures certain important aspects of intellectual development, none capture its entirety.

The psychometric approach, while failing to specify actual developmental mechanisms, provides a clear picture of the abilities that may be important at different ages and characterizes individual differences at different ages. For example, the distinction between crystallized and fluid intelligence is extremely valuable when considering the best methods of teaching older adults. It has led to research that considers how older adults use, and can be taught to use, crystallized knowledge to compensate for decreases in fluid intelligence. There is also some suggestion that fluid intelligence in adults can be increased to a certain extent with training. The psychometric approach has yielded a variety of measures of intelligence that have proven to be valuable predictors of success in school.

The Piagetian approach suggests that there may be important qualitative differences in how children and adults think. For example, young children may not understand basic concepts such as conservation and reversibility. Recognizing these differences, an educator may take them into account in trying to teach young children concepts that may require such understandings. Piaget has offered a mechanism of cognitive change in which a child is an active learner who is forced to develop new logical structures when he or she encounters information that conflicts with current schemata. Hence, one way teachers can encourage cognitive development is by providing the child with materials and tasks that will allow the child to encounter such disequilibrium.

The information-processing perspective pinpoints particular focuses of intellectual development, such as changes in strategy use, memory, and representation, identifying the limitations that children and aging adults face at different points in the lifespan. This approach offers concrete suggestions for improving intellectual performance, such as teaching children and older adults appropriate strategies and how to monitor their performance. For instance, it appears that young children's memories can be improved by teaching them strategies such as rehearsal and elaboration. Similarly, such an approach pinpoints where elderly adults may have greatest difficulties, such as on tasks that require speed in processing, and identifies alternative strategies they may use to compensate for such deficits. When used to study individual differences, this approach allows researchers to draw much more specific conclusions than those drawn by researchers in the psychometric tradition.

The learning approach acknowledges the importance of the information and knowledge processed, and the importance of expertise for intellectual performance. This approach suggests that people may perform well in areas in which they possess expertise, regardless of their age. Such an approach suggests that teachers must remember that children from different backgrounds and different ages may have different knowledge in certain areas and may therefore appear more able. It also points out that children may be able to think in much more sophisticated ways, and to learn new concepts more easily, in domains where they have previous knowledge and a certain amount of expertise. This kind of approach also recognizes both the advantages and disadvantages in having a large knowledge base that adults may encounter as they age.

Finally, the contextual approach acts as a corrective to the other approaches, cautioning against conclusions about universal developmental pathways, and urges that context and culture be taken into account. It indicates that students who show little expertise in some areas may demonstrate extremely sophisticated performance in other areas of life, and that it may not be appropriate to assess the development of all children on one specific continuum that was developed for studying middle-class children in Western countries. Similarly, it argues that although the elderly may demonstrate declines in performance on some educational tasks, they may continue to show sophistication on tasks that they encounter in their daily lives, and urges that the changing context in which intelligence is displayed throughout the lifespan be taken into account.

Taken together, research from all of these approaches begins to provide researchers with a rudimentary picture of how intelligence changes over the lifespan, and how educators can best understand the intellectual capabilities of their students.

See also: Human Development; Human Development: Aging; Lifespan Development; Lifespan Development: Phases; Adult Learning: An Overview; Development of Learning Across the Lifespan; Environments for Learning; Individual Differences, Learning, and Instruction

References

Brown A, DeLoache J S 1978 Skills, plans and self-regulation. In: Siegler R S (ed.) 1978 *Children's Thinking: What Develops?* Erlbaum, Hillsdale, New Jersey

Case R 1985 *Intellectual Development: Birth to Adulthood.* Academic Press, Orlando, Florida

Ceci S J 1990 *On Intelligence . . . More or Less: A Bioecological Treatise on Intellectual Development.* Prentice-Hall, Englewood Cliffs, New Jersey

Charness N, Bieman-Copland S 1992 The learning perspective: Adulthood. In: Sternberg R J, Berg C A (eds.) 1992 *Intellectual Development.* Cambridge University Press, New York

Charness N, Bosman E A 1990 Expertise and aging: Life in the lab. In: Hess T M (ed.) 1990 *Aging and Cognition: Knowledge Organization and Utilization.* Elsevier, North-Holland, Amsterdam

Chi M T H 1978 Knowledge structures and memory development. In: Siegler R (ed.) 1978 *Children's Thinking: What Develops?* Erlbaum, Hillsdale, New Jersey

Cornelius S W, Caspi A 1987 Everyday problem solving in adulthood and old age. *Psychology and Aging* 2 (2): 144–53

Hofstaetter P R 1954 The changing composition of intelligence: A study of the t-technique. *J. Genet. Psychol.* 85: 159–64

Keil F C, Batterman N 1984 A characteristic-to-defining shift in the development of word meaning. *J. Verbal Learn. Verbal Behav.* 23 (2): 221–36

Kliegl R, Smith J, Baltes P B 1990 On the locus and process of magnification of age differences during mnemonic training. *Dev. Psychol.* 26: 894–904

Laboratory of Comparative Human Cognition 1982 Culture and intelligence. In: Sternberg R J (ed.) 1982 *Handbook of Human Intelligence.* Cambridge University Press, Cambridge

McCall R B, Eichorn D J, Hogarty P S 1977 Transitions in early mental development. *Monogr. Soc. Res. Child Dev.* 42 (3): 108

Salthouse T A 1991 *Theoretical Perspectives on Cognitive Aging.* Erlbaum, Hillsdale, New Jersey

Schneider W, Korkel J, Weinert F 1989 Expert knowledge and general abilities and text processing. In: Schneider W, Weinert F (eds.) 1989 *Interactions Among Aptitudes, Strategies, and Knowledge in Cognitive Performance.* Springer Verlag, New York

Sincoff J B, Sternberg R J 1989 The development of cognitive skills: An examination of recent theories. In: Colley A M, Beech J R (eds.) 1989 *Acquisition and Performance of Cognitive Skills.* Wiley, Chichester

Sternberg R J, Powell J S 1983 The development of intelligence. In: Flavell J, Markman E (eds.) 1983 *Handbook of Child Psychology*, Vol. 3. Wiley, New York

Willis S L, Schaie K W 1986 Practical intelligence in later adulthood. In: Sternberg R J, Wagner R K (eds.) 1986 *Practical Intelligence: Nature and Origins of Competence in the Everyday World.* Cambridge University Press, New York

Further Reading

Cornelius S W 1990 Aging and everyday cognitive abilities. In: Hess T M (ed.) 1990 *Aging and Cognition: Knowledge Organization and Utilization.* North-Holland, Amsterdam

Sternberg R J, Berg C A (eds.) 1992 *Intellectual Development.* Cambridge University Press, New York

Lifespan Development: Memory

W. Schneider

Since the 1970s, a new interest in the development of memory has stimulated numerous research activities. These have led to a complex pattern of findings.

Although the majority of studies address memory development in children, use of a lifespan perspective has also attracted much attention. This entry will present the most important outcomes of research on memory processes, in both children and adults.

1. Sources of Memory Development in Children

According to most researchers, changes in basic capacities, memory strategies, metacognitive knowledge, and domain knowledge all contribute to children's memory development (Bjorklund 1990, Schneider and Pressley 1989, Siegler 1991). There is also broad agreement that some of these sources of development contribute more than others, and that some play an important role in certain periods of childhood but not in others.

1.1 The Role of Basic Capacities

One of the earliest views of memory development relied heavily on the concept of "capacity." In its simplified version, memory development was exclusively seen as a function of memory capacity: according to this model, what develops in memory is the hardware of the memory system conceptualized as absolute capacity, rather than its software, that is, specific processes or procedures to memorize materials. Of course, such a simplified view is incompatible with the memory data.

Dempster (1985) reviewed in detail potential sources of development for short-term capacity. Taken together, the data from numerous studies show that age-correlated performance increases in memory span should not be interpreted as enlargement of some biologically determined capacity, particularly when memory development during the preschool years and thereafter is considered. It is only during early infancy that the effects of structural changes and basic processes seem to be large and direct contributors to memory performance (Siegler 1991). Factors that may contribute to developmental increases in memory span from the preschool years onward include: (a) speed of information processing; (b) automatic item processing.

In sum, then, it appears that *intra-individual* changes in children's memory capacity contribute little to memory development. As was pointed out by Siegler (1991), these basic processes are present at a very early age and function well even in very young children. Although basic processes are essential for memory, they do not contribute much to improvements in memory with age.

1.2 Effects of Memory Strategies

"Memory strategies" have been defined as mental or behavioral activities that achieve cognitive purposes and are effort-consuming, potentially conscious and controllable (Flavell 1985).

Since the early 1970s numerous studies have investigated the role of strategies in memory development.

Particularly in the 1970s individual differences in the use of memory strategies were conceived of as the major source of developmental differences in memory development (Weinert and Perlmutter 1988). The majority of studies on the development of strategies investigated children's use of rehearsal, organization, and elaboration strategies in laboratory tasks. Typically, these strategies were not observed in children younger than 6 or 7. This absence of strategic behavior was attributed to a "production deficiency" (Flavell 1985). That is, young children do not engage in memory strategies because they simply do not know how and when to do so. However, more recent research has shown that the ages of strategy acquisition are relative, and variable between and within strategies. Even preschoolers and kindergarten children are able to use intentional strategies, both in ecologically valid settings such as hide-and-seek tasks, and in the traditional context of a laboratory task (see Schneider and Pressley 1989).

In general, the use of creative, natural-tasks settings in studies conducted mainly in the 1980s and early 1990s has clearly shown that young children's strategic competencies have been underestimated for a long time. Despite this recent change in perspective, there seems little doubt that the most dramatic developmental changes in children's strategy use can be observed during the elementary school years.

Taken together, the findings from studies demonstrate that strategy development in children is more continuous than was originally assumed. They also show that use of encoding and retrieval strategies must be considered in interaction. New methodologies (e.g., mathematical modeling) permit sophisticated analyses of encoding versus retrieval (for a review see Brainerd 1985). Even more importantly, there is now an increasing realization that the use of encoding and retrieval strategies largely depends on children's strategic as well as nonstrategic knowledge. There is impressive evidence that individual differences in metacognitive and domain-specific knowledge may have a strong impact on how well strategies are executed, and on how much children recall in a memory task. Given these findings, the earlier belief that individual differences in memory strategies represent the most important source of memory development no longer seems tenable. There is now broad consensus that the narrow focus on developmental changes in strategy use should be replaced by an approach that takes into account the effects of various forms of knowledge on strategy execution.

1.3 The Role of Metacognitive Knowledge

One knowledge component that has been systematically explored since the early 1970s concerns children's knowledge about memory. Flavell and Wellman (1977) coined the term "metamemory" to refer to a person's potentially verbalizable knowledge about memory storage and retrieval, and developed a taxonomy that parsed metamemory into two main categories, "sensitivity" and "variables." The sensitivity category included knowledge of when memory activity is necessary (i.e., memory monitoring). The variables category included a person's mnemonic self-concept, characteristics of a task relevant to memory, and knowledge about potentially applicable memory strategies (see Schneider and Pressley 1989 for an overview of conceptualizations of metacognitive knowledge).

Empirical research exploring the development of different aspects of metacognitive knowledge revealed that children's knowledge of facts about memory increases considerably over the primary-grade years, but is incomplete by the end of childhood. Most studies showed impressive increases in knowledge about strategies with increasing age, a finding that was paralleled by the development of strategic skills. Thus an important aim of most empirical studies was to demonstrate that there are close relationships between metamemory and memory behavior.

Evaluating the outcomes of research dealing with metamemory–memory behavior relationships is a complicated task. Whereas the first generation of studies found only weak relationships between knowledge about strategies and strategy use, a second generation of studies indicated a more positive pattern of results. In a meta-analysis of studies containing metamemory–memory relationship data, Schneider and Pressley (1989) reported an overall correlation of 0.41 based on a large set of studies. Accordingly, a significant statistical association between metamemory and memory was found, particularly when the relationship between knowledge about strategies and the use of memory strategies was concerned. What children know about their memory obviously influences how they attempt to remember. Given the diversity of findings, however, much more needs to be known about the interplay between metacognitive knowledge and strategic behavior in various memory situations.

1.4 The Impact of Domain Knowledge

Since the late 1970s, there has been increasing evidence for the striking effects of domain knowledge on performance in many memory tasks. In numerous studies, it has been shown that domain knowledge influences how much as well as what children recall (Chi and Ceci 1987). Research on the interaction of domain knowledge and specific memory strategies indicates that there are at least three ways in which the knowledge base relates to strategy use (Pressley et al. 1987): knowledge can (a) facilitate the use of particular strategies, (b) generalize strategy use to related domains, or (c) even diminish the need for strategy activation.

1.4.1 Knowledge and the use of particular strategies. The assumption that rich knowledge enables competent strategy use has been confirmed in numerous studies. Most of these studies focused on the effects of conceptual or semantic knowledge on the use of organizational strategies in sort–recall tasks. Experimental manipulations concerned children's knowledge of categorical relationships among items in terms of "category typicality" or "interitem associativity." Taken together, this research clearly showed that differences in the meaningfulness of words considerably influences strategic processing, particularly in young school children. Strategic effects of the knowledge base are not restricted to categorization tasks but have been observed in other memory paradigms as well (Pressley et al. 1987).

1.4.2 Knowledge strategy use and related domain. Several researchers (e.g., Best and Ornstein 1986, Bjorklund 1987) have proposed that semantic organization initially seen in the recall of young school children is mediated not by a deliberately imposed strategy but by the relatively automatic activation of well-established semantic memory relations. As they automatically process highly related items in a categorical fashion, children may notice categorical relations in their recall. They may then realize that categorization is a good learning strategy.

1.4.3 Nonstrategic effects of the knowledge base. Evidence that rich domain knowledge can diminish the need for strategy activation has been convincingly demonstrated in developmental studies using the expert–novice paradigm. Studies comparing experts and novices in a given domain (e.g., chess or soccer) on a memory task related to that domain provided evidence that rich domain knowledge enables a child expert to perform much like an adult expert and better than an adult novice—thus showing a reversal of usual developmental trends. Moreover, these studies also confirmed the assumption that rich domain knowledge can compensate for low overall aptitude on domain-related cognitive tasks, as no differences were found between high- and low- aptitude experts on the various recall and comprehension measures.

Taken together, these findings indicate that domain knowledge increases greatly with age, and is clearly related to how well children remember. Domain knowledge also contributes to the development of other competencies that have been proposed as sources of memory development, namely basic capacities, memory strategies, and metacognitive knowledge. Accordingly, it seems evident that changes in domain knowledge play a large role in memory development.

2. Memory Development in Adults and the Elderly

Assessments of memory development between late adolescence and late adulthood have not revealed any substantial changes in memory performance as a function of capacity, strategies, or knowledge. Obviously, interindividual performance differences remain stable, and intra-individual changes over time seem negligible during this time period. On the other hand, numerous studies have identified declines in memory performance in the elderly. Attempts to locate the sources of memory losses in old age have relied on the four components already outlined above.

2.1 The Influence of Basic Capacities

Study of memory in the elderly is made difficult by the problem of recruiting representative subjects. This makes it difficult to judge the importance of cognitive capacity as an explanatory factor. However, even studies that used healthy and intelligent old people as subjects found that information–processing speed was generally reduced in the elderly (see reviews by Knopf 1987, Light 1991). Training studies focusing on "developmental reserve capacity" (e.g., Baltes and Kliegl 1992, Kliegl et al. 1989) revealed that although elderly persons could considerably increase their memory performance as a function of cognitive training, none of the older adults reached a level of performance approaching the average of (trained) young adults. There is reason to assume that the negative age difference found in these studies is due to neurobiological constraints leading to a reduction of mental capacity.

2.2 The Impact of Memory Strategies

According to the often invoked "disuse hypothesis," older people should use memory strategies less frequently than young adults because they are no longer capable of complex memory tasks. By and large, however, there is little evidence to support this assumption. For example, Knopf (1987) did not find any differences between young adults and the elderly in the use of grouping strategies. Regardless of age, most subjects were able to use organizational strategies facilitating the recall of long wordlists. On the other hand, effects of strategy use on memory performance seemed to decrease with increasing age. Whereas these and many other findings provide strong evidence against the "disuse hypothesis," they are in accord with the assumption that memory loss in old age is related to decreases in mental capacity and information-processing speed.

2.3 The Role of Knowledge Components

The results of most studies assessing age differences in metacognitive and domain-specific knowledge do not indicate any decline in these knowledge components as a function of age. Although metacognitive knowledge seems to remain stable in old age, its relation to memory performance decreases with increasing age (see Knopf 1987). Regarding the impact of domain-specific knowledge, several findings support a "compensation hypothesis" in that older subjects can use their particularly rich knowledge in many domains to compensate for deficiencies resulting from slower information-processing (Salthouse 1991).

3. Conclusion

Generalizations in the field of memory research are difficult given the great variability of memory phenomena, attributes, modalities, and contents. Given the evidence of several studies, however, it appears that the knowledge base and metacognitive knowledge are major sources of interindividual differences in memory performance, regardless of chronological age. Remarkable intraindividual changes in memory development are apparent during the elementary school years and in old age. Young children's memory gains can be attributed to the joint development of strategies and knowledge. Decreases in memory functions observable in very old adults point to neurobiological constraints that could be due to both a genetically determined program of biological aging as well as to a neurophysiological substrate resulting from a lifetime of experience and cognitive activity (Baltes and Kliegl 1992).

See also: Adult Learning: An Overview; Development of Learning Across the Lifespan; Psychology of Adult Education

References

Baltes P B, Kliegl R 1992 Further testing of limits of cognitive plasticity in old age: Negative age differences in a mnemonic skill are robust. *Dev. Psychol.* 28(1): 121–25

Best D L, Ornstein P A 1986 Children's generation and communication of mnemonic organizational strategies. *Dev. Psychol.* 22(6): 845–53

Bjorklund D F 1987 How age changes in knowledge base contribute to the development of children's memory: An interpretive review. *Dev. Rev.* 7(2): 93–130

Bjorklund D F (ed.) 1990 *Children's Strategies: Contemporary Views of Cognitive Development.* Erlbaum, Hillsdale, New Jersey

Brainerd C J 1985 Model-based approaches to storage and retrieval development. In: Brainerd C J, Pressley M (eds.) 1985 *Basic Processes in Memory Development.* Springer Verlag, New York

Chi M T H, Ceci S J 1987 Content knowledge: Its role, representation, and restructuring in memory development. In: Reese H W (ed.) 1987 *Advances in Child Development and Behaviour.* Academic Press, San Diego, California

Dempster F N 1985 Short-term memory development in childhood and adolescence. In: Brainerd C J, Pressley M (eds.) 1985 *Basic Processes in Memory Development.* Springer Verlag, New York

Flavell J H 1985 *Cognitive Development,* 2nd edn. Prentice-Hall, Englewood Cliffs, New Jersey

Flavell J H, Wellman H M 1977 Metamemory. In: Kail R

Hagen J W (eds.) 1977 *Perspectives on the Development of Memory and Cognition*. Erlbaum, Hillsdale, New Jersey

Kliegl R, Smith J, Baltes P B 1989 Testing-the-limits and the study of adult age differences in cognitive plasticity of a mnemonic skill. *Dev. Psychol.* 25(2): 247–56

Knopf M 1987 *Gedächtnis im Alter*. Springer Verlag, Berlin

Light L L 1991 Memory and aging: Four hypotheses in search of data. *Annu. Rev. Psychol.* 42: 333–76

Pressley M, Borkowski J G, Schneider W 1987 Cognitive strategies: Good strategy users coordinate metacognition and knowledge. In: Vasta R (ed.) 1987 *Annals of Child Development*, Vol. 5. JAI Press, New York

Salthouse T A 1991 *Theoretical Perspectives on Cognitive Aging*. Erlbaum, Hillsdale, New Jersey

Schneider W, Pressley M 1989 *Memory Development Between 2 and 20*. Springer Verlag, New York

Siegler R S 1991 *Children's Thinking*, 2nd edn. Prentice-Hall, Englewood Cliffs, New Jersey

Weinert F E, Perlmutter M (eds.) 1988. *Memory Development: Universal Changes and Individual Differences*. Erlbaum, Hillsdale, New Jersey

Further Reading

Charness N (ed.) 1985 *Aging and Human Performance*. Wiley, Chichester

Kail R V 1990 *The Development of Memory in Children*, 3rd edn. Freeman, New York

Kausler D H 1991 *Experimental Psychology, Cognition, and Human Aging,* 2nd edn. Springer Verlag, New York

Schneider W, Körkel J, Weinert F E 1990 Expert knowledge, general abilities, and text processing. In: Schneider W, Weinert F E (eds.) 1990 *Interactions among Aptitudes, Strategies, and Knowledge in Cognitive Performance*. Springer Verlag, New York

Lifespan Development: Phases

A. W. Fales

Two major approaches have been used to characterize learning over the lifespan. Life phase approaches divide the lifespan into age-specific phases characterized by particular normative life events (such as marriage, occupational identification, retirement) and psychosocial tasks (such as developing intimacy, letting children go, mentoring) which are believed to have substantial effects on the individual's learning needs, motives, and behavior. Various theories of psychological development over the lifespan (Loevinger 1977, Kohlberg 1973, Perry 1970) propose a series of hierarchical, sequential, qualitative changes in the psychological structures within the individual. These structural changes are age-related only in that each more advanced stage depends on the prior stage having been completed. The major implication of developmental approaches for learning over the lifespan is that learning processes, goals, and strategies are qualitatively different in the various developmental stages. In general, the literature and practice relating adult learning to life phases or developmental stages have used the two approaches synonymously or interchangeably rather than interactively, or have reflected a lack of awareness of the developmental stage viewpoint altogether. Some researchers (Cross 1981, Chickering et al. 1981, Weathersby 1978) have begun, however, to provide a basis for a more comprehensive understanding of the effects of the interaction of life phase events and developmental stage characteristics on adult learning processes and thereby to identify instructional strategies appropriate to different phase—stage life positions.

1. Life Phase Approaches

The idea of life phase has intuitive merit and has been used throughout history to describe the human journey from birth to death. Shakespeare's seven ages of man and the ancient tarot represent diverse examples. Research on phases of adult life and learning has, however, a rather brief history beginning in the 1930s. Early research focused on the patterns of life goals, psychosocial tasks, mastery styles, and intrapsychic changes (Havighurst 1973).

Many of the early researchers related the life phases they identified to changes in learning needs, goals, and processes. More recently a number of researchers have presented life phase models in which common psychosocial tasks are specified for relatively specific chronological periods.

The various studies of life phases use different research methods and are based on small, nonrepresentative samples of, for the most part, white, middle class, American males. Each presents a slightly different breakdown of chronological periods and key issues in each period. In general, however, the phases identified can be described as follows:

(a) Separating from family of orientation (late teens to early 20s). Tasks include becoming self-supporting, forming attachment with peers, separating emotionally from parents, and forming an identity.

(b) Provisionsl adulthood (early to late 20s). Tasks include selection of a mate and intimacy, forming a family, deciding on life-style, forming an occupational identity, mastering what one is "supposed" to be in life.

(c) Thirties transition (late 20s and early 30s). Tasks include evaluating and exploring alternatives to choices in phase (b), and establishing an adult relationship with parents.

(d) Thirties stabilization (early to late 30s). Tasks include succeeding at phase (c) choices, solidifying a sense of self, increasing the attachment to the family of procreation, and giving up mentors.

(e) Forties (mid-life) transition (late 30s and early 40s). Tasks include re-evaluating the "dream" of the first half of life, restructuring the time perspective, establishing a sense of meaning, establishing generativity, and expanding emotional repertoire.

(f) Restabilization (middle 40s and middle 50s). Tasks include succeeding at phase (e) choices, developing self-acceptance, maintaining growth and flexibility emotionally and intellectually, and grandparenthood.

(g) Preparation for retirement (late 50s to middle 60s). Tasks include developing adult relationships with children, preparing for the end of an occupational role, and developing alternative sources of self-esteem.

(h) Young old period (middle 60s to late 70s). Tasks include exploring uses of leisure, consolidating a sense of self as continuous, maintaining health, income, social relations, and emotional attachments, re-evaluating meaning, and developing spirituality.

(i) Old old period (late 70s to death). Tasks include establishing self-acceptance, a life review, maintaining emotional attachments, adjusting to declines in health, relationships, and mental functions, facing death, and providing for generational continuity.

While the notion of life stages has been eagerly adopted by some as a basis for adult education program development (see, for example McCoy 1977, Knox 1979), others caution that research has shown that the stage characteristics may not be valid for even a majority within a specified chronological range, and certainly may not apply to any given individual (Kummerow 1977).

2. Psychological Development Approaches

Development theories have been central to an understanding of children's learning [development being the acquisition of new psychological structures or the change from an old structure to a new one Loevinger 1977 p. 32)]. It is only fairly recently, however, that theories of cognitive (Perry 1970), moral (Kohlberg 1973), and ego (Loevinger 1977) development have been seen as having relevance to understanding adult learning (Cross 1981, Merriam and Caffarella 1991). Developmental theories are presented in terms of stages, which are hierarchical, proceed by gradual step-wise integrations, and are irreversible. These stages may be maturationally related but in adulthood are more likely to be related to the acquisition and integration of experience. Loevinger's theory of ego development incorporates the domains of cognitive, moral, interpersonal, and conscious preoccupation development within an integrated framework and postulates six major stages with three transitional stages. The stages are only minimally age-related and, with the exceptions of the first two, all can be found in "normal", functioning adults. Progression through the stages and the events or experiences which result in transition from one stage to the next are not well-understood. However, the structural transition from one ego stage to another must, theoretically, result in changed perceptions of self, other, knowledge, relationship, feeling, justice, and sources of meaning.

3. Implications for Adult Learning

Life phase and developmental stage theories each have distinct implications for the design and facilitation of adult learning. Table 1 presents examples of some implications for facilitation and the content/interest aspects of adult learners in three life phases for three ego development levels. The three life phases are (a) the phase of separation from the family, (b) the phase of early middle age (the 30s), and (c) the phase of preparation for retirement. From the standpoint of such a theory as Loevinger's, it is possible to identify the three levels or phases of ego development as the conformist, the conscientious, and the autonomous. At the conformist level, the individual's self concentrates on adhering to the rules and tenets of the immediate social environment. In the conscientious phase, the emphasis is on doing a good job and personally assessing one's own achievement. In the autonomous phase the emphasis is on respect for autonomy and independence, yet concern for interactions with others. As Table 1 shows, each ego-development level can be related to each of the three selected life stages in terms of implications drawn about the ways adult education can be facilitated and about the typical content that is of interest to persons at that particular developmental life stage.

Many more specific implications could be gleaned from a close examination of the literature. The examples in the table may suffice to illustrate the kinds of approaches an educator of adults might use for adults in different life phase/developmental stage categories.

Table 1
Implications for adult education of ego-development levels for three selected life phases.

Levels of ego development	Implications	Three selected life phases		
		1. Separation from family	2. Early middle age	3. Preparation for Retirement
Conformist Conformity to external rules; belonging; social acceptance; conceptual simplicity	Facilitation	Reward through approval. Provide structured resources and content. Guidance re. choosing from established work and lifestyle options	Reward through recognition/status. Provide structured resources and content. Guidance re. assessment of self in relation to progress of peers, status	Attention to aging effects, e.g., lighting, speed of concept presentation, building self-esteem as learner. Permission to change. Emphasis on association of new material to existing concepts. Concrete and directed method. Provide structure. Reward through approval/recognition. Provide emotional support
	Content/interest	Competence in expected adult roles; work, skills, parenting, childbirth, nutrition, literacy	Appropriate role-related progression, e.g., children's sport leadership, financial management, "normal" occupational progression. Current leisure or social fads, e.g., fitness, conservation. Intergenerational activities	Maintenance of self-esteem. Expansion of peer-accepted leisure interests, hobbies, volunteer activities. Relationships with adult children. New vocational skills for post retirement use. Financial and life planning. Understanding social change. Health and fitness
Conscientious Self-evaluated standards; mutual relationships; differential feelings; conceptual complexity	Facilitation	Incorporate interpersonal interaction. Guidance in selection of learning goals (long-term) consistent with self-expectation. Include opportunity for self-evaluation	Incorporate interpersonal and group interaction, and intentional affective learning. Structured, self-directed learning modes appropriate. Guidance in use of self-assessment and evaluation within established contexts. Reward through social interaction and self-approval	Emphasize communication skills. Cross-generational groupings. Use of reflection and introspection for self-assessment and future goal identification. Conscious attention to philosophical issues relative to content. Encourage independence in females and affectivity in males
	Content/interest	Achievement of personally valued competence in work and interpersonal relations. Alternative life-style options. Role and social relationships. Concern with social issues	Exploration and testing of alternative life-styles to own. Perceptions of how to link early choices with possible changes in occupation and lifestyle. Conscious assessment of self in relation to parents' values. Stress management. Coping with divorce	Alternative post-retirement roles and relationships. Maintenance of physical, mental, and economic well-being. Skills in interpersonal relating intergenerationally

Levels of ego development	Implications	Three selected life phases		
		1. Separation from family	2. Early middle age	3. Preparation for Retirement
Autonomous Conformist level and conscientious level plus: coping with conflicting inner needs; respect for autonomy and interpersonal interdependence; vivid expression of feelings; integration of physiological, psychological, and social aspects of self; self-fulfilment; increased conceptual complexity; complex patterning and tolerance for ambiguity	Facilitation	Autonomous stage probably not attained by this life phase	Autonomous stage still rare by this life phase. Largely self-directed learning modes and self-planned activity. Opportunity for individual work with group sharing. Life experience assessment for educational credit. Self-based rewards. Reflection as integrative learning tool. Use of imagery, physical activity, creative integrative techniques. Presentation of multiple perspectives	Use of reflection for integrative learning, identification of complex patterns, linking of new understandings with old. Largely self-directed learning modes, and self-planned activity. Provide opportunity for sharing cross-generationally as well as with own life phase cohort. Provide opportunities for expression of complexity of patterns and recognition of value of multiple perspectives. Use in guidance roles with other group members
	Content/interest		Self-discovery. Facilitating others' growth. Freedom and responsibility. Solving social and moral problems. Leadership in areas of ethical and moral concern. Applying coping skills to life planning. Creative stress management. Non-traditional life-style choices	New avocational roles through which self can be expressed. Existential philosophical approaches to knowledge, human problems, and spiritual understanding. Maintenance of physical, mental, and social capacity in integrated form. Expression of own complexity of understanding–wisdom. Welfare of humanity. Biography, mythology, history, spiritual growth

In actual program design and facilitation, the educator often applies an implicit understanding of these interactions in how he or she individualizes instruction, develops materials, and plans program format. In some cases program evaluation research has confirmed the value of use of techniques relevant to the developmental stage/life phase of the learners. For example, a study of the use of demonstration plots in conjunction with literacy training in Iran found that older autonomous farmers benefited significantly from the use of both methods while younger farmers without access to their own land did not (UNFAO 1975). Although such findings do not directly test the relevance of life phase approaches to design and facilitation, they do imply that attention to these factors would produce significant gains in learning.

The practical reality of adult education is usually that the teacher/facilitator does not know the developmental level of his/her students, although the life phase may be easier to estimate. Nevertheless, a little thought can increase provision of alternative learning modes appropriate to different developmental levels. For example, behavioral learning techniques can be used in a teacher-directed or a self-directed manner; skill learning (such as typing or memorization of the alphabet) can be rote learning or can be taught with an emphasis on understanding underlying principles (appropriate to a higher level of cognitive development). Learners in the same classroom can be allowed to choose whether they prefer to learn from the teacher (conformist ego stage), through small group interaction (conscientious ego stage), or independently with group sharing (autonomous ego stage). Thus these concepts can be applied even when the planner or facilitator does not have complete knowledge of the phases/stages of the learners.

If the facilitator perceives his/her role as one of assisting the learner to attain his/her fullest potential, the facilitative techniques used may be intentionally chosen to create a situation where the learner must go beyond his/her usual developmental stage response and will be more likely to produce behaviors appropriate to a level above his/her actual level. The life-phase transitions appear to provide natural "teachable moments" for this type of developmental stage transition, and the experience of a new learning mode which helps resolve or restructure a critical life event during a transitional phase can be a powerful catalyst for progression to the next developmental stage.

See Also: Human Development; Lifespan Development; Lifespan Development: Problems and Crises; Development of Learning Across the Lifespan; The Implications for Educators

References

Chickering A W 1981 *The Modern American College: Responding to the New Realities of Diverse Students and a Changing Society.* Jossey-Bass, San Francisco, California

Cross K P 1981 *Adults as Learners: Increasing Participation and Facilitating Learning.* Jossey-Bass, San Francisco, California.

Havighurst R J 1973 History of developmental psychology: Socialization and personality development through the life span. In: Baltes P B, Schaie K W (eds.)1973 *Life-span Developmental Psychology: Personality and Socialization.* Academic Press, New York

Knox A B (ed.) 1979 *Programming for Adults Facing Mid-life Change* Jossey-Bass, San Francisco, California

Kohlberg L 1973 Continuities in childhood and adult moral development revisited. In: Baltes P B, Schaie K W (eds.) 1973 *Life-span Developmental Psychology: Personality and Socialization,* Academic Press, New York.

Kummerow J M 1977 Developmental theory and its application in guidance programs. *Pupil Person. Serv. J.* 6(1)

Loevinger J 1977 *Ego Development: Conceptions and Theories.* Jossey-Bass, San Francisco, California.

McCoy V R 1977 Adult life cycle change: How does growth affect our education needs? *Lifelong Learning* 1: 14–18, 31

Merriam S B, Caffarella R S 1991 *Learning in Adulthood. A Comprehensive Guide.* Jossey-Bass, San Francisco, California

Perry W G Jr 1970 *Forms of Intellectual and Ethical Development in the College Years: A Scheme.* Holt, Rinehart and Winston, New York

United Nations Food and Agriculture Organization (UNFAO) 1975 The bramble bush of literacy. *Ideas and Action* 105: 5–6

Weathersby R 1978 Life stages and learning interests. *The Adult Learner: Current Issues in Higher Education.* American Association for Higher Education, Washington, DC

Further Reading

Tuijnman A C, van der Kamp M (eds.) 1992 *Learning Across the Lifespan: Theories, Research, Policies.* Pergamon Press, Oxford

Lifespan Development: Problems and Crises

L. Montada

Most problems in human development belong to one of three categories: (a) a desired or prescribed goal cannot be reached by using well-established routines, and new solutions, new insights, new skills, or new knowledge are required; (b) goals that have been pursued must be abandoned because of losses, failures, or constraints, and alternative goals must be chosen or established; and (c) two goals are incompatible and a decision that the less favored goal has to be abandoned is required. In short, many developmental problems can be conceptualized as discrepancies or incompatibilities between goals, opportunities, demands, capacities, and resources. A special case is the lack of or loss of goals to motivate commitments. The concept of "crisis" is used when a person is not easily able or prepared to do what is required in a situation, but is also emotionally affected by the existing problem.

Developmental problems and crises are those that affect a person's life-course and life plans. These problems or crises are frequently remembered as major challenges or turning points, or as traumatic events that demand a readjustment, perhaps requiring new goal decisions, the reorganization of life plans, the acquisition of new competencies, or a change of the self-concept and of views about the world. The changes may result in developmental gains or in disorders. Gains are expected to result from the mastery of problems and crises. It is a common idea that major changes and growth in human development result from struggling with problems and crises and that a new level of intellectual, social, and personal organization will be gained by overcoming them.

Most of the relevant knowledge is documented in the literature concerning developmental tasks, normative life crises, and critical life events. While the sequence of developmental tasks is conceived of as being more or less age normative (i.e., a majority of individuals in a population are confronted with the same class of tasks within a specific period of life), critical life events occur more or less incidentally or accidentally at various points within a lifetime, although they may have a decisive impact on future life and development.

1. Age-normative Crises and Tasks

1.1 Stage Models

Stage models of human development usually entail the metaphor of a crisis of transition from one level to the next, with the transition triggered by problems or conflicts that cannot be solved at the lower stage (see *Lifespan Development: Phases*). The organismic assumption is that problems result from universal maturational or developmental changes within the organism allowing new cognitions, experiences, and interactions. Piaget's stages of cognitive development in 1970 and Freud's sequence of psychosexual conflicts in childhood and adolescence (Freud 1938) are classic examples. In contrast, in dialectic, interactional, or transactional approaches, both the subjects and the various life contexts contribute to the generation and solution of problems and crises, and, because both subjects and contexts exhibit large differences and are continuously changing, neither a universal sequence of problems nor a universal sequence of outcomes is expected.

Erikson's theory of personality development (1968) is a prominent example of the organismic tradition. There are eight major stages throughout the life-course, each characterized by a specific conflict or crisis. The central issues of the crises or the stage-specific conflicts are trust versus mistrust (first year of life), autonomy versus shame and doubt (third year), initiative versus guilt (fourth and fifth year), industry versus inferiority (middle childhood), identity versus role diffusion (adolescence), intimacy versus isolation (early adulthood), generativity versus stagnation (middle adulthood), and ego integrity versus despair (later adulthood). The crisis in adolescence concerning the issue of identity versus role diffusion is well-known. The adolescent has to build up facets of a self concerned with gender, familial background, religion, moral values, educational and professional aspirations and capacities, political attitudes, and so forth and to integrate them into a consistent personal identity. Failures to construct an identity result in "role diffusion," characterized by an imbalance of attitudes and values, goal instability, and sometimes ideological one-sidedness, unrealistic expectations, superficial and unstable commitments, or drug abuse. Failure to master the stage-typical crises results in lasting personality disorders. The postulated universality of these stages is, however, open to question.

1.2 Developmental Tasks

Like Erikson, Havighurst structured the life-course along a sequence of problems that he labeled developmental tasks. However, he adopted a more explicit dialectical perspective, bridging biological, sociological, and psychological approaches. Taxonomies list numerous specific developmental tasks in each life period that may be subsumed under some general concerns like "making the most of disengagement" in the seventh decade. Developmental tasks for the elderly, for instance, are mastering retirement from professional roles, health problems, or loss of partners, and accepting one's own life history, a decline in physical and mental abilities, and the finiteness of human life.

Havighurst's sequence of developmental tasks was considered widespread in Western societies. There are other tasks that are not statistically normal and age bound, which, nevertheless, may have a decisive influence on the future course of life. In fact, in life retrospectives focusing on major turning points, milestones, transitions, and stressful or traumatic experiences, the postulated age-normative tasks and crises do not constitute the majority of reported memories (Thomae and Lehr 1986).

Havighurst (1972) suggested three broad sources of developmental tasks throughout the life course: biological changes within the organism such as puberty and menopause, tasks set by society (e.g., in education and professional life), and values, aspirations, and goals of the developing individual. For instance, upward mobility depends on biological factors such as mental and physical health; on psychological factors such as individual aspirations, capacities, and education; on social context factors such as job aspirations of the family; on societal factors such as availability of occupational positions, possibly affirmative actions for hitherto underpriviledged subpopulations; and on cultural factors such as the general valuation of upward mobility or informal normative constraints for subpopulations. Thus, the chances for optimal development may vary considerably between birth cohorts, families, and individuals.

This is the view of modern conceptions of human development (e.g., Lifespan Developmental Psychology, see Baltes et al. 1980), that use interactional models and postulate reciprocal influences between individuals, members of social networks, and cultural and societal opportunities, demands, and resources, and assume that subjects are active agents in their own development who have long-term commitments, and select goals, settings, and contexts. Development is expected to take differential and individual trajectories. One example of the differential impact of the same context conditions illustrates this conception. According to Elder's studies, the Great Depression of the 1930s had greatly varying effects on children depending on their age. For younger children of unemployed fathers the experience of familial conflict and poor parenting caused by the economic problems had long-lasting negative effects on personality and achievement. For the adolescent sons, however, this was an opportunity to assume some responsibility for the support of the family and the experience had long-lasting positive effects on their personality, and social and professional development (Elder 1974).

2. Critical Life Events

Events such as the birth of a sibling; parents' divorce; moving to another school or residence; marriage; becoming a parent; getting, changing, or losing a job; serious health problems; becoming a victim of crime; the death of a close one; accidents; a natural catastrophe; or economic losses are breaks in the course of life that require (or permit) changes in roles, goals, or the organization of one's life, and that quite frequently lead to the acquisition of new abilities, knowledge, attitudes, or affiliations. Such events generate problems, which either constitute challenges for growth or risks of maladjustment and disorders.

A broad range of criteria have been used to assess the consequences of critical life events and of struggling with their associated problems. The risk of pathogenetic stress that resulted in mental or psychosomatic illness has been investigated from a clinical perspective. Effect variables such as negative emotions (e.g., strong fears following traumatic threats, resentment toward a victimizer, or mourning following bereavement), loss of self-esteem and helplessness following failure, loss of interpersonal trust following betrayal, and loss of belief in a just world following uncompensated and unpunished victimization are specific types of problems. The continuation of these effects for a prolonged period of time is an indicator of impaired mental health or personality disorder. Developmental gains may include a positive self-concept including self-efficacy, acquired belief in one's own invulnerability, the capacity to cope with loss, and various problem-solving strategies and skills.

Early research was focused on the impact of critical life events on mental and physical health. The hypothesis was—in analogy to the stress concept—that the number and amount of life changes caused by an event would be the most important risk factor. Therefore, an accumulation of events was expected to increase the risk of failing to solve the multiple associated problems. After extensive research through the 1970s and 1980s it became evident that for the population as a whole, the impact of events is not as large as was expected and explains no more than 10 percent of the variance of health scores and mortality. Whereas most people recover and adjust quite quickly after having experienced a critical event, some do not. This has been shown for a variety of event types, even including the death of a close one, serious injuries, and illnesses. Research is required to identify the factors that explain or predict both successful problem-solving and adjustment and failures to adjust adequately. Specifically, can dimensions be identified along which an event risk varies? Are strategies and interventions available to prevent poor adjustment? What are the major differences between people who show good and poor adjustment?

2.1 Relevant Dimensions of Events

The hedonistic value of events varies considerably. Some events are generally experienced as desirable (e.g., marriage, birth of a child, getting a job), others as undesirable, implying adversity or losses. However, the evaluation of the same class of events typically varies among individuals. The birth of a child, for instance, might be a burden for some, interfering with a professional career; the death of a spouse might mean liberation for some; injuries and illness might serve as an excuse for professional failure or as an atonement for guilt. What is relevant is the subjective valuation, not the normative one. Life changes that are caused by an event may be more or less appreciated, taken for granted, regretted, resented, or hated. Negative effects are more likely with negatively valued changes. The extent of change per se is not necessarily distressing, but may, instead, be challenging.

A significant factor is how many members of a population are confronted with a critical event. If many members of a population are affected, as is the case with some historically graded events such as major economic depressions, wars, or natural or technical catastrophes, the psychological and social experience is different from cases where only single individuals are affected, such as accidents, criminal victimizations, or bereavements. Problems and losses that are widespread within a population are presumably less likely to be perceived as unjust, society is more inclined to respond with sympathy to victims and to provide support, and negative social reactions are less probable because ascriptions of responsibility to victims are less likely. For the same reasons, transitions (such as pregnancy, retirement, marriage) which are "in-time" (that is, within the normal age range) are easier to cope with than "off-time" transitions that bear a higher risk of social critique and subjective shame.

2.2 Subjective Interpretations

The psychological impact of events is largely derived from their subjective interpretation. For instance, the impact of becoming physically handicapped as a result of an event varies widely depending on subjective views of the event. Two categories of interpretation are particularly relevant: (a) attributions of causation and responsibility, and (b) views about the meaning.

For instance, the distress caused by serious injury depends a good deal on whether it was considered to be caused by natural processes, to be simply one's fate, to be caused by a responsible agent, or to be personally caused. These different views elicit different emotional responses: guilt if the subject feels personally responsible, outrage if others are responsible. In many cases, victims may ascribe some causal responsibilities to themselves which might help them to avoid feelings of resentment against others and feelings of helplessness or lack of control in similar situations. For some victims it might be easier to find an emotional balance if nobody is to blame, because the injury is viewed simply as the result of bad luck.

Yet this is not true for all those who consider the question "Why me?". They are searching for meaning, explanations, or responsibilities. Bad luck makes the injury meaningless, and undeserved bad luck undermines their belief in a just and controllable world. Injuries resulting from intentional attacks, a suicide attempt, or risky adventures are not meaningless because reasoned actions which resulted in the injury can be perceived. A second category of meaning may be found in positive consequences of events such as the experience of mastering serious problems, the experience of solidarity by members of a social network, or the reordering of life priorities. The search for meaning, and explanations and attributions of responsibility, can be considered as ways of coping with an event and with associated problems.

2.3 Ways of Coping

Research on coping has identified a variety of ways to deal with adversity, for instance, ruminations about threats and losses, positive illusions about the future, palliative views (such as "downward" comparisons with those who are still worse off, minimization of problems, positive illusions about the future), seeking help and support, efforts to find concrete solutions for problems, and so on.

The various ways of dealing with problems are not uniform in their effectiveness; rather, the effectiveness depends on the particular case, perhaps with the exception that continuous contemplation neither solves the problem nor changes its perception, but merely stabilizes the awareness of adversity. Moreover, continuing to ruminate will frequently reduce the readiness of social network members to extend social support.

Palliative views reduce negative emotions such as fear, resentment, and depression. They seem to be a good choice for instances such as illnesses where a realistic appraisal is neither helpful in solving the problem nor in avoiding further negative consequences. There are, however, cases when a realistic appraisal is needed to motivate decisions which might be adequate to solve the problem (e.g., in the case of unemployment by either applying for jobs or starting a training for a new career).

Constructive problem-solving is widely considered to be the ideal coping strategy. This may be true in cases when problems can be solved without exhausting all resources, without interfering with other important goals, without producing strain, and without bearing the risk of side-effects. In some cases a better strategy may be to accept losses, or to reorganize goal priorities to make them fit the opportunities, capacities, and resources. Brandtstädter and Renner (1992) made an important distinction between tenacious goal pursuit and goal accommodation. They found that elderly people who used an accommodative strategy in coping with age-bound losses had less depressive symptoms than those using a goal pursuit that might eventually fail.

2.4 Protective Factors

Research on the issue of critical events has addressed the question of whether vulnerability or protective factors exist beyond effective ways of coping. This research has identified biological, psychological, and sociological factors.

On a psychobiological level is Dienstbier's concept of toughness. Toughness can be trained (e.g., by aerobic training or by engaging in a reasonable number of challenging tasks). "Toughening up" means a relative strengthening of the "softer" peripheral catecholamine-bound arousal system as compared to the more "aggressive" central cortisol-bound arousal system. Toughened individuals are therefore better equipped to meet stressors without undue physiological arousal (Dienstbier 1992).

On the psychological level, traitlike personality features like Kobasa's concept of hardiness (Kobasa 1982), as well as the experience-based confidence to cope with critical situations, are noteworthy, as are self-efficacy or internal control beliefs and a broad repertoire of possible approaches to problems.

On the social level, a large body of research suggests that social support is a protective factor and negative social reactions are risk factors. Received social support is helpful in many cases, but can also interfere with the development of self-efficacy and competence in problem-solving. While the effects of social support are not always positive, the effects of negative social reactions like derogating and blaming victims constitute secondary problems and are consistently related to maladjustment.

3. Implications for Education and Counseling

Taking an interactional perspective implies taking several possible sources of the generation of problems and crises into account: individuals with their goals, aspirations, and abilities; social networks with their aspirations, normative constraints, and resources; and society with its demands, opportunities, and subserviences. Problems are constituted as incongruencies and incompatibilities between goals, aspirations, demands, resources, and so on. Consequently, the prevention or the solution of problems may take different approaches, focusing on different sources. The choice of an approach in actual cases depends not only on its feasibility but, within an educational perspective, has to be based on criteria for optimal development. Priority should be given to approaches that give individuals

opportunities to build up abilities, protective traits, and convictions that will help them to cope better with future problems and crises (see *Student Counseling*). The experience of mastering crises may strengthen confidence in self-efficacy. Building up a repertoire of coping strategies and of rules for adequately using them in different situations may contribute to stress immunization. Since the life-course may be conceived of as a series of problems it seems appropriate to perceive every problem (from daily hassles to big losses) as a potential challenge and an occasion for learning and gaining new insights.

See also: Lifespan Development: Phases; Development of Learning Across the Lifespan; Study and Learning Strategies; Teaching Methods: Individual Techniques; Student Counseling; Student Support Systems

References

Baltes P B, Reese H W, Lipsitt L P 1980 Life-span Developmental Psychology. *Annu. Rev. Psychol.* 31: 65–110
Brandtstädter J, Renner G 1992 Coping with discrepancies between aspirations and achievements in adult development: A dual process model. In: Montada L, Filipp S H, Lerner M J (eds.) 1992 *Life Crises and Experiences of Loss in Adulthood.* Erlbaum, Hillsdale, New Jersey
Dienstbier R A 1992 Mutual impact of toughening on crises and losses. In: Montada L, Filipp S H, Lerner M J (eds.) 1992
Elder G H Jr 1974 *Children of the Great Depression.* University of Chicago Press, Chicago, Illinois
Erikson E H 1968 *Identity, Youth and Crises.* Norton, New York
Freud S 1938 *Abriss der Psychoanalyse.* Fischer, Frankfurt
Havighurst R J 1972 *Developmental Task and Education.* McKay, New York
Kobasa S C 1982 Commitment and coping in stress resistance among lawyers. *J. Pers. Soc. Psychol.* 42: 707–17
Thomae H, Lehr U 1986 Stages, crises, and life span development. In: Sorensen A B, Weinert F E, Sherrod L R (eds.) 1986 *Human Development and the Life Course.* Multidisciplinary Perspectives. Erlbaum, Hillsdale, New Jersey

Further Reading

Brandtstädter J, Gräser H (eds.) 1983 *Entwicklungsberatung.* Hogrefe, Göttingen
Datan N, Ginsberg L H (eds.) 1975 *Life Span Developmental Psychology, Normative Life Crises.* Academic Press, New York
Filipp S H (ed.) 1990 *Kritische Lebensereignisse.* Psychologie Verlags Union, Munich
Fisher S, Reason J (eds.) 1988 *Handbook of Life Stress, Cognition and Health.* Wiley, New York
Kessler R C, Price R H, Wortman C B 1985 Social Factors in Psychopathology: Stress, Social Support, and Coping Processes. *Annu. Rev. Psychol.* 36: 531–72
Montada L, Filipp S H, Lerner M J (eds.) 1992 *Life Crises and Experiences of Loss in Adulthood.* Erlbaum, Hillsdale, New Jersey

(b) Adult Learning

Adult Learning: An Overview

S. D. Brookfield

Adult learning is frequently spoken of by adult educators as if it were an entirely discrete domain, having little connection to learning in childhood or adolescence. This entry will examine this claim critically by exploring four major research areas: self-directed learning, critical reflection, experiential learning, and learning to learn. Each of these has been proposed as representing a unique and exclusive adult learning process.

1. Issues in Understanding Adult Learning

Despite the plethora of journals, books, and research conferences devoted to adult learning across the world, there is no universal understanding of this process. Even though warnings are frequently issued that at best only a multitude of context and domain-specific theories are likely to result, the energy expended on developing a general theory of adult learning shows no sign of abating. Judged by epistemological, communicative, and critically analytic criteria, theory development in adult learning is weak and is hindered by the persistence of myths that are etched deeply into adult educators' minds (Brookfield 1992). These myths (which, taken together, comprise something of an academic orthodoxy in adult education) hold that adult learning is inherently joyful, that adults are innately self-directed learners, that good educational practice always meets the needs articulated by learners themselves, and that there is a uniquely "adult" learning process as well as a uniquely adult form of practice. This entry argues that it is a grave error to attempt to construct an exclusive theory of adult learning; namely, one that is distinguished wholly by its total exclusion of what is known about learning at other stages in the lifespan. Indeed, a strong case can be made that as learning is examined across the lifespan, the variables of culture, ethnicity, personality, and political ethos assume far greater significance in explaining how learning occurs and is experienced than does the variable of chronological age of the learner.

2. Major Areas of Research on Adult Learning

The four areas discussed below represent the postwar preoccupations of adult learning researchers. Each area has its own internal debates and emphases, yet the concerns and interests of those working within each of them overlap significantly with those of the other three. Indeed, several researchers have made important contributions to more than one of these areas. Considered as a whole, these areas of research constitute an espoused theory of adult learning that informs how many adult educators practice their craft.

2.1 Self-directed Learning

Self-directed learning focuses on the process by which adults take control of their own learning, in particular how they set their own learning goals, locate appropriate resources, decide on which learning methods to use, and evaluate their progress. Work on self-direction is so widespread that it warrants an annual international symposium devoted solely to research and theory in the area (see *Self-directed Learning*). After criticisms that the emphasis on self-directed learning as an adult characteristic was being uncritically advanced, that studies were conducted mostly with middle-class subjects, that issues concerning the quality of self-directed learning projects were being ignored, and that it was treated as disconnected from wider social and political forces, there have been some attempts to inject a more critical tone into work in this area. Meta-analyses of research and theory conducted by Australian, Canadian, and American authors have raised questions about the political dimension to self-directedness and the need to study how deliberation and serendipity intersect in self-directed learning projects (Collins 1988, Candy 1990, Brockett and Hiemstra 1991). There has also been a spirited debate concerning Australian criticism of the reliability and validity of the most widely used scale for assessing readiness for self-directed learning (Field 1991). At least one book, developed in the South African adult educational experience, has argued that self-direction must be seen as firmly in the tradition of emancipatory adult education (Hammond and Collins 1991).

A number of important questions remain regarding the understanding of self-direction as a defining concept for adult learning. For example, the cross-cultural dimension of the concept has been almost completely ignored. More longitudinal and life-history research is needed to understand how periods of self-directedness alternate with more traditional forms of educational participation. Work on gender has criticized the ideal of the independent, self-directed learner as reflecting patriarchal values of division, separation, and competition. The extent to which a disposition to self-directedness is culturally learned, or is tied to personality, is an open issue. Researchers still struggle to understand how various factors—the adult's previous experiences, the nature of the learning task and the domain involved, the political ethos of the time—affect the decision to learn in this manner. There is also a need to know more about how adults engaged in self-directed learning use social networks and peer support groups for emotional sustenance and educational guidance. Finally, work is needed on clarifying the political dimensions of this idea; particularly on the issues of power and control raised by the learner's assuming responsibility for choices and judgments regarding what can be learned, how learning should happen, and whose evaluative judgments regarding the quality and effectiveness of learning should hold sway. If the cultural formation of the self is ignored, it is all too easy to equate self-direction with separateness and selfishness, with a narcissistic pursuit of private ends in disregard to the consequences of this for others and for wider cultural interests. A conception of learning that views adults as self-contained, volitional beings, scurrying around engaged in individual projects, is one that works against cooperative and collective impulses. Citing self-direction, adults can deny the importance of collective action, common interests, and their basic interdependence in favour of an obsessive focus on the self.

2.2 Critical Reflection

Developing critical reflection is probably the main idea for many adult educators who have long been searching for a form and process of learning that could be claimed to be distinctively adult. Evidence that adults are capable of this kind of learning can be found in developmental psychology, where a host of constructs such as embedded logic, dialectical thinking, practical intelligence, reflective judgment, postformal reasoning, and epistemic cognition describe how adults come to think contextually and critically (Brookfield 1987, 1991). As an idea critical reflection focuses on three interrelated processes: (a) the process by which adults question and then replace or reframe an assumption that up to that point has been uncritically accepted as representing commonsense wisdom; (b) the process through which adults take an alternative perspective on ideas, actions, forms of reasoning and ideologies previously taken for granted; (c) the process by which adults come to recognize the hegemonic aspects of dominant cultural values and to understand how self-evident renderings of the "natural" state of the world actually bolster the power and self-interest of unrepresentative minorities. Writers in this area vary according to the extent to which critical reflection should have a political edge, or the extent to which it can be observed in domains of adult life such as personal relationships and workplace actions. Some confusion is caused by the fact that psychoanalytic and critical social theoretical traditions coexist uneasily in many studies of critical reflection.

The most important work in this area is that of Mezirow (1991). Mezirow's early work (conducted with women returning to higher education) focused on the idea of perspective transformation, which he understood as the learning process by which adults come to recognize and reframe their culturally induced dependency roles and relationships. More recently he has drawn strongly on the work of Jürgen Habermas to propose a theory of transformative learning "that can explain how adult learners make sense or meaning of their experiences, the nature of the structures that influence the way they construe experience, the dynamics involved in modifying meanings, and the way the structures of meaning themselves undergo changes when learners find them to be dysfunctional" (Mezirow 1991 p. xii). Applications of Mezirow's ideas have been made with widely varying groups of adult learners such as displaced homemakers, male spouse abusers, and those suffering ill health, though his work has been criticized by educators in Nigeria, the United States, New Zealand, and Canada for focusing too exclusively on individual transformation (Collard and Law 1989, Ekpenyong 1990, Clark and Wilson 1991).

Many tasks remain for researchers of critical reflection as a dimension of adult learning. A language needs to be found to describe this process to educators which is more accessible than the usual psychoanalytic and critical theory terminology. More understanding of how people experience episodes of critical reflection (viscerally as well as cognitively), and how they deal with the risks of committing cultural suicide that these entail, would help educators respond to fluctuating rhythms of denial and depression in learners. Much research in this area confirms that critical reflection is context- or domain-specific. How is it that the same people can be highly critical regarding, for example, dominant political ideologies, yet show no critical awareness of the existence of repressive features in their personal relationships? Theoretical analyses of critical reflection (frequently drawn from Habermas's work) outweigh to a considerable degree the number of ethnographic, phenomenological studies of how this process is experienced. Contextual factors surrounding the decision to forgo or pursue action after a period of critical reflection are still unclear, as is the extent to which critical reflection is associated with certain personality characteristics.

2.3 Experiential Learning

The emphasis on experience as a defining feature of adult learning was expressed in Lindeman's frequently quoted aphorism that "experience is the adult learner's living textbook" (1926 p. 7) and that adult education was, therefore, "a continuing process of evaluating experiences" (p. 85). This emphasis on experience is central to the concept of andragogy that has evolved to describe adult education practice in societies as diverse as those of the United States, the United Kingdom, France, Hungary, Poland, Russia, Estonia, the former Czechoslovakia, Finland, and the former Yugoslavia (Savicevic 1991, Vooglaid and Marja 1992). The belief that adult teaching should be grounded in adults' experiences, and that these experiences represent a valuable resource, is considered as crucial by adult educators of every conceivable ideological hue (see *Experiential and Open Learning*). Of all the models of experiential learning that have been developed, David Kolb's has probably been the most influential in prompting theoretical work among researchers of adult learning (Jarvis 1987). But almost every textbook on adult education practice affirms the importance of experiential methods such as games, simulations, case studies, psychodrama, role play, and internships, and many universities now grant credit for adults' experiential learning. Not surprisingly, then, the gradual accumulation of experience across the contexts of life is often argued as the chief difference between learning in adulthood and learning at earlier stages in the lifespan. Yet an exclusive reliance on accumulated experience as the defining characteristic of adult learning contains two discernible pitfalls, as follow.

First, experience should not be thought of as an objectively neutral phenomenon, a river of thoughts, perceptions, and sensations into which we decide, occasionally, to dip our toes. Rather, experience is culturally framed and shaped. How events are experienced and the readings made of them are problematic; that is, they change according to the language and categories of analysis used, and according to the cultural, moral, and ideological vantage points from which they are viewed. In a very important sense experience is constructed: how we sense and interpret what happens to us and to the world around us is a function of structures of understanding and perceptual filters that are so culturally embedded that we are scarcely aware of their existence or operation.

Second, the quantity or length of experience is not necessarily connected to its richness or intensity. For example, in an adult educational career spanning 30 years the same one year's experience can, in effect, be repeated 30 times. Indeed, one's "experience" over these 30 years can be interpreted using uncritically assimilated cultural filters in such a way as to prove to oneself that students from certain ethnic groups are lazy or that fear is always the best stimulus to critical thinking. Because of the habitual ways in which meaning is drawn from experiences, these experiences can become evidence for the self-fulfilling prophecies that stand in the way of critical insight. Uncritically affirming people's histories, stories, and experiences risks idealizing and romanticizing them. Experiences are neither innocent nor free from the cultural contradictions that inform them.

2.4 Learning to Learn

The ability of adults to learn how to learn—to become skilled at learning in a range of different situations and through a range of different styles—has often been proposed as an overarching purpose for those educators who work with adults (see *Learning to Learn*). Like its sister term of "metacognition," learning how to learn suffers for lack of a commonly agreed on definition, functioning more as an umbrella term for any attempts by adults to develop insight into their own habitual ways of learning. Most research on this topic has been conducted by Smith (1990) who drew together educators from the United States, Scotland, Australia, Germany, and Sweden to work on theory development in this area. An important body of related work (focusing mostly on young adults) is that of Kitchener and King (1990) who propose the concepts of epistemic cognition and reflective judgment. These authors emphasize that learning how to learn involves an epistemological awareness deeper than simply knowing how one scores on a cognitive-style inventory, or what is one's typical or preferred pattern of learning. Rather, it means that adults possess a self-conscious awareness of how it is they come to know what they know—an awareness of the reasoning, assumptions, evidence, and justifications that underlie our beliefs that something is true.

Studies of learning to learn have been conducted with a range of adult groups and in a range of settings such as adult basic education, the workplace, and religious communities. Yet, of the four areas of adult learning research discussed, learning how to learn has been the least successful in capturing the imagination of the adult educational world and in prompting a dynamic program of follow-up research. This may be because, as several writers have noted, in systems of lifelong education the function of helping people learn how to learn is often claimed as being more appropriate to schools than to adult education. Many books on learning to learn restrict themselves to the applicability of this concept to elementary or secondary school learning. While it is useful to acknowledge the school's foundational and formational role in this area, it is also important to stress that developing this capacity is too difficult to be left solely to primary and secondary education. Learning to learn should be conceived as a lifelong learning project.

Research on learning to learn is also flawed in its emphasis on college students' metacognition and by its lack of attention to how this process manifests itself in the diverse contexts of adult life. That learning to learn is a skill that exists far beyond academic boundaries is evident from the research conducted on practical intelligence and everyday cognition in settings and activities as diverse as grocery shopping and betting shops (Brookfield 1991). The connections between a propensity for learning how to learn and the nature of the learning task or domain also need clarification. Learning how to learn is referred to much more frequently in studies of clearly defined skill development or knowledge acquisition than in studies examining emotional learning or the development of emotional intelligence.

3. Emergent Trends

Three trends in the study of adult learning that have emerged during the 1990s, and that promise to exercise some influence into the twenty-first century, concern: (a) the cross-cultural dimensions of adult learning; (b) adults' engagement in practical theorizing; and (c) the ways in which adults learn within the systems of education that are linked to technological advances (e.g., distance education, computer-assisted instruction, and open learning systems).

3.1 Cross-cultural Adult Learning

Although the literature in the area of cross-cultural adult learning is sparse, there are indications that the variable of ethnicity is being taken with increasing seriousness (Cassara 1990, Ross-Gordon 1991). As China opened its borders to adult educators in the 1980s, research on Chinese conceptions of adult learning started to emerge (Pratt 1992). As literature in this area makes clear, framing discussions of cultural diversity around a simple dichotomy of White and non-White populations vastly oversimplifies a complex reality. Among ethnic groups themselves there are significant intra- and intergroup tensions. In the United States, for example, Black, Hispanic, and Asian workers have points of tension between them. Within each of these broad groupings there is a myriad of overlapping rivalries; between African-Americans and immigrants from the British West Indies; between Colombians, Puerto Ricans, Cubans and Dominicans; between Koreans, Vietnamese, Cambodians, and Hmong tribespeople. Moreover, the tribal cultures of Native Americans cannot be conceptualized as a culturally homogeneous block.

Two important insights for practice have been suggested by early research into cross-cultural adult learning. First, adult educators from the dominant American, European, and Northern cultures will need to examine some of their assumptions, inclinations, and preferences about "natural" adult learning and adult teaching styles (Brookfield 1986). For the Hmong tribespeople from the mountains of Laos who are used to working cooperatively and to looking to their teachers for direction and guidance, ways of working that emphasize self-directedness and that place the locus of control with the individual student will be experienced, initially at least, as dissonant and anxiety-producing (Podeschi 1990). However, their liking for materials that focus on personal concrete experience fits well with the adult education practices that emphasize experiential approaches. Second, "teaching their own" is a common theme in case studies of multicultural learning. In other words, when adults are taught by educators drawn from their own ethnic communities they tend to feel more comfortable and to do better. Ethnocentric theories and assumptions regarding adult learning styles underscore the need for mainstream adult educators to research their own practice with native and aboriginal peoples. This will require a critically responsive stance toward their practice (Brookfield 1990) and a readiness to examine some of their most strongly held, paradigmatic assumptions (Brookfield 1987).

3.2 Practical Theorizing

Practical theorizing is an idea most associated with the work of Usher (Usher and Bryant 1989) who has focused on the ways in which educational practitioners—including adult educators—become critically aware of the informally developed theories that guide their practice. Practical theorizing has its origins in practitioners' attempts to grapple with the dilemmas, tensions, and contradictions of their work. Actions that educators take in these situations often appear instinctual. Yet, on reflection, these apparently instinctive reactions can be understood to be embedded in assumptions, readings, and interpretations that practitioners have evolved over time to make sense of their practice.

Practitioners seem to arrive at a more informed understanding of their informal patterns of reasoning by subjecting these to critical review, drawing on two important sources. First, they compare their emerging informal theories to those of their colleagues. This happens informally in individual conversations and in a more structured way through participation in reflection groups. Colleagues serve as mirrors in these groups; they reflect back to the practitioner readings of his or her behavior that come as an interesting surprise. As they describe their own reactions and experiences dealing with typical crises, colleagues can help the individual worker reframe, broaden, and refine his or her own theories of practice. Second, practitioners also use formal theory as a lens through which to view their own actions and the assumptions that inform these. As well as providing multiple perspectives on familiar situations, formal theory can help educators "name" their practice by illuminating the general elements of what were thought of as idiosyncratic experiences. These two sources—colleagues' experiences and formal theory—intersect continuously in a dialectical interplay of particular and universal perspectives.

3.3 Distance Learning

In contrast to its earlier equation with necessarily limiting correspondence study formats, distance education is now regarded as an important setting within which a great deal of significant adult learning occurs (Gibson 1992). Weekend college formats, multimedia experimentations, and the educational possibilities unleashed by satellite broadcasting have combined to provide learning opportunities for millions of adults across the world. That adult educational themes of empowerment, critical reflection, experience, and collaboration can inform distance learning activities is evident from case studies of practice that have been emerging. Modra (1989) provides an interesting account of how she drew on the work of radical adult educators such as Freire, Shor, and Lovett to use learning journals to encourage adults' critical reflection in an Australian distance education course. Smith and Castle (1992) propose the use of "experiential learning technology, facilitated from a distance, as a method of developing critical thinking skills" with "the scattered, oppressed adult population of South Africa" (p. 191).

4. Further Research

Ten important issues need to be addressed if research on adult learning is to have a greater influence on how the education and training of adults is conducted.

First, much greater definitional clarity is needed when the term "learning" is discussed, particularly as to whether it is being used as a noun or verb and whether it is referring to behavioral change or cognitive development (Brookfield 1986). Many writers speak about adult learning systems when they are really referring to adult educational programs. Although learning often occurs in an adult educational program, it is not a necessary or inevitable consequence of such a program.

Second, the interaction of emotion and cognition in adult learning needs much greater attention. For example, can we speak of the emotional intelligence adults develop? Classificatory schema and conceptual categories dealing with adult learning tend to focus on settings for learning (communities, schools, religious communities, the workplace, and so on), or on externally observable processes (self-directed learning, collaborative learning, and so on). Emotional dimensions to conceptual or instrumental learning, or understanding how adults learn about their own emotional selves, are matters that are rarely addressed. More attention is needed to how making meaning, critical thinking, and entering new cognitive and instrumental domains are viscerally experienced processes.

Third, adult learning needs to be understood much more as a socially embedded and socially constructed phenomenon (Jarvis 1987). Research on adult learning draws almost exclusively from psychologistic sources. It is easy to forget that the "self" in a self-directed learning effort is a socially formed self and that the goals of adults' self-directed learning can therefore be analyzed as culturally framed goals. Learning is a collective process involving the cultural formation and reproduction of symbols and meaning perspectives. It should not be understood or researched as if it were disconnected, idiosyncratic, and wholly autonomous.

Fourth, many more cross-cultural perspectives are needed to break the Eurocentric and North American dominance in research in adult learning and to understand intercultural differences in industrialized societies. Blithe generalizations about "the adult learner," "adults as learners," or "the nature of adult learning" imply that people over 25 form a homogeneous entity simply by virtue of their chronological age. Yet the differences of class, culture, ethnicity, personality, cognitive style, learning patterns, life experiences, and gender among adults are far more significant than the fact that they are not children or adolescents. It is necessary to be much more circumspect when talking about adults as if they were an empirically coherent entity simply by virtue of the fact that they are no longer in school. In particular, it is necessary to challenge the ethnocentrism of much theorizing in this area, which assumes that adult learning as a generic phenomenon or process is synonymous with the learning undertaken in university continuing education classes by White American middle-class adults in the postwar era.

Fifth, the role played by gender in learning is as poorly understood in adulthood as it is at other stages in the lifespan. It is still an open question as to whether the forms of knowing uncovered in some studies of adult women learners are solely a function of gender, are connected to the developmental stages of adulthood, or are culturally constructed.

Sixth, the predominant focus in studies of adult learning on instrumental skill development needs widening to encompass work on spiritual and significant personal learning and to understand the interconnections between these domains. This is particularly so given the fact that in surveys of adult learning most people point to learning in workplaces, families, communities, and recreational societies to be more prevalent and significant than learning undertaken within formal education.

Seventh, a way should be found to grant greater credibility to adults' renderings of the experience of learning from the "inside." Most descriptions of how adults experience learning are rendered by researchers' pens, not learners themselves. More phenomenographic studies of how adults feel their way through learning episodes, given in their own words and using their own interpretations and constructs, would enrich our understanding of the significance of learning to adults.

Eighth, the growing recognition accorded to qualitative studies of adult learning should be solidified. In speaking of research that has influenced their practice, adult educators place much greater emphasis on qualitative studies as compared to survey questionnaires or research through experimental designs.

Ninth, research on adult learning needs to be in tegrated much more tightly with research on adult development and adult cognition. With a few notable exceptions (Tennant 1988, Merriam and Caffarella 1991) these two strongly related areas exist in separate though parallel compartments, possibly because of adult educators' self-effacing refusal to become involved with what they see as academically "pure" research. There is also a belief held by many adult educators that theirs is a field of applied practice and that questions of theoretical and conceptual import should therefore be left to academics working within universities.

Finally, the links between adult learning and learning at other stages in the lifespan need much more attention (Tuijnman and van Der Kamp 1992). To understand adult learning it is necessary to know about its connections to learning in childhood and adolescence and to the formation during these periods of interpretive filters, cognitive frames, and cultural rules.

See also: Psychology of Adult Education; Human Development; Lifespan Development: Intelligence; Approaches to Learning; Individual Differences, Learning, and Instruction; The Implications for Educators

References

Brockett R G, Hiemstra R 1991 *Self-direction in Adult Learning: Perspectives in Theory, Research, and Practice.* Routledge, New York

Brookfield S D 1986 *Understanding and Facilitating Adult Learning: A Comprehensive Analysis of Principles of Effective Practices.* Jossey-Bass, San Francisco, California

Brookfield S D 1987 *Developing Critical Thinkers: Challenging Adults to Explore Alternative Ways of Thinking and Acting.* Jossey-Bass, San Francisco, California

Brookfield S D 1990 *The Skillful Teacher: On Technique, Trust, and Responsiveness in the Classroom.* Jossey-Bass, San Francisco, California

Brookfield S D 1991 The development of critical reflection in adulthood. *New Educ.* 13(1): 39–48

Brookfield S D 1992 Developing criteria for formal theory building in adult education. *Adult Educ. Q.* 42(2): 79–93

Candy P C 1990 *Self-direction for Lifelong Learning: A Comprehensive Guide to Theory and Practice.* Jossey-Bass, San Francisco, California

Cassara B (ed.) 1990 *Adult Education in a Multicultural Society.* Routledge, New York

Clark M C, Wilson A L 1991 Context and rationality in Mezirow's theory of transformational learning. *Adult Educ. Q.* 41(2): 75–91

Collard S, Law M 1989 The limits of perspective transformation: A critique of Mezirow's theory. *Adult Educ. Q.* 39(2): 99–107

Collins M 1988 Self-directed learning or an emancipatory practice of adult education: Re-thinking the role of the adult educator. *Proc. 29th Annual Adult Education Research Conference.* Faculty of Continuing Education, University of Calgary

Ekpenyong L E 1990 Studying adult learning through the history of knowledge. *Int. J. Lifelong Educ.* 9(3): 161–78

Field L 1991 Guglielmino's self-directed learning readiness scale: Should it continue to be used? *Adult Educ. Q.* 41(2): 100–03

Gibson C C 1992 Distance education: On focus and future. *Adult Educ. Q.* 42(3): 167–79

Hammond M, Collins R 1991 *Self-directed Learning: Critical Practice.* Kogan Page, London

Jarvis P 1987 *Adult Learning in the Social Context.* Croom Helm, London

Kitchener K S, King P M 1990 The reflective judgment model: Transforming assumptions about knowing. In: Mezirow J (ed.) 1990 *Fostering Critical Reflection in Adulthood: A Guide to Transformative and Emancipatory Learning.* Jossey-Bass, San Francisco, California

Lindeman E C L 1926 *The Meaning of Adult Education.* New Republic, New York

Merriam S B, Caffarella R S 1991 *Learning in Adulthood: A Comprhrehensive Guide.* Jossey-Bass, San Francisco, California

Mezirow J 1991 *Transformative Dimensions of Adult Learning.* Jossey-Bass, San Francisco, California

Modra H 1989 Using journals to encourage critical thinking at a distance. In: Evans T, Nation D (eds.) 1989 *Critical Reflections on Distance Education.* Falmer Press, London

Podeschi R 1990 Teaching their own: Minority challenges to mainstream institutions. In: Ross-Gordon J M, Martin L G, Briscoe D (eds.) 1990 *Serving Culturally Diverse Populations.* Jossey-Bass, San Francisco, California

Pratt D D 1992 Chinese conceptions of learning and teaching: A Westerner's attempt at understanding. *Int. J. Lifelong Educ.* 11(4): 301–20

Ross-Gordon J M 1991 Needed: A multicultural perspective for adult education research. *Adult Educ Q.* 42(1): 1–16

Savicevic D M 1991 Modern conceptions of andragogy: A European framework. *Studies in the Education of Adults* 23(2): 179–201

Smith J E, Castle J 1992 Experiential learning for critical thinking: A viable prospect for distance education in South Africa? *Int. J. Lifelong Educ.* 11(3): 191–98

Smith R M (ed.) 1990 *Learning to Learn Across the Lifespan.* Jossey-Bass, San Francisco, California

Tennant M 1988 *Psychology and Adult Learning.* Routledge, London

Tuijnman A, van Der Kamp M (eds.) 1992 *Learning Across the Lifespan: Theories, Research, Policies.* Pergamon Press, Oxford

Usher R S, Bryant I 1989 *Adult Education as Theory, Practice and Research: The Captive Triangle.* Routledge, New York

Vooglaid Y, Marja T 1992 Andragogical problems of building a democratic society. *Int. J. Lifelong Educ.* 11(4): 321–28

Approaches to Learning

J. B. Biggs

Approaches to learning refer to the ways and strategies in which students go about their learning tasks, thereby affecting the nature of the learning outcome. "Approach to learning" is often used interchangeably with "learning style," but these terms are quite distinct, as will be discussed below. This general area of student learning has been investigated using four distinct frameworks, deriving from personality, information-processing, phenomenographic theories, and systems theories.

There are thus four models relating to students' approaches to learning, each variously emphasizing the different components in the total teaching–learning context: the person, the teaching context, the learning processes used, and the learning outcome. The nature and measurement of approach to learning thus depends on which of these aspects the model addresses. This entry addresses each model in turn, then examines the relationship between approach and outcome.

1. The Personal Styles Model

The styles model focuses on stable individual traits, such as cognitive style or learning style, that are thought to affect the nature of the outcome and which transcend particular learning contexts or content domains and are independent of general ability.

Cognitive style research commenced in the 1950s and proliferated in the next 10 to 15 years; learning styles replaced and subsumed cognitive styles around the 1970s and later, because learning styles were thought to be more applicable to adult education and training (Riding and Cheema 1991). Cognitive and learning styles originate in a person's psychodynamic history, and reflect consistent individual differences in the way the world is perceived, how tasks are learned, and how problems are solved (Gardner et al. 1959).

People are classified as "high" or "low" on a style according to their performance on a given criterion task or test, and then compared on how they handle other, especially educational, situations. At least 20 such styles have been reported, but Riding and Cheema (1991) pointed out that both conceptually and empirically cognitive and learning styles may be grouped into two main families: (a) holist–analytic—including field-dependence/independence, reflection–impulsivity, leveling–sharpening, and holist–serialist; (b) verbalizer–imager, which reflects the preferred modality for handling information.

One major difficulty with such styles is that they are conceived as bipolar (e.g., field-dependent vs. field-independent) and as independent of context. For example, field-independent individuals are said to be able to separate relevant from compelling irrelevant cues, and are therefore good at finding simple figures embedded in more complex ones, but manifest poor social skills, such as facial recognition. Cross-cultural studies show, however, that people in highly collectivist societies (requiring field dependence), and which use a character writing system (requiring field independence), such as Japanese and Chinese, manifest a high degree of both field-dependent and field-independent skills (Hansen-Strain 1989). But if a "style" operates according to the specific context in which it is applied, it is no longer a general style, and its unique meaning is lost.

Two other approaches to learning style have been influential, those derived by Pask (1976) and by Kolb (1976). Pask found that students in classification experiments used two basic strategies: testing one limited hypothesis at a time ("serialist"), and testing more complex hypotheses simultaneously ("holist"). When students *habitually* adopted a particular strategy, he said they exhibited a "style" of learning. "Versatile" students were those who switched strategy as appropriate to the task, but those who stuck to one style to the exclusion of the other displayed the pathologies of "improvidence" (excessive use of the serialist strategy, resulting in the student being unable to relate elements to form a whole), or "globetrotting" (excessive use of the holist strategy, resulting in premature conclusions or unjustified overgeneralizations). Riding and Cheema (1991) saw these styles as belonging to their overriding holist–serialist group, but in view of their derivation and theory of application, the measurement of Pask's "styles" are considered with Entwistle and Ramsden's (1983) "Approaches to Study Inventory" (Sect. 4 below).

Kolb's (1976) theory of learning styles is based on an "experiential" learning theory requiring four abilities: to experience, to reflect, to conceptualize, and to experiment. These abilities are based on two bipolar dimensions, concrete–abstract and active–reflective, which intersect to yield four quadrants. Learning styles are said to result from the particular quadrant in which a person's cognitive strengths lie: abstract–active yields the "converger," concrete–reflective, the "diverger," abstract–reflective, the "assimilator," and concrete–active, the "accommodator." Optimal performance in different academic subjects is said to require one such style over another (see *Study and Learning Strategies; The Implications for Educators*).

The styles are measured by the Learning Style Inventory (LSI) (Kolb 1976), but Hudak (1985) in a review concluded that reliabilities were low, and validity questionable. Indeed, he concluded that "the onus is to demonstrate that the construct 'learning style' has reality and relevance" (p. 409). Honey and Mumford (1986) produced the related Learning Style Questionnaire (LSQ), which renames the styles as "activist," "reflector," "theorist," and "pragmatist." The LSQ is rather more reliable than Kolb's LSI, but appears to measure abilities rather than styles (Allinson and Hayes 1990).

In all, the educational value of the styles model is problematic. Styles owe neither their genesis nor their development to interaction with teaching contexts, so that while the verbalizer–imager styles appear to relate to verbal (written directions) versus visual (maps) modes of presentation (Kirby et al. 1988), such relationships are less consistent in the cases of the holist–serialist family (Riding and Cheema 1991) and of Kolb's styles (Curry 1991).

2. The Information-processing Model

The information-processing model is based on the assumption that "learning style assessed from a behavioral-process orientation is more likely to be useful than one based purely on a personality-or cognitive-style orientation" (Schmeck et al. 1977 p. 413). Writers in this tradition are interested in the efficiency with which basic cognitive strategies are deployed; they draw on levels of processing theories of memory, and work on cognitive and metacognitive strategy use (Moreno and DiVesta 1991, Schmeck et al. 1977, Weinstein et al. 1987). The emphasis here is less on unchanging characteristics as upon the "on-line" cognitive strategies that students use when handling tasks. There is, however, some ambiguity due partly to the method of operationalizing strategy use: self-report questionnaires, which typically ask how students *usually* adopt this or that strategy, or would *prefer* this or that strategy, almost inevitably access the domain of personal traits, not the process domain that would seem required by cognitive theory (Biggs 1993).

Measurement of information-processing-based approaches to learning is typically by questionnaire, such as the Inventory of Learning Processes (ILP) (Schmeck et al. 1977, Schmeck et al. 1991), and the Learning and Study Strategies Inventory (LASSI) (Weinstein et al. 1987). These instruments have good psychometric properties, but their construct validity is open to question to the extent that they have been validated by reference to laboratory tasks, not to teaching contexts.

The information-processing model is similar to a learning style in that information-processing strategies are conceived as being context-free, with elaboration, imaging, rehearsal, and the like operating in much the same way whether the material that is being elaborated or rehearsed is being prepared for an examination or for a laboratory experiment. An important difference

is that information-processing theorists suggest that students be trained in the effective use of information-processing strategies (Weinstein and Mayer 1984). This work has achieved some success, but the extent to which training in strategy use transfers to the teaching–learning context is a matter of considerable debate. Phenomenographers (Sect. 3 below) and systems theorists (Sect. 4 below) argue that poor study skills in most cases result from a mismatch between teaching and application, and should be addressed within the teaching context rather than by intervention (such as skill training) outside it; otherwise intervention could actually increase the use of low-level study strategies (Ramsden et al. 1986) (see *Study and Learning Strategies*).

3. The Phenomenographic Model

Phenomenography is a highly influential methodology in the student learning literature, and is represented in the work of Marton and his team at the University of Gothenburg (Marton 1988), of which Marton and Säljö's (1976) study of surface and deep approaches to learning, and their relationship to the quality of the outcome, is a much-quoted source. Learning is studied from the perspective of the learner, not that of teacher or researcher; the object is to see how students construe the content, expressed as the form of the relationship the knower sets up with the known. Usually such constructions or conceptions can be expressed in a limited number of hierachically ordered ways; some learners have partial or distorted conceptions of the intended topic, while others have sophisticated ones. Learners may "comprehend," more or less, the teacher's perspective, but they genuinely *learn* only what they construct from their own perspective. Their approach to learning is how they go about that construction.

In the Marton and Säljö (1976) study, students were asked to read academic articles and then to describe what they had learned, and how they had gone about learning it. The "what" was classified in terms of their conception of the topic, and it soon became clear that the level achieved depended on what the learner intended to gain from the article. Students generally expressed one of two major intentions: either to understand the author's intended meaning, or to recall key terms or memorize details as accurately as possible, in anticipation of subsequent questions. Those having the first intention processed the text for meaning, focusing on themes and main ideas; those having the second, focused on words and sentences. These intentions and methods of reading came to be called the "deep" and "surface" approaches respectively (not to be confused with Schmeck's entirely different derivation from levels of processing). The deep approach was associated with abstract, high-level, accounts of the passage, with the details being used for illustration and support, while the surface approach was associated with simple, factual statements that overlooked interconnections between aspects of the passages, and which usually missed the author's point.

In this view, then, an approach is intricately bound up with the task, its context, and the nature of the outcome, so that teaching "deep strategies," in the way recommended by information-processing theorists, is seen to be at best irrelevant, and could even be counterproductive, "technifying" learning such that deep-seeming strategies would produce surface-type outcomes, similar to that which occured in the study skills intervention conducted by Ramsden et al (1986).

The measurement of approaches to learning in the phenomenographic school is almost always by interview or by analysis of open-ended written statements, gathered in connection with a particular task. Thus, there is no "instrument" as such for measuring deep and surface approaches in Marton's sense, although the inventories produced by both Biggs (1987) and Entwistle and Ramsden (1983) have been heavily influenced by the work of the phemonenographers.

4. The Systems Model

In the systems model, personal traits, contextual factors, level of processing, and quality of outcome, are seen as forming an open-ended and recursive system, in which individuals adjust their intentions and processing strategies to their view of the task demands (Biggs 1993). In other words, students tend to enter courses with overall goals (to aspire to top grades and pass with minimal effort), and with stable characteristics such as particular abilities, cognitive styles, preferred ways of learning, etc. Depending on how the teaching context is structured, and how they see themselves as succeding or failing (and to what reasons they attribute their performance), they tend to adjust their approach to learning as a relatively stable way of handling a particular set of teaching demands. If those demands change, then the individual should readjust. An approach in this view differs from information-processing by including motivational and contextual components, and from phenomenography by recognizing the role of personality factors. Three approaches have been commonly identified in the systems model: surface and deep (as in the phenomenographic model) and achieving (Biggs 1987, Entwistle and Ramsden 1983).

A surface approach is based on a motive or intention that is extrinsic to the real purpose of the task. The strategy arising from that is "satisficing," but not satisfying, task demands by investing minimal time and effort consistent with appearing to meet requirements. In the academic learning context, the strategy of rote learning of selected content without understanding it is one of the commonest ways of doing this, but it is not the only way. By the same token, the presence of rote learning does not in itself mean that the student is adopting a surface approach.

A deep approach is based on a felt need to engage the task appropriately, which in the academic context usually means to maximize understanding. The focus is thus on underlying meaning rather than on the literal aspects of the task, but the particular strategies that are optimal for doing that would depend on the task in question. It is thus not possible to say what "the" deep approach is, but a common feature would be to process at a high level of generality, such as main ideas, themes, and principles, rather than as conceptually unsupported specifics.

An achieving approach is based on the ego-enhancement that comes out of visibly achieving, in particular through high grades. The focus is on the recognition gained from top performance, the main strategy to organize time, working space, and syllabus coverage cost-effectively, with much use of cue-seeking, systematic use of study skills, planning ahead, and allocating time according to task importance.

Of these approaches, only the deep is task-focused or "natural." Surface and achieving are institutional creations, sanctions, and rewards shifting the focus from the task itself to ways of maximizing the rewards and minimizing the sanctions associated with successful or unsuccessful completion of the task. A deep-achieving approach appears to be the most adaptive institutionally (Biggs 1987).

Approaches in the systems model differ from the phenomenographic meaning in that they refer both to the motives and preferred ways of learning that the student has presently achieved, and to the strategies used in handling specific tasks. Approaches in the phenomenographic sense, on the other hand, refer only to the latter: the way a particular task is currently handled in line with the learner's immediate intentions. The former meaning is used in a predispositional or presage sense; the latter in an ongoing process sense.

Approaches to learning in the systems model are measured by questionnaire, but differ from questionnaires deriving from information-processing theory in at least two respects. First, approaches in the systems framework include affective as well as cognitive aspects, while information-processing theorists focus only on cognitive ones. Second, approaches to learning are derived bottom-up, hence the emphasis on affect and context, which students perceive as important in determining how they learn, while information-processing derivations come top-down, from pre-existing theory, which is rarely derived from educational contexts.

The Approaches to Study Inventory (ASI), developed in the United Kingdom for tertiary students by Entwistle and Ramsden (1983), has 64 items across 16 subscales defined from the work of Marton, Pask, and others, which are reduced by higher order factor analysis to four domains: meaning, reproducing, and achieving orientations, and Pasks' learning styles. The internal consistencies of the subscales range from 0.32 to 0.78, while the domains have a median internal consistency of 0.72.

The Learning Process Questionnaire (LPQ) and the Study Process Questionnaire (SPQ) were developed in Australia by Biggs (1987) for adolescent and adult learners respectively, with subsequent translation, revision, and norming for Hong Kong students (Biggs 1992). The LPQ and SPQ are based on a common model of motive–strategy congruence, according to which a student's predominant motives for learning will determine appropriate strategies for learning; separate motive and strategy subscale scores are available (comprising six items in the LPQ and seven items in the SPQ), which combine to form surface, deep, and achieving approach scale scores (Biggs 1987). Subscale internal consistencies range from 0.51 to 0.77, and approach scales from 0.60 to 0.81.

The ASI and LPQ/SPQ scale scores are intended to reflect how individual students have struck a "steady state" in terms of their motives and preferred strategies for learning within a given teaching context. Mean scores for a whole class thus indicate how a class as a whole has adapted to a given mode of teaching; these instruments accordingly have been widely used for indexing and developing the quality of teaching. A summary of some of this work is given in Biggs (1993).

5. The Relation between Approach and Outcome of Learning

Both phenomenographic and systems models specify an intrinsic relationship with the learning outcome, in that the approach describes how the outcome is constructed by the learner. The acquisition of competence in taught content may be regarded as occurring in two main ways; as an increase in the quantity of learned data, and as a change in the nature of what is learned. For various historical and technical reasons, formal assessments of learning have tended to emphasize quantitative growth in competence, so that relationships between especially deep approaches to learning and institutional assessments have not been as clear-cut (and have even been negative in some courses) as when qualitative assessments have been made (Trigwell and Prosser 1991).

Qualitative assessment of learning outcomes involves showing that the nature of what is learned changes as learning progresses, which is at the heart of phenomenography and of the vast amount of work done on children's understandings of natural phenomena (e.g., White 1988). There appears to be a limited number of these naive understandings, which frequently stack hierarchically until they coincide with the kind of understanding that is required in the official curriculum. These outcomes relate strongly to the kind of approach used during learning (Marton 1988, Marton and Säljö 1976). However, the assessment of outcomes in terms of these hierarchies requires that they are researched on a topic by topic basis.

An alternative approach is to search for aspects associated with increasing competence that generalize across content areas. Two such aspects are the accrual of task-relevant detail in a quantitative sense, and the increasing salience of the learner's construction in which the detail becomes structured. On this basis, a generalizable five-stage hierarchical structure can be found, expressed in the SOLO taxonomy (Biggs and Collis 1982), the first three stages of which (prestructural, unistructural, and multistructural) describe the accrual of detail, and the top two (relational and extended abstract), the nature of the structuring undertaken by the student. The first three stages are associated with surface, and the higher two with deep, approaches to learning (Biggs 1979, Trigwell and Prosser 1991).

If one important outcome of teaching is to encourage deep approaches to learning, and to discourage surface learning, it becomes important that assessment technology generates task demands that cannot be met by technified or surface approaches to the task. Approaches to learning, as both predispositions and on-line ways of handling given tasks, ought not to be considered simply as given styles or personality traits on the one hand, or as detachable cognitive strategies on the other, but as deriving their meaning and function from the student's perceptions of their task demands. Where teaching and particularly assessment methods convey the sense that competence lies solely or even mainly in the accrual of unstructured data, students will adjust their orientations, motivations, and strategies for learning in line with a surface approach. Thus the notion of approach to learning is not simply an interesting application of personality or of information-processing theory, but an integral part of teaching, learning, and assessment.

See also: Adult Learning: An Overview; Individual Differences, Learning, and Instruction; Study and Learning Strategies; The Implications for Educators

References

Allinson C, Hayes J 1990 Validity of the learning styles questionnaire. *Psychol. Rep.* 67: 859–66
Biggs J 1979 Individual differences in study processes and the quality of learning outcomes. *High. Educ.* 8: 381–94
Biggs J 1987 *Student Approaches to Learning and Studying.* Australian Council for Educational Research, Hawthorn
Biggs J 1992 *Why and How do Hong Kong Students Learn?* Faculty of Education, University of Hong Kong, Hong Kong
Biggs J 1993 What do inventories of students' learning processes really measure? A theoretical review and clarification. *Br. J. Educ. Psychol.* 63: 1–7

Biggs J, Collis K 1982 *Evaluating the Quality of Learning: The SOLO Taxonomy*. Academic Press, New York

Curry L 1991 Patterns of learning style across selected medical specialties. *Educ. Psychology* 11: 247–77

Entwistle N, Ramsden P 1983 *Understanding Student Learning*. Croom Helm, London

Gardner R, Holzman P, Klein G, Linton H, Spence D 1959 Cognitive control: A study of individual consistencies in cognitive behavior. *Psychol. Iss.* 1(Monograph 4)

Hansen-Strain L 1989 Student and teacher cognitive styles in second language classrooms. In: Bickley V (ed.) 1989 *Language Teaching and Learning Styles within and across Cultures*. Institute of Language in Education, Hong Kong

Honey P, Mumford A 1986 *The Manual of Learning Styles*. Peter Honey, Reading

Hudak M 1985 Review of *Learning Styles Inventory*. In: Keyser D, Sweetland R (eds.) 1985 *Test Critiques*, Vol. 2. Test Corporation of America, Kansas City, Kansas

Kirby J, Moore P, Schofield N 1988 Verbal and visual learning styles. *Contemp. Educ. Psychol.* 13: 169–84

Kolb D 1976 *Learning Style Inventory: Self-scoring Test and Interpretation Booklet*. McBer and Company, Boston, Massachusetts

Marton F 1988 Describing and improving learning. In: Schmeck R (ed.) 1988 *Learning Strategies and Learning Styles*. Plenum, New York

Marton F, Säljö R 1976 On qualitative differences in learning, I: Outcome and process. *Br. J. Educ. Psychol.* 46: 4–11

Moreno V, DiVesta F 1991 Cross-cultural comparisons of study habits. *J. Educ. Psychol.* 83: 231–39

Pask G 1976 Styles and strategies of learning. *Br. J. Educ. Psychol.* 46: 128–48

Ramsden P, Beswick D, Bowden J 1986 Effects of learning skills interventions of first year university student's learning. *Human Learning* 5: 151–64

Riding R, Cheema I 1991 Cognitive styles: An overview and integration. *Educ. Psychology* 11: 193–215

Schmeck R, Geisler-Brenstein E, Cercy S 1991 The Revised Inventory of Learning Processes. *Educ. Psychology* 11: 343–62

Schmeck R, Ribich F, Ramanaiah N 1977 Development of a self-report inventory for using individual differences in learning processes. *Appl. Psychol. Meas.* 1: 413–31

Trigwell K, Prosser M 1991 Relating approaches to study and quality of learning outcomes at the course level. *Br. J. Educ. Psychol.* 61: 265–75

Weinstein C, Mayer R 1984 The teaching of learning strategies. In: Willrock M (ed.) 1984 *Handbook of Research on Teaching*. Macmillan Inc., New York

Weinstein C, Schulte A, Palmer D 1987 *Learning and Study Strategies Inventory (LASSI)*. H&H Publications, Clearwater, Florida

White R 1988 *Learning Science*. Blackwell, Oxford

Further Reading

Marton F, Hounsell D, Entwistle N (eds.) 1984 *The Experience of Learning*. Scottish Universities Press, Edinburgh

Ramsden P (ed.) 1988 *Improving Learning: New Perspectives*. Kogan Page, London

Schmeck R (ed.) 1988 *Learning Strategies and Learning Styles*. Plenum, New York

Development of Learning Across the Lifespan

M. J. A. Howe

There can be few if any days in a person's life in which no learning takes place. Throughout an individual's life, learning provides important functions. It is important to bear in mind that the single term "learning" covers a range of diverse phenomena, many of which have little in common with one another beyond the fact that they all involve some kind of broadly adaptive change occurring. In the case of most varieties of learning developmental improvements are observed in the speed or efficiency with which learned capabilities are acquired, but there are exceptions. For example, in some kinds of simple conditioning it is hard to discern differences between young children and adults (Estes 1970). It would be an oversimplification to say that development directly causes improved learning, and more accurate to state that increased age merely provides time for events or processes to take place which make certain kinds of learning more likely. With the onset of adulthood, most people do not experience sudden or sharp changes in learning ability, but some decline may be observed in old age.

1. Timing and the Notion of Critical Periods

Contrary to a widely held belief, there are no sharply defined "critical periods" during which particular skills or abilities have to be acquired if they are to be gained at all. Even in the case of language acquisition, which is thought by most psychologists to depend to a considerable extent on innate characteristics that are unique to humans, it has been found that full recovery may take place following the most severe deprivation of learning experiences (Koluchova 1976). And early deprivation of opportunities for social learning does not, on its own, render impossible the eventual normal development of social skills and abilities (Schaffer 1990).

Moreover, critics of Piagetian theories have gone

beyond challenging the notion of critical developmental periods in learning and have increasingly questioned the view that learning capabilities are closely tied to the stage of intellectual development that a child has reached. For some researchers (Brainerd 1977), the valid uses of such stages are restricted to ones that simply describe children's performance rather than claiming to identify the underlying structures that constrain and account for the observed level of performance. There is evidence to show that some of the children's errors which a Piagetian interpretation would ascribe to childlike or restricted reasoning processes are actually caused by specific deficits in linguistic and semantic knowledge (Donaldson 1978).

That is not to say that the developmental phasing and sequencing of learning experiences is by any means unimportant. On the contrary, it can be vital. A good illustration of the crucial nature of the sequence in which different subskills are gained is provided by some experiments on learning in infants that were conducted by White (1971). He was interested in trying to accelerate the kinds of learning that result in young babies becoming able to reach out for objects and pick them up. His first efforts succeeded in improving visual attending skills, which he knew to be an important component of the reaching behavior he wished to accelerate. However, to White's surprise, that intervention delayed rather than brought forward the infants' ability to reach out for objects. Further investigations established that the reason for this apparently paradoxical finding was that White's successful efforts to improve visual attending had the additional, unanticipated, effect of distracting infants from a crucial behavior which normally occurs at around the same time, that of simply observing one's own hands. It turned out that the latter behavior makes a key contribution to the learning of reaching skills, and that the reason for the failure of White's attempt to accelerate reaching was that his intervention disrupted the sequence in which the subskills which lead to that ability are normally gained.

Even when the precise timing and sequencing of learned skill elements is not an issue and no age-related differences in learning ability are involved, age-related factors can still exert a large influence on what a learner actually achieves. For example, in order to reach the highest levels of excellence as a musical performer it may be highly advantageous to begin learning before the end of childhood, if only because an individual who commenced learning as an adult would find it extremely difficult to devote the time and sustain the high level of motivation and concentration necessary in order to achieve the highest levels of performance as an instrumentalist. This may demand as much as 20,000 or 30,000 hours, or around eight hours per day for 10 years. Similarly large amounts of time are needed to reach the highest levels of ability at other areas of achievement, such as chess (Simon and Chase 1973, Howe 1990). And in the case of the skill of composing music, it has been established that no musical works that are now regarded as being of major importance have been produced prior to the composer having devoted around 10 years to concentrated training in composing, typically following many years devoted to the acquisition of basic musical abilities (Hayes 1981).

A number of investigations have examined the relationships between age and achievement at various abilities. Intellectual achievements tend to peak around the third, fourth, and fifth decades of life, earlier in some areas of achievement, such as mathematics, and later in others (Simonton 1992). But this does not necessarily mean that ability to learn as such is closely related to age: in most instances a more likely explanation is that the age-related variations in achievements are largely accounted for by other reasons. One is the simple fact that it can take many years to gain the skills necessary for the highest levels of performance. A second reason is that the circumstances and commitments of an older person's life may make it hard to maintain the single-mindedness and the concentrated effort directed to a specialized sphere of excellence that is usually necessary for reaching the highest peaks of human achievement.

2. Developmental Learning Differences

Although learning does not exhibit the kinds of clear developmental changes that would be found if there were universal age-related changes in the kinds of learning or the rate of learning that are possible at different ages, learning and age are by no means unrelated. Older children and adults outperform younger children at a wide range of learning activities, including most of the kinds of learning that receive prominence in school curricula, and especially those learning tasks that are relatively complex or abstract, or which necessitate the learner depending to a marked extent on previously acquired knowledge or skills.

Why is it that, compared with adolescents and adults, young children are often at a disadvantage when confronted with learning tasks? Simply to say that learning ability has or has not "developed" does not really answer the question: it is necessary to know what changes, and how it changes, in order to bring about the age-related improvements. One possibility is that physical development provides the explanation, via, for example, improved conductance of chemico-electrical impulses in the cortex as a result of increased myelinization. Alternatively, changes in the number or size of brain cells, or in their physical structure, could account for the older child's greater success as a learner.

However, although physical changes in the brain do play a part in the development of learning during the very earliest years, from toddlerhood onward such changes cease to be a cause of age-related variability in learning, and therefore other causes must be found. The kinds of changes that do continue to affect learning, and largely account for the improvements in learning and remembering that are observed as children get older form three broad (and overlapping) categories. These are, first, increases in knowledge; second, the increased use of skills, strategies, and metaskills; and third, a range of influential habits and attributes that are broadly related to motivation, personality, and the directing of attentional resources.

2.1 *The Influence of Existing Knowledge*

A crucial influence on many kinds and forms of learning is exerted by the learner's existing knowledge, that is to say, what the person already knows. Simply as a result of having lived longer, older people know more than young children, and their increased knowledge may facilitate learning in any situation in which the information or skills that are to be acquired are in any way related to information or skills which the learner already possesses.

A good way to demonstrate the influence of a person's existing knowledge on new learning is to compare children and adults in situations where, in contrast to what is usual, the children happen to be more rather than less knowledgeable than the adults within the domain of knowledge relevant to the task. For example, Chi (1978) has found that 10-year olds are comparable with adults at tasks involving their retaining lists of verbal and numerical information. However, when the information to be retained takes the form of chess pieces arranged on a chessboard in legitimate positions that might occur in a game of chess, and the children are good chess players whereas the adults are merely competent at the game, the 10-year olds consistently outperform the adults. Similarly, Ceci and Howe (1978) found that in a study of word learning, 13-year olds were initially much more successful than 10-year olds, who in turn were better than children aged 7. However, when the experimenters carefully adapted the task to ensure that all the words were familiar to even the youngest children, so that they were capable of perceiving the relationships between the words to be learned and some other words that were provided as "cues" to guide recall, the age differences completely disappeared. In other words, the outcome of ensuring that the youngest participants possessed all the relevant knowledge about the task items that was available to the oldest participants completely eradicated (in the latter study) or reversed (in the previous study) the usual age-related difference in performance.

Knowledge may be an important cause of developmental differences in learning even in situations where it appears that many causes are involved. For instance Carey (1985) studied children's understanding of the concept of "being alive." Traditionally, confusions in relation to this are assumed to reflect a fundamental limitation in "animistic reasoning," but Carey found that, contrary to this belief, children's ability to understand the concept—as it relates to humans and other species—depends very heavily on the knowledge they have acquired. Their confusions about the concept, which young children may regard as being a property of children but not of animals, follow directly from their lack of biological knowledge concerning processes such as sleeping, breathing, and eating. As far as the ability to learn is concerned, these findings clearly contradict the view by which "mere knowledge" is seen as having only limited importance.

Even in situations where it at first seems very unlikely that difference between people could be the cause of differences in performance at tasks which involve learning, it may nevertheless turn out that people's existing knowledge is very important. For instance, even when the materials used in a study of learning are chosen to be highly familiar to all participants, there may be differences between participants in the way in which their knowledge in relation to the materials is actually represented, structured, and connected. That is so in the case of simple items such as digits, for example. Although all digits may be familiar to even the younger children in a learning experiment, individuals of different ages still differ in their knowledge about various aspects of the digits that make them meaningful and have implications for learning. Thus, although the number 2 may be highly familiar to younger children as well as older people, learning that involves that number may also be facilitated by knowledge about the digit which is possessed by older but not by younger learners, such as the facts that 2 is a prime number and the square root of 4 and the cube root of 8 (Chi and Ceci 1987).

2.2 *Learning Skills and Strategies*

Even when there is no conscious intention to learn, the extent to which a person retains new information is strongly affected by the kinds of mental processing that occur at the time the new information is perceived (Craik and Lockhart 1972, Craik and Tulving 1975). As young people get older, partly but not wholly as an outcome of schooling, they become increasingly adept at a range of mental activities and strategies that have the effect of magnifying a person's ability to profit from learning. In the case of certain skills, such as reading, the effect of mastering it is radically to transform the learner's potential for new learning, by opening windows onto experiences that were previously inaccessible and making numerous new opportunities available. With narrower skills and strategies the effects are more specific and circumscribed, but the possibility of magnifying the power of learning activities and opening up previously unavailable opportunities to gain new capabilities still remains.

Each of a large variety of skills and strategies can contribute to learning. Some strategies, such as rehearsal and self-testing, exert a positive influence on learning by ensuring that information to be learned is effectively repeated a sufficient number of times to ensure that it can be adequately processed. Other strategies, such as ones that necessitate the learner organizing or elaborating or categorizing new material, are effective largely because they ensure that there are adequate conceptual links between the new material and existing knowledge or by forming stronger links and connections within the body of information that is to be acquired. Yet other strategies, such as ones that incorporate rhythms or rhymes or the meaningful verbal narratives that are sometimes introduced to facilitate the learning of otherwise unrelated lists of items (such as the initial-letter mnemonic *R*ichard of *Y*ork *G*ave *B*attle *I*n *V*ain, which is introduced in order to help English schoolchildren learn the colors of the rainbow), are effective partly because they provide connections between items which are otherwise separate. (People find it hard to learn large numbers of entirely separate items of information, and a strategy that effectively reduces the number of separate elements to be acquired will often make learning easier.) Other strategies which are often effective involve the learner forming visual images that represent items to be learned and sometimes link them together. The (learned) skills, strategies, and other devices that can be introduced to facilitate learning vary considerably in their complexity and in their range of application. The word "mnemonic" is sometimes introduced as a descriptive term for strategies and devices designed to help the learner recall new or unfamiliar information.

Generally speaking, as they get older young people become increasingly prone to making use of appropriate strategies for learning, and also increasingly adept at using strategies, and they develop a widening repertoire of learning skills. They also gain more sophisticated metaskills. That is, they become better at being aware when new learning is necessary, knowing when it is appropriate to introduce a skill or strategy that will facilitate learning, and choosing a strategy that is maximally effective for a particular task, or, if necessary, adapting an existing strategy in order to deal with an unfamiliar situation.

2.3 Motivational and Other Influences

Both knowledge and mental skills form distinctly cognitive influences upon learning, but it would be wrong to assume that all the important determinants that contribute to age-related differences in the effectiveness of individuals' efforts to learn are exclusively cognitive ones. Throughout life, learning is also affected by a variety of factors that are either not cognitive at all or cognitive only in the broadest sense. These form a mixed bag, and include influences that have more to do with motivation and personality than with cognition as such. They include temperament, attentiveness, perseverance, determination, fatigue, distractibility, enthusiasm for learning, self-confidence, impulsiveness, sense of being in control, feelings of autonomy, feelings of success and optimism, as against fear of failure, independence, and self-directedness. The precise effects of these can be highly specific to the particular learning task involved, and in any person each of them alter from one day to the next.

There is no straightforward developmental progression in the manner in which these extracognitive factors exert an influence on learning, although there are some general trends. For example, compared with children, older individuals are often, but not always, less impulsive and distractible, and better at maintaining their concentration. However such changes are largely the result of a person's experiences and educational history than of any universal developmental change. Some individuals never gain the habit of giving the concentrated attention to verbal materials that is necessary for the kinds of successful learning that enable a child to become an educated adult. Some of the above factors are fairly closely linked to particular phases of life. For example, it is clear that, while motivational influences on learning are important throughout the lifetime, the direction and form of motivational influence changes between childhood and adulthood. And compared with older people adolescents seem to experience particular difficulties with sustaining the relatively solitary learning activities that form a necessary part of life as a successful student (Csikszentmihalyi and Larson 1984).

3. Learning in the Older Person

Following early adulthood, although continued cognitive development can and does occur, its form and direction in any person depends very largely on the particular circumstances of the particular individual (Labouvie-Vief and Chandler 1978).

With old age, there may be some deterioration in the physical variables that can affect learning (e.g., hearing and eyesight) and in the motivational influences (e.g., reduced incentives to learn or, in some people, deteriorating self-confidence as a learner), and some forms of learning may be hampered by changes in mental processing activities. Some investigations have reported decrements in old age in recall and learning of verbal information. However, for many older learners, their effectiveness at utilizing existing knowledge and learning strategies will compensate in full or in part for any negative changes that take place. Consequently, when the information is highly meaningful, researchers undertaking experiments on learning and remembering have observed no deterioration in the performance of older people, compared with young adults (Hultsch and Dixon 1984). Age differences favoring younger people are either small or nonexistent when the learner has prior knowledge about the topic, is well-motivated, and when the material to be acquired is well-organized.

See also: Human Development: Aging; Lifespan Development; Lifespan Development: Phases; Self-directed Learning

References

Brainerd C J 1977 Cognitive development and concept learning: An interpretative review. *Psych. Bull.* 84(5): 919–39

Carey S 1985 Are children fundamentally different kinds of thinkers and learners than adults? In: Chipman S F, Segal J W (eds.) 1985 *Thinking and Learning Skills. Vol. 2: Research and Open Questions.* Erlbaum, Hillsdale, New Jersey

Ceci S J, Howe M J A 1978 Semantic knowledge as a determinant of developmental differences in recall. *Journal of Experimental Child Psychology* 26(2): 230–45

Chi M T H 1978 Knowledge structures and memory development. In: Siegler R (ed.) 1978 *Children's Thinking: What Develops?* Erlbaum, Hillsdale, New Jersey

Chi M T H, Ceci S J 1987 Content knowledge: Its role, representation, and restructuring in memory development. *Advances in Child Development* 20: 91–142

Craik F I M, Lockhart R S 1972 Levels of processing: A framework for memory research. *J. Verbal Learn. Verbal Behav.* 11(6): 671–84

Craik F I M, Tulving E 1975 Depth of processing and the retention of words in episodic memory. *J. Exp. Psychol. Gen.* 104(3): 268–94

Csikszentmihalyi M, Larson R 1984 *Being Adolescent: Conflict and Growth in the Teenage Years.* Basic Books, New York

Donaldson M 1978 *Children's Minds.* Fontana, London

Estes W K 1970 *Learning Theory and Mental Development.* Academic Press, New York

Hayes J R 1981 *The Complete Problem Solver.* Franklin Institute Press, Philadelphia, Pennsylvania

Howe M J A 1990 *The Origins of Exceptional Abilities.* Blackwell, Oxford

Hultsch D F, Dixon R A 1984 Memory for text: Materials in adulthood. In: Baltes P B, Brim O G (eds.) 1984 *Life-span Development and Behavior 6.* Academic Press, New York

Koluchova J 1976 Severe deprivation in twins: A case study. In: Clarke A M, Clarke D B (eds.) 1976 *Early Experience: Myth and Evidence.* Open Books, London

Labouvie-Vief G, Chandler M J 1978 Cognitive development and life-span developmental theory: Idealistic versus contextual perspectives. In: Baltes P B (ed.) *Life-Span Development and Behavior 1.* Academic Press, New York

Schaffer H R 1990 *Making Decisions about Children: Psychological Questions and Answers.* Blackwell, Oxford.

Simon H A, Chase W G 1973 Skill in chess. *Am. Sci.* 61(4): 394–403

Simonton D K 1992 Leaders of American psychology, 1879–1967: Career development, creative output, and professional achievement. *J. Pers. Soc. Psychol.* 62(1): 5–17

White B L 1971 *Human Infants: Experience and Psychological Development.* Prentice-Hall, Englewood Cliffs, New Jersey

Further Reading

Coles G 1987 *The Learning Mystique: A Critical Look at Learning Disabilities.* Fawcett Columbine, New York

Ericsson K A, Smith J (eds.) 1991 *Toward a General Theory of Expertise: Prospects and Limits.* Cambridge University Press, Cambridge

Howe M J A (ed.) 1977 *Adult Learning: Psychological Research and Applications* Wiley, London

Environments for Learning

A. Collins, J. G. Greeno and L. B. Resnick

There has been a shift in perspective in educational psychology from teaching to learning. The change is subtle and reflects a move away from an information transmission view to a constructivist view of education. Because of the shift in perspective, this entry is called environments for learning rather than teaching methods. Another shift in perspective involves recognizing that learning and work are not separate activities. In fact, learning takes place both in and out of school, and students' activity in school is a form of work. Resnick (1987) pointed out four contrasts between typical in-school and out-of-school learning: (a) individual cognition in school versus shared cognition outside; (b) pure mentation in school versus tool manipulation outside; (c) symbol manipulation in school versus contextualized reasoning outside; (d) generalized learning in school versus situation-specific competencies outside. The discussion of learning environments will consider those outside as well as within schools, keeping in mind the characteristics to which Resnick has called attention.

In looking broadly at different kinds of learning environments, there are three observable general functions that support different environments: (a) participating in discourse; (b) participating in activities; (c) presenting examples of work to be evaluated. Environments themselves may be divided into six kinds, two relevant to each general function:

(a) (i) communication environments, where learners

participate in discourse by actively constructing goals, problems, meanings, information,
and criteria of success;

(ii) information transmission environments, where
learners participate in discourse by receiving
information;

(b) (i) problem-solving environments, where learners
work on projects and problems;

(ii) training environments, where learners practice exercises to improve specific skills and
knowledge;

(c) (i) evaluative performance environments, where
learners perform for an audience;

(ii) recitation and testing environments, where
learners demonstrate their ability to work problems or answer questions.

Most teaching and learning environments contain elements of all six types. The most effective learning
environments combine the advantages of each type.
Each of the following sections will discuss a particular
type of environment.

1. Communication Environments

Constructivist views of education stress communication among students. In communication environments
the goal is for people jointly to construct understandings of different ideas. Four kinds of communication
environments can be distinguished, based on the following activities: discussion, argumentation, inquiry
teaching, and brainstorming.

Discussion occurs when groups talk about some
topic. In the context of schooling and adult education,
discussions often take place concerning a text everyone has read or a video everyone has seen. Discussions
are probably the most powerful medium for learning.
Some discussions that are formally constituted, such
as business meetings, convey information about social roles, provide occasions for individuals to report
results of their work and to present proposals, and
often result in shared commitments to action. Informal
discussions by groups of friends are occasions for
constructing shared attitudes, opinions, understandings, and norms of behavior (see *Group Learning*).

The Computer Supported Intentional Learning Environment (CSILE) developed by Scardamalia and
Bereiter (1991) is a discussion environment where
learners communicate in writing over a computer
network. They first formulate questions they want to
investigate (e.g., "Why can humans speak when apes
cannot?") and then each learner in the group makes
a conjecture. Then they all begin to investigate the

question, finding whatever relevant information they
can from source materials and typing it into the system for others in the group to read. Through written
discussions, they refine their theories for publication
in the system. Other experimenters are exploring the
potential for students at remote locations to learn
through exchanges of electronic messages.

Argumentation is another important learning method. It has had limited use in school, even though it
is pervasive in business, law, and adult education and
training. Argumentation involves making a case for
a particular idea or decision, and counterarguments
against possible alternatives. Debate teams foster argumentation in school settings, but debates are usually
an extracurricular activity. Presentations of arguments
are an integral part of activity in some discussion environments, including the Itakura method (Hatano and
Inagaki 1991) and Lampert's (1990) conversational
teaching. Being persuasive is an important skill. Argumentation as a learning experience may be mistakenly
undervalued.

Inquiry teaching is characterized by a teacher asking
questions to help students construct a theory or design.
The theory constructed may be one the teacher already
had in mind, or it may be a novel theory. Inquiry teachers use systematic strategies for selecting cases (e.g.,
counterexamples) and for asking questions (Collins
and Stevens 1983). The goal of inquiry teaching is to
foster thinking and understanding by the learners.

Brainstorming is common in business and academia,
but often missing from school and adult education. The
goal is for a group to generate ideas without trying
to critique the ideas. Participants try to generate new
ideas and to reformulate, extend, and synthesize other
people's ideas. Brainstorming is a powerful learning
method for adult education and training.

2. Information Transmission Environments

Traditional schooling stressed the transmission of
knowledge and skills to students. These information
transmission environments include reading and lectures as well as newer media formats such as broadcast
radio and television, videotape, and film.

Reading is probably one of the two most common
ways to learn through acquiring information (the other
is television). Widespread schooling and self-directed
learning are built upon the book: printing changed the
ways by which humans understand the world, because
of the permanence and transportability of the printed
word. It is probably the most effective way to become
exposed to a wide variety of viewpoints, and has
played a crucial role in movements of social change.
At the same time, however, reading faces competition
from the visual media, because of higher bandwidth
and their wider scope.

Attending lectures differs from reading in that the
sequence and pace are controlled by a speaker rather

than the learner, and the information is spoken rather than written. Active interaction with a text includes rereading and searching for specific information. It is often possible to ask questions of a lecturer, although it is much more common for conversational interactions to be limited to the lecturer presenting questions to students to monitor their attention and understanding. Like reading, lecturing may ultimately be replaced by visual media.

Broadcast television and radio are the most passive of the information transmission media, but television has higher bandwidth than reading or lecturing. This allows it to capture significant aspects of the context of a situation, which can be critical to understanding. If a person is confused, however, it is not possible to ask questions (except to other viewers). It is not even possible to stop and resume study later unless an electronic record is made—a feature television shares with lectures. For this reason, it is much less likely to become an important learning environment than the next two media to be considered. Nevertheless, television shows have been major vehicles for learning around the world (see *Distance Education*).

Videotape and film have the wide bandwidth of television, but also have the flexibility for stopping or replaying sections of the tape. They are under the learner's or teacher's control, and so can be scheduled whenever time allows. Stopping allows a group of viewers to mix discussion with viewing. Replaying allows the group to clarify misunderstandings, look for specific information, and call attention to items of information that support alternative interpretations of the material. Much of the world's collected knowledge will eventually be stored on film, so this is likely to be one of the most important learning environments of the future.

Interactive video, based on laserdisc technology, has the wide bandwidth of the visual media, together with the capability to access any piece of the video instantaneously. Two seminal uses of this technology are the Aspen video, with which a person can simulate a drive around the town of Aspen, Colorado, turning right or left at any cross street, and the Palenque video, with which one can walk through the Mayan ruin at Palenque in Mexico and ask for guidance at different points from an anthropologist. Interactive video is merging with intelligent tutoring system technology to provide even more powerful learning environments.

3. Problem-solving Environments

With the renewed emphasis on thinking in the curriculum, there has been a stress on creating different kinds of problem-solving environments. There are several kinds of environments where problem-solving is the focus; namely, environments dedicated to problem-solving, apprenticeship, and adult learning projects.

Problem-solving in school differs from problem-solving in other activities. Lave (1988) pointed out that school problems tend to be well-defined, have one correct answer, and a correct solution method. Problems that arise in life, which Lave called dilemmas, tend to be ill-defined, often unrecognized as problems, and have many possible solutions and solution methods. Schoenfeld (1985) identified many beliefs that students derive from school math problems: for example, that if the answer is not an integer, it is probably wrong; that all the problems at the end of a chapter use the methods introduced in the chapter; that if you cannot solve the problem in five minutes, you are not using the correct method, etc. Schoenfeld argued that most of these beliefs are counterproductive for problem-solving in life.

Apprenticeship occurs in work environments where apprentices are supervised by masters. In successful apprenticeship learning, masters teach by showing apprentices how to do a task (modeling), and then helping them as they try to do it on their own (coaching and fading). Lave and Wenger (1991) described four cases of apprenticeship and emphasized how productive apprenticeship depends on opportunities for the apprentice to participate legitimately, albeit peripherally, in work activities. Becoming a more central participant in a community of practice can provide a powerful motivation for learning, although what is learned in apprenticeship may not generalize easily to other contexts. Collins et al. (1989) characterized how the modeling, coaching, and fading paradigm of apprenticeship might be applied to learning the cognitive subjects of school in an approach they term "cognitive apprenticeship."

Simulation environments are an attempt to create situations that have significant features of authentic problem-solving. There have long been attempts to create simulated learning environments. For example, in one Massachusetts school, students spend half of each day running a legislature, courts, businesses, and media. This serves as a context for learning the skills of citizenship, reading, writing, calculating, and thinking.

Video and computer technology have enhanced the ability to create simulation environments where students are learning skills in context. A novel use of video technology is the Jasper series developed by the Cognition and Technology Group (1990) at Vanderbilt University. In a series of six 15-minute videos, students are put into various problem-solving contexts. The problems reflect the complex problem-solving and planning that occur in real life.

There has been a proliferation of computer simulation environments for learning. For example, simulations let students control objects in a simulated Newtonian world without friction or gravity, or prices in a simulated economy. One series of simulations allows students to run a city, a planet, or an ant colony. Simulation allows students to gain knowledge and skills in contexts in which they could never participate naturally, to see features that are invisible in real environments (e.g., the center of mass, the inside of the human body), and to control variables that cannot be controlled in life.

4. Training Environments

People engage in adult education and training to develop skills they believe are valuable, either in themselves or as components of some other activity. In the traditional training environments—drill, rehearsal, and practice—there is an emphasis on skills and procedures rather than ideas, facts, concepts, and theories. Three kinds of training environments that focus on the skills of solving problems are programmed instruction, homework, and intelligent tutoring systems.

Drill involves repetitive training designed to achieve automaticity in a particular skill (Schneider and Shiffrin 1977). It is most commonly used to teach arithmetic and phonics, though Schneider has shown that it can be used to teach other skills, such as recognizing electrical circuits. Repetition helps master routine parts of performance, freeing capacity to concentrate on decision-making aspects of performance.

Rehearsal involves practicing scripted activities in preparation for a performance. While it teaches strategies for mounting a polished performance, the rehearsed activities may not be applicable beyond the performance, which limits the value of rehearsal as a general learning approach.

Practice emphasizes the conceptual and strategic as well as the routine, and can be carried out with or without a coach watching and guiding the practice. Practice is critical to gaining expertise, and successful techniques such as Reciprocal Teaching (Palincsar and Brown 1984) embody a strong practice component. Central to the whole notion of practice, however, is an ultimate performance. The major motivation for practice in school is to do well on tests, but many young people show growing aversion to tests.

Programmed instruction was developed by Skinner and reflects his emphasis on training and positive reinforcement. The tasks given are easy at first, so that students are likely to succeed and be reinforced for their success. There is an emphasis on repetition with variation to ensure practice, but more complex material is slowly introduced to ensure that students are dealing with new problems and tasks.

Intelligent tutoring systems are the latest attempt to create environments that combine training and problem-solving. For example, the geometry, algebra, and computer language tutors developed by Anderson and his colleagues (e.g., Anderson et al. 1985) start students with easy problems and slowly increase the complexity. Though the domain of intelligent tutoring systems may appear limited, they can be built on top of any simulation program (see above) to provide appropriate tasks and guidance for the learners. They are, however, expensive to build and it remains to be seen whether they will be cost effective.

5. Performance Environments

Learning takes place not just in practicing for performances, but also during performances themselves. Most performances can be distinguished from contests such as sporting events. Performances are high-stakes events where there is an audience, either live or present via a communication medium. Because the stakes are high, people are motivated to do well; performance, therefore, is the stimulus for most practice. To the degree teachers encourage performance, it is likely to provide a powerful motivation for students. The wide availability of recording technology makes performances easier to produce and to reflect upon. For example, students can now produce their own news broadcasts, musical performances, or plays, either on audiotape, videotape, or cable television. Furthermore, they can play these back, reflect upon them, and edit them until they are polished. One of the best examples of the use of technology for recording performances has been in Arts Propel (Gardner 1991) with its cycle of performing, reflecting upon the performance in terms of a set of criteria, and then reperforming.

Contests differ from performances in that winning or losing provides an ultimate criterion for judging performance. Films and statistics are important ways to track performance during contests. As well as providing the basis for making important decisions with regard to future contests (who to start, where they should play), they help to guide practice. By designating certain characteristics to track, statistics provide important indicators of what is valued.

6. Conclusion

Participation in discourse, participation in activities, and presentation of work for evaluation are all essential to learning. Traditional schooling has emphasized reading and the lecture, problem-solving, drill and practice, homework, and recitation and testing as learning environments. In the shift from traditional learning environments to more constructivist learning environments, there has been a parallel shift to incorporate some of the characteristics of work environments, such as shared cognition, tool manipulation, and contextualized reasoning (Resnick 1987).

See also: Human Development; Adult Learning: An Overview; Experiential and Open Learning; Group Learning; Learning to Learn; Concepts of Educational Technology; Student Support Systems; Distance Education

References

Anderson J R, Boyle C F, Reiser B J 1985 Intelligent tutoring systems. *Science* 228: 456–62
Cognition and Technology Group at Vanderbilt 1990 Anchored instruction and its relationship to situated cognition. *Educ. Researcher* 19(6): 2–10

Collins A, Brown J S, Newman S 1989 Cognitive apprenticeship: Teaching the crafts of reading, writing, and mathematics. In: Resnick L B (ed.) 1989 *Knowing, Learning, and Instruction: Essays in Honor of Robert Glaser.* Erlbaum, Hillsdale, New Jersey

Collins A, Stevens A L 1983 A cognitive theory of inquiry teaching. In: Reigeluth C M (ed.) 1983 *Instructional Design Theories and Models: An Overview of Their Current Status.* Erlbaum, Hillsdale, New Jersey

Gardner H 1991 Assessment in context: The alternative to standardized testing. In: Gifford B, O'Connor C (eds.) 1991 *Future Assessments: Changing Views of Aptitude, Achievement, and Instruction.* Kluwer, Boston, Massachusetts

Hatano G, Inagake K 1991 Sharing cognition through collective comprehension activity. In: Resnick L, Levin J, Teasley S D (eds.) 1991 *Perspectives on Socially Shared Cognition.* American Psychological Association, Washington, DC

Lampert M 1990 When the problem is not the question and the solution is not the answer: Mathematical knowing and teaching. *Am. Educ. Res. J.* 27(1): 29–63

Lave J 1988 *Cognition in Practice: Mind, Mathematics, and Culture in Everyday Life.* Cambridge University Press, Cambridge, Massachusetts

Lave J, Wenger E 1991 *Situated Learning: Legitimate Peripheral Participation.* Cambridge University Press, Cambridge

Palincsar A S, Brown A L 1984 Reciprocal teaching of comprehension-fostering and monitoring activities. *Cognition and Instruction* 1(2): 117–75

Resnick L B 1987 The 1987 Presidential address: Learning in school and out. *Educ. Researcher* 16(9): 13–20

Scardamalia M, Bereiter C 1991 Higher levels of agency for children in knowledge building: A challenge for the design of new knowledge media. *Journal of the Learning Sciences* 1(1): 37–68

Schneider W, Shiffrin R M 1977 Controlled and automatic human information processing, I: Detection, search, and attention. *Psychol. Rev.* 84(1): 1–66

Schoenfeld A H 1985 *Mathematical Problem Solving.* Academic Press, New York

Experiential and Open Learning

R. H. Paul

The concepts of experiential and open learning are increasingly having an impact on formal education. In university adult education, the previously strong distinctions between "on" and "off" site learning are being blurred as adults return ever more frequently to part-time study, and as institutional programs increasingly integrate off-site and experiential activities into the curriculum. As education increasingly becomes a lifelong activity, flexible and open learning systems become essential means of responding to the tremendous learning needs of the adult population. This entry discusses the principles and applications of open and experiential learning, their importance to adult education, and their implications for educational development.

1. Open Learning

Open learning is a rapidly evolving concept which has had a major impact on the development of new adult education institutions and programs throughout the world since about 1970. In its application to higher and adult education, the term originated and is most widely applied in the United Kingdom.

Open learning is usually characterized by a commitment to assist students, especially adults, in overcoming deterrents to participation in adult education. Examples of such barriers are (Cross 1981; Martindale and Drake 1989):

(a) Prior educational credentials. The following strategies are used in helping adults who lack certified prerequisite knowledge: open admissions policies, accreditation of relevant experience through specific examinations, prior learning assessment, educational contracting, reduced or no requirements, and generous credit transfer arrangements.

(b) Time constraints. These can be overcome by, for example, flexible and individualized timetabling to permit students to study in their own time and at their own pace.

(c) Physical location. Various distance delivery systems are employed to serve the student in his or her own locale (home, workplace, or regional center).

(d) Financial constraints. Apart from instituting special arrangements for reducing the cost burden on adult students, the deterring effect of insufficient financial support can be reduced by using flexible timetabling and distance delivery making it possible for the student to study while working full-time.

(e) Irrelevance of curriculum materials. Open learning strategies are explicitly intended to overcome this barrier by designing learner-centered curricula, putting emphasis on the student's experience and responsibility for his or her own

393

learning, and encouraging that learning needs identified or negotiated by the students are addressed.

(f) Intrinsic personal barriers. The anticipated negative effects may be lessened if the students are encouraged to define their own educational goals, develop self-confidence, and are informed about the advantages of efficient time management and study skills.

(g) Social and cultural bias. A learner-centered focus, which is a common feature of open learning systems, helps in reducing bias by relating to the student's own culture and experience.

In focusing on the removal of barriers, the concept of open learning tends to be critical of traditional forms of educational provision. It takes account of John Dewey's theorizing as to the relationship between personal experience and education.

Unlike learning theories based on research done primarily with children, open learning has received its impetus from adult education. This is not surprising, given its emphasis on prior experience. As such, it is a logical manifestation of available research on adult development and its implications for adult education (see *Adult Learning: An Overview*).

Open learning can usefully be thought of as a paradigm against which other approaches to learning can be assessed. A model developed by Lewis (1990) provides nine criteria for assessing the orientation of a learning activity. Lewis takes into account Rumble's (1989) concern that open learning is increasingly being used to describe systems which are anything but open. Hence, one program may be relatively open in access but closed in content, while another may be more restricted as to who is admitted but more flexible as to what is learned.

However, even Lewis's model can hide more subtle barriers to openness, a point central to the work of Harris (1988), who focuses on what he terms the "micro-politics" of open learning. Since formal education commonly involves some assessment of acquired knowledge, the degree of openness of learning systems is by necessity relative, and can vary from student to student. Open learning and experiential learning are related because both emphasize the need of adapting the learning process to social, cultural, and personal variables.

2. Experiential Learning

Like open learning, experiential learning incorporates a wide range of concepts, from highly theoretical ones to the simplicity of "learning by doing." The concept is based on the traditional apprenticeship model. It acquired increased importance in the nineteenth century in response to criticism in the sciences and professions

like medicine of the strong emphasis on abstract learning in formal education. Weil and McGill (1989) argue that the concept is being advocated for quite different reasons. Advocates mention the need to shift from an undue emphasis on cognitive aspects to more holistic or humanistic notions of human development, and the necessity of developing cost-efficient and flexible means of offering a relevant education to adult learners.

In the United States, John Dewey (1938) was particularly influential in emphasizing the role of experience in learning, starting from the premise of an intimate and necessary relation between the processes of actual experience and education. The challenge was to find ways to apply the lessons of the past to the problems of the present and future. Recognition of the value of experience became a practical challenge with the return of Second World War veterans who sought to make up for missed educational opportunities. This directed attention to devising processes which encouraged individuals to "make sense" of their experiences in a manner that would facilitate their return to formal education.

Experiential learning received additional impetus from the seminal UNESCO publication *Learning to Be* (Faure et al. 1972), which emphasized lifelong learning as a prerequisite for establishing the knowledge society. A radical idea at the time, lifelong learning has since been widely accepted. A central principle of lifelong learning is to incorporate the student's own experiences and aspirations and to recognise the cultural aspects of learning. As individuals mature, the richness of their experiences provides not only a basis for their own learning but also for assisting others. The challenge for educators is to help the learner to integrate personal experience into current learning activities.

Perhaps the best-known model for experiential learning is that developed by Kolb (1984), which depicts learning as a four-stage cycle. The learner: first, undergoes a concrete personal experience; second, re-examines and reflects on that experience; third, formulates abstract concepts and generalizations; and fourth, tests these in new situations. Individuals have different learning styles and one person may have different styles for different tasks. Hence, the learning cycle can be entered at any of its four stages. Whereas traditional learning models typically start with abstractions which may or may not bear any relationship to the student's experience, experiential learning in adult education emphasizes starting with concrete experience. Although Kolb's (1984) theory of the learning cycle seems relevant, in particular for designing learning environments for adults, it does not yet have an adequate empirical basis in research (see *Approaches to Learning*).

Tough (1971) notes that adults engage in many learning projects, but that formal education is concerned with conscious attempts to learn. In such cases, the challenge is to recognize learning activities through formal assessment. There are a number of responses to this challenge, the best-known being cooperative education, educational contracting, and prior assessment schemes (see Peruniak 1991).

3. Open and Experiential Learning Systems

Examples of "new" approaches to learning since the 1960s are progressive education, deschooling, experiential learning, prior learning assessment, competency-based education, contractual learning, self-directed learning, and cooperative education. These approaches have in common an attempt to democratize formal education and to make it more meaningful or relevant. Perhaps the most universal is the development of open learning systems (Thorpe and Grugeon 1987).

The pioneer in the United Kingdom was the National Extension College, a cost-efficient learning resource centre which provides centrally designed learning materials to institutions throughout the country, notably through its Flexistudy program which enables local authorities to adapt them to local needs. This led the former Manpower Services Commission to introduce its Open Tech program which provided seed money for similar ventures to apply new technologies to various delivery projects in technical and vocational open learning.

The primary motivation for the development of the United Kingdom's Open University (OU) was the democratization of higher education and, while it has been less successful than hoped in attracting students from disadvantaged backgrounds, it has been an international success in establishing the credibility of open education, including open admissions and distance education. It has spurred similar developments in most world regions (see *Adult Tertiary Education; Open University; University Adult Education*).

While there is widespread networking across the various open learning institutions, notably through the International Council for Distance Education (ICDE) and similar regional bodies, it would be misleading to suggest that they are replicas of the Open University. In fact, each takes on manifestations of its own culture and rationales and processes vary considerably across national boundaries. Comparisons on Lewis's (1990) scales would reveal strong differences in the extent to which they are truly "open" (see *Distance Education*).

The more decentralized and diversified system in the United States has not found it necessary to create open universities, but there are many examples of institutions which provide credit for prior learning and which use new technologies to offer educational accreditation at a distance. The United States has been a leader in correspondence education for a long time, having fostered many entrepreneurial and commercial institutions with a strong emphasis on practical learning schemes. It has also been a pioneer in the application of new technologies to increase the interactive nature of distance delivery through computer-assisted learning, interactive video, and cooperative satellite systems (eg., National Technological University, International Universities Consortium, and University Without Walls).

Institutions in the United States like Antioch, Goddard, and Empire State colleges have been leaders in the development of experiential learning, notably through cooperative education and/or contract learning, which use carefully designed assessment schemes to overcome concerns about the academic value of prior experience. The establishment, in 1974, of the Cooperative Assessment of Experiential Learning (CAEL) has given legitimacy to the concept (Gamson 1989). Now standing for Council for Adult and Experiential Learning, CAEL has evolved into a freestanding nonprofit organization to promote experiential learning as an important component of higher education, primarily through formalized procedures of prior learning assessment. Its 1990 directory listed almost 300 institutional members.

Experiential learning programs have since been adopted not only in highly industrialized countries such as Japan, the United Kingdom, and Sweden and Denmark, but also in parts of Southeast and East Asia and in Eastern Europe.

4. Issues and Trends

Open and experiential learning systems have undoubtedly enhanced adult opportunity to learn. Caution is urged, however, to avoid exaggerated claims for their success. Adult education offerings tend to be mainly directed to the confident, highly motivated, and experienced adult. Many such adults have benefited from open learning institutions, primarily because of open admissions, but the majority of adult learners need far more institutional support and are not necessarily any more successful in open learning institutions than they are in more traditional ones. The real challenge is to find ways of teaching adults how to learn, and how to wean them from dependency on the student support systems which often appear essential to their success (see *Student Counseling; Student Support Systems*).

Moreover, the reliance of open learning systems, particularly those using distance education, on behaviorist principles and centrally controlled course packages can undermine the supposed openness of programs. The theme of putting more control into the hands of the learner is common to many innovative approaches, but controversy over academic credibility remains an important obstacle to realizing open learning.

One danger is that innovative approaches to adult

education such as open and experiential learning eventually will become so institutionalized as to represent a "new" orthodoxy and that, despite open admissions and efforts to remove barriers to adult learning, they will simply perpetuate existing educational gaps, whereby those who already have obtained a higher education continue to be those most apt to take advantage of such opportunities. The effective application of new technologies such as computer-assisted learning, and interactive video, and satellite systems, may improve opportunities for interactive learning at a distance, but, again, the educational gap may be widened by the relative inaccessibility of such technologies to the disadvantaged.

5. Suggestions for Research

Much research is needed into topics such as how one encourages "self-directed," "independent," or "interdependent" learners—individuals whose previous exposure to formal education weans them from dependency on such systems in the true spirit of lifelong learning.

Experiential learning has opened up new perspectives on education, as significant differences are found in the ways that individuals perceive the world, notably as influenced by such variables as gender, age, and cultural identity. Further research on gender, in gerontology, and on cross-cultural issues may not only have an impact on adult education strategies but may also affect the way learning processes themselves are interpreted and evaluated.

6. Conclusion

The ideal combination of experience and education held out by Dewey in 1938 remains a laudable goal but its realization is still far from satisfactory. As education to the highest levels is extended to a wide audience, the complexities of overcoming both extrinsic and intrinsic barriers to learning are increasingly recognized. Nevertheless, as more and more adults demonstrate that they can learn when freed from traditional institutional restraints, open learning is gaining more acceptance and credibility.

See also: Adult Learning: An Overview; Approaches to Learning; Development of Learning Across the Lifespan; Self-directed Learning; The Implications for Educators

References

Cross K P 1981 *Adults as Learners: Increasing Participation and Facilitating Learning.* Jossey-Bass, San Francisco, California
Dewey J 1938 *Experience and Education.* Macmillan, New York
Faure E et al. 1972 *Learning to Be.* UNESCO, Paris
Gamson Z F 1989 *Higher Education and the Real World: The Story of CAEL.* Longwood, Wakefield, New Hampshire
Harris D 1988 The micro-politics of openness. *Open Learning* 3(2): 13–16
Kolb D A 1984 *Experiential Learning: Experience as the Source of Learning and Development.* Prentice-Hall, Englewood Cliffs, New Jersey
Lewis R 1990 Open learning and the misuse of language: A response to Greville Rumble. *Open Learning* 5(1): 3–8
Martindale C J, Drake J B 1989 Factor structure of deterrents to participation in off-duty adult education programs. *Adult Educ. Q.* 39(2): 63–75
Peruniak G S 1991 *Prior learning assessment: Challenges to the integrity of experiential learning.* Paper presented at the 10th Annual Conf. of the Canadian Association for the Study of Adult Education, Kingston, Ontario, June
Rumble G 1989 "Open learning," "distance learning," and the misuse of language. *Open Learning* 4 (2): 28–36
Thorpe M, Grugeon D (eds.) 1987 *Open Learning for Adults.* Longman, London
Tough A M 1971 *The Adult's Learning Projects: A Fresh Approach to Theory and Practice in Adult Learning.* OISE, Toronto
Weil S W, McGill I (eds.) 1989 *Making Sense of Experiential Learning: Diversity in Theory and Practice.* Open University Press, Milton Keynes

Further Reading

Boud D, Keogh R, Walker D (eds.) 1985 *Reflections: Turning Experience into Learning.* Kogan Page, London
Keeton M T (ed.) 1976 *Experiential Learning: Rationale, Characteristics and Assessment.* Jossey-Bass, San Francisco, California
Paul R H 1990 *Open Learning and Open Management: Leadership and Integrity in Distance Education.* Kogan Page, London
Sansregret M 1988 *La Reconnaissance des Acquis.* Hurtubise, Montreal
Torbert W R 1972 *Learning from Experience: Toward Consciousness.* Columbia University, New York
Whitaker U 1989 *Assessing Learning: Standards, Principles and Procedures.* Council for Adult and Experiential Learning, Philadelphia, Pennsylvania

Group Learning

G. G. Darkenwald

This entry deals with the discussion group as a means of facilitating individual learning. Groups concerned with problem-solving or with decision-making are not discussed.

1. Theories of Group Behavior

The goal of establishing a general theory of group behavior has yet to be attained (Levine and Moreland 1990). As Cartwright and Zander noted as far back as 1968 (p. 24), many classificatory schemes have been proposed, typically by selecting a few properties (e.g., size, level of intimacy) "to define 'types' of groups on the basis of whether these properties are present or absent . . . Usually only dichotomies have resulted: formal–informal, primary–secondary, . . . temporary–permanent, consensual–symbiotic." Such classifications seem of little value for furthering our understanding of adult learning in groups.

Theoretical approaches to the study of group dynamics may have greater utility for contributing to our understanding of learning in groups than classification schemes. Among the orientations described by Cartwright and Zander (1968 pp. 26–27), field theory, interaction theory, and systems theory are particularly germane to a basic understanding of the structure and process dimensions of learning groups. Nonetheless, it must be concluded that neither general theoretical typologies nor orientations offer much in the way of guidance for practitioners concerned with adult learning groups.

2. Learning in Groups

Nearly all organized adult learning occurs in some kind of group—classes, workshops, conferences, symposia, and so on. Each of these forms of group learning is appropriate and effective for achieving certain educational purposes, such as information transmission, problem-solving, and clarifying issues or problems. However, the concern here is with the small, participatory learning group, namely the discussion group. A defining characteristic of the discussion group is mutual education through the free and open sharing of ideas, feelings, and attitudes with respect to a specific issue or topic. Small groups of an instrumental, rather than strictly educational nature, do not fall within the scope of this entry's concerns. They include problem-solving groups, planning groups, and decision-making groups, among others. Admittedly, adults can and do learn through participation in instrumental groups, but learning is incidental to the principal purposes of such groups.

2.1 Affective and Cognitive Learning

Adult learning groups provide opportunities for both affective and cognitive learning. Typically, these two dimensions of learning are intertwined. This is particularly so in discussion groups, where cognitive learning, such as clarification of concepts or issues, is primary and is often accompanied by changes in members' attitudes.

One variant of the discussion group is primarily geared to attitude and behavioral change. Of course, cognitive learning occurs in such groups, but is merely instrumental, not an end in itself. Brookfield (1985 p. 58) makes a critical observation that "discussions of this nature seem to contradict the essential condition of discussion in that they are undertaken in order to achieve previously specified objectives. To this extent, they are not free or open discussions but exercises in attitudinal manipulation."

3. Group Discussion

Bormann (1975 p. 3) defines group discussion as "one or more meetings of a small group of people who thereby communicate, face to face, in order to fulfil a common purpose and achieve a group goal." Zander (1982 p. 30) further observes that "in a group discussion it is assumed that one does not learn from personal experiences simply by having them; one learns from hearing about the lives or ideas of others . . . Each member integrates others' thoughts with his own views in whatever way he finds sensible for him."

The specific aims or purposes of group discussion have been conceived in a variety of ways, but in general such formulations are similar. The following list, proposed by Zander (1982 p. 31), is offered here as illustrative. According to Zander, five purposes are served by group discussion:

(a) It helps members recognize what they do not know but should.

(b) It is an occasion for members to get answers to questions.

(c) It lets members get advice on matters that bother them.

(d) It lets persons share ideas and derive a common wisdom.

(e) It is a way for members to learn about one another as persons.

Other purposes commonly noted in the literature are

to clarify complex concepts, issues, or problems, and gain a deeper understanding of them.

One of the principal advantages of learning by discussion is that it aids the participant to "interpret and evaluate the subject matter in terms of his or her own emotional and intellectual experience, and his or her own abilities and needs. . . . Learning achieved through the discussion method is [therefore] not only more complete, but also more immediately usable and more readily retained, because the material has pertained directly to, and become a part of, discussants' lives (Harnack et al. 1977 pp. 27–28).

The degree to which the teacher or leader exerts control over the group is perhaps the most salient factor in determining the nature and outcomes of group activities. Leader control is best conceived as a continuum ranging from virtually complete control —"teaching in which students may raise questions or comment, but the general direction is under the strict control of the teacher" (Bligh 1972 p. 150)—to total abandonment of control, resulting in a self-directed learning group. The definition of group discussion set forth above is incompatible with strict teacher control. The self-directed learning group, on the other hand, comes closer to the ideal. Although doctrinaire, the following observation (Brookfield 1985) bears directly on this issue:

A necessary condition of discussion is that there be no preconceived agenda, no cognitive path to be charted, no previously specified objectives. . . . Hence guided discussion is conceptual nonsense in that discussion is free and open by definition. (p. 57)

The position taken in this entry is that strict leader control is the equivalent of didactic teaching and thus incompatible with the fundamental nature of group discussion. Guided discussion that is not strictly leader controlled does, however, qualify as a variant of the discussion method. Furthermore, as noted below, the discussion leader plays a key role in any discussion group, including those that eventually become totally self-directed.

4. Discussion Leadership

In any kind of group, the leader, if only in the initial stages designed to lead to total group self-direction, must be able to balance initiating behaviors (task orientation) with supportive behaviors (group maintenance or strengthening). The task function involves coordinating and facilitating group activities to enhance goal achievement. The maintenance function is concerned with strengthening relationships among members by "providing warmth, friendliness; conciliating, resolving conflict, relieving tension, providing personal help, counsel, encouragement; showing understanding, tolerance of different points of view . . ." (Newcomb et al. 1965 p. 481).

Thibaut and Kelley (1959) raise the question of whether task and maintenance functions can or should be performed by the same person. They conclude, based on the research evidence, that for most groups, performance of these functions by different individuals enhances group functioning. Pankowski (1984 p. 21) points out that self-directed groups are almost always characterized by a member who presses for task accomplishment and another who performs the maintenance role, pressing for the satisfaction of the emotional/affective needs of group members.

Space precludes a discussion of the literature concerning the specific responsibilities and roles of discussion group leaders. Zander (1982 p. 31) stresses the leader's role in handling three procedural problems: "reluctance of members to take part; members' lack of ideas during discussion; and conditions in the group that restrain ready give and take." With respect to the first procedural problem, Zander (1982 p. 21) points out that "a leader need not try to get everyone talking; generally only 30 percent of those present do most of the commenting in a comfortable and efficient group." One would expect a higher participation rate than 30 percent in leaderless or self-directed discussion groups, unless broader participation is precluded by group size.

Many experts in group discussion methods stress a different perspective on the leader's principal responsibility, which, in short, is gradually to abandon the leadership role and become just another member of a self-directed discussion group. Haiman (1955 p. 9) succinctly summarizes this viewpoint: "The ultimate aim of a discussion leader in a learning situation should be to gain full status as a *member* of the group by working himself out of the leader's role."

The functioning and effectiveness of discussion groups are influenced significantly by factors other than leadership. These factors have to do with variations in the characteristics of attributes of discussion groups as described below.

5. Salient Attributes of Discussion Groups

All groups possess certain general properties or attributes that have profound effects on the manner in which they function and on the quality of group interaction and outcomes. The following attributes are discussed briefly below: composition, size, and cohesion.

5.1 Composition

Homogeneous groups, those whose members share similar characteristics, tend to foster member satisfaction and a group sense. Zander (1982 p. 3) asserts that persons whose values and beliefs "do not fit together will have a hard time forming a strong group." Common sense suggests, however, that too much homogeneity can have the undesirable effect of minimizing the divergent experiences and viewpoints so central to effective group discussion.

5.2 Size

In a research review, Levine and Moreland (1990 p. 593) conclude that "as a group grows larger, it also changes in other ways, generally for the worse. People who belong to a larger group are less satisfied . . ., participate less often . . ., and are less likely to co-operate with one another." Zander (1982 p. 34) notes that "the size of a group greatly affects how often a member can talk and how much he expects others will contribute . . . It is hard to develop a full discussion in a meeting of more than twenty-five members; discussion proceeds better in a group of closer to seven or so." Practical experience suggests that groups of fewer than six or seven are too small to sustain a productive group discussion, whereas seven to twelve seems to be the optimal group size.

5.3 Cohesion

Research has found "group effectiveness to be related to cohesiveness, which is reflected in such things as mutual liking among group members, member satisfaction, and other positive reactions to the group" (Pankowski 1984 p. 18). Zander (1982 pp. 4–5) defines group cohesiveness as "the strength of members' desire to remain members," adding that "as cohesiveness becomes stronger in a group, members talk more readily, listen more carefully, influence one another more often, volunteer more frequently, and adhere to group standards more closely."

Composition, size, and cohesion are interrelated attributes of discussion groups. They reinforce one another to promote or hinder group functioning and outcomes.

6. Problems and Issues

Only one source (Brookfield 1985) could be located that provided a thoughtful critique of the assumptions and practices central to group discussion. According to Brookfield, three cognitive outcomes are generally assumed to result from the use of the discussion method. They are: development of powers of analytic clarity, increased appreciation of the complexity of a topic gained by listening to differing viewpoints, and increased identification with the subject matter through stimulation of interest. Brookfield asserts that these outcomes are seldom realized in actual practice. He argues, for example, that clarification of thought is contingent on discussion occurring under emotionally stable circumstances, but for many adults discussion is extremely threatening. Appreciation of the complexities of a topic or issue is often precluded by the rapid pace of many discussion groups, which can lead to confusion rather than enlightenment. Brookfield's thesis is that many of the claims made with respect to the cognitive outcomes of discussion are unsubstantiated. Other concerns raised by Brookfield (1985) include the often low quality of participants' contributions with respect to their relevance to the topic or issue under consideration, the lack of coherent, cumulative learning over time, and the many dysfunctional aspects of the psychodynamics of discussion groups.

Brookfield (1985) proposes four conditions that, if met, are likely to foster meaningful and productive discussions:

> First, group members need to devise and to subscribe to an appropriate moral culture for group discussion . . . This means that the group must spend some time agreeing upon a set of procedural rules concerning the manner in which equity of participation is to be realized. Second, discussion leaders can exercise a degree of forethought regarding the selection of materials that are to form the substantive focus of group discussions . . . Third, the leader should be well versed both in the subject matter to be covered and in the principles of group dynamics . . . Fourth, discussion participants can be prepared for discussion . . . through the development of reasoning skills (so that inconsistencies and ambiguities in argument can be detected) and through the improvement of communication abilities (so that ideas can be articulated accurately). (p. 65)

Despite the problems and shortcomings identified by Brookfield, group discussion, properly conducted, can be a powerful tool for promoting adult learning. In best practice, as he himself asserts, it may well be the adult education method *par excellence*.

See also: Adult Learning: An Overview; Environments for Learning; Individual Differences, Learning, and Instruction; Self-directed Learning

References

Bormann E 1975 *Discussion and Group Methods: Theory and Practice*. Harper and Row, New York

Bligh D A 1972 *What's the Use of Lecturers?* Penguin, Harmondsworth

Brookfield S D 1985 Discussions as an effective educational method: In: Rosenblum S H (ed.) 1985 *Involving Adults in the Educational Process*. Jossey-Bass, San Francisco, California

Cartwright D, Zander A 1968 *Group Dynamics: Research and Theory*. Harper and Row, New York

Haiman F S 1955 The leader's role. In: Adult Education Association of the USA (eds.) 1955 *How to Lead Discussions*. Adult Education Association of the USA, Washington, DC

Harnack R K, Fest T B, Jones B S 1977 *Group Discussion: Theory and Technique*, 2nd edn. Prentice-Hall, Englewood Cliffs, New Jersey

Levine J, Moreland R 1990 Progress in small group research. *An. Rev. Psychol.*: 41:593

Newcomb T M, Turner R H, Converse P E 1965 *Social Psychology: The Study of Human Interaction*. Holt, Rinehart and Winston, New York

Pankowski M L 1984 Creating participatory, task-oriented learning environments. In: Sork T J (ed.) 1984 *Designing and Implementing Effective Workshops*. Jossey-Bass, San Francisco, California

Thibaut J W, Kelley H H 1959 *The Social Psychology of Groups*. Wiley, New York

Zander A 1982 *Making Groups Effective*. Jossey-Bass, San Francisco, California

Further Reading

Berkowitz L (ed.) 1978 *Group Processes: Papers from Advances in Experimental Social Psychology*. Academic Press, New York

Cranton P A 1989 *Planning Instruction for Adult Learners*. Wall & Thompson, Toronto

Hill W F 1969 *Learning thru Discussion*. Sage, Beverly Hills, California

Houle C O 1972 *The Design of Education*. Jossey-Bass, San Francisco, California

Hyman R T 1980 *Improving Discussion Leadership*. Teachers College Press, New York

Legge D 1971 Discussion methods. In: Stephens M D, Roderick G W (eds.) 1971 *Teaching Techniques in Adult Education*. David and Charles, Newton Abbot

Rogers J 1971 *Adults Learning*. Penguin, Harmondsworth

Slavin R E 1983 *Cooperative Learning*. Longman, London

Individual Differences, Learning, and Instruction

R. E. Snow

Individual differences among learners present a pervasive, profound problem to educators. At the outset of instruction in any topic, students of any age and in any culture will differ from one another in various intellectual and psychomotor abilities, in both general and specialized prior knowledge, in interests and motives, and in personal styles of thought and work during learning. These differences, in turn, often relate directly to differences in students learning progress. These relations identify individual predispositions that somehow condition students' readiness to profit from the particular instructional conditions provided. Educational theorists and practitioners have long noted these relations; some have sought to adapt instruction to individual differences so as to reduce the relations. However, in most places and in most times actual instructional practice has remained basically fixed and nonadaptive. Students usually must fit the system; some learn more, some less, some not at all, and some drop out, no matter what instructional system is chosen.

As one of its central concerns, research on instruction seeks to understand the sources, development, malleability, and manifestations of individual differences in learning, to recommend and help develop improvements in education for all students. Psychology's first major contribution to education—the technology of mental testing—was motivated by this goal. Ability tests remain one of its most successful and influential but also most controversial and criticized contributions. Unfortunately, the controversies often overshadow not only the value of mental tests when properly used and interpreted, and the importance of continuing research with them, but also psychology's contribution to the measurement and understanding of the many other kinds of individual differences important in education.

This entry examines the state of knowledge about student individual differences, emphasizing the substantive understanding, management, and use of such differences in relation to instruction. It also notes further research that is needed. It does not review the technology of testing, the controversies surrounding it, or many other issues concerning measurement of individual differences in education.

1. Categories of Individual Difference Constructs

The psychology of individual differences is a diverse field, addressing a variety of problems in different contexts using an assortment of methods. Cronbach (1957) likened it to the Holy Roman Empire: a loose network of far-flung provinces containing many subcultures, often with insufficient contact. Differential psychologists study intelligence; a variety of special abilities and talents; creativity; cognitive, motivational, and learning styles and strategies; interests; values; attitudes; and all of human personality, both "normal" and "abnormal." They also study physical, sensory, perceptual, and psychomotor skills, as well as biological and biochemical variations. Differences associated with gender, ethnicity, and socioeconomic status have also been a focus of study. Furthermore, psychologists who compare age groups, cultures, or different sorts of brain damage, or experts and novices in some field would not call themselves "differential psychologists," but they nonetheless contribute to the psychology of individual differences (see *Psychology of Adult Education*).

To amass the full catalog of distinguishable individual differences of potential relevance to some aspect of instruction would require a cumulative review across a great many sources (e.g., Anastasi 1958, Carroll 1993, Cattell 1971, Cronbach and Snow 1977, Eysenck and Eysenck 1985, Flammer 1975, Guilford 1959, 1967, Jäger 1984, Meili 1981, Pervin and Lewis 1978).

There are literally hundreds of individual difference constructs. Also, some topics that come under "individual differences" need separate special treatment; for example, developmental disabilities and special needs education.

This entry concentrates on the categories of individual differences judged most important for research and development in education: cognitive abilities and prior knowledge, learning strategies and styles, and achievement-related motivation, volition, and interest. Some related kinds of differences are discussed within each of these categories and a catchall category is added to note briefly many other constructs, both new and old, that also deserve assessment and research attention. It then examines how improved understanding of such differences leads to instructional improvements.

For short, but also for theoretical reasons, all individual-difference constructs relevant to learning from instruction are here called "aptitudes," to signify aspects of the present state of a person that are propaedeutic, that is, needed as preparation for some future learning project (Snow 1992). Education is viewed as an aptitude development program in the sense that its primary concern is human preparedness for later states of life. The educational improvements of most importance, therefore, are those that make education adaptive to aptitude differences at the start of instruction and promotive of aptitude developments through and beyond it (Corno and Snow 1986).

2. Cognitive Abilities and Prior Knowledge

2.1 A Taxonomy of Ability Factors

Because an early priority in any science is taxonomy, much research in the twentieth century has sought to build a taxonomy of human abilities, based on intercorrelations among the many cognitive measurements that have been collected. Contemporary studies and reanalyses of old data using modern methods now give a coherent picture (see Carroll 1993, Gustafsson 1984). The distinguishable ability factors emerging from this research can be arranged in three levels of hierarchical order (see *The Development of Competence: Toward a Taxonomy*).

General intelligence (G) is at the top of the hierarchy (the third order), implying that this central ability is involved in all cognitive test performances. Three firmly demonstrated second-order factors are linked directly beneath G: fluid intelligence (G_f), or analytic reasoning ability; crystallized intelligence (G_c), or generalized educational achievement; and general visual perception (G_v), reflecting ability in cognitive tasks that impose figural–spatial imagery demands. Also on this second level is general idea production (G_i), retrieval, or fluency, the ability factor most closely associated with creative intellectual performance. Three other second-order factors represent auditory perception, memory, and speed; these factors have been less studied and are therefore less well-understood in relation to learning from instruction, but they should not be ignored. Beneath each second-order factor, the names of its subordinate, first-order ability factors could be listed. Under G_c, for example, such primary factors as verbal comprehension, word knowledge, and grammatical sensitivity would appear. Under G_v, spatial relations, visualization, and the closure factors would be distinguished. G_f would include inductive and deductive reasoning factors; there is also strong evidence that G, G_f, and Thurstone's primary induction factor are identical in a hierarchical model (see also Gustafsson 1984). The primary level distinctions are not further discussed here (see Carroll 1993).

2.2 Ability–Learning Relation

The research evidence indicates many relations between the major abilities and learning performance. G and G_c are most often found to be highly correlated with learning from conventional instruction. Different subjects call different mixes of ability into play, and the mixes change as students progress in a subject. For example, mathematics may require visual perceptual discriminations as well as memory facilities in the early stages. Reasoning skills are also demanded, together with verbal comprehension and word knowledge, when instruction emphasizes explanation and problem-solving. Most learning demands both G_f and G_c abilities. Especially as learning tasks and teaching methods build closely on prior instruction, crystallized ability and prior knowledge will predominate as aptitude. Whether more general crystallized knowledge or more specific prior knowledge is the dominant factor is often disputed; some research seeks to improve the assessment of prior knowledge and to pin down the conditions under which general versus specific aptitudes are important (Dochy 1992, Schneider and Weinert 1990). Clearly there are subject-matter differences as well as student differences in the degree to which given instructional material will be novel versus familiar. Novel content seems to call more general knowledge and fluid reasoning into play. Visual–spatial abilities appear to move in and out of relevance as spatial reasoning and other operations with visual images are required by chosen materials, problems, or forms of teaching. Visual–spatial abilities have been associated with learning in art, architecture, dentistry, and technical courses, such as carpentry, mechanics, and engineering design. Whether such ability is relevant to problem-solving in mathematical topics, such as geometry, or in aspects of science, depends on topic but also on individual teacher or learner strategy; average correlations here are rarely strong. It is important to realize that superficially spatial–figural tasks do not necessarily require spatial ability.

Instructional method differences can also moderate the correlation between cognitive measures and achievement. There is substantial evidence that less able learners do better when instruction is tightly structured, lessons are broken down into a sequence of simplified units, and teachers or instructional conditions exercise control over minute-to-minute activities and provide frequent feedback. Less able learners do less well in conventional instruction or in environments in which independent activity by learners is required to fill in gaps left by incomplete or less structured teaching; discovery learning would be an example. In these situations, more able learners excel; they often do not benefit particularly from tightly structured teaching (Snow 1982, Snow and Lohman 1984). Again, novelty challenges more able and taxes less able learners. Unfortunately most research does not explicitly distinguish stages of learning and instruction in these terms, and ability–learning relations change with experience in the learning situation. Aptitude differences need to be studied in relation to instructional structure and novelty, as well as other learning task variables, across time and familiarity in particular instructional situations.

In short, general measures of ability regarded as indicators of aptitude correlate strongly with learning achievement and appear to correlate more strongly in some instructional environments than in others: notably those characterized as relatively novel, unstructured, and incomplete. More specialized ability constructs also show some differential validity across different subjects or instructional methods. Just what conditions generate each of these kinds of aptitude-treatment interactions is difficult to determine; there are many subtle variations across situations (Cronbach and Snow 1977, Snow 1977). It is clear that cognitive aptitude differences among learners must be included in evaluation studies to gain a full view of instructional effects.

2.3 Ability Development

Although genetic factors influence ability development, no ability delineated above should be regarded as fixed. The development and differentiation of abilities is significantly a function of the accumulation and specialization of experience before and during education and work (Anastasi 1970). Substantial advances have been made in analyzing the nature of nurture, particularly with respect to general intellectual development. However, the conditions under which particular abilities develop and the means for promoting such development are not well understood. Research is attacking this need, and bringing differential, developmental, and instructional research into intersection (Case and Edelstein 1993). Two programs provide examples. In one, longitudinal patterns of ability differences (Demetriou and Efklides 1987) are related to differences in learning activities and interests (Undheim and Gustafsson 1989), to direct training and transfer effects (Gustafsson et al. 1989), and to

different domains of educational achievement (Balke-Aurell 1982, Gustafsson and Balke-Aurell 1989). The results, though complicated, support Ferguson's (1954, 1956) theory of differential ability development through specializations of learning and transfer over time. G is here interpreted as reflecting cognitive processing complexity; a view consistent with other theories (Snow and Lohman 1984). The other program studies cognitive, motivational, and social development and individual differences longitudinally across a number of years (Weinert and Schneider 1991). Of particular concern are interactions among aptitudes, knowledge, and strategies within particular instructional contexts (Schneider and Weinert 1990).

Distinctions between fluid and crystallized abilities or verbal and spatial abilities appear in the developmental evidence. G_c appears to develop through formal educational experience in learning and transfer of organized knowledge, skills, and processing strategies. Fluid ability presumably develops more through experience in adapting to novelty in the natural world. One theory suggests that fluid ability develops earlier in life and then is invested in formal instructional learning to produce crystallized ability (Horn 1978). Verbal-crystallized ability does appear more influenced by verbal emphasis in educational programs whereas spatial ability is promoted by more technical instruction (Balke-Aurell 1982). In general, less is known about the development of visual–spatial abilities; one hypothesis suggests that early emphasis on verbalization inhibits growth in these abilities.

Direct attempts to improve abilities through instruction have met with mixed but promising results. Some broad interventions have had positive effects on ability development. Some have shown initial improvements that later diminish. Some appear to have positive effects on crystallized skills and negative effects on fluid skills (Detterman and Sternberg 1982, Snow 1982). Some important successes have come from extremely early or intensive interventions (Feuerstein 1979, McKay et al. 1978). Other successes are based on detailed analyses of constituent thinking and reasoning skills and strategies involved in performance (see Baron and Sternberg 1987, Chipman et al. 1985, Nickerson et al. 1985, Resnick 1987, Segal et al. 1985). Examples of success in training G_f skills directly are available (Budoff 1987, Campione and Brown 1987, 1990, DeLeeuw et al. 1987, Feuerstein et al. 1987, Klauer 1990). G_v skills also seem to be trainable (Ben-Chaim 1988, Lajoie 1986). Components of verbal and reading abilities can also be trained (Calfee 1982, Frederiksen and Warren 1987, Perfetti 1985).

2.4 Content and Process Analyses

Cognitive psychology provided new methods for analyzing ability differences to reach more detailed models of information processing for each task.

This helped build theories of abilities that identify component processes, metacognitive skills and strategies, knowledge structures, and sequences of such components involved in individual performance, and thus new interpretations of individual differences in ability.

Initially focused were tasks like those used to represent ability factors; many of these have now been studied. The results provide process models of various reasoning and problem-solving abilities, verbal and reading abilities, mathematical and spatial abilities, and second-language learning abilities (Sternberg 1985a, 1985b). More comprehensive, process-based theories of the cognitive ability hierarchy now seem possible. This supports related research steps. First, analyses of ability task performance suggest how improved assessment measures might be designed. Conventional cognitive tests have not been notably useful for diagnostic purposes. Second, this work supports new attempts at direct training by focusing on diagnosed constituent processes, as suggested in the previous section. Third, research can trace the role of these constituent processes, skills, and strategies in learning particular subject matters. Students clearly differ in strategy selection and adaptation of processing during complex cognitive performance; the problem is to understand this processing in interaction with domain knowledge and the subject matter and instructional context. Finally, developmental studies can track the emergence of component processes involved in various abilities across ages, so ability development may also be describable in process terms. (For reviews of related work see Lohman 1989, Snow and Swanson 1992, Ackerman 1989, Kyllonen and Christal 1990, Frederiksen et al. 1990, Lidz 1987, Snow and Lohman 1989).

Analysis of individual differences in particular subject matter domains is most advanced in mathematics and increasingly in natural science. Mayer (1985) showed mathematical problem-solving to involve individual differences in knowledge related to problem representation, translation, and schema identification; strategy differences in solution planning; and computation automaticity in reaching solutions. Resnick and Omanson (1987) reviewed research on arithmetic understanding to emphasize interplay between reflection on principles, invention, and automatization of procedure. De Corte and Verschaffel (1987) identified many component skills and strategies already apparent among first graders. Gelman and Greeno (1989) analyzed preschool mathematical competence to suggest that children bring implicit principles as initial states to instruction. Thus, although components of mathematical performance have been regarded as skills to be trained onto everybody's blank slate, some children clearly have intuitive concepts of counting, numbers, and sets even before school begins; this early principled knowledge tunes selective attention and allows learning to be generative, not just receptive,

from the start. In effect, early principles are constraints that help some learners assemble and monitor successful performance plans, including novel plans. New meanings and principles can be built onto this basic structure, allowing broader transfer as new tasks appear. Other learners clearly start without this basic structure. It follows that assessment of initial states in mathematics should be geared to detect understanding of these principles; new instruction should relate to them meaningfully when they are present, and construct them when they are not. Such assessment and instruction concerns not just what students already know; it also addresses what students can perceive in novel situations and generate as mental models for reasoning therein. Also important is work that identifies the perceptual and spatial thinking skills involved in such situations (Leushina 1991, Yakimanskaya 1991).

3. Learning Strategies and Styles

3.1 Learning Strategies

Ability and knowledge differences are presumably manifested in observable differences in learning strategies and tactics. Thus, when direct training supplants ineffective strategies with effective ones, the hope is that deeper inaptitudes, or at least their effects, are being removed. Dozens of learning strategy constructs have now been defined. Many reflect rehearsal, elaboration, organizational, monitoring, or motivational activities during learning or studying. Some concern use of global planning, heuristic, or mnemonic devices; some are mapping and structuring tactics using cues detected in reading or listening; and some promote metacognitive processes of comprehension monitoring or hypothesis generating and testing while learning. An important general distinction concerns whether individual strategies lead to deep (versus surface) processing during learning (Marton et al. 1984, Entwistle 1987, Ferguson-Hessler and deJong 1990). Depth of processing may be a core construct to which ability and knowledge, as well as many surface strategy distinctions, connect (see *Approaches to Learning*).

3.2 Strategy Development

Strategies can be directly trained, although such training can sometimes be situation or treatment specific. It also can be dysfunctional; for learners with some ability profiles, the new strategy to be learned is (at least temporarily) in conflict with strategies already automatic. Lohman (1986) explained these interference effects using a production system account of skill acquisition, and predicted failure for skill and strategy training whenever it ignores the particulars of G_f or G_c strengths.

Training design clearly requires careful analysis

of poor learning strategies in comparison with able learners to allow point by point incrementation toward more effective performance (Case and Bereiter 1984). Learners can be helped through a graduated scaffold of tutorial hints and demonstrations to model and eventually internalize the learning strategies of able performers (Campione and Brown 1990). If done well the result is a repertoire of multiple strategies, skill in their use, and flexibility in adaptation to instructional opportunities and demands. Research shows that some learners develop multiple strategies for a task and shift among them during performance (Kyllonen et al 1984, Ohlsson 1984a, 1984b). Flexible strategy shifting seems to be a hallmark of able learning, whereas rigid strategies or random shifting suggest low ability. Work on learning strategies for arithmetic (Siegler and Campbell 1990) further suggests that confidence in retrieved answers is a key individual difference controlling strategy use (see *Study and Learning Strategies*).

3.3 Styles

When strategic differences appear deeply rooted in learner personality, they may be conceptualized as more pervasive learning or cognitive styles (Schmeck 1988). Some style constructs may capture important ability–personality interactions. Some may reflect cognitive organizational differences between subject-matter domains. For example, Pask and Scott (1972) distinguish holist and serialist styles of knowledge organization; although persons habitually prefer one or the other style, it also seems that domains like physics and mathematics call for serialist structure, whereas history is better served by holist structure.

The list of style constructs and associated assessment instruments is lengthy and unorganized (Keefe 1987, Schmeck 1988); it includes many hypothesized habits and preferences as distinct styles, as well as traditional ability and personality constructs. In the 1990s, evidence is still inadequate to judge the validity of style measures or their usefulness in adapting instruction to individuals; some have been called into serious question (Tiedeman 1989).

4. Achievement-related Motivation, Volition, and Interest

Adding style constructs as aptitudes for learning introduces the complex categories of conative and affective individual differences including many kinds of personal needs, motives, goals, and interests relevant to learning. However, these differences have been less well studied and understood in relation to adult learning. Only a few prominent constructs are reviewed here.

There are attempts to bring disparate aspects of motivational and volitional differences together, consider them jointly with cognitive abilities in learning,

and derive adaptive instructional design implications. Most notable are programs by Lepper (1988, Lepper et al. 1990) and Kanfer and Ackerman (1989). Lepper integrated various contrasting student orientations under the general heading of intrinsic versus extrinsic motivation and devised principles for promoting intrinsic motivation in learning. Of particular interest are findings that expert tutors use these principles subtly and adaptively while preserving the student's sense of control. The Kanfer–Ackerman model of ability–motivation interaction concerns attention resource capacity differences. Results show that motivational interventions can impede learning by diverting attention to self-regulatory activities in early stages of skill acquisition depending on ability; in later stages, the same interventions can facilitate performance. Much work in the early 1990s focuses on improving the measurement of cognitive motivational interaction in learning.

4.1 Anxiety and Achievement Motivation

Test anxiety is the most studied motivational aptitude. It interacts with instructional treatment just as G does; high structure is best for more anxious and low structure is best for less anxious students, but ability and anxiety also interact (Snow 1989). Research continues on the information-processing model of anxiety effects in learning, the development of anxiety, and its amelioration by direct intervention.

As Rand et al. (1989) point out, however, test anxiety (or fear of failure) is but half of the traditional theory of achievement motivation and should be studied together with need for achievement as well as ability measures. Lens's (1983) research has shown that need for achievement and anxiety measures can both yield curvilinear relations with instructional achievement. Thus an intermediate level of both kinds of need provides optimal performance; too much or too little of each can be counterproductive. Lens and DeCruyenaere (1991) have also shown that different measures of achievement motivation, anxiety, intrinsic motivation, causal attributions, and expectancy-value instrumentality all yield similar, strong relations with judgments of learning motivation. Boekaerts (1987), however, notes that general measures can miss important situation and task differences.

Also noteworthy are differences in goal orientations and attitudes toward the future. Van Calster et al. (1987) found interactions suggesting that achievement and study motivation depend on future attitudes about goals as well as perceived instrumentality of performance for goals. Dweck and Leggett (1988) found that learners differ in their conceptions about ability development, which then influence motivational orientation to learning; mastery-oriented students believe ability improves with learning and direct their actions toward this end, whereas performance-oriented students think of ability as fixed and direct their actions toward teacher evaluations. Performance goal orientation limits achievement, particularly for learners with low self-perceived ability (see *Participation: Role of Motivation*).

4.2 Interest

A closely related line focuses on interest as both aptitude and task characteristic. Some effects of interest differences on learning rival those of ability differences. There are also qualitative differences in cognitive processing in learning that accrue from interest (see Hidi 1990, Renninger et al. 1992), and related content motivations (see Nenniger 1987). Research aimed at detailing the kinds of variation in subject-specific interests that influence adult learning could be uniquely important for improving instruction.

4.3 Self-efficacy and Effort Investment

Self-perceptions of ability are known to influence choice of learning activities, strategies, and effort investment, as well as short-term achievement. Such differences among self-efficacy also have direct effects on effort investment across semester-long courses (MacIver et al. 1991). Other work shows long-range relations among self-concept of ability, effort, and achievement (Boekaerts 1988). Self-concept research ought to be integrated with the constructs of self-efficacy, effort, and metacognitive strategy. Metacognitive strategy in learning also implies awareness or mindfulness; mindful learning in turn requires the investment of mental effort (Salomon and Globerson 1987). Individual differences in effort investment can appear in the extreme as pathological effort avoidance (Rollett 1987).

4.4 Self-regulation and Action Control

Self-regulation is action control, but the category includes other volitional constructs reflecting purposive striving and persistence. Some learners display state orientation, wherein attention perseverates on present concerns; failures lead to an inability to concentrate on intentions to continue work and perform well. The contrast is action orientation, in which attention is focused on strong intention–action relationships. Action-oriented learners use control strategies to protect their intention–action sequence from competing tendencies; they persist in learning despite momentary difficulties and distractions (Kuhl 1990, Corno 1986, McCombs and Whisler 1989, Simons and Beukhof 1987).

4.5 Achievement via Independence and Achievement via Conformity

Still another construct contrasts persons who are motivated toward learning achievement through independence, who describe themselves as self-sufficient and mature, versus those motivated toward learning achievement through conformity, who characterize themselves as responsible, organized, and attentive to others' expectations. Conforming students show higher achievement when instruction is highly structured with imposed objectives and procedures, whereas students high in independence are better off with low-structure instruction where they can exercise their own initiative (Snow 1977).

5. Other Individual Difference Constructs

Many other individual difference constructs might be included here. In any particular instructional situation, unique combinations of student differences may come into play. Although instructional situations often call upon the major aptitudes discussed above, other differences may illuminate or qualify their functioning in higher-order interactions. Thus, individuality in learning is rich with structure, and there are many faceted contrasts yet to be explored in a systematic, coordinated way in relation to instruction. Some of the personal constructs that deserve such attention are self-perceptions as a learner in relation to perceptions of different instructional environments; interpersonal styles and social competence; the qualitative character of one's conceptions and misconceptions about the physical and social world; and all of the temperaments, attitudes, and emotions that may be connected to these conceptions or to educational conditions directly.

6. Instructional Research, Development, and Evaluation

There are many uses for individual difference information in the study of instruction and the pursuit of its improvement. Those considered here are student selection, instructional system adaptation, individual teacher adaptation, and instructional evaluation in general.

6.1 Student Selection and Advanced Placement

Measures of ability predict future academic achievement and so are used in conjunction with other information to select students for admission to advanced instructional programs. Available evidence supports the validity of this use; it benefits both institutions and individuals by reducing failure rates. Selection by ability is particularly valued where educational resources are scarce or expensive, or where prior academic record is an inadequate predictor. However, selection based only on ability or prior achievement neglects the need for advanced programs to diversify student talents and personal qualities. This argues for a larger future role for research on individual differences in

405

relation to instruction. Optimal diversity of personal qualities in university and college environments has not been a research target.

Ability measures are also used to identify students for development of special aptitudes. Programs for pre-university students who show advanced mathematical abilities offer one example (Stanley et al. 1978, Stanley and Benbow 1983). Many universities also now use special assessments for advanced course placements. These uses contribute to instructional systems aimed at individual goal attainment.

6.2 Instructional System Adaptations

Although these uses are important, the achievement of common goals for all students is the major concern for much instructional research, development, and evaluation. This requires adapting instruction to student differences. Many teacher and instructional system adaptations to individual differences have been studied, operating on minute-to-minute, unit-to-unit, month-to-month, or year-to-year bases. It is easiest to imagine first an ideal system and then to examine some instructional designs and teacher adaptations as examples.

Ideally, an adaptive system aimed at enabling all students to reach common goals includes two kinds of instruction. One provides direct aptitude development for students in need of focused training or remediation as preparation for regular further instruction. The other provides alternative instructional paths toward the same common goals, with paths designed to circumvent present inaptitudes by capitalizing on present aptitudes. Periodic assessments decide the alternation of direct aptitude training and instruction that proceeds toward goals by circumventing inaptitudes. Both aspects of instruction are designed and evaluated with particular kinds of student need as targets (Glaser 1977).

For example, students low initially in reading comprehension skills might receive direct training on these skills while in parallel they pursue goals in mathematics or science instruction that do not place heavy demands on such skills. Perhaps this instructional alternative capitalizes instead on visual–spatial abilities by substituting work with concrete, figural–pictorial materials in place of complex verbiage. Similarly, students high in test anxiety might be given direct help in reducing its debilitating effects while also pursuing instruction designed to provide clear, tight, encouraging structure with minimum stress. Although all possible treatments cannot be provided for all possible individuals in such a system, adaptations for the most important aptitude problems can be planned, and some treatments might reasonably serve more than one kind of student. For example, given previous evidence, a highly structured instructional path might serve students low in crystallized ability, or high in anxiety, or low in independence relative to conformity.

A less structured path might serve students with the opposite profile. Students could switch paths or move to still other treatments as their progress indicated.

Some instructional systems exist that incorporate parts of this ideal. Among them are the Adaptive Learning Environments models, Individually Guided Education, Mastery Learning and the Program for Learning in Accordance with Needs (see Corno and Snow 1986 for detailed references). These systems individualize instructional pace as well as activities and materials. They do not reach the ideal, and have not been sufficiently evaluated with respect to the major aptitudes discussed here, but existing evidence suggests them as starting forms to which other kinds of adaptation and increasingly detailed knowledge about individual differences in learning can be added. Future research should provide detailed analyses, particularly of ability, anxiety, achievement motivation, and subject-specific interests, in close connection with the sorts of direct training and alternative instructional conditions possible in these or similar systems.

New forms of adaptive instructional design and aptitude assessment aim at bringing deeper and more diagnostic perspectives into instructional research. Some new systems use computer-based intelligent tutoring to adapt subsequent instruction to the details of previous performance. Another approach involves a hint hierarchy and transfer tasks with human tutors to gauge learning differences and provide instruction simultaneously. So far, these assessments and adaptations do not use aptitude information from outside their instructional systems. (See Frederiksen et al. 1990, Glaser and Bassok 1989, Snow and Swanson 1992 for details on these and other systems.)

6.3 Individual Teacher Adaptations

Individual teachers adapt to individual differences whenever they tailor choices of group learning activities, reading materials, or personal handling of different students, based on knowledge of student characteristics. This knowledge may come from formal assessments, but effective teachers also gauge each student's strengths and weaknesses, interests, styles of thought, and prior relevant knowledge through careful observation outside as well as inside the classroom. Some teachers devise alternative learning projects to help discover students' particular strengths and weaknesses. Others may use student learning style questionnaires. These are forms of aptitude assessment, though they may not be standardized or systematic. Based on them, alternative instructional treatments may be chosen or designed to use students' strengths to help overcome students' weaknesses.

Research on teaching has identified teacher decisions and actions that appear to influence average student learning. But few studies focus on differential teaching styles as adaptations to different student characteristics. Some studies match teacher styles and student characteristics that work well or poorly by influencing teacher expectations (Brophy and Evertson 1981). Hummel-Rossi (1981) identified eliciting–permissive versus directing–monitoring styles that teachers applied with success to students who appeared to differ in ability and anxiety. There are methods teachers use to adapt repetition and tutoring time for students differing in ability (Fisher and Berliner 1985). Tutoring has also been studied to define adaptive interactions that work well (see Snow and Swanson 1992). Cole (1985) gave examples of adaptive teaching in culturally diverse classrooms. Styles of discourse already part of a person's culture outside of the learning environment can be used as a bridge to shape the learning encounter.

6.4 Instructional Evaluations

Beyond helping to invent adaptations of instruction to individual differences, differential approaches can test whether existing educational practices are maladaptive and can suggest alternatives. The classic example is ability grouping.

In school education, but not usually in adult basic and secondary education, student abilities reflected in test scores, grades, or teacher observations are used to classify students into homogeneous ability groups or tracks for different instructional treatments. This practice may be maladaptive unless all students' chances to reach the common goals of instruction are improved thereby. Although the intent may be to adapt instruction to different ability levels, such grouping often results in slower pace and lower goals for lower ability students. Placement in lower ability groups can diminish student achievement by reducing opportunities to learn (see Peterson et al. 1984).

Ability tracking may pose more serious problems than within-class grouping. Individual teachers can create and change temporary groups as learning progresses, and they can use observed differences in interests or anxiety as well as ability to form groups. Assignment to different educational programs based on ability, however, may make the disadvantages of homogeneous grouping permanent. Yet ability tracking based on career choice is very common in adult education and training. Classification based on career interests is not problematic, so long as ability and interest development have not been foreclosed prematurely by inadequate earlier instruction or counseling. Such classification may be maladaptive if it forces lower common goals on students in slower tracks. The point is controversial. Some research suggests that the effects of ability grouping and tracking are essentially zero. But this conclusion is contrary to much literature indicating the low quality of instruction in low achievement groups and the negative impact of ability grouping on the motivation and self-esteem of students assigned to low groups. Unfortunately most research on ability grouping still leaves the nature of

instruction in different groups out of consideration and fails to evaluate outcomes with respect to initial ability differences (Cronbach and Snow 1977).

Work on cooperative and open learning has suggested alternative ways to use ability grouping to advantage. Webb (1982) showed that using ability information to create systematically heterogeneous groups helps both the more and the less able learners when they are grouped together, especially if the able students act as tutors and the less able students are prompted to ask questions. Other forms of peer cooperative learning in groups and cross-age tutoring have also been found to be effective, though these are not often evaluated with respect to individual differences. Continuing research on the interaction of aptitudes and teacher grouping practices may yet turn prevalent maladaptations into effective adaptations (see Snow and Swanson 1992).

7. Conclusion

The broad review attempted here cannot be briefly summarized. It does support the conclusion that research on individual differences has made and can continue to make important contributions to instructional improvement for children and adult learners. To promote more and better improvements in the future, research needs to integrate knowledge about the many kinds of important individual differences and connect it directly to the design of adaptive educational systems, teacher training programs, and diagnostic assessment devices. Many examples used here identify important points for research and development investment in this connection.

However important the contribution of research on individual differences may be to the design and implementation of particular instructional procedures, the most lasting contribution may be in the enriched conceptions of human diversity it provides to educators who care about evaluating their efforts in this light. A demonstration that a particular procedure is maladaptive for some students may be as important in this regard as a demonstration that some other procedure works well for others. Implicit in this review is the idea that aptitude differences are a function of person–situation interaction, both in the instant and over time; they are thus particular to local conditions. Aptitudes do not simply reside inside individuals as a list of independent, fixed, ever-present traits. Rather, they are exhibited in consort as resultant strengths or weaknesses relative to present and past conditions. Educators who can adopt this view will investigate success and failure in the person–situation interaction, rather than attributing either to the person alone, and manipulate conditions and environments for learning accordingly. Fully articulated, studied, and applied, such a view would represent a true paradigm shift in educational theory, research, and practice with respect to individual differences in learning.

See also: Psychology of Adult Education; Human Development; Approaches to Learning; Environments for Learning; Group Learning; Learning to Learn; Learning Transfer; Self-directed Learning; Study and Learning Strategies; The Implications for Educators; Instructional Design: Guidelines and Theories; Instructional Design: Models; Teacher Roles and Teaching Styles; Teaching Methods: Individual Techniques

References

Ackerman P 1989 Individual differences and skill acquisition. In: Ackerman P L, Sternberg R J, Glaser R (eds.) 1989 *Learning and Individual Differences.* Freeman, New York

Anastasi P 1958 *Differential Psychology.* Macmillan, New York

Anastasi P 1970 On the formation of psychological traits. *Am. Psychol.* 25: 899–910

Balke-Aurell G 1982 *Changes in Ability as Related to Educational and Occupational Experience.* Acta Universitatis Gothoburgensis, Goteborg

Baron J, Sternberg R J 1987 *Teaching Thinking Skills.* Freeman, New York

Ben-Chaim D, Homang R T, Lappan G 1988 The effect of instruction on spatial visualization skills of middle school boys and girls. *Am. Educ. Res. J.* 25(1): 51–71

Boekaerts M 1987 Situation-specific judgments of a learning task versus overall measures of motivational orientation. In: De Corte E, Lodewijks H, Parmentier R, Span P (eds.) 1987 *Learning and Instruction. European Research in an International Context*, Vol. 1. Pergamon Press, Oxford

Boekaerts M 1988 Emotion, motivation, and learning. *Int. J. Educ. Res.* 12(3): 227–345

Brophy J E, Everston C M 1981 *Student Characteristics and Teaching.* Longman, New York

Budoff M 1987 The validity of learning potential assessment. In: Lidz C S (ed.) 1987

Calfee R C 1982 Cognitive models of reading: Implications for assessment and treatment of reading disability. In: Malatesha R N, Aaron P G (eds.) 1982 *Reading Disorders: Varieties and Treatments.* Academic Press, New York

Campione J C, Brown A L 1987 Linking dynamic assessment with school achievement. In: Lidz C S (ed.) 1987

Campione J C, Brown A L 1990 Guided learning and transfer: Implications for approaches to assessment. In: Frederiksen N, Glaser R, Lesgold A, Shafto M (eds.) 1990

Carroll J B 1993 *Human Cognitive Abilities.* Cambridge University Press, Cambridge

Case R, Bereiter C 1984 From behaviorism to cognitive behaviorism to cognitive development: Steps in the evolution of instructional design. *Instructional Science* 13: 141–58

Case R, Edelstein W (ed.) 1993 *The New Structuralism in Cognitive Development: Contributions to Human Development*, Vol. 23. Karger, Basel

Cattell R B 1971 *Abilities: Their Structure, Growth and Action.* Houghton Mifflin, Boston, Massachusetts

Chipman S F, Segal J W, Glaser R (eds.) 1985 *Thinking and Learning Skills*, Vol. 2. Erlbaum, Hillsdale, New Jersey

Cole M 1985 Mind as a cultural achievement: Implications for I Q testing. In: Eisner E (ed.) 1985 *Learning and Teaching the Ways of Knowing.* National Society for the Study of Education, Chicago, Illinois

Corno L 1986 The metacognitive control components of self-regulated learning. *Contemp. Educ. Psychol.* 11(4): 333–46

Corno L, Snow R E 1986 Adapting teaching to individual differences among learners. In: Wittrock M C (ed.) 1986 *Handbook of Research on Teaching.* Macmillan, New York

Cronbach L J 1957 The two disciplines of scientific psychology. *Am. Psychol.* 12: 671–84

Cronbach L J, Snow R E 1977 *Aptitudes and Instructional Methods: A Handbook for Research on Interactions.* Irvington, New York

De Corte E, Verschaffel L 1987 Children's problem-solving skills and processes with respect to elementary arithmetic word problems. In: De Corte E, Lodewijks H, Parmentier R, Span P (eds.) 1987 *Learning and Instruction. European Research in an International Context*, Vol. 1. Pergamon Press, Oxford

DeLeeuw L, Van Daalen H, Beishuizen J J 1987 Problem-solving and individual differences: Adaptation to and assessment of student characteristics by computer-based instruction. In: De Corte E, Lodewijks H, Parmentier R, Span P (eds.) *European Research in an International Context*, Vol. 1. Pergamon Press, Oxford

Demetriou A, Efklides A 1987 Towards a determination of the dimensions and domains of individual differences in cognitive development. In: De Corte E, Lodewijks H, Parmentier R, Span P (eds.) 1987 *Learning and Instruction. European Research in an International context,* Vol. 1. Pergamon Press, Oxford

Detterman D K, Sternberg R J (eds.) 1982 *How and How Much Can Intelligence Be Increased.* Ablex, Norwood, New Jersey

Dochy F R C 1992 *Assessment of Prior Knowledge as a Determinant for Future Learning.* Uitgeverij Lemma B V, Utrecht

Dweck C S, Leggett E L 1988 A social-cognitive approach to motivation and personality *Psychol. Rev.* 95(2): 256–73

Entwistle N 1987 Explaining individual differences in school learning. In: De Corte E, Lodewijks H, Parmentier R, Span P (eds.) 1987 *Learning and Instruction: European Research in an International Context*, Vol. 1. Pergamon Press, Oxford

Eysenck H J, Eysenck M W 1985 *Personality and Individual Differences: A Natural Science Approach.* Plenum Press, New York

Ferguson G A 1954 On learning and human ability. *Canadian Journal of Psychology* 8: 95–112

Ferguson G A 1956 On transfer and the abilities of man. *Canadian Journal of Psychology* 10: 121–31

Ferguson-Hessler M G M, deJong T 1990 Studying physics texts: Differences in study processes between good and poor performers. *Cognition and Instruction* 7(1): 41–54

Feuerstein R 1979 *The Dynamic Assessment of Retarded Performers: The Learning Potential Assessment Device, Theory, Instruments, and Techniques.* University Park Press, Baltimore, Maryland

Feuerstein R, Rand Y, Jensen M R, Kaniel S, Tzuriel D 1987 Prerequisites for assessment of learning potential: The LPAD model. In: Lidz C S (ed.) 1987

Fisher C W, Berliner D C (eds.) 1985 *Perspectives on Instructional Time.* Longman, New York

Flammer A 1975 *Individual Unterschiede im Lernen*. Beltz Verlag, Weinheim

Frederiksen J R, Warren B M 1987 A cognitive framework for developing expertise in reading. In: Glaser R (ed.) 1987 *Advances in Instructional Psychology*, Vol. 3. Erlbaum, Hillsdale, New Jersey

Frederiksen N, Glaser R, Lesgold A, Shafto M 1990 *Diagnostic Monitoring of Skill and Knowledge Acquisition*. Erlbaum, Hillsdale, New Jersey

Gelman R, Greeno J G 1989 On the nature of competence: Principles for understanding in a domain. In: Resnick L B (ed.) 1989 *Knowing, Learning, and Instruction: Essays in Honor of Robert Glaser*. Erlbaum, Hillsdale, New Jersey

Glaser R 1977 *Adaptive Education: Individual Diversity and Learning*. Holt, Rinehart and Winston, New York

Glaser R, Bassok M 1989 Learning theory and the study of instruction. *Annu. Rev. Psychol.* 40: 631–66

Guilford J P 1959 *Personality*. McGraw-Hill, New York

Guilford J P 1967 *The Nature of Human Intelligence*. McGraw-Hill, New York

Gustafsson J-E 1984 A unifying model for the structure of intellectual abilities. *Intelligence* 8: 179–203

Gustafsson J-E, Balke-Aurell G 1989 General and special abilities in the prediction of school achievement. (Unpublished manuscript, University of Goteborg)

Gustafsson J-E, Demetriou A, Efklides A 1989 Organization of cognitive abilities: Training effects. Paper presented at the European Association for Research on Learning and Instruction, Madrid

Hidi S 1990 Interest and its contribution as a mental resource for learning. *Rev. Educ. Res.* 60: 549–71

Horn J L 1978 Human ability systems. In: Baltes P B (ed.) 1978 *Lifespan Development and Behavior*, Vol. 1. Academic Press, New York

Hummel-Rossi B 1981 Aptitudes as predictors of achievement moderated by teacher effect. *Measuring Human Abilities: New Directions for Testing and Measurement*. 12: 59–86

Jäger A O 1984 Intelligenzstrukturforschung: Konkurrierende Modelle, neue Entwicklungen, Perspektiven *Psychol. Rundsch.* 35(1): 21–35

Kanfer R, Ackerman P L 1989 Motivation and cognitive abilities: An integrative/aptitude-treatment interaction approach to skill acquisition. *J. Appl. Psychol. Monogr.* 74(4): 657–90

Keefe J W 1987 *Learning Style Theory and Practice*. National Association of Secondary School Principals, Reston, Virginia

Klauer K J 1990 Paradigmatic teaching of inductive teaching. In: Mandl et al. (eds.) 1990 *Learning and Instruction: European Research in an International Context*. Pergamon Press, Oxford

Kuhl J 1990 Self-regulation: A new theory for old applications. Invited address to the International Congress of Applied Psychology, Kyoto

Kyllonen P C, Christal R E 1990 Reasoning ability is (little more than) working-memory capacity? *Intelligence* 14(4): 389–433

Kyllonen P C, Lohman D F, Woltz D J 1984 Componential modeling of alternative strategies for performing spatial tasks. *J. Educ. Psychol.* 76(6): 1325–45

Lajoie S P 1986 Individual differences in spatial ability: A computerized tutor for orthographic projection tasks. (Unpublished doctoral dissertation, Stanford University, Stanford, California)

Lens W 1983 Achievement motivation, test anxiety, and academic achievement. *Psychol. Rep.*

Lens, W, DeCruyenaere M 1991 Motivation and de-motivation in secondary education: Student characteristics. *Learning and Instruction*. 1(2): 145–59

Lepper M R 1988 Motivational considerations in the study of instruction. *Cognition and Instruction* 5: 289–309

Lepper M R, Aspinwall L C, Mumme D L Chabay R W 1990 Self-perception and social perception processes in tutoring: Subtle social control strategies of expert tutors. In: Olson J, Zanna M P (eds.) 1990 *Self Inference Processes: The Ontario Symposium*, Vol. 6. Erlbaum, Hillsdale, New Jersey

Leushina A M (ed.) 1991 *Soviet Studies in Mathematics Education, Vol. 4: The Development of Elementary Mathematical Concepts in Preschool Children*. National Council of Teachers of Mathematics, Reston, Virginia

Lidz C S (ed.) 1987 *Dynamic Assessment*. Guilford Press, New York

Lohman D F 1986 Predicting mathemathanic effects in the teaching of higher-order thinking skills. *Educ. Psychol.* 21(3): 191–208

Lohman D F 1989 Human intelligence: An introduction to advances in theory and research. *Rev. Educ Res* 59(4): 333–73

MacIver D J, Stipek D J, Daniels D H 1991 Explaining within-semester changes in student effort in junior high school and senior high school courses. *J. Educ. Psychol.* 83(2): 201–11

Marton F, Hounsell D, Entwistle N 1984 *The Experience of Learning*. Scottish Academic Press, Edinburgh

Mayer R E 1985 Mathematical ability. In: Sternberg R J (ed.) 1985b

McCombs B L, Whisler J S 1989 The role of affective variables in autonomous learning. *Educ. Psychol.* 24(3): 277–306

McKay H, Sinisterra L, McKay A, Gomez H, Lloreda P 1978 Improving cognitive ability in chronically deprived children. *Science* 200(4339): 270–78

Meili R 1981 *Struktur der Intelligenz: Faktorenanalytische und denkpsychologische Untersuchungen*. Huber, Bern

Nenniger P 1987 How stable is motivation by contents? In: De Corte E, Lodewijks H, Parmentier R, Span P (eds.) 1987 *Learning and Instruction: European Research in an International Context*, Vol. 1. Pergamon Press, Oxford

Nickerson R S, Perkins D N, Smith E E 1985 *The Teaching of Thinking*. Erlbaum, Hillsdale, New Jersey

Ohlsson S 1984a Attentional heuristics in human thinking. *Proc. 6th Conf. Cognitive Science Society*. Boulder, Colorado

Ohlsson S 1984b Induced strategy shifts in spatial reasoning. *Acta Psychol.* 57: 47–67

Pask G, Scott B C E 1972 Learning strategies and individual competence. *International Journal of Man-Machine Studies* 4(3): 217–53

Perfetti C A 1985 *Reading Ability*. Oxford University Press, New York

Pervin L A, Lewis M 1978 *Perspectives in Interactional Psychology*. Plenum Press, New York

Peterson P, Wilkinson L C, Hallinan M (eds.) 1984 *The Social Context of Instruction: Group Organization and Group Processes*. Academic Press, New York

Rand P, Lens W, Decock B 1989 *Negative Motivation is Half the Story: Achievement Motivation Combines Positive* and Negative Motivation. Report No. 2. Institute for Educational Research, University of Oslo

Renninger K A, Hidi S, Krapp A (eds.) 1992 *The Role of Interest in Learning and Development*. Erlbaum, Hillsdale, New Jersey

Resnick L B 1987 *Education and Learning to Think*. National Academy Press, Washington, DC

Resnick L B, Omanson S F 1987 Learning to understand arithmetic. In: Glaser R (ed.) 1987 *Advances in Instructional Psychology*. Erlbaum, Hillsdale, New Jersey

Rollett B A 1987 Effort avoidance and learning. In: DeCorte E, Lodewijks H, Parmentier R, Span P (eds.) 1987 *Learning and Instruction: European Research in an International Context*, Vol. 1. Pergamon Press, Oxford

Salomon G, Globerson T 1987 Skill may not be enough: The role of mindfulness in learning and transfer. *Int. J. Educ. Res.* 11(6): 623–37

Schmeck R R (ed.) 1988 *Learning Strategies and Learning Styles*. Plenum Press, New York

Schneider W, Weinert F E (eds.) 1990 *Interactions Among Aptitudes, Strategies, and Knowledge in Cognitive Performance*. Springer-Verlag, New York

Segal J W, Chipman S F, Glaser R (eds.) 1985 *Thinking and Learning Skills*, Vol. 1. Erlbaum, Hillsdale, New Jersey

Siegler R S, Campbell J 1990 Diagnosing individual differences in strategy choice procedures. In: Frederiksen N, Glaser R, Lesgold A, Shafto M (eds.) 1990

Simons P R J, Beukhof G (eds.) 1987 *Regulation of Learning*. Instituut voor Onderzoek van Het Onderwijs SVO, The Hague

Snow R E 1977 Research on aptitudes: A progress report. In: Shulman L S (ed.) 1977 *Rev. of Research in Education*, Vol. 4. Peacock, Itasca, Illinois

Snow R E 1982 Education and intelligence. In: Sternberg R J (ed.) 1982 *Handbook of Human Intelligence*. Cambridge University Press, London

Snow R E 1989 Aptitude–treatment interaction as a framework for research on individual differences in learning. In: Ackerman P L, Sternberg R J, Glaser R (eds.) 1989 *Learning and Individual Differences: Advances in Theory and Research*. Freeman, New York

Snow R E 1992 Aptitude theory: Yesterday, today, and tomorrow. *Educ. Psychol.* 27(1): 5–32

Snow R E, Lohman D F 1984 Toward a theory of cognitive aptitude for learning from instruction. *J. Educ. Psychol.* 76: 347–76

Snow R E, Lohman D F 1989 Implications of cognitive psychology for educational measurement. In: Linn R L (ed.) 1989 *Educational Measurement*, 3rd edn. Macmillan, New York

Snow R E, Swanson J 1992 Instructional psychology: Aptitude, adaptation, and assessment *Annu. Rev. Psychol.* 43: 583–626

Stanley J C, Stanley W C, Solono C H (eds.) 1978 *Educational Programs and Intellectual Prodigies*. Johns Hopkins University, Baltimore, Maryland

Stanley J C, Benbow C P 1983 *Academic Precocity, Aspects of its Development*. Johns Hopkins University, Baltimore, Maryland

Sternberg R J 1985a *Beyond IQ: A Triarchic Theory of Human Intelligence*. Cambridge University Press, Cambridge

Sternberg R J (ed.) 1985b *Human Abilities: An Information Processing Approach*. Freeman, New York

Tiedeman J 1989 Measures of cognitive styles: A critical review. *Educ. Psychol.* 24: 261–75

Undheim J O, Gustafsson J-E 1989 Development of broad and narrow factors of intelligence as a function of verbal interests and activities. Paper presented at the European Association for Research on Learning and Instruction, Madrid

Van Calster K, Lens W, Nuttin J 1987 Affective attitude toward the personal future: Impact on motivation in high school boys. *American Journal of Psychology* 100(1): 1–13

Webb N M 1982 Group composition, group interaction, and achievement in cooperative small groups. *J. Educ. Psychol.* 74: 475–84

Weinert F E, Schneider W (eds.) 1991 *The Munich Longitudinal Study on the Genesis of Individual Competencies (LOGIC) Report No. 7: Assessment Procedures and Results of Wave Four*. Max-Planck-Institute for Psychological Research, Munich

Yakimanskaya I S 1991 *Soviet Studies in Mathematics Education, Vol. 3: The Development of Spatial Thinking in School Children*. National Council of Teachers of Mathematics, Reston, Virginia

Learning by Contract

A. D. Rose

Contract learning has grown in acceptance over the past twenty years. While by no means universally accepted, this approach to learning merges several streams of thought. On one level it represents a profound effort to shift authority and responsibility for learning from bureaucracies to individuals, but it also embodies much of the research on the individualization of learning that took place in the 1960s. Both of these strands are connected to research on self-directed learning, learning-how-to-learn and changing models of reflective practice.

1. Definition and Models of Contract Learning

At its simplest level a learning contract is an agreement drawn up between two persons (usually a learner and an instructor) that stipulates what learning is to be attained (learning objectives); how these objectives are to be reached (learning resources and strategies); the completion date; what evidence will be provided that objectives have been met; and the criteria for judging this evidence (Knowles 1986).

Behind this rather vague definition, contract learning is often put forward as an important innovation which could play a role in changing educational institutions. In North America, in particular, the use of the contract was initially seen as a way of individualizing higher education and allowing for greater student–faculty contact while also establishing a framework for the provision of a more meaningful educational experience.

1.1 Approaches to Contract Learning

According to Knowles (1986 p.39), "Contract learning is, in essence, an alternative way of structuring a learning experience: It replaces a content plan with a process plan. Instead of specifying how a body of content will be transmitted (content plan), it specifies how a body of content will be acquired by the learner (process plan)."

There are three types of contract learning: contracting for grades; contracting for one component of study within a traditional program (independent study); and contracting for a complete educational experience or program. In all of these a legalistic (but not legally binding) contract stipulates all aspects of the learning enterprise and each participant enters it with a surer understanding of expectations (Berte 1975).

Contracting for grades is the least nontraditional of the three types. Involving an agreement between the student and instructor about the kind and amount of work required in order to achieve a particular grade, such a contract represents an attempt to make the evaluation process more explicit and fair, while allowing the instructor to retain complete autonomy in evaluating and constructing the learning experience. The key to this type of contract is the level of learning attained and the relationship that this has to the awarding of a particular grade. While related to what is usually included within the traditional North American course syllabus, a contract for grades permits students to understand the grading process and to work towards a particular grade rather than simply completing all requirements and waiting to see what grade will be awarded. In nursing, for example, which is an area which seems to have adopted many aspects of contract learning, students may opt for passing a course at a safe level of practice or they may choose to carry out supplementary activities for a higher grade (McFarland 1983).

The second kind of contract focuses on independent study. Dressel and Thompson (1973 p.1) define independent study as ". . . the student's self-directed pursuit of academic competence in as autonomous a manner as he is able to exercise at any particular time." Independent study is both a goal and a technique

(see *Self-directed Learning*). Historically, independent study was developed in the 1920s for honor students. Today it is seen as a means for allowing students to develop their own topics of inquiry, while working collaboratively with a faculty member. Advocates maintain that even when incorporated within a traditional college program, independent study still allows students to control their learning experience.

Finally, independent study may serve as the foundation for an entire degree program. Not only will a student contract for a particular course, but the entire curriculum will be contracted. Students and advisers will devise their own requirements and will implement these through a variety of strategies. Such programs are based on attitudes towards the learner and especially the adult learner which were popularized in the 1970s. Students are considered to be self-directing and skilled in the task of organizing and planning their own learning. If they are not, then a significant part of their learning task may be to gain the skills necessary to continue.

1.2 Examples of Contract-based Degree Programs

Within higher education, individualization and contract learning grew in the 1970s. While many colleges now regularly include an option of a nontraditional degree, the number of institutions that are primarily committed to such an approach are few. Empire State College (ESC), a part of the State University of New York is one institution that has been able to sustain its mission until the present. ESC is entirely contract-based. Students develop their own programs of study with a faculty mentor and they write contracts for each individual component. Students may choose to take a traditional course or they may write an individualized learning contract with either a faculty member or outside expert. ESC embodies several of the advantages seen to accrue to the contract-based institution. It offers flexibility of access, a broad use of community resources, and the possibility of independent study, all of which can be important to adults. Initially the founders of ESC examined alternative approaches, especially the plans for the Open University in the United Kingdom (see *Open University*). It was decided however that while issues of access were important and the mode of presentation exciting, the basic premises surrounding the organization of knowledge was not innovative enough. The contract model allowed for greater flexibility and more learner control over the curriculum (Hall and Bonnabeau 1993).

Another model, this one in graduate study, has been tried within an Adult Education graduate program at Teachers College, Columbia University. While the development of the degree program itself is more limited with the Adult Education Guided Independent Study (AEGIS) program than at Empire State College, the program does try to allow for flexibility in each component through the development of individual

learning contracts. The purpose is to help participants develop their own self-direction. This is done
by helping students change their perception of the
learning process; transferring responsibility for the
design, conduct and evaluation of their own learning
to the participants; facilitating the growth and critical
abilities; and assisting participants in becoming aware
of the theoretical contexts of problems in the field
and promoting interest and skills in disciplined inquiry
(Bauer 1985).

In both of these programs, problems have surfaced
because the level of self-direction has never lived up
to what was expected. Findings for programs such
as these report that students have differing needs for
structure and their competencies in learning strategies
vary profoundly (see *Study and Learning Strategies*).
It does not necessarily follow that because an adult is
successful in a job that he or she will have the skills
necessary to take advantage of this type of learning
environment (Bauer 1985, Rose 1988).

1.3 Professional Training and Contract Learning

An interesting phenomenon has been the adoption
of contract learning in specific areas of professional
training. Of these nursing seems to have embraced
facets of contract learning most completely and in
fact is found in countries outside of North America.
Nursing education, like other professional fields, was
profoundly influenced by the behavioristic approach
to the design of learning processes. This not only
focused on the particular skills or competencies to be
acquired, but formulated a particular learning methodology laying out the process of this acquisition. In
the 1980s, a more humanistic approach gained favor,
focusing on the development of the whole person. But
this approach still needed to be cognizant of the need
for specific skills. The contract appears to be one
way that nursing educators are balancing both of these
concerns (Byrnes 1986, Sutcliffe 1993). Reactions
among nursing students often varied. Some found the
process difficult, while others found it exhilarating.
As with the overall degree programs, researchers have
found that the contract approach, precisely because it
individualizes, is extremely labor intensive and what
were once adequate workloads become onerous. This
issue has been addressed repeatedly at all levels in
which contract learning have been used (Richardson
1987, Hall and Bonnabeau 1993).

The use of contract learning in individual professional courses serves several functions. It allows
students to pursue their own interests in greater depth
than an instructor would normally require. It gives
students some control over what is being and allows
them some choices, even within the most formally
structured programs. Additionally it allows for greater
synthesis and integration of knowledge. While there is
some evidence that students gain in their ability to synthesize information, what little research has been done

in this area indicates that in fact students do not gain in
self-directedness simply by engaging in contract study
(Caffarella and Caffarella 1986, Waltho 1987).

2. Contract Learning—Conceptual Framework

Contract learning is usually placed within a matrix of
connected issues concerned with what has come to be
called nontraditional education. Nontraditional education is defined as a "... set of learning experiences
free of time and space limitations" (Hartnett 1972
p.14). Many different methods and approaches have
been developed but they all share a common emphasis
on what the student knows and not where or how it is
learned (Cross and Valley 1974).

The nontraditional approach embodies many different methods and formats such as: individualization
through the use of learning modules, contract learning, and cassette instruction; credit for prior learning;
proficiency examinations; distance learning; and external degree programs. The Open University in the
United Kingdom is an example of an institution
that pioneered the promulgation of many of these
innovations, including distance education, the use of
small groups, and individual tutorials. There is, however, little individualization of the curriculum itself
(Campbell 1984).

Part of the rationale for introducing these innovations is the democratization of education; that is the
expansion of higher education beyond its traditional
base. Yet many of these approaches have proved to
most applicable to adults who are seeking to continue
their education while facing many social, financial,
and time constraints. In particular contract learning
frees institutions dealing with adults from some of
the constraints of the traditional classroom while encouraging independent study and the enhancement of
self-directed learning skills.

2.1 Individualizing the Curriculum

One of the driving forces behind the growth of contract
learning was the growth of interest in individualizing
education at all levels, but particularly higher education. Individualization has become a principal component of educational reform since the 1960s. Musgrave
wrote in 1975, "Complete individualization is a goal
for educators much as democracy is a goal for Americans or Christianity a goal for Christians."(p.x)

Despite the near universal acceptance of the goal
of individualization for all educational levels, there
is little agreement on its means or how it should
be operationalized. For some individualized education must include some aspect that is at least in
part self-initiated and self-directed. Any educational intervention would be appropriate here because
the emphasis is on student participation and choice
(Hodgkinson 1975).

For others, particularly educators of children, individualization has come to mean the adoption of a particular technique within the context of a traditionally-organized curriculum. This often means adapting teaching approaches to particular student learning styles, backgrounds, or interests. Such adaptations also frequently include the development or use of computer-assisted instruction where students can follow a set curriculum, but proceed at their own pace.

In addition to the cognitive issues affecting the individualization of the curriculum, this movement also embraces political concerns. For some educators, individualization is a means of transferring power from a bureaucratic institution to students and faculty. Such a transfer involves a reassessment of traditional disciplinary distinctions and of the very structure of knowledge itself. Thus students create their own meaning from material, make their own connections and embark on a personal and meaningful intellectual journey (Feeney and Riley 1975).

2.2 Individualizing the Curriculum in Adult Education

Many of the basic premises of adult education are congruent with the movement to individualize the curriculum. According to Malcolm Knowles (1986 p.43) who popularized the North American definition of andragogy as the "art and science of teaching adults," certain assumptions can be made about adult learners and these assumptions call for a radically different approach to structuring adult learning situations (see *Andragogy*). Indeed, according to Knowles, (1986 p.41) contract learning is an approach, the ". . . most congruent with the assumptions about learners on which the andragogical model is based." These include:

1. Learners need to understand why they need to learn something;
2. Learners have a need to be self-directing;
3. Learners' need to take their experiences and background into account;
4. Learning needs to be oriented to each individual's life situation and readiness to learn;
5. Learning needs to be organized around life tasks or problems; and
6. Learning needs to draw from the learners's intrinsic motivations.

Knowles' interest in contract learning shifts some of the intellectual emphasis of this approach. While a transfer of authority is still the principal objective, the purpose is no longer a redefinition of knowledge, but rather the development of a method for personal development. Thus the scope becomes somewhat more limited.

3. Conclusion

Contract learning has grown in popularity in recent years. It has particularly taken hold in certain aspects of professional education and within continuing professional education. Within these spheres, however, the wider potential of student control over objectives has sometimes been lost. Instead the focus has often been on how students can achieve pre-stated objectives in a meaningful fashion. These approaches often embrace facets of humanistic and experiential education, but they fail to address the broader political issues related to a complete transfer of responsibility for the learning process. To a large extent proponents have underestimated the difficulty of helping individuals become self-directed students. Contract education has proven to be an interesting technique, but its efficacy, particularly in terms of the broader implications need to be more carefully researched.

See also: Adult Learning: An Overview; Environments for Learning; Experiential and Open Learning; Self-directed Learning; Study and Learning Strategies

References

Bauer B 1985 Self-directed learning in a graduate adult education program. In: Brookfield S (ed.) 1985 *Self-Directed Learning: From Theory to Practice*. New Directions for Continuing Education, No. 25 Jossey-Bass, San Francisco, California.
Berte N R 1975 Individualizing education through contracting. In: Berte N R (ed.) *Individualizing Education through Contract Learning*. The University of Alabama Press, Tuscaloosa, Alabama
Byrnes A K 1986 Bridging the gap between humanism and behaviorism in nursing education. *Journal of Nursing Education* 25 (7): 304–305
Caffarella R S, Caffarella E P 1986 Self-directedness and learning contracts in adult education. *Adult Educ. Q.* 36 (4): 226–234
Campbell D D 1984 *The New Majority: Adult Learners in the University*. The University of Alberta Press, Edmonton, Alberta
Cross K P, Valley J R 1974 Non-traditional study: an overview. In: Cross K P et al. (eds.) 1974 *Planning Non-traditional Programs*. Jossey-Bass, San Francisco, California
Dressel P, Thompson M M 1973 *Independent Study: New Interpretations of Concepts, Practices, and Problems*. Jossey-Bass, San Francisco, California
Feeney J, Riley G 1975 Learning contracts and New College, Sarasota, In: Berte N R (ed.) 1975 *Individualizing Education through Contract Learning*. The University of Alabama Press, Tuscaloosa, Alabama
Hall J, Bonnabeau R 1993 Empire State College. Important Lessons from Innovative Colleges and Universities. *New Directions in Higher Education* 82 (Summer): 55–66
Hartnett R T 1972 Non-traditional study: An overview. In Gould S B, Cross K P (eds.) 1972 *Explorations in Non-traditional Study*. Jossey-Bass, San Francisco, California

Hodgkinson H I 1975 Evaluation of individualized learning. In: Berte N R (ed.) 1975 *Individualizing Education through Contract Learning*. The University of Alabama Press, Tuscaloosa, Alabama

Knowles M 1986 *Using Learning Contracts*. Jossey-Bass, San Francisco, California

McFarland M B 1983 Contract grading: An alternative for faculty and students. *Nurse Educator* 8 (4): 3–6

Musgrave G R 1975 *Indivualized Instruction: Teaching Strategies Focusing on the Learner*. Allyn and Bacon, Boston, Massachussetts

Richardson S 1987 Implementing contract learning in a senior nursing practicum. *Journal of Advanced Nursing* 12: 201–206

Rose A D 1988 The individualized bachelor's degree: some reconsiderations. *Innov. Higher Educ.* 13 (1): 38–46

Sutcliffe L 1993 Leaps of knowledge. *Nursing Times* 89 (42): 34–36

Waltho B T 1987 Contract learning—a students' perspective. *Senior Nurse* 7 (6): 28–29

Further Reading

Candy P C 1991 *Self-direction for Lifelong Learning: A Comprehensive Guide to Theory and Practice*. Jossey-Bass, San Francisco, California

Hiemstra R, Sisco B 1990 *Individualizing Instruction: Making Learning Personal, Empowering, and Successful*. Jossey-Bass, San Francisco, California

Learning in the Workplace

J. Lowyck

This entry reviews briefly the following topics: (a) organizational characteristics and goals; (b) theories of informal learning at work; (c) conceptions of training and development; and (d) training methods and supportive learning environments. These issues evidently are interdependent since environment, human behavior, and behavioral change or learning are strongly interconnected. As industry is influenced by multiple and fast changes in the social, political, ethical, technological, demographical, cultural, and ecological domains, rapid and complex evolutions within industry itself constantly occur, which necessitate corresponding high-level behaviors of individuals and groups. This, in turn, requires increased training and organizational strategies focused on optimal learning output.

1. Organizational Characteristics and Learning

Developing and maintaining competitiveness, managing human capital, optimizing organizational structures, restructuring work, maximizing use of technology, creating effective work environments, improving products and services are all required for the survival of modern industry (Offermann and Gowing 1990). While many routine or repetitive tasks have decreased at the workplace, more complex tasks are left to the employee who needs a more elaborated conceptual framework about the task environment and higher-order cognitive activities (Howell and Cooke 1989). Undoubtedly, evolutions within industrial settings highly influence learning needs, learning processes, and support for learning. If one focuses on learning in industrial settings, it is necessary to consider the complex environment in which both learning and training take place. The training–learning model, then, depends on several characteristics of the organization, such as the availability of a qualified workforce, type of tasks to be executed, personnel and financial conditions for learning support, organizational goals, predictability and constancy of job execution, and training as a management tool. Romiszowski (1990), for example, distinguished the following models of a work organization and the concomitant training requirements.

In a "production-line" model the line manager is equally a trainer who demonstrates the task execution, observes and corrects the trainee's actions, and measures and controls the trainee's performance. It is an apprenticeship-like training. Productivity criteria are derived from extended task analyses defined by means of work studies and meticulous time measurement. Training is highly formulated in terms of lower-level tasks and routinization.

As a result of mechanization and automation the number of repetitive, high-speed manufactory and assembly tasks drastically shrinks. Additionally the multidimensionality of the industrial organization in terms of the participation by workers, job mobility among managers, internationalization, and greater public ownership of industry all necessitate a better preparation of executive staff in order to manage the workforce. Instead of a "production-line" model, a "humanistic" model is promoted, which perceives any organization as the cooperative effort of workers and management toward the attainment of common organizational goals. Optimizing the use of human resources capital and raising social skillfulness become main functions of management training. However, as Goldstein (1980) observed, "managers only utilized skills developed in training when the organizational climate was favorable" (p.233).

414

The isolation of individual training efforts from the organization together with the lack of measurement of training effectiveness give rise to an "organization" model. As an answer to the estimated ineffectiveness of management training, organization development starts from a commitment of the top management. By first drawing up a plan for the organization as a whole, goals are subsequently derived for all subparts of the organization. At any level teams and quality circles focus on reaching the organizational goals. Training within this perspective is a very practical, job-related, and process-oriented endeavor. Moreover, in order to keep a "competitive edge" corporations can no longer afford to tolerate suboptimal performance of their human capital and they originate efforts to assess organizational performance carefully. Using performance technology as a strategy, the causes of any under-performance of individuals and groups on specific tasks are diagnosed and multifaceted solutions implemented, such as job redesign, altered reward systems, new information systems, and other recruitment and selection methods (Geis 1986). Training is no longer the exclusive solution for perceived performance shortage.

The introduction of information technology in almost all sectors of industry encourages not only better performance of existing tasks, but even the creation of new activities as a consequence of knowledge handling. It is the "knowledge" model that is now most dominant. As computers take over an increasing part of routine, the focus is on higher-order cognitive processes, such as problem-finding, problem-solving, and decision-making. The metaphor of a "learning organization" has become a powerful perspective on learning in industrial settings, referring to the complex interaction of organization, training, and learning aiming at both innovative processes and the maintenance of identity (see Senge 1990, Pedler et al. 1991).

2. Learning Theories

Although research in educational psychology may be expected to contribute to the foundation of training and development in industrial settings, it has been observed by most reviewers that very little integrative literature is available to work with since both domains exist side by side. Understanding learning theories, however, is essential for any training design and development if at least a systematic and controllable approach is aimed at. Though learning models and theories are developed independently from organizational models, they nevertheless show interesting common characteristics.

2.1 Behaviorist Conceptions

Behaviorist conceptions of learning have been for a long time predominant in training development (Howell and Cooke 1989). Observable behavior is tied to environmental stimuli using reinforcement as the main paradigm. Learning requires the sequential mastery of behavioral elements. Therefore, complex knowledge or skills are subdivided into smaller parts and success in each step of the learning process is conditional for further progress. It is assumed that the accumulation of partial facts and skills can lead to the mastery of more encompassing domain knowledge and skills. Howell and Cooke (1989) observed that "the predominant educational philosophy underlying today's training programs derives from the behavioristic tradition that dominated the psychology of learning until the 1960s" (p.123). When tasks for job execution required relatively limited cognitive activity, and usable tools were available for validating training programs, this strict empiricism was not perceived as a handicap, and some demonstrably successful programs have evolved. The mere use of behaviorist learning principles, however, caused both conceptual and pragmatic problems in contexts involving higher cognitive demands. This forced those responsible for training to accept the importance of cognitive processing in most of the learning processes.

2.2 Cognitive-oriented Conceptions

Cognitive-oriented training conceptions emphasize the continuous and complex interaction between learner characteristics (prior knowledge, cognitive and metacognitive strategies), complex and context-bound tasks, cognitively powerful learning environments, and assessment of learning outcomes in terms of learner control or self-regulation, (meta-) cognitive activity, and transfer. Instead of being seen as a series of elementary subprocesses, learning is conceived in terms of information-processing, interpretation of new information, and reorganization of knowledge by the learner. Moreover, the context or situation is intrinsically part of any learning activity. Learning, within this view, is active, constructive, cumulative, self-regulated, and goal-oriented (Shuell 1986).

"Integrated," "situated," or "active" knowledge highly corresponds with the actual needs of industry since employees need to understand their own behaviors in effectively dealing with complex situations, taking simultaneously technological, organizational, and business aspects into account. This is process-oriented learning and not simply product-oriented learning in terms of isolated outcomes connected to a peculiar situation or task. Knowledge can no longer be perceived as the sum of isolated skills but as a "proactive" competency, oriented toward yet unforeseen situations and tasks (Nyhan 1991). This evidently refers to the problem of transfer.

2.3 Transfer of Training

Training undoubtedly aims at providing usable and adaptive knowledge and skills for future use. However, mainly due to difficulties of measurement, transfer in industrial settings is not well studied. In training for transfer, a distinction is often made between near and far transfer. Near transfer occurs when performance on the job meets the criteria of the task and the setting defined by the training. Far transfer requires the trainee to use learned skills for tasks and settings that differ highly from the training context. As Clark and Voogel (1985) contended, the dilemma is that when one acquires a near-transfer skill it seems to be at the expense of far-transfer generalizability of that skill. Indeed, most training in industrial settings focuses more on procedural and near transfer than on declarative and far transfer, though the importance of far transfer is acknowledged by almost all those responsible for training. This problem of inconsistency increases when emphasis is laid on on-the-job training for specific tasks, since learning of specific procedures on the job is highly contextualized which consequently inhibits transfer (see *Learning Transfer*).

The outcomes of transfer can be studied from three different angles: (a) the similarity of "the source" and "target" situation (identical elements hypothesis); (b) the significance of general strategies for transfer; and (c) support of transfer by situated cognition. The behaviorist approach of the identical-elements approach raises problems. First, not the surface or objective similarity between "the source" and "the target" is important but the similarity as perceived by the trainee. A second problem is the difficulty of an alignment of the learning context with the functional context due to both the different functions and constraints of both situations and the difficulty of determining exactly all task features of a functional context. Considering the general strategies as defined in the so-called key qualifications, the assumption is that the new requirements of the target situation can be met by means of general or domain-undependent strategies (Mandl et al. 1991). In the case of situated cognition, transfer only takes place under the condition that the learned knowledge and skills are decontextualized by sequencing principles, emphasis on multiple perspectives, and cooperation between trainees and trainers. Examples of methods of training for transfer in industrial settings are the "learning workbench," the "cooperative self-qualification," the "autodidactic learning at the workplace," and "project-oriented learning" (see Mandl et al. 1991).

3. Training and Development: Evolution of the Field

In the *Annual Review of Psychology* an interesting series of reviews on training and development has appeared which reflects the evolution of the domain (Campbell 1971, Goldstein 1980, Wexley 1984, Latham 1988, Tannenbaum and Yukl 1992). Two main observations are the shift from the training of observable behavior to more encompassing, cognitive activities, and the gradual integration of (re-) training efforts in the organization as a whole.

In an early review, Campbell (1971) showed pessimism about the theoretical and empirical basis of training and human resource development: "By and large, the training and human resource development literature is voluminous, nonempirical, nontheoretical, poorly written, and dull" (p.565). In his recommendations, he focused on systematic behavior changes that can result from a systems approach, behavior modification methods, programmed instruction, and differential evaluation techniques.

Goldstein (1980) contended that "while the vast majority of writing in this area is not empirical, theoretical, or thoughtful, there is a small but increasingly significant literature that focuses on important issues" (p.262). In his opinion, more emphasis needs to be given to needs assessment techniques, creative development of evaluation models, embedding training in the organization, and empirical investigations that examine the usefulness of training techniques.

Wexley (1984) pointed to an increasing research effort: since Goldstein's review "much research on training and development has taken place. Training is here defined as a planned effort by an organization to facilitate the learning of job-related behavior on the part of its employees" (p.519). He referred to the shift from training to retraining, mainly due to the impact of new technologies. Moreover, training is not a stand-alone activity, but is highly influenced by internal organizational variables and the changing outside environment. While training currently is designed for well-defined tasks, this becomes problematic since there is a need for open and context-bound competencies and for complex skills in supervision and management. Training is no more perceived in terms of behavioral change, but as the multiplicative result of an individual's ability and motivation.

Latham (1988) restricted his review to scholarly journals. He described the following developments. First, training is increasingly linked to the business strategy of firms. Realizing compatibility between the training plan and the business plan is the responsibility of top management. Second, there is a shift from an almost exclusive focus on the training needs of the individual employees to that of the training needs of specific target groups and work teams. Third, training has become less determined by the job-specific behaviors of workers and more by their cognitive abilities and judged learning potential. Finally, in terms of content there is now more attention for learning in and about other cultures.

Tannenbaum and Yukl (1992) examined whether insights contributed by cognitive and instructional psychology were being used in the design of training programs. They noted in particular that effective training depends not only on the training program itself but also on pre- and posttraining environments.

4. Training Methods and Learning Environments

Campbell (1988) pointed to the unavailability of precise training guidelines based on well-validated training principles. However, he remarked that the usual practice in industrial training could gain efficiency if the following guidelines were used as heuristics for organizing training: (a) consistency between training methods and learning processes; (b) activation of the trainee in order to reach the required performance level; (c) use of all available sources of feedback; (d) enhancement by instructional processes of the trainee's self-efficacy and self-confidence; and (e) adaptation of training methods to differences in aptitudes and prior knowledge.

Reviewing off-site training, several methods have been elaborated and their effectiveness measured. Campbell (1988) noted that most studies involve comparisons of one single method with another method or with a control condition with no training. However, it has been shown that the effectiveness of a training method is dependent upon training purposes, characteristics of trainees, and effectiveness criteria used. Reviewing more specific training methods, Tannenbaum and Yukl (1992) concluded that: "In summary, some of the same concerns can be expressed regarding the research on simulations, high-technology methods and behavior modeling. Each training method has demonstrated some utility, but more research is needed to determine the types of content for which a training method is appropriate and to discover how different aspects of the training method affect training outcomes" (p.412).

The emphasis on off-site training reveals another problem. Training decisions often focus on short-term effects, claiming that this is quicker, more productive, and more cost-effective. In this case, training is organized in settings that cause training programs to precede, interrupt, conflict with, or follow learning that occurs on the job (see Gery 1989). In short, this kind of training is seldom "just-in-time."

The importance of on-the-job or on-site training is claimed by many companies and it constitutes an important part of the total training effort. In the literature the findings on effectiveness of on-the-job training are often contradictory. Sometimes it is asserted that in the workplace skills are learned faster, retained longer, and result in greater productivity gains than skills learned in classroom settings. Others, on the contrary, contend that on-the-job training is less effective than off-site training. One of the reasons for this controversy is the fact that the unstructured form of on-the-job training often serves as a control condition. It seems as if the criticism about the measurement of effectiveness in off-site training expressed by Tannenbaum and Yukl (1992) applies to studies of on-site training as well. The need for a precise identification of the main dimensions of any training context and function is clear.

5. Conclusion

This review of learning in industrial settings reveals the complexity of the domain. First, learning and training issues focus on the discrepancy between the expected competencies of employees and their actual competence. If there is a mismatch between necessary knowledge, skills, and attitudes, training and learning support seem necessary. Second, training is dependent upon the overall strategy of an industrial organization and it represents only one possibility to solve an organizational problem since other measures such as selection, career development, reward systems, job redesign, and high-technology support are likely to be important for reaching organizational aims. Third, despite some progress in more basic research, mostly in the domain of cognitive psychology, there is a lack of instrumentation of adapted training methods. Indeed, most training design is still embedded in a behaviorist approach for off-site training contexts. Fourth, a developmental approach of learning and training is lacking. In no study are the transition steps from a highly structured environment toward an open environment covered; nor is the adaptation of the environment to the aptitudes of trainees taken seriously. These are consequences of the narrow scope of most training decisions, which focus on one specific type of training. Seldom are combinations of methods and contexts studied, such as systematic support of on-the-job training or explicit trainee-controlled off-site training. Lastly, research on training and development is often blurred by literature of a nonempirical character and there is a lack of conceptual frameworks for communication and cooperation between researchers and practitioners in the field of industrial training.

See also: Training on the Job; Adult Learning: An Overview; Job and Task Analysis; Program Design: Effectiveness; Evaluation of Industry Training: Cost-Effectiveness; Measurement of Industry Training

References

Campbell J P 1971 Personnel training and development. *Annu. Rev. Psychol.* 22: 565–602

Campbell J P 1988 Training design for performance improvement. In: Campbell J P, Campbell R J 1988 *Productivity in Organizations: New Perspectives from Industrial and Organizational Psychology*. Jossey-Bass, San Francisco, California

Clark R E, Voogel A 1985 Transfer of training principles for instructional design. *Educ. Comm. & Tech. J.* 33(2): 113–25

Geis G L 1986 Human performance technology: An overview. In: Smith M E (ed.) 1986 *Introduction to Performance Technology*. National Society for Performance and Instruction, Washington, DC

Gery G J 1989 Training vs. performance support: Inadequate training is now insufficient. *Performance Improvement Quarterly* 2: 51–71

Goldstein I L 1980 Training in work organizations. *Annu. Rev. Psychol.* 31: 229–72

Howell W C, Cooke N J 1989 Training the human information processor: A review of cognitive models. In: Goldstein I L et al. (eds.) 1989

Latham G P 1988 Human resource training and development. *Annu. Rev. Psychol.* 39: 545–82

Mandl H, Prenzel M, Gräsel 1991 The problem of transfer in vocational training. Paper presented at the Fourth European Conference for Research on Learning and Instruction, University of Turku

Nyhan B 1991 *Developing People's Ability to Learn: European Perspectives on Self-learning Competency and Technological Change.* European Interuniversity Press, Brussels

Offermann L R, Gowing M K 1990 Organizations of the future: Changes and challenges. *Am. Psychol.* 45(2): 95–108

Pedler M, Burgoyne J, Boydell T 1991 *The Learning Company: A Strategy for Sustainable Development.* McGraw-Hill, London

Romiszowski A J 1990 Trends in corporate training and development. In: Mulder M, Romiszowski A J, van der Sijde P C (eds.) 1990 *Strategic Human Resource Management.* Swets and Zeitlinger, Amsterdam

Senge P M 1990 *The Fifth Discipline: Mastering the Fine Practices of the Learning Organization.* Doubleday, New York

Shuell T J 1986 Cognitive conceptions of learning. *Rev. Educ. Res.* 56(4): 411–36

Tannenbaum S I, Yukl G 1992 Training and development in work organizations. *Annu. Rev. Psychol.* 43: 399–441

Wexley K N 1984 Personnel training. *Annu. Rev. Psychol.* 35: 519–51

Further Reading

Goldstein I L et al. (eds.) 1989 *Training and Development in Organizations.* Jossey-Bass, San Francisco, California

Patrick J 1992 *Training: Research and Practice.* Academic Press, London

Resnick L B 1991 Situations for learning and thinking. Address presented at the Annual Meeting of the American Educational Research Association, Chicago, Illinois

Learning to Learn

R. M. Smith

Long proposed as a major goal for formal education, learning to learn has increasingly become an object of systematic inquiry and experimentation. While much of the expanding body of relevant information pertains to the pre-adult years, the emphasis here is on learning to learn in adulthood.

1. Definition

Learning to learn is understood to be a complex, lifelong process—or a constellation of processes—through which people acquire and modify their skills and capacities for knowledge acquisition, problem-solving, and the extraction of meaning from experience. It refers to learning about learning itself. Conceptually, the idea subsumes the more specific notion of "metacognition" ("knowing about knowing" or "thinking about thinking").

There is no consensus definition of "learning to learn" (nor of "learn how to learn," a frequently used alternative term). Candy (1990) defines it discursively as follows:

(a) It is a developmental process in which people's conceptions of learning evolve and become consciously available to systematic analysis and review.

(b) It involves the acquisition of a repertoire of attitudes, understandings, and skills that allow people to become more effective, flexible, and self-organized learners in a variety of contexts.

(c) It occurs both prior to, and coincidental with, learning endeavors.

(d) It may be enhanced through processes of formal schooling and the way in which the curriculum is constructed and is therefore a viable—perhaps crucial—objective for educational systems at all levels.

(e) It involves entering into the deep meaning structures of material to be learned and, in its most advanced forms, may lead to critical awareness of assumptions, rules, conventions, and social expectations that influence how people perceive knowledge and how they think, feel, and act when learning.

(f) It has both generic and context-specific components.

(g) It is a multidimensional entity whose meaning varies according to the meaning given to the word learning. (pp. 34–35)

An unresolved issue of definition is the relationship between learning to learn and "critical reflection." Mezirow et al. (1990) states that critical reflection, or critical reflectivity, is a process of testing the validity or justification of one's "taken-for-granted premises" and that adult educators have a special responsibility for its fostering and for helping learners plan to take action. The process is said to involve becoming open to alternative perspectives, recognizing and questioning one's implicit assumptions, and becoming less fearful of change: "becoming reflective of the content, process, and especially the premises of one's prior learning is central to cognition for survival in modern societies" (p. 375). Brookfield (1990 p. 332) posits "reflecting on reflections" as the "same kind of psychological processes as learning to learn." However, there appears to be some danger here of a reductionist point of view that may vitiate the impact of an overall concept of learning to learn that accommodates to such disparate matters, among many, as study skills enhancement, training for independent or collaborative learning, and enhancing holistic learning capacity. There clearly is more to learning to learn than becoming critically reflective.

2. How People Learn to Learn

Learning to learn is a matter of both aptitude and personal experience, and people can typically be said to learn to learn in a relatively haphazard manner. From in-school and out-of-school experience, people constantly acquire new information and behaviors. While so engaged, they gradually develop personal learning strategies and personal knowledge about the optimum conditions for learning. Each person develops a concept of "self-as-learner." The learning to learn process is understood as haphazard because it results not so much from deliberate interventions on the part of teachers or trainers to improve learning capacity and performance as from personal interpretations over time of learning-related experience. These interpretations often prove dysfunctional as far as becoming an active, flexible, confident learner in a variety of contexts is concerned. Hence the growing interest in the deliberate enhancement of learning capacities, dispositions, and strategies through such means as curriculum planning, instruction, and training (Candy 1990).

One perspective on the issue of how people learn to learn comes from identifying what are believed to be the most important factors leading to effectiveness in lifelong learning. Among these there is considerable agreement about the importance of awareness, reflection, and self-monitoring. The three concepts exhibit an interactive and mutually re-enforcing relationship. "Awareness" refers to insight into self-as-learner and to understandings about education, learning, and learning-related processes.

Effective learners are usually able to describe their preferred ways of taking in and processing information or receiving instruction and undergoing evaluation as well as their preferred environments for learning (i.e., their learning styles). They tend to be more aware of their motives, purposes, and goals for learning. They understand that to learn may be variously to memorize pieces of information, to acquire knowledge for practical application, to abstract meaning from experience, or even to re-interpret reality. They are sensitive to a difference between learning and being taught. They possess reasonably accurate perceptions of the extent of their knowledge and their capabilities. They are also aware of the in- and out-of-school opportunities and resources for learning available to them, which are relatively rich in most industrialized societies. It has also been shown to be useful for the individual to develop something of a sophisticated concept of knowledge, one that acknowledges differences between official, unofficial, and personal knowledge and all that have value—that a person may think relativistically about one domain of knowledge and narrowly or rigidly about others, and that many problems have more than one "correct" answer. People thus learn to learn more effectively as they develop awareness as learners. Self-monitoring and reflection drive this development.

3. Facilitation

Facilitation takes two primary forms: either (a) building a learning to learn dimension into programming and instruction—for example, teaching a subject from a learning to learn stance and perspective; or (b) designing and conducting distinct, discrete events aimed at learning proficiency enhancement—such as a workshop on coping with examinations or on group problem-solving strategies. The latter type of intervention is frequently labeled "training." Approaches and resources for facilitation are discussed in Smith (1982) and Gibbs (1981, 1992).

Facilitators are usually advised to expect resistance and difficulties in helping people to externalize, examine, and modify assumptions and habits related to learning, study, and knowledge. It is recommended that they (a) find ways to make process training palatable and understandable; (b) maintain a climate conducive to behavioral change; (c) carefully adapt approaches and materials to different audiences; and (d) seek ways of continually strengthening activeness, self-awareness, and reflection in learning (Smith 1982, 1992)

Hammond (1990) describes and evaluates five comprehensive approaches for enhancing effectiveness in learning and states that such programs are likely to be effective and gain acceptance to the extent that they include a credible theoretical base, undergo field testing and evaluation, provide practice and application activity and support in the employment of new behaviors, make available useful materials for both facilitator and learner, and provide training for facilitators if needed.

The role of the facilitator in problem-based learning (Barrows and Tamblyn 1980) has been carefully analyzed and described in Barrows (1988), the principal advocate of an approach intended to place active, independent learning and problem-solving at the center of medical education and continuing education for physicians. Meeting in small groups with a "tutor," participants work at simulated problems drawn from everyday practice:

> The tutor . . . facilitates student learning through guidance at the meta-cognitive level. . . . It is the tutor's expertise in this process, not in the content areas in which the students are studying, that is important. The students are expected to acquire the knowledge they need from content experts . . . who serve as consultants, as well as books, journals, and automated information sources. . . . The tutor guides the students through repeated practices in reasoning and self-directed study, improved through their increasing skills in self-assessment. Although the tutor may be more directive initially and closely models the reasoning processes and information seeking processes he hopes the students will acquire, he eventually withdraws from the group as they learn to take on responsibility for their own learning. (p. 50)

Among the facilitative strategies employed by the tutor with this approach are modeling, climate setting, the asking of probing questions, suggesting resources, challenging group members to substantiate their statements, concensus testing, monitoring of group members' educational progress, and "interventions necessary to maintain an effective group process in which all contribute" (p. 20). Problem-based learning has also been applied in corporate training and faculty development as well as business, professional, and liberal arts courses in higher education institutions (see *Group Learning*).

4. Methods and Applications

There has been considerable interest in the feasibility of helping people to learn more meaningfully—to move from a superficial or "surface" approach (e.g., rote memorization) to the learning of subject matter toward a so-called "deep" approach that results in better understanding of what is learned. Research in several countries has found the use of the surface approach to be common in courses with heavy workloads, little opportunity for in-depth pursuit, little learner input into topics or methodology, and anxiety-producing assessment systems. Those who employ a deep approach understand more and produce superior written work, remember better, and receive higher marks than those employing a surface approach (Gibbs 1992).

A comprehensive national study in the United Kingdom, the "Improving Student Learning Project," identified nine elements which foster a deep approach. The elements, with some examples of appropriate methods are as follows: (a) encouraging independent learning (learning contracts); (b) supporting personal development (intensive group work); (c) presenting problems (exploring "real world" issues); (d) encouraging reflection (learning diaries or journals); (e) independent group work (peer tutoring); (f) learning by doing (simulations, games); (g) helping learners become more aware of task demands and purposes for learning; (h) project work (individual or group); and (i) fine tuning—minor modifications of conventional methods (making lectures more "interactive").

The above elements emerged from case studies of innovation projects undertaken by volunteer instructors of conventional and extramural courses at 10 colleges under the leadership of the Oxford Centre for Staff Development, which now offers faculty training workshops and consultation to academic departments and institutions. The project demonstrated that significant improvements in the quality of student learning are possible within existing course restraints through appropriate modifications in instructional design and delivery. Optimum results require comprehensive changes involving staff teams, appropriate staff development activity, and usually a modification of assessment systems (Gibbs 1992).

Successful applications of the learning to learn concept in North American colleges and universities are described in Schlossberg et al. (1989). A few institutions have undertaken to integrate learning to learn philosophy and related activity into either the overall college curriculum or in special baccalaureate degree programs for the "returning student." Among these are Alverno College (Milwaukee) and Depaul University (Chicago). Almost 80 percent of 2,600 higher education institutions surveyed in 1985 reported offering a credit or noncredit course on the topic of coping with college—employing such methods as support groups, diagnostic instruments, self-assessment, training in self-monitoring, and autobiographies describing learning experiences. In some instances, substantially superior academic performances of course participants have been documented through research as well as positive effects on intellectual, interpersonal, political, and civic development. In addition, most institutions maintain learning centers or academic support services for students seeking to improve competence in learning.

5. Fostering Autonomy in Learning

The acquisition of learning strategies, listening and viewing comprehension, and the fostering of autonomy and self-direction in learning are among the topics investigated at the Center for Research and Pedagogical Applications at the University of Nancy, France. Holec (1985) states the following with regard to self-direction and autonomy in learning (an "autonomization" process):

> The acquisition of autonomy by the learner is the fundamental goal in the C.R.A.P.E.L. approach, and it is important

to underline from the outset that it is a tendency, a dynamic process with a future, not a stable condition, something which develops—hence the neologism "autonomization." This process can be seen from three different points of view: From the point of view of the learner, it is a matter of acquiring those capacities which are necessary to carry out a self-directed learning programme. From the point of view of the teacher, it is a matter of determining those types of intervention which are conducive to the learner's acquiring those capacities. From the institutional point of view, it is a matter of creating those conditions which allow the learner and the teacher to put these aims into practice. (p. 180)

The necessary learner competencies have been found to lay in the defining of objectives, content, materials, and techniques; defining the place, time, and pace of learning; and evaluating what one has learned. Since very few people possess such knowledge and skill, it becomes necessary to learn to learn—a process requiring a radical change in the role of the learners and their perception of that role. Individuals need to be disabused of the notion that they can learn only from experts and usually have to modify their notion of what learning is. Considerable self-examination is involved.

Teachers foster the autonomization process by providing two kinds of support "continuously adapted to the learner's state at any given moment" (Holec 1985 p. 184): technical support and psychosocial support. The former involves providing help as needed in the learner's analysis and making of instrumental decisions and the surfacing of personal "theory" informing one's actions (e.g., in choice of objective, learning resource, or strategy). Psychosocial support takes the form of encouraging learners' commitment to the acquisition of autonomy and to the gradual development of the requisite confidence and skills. Among the potential problems are allowing the learner to become overly dependent on the teacher and the providing of more or less support than is needed. Like the learners, the teachers usually have to examine or modify their conceptions of teaching and learning.

6. *Learning to Learn in the Workplace*

Interest in learning to learn in the workplace stems from such factors as increased concern for organizational productivity, organizational renewal, and the role of managers as learners and teachers. Mumford (1986 p. 8) carefully examined programs and publications in the area of learning to learn for managers in the United Kingdom and the United States, citing, among others, such potential benefits as the following:

(a) an increase in the capacity of individuals to learn;

(b) a reduction in the frustration of being exposed to inefficient learning processes;

(c) an increase in motivation to learn;

(d) development of learning opportunities well beyond formally created situations;

(e) a multiplier effect for the manager in his or her developmental relationship with his or her subordinates;

(f) the reduction of dependence on an instructor;

(g) the provision of processes which carry through beyond formal programs into on-the-job learning;

(h) the better identification of the role of learning in effective managerial behavior, for example, in problem-solving or team work;

(i) the development of more effective behavior in relation to the crucial subject of change.

Mumford (1986) concluded, however, that the capacity to learn effectively is not a priority for most managers and that learning to learn should be integrated with something they are concerned with, such as developing a specific competence. He found relatively little treatment of the topic of the manager as learner and even less concerning how managers learn to learn, but remained convinced that organizations and human resource personnel cannot afford to ignore this area. Mumford also identified some key factors influencing learning to learn—job content, motivation and personal blockages to learning, influence of superiors and subordinates, and organizational climate—and he provided examples of different approaches to helping managers to learn more effectively.

Marsick (1990) advocates wider use of action learning programs such as those developed at Sweden's Management Institute in Lund in order to foster critical reflectivity, suggesting that these are superior to the quality circles for this purpose. Small group problem-solving workshops through projects linked to taking action on organization-specific issues are central to action learning.

Some publications describe and discuss the broader topic of the relevance of learning to learn initiatives directed to all levels of personnel in the organization and ways to foster development of the "learning organization" (Cheren 1987, 1990, Argyris 1982). Learning to learn efforts include study strategy workshops and interactive video courses; orientation to in-house and outside educational opportunities; and the establishment of corporate learning centers for help with personal learning projects, self-assessment, and answers to reference questions.

Cheren (1990) sees learning to learn applications in the workplace as processes to be built into the formal training activities (e.g., enhancing strategies required for a particular course) and, perhaps more important, a dimension of day-to-day activity. Human resource and training professionals are urged to take the lead in improving problem-solving by individuals and work-station groups, establishing in-house learning resource centers, supporting the employee's personal development plans, and designing record keeping and evaluation systems that credit and reward informal and formal efforts to learn. He suggests "learning management" as a preferred conceptual rubric in the workplace.

7. Conclusion

The viability and utility of the concept of learning to learn now appears to be reasonably well-established despite the complexities of the phenomena involved and the challenges posed by implementation. It seems likely that teaching and learning and learning to learn will henceforth tend to be understood as interacting and interdependent processes. People learn to learn effectively through educational experiences and training that result in flexibility and awareness as well as the development of a repertoire of appropriate strategies for various learning contexts. Self-monitoring and reflective capacities tend to govern people's development as learners and problem-solvers. Theory regarding the facilitation of learning capacities is emerging from research and experience in a variety of contexts, and useful training resources and techniques are becoming available. Dissemination of this information needs to become more systematic and widespread.

See also: Adult Learning: An Overview; Approaches to Learning; Experiential and Open Learning; Learning in the Workplace; Learning Transfer

References

Argyris C 1982 *Reasoning, Learning, and Action: Individual and Organizational*. Jossey-Bass, San Francisco, California

Barrows H S, Tamblyn R M 1980 *Problem-Based Learning: An Approach to Medical Education*. Springer, New York

Barrows H S 1988 *The Tutorial Process*. Southern Illinois School of Medicine, Springfield, Illinois

Brookfield S D 1990 Expanding knowledge about how we learn. In: Smith R M (ed.) 1990

Candy P 1990 How people learn to learn. In: Smith R M (ed.) 1990

Cheren M 1987 *Learning Management: Emerging Direc-*
tions for Learning to Learn in the Workplace. National Center for Research in Vocational Education, Ohio State University, Columbus, Ohio

Cheren M 1990 Prompting active learning in the workplace. In: Smith R M (ed.) 1990

Gibbs G 1981 *Teaching Students to Learn*. Open University Press, Milton Keynes

Gibbs G 1992 *Improving the Quality of Student Learning*. Technical and Educational Services, Bristol

Hammond D 1990 Designing and facilitating learning-to-learn activities. In: Smith R M (ed.) 1990

Holec H 1985 Autonomous learning schemes: Principles and organization. In: Riley P (ed.) 1985 *Discourse and Learning: Papers in Applied Linguistics and Language Learning from the CRAPEL*. Longman, London

Marsick V J 1990 Action learning and reflection in the workplace. In: Mezirow J et al. 1990

Mezirow J et al. 1990 *Fostering Critical Reflection in Adulthood*. Jossey-Bass, San Francisco, California

Mumford A 1986 Learning to learn for managers. *J. European Industrial Training* 10(2): 3–28

Schlossberg N K, Lynch A Q, Chickering A W 1989 *Improving Higher Education Environments for Adults: Responsive Programs and Services From Entry to Departure*. Jossey-Bass, San Francisco, California

Smith R M 1982 *Learning How to Learn: Applied Theory for Adults*. Cambridge University Press, New York

Smith R M 1992 Implementing the learning to learn concept. In: Tuijnman A C, Van Der Kamp M (eds.) *Learning Across the Lifespan: Theories, Research, Policies*. Pergamon Press, Oxford

Further Reading

Boud D J, Keogh R, Walker D (eds.) 1985 *Reflection: Turning Experience into Learning*. Kogan, London

Brown A 1987 Metacognition, executive control, self-regulation and other more mysterious mechanisms. In: Weinert F E, Kluwe R H (eds.) 1987 *Metacognition, Motivation and Understanding*. Lawrence Erlbaum Associates, Hillsdale, New Jersey

Cell E 1984 *Learning to Learn From Experience*. State University of New York Press, Albany, New York

Novak J D, Gowin D B 1984 *Learning How to Learn*. Cambridge University Press, New York

Smith R M (ed.) 1988 *Theory Building for Learning How to Learn*. Educational Studies Press, Northern Illinois University, Department of Leadership and Educational Policy Studies, DeKalb, Illinois

Smith R M (ed.) 1990 *Learning to Learn Across the Lifespan*. Jossey-Bass, San Francisco, California

Learning Transfer

D. N. Perkins and G. Salomon

Transfer of learning occurs when learning in one context or with one set of materials impacts on performance in another context or with other related materials. For example, learning to drive a car helps a person later to learn more quickly to drive a truck, learning mathematics prepares students to study physics, learning to get along with one's siblings may prepare one for better interaction with others, and experience in playing chess might conceivably make a person a better strategic thinker in politics or business. Transfer is a key concept in education and learning theory because most education and training aspires to transfer. Usually the context of learning (classrooms, exercise books, tests, simple streamlined tasks) differs markedly from the ultimate contexts of application (in the home, on the job, within complex tasks). Consequently, the ends of education and training are not achieved unless transfer occurs. Transfer is all the more important in that it cannot be taken for granted. Abundant evidence shows that very often the hoped-for transfer from learning experiences does not occur. Thus, the prospects and conditions of transfer are crucial issues for school and adult education.

1. Transfer Defined

1.1 Transfer versus Ordinary Learning

In a sense, any learning requires a modicum of transfer. To say that learning has occurred means that the person can display that learning later. Even if the subsequent situation is very similar, there will be some differences, perhaps time of day or the physical setting. Thus, no absolute line can be drawn between ordinary learning and transfer.

However, transfer only becomes interesting as a psychological and educational phenomenon in situations where the transfer would not be thought of as ordinary learning. For example, an adult learner may show certain grammar skills on an English test (ordinary learning) but not in everyday speech (the hoped-for transfer). The student may solve the problems at the end of the chapter (ordinary learning) but not similar problems when they occur mixed with others at the end of the course (the hoped-for transfer). In other words, talk of transfer is always at least implicitly contrastive: it assumes learning within a certain context and asks about impact beyond that context.

1.2 Positive versus Negative Transfer

Positive transfer occurs when learning in one context improves performance in some other context. For instance, speakers of one language find it easier to learn related than unrelated second languages. Negative transfer occurs when learning in one context impacts negatively on performance in another. For example, despite the generally positive transfer among related languages, contrasts of pronunciation, vocabulary, and syntax generate stumbling blocks. Learners commonly assimilate a new language's phonetics to crude approximations in their native tongue and use word orders carried over from their native tongue.

While negative transfer is a real and often problematic phenomenon of learning, it is of much less concern to education than positive transfer. Negative transfer typically causes trouble only in the early stages of learning a new domain. With experience, learners correct for the effects of negative transfer. From the standpoint of education in general, the primary concern is that desired positive transfers occur. Accordingly, the remainder of this entry focuses on positive transfer.

1.3 Near versus Far Transfer

Near transfer refers to transfer between very similar contexts, as for instance when distance learners taking an exam face a mix of problems of the same kinds that they have practiced separately in their homework, or when a garage mechanic repairs an engine in a new model of car, but with a design much the same as in prior models. Far transfer refers to transfer between contexts that, on appearance, seem remote and alien to one another. For instance, a chess player might apply a basic strategic principle such as "take control of the center" to investment practice, politics, or a military campaign. It should be noted that "near" and "far" are intuitive notions that resist precise codification. They are useful in broadly characterizing some aspects of transfer but do not imply any strictly defined metric of "closeness."

2. Prospects of Transfer

As noted above, transfer is especially important to learning theory and educational practice, since very often the kinds of transfer hoped for do not occur. The classic investigation of this phenomenon was conducted by the renowned educational psychologist E L Thorndike in the first decades of the twentieth century. Thorndike examined the proposition that studies of Latin disciplined the mind, preparing people for better performance in other subjects. Comparing the performance in other academic subjects of students who had taken Latin with those who had not, Thorndike (1923) found no advantage whatsoever in Latin studies. In other experiments, Thorndike and Woodworth (1901) sought, and generally failed to find, positive impact of one sort of learning on another. Thorndike concluded that transfer depended on "identical elements" in two performances and that most performances were simply too different from one another for much transfer to be expected. In terms of the rough near–far distinction, near transfer is much more likely than far transfer.

Thorndike's early disturbing findings have resurfaced repeatedly in other investigations. For instance, the advent of computer programming gave rise to the notion that computer programming developed general problem-solving skills, much as Latin was thought to cultivate mental discipline. Unfortunately, several experiments seeking a positive impact of learning to program on problem-solving and other aspects of thinking yielded negative results (see Pea and Kurland 1984, Salomon and Perkins 1987).

Another learning experience that might be thought to impact broadly on cognition is literacy, the mastery of reading and writing. Wide-ranging transfer might be expected from experience with the cognitive demands of reading and writing and the cognitive structures that text carries. However, Scribner and Cole (1981) reported a study of an African tribe, the Vai, with an indigenous form of writing not accompanied by schooling. Using a variety of general cognitive instruments, they found no differences between Vai who had mastered this script and others who had not. They argued that the impact of literacy depends on immersion in diverse activities surrounding literacy, not on acquisition of reading and writing per se. The Vai only employed their script in a very specific way, in contrast with the diverse uses of literacy apparent in many cultures (see *Anthropological Study of Literacy and Numeracy*).

For yet another example, researchers have looked for transfer effects between puzzles or games that are isomorphs of one another, sharing the same logical structure but presented or described in very different physical terms. For example, some research has focused on the well-known Tower of Hanoi puzzle, which requires moving three (or more) rings of different sizes between three pegs according to certain rules. One isomorph involves a story about three extraterrestrial monsters, each holding a crystal globe of a different size. The rules for the monsters passing the globes to one another are logically equivalent to the rules for moving the disks from peg to peg.

It is not clear whether study of problem isomorphs should be regarded as near or far transfer, because isomorphs are nearly identical structurally but very different in external trappings. In any case, subjects usually do not recognize the connection between one isomorph and the other and hence do not carry over strategies they have acquired while working with one to the other. However, if the relationship is pointed out, then the learners can transfer strategies fruitfully (Simon and Hayes 1977).

While the preponderance of results concerning transfer appears to be negative, it is important to recognize that occasional positive findings have appeared. For instance, Clements and Gullo (1984) and Lehrer et al. (1988) achieved positive transfer from engagement in LOGO computer programming to certain cognitive measures, including measures of divergent thinking. Brown (1989) reported a series of studies showing positive transfer by preschool children of abstract concepts, for instance the idea of stacking objects to climb on to reach something, or the idea of mimicry as a defense mechanism in animals. Campione et al. (1991) report that when children are taught to self-monitor

and self-direct themselves during reading in what has been called "reciprocal teaching," this transfers also to learning in other text-mediated areas of learning such as social studies and mathematics. Salomon et al. (1989) showed that students can transfer from a computer program designed to make them more strategic readers to their performance a while later on in writing, suggesting that what the students acquired was transferable tendencies to self-monitor and self-direct.

3. Transfer and Local Knowledge

Near transfer seems to have much better prospects than far transfer. Not only does this trend appear in the empirical findings, but it also makes sense in terms of contemporary research on "expertise." Since the 1970s, a number of investigators have built a case for the importance of "local knowledge" (with knowledge taken in a broad sense to include skills, concepts, propositions, etc.). In areas as diverse as playing chess, problem-solving in physics, and medical diagnosis, expert performance has been shown to depend on a large knowledge base of a rather specialized kind (see Ericsson and Smith 1991). General cross-domain principles, it has been argued, play a rather weak role. In the same spirit, some investigators have urged that learning is highly situated, that is, finely adapted to its context (Brown et al. 1989, Lave 1988) (see *Environments for Learning*).

A strong local knowledge position would predict little far transfer under any conditions, because knowledge in one context would not be very relevant to others. However, the research on expertise does not really bear this assumption out: the importance of local knowledge does not imply the unimportance of rather general knowledge that works in conjunction with local knowledge (Perkins and Salomon 1989). Moreover, the idea of situated learning does not necessarily imply that the prospects of transfer are limited. Greeno et al. (1993) offer a situated learning view of transfer in which transfer depends on similar opportunities for action across situations that may be very different superficially. In sum, a monolithic local knowledge position is difficult to sustain.

4. Conditions of Transfer

Positive findings of transfer, both near and far, suggest that it is too simplistic merely to ask whether transfer occurs. It can, but often does not; the important question is under what conditions transfer appears.

4.1 Thorough and Diverse Practice

The question of literacy may be considered once more. In a classic study of the impact of literacy and education in the former Soviet Union, Luria (1976) found major influence on a number of cognitive measures. His results concerned a population where reading and writing played multiple roles. The contrast between Luria's and Scribner and Cole's findings suggests that transfer may depend on extensive practice of the performance in question in a variety of contexts. This yields a flexible, relatively automatized bundle of skills easily evoked in new situations.

4.2 Explicit Abstraction

Transfer sometimes depends on whether learners have abstracted critical attributes of a situation. In one demonstration, Gick and Holyoak (1980, 1983) presented subjects with a problem story that allowed a particular solution. From subjects who solved the problem, they elicited what the subjects took to be the underlying principle. They then presented the subjects with another, analogous problem that invited a similar approach. Those subjects who had the fullest and soundest basic grasp of the principle for the first puzzle were most successful with the second. These and other results suggest that explicit abstractions of principles from a situation foster transfer.

4.3 Active Self-monitoring

Similarly, metacognitive reflection on one's thinking processes appears to promote transfer of skills. This contrasts with the explicit abstraction category above, in that abstraction focuses on the structure of the situation whereas self-monitoring focuses on one's own thinking processes. Belmont et al. (1982) undertook a synthesis of a number of efforts to teach retarded persons simple memory strategies and to test whether they would apply these in slightly different contexts. Many of these studies showed no transfer, while a few revealed some. The researchers isolated the factor that appeared to account for success: teaching the subjects not just to apply the strategy but to monitor their own thinking processes in simple ways. Presumably, this activation of self-monitoring helped them later to recognize when they might apply the strategy they had learned.

4.4 Arousing Mindfulness

Mindfulness refers to a generalized state of alertness to the activities one is engaged in and to one's surroundings, in contrast with a passive reactive mode in which cognitions, behaviors, and other responses unfold automatically and mindlessly (Langer 1989). Mindfulness is more encompassing than either explicit abstraction or active self-monitoring, but would have the effect of fostering both.

4.5 Using a Metaphor or Analogy

Transfer is facilitated when new material is studied in the light of previously learned material that serves as an analogy or metaphor. Things known about the "old" domain of knowledge can now be transferred to a "new" domain, thereby making it better understood and learned. For example, students may initially understand the idea of an atom better by thinking of it as a small solar system, or how the heart works by thinking of it as a pump. Of course, most such analogies are limited and need elaboration and qualification.

5. Mechanisms of Transfer

Why do factors of the kind identified above encourage transfer? An answer can best be provided by an examination of the mechanisms of transfer, the psychological paths by which transfer occurs.

5.1 Abstraction

It is still possible to concede Thorndike's point that identical elements underlie the phenomenon of transfer. However, research suggests a more complex picture of how identical elements figure in the process of transfer. An identity that mediates transfer can reside at a very high level of abstraction. Phenomena such as the branching of arteries and that of electrical power networks can evince the same deep principle (the need to deliver something to a region point by point) with great differences in what constitutes a conduit (arteries versus wires) and in what is being carried (blood versus electricity). Such a degree of abstraction helps to account for far transfer, because highly abstract identical elements can appear in very different contexts.

5.2 Transfer by Affordances

Writing from the perspective of situated cognition, Greeno et al. (1993) argue that transfer need not depend on mental representations that apply to the learning and target situations. Rather, during initial learning, the learner may acquire an action schema responsive to the affordances—the action opportunities—of the learning situation. If the potential transfer situation presents similar affordances and the person recognizes them, the person may apply the same or a somewhat adapted action schema there. External or internal representations may or may not figure in the initial learning or the resulting action schema.

5.3 High Road and Low Road Transfer

Two studies (Salomon and Perkins 1989, Perkins and Salomon 1987) synthesized findings concerned with transfer by recognizing two distinct but related mechanisms, the "low road" and the "high road." Low road transfer happens when stimulus conditions in the transfer context are sufficiently similar to those in a prior context of learning to trigger well-developed semiautomatic responses. In keeping with the view of Greeno et al. (1993), these responses need not be mediated by external or mental representations. As a relatively reflexive process, low road transfer figures most often in near transfer. For example, when a person moving house rents a small truck for the first time, they find that the familiar steering wheel, shift, and other features evoke useful car-driving responses. Driving the truck is almost automatic, although it is a different task in several minor ways.

High road transfer, in contrast, depends on mindful abstraction from the context of learning or application and a deliberate search for connections: What is the general pattern? What is needed? What principles might apply? What is known that might help? Such transfer is not in general reflexive. It demands time for exploration and the investment of mental effort. It can easily accomplish far transfer, bridging between contexts as remote as arteries and electrical networks or strategies of chess play and politics. For instance, a person new to politics but familiar with chess might carry over the chess principle of control of the center, pondering what it would mean to control the political center.

In particular cases of transfer, the two roads can work together: some connections can occur reflexively, while others are sought out. In principle, however, the two mechanisms are distinct.

This framework accords well with a number of the points made above. It acknowledges that transfer is sometimes stimulus driven, occurring more or less automatically as a function of frequent and diverse practice (the low road). On the other hand, transfer sometimes involves high levels of abstraction and challenges of initial detection of possible connections (the high road). The framework allows for identical elements in Thorndike's original sense —identities that the organism simply responds to (the low road)—but insists on the importance of identities discovered and exploited by mindful exploration (the high road).

This analysis, along with the views and findings of Luria, Scribner and Cole, Greeno, and others, emphasizes that the conditions for transfer are stringent. Reflexive (low road) transfer requires well-automatized patterns of response that are thus easily triggered by similar stimulus conditions, and it requires stimulus conditions sufficiently similar to prior contexts of learning to act as triggers. Many learning situations offer practice only for a narrow range of examples and not enough practice to achieve significant automaticity, providing a poor basis for reflexive transfer. Mindful (high road) transfer requires active abstraction and exploration of possible connections. Many learning situations do not encourage such mental investments, although people more inclined to mindfulness or metacognition are by definition more likely to make them.

6. Teaching for Transfer

The observations above about mechanism clarify why transfer does not occur as often as would be wished. They also provide guidelines for establishing conditions of learning that encourage transfer.

In many situations, transfer will indeed take care of itself: situations where the conditions of reflexive transfer are met more or less automatically. For example, instruction in reading literacy normally involves extensive practice with diverse materials to the point of considerable automaticity. Moreover, when students encounter reading situations outside of the literacy class—newspapers, books, assembly directions, and so on—the printed page provides an overt stimulus to evoke reading skills.

In contrast, in many other contexts of learning, the conditions for transfer are less propitious. For example, social studies are normally taught with the expectation that history will provide a lens through which to see contemporary events. Yet the instruction all too commonly does not include any actual practice in considering current events from a historical perspective. Nor are learners encouraged to reflect upon the eras they are studying and extract general widely applicable conclusions, or even questions. In other words, the conventions of instruction work against both automatic (low road) and mindful (high road) transfer.

In response to such dilemmas, two broad instructional strategies to foster transfer may be defined: hugging and bridging (Perkins and Salomon 1988). Hugging exploits reflexive transfer. It recommends that instruction directly engage the learners in approximations to the performances desired. For example, a job counselor might engage students in simulated interviews rather than just discussing good interview conduct. The learning experience thus "hugs" the target performance, maximizing the later likelihood of automatic low road transfer.

Bridging exploits the high road to transfer. In bridging, the instruction encourages the formulation of abstractions, searches for possible connections, mindfulness, and metacognition. For example, a job counselor might ask students to reflect on their strengths and weaknesses and devise a plan to highlight the former and downplay the latter in an interview. The instruction thus would emphasize deliberate abstract analysis and planning. Of course, in the example of the job interview, the teachers might employ both hugging and bridging. Instruction that incorporates the realistic experiential character of the former and the thoughtful analytic character of the latter seems most likely to yield rich transfer.

In summary, a superficial look at the broad conclusions drawn by research on transfer is discouraging: the great majority of studies suggest that transfer is not easily achieved. However, a closer examination of the conditions under which transfer does and does not occur and the mechanisms at work presents a more positive picture: education can achieve abundant transfer if it is designed to do so.

See also: Approaches to Learning; Environments for Learning; Individual Differences, Learning, and Instruction; Learning to Learn; Study and Learning Strategies

References

Belmont J M, Butterfield E C, Ferretti R P 1982 To secure transfer of training instruct self-management skills. In: Detterman D K, Sternberg R J (eds.) 1982 *How and How Much can Intelligence be Increased?* Ablex, Norwood, New Jersey

Brown A L 1989 Analogical learning and transfer: What develops? In: Vosniadou S, Ortony A (eds.) 1989 *Similarity and Analogical Reasoning.* Cambridge University Press, New York

Brown J S, Collins A, Duguid P 1989 Situated cognition and the culture of learning. *Educ. Res.* 18(1): 32–42

Campione J C, Brown A L, Reeve R A, Ferrara R A, Palincsar A S 1991 Interactive learning and individual understanding: The case of reading and mathematics. In: Landsmann L T (ed.) 1991 *Culture, Schooling, and Psychological Development.* Ablex, Norwood, New Jersey

Clements D H, Gullo D F 1984 Effects of computer programming on young children's cognition. *J. Educ. Psychol.* 76(6): 1051–58

Ericsson K A, Smith J (eds.) 1991 *Toward a General Theory of Expertise: Prospects and Limits.* Cambridge University Press, Cambridge

Gick M L, Holyoak K J 1980 Analogical problem solving. *Cognit. Psychol.* 12(3): 306–55

Gick M L, Holyoak K J 1983 Schema induction and analogical transfer. *Cognit. Psychol.* 15(1): 1–38

Greeno J G, Smith D R, Moore J L 1993 Transfer of situated learning. In: Detterman D, Sternberg R (eds.) 1993 *Transfer on Trial.* Ablex, Norwood, New Jersey

Langer E J 1989 *Mindfulness.* Addison-Wesley, Reading, Massachusetts

Lave J 1988 *Cognition in Practice: Mind, Mathematics and Culture in Everyday Life.* Cambridge University Press, New York

Lehrer R, Guckenberg T, Sancilio L 1988 Influences of Logo on children's intellectual development. In: Mayer R E (ed.) 1988 *Teaching and Learning Computer Programming: Multiple Research Perspectives.* Erlbaum, Hillsdale, New Jersey

Luria A R 1976 *Cognitive Development.* Harvard University Press, Cambridge, Massachusetts

Pea R D, Kurland D M 1984 On the cognitive effects of learning computer programming. *New Ideas in Psychology* 2(2): 137–68

Perkins D N, Salomon G 1987 Transfer and teaching thinking. In: Perkins D N, Lochhead J, Bishop J (eds.) 1987 *Thinking: The Second International Conference.* Erlbaum, Hillsdale, New Jersey

Perkins D N, Salomon G 1988 Teaching for transfer. *Educ. Leadership* 46(1): 22–32

Perkins D N, Salomon G 1989 Are cognitive skills context bound? *Educ. Researcher* 18(1): 16–25

Salomon G, Globerson T, Guterman E 1989 The computer as a zone of proximal development: Internalizing reading-related metacognitions from a Reading Partner. *J. Educ. Psychol.* 81(4): 620–27

Salomon G, Perkins D N 1987 Transfer of cognitive skills from programming: When and how? *Journal of Educational Computing Research* 3(2): 149–69

Salomon G, Perkins D N 1989 Rocky roads to transfer: Rethinking mechanisms of a neglected phenomenon. *Educ. Psychol.* 24(2): 113–42

Scribner S, Cole M 1981 *The Psychology of Literacy.* Harvard University Press, Cambridge, Massachusetts

Simon H A, Hayes J R 1977 Psychological differences among problem isomorphs. In: Castelan N J, Pisoni D B, Potts G R (eds.) 1977 *Cognitive Theory,* Vol. 2. Erlbaum, Hillsdale, New Jersey

Thorndike E L 1923 The influence of first year Latin upon the ability to read English. *School Sociology* 17: 165–68

Thorndike E L, Woodworth R S 1901 The influence of improvement in one mental function upon the efficiency of other functions. *Psychol. Rev.* 8: 247–61

Further Reading

Cormier S M, Hagman J D (eds.) 1987 *Transfer of Learning: Contemporary Research and Applications,* Academic Press, New York

Detterman D, Sternberg R (eds.) 1993 *Transfer on Trial.* Ablex, Norwood, New Jersey

Vosniadou S, Ortony A (eds.) 1989 *Similarity and Analogical Reasoning.* Cambridge University Press, Cambridge

Self-directed Learning

R. Hiemstra

Most adults spend a considerable time acquiring information and learning new skills. The rapidity of change, the continuous creation of new knowledge, and an ever-widening access to information make such acquisitions necessary. Much of this learning takes place at the learner's initiative, even if available through formal settings. A common label given to such activity is self-directed learning. In essence, self-directed learning is seen as any study form in which individuals have primary responsibility for planning, implementing, and even evaluating the effort. Most people, when asked, will proclaim a preference for assuming such responsibility whenever possible.

Interest in self-directed learning considerably increased around the world during the 1980s. Few topics, if any, have received more attention by adult educators than self-directed learning. Numerous new programs, practices, and resources for facilitating self-directed learning have been created, and many studies have been undertaken. This entry extracts some meaning from all this information.

1. What is Self-directed Learning?

Several things are known about self-directed learning:

(a) Individual learners can become empowered to take increasingly more responsibility for various decisions associated with the learning endeavor.

(b) Self-direction is best viewed as a continuum or characteristic that exists to some degree in every person and learning situation.

(c) Self-direction does not necessarily mean that all learning will take place in isolation from others.

(d) Self-directed learners appear able to transfer learning, in terms of both knowledge and study skill, from one situation to another.

(e) Self-directed study can involve various activities and resources, such as self-guided reading, participation in study and tutorial groups, internships, electronic dialogues, and reflective writing activities.

(f) Effective roles for teachers in self-directed learning are possible, such as dialogue with learners, securing resources, evaluating outcomes, and promoting critical thinking.

(g) Some educational institutions are finding ways to support self-directed study through open learning programs, individualized study options, nontraditional course offerings, and other innovative programs.

This latter component—educational institutions developing innovative responses to self-directed learning preferences—has spawned several unique programming efforts. For example, establishment of the Open University in England in 1969 generated similar efforts around the world. St Francis Xavier University (Antigonish, Nova Scotia), Teacher College (Columbia University, New York City), NOVA Southeastern University's nontraditional doctoral program (Fort Lauderdale, Florida), Syracuse University's Instructional Design Program (Syracuse, New York), and the Ontario Institute for Studies in Education (Toronto, Canada) have incorporated self-directed learning principles into various of their adult education efforts.

These latter two (Syracuse University and Ontario Institute) have assimilated some computer-mediated instruction into their programs.

Brookfield (1986) describes other higher education efforts where individualized, self-directed learning opportunities exist, including locations in Germany, Denmark, and Eastern Europe. Brockett and Hiemstra (1991) describe several self-directed efforts in China, Indonesia, Japan, Norway, Russia, Saudi Arabia, Sweden, and Tanzania. Knowles (1984) describes various self-directed learning efforts in various government, industry, health, religious, and military settings.

1.1 History of Self-directed Learning

Self-directed learning has existed even from classical antiquity. For example, self-study played an important part in the lives of such Greek philosophers as Socrates, Plato, and Aristotle. Other historical examples of self-directed learners include Alexander the Great, Julius Caesar, Erasmus, and Descartes. Social conditions in countries under foreign rule, in Africa, Asia, and even in colonial America, and a corresponding lack of formal educational institutions necessitated that many people learn on their own.

There were early scholarly efforts to understand self-directed learning in the nineteenth-century United States. Craik (1840) documented and celebrated the self-education efforts of several people. About the same time in the United Kingdom, Smiles (1859) published a book entitled *Self-Help*, that applauded the value of personal development.

However, it is since the 1960s that self-directed learning has become a major research area. Groundwork was laid through the observations of Houle (1961). He interviewed 22 adult learners and classified them into three categories based on reasons for participation in learning: (a) goal-oriented learners, who participate mainly to achieve some end goal; (b) activity-oriented learners, who participate for social or fellowship reasons; and (c) learning-oriented learners, who perceive of learning as an end in itself. It is this latter group that resembles the self-directed learner identified in subsequent research (see *Participation: Role of Motivation*).

The first attempt to understand learning-oriented individuals better was made by Tough, a Canadian researcher and one of Houle's doctoral students. His dissertation effort to analyze self-directed teaching activities and subsequent research with additional subjects resulted in a book called *The Adult's Learning Projects* (Tough 1979). This work has stimulated many similar studies with various populations in different locations.

In parallel scholarship during this same period, Knowles popularized in North America the term "andragogy" with corresponding adult instructional processes. His *Self-directed Learning* (1975) provided foundational definitions and assumptions that guided much subsequent research: (a) self-directed learning assumes that humans grow in capacity and need to be self-directing; (b) learners' experiences are rich resources for learning; (c) individuals learn what is required to perform their evolving life tasks; (d) an adult's natural orientation is task- or problem-centered learning; and (e) self-directed learners are motivated by various internal incentives, such as need for self-esteem, curiosity, desire to achieve, and satisfaction of accomplishment (see *Andragogy*).

Another important research effort was Guglielmino's (1977) Self-directed Learning Readiness Scale (SDLRS), an instrument subsequently used by many researchers to measure self-directed readiness or to compare various self-directed learning aspects with numerous characteristics. Spear and Mocker's (1984) work on organizing circumstances showed how important it is to understand a learner's environmental circumstances in promoting self-directed learning.

Establishment of an annual International Symposium on Self-directed Learning in 1987 by Long and his colleagues completes this historical picture. These symposia have spawned many publications, research projects, and theory-building efforts by researchers throughout the world.

1.2 Competing Concepts

As with the development of many new ideas, self-directed learning has created some confusion in that many related concepts are often used interchangeably or in similar ways. Examples include self-directed education, self-planned learning, learning projects, self-education, self-teaching, autonomous learning, "autodidaxy," independent study, and open learning. Yet these terms typically offer varied, though sometimes subtly different, emphases. To illustrate some of these differences, some competing terms will be examined. Section 1.4 provides a conceptual model and corresponding definition of self-directed learning.

Self-planned learning. Tough's research on people engaged in learning projects involved obtaining information on "a series of related episodes, adding up to at least seven hours" where "more than half of the person's total motivation is to gain and retain certain fairly clear knowledge and skill, or to produce some other lasting change" (1979 p. 7). Tough used the seven-hour parameter because he felt it approximated a typical working day and separated brief learning activities from more major endeavors. Actually, he and many others have found that most learning projects far exceed the seven-hour minimum. Nearly 100 learning project surveys with various groups in 10 countries have confirmed that approximately 90 percent of adults conduct at least one intentional learning project annually. A typical adult spends about 500 hours a year in such learning with approximately 70 percent

planned by the learner. This self-planning predominance spawned considerable research on self-directed learning.

Autonomous learning. Autonomy is often associated with independence of thought, individualized decision-making, and critical intelligence. Gibbs (1979) notes that this concept "is probably the most familiar, for it is part of an individualistic, antiauthoritarian ideology . . . deep-rooted in Western capitalistic democracies" (p. 121). Chene (1983) suggests autonomy stands for psychological and methodological learning dimensions. Boud (1988) provides several ideas on developing student autonomy. Candy (1991) suggests that continuous learning is a process in which adults manifest personality attributes of personal autonomy in self-managing learning efforts. He also profiles various autonomous learner characteristics (pp. 459–66).

Autodidaxy. Candy (1991) urges that self-direction be differentiated as a goal for learner control of decision-making from an educational method in which teachers use processes for promoting self-direction. He proposes "autodidaxy" as a term for referring to self-instruction which takes place outside of formal institutional settings.

Self-education. Self-directed learning can be called something else from country to country or culture to culture. For example, in Russia it is known as self-education:

> The role of self-education naturally increases in adults, for the potential possibilities of the personality are extremely great, and the formed world outlook . . . will make it possible to develop one's abilities more successfully, systematically and comprehensively. This is especially true since life does not stand still and society is developing scientifically and technically. Anyone who does not engage in self-education, voluntarily or not, lags behind the demands of the time. (Ruvinsky 1986 p. 31)

Ruvinsky also describes several Russians who engage in self-education.

Open learning. Individualized study is often associated with external degree, open learning, or nontraditional programs where most learning takes place outside formal classrooms. One of the most widely known is the United Kingdom's Open University, started in 1969, and emulated since in many countries. Currently, development of many distance education efforts using computer-assisted learning is necessitating new research and understanding regarding how technology can enhance self-directed learning (Hiemstra 1994a) (see *Experimental and Open Learning*).

Empowerment. A concept gaining cogency in current literature is the notion of an empowered learner, person, or employee who assumes increasing personal responsibility for decisions associated with education, life, or job. For example, business and industrial organizations are beginning to develop self-directed work teams (Osburn et al. 1990) and many efforts to use self-directed learning and the promotion of personal empowerment for enhancing performance in a variety of occupational situations are underway (Durr et al. 1994, Piskurich 1993, 1994).

1.3 Synthesizing Relevant Research

There have been many overviews of self-directed learning research (Brockett and Hiemstra 1991, Caffarella and O'Donnell 1987, Candy 1991, Hiemstra 1992, Merriam and Caffarella 1991).

Confessore and Confessore (1992) conducted a 3-iteration Delphi study involving 22 self-directed learning experts from several countries. Consensus was reached in several areas, such as the most important self-directed learning research findings, research trends, practical applications, and published works.

Based on such literature and research, five major findings can be extracted: (a) several instruments for measuring some self-directed learning aspects have been developed; (b) self-directed learning readiness has been associated with various performance, psychological, and social variables; (c) a majority of self-directed learning research efforts have been qualitative in nature; (d) practice implications and techniques for facilitating self-directed learning are being devised; and (e) a coherent self-directed learning theory has not yet been developed.

1.4 Toward a Theory of Self-directed Learning

Candy (1991) outlines some useful dimensions of a theory and cautions about the often unrecognized dichotomy that exists between self-directed learning as a process and as a goal. Long (1989) also urges that any self-directed learning theory building be examined in terms of sociological, pedagogical, and psychological dimensions.

Brockett and Hiemstra (1991) synthesized different aspects of knowledge about the topic and conceptualized the Personal Responsibility Orientation (PRO) model. This model recognizes both differences and similarities between self-directed learning as an instructional method and learner self-direction as a set of personality characteristics. As can be seen in Fig. 1, the point of departure for understanding self-direction is personal responsibility. Personal responsibility refers to individuals assuming ownership for their own thoughts and actions. This does not necessarily mean control over all personal life circumstances or environmental conditions, but it does mean people can control how they respond to situations.

In terms of learning, it is the ability or willingness of individuals to take control that determines any potential for self-direction. This means that learners have choices about the directions they pursue. Along with this goes responsibility for accepting any conse-

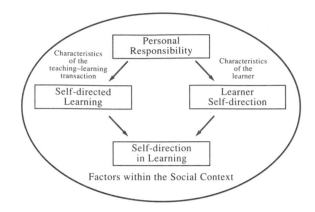

Figure 1

The PRO (Personal Responsibility Orientation) Model
(Brockett T G, Hiemstra R 1991 *Self-direction in Adult Learning.*
©Routledge, London. Reproduced with permission.)

quences of one's thoughts and actions as a learner.

Brockett and Hiemstra (1991) interpret self-directed learning (see Fig. 1) as an instructional process centering on such activities as assessing needs, securing learning resources, implementing learning activities, and evaluating learning. Hiemstra and Sisco (1990) refer to this process as individualizing instruction, a process focusing on characteristics of the teaching–learning transaction. In essence, this aspect of self-direction centers on those factors external to the individual.

While much early research and seminal thinking (see Sect. 1.1) focused on this process orientation, more recent research has related to better understanding the various personal or personality characteristics of successful self-directed learners. Self-concept, readiness for self-direction, the role of experience, and learning styles have been some of the characteristics studied. This emphasis on a learner's personal characteristics or internal factors is shown in Fig. 1 as learner self-direction. In essence, learner self-direction refers to those individual characteristics that lead to taking primary responsibility for personal learning.

Consequently, self-direction in learning is a term recognizing both external factors that facilitate a learner taking primary responsibility, and internal factors that predispose an adult accepting responsibility for learning-related thoughts and actions. At the same time there is a strong connection between self-directed learning and learner self-direction. Both internal and external aspects of self-direction can be viewed on a continuum and optimal learning conditions exist when a learner's level of self-direction is balanced with the extent to which self-directed learning opportunities are possible.

The PRO model's final component is represented by the circle in Fig. 1 that encompasses all other elements.

While the individual's personality characteristics and the teaching and learning process are starting points for understanding self-direction, the social context provides an arena in which the learning activity or results are created. To fully understand a self-directed learning activity, the interface existing between individual learners, any facilitator or learning resource, and appropriate social dimensions must be recognized. Thus, Brockett and Hiemstra (1991) recommend that self-direction in learning be used as an umbrella definition recognizing those external factors facilitating adults taking primary responsibility for learning and those internal factors or personality characteristics that incline one toward accepting such responsibility.

2. Usefulness of Self-directed Learning Approaches

Formal education and schooling remain highly valued in most societies, and many educators, employers, policymakers, and ordinary citizens find it difficult to place high value on what is learned on their own and outside the formal system. However, adult educators have shown how nontraditional programs, distance education, and self-directed learning efforts can meet many challenges associated with keeping up to date on constantly changing knowledge. Self-directed learning researchers have challenged the assumption that adult learning can take place only in the presence of accredited teachers. In addition, because people can carry out self-directed learning outside of training organizations or formal schools, many administrators are beginning to look toward such learning as a means for stretching scarce education funds.

Several researchers have also demonstrated that giving some learning responsibility back to learners in many instances is more beneficial than other approaches. For example, in the workplace employees with busy schedules can learn necessary skills at their own convenience through self-study. Some technical staff in organizations who must constantly upgrade their knowledge can access new information through an individualized resource center.

Perhaps most important of all, self-directed learning actually works. Many adults succeed as self-directed learners when they could not if personal responsibility for learning decisions had not been possible. Some will even thrive in ways never thought possible when they learn how to take personal responsibility. In many respects, future learners will need to become self-directed throughout their lives just to cope with the huge quantity of information available to them.

3. Self-directed Learning Controversies

There have been several associated controversies. Many sources shown in the bibliography discuss them. Three of the most prominent in the literature will be discussed in this section.

Brookfield (1988) provided several critical reflections on self-directed learning. For example, he suggested that the preoccupation of many adult educators with self-directed learning is unwise because of its inadequate theoretical base. He also suggested that research on self-directed learning up to 1988 had been carried out mainly with middle-class, White subjects. Another concern was his perception that research on self-directed learning had been primarily quantitative in nature.

As discussed elsewhere in this entry there continues to be a need for more adequate theory pertaining to self-directed learning. Brockett and Hiemstra (1991) and others have been working toward that end. Groups traditionally viewed as hard-to-reach or outside the middle-class mainstream have actually been studied more widely than suggested by Brookfield. Regarding his concern about excessive use of quantitative research, Long (1989) and others have discovered that the majority of research efforts in this area have actually been qualitative in nature.

Another major controversy has centered on Guglielmino's (1977) SDLRS, an instrument used in many studies on self-directed learning. It has been criticized as difficult to use with certain groups, without appropriate validation, and both conceptually and methodologically flawed (Bonham 1991; Field 1989, 1991). Guglielmino et al. (1989) and McCune and Guglielmino (1991) are some of the people who have refuted the criticisms in subsequent publications. The instrument appears to have some limitations in terms of with whom and how it is used, but if employed appropriately is helpful for achieving a better understanding of aspects of self-directed learning. However, additional instruments are needed for future quantitative research.

Candy (1991) suggests that research on self-directed learning has been stalemated in recent years because of the absence of a consistent theoretical base, continued confusion over the term's meaning, and the use of inappropriate research paradigms. His criticisms seem consistent with what others have reported and have already prompted new thinking and research. For example, a staged model has been developed that matches appropriate learning and teaching with self-directed learning abilities (Grow 1991, 1994, Tennant 1992).

4. Emerging Trends and Issues

A number of trends are emerging from the research on self-directed learning. Confessore and Confessore's (1992) Delphi study also obtained consensus views on several trends. Three significant trends are:

(a) research on the feasibility of self-directed learning meeting some job-related training needs in industry (Hiemstra 1994b, Ravid 1987);

(b) efforts to better understand the role of educational technology in self-directed learning and distance education (Hiemstra 1994a);

(c) researchers' focus on enhancing self-directed learning by better understanding environmental factors (Spear and Mocker 1984). For example, Hiemstra (1991) and his colleagues describe various ways physical, social, and psychological aspects of the learning environment can be affected.

4.1 Future Research Issues

Even though several research trends are observable, there still remains much work to be done.

(a) Additional research is required to test conceptual ideas like the PRO model (Brockett and Hiemstra 1991), and other emerging ideas to ensure the evolvement of a theory of self-directed learning.

(b) Ways need to be found whereby organizations and educators can facilitate self-directed learning and enhance critical thinking skills without impinging on the value of self-directed or spontaneous learning (Garrison 1992). For example, Smith (1990) describes how learners can be helped to learn, ask critical questions, and reflect on what they are learning.

(c) It is important that better ways of incorporating computer technology and electronic communication into self-directed learning be determined as more distance education programs are created.

(d) Future research is needed on such issues as expanding the repertoire of design and methodology for studying self-directed learning, how competencies necessary for effective self-directed learning are developed, and how the quality of self-directed learning resources can be measured.

(e) Ways of measuring and maintaining quality in self-directed learning need to be determined.

(f) The most appropriate roles for educators and educational organizations in relation to self-directed learning need to be found.

(g) Ways of better delineating micro-elements of the teaching and learning process so that learners can become self-directed in any part of the process (Hiemstra 1994b).

(h) Finally, ways for learners and others to evaluate the value and effectiveness of self-directed learning need to be developed.

See also: Adult Education: An Overview; Distance Education; Experiential and Open Learning; Study and Learning Strategies; Learning to Learn

References

Bonham L A 1991 Guglielmino's self-directed learning readiness scale: What does it measure? *Adult Educ. Q.* 41(2): 92–99

Boud D (ed.) 1988 *Developing Student Autonomy in Learning*, 2nd edn. Kogan Page, London

Brockett R G, Hiemstra R 1991 *Self-direction in Adult Learning: Perspectives in Theory, Research, and Practice.* Routledge, London

Brookfield S D 1986 *Understanding and Facilitating Adult Learning: A Comprehensive Analysis of Principles and Effective Practices.* Jossey-Bass, San Francisco, California

Brookfield S D 1988 Conceptual, methodological and practical ambiguities in self-directed learning. In: Long H B (ed.) 1988 *Self-directed Learning: Application and Theory.* Department of Adult Education, University of Georgia, Athens, Georgia

Caffarella R S, O'Donnell J M 1987 Self-directed adult learning: A critical paradigm revisited. *Adult Educ. Q.* 37(4): 199–211

Candy P C 1991 *Self-direction for Lifelong Learning: A Comprehensive Guide to Theory and Practice.* Jossey-Bass, San Francisco, California

Chene A 1983 The concept of autonomy in adult education: A philosophical discussion. *Adult Educ. Q.* 34(1): 38–47

Confessore G J, Confessore S J 1992 In search of consensus in the study of self-directed learning. In: Long H B (ed.) 1992

Craik G L 1840 *Pursuit of Knowledge Under Difficulties: Its Pleasures and Rewards.* Harper and Brothers, New York

Durr R, Guglielmino L, Guglielmino P 1994 Self-directed learning readiness and job performance at Motorola. In: Long H B (ed.) 1994

Field L 1989 An investigation into the structure, validity, and reliability of Guglielmino's Self-Directed Learning Readiness Scale. *Adult Educ. Q.* 39(3): 125–39

Field L 1991 Guglielmino's self-directed learning readiness scale: Should it continue to be used? *Adult Educ. Q.* 41(2): 100–103

Garrison D R 1992 Critical thinking and self-directed learning in adult education: An analysis of responsibility and control issues. *Adult Educ. Q.* 42(3): 136–148

Gibbs B 1979 Autonomy and authority in education. *J. Phil. Educ.* 13: 119–32

Grow G 1991 Teaching learners to be self-directed. *Adult Educ. Q.* 41(3): 125–149

Grow G 1994 In defense of the staged self-directed learning model. *Adult Educ. Q.* 44(2): 109–114

Guglielmino L M 1977 Development of the self-directed learning readiness scale (Doctoral dissertation, University of Georgia) *Dissertation Abstracts International* 1978 38: 6467A

Guglielmino L M, Long H B, McCune S K 1989 Reactions to Field's investigation into the SDLRS. *Adult Educ. Q.* 39(4): 235–45

Hiemstra R (ed.) 1991 *Creating Environments for Effective Adult Learning.* New Directions for Adult and Continuing Education, No. 50. Jossey-Bass, San Francisco, California

Hiemstra R 1992 Individualizing the instructional process: What we have learned from two decades of research on self-direction in learning. In: Long H B (ed.) 1992

Hiemstra R 1994a Computerized distance education: The

role for facilitators. *The MPAEA Journal of Adult Education*. 22(2): 11–22

Hiemstra R 1994b Helping learners take responsibility for self-directed activities. In: Hiemstra R, Brockett R G (eds.) 1994 *Overcoming Resistance to Self-direction in Learning*. New Directions for Adult and Continuing Education, No. 64. Jossey-Bass, San Francisco, California

Hiemstra R, Sisco B 1990 *Individualizing Instruction: Making Learning Personal, Empowering, and Successful*. Jossey-Bass, San Francisco, California

Houle C O 1961 *The Inquiring Mind*. University of Wisconsin Press, Madison, Wisconsin

Knowles M S 1975 *Self-directed Learning: A Guide for Learners and Teachers*. Follett Publishing Co., New York

Knowles M S (ed.) 1984 *Andragogy in Action*. Jossey-Bass, San Francisco, California

Long H B 1989 Self-directed learning: Emerging theory and practice. In: Long H B (ed.) 1989 *Self-directed Learning: Emerging Theory and Practice*. Oklahoma Research Center for Continuing Professional and Higher Education, University of Oklahoma, Norman, Oklahoma

Merriam S B, Caffarella R S 1991 *Learning in Adulthood: A Comprehensive Guide*. Jossey-Bass, San Francisco, California

McCune S L, Guglielmino L M 1991 The validity generalization of Guglielmino's self-directed learning readiness scale. In: Long H B (ed.) 1991

Orsburn J D, Moran L, Musselwhite E, Zenger J H 1990 *Self-directed Work Teams: The New American Challenge*. Business One Irwin, Homewood, Illinois

Piskurich G M 1993 *Self-directed Learning: A Practical Guide to Design, Development, and Implementation*. Jossey-Bass, San Francisco, California

Piskurich G M 1994 The current state of SDL in business and industry. In: Long H B (ed.) 1994

Ravid G 1987 Self-directed learning in industry. In: Marsick V J (ed.) 1987 *Learning in the Workplace*. Croom Helm, Beckenham

Ruvinsky L I (trans. Sayer J) 1986 *Activeness and Self-education*. Progress Publishers, Moscow

Smiles S 1859 *Self-Help*. John Murray, London

Smith R M (ed.) 1990 *Learning to Learn Across the Life Span*. Jossey-Bass, San Francisco, California

Spear G E, Mocker D W 1984 The organizing circumstance: Environmental determinants in self-directed learning.

Adult Educ. Q. 35(1): 1–10

Tennant M 1992 The staged self-directed learning model. *Adult Educ. Q*. 42(3): 164–166

Tough A 1979 *The Adult's Learning Projects: A Fresh Approach to Theory and Practice in Adult Learning*, 2nd edn. University Associates (Learning Concepts), San Diego and Ontario Institute for Studies in Education, Toronto

Further Reading

Brockett R G, Hiemstra R 1993 *El aprendizaje autodirigido en la educacion de adultos: Perspectivas teoricas, practicas y de investigacion*. Paidos Ediciones, Barcelona

Confessore G J, Confessore S J (eds.) 1992 *Guideposts to Self-directed Learning*. Organization Design and Development Inc., Pennsylvania

Long H B (ed.) 1990 *Advances in Research and Practice in Self-directed Learning*. Oklahoma Research Center for Continuing Professional and Higher Education, University of Oklahoma, Norman, Oklahoma

Long H B (ed.) 1991 *Self-directed Learning: Consensus and Conflict*. Oklahoma Research Center for Continuing Professional and Higher Education, University of Oklahoma, Norman, Oklahoma

Long H B (ed.) 1992 *Self-directed Learning: Application and Research*. Oklahoma Research Center for Continuing Professional and Higher Education, University of Oklahoma, Norman, Oklahoma

Long H B (ed.) 1993 *Emerging Perspectives of Self-directed Learning*. Oklahoma Research Center for Continuing Professional and Higher Education, University of Oklahoma, Norman, Oklahoma

Long H B (ed.) 1994 *New Ideas about Self-directed Learning*. Oklahoma Research Center for Continuing Professional and Higher Education, University of Oklahoma, Norman, Oklahoma

Long H B, Confessore G J 1992 *Abstracts of Literature in Self-directed Learning 1966–1982*. Oklahoma Research Center for Continuing Professional and Higher Education, University of Oklahoma, Norman, Oklahoma

Long H B, Redding T R 1991 *Self-directed Learning Dissertation Abstracts 1966–1991*. Oklahoma Research Center for Continuing Higher and Professional Education, University of Oklahoma, Norman, Oklahoma

Study and Learning Strategies

N. J. Entwistle

It is commonly accepted that many students entering adult education from school are not well-prepared for the different types of learning and studying required of them. In school, students tend to be dependent on teachers to organize their studying for them through regular assignments or homework, and the material they have to learn is generally presented in a carefully packaged form. In adult education, students are given much more freedom to plan their own work, and they also have to extract what has to be learned from lectures and books. Thus independent studying becomes an important determinant of progress in adult education (Raaheim et al. 1991, Rohwer 1984). This entry focuses on independent studying, seen in a broad perspective, including the ways in which students learn in higher and adult education, and the influences on those ways of learning. Improving the quality of learning, then, becomes the major focus, rather than simply training students in effective study methods.

Attempts to help adults to become more effective learners have drawn on many different sources of ideas. Traditional study skills training has been based on personal experience, often substantiated through selected findings from psychological research. In comparatively recent years, however, there has been more systematic research drawing both on cognitive theories and student surveys. The work derived from cognitive psychology has been conducted mainly in North America, and has relied on quantitative research methods. Some of these studies have been experimental. Students trained in particular ways are compared with those who have followed their normal study practices. Other studies have used surveys, with items based on psychological concepts, to investigate the ways students learn. In Europe, a rather different tradition has developed. Interviews and naturalistic experiments have been used to identify concepts and categories which describe the everyday study activities of adult learners. These qualitative analyses have been supplemented by surveys, but with items derived from interviews with students. Fortunately, these contrasting methodologies have produced findings which are to a large extent complementary, although there is less agreement about the interventions which should be used to improve study strategies.

This review of study skills and strategies will pay little attention to traditional study skills training, which has already been extensively reviewed (e.g., Maxwell 1979, Hills 1979, Armbruster and Anderson 1981). It will concentrate, instead, on more recent research and development work, indicating the theoretical rationale on which each is based, an indication of some of the training methods typically used, and a discussion of the effectiveness of different intervention strategies. The first few sections concentrate on the rationales, theories, and empirically derived concepts and categories, used to describe the ways in which adult students learn and study. In these sections, interventions are mentioned to illustrate the procedures involved. A more thorough consideration of ways of supporting student learning and studying will be discussed later.

1. Traditional Study Skills Training

The rationales provided for the study skills materials that have been used in higher and adult education rely partly on psychological justifications, but these are all too often flimsy. For example, many "how to study" manuals provide advice about how to deal with notes by reading the material at the end of the day, at the end of the week, and again in preparation for termly tests. The basis of the advice seems to derive from Ebbinghaus's work on learning material and the advice itself is totally unrealistic, creating a workload of overlearning which no student could maintain (Gibbs 1981). Again, such manuals often suggest an attention span in lectures of some 15 minutes. Tracing the source of this evidence back, it seems to lie in work with servicemen on tasks quite dissimilar to lectures. Many of the study skills manuals were written at a time when psychologists believed that it would be possible to establish general laws governing behavior. Thus evidence from any context, and even from different species, could be used to explain student behavior. Nowadays, such claims are less frequently made, although enthusiastic extrapolation from contrived laboratory experiments to everyday studying is still commonplace. The use of psychological theory to develop interventions in helping students to study is legitimate insofar as the procedures are appropriate to the context of everyday studying. However, many "how to study" manuals continue to use psychological evidence selectively to justify practices which are, in actuality, derived from personal experience or which rely more on logic or commonsense views (Nisbet 1979).

Study skills manuals contain chapters dealing with specific techniques of studying, and these indicate the rationale which typically underlies them. Most manuals deal with topics such as: finding a place to work which is physically conducive to study, maintaining motivation and concentration, strengthening the memory, improving speed in reading, note-taking, essay-writing, organizing work schedules, revising, and taking examinations. The advice is often presented in the form of mnemonics and recommends mechanical procedures which students are expected to follow. The advice also often portrays the student in an adversarial role in relation to teachers and facilitators of adult learning. It rarely implies that studying is a way of acquiring useful knowledge, gaining understanding, or developing as a person. Study strategies are seen as a way of coping with the system, rather than as a component of generic intellectual skills which will be important throughout life.

Many of the procedures described in study skills manuals will be valuable, but only if they are applied in appropriate ways. Nisbet and Shucksmith (1986) draw an analogy with soccer training. To play soccer it is necessary to develop ball skills, and without them no player can be considered skilled, but these skills are not sufficient in themselves. They have to be brought into play at the right time, and players need to "read" the game by looking ahead and anticipating what will be required. This emphasizes the idea of orchestrating skills into strategies or habitual patterns of behavior directed toward the purposes of the game. Beyond strategies, teams also need a flexible game plan which integrates strategies into ways of achieving the goal—literally, within the analogy. In studying, it is equally important to be able to apply study skills appropriately and to build a range of effective strategies. Beyond that, students also need a sense of purpose which is equivalent to a "game plan." Study skills manuals often fail to provide the link into the reality of everyday studying and so leave the students unable to apply even sound advice in effective ways.

Most of the traditional study skills manuals suggest specific ways to tackle demanding learning tasks. For example, speed-reading may be encouraged to allow students to cover their required reading textbooks more quickly, but speed-reading may also deflect students from reading for meaning. In one much-quoted study, Perry (1959) trained students to read more quickly using one of these procedures. He then asked them to apply those skills in reading a chapter from a book, and stopped them after 20 minutes. He was impressed by the amount students had read, and also by their ability to answer detailed questions about the material, but he then asked them what the chapter was about. Only one student out of 115 could tell him! Perry argued that the students had fallen into a trap of "obedient purposelessness" and concluded that training in the mechanics of reading alone may be worse than useless: students may afterwards be *less* effective in reading for understanding than before, although they will probably cover more ground.

Another feature of much traditional advice is to suggest how to become better organized in studying. Some of the suggestions are valuable, but the danger is that they are presented as if there is just one way to be well-organized. Often students reject the advice because it feels "uncomfortable," and yet are left with a belief that they are deficient through not being able to follow that advice. It is probably one of the best-established research findings in this field that successful learners are better organized than those who do less well, but their ways of being organized are often very different. In a comparison of the comments of contrasting groups of Australian university students, Pond (1964) found that "high achievers" had organized their studying and time allocations, worked during free periods, decided their priorities, and tried to improve their study techniques. In contrast, "low-achievers" considered such habits of little importance, attributing their poor performance to circumstances beyond their control such as inadequate study facilities or scarcity of books. Although the successful students were better organized, the form of that organization was varied, even idio-syncratic. Individual differences in effective study strategies thus make prescriptive advice on organization potentially damaging, if it interferes with existing idiosyncratic, but effective, study methods (see *Individual Differences, Learning, and Instruction*). It is important to discover what strategies successful students use, but the advice provided needs to be well-supported by research evidence of its effectiveness. Above all, the early attempts at study skills training lacked any theoretical basis or empirical support. In a variety of different ways, such under-pinning is now increasingly being provided.

2. Strategy Training

Strategy training is based on the observation that learning in higher and adult education requires the use of fairly general skills and strategies which are rarely explicitly taught to students during normal periods of instruction. It is believed that by making these strategies explicit, students will develop more effective ways of learning and applying the information presented in books or lectures (Dansereau 1985). The strategies taught have to have fairly wide applicability, and yet be specific enough for students to see their relevance to their own course of study. Strategy training involves giving students a set of logical procedures to follow which provide initial props in tackling typical learning tasks.

One of the early forms of strategy training was developed by Robinson (1946) in the SQ3R method of helping servicemen read more effectively during their short, intensive college courses in wartime. Subsequently, the method attracted a good deal of interest and was widely used. Students were required to follow a set procedure in reading. They had to survey (read topic headings and summary), question (turn topic headings into questions), read (to answer the questions), recite (try to recall the answers to questions without checking back), and review (check the accuracy of the answers by looking back over the test). The method has theoretical justifications from psychological theory and can be useful for students with severe difficulties (Maxwell 1979), but it is also time-consuming and inflexible.

The SQ3R method was a first step toward more thoroughly researched strategy training. With the advent of information-processing theories in psychology, strategy research has burgeoned in North America. The research methodology used in these studies has its origins in the systematic experimental investigations developed within behaviorist psychology, which was subsequently extended into work on cognitive processes. A variety of such methods—their theoretical bases and empirical support—have been discussed in detail in a publication by Weinstein et al. (1988). Here particular examples of these methods will be used to illustrate the general approach.

In developing some quite elaborate sets of strategy training procedures, Dansereau (1985) has distinguished between primary and support strategies. Primary strategies describe the cognitive processes involved in learning itself, while support strategies indicate those activities of organization and concentration which enable learning to continue efficiently. This system of strategies is taught to students using the mnemonic MURDER: setting the *mood* for studying; reading for *understanding; recalling* what has been learned and correcting that recall; then amplifying and storing it so as to *digest* it thoroughly; *expanding* that knowledge by self-questioning; and finally *reviewing* performance on tests to learn from mistakes. The learning processes which underpin the primary strategies are taught by suggesting a variety of techniques which will strengthen recall, such as the use of vivid imagery associated with the information to be stored, networking which produces concept maps to indicate relationships between main concepts, and the more detailed analysis and definition of key concepts. Support strategies also have techniques associated with them. Students use a workbook to specify long- and short-term goals, and to schedule their time. They are also taught relaxation techniques, along with self-talk, to help them set and maintain an appropriate mood for studying.

Evaluations of the effectiveness of strategy training, using experimental designs, have indicated that students using the MURDER strategies perform better on tests of the material learned, and also have better attitudes to the work, than students using their normal study methods (Dansereau 1985). There is some evidence that the effects of strategy training may be enhanced by including in the procedure cooperative learning in which the reading is done in pairs of students. One student in each pair then recalls what has been read, while the other listens and criticizes. In subsequent work, Dansereau (1988) and his colleagues have explored a variety of ways in which cooperative learning might be used to enhance strategy training. They conclude, from a series of experiments, that critical listening enhances immediate recall, but elaboration techniques facilitate transfer (see *Learning Transfer*).

Other research on strategy training has concentrated on particular tasks, such as reading texts (Mayer 1984) or note-taking (Kiewra 1989), where information-processing theories provide a rich variety of research hypotheses on the efficacy of various strategies. All too often, however, such research seems to have been driven by the theory and fitting study behavior into the theory, rather than by attempts to improve the efficacy of student learning. As a result, it often lacks realism and practicality. To intervene effectively it is crucial to be able to describe accurately the everyday study behavior of adult learners.

3. Study Strategy Inventories

Running in parallel with the strategy training, research surveys have been used systematically to map out the processes used by adults in their everyday studying, as a first step toward providing more adequate advice on studying. This questionnaire methodology has its theoretical and methodological origins in psychological research on individual differences and sets out

to define coherent scales which indicate the relative strengths and weaknesses of individual students (see *Individual Differences, Learning, and Instruction*). It is now clear that studying can be described in terms of perhaps four main components, which recur in several different instruments.

3.1 Characteristics of Successful Adult Learners

One approach that has been used in developing study strategy inventories is to identify the characteristics of successful students. This procedure was used to produce the *Manual of the Survey of Study Habits and Attitudes* (Brown and Holtzman 1966) which was one of the first inventories to be widely used in higher education. It describes four attributes of successful students: work methods (effective study procedures); delay avoidance (promptness in completing work); teacher approval (favorable opinions about teachers); and educational acceptance (approval of educational objectives). This early inventory concentrated partly on study methods and partly on attitudes and evaluations of the courses attended. Each of these aspects have subsequently been developed further, with those related to perceptions of courses becoming somewhat separate from the mainstream of study strategy inventories. These will therefore be discussed in a subsequent section.

The item pool used by Brown and Holtzman was derived mainly from traditional study skills manuals and courses, and these have also been used to develop more extensive sets of categories describing aspects of studying. The *Learning and Study Strategies* inventory (Weinstein et al. 1988) was developed initially in this way, supplemented by ideas from cognitive psychology. It contains ten scales which cover four domains. The first domain describes attitudinal or emotional correlates: anxiety, motivation, and attitudes to education. The second represents learning skills: information processing (e.g., reasoning and the elaboration of ideas through the use of images or analogies); and selecting main ideas (identifying the key points in lectures or in a book). The third domain describes systematic or organized study methods, including time management, concentration, and study aids (practice exercises and memory support). Finally, two scales relate to assessment strategy: self-testing and test strategies (preparation and integration).

3.2 Concepts from Cognitive Psychology

A second source of items for study strategy inventories has been cognitive psychology. Taking descriptions of learning provided by theorists, it is possible to use these as a way of categorizing study processes. The cognitive theories, however, describe learning under controlled laboratory contexts, and thus additional items are required to cover the full range of adult study. One concept which has particularly influenced the design of inventories has been that of depth of processing. This idea was introduced by Craik and Lockhart (1972) to describe contrasting stages in information processing in the memory. Information enters as perceptions which are initially reviewed and interpreted through matching with existing schemata. This is shallow or surface-level processing. Subsequently, a deeper level of processing may be used which involves linkages being established with other images or concepts through elaboration or extension (see *Learning Transfer*).

Schmeck (1983) used this theory to derive items for his Inventory of Learning Processes which was found to contain four distinguishable sets of items. He described three scales as contrasting learning processes: deep processing (analytic thinking), elaborative processing (using analogies and images), and fact retention, which relied on the memorizing or overlearning expected to occur within surface-level processing. The final scale was composed of items describing study methods.

Information processing implies a temporal sequence of increasingly complex memory processes, as information is transformed from the initial perceptions into semantic material retained in long-term memory. This type of sequence has been used by Thomas and Rohwer (1989) to categorize items in their Study Activity Survey. They suggest a temporal and developmental sequence from the simplest to the most elaborate cognitive study activities. Thus, basic encoding is followed by selection activities, memory augmentation, integration, and extension, and each process depends on the successful acquisition of the previous one. This series can also be taken to represent a developmental progression among students as they become more mature and sophisticated in their learning projects. This list extends Schmeck's three learning processes and parallels the learning skills included in Weinstein et al.'s inventory. Thomas and Rohwer also describe a hierarchy of "effort-management" study activities which begins with monitoring, and progresses through self-regulation, planning, and evaluation. Again some overlap can be seen with both Schmeck's and Weinstein et al.'s scales relating to organized studying.

3.3 Concepts from Research on Learning

The identification of the concepts of approaches to learning (deep/surface/strategic; see Sect. 4.2 below) and styles of learning (holist/serialist; see Sect. 4.3 below) led to the development of an Approaches to Studying Inventory (ASI) to measure them (Entwistle and Ramsden 1983). This inventory also contained scales previously used as indicators of different forms of motivation, study methods, and attitudes (Entwistle and Wilson 1977). A very similar inventory, the Study Processes Questionnaire (SPQ), was developed independently by Biggs (1978, 1987). Both inventories,

from factor analysis, typically produce three main factors in which an approach to learning is supported by a distinctive form of motivation. The deep approach, with the intention to understand what is being learned, is found to be closely linked to intrinsic motivation (interest in the subject matter itself). In contrast, the surface approach, which is concerned with reproducing what faculty require, is associated with either instrumental motivation or fear of failure. Finally, the strategic approach, with the intention to obtain the highest possible grades, not surprisingly correlates with the competitive form of motivation described as "need for achievement" (Entwistle 1988). The ASI sometimes produces a fourth factor which can be seen as a nonacademic orientation to studying defined in terms of negative attitudes, disorganized studying, and learning pathologies, but in other analyses these scales load negatively with the strategic approach.

Recently, attempts have been made to apply factor analysis to a pool of items drawn from both the ASI and the Schmeck inventory. In spite of their very different theoretical origins, there proved to be considerable commonality, with the simplest interpretation suggesting four main dimensions: deep analytic, deep elaborative, surface, and organized studying (Schmeck 1988, Entwistle and Waterston 1988). Schmeck suggests additional dimensions of self-confidence, and both analyses hinted that Pask's holist and serialist categories might be separate, although there were overlaps with "deep elaborative" and "deep analytic" factors respectively. Evidence suggests that consistent preferences for holist or serialist strategies may be stable individual differences (Pask 1988), while approaches to studying are more likely to vary according to the particular learning context or even the particular task (Calder 1989). There is certainly evidence that adult students adjust their approach to learning in response to different forms of assessment. Factual multiple-choice or short-answer questions push all students, in different degrees, toward a surface approach to learning, while more open questions encourage a deep approach (Thomas 1986) (see *Approaches to Learning*).

4. Research on Student Learning

The main characteristic of the quantitative studies has been to try to identify component parts of studying which may then be trained or taught. In contrast, the qualitative research originating mainly in Europe has attempted to describe study processes as a whole, although again important concepts and categories have been identified in order to facilitate the communication of the findings. The educational philosophy and research methodology from which these studies derive are, however, in marked contrast to the North American work. A series of concepts has been derived directly from the experiences of students which allow study activities to be described as they apply to everyday learning situations in adult and higher education. These concepts can be seen as a hierarchy from broad and inclusive ones to those which describe reactions to specific tasks. Taken as a whole, they also have a coherence which is useful in considering interventions to improve the quality of student learning in adult education.

4.1 Orientations and Conceptions

Adults vary markedly in their goals and purposes, and it is only through a recognition of those individual purposes that the effort and direction of students' studying can be understood. From an interview study, Taylor (see Gibbs et al. 1984) suggested that four distinct educational orientations could be identified: academic, vocational, personal, and social. By orientation, she meant the overall set of motives and purposes which described students' attitudes to the course of study they were taking. Taylor found that each of the first three orientations could be directed either intrinsically toward aspects of the course content or extrinsically toward the qualifications or satisfactions which were associated incidentally with that content. From her interview study, she also found that students had what could be called a "study contract" with themselves. They knew what they were aiming for, and their satisfaction with the course depended more on their progress toward fulfilling that contract than on the lecturers' requirements for demonstrating excellence (see *Learning by Contract*).

Students' predominant educational orientation seems to affect strongly both the effort they put into studying and its quality. How they study also depends on what they believe the learning project to require of them. Säljö interviewed a group of Swedish adults to find out what "learning" meant to them. He identified a hierarchy of conceptions of learning at increasing levels of sophistication (see Marton and Säljö 1984). Learning, at its simplest, was seen as increasing knowledge, as memorizing, or as acquiring facts. In contrast, the more sophisticated learners saw learning as requiring the abstraction of meaning or the interpretative understanding of reality. Students will go about their studying in very different ways if, on the one hand, they believe learning to involve memorizing information or, on the other, they see it as requiring the abstraction of meaning and the development of personal understanding. This is indeed what has been found (Van Rossum and Schenk 1984).

4.2 Approaches to Learning

Marton, working in the University of Gothenburg, carried out qualitative analyses of a naturalistic experiment in which students were asked to read a nontechnical text and to be ready to answer questions afterwards. In the subsequent interviews, Marton found that adults differed in the level of understanding they displayed as a consequence of what he termed their "approach to learning" (see Marton and Säljö 1984). Students adopted either a deep or a surface approach to the reading, and the concept has since been extended to describe how students tackle many other learning tasks in lectures, essay writing, and problem solving (Marton et al. 1984).

The crucial defining feature of the approach lies in the contrasting intentions shown by students. A deep approach depends on an intention to reach a personal understanding of the material presented. It appears that this approach has its roots in an intrinsic educational orientation and a sophisticated conception of learning. In adopting a deep approach, the student has to interact critically with the content, relating it to previous knowledge and experience, as well as examining evidence and evaluating the logical steps by which conclusions have been reached. In contrast, a surface approach derives from an extrinsic orientation and a simple conception of learning as memorization. It involves an intention merely to satisfy task or course requirements, seen as external impositions largely remote from personal interests. The surface approach can still be active, but it relies on identifying the elements within the task most likely to be assessed, and then memorizing those details (see *Approaches to Learning*).

Marton's conclusion was drawn from the specific task of reading a nontechnical article as part of a laboratory experiment. The task was divorced from the conceptual and assessment demands of everyday studying, but subsequent research has confirmed just how important the initial intention is (Marton et al. 1984). The influence of assessment on approach also has a crucial effect in everyday studying. Indeed both Ramsden (1981) and Biggs (1978) independently found that the pervasive influence of assessment necessitated the description of another approach to learning—"strategic" (Ramsden) or "achieving" (Biggs)—with its own characteristic intention. In this approach, the student adopts deep and surface approaches in combination so as to achieve the highest possible marks. The approach involves using well-organized study methods and careful time management (Entwistle and Waterston 1988), but there is also an alertness to any cues given by tutors about what they are looking for in their judgments of performance, or what questions they are going to set in the examinations. It is as if the students are conscious of two separate foci of attention: the content and the teacher's reward system (Entwistle and Entwistle 1991). Approaches to learning are strongly affected by other aspects of the learning environment (see *Environments for Learning*).

4.3 Styles of Learning

Whereas Marton left the task requirements deliberately vague, Pask (1976) required students to develop conceptual understanding. Even with this restriction, adult learners still showed different learning strategies in seeking understanding. They had distinct preferences in the styles of learning they adopted. Some students adopted a holist style in which, right from the start, they tried to see the task in the widest possible perspective, establishing an overview which went well beyond the task itself. Their learning process involved the use of illustrations, examples, analogies, and anecdotes in building up an idiosyncratic form of understanding deeply rooted in personal experience and beliefs. Other students preferred a serialist style in which they began with a narrow focus, concentrated on details and logical connections in a cautious manner, and looked at the broader context only toward the end of the topic. Extreme holists were impulsive, even cavalier, in their use of evidence, tending to generalize too readily and to jump to unjustified conclusions. Extreme serialists were often too cautious, failing to see important relationships or useful analogies, thus leaving their understanding impoverished.

Pask (1976) found that students matched with learning materials of their own style learned faster and more fully than students who were mismatched. As lecturers and textbooks adopt varying styles of presentation, however, there seems to be an advantage in everyday studying of being able to switch readily between styles, adopting what Pask describes as a versatile style. It may be possible to help students to become more versatile by deliberately adopting their weaker style in some tasks (Pask 1988), but stylistic preferences seem to be extremely strong. There is a continuing debate about their origins with a suggestion that they may reflect cerebral dominance of left (serialist) or right (holist) hemispheres of the brain, associated with firmly established personality characteristics of the individual. Their modifiability may thus be limited, implying that students need opportunities to choose materials and methods conducive to their own styles of learning (see Entwistle 1988) (see *Teacher Roles and Teaching Styles*).

5. Influences of the Context

To fully understand the reasons why students study in the ways they do, it is essential to consider learning and study strategies in relation to the whole learning environment that they experience. Their ways of studying depend on their perceptions of what they are required to do or of what "pays off" in assessment terms (Becker et al. 1968). It has been the lack of this component in the study skills equation which has left those forms of advice unrealistic and often inapplicable.

5.1 Perceptions of Courses

Research has begun to explore the influences of perceptions of the environment on approaches to learning and studying. The strongest and most pervasive influence on approaches to learning seems to be the assessment procedures, and how they are perceived by students. Even totally incorrect beliefs about those procedures influence study behavior (Gibbs 1981). It now appears that essay questions, problem solving, or project reports are most likely to promote deep approaches to learning, whereas factually oriented short-answer or multiple-choice questions cause adult learners to opt for surface approaches (Thomas 1986). Ramsden developed a Course Perceptions Questionnaire (Entwistle and Ramsden 1983) to describe the main components of students' perceptions of the courses they were taking. The scales included in that questionnaire were: clear goals and standards, formal teaching methods, workload, vocational relevance, good teaching, freedom in learning, openness to students, and social climate. Ramsden was able to show that good teaching and freedom in learning were the perceived characteristics of educational programs enrolling higher proportions of students using deep approaches, while a heavy workload was the main factor associated with a dominant surface approach (Entwistle and Ramsden 1983).

5.2 Individual Differences in Perceptions

In the above study, perceptions of programs were based on consensus among the students. There may be some aspects of the learning context about which there is considerable agreement among students (e.g., the assessment procedures), but Meyer (1988) has argued that there should be qualitative differences between students in their perceptions of most other aspects of the environment. For example, how students perceive teaching will logically depend on their own educational orientations—that is, what they want to gain from the course. Meyer has suggested that the lack of associations between course perceptions and approaches to learning at the individual level may have been not only a function of the type of question asked, but also a function of the correlational techniques of analysis used. He has since demonstrated, using a form of multiple-dimensional scaling called "unfolding analysis," that areas of space can be defined in which are located both approaches to learning and associated perceptions of the learning environment (Meyer and Muller 1990). Exploring Meyer's ideas further, Entwistle and Tait (1990) have also shown that items describing students' preferences for different types of teaching and courses bring out close associations with the equivalent approaches to learning. While this is hardly a surprising finding, it does have important implications. Students evaluate more positively teachers and facilitators who teach in the way they prefer. Thus, for example, students using surface approaches rate highly teachers who "spoon-feed" them, while students adopting deep approaches prefer clear explanations and challenging ideas. Evaluations of teaching which ignore these differences, as would be true of most student feedback questionnaires (Marsh 1987), thus produce essentially uninterpretable evidence, at least where differences between students' perceptions are marked (see *Teaching Methods: General*).

5.3 Perceptions of Failing Students

Besides showing that unfolding analysis can be used to provide evidence of associations between perceptions of the learning environment and approaches to learning, Meyer has also shown that there are some students who do not show the expected linkages in their inventory responses. Unfolding analysis not only locates inventory scales within two- or three-dimensional space, it also positions students within the same space. Some students occur as "outliers" or are even so disparate in their responses that they have to be omitted from the analysis in order to produce effective solutions. It has been shown, in two very different samples, that a high proportion of students who make uninterpretable linkages in their inventory responses also fail to meet the program evaluation requirements (Meyer et al. 1990, Entwistle et al. 1991). Preferences for clear explanations in lectures or open-ended essay questions are associated by these students not with a deep approach to learning, but rather with a surface approach. The full implications of this finding are far from clear, but they need to be considered alongside similar evidence from Biggs (1985) that adult learners who were not prepared to take personal responsibility for poor performance (making external attributions) showed no clear factor structure in their responses to his study processes questionnaire (SPQ).

6. Improving Learning and Studying

The purposes of the research reported above are to try to provide a sounder and more coherent basis on which to help students to overcome difficulties in studying, and to use learning strategies directed toward the development of understanding. It is now possible to evaluate recommended intervention procedures in this light. The research on adult learning also provides a set of concepts and categories which may be used to describe studying in more precise terms, and yet without relapsing into a jargon inaccessible to nonspecialists. Moreover, the research emphasizes a coherence singularly lacking within the language of study skills training and also provides an emphasis on individual purposes in studying which is in tune with adults' own experiences.

6.1 Strategy Training and Metacognitive Awareness

One of the main contrasts in the various forms of intervention used to help with study skills and strategies is between researchers who rely on strategy training and those who try to increase students' metacognitive awareness of their own intentions and learning processes. Many United States educational psychologists have argued for what amounts to prescriptive strategy training as the most efficient way of improving study methods (e.g., Rohwer 1984, Pressley and Levin 1987). There has been a parallel concern in trying to develop thinking skills with emphasis on the development of critical thinking, informal logic, creative thinking, and brainstorming, applied in a variety of course settings (e.g., Baron and Sternberg 1987, Nickerson 1988, Resnick 1987). All of these methods emphasize the process of learning (Glaser 1984), but they are sometimes presented as set routines to be followed. As McKeachie (1988) comments, there is a danger that students will try to follow such procedures without recognizing individual differences. Strategy training does not necessitate prescription, but it does tend to leave that impression. At best, students are provided with a set of strategies which help them decide under what conditions and for what purposes each strategy will be most useful. It is the researcher who is describing the strategies, however, often on the basis of psychological theory: the adult learners are being offered received wisdom.

Other attempts at improving student learning have taken an entirely different path. They have sought to develop "skill in learning," meaning expert performance, as opposed to training in specific study skills (Svensson 1984). The essence of this approach is reflection (Boud et al. 1985), as a process of developing greater self-awareness in tackling academic tasks. Again, metacognition is seen as important, but the individual is given more freedom to explore ways of achieving it. In practice, this may involve encouraging students to discuss among themselves their different ways of studying, and from those discussions to decide which strategies are most effective. This technique draws heavily from the ideas of Rogers (1969) who attacks the model of the teacher as instructor, and presents an alternative image of the teacher as a facilitator of learning (see *Self-directed Learning; Teacher Roles and Teaching Styles*).

A typical procedure would start by asking students, in pairs, to discuss their own experiences of learning which proved easy or very difficult (Gibbs 1981). The discussion is then broadened in steps to groups of four, then eight, finishing with a plenary session in which the workshop leader structures the various conclusions and comments on them. The students are then left as the "owners" of the ideas generated, rather than the recipients of other people's theories and practical tips. Rogers sees the sense of ownership as critical to the adoption of suggestions about learning, and the lack of such involvement could be a serious disadvantage to strategy training. However, it could be argued that strategy training offers alternative ways of studying that have been substantially researched, and which have been proved to be effective. Why should such ideas and evidence be withheld from students? In a comparison of conventional study skills training and "learning to learn" discussion workshops, Martin and Ramsden (1987) found that students initially resented the lack of information provided in discussion groups, but ultimately came to the conclusion that the experience had led to profound changes in the ways in which they conceptualized their learning. The students following the conventional program reacted in the converse way, at first feeling that the strategies were valuable, but later admitting that they were unable to use them in everyday studying (see *Group Learning*).

6.2 Developmental Differences in Study Processes

Rather than seeking to decide between strategy training and "learning to learn" discussion groups, it will be more fruitful to consider for which students, and for what purposes, the contrasting procedures might be of most value. A starting point may well be the observation that students who fail often seem to lack any coherence in their perceptions of the links between the learning context and their approaches to learning. Other weak students seem to have an orientation to their courses which is extrinsic, and a dualistic conception of learning as reproducing the information presented. They may also make inappropriate attributions for the causes of their poor performance by blaming "the system," or their own lack of ability, rather than recognizing weaknesses in themselves which can be overcome by changing their learning strategies. Biggs (1987) suggests a hierarchy of interventions which should be matched with the developmental stage of the learner. He suggests that prescriptive "props," in the form of direct strategy training, may be necessary for students who are having substantial difficulties with studying. As those strategies begin to work, adult learners will gain in confidence and so be ready for a reappraisal of their orientations and conceptions through discussions. At this stage, the students will also be more receptive to considering the research evidence which underpins the various recommended strategies. It is thus possible to envisage an overall procedure which might bring together various interventions in a complementary fashion.

First, it would be necessary to identify students with problems in studying, and the probable reasons for those difficulties. This might involve an initial use of inventories, supplemented by individual counseling where difficulties were not easy to diagnose. Students who showed evidence of inappropriate attributions could be helped to alter them. Van Overwalle et al. (1989) have used videotapes in which second-year university students describe experiences which led them to make external attributions, subsequently finding study strategies which allowed them to perform more effectively. There was evidence that the weakest students benefited substantially from viewing these videotapes. However, attempts to supplement the tapes with study skills training provided no additional

benefit, but the form of that training may have been inappropriately matched to the needs of those students.

Students whose conceptualizations of teaching and learning in higher and adult education are incoherent would probably benefit from individual counseling to encourage a reintegration of their perceptions of the learning context. This process might also be encouraged through facilitators being more open in explaining to the class in which particular ways their teaching methods are intended to facilitate learning, and also by "modeling" the forms of thinking they wish to encourage. Students whose inventory responses indicate no severe problems might be asked to attend workshops which began with open discussions, but which led on to a presentation of research findings and alternative strategies, held together by continuing discussions about individual purposes and idiosyncratic forms of study organization. Already an extensive series of workshops linked to inventory responses has been developed in Texas (Weinstein 1988) with considerable success. One remaining difficulty, however, in introducing effective general strategy training is that different subjects make rather different intellectual demands on the student. Thus, whereas some general principles and strategies may be relevant, the way of applying them may be sufficiently different in each faculty to create confusion in the student. It is, therefore, essential to provide additional study skills support within adult education programs or within major course areas (Tabberer and Allman 1983).

Looking to the future, microcomputer-based inventories could be used both to predict possible failure and to diagnose specific learning difficulties. It is also possible to develop microworlds which mimic learning environments and allow students to explore alternative study strategies in relation to outcomes predicted from research findings (Entwistle et al. 1988) (see *Environments for Learning*).

6.3 Other Influences on Learning and Studying

As already indicated, students direct their study strategies to achieving the goals they set, and their learning is also strongly influenced by the teaching they experience and other learning resources provided by their teaching departments. Offering conventional study skills courses, within conventional assessment systems, often leads to students applying a surface approach more strategically, as understanding is not a perceived requirement. If, therefore, the intention of faculty is to encourage a deep level of understanding of the subject or profession, an environment has to be provided which supports a deep approach to learning in a variety of ways.

There have also been other interventions which have changed the curriculum, in ways intended to change the student's ways of learning and studying, in particular through developing a problem-based curriculum (in medicine, for example) or through encouraging problem-solving in case studies (in law or business studies) (see Boud 1985). It appears that interventions which are directed solely at influencing study strategies may have locally beneficial effects, but if the overall quality of student learning in higher and adult education is to be substantially improved, a systems analysis, at program, course, and institutional level, will be required (Entwistle et al. 1992).

See also: Adult Learning: An Overview; Approaches to Learning; Environments for Learning; Individual Differences, Learning, and Instruction; Learning to Learn; Learning Transfer; Student Counseling; Student Support Systems; Third-age Students in Higher Education; Teaching Methods: Individual Techniques; Adult Tertiary Education; University Adult Education

References

Armbruster B B, Anderson T H 1981 Research synthesis on study skills. *Educ. Leadership* 39: 154–56

Baron J B, Sternberg R J (eds.) 1987 *Teaching Thinking Skills: Theory and Practice.* Freeman, New York

Becker H S, Geer B, Hughes E C 1968 *Making the Grade.* Wiley, New York

Biggs J B 1978 Individual and group differences in study processes. *Brit. J. Educ. Psychol.* 48: 266–79

Biggs J B 1985 The role of metalearning in study processes. *Brit. J. Educ. Psychol.* 55: 185–212

Biggs J B 1987 *Student Approaches to Learning and Studying.* Australian Council for Educational Research, Hawthorn

Boud D (ed.) 1985 *Problem-Based Learning in Education for the Professions.* Higher Education Research and Development Society of Australasia, Sydney

Boud D, Keogh R, Walker D (eds.) 1985 *Reflection: Turning Experience into Learning.* Kogan Page, London

Brown W F, Holtzman W H 1966 *Manual of the Survey of Study Habits and Attitudes.* Psychological Corporation, New York

Calder I A 1989 *The study and learning strategies of students in a New Zealand tertiary institution.* Unpublished doctoral thesis, University of Waikato

Craik F I M, Lockhart R S 1972 Levels of processing: A framework for memory research. *J. Verb. Learn. Verb. Behav.* 11: 671–84

Dansereau D F 1985 Learning strategy research. In: Segal J W, Chipman S F, Glaser R (eds.) 1985 *Thinking and Learning Skills,* Vol. 1. Erlbaum, Hillsdale, New Jersey

Dansereau D F 1988 Cooperative learning strategies. In: Weinstein C E, Goetz E T, Alexander P A (eds.) 1988

Entwistle N J 1988 *Styles of Learning and Teaching.* Fulton, London

Entwistle N J, Wilson J D 1977 *Degrees of Excellence: The Academic Achievement Game.* Hodder and Stoughton, London

Entwistle N J, Ramsden P 1983 *Understanding Student Learning.* Croom Helm, London

Entwistle N J, Odor J P, Anderson C 1988 Encouraging reflection on study strategies: The design of a computer-based adventure game. In: Ramsden P (ed.) 1988 *Improving Learning: New Perspectives.* Kogan Page, London

Entwistle N J, Waterston S 1988 Approaches to learning and levels of processing in university students. *Brit. J. Educ. Psychol.*: 58: 258–65

Entwistle N J, Tait H 1990 Approaches to learning, evaluations of teaching, and preferences for contrasting academic environments. *Higher Educ.* 19: 169–94

Entwistle N J, Entwistle A C 1991 Contrasting forms of understanding for degree examinations: The student experience and its implications. *Higher Educ.* 22: 205–27

Entwistle N J, Meyer J H F, Tait H 1991 Student failure: Disintegrated perceptions of studying and the learning environment. *Higher Educ.* 21: 249–61

Entwistle N J, Thompson S, Tait H 1992 *Guidelines for Promoting Effective Learning in Higher Education.* Centre for University of Edinburgh, Edinburgh

Gibbs G 1981 *Teaching Students to Learn.* Open University Press, Buckingham

Gibbs G, Morgan A, Taylor E 1984 The world of the learner. In: Marton F, Hounsell D J, Entwistle N J (eds.) 1984

Glaser R 1984 Education and thinking: The role of knowledge. *Am. Psychol.* 39: 93–104

Hills P J (ed.) 1979 *Study Courses and Counselling: Problems and Possibilities.* Society for Research into Higher Education, Guildford

Kiewra K 1989 A review of note-taking: The encoding-storage paradigm and beyond. *Educ. Psychol. Rev.* 1: 147–72

Marsh H W 1987 Students' evaluations of university teaching: Research findings, methodological issues, and directions for future research. *Int. J. Educ. Res.* 11(3)

Martin E, Ramsden P 1987 Learning skills or skill in learning. In: Richardson J T E, Eysenck M W, Warren Piper D (eds.) 1987 *Student Learning: Research in Education and Cognitive Psychology.* Open University Press, Buckingham

Marton F, Hounsell D J, Entwistle N J (eds.) 1984 *The Experience of Learning.* Scottish Academic Press, Edinburgh

Marton F, Säljö R 1984 Approaches to learning. In: Marton F, Hounsell D J, Entwistle N J (eds.) 1984

Maxwell M 1979 *Improving Student Learning Skills.* Jossey-Bass, San Francisco, California

Mayer R E 1984 Aids to text comprehension. *Educ. Psychol.* 19: 30–42

McKeachie W J 1988 The need for study strategy training. In: Weinstein C E, Goetz E T, Alexander P A (eds.) 1988

Meyer J H F 1988 Qualitative differences in students' perceptions of learning environments. In: Knapp C A (ed.) 1988 *The Development of Learning and Thinking Skills in Students: Implications for Instructional Development.* Bureau for University and Continuing Education, University of Stellenbosch, South Africa

Meyer J H F, Muller M M 1990 An unfolding analysis of the association between perception of learning context and approaches to studying. *South African J. Higher Educ.* 4: 46–58

Meyer J H F, Parsons P, Dunne T T 1990 Individual study orchestrations and their association with learning outcome. *Higher Educ.* 20: 67–89

Nickerson R S 1988 On improving thinking through instruction. *Rev. Res. Educ.* 15: 3–57

Nisbet J D 1979 Beyond the study methods manual. In: Hills P J (ed.) 1979

Nisbet J D, Shucksmith J 1986 *Learning Strategies.* Routledge, London

Pask G 1976 Learning styles and strategies. *Brit. J. Educ. Psychol.* 46: 4–11

Pask G 1988 Learning strategies, teaching strategies, and conceptual or learning style. In: Schmeck R R (ed.) 1988

Perry W G 1959 Students' use and misuse of reading skills. *Harvard Educ. Rev.* 29: 193–200

Pond L 1964 A study of high-achieving and low-achieving freshmen. *Aust. J. Higher Educ.* 2: 73–78

Pressley M, Levin J R 1987 Elaborative learning strategies for the inefficient learner. In: Ceci S J (ed.) 1987 *Handbook of Cognitive, Social, and Neurological Aspects of Learning*. Erlbaum, Hillsdale, New Jersey

Raaheim K, Wankowski J, Radford J 1991 *Helping Students to Learn at University*, 2nd edn. SRHE/Open University Press, Buckingham

Ramsden P 1981 A study of the relationship between student learning and its academic context. Unpublished doctoral thesis, University of Lancaster

Resnick L B 1987 Instruction and the cultivation of thinking. In: De Corte E, Lodewijks H, Parmentier R, Span P (eds.) 1987 *Learning and Instruction: European Research in an International Context*. Pergamon Press, Oxford

Robinson F P 1946 *Effective Study*. Harper and Row, New York

Rohwer W D Jr 1984 An invitation to a developmental psychology of learning. In: Morrison F J, Lord C A, Keating D P (eds.) 1984 *Aptitude, Learning, and Instruction: Cognitive Process Analyses of Aptitude, Learning, and Problem Solving*, Vol. 1. Erlbaum, Hillsdale, New Jersey

Rogers C R 1969 *Freedom to Learn*. Merrill, Columbus, Ohio

Schmeck R R 1983 Learning styles of college students. In: Dillon R, Schmeck R R (eds.) 1983 *Individual Differences in Cognition*. Academic Press, New York

Schmeck R R (ed.) 1988 *Learning Strategies and Learning Styles*. Plenum Press, New York

Svensson L 1984 Skill in learning. In: Marton F, Hounsell D J, Entwistle N J (eds.) 1984

Tabberer R, Allman J 1983 *Introducing Study Skills: An Appraisal of Initiatives at 16+*. NFER/Nelson, Windsor

Thomas J W, Rohwer W D Jr 1989 Hierarchical models of studying. Paper presented at the Annual Meeting of the American Educational Research Association, San Francisco, California

Thomas P R 1986 The structure and stability of learning approaches. Unpublished doctoral dissertation, University of Queensland

Van Overwalle F, Segebarth K, Goldchstein M 1989 Improving performance of freshmen through attributional testimonies from fellow students. *Brit. J. Educ. Psychol.* 59: 75–85

Van Rossum E J, Schenk S M 1984 The relationship between learning conception, study strategy and learning outcome. *Brit. J. Educ. Psychol.* 54: 73–83

Weinstein C E 1988 Assessment and training of student learning strategies. In: Schmeck R R (ed.) 1988

Weinstein C E, Goetz E T, Alexander P A 1988 *Learning and Study Strategies*. Academic Press, New York

The Implications for Educators

D. Mackeracher and A. C. Tuijnman

Adult learning involves a complex and dynamic interaction among a variety of physiological, personal, and environmental factors. The study of the adult learning process is informed by many theories and findings contributed by different science and social science disciplines ranging from medicine and neurology to psychology and education. This multidisciplinary body of knowledge, while being far from complete, provides useful insights into questions such as whether, why, and how adults change and learn over the lifespan.

The aim of this entry is to describe some important theories, perspectives, and research findings on the adult learning process insofar as these inform the study and practice of adult education. Hence the focus is on the implications for educators and others involved in adult learning, such as administrators, counselors, and program designers.

The topics dealt with include the capacity of adults to learn, learning styles, conditions and factors influencing learning, and motivation. The role of educational technology and open learning networks in facilitating adult learning is also discussed. The entry does not deal, at least not explicitly, with sequential perspectives of adult development over the lifespan, such as functional or structural stage models and postformal theories of cognitive development.

1. The Learning Process

Research studies on the learning of adults generally describe a cyclical sequence of learning activities (Kolb 1984, Brookfield 1986, Mines 1986, Kitchener and King 1990). There is some disagreement on the nature, order, and importance of these learning activities, and on their implications for effective adult learning (Hiemstra 1991). However, there is evidence that the importance of each activity varies with the situation and goals of learning; that the nature and order of activities vary between situations and learners; and that the nature of the learning activity is less important to the learner since the sequence is repetitive, but may be important to the educator in developing strategies for instruction or facilitation (Cross 1981). This interpretation of the adult learning process draws heavily on cognitive and information-processing theories, where the process is viewed as involving a complex interaction among cognitive, affective, psychomotor, and social behaviors and processes.

The basic activities in the learning process include some which are internal to the individual—taking in information, searching for and assigning meaning and value to information, utilizing information, making decisions, acting, and receiving feedback from internal sources on the consequences of actions—and some which involve the external environment—receiving feedback from external sources about the consequences of actions, interacting with objects and other persons, and having access to additional sources of new information.

The learner takes in information through sensory receptors from both internal and external sources. The richness and accuracy of this information are directly limited by the acuity of the learner's sensory receptors, focus of attention, and personal expectations; and indirectly affected by physical and emotional well-being, cognitive style, and previous experience. The observed information can be selectively controlled by the learner in spite of the quality and quantity of information actually available. By implication, what is learned is not necessarily the same as that presented by the educator. Hence the educator should pay attention to the assessment of learning outcomes.

The learning process continues as the individual searches for and assigns meaning and value to information (Torbert 1972, Hayes 1989). Personal meanings and values are often idiosyncratic and emerge from the ways in which an individual makes sense of direct personal experience. Social meanings and values are acquired throughy socialization and make it possible for the members of the same group to communicate. When created through shared interpersonal activity, meanings and values are both social and personal, and make sense to all individuals who participated in the creation process (Brim and Wheeler 1966). The implication is that learners should be helped to relate new subject matter to previously acquired experience as well as to their current knowledge base.

Information is used in various cognitive activities such as analyzing, comparing, inventing, and organizing. The outcome of these activities is the development of a personal system for making sense of reality and for determining action strategies. The system is flexible, dynamic, and open to change. Conscious cognitive activities involve the use of words, images, sounds, and felt sensations as representational markers for meanings and values. Unconscious activities usually involve nonverbal representational markers and may be raised to consciousness through such processes as thinking, reflecting on experience, and meditating. Emotions modify both conscious and unconscious cognitive activities.

When an individual learns in personal interaction with other persons, whether teachers or learners, there are general social expectations that cognitive and emotional processes will be made explicit, usually by formulating them into words. In this way, the individual's learning activities can be shared with, or assessed by, others.

Information manipulation results in the individual making decisions to act, which may be as unconscious and fleeting as shifting the focus of the eyes, or as conscious and extensive as migrating to a new country. The individual acts in ways which are intended, at least at the conscious level, to be congruent with decisions. Transactions, particularly those intended to change internal conditions, may not be apparent to others, but always provide the individual with new information about the action and its consequences through internal sensory feedback. Actions which involve the external environment provoke a response from persons or objects which, through feedback, also provide the learner with information about the consequences of actions. Responses can vary from silence and immobility to complex dialogues. By this means, an interactive system is established between the learner and both internal and external environments. The educator may be an important component in this interactive system.

The learning process can begin with any activity in the general learning sequence. For example, if the individual is presented with wholly new information, learning may begin with attempts to make sense of information on the basis of personal or social meanings and values. Learning may then occur with changes in information utilization. If the learner receives information or feedback which is contrary to expectations, learning may begin with attempts to develop new strategies for coping and for reducing anxiety associated with the experience.

Educators, those who facilitate the learning process, can do so directly through presenting information of varying quality and quantity at an appropriate speed, allowing for adequate response time, using recognition rather than recall techniques, providing adequate feedback on actions taken by the learner, and interacting with the learner through an exchange of meaning; and indirectly by monitoring internal activities as these are made public by the learner. Facilitation of internal activities is always limited by the learner's willingness to make these public and the ability to describe them accurately.

2. Capacity to Learn

Until the 1970s, it was commonly believed that the learning capacity of people increases until their early twenties, after which there would be a decrease during the remainder of the lifespan. There are different, often hypothesized explanations for this decrease; for example, the speed of peripheral sensory or motor processes would decline with increasing age because of neuronal loss or a general decline in the physiological system, or cognitive performance would decrease because certain functions would be less used with increasing age. Although there is some evidence that cognitive performance declines with increasing age, research studies show that intelligence is not an obstacle to learning at an old age (Peterson 1983). Even though studies have generally demonstrated the ability of most people to learn throughout life, an important role of the educator is to actively encourage a belief in personal learning capacity.

Lohman (1989) summarizes the advances in three traditions of research on human intelligence: trait theories, information-processing theories, and general theories of thinking. Of special interest here is the trait theory of fluid and crystallized abilities (Snow 1981). Crystallized intelligence depends on sociocultural influences; it involves the ability to perceive relations, to engage in formal reasoning, and to understand one's intellectual and cultural heritage. In general, crystallized intelligence continues to grow slowly throughout adulthood as the person acquires increased information and develops an understanding of the relation among various facts and constructs. Fluid intelligence, in contrast, is not closely associated with acculturation. It is generally considered to be independent of instruction or environment and depends more on genetic endowment. It consists of the ability to perceive complex relations, use short-term memory, create concepts, and undertake abstract reasoning. Fluid intelligence involves those abilities that are the most neurophysiological in nature. These are generally assumed to decline after the person reaches maturity.

Lohman and Scheurman (1992) present several conclusions with major implications for adult education:

(a) Intelligence and capacity to learn at all ages are in significant measure the product of education and experience.

(b) Those who view cognitive ability as a reflection of the biological integrity of the organism naturally look for biological causes for the observed decline in general fluid abilities over the lifespan. However, other explanations are equally plausible, including the dispersion in attentional resources brought about by an increase in knowledge, and the relative decline of such abilities through disuse.

(c) Education has traditionally sought only to develop crystallized abilities and has presumed that fluid abilities were unalterable. However, there is some indication that fluidization is encouraged when adults are asked to stretch their knowledge to solve increasingly unfamiliar problems or to organize concepts in new ways.

(d) Fluid abilities are at once both the most important products of education as well as the most important aptitudes for learning in that medium.

(e) Adults continue to develop those abilities that they use; abilities that show decline in the later adult years either emphasize speed or require the solution of novel problems. In both cases, disuse may be a significant factor in explaining the decline.

In conclusion, it appears that learning abilities are determined more by previous experience of education and experience of work than by age. Moreover, differences in learning abilities seem to be larger within than between age cohorts. Older people tend to learn a little slower, but often learn more meticulously and with more intensity than young people.

3. Adult Learning Styles

There are indications that adults exhibit diverse learning styles—that is, the unique ways and means by which they gather, process, and internalize information (see *Approaches to Learning; Individual Differences, Learning, and Instruction; Study and Learning Strategies*). A theory on the learning styles of adults has been proposed by Kolb (1984). The point of departure is a dialectic model of learning. A two-way matrix is hypothesized based on the following dimensions: concrete versus abstract learning, and active versus reflective learning. Learning is assumed to occur in a field of tension formed by these categories which, according to Kolb, are cyclically arranged. The notion of a "learning circle" is at the heart of the theory. It is postulated that in learning, adults proceed through the four stages of the learning circle. Experience lies at the basis of perception and reflection ("what was good, what was wrong?"). The learner "collects" observations and "translates" them into a "theory." Hypotheses can be derived from this body of ideas, and these are tested in practice by action. This eventually results in new experience.

According to Kolb (1984), four kinds of ability are needed for optimal learning. These are in the domains of experience, reflective observation, abstract concept formation, and active experimenting. However, people usually do not perform equally well in all four domains. One or two may stand out. Adult learning can be particularly effective if the preferred learning ability or mode is employed. Kolb distinguishes four such learning styles, namely: the diverger, the assimilator, the converger, and the accommodator (Van Der Kamp 1992).

The implication could be that the differences in cognitive or learning styles among adults have to be matched with differently designed and paced systems of instruction. Although it is generally assumed that the matching of learning styles with specific instructional methods will enhance both the ability and motivation to learn and, hence, improve learning outcomes, a review of empirical studies by Cohen et al. (1989) found little evidence to support this hypothesis. The apparent absence of a clear link between learning styles, tailored instructional methods, and learning outcomes does not necessarily imply that the concept of learning styles is invalid. Knowledge of the preferred learning modes of adults can be useful in the design of learning environments. There is a realization that good practice in adult education often depends on the application of methods that give attention to individual learner needs and match preferred learning styles.

4. Conditions for Learning

Various writers agree that several conditions are essential for facilitating the learning process. First, the individual must have access to sufficient information from direct experience or secondary sources, with enough variations on themes, presented through a variety of media, to allow similarities and differences to be perceived and patterns of meaning to emerge. Second, the learner must have enough time and freedom from threat to allow learning to proceed naturally, without anxiety or undue stress. Third, the learner must proceed through an appropriate learning "gradient" —the stepwise progression or "pacing" from easy to difficult. Four, effective learning is linked to a positive self-concept and self-evaluation as a learner.

A further condition is assumed to be of importance for adult learners: that sufficient and effective patterns of meaning and strategies for learning must have already developed if the individual is to be a competent learner. While children are usually given the time and assistance needed to develop these basic patterns and strategies, adults are generally assumed to have developed them in earlier years, an assumption which is sometimes false and can create obstacles in the learning process. Learning how to learn is increasingly viewed as an essential component and precondition for competent adult learning. Smith (1990) notes that the concept of "learning to learn" in adult education refers to the knowledge, processes, and procedures that people acquire through assistance to make appropriate educational decisions and carry out instrumental tasks associated with successful lifelong learning (see *Learning to Learn*).

5. Factors Influencing Learning

Factors which influence the learning process include, among others, whether learning occurs when the individual is acting alone, interacting with objects, or engaged in social interaction (Cross 1981); whether learning is based on information from personal experience or from secondary sources, such as opinions of others or factual data (Kolb 1984); whether learning focuses on new meanings, values, skills, or strategies, or on the expansion or transformation of those which already exist (Brim and Wheeler 1966); whether the learner's learning strategies and communicating skills work; and whether the educator's strategies and skills are effective.

Developmental tasks are important factors in adult learning to which educators must be attentive. Havighurst (1953) described the concept as follows:

> [A developmental task is] a task which arises at or about a certain period in the life of the individual, successful achievement of which leads to his happiness and to success with later tasks, while failure leads to unhappiness in the individual, disapproval by the society, and difficulty with later tasks. (p. 2)

Developmental tasks can be seen as arising from three sources: physical maturation, cultural pressure resulting from the expectations of the community and society, and aspirations in relation to individual values and needs. These vary according to lifespan phases and the general and specific problems which individuals face during moments of major transition. An elaborate example of the developmental tasks which individuals in Western societies face as they grow older is presented by Fales (1985) (see *Lifespan Development: Phases*).

Theories of lifespan development describe one or more additional stages of development that go beyond the level of formal operations described in Piaget's theory. These stages are characterized by an understanding of knowledge as constructed rather than as given, as contextual rather than as absolute, and as mutable rather than as fixed (Lohman and Scheurman 1992). The implications are that, since individual responses vary even in the case where a similar developmental task is confronted, the individual learning needs of adults need to be taken into account in the design of learning environments. Learning activities and instructional approaches should be based on learners' needs and interests, which are not constant but change with advancing age. Moreover, effective learning environments require that educators be conscious of various social or cultural impediments that might affect adult learning activities (see *Environments for Learning*).

Several additional factors critical to effective adult learning, especially insofar as these have implications for adult educators, are considered below.

5.1 Personal Learning System

Each individual's system of personal structures (such as meanings and values) and information processing capacity can be viewed as having cognitive, affective, and physical components, which determine what information is attended to and taken in, how it is processed and stored, and how selected information is interpreted. These individually based organizing structures and processes may facilitate or inhibit learning. Educators therefore have to pay attention to the individual's preferred cognitive or learning styles, decision-making and problem-solving strategies, action tendencies, and feedback requirements. In general, changing the structures of the learning system is easier than changing the processes. With the passage of time, individuals appear to maintain consistency and continuity in their learning styles (Cross 1981), but do change their interpretation of meanings and values. The major organizing structures of the learning system may change as a consequence of developmental transitions and major life events or crises (Commons et al. 1989, Smith and Baltes 1990).

It follows that adults enter a learning activity with established preconceptions of experience which provide predefined meanings and values even for a wholly new experience. The educator must be prepared to acknowledge each learner's personal system as viable for that individual and as a valued and unique source that influences further learning. Since personal systems become increasingly established as individuals age, older learners may need to be acknowledged and affirmed even more than younger learners (Peterson 1983).

5.2 Feedback

Feedback mechanisms are those processes which provide information to the learner on the actual consequences of personal activity in relation to intended consequences or goals. Feedback may come from three basic sources. First, internal sensory receptors throughout the body provide immediate reflexive feedback about an activity as it occurs. Second, external sensory receptors such as the eyes and ears offer slightly delayed information about the acting self as an object of one's own perception. It may be noted here that older people are more likely than younger people to have difficulty in remembering recently acquired information. Whereas hearing loss appears to be closely associated with difficulties of long-term memory recall, decline in visual perception is more closely associated with problems in short-term memory. Third, other objects and persons in the external environment give delayed feedback by responding to the activity of the learner. As feedback is increasingly delayed, its impact on the learner and potential effect on learning is correspondingly diminished. An individual learner is moreover free either to ignore or attend to any source or type of feedback. The implication is that educators, in designing a learning environment for adults, may well try to appeal to several senses and to incorporate sufficient moments for external feedback.

5.3 Arousal

Arousal is essential to learning and is stimulated by novelty and uncertainty. As arousal levels increase, learning becomes more efficient and effective until optimal conditions are achieved. These conditions are framed by emotions, however, which are arousal states in which both internal and external factors are given meaning based on the current situation, past experience, and expectancy with respect to the future. Thus arousal is accompanied by specific meanings, values, and action tendencies which are learned through experience and conditioned by both the actual learning situation and the learner's expectations as to the outcome. Encouraging the learners to connect new concepts and information with their personal experience, and to intersperse instruction with concrete examples that have emotional value and are familiar to the learners, are some steps that may be taken to facilitate the learning process. Accordingly, to assist the learner to establish or re-establish connections among personal experiences, meanings, and new information is an essential function of the educator of adults. This may be done by using mindmaps and knowledge bridges often and in different ways.

5.4 Stress, Anxiety, and Resistance

Stress, an arousal state which is nonspecific, is a response to a real or perceived, but identifiable, threat to personal security. Anxiety is a stress-like response in which the threat remains unidentified. Adult learning can be hindered by stress and anxiety, for example, when unpleasant memories of school emerge or when previously acquired knowledge is unsettled. Fear of failure in front of a group is another factor that may lead to resistance and lack of initiative. These examples show that there are not only many external barriers to adult learning, such as high costs or work-specific impediments, but also many personal barriers (see *Experiential and Open Learning*).

Educators should attempt to maintain a learning environment which is free from threat and assist learners to identify unlabeled fears and anxieties. Correspondingly, educators can work to enhance self-confidence in learners by diminishing the possibility to fail or to make grave errors, and by reducing time pressure. Self-pacing may be a desirable method, especially in instructing older adults, because it usually guarantees that the allocation of time for learning is adequate.

Too little information, repetitive and unproductive learning activities, or any condition which reduces the arousal level of the learner can result in sensory deprivation, boredom, and inactivity. Too much information, arousal, or anxiety can result in disorganized learning responses, selective inattention, or distorted perceptions. Optimal levels of arousal and information are individually determined and fluctuate over time and in idiosyncratic ways. Educators must be prepared to respond to individual needs for arousal and information, and to be attuned to changes in these needs over time.

5.5 Motivation and Action Tendencies

"Motivation," as defined by psychologists, generally refers to factors influencing the initiation and direction of behavior. The term thus refers to subjective "sources of organized activity"—drives, urges, emotions, needs, and other states of individuals that impel, move, push, or otherwise make them sensitive to their environment and direct their subsequent behavior (Hewitt 1988). The expectancy/valence theory, as as applied to adult education by Bergsten (1977), provides an explicit formulation of the relationships among variables such as personal meanings and values, self-esteem, context and situation, and expectancy in influencing motivation as a cause of engagement in self-directed learning or of participation in organized adult education.

Apart from expectancy/valence tendencies, orientations which relate to learning can also be described in other terms, such as: "approach/avoidance tendencies," "internal/external locus of control," "achievement/affiliation needs," "active/passive orientations to information use," "coping/irrelevant responses," and so on. A useful way to approach motivation in relation to adult learning is to view learning-associated behaviors as expressions of the individual's wish to master a developmental task or subject and the desire to identify with a group or with significant others (see *Participation: Role of Motivation*).

The task facing the educator is to make sense of motivation to learn and the corresponding action tendencies exhibited by the learners, and to develop a preparedness and strategies for enhancing or blocking specific tendencies (see *Instructional Design: Guidelines and Theories*). Educators can enhance a desire to learn and mastery by creating high expectations about the learning outcomes, heightening self-esteem, and ensuring respect through accepting and confirming the viability of the learner's self-identity and perceived reality, and through making the learning situation controllable by the individual learner. Using discovery teaching techniques is a useful way to involve and motivate learners. Since many adults are goal-directed, providing explicit instructional objectives is another useful strategy. A third way is to encourage learners to be self-directed in devising their own personal goals, learning approaches and styles, and resource needs (Hiemstra and Sisco 1990) (see *Self-directed Learning*).

In a similar way, educators can enhance action tendencies toward belonging by reducing potentially threatening situations, by utilizing personal biographies and the past experience of learners as resources for learning activities, and by promoting group interactions. Moreover, the educator can use discrepancies between past and current learning experiences as a theme to encourage group interaction, as such interaction has value as a learning motivator and serves a purpose as a means for analyzing individual and group needs (see *Group Learning; Individual Differences, Learning, and Instruction*).

6. New Directions

Some promising innovations in adult education, which to an extent are based on recent insights into the factors that optimalize adult learning, are described below. Attention is given, first, to the possible applications of new information technology and, second, to the idea of open learning which is considered to hold great potential for development.

6.1 Personalized Instruction

Personalized systems of instruction that allow the learner to pace the learning encounter are generally considered effective; according to some authors they may increase retention and the satisfaction of adults with the learning encounter. "Computer-based training" is a concept being used at present to denote the entire range of information technologies and programmed instructions applied to adult learning (see *Teaching Methods: Individual Techniques*).

Adult learning through technology makes use of a variety of approaches (for an overview, see Bainbridge and Quintanilla 1989). Examples are "traditional" media, such as broadcasting and audiocassettes; and "innovative" media, such as preprogrammed computer-based learning, computer-based communications, interactive video, tutorial systems, and simulation programs. Interactive videodisk training, for example, is increasingly being used in learning environments where an error in decision-making would be too dangerous or costly. These new educational technologies, which are directed toward the individual learner, offer not only an instructional advantage but may also improve feedback by enhancing the opportunities for self-assessment. New technologies are important, potentially at least, in enhancing learning in the workplace. They not only make further education and training a necessity but also change the context in which learning takes place (Marsick 1987). For example, new information technologies put a demand on the preciseness of the learning task and its objectives, and pose new problems for communication. This has, of course, repercussions also on the competence required of educators.

The new media in education have provided an impetus for the development of new strategies of adult learning. Two examples are "integrated learning" and "accelerated learning." The first refers to a cooperative approach where instructors work in "corporate classrooms." It is essentially based on complete job analysis, after which learning modules for specific skills are developed (see *Job and Task Analysis*). Instructors work together with employees in developing activity guides, job-plan sheets, and other instructional materials. Accelerated learning is another innovative concept. Some general principles for achieving accelerated learning can be found in the research literature.

6.2 Open Learning

Open learning refers to a principle of "learner-centeredness" and "open access" to learning opportunities. Paine (1989 p. ix) describes the term as referring to "learning which allows the learner to choose how to learn, where to learn, when to learn and what to learn as far as possible within the resource constraints of any education and training provision."

New directions for open learning have opened up as a consequence of the development of educational technology and its application to adult education, especially by open universities and other institutions for distance learning (see *Educational Technology in Distance Education*). However, relying only on the application of educational technology may limit the contribution of the open learning concept to the design of environments for effective adult learning (see *Experiential and Open Learning; Study and Learning Strategies*). The main characteristics of open learning are (Van Der Zee 1989, Van Der Kamp 1992):

(a) It is learner-centered, rather than institution-centered.

(b) It provides a means of equipping adults for self-directed learning.

(c) It implies informal learning and the use of a wide range of teaching/learner strategies.

(d) It helps in removing barriers to learning, particularly those barriers inherent in the established patterns of education and training.

(e) It gives the adult learner more choice by creating a diversity of individual opportunity.

(f) It is user-friendly, bringing education closer to the learner, who decides on when and how to engage in the learning task.

(g) It is in sharp contrast to a supplier-oriented approach to adult education; hence it has much to offer in designing powerful learning environments.

7. Facilitating Adult Learning: Conclusions

This overview has shown that there is a growing body of information about how to facilitate adult learning and which factors improve the effectiveness of the learning process. It is also evident that the development of powerful learning environments for adults needs to be based in adequate theories, methods of instruction, and new insights into how people organize their own personal learning projects. Promising theories and insights are offered by authors such as Darkenwald and Merriam (1982), Knowles (1984), Brookfield (1986), Caffarella and O'Donnell (1987), Brockett and Hiemstra (1991), Candy (1991), and Van Der Kamp (1992).

Key observations contributed by these authors are: that the readiness and capacity to learn is influenced, both positively and negatively, by previous experiences of learning; that adults generally want to learn, and that they learn most effectively when they have strong intrinsic motivation; that adults generally wish to assume considerable responsibility for their own learning—conversely, they may resist learning when they are told precisely what and how to learn; that adults tend to learn effectively if they consider material relevant to their personal needs and interests; that adults seek to learn what can be applied—they are generally problem-oriented learners; that adults value information which is meaningful and useful to them—information related to their expectations and previous experience; and that adults want to know the outcomes of their learning efforts—they require positive reinforcement and performance feedback.

See also: Lifespan Development; Lifespan Development: Intelligence; Adult Learning: An Overview; Approaches to Learning; Study and Learning Strategies; Instructional Design: Models; Teacher Roles and Teaching Styles; Teaching Methods: General; Teaching Methods: Individual Techniques

References

Bainbridge L, Quintanilla S A R 1989 *Developing Skills with Information Technology*. Wiley, Chischester
Bergsten U 1977 *Adult Education in Relation to Work and Leisure*. Almqvist and Wiksell, Stockholm
Brim O G, Wheeler S 1966 *Socialization After Childhood: Two Essays*. Wiley, New York
Brockett R G, Hiemstra R 1991 *Self-direction in Adult Learning: Perspectives on Theory, Research and Practice*. Routledge, London
Brookfield S 1986 *Understanding and Facilitating Adult Learning: A Comprehensive Analysis of Principles and Effective Practice*. Jossey-Bass, San Francisco, California
Caffarella R S, O'Donnell J M 1987 Self-directed adult learning: A critical paradigm revisited. *Adult Educ. Q.* 37(4): 199–211
Candy P C 1991 *Self-direction for Lifelong Learning: A Comprehensive Guide to Theory and Practice*. Jossey-Bass, San Francisco, California
Cohen S A, Hyman J S, Ashcroft L, Loveless D 1989 Comparing effects of metacognition, learning styles, and human attributes with allignment. Paper presented at the annual conference of the American Educational Research Association, March

Commons M L, Sinnott J, Richards F A, Armon C (eds.) 1989 *Adult Development: Comparisons and Applications of Developmental Models.* Praeger, New York

Cross K P 1981 *Adults as Learners: Increasing Participation and Facilitating Leaving.* Jossey-Bass, San Francisco, Calfornia

Darkenwald G G, Merriam S B 1982 *Adult Education: Foundations of Practice.* Harper and Row, New York

Fales A W 1985 Learning development over the lifespan. In: Husén T, Postlethwaite T N (eds.) 1985 *The International Encyclopedia of Education,* 1st edn. Pergamon Press, Oxford

Havighurst R J 1953 *Human Development and Education,* rev edn. of *Development Tasks and Education.* Longman, New York

Hayes E R 1989 Insights from women's experiences for teaching and learning. In: Hayes E R (ed.) 1989 *Effective Teaching Styles.* Jossey-Bass, San Francisco, California

Hewitt J P 1988 *Self and Society: A Symbolic Interactionist Social Psychology,* 4th edn. Allyn and Bacon, Newton, Massachusetts

Hiemstra R (ed.) 1991 *Creating Environments for Effective Adult Learning.* Jossey-Bass, San Francisco, California

Hiemstra R, Sisco B 1990 *Individualizing Instruction: Making Learning Personal, Empowering and Successful.* Jossey-Bass, San Francisco, California

Kitchener K S, King P M 1990 The reflective judgment model: Ten years of research. In: Commons M L et al. 1990 *Adult Development: Models and Methods in the Study of Adolescent and Adult Thought.* Praeger, New York

Knowles M 1984 *The Adult Learner: A Neglected Species,* 3rd edn. Gulf Publishing, Houston, Texas

Kolb D A 1984 *Experiential Learning.* Prentice-Hall, Englewood Cliffs, New Jersey

Lohman D F 1989, Human intelligence. An introduction to advances in theory and research. *Rev. Educ. Res.* 59(4): 333–73.

Lohman D F, Scheurman G 1992 Fluid abilities and epistemic thinking: Some prescriptions for adult education. In: Tuijnman A C, Van Der Kamp M (eds.) 1992 *Learning Across the Lifespan: Theories, Research, Policies.* Pergamon Press, Oxford.

Marsick V J 1987 *Learning in the Workplace.* Croom Helm, New York

Mines R A (ed.) 1986 *Adult Cognitive Development: Methods and Models.* Praeger, New York

Paine N (ed.) 1989 *Open Learning in Transition. An Agenda for Action.* Kogan Page, London

Peterson D A 1983 *Facilitating Education for Older Learners.* Jossey-Bass, San Francisco, California

Smith J, Baltes P B 1990 Wisdom-related knowledge: Age/cohort differences in response to life-planning problems. *Dev. Psychol.* 26(3): 494–505

Smith R M (ed.) 1990 *Learning to Learn Across the Lifespan.* Jossey-Bass, San Francisco, California

Snow R E 1981 Toward a theory of aptitude for learning: Fluid and crystallized abilities and their correlates. In: Friedman M P, Das J P, O'Connor N (eds.) 1981 *Intelligence and Learning.* Plenum Press, New York

Torbert W 1972 *Learning from Experience: Toward Consciousness.* Columbia University, New York

Van Der Kamp M 1992 Effective adult learning. In: Tuijnman A C, Van Der Kamp M (eds.) 1992 *Learning Across the Lifespan: Theories, Research, Policies.* Pergamon Press, Oxford

Van Der Zee H 1989 Developing the educational potential of public libraries. In: Goffree F, Stroomberg H (eds.) 1989 *Creating Adult Learning.* SMD, Leiden

Further Reading

Boucouvalas M, Krupp J A 1990 Adult development and learning. In: Merriam S B, Cunningham P M (eds.) 1990 *Handbook of Adult and Continuing Education.* Jossey-Bass, San Francisco, California

Birren J E, Schaie K W 1985 *Handbook of the Psychology of Aging,* 2nd edn. Van Nostrand Reinhold, New York

Kohlberg L, Armon C A 1984 Three types of stage models used in the study of adult development. In: Commons M, Richards F A, Armon C A (eds.) 1984 *Beyond Formal Operations: Late Adolescent and Adult Cognitive Development.* Praeger, New York

Merriam S B 1987 Adult learning and theory building: A review. *Adult Educ. Q.* 37(4): 187–98

Weinert F E, Kluwe R H (eds.) 1986 *Metacognition, Motivation, and Understanding.* Erlbaum, Hillsdale, New Jersey

SECTION IV

Educational Technology

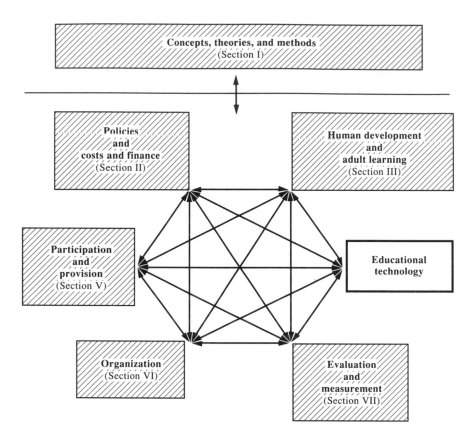

Figure 1
Schematic representation of Section IV in relation to the other Sections

SECTION IV

Educational Technology

Introduction

A. C. Tuijnman

Section IV of the *Encyclopedia* deals with a substantive area of knowledge of adult education and training, namely the design and implementation of resources and environments conducive to effective adult learning. Because of the recent advances achieved in fields such as cognitive and instructional psychology, and not least because of the relative speed of technological change, educational technology is among the most innovative and, therefore, exciting areas in the theory and practice of adult education.

1. Why Use Educational Technology?

Educational technology is a term used to describe the relatively new field dedicated to the design, implementation, and evaluation of environments, processes, and resources for learning. The latter concepts, which draw attention to the distinction between technology *in* education and technology *of* education, are described in the first entry in this section, which is written by Eraut. Today, educational technology may be defined as the systematic way of designing, implementing, and evaluating the total process of learning and teaching in terms of specific objectives, based on research in human learning and communication, and employing a combination of human and nonhuman resources to bring about effective instruction.

The use of the term "educational technology" in the heading of Section IV may strike some readers as an unnecessary provocation. Granted, the term is a little awkward. Yet it also has certain advantages, for example in that it calls attention to the *purposefulness* of learning and teaching; the *systematic design*, implementation, and evaluation of learning and teaching processes; and the *effectiveness* of instruction as a criterion for evaluation. In adult education and training, the applicability and importance of these three key concepts of educational technology—purposefulness, systematic design, and effectiveness—have traditionally been questioned. Many authors in the field have tended to emphasize other, apparently opposed

concepts, such as facilitation vs. purposive teaching, self-directedness vs. systematic design, and openness vs. effectiveness. These central principles of modern practice in adult education and training must be protected and further developed. But at the same time, the field of adult education must take account of recent innovations in educational technology. This is all the more important because not all adult education and training programs build on the application of open and self-directed modes of learning. Many—if not most—education and training programs for adults are designed to serve explicit learning objectives, and they involve the purposeful creation of active learning environments for the facilitation of effective instruction.

Questions about the curriculum and the design of environments for instruction and facilitation have received only piecemeal attention in the field of adult education. For example, although the seminal volume, *Lifelong Learning for Adults: An International Handbook* (Titmus 1989) did include one entry dealing with the curriculum and two others concerned with teaching methods in adult and education, these entries were presented in different sections of the *Handbook*. The handbooks on adult and continuing education, which have been published about once every decade since 1934 by the American Association for Adult and Continuing Education, demonstrate a similar lack of attention to major aspects of educational technology, such as the curriculum and the systematic requirements of the design, implementation, and evaluation of learning environments for adults. Even the most recent volume, the impressive 48-chapter *Handbook of Adult and Continuing Education* (Merriam and Cunningham 1989) only mentions in passing central concepts such as the intended, implemented, and attained curriculum, teaching methods, and the design, implementation, and evaluation of learning environments, learning resources, and learning processes. Yet an innovative aspect of Merriam and Cunningham's acclaimed *Handbook* is the inclusion—apparently for the first time in a publication of this kind—of a chapter entitled "New Educational Technologies for the Future." This chapter, which can be seen as a hallmark of its time, nevertheless sets an important precedent, perhaps less because of its content, but because it marks the insertion of the concept of educational technology into the mainstream vocabulary of adult education. The term "educational technology" is used as the label for Section IV of *The International Encyclopedia of Adult Education and Training* because it offers a means of drawing the attention of the reader to the perceived need of developing a new understanding of the role of technology *of* education, in particular the technology of designing learning resources and implementing learning processes in adult education and training. The second purpose is to highlight the increasingly important role of technology *in* adult education and training. The fact that the information society is advancing rapidly, at least in the more affluent parts of the world, raises many questions about the development of adult education and training systems in lifelong learning societies. It can reasonably be assumed that educational technology will have a large influence on the future of adult education and training systems—although its impact will be uneven and not always beneficial. Therefore, writers, researchers, and especially the practitioners in the field, should examine such technologies critically, so that, hopefully, pitfalls can be avoided and the promises fulfilled.

2. How the Entries are Organized

The entries included in this section are organized as follows. First, Eraut describes the principles, scope, and evolution of educational technology, which emerged as a field of study in the early 1960s. At that time, audiovisual education and programmed learning were at the center of attention. Much ground was covered during the 1970s, when new concepts such as learning resources, individualized instruction, and not least the systems approach to curriculum development were explored. As concepts such as open and experiential learning, cooperative learning, accelerated learning, and self-directed learning became increasingly prominent in the field during the 1980s, a problem-solving approach to the design of learning resources and processes became the mainstay of educational technology. With the advent of the information society, communicative and interactionist models of educational technology have become key concepts in the 1990s.

The first, very substantive essay by Eraut is followed by an entry addressing issues in the design of curricula in adult education and training. Streumer and Tuijnman offer several reasons for the attitude of indifference, on the part of many researchers and practitioners in the field, to the analysis of "formal" curricula in adult education and training. But Streumer and Tuijnman also note that the situation is gradually, albeit slowly, changing. Concepts of curriculum,

and approaches and models of curriculum development, are also discussed in this entry. Streumer and Tuijnman do not address questions about the content of adult education and training, since this content is highly varied and depends on both purposes and practices. In the next entry, Kamper examines issues and trends in the design of curriculum and resource materials for one specific area of practice, namely adult literacy. Materials for literacy work that are currently in use in both developing and developed countries are described, and examples given of actual practices in four countries: Germany, Indonesia, Namibia, and the Netherlands.

Two entries look at particular aspects of the role and application of educational technology in adult education and training. In the first of these, Bates examines the relationship between educational technology and the organization of distance education, and the issues of approach and style arising from the use of technology for the administration, development, production, and delivery of learning resources through distance education. Bates pays particular attention to the use of multimedia systems and two-way interactive technologies in distance education. Options and dilemmas for program delivery, for example concerning the choice of classroom instruction vs. instructional design approaches, are also described. In a related entry, Roth discusses the application of educational technology in two other areas of practice: initial vocational education for youth and continuing vocational training for adults. Roth looks into the uses of educational technologies in integrating academic and vocational curricula, and examines the role and usefulness of modern technologies such as integrated learning systems, interactive television systems, microcomputers, and computer-based training systems.

Design is the subject of the next cluster of six entries. Reigeluth introduces the main theories and principles of instructional design. The question that occupies instructional designers most is how to identify the learning resources and the methods of instruction that are most likely to work effectively in a variety of settings. Reigeluth notes that instructional design theory is different from, but related to, learning theory. Design theory is focused on the methods that may facilitate effective instruction, whereas learning theory is concerned with the process factors by which people learn. Next, Gustafson presents a series of instructional design models that can be applied for different purposes and in different settings. The author also describes an instructional design model that establishes common ground among the various approaches and models. For example, a common feature of most design models is that they begin the design cycle by defining the learning needs of adults and, thus, by establishing priorities. This is followed by a developmental stage, in which the learning objectives are specified and the appropriate learning resources chosen. It follows that the identification and assessment of learning needs are major problems for instructional designers. Kessels and Smith focus on one particular aspect of needs assessment, namely job and task analysis in firm-based education and training. The authors note that although job and task analysis are generally considered as belonging to the problem identification stage that preceeds the design stage, it is not always clear whether job analysis should be considered as a part of needs assessment or of instructional design. Kessels and Smith offer not only definitions of needs assessment and job and task analysis, but also descriptions of the most common methods and techniques that may be used, as well as the underlying assumptions and the limitations arising from them. In a subsequent entry, Howieson discusses the main purposes, principles, characteristics, applications, and criticisms of modularization in adult education and training. Howieson concludes that the modular approach holds great promise for the building of a lifelong learning society, mainly because it discourages a "terminal" perspective on education and training, and encourages a systems view in which all programs lead on to other programs in either a horizontal or vertical modular structure.

The determinants of effective adult education and training programs are discussed by Mulder. The focus is on the contribution of program design and implementation to successful outcomes. The human resource results model is considered especially promising in this respect. Approaches to training evaluation are reviewed, and a number of questions for future research and evaluation studies on the characteristics of effective provision posed. Smith and Marsiske propose several ways of looking at taxonomies of adult skills and competencies. Given that needs assessment and job and task analysis generally precede the development of learning environments and the design of learning resources, and also given that notions about the hierarchical ordering of skills and competencies influence the approach to evaluation and assessment that is commonly taken, the entry contributes a number of important insights with implications for the successful application of educational technology to adult education and training.

The last four entries in Section IV deal with the various aspects of teaching methods and teacher education. First, Brookfield discusses the concepts of role and style in the teaching of adults. A distinction is made between the multiple roles for adult teachers, including those as diverse as counselor, analyst, resource, model, mediator, and facilitator. Brookfield notes that the concept of teaching style evades clear definition, and he offers no definitive statements about uniquely adult teaching styles. Yet it is clear that the teaching of adults differs in some respects from the teaching of children. Maturity, voluntariness, and self-directedness are among the distinctive aspects that shape the learning environment in adult education. Many adult education and training programs require the teachers to set learning objectives, define content, administer learning stimuli, and assess the outcomes against predefined criteria. In this case the trainers tend to be recruited not on the basis of their teaching ability but on grounds of their competence in and knowledge of the subject at hand. The role of the teacher can be quite different in consumption-oriented forms of adult education, such as personal perspective-change programs, where performance evaluation does not play a significant part. In the liberal tradition of adult education, in contrast, the teachers tend to be defined more as resource persons and helpers than as instructors. This distinction draws attention to the interchangability of teaching and learning roles, where facilitators will assist rather than direct the learners. This perception of the role of the facilitator or the instructor will influence the choice of teaching methods and resource materials. Stephens reviews what is currently known about such methods and resources for the teaching of adults. Individual methods and techniques for teaching and learning in adult education are discussed by Romizowski. Finally, Jarvis and Chadwick review the history as well as the recent trends and issues in the training of adult educators in Europe and other world regions.

References

Merriam S B, Cunningham P M (eds.) 1989 *Handbook of Adult and Continuing Education*. Jossey-Bass, San Francisco, California

Titmus C J 1989 *Lifelong Education for Adults: An International Handbook*. Pergamon Press, Oxford

Concepts of Educational Technology

M. Eraut

Educational technology emerged as a field of study and occupational category in the early 1960s. One constituent, audiovisual education, was expanded into a tradition of applying within education the technologies developed outside it for entertainment, information handling, and communication. Another constituent, programmed learning, led to an applied behavioral science concept of learning design. Common ground was established around concepts of learning resource, individualized learning, and the systems approach. These were often combined into a single process of instructional development, though many practitioners were forced to adopt a more piecemeal approach. A problem-solving concept of educational technology became more attractive as the applied science claims declined in credibility. Improved access to learning was achieved through distance education, supported self-study, and new communication interfaces for the physically disabled. Increasing recognition of the power of mass communications led to concern about their control, while research into mass media provoked more critical approaches to learning resources. The emergence throughout the 1980s of interactionist concepts of educational technology is reviewed, distinguishing between interaction embedded in learning resources and interactive settings for using such resources. Research suggests that educational technology needs to give as much attention to interactive settings as it does to interactive resources. Finally, the implications of the developing information society are discussed for rethinking educational goals and the role of educational technology in facilitating their achievement.

1. Introduction

Educational technology came into existence as an occupational category during the 1960s. Prior to that time people were engaged in jobs and activities which are now regarded as pertaining to educational technology, without being labeled as educational technologists, and this situation still persists in the 1990s. Even in the United Kingdom and the United States only a small proportion of those people whom even a cautious analyst would describe as working in the field of educational technology call themselves educational technologists (Saettler 1990). The field of educational technology is scarcely recognized in Europe outside the United Kingdom (Plomp and Pals 1989), or even in Japan (Sakamoto 1989). While the same kinds of activities are pursued, the research aspects are still mainly linked to the older academic disciplines, and practical skills are developed by on-the-job training rather

than higher education courses. Nevertheless, there is strong multinational representation at international conferences on educational technology. Conceptual frameworks are shared, if not always agreed; and the factions, debates, and paradigm conflicts which characterize any significant field of study transcend national boundaries.

This entry will confine itself to conceptual frameworks used or advocated by people describing themselves as educational technologists. Most of these frameworks are often treated as occupationally specific, although this is rarely the case. Many have been imported and adapted, and some are still shared with other occupations. There is also a more philosophical line of thinking which examines the idea of educational technology in the context of knowledge claims in general, the impact of the social and natural sciences, and the nature and historical significance of technology. This proceeds with only token attention to the occupational niches taken up by people calling themselves educational technologists. However, this apparently disinterested pursuit of philosophical argument may also serve important political purposes. Educational technologists can be viewed as an interest group whose conceptual frameworks are intended not only to guide and describe practice but also to gain political or academic credibility. Thus, claims about the effectiveness and utility of educational technology serve an important political purpose in attracting resources and sponsorship, and claims about the theoretical foundations of educational technology play an important part in justifying its academic status, for which criteria related to disciplined and research-based study usually count for more than those related to utility.

2. Early Developments

The history of educational technology is so short that an account of how various occupations and patterns of thinking were brought together to create the field of educational technology is essential for understanding the situation in the 1990s. Indeed, the conceptual frameworks evolved during the 1960s still inform what is taught as educational technology in the 1990s, even though they have undergone considerable modification.

Entrants to educational technology during the 1960s usually arrived by one of two routes—audiovisual education or programmed learning. Each was associated with a number of possible conceptual frameworks, which practitioners adopted according to the nature of their job, their training, and their personal preference. However, while programmed learning could be viewed as theory-driven in its initial stages, audiovisual education found it difficult to formulate any theoretical basis for its practice. In contrast, audiovisual educators could easily link their expertise to the accumulated professional experience of classroom teachers, while programmed learning specialists tended to criticize teachers with a detachment that did little to promote mutual understanding.

Most audiovisual specialists saw themselves solely as practitioners: advisers to teachers, trainers of teachers, and providers of learning resources for use by teachers. Insofar as they had a theoretical base it consisted of two assumptions: (a) that stimulus richness and variety would enhance attention and motivation; and (b) that degree of abstraction was a critical variable in learning. Dale's "Cone of Experience," with "direct purposeful experience" at the base and "verbal symbols" at the apex (Dale 1969), was probably the most frequently cited conceptual model. Although there were always provisos about appropriateness, quality, and effectiveness, it was generally believed that the more audiovisual materials used the better; and that students needed to spend a significant amount of time in contact with "the real world" or with lively mediated representations of it—for example, motion pictures. Neither of these assumptions is theoretically tenable today, but they are not without merit as "rules of thumb."

Communication theorists have shown that there is a limit to the amount of information that can be received and processed at any one time, and that multiple channel communication can be disadvantageous (Travers 1970), but the average classroom remains a long way from media saturation. The conclusion seems to be that, in using audiovisual materials to enhance richness and variety, basic principles of message design such as simplicity, clarity, and logical organization need to be carefully observed.

Similarly, the notion of "authentic reality" inherent in Dale's cone of experience has been undermined by perception theorists' demonstration that much of what people see and hear is framed by their preexisting cognitive/perceptual schemata. It is not just experience but its interpretation that is crucial. Nevertheless, the problem of abstraction is still recognized by developmental psychologists who stress the role of concrete–operational experience for young children and distinguish between concrete, iconic, and symbolic modes of representation (Bruner 1966). The audiovisual specialists' concern with "real experience" can also be reformulated in terms of the sociology of knowledge, with attention being focused on the tensions and barriers to learning which arise from the gap between school knowledge and knowledge that has currency in the students' lives outside school.

How then did the move toward educational technology begin? One of the key individuals was Dr

James Finn, who became president of the Division of Audiovisual Instruction (DAVI), the United States media specialists' professional association, in 1960. His seminal paper *Technology and the Instructional Process* (Finn 1960) examined the possible relations of technology with education, but set this in the context of a general discussion of the role of technology in society. His main argument was that many areas of North American society were being transformed by technology, and that it was inevitable that education would eventually undergo a similar transformation. Moreover, although technological change might be led by changes in instrumentation, it was never limited to that. The transformation would involve organizational and cultural changes so radical that it was impossible to predict them. At that time two major trends were discernable but they led in opposite directions: one was the trend toward mass instructional technology, as exemplified by the new prominence of television; the other was a trend toward individualization, of which programmed learning provided a new example. The concept of programming was central to both these trends.

Finn's argument included some hard political advice. Recent highly publicized experiments in instructional television had bypassed the audiovisual specialists, and this could happen again with teaching machines. "How many of us," he asked "will go overboard and sink with the old concepts that will be absorbed or outmoded and tossed to the sharks by the new technology?" The concept of audiovisual education may go "down the drain, or it may not, depending on whether or not it can be redefined acceptably." Referring to teaching machines, he added:

It is my position that the audio-visual field is in the easiest position to help integrate these mechanisms properly into the instructional process. They are not primarily audio-visual; they are primarily technological. The audio-visual field, I think, must now suddenly grow up. The audio-visual specialists, are, of all educational personnel, the closest to technology now; we have, I think, to become specialists in *learning technology*—and that's how I would redefine audio-visual education. (Finn 1960 pp. 393–94)

Significantly, DAVI published a major sourcebook, *Teaching Machines and Programmed Learning*, edited by Lumsdaine and Glaser, the same year. Apart from a shortened version of Finn's paper, it was written entirely by psychologists. Finn explained the reasons for DAVI sponsorship in a foreword, stating: "the audiovisual professional, as a technologist of the teaching profession, must relate to fields like psychology exactly as the medical doctor relates to his basic sciences." The editors' concluding remarks suggested that psychologists were now ready to play their part:

It seems to us that the numerous contributors whose writings have produced this volume have reflected one dominant idea. This is the concept that the processes of teaching and learning can be made an explicit subject matter for scientific study, on the basis of which a technology of instruction can be developed. (p. 563) . . . As we learn more about learning, teaching can become more and more an explicit technology which can itself be definitively taught. (Lumsdaine and Glaser p. 564)

The basis for consistent improvement in educational methods is a systematic translation of the techniques and findings of the experimental science of human learning into the practical development of an instructional technology. To achieve the full benefits inherent in this concept, instructional materials and practices must be designed with careful attention to the attainment of explicitly stated, behaviorally-defined educational goals. Programmed learning sequences must be developed through procedures that include systematic tryout and progressive revision based on analysis of student behavior. (Lumsdaine and Glaser p. 572)

This introduces two new concepts, which were to be of seminal importance. First, there is the concept of instructional technology as applied learning theory. Second, there is the idea of product development through the systematic testing and revision of learning materials. Though familiar in industry, it appears that the idea of product development was rediscovered in education almost by accident: "An unexpected advantage of machine instruction has proved to be the feedback to the programme" (Skinner 1968 p. 49). Linking the two concepts gives the idea of scientific research leading to technological development which gradually evolved among psychologists between 1954 and 1964. Indeed, associations between science and technology, research and development, and psychology and education provided an attractive platform for expanding psychological research during the 1960s, without the precise nature of the linkages and dependencies needing to be agreed.

At least three different perspectives on this issue can be discerned in the psychological writings of the period:

(a) Technology is seen as the direct application of the findings of instructional scientific research. Laboratory-derived procedures need only minor modification to fit them for general use in education. The psychologist's expertise is paramount (Skinner 1958).

(b) Technological research and development is needed to combine findings from learning research with other forms of knowledge. Research and development centers are needed to accomplish the often major modifications that are required to put theory into practice. These should be run by a partnership of psychologists and educators (Hilgard 1964, Glaser 1965).

(c) Science and technology proceed in parallel. Each is capable of contributing to the other, especially if mutual communication is improved. Education

is not just the straightforward application of learning theory, and psychological research has generated no more than "islands of knowledge and understanding within the science of learning" (Melton 1959).

The third perspective uses the term "technology" descriptively, much as social anthropologists would use it; but the first two perspectives use the term prescriptively, with an aspirational futurist connotation. Thus Melton would describe current educational practice as technologically primitive, while Skinner and Hilgard describe it as nontechnological.

On the whole, these psychologists saw educational technology being developed within the educational sector, though very closely linked to training technology in the industrial and military sectors. But Finn et al. (1962) saw it coming mainly from the outside:

Education, as a sector of national life, has, for the most part, been cut off from technological advances enjoyed by industry, business, military establishments, etc. The American educational enterprise exists out of technological balance with great sectors of the society. As such, it can be viewed as a relatively primitive or under-developed culture existing between and among highly sophisticated technological cultures. (Finn et al. 1962)

Finn was overtly skeptical about the psychologists' claims that a science of learning was almost developed (Finn 1968).

Many writers confuse these different meanings of the term "educational technology" or simply choose the one that best suits their argument. For easy reference, they have been depicted in Fig. 1. The descriptive categories (1 and 3) have been expanded to include educators' common concern with disseminating practices developed in one place and thought to be improvements on tradition. Box 4 includes both the psychological perspectives described above: the "strong" applied science of Skinner and Lumsdaine, and the weaker "technological research and development" perspectives of Hilgard. Box 3 could also have been subdivided between those who extrapolate from existing trends (the prophets) and those who have advocated redesigning the educational system from a new set of "first principles" (the utopians), but this is probably too fine a distinction.

Lumsdaine (1964) made a widely quoted distinction between "educational technology 1," the application of physical science and engineering technology to the design of instructional devices (corresponding with Box 1 in Fig. 1 above), and "educational technology 2," the application of the behavioral sciences to create a technology of learning (corresponding with Box 4 in Fig. 1); but somewhat marred the discussion with the implication that a technology was dependent upon rather than interdependent with its "underlying" sciences—an unfortunate misapprehension when technological developments such as paper, ink, and movable type are discussed, which preceded

	Imported into education and adapted	Developed within the educational sector
Description and dissemination of good current practice	(a) Use of existing devices, mainly developed outside education (Audiovisual education)	(b) Currently used teaching techniques and educational practices (teacher as educational technologist)
Prescription for and prediction of future practice	(c) Wholesale use of post-industrial instruments, techniques, and organizational patterns (Educational futures)	(d) Results of massive investment in research and development (Technological research, applied science)

Figure 1
Conceptions of educational technology

scientific understanding of the phenomena by several centuries. More significant for the future, perhaps, was Lumsdaine's generic definition of a program;

> An instructional program is a vehicle which generates an essentially reproducible sequence of instructional events and accepts responsibility for efficiently accomplishing a specified change from a given range of initial competences or behavioral tendencies to a specified terminal range of competences or behavioral tendencies. (Lumsdaine 1964 p. 385)

This goes beyond the idea of a program as a reproducible presentation to the idea of a program as guaranteed learning, with the programmer accepting responsibility for student learning whenever the conditions meet the original specifications. This concept of a validated learning package neatly combined the scientist's need for reproducibility with the technologist's practice of empirical development to meet specified criteria, and provided the cornerstone for several important future developments.

Finn also identified programming as a central concept, but for a different reason. In noting that programming was common to several new technological developments—both in mass communication and in individualized learning—he added: "The heartland is programming. He who controls the programming heartland controls the educational system" (Finn 1960 p. 393) Moreover, the economics of program production demanded thinking about learning resources on a larger scale; for only then could the high production costs of television or the high development costs of programmed learning be justified.

3. The Systems Approach

The term "system" appeared fairly regularly in the early writings on educational technology referred to above, but did not immediately become part of

people's central conceptual frameworks. The Oxford English Dictionary gives it two main types of meaning:

(a) "An organized or connected group of objects; a set or assemblage of things connected, associated, or interdependent, so as to form a complex unity; a whole composed of parts in orderly arrangement according to some scheme or plan"

(b) "A set of principles, etc.; a scheme, method."

The physical, biological, and social sciences used it only in the first sense, but the influential new field of systems engineering began to use it in the second sense as well. The fields having the most immediate impact on the thinking of educational technologists were those of man–machine systems, management, and systems engineering.

The central concept of thinking about man–machine systems was that it made little sense to design machines without also thinking about their human operators, or to design human jobs without considering whether some tasks were more appropriately delegated to machines than others. It was the system as a whole which needed to be optimized. These ideas were developed in military and industrial contexts, where the use of machines was taken for granted; and resulted in the coordination of the previously separate fields of personnel selection, training, and equipment design. Its attractiveness to educational technologists was that it addressed one of their most pressing problems, the respective roles of classroom teacher and mediated instruction. This recurrent issue was highlighted by early experiments with closed circuit television and programmed instruction. The consequence, as Heinich (1968) persuasively argued, was the need for media specialists to reconceptualize their role. Decisions about the use of machines and materials needed to be

459

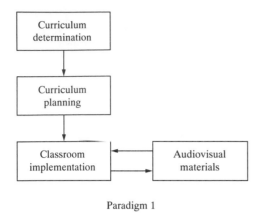

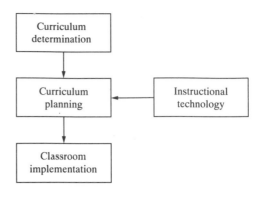

Figure 2
Two paradigms for educational technology
Source: Heinich 1968

made at the curriculum planning rather than the classroom implementation stage, according to Paradigm 2, rather than Paradigm 1, in Fig. 2.

Hoban added a further strand to the reconceptualization process when he emphasized the need for a management of learning perspective:

> When we consider the part machines play in education, we are forced into a consideration of man/machine systems. When we consider man/machine systems, we are forced into a consideration of technology . . . technology is *not* just machines and men. It is a complex, integrated organization of men and machines, of ideas, of procedures, and of management. (Hoban 1965 p. 242)

> The central problem of education is not learning but the management of learning . . . No matter which of the new educational media is introduced, the situation into which it is introduced is transformed by the introduction. Acceptance of management of learning as a central problem of organized and institutional education would, at least, permit the admission of a wider range of alternative procedures, techniques, and methods in teaching—without threatening or substantially altering the critical functions of education, teaching, or learning. (Hoban 1965 p. 244)

By this time systems thinking had become an important aspect of the field of management. The initial influence came not from engineering but from biology, where von Bertalanffy (1950) first formulated his theory of open systems. The theory was taken up and further developed by organization theorists during the 1950s and early 1960s (Griffiths 1964), though their prime concern was not with designing new systems but with analyzing and improving existing systems, and not with man–machine systems but with social systems. In particular, the systems concept drew attention to an organization's interaction with its environment and to the interplay between and coordination of its various subsystems. For the educational technologist intimately concerned with the problem of change this kind of understanding was crucial, and so was the growing body of research on innovation which followed it, but this particular strand of systems thinking had relatively little influence for some considerable time, because it was overshadowed by the impact of the systems engineers.

Systems engineering (sometimes described as operations research) evolved during the Second World War as a field concerned with the design of large-scale technical systems. Its reputation was based on successes in the military and aerospace sectors but it also found increasing application in sections of industry. Ramo defined it as follows:

> The systems approach is a technique for the application of a scientific approach to complex problems. It concentrates on the analysis and design of the *whole*, as distinct from the components or the parts. It insists upon looking at a problem *in its entirety*, taking into account all the facets and all the variables, and relating the social to the technological aspects. (Ramo 1973 p. 15)

He illustrated his argument with a comparison between telephones and automobiles. The telephone system was designed as a system from the outset and provided a closely integrated network of people and equipment that handled a wide range of demands with considerable efficiency. The automobile system was never designed as an integrated system, its subsystems (e.g., roads, repair, manufacture, insurance, parking, etc.) were uncoordinated, and it was extremely inefficient. Media specialists had no difficulty in identifying the "audiovisual system" with the latter, for it suffered from an equally frustrating lack of coordination between such aspects as hardware manufacture, building design, teacher training, and software production and

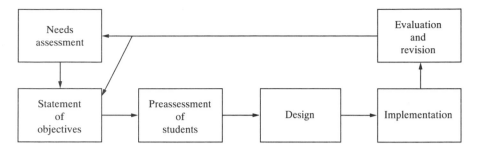

Figure 3
A general model of instructional development
Source: Diamond 1989 p. 330

distribution. The message was to "think big," and throughout the 1960s it seemed that systems engineers were waiting for the opportunity to redesign the United States educational system from the beginning.

Thinking big was also a popular pastime for educators in the late 1960s and the early 1970s, and there were sufficient examples of large-scale applications of educational technology—Oakland Community College, Oklahoma Christian College, Project PLAN, Oakleaf School, the Open University, Televised Primary Education in the Côte d'Ivoire, IMU Mathematics in Sweden, and many others—to capture the imagination of educational technologists and nurture their ambitions. Even then, however, few working educational technologists had the opportunity to work on a large scale. They could apply systems thinking to the analysis of their working contexts in order to optimize project selection and choose appropriate innovation strategies (Diamond 1989), but they were unable, except on paper, to consider solutions which changed significant organizational norms—for example, the organization of schools into standard size classrooms, or the promotion of university staff for research rather than teaching. While there might have been a "promising" innovation somewhere else in the world they were unlikely to survive in employment unless they got something done within the constraints of their own institutional context.

The principle arena for applying what was known at the time as the "systems approach" was higher education. In addition to the rapid growth within higher education of media production and service units, groups began to appear who sought to apply the programming approach identified by Lumsdaine to the development of courses and modules. The course, it was argued, was a sufficiently autonomous entity to be treated as a distinct instructional system; and a systematic approach to the development of courses should take into account both the potential of audiovisual media and the power of a programming process which analyzed learning objectives, prepared valid instruments of assessment, and refined its prototype

design by systematic tryout and revision. A proliferation of models for the development of instructional systems flooded the literature between 1965 and 1975, most of which shared the features of the general model presented in Fig. 3 (taken from Diamond 1989).

Conceptually, many of these models subtly changed the meaning of the word "system" from the first dictionary definition, associated with looking at complex situations holistically, to the second definition, a set of design principles. For some a "systems approach" came to mean a "systematic approach," while for others the issue of fitness for purpose within a larger institutional or social context remained a dominant concern. Politically, the more task-oriented models (Andrews and Goodson 1980) held a short-term advantage for four main reasons:

(a) They were less likely to challenge some of the prevailing institutional norms, although they did challenge the role and autonomy of individual professors and lecturers.

(b) Although insisting on detailed specification of objectives and preordinate evaluation, these models still allowed considerable flexibility of interpretation.

(c) The tightly coupled objectives–evaluation framework gave sufficient sense of a scientific approach to remain attractive both to psychologists and to politicians concerned with accountability.

(d) The product orientation and often implicit promise of a multimedia approach gained the allegiance of media specialists.

4. Consolidation

The period between 1967 and 1972 can be regarded as a period of consolidation. "Educational technology" became a recognized term and people began to accept

461

it as an occupational definition which covered a range of jobs in all sectors of education. The early conceptual frameworks were tried, developed, and modified according to three main criteria: (a) Did they provide a credible rationale for a newly emerging field? (b) Did they define a distinguishable set of activities as being primarily the concern of educational technologists? (c) Did they create a boundary for the occupation that was politically defensible?

The first official endorsement of a field called educational technology may well have been the establishment in the United Kingdom of the National Council for Educational Technology in 1967. This followed the report of a committee on audiovisual aids in higher scientific education, which only used the term in its concluding section. The United Kingdom Association for Programmed Learning promptly added "Educational Technology" to its title in 1968, while in the United States the Department of Audiovisual Instruction of the National Education Association changed its name to Association for Educational Communications and Technology in 1970. This coincided with the publication of a major report by a Commission on Instructional Technology appointed by Congress, and anticipated the creation of a National Center for Educational Technology within the National Institute of Education at Washington. A conference was held by UNESCO on "Training Programmes for Educational Technologists", in June 1970, and the International Bureau of Education published an important bibliography of educational technology later that year (Huberman 1970). Though the first periodical, *Educational Technology*, had been founded in the United States in 1960, it was some time before the second journal, *Programmed Learning and Educational Technology*, added the term in 1967.

As official recognition grew, the problem of defining educational technology became acute. The National Council for Educational Technology (UK), when it first met in 1967, stated that "Educational technology is the development, application and evaluation of systems, techniques and aids to improve the process of human learning" (NCET 1969). This compromise has stood the test of time because it allowed all the appropriate interest groups to identify with it without appearing too threatening to the others. The United States Commission on Instructional Technology showed a similar concern for reconciling the aspirations of educational technologists with the beliefs and expectations of educators and politicians:

Instructional technology can be defined in two ways. In its more familiar sense, it means the media born of the communications revolution which can be used for instructional purposes alongside the teacher, textbook, and blackboard. In general, the Commission's report follows this usage. In order to reflect present-day reality, the Commission has had to look at the pieces that make up instructional technology: television, films, overhead projectors, computers, and the other items of "hardware" and "software" (to use

the convenient jargon that distinguishes machines from programs). In nearly every case, these media have entered education independently and still operate more in isolation than in combination.

The second and less familiar definition of instructional technology is more than the sum of its parts. It is a systematic way of designing, carrying out, and evaluating the total process of learning and teaching in terms of specific objectives based on research in human learning and communication, and employing a combination of human and nonhuman resources to bring about more effective instruction. The widespread acceptance and application of this broad definition belongs to the future. Though only a limited number of institutions have attempted to design instruction using such a systematic, comprehensive approach, there is reason to believe that this approach holds the key to the contribution technology can make to the advancement of education. It became clear, in fact, as we pursued our study, that a major obstacle to instructional technology's fulfillment has been its application by bits and pieces. (Tickton 1970 pp 21–22)

More useful, perhaps, is the much longer definition statement produced by AECT in 1972, which included a rationale for the field of educational technology, a description of what people in the field do, and a discussion of its social and professional context (Ely 1973). The rationale section identified the uniqueness of the field with three major concepts and their synthesis into a total approach. These were "the use of a broad range of resources for learning, the emphasis on individualized and personalized learning, and the use of the systems approach." The development of each of these concepts during the consolidation period is discussed below.

The concept of "resources for learning" was a useful expansion of the earlier term "audiovisual materials," because it incorporated printed resources and could also be interpreted as including environmental resources (school trips and visits) and resource people (visitors). Although some resource production was integrated with curriculum development in the manner envisaged by Heinich's Paradigm 2 (see Fig. 3), most of it remained only loosely coordinated with the curriculum. Hence the teacher retained a major role in the selection of learning resources, and considerable attention was given to resource management, distribution, and utilization. Indeed, the teacher was often referred to as a manager of learning resources (Taylor 1970), an idea suggesting that every teacher was an educational technologist (Fig. 1 Box 3) and that teacher education, therefore, was the highest priority (Witt 1968). Resource production was assumed to be a shared responsibility. Some would be produced by commercial firms, some would be produced by locally based educational technologists, and some would be produced by the teachers themselves, preferably with technical and advisory support from educational technologists.

The associated term "resource center" also came

into common currency, combining a number of functions now considered essential for the teacher's role as a manager of resources. Thus a teachers' resource center was a place where teachers could select from a collection of existing resources, make multiple copies of a resource, produce their own resources, or even commission others to produce resources for them. Similar facilities could also be envisioned for pupils, for whom the term "learning center" or "pupils' resource center" was sometimes used.

The resources concept raises the issue of the respective roles of educational technologist and librarian; and in most countries there is now a long history of interprofessional discussion and mutual accommodation. It has become increasingly common for simple audiovisual materials to be stored in libraries and for pupils to have access to them there, while production facilities are usually found in educational technology units. Arrangements for storing complex software such as film or videotape and for managing the audiovisual equipment used in classrooms are much more varied, with reprographic equipment often being lodged with the administration.

Attention to individualized learning was not a new concept, but the idea was given a considerable boost by the advent of programmed learning. Earlier initiatives such as the Dalton and Winnetka plans were revived and redeveloped under the influence of behavioral psychologists to incorporate tightly specified student assignments, programmed learning sequences, and criterion-referenced tests (Weisgerber 1971). Most of these systems individualized only the pace at which students could learn, but some, such as the IMU in Sweden or Project PLAN in the United States, introduced assignments of different levels of difficulty, the latter backed by a computer-based record-keeping and advisory system. Later, terms such as "mastery learning," "modular instruction," "audiotutorial systems," and "personalized systems of instruction (PSI)" came to be associated with this line of development;

these are discussed elsewhere in this *Encyclopedia*. On the whole, mastery learning and PSI came to be associated with specific objectives and repetition of units by students who failed to get high scores on criterion-referenced tests, while modular instruction and audiotutorial systems allowed a looser interpretation of the systems approach and put more emphasis on the use of nonprint media. Some systems incorporated short tutorials and even some group teaching into what remained basically individualized systems.

The third key concept in this first AECT definition statement was the systems approach, whose origins were discussed above. Its main areas of application were in course development in higher education and in training development in industry and the armed services. In North America both were subsumed under the generic title of "instructional development;" but in European higher education the term "educational development" became more popular because "instruction" carried negative connotations of learner passivity.

At school level, a different problem arose. The systems approach to instructional development closely resembles the Tyler/Bloom model of curriculum development; and when Bloom began to advocate mastery learning even the element of individualization ceased to be unique to people claiming expertise in educational technology. Recognizing this lack of product differentiation, Rowntree (1974) adopted the title *Educational Technology in Curriculum Development* for his popular book on the subject. Thus, apart from a few nationally funded projects which carried an educational or instructional technology label, the term "educational technology" usually referred to the design, production, and utilization of learning resources which incorporated audiovisual and/or electronic media.

It is also worth noting that the term "resources" in the AECT definition (Fig. 4) is used in a broad sense that includes both people (human resources) and settings (the resources of the organization and

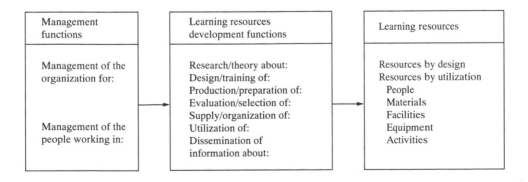

Management functions	Learning resources development functions	Learning resources

Management of the organization for:
 	
Management of the people working in:
	Research/theory about:
	Design/training of:
	Production/preparation of:
	Evaluation/selection of:
	Supply/organization of:
	Utilization of:
	Dissemination of information about:
		Resources by design
		Resources by utilization
		  People
		  Materials
		  Facilities
		  Equipment
		  Activities

Figure 4
The domain of educational technology
Source: Adapted from Ely 1973

its environment). This usage is similar to that of economists and planners, but wider than the educators' meaning which generally refers only to materials and equipment. Thus educational technologists could negotiate local meanings in their own work settings, according to what they felt was feasible and appropriate.

5. Development and Criticism of the Early Frameworks

A social historian could cite the early development of educational technology as a prime example of the centralist approach to reforming society which persisted throughout the 1960s and early 1970s. In the United States, the post-Sputnik period was characterized not only by the space race but by substantial federal spending on education. The 1958 National Defense Education Act (NDEA) was responsible for a wave of spending which launched educational technology into the schools, and basic research received generous funding from the federal government throughout the 1960s. While other nations spent on a much smaller scale, their mood was not substantially different. Moreover, UNESCO funded substantial projects in educational television in less-developed countries, where the scarcity of trained teachers was seen as offering even greater potential for gaining benefits from the use of technology. In the United Kingdom the idea of a technology-based Open University featured prominently in the successful election campaign of Harold Wilson in 1964.

The initiatives of the 1960s, however, were not based only on expanding the use of technology. They were also characterized by a social engineering approach which claimed to be based on the emergent social sciences. At no time, before or since, have the social sciences been held in such high regard. They saw themselves as extending the physical sciences into the realm of human behavior, presented a strongly positivist image, and claimed to be culturally neutral and value free. It is surely no coincidence that Lumsdaine's (1964) distinction between a technology-based Educational Technology 1 and a behavioral science-based Educational Technology 2 reflected so precisely the technological futurism and social engineering ideologies which prevailed in Western society at that time.

The term "engineering" itself carries a relevant range of meanings. First, branches of engineering are distinguished by the nature of their product—aeronautical, civil, electrical, mechanical, production, systems, transport, and so on—and there is a debate about how much these branches have in common. Within educational technology, the broadcasters and moving picture producers have remained separate, but the urge to present a united front has sometimes prevented sufficient articulation of the effect of different

kinds of product, both on the design process itself and on the knowledge requirements for the producer (Eraut 1988). Second, while engineers sometimes emphasize their knowledge base and denote themselves as applied scientists, they also stress their experience and pragmatism and describe themselves as problem solvers. The balance can vary considerably, according to whether they are mainly concerned with applying existing knowledge to tasks only marginally different from those encountered previously or with creating a new design to solve a problem with many novel features.

This last distinction, in particular, has been recognized by two widely quoted typologies of educational technology. Davies (1981) refers to three archetypes —the audiovisual, the engineering, and the problem-solving. Under audiovisual he includes both the use of learning resources and mass communications; engineering refers both to applied behavioral science and systematic instructional development; problem-solving is a more creative approach to design which he identifies with the notion of instructional development as an art. Romiszowski (1981) presents a similar three-fold distinction. Like Davies, his third archetype is concerned with problem-solving, though he also links it to the more holistic type of systems approach. His first two concepts are inappropriately named product and process, even though his explanations suggest a view almost identical to that of Davies. It is a common fallacy to suggest that learning resources are not developed by a process, even when it does not closely resemble that advocated by instructional developers; and equally fallacious to imply that instructional development does not yield a product, even though it may not be a learning resource. Some authors even suggest that following their instructional development blueprints will necessarily lead to success. However, there are no guaranteed routes to good design, precisely because it cannot be reduced to an applied science.

The articulation of a problem-solving concept of educational technology can be viewed as an attempt to introduce greater flexibility and creativity into the design processes in which many educational technologists were engaged. Whereas in the mid-1960s people thought that learning resource production and course development could benefit by being made more systematic and incorporating formative evaluation, by 1980 the situation had changed and the danger appeared to come from those who thought all the relevant expertise would be encapsulated in simplistic instructional development manuals. The problem-solving concept also helped to distance educational technologists from their behavioral science origins at precisely the time when the behavioral sciences were coming under increasing criticism.

Until the mid-1970s, research into the use of media in teaching was dominated by media comparison studies which yielded little information of practical or theoretical use (Clark 1983). Hence there was a need to examine the links between media and learning at a more micro level with greater attention to identifying critical media attributes and the ways in which they affect a learner's cognition (Salomon 1979). This second phase of more cognitively oriented media research was reviewed by Clark and Salomon, who concluded as follows:

> Generally, it appears that media do not affect learning in and of themselves. Rather, some particular qualities of media may affect particular cognitions that are relevant for the learning of the knowledge or skill required by students with specific aptitude levels when learning some tasks. These cognitive effects are not necessarily unique to one or another medium or attribute of a medium The same cognitive effect may often be obtained by other means, which suggests a measure of "functional equivalence". This implies that there may be "families" of functionally equivalent but nominally different instructional presentation forms. (Clark and Salomon 1986)

The modesty of this analysis may not yet be typical of the social sciences, but it is an excellent example of the retreat from the sweeping generalizations to which their predecessors aspired. It also suggests that the knowledge base for the media selection aspects of instructional design is both complex and of limited scope. Other criticisms of the audiovisual or technology-driven archetype can be found in Sects. 6 and 7 below.

Criticism of the engineering archetype has been more vociferous, because of its more overtly positivist stance (it was only the research side of the audiovisual archetype which began in such a positivist way). The major focus of debate has been the use of behavioral objectives. They have been criticized (a) for imposing an atomistic interpretation of the learning process and (b) for creating impoverished representations of the relevant knowledge domains. Both arguments have been more strongly supported in Europe than North America: reductionism had already permeated North American practice through the widespread adoption of multiple-choice and short-answer tests, so using behavioral objectives had less effect on existing learning goals. By the mid-1970s, many instructional developers had ceased to define objectives at the behavioral level and were somewhat irritated by critics who failed to distinguish between general and specific objectives (see Eraut 1989b for a review of this whole debate). Some even began to use alternative modes of knowledge representation alongside more general statements of goals (Rowntree 1981). In doing so, however, they had effectively abandoned the applied science approach of those like Gagné and Briggs (1974) who continued to advocate design principles based on inferring learning categories from behavioral objectives, then shaping instructional plans to fit those categories. While theoretically sound within its own terms of reference, this approach has gradually lost credibility through lack of evidence that its products have had any demonstrable advantage.

The problem-solving concept of educational technology has not been much criticized but neither has it been greatly clarified. What, for example, is the role envisaged for an educational technologist working in this way? Two answers are possible: one is the role of a process consultant (Hewton 1989), another is that of a specialist member of a problem-solving team which also includes other specialisms. In practice, many people attempt to combine the two although there are inherent dangers in such a dual role. Educational technology has been, often justifiably, accused of being a solution in search of a problem. What then is the nature of the educational technologist's expertise? Consultancy requires many interpersonal skills and an ability to conduct analyses of problems and situations and to search for knowledge of possible relevance to developing an appropriate response. Knowledge of educational technology practice and methodology has to be shared with others in a manner which does not jeopardize their ownership of the problem. Beyond this level of competence, however, much of the expertise is tacit. The expert educational technologists in this problem-solving tradition are pragmatic, well-informed people, who know their theory but rely even more on accumulated professional experience. Schon (1983) calls such people "reflective practitioners," and contrasts them with professionals in the "technical rationality" tradition who claim that their expertise is based upon applied science.

Criticism of the conceptual frameworks of educational technology has also developed at a deeper level, reflecting the growing debate within the social sciences between the positivist and interpretative paradigms. Eraut summarizes the position in the following terms:

> The positivist paradigm has played an important part in the field of educational technology. It is strongly research-based and incorporates two major research traditions. The experimental tradition is rooted in behavioural psychology and is associated with small-scale experiments under controlled conditions. The correlational tradition forms the basis of much educational research and is associated with large field samples and the use of statistical techniques to ascertain the relative significance of various personal and situational factors. In both traditions the purpose of theory is to explain, generalize and predict. Hence the positivist paradigm is associated with strong knowledge claims.

> The interpretative paradigm starts from a different view of theory. Theories are not part of some natural truth waiting to be discovered, they are invented by people in order to interpret and make sense of their world. Empirical evidence affects whether people find a theory adequate for this purpose, but so also do other considerations. The purpose of a theory is not to provide a causal explanation of a situation or sequence of events but rather to add to one's understanding of it. Moreover, it is expected that people's understandings of any given social situation will differ according to their role, their interest, and their knowledge; so it is important for one's own understanding to know how other people perceive the situation. Hence

there is a strong emphasis on qualitative methods and case study research, though not to the exclusion of quantitative data. Knowledge claims in this paradigm tend to be rather weaker than those in the positivist paradigm because they are believed to be more situationally and culturally specific.

Within the field of educational technology, both paradigms can be found in abundance. However their distribution is not at all even. Positivist approaches are stronger in instructional design, interpretative approaches in utilization. Positivist approaches are more readily found where there is political power and in large-scale developments, interpretative approaches where there is little power and the enterprise is small-scale and local. Positivist approaches are stronger in North America, interpretative approaches in Europe. Positivists believe in expertise, interpretativists in wisdom (Eraut 1989a p. 4).

Hawkridge (1993) also gives considerable attention to criticism derived from a third social science paradigm, based on critical theory. This has become quite prominent among philosophers and sociologists of education, and is increasingly used in research into mass communications. Hitherto it has received limited attention in educational technology, but that may well change during the 1990s.

A contrasting perspective is provided by Heinich (1984). He argues that educational technologists have been too pragmatic, are tackling the wrong problems, and have grown used to thinking too small. They have been oversocialized into the prevailing norms of their host cultures in schools and higher education, and thus have lost sight of the potential of technology to transform those institutions. There is surely some truth in this criticism: much may have to be challenged if progress is to be made. To effect change from the outside, however, requires either power or an alliance with powerful people who have other agendas for change; and to effect change from the inside requires a normative–re-educative approach through staff development, which Heinich regards as a diversion. The primary effort, he argues, should be devoted to "the development of more powerful technologies of instruction along with the development of organizational structures that facilitate their use," because "the basic premise of instructional technology is that all instructional contingencies can be managed through space and time (i.e. they can be incorporated into the interface between student and material and/or device). Our inability to do so in any given situation is viewed as a temporary deficiency in our knowledge base." It is precisely this premise that most educational technologists have long since abandoned, and attempts to revive it under the label of information technology have been treated with a degree of skepticism.

6. Mass Communications, Access, and Control

A major feature of educational technology since the 1950s has been the regular stimulus of technological innovation. Each new medium to arrive on the scene has raised hopes for an impact on education similar to that achieved in the entertainment, communication, and information-handling aspects of society; and these hopes have been encouraged by industries anticipating sales of new media to schools. However, the investment in software development and training has rarely been sufficient to realize the potential of the new medium, and the evidence for imposing a new burden on hard-pressed education budgets has not been convincing. Resources have gradually accumulated in richer countries and districts lucky enough to be the recipients of pilot projects, but coherent long-term policies have been lacking.

The more successful media have developed their own specialist communities of producers, publishers, designers, and so on, whose criteria for success have had little connection with education. Broadcasters, for example, derive their criteria from (a) aesthetic criticism of peers and critics and (b) their ability to attract and hold an audience (not to teach a captive audience). Designers of computer software also derive their success criteria from their peers, but are mainly judged by their ability to sell their programs to a business-dominated market. There are some specialist education producers in both broadcasting and computing but they are a small group, sandwiched between the norm-determining commercial or public service community and a conservative and penurious educational system. Some are qualified teachers and value the opinions of other teachers as well as anxiously watching their sales and popularity. Thus the needs of education have a small impact on software development but virtually none on hardware development.

Of equal importance is the burgeoning academic field of communication or media studies, which combines the artistic approach of the critic (as in literature and painting) with an essentially social scientific study of the role and impact of mass communication in modern society. Although communication models were frequently cited by media specialists during the formative period of educational technology, they were discussed only in the most general terms. However, the development of research in related fields suggests

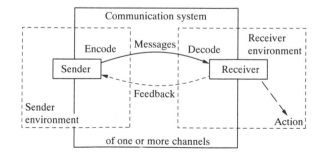

Figure 5
A composite communication model

that communication theory concepts could have more direct application in the 1990s. Since communication theory models have as many variants as systems models, a composite model is presented in Fig. 5 to show the main features of this approach.

Traditional educational technology research focused primarily on the interaction between message characteristics and subsequent receiver action, and was thus dependent on the constructs available for describing them. Neither simple media distinctions nor the simple "types of learning" classifications of the behavioral psychologists have provided adequate descriptions of messages, and this is now recognized as a much more complex problem to which linguistics, visual communication, semiotics, cognitive psychology, and the relevant content specializations also have to contribute. The characterization of receiver action also poses problems when it has to be elicited by some kind of achievement test which fails to recognize emotions, motivation toward the subject matter of the message, or transfer to "real" action in subsequent situations. Receiver actions have to be understood as part of their ongoing interaction within their environment in which some messages and some actions are given greater priority than others, so receiver behavior cannot be interpreted in terms of the communication system alone.

Even in culturally familiar settings the sender often lacks appreciation of the receiver's environment and encodes the message in some inappropriate way or misinterprets the feedback he or she received, and this problem is magnified as the cultural gap between senders' and receivers' environments widens. The often unconscious influence of the senders' attitudes and beliefs is being increasingly researched, as also is the influence of the politics of the senders' environment on message selection. This raises the issues of who controls the communication system and whose interests it serves, a major concern when systems have a monopoly or are largely controlled by a single interest group.

One positive aspect of mass communication technology has been its contribution to the problem of access. Sometimes this is interpreted in terms only of access to products, so debate is focused around the extent to which products such as broadcast programs and learning resources can be made more widely available by extending communication and distribution networks and/or reducing the cost. Both raise financial issues familiar to those in public broadcasting, adult education, and library services. Access to products, however, does not guarantee access to learning. There have been a few dramatic examples of unaccompanied products making a difference, such as the *Sesame Street* series, which helped to increase access to learning opportunities for the vitally important preschool population, but even these have not taken on the sole responsibility for taking a cohort of learners to specified learning goals. Most individuals in most situations require learning packages rather than single resources, and human support systems as well. How then has educational technology helped to improve access to learning?

The best-known contribution of educational technology to access has probably been the development of distance education systems. The Open University in the United Kingdom made a dramatic impact in this field, through its ambitious planning, high-quality products, political backing, and association with high-status institutions such as the BBC. It also used product development methods derived from educational technology, as well as a multimedia approach; and it made proper provision for a human support system for its students. The consequent opening up of educational opportunities for adults is well-documented.

Less dramatic but not insignificant has been the growth of supported self-study within educational institutions. Though sometimes used to deliver the normal curriculum in the manner of the individualized learning systems reported above, its contribution to access has been to make it possible to run smaller classes than would otherwise be considered viable, to overcome a shortage of specialist teachers, by using them as visiting consultants rather than class teachers, and to enhance the feasibility of drop-in learning systems, which learners can attend flexibly at their own convenience. Often it is possible to construct learning packages around existing resources of a conventional kind, rather than design complete new systems which takes longer and costs much more.

The third major contribution has been the development of technological support for people with physical disabilities. Some members of this group have been emancipated by new technology to a quite remarkable extent, though many others have yet to benefit because of the cost. The arrival of personal computers and the development of a range of purpose-designed interfaces has provided communication with wider society of a quality that had been previously considered impossible (Hawkridge and Vincent 1992).

The limits on the access developments reported so far are largely financial, but finance is not the only form of control. One has only to ask what products and messages are available for people to access, to recognize that control has other dimensions. Not only is there control over the selection of programs for production and dissemination but there is also control over how these programs are conceived and framed. While bias is not always intended, a degree of cultural and ideological framing is unavoidable. Both mass communication systems and school systems present similar problems, and their messages have been known to reflect the views of their controllers on such critical issues as gender, class, and ethnicity, even when overt political agendas have been carefully balanced.

One partial remedy for the problem of minimal influence on these systems is access to alternative channels of communication. The possibilities opened up by desktop publishing, cheap video equipment, and cable networks make this much more feasible than even in the 1980s. Hence an important role for educational technologists could be to provide sufficient education, training, and facilities for local and minority groups to be able to produce and distribute their own learning resources. Not only should one consider access to programs and access to learning, but also access to the means of production and channels of communications.

7. Interactionist Concepts of Educational Technology

Both technological and theoretical developments have brought interactionist concepts of educational technology into greater prominence during the 1980s and early 1990s, but while interactivity is applauded as desirable, there are divergent perspectives about what it means. Hence it is useful to make certain distinctions. First, interactivity may be either situated within a learning resource or viewed as a characteristic of the setting in which the resource is used. Second, although interactivity usually refers to the learning process, the concept is sometimes extended to encompass learning goals as well. However, even when people share the same definition they may have different perspectives about the level of interaction which actually occurs (depending no doubt on their personal norms and expectations), and about the potential for interactivity inherent in any particular resource or setting. Hence claims for interactivity need careful examination.

Two kinds of interactivity may be built into a resource—that which facilitates the use of the resource as a tool and that which attempts to build a tutoring function into the resource. Thus the computer is regarded as the interactive tool *par excellence* because it allows people to prepare texts, designs, or programs by the interactive processes of trial and error and successive approximation. It is the ability to see what has been done and change it that makes the computer so valuable as a tool. There is an important distinction to be made, however, between using a computer successfully to complete a task and learning the concepts embedded within that task. This latter goal has been approached either through tutoring or through designing what has come to be called a learning environment.

The concept of a learning environment controlled by a computer probably originated with Moore who designed a computer-controlled "talking typewriter" to teach children to read. He described it as one example of an "autotelic responsive environment." He defined as autotelic any activity in which one engages for its own sake and not for obtaining some external reward, and a responsive environment as one which satisfies the following conditions:

(a) It permits the learner to explore freely.

(b) It informs the learner immediately about the consequences of his or her actions.

(c) It is self-pacing, that is, events happen within the environment at a rate determined by the learner.

(d) It permits the learner to make full use of his or her capacity for discovering relations of various kinds.

(e) Its structure is such that the learner is likely to make a series of interconnected discoveries about the physical, cultural, or social world (Moore 1968).

Papert's work with LOGO-based microworlds embraces a similar rationale, though subsequent research has revealed a major problem with the fifth principle. Like other contexts designed to promote discovery learning, students do not necessarily learn all the concepts built into their design. Thus Hoyles and Noss, in a review of learning in mathematical microworlds, drew attention to "the inescapable and perhaps unpalatable fact that simply by interacting in an environment, children are unlikely to come to appreciate the mathematics which lies behind its pedagogical intent." Their observations suggest that:

> pieces of knowledge are appropriated (or not) depending upon pupils' own agendas, how they feel about their participation, teacher intervention, and above all, the setting in which the activities are undertaken. Thus it is misguided to argue that simply by interacting with the computer, children are in general likely to 'acquire' specified mathematical ideas. (Hoyles and Noss 1992 p. 31)

They still regard interactive software as a valuable learning resource, but argue that achievement of the intended learning goals also requires a teacher and benefits from interaction with peers. An interactive setting is needed as well.

Attempts to build a tutoring function into learning resources also have a long history. In the 1960s the term in favor was "adaptive programming." The goal was that of adapting the messages presented by an interactive resource to fit the requirements of the learner at that particular time. In the 1990s it is called "intelligent tutoring" and its purpose is to build a tutoring system around knowledge of the subject, knowledge of the system, and knowledge of how to help the student learn (Sleeman and Brown 1982). Each of these three subgoals presents major problems, which derive not so much from the technology as from the positivist and reductionist view of knowledge upon which any operational version of intelligent tutoring must ultimately depend. First, there are considerable doubts as to whether the knowledge representation problem is solved (Dreyfus and Dreyfus 1986, Self 1987). Second, it is now abundantly clear from decades of psychological research that the difficulties of characterizing individual students according to some manageable set of variables, incorporating subtle distinctions of mental abilities, cognitive style, and other personality variables are quite intractable. Third, the possibility of making links between student characteristics and machine decisions that are valid at the individual level is rapidly receding as research into aptitude–treatment interaction struggles to find barely significant correlations at the level of groups. Little has been achieved beyond analyzing student responses to a small number of test items and tasks, and arranging the next presentation accordingly. Even then the decision rules are primitive and there is little evidence for more than a marginal improvement in learning.

The above discussion suggests that there has been a tendency for the introduction of interactive learning resources to be accompanied by extravagant claims, and that this has not been helped by the use of metaphors like "environment," "intelligent," and "tutor." This contrasts with the relative neglect by educational technologists of the role of interaction with peers and teachers in settings designed to promote learning. Perhaps this is due to their early preoccupation with behavioral psychology at the expense of cognitive psychology and social psychology.

The processes by which learning goals and achievements are defined, accepted, or negotiated by learners have a profound effect on learning. This led Flechsig (1975) to argue that the interactionist concept of educational technology "is characterized by the principle that learners take over the control over their learning processes, whereas the three other concepts—explicitly or implicitly—locate the control functions within the teacher or the teaching system" (p. 8). Meanwhile Azuma, following Moore's autotelic principle, was making a similar argument:

> An important problem we have to recurrently rethink during this coming decade is the proper balance of the two approaches which we have seen in technological development over the two preceding decades. One is the effort to improve the effectiveness of mastering externally defined learning tasks, the other is an orientating towards providing a learning environment wherein learning is intrinsically motivated and self-directed. (Azuma 1977 p. 3)

This attractive argument was to be heard throughout the 1980s, particularly by the followers of Papert (1980), but it neglects the fundamentally social nature of human beings. Irrespective of formal statements of purpose, social interactions with teachers, peers, families, and significant others profoundly affect what is considered valid, meaningful, or useful knowledge, and what is to count as good or acceptable progress in learning. Nevertheless, within such a context and working toward their future needs, societies are increasingly looking to their education systems to develop independence and collaboration, and the appropriate use of learning resources can play an important part in pursuing this purpose.

One important perspective on this issue concerns the ownership of learning goals. It is argued that the greater the involvement of learners in the determination of goals, the more they will be committed to pursuing those goals. Since goals also require social approval to be accepted as meaningful, this implies a process of negotiation which allows learners to combine a sense of self-direction and efficacy with the reassurance of social approval. In some settings, for example where there is project work or contract learning, learners will have a major say in goal determination. In others, goals will be negotiable only at the level of detail or the order in which they are tackled within a tightly specified formal curriculum. However, even at this level negotiation can have a significant impact on gaining acceptance of goals and cultivating a sense of ownership, provided that the purpose and importance of the externally determined goals is clearly communicated.

A framework for conducting such negotiations and giving reality to their implementation was introduced by the Technical and Vocational Education Initiative (TVEI) of the United Kingdom Department of Employment during the late 1980s under the heading of "flexible learning." It sought to combine the advantages of resource-based learning with the notion of action planning, a concept derived from management theory (Eraut et al. 1990).

The framework involves learners or groups of learners negotiating learning targets with their teachers then planning their own learning pathways to include an appropriate combination of learning resources and experiences. By including groupwork and experiential learning within its remit it avoids the isolationism which often limits resource-based learning, and is much better suited to goals involving practical and interpersonal skills. In practice, three major constraints tend to operate: tightly specified curricula can so reduce the opportunity for negotiating goals that little sense of ownership is developed, learning paths may be constrained by lack of sufficient resources, and the difficult tutoring role may be too demanding of some teachers' subject and pedagogic expertise, and possibly also of their available time.

Conceptual constraints arise because learning is not simply a matter of assimilating new information, but also involves the development and modification of conceptual frameworks for structuring and organizing information. Theories of cognitive development suggest that it results from learners struggling to construct their own knowledge base in order to make sense of a world that is constantly being revealed to them through interaction with their social and physical environment. While a person's knowledge base will have many similar features to those of others as a result of continuing social communication, facilitated in most cases by use of a common language, it still remains personalized; and it is important for a person's learning as well as their sense of identity that the personal nature of their knowledge is recognized.

Comparatively recent thinking has brought together

previously separate developments in cognitive and social psychology, as research in Geneva by Doise, Mugny, and Perret-Clermont has shown that cognitive development of the kind characterized by Piaget is facilitated by peer interaction (Light and Blaye 1990). These findings have been interpreted in terms of sociocognitive conflict: divergent views are more effective in promoting development when held by different people than when left for resolution by purely internal argument as a result of cognitive dissonance. The Russian psychologist Vygotsky, however, whose work is being increasingly recognized as of major importance, put more stress on what has come to be called "guided intervention." In particular he developed the concept of a "zone of proximal development" to describe "the distance between the actual developmental level as determined by individual problem solving and the level of potential development as determined through problem solving under adult guidance or in collaboration with more capable peers" (Vygotsky 1978 p. 86).

Teaching is then characterized in terms of helping learners to bring within their individual capability that for which they previously required assistance, and a major role for either a teacher or a more capable peer is that of providing the cognitive "scaffolding" to support this transition. Such scaffolding comes from a deeper understanding of the problems encountered and the possession of conceptual frameworks of which the learner is as yet only dimly aware. All the evidence so far is that the process of assisting the learner through the zone of proximal development requires interaction with a teacher and/or capable peers, even when interactive learning resources are used (Hoyles and Noss 1992, Eraut and Petch 1994).

While some educational technologists are beginning to give more attention to cognitive psychology, most still seem reluctant to come to terms with its implications, perhaps because they find the underpinning constructionist epistemology deeply unsettling and the more extravagant claims of the artificial intelligence field somewhat suspect. However, they cannot afford to remain content with a view of learning which can account only for the assimilation of new information to existing cognitive frameworks. Nor should they continue to treat interaction with teachers, peers, and significant others as irrelevant to the design and use of interactive learning resources.

8. Information Technology and the Information Society

What is often referred to as new information and communications technology (NICT) has dominated educational technology throughout the 1980s and 1990s. With it has come a return to the atmosphere of the 1960s when the dominant issue for laypeople, if not for all educators, was how to use NICT for the improvement of education. People have been carried away by inflated claims, treated pockets of innovation as normal practice, and ignored decades of research on the process of planned change. However, there is one important difference. Finn's (1960) prediction that new technology would bring about organizational and cultural changes which would transform society is no longer regarded as mere futurism; it has become part of the conventional wisdom about information technology. So alongside the other concern with using NICT to promote learning is a newer concern with preparing learners for a future in which new technology will play a dominant role in society.

One indication of the growing significance of the challenge posed to education by this development was the dedication of the 1989 biannual meeting of the Council of Europe's Standing Conference of Ministers of Education to the theme of "Education and the Information Society." The conference noted that:

The gradual development of an information society is giving rise to a number of tensions which need to be resolved in policy and practice. These include:
1. The tension between past and future, i.e. between traditional culture and new habits and attitudes.
2. The tension between preparing pupils as citizens who will contribute to creating the future and qualifying them for future employment according to externally determined predictions of need.
3. The tension between the formal curriculum of the school and the 'informal curriculum' available outside it.
4. The tension between teaching pupils about NICT and making the use of NICT part of school life.
5. The tension between responding to vociferous demands from pupils and parents and ensuring equality of access for all pupils. (Eraut 1991 p. 13)

These are deep issues whose complexity indicates that the use of NICT is far from being a simple matter of finding the money and training the teachers.

In an expert paper prepared for the conference, Eraut drew attention to seven types of educational aim which had been advocated in connection with using NICT in education and in wider society, as follows:

1. The more effective achievement of existing goals by using new methods such as video presentation or computer-assisted learning.
2. Enabling new goals to be taught within the current curriculum framework of subjects. For example, the vicarious experience brought into the classroom by television, the information-processing potential of computerized databases and the modelling capacity of new interactive software have significantly changed what can be taught in subjects like science and geography.
3. Learning about society and its technology. The onset of the information society must have a major effect on what is taught in the social science and science/technology areas of the curriculum. One major issue is the extent to which this should have a future orientation.
4. Learning to use new information and communication technologies as part of a general programme for developing information-handling and communication skills. This

can be taught either as a separate subject, or as part of a cross-curricular approach like study skills. The most ambitious claims in this area relate to the use of computers in developing metacognitive or thinking skills.

5. Learning knowledge and skills appropriate for some specialist occupation. This would be a form of prevocational or vocational education. Computer science, technical graphics and office skills are common examples.

6. Learning to criticize the programmes and products of NICT. The purpose is to develop a more critical approach from a variety of perspectives. Media studies has tended to follow the tradition of art or literary criticism, while consumer education has focused more on technological or economic aspects. The appraisal of computer software could profitably draw on both traditions.

7. Creative use of NICT for purposes defined by the students themselves. The assumption is that students should not be only at the receiving end of other people's communications. They should learn to produce communications of their own, e.g. class newspapers, videos, computer programs, partly to improve their understanding of the various media and genres but also to develop their enterprise and initiative; and to counteract any monopolistic tendencies in public communications facilities. (Eraut 1991 pp. 165–66)

These aims penetrate into almost every section of the school curriculum, so what is eventually needed is a reappraisal of the shape and scope of the whole curriculum and the balance and emphasis within each part of it. In the meantime, hard thinking is needed about priorities and about the realities of implementation.

The process of change will remain gradual. Hawkridge (1993) argues in his analysis of the challenges to educational technology coming from cognitive science, information technology, and critical theory, that the field of educational technology itself needs modernizing, but it should be done without any utopian aspirations. The history of educational technology provides many examples of limited theories, poor quality products, and naive approaches to implementation. New generations of policymakers and educational technologists ignore the lessons learned from such experience at their peril.

References

Andrews D H, Goodson L A 1980 A comparative analysis of models of instructional design *J. Instr. Dev.* 3(4): 2–16

Azuma H 1977 The third decade of educational technology. *Educ. Tech. Res* 1: 1–4

Bruner J R 1966 *Towards a Theory of Instruction*. Belknap Press, Cambridge, Massachusetts

Clarke R E 1983 Reconsidering research on learning from media. *Rev. Educ. Res.* 53(4): 445–60

Clark R E, Salomon G 1986 Media in teaching. In: Wittrock M C (ed.) 1986 *Handbook of Research on Teaching*, 3rd edn. Macmillan, New York

Dale E 1969 *Audio Visual Methods in Teaching*. Holt, Rinehart, and Winston, New York

Davies I K 1981 Instructional development: Thematic, archetypes, paradigms and models. In: Dill C E (ed.)

1981 *Instructional Development: The State of the Art*, Vol 2. Association for Educational Communications and Technology, Washington, DC

Diamond R M 1989 Systems approaches to instructional development. In: Eraut M (ed.) 1989a

Dreyfus H L, Dreyfus S E 1986 *Mind over Machine*. Blackwell, Oxford

Ely D P 1973 The field of educational technology: A statement of definition. *Audio Visual Instruction* 18(3): 52–53

Eraut M 1988 What has happened to learning design? In: Mathias H, Rushby N, Budgett R (eds.) 1988 *Designing New Systems and Technologies for Learning*. Aspects of Educational Technology 21. Kogan Page, London

Eraut M (ed.) 1989a *The International Encyclopedia of Educational Technology*. Pergamon Press, Oxford

Eraut M 1989b Specifying and using objectives. In: Eraut M (ed.) 1989a

Eraut M (ed.) 1991 *Education and the Information Society*. Cassells, London

Eraut M, Nash C, Fielding M, Attard P 1990 *Flexible Learning in Schools*. Employment Department, London

Eraut M 1995 Groupwork with computers in British primary schools. *J. Educ. Computing Res.* 13(1): 61–87

Finn J D 1960 Technology and the instructional process. In: Lumsdaine A A, Glaser R (eds.) 1960

Finn J D, Perrin D G, Campion L E 1962 *Studies in the Growth of Instructional Technology I: Audiovisual Instrumentation for Instruction in the Public Schools, 1930–60—A Basis for Take-Off*. Department of Audiovisual Instruction, National Education Association, Washington, DC

Finn J D 1968 The emerging technology of education. In: Weisgerber R A (ed.) 1968 *Instructional Process and Media Innovation*. Rand McNally, Chicago, Illinois

Flechsig K H 1975 *Towards a Critical Appraisal of Educational Technology Theory and Practice*. Steering Group on Educational Technology, Council for Cultural Cooperation, Council of Europe, Strasbourg

Gagné R, Briggs L J 1974 *Principles of Instructional Design*. Holt, Rinehart, and Winston, New York

Glaser R 1965 Toward a behavioral science base for instructional design. In: Glaser R 1965 *Teaching Machines and Programmed Learning, II*. Department of Audiovisual Instruction, National Education Association, Washington, DC

Griffiths D E 1964 Administrative theory and change in organizations. In: Miles M B (ed.) 1964 *Innovation in Education*. Teachers College Press, New York

Hawkridge D 1993 *Challenging Educational Technology*. Athlone Press, London

Hawkridge D, Vincent T 1992 *Learning Difficulties and Computers: Access to the Curriculum*. Jessica Kingsley, London

Heinich R 1968 The teacher in an instructional system. In: Knirk F G, Childs J W (eds.) 1968 *Instructional Technology*. Holt, Rinehart, and Winston, New York

Heinich R 1984 The proper study of instructional technology. *Educational Communications Training Journal* 32(2): 67–87

Hewton E 1989 Higher education consultancy. In: Eraut M (ed.) 1989a

Hilgard E R 1964 A perspective on the relationship between learning theory and educational practices. In: Hilgard

E R (ed.) 1964 *Theories of Learning and Instruction*, 63rd NSSE Yearbook Part I. University of Chicago Press, Chicago, Illinois

Hoban C F 1965 From theory to policy decisions. *Aud. Vis. Commun. Rev.* 13(2): 121–39

Hoyles C, Noss R 1992 A pedagogy for mathematical microworlds. *Educ. Stud. Math.* 23(1): 31–57

Huberman M 1970 Educational technology, a bibliography. *Bull. Int. Bur. Educ.* 177: 263–309

Light P, Blaye A 1990 Computer-based learning: The social dimensions. In: Foot H C, Morgan M J, Shute R H (eds.) 1990 *Children Helping Children*. Wiley, Chichester

Lumsdaine A A 1964 Educational technology, programmed learning and instructional science. In: Hilgard E R (ed.) 1964 *Theories of Learning and Instruction,* 63rd NSSE Yearbook Part I. University of Chicago Press, Chicago, Illinois

Lumsdaine A A, Glaser R (eds.) 1960 *Teaching Machines and Programmed Learning*. Department of Audiovisual Instruction, National Education Association, Washington, DC

Melton A W 1959 The science of learning and the technology of educational methods. *Harv. Educ. Rev.* 29: 96–106

Moore O K 1968 Autotelic responsive environments and exceptional children. In: Weisgerber R A (ed.) 1968 *Instructional Process and Media Innovation*. Rand McNally, Chicago, Illinois

National Council for Educational Technology 1969 *Towards More Effective Learning*. The Report of the National Council for Educational Technology 1967–1968. NCET, London

Papert S 1980 *Mindstorms: Children, Computers and Powerful Ideas*. Basic Books, New York

Plomp T, Pals N 1989 Continental European perspectives. In: Eraut M (ed.) 1989a

Ramo S 1973 The systems approach. In: Miles R F (ed.) 1973 *Systems Concepts*. Wiley Interscience, New York

Romiszowski A J 1981 *Designing Instructional Systems*. Kogan Page, London

Rowntree D 1974 *Educational Technology in Curriculum Development*. Harper and Row, London

Rowntree D 1981 *Developing Courses for Students*. McGraw-Hill, Maidenhead

Saettler P 1990 *The Evolution of American Educational Technology*. Libraries Unlimited, Englewood, Colorado

Sakamoto T 1989 Asian perspectives. In: Eraut M (ed.) 1989a

Salomon G 1979 *Interaction of Media, Cognition and Learning*. Jossey Bass, San Francisco, California

Schön D 1983 *The Reflective Practitioner: How Professionals Think in Action*. Temple Smith, London

Self J 1987 IKBS in education. *Educational Review* 39(2): 147–54

Skinner B F 1958 Teaching machines. *Science* 128: 969–77

Skinner B F 1968 *The Technology of Teaching*. Prentice-Hall, Englewood Cliffs, New Jersey

Sleeman D, Brown J S (eds.) 1982 *Intelligent Tutoring Systems*. Academic Press, London

Taylor G (ed.) 1970 *The Teacher as Manager*. NCET, London

Tickton S G (ed.) 1970 *To Improve Learning, An Evaluation of Instructional Technology*. Bowker, New York

Travers R M W 1970 *Man's Information System: A Primer for Media Specialists and Educational Technologists*. Chandler, Scranton, Pennsylvania

von Bertalanffy L 1950 The theory of open systems in Physics and Biology. *Science* 111: 23–29.

Vygotsky L S 1978 *Mind in Society: The Development of Higher Psychological Processes*. Harvard University Press, Cambridge, Massachusetts

Weisgerber R A (ed.) 1971 *Developmental Efforts in Individualized Learning*. Peacock, Itasca, Illinois

Witt P W F (1968) Educational technology: The education of teachers and the development of instructional materials specialists. In: Witt P W F (ed.) 1968 *Technology and the Curriculum*. Teachers College Press, New York

Curriculum in Adult Education

J. N. Streumer and A. C. Tuijnman

This entry deals with the curriculum in adult education. The central argument in the first part is that, despite the increasing professionalization and the growing share of continuing vocational training in total provision, the discussion of theories and aspects of curriculum in adult education continues to be neglected. Some reasons for the indifference to curriculum development in adult education are also mentioned. The second part describes a number of ways in which the curriculum can be defined and analyzed. Whereas curriculum concepts are not specific to adult education, their interpretation differs according to the purposes which the curriculum is supposed to serve. This part therefore pays attention also to the role of values in curriculum development, and draws out the importance of adult education theory.

The content of adult education is only touched upon briefly in the third part. It is noted that the content of adult education is extremely varied, and that it must be reviewed in relation to both purpose and practice.

The final part occupies the largest space. It describes different approaches to the development of curricula in adult education, discusses features of major curriculum design models, reviews their usefulness and provides a practical example, and summarizes the criteria for selecting designs for curriculum development in adult education.

1. The Neglected Curriculum

In many countries only little systematic attention has been paid to the curriculum in adult education. Opposition to the development of explicit curricula has been particularly strong in countries where teachers and policymakers have emphasized the nonformal character of adult education.

1.1 Reasons for Indifference

Indifference to the development of formal curricula in adult education can be explained in several ways, for example:

(a) In most countries, adult education has evolved in a spontaneous and sporadic way in response to both private demands and public needs; and institutions of adult education have long enjoyed virtual autonomy in deciding about the purpose, goals, and content of their offerings, which accordingly have varied greatly.

(b) The idea that adults, as voluntary and self-directed learners, ought to be free to choose the competencies and the body of knowledge they wish to master as well as the teaching and learning methods most suited to that task, has provided legitimacy for the "open curriculum," which is co-determined by the participation of mature students, as a central principle in the practice of adult education.

(d) The notion that adult education ideally involves learning for its own sake has moreover favored the humanities and social sciences, to the detriment of other subjects which are seen as being primarily linked to job training and that have a tendency to put stricter demands on both content and sequencing in the curriculum.

(e) Accordingly, whereas curricula in the regular education system are usually focused on subject-bound knowledge, those in adult education assign a comparatively greater weight to noncurriculum-bound skills and competencies.

1.2 Changing Perspectives

Although opposition to the development of formal curricula in adult education is still strong among certain groups and in some countries, in others the position seems to be changing, albeit slowly. The integration of some adult education programs into the formal system, and the expansion of publicly funded, credential adult education, have raised the demands placed on the content of adult education, particularly on programs that carry a degree of formal equivalency in the regular system. Increased institutionalization and especially the weakening of the liberal tradition in adult education have also led to increased control and a greater degree of curriculum determination by external agencies. Increased attention for curriculum theory in the training of adult educators can also be explained, at least partly, as a by-product of the growing weight of vocational education and training in total provision, as training in business and industry has long relied on methods such as job and task analysis and technologically based curriculum development. The growth of continuing vocational training has led to a situation where criteria such as accountability, cost-effectiveness, and performance evaluation are increasingly applied also to general adult education provision.

1.3 Professionalization

Professionalization is a common trend in adult education in many countries (see *Professional Associations*). This trend is not altogether uncontroversial, however, as it is inevitably linked with questions about standards and criteria, for example, in relation to the definition and certification of the prerequisite knowledge, skills, attitudes, and behaviors needed to achieve professional identity and status as an adult education practitioner.

The competencies needed by adult educators have been the subject of several studies undertaken during the 1960s and 1970s. Galbraith and Zelenak (1991) review some of these studies and note that the majority are concerned with the identification of specific roles or settings in adult education; few have attempted to describe the generic competencies and proficiencies all practitioners in the field reasonably should possess. Knowledge of the principles of curriculum design and evaluation typically was not mentioned in these studies as an essential proficiency needed by all practitioners regardless of institutional affiliation or teaching role. This partly reflects a situation where, as a rule, the average teacher or planner in adult education ". . . is new to the position, has little or no coursework in adult education, comes from a field outside of adult education, and is likely to leave it in five years, and works very hard" (Hartman 1983 p. 4; quoted in Galbraith and Zelenak 1991 p. 125). Even the practitioners in the field who have received some form of on-the-job or inservice training, and the minority who have acquired professional training by means of undergraduate or graduate degree programs in adult education, in the past tended to have had little exposure to curriculum theory and the principles of curriculum design and evaluation.

The idea that systematic attention must be given to curriculum theory and design in the professional development of practitioners is gaining recognition as a consequence of professionalization and the growth of credential programs in adult education during the 1980s, especially in North America. To an increasing extent, it is now being recognized that participants in adult education programs can benefit from systematic curriculum development. Yet the situation is far from ideal. It is significant in this respect that the term "curriculum" does not appear in the subject index of the

48-chapter *Handbook of Adult and Continuing Education* edited by Merriam and Cunningham (1991) for the American Association for Adult and Continuing Education.

2. Concepts of Curriculum

Jackson (1992) notes that a look at the entries under the heading "curriculum" in any of the annual volumes of *Education Index* reveals two major kinds of writing on the subject. One is narrowly focused, forming the bulk of the entries, and is mostly concerned with the introduction and evaluation of specific subject matter in the curriculum of an educational institution. The second, more broadly focused category deals with topics such as ". . . the construction of general theories of curriculum development or broad perspectives on the curriculum as a whole or on the status of curriculum as a field of study" (Jackson 1992 p. 3).

2.1 Descriptions and Definitions

Many authors agree that the field often described as curriculum studies in education is beset by both conceptual and methodological problems (Olivia 1982, Goodlad 1985). The parameters delineating this domain of study are not yet clearly identified; research studies often appear fragmented and lack a developed theoretical basis. One explanation is that the field is still young; another that different value orientations and theoretical perspectives are brought to bear on the curriculum, which therefore by definition is a contested area of research.

Olivia (1982 pp. 5–6) illustrates "the amorphous nature of curriculum" using a range of definitions and interpretations gleaned from different sources:

(a)   Curriculum is a set of subjects.

(b)   Curriculum is content.

(c)   Curriculum is a set of materials.

(d)   Curriculum is a set of performance objectives.

(e)   Curriculum is experience of guided learning.

(f)   Curriculum is everything that goes on within or is directed by an educational institution, including student guidance and interpersonal relationships among teachers and students.

The notion "curriculum" can apparently be interpreted in different ways, from a subject to be taught, to all the experiences of learners both within and outside an educational institution. Through the years, the preferred definition of curriculum has placed an increasing emphasis upon the experiences of learners, regardless of whether these are consciously directed or indirect. The latter are a product of activities which are not formally planned or evaluated by the educational institution. In this context, the term "hidden curriculum," a curriculum which is not explicitly endorsed, is often used. Directed learning experiences, in contrast, are realized through systematically planned curricula.

In researching definitions of curriculum, Olivia (1982) concludes that differences in substance are not as great as differences in inclusiveness. Some writers combine elements of instruction and curriculum, whereas others define a curriculum just as arbitrarily, for example, by (a) dealing with purpose—what a curriculum does or should do; (b) describing the context in which it is shaped; and (c) equating it with instructional strategy.

2.2 Link between Curriculum and Instruction

It can be concluded from the above that the relationship between curriculum and instruction can be interpreted in different ways. These perspectives can be described as the dualistic, interlocking, concentric, and cyclical views.

In the dualistic view, curriculum and instruction are conceived as two entities. The curriculum planners ignore the instructors and in return instructors ignore curriculum planners. This situation is partly due to the difficulty of designing curricula. Curriculum documents must possess sufficient clarity and specificity, be attractive and helpful, and allow for a variety of settings and circumstances, while at the same time they must retain the widest possible acceptability. In contrast, the interlocking view posits an integrated relationship between curriculum and instruction.

The concentric view appears in two forms: one that considers instruction as a subsystem of curriculum, and another that subsumes curriculum as a part of instruction. In both versions, a hierarchical relationship is posited in which one entity is part of the other. Finally, in the cyclical view the element of feedback is stressed. Curriculum and instruction are seen as entities with a continuing circular feedback.

2.3 Values and Curriculum

A common element runs through the approaches discussed above, namely that values are considered to be important for the design of adult education curricula. Norms and values are central to the thought and action of adult educators, program managers, training coordinators, and course leaders. These values are reflected not only in differences among perspectives on curriculum, but also by the existence of a diverse array of adult education institutions serving dissimilar purposes and teaching a widely different content.

Ornstein and Hunkins (1988) distinguish between educational philosophies and approaches to curriculum. Educational philosophies, which have their roots in one or more philosophical tradition such as idealism, realism, pragmatism, and existentialism, guide the design of curricula. Curriculum approaches are interpreted as meta-orientations, which encompass values, distinct knowledge areas, and curriculum principles.

2.4 The Role of Theory

Streumer (1990) draws a line between curriculum concepts and ideas of education and training. Whereas the latter are similar to what Ornstein and Hunkins refer to as "philosophies of education," curriculum concepts are defined as the rationales upon which curricula are built. In a curriculum concept, the first rough outline of an idea about adult education or training is encountered. At this stage, choices about curriculum content and form have not yet been made. Rather, the points of departure contained in notions of adult education and training are transferred onto a curriculum level. These orientations guide decision-making concerning objectives, content, and instructional strategy.

Since theory can serve a heuristic function, the formulation of an explicit theory of adult education is often considered as the first activity in the curriculum development process. The next step is recognition of a curriculum approach, which guides decisions concerning learning needs assessment, the specification of objectives, the formulation of design specifications, and the production, implementation, and evaluation of curriculum materials. This sequence does not negate the possibility that curriculum designers only become aware of the role of theory in adult education at a later phase in the development process. This may result in an adjustment of the original perspective.

Apart from providing legitimacy for a curriculum by justifying the choices that are made during the development process, theories also serve an innovative function, because the perspectives of adult educators are confronted with other views during an initial stage in the development of the curriculum. Such a confrontation may lead to a situation in which opinions can be discussed, standpoints revised, and compromises made.

3. Curriculum Content

The content of adult education is as widely diverse as its purposes, goals, and institutional arrangements.

Different people adhere to different views of the purposes of adult education. These differences relate to distinctions such as those between teacher-centered and learner-centered approaches, subject-based versus experience-based knowledge, and learning for its own sake versus instrumental adult education. These differences are naturally reflected in controversy over content, and have major consequences for the development of curricula in adult education. For example, people who view adult education as an essentially voluntary, self-directed learning activity are more likely to stress the principle of an "open curriculum" than those favoring an instrumental approach, and this attitude necessarily has implications for the specification of objectives, choice of subject-matter, application of instructional media, and the use of evaluation.

In theory it should be possible to describe different content domains in adult education, for example, according to whether the education is considered "for its own sake," as a means of coping with lifespan transitions or developmental tasks, or as preparation for a current or future job (see *Lifespan Development: Intelligence; Lifespan Development: Phases; Lifespan Development: Problems and Crises*).

Education for lifespan development concerns the provision of learning opportunities to adults facing a given developmental task in relation to changes that occur either in private life, such as getting married or divorced, becoming a parent, or entering retirement, or at large in society, for example, environmental change, political movements, religious and cultural transition (cf. Havighurst 1948, Heymans 1992). In this category, the content is non-job-related, although it may result in an enhancement of performance on the job. The learning activity may involve formal education, but is most often accomplished through informal, learner-centered activities. Adult educators supporting human development tend to view the process as essentially voluntary and self-directed, and are likely to emphasize the notions of "experiential learning" and "open curriculum" (see *Experimential and Open Learning; Self-directed Learning*).

The purpose of much adult education is to assist the learner to prepare for further education or for a future job. The content can, in this case, be both academically, subject, or vocational oriented. It is often difficult to draw a line between the latter type of adult education and continuing professional education. Common also is the provision of formal education for adults seeking to enter employment or to enhance their career prospects. These learning activities are instrumental in character and are usually well-planned and structured.

It can be inferred from the above that, although it should be possible to classify on the basis of empirical observation the major themes and content domains that are currently being covered in adult education—in fact, classifications based on an interpretation of the formal syllabuses of adult education institutions in the United States have been proposed by several authors—the value of time spent on such an exercise may seem in doubt if it were not matched by a thorough, comprehensive analysis of the relationships between, first, purpose and content and, second, practice and content (Jarvis 1989). Such an analysis cannot be attempted here.

Finally, a discussion of curriculum content in adult education should also pay attention to models of lifelong learning. In this perspective, curricula in adult education are grounded in school-based curricula. The expansion of adult education as an essential component of lifelong learning therefore has implications for school-based curricula. For example, since schooling is no longer aimed at providing young people with sufficient knowledge and skills they need for the rest of their life but aims to prepare youth for a life of active learning, the differentiation of students into qualitatively dissimilar programs may have to be delayed, and overspecialized vocational education at the secondary level avoided.

4. Curriculum Development

The diversity of goals and the heterogeneity of demands on curricula in adult education commonly require the use of a combination of approaches and methods of curriculum development. Several approaches to curriculum development are introduced briefly in the paragraphs that follow. Some attention is subsequently given to curriculum models and especially to modular and technology-based approaches to curriculum design.

4.1 Approaches to Curriculum Development

Eisner and Vallence (1974), McNeil (1981), and Miller and Seller (1985) discuss different approaches to curriculum design. Saylor and Alexander (1974), and Saylor et al. (1981) describe several approaches based on the predominant source of the data from which the objectives are derived: subject matter, competencies, human traits, social functions and activities, and individual needs.

In the subject matter approach, the structure and content of an (academic) discipline strongly influence the development of a curriculum. It has the advantage that development appears to proceed orderly: the relevant subject matter is divided according to learning needs and age-related changes in cognitive functioning. A problem is that the content must be selected carefully to illustrate and clarify the structures of a discipline. Another drawback is that the huge increase in available information at the different levels of understanding is difficult to handle.

The technology-based approach to curriculum development is sequential–analytic: it assumes a direct, causal relationship between goals, planned learning activity, and eventual performance. The match between the learning activities of adults and the actual tasks they perform in the course of everyday life, at home or at work, is at the heart of this systems-based approach. Job and function analysis are used in deciding upon the goals and learning objectives, content, media of instruction, and evaluation. The approach neglects learning for the sake of learning and reduces the scope for self-determination by learners; it is usually applied only to vocational training in business and industry.

The human traits-based approach to curriculum development has two main features (Saylor et al. 1981 p. 222). First, the development of desirable traits, such as initiative, self-confidence, creativity, capacity for effective communication, problem-solving, and decision-making, is the central goal. Second, the curriculum is deliberately chosen so as to facilitate the realization of this goal. The limitations concern the difficulty of anticipating and evaluating traits that are in a process of continuous development and, thus, the difficulty of planning for an educational experience.

Another approach emphasizes the influence of social and cultural factors on the curriculum. Clusters of social activities or problems are the organizing elements in this approach, for example, consumerism, the environment, the quality of rural life, apartheid. This approach is highly popular in adult education, because it uses materials based on real-life activities and also because it addresses issues to which the development of social competence is central.

A fifth approach to curriculum development focuses on the adult learners' individual needs and interests. It implies that needs and interests be systematically studied, and priority be given to individual guidance. The approach is flexible because the learners can influence aspects of curriculum such as the objectives, content, and the choice of media. Possible limitations can be overcome by grouping adult learners according to their special interests (see *Group Learning*).

4.2 Usefulness of Design Models

There are different approaches to curriculum development; some of these involve the use of explicit design models. A model is a simplified representation of an actual process in which the main components and their interrelationships are schematically presented. Curriculum design models not only describe a sequence of central phases or activities, but also indicate the procedures that can be applied in curriculum development. Methods and techniques, as opposed to procedures, mostly involve a further specification of the model. Ori (1989) mentions several advantages of using design models in the development of curricula. Models:

(a) are a device for systematic problem-solving;

(b) reduce the chance that essential activities or elements are overlooked in the development process;

(c) increase the probability of finding a correct solution;

(d) encourage preliminary research and the evaluation of alternative solutions;

(e) increase efficiency, since the steps to be taken are clear from the outset;

(f) improve the transparency of communication and decision-making.

There are also writers who question the value of using models for the design and implementation of adult education and training programs. A common criticism is that models imply reductionism.

Verhoeven (1986), for example, notes that most users of design models are insufficiently aware that such models are not based on empirical facts but on heuristics, so that the personal characteristics of planners determine the final product regardless of the model used. While this may be partly true, design models nevertheless serve a useful purpose, since they imply a systematic approach to the development, production, evaluation, and implementation of complete curricula, including the arrangements for instruction and interaction among learners in a group.

Curriculum development involves clarification and decision-making concerning the interests and learning needs of adults, institutions, communities, and society; the institutional factors conditioning the adult education or training event; the target group; the goals and instructional objectives; the choice of subject matter, teaching methods, and media; and the form of learning outcomes and transfer. Curriculum design models, as sources of inspiration, can assist the planner or teacher in deciding upon these issues, while taking into account the context within which a learning activity is situated.

4.3 Levels of Curriculum Design

Romiszowski (1981) distinguishes between four levels of curriculum design: the course or program, the lesson, the instructional event, and the learning step. At the course level, the focus is on the specification of the goals and the envisaged results: learning needs are identified, prioritized, and transformed into problem definitions; it is determined whether an adult education or training program offers a solution to the perceived problem; the organizational context of the problem is described; the institutional and organizational limitations are surveyed; implementation possibilities are explored; and the learning system to be developed is defined in terms of general goals. At the next level, the structure, number, and sequence of the lessons is determined. Detailed specification occurs at the level of the instructional event: the general goals are translated into learning objectives; the lesson plan is created; the prerequisite knowledge of the course participants is defined; the desirability and method of performance testing is agreed upon; and the form and content of the lesson is decided. Decisions as to how and by what means the instruction will proceed from one learning activity to the next are taken at the last level, that of the learning step.

4.4 Design Models in Context

Andrews and Goodson (1980), in discussing the criteria for judging the usefulness of different models for curriculum development, concluded that it is important to carefully study the match between the specific features of a design model and the context within which it is to be applied. Gustafson (1981) distinguishes four model features, according to whether the focus is on the learning situation, the means of learning, the instructional system, or organizational development.

Models in the first category are mostly used in improving an actual learning situation. Models in the second group are intended for the development of specific learning materials, such as a course packet, module, CAI program, or an AV production. Models aimed at improving the instructional system commonly rely on context and problem analysis. Human resource development as a principal means for achieving change in an organization is characteristic of the approach inherent in models for organizational development (Nadler 1980) (see *Human Resource Development; Evaluation of Industry Training: Cost-Effectiveness*).

4.5 A Model in Practice: The Twente Model

A curriculum design model developed at the University of Twente in the Netherlands is globally described in Fig. 1. Although the model is intended as an aid in developing mainly vocationally oriented programs, some parts are also applicable to the design of more generally or academically oriented programs in adult education.

The Twente model is intended for the development of modular curricula. A "module" is defined as a complete unit, in which elements such as learning goals, the subject matter or course materials, the instructional strategies and media to be used, and a procedure for performance testing are described.

Compared with "traditional" curricula, a modular design makes it easier to create new study routes, integrate new adult learners, update subject matter in the form of adding or revising modules, improve the motivation of those engaged in the planned learning activity, and increase flexibility both of the curriculum itself and of responding to differences in individual adults' interests and learning capacity.

The Twente model begins with the analysis of a job or function profile, followed by defining the prerequisite knowledge, skills, and attitudes for that function. Figure 1 shows the phases that subsequently are distinguished: studying the knowledge, skills, and attitudes of the students; deciding on the rough structure of the module system; making an inventory of existing training materials and evaluating their adequacy; developing modules; evaluating the product —a curriculum document—and deciding on its implementation (Streumer et al. 1991).

4.6 Selection of Design Models

When someone decides to use one or more models in developing an adult education curriculum, then it is important to determine which design levels are implicated, how the design setting can be characterized,

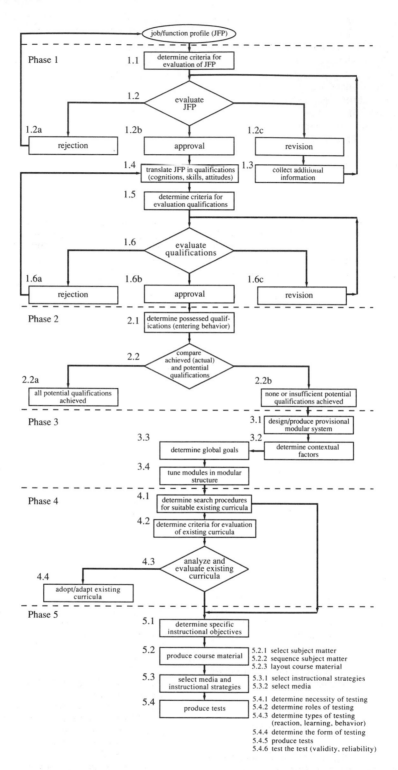

Figure 1
Twente Model for Curriculum Development (Streumer et al. 1991 pp. 6–7)

and which development phase needs priority. Besides these considerations, the size and the lifetime of the future curriculum, the characteristics and size of the target group, the noncompletion risk, and the degree of detail all play a role.

The size of the curriculum refers to the time needed when using the curriculum. This can vary from a few hours to a number of months. The lifetime of a curriculum refers to the number of times that the curriculum will be used. The size of the target group refers to number of students that will use the curriculum in the course of its lifetime. The non-completion risk refers to the actual necessity of a curriculum. A curriculum with a high non-completion risk implies negative consequences for students or organizations of not completing the curriculum. Finally, the degree of detail concerns the system level at which the curriculum must be developed. An appropriate model must be chosen in accordance with the degree of detail. All these factors influence the choice whether and how a model or parts of a model will be used in designing a curriculum.

5. Conclusion

Several years ago, Colin Titmus wrote the following words in the introductory chapter to the volume, *Lifelong Education for Adults: An International Handbook:*

> ... There has indeed been little study of curriculum to back up animated discussion founded purely on value judgements. The principle that each person should be free to choose what he or she studies has obscured to some degree the possibility that free choice may not result in what the individual or society most needs. In some fields, work has been done in curriculum studies, but the question of the content of adult education requires further study. (Titmus 1989 p. xxxii)

It can be concluded on the basis of the overview presented in this entry that—despite the important contributions that have been made by authors in specialized fields such as human resource development and curriculum technology—the question both of the content and the curriculum in adult education remains in need of serious research attention.

See also: Adult Learning: An Overview; Concepts of Educational Technology; Instructional Design: Models

References

Andrews D H, Goodson L A 1980 A comparative analysis of models of instructional design. *J. Instr. Dev.* 3(4):2–16

Eisner E, Vallence E (eds.) 1974 *Conflicting Conceptions of Curriculum.* McCutchan, Berkeley, California

Galbraith M W, Zelenak B S 1991 The education of adult and continuing education practitioners. In: Merriam S B, Cunningham P M (eds.) 1991

Goodlad J I 1985 Curriculum as a field of study. In: Husén T, Postlethwaite T N (eds.) 1985 *International Encyclopedia of Education*, 1st edn. Pergamon Press, Oxford

Gustafson K L 1981 *Survey of Instructional Development Models.* ERIC Document Reproduction Service No. ED 211 097. National Institute of Education, Washington, DC

Hartman M 1983 Some surprises found in national survey of adult educators. *The Learning Connection* 5(1):4–6

Havighurst R 1948 *Developmental Tasks and Education.* University of Chicago Press, Chicago, Illinois

Heymans P G 1992 Lifespan learning: Developmental tasks and their management. In: Tuijnman A C, Van der Kamp M (eds.) *Learning Across the Lifespan: Theories, Research, Policies.* Pergamon Press, Oxford

Jackson P W 1992 Conceptions of curriculum and curriculum specialist. In: AERA 1992 *Handbook of Research on Curriculum.* Macmillan, New York

Jarvis P 1989 Content, purpose, and practice. In: Titmus C J (ed.) 1989 *Lifelong Education for Adults: An International Handbook.* Pergamon Press, Oxford

McNeil J D 1981 *Curriculum: A Comprehensive Introduction.* Little, Brown and Co., Boston, Massachusetts

Merriam S B, Cunningham P M 1991 (eds.) *Handbook of Adult and Continuing Education.* Jossey-Bass, San Francisco, California

Miller J P, Seller W 1985 *Curriculum: Perspectives and Practice.* Longman, New York

Nadler L 1980 *Corporate Human Resources Development: A Management Tool.* Van Nostrand Reinhold, American Society for Training and Development, New York

Olivia P F 1982 *Developing the Curriculum.* Little, Brown and Co., Boston, Massachusetts

Ori H R 1989 *Het projectmatig ontwerpen van curricula voor bedrijfsopleidingen.* Philips Components, Eindhoven

Ornstein A C, Hunkins F P 1988 *Curriculum: Foundations, Principles, and Issues.* Prentice Hall, Englewood Cliffs, New Jersey

Romiszowski A J 1981 *Designing Instructional Systems: Decision Making in Course and Curriculum Design.* Kogan Page, London

Saylor J G, Alexander W M 1974 *Planning Curriculum for Schools.* Holt, Rinehart and Winston, New York

Saylor J G, Alexander W M, Lewis A J 1981 *Curriculum Planning for Better Teaching and Learning.* Harcourt Brace Jovanovich, New York

Streumer J N 1990 Onderwijs en opleidingsconcepties. In: Creemers B (ed.) 1990 *Nieuw Losbladig Onderwijskundig Lexicon.* Samson Uitgeverij, Alphen aan den Rijn

Streumer J N, Thijsen J A, Nijhof W J 1991 *Contractonderwijs in ontwikkeling. Van opleidingsvraag naar gemoduleerd cursusaanbod.* ACON, Woerden

Titmus C J 1989 Introduction. In: Titmus C J (ed.) 1989 *Lifelong Education for Adults: An International Handbook.* Pergamon Press, Oxford

Verhoeven W F J 1986 Bedrijfsopleidingen: What business are we in? In: Plomp Tj, Thijssen J G L (eds.) 1986 *Curriculumontwikkeling van beroeps- en bedrijfsopleidingen.* Swets en Zeitlinger, Lisse

Further Reading

Apple M W 1979 *Ideology and Curriculum*. Routledge and Kegan Paul, London
Aronowitz S, Giroux H A 1991 *Postmodern Education: Politics, Culture and Social Criticism*. University of Minnesota Press, Minneapolis, Minnesota
Carnevale A P, Johnston J W 1989 *Training America:* *Strategies for the Nation*. National Center on Education and the Economy, American Society of Training and Development, Alexandria, Virginia
Jarvis P (ed.) 1992 *Perspectives on the Education and Training of Adults in Europe*. National Institute of Adult Continuing Education, Leicester
Paterson R W K 1979 *Values, Education and the Adult*. Routledge and Kegan Paul, London

Curriculum in Adult Literacy

G. Kamper

This entry offers a brief overview of some of the factors that influence the design of curricula for adult literacy programs. Materials for literacy work that are currently in use in some developing and industrialized countries are described. Examples are given of practice in Indonesia, Namibia, Germany, and the Netherlands.

1. Orientations of Literacy Programs

Educational programs for illiterate and semi-illiterate adults follow different philosophies, goals, and objectives. Some programs are initiated by grassroots organizations, some by (national) liberation movements, and others by central or local governments and international agencies. Many literacy programs in the developing countries are intended as a means for consciousness raising and promoting social and political change. Others may respond to the needs of nonliterate immigrants in industrialized countries, or serve people who cannot sufficiently read and write despite having attended the compulsory school.

Adult literacy curricula reflect in scope, goals, contents, and teaching methods the main principles of the different underlying philosophies of human development and education. Certain trends can be noted, however. The development has been from a rather academic view of literacy to a functional understanding of it in relation to basic vocational skills. There is also a cultural and emancipatory view of literacy. Since all programs have certain elements in common it is very difficult to draw an exact demarcation line between curricula for adult literacy, adult basic education, and postliteracy programs (see *Curriculum in Adult Education*).

2. Factors Influencing Curriculum Design

Various beliefs and decisions influence the design of curriculum materials for adult literacy. Among these mutually dependent factors are:

(a) *Language policy*. A country can be monolingual, or supposed to be monolingual, or a variety of languages can be accepted. Policy defining the kind of relations between the languages of native and immigrant minorities and the mainstream language, or between people's mother tongues and an official language—in former colonies a foreign language is often the official one—influences not only questions of initial literacy, its curricula and materials, but also the system of general education.

(b) *Adult education policy*. Literacy learning can be embedded in different contexts, for example, individual personal development or assimilation and integration in a society, or promotion of social activity and change in the community. Literacy classes can also be considered merely as a starting point for, or lowest level of, adult basic education programs with an emphasis on social integration or vocational training programs. A literacy campaign is often part of the political education activity and cultural policy of a liberation movement or a government. Depending on these possibilities literacy education can be organized in rather nonformal or more formal ways. This has implications for the development of curricula.

(c) *Linguistic features of the language*. Many languages use an alphabetic script. Others use pictographic scripts or have signs for syllables or employ mixed systems. Some languages have regular consonant–vowel sequences that are easy to analyze even for beginning learners, while others have difficult consonant clusters. Some of the languages which use an alphabetic system follow mainly the phonological principle. In this case clear sound–letter correspondences make it comparatively easy to transcribe spoken language into written form. Reading, and particularly spelling, is made much more difficult if a language is characterized by a complicated hierarchy of phonological, morphematic, and historic principles. Curricula and materials have to respond to this.

(d) *Teaching methods*. Teaching methods depend on the linguistic features of the language and rely on knowledge or beliefs about learning processes. Methods range from highly structured approaches that use standardized workbooks or primers ("pure literacy methods") to less formalized ones. In the latter situation, students' participation in choosing subjects and topics for discussion, reading, and writing, are emphasized (c.g., "learner-centered methods," "experiental learning," "critical thinking").

(e) *Staff policy*. Some programs work with untrained or unsupervised volunteers in one-to-one tutorial settings. Mass campaigns can mobilize a virtual "army" of volunteers to teach illiterates throughout an entire country for a short period of time. Programs can also rely on teachers recruited from primary or secondary schools. Many programs employ only a few tenured staff members, who may or may not have specific qualifications. They perform tasks such as fund raising, program management, curriculum development, tutor training, and supervision along with volunteers who then do the actual teaching. Who produces and provides materials in what quality according to a chosen or given curriculum is closely connected with questions of staff policy.

3. Approaches and Inconsistencies

3.1 Trends

A generally recognized principle is that adult learning is supposed to be different from children's learning in many ways, and that the materials used for child instruction in the formal school system cannot readily be used for adult literacy purposes. Yet the intellectual content of traditional school education still influences, and in part determines, current approaches to adult literacy. Vocational elements have increasingly entered the literacy curricula used in the different countries. New subjects such as environmental education, population, and peace education have also had an impact on literacy curricula. Where emancipatory literacy and learner-centered philosophies are claimed, adequate curricula are necessary to put them into practice. The gaps and inconsistencies between learning needs, objectives, and curriculum content have not been solved, however, despite attempts to develop innovative curricula for adult literacy.

Sometimes no general curriculum exists. This is often the case, particularly in industrialized countries where small-scale literacy work is initiated and run by grassroots organizations. The philosophy of the "Open Curriculum" holds that learning objectives are totally personal and that the needs, experiences, and ideas of the individual students, are the only guidelines for choosing topics and contents. If government money or other public funds are provided, then these literacy programs are usually also given some formal objectives and a partly prescribed curriculum. Thus a variety of literacy methods and curricula, ranging from open to entirely prescribed ones, may coexist in one and the same country or region. This is the case in the United States, for example. The extent to which innovative ideas are put into practice depends, however, on the dedication and competency of tutors in teaching and animating adult learning.

3.2 Examples

The Laubach Method. There is a historical development of methods following the strategic progression from the traditional "pure" literacy, through functional literacy, to literacy for empowerment. But previously prevalent methods have not been fully supplanted or replaced. An example of the "pure literacy method" associated with the "traditional" view of literacy is the Laubach Method. It was developed by Gray and Laubach and has now been spread throughout the world by a specialized institution—Laubach Literacy International. It is particularly known and still employed in the United States and Canada, and it was the method used by the American Peace Corps. The Laubach method uses a highly structured curriculum and standardized teaching materials. The basic Laubach teaching tool is a pre-designed picture–letter–word chart. Each picture on the chart has been carefully chosen to represent both the shape of the letter to be learned and a word that begins with that letter (Comings and Kahler 1984 p. 20).

The main criticisms of approaches of this kind concern the fact that they do not take into account the students' life circumstances, their motives for learning, nor the possible use of newly acquired skills. In short, they do not pay attention to the needs of learners or the demands for economic or social change. The neglect of these factors is not only a moral question, but also limits success.

The Paulo Freire Approach. A specific approach to adult basic education is associated with the name and the political–theoretical work of the Brazilian theologian and popular educator Paulo Freire. The main objective is social change gained by consciousness raising (conscientization) and appropriate action. This means that students, with the help of a facilitator or teacher, discuss their problems ("Dialogic Method"), find solutions, and put these into action. Problems can range from why and how to improve the water supply in the village to questions of how the big landowners exploit and oppress the peasants. Solutions can accordingly range from building a latrine to registering as voters. According to Freire (1985), the method consists of: (a) carrying out an investigation into the actual problems of the people who shall participate in a literacy program, (b) making decisions on a set of keywords ("generative words") that allow discussions of the problems to start and provide syllables, (c) designing picture-posters which "encode" the keywords, (d) discussing community problems shown in the pictures, (e) analyzing the syllables of the generative word, (f) connecting spoken and written syllables and identifying the single letters in the written syllables, (g) writing and reading new words with the learned syllables and letters, and (h) acting according to the discussed problem-solution. The main materials for this literacy work are therefore the pictures which "encode" the keywords. These are accompanied by cards with syllables and letters and often teachers' manuals or textbooks which give the contents and the sequence of the lessons.

Liberation movements and revolutionary governments throughout the world have often appreciated and adopted this approach. Examples include Nicaragua's "Literacy Crusade" under the Sandinista government and the SWAPO literacy campaign in Namibia's refugee camps. In cases of mass campaigns it has happened that problem situations and keywords taken from a particular situation did not fit when applied to other people. On occasion some of the teachers were either not inspired to liberate the poor or they themselves lacked the required analytical skills and, hence, applied the method in a mechanical way. There has also been some criticism of Freire's naive faith in the degree of social justice which actually occurs as a result of the application of his theory (see Lind and Johnston 1990).

Freire's approach has also aroused strong interest among intellectuals in industrialized countries. The idea of "learner-centeredness" has been adopted by literacy programs in Europe and North America. However, there are very few examples of projects outside of the developing countries where this method was explicit and successfully implemented. According to Kirkwood and Kirkwood (1989), Scotland may be an exception.

4. Literacy Materials

Philosophies and objectives need to be transformed into curricular principles. On the one hand, adult education laws and provision of the necessary funds determine the extent to which these principles are put into practice. But on the other hand, the kind and quality of teacher and tutor training and of the materials in use determine the extent to which curricular principles are realized in the actual teaching process in literacy classes.

Manuals, collections of worksheets, textbooks, and

so on are often the only guides teachers can refer to after their initial training. Sometimes they even have to work without initial training. The more competent teachers are—by training or experience—the closer they will tailor the teaching process and the use of materials to the needs and experiences of their students. The less competent they are, the more they will depend on manuals and other given materials. The more institutionalized the literacy programs are, the more they seem to provide their teachers and learners with structured curricula and standardized materials. The less institutionalized the literacy work is, the more frequent the use of "Open Curricula," and the stronger the demands on tutors and teachers to produce their own materials, preferably in a dialogue with their students. In these cases standardized material—if it exists at all—can be confined to a manual on how to explore the needs of students and how to produce worksheets and collections of reading materials.

4.1 Developing Countries

In the long-lasting efforts to promote literacy in developing countries, the weight of materials and media "has been given so much importance that for a long period the literacy curriculum was limited to the design and production of instructional materials" (Giere et al. 1990 p. 119). Dave et al. (1988), in a study on postliteracy in 24 countries, identified many categories of materials, media, techniques, and resources: newspapers and wall-newspapers, posters, and magazines; textual materials; supplementary reading materials; extension literature produced by development agencies such as health departments and agricultural extension services, and so on; libraries, mobile exhibitions, and museums; correspondence courses; radio, television, and video (modern electronic and audiovisual media); traditional and folk media; and sports, games, and physical culture.

A distinction is usually made between literacy material for beginners and follow-up materials for neo-literates, which are intended to prevent them from relapsing into secondary illiteracy because of lack of practice. The materials used for many initial-level literacy projects range from primers and syllabuses to simple, broadly formulated curricular frames, which are based on predetermined content areas. These didactic materials cover areas such as literacy (mother tongue), numeracy, vocational skills, citizenship training, environmental orientation, and so forth. Topics covered by postliteracy materials often include health, nutrition, child rearing, and new agricultural techniques. These materials can also provide possibilities for the newly literate to express and exchange ideas and thoughts on their own issues in local or regional newsletters. Materials may also deal with subjects thought to facilitate transmission to formal education, such as political education, mathematics, history, political economy, geography, the country's language, and a foreign language (Giere et al. 1990 pp. 120–121).

4.2 Industrialized Countries

In traditional countries of immigration like Canada or the United States literacy work among immigrants has a long tradition. But the existence of nonliterate or not functionally literate people among the autochthonous population in all industrialized countries was hardly publicly recognized prior to the 1970s. The number of people concerned is in relative terms much smaller than in the developing countries, and governments do not take it as an equally important problem.

While initial attempts were made to use children's primers "it was soon recognized that learning materials for adults had to take into account life experiences, situations and words of the adult world, both to avoid memories of frustrating school experiences and to increase motivation through a strong link with the realities of adult life and interest" (Giere 1987 p. 66). Materials vary from professionally printed textbooks produced by publishing companies and literacy institutions to collections of worksheets, mimeographed authentic materials, and student writings published in newsletters and booklets. The approaches taken may to a varying degree be grammatically oriented, learner-centered, or topical–functional, for example, how to cope with matters related to the post office, trains, and shops, or how to fill in various forms. "Creative writing" and publishing as a means of achieving personality growth and social communication is also practiced.

5. Some Examples

5.1 Indonesia

The learning program Kejar Packet A from Indonesia is designed to meet the minimum essential learning needs of the people "plus–minus" the curriculum of the primary school.

The basic materials of Learning Package A are 100 booklet titles, 20 of which contain integrated basic lessons in reading, writing, arithmetic, and Bahasa Indonesia. The next 40 booklets continue this and contain additional information on basic knowledge and skills. The remainder contain information on wider life skills. The design of this package provides space for various ways of studying by different participants. Audiovisual aids such as taped cassettes and drawings are attached to the packet in order to help involve illiterate adults (UNESCO 1984 pp. 22–23).

5.2 Namibia

In 1986 the South West Africa People's Organization (SWAPO) of Namibia published a *Literacy Promoter's Handbook* related to Stage I of the SWAPO Literacy course. This introductory course was intended to give participants a basis for developing fluent reading and writing skills needed in order to follow the literacy programs of Stages 2 and 3. The history of the handbook goes back to some Namibians who attended a literacy course in Zimbabwe and then produced a set of literacy materials for use in SWAPO's refugee settlements in Angola and Zambia. They used the Paulo Freire method, which proved effective.

The first part of the book explains the theory and practice of literacy work aiming at "a liberating methodology of adult education and community work," using a combination of text and cartoon-style drawings. The second part is a detailed set of lesson plans. It provides pictures representing a problem common to the adult learners ("codes"), keywords, questions for discussions, and suggestions for reading and writing with syllables. The content is "based on the experiences Namibians have strong feelings about: hunger, bad water, exploitive labour, poor housing, and brutal policing, for instance" (SWAPO 1986). While the handbook is written in English, the keywords and syllables are given in Oshiwambo. The book was designed to be used in the training of literacy promoters who would use it afterwards in preparing their daily work. It was also intended as a guide for untrained promoters. The handbook was retained after Namibia gained its independence in 1990, although its form was adapted to the new situation.

5.3 The Netherlands

In the Netherlands a new effort was begun in the 1970s to develop literacy work and basic education with Dutch-speaking and non-Dutch-speaking adult residents of the country. The development from the initially spontaneous to a broader and more institutionalized adult basic education provision in the beginning of the 1990s brought a shift from a formerly more or less totally open curriculum to a complex concept of curriculum. It takes into account different subjects on different levels which are defined in accordance with the needs of different target groups. In the beginning phase of the Dutch literacy programs there was a strong belief that according to the theories of experiential learning and student-centeredness, the best learning material would be developed in cooperation between the tutor and the students. Standardized learning materials were therefore uncommon. In 1990 the development of concrete learning materials began (Hamminck 1990). In addition to these activities, national and local agencies have been producing easy-to-read materials for beginning readers since about 1982. The development of computer-aided learning was still in the experimental stage in the early 1990s.

5.4 Germany

The German efforts to establish literacy programs for adults with German as the mother tongue started in the late 1970s and early 1980s. Campaigns and concepts borrowed from British and Dutch adult literacy programs were relevant influences. Although there was some interest in Freire's ideas at the outset, soon an "Open Curriculum" approach was followed. The language experience approach was promoted and methods that could relate to the morphological aspects of the German language and its spelling were discussed. Experienced tutors held workshops on how to produce one's own materials. Collections of worksheets were circulated and a few handbooks written by tutors and storybooks written by students published.

Nearly all German adult literacy learners had previously attended compulsory school and experienced learning difficulties there. There is a risk that these are repeated in literacy classes. An explicit counseling approach—based on Alfred Adler's psychoanalytical social psychology—which is now part of the curriculum was therefore developed. The specific materials are descriptions of personal experiences by counselors (see Fuchs-Brüninghoff et al. 1990). To a limited degree perceptive and cognitive functions are also regarded as part of the curriculum (see Kamper and Rübsamen 1990). However, the fairly large and well-developed program "German for workers from abroad" makes only a minor provision for illiterates. Among the materials for the general program are a few collections of worksheets that are specifically designed for illiterates. They are similar to those for German illiterates but they take into account the differences in living conditions and orientations.

6. Conclusion

Although curricula and materials are not in the foreground of the international debate on adult literacy there is some consensus that, in order for programs to be successful, they have to be tailored as closely as possible to the students' needs. The possibilities depend on the overall goals of the programs as well as on the available funds, and they are influenced by the underlying philosophies. Within the framework of this consensus, curricula and materials for adult literacy are in format and content as varied as the educational and labour market policies they seek to facilitate. Another common feature is that there are inconsistencies and tensions between claimed goals, the reality of literacy programs, and their outcomes.

In the period subsequent to UNESCO's International Literacy Year and the World Conference on Education for All, which both took place in 1990, public awareness of the need for adult basic education, including adult literacy, has risen. The main issues of discussion at present are the role of communication skills and, in particular, literacy skills for economic growth in both developing and industrialized countries; the relevant target groups and their needs; and the costs of programs. The topic of improving national primary school systems to avoid later adult illiteracy, however, often pushes questions of adult literacy to the sidelines.

See also: Literacy and Numeracy Models; Anthropological Study of Literacy and Numeracy; Adult Literacy in the Third World; Postliteracy; Curriculum in Adult Education; Asia, Southeast: Literacy

References

Comings J, Kahler D 1984 *Peace Corps Literacy Handbook: Appropriate Technologies for Development*. Peace Corps, Washington, DC

Dave R H, Ouane A, Perera D A 1988 *Learning Strategies for Post-Literacy and Continuing Education: A Cross-National Perspective*, 2nd edn. UNESCO Institute for Education, Hamburg

Freire P 1985 *The Politics of Education: Culture, Power and Liberation*. Macmillan, London

Fuchs-Brüninghoff E, Pfirrmann M (eds.) 1988/90 *Lernprobleme–Lernberatung*. Deutscher Volkshochschul Verband, Bonn

Giere U 1987 *Functional Illiteracy in Industrialized Countries: An Analytical Bibliography*. UNESCO Institute for Education, Hamburg

Giere U, Ouane A, Ranaweera A M 1990 *Literacy in Developing Countries: An Analytical Bibliography*. UNESCO, Paris

Hamminck K 1990 *Functional Illiteracy and Adult Basic Education in the Netherlands*. UNESCO Institute for Education, Hamburg

Kamper G, Rübsamen H 1990 Basic skills involved in learning to read and write, or two literacy teachers take research into their own hands. In: Hautecoeur J-P (ed.) 1990 ALPHA 90: *Current Research in Literacy*. UNESCO Institute for Education, Hamburg

Kirkwood G, Kirkwood C 1989 *Living Adult Education: Freire in Scotland*. Open University Press, Milton Keynes

Lind A, Johnston A 1990 *Adult Literacy in the Third World: A Review of Objectives and Strategies*. Swedish International Development Authority, Stockholm

SWAPO Literacy Campaign 1986 *Literacy Promoter's Handbook*. SWAPO of Namibia, Luanda

UNESCO 1984 *Literacy Situation in Asia and the Pacific—Country Studies: Indonesia*. UNESCO Regional Office for Education in Asia and the Pacific, Bangkok

Further Reading

Archer D, Cottingham S 1995 *Reflect, Regenerated Freirean Literacy through Empowering Community Techniques*. Actionaid, London

Ouane A, Sutton P T (eds.) 1991 Language Policy and Education. *International Review of Education*. 37(1): 1–187

Educational Technology in Distance Education

A. W. Bates

Modern distance education systems depend on technology for the administration, development, production, and delivery of teaching materials, and increasingly for student–teacher interaction. This entry discusses the relationship between technology and the organization of distance education, and issues of pedagogy arising from the use of technology for distance education.

1. Media and Technology in Distance Education: Some Definitions

It is useful to make a distinction between media and technology. The term "media" is used in this entry to describe generic forms of communication associated with particular ways of representing knowledge. Each medium not only has its own unique way of presenting knowledge, but also of organizing it, often reflected in particular preferred formats or styles of presentation. A single medium such as television may be carried by several different technologies (satellite, cable, video cassette, etc.). In distance education, the most important four media are text, audio, television, and computing.

While certain technologies are closely associated with each medium, a variety of different technologies may be used to deliver these media, as Table 1 indicates.

It can be seen that media can usually be carried by more than one technology, and certainly these distinctions will become less meaningful as media and technologies become integrated into single machines

or transmission systems. Nevertheless, there are still significant differences in the bandwidth required for different media (uncompressed television requires 1,000 times the bandwidth capacity of an audio telephone call), and in the educational applications associated with different technologies.

A second major distinction is between technologies that are primarily one-way and those that are primarily two-way. Table 2 summarizes the distinctions.

The significance of two-way technologies is that they allow for interaction between learners and instructors or tutors, and—perhaps even more significantly—for interaction between the distance learners themselves.

2. Technological Development and Forms of Distance Education

Distance education takes many forms, but it can be roughly classified into three stages of development, or "generations" (Kaufman 1989), each reflecting major technological innovations.

The first generation is characterized by the predominant use of a single technology (initially correspondence by mail, subsequently radio, then television), and lack of direct student interaction with the teacher originating the instruction.

Second-generation distance education is characterized by a deliberately integrated multimedia approach, with learning materials specifically designed for study at a distance, but with two-way communication still mediated by a third person (a tutor, rather than the originator of the teaching material).

Table 1

The relationship between media, technology, and distance education applications of technology

Media	Technologies	Distance education applications
text (including graphics)	print computers	course units, supplementary materials, correspondence tutoring, data bases, electronic publishing
audio	cassettes, radio; telephone	programs, telephone tutoring; audio-conferencing
television	broadcasting, videocassettes, videodiscs, cable, satellite, fiber optics, ITFS, microwave	programs, lectures, video-conferencing
computing	computers, telephone, satellite, fiber optics, ISDN, CD-ROM, videodisc	computer-aided learning (CAI, CBT), e-mail, computer-conferencing, audio-graphics, databases, multi-media

Third-generation distance education is based on two-way communications media which allow for direct interaction between the teacher who originates the instruction and the remote student, and often between remote students, either individually or as groups.

Kaufman (1989) characterizes the three generations as a progressive increase (from first to third generation) in learner control, opportunities for dialogue, and emphasis on thinking skills rather than mere comprehension (see *Distance Education*).

2.1 First Generation: Single Media

Correspondence teaching can be traced back at least as far as St Paul's epistles. In its modern form, correspondence teaching began in the nineteenth century, it relied on the postal service, and was characterized by little or no production of materials. Rather, students were given a reading list and a set of sample questions, which correspondence tutors marked. The student may have received some helpful comments from the tutor, before sitting the same examination as full-time, internal students. Many thousands of students in British Commonwealth countries, for instance, took the London University external degree in this way. The distinctive characteristic of such education was, in general, its very low completion rates (Glatter and Wedell 1971).

Educational broadcasting aimed at a general public can also be considered a form of distance education. The mandate of public broadcasting organizations in Europe and some British Commonwealth countries includes education; public broadcasting organizations in most West European countries have educational departments (e.g., *Teleac* in Holland, *Utbildningsradion* in Sweden). The BBC introduced adult education radio programming as early as 1924, with the program *Insects in Relation to Man* (Robinson 1982). Similarly

Table 2
One-way and two-way technology applications in distance education

Media	One-way technology applications	Two-way technology applications
text	course units, supplementary materials	correspondence tutoring
audio	cassette programs; radio programs	telephone tutoring, audio-conferencing
television	broadcast programs; cassette programs	interactive television (TV out, telephone in), video-conferencing
computing	CAL, CAI, CBT databases, multimedia	e-mail, computer-conferencing

with television: both the BBC and commercial television companies in the United Kingdom produce and transmit substantial amounts of educational television for schools and adults (Bates 1984).

Programs produced by broadcasting organizations are characterized by high production standards, which attempt to exploit the unique presentational characteristics of broadcasting. However, while the broadcasts are often accompanied by other media, such as print, and may even be linked to local face-to-face classes, there is little or no tutoring at a distance. Choice of medium is determined by the nature of the originating organization, rather than by curriculum design, and broadcast-based courses are rarely linked to the acquisition of formal qualifications.

In North America, several distinct forms of educational broadcasting have developed, all of which can be considered as first-generation distance education. Programs produced and/or distributed through the Public Broadcasting System (PBS) are not too dissimilar from educational broadcasting in Europe. Examples which may be cited here are *Sesame Street* for children and *Nova* (a science series) for adults. As well as commissioning or purchasing original productions, again using high production standards, the PBS system also buys in material from other countries. There is a much broader definition of "education" than in Europe, and educational broadcasting includes cultural and even "high-quality" entertainment programs with an implicit cultural emphasis (such as the British costume drama *Upstairs, Downstairs* about life in an upper-middle- class Edwardian household). Not only do many of these series result in the publication of glossy, well-produced "coffee-table" books, which can be purchased by the public, but many colleges also offer credit courses built around the programs.

For many years, Chicago TV College delivered "lectures" by television to home-based adult students who registered with the City Colleges of Chicago and took their examinations. In contrast, the program "Sunrise Semester," originated by New York University, provided general adult education programs in the forms of interviews and lectures by distinguished academics, but not for credit.

2.2 Second Generation: Multimedia Distance Education

The Open University, established in the United Kingdom in 1969 to produce fully qualified graduates, adopted an integrated multimedia approach to distance education, even though the predominant teaching medium was, and remains, print (Perry 1976) (see *Open University*).

The Open University was the first incarnation of what Peters (1984) has described as the "industrial" model of distance education. This is typified by the continued use of "one-way" media (print, broadcasting, cassettes) with "two-way" communication provided by correspondence tutors, and sometimes supplemented with face-to-face tutorials. Much emphasis is given to curriculum design, to ensure that the materials facilitate independent study, and that there is an integration of the different media used. Materials are produced by a team that includes, as well as several subject specialists, television producers, book editors, a representative of the regional (tutorial) staff, and educational technologists (instructional designers). Courses often take two or more years to develop before they are offered to students. Another characteristic of the industrial model is its high fixed costs—associated with developing the courses—and low variable costs —the cost of each additional student is low once materials have been created. Large numbers of students are required to justify the high fixed costs.

The Open University, and many similar institutions created since, are autonomous, insofar as they award their own qualifications; they often cover an entire country (e.g., Allama Iqbal Open University in Pakistan) or even a whole region (e.g., University of the South Pacific); and they are solely dedicated to distance education (i.e., single-mode institutions). By contrast, in countries such as Australia, Canada, France, Sweden, and the United States, the predominant form of distance education is the dual-mode institution which, as well as teaching on campus, also offers courses at a distance. Dual-mode institutions have had a harder struggle in providing courses based on the industrial model of distance education, not only because of the far smaller student enrollments for distance courses than in single-mode institutions, but also because of the lower priority or status often given to distance education in these institutions. Such institutions usually arrange for the professor who delivers similar programs on campus to design relatively low-cost, print-based materials in conjunction with an instructional designer/developer from the distance education branch of the institution.

Despite—or perhaps because of—these difficulties, dual-mode institutions have often been more ready than single-mode institutions to use interactive technologies as a central part of their distance teaching, and they have placed less emphasis on high-cost print and television production, and more on bought-in or adapted print materials, or low-cost local print production.

2.3 Third Generation: Two-way Interactive Technologies

Third-generation distance education is based on the use of electronic information technologies, but not just in the "one-to-many" form of print and broadcasting (Pelton 1990). These third-generation technologies, based on telecommunications and computers, provide far greater facility for two-way communication, and result in much more even communication between student and teacher (and also between students). Typical technologies are computer-conferencing or computer networking, and audio- and video-conferencing (including audio-graphics). Pelton (1990) also includes in third-generation distance education the use of television to relay lectures from one site to students at a distant or remote site, with the opportunity of two-way communication between students and the 'distant' teacher, using either two-way television or voice telephone.

There are many examples of such forms of distance education in the United States. The use of television for such two-way systems has until recently been restricted to satellite, cable, or specialist transmission frequencies (such as Instructional Television Fixed Services—including the Indiana Higher Education Telecommunications System), and has been used primarily to relay lectures from one campus to others. There is usually some form of two-way communication (mainly via telephone) from the remote sites (Lewis 1983).

The National Technological University provides mainly postgraduate master's courses in engineering, computer sciences, and business management to students in member institutions, including business sites. In 1990-91, programs were originated from 23 different institutions with "leading edge" researchers and instructors, then the programs were re-broadcast via satellite to over 300 reception sites across the United States (NTU 1991). Students generally interact by telephone with the remote teacher, and sometimes also through computer networking. EuroPace offers a similar type of program via satellite in Europe.

Television-based distance teaching, used for delivering lectures to remote sites, has received a considerable boost as a result of technological developments. One of the main inhibitors to greater use of television for relayed lectures has been the high transmission costs arising from the bandwidth required. Compressed video technology, however, is reducing the bandwidth (and hence transmission costs) by a considerable factor (compression ratios of 100:1 at the time of writing). Fiber optic and satellite technology developments, as well as compressed video, are all increasing telecommunications transmission capacity in the United States. Providers of cable and satellite services are therefore looking for new uses for television, and distance education is seen by suppliers as a large potential market.

However, television is by no means the only medium used for this kind of teaching. One of the major distance teaching institutions in the United States is the University of Wisconsin, which has a state-wide audio-teleconferencing network, enabling professors at one site to deliver lectures to multiple classroom sites around the state, and facilitating two-way communication between professor and students at the remote sites through the telephone system (Parker and Olgren 1980). The system has been augmented with a number of devices (including slow-scan television and audio-graphics) to provide graphical support for the lectures (Winders 1988).

A third technology associated with third-generation distance education is computer networking. This allows text and graphics generated at a computer workstation to be communicated to any other workstation connected to the network. This can be transmitted through public data networks, over the standard telephone system, to virtually anywhere in the world.

The Open University in the United Kingdom has used computer networking as part of a course which also uses printed texts, television broadcasts, and audio cassettes. This course, on information technology, required all students to have a microcomputer. The network linked 1,500 remote students each year with their local tutors and their central academic staff, and computer conferencing was used for discussion of course topics, and to generate assignments and practical work for the course (see Mason and Kaye 1989). The University of Phoenix, Arizona, in the United States uses computer networking for the delivery of postgraduate business courses, requiring students to work in small groups, but remote from the central site (see Harasim 1990).

Courses based on these technologies are characterized by relatively low fixed costs, since they provide easy access to teachers without the need for high-cost development of materials, yet relatively high marginal costs, since telecommunications and teacher costs increase in proportion to the number of students (if a high degree of interactivity is to be maintained). For this reason, third-generation technologies allow courses to be tailored to fit the needs of comparatively small numbers, and consequently are proving particularly appealing to dual-mode institutions, especially since the technologies involve only minor changes in teaching behavior.

3. Pedagogic Issues

3.1 Access versus Advanced Technology

In general, distance education has been limited to relatively few technologies: print; broadcast television; radio; audiocassettes and videocassettes; and the telephone. The reason for this is that students are likely to own or have access at home to such technologies. Thus, the use of computers has been restricted to certain courses, such as computer sciences, where computing is the subject of study, and students are therefore expected already to have access to such equipment.

Distance education course designers are reluctant to use technologies that are not accessible to nearly all the potential students, because that limits access to courses, particularly for the more economically disadvantaged students, for whom distance education and open learning may be the only practical educational option. Experience has also shown that if parts of the course associated with the use of a particular technology are optional, nearly all students—even those with access to the technology—avoid that part of the course.

In order to find ways of employing more advanced technologies, such as computer-based multimedia, interactive videodisc, and two-way video communication such as video-conferencing, a number of distance teaching institutions, such as the Dutch Open University, have established local learning centers, where students can access equipment not available at home or work (Beijderwellen 1990). Also, as open learning and distance education begins to reach into the workplace, technologies such as computers and even video-conferencing become more accessible.

However, the requirement to attend a learning center in order to access essential learning material reduces the flexibility of the course, and may therefore restrict access for certain potential students. Also, it is a relatively untested assumption that advanced technologies, such as computer-based multimedia or video-conferencing, are pedagogically more effective than older—and generally cheaper—technologies such as print or audiocassettes.

3.2 Pedagogical "Equivalence" versus Unique Teaching Functions

There is a widespread belief, particularly in the United States (see Clark 1983), that there are no significant pedagogic differences between media (e.g., a lecture delivered by television is just as effective as one delivered face to face). If this is so, then the main criteria for choosing a medium would be cost, administrative convenience, or student access.

However, there is evidence that shifting even the same medium (e.g., television) from one technology to another (e.g., from broadcast to videocassette) has significant pedagogic implications in a distance education context. For instance, Bates (1984) listed some of the learning implications of using cassettes rather than broadcasting and drew the following conclusion: "Broadcasts appear to be much weaker instructionally than cassettes in terms of integration with other material, ease of recall, mastery learning, deep thinking and possibly creative thinking" (pp. 272–313). In addition, of course, cassettes give students much more flexibility, in that they do not have to view at a set time. While Bates's comments were directed at broadcast television programs, the same conclusions would apply to the use of television to relay live lectures, compared with making recordings of the lectures available on cassettes.

Other researchers at the Open University in the United Kingdom (Durbridge 1983, Brown 1984, Crooks and Kirkwood 1988) have also pointed out that changing from one technology to another has profound implications for the design of the teaching materials. With cassettes, for instance, the teaching material need not be continuous (as with a broadcast or lecture), pauses could be added, and questions inserted to increase student activity.

A common factor, of course, is that modes of design associated with an "old" technology tend to be carried over to a newer one, even though the new technology may have inherent design advantages over the old. Thus, in many institutions audiocassettes are used merely to record "continuous" lectures, and videocassettes are used to distribute broadcast programs. However, the Open University in the United Kingdom found that designing audiocassettes in a way that utilized their unique features led to greater student interaction and higher student ratings of the material, compared with radio broadcasts (Bates et al. 1981).

This is not an argument against the use of broadcasting; Bates identified a large number of unique teaching functions for both broadcast television and radio (Bates 1984). It does indicate, though, that there appear to be profound pedagogical differences between media that need to be identified, and that media should be used carefully to exploit their strengths and avoid their weaknesses, rather than just relaying a predominant mode of delivery, such as a lecture or broadcast.

3.3 "Live" Interaction versus Flexibility

One common criticism of distance education, particularly from campus professors, is that distance education is inferior to campus-based instruction because it uses technology merely to deliver information rather than develop understanding or the ability to think critically (Harris 1987). One of the strong arguments for third-generation distance education, being based on interactive technologies, is that it more closely resembles face-to-face teaching, and hence leads to a higher quality of distance education than second-generation distance education. For instance, Garrison (1989 p. 69) states:

> Teleconferencing represents a paradigm shift in facilitating and supporting learning at a distance . . . Of all the means used to support distance education, teleconferencing most closely simulates the transaction between teacher and students in a contiguous or conventional form of education. The exchange is conversational in nature, it may be spontaneous, and it is immediate.

Garrison argues that because teleconferencing (in fact, in this context he is referring to audio-conferencing) allows classroom-style instruction to be extended beyond the classroom and across distances, it is therefore superior to print-based forms of distance education, even when mediated by correspondence tutoring. This results from his belief that:

> Dialogue and negotiation are essential . . . Interaction to facilitate and support the educational process must be

seen as the central feature of any educational transaction *including* distance education . . . the relative advantage of audio-teleconferencing is a consequence of the quality of interaction and support it affords. (Garrison 1989 pp. 66–68)

The argument that true knowledge can come only through questioning and dialogue is as old as Plato and the Socratic dialogues. Holmberg (1990 p.53), however, has challenged Garrison's claim that this can be achieved in distance education *only* through the use of telecommunications technologies. He claims that: "Distance education can be—and often is—exclusively based on *non*-contiguous communication and wholly individual study." Holmberg (1984) has argued that well-designed print materials "simulate" a dialogue between teacher and learner, for instance.

A more pragmatic criticism of making telecommunications the main or sole means of delivery for distance education is that they reduce flexibility for the distance learner. This is one advantage of computer-conferencing over audio-conferencing, since students can study asynchronously from home, provided they have access to a computer.

3.4 Classroom Instruction versus Instructional Design

Garrison's arguments reflect a view of distance education that is much more common in North America and Australia, where distance education is conducted mainly by dual-mode institutions, than in Europe or Asia, where distance education is designed and delivered by autonomous distance teaching institutions. Put simply, the North American view is that the traditional form of group face-to-face instruction is the preferred and most effective form of higher education, and that the closer distance education can directly imitate this, the more effective it will be.

European and Asian distance education experts on the other hand, have designed and developed forms of distance education that emphasize the need for flexible learning opportunities that provide independence for learners. They have tried to develop forms of teaching that are quite different from the traditional face-to-face approach of classroom teaching. Courses from autonomous distance teaching institutions are based on breaking down instructional and learning requirements, and allocating different tasks to different technologies, such as print, telephone, and correspondence.

There are good reasons why the two approaches to distance education are so different. There has been a much greater tradition in North American colleges and universities of providing off-campus teaching as an extension of the traditional college. In addition, North American colleges have been more flexible in providing opportunities for more mature students. By contrast, the target group for open universities in both Europe and Asia is quite different: namely, mature adults who are no longer engaged in full-time education, most of whom have families, and who are in employment. The prime concern of open universities is to provide learning opportunities that fit the lifestyle of mature adults; the greater the flexibility, the better. There was therefore no need to aim to "extend" classroom teaching to distance learners; indeed, this was seen as likely to be more of a handicap than an advantage.

The autonomous distance teaching institutions try to provide interaction in a variety of ways: design of print material that encourages interaction and questioning by the individual learner in isolation; use of postal services, and increasingly the telephone, for individual tutor–student communication; and a variety of group, face-to-face arrangements, such as evening classes, weekend day-schools, and week-long residential summer schools.

Extending classroom lectures to remote sites, on the other hand, can suffer from a lack of preparation and curriculum design. If the total number present at the same time at all sites is not kept low, opportunities for meaningful interaction diminish rapidly.

In essence, this is not an "either/or" scenario. Distance education students need opportunities both for individual study, and for group study and interaction with teachers. Modern technologies allow for both, but require a combination of different technologies. This combination will differ depending on the context.

Thus Garrison is right to assert that, in the Canadian context of courses with small numbers of students, relatively efficient telephone networks, and relatively affluent students or institutions able to bear the costs of telephone lines and on-line tutors, audio-conferencing can play a more central role in distance teaching. Yet even in these circumstances, it is important to use audio-conferencing in conjunction with other media, such as printed material.

In other contexts, and particularly, if large numbers of students are to be taught at a distance, or if the telephone system is not efficient, or if tutors are not skilled at designing and conducting conferences that encourage and support student interaction, then other forms of communication such as correspondence or mail are likely to be essential, and indeed more appropriate.

4. The Need for More Research and Theory Building

In general, while there has been an enormous amount of comparative research into the relative effectiveness of distance teaching using technological delivery compared with conventional classroom teaching, the most common results from well-conducted studies have shown no significant differences. Even if differences were to be found, this research would not be helpful since, for many distance learners, face-to-face tuition at a regular institution is not an option. More importantly, there has been little systematic research into either the effectiveness of different distance teaching approaches using technology, or the relationship between different forms of learning and the use of different distance teaching technologies.

Where research has been conducted, it has concentrated on differences in comprehension; where differences have been found, they are often heavily outweighed by many other factors, such as the quality of the teaching and the appropriate use of technology. As long ago as 1977, Schramm was suggesting that what was needed were studies into how a medium is used and into the content of media (Schramm 1977).

Moreover, there has been little development of pedagogic theories of teaching and learning through the use of technology, although considerable practical experience has been amassed.

Lastly, much more needs to be known about the relative costs of different technologies. The cost structure of distance education is quite different from that of conventional education. Furthermore, the cost structure of the technologies used in distance education is quite complex: some technologies are much more cost-effective with large numbers than with small numbers of students per course, for instance; the reverse is true for other technologies.

As a consequence, a great many questions remain unanswered about the relative effectiveness of different technologies in different distance education contexts. What is clear is that technology will become an even more critical issue for distance education in the future, and wise decisions are unlikely to be reached without a better understanding of the relationship between different technologies and distance learning.

See also: Distance Education; Open University; Evaluation of Distance Education: Cost-Effectiveness

References

Bates A W et al. 1981 Radio: The forgotten medium? Papers on Broadcasting 185, Institute of Educational Technology, Open University, Milton Keynes (mimeo)

Bates A W 1984 *Broadcasting in Education: An Evaluation.* Constables, London

Beijderwellen W 1990 Interactive video in geology at the Open University of the Netherlands. In: Bates A W (ed.) 1990 *Media and Technology in European Distance Education.* European Association of Distance Teaching Universities/Open University, Milton Keynes

Brown S 1984 Video-cassettes. In: Bates A W (ed.) 1984 *The Role of Technology in Distance Education.* Croom Helm, London

Clark R 1983 Reconsidering research on learning from media. *Educ. Res.* 53(4): 445–59

Crooks B, Kirkwood A 1988 Video-cassettes by design in Open University courses. *Open Learning* 3(3): 13–17

Durbridge N 1983 Design implications of audio and video-cassettes. Papers on Broadcasting 222, Institute of Educational Technology, Open University, Milton Keynes (mimeo)

Garrison D R 1989 *Understanding Distance Education: A Framework for the Future*. Routledge, London

Glatter R, Wedell E G 1971 *Study by Correspondence: An Enquiry into Correspondence Study for Examinations for Degrees and other Advanced Qualifications*. Longman, London

Harasim L (ed.) 1990 *On-Line Education: Perspectives on a New Environment*. Greenwood, New York

Harris D 1987 *Openness and Closure in Distance Education*. Falmer Press, London

Holmberg B 1984 Guided didactic conversation in distance education. In: Sewart D, Keegan D, Holmberg B 1984 *Distance Education: International Perspectives*. Croom Helm, London

Holmberg B 1990 A paradigm shift in distance education? Mythology in the making. ICDE *Bulletin* 22: 51–55

Kaufman D 1989 Third generation course design in distance education. In: Sweet R (ed.) 1989 *Post-secondary Distance Education in Canada: Policies, Practices and Priorities*. Athabasca University/Canadian Society for Studies in Education, Athabasca

Lewis R 1983 *Meeting Learners' Needs through Telecommunications: A Directory and Guide to Programs*. American Association for Higher Education, Washington, DC

Mason R, Kaye A (eds.) 1989 *Mindweave: Communication, Computers and Distance Education*. Pergamon Press, Oxford

National Technological University (NTU) 1991 *National Technological University Annual Report 1990–91*. NTU, Fort Collins, Colorado

Parker L, Olgren C H 1980 *Teleconferencing and Interactive Media*. University of Wisconsin–Madison, Madison, Wisconsin

Peters O 1984 Distance teaching and industrial production: A comparative interpretation in outline. In: Sewart D, Keegan D, Holmberg B 1984 *Distance Education: International Perspectives*. Croom Helm, London

Pelton J 1990 Technology and education: Friend or foe? In: Croft M et al. 1990 *Distance Education: Development and Access*. International Council for Distance Education/Universidad Nacional Abierta, Caracas

Perry W 1976 *The Open University: A Personal Account*. Open University Press, Milton Keynes

Robinson J 1982 *Learning Over the Air: 60 Years of Partnership in Adult Learning*. BBC Books, London

Schramm W 1977 *Big Media, Little Media: Tools and Technologies for Instruction*. Sage, Beverley Hills, California

Winders R 1988 *Information Technology in the Delivery of Distance Education and Training*. Peter Francis, Ely

Educational Technology in Vocational Training

G. L. Roth

Maintaining a competitive workforce is a major concern for policymakers of most industrialized nations. Several strategies are used to train prospective workers effectively and retrain current workers. Many workers need up-skilling to succeed in workplaces characterized by increasing levels of complexity and ambiguity. This entry discusses: (a) the dynamic constructs of workforce preparation; (b) applications of educational technologies in technical training for youth and adults; and (c) preparation of workers for future work settings with educational technologies. This entry converges select issues contained within the literature bases of workforce preparation and educational technology.

1. The Dynamic Constructs of Workforce Preparation

For many years corporations considered workplace automation and other technological advantages to be the best defense against production complacency. However, in today's global marketplace, contemporary technology is available to any international competitor with the resources to buy it. What, then, provides competitive advantages for one international firm as compared to another? Enlightened corporate leaders and national policymakers recognize that the collective abilities of the workforce constitute either a key advantage or an urgent liability in the global arena of economic competition.

K T Li, senior adviser to the President of the Republic of China, described the significance of preparing workers for the demands of the workplace: "In a future of rapid international change and accelerated advances in science and technology, how to effectively develop scientific and technical manpower to meet the needs of economic and scientific development will be a very important task for human resources planning" (Li 1992 p. 30).

National policymakers and other officials are examining strategies for preparing individuals for the workplace. Content, methods, policies, and procedures for traditional vocational education programs have experienced close scrutiny. Technical training strategies such as work-based learning and apprenticeship are being appraised by countries such as France and the United States, where these approaches are not predominant. Curriculum innovations within vocational education, for example integrative curriculum and tech prep (as explained below), are also being explored: Within these fluid contexts of workforce preparation linger potential roles for educational technologies. The following four subsections explore select topics that are affecting the nature of workforce preparation.

1.1 Apprenticeship

Although apprenticeship dates back several centuries as a means for preparing workers, it is receiving renewed international attention as a school-to-work strategy for young adults. In contemporary practice, apprenticeship has two components: on-the-job training that is provided by the private sector; and related instruction that is typically provided by public schools. Apprenticeship is an effective method for increasing collaboration between public schools and the private sector. Such partnerships are needed to ensure a young person's smooth transition from school to work.

Apprenticeship systems are the mainstays of the educational systems of countries including Germany, Austria, and Switzerland. In Switzerland, in particular, there is undoubtedly a connection between this form of training, the low volume of youth unemployment, and the country's widely admired economic performance (Silvestre 1991).

In all three countries, young people leave compulsory secondary education at about age 16 and enter the workforce. The workplace gradually supplants classroom learning. These apprenticeship systems prepare young adults for futures of increasing responsibility, skills, recognition, income, and independence (Nothdurft 1990). The European apprenticeship model helps youth to develop the kind of worker virtues and adult responsibilities that employers readily seek. Sohngen (1989) cited several positive aspects of the German apprenticeship system, such as providing an optimal mix between theoretical and practical learning, exposing learners to a broad array of work-based learning experiences, and presenting trainees with state-of-the-art technology.

1.2 Vocational Education and Curriculum Integration

Historically, vocational education students who were aptly grounded in mathematics, science, and communications have fared well in the workplace. There is logic in the marriage of academic and vocational education subject matter. This connection is prevalent in Japan, where vocational students study mathematics, Japanese literature, English, history, and general science (Dore and Sako 1989). Salmi (1991) assessed vocational education in Algeria, Egypt, and Morocco, and observed complex relationships between general and vocational education. He deemed it inappropriate to isolate vocational education from general education.

A curriculum strategy that is gaining momentum in the United States is the integration of academic and vocational education. This approach implies that teachers should work across disciplines using themes related to real-world situations. Integration of academic and vocational education may be defined as the meshing of academic content and methods with applied vocational instruction to increase levels of student achievement.

Why has interest emerged for integrating academic and vocational education? Educators began to question the validity of teaching subject areas in isolation from one another. An integrated curriculum can enhance the relevance of subject matter through connections rather than confusing its purpose through isolation (Jacobs 1989). Vocational educators in the United States are being encouraged to work with academic teachers on interdisciplinary projects that integrate mathematics, communications, and science topics into technical courses. The durability of this integrated knowledge is considered greater for learners than the mere memorization of isolated chunks of information (Kersh 1989).

1.3 Tech Prep

Tech prep is a curricular innovation in the United States that features an interdisciplinary approach for curriculum and instruction. Tech prep connects academic content and methods with applied vocational instruction to increase levels of student achievement. Tech prep programs have several characteristics worth noting: (a) secondary and post-secondary programs are linked to lead students to an associate degree or a two-year certificate; (b) technical preparation is provided in fields such as engineering technology, applied science, practical arts or trades; (c) competence is stressed in mathematics, science, and communications; and (d) job placement is the ultimate intention. Tech prep is intended to prepare youth for careers that have high levels of technological content. Primary features of these programs include integration of academic and vocational education, partnerships between educators and private sector representatives, and articulation between secondary and postsecondary institutions.

1.4 Workforce Competencies

Research has been conducted to determine the workforce competencies that employees need in order to achieve success in a technologically, complex work setting. In the United States relevant studies were conducted by Carnevale, Gainer, and Meltze in 1991 and the Secretary's Commission on Achieving Necessary Skills or "SCANS Report" (1991).

Carnevale and colleagues outlined a set of workplace skills that employers view as essential worker attributes: (a) learning to learn; (b) reading, writing, computation; (c) communication—listening and oral communication; (d) creative thinking and problem-solving; (e) self-esteem and goal setting, motivation/employability, career development; (f) interpersonal skills, negotiation, and teamwork; (g) organizational effectiveness and leadership.

The SCANS Report (1991) identified skills that individuals should possess for successful employment.

The Commission that authored the report identified five competencies and a three-part foundation of skills and personal qualities that are central to job performance.

The five competencies are:

(a) resources: identifies, plans, and allocates resources;

(b) interpersonal: works well with others;

(c) information: acquires and uses information;

(d) systems: understands complex interrelationships;

(e) technology: works with a variety of technologies.

The three-part foundation consists of:

(a) basic skills: reads, writes, performs arithmetic and mathematical operations, listens, and speaks effectively;

(b) thinking skills: thinks creatively, makes decisions, solves problems, visualizes, knows how to learn, and reasons;

(c) personal qualities: displays responsibilities, self-esteem, sociability, self-management, integrity, and honesty.

There are commonalities as well as variances in the workforce competencies cited by these two sources. However, the content of the aforementioned workforce competencies comprises only one piece of the puzzle of workforce preparation. Strategies for preparing younger workers with these skills and abilities remain significant issues. The United States General Accounting Office (1990) compared the national policies for employment preparation of noncollege youth in England, Germany, Japan, and Sweden. The study cited several approaches shared by some or all of the countries:

(a) Schools emphasize student effort rather than ability and, therefore, expect all students to attain the academic skills necessary to perform effectively in postsecondary education or the workplace. The schools do not take it as a matter of course that many students will lag behind.

(b) Schools and the employment community play a more active role in guiding the transition from school to work, including an orientation to the world of work built into the school curriculum.

(c) Training is accompanied by certification of achievement of competency on nationally determined skill levels.

(d) Governments make extensive investment in remedial education, training, or job placement for jobless out-of-school youth.

Policies, content, and processes for fitting young adults into the workplace are being realigned in many countries. Leaders are looking at each other's systems of workforce preparation in search of solutions that might be adapted to fit their country's needs. In this search, educational technologies are being critiqued for roles they might play in technical training for youth and adults.

2. Roles of Educational Technologies in Technical Training for Youth and Adults

The preceding paragraphs have portrayed the dynamic constructs of school-to-work transition for young adults. Changes are occurring across three educational fronts. Contexts are being reconsidered, with apprenticeship training systems and other forms of work-based learning receiving increased international attention. Content of instruction is being aligned with workplace needs, and workforce competencies and strategies for providing them are being established. New processes for workforce preparation are emerging, and approaches such as tech prep and curriculum integration are evolving.

These changing forces provide the backdrop for current and potential roles of educational technologies in technical training for youth and adults. Recognition of this backdrop is crucial, for it provides a glimpse of the situations, their complexities, and images of solutions found in the initial training and retraining of workers. By gaining an understanding of these scenarios, one can begin to visualize the educational problems encountered in workforce preparation. Awareness of these problems is critically important. A basic premise regarding the use of educational technologies is that they should be applied in response to an appropriate educational problem (Ely and Plomp 1989). Contrary to this desirable practice, educators often begin with the inclination to use an educational technology and then search for a problem to which it may be applied.

There is no shortage of educational problems confronting practitioners who provide technical training for youth and adults. However, there is a shortage of definitive answers regarding the effectiveness of educational technologies used in response to those problems. Vocational and technical education is burdened with the malaise that afflicts education in general. That is, limited research findings hinder practitioners and theorists in their quest to assess the effectiveness of educational technologies.

Scant research evidence has restricted the conclusions and recommendations that researchers are willing to assert regarding applications of educational technologies. As an example, Robyler in 1990 alluded to this problem in the United States in her meta-analysis of computer applications in schools. She noted that, after nearly 25 years of using computers in schools, including nearly a decade of microcomputers, the effects of this technology on measures such as student achievement, attitudes, dropout rates, and learning time were mostly undetermined. Robyler lamented:

> The single greatest problem facing a systematic assessment of the impact of the microcomputer revolution on teaching and learning is the lack of sufficient numbers of studies in key areas. Findings indicate that computer applications have an important role to play in the future of education, but the exact nature of that role has only begun to be explored. Opportunities for using technology to make an impact on education have never been greater, and neither have opportunities for research. The next decade must be a time for taking full advantage of both. (p. 55)

Although conclusions regarding the effectiveness of computers and other educational technologies may be nondescript, ideas abound for their potential applications. Ideas are spawned from questions posed by the unique educational problems of workforce preparation. A sampling of questions includes:

(a) How can educational technology enhance the integration of vocational and academic education?

(b) How can educational technology link classroom and work-based learning?

(c) In what ways can educational technology enhance apprenticeship systems?

(d) How can educational technology foster partnerships between the private sector and public schools?

(e) How can educational technology replicate learning environments or situations that would otherwise be too dangerous, costly, or time-consuming for learners?

(f) How can educational technology prepare learners for ambiguous and ill-structured work settings?

(g) How can educational technology increase access to technical training programs?

(h) How can educational technology efficiently enhance people's learning skills?

Although there is a shortage of answers, insight into these questions may be found by reviewing current applications of educational technologies. Examples of applications are outlined in the following paragraphs.

2.1 Integrated Learning Systems

Integrated learning systems are courseware and management software that operate on networked hardware. Rather than being deployed as stand-alone entities like most hardware and software products, these systems include a comprehensive curriculum package. Integrated learning systems use microcomputers and other related pieces of hardware, but they are used in a manner different from the way in which microcomputers have traditionally been used in schools (Gooler and Roth 1990). A hardware configuration for a classroom fitted with an integrated learning system typically includes 30–35 student work stations, each containing a microcomputer, earphones, CD-ROM drive, mouse, and other student peripherals. Each student work station is connected via a file server and an instructor work station. The unique aspect of this assemblage of technology, however, rests with the quality of the instructional content that can be delivered through the system.

Integrated learning systems provide comprehensive curriculum packages, not merely a collection of unrelated educational programming. Integrated learning systems feature curriculum content, instructional and assessment strategies, and a means for managing the teaching and learning processes within the system (Gooler and Roth 1990). These commercial products are created with the input of teachers, content experts, curriculum writers, and instructional designers. The systems are designed to emphasize the strengths of each respective technology.

How might an integrated learning system be applied to the challenges of workforce preparation? Current applications include adult basic education and pilot training. If the appropriate curricular packages were developed, integrated learning systems could provide a powerful strategy for integrating academic and vocational education. Integrated learning systems could feature interdisciplinary curriculum packages to help vocational education students sharpen their skills in science, mathematics, and communications.

2.2 Interactive Television Systems

Television is recognized for its capability as an instructional medium. Over the years commercial television has brought viewers a variety of learning opportunities, from university courses for adult learners to messages from Big Bird and other Sesame Street characters for younger learners. With the advent of videocassettes, learners can receive instruction on a broad range of topics, including fitness and health, sports and recreation, religion, literacy, foreign languages, and finance.

A traditional limitation of television as an educational medium has been its lack of interactivity with learners. Traditional television and video viewing place learners in predominantly passive roles.

Interactive television systems have been created to provide more powerful connections for learners with this medium. These systems allow students to interact with their television teachers, with students at other sites, and with experts or guest speakers at distant locations. Interactive television systems permit learners to interact electronically with one another at a distance in a similar manner to that achieved through face-to-face instruction. Winger (1991) explained three realms of development for interactive television:

of time, by offering educational and training activities by direct reception or for recording 24 hours a day;

of space, by being accessible in the workplace, the school, and the home;

of subject, by allowing access to a multitude of information, courses, and data banks. (Winger 1991 p. 22)

How can interactive television systems support workforce preparation programs? These systems electronically interconnect schools and school districts—a feature especially appealing to rural schools, which suffer from teacher shortages and diminishing learning opportunities (Gooler and Roth 1990). These systems have the potential to increase access for learners to higher cost, vocational programming at locations that traditionally have low enrollments. Furthermore, students at multiple locations can simultaneously and collectively work on team assignments and shared projects. Interactive television connections to workplace settings can allow students to learn from expert workers and observe actual work settings.

2.3 Computer-based Training Systems

Whereas the preceding two examples refer to school settings, educational technologies fulfill many training roles in business, industry, and nonprofit-making organizations. Applications of educational technologies that fulfill training needs in the private sector provide insight for potential applications to vocational and technical education. The following examples represent educational technology applications in the technical training of nuclear personnel.

(a) A competency-based and computer-based training program is used to help nuclear support personnel pass a nuclear safety and evacuation test.

(b) Interactive videodisk technology is used to train personnel about locations and components of a nuclear plant that generally are not accessible to workers. Surrogate tours permit operators, security guards, and maintenance workers to learn design and component locations that they may not be able to access because of radiological constraints.

(c) Expert systems are used in the nuclear industry to capture the knowledge and logic of an expert on specific work topics. This permits the specific knowledge of the expert to be applied to problem situations without the physical presence of the specialist.

(d) Computer simulations have been used in a variety of fields to replicate real work settings that could otherwise not be accessed because of unsafe conditions, cost, time factors, or distance. The nuclear industry relies heavily on computer simulations to train reactor operators. Full-scope

simulators are meticulous replications of the control room of a nuclear plant. Through the use of sophisticated software and complex mathematical models the simulator duplicates actual plant responses to normal, abnormal, and emergency conditions.

Computer-based training systems are prevalent in numerous manufacturing, service, and governmental environments. They bring to each training situation certain assets and limitations.

2.4 Applications of Microcomputers in Vocational Education

A few studies are worth noting that examine applications of microcomputers in vocational education. Tesolowski and Roth (1988) conducted a survey in the United States to ascertain the relative importance of 47 competencies for applying microcomputers in vocational education. A structured brainstorming process with a panel of recognized computer-using vocational educators resulted in an initial competency profile. After a refinement process, the competencies were clustered into five categories: (a) developing a personal plan for microcomputer competency (8 competencies); (b) integrating computer-based instruction (CBI) into vocational curricula (8 competencies); (c) planning, executing, and evaluating CBI (14 competencies); (d) planning and organizing the vocational education learning environment for CBI (7 competencies); and (e) performing classroom management functions with CBI (10 competencies).

Schell and Hartman in 1992 described possible roles of microcomputers and hypertext software in conjunction with flexible cognition theory for advanced vocational educational learning. They cited seven dependent elements commonly found in the literature on flexible cognition theory: multiple representations, learning in context, transfer of learning, ill-structured settings, variable knowledge assemblies, metaphors for complex ideas, and exceptions to the rules. The authors cited two capabilities of hypertext software that make it a good match for flexible cognition theory: (a) the ability to branch and connect pieces of information and (b) the ability to connect the strengths of multimedia. They described hypertext as a tool that may be used in conjunction with flexible cognition to help vocational students apply knowledge to authentic workplace problems.

3. Educational Technologies, Workforce Preparation, and Learning Organizations

Various writers have posed perspectives of the future development of human capital in the workplace. Their viewpoints cite the creation and transmission of knowledge as primary functions of work organizations. Learning is considered by several writers to be the foundation of future work settings. Technology will increasingly impact on the learning that occurs within organizations. Perelman (1991) asserted that combined advances in computer science, cognitive science, neuroscience, phototonics, mathematics, and other fields are dramatically altering the roles of learning in a number of contexts.

The importance of learning in work settings has caused a descriptive term to emerge—the "learning organization." Senge (1990 p.3) described learning organizations as those "where people continually expand their capacity to create the results they truly desire, where new and expansive patterns of thinking are nurtured, where collective aspiration is set free, and where people are continually learning how to learn together." Woolner (1991) described organizational learning as an on-going, systematic integration of work and learning at three levels—the individual, the work group, and the whole organization.

Leonard-Barton in 1992 cited her ideas regarding the factory as a learning laboratory. She described learning laboratories as "complex organizational ecosystems that integrate problem-solving, internal knowledge, innovation and experimentation, and external information." She summed up the learning laboratory as an organization dedicated to knowledge creation, collection, and control. Drucker extended the role of knowledge beyond the workplace by describing it as the primary societal resource for individuals and the economy. He stated that: "the purpose and function of every organization, business and non-business alike, is the integration of specialized knowledges into a common task" (Drucker 1992 p. 96).

The preceding viewpoints depict the important roles that knowledge and learning will play in work organizations of the future. What roles will educational technologies fulfill in training and retraining workers for learning organizations? The augmentation of human performance through technology is a probable answer.

Smith and Sheppard (1990) defined human augmentation as extending the capabilities of human workers by teaching them how and when to apply technological tools to a problem that is understood. They described human augmentation in the context of vocational education as an empowering process that can enhance the optimal productivity of students equipped with technological tools.

Technology will serve a variety of functions to enhance the performance of workers in future work settings. Carr (1992 p. 32) used the term "performance support system" to describe electronic systems that use computers and associated technology "to provide just the help a performer needs to do a job, just when the performer needs it, and in just the form in which he or she needs it." He outlined four roles that a performance support system might fulfill (Carr 1992 p. 33):

(a) the librarian, helping the performer find and use information quickly and accurately;

(b) the advisor, providing guidance and expert advice to the performer;

(c) the instructor, providing the performer with on-demand training about specific points;

(d) the dofer (a term coined by Anthony Putman), who does as much of the routine work of the job as possible, letting the performer concentrate on more important tasks.

Merging the concepts that undergird learning organizations with the tenets espoused by Carr about performance support systems can result in powerful visions of the roles of educational technologies in future work settings. In such settings, distinct dichotomies between technology as the object of instruction and technology as the process of instruction will dissipate. People receiving technical training will be learning about and with technology. Applications of performance support systems in learning organizations represent a future bond between educational technology and the curricula of technical training.

4. Conclusion

Explicit roles of educational technologies in workforce preparation cannot be generalized across national boundaries. Educational technologies should be used to solve specific instructional problems. Such problems vary from one part of the world to the next. Content, context, methods, and processes of technical training for youth and adults differ across disciplines as well as borders. Educational technologies fulfill specialized needs in response to unique learning problems encountered in workforce preparation programs.

The roles of educational technologies in technical-skills training for youth and adults are largely a function of the dynamic constructs of workforce preparation. These roles are in a state of flux as countries as well as corporations alter policies, procedures, and actions for the training of initial workers and the retraining of current workers. In general terms, educational technology systems are used to increase access to programs, improve the effectiveness of programs, and enhance the quality of programs.

The most interesting aspects of educational technologies and their roles in workforce preparation are likely to be found in the future. Technologies will increasingly be used to improve and extend the performance of humans at work. Learning and knowledge will comprise critical elements of work environments. Future roles of educational technologies will be woven into the fabric of work. Learners receiving technical training will be unable to distinguish whether a technology is the object of instruction, the process of instruction, or both. Educational technology within technical skills training will become a transparent learning prosthesis.

See also: Technical and Vocational Education and Training; Market Failure in Adult Education and Training; Demand, Supply, and Finance of Adult Education; Concepts of Educational Technology; Job and Task Analysis; Program Design: Effectiveness

References

Carr C 1992 PSS! Help when you need it. *Training and Development* 46(6): 30–38

Dore R P, Sako M 1989 *How the Japanese Learn to Work.* Routledge, London

Drucker P F 1992 The new society of organizations. *Harv. Bus. Rev.* 70(5): 95–104

Ely D, Plomp T 1989 The promises of educational technology: A reassessment. In: Forester A (ed.) 1989 *Computers in the Human Context.* Blackwell, Oxford

Gooler D D, Roth G L 1990 *Instructional Technology Applications in Vocational Education: A Notebook of Cases.* Illinois State Board of Education, Springfield, Illinois

Jacobs H H 1989 *Interdisciplinary Curriculum: Design and Implementation.* Association for Supervision and Curriculum Development, Alexandria, Virginia

Kersh M 1989 Integrative curricula for the twenty-first century. *Educational Horizons* 68(1): 2

Li K T 1992 Challenges and opportunities of human resources development. *Industry of Free China* 78(5): 29–33

Nothdurft W E 1990 *Youth Apprenticeship, American Style: A Strategy for Expanding School and Career Opportunities.* Consortium on Youth Apprenticeship, Somerville, Massachusetts

Perelman L J 1991 *The Technology Connection: A Business Action Plan for Increasing Technology and Productivity.* Center for Workforce Preparation and Quality Education, University of Pennsylvania, Philadelphia, Pennsylvania

Salmi J 1991 Issues in strategic planning for vocational education: Lessons from Algeria, Egypt, and Morocco. *J. of Ind. Teach. Ed.* 28(3): 46–62

Secretary's Commission on Achieving Necessary Skills (SCANS) 1991 *What Work Requires of Schools.* United States Department of Labor, Washington, DC

Senge P M 1990 *The Fifth Discipline: The Art and Practice of the Learning Organization.* Doubleday/Currency, New York

Silvestre J J 1991 Schooling and vocational training in Switzerland. OECD *Observer* 170: 28–31

Smith D C, Sheppard R W 1990 The augmentation quotient: The challenge for vocational education. In: Frantz N, Miller M (eds.) 1990 *A Context for Change: Vocational–Technical Education and the Future.* University Council for Vocational Education, Macomb, Illinois

Sohngen B 1989 The dual system of vocational training in West Germany. Paper presented at the Workforce 2000 Conference, Pittsburgh, Pennsylvania

Tesolowski D G, Roth G L 1990 A comparison of the importance of competencies for applying microcomputers in vocational education. *Journal of Research on Competencies in Education* 20(3): 271–86

United States General Accounting Office 1990 *Training Strategies: Preparing NonCollege Youth for Employment in the U.S. & Foreign Countries.* United States General Accounting Office, Washington, DC

Winger M 1991 How the new media are developing the field of education and training. *Educational Media International* 28(1): 20–22

Woolner P 1991 Integrating work and learning: A developmental model of the learning organization. Paper presented at the AAACE Annual Conference, Montreal, Quebec

Further Reading

Andrews D H 1988 Relationships among simulators, training devices, and learning: A behavioral view. *Educ. Technol.* 28(1): 48–54

Bailey G D 1992 Wanted: A road map for understanding integrated learning systems. *Educ. Technol.* 32(9): 3–5

Carnevale A 1990 *Workplace Basics: The Essential Skills Employers Want.* Jossey-Bass, San Francisco, California

Carr C 1989 Using expert system job aids: A primer. *Educ. Technol.* 29(6): 18–22

Compton-Hall M 1990 The future of CBT. *Interactive Learning International* 6(1): 35–37

Gredler M B 1986 A taxonomy of computer simulations. *Educ. Technol.* 26(4): 7–12

Johnston W B, Packer A E 1987 *Workforce 2000: Work and Workers for the 21st Century.* Hudson Institute, Indianapolis, Indiana

Liebowitz J 1989 Expert systems technology for training applications. *Educ. Technol.* 29(7): 43–45

Wilson J, Pickard D 1989 Interactive training—Planning for success. *Interactive Learning International* 5(1): 3–8

Instructional Design: Guidelines and Theories

C. M. Reigeluth

Instructional design (ID) is concerned with discerning the methods of instruction that are most likely to work best for different situations. This entry will begin by exploring the idea of ID. Elaborations of the definition will include a description of the conditions–methods–outcomes nature of ID theories and contrasts between

ID and learning theories, between prescriptive and descriptive theories, between pragmatic (or eclectic) and ideological views of instruction, between validity and superiority as criteria for judging ID theory, between general and detailed theories, and between ID theories and ID process models. The entry will then present a brief history of ID theories and project their future evolution to meet the needs of a post industrial, information-based society. Finally, there will be a discussion of trends and issues relating to the emergence of a new paradigm of instruction to meet the needs of the information-age society, including the need to develop prescriptions for the use of adaptive strategies, advanced technologies, constructivist strategies, minimalist instruction, affective learning, and systemic change.

Any attempt to understand education is enlightened by the recognition that education is a system; namely, that it is comprised of many interacting elements, and that the effects of each element are dependent to a great extent upon other elements of the system. Banathy (1991) has identified four levels of educational systems: (a) the learning-experience level; (b) the instructional system that implements those learning experiences; (c) the administrative system that supports the instructional system; and (d) the governance system that owns, rules, and funds the entire educational or training enterprise. Separate fields have arisen for each level, including learning theory, instructional and curriculum and counseling theories, administrative studies, and policy studies, respectively. Interdisciplinary linkages are woefully deficient in most cases. This entry will focus on the instructional level of educational systems.

Within the instructional level, there are many theoretical approaches, each oriented around a different type of decision-oriented activity. Curriculum theory and theories of front-end analysis inform decisions about what to teach. Instructional design theory addresses decisions about how to teach it. Instructional mediation (or instructional development) theory is concerned with how to take the designs (or blueprints) for the instruction and make them a reality on the most appropriate media. There are also theories for instructional evaluation, dissemination/implementation/change, and management. This entry only addresses instructional design theory.

1. Characteristics of ID Theories

An ID theory is a set of guidelines that indicate what methods of instruction are most likely to work best for different situations. Just as a carpenter uses different tools for different situations, so a person who creates instruction must use different tools to facilitate learning under different situations. ID theory is accumulated knowledge about which methods work best for which situations.

1.1 Conditions–Methods–Outcomes

It is helpful to think of two aspects of the teaching "situation" that will influence which methods will work best: desired instructional outcomes and instructional conditions. Desired instructional outcomes include the effectiveness of the instruction (which is based on learning outcomes), the efficiency of the instruction (as indicated by learning time and/or cost of the instruction), and the appeal of the instruction (the extent to which the learner enjoys it).

Instructional conditions include some aspects of the learner (such as relevant prior knowledge, ability, motivation, and learning styles), some aspects of what is to be learned (such as whether it requires application, understanding, or simple memorization), some aspects of the learning environment (such as instructional resource and time constraints), and even some aspects of the instructional development process (such as development resource and time constraints).

Of course, different aspects of an instructional situation will influence how well different kinds of methods, or "tools," will work. Hence the basic form of instructional theory is "if–then" statements—often called "prescriptions" or "guidelines"—in which a method appears in the "then" part and relevant aspects of a situation appear in the "if" part of the statement. If a prescription is very narrow, prescribing a single method variable, it is usually called a "principle of instruction." A theory is much broader in scope: an integrated set of method variables—a package deal—is prescribed, rather than just a single method variable.

A few additional distinctions will assist in clarifying what ID theory includes and excludes.

1.2 Instruction versus Learning

ID theory is different from, but related to, learning theory. ID theory focuses on methods of instruction and facilitation—what the teacher or other learning resource does—whereas learning theory focuses on the learning process—what happens inside the learner.

1.3 Prescriptive versus Descriptive

Simon (1969) has distinguished between the natural sciences, which are descriptive, and the design sciences (or sciences of the artificial), which are prescriptive. The natural and design sciences are usually closely related, as in the case of biology and medicine, physics and engineering, and learning and instruction. Banathy (1991) made the same distinction under the rubrics of conclusion-oriented and decision-oriented disciplines.

ID theory, as a design science, is prescriptive, or decision-oriented, but it is closely related to learning theory. There is a common misconception that descriptive theory must precede prescriptive theory—that learning theory must precede ID theory. In reality, throughout the history of science, from the steam engine to superconductivity, the prescriptive has often preceded the descriptive. Someone has discovered that a certain technique (or tool or method) works; others then set about trying to determine why. Although this has often been true with ID theory, it is also true that instructional tools have been invented and prescriptions have been developed based on a new learning theory.

1.4 Pragmatic (Eclectic) versus Ideological

It seems fair to say that all descriptive theories contribute something useful, no matter how inadequate they may be overall. As Snelbecker (1987) has pointed out, descriptive theorists strive for theoretical purity, adopt a single perspective or view of the world, and put their theories up to compete against other theories. Their primary concern is whether their theory is ideologically pure and conceptually consistent.

But practitioners need to address all aspects of a problem and multiple kinds of problems. Their primary concern is how well a prescriptive theory attains their practical goals. Therefore, they need multiple perspectives, and frequently develop solutions that are based on, or can be explained by, several different descriptive theories. Therefore, prescriptive theorists tend to take a pragmatic view that integrates useful contributions from a variety of theoretical perspectives.

1.5 Validity versus Superiority

For descriptive theories, the major scientific concern is validity—how well they describe reality. But for prescriptive theories, since they are goal-oriented, the major scientific concern is superiority (or optimality) —how well they attain the goal. There are usually many ways to attain a single goal, but some are better than others. The goal of prescriptive theory is not to find out if a given method works; it is not just to identify a method that "satisfices," but to identify the method that is better than the other known alternatives for each set of conditions. Of course, the efficiency (based on time and/or money) and appeal of a method are important criteria, as well as its effectiveness. The goal of prescriptive theory is also to improve the best available methods continually. This is significant, because it requires a completely different paradigm of research than does descriptive theory—a paradigm that is coming to be called "formative research" (Newman 1990, Reigeluth 1989).

1.6 Level of Detail or Generality

Prescriptive theories, like descriptive theories, can be very detailed, very general, or anywhere between. The more general an ID theory is, the broader it will be (i.e., the more situations in which it will apply), but the guidance it will provide to an instructional designer will be reduced. For example, "To improve learning and motivation, have the learner actively engaged," applies to almost all instructional situations, but it provides little guidance to a designer or teacher as to exactly what the instruction should be like for their particular situation. More guidance makes the designer's work easier and quicker, but it also takes more time and effort for the designer to learn initially.

If a designer does not have formal training in instructional theory, he or she will invent their own, but it may differ considerably from the accumulated experience of researchers and practitioners as represented by the current knowledge base of prescriptive theory.

1.7 Product versus Process

Finally, it is helpful to consider the distinction between ends and means, or product and process. ID theory is that knowledge base that deals with the ends or products (using that term loosely)—what the instruction should be like (after it has been designed). Instructional development models, on the other hand, deal with the means or process—what an instructional designer should do to plan and create the "products." Typical development models specify activities for a developer to perform to analyze (needs, tasks, content, learners, and more), design, produce, evaluate, implement, and manage an instructional system or "product." ID theories specify instructional methods for a teacher (or other learning resource) to use to help a learner learn. This is a very important, yet often overlooked, distinction.

For a concise description of some modern ID theories see Reigeluth (1983), in which eight theorists describe their respective ID theories. In another volume (Reigeluth (1987) the same theorists illustrate their theories through a sample lesson.

2. History of ID Theories

Like most fields, ID theory began by investigating general instructional variables, such as expository vs. discovery, lecture vs. discussion, and media-based vs. traditional methods. It was soon realized that two discovery methods could differ more from each other than do a discovery and an expository method. The field then gradually entered an analysis phase in its development (which began to gain visibility in the late 1950s with B F Skinner's work). The research objective was to break a method down into elementary components and discover which ones made a difference. Instructional researchers then proceeded to build a considerable knowledge base of validated prescriptions, primarily for the simpler types of learning, for which the behaviorist paradigm was fairly adequate.

Researchers have since found that the effects of each component are often influenced considerably by which other components happen to be present in the in-

Table 1
Major differences between the industrial age and the information age that affect education

Industrial age	Information age
Adversarial relationships	Cooperative relationships
Bureaucratic organization	Team organization
Autocratic leadership	Shared leadership
Centralized control	Autonomy with accountability
Autocracy	Democracy
Representative democracy	Participative democracy
Compliance	Initiative
One-way communications	Networking
Compartmentalization (division of labor)	Holism (integration of tasks)

struction. Furthermore, researchers have realized that practitioners need to think holistically; in other words, they need to identify the best *combination* of method components for a given situation. Hence, the field entered into a synthesis phase, which began to gain visibility in the 1980s with the publication of Reigeluth's (1983) edited volume *Instructional Design Theories and Models*, in which the focus is on building components into optimal models of instruction for different situations. The research objective is to improve a given model or theory.

Aside from this developmental process that most fields and disciplines seem to go through, another historical trend has strongly influenced the development of ID theories: the ongoing transformation from the industrial age to the global information age. Certain general characteristics prevailed during the industrial age that are giving way to new characteristics in the information age (Reigeluth 1992a). Some of those changes have particularly important implications for a new paradigm of education (see Table 1).

Perelman (1987) documented many characteristics of the current paradigm systems of education. In the United States and many other industrialized countries, consolidated districts are highly bureaucratic, centrally controlled autocracies in which students receive little preparation for participating in a democratic society. They frequently exhibit adversarial relationships, not only between teachers and administrators but also between teachers and students, and even between teachers and parents. Leadership is vested in individuals according to a hierarchical management structure, and all those lower in the hierarchy are expected to obey those above. Learning is highly compartmentalized into subject areas. Students are often treated as if they are all the same and are all expected to do the same things at the same time. They are also usually forced to be passive learners and passive members of their school community. These characteristics are all incompatible with society's needs in the emerging information age, and changes in this paradigm are beginning to emerge. Those

changes will have very important implications for ID theory.

3. Emergent Trends and Issues

Most current ID theories were developed for the industrial-age paradigm of education and training. Just as mass production in business is giving way to customized production (Reich 1991) and mass marketing is giving way to targeted marketing (Toffler 1991), so mass teaching is giving way to personalized teaching. These changes in all of these sectors (and others) are made possible by information technology. Every year teachers are acquiring more and more powerful tools with which to facilitate learning. Those tools require the use of new instructional methods to take full advantage of their expanded capabilities. Hence, ID theories must offer guidance for the use of such new instructional methods. These information-age ID theories are likely to incorporate prescriptions for the use of adaptive strategies, advanced technologies, constructivist strategies, minimalist instruction, and systemic change, to name but a few of the emerging ideas. Each of these will be briefly described.

3.1 Adaptive Strategies

Whereas conformity was one of the general characteristics of the industrial age, diversity is emerging as a hallmark of the information age. Different students increasingly have very different learning needs, interests, goals, abilities, prior knowledge, and so forth. It is therefore increasingly important to adapt instruction —both content and methods—to each learner's needs and interests. Advanced technologies are gradually providing more powerful and cost-effective means for such adaptations.

3.2 Advanced Technologies

There are two important ways in which advanced technologies are influencing the future development of ID theories: through their use as tutors and tools for learners and their use as tools for instructional designers.

As tutors new technologies offer new capabilities that require new instructional strategies to take appropriate advantage of them. Dynamic media require guidelines as to when and how to use motion in instruction. Interactive media require prescriptions as to what kinds of learner activities to elicit when, and when and how to respond to each kind of learner activity. Massive memory storage capabilities require guidelines as to when and how to utilize them best in instruction. Hypertext and hypermedia require guidelines as to when and how their unique capabilities can best be utilized to facilitate learning. Multimedia, expert systems, artificial intelligence, computer-based simulations, and virtual reality represent but a few of the additional technologies for which guidelines are sorely needed. The increasingly more powerful and cost-effective capabilities of these advanced technologies all require guidelines as to when and how best to use them to facilitate learning.

3.3 Constructivist Strategies

Constructivism offers some practical instructional strategies that have much to contribute to the new paradigm of education for the information age. Some of its strategies are fairly uniformly applicable to most kinds of learning, but others are only applicable to higher-level learning in ill-structured domains.

At the heart of constructivism is the belief that each learner must construct his or her own knowledge and therefore that instruction must create an active role for the learner (see, e.g., Brown et al. 1989, Perkins 1992). It also prescribes that learning should be situated in authentic activities. Slightly less broadly applicable is the prescription that instruction should facilitate the construction of meaning, or sense making. This is accomplished primarily through such strategies as learning in context, modeling, and coaching, but it is not appropriate for all learning situations.

Perhaps the most valuable contributions of constructivism are considerably less broadly applicable: those for facilitating higher-level learning in ill-structured domains. Some useful instructional strategies include: generative tasks, learner exploration, analogical transfer, and the fostering of multiple perspectives.

3.4 Minimalist Instruction

Carroll (1990) has developed the idea of "minimalist instruction" for teaching people "what they need to learn in order to do what they wish to do" (p. 3). It is similar to the notions of just-in-time training and on-line help systems. At its heart is the idea of not teaching people things that they do not yet have to know. This seems most appropriate for training situations, such as training people to use desktop computer systems, where it is relatively easy to determine what one needs to learn at a given point in time. Another important aspect of minimalist instruction is "to design instruction to suit the learning strategies people spontaneously adopt" (p. 3) and the relevant knowledge they have already acquired. Both of these require that the instruction be highly adaptive, and utilize advanced technology and some constructivist strategies.

Specific instructional prescriptions include the following. First, all instruction should occur with real tasks that are meaningful to the learner, so that the learner is motivated. Second, the "training wheels" approach should be used so as to pick a version of the meaningful task that is simple enough not to overwhelm the beginner. For example, a real word-processing task might be selected that requires the use of only a small subset of the capabilities of the system. This is similar to the Elaboration Theory's "simplifying conditions method" approach to sequencing (Reigeluth 1992b). Some artificial simplifying conditions can also be instituted, such as disabling certain functions of the system, so that the learner cannot yet make certain types of errors. As the learner progresses, the meaningful tasks become gradually more complex until the learner has mastered all that he or she needs to learn.

Third, the learner should be helped to understand meaningfully what he or she is doing. Reasoning is very important for this process, and the learner's prior knowledge must be diagnosed and utilized. Fourth, reading materials and other passive activities should be reduced to a minimum, and largely replaced with discovery activities. The reading materials should be designed for random access and to be read in any order, and they should have strong linkages to different parts of the real, meaningful task. Fifth, emphasis should be placed on helping the learner to recognize and recover from errors so that errors become triggers for positive learning experiences.

3.5 Affective Learning

The affective domain (Krathwohl et al. 1964) has received relatively little attention from instructional theorists, but it is emerging as an important area of human development for the information age. Martin and Briggs (1986) conducted a comprehensive review of ID theories in this domain, and identified three major dimensions that appear to require different models of instruction: attitudes and values, morals and ethics, and self-development. They also identified a variety of other dimensions of the affective domain: emotional development and feelings, interest and motivation, social development and group dynamics, and attributions. The most advanced ID theories are in the dimension of attitudes and values and include the Yale Communication and Attitude Change Program, Dissonance Theory, Cognitive Balancing Theory, Social Judgment Theory, and Social Learning Theory (see Martin and Briggs 1986 for a summary).

One of the most promising new developments in this domain is an ID theory for attitudes being developed by Kamradt and Kamradt (in press). Based on the notion that attitudes have a tripartite composition of feelings, cognitions, and behaviors, they have developed a set of guidelines for systemically influencing all three through a systematic process that moves the learner just outside of his or her comfort zone one step at a time in the direction of the desired attitude. First, role-playing is used to force a new behavior more consistent with the target attitude. This creates a dissonance or discomfort which serves as a trigger event to influence the cognitive element through discussion and persuasion. Finally, reinforcement techniques are used to change the feelings associated with the new behavior and new thinking. After this small shift in attitude has been consolidated, the learner is ready for another round of this three-part strategy. Ethical issues are particularly important in the affective domain, and the Kamradts advocate that no attempts be made to change a learner's attitude without the knowledge and consent of the learner.

3.6 Systemic Change

It seems highly likely, given the different educational needs of the information age, that ID theories will adapt to meet the needs of a new paradigm of education and training, and that those changes will incorporate the use of adaptive strategies, advanced technologies, constructivist strategies, and minimalist instruction. However, this new paradigm of instruction will be of little value if the larger system within which it is embedded remains rooted in the industrial age. Referring back to Banathy's (1991) four levels of educational (and training) systems (learning-experience, instructional, administrative, and governance), this entry has focused on theory for prescribing the instructional system that will support a new paradigm of learning to meet the radically different education and training needs and conditions of the emerging information society. But unless a compatible paradigm shift is also effected at the administrative and governance levels, the new instructional paradigm will be ineffective and short-lived. Instructional designers and ID theorists alike must begin to view themselves as concerned with educational systems design—spanning all four levels of the system—not just with instructional systems design—focusing on just one of those levels. (For further information, see, e.g., Reigeluth and Garfinkle 1992.)

4. Conclusion

ID theory is still a relatively young field. Much remains to be learned about how to facilitate learning, especially more complex kinds of learning in ill-defined domains (including thinking skills) and the affective domain (including attitudes and values). In addition, massive changes in society are forcing the development of a new paradigm in ID theory for even the least complex kinds of learning. The need for more adaptive instruction, combined with the development of far more powerful technological tools for learning, have created entirely new horizons for ID theory.

See also: Approaches to Learning; Individual Differences, Learning, and Instruction; Study and Learning Strategies; Concepts of Educational Technology; Instructional Design: Models

References

Banathy B H 1991 *Systems Design of Education*. Educational Technology Publications, Englewood Cliffs, New Jersey
Brown J S, Collins A, Duguid P 1989 Situated cognition and the culture of learning. *Educ. Researcher* 18(1): 32–42
Carroll J M 1990 *The Nürnberg Funnel: Designing Minimalist Instruction for Practical Computer Skill*. MIT Press, Cambridge, Massachusetts
Kamradt E M, Kamradt T F in press A systematic approach for attitude development. *Educ. Technol.*
Krathwohl D R, Bloom B S, Masia B B 1964 *Taxonomy of Educational Objectives: The Classification of Educational Goals. Handbook II: Affective Domain*. McKay, New York
Martin B L, Briggs L J 1986 *The Affective and Cognitive Domains: Integration for Instruction and Research*. Educational Technology Publications, Englewood Cliffs, New Jersey
Newman D 1990 Opportunities for research on the organizational impact of school computers. *Educ. Researcher* 19(3): 8–13
Perelman L J 1987 *Technology and Transformation of Schools*. National School Boards Association, Alexandria, Virginia
Perkins D N 1992 Technology meets constructivism: Do they make a marriage? In: Duffy T M, Jonassen D H (eds.) 1992 *Constructivism and the Technology of Instruction*. Erlbaum, Hillsdale, New Jersey
Reich R B 1991 *The Work of Nations*. Knopf, New York
Reigeluth C M (ed.) 1983 *Instructional-Design Theories and Models: An Overview of their Current Status*. Erlbaum, Hillsdale, New Jersey
Reigeluth C M (ed.) 1987 *Instructional Strategies in Action: Lessons Illustrating Selected Theories and Models*. Erlbaum, Hillsdale, New Jersey
Reigeluth C M 1989 Educational technology at the crossroads: New mindsets and new directions. *Educ. Tech. Res. Dev.* 37(1): 67–80
Reigeluth C M 1992a The imperative for systemic change. *Educ. Technol.* 32(11): 9–13
Reigeluth C M 1992b Elaborating the elaboration theory. *Educ. Tech. Res. Dev.* 40(3): 80–86
Reigeluth C M, Garfinkle R J (eds.) 1992 Systemic change in education (special issue). *Educ. Technol.* 32(11)
Simon H A 1969 *The Sciences of the Artificial*. MIT Press, Cambridge, Massachusetts
Snelbecker G E 1987 Contrasting and complementary approaches to instructional design. In: Reigeluth C M (ed.) 1987

Toffler A 1991 *Power Shift*. Bantam Books, New York

Further Reading

Bloom B S (ed.) 1956 *Taxonomy of Educational Objectives: The Classification of Educational goals. Handbook I: Cognitive Domain*. McKay, New York

Gagné R M, Briggs L J, Wager W W 1988 *Principles of Instructional Design*, 3rd edn. Holt, Rinehart, and Winston, New York

Skinner B F 1965 Reflections on a decade of teaching machines. In: Glaser R (ed.) 1965 *Teaching Machines and Programmed Learning, II*. National Education Association, Washington, DC

Instructional Design: Models

K. L. Gustafson

Instructional design models are popular for depicting the systematic process of developing education and training. Various forms of models exist that can be best applied for different purposes and in different settings. Characteristics of these models and where and how they may be used are discussed in this entry.

1. A Definition of Instructional Design

Before discussing instructional design models, it is necessary to define the term "instructional design" and related terminology. Unfortunately, over time authors in the field have been inconsistent in their use of several terms including instructional design, instructional development, systems approach, and instructional technology. There have been periodic attempts to develop standard terminology (e.g., Association for Educational Communication and Technology [AECT] 1977), but this work has been largely ignored. These terms are used interchangeably by some authors, in completely opposite ways by others, and still others have used first one and then another in their various writings. Thus, it becomes difficult to comprehend the literature unless one consciously poses the question: "What does this author mean when using this term?" The reader can then match the concept with that author's usage of it.

For the purposes of this entry, the term "instructional design" will be used to describe the complete process of: (a) analyzing *what* is to be taught/learned; (b) determining *how* it is to be taught/learned; (c) conducting *tryout* and *revision*; and (d) assessing *whether* learners learn. Some authors would add to this list a step involving implementation of the resulting product or system in the intended setting or marketing it commercially according to their distribution plan (see *Concepts of Educational Technology*).

2. A Representative Instructional Design Model

An example of a widely distributed design model that contains all of the aforementioned core elements is the one that was developed by the National Special Media Institutes in the United States (see Fig. 1). Called the Instructional Development Institutes (IDI) model, it contains three phases: design, develop, and evaluate. Each phase is divided into three steps and each step is further divided, resulting in a total of 27 elements. The elements are to be executed in more or less linear fashion with the result being an instructional system for full implementation in the designated environment.

Instructional design models have become very popular among instructional designers since the mid-1960s. They regularly appear in one form or another in virtually all of the major publications in the field. These models originated from an interest in applying concepts from general systems theory to the design of education and training (see, e.g., Barson 1967, Branson 1975, Branson et al. 1975, and Silvern 1965). They have additional roots in job and task analysis (Bobbitt 1918), in Tyler's (1969) and later Mager's (1984) advocacy of instructional objectives stated in terms of learner behavior, and in programmed instruction (Lumsdaine and Glaser 1960), the last having its roots in behavioral psychology and formative evaluation and testing. In the early 1990s cognitive theories received much attention, but there has been little resulting impact on instructional design models. Early models continued to be described in later literature (see, e.g., Seels and Glasgow 1990). Later models (e.g., Gerlach and Cooper 1985) are similar in structure and content to earlier models. Although most of the design model building has occurred in the United States, scholars in other countries have also published models that are essentially similar in form and content (Plomp 1982, Romiszowski 1981) (see *Curriculum in Adult Education*).

Instructional designers' fascination with models seems to have its roots in model-building in the physical and natural sciences. In those sciences, models serve multiple purposes including theory building

Instructional Development Model

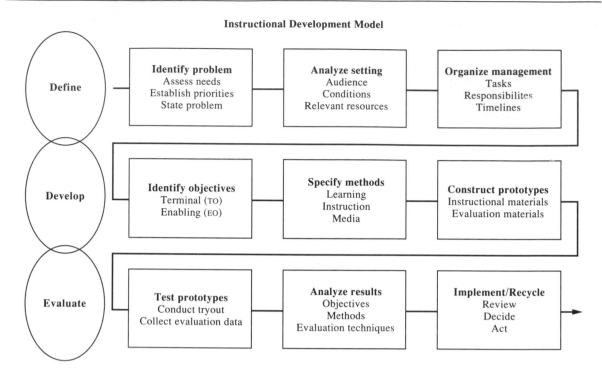

Figure 1
The Instructional Development Institutes (IDI) model
Source: University Consortium for Instructional Development and Technology

and testing, explaining, or describing observed phenomena, and predicting future events. Instructional designers, however, seem to have more limited goals in mind when constructing and presenting their models. With only a few exceptions, their models serve as process guides for practitioners. Their primary, if not sole, purpose is to depict a set of events or activities that the model's author believes is necessary for designing effective, efficient, and relevant instruction. As guides, they may be useful in: (a) project planning and management; (b) communicating with clients, subject-matter experts and other interested parties; and (c) aiding decisions on how to organize and structure the content and learning activities. Most models do not attempt to serve all of three of these purposes. The most popular use of models is to plan projects; communication with clients and others is a close second. That instructional design models serve only one or two purposes is not surprising. If a model is to communicate with unskilled clients, it must not be filled with jargon and so much detail that it overwhelms them. On the other hand, if it is to provide guidance concerning specific features of the instructional design, it must contain extensive detail to account for the many different kinds of content, learners, and delivery settings.

3. A Brief History of Models of Instructional Design

Determining a starting date for any educational concept is arbitrary and subject to debate. Silvern (1965) is often credited with first attempting to apply the concepts of General Systems Theory (GST) to design of training for the military and aeronautics industry in the United States. He proposed that several fundamental concepts from GST (e.g., open/closed, interdependent elements, cybernetic loops, etc.) should provide the basis for a scientific approach to designing training. His work was also heavily based on behavioral theories of learning and emphasized detailed analysis and reduction of complex content into its elemental parts.

One of the early attempts to apply these same concepts in an educational setting was made by Barson at Michigan State University and teams at three other universities. Barson (1967) and his associates used the term "instructional development" to describe the systematic design process and accompanying model they envisioned. Barson's model is no longer being referenced in the literature, but remains noteworthy in that it is one of very few that have ever been rigorously tested in multiple settings. His team also developed a set of heuristics describing how the development process might best be conducted in higher education. These heuristics have formed the basis for considerable research concerning the design process.

For some time, the term "instructional development" dominated the literature and in professional associations. For example, the *Journal of Instructional Development* was published by AECT for over 10 years before it was combined with another AECT journal into what is now *Educational Technology Research and Development*. That same association still contains a large and active Division of Instructional Development indicating the staying power of this term.

Another influential early model by Hamreus (1967) also used the term. Hamreus's model is noteworthy in that it existed at varying levels of detail from a "mini-model" containing only a few steps to a "maxi-model" that was much more detailed. Hamreus's approach has the advantage of providing a simple structure for communicating with clients coupled with detailed guidance for the instructional designer. Other influential early models were created by Branson et al. (1975) for the United States military, Briggs (1977) aimed at individual teachers in education, and Banathy (1968) aimed at both education and training.

The intellectual base of instructional design was, at first, founded on GST and behavioral psychology. However, in 1990 Salisbury reviewed several major textbooks in the field and concluded that few general systems concepts had been explicitly described or incorporated. This is partially due to a metamorphosis of the terms and partially that the field has moved to a highly analytic approach to the design process. This latter development is noteworthy in that, while early approaches did consider analysis to be an essential part of the process, later writers have elevated it to primary importance. This focus has resulted in a diminished emphasis on the actual design of the instruction. It is somewhat ironic that while the term "design" is gradually replacing "development" as the preferred term in the profession, there is increased interest in analyzing *what* (if anything) needs to be learned with less attention being paid to *how* it is to be learned.

4. A Model Classification Schema

The instructional design literature is replete with models. However, close examination will reveal that the differences between later models and their predecessors are generally quite small and usually reflect only minor word changing and differing amounts of emphasis on specific parts of the process. Gustafson (1991) has advanced a three-part classification scheme (see Fig. 2) that can be used to compare and contrast the various models. This classification scheme also can be used to simplify the task of determining what assumptions the model's creator has made, but often left unstated, concerning when, where, and how it might be used. The importance of determining an

author's unstated assumptions cannot be overstated. Many models may be useful for a specific situation, but be completely inappropriate and ineffective elsewhere. However, authors are generally remiss in not stating the assumptions and limitations associated with their models. Some even imply that their models would be useful for virtually any set of conditions. This view is not unlike that of early physicians who treated all illness in the same way due to a lack of alternatives. When examining the attributes of various models and relating them to the scheme, it is important to keep in mind that the scheme is not a taxonomy in the sense used by scientists in the physical or biological sciences. That is, there is no hierarchy implied among its categories and they are not mutually exclusive. This latter point is particularly important to note. Many of the models can be and have been used in varied settings. Thus, it is how they are used and for what purposes at any given time that best categorize them for that user. The scheme should be used only for highlighting the model's assumptions and how they are typically used.

The model classification scheme is based on the primary focus of the instructional design effort. Three distinctly different foci seem possible: (a) a classroom orientation; (b) an instructional product orientation; and (c) an instructional system orientation. Across these categories one can then examine a number of variables including: typical outputs of the design effort; amount of resources typically committed to the effort; whether it is a team or individual effort; whether the emphasis is on selecting from existing materials or creating new ones; the amount of analysis done (and why) before actual design begins; how much if any formal tryout and revision occurs; and whether distribution to a specific target audience is of concern. By asking questions associated with each of these variables, the essential characteristics and assumptions of any design model become visible. (For a more detailed discussion of this scheme and a number of specific instructional design models see Gustafson 1991.)

5. Classroom Models

Only a few models exist that focus on classroom teacher-based instruction (e.g., Gerlach and Ely 1980, Heinich et al. 1988, Dick and Reiser 1989, Kemp 1985). This lack of models probably helps explain why instructional design has had so little influence on public education and is not readily accepted by most classroom teachers. The fact of the matter is that the underlying concepts of both product- and systems-oriented models do not relate well to the world of practicing classroom teachers. Typical classroom teachers have several different preparations to make each day, very limited amounts of resources available for design, and no help in planning their instruction. Additionally, teachers usually work from a predetermined curriculum; must select only from instructional materials that are readily available; will not teach the same content again for another full year; and share few of their experiences with other teachers. Teachers also tend to be very resistant to external evaluation of their effectiveness because they are wary of being held accountable for student learning without being given anything near an adequate amount of resources or design time. As one perceptive observer has commented, if teachers were to use the extensive and time-consuming design processes depicted by most models for designing their instruction, and used the often-cited figure of 500 hours to develop one hour of instruction, that means that if they worked full-time all summer they would have one hour of instruction prepared to deliver in the fall! Even if they were really efficient and could reduce the ratio to 100:1, they would still only have amassed enough instruction for the first day of school. Clearly teachers can use only instructional design models that emphasize materials selection; little or no analysis, tryout, or revision; and do not require a team of "experts" to implement.

6. Product Models

Product design models are oriented toward producing specific instructional products either for specific clients or for commercial marketing. An example of the former would be for a company to develop a prepackaged training program for newly hired personnel to assure that everyone receives exactly the same information and that training is readily available whenever someone is hired. These products are often print-based, but technology-based packages are becoming more popular. Examples of commercially marketed products abound for both education and training. Naturally these products vary widely in their effectiveness and in the amount of rigor with which they were developed and tested (despite claims often made by their producers). Products are usually self-instructional, although this is not a requirement. Typically, considerable resources are committed to their design which is done by a team. The amount of "front-end" analysis conducted varies widely, as does the amount of tryout and revision. Usually great attention is paid to how the instructional product will be distributed or marketed. However, many large companies have found to their dismay that regional units do not readily accept centrally developed training and may even misuse it through malice or lack of knowledge. Examples of product-oriented instructional design models include Bergman and Moore (1990) and van Patten (1989).

7. Instructional Systems Models

Instructional systems-oriented models and product design models share many assumptions with one of the principal differences being the size and scope of the design effort. Product models usually focus on only

	Typical outputs	Resources committed to dev. process	Team or individual dev.	Emphasis on dev. or select materials	Amount front-end analysis/needs assessment	Amount tryout and revision	Distribution/ dissemination
Classroom orientation	Hour of instruction	Very low	Ind.	Select	Low	Low to med.	None
Product orientation	Self-instructional package	High	Ind. to team	Dev. or select	Low to med.	Very high	High
System orientation	School or military college course	High	Team	Dev.	Very high	Med. to high	Med. to high

Selected characteristics (column group); Focus of models (row group)

Figure 2
A taxonomy of instructional development models based on selected characteristics
Source: ERIC Clearinghouse on Information Resources 1991 *Survey of Instructional Design Models*

one package at a time whereas systems models tend to focus on large-scale efforts in which multiple products may be simultaneously designed so as to become an integrated "system" (see *Approaches to Learning*).

Additionally, systems design models always require a team effort due to the complexity of the design and the magnitude of the projects. An example of an instructional system is a complete college course in elementary biochemistry to be taken by thousands of university students. A ten-week training program for equipment repair in the military or a sales training course in industry are other examples of design at the instructional systems level. Obviously, to engage in projects of this size requires extensive resources, the amount of front-end analysis is often extensive, and tryout and revision are common. Distribution or dissemination of the instructional system may or may not be included as a step in the design model although it is always expected to occur. Examples of systems-oriented models include National Special Media Institute (IDI) (1971), Branson et al. (IPISD) (1975), Dick and Carey (1990), Seels and Glasgow (1990), and Briggs et al. (1991).

8. Trends and Issues

Since the history of instructional design models began in the 1960s, several attempts have been made to identify trends in terms of form, style, and content (Stamas 1973, Andrews and Goodson 1980, Gustafson 1991). None of these reviews has detected any clear trends indicating a maturation and elaboration of the fundamental concepts contained in the original models. Given the rapid advances witnessed in instructional delivery technology, this finding might seem surprising. However, when one considers how slowly practical knowledge has accrued on how human learning takes place, this result is understandable. With a few exceptions, the underlying concepts driving the field of instructional design can be traced to the original models cited earlier. This failure to make substantial enhancements in professional practice points out a clear shortcoming of the field; namely, few professionals are actively attempting to refine and enhance knowledge of the instructional design process. The most notable exceptions are Merrill and Reigeluth. Working together and independently, they have attempted to enhance and inform practice. For a comprehensive review of their attempts (and those of others) to apply psychological theory to the design process, see Reigeluth's seminal work (1983).

Since the late 1980s, Merrill has directed most of his efforts toward designing an automated system for conducting instructional design. The aim of this system which is called "ID Expert" (Merrill et al. 1990), is to develop an expert system shell that can make instructional design decisions based on information provided to the shell by a subject-matter expert. While success

has been limited, Merrill has remained optimistic that what they are attempting is both possible and practical. Should his optimism be confirmed, this approach would have a profound impact on the practice of instructional design and the models used to depict the process. Others have also been experimenting with how to enhance learning and performance.

In the world of military and industrial training, work is being done in the area of performance support systems, or PSS (e.g., Gery 1991). Much of the impetus for this work is the recognition that in a rapidly changing work environment it is becoming impossible to train workers in traditional ways. The cost of removing them from productive work to receive training that they may not yet need is costly and inefficient. Rather than provide training, the goal of PSS is to provide direct support and assist workers to perform competently. An example would be to develop a PSS for inventory managers that would integrate data from the inventory database into a shell that would assist individuals in deciding what needed to be purchased, rotated out of stock, or eliminated entirely. Gery has reported instances in which the cost of developing PSSs was quickly recovered by companies, making them eager to look for other potential applications of this approach to worker performance improvement (Gery 1991). Gustafson and Reeves (1990) have devised a prototype of a PSS for instructional designers. Unlike Merrill's approach, which is to eliminate the designer, Gustafson and Reeves have been examining how to help novice designers, and even subject-matter experts having no formal instructional design training, to develop reasonably effective instruction. If any of these efforts is even modestly successful in a variety of settings, the practice of instructional design will undergo dramatic change.

Hypermedia is another area generating considerable excitement and exploration, and will likely have significant implications for how instruction is designed. Hypermedia is a form of information storage and retrieval quite unlike the highly structured and often hierarchical forms preferred by instructional designers. Examples include programs such as Election 88 developed by ABC Interactive, and a product from IBM named Illuminated Manuscripts. These packages contain multiple, rich sources of information in many forms, including video, audio, photographs, graphics, text, and databases. Users are free to explore these extensive resources in almost any fashion they wish. The underlying "theory" is that people construct their own knowledge links and thus the programs allow them to make whatever links make sense to them. The word "theory" is placed in quotation marks to indicate most of the designers of these programs are not working from a theoretical framework. Rather, they are skilled artists and programmers who are "doing what feels right." Now that a sufficient number of these packages exist, researchers are beginning to examine how they are actually being used and with what effects.

Constructivism is yet another area that is likely to change the instructional design process and its accompanying models. It has gained considerable attention from educators dissatisfied with behaviorism and cognitive psychology. While it is not possible to elaborate on constructivism here, suffice it to say that it is based on the belief that individuals construct their own reality. In that sense it is in sharp contrast to logical positivism that has been at the heart of instructional design since its earliest days. Like expert systems, PSS, and hypermedia, its future impact on the design of teaching and learning is unclear. However, students of the instructional design process are well advised to monitor developments in this area.

See also: Psychology of Adult Education; Approaches to Learning; Individual Differences, Learning and Instruction; Concepts of Educational Technology; Curriculum in Adult Education; Instructional Design: Guidelines and Theories

References

Andrews D, Goodson L 1980 A comparative analysis of models of instructional design. *J. Instr. Dev.* 3(4): 2–16

Association for Educational Communication and Technology (AECT) 1977 *The Definition of Educational Technology.* AECT, Washington, DC

Banathy B 1968 *Instructional Systems.* Fearon, Belmont, California

Barson J 1967 Instructional systems development. A demonstration and evaluation project: Final report. ERIC Document Reproduction Service No. ED 020 673, Washington, DC

Bergman R, Moore T 1990 *Managing Interactive Video/Multimedia Projects.* Educational Technology Publications, Englewood Cliffs, New Jersey

Bobbitt J F 1918 *The Curriculum.* Houghton Mifflin, Boston, Massachusetts

Branson R 1975 *Interservice Procedures for Instructional Systems Development.* Florida State University, Center for Educational Technology, Tallahassee, Florida (National Technical Information Service, 5285 Port Royal Rd, Springfield, Virginia 22161; Document Nos. AD-A019, 486 to AD-A019 490)

Branson R et al. 1975 Interservice procedures for instructional systems development. ERIC Document Reproduction Service Nos. ED 122 018–122 022

Briggs L (ed.) 1977 *Instructional Design: Principles and Applications.* Educational Technology Publications, Englewood Cliffs, New Jersey

Briggs L, Gustafson K, Tillman M 1991 *Instructional Design.* Educational Technology Publications, Englewood Cliffs, New Jersey

Dick W, Carey L 1990 *The Systematic Design of Instruction*, 3rd edn. Scott, Foresman/Little, Brown Higher Education, Glenview, Illinois

Dick W, Reiser R 1989 *Planning Effective Instruction.* Prentice-Hall, Englewood Cliffs, New Jersey

Gerlach V, Cooper M 1985 A model for the development of computer instructional specifications. ERIC Document Reproduction Service No. ED 270 097, Washington, DC

Gerlach V, Ely D 1980 *Teaching and Media: A Systematic Approach*, 2nd edn. Prentice-Hall, Englewood Cliffs, New Jersey

Gery G 1991 *Electronic Performance Support Systems.* Weingarten, Boston, Massachusetts

Gustafson K 1991 Survey of instructional development models, 2nd edn. ERIC Clearinghouse on Information Resources. Syracuse University, Syracuse, New York

Gustafson K, Reeves T 1990 IDioM: A platform for a course development system. *Educ. Technol.* 30(3): 19–25

Hamreus D 1967 The systems approach to instructional development. In: *The Contribution of Behavioral Science to Instructional Technology.* Teaching Research Division, Oregon State System of Higher Education, Monmouth, Oregon

Heinich R, Molenda M, Russell J 1988 *Instructional Media and the New Technologies of Instruction*, 3rd edn. Macmillan Inc., New York

Kemp J 1985 *The Instructional Design Process.* Harper and Row, New York

Lumsdaine A, Glaser R (eds.) 1960 *Teaching Machines and Programmed Learning: A Source Book.* Department of Audio-Visual Instruction, National Education Association, Washington, DC

Mager R 1984 *Preparing Instructional Objectives*, 2nd edn. Pitman Management and Training, Belmont, California

Merrill M D, Li Z, Jones M 1990 The second generation instructional design research program. *Educ. Technol.* 30(3): 26–31

National Special Media Institute 1971 *What Is an IDI? Michigan State University, East Lansing, Michigan*

Plomp T 1982 *Onderwijskundige Technologie: Enige Verkenningen.* University of Twente, Enschede

Reigeluth C 1983 *Instructional-design Theories and Models: An Overview of their Current Status.* Erlbaum, Hillsdale, New Jersey

Romiszowski A 1981 *Designing Instructional Systems: Decision-making Course Planning and Instructional Design.* Kogan Page, London

Seels B, Glasgow Z 1990 *Exercises in Instructional Design.* Merrill, Columbus, Ohio

Silvern L C 1965 *Administrative Factors Guide to Basic Analysis.* Education and Training Consultants, Los Angeles, California

Stamas S 1973 A descriptive study of a synthesized operational instructional development model, reporting its effectiveness, efficiency, and cognitive and affective influence of the development process on a client. (Doctoral dissertation, Michigan State University) *Dissertation Abstracts International* 34 (University Microfilms No. 74–6139)

Tyler R W 1969 *Basic Principles of Curriculum and Instruction.* University of Chicago Press, Chicago, Illinois

van Patten J 1989 What is instructional design? In: Johnson K, Foa L (eds.) 1989 *Instructional Design: New Alternatives for Effective Education and Training.* Macmillan Inc., New York

Further Reading

Diamond R 1989 *Designing and Improving Courses and Curricula in Higher Education: A Systematic Approach. Jossey-Bass, San Francisco, California*

Flechsig K 1989 *A knowledge-based system for computer-aided instructional design. Education and Informatics.*

Paris: Unesco: 400–403

Gagné R, Briggs L, Wager W 1988 *Principles of Instructional Design*, 3rd edn. Holt, Rinehart and Winston, New York

Hannifin M, Peck K 1987 *The Design, Development, and Evaluation of Instructional Software*. Macmillan Inc., New York

Leshin C, Pollack J, Reigeluth C 1992 *Instructional Design Strategies and Tactics*. Educational Technology Publi-cations, Englewood Cliffs, New Jersey

Richey R 1986 *The Theoretical and Conceptual Bases of Instructional Design*, Nichols, New York

Rosendaal B, Schrijvers J 1990 De eerste stappen naar een geïntegreerd ondersteuningssysteem voor cursusont-werp. *Opleiding en Ontwikkeling* 3(11): 8–14

Salisbury D 1990 General systems theory and instruc-tional systems design. *Performance and Instruction* 29(2): 1–11

Job and Task Analysis

J. W. M. Kessels and C. A. Smit

Job analysis is an important aspect of human performance technology and its methods and techniques are widely used in recruiting, selecting, job design, appraisal, and organizational development. There is a growing view that it is an indispensable form of analysis in the design process of instructional systems. Numerous textbooks on instructional design stress its importance (Romiszowski 1981, Tracey 1984, Nadler 1982, Foshay et al. 1986, Davis 1971, Rothwell and Kazanas 1992); however, in daily practice job analysis is rarely carried out. Spurgeon et al. (1984), cited in Patrick (1991), report on a national survey in the United Kingdom which found that less than 20 percent of the employers of computer personnel had carried out any formal analysis of the jobs of programmer, systems analyst, and analyst programmer before developing training provisions. Meanwhile, in the United States, 62 percent of the trainers interviewed did not conduct a structured and systematic needs assessment for design purposes (Pieters 1992 citing *Training*, Oct. 1985). A multiple case study on 17 training programs in the Netherlands, examining nine successful and eight unsuccessful cases, found no occurrence of systematic needs assessment, job, or task analysis (Kessels 1992). The question which naturally arises is whether job or task analysis is actually as indispensable as argued for in literature, or whether the training design practice itself is still in a developmental phase.

1. Terminology and Definitions

Though the practical application of job or task analysis is apparently scarce, the nomenclature is, in contrast, abundant. Some writers try to distinguish precisely the differences between the following types of analysis: occupational, job, work, performance, task and subtasks, duty, skills; and that of elements, subject matter, and content analysis (Tracey 1984, Rossett 1992). Subsequently, clear definitions of the terms oc-cupation, job, performance, and so on are needed. On the other hand, job, task, and skills analysis are used interchangeably (Patrick 1991). In the description of the types of analysis needed in the design, develop-ment, and implementation of training interventions, this entry does not focus on the *object* of analysis as a determinant, but on the *purpose* served by the analysis, gathering information on the gap between what is and what should be (Kaufman 1990). Thus, it is not only important to analyze the performance, action, and behavior of employees but also their results and accomplishments: data on sales, services delivered, absenteeism, accidents, customer satisfaction, sick leave, time between machine break-down, scrap, and so on. This type of analysis, called "extent data analy-sis" by Rossett (1987), should also be included in the initial needs analysis and is part of job analysis.

Most authors consider job analysis as belonging to the front-end analysis phase preceding the design and development phases: however, it is not always clear whether or not job analysis is part of needs assessment. Needs assessment ascertains whether a perceived problem can or cannot be resolved by training interventions. If training is appropriate, which means that part of the solution to the problem can be achieved by means of the results of learning processes, then job analysis provides further information on what the requirements are for closing the gap between what is and what should be. These requirements are constituted not exclusively of skills and attitudes, but also of favorable conditions in the work environment. Separating needs assessment and job analysis is not recommended for the following reason: needs assess-ment and job analysis methods are very similar, in that both use interview, observation, document search, group activity, and survey techniques. It could be argued that it is not cost-effective to start extensive and time-consuming job analysis while the role of training as part of the solution remains undecided. From a systemic point of view, performance is seen as the result of a number of influencing variables in a larger system of which training and development

509

form merely a part. Before appropriate interventions are selected and deployed, analysis should not only reveal whether employees lack skills or knowledge, but also whether the environment is a barrier, how incentives operate, and how management support and motivation affect performance (Stolovitsch and Keeps 1992, Rossett 1992, Mager and Pipe 1991, Gilbert 1978, Romiszowski 1981). This must lead to the conclusion that, from the wider perspective of human performance technology, the perceived problem ought to be analyzed regardless of whether or not training is involved. Therefore, instead of separating job analysis from training needs assessment, there may be a reason for conducting a multidisciplinary needs assessment, in which training technologists will participate, and will carry on with dedicated analysis as soon as explicit training interventions are agreed upon.

It is also recommended that job analysis should not be restricted only to the initial stage of the design process for the following reasons: (a) it may lead to incomplete information, because very often at the beginning it is not clear at all what the developer should be looking for during the analysis, in spite of careful planning; (b) it may lead to vast analysis activities, stemming from a fear of overlooking critical elements, resulting in an overload of detailed data, that is unlikely to be used. Therefore, it is important to integrate job analysis not only into the needs assessment phase but in all the activities concerning design, development, and implementation. Since each phase requires new and specific information, additional analysis is needed and job analysis continues throughout the training process. The information needed for stating relevant instructional objectives and setting criterion measures is of a different nature from the information on the basis of which training strategies are chosen, training materials developed and trainers selected. Subsequently evaluation of performance and of impact on the organization could be considered as the last form of job analysis in the total process. Thus, job analysis should be an iterative activity throughout the design and development process and be given a wider application, not simply limited to the initial stage of the project.

Unfortunately, job analysis is often associated with the time and motion studies that were introduced along with scientific management. This negative connotation gives rise to ideas such as: (a) job and task analysis is restricted to visible tasks and the main analysis technique is observation (Rossett 1987); (b) job analysis is only applicable to the technical tasks of blue collar workers and only as far as psychomotor skills are involved, so conducting job analysis does not apply to designers of management development programs and problem-solving workshops; (c) job analysis focuses on a single incumbent interacting with his or her surrounding equipment and materials, and not on members of a group interacting with each other, with clients and customers, with ideas and problems; (d) job

analysis offers simply a description of the actual performance and not of what should be. Thus, job analysis would have no value for training and development programs geared toward improvement, organizational change, or in a learning organization.

In spite of the above misinterpretations, in corporate education, job analysis is increasingly considered as one of the few guarantees that a training program is performance-oriented, even for programs on management development, problem-solving, customer satisfaction, and quality improvement.

Annett et al. (1971 cited in Patrick 1991 p.132) focus on the decision-making process in training and define job analysis as the process of collecting information necessary to reach decisions about what, how, even how thoroughly, to train and perhaps how much to invest in training.

As previously advocated, a wider application of job analysis beyond the initial phase of training design is necessary and, considering the amalgam of labels used, job analysis in this context can be described as a group of information collection methods and techniques that claim to provide a valid basis for the design, development, and implementation of performance-oriented, cost-effective, and efficient training activities.

2. Purposes of Job Analysis

The need for job analysis grows when training programs drift away from performance and become too content-oriented. As a result, they lose their focus on the skills needed and on the problems to be resolved in the work environment. The basis of mismatched programs lies mainly in existing textbooks, management theories, concepts originated in the group dynamics laboratory, technical specifications, and so on. The content becomes an end in itself. There may exist a superficial relationship with the subject matter essential for the job, but very often this concerns only the names and labels used. The content is merely information to be transmitted without subject matter expertise. Programs based on this type of information tend to focus strongly on dissemination of knowledge, whether it is relevant for a given performance problem or not. Job analysis is an intervention to direct and redirect programs toward performance improvement.

In the design and development process, job analysis should provide the basic information for:

(a) Reaching a conclusion on whether training is needed or not, and on what interventions should be implemented in order to support the training provisions.

(b) Stating the training objectives. In addition to task-oriented information on the content of the target skills, psychological information is needed to enable skills to be classified as cognitive, inter-active, reactive, or psychomotor (Romiszowski 1981, Patrick 1991).

(c) Stating realistic criteria for learning results, performance improvement, and impact to be achieved, and for constructing matching assess-ment instruments.

(d) Selecting training strategies and planning se-quence. For training design purposes, the follow-ing aspects are very important: what is difficult in the job, what is easy, what the job incumbent is afraid of (something that might happen), what is critical, what is particularly difficult for new-comers, what in the job is tiring or annoying, rewarding or motivating.

(e) Selecting subject-matter information, real-life examples, case studies, and exercises to support the learning process.

(f) Generating relevant assignments and projects.

(g) Organizing local support.

(h) Selecting experienced trainers and coaches.

(i) Selecting trainees.

(j) Assessing results.

Each product in the design and development process requires a different kind of information and different questions to be answered by means of additional analy-sis. Therefore, it is doubtful that a single database, with global statements on behavior, standards, and conditions for all the human resource areas, will serve the many and different job analysis purposes as men-tioned above. The simple job analysis as suggested by Dennis and Austin (1992) in their "Behavioural Analy-sis and Standards for Employees (BASE)" is not likely to provide the variety of information needed in the diverse domains of recruiting and selection, training, performance, and competency assessment.

Besides these information-gathering purposes, job analysis serves to establish local and top management support for a training program. During the analysis process many representatives of the hierarchal struc-ture are involved in the various cycles of information gathering, feedback, and agreement sessions. Their investment in time and effort often turns into com-mitment as soon as they perceive these efforts as beneficial to their own interests. Involvement in job analysis is not limited to members of the organization. Clients and customers can contribute with valuable information on the expected level of quality in services and products. Besides the valuable information on actual and desired performance, such an invitation to participate will result in reinforced relationships.

The process of needs and job analysis is in itself an important learning process for the organization. Job analysis can be considered as a feedback mechanism that offers information on what is, and that tries to find out what should be. To benefit from this learning process, job analysis should be carried out by a project group or task force including responsible managers and influential stakeholders.

3. Methods and Techniques

Literature and practice offer a wide array of meth-ods and techniques used for job analysis purposes. Most methods used are based on commonly known information-collection techniques like interview, ob-servation, group techniques, survey, and document search. Tracey (1984), Zemke and Kramlinger (1982), Rossett (1992), and Carlisle (1986) stress a systematic organization and application of the analysis: it should have a purpose, clear goals, carried out according to a plan, using methods and data collection techniques that are appropriate for the type of information sought for, and the results should be reported on accurately.

In addition to the general information-collection techniques mentioned above, job analysts have de-veloped dedicated methods for specific application. Flanagan (1954) focused on the critical incidents tech-nique. This technique collects typical behaviors and practices, ranging from highly desirable and effective to highly undesirable and ineffective.

Other tailored job analysis methods include:

(a) Focus groups: for comparing and contrasting in-tangible aspects of jobs and attitudes of high and low achievers (Zemke and Kramlinger 1982).

(b) Adoption by training staff: trainers adopt a new plant, department, or system to experience and investigate the qualifications that are required for running it (Kessels and Smit 1989).

(c) Simulation: new tasks, approaches, and pro-cedures are tried in a mock-up or in a virtual reality situation in order to examine the job requirements (Kessels and Smit 1989).

(d) Job comparison: the requirements of future jobs and tasks can be identified by comparing the requirements of familiar jobs and cognitive op-erations used in one context to those needed in a new context. For example, the requirements of the new traffic control function in the naval context can be identified to some extent by com-paring the requirements of air traffic and railroad traffic control functions and examining the spe-cific context differences (Kessels and Smit 1989).

(e) The jury of experts: contradicting opinions and conflicting performance and quality standards found during the job analysis can be submitted to a jury of experts who judge the desired objectives for the training program (Kessels and Smit 1989). Besides the jury of experts contributing to the necessary involvement of line managers and subject-matter experts, this often reveals inconsistencies in organization behavior that cannot be solved through training.

Patrick (1991) distinguishes between three major types of analysis:

(a) The task-oriented approaches include the hierarchical task analysis and the critical incidents technique. These approaches serve the identification of training needs, the specification of training objectives, and the identification of training content.

(b) The psychological taxonomies include information-processing requirements, ability/aptitude requirements, and the types of learning. These taxonomies help to improve the selection of trainees, to design the training, and to elaborate the content of cognitive complex tasks.

(c) The third set of analysis concerns knowledge representation. This set should enable the analysis of complex cognitive tasks and provide a framework of the different kinds of knowledge used during expert performance. However, no strong generalizations emerge concerning how to analyze complex tasks and much improvisation and ingenuity is required by the analyst (Patrick 1991).

4. Expertise of the Job Analyst

A concise description of the expertise of the job analyst can be found in Tracey (1984):

> Analysts should have a general knowledge of the job categories to be studied and should be capable of avoiding bias. They should have the mental ability and insight required to probe for and elicit information in a systematic manner, and to recognize commonalities and variations in specific jobs. In addition, job analysts should be articulate and methodical; be able to write reasonably well, to observe astutely, and to attend to detail for relatively long periods of time; and, of course, be interested in people and jobs. (p.98)

In addition to Tracey's characterization of the job analyst, it is important to acknowledge a practical dilemma; often the training designer is an experienced employee or subject-matter expert whose involvement in the design and development process of new training programs follows on from an initial interest in moving into training. Conducting task analysis presumes that the analyst can be completely uninhibited in asking questions such as: "Why do you do this, in that way?"; "How do you know that you should alert X in this situa-

tion?"; "What do you find difficult when a problem like this arises?" and so on. This attitude, combining innocence or naivety with integrity and security, is essential for obtaining information that is high in both quality and quantity. However, it is impossible for an experienced colleague or subject matter expert who is designing a training program for his or her own field of expertise to ask this kind of question and to pretend to have a naive attitude. The experienced employee is both inhibited by his or her own competence and by the fear of losing face in front of colleagues. This is often the reason why training staff do not conduct front end analysis. In fact, the nature of job analysis is one of "professional illiteracy": a skilled information-gathering process, pretending ignorance, thus evoking critical, though often unconscious, know-how. This attitude cannot occur between colleagues. It is therefore recommended that job analysis be conducted partially in couples in which both subject-matter and training design expertise are represented. Where the analyst whose contribution stems from training expertise can play the role of "professional illiterate," that role will be accepted by the job holders. Job holders even appreciate the interest an "outsider" shows in their work. This positive and nonthreatening climate during the data-collection process is of great value regarding the quality of information sought.

5. Discussion of Underlying Assumptions

In general, instructional designers like to do job and task analysis, once they have experienced it; it brings them out of their potentially limited world and initiates them into the real action of an organization. However, many get caught up in piles of collected data, ending up stating hundreds of instructional objectives that will never be used. Managers feel uneasy with this kind of time- and cost-consuming activity that, in their opinion, does not contribute a great deal. Swanson and Gradous (1986 p.239) warned against this paralysis through analysis. For Hiebert and Smallwood (1990) it is one of the reasons to suggest a completely different look at needs analysis. As opposed to the objectivist tradition, they introduce an interpretative approach. Unlike the objectivist approach, the interpretative does not assume that an objective set of training needs exists. The one chosen depends on experience, knowledge, skills, and preferences. The environment consists of a dynamic flow of information and since the analyst is part of that environment there is no such thing as an objective observer. Meanings, interpretations, and training needs, are socially and culturally determined. They can be negotiated and renegotiated. Thus, needs and job analysis is a negotiating and agreement process in which the analyst is a major stakeholder.

Finally, Hiebert and Smallwood (1990) introduced the integrative approach as a compromise between the positions of the objectivist and interpretative mode. It employs parts of both. The goal of the integrative approach is to use objectivist language and processes while thinking in the interpretative mode and concurrently moving participants to recognize the value of new approaches.

See also: Curriculum in Adult Education; Educational Technology in Vocational Training; Instructional Design: Models; Modularization in Adult Education and Training; The Development of Competence: Toward a Taxonomy; Teaching Methods: Individual Techniques

References

Annett J, Duncan K D, Stammers R B, Gray M J 1971 *Task Analysis*. Training Information No. 6. HMSO, London
Carlisle K E 1986 *Analyzing Jobs and Tasks*. Educational Technology Publications, Englewood Cliffs, New Jersey
Davis I K 1971 *The Management of Learning*. McGraw-Hill, London
Dennis J, Austin B 1992 A BASE(ic) course on job analysis. *Training and Development*. July. p. 67–70
Flanagan J C 1954 The critical incident technique. *Psychol. Bull.* 51: 327–58
Foshay W, Silber K, Westgaard O 1986 *Instructional Design Competencies, The Standards*. The International Board of Standards for Training, Performance, and Instruction. University of Iowa, Iowa City, Iowa
Gilbert T 1978 *Human Competence: Engineering Worthy Performance*. McGraw-Hill, New York
Hiebert M B, Smallwood W N 1990 Now for a completely different look at needs analysis. In: Allen E L (ed.) 1990 *Needs Assessment Instruments: ASTD Trainer's Toolkit*. ASTD-Pfeiffer
Kaufman R 1990 A needs assessment primer. In: Allen E L (ed.) 1990 *Needs Assessment Instruments: ASTD Trainer's Toolkit*. ASTD-Pfeiffer
Kessels J W M 1992 Towards design standards in corporate education. Paper delivered at ECER'92, Twente University, Enschede
Kessels J W M, Smit C A 1989 *Opleidingskunde, een bedrijfsgerichte benadering van leerprocessen*. Kluwer, Deventer
Mager R F, Pipe P 1991 *Analyzing Performance Problems*. Kogan Page, London
Nadler L 1982 *Designing Training Programs: The Critical Events Model*. Addison-Wesley, Reading, Massachusetts
Patrick J 1991 Types of analysis for training. In: Morrison J E (ed.) 1991 *Training for Performance: Principles of Applied Human Learning*. Wiley, Chichester
Pieters J M (1992) Behoefteanalyse. In: Plomp T, Feteris A, Pieters J M, Tomic W (eds.) 1992 *Ontwerpen van Onderwijs en Trainingen*. Uitgeverij Lemma, Utrecht
Romiszowski A J 1981 *Designing Instructional Systems: Decision-making in Course Planning and Curriculum Design*. Kogan Page, London
Rossett A 1987 *Training Needs Assessment*. Educational Technology Publications, Englewood Cliffs, New Jersey
Rossett A 1992 Analysis of human performance problems. In: Stolovitch H D, Keeps E J (eds.) 1992 *Handbook of Human Performance Technology: A Comprehensive Guide for Analyzing and Solving Performance Problems in Organizations*. Jossey-Bass, San Francisco, California
Rothwell W J, Kazanas H C 1992 *Mastering the Instructional Design Process: A Systematic Approach*. Jossey-Bass, San Francisco, California
Spurgeon P, Michael I, Patrick J 1984 *Training and Selection of Computer Personnel*. Research and Development no. 18. Manpower Services Commission, Sheffield
Stolovitsch H D, Keeps E J 1992 What is human performance technology? In: Stolovitch H D, Keeps E J (eds.) 1992 *Handbook of Human Performance Technology: A Comprehensive Guide for Analyzing and Solving Performance Problems in Organizations*. Jossey-Bass, San Francisco, California
Swanson R A, Gradous D 1986 *Performance at Work: A Systematic Program for Analyzing Work Behavior*. Wiley, New York
Tracey W R 1984 *Designing Training and Development Systems*, rev. edn. American Management Associations, New York
Zemke R, Kramlinger Th 1982 *Figuring Things Out: A Trainer's Guide to Needs and Task Analysis*. Addison-Wesley, Reading, Massachusetts

Further Reading

Benjamin S 1989 A closer look at needs analysis and needs assessment: Whatever happened to the systems approach? *Performance and Instruction* 28(9): 12–16
Gael S (ed.) 1988 *The Job Analysis Handbook for Business, Industry and Government*, Vols. 1 and 2. Wiley, New York
Kirwan B, Ainsworth L K 1992 *A Guide to Task Analysis*. Taylor and Francis, London
McCormick E J 1979 *Job Analysis: Methods and Applications*. AMACOM, New York
Newstrom J W, Lilyquist J M 1990 Selecting needs analysis methods. In: Allen E L (ed.) 1990 *Needs Assessment Instruments: ASTD Trainer's Toolkit*. ASTD-Pfeiffer
Patrick J 1992 *Training: Research and Practice*. Academic Press, London
Peterson R 1992 *Training Needs Analysis in the Workplace*. Kogan Page, London

Modularization in Adult Education and Training

C. Howieson

This entry discusses the trend in a number of countries to restructure education and training, including provision for adults, on a modular basis. It describes the main features of modularized provision, outlines the reasons for the adoption of a modular approach and its perceived advantages and disadvantages, and considers some of the issues that have arisen in practice when adult education and training provision has been modularized. Any general discussion of modularization, however, encounters a number of problems: the lack of a single definition of modularization; the variety of models of modular systems that exist; the tendency for modularization to be introduced as part of wider reforms, and related to other innovations; and a relative lack of research evidence about the implementation of modular reforms.

1. Definition and Main Features

The concept of modularization evolved in higher education in the United States in the second half of the nineteenth century; the Harvard system of elective courses is commonly cited as one of the major influences on the development of a modular or elective system (Theodossin 1986). Interest in modularization in vocational training is more recent; for example, in the United Kingdom the introduction of a modular system for craft training by the Engineering Industry Training Board in 1968 marked the start of this approach to vocational training which was copied in many other industries (Roberts 1987). The extensive International Labour Organisation (ILO) project on "modules of employable skills" (MES) from the mid-1970s onwards, aimed at workers in developing countries, was a particularly significant initiative in promoting a modular approach to training (ILO 1984).

The scale of modularizing training provision varies from the modularization of particular courses or programs through to reforms that are national and international in their scope. The strategy adopted also varies, such as the degree of standardization in the design of modules. For example, in the Netherlands, although most apprenticeship branches are modularizing their provision, each is doing so independently. This compares with Scotland which modularized all of its national system of craft and technician level training in 1984 on the basis of a single, uniform type of module (SED 1983). Another approach is the ILO's MES project which is international in its scope and uses a standard format but focuses on only five major occupational areas.

Definitions of "a module" and "modularization" are as varied as they are numerous. Other terminology such as "component," "unit," "element," or "segment" is sometimes used instead of, or interchangeably with, the term module. The definition of the Australian Committee for Training Curriculum is one that reflects the most common definitions:

A module is a specific learning segment complete in itself, which deals with one or a number of aspects of vocational education at a given level of understanding or skill performance in accordance with stated aims and objectives. A module must be capable of being separately assessed and be capable of standing on its own or being linked to other modules in the same or related study areas. (Innes 1992)

In some systems definitions include a notional time element, for example, in Scotland, National Certificate modules are defined as "individual units of study which have a notional 40-hour duration (SCOTVEC 1991 p. 1). In other cases, while the module is an assessable element in itself, it is defined as part of a total program (de Bruijn 1992). The issue of separate assessment during or soon after a module's completion is fundamental to modular systems; this is described by Theodossin as

The defining characteristic which distinguishes modular from traditional course structures . . . . Without terminal assessment the module would remain another variation of the traditional course (Theodossin 1986 p. 1).

A number of other characteristics are frequently associated with modular systems: defined objectives in terms of the skills and knowledge against which attainment can be measured (learning objectives); greater choice and flexibility in the selection of courses and in study patterns; nontraditional pedagogy; greater emphasis on individualized learning and opportunities for credit accumulation and transfer. For example, in Germany, the limited use of modules in initial vocational education has largely been in the context of the development of project-based, activity-orientated, self-regulated learning (Jordan et al. 1992). The association of modularization with nontraditional pedagogy is common in many countries. Nevertheless, modularization as such does not necessarily dictate particular pedagogical approaches or other aspects such as content or curricular progression; Theodossin (1986) describes modules as neutral devices for curricular accounting.

In a number of countries, especially since the early 1980s, the development of modular provision has been associated with efforts to design training on the basis of identifiable and usually nationally agreed standards of competence. This approach has been particularly evident in England, Scotland, Australia, and New Zealand. Definitions of "competence" vary although they commonly incorporate ideas about the specification of the knowledge and skill and the application of that knowledge and skill to the standard of performance required in the workplace. Competency-based training is concerned with training to industry-specific standards and is partly a reaction to assessment of much traditional adult education and training which, in its emphasis on knowledge and content, failed to provide an adequate assessment of students' ability to perform their work roles successfully (Hodkinson 1991, Jessup 1991). Competency-based vocational education and training and modular approaches usually go hand-in-hand; Candy and Harris note that the modularization of the curriculum is one of the distinctive characteristics of competency-based systems (Candy and Harris 1990) (see *Recognition and Certification of Skill*).

The specification of defined learning objectives for modules, especially if they are competency-based, has various implications for modular training provision. It means that, in theory, modules need not have any fixed time or length: students take the time they need to achieve the learning outcomes although for financial and resource reasons, the approach is frequently to indicate a notional time base. The principle that students work towards the modules' learning objectives at their own pace means that modular systems tend to emphasize individualized, self-directed study. A group of students may therefore be studying different modules or be at different stages of the same module (ILO 1984, de Bruijn 1992, Black et al. 1991). Self-paced learning has major implications for both students and teachers/trainers.

The emphasis in modular systems on learning objectives (especially expressed in terms of competencies), as well as their unit structure, also implies that learning can take place in a range of environments and through various delivery modes. For example, in Scotland, National Certificate modules can be delivered on a part-time or full-time basis, in schools and colleges as well as in the workplace or by distance and open learning. In the United Kingdom there has been considerable interest in work-based learning and the development of workplace-assessed units. The accreditation or recognition of prior learning is also facilitated by modules' specified learning objectives, that is, the formal recognition of students' competencies and skills no matter where they have been acquired, whether through formal or informal training, work activities, or life experiences (Jessup 1991, VEETAC 1991).

2. Reasons and Objectives of Modularization

2.1 Responsiveness to Industrial Change

Why has a modular approach been adopted in some parts of the training system? The traditional structure of such systems has been linear or grouped; this is still the dominant type of course structure in, for example, continental Europe, although certain countries including The Netherlands, France, and Sweden are moving toward a more modular approach. In a linear or grouped system, courses are designed specifically for each area of training or line of study (e.g., plumbing, butchery); students on a course are usually required to take particular groupings of subjects in a prescribed sequence within a set time period; they usually spend most of their time in the same student group and certification is based on simultaneous terminal examination of the required subjects (Russell 1986). While this approach has various strengths, such as complete and continuing concentration on a particular area of work, it also has major shortcomings which underlie the shift

from linear to modular structures (OECD 1989).

A linear approach is most relevant where jobs are relatively stable in content and process, well-defined, and clearly demarcated horizontally from other jobs and stratified vertically in terms of the levels of job. In these circumstances structuring training on the basis of specific lines and levels of study which correspond to distinct and stable structures of employment is a rational approach. As the structure of the labor market changes and becomes more blurred and fluid then linear systems become less appropriate:

> Technical and organizational changes at work have made a great difference to the organization and content of vocational education in the 1970s and 1980s. The modular principle can be seen as a reflection of new production concepts in industry . . . the automated production of the 1980s is accompanied by broad-based skills. The vocational lines of the upper secondary school are too rigid and narrow to fit in with the demands of the 1980s for diversity and preparedness for change in the skills context. . . . The skills requirements of the 1980s also mean less emphasis on manual skills and more on systematic understanding and capacity for learning. (OECD 1989 p. 60)

In a modular system, programs of modules can be put together to give the most appropriate profile for a particular occupation or job and programs can be adapted quickly to meet changing requirements without revising the entire curriculum.

2.2 Increasing Participation Levels

Another common thread in moves toward modularization is the perceived need to raise the skill levels of the workforce through improving participation levels in all sectors of education and training (SED 1983, de Bruijn 1992, New Zealand Ministry of Education 1990). Modularization is seen as a way to increase participation rates by giving individual students greater opportunities to select their program of study and to vary their rate of progress; by facilitating access through short "stand alone" units which receive credit instead of long courses with no intermediate credits; and by providing multiple entry and exit points that accommodate interruptions to study, changes of direction, and progression with credit (credit accumulation and transfer).

Modularization has frequently been seen as a particularly relevant approach to improve the participation of the new groups in need of adult education and vocational training because of rising unemployment and changes in work practices. Its short-term goals and the opportunity to move in and out of the education and training system with credit are seen as a way to encourage them to participate, while the division of the curriculum into more "manageable" chunks and the innovative pedagogy often associated with modularization should provide a more positive learning experience and retain them in the system. The short courses introduced in the Netherlands in 1979 for young people unable to obtain an apprenticeship because of economic recession, or unable to meet the admission requirements for the longer vocational courses or for apprenticeships, are one example of this thinking (de Bruijn 1992).

2.3 Coherence and Efficiency

Modularization is seen as a means to promote coherence in adult education and training systems. In modular systems the clear specification of learning objectives should prevent the duplication of provision; it provides the basis for identifying study pathways between courses (articulation), for mutual recognition of training levels and enabling students to plan their route through the system. Modularization thus provides a "common currency of qualifications" which can offer both coherence and flexibility (OECD 1989). This common currency can function in terms of credits where a standard currency of credits is agreed for different modules of varying sizes and levels used by different institutions or, more radically, by adopting a common type of module throughout the system. The latter approach was taken in Scotland: all craft and technician level vocational courses were replaced by a common, national system of modules each accredited by a single National Certificate to facilitate integration and progression across different institutions (Howieson 1992).

A more coherent and integrated training system also means a more cost-effective system, and the efficient use of resources has figured in moves towards modularization including avoiding duplication of provision. For example, when apprenticeship training in the metal industry in the Netherlands was modularized, 20 separate courses were merged into three groups (Streumer 1991).

The attention to increased efficiency has overlapped with a desire, in a number of countries, to make training itself more business-like. This is illustrated in the change to business terminology with the use of words such as "efficiency," "clients," and "the market-place" (Theodossin 1986, Netherlands Ministry of Education and Science 1991). Modularization and credit transfer are part of this market-oriented approach; they can be seen as devices to respond to the needs of clients (employers, governments, and students), to bring in more business, and to ensure efficient and cost-effective operations.

3. Criticisms of Modularization

3.1 Fragmentation

While modularization has increasingly been seen as a relevant approach to the changing demands on the subsystem for adult education, it has been subject to various criticisms. The most common center on the

dangers of the fragmentation of learning if the curriculum is divided up into free-standing units and of the possibility that students will end up taking incoherent groupings of modules (Jonathan 1987). In vocational education and training, concern about the fragmentation of the curriculum has additional dimensions. One relates to the role of training in the occupational socialization of young workers which is seen as requiring relatively stable groups of students who share a distinct occupational identity. Another dimension is the need in various occupational areas to build up adequate levels of competence; this implies continuity and coherence in courses, especially where skills have to be "confirmed" (i.e., practiced and overlearned) and not just acquired (Squires 1987). Theodossin (1986) however, citing a multidimensional taxonomy of coherence, suggests that the issue is such a complex subject that sweeping statements about coherence or incoherence are ill-conceived. Moreover, he argues that nonmodular courses which are defended as coherent in theory may not always be so in practice.

Yet, despite the widespread criticism of modularization and fragmentation of learning, modularization does not necessarily preclude coherence. Although the notional duration of a module may be, for example, 35 hours, half, double, or treble modules may be constructed if this is more appropriate to the subject matter. This is a common approach in much modular provision. Various strategies can be used to make clear the interrelation of related modules such as the simultaneous delivery of several modules in a particular area of study; the use of "integrative" modules that emphasize synthesis; and by work experience (SOED 1991). There are also various strategies that can be used to create a sense of occupational identity and purpose among students, for example, through project work, guidance and counseling, and the creation of core-building student groups (Russell 1986).

3.2 Assessment

Other criticisms center on assessment in modular provision. The principle of carrying out assessments at the end of each module is seen as adding to the risk of fragmentation, as well as the possible overassessment of students if they are taking a number of modules simultaneously. While terminal assessment can fragment the learning experience—this was one of the findings of an official evaluation of the modular system in Scotland (SOED 1991)—it is not inevitable. Although the evaluation criticized the approach in some subject areas of teaching and testing each learning objective of each module separately, in other areas this had been avoided by, for example, assessing performance as it occurred in the learning process or by assessing a number of learning objectives of several modules through one assessment instrument. Assessment is certainly an area where extensive staff development is required when provision is modularized (Candy and

Harris 1990, SOED 1991, de Bruijn 1991).

Another commonly perceived disadvantage of assessment in modular systems is that it can result in a short-term approach to learning, that once students have been assessed in a particular module, they have little incentive to retain what they have learned. There seems to be little research to prove or disprove this assertion. The evaluations that have been carried out have generally focused on the opinions of staff, students, and employers rather than measuring how much students learn and retain. Research in Scotland found that students, employers, and staff had sharply contrasting views of assessment; students and employers were more positive than the staff (Black et al. 1991). The study also highlighted a number of ways that retention can be encouraged: such as special integrative modules that bring together some of the key learning objectives of a program of modules and better specification of learning objectives of modules to ensure that they demand more than "short-term storage" from students.

4. The Experience of Modularization

4.1 Coherence Versus Choice

Possibly much of the criticism that modularization results in incoherence stems from an overemphasis on its potential for choice and flexibility. Taken to its extreme of unfettered choice from a wide array of modules, modularization might result in incoherence but, in practice, few systems have adopted this approach. Most are based on some degree of restriction, for example, setting entry requirements to some modules; identifying compulsory "core" modules; limiting the range of optional modules; and specifying the sequencing of modules. The balance of choice and restriction generally varies; for example, occupations differ in the extent to which core modules are required or in the necessity to sequence modules. Individual needs also vary so that a limited core and more extensive range of optional modules is more appropriate for someone not completely committed to a particular occupational area.

In modular provision in adult education and training compared with that in general education, there is much more emphasis on identifying groups of modules that have to be taken because certain skills and knowledge are deemed necessary for occupational competence. For example, in the Netherlands, as the apprenticeships branches have modularized their training, much attention has been given to designing "clusters of modules" and although apprentices generally have some choice about when to study some of their modules they have little choice about which modules to take. Fragmentation is thus not a problem although student choice is limited.

Even where modularization has been introduced on a more general basis, across all occupational areas, the tendency is towards recognized groupings of modules. This has proved to be the case in Scotland (SOED 1991, Howieson 1992). The Scottish modular system is one which comes closer in its design than most others to the stereotype of modularization as a cafeteria "pick and mix" system. A National Certificate is awarded for the completion of even one module and for the first six years of its operation (1984–1990), awards for groups of modules were not made. Nevertheless the demands of employers and industry groups meant that, in practice, standard packages of modules were frequently studied and since 1990 group awards for specific groups of modules have been made.

The tendency to specify packages of modules may help to avoid fragmentation and is more likely to create a sense of occupational identity and purpose. Nevertheless, coherence and continuity may well be achieved at the expense of flexibility and choice, especially that of students. Flexibility and choice are generally seen as among the benefits of modularization but there is a potential tension between flexibility and choice for industry and for students. For industry, flexibility means the ability to tailor training more closely to their requirements and to enable it to respond quickly to changing skill needs; for students, flexibility and choice is related to greater opportunities to select their own programs of study, to vary their rate of progress, and to change their direction of study (Howieson 1992). It seems that, in practice, it is flexibility for industry that predominates in modular training provision.

4.2 Changing Staff Roles

Where adult education and training have been modularized, the new system has made major demands on staff and resulted in radical changes to their role. It has meant much less formal teaching and much more "administration and assessment together with the responsibility of designing and facilitating learning as well as increased responsibility for student counseling" (Hodkinson 1991 p. 29). Terms such as "facilitator," "manager," "guide," and "counselor" tend to be used in descriptions of the new roles of staff in modular systems (ILO 1984; Howieson 1992; de Bruijn 1991, 1992; Jordan et al. 1992). These studies all note that modularization and its associated features have moved the emphasis in teaching/training from a collective to an individual approach, in which students are encouraged to take responsibility for their own learning, to take a more active role, and to work at their own pace towards defined learning objectives. Rather than instructing a group or class of students, the teacher's/trainer's role becomes one of advising and guiding students through their training. Staff need to develop counseling skills and new types of teaching skills as well as expertise in new methods of assessment. Timetabling and organizational techniques also need to be developed to deal with the organization of modular programs and with individualized learning within student groups. Where a modular approach has been introduced, the consequent need for extensive staff development has been obvious. The development of training materials for instructors was an integral part of the ILO's MES project (see *Teacher Roles and Teacher Styles*).

The move to modularization is demanding and challenging for staff; staff themselves seem to vary in their opinion as to whether the change is beneficial or not in professional terms. Some see it as requiring them to extend their professional expertise, for example, in the organization of the learning process and in helping students integrate their learning. Others think that their role has been devalued and limited, in particular, by the prestructuring of what is to be learned and assessed through the specification of learning objectives for each module. Experience from Scotland indicates that where module specifications are very tight this does tend to inhibit staff in their teaching and assessment (Black et al. 1991).

As well as extending teachers'/trainers' counseling skills, modular systems also imply the need for more systematic attention to guidance if potential students are to access the system and to plan a coherent path through it.

5. Conclusion

While the extent and pace of modularization vary across different countries, several objectives underlie most modular reforms. They relate mainly to the perceived need to improve subsystems of adult education and training to meet the changing skill needs arising from changes in occupational practice and the structure of the labor market. Modularization is thus related to the level of satisfaction or dissatisfaction with existing subsystems. The extent and scope of modular reforms in different countries tend to be determined by the degree to which current training is thought to meet the needs of particular sectors or particular client groups.

Modularization has usually been part of wider reforms and intended either to promote or reinforce them. As well as accompanying wider reforms, modular systems seem to be more responsive to the need for further change. This is evident in those countries which have had modular provision for some time, where modularization has been able to meet new objectives and facilitate the introduction of other education and training initiatives. Modular systems tend to change and develop faster and to a greater degree than traditional vocational education: where modular reforms have been introduced, it has generally turned out to be a continuing process of reform rather than a one-off event (Raffe 1992).

There is a strong interest amongst policymakers in many countries which have little experience of modularization in learning from those with longer standing or more extensive modular provision. For example, in the mid-1990s, there is interest in the European Union in the potential of modular forms of training including the development of transnational modules. The potential of modular approaches to contribute to the integration and training of increasingly heterogeneous populations caused by higher levels of migration (whether from necessity or choice) is a relevant issue also for other countries and continents.

See also: Recognition and Certification of Skill; Demand, Supply, and Finance of Adult Education; Approaches to Learning; Curriculum in Adult Education; Educational Technology in Vocational Training; Job and Task Analysis; The Development of Competence: Toward a Taxonomy; Teacher Roles and Teacher Styles

References

Black H, Hall J, Martin S 1991 *Modules: Teaching, Learning and Assessment*. Scottish Council for Research in Education, Edinburgh

Candy P, Harris R 1990 Implementing competency-based vocational education: A view from within. *Journal of Further Higher Education* 14(2): 38–58

de Bruijn E 1991 *The Modular Approach in the Apprenticeship System*. Centre for Educational Research (SCO), University of Amsterdam, Amsterdam

de Bruijn E 1992 *The Effectiveness of New Curriculum Models for Initial Vocational Training: Modularization*. Centre for Educational Research (SCO), University of Amsterdam, Amsterdam

Hodkinson P 1991 NCVQ and the 16–19 curriculum. *British Journal of Education and Work* 4(3): 25–39

Howieson C 1992 *Modularization in Initial Vocational Training*. Centre for Educational Sociology, University of Edinburgh, Edinburgh

Innes R 1992 Personal correspondence. Department of Employment, Vocational Education, and Training, Perth

International Labour Organisation 1984 *Final Report on the ILO/SIDA Research and Development Project in Vocational Training Methods and Techniques*. ILO, Geneva

Jessup G 1991 *Outcomes: NVQs and the Emerging Model of Education and Training*. Falmer Press, Basingstoke

Jonathan R 1987 The case for and against modularisation. *Scottish Educational Review* 19(2): 86–97

Jordan S, Manning S, Weissflog I 1992 *The Effectiveness of New Curriculum Models for Initial Vocational Training —Modularisation*. Research Forum Education and Society (WiFo), Berlin

Netherlands Ministry of Education and Sciences 1991 *Main Reforms and Debates*. Dutch Report to the OECD. Ministry of Education and Sciences, Zoetermeer

New Zealand Ministry of Education 1990 *Tomorrow's Standards*. Learning Media. Ministry of Education, Wellington

Organization for Economic Cooperation and Development 1989 *Pathways for Learning*. OECD, Paris

Raffe D (ed.) 1992 *Modularisation in Initial Vocational Training: Recent Developments in Six European Coun-*

tries, Centre for Educational Sociology, University of Edinburgh, Edinburgh

Roberts I 1987 Modular structures: Their strengths and weaknesses. In: Twining J, Nisbet S, Megarty J (eds.) 1987 *World Yearbook of Education*. Kogan Page, London

Russell R 1986 Grouped versus modular courses. In: Farley M (ed.) 1986 *Modularization and the New Curricula*. Further Education Staff College, Coombe Lodge, Bristol

Scottish Education Department (SED) 1983 *16–18s in Scotland: An Action Plan*. Scottish Education Department, Edinburgh

Scottish Office Educational Department (SOED) 1991 *Six Years On*. HMSO, Edinburgh

Scottish Vocational Education Council (SCOTVEC) 1991 *Guide to Scotvec Procedures*. SCOTVEC, Glasgow

Squires G 1987 *The Curriculum Beyond School*. Hodder and Stoughton, London

Streumer W 1991 *The Development and Implementation of a Modular System in Vocational Education and Training: Practical Problems*. PCBB, s'Hertogenbosch

Theodossin E F 1986 *The Modular Market* Further Education Staff College, Coombe Lodge Bristol Vocational Education and Training Accreditation Board (VEETAC) 1991 *Interim Guidelines for Accreditation*. VEETAC, Melbourne

Program Design: Effectiveness

M. Mulder

Countries and organizations invest substantial sums in the further education and training of their workforce. This investment in human resources is motivated by a desire to develop the required level of competence in the organization. In return for this investment, organizations naturally want successful training programs—programs that enhance the competence of workers and that contribute to attaining the general goals of the organization. But what are the factors that contribute to the success of training programs?

Determinants of successful training programs are discussed in this entry. Several models for the design of training programs are described, and the functionality of such models for establishing successful programs is stressed. Approaches to and questions for effectiveness evaluation are presented, and transfer studies as well as management activities that can enhance the transfer of training are reviewed.

1. Definitions

Nadler (1984 p. 1.16) distinguishes "training," "education," and "development" as activities of human resource development. "Training" is aimed at creating learning processes that are relevant for the present job, "education" is aimed toward a different but identified job, and "development" is aimed at the growth of the individual but not related to a specific present or different job, thus enhancing the flexibility of the individual and the organization. An important additional difference between "training" and "development" consists of the intentionality of the training intervention. "Training" is preplanned and goal-oriented, whereas "development" may be incidental. In this entry, "training" is defined as the provision that is aimed at creating intentional learning processes that contribute to improving the performance of workers in their present job (Mulder 1992).

2. Systems Design Models

Training is often conceptualized as a systems design model. Such models represent important components of the preparation stage of the training process, training delivery, and post-training activities. Andrews and Goodson (1980) describe about 40 systems design models that were developed during the 1960s and 1970s. They conclude that there is wide variety in the scientific basis, the context of application, and the documentation of these models, but that the major components of the systems design models are identical, and that the systems philosophy in training design is well proliferated. The common elements in the models can be summarized as the input, process, output, and context elements.

An important systems design model has been developed by Romiszowski (1981). This model is characterized by three design dimensions: (a) the stage in the systems approach, (b) the design level, and (c) the kind of activity that is performed in the design project. There are, moreover, five design stages: problem definition, problem analysis, design or development of a solution, implementation, and control or evaluation. The following design levels are distinguished: (a) the course level, (b) the module level, (c) the lesson plan level, and (d) the activity level. The kind of activities are: (a) analysis activities, (b) synthesis activities, and (c) evaluation activities. A further characteristic is that the design activities relate to one another in a nonlinear fashion. Figure 1 shows this nonlinearity in instructional design, and can be conceived as a representation of the instructional design nucleus at all design levels. The main stages of instructional design are positioned in the outer shell, whereas the character of the instructional design activities are placed in the center.

The tools that are described in the work of Romiszowski are interpreted as heuristics, since in

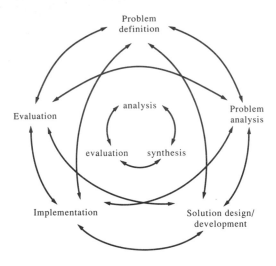

Figure 1
The instructional design nucleas at all system levels

most cases there is no single right answer to performance problems in organizations. Training program designers can therefore only create the best solutions in the given circumstances. The assumption is that employing training design models enhances the fit of the solution to the performance problem encountered.

During the first stages of the training design project the designer should decide whether training is the solution to a given problem. The designer must analyze the performance problem thoroughly because such problems are not only caused by skill insufficiencies, but also by, for example, problems of incentive, motivation, organization, ergonomics, and safety. The first question the designer should answer is whether a prospective trainee lacks the necessary knowledge, skills, and attitudes. The next question is whether the knowledge, skills, and attitudes can be systematically taught. If there are other causes of the performance problem, the training designer may propose (or be invited to participate in) an interdepartmental project, of which training is part of the solution. Various studies have been conducted to analyze the relationships between design variables and training effects.

In a recent study Kessels (1993) stressed the importance of combining the so-called systematic and relational approach in designing effective training programs. The systematic approach refers to the application of systems theory in program design. The relational approach refers to the communication between all stakeholders in the design project by which consensus is achieved about the purpose and implementation of the program. Krijger and Pol (1995) conducted a study in which they tested a design model that enhances lasting effects in changing leadership style of managers. In their study they found that

the following variables were influential: concrete and intensive feedback about the effects of behavior in situations with a large similarity to job performance, skills and insight in emotional processes, concrete and precise formulation of objectives, and providing follow-up activities. These are only two examples of studies in which the relationships between training design and effects are explored. Russ-Eft and Zenger (1995) have reviewed a large number of these studies in the field of behavior modeling in North America (see *Instructional Design: Guidelines and Theories; Instructional Design: Models*).

3. The Human Resource Results Model

In a comprehensive study of the American Society for Training and Development, various areas that are related to training are distinguished in a so-called "Human Resource Wheel" (McLagan and Suhadolnik 1989). The basis of this Human Resource Results model is that Human Resource (HR) related systems and interventions are distinguished on the one hand, and HR-related outputs on the other (see Fig. 2).

It can be seen from Fig. 2 that HR-related systems and interventions consist of three components: HR Environment, HR Development, and HR Support. HR Development consists of:

(a) Training and development: identifying, assuring, and—through planned learning—helping in developing the key competencies that enable individuals to perform current or future jobs.

(b) Organization development: assuring effective inter- and intra-unit relationships and helping groups in initiating and managing change.

(c) Career development: assuring an alignment of individual career planning and organization career management processes in order to achieve an optimal match of individual and organization needs.

HR Environment consists of:

(a) Organization/job design: defining how tasks, authority, and systems will be organized and integrated across organizational units and in individual jobs.

(b) Human resource planning: determining the organization's major human resource needs, strategies, and philosophies.

(c) Performance management systems: assuring that the goals of individuals and the organization are aligned and that the goals of the organization are supported by the tasks the individuals perform at work.

(d) Selection and staffing: matching people and their career needs and capabilities with jobs and career paths.

HR – Related systems   HR – Outputs
and interventions

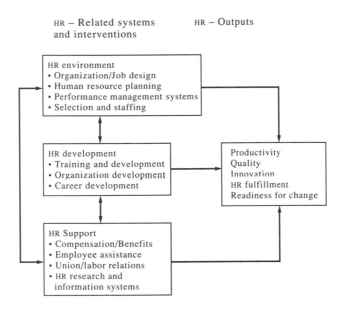

Figure 2
Human resource results model

HR Support consists of:

(a) Compensation/benefits: assuring fairness and consistency in the provision of compensation and benefits.

(b) Employee assistance: providing personal problem-solving assistance and counselling to individual employees.

(c) Labor relations: assuring good relationships between the labor unions and the organization.

(d) Research and information systems: assuring the development and operation of a human resource information base.

All of these HR areas should result in the following HR-related outputs: Enhanced productivity, quality, innovation, HR fulfillment, and readiness for change. If these outputs are the main criteria for successful performance in organizations, then training programs should contribute to these criteria. This philosophy is often referred to as the "training-as-a-tool-of-management" philosophy.

4. Approaches to Training Evaluation

Training can be conceptualized at different levels in the organization. Romiszowski (1981) distinguishes between the macro level and the micro level. The macro level is the level of the organization. At that level, performance problems are analyzed and solu-

tions defined. Criteria for success are those human resource results that are distinguished by McLagan and Suhadolnik (1989). The micro level is the training design level, which consists of the design stages described above. Achievement is the principal success criterion at that level; for example, measured in terms of increased knowledge and skills.

The outcomes of the problem analysis stage at the macro level serves as the input into the needs analysis at the micro level. The output of the micro level (increased knowledge, skills, and attitudes) serves as input for the implementation stage of the training outcomes at the macro level. The meso level and the supra level can be added to the macro and micro levels. The meso level is the level of the training department within the organization, and the supra level is the business environment. Outputs of these levels can also contribute to variation in performance criteria such as productivity, quality, and innovation.

Hinrichs (1983) relates the concept of the supra-system to the system of interest: the individual trainee, the training department, and executive management. For the individual trainee, the training department is the supra-system. Formal achievements of the individual trainee are learning and altered behavior. Trainees' needs are satisfied by the personal growth of individuals and the sense of increased competence. For the training department, executive management is the supra-system. Formal achievements of the training department are the determination of specific training needs, program design and implementation, and identification of the individuals to be trained. The training department's needs are satisfied by recogni-

521

tion of successful programs and objectives achieved, and by continuing demand for training programs. For the executive management, the business society is the supra-system. Formal achievements of executive management with respect to training are the setting of policy and the objectives for training, and the allocation of resources to training vis-à-vis other strategies. Executive management's needs are satisfied by organizational success in meeting the overall objectives. The work of Kirkpatrick (1994) on training evaluation has become very well known, and is applied on a broad scale. His classification of training effects goes back to the 1950s, and boils down to four levels of evaluation; (a) the reaction of the trainees; (b) the learning results; (c) the change of work behavior; and (d) the benefits for the organization. Various authors have developed or used similar categories of training effects.

5. Questions for Training Evaluation

Training results can be categorized at each of the systems levels identified above. Beyond the evaluation of training system characteristics, Brinkerhoff (1987 p. 16) distinguishes between three categories of questions for training effectiveness evaluation in relation to the human resource development decision cycle, which in fact should be analyzed at different systems levels:

(a) The trainees exit with new knowledge, skills, and attitudes; sufficient human resource development has taken place. In this case the relevant questions are: Who has not acquired the specified knowledge, skills and attitudes? What else was learned? Are the acquired knowledge, skills, and attitudes sufficient for effective on-the-job usage?

(b) The trainees use newly acquired knowledge, skills, and attitudes on the job or in personal life; reactions to human resource development are sustained. Possible questions are: Have the training effects lasted? Who is using the new knowledge, skills, and attitudes? Which skills and attitudes are being used and which are not? How are the skills and attitudes being used? How well are the skills and attitudes being used?

(c) The usage of the newly acquired knowledge, skills, and attitudes benefits the organization; original human resource development needs are sufficiently diminished. Relevant questions are: What benefits are occurring? What benefits are not occurring? Are any problems occurring because of the use or non-use of new knowledge, skills, and attitudes? Should human resource development be continued? Should less be done, or more? Are revisions needed? Was it worth it?

Questions as to whether any learning took place can be answered at the micro or individual trainee level. Questions as to whether the trainees use new knowledge, skills, and attitudes can be analyzed at the macro or the (executive) management level, or at the level of job performance. In the process of answering these questions supervisors' perceptions of the trainee are at stake. The evaluator should contact management in an early stage of the training design process to establish the commitment of the management to evaluation. Questions with respect to the effects of training at the organizational level should also be analyzed at the macro or (executive) management level. However, questions concerning the organizational impact of training are not easy to answer. Management has several human resource strategies at its disposal, as described earlier, and the effects of different strategies will interact. Because of this complexity, little is known about the direct and indirect effects of human resource interventions.

6. Learning Results and Transfer

The success of training programs can be assessed at both the micro level and the macro level. At the micro level learning results are the main objective of the training effort, whereas at the macro level performance change is the ultimate objective. The transfer of training facilitates performance change.

Previous research has contributed to an understanding of success and failure factors in training design. Useful reviews of previous studies are presented by Campbell (1971), Goldstein (1980), and Wexley (1984). Campbell reviews 213 publications in the training field on a wide variety of topics. He concludes: "In sum, we know a few things but not very much" (Campbell 1971 p. 593). Goldstein analyzes more than 250 studies on various training issues. He presents a more optimistic conclusion than Campbell, and contends that whereas ". . . the vast majority of writing in this area is not empirical, theoretical, or thoughtful, there is a small but increasingly significant literature that focuses on important issues and raises the expectations of this reviewer about future possibilities" (Goldstein 1980 p. 262). Wexley (1984) discusses the results of about 150 empirical and theoretical studies on the outcomes of training programs. He finds that the fit of training programs to the trainees and their jobs is a major success criterion. Some studies also show that specific interventions resulted in training time reduction. This is an important finding, as the cost of training is to a large extent determined by the cost to the organization of a reduction in the trainees' worktime (see *Measurement of Training Costs*). On the basis of the above reviews it can be concluded that the results of studies tend to be contingent upon particular situations and circumstances, for example, with respect to the branch and type of organization in which the training activity took place.

Baldwin and Ford (1988) analyze 70 studies of training transfer. The authors propose a conceptual model that consists of training inputs, training outputs, and conditions for transfer. Training inputs are divided into three clusters of variables: (a) trainee characteristics, such as ability, personality, and motivation; (b) training design, for example, in relation to principles of learning, sequencing, and training content; and (c) work environment, such as support and opportunity to use training results. The hypotheses are, first, that training design, trainee characteristics, and work environment directly influence learning and retention; and second, that learning and retention, trainee characteristics, and the work environment influence generalization and maintenance of the learning results.

Baldwin and Ford (1988) conclude that some studies show that improved training design results in improved transfer. Correspondence between training elements and the work setting, the teaching of general principles instead of specifics, stimulus variability, and specific conditions for practicing learning tasks are some of the factors that appear to enhance transfer. But the results also indicate that the outcomes of training are contingent upon training task and training recipient. The studies on trainee characteristics show conflicting results. In some studies relationships are found between trainee selection and the prediction of trainability, but in other studies this is not the case. Several studies report significant effects of motivational factors on transfer. The number of empirical studies on the relationships between characteristics of the work environment and transfer is limited. However, one research study shows that pre-training discussion with supervisors and subsequent supervisors' sponsorship contributes most to successful skills transfer.

7. Conclusion

General answers to the question as to what are the determinants of successful training programs cannot be given. Theoretically one can expect that the characteristics of trainer, trainee, training program, and management are important determinants. The International Board of Standards for Training, Performance, and Instruction has published four reports that list the kind of competencies training managers, trainers, and instructional designers should have acquired in order to manage, design, develop, implement, and evaluate training programs. Broad and Newstrom (1992) mention a long list of management activities that support training transfer. Particularly important are management involvement in pre-training decisions, support during the training activity, job linkage for pre-entry into the work situation, active stimulation of application of learning results, and follow-up. As the research basis of training design is generally weak, training

practice rests in the main on conceptual training models.

See also: Human Resource Development; Economics of Adult Education and Training; Instructional Design: Guidelines and Theories; Instructional Design: Models; Evaluation of Distance Education: Cost-Effectiveness; Evaluation of Industry Training: Cost-Effectiveness; Evaluation of Public Training: Cost-Effectiveness; Measurement of Industry Training

References

Andrews D H, Goodson N D L 1980 A comparative analysis of models of instructional design. *J. Instructional Development* 3(4): 2–16
Baldwin T T, Ford J K 1988 Transfer of training: A review and directions for future research. *Personnel Psychology* 41: 63–105
Brinkerhoff R O 1987 *Achieving Results from Training. How to Evaluate Human Resource Development to Strengthen Programs and Increase Impact*. Jossey-Bass, San Francisco, California
Broad M L, Newstrom J W 1992 *Transfer of Training. Action-packed Strategies to Ensure High Payoff from Training Investments*. Addison-Wesley, Reading
Campbell J P 1971 Personnel training and development. *Annual Review of Psychology* 22: 565–602
Goldstein I L 1980 Training in work organizations. *Annual Review of Psychology* 31: 229–72
Hinrichs J R 1983 Personnel training. In: Dunnette M D (ed.) 1983 *Handbook of Industrial and Organizational Psychology*. Rand McNally, Chicago, Illinois
Kessels J W M 1993 *Towards Design Standards for Curriculum Consistency in Corporate Education*. FCE, Terschuur
Kirkpatrick D L 1994 *Evaluating Training Programs. The Four Levels*. Berret-Koehler, San Francisco, California
Krijger N L, Pol S M 1995 Changing leadership style: A training model for lasting effects. In: Mulder M, Nijhof W J, Brinkerhoff R O (eds.) 1995 *Corporate Training for Effective Performance*. Kluwer Academic Publishers Boston, Massachusetts
McLagan P A, Suhadolnik D 1989 *Models for HRD Practice. American Society for Training and Development*, Alexandria, Virginia
Mulder M 1992 Toward a comprehensive research framework on training and development in business and industry. *Int. J. Lifelong Education* 11 (2): 139–55
Nadler L (ed.) 1984 *The Handbook of Human Resource Development*. John Wiley, New York
Romiszowski A J 1981 *Designing Instructional Systems*. Kogan Page, London
Russ-Eft D F, Zenger J H 1995 Behavior modeling training in North America: A research summary. In: Mulder M, Nijhof W J, Brinkerhoff R O (eds.) 1995 *Corporate Training for Effective Performance*. Kluwer Academic Publishers, Boston, Massachusetts
Wexley K N 1984 Personnel training. *Annual Review of Psychology* 35: 519–51

Further Reading

Basarab D J Sr, Root D K 1992 *The Training Evaluation Process. A Practical Approach to Evaluating Corpo-*

rate Training Programs. Kluwer Academic Publishers, Boston, Massachusetts

Bramley P 1992 *Evaluating Training Effectiveness. Translating Theory into Practice.* McGraw-Hill, London

Camp R R, Blanchard P N, Huszczo G E 1986 *Toward a More Organizationally Effective Training Strategy and Practice.* Prentice-Hall, Englewood Cliffs, New Jersey

Craig R L (ed.) 1987 *Training and Development Handbook. A Guide to Human Resource Development.* MacGraw-Hill, New York

Hamblin A C 1974 *Evaluation and Control of Training.* MacGraw-Hill, London

International Board of Standards for Training, Performance, and Instruction 1986 *Instructional Design Competencies. The Standards.* University of Iowa, Iowa City, Iowa

International Board of Standards for Training, Performance, and Instruction 1988 *Instructor Competencies. The Standards*, Vol. 1. IBSTPI, Evergreen Park, Illinois

International Board of Standards for Training, Performance, and Instruction 1989 *Training Manager Competencies. The Standards.* Altschuler, Melvoin and Glasser, Chicago, Illinois

International Board of Standards for Training, Performance, and Instruction 1991 *Instructor Competencies. The Standards*, Vol. 2. A M & G Consulting Services, Chicago, Illinois

May L S, Moore C A, Zammit S J (eds.) 1987 *Evaluating Business and Industry Training.* Kluwer Academic Publishers, Dordrecht

Mulder M 1990 Training and development in organizations: An international research perspective. In: Mulder M, Romiszowski A J, Van der Sijde P C (eds.) 1990 *Strategic Human Resource Management.* Swets and Zeitlinger, Amsterdam

Phillips J J 1993 *Training Evaluation and Measurement Methods.* Kogan Page, London

Smith M E 1987 Measuring results. In: Craig R L (ed.) 1987 *Training and Development Handbook. A Guide to Human Resource Development.* 3rd ed. McGraw-Hill, New York

Tracey W R (ed.) 1985 *Human Resources Management and Development Handbook.* American Management Associations, New York

The Development of Competence: Toward a Taxonomy

M. Marsiske and J. Smith

This entry is meant to serve as a bridge between the elements of human development, cognitive functioning, and learning which have been discussed throughout this Section. The goals of this entry are firstly to summarize current knowledge about cognitive development over the lifespan, and secondly to explore the implications of these findings for the design of adult learning environments, and more particularly, training programs. Two categories of intellectual functioning are distinguished (Baltes 1993), one reflecting the "mechanics" of the cognitive system (e.g., processing speed, reasoning, working memory capacity) and one reflecting the "pragmatics" (i.e., the application of knowledge acquired through acculturation, education, and training). It is suggested that different job-related tasks and contexts require different competencies, and that designers of adult education and training programs must carefully consider those skills and abilities which are relevant to a particular work environment, an individual's prior experience with a particular job or occupational setting, and an individual's placement within the life course (i.e., chronological age). To illustrate this perspective, this entry briefly considers the research dealing with lifelong learning and the acquisition of expertise. Although the focus in this entry is mainly on work-relevant knowledge and skills, findings regarding the adult development of intellectual competencies are applicable to the broad range of contexts in which adults find themselves facing learning tasks.

1. Cognitive and Intellectual Development Across the Lifespan

Throughout much of the twentieth century, researchers have been interested in the patterns and processes underlying intellectual development in adulthood and old age (see *Human Development: Aging; Self-directed Learning*). For most of this time, researchers have been concerned with the development of psychometric intelligence (e.g., Schaie 1994), although more recent scholarship has also been concerned with the adult developmental trajectories of basic cognitive processes like working memory and speed of processing (e.g., Lindenberger and Baltes in press, Salthouse 1991).

The data suggest that, contrary to stereotypes, adult intellectual and cognitive development cannot be characterized as a period of general decline. As Baltes (1993) has noted, lifelong development, including intellectual aging, always consists of the joint occurrence of gain and loss. To summarize this gain–loss dynamic, Baltes and his colleagues have proposed a "dual process" conception of intellectual development (Baltes 1993). It combines psychometric conceptions of the multifactorial structure of intelligence with cognitive and evolutionary psychological perspectives. The first process, the cognitive *mechanics*, is thought to reflect the neurophysiological functioning of the brain and central nervous system. The second process, the cognitive *pragmatics*, is thought to reflect knowledge that individuals acquire from their culture and immediate life environments as they engage in transactions with it.

The two different aspects of cognitive and intellectual functioning generally show different developmental trajectories. Specifically, cognitive activities associated with the pragmatics of intelligence seem to show stability or growth until advanced old age, while the cognitive mechanics are thought to show relatively normative patterns of decline by about the sixth decade of life (Baltes 1993, Horn and Hofer 1992, Schaie 1994, Salthouse 1991). Of course, these general patterns address only average trends; there are wide individual differences in the timing, magnitude, and nature of intellectual changes. Indeed, it is suggested below that experience in work environments may be one major source of individual differences.

1.1 Individual Differences in Intellectual Development: The Role of Context

The overarching conclusion from both cross-sectional and longitudinal research on intellectual development is that, throughout most of the typical occupational work life, there is little meaningful decline in relevant cognitive abilities. By the end of the work career, however, some decline is noticeable in elements of the cognitive mechanics like attentional capacity, speed of processing, working memory, and reasoning and spatial ability (Craik and Jennings 1992, Salthouse 1991).

It is in the cognitive pragmatics that the greatest potential for selective growth in adulthood and old age seems to reside. The experiential benefits accrued from living longer, practicing particular performances more, and having encountered a broader range of situations and conditions are hypothesized to have positive consequences for intellectual functioning. Psychometric evidence regarding the age-related maintenance of knowledge-based functioning comes from studies of psychometric intelligence which included measures of world knowledge, practical knowledge, and verbal knowledge (e.g., Horn and Hofer 1992, Schaie 1994).

More recent research has emphasized the fact that knowledge-based functioning may be most preserved in those domains where it is actually used and applied. The prototype of this idea comes from the study of expert systems (e.g., Ericsson and Charness 1994, Ericsson and Smith 1991). In studies of diverse expert groups, including typists (Salthouse 1984), and pianists (Ericsson et al. 1993), results have suggested that older experts can generally demonstrate levels of domain-relevant performance proficiency equal to, or greater than, that of younger experts. Although the evidence suggests that older experts encounter the same age-related losses in the mechanics of cognition as other older adults, the experts seem to use their pragmatic knowledge of optimal performance strategies to

ensure continued high-level performance. Indeed, accumulated procedural and declarative knowledge may sometimes be used to compensate for losses in the cognitive mechanics (Baltes, 1993).

Thus the expertise research suggests that in those domains in which adults have the most practice and familiarity there may be continued preservation or even growth of functioning. This has positive implications for the workplace competence of older workers. As long as workers update and revise their knowledge bases to guard against obsolescence (e.g., Featherman et al. 1990, Willis and Dubin 1990), workers with more on-the-job experience may be expected to have higher levels of job relevant knowledge, and that knowledge may be more elaborated, complex, and tested by a broader range of problem situations. In other words, in work environments which foster and support the updating and revision of skills, and which expose workers to a variety of work challenges, on-the-job practice may be one of the best sources of job-relevant learning.

1.2 Modifiability and Plasticity of Intelligence

Expertise research generally focuses on the knowledge and skills that individuals acquire in the course of experience and practice in particular domains, like particular occupations. Not all adult learning can occur "on the job," of course. Employers may require employees to take courses in order to acquire new skills and knowledge (particularly with regard to the introduction of new technologies), and adults themselves may also pursue continuing education for personal reasons. In addition, career retraining may become important when individuals are between occupations. Lifespan research on the modifiability of intellectual and cognitive performance has been encouraging with regard to adults' potential for acquiring new knowledge and skills via such formal training programs.

In general, the literature suggests that many adults have a sizable *cognitive reserve capacity* (Kliegl et al. 1989) but there may be age-related limits on these reserves. The notion of reserve capacity reflects the idea that individuals can grow and change, but there may also be individual differences in how much change is possible. Indeed, the data suggest that even adults in the postretirement years continue to have substantial levels of cognitive reserves. Baltes, Willis, and their colleagues have conducted a series of investigations designed to assess the modifiability, or plasticity, of older adults' intellectual performance (e.g., Baltes and Lindenberger 1988, Willis 1987). The results of these studies have suggested that the provision of practice and/or training with tests of fluid intelligence (thought to be prototypical of the mechanics of intelligence) could lead to improvements of 0.5 to 1 standard deviation units, on average, in adults aged approximately 60 to 90 years of age. Such gains tended to be highly specific (to the ability trained), but long lasting (Willis and Schaie in press) (see *Individual Differences, Learning, and Instruction*).

Of course, it is important to acknowledge that reserve capacity may itself change over the course of adulthood and that there may be some age-associated losses in plasticity and performance potential. Using a research strategy called "testing the limits" (Kliegl et al. 1989), investigators have compared adults' performance on cognitive tasks under supportive conditions (e.g., following training and practice, and in easy task conditions) with performance in nonsupportive conditions (e.g., at fast speeds). In one set of studies (Baltes and Kliegl 1992, Kliegl et al. 1989) both younger and older adults were trained to use a mnemonic (Method of Loci) to serially recall a list of words. Instruction in the mnemonic substantially improved the memory performance of both younger (20–24 years old) and older (60–75 years old) adults; older adults went from a baseline recall of 5–7 words to a mean of about 15 words in correct order. Despite having acquired the Method of Loci, however, under high-challenge conditions of high speed, the lowest functioning members of the young group were typically still outperforming the highest functioning older adults. These findings suggest that plasticity in the cognitive mechanics of older adults cannot completely compensate for age-related restrictions in maximum performance potential under high-challenge conditions.

By extrapolation, these cognitive intervention findings suggest that inservice and work-relevant education may be effective throughout the work career. At the same time, the results also suggest that worker age may be an important moderator of the effectiveness of training (especially when high performance demands, like speediness, are imposed), and training programs may need to consider the special needs of older workers—a point which is examined below. Results from computer-training literature offer a useful example in that older adults have been found to benefit from training in the use of computer software (e.g., Charness et al. 1992, Garfein et al. 1988). On the one hand, this literature shows that older and younger workers can demonstrate substantial positive performance gains in their use of software at the conclusion of training. On the other hand, the results also suggest that older adults require much longer than younger adults to learn to use new software, that they make more errors and that more effort may be needed to effectively train them (Charness and Bosman 1990).

2. Workplace Variability in Skill Demands

Job performance is a multidimensional concept; different jobs are composed of many different tasks, and the importance of particular tasks may vary across individuals within the same nominal occupational category (see *Job and Task Analysis*). Not all job tasks require the same configuration of mechanic or pragmatic abilities. Moreover, different abilities may be required by

persons in a particular profession at different stages of the occupational career. In the initial job-learning phase, abilities predictive of learning and adaptation may be most important. Later in the career, however, specific job knowledge and skills (and not general intellectual competencies) may be the best predictors of future job performance.

In designing training and learning environments, then, it is important to consider the needs of the learner. What are the relevant knowledge and skills workers need to improve performance? Some jobs (e.g., pilots, air traffic controllers) may require high levels of cognitive mechanics, especially reasoning and spatial ability (Ackerman and Kanfer 1993). Many other occupations, however, may place a higher demand on the development of occupation-specific knowledge.

With regard to the acquisition and use of this domain-specific knowledge, the expertise approach mentioned above has constituted a primary paradigm for psychological investigation. The major contribution of research in various domains of expertise (e.g., Chi and Glaser 1988, Ericsson and Smith 1991) has been to emphasize: (a) the importance of careful task analysis to illustrate the diversity of domain-specific knowledge (both factual and procedural) needed in different performance domains; (b) sources of individual differences in terms of knowledge acquisition and application; and (c) the necessity of examining the dialectics and dynamic interactions between individuals and their work environment over time.

With regard to this last point, an important aspect of the relationship between job demands and cognitive competencies is the role of career history or prior work experience. An accumulating body of research suggests that the predictive salience of intellectual abilities, especially cognitive mechanics such as speed and working memory capacity, changes over the working life. In the industrial–organizational literature, this is discussed as the "changing validities" of predictor tests (Henry and Hulin 1989). In longitudinal investigations of the relationship between various cognitive screening inventories and job performance, the usefulness of early measures of general cognitive competencies for predicting job performance decreases as time goes on. Drawing from experimental research on the predictors of motor skill performance over many training and practice trials, Ackerman (1992) has offered a model of why such predictive validities might decline. With regard to perceptual motor tasks, Ackerman suggests that initial learning of the task requires general intellectual and problem-solving abilities. With increased task-specific practice, individuals begin to automate aspects of the task. Eventually, individuals reach an asymptotic performance plateau (the point at which the task has been automatized, and no more improvements are observed); at this point, Ackerman reports that individual differences in performance are best predicted by indicators of psychomotor speed.

Extrapolating from this line of research, the argument is that early job performance places a major emphasis on learning (identifying and understanding relevant features of the job, its duties, and useful resources). Consequently, general intellectual abilities (particularly the mechanics of intelligence, which were designed as predictors of the ability to profit from educational experiences) may be the best predictors of performance in this early phase of the work career. As knowledge is acquired, however, the amount and complexity of one's job-related knowledge may become more important. As one automates work routines, it is this explicit and tacit knowledge (Sternberg and Wagner, 1993) which becomes more important as a predictor of job performance.

Some job-related tasks at high levels of difficulty may be relatively more difficult to automate. Air traffic controllers and radar operators, for example, who may need to continuously and rapidly scan dynamic visual displays, may only be able to automate general performance strategies. They must continually adapt, however, to the changing nature of the display. This is not to imply that air traffic controllers cannot develop expertise, but only that the nature of that high-challenge profession may limit the amount of task automation that is possible. Other jobs with a high degree of task variety (i.e., jobs in which the same task may not be repeated very often) would also be less likely to draw upon automated skills. For such professions, general intellectual and cognitive abilities may remain important throughout the work career.

3. Expertise as a Prototype of Adult Cognitive Development

The term "expertise," it has been argued, is associated with the long-term accumulation of an extensive, highly organized and integrated factual and procedural knowledge base and with high-level performance (Chi and Glaser 1988, Ericsson and Smith 1991). In the course of adult activities (related not only to work, but also family, leisure, interpersonal contexts, and idiosyncratic interests) and by virtue of living longer, individuals have the opportunity to accumulate knowledge in a variety of domains. The extent to which these opportunities are realized will vary between individuals. Only some individuals, by virtue of their particular life ecology or their self-motivated concentration and specialization in one (or more) domains, may develop areas of expertise and reach the status of a recognized *expert* in a domain. Although relatively few individuals may reach this recognized status, expertise development may constitute a general process which characterizes most adults' accumulation of knowledge and skills which are relevant to their life tasks.

Research on expertise and expert knowledge has attempted to determine differences in the amount and organization of knowledge between experts and semi-novices (e.g. chemistry professors vs. chemistry students). These comparisons suggest that, beyond the amount of knowledge and practice, experts differ from novices in the nature in which their knowledge is organized (Glaser 1984). As Glaser noted, "the knowledge of novices is organized around the literal objects explicitly given in a problem statement. Experts' knowledge, on the other hand, is organized around principles and abstractions that subsume these objects" (p. 98). In part, knowledge organization differences may reflect the operation of metacognitive knowledge, another central feature of the pragmatics of intelligence. Compared to novices, experts are more likely to discontinue an unsuccessful problem-solving strategy, to be more accurate in judging the difficulty of new problems and tasks, and are better able to estimate the amount of time and effort to complete a task (Chi et al. 1982).

The literature on expertise also highlights the important role of continued practice, challenge, and updating of knowledge for the maintenance of expert performance. The work environment offers many different opportunities to apply the skills and knowledge acquired in adolescence and early adulthood, to specialize and extend these skills, and to acquire new skills. Indeed, it may be day-to-day work experience that offers the best training opportunities for most adults.

4. Implications for Designing Learning Environments for Adults

In this final section, the implications of adult developmental ideas are considered with regard to the design of learning environments for older workers. Although these ideas emerge from lifespan development and cognitive psychology, they are not unlike the principles of adult learning discussed in the previous entries (see *Lifespan Development: Intelligence; Development of Learning Across the Lifespan; Environments for Learning; Study and Learning Strategies; Instructional Design: Guidelines and Theories*).

(a) *Learners have pre-existing knowledge.* Knowledge acquisition will be facilitated to the extent that it can be integrated into pre-existing knowledge structures. Adult learners, particularly those with extensive experience in their field, will have substantial bodies of factual and procedural knowledge relevant to their professional practice. The most effective learning will draw upon transfer from prior knowledge. Application of material to-be-learned to familiar problems, and encouraging student questions and concerns to guide the presentation of material can be very useful in fostering the integration of new knowledge.

(b) *Learners need opportunities for real-world practice.* Didactic transmission of information is unlikely to yield long-term training gains. The natural learning of new material relies on extensive (and deliberate) practice of domain-relevant skills (Ericsson et al., 1993) When new knowledge can be applied to familiar problems (ideally within the context in which the new learning is to be applied), and when corrective feedback is immediately available, learning is most likely to be effective.

(c) *Contextual relevance aids learning.* Related to the previous point, knowledge that is tangential to the concerns of learners is unlikely to be integrated or retained in the knowledge system. When new technologies or job demands are introduced to workers, training is likely to be most effective when it incorporates many practice opportunities, ideally directly relevant to daily job tasks. As an example, a general training program (e.g., in "night school") in the use of a particular computer program is likely to be less effective than a course in which the software is applied on-the-job, on the particular computer system and using the specific work materials that the individual faces every day. Opportunity to practice in situ, ideally with the availability of contingent feedback, is likely to be most effective in helping individuals integrate new technology into the activities of their daily lives.

(d) *There is variability in cognitive plasticity.* There will be individual differences in the ability to acquire and use new information. With advancing age, there may also be some increased difficulty for older learners to acquire new knowledge at the same speed and level of instruction as younger learners. Reduced instructional speed and extensive practice opportunities may be important to facilitate the knowledge acquisition of learners at lower levels of cognitive plasticity. Of course, under supportive low-challenge conditions, few age-group differences in the capability for learning should be expected.

(e) *Contact between experts and novices may be mutually beneficial.* Beyond organized training programs, arranging for contact between experts and novices may be one highly efficient mechanism of job-relevant training. For experts, the communicative demands of instructing novices may facilitate knowledge organization. For novices, the ability to observe and learn the heuristics which guide the high-level performances of experts may accelerate their own organization and integration of knowledge.

Work-related training that is not tailored to the needs and capacities of the trainees may be less effective in moderating the maintenance and updating of expertise. Indeed, within organizations, training opportunities are often only made available to young employees on the assumption that the cost of provision to middle-aged and older workers would not be recovered in subsequent performance. Such a restriction of the opportunities of older workers ignores a vast body of literature which suggests that older workers can profit substantially from training interventions, and that older workers (by virtue of their highly elaborated, domain-specific knowledge bases) may be among the most valuable human resources for many occupational settings.

See also: Human Development; Lifespan Development; Adult Learning: An Overview; Development of Learning Across the Lifespan; Environments for Learning; Learning in the Workplace; Instructional Design: Guidelines and Theories; Instructional Design: Models; Job and Task Analysis

References

Ackerman P L 1992 Predicting individual differences in complex skill acquisition: Dynamics of ability determinants. *J. Appl. Psychol.* 77: 598–614

Ackerman P L, Kanfer R 1993 Integrating laboratory and field study for improving selection: Development of a battery for predicting air traffic controller success. *J. Appl. Psychol.* 78: 413–32

Baltes P B 1993 The aging mind: Potentials and limits. *Gerontologist* 33: 580–94

Baltes P B, Kliegl R 1992 Further testing of limits in cognitive plasticity in old age: Negative age differences in a mnemonic skill are robust. *Dev. Psychol.* 28: 121–25

Baltes P B, Lindenberger U 1988 On the range of cognitive plasticity in old age as a function of experience: Fifteen years of intervention research. *Behavior Therapy* 19: 283–300

Charness N, Bosman E A 1990 Human factors and design for older adults. In: Birren J E, Schaie K W (eds.) 1990 *Handbook of the Psychology of Aging,* 3rd edn. Academic Press, New York

Charness N, Schumann C E, Boritz G M 1992 Training older adults in word processing: Effects of age, training technique, and computer anxiety. *International Journal of Technology and Aging* 5: 79–106

Chi M T H, Glaser R, Rees E 1982 Expertise in problem solving. In: Sternberg R J (ed.) 1982 *Advances in the Psychology of Human Intelligence,* Vol. 7. Erlbaum, Hillsdale, New Jersey

Chi M T H, Glaser R 1988 *The Nature of Expertise.* Erlbaum, Hillsdale, New Jersey

Craik F I M, Jennings J M 1992 Human memory. In: Craik F I M, Salthouse T A (eds.)1992 *The Handbook of Aging and Cognition.* Erlbaum, Hillsdale, New Jersey

Ericsson K A, Charness N 1994 Expert performance: Its structure and acquisition. *Am. Psychol.* 49: 725–47

Ericsson K A, Krampe R Th, Tesch-Römer C 1993 The role of deliberate practice in the acquisition of expert performance. *Psychol. Rev.* 100: 363–406

Ericsson K A, Smith J 1991 *Toward a General Theory of Expertise: Prospects and Limits.* Cambridge University Press, Cambridge, Massachussetts

Featherman D L, Smith J, Peterson J G 1990 Successful aging in a "post-retired" society. In: Baltes P B, Baltes M M (eds.) 1990 *Successful Aging: Perspectives from the Behavioral Sciences.* Cambridge University Press, New York

Garfein A J, Schaie K W, Willis S L 1988 Microcomputer proficiency in later-middle-aged and older adults: Teaching old dogs new tricks. *Social Behaviour* 3: 131–48

Glaser R 1984 Education and thinking: The role of knowledge. *Am. Psychol.* 39: 93–104

Henry R A, Hulin C L 1989 Changing validities: Ability-performance relations and utilities. *J. Appl. Psychol.* 74: 365–67

Horn J L, Hofer S M 1992 Major abilities and development in the adult period. In: Sternberg R J, Berg C A (eds.)1992 *Intellectual Development,* Cambridge University Press, New York

Kliegl R, Smith J, Baltes P B 1989 Testing-the-limits and the study of age differences in cognitive plasticity of a mnemonic skill. *Dev. Psychol.* 25: 247–56

Lindenberger U, Baltes P B in press Intellectual aging. In

Sternberg R J et al. (eds.) in press *Encyclopedia of Intelligence.* Macmillan, New York

Salthouse T A 1984 Effects of age and skill in typing. *J. Exp. Psychol. Gen.* 113: 345–71

Salthouse T A 1991 *Theoretical Perspectives on Cognitive Aging.* Erlbaum, Hillsdale, New Jersey

Schaie K W 1994 The course of adult intellectual development. *Am. Psychol.* 49: 304–13

Sternberg R J, Wagner R K 1993 The g-ocentric view of intelligence and job performance is wrong. *Psychological Science* 2: 1–5

Willis S L 1987 Cognitive training and everyday competence. In: Schaie K W (ed.) 1987 *Annual Review of Gerontology and Geriatrics,* Vol. 7 Springer, New York

Willis S L, Dubin S S 1990 *Maintaining Professional Competence: Approaches to Career Enhancement, Vitality, and Success Throughout a Work Life.* Jossey-Bass, San Francisco, California

Willis S L, Schaie K W in press Cognitive training in the normal elderly. In: Boller F (ed.) in press *Cerebral Plasticity and Cognitive Stimulation.* Springer, New York

Teacher Roles and Teaching Styles

S. D. Brookfield

The concepts of role and style in teaching have evolved as researchers try to make sense of the ways in which teachers of adults habitually practice their craft, and as they try to understand the learned, seemingly instinctual, responses that teachers develop to the constant dilemmas and tensions of practice. On closer examination, however, the concepts of role and style can be seen not as static constructs through which we can understand the essential nature of teaching, but rather as contextually bound, fluid and capable of multiple interpretation.

The experience of teaching is reported by teachers as being one of sustained ambiguity. In ethnographic studies of teachers' learning and thinking (Calderhead 1987, 1989), teaching is spoken of as multifaceted, contextual, and even chaotic. Given this phenomenological reality, proposing neat delineations of adult teachers' roles and fixed concepts of teaching styles becomes problematic. The roles which teachers of adults can play in particular settings are inevitably constrained by a host of contextual variables. These can be as diverse as the political ethos of the educational institution and of the wider society, the expectations, motives and experiences of the learners involved, or individual teachers' own personalities. Similarly, what can be described as a particular teacher's style is not a static, discrete phenomenon. It is true that teachers of adults may have political orientations, habitual ways of practicing, deeply-etched personality traits, and clear philosophical rationales, all of which frame how they approach their practice. However, the extent to which these elements comprise a distinctive style, and the extent to which any such style can be imposed or allowed, depends greatly on the shifting contexts, constraints, and distortions of practice.

1. Teacher Roles

Multiple roles have been proposed for adult teachers, including those as diverse as counselor, analyst, resource, model, and mediator. Most roles fall into one or other of two distinctive categories representing the liberal and critical traditions in the field. These approaches are those of teachers as facilitators and teachers as critical animators.

1.1 Teachers as Facilitators

The concept of adult teachers as facilitators is prominent in the literature of adult education (Brookfield 1986, 1989, Galbraith 1991). The concept has its roots in the ideas of Carl Rogers which have been interpreted for a wide audience by Knowles (1984). Teaching as facilitation is a role description which emphasizes the pre-eminence of student learning and the development of student self-insight. It regards as suspect the promulgation of teachers' agendas and the notion of the teacher as a repository of approved knowledge. The teacher's role becomes that of process analyst rather than content expert, and there is an assumption that good adult educational activities attempt to meet learners' needs as these are felt and expressed by the learners themselves. Three interpretations of the function of the teacher as facilitator are evident in the literature of adult education: the teacher as facilitator of self-directed learning, the teacher as andragogue, and the teacher as learning analyst.

The teacher as facilitator of self-directed learning is a role designation which has had an enormous impact on adult education practice (Candy 1991, Brockett and Hiemstra 1991). According to this conception, the teacher's task is to act as a nondirective resource person. Those who consider themselves as facilitators of self-directed learning seek to honor learners' wishes. The development of self-confidence, which accompanies the attempt by learners to exert control over the planning, conduct, and evaluation of their learning activities, is the objective. The concept of self-directedness has been criticized for its practical, conceptual, and methodological ambiguities (Brookfield 1988) and for its avoidance of social commitment (Collins 1991).

The teacher as andragogue is a concept that is associated with Knowles's work (1984), and it focuses on the importance of teachers working cooperatively with learners to develop methods and curricula which are grounded in the needs and experiences of adults. Teachers and learners are seen as equals and there is an emphasis on consensus building, rather than conflict, and on the liberating aspects of learning rather than on the difficulties learning often involves. The importance of connecting education to the circumstances and problems of adult life is stressed, and there is an acknowledgement of the integrity and educational value of learners' past experiences. Proponents of these ideas have been criticized for adopting an overly technicist approach to teaching adults, for decontextualizing adult education from wider political issues, and for oversimplifying the complex nature of educational and learning processes (Hartree 1984, Tennant 1986).

The teacher as learning analyst is a role designation which focuses on teachers helping learners to understand their own learning patterns and processes so that they can overcome certain habits, inclinations, and dispositions that are harmful or constraining. In adult education this approach to facilitation has come to be associated chiefly with the work of R M Smith (1990). Smith (1990 p. 4) lists nine activities which can be considered as learning to learn, including increasing the capacity for self-reflection, broadening people's repertoires of learning styles, and helping learners make informed choices from the range of educational options available. As is the case with andragogy, the conceptual and practical components of this idea tend to proliferate and overlap with those of allied concepts such as metacognition, reflective judgement, and learning style.

1.2 Teachers as Critical Animators

The adult teacher as critical animator is a role conception which is grounded in a very different intellectual tradition to that of teachers as facilitators. The concept of facilitation is primarily psychological, whereas the concept of critical animation draws from a stream of sociological and political analysis. Politically, facilitation might be thought of as a liberal concept and critical animation as a socialist concept. It is no surprise, therefore, that political cultures in which socialist ideas are an accepted part of normal political discourse (even if a majority of people do not subscribe to these) tend to be those in which many adult educators are likely to regard their role as that of critical animator.

Those teachers of adults who see their role as being that of a critical animator share three basic assumptions about the practice of adult education. The first of these is that teachers should encourage learners to engage in critical thinking; that is, to scrutinize carefully their taken-for-granted assumptions, to consider alternative ways of interpreting and living in the world, and to become aware of how oppressive economic, political, and social structures do psychological, economic, and physical violence to human beings. A second assumption is that the critical animator should encourage learners to engage in a praxis of action and reflection, that analysis by itself is not enough. Finally, animators regard their practice as geared toward the realization of egalitarian values and structures, often of a democratic socialist nature.

Two clear strands of writing are evident in the critical animation tradition. The first of these draws upon the work of the Frankfurt school of critical social theory (Collard and Law 1991, Collins 1991) and upon the ideas of Antonio Gramsci, the Italian political economist (Armstrong 1988). This stream of thought emphasizes the crucial role of education in social transformation and interprets the adult teacher's role in an activist sense. The teacher's role is to educate in, and for, social action, so that social movements stand a better chance of breaking down oppressive structures. This emphasis on teaching as a component of social action is evident in the lives and ideas of Horton and Lindeman in the United States, Coady in Canada, Grundtvig in Denmark, Tawney and Williams in the United Kingdom, Freire in Brazil, Lovett in Northern Ireland, and in workers and trades union education movements throughout the world. Although the relative emphasis on either socialism or social democracy would vary among these figures and movements, all involved see adult education's basic justification as being that it is a force for fundamental social change.

The second strand of writing in this tradition acknowledges the importance of social transformation but, in addition, interprets critical thinking as occuring in contexts other than the purely political, such as personal relationships, the workplace, and interactions with the media (Brookfield 1987, Marsick 1988, Mezirow 1991). The teacher's role is to assist learners to recognize the epistemic, psychological, and political constraints which prevent them from living their lives according to their own, clearly realized, sense of rightness. These writers share many of the ideological biases of the social transformation stream of animation and they frequently stress the need for teachers to become involved in collective social action. But they argue that teachers of adults can also help to engender significant personal or small group transformations which do not necessarily have to be part of a major social action movement. This form of practice has been criticized for appearing to be more radical than it really is, and for being an essentially liberal, rather than socialist, perspective on transformative practice (Griffin 1988).

2. Teaching Style

As an anthology on teaching style in adult education recently acknowledged (Hayes 1989), the concept of teaching style eludes clear definition. At the core of most treatments of this concept is the idea that a style comprises a set of habitual dispositions— typical ways of approaching practice and of working through tensions and dilemmas—which can be observed over time. Sources which can be seen as framing teaching style range from personality, gender, culture, and class to the espoused theory, values, and political ethos of a field of practice. All of these are interpreted in the context of teachers' daily classroom experiences. In explorations of teacher learning and thinking (Calderhead 1987, 1989) teachers report that while they may begin their careers with firm philosophical and methodological preferences, the contextual realities and constraints of practice mean that these are usually substantially modified. Indeed, teachers' biographies often record either a detaching from a deeply-etched style, or a broadening of typical ways of practicing. Pratt (1989) has observed how the changing perspectives which teachers take on their practice, and the transitions in self-concept they experience, can be understood as recognizeable developmental stages. Teaching becomes a journey into ambiguity, in which teachers pass through an initial period of regarding teaching as the mastery of skills and procedures, followed by an increased emphasis on clinical problem-solving, until they come to incorporate as a permanent feature of their practice some critical reflection on the problematic nature of their activities. In this regard what might, in the early stages of a teacher's life, be viewed by the teacher as the reassuringly fixed components of his or her style can, over time, be reinterpreted as a constraining dependence on inappropriate, uncritical, habitual reactions. The ways in which teachers change their conceptions of practice can thus be interpreted as an adult learning process characterized by dialectical thinking, reflective judgment, and critical analysis.

2.1 Teaching Style as Practical Theory Development

One useful perspective on the development of teaching style is to interpret this as a process of what has been described as "practical theory development" (Usher and Bryant 1989).

Practical theory originates in situationally based insights regarding problems, tensions, and dilemmas of adult education practice. All practitioners develop informal, contextually grounded theories of practice to help them understand their work environment. Sometimes, however, the opportunity arises to subject such theories to critical analysis. Without this critical analysis informal theories risk remaining at the level of anecdotal, idiosyncratic reminiscence. They are little more than a collection of unconnected experiential travelers' tales from the front lines of practice. Those adult educators who do undertake a critical analysis of their informal theories can accomplish this in two ways. First, they can engage in a form of collaborative experiential scrutiny in which their hunches, instincts, and intuitions (i.e. their informal theories in use) are compared to those of other educators working in similar and allied contexts. Second, these evolving, informal theoretical tenets can be reviewed through the perspectives embedded in formal theories.

Consequently, the process of practical theory development is one in which informal theories are continuously subjected to particular and universal analysis. Particular analysis comprises the experiential comparisons mentioned earlier. Universal analysis comprises the comparison to formal theory. This constant interplay between the particular and the universal can be described as a "reflexive" or dialectical process. The evolution of a teaching style can be viewed as a form of practical theory development in which teachers' methodological preferences and philosophical inclinations are critically reinterpreted over time. Accompanying the recognition that teachers have developed a reliance on habitual ways of practicing, comes the realization that these may not always be appropriate. As teachers encounter the constraints and dilemmas of practice they learn to distrust some of their habitual, instinctive reactions and to adopt a more contextual approach. The development of this kind of insight is a gradual process distinguished by a continual praxis of experimentation, reflection, formal review, and experiential comparison. This is in marked contrast to the idea that style is a stable construct— a fixed pedagogic genetic trait or a way of practicing learned during a period of professional preparation—which is consistently applied to the world of practice.

2.2 Teaching Style and Learning Style

Many analyses of teaching style explore the connections between this concept and that of learning style. Teachers' practices can be reviewed regarding the extent to which these match the various learning styles of their students. Teachers' own teaching styles can also be analyzed for the extent to which they are grounded in their own personal learning styles.

Some interesting work has been done on the intersection of adult teaching styles and adult learning styles (Conti 1985, 1989), particularly the extent to which an andragogical or collaborative style of teaching is most suited to adult learners. Studies have been conducted on whether or not a collaborative teaching style is correlated with higher levels of student attendance (Beder and Carrea 1988), on the extent to which students with certain learning styles deliberately choose certain kinds of educational programs (Loesch and Foley 1988), and on cross-cultural differences and similarities in preferred teaching and learning styles (Pratt 1988). No clearly definitive picture emerges from this research regarding the desirability of matching one uniquely adult teaching style to the diverse styles of adult learners. Indeed, a strong personal and social case can be made that at times it is as important to teach against students' preferred learning styles as it is to teach to them (Brookfield 1990 p. 67–70).

Teachers' own teaching styles can also be investigated regarding the extent to which these develop, sometimes unconsciously, out of teachers' own experiences. Those teachers who study their own histories as learners, and who explore the manner in which their experiences as learners have shaped their practices as teachers, may well be surprised to discover just how much of what they imagined to be their objective, rationally applied pedagogy actually reflects their own autobiographies (Tripp 1987). In fact, one fruitful but neglected approach to faculty development is to encourage teachers to place themselves regularly in the role of a learner who is trying to learn something new and difficult, to reflect on what was affirming and demeaning about this experience, and to review their own teaching practice from this unfamiliar phenomenological perspective (Brookfield 1990 pp. 40–42).

3. Adult Teaching Styles

Although no clearly definitive statement is possible concerning uniquely adult teaching styles, three observations can be made. The first concerns the contextual ambiguity of adult teaching and the essentially fruitless nature of any quest to discover all-embracing, context-free styles. What is likely to be more useful is to study how teachers' styles evolve as a process of practical theory development with emerging insights examined critically through comparison with the experiences of others in allied contexts and reviewed through the perspective of formal theory. Second, analyzing the link between teachers' evolution of certain styles and their own personal histories as learners could reveal some important but hitherto neglected connections. The ways in which teaching styles are influenced by, or are an outgrowth of, teachers' own preferred learning styles is an important area for research. An important practice connection could be the development of inservice and initial preparation programs which use teachers' own experiences of learning as the means for prompting them to review their own teaching practice. Third, of overarching concern to adult learners seem to be the questions of teacher credibility and teacher authenticity. More important to learners than individual variations in teaching role or teachers' styles are the fundamental ethical and moral questions learners ask concerning their teachers: Can I trust this person? What does this person stand for? Is it worth my while being in this person's presence?

4. Teacher Credibility and Authenticity

In an integrative summary of research on the ways in which adults experience formal education (Brookfield 1990) the fundamental significance to learners of teachers being perceived as both credible and authentic was highlighted. It seems as if adults can tolerate wide variations in teaching roles and styles if, at a fundamental level, they trust their teachers to be credible and authentic. In programs of inservice, professional development, and also during periods of initial preparation, much greater attention needs to be paid to helping teachers of adults examine their own practice for the extent to which credibility and authenticity are evident. When learners perceive these qualities to be in place, the trust in teachers that is so fundamental to significant learning stands a much greater chance of being developed.

"Credibility" refers to the sense that learners report of feeling that it is in their own best interests to be in the presence of a particular teacher. Teacher credibility is, not surprisingly, reported to be of greatest significance to those adults for whom a learning activity represents an anxiety-ridden journey into unfamiliar territory. The indicators of credibility most frequently cited by adults are: (a) the teacher's demonstrable subject, content, or skill expertise; (b) the length, breadth, depth, and intensity of a teacher's experience; (c) the sense learners have that a teacher's actions are guided by a well-thought through rationale; and (d) the perception that teachers stand for something, that is, that they have a confident belief in the value of what they teach and the importance of the tasks they ask students to undertake. This emphasis on credibility contradicts much writing on the role of teacher as facilitator, which tends to downplay the significance of the teacher's actions within the learning group, preferring instead to conceptualize the teacher as one among equals. In contrast, the critical animation tradition is one which acknowledges the teacher possessing a declared moral vision, that is, having an explicit commitment to certain social values and political ideals. As Freire comments, adults have a right to expect "critical competence" in their teachers (Shor and Freire 1986 p. 172).

"Authenticity" refers to the sense that students report of perceiving their teachers as being honest and open with them. Five indicators of trustworthy, authentic behaviors that are frequently mentioned are: (a) an observed congruence between teachers' words (especially their espoused philosophical beliefs about education) and their actions; (b) teachers' readiness to allow aspects of their personalities outside of their educational role to show themselves in their practice; (c) a readiness to listen to students' voices and to be open to changing practice as a result of students' suggestions; (d) teachers' attempts to make full, repeated disclosure of their agendas and expectations so that learners do not feel they are subject to arbitrary decisions or evaluative criteria which are kept secret until the last minute; and (e) teachers' readiness to admit to errors. Regarding this last indicator, it is interesting to note the crucial importance of timing for such admissions of teacher error. When teachers speak about their own mistakes, errors, and inadequacies at the outset of a class then students report that their own anxieties are raised to an almost unendurable pitch. However, once students trust the teacher's essential credibility, then perceiving a teacher's fallibility is symbolically powerful for many adults. It induces a sense of relief and release, a feeling that making mistakes is a normal part of learning and that learners do not have to exemplify perfection to gain teacher approval.

Striving to establish credibility and authenticity is both risky and riven with potential contradictions. In overemphasizing the components of their credibility teachers may be perceived as engaging in an arrogant and boastful display of their skill, knowledge, and experience. In striving to be authentic by admitting to error teachers risk leaving students with a perception that the most distinguishing characteristic of their teaching is its ineptness. So of all the complex balances teachers try to attain, maintaining credibility and authenticity in a point of congenial tension is one of the most problematic. However, striving for this balance, even with the realization that it can never be satisfactorily realized, means that adult teachers' efforts stand a much better chance of creating in learners the trust that is such an essential underpinning of significant learning in adulthood.

See also: Adult Learning: An Overview; Individual Differences, Learning, and Instruction; Self-directed Learning; Teaching Methods: General

References

Armstrong P F 1988 L'Ordine Nuovo: The legacy of Antonio Gramsci and the education of adults. *Int. J. Lifelong Educ.* 7(4): 249–59

Beder H, Carrea N 1988 The effects of andragogical teacher training on adult students' attendance and evaluation of their teachers. *Adult Educ. Q.* 38(2): 75–87

Brockett R G, Hiemstra R 1991 *Self-Direction in Adult Learning: Perspectives on Theory, Research and Practice*. Routledge, London

Brookfield S D 1986 *Understanding and Facilitating Adult Learning: A Comprehensive Analysis of Principles and Effective Practices*. Jossey-Bass, San Francisco, California

Brookfield S D 1987 *Developing Critical Thinkers: Challenging Adults to Explore Alternative Ways of Thinking and Acting*. Jossey-Bass, San Francisco, California

Brookfield S D 1988 Conceptual, methodological and practical ambiguities in self-directed learning. In: Long H B (ed.) 1988 *Self-Directed Learning: Application and Theory*. Department of Adult Education, University of Georgia, Athens, Georgia

Brookfield S D 1989 Facilitating adult learning. In: Merriam S B, Cunningham P M (eds.) 1989 *Handbook of Adult and Continuing Education*. Jossey-Bass, San Francisco, California

Brookfield S D 1990 *The Skillful Teacher: On Technique. Trust and Responsiveness in the Classroom*. Jossey-Bass, San Francisco, California

Calderhead J (ed.) 1987 *Exploring Teachers' Thinking*. Cassell, London

Calderhead J (ed.) 1989 *Teachers' Professional Learning*. Falmer Press, London

Candy P C 1991 *Self-Direction for Lifelong Learning: A Comprehensive Guide to Theory and Practice*. Jossey-Bass, San Francisco, California

Collard S, Law M 1991 The impact of critical social theory on adult education: A preliminary evaluation. Proc. Adult Education Research Annual Conference No. 32. Center for Continuing Education, University of Oklahoma, Norman, Oklahoma

Collins M 1991 *Adult Education as Vocation: A Critical Role for the Adult Educator*. Routledge, London

Conti G J 1985 The relationship between teaching style and adult student learning. *Adult Educ. Q.* 35(4): 220–28

Conti G J 1989 Assessing teaching style in continuing education. In: Hayes E (ed.) 1989

Galbraith M W (ed.) 1991 *Facilitating Adult Learning: A Transactional Process*. Krieger, Malabar, Florida

Griffin C 1988 Critical thinking and critical theory in adult education. In: Zukas M (ed.) 1988 *Papers from the Transatlantic Dialogue*. School of Continuing Education, University of Leeds, Leeds

Hartree A 1984 Malcolm Knowles' theory of andragogy: A critique. *Int. J. Lifelong Educ.* 3(3): 203–10

Hayes E (ed.) 1989 *Effective Teaching Styles*. Jossey-Bass, San Francisco, California

Knowles M S (ed.) 1984 *Andragogy in Action*. Jossey-Bass, San Francisco, California

Loesch T, Foley R 1988 Learning preference differences among adults in traditional and nontraditional baccalaureate programs. *Adult Educ. Q.* 38(4): 224–33

Marsick V J 1988 Learning in the workplace: The case for reflectivity and critical reflectivity. *Adult Educ. Q.* 38(4): 187–98

Mezirow J M 1991 *Transformative Dimensions of Adult Learning*. Jossey-Bass, San Francisco, California

Pratt D D 1988 Cross-cultural relevance of selected psychological perspectives on learning. In: Zukas M (ed.) 1988 *Papers from the Transatlantic Dialogue*. School of Continuing Education, University of Leeds, Leeds

Pratt D D 1989 Three stages of teacher competence: A developmental perspective. In: Hayes E (ed.) 1989

Shor I, Freire P 1986 *A Pedagogy for Liberation: Dialogues on Transforming Education* Bergin and Garvey, South Hadley, Massachussetts

Smith R M (ed.) 1990 *Learning to Learn Across the Lifespan*. Jossey-Bass, San Francisco, California

Tennant M 1986 An evaluation of Knowles' theory of adult learning. *Int. J. Lifelong Educ.* 5(2): 113–22

Tripp D H 1987 *Theorizing Practice: The Teacher's Professional Journal*. Deakin University Press, Victoria, Australia

Usher R S, Bryant I 1989 *Adult Education as Theory Practice and Research: The Captive Triangle*. Routledge, London

Teaching Methods: General

M. D. Stephens

In the teaching of adults there is a gap between most practice and fashionable theory. Knowles (1975) stressed that adult education should be learner-centered, not teacher-centered; because the teacher was only one resource among many, he or she should be a facilitator and resource; the teacher and learner should be in partnership with the possibility of formal contracts being made; learning methods should be largely self-directed and draw heavily on the learner's experience; and that the curriculum should be based on issues and problems, rather than academic subjects. In reality most adult education is lecture-based and fixed within the area of a discipline. In the early 1990s, resources and expertise do not yet match the more demanding approach to the teaching of adults. The following themes reflect the state of the art (for it remains far from a science). Besides short descriptions of learning theories and various teaching methods, this entry will also deal with issues and trends in the teaching of adults.

1. Teaching the Adult

It used to be the belief that mental abilities reach a peak of development and then decline. This idea has increasingly been challenged by research (see *Human Development: Aging; Lifespan Development: Intelligence*). For example, there is little evidence to support the contention that in adulthood there is a decrease in the potential for new learning. While physical capacity may decline, learning potential should not. And writers like Mackenzie (1991) have noted there are dangers in taking the average. There is a wide range of individual differences. Some older adults will do better than younger men and women, some will perform less well, and some will be the same.

Success encourages further effort in adults. An ability to master learning material is rewarding, while a teacher's praise can shape further learning. There is also a need to recognize what the adult has acquired from his or her previous, often very rich and extensive experience, and to build upon it. New learning can be negated by apparently being in conflict with things previously learned. Similarly, an adult student's prejudices can get in the way of learning. Many adults also have a fear of failure which may make them try to avoid new learning. As in most things, those who enjoy what they are learning are likely to be the most successful.

There are numerous ways of approaching the characteristics of adult learners. The most effective are usually those based on common sense. For example, Pratt (1988) looked at the teaching of adults in terms of the support and direction they may require and came up with four categories. There are learners who need substantial direction and support; those who just need direction; those who are largely self-directing, but need support; and those who are self-directing and need little support. Of course many adults expect to assume responsibility for themselves, and often find being told what to do by a teacher an unfamiliar experience. They are used to dealing with concrete situations and establishing their own goals. The formal learning situation and its unfamiliarity may lead them to underestimate their own abilities and to display a lack of confidence. Unlike the child at school, the adult usually works at his or her own pace and will tend to react negatively to completing tasks within pressured time. However, the adult learner has a different time perspective to the child, with value given to the more immediate rather than the long-term.

Daines and Graham (1988) make much of the adult student's expectations. Among these they list the fact that many adults expect education to be similar to their school experience where they recall being "talked at" and will assume that such rigid methods are still in use in adult education. They therefore may be surprised when asked to take part in group activities, and to offer their own experiences and knowledge. They will assume that the teacher has a good grasp of his or her subject matter, and that there will be a competent use of a number of teaching approaches and aids. Teacher competence will be anticipated, and he or she will be expected to be a model of good practice. Daines and Graham (1988) suggest that adults expect to be made to work and will be disappointed if they do not achieve something as a result of attending a course. They may complain of the effort demanded of them, but they do not expect adult education to be easy. Few adults attend a class for social reasons alone. They also can be offended if their adult status is not recognized. While they can accept constructive criticism of their performance and progress they are, in certain respects, more sensitive than children and will not tolerate being patronized, or being subjected to harsh criticism or humiliation. They may well react against what they see as neglect by the teacher.

2. Learning Theories Relevant to Choice of Method

What has frequently happened in the education of adults is that experienced teachers seek out learning theories to help justify teaching techniques which they have found to be effective with their students. This is unsurprising as, despite the contribution of the major theories, understanding of the subject has not yet reached a degree of sophistication where a teacher's decision on which teaching method to use is determined more by information on adult learning than the teacher's rule-of-thumb experience. Such learning theories range from Skinner's (1953) work on operant conditioning to Rogers' (1963, 1983) person-centered, humanistic focus, from Maslow's (1968) self-actualization to Wildemeersch's (1991) learning from regularity, irregularity, and responsibility.

Work on the major learning theories and associated teaching methods which had emerged by the mid-1970s was summarized by Entwistle and Hounsell (1975). They saw the humanist theories of Rogers and Maslow supporting the use of leaderless discussion groups, cooperative projects, and the exploratory reading programs, while the cognitive theories of for example, Bruner et al. (1962) would relate to individual project work. Pask and Scott's (1971) work provided information processing theories and would be associated with such techniques as computer-managed learning or handouts and guided reading. Similarly, Skinner's (1953) behaviorist approach would underpin programmed learning methods. Each established or new learning theory can be associated with one or more teaching methods.

Since the 1970s there has been an increasing output of research and information and a tendency for a number of rival camps supporting differing learning theories to emerge. Besides the over-familiar debate about whether adult learning should be differentiated from child learning by using the term (first established in Europe) of "androgogy" rather than "pedagogy," there are also such discussions as the behavioral versus the normative paradigm, or the traditional didactic approach versus the communication model. Innumerable other rivalries are to be found within the theories of adult learning and adult teaching methods. While this points to an encouraging richness of intellectual development, there is much new thinking based on an awareness of the limitations of the human capacity to acquire an overall knowledge of the whole truth and to develop an adequate all-pervading plan for aiding human learning. The most lauded of sciences is only partly aware of the interacting variables in what is a very complex world.

The teaching methods favored on a program can be influenced by the adult's reasons for wanting to learn. These will be complex, but may include being attracted by the qualification offered, a wish to acquire a new skill, to seek intellectual or technical stimulation, or to gain new ideas or, to the contrary, to have prejudices confirmed. A student's motivation may include social considerations such as a desire to join old friends in a class or because he or she is lonely. In teaching, the more information the teacher has about the students the more likely he or she can make effective the adult student's learning.

Adults' motivation can be hindered by a number of considerations over which the teacher is likely to have some impact. Adults do not like to be talked down to as if they were young children in a classroom. However, like children they do respond to encouragement and praise. They must be given realistic goals as morale drops when they fail to make progress. They appreciate individual attention and a good atmosphere in the group. A common problem in adult classes which can undermine morale and lead to irritation is a student who dominates. Teachers are often judged by how well they handle such a problem. Similarly, the course must be well-organized and the environment in which the group meets comfortable. Perhaps the most common compliment about effective teachers of adult classes is that they are "enthusiatic" about their subject. With this normally goes deep interest and concern that the students should share that enthusiasm.

3. Teaching Methods

If possible, before a program begins it is important for the teacher and the adult students to discuss and agree the aims and objectives of the course. The aims of the course will be the general intentions (e.g., the imparting of knowledge, ideas, and information, or to encourage a change in behavior, improve skills, or modify attitudes) while the objectives are the various stages leading to the course aims. The teacher will have to know before each meeting with the students what he or she will want the students to be able to achieve by the end of the session. Such objectives should be easy to assess.

3.1 Teaching Techniques

Teaching techniques themselves come into three broad categories: expository methods where a tutor presents the content to an adult learner (such as a lecture or talk, lecture or talk with group participation, or a demonstration); direction methods where teachers organize and structure a program so the adult learner arrives at a set of predetermined objectives (as with most discussion methods, group tasks and activities, brainstorming, skills practice, buzz groups, question and answer sessions, role playing, and visits and field trips); and discovery methods where the learners pursue a process of intellectual exploration (most notably through self-directed learning, but also through some forms of gaming and simulation). The methods favored will be those which can be matched to the learning which is to be achieved. Usually a mixture of techniques will succeed best with adults so that the student's interest is maintained.

3.2 The Lecture

Despite many critics over the years, the lecture, talk, address, or speech is probably used more than any other vehicle for encouraging learning among adults. This can take many forms besides the one-hour lecture, ranging from the uninterrupted talk, to the lecture with group participation, to coaching and showing, to debate. The appeal of the lecture is that it permits the speaker to present it to a small audience or a large one. There is often an assumption that it is a cheap way of teaching. Unfortunately the stimulus to learning can be very limited, particularly if members of the audience have no opportunity to enter into a discussion on the points made. The forms of teacher presentation which revolve around demostration are invariably more effective and include numerous models from those seen in keep-fit classes to the adult education tutorial class with its small membership (rarely more than 15 students), the presentation of a paper by the teacher for discussion by the students, and directed reading and writing by the students outside of the class time.

3.3 The Discussion

Usually more favored by both teachers and students in adult education have been various forms of discussion. Such discussion groups may be teacher-led, teacher-advised, or without a teacher. All three forms were to be found as early as the nineteenth century. At that time tutorless discussion groups often resulted because there was no teacher available, or the services of a teacher could not be afforded. Often in the twentieth century a formal decision has been taken by the adult students not to have a teacher. These tutorless groups were much explored by students who felt that what was important in their learning was not what they learned, but how they learned it. Another school of thought was taken up with using discussion as a way of releasing and understanding feelings and often a teacher was felt to get in the way rather than help the learning process. Discussion groups can be used just for discussion, or for problem-solving, group tasks and activities, negotiation, skills practice, projects, case studies, role playing, gaming, or simulation. There are specific forms of discussion groups such as those for brainstorming or buzz groups, or of distinctive organization like study circles (see *Study Circles*).

Discussion can deteriorate easily into a somewhat aimless activity. The group purpose needs to be well-defined before it is used as a teaching method. Back-up materials (from books to videotapes) need to be available. Whether there is a teacher or not there remains the problem of encouraging the less articulate, curbing the over-talkative, and ensuring that there are opportunities for discussion.

3.4 Self-directed Learning

There is also independent or individual learning, sometimes called "self-education" or "individual transactions," with its methods of reading, individual practice, various tasks and activities, homework, and such techniques as diary keeping (preferably kept with a specific theme in mind). Such writers as Brookfield (1981) have defined independent learning as that which takes place in the natural societal setting and independent of a teacher's direction or institutional accreditation. Tough (1967, 1980) used the term "self-teaching" for an adult who takes major responsibility for planning his or her learning, and making sure motivation is maintained, and that all things necessary for learning success are covered (see *Self-directed Learning*).

3.5 Good Practice

Good practice in all forms of adult education seems generally agreed and international in its acceptance. For example, the learning situation created, whatever it is, should take account of individual differences within the adult students. The adult student's present knowledge and attitudes must be taken into account, and the learner must be motivated to learn. It is best if the learning situation gives scope for practice and for the learning to be reinforced. The adult student should be an active participant in the learning, that is, not just a listener. The learning to be covered should be in paced and digestible amounts. The learning should be meaningful to the adult student. Even for the self-directed learner, coaching and guidance is of value in the acceptance of new theories, ideas, and information.

There is a rich array of other than human learning resources available in the teaching of adults. Written resources range from books and articles to promotional material, catalogs, photocopies, handouts, and newspapers. Many classes need to be enriched by bringing in specimens, samples, and models. A policeman explaining his job to a class studying local crime should enhance an adult learner's understanding and provide that element of variety which helps to avoid a group becoming stale.

Local or national events should also be seen as learning resources available to the adult student. The list is potentially enormous and covers visits, conferences, exhibitions, field trips, sports events, cinemas, theaters, public lectures, social gatherings, and so on. Most areas of interest to the adult learner will have some public function available which can be used to enrich a course.

In his article on "The Psychological Characteristics of Students in Adult Colleges and Universities" in China, Zhao An Xiang (1992) notes that adult students have strong views on all kinds of things, and rarely follow others blindly. They like querying things, and want to know why, as well as what. They appraise teachers according to both their words and actions. They dislike teaching methods which attempt to cram students with information, but like discussion and heuristic (i.e., allowing or assisting to discover) techniques. Adults favor absorbing theoretical knowledge according to their work experience. Such students have well-developed abilities in observation, analysis, and solving problems, and are rich in life experience. The things they meet they think about and compare with what they already know. They observe matters from all sides, sum up while drawing on their experience, and then make a judgment of their own. They usually have strong self-esteem and often dislike answering questions in class, preferring to exchange what they have learned in discussion.

4. Audiovisual Aids

The technology which has become available to adult educators since the 1960s is impressive. As always there is a need to retain those aids which have worked well in the past while taking advantage of new possibilities. Adults are more likely to learn effectively if more than one sense is utilized. While hearing is the sense most used, this dominance needs to be challenged by the adult student having much to see. In some adult classes, smell and taste can also be important in the pursuit of learning.

Where distance education has developed, most findings suggest that a complete reliance upon radio and television broadcasts does not lead to substantial learning. The ideas on correspondence education which

first appeared in the nineteenth century have continued to provide the most effective material for distance learners. A majority of schemes use broadcasts as a supplement to the printed material and exercises sent to the student by post. Similarly, effort is made to have local centers to which the distance education student may go for some face-to-face teaching. In an institution such as Japan's University of the Air the broadcasts act as audiovisual aids.

Although television represents a highly sophisticated form of audiovisual aid the teacher of adults is more likely to use other ones to help people learn. Such aids must not get in the way of the adult student's understanding so usually those which are clear and simple are best. Daines and Graham (1988) list writing boards, charts, posters, diagrams, flip charts, display boards, flannel boards, magnetic boards, tape recorders, record players, radios, televisions, video recorders, slide projectors, film projectors, overhead projectors, epidiascopes, and microscopes. These are usually easy to make or readily available. The invention of the overhead projector and its wide dissemination has made the presentation of such things as figures on a transparency much easier and usually less crude than earlier technology such as the chalk board or the flip chart.

For those who teach adults in well-resourced institutions such as universities the range of audiovisual aids available will be much more extensive and will include computer-assisted instruction, developments in programmed learning, and gaming simulation. However, when planning adult learning the choice of audiovisual aids has to be carefully integrated. The use of, say, computer-assisted instruction can become a rival diversion to the adult learners. It is easy to swamp a session with an inept use of audiovisual aids so that the learning objectives are lost.

5. Evaluation and Assessment

A belief that course evaluation is a key element in the planning of any adult education is now common in many countries. Alongside the evaluation of the course there should be an assessment of the adult student's learning and the teacher's teaching. The questions such evaluations and assessments attempt to answer include: have the course aims and objectives been fulfilled? Have the students achieved substantial learning and their needs and wants been met? Was the program well planned, and managed? Did the teacher display good practice? Was there plenty of feedback? Was it time well-spent and resources well-used? Within such evaluation and assessment the choice of teaching methods and their effective use hold a central role.

The use of evaluation and assessment is a teaching method in itself. The adult students should be involved in the process as it provides opportunities for learning of notable importance. While most adults are reluctant to discuss directly the teacher's role they will respond to questions about what they liked on the program, or those aspects which could usefully be changed. Too often requests for direct criticism will lead the adult learner to speak only of the good points. Anonymous reports from members of a group at the end of a course can be helpful. Such questionnaires can invite the adult student to make any comments he or she wishes, or can include responses to a series of carefully worded items of the style: "I found the most useful/least useful part of the course to be . . ."

A final evaluation session can be a helpful way to introduce adult students to unfamiliar teaching methods such as buzz groups (where the group is divided up into subgroups or pairs to discuss briefly a topic, having the great advantage of involving all the students), brainstorming (where the class pools its ideas), or small groups reporting back. Self-evaluation, with carefully agreed questions, can also be a useful exercise for adult learners.

6. Conclusion

When advising on the complex issue of effectively teaching adults there is a need to generalize. Alas, each adult, whether student or teacher, is a unique assemblage of characteristics. This being the case there are no universal methods of teaching adults. Each different technique can be appropriate on the right occasion. Even the often maligned one-hour lecture well-presented at the opportune moment has inspired adults to pursue a lifetime's study of a particular subject. As has already been noted, usually a variety of methods helps to maintain interest and motivation. Used with imagination such teaching methods will let the adult student listen, look, talk, and practice, and thus ensure effective learning.

See also: Individual Differences, Learning, and Instruction; Development of Learning Across the Lifespan; Study and Learning Strategies; Teaching Methods: Individual Techniques

References

Brookfield S D 1981 Independent adult learning. *Stud. Adult Educ.* 13(1): 15–27

Bruner J S, Goodnow J T, Austin G A 1962 *A Study of Thinking.* John Wiley, New York

Daines J, Graham T B 1988 *Adult Learning: Adult Teaching.* University of Nottingham, Department of Adult Education, Nottingham

Entwistle N, Hounsell D (eds.) 1975 *How Students Learn.* University of Lancaster, Lancaster

Knowles M 1975 *Self-directed Learning: A Guide for Learners and Teachers.* Associated Press, Chicago, Illinois

Mackenzie A M 1991 *Adult Age Differences in Memory.* University of Nottingham, Department of Adult Education, Nottingham

Maslow A H 1968 *Toward a Psychology of Being*, 2nd edn. Van Nostrand, New York

Pask G, Scott B C E 1971 Learning strategies and individual competence. *International Journal of Man-Machine Studies* 4(3): 217–53

Pratt D D 1988 Andragogy as a relational construct. *Adult Educ. Q.* 38(3): 160–72

Rogers C R 1963 *Freedom to Learn.* Constable, London

Rogers C R 1983 *Freedom to Learn for the Eighties*, rev. edn. Merrill, Columbus, Ohio

Skinner B F 1953 *Science and Human Behaviour.* Macmillan, New York

Tough A M 1967 *Learning Without a Teacher: A Study of Tasks and Assistance during Adult Self-teaching Projects.* Ontario Institute for Studies in Education, Toronto

Tough A M 1980 *Expand Your Life.* College Entrance Examination Board, New York

Wildemeersch D 1991 Learning from regularity, irregularity and responsibility. *Int. J. Lifelong Educ.* 10(2): 151–58

Zhao A X 1992 The psychological characteristics of students in adult colleges and universities. In: Zhang X D, Stephens M D (eds.) 1992 *Adult Higher Education in China.* Shandong Publishing Company, Jinan

Further Reading

Bornstein M H, Bruner J S (ed.) 1989 *Interaction in Human Development.* Erlbaum, Hillsdale, New Jersey

Engestrom Y 1987 *Learning by Expanding.* Orienta-Konsultit Oy, Helsinki

Gagné R 1985 *The Conditions of Learning and Theory of Instruction*, 4th edn. Holt, Reinhart and Winston, New York

Hiemstra R, Sisco B 1990 *Individualizing Instruction: Making Learning Personal, Empowering and Successful* Jossey-Bass, San Francisco, California

Rogers A 1986 *Teaching Adults.* Open University Press, Milton Keynes

Stephens M D 1991 *Education and the Future of Japan.* The Japan Library, Sandgate

Walkin L 1990 *Teaching & Learning in Further & Adult Education.* Stanley Thornes, London

Teaching Methods: Individual Techniques

A. J. Romiszowski

It could be said that all learning is individual. After all, nobody, not even teachers, can learn in place of a learner. Teachers can, however, help learners to learn, and in a variety of ways. They may offer guidance or counseling, remove obstacles to efficient learning, or provide extra resources. To the extent that they do this on a differentiated, individual basis, their teaching methodology can be said to be individualized.

In preindustrial society, most teaching was individualized. In the nineteenth and twentieth centuries, however, the majority of instruction ceased to be one-to-one, or based on small groups, and became based instead on large groups. It became increasingly difficult for teachers to give individual attention to every learner, and this situation gave rise to a search for new systems of instruction to facilitate the individual treatment of individuals.

Arguments for breaking down uniformity of instruction also gained support from research on individual differences and the development of instruments for measuring human abilities. It became clear that students differ not only in intelligence, but also in creativity (Wallach and Kogan 1965), and in various elements of intellect (Guilford 1967). It also emerged that great differences between competence and performance are possible, and that inequalities in intellect, physical ability, and social behavior—marked in childhood—increase as students move through the grades (Thomas and Thomas 1965).

In the 1970s and 1980s further support for individual treatment of individual learners came from several areas. Theoretical studies on the special characteristics of the adult learner led to an increasing emphasis on involving learners in the planning and direction of their own learning programs (Knowles 1975). Practical issues of delivering quality instruction to an ever-growing population of students led to the increasing use of peer tutoring as an individualization strategy (Goodlad and Hirst 1989). Growth in the acceptance of theories (or, rather, philosophies) of learning such as reflection-in-action (Schon 1991), situated cognition (Collins et al. 1989, Streibel 1991) and constructivism (Duffy and Jonassen 1991) has emphasized the role of learners as individual "creators" of knowledge. It is fostering a "minirevolution" in the design and development of learning materials, particularly computer-based courseware.

1. Approaches to Individualization

1.1 Early Examples

The development of individualized instructional programs began in the latter part of the nineteenth century (Harris 1960), since when an increasing number of programs allowing for differences among students have been proposed and developed (De Haan and Doll 1964, Shane 1962). In the United States Search had initiated the Pueblo Plan by 1888, a laboratory scheme permitting students to pace their own coverage of their course (Search 1894). Parkhurst's (1922) Dalton Laboratory Plan presented self-instructional units that students worked through at their own pace. In the United Kingdom elements of individualization were introduced as early as the eighteenth century, with the monitorial system and a variety of peer-tutoring schemes (Salmon 1932).

1.2 Self-instructional Approaches to Individualization

With the boom of programmed instruction in the early 1960s another interpretation of individualization began, as self-paced individual study of prescribed material (usually common to all students in a group). This trend continued with the development of computer-based learning systems, which started as drill-and-practice programs covering routine skills and progressed to more sophisticated "programmed tutorial" courseware and thereafter to computer-based systems that simulate real-life situations, such as the science laboratory or business and social problems. In the early 1990s computer-based "conversational tutorials" were developed, which enabled the simulation of the open one-to-one tutorial situation where both participants may initiate interactions (Romiszowski and Chang 1992).

Another development is hypertext or hypermedia, which utilizes the power of computers and telecommunications to give the individual learner access to a network of information, so designed that each user will be able to access material that is: (a) relevant to that individual's current interests; (b) as detailed or general as the individual desires; and (c) supported by as much background or prerequisite information as the individual needs in order to understand fully the topic of interest (see Jonassen and Mandl 1990).

This trend is apparently based on popular learning-theory positions, such as learner control and constructivism. In practice, however, the development of a hypermedia knowledge base on a subject is closer to librarianship than to teaching. It focuses on "facilitating access to information" rather than on "causing learning to occur." In the long term, hypermedia information systems will probably be seen for what they are: as a possible element in an individualized teaching system, but not as a complete teaching system in their own right. It is possible, however, that a fusion of work on hypermedia systems with work on conversational tutorial systems may provide a basis for a new generation of powerful, media-based, individualized teaching systems.

1.3. Group-instructional Approaches to Individualization

Another category of approaches to individualization has been the utilization of techniques that may make the conventional teaching process more responsive to the needs of individual students. Techniques such as independent study, project-based work, small-group activities, and student-directed learning have been implemented in a variety of different ways, following a variety of different educational philosophies.

Many specific types of group situations have

been developed with the individual in mind. An early example is the "T-group", which is used to enable individuals to learn to react appropriately to other individuals (Lewin 1952). Role-playing and other simulation techniques have been employed in a variety of contexts as a way of involving all the individuals in a group and building on the individual personal experience of the participants (Megarry 1979, Greenblat and Duke 1981). Games are now commonly employed as instructional techniques, not only in elementary schools, but throughout the school system, into university, business, and the professions (Ellington et al. 1984, Christopher and Smith 1987). A well-structured instructional game ensures that each individual engages in learning-directed activities, while involved in a group situation.

The adult learning movement, with its emphasis on self-directed learning, offered yet another methodology for individualization in the form of "learning contracts" (Knowles 1975). A learning contract is an individually "negotiated" agreement between learner and teacher, defining the objectives, methods and resources, timelines, evaluation criteria, and methods of a proposed course of study. Learning contracts introduce elements of "management by objectives" into the context of learning and teaching. The implementation of individualized teaching, based on learning contracts, follows a cyclical instructional process model and utilizes a variety of student-completed instrumentation for course planning, control, and evaluation (see Hiemstra and Sisco 1990).

Yet another growing trend has been toward the organization of individualized teaching by sharing the responsibility for teaching with the learners, through a variety of peer-tutoring methodologies. Goodlad and Hirst (1989) traced the origins of peer tutoring back to the eighteenth century and earlier in British education, and outlined the growth of this approach in the United States in the twentieth century, both in terms of frequency of utilization and increasing sophistication and systematization of the approaches and models employed.

2. Classifying Approaches to Individualization

With so many approaches to the individualization of instruction, it is useful to develop a way of classifying and describing them. Four relevant questions can be asked of any teaching model that purports to be individualized: (a) What aspects are in fact individualized? (b) When (at what level) does the course adapt to the individual? (c) Who decides? (d) How does the system adapt to the individual?

2.1 What may be Individualized?

Some of the more obvious and more important characteristics that may be individualized include:

(a) pace of study: students may be constrained to learn at a predetermined pace, or they may be allowed to work at varying paces;

(b) materials or media: students may be allowed to choose alternative versions of a lesson in different media.

(c) methods of study: students may receive alternative lessons differing in the instructional strategy and/or in the detailed tactics of instruction.

(d) content of study: students may receive alternative lesson content, either as a means of tailoring a course to the individual's own objectives or as a means of selecting material familiar or interesting to the individual;

(e) objectives of study: course objectives may be varied in order to adapt courses to the different aptitudes of individuals or their different needs;

(f) evaluation methods: different students may be assigned (or may select) different tasks to demonstrate what they have learned;

(g) evaluation criteria: different students may elect to aim for different levels of mastery of a skill, or coverage of a domain of knowledge, and would therefore be evaluated according to different sets of standards.

2.2 When does Individualization Take Place?

The present author (Romiszowski 1984) has suggested a four-level model of classification, depending on whether individualization decisions are taken:

(a) at the course level: do students simply exercise their option to take or not to take a given course? —this is a characteristic of most credit-unit systems, as in United States degree courses, for example;

(b) at the course unit level: options are offered in terms of the overall objectives, the overall study methods, and the resources, to suit the individual needs, interests, or abilities of the participants;

(c) at the lesson level: sequence, content, amount of practice, and media, may be individualized;

(d) at the individual exercise or step level: this is a feature of fully interactive instructional systems.

2.3 Who Decides?

The decisions to individualize may be taken by:

(a) the students themselves, when they choose a particular course option or a particular textbook;

(b) the teacher, who may prescribe individual objectives or media or extra content;

(c)   an automated system, which may have built into it a diagnostic device that automatically adapts the presentation to the individual student;

(d)   any combination of the above: this is the negotiated situation, involving a joint decision between student and teacher, taken in the context of information generated by the system.

2.4 How Does the System Adapt to the Individual?

Two factors are identified as of importance: first, the style and type of instructional materials employed in the system, and the way in which the learners select and have access to the materials; second, the role of the tutor or instructor (if there is one) in the system, both as a medium of instruction and as a medium for management and control.

It is apparent that there are innumerable different ways of answering the "how" question. In practice, a reply generally requires a detailed description of the system in question. The "what," "when," and "who" questions may, however, be used to compare the general structure and philosophy of different systems of individualized teaching, before embarking on the detailed analysis of the "how" (see Romiszowski 1984 for examples).

3. Successes and Failures of Individualization

Many specific plans and systems for individualization have been devised and implemented since the 1960s. Most of these have not withstood the test of time.

Individually Prescribed Instruction (IPI) was a widely implemented plan that utilized carefully designed diagnostic tests to select specific modules of programmed self-instructional materials for individual students. It was the basis of a long-term research program of the University of Pittsburgh, which demonstrated the effectiveness and the efficiency of the plan as compared to most conventional approaches to the teaching of mathematics. However, by the 1980s very few American schools were utilizing the IPI materials and methods.

Project PLAN was an ambitious project that intended to apply the power of the computer to the management of individualized classroom-based instruction across the whole of the United States. Launched in 1967, it had almost completely disappeared from American schools by the early 1970s, when funding ran out. It is surprising, however, that it has not been revived now that the computing and telecommunications power necessary to make it operational are infinitely cheaper than when the project started.

Other plans of the 1970s also vanished without a trace through the 1980s. A variety of "learning resource centers" in the United States and "learning by appointment centres" in the United Kingdom

flourished for a decade but then experienced a decline. Other innovative plans, such as the "Learning Activity Pack" (LAP) movement, the Audio-tutorial method and the highly individualized and well-designed Swedish "IMU" system of mathematics teaching all flourished briefly, only to sink into oblivion.

A plan that showed particular promise was the so-called Personalized System of Instruction (PSI), or more colloquially the "Keller Plan." Keller developed a system for the teaching of his undergraduate psychology courses that was a combination of modularized self-study materials and peer teaching (Keller and Sherman 1974). The plan, first developed in the United States, was most successfully implemented and disseminated in Brazil, whence it spread to most Latin American countries.

The overall philosophical model underlying the system was "mastery learning." Students would work through a sequence of modules, achieving minimum criteria of mastery on one module before proceeding to the next. The course teacher would evaluate and if necessary tutor the faster students to help them achieve mastery and would then employ them as peer tutors to help the slower students (Keller 1968, Keller and Sherman 1974).

The effectiveness of the Keller Plan was demonstrated in many experimental applications. Interest grew throughout the 1970s to the extent that, in several countries (notably Brazil and Venezuela), whole departments and even whole universities remodeled themselves to operate according to this plan (Sherman 1974). It is interesting to speculate why, in the 1990s, hardly any trace of the Keller Plan survives in North American higher education, or in other countries that adopted it enthusiastically in the 1970s.

The reasons for so many failures may be related to the philosophies underlying the individualization plans of earlier decades. The move toward learner-directed learning as opposed to system-prescribed learning inevitably made obsolete several of the earlier plans. Equally, the reasons may in part be administrative, related to the transient nature of funding for special projects in education. However, it is significant that very few of them built up sufficient momentum and grass-roots acceptance to become an integral part of the educational landscape. Finally, some of the reasons may be systemic, attributable to the resistant nature of most systems, including educational ones, when faced with innovation and change.

Several new individualization projects do appear to be taking root. In the United States in the name of "restructuring the school system," a host of mainly technology-based, instructional innovations are being developed and experimentally implemented, many financed by a consortium of private businesses that have founded the New American Schools Development Corporation (Rundell 1992). The leading computer manufacturers—Apple, Amiga, and IBM in particular—are promoting "interactive multimedia" as the new road to educational excellence through individualization. In a similar way, the DELTA initiative in Europe is placing many of its eggs in the information technology basket.

Will these new technological initiatives succeed where many of the earlier plans and systems largely failed? Or, as Hiemstra and Sisco (1990) suggested, is the route to individual treatment of the individual learner rather to be achieved through improvement of the skills of the teaching profession in the area of "making learning personal, empowering and successful"? Finally as Boud (1988) suggested, is the most effective route, at least in part, to be sought through improving the skills of the learners themselves and empowering them to exercise their options as autonomous participants in the teaching–learning process?

It is probable that successful and long-term educational innovations will be based on a combination of these three strands of current developments. How to interweave them in order to create a permanent improvement in the fabric of education will also depend on the ability of planners to adopt a systemic view of the complexity that faces them and implement a systematic strategy of planned change.

See also: Approaches to Learning; Development of Learning Across the Lifespan; Individual Differences, Learning, and Instructional Design: Guidelines and Theories; Instructional Design: Models; Program Design: Effectiveness; Teacher Roles and Teaching Styles

References

Boud D J (ed.) 1988 *Developing Student Autonomy in Learning*, 2nd edn. Kogan Page, London
Christopher E M, Smith L E 1987 *Leadership Training Through Gaming: Power, People and Problem Solving*. Nichols, New York
Collins A, Brown J S, Newman S E 1989 Cognitive apprenticeship: Teaching the crafts of reading, writing, and mathematics. In: Resnick L B (ed.) 1989 *Knowing, Learning, and Instruction: Essays in Honor of Robert Glaser*. Erlbaum, Hillsdale, New Jersey
De Haan R F, Doll R C 1964 Individualization and human potential. In: Doll R C (ed.) 1964 *Individualizing Instruction*. Association for Supervision and Curriculum Development, Washington, DC
Duffy T M, Jonassen D H 1991 Constructivism: New implications for instructional technology? *Educ. Technol.* 31(5): 7–12
Ellington H I, Addinall E, Percival F 1984 *Case Studies in Game Design*. Kogan Page, London
Goodlad S, Hirst B 1989 *Peer Tutoring: A Guide to Learning by Teaching*. Kogan Page, London

Greenblat C S, Duke R D 1981 *Principles and Practice of Gaming-Simulation*. Sage, Beverly Hills, California
Guilford J P 1967 *The Nature of Human Intelligence*. McGraw-Hill, New York
Harris C W (ed.) 1960 *Encyclopaedia of Educational Research*. Macmillan Inc., New York
Hiemstra R, Sisco B 1990 *Individualizing Instruction: Making Learning Personal, Empowering, and Successful*. Jossey Bass, San Francisco, California
Jonassen D H, Mandl H (eds.) 1990 *Designing Hypermedia for Learning*. Springer-Verlag, Berlin
Keller F S 1968 Goodbye teacher. *J. Appl. Behav. Anal.* 1: 79–89
Keller F S, Sherman J G 1974 *The Keller Plan Handbook: Essays on a Personalized System of Instruction*. Benjamins, Merlo Park, California
Knowles M S 1975 *Self-Directed Learning: A Guide for Learners and Teachers* Association Press, New York
Lewin K 1952 *Field Theory in Social Science: Selected Theoretical Papers*. Tavistock Publications, London
Megarry J 1979 Developments in simulation and gaming. In: Howe A, Romiszowski A J (eds.) 1979 *International Yearbook of Educational and Instructional Technology 1978/79*. Kogan Page, London
Parkhurst H 1922 *Education on the Dalton Plan*. Chivers, Bath
Romiszowski A J 1984 *Producing Instructional Systems: Lesson Planning for Individualized and Group Learning Activities* Kogan Page, London
Romiszowski A J, Chang E 1992 Hypertext's contribution to computer-mediated communication: In search of an instructional model. In: Giardina M (ed.) 1992 *Interactive Multimedia Learning Environments: Human factors and Technical Considerations on Design Issues*. Springer-Verlag, Berlin
Rundell C R 1992 To start a school: NASDC as a catalyst for systemic change. *Educ. Technol.* 32(11)
Salmon D (ed.) 1932 *The Practical Parts of Lancaster's "Improvements and Bells Experiment"*. Cambridge University Press, Cambridge
Schon D A 1991 *The Reflective Practitioner: How Professionals Think in Action*. Avebury, Aldershot
Search P 1894 The Pueblo Plan of individual teaching. *Educational Review* 8
Shane H G 1962 The school and individual differences. In: Henry N B (ed.) 1962 *Individualizing Instruction*. University of Chicago Press, Chicago, Illinois
Sherman J G 1974 PSI Personalized System of Instruction: 41 Germinal Papers. Benjamins, Merlo Park, California
Streibel M J 1991 Instructional plans and situated learning: The challenge of Suchman's theory of situated action for instructional designers and instructional systems. In: Anglin G J (ed.) 1991 *Instructional Technology: Past, Present and Future*. Libraries Unlimited, Englewood, Colorado
Thomas R M, Thomas S M 1965 *Individual Differences in the Classroom*. McKay, New York
Wallach M A, Kogan N 1965 *Modes of Thinking in Young Children*. Holt, Rinehart and Winston, New York

Training of Adult Educators

P. Jarvis and A. Chadwick

The form and structure of adult education is diffuse; some of it is controled by the professions and occupations, some established by the state, some organized by voluntary groups, and so on. Consequently, the training of adult educators is not systematized in any country, as Jarvis and Chadwick (1991) show for Western Europe. While much of the material for this entry is drawn from the above study, reference is made beyond Europe in order to demonstrate both the complexity of the situation and some of the issues involved in it.

This entry commences with a brief history of training in the United Kingdom where the efforts to introduce training have been sustained for more than half a century. Thereafter, the second section deals with different types of training and trainees; the third examines licensing and qualifications; and the final section considers some of the trends that emerge.

It will be seen in this entry that both the theory of adult education and training in teaching skills are included. The former is as prevalent as the latter and this may be due to the significant and growing role the universities have played over time.

1. History of Training

The origins of adult education inevitably differ from country to country both in chronology and focus, although some transnational influences of varying authenticity may be discerned. Similarly, any consideration of formally provided training programs must recognize a similar pattern, while acknowledging the existence of informal "self-help" training.

In some countries, the provision of training courses for adult educators commenced in the period following the Second World War. In Norway, for example: "Since the late 1950's the training of adult educators has been continuously discussed . . . leaders of adult education realised the needs for providing training for workers in the field, and thus also for establishing adult education as an academic discipline" (Brattset 1991 p. 173).

If vocational education in the United States is taken into account, problems associated with vocational education and training were being addressed as early as the 1870s. From 1914–17, vocational training received a boost from the federal government through the Smith-Lever Act of 1917, for example, which established agricultural extension. Under such momentum, irrespective of a comparable lack of support for liberal studies, vocational training for adults "became in a short time the principal constituent of adult education" (Grattan 1959).

Houle (1964) notes that Teachers College, Columbia University, introduced the first graduate programs in the United States in the early 1930s. Nevertheless, opportunities for training adult educators up to and including the 1940s were few in the United States, leading a contemporary observer to indicate "that the present rewards for service in this field do not encourage training programs" (Starr 1943 p. 90). Training courses in existence at that time were chiefly concerned with agricultural extension workers, although Houle is quoted as suggesting that other kinds of adult education, as they expanded, might well attack the problem of training "by developing an integrated program of preservice, induction and in-service education" (Starr 1943 p. 91).

It is, however, from the United Kingdom that the following illustrations are drawn because it has a long history of training for adult educators. The first comprehensive steps concerning the training of tutors were taken during the 1920s and 1930s. Those practitioners with managerial responsibility were to wait until the recent past for recognition of their training requirements.

"All the evidence . . . suggests the need for some definite provision for the training of tutors for adult classes." Thus opens the chapter on the training of tutors in an important 1928 report *The Tutor in Adult Education* (The British Institute of Adult Education and the Tutor's Association 1928 p. 62). There is some evidence to suggest that the earliest formal provision of training for adult educators had taken place nearly 200 years earlier under the overall guidance of Griffiths Jones, founder of the Welsh circulating charity schools (Kelly 1950 p. 42). However, the first major perception of the value of training which formally recognized the importance of both content *and* process skills was that suggested in the influential "*1919 Report*" (Ministry of Reconstruction 1919 pp. 137–39).

This led to the production of a 1921 report which concluded that universities should arrange training courses "in the preparation of material, the practice of lecturing, and the conduct of classes and discussion" (Board of Education 1921 p. 20). The 1928 report, financially assisted by the Carnegie United Kingdom Trustees, provided a substantial stimulus to the topic. However, by 1934 it was asserted that: "Very little has been done hitherto in the way of providing specific courses for the training of tutors engaged in adult education" (Silverman 1934 p. 180). Nevertheless, a number of experiments in training tutors were undertaken, with the emphasis being placed more on subject knowledge than on teaching methods. Among principal experiments in the provision of formal training courses was an Oxford University three-week course held in 1926. The program included "lectures on the principles of teaching, practice classes and group meetings for instruction in the drafting of syllabuses, in the preparation of lectures etc." (Silverman 1934 p. 187).

Other courses included a summer school for training tutors which first commenced in 1920 and was provided by the Workers' Educational Association under the supervision of an Oxford University Board of Studies. The Association of Tutors in Adult Education organized a course in 1932 which, although deemed to have been successful by participants, met with a degree of criticism by those members of the Association who viewed the outcome of a formal training scheme as stereotyping teaching methods. It should be added that the full-time training courses offered during this period were those held by the then University College, Nottingham, which offered a certificate and a one-year graduate Diploma in Adult Education, albeit with few applicants. The courses ceased with the advent of the Second World War.

At this stage in the development of training in the United Kingdom it was conceded "that the whole problem of training for adult education is one of some difficulty, and the work is still at the experimental stage" (Silverman 1934 p. 187). Yet there were opportunities for further initiatives and the Association of Tutors in Adult Education, despite misgivings in some quarters, had cooperated with the British Institute of Adult Education to produce the 1928 report identified above. It also produced material for use by tutors and students such as bibliographies in a range of subjects, co-published a series of introductory books, and produced teaching aids. By 1944, the Association was able to declare "that there is widespread agreement amongst both tutors and the bodies concerned with adult educational provision as to the need for the training of tutors, both those working full-time and those working part-time." Furthermore, the majority of tutors "have had no formal training and have had to find their way to a more or less adequate technique by a lengthy and arduous process of trial and error" (Executive Committee of the Association of Tutors 1944 p. 21). A recommendation was made that three types of training course be offered, namely a full-time course for intending full-time teachers of adults, a part-time course for intending teachers, and a part-time course for "occasional speakers and pioneer lecturers."

Despite the sanguinity of the Association's pronouncement, a high degree of skepticism and hostility remained regarding the training of teachers in adult education. Adult educators were assumed to be born not made, and training in methodological skills was thought, at best, to be unnecessary. Therefore, the debate surrounding the value of training was to continue into the 1950s. A number of perennial concerns such as the "status" of the work, employment prospects,

and training which could create an over-formal rigidity and too systematic approach have continued to be discussed. Yet a Ministry of Education pamphlet issued in 1947 observed that there was scope for full- and part-time teachers of adults to undertake short courses in teaching methods; furthermore, the Ministry of Education wished to encourage an expansion of such courses which had been run by local education authorities and the universities.

One early initiative in the immediate postwar period commenced in 1949 where a University of Manchester course of 20 meetings on teaching adults attracted a wide variety of participants. It was to be held annually thereafter. This series was to lead to the provision of a certificate course in 1955, and a Diploma in Adult Education as from 1961. This course was followed by a similar offer from Nottingham some five years later.

Simultaneously, opportunities for the wider preparation of and support for adult educators were still slowly developing, if only through occasional one-day or weekend schools or summer school provision (Legge 1951 p. 1).

Despite continuing opposition, the rise in the number of full-time teachers in the further education sector provided a momentum for training. During the 1950s and 1960s, the City and Guilds of London Institute began to contribute to the training of adult educators through a series of certificates such as the Technical Teachers Certificate in 1953 and the Further Education Teachers Certificate in 1968. These awards were to lead to the current provision of the Further and Adult Education Teachers Certificate.

Other influences for the development of training provision came from the youth service where the Albemarle Reports of 1960 and 1966 advocated systematic methodological training, and from the four technical teacher-training colleges in Bolton, Huddersfield, London, and Wolverhampton. Similarly, Her Majesty's Inspectorate, through a group of specialists, produced a number of surveys and, in 1963–64, undertook a national enquiry of full- and part-time training for teachers of adults. A Department of Education and Science report, produced in 1965, was made available to universities in the United Kingdom and the Workers' Educational Association. Reference was made to it in the National Institute of Adult Education's 1966 "Recruitment and Training" enquiry. Elsdon (1975) notes that a similarly important exercise was the international course on the status, recruitment, and professional training of workers in adult education promoted by the Council of Cultural Co-operation of the Council of Europe in 1965. The reports emanating from this course "influenced administrative and field practice through participants and readers both in England and abroad; training schemes in Belgium, Denmark, Germany, Holland, Switzerland, and to some extent in France, as well as in England, bear a clear relationship to the Reports' recommendations . . . it was the first official report to lend its support to the concept that the training of all teachers should be broadened to secure a further understanding of the links and continuity in education from the schools to, and across, the whole of the post-school education field" (Elsdon 1975 p. 18).

In 1973 a report on adult education recognized that there had been a "commendable development" of training specifically for work in adult education, but echoed the view expressed almost 40 years earlier that training was still "only at an experimental stage." Nevertheless, the authors of the report recommended a number of developments by which training could be furthered (Department of Education and Science 1973).

During the 1970s, a series of reports emanating from the Advisory Committee for the Supply and Training of Teachers (ACSTT) addressed full-time and part-time teachers and, unusually, those with managerial responsibilities (ACSTT 1975, 1978a, 1978b). During this period, a key volume was published (Elsdon 1975) in which training was discussed within a framework of practice, philosophy, structure, and organization, which usefully widened the debate through references to texts drawn from various parts of the world.

The growth of training provision has been characterized by its slow pace, varying degrees of opposition, and lack of resources. There has also been a growing belief that the importance attached to assisting adults to learn can bring with it a recognition that the adult educator can become a more effective practitioner as a result of training (Graham et al. 1982 p. 195). Some of the major elements associated with training are discussed below.

2. Form and Structure of Training

The types of training for educators of adults are as diverse as the practice of educating adults, and the extent to which adult education as a single profession is debatable. Indeed, it is probably best regarded as a functional occupation which may be practiced in a variety of different occupations and professions, including medicine, nursing, and engineering (Legge 1982). Hence there are educators of adults practicing as vocational educators, human resource developers, trainers, and even teacher practitioners; some, but by no means all, of these groups receive preparation for their teaching role to a certain extent.

However, the introduction of training has not been particularly straightforward because the study of the field of practice was contemporaneous with the actual training for practice; indeed, the study of the field was sometimes regarded as an aspect of the training. This study probably began in the United Kingdom and the United States long before the pedagogic element was introduced, since some of the universities introduced award-bearing courses, such as diplomas and masters degrees, many years before there was a great deal of preparation for the teaching of adults. One of the reasons for this was the assumption that anybody could teach provided that they were qualified in their subject. Such a view is still to be found in a number of countries in the world, and with politicians in almost all countries. It is only more recently that the actual techniques of teaching have begun to play a more significant role in training.

As a result of early initiatives in studying the field rather than in teaching about the educational processes, four distinct forms of training can now be distinguished: training in the performance of the educational functions, such as teaching techniques; curriculum and program planning; academic study of the field, usually for a diploma or a higher degree; a combination of the two previous forms; and research and development. However, there are a number of other variables in this analysis: the training might be full-time or part-time, conducted as pre-service or inservice, organized at the local level or at a regional or national one, organized by an adult educational organization or by a vocational or professional body, and certified or uncertificated. There are also a few instances where training is mandatory for practice, and they relate to certain forms of vocational preparation, such as nursing education in the United Kingdom and teaching in folk high schools and adult education centers in Finland (Yrjola, 1991).

Arguably, one of the most comprehensive systems of providing training in the performance of educational functions was introduced in the United Kingdom in the late 1970s. As indicated above, three reports were published by the Advisory Committee for the Supply and Training of Teachers (ACSTT). The second report, *The Training of Adult Education and Part-Time Further Education Teachers*, proposed three stages of training, with each stage containing a range of modules designed to meet the varied needs of part-time workers concerned with different subjects, different levels of work, and dissimilar age groups.

It was envisaged that the first two stages should be widely available and taken by all newly appointed part-time adult educators who taught regularly and had not already trained as school teachers. The first two stages were to involve some 100 hours of course attendance. In addition, some 30 hours of teaching practice were to be undertaken. Stage one training provided an introduction to basic teaching skills. The second stage extended the basic topics contained in the initial course, while the final stage provided an opportunity for those completing the first two stages to undertake training leading to full certification. Although this report was never officially recognized, it gave major impetus to the training of part-time field workers which, in partnership with the City and Guilds of London Institute, continues to flourish.

There are now many countries where short inservice courses and seminars are offered for adult educators.

In some cases the programs are systematic. But in Greece, for instance, the programs, financed by the European Social Fund, were not even planned to be systematic, but merely to introduce practicing adult educators to some aspects of pedagogy (Vergidis 1991). In contrast to this, some European universities offer five-year degree-level courses which are pre-service and full-time. The University of Leuven in Belgium, for instance, offers a full-time five-year degree course in social pedagogy for those people about to enter adult education, youth, or community work.

In the United States, on the other hand, there is still relatively little pre-service training (Caldwell 1981), and, initially, the emphasis was upon the academic study of the field, usually of a part-time and inservice nature, at graduate level in order to train leaders in the field. From the early 1930s onwards, the number of universities offering such programs has grown considerably, with both master's and doctoral programs (sometimes both an EdD and a PhD program in the same university) being available. These programs are usually part-time, although some have a full-time residence requirement; they rarely require time spent in practice. However, in the United States, it was apparent that the teachers as well as the leaders needed training, and short practical courses were introduced for practitioners—often by colleges of agriculture preparing agricultural extension agents for their work (Houle 1964). Often these courses were uncertificated.

More recently, there have been a number of part-time certificate and diploma courses introduced by a variety of universities. For example, a Certificate in the Education of Adults has recently been introduced by the University of the West Indies, initially on its Mona campus in Jamaica. By contrast to this, Vergidis (1991) suggests that the universities in Greece have no contact with adult education.

Few universities or colleges have attempted to offer pre-service or inservice training for teachers of adults irrespective of what profession the teachers were about to enter. A notable exception to this has been the University of Surrey in the United Kingdom, which introduced a one-year full-time or two-year part-time course leading to the award of a Post-Graduate Certificate in the Education of Adults. This was made possible only because of the fact that the profession of nursing in the United Kingdom requires its teachers to be qualified in education as well as in nursing; thus a course, though designed for nurse educators, could also be one on which other practitioners could enroll. Now there are a number of similar courses being run in the United Kingdom. Additionally, the same university offers a part-time master's degree course for educators of adults irrespective of the field in which they teach, and this is similar to that offered by universities in many countries in the world. More recently, the same university has pioneered a master's degree course in the practice of education by distance learning, which is open to educators of adults in whatever profession they teach anywhere in the world. In this instance, it is the first time that an attempt has been made to utilize this mode of education in the practice of postcompulsory education, and its aim is to produce reflective practitioners through their continuing ability to relate practice to theoretical insights contained in course material.

2.1 Curricula/Competencies

From the discussion above, it is clear that a large variety of different forms of training exist, some being aimed at "knowledge how" while others are more concerned with "knowledge that" questions (Ryle 1963, Jarvis 1991a). This distinction actually poses a major problem for adult education, one which has been implicit throughout this entry: adult education is both a field of practice and a field of study, so that it is possible to see three distinctly different forms of training: actually being in the practice situation (e.g., teaching/professional practice); learning knowledge about how to practice (e.g., program planning, curriculum studies, pedagogics); and learning knowledge about the field itself (e.g., philosophy of adult education, psychology of adult learning). Hence, it may be seen that there are two different forms of theory (Jarvis 1991b)—one of practice and one about practice—and both may be found in different training courses.

Some of the short courses are organized with the specific intention of focusing upon practical knowledge, such as workshops on program planning. An example of this is the Diploma of Adult Education offered by the University of British Columbia and taught in Hong Kong and Singapore, which includes the following modules: institutions of adult education; community practice of adult education; introduction to educational psychology; instructional techniques and teaching aids; developing short courses, workshops, and seminars; instructional design; institutional research and evaluation for program managers in adult education; and diploma seminar and internship.

The courses of a long duration are much more complex, with many of the taught master's degree courses focusing upon "knowledge that" topics, such as philosophy and sociology of adult education. A five-year degree course in Belgium combines the two approaches covering a variety of subjects, including social pedagogics; theories of agology; theories of neighborhood work and community development; planning and curriculum development, methods, and techniques; group work; theories of organizations; and systems and government policy (Hinnekint 1991). It will be seen from this wide coverage that this course is designed not only for adult educators, but community development workers and those who assist young adults to learn.

It is immediately apparent that there are different competencies being emphasized in these courses, which reflects the fact that both the occupational role of the adult educator and the study of adult education differ in different cultures. However, it also raises quite significant questions about the nature of the study of adult education and, therefore, the automatic application of theoretical perspectives from one culture to the practice in another. Alternatively, it suggests that since the role differs from one culture to another, there can be no common curriculum across countries in the training of adult educators. Questions may also be posed as to whether there are core skills, or competencies, that are generic.

No consideration of the form and structure, curriculum issues, and competencies relating to training can neglect the participants. With regard to the trainees it is necessary to consider, for example, who employs them and in what capacity (i.e., voluntary, part-time or full-time); similarly, under what terms are they employed and what functions do they perform. It has been observed elsewhere that there exist many analyses and typologies of adult educators and their training needs. One such classification relating to Asia and the Pacific (Duke 1989) identifies five categories as related to functions and training requirements:

(a) teaching personal (the great majority, including voluntary and part-time workers);

(b) policymakers and others mainly in administration;

(c) facilitators or *animateurs*, such as supervisors and course designers;

(d) the teachers of adult educators (trainers of trainers); and

(e) research and evaluation personnel.

However, as previously indicated, individual countries have their own perceptions of what constitutes adult education with the concomitant implications for training provision. In Finland, for example, the system of adult education comprises three sections, namely liberal, vocational, and other forms. This latter group includes universities, radio and television, private schools, and colleges, but excludes social, health and religious, or voluntary workers. Finnish training provision ranges from master's degree study in adult education to the necessity of practical training if one seeks permanent employment in a folk high school. In terms of vocational education, 42 centers exist and the majority of their teachers undertake training in pedagogy or andragogy, together with a short program of practice training. Other training provision includes two private organizations. One of these, the Association of Training Managers, has established a sound reputation among training managers in the business community. The State Training Center provides training programs for civil servants, while in liberal adult education, leaders of study circles are assisted to gain greater professional knowledge through provision by study centers (Yrjola 1991).

The growing importance of adult education in all its forms has resulted in increased numbers of individuals becoming actively involved. As Frank (1989) suggests:

> These increasing numbers have involved both the highly qualified and amateurs with only limited experience and qualifications. It has taken place in employment in statutory authorities, voluntary organisations, and combined systems involving radio and correspondence, in areas of both vocational re-training schemes and "cultural" programmes. (p. 101)

Thus, among roles performed within a broad definition of adult eduction are those of teachers, lecturers, instructors, and trainers, organizers, managers and administrators, and training officers, and counsellors.

Many other participants may be involved, although there are those who do not see any part of their roles as relating to adult education and, therefore, do not accept or seek training opportunities. In the field of medicine, doctors, nurses, health visitors, and midwives can be cited as examples. Similarly, social workers or members of religious orders may also take on adult educational roles, while ancillary workers, secretaries, or clerks, for example, who work in the field might benefit from some form of training. Additionally, the research worker may require training in terms of research methods, but also in gaining knowledge about the diverse field of adult education. There are also "special needs" areas such as those concerning adult literacy and basic skills or those relating to work with adults who have various impediments. Additionally, the training requirements of unemployed adults are demanding increasing attention.

These latter examples, among others, raise the vexed question of whether different subjects and types of student personnel require differently trained teachers. Some argue for a generic approach, while others assert the speciality of their own subject and student group.

3. Licensing and Qualification

There appears to be an increasing call for the provision of training programs for adult educators, teachers, and managers alike at both national and international level, although there is still a lack of systematic training schemes. The introduction of training is a sign of increasing professionalization of adult education, but because the education of adults occurs in a variety of sectors of society it is not possible to consider it as a single profession. Consequently, while there may be some movement along the path to professionalization, this can only be achieved in terms of the functions of the educator and manager, rather than in the direction of a single structural profession seeking to take control of its own licensing procedures. Such a conclusion is contrary to that reached by Boshier, who suggested that "it should be possible to train practitioners without creating a self-serving profession" (1985 p. 5). He clearly implies that there is potentially a single profession, and that it is necessary to unify the field. Fordham and Fox (1989 p. 204) claim that, in Africa, adult educators are not yet a single "coherent professional group," but they also imply that at some time in the future adult education might become unified. However, it is suggested here that this is not possible given the diversity of practice. It might be argued, therefore, that the traditional model of professionalization is inappropriate.

The fact that adult education is so diverse means that it can never control entry into a single occupation of the education of adults, although individual professional groups can license their own educators. For instance, in the United Kingdom, nursing controls the entry into nurse education and insists that nurse educators be trained in education; similarly, midwifery has also licensed its own teachers and organized its own training and mandatory refresher courses for its educators for many years. In precisely the same way, in the United Kingdom, there is evidence to indicate that a substantial number of voluntary bodies, independently of each other, provide training for their own part-time teachers (ACACE 1983 pp. 1–27).

Consequently, it is recognized here that since adult education in its widest sense is not a single profession, it will always be impossible for it to control itself in the way that other professions do. Hence, it will never have the power to license its own practitioners nor to award certificates and qualifications. Even so, many universities throughout the world offer award-bearing courses in adult education for those who teach adults. Some offer first degrees (e.g., the University of Zimbabwe and the University of Technology in Sydney) and many offer higher degrees, while others offer certificates and diplomas. One of these is the Pontifical University of Salamanca in Spain, which offers a Diploma in Adult Education course, but only to those who are already qualified teachers and university graduates.

In contemporary society, however, qualifications are playing an increasingly important role. In Finland, for example, it is not possible to get a permanent position in a folk high school without having studied adult education (Yrjola 1991 p. 167). In a similar manner, it is possible for a government to insist that, for example, all literacy workers in its employ be trained but, significantly, the Spanish government insists that literacy workers in the permanent adult education program should be trained as primary school teachers (Cabanas and Amador 1991 p. 115). The logic behind this requirement is that since the literacy level of the adults being taught is the same as that of primary schools, the training should be the same. While the insistence on training is to be applauded, it might be argued that the emphasis on educational outcomes rather than upon the types of student being educated is a false logic that has resulted in a form of training that does not necessarily best prepare these adult educators for their work. It is also of interest to note that writers of distance education materials in the Netherlands are expected to hold appropriate teaching qualifications (Bolhuis and Wagenaar 1991 p. 39). Additionally, Vergidis (1991 p. 101) reported that, in Greece, the lack of adult educators with formal professional qualifications is a major impediment to the improvement of popular education programs. However, there is a continuing debate about the effectiveness of such training.

The relationship between the training of educators of adults and school teachers has been problematic for some time. In Belgium, for example, little or no consideration is given in teacher-training provision for the preparation of adult educators, while in Ireland some school teacher-training courses are now beginning to offer some modules in adult education. In Cyprus, however, it is expected that future school teachers should be willing to work as adult educators or community leaders (Symeonides 1991 p. 226).

4. Trends in the Training of Adults

It is naturally difficult to isolate trends in such a diverse set of international practices. However, an increasing acceptance that adults need to have their education continued beyond school does mean that the education of adults will continue to expand, with a comcomitant demand for the training of adult educators. Since a great deal of that education is undertaken by volunteers and part-time workers, training, where it occurs at all, is still likely to take the form of short practical and intensive seminars and workshops covering the pedagogic and personal skills necessary for working in an everyday situation.

There has been a growing recognition that Human Resource Development (HRD) is important to industry and commerce, and certificated courses for trainers have been introduced, such as those offered by the City and Guilds of London Institute. This trend will no doubt continue with higher-level courses, such as master's degrees in HRD, assuming considerable importance. In some universities in the United States, it is possible to study both HRD and adult education together, and this might well be a trend that other countries will follow. In addition, with the increasing emphasis on the importance of practice, there might well be an increase in training mentors (Deloz 1984) and even teacher practitioners (Jarvis and Gibson 1985). It is perhaps significant to note that nursing in the United Kingdom has for many years trained its experienced workers as teacher practitioners so that they can teach recruits in their professional practice situations. Indeed, there is a possibility that in times of economic stringency when the wisdom of training teachers in the theory of education is called into question, the use of mentors, and therefore mentor training, may assume greater importance.

In contrast, many adult education courses are necessarily practice-based, but this might be a precursor to an increase in the academic study of adult education. Hence, the growth in theory courses at master's degree level is a genuine possibility in some countries of the world. At the same time, the development of distance education makes it possible for the theory of adult education to be taught at a distance.

Another trend that is occurring in Europe, with the emergence of the single market, is student mobility, with schemes already in operation whereby European universities are cooperating together to give their students a wider experience of the theory and practice of adult education. Already some universities, notably in Aachen (Germany), Barcelona (Spain), Leuven (Belgium), Nijmegen (the Netherlands), and Surrey (the United Kingdom), conduct a joint teaching program in adult education, and this might eventually lead to a joint award. With the emergence of credit transfer, it should be increasingly possible to gain credits in different countries that will contribute to a joint award.

See also: History of Adult Education; Adult Education: Concepts and Principles; Adult Education: Disciplinary Orientations; Professional Associations

References

ACACE 1983 *Teachers of Adults: Voluntary Specialist Training and Evaluating Training Courses.* Advisory Council for Adult and Continuing Education, Leicester

ACSTT (Adult Committee of Supply and Training of Teachers) 1975 *The Training of Teachers for Further Education.* ACSTT, London

ACSTT 1978a *The Training of Adult Education and Part-time Further Education Teachers.* ACSTT, London

ACSTT 1978b *The Training of Teachers for Education Management in Further and Adult Education.* ACSTT, London

Board of Education, Adult Education Committee 1921 *The Recruitment, Training and Remuneration of Tutors*, Paper 2. HMSO, London

Bolhuis S, Wagenaar J 1991 Adult education in the Netherlands. In: Jarvis P, Chadwick A (eds.) 1991

Boshier R 1985 A conceptual framework for analysing the training of trainers and adult educators. *Convergence* 18(3–4):3–22

British Institute of Adult Education and the Tutor's Association 1928 *The Tutor in Adult Education* Carnegie UK Trust, Dunfermline

Brattset 1991 The training of adult educators in Norway. In: Jarvis P; Chadwick A (eds.) 1991

Cabanus J Q, Amader J V 1991 Training of adult educators in Spain. In: Jarvis P, Chadwick A (eds.) 1991

Caldwell P 1981 Preservice training for instructors of adults. In: Grabowski S M et al. (eds.) 1981 *Preparing Educators of Adults.* Jossey-Bass, San Francisco, California

Deloz L O 1984 *Effective Teaching and Mentoring.* Jossey-Bass, San Francisco, California

Department of Education and Science 1973 *Adult Education: A Plan for Development.* HMSO, London

Duke C 1989 Training of adult educators. In Titmus C J (ed.) 1989 *Lifelong Education for Adults.* Pergamon Press, Oxford

Elsdon K T 1975 *Training for Adult Education.* University of Nottingham or the National Institute of Adult Education, Nottingham

Executive Committee of the Association of Tutors 1944 *The Future of Adult Education.* Association of Tutors, Bradford

Fordham P, Fox J 1989 Training the adult educator as professional. *International Review of Education* 35(2): 197 212

Frank E 1989 The educators. In: Titmus J (ed.) 1989 *Lifelong Education for Adults. Pergamon Press, Oxford*

Graham T B, Daines J M, Sullivan T, Harris P, Baum F E 1982 *The Training of Part-time Teachers of Adults.* Department of Adult Education, University of Nottingham, Nottingham

Grattan C H (ed.) 1959 *American Ideas about Adult Education, 1710–1951.* Teachers College, New York

Hinnekint H 1991 *The training of adult educators in Belgium.* In: Jarvis P, Chadwick A (eds.) 1991

Houle C O 1964 The emergence of graduate study in adult education. In: Jensen G, Liveright A A, Hallenbeck W (eds.) 1964 *Adult Education: Outline of an Emerging Field of Study.* Adult Education Association of the USA, Chicago, Illinois

Jarvis P (1991a) Practical knowledge and theoretical analyses in adult and continuing education. In: Friedenthal-Hasse H et al. (eds.) 1991 *Erwashsenenbilding in Kontext.* Klinkhart, Bad Heilbrunn

Jarvis P (1991b) Towards a Theoretical Rationale. In: Jarvis P, Chadwick A (eds.) 1991

Jarvis P, Chadwick A (eds.) 1991 *Training Adult Educators in Western Europe.* Routledge in association with the European Bureau of Adult Education, London

Jarvis P, Gibson S 1985 *The Teacher Practitioner In Nursing, Midwifery and Health Visiting.* Croom Helm, London

Kelly T 1950 *Griffith Jones Llanddowror Pioneer in Adult Education.* University of Wales Press, Cardiff

Legge C D 1951 The Training of Tutors in Adult Education Report on Training Schemes. University Council for Adult Education, London

Legge D 1982 *The Education of Adults in Britain.* Open University Press, Milton Keynes

Ministry of Reconstruction, Adult Education Committee 1919 *Final Report.* HMSO, London

Ryle G 1963 *The Concept of Mind.* Penguin, Harmondsworth

Silverman H A 1934 The tutor in adult education. In Peers R (ed.) 1934 *Adult Education in Practice.* Macmillan London

Starr M 1943 Training of teachers for adult education. Teach. Educ. J. (December)

Symeonides K 1991 Training adult educators in Cyprus. In: Jarvis P, Chadwick A (eds.) 1991

Vergidis D 1991 Training adult educators in Greece. In: Jarvis P Chadwick A (eds.) 1991

Yrjola P 1991 The training of adult educators in Findland. In: Jarvis P Chadwick A (eds.) 1991

SECTION V

Participation and Provision

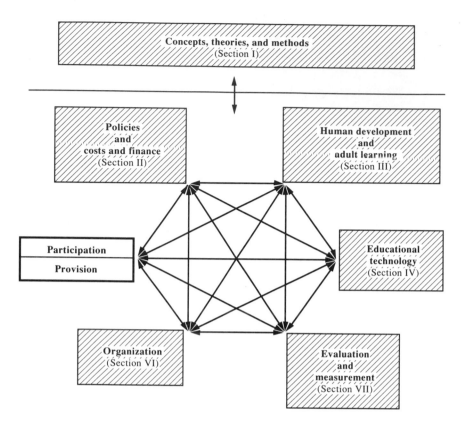

Figure 1
Schematic representation of Section V in relation to the other Sections

Participation and Provision

Introduction

D. Hirsch and A. C. Tuijnman

Interest in the factors that influence the demand for adult learning across the whole lifespan, and in the way adults manage their personal development and choose among learning options, has mounted as a result of a new recognition of the centrality of a lifelong learning philosophy. While lifelong learning is gaining momentum, the governments of both industrialized and developing countries seem to be opting for a strategy in which increased provision relies, in the main, on the strength of private initiative. Informal learning at home and in the work place in particular is being given increased attention by researchers and policymakers. This situation raises a number of questions concerning the determinants, the nature and distribution of adults' opportunity to learn. The increased reliance on nonformal and informal approaches to adult learning brings to the fore the role of public policy in influencing opportunity and promoting lifelong learning, rather than providing it directly.

Children are sent to school; for adults, education and training are mostly voluntary activities. Therefore both the quantity and nature of organized adult learning are variable, depending on a match between individuals' desire to learn and the availability of learning opportunities. It can be useful to examine this matching condition in terms of demand and supply, particularly at the end of the twentieth century, a time when both the nature of demand for adult learning and the potential delivery modes of education and training are rapidly evolving. This introduction considers the principle of demand and supply in adult education, looks at how both sides of the "market" are developing, and suggests how policymakers and others might approach the task of improving the match between demand and supply.

Two sets of entries in Section V describe aspects of demand and supply relationships in adult education. The first group of entries deals with the demand characteristics of adult learners. It also examines the determinants of and barriers to participation in adult learning activities. Student counselling and other support systems that might be effective in stimulating broad participation and preventing dropout are also given attention. The second cluster of entries describes some of the defining characteristics of a range of institutions offering adult education and continuing vocational training.

1. The Principle of Demand and Supply

The demand-supply metaphor can add value to discussions about educational provision, despite important dissimilarities between educational activity and a commercial market. While there are many cases in which education and training are sold at market prices to consumers, there are many more in which they are paid for by a government, an employer, or someone else other than the individual learner. The main interest in paying attention to demand, however, lies not in predicting how much "learning" will be bought at a given price (the pure economic approach), but rather in identifying the needs, desires, and behavioral inclinations of individual learners. This is particularly significant in the case of adults, for two reasons. First because the nature of courses and other learning opportunities ("supply") needs to be linked to what learners want and to what they will participate in. Secondly because participation is most likely to lead to effective learning where participants are strongly motivated.

The potential demand for education and training is becoming both greater and more heterogeneous than it has ever been in the past. It is widely acknowledged that lifelong learning for all citizens is desirable in today's societies. Advanced information technologies have helped create a more complex use of knowledge at work and in daily life, making it desirable that all adults are adaptable, capable of applying literacy skills and able to learn continuously. Furthermore, decentralized democratic processes and a greater stress on choices by consumers of products and services assume functional literacy levels that appear not to have been attained by a significant proportion of adults in advanced societies.

But to create universal access to learning it is necessary to cater for the varying needs of a wide range of groups, particularly those that have been disadvantaged in the past. Responding to demand may mean re-examining methods and institutions that have traditionally resulted in educational participation being highest among adults who are already well educated.

Fortunately on the supply side too, there is much potential for change. New computer and communications technologies raise the prospect of new kinds of access to information and instruction, both for distance learners and for students on-campus. Some institutions are becoming more open and flexible, and competition for students among various public and private institutions can in some cases help break down old barriers to access. The location of learning is also becoming more flexible: the merits of "situated" learning are becoming widely recognized, and partnerships between educational institutions and others is making it easier to combine classroom-based with experiential learning.

In developing a closer fit between demand and supply, policymakers and others need to take account of one further aspect of learning that makes it unlike a commercially traded product. The supply process is intimately connected with the character and expression of demand. Teachers and facilitators can provide instruction, but learning must effectively be "coproduced" with students. This is particularly true in the case of adults, who tend to learn most effectively when they play an active, self-directed role in the learning process. So at the micro level, it is necessary for learning to be designed in partnership with those demanding it, rather than simply supplied to them in the form of instruction defined "from above."

2. Sources of Demand and Participation

Access to education for all adults, in many countries, first became part of a political agenda in the 1970s, with calls to make recurrent education a basic right. Technological and structural economic changes in the 1980s created a more instrumentalist rationale for lifelong learning: the need to ensure that workers acquire the skills and flexibility needed to make the most of an information-based economic system. Such motives have led to various forms of demand for lifelong learning at a macro level, differing from one country to another.

In Japan, for example, a strong emphasis has been put on "learning as consumption": the encouragement of learning activities for their own sake rather than as part of the production process. Most other OECD countries on the other hand, and particularly the United States, are tending to emphasize the "investment" possibilities of learning, as a route to extra income for the individual and to extra prosperity for society as a whole. Such respective rationales, however, must be seen in the context of existing learning cultures and

systems. In Japan, there is already a well-functioning system for workers to learn in ways that enhance production, within the extensive education and training structures of large enterprises. Nordic countries on the other hand, which have stressed the improvement of work-related learning, already have long-established traditions of learning for leisure. Among these long-standing traditions are the study circles and the folk high schools, which are described in the entries by Byström, and Arvidson and Gustavsson.

Compared with the 1970s and 1980s, there would now seem to be more appreciation of the fact that adult learners are inherently different. It is now also generally recognized that the contexts in which adults decide to engage in learning tasks are not invariant but change over time. Populations vary from migrants, dropouts, and out-of-school youth to unemployed workers, engineers, scientists, and older adults. Forms of outreach and educational delivery differ as well. These range from classroom learning to collaborative group learning and independent or self-directed learning at work or at home.

The question why these diverse groups of people participate in organized adult education or engage in self-directed learning activities is at the heart of a well-developed line of research in adult education. Different theories of participation have been developed that employ frameworks derived from related work in psychology, sociology, and economics, and a number of variables that exert significant effects on the decision of adults to engage in a learning task have been identified. Two premises guide this line of research. The first is that learning is mostly voluntary. The second postulate is that the characteristics of adult learners, their reasons for study, and the programs they attend are highly variable. These premises are examined in two entries. The first, by van der Kamp, deals with the determinants of participation while the second, by Deshler, considers the issue of participation motivation in adult education.

The heterogeneity and the voluntary nature of most participation pose problems in both policy-making and for research into adult education. The heterogeneity of provision and participation is a political issue because statistics on the extent and patterns of participation by different social groups reveal large disparities in many countries. This is true even of Sweden, a country where a deliberate policy of equalizing opportunity to learn as well as actual participation was implemented during the 1970s and 1980s. Problems for research arise because it is very difficult to generalize across research studies, since most studies examine the recruitment policies and enrolment profiles of specific institutions or programs, or have focused on the participation of specific groups of people who share certain characteristics.

Against the overall background of societies wishing for various reasons to make adult learning more extensive, it is possible to identify a variety of groups with specific learning needs which are becoming increasingly apparent. As noted by Tuijnman in the first entry, these groups include many categories of adults. Because the categories overlap greatly, they are not covered in separate entries. However, exceptions are made in two cases: women, who are dealt with in the two entries contributed by Goodale and Oglesby; and third-age students in higher education, who are discussed in an entry written by Hore. Other major categories of adult learners comprise:

(a) Immigrants who need to learn language and cultural skills in relation to their host country.

(b) Ethnic and other minorities who have hitherto been alienated from mainstream education.

(c) Dislocated workers who need to learn new skills because those they once learned in school have become redundant.

(d) Long-term unemployed people who have to relearn basic work skills.

(e) Other categories of people with low previous educational attainment who are looking for a "second chance" to learn.

(f) Better-educated groups who nevertheless need constantly to update and develop their skills and knowledge.

(g) Older people who, regardless of former levels of education, wish to make learning an important activity in retirement.

Although the learning needs of all these categories of people may be relatively easy to identify, need does not automatically translate into demand. In their entries, Van der Kamp and Deshler show that the inclination to participate in organised learning activities depends on a variety of factors, including financial and time constraints, the existence or otherwise of obvious opportunities to apply what is learned, and the quality of information about what is on offer. It seems reasonable to assume, however, that there is a high degree of *latent* demand, which will be translated into participation if the supply of opportunities is well-designed to meet the constraints of the target group. This is the thrust of the arguments presented in the entry on participation motivation by Deshler and the entry on student outreach contributed by Osborn. Moreover, the entries by Potter on student counseling, Healy and Martin on student support systems, and Garrison on preventing student dropout paint a convincing picture of the need to pay close attention to the specific learning needs of adults even after they become engaged in structured adult learning. Student support systems can be effective not only in attracting adults who seem less inclined to follow an educational program voluntarily, but also in helping learners to persist once they have embarked on a learning task.

In conclusion, the heterogeneity of the clientele of adult education and training makes it difficult to generalize about the "productive" factors that influence participation, and by implication underscores the importance of ensuring a flexible and diverse provision so that the differing learning needs of adults can be taken into account.

3. Modes of Supply and Provision

It is difficult to summarize the structure of education and training provision for adults in an international framework, as different countries have very different structures. Tuijnman, in the first entry in this cluster, offers an attempt to organize the important characteristics of providers of adult education and training using specific taxonomies as well as on the basis of the International Standard Classification of Education (ISCED). The following three broad categories of supply may be distinguished:

(a) Education and training institutions specifically designed to cater for adults, defined as people returning to study after a break from initial education. This includes what in many countries is referred to as formal adult education. Adult basic education, described by Kutner, and adult secondary education, presented by Martin, are two examples of provisions that fall into this category.

(b) Postsecondary institutions with provision for adults as well as for students who are continuing studies immediately after school. Although a common form of provision for adults by these institutions has been university extension, the participation by adults in postsecondary education—whether full-time or part-time, face-to-face or at a distance—has been growing rapidly. This category of provision is dealt with in the entries by Duke on adult tertiary education, Cohen on community colleges, Watson on polytechnical education, and Kasworm on university adult education.

(c) Learning that is mainly detached from formal educational institutions, including work-based education and training, informal study circles, voluntarily-organized "universities of the third age," and informal learning based around community activities. Provision in this category is covered in entries by Lowerie on libraries as learning resources, de Wolf on distance education, Holmberg on the open university, Arvidson and Gustavsson on folk high schools, and Bryström on study circles. The concepts of community education and popular education are dealt with in entries by Cunningham and Evans included in Section I.

In order to make both education for leisure and education for investment a reality for all people regardless of prior experience of learning, sex, age, and life career, some coherence is needed among the diverse and ad hoc approaches to initial and adult education that characterize current provision. Here a dilemma arises. Since the learning needs of adults are highly differentiated, the strategies to be followed will have to be diversified as well. Hence the wide variation in the types of institutions that sponsor and offer adult education and training.

4. Trends in Adult Learning

There is a considerable extent to which the boundaries between these learning modes are breaking down. A number of postsecondary and adult education institutions are trying to establish better links with community groups and employers, and to design course structures around the needs of learners rather than institutions. The following trends, although by no means universal, have the potential to transform adult learning in ways that make it more sensitive to the needs and aspirations of various user groups:

(a) Increased possibilities to learn at a place remote from the teaching institution. Distance learning, whose possibilities are enhanced by various new communication technologies, removes physical constraints not just for those who live in remote areas but also for those whose work or family commitments constrain travel to a place of learning. Having originally been a mode used mainly by specialist institutions, distance learning is becoming an important part of the activities of mainstream institutions as well.

(b) Increased opportunities to learn at a time convenient to the learner. This is a product both of institutional change (e.g., the provision of more short-duration and part-time courses) and of technological development. The intelligent use of computer software can reduce the necessary contact time with teachers and other pupils, and thus allow study to take place to a greater extent at a time determined by the learner.

(c) A more interactive mode of learning in which the teacher becomes a resource and a facilitator rather than merely an instructor. This trend is also facilitated by computer technology that allows a greater range of teaching modes than an instructor lecturing to a class. It is a particularly valuable development in the context of a diverse set of adult learners each with particular needs.

(d) A greater stress on applied or "situated" learning rather than theoretical instruction. Where learning is intended as an agent of change, it can be unhelpful to externalize it from the context of its eventual application. Thus firms often find that sending workers on courses is not as effective in improving performance as internal group learning activities addressing the organization of work. Many educational institutions are trying to play a role in facilitating "situated" learning, at work or in the community, rather than seeing it merely as a challenge to their own campus-based services.

(e) The development of informal learning opportunities. Where a museum sets up an education room, a fire station has an open day to tell the public of its activities, or a neighborhood group organizes classes enabling nonteachers to pass on literacy skills, learning becomes a more significant part of everyday life. It is hard to define the boundaries of informal learning, or to demonstrate that it is necessarily a growing phenomemon. But movements for lifelong learning have consciously attempted to increase the possibilities for learning informally, for example by encouraging public and private organizations to explain their activities to the general public.

Although the existence of new technologies provides valuable tools for such improvements in the flexibility of supply, it does not make change inevitable. More open, diverse, and flexible learning opportunities for adults also depend crucially on change in education and training cultures. Old teaching methods, relationships between teachers and students, and the structure of institutions are not always easily reformed. Change depends partly on the ability of teachers to learn new methods, through inservice training or otherwise, but also on the institutional and funding context in which they operate. Public funding mechanisms often favor a particular type of learning, depending for example on the weighting they give to full-time or part-time students, and to on-site versus off-site instruction.

5. Some Implications for Policy

The supply of learning opportunities to adults, unlike the supply of schooling to children, cannot be based entirely on some form of "universal" public provision. The heterogeneous characteristics and needs of adult learners make it inevitable that opportunities will depend on a combination of public, private, and not-for-profit providers, as well as on self-organized activity. In any case fiscal constraints severely limit the prospects of public funds being devoted to mass provision on the same scale as schools and initial higher education.

The state can therefore best play a strategic role in attempting to create a better match between the demand for and the supply of adult learning opportunities. Potentially the most active role for public policy is in the following three areas:

(a) The coordination of strategies or coalitions that aim to enhance adult learning. Partnerships between different providers in the public and private sectors can help to create a more coherent framework of opportunities for the individual to select, preventing unnecessary overlap and creating linkages between various activities. At the local level in particular, public authorities can potentially play a key role as the convenors and coordinators of networks, as well as acting as the provider of some opportunities for adult learning, on which others can build.

(b) The provision of an infrastructure that makes it easier for demand and supply to be matched. Two particularly important aspects of this infrastructure are qualifications and information. Recognized qualifications, that can only be established centrally (although potentially by a partnership of governments and others), create essential incentives for many kinds of learning, in particular those that aim to enhance employment prospects. Information is also a key service in a pluralistic framework of provision, which can too easily represent a maze to users. A third and newer aspect of learning infrastructure that can potentially be enhanced by government is communication and information technology. Although many developments are in the hands of private operators, government might consider means of encouraging intelligent educational uses of new hardware, for example by reconsidering teaching structures in publicly controlled institutions.

(c) The establishment of clear and consistent financing principles. This aspect of policy is the most fraught with difficulties, and a a number of issues remain unresolved in many countries. For example, countries that have adopted the ethos of choice for the individual learner remain unwilling to give fully-flexible vouchers to students to select exactly what, when, and where they study. There is a continuing conflict between the desire of such governments to allow individual demand to express itself and the existence of government preferences—a form of macro demand, usually concentrated on vocational courses creating skills that are likely to improve overall economic performance. The structure of financing has important implications for the nature and behavior of public postsecondary institutions in relation to adults. A more "market" oriented model in which funding is directly linked to enrolments may encourage institutions to see themselves as competitors with private organizations and to analyze demand in terms of identifying new markets. On the other hand a more traditional system of core funding for each institution or course encourages more detached judgments about the value of courses to different user groups, made by policymakers or the managers of institutions.

Thus even though governments should not seek to control the overall level of adult learning opportunities, they can exercise considerable influence. Where there is genuine public concern that demand is going unmet, the exercise of such leverage may be considered a significant priority of education policy.

(a)   Participation

Clienteles and Special Populations

A. C. Tuijnman

The purpose of this entry is to discuss some characteristics of populations and special clientele groups in adult education. The participation concept is briefly introduced, factors influencing participation in adult education are discussed, and the characteristics and learning needs of special clienteles are described.

Starting with the seminal publication, *Handbook of Adult Education in the United States* (Rowden 1936), nearly all comprehensive handbooks on adult, continuing, and lifelong education that have been published in the twentieth century have included separate entries offering exhaustive descriptions of participant groups in adult education (Knowles 1960, Smith et al. 1970, Boone et al. 1980, Titmus 1989, Merriam and Cunningham 1991). This *Encyclopedia* departs from this practice. With the exception of the two entries on women in adult education and third-age and part-time students in higher education, the audiences and special clienteles of adult education are discussed in the entries describing specific program areas (see *Providers of Adult Education: An Overview*).

1. Concept of Adult Education

A broad concept of adult education is used in this entry. Consistent with the definitions presented elsewhere (see *Adult Education: Concepts and Principles*), adult education is defined as referring to any learning activity or program deliberately designed to satisfy learning needs or interests that may be experienced at any stage in their lives by persons whose major social roles are characteristic of adult status and whose principal activity is no longer in education. Its ambit thus spans vocational and general education, formal and nonformal education, continuing vocational training, as well as education with a collective, social purpose.

2. The Participation Theme

The notion of "participation" is important in adult education. Since the 1960s many research studies have been carried out to explain the participation of adults in organized learning activities. Whereas some of these studies have been sociological in orientation and used the sample survey approach to examine how many adults in a population take part, who they are, and in what kinds of programs they enroll, the majority of studies have been conducted within the psychological paradigm.

Research studies investigating participation in adult education have been mostly of a descriptive kind. Even when numerical information was collected and analyzed, there was a tendency to use the data as anecdotal evidence and as illustrations of the types of programs offered, the characteristics of participants, and the patterns of enrollment in different institutions. Compared with the research on student learning and initial educational attainment, relatively few studies systematically investigated the antecedent factors of participation in adult education. This scarcity of studies is relative, however, because participation research has featured prominently compared to research on other themes in the field (Boshier and Collins 1984).

The results of empirical studies indicate many factors which influence the decision to take part in adult education. The evidence generally shows that the following demographic, sociological, psychological, and economic variables are related to participation: home background, age, sex, ethnicity, previous educational attainment, conditions of employment, occupational status, and income. Other variables that influence motivation and participation are social roles, social contact, area of residence, community involvement, marital status, household composition, and especially the presence of school-age children in the family.

In research studies investigating the learning pursuits of adults a distinction is often made between two categories of adults: those who participate and those who do not. For reasons such as data availability and the role of institutions in initiating or financing studies, the orientation of the research has been mostly on the first category, the participants. However, once it had been determined that only a minority of adults tended to take part in organized learning activities, and that nonparticipation implied a social and economic cost, the interest of research workers shifted to the reasons why certain people do not take part. A number of barriers to participation have been identified in this line of research. Cross (1981) and others group these into three categories: situational, institutional, and dispositional barriers (see *Participation: Antecedent factors; Participation: Role of Motivation; Experiential and Open Learning*).

3. "Targeting" Adults for Intervention

Populations that experience a special situation or economic or social disadvantages have long been designated as "target groups" in the field of adult education. Various criteria have been used to define groups of adults who constitute a target group. Examples are variables such as the level of initial education, unemployment, and the ability to speak the national language. Because direct assessments of, for example, the basic literacy skills in a population were until recently not generally available, policymakers and program designers have had to identify target groups by means of indirectly measured and therefore imprecise selection criteria.

The fact that "target group" is a widely used and generally accepted concept in adult education gives two important clues to understanding the field. First, it indicates a firm belief among practitioners that adult education can contribute to achieving desired objectives such as reducing marginality and social or economic disparities. Second, the notion implies adherence to certain values—democracy and social equality—as well as a degree of acceptance of political attitudes, for example, those associated with social activism and interventionism (see *Recurrent Education*). Rubenson (1987) states the position succinctly:

> Unless special measures are taken to support underprivileged groups, an expanded system of recurrent education is very likely to increase the differences between generations . . . The right to educational leave is a fundamental prerequisite in the development of a system of recurrent education. This right has already been established in many OECD countries, either by law or by virtue of collective bargaining. It is too early yet to comment on the effects of this reform, but the available information suggests that women and the educationally underprivileged make the least use of the right (OECD 1977–81) . . . To correct the social bias of recruitment, a system of recurrent education needs to include positive discrimination in favour of the educationally weakest groups. (Rubenson 1987 p. 39)

Because research studies have consistently shown that certain groups are underserved in adult education and training, and that this lack of participation can result in an accumulation of disadvantages (Tuijnman 1991), "affirmative action" is widely seen as a strategy for equalizing opportunity and access in adult education. Affirmative action can of course be directed not only at the obviously disadvantaged, but in principle at all social groups who are shown in statistical surveys to be underserved in certain programs of adult education.

Research efforts have been devoted to finding ways of reducing or overcoming barriers to participation. However, the experience of employing active recruitment strategies and intervention policies designed to encourage the participation of underprivileged adults is mixed. Because the people who are targeted for intervention through adult education tend to be difficult to recruit, successful strategies for reaching them require community-based action as well as broad political support. Not surprisingly, this support is often lacking. There are, however, also many examples of success in outreach work. The mass literacy campaigns conducted during the 1960s and 1970s in some countries in Latin America and Asia stand out in this respect.

It can be concluded that notions such as positive discrimination and affirmative action have a long history in adult education, and that outreach and negotiated programs focused on the learning needs of audiences such as minority groups, women, working-class people, and immigrants are typical of adult education work (see *Student Counseling; Student Outreach; Student Support Systems*).

4. Opportunity and Outcomes

Underlying the participation theme in adult education is a dilemma concerning the implementation of policy to enhance equality of opportunity vis-à-vis equality of outcomes. The widely shared position that society has a duty to assist disadvantaged adults by offering learning opportunities that may help them to improve their situation implies an acceptance of the necessity of public intervention in adult education. The question, however, is where the line for intervention should be drawn. Research studies show that merely offering opportunities is not likely to result in equal participation, and that equal participation is unlikely to yield equal outcomes for different participants. Thus, without public intervention, spending on adult education and training is likely to be mainly used for creating learning opportunities for those who have received an above- average initial education. The social and economic value of this human capital investment will become increasingly unequally distributed among social groups, thus reinforcing the cycles of "accumulation" (Tuijnman 1991) and "resource conversion" (Tuijnman et al. 1988) which characterize the function of adult education in social stratification. The policy dilemma implied in the above argument can be usefully illustrated with a brief look at the experience of Sweden, a country that historically has played a major role in the development of Western adult education.

In Sweden, during the 1970s and 1980s, the goals of formal adult education were specified in terms of the development of both the individual and the society (Sweden 1985).

(a) It should reduce the gaps in educational opportunity as well as educational attainment between generations and social groups.

(b) It should increase the ability of citizens to become involved in and to influence the development of society.

(c) It should contribute to occupational training while also enabling workers to influence working conditions and the work environment, thereby contributing to employment and progress in society.

(d) It should fulfill adults' individual wishes for education, giving them opportunities for supplementing their initial, formal education.

It is significant to note that the first goal mentions not only equal opportunity but also equal outcomes. This idea was strongly advocated by interest groups in Swedish society during the mid-1970s, particularly by the popular movements, the study associations, and the workers' trade union (*Landsorganisationen i Sverige*, LO). It was claimed that publicly subsidized adult education, especially municipal adult education, should be targeted to adults with only six or seven years of initial, formal schooling. Other target groups were also identified: for example, those in the workforce either being made redundant or being employed in a sector subject to major restructuring; adults with reading and writing difficulties; adults seeking to enhance their civic and political capacities; and young adults lacking a start qualification, for example, a certificate of completed studies at the upper secondary level. Unemployed adults were targeted through programs offered by the former National Labor Market Board (Rubenson 1989).

Ironically, while during the 1980s and 1990s an increasing number of people in various countries had become interested in the Swedish experience of designing outreach programs and implementing policies designed to equalize not only opportunities but also the eventual outcomes associated with youth and adult education, in Sweden after a change in government in the early 1990s the importance not only of social intervention by means of adult education but also of public adult education per se was de-emphasized (Sweden 1992). The swiftness with which this dramatic policy change was implemented illustrates the extent to which public intervention strategies had become discredited during the 1980s. It also shows that policy to enhance equality of opportunity and outcomes by means of second chance education for adults requires broad political support in the community.

In conclusion, the learning needs of special audiences are often mentioned in the national goals for adult education in countries where such goals have been formulated. However, the goals for adult education rarely differentiate between opportunity and outcome. A focus on equal outcomes will clearly require backing from the general population and the government. While many adult education practitioners take the notion of affirmative action or positive discrimination for granted, this is certainly not true for the community as a whole. This difference in a way sets adult educators apart, and may explain the weak position of public adult education in Western societies in the early 1990s. This contrasts with the position in some developing countries, where the inequality-reducing objective of adult education has been enshrined in state policy.

5. Extent of Participation

Statistical offices in many countries gather some information about participation in adult education. Two types of information are collected: institutional and survey-based statistics. Because it has been more common for the data to be collected from the registers of institutions offering adult education than for the data to be collected directly through household surveys, data about publicly supported, formal adult education tend to be more often available, and in greater detail, than data concerning the nonformal and informal learning activities of adults. The disadvantages of register-based data collection are that double counting is unavoidable, that no data is available about the nonparticipants, and that there tends to be wide variation among the institutions in the kinds of additional information about participant characteristics that are entered into the books and from which aggregate indicators can be derived (see *Measurement of Adult Education; Measurement of Industry Training*).

The limitations of a data collection strategy that depends on institutional statistics are increasingly being recognized, and as a result more countries now undertake surveys to discover what types of organized learning opportunity for adults are being offered, and who benefits from them. Such surveys have yielded useful information about the characteristics of both participant and nonparticipant groups.

6. Populations with Special Learning Needs

The variables commonly examined in surveys of adult education participation are discussed in greater detail below. The purpose is to describe the distribution of learning opportunities in a population. The characteristics of adults with special learning needs are also described.

6.1 Age Groups

Surveys in the industrialized countries have generally found a marked bias in the age distribution of participants in adult education and training in favor of younger adults. For example, in Australia in the late

1980s, the number of employees undertaking some form of continuing education or training decreased with age from 93 percent of persons aged between 15 and 24 years to 49 percent of employees aged 55 to 64 years (ABS 1992). The case of Australia is not atypical; similar patterns also exist in other countries.

Age groups in adult education can be divided in various ways, for example, intervals according to labels such as young adult, middle adult years, seniority, and old age. The period of life following adolescence is often denoted with the term "young adulthood." Depending on the society concerned it refers to the period from about 18 to 24 years. Young adulthood is characterized by the separation from the family of orientation and the searching and testing of social and occupational roles, involving a choice of life-style, educational career, labor market entry, or partner and family.

In some societies the vast majority of young adults are in full-time schooling; in others they are mostly in the workplace. The responsibilities and subcultures are different, as are the roles for adult education. The continued involvement of a large group of young adults in education and training in fact determines much of the social environment and learning culture in higher and adult education. By comparison, young adults in the workplace are given time to explore social roles only within strict limits, and instead of being able to procreate their own learning environment, they frequently have to adapt to prescribed rules.

The young adult period of exploration is followed by a period of review, after which, at the age of about 30 to 35, the person moves on to stabilization. The middle adult years, ranging from about age 35 to 55, are for many people a time of total immersion in family, career, and community affairs. Fales (1989) subdivides the period into three phases: (a) 30s stabilization, in which developmental tasks such as choosing among career opportunities, solidifying a self-concept, establishing an adult relationship with parents, and increasing attachment to one's own partner and family are accomplished; (b) 40s transition, where the main tasks include a re-evaluation of goals and expectations developed during a previous period and a restructuring of the time perspective; (c) restabilization (middle 40s to middle 50s), involving tasks such as developing self-acceptance in work, family, and community and maintaining growth and flexibility intellectually and emotionally. These transitions, and the developmental tasks that characterize them, pose challenges to adult education.

Kennedy (1989) notes that, until the 1960s, adults were seen as moving straight from the struggles of work to the status of old age, at about age 50 to 55. A rise in welfare, health, and life expectancy, coupled with social and cultural changes, enables adults aged 50 to embark on developmental projects, and to acquire new social and psychological experiences. The consequence is increased variety in role sequences and role complexity, which accompany changes in work patterns and family composition. It therefore seems justified to consider the period from about 50 to 65, or retirement age, as a distinct period denoted with the term "adult maturity." Specific learning demands arise as people embark on a new phase in their life career, form new relationships with their grown-up children, engage in community work, and take up caring for their own, elderly parents.

Preretirement education forms another important aspect of provision for this group. This can be defined as "the acquisition of information, understanding, and appreciation which will assist in facilitating personal adjustment and self-fulfillment after retirement from the labor force at whatever age this occurs" (Withnall and Kabwasa 1989 p 320). Preretirement education is often organized through study circles and self-help groups.

The importance of offering systematic learning opportunities for "senior citizens," a term used in Asian societies to denote people in retirement and older adults, increases concomitantly with the aging of the populations of the more affluent societies. As more courses are specifically designed to suit the learning capacity and the special interests of older adults—for example, local history, arts, religious education, nutrition, sex and "death" education, physical fitness programs—the participation rate increases. Although older adults are still underserved, the situation appears to have improved. In the United States, the establishment within community colleges, folk high schools, universities and other institutions of programs catering for specific learning demands of older adults—Elderhostel and Seniornet are two examples—might serve as models for development elsewhere (Hiemstra 1992). A survey among the senior citizens of Japan suggests that, for this group, the learning demand is not satisfied yet (Kawanobe et al. 1993) (see *Third-age Students in Higher Education*).

A long-standing debate concerns the question whether programs should be targeted especially to older adults, or whether elderly people should be accommodated in the same programs that are attended by younger learners. Some countries—for example, the Netherlands and Sweden—appear to have adopted a policy of promoting adult participation in youth and young adult-dominated upper secondary schools, colleges, and universities. While economic arguments have played a role in this decision—no separate programs or institutions would be needed—pedagogical arguments have also been used. Withnall and Kabwasa (1989) conclude that the few research studies there are on this question suggest that older people dislike segregation, but that there are certain situations where age-segregated classes may be preferable.

In conclusion, age in relation to developmental tasks is often used as a criterion for judging whether affirmative action in adult education is needed. The above discussion also makes it clear that theories about lifespan development need refinement, since the division of life career into the broad phases outlined above is incomplete (see *Human Development: Aging; Lifespan Development: Phases; Lifespan Development: Problems and Crises*).

6.2 Gender

Learning opportunities for adults have been extended in many countries during the 1970s and 1980s. For example, in the Netherlands, overall participation increased by 38 percent from 1979 to 1988 (Cramer and Van der Kamp 1991 p. 11 Table 2). Despite this increase, the marked degree of imbalance in the participation rates of men and women has generally not been diminished. Figure 1 presents the position in the Netherlands during the 1980s. While aggregate participation increased, the share of women in the total actually decreased, because the number of male participants in adult education grew more rapidly than the number of women. The expansion of continuing vocational education since the early 1980s provides a part of the explanation. It should be noted that on-the-job training is not included in the data on which Fig. 1 is based. If comparable time-series were available and on-the-job training included, then the sex differences in participation would be even more dramatic since, compared to women, men tend to be overrepresented in firm-based occupational training (Tuijnman 1992). In contrast, women tend to be overrepresented in liberal arts and recreational courses. Thus, while women may form a target group in occupational training, because they tend to be underrepresented compared to men, the latter may constitute the target group for delivery programs in community development (see *Women and Access to Vocational Training; Women and Adult Education*).

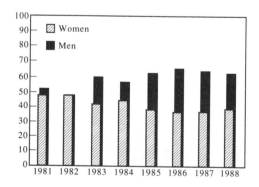

Figure 1
Share of women and men in adult education participation in the Netherlands (aggregate of all adult education and training, excluding on-the-job training)
Source: Dutch Central Bureau of Statistics and Cramer and Van Der Kamp (1991)

6.3 Ethnicity

Multicultural perspectives on adult education provision have grown in importance during the 1980s, as continued migration and demographic changes have profoundly affected the cultural fabric of societies in both the developing and developed countries. In surveys of provision and participation, cultural, ethnic, linguistic, and racial minority groups have consistently been found to be underserved, with the exception of programs especially targeted at these groups (Ross-Gordon et al. 1990). For example, in Australia, those in the age group 15 to 64 years who were born in the country were more likely to be attending an educational institution in May 1991 (the date of the education survey) than overseas-born persons in the same age group. At that time 18 percent of the Australian-born population was enrolled in an educational institution, compared to 13 percent of the overseas-born population (ABS 1992). The evidence may suggest that there is a need for designing educational programs to cater specifically for the learning needs of ethnic and cultural minority groups. This also applies to other socially isolated groups, such as disabled adults and prison inmates.

6.4 Previous Educational Attainment

A survey conducted in the United States in 1963 found that the level of formal education initially acquired is the most important determinant of participation in adult education (Johnstone and Rivera 1965). Since then this finding has been replicated in surveys in many different countries. However, in a longitudinal study of a group of Swedish men, Tuijnman (1991) found that the effect of initial education on the likelihood of participation in adult education decreased not only with increasing age but also with previous occurrences of participation. In fact, the results showed that initial educational attaintment was a highly important determinant of first-time participation. But, in later stages, previous participation in adult education explained more of the variance in participation than schooling background.

6.5 Employment and Occupational Status

The quality of initial schooling and the level of formal education reached by a person before entering the job market is a very powerful predictor not only of recurrent participation in organized learning activities but also of employment status, occupational mobility, and life career attainment. The strong correlation between unemployment incidence and educational attainment has led governments to target unemployed adults for intervention through adult education and training. Public training programs for the unemployed form a large and important component of adult education provision in many countries (see *Government Role in Adult Education and Training*).

An above average level of initial education increases the likelihood of obtaining an above average job. Occupations and jobs also differ in terms of the frequency and quality of learning opportunities that are offered. Adult education and training therefore tend to benefit higher-level workers more than lower-level workers. Table 1 shows that this observation held in some European countries in the mid-1980s (see *Training on the Job*).

Above-average levels of educational attainment are also consistently associated with above-average earnings. Adult education is implicated in this relationship in two ways. First, given that adult education carries both an opportunity and a direct cost to the individual who takes part, the economic barrier to participation is likely to be lower the higher the level of income. The other side is that adult education is also an economic variable. It contributes to human capital formation, thus facilitating occupational mobility. Further education and training is therefore not only more affordable for people with well-paying jobs, but it may also carry additional economic benefits for this group. Above-average earnings are moreover associated with above-average levels of participation in "high" culture, active leisure pursuits, as well as residential segregation—additional variables known from research studies to covary with adult education participation.

7. Participation in a Learning Society

This entry has presented arguments in favor of a policy for equalizing the distribution of learning opportunities for adults. But these imperatives are, in the mid-1990s, unevenly matched both by the supply of learning opportunities and by the aspirations of individuals and communities (OECD 1991). Few people doubt that, on the whole, the educational aspirations of adults in both the developing and the developed countries have tended to rise over time. This increase in demand is expressed by people seeking to influence the development of their local community, by women's groups seeking to achieve cultural and economic emancipation, and by minorities and trade unions who regard education and training as a means of achieving their objectives. The demand for learning is influenced by factors such as a secular rise in the level of initial education, a general rise in nonwork time, and demographic developments ranging from migration to changes in the composition of families and households (Schuller 1992). These changes are significant because they reinforce trends toward the establishment of the learning society.

New learning needs and demands arise from many factors. A group of Japanese researchers group these into three categories, relating to changes in the work environment, changes in the living environment, and ecological changes in the global environment (Kawanobe et al. 1993). Changes in the professional environment and the workplace, which have amplified the need for further education and training, have triggered a new debate about recurrent education policy (OECD 1992). However, workplace-related changes are not the only reason behind the demand for a lifelong learning policy. Although lifelong learning policies and programs are heavily influenced by the emphasis on skills improvement, the nonvocational aspects are also receiving increased attention. Changes in the living environment, which relate to the aging of the population and the way leisure time is being spent, tend to increase the demand for adult education.

The notion of a learning society (Husén 1974, 1986) is central to the concept of lifelong learning, as it has been promoted since the 1960s (see *Lifelong Learning*). It should be noted, however, that the situation in the 1990s differs in some respects from that prevailing during the 1960s. At that time the concept of lifelong learning was promoted by social scientists and policy analysts in international organizations such as OECD and UNESCO but failed to catch on in practice, mainly because the preconditions for reform—high level of initial education, democratization of work, leisure time, and so on—were not yet in place. An increasing number of governments are likely to proclaim an interest in the learning society as these conditions will be increasingly met.

It is interesting to note that efforts to create a "lifelong learning culture" are under way all over the world, in cities as diverse as Adelaide, Göteborg, Los Angeles, Mexico, Pittsburgh, and Vienna. This devolution can be explained in several ways: first, because people relate their learning activities to the community that constitutes their immediate environment; second, because of the community-based character of much

Table 1
Variation in employer-sponsored adult education and training by occupational groups (percent receiving training[a])

| Country | High % | Occupational Categories[b] | | | |
		M+ %	M %	M− %	Low %
Germany[c]	31	38	26	15	3
France[c]	46	49	27	22	12
Netherlands[c]	34	32	26	11	5
Sweden[d]	37	39	27	18	12

a Because the training definitions vary the estimates are not comparable in a strict sense   b Socioeconomic categories are defined as follows: High = professionals, managers and administrators; M+ = lower grade professionals, technicians, and supervisors of nonmanual workers; M = routine nonmanual workers in sales, commerce and administration, including rank-and-file service workers; M− = lower grade technicians, supervisors of manual workers and skilled manual workers; Low = semi- and unskilled manual workers   c 1985–87 data, EC labor force surveys, participation in job training schemes in the last 12 months. Source: CEDEFOP (1990)   d Quality of living survey, ULF 1986–87, employer-sponsored training course in the last 12 months.

adult education; and third, because of the importance of creating some coherence among the large number of actors involved in the provision of learning opportunities for adults.

The democratization of education for youth was given high priority in many countries during the 1950s and 1960s. This followed on from a heated debate concerning the reserve of talent. Research studies now indicate that there may also be a large untapped learning reserve as regards the education of adults.

See also: Government Role in Adult Education and Training; Legislation in Adult Education; Time, Leisure and Adult Education; Demand, Supply, and Finance of Adult Education; Study and Learning Strategies; Student Support Systems

References

Australian Bureau of Statistics (ABS) 1992 *Education and Training in Australia* (Catalogue Number 4224.0). Commonwealth Government Printer, Canberra

Boone E J, Shearon R W, White E E (eds.) 1980 *Serving Personal and Community Needs Through Adult Education.* Adult Education Association Handbook Series in Adult Education, Jossey-Bass, San Francisco, California

Boshier R W, Collins J B 1984 The Houle typology after twenty-two years: A large-scale empirical test. *Adult Educ.* 35(3): 113–30

CEDEFOP 1990 *Vocational Training News Flash, 1990 No. 2.* European Center for the Development of Vocational Training, CEDEFOP, Berlin

Cramer G, Van Der Kamp M 1991 *Feiten en Cijfers over de Volwasseneneducatie: Trends in de Periode 1979–1988.* Dutch Advisory Council for Adult Education, Utrecht

Cross K P 1981 *Adults as Learners.* Jossey-Bass, San Francisco, California

Fales A W 1989 Lifespan learning development. In: Titmus C J (ed.) 1989

Hiemstra R 1992 Ageing and learning: An agenda for the future. In: Tuijnman A C, Van der Kamp M (eds.) 1992 *Learning Across the Lifespan: Theories, Research, Policies.* Pergamon Press, Oxford

Husén T 1974 *The Learning Society.* Methuen, London

Husén T 1986 *The Learning Society Revisited: Essays.* Pergamon Press, Oxford

Johnstone J W, Rivera R 1965 *Volunteers for Learning: A Study of the Educational Pursuits of American Adults.* Aldine, Chicago, Illinois

Kawanobe S et al. 1993 *A Study on Lifelong Education in Selected Industrialized Countries.* National Institute for Educational Research and Monbusho, Tokyo

Kennedy C E 1989 Adulthood. In: Titmus C J (ed.) 1989

Knowles M S (ed.) 1960 *Handbook of Adult Education in the United States.* Adult Education Association of the USA, Washington, DC

Merriam S B, Cunningham P M (eds.) 1991 *Handbook of Adult and Continuing Education.* Jossey-Bass, San Francisco, California

Organisation for Economic Co-operation and Development 1977 *Learning Opportunities for Adults. Vol. 1: General Report.* OECD, Paris

Organisation for Economic Co-operation and Development 1979 *Learning Opportunities for Adults. Vol. 2: New Structures, Programmes and Methods.* OECD, Paris

Organisation for Economic Co-operation and Development 1979 *Learning Opportunities for Adults. Vol. 3: The Non-Participation Issue.* OECD, Paris

Organisation for Economic Co-operation and Development 1979 *Learning Opportunities for Adults. Vol. 4: Participation in Adult Education.* OECD, Paris

Organisation for Economic Co-operation and Development 1981 *Learning Opportunities for Adults. Vol. 5: Widening Access for the Disadvantaged.* OECD, Paris

Organisation for Economic Co-operation and Development 1991 *The Lifelong Learner in the 1990s.* OECD, Paris

Organisation for Economic Co-operation and Development 1992 *High-Quality Education and Training for All.* OECD, Paris

Ross-Gordon J M, Martin L G, Briscoe D (eds.) 1990 *Serving Culturally Diverse Populations.* Jossey-Bass, San Francisco, California

Rowden D (ed.) 1936 *Handbook of Adult Education in the United States.* American Association for Adult Education, New York

Rubenson K 1987 Participation in recurrent education: A research review. In: Schütze H G, Istance D (eds.) 1987 *Recurrent Education Revisited: Modes of Participation and Financing.* Almqvist and Wiksell, Stockholm

Rubenson K 1989 Swedish adult education policy in the 1970s and 1980s. In: Ball S J, Larsson S (eds.) 1989 *The Struggle for Democratic Education: Equality and Participation in Sweden.* Falmer Press, London

Schuller T 1992 Age, gender, and learning in the lifespan. In: Tuijnman A C, Van der Kamp M (eds.) 1992 *Learning Across the Lifespan: Theories, Research, Policies.* Pergamon Press, Oxford

Smith R M, Aker G F, Kidd J R (eds.) 1970 *Handbook of Adult Education in the US.* Macmillan, New York

Statistics Sweden (SCB) 1990 Personalutbildning 1975–1989. Statistics Sweden, Stockholm

Sweden, Ministry of Education 1985 *Vuxenutbildningens 1970-talets reformer: En utvärdering.* Allmänna Förlaget, Stockholm

Sweden, Ministry of Education and Science 1992 *The Swedish Way Towards a Learning Society: Report to OECD.* Swedish Ministry of Education and Science, Stockholm

Titmus C J (ed.) 1989 *Lifelong Education for Adults: An International Handbook.* Pergamon Press, Oxford

Tuijnman A C 1991 Lifelong education: A test of the accumulation hypothesis. *Int. J. Lifelong Educ.* 10(4): 275–85

Tuijnman A C 1992 The expansion of adult education and training in Europe: Trends and issues. *Int. Rev. Educ.* 38(6): 673–92

Tuijnman A C, Chinapah V, Fägerlind I 1988 Adult education and earnings. *Econ. Educ. Rev.* 7(4): 423–37

Withnall A M E, Kabwasa N O 1989 Education for older adults. In: Titmus C J (ed.) 1989

Participation: Antecedent Factors

M. Van der Kamp

Adult education gives people new chances on the labor market and opportunities for social–cultural development. Yet certain people take part in adult education while others do not. What are the factors influencing participation? This entry discusses three research traditions in participation research and their main findings. In the conclusion an integrative, multilevel approach is suggested for future research.

1. Definition and Context

Participation research forms a "classical" theme in adult education. To understand this kind of research it is important to realize that for most adults learning is voluntary. In addition, the characteristics of adult learners, their reasons for study, and the programs they attend are highly variable. This heterogeneity and the voluntary nature of participation pose problems for researchers and decision makers. Participation in adult education is unequally distributed in society, which also makes it a political issue.

The aim of this entry is to gain insight into the major antecedent factors influencing participation in adult education. Participation is considered here as the decision process that determines whether or not individuals take part in structured adult education programs. Hence self-directed and independent learning are beyond the scope of this entry (see *Self-directed Learning*). This also applies to specific research themes such as needs assessment and dropout (see *Student Outreach*).

2. Developments Relevant to Participation Research

Three developments are relevant to participation research. First, adult education has been considered as an instrument for raising the economic level of a nation, particularly since the mid-1980s. Second, there is a belief that demographic and technological developments and their impact on labor markets have made the permanent training and retraining of the labor force essential. Politicians speak in this connection of underinvestment in adult education (Ritzen 1989). A third development is the tendency to consider adult education as a "market" governed by relations between supply and demand. Insight into the characteristics, needs, and preferences of the "buyers" and "sellers" of education is necessary for an understanding of the functioning of this market. Knowledge about "inputs" is also a precondition for an assessment of "outputs," that is, the effects of adult education (see *Economics of Adult Education and Training*).

3. Different Traditions in Research on Antecedents

For a long time empirical research on the antecedents and effectiveness of adult education was rather inadequate. Most studies were of a descriptive kind, and explanatory research based on theoretical models was rare. Sociologists and psychologists, educationalists and economists sparsely and separately worked on different aspects of adult education. As a consequence, there was no unified theoretical perspective. Another reason for the underdevelopment of empirical research was the low priority of adult education on the political agenda. That adult education gained in importance during the 1970s can be inferred from a sharp increase in the efforts devoted to participation research during this period. After a period of consolidation in the early 1980s there was growth again in the late 1980s.

Previous investigations into the factors influencing participation have tended to use a sociological, psychological, or economic frame of reference (Tuijnman and Fägerlind 1989). The distinctions are not clearcut, but in the sociological tradition the attention is mainly focused on the influence of socio-demographic variables such as sex and age, home background, previous educational career, social roles and positions, and characteristics of institutions and their provisions. The focus in the psychological tradition is on personality traits, intellectual abilities, and a host of attitudinal dispositions such as motivational orientations, expectations, intentions, and attitudes. Research in economics has so far played a rather modest role in participation research.

4. Sociological Factors

4.1 Youth Educational Attainment

Youth or initial educational attainment is the antecedent variable consistently observed as the most powerful predictor of participation. By controlling for initial attainment, the independent effects of age and measures of social position have in some studies been reduced to nonsignificance (Cookson 1986). The relationship between initial and adult education explains to some extent the lesser participation of people from lower status homes compared with people with a middle-class background. Educational experiences gained during one's career are to an extent cumulative. A traumatic experience of school, lack of motivation, and low performance during initial education may lead to lack of motivation to learn as an adult, whereas much adult education is oriented toward highly motivated and self-confident people. For this reason many observers claim that as long as opportunities in school education are unequally distributed, there is little hope that the gap between the well- and poorly educated can be bridged by means of adult education (Houtkoop 1985).

4.2 Previous Participation in Adult Education

The cumulative effect is reinforced because experience of participation in adult education increases the chance of subsequent participation. Many participants have a long history of participation in adult education behind them (Bergsten 1980). If unchallenged, the will and capacity to learn can diminish or even disappear. "Positive" experiences of learning have the opposite effect. Bergsten (1980) emphasizes the independent influence of previous participation and stresses the importance of "first recruitment."

4.3 Social Roles: Work and Leisure

Darkenwald and Merriam (1982) have coined the expression "learning press." It refers to the extent to which one's current environment requires or encourages further learning. Work is an important factor. Studies investigating the relationships between work and education reveal a cluster of factors determining the chance of receiving continuing education and training. Prominent among these are work roles, labor market segments of employment, the size of the firm, main areas of production, the use of technology, the degree of market competition and the extent to which workers are organized (Tuijnman 1989).

Certain roles offer a better chance of access to education. According to Rubenson (1990), in the United States workers with a university background are 15 times more likely to receive job training than those with only elementary education. People in higher positions take longer external courses, those in lower positions are more involved in short-term on-the-job training. People in higher positions also have more possibilities for informal learning at work. The consequence is a polarization: some employees work in an environment where new skills are constantly required, whereas others end up in a situation of gradual dequalification. New technology may reinforce this development.

The interest people have in adult education for their job is positively related to work satisfaction. Bergsten (1980) opposes the notion that participation could be a compensation for boring and monotonous work. Challenges in the work place can lead to activities in other fields. In general, participation in educational activities correlates positively with leisure and cultural activities (Bergsten 1980, Cookson 1986).

4.4 Gender

The remarks made above about the importance of the work role for participation apply mainly to men. Because of the traditional division of labor, men and women tend to hold different positions in the labor market. Woman often have a lower labor force participation rate than men. These sex differences are reflected in the differential pattern of participation in adult education. However, the share of women in overall enrollment has increased since the 1970s. In some programs women are now in a majority position, at least with respect to their number.

There are several possible explanations. Because the enrollment rate in secondary and tertiary education has for a long time tended to be lower for girls than boys, there was a largely untapped reserve of talent among women, especially among the older generation. For the incoming generations the disadvantage is of a more qualitative nature. Part of the "learner reserve" has been tapped by the feminist movement and by an improvement in the material living conditions of women. Educational provisions for women have also improved. The removal of some external barriers and the creation of new learning opportunities has benefited women more than any of the other groups underrepresented in adult education (Cross 1984). As a group, however, women have tended to participate mainly in general and leisure-oriented educational activities that hardly improve access to the labor market.

4.5 Age

There is a relationship between age and participation. For a long time it was assumed that the ability to learn reached a maximum during early adulthood, and then decreased rapidly. However, research showed that differences within age cohorts are much larger than differences between age cohorts. Learning abilities are determined more by previous educational level and occupational status than by age. Older people tend to learn a little slower, but often learn more meticulously and with more intensity than younger people (*Lernfähigkeit* 1979). However, old age is often confounded with a constellation of conditions unfavorable to participation, such as a low level of initial schooling and few occupational opportunities (Schulenberg et al. 1978). In addition, different educational needs are associated with different stages in life career. For example, job training or study for new instrumental qualifications are often not relevant for the elderly. In general, the share of older participants is increasing. This is partly due to change in provision, but also to the fact that the new generations of older people are better educated than previously (Van der Kamp 1990).

5. Psychological Factors

5.1 Deterrents to Participation

Cross (1984) made a distinction between three categories of deterrents to participation: situational, institutional, and dispositional barriers. Situational barriers arise from one's situation in life at a given time. Lack of money and lack of time are prime examples. Institutional barriers arise from characteristics of the educational establishments, for example, accessibility, recognizability, and attractiveness. Dispositional barriers arise from psychological characteristics. Darkenwald and Merriam (1982) added a fourth category, namely, information barriers.

Darkenwald and Valentine (1985) developed the Deterrents to Participation Scale (DPS) in which six clusters are identified: lack of confidence, lack of relevance, time constraints, low personal priority, costs, and personal problems. Time factors were found to be the overarching deterrent. There are obvious differences with Cross's analytical distinction. Situational barriers are divisible into time constraints, costs, and personal problems; institutional barriers are restricted to the lack of relevance of the program; and dispositional barriers to lack of confidence. The DPS has been widely used as a basis for research (Blais et al. 1989, Martindale and Drake 1989).

Rubenson (1987) suggests that the most powerful impediment is the individual's expectation that participation will not result in improved living conditions or labor market position. There is a clear parallel with the "lack of relevance" factor from the DPS.

5.2 Characteristics of Provision

Institutional barriers in a broader sense refer to characteristics of the provision. Participation in adult education programs does not occur in a social or institutional vacuum. The nature of provision at present is much in accordance with the rules of the marketplace: provisions attracting the largest number of people with the minimum of cost are considered the most successful. This leads to a certain imbalance in provision. According to Schulenberg et al. (1978) provisions are geared to people with explicit motivations and manifest needs.

Rubenson (1990) notes that a delivery system that takes for granted that the adult is a self-directed individual in possession of the instruments vital to making use of the available possibilities for adult education—in other words, a system that relies on self-selection in recruitment—will by necessity create inequality in a society.

5.3 Personality Traits and Cognitive Abilities

Research into the relationship between participation and personality traits and cognitive abilities is relatively rare. Rubenson (1987) stresses the importance of self-evaluation and related concepts such as self-perception, self-reliance, and self-confidence. Adults with a positive self-evaluation are more likely to succeed in achievement-oriented situations than those with a negative self-evaluation.

Tuijnman (1989) included measures of cognitive ability in a model examining the effects of recurrent education, using data from the Swedish Malmö study. It turned out that cognitive ability has an independent influence on participation in adult education. Cognitive ability exerts a positive effect on the cumulation of learning experience, independent of initial educational attainment.

5.4 Motivational Orientations

A central theme of research is concerned with "motivational orientations" to both predictor and outcome variables.

Houle (1961) created a theoretical typology on the basis of indepth interviews. He proposed that participants in adult education are either goal-, activity-, or learning-oriented. The goal-oriented were purported to use education as a means of accomplishing fairly clear-cut objectives; the activity-oriented were those who took part because they found a meaning in the circumstances of the learning which had no necessary connection with the content or announced purposes of the activity; the learning-oriented sought knowledge for its own sake, as a more or less constant activity.

Houle's construction led to a vast number of empirical studies to test the validity of the typology and to the construction of standardized instruments like the Education Participation Scale (EPS) developed by Boshier.

Boshier and Collins (1985) re-analyzed data from more than 12,000 learners in different parts of the world and concluded that six learning orientations can be distinguished: social contact, social stimulation, professional advancement, community service, external expectations, and cognitive interest. Cognitive interest (learning orientation) and professional advancement (goal orientation) can be clearly distinguished. The other factors are "a murky fruit salad" (Boshier and Collins 1985 p. 129). In several surveys socioeconomic and life cycle variables explained part of the variance in motivation. Significant relationships were found with, for example, socioeconomic status and earnings, sex and age, marital status, and previous participation in adult education, but the amount of explained variance was usually small. A shortcoming of research on motivational orientations is the lack of clarity about the relationship between orientations and actual participation.

5.5 Attitudes

Houle (1961 pp. 15–16) pointed at the importance of attitudes toward adult education: "every adult has a basic orientation to education, an underlying conviction of its nature and value which influences his or her opinion about participation and learning" (also quoted in Hayes and Darkenwald 1990). Darkenwald and Hayes (1988) developed the Adult Attitudes toward Continuing Education Scale (AACES). They found a strong relationship between (positive) attitudes and participation. Women and people with a higher level of initial education show a more positive attitude toward adult education than men and the poorly educated.

The underlying dimensions of the AACES show some similarities with the motivational orientations mentioned before. Three basic attitudes are distinguished: enjoyment of learning, importance of adult education, and the "intrinsic value" of learning. It appears that a positive perception of the importance of adult education is more decisive for participation than a positive perception of the enjoyment of learning or its intrinsic value. According to Bergsten (1977) there are differences between social groups in this respect, as positive perceptions of the intrinsic value of adult education are linked to a leisure style usually found in the middle and upper classes.

5.6 Intentions

It is generally difficult to demonstrate a strong correspondence between attitudes and the performance of specific behavior. The theory of reasoned action of Ajzen and Fishbein has been applied to participation in adult education by Pryor (1990) and was proven successful. The theory postulates that a given behavior is determined by an intention to perform that behavior. Intention is determined by an attitude toward the behavior and a perception of social pressure to perform the behavior. Pryor (1990) found that the intention to participate was largely predicted by attitudes toward adult education. Differences in attitudes between those who intend to participate and those who do not are explained by differences in the strength of the belief in the outcomes of participation and a corresponding evaluation of each outcome. In this case belief in an improvement of professional behavior by means of adult education predicted a positive attitude toward participation.

6. Economic Factors

The research from an economic perspective has mainly been concerned with (a) the assessment of the economic barriers to participation, such as the effect of different means of educational financing on participation rates; and (b) the estimation of costs and benefits of adult education.

6.1 Costs as Barriers

Costs are often mentioned by respondents as barriers to participation. This variable, together with lack of time, is more frequently noted in self-report surveys than other types of barriers. But such results are difficult to interpret. People often have no idea about the actual costs of courses and alternatives. In fact, the ability to pay does not usually coincide with the willingness to pay. However, there is more empirical evidence. Cross (1984) mentions programs where the withdrawal of funds or the loss of financial benefits led to a dramatic fall in participation. De Groot (1984) did a time-series analysis of the relation between participation and price increases in Dutch evening classes. A rather strong increase in prices led to a decrease in participation. So it seems that the cost of education does have an impact on participation.

6.2 Participation as Investment

The decision to participate is often interpreted as being governed by an anticipation of the costs and benefits of the activity. Some economists assume that people invest in themselves by education and training to maximize their life-time earnings. Empirical research in this field is mostly restricted to the field of industrial training. There is evidence that investment in adult education does have a payoff to the individual and the enterprise (Mincer 1989). However, there is also an indication of underinvestment generally, and for certain groups in particular (Ritzen 1989). Yet educational activities are also risky investments and the benefits are often unclear in advance. In such situations people tend to be risk adverse and hence refrain from participation (Levhari and Weiss 1974).

When people participate in education, other values are taken into account as well. Groot et al. (1990) found only a small positive effect of expected life-time earnings on the probability of receiving training. They conclude that the anticipation of an increase in earnings is not all that important as an antecedent factor. Context factors and individual characteristics seem to have a greater influence on decisions to participate than considerations of costs and benefits. People in certain labor markets and large firms participate more than workers in small and medium-size firms. The same applies to young people, especially men with prestigious and full-time jobs and high levels of initial education (Bishop 1985, Mincer 1989).

So far, a disadvantage of the economic perspective is that our knowledge about the nature of the decision-making process leading to participation is very limited. Wong and Siegerist (1989) questioned workers about their (intended) participation in training. In general there was a great preparedness to take up training. The actual decision was governed by a weighing of the demands of the working place and an estimation of one's own capabilities and expected benefits. These factors have a different weight for people with different personal characteristics such as age, sex, social position, and educational level. To keep on learning, or in the words of Wong and Siegerist, "to remain in the circuit of permanent education" (p. 4), experiences of educational success are necessary.

7. Models of Participation

Most of the research described so far made use of cross-sectional data gathered at only one moment in time. A great improvement is the use of longitudinal data to explain participation in adult education. Tuijnman (1989), who used data from the Malmö cohort of Swedish men, found significant differences between the men who took part and those who did not, with regard to variables such as home background, initial educational attainment, cognitive ability, and occupational status. The effect of job status on participation was estimated at successive moments in time. The effect of job level on participation increased with advancing age, whereas the effect of initial education decreased. Tuijnman and Fägerlind (1989) infer that the direct effect of youth education on adult education becomes mediated and reinforced by the occupational positions held. From the results it is also clear that cognitive factors play an important and independent role in influencing participation. This finding sets limits to the applicability of corrective policy intervention.

An interesting feature of Tuijnman's study is that different types of variables—psychological, sociological, and economic—are examined by means of structural relations (path) analysis. There is a need to develop multilevel explanatory models of participation in adult education. Rubenson (1987) puts it as follows: ". . . Thus analysis of recruitment has to consider both the macro and the micro levels, i.e. both structural conditions and individual psychological factors and, in addition, the link between them" (p. 41). Rubenson proposed such a model based on the "expectancy–valence" theory, in which "valence" expresses an affective attitude to the result of an action and "expectancy" expresses the individual's expectations of being able to participate in and complete the activity. These together exert a force that determines whether an individual is likely to participate in an educational activity. Unfortunately, only parts of this multilevel model have so far been empirically tested. The overall check still remains to be done. This also applies to the model described below.

In the model proposed by Cookson (1986) participation is seen as the outcome of influences exerted by external context-variables, social background and social role, personal characteristics and cognitive abilities, attitudinal dispositions, retained information and situational factors. This model is labeled ISSTAL after its key descriptors: interdisciplinary, sequential-specificity, time-allocation, and life span perspective. The lifespan perspective gives the model currency, as participation is viewed in relation to different social roles adopted in the life span. According to Cookson, participation in adult education shows synchronic and diachronic covariation. Not only does an individual's participation in adult education activities have implications for other types of social activity, but patterns of participation synchronically covary with other types of socially valued activities. Participation in adult education is thus conceptualized as part of broader behavior of social participation. The life span hypothesis of the ISSTAL model postulates that social participation fits into "lifelong patterns," exhibiting diachronic covariation. Accordingly, compared with others in the same age cohort, people who exhibit higher levels of participation in their thirties may be expected to display similarly higher levels in their forties, fifties, and sixties.

The models proposed by Rubenson and Cookson, and also those developed by others such as Darkenwald and Merriam (1982) and Pryor (1990) are valuable as heuristic schemes and as agenda for research. With the help of these models future research could be focused on variables suitable for policy intervention. However, the models have not reached the status of tested theories yet. A precondition for modeling and explanatory participation research is the availability of extensive, multilevel data. Even though analyses of longitudinal data sets such as those by Tuijnman (1989) and Van Leeuwen and Dronkers (1992) are an improvement, they do not take into account the multilevel character of variables influencing participation. Accordingly, a high priority for future research is the collection of large-scale (comparative) survey data at both the institutional and individual level. The development of participation (and effectiveness) research depends on the availability of such data. This does not deny the importance of descriptive research which, as can be inferred from the above review of previous studies, has yielded a certain "map" of factors influencing participation in adult education.

References

Bergsten U 1977 *Adult Education in Relation to Work and Leisure. A Cross-Sectional Study of Adults with Short Previous Formal Education.* Almqvist and Wiksell, Stockholm

Bergsten U 1980 Interest in education among adults with short previous formal schooling. *Adult Educ.* 30(3): 131–51

Bishop J 1985 *Preparing Youth for Employment.* The National Center for Research in Vocational Education, Ohio State University, Columbus, Ohio

Blais J, Duquette A, Painchaud G 1989 Deterrents to women's participation in work-related educational activities. *Adult Educ. Q.* 39(4): 224–34

Boshier R W, Collins J B 1985 The Houle typology after twenty-two years: A large-scale empirical test. *Adult Educ. Q.* 35(3): 113–30

Cookson P S 1986 A framework for theory and research on adult education participation. *Adult Educ. Q.* 36(3): 130–41

Cross K P 1984 *Adults as learners.* Jossey-Bass, San Francisco, California

Darkenwald G G, Hayes E R 1988 Assessment of adult attitudes towards continuing education. *Int. J. Lifelong Educ.* 7(3): 197–204

Darkenwald G G, Merriam S B 1982 *Adult Education: Foundations of Practice*. Harper and Row, New York

Darkenwald G G, Valentine T 1985 Factor structure of deterrents to public participation in adult education. *Adult Educ. Q.* 35(4): 177–93

De Groot H 1984 *De prijs van avondonderwijs*. Sociaal en Cultureel Planbureau, Rijswijk

Groot W, Hartog J, Oosterbeek H 1990 Training choice and earnings. *Research memorandum 9027*. University of Amsterdam, Amsterdam

Hayes E R, Darkenwald G G 1990 Attitudes toward adult education: An empirically-based conceptualization. *Adult Educ. Q.* 40(3): 156–68

Houle C O 1961 *The Inquiring Mind*. University of Wisconsin Press, Madison, Wisconsin

Houtkoop W 1985 Volwasseneneducatie en de ongelijke verdeling van educatieve kansen, In: Peschar J L, Wesselingh AA (eds.) 1985 *Onderwijssociologie: Een inleiding*. Wolters Noordhoff, Groningen

Lernfähigkeit und Lernverhalten von Erwachsenen 1979 Pädagogische Arbeitsstelle des DVV, Frankfurt

Levhari D, Weiss Y 1974 The effect of risk on the investment in human capital. *Am. Econ. Rev.* 64: 950–64

Martindale C J, Drake J B 1989 Factor structure of deterrents to participation in off-duty adult education programs. *Adult Educ. Q.* 39(2): 63–75

Mincer J 1989 Human capital and the labour market: A review of deterrents to participation in off-duty adult education programs. *Educ. Researcher* 18: 27–34

Pryor B W 1990 Predicting and explaining intentions to participate in continuing education: An application of the theory of reasoned action. *Adult Educ. Q.* 40(3): 146–57

Ritzen J M M 1989 Government and job training. The Eric John Hanson memorial lecture series, Vol. 4 University of Alberta, Alberta

Rubenson K 1987 Participation in recurrent education: A research review. In: Schütze H G, Istance D (eds.) 1987 *Recurrent Education Revisited: patterns of Participation and Financing*. Almqvist and Wiksell, Stockholm

Rubenson K 1990 Participation in adult education and training—between market and policy. Paper presented at the Conference "Investing in Human Resources," Amsterdam 10–11 December, 1990. Dutch Advisory Council for Adult Education and Training, Utrecht

Schulenberg W, Loeber H B, Loeber-Pautsch U, Pühler S 1978 *Soziale Faktoren der Bildungsbereitschaft Erwachsenev*. Klett-Costa, Stuttgart

Tuijnman A 1989 *Recurrent Education, Earnings and Wellbeing: A Fifty-year Longitudinal Study of a Cohort of Swedish Men*. Acta Universitatis Stockholmiensis. Almqvist and Wiksell, Stockholm

Tuijnman A, Fägerlind I 1989 Measuring and predicting participation in lifelong education using longitudinal data. *Scand. J. Educ. Res.* 33(1): 47–66

Van der Kamp M 1990 Education for older adults in Europe: A common problem, different solutions? In: Wellings A (ed.) 1990 *Towards 1992. Education of Adults in the New Europe*. SCUTREA, University of Sheffield, Sheffield

Van Leeuwen S, Dronkers J 1992 Effects of continuing education: A study on adult education, social inequality and labour market position. *Int. J. Educ. Res.* 17(6): 609–24

Wong R, Siegerist E 1989 *Werk hebben, werk houden*. OSA-voorstudie V-34. OSA, The Hague

Further Reading

Boshier R W 1989 Participant motivation. In: Titmus C J (ed.) 1989 *Lifelong Education for Adults: An International Handbook*, Pergamon Press, Oxford

Bronneman-Helmers R 1988 *Samenhang rond volwasseneneducatie*, Vol. 1. Sociaal en Cultureel Planbureau, Rijswijk

Caffarella R S, Caffarella E P 1986 Self-directedness and learning contracts in adult education. *Adult Educ. Q.* 36(4): 226–34

Groot W 1991 Scholing, arbeidsmarkt en economische ontwikkeling, Een overzicht. Ministerie van Sociale Zaken en Werkgelegenheid, The Hague

Houtkoop M, Van der Kamp M 1992 Factors influencing participation in continuing education. *Int. J. Educ. Res.* 17(6): 537–48

Nordhaug O 1983 Distribution of adult education: The Norwegian case. *Adult Educ. Q.* 34(1): 29–37

Scanlan C L, Darkenwald G G 1984 Identifying deterrents to participation in continuing education. *Adult Educ. Q.* 34(3): 155–66

Schütze H G, Istance D 1987 *Recurrent Education Revisited: Modes of Participation and Financing*. Almqvist and Wiksell, Stockholm

Valentine T, Darkenwald G G 1990 Deterrents to participation in adult education. *Adult Educ. Q.* 41(1): 29–43

Participation: Role of Motivation

D. Deshler

This entry discusses theories and explanations concerning participation motivation in adult education. The discussion is focused on the multiple context factors that motivate or deter participation.

1. Variation in Participation Levels

Participation in adult education varies among coun-

tries. In some countries, public authorities and institutions provide extensive learning opportunities for adults, while in others the provision of adult education is primarily the domain of nongovernmental organizations, including business, industry, voluntary agencies, and self-help groups. Some political systems have discouraged popular education and literacy efforts among the masses, while others have actively engaged in literacy campaigns. Obligatory education and training for different categories of professionals and workers is extensive in the industrialized countries.

Participation rates are usually lower for rural people and for those at the bottom of the social and economic hierarchy. In many countries, there is considerable disparity between participation rates for women in comparison to men as well as disparities among ethnic and racial groups. The distribution of adult education participation also varies according to subject matter categories.

The two categories of general adult education and continuing vocational training account for the major part of total participation in organized adult education in the industrialized countries. However, participation in adult learning that is not sponsored by agencies is even more extensive than organized adult learning. A significant part of adult learning occurs in the form of self-planned learning projects rather than as group learning organized by institutions (Tough 1982). The extent of participation and persistence in sponsored adult education has been extensively surveyed in North America and Europe since 1965. It has generally been less studied by means of large-scale surveys in countries in Africa, Asia, and Latin America.

Explanations for participation motivation in adult education are diverse. No comprehensive theories exist, although Rubenson (1987) mentions three approaches to model building. The first focuses on the individual's (cognitive) reasons for participation. The second emphasizes adult education as a societal process which influences the individual. The third approach looks into the interaction between individuals and social forces. The research in North America began with an emphasis on the learner's motivation for participation and later added societal factors as explanations. In Europe, particularly in the Nordic countries, the focus of research studies has mostly been on societal influences, especially public policy (Nordhaug 1991).

2. Explanations Based on Adult Learner Motivation

North American researchers, influenced by educational psychology, have traditionally focused on the individual adult learner for motivational explanations. "Motivation" has been defined as a general state of readiness, in this case, to learn. The interest has been to discover the main personal incentives of adults for pursuing education. This research was to produce an understanding of the factors that motivate adults to engage in voluntary learning projects.

Maslow's (1954) hierarchy of needs theory provided an initial conceptualization for participation studies. A motivating force was theorized to emerge when each subordinate need was satisfied. The lower order (life-chance, deficiency) needs for survival were

hypothesized to be met before the higher order (lifespace, personal growth, the development of leisure) needs would be addressed by persons. According to this theory, persons with "low" levels of education were more inclined to enroll in adult education for professional advancement, social contact, and social stimulation. In contrast, persons with "high" occupational status were more inclined to enroll for "cognitive" reasons.

Rubenson (1975, 1987) and Howard (1989) developed the "expectancy–valence" model. The theory behind this model holds that an anticipation of rewards from learning "energizes" individual behavior, that perceived value of various outcomes gives direction to behavior, and that learned connections develop between behavior and outcome expectancy.

Other theories hold that participation in adult education is motivated in response to various changes that occur across the life span. Drawing upon the work of developmental psychologists, researchers have found evidence that participation in adult learning tends to be related to cognitive development and life stages or phases (Thorndike et al. 1928, Havighurst 1972, Houle 1984, Lasker et al. 1980). Aslanian and Brickell (1980) report that life span transitions are accompanied by active learning efforts and that significant "trigger" events associated with life transitions, such as getting married, obtaining or losing a job, having children, getting divorced or retired, losing a relative, and so on "activate" incentives and motivation to learn. Studies on adults who returned to school or pursued higher education after an interruption in their study program, indicate that a major reason for undertaking continuing education is to clarify self-identity and to explore new interests and careers (Chickering and Havighurst 1981).

In addition, it is found that many adults have been "educationally deformed," "vaccinated against," or "turned-off" by their previous experiences in formal education and that, for many, participation in adult education requires "educational reformation" and "transformation" through emancipatory adult education to overcome negative socialization, alienation from elitist educational institutions, lack of peer support, psychological passivity and fatalism, or lack of self-confidence (see *Psychology of Adult Education*).

3. Explanations Based on Social Contexts

The research on participation motivation of individuals cited above has uncovered internal psychological aspirations, barriers, and developmentally related motivations. However, it has also led to an appreciation of the importance of various social factors, such as political systems, government resources, economic opportunity, labor market structures, social class, age, and gender socialization, that exert external influences on participation that can no longer be ignored.

Participation, according to this sociological perspective, depends upon several structural factors, including home background, previous educational attainments, and occupational status (Anderson and Darkenwald 1979, Tuijnman 1989). Government language policies, such as offering instruction in only official languages or the provision for education in indigenous or nondominant languages, also affect motivation for participation in recurrent education. Participation is also affected by government labor market policies that require certification or provide financial incentives or mandates to businesses and industries to educate workers.

It is suggested by Quigley (1990) that many adults actively resist participation in adult education as a political boycott against educational providers who do not share similar values or visions of a future society. The fact that most adult education teachers are drawn from the middle class and are often of a different race or culture than many of their learners must also be taken into account in understanding initial motivation for participation as well as dropout or boycott behavior (see *Student Dropout*). More recently, feminist researchers have pointed out that aspirations of women are different than those of men, and that participation in adult education is related to gender socialization and the influence of religious or cultural norms that either encourage or discourage women from participation in adult education (Belenky et al. 1986, Lutrell 1989). Clearly, social structures of society as well as cultural norms facilitate or discourage participation (see *Sociology of Adult Education*).

Freire (1973) gave recognition to the power of a hegemonic culture to silence the poor and to reduce their educational aspirations and participation in learning. He suggested that a powerful explanation for nonparticipation on the part of the oppressed was that often dominant cultures promote ideologies and beliefs that undermine the confidence of the poor. This is reinforced by government policies and the curricula content of adult education. Popular education participation is based on the assumption that the oppressed can overcome their silence and limited educational aspirations through opportunities to critically reflect and be emancipated from a dominant hegemony that reproduces social injustice. Participation or nonparticipation, according to this view, can be explained by the extent of political repression or democratic egalitarian social space, by public educational support or neglect, or by the activism of popular movements (see *Popular Education and Conscientization*).

The presence or absence of nongovernmental organizations dedicated to adult education can affect participation. In addition, the nature and philosophy of provider organizations toward participant roles in decision making can either motivate or discourage participation. Popular participation in development programs is negatively affected by overcentralized planning, inadequate delivery mechanisms, lack of local coordination, inappropriateness of project technology, irrelevant project content, lack of local structures, and ideological differences. According to a sociological perspective, unequal access to and control over societal wealth and power is the primary explanation for lack of participation motivation (see *Community Education and Community Development*).

4. Explanations Based on Learner Interaction with Social Influences

Explanations for participation motivation based on individual learner characteristics and external social influences are both essential, but neither is sufficient in isolation from the other. A number of theories, based on inclusion of social as well as personal variables and their interaction, have been proposed. Participation motivation appears to be recurrent, cumulative, and complex. The power–load–margin model of McClusky (1963) was one of the first of these explanations that presented a "personal, social interactive" model. "Load" represents the demands made upon the individual by self and society, while "power" represents a combination of interacting forces available to the individual to sustain the load. The ratio of load to power is defined as the "margin" of power available to engage in adult education.

Another early model was proposed by Miller (1967), who linked the motivational needs hierarchy of Maslow (1954) with the force field analysis model of Lewin (1947). Miller predicted that when personal needs and social forces are strong in the direction of an educational objective, participation will be high. The opposite would be true if the personal needs and social forces contradict each other. The social forces were hypothesized to be different according to social class and, therefore, to present different force fields for participation.

Houle (1961) created a typology of adult learners based on personal orientations toward learning: the goal oriented, the activity oriented, and the intrinsic learning oriented. A number of studies followed that tried to test this typology and correlate orientation scores with a variety of sociodemographic and life-cycle variables. The best known of these is Boshier's congruence model (1971, 1982; Boshier and Collins 1985), which is based on the idea of congruence between interacting internal (self) and external (environmental) variables. The theory holds that the greater the incongruence experienced by an individual between the actual and perceived notions of self, others, and his or her educational environment, the greater the likelihood of nonparticipation or dropout. The theory moreover holds that people are either primarily growth-motivated or deficiency-motivated. Instead of Houle's three orientations, the theory proposes six factors that explain enrollment: social contact, social stimulation, professional advancement, community service, external expectations, and cognitive interest. Boshier hypothesized that people move from deficiency-oriented to growth-oriented motivation as they get older or increase their socioeconomic status. The education participation scale (EPS), an instrument developed by Boshier and colleagues to measure the factor structure of motivational orientations, contains 40 items, cast on a 4-point Likert scale. The testing of the theory using the EPS instrument has provided evidence that, although the correlations between motivational orientation scores and "antecedent" variables usually attain statistical significance, the amount of unexplained variance usually exceeds the explained variation. Participants with "low" education, occupational status, and income are more often inclined to be enrolled for social contact, social stimulation, community service, and external expectation reasons than people with a relatively high level of educational attainment, occupational status, and income. The most powerful predictor found in Boshier and Collins's study (1985) is occupational status. Boshier and Collins (1985) conclude that more is known about what motivates adults to continue learning than what impels them to enroll.

Rubenson (1975) also combined the perspectives of the learners with the effects of environmental factors, and their socialization by family, school, and work, in his expectancy–valence model. The theory holds that learners will participate and persist if a learning activity is consistent with their current needs. Yet running parallel to these needs are forces of socialization and structural factors that determine positive, negative, or neutral valence toward proposed adult education. Since structural and cultural factors are different, according to social class, the theory suggests different outcomes according to class.

Cross (1981) suggests in her chain-of-response model that anticipation of learning is not an isolated act, but one that is critically related to a complex chain of responses to an individual's position in society. Participation is influenced by factors along a continuum, beginning at one end with individual self-evaluation and attitudes towards education, then moving toward the importance of goals and expectations about learning in relation to life transitions, and then influenced by available information and environmental opportunities or barriers.

Darkenwald and Merriam (1982) restructured the psychosocial interaction model developed by Cross (1981), theorizing that the probability of participation depends on socioeconomic status, learning press, perceived value and utility of adult education, readiness to participate, participation stimuli, and environmental and personal barriers.

Tuijnman and Fägerlind (1989) report on a longitudinal study of antecedents to participation in adult education using longitudinal data collected from 834 Swedish men over a 50-year period. This study in-

vestigated the effects of home background, cognitive ability, initial educational attainment, socioeconomic status, general attitude toward education, and specific interests in adult education. They report that collectively these variables explain no more than between 10–26 percent of the variance in the participation variable. However, the results also indicate that the effects of initial educational attainment on adult education participation, with increasing age, becomes increasingly mediated by their occupational positions in the labor market. The study to some extent supports the hypothesis undergirding the resource conversion theory, namely that the assets an individual has access to in childhood, such as the environmental resources of the home and personality attributes, are converted into marketable assets, particularly through formal education. The interaction of these resources constitutes a force, the strength of which determines, among other things, the likelihood of continued participation in adult education (Tuijnman and Fägerlind 1989 p. 49).

The most recent line of theory building has focused on the concept of deterrents to participation. Scanlan and Darkenwald (1984) created a "deterrents to participation scale" (DPS). This instrument has been used in modified form in several research studies. For example, Reddy (1991) found in South Africa that the major categories of deterrents to participation, including dispositional constraints, personal constraints, lack of infrastructural support, lack of course relevance, work constraints, and information barriers, were cross-nationally relevant. However, there were many context-sensitive deterrents that could not be generalized across cultural, class, and racial lines, even if examined within one single and limited geographic area.

Efforts to build generalizable models have contributed to an awareness of the complexity associated with the concept of participation motivation, and to an appreciation of the diversity of specific political, economic, social, and cultural deterrents in unique historical contexts. Although several theoretical models have been generated, most have not been tested cross-culturally. The few rigorous statistical studies that exist suggest that the probability of acquiring a substantial amount of adult education is greater "the higher the level of parental education, the higher the interest taken in education by a person's parents during childhood, the higher the initial level of formal educational attainment, and the higher the prestige of the occupational positions a person has held in the labor market" (Tuijnman and Fagerlind 1989 p. 63).

5. *Future Research: Outstanding Issues*

Research on participation motivation in adult education is still in its theoretical development stage. Explanations for participation motivation in adult education continue to emerge from quantitative studies, although very few such studies have sought generalizable knowledge across cultures. Qualitative participation studies that document unique historical situations and particular political, social, and cultural situations should also be encouraged. In addition, life span narrations of the participation of individuals can be helpful in integrating the findings of sociological and psychological studies. The predictive capacity of early experiences in formal education for participation in continuing education needs to be further researched along with the role of critical incidents and major life transitions in fostering adult learning.

A distinction should be made between initial participation and persistence in participation. How does motivation change as a consequence of participation? How does participant motivation vary in relation to learning environments and instructor learning styles of specific providers? How do various cultural factors affect the socialization process that influences participation in adult education? Nonparticipants should be studied to more fully understand resistance to participation particularly in workplace training programs.

Researchers know far too little about the way that government policy and educational organizations shape participation in adult education. How do the politics of the provision, purpose, and content of adult education influence the participation of specific groups in society? What are the effects of the mass media and the provision of distance education on participation?

Whether the focus of research at the outset is on the individual; the educational provider; the employer; or the social, political, economic, or historical context, it is clear that research on participation motivation will be enhanced by taking a multidisciplinary approach.

See also: Clienteles and Special Populations; Participation: Antecedent Factors; Student Counseling; Study and Learning Strategies

References

Anderson R, Darkenwald G 1979 *Participation and Persistence in American Adult Education.* College Board Publications, Princeton, New Jersey

Aslanian C B, Brickell H M 1980 *Americans in Transition: Life Changes as Reasons for Adult Learning.* The College Board, New York

Belenky M F, Clinchy B M, Goldberger N R, Tarule J M 1986 *Women's Ways of Knowing: The Development of Self, Voice and Mind.* Basic Books, New York

Boshier R W 1971 Motivational orientations of adult education participants: A factor analytic exploration of Houle's typology. *Adult Educ.* 21(2): 3–26

Boshier R W 1982 *Education Participation Scale.* Learning Press, Vancouver

Boshier R W, Collins J B 1985 The Houle typology after 22 years: A large scale empirical test. *Adult Educ.* 35(3): 113–30

Chickering A, Havighurst R 1981 *The Modern American College.* Jossey-Bass, San Francisco, California

Cross K P 1981 *Adults as Learners: Increasing Participation and Facilitating Learning.* Jossey-Bass, San Francisco, California

Darkenwald G G, Merriam S B 1982 *Adult Education: Foundations of Practice.* Harper and Row, New York

Freire P 1973 *Education for Critical Consciousness.* Continuum, New York

Havighurst R J 1972 *Developmental Tasks and Education,* 3rd edn. D. McKay Co., New York

Houle C 1961 *The Inquiring Mind.* University of Wisconsin Press, Madison, Wisconsin

Houle C 1984 *Patterns of Learning: New Perspectives on Life Span Education.* Jossey-Bass, San Francisco, California

Howard K W 1989 A comprehensive expectancy motivation model: Implications for adult education and training. *Adult Educ. Q.* 39(4): 199–210

Lasker H M, Moore J F, Simpson E 1980 *Adult Development and Approaches to Learning.* US Department of Education, Office of Educational Research and Improvement, NIE, Washington, DC

Lewin K 1947 Frontiers in group dynamics: Concept, method and reality in social science. *Human Relations* 1: 5–41

Lutrell W 1989 Working-class women's ways of knowing: Effects of gender, race and class. *Sociology of Education* 62: 33–46

Maslow A H 1954 *Motivation and Personality.* Harper and Row, New York

McClusky H Y 1963 The course of the adult life span. In: Hallenbeck W C (ed.) 1963 *Psychology of Adults.* Adult Education Association, Washington, DC

Miller H L 1967 *Participation of Adults in Education: A Force Field Analysis.* Center for the Study of Liberal Education of Adults, Boston, Massachusetts (ERIC No. ED011996)

National Center for Education Statistics (NCES) 1987 *Trends in Adult Education 1969–1984.* NCES Publication No. CS 87-307. US Government Printing Office, Washington, DC

National Institute for Adult Continuing Education 1990 *Education's for Other People: Access to Education for Non-Participant Adults.* National Institute for Adult and Continuing Education, Leicester

Nordhaug O 1991 Sociological adult education research in Norway: Status and directions. *Scandinavian J. Educ. Res.* 35: 57–68

Quigley B A 1990 Hidden logic: Reproduction and resistance in adult literacy and adult basic education. *Adult Educ. Q.* 40(2): 103–15

Reddy K B 1991 Perceived deterrents to participation in compensatory education by educationally disadvantaged adult South Africans. Unpublished doctoral dissertation, Cornell University, Ithaca, New York

Rubenson K 1975 *Participation in Recurrent Education.* CERI, OECD, Paris

Rubenson K 1987 Participation in recurrent education: A research review. In: Schutz H G, Istance D (eds.) 1987 *Recurrent Education Revisited: Modes of Participation and Financing.* Almqvist and Wiksell, Stockholm

Scanlan C, Darkenwald G G 1984 Identifying deterrents to participation in continuing education. *Adult Educ. Q.* 34(3): 155–66

Thorndike E L, Bregman E O, Tilton J W, Woodyard E 1928 *Adult Learning.* Macmillan, New York

Tough A 1982 *The Adult's Learning Projects: A Fresh Approach to Theory and Practice in Adult Learning.* Ontario Institute for Studies in Education, Toronto

Tuijnman A 1989 *Recurrent Education, Earnings, and Well-Being: A Fifty-Year Longitudinal Study of a Cohort of Swedish Men.* Almqvist and Wiksell International, Stockholm

Tuijnman A, Fägerlind I 1989 Measuring and predicting participation in lifelong education using longitudinal data. *Scandinavian J. Educ. Res.* 33(1): 47–66

Further Reading

Courtney S 1991 *Why Adults Learn: Towards a Theory of Participation in Adult Education.* Routledge, Chapman and Hall, Inc., New York

Darkenwald G G, Valentine T 1985 Factor structure of deterrents to public participation in adult education. *Adult Educ. Q.* 35(4): 177–93

Jarvis P 1987 *Adult Learning in the Social Context.* Croom Helm, London

Merriam S B, Caffarella R S 1991 *Learning in Adulthood: A Comprehensive Guide.* Jossey-Bass, San Francisco, California

Tenent M 1988 *Psychology and Adult Learning.* Routledge, London

Hayes E R 1987 Low-literate adult basic education student perception of deterrents to participation. Unpublished doctoral dissertation, Rutgers University, New Brunswick, New Jersey

Houtkoop W, van der Kamp M 1992 Factors influencing participation in continuing education. *Int. J. Educ. Res.* 16

Student Counseling

J. Potter

The counseling of learners—or potential learners—is a vital activity within adult education and one which is integral to its philosophy and goals. Although considerable ground has been gained in promoting an understanding of counseling for adult learners and in establishing these services, many challenges remain. This entry provides a discussion of the nature and importance of counseling for adult learners, and reviews selected emerging issues.

1. Concepts and Definitions

Woolfe et al. (1987) describe counseling as being "about helping people to help themselves to live their lives more effectively" (p. 35), and as involving four stages—exploring, understanding, decision-making, and acting. But what does this mean for adults in an educational context? The answer is not a simple one nor is it a singular one.

Adult learners or potential learners bring many strengths to an educational setting as a result of life experience. That same complexity and richness, however, also implies that they present a variety of needs which may include the need for information about learning opportunities; for help in overcoming the residual pain of previous encounters with the educational system; for assistance in determining career and learning directions; for financial assistance; for help in learning how to learn; for help with personal or family concerns; for assistance in dealing with the educational system; or for emotional or psychological support. Counseling in an adult education context, then, may involve any of these activities and more, and may take place at any stage in the learning process—

pre-entry, entry, during, or at exit (Schlossberg 1984a, Lynch and Chickering 1984).

Considerable variation exists in terminology used to articulate this helping function. "Guidance" and "counseling" are the two most common terms and are, on occasion, used interchangeably as, for example, by the Council for Cultural Cooperation (1982); frequently, however, distinctions are drawn. Woolfe et al. (1987) are among the clearest in distinguishing between two approaches. Guidance, according to them, emphasizes advice-giving and is advisor-directed; the major concern is with the decision or product which is specific to the situation at hand. Counseling, on the other hand, is more concerned with the process of decision-making and assumes that learning from one situation can be transferred to another. This activity is more nondirective and client-driven, with the counselor acting as an enabler or facilitator. Paulet (1988) draws a similar distinction between advising and counseling. Others (e.g., Brown 1991) use "guidance" as the more generic term and list "counseling" as a specific activity within a framework which also includes informing, advising, assessing, enabling, advocating, and feeding back.

2. Functions of Counseling

Educational counseling may serve a number of important functions for the individual, the institution, and for adult education in general. In broadest terms, counseling helps to remove or reduce barriers for the individual, barriers which may be informational, dispositional, situational, or institutional in nature. As a result, counseling provides improved access to

575

educational opportunities for adults and increases the likelihood of successful completion. As recognized by the Council for Cultural Cooperation, adult education is still largely a privilege of the already educated; educational guidance and counseling, therefore, have an outreach function to help extend equality of opportunity to underserved groups. The Council report (1982) refers to guidance and counseling as the "hinge-pin" between supply and demand in adult education.

Counseling can also be vital in helping adults deal with change. Schlossberg (1984b) builds upon earlier research by Aslanian and Brickell which indicated that a high proportion of adults seeking to continue their education are facing a transition in their lives. She offers a model for helping adults which assists them in exploring their transition, in understanding their resources, and in coping with the process of change. In a later work (Schlossberg et al. 1989), she applies the notions of adults in transition to the institutional setting and develops comprehensive recommendations for improving educational environments for adults. Woolfe et al. (1987) examine the risks, uncertainties, and grieving associated with change and suggest that counseling in adult and continuing education is frequently directed toward helping adults cope with change.

With the increased complexity of choice faced by adults, guidance and counseling can also provide assistance with decision-making as well as with helping students or prospective students to make necessary linkages. Active mediation is also an important function in helping adult learners, both within institutions and the larger community.

Guidance and counseling services for adult learners can also provide major benefits for educational institutions by attracting and retaining highly motivated nontraditional students. Adult education, as a whole, benefits from the important information about adults' needs and preferences gained through the counseling process—information that can be used in planning adult education programs and services.

The growth in and concern for counseling of adult learners is evidenced by national and international movements as well as by an expanding literature base. A 1981 study sponsored by the Council for Cultural Cooperation, for example, investigated the provision of information, guidance, and counseling in adult education throughout Germany, Denmark, France, Italy, the Netherlands, Portugal, Spain, Sweden, the United Kingdom, and Northern Ireland. In the United States, the National Association of Educational Guidance Services initiated a Task Force on Advising Adult Learners in 1986 which resulted in a report and list of recommendations (Polson 1986). Many writers indicate a lack of satisfaction with the recognition of the need for guidance and counseling services for adult learners. The expanding number of issues related to educational guidance and counseling for adults represented in the literature, however, indicate the growth and development of this aspect of adult education. The remainder of this entry reviews a number of these issues.

3. Settings and Structures

Educational counseling for adults may be offered in a variety of settings and through a range of agencies. Woolfe et al. (1987) list adult education centers, institutions of further and higher education, government training centers, community development centers, workplaces, and voluntary organizations as possible providers.

Institutionally based counseling for adults appears to be more the norm in North America than elsewhere. Polson (1986) reports that 79 percent of institutions responding to a national survey indicated the provision of special advisory services for the adult population. These services are generally available during regular working hours; slightly more than one-half of the respondents, however, provide office hours at nontraditional times. Although these services are primarily offered on campus only, about 40 percent indicated that similar services are available in off-campus locations. The counseling services provided by tutors in the United Kingdom's Open University are another example of a means of delivering institutionally based programs. Based on its investigation, however, the Council for Cultural Cooperation (1982) recommends that educational counseling services should remain independent of educational institutions because of the likelihood that the providers will offer biased advice.

Levine and Piggins (1981) explore the issue of counseling available in the workplace and conclude that there is a need for greater flexibility in the variety of courses and programs that will be supported by employers and unions and that more attention must be paid to enabling services such as childcare. Similar criticisms are raised concerning government counseling services; for example, in reviewing educational counseling provided by the Canada Employment Centre, Edwards (1991) questions whether it is the requirements and interests of the client that are being served or rather the government's agenda.

Ironside (1981) reports on four models for community counseling for adults and describes the strengths and weaknesses of each. These include the institution-based model (Women's Resource Centre, Vancouver, Canada); the community council/consortium model (Education Information Centre, Brantford, Canada); local government model (Education Advice Centre, Cologne, Germany); and the brokerage model (Belfast Educational Guidance Service).

There is, therefore, little consistency in re- commendations regarding a "best" model. Whatever the structure for delivery, writers largely agree that the need for counseling and guidance services for adult learners is not sufficiently recognized and that these services are not adequately funded.

4. Roles of Educational Counselors and Advisors

Counselors and advisors of adult learners are called upon to play many roles. The role of provider of up-to-date information is, of course, central. The counselor may also be called upon to help clients assess their current skill levels. The description of "counselor-as-advocate" appears frequently; Woolfe et al. (1987), for example, suggest that the counselor must be concerned with not only the student/client but also with the system. Schlossberg (1984b) recommends an ecological approach in which the counselor is more than a good listener, but is also a broker, an advocate, and a linker. In another work (Schlossberg 1984a), it is suggested that counselors of adults in transition move from thinking of themselves as therapists and take on the role of environmentalist to build a supportive climate and collaborative community. This theme is carried forward by Lynch and Chickering (1984) who point out that the influx of adult learners to traditional higher education settings demands new roles for student development specialists; their list of potential roles includes ecology manager/consultant, resource person, mentor/educator, facilitator, and advocate. The theme of "counselor-as-educator" also runs through the work of several authors. Students need to learn how to learn (Gelatt 1984) as well as how to transfer the learning from one life situation to others.

5. Professionalization

What are the elements which make for an effective educational counselor or advisor of adults? Considerable concern is in evidence regarding issues of qualifications and professional training for counselors of adult students. Several authors, Imeson (1991) for example, view educational guidance for adults as a relatively uncharted movement and raise questions about the necessary knowledge and skills. Schlossberg (1984b) maintains that knowledge of adult development is as essential as are process skills in helping adults. Her model for helping adults in transition depends on the integration of content and process.

An ambitious project carried out in the United Kingdom by the Unit for the Development of Adult Continuing Education (UDACE), and funded by the Further Education Unit (FEU) of the National Institute of Adult Continuing Education (NIACE), took as its objective the development of a list of competencies for counselors of adult students (Oakeshott 1991). As a basis for this work, which measures competencies as outcomes rather than as methods or processes, four major objectives for educational guidance are identified: it should help potential adult learners to identify their learning requirements and interests, to make decisions appropriate to their requirements, to pursue strategies to meet these requirements in relation to opportunities available or negotiable, and to evaluate their own learning and decision-making processes. The report identifies three major work roles for the educational advisor: to provide a service offering educational guidance to adults, to deliver educational guidance to adults, and to provide feedback on clients' requirements to agencies concerned with adults' learning. The report also defines concomitant subtasks which can be used to develop education/training standards and to assess performance. By the project officer's observation, however, there is a need to find better ways to assess competence in interpersonal fields.

Woolfe et al. (1987), working from a philosophy of counseling as an educational process and from an acceptance of the counselor's role as one of helping the student or client to understand the learning process and to transfer it from one situation to another, suggest a number of agenda items for a potential training program for helpers of adults. They recommend that counselors need to be trained in the following: to understand adult life as a process of change and development; to understand the motivation behind and the nature of adult learning; to understand cultural, social, and economic influences on adult learning; to develop bridges between educational, work, and personal lives of adults; to work within systems to promote organizational change; to understand the importance and complexity of interpersonal relationships in learning; to use basic counseling skills; to recognize the open-ended nature of the helping process; and to recognize the need for accepting personal responsibility for one's own development.

Lynch and Chickering (1984) cite many of the same recommendations for the professional development of institutional student development specialists working with adult learners. Because of the increasing use of technologies for the counseling of adults, especially those studying through distance education, they add the need for training and skill development in these new technologies.

Training opportunities for counselors of adults remain limited. To promote the professional development of counselors of adult learners, the Council for Cultural Cooperation Report (1982) points to the need for increased exchange of experience through international, national, and regional meetings, through writing, and through study visits. A cautionary note regarding the professionalization of counseling for adult learners is struck by the Council as well as by Woolfe et al. (1987); they warn that this function ought not to be limited to professionals only, but that teachers of adults must continue to view themselves as having a vital counseling role.

6. Models and a Theory Base for Counseling Adult Learners

The deficit of comprehensive theory to support the growing practice of counseling adult learners remains a concern. Adult development writing is rich, but there are still many unanswered questions and much potential for investigation remains to challenge adult education theorists. However, adult development theory is acknowledged widely as fundamental to counseling practice.

Schlossberg (1984b) provides one of the most fully developed frameworks for counseling adults in transition. Her model proposes three primary goals for this type of counseling—to explore, to understand, and to cope—and outlines for each goal a knowledge component and a skills component. Exploring, for example, requires a knowledge of the transition, its type, content, and impact, and calls for listening, responding, attending, and focusing skills. Likewise, to accomplish the second goal of helping the client to understand, the counselor uses knowledge concerning the interactions among the individual, the transition events, and her or his environment to determine coping resources, and also uses helping skills of interpreting, identifying themes, confronting, and presenting information in order to provide a new perspective. Coping, the third helping goal, requires knowledge of the stages in the transition process as well as the skills to help the client decide on a course of action (or inaction).

Several authors contribute to the formulation of a theory base for educational guidance and counseling for adults. Woolfe et al. (1987) build a framework using concepts of adult development and principles of counseling. They offer strategies for particular applications, for example, in working with the unemployed, the retired, or with students at a distance. Marsick (1985) describes a specific application, re-evaluation counseling, which is used to examine and work through internalized patterns and preconceptions to improve learning. Developmental academic advising (Thomas and Chickering 1984), which is based on solid adult education principles, encourages advisors of students of all ages to view students as whole persons and to understand their needs using various development theories, including intellectual, moral reasoning, and life-cycle theories. Other specialized bodies of literature, in learning and career counseling to name but two examples, add to the richness of resources for the counseling of adult learners.

7. Use of Technology

Computer technology has been used extensively and for some time to assist with career counseling, with programs such as Choices, DISCOVER, and SIGI PLUS; these tools can help clients to assess interests and examine values as well as to identify and explore options. More recently, with the proliferation of personal computers in homes, libraries, workplaces, educational institutions, and so on, this medium is being used to disseminate up-to-date information about educational opportunities through computer networks;

a project initiated by the Open Learning Agency in British Columbia is an example of this kind of service. A range of technologies, including telephone, television, cable, satellites, computers, electronic mail, videotapes, cassettes, and videodiscs provide assistance in various aspects of counseling, for example, record keeping, information provision, making assessments, and academic skill development (Lynch and Chickering 1984).

Technology is also playing an important role with a specific group of learners that are gaining greater recognition, that is, those studying through distance education formats. Woolfe et al. (1987) devote a chapter to means of counseling adult learners at a distance. Paulet (1988) points out that the significance of counseling and related support services for campus-based postsecondary education is well recognized; questions are now appearing about the need for such opportunities for distance education students as well. Paulet reminds practitioners about the social aspect of learning and about the concept of a community of scholars which still pertains to those learning away from a main campus setting. Distance education students, with their diverse backgrounds, lack of familiarity with new learning formats, and multitude of competing life concerns, need a support system as well as current and accurate information. Some services—for example, the provision of information—are being provided through nontraditional methods such as written communication, telephone, audiocassette, radio, and television, but the range of counseling content is limited. Distance education students also require help with goal-planning and decision-making skills as well as in making personal, social, and intellectual adjustments. In some cases, tutors or community representatives are employed to assist adult learners in their local communities.

Cooper (1991) raises a similar concern about the isolation which may be felt by individuals taking advantage of flexible learning alternatives such as modularization, accreditation of prior learning, and open learning as well as distance learning. He warns of the potential for a growing sense of confusion rather than empowerment and the risk of deterioration of needed support systems. Educational guidance and counseling, either through institutionally based or community-based services, are important for providing coherence of information, helping with decision-making and the acquiring of necessary skills, and providing a sense of connectedness.

8. Ethical Issues

Little writing appears on ethical issues specifically related to the educational counseling and advising of adults. Day (1988) reminds educational advisors of the responsibility which is part of providing choice options for adult learners. He uses the examples of Eliza Doolittle in *Pygmalion* and Rita in the film *Educating Rita* to reinforce his assertion that the increase in choices brought about through learning may have significant implications for other aspects of the learner's life, such as for one's personal relationships. He suggests that educational counselors, in their role as educators, have a responsibility in helping learners to understand that learning cannot be viewed in isolation from the wholeness of their lives, but that it has consequences.

Oakeshott (1991) acknowledges the need to recognize the importance of adhering to professionally recognized ethical principles in competence statements for educational advisors, but admits uncertainty in determining ways to do so.

9. Evaluation and Research

The need for further research in the field of educational counseling and guidance for adults is noted by several authors. Knox (1981), for example, suggests that the evaluation of these services for adults requires investigation. Likewise, Oakeshott (1991), as a result of his competence project, identifies the need for research into the relationship between guidance activities and outcomes for clients. He also recommends the continuation of the work begun in this project (i.e., the identification of the competencies required by effective advisors). He also suggests that, because the effectiveness of educational guidance cannot be fully gauged simply by measuring outcomes for clients, new techniques must be developed to assess interpersonal elements of the counseling interaction.

Despite impressive developments in the counseling aspect of adult education, many writers warn that counseling is still viewed as a marginal enterprise with inadequate policies and precarious funding. Particularly in recessionary times, the message is clear that these services have a vital contribution to make to individual, social, and economic renewal.

See also: Study and Learning Strategies; Participation: Role of Motivation; Student Support Systems; Student Outreach

References

Brown J 1991 What is educational guidance? *Adults Learning* 2(10): 277–78
Cooper R 1991 Educational guidance and flexible learning. *Adults Learning* 2(10): 284–85
Council for Cultural Cooperation 1982 *Information, Guidance and Counselling in Adult Education.* Report of the seminar held in Soest, Germany, September 22–24, 1981. Council for Cultural Cooperation, Strasbourg
Day M 1988 Educational advising and brokering: The ethics of choice. In: Brockett R (ed.) 1989 *Ethical Issues in Adult Education.* Teachers College, Columbia University, New York
Edwards R 1991 Guidance and unemployment in Canada. *Adults Learning* 2(10): 279–82
Gelatt H B 1984 Excellence, equality and education: A future for counselling. *New Perspectives on Counseling Adult Learners.* In: Council for the Advancement of Experiential Learning 1984. National Institute of Education, Washington, DC
Imeson R 1991 The great training debate. *Adults Learning* 2(10): 283
Ironside D 1981 Community counseling for adults. In: DiSilvestro F (ed.) 1981
Knox A 1981 Emerging issues in counseling adult learners. In: DiSilvestro F (ed.) 1981
Levine H, Piggins D 1981 Workplace counseling: The missing link. In: DiSilvestro F (ed.) 1981
Lynch A, Chickering A 1984 Comprehensive counseling and support programs for adult learners: Challenge to higher education. In: Council for the Advancement of Experiential Learning 1984 *New Perspectives on Counseling Adult Learners.* National Institute of Education, Washington, DC
Marsick V 1985 Working with adult learners in higher education: Going against internalized norms. Paper presented at the Conference of the American Association for Adult and Continuing Education, Milwaukee, Wisconsin November 6–10, 1985
Oakeshott M 1991 *Educational Guidance for Adults: Identifying Competences.* National Institute of Adult Continuing Education, Leicester
Paulet R 1988 Factors influencing successful counseling in selected distance education programs. *J. Res. Dev. Educ.* 21(3): 60–64
Polson C 1986 Advising adult learners. National Academic Advising Association Task Force Report presented at the National Conference on Academic Advising, Seattle, October 12–15, 1986
Schlossberg N 1984a *Caught in a Dilemma: Adults as Learners.* New Perspectives on Counselling Adult Learners. National Institute of Education, Washington, DC
Schlossberg N 1984b *Counseling Adults in Transition: Linking Practice with Theory.* Springer, New York
Schlossberg N, Lynch A, Chickering A 1989 *Improving Higher Education Environments for Adults.* Jossey-Bass, San Francisco, California
Thomas R, Chickering A 1984 Foundations for academic advising. In: Winston R et al. 1984 *Developmental Academic Advising: Addressing Students' Educational, Career and Personal Needs.* Jossey-Bass, San Francisco, California
Woolfe R, Murgatroyd S, Rhys S 1987 *Guidance and Counselling in Adult and Continuing Education: A Developmental Perspective.* Open University Press, Milton Keynes

Further Reading

Allman P 1983 The nature and process of adult development. In: Tight M (ed.) 1983 *Education for Adults: Adult Learning and Education.* Croom Helm, London
Bitterman J 1985 Academic advising and adult education: An

emerging synthesis. NACADA J. 5(2): 29–33

Dean G et al. 1987 Adults in mid-career change: Case studies for advisors. NACADA *J.* 7(1): 16–26

DiSilvestro F (ed.) 1981 *Advising and Counseling Adult Learners.* Jossey-Bass, San Francisco, California

Egan G 1982 *The Skilled Helper.* Brooks–Cole, Monteray, California

Friesen J 1986 Systems approach to adult counselling. *Guidance and Counselling* 1(3): 10–15

Marton F, Hounsell D, Entwistle N (eds.) 1984 *The Experience of Learning.* Scottish Academic Press, Edinburgh

Moore G, Waldron M 1991 *Helping Adults Learn: Course Planning for Adult Learners.* Thompson Educational Publishers, Toronto

Murgatroyd S 1985 *Counselling and Helping.* British Psychological Society, Leicester

Payne J 1985 Educational guidance services and the provision of adult education. *Int. J. Lifelong Education* 4(1): 35–54

Thomas N, Majnarich B, Lobes D 1982 Educational information centres: One answer for adults. *New Directions for Experiential Learning* 16:75–85

Student Dropout

D. R. Garrison

A common understanding of dropout is that it is a purposeful withdrawal from attending a course of studies resulting in a failure to meet the course objectives. The purpose of this entry will be to identify and order some of the factors and variables associated with dropout. At the same time, however, it will be seen that usually only a small percentage of the dropout variance (typically 15–20%) is accounted for in the best of studies. This is a clear indicator of the complexity of the problem.

1. An Overview of Dropout Research

In an early comprehensive review of dropout research in adult education, Verner and Davis (1964) classified reasons for dropout into personal factors (socioeconomic and psychosocial) and situational factors (institutional and noninstitutional). They concluded that 26 personal factors had been tested with inconclusive results, although "age, education, marital status, occupation income, and rate of social participation appear to be related to persistence of attendance" (p. 172). Similarly, none of the 18 situational factors had been tested conclusively. They concluded that future research should collect data before discontinuance occurs. This would reduce the validity and reliability problems associated with after-the-fact responses. However, a priori data collection also carries with it the difficulty of accounting for events between assessment and dropout.

A more recent synthesis of research and theory related to adult dropout was presented by Darkenwald (1981). He found that the quality and quantity of dropout research had improved since Verner and Davis's (1964) review. With regard to socioeconomic variables, Darkenwald (1981) found most "to be at best only weakly related to dropout behavior" (p. 11). Particular emphasis was given to a national sample of 9,173 adult part-time learners studied by Anderson

and Darkenwald (1979). Using multivariate methods of analysis, Anderson and Darkenwald controlled for spurious findings, but less than 2 percent of the dropout variance was accounted for by sociodemographic variables such as age and educational attainment.

1.1 Psychological Variables

In terms of the educational process, Darkenwald (1981) looked at psychological variables such as intelligence and personality (e.g., adjustment, autonomy, need for achievement) and stated that few firm generalizations are warranted. He suggested that "psychological measures, especially of ability, would seem to be important to include in future dropout research to gauge their effects in conjunction with other kinds of variables" (Darkenwald 1981 p. 12). However, in a series of studies of adult high school students, Garrison (1983, 1985, 1987) examined psychological variables, including ability as well as situational variables, and found no significant direct relationship between ability and dropout behavior. Factors found to be significant discriminators between persisters and dropouts were psychological variables such as self-control and self-confidence as well as situational variables such as life changes and high cost. However, Garrison (1985) found an interaction effect in that lower ability students appear to "set unrealistic goals for themselves and have unrealistic expectations of the program resulting in an incongruence leading to dropout" (p. 36).

1.2 External Situational Variables

The next category of variables reviewed by Darkenwald (1981) were external situational variables (i.e., not related to individual characteristics or to the educational process). While these factors are typically cited as reasons for dropping out in after-the-fact studies, some believe these respondents are giving socially acceptable and "ego sustaining" responses (Boshier 1973). Darkenwald (1981) concluded that the "point is not that situational factors are unrelated to dropout behavior—they definitely are. In most cases, however, bad weather, child care problems, illness in the family, and other external situational variables are best seen as contributing to dropout rather than directly 'causing' it" (p. 12). Darkenwald goes on to say that such situational factors have a particularly adverse effect on adult basic education (ABE) and high school programs. This was confirmed by Garrison (1983, 1985) in two longitudinal studies that avoided the charge of after-the-fact rationalizations. In these studies, financial concerns and life changes were significant predictors of dropout for adult students in high school completion programs.

1.3 Program Variables

Another category of predictor variables concerns the administrative and organizational properties of educational programs. Some evidence exists linking dropout to length of the program. It is suggested by Darkenwald (1981) that retention can be facilitated by reducing the disruption of daily routine. Also relevant is the dropout research in distance education, since this supposedly causes the least disruption to the adult's routine. However, dropout statistics in distance education range from less than 10 to over 90 percent, dependent on the program. This suggests there may be other important variables involved in the decision to drop out, such as the frequency and quality of interaction among people. If classroom interaction and integration are high, then tolerance to disruption of the adult's routine becomes greater and dropout less likely.

1.4 Teaching–Learning Variables

Teaching–learning variables have been reported by Darkenwald (1981) as being "far more important than others in accounting for dropout extent to which a course or other organized learning activity is relevant to, or congruent with, student needs, and are probably the major determinants of persistence" (p. 14). However, teaching and learning variables interact with nonschool factors. Borgström (1980), in a large study of Swedish adults, found that dropout was due to a combination of variables. External variables such as illness merely served as a trigger or the last of a number of difficulties. The teacher was an important factor, and lack of community support and classroom integration was a problem for those who dropped out. Borgström (1980), moreover, reported that "most of the drop-out students followed up did not resume their studies within two years after leaving their courses" (p. 124).

More specific to the teaching situation, Darkenwald (1981) reports that few dropout studies have looked at teacher behavior. One study at the Chinese University of Hong Kong reported that students attend class more regularly if the teacher was perceived as approachable, had opportunities to clarify doubts, and participated in discussions (Lam and Wong 1974). A more recent study by Sullivan (1984) hypothesized that the rate of dropout is related to teacher performance. Dropouts were seen as both temporary and permanent absentees. Sullivan (1984) found that for both temporary and permanent absences, "there is no statistically significant association between absence and our six teacher characteristics" (p. 180).

In summary, it is concluded that the variables that are known from research studies to be associated with dropout account for a small but significant amount of variance. Among the better predictors of dropout appears to be congruence of institutional and student goals. Socioeconomic variables such as financial and family responsibilities may be particularly associated with dropout in adult basic education, while psychological variables such as self-confidence and self-other congruence may be more highly associated with dropout in higher education.

2. Theoretical Issues

The importance of theoretical models and frameworks to guide and interpret research on dropout cannot be overemphasized. Equally important is the need to verify these models with systematic and sustained research programs. Unfortunately, models of dropout in adult education have not contributed much to the prediction of adult dropout. Compounding this problem is the apparent reduction of reported research on adult dropout in the literature.

Perhaps the best known model of dropout in adult education is Boshier's (1973) congruence model. It purports to explain both participation and dropout behaviour. There are two components to the model; the first is concerned with growth and deficiency motivation for participation as measured by the Education Participation Scale, while the second component, tenuously linked to the first component, cover aspects of self incongruence as measured by Personality and Educational Environment Scales. Boshier views dropout as an extension of nonparticipation, and both result from enrollment for deficiency reasons. The congruence model is built largely upon self-concept and psychological discontent theory, where the adult learner's two primary concerns are "maintaining inner harmony with himself and with the environment" (Boshier 1973 p. 259). The two primary measures are self-ideal and self-other incongruence, which essentially reduces the model to a few psychological variables. It has been argued that the model is based largely on a measure of global self-esteem (Garrison 1987).

Rubenson and Höghielm's (1978) expectancy–valence model of adult dropout behavior was developed specifically in the context of adult education and, like the congruence model, attempts to explain both participation and dropout. The expectancy–valence model relates cognitive and social or environmental variables to explain decisions regarding participation or dropout. Expectancy is a result of a belief that education will have desirable consequences and that there is a good chance of completing the program and achieving a successful outcome. Valence is the degree to which participation in adult education will meet or satisfy certain needs. The likelihood of completing a course is a product of expectation and valence. While this model shows promise, little work has been done to validate it.

Any discussion of theoretical models of dropout in adult education must include Tinto's model, since it has been used as a basis for many empirical studies. It was developed to predict dropout behavior of residential college students, but has also been used to study adult populations. The key factors in this model are goal commitment and institutional commitment which lead to academic and social integration and, in circular fashion, lead to greater goal and institutional commitment. Through increased integration and commitment the likelihood of dropout is reduced. Although context variables are considered in the model, Tinto (1975) believes that their impact "will be best observed through the person's changing evaluations of his commitments to the goal of college completion" (p. 97). That is, background variables will be reflected in levels of commitment and integration and need not be measured directly.

Tinto's model has been used in adult education for the study of institutional commitment and social integration. It has been argued that for adult students who live away from the institution, social integration may not be an important correlate of dropout. However, several studies have shown that the two are related (Cleveland 1989, Garrison 1985, Martin 1988). It has also been shown that socioeconomic variables are important, along with social integration variables. This led Garrison (1988) to conclude that integration must occur in both directions. That is, the adult student should be integrated into the school community but also the school must be integrated into the adult student's life. In short, it would appear that Tinto's model has potential in explaining dropout decisions, but perhaps should be enhanced by considering the nonschool role responsibilities that most adults have assumed.

3. Student Retention

Understanding why adult students drop out is only the first stage in addressing a serious problem in adult education. The next step is to know which intervention strategies might reduce unnecessary dropout. Strategies may be directed toward three categories of factors associated with dropout—environmental constraints, institutional support, and classroom integration.

Constraints such as lack of funds and family responsibilities have consistently been shown to be associated with dropout. Student support services that provide assistance in areas of financial aid and day care will thus go a long way in preventing dropout. Academic and career counseling is also a needed service that can effectively increase retention. In particular, clarity of student needs, goals, and course relevancy are issues that should be explored with returning adult students who may be unrealistic or uncertain as to their needs and goals.

It may also be important to improve the fit between school life, and to ensure that the student is integrated both academically and socially into the educational setting. Teachers must create a supportive yet academic challenging and interesting learning climate. This can be done by facilitating two-way communication between the teacher and the student as well as among the students. Citing a variety of sources, Gordon (1985) states that is has "been demonstrated that quantity and quality of faculty–student interaction has a direct impact on retention" (p. 127). Through academic and social integration students gain confidence and increase their motivation. Institutions must provide inservice training to prepare teachers to deal with student needs and expectations.

4. Conclusion

As a result of the complexity of the problem of adult dropout behavior, our understanding of the phenomenon is at best tentative. Few models specific to adult education have been proposed that have adequately dealt with the complex array of variables associated with dropout behavior. While the development and testing of theoretical models is a high priority, the focus should also be upon applying these theoretical models. The continued development of our understanding and prediction of dropout in adult education will proceed with the validation of situation-specific models.

See also: Participation: Antecedent Factors; Participation: Role of Motivation; Student Counseling

References

Anderson R, Darkenwald G 1979 *Participation and Persistence in American Adult Education*. Direction papers in lifelong learning. College Entrance Examination Board, New York

Borgström L 1980 Drop-out in municipal adult schools in the context of allocation policy. In: Höghielm R, Rubenson K (eds.) 1980 *Adult Education for Social Change: Research on the Swedish Allocation Policy*. Stockholm Institute of Education, Stockholm

Boshier R W 1973 Educational participation and dropout: A theoretical model. *Adult Educ.* 23(4): 255–82

Cleveland M 1989 Adult student attrition at post-secondary institutions. In: Bédard R (ed.) 1989 *Proceedings of the 8th Annual Conference of the Canadian Association for the Study of Adult Education*. Tele-Université, Quebec

Darkenwald G 1981 *Retaining Adult Students*. National Center for Research in Vocational Education, Ohio State University, Columbus, Ohio

Garrison D R 1983 Psychosocial correlates of dropout and achievement in an adult high school completion program. *Alberta J. Educ. Res.* 29(2): 131–39

Garrison D R 1985 Predicting dropout in adult basic education using interaction effects among school and nonschool variables. *Adult Educ. Q.* 36(1): 25–38

Garrison D R 1987 Dropout prediction within a broad psychosocial context: An analysis of Boshier's congruence model. *Adult Educ. Q.* 37(4): 212–22

Garrison D R 1988 A deductively derived and empirically confirmed structure of factors associated with dropout in adult education. *Adult Educ. Q.* 38(4): 199–210

Gordon V N 1985 Students with uncertain academic goals. In: Noel L, Levitz R, Saluri D (eds.) 1985 *Increasing Student Retention*. Jossey-Bass, San Francisco, California

Lam Y, Wong A 1974 Attendance regularity of adult learners: An examination of content and structural factors. *Adult Educ.* 24(2): 130–42

Martin L G 1988 A test of Tinto's model of attrition: As applied to an inner-city adult literacy program. In: Zukas M (ed.) 1988 *Transatlantic Dialogue: A Research Exchange*. University of Leeds, Leeds

Rubenson K, Höghielm R 1978 *The Teaching Process and Study Dropouts in Adult Education: Theoretical Premises and Structure of the Project* (Report #3). Stockholm Institute of Education, Stockholm

Sullivan T 1984 Dropouts and training. *Int. J. Lifelong Educ.* 3(3): 163–91

Tinto V 1975 Dropout from higher education: A theoretical synthesis of recent research. *Rev. Educ. Res.* 45: 89–125

Verner C, Davis G 1964 Completions and dropouts: A review of research. *Adult Educ.* 14(3): 157–76

Further Reading

Darkenwald G, Gavin W J 1987 Dropout as a function of discrepancies between expectations and actual experiences of the classroom social environment. *Adult Educ. Q.* 37: 152–63

Houtkoop W, Kamp M van der 1992 Factors influencing participation in continuing education. *Int. J. Ed. Res.* 17(6): 537–48

Langenbach M, Korhonen L 1988 Persisters and nonpersisters in a graduate level, nontraditional, liberal education program. *Adult Educ. Q.* 38(3): 136–48

Tinto V 1982 Defining dropout: A matter of perspective. In: Pascarella E T (ed.) 1982 *Studying Student Attrition*. Jossey-Bass, San Francisco, California

Student Outreach

M. Osborn

This entry explains the term "outreach," describes outreach programs and methods, mentions some of the main target groups, and provides some examples of outreach activities that have been conducted in different, mainly industrialized countries.

1. Definition and Approach

The term "outreach" describes the provision of mainly postinitial education for adults targeted at particular social groups who might not otherwise participate in educational activity. It refers to a strategy which is intended to compensate for the limitations of an institution or center-based service.

The term "outreach" became popular in the 1960s and 1970s when research findings indicated that, far from providing a second chance for adults who had received little formal education initially, adult education often reinforced the advantage gained by those who had already succeeded in education. Thus the challenge is to devise and implement outreach programs and methods which will attract those who do not participate in adult education and, in particular, to involve the socially and economically disadvantaged sections of the population, and to make available educational resources to them.

A problem is that some versions of outreach may still be seen by potential participants to be institutionally or officially dominated even when they use noninstitutional settings and locations and flexible timings (Watts and Knasel 1985). More unconventional approaches to outreach will involve participants not only in attending, but also in jointly planning and controlling learning activities that are relevant to their needs. A common feature of all outreach activities is that the learners themselves control the experience, deciding for themselves what is learned, how it is learned and through whom learning takes place (see *Experiential and Open Learning*).

2. Target Populations and Methods

Outreach programs may be aimed not only at the working class and those who may be termed "educationally disadvantaged," but also at other groups who may have particular problems and needs, and who do not participate in center-based activities for a variety of reasons. These include, for example, the elderly, the unemployed, those from ethnic minorities, Gypsies, and the mentally and physically handicapped. Another potential target group is housebound women with young children.

Outreach activities tend to take one of two main forms. First, it may be an activity at the level of the local community, often involving personal recruitment either individually or through contact with existing local groups and networks. An example is presented by the Swedish outreach experiments which recruited participants at their place of work and in their local housing areas. Second, it may be an activity at a national level in the form of "distance education" involving the use of the media and printed materials supplemented by locally based teaching groups. An example is the United Kingdom's Open University community education program. Various combinations of the two forms may also occur. For example, at a national level the media may be used to arouse initial interest which is then built upon at a local level as in the United Kingdom adult literacy program.

3. Programs for Working-class and Educationally Disadvantaged Groups

Attempts to reach working-class adults in a disadvantaged area in Liverpool have been described by Lovett (1975). The tutors, acting as resource agents, educational guides, and teachers, made themselves aware of the problems and needs of people in the community, and encouraged them to engage in educational activities. Methods used included a house-to-house survey of a street, involvement of the leadership of various local groups, and the use of local radio. Another outreach project in the United Kingdom began with a community study of Leigh Park, a large overspill housing estate, and then set out to widen the take-up of educational activities (Fordham et al. 1979). Through its community involvement, the project became the facilitator and often the initiator of a wide variety of socially based learning groups forming a network.

In the Swedish outreach experiments, participants were contacted individually, either in their workplace by trades union organisers or in their local housing areas, and were encouraged to join study circles (Rubenson 1979). Courses and materials were free and some expenses were covered. Interviews with those involved demonstrated that many would not have participated if they had not been contacted in the way they were. A significant distinguishing feature of the Swedish experiments was that the outreaching activity was given a more established form and organization on the basis of earmarked state funds. Selectivity concerning who was approached and the advantageous enrollment conditions contributed to the success of the strategy.

Many of the notable early outreach initiatives have been part of adult literacy movements. Lovett (1988) describes Third World initiatives in adult literacy such as the Nicaraguan Literacy Crusade where thousands of young people were sent out into the countryside for a six-month period, turning the whole country into one large literacy school (see *Adult Literacy in the Third World*).

4. Outreach, Distance Education, and the Media

Distance learning methods are a major form of outreach activity. Learning methods normally combine the use of printed materials with the use of television and radio for publicity and motivational purposes as well as direct teaching. Case studies of the use of distance teaching methods for adult basic education in Europe are described by Kaye and Harry (1982). Some are regional projects while others provide coverage at a national level. In all these projects the most important elements are personal contact, the use of specially prepared printed materials and to varying degrees, the use of the media. In countries as diverse as Jamaica, Tanzania, and Egypt use has been made of local "listening" or "viewing" centers which are sometimes attended by support staff.

At the level of higher education, the Open University in countries such as Germany, Indonesia, India, the Netherlands, and the United Kingdom makes use of such methods not only to reach the mass of its students, but also to reach those who are disadvantaged by physical handicap, by being in prison, or by living in remote areas. An extension of distance methods—telephone and on-line computer-aided teaching—has been a successful means of helping the geographically isolated. In general, research suggests that television and radio provide the essential spark, or a central role in recruiting, but there is little evidence that broadcasts unaccompanied by other methods have a lasting effect after the series has finished (see *Distance Education*).

5. Outreach, the Elderly, and the Housebound

There are numerous examples of novel and innovatory programs for older adults in countries such as France, the United Kingdom and the United States. One example, which makes use of outreach methods in combination with institutionally based services is the University of the Third Age. Research findings have highlighted the need for interagency cooperation and the development of learning opportunities by negotiation with older people themselves (Withnall 1990). In a number of countries there are outreach schemes that are designed to involve housebound learners by using trained volunteers to attend special classes and then to visit the housebound person at their home and share what they have learned in the class.

6. Outreach and the Unemployed

Many providers of programs for the unemployed report difficulties in reaching the unemployed and encouraging them to participate, in particular in recruiting the very groups which need assistance most—those with the poorest education as well as older people and the youth dropouts. Two schemes in Belgium have made particular efforts to reach these nonparticipants. At Canal-Emploi, cable television and face-to-face workshops were used to help participants to understand their social and economic situation and to give them the necessary confidence and basic skills to go on subsequently to professional training courses organized by other bodies. Another project aimed particularly at the unemployed aged below 35, centered learning activities on groups of 12 to 15 people, and used local people as tutors with the aid of initial training and monthly evaluation training sessions.

Reaching out to unemployed adults in their communities has become a key component in strategies to combat unemployment in the industrialised countries. For example, in Cleveland in the United Kingdom, the "Outreach College" project took outreach modules (short courses of one term or less) out to unemployed people in community-based local learning centers. An important feature of such initiatives for the unemployed was the creation of self-learning, self-determining, and self-sustaining groups (Portwood 1988).

7. Outreach in Educational Guidance and Counseling

A core feature of guidance programs for adults is that they should be open and accessible to adult clients at times and places convenient for them. This involves two separate issues: first, bringing to the attention of the general public the facilities available in ways which are not conventional; and second, reassessing the forms and types of provision in response to the expressed wishes of a public hitherto not using the adult education service.

In the first type, various institutions offer "open days" which are extensively advertised locally and which provide information that enables people to discuss various options, to receive advice, and perhaps make further arrangements for educational guidance. In Sheffield in the United Kingdom, successful work of this type was done from a mobile caravan on housing estates, and in a factory. A number of community colleges in Ontario have established store-front centers on a main downtown street. In the United Kingdom, "shop-front" premises have been used in a similar way to provide information. In Australia, the Learning Exchange in Melbourne provided an enquiry service, information on local community resources, a newspaper which enabled people to initiate discussion and activity groups, a place to meet, a library, and

research projects on alternative ways of using community resources. Other local learning exchanges in the United States, Canada, Australia, Sweden, and the Netherlands provide information by mail, telephone, and personal visits about many study opportunities available to adults (see *Student Counseling; Student Support Systems*).

8. The Outreach Worker

The outreach worker's role is often that of a facilitator, empowering community groups, putting them in contact with one another, providing them with the resources and professional support they need, and helping them to define clear goals and objectives. Outreach workers or tutors are often women working part-time and in some isolation with little or no job security. In an attempt to meet the support needs of outreach staff, a project in mid-Glamorgan, Wales offers the tutors themselves initial training, management support, peer support, staff development opportunities, and a resource base.

9. Conclusion

In summary, the aim of outreach programs is to eliminate the obstacles which prevent adults with brief and inadequate schooling and others with particular disadvantages, from participating in learning activities and using the educational resources provided by society. Rubenson (1979), in considering future developments in outreach, suggests that in order to bring about changes (in provision and organization), the outreaching activity must act as a two-way communication. Thus the information obtained by outreach workers and organizers should be fed back systematically into the organization and should build a foundation on which to evaluate the activity and consequent changes. This process, sometimes identified as "inreach" should be a process of mutual involvement and learning contributing to curriculum planning and development (Krafchik and Warke 1987).

See also: Clienteles and Special Populations; Student Support Systems

References

Fordham P, Poulton G, Randle L 1979 *Learning Networks in Adult Education: Non-formal Education on a Housing Estate*. Routledge and Kegan Paul, London
Kaye A, Harry K (eds.) 1982 *Using the Media for Adult Basic Education*. Croom Helm, London
Krafchik M, Warke S 1987 *Educational Outreach and Unemployment Groups*. Centre for Unemployment Studies, Wolverhampton Polytechnic, Wolverhampton
Lovett T 1975 *Adult Education, Community Development and the Working Class*. Ward Lock Educational, London
Lovett T (ed.) 1988 *Radical Approaches to Adult Education: A Reader*. Routledge, London

Portwood D 1988 *Outreach and Inreach: Colleges and Unemployment Groups.* Further Education Unit, London

Rubenson K 1979 *Recruitment to Adult Education in the Nordic Countries: Research and Outreaching Activities.* Stockholm Institute of Education, Stockholm

Watts A G, Knasel E G 1985 *Adult Unemployment and the Curriculum: A Manual for Practitioners.* Further Education Unit, London

Withnall A 1990 Education and older adults: A state-of-the-art review. *Adults Learning* 1(9): 255–57

Further Reading

Edwards R 1991 The politics of meeting learning needs: Power, subject, subjection. *Studies in the Education of Adults* 23(1): 85–97

Glendinning F (ed.) 1980 *Outreach Education and the Elders: Theory and Practice.* Seminar Papers, Beth Johnson Foundation, Stoke-on-Trent

Groombridge J (ed.) 1987 *Learning for a Change.* NIACE/Replan, Leicester

Romiszowski A J 1981 *Designing Instructional Systems: Decision Making in Course and Curriculum Design.* Kogan Page Nichols Publishing, London

Saylor J G, Alexander W M 1974 *Planning Curriculum for Schools.* Holt, Rinehart and Winston, New York

Saylor J G, Alexander W M, Lewis A J 1981 *Curriculum Planning for Better Teaching and Learning.* Harcourt Brace Jovanovich, New York

Thompson J (ed.) 1980 *Adult Education for a Change.* Hutchinson, London

Student Support Systems

C. Healy and H. Martin

The demand for, and expansion of, adult education is greater than ever. Due to their special needs, adults often require as much or more support than younger learners. Arrangements to promote and reinforce adult efforts to intiate and continue learning activities are taking increasingly varied forms and are incorporating many functions of traditional services such as advising, counseling, tutoring, orientation, financial assistance, and peer support networks. However, the forms for rendering these functions may differ because they evolve from the matrix of challenges and resources in the adult learners' contexts. These support systems are increasingly dependent on personnel who are not trained in traditional support or personnel services. By recognizing that counseling helps adult learners on two levels, first to assimilate or engage in the new experiences, and second to accommodate or develop changed perspectives and behaviors from processing new experiences, one can realize that untrained personnel can assist in the first function, while the second, more complex function can be addressed by trained personnel. Examples of governmental and collaborative support systems are given now. They are intended to illustrate the range of systems which are coming into existence to support adult learning. The development of such support systems depends on alliances between educational, economic, and political entities.

1. Background and Philosophy of Support Systems for Adult Learners

In spite of philosophical and pragmatic arguments in favor of adult education, one cannot deny that institu-tions for adult education and training provision have generally attracted only a minor portion of their potential audience, even when there were few economic constraints. Perhaps more disheartening is the problem of retaining adult learners. Many adult education programs suffer from high attrition due to an array of problems which confront the students. Although support systems have been shown to promote enrollment and retention, there has been a general failure to offer support systems, much less integrate them with recruitment and provision.

Adult learners usually face multiple barriers to resuming their education. The need to attend to family obligations and the lure of other activities competes for both time and energy. Success is far more likely when learners have the active support of employers and others significant to them. Long absences from school may also have created anxieties about the capacity to continue learning across the whole lifespan, and impatience with pedagogy that fails to take into account the differences between the young and older learners. In addition, the competence of adult learners must be acknowledged and they must be allowed to play a more active role in the development of course syllabi and goals. Moreover, they may need active intervention with instructors, employers, and others, and support from counselors and tutors (Chuma 1991). Services may also need to enlighten employers about absorbing more women and retrained older workers into the workforce and about underwriting their employees who are engaged in adult education (Gooderham 1991).

Unfortunately, heightened appreciation of the importance of adult education coincides with financial crises befalling most of the world's educational systems. The specter of reduced educational budgets and resources underscores the need to promote andragogical innovations as well as systems to support them. Approaches which are the most systemic and involve the largest network should go the furthest in securing the educational goals of all concerned. And the more integrated the support systems, both horizontally and vertically, the higher the likelihood of success.

2. Student Support Systems at the Government Level

Some types of support by central or local governments enjoy almost universal appeal. Examples of these are: paid educational leave, state-sponsored childcare, scholarships, guarantees of employment following formal studies, vocational training on apprenticeships, and linking employment and education through cooperative education. Also important in supporting adult education is the provision of multiple options, alone or in concert with industry. One may even view increasing accessibility as a major support system in itself. The People's Republic of China, for instance, offers one of the most comprehensive systems for facilitating access. Prospective learners may choose to study independently, via correspondence or televised courses, part-time or full-time at an established residential college, or through workshops in the factory or farm. About half of the workers in industrial and commercial enterprises attend short-term training courses (see *China, People's Republic*).

Outside of Europe, national sponsorship of free education has led to increased access, but there has been diminishing attention or resources expended in support of efforts beyond the narrow context of institutional, classroom-based supervision. Some exceptions can be found in nations as diverse as the United States (where substantial aid is given to categories of adults on the basis of factors such as financial need), France (liberal work-study programs), and Singapore (scholarships and loans are available for poor students if they pursue need-driven academic majors) (Salmi 1992).

2.1 Efforts in Rural Areas

Governmental systems have long been a feature of agricultural education. These efforts often illustrate one of the few instances of true long-range thinking in the provision of education for adult learners. In the United States, agricultural extension guidance, publications, and experimental farms have been an integral part of many public universities since their initial establishment.

It is crucial that the instruction does not occur in a vacuum. Appreciation for the more conservative audiences found in rural areas needs to take the form of teaching within the context of local traditions and with the support of individuals who command respect within the smaller community (Roberts 1989). Indonesia's *Dikmas* program exemplifies a large-scale approach that integrates literacy, vocational education, and exposure to developments occurring in the more sophisticated parts of the nation (see *Asia, Southeast: Literacy*). Elsewhere in Asia, Thailand's *Khit-Pen* and Japan's *Kominkan* programs are similarly attuned to enhancing the general educational level of rural communities (Duke 1989). Amongst African countries, rural adult education is offered full-time development workers who provide instruction and support the establishment of women's clubs at the village level. These clubs meet twice weekly to upgrade the quality of life in a variety of spheres, e.g., home economics, child rearing, and agricultural production, and are often dependent on self-help principles (Kamfwa 1992).

2.2 Regional Centers

Governments have established centers in support of adult learners who are beyond the reach of conventional institutions. Some centers are rather modest in scope. One in Papua New Guinea, for example, simply offers weekly tutorial services for extension students enrolled in correspondence courses. A better funded example is Malaysia's Center for Off-Campus Studies. The "Center" has an umbrella of 12 regional centers which support a Distance Education program by providing tutors, technical receivers and transmitters, meeting venues for student discussions, and laboratory equipment. Each center's operation is integrated with, and supported by, the local secondary school and regional library, as well as the Universiti Sains Malaysia, and presents a model which other tertiary learning programs may wish to emulate (Indrus and Zin 1992).

Spain's Popular Universities, which have counterparts in Latin America, illustrate a more eclectic system in support of adult education. In 1990 some 500,000 adults either enrolled in one of the 87 sites' 2,000 courses, or participated in one of the 4,000 cultural events offered. Depending on local needs, the Popular Universities also include as part of their offerings social intervention and back-up educational programs, creation of cooperatives and small businesses in rural areas, and training for entry into the job market. The ability to respond to a variety of adult learner needs is due, in part, to each site's varied infrastructure and variable teams of instructors, which facilitates adaptability (Lopez 1992).

2.3 United States Community Colleges

Integrated support systems are found in many of the North American Community Colleges (also known as Two-Year or Junior Colleges). Although these institutions traditionally fall under the public school system, the range of support services goes well beyond the expectations of adolescents. The Community College usually makes available a comprehensive range of services provided by trained professionals housed within a division known as Student Services or Student Affairs. These are usually available to students and include not only personal, financial, and academic counseling, but also services which address health and disability problems, childcare for dependents, social interests, employment referral, and career guidance.

3. Cooperative Support Systems

One of the most cost-effective models for adult education is the Study Circle. These consist of populist learning activities which link clusters of individuals in the community, educational associations, firms, and public institutions. Although common primarily in the Nordic countries, Germany, and Japan, variants can also be found in Tanzania and other developing nations.

In Sweden, where it has reached its fullest development, the study circle brings together 5–20 friends or associates. Under the direction of one of the group's members, they assemble a planned study of a subject or problem area. One of 10 national associations then sanctions the plan and the leader, and makes the study circle eligible for state funding. There have been more than 300,000 study circles in Sweden alone, which have run the gamut from studying the theater, union education, aesthetics, immigrant language skills, and international studies. There have even been 4,000 study circles at the university level (see *Study Circles*).

Similar to the Study Circle are "self-help" groups organized at the work site. These generally meet on a regular basis following initial assessment and identification of needs by outside educators or consultants in collaboration with the management. Employer support can take the form of paying start-up costs, allowing the use of premises, and paid release time. However, it is unusual for employers to pay for formal support services such as counseling.

In the United Kingdom a major component of continuing vocational education is known as PICKUP (Professional, Industrial, and Commercial Updating). It was stimulated by the Thatcher government's desire to see education take a more "free market" stance by making itself self-financing or at least cost covering. The basic premise is that by increased private sector involvement the full expertise of the universities can be made available to the various professions, industry, and commerce (Hester 1991). Implicit in such models with strong employer involvement is the expectation that the learners' studies are linked directly to their current employment.

Throughout the world employees find themselves engaged in on-the-job training. In the United States it has been estimated that business and industry spends between US $40–200 billion on employee training and development—more than equal to the annual budget of all United States postsecondary institutions combined. North American businesses now teach over a thousand college credit courses and some even offer degree programs (Smith 1984). For the most part, what is known as market financed or Industry-Based Training (IBT) is provided by professional trainers within the organization, or by educators brought in from outside. The curriculum is driven by the needs which the employer perceives. The high level of employer support and commitment for the programs is attested to by the fact that employers nearly always pay the full cost (Dahlgren and Stone 1990). However, these expenses seldom include student support beyond formal teaching (see *Measurement of Training Costs*).

An interesting example of market financed education exists in Finland. The employers' "cash-for-services" approach consists of an initial analysis of educational needs, and then a demand for as local a level as possible of educator customization of curriculum, and procurement of materials and teachers (Marjomaki 1990).

Such training is naturally more reflective of worker needs and more state-of-the-art since traditional academic criteria—for example, prerequisites, credentialing, academic periods, and degree objectives—do not delimit the trainer. Lessons can be "sandwiched" between periods of employment, or conducted on-the-job. Greater success can be achieved when these efforts are backed by systems which support the learners in getting the most out of the instruction. This trend may also help stem the current imbalance in many parts of the world between overeducation in low-demand fields and undereducation in high-demand ones, for example, in Indonesia, Morocco, and Thailand (Salmi 1992) (see *Overeducation*).

4. Conclusion

Considering diminishing budgets for education together with demands for the retraining or upgrading of adult learners, it seems inevitable that alliances between educators and employers will have to be made. These alliances, however, will also need to integrate input from professional associations and/or trade unions affiliated with the skills at issue. Each entity has a vested interest that goes beyond the narrower focus of any single private or public employer (Knox and McLeish 1989). In the United States, union-sponsored efforts for its members illustrate benefits which include not just the individual worker, but the family and local educational institutions, as well as the employer.

In many parts of the world the endorsement or active participation of religious leaders or agencies may also help to encourage reluctant or apprehensive workers to change old ways to suit new market conditions and to accommodate modernism. In short, efforts to support the adult learner need to include diverse groups and be integrated with one another at all levels. This is demanded not only because it represents the most efficient delivery of services, but because societies can ill afford to squander their human resources.

See also: Student Counseling; Student Outreach

References

Chuma P 1991 People's participation in continuing education: A case study of extension studies of the University of Zambia. *Int. J. Univ. Adult Educ.* 30(2): 35–40

Dahlgren J, Stone J R 1990 Industry perceptions of industry-based training provided by technical colleges. *J. Voc. Tech. Educ.* 7(1): 46–56

Duke C 1989 Provision in Southeast Asia. In: Titmus C J (ed.) 1989 *Lifelong Education for Adults: An International Handbook*, Pergamon Press, New York

Gooderham P 1991 Socioeconomic outcomes from adult education. *Adult Educ. Q.* 41(4): 203–16

Hester M 1991 The changing face of British university adult education—with specific reference to Exeter University. *Int. J. Univ. Adult Educ.* 30(3): 55–70

Idrus R, Zin A–R 1992 Supporting adult learners in distance education at the centre for off-campus studies, Universiti Sains Malaysia, Malaysia. *Int. J. Univ. Adult Educ.* 30(1): 51–62

Kamfwa F 1992 Contributions of women's clubs to rural development in ndola rural east. *J. Adult Educ.* 1(1): 42–54

Knox A B, McLeish J A B 1989 Continuing education of the professional. In Titmus C J (ed.) 1989 *Lifelong Education for Adults: An International Handbook* Pergamon Press, New York

Lopez V 1992 Popular universities in Spain. *Int. J. Univ. Adult Educ.* 31(2): 1–7

Marjomaki V 1990 Towards market financed education. *Adult Educ. in Finland* 27(2): 35–38

Roberts H W 1989 Integrated rural developments: Special-ized training programs. In Titmus C J (ed.) 1989 *Lifelong Education for Adults: An International Handbook*. Pergamon Press, New York

Salmi J 1992 The higher education crisis in developing countries: Issues, problems, constraints and reforms. *Int. Rev. Educ.* 38(1): 19–33

Smith W 1984 The future impact of lifelong learning. *Standard Education Almanac*. Professional Publications, Chicago, Illinois

Further Reading

Bojuwoye O 1992 The role of counselling in developing countries: A reply to Soliman. *Int. J. for the Advancement of Counseling* 15(1): 3–16

Dominice P 1992 Continuing education and the burden of schooling. *European Educ.* 24(1): 55–67

Garry A, Cowan J 1992 Opinion: Self-help continuing professional development groups in the workplace—A case study to determine their potential and viability. *Educational and Technology Int.* 29(1): 6–27

Gibson C 1992 Current trends and social issues: Alphabet soup is coming your way. *Adult Learning* 4(2): 18–9

Hill N 1991 AISES: A college intervention program that works. *Change* 23(2): 24–6

Kaeley G 1991 Break in studies and post secondary mathematics performance. *Int. J. Univ. Adult Educ.* 30(2): 49–64

Kamvnema A 1982 A study of the low attendance and performance of adults in high schools. *J. Adult Educ.* 1(1): 60–72

Kuh G, Schuh J, Whitt E 1991 Some good news about campus life: How "Involving Colleges" promote learning outside the classroom. *Change* 23(5): 48–55

Mohle H 1992 The development of adult distance education: The 15th world conference on distance education, Cavacus 1990 *Int. Rev. Educ.* 38(2): 189–93

Soliman A M 1991 The role of counseling in developing countries. *Int. J. for the Advancement of Counseling* 14(1): 3–14

Third-age Students in Higher Education

T. Hore

Higher education is in the midst of a quiet revolution. The increasing number of third-age students entering higher education is forcing institutions to change their administrative arrangements and methods of teaching and even to call into question their fundamental purposes as higher education institutions and their relationship to the society in which they are embedded. This entry will examine these changes.

The quietness of this revolution has affected the chances to assess it. First, there has been little official reaction to it in its early stages either at government or institutional level. This has meant that the data collections about adult students are inadequate and in some cases nonexistent. Where databases do exist different definitions of "nontraditional" make cross-cultural comparisons difficult. Second, research on nontraditional students, while it has grown rapidly since the early 1970s, has been local rather than national in scope.

Because of the general dearth of national studies and national databases this entry will focus on Australia (where there have been national studies on third-age and part-time students), and where possible, it will compare the Australian data with information from the United Kingdom. The choice of these two countries will highlight the phenomenon of the nontraditional student because the supply of higher education is more strictly rationed in those countries than in Canada and the United States, for example.

There have always been nontraditional students in higher education, if traditional students are defined as those who enter higher education straight from school at the age of about 18 years. Apart from military personnel returning to study after war service, the numbers of nontraditional students have been relatively small. This entry will not concentrate on the nontraditional students who entered immediately after the Second World War, as they are not typical of the more recent wave of entrants which started to build in the early 1970s. The veterans were mainly male and entered as a result of government rehabilitation legislation. They were easily identifiable and the literature on their progress and performance is extensive, particularly in North America (Frederiksen and Schrader 1950). For the purpose of this entry, the nontraditional student will be defined as the mature-age student entering higher education to obtain a degree, and will therefore concentrate primarily on the formal higher education system. Toward the end of the entry there will be a brief examination of a more informal educational development—the University of the Third Age (U3A).

A description of the phenomenon of recent nontraditional entrants should illuminate the changes in the social mores and the subsequent reactions of governments and institutions.

1. The Mature Student

As this entry will concentrate on the nontraditional mature-age student, it is necessary to define what is meant by "mature." In the United Kingdom the criterion is usually over 21 years of age on commencement of tertiary study, whereas in Australia the dividing line in most research studies is usually drawn at 25 years and over. Roderick et al. (1982) pointed out that there is no nationally agreed definition of mature-age students in the United Kingdom. The same is true in Australia where practice varies between institutions. The defining ageline is drawn completely arbitrarily and the different definitions make direct comparisons difficult.

1.1 Critical Mass

Why has there been an upsurge across the Western world in higher education literature concerning the mature-age student phenomenon? (see, e.g., Hore and West 1980, Smithers and Griffin 1986, and Apps 1981, for descriptions in Australia, the United Kingdom, and the United States respectively). The first

reason is that they have become a group large enough to be noticed and to arouse the curiosity of the researchers interested in such questions as: who are these students and why are their numbers increasing? At Monash University in Melbourne, questionnaires are given to all entering first-year students every second year. The questionnaires contain detailed questions about the socioeconomic backgrounds of the respondents. In the early 1970s the numbers of students over the age of 25 years began to increase significantly.

By 1978 in Australia, 32.7 percent of students in universities and 21.4 percent of students in colleges of advanced education were over the age of 25 years when commencing a higher education course for the first time. By 1982, these percentages had increased to 36.0 and 26.3 respectively (Australian Bureau of Statistics 1983). After 1987 the definition of "commencing student" was changed in the Australian higher education statistics collection and from that date a commencing student was one who had enrolled for the first time in a given course.

It will be shown later in this entry that higher education is a route to upward social mobility for mature females in both societies in question. The Australian Higher Education Statistics for 1988 (Department of Employment, Education, and Training 1988) provide some interesting figures on women commencing full- and part-time education on campus (excluding external or correspondence students). In full- and part-time studies female commencers outnumber males by the same proportion in both modes of study—53 percent female to 47 percent male. The gender split by age figure is not given, but 35 percent of the commencing students overall are over the age of 25 years.

In the United Kingdom, the Department of Education and Science in 1988 issued a Statistical Bulletin on mature-age students in higher education from 1975 to 1986. Unfortunately the collection was restricted to first-year students and did not differentiate between those students who were entering higher education for the first time and those who were commencing a second degree or a graduate degree. The Department of Education and Science defined mature students as those over 21 years of age commencing a first degree or subdegree program, or over 25 years if commencing a graduate course. While there can be no direct comparison, some of the trends identified in the Statistical Bulletin are similar to those identified in the Australian research. For example: the number of mature-age students was increasing; the number of mature-age women students was increasing faster than that of men; only a small proportion of mature-age students were studying the science-based offerings; and the majority of mature-age students were studying part-time.

By the mid-1970s, when the trend lines in Australia showed that the over 25-year olds commencing

Table 1
Demographic background variables: proportions for each type of mature-age student

	Median age (years)	Female (%)	Married (%)	Divorced/separated (%)
Early school-leavers	33.8	59.5	72.8	14.8
Recyclers (a)	31.6	61.8	74.3	9.4
Recyclers (b)	32.5	47.2	75.2	10.3
Returners	31.0	39.5	69.5	12.9
Deferrers	29.8	48.9	67.4	13.5
Total sample	32.4	54.0	72.5	12.2

as undergraduate students were increasing for no obvious reason (there had been no government initiative at that time encouraging such students), researchers began to seek reasons for this perturbation in the standard pattern.

1.2 Description of Entrants

Mature-age students are not a homogeneous group; different types of people enter, using different methods of entry and with different reasons for doing so. One useful classification of types of mature-age students was based upon their educational starting points (Hore and West 1980). There are early school-leavers, that is, those who left school early without the qualifications required for entry into higher education; recyclers, who had previously completed a postsecondary school qualification (this group further divides into those who are (a) upgrading their qualifications in the same discipline, and (b) entering a different discipline); returners, who discontinued a previous higher education course and have now decided to return; and deferrers, who qualified at school to enter higher education but who did not do so at that time. An Australian national study of over 2,200 mature-age students (West et al. 1986) yielded the following percentages for each of the above classifications: early school-leavers 34.2; recyclers (a) 22.4, recyclers (b) 24.6; returners 11.0; and deferrers 7.8 percent.

Some brief quotations from typical members of each of the above groups may assist the reader in understanding the diversity of background and motivation which these mature entrants bring to higher education. (All of these extracts come from Hore and West 1980 Chap. 5.) Early school-leavers: "My parents were in the lower income bracket and higher education was not considered an option for me. Boys in our group would have been considered, because they were seen as the future breadwinners, but not a girl. I grew up with the idea that I would leave school at 16 and work in an office as it had been 'good enough for my mother.'" Recyclers (same discipline):

"It will upgrade my teacher's qualification, thereby creating greater job security and promotion opportunities." Recyclers (new discipline): "I will have a social work degree and hopefully will be able to practice in that area instead of being a mentally frustrated nursing sister." Returners: "I had to drop out of study because of family pressures and the need to earn some money." Deferrers: "My parents were extremely poor and to go on to the final years of high school would have meant that I had to change schools. This meant new uniforms, books, fares, and so on. I was capable at this stage of getting a job, having been turned out of the process line of 'commercial students.'"

There are significant differences in the backgrounds of the mature-age students in each of the groups mentioned above. To return to the data from the national study (West et al. 1986 p. 17), one can see those differences in a number of variables (see Table 1). As one might expect from the brief descriptions of the people in each of the groups, the early school-leavers and the recyclers upgrading in the same discipline contained the majority of female students.

The predominance of women in the early school-leaver group can be better understood if one places it against the expansion of secondary retention that

Table 2
Some socioeconomic background variables: percentage proportions for each type of mature-age student

	Student's previous employment in professional occupations	Father's occupation Professional or managerial	Skilled or semiskilled
Early school leavers	14.9	28.2	40.4
Recyclers (a)	81.4	38.3	28.6
Recyclers (b)	69.8	47.4	25.1
Returners	25.4	49.8	26.4
Deferrers	21.1	43.2	24.6
Total sample	45.1	38.8	31.1

occurred in Australia in the 1960s and 1970s. In the 1950s in Australia less than 10 percent of children commencing secondary school at the age of 11 years stayed on to the final year of school some six years later. This meant that those children who left school early did not have the qualifications necessary for entering tertiary education. This group contained more girls than boys since their retention rates had always been lower and initially grew more slowly. The rate of retention in secondary schools in the early 1990s is around 50 percent, so that these students leaving school in the 1960s and 1970s were, in a real sense, disadvantaged compared with students 20 to 30 years on. The recyclers returning to upgrade their initial qualifications were mainly female because many of the professions which previously required subdegree qualifications, for example, diplomas in nursing, primary-school teaching, and librarianship, now required degrees. These professions were staffed predominantly by females. Many women who had taken time out of their profession for child rearing, and sought later to return, were caught by this qualification inflation, by which they were then deemed unqualified to re-enter their profession. The issue of divorce/separation will be discussed in greater detail later to question whether study is harmful or helpful to a relationship.

The paternal occupational level is an often-used, though crude, measure of socioeconomic status, as is illustrated in Table 2, but since these students are themselves adults, their own occupational levels are also included for reference. From the occupational levels it can be seen that the various schemes to allow the entry of early school-leavers into higher education provide a route for the upwardly mobile female to break through the class barrier.

The method of qualifying to enter higher education, particularly in countries like Australia and the United Kingdom where the supply of places in higher education is closely rationed, becomes a critical factor. While some institutions have reserved places (especially for mature students) and relaxed the entry requirements it would be wrong to think that the majority of mature students enter through the various "special entry" schemes, for many will seek to enter by jumping the same hurdles as the normal-age student: the Higher School Certificate, which acts, like the British General Certificate of Education A levels, as the selection filter for higher education. A similar picture emerges in the United Kingdom, where over half of the mature students entered on the strength of their General Certificate of Education results (Smithers and Griffin 1986).

In summary, mature-age students are not a homogeneous group. They are made up of several subgroups of adults who have quite different backgrounds and quite different motivations for entering higher education. A major result of the contemporary phenomenon of mature-age entry into higher education

has been changed community attitudes to education, particularly toward women.

So far this entry has focused on people's personal reasons for entering higher education, mirroring the origins of mature-age education itself, but this groundswell prompted political action, in part reflecting the changing social mores. This action was not initially altruistic as it was prompted more by demographic predictions and labor market needs than considerations of social justice. Later, governments in both countries reacted by issuing Green and White Papers stressing the need to increase access for groups previously underrepresented, members of the lower socioeconomic groups, particularly women, and other groups seen as disadvantaged. In Australia the disadvantaged groups included people from rural and isolated areas and Aboriginal people.

Some statements from the White Papers from both countries will highlight the policies being announced to increase access. The United Kingdom White Paper (DES 1987 para 2.14) invited institutions "to consider carefully the steps necessary to secure increased participation by both young and older people, and to act accordingly." Similarly, the Australian White Paper (1988 para. 2.2) focused on national equity goals which espoused the principle that it was inefficient to have barriers to higher education which prevented access to the system or to parts of that system. This latter point addressed the concentration of women in a narrow range of courses and disciplines. However, Powles (1987), examining Australian statistics 1976–83, noted that there had been large increases in the proportion of both full-time and part-time female students in the 23- to 29-year old age group despite the fact that these are the years in which childbearing and rearing are most common. In the United Kingdom, open-access courses attract women students because they provide access to personal growth and self-discovery as well as a path to higher education (Hutchinson and Hutchinson 1986). These are important aspects of the changing social scene which made it more acceptable for women to return to study and also to do so for other than purely vocational reasons.

The majority of Australian mature-age students entering higher education for the first time enroll in the areas of humanities and social sciences. There are two main reasons for this: first, they usually do not have the prerequisite background in mathematics and the sciences to enter the faculties of science, medicine, or engineering; second, they seek areas of study which will enable them to use their life experiences. When one looks at the field of study for mature-age students by gender it parallels the gender split for normal-age (i.e., straight from school) students. For example, more women than men are studying humanities (65% to 35%). More men than women are studying economics or business (24% to 7%). The picture is not one of women moving into the male-dominated areas but it does portray an increase in the general educational level of women and, as will be seen in the section on employment, greater employment opportunities. The United Kingdom scene reflects this situation, except that many United Kingdom institutions provide "access" courses which attempt to provide the missing background knowledge and overcome the barriers formed by strict prerequisites (Lucas and Ward 1985, Woodrow 1988).

The ethnic composition of the mature student population cannot be ascertained from the existing databases in either country. One study in the United Kingdom (Millins 1984) showed that most students on access courses were British Black or Caribbean (54%); 75 percent were female, and 63 percent were from the lower occupational groups. In Australia, ethnic identity becomes blurred in data collections, such as the Census, as immigrants become citizens (see Foster 1989) and while second-generation immigrants are attending higher education institutions in greater numbers they do so as traditional rather than nontraditional students.

1.3 Progress and Performance

By the 1980s it had been established that the mature student was a good performer academically (see Barrett 1976, Brennan 1986, Kilminster and Miller 1989, Walker 1975). These findings were repeated worldwide with researchers advancing two main reasons to account for this success, namely, greater levels of motivation and maturity (Apps 1981, Graham 1989). Life experience has academic value, particularly in the subjects favored by the mature entrants, that is, humanities and social sciences. This is not to say that mature students do not drop out of their studies—they do, at about the same rate as normal-age students. The significant difference between the mature and the younger groups' attrition is the type of reason advanced for dropping out. The mature students' reasons are indicative of a crisis within the family, usually to do with finance or the health of themselves or their children. Women revert to the role of the primary care-giver whenever any crisis arises, even though they may be living in an intact relationship with a male partner or husband. Students who are also single parents do not usually have the choice to remain in higher education.

2. On Completion of Higher Education

Mature-age students had been studied extensively in Australia by the early 1980s (e.g., Barrett 1976, Barrett and Powell 1980, Hore and West 1980, McDonald and Knights 1982) and in the United Kingdom (e.g., Roderick et al. 1982, Phillips 1986, Smithers and Griffin 1986). Much was known about mature-age students: who they were, why they entered higher education, and how well they performed once

they got there, but little was known about what happened to them after graduation. How had the experience of higher education affected them as people and what effect had it upon their subsequent careers? Two studies have been published which address these issues, one in Australia (West et al. 1986) and one in the United Kingdom (Graham 1989). Data from both of these studies will be used here to illustrate the changes which have occurred in the lives of mature-age graduates.

2.1 Changes to the Graduate as a Person

Graham discusses three factors which were mentioned most frequently by mature graduates in surveys carried out by the Central and West London Open College in 1986 and the Open University in 1987: (a) growth in self-confidence; (b) wider horizons; and (c) capability in work. Many older students begin their courses with a very low self-image and a burden of doubts about their ability to succeed. Initial success is often regarded as a fluke, but as this becomes consistent, students begin to take a delight in their achievements. In addition to the specific information about their chosen discipline, mature graduates value the experience of encountering other points of view, challenging them, and in so doing questioning their own prejudices and permitting further personal growth. One of the respondents put it so well that her comments are included as they appeared in Graham:

> It would be almost impossible to overstate the profound effect on my life which acquiring my degree has had. It fostered a critical analysis of my life, contributed to my maturity of thought, created a wider toleration of people and events, reinforced and highlighted aspects of identity and self-awareness . . . Above all, it has deeply enriched my quality of life, and when I consider its impact, I feel that its overall effect has been little short of dramatic. (Graham 1989 p. 37)

Having reached a new plane of achievement, older graduates wish to be employed in work commensurate with their demonstrated capabilities. Typically, they see their worst fate as being under-utilized or condemned to unrewarding or undemanding tasks.

The study by West et al. (1986) was a national study funded by the Australian Government to look at the impact of higher education on those people who had entered it as mature-age students (over 25 years of age). Ideally the preferred research strategy would have been to follow a cohort of entering students throughout their years of study and into the early years of employment, but, because of the high cost and the time lag before the results are available, it is difficult to persuade funding agencies that they should support such extended studies. The strategy adopted in the West et al. study was to ask respondents to describe aspects of their personal life and employment both now and six months before they began their degree. The six-month-before period was used to allow for the inclusion of temporary jobs taken to earn money before commencing the course. This strategy was employed to examine both the effects on the person and their employment.

There are problems of validity in inferring impact from change, because one cannot be sure whether the observed changes are due to "maturation," that is, the passage of time itself, or to "history," that is, those events, other than higher education, during the time period which may have caused the change. In order to provide at least some form of control to account for the effects of maturation and history in the West et al. (1986) study, comparisons were made between those mature students who graduated and those who withdrew during the first year of study. In every case where change was observed, both in the employment and the personal variables, the change was greater for graduates than for first-year withdrawers.

The findings of the West et al. study concerning changes to the person can be summarized as follows: very large increases in their communication skills, academic ability, and leadership skills; large increases in their academic interests and self-esteem; medium increase in their intellectual interests, social liberalism, attitudes toward feminism, altruistic orientation, and overall life satisfaction; and a large decrease in dogmatism.

There is surprisingly little research on the impact that being a mature student has on the relationship between the students and their partners. Data from the West et al. study show that there is an increase in the proportion divorced or separated and a decrease in the proportion never married during the period covered by the study. The respondents were asked specifically about the impact of studying on their relationship. The most noteworthy of the results indicate the high number of respondents who claimed that their relationship had been enriched by being a student (41.2%). Being a student also caused problems in the relationships of 31.8 percent of the respondents but 28.9 percent overcame these problems and only 2.9 percent parted. On the other hand, 14.2 percent reported that being a student aggravated existing problems and that the relationship ended. While these figures do not support the view commonly held by researchers in this field that being a student leads to marriage/relationship breakdown, it is true that for a minority (17.1%) being a student does create or aggravate existing problems and end relationships.

2.2 Changes to the Graduate as Employee

Taking the whole group of mature graduates surveyed by West et al., the differences in occupational level before and after entering higher education are dramatic. For example, 14.9 percent of respondents were in the upper professional category before beginning their course and 32.8 percent at the time of the survey. Significant moves in occupational level occurred for all types of mature-age students. For the early school-leavers, returners, and deferrers, of whom relatively few were in professional or managerial categories (25.7, 39.7, and 37.1% respectively), the situation improved considerably to 56.4, 73.8, and 56.8 percent respectively. For both groups of recyclers, which already had large numbers in the upper employment categories, the shifts were much smaller but still substantial. The changes were particularly great for females. Before starting their course only 9.4 percent of women were in the upper professional occupations, compared with 28.3 percent after graduation. A particularly interesting group of women is the one containing those who were previously involved in home duties. The occupational destinations of 286 of the 300 females who were housewives before commencing study show that latterly over 50 percent were employed in professional occupations and nearly three-fourths were in paid employment. Twenty-six percent remained in the home duty category after graduation.

To summarize the findings from the 2,200 respondents, it can be stated that, from the employment perspective, undertaking higher education was very advantageous. The graduates markedly improved their occupational status and their job prospects, and showed substantial increases in their work satisfaction. They felt the work to be more challenging, stimulating, responsible, and important, albeit marginally more stressful. For the mature graduate, higher education had a significant impact upon employment.

2.3 Reactions of Employers to Older Graduates

Graham (1989) has summarized employers' perceptions of the assets and liabilities of older graduates. Employers who had recruited mature graduates or were seriously considering doing so commented on the sense of commitment and determination displayed by the older graduate. They saw the older entrant as having a more realistic and balanced approach to business problems and being less likely to react impetuously in a difficult situation. Older entrants had the advantage over younger staff in terms of skill in handling people. Transferable skills or relevant work experience were seen by employers as a bonus which would make up for older graduates' later entrance into academic studies. There are certain limitations which may apply more to older rather than younger applicants. For example, family commitments may be a problem if the job requires frequent moves around the country. Some older graduates have higher salary expectations and not all are skilled at handling people, thus possibly finding it difficult to combine seniority of years with junior status in the organization. Graham reiterated the point that while older graduates are not a homogeneous group there are certain positive traits of maturity such as realism and self-knowledge which make them serious-minded about the jobs for which they apply and their employers are repaid by them with loyalty and commitment.

3. Social Class

Despite the influx of mature-age students into the system in both Australia and the United Kingdom since the early 1970s, both systems of higher education remain elitist (Neave 1985). In the United Kingdom, Smithers and Robinson (1989), using occupation of head of the household as the measure, showed that two out of three normal age entrants to higher education came from social classes 1 and II (professional and managerial groups). Only 1 in 200 came from social class V (unskilled manual workers). For mature entrants to higher education, using their own occupation as the indicator, the social class which predominates is IIIA (skilled nonmanual workers). In Australia, there are no national figures on the social class composition of university entrants, so one has to rely on the collections which are available from individual universities. In Melbourne, Monash University's 1986 data show that, of the students entering a bachelor's degree course at first-year level, 69.7 percent came from the equivalent of the British social classes I and II. The social class composition of mature-age entrants indicates that 45.1 percent of that group were from social classes I and II, but note the variation between the types of mature students: for the early leavers, only 28.2 percent had fathers from the professional occupations as compared to 49.8 percent for the returners. One way to improve the number of students from the lower social classes would be to change the aspirations of students early in their high-school years. This has been shown to work (Hore and Barwood 1989), but its study falls outside the brief of this entry.

4. Impediments to Change

4.1 Finance

One of the reasons why there was an increase in the number of mature students entering higher education in Australia in the mid-1970s was that the Commonwealth Government took over total funding responsibility for higher education. Prior to this time students had to contribute 15–20 percent of the costs, although a number of full-time students were on scholarships. The abolition of fees had two effects, first, an increase in the Commonwealth Government's accountability measures and second, a rise in the labor needs aspects of the production of university graduates. For mature students from lower socioeconomic backgrounds, the abolition of fees meant that they could attend higher education without tuition costs. The major conclusion from a study investigating the social composition of the student population after the abolition of fees

was that the effect was small. However, the majority of individuals who were affected were disproportionately from the lower socioeconomic and other under-represented groups, that is, women, migrants, older people, and the rural community (Anderson et al. 1980). At first glance it appears that the abolition of fees had little effect on the numbers of mature students but the study was confounded by another event—the abolition of teacher-training scholarships—which required the student to work for the granting body for a period of time after graduation. The scholarships, for many students from the lower socioeconomic groups, were a significant channel of upward mobility.

The trend lines from the Monash University database following the abolition of fees indicated an increase in the numbers of students over 25 years of age on entry from under 13 percent in 1975 to a peak of 15.2 percent in 1982, and two-thirds of these were women. It must be concluded that the abolition of fees was an incentive for the mature-age student, particularly the single mother or the wife with a spouse who was uncommitted to his wife's introduction to higher education.

Moves in the United Kingdom in the early 1990s to introduce full-cost fees and the introduction in Australia in 1987 of the Administrative Charge and in 1989 of its replacement, the Higher Education Contribution Scheme, have rationed access to higher education by price. Under the Australian scheme all students inherit a tax debt (in 1996 each full-time student faced a debt of A$2,424) to be paid back when they earn more than A$27,675 a year. Alternatively, they can pay A$1,818 on commencement and avoid a tax debt. Since the majority of students come from the upper socioeconomic classes, it is not surprising that in 1989 over 20 percent paid at the start of their studies, and the Minister expected that the scheme would settle down with more students paying "upfront." This appears not to be the case, e.g., in 1996, only 16 percent of students at Monash University (with approximately 45,000 students) have paid up front. From the mature student's point of view, as the Higher Education Contribution Scheme does not require payment on commencement, it did not have the deterrent effect of either the Administrative Charge or any other loan scheme without an associated grant or scholarship to ameliorate prestudy payments.

4.2 Institutional Responses

Fulton and Ellwood (1989) summarized the United Kingdom scene of the late 1980s when a number of different influences began to emerge to create a strong movement toward the expansion of access. These included: patterns of demand and demography; pressures for social equality; changes in secondary education; patterns of employment; and the declining credibility of the A-level examination on which selection into higher education was based.

Despite these influences, which are also at work in Australia, most tertiary institutions sought to increase their market share from the pool of qualified school-leavers rather than look for students in the nontraditional groups such as older women and members of the disadvantaged social classes. On the whole, the more popular the institution and the stronger it was in attracting the traditional school-leaver, the less likely it was to adopt access initiatives. As far as this group of institutions was concerned, the cost of access programs was not tenable from an economic point of view, but was advantageous as a political and educational statement. It appears that those with a strong position in the more traditional market will require other incentives to broaden the social composition of their student body.

Changes in the secondary education of both countries, in both cases toward a common curriculum, may loosen the link between age and a particular level of performance. In turn, this will redefine, or render invalid, any age-related concepts or definitions about who is "nontraditional." It is possible that a future nontraditional group could be the young or very young, rather than the mature, because performance will be based on the achievement of criteria irrespective of age. Already these young students are entering universities in both Australia and the United Kingdom, in some cases in spite of expectations, if not regulations, prohibiting early entry.

5. Effects on Higher Education of the Aging Population

There are two other currents which together form a new wave in higher education (Weinstock 1978). The first is the shift in demography which shows an increase in the number of older people, and the second, the recognition that education is as much a need for the old as it is for the young. Development is not something which only happens in childhood and researchers are now discussing it as a life-long feature (e.g., see Birren et al. 1981). Until comparatively recently, people in the later years of life were not visible on the campuses of higher learning, and they still have not reached the critical mass level. This level may be reached with the introduction of various laws preventing discrimination on the basis of age. Until that point, however, the older, retired members of the population in both the United Kingdom and Australia have to find an alternative method of education.

5.1 The University of the Third Age

Adult education is nonformal and does not usually provide an award although this distinction is blurred in Australia and the United Kingdom as adults do study secondary-school level courses to enable them to enter higher education or undertake certificate courses upgrading their vocational skills. The comments made earlier about the dearth of systems to collect data on nontraditional students are also true of the adult education activity.

A rapidly growing addition to the extensive provision of adult education in Australia has been the introduction of Universities of the Third Age (U3A). The concept of the University of the Third Age originated in France in 1973 when established universities began to be involved in the education of people in the third age of their life, or "active retirement." (The two preceding ages are "childhood" and "active working life" and the fourth age is "senility and dependence.") According to Midwinter (1984) France has two-thirds of the world's U3As. The United Kingdom has about 50, the first of which began in 1982 at Cambridge though it has no official connection to the University of Cambridge (Norton 1984). As with the U3A movement in the United Kingdom whic ". . . defiantly lacks a rigid form" (Midwinter 1984 p. 6), the Australian scene is difficult to quantify, but there are about 27 U3As within the State of Victoria and another 20 in the remaining states. The Australian and United Kingdom versions of the U3A are self-help organizations where no distinction is made between those who teach and those who learn, and education is given freely by members to their colleagues (Greengross 1985). The primary aim of the U3A movement is to stimulate mental activity and provide the opportunity for the pursuit of education for its own sake, and not for qualifications or as preparation for employment. There are no prerequisites at the beginning and no qualifications at the end.

The U3A movement appeals to the active retired members of the community for many reasons. It offers: the chance to make up for educational opportunities lost due to the Second World War, family, or job commitments; arrangements whereby the classes are held locally (avoiding problems of transport), and during the day (avoiding having to travel at night); classes where the content and method are negotiated between the tutor and the class members and where the environment is nonthreatening and nonexamination oriented; and classes where there is a wide range of choice from the esoteric to the mundane. Two other important aspects are the sense of independence in determining what is provided in a cooperative environment, and the idea that exercising this choice in a group of one's age peers is a relaxed way to learn. The University of the Third Age has much to teach those who participate in traditional and nontraditional education.

6. Conclusion

In preparing this entry it has become clear that future cross-cultural research on the nontraditional student will continue to be handicapped unless governments and academic communities agree on standard definitions and to maintain databases which enable researchers to explore basic demographic variables.

See Adult Tertiary Education; University Adult Education; Human Development: Aging; Lifespan Development: Problems and Crises

References

Anderson D S, Boven R, Fensham P J, Powell J P 1980 *Students in Australian Higher Education: A Study of their Social Composition Since the Abolition of Fees.* Education Research and Development Committee Report No. 23, Australian Government Publishing Service, Canberra

Apps J W 1981 *The Adult Learner on Campus: A Guide for Instructors and Administrators.* Follett, Chicago, Illinois

Australian Bureau of Statistics 1983 *Bulletin* 4208.0

Australian White Paper 1988 *Higher Education: A Policy Statement.* Australian Government Publishing Service, Canberra

Barrett E M 1976 Mature age unmatriculated students. *Aust. Educ. Res.* 3: 15–22

Barrett E M, Powell J P 1980 Mature age unmatriculated students and the justification of a more liberal admissions policy. *Higher Educ.* 9(4): 365–83

Birren J E, Kinney D K, Warner Schaie K, Woodruff D S 1981 *Developmental Psychology: A Life-span Approach.* Houghton Mifflin, Boston, Massachusetts

Brennan J 1986 Student learning and the "capacity to benefit": The performance of nontraditional students in public sector higher education. *J. Access Studs.* 1(2): 23–32

Department of Education and Science (DES) 1987 (White Paper) *Higher Education: Meeting the Challenge.* HMSO (Cmnd 114), London

Department of Education and Science 1988 *Mature Students in Higher Education 1975–1986.* Statistical Bulletin No. 11/88 DES, London

Department of Employment, Education, and Training 1988 *Selected Higher Education Statistics.* Canberra

Foster L E 1989 *Diversity and Multicultural Education.* Allen and Unwin, Sydney

Frederiksen N, Schrader W B 1950 *Adjustment to College: A Study of 10,000 Veteran and Non-veteran Students in Sixteen American Colleges.* ERIC Document Reproduction Service No. ED 058856, Washington, DC

Fulton O, Ellwood S 1989 Admissions access and institutional change. In: Fulton O (ed.) 1989

Graham B 1989 *Older Graduates and Employment.* Association of Graduate Careers Advisory Services, Manchester

Greengross S (ed.) 1985 *Aging: An Adventure in Living.* Human Horizons Series. Souvenir Press, London

Hore T, Barwood B 1989 Strategies for improving access. *Aust. Univ. Rev.* 32: 2–5

Hore T, West L H T 1980 *Mature Age Students in Australian Higher Education.* Monash University, Clayton, Victoria

Hutchinson E, Hutchinson E 1986 *Women Returning to Learning.* National Extension College, Cambridge, Massachusetts

Kilminster S, Miller A 1989 The student progress and performance study 1975–1988. *Aust. Univ. Rev.* 32(1): 17–21

Lucas S, Ward P 1985 *A Survey of "Access" Courses in England.* University of Lancaster, Lancaster

McDonald R, Knights S 1982 Experiences of adult students at Murdoch University. In: Teather D C B (ed.) 1981 *Towards the Community University.* Kogan Page, London

Midwinter E (ed.) 1984 *Mutual Aid Universities.* Croom Helm, London

Millins P K C 1984 *Access Studies to Higher Education September 1979–December 1983: A Report.* Roehampton Institute, London

Neave G 1985 Elite and mass higher education in Britain: A regressive model? *Comp. Educ. Rev.* 29(3): 347–61

Norton D 1984 The University of the Third Age—Nationwide. In: Midwinter E (ed.) 1984

Phillips C J 1986 Full-time mature students in higher education: A survey of their characteristics, experiences and expectations. *Brit. Educ. Res. J.* 12(3): 289–308

Powles M 1987 *Women's Participation in Tertiary Education: A Review of Recent Australian Research.* University of Melbourne, Melbourne

Roderick G W, Bilham T, Bell J 1982 Supply and demand: Mature students at British universities. *Higher Educ. Rev.* 15(1): 29–45

Smithers A, Griffin A 1986 *The Progress of Mature Students.* Joint Matriculation Board, Manchester

Smithers A, Robinson P 1989 *Increasing Participation in Higher Education.* British Petroleum Education Department, London

Walker P 1975 The university performance of mature students. *Res. Educ.* 14: 1–13

Weinstock R 1978 *The Graying of the Campus.* Educational Facilities Laboratories, New York

West L H T, Hore T, Eaton E G, Kermond B M 1986 *The Impact of Higher Education on Mature Age Students.* Commonwealth Tertiary Education Commission, Monash University, Melbourne

Woodrow M 1988 The access course route to higher education. *Higher Educ. Q.* 42(4): 317–34

Further Reading

Duke C 1989 Creating the accessible institution. In: Fulton O (ed.) 1989

Fulton O (ed.) 1981 *Access to Higher Education.* Society for Research into Higher Education, Guildford

Fulton O (ed.) 1989 *Access and Institutional Change.* Society for Research into Higher Education/Open University Press, Buckingham

Millar T B 1987 *Higher Education Policy in Britain and Australia.* University of London, Australian Studies Centre, Institute of Commonwealth Studies, London

Woodley A, Wagner L, Slowey M, Hamilton M, Fulton O 1987 *Choosing to Learn: Adults in Education.* Society for Research in Higher Education/Open University Press, Buckingham

Women and Access to Vocational Training

G. Goodale

Female access to adult education and vocational training is directly related to women's labor market situation. Labor economists have measured this relationship in terms of earnings and suggested, in human capital theory, that greater investments in education and training would yield higher wages, among other things. However, when one compares the effect of education and training on earnings for women and men, the theory falls short in accounting for the wage gap. Women consistently do not earn as much as men with comparable levels of education and training (Reskin and Hartmann 1986, Harlan and Steinberg 1989).

Why is this the case? Despite the substantial increase in the proportion of women in the labor force worldwide, occupational segregation by sex has persisted. Occupational segregation not only accounts for a large proportion of the wage gap between full-time working women and men, it is also linked to the perpetuation of poverty in many female-headed households. A report cites childhood poverty in the United States as almost "inescapable" in single-parent families headed by women without high school diplomas (AAUW/NEA 1992 p. 5).

It is important to recognize the forces and processes which place women at a disadvantage so that policies may be formulated and implemented to influence the main areas of discrimination. And within this context, the implications for adult education and training, and what women are being educated and trained to do, must be examined.

The concept of adult education and training as an enabling factor for achieving equality is based on the belief that economic and social inequality between women and men is linked to women's lack of occupational qualifications. Policies and programs often assume that "open access" is the key to guaranteeing equality in education, training, and employment or economic outcomes. But are these views warranted?

This entry suggests that it is more useful to identify the ways in which education and training determine and indeed limit women's opportunities. It builds on the view that adult education and vocational training contribute to women's disadvantaged position in the labor market and argues that "fitting them into" the current system would only serve to perpetuate existing inequalities.

The relationship between training and occupational segregation by sex is complicated. On the one hand, training systems could be characterized as a source of occupational segregation by influencing women's occupational preferences and preparing millions of women for traditional female-dominated occupations. On the other, training responds to the demands of the

market. Thus training systems and the labor market interact and mutually reinforce the barriers which serve to relegate women to a limited number of occupations and, therefore, lower wages, less occupational mobility, and job security, and reduce women's capacity to achieve self-reliance (Harlan and Steinberg 1989 pp. 35–36).

From this perspective, "access" alone is not enough. An exclusive focus on access to existing provisions may in fact contribute to inequality of outcomes. The extent to which vocational education and training are able to contribute to greater labor market equality for women depends on whether the training and educational processes and structures which place women at a disadvantage are changed. Males and females do not have the same educational and training experiences, and as one study puts it, public education and training systems "shortchange" girls (AAUW/NEA 1992).

This entry briefly reviews the relationship between adult education and training for women and labor market outcomes in terms of occupational segregation. Elements of a framework for considering the constraints women face in gaining access to and participating in adult education and training will then be suggested, followed by examples of measures and programs which have been effective in overcoming some of these barriers.

1. Occupational Segregation by Sex and its Consequences

The distribution of economically active females and males has remained remarkably stable despite significant and unprecedented changes in the structure of economies and the turnover of occupations, the increased employment of women, the narrowing of educational and training differentials between men and women, and the increasing similarity of work patterns of men and women over their lifetimes (Reskin and Hartmann 1986). A review of changes in the labor market position of women in the former 12 European Union states (Marvani 1992) concludes that the persistence of occupational segregation and the rigidity it generates remain the underlying causes of the inequality women suffer in employment, job status, and pay. Even more alarming is the fact that this segregation has remained virtually unchanged despite explicit policies to achieve equal opportunities and treatment through provisions associated with equal pay, legislation prohibiting direct discrimination in recruitment, promotion, dismissal, and training.

A review of worldwide trends in education (Kelly

1990) indicates that impressive progress has been made since the early 1970s in achieving equality of access for women. In 1960, gender was the greatest predictor of educational access worldwide. Has increased educational provision served to eliminate gender-based inequalities in the workplace, the family, the community, and the political system? The study concludes that differences in the proportion of women educated and the amount of education they received have resulted in few changes in their rate of entry into the workforce for a wage, the degree of gender segregation, their income relative to men's, and their access to political power.

However, if increased provision has not had the desired effect on training outcomes, the type of education and training followed by girls and young women does appear to influence their levels of labor-force participation, job loss, and income earned in both wage and self-employment. One study (Paukert 1984) concludes that by virtue of the subjects they take in school and the narrow range of traditionally "female" occupations they follow in training, girls' future employability is limited and they are at a disadvantage compared with boys in getting jobs, particularly in periods of economic expansion when restructuring is likely to call for new types of skills, usually of a technical nature. Equality of access has in practice meant access to "gendered subjects," with engineering, hard sciences, and technical subjects male domains in which women have made few inroads. A study of job training in the United States concludes that vocational education and job-related training programs, highly partitioned by sex, provide some of the most direct evidence of the linkage between vocational education and training systems and occupational segregation. Rather than counteracting occupational segregation, vocational training reinforces it by preparing women for lower-paying, sex-typical occupations (Harlan and Steinberg 1989).

Patterns of female participation in training may be understood by tracing the development of training systems. Assumptions concerning women's domestic roles often become the rationale for laws and policies requiring specific curricula for girls and women. These measures can result in several trends. First, men and women will be differentially distributed across vocational courses, with women predominantly in health, home economics, and office and business programs, and men in technical preparation, the trades, and agriculture. Second, there may be noticeable differences in the location of training for women and men. Classroom training is typically the predominate training ground for "female" occupations, while on-the-job training and apprenticeships are generally the means of qualifying for male-dominated technical jobs (Harlan and Steinberg 1989). Finally, the administration of training programs can influence women's enrollment opportunities. For example, federally funded training initiatives may target men or limit the enrollment to one person per household, a practice which reflects a concern for preserving the male-headed household and the authority of the male family head by maintaining his status as principal wage earner (Harlan 1989).

2. Obstacles to Female Access to Adult Education and Vocational Training

2.1 Prevailing Views

The issue of female access to training is often conceptualized in terms of enrollment patterns by level and across programs, and the extent and adequacy of educational and training facilities. In this context, increased access for females is generally linked to expanding the infrastructure; improving the availability and quality of facilities; increasing the provision of equipment and materials; improving support services such as accommodation, transportation, and other sex specific facilities; increasing the numbers and percentage of female staff; and eliminating gender biases and improving the relevance of curricula, materials, and counseling and training methods. The solution is seen as a technical one, although family level considerations such as parents' perceptions of the opportunity costs of educating and training girls, family income levels, labor needs, and parents' educational levels may also be acknowledged.

Valuable information has been gleaned from this approach. For example, a review of girls' access to education, including vocational education, in sub-Saharan Africa (Hyde 1989) identified school-based, family, and societal factors which influenced girls' participation. The first comprised poor quality of schools, in particular the tendency to encourage girls to enroll in domestic science; inadequate equipment and facilities for science and mathematics; lack of role models for girls both in materials and among teaching staff; mismatch between the provision of vocational training and employment options; and teachers' attitudes toward girls' capabilities. Family level factors included income and labor requirements; parental attitudes on the acceptability of training girls in certain subject areas. Societal factors comprised activities which competed for girls' time, such as marriage and child-rearing, customary rites, and income-earning activities. The study concluded that expanding the system may have been successful in increasing girls' participation but it has not reduced or eliminated the gender differentials found at all levels and across programs.

Expanding the system therefore is not sufficient. Other studies (Bellow and King 1990) focus on the issue of demand for women's training and adult education and suggest that entry level barriers may be substantially reduced by lowering the cost of education and training and by raising the benefits. This latter point links the provision of training with educational and training outcomes and the failure of many policies and programs to lead to women's employment or to raise their incomes and productivity. Training for growth sectors of the economy might influence perceptions of the benefits of investing in females; however, at the same time, discrimination in the labor market which leads to women's lower wages relative to men's must be eliminated and vocational education and training supplemented with reliable and unbiased career guidance and placement services.

2.2 A Broader Framework

Training policy is not a technical issue dealing only with training systems and institutions. It is an inherently political issue and reflects the extent to which training is influenced by its environment. The problem of women's access to adult education and training should be treated as the complex social, economic, and political issue it is. A technical approach which focuses exclusively on women's lack of skills and on "fitting" women into the system assumes a world in which women's disadvantages in training and employment can be attributed to technical factors and "fixed" by technical inputs. This view is reminiscent of the 1950s and 1960s when it was thought that the provision of education and training would enable women to participate in and benefit from social and economic development on an equal basis with men.

It is clear, however, that the provision of more skills without due consideration of the processes which place women in a disadvantaged position does little to redress or eliminate women's past, present, and future inequalities. Taking a broader view of women's access to adult education and training therefore has implications for policy formulation and implementation. In particular, it requires a fundamental shift from providing compensatory measures for women to changing the system and the policies, structure, and practices which serve to perpetuate those inequalities which are found in the household division of labor and which subsequently place women at a disadvantage in the labor market.

From this perspective, a number of factors may be identified which influence female participation in and benefits from adult education and training.

2.3 Data Collection, its Use and Female Participation

The kinds of data collected, by whom and with what methods, and the use of this data have considerable bearing on the extent to which training programs will reach women and meet their gender-specific needs. By disaggregating baseline data by sex (and class and race) and applying gender as an analytical factor in problem identification, it is possible to assess with greater accuracy the obstacles to women's access to training and employment and the processes which put them at a disadvantage in the household, the training/educational setting, and the workplace.

The methods by which data are collected can also influence the effectiveness and relevance of training programs. In particular, research methods need to clarify the perspectives of the women concerned and of the various groups whose decisions may influence them. By involving them in the definition of the problem and the solution, program effectiveness may be increased and accountability among key individuals and groups fostered. However, participatory methods for defining training and other related needs will not automatically yield information on women. Specific steps must be taken to ensure their involvement. Female field agents, researchers, and training staff having sensitivity to gender issues have been found to be especially effective in gaining access to poor rural and urban women, and research methods which employ problem-solving approaches can provide data while serving to build confidence and group solidarity which is important for subsequent training program implementation.

2.4 Policy Goals, Legislation and their Implementation

Gender stereotypes and ideologies concerning women's roles, capabilities, and career aspirations shape educational policies and determine the extent and use of resources allocated to improving women's access to adult education and training. The structure of training systems reflects to a great extent the structure of the labor market. Prevailing patterns of sex segregation by work type, level, and characteristics have been widely used by planners and trainers to justify not only sex segregation in the provision of vocational training but lower investments in skilled and technical level education and training for females and the discouragement of females to enroll in vocational training (Byrne 1980). Measures to eliminate discrimination and counteract inequality must therefore be rooted firmly in planning and structures, so that sex equality goals are explicit objectives of training policy.

This points to the importance of comprehensive legislation to promote equal opportunities for women in vocational training and employment. A 1989 study in the United States concludes that nothing would have changed in terms of vocational education opportunities for women without the passage of legislation which prohibited discrimination on the basis of sex in all education programs which received federal assistance and included provisions aimed at overcoming sex discrimination, bias, and stereotyping (Vetter 1989 p. 109). Strong policies and legislation explicitly promoting women's employment in nontraditional occupations and seeking nondiscrimination in employment and wages also appear to provide incentives to women, parents, and training providers, including employers.

Training and educational policymakers and planners must be held accountable for the achievement of sex equity objectives and for monitoring progress on a regular basis. Since opening programs to females does not in itself achieve equal enrollments, positive measures are required to attract and support girls. However, special provisions to achieve equal opportunities for women risk being conducted as pilot programs outside mainstream training programs, thereby reducing their capacity to influence the general provision of adult education and training. This problem can be reduced if policymakers ensure from the outset that positive action strategies are routinely pursued in all major programs with targets and timetables to monitor achievement. It is important in this context to refer to recent work in the field of organizational theory which demonstrates that women's opportunities and experiences are influenced by the "male bias" which prevails in many, if not most, organizations (Mills and Tancred 1992).

A framework for conceptualizing these barriers to women's access and achievement in vocational training might include: an analysis of processes which create divisions on the basis of sex; institutional values, culture, and image; and interaction between different interest groups (Acker 1992).

2.5 Processes which Divide an Organization on the Basis of Sex

Sex differences in participation in adult education and training programs are related to variables such as the differential and selective recruitment and promotion of women; the nature of the organizational structure and hence the structure of power and authority; and the rules, regulations, and working arrangements which prescribe workplace behavior and the relationship between workplace and household.

Recruitment and promotion criteria and procedures have been specifically mentioned in studies of the status of women in further training (Gaynor 1990, Warwick 1990). Existing practices may serve to recruit women at low levels in the structure, where entry level wages are low and training and occupational mobility prospects are limited. The lack of women in positions of authority in training institutions also results in a lack of role models for female students and confirms assumptions and sex-role stereotypes that women should not or cannot hold positions of authority.

Low proportions of women in training systems contribute to the problem of "critical mass" which Byrne (1991) suggests influences the extent to which females, as a minority in a course, a discipline, or an institution, are viewed as "normal" or "abnormal and unfeminine." These perceptions serve to "filter out" girls' from certain vocational and technical fields.

Other organizational practices which create obstacles for women by producing divisions on the basis of sex include vocational guidance, counseling, and job placement programs that provide biased and inaccurate information about the job market, convey gender stereotypes as regards "appropriate" occupations for women, and channel girls (and boys) into specific subject and vocational areas.

New forms of work organization which represent an alternative to prevailing hierarchical arrangements can promote more participatory decision-making and greater teamwork and cooperation. Such changes have been found effective in removing some of the barriers to women's participation. Group approaches which promote peer support and solidarity and use problem-solving methods, have helped women overcome barriers associated with entry and the isolation they experience in nontraditional fields.

Organizational arrangements and rules reflect expectations and assumptions about the relation between training or the workplace and the family. These can present obstacles to women in terms of making their daily lives fit the requirements of the institution. Arrangements which do not discriminate against pregnant students, trainees, or staff; which provide re-entry schemes, childcare facilities, and assistance to both parents and not just women with family responsibilities, contribute to facilitating female participation in training and employment.

2.6 Image Problems

The "image" of adult education and vocational training influences the participation of females. This problem has been characterized broadly as an issue of "institutional ecology" (Byrne 1991) and involves the climate of a department or school, confirmed through its educators and trainers, the language and discourse used, and the teaching style, and played out in interpersonal relations and in sex differentiation in language, curricula, and materials. These factors give a message of "male dominance and preference" and produce a learning environment which is alienating for girls (and some boys).

A related issue is employers' attitudes toward women's capabilities, roles, and motivations. A study of women in electronics in Australia found that the definition of male and female jobs was based on "notions" of employers and training providers about skilled jobs, training, and rewards in terms of pay and status. Men worked at skilled levels and received external technical and trade training which resulted in qualifications recognized throughout the industry. Women were found at unskilled or semiskilled levels and received in-house, task-specific training, the standard of which varied extensively between enterprises and was not formally recognized (Windsor 1989).

2.7 Gender Bias in Group Interaction

The nature of the interaction between trainers and counselors and their female students and between female students and their peers influences girls' instructional opportunities, their access to equipment and facilities, and the support, attention, and instructional time they receive (Adams and Kruppenbach 1986). One project in the Nordic countries (Ahlgreen 1990) introduced new pedagogical methods geared to the background of girls and women and aimed at making vocational education more experience-related and improving their motivation and personal development. Due to their feelings of loneliness and isolation in nontraditional occupations, girls needed help in coping with discrimination and sexual harassment. Trainers and counselors were also assisted in identifying discrimination and gender biases in their language, attitudes, and behavior. Other similar experiences demonstrate that due to discriminatory behavior and harassment by male students, training programs should routinely provide measures to raise awareness among boys of these issues and of the legitimacy and value of women entering traditionally male vocations.

3. Strategies for Change

Sex segregation in the labor market and the way training contributes is not "a woman's problem" resolved through the provision of skills and knowledge to enable women to "catch up with men" and "fit" into the system. What is required is an integrated strategy aimed at the education, training, and employment sectors; those interest groups whose attitudes, actions, and decisions influence the opportunities open to females; and women as active agents of change and not passive recipients of skills.

A three-year program in South Asia (involving Bangladesh, India, Sri Lanka, and Pakistan), for example, combined the efforts of governmental and nongovernmental organizations engaged in formal and nonformal adult education provision, employers, trade unions, and women's groups to identify the obstacles to women's entry into nontraditional occupational areas for wage and self-employment and to formulate policies and programs to improve the situation. The acceptability of any new national-level strategy was found to be contingent on the active engagement, from the outset, of these different interest groups. While legislation on equality of opportunity and treatment in training and employment was deemed necessary in all countries, it was clearly not sufficient for a variety of socioeconomic, cultural, and political reasons and needed to be supplemented by broad-based developmental efforts aimed at involving family members, training personnel, and employers.

A four-pronged approach was developed focusing on: (a) the adult education system, in particular improving the accessibility and relevance of training for women for both self-employment and wage employment; (b) providing women with personal development programs, and improving vocational guidance; (c) employment promotion, including job placement, work-study, and apprenticeship schemes for women;

and (d) the provision of support measures to women in both training and employment context, such as insurance coverage, adequate childcare, safe hostel accommodation, providing incentives to employers, and trade union support for training women and the implementation of equal opportunities programs. A similar integrated approach has been developed in Ireland by the Employment Equity Agency.

A discussion of partnerships and integrated strategies to improve women's employment situation through training efforts would not be complete without underscoring the role of women in defining and implementing these measures. Several decades of international development assistance have produced a litany of failures as regards reaching and benefiting women and eliminating the factors which place them at a disadvantage in training and employment. Much of this failure might have been avoided had the situation, needs, and interests of women been accurately defined at the outset and assistance been designed and delivered through processes which involved women and the organizations which assist them. Planning and management procedures of adult education and training must be restructured, resources reallocated, and staff retrained to make the efforts aimed at improving the access of women more than mere window-dressing. It may be rhetorical, but women must be seen as actors, as leaders and agents in the change processes if training is to contribute to the achievement of equality rather than inequality of women in the labor market.

See also: Clienteles and Special Populations; Women and Adult Education

References

Acker S 1992 Gendering organisational theory. In: Mills A J, Tancred P (eds.) 1992. *Gendering Organisational Analysis.* Sage, London,

Adams M A, Kruppenbach S E 1986 *Some Issues of Access and Equity in the Education of African Females: Progress and Prospects.* Michigan State University, East Lansing, Michigan

Ahlgreen M (ed.) 1990 *The Nordic* BRYT—*Project: Final Report.* Nordic Council of Ministers, Copenhagen

American Association of University Women (AAUW) 1992 *How Schools Shortchange Girls.* AAUW Education Foundation, Washington, DC

Bellow R, King E M 1990 *Promoting Girls' and Women's Education: Lessons from the Past.* World Bank, Washington, DC

Byrne E M 1980 Technical and vocational education for women—The way ahead. Document ED/80/CONF. 401/3 presented at the International Congress on the Situation of Women in Technical and Vocational Education, Bonn, June 9–12. UNESCO, Paris

Byrne E M 1991 *Investing in Women: Technical and Scientific Training for Economic Development.* ILO, Geneva

Gaynor C 1990 *The Status of Women Teachers in Southern Africa.* Working Paper SAP 4.5/WP.37 ILO, Geneva.

Harlan S L 1989 Women and federal job training policy. In: Harlan S L, Steinberg R J (eds.) 1989 *Job Training* for Women:*The Promise and Limits of Public Policies*. Temple University Press, Philadelphia, Pennsylvania

Harlan S, Steinberg R J 1989 Job training for women: The problem in policy context. In: Harlan S, Steinberg R J (eds.) 1989 *Job Training for Women*. Temple University Press, Philadelphia, Pennsylvania

Hyde K A L 1989 *Improving Women's Education in Sub-Saharan Africa: A Review of the Literature*. World Bank, Washington, DC

Kelly G P (ed.) 1990 *International Handbook of Women's Education*. Greenwood Press, Westport, Connecticut

Marvani M 1992 *The Position of Women in the Labour Market*. Women of Europe Supplements, No. 36. Commission of the European Communities, Brussels

Mills A J, Tancred P (eds.) 1992 *Gendering Organizational*

Analysis. Pergamon Press, Oxford

Paukert L 1984 *The Employment and Unemployment of Women in OECD Countries*. OECD, Paris

Reskin B F, Hartmann H I (eds.) 1986 *Women's Work, Men's Work: Sex Segregation on the Job*. National Academy Press, Washington, DC

Vetter L 1989 The vocational education option for women. In: Harlan S L, Steinberg R J (eds.) 1989 *Job Training for Women. Temple University Press*. Philadelphia, Pennsylvania

Warwick J 1990 *Planning Human Resources Development Through Equal Opportunities (Gender): A Handbook*. Further Education Unit, London

Windsor K 1989 *Shortcircuiting, Women in Electronics: Skills, Training and Working Practices*. Department of Employment, Education and Training, Canberra

Women and Adult Education

K. L. Oglesby

The United Nations (UN) International Women's Year of 1975, together with its Decade for Women 1976–85, encouraged those involved in adult education to bring women's educational needs to the forefront and specifically design programs, promote courses, or institute references to women's role in society in their policy statements. The UN's 1975 World Plan of Action for the Decade of Women listed minimum objectives which governments were urged to adopt in relation to education, employment, health and welfare, and the social, political, and economics spheres.

Various international organizations responded to the UN call in different ways but almost all emphasized the need for education and training for women. The International Council for Adult Education (ICAE) in 1979 proposed a five-year plan to increase women's participation in adult and nonformal adult education programs. The International Labour Organisation (ILO) medium-term plan of 1982–87 gave prominence to the problem of working women, and was concerned with the impact on their work, incomes, and roles in society of the changes occurring in the economy and labor market at the national and international level. The ILO envisaged that in the developed countries in the 1980s a process of economic reconstruction would involve a reduction of those industries in which women were predominantly employed, and that in the developing countries modernization and technological change would seriously threaten the already low incomes of rural women.

In the light of that prediction it is interesting to note that, despite the achievements of the UN Decade of Women (1975–85), it appears that the majority of women in the developing countries were worse off educationally and economically in 1989 than they

were at the start of the UN Decade, and the progression picture for women in the developed countries is patchy. The 1980s were characterized by economic recession, famine, food crises, and international debts which led to a halt in material and social improvements on many fronts. They also brought major changes to the world's political and social scene, with, amongst others, the breaking down of political barriers in Europe, the strengthening of Islamic movements in the east and south, the emergence of steps towards black empowerment in South Africa, and ethnic and political empowerment in the Americas. The early 1990s depict major changes in welfare and educational policies, reflecting the prevailing economic ethos and demographic trends. With the notable exception of Ireland, the proportion of all those under the age of 25 has declined in all countries in Western Europe. There have been marked shifts in occupational growth and decline, with an increasing rate of job obsolescence in Eastern Europe and a growth of part-time work in Western Europe. Unemployment has risen very significantly in regions such as Europe where the picture used to be very much healthier than in other areas of the world. The international debt crisis has also led the governments of developing countries to cut back on health, education and employment opportunities generally. Throughout most of Africa and much of South America, average incomes have fallen by 10–25 percent during the 1980s. In the 37 poorest nations spending on education has fallen by 25 percent.

These movements have led to major changes in educational policies in many countries, with a prevailing emphasis being laid on education for industrial and commercial objectives and a reduction of the resources allocated to adult education provision which is not geared to economic ends. This, in turn, has had an effect on women's adult education provision.

1. Participation in Adult Education Programs

Before the early 1970s, evidence of women's participation in adult education programs had to be searched for among the general material published on adult education developments. Even by 1985 there were very few large-scale projects cataloging evidence of the extent of women's participation. More extensive studies have been published since, and in both the developed and developing countries there are a number of studies which plot the position of women in specific areas of adult education development. However, it still remains the case that no comprehensive international review of the position of women in adult education has been published, although there has been an increase in the number of publications which chart the position of women in adult education programs on a regional basis (EBAE 1991).

Reports on women's programs fall into two categories: those that are analytical and contain useful theoretical and practical insights for practitioners (the number of these has increased since the late 1980s); and those which provide interesting descriptions of projects but little in the way of analytical thought or impetus for further development. Explanations of women's participation in varying types of programs are many and vary both in their nature and conceptual level and in the degree to which they are governed by the prevailing social, cultural, economic, and political climate of particular societies.

Women participate in programs to different extents in different countries according to their immediate and long-term needs. The reasons why they participate fall into four classes: social (meeting and mixing with people); remedial (completing their education or taking second chance opportunities to recover lost educational ground); compensatory (to counterbalance felt deficiency in their life-style); and occupational mobility (education for entering or re-entering the labor market or for moving into a different occupational field for which their existing educational attainment level is inadequate). In the survey which follows of adult education for women in the developed and developing countries some indications will be given of the programs in which women currently participate with emphasis on particular developments in general education, income generation, and literacy programs.

2. Adult Education for Women in the Developed Countries

The provision of general educational programs for adults in the developed countries tends to fall into two categories: the liberal education courses, including subjects concerned with civic and political education, the arts, language, literature, and recreational topics; and basic education courses of a remedial kind for literacy and numeracy subjects. The general educational programs may be entered by women on the basis of straightforward subject interests or they may have a vocational aim in mind and be seeking to improve their initial educational qualifications prior to entering vocational courses or reentering the labor market. Courses offering re-entry to study tend to provide a broadly based program for those students who wish to reappraise their general educational levels, improve them, and consider new avenues of personal development, or career development. They enable students either to obtain the necessary entry qualifications for university or college or provide those institutions with evidence that these students can be admitted to degree courses under alternative entry schemes.

Research studies have shown that the main motives for women's participation are social security, independence, a wish to be of help to others, to be generally better educated, and to further their personal development, which includes the possibility of furthering their professional or occupational interests. In studies in the United Kingdom (ACACE 1982, Sargant 1991) women showed a wider range of motives for studying than men, but there was no fundamental difference between their attitudes toward adult education. The main differences arose in their respective participation rates in courses which do not lead to qualifications, where the women predominate by a factor of three to one. Whatever the particular motivation, the underlining fear of inadequacy, whether socially or educationally based, is usually common to both. One important feature of adult education programs for women is that they usually help to enhance their self-confidence and self-esteem, as well as developing their intellectual and practical skills.

Adult education provision in Western European countries has reflected the growing concern for equal access to employment and education fields for men and women, and EU programs have emphasized this concern (Oglesby 1991). These concerns have also been echoed in Central and Eastern Europe where political and social developments have astounded with the speed with which they have occurred. From these countries is now emerging evidence of the life-styles of and working conditions for their women. The main concerns include:

(a) the role of adult education and political education in helping to reformulate new forms of government akin to the western systems and building a new social order;

(b) building new economic growth through the training and retraining of workers;

(c) levels of functional literacy;

(d) approaches which might help the plight of the currently unemployed and those for whom the prospect of unemployment looms large. Guidance and counseling for adults are coming more to the fore in the East as the automatic expectation of a job is being rapidly undermined;

(e) work connected with the immigrant and ethnic minority population.

However there is a fear in Eastern European countries that in a rush to overthrow the old political order and adopt Western approaches, the socialist principles which guarded the basic rights for women will be eroded and their life choices and quality of life will be constrained. The women in the East have experience of doing jobs which in the West are classified as nontraditional. With the advent of Westernization such women are being offered retraining for a much narrower range of occupations, such as office work.

The East has a marked tradition of viewing adult education as an integral tool of planned social and economic change. East Europeans are very concerned with the role of adult education in political education, with building a new social order, and with building new economic growth through the training and retraining of workers. One of the main roles for adult education in Europe is to enable both halves of its population to learn, to encourage their creativity, and to contribute to their general cultural development as well as having regard for the economic necessities.

3. Adult Education for Women in Developing Countries

Jayaweera (1979) considered that socioeconomic conditions in less developed countries and the inadequacy of welfare services made it imperative for nonformal education programs to focus on the satisfaction of basic needs, and it would appear that the situation has not changed. The immediate problems for the women include poor environmental sanitation and health standards, maternal and infant mortality, and malnutrition and short life expectancy. The adult education provision in the poorest developing countries reflects their basic needs, with the majority of programs falling into three categories: health education, including family planning; education for income generation; and literacy programs.

3.1 Health Education

Maternity and childcare clinics have been established in many countries to serve rural areas, but often without adequate resources and staff, and not within easy access for many villages. Preventative health measures

and family planning are seen as an intrinsic part of most clinics' programs, although the latter depends considerably for acceptance on cultural practices and religious beliefs. Where possible, and particularly through paraprofessional and/or village workers, the maternity and childcare clinics provide education in disease prevention and hygiene, food and nutrition, safe drinking water, methods of processing foods, the reason for inoculations, improved sanitation practices, and the benefits to mothers and children of spaced childbirth. Health and nutrition are also covered in nutrition rehabilitation units which may be attached to maternal and child clinics set up as a separate hospital ward. However, these forms of education usually only reach a small proportion of rural women because of the urban bias in the allocation of health services (Loutfi 1980).

3.2 Education for Income Generation

Despite the great diversity of the economic, political, and cultural systems, the factor affecting motivation to attend courses which is common for women in the developing countries of Asia and Africa is the overriding need for vocational education which is designed to generate more income. However, the impact of such programs on living standards and income generation seems to have been limited and they appear not to have reached the poorest and most educationally disadvantaged women for a number of reasons. The educational background of women raises barriers for them. The curriculum considered suitable for women in schools, universities, and vocational institutions limits the range of vocational skills and choices available to them. Training and employment opportunities for women can be seen as of marginal importance in view of the massive unemployment situation in many countries. It is also suggested that the socialization process has conditioned many women to accept their cultural roles and match their career aspirations accordingly (see *Women and Access to Vocational Training*).

In common with women in the developed countries, women in the developing countries have to balance the demands of their working day between their agricultural or industrial work and the care of their families. As in the developed countries, poor transport facilities in the rural areas restrict access to courses. The living conditions of women from low income families in rural areas are particularly hard, with heavy demands being made on their time in the collection of water, fuel, and food, which has meant they have little time available to undertake courses. Most of these reasons are broadly similar to those behind the low participation rates of women in developed countries but with one major difference: very few women or men have completed a full primary education and the highest illiteracy rates in the world are for women in the developing countries.

3.3 Agricultural Extension Programs

There is extensive participation by women in agriculture, but preference is usually given to men in any agricultural education and extension programs on modern techniques and technological innovations. Where provision is made for women they tend to be offered programs relating to women's traditional domestic roles. Although such programs produce high dropout rates they continue to be promoted by international agencies and state institutions (see Oglesby et al. 1989).

For those developing countries where the economic situation has progressed further the emphasis is now tending to lie with community development projects through education, and these appear to be more successful in maintaining participation rates. The Rose Hall Project in St Vincent in the Caribbean is a project to improve the economic, social, and educational status of women. The three main objectives of this pilot project are: to develop and influence government policy on women and development issues, to develop and test the participatory training methodology for use by workers in rural communities, and to develop a model for the participation and integration of women in rural development. A number of activity programs have evolved in response to local needs: for example, a farmers group, a chemical and seed shop, sewing, clothes-making, fruit preservation, adult basic education, preschool activities, and the establishment of a multipurpose community center (Leicester 1991).

3.4 Firm-based Education and Training

One interesting development for assisting women in developing countries has been the Women's World Banking Organization which loans women the money to start their own businesses. One principle for making such loans is the belief that a woman in business changes a family's standard of living, the woman's self-respect, the literacy rate, the environmental conditions and, ultimately, a country's credit rating. Another principle underlining the loan system is that by attacking the problem of poverty one attacks the underpinning problem.

Women's World Banking officially started in 1980 from an idea that was floated at the 1975 conference marking the start of the United Nations Decade for Women. It makes loans on the basis of character rather than financial collateral and undertakes to guarantee half of whatever loan a woman requires, and the local affiliation of the Women's Bank guarantees another 25 percent. The regular state and private bank is asked to take a chance on only 25 percent of the amount of the requested loan. Women's World Banking works with local banks and tries to encourage women to use these instead of the local money lenders. An extensive training program is also provided to teach women accounting and book-keeping as well as management techniques and an affiliation sends experienced members to assist new members. One example of the Bank's work was a loan to a woman in Colombia in 1982 who wished to start a bicycle repair shop: the woman now has 2 shops, 13 employees, and a factory.

Many of the women who take out loans from Women's World Banking cannot complete loan forms because they are illiterate. However, experience with the scheme has established that, once a woman produces income of her own, one of the first things she will do is to make sure the children are in school, and stay there, and she will learn to read herself.

4. Literacy Programs for Women

Female illiteracy is deemed to have adverse effects not only on the well-being of families and their children's level of education but also on their prospects of labor force productivity. Different countries have adopted differing approaches to the problem but on the whole programs tend to use either the political, economic, population, cultural, or religious approaches (see Oglesby et al. 1989).

UNESCO has provided an important framework of instruments to ensure equal treatment for men and women and to combat discrimination. Although it addresses the issues through many forms of adult education projects, a major effort is made through programs for combating illiteracy, and for reinforcing postliteracy adult and basic education. Most of these programs intend to provide illiterate women and girls with basic education literacy, numeracy, knowledge of child care, health, sanitation, stimulate income generating activities and provide elements of specific education. This is a relatively new aspect which was introduced in a literacy program in the late 1980s and which aims at giving poor and illiterate women some notion of their civic rights, labor and agricultural rights, and to make them aware of their position and role in the society. Several projects of this kind are being carried out on a national and subregional basis. A particularly successful one was carried out in India in 1989 which succeeded in raising civic and social awareness in women by mobilizing them through cooperatives in various socioeconomic activities. Project materials were produced concerning concepts and topics such as the constitutions, citizenship, rights and responsibilities, family and community concerns, international relations, and international and national actions to improve the status of women. To reinforce the literacy skill levels required, other materials on the same themes for neoliterate women were elaborated and diffused through regional and local networks while rural libraries were organized and made available to them. Between June 1987 and May 1990 UNESCO cooperated with many agencies on pilot projects such as: the production of training handbooks in Arabic on literacy, postliteracy and civic education for women in rural areas, including parent education, the division of labor in the family between children and adults, and the concept of shared responsibility; solar irrigation systems in the Sudan; women, power, and peace in Malta; a survey on the ways in which the attitudes of the teachers affect the schooling of girls; seminars on equality and educational opportunity for girls and women in Bangladesh; an educational project in 30 villages in India to strengthen women's organizations and cooperatives; and hygiene and health projects, all linked with literacy classes.

The 1990 World Charter on Education states that of more than 960 million adult illiterates two thirds are women, and functional illiteracy is a significant problem in all countries of the world. UNICEF supports this contention and estimates that there has been an acceleration in the growth of illiteracy. UNESCO estimates that by the year 2000 there will be 1 billion illiterates. Even though the overall percentage of adult illiterates may be declining (one estimate is from 40 percent in 1960s to 28 percent at the beginning of the 1990s) the absolute number of illiterates continues to increase because of population growth. In a concerted world effort to address the worsening situation, the United Nations declared 1990 to 2000 the UN Literacy Decade and 1990 as the Year of Literacy.

Within these global figures lies the fact that in 1985 63 percent of illiterates were women and that proportion is rising. The rate of increase is largest in Africa where 54 percent of the adult population are estimated to be illiterate, although the greatest numerical increase is in Asia. There are also striking disparities between the rural and urban areas. The illiteracy rates for women in Pakistan and India are respectively 92.7 percent and 82.4 percent in rural areas and 65.3 percent and 48.1 percent in urban areas (UNESCO 1988). The illiteracy rates in Argentina are about 61 percent of the female population. China is estimated as having 150 million nonliterate women who account for 30 percent of the total female population. Statistics and data repeatedly confirm that the majority of those who have been systematically denied opportunities in education are girls and women. It is also well known that the causes for this are rooted in economic situations as much as in cultural and societal prejudices. This is true for women in all societies from the least developed to the most industrialized with differences being purely relative in degree.

However, most industrialized countries will today admit, more explicitly, that part of their adult population is illiterate and that these are overrepresented among the unemployed, since although a high level of education is not a guarantee of employment in the economic climate of the early 1990s, it is nevertheless a prerequisite for entry into a secure and well-paid profession. However, even where the existence of the problem is acknowledged, very few studies have been carried out to estimate its actual extent and fewer still to analyse its causes.

Illiteracy statistics in the United States range between 27 and 59 million. Its basic literacy programs are well regarded but it has problems in supporting progression at the upper levels of literacy as job requirements and changes become increasingly more demanding. The reason cited for this state of affairs is that 90 percent of jobs require reading and writing for an average of two to three hours per day while a high school program only requires reading and writing for an average of one to two hours a day. Three fourths of the unemployed do not have the basic reading skills required for high technology jobs and new standards are increasingly being introduced for high school graduates to put them in a position to compete successfully with students from East Asia and Europe. Illiteracy among Blacks and Hispanics is two to three times greater than the national average (Ntiri 1991).

4.1 Functional Literacy

The problem of assessing the extent of illiteracy in industrialized countries is complicated by the varying levels of functional literacy required by societies and which is difficult to evaluate statistically by census alone. Functional illiteracy is a term which covers all those who in certain countries are designated as being below the educational levels required to operate in society. Few industrialized countries have a comprehensive literacy education policy for their indigenous population and/or immigrant workers.

Rising functional literacy levels are a problem in European countries also. Industrialists in Ireland express dissatisfaction with the standard of written or oral skills of school leavers and the government has identified a particular need for adult education provision in general adult education studies for students between the ages of 17 and 22. However, most of the money is directed toward training which does not necessarily include basic education.

Australia had to undertake a program of basic education in the 1970s in order to enable a considerable percentage of the workforce, including women, to participate in training courses when it was discovered that 55.8 percent of its non-English population was functionally illiterate. By defining illiteracy as the inability to read and write in Japanese, Japan estimated that approximately 3 percent of its entire population was illiterate. In Canada 60 percent of offenders who enter the federal prison system are functionally illiterate. In the United States the rate is as high as 75 percent.

4.2 Literacy Programs for Women: The Challenges

Women have often been subject to literacy programs not planned by them or reflecting their needs: consequently there is a high dropout rate and poor program results. It would appear from the literature that the challenges to be addressed include practical, educational, and sociocultural aspects. Practical problems include (a) lack of time; (b) location of classes entailing traveling difficulties; (c) lack of practical special provisions to help women concentrate on literacy (e.g., childcare assistants). Educational problems include (a) the available reading materials are not designed for women; (b) promotion of literacy is linked to projects for income generation which may fail; (c) technical skills programs can simply add to women's existing workload. Sociocultural problems include (a) little exposure to popular languages other than the mother tongue, particularly in rural areas; (b) women's isolation from literate environments; (c) cultural attitudes (e.g., men forbidding women to visit literacy classes); (d) failure of most programs to integrate literacy down to the village level. Most African women, for example, have not been able to attend school and school still looks alien to African societies which function according to the norms and tempos of village traditions.

Literacy does not automatically empower women but it does offer keys for unlocking closed doors. In Eastern Africa women are participating more in literacy programs possibly because of changes in the social and rural environment for men and women. Common motivating factors appear to include (a) a desire to help their children study; (b) the prospect of greater self-reliance and control over their personal life; (c) a wish to participate in society in the same way as men; (d) clearly apparent practical benefits, such as links between literacy and health through nutrition and hygiene; (e) the development of skills in organization, marketing, and in accessing credit; (f) a productive outcome in terms of income generation which is the usual basis on which the worth of programmes is measured by the participants; (g) clearer monitoring of financial affairs (Gugnani and Dikshit 1991).

Although the acquisition of literacy skills may not always contribute to material improvements, its help in personal development has been clearly documented. It is evident that attending literacy classes helps to build a positive self-image through the women's increasing confidence in taking their own decisions in family matters such as their children's education, and their attendance at woman and child welfare centers.

The positive factors which promote and increase the chances of successful literacy programs include:

(a) community support from local leaders;

(b) the curriculum relevantly related to the social and political context into which the women are working;

(c) a component for the education of men and other members of the family and society in general;

(d) programs which promote confidence in the women;

(e) teacher training, material design, and learning strategies which address the particular needs and learning difficulties faced by women and girls;

(f) mobilization of and commitment to the programs at a small local level;

(g) creative organization approaches;

(h) awareness-raising on civic and social rights;

(i) clearly defined priorities and objectives.

Literacy is a potentially empowering tool but it is not a simple way out of dealing with the problem of women's position in society. There are two main challenges to literacy programs. One is to facilitate and sustain participation: motivation is essential, but that is seldom the problem. The second main challenge is to overcome the barriers of local cultural attitudes, practical constraints connected with the organization of courses and those structural barriers relating to the position of women within their societies.

4.3 Postliteracy Programs

The causes of relapse into illiteracy are various. Unfavorable environmental conditions produce situations which do not foster literacy and even discourage written communication in sectors of the population. Because of the ground which has been lost following literacy campaigns there has been an increasing emphasis in recent years on projects which include postliteracy developments.

Following the well-publicized and well-documented rural development and literacy campaign of 1972–75 in Somalia, literacy among the adult population rose from less than 5 percent to almost 15 percent (49% men and 51% women). However, this achievement collapsed almost immediately for two main reasons: first, because of inflation, the international economic situation, and recurrent droughts and wars, the available funds were directed elsewhere away from education; second, the concept of literacy employed was largely one isolated from the communities, unrelated to the daily lives of the learners, and with virtually no follow-up on literacy activities. A Ministry of Education evaluation carried out in 1977 revealed that most of the learners had lost the skills they had acquired. In the south agricultural zone 45–50 percent of the learners had relapsed into illiteracy. Elsewhere the percentage of illiterates fluctuated between 30 percent in the towns and 80 percent among the nomads. It has now been estimated that the illiteracy position is worse than before the 1972–75 campaign and it is particularly poor among women.

In order to rescue the situation the refugee adult

education unit in Somalia decided to offer a program in three phases: preliteracy, basic literacy, and postliteracy/continuing education. The content of the program would be general health, agriculture, and small-scale business management. The vast majority of learners, that is, over 90 percent, were women. It was believed that literacy would have a beneficial effect on these women and their communities, especially as most of them were household heads. The outcome so far appears to be a successful one (Macharia 1990).

Despite concentrated effects on literacy levels for women, adult education literacy programs can prove problematic in India. Indian women of certain castes and social–cultural influences consider themselves to be nonlearners and are brought up to believe that any matter which takes them away from the home may result in condemnation from the family and the community. One attitude in such communities is that education would help women to see themselves as individual entities and therefore question their expected dedication to others (Sahasrabudhe 1992).

5. Conclusion

One of the principal historical reasons given for the submergence of women's interests and needs in the adult education field and for the lack of concern in its literature is that education and its systems reflect male thinking and have been designed primarily for the needs of a dominant socioeconomic group in society. The problems for women in relation to such programs stem from the fact that it is not organizationally acknowledged that although women share equally with men the problems associated with modernization and technological change, and the dependency and exploitation resulting from poverty, they are, in addition, subject to the cultural and social pressures of being women.

Two of the major premises which seem to underlie adult education literature and programs for women's development are that economic growth and development are sufficient conditions for the advancement of women; and that improvements made in women's standing in education and employment terms will have a spin-off in political and social terms which will enable women to effect permanent improvements to their lives and standing in society. In the light of the evidence these premises would appear to be in need of questioning and re-evaluation.

Evidence from successful projects which have evaluated the outcomes indicate that those adult education programs for women which stand the greatest chance of making valuable and lasting impacts on the lives of the women learners are those which

(a) value and draw on women's experience and seek to develop their self-motivation and self-confidence;

(b) employ and promote cooperative learning rather than hierarchical teaching approaches;

(c) acknowledge the practical constraints under which the women are attempting to learn and accommodate these in the education format adopted;

(d) acknowledge the women's previous education experiences and attempt to compensate for these;

(e) work through the women's own social networks. The major success of informal learning is due to women taking responsibility for their own learning and learning from each other, for example, the Women's Institute movement in the United Kingdom and elsewhere.

It remains a crucial function for adult educators to ensure that educational opportunities are maximized and widened to enable greater choice and greater freedom of choice for women, whether facilitated through the formal, nonformal, or informal adult education learning systems.

See also: Women and Access to Vocational Training; Community Education and Community Development; Adult Education for Development; Adult Literacy in the Third World

References

Advisory Council for Adult and Continuing Education (ACACE) 1982 *Adults: Their Educational Experiences and Needs: The Report of a National Survey.* ACACE, Leicester.
European Bureau of Adult Education (EBAE) 1991 Grassroots Education for Women in Europe. EBAE, Amersfoort
Gugnani H R, Dikshit S D 1991 Evaluation on literacy and the empowerment of women. *Adult Education and Development* 37: 183–93
Jayaweera S 1979 Programmes of non-formal education for women. *Convergence* 12(3): 42–54
Leicester M 1991 Community development and women's education. *Commonwealth Association for the Education and Training of Adults Newsletter* January
Loutfi M F 1980 *Rural Women: Unequal Partners in Development.* International Labour Organization, Geneva
Macharia D 1990 The education of adult refugees in Somalia. *Convergence* 23(3): 11–22
Ntiri D W 1991 Literacy and workplace democracy in the US. *Education for Critical Democratic Citizenship 4*
Oglesby K L 1991 Women and Education and Training in Europe: issues for the 90s. *Studies in the Education of Adults* 23(2): 133–44
Oglesby K L, Kranjc A, Mbilinyi M 1989 Adult education for women. In: Titmus C J (ed.) 1989 *Lifelong Education for Adults: An International Handbook.* Pergamon Press, Oxford.
Sahasrabudhe A 1992 Failure of women's adult education in India—Some sociocultural constraints and possible remedial measures. *Adult Education and Development* 38: 225–33

Sargant N 1991 *Learning and Leisure*. National Institute of Adult Continuing Education, Leicester

Further Reading

Gayfer M 1980 Women speaking and learning for ourselves. *Convergence* 13(1–2): 1–13
James D et al. 1989 *Adults in Higher Education*. National Institute of Adult Continuing Education, Leicester
Kabeer M 1991 Keeping women out. Community develop-ment and women's education. *Commonwealth Association for the Education and Training of Adults Newsletter* January
Phiri S 1992 Women and literacy. *Adult Education and Development* 38: 217–23
Ramdas L 1990 The world charter for education—literacy: The critique from below. *Voices Rising* 4(2)
Stromquist M 1990 Women and illiteracy: The interplay of gender subordination and poverty. *Comp. Educ. Rev.* 34(1): 95–111

(b) Provision

Providers of Adult Education: An Overview

A. C. Tuijnman

In this entry the important characteristics of providers of adult education are discussed. Although the focus is mainly on institutions engaged in the organized and systematic provision of adult education, the role of some other crucial providers, such as public libraries, museums, and religious institutions, is also considered.

The variables useful in classifying the institutional providers of adult education are presented in a first part of this entry. Typologies of adult education institutions that have been proposed by various authors in the field are briefly reviewed. Next, the use of the International Standard Classification of Education for the purpose of classifying the institutions and agencies offering adult education is discussed.

Four main categories of adult education providers are identified and several examples of each are given in the second part of the entry. Adult basic education agencies and colleges for further education are seen as examples of a providers' category termed "formal-equivalency public adult education." Mandatory continuing education is also considered an element in this category. Nonformal, mostly publicly supported, adult education constitutes a second category. Within it, the role in adult education of "correctional" institutions, the military, agricultural extension, public libraries, museums and galleries, and community-based adult education in public schools are discussed. The third category comprises nonprofit-oriented and mostly self-supporting forms of adult education provision. Examples are the Chautauqua movement, religious institutions, integrated rural development, sociocultural animation, and the activities of consumer cooperatives. For-profit providers of adult education are grouped in the last category. Private correspondence schools, proprietary schools, and various for-profit consulting firms and training agencies are among the examples. For-profit adult education is, however, not discussed in detail in this entry.

The third part of the entry deals with major trends in the provision of adult education. Attention is paid to the changing policy context of adult education, and the way this is influencing salient features of provision.

1. Typologies

In most countries there is wide variation in the types of institutions that sponsor and offer adult education. In an international perspective, this variety is nearly bewildering. It is therefore appropriate to focus on a limited number of classification variables or descriptors that can be used to simplify the picture.

Schroeder (1970) identified four types of adult education providers in North America. "Type I providers" refers to institutions that are established specifically for the purpose of offering organized adult education. Examples are correspondence education institutions established in Austria, Germany, and Switzerland; adult basic education centers in the United States; and the residential folk high schools in the Nordic countries. "Type II providers" are classified as institutions that were initially created to serve the educational needs of youth or young adults but were later also given some responsibility for the teaching of adults. Examples would be public schools, junior colleges, and university extension. "Type III providers" are institutions that have a function which is wider than that normally associated with the teaching of adults. Libraries, museums, and galleries are examples given by Schroeder (1970). "Type IV providers," finally, are described as institutions for which adult education is a means toward achieving the goals of the organization. Appropriate examples in this case are professional and voluntary organizations, labor unions, cooperative groups, and agencies involved in integrated rural development. Religious institutions, agricultural extension, and the armed forces are additional examples.

Another relevant typology is the one proposed by Coombs (1973), who distinguished between formal, nonformal, and informal learning (see *Formal, Nonformal and Informal Education*). Hutchinson and Townsend Coles (1985) discuss three ways in which contemporary providers of adult education can be classified: (a) by distinguishing between governmental and nongovernmental organizations; (b) by considering the degree of involvement of the organizations—

which mainly refers to whether they were established with the explicit purpose of offering adult education; and (c) by determining whether the organizations principally aim at making a profit.

Apps (1990) presents an integrated framework of adult education providers that incorporates a variety of models previously developed in the field. It features four categories: (a) fully or partially tax-supported adult education institutions; (b) nonprofit, self-supporting institutions; (c) for-profit providers; and (d) nonorganized learning opportunities for adults. Examples of providers in category (a) are public school adult education, community and technical colleges, the armed forces, and public libraries and museums. Category (b) includes health and community-based agencies, worker education programs, voluntary organizations, and religious institutions. Category (c) comprises providers such as for-profit, degree granting colleges and universities, correspondence and proprietary schools, and agencies and firms specializing in human resource development. Finally, examples of category (d) institutions are the mass media, the family, and the workplace.

2. Alternative Classification Criteria

It may be noted that many providers cannot be appropriately described with the use of dichotomous, two-category variables. For example, programs are seldom entirely publicly or privately funded. Similarly, institutions can only rarely be described as being fully nonprofit or for-profit. The use of continuous variables implies recognition of the fact that most providers tend to differ on classification criteria *only in degree*.

Alternative criteria for the ordering of adult education institutions are plentiful. In selecting worthwhile criteria, one can usefully start from the premise that variables that are known from previous research studies to show high variation among providers are in principle relevant. Apart from the criteria already mentioned above, the institutions offering adult education can thus be studied in terms of their size; recruitment strategy; certification practice; staff profile; modalities of teaching and learning (such as the degree of openness and the application of instructional technology); the distribution of costs, expenditure, and income; and degree of community involvement.

Another group of relevant variables can be derived from characteristics of the participants of the programs and the mainly demographic variables that describe them, for example: initial educational attainment, age, sex, ethnicity, household composition, employment situation, occupational status, income situation, motivational orientations, and leisure and career orientation (see *Clienteles and Special Populations*).

3. International Standard Classification of Education

The distinction between formal and nonformal modes of learning contributed by Coombs (1973) and other authors offers another way of classifying the main providers of adult education. An interesting option is to establish the formal equivalency level of adult education courses and programs according to the types and levels of formal and nonformal education as defined in the International Standard Classification of Education (ISCED).

The ISCED system is intended to facilitate the identification of courses, programs, and fields of education according to their level and content. It was formally adopted by the International Conference on Education at its 35th Session in September 1975, and, despite its shortcomings, has since been widely used as a basis for improving the international comparability of education statistics by UNESCO, the Organisation for Economic Co-operation and Development (OECD), and the statistical office of the European Union (EUROSTAT) (see *Statistics of Adult and Nonformal Education*).

From the outset, there has been much concern about the application of ISCED to adult education. In various documents (UNESCO 1978, Gupta 1985) it is mentioned that ISCED covers all "organized and sustained communication designed to bring about learning" and that involves "an organized educational agency." Adult education (which is defined not in reference to an age criterion, but as part-time education) is regarded as separate from regular education offered on a full-time basis. Difficulties of interpretation notwithstanding, the ISCED system can be used as a means of identifying the institutional providers of adult education.

The formal equivalency level in ISCED courses for adults can often be readily determined. The level of an adult education course can, in some cases, be recognized even if it does not confer a certificate or qualification that corresponds to a formal grade in the regular system (e.g., because it allows the learners to transfer to the regular system or to take up an occupation that—according to the International Standard Classification of Occupations (ISCO)—presupposes a certain highest level of formal educational attainment). Such programs and services for adults that are not part of the regular system, but that nevertheless can be assigned an equivalency level in ISCED, can be referred to as "para-formal education."

There are, of course, also adult education programs for which a formal equivalency level cannot be decided in an unambiguous way. This may be the case with educational activities organized by nonprofit, self-supporting agencies such as religious institutions, labor unions, and voluntary educational associations. Some publicly supported institutions also fall into this group—for example, the armed forces, agricultural extension, museums, libraries, and houses of culture (see *Formal, Nonformal, and Informal Education*).

4. Formal and Public Adult Education

Some examples of publicly supported institutions offering formal or para-formal adult education are discussed in this section. Although the boundary between formal and para-formal, on the one hand, and nonformal on the other, is not always clear, in the main the courses offered in adult basic education, adult secondary education, adult tertiary education, as well as those organized as a consequence of the mandatory continuing education for professionals, may be considered formal or para-formal because they tend to confer credentials and qualifications that are recognized in the regular system of education.

4.1 Adult Basic Education

Adult basic education generally comprises functional literacy programs and life-skills training courses for adults. Such programs, which are mostly associated with ISCED levels 1 and 2, usually aim to impart: (a) communication skills—language, numeracy, and social skills, including general civic, scientific, and cultural knowledge, and democratic attitudes and values; (b) life skills—knowledge of health, sanitation, nutrition, family planning, and the environment; and (c) basic work skills—problem-solving, practical, social-communicative, leadership, and literacy and numeracy skills.

Examples of adult basic education are the GRUNDVUX program in Swedish municipal adult education (now KOMVUX)and similar programs offered in public schools and community colleges in North America and in centers for adult education in Denmark. The adult basic education centers in the Netherlands were established in 1987, when the government decided to create a new institution by merging public agencies such as the Dutch open schools, the informal education centers for young adults, and literacy and language classes for immigrants, ethnic minorities, and people with an initially low level of formal schooling (see *Adult Basic Education*).

4.2 Adult Secondary Education

Postliteracy programs may be classified as "lower-secondary education" (ISCED 2), whereas "adult secondary education" is mainly intended for people who have completed at least 9 years (but fewer than 12 years) of schooling (ISCED 3). In Sweden, municipal adult education (KOMVUX) and folk high schools offer courses at this level, as do the *Volkshochschulen* in Germany. In France, adult secondary education is offered through the *Centre National D'énseignement à Distance* and the *Groupements d'établissements de l'éducation Nationale*. In the United States, approaches to adult secondary education may involve traditional day and evening schools, diploma and alternative high school programs for adults, competency-based educational (CBE) programs, and the General Education Development (GED) test program (see *Adult Secondary Education; Postliteracy*).

Two-year community colleges in North America, the colleges for further education in the United Kingdom, and both French agencies mentioned above are examples of institutions offering both technical–vocational, remedial, and general or liberal education for adults that are intended to offer a bridge between high school and four-year colleges and universities. More than half of the students who attended community colleges in the United States at the end of the 1980s were enrolled part-time, and many of these were adults (ACCT 1988). Depending on their orientation, such programs may be classified as "upper-secondary education" (ISCED 3) or as "non-university tertiary education" (ISCED 5). The same applies to the *folkehöjskoler* existing in Denmark and the other Nordic countries (see *Community Colleges; Folk High Schools*).

4.3 Adult Tertiary Education

Adult tertiary education is offered by a range of institutions—for example, regular and open universities, polytechnics, people's and worker's universities, university extension programs, and distance education institutions. A sizeable part of the student body in tertiary-level educational institutions around the world consists of adults aged 25 and over. These people may be enrolled in for-credit higher education programs corresponding to levels 5, 6, and 7 in ISCED, or they may attend noncredit professional or other refresher courses of a brief duration at either the undergraduate or graduate level.

Adult tertiary education is a rapidly expanding sector of provision. The demographic situation in some of the industrialized countries characterized by high life-expectancy, increased leisure time, and large numbers of comparatively well-educated and wealthy pensioners, reinforces the social demand for higher education among older adults. This increase in demand is reflected in the rapid spread of the Elder Hostel Movement in the United States, which refers to a confederation of mainly colleges and universities offering educational programs and services especially targeted at people over 60 years of age (see *Third-age Students in Higher Education; Adult Tertiary Education; University Adult Education*).

4.4 Continuing Professional Education

Whereas lifelong learning is still considered a utopian idea by some policymakers and educators, it has already become an undeniable reality in some professions. The purpose of continuing professional education is the improvement of work skills and the enhancement of career development. In most professional fields, continuing education activities are conducted by four main types of providers: higher education institutions, professional associations, employers, and for-profit consultancy firms (Knox and McLeish 1985).

As is the case with adult education more generally, continuing professional education is based on the principle of voluntary participation, at least in theory. However, as a result of rapid technological change, job competition, and strong advocacy of groups demanding that citizens need to be protected by laws requiring professionals to study annually for a certain minimum number of hours, continuing professional education has become mandatory for a minority of professional workers.

"Mandatory continuing education" refers to organized and comprehensive further education programs in fields such as law, navigation, medicine, pharmacy, and engineering, that have been made compulsory by law or through a binding regulation, usually because a national government or professional association has made attendance a prerequisite for continued membership in a professional club or for maintaining a licence for practice. It is generally provided by universities and professional colleges, although it may also be offered by professional associations and for-profit consultancy firms and other independent providers.

According to Apps (1985 p. 70), the advantages of mandatory study are usually summarized as those of stimulating advanced study, improving the "public image" of an occupation, providing guaranteed funding for continuing professional education, enforcing a minimum standard of performance, and improving cost-effectiveness by enhancing the quality of professional services while reducing the number of costly malpractice suits. There was a lively debate about the perceived advantages and disadvantages of mandatory professional education during the 1970s and early 1980s. Controversy around this issue seems to have subsided since then, in part because in some countries continuing education has expanded to a point where the large majority of professional workers take part at a level much above the minimum requirement (see *Lifelong and Continuing Education*).

5. Nonformal Public Adult Education

The programs referred to above generally receive some public funding and confer qualifications that carry formal equivalency in the regular system. Many public institutions also offer programs of a nonformal type, which cannot readily be accommodated in the ISCED system. A total of six examples of public agencies that offer adult education on a vast scale are given below: prisons, the armed forces, agricultural extension, public libraries and museums, public schools, and institutions offering primary healthcare education for adults. Government-supported literacy campaigns are not discussed in this entry (see *Adult Literacy in the Third World*).

5.1 Prisons

Public authorities in many countries organize "correctional" education and training designed for imprisoned adults. Although the programs are usually separately administered and funded, they may be seen as an extension of public adult education. Forster (1985) describes management systems for prison education in different countries. He concludes that some carefully separate the penal system from the judiciary, while others see the two as complementary; some are heavily centralized, whereas others are invested with a degree of autonomy. It is therefore difficult to generalize about the learning opportunities offered to imprisoned adults in an effort to change deviant behavior and faciliate a future re-entry into society.

5.2 Armed Forces

Continuing education organized by the armed forces is a second example of mainly nonformal public provision. In many countries, the military account for a large share of total provision. Some countries in Europe and North America have developed an elaborate system of educational credits, so that the further education received by army personnel can be recognized in the regular system. The latter type of provision therefore belongs to the para-formal system.

Much of the writing on the adult education efforts of the armed forces has originated in the United States. An useful overview is presented by Veeman and Singer (1990). It is certain, however, that the military in other countries such as the People's Republic of China, Germany, France, and the Koreas have also developed extensive adult education services. The main categories are the inservice training of enlisted recruits, the further education of officers, and the continuing vocational and professional training of permanent staff (Castrovilli 1988). Military personnel have also been used as teachers in literacy campaigns in Indonesia, Iran, and some countries in Sub-Saharan Africa.

5.3 Cooperative Extension

The cooperative extension services that are organized by government authorities in many developing and industrialized countries constitute a third example of mainly nonformal public adult education. The extension services are especially common in the agricultural sector, where they involve instruction and practical demonstrations in subjects such as farming, fishery, home economics, water supply, energy, and the protection of the environment. The cooperative extension services are often considered to be a part of the adult education system. The United States has an active cooperative extension program, which not only aims at disseminating information about new products, markets, and innovations in production techniques to individuals, families, and communities who can apply these new ideas to increase quality and yield and improve marketing and enhance profitability, but also at creating and strengthening an understanding of public policy toward farming (Blackburn 1989).

5.4 Libraries, Galleries, and Museums

Public libraries, galleries, and museums offer a natural setting for adult classes, study circles, and self-directed learning. They play an important role in nonformal adult education by supporting voluntary learning for reasons of recreation, personal development, or the improvement of occupational skills. Self-directed inquiry is enhanced as a result of advances in the programming of exhibitions and the design of displays. Public libraries and museums often function as community information centers, and they play a part in the recruitment strategies of agencies organizing adult education (e.g., by providing library-based guidance and tutorial support for adults who need help in devising personal learning projects).

Libraries and museums as learning resource centers increasingly offer special documentation services and low-cost access to multimedia packages, electronic databases, and open learning networks.

The "houses of culture" are an important historical antecendent of public libraries and museums as places catering for the general cultural and educational needs of the whole population, as well as serving the socialization and cultural needs of local communities and the state. The houses of culture were widespread in the former Soviet Union, and in some countries in Central and Eastern Europe. They still serve an important function in adult education in Asia (e.g., in the People's Republic of China). In Japan, the Social Education Law of 1949 states that national and local public agencies must promote an environment congenial to the cultural and intellectual enhancement of all citizens. The law authorized the *Kominkan* (citizen's public hall) to be the main facility for promoting social and cultural education in Japan (see *China, People's Republic; Japan: Social and Adult Education*).

5.5 Public Schools and Community Education

The role of public schools in community education has long fascinated adult educators. Whereas public schools organize courses (e.g., in adult basic education) that may be considered part of the formal or para-formal system, in many countries they also provide nonformal, community-based programs. "Community education" is an umbrella concept for a variety of local programs intended for adults as well as children, that range from school–business partnerships and at-risk youth programs to specific activities such as environmental, peace, and population education. By strengthening the ties between the local school and the surrounding community, it is hoped that public schools can become a unifying factor and serve as a catalyst for community problem-solving (Delargy 1991). Additional goals are to enhance parental involvement and to encourage public schools to draw more effectively on available community resources (see *Community Education and Community Development; Partnership: Initial and Adult Education*).

5.6 Primary Healthcare

The last example given in this entry concerns the provision of primary healthcare programs for adults by professional or voluntary adult educators who collaborate with medical personnel in bringing healthcare as close as possible to where people live and work. Agencies such as the World Health Organization (WHO) and the United Nations Children's Fund (UNICEF) put high value on nonformal ways of spreading primary healthcare among households and communities because these methods are considered cost-effective in bringing people into first contact with the national healthcare system. They aim at prevention as well as cure and care, and build on local participation and voluntary, self-directed learning (Stensland 1985).

6. Nonformal, Self-supporting Adult Education

As societies and their educational systems have grown more complex with the advance of time, adults have gradually been offered an increasingly varied supply of organized learning opportunities. So far the focus has mostly been on publicly supported institutions and agencies. Another important provider group that has a long tradition in nonformal education for adults includes a number of nongovernmental, and mainly self-supporting, institutions, associations, and cooperatives. There are five examples given below, ranging from the historically important Chautauqua movement to religious institutions, labor unions, and integrated rural development programs. It is acknowledged that these examples, although undeniably important, are only a selection.

6.1 Religious Institutions

Religious education is one of the most widespread forms of nonformal education all over the world (Thomas 1985). It is inherent to all world religions; is organized in schools, monastries, local churches, theological centers and libraries, mosques, prayer halls, temples, and synagogues; is offered in a variety of forms—lectures, classes, weekend schools, study circles and discussion groups, festivals, periodic retreats, and tours of pilgrimage; is typically financed by private donations or from institutional funds, and is offered to the learners at low or virtually no cost (Beatty and Hayes 1991). The following goals usually apply:

(a) to strengthen faith by teaching an understanding of religious history, content, and literature;

(b) to maintain tradition by teaching individuals and communities how to apply religious commandments, observances, and ceremonies;

(c) to establish personal morality and social ethics;

(d) to develop an attitude of respect and concern for others; and

(e) to encourage and teach people how to let others share in their faith.

6.2 The Chautauqua Movement

The late nineteenth and early twentieth century was the heyday of the Chautauqua movement, a community-based network for adult education in the United States that has played a catalyst role in adult education (see *History of Adult Education*). It was named after the Chautauqua Lake in New York, where activities began in 1874 when John Vincent, a liberal educator, started his home-reading circles as a Sunday school assembly for adults (Bestor 1936). It rapidly expanded into a full-fledged educational movement that brought popular culture and thought, and programs on music, arts, and drama (and later also secondary and higher education) to people living in remote areas on the United States frontier with Canada.

The Chautauqua Institution provided residential education, whereas the College of Liberal Arts of Chautauqua University (which as a result of the pioneering efforts of William Harper had received its charter in 1883), was one of the first correspondence schools in the United States. This institution became a model for distance education in North America and Europe. It extended into remote rural areas by relating correspondence study to discussion groups organized through the Chautauqua Literacy and Scientific Circles. These circles, which brought many Americans into contact with new scientific, cultural, and political ideas, were the source of inspiration for Oscar Olsson, a Swedish school teacher who, in 1902, organized the first study circles at Lund in Sweden (see *Study Circles*).

6.3 Integrated Rural Development

The concept and policy of "integrated rural development" began to make headway in the late 1960s and early 1970s, especially in Southeast Asia and Sub-saharan Africa. The agricultural, health, and community development education programs set up in Latin America since the 1960s warrant a case study by themselves (see *Latin America: Adult Education*).

"Rural integrated development" is generally understood to refer to a "total" policy strategy in which rural adults—in particular marginalized groups such as landless and often poor peasant workers, women, functional illiterates, the elderly, and the unemployed —instead of being the passive recipients of local support and perhaps foreign aid, are targeted as the focal groups in concerted development efforts aimed at promoting self-reliance and liberation from poverty and social oppression (see *Adult Education for Development*). The main objective of the development strategy was to alleviate rural poverty through self-help and —by improving the conditions of employment, education, and health care in rural communities—to halt the ongoing process of migration from rural to urban areas. Agricultural extension, literacy, and life-skills training, and community-based adult education in subjects such as hygiene, healthcare, and nutrition, are at the heart of the strategy (Food and Agriculture Organization 1979).

The integrated approach to rural development, which demands a total commitment from national political and administrative bodies as well as extensive interagency cooperation in policy planning and implementation, can be described as a holistic strategy for promoting the self-reliance of local communities. It was proposed not only by social scientists and policymakers critical of the Western concept of modernization—which would involve industrialization, urbanization, and a commodity-based and export-led path to economic development—but also by economists and experts associated with aid agencies, who felt that this approach would make it possible to draw most efficiently on resources and expertise available in different areas (e.g., agricultural extension, primary healthcare, nutrition, sanitation, and literacy).

The strategy, which appeals to socialist ideologies, is based in a broad program of educational reform involving widespread community participation in nonformal education and literacy campaigns, as well as in social reform and economic restructuring involving land reallocation and the establishment of agricultural collectives. The Ujamma scheme in Tanzania, which incorporated nonformal education in a program of forced collectivization of agricultural production in planned villages and 10-family cells, is a prime, although often severely criticized, example (Roberts 1985).

Another much discussed example, which compared with the Ujamaa scheme is more grassroots-based, is that of the *Sarvodaya Shramadana* movement in Sri Lanka. The word "*Sarvodaya*" was defined by Mahatma Gandhi as the well-being of all—as different from the well-being of the few or even of the majority—and "*Shramadana*" refers to the sharing of time, thought, and effort for the well-being of others (Ariyaratne 1985). The movement initially drew its inspiration from the Intensive Agricultural District Program conducted in India in the early 1960s in the first instance and, secondly, from agricultural projects run in the People's Republic of China since its creation in 1949 (Kidd 1979). Over the years, the movement evolved numerous local community development programs based on a distinct, Buddist-inspired philosophy emphasizing compassion and respect for life, action preparedness, altruism, and self-determination

(Ariyaratne 1985). A key activity is the provision of education and training for youth and adults through its several hundred institutions spread through all districts in Sri Lanka. The following subjects are included in the curriculum: maternity and primary healthcare, nutrition, sanitation, agriculture, small-scale industrial activity, community leadership, organization of *Shramadana* camps and libraries, crafts, engineering, and the maintenance of water supply.

6.4 Sociocultural Animation

The ideas supporting sociocultural animation originated in North America, but also spread to European countries such as Belgium, France, Switzerland, and the Netherlands. By the mid-1960s, the terms "*animation socioculturelle*" and "*animateur*" had become established in Francophone vocabulary (Simpson 1985). Whereas integrated rural development aims at alleviating rural poverty and building self-reliant local communities, "sociocultural animation" refers to a set of grassroots activities intended to alleviate poverty in a cultural and community sense, especially in urban areas. As with integrated rural development, the term has strong egalitarian and normative connotations; however, while the former concept refers to policy for promoting social and economic democracy, sociocultural animation seeks to establish cultural democracy. The latter refers, not to the popularization of heritage arts and "high" culture, but to the energizing of the local population to participate actively in community and neighborhood events. The movement seeks to encourage community members to escape from the mass media and commercially produced mass culture by organizing local "action" groups and manifestations, and by offering community-based adult education, especially in the arts (see *Community Education and Community Development*).

6.5 Unions, Cooperatives, and Consumer Groups

The role in nonformal adult education of indigenous mass organizations (e.g., trade unions, youth and women's associations, and consumer cooperatives) is very important in many countries in Africa, Asia, Europe, and Latin America. Most countries have their own, typical examples. The function of such organizations tends to change over time, as some disappear and others emerge.

The *Znanie* (Knowledge) Society, which was established in the former Soviet Union in 1947, and which spread to the countries of Central and Eastern Europe during the early 1950s, is a case in point. The knowledge societies were formed by scientists and other members of the intelligentsia who were expected by the state and the Communist Party to give public lectures and to teach popular courses. The *Znanie* societies lost much of their appeal as a result of the political upheavals during the late 1980s and early 1990s, and other forms of voluntary and popular adult education have assumed a more prominent role.

Japan presents another interesting case study. Here, the provision of social education for adults is extremely diverse and multifaceted. A large part of the social education system is publicly supported, but there is also vigorous voluntary activity. The role in provision played by the various nongovernmental organizations is in fact characteristic of Japanese social education. There are three large organizations—the *Seinendan* (community youth association), *Fujinkai* (community women's association), and the parent–teacher association—each of which held a membership of over 5 million in the early 1970s (Moro'Oka 1985). This membership has declined since, however, and new, smaller associations and cooperative societies have sprung up, especially in the large cities. These are concerned with a wide range of topics—for example, consumer rights, the preservation of the environment, and international affairs. The decline of traditional organizations offering social education for adults also besets the *Kominkan*, which have increasingly come under competition from efficiently run, private, and for-profit "culture centers," which aim to satisfy the increased public demand for meaningful leisure time and recreation (see *Japan: Social and Adult Education*).

7. Major Trends in Provision

The policy context of adult education provision has changed remarkably since the 1970s. A comparison of the strategies proposed at that time (see Lowe 1982) with those gaining currency since the late 1980s clearly bear this out (see Tuijnman 1992). The following trends are among the most salient ones:

(a) During the 1980s, the tendency was to strengthen the development of continuing vocational training, especially job training in industry sponsored by employers, rather than postcompulsory, formal adult education in institutions fully or partly financed from the public education budget (see *Recurrent Education*).

(b) The notion that work ought to be alternated on a recurrent basis with formal education has been replaced by strategies to provide workers with the appropriate learning opportunities while remaining part of the labor force, for example, by offering on-the-job training, distance education, and refresher courses of a brief duration— programs that tend to be financed by firms and the individual adult learner rather than by public authorities (see *On-the-job Training*).

(c) Formal arrangements for study leave, such as those originally envisaged in the 1970s by the

International Labour Office and the OECD, have not been legislated for in the majority of countries (see *Paid Education Leave and Collective Bargaining*). Instead, the tendency has been for governments to rely on partnerships with employers and on the initiative of individual adult learners (see *Partnerships: Initial and Adult Education*).

(d) Despite the changes already mentioned, the overall level of participation in organized adult education seems to have increased in many industrialized countries during the 1980s. The main factors behind this are the increased demand for education by adults, who are often prepared to make a contribution toward the costs of such provision, and the expansion of investment by the private sector (see *Demand, Supply, and Finance of Adult Education*).

(e) There is a tendency to assign priority to literacy programs and vocational and technical courses in adult education, supplanting the previous "academic" hallmark and general character of many adult education programs. There is no doubt that decision-makers now put emphasis on "employable skills" syllabuses (i.e., on programs conferring instrumental qualifications either for the present job or for a future occupation) (see *Economics of Adult Education and Training*).

(f) In many countries, stagnation or even a relative decline in the amount of public resources for general or "liberal" adult education is matched with a devolution of responsibility for decision-making from the central government to institutions and individuals (see *Legislation in Adult Education*).

(g) The demand for accountability is a general phenomenon in education. It constitutes a key factor in an explanation of the tendencies mentioned above. Accountability arose in part from the "new consumerism" of the 1980s; the "consumer" of adult education—the individual learner, firms, and local communities—were seen as demanding "value for money." The "buying" and "selling" of adult education and training on competitive markets are considered essential ingredients in a strategy aimed at ensuring quality control and meeting the demand for accountability (see *Market Concepts in Provision; Market Failure in Adult Education and Training*).

(h) The range and variants of learning possibilities have generally increased in many countries. They now vary from classroom learning to collaborative "group learning" and "open learning" networks. New programs have been added on top of already existing ones. This fragmentation in adult education makes the choice of the "right" learning strategy increasingly impor-

tant, but also increasingly difficult (see *Student Counseling; Student Support Systems*).

(i) Concomitant with the above, the notion "social demand" seems to have been replaced with "individual demand" as a determinant of adult education provision. The primary responsibility for organizing a learning encounter is increasingly seen as resting with the individual adult learner. This has implications for equity, since people with a short initial education may become increasingly disadvantaged (see *Participation: Antecedent Factors*).

(j) Professionalization is another salient trend in adult education. It has been promoted by new advances in theory and practice, and by innovative research studies conducted especially in related social science disciplines, as well as by the creation and expansion of specialist training centers for the educators of adults (see *Training of Adult Educators*).

See also: Adult Education: Concepts and Principles; Clienteles and Special Populations

References

Apps J W 1985 Mandatory continuing education. In: Husén T, Postlethwaite T N (eds.) 1985 *The International Encyclopedia of Education*, 1st edn. Pergamon Press, Oxford

Apps J W 1990 Providers of adult and continuing education: A framework. In: Merriam S B, Cunningham P M (eds.) 1990 *Handbook of Adult and Continuing Education.* Jossey-Bass, San Francisco, California

Ariyaratne A T 1985 Integrated rural development: Sarvodaya movement. In: Husén T, Postlethwaite T N (eds.) 1985 *The International Encyclopedia of Education*, 1st edn. Pergamon Press, Oxford

Association of Community College Trustees (ACCT) 1988 *Fact Book on Community Colleges.* American Association of Community and Junior Colleges, Washington, DC

Beatty P T, Hayes M J 1991 Religious institutions. In: Merriam S B, Cunningham P M (eds.) 1991 *Handbook of Adult and Continuing Education.* Jossey-Bass, San Francisco, California

Bestor A E Jr 1936 The Chautauqua movement. In: Ely M L (ed.) 1936 *Adult Education in Action.* American Association for Adult Education, New York

Blackburn D J (ed.) 1989 *Foundations and Changing Practices in Extension.* Media Distribution, University of Guelph, Ontario

Castrovilli M (ed.) 1988 *Army Continuing Education.* School Guide Publications, New York

Coombs P H 1973 *New Paths to Learning.* International Council for Educational Development, New York

DeLargy P F 1991 Public schools and community education. In: Merriam S B, Cunningham P M (eds.) 1991 *Handbook of Adult and Continuing Education.* Jossey-Bass, San Francisco, California

Food and Agriculture Organization 1979 *World Conference on Agrarian Reform and Rural Development.* Food and Agriculture Organization of the United Nations, Rome

Forster W 1985 Adult education in prisons. In: Husén T, Postlethwaite T N (eds.) 1985 *The International Encyclopedia of Education*, 1st edn. Pergamon Press, Oxford

Gupta H 1985 *Manual for Statistics on Adult Education* Preliminary draft. (ST. 86/WS/2) UNESCO, Division of Statistics on Education, Office of Statistics, Paris

Hutchinson E M, Townsend Coles E K 1985 Providers of adult education. In: Husén T, Postlethwaite T N (eds.) 1985 *The International Encyclopedia of Education*, 1st edn. Pergamon Press, Oxford

Kidd J R 1979 A China plant and an Indian cane: Adult learning programs in India and China. *Indian J. Adult Educ.* 40(1): 9–36

Knox A B, McLeish J A B 1985 Continuing education of the professional. In: Husén T, Postlethwaite T N (eds.) 1985 *The International Encyclopedia of Education*, 1st edn. Pergamon Press, Oxford

Lowe J 1982 *The Education of Adults: A World Perspective*, 2nd edn. UNESCO, Paris

Moro'Oka K 1985 Nonformal education in Japan. In: Husén T, Postlethwaite T N (eds.) 1985 *The International Encyclopedia of Education*, 1st edn. Pergamon Press, Oxford

Roberts H W 1985 Integrated rural development: Specialized training programmes. In: Husén T, Postlethwaite T N (eds.) 1985 *The International Encyclopedia of Education*, 1st edn. Pergamon Press, Oxford

Schroeder W L 1970 Adult education defined and described. In: Smith R M, Aker G F, Kidd J R (eds.) 1970 *Handbook of Adult Education*. Macmillan, New York

Simpson J A 1985 Sociocultural animation. In: Husén T, Postlethwaite T N (eds.) 1985 *The International Encyclopedia of Education*, 1st edn. Pergamon Press, Oxford

Stensland P G 1985 Primary health care and adult education.

In: Husén T, Postlethwaite T N (eds.) 1985 *The International Encyclopedia of Education*, 1st edn. Pergamon Press, Oxford

Thomas R M 1985 Religious education. In: Husén T, Postlethwaite T N (eds.) 1985 *The International Encyclopedia of Education*, 1st edn. Pergamon Press, Oxford

Tuijnman A C 1992 Paradigm shifts in adult education. In: Tuijnman A C, Van Der Kamp M (eds.) 1992 *Learning Across the Lifespan: Theories, Research, Policies*. Pergamon Press, Oxford

UNESCO 1978 Revision of the recommendation concerning the International Standardization of Educational Statistics. (ST. 77/WS/12) UNESCO, Paris

Veeman F C, Singer H 1990 Armed forces. In: Merriam S B, Cunningham P M (eds.) 1990 *Handbook of Adult and Continuing Education*. Jossey-Bass, San Francisco, California

Further Reading

Bhola H S 1989 *World Trends and Issues in Adult Education*. Jessica Kingsley, London

Boyd R D, Apps J W (eds.) 1980 *Redefining the Discipline of Adult Education*. Jossey-Bass, San Francisco, California

Rassekh S 1991 *Perspectives on Literacy: A Selected World Bibliography*. UNESCO, International Bureau of Education, Geneva

Schroeder W L 1980 Typology of adult learning systems. In: Peters J M (ed.) 1980 *Building an Effective Adult Education Enterprise*. Jossey-Bass, San Francisco, California

Titmus C J (ed.) 1989 *Lifelong Education for Adults: An International Handbook*. Pergamon Press, Oxford

Adult Basic Education

M. A. Kutner

"Adult basic education" may be broadly defined as involving reading, writing, and mathematical skills necessary for adults to be literate. Participants in adult basic education include adults who have not completed secondary school and who are past the age of compulsory education, adults whose first language is different from the nation's first language, and adults who have completed their secondary education but do not possess sufficient basic education skills. In this entry, policies and programs intended to address adult illiteracy in industrialized countries are examined through a brief survey of ways in which some countries—including Australia, Canada, France, Germany, Sweden, the United Kingdom, and the United States—have recognized and address this problem. These countries were chosen as examples rather than exemplars of adult basic education, since a compre-

hensive survey including all countries has not yet been conducted.

A number of points must be understood when undertaking a comparative examination of adult basic education. Countries interpret literacy differently and acceptance of illiteracy as a problem has been varied, as are the goals of adult basic education in different countries. Also, limited research has been conducted about the problems of adult illiteracy, measurements of the scope of the problem, and effective instructional methods. Nevertheless, examining adult basic education programs in different nations is informative for practitioners and policymakers.

First, this entry examines the scope of the literacy problem and the manner in which it was initially recognized. Next, the ranges of services and programs offered are described and compared. Finally, sugges-

619

tions for improving services for illiterate adults are presented.

1. Adult Illiteracy in Industrialized Countries

Before adult illiteracy is addressed it must first be recognized as a problem, something that most countries have often been slow to do for a number of reasons: (a) illiteracy was generally believed to apply to a small segment of the population, such as immigrants, and was not considered to be a major concern (Benton and Noyelle 1992, Hammink 1990); (b) comparatively low unemployment rates had not given sufficient cause to question the literacy skills of the workforce as long as it was relatively easy for people with little initial schooling to find employment; and (c) compulsory schooling requirements lulled policymakers into a false belief that illiteracy was a problem faced by only a small segment of the country's population (see *Postliteracy*).

1.1 Definitions of Literacy

Recognizing illiteracy as a problem has also been complicated by the different ways in which literacy may be defined. Definitions of literacy have changed over the years, with the grade-level equivalency definition used for elementary and secondary education now generally considered to be inappropriate for adults (see *Literacy Research and Measurement*). Indeed, only a small portion of a population is illiterate if one holds to "academic" definitions of illiteracy (Wagner 1985). However, such a limited view does not consider the fact that the level of basic skills that people need is not stable but increases with social and economic development. It is no longer the case that completing the primary grades provides sufficient skills for workers to succeed in the workplace and be productive members of society even though they may possess minimal reading, writing, and arithmetic skills. New technologies and skill-intensive methods of production require that even workers with a secondary or tertiary education should undertake further education and training (Ryan 1991). A functional definition of literacy is more appropriate for adult basic education. "Functional literacy" is defined in terms of the skills that all adults need rather than as a grade-level reading equivalent that is used to assess the literacy levels of school-aged children. These skills may include balancing a checkbook, reading a bus schedule, or understanding an instruction manual. The concept of functional literacy has now achieved widescale acceptance, although a universal definition of literacy has not been established.

1.2 Recognition of Widespread Illiteracy

Industrialized countries began to consider adult illiteracy as a significant problem during the late 1960s.

The United States was first to take legislative action, by enacting (in 1966) the Adult Education Act, designed to provide financial support for adult basic education. Shortly afterwards, in 1967, municipal adult education in Sweden was formally structured by the national legislature. Adult literacy training was developed under the administration of municipal adult education in the 1970s (Larsson and Fransson 1991).

The United Kingdom in 1975 implemented a three-year national literacy plan led by the British Broadcasting Company (Benton and Noyelle 1992); while Belgium and the Netherlands followed some years later (Limage 1990, Hammink 1990). Germany and France were comparatively late in taking action: between 1979 and 1982, German state governments began to back literacy instruction programs, and France officially recognized adult literacy as a problem with the publication of the *Oheix Report* on poverty.

2. Programs and Services for Illiterate Adults

Countries vary in the degree to which they use a national, public system or a mix of public and private approaches to provide adult basic education services. In some cases, adult basic education is provided through a national public system. In other cases, voluntary organizations take the lead. Generally, a combination of public and private ventures address adult basic education needs.

2.1 Public Programs

Efforts by public authorities to offer educational programs for illiterate adults are generally limited by lack of funding and by not being targeted on those in need. Although there are laws or other regulations in support of adult basic education in most European countries, they are often focused on services for immigrants and are not designed in response to specific concerns about the implications of functional illiteracy (e.g., France and Sweden) (Brand 1987). Public programs in the United States, Canada, and Australia also target native language speakers.

In Sweden and the Netherlands, national governments have assumed primary responsibility for adult basic education. The Swedish government operates a comprehensive adult education system with close coordination between local and national governments (Ericson 1991). The national government manages the formal adult basic education system and subsidizes popular adult education activities. Formal adult basic education has been composed of GRUNDVUX, or basic education up to Grade 6, and KOMVUX, or municipal adult education from Grades 7 to 9. Beginning in July 1992, GRUNDVUX was replaced by a program designed to provide adults with literacy skills through to Grade 9. All municipalities must provide this instruction and all citizens must be served if they wish. Informal adult education, or "popular education" in Sweden, is partially financed by the federal government but administered independently through voluntary educational associations. Adults wishing to participate in adult education are supported, both financially and legally, by the government (Swedish Ministry of Education and Science 1992) (see *Europe, Nordic Countries*).

In the Netherlands, the Ministry of Education endorses five types of adult education programs and provides funding; however, adult basic education services are planned at the municipal level (Hammink 1990). Adult basic education encompasses five types of programs: adult literacy for native Dutch speakers, language courses for non-Dutch speakers, open school, informal education for young adults, and household information in the countryside. National rules for adult basic education, established in 1987, brought together the five adult basic education programs, previously operated by a number of ministries and agencies, and established the foundation for new adult basic education legislation. In all five adult education programs, the central government supports or guides the programs, and services are provided by a mix of volunteers and professionals (see *Europe, Western and Southern*).

In other countries, such as Australia and the United States, both the federal and the state governments are important sources of support for adult basic education services. Adult literacy programs in Australia, for individuals over 15 years of age, are supported by both state governments and the Commonwealth Department of Education. A 1980 survey identified 179 Australian adult education programs, three times the number of programs operating 15 years previously (Anderson 1985). Almost half of these programs were supported with state government funds and one-sixth with funds from the Commonwealth Department of Education. The remaining programs were supported through community-based organizations, volunteer agencies, and prisons (see *Australia and New Zealand*).

In the United States, the federal government is the principal funder of adult basic education. Federal funds, primarily through the Adult Education Act, are distributed through states to local agencies including school districts, community colleges, and community-based organizations. States are responsible for administering and supplementing federally funded adult education services. Although local adult education programs receive training and technical assistance from and submit reports to state agencies, they generally have considerable autonomy in determining the structure and content of the program. Other federal programs such as the Job Training Partnership Act (JTPA) and the Jobs and Basic Skills Training Program (JOBS) support adult basic education services, although these programs are typically more employment oriented than services provided through the Adult Education Act (Kutner et al. 1990) (see *North America*).

In Canada and Germany, there is little centralized support for adult basic education; most of the responsibility lies with the provincial or state governments. In Canada, the central government finances selected projects such as the Frontier College, which has worked to improve literacy skills of workers and disadvantaged groups since 1899, and provides services such as the national literacy survey which are too large to be managed by the provinces. During the late 1960s and early 1970s, the Canadian central government was the primary sponsor of literacy education and training for unemployed workers. Provincial governments became involved with literacy training as national efforts declined. Traditionally, adult education in Canada is provided through community colleges, although many provinces rely upon, or are turning to community-based groups. British Columbia and Quebec have comparatively well-developed adult basic education programs. Since about 1980, adult literacy has been a policy priority in British Columbia, with the province providing funding and support for research and development. Quebec supports the literacy activities of voluntary organizations and is considered to be the Canadian province with the greatest commitment to adult basic education.

The German federal government became involved in adult literacy in October 1982 by providing literacy services at high schools across the country (Drecoll 1985). These efforts, however, are apparently quite limited, a situation which is compounded by the weak tradition of volunteer literacy activities compared to those in other countries. In Germany, adult education institutes have offered literacy, in addition to the more traditional vocational and general education, since the late 1970s. Some state governments and the German Adult Education Association support these literacy education efforts, but the institutes are funded primarily through their constituencies.

As in Canada and Germany, the central governments of France and the United Kingdom have assumed limited roles; predominately local agencies and community groups coordinate and provide adult basic education services. In France, the government has so far played a minimal role in promoting literacy education. The Interministerial Committee was established to research and coordinate literacy efforts; however, it is poorly funded, cannot sponsor major new programs, and has little connection to the Ministry of Education. Generally, adult basic education in France has been provided for immigrants by volunteer organizations.

Adult literacy activities in the United Kingdom date to 1975 when a temporary Adult Literacy Unit was established. The Unit oversaw a three-year campaign promoted by the British Broadcasting Company (BBC) and supported by national funds distributed to local literacy programs. Approximately 155,000 adults participated during this period (Limage 1990). In 1978, the Adult Literacy and Basic Skills Unit (ALBSU) was formed to coordinate literacy efforts. It operates under a short-term budget and mandate, and has cooperated with the BBC to develop a Basic Skills Accreditation for adult students (see *Recognition and Certification of Skill*).

2.2 Volunteer and Community-based Programs

Educational programs for illiterate adults are often provided through voluntary, community-based organizations. In France, Germany, and the United Kingdom, such volunteer organizations represent the primary mechanism of support for adult literacy activities. Beginning in 1977, French NGOs (notably the ATD Fourth World movement) launched a large-scale campaign. Most voluntary organizations in France target their services to language training for immigrants. The German national government does not fund or supervise adult education; each adult education institute is funded by the community. Drawing on its longstanding tradition of volunteerism, the United Kingdom relies heavily on volunteers for organizing literacy education.

In Canada and the United States, a substantial network of community-based organizations complements the services provided through public agencies. In Canada adult literacy services are offered by Community Councils for Literacy, the Movement for Canadian Literacy, and the Association of People's Literacy Groups, as well as two organizations with roots in the United States—Literacy Volunteers of America and Laubach Literacy of Canada. The latter two organizations also play a major role in adult basic education in the United States. Both recruit and train literacy tutors who provide services at one of the local affiliates or in conjunction with adult education services funded through government agencies. Adult literacy work in the United States is also promoted by libraries, churches, and other community institutions.

3. Future Directions

Adult basic education has generally not been a high priority for the industrialized nations discussed in this entry. Increased government support for adult basic education in the industrialized nations has generally been preceded by concerns that adult illiteracy, as defined in a functional or applied context, constrains economic growth. Additional government support for adult basic education programs in industrialized nations is likely to be contingent on the acceptance by policymakers that economic growth will continue to be impeded by an inadequately prepared workforce and that, due to technological advances, the completion of primary grades does not provide workers with sufficient skills to succeed. Consequently, expanded adult basic education will probably focus on basic skills related to the workplace, including skills which are transferable from job to job and skills which enable workers to adapt to changing demands.

Industrialized nations face a number of challenges. Increased funding for adult basic education is important but not at the expense of support for primary or secondary education or from other social services which benefit disadvantaged populations. There is also a need to develop effective systems for providing adult basic education services which accommodate the competing demands on adult learners, such as job requirements and family responsibilities, and to provide instruction in a format appropriate for adults.

See also: Literacy and Numeracy Models; Postliteracy; Adult Secondary Education; Literacy Research and Measurement

References

Anderson J 1985 Literacy in Australia. In: Malmquist E (ed.) 1985 *The Right to Read: Literacy Around the World.* Rotary International, Evanston, Illinois

Benton L, Noyelle T 1992 *Adult Illiteracy and Economic Performance in Industrialized Countries.* OECD, Center for Educational Research and Innovation, Paris

Brand E 1987 Functional illiteracy in industrialized countries. *Prospects* 17(2): 201–11

Drecoll F 1985 Adult literacy in the Federal Republic of Germany. In: Malmquist E (ed.) 1985 *The Right to Read: Literacy Around the World.* Rotary International, Evanston, Illinois

Ericson B 1991 Introduction. In: Ericson B (ed.) 1991 *Swedish Aspects on Literacy. Selected Papers from the 13th World Congress on Reading.* Swedish National Board of Education, Stockholm

Hammink K 1990 *Functional Illiteracy and Adult Basic Education in the Netherlands.* UNESCO Institute for Education, Hamburg

Kutner M A, Furey S, Webb L, Gadsden V 1990 *Adult Education Programs and Services: A View From Nine Programs.* Pelavin Associates, Inc., Washington, DC

Larsson S, Fransson A 1991 Who takes the second chance? Implementing educational equality in adult basic education in a Swedish context. In: Ericson B (ed.) 1991 *Swedish Aspects on Literacy. Selected Papers from the 13th World Congress on Reading.* Swedish National Board of Education, Stockholm

Limage L 1990 Adult literacy and basic education in Europe and North America: From recognition to provision. *Comp. Educ.* 26(1): 125–40

Ryan P 1991 *Adult Learning and Work: Finance, Incentives and Certification.* National Center on Adult Literacy, University of Pennsylvania, Philadelphia, Pennsylvania

Swedish Ministry of Education and Science 1992 *The Swedish Way Towards a Learning Society.* Utbildningsdepartementet, Stockholm

Wagner S 1985 Illiteracy and adult literacy teaching in Canada. *Prospects* 15(3): 407–17

Further Reading

Abrahamsson K 1991 Reading our future—Swedish policies for adult literacy, work transformation and active citizenship. In: Ericson B (ed.) 1991 *Swedish Aspects on Literacy. Selected Papers from the 13th World Congress* on Reading. Swedish National Board of Education, Stockholm

Chisman F P 1989 *Jump Start: The Federal Role in Adult Literacy. Final Report of the Project on Adult Literacy.* Southport Institute for Policy Analysis, Southport, Connecticut

Esperandieu V, Lion A 1984 *Des illettres en France: rapport au Premier ministre 1984.* La Documentation Francaise, Paris

Goffinet S, Loontjens A, Loebestein A, Kestelyn C 1986. *Les itinéraires d'analphabétisme, Recherche pour la Commission des Communautés Européennes.* Office des publications officielles de Communautés Européennes, Brussels

Harman D 1987 *Illiteracy: A National Dilemma.* Cambridge Books, New York

Hunter C S, Harman D 1979 *Adult Literacy in the United States.* McGraw-Hill, New York

Kirsch I, Jungeblut A 1986 *Literacy: Profiles of America's Young Adults.* Educational Testing Service, Princeton, New Jersey

Nesbitt P 1987 *Literacy in Canada: Southam Literacy Study.* Creative Research Group, Toronto

Taylor M C 1990 Adult basic education. In: Merriam S B, Cunningham P M (eds.) 1990 *Handbook of Adult and Continuing Education.* Jossey-Bass, San Francisco, California

Tuijnman A C, Kirsch I S, Wagner D A (eds.) 1995 *Adult Basic Skills: Advances in Measurement and Policy Analysis.* Hampton Press, New York

Wells A 1987 Adult literacy: Its impact on young adults in the United Kingdom. *Prospects* 17(2): 259–65

Adult Secondary Education

L. G. Martin

Adult secondary education (ASE) is comprised of educational programs which provide adult secondary school noncompleters with opportunities to obtain certifications of secondary school completion. Although secondary educational opportunities for youth are broadly available in the world community, the most deliberate efforts to develop and maintain ASE programs can be found in the most highly industrialized countries. While it is often equated with advanced literacy skills for functionally illiterate adults, ASE remains a marginal part of the system of education with regard to both the dominant youth-based systems of secondary education and other provisions of adult education and training.

1. Trends Toward Increasing Skill and Credential Requirements

Historically, most industrialized countries have long required compulsory schooling through the initial years of secondary school. These requirements have boosted the literacy rates of such countries to over 90 percent of their populations. However, during the 1970s and 1980s, several social, economic, and demographic trends have stimulated concerns for the educational needs of school noncompleters. First, a concern for the quality of education is widespread. In many countries, the level of educational attainment is rising as an increasing number of young people complete secondary schooling. However, since attainments are not rising as fast as expectations, widespread frustrations with regard to standards of educational achievements can be noted (Kairamo 1989).

Second, declining birthrates in many industrialized countries, and the increased immigration of often low-skilled and poorly educated minorities of diverse cultural backgrounds, have combined with native-born school noncompleters to increase the percentage of low literates among each country's population. In the United States, the rapid increase in minority participation in the workforce parallels a significant decline in the proportion of White male workers and portends significant changes for numerous occupations (Martin 1990). Third, advanced technology and increased economic competition in a global market have increased the demands among employers for much higher skill levels for available jobs. For example, Goddard (1989) predicts that by the year 2000 the majority of all new jobs in the United States will require a postsecondary education.

For industrialized nations, the completion of secondary school has become a benchmark definition of functional literacy and a minimum standard for the development of human capital. The citizens and policymakers in these countries believe that improved academic performance by students and increased levels of school completion will bring about continued economic development and social progress. As school noncompleters in each country struggle to compete for jobs that reflect the credential inflation brought on by technological developments and job restructuring, ASE programs provide the credentials most in demand for either entering employment or furthering educational opportunities (see *Postliteracy*).

2. Nature and Scope of Provision and Offerings

The type of opportunity structures created for school noncompleters who seek to return to the educational system varies in accordance with the structures of conventional secondary education in different countries, and with the purposes envisioned for the role of education in those societies.

2.1 Adult Secondary Education in Decentralized Systems: The United States and the United Kingdom

In both the United States and the United Kingdom, ASE programs run on federal, state, and local funding. Although state education agencies are ultimately responsible for the administration and supervision of all ASE programs within the state, county, or municipality —including teacher training, curriculum selection and development, evaluation, and fiscal accountability— decentralization and local autonomy are the rule rather than the exception. Local programs are diverse, but the majority use local school facilities and tend to reproduce with adults the atmosphere and practices of traditional schools.

As they matriculate through four grades of secondary school, students in the United States receive a "diploma" when they have acquired a specified number of "credits." However, during the 1980s, between 25 and 30 percent of secondary school students did not graduate with their grade cohorts (Martin and Fisher 1989).

Although United States citizens have had access to obtaining a high school equivalency diploma since the 1940s via the General Educational Development (GED) tests, it was not until the passage of the 1966 Adult Education Act that it was specifically targeted for funding via federal legislation. Adult learning centers, postsecondary vocational institutions, community colleges, youth-based high schools, correctional facilities, the military, large employers, and government training programs provide educational access to adult school noncompleters (see Kurian 1988b).

In the United Kingdom, progress through school depends chiefly on age rather than attainment: there is no grade system, nor is there a secondary school diploma (Booth 1985). Students who do well in secondary school tend to take the General Certificate of Secondary Education (GCSE) examination at age 16. The same category of students two years later will take the General Certificate of Education (GCE) A ("advanced")-level examinations. Universities frequently require that a candidate have three A-level passes for admission. Students take GCSEs and A-level examinations in as many subjects as they wish, and, receive a "pass" or "fail" for each examination. However, statistics suggest that at age 16 there is a huge dropout of students. In 1992, some 35 to 40 percent of the 16-year olds were still in school or in full-time courses in colleges of further education (Male 1988).

Colleges of further education (or polytechnical colleges) and the National Extension College (via correspondence courses) offer secondary education

to persons aged 16 years and older. Some academic courses are offered to a minority of the students who wish to prepare for GCSEs or A-level examinations. Many of the students taking the vocational courses are employed by factories and firms and are given "day release" several hours each week to attend classes in the colleges of further education, which also have full-time students.

2.2 Highly Centralized System of Secondary Education: France

France's highly centralized system of education is administered by the Ministry of Education and the Ministry of Universities. The government also exerts considerable indirect influence over private schools through a system of national examinations and certificates, making it necessary for them to conform to public school criteria. The educational budget is incorporated into the national budget. However, about 10 percent of educational expenditures are borne by local government (Kurian 1988a). The vocational part of the second cycle of secondary education and other forms of technical and vocational education are partly financed by an "apprenticeship tax" levied on all commercial and industrial organizations.

Secondary education is divided into two cycles: first cycle—grades six to nine, and second cycle—grades 10 to 12. The *baccalauréat* is the highest step in French secondary education. It is both a school-leaving examination and an automatic passport to higher education. It is a grueling ordeal with a high failure rate of 30 to 35 percent. The pass rate is 10 out of every 20 in every subject. Consequently, large numbers of French youth stop their schooling when they reach the limit of compulsory education at age 16. Fewer than 10 percent of the eligible group have completed their secondary education (Kurian 1988a).

For school noncompleters, the regular program of the secondary schools as well as some vocational programs can be taken by means of correspondence courses, which in 1982 enrolled over 230,000 pupils. These courses are provided free by the *Centre d'Enseignment par Correspondance* (National Correspondence Course Center, or CNEC) which runs and coordinates six institutions (Kurian 1988a). Adult education aimed at enhancing the functional literacy of the already literate is sponsored by the *Association Nationale pour la Formation Professionelle des Adultes* (AFPA). The Ministry of Education is involved in this area through the *Conservatoire National des Arts et Metiers* (CNAM) founded in 1819. This institution, with 36 outposts, runs lecture courses and practical training, mostly through evening classes, and awards diplomas on their completion.

2.3 Education and Industry Partnership: Germany

In Germany, academic administration is centralized at the state level and each state issues a detailed course of study and conducts state examinations at the end of the secondary school level. The states are involved in curriculum revision and take an active part in approving textbooks. Teachers are usually members of the state civil service. Specific responsibilities for educational administration have been delegated by the states to the cities and counties. The local level is usually responsible for school buildings and equipment, with financial help from the state as necessary. The costs of education are covered by general taxes collected by the state and municipality (Rust 1988).

Completion of Grade 13 of the *Gymnasium* (grades 5–13) entitles a student to sit for the *Abitur* (a state-administered examination), which entitles a student to enroll in the university. The vocational school (*Berufsschule*) is attended primarily by main-school leavers who are required to remain part-time in school while preparing for an occupation. This training takes place in a dual system of vocational training which combines training programs in companies and school-based instruction in vocational schools over an average of three years. Middle-school leavers are able to enroll in a senior technical school. Almost two-thirds of an age cohort undergo training that leads to qualifications as a skilled worker in over 400 officially recognized occupations. Under this system, examinations are conducted to determine whether the trainee has acquired the necessary knowledge and skills. The overall passrate for these examinations is between 85 and 96 percent (Kairamo 1989).

For school noncompleters, "Second Way" schools are available. They include the academic secondary evening school (*Abendgymnasium*) or a special university preparatory school for adults, called the *Kolleg*. The former offers regular *Gymnasium* courses in the evening. The latter has developed intensive full-time courses of two to three years' duration. Entrance requirements may be met by completion of the middle school or some vocational schools, entrance examinations, or combination of these. Substantial consideration is given to work experience. Both schools lead to the *Abitur* examination. Average grade points and *Abitur* examination marks are the primary admissions criteria used by universities and equivalent institutions.

Germany has also established a tradition of sponsoring education through the media (Rust 1988). The third television channel of the country offers courses under the name *"Telekolleg"* (TV courses). These courses enable students ultimately to obtain the middle-school level qualifications through a combination of viewing, work with TV program printed materials, and attendance at regular meetings.

3. Characteristics of School Noncompleters

The majority of persons who have difficulty functioning in advanced societies are assumed to be found in that portion of the population that did not complete secondary school. Native-born adults failed or were failed in their first encounter with the educational system, and immigrants often arrive with low levels of education from their countries of origin. Therefore, school noncompleters tend to be from among those persons who are included in statistics on nearly every measure of major social or economic disadvantage—poverty and social dependency, unemployment, racial or ethnic discrimination, inadequate housing, deteriorating communities, lack of access to health services, and so forth. The lack of ability to perform literacy-related tasks or the failure to possess credentials are lower on their list of priorities than resolving immediate problems. Consequently, the piecemeal approaches employed by ASE programs to address the learning needs of noncompleters fail to recognize the multifaceted nature of their life experiences. Therefore, these programs fail to enroll a substantial proportion of those in need of literacy services. For example, fewer than 10 percent of the target population in the United States are served annually by such programs (Martin and Fisher 1989).

4. Nature of Access

The service delivery system of ASE programs consists of a network of different types of programs that are defined largely by the prerogative of individual countries and their educational governance systems. Although situated in different settings, there are essentially two major alternatives for adults to complete secondary school: acquire a secondary school diploma or pass an examination.

The "Adult Secondary School" provides the traditional secondary school curriculum via evening classes for noncompleters to obtain the credits required for completion of a secondary school diploma. "Alternative High School Diploma" programs tend to combine somewhat traditional graduation requirements with credit for informal learning experiences and flexible structures that allow choices in content and scheduling.

"Competency-based Education" programs utilize adult-oriented assessment instruments to test functional competencies of learners. Credentials of secondary school completion are awarded when learners can demonstrate, via tests, log books, demonstrations, and so on, that they have mastered the minimum competencies expected of secondary school completers. "Examination" programs utilize commercially published workbooks and texts, and teacher-made materials, to prepare learners to pass exit examinations such as the General Educational Development (GED) tests in the United States, the GCSE in the United Kingdom, or the *Abitur* in Germany.

5. Methods and Materials

The types of learning materials used in ASE programs are largely a function of the goals of the programs. In examination programs, the primary criterion for the selection of materials is the ability to facilitate the passing of the tests. In the adult secondary school, materials selected closely parallel those used in the traditional secondary school. The materials that provide the instructional content vary from published workbooks, tests, and other assigned readings, to audiovisual and video sources. Instructional approaches include individualized instruction via workbooks and computers, and small and large groups.

6. Staffing

The credential requirements of ASE staff vary in accordance with the sponsorship of the programs. For example, when programs are under the jurisdiction of the public school system, the administrative, instructional, and counseling staff are subject to the credentialing requirements of that system. Adult secondary education programs are typically staffed by part-time instructors and volunteers. However, most countries have laws or regulations allowing for preservice or inservice training for full- or part-time staff.

7. General Trends and Issues

Several trends and issues will likely determine the focus and direction of ASE programming in the 1990s and beyond. These include:

(a) *Educational leave for working adults.* Provisions for educational leave with or without pay (but guaranteeing return to employment without loss of rights or status) could be an enormous factor in the further development of ASE. For example, Sweden in 1975 passed the "Act Concerning an Employees's Right to Educational Leave" to provide grants for adults to claim (unpaid) leave for study. Only two other countries—France (the Law of July 1971) and Belgium (1973)—have broad-based liberal laws of educational leave which could allow for general or vocational ASE (Brookfield 1985) (see *Paid Educational Leave and Collective Bargaining*).

(b) *Competency-based programs for workplace training.* Adult secondary education programs have traditionally relied on the youth-based secondary system for the criteria against which to judge the academic performance of adults. Since the 1970s, researchers and practitioners in the United States have been developing assessment instruments and curricula based on the functional competencies involved in adult-oriented tasks. Because these instruments and their accompanying curricula are based on the functional context of adults' life experiences, they are likely to be more useful than school-based examination for assisting learners in the workplace (see *Recognition and Certification of Skill*).

(c) *Competition for funds.* To become a more effective vehicle of educational access for school noncompleters, ASE programs must compete more effectively for those funds allocated to education. As a marginal educational entity, it lags behind nearly all other categories of educational systems in funding. The most effective avenue to obtain increased funding is to increase demands from school noncompleters. Therefore, practitioners should be more attentive to developing and marketing programs directed toward specific segments of potential learners.

8. Conclusion

Adult secondary educational systems tend to be the manifestation of efforts to improve the human capital resources of the various countries involved. While this motive neglects the needs of school noncompleters for personal empowerment, it does stimulate the development of opportunity structures which provide access to education.

See also: Clienteles and Special Populations; Providers of Adult Education: An Overview; Adult Basic Education; Postliteracy

References

Booth C 1985 United Kingdom: System of Education. In: Husén T, Postlethwaite T N (eds.) 1985 *The International Encyclopedia of Education, 1st edn.* Pergamon Press, Oxford
Brookfield S 1985 Adult education in public schools. In: Husén T, Postlethwaite T N (eds.) 1985 *The International Encyclopedia of Education, 1st edn.* Pergamon Press, Oxford
Goddard R W 1989 Work force 2000. *Personnel J.* 68 (2): 65–71
Kairamo K 1989 *Education for Life: A European Strategy.* Butterworths, London
Kurian G T 1988a France. In: Kurian G T (ed.) 1988, Vol. 1
Kurian G T 1988b United States. In Kurian G T (ed.) 1988, Vol. 3
Male G A 1988 United Kingdom. In: Kurian G T (ed.) 1988, Vol. 3
Martin L G 1990 Facilitating cultural diversity in adult literacy programs. In: Ross-Gordon J M, Martin L G, Brisco D B (eds.) 1990 *Serving Culturally Diverse Populations.* Jossey-Bass, San Francisco, California
Martin L G, Fisher J C 1989 Adult secondary education. In: Merriam S B, Cunningham P M (eds.) 1989 *Handbook of Adult and Continuing Education.* Jossey-Bass, San Francisco, California
Rust V D 1988 West Germany. In: Kurian G T (ed.) 1988b, Vol. 3

Further Reading

Betson L, Noyelle T 1992 *Adult Illiteracy and Economic Performance.* CERI[2u]/[1u]OECD, Paris
Kurian G T (ed.) 1988 *World Education Encyclopedia.* Facts on File, New York

Legge D L 1982 *The Education of Adults in Britain.* Open University Press, Milton Keynes
Jourdan M 1981 *Recurrent Education in Western Europe: Progress, projects and trends in recurrent, lifelong and continuing education* NFER-Nelson, Windsor

Adult Tertiary Education

C. Duke

The 1980s have seen a significant growth in the proportion of adults enrolled in tertiary education institutions in many societies. The expansion of adult and continuing education is, however, a complex phenomenon reflecting diverse social, economic, and cultural changes, needs of societies, and aspirations of individuals. An adult education tradition found in many countries values a second chance for the socially and educationally disadvantaged, equality of access if not of outcome and social change as well as individual advancement. Adults in tertiary-level education may follow established or specially created degree and other award-bearing courses, or special-purpose, usually nonaward-bearing, short courses designed to meet particular needs. These categories are frequently distinguished for administrative and financial purposes as well as in terms of intent, yet the distinction between them, and from regular tertiary education immediately following upper-secondary schooling, is often blurred.

The newer theories and philosophy of lifelong learning and recurrent education are distinct from this adult education tradition, and reflect a need to continue learning and to return periodically to education throughout life in order to cope with rapid technological and other changes. The expansion of adult and continuing higher education must be seen in the context of a general shift from elite toward mass higher education, with a changing role for higher education, especially universities. In principle this change makes the notion of substantial and varied adult and continuing education within higher education easier. There is regional and national diversity within these broad trends, but with a common tendency toward significant numbers of adults in higher education, especially throughout the advanced industrialized world.

1. Adult Education

The term "adult education" has been the subject of much attention in an attempt to reach an agreed definition. Many definitions of, and claims for, adult education are, however, infused with a set of values which contain frequent reference to an adult education movement (see Taylor et al. 1985). These values are broadly liberal and reformist. They reflect concern with social injustice, inequality, and lack of opportunity for the socially and economically disadvantaged, who were originally mainly working-class people, and later especially women and members of minority ethnic groups, together with other categories of disadvantage such as the physically and mentally handicapped and prisoners. Adult education may also be seen simply as an administrative category referring to resources, teachers, and students outside the regular school system, which encompasses all teaching-learning objectives and subject matter. Some writers refer instead to the education of adults in order to avoid the connotations of adult education, which include a liberal, usually nonvocational and often nonassessed, voluntary character as well as aspirations to social or civic amelioration (see *Adult Education: Concepts and Principles*).

1.1 "Adult" within Tertiary Education

The sense of social purpose, which has made adult education in part a movement, also influenced the development of adult education within the growing university system, notably in both the United Kingdom and the United States. The extension movement in the United States represented a commitment to community service which has built an extra dimension into the mission of United States universities, namely community service alongside teaching and research (Rockhill 1983). In contrast, European universities developed with a strong emphasis on only the third of these functions. In the United Kingdom the reform of the older universities and the development of new civic universities in the major industrial centers was accompanied by a sense of mission, to extend the benefits of scholarship to members of the working classes. University extension originated at Cambridge and Oxford in the 1870s and was added to the functions of most universities in the first part of the twentieth century, usually via extramural departments (Blyth 1983, Marriott 1984).

2. Continuing Education

The term "continuing education" was originally restricted mainly to relatively high-level, often graduate as well as postexperience, vocational education. This might be of a refresher, updating, or upgrading nature, or designed to add new skills and qualifications, for example in management, to a prior qualification in another specialized field. It is argued that the resources for such high-level specialized work reside logically and perhaps uniquely within higher education, thereby incidentally exaggerating the elitist or inegalitarian tendencies latent in adult continuing education whereby those with most initial education most energetically seek further education throughout life. However, other large organizations and corporations, especially in the private sector, have increasingly become providers of specialized updating education for their own workforces, thereby entering into competition for what may be seen as lucrative high-revenue work.

Continuing education has increasingly acquired a broader meaning, encompassing all forms of post-initial education for adults. According to this definition, in many societies the majority of students in tertiary education are also in continuing education, in that they have returned to study after a break from initial continuous education (Abrahamsson 1986, Abrahamsson et al. 1988, Campbell 1984). Their study may be full-or part-time; on an award-bearing or a nonaward-bearing, or "short" course; and for vocational, community, or personal development purposes. The use of the term "continuing" within tertiary education may thus stress the high level of the work, appropriate to a university, or it may rather be deliberately eclectic and encompassing, stressing the scale, scope, and significance of the work (see *Lifelong and Continuing Education*).

3. Change in Tertiary Education

Adult and continuing education is expanding within tertiary education while the growth of in-company refresher and updating programs on a large scale in advanced industrialized countries means a massive increase also in continuing education outside the recognized tertiary education system. Meanwhile, industrial societies demand higher levels of formal pre-experience educational attainment, reflected in increasingly high retention through upper-secondary education and higher participation rates in tertiary education. Universities and colleges are thus experiencing greater diversification as well as expansion of clientele, in terms of school- and junior college-leavers as well as older adults. The rapid expansion of continuing education within tertiary education is one aspect of a major transformation, as tertiary education is pushed from an elite toward a mass model (Roderick and Stephens 1979). While the same phenomena can be identified in most societies, they are most advanced in the United States, with Sweden, Canada and other European and non-European countries following at different rates (OECD 1974).

4. Major Program Areas

Different typologies are used to analyze and describe adult and continuing education, none of them entirely satisfactory (Duke 1986). Some concentrate on the different categories of learners, or target groups, others on different teaching-learning arrangements and technologies such as discussion or study groups, distance or self-directed learning. The categories most commonly used are based on the known or supposed purposes and intentions of the educational institution and/or the learner. A fourway categorization distinguishes between basic or remedial education; vocational or refresher education (continuing education in the restricted sense); civic, political, or community education; and liberal education, where personal development is the main objective. A fifth, somewhat different, category is found in the tertiary education systems of most countries, and treated differently among them. This is the teaching or training of adult educators, together with research and scholarship in this field.

4.1 Continuing Professional Education

The largest and most rapidly growing category of continuing education, probably in all societies, is that concerned with upgrading and updating the knowledge, skills, and competencies of people in their occupational roles. This type of education is known as continuing professional education (CPE). Governments and large employers are generally aware of the rate of obsolescence of knowledge and of skills. There may be skepticism and uncertainty about the value and rate of return to society, but vocational updating, being more specifically fashioned to employer needs, is widely regarded as important. It has become mandatory in a number of key occupations, and may become an intrinsic part of plans for organization and staff and career development (see *Providers of Adult Education: An Overview*).

Continuing professional education is a large-scale social enterprise, partly within and partly outside tertiary education. Large budgets are involved, and high fees can be charged for parts of the work. Continuing professional education can, therefore, be an area of intense competition, particularly since constraint on public expenditure (a factor common to most planned and free market economies, developing as well as industrialized) means contraction of public funds going to higher education and pressure to generate income from other sources. Different views prevail within different political systems as to who should pay for CPE–

the individual beneficiary, the employer, or the wider community through the public revenue system. Devices such as tax relief may obscure the actual division of costs among these three. In the United Kingdom a trend away from high income tax and a strong welfare state toward lower taxation and a contracted welfare state is reflected in the government's assertion that employers and individuals should pay for continuing professional education. Substantial funds can, however, be attracted from different public sources in different ways for some CPE programs, and different kinds of developmental grants are also made by several government departments and agencies. Employers in the United Kingdom have argued that the taxation system lacks the incentives, available elsewhere, to spend on CPE. One difficulty associated in many countries with the self-financing character of CPE is that those institutions providing CPE may only be able to offer such courses at high fees to those who can afford to pay. Less wealthy employers managing small enterprises, the self-employed, and public-sector organizations may have equally great needs, yet may be unable to afford access to continuing education.

4.2 Political and Civic Education

Traditionally, adult educators have been concerned about the nature of society and frequently committed to social change or amelioration through adult education (Thompson 1980). Such commitment continues to characterize radical adult educators and a number of those who define themselves in this way are found working as educators within institutions of higher education. Discussion and writing about adult education tends to over-represent the significance of this strand of adult education, especially within tertiary education. The trend toward mass tertiary education, and demands for more vocationally relevant education, have reinforced a tendency away from radical social criticism in universities, following the crisis in tertiary education experienced in many Western countries in the early 1970s (Duke 1988), Taylor et al. 1985. McIlroy and Spencer 1988). Courses concerned with social and political issues play a minor part in most continuing education programs although this may be balanced in part by civic role education, for example, to be a lay magistrate, trade union or voluntary group leader, or a school governor. There are also signs that consumer, environmental, peace, women's, and other movements may represent a renewal of popular political education, and that this may be finding support and expression in some areas of tertiary education.

4.3. Liberal Adult Education

Over the past 40 years education for leisure, personal development, and self-expression has been a major growth area, especially among the more affluent middle classes of Western and westernized societies. Characteristically, university programs reflect middle-class intellectual and leisure interests. History, literature, natural history, and the fine arts are major program areas; many universities offer a wide range of study tours where recreation on vacation is combined with well-informed study guidance. The widening gap between rich and poor, discernible in many countries in the 1980s, appears to have benefited this program area of continuing education, since those classes and groups which tend to seek liberal adult education within tertiary education also tend to have more disposable income.

4.4 Teaching and Research in Continuing Education

Most countries have arrangements within their tertiary education systems for the training of adult educators as an area of professional work, and for research and development in continuing education as a field of study. Such work is most commonly separated from the direct provision of continuing education. The latter is often known as "extension." This form of continuing education is organized at least in part through distinct extension or continuing education schools or divisions. Teaching and research in continuing education may usually be found as part of a professional school of education, possibly associated with tertiary education, or with educational administration. In North America, in particular, there are substantial graduate training and research programs preparing and informing continuing educators to work within the schools, community, or the tertiary education system, or to go into a specialized area such as agricultural extension, health education, or professional continuing education for lawyers, doctors, or engineers. In some countries, separate teaching or research institutes concentrate exclusively on training or research in the education of adults. (see *Training of Adult Educators*).

5. Institutional Considerations

5.1 Organization and Management

One strand of adult education scholarship has emphasized its marginality within tertiary education. In the traditions of the United Kingdom and the United States separate units or departments have been charged with design and delivery of continuing education. In North America extension and continuing education structures exist, often on a massive scale, as largely distinct administrative and budgetary systems, although adults taking degree courses may be fully integrated into regular teaching and administrative arrangements. In the United Kingdom the tradition of separate funding and administration has protected liberal adult education within a number of universities, though at a cost of separation and limited influence from the main councils determining the mission of the university as a whole (McIlroy and Spencer 1988, Marriot 1984). A number of changes have led to the removal of this special separate funding of university adult education and there is much discussion about and experimentation with the most effective means of taking continuing education into the mainstream of university planning and provision (see NIACE 1989). The trend is toward smaller specialized continuing education departments which are partly direct providers of courses and partly catalysts and proponents for continuing education throughout the university. The diversity of continuing education, however, can pose problems for course delivery.

5.2. *Finances and Resources*

The cost of separate specialized departments is one aspect of the financing of continuing education. More fundamental is the question of who should pay—the state or community through public revenues, the employer as major economic beneficiary, or the individual who may benefit in an economic as well as a personal sense. Many governments are preoccupied with constraining public expenditure. This inclination is accentuated by demographic changes, with an increasingly large dependent older population and a declining young population in industrialized societies. Expansion of tertiary education implies reducing costs per person-place, and puts more pressure on continuing education to be paid for privately, whether by employer or individual. Continuing education fees are seen as a source of income in subjects having direct economic value. Whereas much of this work has traditionally been costed marginally and carried in part as a public or community service, close scrutiny reveals that even apparently economically viable courses cost the institution money, when hidden or infrastructure costs are identified. As continuing education expands as a proportion of all tertiary education, it becomes harder to carry and hide costs in this way.

5.3 *Curriculum and Staff Development*

Differences between adult and young learners have been studied, and the term "andragogy" created to emphasize the different teaching methods required. Where adults are taught separately from younger students, for instance on openly recruited or specially designed, "tailor-made," short courses for occupational groups or particular employers, suitable curricula and teaching methods can be devised and negotiated relatively freely. Much fruitful innovation in curriculum design and teaching methods occurs within continuing education, encouraged by the knowledge that dissatisfied learner-clients, and their sponsors, will act in their own interests and take their business elsewhere.

Adult students permeate the whole of tertiary education in many countries, and course structures are altered, for instance through modularization and the introduction of more flexible distance and open learning delivery systems, including distinct open universities and colleges. Questions posed about appropriate learning needs and styles, and about teaching methods, have tended to spill over and to permeate curriculum development more generally. Other pressures are experienced, as tertiary education is forced to become more cost-effective and to enroll larger numbers of students with different backgrounds, aspirations, and abilities, while receiving little or no increase in resources. Staff training and development may be unimportant in times of stability or gradual change. Where change is rapid, the need for staff appraisal and development becomes acute. Thus, continuing education, representing new clienteles with different learning needs, tends to be placed at the forefront of both curriculum and staff development within tertiary education, and to be a testing ground for innovations which may then pervade the institution more widely.

5.4 *Permeable Boundaries*

Most tertiary education institutions have been conceived and managed as separate, distinct communities, at times almost as closed institutions in the sense established by Erving Goffman writing of "total institutions" in *Asylums* (1961). Academic gowns and teaching terms with residence symbolized the separation. The term "ivory tower" was coined in negative reference to this separateness. The late twentieth century has seen loss of confidence in and respect for tertiary education in many countries, for both sociocultural and economic reasons, and more demand for service, relevance, and utility. Continuing education is at the forefront of innovations and trends toward closer university-community links, and it plays a major part in the process of boundary permeation which is changing the character of tertiary education. (Duke 1988). Continuing education courses are negotiated, in particular, with nonacademic partners outside the university environment. Continuing education students occupy other dominant roles (as workers, citizens, parents, etc.) not shared by the traditional young full-time student.

6. *Future Prospects*

Continuing education within tertiary-level institutions is in the forefront of institutional adaptation. It is both a testbed and a cutting edge for changes which are transforming tertiary education. Within this sector the familiar "front-end" model of education still persists, as it does among most educational planners (Abrahamsson 1988). The rationale for change provided by theorists of lifelong learning and recurrent education is still little used. However, it is likely that, as continuing education expands and plays a lead in reshaping and relocating higher education in the social and economic structure, these concepts will be used to explain and make more comfortable a transformation that has already largely occurred. Within this systemic shift in tertiary education, different societies will come to different arrangements for integration and differentiation, so that some institutions will be permeated by continuing education work, others will contain it in different ways, and again others may continue to concentrate on research, or on initial high-level education for a small elite.

See also: Community Colleges, Distance Education, Open University, University Adult Education, Third-age Students in Higher Education

References

Abrahamsson K (ed.) 1986 *Adult Participation in Swedish Higher Education: A Study of Organisational Structure, Educational Design and Current Policies.* Almqvist and Wiksell, Stockholm

Abrahamsson K (ed.) 1988 *Implementing Recurrent Education in Sweden: On Reform Strategies of Swedish Adult and Higher Education.* Swedish National Board of Education, Stockholm

Abrahamsson K, Rubenson K, Slowey M 1988 *Adults in the Academy. International Trends in Adult and Higher Education.* Swedish National Board of Education, Stockholm, Sweden

Blyth J 1983 *English University Adult Education 1908–58: The Unique Tradition.* Manchester University Press, Manchester

Campbell D 1984 *The New Majority: Adult Learners in the University.* University of Alberts, Edmonton

Duke C (ed.) 1986 *Adult Education: International Perspectives from China.* Croom Helm, Beckenham

Duke C 1988 The Future Shape of Continuing Education and Universities: An Inaugural Lecture. University of Warwick, Coventry

Goffman E 1961 *Asylums: Essays on the Social Situation of Mental Patients and Other Inmates.* Anchor Books, Doubleday and Co. New York

McIlroy J, Spencer B 1988 *University Adult Education in Crisis.* Department of Adult and Continuing Education, University of Leeds, Leeds.

Marriott S 1984 *Extra-Mural Empires: Service and Self-Interest in English University Adult Education 1873-1983* Department of Adult Education, University of Nottingham, Nottingham

National Institute for Adult Continuing Education (NIACE) 1989 *Adults in Higher Education. A Policy Discussion Paper* (NIACE) Leicester

Organisation for Economic Co-operation and Development (OECD) 1974 *Policies for Higher Education* OECD, Paris

Rockhill K 1983 *Academic Excellence and Public Service: A History of University Extension in California* Transaction Books, New Brunswick, New Jersey

Roderick G,. Stephens M (eds.) 1979 *Higher Education for All?* Falmer Press, Brighton

Taylor R, Rockhill K, Fieldhouse R 1985 *University Adult Education in England and the USA: A Reappraisal of the Literal Tradition* Croom Helm, Beckenham

Thomson J (ed.) 1980 *Adult Education for a Change* Hutchinson, London

Further Reading

CERI 1987 *Adults in Higher Education.* OECD, Paris

Crombie A D, Harries-Jenkins G 1983 *The Demise of the Liberal Tradition, Two Essays on the Future of British University Adult Education* Department of Adult and Continuing Education, University of Leeds, Leeds

Cross K P 1978 *The Missing Link: Connecting Adult Learners to Learning Resources.* College Entrance Examination Board, New York

Fordham P 1983 A view from the walls: Commitment and purposes in university adult education. *Int. J. Lifelong Educ.* 2 (4): 341–54

Jepson N 1973 *The Beginnings of English University Adult Education: Policy and Problems.* Michael Joseph, London

McIlroy J 1987 Continuing education and the universities in Britain: The political context. *Int. J. Lifelong Educ.* 6(1): 27–59

Midwinter E 1984 *Mutual Aid Universities.* Croom Helm, Beckenham

Schlossberg N K, Lynch A Q, Chickering A W 1989 *Improving Higher Education Environments for Adults.* Jossey-Bass, San Francisco, California

Stern M R (ed.) 1983 *Power and Conflict in Continuing Professional Education.* Wadsworth, Belmont, California

Williams G 1979 *Towards Lifelong Education: A New Role for Higher Education Institutions.* UNESCO, Paris

Woodley A, Wagner L, Slowey M, Hamilton M, Fulton O 1987 *Choosing to Learn: Adults in Education* SRHE/Open University Press, Milton Keynes

Community Colleges

A. M. Cohen

Educational systems in all nations are called on to accommodate people who are past the age of compulsory schooling but who desire continuing education that is not provided by the traditional universities. That group includes students seeking preparation for jobs or low-cost access to prebaccalaureate studies, and adults who want culturally and socially relevant continuing education. The systems are also expected to supply properly trained workers for the nation's business and industry, and to retrain the workforce to meet the demands of emerging technologies. These challenges have led many countries to develop various forms of schooling in which one or a combination of these functions are carried out.

1. Scope and Definition

The postcompulsory, nonuniversity sector includes structures organized in association with the nation's formal school system as well as numerous unique enterprises standing apart. Although this area of education is a loosely defined sector, its outlines can be traced in the formally recognized institutions that perform its functions in the nations of Asia, Europe, and North America where the concept is most generally recognized.

The names applied to the institutions in this sector suggest its multiple purposes. In the United States, the term "community college" is used generically for all publicly supported institutions accredited to award the associate degree as their highest degree. Elsewhere these institutions may be known as "junior colleges" (still used in the United States for some privately supported colleges), regional or district colleges, technical or technological institutions, or by a number of other names, as shown in Table 1. "Short cycle institution" is sometimes used in Europe to encompass the entire group of of postsecondary schools that do not award baccalaureate degrees. But in this entry "community college" is used as the collective term.

Distinctions within the category may be made by reference to curricular classifications or modes of institutional organization. The colleges may offer general or foundation studies, pre-university courses, technical and vocational programs, and cultural and social education. None of these terms is definitive and the same institution may provide several types of curricula, with overlaps among them. The colleges may be organized as branches of a university, locally governed schools, or as independent state or national systems. In some nations, specialized curricula are provided in two or three types of community colleges, each governed and funded differently.

Overall, community college education is less a definable institutional sector than an area of education that serves several purposes in the interstice between compulsory and higher education or, in some cases, after higher education. It tends to follow patterns of workforce differentiation and is more generalized in countries where student tracking is delayed (as in the United States), and more specialized where streaming students according to their likely place in the workforce is made earlier (as in some Northern European countries).

Nevertheless, the community colleges worldwide share certain characteristics. Their fees are usually lower than those charged by universities, and students may enroll without satisfying the rigorous requirements that many university systems impose. The institutions employ large numbers of part-time faculty members. They may provide undergraduate studies that can be used as credits toward baccalaureate degrees if the student eventually gains admission to the university, a function that is especially prominent in the United States and Canada. Where educational expectations are expanding they relieve the pressure placed on university systems by people seeking admission for postsecondary studies. And they act as flexible institutions that can organize programs to resolve short-term problems of language preparation for immigrant groups, workforce retraining in the face of technological change, and community expectations for ad hoc postsecondary education of general interest to the local populace.

2. Development of Community Colleges

The development of community colleges in the various nations has followed different patterns. In the United States, where 1,250 community colleges serve more than 5.5 million students, the institutions date from the early years of the twentieth century. As long ago as 1930, community colleges were operating in nearly every state. The general expansion of postsecondary education that began in the 1940s led to rapid growth as institutions were organized to provide first-year and second-year courses for students for whom the universities had no space. Many additional students appeared who either were not qualified for university entrance because of their poor prior academic preparation, or who could not afford the higher tuition charges. The colleges also grew because they organized programs to prepare people for middle-level or semitechnical occupations that the universities had ignored. These two central functions, prebaccalaureate and technical training, were subsequently joined by two others: cultural and educational programs for lifelong learning, in which people might participate for their personal interest, and remedial courses for the students who failed to learn basic literacy skills during their previous schooling. By the 1980s nearly half the undergraduates enrolled in publicly supported higher education in the United States were in community colleges, found now in all 50 states. And if the proprietary trades schools are added to the category, the number of students in community colleges exceeds the total enrolled in universities.

Although the community colleges in other nations are not as comprehensive or ubiquitous, they share many of the same developmental characteristics. Canada's were founded in each province to meet rising demands for access to postsecondary studies, workforce preparation, and adult education. The Republic of China's (Taiwan) junior colleges, organized in the late 1970s, provide programs that vary in length from 2 to 5 years, with the latter accepting students from middle schools (Ministry of Education 1990). The Swedish system was reformed in 1970 when pre-university preparatory schools were combined with vocational programs to form single upper-secondary schools. The University Institutes of Technology (IUTs) were founded in France in the 1960s in an attempt to channel more students into programs connected with the workplace. Their selective admissions policies and technological emphases differentiate them from that nation's higher technicians' sections which are more nearly terminal vocational schools.

3. Goals and Functions

The emphasis placed on the functions assigned to community colleges varies considerably. Occupationally related studies are prominent in many systems. Some of the community colleges in the United States provide vocational and technical programs exclusively, and a few states have organized dual systems, with university branches providing the general education and technical institutes, the occupational studies. Sweden's upper-secondary schools integrate general subjects with vocational training that includes a workplace-based component. Vocational courses are also featured in the regional technical college system in Ireland, the Japanese special training schools, and the junior colleges in the Republic of China (Taiwan).

Pre-baccalaureate programs are prominent in community colleges in nations where the universities have been unable to matriculate a rising number of degree seekers. Colleges in the United States enroll sizable numbers of students who seek the first 2 years of a bachelor's degree program. Such students form a high proportion of the enrollment in numerous institutions, especially in states such as Kentucky and Wisconsin where the colleges were organized as branches of the state university, and in states where the public universities' first-year class is kept deliberately small so that the community colleges serve as feeders to the upper division; Arizona, California, and Florida are notable

Table 1
Institutions providing community college functions

Institution	Country
College of Advanced Education	Australia
College of Applied Arts and Technology	Canada
Collége d'Enseignment Général et Professionnel (CEGEP)	Canada
College of Further Education	Australia
	United Kingdom
Community College	Canada
	New Zealand
	United States
Fachhochschule	Germany
Folk High School	Denmark
Higher Technicians' Section	France
Institut Teknologi	Malaysia
Junior College	Japan
	Republic of China
	United States
Regional (or District) College	Norway
	Israel
Regional Technical College	Ireland
Special Training School	Japan
Technical College (or Institute)	United States
	Malaysia
	New Zealand
Technological Education Institution	Greece
Two-year Vocational University	People's Republic of China
University Institute of Technology (IUT)	France
Upper Secondary School	Sweden
Volkhochschule	Germany
Workers' College	People's Republic of China

examples. The credits earned in the Canadian community colleges and in the Japanese junior colleges can also typically be applied to the baccalaureate degree, but this feature is rare in other nations.

The cultural and social education of adults, often called "lifelong learning," is emphasized in the regional colleges in Norway, the *Volkshochschulen* in Germany, the folk high schools in Denmark, and the colleges of further education in the United Kingdom and Australia. The lifelong learning programs in these institutions have a widespread scope. Cultural and leisure-time activities are a part, along with programs that are attentive to social objectives in the local communities. The British and Australian systems rely heavily on open or distance learning provided through electronic media. Table 2 displays the major emphases and orientations of community colleges in different countries.

4. Organization

Governance and organizational patterns vary. United States community colleges were formed originally by public school districts, churches, independent agencies, universities, or under special state authorization, with the state-coordinated system gradually becoming the prevalent pattern. In Austria, Denmark, Indonesia, Sweden, and, more recently, France, short-cycle postsecondary programs were attached to the secondary school system. In South America, the colleges were more likely to be founded as branches of the university or the polytechnic colleges. Separate systems were developed to govern community colleges in Canada, and New Zealand has formed a technical

institute system to link its community colleges with its polytechnics and technical institutes (Kintzer 1990). Japan's junior colleges and special training schools are privately supported in the main, but there is also a small system of public technological colleges. Norway's short-cycle programs are conducted through district colleges, Israel's through regional colleges, Germany's through *Fachhochschulen*, nationally coordinated but with a strong component of local governance.

The age limits for compulsory schooling affect the way community colleges are organized. In nations where the compulsory years end early, the community college may take the form of an institution offering programs that extend for 4 or 5 years. The programs in these institutions serve upper-secondary as well as early collegiate functions. But where the students are obliged to attend school for 10 years, the community colleges operate as postsecondary institutions offering prebaccalaureate, occupational, and/or leisure-oriented studies. Such programs may be of only 1 or 2 years' duration, or even shorter in the case of specific occupational-certificate programs.

The formation of community colleges usually follows the recommendations of some state or national body commissioned to study ways of accommodating the rising demand for postsecondary studies and for relevant occupational and technical training. These types of commissions were organized in numerous countries in response to the population bulge of the 1960s. During that decade, 50 community colleges a year opened in the United States. The Israeli colleges, along with those in such African countries where they have been developed, also date from that time. The colleges in Scandinavia grew out of the older, locally

Table 2
Major emphases of institutions providing community college functions

	General	Pre-university	Technical	Vocational	Cultural/Social
Australia					×
United Kingdom					×
Canada	×	×	×	×	
Denmark					×
France			×	×	
Germany					×
Greece			×		
Ireland				×	
Israel	×		×		
Japan	×	×	×	×	
Malaysia				×	
New Zealand			×	×	
Norway		×		×	
People's Republic of China			×	×	
Republic of China			×	×	
Sweden	×			×	
United States	×	×	×	×	

governed adult schools but those systems, too, have been broadened since the 1960s.

The community colleges may be integrated into a single postsecondary system that includes the universities; they may be extensions of the secondary school system; or increasingly, they may take form as separately organized postsecondary structures. Most of the community colleges in the United States are governed by state or local boards of trustees and local boards are influential in the German and Scandinavian systems. In general, the community colleges operate under state or national laws with local boards more prominent than they are in the university sector.

5. Clientele

Enrollments in each nation's community colleges vary greatly depending on the level of institutional development, especially the number of sites, and the accessibility of the universities. Since the 1970s enrollment growth worldwide has been greater in the community colleges than in the universities. In Australia and the United Kingdom, further education enrolls twice as many students as the universities. In some of the states in the United States where a campus is within reasonable commuting distance for nearly the entire population, as many as 85 percent of the students who begin higher education do so in a community college. But the proportion of postsecondary enrollment in community colleges in France, Israel, and Italy is considerably lower, principally because the universities are open to a broader range of matriculants.

The people attending community colleges tend to reflect the characteristics of the adult population in the districts where the colleges are located. Their ages range from upper teenage all the way to the most elderly, with the former concentrated in the prebaccalaureate programs and the latter in leisure-oriented education. Half the students in the United States community colleges are aged 25 or younger, and one-third of them are under age 22 (Cohen and Brawer 1989). In systems where lifelong learning is emphasized, the median student age is higher.

Most community college students attend on a part-time basis, commuting from their nearby residences. The students' aspirations and age affect their attendance patterns. The younger students, typically enrolled in vocational entry or prebaccalaureate programs, are more likely to attend full-time. Most of the older students who enroll in education for their personal interest or in occupational recertification or career upgrading courses are employed in local business, industry, or service occupations and attend part-time.

Data on the positions held by the students after they leave the community colleges are difficult to aggregate because the institutions serve as continuing learning centers with sizable numbers of students entering and leaving as their educational aspirations and life circumstances shift. Nearly one-third of the students receiving a university diploma of technology from a French IUT, and two-thirds of those obtaining associate in arts or sciences degrees from United States community colleges matriculate at universities. But these figures are misleading because most of the community college attendees do not complete the degree programs, and many of the programs in all systems lead to certificates that do not qualify the holder for university study. Similarly, the figures on job entry are unclear. Many students already hold jobs and use the colleges for further education qualifying them for advancement. The data that are available suggest that as many as 90 percent of the graduates of programs leading to positions in selective-entry fields, such as the health and engineering technologies, obtain employment, whereas as few as 20 or 30 percent of the students who are prepared as office workers or sales personnel gain immediate employment. The job market in a college's locality constitutes a major variable.

6. Finance and Facilities

The financing of community colleges is varied, ranging from full support by national governments to a majority of support coming from local communities. Many systems are funded by monies coming from a combination of sources. The pattern in the Nordic countries is for the national government to fully support the institutions, whereas in Japan tuition paid by the students accounts for a sizable proportion of the funding. Community colleges in the United States receive practically no money from the federal government except for that which is paid on behalf of students who receive federal grants and loans. Overall public community colleges in the United States receive 10 percent of their income from the federal government whereas tuition and fees account for 16 percent, local aid 17 percent, and state aid 47 percent (Cohen and Brawer 1989). The junior colleges in Japan receive 9 percent of their income from the government, 62 percent from student fees, 10 percent from endowments, and 11 percent from loans (National Institute for Educational Research 1990). In both nations, auxiliary services and private gifts and grants account for the remainder.

The cost per student per credit hour is from one-third to one-half as much as in universities, with the difference a result of many factors. The faculty in community colleges teach longer hours and are paid less, the libraries and laboratories are considerably more modest, and class size is larger on average. The tendency in most nations is for the community colleges to have limited facilities, often to have no exclusive campuses of their own. They offer courses in school buildings, in public administration facilities, and in businesses and factories, especially for the people working there. However, although the community colleges of the United States and Canada often started in such donated and rented facilities, in the early 1990s most of them now have developed full-service campuses.

7. Faculty and Staff

The community college faculty have more in common with secondary school teachers than with university professors. They rarely engage in research or scholarly publication. Their credentials may be trades experience or baccalaureate degrees for those teaching the vocational courses, and masters degrees for those teaching in prebaccalaureate programs. Some, such as the Danish folk high schools operate with noncertificated faculty. The part-time instructors in United States community colleges outnumber the full-timers by 58 to 42; just under one-fourth of the instructors hold a doctoral degree. The doctorate is even less common among community college instructors in other countries where continuing and vocational studies are more prevalent.

The faculty often have close ties with local industries or governments, working in the plants or agencies and teaching during off hours. The full-timers teach for more hours (12–20 per week) and are paid less than the university professors. The part-timers are on hourly pay scales and usually have little security of employment. Instructional innovation is encouraged and community college systems around the world rely heavily on cooperative learning, multimedia presentations, peer tutorials, and open-broadcast output, as well as on traditional classroom activities.

8. Curriculum

Each of the curricular areas—general, pre-university, technical, vocational, and cultural–social—covers a broad scope. General studies include reading, writing, and arithmetic for students who passed through the compulsory school years without being adequately prepared for life in the community, or who dropped out of secondary school before completing the requirements for a diploma. The programs may also emphasize rudimentary work habits, study skills, and personal hygiene and social practices.

The pre-university curricula feature introductory courses in the sciences, social sciences, mathematics, humanities, and fine arts, often arrayed in two-year programs leading to a university specialization. They are heavily influenced by the university faculty who often have authority over which courses are acceptable for credit toward the baccalaureate; therefore the courses rarely deviate greatly from the content and text of their university counterparts.

Technical studies apply science to the workplace.

Most of the health fields fall in this category, along with engineering, some mechanical operations, business management, information processing, and professional support areas such as laboratory technician training. In nations where teacher education does not require a bachelor's degree, those studies are provided through the community colleges.

Vocational studies prepare people for jobs in factories, offices, and farms. They center on specific workplace functions and may be provided through programs that take only a few months to complete. The type of vocational study that is offered varies with labor force demands in the college's vicinity and the programs often have direct links with local employers or labor organizations.

Cultural and social studies are provided for adults who may or may not have participated in prior postsecondary education. The courses are often presented as short, discrete offerings for a few days or months, with a focus on specific topics; for instance, child care, art appreciation, cooking, foreign languages, labor union or small business management, civic issues, and consumer education. Certificates of completion may also be awarded.

9. National Profiles

As the following profiles illustrate, the organization and operation of community colleges in the various nations takes different forms. The curricular emphases, control, and student populations are the major differences. However, the absence of a community college system or of a particular curricular function within one does not necessarily mean that the function is not offered; it may be provided by that nation's university or adult school system.

9.1 People's Republic of China

The two-year vocational or polytechnic institutions in the People's Republic of China were developed in the 1970s and 1980s, initially under World Bank financing. By 1982, 53 such institutions were in operation, offering courses in secretarial work and accountancy. Adult education through various inservice courses and two-year and three-year vocational courses presented through the universities are also provided, but the tendency is to promote more two-year vocational schools. In general, the workers' colleges provide the technologies, especially engineering, while the two-year vocational universities are directed toward local community requirements for vocational studies (Shiqi 1984) (see *China, People's Republic*).

9.2 Germany

The *Volkshochschulen* began in the nineteenth century as open-access, low-cost institutions. They now total

900 institutions offering a varied curriculum including language training for foreigners, personal interest courses in the arts and humanities, and a potpourri of courses and activities relating to local community social objectives. They tend to operate without permanent campuses, and with courses taught by part-time instructors in various types of facilities. Local governance is strong in their operation, but they are funded by a combination of state and national monies (Bogart 1985).

9.3 Japan

Japan's 561 junior colleges, 3,152 special training schools, and 62 technical colleges together enroll more than 25 percent of the students who graduate from high school. This compares with less than 19 percent who go to the universities. Women form 91 percent of the junior college students, but men form the majority of the students in the special training schools. Beginning in 1976, the latter schools have taught technologies, paramedical fields, business, accounting, and foreign languages. The junior colleges are heavily weighted toward the liberal arts, with more than 70 percent of the students majoring in humanities, home economics, or education (National Institute for Educational Research 1990). There is little transfer to the universities from either set of institutions. As compared with the universities, the colleges enroll students from the lower socioeconomic groups and their programs lead to less prestigious employment. Adult education is not featured, but is provided instead through locally organized social education centers. General vocational studies are undertaken in more than 3,000 miscellaneous postsecondary schools privately organized to offer business and health-related studies and to prepare students for the university examinations (Abe 1989) (see *Japan: Social and Adult Education*).

9.4 New Zealand

The 20 technical institutes and community colleges in New Zealand enroll 80 percent of all students in higher education in that nation. They offer short courses in business for local interest to a population comprising mainly part-time students. Certificate programs in nursing and applied sciences are also offered by a faculty made up of approximately equal numbers of full-timers and part-timers (Kennedy 1981).

9.5 Norway

The Norwegian regional colleges enroll just over 6 percent of all students in higher education in that nation. They tend to be more vocationally oriented than the universities but they do offer certain courses which can be credited toward traditional university degrees. Some 70 percent of the students are in vocational programs, and 20 percent in university preparation. Funding was originally based on local sources for buildings and national sources for operations, but the colleges have since become totally funded by the government (Kyvik 1981).

10. Trends and Issues

The worldwide expansion of postcompulsory, nonuniversity education will continue as national development, technological change in the workplace, and rising demand for further education focus attention on this sector. The major inhibitors to this expansion are competition from the universities and the lower school systems, and limitations on public finance of education. In most nations the tendency is for technological studies and vocational education to be provided at public expense while cultural and social education is often seen as a consumption item to be paid for by the participants. Free or heavily subsidized postcompulsory education for everyone on a recurrent basis is not feasible; therefore, cooperative arrangements, with financing and facilities provided in cooperation with local industries, continue to be sought so that the burden of paying for the instruction can be shared.

Issues of national planning versus local option come continually into play. In many nations the central agencies attempt to anticipate workforce needs and to encourage development of programs that prepare people in those specialty areas. At the same time, the locally based community colleges value their ability to respond to local demands on the part of industries that need especially trained workers and individuals who want access to programs of their choice. The organization of the community colleges within national education systems often conflicts with these local and individual expectations.

Within the community colleges the necessity of serving masses of people economically and sustaining curricular relevance make for continual modifications. Instructional systems that differ from the traditional labor-intensive teaching are sought and the proper training for instructors is always a concern. The amount of credit that should be awarded for work experience is an issue, along with the capacity of the institutions to maintain control over their own curricula while not jeopardizing their students' ability to transfer credits to other postsecondary institutions.

The various types of institutions that make up the community college sector in any nation present a problem of coordination. Duplicating and competing systems magnify problems of finance and articulation. The United States has publicly funded community colleges, private junior colleges, and proprietary trade schools. Japan has private junior colleges, national technological institutes, and special training schools with a strong component of local governance. The lines between France's university institutes of technology and higher technicians' sections are not clearly drawn. And within every nation institutional drift occurs continually as the local colleges become regional, the specialized institutes become comprehensive, and the competition for students and funding leads all of them to organize new programs continually.

The community college sector attempts to retain its flexibility so that it can respond to changing student populations and labor force demands. But this flexibility and the absence of familiar academic degrees results in the public's holding a murky view of what the institutions are. Institutional evaluation is often misguided because traditional paradigms of educational research focus on degree attainment and students' cognitive learning developed through sequentially organized programs, neither of which is a feature of community college education.

In the nations where the community colleges have not developed, studies repeatedly point to the need for some type of institution to perform the functions that could be provided by this sector. In Italy, for example, where the universities have been open to all petitioners, the need for two-year vocational programs and other types of intermediate diploma-related activities is apparent. In the United Kingdom, where the proportion of 18-year olds entering higher education continually expands each year, the case for an increase in the number of two-year diploma courses and for a breakdown in the barriers between the universities and the community colleges can be recognized. In general, expansion of the community college sector is assured because of rising demand worldwide for further education at reasonable cost.

See also: Lifelong and Continuing Education; Recurrent Education; Third-age Students in Higher Education; Providers of Adult Education: An Overview; Adult Tertiary Education

References

Abe Y (ed.) 1989 *Non-university Sector Higher Education in Japan.* Hiroshima University Research Institute for Higher Education, Hiroshima

Bogart Q J 1985 The community college and the Volkshochschule: An international comparison of leadership objectives in the adult teaching/learning process. Paper presented at the Annual National Convention of the American Association of Community and Junior Colleges, San Diego, California

Cohen A M, Brawer F B 1989 *The American Community College,* 2nd edn. Higher Education Series. Jossey-Bass, San Francisco, California

Kennedy P J 1981 *New Zealand: A Study of the Educational System of New Zealand and a Guide to the Academic Placement of Students in Educational Institutions of the United States.* World Education Series. American Association of Collegiate Registrars and Admissions Officers, Washington, DC

Kintzer F C 1990 Education for employment: An international perspective. *Higher Educ. Eur.* 15 (4): 97–104

Kyvik S 1981 *The Norwegian Regional Colleges: A Study of the Establishment and Implementation of Reform in Higher Education.* Studies in Research and Higher Education. Norwegian Research Council for Science and the Humanities, Oslo

Ministry of Education, Taiwan 1990 *Educational Statistics of the Republic of China, 1990.* Ministry of Education, Taipei

National Institute for Educational Research 1990 *Basic Facts and Figures About the Educational System in Japan.* National Institute for Educational Research, Tokyo

Shiqi H 1984 On some vital issues in the development and reform of higher education in the People's Republic of China. Paper presented at the World Congress on Comparative Education, Paris

Further Reading

Assefa A M 1988 *France: A Study of the Educational System of France and a Guide to the Academic Placement of Students in Educational Institutions of the United States.* World Education Series. American Association of Collegiate Registrars and Admissions Officers, Washington, DC

Dennison J D, Gallagher P 1986 *Canada's Community Colleges: A Critical Analysis.* University of British Columbia Press, Vancouver

Furth D 1973 *Short-cycle Higher Education: A Search for Identity.* OECD, Paris

Gilliland R J 1986 Folkhighschool: The people's college of Scandinavia. *Community Tech. Jr. Coll. J.* 56(5): 22–25

Kintzer F C 1984 Short-cycle higher education: Purposes and issues. *Higher Educ.* 13: 305–28

Organisation for Economic Co-operation and Development 1985 Educational reforms in Italy. In: OECD (eds.) 1985 *Reviews of National Policies for Education.* OECD, Paris

Squires G 1987 *Education and Training after Basic Education: Organisation and Content of Studies at the Post Compulsory Level. General Report.* OECD, Paris

Distance Education

H. C. de Wolf

Distance education is encountered all over the world. It developed in response to difficulties faced in bringing traditional face-to-face education to certain students. It is offered at all levels, from primary to university, for general education, training, and retraining. Its importance is growing, partly because it meets current societal needs and partly because technological developments have widened its applicability. The number and size of institutions dedicated to distance education is increasing, and more and more conventional institutions are using techniques "borrowed" from distance education to make their own teaching more effective, efficient, or flexible.

This entry defines distance education and compares it with more traditional face-to-face education as well as open education. The history, development, use, functions, and practices of distance education are also discussed.

1. Definition

Distance education is described by a variety of labels, such as "correspondence education," "home study," "independent study," "external studies," "distance teaching," and "open learning" (Keegan 1988 p. 26). A more or less generally accepted definition of distance education is proposed by Holmberg (1990 p. 1):

> The term distance education covers the various forms of teaching and learning at all levels which are not under the continuous, immediate supervision of tutors present with their students in lecture rooms or on the same premises but which nevertheless benefit from the planning, guidance and tuition (i.e. tutoring, teaching) of the staff of a tutorial organization. Its main characteristic is that it relies on noncontiguous, i.e. mediated, communication. Distance study denotes the activity of the students, distance teaching that of the tutorial organization.

2. Distance Education versus Face-to-Face Education

The objectives for distance education often correspond to those of face-to-face education. The main difference is that distance education does not, as a rule, expect the students to attend classes at a particular place and time. Thus there usually is no face-to-face contact between the teacher and the student. The latter works with printed and/or interactive electronic study material. Should contact between the student and the teacher still be necessary, it is not normally immediate in the physical sense. Written or telephone contact is often used, as well as more modern media such as radio, television, and electronic networks. Students may receive written assignments, return the completed work to the tutor, and receive suggestions for further study through the mail or electronic networks (Keegan 1990).

Large institutions for distance education may also provide opportunities for direct contact between tutor and student, for example, in study centers. In such centers, students not only receive advice concerning the program, but can also consult tutors on specific study problems.

3. The Openness of Distance Education

The extent to which distance education is "open" may vary in a number of respects (Harris 1987, Hodgson et al. 1987). Distance education is always open, however, in the sense that establishments do not dictate where study must take place.

Some forms of distance education require that a program has to be followed at a certain pace with fixed moments of instruction and assessment. Other forms of distance education offer the student much freedom of choice not only in terms of the study venue, but also in terms of the pace, time, and composition of the study program. Thus openness can be considered in relation to both content and didactic approach. Some distance education programs set formal entry requirements for prospective students, whereas others admit all applicants. Openness can therefore also be measured in terms of accessibility.

These various forms make special demands on the type of education provided. Partly because of this, distance education in its most advanced form has become "industrialized" in how it produces and offers education. Effort is made to determine who the students are, what the study objectives are, and which resources are available. The most suitable form of distance education may then be organized in a rational way.

4. History of Distance Education

4.1 Distance Education in the Absence of Other Options

Distance education developed where face-to-face education was, for one reason or another, not feasible, for example, because certain students could not attend school. Generally, such students were given written material to study on their own, with teachers periodically checking on their progress. Assignments and directions for further study would be given immediately, either during incidental contact or in writing. Advances in printing techniques and the development of textbooks greatly increased the feasibility of this approach. The emergence of efficient postal systems has enormously increased the scope for education through written communication.

The first distance education institutions were established in the latter half of the nineteenth century. These were often known as "correspondence schools." For example, correspondence schools for out-of-school children were started in Australia, where some outlying "stations" were situated a long distance from the nearest town or village. Distance education correspondence schools also developed in the more sparsely populated regions of Canada and New Zealand. Gradually, in certain densely populated areas, distance education techniques were adopted for use by schools in cases where capacity problems occurred. A recent trend is the adoption of distance education in places suffering from serious traffic congestion. In these circumstances, distance education is a supplement to face-to-face education, providing a solution to a specific problem (Evans and King 1991).

In the examples given above, distance education is regarded as a replacement for face-to-face education: the next best solution. The tendency in such circumstances is for distance education, as it struggles to be valued alongside face-to-face education, to try to emulate face-to-face education.

4.2 Distance Education as the Most Suitable Form of Education

The origin of distance education can be linked to the existence of students wishing to realize specific study objectives (i.e., gain specific qualifications or skills). For instance, for adults who did not receive a diploma when they were at school but who still want to obtain one, distance education can be second-chance education. There are also people who for professional reasons seek to update their knowledge or skills. Distance education is an efficient and effective option for this clientele.

5. Development of Distance Education

As a result of improved educational technology, distance education has become a highly efficient form of provision. It has even been described as the beginning of a "Copernican revolution" in education (Moore 1988 p. 68). The "next" educational world no longer revolves around teachers, teaching programs, and educational materials, but around students, their study objectives, circumstances, prior knowledge, and the learning experiences that are designed accordingly. Development toward such a future began approximately 30 years ago.

During the first half of the twentieth century, distance education was generally nothing more than the dissemination of letters and eventually printed materials. Eventually, especially during the 1960s, distance education began the transformation into an authentic and advanced form of education. The impetus for this change came from different factors, for example, technological development and the establishment of open universities throughout the world. During the 1960s, the view became widespread in the developed countries that universities should admit a wider group of students. This was driven not only by a desire for equal opportunities, but also by a belief that modern societies need large numbers of highly educated people. Many adults had not experienced secondary or higher education in their youth and could not be expected, at their age and position in life, to be able to enter conventional universities, or to wish to do so. Consequently, open universities were set up. Being universities, they

tended to enjoy a high status. Established at a time when radio and television were already widespread and set up as national institutes in a number of countries, the open universities were an influential factor in the development of distance education. In recent years, distance education is increasingly seen as an effective way of meeting the rising demand for adult education and continuing vocational education.

6. Distance Education: Provision

6.1 Primary Education

Distance education has been used in primary education for many years, especially in sparsely populated areas, for children living great distances from schools. In many cases, it is organized by traditional schools which provide first and foremost face-to-face education. Printed material, telephone or radio contact, and occasionally computers are used in the educational process. Parents are sometimes called upon to help supervise their children's study. Much emphasis is put on giving children the impression that they belong to a real school with a teacher who feels a responsibility toward them. A recent example of distance education at the primary level for adults is the ACPO (*Accion Cultural Popular*) program in Colombia. It was the first of many radio school systems in Latin America with courses covering the whole primary curriculum (Young 1990 p. 184). Radio schools combine daily radio programs with printed materials and group discussions (see *Adult Basic Education*).

6.2 Secondary Education

The situation for secondary education is very similar to primary education. However, in addition to the schools described above, there are also institutions offering distance courses to adults unable to attend face-to-face education courses. These courses tend to rely on printed materials, solitary telephone contact, group telephone classes, and occasionally computers. Some countries organize radio and television courses for adults seeking a secondary education. Such programs are popular in Asian countries (Asian Development Bank 1987) (see *Adult Secondary Education*).

6.3 Tertiary Education

At the tertiary level, distance education is dominated by open universities. While they continue to offer a second chance for a degree, they are increasingly offering training and retraining courses. In doing so, they keep in step with the learning society. Distance education courses are also offered by traditional universities and colleges to both part-time and full-time students facing difficulties in attending lessons. Staff shortages and accommodation problems also motivate institutions to use distance education in place of face-to-face education (Reddy 1988) (see *Adult Tertiary Education*).

6.4 Continuing Education and Training

At all levels, distance education is frequently used for continuing education and training, for example, teacher training. In certain developing countries, for example, Guyana and Zimbabwe (Brophy and Dudley 1990, Gatawa 1990 p. 99), a new generation of teachers able to educate the populace on a higher professional and cultural level has been trained using distance education (see *Lifelong Learning and Continuing Education; Technical and Vocational Education and Training*).

6.5 A Systems Perspective

Most institutions offering distance education are integrated into national education systems. This means not only that much of the finance comes from public sources, but also that many courses lead toward qualifications that fit into the national system. Government control of course content and public monitoring of the educational process are other consequences. This, however, is not always the case. Much distance education is private and does not necessarily involve officially recognized qualifications.

7. Functions of Distance Education

Distance education methods were initially very similar to face-to-face education methods. Gradually, however, it became clear that distance education was different and demanded other didactic approaches (Holmberg 1989). In face-to-face education, the essential functions are united in the teacher, who instructs, guides, and assesses groups of students within a curriculum framework. In distance education these tasks are separate. Indeed, the division of such tasks is not only different from the teacher's point of view, but also from the student's. The essential educational functions in an institution offering distance education may be divided into three groups: developing and producing programs and courses; advising and guiding students; and evaluating study results and awarding certificates, diplomas, and other qualifications.

Each of these functions may be considered as a subsystem; the first dealing with courses—covering their design, development, production, and distribution. The second subsystem concerns the students, and covers admission, the allocation of students to courses, counseling, the assessment of students, and certification. The third subsystem evolves around resources —information, finance, staff, and equipment. Taking these three subsystems or functions as a basis, one can examine distance education in theory and practice, as is done below.

8. Distance Education in Practice

8.1 Programming

Distance education programs are developed via the following stages. First, consideration is given to the choice of disciplines and disciplinary orientations in which education is to be offered. Second, in deciding whether or not to opt for distance education, consideration is given to the feasibility of recruiting capable staff. Third, decisions are made with respect to the preferred type of final objective, the certification system, and the diplomas to be awarded. Should, for example, the diplomas be similar to those awarded by conventional institutions or should they recognize specific areas of competence associated with a particular profession? Fourth, a choice is made between fixed programs spread over one or several years, on the one hand, and an approach based on modules that can be strung together in various ways to form study programs leading to a diploma, on the other. Much of today's secondary and tertiary distance education is modular in orientation. Course length varies from several weeks to several months, and courses are designed to allow students to follow, either simultaneously or consecutively, other courses. A student may follow a degree program or may take single courses. A last important decision concerns the choice of the media to be used. Some distance education institutions are primarily purveyors of printed education. Others concentrate on radio, television, or newer, more interactive, media.

8.2 Course Development

As soon as programs have been decided upon, courses have to be developed (Parer 1989). Distance education courses may consist of printed material, electronic courseware, distance instruction via interactive or noninteractive media, and distance or face-to-face guidance. This is referred to as the "media mix." Many establishments prioritize the media in the order listed above. Printed material is included as a matter of course. Electronic media are used wherever possible and suitable, usually in situations where printed materials fall short of reaching a prescribed objective. Direct contact between students and tutors is minimal, and used only when "all else fails."

There are, however, establishments that take a different line. The distance education department at Empire State College in the United States makes extensive use of direct, albeit telephone, contact between mentors and students. Other institutions place great emphasis on radio and television lessons, with less attention being given to printed self-study materials.

The difference between study materials for distance

education and those for traditional education is that the former are developed to enable students to learn without direct teacher support or prior introduction in a lesson, whereas the latter rely upon direct study assistance. Printed materials for distance education thus have to include guidelines for study, self-tests, explanations and examples to ensure accessibility, and sufficient study stimuli. With face-to-face education, these aspects tend to be provided primarily by the teacher.

The way in which the materials are developed depends upon the designated level of education to be reached, the quality requirements, and on the extent of face-to-face contact that can be realized. An institution seeking to be much like its counterparts is more likely to give content experts—who will be viewed as teachers—the freedom to choose or develop materials themselves. Where this is not the case, course development is more likely to be placed in the hands of educational technologists and content experts.

8.3 *Curriculum Materials and Didactic Approaches*

In recent decades, a great deal of high quality printed materials have been developed for distance education. However, the content, methods, and didactic approaches used in these materials differ widely. One can distinguish among three basic variants. The first is the integrated course model in which the content and the didactic approach are interwoven, and where the student makes staged progress through a series of small units. In a second variant, which is common in higher distance education, a textbook or other thorough coverage of the subject-matter is accompanied by a study guide which helps students in organizing their studies. A third, even simpler variant consists of a reading list accompanied by study directions.

The first option allows the institution to achieve a maximum amount of guidance in the materials. The content and the didactics are interwoven throughout the materials and it is difficult for the student to make use of one while disregarding the other. In the second, the didactics and the content are divorced from each other. Although it is possible to attempt to exert an equal amount of guidance here as in the former, both in quantity and quality, the fact that the guidance in this variant is physically separate from the content makes it easier for the student to choose his or her own study strategy. The third variant offers the student the greatest amount of freedom in that the instructions are often of a more general, strategic nature than those encountered in the other two. The students are more or less forced to seek their own way through the materials.

The choice of one or another of these approaches depends on both didactic and nondidactic factors. An example of the former could be the wish to reduce the extent of explicit study guidance, so that students "learn to learn." Courses for beginning students might use the first, interwoven variant; intermediate courses the second, divorced option; and advanced courses the third, more strategic approach. Examples of nondidactic factors are time and money. If constraints beset these factors, then an institution might opt for the second or third variant, both of which often require less time and resources than the first.

8.4 *Evaluating the Quality of Study Materials*

Because study materials play such an important role in distance education, a great deal of attention is paid to their development, production, and evaluation. In consequence, the quality of distance education is generally high.

Quality control is inherent in distance education, since all aspects of the learning process are carefully considered. Before course development is begun, much effort goes into designing the methods, coverage, and presentation of the subject matter. Distance education is moreover always on public display. There is no teacher operating behind closed doors providing education without a check as to its quality. Another important factor is the "market" for adult education. Heavy investment in study materials can only be recovered by large student enrolment. Thus the providers of distance education are obliged to provide a quality product to win customers. The quality of distance education is further enhanced by the wish to establish parity of esteem with other, more traditional institutions. Distance education tends to try to shake off its "second best" image by producing first-rate study materials. Furthermore, the design of distance education material often depends on the cooperation and involvement of a team of many people, such as authors, the chairperson, and educational technologists. It also depends on developmental testing with sample populations of prospective students. Since the development of distance education materials usually occurs in stages, testing can be done stepwise.

One type of developmental testing is the testing of first draft materials. The materials are far from "finished," but give a fairly good idea of what the final materials will contain, and which didactic method may be pursued. The goal of first draft testing is to discern whether a chosen, sometimes novel, didactic approach or content structure actually works. If a course team identifies major problems at this stage, the necessary adjustments can readily be made. Subsequent to this comes final draft testing. The materials bear a great resemblance to the final materials with respect to content, didactics, and form (thanks to desktop publishing). This form of testing is used to rid materials of smaller, yet important, problems which often go unnoticed by the course team. It is also helpful in discerning whether actual study time needed by students corresponds to the nominal study time estimated by the developers. A third type of developmental testing is experimental edition testing. Here, an experimental version of the completed manuscript, complete with all other media to be used, including tutor guidance, is made available to either the general public or a sample thereof. Tutors often function to log the problems that need to be revised by the course team after the experimental version is released. This form of testing is much more laborious than the previous two, and increases the duration of the developmental process greatly.

In addition to newly developed materials, already existing materials (e.g., textbooks) can also be scrutinized to determine whether these can be used for distance education. This type of developmental testing yields information both on the suitability of the material, and on the amount and type of extra study guidance that may be needed in a distance education setting.

8.5 Electronic Media and Distance Education

Distance education has long experimented with a variety of electronic materials and media (Bates 1990, Mason and Kaye 1989). Radio and television courses exist all over the world, many of which form part of distance education programs. The instructive value of radio and television programs is questioned in developed countries. Their usefulness is limited because they are transmitted at fixed, often unfavorable, times. Another problem is that the students can only listen or watch—they are mostly passively involved. Experience has shown that the primary function of television courses is to make people aware that a given subject area exists and that they can learn more about it by following a course at a certain institution. In less-developed countries with widely dispersed populations, the radio tends to be more important. Indonesia is a good example. There, the spoken word is more important than the printed word. The country has a surfeit of portable radios and a dearth of good printed materials, telephone links, televisions, and computers.

The situation for audio and video differs somewhat from that of radio and television. Audiocassette recorders are available all over the world, so frequent use is made of them in distance education. Video recorders tend to be commonplace mainly in developed countries. This is less true of videodisc equipment, although it is attractive from a didactic viewpoint. The advantage of videodisc technology, backed up by computer software, is that it facilitates the use of interactive materials.

Computers are gradually beginning to play a greater role in all education. When it comes to making use of computers, distance education does not lag behind other forms of education. Computer-aided instruction is common in distance education. Students without access to computers at home can often make use of those provided in the study centers. It may be argued, however, that this is contrary to the basic principle of distance education, which holds that students should be able to study at home or at some other place of their own choice. Computer networks offer many new opportunities for distance education. In practice, however, this type of technology tends to be used mainly in developed countries and mostly for students in higher education courses who already have an independent income.

8.6 Production and Distribution of Courses

In all forms of distance education, the actual production and distribution of course materials are possibly the most important operational considerations once the materials have been developed. Some institutions, particularly open universities and those providing printed materials for adult education, work with attractive but expensive publications. Others make do with textbooks produced elsewhere, accompanied by simply type-set guidance materials. The development of desktop publishing methods has, on the whole, led to increased quality and a reduction in the time needed for production.

9. Guidance, Counseling, and Evaluation

9.1 Student Guidance

Advising and providing guidance to students is the second essential function of every distance education institution. Most open forms of distance education allow students a great deal of freedom to arrange their study according to personal preferences and possibilities. Education can therefore be regarded as student-influenced, yet guided, self-study. This presupposes that the student is able to cope with "independent learning." The absence of a teacher providing direct leadership in the educational process requires the student to be independent. Because distance education allows considerable freedom and does away with permanent direct contact between teacher and student, it is often more suitable for adult education than adolescent or child education. Distance education is only appropriate for children when special measures are taken, for example, that decision-making and guidance be made the responsibility of adults. In practice, only fairly "closed" forms of distance education are used for children, and even then only where face-to-face education is not a realistic option. Most distance education is aimed at adults.

9.2 Student Counseling

Even before students enroll, they are likely not only to need information but also advice. Institutions offering distance education generally advertise their courses and emphasize the quality of the education they provide. Study advice is subsequently provided via the most convenient channels, usually post and telephone. As previously mentioned, large institutions, such as open universities, also tend to have study centers which fulfill a number of functions, including providing advice to students. However, students of many smaller institutions seeking help with their studies can only do so in person at the organization's headquarters. The fewer the entry requirements imposed, the more important the study advice becomes. If prior educational qualifications are required, students can by and large decide for themselves whether they can expect to cope with the course they consider. Many institutions, however, are open in the sense that anyone who wants to enroll may do so. It is therefore important to determine the student's prior knowledge and study skills. It is no coincidence that distance education institutions take much trouble to develop and implement entry tests for students to assess their prior skills and experience.

Study guidance falls into a number of general categories. In some places, every student has access to the services of a mentor. A mentor is someone who follows students' progress throughout the duration of their studies. A mentor is not only available for consultation on subject-related topics, but also takes the initiative to guard and encourage the students' progress, for instance, by seeking contact whenever the student is in danger of falling behind. Other institutions employ both counselors, who provide general advice whenever needed, and tutors, one for each course, whom students may approach if study problems are encountered. Another approach involves having an expert teacher for each course and leaving it largely to them to decide how best to guide students toward attaining their objectives.

9.3 Formative and Summative Evaluation

Students in distance education are, to a considerable extent, left to their own devices. Thus it is important that they know whether they progress with their studies. Because there is no teacher present to ascertain that progress takes place, the students need to be able to test themselves. Consequently, many distance education materials feature progress tests (formative evaluation). Some distance education institutions also give students the opportunity, or even require them, to complete one or more assignments during a course which are then assessed by someone within the institution. The way in which the examination system (summative evaluation) in distance education is organized depends to a great extent on whether the program has a face-to-face counterpart. In this case, there are likely to be rules to ensure that examinations and diplomas are equivalent to those provided by these counterparts.

10. Conclusion

There are substantial differences between distance education and face-to-face education in the organization of duties and responsibilities. In face-to-face education the teachers are central; they not only instruct as experts on the subject, but also guide students through their studies and assess their achievement. In distance education, instruction, guidance, and assessment are either provided through the materials or at a distance by specialists. This requires another type of logistic management. The possibilities often depend on the financial arrangements. In face-to-face education the principal costs are for teachers and equipment, including accommodation. More students require more teachers, more classrooms, and more equipment. In distance education the main cost is incurred for course development. Once the course is ready, duplication and distribution is relatively inexpensive. The intake capacity of distance education is therefore great, with the average cost per student falling as their numbers rise. This is why distance education tends to be used when student numbers are high, and why conventional establishments sometimes (must) adopt distance education techniques.

Influenced by the recent, rapidly growing importance and availability of information-technology a convergence of face-to-face education and distance education can be seen. Institutions dedicated to face-to-face education are discovering that the educational approach intrinsic to distance education and its accompanying organizational structure provides experiences and expertise useful for innovating their own educational system with respect to both the redesign of its tasks and the responsibilities of its employees and students. At the same time, institutions for distance education are confronted with the new and existing possibilities of real time contact between teachers and students at a distance and new techniques of developing, producing, and exploiting course materials (Lockwood 1995). Face-to-face education and distance education are merging and a new generation of the latter is coming into existence.

See also: Educational Technology in Distance Education; Evaluation of Industry Training: Cost-Effectiveness; Open University; Experiential and Open Learning

References

Asian Development Bank 1987 *Distance Education*, vols 1–3. Asian Development Bank, Manila
Bates A W (ed.) 1990 *Media and Technology in European Distance Education. Proceedings of the EADTU Workshop on Media, Methods, and Technology.* Open University Press for the European Association of Distance Teaching Universities, Milton Keynes
Brophy M, Dudley B 1990 Emergency Science Programme, Guyana. In: Koul B N, Jenkins J (eds.) 1990

Evans T, King B (eds.) 1991 *Beyond the Text: Contemporary Writing on Distance Education*. Deakin University Press, Geelong

Gatawa B S M 1990 The Zimbabwe Integrated National Teacher Education Course, Zimbabwe. In: Koul B N, Jenkins J (eds.) 1990

Harris D 1987 *Openness and Closure in Distance Education*. Falmer Press, Lewes

Hodgson V E, Mann S J, Snell R 1987 *Beyond Distance Teaching—Towards Open Learning: The Society for Research into Higher Education*. Open University Press, Milton Keynes

Holmberg B 1989 *Theory and Practice of Distance Education*. Routledge, London

Holmberg B 1990 *Perspectives of Research on Distance Education*, 2nd edn. Zentrales Institut für Fernstudienforschung, Hagen

Keegan D J 1988 On defining distance education. In: Sewart D, Keegan D, Holmberg B (eds.) 1988

Keegan D J 1990 *The Foundations of Distance Education*, 2nd edn. Routledge, London

Lockwood F (ed.) 1995 *Open and Distance Learning Today*. Studies in Distance Education. Routledge, London

Mason R, Kaye A (eds.) 1989 *Mindweave: Communication, Computers, and Distance Education*. Pergamon Press, Oxford

Moore M 1988 On a theory of independent study. In: Sewart D, Keegan D, Holmberg B (eds.) 1988

Parer M S 1989 *Development, Design and Distance Education: A Project Initiated at the Thirteenth World Congress of the International Council for Distance Education* Centre for Distance Learning, Gippsland Institute, Churchill

Reddy G Ram 1988 *Open Universities: The Ivory Towers Thrown Open*. Sterling, New Delhi

Young M 1990 Accion Cultural Popular, Colombia. In: Koul B N, Jenkins J (eds.) 1990

Further Reading

Asian Association of Open Universities 1989a *Proceedings of the Round Table Conference on Distance Education for South Asian Countries, November 6–8, Islamabad*. Asian Association of Open Universities, Nonthaburi

Asian Association of Open Universities 1989b *Proceedings of the Seminar on Open Universities of Asia: Problems and Prospects, November 10–11, Allama Iqbal Open University, Pakistan*. Asian Association of Open Universities, Nonthaburi

Doerfert F et al. 1989 *Short Descriptions of Selected Distance Education Institutions*. Zentrales Institut für Fernstudienforschung, Hagen

Harry K 1991 Distance education: A survey of the current literature. *British Book News* (April): 230–35

Holmberg B 1981 *Status and Trends of Distance Education*. Lector, Lund

Koul B N, Jenkins J (eds.) 1990 *Distance Education: A Spectrum of Case Studies*. Kogan Page, London

Moore M G, Clark G C (eds.) 1989 *Readings in Distance Learning and Instruction*. Pennsylvania State University, University Park, Pennsylvania

Ross H P 1990 *Open Learning and Open Management: Leadership and Integrity in Distance Education*. Kogan Page, London

Peters O 1973 *Die didaktische Struktur des Fernunterrichts, Untersuchungen zu einer industrialisierten Form des Lehrens und Lernens*. Beltz, Weinheim

Sewart D, Keegan D, Holmberg B (eds.) 1988 *Distance Education: International Perspectives*. Routledge, London

Folk High Schools

L. Arvidson and B. Gustavsson

This entry deals with the folk high schools in four of the Nordic countries—namely Denmark, Finland, Norway, and Sweden. Folk high schools in Poland are also considered. The first folk high school was founded by N F S Grundtvig in Denmark in the mid-nineteenth century. Since then many changes have taken place.

Folk high schools now offer general civic and political education as well as vocational education and preparation for higher studies. In many countries, folk high schools receive government grants, above all to cover tuition costs. Despite public funding, the schools are not bound by strict regulations as to the content of their educational program and the recruitment of students and teachers.

The term "folk high school" denotes a normal-ly residential college offering nonformal, mainly nonvocational, usually full-time and long-term adult education courses. The term gives rise to various misunderstandings. The folk high school differs from the high schools existing, for example, in the United States which offer a formal education to adolescents and young adults. They also differ from the German *Volkshochschulen* which offer both formal and nonformal adult education, often on a part-time basis. (The Nordic folk high school is in Germany a *"Heimvolkshochschule."*) In some countries other terms have been introduced. "Folk schools" is used in the United States. Folk high schools are known as "popular universities"—*Uniwersytety Ludowe*—in Poland, and in Tanzania the term "folk development college" has currency.

Table 1
Characteristics of folk high schools

Country	Founding year of first folk high school	Number of schools in 1991	Number of students in 1991[a]	Lowest age of admission
Denmark	1844	101	14,000	17½
Norway	1864	84	6,700	17
Sweden	1868	132	20,000	18
Finland	1889	93	6,100	16
Poland	1900	—	—	—

a In long-term courses (16 weeks or more)

1. Historical Background

The following paragraphs describe the historical development of the Nordic folk high school, and present some basic traits that are common to folk high schools in different countries. Some important differences between folk high schools in Denmark, Finland, Norway, Sweden, and—of interest especially for ideological reasons—Poland are pointed out.

Denmark is generally regarded as the originator of the folk high school, and Nikolaj Frederik Severin Grundtvig (1783–1872) as its founder. There are good reasons for this, since Grundtvig was the first to present the idea of a "people's high school." However, the Dane Christian Kold was the man to implement the idea.

Grundtvig was a Lutheran pastor, poet, politician, and eminent personality in Danish culture during the nineteenth century. The key concepts in his enthusiastic endeavor to create the folk high school were "*folkelighed*" (rootedness in the spirit of the people) and "*Livsoplysning*" (enlightenment for life). The implication is that the studies have to start from the people's own life conditions and experiences. Their local culture and their own language, not classic culture and Latin, ought to be at the center of all educational work. The great importance Grundtvig attributed to Danish culture has its explanation in the fact that Denmark had been at war with its southern neighbor, and that, as a result, German had been the official language in some parts of historical Denmark. In spite of many changes, Grundtvig's original ideas still have much currency. In Denmark, Norway, and Finland several folk high schools characterize themselves as Grundtvigian. There are about 30 such schools in Finland (Slumstrup et al. 1983).

Grundtvig's ideas were not equally important in all countries where folk high schools were established. Nor were they the sole basis for all folk high schools in Denmark. As Borgen (1981) rightly observes, "Grundtvig's ideas can be sown like seeds and grow elsewhere, but they cannot be directly transferred to other countries." This observation is strongly supported by the fact that folk high schools in the other Nordic countries differ from the Danish folk high school in many respects, even though the first schools in these countries were founded rather soon after the development began in Denmark. Table 1 shows the founding year of the first folk high school in each of the Nordic countries and Poland. The number of schools and students enrolled in 1991 is also indicated.

2. Situation at Present

A common feature of folk high schools in the Nordic countries is that their educational work is not regulated by curricula established by the public authorities. Yet in Scandinavia public financial support is given not only to cover teachers' salaries, but also for school buildings. These grants are secured by special laws or acts. Furthermore, the students can receive government grants and loans. Swedish folk high schools also receive substantial financial assistance from the regional and local education authorities.

2.1 Denmark

The Danish folk high schools are characterized by a great variety of courses, differing in duration as well as content. Mostly the courses last for between four and six months, beginning in January or August. They aim at providing nonformal and general adult education (noncredit courses). The number of courses of brief duration is growing. Some schools promote specializations such as languages, music, art, and "social pedagogy," thus creating courses with a particular profile. Other folk high schools may train youth and sports leaders. Although there are no formal examinations, some courses qualify for access to regular higher education.

2.2 Norway

About 35 of the Norwegian folk high schools belong to different Christian congregations and are members of Norway's Christian Folk High School Association. The remaining 49 schools are members of the

Norwegian Folk High School Association. Almost all schools arrange (non-credit) winter courses lasting 33 weeks. All of them are residential schools, and most teachers live on the premises. Both practical and theoretical subjects are optional. A number of schools have advanced courses designed for participants with university or other higher education.

2.3 Sweden

In Sweden, the folk high school teachers and, during the last decades, their trade union, have traditionally exercised a decisive influence on the development of popular education. More than half the folk high schools in this country are owned by the so-called "popular movements", and most of the remaining schools by county councils. Most schools have residential facilities, but typically only half of the students live there. Some schools are even "day folk high schools," with no residential facilities. To qualify for government support, a folk high school must arrange at least one general course lasting for 30 weeks (alternatively 15+15 weeks). Apart from these courses, most schools offer specialized courses on subjects such as music, handicrafts, Third World problems, drama, mass media, and so forth. Some courses are equivalent to secondary education, and qualify for admission to university. A number of schools arrange a two-year course for "*fritidsledare*" (organizers of leisure time activities and youth leaders), which are considered to be equivalent to two years of university education.

2.4 Finland

Finland is a bilingual country (Finnish and Swedish), and this influences its folk high schools—four-fifths of the schools are Finnish-speaking, and the rest Swedish-speaking. All of them are residential schools, annually arranging one or more courses of 30–40 weeks duration. The schools provide general as well as vocational education, but they also offer courses following the lower- and upper-secondary curricula. Several folk high schools moreover offer special preparatory courses for higher vocational or professional education in universities.

In terms of their orientation, the Finnish folk high schools fall into three groups: Grundtvigian folk high schools, Christian folk high schools, and folk high schools run by political parties and organizations. A small number of schools are owned by municipalities.

2.5 Poland

The first Polish folk high schools were created in 1900, based on a nationalistic ideology. A greater number of schools were founded after the First World War. In the period up to 1940, some 80 agricultural schools and folk high schools were started. The Nordic inspiration is unquestionable in this period. The first translation into Polish of Grundtvig's writings was published in 1922.

After 1945, the new regime reduced the number of folk high schools to nine, and later—during the Stalinist period—to just one, which reported directly under the Communist Party. In modern Poland, different movements have reopened folk high schools and started new ones. In the early 1990s, only one group of folk high schools received government grants, namely the institutions offering leadership training to special constituencies.

The Catholic Church is planning to open folk high schools, and so are groups connected with the Solidarity Movement. A Cooperative folk high school is operating, and there are several "Sunday folk high schools," with historical and ideological links to the folk high schools of the 1920s and 1930s which were predominantly inspired by the Danish tradition.

3. General Characteristics

Folk high schools are usually institutions offering nonformal education to adults. They are independent of the school system, but not independent of government financial support. The folk high school normally enjoys freedom to decide on the general profile of the school, the orientation of its educational program, the curricula, working methods, and the recruitment of teachers and students.

Some basic traits of a common folk high school ideology can be found in different countries, although many differences exist as well. Controversy surrounds the debate on the essential questions, for example:

(a) civic education *or* vocational training?

(b) inspiration *or* instruction?

(c) the spoken word *or* the printed book as the main source?

(d) residential *or* nonresidential?

One of the main aims of the Danish folk high school was to instill in young people an appreciation of Danish and local culture. By contrast, in Sweden, "Scandinavism" was predominant at the time when the first folk high schools were founded. The folk high school became a Citizenship Training School for the sons of landowners and farmers, although the courses also offered relevant vocational training (Simon 1960, Burgman 1968). "Enlightenment" and "Revival" were other central concepts of the pioneer days of the Danish folk high school. The Swedish folk high school stressed the importance of teaching based on sound scientific knowledge. A fundamental difference between, on the one hand, the Danish and the Norwegian folk high schools, and the Swedish ones on the other, is that the former were mainly "oral," while the latter were more oriented toward books and self-education (Burgman 1968). Later on, various other methods were implemented in Sweden as in other countries (e.g., project studies and thematic studies) (Sundgren 1986).

Flexibility is one of the characteristics of the folk high school. This is one of the factors explaining the differences between folk high schools in different countries. To give just one example: in Finland, vocationally oriented courses have been of considerable importance. Danish folk high schools differ from the rest of the Nordic folk high schools by virtue of their having a greater variety. In Denmark, many folk high schools have been closed, although new ones have also appeared. In the other countries, the folk high schools have acquired a more stable, institutional character. A folk high school will rarely be closed.

The freedom of the folk high school is reflected by the variation existing within the different countries. This variety is in accordance with Grundtvig's fundamental concept "*folkelighed*." The meaning of this concept is that all activities should originate not only in the culture of one's own country, but in that of one's own province or village. Thus far, then, the development of the folk high school has followed Grundtvig's intentions.

4. Training of Folk High School Teachers

The education and training of teachers differs among the Nordic countries. Sweden has a one-year full-time university course in andragogy, didactics, and applied teaching methods. Denmark has a "Free Teacher Training College"; however, only a very limited number of folk high school teachers have attended that college. The decisive criterion for a post at a Danish folk high school lies in the candidate's personality; formal qualifications are less important. The other countries do not organize special training for future folk high school teachers. In Norway, folk high schools employ trained primary and secondary school teachers, with a differentiation in salaries according to academic qualifications.

5. Governance of Folk High Schools

The relationship between the folk high school and the government has changed in all Nordic countries during the 1980s and early 1990s. In Denmark, a new Act on the day folk high school has been adopted. It stipulates that special commissions should advise the municipal authorities, who decide on financial matters. In Finland, the folk high schools are governed by laws very similar to those governing other kinds of adult general and vocational education. In Norway, the Folk

High School Law of 1984 grants the folk high school continued independence.

In Sweden an independent Council for Nonformal Adult Education has been established to distribute the funds that Parliament has set aside for NFAE providers. Appropriations are influenced by an evaluation of the work of the folk high schools and the study associations. Each folk high school is obliged to state its aims and the objectives of its program so as to facilitate external performance assessment.

6. Trends and Developments

In Sweden, the establishment of the independent NFAE Council, entrusted with the distribution of government funds for popular adult education, can be seen as a reflection of a strong tendency in politics and society toward privatization. Another aspect of this trend are the attempts of several county authorities to hand over their folk high schools to different private groups and voluntary organizations. This situation has repercussions on the organization of the activities of folk high schools—for example, through effects on the residential character of such schools.

In Denmark, all folk high schools are residential ones. Students as well as teachers live on the premises, and the principal (or the principals, often husband and wife) have a very important part to play in the life of the school. The Danish folk high school presents itself as a "way of life."

In other countries, especially in Sweden, there is a pronounced change in the residential character of the folk high school. A considerably smaller portion of the teachers live on the school premises. A number of schools without boarding facilities have been established. And in schools with boarding, there is a trend to use it less and less. An increasing number of students live, for a major part of their studies, in their respective homes. Many schools establish day folk high schools as their branches. This change seems to have considerable influence on informal out-of-lessons learning (Svanberg Hård 1992).

Another development is that compared with the original idea of providing a *general* civic education following a more or less uniform syllabus, one can now note a great number of special courses or "courses with a special profile." The specializations may include music, sports, tourism, and bible studies, among others.

A third noteworthy change is that an increasing portion of the total folk high school courses tend to be of a brief duration, often lasting only for a few days. These courses are usually arranged in cooperation with voluntary educational organizations of different kinds, but also with municipal and other authorities, and with trade unions and employers.

Taken together, the changes mentioned above give rise to the question as to whether the traditional notion of "*folkelighed*" is losing ground to more utilitarian concepts, and whether in future people will enroll in folk high schools for reasons relating to career development rather than personal development, which used to be an important criterion.

See also: Study Circles; Europe: Nordic Countries; Community Colleges; History of Adult Education

References

Borgen S 1981 *Dialogen i voksenundervisningen.* Forlaget Forum, Copenhagen
Burgman H 1968 Folkhögskolan och den pedagogiska utvecklingen 1868–1918. In: Degerman A (ed.) 1980 *Svensk folkhögskola 100 år, del 3.* Liber, Stockholm
Simon E 1960 *Réveil national et culture populaire en Scandinavie. La genèse de la højskole nordique 1844–1878.* Scandinavian University Books. Gyldendal, Copenhagen
Slumstrup F et al. 1983 *Grundtvigs oplysnings-tanker og vor tid.* Nordiska folkhögskolerådet, Kungälv
Sundgren G 1986 *Folkhögskolepedagogik mellan myndighet och medborgare: en studie av ett forsknings- och utvecklingsarbete på fem folkhögskolor 1975–1978.* Department of Education, University of Stockholm, Stockholm
Svanberg Hård H 1992 *Informellt lärande på folkhögskola.* Department of Education and Psychology, Linköping University, Linköping

Further Reading

Berndtsson R 1992 *Det nya kortkursprojektet.* Department of Education and Psychology, Linköping University, Linköping
Borish S M 1991 *The Land of the Living. The Danish Folk High Schools and Denmark's Non-violent Path to Modernization.* Blue Dolphin, Nevada City, California
Kühn A D 1990 *Geschichte und gegenwärtige Situation der schwedischen Volkshochschule.* Eberhard-Karls-University, Tübingen
Paulston R 1980. *Other Dreams Other Schools. Folk Colleges in Social and Ethnic Movements.* University Center for International Studies, University of Pittsburgh, Pittsburgh, Pennsylvania
Rørdam T 1980 *The Danish Folk High Schools.* Danske selskab, Copenhagen
Ueberschlag G 1981 *La Folkhögskola. Etude l'évolution historique idéologique et pédagogique des écoles supérieures d'adultes en Suède 1868–1945.* University of Paris IV, Paris

Libraries as Learning Resources

B. Woolls

Libraries are repositories of important information available as learning resources for adult students, professionals, researchers, and the public at large. This entry deals with all types of libraries—academic, public, school, and special libraries—their collections and services, and the users who learn from them.

1. The Educational and Research Functions of Libraries

In the late twentieth century, libraries serve many functions, meeting the archival, educational, recreational, reference, research, and social needs of users. Public libraries are more likely to cater for modest research needs and provide for social functions, such as providing responses to short reference questions, recreational reading, and details of programs (films, colloquia.) For academic, research, and school libraries, the major purpose is to support education and research, while special libraries house research information and archives for their parent institutions or agencies.

As libraries provide for their educational and research function, learning resources are added to library collections, and information dissemination begins to meet the identified learning needs of users. Levels of study range from very basic education, including beginning literacy, to advanced study. Motivation includes simple enjoyment through to self-fulfillment or career enhancement. The media used may include a wide range of formats, such as books, magazines, microfilm, video, films, various types of recordings, and computers and their links to a variety of electronic databases or communication devices.

Learners requiring library services for their formal education or library research plans range from beginning readers to working adults, highly educated professionals, and retired persons. Those who are not completing a formal course of study may be pursuing informal or self-directed learning projects. The level of initial educational attainment and previous learning experience range from the most basic to an advanced level, including academic researchers. Librarians are faced with the difficult task of anticipating and analyzing the level of learning and the information needs

649

of the clients, as well as offering advice and guidance in the choice of the most appropriate learning resource. How well they accomplish these tasks, and the impact of the services they provide are difficult to determine.

Some studies have dealt with these questions. For example, Butler (1988) described the establishment of the Educational Advisory Services Project (EASP) in the United Kingdom in 1980 as a means to determine how public libraries offered educational guidance for their users. One finding of the study was that libraries and users placed "high value" on personal contact. In another study, Smith (1987) identified methods to improve services to meet the needs of several specific groups of library users including "serious learners engaged in sustained study, research, or self-training."

Providing learning resources to meet research and learning needs is not a new function of libraries. Allred (1985) noted that in Europe in the Middle Ages, monks used their monastic libraries to pursue their studies, and libraries during the Reformation were relied upon during the implementation of educational programs. Libraries, freely available to users, have served as information sources in times of economic and social stress, providing resources for learning and self-improvement.

Shuman (1992) suggested that when societal and economic factors in the United States limited students' attendance in formal education at an early age, the public library became "the people's university." This facility provided individuals with a place to study what they wished, when they wished, and when they had sufficient time. The possibility of freely determining the time, place, and subject has been helpful to those seeking information and knowledge. A study from the United States described literacy education as providing "learning opportunities for adults sixteen and over who are not enrolled in secondary school. The opportunities include the range from initial acquisition of basic reading ability through the threshold of functional literacy in home, work and community" (United States Office of Education 1988 p. 62).

Literacy has moved beyond the ability to read and write. Now it is necessary to become information literate. Information literacy is: "a) a survival skill in the information age, b) the ability to acquire knowledge and use it, c) the ability to find information necessary for any task or decision at hand. Who are the information literate? Those who have learned how to learn" (Pelzman 1989 p. 82). Information literacy is rapidly translating into a demand for electronic information technologies. To be truly successful in this quest, literate readers and library users demand that libraries are transformed into learning resources. Changes in technology create demands for new learning and retraining just to stay employed. Basic computer literacy for today will be outmoded tomorrow. Learning resources in libraries must help individuals understand what is being developed and how they can strive to keep up with change.

2. Libraries as Learning Resource Centers

In the early 1960s, particularly in the United States, some university and college libraries were renamed "Learning Resource Center." According to Ellison (1972), the primary functions of this kind of center were to facilitate learning by students, to supply students and faculty with resources, and to provide materials that would contribute to the curriculum and to the learning experiences of students.

These learning resource centers provided expanded services, including instructional research, evaluation of learning, course development, training services, production of instructional materials, instructional experimentation and demonstration, in addition to the library and audiovisual services that libraries traditionally had offered, such as consultation, selection, dissemination, distribution, and use of all instructional materials, information sources, and facilities. The ultimate goal was to improve student learning by helping faculty review research results and choose the best instructional methods and the most effective materials with which to teach.

The concept of learning resource centers changed the organization of information and the management of libraries from a print-only environment into one with nonprint materials and ultimately all newer technologies, including machine-readable records, database searching, CD-ROM and videodisks. Through new resources and services, librarians could help faculty review their methods of instruction and suggest more creative practices. The preparation of new learning materials, the provision of audiovisual materials and equipment to support courses, and the operation of autotutorial laboratories became one program with the existing library collection and reference services. Instructional responsibilities for the librarian expanded beyond teaching library research skills to new students.

Management of libraries changed as new types of personnel were added to existing staff. Personnel were needed whose skills included instructional design, preparation of learning materials, on-line database searching into machine readable (computer) records. Technical staff was needed to keep the hardware (equipment) functioning.

Training of staff in libraries is varied. In many countries, persons appointed to library positions are trained on-the-job. Formal training in an academic setting is given in two-year "technical" programs. Another model is the four-year program for a degree. In some countries, education for librarianship is a postgraduate experience. The expansion of information formats and the need for experienced technical staff to maintain equipment, as well as the increased skills needed for both librarians and patrons of libraries who have access to electronic information, means that the training of staff and patrons never ends. As job descriptions for staff are updated with each new technology, the retraining cycle continues. Patrons, often reluctant to accept change, must be introduced to each new form of information if they are to maximize the use of a library's learning resources.

Whether or not a library is renamed "learning resource center" or remains a "library," the education function—to facilitate learning—continues to be the major mission of all types of libraries providing learning resources for their users.

3. Information Formats for Learning Resources

Traditionally libraries have provided printed materials, books, magazines, newspapers, pamphlets, reports, maps, and microforms among other printed items. With the advent of the resource center and the expansion of audiovisual technologies, these resources expanded to include films, filmstrips, records, tapes, videotapes, three-dimensional models, and the equipment to produce even more learning materials, such as cameras, videocameras, dry mount press, and laminating machines. Since most audiovisual materials require equipment to play or project items, librarians have added acquisition and maintenance of necessary hardware to their responsibilities.

As newer technologies evolved, even more equipment was needed and most was computer-related. A new staff member, the computer technician, was added. These technologies included new and repackaged published information and new formats such as videodisks, CD-ROM, and computer software programs. Also included in these technologies were on-line public access catalogs (OPACs) replacing traditional card catalogs and allowing access to the holdings of libraries by interested users in remote locations. Computer software programs such as word-processing, database creation, and spreadsheets with dot matrix and laser printers helped create new information resources within and between libraries. Yet other computer programs required telecommunications connections including those for on-line searching capabilities, INTERNET, telefacsimile, E-mail, and bibliographic utilities.

Bibliographic utilities—that is, centers storing citations of information and records of the location of that information—assisted with the cataloging of materials and making their location and the actual items themselves accessible to all types of libraries. These machine-readable records allow users in one library to seek information from other libraries and subsequently borrow materials through interlibrary loan. Knowing electronically what is available in libraries has made it faster and easier for library users to access information.

The learning resources of libraries also include study and meeting facilities. For some users, the library represents the only place in their daily lives available for quiet study. This was a traditional characteristic of libraries, but reference areas now sometimes have banks of computers for use in the search for information.

Librarians now must provide guidance and support in the choice of the appropriate format of information from the vast array available. This has created a new challenge because the users must be made aware of the availability of a wider array of knowledge and often need to be shown how to access the information.

4. Users of Learning Resources

The users of libraries are often independent learners. In colleges and universities, students are given assignments that suggest library research, but when and how this research is conducted are dependent upon the student's motivation. They have become independent users of the library. Public librarians have always been responsible for encouraging users to take advantage of their facilities. Librarians in special libraries may also be required to "sell" their services. These independent users with lifelong learning needs may not be readily recognized as different from social users.

To be helpful in the process of identifying these learners, Fisher (1988) has provided characteristics of independent users including how they work. Such users may be individuals or in groups—a family, a club, or a community group. The place of learning may be in the library, but it can also be at home, at work, in a hospital, or elsewhere. The social or domestic situation includes persons who are students, but also those who are retired, unemployed, single, or with particular financial or family problems, or with physical disabilities. Independent learning may be for leisure, hobby or travel, or necessity, such as gaining information related to house purchase or a combination of leisure and necessity.

5. Teaching Users of Learning Resources

The need for user education has become critical with the changes in technologies. It is no longer possible for someone to use libraries effectively if all they understand is the card catalog, call number, and use of call number to locate a book on the library shelf. Communication technology provides access to information concerning the holdings of the world's library collections, and patrons are being taught to use these electronic databases so that they no longer need the intermediary librarian. Previously, because of the costs involved, trained librarians conducted on-line searching for their clients. However, CD-ROM technologies, providing similar access to information without long-distance communication costs, allow users to learn how to conduct their own searches. Training users to access these databases as well as on-line public catalogs means that instruction must be provided for all, including "technophobics" (those who resist technology). This is very different from lecturing users on finding items in the card catalog. When access to information goes beyond the library's walls, experienced print users must adapt to new formats. Encouraging those who are computer literate but unaware of the expanding resources available through the library, but not physically in the building, becomes a part of teaching information literacy.

Further, librarians must help users become discriminating in their choices of where to search and how to sift through the quantities of information they may locate. Because of the expansion of access to information, users must learn to make choices quickly from the variety of sources and resources or they can become overwhelmed by the sheer quantity of information provided in response to their queries. This additional component of information literacy is a new responsibility for librarians.

6. *Learning Resources by Types of Libraries*

Many similarities exist between types of libraries, but there are also many differences. Academic, research, and school libraries are attached to educational institutions and have as their mission the provision of learning resources to support the needs of primary users. School libraries have books to interest new readers and others trying to improve their skills in reading and comprehension so that they will enjoy reading. They also have information with which to expand classroom activities and to encourage the students to undertake independent research and learning. School library collections are usually focused on the actual curriculum being taught. Their collections vary just as the sizes of the schools vary.

Smaller technical schools and schools with two-year training programs are less likely to have the larger collections found in four-year institutions and those colleges and universities offering advanced degrees in a wide variety of fields. Resources focus on what is being taught and the numbers of students and demands of faculty in each area. A research institution with a strong fine arts component and a large number of students enrolled will collect information on artists, musicians, and literary figures, including recordings, music scores, art prints and slides. Agriculture schools or trade institutes will have information on agriculture or information on the particular trade being taught. Small liberal arts universities will have broad collections while universities with medical schools will have extensive medical collections.

Public libraries serve the public that supports them.

The term "public" library does not necessarily mean that a collection is open to all. Since they are supported by local, state, or national governments, governments may dictate use of and limit access to the collections. Public libraries usually provide collections of wide interest to match the diversity of their users. Public libraries found in larger cities are also considered to be research libraries and will have extensive reference collections on specific topics. Most public libraries serve a smaller population and they meet recreational needs as well as other information demands of their communities. When the library is in a rural area, information on agriculture and materials on operating a small business may be in heavy demand while gardening books may be more useful for clientele living in the suburbs.

National libraries house large research collections and offer access to a wealth of information. If a national government has a publishing policy, copies of each item published within the country may be deposited in the national library. National libraries may also acquire materials from other countries. Information in national libraries may be open to all as in Tokyo, Japan, where their national library, the National Diet Library, displays many of the aspects of a very large public library and is heavily used by students and others. In contrast, the British Library in London and the Library of Congress in Washington, DC, require applications from those who wish to make extensive use of the collections and only grant access to those whose needs cannot be met elsewhere.

Rules and regulations range from open access to all to very restricted access. When a library is a private institution, regulations will be established by the institution and access restricted to those paying tuition or fees for use. When school, college, university, research, and public libraries are funded by government, regulations are established by that government. Citizens of a particular state may have access by virtue of being citizens of that state.

Special libraries serving as learning resources have not yet been discussed because of their very special nature. These libraries exist in businesses and corporations and have a more commercial rather than learning role, although special collections in other types of libraries may be described as "special libraries." Having narrowly focused collections to meet the specialized needs of their users, use of specialized collections depends upon policies, established by the management of the corporation or institution to which they are attached. If the corporation housing a special library is engaged in competitive enterprise, it is likely that the library will be closed to those outside the corporation. Information being collected within the library might be a clue to the research being conducted for new products or applications for new products to market. Corporations thus limit library use to prevent discovery of their research directions.

It is doubtful that any single library has ever met

all the needs of its users. In the early 1990s the ever-increasing sources of information and the electronic methods linking information providers have greatly expanded the availability of learning resources for all.

7. Conclusion

Libraries have always been repositories of learning resources. From earliest times, they have provided access to information for scholars. The constantly increasing amount of information being generated and published, the expanding formats of information storage and retrieval, and the ever-changing education needs of library users make it difficult for any library to be an effective learning resource. Because information continues to expand and information needs continue to change, the challenge to maintain libraries as viable learning resources remains an exciting opportunity.

For example, the widespread use of electronic "E-mail", among other new forms of information sources, is changing the amount of information available to library users as well as the amount of information any library needs to store. Users are no longer concerned exclusively with where information is found, they are only interested in getting correct and complete information. If library collections can be accessed through electronic searching of the OPAC and if information can be requested for transmission through telefacsimile machine some users may not visit a library at all. Yet the need remains for a location at which to collect information so that it is available to users who need learning resources.

References

Allred J 1985 Libraries and adult education. In: Husén T, Postlethwaite T N (eds.) 1985 *The International Encyclopedia of Education*, 1st edn. Pergamon Press, Oxford

Butler L 1988 *The Role of Public Libraries in the Provision of Educational Guidance for Adults* British Library Research and Development Department, London
Ellison J W 1972 The identification and examination of principles which validate or refute the concept of college or university learning resource centers, (Doctoral dissertation, Ohio State University)
Fisher R K 1988 *Library Services for Adult Continuing Education and Independent Learning: A Guide*. Library Association Publishing, London
Pelzman F 1989 Washington observer: Information literacy —a common ground. *Wilson Library Bulletin* 63: 82
Shuman B A 1992 *Foundations and Issues in Library and Information Science*. Libraries Unlimited, Englewood, Colorado
Smith V 1987 *Public Libraries and Adult Independent Learners: A Report* Council for Educational Technology, London
United States Office of Education 1988 *Libraries and Literacy Education: Comprehensive Survey Report*. United States Department of Education, Office of Educational Research and Improvement, Library Programs, Washington, DC

Further Reading

Bender D 1980 *Learning Resources and the Instructional Program in Community Colleges* Library Professional Publications, Hamden, Connecticut
Birge L E 1979 The evolution of American public library services to adult independent learners. (Doctoral dissertation, Arizona State University)
Crawford W 1988 *Current Technologies in the Library: An Informal Overview*. Hall, Boston, Massachusetts
Krashen S 1992 *The Power of Reading: Insights from the Research*. Libraries Unlimited, Englewood, Colorado
Library Association 1980 *Adult Education and Public Libraries in the 1980s: A symposium. Papers Given at a Special Conference Organised by the Library Association on 21 February 1979*. Library Association, London
UNESCO 1990 *Compendium of Statistics on Illiteracy*. UNESCO, Division of Statistics on Education, Paris
UNESCO 1993 *World Education Report*. UNESCO, Paris

Open University

B. Holmberg

This entry discusses the open university concept and its application in various parts of the world. Although open universities rely largely—or almost exclusively —on distance education as their mode of teaching, the entry does not deal exclusively with distance education. The procedures of distance education are examined only in so far as they are relevant to open university work.

Both the independent open universities and a number of other organizations which do similar work are included. The educational characteristics, organization, evaluation and economics of open university work are analyzed. The student bodies are described and the problem of completion and dropout is discussed on the basis of empirical studies. Reference is also made to research on open university work, its organization in open universities, and to the expected development of independent open universities as well as of parallel work more closely related to the mainstream of university education.

1. The Open University Concept

The term "open university" was introduced when, under the name of the Open University, a distance-teaching university with open access was founded in the United Kingdom in 1969. The adjective "open" in this context has been variously interpreted. In modern usage distance-teaching universities are usually called open universities even if, as far as access is concerned, they are no more open than traditional universities. This applies, for example, to the *FernUniversität*, which has the same rules for student enrollments as other German universities (to be accepted as degree students applicants must have passed the *Abitur* or a corresponding university entrance examination).

However, if openness in education is taken to mean a maximum of choice and control left to the students, openness with regard not only to admission and place and time of learning, but also openness with respect to content and mode of learning, it is not in the "open universities" that its most notable examples are found, but rather in the higher education institutions which make provision for "contract learning," such as the English Polytechnic of East London and the Empire State College in the state of New York (Hinds 1987, O'Reilly 1991, Worth 1982).

It has been argued that distance education is always to some extent open as it allows students to learn when and where it suits them. Distance education, which is the principal mode of teaching and learning of open universities, is taken to cover the various forms of study which are not under the continuous, immediate supervision of teachers present with their students in classrooms but which, nevertheless, benefit from the planning, guidance, and teaching of a supporting organization. The clientele of open universities are usually adult, individual students (see *Experiential and Open Learning*).

2. The Development of Open University Systems

If distance teaching universities are regarded as open universities, the oldest open university is the University of South Africa, originally founded as an examining body (like London University) and starting teaching at a distance in 1946 (Boucher 1973). With this exception the other open universities started their work in the 1970s, 1980s, and 1990s. The Open University in the United Kingdom presented its first course in 1971.

The following are well-known open universities in 1992 (with the year when they began teaching students):

Allama Iqbaal Open University, Pakistan (1975)
Andhra Pradesh Open University, Hyderabad, India (1982)
Athabasca University, Alberta, Canada (1975)
Central Broadcasting and Television University, China (1979)
FernUniversität, Germany (1975)
Indira Gandhi National Open University, New Delhi, India (1985)
Korea Air and Correspondence University, South Korea (1982)
Kota Open University, Rajasthan, India (1987)
Kyongi Open University, South Korea (1982)
Nalanda Open University, Bihar, India (1987)
The National Open University of Taiwan (1987)
Open Universiteit, the Netherlands (1980)
The Open University, the United Kingdom (1971)
The Open University of Israel, Tel-Aviv (1976)
Ramkhamhaeng University, Thailand (1972)
Sri Lanka Institute of Distance Education (1978)
Sri Lanka Open University (1980)
Sukhothai Thammathirat Open University, Thailand (1978)
Télé-Université (part of the network of the University of Québec), Canada (1972)
Unisur (Unidad Universitaria del Sur de Bogotá), Colombia (1981)
Universidad Estatal a Distancia, Costa Rica (1978)
Universidad Nacional Abierta, Venezuela (1977)
Universidad Nacional de Educación a Distancia, Spain (1973)
Universidade Aberta, Portugal (1990)
Universitas Terbuka, Indonesia (1984)
University of the Air, Japan (1985)
University of South Africa, Pretoria (1946)
Yashwantrao Chavan Maharashtra Open University, Nashik, India (1989).

There are a number of organizations which do work similar to that of these universities and which might have been included in the list, among them:

The National Distance Education Centre, Ireland
The International University Consortium, Maryland, USA
North Island College, British Columbia, Canada
The Open Education Faculty of Anadolu University, Turkey
The Open Learning Agency, British Columbia, Canada
The Open Learning Institute of Hong Kong.

Mention should also be made of the so-called dual-mode universities with special commitments to open learning, which have spread in Australia. Since 1989 there have been eight Australian distance education centers, namely Deakin University and Monash University in Victoria, the University of New England and Charles Stuart University in New South Wales, the University College of Central Queensland and the University College of Southern Queensland, the University of South Australia, and the Western Australian Distance Education Centre (Murdoch University).

A great number of other private, state-owned, church- or foundation-financed organizations, university departments, colleges of advanced education, and schools serving open learning are active in various parts of the world. Some of them are members of national and/or multinational professional bodies, such as the International Council for Distance Education (ICDE), the Asian Association of Open Universities (AAOU), the Association of European Correspondence Schools (AECS), the European Association of Distance Teaching Universities (EADTU), the Distance Education and Training Council based in the United States, and the Open and Distance Learning Association of Australia, until 1993 called the Australian and South Pacific External Studies Association (ASPESA).

As evident from the above list of open universities some developing countries make consistent use of open university approaches to higher education. In others traditional universities use open learning methods to a limited extent, for example, in Kenya and Zimbabwe. Plans for new open universities have been developed for Southern Africa and Vietnam. Teacher training, the training of paramedics, and basic business administration are common fields of open learning activities in developing countries. Much experience of this has been gained, for example, in East Africa and Latin America.

Many open universities are very large. The British Open University and the German *FernUniversität* have student bodies of between 120,000 and 40,000 students, the French *Centre National d'Enseignement à Distance* has more than 250,000 students enrolled and the open universities in Thailand and China work with even larger numbers of students (700,000 to a million students in each of these countries).

3. Educational Characteristics of Open Universities

The application of distance education methods to open learning usually means that two components characterize the teaching of open universities: (a) the presentation of subject matter in preproduced, in most cases printed, courses; and (b) mediated interaction between students and tutors in writing (correspondence), on the telephone, or by other media. The latter is part of the student-support activities that are usually considered necessary; these also include counseling (see *Student Support Systems*).

Electronic mail and telefax are used to some extent in developed parts of the world to speed up communication. Tutor–student interaction in most open universities is also effected by supplementary face-to-face sessions, usually in regional and local study centers. However, some universities have no mediated person-to-person interaction and replace this by self-checking exercises, interaction with computer programs, and face-to-face tutorials. The Open Universiteit in the Netherlands and Unisur in Colombia are examples of this approach.

Radio, television, and satellite communication are available in many areas (not only in the developed parts of the world), and serve mass audiences. This applies to a very great extent to China, for example. While most open university students learn entirely individually there are examples of group learning. This can be—and is to an increasing extent—brought about by tele and computer conferencing (see *Group Learning*).

4. The Organization of Open University Teaching

From an organizational/typological point of view a distinction should be made between independent organizations and organizations which are part of and dependent on larger units. A third type can be described as networks. The higher education institutions called open or distance teaching universities and their foundation-owned or commercial counterparts as a rule belong to the independent type. Well-known examples of the second type are the extra-mural departments of United States and Canadian universities; so are university providers of Australian external study, and East European distance teaching. Examples of networks occur in England, Germany, and Norway.

The independent organizations decide on their own course provision and teaching methods and, if they are official universities, on their own curricula, examinations, and degrees to the extent that national regulations allow. Open learning departments of conventional universities, on the other hand, do some of the same teaching as that given face-to-face by the parent organizations. The typical open learning service of an Australian dual-mode university is run by an administrative unit which relies on regular university staff to develop courses for and teach open learning students. These students are given the same learning content, study—as far as individual courses are concerned—within the same time limits, and are examined in the same way and at the same time as regular students.

The distinction between independent organizations and those belonging to larger units overlaps with a dichotomy between large-scale and small-scale systems of distance education. The former develop large editions of each course, sometimes for several thousand students and often by team work, and engage a sufficient number of tutors (who need have nothing to do with course development) to comment on students' assignments and teach in other ways. The small-scale approach involves teachers in developing courses exclusively for their own students, so that the course writer is identical with the tutor. The large-scale organizations, as typically represented by, for example, the British Open University and the Spanish *Universidad Nacional de Educación a Distancia*, can be regarded as innovations outside the traditional educational systems. The small-scale organizations, on the other hand, find it important to keep within the mainstream of education. The Australian University of

New England in Armidale, New South Wales, is often referred to as a prototype.

The networking bodies, the third type, have co-ordinating functions and supplement the course provision of other open learning agencies. *Norsk Fjernundervisning* in Norway is an example, as is the Canadian Knowledge Network in British Columbia, which synthesizes "the experiences of open learning systems and educational television networks" (Forsythe 1982 p. 283). The German DIFF (*Deutsches Institut für Fernstudien*) at Tübingen University is a further and somewhat special kind of network. Among other things it develops courses for use by other institutions, runs a department for research on the psychology of learning, and offers a documentation service. A further example of networking is "Flexistudy," associated with the National Extension College in Cambridge, England. This term refers to flexible arrangements not only for individual learning based on preproduced course materials but also for teacher-contact time and the use of other resources.

5. Open University Students

Open university students can by no means be described as a homogeneous group. The only common factor is that these students are usually adults and gainfully employed and/or looking after their families. The 25–35 age group seems to be the largest in most open universities. The reasons why adults choose open learning are primarily the availability, convenience, flexibility, and adaptability of this mode of education to individual needs. A predilection for entirely individual work is frequently mentioned. In a Swedish study, including students at the British Open University, 63 percent of the population (about 4,000) stated their preference for working on their own at the same time as they stressed the importance of the support given by their teaching organization. Free pacing, a privilege given only to a limited extent to open university students, was mentioned as an even more important argument in favour of open learning (Flinck 1980 pp. 6–9) (see *Evaluation of Distance Education: Cost-Effectiveness*).

There are indications that open university students consider themselves independent and capable. An investigation reporting on interview studies of more than 500 *FernUniversität* prospective and enrolled students in Germany showed that these "saw themselves as more competitive, achievement oriented and assertive" than the average general population and student groups investigated. "Only small differences were found between dropouts and persisters . . .; the persisters (before enrollment) had portrayed themselves as more competent and successful in coping with academic and social demands" (Göttert 1983). Nevertheless, quite a few open university students seem to doubt their ability to cope, which necessitates intensive counseling activities (see *Student Counseling*).

6. Completion and Dropout

While some open universities have succeeded in taking most of their students to successful completion in the form of degree examinations (this is above all true of the United Kingdom Open University), it is nevertheless a fact that, on the whole, the completion rate in open learning and distance education generally is fairly low. It would not be correct invariably to regard discontinuance as a sign of failure, however, as open university courses are often used by individual students who do not declare either their ultimate goals or the period over which they intend to spread their study. Thus it is often impossibile to say for certain whether noncompletion means interruption, or dropout in the sense of failure, or if it accords with students' intentions or plans. It is also something of a problem how to regard nonstarters, that is, those who have registered as students but show no signs of actual study. "When nonstarters . . . are included among noncompleters, dropout rates around 50 percent are not unusual . . . Nonstarters are sometimes as frequent as—or even more frequent than—'real' dropouts" (Bååth 1984 p. 32).

A general characteristic is that dropout, when it occurs, usually happens at the beginning of study. It makes sense to regard the first few months of study as a trial period. The Open University in the United Kingdom requires an introductory period of study and, after this period, a reconfirmation of study intentions before a student is regularly registered. Those who drop out during the introductory period are not included in the university statistics.

Several scholarly studies of the causes of dropout and the possibilities of improving completion have been carried out (Bååth 1984, Cookson 1990; Schuemer and Ströhlein 1991). The agreement between personal interest and courses offered as well as inclinations for individual rather than collective work have been found to favor completion (Bartels 1983), as have learning matter presentation and tutor–student interaction characterized by an empathy approach (Holmberg 1989, 162 ff.). However, the only really safe general conclusion to be drawn from the studies carried out is that individual study motivation is the most decisive factor. It is evident that "neither age nor distance nor domestic environment nor any other quantifiable term stands out as a salient feature. It is motivation above all else which, despite physical and general social and environmental problems, brings success" (Sewart 1988 p. 168).

7. The Evaluation of Open University Work

The amount of prestige conferred on open universities varies a good deal. In the United Kingdom the Open University, although it has its own specific degree structure and prepares students for less specialized degrees than traditional universities, has acquired general recognition. In Germany and Spain the open universities, which apart from their use of distance education methods, are basically traditional universities, enjoy much prestige for their high standards of teaching and research. Whereas this reflects the situation in some parts of the world the situation is different in others, where open universities represent only the second best. In some countries (Thailand may be an example) open universities appear to act as safety valves by expanding the intake of higher education students and thus absorbing youths for whom there are no jobs, while traditional universities are considered more prestigious. Limitations of the opportunities for tutor-student interaction, mediated or face to face, and also pure prejudice in some countries, make politicians and educationists query the quality of open learning.

If and when weaknesses of the kind indicated occur counter measures are possible. Improvements can be brought about along the lines of well-established and successful open universities. The most successful of them all seems to be the United Kingdom Open University, which during the first 20 years of its existence produced more than 120,000 graduates.

Systematic course and systems evaluation has proved very helpful. In this context "course" denotes not only the course materials but the whole process of interaction between students and tutors, counselors, and other representatives of the teaching organization. Measurement techniques have been developed for the assessment of students' achievements and the evaluation of courses and programs. A study of the practices in this respect of 16 distance teaching organizations is given in Chia (1990). Formative evaluation investigating teaching and learning with a view to improving courses can be of decisive importance for the quality of open learning. Developmental testing of the kinds carried out at, for example, the Open University in the United Kingdom and the *FernUniversität* in Germany has exerted much valuable influence. This applies even more to an evaluation approach developed at the Open University of Israel (based on Guttman's facet theory which is well known to statisticians). "Specification of course content and its instructional objectives in 'course maps' served as a basis for preparing a teaching syllabus, establishing a computerized bank of questions and assessing all course components" (Ganor 1990 p. 80). The information thus collected is used as a foundation for staff development.

8. The Economics of Open Universities

Open universities differ in the ways they work and thus in their economy. The United Kingdom Open University includes the use of television and radio for its teaching, whereas the German *FernUniversität* does so only marginally. Both these universities run a number of study centers where students are offered tutorials and various media facilities. This type of service is not provided everywhere. Some open universities and other higher education institutions offering open learning facilities make use of the telephone for oral tutorials, whereas others do not. Some make use of advanced information technology; others limit themselves to presenting learning matter in print and interacting with students by written correspondence. In the Australian New England system parallelism with on-campus study has gone so far as to include the same student-staff ratio as conventional university teaching. This makes for a financial situation which is very different from that of large-scale open universities, which produce courses in large editions and use various kinds of technology, labor-saving devices, and division of labor to attain economies of scale.

The economics of open universities and similar organizations have been subjected to a series of careful investigations (see Rumble 1986, Keegan 1990). A safe conclusion is that open university teaching is characterized by very favorable cost-benefit relations if the distance education element consistently predominates. It is primarily arrangements for face-to-face sessions (study centers, residential schools, and classes of various kinds) and to some extent the use of very sophisticated technology, that may modify the validity of this statement. Nevertheless, the average cost per graduate in the United Kingdom Open University, which makes extensive use of both study centers, other face-to-face facilities, and advanced technology, is below half of that at conventional universities (Wagner 1977 p. 365).

9. Research on Open University Work

Some kind of institutional research occurs at most open universities and other organizations offering open learning facilities in higher education. This institutional research is usually combined with course evaluation. Investigations of more general conditions of open learning, development and testing of theories relevant to open university work, and studies on media and methods are continuously being carried out at some open universities. The German *FernUniversität* and the Dutch Open University have both an institute for institutional research, evaluation, and development work serving the disciplinary faculties and an independent institute for research on distance education and open learning. Much scholarly literature on the subject has been published although it is fairly new area of research. A selective bibliography lists some 1,500 titles divided into 36 specific areas of study (Holmberg 1990). There is an International Centre for Distance Learning based at the United Kingdom Open University which collects and disseminates information worldwide using two computerized databases.

10. The Future

There is a strong tendency toward further growth. New open universities and other new applications of open university principles are constantly being discussed or planned in most parts of the world. To what extent new activities will tend to develop along the lines of the independent large-scale open universities or move in the direction of the mainstream of university education is uncertain. The same uncertainty prevails as to some of the present open university activities. The two opposite approaches reflect an ideological issue as to student autonomy and respect for the individual student's predilections on the one hand and the appreciation of social elements (personal meetings, and peer-group interaction) and of traditional teacher-student relations on the other hand. This is related to an early discussion as to whether open learning and distance education represent a mode of education in its own right or is merely a substitute for conventional education when "regular" teaching is not available. The former view was developed as early as 1973 in an analysis of distance education as an industrialized form of teaching and learning (Peters 1989). For discussions of these issues see Garrison (1989), Holmberg (1986, 1989 p. 150 ff.), Peters (1989), Smith and Kelly (1987).

Most probably the future will see a further strenghtened open university movement with applications of different kinds stressing to varying degrees the values and views indicated.

Considering the relative newness of open universities further research on practically every point is desirable. This includes instructional design, mediated student-tutor interation, the potentials of modern information and communication technology and organizational-administrative concerns as well as theory building and the testing of possible predictive theories.

See also: Distance Education; Educational Technology in Distance Education; University Adult Education; Evaluation of Distance Education: Cost-Effectiveness

References

Bååth J A 1984 Research on completion and discontinuation in distance education. *Epistolodidaktika* 1–2: 31–43

Bartels J 1983 *Studienabbrecher.* FernUniversität, ZFE, Hagen

Boucher M 1973 Spes in Arduis—A history of the University of South Africa. University of South Africa, Pretoria

Chia N 1990 Measurement techniques in distance education: Definition, classification, characteristics, selection and application. *Epistolodidaktika* 2: 51–93

Cookson P S 1990 Persistence in distance education—a review. In: Moore M G (ed.) 1990 *Contemporary Issues in American Distance Education.* Pergamon Press, Oxford

Flinck R 1980 The research project on two-way communication in distance education: An overview. *Epistolodidaktika* 1–2: 3–10

Forsythe K 1982 Knowledge network—a new hybrid for learning systems. *Distance Educ.* 3(2): 283–92

Ganor M 1990 On the structure of evaluation at a distance. In: Croft M, Mugridge I, Daniel J, Hershfield A (eds.) 1990 *Distance Education: Development and Access.* International Council for Distance Education (ICDE) Universidad Nacional Abierta, Caracas

Garrison D R 1989 *Understanding Distance Education. A Framework for the Future.* Routledge, London

Göttert R 1983 Fernstudieninteressenten. Ihr Selbstbild und weiterer Studienverlauf. ZIFF-*Papiere* 47 Fern Universität, Hagen

Hinds E 1987 The school for independent study and international links. ZIFF-*Papiere* 69 FernUniversität Hagen

Holmberg B 1986 *Growth and Structure of Distance Education.* Croom Helm, London

Holmberg B 1989 *Theory and Practice of Distance Education.* Routledge, London

Holmberg B 1990 *A Bibliography of Writings on Distance Education.* FernUniversität, ZIFF, Hagen

Keegan D J 1990 *Foundations of Distance Education.* Routledge, London

O'Reilly D 1991 Developing opportunities for independent learners. *Open Learning* 6(3): 3–13

Peters O 1973 *Die didaktische Struktur des Fernunterrichts. Untersuchungen zu einen industrialisierten Form des Lehrens und Lernens.* Tübinger Beiträge zum Fernstudium 7 Beltz, Weinheim

Peters O 1989 The iceberg has not melted: Further reflections on the concept of industrialization and distance teaching. *Open Learning,* 4(3): 3–8

Rumble G 1986 *The Planning and Management of Distance Education.* Croom Helm, London

Schuemer R, Ströhlein G 1991 Diagnosis and therapy: Theoretical and methodological aspects of drop-out research. In: Holmberg B, Ortner G E (eds.) 1991

Sewart D 1988 Students and their progress. In: Sewart D, Keegan D, Holmberg B (eds.) 1988 *Distance education: International Perspectives.* Croom Helm, London

Smith P, Kelly M (eds.) 1987 *Distance Education and the Mainstream. Convergence in Education.* Croom Helm, London

Wagner L (1977) The economics of the Open University revisited. *High. Educ.* 6(3): 359–81

Worth V (1982) *Empire State College/State University of New York Center for Distance Learning: A Care Study.* The Open University, Milton Keynes

Further Reading

Boot R L, Hodgson V E 1987 Open learning: Meaning and experience. In: Hodgson V E, Mann S J, Snell R 1987 (eds.) *Beyond Distance Teaching—Towards Open Learning* Open University Press, Milton Keynes

Casas Armengol M 1986 *Universidad sin clases. Education a distancia en América Latina.* Universidad Nacional Abierta, Caracas

Foks J 1987 Towards open learning. In: Smith P, Kelly M (eds.) 1987 *Distance Education and the Mainstream.* Croom Helm, London

Henri F, Kay A 1985 *Le savoir à domicile. Pédagogie et*

problématique de la formation à distance. Presses de l'université de Québec, Télé-université, Québec

Holmberg B 1989 The concepts and applications of distance education and open learning. Int. J. Innovative Higher Educ. 6(1,2): 24–28

Holmberg B, Ortner G E (eds.) 1991 *Research into Distance Education/Fernlehre und Fernlehrforschung*. Peter Lang, Frankfurt

Kaye A, Rumble G (eds.) 1981 *Distance Teaching for Higher and Adult Education*. Croom Helm/Open University Press, London

Ortner G E, Graff K, Wilmersdoerfer H (eds.) 1992

Distance Education as Two-way Communication. Essays in Honour of Börje Holmberg. Peter Lang, Frankfurt

Perry W 1976 *Open University: A Personal Account*. The Open University, Milton Keynes.

Rumble G, Harry K (eds.) 1982 *The Distance Teaching Universities*. Croom Helm, London

Verduin J R, Clark Th A 1991 *Distance Education. The Foundation of Effective Practice*. Jossey Bass, San Francisco, California

Vertecchi B (ed.) 1988 *Insequare a distanza*. La Nuova Italia Editrice, Florence

Polytechnical Education

L. J. Watson

Historically, the term "polytechnic" has proved to be formidably protean. The elasticity of the polytechnical objective in education is instanced by the gulf between what are arguably its two best known exemplars: the unique *Ecole Polytechnique* in Paris, and the dynamic sector of British higher education formed by 40 polytechnics and analogous institutions. Yet despite the diversity which lies behind the term "polytechnic," it is manifestly the case that in almost all countries one of its major implications has been a commitment to adult education—of a different order from that applying to the university sector. Polytechnics almost everywhere have played a significant role in organizing extension education for adults who, for whatever reason, have not transferred to traditional universities after completing upper-secondary education. A comprehensive comparative survey of the relationship between adult education and the polytechnic mission in all the relevant countries is beyond the scope of this entry. Indeed it remains a cause for dismay that a study of polytechnical education worldwide has itself yet to be written. Attention here is focused upon some problems of definition, upon the historical context, and upon some current challenges. The experience of the polytechnics in the United Kingdom is treated as a paradigm partly because of the large size of the sector in the United Kingdom, but also because it has demonstrably served as a role model for other countries.

1. Concepts and Definitions

The *Ecole Polytechnique* has, for a long time, enshrined, as no other institution, several aspects of polytechnical education: inculcation of applicable knowledge at the leading edge of technological advance, relevance to the needs of the nation and society, and access based on merit rather than privilege.

It is interesting to note, however, that Napoleon Bonaparte had founded the *Ecole* with a narrow view

as to its applicability—the school was to provide an elite corps of engineers for the imperial army. From the start, despite the commitment to merit-based entry, there was little emphasis on opening alternative routes to higher education. More central was the conviction that traditional universities simply could not meet the technological needs of a modern nation. Effectively ceasing to be a military academy, the *Ecole* eventually became one of the chief providers of France's leading politicians, technocrats, and top-grade industrialists —its often envied graduates, *"les X,"* influencing decision-making at the highest level. The special entry requirements to the institution have spawned numerous expensive crammers making it a byword for exclusiveness (see Halls 1976). Nevertheless, despite this paradox, the prestige of the *Ecole Polytechnique* certainly played some part in determining the nomenclature of institutions as diverse as Virginia Polytechnic Institute (founded in 1872) and California State Polytechnic University in the United States; or, in the United Kingdom, The Polytechnic, Regent Street, (founded in 1838); or the National Polytechnic Institution of Athens; or the National Polytechnic Institute in Mexico; or the Soviet polytechnics, set up in the interwar years.

However, it was at least as much the criterion of practical usefulness, as any desire to bathe in the reflected glory of the Parisian polytechnic, that seems to have predominated in the choice of the term and to have encouraged its proliferation—a point famously underscored by George Bernard Shaw's Straker in *Man and Superman* of 1903:

> Very nice sort of place Oxford, I should think for people that like that sort of place. They teach you to be gentlemen there. In the polytechnic they teach you to be an engineer or such like.

In contrast, the *Ecole Polytechnique* had taken its title in deference to the organic and fruitful interrelationship of the arts and sciences that was imagined, in a period of neoclassicism, to have existed in Greek civilization; a motivation that was humanistic rather than utilitarian.

2. Historical Development

2.1 France

In its atypical way, the *Ecole Polytechnique* had only indirectly encouraged the development of adult education. In the altruistic aftermath of both the revolutions of 1830 and 1848, the *Association Polytechnique* (made up of staff, students, and graduates of the *Ecole*) set up evening classes in technical subjects and mathematics for working-class students. These classes were to endure and expand through the century, but always outside the *Ecole* proper (see Capelle 1967). Conversely, the handful of polytechnics in Victorian and Edwardian England were seen primarily as extension colleges for adults in employment. They offered evening and day-release courses, although they also began to accept young people into full-time vocational education (see Robinson 1968).

2.2 Soviet Union

In the Soviet Union, the polytechnical framework for education espoused by Lenin after 1918 (and developed by Krupskaya) was to be indebted to both the French and British models. The Soviet polytechnic principle reflects Marx's admiration for the French attachment to the integration of theoretical knowledge (across the humanities, science, and technology) with practical application. It also echoes Lenin's (and Krupskaya's) rather Victorian-sounding belief that polytechnical education should be firmly based on work training.

Confusion is frequently caused by the fact that the Soviet term "polytechnical" is most often applied to secondary (and even some primary) rather than tertiary education. Polytechnical education in the "unified labor" schools aimed to discourage elitism and was to be a functional preparation fulfilling the prescribed norms of the economy as envisaged by the State Planning Commission. Whereas the 68 tertiary polytechnic institutes that were gradually created, although retaining the polytechnical commitment to practicality, have trained elite personnel for key engineering and technological posts. Despite also being leading research centers, they have a tradition of accepting a high proportion of adults on to full-time programs and also offer wide-ranging programs of quinquennial inservice courses for teachers, scientists, and engineers (see Korol 1957).

2.3 China

Not least because of its Marxist–Leninist pedigree, the term "polytechnical" was eagerly taken up by the Chinese educational authorities after 1949, although

less often applied to school education than in the Soviet Union. One major aim of the Chinese reorganization of tertiary education was to create a network of complementary institutions in each of a number of regional centers. In such locations there would be an academy of medicine, a teacher-training institution, specialized institutions meeting specific local priorities, a general university, and a polytechnic. There is no doubt that Chinese polytechnics, like their Soviet models, were regarded as truly university-level institutions specializing in engineering and technology (and to be compared in this respect with the institutions of technology in Australia or the United States). Chinese polytechnics also imitated their Soviet precursors in providing inservice training and continuing education (see Price 1970).

2.4 United Kingdom

Despite the admiration of some observers, such as Dewey, the Marxist connotation of polytechnical education actually seems to have retarded its development outside the Communist bloc. In this respect, the creation in the United Kingdom between 1969 and 1973 of the vibrant new polytechnic sector in higher education proved to be a vital turning point.

From the start, the remit of these institutions was to maintain close links with industry, commerce, the professions, and public service—and all this with special regard to the immediate geographical region in which they were located. Significantly, the establishment of the new polytechnics was also construed as an attempt to meet the needs of part-time students and as an embodiment of a commitment to widening access to higher education: two areas in which the traditional universities were perceived as having largely failed.

The setting up of the new sector was one direct consequence of the plea made in the *Robbins Report* of 1963 for a large-scale and rapid expansion of British post-compulsory education, subsequently fleshed out in a government White Paper of 1966. The particular contribution of the 1966 White Paper was to determine that new institutions would be formed by amalgamating existing colleges maintained by local authorities (see Anon 1966).

For a variety of motives, the White Paper of 1966 and subsequent legislation elected to leave the polytechnics outside the university sector. The positive intention at the time was to stress the distinctive practicality and the innovative character of the new institutions. Nevertheless, there is good reason to believe that negative considerations weighed more heavily. Local authority control, an option open for the administration of polytechnics but not universities, meant a lighter direct burden on central government expenditure.

In such circumstances the polytechnics in the United Kingdom, unlike their homonyms in France, the United States, the Soviet Union and China, had little choice but to carve out their own destiny, succeeding from the start in balancing the quest for academic credibility against a genuine commitment to their special remit. The latter was wholeheartedly accepted. Vocational and applied aspects of study were stressed. Structured provision for moving from subdegree diploma and certificate courses on to degree programs exemplified the much needed flexibility. Sizable periods of paid work experience were an essential ingredient of many degree programs, ensuring the long-delayed bonding between higher education and the world of commerce and industry. The resulting "sandwich" model is one of the most distinctive and admired features of British education. The highly desirable equal ratio of male and female students was achieved. As many as one-third of polytechnic full-time entrants were mature students.

Undoubtedly, the discernibly practical value of most polytechnic courses and the excellent employment prospects of polytechnic graduates played a large part in drawing into higher education students from previously under-represented sections of the population. Students themselves, and sponsoring employers, could think in terms of a return on their investment of time and/or money. Polytechnics enabled students not just to undertake diploma, degree, and graduate courses, but to prepare for major professional qualifications. The attractiveness of the polytechnic ethos was not, however, the only factor in their broadening of the profile of the higher education population. The institutions themselves adopted a proactive stance by devising foundation programs for mature students who had left school without the relevant formal qualifications. They developed associate studentships that enabled students to combine periods of varying intensity of part-time attendance, and even part-time with full-time study, so that the opportunity for study could be fitted to the rhythm of the students' work and domestic lives. Particular thought was given to ways of enabling mature women to enter higher education —some skills acquisition and training programs were designed specifically for them.

While it remained true that the majority of polytechnic students in the United Kingdom were school or college leavers, the institutions came to be regarded as centers of expertise in meeting the needs of adult learners. Most mature students wishing to add to existing qualifications or to acquire formal qualifications for the first time chose to do so at a polytechnic. By August 1991, approximately 80 percent of students in the United Kingdom in the age range of 21 to 44 studied at polytechnics. Over three-fourths of part-time places were filled by mature students (see Anon 1991).

The growing number of specially designed "access" courses have been of particular help to mature students, being run in association with a wide range of educational establishments, including further and higher education colleges.

This successful combination of academic and vocational goals did not go unnoticed elsewhere in Europe. In pressing their claims for wider recognition, institutions such as the German *Fachhochschulen* (although dissimilar to polytechnics in the United Kingdom in not preparing students for higher degrees) have in effect formed a pan-European polytechnical sector.

3. Current Challenges

3.1 International Students and Adult Education

Without being satisfied that at home they had entirely succeeded in discarding their image of "second best," polytechnics in the United Kingdom could, by 1990, point to an enviable record of achievement both at home and in the European Community. By 1991, polytechnics were participants, for example, in the majority of the 392 ERASMUS Interuniversity Cooperation Programs involving the United Kingdom. Though sharing with the university sector a legitimate mix of financial and educational motives, polytechnics sought to increase and diversify their recruitment of students from overseas.

Polytechnic activity in overseas recruitment had a direct and influential bearing on adult education in at least two senses. First, the majority of overseas students were "mature" by the customary definition. They had only recently begun to build up a profile of qualifications permitting entry to higher education after having left school to go directly into employment, usually through part-time study. Second, whether or not they were mature, overseas students usually lacked familiarity with the teaching and learning methods pertaining in the institutions in the United Kingdom which they were entering. A correct perception developed that levels of responsiveness, care, and learning support required by overseas students were not dissimilar from those needed by home adult learners. An element of cross-funding became possible whereby adult education initiatives within a polytechnic could be financed by income from overseas student fees. In some polytechnics, those responsible for facilitating the admission of adult learners and of overseas students, and those charged with the ongoing support of both categories of student, were located in the same unit, pooling expertise.

3.2 University Status

It was in international work, more than perhaps in all other areas, that the withholding of the university title from polytechnics proved a serious handicap. In many countries, the word "polytechnic" meant nothing at all; in others the term "polytechnic" was used, but in a different and unhelpful way. Problems could even arise in countries where polytechnics had been specifically set up with the British model in mind.

The two Hong Kong polytechnics, founded in 1972 and 1984, have an excellent track record in adult education, and have long made it possible for students to acquire higher diploma qualifications through flexible modes of day-release and part-time study, with work being undertaken at linked colleges where appropriate. However, despite an enviable reputation for quality, they found it difficult to win the right to prepare students for degrees. Eventually, sweeping reforms have actually subtracted out all work classified as "subdegree" from the two polytechnics to vocational colleges. The polytechnics will, however, continue to operate important divisions of continuing education and extramural departments, and not just at degree level but also in the areas of professional development for teachers, social workers, and others.

Polytechnical education in New Zealand is a significant growth area commencing only two years after the creation of the United Kingdom sector. Of the two dozen polytechnics in New Zealand, five have recently gained the right to award degrees (in vocational subjects largely unavailable at universities), but this will not be the major focus of their work. This remains the provision of nondegree vocational education, more often than not to adult leavers drawn from the immediate region in which the institution is located. Most part-time programs have no formal entry requirements, and anyone can enroll. Priority is explicity given to second chance education, upgrading of skills, training, and community studies.

Perhaps following the Antipodean rather than the British example, the Singapore government went one step further, by not only keeping its own polytechnics firmly within the nondegree sector but by refusing to accept the compatibility of United Kingdom polytechnic degrees with those awarded by the traditional universities. In countries as different as Indonesia and Portugal, the world "Polytechnic" is used to refer to further rather than higher education, often for the 16 to 18 age range.

The probable loss of overseas market opportunity was not least among the United Kingdom government's reasons for deciding, in 1990–91, to unleash a series of far-reaching reforms (although a wider commitment to fair competition undoubtedly played a part): an amount of research funding formerly given straight to the universities was opened for bidding from polytechnics; a process was begun for merging the Polytechnic and Colleges Funding Council with the University Funding Council; most crucially, in May 1991 it was announced, with all-party support, that polytechnics would be empowered to award their own degrees and, if they wished, to use the title of universities. All have decided to follow the latter course of action; at the time of writing (May 1992) most polytechnics had already begun to use their new titles in advance of the formal passage of the required legislation. So problematic had the word "polytechnic" proved to be, that it is believed that none have opted to use it, even adjectivally, as part of their university title.

4. Conclusion

Whatever the case, it should be stressed that the change of name in the United Kingdom has not brought with it a change of ethos. The British polytechnics have not allowed excitement at their rapid expansion to diminish commitment to access: despite the absence of tangible financial benefits, they have ensured that the number of part-time students has kept pace with the growth in the full-time student population; and investment in access departments of various kinds continues to increase in order to facilitate the entry of under-represented sections of society into higher education. The institutions remain proud of their distinctive polytechnical role, which is pre-eminently exemplified by their commitment to adult education, even if they are relieved to be no longer encumbered by a troublesome title.

Now that their erstwhile counterparts have become university institutions, the German *Fachhochschulen*, the Belgian technical higher education institutions, the Irish regional training colleges, and the HBO institutions in the Netherlands, and others like them, may feel that they have been cast adrift. Alternatively, they may decide to cite the metamorphosis of the polytechnics in the United Kingdom in a bid of their own for university status. They will be able to argue from the British experience that such a tranformation does not undermine support for adult education and continuing professional development.

See also: Third-age Students in Higher Education; Adult Tertiary Education; University Adult Education

References

Anon 1966 *A Plan for Polytechnics and Other Colleges.* HMSO, London
Anon 1991 *Higher Education in Britain: The Polytechnics.* British Council, London
Capelle J 1967 *Tomorrow's Education: The French Experience.* Pergamon Press, Oxford
Halls W D 1976 *Education, Culture and Politics in Modern France.* Pergamon Press, Oxford
Korol A G 1957 *Soviet Education for Science and Technology.* Greenwood Press, Greenwich, Connecticut
Price R F 1970 *Education in Communist China.* World Education Series. Praeger, New York
Robinson E 1968 *The New Polytechnics.* Penguin, Harmondsworth

Further Reading

Burgess T, Pratt J 1974 *Polytechnics: A Report.* Pittman, London
Donaldson L 1977 *Policy and the Polytechnics: Pluralistic Drift in Higher Education* Lexington Books, Lexington, Massachusetts

Harris W J A 1980 *Comparative Adult Education: Practice, Purpose and Theory*. Longman, London
Kogan M C 1971 *The Politics of Education*. Penguin, Harmondsworth
Richmond W K 1978 *Education in Britain since 1944: A Personal Retrospect*. Methuen, London

Study Circles

J. Byström

A study circle is a circle of friends or associates assembled for common and planned study of a predetermined subject or problem area. The study circle is a form of education capable of attracting people with a short previous education who are often unaccustomed to taking part in adult education programs.

The study circle is now generally recognized as a modern method of adult education and has even drawn attention from areas outside of popular education, for example, in the case of industry training circles in large firms in Germany and Japan. Study circles have their roots in the inadequacies prevalent in nineteenth-century society in Sweden. They developed alongside the popular movements that emerged at that time.

This entry describes the historical background and the development of the study circle, and discusses its ideology and pedagogical ideas. The study circle is a part of popular education in all Nordic countries, but there are differences in historical development and in how the study circles are organized. This entry deals primarily with Sweden, a country where roughly one-fourth of the adult population takes part in study circles each year.

1. Definition

The study circle is a small group of people (normally between 5 and 12), who over an extended period of time, and on a regular basis, meet to study or to take part in a cultural project under the guidance of a leader. Most study circles last two or three months, during which time the participants normally meet once a week for two to three hours (see *Group Learning*).

2. Historical Background

2.1 The Growth of the Popular Movements

During the second half of the nineteenth century so-called "popular movements" emerged in the Nordic countries. First came the free Church movement followed by the temperance movement and the labor movement. Lack of knowledge was seen as an impediment to organizational development and to the desired transformation of society. The knowledge needed for bringing about radical social change was not offered as part of the traditional school curriculum. Despite inauspicious circumstances, many workers studied on their own. The study circles offered not only an opportunity for learning, but they also played an important role in establishing social and cultural networks.

2.2 Orientation of Study Circles

The study circles served mainly two goals, although in practice these were often combined. First, the education offered by the circles was seen as "ammunition" for the trade unions and the political movement—a means of engaging in, and preparing for, class struggle and social transformation. Second, the circles were intended as a means of raising the level of general education of the working class.

Both goals are reflected in the arrangement and methods of the studies, which can be summarized as follows:

(a) People studied in small groups, often in their homes.

(b) They had little to draw on in the way of study materials.

(c) They had no teachers, nor did they feel the need for any. The leader of the group was primarily an organizer and administrator with no special theoretical qualifications.

(d) To supplement their studies, people would attend lectures or meetings.

(e) The people who studied in this way had no academic background, but they had acquired an abundance of practical experience.

(f) People learned to discuss, to argue, to show consideration for others, to accept defeat, and share responsibility.

(g) They experienced a sense of solidarity and community.

(h) The knowledge they acquired was immediately relevant and applicable to everyday life.

(i) They began studying at their own level, and the studies were directed by their own needs.

The form of education which thus evolved within the popular movements later provided the foundation of what came to be known as the "study circle". The first real study circle is customarily said to have been founded in 1902 by Oscar Olsson, a keyperson in the temperance movement. He was inspired by a visit to the United States and observation of the successful Chautauqua movement (see *Community Education and Community Development*).

2.3 State Grants

At a very early stage, each of the popular movements developed special organizational arrangements for educational activities—usually in the form of an adult education association. In Sweden, the activities of these associations are mainly financed by grants from the state and the municipal authorities. As early as 1912, the Swedish Parliament voted to give grants for the purchase of books.

State funding of study circle activities, which was introduced in 1947, has played a vital role in enabling Swedish popular education to develop. For example, during the 1970s, the number of study hours qualifying for public aid rose from 5.5 million to 12 million. At the same time as these grants were introduced, rules and conditions were drawn up which gave a definition of the study circle with the aim of preserving its distinctive character.

From the 1960s onwards, public institutions have often chosen to distribute information on vital social issues through the organized adult education associations.

3. The Pedagogy of the Study Circle

3.1 Philosophy

Study circles make use of a great variety of methods and subjects. It is therefore relevant to ask whether the study circle demands special teaching and learning methods.

There is a basic study circle philosophy which is close to Paulo Freire's ideas concerning the pedagogy of the oppressed (see *Popular Education and Conscientization*). The views of the popular movements concerning society, people, and knowledge govern the choice of methods in the study circles. This pedagogy is based on the ideals of community development and principles of emancipatory democracy involving the struggle for freedom, justice, and equality. Study circles therefore seek to establish an environment which is conducive to personal development and the enhancement of inner creative abilities.

3.2 Context

A fundamental idea in the pedagogy of the study circle is that people have an innate desire to learn.

Educational efforts do not necessarily demand a monetary or nonmonetary reward. The new knowledge the participants acquire will be important insofar as it enriches their everyday lives. This is why the precise cognitive targets of the study circle cannot be defined in advance.

Instead, the common efforts of the members, as well as the use of the acquired knowledge, indicate new needs and problems to be dealt with. The study circle must have sufficient flexibility to adjust its activities in accordance with the resulting redefinition of learning goals to be attained. Through their studies, the members must be enabled to view their own lives in a wider social context. This means that the members of the study circle must learn how to deal with problems through their studies and how to work out solutions to problems that cannot be foreseen in advance by the producers of study materials, the study circle leader, or the circle members themselves.

3.3 The Common Goal

Characteristic of the study circle is the collective nature of learning. In dialogue with others, the participants constantly appraise their knowledge, comparing notes and helping each other to discover new insights and to find new knowledge. In order for a study circle to function adequately, certain principles have to be observed by all its members, including the leader. Above all, everyone must be actively engaged in pursuing the common learning goals. It is only then that dialogue and equal participation, as well as sharing of responsibility, can exist.

The knowledge and experience is used as an input into the learning activity, but it is not enough. New information is also required in order to progress. All members of the study circle share a responsibility for ensuring that studies are meaningful. Even if the leader's knowledge of the subject is an asset, the leader should not assume the traditional role of a teacher. It is his or her job to assist the participants by providing information, indicating means of problem solving, and ensuring the active participation of all members.

The learning process within the study circle builds on the participants' knowledge, experiences, and perceived learning needs. Members are not only reponsible for themselves, but also for the learning progress achieved by the other members of the study circle. However, the knowledge communicated in the study circle is not universal and common to all. All participants receive and process the material in accordance with their own needs. Hence no two study circles are alike, nor should they be.

4. Trends and Developments

4.1 Freedom from Rules

In Sweden, during the 1980s, demands grew stronger

for abolishing the formal rules that had been associated with the system of state grants since 1947. In order to meet future challenges, the educational associations required continued freedom to develop the study circle approach. Since the early 1990s, the state no longer sets formal regulations for the study circles: only some basic goals are defined.

4.2 International Scope

Interest in the study circle has increased even outside the Nordic countries. The study circle approach is gaining recognition in Canada and the United States. The Nordic educational associations are engaged in development projects in Central and Eastern Europe. There is also an interest in the Scandinavian experience of popular education in Latin America. FoNoLa (The Society for Exchange of Popular Education Scandinavia–Latin America) is one of the organizations that supports developments involving study circles.

See also: Europe: Nordic Countries; Folk High Schools; Experiential and Open Learning; Group Learning; Community Education and Community Development

Bibliography

Arvidson L 1985 *Folkbildning i rörelse*. Liber Förlag AB, Malmö
Arvidson L 1989 Popular education and educational ideology. In: Ball S, Larsson S (eds.) 1989 *The Struggle for Democratic Education: Equality and Participation in Sweden*. Falmer Press, London
Arvidson L 1991 *Folkbildning och självuppfostran*. Tidens Förlag, Stockholm
Byström J 1983 *Studiecirkelns pedagogik*. Brevskolan, Stockholm
Freire P 1970 *Pedagogy of the Oppressed*. Continuum, New York
Ginner T 1988 *Den bildade arbetaren*. Linköping University, Linköping
Oliver L P 1987 *Study Circles: Coming Together for Personal Growth and Social Change*. Seven Locks Press, Washington, DC

University Adult Education

C. E. Kasworm

Historically, the university has been defined as a community for advanced knowledge creation and for the instruction of an elite group of youth. However, since the 1960s, many universities and higher education institutions have questioned this belief. They have redefined the relationship between the university, the adult learner, and the society. Rather than selective instruction solely focused on young adults, university adult education reflects the necessity of qualified adult learner access and involvement in university instruction. Mature adult participation in university studies is based on the need for continuous development of advanced specialized knowledge across the adult lifespan. In addition, there are a number of other societal issues which have advanced this concern for university adult education. These international issues and trends reflect changing demographic patterns, the increased learning needs of the workforce, and the growth of knowledge in an information-based society. Of growing importance, many countries have also supported university adult education due to pressures of educational equity, with particular concerns for women, workers, and disadvantaged socioeconomic groups.

1. Definitions and Terms

Due to its recent development, university adult education is characterized by diverse definitions and classifications. It is most often defined by a description of its student group, the adult undergraduate in university studies, or by a description of a particular policy or academic program specifically oriented to adult access to university studies.

Within the literature, adult learners in university adult education may be referred to as "mature students," "re-entry students," "part-time students," "continuing extension education students," "second-chance students," "older adult students," as well as "school leavers." These varied terms each reflect the following key elements:

(a) adult students who enter or re-enter higher education with a past major interruption in their formal involvement in learning. These individuals seek a focused academic study, an assessment of advanced knowledge, and subsequent award of a degree, certificate, or credential of advanced specialized expertise.

(b) adult students who enter higher education with mature life experiences due to major full-time past responsibilities in work roles, in family provider/sustainer roles, in apprenticeship training, or in military service roles.

(c) students enrolled in academic studies who represent specific chronological age categories, most often defined by a lower age limit of 21, 25, or 30 years of age or older. This age categorization for university adult students is somewhat arbitrary. However, it is often used to identify groups of adult students who have interrupted their "schooling" and pursued adult roles outside the university tradition.

(d) adult students who completed one university degree of studies, left the university, and who re-entered to pursue a second academic course. These students may be described as second degree seekers, certificate-seekers, or professional development oriented students.

In addition, university adult education can also offer specialized access and programs for senior adults (50 years of age and over). These provide access to university studies, either through the normal route of admission or in academic programs designed for older adult populations. As an example, over 260,000 students aged 50 and over in the United States participate in university degree programs or select courses. Further discussions of definitions and characterizations of students are given in Schütze (1988), West and Hore (1989), Cross (1981), Schlossberg et al. (1989), Abrahamsson (1986), and in the Woodley et al. (1987).

Beyond the characterization of adult university students, university adult education is often defined through a particular policy, program, instructional delivery system, or strategy supporting adult access and participation. The international terms for university adult education include "recurrent education," "adult higher education," "further education," "extramural education," "open university" (distance higher education), and "extension (university) education." These terms reflect a belief that advanced specialized knowledge should be accessed by competent and motivated adults of any age.

University adult education is a movement away from a "front-loading" model of education toward a "continuous" model of lifelong learning. It also reflects an increasing lack of distinction and separateness between formal academic programs and nonformal continuing education programs for adult learners.

2. National Enrollment Patterns

To understand the presence and growth of university adult education from an international perspective, Table 1 presents enrollment data for a number of countries. The estimates show the extent of the enrollment of adult students (aged 25 or older) in undergraduate university programs in proportion to total national university enrollment.

The data in Table 1 generally suggest growth in

Table 1
Representative enrollment statistics of university adult education

	1981–82	Most recent statistics
Australia	32.1	40.3% (1987)
Austria	4.8	44.8%[a] (1989–90)
Belgium		4.8% (1984)
Canada	10.0	37.0% (1990–91)
China		49.0% (1988)
Denmark		9.1%[a] (1988–89)
Finland	19.6	47.2% (1989–90)
France	9.2	16.2% (1989–90)
Germany	8.7	50.6%[a] (1989–90)
Israel		30.7% (1988–89)
Norway		45.0% (1987)
Spain		23.5% (1989–90)
Sweden	54.6	65.9% (1986)
United Kingdom	16.7[b]	31.8% (1983–84)
United States	24.0	41.0% (1989)
Venezuela		7.3% (1985)

Sources: The 1981–82 statistics are an adaptation from Abrahamsson et al. 1988. The most recent statistics were either reported by the OECD, a national policy body, or were extrapolated from projections of enrollments (Kasworm 1994)
a Includes ISCED levels 5,6,7—postsecondary, undergraduate, and graduate studies   b Excludes Open University students

adult student enrollments within nations supportive of the concepts of lifelong learning and human resource development in the workplace, or that actively seek to educate the citizenry through university adult education. The countries where adults account for 30 percent or more of participation in university adult education have specific national policies to encourage adult access and participation in universities and national open university systems. Such countries may also have strong decentralized commitment on the part of universities to admit adult students.

3. Characteristics of University Adult Education

A number of major aspects characterize university adult education in an international perspective.

3.1 Admission Standards and Open Access Standards

There is a growing belief that capable individuals, no matter what their age, position in society, or current life commitments, should have the opportunity to access university studies. Some universities therefore modify conventional admission procedures for adult applicants. For example, Sweden has the 25/4 rule (see Kim 1982). In Israel, the Israeli Council amended their requirement for a *Bagrut* matriculation certification for individuals who were over the age of 30. In the United States, 92 percent of the higher education institutions offer alternative mechanisms for adult student entry without the requirement of a high school diploma. In addition, there are many notable activities to admit adults lacking the prerequisite educational qualifications.

3.2 Part-time Study Options and Alternative Learning Formats

University adult education assumes that adults can gain academic proficiency through part-time studies and through alternative learning formats beyond the usual classroom or tutorial system. Three-fourths of all part-time students in Canada are adult students, with four out of every five adult students pursuing part-time studies. In the United States, over 60 percent of all college/university students are in part-time studies, with estimates that over 75 percent of the enrolled adult students are in part-time studies. Many national university systems have supported the redefinition of degree programs into courses or single-subject studies. Part-time involvement also suggests the provision for accumulation of course credits or certificates and transferability of course credits between institutions. Alternative learning formats for university adult education students present more flexible and convenient time, location, and student–professor interactions in university studies (see *Time Policies and Lifelong Education*).

3.3 Adult Life Experiences and Assessment

University adult education programs presume that the past and current life experiences of adults are a significant variable in the instructional process. Certain university adult education programs require specific adult life experiences for admission into academic programs. For example, some academic programs require a specific number of years and level of experience in business to enter into a university adult degree program in business. Many academic programs create instructional designs which incorporate and build upon adult life experiences of their university adult education students. There are also a number of policies and university programs which feature specialized assessment strategies. These assessment efforts examine prior learning experiences as potentially equivalent to academic knowledge. Sweden, Canada, the United Kingdom, the United States, and other countries (with open university systems) have varied possibilities for the accreditation of experiential learning from nonformal or training settings.

3.4 Financial Support

Many nations, for example France and Sweden, have created schemes for the financial support of adult university students. Denmark provides state grants covering 80 percent of costs for vocationally quali-fying part-time higher education for adults. Finland has specific provision for financial aids for mature students, but with specific limits on age range, length of time, and amount of aid in relation to monthly work income. National funding of adult students is under discussion in Australia, Canada, Norway, and the United States. Moreover, many firms and labor unions in Canada and the United States provide tuition reimbursement plans for employees who successfully complete approved university studies.

3.5 Alternative Teaching and Learning Models

University adult education not only relies on open university and distance learning systems, but also confers recognition on alternative systems for educational delivery, including skills assessment and validation schemes. Certain forms of university adult education employ methods of instruction based on andragogical learning models (see *Andragogy*). A few programs utilize learning contracts and independent learning based in self-directed and self-regulated study. Many university adult education instructional programs incorporate experiential and cooperative group learning strategies (see *Experiential and Open Learning*).

4. Policy Support Structures

University adult education is very heterogeneous in form and function. There appear to be three basic international patterns of university adult education. The first reflects a national commitment to higher education policy devoted to adult programs or adult access to university systems. A second pattern represents a minimal national commitment, with emphasis on university-level policy for the integration of all students, combining adult and young adult, in adapted structures and forms of university studies. The third pattern reflects specialized adult learner programs or structures. In this pattern, there may be a national commitment to an exclusive "national adult-oriented university." Another possibility focuses upon a university-level policy supportive of segregated university adult education for adults.

4.1 National Policies for University Adult Education

Sweden best exemplifies the first pattern. It has a national policy of higher education to support recurrent education. Several key features of this policy include a specific admissions scheme for adults, often denoted as the 25/4 rule. This rule specifies that a person must be at least 25 years of age, have 4 years of work or related life experience, and must have certified prerequisite knowledge and competence in subject areas essential to the study program. Sweden supports single-subject studies, part-time and evening studies, provisions for distance learning, integration of vocational and academic courses, consideration of credits for experiential learning, and concern for equity and efficiency in educating their entire population (Abrahamsson 1986).

Through the Norwegian Adult Education Act of 1976, Norway has also set out to provide alternative ways of admitting adults to the university. In Norway, the so-called "regional colleges" have been made responsible for adult education, conferring a first degree, as well as for the provision of inservice and refresher programs. Alternative degree credit courses, the breaking up of degree courses into modules, and the encouragement of part-time studies also reflect these changes (Aamodt 1990, Kulich 1985). China is another country that has created a separate, national adult higher education system (Bo and Yan 1988) (see *China, People's Republic*).

4.2 University Policy for Admitting Adults

The second pattern focuses upon university policy to provide for the integration of adults. Although national policy may support these efforts, it is not a force for innovation in this area. Rather, university policy has shaped admission policies or structures which support adult access. These are mostly in the form of part-time university studies and evening, weekend, or summer studies to accommodate both young, traditional-aged university students as well as university adult education students.

As an example, the Council for National Academic Awards (CNAA) in the United Kingdom has supported a significant increase in part-time degree programs, encouraged credit accumulation and transfer schemes between polytechnics and colleges of higher education, and supported mature-student entry admission schemes (see *Polytechnical Education*). A number of universities even "modularize" their academic programs. This refers to the dividing of a program into smaller units of study that may be seen as semi-independent, such as in certificate programs or "phased exit" programs.

Many universities also offer distance or open learning opportunities, as well as methods for assessing the relevant experience of the adult learners. This approach is characterized by a policy of supporting the adaptation of existing university programs to the special needs of adult learners. In differing ways, many universities in Australia, Canada, Finland, the United Kingdom, Israel, Spain, and the United States follow this approach to the programmatic inclusion of adults into regular university programs.

4.3 Policies for Specialized Adult Learner Access

This third pattern reflects a policy, university structure, or academic program designed to solely serve adult learners. This pattern is often supported at the national level by a designated university for adult

learners. A dominant form of this pattern reflects the prototype of the Open University in the United Kingdom and the subsequent proliferation of open and distance education universities around the world (see *Open University*). As examples of major activity, many countries in all world regions feature national open universities to serve adult learners. In addition, there are specialized open universities designated by region or by institution, such as Athabasca University in Canada or Deakin University in Australia. In cases where national support for an adult-oriented university is lacking, university adult education may be offered through specialized programs based in distance education delivery systems, but which are not officially classified as open universities. Two examples of national delivery systems in the United States are the National Technological University which delivers undergraduate and graduate instruction via satellite from a number of universities, and the Electronic University, which is an educational communications system of computer courses linking students and instructors from various universities.

5. Trends and Developments

Both national governments and individual universities have created opportunities to serve the part-time adult student. In certain countries, academic programs for adults occur through evening, weekend, or summer schools, as well as through programs of a brief duration.

Finland has established further education centers with the universities. The country also offers extramural instruction in cooperation with nonacademic institutions that adhere to the principles of the open university. In a focused concern for enhancing the learning opportunities of the workforce, Denmark adopted the Open Education Act in 1990. This has established national support for vocationally oriented, qualifying, and part-time education designed for adults. According to the Act, the Ministry of Education should endorse the courses offered by the various universities and other institutions. The Act also regulates employer involvement in planning and financing. In addition, the Act requires access to courses after work hours, examinations to include external evaluation, and the option to transfer credit to a full-time course of education. Employers may also purchase Open Education courses as part of a staff training program.

In Venezuela, the University of Simon Bolivar features an andragogical model of instruction and individualized learning experiences in collaboration with instructional faculty. This instruction is also offered in a distance education format with regional study centers and a program of assessment for validating past learning experiences.

In the United States, there are over 120 adult degree programs and over 350 external degree programs which predominantly serve adult learners. One type of adult degree program is represented in the United States by Empire State College, Thomas Edison College, and Metropolitan State College. These three institutions are "universities without walls"—offering a decentralized, nonresidential, and innovative higher education program. Their curricula are individualized, with instruction and assessment of instruction offered in an open learning philosophy. Students participate at their own rate of desired involvement. An important aspect is the assessment of learning experience gained either through individualized instruction or through work and life experience. Two highly different examples of competency-based models are presented by Regents College (New York) and Alverno College (Wisconsin). Within these programs, specialized assessment and validation processes examine life experiences as reflective of equivalent academic learning experiences, as well as assessment of knowledge and skill through alternative experiential activities both within and outside the classroom.

A growing trend in a number of adult degree programs are specialized cooperative arrangements between a business organization and a university. These formal agreements represent both worksite course offerings and jointly sponsored degree programs. For example, 47 percent of the colleges and universities in the United States offer credit courses for business employees at business locations; 19 percent of the offerings are jointly developed and sponsored degree programs. In addition, the United States also features 15 "corporate colleges"—business corporations which have established academic university degree programs to serve their adult workforce. These degrees are predominantly focused upon high technology subject matter and are offered only to employees at the worksite. Canada has also reported such cooperative activities. In 1985, Canadian employers provided 34 percent of adult part-time courses, while universities provided only 17 percent of such courses.

6. Conclusion

University adult education has become a recognized element of international higher education. However, because of its recent development within divergent systems of higher education, there is significant heterogeneity of form, function, and terminology. International enrollment trends and the proliferation of specialized institutions and academic programs suggest continued growth of university adult education. Future efforts will focus on innovative structures, national policies, and adult-oriented instructional strategies for greater access and participation of the adult community in university life.

See also: Third-age Students in Higher Education; Adult Tertiary Education; Open University

References

Aamodt P O 1990 A new deal for Norwegian higher education? *European J. Educ.* 25(2): 171–86

Abrahamsson K 1986 *Adult Participation in Swedish Higher Education: A Study of Organizational Structure, Educational Design and Current Policies*. Studies in Higher Education in Sweden Series No. 7. Almqvist and Wiksell International, Stockholm

Abrahamsson K, Rubenson K, Slowey M (eds.) 1988 *Adults in the Academy: International Trends in Adult and Higher Education*. Swedish National Board of Education, Stockholm

Bo Yu, Yan Xu Hong 1988 *Adult Higher Education: A Case Study on the Workers' Colleges in the People's Republic of China*. UNESCO, International Institute for Educational Planning, Paris

Cross K P 1981 *Adults as Learners: Increasing Participation and Facilitating Learning*. Jossey-Bass, San Francisco, California

Kasworm 1994 Adult higher education from an international perspective. *High. Educ* 25(4): 411–23.

Kim L 1982 *Widened Admission to Higher Education in Sweden: (The 25/5 Scheme). A Study of the Implementation Process*. National Board of Universities and Colleges, Stockholm

Kulich J 1985 University level adult education in Scandinavia. *Can. J. University Continuing Education* 11(2): 33–63

Schlossberg N, Lynch A, Chickering A 1989 *Improving Higher Education Environments for Adults: Responsive Programs of Services from Entry to Departure*. Jossey-Bass, San Francisco, California

Schütze H G 1988 The context of adult participation in higher education: An overview of the CERI/OECD project. In: Abrahamsson K, Rubenson K, Slowey M (eds.) 1988

West L, Hore T 1989 The impact of higher education on adult students in Australia, Part 1. Employment. *High. Educ.* 18: 341–52

Woodley A, Wagner L, Slowey M, Hamilton M, Fulton O 1987 *Choosing to Learn*. The Society for Research into Higher Education/Open University Press, Milton Keynes

Further Reading

Apps J W 1988 *Higher Education in a Learning Society: Meeting New Demands for Education and Training*. Jossey-Bass, San Francisco, California

Duncan D D (1984) *The New Majority: Adult Learners in the University*. University of Alberta Press, Edmonton

Eurich N P 1985 *Corporate Classrooms—The Learning Business*. Carnegie Foundation for the Advancement of Teaching, Princeton, New Jersey

Hall J W 1991 *Access Through Innovation: New Colleges for New Students*. National University Continuing Education Association, American Council on Education/Macmillan, New York

Panhelainen M 1991 Universities in the adult education market. *Life and Education in Finland* 28(2): 46–48

Schütze H G (ed.) 1987 *Adults in Higher Education. Report for CERI/OECD*. Almqvist and Wiksell International, Stockholm

Worker Education and Labor Education

N. Eiger

This entry focuses on the development and current status of diverse labor education systems in four industrialized countries: the United States, the Federal Republic of Germany, Sweden and the United Kingdom. These systems are selected because they have influenced labor education activities in many parts of thc world.

1. Definition

Since there has been much confusion over terms, with "labor education" simply being subsumed under "adult education" or "vocational education," it is appropriate at the outset to clarify its defining characteristics. "Labor education" can be defined as a multidimensional, multilevel set of activities conducted largely by trade unions, worker education associations, and universities and colleges. Its participants are primarily blue- and white-collar workers who most often are recruited through their trades union organizations. However, labor education does not necessarily reach out only to organized employees.

One of its aims is to educate workers for effective participation in their collective organizations. A second aim is to strengthen trades union organizations by preparing skilled leadership capable of analyzing and responding to changing social and economic environments. A third dimension, that has generated considerable controversy, involves ideological values and the recurrent tension over education for social transformation in contrast to a narrow technical-oriented focus (see *Ideologies in Adult Education*).

Labor education starts with the worker's economic interests and concerns and expands to encompass the broad range of skills and knowledge needed to advance economic interests and develop an effective collective voice. Its content dovetails with the broader category of adult education when it addresses the wide range of educational needs of workers: education for leisure, citizenship, and cultural development. However, we will use the term "worker education" in referring to this broader concept of subject matter.

Despite the fact that all four systems studied here are at similar stages of economic development, they exhibit markedly different models of labor education. Among the factors shaping these differences are the ideologies, culture, and traditions of their labor movements; the economic and cultural history of the nation; government policy; and the labor strategies of employers. The stage of development would be a more central factor in examining labor education programs in less-developed countries.

2. Labor Education in the United States

In most countries labor education can be traced to the beginning of the Industrial Revolution and the sporadic efforts of the early trade unions and working-class political reform movements to provide educational opportunities for workers. The roots of contemporary labor education in the United States, however, can best be traced to the 1920s. That decade witnessed the emergence of labor education as a movement largely outside of the union structure. In a reaction to various anti-union business strategies, reminiscent of the 1980s, independent labor education institutions arose that represented various philosophical currents in the labor movement.

Brookwood Labor College, for example, was a socialist-oriented workers school (Bloom 1990) that challenged the business unionist orthodoxy of the American Federation of Labor (AFL). The labor intellectuals who taught in its classes helped prepare a number of the leaders who became the organizers of the great organizing drives of the 1930s, that succeeded in unionizing the unskilled and semi-skilled mass production workers, long spurned by the old line AFL craft unions. Brookwood represented what can be termed the "organizing-class model." A second model, called the "service-instrumental model," was represented in the 1920s by the Wisconsin School for Workers in Industry (Schultz 1973) which was founded by pro-labor academics interested in providing liberal education for workers. This program evolved into the Wisconsin School for Workers which, however, shifted from liberal education and, since the 1950s, has stressed providing union stewards and officers with technically focused subjects needed to conduct collective bargaining and reach agreements. A third strand of labor education, which encompassed the broader notion of worker education, arose from the pro-labor, social welfare impulse of progressive upper-middle-class individuals. It took the form of uplift-type programs conducted by the National Women's Trade Union League and the establishment at Bryn Mawr College of an annual School for Women Workers in Industry (Schneider 1941). At the same time, state and local labor bodies sponsored over 75 city labor colleges that employed faculty from nearby universities on an ad hoc basis.

Inevitably conflicts grew between the national AFL's ideology of craft unionism and a number of the voluntary independent schools, who saw their mission in more radical social terms and thus gave high priority to promoting industrial unionism. Weakened by these disputes, the voluntary labor education institutions declined in the 1930s, their demise hastened by the economic depression.

Despite the ideological conflicts and general mistrust of what trade unionists felt was the elitist culture and role of the universities (a view shared by all the labor movements discussed in this entry), the leadership of the AFL gradually reached out to universities for labor education services. Spurred by their satisfaction with the University of Wisconsin's School For Workers program (which was highly pragmatic and simply provided the subjects requested by labor), labor organizations began to seek similar models at other universities such as Rutgers, the State University of New Jersey (Levine 1973).

Programs such as these helped to dissipate some of the mutual distrust between the divergent cultures of labor and academia. However, it was not until the period after the Second World War that the seeds planted in Wisconsin and New Jersey sprouted into many state university labor education extension centers. To a large extent these extension programs arose as a public policy response, often mandated by legislation, to the wave of postwar strikes; their aim was to promote labor–management harmony through informed collective bargaining. Today there are 50 such programs affiliated with the University College Labor Education Association in over 25 states reaching some 100,000 workers annually with a variety of educational and research services that go far beyond the original narrow government mandate of the 1940s.

Paralleling this substantial network of union–university and college cooperation is an even larger system of educational activities sponsored directly by union education departments and the AFL. A trend in recent years, despite declining resources, has been the establishment of union-sponsored residential labor schools, the largest of which is the AFL-CIO's George Meany Labor Studies Center in Maryland.

3. The German Model of Labor Education

Since the history and structure of the German and Swedish labor movements are significantly different from that of the American unions, the evolution of their labor education systems is also strikingly different. Labor education in the Federal Republic of Germany and Sweden is sponsored almost exclusively by the trades union movement or institutions closely allied with labor. Unlike the United States' system, universities play hardly any role, some recent exceptions notwithstanding.

Moreover, unlike the predominant business–unionist ideology that pervaded most parts of the American labor movement, German workers in the first three decades of this century and after the Second World War, and Swedish blue-collar workers to this day, viewed their trade unions through the prism of social democratic values. Accordingly, unions were seen as

part of a larger social movement of labor that included the Social Democratic Party, the cooperative movement, and the worker education and cultural associations. This concept of labor as a social movement never crystallized in the United States, for this view of labor as an integrated way of life through which workers and their families could find fulfillment in a wide range of well organized, cultural, educational, and recreational activities was alien to the individualistic culture of the United States and the concomitant perception of its "classless" character. Labor in Europe, in contrast, was seen as a political–cultural movement that counterposed the values of social solidarity, egalitarianism, and economic democracy to the competitive materialism of the market society. Nevertheless, there were efforts among those few American unions adhering to social democratic traditions, particularly in the garment trades, to create a worker culture through educational programs.

The culture of the university was spurned by labor in Germany and Sweden as representing the elitism of the upper classes, and this distrust was reciprocated (Deutscher Gewerkschaftsbund 1973). With the defeat of Nazism in Germany, the tradition of developing labor education opportunities solely through the unions was revived with the rebirth of a powerful and prosperous labor movement. This tradition evolved into the elaborate educational structure that exists today. Although largely furnished through the German Trades Union Federation (DGB) and its independent national affiliates, labor education is also sponsored by such institutions as the Frederick Ebert and Hans Bockler foundations that identify with the labor movement or are closely linked to it.

German labor education is based on a three-level progression that parallels the three levels of administrative organization of the DGB and its affiliates. Union members generally enter the system of labor education at the local union level, either through activities sponsored by local unions or (if they are small and lack resources) by the DGB, and then proceed through a progression of learning options at the district, regional, and national levels. During the 1980s it was estimated that some 400,000 workers took part annually in educational activities organized by the DGB, exclusive of the tens of thousands of enrollees in the DGB's five federal schools and the programs sponsored by individual union affiliates and their labor schools (Eiger 1982).

At the most advanced level of the progression is the opportunity for union officers to attend long-term study programs at the college level offered by three academies that are friendly to, but not controlled by, the unions (Cook and Douty 1958). Graduates of their nine-month to three-year courses of study generally move into the top leadership positions of the unions, the Social Democratic Party, and the government.

Worker education, in the broadest sense of the term, is conducted through *Arbeit und Leben* (Work and Learning), an association similar in some respects

671

to the Worker Education Association of the United Kingdom.

4. The Swedish Model

The vast network of Swedish labor's educational programming started to evolve in its modern form in 1912, when the three major components of the labor movement founded the Workers Education Association (ABF). This added a new dimension to a social movement that comprised the Swedish Labor Union Confederation (LO), the Social Democratic Party (SAP), and the Cooperative Union (KF). This new arm of the labor movement was given the task of coordinating and developing a broad range of labor education, worker education, and cultural activities which it has been doing on an ever-increasing scale until the 1980s when a moderate decline was experienced (Eiger 1988).

Starting out in 1912 with 57 study circles enrolling 785 participants, ABF's programs grew to 91,898 study circles enrolling 789,486 members in 1986, and have since maintained a high level of participation.

Just as the ABF serves the educational needs of its primary base, the 2.2 million members of the LO and their families, the TBV (the Educational Association of Salaried Employees), founded in 1935 by the white-collar unions, was organized to provide educational services to state, local government, and private-sector salaried employees.

Educational outreach and instruction is carried out by a virtual army of labor education practitioners: some 20,000 study circle leaders and at least as many study organizers (Eiger 1981).

The concept of the workplace study organizer is an innovative Swedish contribution that started in the late 1960s as a government subsidized, union experimental program. Today all sections of Sweden's labor movement accept the objective of maintaining at least one active study organizer in each plant, agency, or office. The unions have been successful in negotiating varying generous amounts of paid time off the job, particularly in large firms, for study organizers to carry out their functions of planning, promoting, and recruiting workers for labor and adult education programs (Eiger 1981).

Over and above this system, but paralleling and integrated with it, are the programs carried out directly through the unions aimed at educating members and representatives for the wide range of organizational roles and tasks they are asked to assume. This is carried out through a network of residential labor schools, 20 labor folk high schools, and local union education committees working with the ABF and TBV. Through this elaborate system, the unions claim to reach one out of six of their members each year with some form of educational activity (Eiger 1988) (see *Europe, Nordic Countries; Baltic Countries*).

5. The United Kingdom Model

At the risk of over-simplification, the British system of labor education can be placed somewhere between the Swedish and German models on one side and the North American model on the other, but in recent years it appears to be converging with the latter. As with all labor education systems, its evolution cannot be understood outside of the context of the special history and character of the British labor movement. It is different from the three systems discussed above in the special role played by the estimated 200,000 shop stewards—an institution that has evolved its own traditions and militant culture.

University extension programs with a partial outreach to workers were started as early as 1873 at Cambridge and in 1878 at Oxford. At the turn of the century, workers turned to the wide spectrum of socialist ideas ranging from Fabianism, Christian socialism and social democracy to syndicalism and guild socialism. An opposing ideological approach was the United Kingdom's version of social uplift education for workers, the counterpart of such institutions in the United States as the Bryn Mawr School for Women Workers. This view of education centered on the social sciences and liberal arts and sought to promote social harmony. In the United Kingdom it was represented by Albert Mansbridge who helped found the Workers' Education Association (WEA), a system of liberal education based on the cooperative involvement of universities, Labor Party branches, local unions, and cooperatives.

However, as labor struggles grew in the effort to organize unions, centers were needed to provide more advanced long-term leadership education for trade unionists. Ruskin College in Oxford, founded in 1899, was the first of these pioneering centers (Elvin 1949). To this day it is one of the best-known labor education institutions in the world. Students have a choice of studies lasting one or two years, with most attending the two-year program. Some trade unionists take advantage of obtaining a full four-year university degree by enrolling for an extra two years in one of the colleges of Oxford University (Nash 1980).

After the Second World War the Labour government sought to expand worker education through a system of Local Educational Authorities (LEAs). The growth of the LEAs alongside the worker education services of university extramural departments undercut the functions of the WEA. By 1950, less than 10 percent of WEA classes were specifically held for trade unionists. In 1966, the Trades Union Congress set up an education committee to supervise all labor education it helped subsidize. As a result, the nature of the WEA courses through the unions shifted from broader liberal education themes to a much greater emphasis on labor-requested practical technique or "tool" subjects similar to those demanded by the unions in the United States (McIlroy 1980).

Efforts were made to export the early WEA model

to many of the British Commonwealth countries. In New Zealand, it continues to play a small part in worker education offerings. In Australia, its role has declined even more as the universities, colleges, and state departments of further education have taken on the challenge of providing workers with educational services.

Although attempts were made, starting in 1917 by Albert Mansbridge (general secretary of the WEA in England), to introduce the Workers' Education Association into Canadian cities and some tutorial-type programs were organized for workers, after an early period of growth the WEA never took root in Canada (Verner and Dickinson 1974). Since many of Canada's larger unions were affiliates of American-based unions, Canadian labor education evolved more closely along the direction taken in the United States.

Nongovernmental organizations throughout the world concerned with worker education in the tradition of the WEA formed the International Federation of Worker Education Associations (IFWEA) in 1947, which has grown to embrace member associations in Western Europe, Africa, Asia, and the Middle East. The IFWEA continues to provide opportunities for these associations to exchange information and promote worker education internationally.

Today the central focus of British labor education is on meeting the practical "tool subject" needs of the large shop steward movement (Nash 1980). The growth of shop steward courses can be traced from 155 programs for 2,263 stewards in 1968 to well over 100,000 enrollees in the late 1980s. Another area gaining increased attention is training union officers in recruitment and organizing. This priority is a response to the 22 percent decline in union membership in the years from 1979 to 1987. With these shifts the British system has been brought much closer to the American model than the continental European systems.

The ebbing of union strength has had a marked negative impact on British union and university programs. A number of university extension (extramural) programs have been terminated during the 1980s as funding from the Department of Education was sharply cut back, and those that remain now give a lower priority to labor education.

6. The Content of Labor Education

The content of labor education reflects the wide range of needs, interests, and philosophies of trade unionists and their organizations. In all the countries studied a central focus is on basic trades union education courses that equip members to participate effectively in their unions and prepare leaders for the multiplicity of roles they must play. Beyond these core courses, differences in subject priorities emerge based on the differences among the organizations in their strategies and goals.

Sweden's system of worker education activities was given a particular impetus in recent decades by at least two labor movement priority goals: (a) a commitment to further workplace transformation through democratization as a central aim of industrial relations policy; and (b) the promotion of greater equality and social justice by bridging the education gap between classes.

The first goal of workplace democratization has had a special impact on the content and scope of labor education in Sweden and Germany in the 1970s and 1980s. Indeed, the most innovative and expansive periods in the development of Swedish and German labor education occurred in the 1970s (as early as the 1950s in Germany) when both labor movements pursued an enlargement of worker participation in workplace decisions through legislative reforms. As a result of these reforms, often referred to as "codetermination," both labor movements had to meet the challenge of training thousands of worker representatives that were mandated by law to sit on company boards (Eiger 1982). Beyond this group, 150,000 work councillors and a parallel structure of union shop stewards had to be trained in Germany; in Sweden, thousands of new members of codetermination committees, stewards, union ombudsmen, and working environment representatives had to be trained as well.

Since in the United States and the United Kingdom there are no legislated frameworks for various forms of codetermination or worker involvement in workplace decisions, there is nothing comparable to Sweden in terms of the emphasis on education for workplace democratization.

7. Current and Future Trends

The decline of the American labor movement during the last two decades has required labor educators to stress programs that strengthen the organizational framework of unions. A growing emphasis is placed on internal and external organizing and membership involvement. Organizational development seminars are another important response to this problem; since 1980 in the United States this has included introducing trade unionists to strategic planning.

In response to large-scale changes in the demographic composition of the workforce and the need to have the various levels of labor's organizational structure reflect the gender and ethnic changes that have taken place, labor educators are devoting increased resources to leadership development programs among women and minority group workers. In addition, all the labor movements discussed have a serious generational problem in trying to reach and integrate young workers. Labor education aimed at young workers is a growing priority.

In response to the needs generated by the pace and nature of technological change, labor educators are beginning to focus on the ends to which it is put and the values and policy choices that drive it. Educational programs that diffuse knowledge of the new production systems also explore how they can be made human-centered rather than alienating.

In responding to new information technology, workers not only need to have access to the many new sources of information but also to avoid being overwhelmed. Toward this end, labor educators are challenged to develop the capacity among workers for critical inquiry and self-directed learning.

Possibly the most important challenge arises from the globalization of the economy. Capital is organized across national frontiers and is highly mobile, while labor is still organized along national lines and is relatively immobile. Labor educational programs will have to focus increasingly on international issues and the strengthening of international labor relationships and strategies.

Labor educators are required to challenge the view that cultural activities are an elite form of expression to be enjoyed by the privileged few. Counterposed to such an elitist view are worker education programs sponsored by labor unions such as the Bread and Roses project in the United States and the Art Promotion Society in Sweden. Many unions throughout the world have sponsored programs inspired by these models.

8. Labor Education Methods

The methods of labor education are highly participatory, problem-centered and action-oriented. This methodology is not only a means of accommodating different adult learning styles, but also based on an awareness among labor educators that democratic political and economic ends require means that are consistent with those ends. For example, Sweden's worker education movement developed the innovative concept of the study circle as early as 1902, inspired by the Chautauqua adult education circles in the United States (see *Study Circles*). The various forms assumed by tens of thousands of these study circles each year are much more participatory than traditional adult education classes (Blid 1990). The concept of the study circle has made inroads in the United States, as evidenced by the adoption of this method in a nationwide educational program sponsored by the Bricklayers Union.

Labor education programs in all countries make great use of role-playing, simulations, critical analysis of case studies, and action research.

9. Financing and Accessing Labor Education Opportunities

The many ways labor education programs are funded reflects the traditions of each national labor movement and the degree of influence it has on company and government policy. In the United States, the pendulum of government assistance has shifted with each back and forth swing from liberalism to conservatism. Today, with the pendulum stuck in more than a ten-year conservative cycle, there is little direct support for labor education.

Nevertheless, as was pointed out earlier, some 50 state universities and community colleges still conduct a wide range of labor education programs through unions using partial subsidies from state appropriations. Today, as a result of federal cuts in revenues to the states deepening the fiscal crisis experienced by most states, shrinking subsidies to university labor education are being further cut back.

The North American approach to overcoming the barriers preventing access to worker education is based on the principle of *laissez-faire*, that is, to leave it to the labor market parties to negotiate such issues as educational leave for workers and educational funds jointly administered by companies and unions. Since the 1970s, a number of unions have negotiated various contractual provisions for tuition refund programs and educational funds based on a percentage of hourly earnings. Despite this approach, or perhaps because of it, a very small percentage of workers are covered and an even smaller percentage take advantage of the opportunities for further education that is offered. The most extensively financed programs in the United States are found in the car manufacturing industry, as a result of jointly negotiated union and company education funds.

The Swedish example represents a completely different approach to the problem of eliminating access and financial barriers; government education policy in Sweden is geared to eliminating each of the obstacles. The obstacle of the lack of opportunities is addressed not only with full subsidization of higher education, but also with generous government financing, with few strings attached, of tens of thousands of study circles conducted by the Workers Education Association, the trade unions, and the adult education programs of ten other voluntary educational associations, as well as the municipal adult education authorities. The obstacle of obtaining time off from one's job for short-and long-term study is addressed through Swedish legislation that offers a general entitlement to educational leave. Although the employer cannot deny such leave or choose the precise course of study, the leave can be deferred for up to a maximum of six months. The worker's problem of financing the studies is often met, particularly for workers who have educational disadvantages, through a variety of available benefits and stipends.

In Germany, the labor movement has fought to get paid time off for study since 1963. Initially, as in the United States, this goal was pursued through collective bargaining. Dissatisfied by the slowness of the process, the German Trades Union Federation, like its Swedish counterpart, took the legislative route, with only partial success, in order to mandate such leaves in several *Länder* (Von Moltke and Schneevoigt 1977).

In the United Kingdom, the unions used collective bargaining to obtain what they referred to as "day release" for shop steward and union member education. As a result of these day release agreements with the Employers' Confederation, large firms, starting in 1969, began releasing stewards from their jobs with pay to attend one-day programs each week for five weeks. Labor educators in the United Kingdom attribute much of the expansion of shop steward training to these day release opportunities. In Sweden, the Union Representative Act passed in 1976 has encouraged even more far-reaching forms of paid time off for union education. Other financial barriers were addressed in a limited way in the United Kingdom through large grants from the government to hire tutors for labor education courses. Since the 1950s, an important source of funding for labor education in Latin American, African, and Asian countries is through the various international outreach agencies of the American, Swedish, and German labor movements. A significant role in supporting labor education in these regions is also played by the International Labour Organisation and international labor bodies such as the International Confederation of Free Trade Unions. Labor education programs in the less-developed countries understandably emphasize nation-building priorities through study of economic planning, development of cooperatives, as well as organizational and leadership skills.

10. Conclusion

Our brief journey through the development of labor education and worker education in four countries pointed up the ideological and historical threads woven through decades of development in each system along with an overview of their methodology, structure, and changing content.

The differences between the various systems of labor education not only reflect different national environments but also the philosophical differences that were placed into three categories: the organizing—class model, the servicing—instrumental model, and the labor—management partnership model. Although in the past there were tensions and debates among these different views of the mission of labor and its educational programs, there has in recent years been a trend toward the convergence of these models. Faced with similar challenges arising out of the globalization of capital and technological change, the three models are increasingly seen as not mutually exclusive, but capable of being combined in varying degrees depending on the particular situations and challenges confronting the trade unions.

See also: History of Adult Education; Technological Change and Education; Paid Educational Leave and Collective Bargaining

References

Blid H 1990 *Education By the People—Study Circles.* ABF/Workers Education Association, Brunsvik, Ludvika
Bloom J D 1990 Brookwood Labor College. In: London S H, Tarr E R, Wilson J F (eds.) 1990 *The Re-education of the American Working Class.* Greenwood Press, New York
Cook A H, Douty A M 1958 *Labor Education Outside the Unions.* A Review of Post war Programs in Western Europe and the United States. Cornell University, New York
Deutscher Gewerkschaftsbund (DGB) Ebert Stiftung 1973 *The German Labor Movement.* Druckhaus Deutz, Frankfurt
Eiger N 1981 Labor education and democracy in the workplace. *Working Life in Sweden* 22(11)
Eiger N 1982 Labor education through the West German Federation of Trade Unions. *J. Br. Soc. Ind. Tutors* 3(7): 7
Eiger N 1988 Worker education in Sweden: A force for extending democratic participation. *Scandinavian Review* 76(1): 81–89
Elvin L 1949 *The Story of Ruskin College 1899–1949.* Oxford University Press, Oxford
Levine H A 1973 Union-university and inter-university cooperation in the US. In: International Labour Office 1973 *The Role of Universities in Workers' Education.* International Labour Office, Geneva
McIlroy J A 1980 Education for the labor movement: United Kingdom experience past and present. *Lbr Studies J.* 4 (3): 208–11
Nash A 1980 British and American labor educators: A comparative analyses. *Lbr Studies J.* 4 (3): 250–57
Schneider F H 1941 *Patterns of Workers' Education: The Story of the Bryn Mawr Summer School.* American Council on Public Affairs, Washington, DC
Schultz D 1973 *The changing political nature of worker education: A case study of the Wisconsin School for Workers* (Doctoral dissertation, University of Wisconsin). University Microfilms, Ann Arbor, Michigan
Verner C, Dickinson G 1974 *Union Education in Canada.* Vancouver Adult Education Research Center, University of British Columbia, Vancouver
Von Moltke K, Schneevoigt N 1977 *Educational Leaves for Employees: European Experience for American Consideration.* Jossey-Bass, New York

Further Reading

Altenbaugh R J 1990 *Education for Struggle. The American Labor Colleges of the 1920's and 1930's.* Temple University Press, Philadelphia, Pennsylvania
Blyth J A 1983 *English University Adult Education, 1908–1958: The Unique Tradition.* Manchester University Press, Dover, New Hampshire
Denker J 1981 *Unions and Universities: The Rise of the New Labor Leader.* Allanheld Osmun and Company, Montclair, New Jersey
Griggs C 1983 *The Trades Union Congress and the Struggle for Education, 1868–1925.* Falmer Press, Bavcombe

Hansome M 1963 *World Workers Education Movements: Their Social Significance.* AMS Press, New York

International Labour Office 1974 *The Role of Universities in Workers Education.* International Labour Office, Geneva

Levine H A 1973 Labor management policies on educational opportunities. Unpublished paper presented at Recurrent Education Conference, March 21, 1973, Georgetown University (minor) DHEW/OECD (CERI)/PSL-GV

London S H, Tarr E R, Wilson J F (eds.) 1990 *The Re-Education of the American Working Class.* Greenwood Press, New York

Rogin L, Rachlin M 1968 *Survey of Adult Education Opportunities for Labor: Labor Education in the United States.* National Institute of Labor Education, Washington, DC

Wertheimer B M (ed.) 1981 *Labor Education for Women Workers.* Temple University Press, Philadelphia, Pennsylvania

SECTION VI

Organization

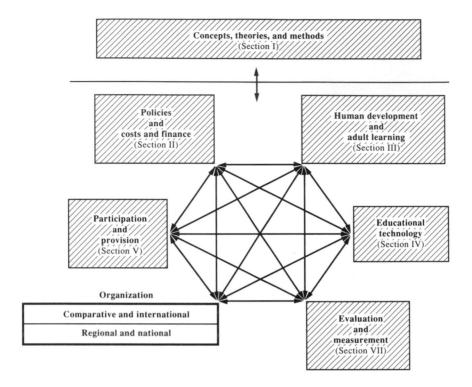

Figure 1
Schematic representation of Section VI in relation to the other Sections

SECTION VI

Organization

Introduction

A. C. Tuijnman

Whereas some aspects of adult education organization and provision are unique to a given region or country, there are also many common characteristics in many parts of the world. The purpose of Section VI is to describe the international, regional and, in some cases, the national dimensions of adult education and training. The schema (Fig.1) shows the relationship of Section VI to the other sections of the *Encyclopedia*.

1. Comparative and International Organization

International adult education can be seen as a process whereby people take part in learning activities that increase their sensitivity, understanding, and knowledge of other cultures and societies. The term can also refer to the systematic study of the processes of adult education and training as they take place in other countries. Comparative adult education, in contrast, is described as an area of study focused on the organization and provision of learning opportunities for adults in an international perspective, and is one that uses a comparative and empirical approach to the collection and analysis of data. If comparative adult education is understood to refer to research studies that employ data, whether qualitative or quantitative, from one or more countries or regions to establish general statements about adult education and training that are valid for more than one country, then many of the entries included in Section VI illustrate that the field generally has not advanced beyond the initial stages of development, which involve descriptions of international cooperation and accounts of regional forces and factors in the development of adult education and training. A similar conclusion was reached by Kidd and Titmus in 1985, when the first edition of the *International Encyclopedia of Education* appeared in print.

The above conclusion notwithstanding, much has happened in comparative adult education during the period since 1985. While theoretically inclined writers constructed a conceptual framework for comparative adult education, others pursued new work on the development of internationally transparent and consistent definitions of adult education and training. Progress has also been made in the area of comparative research methodology. A third aspect of growth is that a degree of consensus about the aims, means, and ends of international data collection on adult education emerged during the early 1990s.

In a sense, 1995 may well come to be seen as marking a crucial moment in the development of comparative adult education. That year saw the publication of the first internationally comparable indicators of participation in adult education and training by the Organisation for Economic Co-operation and Development (OECD). The first *OECD Draft Manual for International Training Statistics* was also published in that year. A third noteworthy development in 1995 was the inclusion, for the first time, of categories of public and private spending on adult education and training in the joint UOC questionnaires, which are used by UNESCO, OECD, and the European Union to collect comparable data on educational finance and expenditure. Also in 1995, UNESCO embarked on the difficult task of revising the International Standard Classification of Education (ISCED), with the aim of expanding the scope of the international data system by including variables on adult education, distance education, nonformal education, and continuing vocational training. While the fruits of this effort still lie in the future, 1995 also saw the conclusion of two comparative studies that had involved—for the first time in the history of the field—large-scale and common data collections from internationally defined samples of adults in different countries. The first, the Continuing Vocational Training Survey (CVTS), was undertaken by the countries belonging to the European Union. The second, the International Adult Literacy Survey (IALS), was a large-scale survey of the basic literacy skills of the adult populations in seven industrialized countries.

The initiatives mentioned above were only possible because governments and international organizations had assigned priority to the development of a comparative knowledge base in adult education and training. That so much was achieved so quickly shows that the field of adult education has moved closer to the mainstay of both educational policy-making and research by the mid-1990s. Much can be achieved in the coming years if the interests of the policymakers, researchers, and the public can be sustained. However, a cautionary note must be inserted here because, despite the successes booked in recent years, the field of comparative adult education is still in its infancy with respect to both data collection and the effort to use the information as a basis for generalization. This is the central conclusion emerging from the first two entries in Section VI, namely Titmus' review of comparative adult education, and Wilson's overview of comparative studies in the field of vocational education and training.

The entries by Titmus, Wilson, Imel, Duke, Khalil-Khouri, Salt and Bowland, Comings, Long, and Bélanger and Mobarak make it clear that several international organizations, nongovernmental and professional associations, and specialized agencies have long played an important role in facilitating the development of adult education and training, for example by encouraging theoretical and conceptual work and by focusing the efforts to clarify definitions, promote competence building, stimulate the exchange of knowledge about promising practices, and manage the compilation of statistical information about finance, provision, and participation. Organizations belonging to the United Nations family, such as the United Nations Educational, Scientific and Cultural Organization (UNESCO), the International Labour Organization (ILO), the World Health Organization (WHO), the Food and Agricultural Organization (FAO), and the United Nations Children Fund (UNICEF) have been among the principal actors in adult and nonformal education worldwide. The UNESCO World Conferences on Adult Education, through the UNESCO Recommendations for Adult Education, were particularly instrumental in proposing a standard terminology and formulating concrete policies for the expansion of adult education and training within the context of national plans for educational development. Other agencies such as the Council of Europe, the Organisation for Economic Co-operation and Development, the World Bank, the European Union, the Arab Region Literacy Organization (ARLO), and the Asian-Pacific Education Council (APEC) have also made significant contributions in areas such as lifelong learning, recurrent education, continuing vocational training, adult literacy, and nonformal education.

Nongovernmental organizations, popular movements, and networks operating at the international, regional, and national levels have traditionally also played a critically important role in the development of adult education, particularly in areas such as literacy and popular education. Comings, in an entry describing the main nongovernmental organizations active in the field of adult education, points out that such organizations play an important role in supplementing

the efforts of others, and that they can be successful in ways that governments can not. Khalil-Khouri, for example, describes how the International Council of Adult Education (ICAE) was established in Toronto in 1973 by the Canadian educator and scholar J. Roby Kidd, and what contributions ICAE has since made to the fields of adult education, literacy, and nonformal education. Additional dimensions of international adult education are discussed in the entries by Long on professional associations and by Imel on information sources in adult education.

2. Regional and National Studies

As previously noted, whereas there is a dearth of rigorously comparative studies in adult education at the international level, there are numerous publications in which useful descriptions are given of policies, programs, and practices of adult education in different countries. The entries grouped together in this subsection present numerous case studies of adult education and training in all world regions and, in a few cases, of the experience of a single country.

Some attention is given to the uses of the terminology of adult education in each region. Specific concepts and theories are explained if they are considered crucial for an understanding of the history and practice of adult education and training in the region concerned. The entries furthermore offer a brief history of adult education in the regions, mention the scope, orientation, and main goals of adult education, and describe the structural characteristics of the delivery systems in the countries of the region. Some indications of the extent and social distribution of participation, and aspects of control, legislation, and finance are also offered. Many entries also describe recent and emerging issues that pose challenges for policy, research, and practice.

Readers will note that more attention is devoted to some world regions or groups of countries than to others. One constraint was posed by the number of entries that could be devoted to Section VI. A second, less obvious limitation was posed by the difficulty of reviewing developments in some regions and countries undergoing rapid political and social change. These limitations notwithstanding, most world regions and groups of countries are covered in the 20 entries included in this subsection.

Okedara deals with the theory and practice of adult education in English-speaking, bilingual or multilingual countries in Africa. The countries covered by Okedara lie mostly in Sub-Saharan Africa and share cultural experience with the United Kingdom through their colonial history. The entry also treats adult education in Ethiopia and Liberia—two countries that are English-language oriented even though they never were under British rule. In the next entry, Ouane concentrates on adult education in the countries in mostly Western Africa. The focus of the entry is on the characteristics and other specificities of adult education and training in what is termed "Francophone Africa," a region molded by a common history and a context shaped by the experience of French colonialism.

Algeria, Tunisia, Morocco and other countries in Northern Africa that to an extent share the experience of French administration are not discussed by Ouane. Instead these countries are covered in a subsequent entry by Massialas, who deals with adult education and training in the Arab States. Massialas explains why the organization and provision of adult education pose pressing problems for many of the 22 countries making up the large and varied Arab world.

Turning to the Asian and Pacific region, Cheng, Wong, and Zhou describe the characteristics of the organization and provision of adult education in numerous countries in East and Southeast Asia. The authors note that the development of adult education in this vast region is influenced not only by economic development priorities, but also by values and expectations about the functions of education in society, which form part of the distinct cultural heritages of the region. Napitupulu, in the next entry, offers an overview of literacy education in countries in Southeast Asia, in particular Indonesia, Malaysia, the Philippines, Thailand, and Vietnam. Adult education and training in the People's Republic of China are the subjects of a separate entry. Chuan discusses the following aspects of Chinese adult education: concepts and principles, history, functions, organization and modes of provision, and administration. Adult education policy and research are given special attention. Two entries are devoted to the Japanese situation and experience of adult education and training. The first, by Miura, considers social education and adult education for the development of culture and leisure. Training and other forms of adult education "for investment" are the subject of a second entry contributed by Sako. Caldwell, finally, reviews the developments and position of adult education and training in Australia and New Zealand, two countries that increasingly seek to define their place and future in relation to other countries located in the Asian and Pacific region.

The principles, functions and organization of adult education and training in countries in or near the Indian Subcontinent are discussed by Tilak, who notes that the promotion of adult education and especially literacy should be a high priority for the governments in the region. Not only are the adult literacy rates low, but even primary education is far from universal in Bangladesh, India, Nepal, Pakistan, and other countries in the region.

Four entries are devoted to adult education and training in the Americas. Grossi and Palma describe the history and current situation of adult education in Latin America. Ducci, in the next entry, concentrates on the National Training Agencies in Latin America. By educating and training significant portions of the labor force, these agencies play a very important role in social and especially economic development. Giere, Hielscher, and Ramesar introduce the rich and diverse experience of adult education and training in Central America and the Caribbean. The authors cover not only Cuba, Nicaragua, and Mexico, but also a host of other, usually smaller, nations in the Caribbean archipelago. Examples are Haiti, Trinidad and Tobago, Curacao and Aruba, and mainland countries such as Guyana, Surinam, and Belize. Finally, adult education in North America is the subject of an entry contributed by Griffith. He notes that emphasis is placed on the goals and scope of adult education and training in Canada and the United States. Significant organizations and associations, financing, and research orientations are also addressed.

This *Encyclopedia* devotes five entries to the highly varied experience in adult education and training of the European countries. Märja and Vooglaid review the history, needs, and priorities of adult education in three newly independent Baltic countries: Latvia, Lithuania, and Estonia. Kranjc reviews the development of adult education in the Central and Eastern European countries, the focus being on Albania, Bulgaria, the Czech Republic, Hungary, Moldavia, Poland, Romania, and the Slovak Republic. Adult education and training in the Nordic countries of Denmark, Finland, Iceland, Norway, and Sweden are the subject of the entry by Wahlgren. The fourth entry, by Houtkoop, deals with adult education in the European Union countries in Western and Southern Europe. Walther, in the last entry of this cluster, describes a number of European Union initiatives in adult education and continuing vocational training.

(a)   Comparative and International Organization

Comparative Studies: Adult Education

C. J. Titmus

Little attention has been devoted in comparative education studies to adult education, no doubt because it was long considered a marginal area. For this reason, as educational opportunities have taken on global significance, adult educators have developed comparative studies in this field independently of the mainstream of comparative education. This situation has had certain advantages, for example, in terms of promoting a common understanding of concepts and cementing networks, but there are also disadvantages. One important disadvantage is that this separation has led to a neglect of empirical, positivist studies in comparative adult education.

In this entry the development, purposes, forms, topics of study, problems, and issues of comparative adult education are considered, together with the added dimensions of lifelong learning and recurrent education.

1. Development

From a relatively early stage in its history adult education acquired an international dimension. In the nineteenth century there was much borrowing of practices between countries. From 1925 to the Second World War the World Association for Adult Education attracted into membership most of the countries in which the education of adults was then established on any substantial scale. After 1945 its work was taken over by a number of world and regional organizations. Several United Nations agencies, the World Bank, OECD, and other bodies which have contributed to the worldwide spread of adult education, became involved in international studies of the educational needs and realizations of adults.

Additionally, at regional level, the Council of Europe, the European Community, and the Organization of American States have played a similar role. A number of nongovernmental organizations have been formed. These include the Asian and South Pacific Bureau of Adult Education (ASPBAE), the African Adult Education Association (AAEA), the European Bureau of Adult Education (EBAE), and, since 1973, a world association, the International Council of Adult Education (ICAE), all established as a result of interest in international development and all stimulating it through their meetings and publications.

The work of these organizations has helped to create a demand for more effective ways of comparing adult education activities in different countries. The First International Conference on the subject was held at Exeter, New Hampshire, in 1966, on the initiative of the International Congress of University Adult Education (ICUAE). Other meetings have followed, including one in 1991 in Ibadan, Nigeria, under the auspices of the Committee for the Study and Research in Comparative Adult Education (CSRCAE), which was formed jointly by ICAE and ICUAE.

The growth of interest in the field is demonstrated by the number of journals which have been founded to offer forums for discussion and to report research. Among them are *Convergence*, published in Canada for ICAE, and the *International Journal of University Adult Education*, now over 30 years old and edited in the United Kingdom for ICUAE. From Germany have come *Adult Education and Development*, a publication in English of the German Adult Education Association, which concentrates on the Third World, and the *Internationales Jahrbuch der Erwachsenenbildung*. This last journal, like the British periodical, the *International Journal of Lifelong Education*, is not a product of an association, but an independent initiative of the editor(s).

Although adult educators have to some extent learned their lessons from work already conducted in comparative education (Bennett et al. 1975), a number have been wary of following mainstream ideas too slavishly. Comparative education concerns itself for the most part with school and higher education systems, although it has begun to make ritual obeisance to adult education. Its theories and practices, comparative adult educators have argued, take no account of the specific nature and circumstances of their field. Therefore it should not be assumed uncritically that the experience of comparative education applies to adult education.

2. Purposes

Most comparative adult educators would agree that their primary goals were the orthodox ones of comparative education, namely, studying other societies' practices to understand better one's own (Bennett et al. 1975 p.10). Certain scholars have also been inspired by the belief that it would be possible to arrive at a coherent, global theory of adult education with the help of comparative studies. At a more immediately practical level it has been argued by some scholars that a general map of the whole territory of adult education should be drawn up, so that meaningful comparison of parts of it would be possible.

There has been some disagreement on the relative priority to be given to macro versus micro studies and, not surprisingly, some discussion of method. Consideration of method has generally been at a less theoretical level than in comparative education, the methodological ideas of which, with some exceptions, have generally been followed (Lichtner 1989).

On the whole, however, comparative adult education has been closely concerned with the practical needs of the field. Adult educators have not been reluctant to engage in cultural borrowing and their interest in what colleagues elsewhere have been doing has always been largely inspired by the underlying hope of importing or exporting successful practices. Indeed, the worldwide spread of adult education since the Second World War has been a large-scale example of cultural borrowing and imposition (see *Adult Education: Concepts and Principles*). It was undertaken in its early years on the basis of faith rather than study of the contexts involved, not always with the best results, but in later years more critical comparative approaches have been adopted, for example, by the People's Republic of China (Duke 1987).

Comparative adult educators have found themselves obliged to conduct studies of immediate relevance, if not to cultural borrowing, then certainly to decision-making concerning policies and practice. It is for these that funding, limited as it is, is most readily available. For example, the increasing perception that education contributes to the ability of countries to compete with others economically has led to attempts to design education to support economic growth. In Europe particularly, the ever closer relations between states of the European Community has caused governments to commission studies of the continuing education of their rivals (e.g., Bayerisches Staatsinstitut für Hochschulforschung und Hochschulplanung 1989).

3. Forms of Study

The worldwide growth of adult education and the development of identifiable national patterns of provision is relatively recent. Hence, of necessity, there is a continuing flow of basic single-nation studies. Most are factual descriptions of what is done and how it is organized, notably those that are sponsored or published by government agencies, for example, those of Scandinavian countries. Between 1977 and 1984 the European Center for Leisure and Education in Prague, with UNESCO financial support, commissioned and published 14 studies of individual states, in both Eastern and Western Europe (ECLE 1977–84). Each was written by a native of the country, but for a comparative perspective in single-nation studies particularly valuable contributions have been made by foreigners, usually Americans or Europeans (e.g., Kunzel 1974, Hunter and Keehn 1985).

Single-nation studies and collections of individual nation studies drawn up according to a common framework provide the materials for comparison. This juxtaposition constitutes the common form adopted by intergovernmental organizations for their reports, whether of national systems as a whole or of kinds of provision within those systems (e.g., UNESCO 1984).

Works which actually compare one country with others, if only to identify differences and similarities between them, are rare. Those that attempt some investigation of the reasons behind these differences and similarities are even rarer. The European Center for the Development of Vocational Training (CEDEFOP), set up by the European Communities, has published some valuable work. For the most part, attempts at interpretative comparison have been left in the hands of individual scholars, more of whom are showing the confidence to engage in such work (Titmus 1981).

The form of study specially favored in adult education is the overview. Instead of comparing individual states, a group of countries are examined with a view to identifying common features of all or part of their adult education provision, although in some projects individual deviations from the norm are also noted. Groups are not chosen at random, but for geographical proximity or shared characteristics of their culture which appear to exert a significant influence on their adult education. Most frequently the basis of selection has been regional (Gajardo 1983), but there are also studies of countries at a similar level of economic development (Vélis 1990). In addition, common religion or political systems may form the criteria for choice, or age groups—young adults or the elderly, for example—although these are usually combined with others, such as regional ones. Potentially the range of groups is very wide. There have been global overviews, commissioned by UNESCO (e.g., Lowe 1982, Bhola 1988), or undertaken by individuals on their own initiative (Hopkins 1985).

Interest in overviews appears to indicate an awareness that, while adult education is still organized in discrete national units, it is less uniquely a product of the state in which it is provided than schools or higher education are, and that it derives its character to a far greater extent than these forms of education from forces that transcend any distinctive national society. Overviews seem to confirm this perception and indicate that international and transnational influences are becoming more significant.

Understanding the ways in which the international context impacts on adult education requires further investigation, but existing comparative studies suggest some possible contributory factors. The state apparatus has played a minor role in adult education until recent times. The growth in adult education owes much to the provision made by private organizations—religious, social, or political associations, or commercial and industrial companies—operating for their own ends. Many of these organizations are international or have strong international links and their perspective is frequently wider than that of the nation-state. Adult education, being less institutionalized, is less enclosed within state boundaries than formal education. Unlike formal schooling, a primary aim of which is long-term socialization into a specific state, adult education, in fact if not in principle, largely serves limited, short-term educational needs of the present or the immediate future, which are not necessarily deeply rooted in the culture of the society in which it occurs.

4. Subjects of International and Comparative Study

Apart from the continuing production of general surveys of adult education in individual states, most comparative work has been devoted to those adult education activities which globally have attracted the most extensive provision. These include efforts to eradicate illiteracy, to which a number of UNESCO agencies, the World Bank, and other national and international agencies have devoted considerable resources and adult vocational education. Attempts to achieve universal literacy have involved workers indigenous to the countries in which action has been taken, as well as outside experts. Such programs have covered almost all the developing world and have provided examples of measurable inputs, applied simultaneously to a number of national situations, thereby creating cases more than usually favorable to comparative study. Indeed, many reports of campaigns in individual countries and in groups of countries, and of global studies have been generated from the research associated with these activities (UNESCO 1976).

In the late 1970s and the 1980s industrialized countries openly recognized that adult illiteracy and lack of basic education were not purely problems of the Third World. This common awareness, in turn, inspired an international sharing of experiences resulting in a number of comparative studies (Vélis 1990).

The importance accorded to the eradication of illiteracy is linked to a concern for vocational education for adults. In the 1970s UNESCO published a series of reports on developing countries including Botswana, Egypt, Argentina, and the Republic of Korea from which a number of regional overviews have appeared. The European Center for the Development of Vocational Training has been particularly active in sponsoring studies of adult education provision and needs in Europe. Among its publications have been reports on youth unemployment and vocational training, the financing of vocational training, and the training of vocational educators (Théry 1984) and of migrant workers.

Topics in adult education which have resulted in extended international or cross-national study are usually those that have succeeded in attracting the attention of an international governmental or nongovernmental organization as a result of having some immediate relevance for policy. Therefore, funds have usually been made available for the study of such topics. The OECD has sponsored reports on learning opportunities for adults and adult participation in study. UNESCO has sponsored work on lifelong education and adult education terminology (see *Adult Education: Concepts and Principles*). The European Bureau of Adult Education has specialized in collating and reviewing legislation (EBAE 1985) and terminology.

Comparative adult education has tended to reflect the changing preoccupations of national and international authorities rather than of people at the grassroots level. For example, interest in paid educational leave, which was strong in the 1970s, has faded to some extent, as hopes of achieving it as a universal right of adults have declined (see *Paid Educational Leave and Collective Bargaining*). In the 1980s wider access, particularly nonconventional access, of adults to higher education became a significant issue of policy and practice in a number of countries. A belief that such access was a topic of international concern led to the introduction of a comparative dimension in a number of studies on access (Schütze et al. 1987). Nonformal education and the development needs of the Third World have repeatedly been under investigation.

Some topics have, by virtue of their wide appeal, gained their own momentum. Women's education is a theme to which many articles and books have been devoted (see *Women and Adult Education*). The literature of correspondence and distance education overlaps with examinations of the use of mass media in adult education and of open learning systems (see *Concepts of Educational Technology*). The experience of other countries in the training of adult educators is seen to be of importance as the field has become more professionalized (Théry 1983).

5. Comparative Studies in Lifelong Learning and Recurrent Education

Comparative studies, like other enquiries into adult education, increasingly adopt a lifelong perspective, although for the most part they do not place their topics explicitly within the framework of lifelong education. The distinction between youth and continuing education is rather more blurred in developing countries, and studies of literacy campaigns, nonformal education, and integrated rural development are necessarily conducted within a "cradle to grave" framework. In advanced states adult or continuing education is still perceived and studied, in practice if not in theory, as a distinct sector. There is a tendency to include the words "lifelong learning" or "recurrent education" in the titles of publications without giving those concepts much attention in the contents.

The fate of lifelong education is an example of changing fashion in comparative adult education. For a number of years the Council of Europe conducted an enquiry into the extent to which permanent or lifelong education was being achieved in its member states, and followed it up with several experimental projects in permanent education. The UNESCO Institute for Education, in Hamburg, also addressed lifelong education, but its case studies were mainly school-oriented and gave limited influence to postinitial education. Since the 1970s, however, the number of comparative or international studies explicitly devoted to the subject has declined. Progress may be being made toward lifelong education, but it is no longer discussed to the same degree in those actual terms (see *Lifelong and Continuing Education*).

The concept of recurrent education—the alternation of periods of education with periods of work or other activity throughout life—has attracted study because it is more clearly understandable than lifelong education. Recurrent education is already realized, in some measure, in adult education and is linked to the issues of paid educational leave. However, few comparative studies have been devoted specifically to recurrent education, and it tends to be considered, if at all, under the more general headings of adult or continuing education (see *Recurrent Education*).

6. Comparative Adult Education in the World

Work in comparative adult education began in North America and Europe. It would appear that more research is still conducted in these regions than anywhere else, particularly in the English-speaking countries. An important factor in this predominance may be the common language. Scholarly access to foreign education is difficult for those who do not understand the language of the countries being investigated. Since English is an official language of a larger part of the globe than any other tongue, people who only speak English have immediate access to more countries than those who are limited to any other single language. In addition, they have the advantage that the United Kingdom and the United States have been involved in the life of other regions for longer than most other countries.

References in this entry indicate, however, a growing interest by many countries in comparative studies—not only European countries, such as the Federal Republic of Germany, Sweden, and Italy, but countries in parts of the developing world. Further evidence of the value of a common language (Spanish, except in Brazil) as a facilitator of comparative investigation is provided by the number of published works dealing with aspects of adult or popular education in the Latin American region (see *Latin America: Adult Education*). The growing sense of common interest among countries of the Pacific Rim is beginning to stimulate comparison and overview in that region. African scholars are relating their contemporary adult education to that of the former colonial powers, which introduced it to the Continent (see *Africa, Anglophone; Africa, Francophone*).

7. Issues Confronting Comparative Adult Education

The scope for comparative research into adult education is vast, not merely because systematic work in it only began quite recently, but because the field itself has become so large. Although the progress being made does credit to the scholars engaged in it, they are few and the resources made available to them are small. Lack of opportunities for research training in comparative investigation and lack of confidence, both on the part of educational researchers and potential sponsors, in the validity of comparative studies in adult education are other contributory factors to the limited amount and quality of comparative research.

To compare phenomena in this field is particularly difficult because of the breadth and diversity of what is comprehended within the term "adult education," and because of the variations in the meaning attaching to it from country to country. The field is rich, but not precise, in its terminology and the connotations of its terms need to be made culturally specific. Some progress has been made toward a common international understanding of adult education by the compilation of international glossaries, by the EBAE (EBAE 1980) and by UNESCO (Titmus et al. 1979). Both these works have inspired offshoots, but their interpretations lag behind changes in usage.

In most countries initial education has a common

institutional framework to which national systems either conform or aspire. Adult education is still largely unstructured throughout the world, or alternatively the structure is complex and the patterns have yet to be identified with confidence. It is becoming more institutionalized, but still features initiatives undertaken outside formal structures to meet temporary needs, which last only as long as the need (or, unfortunately, only as long as financing) is present.

The fragmentation, lack of organization, and ephemeral nature of a considerable portion of adult education and a traditional reluctance to attribute much importance to quantification have meant that statistics have either not been compiled or have not been presented in usable forms (see *Measurement of Adult Education; Statistics of Adult and Nonformal Education*). This is true even of countries and areas of provision where adult education is most highly structured. For example, in the former Federal Republic of Germany there are no national records of the number of participants in adult education provided by institutions of higher education, or by employers. Some attempts have been made to encourage the collection of data which is comparable internationally (UNESCO 1975), but without significant success. However, some new work was undertaken recently under the auspices of the OECD, in which the first comparable indicators were constructed in the areas of job-related adult education and training (Borkowsky et al. 1995), and adult literacy (Tuijnman et al. 1995). It is too early, however, to evaluate the significance of these new efforts.

Not only comparative adult educators, but also adult educators in general, have not shared the belief in the primacy of quantitative research which dominated the general field of comparative education in the 1970s. Nevertheless, there is a growing sense that qualitative studies, of the kind common in the past, would be strengthened by a quantitative dimension. Until reliable and comparable data become available, the possibilities open to comparative adult education will remain restricted.

See also: Comparative Studies: Vocational Education and Training; International Adult Education; International Council for Adult Education; UNESCO and Adult Education; Statistics of Adult and Nonformal Education; Statistics of Employee Training

References

Bayerischers Staatsinstitut für Hochschulforschung und Hochschulplanung (ed.) 1989 *Wissenschaftliche Weiterbildung in sieben westlichen Industrieländern.* Bundesminister für Bildung und Wissenschaft, Bonn

Bennett C, Kidd J R, Kulich J (ed.) 1975 *Comparative Studies in Adult Education: An Anthology.* Syracuse University, Syracuse, New York

Bhola H S 1988 *World Trends and Issues in Adult Education.* Jessica Kingsley/UNESCO, London

Borkowsky A, van der Heiden M, Tuijnman A C 1995 Indicators of continuing education and training. In: *Education and Employment.* OECD, Paris

Duke C 1987 (ed.) *Adult Education: International Perspectives from China.* Croom Helm, London

European Bureau of Adult Education (EBAE) 1980 *The Terminology of Adult Education/Continuing Education.* EBAE, Amersfoort

European Bureau of Adult Education 1985 *Survey of Adult Education Legislation.* EBAE, Amersfoort

European Centre for Leisure and Education (ECLE) 1977–84 *Adult Education in Europe: Studies and Documents. Vol. 1: Czechoslovakia; Vol. 2: France; Vol. 3: Hungary; Vol. 4: Yugoslavia; Vol. 5: German Democratic Republic: Vol. 6: Poland; Vol. 7: Austria; Vol. 8: Federal Republic of Germany; Vol. 9: United Kingdom; Vols. 10–11: Italy; Vol. 12: Bulgaria; Vol. 16: Portugal; Vols. 19–20: USSR; Vols. 21–22: Ireland.* ECLE, Prague

Gajardo M 1983 *Educación de Adultos in América Latina: Problemas y Tendencias (apartes para un debate).* UNESCO/OREALC, Santiago

Hopkins P G H 1985 *Workers' Education: An International Perspective.* Open University Press, Milton Keynes

Hunter C St J, Keehn M M (ed.) 1985 *Adult Education in China.* Croom Helm, London

Kunzel K 1974 *Universitätsausdehnung in England.* Klett, Stuttgart

Lichtner M (ed.) 1989 *Comparative Research in Adult Education: Present Lines and Perspectives.* Centro Europeo dell'Educazione, Frascati

Lowe J 1982 *The Education of Adults: A Worldwide Perspective,* 2nd edn. UNESCO, Paris

Schütze H G (ed.) Slowey M, Wagner A, Paquet P 1987 *Adults in Higher Education: Policies and Practice in Great Britain and North America.* Almqvist and Wiksell (for CERI), Stockholm

Théry B 1983 *Professional Situation and Training of Trainers in the Member States of the European Communities. Synthesis Report.* CEDEFOP, Berlin

Titmus C 1981 *Strategies for Adult Education: Practices in Western Europe.* Open University Press, Milton Keynes

Titmus C, Buttedahl P, Ironside D, Lengrand P 1979 *Terminology of Adult Education.* UNESCO, Paris

Tuijnman A C, Kirsch I S, Wagner D A (eds.) 1995 *Adult Basic Skills: Advances in Measurement and Policy Analysis.* Hampton Press, New York

UNESCO 1975 *International Standard Classification of Education (ISCED).* UNESCO, Paris

UNESCO 1976 *The Experimental World Literacy Programmer: A Critical Assessment.* UNESCO, Paris

UNESCO 1984 *Literacy Situation in Asia and the Pacific. Country Studies: Bangladesh, India, Pakistan, Nepal, Sri Lanka.* UNESCO, Bangkok

Vélis J-P 1990 *Through a Glass Darkly: Functional Illiteracy in Industrialized Countries.* UNESCO, Paris

Further Reading

Titmus C (ed.) 1989 *Lifelong Education for Adults: An International Handbook.* Pergamon Press, Oxford

Comparative Studies: Vocational Education and Training

D. N. Wilson

1. Introduction

The comparative examination of specialized subsystems of national educational systems includes the study of the training components of both the secondary and postsecondary levels of education. At the secondary level, delivery is usually by means of separate technical, vocational, or industrial tracks. At the postsecondary level, delivery takes place in polytechnics, technical institutes, or colleges of technology which confer certificates or diplomas to skilled workers, technicians, and technologists. In addition, many countries deliver training in nonformal modes, such as National Youth Services. Technical and vocational education systems are typically under the jurisdiction of the Ministry of Education or the Ministry of Labor, although in some countries they may be private or nongovernmental, such as the National Industrial Learning Service of Brazil (SENAI), which is under the aegis of the Federation of Industries.

The distinguishing feature of training systems is their focus upon relationships between education and the economy, and employment and industry. The majority of available studies, unfortunately, examine training in single countries, with few binational or multinational comparative studies. Bereday (1964 p. 22) labels national studies "area studies," but also considers them comparative since they facilitate comparisons "in the mind of the reader" with his or her own system. An examination of national studies indicates that the majority are evaluative reports designed to improve these national systems.

The activities of bilateral and multilateral technical assistance agencies have enriched comparative studies with both national and transnational subject-specific reports largely written, as in the case of national studies, by other than comparative educators. At the international level, responsibility for providing information on training has been shared by UNESCO and the International Labour Organisation (ILO). In addition, the World Bank and regional development banks have been active in both the study of, and investment in, adult education and training, particularly in Less Developed Countries (LDCs).

1. The Evolution of Comparative Studies

The history of comparative studies in the fields of adult education and technical and vocational training parallels the evolution of comparative education. The "travellers' tales" era included anecdotal and informal studies of other countries' systems intended to discover and adopt better methods of delivering training in the author's nation. The late nineteenth century witnessed the dissemination of training innovations at international expositions: for example the Task Analysis Method of curriculum development introduced by Victor della Vos, Principal of The Moscow Imperial Technical Institute, at the 1884 Philadelphia Exposition. Recent comparative studies of training have reflected the advance of social sciences methods (e.g., Foster 1987, Schiefelbein 1979).

The historic focus of comparative studies was on European nations such as Germany, the United Kingdom, and Sweden. However, the past three decades have seen a shift in interest toward innovative training systems found in some newly industrialized countries, for example, Israel, Brazil, Singapore, and Colombia, that have become the newer models of relevance for the LDCs.

A number of quantitative studies have been undertaken by educational economists comparing rate-of-return on investments in technical and vocational education. Other research themes found in comparative studies focus on the transfer of innovations, the impact and influence of international agencies, the diffusion or transfer of technology, policy studies, system reform, and so on.

A related development appears to be the proliferation of education sector and policy studies undertaken by most bilateral (country-to-country) and multilateral (international organization) donor agencies and development banks. Individual national sector studies have been undertaken to describe the status and role of education and to identify future developmental options. Such studies do not purport to be comparative but, as noted above, facilitate readers' comparisons with those educational systems with which they are familiar. At a more global level, education sector policy studies have applied findings from comparative studies to identify future development alternatives in the developing member countries (DMCs) of the regional development banks.

Two trends discernible in comparative studies of technical and vocational education and training are *regionalization* and *vocationalization*. Wilson (1991) noted the trend toward regionalization in South East Asia with the establishment of the South East Asia Ministers of Education Organization (SEAMEO) Regional Center for Vocational and Technical Education in Brunei. This center complements regional centers established in Latin America (CINTERFOR) and in Africa (CIADFOR) by the ILO; in Europe by the Organisation for Economic Co-operation and Development

(OECD), the *Centre Européen pour le Développement de la Formation Professionelle* (CEDEFOP), and the European Union; and in the United States at Ohio State University Center on Education and Training for Employment. Numerous comparative studies on technical and vocational education and training have been published by these organizations (see *European Union: Continuing Vocational Training*).

Vocationalization as a trend, as Lauglo and Lillis (1988 p. 8) note, "transcends the divide between rich and poor countries, and between different political systems." These authors also observe that "the current wave of interest in vocationalization is not rooted in ideological revival but in political and economic conditions" and "are ideas which are 'actualized' by political and economic circumstance".

2. Taxonomy of Comparative Studies

An examination of the available literature suggests that pragmatic studies of technical and vocational education and training far outweigh those which are theoretical in orientation, a result attributed to the occupation-specific nature of such training. This condition may also reflect the commissioning and undertaking of most such studies by *practitioners* (including donor agencies) rather than researchers. Of course, many general comparative studies also include a training component, but they are excluded from examination in this entry. Rather than list all available comparative studies, exemplar studies have been organized in a taxonomy which lists them according to selected attributes.

2.1 Systems with High Enrollment in Vocational Education

With its secondary enrollment in technical and vocational education at a level consistently over 50 percent, Israel has probably been the subject of more research-based studies than any other nation. These studies include: Kahane and Starr's (1976) examination of the impact of rapid social change upon technological education, Borus's (1977) comparisons of the cost-effectiveness of four training modes, Ziderman's (1988) study of the cost-effectiveness of training, Neumann and Ziderman's (1989) study treating the greater cost-effectiveness of vocational secondary schools as compared with academic secondary schools, and Ayalon's (1990) examination of "second-chance" training programs.

In the former Soviet Union, technical and vocational education and training has also received considerable attention, and provides insights into the structure and operation of the Soviet polytechnical model, but the majority of publications are descriptive rather than research-related. The studies by Zajda

(1979) on labor education and O'Dell (1988) on vocationalization policies evince a more substantive approach. According to Noah and Middleton (1988), China has almost realized plans to vocationalize 50 percent of its upper secondary programs.

2.2 National Case Studies

National studies of technical and vocational training in the 1970s which focused upon LDC development include: Weinberg (1967) on industrial education in Argentina, Fuller (1976) on trades training in India, King (1977) on the Kenyan nonformal training sector; van Rensburg (1977) on the Botswana Brigades, Mmari (1977) on Tanzania's linkage of school and work, and Godfrey (1979) on demand for training in Kenya. These studies range methodologically from van Rensburg's historical–descriptive study to the more analytical studies on Argentina, India, Tanzania, and Kenya, which examine both formal and nonformal delivery modes.

A greater degree of analysis is evident in the comparisons between formal and nonformal training delivery modes undertaken by Corvalan-Vasquez (1981) on INACAP in Chile and by Lehmann and Verhine (1982) in Brazil. Other comparative research includes that of Chapman and Windham (1985) on Somalian academic and vocational policy failures, and Lehmann and Verhine (1988) on technical and vocational education and training and job acquisition in Brazil.

In marked contrast to national case studies, Meghnagi (1989) compared regional systems in Italy, and Leclercq (1989) compared school-based and firm-based training in Japan. The paucity of such microlevel comparative case studies within single nations suggests that this area should receive greater methodological emphasis.

Lauglo and Lillis' volume (1988) included case studies on evaluation of vocational education and training in Trinidad and Tobago, the relation of United States' training to a deep-seated belief in the distributive effects of material success, an examination of curriculum diversification in Sierra Leone, the technical and vocational education Initiative in the United Kingdom, the integration of school and work in Sweden, productive education in Zimbabwe, the relationship between Industrial Education and postsecondary employment in Kenya, and the comparison of work-oriented and education-oriented curriculum diversification in Tanzania. This volume is organized along thematic lines to examine goals and justifications, context of policy formulation, policy implementation and evaluation studies in both developed and developing nations.

The national study which has probably made the greatest impact upon technical and vocational education and training was Foster's (1965) study of secondary education in Ghana that generated his "vocational school fallacy in development planning" article, an idea which was updated somewhat in a 1987 review article. While many educational economists have seized upon Foster's contentions to support investments in "academic" rather than vocational, secondary education, Puryear's excellent "SENA effect" (1979) article on Colombia—which provides evidence favorable to investment in vocational education and training—has not received the attention it deserves.

McMahon (1988), Psacharopoulos and Loxley (1986), Psacharopoulos (1987), and other economists have employed rate-of-return studies from a variety of LDCs to generate policy recommendations favoring investment in general secondary and postsecondary education rather than in vocational education and training. This approach has been criticized by Klees (1986) and Wilson (1990) as misleading and potentially deleterious to the overall LDC national development process. Since training provision is significantly more expensive than other forms of education, the amortization of investment over the lifetimes of graduates will not yield comparatively "better" returns on the initial investment, although Colombian, Israeli, and Indonesian studies suggest that "quality" training systems may do so.

2.3 Two-country Comparative Studies

There is a significantly smaller number of between-country studies comparing specific themes or developments, than within-country studies. Two-country comparative studies include Dryland's (1965) comparison of polytechnical education in the United States and USSR, Titmus's (1972) comparison of adult education and training in France and the United Kingdom, Price's (1974) comparison of labor and education in Russia and China, Iram and Balicki's (1980) comparison of technical and vocational education and training in Israel and Switzerland, Lutz's (1981) comparison of education and employment in France and Germany, Psacharopoulos and Loxley's (1986) comparison of returns to vocational and academic secondary education in Columbia and Tanzania, Gallart's (1988) comparison of the secondarization of technical education in Argentina and the vocationalization of secondary education in Brazil, and Wilson's (1991a) comparison of training reform in Indonesia and Malaysia. From a methodological perspective, the single-country studies comparing technical and vocational education and training subsystems and the two-country comparative studies facilitate *actual* comparisons, rather than what Bereday (1964) called comparisons "in the mind of the reader" (1964 pp. 21–2).

2.4 Regional Comparative Studies

The emergent trend of regionalization is evident in the following studies: Oxtoby's (1977) comparison of training in the Commonwealth Caribbean, Corvalan-Vasquez's (1977) comparison of the replications of the Brazilian SENAI model in 19 Latin American and 2 Caribbean nations, Corvalan-Vasquez (1988) on training trends in Latin America, Tilak (1988) on South Asia, Ducci (1988) on equity and productivity in Latin American technical and vocational education and training, and Wilson's (1991b) comparison of the transfer of SENAI from Brazil to Colombia (SENA) and Costa Rica (INA).

2.5 Transnational Comparative Studies

Several thematic transnational comparative studies reflect the use of social science theories, methods, and approaches. Studies employing perspectives from *economics* include: Zymelman (1976) on the economic evaluation of vocational education and training, Tilak (1988) on the economics of vocationalization, and Middleton (1988) on the implications of changing World Bank investment patterns. Studies focusing comparatively upon *pedagogical* concerns include Lauglo's (1983) comparison of general and vocational curricula in Western industrial countries, Bowman (1988) on links between general education and vocational training, Loose's (1988) comparison of training curricula in seven countries, Follis's (1989) examination of staff development in vocational education, and Jallade's (1989) examination of training trends in the 1980s. Studies from a *sociological* perspective include Ciavatta and De Moura Castro (1983) on the contribution of technical and vocational education and training to Latin American social mobility and Noah and Eckstein (1988) on business and industry involvement with education in the United Kingdom, France and Germany. Comparative *political* perspectives are explored in King (1988) on the politics of training in Africa, Neave (1988) on the European Community's training policies in the run-up to the Maastricht Treaty, and by Oxenham's (1988) multijurisdictional examination of what employers want from education. Finally, transnational comparative studies of training include Chesswas (1968), with its country profiles, and the UNESCO (1978) comparative study of trends and issues, Schiefelbein's (1979) examination of education and employment in 10 Latin American cities, Dore et al's (1976) analysis of training outcome data in 25 countries, Lillis and Hogan's (1983) study of vocational curriculum diversification, Caillod's (1978) comparison of technical and vocational education and training structures, Lauglo's (1983) comparison of vocational training and general secondary curricula in Western nations, and the World Bank (1989) policy study on flexibility, efficiency, and quality in technical and vocational education and training. These studies range from the UNESCO compendia of data to the more sophisticated analyses of transnational data to discern and validate hypotheses on trends in technical and vocational education and training.

3. Methodological Considerations for Studies of Vocational Education and Training

What factors and features make studies in technical and vocational education and training comparative? How can valid comparisons of training systems and structures be made? How should such comparisons be structured? These and other questions are not readily addressed in the literature on comparative methodologies, particularly with respect to the comparison of training subsystems.

3.1 System Description

An important starting point for any study of technical and vocational education and training, as implied in the 1974 UNESCO *Revised Recommendations Concerning Technical and Vocational Education*, is to situate the training subsystem within the context of its national system of education. Technical and vocational education is thus recognized to be: (a) an integral component of general education, (b) a means of preparation for occupational entry, and (c) an aspect of continuing education. Additionally, since systems of technical and vocational education and training are responsible for the preservice education and training of future labor force participants, the national economic, demographic and labor market contexts should also be described. There are sufficient similarities and differences between subsystems of national educational systems to facilitate relevant comparisons. For example, a national study of training can be comparative (Borus 1977, Meghnagi 1989, Leclercq 1989), when different modes of delivering training are compared within the same country.

3.2 Thematic Considerations

A second important methodological consideration is the need for a theme upon which to "ground" the comparative study. Thematic considerations usually include policy considerations, the relationships between technical, vocational and general education, cost considerations, the transfer of models or innovations, curriculum development and innovation, economic and economic development strategies, the use of innovative technologies to deliver technical and vocational education and training, administration and management issues, streaming and tracing issues, issues of equality in access and outcome, and educational system growth and differentiation considerations.

3.3 Data Requirements

The construction of a relevant classification scheme for the study of technical and vocational education and training is facilitated by Chesswas's (1968) UNESCO *Educational System Profile*, which has been adopted (in varying formats) by most development banks and bilateral and multilateral donor agencies.

In addition to the "customary" system-descriptive data requirements, studies of training subsystems should be concerned with the following:

(a) Responsible authority—national training board; ministry of education; ministry of labor; private sector body (e.g., manufacturer's association).

(b) Determination of supply and demand—human resource development policies; manpower survey data; labor force studies.

(c) Access to technical and vocational education and training—demographic; socioeconomic; examination scale quartile of entrants.

(d) Enrollment—continuing students or school leavers; percentage of total in training stream/track; geographic availability; age at which students are streamed/tracked into technical and vocational education and training.

(e) Delivery of training—preservice; inservice; on-the-job; apprenticeship; modular approach; distance delivery.

(f) Class and work group size.

(g) Whether technical and vocational education and training are terminal or progression to post-secondary education is possible.

(h) Curriculum orientation—ratio of theory to practice; industrial practice components; industrial attachments/visits.

(i) Curriculum development process(es)—conventional approach; task/activity analysis; involvement of industry; Modules of Employable Skill (MES) approach.

(j) Technologies utilised—equipment compatibility with industry; use of CAI, videodisc, simulation software; audiovisual aids.

(k) Testing and certification—ministry responsible; recognition; apprenticeship system; instructor certification.

(l) Transition from school to work—industrial practice arrangements; cooperative education; job search strategies; relationship between training received and occupational destinations; opportunities to enter post-secondary education.

(m) Finance—government allocation; industrial "levy" system; cost-recovery mechanisms; polyvalent approach.

(n) Cost components—unit costs; facilities; equipment; training consumables; routine and preventive maintenance.

(o) Instructional personnel—training and certification; industrial experience/qualifications; salary scale equivalence.

4. Likely Future Methodological Trends

With the exception of surveys conducted by the European Union and CEDEFOP, and of unpublished background papers prepared for development bank policy studies, no comparative studies of technical and vocational training have employed the large-scale cross-national statistical studies intended to explore developmental similarities and differences. This constitutes an important methodological lacuna, since such systems appear to amass greater volumes of quantitative data than most other education subsectors. It would be desirable—in light of the current focus upon "technological education," that is, the focus upon science and technology for development—for a transnational study to be undertaken in connection with one or more aspects of technical and vocational education and training. Such a comparative study might focus upon the relationships between upgrading mathematics and science content in curricula and attributes of economic and/or social development.

Additional comparisons of countries with vocational education and training enrollment over 50 percent have been advocated above. In addition, Foster (1987) called for empirical studies to assess the internal and external efficiency of training. Finally, this entry has identified the need for microlevel comparative case studies *within* single nations. This agenda should complement the impressive increase in comparative studies of technical and vocational education and training which has taken place since the mid-1980s.

See also: technical and vocational education and Training; Market Failure in Adult Education and Training; Comparative Studies: Adult Education; International Labour Organisation; European Union: Continuing Vocational Training; Japan: Vocational Education and Training; Latin America: National Training Agencies; Measurement of Industry Training; Statistics of Employee Training

References

Ayalon H (1990) The social impact of nonregular education in Israel, *Comp. Educ. Rev.* 34(3): 302–13

Bereday G Z F 1964 *Comparative Method in Education*. Holt, Rinehart and Winston, New York

Borus M 1977 A cost-effectiveness comparison of vocational training for youth in developing countries: A case study of four training modes in Israel. *Comp. Educ. Rev.* 21(1): 1–13

Bowman M J 1988 Links between general and vocational education: Does the one enhance the other? *Int. Rev. Educ.* 34(2): 149–71

Caillods F 1978 *Analyse comparative des structures d'emploi: Rapport de synthèse interimaire*. International Institute of Educational Planning (IIEP), Paris

Chapman D W, Windham D M 1985 Academic program "failures" and the vocational school fallacy: policy issues in secondary education in Somalia. *Int. J. Educ. Dev.* 5(4): 269–81

Chesswas J 1988 *Methodologies of Educational Planning for Developing Countries*. IIEP, Paris

Ciavatta F M A, De Moura Castro C 1983 La Contribución de la educación técnica a la movilidad social: Un estudio comparativo en América Latina. *Revista Latinoamericana de estudios educativos* 1: 9–42

Corvalan-Vasquez O 1977 *Vocational Training in Latin America: A Comparative Perspective*, University of British Colombia, Vancouver/International Council for Adult Education, Toronto

Corvalan-Vasquez O 1981 *Apprenticeship in Latin America: The INACAP Program in Chile: A Case Study*. Occasional Paper No. 6. Michigan State University East Lansing, Michigan

Corvalan-Vasquez O 1988 Trends in technical–vocational and secondary education in Latin America. *Int. J. Educ. Dev.* 8(2): 73–98

Dore R, Humphrey J, West P 1976 *The Basic Arithmetic of Youth Employment: Estimates of School Outputs and Modern Sector Vacancies for Twenty-five Countries*. ILO World Employment Programme, Geneva

Dryland A R 1965 Polytechnical education in the USA and the USSR *Comp. Educ. Rev.* 9(2): 132–38

Ducci M A 1988 Equity and productivity of vocational training: the latin american experience. *Int. J. Educ. Dev.* 8(3): 175–87

Follis B 1989 Staff development for technical and vocational education: An international perspective. *Compare* 19(2): 69–81

Foster P J 1965 The vocational school fallacy in development planning. In: Anderson C A, Bowman M J (eds.) 1965 *Education and Economic Development*. Aldine, Chicago, Illinois

Foster P J 1987 Technical vocational education in the LDCs. *Int. J. Educ. Dev.* 7(2): 137–39

Fuller W P 1976 More evidence supporting the demise of pre-employment vocational trade training: A case study of a factory in India. *Comp. Educ. Rev.* 20 (1): 30–41

Gallart M A 1988 The secondarization of technical education in Argentina and the vocationalization of secondary education in Brazil. In: Lauglo J, Lillis K (eds.) 1988

Godfrey M 1979 Training in Kenya: Need versus effective demand. *Comp. Educ.* 15(2): 187–95

Iram Y, Balicki C 1980 Vocational education in Switzerland and Israel: A comparative analysis. *Canadian and Int. Educ.* 9(1): 95–105

Jallade J-P 1989 Recent trends in vocational education and training: An overview. *Euro. J. Educ.* 24(2): 103–25

Kahane R, Starr L 1976 The impact of rapid social change on technological education: An Israeli example. *Comp. Educ. Rev.* 20(2): 165–78

King K 1977 *The African Artisan: Education and the Informal Sector in Kenya*. Teachers' College Press, New York

King K 1988 The new politics of job training and work training in Africa. *Int. J. Educ. Dev.* 8 (3): 153–61

Klees S J 1986 Planning and policy analysis in education: What can economics tell us? *Comp. Educ. Rev.* 30(4): 574–607

Lauglo J 1983 Concepts of "general education" and

"vocational education" curricula for post compulsory schooling in Western industrialised countries: When shall the twain meet? *Comp. Educ.* 19(3): 285–304

Lauglo J, Lillis K (eds.) 1988 *Vocationalizing Education: An International Perspective*. Pergamon Press, Oxford

Leclercq J-M 1989 The Japanese Model: School-based education and firm-based vocational training. *Eur. J. Educ.* 24(2): 183–96

Lehman R H, Verhine R E 1982 Contribution of formal and non-formal education to obtaining skilled industrial employment in Northeastern Brazil. *Int. J. Educ. Dev.* 2(1): 29–42

Lehmann R H, Verhine R E 1988 Education and industrial job acquisition in Brazil: Towards an improved causal model. *Int. J. Educ. Dev.* 8(1): 9–24

Lillis K, Hogan D 1983 Dilemmas of diversification: Problems associated with vocational education in developing countries. *Comp. Educ.* 19(1): 89–107

Loose G 1988 *Vocational Education in Transition: A Seven Country Study of Curricula for Lifelong Vocational Learning*. UIE Case Studies 8. UNESCO Institute for Education, Hamburg

Lutz B 1981 Education and employment: Contrasting evidence from France and the Federal Republic of Germany. *Eur. J. Educ.* 16(1): 73–86

McMahon W J 1988 The economics of vocational and technical education: Do the benefits outweigh the costs? *Int. Rev. Educ.* 34(2): 73–94

Meghnagi S 1989 Technical and vocational education in Italy: The state and the regions. *Eur. J. Educ.* 24(2): 159–65

Middleton J 1988 Changing patterns in World Bank investment in vocational education and training: Implications for secondary vocational schools. *Int. J. Educ. Dev.* 8(3): 213–25

Mmari G R V 1977 Attempts to link school with work: The Tanzanian experience. *Prospects* 7(3): 379–88

Neave G 1988 Policy and response: Changing perceptions and priorities in the vocational training policy of the EEC Commission. In: Lauglo J, Lillis K (eds.) 1988

Neumann S, Ziderman A 1989 Vocational secondary schools can be more cost-effective than academic Schools: The case of Israel. *Comp. Educ.* 25(2): 151–64

Noah H, Eckstein M 1988 Business and industry involvement with education in Britain, France and Germany. In: Lauglo J, Lillis K (eds.) 1988

Noah H, Middleton J 1988 *China's Vocational and Technical Training*. World Bank, Policy, Planning and Research Working Papers. World Bank, Washington, DC

O'Dell F 1988 Recent Soviet vocationalization policies. In: Lauglo J, Lillis K (eds.) 1988

Oxenham J 1988 What do employers want from education? In: Lauglo J, Lillis K (eds.) 1988

Oxtoby R 1977 Vocational education and development planning: Emerging issues in the Commonwealth Caribbean. *Comp. Educ.* 13(3): 223–42

Price R 1974 Labour and education in Russia and China. *Comp. Educ.* 10(1): 13–23

Psacharopoulos G 1987 To vocationalize or not to vocationalize: That is the curriculum question. *Int. Rev. Educ.* 33 (2): 187–211

Psacharopoulos G, Loxley W 1986 *Diversified Secondary Education and Development: Evidence from Colombia and Tanzania*. Johns Hopkins University Press, Baltimore, Maryland

Puryear J M 1979 Vocational training and earnings in Colombia: Does a SENA effect exist? *Comp. Educ. Rev.* 23(2): 283–92

Schiefelbein E 1979 Educación y empleo en diez ciudades de América Latina. *Revista del Centro de Estudios Educativos*. 8(3): 126–34

Tilak J B G 1988a Economics of vocationalization: A review of evidence. *Canadian and Int. Educ.* 17(1): 45–62

Tilak J B G 1988b Vocational education in South Asia: problems and prospects. *Int. Rev. Educ.* 34(2): 244–57

Titmus C 1972 Vocational training in the United Kingdom and France: A comparative study. *Stud. Adult Educ.* 4(1): 21–33

UNESCO 1973 *Revision of the Recommendations Concerning technical and vocational education*. UNESCO, Paris

UNESCO 1978 *Developments in technical and vocational education: A Comparative Study*. UNESCO, Paris

van Rensburg P 1977 Combining education and production: Situating the problem. *Prospects* 7(3): 352–54

Weinberg P D 1967 *La ensenanza tecnica industrial en la Argentina 1936–1965*. Instituto Di Tella, Buenos Aires

Wilson D N 1990 The deleterious impact of rate-of-return studies on LDC education policies: An Indonesian case. *Canadian and Int. Educ.* 19(1): 32–49

Wilson D N 1991a Reform of technical–vocational education in Indonesia and Malaysia. *Comp. Educ.* 19(2): 207–21

Wilson D N 1991b Transfer of the SENAI model of apprenticeship training from Brazil to Colombia and Costa Rica. In: De Moura Castro C, Oliveira J B, Wilson D N (eds.) 1991 *Innovations in Educational and Training Technologies*. ILO Turin Centre, Turin

Zajda J 1979 Education for labour in the USSR *Comp. Educ.* 15(3): 287–99

Ziderman A 1988 *Israel's Vocational Training*. World Bank Population and Human Resources Working Paper No. 25. World Bank, Washington, DC

Zymelman M 1976 *The Economic Evaluation of Vocational Training Programs*. Johns Hopkins University Press, Baltimore, Maryland

Further Reading

Dale R (ed.) 1985 *Education, Training and Employment: Towards a New Vocationalism*? Pergamon Press, Oxford

Gorham A 1987 *Education Sector Policy Review: Comparative Data Paper*. Asian Development Bank, Manila

Grubb W N (1985) The convergence of educational systems and the role of vocationalism. *Comp. Educ. Rev.* 29(4): 526–48

King A 1969 Higher technical education and socio-economic development. *Comp. Educ.* 5(3): 263–81

Smart K F 1975 Vocational education in the Federal Republic of Germany: Current trends and problems. *Comp. Educ.* 11(2): 153–63

UNESCO 1983 *technical and vocational education in the World, 1970–1980: A Statistical Report*. UNESCO, Paris

World Bank 1989 *Vocational Education and Training in Developing Countries: Policies for Flexibility, Efficiency and Quality*. World Bank, Washington, DC

Wright C A 1988 Curriculum diversification re-examined: A case study of Sierra Leone. In: Lauglo J, Lillis K (eds.) 1988

Information Sources in Adult Education

S. Imel

Information sources in adult education are expanding at a rapid rate. Not only have the kind and type of information sources changed but there have also been developments in how these sources can be accessed through a variety of information providers. Because it is neither feasible nor desirable to cover exhaustively all the available adult education information sources, the purpose of this entry is to provide a framework for approaching the available sources by describing general types of adult education materials and then discussing how these can be located and accessed. First, some issues associated with the rapid expansion of information resources will be raised.

1. Related Issues

Three issues related to the expansion and availability of information are access and equity, the fragmented nature of information sources, and the selection of the most appropriate information.

1.1 Access and Equity

The issue of access and equity refers to the accessibility of information sources as well as how fairly all perspectives are represented in the information made available. Although information technologies have increased the accessibility of information, not all individuals have access to these technologies. Increased use of such technologies may well widen the gap between those who have access to information and those who do not. The appropriateness of available information is also a part of this issue. The capacity of information providers to make available and disseminate information cannot keep pace with the information growth. Thus, institutional selection criteria determine to what extent information representing a variety of perspectives is accessible to clients (Imel 1989).

1.2 Fragmented Nature of Information Sources

Despite the fact that there is much information available, great fragmentation exists among current providers of adult education information. This issue is particularly acute when viewed from an international perspective. Because of its nature, it would not be feasible for one information provider to serve the entire field of adult education; however, better linkages need to be developed among existing information providers. Such collaboration could minimize duplication of services as well as lead to better information services for adult educators.

1.3 Selecting Appropriate Information

The increasing availability of information combined with its greater accessibility means that individuals must develop skills in selecting the most appropriate information for their needs. They must not only become familiar with methods of accessing information sources, but they must also make decisions about those most appropriate for their needs by becoming knowledgeable about the range of sources available (Imel 1989, 1991). Unfortunately, the fragmented nature of information sources exacerbates this process since individuals are confronted with an increasing array of information providers.

2. Types of Information Sources

Adult education information is available in a variety of forms, the most common being books, periodicals, fugitive literature, and dissertations. These sources are briefly described here with selected illustrative examples. (See Brockett 1991 for discussions of other forms of adult education resources including nonprint materials.)

2.1 Books

Traditionally, books have been the most common and comprehensive source of information in adult education. Because books are durable and because libraries have systematic procedures for collecting and classifying them, much adult education information is available in book format. Unfortunately, due to their specialized nature, most adult education books are only available in university or large public libraries.

Several publications such as *Lifelong Education for Adults: An International Handbook* (Titmus 1989), *Handbook of Adult and Continuing Education* (Merriam and Cunningham 1989), *An International Dictionary of Adult and Continuing Education* (Jarvis 1990), and *International Biography of Adult Education* (Thomas and Elsey 1985) serve as important references to the nature of the field and its contributors. In addition, some of the field's classics such as *The 1919 Report* (Adult Education Committee, Ministry of Reconstruction 1919) and *The Meaning of Adult Education* (Lindeman 1989) have been reprinted by the Department of Adult Education at the University of Nottingham and the Oklahoma Research Center for Adult and Continuing Education, making them more widely available. Despite these advances, much of the book literature remains unavailable to large numbers

693

of adult educators unless they have purchased it for their personal use.

2.2 Periodicals

Periodicals are journals, magazines, and newsletters that are published on a regular basis. Because of the frequency of their publication, periodicals—especially newsletters—are a source of current information. There are literally hundreds of adult education periodicals. Examples of journals include *Convergence*, published by the International Council for Adult Education (ICAE); *International Journal of Lifelong Education*, published by Taylor and Francis Ltd; *Adult Education Quarterly*, published by the American Association for Adult and Continuing Education (AAACE); *Studies in the Education of Adults*, published by the National Institute for Adult and Continuing Education in Great Britain; *Contraste*, published by the *Instituto de Capacitación para Educadores de Adultos* (ICEA); AALAE Journal, published by the African Association for Literacy and Adult Education; and *New Horizons in Adult Education*, an electronic journal available through Nova University's Adult Education Network (AEDNET).

Among the many adult education newsletters, UNESCO's *Adult Education Information Notes* is particularly noteworthy for its excellent coverage of international resources in adult education. Published quarterly in English, French, Spanish, Russian, Arabic, and Chinese, each issue contains abstracts of adult education newsletters, journals, and books from around the world, as well as news of international developments in adult education.

2.3 Fugitive Materials

Many of the resources in adult education are fugitive materials, that is, their availability is not well-known or publicized. Fugitive materials include such items as conference proceedings and papers, pamphlets, brochures, research studies, and reports of government-funded projects. Computerized databases, discussed in the next section, have made fugitive materials much more accessible.

2.4 Dissertations

Particularly in North America where graduate study in adult education has been formalized, dissertations are an important source of adult education information because they frequently represent new developments in research. Information about dissertations is available through such sources as *Dissertations Abstracts International* and *British Education Index*.

3. Accessing Adult Education Information Sources

The adult education sources described above can be accessed through information providers such as libraries, information databases, clearinghouses and resources centers, and organizations. Increasingly, professional networks are serving as important sources of information. These access points are described here using relevant, illustrative examples.

3.1 Libraries

Although there are many fine collections of adult education materials at university libraries, the Syracuse University Library houses the largest collection in the world. Known as the Syracuse University Resources for Educators of Adults (SUREA), it contains a number of special collections, including archival materials from groups and individuals; the largest media collection of adult education materials; and more than 10,000 photographs. A second note-worthy library is that of the UNESCO Institute for Education in Hamburg, Germany.

3.2 Information Databases

Information databases store collections of related information that can be retrieved via computer using information retrieval software. When stored, the materials have usually been indexed or classified using a vocabulary control device that is used to retrieve information from the database. Some information databases are also available in CD-ROM (compact disk-read-only memory) format (Imel 1991).

Among the databases that contain adult education information are the Educational Resources Information Center (ERIC), the Australian Education Index (AEI), British Education Index (BEI), Canadian Education Index (CEI), Dissertation Abstracts Online (DAO), and *Red Latinoamericana de Información y Documentación en Educación* (REDUC).

In North America, the ERIC database is considered to be the primary source of adult education materials because of the comprehensiveness of its coverage and its history of service to the field. Established by the United States Office of Education in 1966, ERIC has focused on collecting and disseminating information about fugitive materials, including English-language adult education materials from around the world. It also indexes the major English-language adult education journals.

A database known as "International ERIC" (consisting of ERIC, BEI, CEI, and AEI) has been created. International ERIC represents a major example of international cooperation and outreach in creating a database of international—rather than national—scope.

Dissertation Abstracts Online provides online access to the same information about dissertations on adult education that appears in the print index *Dissertation Abstracts International*. Since 1988, DAO has expanded its scope beyond North America to include British and European dissertations and master's abstracts.

Red Latinoamericana de Información y Documentación en Educacion is a bibliographic database on education developed cooperatively by 23 associated centers in 17 Latin American and Caribbean nations. Its collection of more than 12,000 documents includes information on nonformal education.

3.3 Clearinghouses and Resource Centers

Clearinghouses and resource centers throughout the world provide information on adult education to a variety of audiences. They perform a number of functions providing access to information databases, information about resources and materials, collections of materials and resources, and referral to other agencies and organizations serving adult learners. Many also develop and disseminate newsletters and free or inexpensive materials on adult education topics. Some of these organizations, such as the ERIC Clearinghouse on Adult, Career, and Vocational Education (ERIC/ACVE), serve international audiences but others are more local in scope. *Directory of National Clearinghouses: Resource Centers and Clearinghouses Serving Adult Educators and Learners* (Clearinghouse on Adult Education and Literacy 1990), *Directory of Adult Education Documentation and Information Services* (UNESCO 1984), and *International Handbook of Resources for Educators of Adults* (Charters and Dengel 1986) contain information about specific adult education clearinghouses and resource centers.

3.4 Organizations

Many organizations also provide access to adult education information, primarily through the production of their own publications but also through the provision of services similar to those of clearinghouses and resource centers. There are numerous organizations worldwide whose special focus is on adult education. Information about many of these groups can be located in the *Yearbook of International Organizations* (Union of International Associations 1991) and *Encyclopedia of Associations. International Organizations* (Irvin 1991).

Whereas most adult education organizations serve national or regional audiences, two that are international in scope have been instrumental in providing access to sources in adult education: UNESCO and the International Council for Adult Education. Both organizations sponsor conferences, develop publications, and work with other adult education organizations throughout the world (Duke 1989).

UNESCO, an intergovernmental organization, produces and disseminates a number of adult education publications. In addition to *Adult Education Information Notes*, the newsletter mentioned previously, UNESCO also publishes the quarterly journal *Prospects*. Although not devoted specifically to adult education, it contains many adult education-related articles. The UNESCO Institute for Education in Germany publishes the *International Review of Education*, which pays attention to issues in adult education and literacy,

and has developed a number of publications on the problems of illiteracy and postliteracy in both the developing and the industrialized countries. The International Bureau of Education (IBE), a UNESCO affiliate in Geneva, publishes bibliographies and directories related to adult education such as the *Directory of Adult Education Documentation and Information Services* (UNESCO 1985) and the *Annotated Bibliography of National Sources of Adult Education Statistics* (UNESCO 1989).

Probably the most influential international organization in adult education is the International Council for Adult Education (ICAE). Publisher of the journal *Convergence*, ICAE also produces the Monographs on Comparative and Area Studies in Adult Education series in conjunction with the University of British Columbia's Centre for Continuing Education.

3.5 Professional Networks

Contact with other adult educators through professional networks is another source of information. Although this type of access may be less formal, it is nevertheless effective. Traditionally, professional networking has occurred through professional associations and conferences (Brockett 1991). International adult education conferences and symposia sponsored by such groups as UNESCO, ICAE, and the International Congress for University Adult Education have been important means of disseminating information about adult education throughout the world.

Examples of more formalized professional networks are two that were developed by the Syracuse University Kellogg Project. The first, the Adult Education Network (AEDNET), is an international electronic network that includes more than 1,200 people in 9 countries in the Americas, Europe, and the Pacific Rim. Its activities include electronic discussions; information exchanges on member inquiries; conference, special event, and publication announcements; and distribution of the electronic journal *New Horizons in Adult Education*. Now operated by Nova University, AEDNET is distributed through BITNET, Internet, NSFNET, CSNET, and NYSERNET.

The International Information Sharing Network (IISN) is the second professional network created by the Syracuse University Kellogg Project. Now administered by Northern Illinois University, IISN fosters information sharing among 350 participants in 75 developing countries through the distribution of a newsletter and by responding to members' requests for information.

4. Conclusion

Currently, adult educators have available a wealth of information sources. However, the extent to which all adult educators can benefit from these sources will depend upon the development of a more holistic, less fragmented system. Systems such as AEDNET and "International ERIC" are indications of movement in this direction. In addition, adult educators need to develop skills that will enable them to be intelligent consumers of the plethora of information available.

See also: International Adult Education; UNESCO and Adult Education; Nongovernmental Organizations

References

Adult Education Committee, Ministry of Reconstruction 1919 *The 1919 Report: The Final and Interim Reports of the Adult Education Committee of the Ministry of Reconstruction.* HMSO, London

Brockett R B 1991 Disseminating and using adult education knowledge. In: Peters J M, Jarvis P (eds.) 1991 *Adult Education.* Jossey-Bass, San Francisco, California

Charters A N, Dengel R E 1986 *International Handbook of Resources for Educators of Adults. English Language Materials.* Syracuse University Publications in Continuing Education, Syracuse, New York (ERIC Document Reproduction Service No. ED 283 971)

Clearinghouse on Adult Education and Literacy 1990 *Directory of National Clearinghouses: Resource Centers and Clearinghouses Serving Adult Educators and Learners.* Clearinghouse on Adult Education and Literacy, Division of Adult Education and Literacy, United States Department of Education, Washington, DC

Duke C 1989 International adult education. In: Titmus C J (ed.) 1989 *Lifelong Education for Adults: An International Handbook.* Pergamon Press, Oxford

Imel S 1989 The field's literature and information sources. In: Merriam S B, Cunningham P M (eds.) 1989 *Handbook of Adult and Continuing Education.* Jossey-Bass, San Francisco, California

Imel S 1991 Information resources for professional development. In: Brockett R G (ed.) 1991 *Professional Development for Educators of Adults*, New Directions for Adult and Continuing Education Series, No. 51. Jossey-Bass, San Francisco, California

Irvin L (ed.) 1991 *Encyclopedia of Associations 1992: International Organizations*, 26th edn. Gale Research, Detroit, Michigan

Jarvis P 1990 *An International Dictionary of Adult and Continuing Education.* Routledge, London

Lindeman E 1989 *The Meaning of Adult Education.* Oklahoma Research Center for Continuing Professional and Higher Education, Norman, Oklahoma

Merriam S B, Cunningham P M (eds.) 1989 *The Handbook of Adult and Continuing Education.* Jossey-Bass, San Francisco, California

Thomas J E, Elsey B (eds.) 1985 *International Biography of Adult Education.* Department of Adult Education, University of Nottingham, Nottingham

Titmus C J (ed.) 1989 *Lifelong Education for Adults: An International Handbook.* Pergamon Press, Oxford

UNESCO 1985 *Directory of Adult Education Documentation and Information Services*, 3rd edn. IBEDATA Series. United Nations Educational, Scientific, and Cultural Organization, Paris (available in English, French, and Spanish editions)

UNESCO 1989 *Annotated Bibliography of National Sources of Adult Education Statistics.* IBEDATA Series. United Nations Educational, Scientific, and Cultural Organization, Paris

Union of International Associations (ed.) 1991 *Yearbook of International Associations.* KGS Verlag, Munich

International Adult Education

C. Duke

Adult education includes all forms of the education and training of adults. In some countries the term "continuing education" is preferred; other countries use the term "nonformal education" in a similarly broad sense. Although there are specialized meanings, in international discourse these terms tend to be used interchangeably (see *Adult Education: Concepts and Principles*).

International adult education refers to those aspects of the education of adults which include some dimension of international exchange or comparison. This includes comparative research studies and aid programs but takes many other forms as well. International efforts in adult education are often intended to inform and improve the practice of adult education, and to increase government interest in and support for adult education programs. Much international adult education activity has the character of a social movement, and is committed to social, and even political, change. Tensions may arise between international adult education and adult education within different countries, where political constraints may be more strongly felt.

The practice of adult education is very specific to the particular social, political, and economic context, whereas international adult education seeks to find and to amplify commonalities. This may enhance tensions between local and international perspectives and activities. On the one hand, adult education may be seen as a subsystem of national education systems. On the other hand, as an international social movement it reflects changes in the wider international scene as well as internationally shared values which underlie the idea that adult education is a movement.

1. The New International Context

International adult education has taken two forms in particular. One is comparative studies, between rather similar or very different countries and systems. These studies may be purely scholarly, but they often have an applied or policy-oriented purpose. The second major form of exchange has focussed on adult education as a form of aid for development. In this sense North–South relations have predominated, with the transfer both of resources, and of ideas and models for adult education, from the North to the South.

Much of the post-Second World War context for international adult education has been one of East–West tension and North–South aid and development relations. Adult education has reflected this international pattern, by seeking to enhance international understanding and exchange between political and economic systems. It has been assisted by the improvement in international communications which is reflected in the phrase "global village," and international adult education has been characterized by a considerable increase in the frequency, scale, and variety of exchanges and of international comparative writing.

The context for international adult education was transformed in the late 1980s by political changes particularly in Eastern Europe and the former Soviet Union. The end of the Cold War changed the political context in which East and West competed for political standing, fostered through aid relations in the South. The attention of Western industrialized nations has shifted politically to the European Union, and economically to investment in Eastern Europe. North–South aid relations appear to be threatened by these developments, and consequently the political and economic basis for more international adult education activity is also eroded. International adult education continues to reflect the international order, resulting in much stress upon exchanges within Western Europe and Europe as a whole, and in concern about the attenuation of North–South relations.

Another manifestation of the new international order is the resurgence of nationalism based on ethnicity in parts of Europe, and possible trends toward a "Fortress Europe" and "Fortress North America" mentality, which takes the form of restricting the movement of people from the South and harassment of minority ethnic groups within different countries. International adult education as a social movement concerned with liberal and human values, and with equity, is influenced by such changes, and its agenda for discussion and action is altered accordingly.

2. Adult Education for Development and as a Movement

UNESCO has periodically convened major international conferences on adult education (e.g., Elsinore in 1949, Montreal in 1960, Tokyo in 1972, and Paris in 1985). In 1985, there were 841 participants from 122 member states, compared with attendance from 25, 70, and 82 member states respectively at the earlier conferences. These events have regularly stressed adult education as a factor in economic, cultural, and social development. Similarly, the large Commonwealth conference on nonformal education for development in New Delhi in 1979 concentrated on the overall standard of living of the most needy sections of society.

The International Council for Adult Education which was created following the 1972 UNESCO conference in Tokyo likewise emphasized adult education in and for development, at its first world conference in Dar es Salaam in 1976. In opening the conference, President Julius Nyerere of Tanzania stated:

> Adult education is not something which can deal with just "agriculture" or "health" or "literacy" or "mechanical skill", etc. All these separate branches are related to the total life a man is living, and to the man he is and will become . . . This means that adult education will promote changes in men and society. And it means that adult education *should* promote change, at the same time as it assists men to control both the change which they induce, and that which is forced upon them . . . (Hall and Kidd 1978 p. 12)

Themes of development and action characterize much of the dialogue on international adult education. This reflects the "social movement" origins of adult education, which may be traced in particular to industrializing British society, where concern for social equality and progress paralleled concern with technical education and retraining to meet economic needs. Adult education as a means of reducing social inequality and initial educational disadvantage is a recurring theme in the literature of the field, as is exemplified by the many studies of participation in adult education. "Radical adult education" is often in tension with "functional adult education", promoted as a means of development of different sectors such as agriculture, industry, health, and population control. International adult education as a social movement strives to combine a concern for equity with efforts for economic development, particularly of the disadvantaged and marginalized groups (see *Critical Approaches to Adult Education*).

Whereas much international education is infused with radical or reformist social purpose, the majority of adult educators work within different countries on programs that lack any clear ideological purpose. They may be concerned with vocational and technical skills and knowledge, or with education for leisure and personal enrichment. International adult education may thus present a challenge to adult educators working at national and local levels, as well as to those who are responsible for policies and resources to support adult education within different countries. Those working on vocational training programs or in general adult education within different countries may feel challenged or offended by the high-minded, yet detached purposes which are commonly discussed at, and transmitted from, international adult education meetings. This tension is periodically polarized, and may take the form of a choice between internationalism and national or local concerns.

3. Roles and Activities of International Bodies

Much international adult education is carried forward on the basis of contacts and networks between individual scholars and practitioners in different countries. Other exchanges occur on a country-to-country basis through national adult education associations or departments of government. A particular and highly visible role is played by international organizations, which may be divided into two broad categories: Intergovernmental organizations (IGOs) and International non-governmental organizations (INGOs). The roles which these kinds of bodies play tend to change quite considerably from time to time, and especially in relation to changes in the international scene. The relationship between IGOs and INGOs, and their complementarity of roles, is also important.

3.1 Intergovernmental Organizations (IGOs)

Since the Second World War the most prominent intergovernmental organization promoting activity and exchange in adult education has been UNESCO (see *UNESCO and Adult Education*). UNESCO had political problems during the 1980s; the United Kingdom and the United States in particular withdrew from membership, with serious effects on the Organization's budget and programs. Education remains a major area of UNESCO activity, however, although its work in literacy, adult education, and rural development has been restricted by budgetary constraints and the contraction of this division. UNESCO generally promotes adult education, especially in the context of development in the South. Apart from its Paris headquarters it works through its regional offices, particularly the Asian and Pacific Regional Office in Bangkok, where adult or nonformal education has been a salient feature of the program over many years.

Apart from the major periodic international conferences in adult education, UNESCO at a General Conference in Nairobi in 1976 produced a commonly quoted definition of adult education which gives the activity a very wide scope (UNESCO 1976). The papers from its fourth international conference (Paris in 1985) tend to be used as a benchmark and agenda in the international adult education community (UNESCO 1985).

As the leading agency of the United Nations concerned with education, UNESCO was a major partner in the work for the UN International Literacy Year, 1990. This took as its theme "basic education for all,"

convening a world conference in Thailand in March of that year (Mayor 1990, UNESCO 1990, Bhola 1990). Also prominent in activity for the International Literacy Year was UNICEF (the United Nations Children's Fund) and the International Bank for Reconstruction and Development (IBRD) (i.e., the World Bank).

In addition to its head office and regional activities, UNESCO supports several specialized institutes promoting aspects of adult education among other international educational activities. These include the International Institute for Educational Planning in Paris and the International Bureau of Education, a documentation center in Geneva. The UNESCO Institute for Education (UIE) in Hamburg concentrates on lifelong education. From the late 1970s to the late 1980s it was preoccupied especially with literacy, but it has broadened its agenda to encompass other areas of adult education and development in the industrialized countries.

Because adult education is a development and support service to many other fields of activity, intergovernmental organizations not primarily concerned with education also become involved in international adult education activities. For example, adult education (or training) may occasionally be encountered on the agenda of the following: The International Labour Organisation (ILO), the Food and Agriculture Organization (FAO), the World Health Organization (WHO), and the United Nations Environment Programme (UNEP). UNICEF has a more obvious interest in the education of adults from a community and nonformal education perspective. Outside the UN family of IGOs, the World Bank becomes heavily involved in adult education from time to time. In addition, regional IGOs play a part in international adult education, and in particular the Organisation for Economic Cooperation and Development (OECD), which includes the world's leading industrialized nations of Europe, North America, and the Pacific Rim, takes a keen interest in the education of adults in a broader economic and social context. The OECD has devoted special attention to promoting and applying the concept of recurrent education, and also sometimes paid educational leave. The reshaping of Europe after 1992 raises questions about the membership and role of both OECD and the European Union, and consequently about the means whereby international adult education will be promoted among industrialized nations within and beyond Europe.

3.2 International Nongovernmental Organizations

The most influential and comprehensive nongovernmental organization (NGO) in the field of adult education is the International Council for Adult Education (ICAE) founded by Dr Roby Kidd following the UNESCO conference in Tokyo in 1972. The majority of the world's nations are members, and the Council has created strong working relations, embedded in its constitution, with the major regional NGOs, most of which have earlier origins (see *International Council for Adult Education*).

Other more specialized NGOs include the older but less active International Congress of University Adult Education which produces the *International Journal of University Adult Education*. This organization, as its name implies, is concerned mainly with adult education within higher education. Another NGO, the International Association of Community Education, embraces school-age as well as adult education.

The British Commonwealth supports a number of professional associations. For example, the Commonwealth Association for the Education and Training of Adults (CAETA), which is formally restricted to member countries and confines its activities to these, was inaugurated in India in 1987 and has subsequently held conferences and workshops in Africa, Asia, and the Caribbean. Like UNESCO and ICAE, it is concerned particularly with promoting and enhancing the practices of adult education as a means of economic and social development. Other associations and networks formed in the 1980s are more concerned with scholarly exchanges or with more specialized areas of adult education, such as its history. Adult education is also used as a campaign tool for furthering the activities of "single issue" NGOs in such areas as consumer education, environmental conservation, and peace (see *Nongovernmental Organizations*).

3.3 Complementary Roles

Intergovernmental and nongovernmental organizations have distinctive strengths and limitations. While cooperation is common, for example over the International Literacy Year in 1990, their roles are often complementary. The major agencies of both kinds share a commitment to adult education oriented toward development, giving a harmony of outlook and purpose among key professional personnel who generally work in close informal cooperation. A third kind of international agency, also frequently involved in informal cooperation, is the aid agency, whether governmental or nongovernmental, which puts resources into adult education. Examples include the Canadian International Development Agency (CIDA), the United States Agency for International Development (USAID), and the W K Kellogg Foundation, all of which have provided substantial support to ICAE over the years. A major European agency is the *Deutscher Volkshochschulverband* (DVV). Its Department for International Cooperation is responsible for substantial German government funds often flowing to NGO projects in the countries of the South. Although DVV enjoys close partnership with NGOs it also works alongside bodies like UNESCO, and produces and disseminates widely its periodical *Adult Education and Development*.

The strength of intergovernmental organizations is that they have the authority of government behind them and, directly or indirectly, can influence the flow of national and international aid funds to enhance programs of adult education in the South. Their conference resolutions carry some authority with their respective member states. Nongovernmental organizations lack this formal authority, although their voices may carry considerable weight. In some countries, the government gives strong and overt support to the work of national, regional, and international NGOs. Elsewhere the involvement and support may be at a lower level of organization, or be restricted entirely to adult educators working in a personal or private capacity. Counterbalancing the restricted formal influence of NGOs is their advantage in terms of flexibility and rapid responsiveness to new situations and new needs. International adult education is thus promoted in different but complementary, and often linked, ways.

4. Major Activities and Trends

4.1 The Exchange of Information

Much of the international activity in adult education is restricted to the exchange of information and experience. This takes place through periodic meetings organized by national, regional, and international bodies. However, because of the cost of travel and shortage of time, much exchange takes the form of published and other written materials. Most of the IGOs and large NGOs have their own media for communication and dissemination of information, and some of these are very widely read and used. Other bodies, particularly universities with an international orientation, promote and publish scholarship in adult education for an international readership. The leading journals and other information services in adult education tend to be much more practical and applied in their orientation. These latter publications thus reflect both the applied orientation toward practitioners of adult education and the particular value orientation of international adult education as a movement.

4.2 Research

Comparative international research also commonly reflects commitment to action and improvement of the adult education service:

> Those who use lifelong education to achieve personal or societal ends can benefit in their planning and execution by some understanding of lifelong education in other countries . . . Studies in comparative adult education that transcend national boundaries should enable educators of adults to use adult education to facilitate people's control of the quality of their lives. (Charters et al. 1981 pp. xii–xiv, 16–17)

Some international studies take an individual theme

and compare practices or case studies in different countries and regions (Duke 1985, Duke 1990). Others may concentrate on the comparison of policy and practice between two or more countries (see, e.g., Schutze et al. 1987). Whereas the movement orientation of international adult education tends to concentrate on development issues and on the South, others, perhaps with a more scholarly than applied interest, attend to themes in the North (Abrahamsson et al. 1988). However, the spectrum of research subjects is wide, ranging from policies, models, and systems of adult education to very specific matters of professional practice (see *Adult Education Research; Comparative Studies: Adult Education; Comparative Studies: Vocational Education and Training*).

4.3 Lobbying

A major purpose behind many international meetings of adult educators, whatever the nature of the sponsorship, is to define and clarify the contribution of adult education in development, and to produce guidelines, statements of policy, and manifestos for action. Such statements may be intended for general clarification of professional issues, and to widen the horizons of adult educators who are restricted and limited by local or national circumstances. A common goal, however, is to inform and persuade government and international agencies of the need to raise the status of adult education and to put more resources into this work as a mode of development. Major meetings of UNESCO, ICAE, and other bodies, together with the ancillary meetings, documentation, and dissemination of proceedings, thus have the clear aim of lobbying for more adult education. Although the UNESCO Recommendation for the Development of Adult Education (1976) has frequently been criticized for its breadth and generality, it has also been used to help adult education associations to persuade their ministries of education to widen the scope of and support for adult education in different member states. Periodic world conferences and assemblies of adult educators, like the similar events arranged at regional level, provide benchmarks and rallying opportunities to enhance the standing of adult education as a development activity, and to stake a claim for more government and international aid agency support.

4.4 Professional Development

Conferences, seminars, and workshops provide an important forum for the professional development of adult education leaders. They may at the very least sustain and raise morale, in cases where adult educators feel isolated and embattled in their domestic situation. They have the capacity to widen professional understanding, enabling practitioners to see their own work in a wider and more comparative way, and so to identify options for development of the service in their different countries. Such activities may foster the practice of educational innovation through workshops and the exchange of practical experience and experimentation. Planned professional development allows adult educators to understand more clearly and in more practical ways the connections between their own work and that of the formal school system; or between adult education and the work of other development departments such as agriculture, forestry, or industry.

Different international bodies sponsor different forms of professional development, not only through periodic conferences but more specifically through workshops, training courses, scholarships, and fellowships, enabling study overseas (see *Professional Associations*). Whereas workshops and conferences may take place in all parts of the world and are usually deliberately rotated between countries and regions, more formal training (e.g., for the attainment of graduate degrees) generally takes place in the countries of the North. This again raises the question of North–South transfer of models and knowledge, and the possibility of cultural domination.

4.5 Aid

National aid agencies, national adult education associations, as well as international governmental and nongovernmental organizations, promote different forms of aid which normally flows from the North to the South. Some aid programs specifically support adult education organizations, but frequently adult education aid takes the form of a component within a broader aid package. Quite small amounts of aid (if handled by adult education associations in the recipient countries), can play a significant role in fostering innovation in adult education, and allowing some freedom for innovation in extremely poor countries with very limited budgets. This form of aid can, however, be politically problematic, where the government concerned is suspicious of the radicalism of local adult education movements. On the other hand, IGO or government-to-government programs of aid tend to reinforce existing power structures and relations, and in turn are subjected to criticism from those in the international adult education movement.

5. Future Prospects

5.1 Achievements

Internationalism, including internationalism in adult education, has advanced considerably since the Second World War. The first adult education landmark was the UNESCO conference at Elsinore, Denmark, in 1949. International adult education has been and continues to be inspired by a set of values which ally it with other movements, notably those centering on women's, peace, and environmental issues. The ICAE, created in 1972, has provided a particular vehicle for the expression of these ideals with their promotion both in the North and more especially for the benefit of the disempowered and underprivileged in the South. Adult education has been written more firmly into the agenda of many governments and departments of education, partly because of the success of international adult education lobbying, and because of demographic and economic imperatives which have made adult education and retraining of greater national importance worldwide.

5.2 Prospects and Tensions

International events at the end of the 1980s appeared to dispel the threat of global nuclear war and to mark the end of 75 years of confrontation, war, and the Cold War, centering on Europe but influencing international relations worldwide. Changes at the end of that decade have meant that international adult education must operate in a very different, perhaps more benign, environment. Reduced military standing might release more resources for education, including adult education, and for North–South development and aid programs. Counterbalancing these prospects, however, are concerns that the wealthy nations will ignore the needs of the South, and concentrate their resources and interest on the economic reorientation and development of Asia and Eastern Europe. The new century would appear to be an era of opportunity but also of new problems for international adult education.

The International Literacy Year in 1990 concentrated attention upon the increasing absolute number of illiterates, a persisting condition despite massive literacy programs in many countries, and proportional reductions in illiteracy. Some adult educators remain concerned that internationally driven campaigns to eradicate illiteracy may be ill-fitted to particular local circumstances and insensitive to particular needs. In extreme cases they may do more harm than good. It also remains the case that adult education and literacy programs cannot alone resolve problems which have political, economic, and other social causes.

Another source of tension for international adult education is between, on the one hand, what might be called the "visionary" tendency within the field and, on the other, the "technical" or "technicist" tendency. Adult education as a movement emphasizes its contribution to social development and transformation, and to the reduction of inequality. It is thus inherently political and ideological in orientation, and yet efforts to professionalize the adult education service customarily place emphasis upon the technical skills related to teaching and facilitating learning, and often tend to be quite apolitical. Allied to this tension is the success with which adult education has come to be recognized and taken into the mainstream of the school-based education service in an increasing number of countries. Both this fact and the universal stress on economic

survival and competition which characterizes the mid-1990s, could threaten those characteristics peculiar to the movement which have distinguished and energized international adult education. On the other hand, old and new needs which require a response from adult education provide a rich agenda for the field. These include the persistence of illiteracy, of social and economic deprivation, and of racism and ethnocentrism in old and new forms. To these may be added the problems of the environment which call for an international and an educational response.

See also: Adult Education: Concepts and Principles; Community Education and Community Development; Adult Education Research; Comparative Studies: Adult Education; International Council for Adult Education; Nongovernmental Organizations; UNESCO and Adult Education

References

Abrahamsson K, Rubenson K, Slowey M (eds.) 1988 *Adults in the Academy. International Trends in Adult and Higher Education.* Swedish National Board of Education, Stockholm

Bhola H S 1990 *Literacy For Survival and For More Than Mere Survival.* International Bureau of Education, Geneva

Charters A N et al. (eds.) 1981 *Comparing Adult Education Worldwide.* Jossey-Bass, San Francisco, California

Duke C (ed.) 1985 *Combating Poverty Through Adult Education: National Development Strategies.* Croom Helm, London

Duke C 1990 *Grassroots Approaches To Combatting Poverty Through Adult Education.* DVV, Bonn

Hall B L, Kidd J R 1978 *Adult Learning: A Design For Action.* Pergamon Press, Oxford

Mayor F 1990 *International Literacy Year: Opportunity and Challenges.* UNESCO, Paris

Schutze H J (ed.) 1987 *Adults in Higher Education: Policies and Practice in Great Britain and North America.* Almqvist and Wiksell, Stockholm

UNESCO 1985 *Fourth International Conference on Adult Education: Final Report.* UNESCO, Paris

UNESCO 1976 Recommendation on the Development of Adult Education. UNESCO, Paris

UNESCO 1990 *Literacy: 1990 International Literacy Year.* UNESCO, Paris

Further Reading

Coombs P H 1985 *The World Crisis in Education: A View from the Eighties.* Oxford University Press, New York

Duke C (ed.) 1986 *Adult Education: International Perspectives from China.* Croom Helm, London

Lowe J 1982 *The Education of Adults: A World Perspective,* 2nd edn. UNESCO, Paris

Titmus C (ed.) 1989 *Lifelong Education for Adults: An International Handbook.* Pergamon Press, Oxford

Titmus C 1991 Adult education a concept and structure: An agenda for research. *Int. J. Univ. Adult Educ.* 30(3): 1–11

International Council for Adult Education

T. Khalil-Khouri

The International Council for Adult Education is the largest and most important international nongovernmental organization dedicated to the education of adults. This entry describes its origin, history, and aims. It also describes the Council's structure and the programs and projects it sponsors.

1. History

International and regional conferences and meetings have special significance for adult education. It was at such a conference that the International Council for Adult Education was born. Discussions about the need for an international and nongovernmental adult education organization took place at UNESCO's World Conference on Adult Education in Elsinore in 1949. Eleven years later, by the time of the second world conference that was held in Montreal in 1960, the debate was still ongoing, with one side saying that such action should be linked to governments or to the UNESCO, and the other arguing that only free voluntary activism could represent the various aspects of the adult education movement. One of the resolutions from the Montreal conference was to urge governments to encourage the development of voluntary organizations.

J. Roby Kidd, a Canadian educator and professor of adult education at the Ontario Institute for Studies in Education (OISE) was one of a small number of educators who had a democratic, progressive, social, and international vision of adult education. He had for some time been promoting the idea of an international organization for adult education built on basic democratic values with its roots in social activism.

It was at the third world conference, in Tokyo in 1972, when a number of developing countries had already begun creating national educational associations and bodies for regional cooperation on educational associations and bodies for regional cooperation on educational matters, that Kidd, through a series of informal talks, received enough support from a number of countries to bring the idea of establishing an international organization to fruition.

Kidd had attended the Tokyo conference as a Canadian observer. Convinced that a permanent coordinating body, such as a Council, would strengthen the already existing regional and national associations, encourage the establishment of new ones, enhance the links among them, and ensure world solidarity, he lobbied for the support of representatives present at the conference, and received initial support from 16 countries. With that support he was able to incorporate the International Council for Adult Education (ICAE) which began operations from its headquarters in Toronto, Canada in 1973, with Kidd as its first Secretary General.

2. Aims and Objectives

The ICAE is the largest international NGO based in Canada. It is also a major international nongovernmental organization working in adult education with consultative status at UNICEF, UNESCO, ECOSOC, ILO, and FAO.

As set out in the Constitution, the Council stresses the importance of adult learning for the healthy growth and development of individuals, communities, and societies, by helping them gain the knowledge, skills, and competency to achieve a just and equitable economic, social and cultural development. The Council is defined in the Constitution as a place for encounter; a means for enhancing international understanding and cooperation; a means for advancing fuller participation by such individuals and groups in the determination of their economic, social, and cultural development by encouraging, supporting, and strengthening the activities of member organizations; by stimulating the establishment, where such do not exist, of national organizations for the further promotion, development, and coordination of education for adults; by cooperating with intergovernmental and international nongovernmental organizations wholly or partly concerned with the education of adults; by encouraging all relevant national organizations to become active and supportive members of their respective and relevant regional organizations having a major concern for the education of adults.

Equally important to its mandate and vision, is the Council's support for international understanding and world peace. The ICAE operates in partnership with adult education and other development organizations around the world, and therefore provides an international forum for debate and dialogue on how adult education can help alleviate entrenched poverty and its resulting forms of exploitation and inequity.

3. Structure of the Council

Today the ICAE is a federation of 107 autonomous national, regional, and sectoral adult education associations from 83 countries. The national organizations have to join the ICAE's member association in their region before applying for membership in the ICAE. Although the Constitution of the Council does not allow for individual members, for a nominal fee, individuals can become "Friends of ICAE" in return for which they would receive ICAE publications.

The Council operates through a Secretariat office in Toronto, Canada, which acts as a support, communications, and information dissemination centre for the membership and the governing structures. There are three major organs that govern the activities and affairs of the Council. These are the General Assembly, the Executive Committee and the Bureau of Officers.

The General Assembly, as defined by the Constitution, is the ". . . gathering together of the whole membership of the Council for the purposes of consideration, evaluation, delineation of the broad lines of policy and development of the Council." The General Assembly is convened at intervals of no longer than four years. It has the responsibility to elect, from among the nominees put forward by ICAE member organizations, the Executive Committee of the Council. The last General Assembly, which met in September 1994 in Cairo, Egypt, voted, in view of the changing global economy and in the interest of efficiency, to reduce the size of the Executive Committee from 33 to 23 members.

The Executive Committee is elected for a four-year term and is made up of the President; the Treasurer; seven Vice Presidents, one from each region (Africa, Arab region, Asia & South Pacific, Caribbean, Europe, Latin America, North America); seven Ordinary Members and seven ex-officio, nonvoting members, who are the secretaries general of the regional member organizations. The Executive Committee appoints the secretary general of the Council, is accountable to the General Assembly and meets once a year.

The third governing body, the Bureau of Officers, is a decision-making body, made up of the President, the Treasurer and a number of Vice Presidents. The Bureau deals with matters requiring the Executive Committee's attention in between the Executive's annual meetings.

4. Affiliations

The ICAE, as an international nongovernmental organization, has been granted consultative status with the United Nations. The ICAE is in consultative status (Category A) with UNESCO; is on the ILO's list of cooperating INGOs; is in associate status with the UN Department of Public Information; and in consultative status (Category 1) with the Economic and Social Council and its various commissions and other subsidiary bodies, such as the Commission for Social Development, the Commission on Human Rights, the Commission on the Status of Women, the Commission on Sustainable Development, the Commission on Crime Prevention and Criminal Justice, and the Regional Economic Commissions.

By virtue of its consultative status, the ICAE attends UN meetings and conferences, suggests items for agendas, makes statements, and submits draft resolutions. Also, the ICAE receives considerable documentation from and has access to UN information, and has the opportunity to participate in the planning and execution of UN programs and activities of interest to its membership and in keeping with its mandate. Like other international NGOs in consultative status, the ICAE keeps the UN informed of its work and acquaints its own members with UN activities and projects of interest to them. The Council also supports, advises and collaborates with the UN in accordance with ICAE's own aims and purposes and within the nature and scope of its competence and activities.

Most recently, the Council was included among the institutional members of a panel of advisers to the International Commission on Education for the Twenty-first Century. The aim of the Commission is to study the challenges facing education and formulate suggestions and recommendations in the form of a report which can serve as an agenda for renewal and action.

5. Programs and Projects

The work of the Council is carried out through its member associations in all regions of the world. It includes advocacy; research; training of trainers and practitioners through the organizing of seminars, workshops, and conferences; information sharing and exchange through the publication of a quarterly journal, *Convergence*; occasional papers, monograms, and reports on activities; and a newsletter, *ICAE News*, in addition to the bulletins and newsletters specific to each of ICAE's four priority programmes. The Secretariat in Toronto also houses a resource centre with an extensive collection of international materials on adult education, literacy, and popular and nonformal education. It is considered one of the largest collection of materials in Canada from and about adult education in Third World countries.

The ICAE's programs respond directly to needs and issues identified by member associations, practitioners, and educators working in the field. In January 1990 a decision was taken by the General Assembly at their meeting in Bangkok, Thailand, to decentralize all of the Council's programs in accordance with the strategies laid out by Kidd in his first report as Secretary General of ICAE in 1973: "To locate the main services of the Council close to where the action is needed." It is the Council's belief that the decentralization of power is one of the best ways of empowering people, promoting participation, and increasing efficiency. The four priority program areas of the ICAE are Literacy (based in Asia), Women's Education (based in Latin America), Education for Environmental Action (was based in Latin America, but is currently operating from

Toronto), and Education for Peace and Human Rights (based in Europe). Additional specialized, decentralized, international networks and working groups have been formed to work on such issues such as education for older adults, education for adults with special learning needs, primary health care, participators research, and transformative research, popular culture, and criminal justice.

6. Information Services of the Council

Much international activity in adult education revolves around the exchange of information and experiences through meetings and conferences, or, more importantly through publications. Another one of the strategies laid out by Kidd in 1973 involved creating a better-functioning information system in several languages. The ICAE's four official languages are Arabic, English, French, and Spanish, and when finances allow it, publications are produced in all four.

The ICAE can be defined as a knowledge-based organization. What ICAE shares with its members is knowledge on eliminating one of the greatest obstacles towards development, illiteracy. It also shares knowledge on fostering democratic participation, and human rights awareness, and knowledge on empowering women. Over the past twenty years the Council has accumulated a vast body of knowledge and experience, and is currently looking toward becoming more proactive in the dissemination and processing of that information.

In order to define its presence in the global context and continue advocating for adult education, the ICAE is endeavouring to build a solid foundation for the creation, movement, and exchange of information and knowledge. Such sharing of knowledge in every direction, South–South, South–North, and North–South, is a key to reducing the economic gap.

The international meetings and conferences organized by the ICAE are used not only as a way of exchanging information, but also as a means to define and clarify the role and contributions of adult education and to produce guidelines, policy statements, and agendas for action. The ICAE has organized a number of specialized conferences, on a regional and an international scale, which have produced statements and recommendations, and has participated, through its regional member organizations and international coordinators of its programs in a number of Preparatory Committee meetings for UN conferences.

7. Conclusion

Currently the Council is actively preparing for the UN World Summit on Social Development (Copenhagen, March 1995), and the UN World Conference on Women (Beijing, September 1995). In September 1994, the ICAE held its Fifth World Assembly in Cairo, Egypt on Women, Literacy, and Development: Challenges for the Twenty-first Century. A meeting of the General Assembly was held in conjunction with the conference.

As a result of the Assembly's recommendations, the Council is currently undergoing an in-depth evaluation and review process to examine the structures and programs of the organization; the efficacy of the programs and the effectiveness of the decentralization process; the relationship between regional and national organizations; the relationship between the regions and the Secretariat and the role and mandate of the Secretariat and the Executive Committee. This process of evaluation and reflection aims at renewing the ICAE's mission and reaffirming its vision to better prepare it to meet the challenges of the next century.

See also: Comparative Studies: Adult Education; International Adult Education; Nongovernmental Organization; UNESCO and Adult Education

International Labour Organisation

A. Salt and D. Bowland

As the United Nations system's specialized agency primarily concerned with bettering the lives of workers, the International Labour Organisation (ILO) has long considered the development of productive skills for employment as one of its central concerns. In operationalizing this concern, the ILO has supplemented its normative or standard-setting activities with a wide range of technical assistance activities aimed at developing national capacity, particularly in developing countries, to plan, program, and deliver employment-related training which both meets the needs of the labor market and satisfies the aspirations of the individual for personal development. This entry traces the evolution of ILO technical assistance in continuing education and vocational training, examines trends in the 1990s, and concludes with a review of priorities and targets for future action in the light of technological and structural change and of regional disparities.

1. *ILO's Involvement in Continuing Education and Vocational Training*

The International Labour Organisation was created in 1919 under the Treaty of Versailles, together with the League of Nations, and outlived that body to become, in 1946, the first specialized agency in the United Nations system. Uniquely among United Nations agencies the ILO is tripartite in composition, meaning that its policy and decision-making organs consist not only of government representatives but also of representatives of employers' and workers' organizations.

The ILO is first and foremost a normative, or standard-setting organization. It seeks to formulate international policies and programs to improve working conditions—as a means of bettering the lives of workers and contributing to peace and social justice—and to develop international labor standards to serve as guidelines for national authorities in putting these policies into action. Once ratified, ILO conventions enter into a country's national legislation, but over and above their immediate legislative effect they also serve to point the way to social progress.

In pursuing the goal of social justice, the ILO has always regarded continuing education and, particularly, vocational training as important concerns, given that they contribute to the development of an individual's productive capacity. Indeed, the preamble to the ILO's Constitution identifies vocational training as one of the means of improving the conditions of work and the welfare of workers. At the normative level, the ILO's concern with vocational training has been reflected in a number of conventions and recommendations on the subject adopted over the years by the tripartite International Labor Conference. The latest, and most specifically focused of these training-related standards, are the Human Resources Development Convention, 1975 and the Human Resources Development Recommendation, 1975 (ILO 1991). These were supplemented by the Vocational Rehabilitation and Employment (Disabled Persons) Convention and Recommendation, 1983 (ILO 1983).

The Human Resources Development Convention 1975 stipulate the adoption of "comprehensive and coordinated policies and programmes of vocational guidance and vocational training, closely linked with employment, in particular through public employment services" (ILO 1991 p. 1). It also specified that such policies should take into account the economic, social, and cultural circumstances of individual countries, and emphasizes the importance of improving the abilities of individuals without any discrimination whatsoever. These broad principles are elaborated in more detail in the Human Resources Development Recommendation, 1975. While economic efficiency is not ignored in these standards, it is worth noting the emphasis given to the rights of the individual and the social objectives of training. The Vocational Rehabilitation and Employment (Disabled Persons) Convention and Recommendation, 1983 set forth basic principles and measures to ensure equality of opportunity and access to services for disabled persons in vocational training as well as employment.

2. *Development of Technical Cooperation*

Following the Second World War and as a result of the need to help displaced persons build new lives and to assist war-damaged countries, especially in Europe, to reconstruct their economies, the ILO became directly involved in vocational training. It did this by engaging in research, information dissemination, and limited, largely short-term, technical assistance. Beginning in the 1950s, however, when the United Nations expanded its development programs and put greater emphasis on the needs of poorer, less developed countries, the ILO has substantially increased its technical assistance, or technical cooperation as it is known today. With the emergence of many former colonies as independent states in the 1960s and the increased availability of funds for economic development from the United Nations and other sources, the ILO became heavily involved in helping the newly independent states, and the focus of its technical cooperation programs shifted primarily to their concerns.

Technical cooperation expenditures grew rapidly during the 1970s and 1980s, reaching a peak of US$152 million in 1990. Table 1 summarizes these trends. Along with the growth in volume, the ILO's technical cooperation program also became more diverse. In addition to standard setting, research, information dissemination, and the provision of long and shorter term expert and advisory services, the ILO became active in equipment procurement, and the organization of fellowship programs and technical meetings. The program's geographical focus also changed. For example, from 1975 to 1990, Africa's share of ILO technical assistance increased from 39 to 53 percent and Asia's from 23 to 25. All other regions declined in relative shares. These shifts reflected, in a large part, the ILO's increasing emphasis on assisting the

Table 1
Annual ILO technical cooperation expenditures

Year	Expenditures (000's of US dollars)
1950–51	341
1960	3,485
1970	29,946
1980	99,392
1985	90,400
1990	152,175

least developed countries, most of which are located in Africa and Asia.

Vocational training has occupied, and continues to occupy, a major place in the ILO's overall technical cooperation program. Since the early 1960s, the ILO has implemented hundreds of vocational training projects in scores of countries around the world. Indeed, those countries where public vocational training systems have not benefitted at some stage from ILO assistance are the exception rather than the rule. From 1950 to around 1972 vocational training projects accounted for approximately half of the ILO's technical cooperation expenditures. Since then, projects primarily concerned with vocational training have declined in relative terms to about one-fifth of the total, as other areas of ILO technical cooperation, such as management development, vocational rehabilitation of disabled persons, workers' education, enterprise and cooperative development, occupational safety, and the hotel and tourism and maritime industries have expanded. Since training is also an important component of these newer technical cooperation activities, however, training as such continues to account for over half of total ILO technical cooperation.

In 1965, the International Training Centre of the ILO began operating in Turin, Italy. The Centre's initial task was to provide advanced training for skilled technicians and instructors, and subsequently to develop and deliver programs for the trainers of instructional staff in training institutions and in industry. It also focused on general management skills and techniques for productivity improvement. By the late 1970s, as national and regional capacities in these topics grew, the Centre shifted its emphasis more toward the management of vocational training, whether at the institutional or system level, skills upgrading for in-plant trainers and supervisors, and the development and testing of new training techniques and methodologies. It also began to reappraise the suitability of "traditional" vocational training approaches for the special needs of the informal sector, and to devise innovative methodologies for these sectors. In many developing countries, the informal sector's large number of microenterprises accounted for a high proportion of goods and services, and also of employment.

During the 1970s and 1980s the ILO provided technical assistance for the development of vocational rehabilitation services and centers, and for the training of rehabilitation personnel, in over 60 countries, particularly in Africa. In many of these countries, the subsequent difficulties of trained disabled persons in finding employment led to a new emphasis in ILO projects, namely on training and assistance for self-employment, particularly in the informal sector. In addition, the development of methods to mobilize community support for the vocational integration of disabled members has become an important component of ILO technical cooperation projects in this field, as is the search for opportunities for disabled persons

to be trained and employed alongside nondisabled people.

In 1992 the ILO implemented approximately 180 vocational training and vocational rehabilitation projects in more than 60 countries. They were funded largely by the United Nations Development Programme (UNDP) and to a lesser extent by the World Bank. In addition, a number of projects were funded by donor countries that channel a portion of their aid funds through the ILO rather than implementing projects directly on a bilateral basis.

3. Trends in ILO Technical Assistance

The early emphasis of ILO vocational training projects was on expanding prevocational training capacity through the formulation of training legislation and policies, the establishment of national training organizations, and the construction of infrastructure. As training systems expanded and matured, and as the demands made on them grew as a result of increasing numbers of new labor market entrants and the rapid pace of technological change, many countries shifted their focus more to increased cost-effectiveness, greater relevancy, establishment of occupational standards and testing systems, and improving on-the-job training. These trends were, however, less pronounced in the least developed countries, many of which still face serious difficulties in establishing basic entry-level vocational training systems and operating them cost-effectively.

As a result of these trends, the focus of ILO technical cooperation activities has also changed. Most significantly, the ILO is placing much greater emphasis on helping member states to establish appropriate policy frameworks. Key components of this strategy are strengthening links with the labor market, improving the efficiency and effectiveness of public sector training systems, and strengthening support to the informal sector. More attention is now being paid to problem solving, and less to starting up new projects. At the International Training Centre of the ILO in Turin, courses are becoming shorter, more specialized, and tailored for trainees with higher levels of education. Whilst training in the management of vocational training systems and institutions continues, this has been supplemented by major new programs on vocational education and training policy and planning and, in the area of training methodologies, programs on the development and application of new training technologies.

These trends have also been reflected in the operating characteristics of ILO vocational training projects. The average size of projects has declined and the average number of international experts and the length of their assignments have fallen in favor of increased use of short-term and national consultants. Projects include relatively smaller equipment components but relatively larger fellowship components. More use is being made of United Nations volunteers. The ILO is also making an effort to encourage technical cooperation among developing countries through regional skills development teams: APSDEP (the Asian and Pacific Skill Development Programme), CIADFOR (*Centre interafricain pour le développement de la formation professionnelle*) and CINTERFOR (Inter-American Vocational Training Research and Documentation Center). Finally, in response to growing pressure on available resources and the emergence of more complex, if smaller, projects, the ILO has increased its emphasis on improved project design, monitoring, and evaluation.

The ILO advocates a broad systems approach to the design and implementation of vocational training. There are several reasons for this. First, experience has demonstrated that concentration on a few selected elements of an instructional system, such as instructor training or materials development, without adequate attention to other elements, such as a national policy framework, instructor salaries, equipment, or trainee motivation, often results in training programs not meeting their goals. An effective training system requires all its components to be efficient and mutually supporting.

Second, in addition to providing job-related skills, training programs frequently have objectives covering educational, social, political, and economic goals. For example, training programs can be designed to facilitate personal growth and occupational advancement; improve the situation of special groups such as refugees, women, disabled persons, or unemployed youths; raise productivity, improve safety, provide remedial education, stimulate rural development, and much more.

Third, training is only one factor, albeit a vital one, influencing human resources and economic development. Failure to take this into account can seriously weaken the impact of training. For example national training programs not linked with employment opportunities and the skills demanded by employers may create social frustration as well as waste resources.

4. Future Directions

Future ILO vocational training policies and programs will be influenced both by changes in the technical cooperation environment and in ILO priorities. First, a new consensus concerning major aspects of human resources development is emerging among the development assistance community. There is increased recognition of the importance of investment in human resources development as one of the critical factors in successful economic development. A second component of the consensus is the importance attached to markets in successful growth strategies. A third element is the advocacy that governments should concentrate on those things which they do best, for example infrastructure and education, and abstain from what they do poorly, such as the operation of industrial enterprises. A World Bank *Policy Paper on Vocational and Technical Education and Training* (to which the ILO contributed) brings many of these concepts to bear on problems of interest to trainers, emphasizing strengthened primary and secondary education as a basis for acquiring labor market skills. It encourages not only the reform of public training systems but also the creation of a favorable policy environment for private sector training, including incentives for employers to provide, and workers to pursue, training (Middleton et al. 1991).

The challenge for the ILO in this new consensus is to identify ways in which the social objectives of training are not lost in the search for greater efficiency. In addition to the changing policy consensus on human resources development, there is a second trend that will influence ILO involvement in technical cooperation. There is a growing feeling (both inside and outside the UN) that technical cooperation projects lack focus and coherence; that they have not contributed sufficiently to building national capacities and self-reliance; that they have not adequately relied on local resources and skills; and that they have focused too little on advice and assistance to policy makers and planners.

These concerns are reflected in a new approach to technical cooperation under which the UNDP, a major funder of ILO training activities, will in the future emphasize the execution of projects by governments themselves rather than by specialized agencies. To achieve greater coherence and impact the UNDP will also stress the planning of technical cooperation at the program level, rather than on the current project-by-project basis. Specialized agencies, such as the ILO, will be encouraged to move away from direct involvement in project implementation to more concern with "up-stream" or preproject activities, such as sector analysis and policy/program formulation in order to provide a framework for a thematically linked group of technical assistance activities supporting national development objectives. The specialized agencies will also be called upon to help governments acquire the skills necessary to manage development projects effectively. One ILO response to these new imperatives has been to work closely with UNDP to develop programs at the ILO Turin Centre on the management of technical cooperation and of field coordination for senior United Nations system representatives at the country level.

In addition to those changes in the external environment for technical cooperation summarized above, a number of internal changes in program priority and administrative arrangements will impact on how the ILO relates to the concerns of its member states. In the first place, the ILO intends to establish a much closer linkage between its technical cooperation activities and the achievement of the basic normative objectives of the Organisation. Standard-setting and technical cooperation activities have always been seen as complementary and mutually supportive activities;

however, this relationship will become more explicit in the ILO's future programs. In addition, the Organisation will give greater responsibilities to its field structure, whose role in programing and management of operational activities in developing countries will increase considerably.

5. *Program Priorities*

While many details are yet to be worked out, it is reasonable to expect that in the future the ILO will focus its training activities on assisting national governments in their efforts to formulate appropriate policies and programs and to manage and evaluate better the effectiveness of their training systems as a flexible response to changing labor market conditions. It can expect to be less involved in managing technical cooperation projects (that will be the responsibility of national governments) even though it will continue to provide technical advice and assistance to those governments and organizations requesting help in project implementation. The new or newly prioritized concerns will be elaborated further within the framework of the relevant mandates of the ILO, building in particular on the Human Resources Development Convention, 1975 referred to earlier.

5.1 *Targets for Action*

The ILO will continue its long-standing concern with on-the-job training, including apprenticeship schemes and continuing training and retraining, and the identification of policies that encourage such training. A particularly important objective will be to encourage workers' involvement in planning enterprise-based training and monitoring its impact, an issue intimately bound up, as noted earlier, with incentives to workers to engage in training.

Existing training systems have not proved effective in reaching workers outside the formal wage sector, yet in many countries most workers are employed in either the informal sector, primarily in urban areas, or in rural communities. Innovative, low-cost, and relevant training techniques must be developed and brought to bear in these areas. In rural communities the ILO will continue to support self-help schemes to enhance income. The ILO will also continue to emphasize improvement of training opportunities for women, unemployed youth, refugees, and other vulnerable groups. Community-based initiatives to identify or create training and work opportunities for disabled youth and adults, especially women, will be promoted and supported.

In the field of instructional technologies, a major challenge for the ILO is in increasing the responsiveness of training systems to changing needs by helping develop flexible training methodologies based on modular training techniques and innovative training approaches, such as computer-based training, distance learning, and interactive video.

Tripartite advisory bodies made up of workers', employers', and government representatives can play an important role in building consensus, recommending training policies, and evaluating training activities. The ILO will assist such bodies by helping train supporting technical staff, providing access to information and developing comparative case studies.

The ILO will strengthen its research capability in support of its new priorities. As new training policy options are explored by national authorities, there will be an important need for targeted research, and the development of practical procedures and guidelines to aid policy makers and training practitioners in assessing options and implementing solutions. A related priority for the ILO is to strengthen its information dissemination role.

5.2 *Regional Strategies*

As stipulated in its Human Resources Development Convention, 1975, ILO training approaches will be tailored to the needs and circumstances of individual countries. This differentiation can be illustrated by examining broad differences in the strategies the ILO will adopt in five major regions. In Africa the ILO will focus on helping countries to improve the efficiency and effectiveness of public training systems. In view of the shortage of wage jobs, emphasis will be given to self-employment and reorientating public training toward the needs of the informal sector. Inclusion of basic skills in training programs will be an important means of supporting regional emphasis on primary education. The involvement of the community, and particularly of disabled persons' organizations, in supporting the integration of disabled persons in local training programs and informal sector work will be important.

In Asia, the ILO strategy is likely to accord higher priority to sectoral policy analysis and training opportunities for disabled individuals, information exchange, new instructional technologies, further education, and rural community development. In the poorest, and most highly populated countries of the region, an important ILO priority will be to help reorientate public sector training systems toward the needs of poor and disadvantaged groups.

In the Arab States, ILO emphasis will be on developing regional networks in vocational training and vocational rehabilitation to share scarce resources and exchange information. In East and Central Europe ILO will focus on training-policy formulation, retraining, and increasing the role of employers' and workers' organizations in human resources planning and development. The ILO will also provide help in development of training legislation, occupational certification, new instructional methodologies, and evaluation of training effectiveness.

In Latin America and the Caribbean, training systems in many countries are well-developed and have established close relationships with industry and the labor market in general. However, as rapid changes in the economic environment confront these training systems with new problems and challenges, the ILO priority will be to serve as a source of information on experiences in other systems. The ILO will continue to place priority on developing community-based approaches to vocational rehabilitation. It will emphasize the inclusion of basic skills in training programs.

It is clear that the principal challenge for the ILO in the coming years will be to maintain its ability to respond to the rapidly changing vocational training needs of its member states in the continuing effort to achieve the Organisation's objectives in line with its core mandate and founding principles.

See also: Technical and Vocational Education and Training; Technological Change and Education; Demand, Supply, and Finance of Adult Education; Comparative Studies: Vocational Education and Training; UNESCO and Adult Education

References

ILO 1983 *Convention Concerning Vocational Rehabilitation and Employment (Disabled Persons)* Convention (No. 159) and Recommendation No. 168. ILO, Geneva

ILO 1991 *Human Resources Development: Vocational Guidance and Training, Paid Educational Leave*. General Survey of the Reports on the Paid Educational Leave Convention (No. 140) and Recommendation (No. 148), (1974), and the Human Resources Development Convention (No. 142), and Recommendation (No. 150), (1975). International Labour Conference Report 78 III, Part 4B, Geneva

Middleton J, Ziderman A, Van Adams A 1991 *Vocational and Technical Education and Training*. A World Bank policy paper. Education and Employment Division, Population and Human Resources Development, Washington, DC

Further Reading

ILO 1980 *Report of the Director-General to the International Labour Conference 6th Session. Part 1: Training: Challenge of the 1980s*. ILO, Geneva

ILO 1991 *Programme and Budget Proposals for the Biennium 1992–93*. ILO, Geneva

ILO 1992 *Adjustment and human resources development, International Labour Conference*, Report VI. ILO Geneva

Kanawaty G, Moura Castro C 1990 New directions for training: an agenda for action *Int. Lab. Rev.* 129(6): 751–71

United Nations *Industrial Statistics Yearbook*. UN Statistical Office, New York

Nongovernmental Organizations

J. P. Comings

This entry looks at the support that the nongovernmental sector provides to adult education. The term "nongovernmental organization" (NGO) defines a range of institutions that include nonprofit agencies, community-based organizations, charities, advocacy groups, private universities, religious institutions, unions, and other formal and informal groups. They are outside of the regular government bureaucracy and employ their revenue not for personal gain, but for the betterment of the constituencies they serve. Nongovernmental organizations contribute to every aspect of adult education but they are thought to have a comparative advantage, in relation to government entities, in some specific ways.

Nongovernmental organizations are seen as having qualities of sensitivity and objectivity that help them serve adult learners. In opposition to government bureaucracies, NGOs are seen as being able to adapt their programs to the needs of individual populations, to use funding more efficiently and effectively, and to gain the trust of adult learner populations that may be outside the mainstream of society (WCEFA 1990 pp. 76–77). There is an opposing point of view that states that adult education, particularly when it focuses on basic skills or secondary school equivalency, should be the responsibility of government. Nongovernmental organizations are seen as a way for government to shirk its responsibility and turn over this area of difficult and important work to groups of underfunded volunteers. A synthesis of these two points of view is emerging that argues that both government and NGOs have roles to play, and that together they can provide better service than either can alone.

1. Developing Countries

In the context of developing countries, the primary nature of NGOs is their quality of nongovernment status. The NGOs provide many of the relief and development services that governments do, including adult education, but they do so outside government programs and priorities. They are viewed as more efficient and effective than government agencies because they are less bureaucratic and political. On the other hand, they are often antagonistic to government policies and may not be integrated into national plans.

In most countries, both local and international NGOs are active. The local NGOs quite often receive most of their funding from sources outside their country, such as multilateral or bilateral development organizations (UNICEF and the Swedish International Development Agency, for example) and from NGOs based in the industrialized world (Oxfam in the United Kingdom, the Bernard von Leer Foundation in the Netherlands, and the Friedrich Naumann Stiftung in Germany, for example). International NGOs are based in industrialized countries with operations in the developing countries (Save the Children in the United States, *Ecoles Sans Frontières* in France, and Action Aid in the United Kingdom, for example).

Most early NGO literacy efforts were based in churches, religious organizations, and missionary groups, but a nonsectarian approach to literacy developed early in the twentieth century. Laubach Literacy International began with the work of Frank Laubach in the Philippines in the 1920s, and World Education began with the work of Mrs Welthy Fisher in India in the 1950s. These two American NGOs have had some influence on the adult education programs in almost every developing country, if not through direct efforts then by assistance with literacy program design. The Summer Institute of Linguistics began work in the 1940s developing writing systems for hundreds of unwritten languages, and, along with translating the Bible, helped support literacy efforts.

In countries with high rates of illiteracy, there are local NGOs that focus on adult education and most NGOs have adult education as an element of their program. The International Institute for Rural Reconstruction was founded in China by an American, Y C James Yen, as a literacy mass movement which later became active in a wide range of activities and moved on to the Philippines. The Dhaka Ahsania Mission, the Bangladesh Rural Advancement Committee, and *Gonoshahajjo Sangstha* are examples in Bangladesh.

2. The Industrialized World

In the industrialized world, the nongovernmental status of NGOs is not always so clear since some NGOs have a large part of their activities funded by government and others are focused exclusively on influencing government action. Most NGOs have funding from several different sources which can include national, state, and local government as well as private individuals, corporations, and foundations. The primary quality of NGOs in the industrialized world is less their nongovernmental status and more their connection to local communities and specific target populations.

In the United States, Laubach Literacy Action (the US wing of Laubach Literacy International) and Literacy Volunteers of America (LVA) have strong volunteer literacy programs operated through state affiliates. These local agencies recruit students and volunteer tutors, train the tutors, and then match a student with a tutor. Both organizations have a systematic approach that is easy for a volunteer tutor to learn and follow.

In North America, most NGOs are small Community-Based Organizations (CBOs). Some of these CBOs focus on specific ethnic populations such as Haitian, Hispanic, or African-American. Some serve a particular geographic community, and others have a religious affiliation. Community-based organizations have a close relationship to the people they serve and are quite often managed and staffed by people from the community.

3. Roles for NGOs

3.1 Funding Adult Education

In both developing and industrialized countries, the demand for adult education and continuing vocational training continues to grow, often outstripping the supply of educational services (see *Demand, Supply, and Finance of Adult Education*). Expecting NGOs to raise sufficient private funds to serve this burgeoning demand for adult learning is unrealistic. In developing countries, the issue of funding becomes even more difficult, since there is already insufficient funding to provide formal education to all children. In the developing countries, there is very little in the way of local private funding for adult education NGOs, and the government is rarely a funder of NGOs. Much of the funding for NGOs comes from international organizations, and this raises the issue of how to sustain their efforts.

Nongovernmental organizations do have resources to contribute to adult education that are in addition to government support. Volunteers are more easily recruited by NGOs, and NGOs are more likely to attract other resources such as free space, free reading materials, cash support from businesses and individuals, and free transportation services. Volunteers can be particularly helpful in adult education. Adult learners may have disabilities or other factors in their lives that make learning difficult, and volunteers can be a useful adjunct to professional teachers. Volunteers can provide additional instructional time.

In the industrialized world, NGOs have a much larger potential pool of resources from which to draw funding and in-kind contributions than in developing countries. Even so, these resources will never be sufficient to address the problem fully and in a meaningful way. For example, the two largest adult education NGOs, Laubach Literacy Action and Literacy Volunteers of America, serve less than 0.3 percent of the people who could benefit from basic literacy services in the United States. These resources are better seen as additional to funding from government.

3.2 Implementing Adult Education

There are adult learners who distrust government. Some people might not use government services or may bring to their classes prejudices that interfere with learning. An NGO program can offer a neutral and more efficient learning environment.

In adult education, "community-based" may be a quality that is more important than nongovernmental status. A study by the Association for Community Based Education (1986 pp. 23–24) pointed out that NGOs are more likely than government programs to be connected to the community they serve, draw staff from that community, provide a learning environment that is comfortable for people from that community, and be willing to modify curriculum and materials to meet the needs of that community. Though there are examples of local government agencies in the United States that are "community-based," this is less true in developing countries because the bureaucratic structure is usually centrally controlled with little delegation of authority and autonomy to local government entities (see *Community Education and Community Development*).

3.3 Designing and Developing Adult Education Efforts

Nongovernmental organizations are thought to have the ability to be creative in ways that government agencies do not. They are more flexible with their policies and procedures, can make decisions quickly, and are able to experiment across a wide range of possibilities. Government agencies are bureaucratic and require time-consuming procedures before policy and funding priorities are changed to meet a new possibility. Government decisions are more likely to be made by people who have little experience in direct implementation of adult education programs.

Nongovernmental organizations take a wide range of approaches and even use materials developed by students themselves. The ability of NGOs to be creative and flexible with curriculum and materials is a clear advantage in adult education where tailoring an approach to a community or group of learners can be the key to success.

In developing countries, governments do have a comparative advantage through economies of scale. Nongovernmental organizations generally serve small populations and can only produce a limited number of copies of materials, while governments can produce millions at a much lowered cost. In Nepal, the government produces a very effective set of literacy materials at a low cost, and NGOs buy them for use in their programs. The NGOs augment these materials with ones they develop themselves to address their specific interests.

3.4 Improving Programs

Government funding agencies have an interest in improving the efficiency and effectiveness of the agencies (both governmental and nongovernmental) they fund to provide adult education. There is a specialized type of adult education NGO, a service agency (Hoxeng 1989), that provides the services needed to improve effectiveness. The System for Adult Basic Education Support (SABES) in Massachusetts, the Adult Literacy and Basic Skills Unit (ALBSU) in the United Kingdom, and the Lesotho Distance Teaching Centre (LDTC) are good examples. These service agencies are technical assistance and training organizations whose mission is to improve the provision of service by both NGOs and local government implementing agencies. They provide staff training to upgrade the skills of both teachers and administrators, offer technical assistance in improvement of curriculum and management, and help to link provider programs to the larger world of knowledge and experience in adult education. An NGO status for service agencies frees them from the bureaucratic control and oversight qualities of government organizations.

3.5 Formulating Policy

National policy is a role set aside for government, but NGOs have a critical role to play in informing decision makers. Since NGOs are more likely to be connected to the clients of adult education programs, they can help make their voice heard in the policy dialogue.

In the United States there are several national NGO advocacy groups. The Southport Institute that published the *Jumpstart* study (Chisman 1989), and the Literacy Network, which is a membership organization, are both active in advocating adult education funding and specific adult education needs. The International Reading Association and the American Association of Adult and Continuing Education are large membership organizations which, among other issues, promote and support adult education in both Canada and the United States. Project Literacy US (PLUS) is a collaboration between the Public Broadcasting Service (PBS) and ABC/Capitol Cities that uses media to advocate literacy and is a major force for bringing the issue of adult illiteracy to the forefront of the national debate. There are similar organizations in other countries: the Movement for Canadian Literacy, the Campaign for Popular Education in Bangladesh, and the Finnish Adult Education Association. Internationally, the International Council on Adult Education, which has separate affiliates in each geographic region, plays this advocacy role.

Even when both governmental and nongovernmental agencies are involved in adult education, NGOs may be in a better position to argue for and against specific policies since their staff are outside the bureaucratic structure. This can be particularly important in developing countries where bureaucracies can be rigid and opportunities for employment outside government can be scarce. In the industrialized world, NGOs are more likely to represent a broad range of political points of view, some of which are not heard much within government.

4. Future Trends

A model where government sets national policy, provides funding, and performs those tasks which can benefit from economies of scale, and where NGOs do what they do best, that is implementation, is developing. The qualities of an NGO are also being taken on by local government agencies which can be more closely connected to a community. Out of an understanding and acceptance of the comparative advantages of national government agencies, local government agencies, national NGOs, and CBOs will come a collaborative approach that will use the best qualities of each.

See also: Adult Education for Development; Professional Associations; Comparative Studies: Vocational Education and Training; International Adult Education

References

Association for Community Based Education 1986 *Adult Literacy: A Study of Community Based Literacy Programs.* Association for Community Based Education, Washington, DC

Chisman F P 1989 *Jump Start: The Federal Role in Adult Literacy.* Southport Institute for Policy Analysis, Southport, Connecticut

Hoxeng J 1989 The service center approach. In: Eddy D, Garb G (eds.) 1989 *Towards a Fully Literate World* World Education Reports, No. 28. World Education, Boston, Massachusetts.

World Conference on Education for All (WCEFA) 1990 *Meeting Basic Learning Needs: A Vision for the 1990s—Background Document.* World Bank, Washington, DC

Further Reading

Drabek A G (ed.) 1987 Development alternatives: The challenge of NGOs. *World Dev.* Vol. 15 (Special issue). Supplement

Hunter C S, Harman D 1979 *Adult Illiteracy in the United States. A Report to the Ford Foundation.* McGraw-Hill, New York

International Council for Adult Education 1991 A world wide review of NGO literacy: View from the grassroots and the shop floor. *Convergence* 24 (1–2)

Korten D C 1990 *Getting to the 21st Century: Voluntary Action and the Global Agenda.* Kumarian Press, West Hartford, Connecticut

O'Neill M 1989 *The Third America: The Emergence of the Nonprofit Sector in the United States.* Jossey-Bass, San Francisco, California

Professional Associations

H. B. Long

Professional adult education associations are found in almost every nation, yet general knowledge of these organizations is limited. This entry is designed to provide systematic information on professional adult education associations through a discussion of eight major topics as follows: (a) history, (b) purpose, (c) description of adult education professional associations, (d) purposes of adult education professional associations, (e) consequences, (f) typology of associations, (g) issues, and (h) needed research.

1. History

Few studies or reports of professional adult education associations exist. Despite the increasing awareness of historical questions concerning adult education, the role of professional associations has received limited attention. Knowles (1962, 1977) is an exception. Based on his doctoral dissertation, Knowles provides one of the few in-depth discussions of the development of adult education associations in the United States. Kelly's (1970) comprehensive history of adult education in the United Kingdom provides limited information about the Workers' Educational Association (WEA). Long (1985) reports a brief description of the American Association for Adult and Continuing Education. More recently, Long (1992) examined the role of major American associations such as the predecessor organizations of the American Association for Adult and Continuing Education (AAACE), as well as the precursors to the National Continuing Education Association (NUCEA) and the Association for Continuing Higher Education (ACHE) in adult education knowledge development. Brockett (1989) provides a scholarly discussion of a variety of topics concerning professional associations for adult and continuing education. Up to the early 1990s, it can be asserted that the treatment of professional adult education associations has been more descriptive than analytical. This entry continues the tradition.

It is not unusual for individuals to form associations to promote or sustain an idea of organization in which they strongly believe. Adult educators are no exception to the practice. Associations formed on behalf of educational activities for adults in the United Kingdom and the United States have existed since the eighteenth century. Frustrated by his unsuccessful efforts to gain membership to a London philosophical society about 1816, Timothy Claxton formed "The Mechanical Institution" in August of 1817 (Long, 1992). The institution was an association of working men who were interested in improving their knowledge and the skills used in their crafts. A few years later his American colleague Josiah Holbrook initiated his ambitious design known as the "American Lyceum," which was based on an hierarchical association structure. The town lyceum was the basic element in a chain that penultimately led to the universal lyceum. In reality, the national organization was the structural capstone in the organization.

The twentieth century also gave birth to a variety of associations that focused on the education of adults. The Association for the Higher Education of Working Men was formed in the United Kingdom in 1903. The name of this association was changed in 1905 to become the Worker' Educational Association (or WEA). Between 1900 and 1930 Americans actively engaged in association forming. Several of the contemporary American adult education associations, such as the American Association for Adult Education, Department of Immigrant Education (later Department of Adult Education) of the National Education Association (formed in 1867), and the National University Extension Association, were formed during that period. A number of associations were formed in other regions of the world following the Second World War.

2. Purpose

This entry is designed to provide a descriptive overview of the range of professional adult education associations, their characteristics and purposes.

However, the achievement of this purpose is limited by several factors. First, the difficulty in identifying all the professional associations and of obtaining descriptive information from them presented an almost impossible task. Second, it is not always easy to distinguish between a professional adult education association and associations that might not be "professional." The differences between consumer associations, professional associations, and quasi-governmental organizations are not always explicit in the available information.

3. Description of Associations

A casual review of associations that exist in the international arena reveals a variety of organizations that are engaged in promoting and sustaining educational opportunities for adults, but which cannot be identified definitively as "professional" associations (Irvin 1992). Many of these are found in Europe, including the European Bureau of Adult Education. The National Institute of Adult Continuing Education (England and Wales and Scotland) is a good example of a quasi-governmental body that performs some of the tasks that are often conducted by professional associations in other nations, such as the American Association for Adult and Continuing Education in the United States.

Professional associations and many of the governmental or quasi-governmental adult education organizations frequently share some common goals. For example, organizations such as the British Standing Conference on University Teaching and Research in the Education of Adults, and the Adult Education Research Conference in the United States, appear to have some similar objectives such as the improvement of adult education knowledge. Yet their membership patterns seem to differ. In turn, the Research Conference is also different in structure and membership from most other adult education organizations in the United States, in that it is sometimes described as a "nonorganization," with its officers limited to a constantly changing steering committee and lacking many of the structures normally associated with associations.

3.1 International Organizations

In addition to the regional organizations, such as AALAE, ASPBAE, CARCAE, EBAE, and CEAAL noted in the next section, there are several international adult education organizations. They include the Commonwealth Association for the Education and Training of Adults based in Zimbabwe; the International Congress for University Adult Education in New Brunswick, Canada; the International League for Social Commitment in Adult Education located in Vancouver, Canada; and the Nordic Folk High School Council in Sweden. Other organizations of an international character not identified by the International Council for Adult Education (ICAE) include the International Association for Continuing Education and Training. While it does not describe itself as an international organization, the American Association for Adult and Continuing Education has in the early 1990s become international in many respects: its membership list includes an increasing number of individuals who do not live in the United States; the *Adult Education Quarterly* published by the association has international subscribers; and its annual conferences feature international topics and exchanges.

Cooperation among professional adult education associations and related bodies has increased greatly since the early 1970s. Joint meetings have been held between American and English associations, and between American and Canadian associations. These cooperative activities contribute to improved understanding of the different national adult education structures, policies, provisions, and problems.

713

3.2 Regional Organizations

A number of regional organizations that include education of adults as a major or minor goal are also found around the globe. They include the African Association for Literacy and Adult Education (AALAE), the Arab Educational, Cultural and Scientific Organization (ALESCSO), the Asian-South Pacific Bureau of Adult Education (ASPBAE), the Caribbean Regional Council for Adult Education (CARCAE), the European Bureau of Adult Education (EBAE), and the *Consejo de Educación de Adultos de América Latina* (CEAAL) in South and Latin America. Many of these groups combine individual membership activities with government support (direct or indirect).

3.3 National Organizations

No complete registry of all national professional associations concerned with adult education is available. The most convenient, if not exhaustive, directory is maintained by the International Council for Adult Education (ICEA). The ICEA *Directory* (1991) lists 90 national organizations from 77 nations that are ICEA members. In addition, the booklet identifies 4 additional national contacts that are not members. It is obvious that this list is only partial. An examination of the members from Canada, the United Kingdom, and the United States quickly reveals that a large number of organizations from these 3 nations are not included in the ICEA membership list. It may be assumed that many professional organizations in the developing countries are not included either. The list contains the Coalition of Adult Education Organizations, which is a coalition of more than 20 other organizations that are involved in adult education in some way. The Canadian membership includes only 3 organizations, whereas at least 12 might qualify as associations with some interests in adult education. Hence, it appears conservative to estimate that at least 150 national adult education associations may exist. These estimates do not include the variety of state and provincial associations found in a number of nations. In the United States alone there are probably at least 100 different state associations. Many of the state associations are associated in some way with national organizations, but the memberships may not always be mutually inclusive.

Space does not permit a complete listing of all the 77 nations with the 90 adult education associations affiliated with the International Council for Adult Education. An illustrative listing that identifies some of the associations from different regions of the world, however, follows: Bahamas Adult Education Association, Bolivia's *Asociación de Instituciones de Promoción y Educación* (AIPE), National Association for Adult Education of China, Association of Finnish Adult Education Organizations, Hong Kong Association for Continuing Education, *Associazione Italina di Educazione degli Adulti* (AIDEA), Korean Association of Adult and Youth Education (South Korea), National Adult Education Association of Liberia, *Programa de Formación en la Acción y la Investigación Social* (PRAXIS), Higher Council for Literary and Adult Education for the Palestinian People, Senegal's *Direction de la Formation Permanente*, and the National Adult Education Association of Uganda.

4. Association Purposes

Given the above description of the numbers of professional adult education associations, it is no surprise to note that professional associations differ in the variety of purposes they have set for themselves. There are some purposes, however, that appear to be common to a majority of the adult education professional associations: publication and dissemination of research and other information, and provision of a conference for members are basic activities. The purposes of these dissemination activities include strengthening theory and the improvement of practice, as well as development of communication networks among practitioners and scholars. Other activities that may be pursued in different countries include lobbying efforts designed to encourage legislative bodies to appropriate funds and to draft "friendly" legislation. Historically, associations, such as Claxton's "Mechanical Institution" referred to above, seem to have been local in nature. Gradually, they enlarged their vision, as in Holbrook's Lyceum that aspired to a universal organization. This process also appears in the twentieth century with associations first having specialized interests and/or national aspirations. More recently, avowed international organizations such as the International Congress for University Adult Education and the ICEA have emerged. Even regional and national organizations such as the European Bureau of Adult Education based in the Netherlands and Spain, and the *Consejo de Educación de Adultos de América Latina*, and national organizations such as the National Institute of Adult and Continuing Education (England and Wales and Scotland) and the American Association for Adult and Continuing Education have broadened the scope of their activities. The literature of the regional and national associations is increasingly available to readers who do not live in the local region or nation. In addition, national and regional conferences often include participants from other parts of the world.

The American Association for Adult and Continuing Education, which traces its roots back to the American Adult Education Association founded in 1926, is one of the oldest and largest professional membership associations. Therefore, the following description of the Association may be illustrative of some of the activities in which professional adult education associations typically engage:

> Provides leadership in advancing education as a life-long learning process. Serves as a central forum for

a wide variety of adult and continuing education special interest groups. Works to stimulate local, state, and regional adult continuing education efforts; encourage mutual cooperation and support; monitor proposed legislation and offer testimony to congress. Conducts special studies; maintains speakers' bureaus and charitable programs; bestows awards. Sponsors National Adult Education and Continuing Education Week. (Irvin 1992 p. 7384).

The American Association for Adult and Continuing Education lists the following publications: *Adult Education Quarterly, Adult Learning Practitioner Journal* (8 times per year), *American Association for Continuing Education—Newsletter–On Line* (10 times per year).

Membership categories include institutional and professional memberships. Membership dues defray a major part of the US$500,000 annual budget. No direct government funds are awarded to the Association, even though the Association occasionally obtains competitive government grants for special research and demonstration projects. The annual conference, which usually attracts approximately 3,000 participants, is another major source of funds.

While differences will be found among professional adult education associations, most of the associations are engaged in many, if not all, of the following activities.

4.1 Knowledge Development

Adult education knowledge development is often among the stated objectives of adult education professional associations. One of the major goals of the American Association for Adult Education when it was formed in 1926 concerned the improvement of adult education knowledge. The Association immediately established various mechanisms to achieve this goal. Annual conferences were initiated to provide practitioners with the opportunity to share their knowledge derived from practice, research projects were encouraged (and sometimes funded), and the journal *Adult Education* was published.

Adult education professional associations in the United States have been actively engaged, since the 1920s, in efforts designed to improve adult education knowledge (Long 1992). As a result of some of these efforts, books on adult education have been published; research findings have been reported in supported journals; and state, regional, and national conferences have provided a forum for the discussion of new research findings. Elsewhere, Long (1992) identifies professional adult education associations in the United States as important contributors to the development of adult education knowledge.

4.2 Professional Development

In addition to publications, such as periodicals, published by a number of associations including the Australian Association of Adult Education, the Canadian Association for Adult Education, the National Association of Adult Education (Ireland), and the Indian Adult Education Association, associations also conduct special professional development workshops. The American Association for Adult and Continuing Education frequently conducts preconference sessions prior to their annual conference on special professional development problems as well as the regular conference sessions.

4.3 Public Awareness

Professional adult education associations are also involved in efforts to create awareness of adult education needs. These efforts include studies that document the educational needs of adults such as literacy, training, professional education, and other concerns according national needs. The development of support for adult education at the grassroots level is often paralleled by association-designed and/or -encouraged efforts to communicate funding needs to governmental leaders. These activities naturally vary from nation to nation according to political realities, planning and budgeting processes, and structural conditions.

4.4 Professional Networks

The creation and development of professional networks is an often unheralded but critical outcome of professional adult education associations. Regular meetings provide professional association members with the opportunity to share ideas and develop support structures.

5. Consequences

Professional associations may have two different kinds of consequences: beneficial and harmful. Brockett (1989) cites three benefits of professional adult education associations: benefits to individuals, benefits to the field, and benefits to society. Brockett cites Darkenwald and Merriam (1982) who suggest that the most important contribution may be opportunities for professional development. Pavalko (1971) identified the professional association as a mechanism for the exchange and dissemination of new information. Ashford (1978) discovered that adult educators employed by higher education institutions turn to professional associations for assistance more frequently than adult educators employed in other settings.

The benefits to the field are often more implicit than explicit. Long (1992) recounts the contributions to the knowledge base, while McClusky (1982 p.8) says the formation of the AAALE "constituted the decisive and formative first step in giving both substantive and programmatic identity to the field." Fellenz (1981) cites professional adult education associations as a critical element in the growth of adult and continuing education. According to Brockett (1989), the benefits to society may be assessed by how well professional adult education associations create "[.] a greater awareness of adult learning throughout the larger society" (p.114).

Potentially harmful consequences may also result from the existence and actions of professional adult education associations. If professional associations have sufficient strength they may stabilize political inequalities, deform civic consciousness, distort the public agenda, and alienate final control (Dahl 1982). Professional associations may also become a political oligarchy that may have oppressive effects upon rank and file members (Long 1989).

6. *Typology of Associations*

Meister (1984) identifies two broad general categories of associations: expressive and instrumental. Griffith (1970) devised a more concrete typology that contains five categories of professional adult education associations: (a) interest in a specific content area such as literacy education; (b) affiliation with a certain type of sponsoring agency, such as military, labor, or a university; (c) emphasis on a particular delivery method such as external degree programs; (d) geographic location, such as a region, state, or metropolitan area; and (e) identification with a specific clientele, such as the aged.

7. *Issues*

Professional adult education associations, especially in democratic societies, play roles that present dilemmas for pluralistic democracies. Some of the potentially problematic consequences of associations are noted above in sect. 5. Associations, by their nature, also introduce controls over their members. These controls may be designed to accomplish a variety of objectives that are acceptable to an association's members, but may not always be in the best interest of all members, or even the majority of them. As suggested by some of the opponents to professional associations, conflicts may exist between the personal interests of association members and the interests of those who should be served by the association. Some association objectives may become highly visible issues, such as the role of associations in professionalizing the field.

"Few issues in adult and continuing education have been more controversial than whether the field should strive toward great professionalization" (Brockett 1989 p. 119). The topic is especially divisive among North American adult educators (Galbraith and Zalenak 1989, Cervero 1987). Brockett (1989 p. 119) says the issue will inevitably be linked to questions such as:

> Should professional associations develop and administer some sort of certification process for adult and continuing educators? If such a process were to be adopted,

which associations would have a role in establishing and enforcing standards? Could increased professional status allow associations to have greater influence in the process of seeking legislative support for adult and continuing education programs?

Other issues related to professionalization include the establishment and enforcement of standards and criteria for association membership. Adult educators, especially in North America, are divided on whether or not professionalization and membership in a professional association contradict the democratic values of many adult educators. Professionalization of the field of adult education is thus often associated with the American Medical Association model, or with what Meister (1984) refers to as an "instrumental association."

Cotton (1968) classified the American adult education literature according to three types: social reformist, eclectic, and professional. According to Cotton, the social reformists and the professionally oriented writers differed on four selected topics: audience for their ideas/literature, purpose of their writing, approach, and extent of need for adult education. The ideas/literature of the social reformists were directed to a national audience, while adult educators with a professional orientation presented their ideas to a restricted audience composed mainly of their professional colleagues. The social reformists wrote to gain public support for adult education, whereas the professionals' literature was designed to clarify the need for adult education. Social reformists took a rational–normative approach in their literature, while the professionals resorted to empirical documentation of the case for adult education. Finally, adult education was crucially needed according to the social reformists. In contrast, the professionals described the need for adult education in less apocalyptic terms. For them adult education was important, but not crucial (Long 1983). Thus, attitudes concerning professionalization and professional associations often go beyond just the issue of forming an association of people with mutual interests. A variety of philosophical values may be involved in discussions of the appropriateness of professional adult education associations. Objections to professional associations of adult educators appear to reflect the position that such associations are composed of an elite who use the organization for narrow personal objectives that are contrary to the best interests of adult education consumers. A counterargument is that consumer-oriented associations are also frequently dominated by reformers who constitute an oligarical elite of another kind.

8. *Needed Research*

The field of adult education would be well-served by at least two kinds of additional research concerning professional adult education associations: sociological and historical. Sociological inquiries into professional adult education are recommended. These investigations may determine the degree to which different associations are expressive–instrumental, if and how oligarchies are formed within the associations, effects of oligarchies upon association goals and activities, and so forth. In addition, historical research may be helpful in illuminating the differences between associations at different times and/or differences within an association over time.

See also: History of Adult Education; Training of Adult Educators; Worker Education and Labor Education; Information Sources in Adult Education; Nongovernmental Organizations

References

Ashford M 1978 A comparative analysis of the perceived importance of selected occupational socialization factors to adult educators. (Unpublished doctoral dissertation, University of Georgia, Athens, Georgia)
Brockett R G 1989 Professional associations for adult and continuing education. In: Merriam S B, Cunningham P M (ed.) 1989 *Handbook of Adult and Continuing Education.* Jossey-Bass, San Francisco, California
Cervero R M 1987 Professionalization as an issue for continuing education. In: Brockett R G (ed.) 1987 *Continuing Education in the Year 2000*, New Directions for Continuing Education, No. 36. Jossey-Bass, San Francisco, California
Cotton W E 1968 *On Behalf of Adult Education: A Historical Examination of the Supporting Literature.* Center for the Study of Liberal Education, Boston, Massachusetts
Dahl R A 1982 *Dilemmas of Pluralistic Democracy: Autonomy vs. Control.* Yale Studies in Political Science, No. 31. Yale University Press, New Haven, Connecticut
Darkenwald G G, Merriam S B 1982 *Adult Education: Foundations of Practice.* Harper & Row, New York
Fellenz R A 1981 The national leadership role belongs to professional adult educators. In: Kreitlow B W (ed.) 1981 *Examining Controversies in Adult Education.* Jossey-Bass, San Francisco, California
Galbraith M W, Zelenak B S 1989 The education of adult and continuing education practitioners. In: Merriam S B, Cunningham P M (eds.) 1989 *Handbook of Adult and Continuing Education.* Jossey-Bass, San Francisco,

California
Griffith W S 1970 Adult education institutions. In: Smith R M, Aker G F, Kidd J R (eds.) 1970 *Handbook of Adult Education.* Macmillan, New York
International Council for Adult Education 1991 ICAE *Directory.* ICAE, Toronto
Irvin L 1992 *Encyclopedia of Associations and International Organizations*, 26th edn. Gale Research Inc., Detroit, Michigan
Kelly T 1970 *A History of Adult Education in Great Britain: From the Middle Ages to the Twentieth Century*, 2nd rev. edn. Liverpool University Press, Liverpool
Knowles M S 1962 *The Adult Education Movement in the United States.* Holt, Rinehart & Winston, New York
Knowles M S 1977 *The Adult Education Movement in the United States*, rev. edn. Krieger, Huntington, New York
Long H B 1983 *Adult Learning: Research and Practice.* Cambridge University Press, New York
Long H B 1985 American Association for Adult and Continuing Education. In: Kent A (ed.) 1985 *Encyclopedia of Library and Information Science*, Vol. 39. Marcel Dekker, New York
Long H B. 1989 Personal/professional politics in the development of adult education knowledge in North America. *Proc. 8th Annual Conf. Canadian Association for the Study of Adult Education*, Cornwall, Ontario, June 1–30
Long H B 1992 Professional associations' contribution to the development of adult and continuing education knowledge. *Context* 4 (2)
McClusky H Y 1982 The legacy of the AEA/USA with implications for the future of adult and continuing education. Part I. *Lifelong Learn.* 6 (1): 8–10
Meister A 1984 *Participation, Associations, Development, and Change* (ed. and trans. Ross J L) Transaction Publications, New Brunswick, New Jersey
Pavalko R M 1971 *Sociology of Occupations and Professions.* Peacock, Itasca, Illinois

Further Reading

Brockett R G (ed.) 1987 *Continuing Education in the Year 2000.* New Directions for Continuing Education, No 36. Jossey-Bass, San Francisco, California
Mackay A F 1980 *Arrow's Theorem: The Paradox of Social Choice: A Case Study in the Philosophy of Economics.* Yale University Press, New Haven, Connecticut
Smith C, Freedman A 1972 *Voluntary Associations: Perspectives on the Literature.* Harvard University Press, Cambridge, Massachusetts

UNESCO and Adult Education

P. Bélanger and H. Mobarak

From its inception in November 1946, the United Nations Educational and Scientific Organisation (UNESCO) has undertaken many initiatives to grasp the reality of adult education, to promote the right to learn of the world's adult population, and to foster inter-

national coorperation in this field. At almost every UNESCO General Conference, one or several resolutions relating to adult education or literacy have been adopted.

However, one cannot review UNESCO's role without

first attempting to reconstruct conceptually a domain operating without clear boundaries and under a variety of institutional arrangements. Indeed, the most important feature of adult education, and hence one of the major difficulties for the analyst, is its diversity: this expanding field of learning is diversified not only through the multiplicity of the educational agents involved, but also in relation to the content of learning and the different patterns of recurrence to learning across the lifespan. Moreover, the concepts and terms used to express this moving reality vary from country to country, as well as between the different sectors of activity. The developments taking place in this regard are often unrelated to one another.

1. Extent of Adult Education in UNESCO

In world public opinion, adult education at UNESCO refers primarily to adult basic education, literacy campaigns, functional literacy projects, and postliteracy activities. This is explainable since the basic learning needs have always been a priority area within the program of the Paris-based UN organization. However, the involvement of UNESCO in adult education goes beyond the activities coordinated by the Basic Education Division, though not always explicitly and often under different names.

The continuous upward trend in the social demand for adult education since the 1970s invites one to review UNESCO's role from such a broader perspective. Indeed, one should note that the definitions of adult education do not operate a semantic exclusion, leaving aside important contributions or hiding significant shortcomings in this domain. The dispersion of activities and responsibilities for adult education is a phenomenon that takes place both at national and international levels; in ministries of education, labor, health, and others; as well as in international organizations such as UNESCO, ILO, OECD, WHO, and others.

The definition retained for the analysis of UNESCO's role is one given by UNESCO itself in the *Recommendation on the Development of Adult Education* in 1976. It offers a common framework encompassing the diversified fields of adult education and training:

> The term "adult education" denotes the entire body of organized educational processes, whatever the content, level and method, whether formal or otherwise, whether they prolong or replace initial education in schools, colleges and universities as well as in apprenticeship, whereby persons regarded as adults by the society to which they belong develop their abilities, enrich their knowledge, improve their technical or professional qualifications or turn them in a new direction and bring about changes in their attitudes or behaviour in the twofold perspective of full personal development and participation in balanced and independent social, economic and cultural development. (UNESCO 1976a p. 2)

It has been suggested (Coombs 1985) that the adoption of such a comprehensive perspective and of an "all-embracing, open-ended definition of adult education" was probably one of the most significant contributions of UNESCO in this domain since the late 1970s, even if the organization's discourse may at times have fallen short of such a broad vision.

The role of the agency is analyzed below, taking into consideration the four dimensions of its mandate: normative action, awareness raising, the promotion of intellectual exchange, and the development of technical cooperation.

2. The Role of UNESCO

2.1 The Normative Role

Because of the marginal status of adult education in most countries, its late recognition as a legitimate field of education, and the low priority it has received in many countries, UNESCO has been invited, since 1960, to elaborate international normative instruments recommending the member states to acknowledge the importance and scope of adult education activities in the context of lifelong learning.

As already mentioned, the major intervention of UNESCO to that effect was the adoption of the *Recommendation on the Development of Adult Education* by the General Conference at its 19th session, held in Nairobi, Kenya, in 1976. After proposing the broad definition quoted above, the *Recommendation* sets forth the general objectives of adult education in a similarly comprehensive perspective and underlines the priority to be given to "educationally underprivileged groups" (UNESCO 1976a). Recognizing a world trend to suppress institutional frontiers between nonformal educational actors and to reassess the role of formal education ministries in their relation to the departments of culture, health, agriculture, or labor, the *Recommendation* devotes two chapters to the importance of specific and flexible approaches and structures required in adult education.

The 1976 *Recommendation* also indicates improvements to be made in the legal status of programs and personnel and proposes a framework for policy developments regarding the relations between adult and youth education on the one hand, and between continuing education and work on the other. The member states are also being asked to recognize the role played by adult educators and literacy workers, and to give them the needed conditions for an efficient implementation of their task. The last chapter suggests orientation for bilateral and multilateral international cooperation, technical assistance, and exchange of information.

The text of the *Recommendation* was adopted in the five official languages used by the General Conference of UNESCO at that time. In 1985, 60 countries sent reports on the development of adult education in the light of the propositions announced in 1976. They reported progress in the institutionalization of adult education through new legislation and policy development, but underlined serious financial difficulties, inadequate recognition of the specificity of adult education, and stressed the priority to be given to adult literacy in rural areas in particular (UNESCO 1985, Conf. 210/4). The real impact of the *Recommendation*, however, can only be assessed in the long term.

Another important text adopted by UNESCO is the declaration of "The Right to Learn" adopted in 1985 at the UNESCO Fourth International Conference on Adult Education. The declaration (UNESCO 1985) states:

> Recognition of the right to learn is now more than ever a major challenge for humanity. The right to learn is: the right to read and write; the right to question and analyze; the right to imagine and create; the right to read about one's own world and to write history; the right to have access to educational resources; the right to develop individual and collective skills . . . The act of learning, lying as it does at the heart of all educational activity, changes human beings from objects at the mercy of events to subjects creating their own history (pp. 67–68)

This text, published and disseminated the world over in all official languages of United Nations, has become a widely used instrument to help people assert their right to learn and to define it in broad terms.

The normative role of UNESCO was also crucial in the recognition by the member states of their mandate to provide literacy education for all. The United Nations system and UNESCO have developed legal instruments to recognize and legitimize the universal human right to read and write. In 1944, in Article 26, the Universal Declaration of Human Rights explicitly recognized the fundamental right to education.

In the very first article of the Constitution establishing UNESCO, paragraph 2(b), a direct reference was made to adult education, asking the new UN organization and the member states to "give fresh impulse to popular education and to the spread of culture . . ."

Following a recommendation made at the Montreal International Conference in 1960 (UNESCO 1960) a UNESCO meeting held in Iran in September 1975 adopted the *Declaration of Persepolis*. This text states that "literacy is not just the process of learning the skill of reading, writing, and arithmetic, but a contribution to the liberation of man and to his full development" (UNESCO 1975). One year later in Nairobi, the UNESCO General Conference adopted the *Recommendation* mentioned above concerning the development of adult education, which puts literacy as an integral part of the educational task recommended to the member states.

The most comprehensive international instrument on literacy is the *World Declaration on Education for All* and the *Framework for Action to Meet the Basic Learning Needs* adopted in Jomtien, Thailand on March 9, 1990 by the World Conference on Education for All (WCEFA) convened jointly by UNESCO, UNICEF, the United Nations Development Program (UNDP), and the World Bank (Inter-Agency Commission 1990).

The *Declaration* represents a new consensus and a declared commitment by the convenors and the national authorities to ensure that "the basic learning needs of all children, youth, and adults are met effectively in all countries." Recognizing that more than "one third of the world's adults have no access to the printed knowledge," the *Declaration* proclaims that "every person—child, youth and adult—shall be able to benefit from educational opportunities designed to meet their basic learning needs," that "basic education should be provided to all children, youth and adults," that "the basic learning needs of youth and adults are diverse and should be met through a variety of delivery systems," and that "knowledge and skills that will enhance the learning environment of children should be integrated into community learning programmes for adults." On the basis of this declared renewed commitment to ensure that the basic learning needs of all children, youth, and adults are met, a *Framework for Action* was also adopted indicating the phasing of implementation during the 1990s, including comprehensive policy reviews at regional and global levels both in 1995–96 and in 2000–01. Although the World Bank and UNDP seem more inclined to frame the issue into a choice between child education and adult literacy and to retain primary formal education as the priority, UNICEF and UNESCO tend to insist on the complementarity and the synergy between formal and nonformal basic education.

UNESCO's commitment to education for all was already apparent in the medium-term plans launched since 1977 (UNESCO 1977, UNESCO 1983), but can be seen most clearly in the third *Medium-Term Plan (1990–1995)* as well as in the biennial programs in 1990–91 and 1992–93 (UNESCO 1989) where, in spite of the financial constraints besetting UNESCO, a clear priority was given to the education of children *and* to adult literacy, as can be observed in the activities coordinated by its Basic Education Division and its Literacy and Adult Education Section.

UNESCO has adopted other normative instruments directly or indirectly related to adult education, like the *Recommendation Concerning Education for International Understanding, Cooperation and Peace and Education Relating to Human Rights and Fundamental Freedoms* (UNESCO 1974), or the *Recommendation on Participation by the People at Large in Cultural Life and Their Contribution to It* (UNESCO 1976b). In this last *Recommendation*, one can grasp UNESCO's understanding of lifelong learning in its relation to cultural life. A review of UNESCO's normative role in adult education cannot leave aside such instruments, nor the texts on museums, libraries, the use of media, and on the democratization of science.

2.2 Awareness Raising

The most visible initiatives taken by UNESCO for the promotion of adult education were the four World

Conferences held in this field since the founding of UNESCO.

The First World Conference on Adult Education took place in 1949 at Elsinore, Denmark. In the immediate aftermath of the Second World War, and so close to the tragic decades of the 1930s and 1940s, the delegates (86% of whom came mainly from the Western industrialized countries) were most concerned by the contribution of adult education to a lasting peace and international understanding. Thus, five objectives were proposed to that end: the creation of a "common culture" to end the opposition between the "masses" and the "elite," the stimulation of a genuine spirit of democracy and tolerance, the development of "hope and confidence" among the youth, the restoration of a sense of community, and the promotion of "an enlightened sense of belonging to a world community" (UNESCO 1949). The Conference resulted in the development of international cooperation in this field through the organization of international seminars, the sending of advisory missions to countries, and the building of professional networks to promote the exchange of information.

The Second World Conference was held in Montreal in 1960 and attended by representatives from 51 countries, including, for the first time, a majority of Southern countries and delegates from Eastern Europe. The main contribution of the Montreal Conference was the clear indication given to member states asking them to treat adult education "as a necessary part of the educational provision of every country" (UNESCO 1960). Concrete strategies were outlined for "strenghtening the position of adult education" at national and international levels. This Conference has given many national delegations the advocacy tools needed to increase governmental contribution to the development of adult education activities and "public" services.

Confirming a pattern of holding a conference at intervals of 10–12 years, UNESCO convened the Third International Conference on Adult Education in Tokyo in 1972 (UNESCO 1972). Among the 400 delegates from 82 countries who came to Tokyo, a "large governmental contingent" was present attesting "the new weight being attached to adult education" (Lowe 1985). The Conference identified important trends since 1960 in adult education: the emergence of a consensus on the importance of adult education, the rapid development of functional literacy and the questioning of its often exclusive relation to economic development, the innovations in educational technology and distance education, the professionalization of the field, the growing recognition of the need for evaluation and assessment, and the expansion of international cooperation. The Conference proposed policy orientations for the further development of adult education, underlining the complementarity between formal and nonformal approaches. The delegates insisted on the importance of developing adult education in accordance with the concept of lifelong learning, recommending a transformation of formal institutions, schools, and universities, in that perspective. However, the Tokyo meeting will be most remembered for its criticism of the limited accessibility of adult education and of the prevailing tendency to provide further education for those who are already educated. "Adult education," said the participants in the final report (UNESCO 1972 pp. 22–23) "is no exception to the rule, for those who most need education have been largely neglected . . . Thus the major task of adult education during the . . . decade . . . is to seek out and serve these forgotten people."

The Fourth International Conference on Adult Education was held in Paris in 1985. The context of this conference was very special because of the economic crisis that had been evident since the late 1970s, forcing many governments to freeze and often reduce their contribution to adult education, and also because of the UNESCO crisis created by the withdrawal of membership by the United States and the notice of possible withdrawal by the United Kingdom. In spite of these constraints, the Fourth Conference was the largest in size with nearly 850 accredited delegates, 122 participating member states, and 59 nongovernmental organizations (NGOs). That in itself was an unexpected indicator of the growing importance of adult education, but also of the semantic ambiguity mentioned above. This problem became central during the discussion since many governments confirmed that, without pledging increases in "adult education budgets," they were getting more and more involved in diverse educational activities for adults: labor force training and retraining, agricultural extension, healthcare, and so on (UNESCO 1985). Confronted by the paradox of the growing demand of adult education as a key dimension of development and the squeeze in the public financial resources allocated to this domain, the participants limited themselves in their final report to underlining the rapid developments that have taken place in formal and nonformal adult education, drawing attention to the democratization of access; referring to the roles of NGOs; and insisting on international cooperation in the domains of legislation and finance, learning/teaching approaches, research and evaluation, and uses of media. Indirectly, this Conference sent national governments and multilateral organizations a signal reminding them that they should adjust to ongoing developments in adult education. Adult education was growing not only through the further development of past trends in that field but also, in a very diversified way, as the learning dimension of many development programs and socioeconomic policies. It is at this Conference that the, previously quoted, Declaration on the "right to learn" was adopted. The role of UNESCO as an international center of information on adult education was also underlined.

It is in the domain of adult literacy within adult education that UNESCO has intervened with the most vigor and constancy for raising awareness. UNESCO has taken many initiatives to continuously remind world public opinion that "illiteracy is one of the great social problems of our time."

In fact, literacy has always been one of the major concerns of the UNESCO delegates at all general conferences held every two years since 1946. However, it was only in 1960, at the Montreal Second International Conference on Adult Education, that a concrete proposal was made to launch a vast campaign for the eradication of illiteracy. This recommendation gained momentum in the 1960s. In 1964, for example, at its 13th session, the General Conference decided to initiate a five-year Experimental World Literacy Program (EWLP) to prepare the campaign. The EWLP Program was prepared by a special conference held in Teheran in 1965: the World Congress of Ministers of Education on the Eradication of Illiteracy. Implemented between 1967 and 1973, the objectives of this experimental program were to test and demonstrate the economic and social returns of literacy and, more generally, to study the mutual relations and influences between literacy education and development.

Furthermore in 1966, UNESCO, in collaboration with the United Nations General Conference, proclaimed September 8 of every year to be International Literacy Day. Every year since then, UNESCO and a growing number of member states have taken the opportunity of this special day to release new data on the situation of illiteracy and to make appeals for the intensification of all necessary actions. It is within this perspective of educating public opinion and promoting literacy that UNESCO awards six International Prizes to recognize the achievements made by governmental and nongovernmental organizations in the campaign against illiteracy every year on International Literacy Day. These six prizes are: the Mohammed Reza Pahlevi Prize awarded by the Government of Iran in 1967, the Nadezhda K Krupskaya Prize donated by the Soviet Union in 1979, the International Reading Association Prize (USA) donated in 1979, the Noma Prize given in 1980 by a Japanese publisher, the Iraqi Prize given in 1981, and the King Sejong Literacy Prize awarded since 1990 by the Government of the Republic of Korea. However, the M R Pahlevi Prize was terminated in 1979, and the N K Krupskaya and the Iraqi literacy prizes were suspended in 1992.

The 1990 International Literacy Year (ILY), proclaimed by the United Nations with UNESCO as the lead organization was certainly one of the most efficient initiatives taken to develop public awareness on the basic learning rights and needs of hundreds of millions of adults and to mobilize resources to meet them. The report prepared by the secretariat of ILY (UNESCO 1991) shows that national committees were formed in 110 countries and all kinds of meetings and conferences were organized to mobilize partners, encourage action, and reinforce international cooperation. One of the welcome changes that happened during that year was

the new approach developed by UNESCO to discard the negative "stigma" of illiteracy and propose a more comprehensive message about women and men who, as adult learners, try to improve their quality of life in different contexts. The scientific community, from linguists to educational psychologists and sociologists, had been in need of such a change from UNESCO in its discourse about literacy for many years. The role of awareness raising is now giving UNESCO the challenge of proposing less simple and more accurate images about literacy, while at the same time monitoring the situations through more adequate indicators —a demand that UNESCO is trying to answer through intellectual cooperation.

2.3 Promotion of Intellectual Cooperation

The third contribution of UNESCO to the development of adult education consists in its diversified activities (conferences, seminars, meetings, publications) which increase the exchange of ideas and experiences in this field between researchers and practitioners, between north and south, east and west. However, in order to find references to these activities, one should examine the full spectrum of UNESCO's programs and actions.

In UNESCO's third *Medium-Term Plan (1990–1995)*, the main contribution to adult education is to be found in the program on Education for All (UNESCO 1989 Chap. 1.1). In this sector of activities, central issues on adult basic education were singled out and explored through seminars, conferences, or commissioned papers and publications on such topics as: the cumulation of privileges in the present economy of adult education, the discussion of the language issue in literacy, the development of legislative measures giving access to adult education, the debate on macro-approaches like national campaigns versus functional strategies, the comparative analysis of illiteracy in industrialized countries and in that of developing countries, the necessary links between literacy and postliteracy, and the relations between primary education and adult literacy. One of the most important issues that UNESCO has raised and developed is the one relating adult education and integral development, stressing the relationships between illiteracy and poverty, and between literacy and community and rural development.

In order to facilitate such intellectual cooperation and to disseminate information on the subject, UNESCO publishes the quarterly newsletter *Adult Education Information Notes*.

UNESCO has also developed, at the UNESCO Institute for Education (UIE) in Hamburg, an Exchange Network on Literacy and Post-Literacy in Developed and Developing Countries. The UIE Network, created in 1988, is an information clearinghouse for the dissemination and exchange of documentation, innovation, research reports, and relevant learning materials concerning adult literacy and postliteracy. The purpose is to foster cooperation in this field between researchers and practitioners in developed and developing countries.

The analysis of UNESCO's *Medium-Term Plan (1990–1995)* indicates that adult education is also present in other educational programs as well as in the programs on science, culture, and communication. Indeed, one can find, in all other sections of the *Medium-Term Plan* (UNESCO 1989), explicit references to adult education:

(a) to environmental education, nonformal education for international understanding, retraining and continuing education, distance education for out-of-school learners, and adult participation in higher education (Chap. 1.2);

(b) to the relation between formal and nonformal education and industry-run learning programs (1.3);

(c) to adult environmental education (2.2);

(d) to out-of school introduction activities to science and scientific education through the media (2.3);

(e) to the promotion of reading, the strengthening of art education in the nonformal sector, and the development of rural sound libraries (3.2);

(f) to the study of the relation between the media and the uses of literacy and the promotion of the educational role of the media (4.3);

(g) to population education for adults (5.2);

(h) to the analysis of the relationship between human resources and development (6.1);

(i) to peace education (7.1);

(j) to the development of adult education statistics (112).

In addition, there is also the mobilizing project "Combating Illiteracy" and the Transverse Theme on Women where attention is given to literacy, vocational training, and access to scientific studies.

Dealing with these issues, thousands of meetings of all sizes are held every year on all continents by UNESCO HQs, as well as by its institutes and regional offices. These meetings gather together planners; governmental and nongovernmental representatives; specialists in the areas of science, culture, and communication; adult and nonformal education leaders; and members of nongovernmental organizations. Through these, one can expect that new approaches for the diversification of strategies and for the evaluation of past experiments are developed, the shifting of priorities prepared, and innovations promoted.

As one of the focal points for research on nonformal and adult education in UNESCO, the UNESCO Institute for Education in Hamburg has been undertaking, since 1980, studies and training programs on adult literacy and postliteracy, on nonformal basic education for out-of-school learners, on evaluation and monitoring, and on adult education policies and strategies.

2.4 Technical Cooperation

The fourth main contribution of UNESCO in adult education is the concrete work it has done in the field of multilateral cooperation. Such cooperation has taken many forms: expert missions, complementary financial support, studies and action research, pilot projects, planning of nonformal education programs, gathering of data or assistance given to member states for the development of national statistics on literacy and the monitoring of nonformal education, training of trainers, building of exchange networks, promotion of interregional cooperation, collaboration with nongovernmental organizations, and so forth.

It is impossible within the limits of this synthesis to summarize all the projects initiated and supported partially or totally by UNESCO since 1960 in the field of adult education. Certainly, literacy has been a high priority in UNESCO technical assistance programs. One should not forget the important Experimental World Literacy Program and the role played by UNESCO in the promotion and critical assessment of actions like mass campaigns or functional programs (Jones 1988).

3. The Changing Role of UNESCO in Adult Education

UNESCO is closely associated with the development of adult education that has taken place in most countries since 1945. The main contribution of UNESCO has been in the promotion of adult education through awareness-raising activities and the adoption and wide dissemination of normative instruments (Bhola 1989 pp.88–97). The contribution of UNESCO to research, though real, has been less prominent. This role will be essential for the further development of international cooperation in this domain.

Following the "silent explosion" and the diversification of adult education activities, it has become necessary to assess the compatibility and comparability of the different terminologies used in various countries and sectors. The ideological tensions and semantic segmentations or exclusions need to be reviewed. Empirical studies are required to reassess the real and changing boundaries between formal, nonformal, and informal education, and between initial and adult education; and to re-evaluate the distinction between childhood, youth, and adulthood (Husén 1990). Comparative analysis is needed to understand the cumulative patterns of recurrent education and lifelong learning (Tuijnman 1989).

One of the challenges will be to develop the conceptual tools needed to monitor and research this expanding and cross-sectorial educational domain, to reconstruct the whole reality of organized adult learning, and to trace it under the various names and different institutional arrangements with which it presents itself. This is important because, through the rapid growth of the various forms of adult education, a new general economy of education is being created. Adult education is now encompassing so many fields of activities, involving a number of actors and ministries, that the role to be played by national bodies for adult education will increasingly have to become a transversal one. The task to be performed by the adult education institutions will be less and less one of providing themselves opportunities for adult learning in the different domains. Instead, they will be called upon to offer these various forms of adult education a common framework of reference, providing them with specific expertise on the learning styles of adults, on conditions of accessibility like leave of absence regulations, on recognition of nonformal or "experiential" learning achievements, on the relations between initial education and further education, on the monitoring of adult education participation and diversified provision, on "adult learning" policy development, and so on.

What is true within national boundaries also holds at the international level. Adult learning can no longer be the sole responsibility of a single UN organization, even though it specializes in education. Adult learning is becoming an intergral part of the strategies of preventive health policies at WHO, of population policies, of environmental world programs, of economic development plans in all UN agencies (ILO, FAO, UNICEF, UNIFEM, UNDP, WHO), not to mention similar trends in the other multilateral organizations like OECD, the European Commission, and the Commonwealth Secretariat. The Fifth International Conference, to be held in 1997, will certainly reflect this trend. It will no longer be possible to organize a World Conference on Adult Education without involving the other multilateral agencies, in the same way as it is no more feasible to organise a comprehensive national conference on adult education without enlisting the active participation of the different ministries and nongovernmental actors that have an interest at stake in the field of adult learning.

See also: Adult Education: Concepts and Principles; History of Adult Education; Comparative Studies: Adult Education; International Adult Education; International Council for Adult Education; International Labour Organisation

References

Bhola H S 1989 *World Trends and Issues in Adult Education.* Jessica Kingsley/UNESCO, London
Coombs P H 1985 Suggestions for a realistic adult education policy. *Prospects* 15(1): 27–38
Husén T 1990 *Education and the Global Concern.* Pergamon Press, Oxford
Jones P W 1988 *International Policies for Third World Education.* Routledge, London
Lowe J 1985 UNESCO world conferences in adult education. In: Husén T, Postlethwaite T N (eds.) 1985 *The International Encyclopedia of Education*, 1st edn. Pergamon Press, Oxford
Inter-Agency Commission 1990 *World Declaration on Education for All/Framework for Action to Meet Basic Learning Needs.* Inter-Agency Commission for the WCEFA, New York
International Council for Adult Education 1986 *Making the Connection: The Adult Education Movement and the 4th UNESCO Conference.* ICEA, Toronto
Tuijnman A 1989 *Recurrent Education, Earnings, and Well Being.* Almqvist and Wiksell, Stockholm
UNESCO 1949 *Summary Report of the First International Conference on Adult Education.* UNESCO, Elsinore
UNESCO 1960 *Report of the Second World Conference on Adult Education.* UNESCO, Montreal
UNESCO 1972 *Report of the Third International Conference on Adult Education.* UNESCO, Tokyo
UNESCO 1974 General Conference on the Recommendation concerning Education for International Understanding, Cooperation and Peace and Education relating to Human Rights and Fundamental Freedoms. UNESCO, Paris
UNESCO 1975 *The Experimental World Literacy Program: A Critical Assessment.* UNESCO, Paris
UNESCO 1976 *Declaration of Persepolis.* International Symposium for Literacy, Persepolis, Tram, 3–8 September 1975. In: Bataille L (ed.) 1976 *A Point for Literacy. Adult Education for Development: The Spirit and Declaration of Persepolis.* Pergamon Press, Oxford
UNESCO 1976a General Conference on the Recommendation on the Development of Adult Education. UNESCO, Nairobi
UNESCO 1976b General Conference on the Recommendation on Participation by the People at Large in Cultural Life and Their Contribution to it. UNESCO, Nairobi
UNESCO 1977 *Medium-term Plan 1977–1982.* UNESCO, Paris
UNESCO 1983 *Second Medium-term Plan 1984–1989.* UNESCO, Paris
UNESCO 1985 *Final Report of the Fourth International Conference on Adult Education.* UNESCO, Paris
UNESCO 1989 *Third Medium-term Plan 1990–1995.* UNESCO, Paris
UNESCO 1991 ILY report. *Source* (23): 7ff

Further Reading

Faure E et al. 1972 *Learning to Be: The World of Education Today and Tomorrow.* UNESCO, Paris
Lowe J 1982 *The Education of Adults: A World Perspective*, 2nd edn. UNESCO, Paris

(b)   Regional and National Organization

Africa, Anglophone

J. T. Okedara

This entry deals with the theory and practice of adult education and training in countries in Anglophone Africa. It presents trends and discusses the state of the art of adult education in English-speaking Africa, especially in relation to the objective of meeting basic learning needs for all by the year 2000 (Inter-Agency Commission 1990).

The English-speaking, bilingual or multilingual countries of Africa include Botswana, Egypt, Gambia, Ghana, Kenya, Lesotho, Malawi, Nigeria, Port-Guinea, Sierra Leone, Somalia, South Africa, Sudan, Tanzania, Uganda, Zambia, and Zimbabwe. These countries share cultural experience with the United Kingdom through their colonial history. Ethiopia and Liberia are also English-speaking, even though they never were under the British rule. The Arab countries of North Africa are not included in the discussion since the emphasis is on adult education and training programs in the following countries in Sub-Saharan Africa: Nigeria, Ghana, Kenya, Uganda, Tanzania, Malawi, Ethiopia, Zambia, and Zimbabwe.

1. Concept of Adult Education

"Adult Education," within the context of this entry, refers to all educational activities arranged for adults without any legal compulsion. These activities are aimed at people who normally are old enough to work, vote, and establish a family. Adult education, which is also referred to as "nonformal education," is provided at all levels of the education system. In Anglophone Africa, "literacy education" is offered at the basic education level. It is referred to as "continuing education" or "extramural studies" when offered at the secondary level. Sometimes the term "remedial education" is used. It refers to adult education offered to those who once dropped out of the regular school system. "Continuing vocational education" mainly refers to programs offered at college level—for example, in teacher training institutions, and technical and trade schools. "External degree programs" are offered to adults at the first degree level. "Correspondence education" and "workers education" are additional concepts of importance.

2. Illiteracy: Scope of the Problem

The area of adult education most often discussed in the developing countries is adult literacy education. It constitutes a foundation for continuing education programs. The map of world illiteracy has been observed to coincide with a map of underdevelopment, as evident in poverty, poor health, and malnutrition (Inter-Agency Commission 1990). The following statements, credited to neoliterates in Ibadan, Nigeria, bear testimony to this relationship (Okedara 1981 pp. 21–39):

"Illiteracy is a state of bondage . . ."
(Mrs Mopelola Akinleye, giving evidence in Yoruba)

"Literacy education is a must for any person who wants to get ahead."
(Mrs Iyabo Oyebisi giving evidence in Yoruba)

"Continuous reading and writing are sure to make one a full person."
(Mrs Agnes Aigbede giving evidence in Edo)

"Literacy education affords participants knowledge of how to achieve a better living standard and a great happiness."
(Mrs O Omokeowa giving evidence in Igbo)

"I feel debased and dehumanized for my literate juniors became my foremen, as hard as I worked . . ."
(Mr Z Adegboyega giving evidence in Yoruba)

Data collected by the UNESCO Office of Statistics in 1989 show that adult illiteracy rates are skewed more to developing countries than to developed countries. One can observe that apart from some areas in Southeast Asia and the Indian subcontinent, countries in Sub-Saharan Africa record the highest rates: 60 percent in 1985, 53 percent in 1990, and an anticipated 40 percent in the year 2000. This shows that adult illiteracy rates in Sub-Saharan Africa are declin-

Table 1
Number of adult illiterates (15 years and over) and rate of illiteracy

Regions	Number of illiterates (million)			Illiteracy rate (%)		
	1985	1990	2000[a]	1985	1990	2000[a]
World	965.1	962.6	942.0	29.9	26.9	22.0
Developing countries broken down as follows:						
Sub-Saharan Africa	133.6	138.8	146.8	59.1	52.7	40.3
Arab States	58.6	61.1	65.8	54.5	48.7	38.1
Latin America and the Caribbean	44.2	43.5	40.9	17.6	15.2	11.3
East Asia	297.3	281.0	233.7	28.7	24.0	17.0
South Asia	374.1	397.3	437.0	57.7	53.8	45.9
Developed countries	57.0	42.0	23.5	6.2	4.4	2.3

Source: UNESCO Office of Statistics (Revised Figures, 1989) a Forecast
b Certain countries were classified as both Sub-Saharan African countries and Arab States

ing, albeit slowly. However, the data can also be taken as indicative of insignificant progress, since in absolute terms, the projected number of adult illiterates is on the increase in the African region: 134 million in 1985, 139 million in 1990, and an expected 147 million by the year 2000. Table 1 presents the global picture. The data show the magnitude and seriousness of the illiteracy problem.

Like other African countries, the English-speaking group has made considerable effort to eradicate illiteracy and thereby promote general development. Basic education, involving primary education and adult literacy, have received much attention, as is evident from Tables 2 and 3. There was substantial growth in primary school and adult education enrollments during the 1960s, 1970s, and 1980s. The gross enrollment rate in primary schooling, which indicates the potential intake of the system in relation to the population concerned, rose from 38 percent in 1960 to 79 percent in 1980. The rate of illiteracy among the population aged 15 and over fell from 71 percent in 1970 to 61 percent in 1980 (Haidara 1990). The story was more pronounced in Tanzania, Zambia, Uganda, Kenya, Lesotho, Zimbabwe, and Botswana than in Malawi, Somalia, Sierra Leone, Sudan, Liberia, Nigeria, and Ghana. As can be seen from Table 2, Tanzania has recorded spectacular adult literacy enrollments.

As in other parts of Africa, the English-speaking countries have not been able to fulfill the objectives advocated in 1961 by the Conference of Education Ministers in Addis Ababa, that called for compulsory primary education throughout the African countries, to be achieved by 1980. The Harare (Zimbabwe) declaration of July 1982, by the Regional Conference of Ministers of Education and Ministers responsible for Economic Planning of Member States in Africa, called for the elimination of illiteracy in all African countries. The aim was "to universalize primary schooling

for children and to promote literacy among young people and adults on a massive scale" (Haidara 1990 p.3). A similar declaration was adopted in relation to postliteracy. The General Conference of UNESCO, at its nineteenth session in Nairobi, Kenya in November 1976 adopted Resolution 1.91, which empowered the Director-General of UNESCO to bring into operation: "a programme of activities with a view ... to encourage strategies and methods for literacy teaching and for post-literacy activities ... calling upon the broadest possible participation of the population concerned."

Again, in a technical meeting in Bamako, Mali in December 1982, the UNESCO Regional Director for Education in Africa (BREDA) called for an intensification of the struggle against illiteracy in Africa, with the goal to eradicate it by the year 2000. Set up to combat illiteracy, BREDA coordinates adult education programs throughout Africa through its regional activities in cooperation with recognized national bodies. It supports the gathering, exchange and dissemination of information; mobilizes awareness; produces and distributes teaching materials; and lends assistance to staff training activities, educational planning, and program evaluation.

To what extent have the various activities been successful in reaching the adult population in the English-speaking African countries? An appraisal of selected efforts in some of the countries can indicate the progress made thus far.

3. Country Experiences

3.1 The United Republic of Tanzania

Tanzania is the leading English-speaking African country that gave urgent attention to the development

Table 2

Demographic and basic education characteristics of English-speaking African countries

	Population (millions) mid-1988	Population Annual growth rates	Primary Enrollment Annual growth rates	Adult Literacy rates male	female
Low-income economies					
Ethiopia	44.7	1.8	4.4	—	—
Malawi	7.9	3.2	4.0	52	31
Tanzania	25.4	3.7	(0.9)	93	88
Zambia	7.9	3.9	4.1	84	67
Uganda	17.2	3.4	9.7	70	45
Somalia	7.1	3.5	(5.7)	18	6
Sierra Leone	3.9	2.4	3.5	38	21
Kenya	23.1	4.1	3.6	70	49
Sudan	23.8	3.0	3.0	33	14
Lesotho	1.7	2.8	4.4	62	84
Nigeria	105.5	3.4	(1.3)	54	31
Ghana	14.1	3.4	(1.3)	64	43
Liberia	2.4	3.2	2.6	47	23
Lower-middle income economies					
Zimbabwe	9.1	3.1	8.9	82	67
Egypt	51.5	2.7	6.1	59	30
Cameroon	10.7	2.7	4.3	68	45
Botswana	1.2	3.6	5.4	73	71
South Africa	33.7	2.2	1.6	—	—

Source: Inter-Agency Commission 1990 Annex 1

of an adult literacy program. Its former President, Julius Nyerere, the initiator of the Tanzanian literacy program had insisted that literacy could not wait for the school-age children to grow up. Consequently, the nationwide literacy campaign in Tanzania was announced on December 31, 1969, and 1970 was

Table 3

Adult education participation in some English-speaking African countries

Country	Year	Adult education enrollment	Population 15 and over (thousands)	No. of adult students per 1,000 population 15 and over	Women as proportion of total enrollment
Low-income economies					
Tanzania	1977	3,567,544	8,904.3	401	37.5
Zambia	1980	19,787	3,052.0	7	42.4
Somalia	1981	24,815	2,717.8	9	35.1
Sierra Leone	1980	11,643	1,949.5	6	—
Sudan	1980	101,336	10,269.4	10	—
Nigeria	1976	201,332	35,859.2	6	—
Liberia	1980	14,660	1,023.8	14	45.4
Lower-middle-income economies					
Zimbabwe	1979	4,065	3,777.6	1	—
Egypt	1982	189,088	26,738.9	7	9.4
Botswana	1978	192	386.8	1	53.1

Source: Inter-Agency Commission 1990 Annex 1

declared the "Adult Education Year." The ruling political party was instrumental in allocating more than 10 percent of the national annual education budget to the program, so that an adequate infrastructure could be established. Also, the Party assisted in mobilizing learners, administrators, supervisors, teachers, and volunteers for the program. As a result of this massive effort, enrollments increased from 261,000 in 1970 to 5,200,000 in 1975, reaching almost 7 million in 1980. However, since then enrollment rate has declined to 4 million in 1988. The country was able to reduce its illiteracy rate from 69 percent (1967 census) to 39 percent in 1975, 21 percent in 1981, 15 percent in 1983, and 10 percent in 1986 (Mpogolo 1990 p.4)

The groundwork was prepared by the UNDP Work-oriented Adult Literacy Pilot Project (WOALPP, which ran from 1968 to 1972) and by its successor, the Tanzania/UNDP/UNESCO Functional Literacy Curriculum, Programmes, and Materials Development Project. As soon as international assistance stopped in 1976, a national literacy center was established, coordinated by the Ministry of Education through its Department of Adult Education. Other ministries, institutions, and organizations participated by offering functional literacy programs. Learning materials were provided free of charge to learners. Adults with poor eyesight were provided with spectacles. Radio programs relevant to all literacy activities were recorded on tapes by education experts and broadcast by Radio Tanzania in Dar-es-Salaam. Both literacy and postliteracy programs were developed as a continuous process. Postliteracy strategies included the provision of textbooks, rural newspapers, and rural libraries, as well as the establishment of correspondence education, broadcast education, and folk development colleges. The Tanzania Institute of Adult Education began offering courses in 1969, producing certified adult educators to coordinate and supervise adult education programs. Moreover, the University of Dar-es-Salaam conducts degree courses for adult education administrators, while teacher-training colleges educate the required teaching staff.

The adult education campaign can be said to have contributed in no small measure to the development of human and material resources in Tanzania. It has facilitated the creation of employment opportunities, and has improved the use of standard Kishwahili among adults (Mpogolo 1990).

3.2 Ethiopia

Ethiopia presents another case study in adult literacy education. At the time of the "Popular Revolution," in 1974, 93 percent of the population was illiterate. Consequently, a national literacy campaign was launched in 1979. By 1983, 6.7 million males and 7.3 million females had been enrolled in the program, of which the majority was made literate. Thus, the illiteracy rate dropped from 93 percent in 1974 to 26 percent in 1990.

The contributing factors included the distribution of primers and other reading materials in 15 national languages. Support services which helped sustain literacy practice included reading rooms and radio transmitters that covered 90 percent of Ethiopia. Community skills training centers, provided by the Ethiopian Government, offered health education; agricultural extension; arts and crafts, such as carpentry, weaving, pottery, and metal work; as well as political education. The country has gained useful experience in functional basic education, literacy, and postliteracy programs as a result of these activities.

3.3 Zimbabwe

Classified as a lower-middle income economy by the World Bank, Zimbabwe has had a unique approach to adult literacy education. The country had an estimated 2.5 million semiliterates and illiterates, representing half of the population in 1980. This figure had risen to an estimated 9.1 million in the late 1980s (see Table 2). The country conducted a literacy campaign from 1983 to 1988. This was organized and administered jointly by the Ministry of Education and the Ministry of Community, Cooperative, Development, and Women Affairs. According to the results of an evaluation of the program carried out in 1987, only about 40,000 adults were made literate. The Ministry of Primary and Secondary Education was then given total responsibility for handling the adult literacy campaign. The unique aspect of the approach subsequently adopted was that each primary school was requested to eradicate illiteracy from its catchment area. Teachers at every primary school were to supervise adult literacy and mass education programs in their vicinity. Others were to serve as instructors in their communities. Moreover, local authority staff were expected to promote literacy education in the area within their jurisdiction. They were to be assisted by specialists in agriculture, primary health care, cooperative farming, and general human resources development. Table 2 shows that the country has made progress in basic education activities, with an annual growth rate of 8.9 percent for primary enrollment and an average of 75 percent for adult literacy enrollment.

3.4 Nigeria

Nigeria has low literacy rates compared to some English-speaking African countries, as revealed in Table 2. However, it has a rich history of adult literacy efforts. Freed slaves, who left Sierra Leone, brought written English literacy to Nigeria by 1841. From 1842 to 1968, many Christian missions taught their converts to read and write in mother tongue and English. The British colonial government launched an adult literacy campaign in 1941 due to the need for literate colonial military personnel during the Second World War. At

727

Table 4
Implications of Jomtien literacy targets: Required annual illiteracy reduction rates for whole population and for women (selected English-speaking African countries with low human development index)

Country	Illiteracy rate, whole population 1985 (%)	Annual % reduction needed to halve it by year 2000	Female illiteracy rate 1985 (%)	Annual reduction needed to reach parity by year 2000	Year in which parity reached if past reduction rate unchanged
Sierra Leone	70	4.97	79	5.70	2072
Somalia	88	4.73	94	5.17	2100+
Sudan	77	4.69	85	5.35	2100+
Nigeria	57	5.10	68	5.25	2051
Kenya	40	5.65	51	7.17	2022

Source: UNDP *Human Development Report* 1990

that time, an adult education department was set up in each of the three regional ministries of education. The Northern Literature Agency was established and it helped in the production, translation, and distribution of literature on adult education. After the Second World War, adult education was established nationwide. The program was supported by the printed media in both the north and the south of the country. By 1960, the mass literacy campaign had been organized in all regions of Nigeria. The campaign contributed to a positive change in attitudes, customs, and habits of many people. The federal government launched a new National Mass Literacy Campaign in 1982. An interim evaluation shows that the average enrollment rate was 2.8 percent of the illiterate population (Okedara 1988). At the same time, dropouts from the primary school-age population increased the number of adult illiterates. The Open University, established in 1983 with the aim of assisting the working class in obtaining a college or university degree, was discontinued in the late 1980s by the Buhari Administration because of insufficient financial resources.

However, the universities in Nigeria run adult education programs offering remedial education, continuing education, and vocational education. Professional adult education courses, designed to prepare workers for the field of adult education and related areas, are also offered. Correspondence education is provided by the University of Ibadan and the Correspondence Open Study Centre at the University of Lagos. The Babangida Administration strengthened the mass literacy campaign in 1987 by providing a timetable for reaching the goal of eradicating illiteracy by the year 2000. This led to the establishment of state agencies for adult and nonformal education throughout the country. As part of the timetable, the National Commission for Adult and Nonformal Education was inaugurated in 1991. The Commission has to be given sufficient resources if it is to succeed in eradicating illiteracy by the year 2051—if progress follows the annual reduction rate suggested in Table 4.

3.5 Liberia

As revealed in Table 2, Liberia is among the least literate of the English-speaking African countries, with an average adult literacy rate of 30 percent and an annual growth rate in primary enrollment of 2.6 percent. In the early years, Christian missions were the main literacy agencies in the country. The Liberian government became interested in adult literacy issues as a result of the so-called Phelps–Stokes Reports of 1922 and 1924. Long before this, in 1814, Dualu Bukate developed a script in his own language, Vai, for the purpose of teaching his people how to read and write. Other ethnic groups, such as Base, Loma, and Kpella, also invented their own scripts. Churches became more and more interested in adult literacy work; teaching was either by means of primers and Bible reading, or through the use of Laubach cards, a traditional adult literacy method (see *Adult Literacy Programs in Developing Nations*).

The Liberian government did not actively campaign against illiteracy until the 1940s, when the governments of Ghana and Nigeria began their adult education campaigns. Dr Frank Laubach was invited to Liberia by the then Tubman Government. Laubach demonstrated how quickly illiterate adults could be taught how to read and write, using his adult literacy cards. The government then allocated funds for the production of adult literacy primers in the principal Liberian languages, including Yai, Kru, and Grebo. A presidential proclamation for the commencement of the National Literacy Campaign in Liberia was issued in 1950, but the effort has dissipated since then.

In 1969, UNESCO launched functional literacy programs in English with the aim of making literate the mixed ethnic target groups working in the main sector of the Liberian economy. The government picked up the interest and declared a commitment to wipe out illiteracy among its populace. Since then, an unfortunate and destructive civil war has delayed the implementation of the national mass literacy campaign in the country.

4. Conclusion

The account thus far shows that, with the notable exception of Tanzania, English-speaking African countries continue to record higher population growth rates than the rates at which illiterate adults are made literate. In particular, the rate of illiteracy is consistently higher among women than among men. Despite this, the enrollment of the illiterate population in adult literacy programs is low: less than 15 illiterates per 1,000 adult population (15-year olds and over) attend literacy classes (see Tables 2 and 3). Table 4 shows that none of the English-speaking African countries, where data are available, is likely to be able to meet the objective of providing literacy to all by the year 2000. The primary school enrollment rates in all countries appear low. At the same time, the dropout rates among primary students and among adult education participants are high.

The Tanzanian experience shows that certain problems can be overcome or greatly reduced through a strong political will, adequate funding, and the establishment of a supportive infrastructure. It also appears that the adult education effort must be seen not as a once and for all affair, but should be sustained, as in the case of the formal school system. This can be achieved by means of a postliteracy program that has yet to be developed. Judging by the paucity of resources available to African countries, it seems doubtful whether they, alone, can overcome the illiteracy problem. They certainly need substantial assistance from the developed countries, as well as from the relevant international organizations.

See also: Adult Education for Development; Africa, Francophone

References

Haidara B 1990 *Regional Programme for the Eradication of Illiteracy in Africa.* UNESCO International Bureau of Education, Geneva

Mpogolo Z J 1990 *A Nationwide Literacy Compaign: The Tanzanian Experience.* UNESCO, International Bureau of Education, Geneva

Okedara J T 1981 *The Impact of Literacy Education in Ibadan, Nigeria.* Ibadan University Press, Ibadan

Okedara J T 1988 An Assessment of the 1982/83 National Mass Literacy Campaign in Nigeria. *Literacy Voices* 1(1)

Inter-Agency Commission (UNDP, UNESCO, UNICEF, and World Bank) 1990. Meeting basic learning needs: A vision for the 1990s. Background document. World Conference on Education for All, March 5–9, Jomtien

Further Reading

Bhola H S 1980 *Programme and Curriculum Development in the Post-Literacy Stages.* DSE, Bonn

Bhola H S 1988 *World Trends and Issues in Adult Education.* UNESCO, Paris

Bown L, Okedara J T 1981 *An Introduction to the Study of Adult Education: A Multi-Disciplinary and Cross-Cultural Approach for Developing Countries.* Ibadan University Press, Ibadan

Dave R H et al. 1985 *Learning Strategies for Post-Literacy and Continuing Education: A Cross-National Perspective.* UNESCO, Hamburg

ERIC Clearinghouse on Adult Education 1968 *Adult Education In Africa.* Current Information Sources, No. 12 ERIC, Washington, DC

Lind A, Johnson A 1986 *Adult Literacy in the Third World: A Review of Objectives and Strategies.* Swedish International Development Authority, Stockholm

Liveright A A 1959 *Strategies of Leadership in Conducting Adult Education Programs.* Harper and Brothers, New York

Mpogolo Z J 1991 The regional construction on post-literacy and continuing education. A paper presented at the World Conference on Comparative Adult Education, University of Ibadan

Okedara J T 1972 *Comparative Study of Adult Education Prospectuses of Some Universities and Colleges in Europe, North America and Africa, 1970–71.* University of Ibadan, Ibadan

Okeem E O 1982 *Adult Education in Ghana and Tanzania, 1945–1975.* University of Nigeria Press, Nsukka

Sheffield, Diejomaoh 1972 *Non-Formal Education in African Development.* African–American Institute, New York

UNESCO 1985 *The Development of Adult Education: Aspects and Trends and Final Report.* Proc. 4th Int. Conf. on Adult Education. UNESCO, Paris

UNDP 1988 *Needs and Strategies for Education and Training in Developing Countries in the 1990s.* UNDP, New York

Wagner D A 1990 *Literacy and Research: Past, Present and future.* UNESCO, International Bureau of Education, Geneva

World Bank 1988 *Education in Sub-Saharan Africa: Policies for Adjustment, Revitalization and Expansion.* The World Bank, Washington, DC

Africa, Francophone

A. Ouane

It is generally admitted that adult education has, in most cases, emerged as a substitute and a complement to the formal, more institutionalized form of education. This dual character is generally reflected in the organizational and structural specificities of adult education and continuing vocational training. Applied to the situation of Francophone Africa, these specificities are molded in a context which shape them to reflect the particular nature of what is broadly termed "Francophone Africa." These characteristics, and their relationships to the organization and provision of adult education in the region, are briefly discussed in this entry.

1. Context

"Francophone Africa" is a generic term coined to designate former French colonies situated in Africa south of the Sahara. In fact, it is in reality spread over a large geographic area encompassing some 25 countries differing considerably in their economic situation and potential, their ethnic texture, and their linguistic configuration. About 185 million inhabitants live in this region. The population ranges from a few thousand in Djibouti to 40 million in Zaire; 91 percent of the population in Burkina Faso live in rural areas, while 60 percent live in urban areas in Côte d'Ivoire; the number of languages ranges from one in Burundi, Madagascar, and Rwanda to more than 250 in Cameroon and Zaire. The literacy rate of the adult population aged over 15 years is very low, varying between 13 and 56 percent.

Some of these differences were widened by the post-Independence path of development of individual countries. According to UNDP (1991 p. 120), apart from Gabon which enjoys a medium human development, all countries in the region have a low Human Development Index (HDI). They rank between 115 and 158 from a total of 160 countries. Their HDI ranges from 0.510 for Gabon to 0.066 for Guinea, as compared to 0.993 for Japan, which heads the list. However, in the field of education, the common colonial past has strongly influenced these countries and is still influencing undertakings in individual countries to an extent that one could speak of a Francophone African "model" or "pattern."

Education in French-speaking Africa can be said to have three dimensions: traditional education, which cannot be separated from training and work, and that encompasses community-based, informal means of transmitting cultural identities, values, and skills; the "modern" formal education—preceded by missionary

schools or Koranic schools, according to the countries concerned; and nonformal education, which started at the adult level as a supportive means for development, and which has been enlarged to include dropouts and out-of-school children.

2. Genesis, Characteristics, and Forms

Emerging adult education activities in the region were influenced by the historical features outlined above. All the countries concerned are experiencing change caused by the related shifts from an oral to a literature-based culture and from a rural culture to an urban one. These shifts create a number of issues which have fundamental consequences for adult education.

Under the umbrella of "adult education," different modalities of learning aimed at providing complementary basic training to the "adult" population (which very often includes the so-called "mature" children aged 9 years and older) are included. In this range are to be found multiple adult literacy activities, extension training in rural areas (rural animation), vocational and income-generating training activities in urban areas (both in the formal and informal sectors of the economy), community development programs, and industrial training programs.

In the mid-1990s the concept of "adult education" is still of recent origin. The activities which are now termed "adult education" were run in a fragmented manner within tightly compartmentalized institutions. Until fairly recently, adult education was equated with adult literacy, focusing more on the age of the clientele and the initial aspect of the learning than on the multivaried nature of the process, its content, and context. As a result, departments of literacy were nominally expanded into departments of literacy and adult education without expanding their scope beyond literacy and postliteracy activities for adults, youth, and out-of school children.

This lack of institutional support is reflected in the absence of formal training structures for adult educators. Moreover, there is up to now no qualification such as an "adult educator," even though this task is being performed by people coming from different walks of life.

2.1 Major Features of Adult Education Programs in Francophone Africa

Adult education in French-speaking African countries is faced with huge tasks. One of them is to eradicate adult illiteracy. Another is to prepare people for

Table 1
Percentage illiteracy rates from 1980 to the year 2000

Countries	1980 Total	1985 Total	Male	Female	1990[a] Total	Male	Female	2000[a] Total	Male	Female
Benin	72.0	81.3	74.0	88.3	76.6	68.3	84.4	65.8	56.3	74.8
Burkina Faso	88.6	85.5	77.0	93.8	81.8	72.1	91.1	72.3	60.9	83.3
Burundi	73.2	57.9	46.6	68.2	50.0	39.1	60.2	34.6	25.4	43.3
Cameroon	51.5	52.0	38.9	64.4	45.9	33.7	57.4	34.0	24.3	43.4
Central African Republic	76.0	68.5	55.0	88.7	62.3	48.2	75.1	49.9	36.5	62.4
Chad	88.2	77.0	66.0	87.5	70.2	57.8	82.1	56.6	43.3	69.4
Congo	59.4	48.3	34.0	61.8	43.4	30.0	56.1	34.1	23.0	44.8
Côte d'Ivoire	65.0	51.3	37.5	65.7	46.2	33.1	59.8	36.5	25.1	48.2
Gabon	57.3	43.9	30.1	56.9	39.3	26.5	51.5	30.7	20.3	40.7
Guinea	75.9	83.2	74.5	91.6	76.0	65.1	86.6	61.5	48.5	73.9
Madagascar	38.8	23.1	14.2	31.6	19.8	12.3	27.1	14.5	9.0	19.7
Mali	90.6	77.3	69.0	84.6	68.0	59.2	76.1	48.0	40.1	55.4
Mauritania	82.6	72.5	60.2	84.2	66.0	52.9	78.6	53.1	39.7	65.9
Niger	90.2	78.5	67.9	88.7	71.6	59.6	83.2	57.7	44.5	70.6
Rwanda	50.3	54.6	40.7	67.9	49.8	36.1	62.9	40.9	28.5	52.8
Senegal	86.9	67.9	54.6	80.7	61.7	48.1	74.9	49.5	36.3	62.2
Togo	84.1	62.1	48.6	74.9	56.7	43.6	69.3	45.6	33.9	56.8
Zaire	45.5	34.1	20.6	46.8	28.2	16.4	39.3	18.3	10.1	26.3

Source: For 1980: BREDA 1986; for 1990 and 2000: UNESCO 1990
a Forecast

jobs which are scarce and most of which do not demand high qualifications. Yet another task is to contribute to the creation, maintenance, and development of a literate and literating environment while addressing overall development issues. Solving the first task has mobilized all resources and energy to the extent that adult education was largely reduced to adult literacy. However, at the practical level, large and various learning activities, both structured and unstructured ones that are addressed to different categories of adults, are taking place. The diffuse nature of these activities is reflected in their categorization as "*éducation populaire*" and "*animation socio-culturelle*." Their vocational orientation and concern for development is translated into extension activities for the rural population and apprenticeship courses for urban dwellers.

The highest illiteracy rates in the world are found in sub-Saharan Africa, more precisely in West Africa's French-speaking countries. Among the 26 countries in the world which have the highest illiteracy rates (i.e., above 70%), 16 are located in sub-Saharan Africa and 12 in West Africa. These countries are also characterized by large differences between men and women with respect to literacy, as can be inferred from Table 1.

The impossibility of rapidly achieving Universal Primary Education (UPE) in such a context is evident. The slow development of agricultural production is also alarming. In addition, due to the multilingual nature of the countries concerned, the language issue is present in all of them, although the way it is addressed varies according to the complexity of the linguistic texture and the place of the French language in national policy.

Although most of the national definitions of adult education seem to be country specific, if not situation specific, a cursory look at those prevailing in this region show them to be the broad, functional categories focusing on the application of literacy skills and its relation to technical progress and economic development. The political dimension and the emancipatory function are less prominent. A philosophy of liberation and a critical understanding of reality are therefore often lacking in these programs. As a corollary to this pragmatic concern, the literacy programs as basic components of adult education are selective.

The structural and institutional framework is another variable influencing adult education endeavors. A common feature is the integration of adult education into development projects. Since the early 1970s, literacy programs have been part of extension activities carried out by development agencies or authorities specialized in particular areas of policy, for example, mining, agriculture, fishery, and so forth. Such extension activities may have both local and nationwide significance.

Another notion currently prevailing is that of animation. Animation is an overall pedagogical principle borrowed from French social pedagogy, which is problem-oriented. It helps participants to identify issues and to tackle them critically through the learning process.

Because of their integration into development projects, and because of the historical existence of juxtaposed dual education systems, two important notions have gained currency in adult education in French-speaking Africa: the transfer or practice of competence and responsibility, and the creation of a literate environment, conducive to adult learning. The practice of competence and responsibility, particularly by the newly literate adult, consists in the application of newly acquired skills in order to assume daily individual and collective responsibilities which his or her previous situation as illiterate or poorly skilled did not permit.

In a situation like the one prevailing in French-speaking Africa, which is characterized by fierce competition with dominant foreign languages, a special effort is required to create, maintain, and protect a literate environment favorable to the use and promotion of the local languages. What is understood by such an environment? How is it to be created? Lazarus (1982) pointed out the following:

> A literate environment implies the development of an infrastructure to ensure, firstly, the easy availability of written material, newspapers, books, pamphlets, leaflets, etc., for the new literates at the level of their understanding; secondly, the possibilities of further education provision through evening schools, correspondence education; etc.; and thirdly, the possibilities of new literates to become their own "agents of change" by using their new skills in work and in their social and personal lives. Thus, a literate environment creates and ensures a cultural, economic and social environment favorable to the retention of literacy. (p. 68)

These tasks have to be supported by policy measures aimed at institution building. The policy aspects involve the formulation of legislation concerning language construction and the role of languages in education in general.

The institution building aspect takes two forms according to the functions these institutions are designed to perform. One set of institutions should produce in quantity and in quality reading materials for neoliterates. These institutions are endowed with policy arrangements to secure a literate environment. The second kind of institution aims at setting up structures providing neoliterates with facilities and motivation to apply their skills for their own benefit and for the larger interest of their group and local community.

Throughout Francophone Africa, the rural or community press has aimed at feeding neoliterates with reading materials, while consolidating the newly established linguistic norms and providing awareness for the promotion and "modernization" of the local languages. The rural press contributes to spreading written messages in these hitherto predominantly oral societies; it allocates space for neoliterates to exercise their writing skills in raising questions to their leaders and to other members of the society. Moreover, it may be noted that rural newspapers are often attached to discussion groups, reading clubs, and so on, that chiefly aim at spreading messages requiring literacy-based actions. The experiences are very rich in this respect. Some of the papers like *Kibaru* in Mali, *Gangaa* in Niger, and *Game Su* in Togo, are known internationally. Their structures, content, functioning, and approaches to evaluation, have been the subject of a number of case studies (Ouane 1982, 1984, Ouane and Amon-Tanoh 1991, Kané 1984, Badiane 1984, Ilboudo 1984).

With continuing democratization, newspaper publishing in local languages is mushrooming, reflecting the spectrum of political opinions. All political parties are discovering the need to address the silenced and voiceless majority which, until recently, was largely ignored.

Prior to this, the activities designed to generate communication in local languages, to practice newly acquired skills, and to sustain the evolving literate environment were developmental in nature and limited in scope.

Village pharmacies, village shops, and small-scale income-generation activities for specific target groups such as farmers, rural women, nomadic tribes, or fisherman, for example, were the prevailing forms of activities in which neoliterates were playing a key role. This literacy environment did not require many high-order communication skills, and only small numbers of learners were motivated to participate in literacy courses.

2.2 An Overview of Selected Activities

The various activities in this region are poorly documented. Specific programs, for example, youth training schemes such as practiced in Burkina Faso, Mali, and Senegal, are an exception in the literature. Another noteworthy exception is INADES/*Formation—Institut Africain pour le Développement Economique et Social* (African Institute for Economic and Social Development). Based in Côte d'Ivoire, it has developed education programs for adults in different African countries —for instance, distance education courses (in national languages) in Burkina Faso, Burundi, Ethiopia, and Rwanda. INADES—"*Initiation au développement*" (Initiation to development) also encourages the formation of study groups, which may include semiliterates and complete nonliterates. Examples of these can be seen in the "collective" correspondence courses for farmers in Burkina Faso, Burundi, and Ethiopia.

2.2.1 Burundi. Very high dropout rates at the primary level of the formal system in Burundi and a high level of grade repetition (more than 40% at Grade 6 of primary school) make it necessary to build up a system of recuperation for those who are not in the formal system. A project involving "*Centres de Formation Polyvalente*," which operate in all parts of the country, seeks to provide vocational training and practical knowledge in agriculture, family economy, masonry, and other fields for school-leavers at different levels.

Different adult education programs, both governmental and nongovernmental ones, also exist. These are mainly aimed at improving the living conditions of their target population. These programs intend to achieve active participation of the adult learners and the mobilization of the whole community. Examples of some of the state initiatives are the literacy program offered by the National Institute for Development (*Institut National pour le Développement*), the programs provided by the Ministry of Social Affairs (*Ministère des Affaires Sociales*), and a project run by the Department of Out-of-School Education (*Départment de l'Education Parascolaire*).

2.2.2 Cameroon.

2.2.2 Cameroon. Different kinds of institutions are providing various forms of adult education in Cameroon. Key notions here are *éducation populaire*, animation, and youths' and farmers' training.

Social groups and organizations are particularly important actors in the process of education/animation of young people. Two institutions can be mentioned: NUFI and PNAJA (*Programme National d'Action en Jeunesse et Animation*—National Action Program in Youth Activities and Animation). The NUFI ("new things") organization has, since 1957, developed literacy programs in national languages. It offers reading, writing, and numeracy classes in more than 50 literacy centers. Political instruction, primary healthcare, history, and other subjects are taught following a functional approach to literacy. Certificates corresponding to primary school leaving diplomas can be obtained. (Datchoua Soupa 1985).

The PNAJA program intends to foster the incorporation of youth into working society through the promotion of community organizations and cooperatives, vocational training of young people, and other educational activities such as literacy, and basic and civic education classes. The main structures established in the frame of this project are the so-called "*Centres de Jeunesse et d'Animation*," where out-of-school vocational training is offered, literacy centers, and centers for recreation and leisure. About 100 of such centers exist, out of which only 3 are sponsored by the government (Ntebe 1985).

2.2.3 Gabon.

2.2.3 Gabon. In Gabon *education populaire* is a pedagogical program which intends to achieve an improved assimilation of development projects by the urban and rural populations and a better integration of workers in industry, especially with respect to the development of new technology and production methods. Literacy is only one component of the educational activities summarized under the concept of popular education. Its main target groups are the out-of-school youth, adults without any schooling, and those with insufficient formal education.

Among the activities of *éducation populaire* in Gabon, the production of educational radio and TV programs in collaboration with the Gabunian radio and TV agency is outstanding. The Department of Production and Technology, part of the *Direction Générale de l'Education Populaire*, produced 6,406 educational radio programs and 174 televisual aids on different subjects in the field of health, agriculture, family education, and others in 1990. About 122 slides have been produced, one serial of 13 episodes, and 7 documentaries on literacy and health.

2.2.4 Rwanda.

2.2.4 Rwanda. There has been a long history of practical complementary education in Rwanda. In addition to the traditional *foyers sociaux* ("social houses"), transformed into social centers for development in 1975, Rwanda has launched and disseminated other types of practical training for young adults who have not had access to school: nutrition centers, female training centers or family sections, rural training centers, and so forth. In multiplying such initiatives, the government aimed at enrolling about 10 percent of the school leavers aged over 6 years or dropouts to complement the other 10 percent that have privileged access to secondary education.

3. Approaches to the Training of Adult Educators

In defining the concept of "adult education," its links with cultural, social, and ecological contexts have been frequently stressed, together with the influences of ideology, educational objectives, the desire for educational reforms, and the prevailing forms of organization. Bhola (1989) mentions

> ... a set of five norms that can be brought to bear on the concept and definition of adult education: (a) the norm of comprehensiveness and continuity; (b) the norm of essentiality; (c) the norm of structural freedom or de-institutionalization; (d) the norm of utility; and (e) the norm of serving people's interests. (p. 16)

Applied to the situation of Francophone Africa, the norm of comprehensiveness is achieved not within individual programs, but as a result of a diversified range of activities. The same is true for continuity, which is provided in individual programs, even though there is a lack of recognition and accreditation of previous learning experience. The other norms are strongly present, particularly that of essentiality, utility, and serving people's interest. Within each of these norms, a large number of functions of pedagogical, managerial, and organizational nature have to be served.

Human resources development is essential for organizational capacity building. The value added to an adult education program can be improved through training and staff development activities. As Boshier (1985) puts it:

> Indeed, in the absence of solid evidence, some people suspect that training has little positive impact on the field especially when linked to credentialling and professionalization. Many workers maintain that no one should be denied an opportunity to practice adult education, because of a lack of training. The "gifted amateur," the mainstay of adult education, should be encouraged. Indeed some say the best adult educators are those who have seen the inside of a teachers' training college or university faculty of education. (p. 4)

In Francophone Africa, different categories of personnel were called upon to teach adults after attending a one-to two-week training course. In the early 1990s, there is a shift from informal, ad hoc approaches to more institutional formal ones. This movement from voluntarism to professionalism is taking place mainly at the middle and national/central levels, where visible structures and institutions offering adult education programs already exist.

As far as the training of adult educators is concerned, informal and institutional modalities exist both at field and intermediate and national levels. However, for the grassroots personnel, the informal modalities are often used as main – and sometimes exclusive – approaches for both initial as well as on-the-job preparation, while for middle-level and national-level adult education workers the informal modalities are only a complementary preparation.

3.1 Informal Approaches

Several approaches fall under this category. Their richness is reflected in the multiplicity of terms currently employed: "sessions," "seminars," "workshops," "orientation," "follow-up training," "operational seminars," "complementary learning through distance education," and so forth.

As already mentioned, these are the main modalities used for the training of grassroots personnel. Up to very recently, there were no institutions that could be entrusted with this task. It should, however, be stressed that several countries in this region, such as Burkina Faso, Central African Republic, Congo, Guinea, Mali, and Senegal, have succeeded in creating large, dynamic literacy programs for adults that were handled by animators and literacy leaders who were prepared for their task on the spot, during short-term, but intensive sessions.

Middle-level and higher-level personnel are also trained through informal ways for the acquisition of knowledge and skills needed for the teaching of adults. Workshops and operational seminars are the predominant forms. In both cases, the guiding principle is to provide training close to actual field situations, and encourage the teachers to produce the tools, methodologies, and concrete materials themselves.

Countries in the region jointly organized a series of operational seminars on themes such as literacy, postliteracy, women's literacy and postliteracy programs, training of personnel, material production, rural and community presses, evaluation, organizing adult education, and cooperation between universities, NGOs, and governments. These seminars are generally known by the names of the cities acting as hosts (Tove, Kita, Sokode, Niamey, Porto-Novo, Lome, Kupela, Conakry, Kaolack, etc.). The Regional Council for Adult Education and Literacy in Africa (CREAA) stemmed from this cooperative effort as a coordinating body for the setting up of an institutional structure for adult education policy and training for adult educators.

3.2 Institutional Approaches

A distinction can be made between institutions in charge of field workers and those catering for the needs of middle- and national-level personnel. The only training institutions for field agents are of a vocational nature. Some of these institutions cater for out-of-school youth and young adults, whereas others focus on people with a short formal education. Apart from their differentiated audience, these institutions also differ according to their orientation: some of them focus on agriculture, while others offer a more polyvalent and comprehensive coverage of content areas.

Taking these characteristics into account, the following institutions are worth mentioning: the CFJA—*Centre de Formation des Jeunes Agriculteurs* (Young Farmers' Training Centers) of Burkina Faso; *les Maisons Familiales Rurales* (Rural Family Houses Promotion) of Senegal; the CPR—*Centres de Promotion Rurales* (Rural Development Promotion Centers), and the CPT—*Centres de Perfectionnement Technique* (Centers for Technical Training) of Niger; the CAR—*Centres d'Animation Rurale* (Animation Centers for Rural Development), and the COP—*Centre d'Orientation Pratique* (Centres for Practical Guidance) of Mali. There are also institutions with a more comprehensive profile, such as the CFP—*Centres de Formation Polyvalente* (Centers for Comprehensive Training) of Burundi; and the CERAI—*Centres Ruraux et Artisanaux Intégrés* (Integrated Centers for Rural Development and Handicraft) of Rwanda; and the *Centres d'Education de Vulgarisation pour l'Auto-développement* (Education and Extension Centers for Self-development) of Zaire.

The location of training institutions is a subject of controversy between those favoring the cities and those advocating settling them in rural areas in order to make the trainees acquainted with the rural context and sensitive to the needs, interests, and priorities of rural populations.

Niger took the initiative in 1977 of setting up a Center for the Training of Literacy and Adult Education Trainers, the CFCA (*Centre de Formation des*

Cadres d'Alphabétisation). The modalities of training are based on action research, in which the trainees are put in a situation where they have to re-invent and re-establish a relationship with the community, the group, and the individual learner. The center deals with the mastery of this methodology and with aspects such as conceptualizing adult education, defining profiles, identifying needs and establishing priorities, preparing participation surveys, and conceptionalizing and producing materials for media learning. In 1982, this center was run by the CREAA and transformed into CERFOCA (Regional Training Center for Higher Level Personnel in Literacy). In 1990, the AALAE (African Association for Literacy and Adult Education) was entrusted by the OAU (Organization of African Unity) to transform the Niger Center into a continental one, the African Institute for Literacy and Continuing Education (INAAEC).

A long-established tradition in this area is the use of formal education personnel and facilities for adult education. This is particularly visible in institutions preparing high-level workers or providing learning for more qualified adult learners. For instance, in Gabon, the personnel working in *éducation populaire* are the officers working at the national and central level and the animators and supervisors who work at the regional and local level. Some 80 percent of the animators are former school teachers who do not have any qualification in *éducation populaire*.

Since 1978 all new animators and supervisors trained for *éducation populaire* programs come from the *Ecole Nationale des Cadres Ruraux* (founded in 1975). They follow a three-year training course, including a one-year specialization in agriculture, cattle raising, and *éducation populaire* (Ndong 1984).

With the development of the demand for adult learning activities, formal education institutions are responding by adjusting their structures and adding new functions to cater for the needs of adult education. In Côte d'Ivoire, Madagascar, Mali, Senegal, and Zaire, new training modalities are being devised in university departments and disciplines, such as social science, applied to development. The CUR—*Centres Universitaires Régionaux* (Regional University Centers) in Madagascar and the ENEA—*Ecole National d'Economie Appliquée* (National High School for Applied Economics) of Senegal have acted in an innovative manner by providing opportunities for adult learners with different experiences of learning related to development work to join formal courses. Likewise, the CUFOP—*Centre Universitaire de Formation Professionnelle* (Continuing Education Center) of the University of Côte d'Ivoire, provides courses for professionals from various backgrounds on cost-effectiveness and productivity in business and industry. Similarly, in Zaire, the INPP—*Institut National de Préparation Professionnelle* (National Institute of Vocational Training) has served the training needs of professional enterprises since 1964, while other employers run their own training centers in their firms.

See also: UNESCO and Adult Education; Africa, Anglophone

References

Badiane F 1984 The development of learning strategies for the post-literacy and continuing education of neo-literates in Senegal. In: Dave R H, Perera D A, Ouane A (eds.) 1984

Bhola H S 1989 *World Trends and Issues in Adult Education.* UNESCO, Paris

Boshier R (ed.) 1985 Conceptual framework for analyzing the training of trainers and adult educators. *Convergence* 18 (3–4): 3–22

BREDA 1986 *Regional Bulletin of Education Statistics.* UNESCO Regional Office for Education in Africa, Dakar

Datchoua Soupa C 1985 L'Enseignement NUFI ou la Problématique de l'Animation. In: 1985 *Actes du Premier Colloque National en Jeunesse et Animation. Centre Universitaire de Dschang du 2 au 7 Septembre 1985.* Ministère de la Jeunesse et des Sports, Direction de la Jeunesse et de l'Animation, Yaoundé

Ilboudo P T 1984 The development of learning strategies for post-literacy and continuing education of neo-literates in Upper Volta. In: Dave R H, Perera D A, Ouane A (eds.) 1984

Kané O 1984 The Lifelong Education Centre (FEP) and other learning strategies for post-literacy in Niger. In: Dave R H, Perera D A, Ouane A (eds.) 1984

Lazarus R 1982 Reflections on creating a literature environment. *Convergence* 15(3): 67–72

Ndong B 1984 Politique et Stratégie du Gabon en matière d'Education Populaire en Milieu Rural et en Milieu Urbain. In: 1984 *Le Formel et le Non-Formel dans l'Education de Masse. Session d'Etude sur les Interactions du Formel et du Non-Formel dans le Contexte d'une Education de Masse. Bamako, 7–9 Mai 1984.* Agence de Coopération Culturelle et Technique, Paris

Ntebe G 1985 L'Action d'Encadrement du Ministère de la Jeunesse et des Sports sur le Terrain. In: 1985 *Actes du premier Colloque National en Jeunesse et Animation. Centre Universitaire de Dschang du 2 au 7 Septembre 1985.* Ministère de la Jeunesse et des Sports, Direction de la Jeunesse et de l'Animation, Yaoundé

Ouane A 1982 Rural newspapers and radio for post-literacy in Mali. *Prospects* 12(2): 243–53

Ouane A 1984 Alphabétisation et formation des formateurs: l'Expérience de l'Afrique Francophone. *Int. Rev. Educ.* 30(3): 329–50

Ouane A, Amon-Tanoh Y 1991 Literacy in French-speaking Africa: A situational analysis. *African Studies Rev.* 33(3): 21–38

UNESCO 1990 *Compendium of Statistics on Illiteracy.* UNESCO Division of Statistics on Education, Office of Statistics, Paris

United Nations Development Program (UNDP) 1991 *Human Development Report 1991.* Oxford University Press, New York

Further Reading

Belloncle G 1984 *La question éducative en Afrique Noire.* Karthala, Paris

Cissé S Y 1985 *L'Education en Afrique à la lumière de*

la Conférence de Harare, 1982. (Etudes et Documents d'éducation 50) UNESCO, Paris

Dave R H, Perera D A, Ouane A 1984 *Learning Strategies for Post-Literacy and Continuing Education in Mali, Niger, Senegal and Upper Volta.* (UIE studies on post-literacy and continuing education 2) UNESCO Institute for Education, Hamburg

Easton P 1984 *L'éducation des adultes en Afrique noire: manuel d'auto-évaluation assistée. Tome 1: Théorie. Tome 2: Techniques.* Karthala, Agence de coopération culturelle et technique, Paris

Hamadache A, Martin D 1986 *Theory and Practice of Literacy Work: Policies, Strategies and Examples.* UNESCO, Paris

Jabre B 1988 *Women's Education in Africa: A Survey of Field Projects in Five Countries.* UNESCO, UNESCO-UNICEF Cooperative Program (Child, family, community. Digest No.26)

Ki-Zerbo J 1990 *Eduquer ou périr. Impasses et perspectives africaines.* UNESCO/UNICEF, Paris

Ouane A 1989 *Handbook on Learning Strategies for Post-Literacy and Continuing Education.* UNESCO Institute for Education, Hamburg

UNESCO 1982 *Employment-oriented National Youth Programmes in Africa: Situations, problems and prospects.* UNESCO, Paris

Arab Countries

B. G. Massialas

The education of adults in the 22 countries comprising the Arab world constitutes a pressing social problem. Given the rapid rate of population growth in the region, Arab governments have by necessity had to concentrate on the education of children and youth. The annual population growth rate in the early 1980s, for example, ranged from 1.8 percent in the People's Democratic Republic of Yemen to 9.2 percent in Djibouti. Egypt, being the most populous Arab state with an estimated population in 1981 of 43.2 million, had an annual population growth rate of 2.7 percent (Environmental Fund 1981). This rapid population growth posed two general problems for governments seeking to supply educational services for all. First, school facilities, additional teaching staff, and other resources were needed in order to accommodate the influx of young children entering the first grade. Second, as the pressure of numbers in the system made it difficult to realize quality improvement, many children dropped out from primary school. The only way these children could be reached was through nonformal education. In Egypt alone it was estimated that almost 50 percent of the primary-school age group dropped out before reaching the intermediate stage.

For a long time, the investment in primary and secondary education was so sizable that few governments could spare resources to finance programs in adult and nonformal education. Yet the magnitude of the potential demand for adult education can be judged against the background that, in the early 1970s, nearly three out of four adults in the Arab countries were illiterate.

1. History and Objectives of Adult Education

Various forms of adult education are deeply rooted in Arab cultures and precede the colonial experience of the nineteenth and twentieth centuries. Examples are the Koranic study circles that existed both in towns and among nomadic groups, and the tradition of teaching philosophy, sciences, and arts to both Arab and foreign students at the ancient universities of Al Azhar, Al Zaytona, and Al Quarawein. In the period following independence (mainly after the Second World War) adult education was seen as an important means of building nation-states. As the economies of the Arab countries developed—especially those of the oil-producing nations surrounding the Gulf—the need to expand rapidly the intake capacity of primary and secondary schools, and the urgency of improving the provision of nonformal education and literacy training for both youths and adults was felt throughout the Arab region.

Many adult education programs in the region are intended to offer basic training for adults—generally the population aged 15 years and over—so that they can acquire literacy, numeracy, and vocational skills and secure gainful employment. Adult education may comprise community development, assistance in agriculture, and instruction in subjects such as health, nutrition, childcare, and family planning. It also refers to programs aimed at personal development and the enhancement of satisfaction and enjoyment in the context of lifelong learning.

Adult education in the Arab countries, as in many other parts of the developing world, has been focused on literacy training. The problem of illiteracy in the region was generally acknowledged in 1964 when the Arab League, under UNESCO auspices, called a conference in Baghdad to discuss education and culture in the Arab region. The decision to establish the Arab League Educational, Cultural, and Scientific Organization (ALECSO) was taken at this important conference. Another major conference, held in Alexandria in the same year, resulted in the creation, in 1965, of the Arab

Literacy Organization (ARLO). This organization was given the responsibility of coordinating the adult literacy efforts among the member countries (Massialas and Jarrar 1983 p. 269).

Successive conferences in Alexandria (1971) and Baghdad (1976) sponsored by ARLO in collaboration with ALECSO and UNESCO's Regional Center for Functional Literacy (ASFEC) sought to renew existing programs, evaluate progress made during this period, and chart a course of action that would eventually result in the reduction of illiteracy in the region. The participants in these meetings recognized that the problem of illiteracy was multifaceted, not resolvable through government declarations offering simplistic remedies. It was also understood that additional financial and human resources were needed in order to design and execute an effective program. The new strategy agreed upon proposed "a global approach to the problem, the development of inter-Arab cooperation, the introduction of compulsory primary schooling, the coordination of literacy training with action to develop primary education, the mobilization of the resources and skills of the people at large, and the continuous assessment of activities carried out in this domain" (Conference of Ministers of Education 1977 p. 9). In implementing the objectives of the Alexandria conferences three stages were envisaged. During the stage of reform initiation (1977–78), ARLO, in collaboration with other international agencies and national governments, was to gather information, train appropriate personnel, and develop appropriate legislation. The goal was that illiteracy would be substantially reduced during the subsequent "implementation stage" (1978–80). During the last period—the "liquidation stage" (1987–91)—all remaining vestiges of illiteracy among the male and female population were to be eradicated, thus enabling the Arab citizenry to participate fully in the social, cultural, and economic development of their nations.

Because assessment data are not generally available, it cannot be known precisely whether and to what extent these desirable but ambitious goals have been realized. There is evidence, however, that much progress has been made, even though there are still problems of support and effective program implementation. One author put it as follows: "While virtually all Arab countries could claim to have devised ambitious plans for eliminating adult illiteracy, almost none had progressed beyond the first stage for lack of funding" (Lucas 1981 p.77).

2. Literacy and Illiteracy in the 1990s

According to UNESCO sources, the illiteracy rate among adults in the Arab countries in 1960 was 81 percent of the population. This amounted to 42.8 million people aged 15 years or more. Since then the situation has improved remarkably. Table 1 gives information on

Table 1
Adult literacy rates by sex in Arab states (percentages)[a]

	1970	1985	1990	2000
Arab states:				
Male	39.5	59.2	64.3	73.1
Female	13.7	31.5	38.0	50.0
Both sexes	26.5	45.5	51.3	62.0
Developing countries:				
Male	57.8	71.1	74.9	80.3
Female	32.6	49.9	55.0	63.2
Both sexes	45.3	60.7	65.1	71.9

Source: UNESCO 1991 p. 97
a Rates for 1990 and 2000 are estimates. Adults are defined as being 15 years or older

literacy trends in the Arab countries and those in the developing countries combined. It can be seen that the literacy rate in the Arab countries increased significantly from 1970 to 1985, from about 27 percent to 46 percent of the adult population. By the year 2000 the literacy rate among adults is expected to be around 62 percent. If accomplished, this target will still leave some 66 million adults illiterate, out of an estimated total of 173 million. Another finding shown in Table 1 is that the Arab countries as a group lag behind the literacy rate achieved by the countries classified as developing. Among these countries only those in sub-Saharan Africa (41%) and in southern Asia (42%) had lower literacy rates than the Arab countries in 1985.

Table 1 shows, moreover, that there is still a substantial discrepancy between the literacy rates of male and female adults. In 1970, for example, the male literacy rate among adult Arabs was 40 percent, while for adult females it was only 14 percent. By 1985 the disparity had decreased, to 59 percent for men and 32 percent for women. It is estimated that the difference will have lessened even more by the year 2000.

Table 2 presents estimates of the rate of adult illiteracy in the individual Arab countries as of 1990. There is a strikingly wide range of adult illiteracy rates in the region, varying from 20 percent in Jordan and Lebanon to 76 percent in Somalia. Absolute figures of the number of illiterates are also given for each Arab country, and the percentage change over a fifteen-year span is noted. It is obvious that there has been an increase in the total number of illiterates in all of the countries, except for Jordan, Lebanon, Saudi Arabia, Tunisia, and Yemen. This indicates that while the percentage of illiterate adults in the population may be gradually lowered, illiteracy can continue to increase in absolute numbers.

737

Table 2
Adult illiteracy rates in the Arab states by country

	Percentage illiteracy rates 1990			Number of illiterates 1990 (in thousands)	Percentage change 1970–90
	Male	Female	Total		
Algeria	30.2	54.5	42.6	6,004	10.6
Bahrain	17.9	30.7	22.6	78	36.9
Djibouti	—	—	—	—	—
Egypt	37.1	66.2	51.6	16,492	27.0
Iraq	30.2	50.7	40.3	4,078	17.9
Jordan	10.7	29.7	19.9	442	−24.0
Kuwait	22.9	33.3	27.0	346	92.3
Lebanon	12.2	26.9	19.9	382	−25.8
Libya	24.6	49.6	36.2	890	23.0
Mauritania	52.9	78.6	66.0	740	23.4
Morocco	38.7	62.0	50.5	7,526	17.9
Oman	—	—	—	—	—
Qatar	—	—	—	—	—
Saudi Arabia	26.9	51.9	37.6	2,897	−0.5
Somalia	63.9	86.0	75.9	3,003	50.3
Sudan	57.3	88.3	72.9	10,061	57.9
Syria	21.7	49.2	35.5	234	20.4
Tunisia	25.8	43.7	34.7	1,761	−9.3
Yemen:					
Former Dem. Yemen	47.2	73.9	60.9	840	28.8
Former Yemen	46.7	73.7	61.5	2,559	−2.6
United Arab Emirates	—	—	—	—	—

Source: UNESCO 1991 pp. 110–13

3. Experiences of Individual Countries

Notwithstanding the difficulties of supporting and coordinating the development of adult education programs, some Arab governments have made sustained and successful efforts to improve the situation. The experience of three countries is described briefly below.

3.1 Iraq

Four years before the war with Iran, in 1976, Iraq embarked on what was called the National Campaign for Literacy and Adult Education. This campaign sought to offer functional literacy programs as well as cultural programs. To accomplish the task of educating one in every six citizens in a population of about 13 million, the government set up the necessary institutions and literacy centers, recruited a large number of instructors, and allocated funds so that the programs could be carried out as planned. There were also volunteers who provided specialized skill training in technical fields. In their training, the special needs of housewives, the military, farm laborers, and industrial workers were taken into consideration. While conditions caused by the Iran–Iraq War of 1980–88 dampened this effort, and even though a systematic program evaluation is not available, the mass literacy campaign in Iraq stands out as a model of what can

be done when a government decides to place a high priority on the effort. Data published by UNESCO (1991) indicate that the illiteracy rate in Iraq was reduced from 82 percent of the adult population in 1960 to 40 percent in 1990.

3.2 Egypt

Egypt is another example of a country where the government has implemented a coherent strategy for addressing the problem of adult illiteracy. In spite of these efforts, 52 percent of the total adult population in Egypt was considered illiterate in 1990. Egypt, as well as Sudan, were placed among the 10 countries in the world with the highest adult illiteracy rates in 1990 (UNESCO 1991 p. 26).

In 1987 a High Council for Adult Education and Elimination of Illiteracy was established in Egypt. It was given the responsibility of organizing the supply of appropriate literacy training. Instructors who offered training as part of their year-long mandatory spell of public service were recruited from among the graduates of postsecondary institutions. Military personnel also offered literacy instruction in the respective governorates in which they were stationed. Various incentives were given to many of these instructors: for example, a reduction in the time required in military service. Regular school teachers were brought into the effort, especially in the training and upgrading of candidate instructors (Jarrar and Massialas 1992 p. 163).

The target population selected for training included young school dropouts (ages 12–15) as well as adults with little or no previous education. Illiterate women were given special attention, not only because they were more numerous than men, but also because the training could help the women to participate more fully in social, cultural, or economic life. Incentives given to women included the opportunity to gain certain vocational skills in conjunction with literacy skills. Special prizes, such as sewing machines, were given to women who successfully completed the program. For males, both employed and unemployed, there was training under programs monitored by the Ministry of Education. Those who were gainfully employed were expected to be trained by their employing agency, in both public and private sectors. The military as well as the ministries of the Interior, Agriculture, and Housing conducted their own training activities. The Ministry of Information provided literacy training through state-controlled radio and television broadcasting.

The government of Egypt devised new ways of delivering adult and nonformal education in order to ensure the spread of literacy among the whole population. For instance, to reduce school dropout among youths, the government reintroduced grade repetition and commenced a program of in-school vocational education for students who were not academically inclined but had the ability to be instructed in a marketable skill. Parent councils were formed to work with schools in promoting and supporting the education of children and youths. The vocational programs instituted in the schools sought to match, in addition to traditional skills in reading, writing, and numeracy, the peculiarities of the local environment (rural–urban) by providing appropriate work tools and work ethics.

Skill training programs sponsored by various agencies were set up in addition to literacy programs for adults. The Ministry of Industry and Natural Resources, for example, through its Productivity and Vocational Training Department, established a network of 37 vocational training institutes, 10 in-plant training centers, and the Instructor Training Institute. Among the training programs offered by these institutions are three-year apprenticeships as well as accelerated courses in 72 different specializations. The apprenticeship program became highly popular among youths.

Given that the scope for public funding is limited, the Egyptian government faces a difficult task in seeking to eradicate illiteracy. Although the country has succeeded in reducing its adult illiteracy rate from about 74 percent in 1960 to 52 percent in 1990, much remains to be done. There is some optimism, however, that the required resources can eventually be raised from international organizations and through revenues from the services fund of each governorate, duties imposed on luxury commodities, and by contributions from citizens, private enterprises, public firms, and political parties. As was mentioned in the introduction, the difficulty in realizing the objective of eradicating illiteracy and offering vocational training stems, in part, from the rapid population increase which averaged 2.7 percent from 1980 to 1990.

3.3 Sudan

Sudan is an Arab-dominated country where nonformal and adult education programs have been given increased attention. At the outset, government policy had a threefold purpose: to eliminate illiteracy, to attend to the education of out-of-school youths and to enhance rural development. The first objective has not been reached, despite the progress since 1960 when, according to World Bank sources, only 2 percent of Sudanese adults were classified as literate. UNESCO estimates that about 17 percent of adults in Sudan were fully literate in 1990. Sudan therefore ranks among the 10 countries with the largest proportion of illiterate adults (UNESCO 1991 p. 26).

The Sudanese government has sought for years to ameliorate the crippling problems of adult illiteracy. In 1972 it enacted the Literacy and Adult Functional Education Law which spearheaded the movement to combat mass illiteracy. A National Council for Literacy and Adult Functional Education was created and was empowered to develop policies, secure financial assistance, and introduce programs for implementation. The Ministry of Education, through its adult education unit, has also been instrumental in planning and executing adult education programs. As in the case of Iraq, a mass mobilization campaign was used as a framework for implementing the objectives pursued by the government. Many programs were implemented through the town and village councils, which were asked to establish literacy and adult functional education committees. Primary school teachers formed the nucleus of the campaign staff. The program comprised two stages. The first sought to assist students in mastering reading, writing, and numeracy skills. Those who successfully completed the program were awarded a certificate of literacy. This certificate was judged to be equivalent to the fourth grade of primary school. The second stage offered extensive training in technical and vocational skills. A wide range of subjects was offered through different programs such as the agricultural program or the industrial program. These activities are in line with the aim of creating incentives for lifelong learning.

4. Institutional Arrangements and Program Development

Adult education programs such as those in Iraq, Egypt, and Sudan have been introduced in virtually all Arab countries, with varying success. Mass mobilization strategies have been used in countries with high rates of illiteracy among adults. In both Iraq and Sudan the mass campaigns signaled a new era in the educational development of the country, creating new prospects and hopes for the future. Due to international conflicts in Iraq and internal strife in the Sudan, the mass campaigns were not afforded the time and resources commensurate with the scope of the objectives. In both cases, even though some success was registered, the benefits never fully materialized.

Both radio and television broadcasting have been extensively used as means of reaching the adult population, especially people living in remote, rural areas. In Tunisia, broadcasts have comprised vocational training programs and information on literacy and other topics such as health, agriculture, and social and cultural affairs. These programs are intended to augment the work of the literacy training and social education centers, as well as the work of grassroots organizations such as the National Union of Tunisian Women, which are spread throughout the country. In Somalia some attempts have been made to use radio to facilitate the work of the National Adult Education and Training Center and the National Women's Education Center. Nomadic education was also part of the overall plan. The broadcasting program of Somalia was short-lived, however, mainly because of technical and administrative problems (Improving the Efficiency of Educational Systems 1984).

Adult education has come a long way in the Arab countries. However, the problem of financing adult education constitutes a perennial concern which has not been solved, especially among the Arab countries outside the Gulf region. Another general problem concerns the recruitment and retention of adult learners. Generally, men are reluctant to participate in adult education programs because they may interfere with employment. Women, being socialized to accept the sole role of housewife, are reluctant to depart from tradition and enroll in an adult literacy program. Resistance is strong, especially in the case of vocational training programs that may lead to gainful employment outside the home.

A research study conducted in Oman has confirmed the general trends set out above. For example, Omani male respondents who were employed indicated that the reasons for not enrolling in adult literacy programs "were mainly those of time limitations caused by the magnitude of job demands or conflict between class and work schedules. Most of those who identified job-related problems believed that their employers were neither sensitive nor appreciative of the employee's efforts to become literate" (Al-Barwani and Kelly 1985 p. 152). Employer insensitivity was particularly pronounced with respect to agricultural workers and others involved in menial jobs, because it was felt that an increase in literacy skills would not raise worker productivity. The main obstacle to the participation of women in adult education programs in Oman was the firm conviction that their main responsibility was to attend to household duties. The idea that "caring for children and going to school are mutually exclusive" was widespread, and formed a powerful barrier to the mobilization of women. In interpreting the results of their study the authors note: "A large portion of the population of Oman still believes that a woman does not need to learn or be educated. Learning and working are still considered to be men's rightful territory. Hence, women do not receive the encouragement and support they need in order to pursue education" (Al-Barwani and Kelly 1985 p. 153).

5. Trends and Policy Implications

A central trend in the development of adult education in the Arab region is that governments have placed an overwhelming emphasis on literacy training. This policy followed the realization, promoted by the Alexandria conferences, that, on average, three-quarters of all Arab adults could not read and write in the 1960s. In some countries, mass literacy campaigns were put in place, usually incorporating a strong element of the ideology of the political party in power. According to the recommendations and agreements reached under the auspices of ARLO, UNESCO, and ALECSO, the literacy programs were to be coordinated by a central agency in each country, but program delivery was to be distributed among a variety of agencies, both public and private.

In addition to literacy, most countries have provided technical and vocational training in the industrial, agricultural, and service sectors of the economy. The trend in adult education for women (especially rural women) has been to provide not only basic literacy training but also topics such as health, nutrition, and family planning.

Another, more indirect, approach to reducing mass illiteracy has been the widespread effort among Arab countries to improve the quality of primary education and to curb school dropout. This effort led to increases in resource allocation and changes in curricula, teaching methods, and the classroom environment. Increased emphasis was put on the perceived needs and interests of the students. This policy has apparently paid off, since gross enrollment ratios for the first level of education in the Arab countries have improved substantially—from 63 percent in 1970 to 83 percent in 1990 (UNESCO 1991 p. 30). Providing primary education for all while preventing school dropout are effective, albeit longterm, ways of reducing illiteracy in a country.

The governments of Arab countries are faced with many policy choices concerning the development of adult education. First, there is the issue of creating and expanding opportunities for women. Unless there is a change in attitude and new legislation is enacted, especially in the traditional Arab countries, adult education programs may well continue to be out of reach for the majority of Arab women. A second major issue concerns the financing of adult education. Although exact figures are mostly unavailable, there is a consensus among regional experts that adult education is not a top priority in the majority of the Arab countries. A study of the factors influencing the provision of literacy training and adult education in the region, concluded that:

> The current level of support is simply not adequate to provide for an effective resolution of the problem. Without the support, techniques for reaching the target population have not been put in place in many of the countries in the region. These techniques include mass mobilization campaigns, distant teaching through radio and possibly TV, community-based programs, the use of mobile units to deliver instruction in isolated areas and other services, etc. (Massialas and Jarrar 1991 p. 63)

Program coordination is a third major element in a strategy for addressing the learning needs of adults in the region. Both intracountry, interagency, and regional coordination are in need of strengthening. Over the years, from the establishment in 1951 of the Arab States Fundamental Education Center in Egypt to the Jomtien Declaration on Learning for All in Thailand in 1990, the majority of Arab countries have tended to supply opportunities for adult learning through a variety of agencies, both public and private. In fact, there has been a proliferation of programs, but little effort to coordinate activities. The inability to supervise and monitor progress in the field has generally contributed to duplication of effort and a weakening of the claims of concerned educators and political leaders for financial support.

At a regional level, the coordination of adult education has entered into an impasse. The absence of a clear, concerted strategy was noted in 1980 at the 11th Arab Summit held in Amman, Jordan. This summit led to the formulation and formal adoption of the First Arab Plan for Obliterating Illiteracy. The plan specified the objectives; presented a strategy and methods of work; defined the three phases of initiation, implementation, and institutionalization; and estimated, for each country, the budget that would be required for meeting the stated objectives. In spite of the achievements, because of political, financial, and technical reasons the plan was never fully implemented. Thus, whereas ARLO and ALECSO have played a key role in the initiation of regional coordinating activities, even more sustained efforts are needed for securing development in the future. One thought is to create a "regional superagency" which would "supervise the recruitment of personnel . . . provide a constant flow of information and technical know-how and monitor

and report on the progress of the relevant programs in the region" (Massialas and Jarrar 1991 p. 63).

The Arab countries still face huge problems in meeting the learning needs of their citizens. Yet there is indication that these needs are increasingly being addressed, particularly through grass-roots strategies. A reordering of priorities may accelerate change to the point where universal literacy and full employment become realistic national and regional goals.

See also: Adult Literacy in the Third World; Asia, Southeast: Literacy

References

Al-Barwani T, Kelly E F 1985 Factors influencing the recruitment and retention of literacy learners in Oman. *Int. Rev. Educ.* 31: 145–54
Conference of Ministers of Education and Those Responsible for Economic Planning in the Arab States 1977 *New Prospects in Education for Development in the Arab Countries.* UNESCO, Paris
Environmental Fund 1981 *World Population Estimates.* Environmental Fund, Washington, DC
Improving the Efficiency of Educational Systems 1984 *Somalia Education and Human Resources Sector Assessment.* Learning Systems Institute, Florida State University, Tallahassee, Florida
Jarrar S A, Massialas B G 1992 Arab Republic of Egypt. In: Cookson P W, Sadovnik A R, Semel S F (eds.) 1992 *International Handbook of Educational Reform.* Greenwood, New York
Lucas C J 1981 Arab illiteracy and the mass literacy campaign in Iraq. *Comp. Educ. Rev.* 25(1): 74–84
Massialas B G, Jarrar S A 1983 *Education in the Arab World.* Praeger, New York
Massialas B G, Jarrar S A 1991 *Arab Education in Transition: A Source Book.* Garland, New York
UNESCO 1991 *World Education Report 1991.* UNESCO, Paris

Further Reading

Abu Nasr J, Lorfing I (eds.) 1988 *Women and Economic Development in the Arab World: A Regional Conference.* Institute for Women's Studies in the Arab World, Beirut University College, Beirut
Al-Abidi S H 1989 The Mosque: Adult education and uninterrupted learning. *Islam Today* 7 (7): 68–77
Kurian G T (ed.) 1988 *World Education Encyclopedia.* Facts on File, New York
Massialas B G 1992 Education in the Middle East and North Africa. *Encyclopedia of Educational Research*, 6th edn. Macmillan, New York
Massialas B G, Jarrar S A 1988 Egypt. In: Kurian G T (ed.) 1988
Sharabi H 1988 *Neopatriarchy: A Theory of Distorted Change in Arab Society.* Oxford University Press, New York

Asia, East and Southeast

Kai-ming Cheng, Suk-ying Wong and Nan-zhao Zhou

Both East and Southeast Asia have seen significant development in adult education since the 1950s, and a wide range of adult education facilities now exist in the region. The philosophies of learning and the structures and modes of delivery vary from country to country. In general, the development of adult education in the region is related to economic development, but it is also influenced by values and expectations as to the functions of education, which form part of the cultural heritage. In the latter context, the countries in the region can be broadly divided into two subregions: East Asia and Southeast Asia. The countries in each subregion share some commonalities amid diversity.

1. Adult Education in East Asia

East Asia is taken to mean societies including China (Mainland), Hong Kong, Japan, Korea (both South and North), Taiwan and, to an extent, Mongolia. Singapore and Vietnam share some of the East Asian characteristics in education, although geographically they belong to Southeast Asia. The societies in the East Asian subregion share some major cultural traditions, which can be conveniently viewed as stemming from a common Confucian heritage. In ancient Confucian communities, education was implemented mainly through the individual study of subject matter specified in a common core curriculum (the Four Books and Five Classics) and learning outcomes were evaluated using a common assessment (the civil examination at the imperial court). On top of some education received at an early age, the students usually studied and took the examination in their twenties or above. In essence, therefore, education in traditional Confucian communities was typically realized in the form of adult education with self-study.

Thus, although the emergence of formal adult education is rather recent in East Asian countries, the notion of adult education has never been foreign. This may help explain the comparative ease with which modern concepts and practices of adult education have been established in these societies. In Japan, for example, nongovernmental organizations began to promote adult educational activities such as the Meirokusha in 1873, and concepts such as "adult education" and "popular education" began to surface. The term "social education" first appeared in local newspapers and magazines in 1883. The first practice of distance education by correspondence was also introduced in that year. In China, to take another example, adult education activities in the modern sense were started as early as the 1840s by Western

missionaries, mainly for vocational training purposes. However, the systematic provision of adult education for the improvement of general literacy skills began much earlier.

1.1 Provision

Mainland China has perhaps the most elaborate system of adult education in the subregion. Adult education in China is offered at three levels: higher education, secondary education, and literacy and primary education. The main providers of adult education within the higher education sector include 40 radio and/or television universities, numerous workers' colleges, peasants' colleges, institutes for administration, colleges of education, and institutions or independent agencies offering correspondence and evening courses covering a full range of disciplines. Secondary education for adults comprises general study programs, vocational training, and courses specifically designed for the dissemination of technology. The latter courses are taught by various institutions using either a distance learning or an inservice mode. Literacy and primary classes for adults are also offered as evening courses attached to formal institutions.

The following figures give an impression of the size of the adult education effort in Mainland China. The number of students in adult higher education courses is in the order of 1.5 million, which can be compared with about 2 million in formal higher education. In addition, there is the newly created Self-study Higher Education Examination system, which attracted an additional 2 million adult learners (see *China, People's Republic*).

To simplify, adult education in Mainland China is developing in dual tracks. In the urban areas, there are programs oriented to formal credentials. These programs are quite similar in scope and organization to those in the other East Asian societies. In the rural areas, by contrast, adult learning programs are more focused on the development of essential literacy skills and training for technology and production. The latter programs are also common in the Southeast Asian countries.

Adult education in North Korea and Mongolia is very similar, in terms of its basic structure, to that in Mainland China, since both mirror the former Soviet model (see *Russian Federation*). Adult education in North Korea is perhaps more structured and planned than its Chinese counterpart, reflecting a higher degree of retention of the Soviet model. The Mongolian system is, however, undergoing reform following the change in the economic system.

In Japan, adult education is largely offered by formal institutions in part-time, evening, or correspondence modes at upper-secondary and higher education level. Formal institutions also offer extension courses which cater for professional upgrading or liberal arts studies ranging from languages to sports. There is the University of the Air, established in 1983, which has a single Faculty of Liberal Arts. Student enrollment in the University of the Air increased by 400 percent from 8,157 in 1985 to 41,468 in 1992. There are also the separate Special Training Schools (*Senshu-gakko*), with a distinct characteristic of offering vocational, technical, and liberal arts studies. Highly important also is Social Education (*Shakai Kyoiku*), which differs from other forms of adult education in that its programs cover elements that are not included in the curricula of institutions of formal education. In conclusion, the number of learners enrolled in adult education programs is comparatively small, but growing rapidly. It should be noted, moreover, that Japan is cultivating a culture of lifelong learning, in which self-study is emphasized in addition to more formal approaches to adult education (see *Japan: Social and Adult Education*).

In South Korea, adult education opportunities are offered by quasi-formal schools which are part of the social education system. Quasi-formal schools include civic schools, which offer an education equivalent to that of primary and secondary schools, trade schools, training institutions attached to industry, and evening classes attached to regular public schools. In addition there are 52 air and correspondence high schools, 6 open colleges, and the Korea Air and Correspondence University. Nonformal and informal adult education is offered through various media, the libraries, and youth organizations.

Adult education in Taiwan is classified under social education which also includes special education and informal educational facilities such as libraries and the media. The largest share in total provision is accounted for by supplementary schools providing remedial classes intended for young and mature adults who seek to take the public examinations that confer the general eligibility for admission to formal education courses at upper-secondary, college, or university levels. Many of the students are already enrolled in education but wish to prepare themselves for public examinations. Taiwan also has a University of the Air, which facilitates distance learning according to a fairly formal curriculum. It has a modest enrollment of less than 20,000 students.

In Hong Kong, adult education is a popular sector with a variety of programs at all levels offered largely by nongovernmental and commercial agencies. Apart from the Open Learning Institute, which specializes in degree-awarding courses for learners over the age of 21 years, numerous foreign institutions also offer "off-shore," distance-learning programs in higher education. The programs can largely be grouped into two

categories: those leading to formal degrees, qualifications, or professional recognitions; those providing recognized skills in, for example, language or secretarial tasks; and those that cater for personal and community development. A high percentage of school leavers and university graduates are engaged in adult education in one way or another.

1.2 Characteristics

East Asia is a subregion with strong traditions in education, regardless of the disparity in the level of economic development and the diversity in ideologies. In the Confucian tradition, the society is seen as a hierarchy where education presents a central means for achieving social mobility. In East Asian communities, the social function of education for qualifying and selecting people is not only a consequence, but rather, the built-in philosophy and aim of education. This underlies the high value people in these societies place on education. However, it also explains the usually rigid structure of the formal education systems, the comparative lack of variety and flexibility in the curriculum, and the tendency to value conformity and competition at the expense of individuality and creativity. These characteristics of education in general also infiltrate into the nonformal sector of education and adult education in particular. However, a large part of adult education in East Asian communities does not possess its own objectives independent from its formal counterparts. This can be seen in the following aspects.

In Mainland China, Japan, South Korea, and Taiwan, the mainstream of adult education at all levels (mostly accredited) admit students by formal entrance examinations. Only the best academically qualified students are selected. The Open University of Taiwan, and the Korea Air and Correspondence University admit, by interview, only high school graduates. In Mainland China, the majority of adult higher education programs admit students through an adult education entrance examination which is a unified national endeavor. Similarly, in the subregion, adult learning facilities at the upper-secondary level require formal academic qualifications. A philosophy of open admission, which is characteristic of much adult education provision in the Western countries, is not in the mainstream of thinking in East Asia. The only exceptions are, perhaps, the University of the Air in Japan, the Open Learning Institute in Hong Kong and the Self-study Examination in Mainland China; both of these are recent endeavors.

The curricula for most East Asian adult education programs follow closely those offered in the formal sector. The assessments that usually mark the end of a course of study are again almost identical with those used in institutions of formal education. Alternative curricula and alternative standards of achievement are nonconcepts in Mainland China. The situation in Taiwan reflects a similar philosophy. Much of what is adult education in Taiwan is offered in supplementary schools which are virtually tutorial schools. Their function is to provide remedial teaching to help students pass examinations, either academically or vocationally in character, which are designed for students in formal institutions.

Correspondence and evening courses are the most frequently used means of adult education in East Asian countries. In Japan, correspondence and evening study projects attract the majority of adult learners. A quota is usually set in regular universities for students seeking to enroll in formal correspondence courses or evening classes. In South Korea, adult education is largely implemented through spare-time attendance and correspondence learning. In Mainland China, students in corresponding and evening programs constitute more than 45 percent of students in all forms of adult higher education. Most of these programs are heavily supported by face-to-face tutorials. In Taiwan, the supplementary school courses are mostly taught in a face-to-face mode either during the day or in the evening. The emphasis on correspondence and face-to-face interactions is compatible with the general notion in the subregion that adult education should be as near to formal education as possible. Following the same notion, course materials in adult learning, even in the distance-learning modes, are not very different from those used in formal programs. A pedagogy of adult learning is yet to emerge in the entire East Asian subregion.

Perhaps the most outstanding feature of adult education in the East Asian subregion is its manpower orientation. In Japan and South Korea, adult education is often seen as a means of improving the quality of the labor force. In a relatively rigid labor market, participation in adult learning is rewarded only when it is sponsored and endorsed by the employer. Some of the adult learning facilities are actually attached to industry and are part of the in-house training mechanism. Free job-hunting or job-mobility achieved through adult education is rare. In Mainland China, North Korea, and Mongolia, the manpower orientation in adult education was reinforced by the socialist manpower planning approach that was inherited from the former Soviet model. In this model, participation in adult education programs requires permission from the work units. Credentials are used for promotion or remuneration purposes only when they fit in with the units' plans. Meanwhile, workers are given paid sabbatical leave to pursue adult education if it is part of the plan. There are workers' colleges in both Mainland China and North Korea which are financed and managed by the industry.

There are a number of corollaries to the manpower orientation in adult education in East Asian societies. First, most of the adult education endeavors in the subregion are financed by the government or by employers. The exception is Hong Kong where most adult learners pay from their private purse. Second,

emphasis and popularity are often with adult learning programs which lead to formal credentials. Third, whereas lifelong learning for cultural and community development is considered important, the notion of lifelong education for self-development and self-interest has, until recently, not been a part of the adult education policies in these countries.

However, with the advent of nontraditional ideologies in the subregion, open education in the international sense begins to emerge in East Asia. First, to various extents, adult education has become a means for job mobility for individuals. In Hong Kong and Taiwan, two examples of Chinese communities which thrive on a free-market economy, adult education is increasingly becoming a major means for individual career mobility and advantage. The establishment of the degree-awarding Open Learning Institute in Hong Kong (in 1989) and the University of the Air—also called the Open University—in Taiwan (in 1986) are symbols of this trend. In Mainland China, the Self-study Higher Education Examination, which requires no entrance qualification and no endorsement from the work unit, has been taken by over 2 million candidates, and their number is on the rise. The self-study examination prospers mainly because of the growing market element in the labor structure. "Open education" is also being introduced in Mongolia, again a reflection of the growth of the market economy.

Second, adult education programs that are not primarily credential or occupational in orientation are beginning to prosper in Hong Kong and Taiwan, where adult learners pursue studies purely for personal development and the satisfaction of leisure interests. In Hong Kong, this track is realized mainly through extramural studies offered by separate divisions of universities. In Taiwan, it occurs in social education which is taken to mean both nonformal and informal education with a strong undertone of moral education. To some extent this is also happening in Japan and South Korea. National education reforms announced by both Japan (in 1987) and South Korea (1987) included lifelong learning as a major objective. Traditionally, such sectors of adult education fall under the category of social education in both Japan and South Korea. Apart from this proliferation of delivery modes, in rural China, adult education usually takes the form of literacy programs, which are increasingly integrated with the dissemination of agricultural technology.

2. Adult Education in Southeast Asia

Southeast Asia consists of a number of highly dynamic societies. Most of the countries in Southeast Asia have seen substantial economic development since the late 1980s and with it has come a rapid development of the educational systems. In the context of a growing demand for education, the development in adult education in this subregion is most spectacular in the realm of distance learning as an alternative to more formal and expensive means of improving education (see *Evaluation of Distance Education: Cost-Effectiveness*).

2.1 Provision

Adult education in Indonesia is administered by the Directorate General of Out-of-School Education, Youth and Sports (*Diklusepora*). There are a large number of *penetarans,* which are short courses run by ministries or other government agencies. There is also the Kejar Program which constitutes the nonformal sector of compulsory education aiming at the improvement of literacy skills for employment and income generation (see *Asia, Southeast: Literacy*). Distance adult education in Indonesia is mainly used for the preparation of primary and junior secondary teachers. Apart from adult learning programs provided by public and private institutions of higher learning, the major provider of distance adult education is the University of Terbuka, established in 1984, which is the only open university in Indonesia. There is no entrance examination and virtually all high school graduates or any associated qualification are recognized. The University of Terbuka has four Faculties: economics, social and political sciences, mathematics and natural science, and teaching and education sciences. The University is a print mode based distance education institution with 96 percent of instruction realized with the help of printed materials. It collaborates closely with local, often private firms in providing on-the-job education and training. While the firms facilitate the teaching/learning process, the University provides the learning material and confers the official accreditation.

Adult education in Laos is placed under the provision of nonformal education by the national ministry, which aims at literacy training for out-of-school youth and adults, especially for those living in villages in rural areas. The ministry is the sole provider of adult education through the broadcast of three educational radio programs for half an hour on Radio Nationale Lao three times each week in the evening. Teacher education, preschool activities, morality, social and physical education, and study skills are the main content areas addressed.

Apart from adult education programs provided by voluntary agencies, distance higher education remains the largest sector in adult education in Malaysia. The largest of such is the Off-campus Program provided by the Universiti Sains Malaysia. Established in 1971, the Off-campus Program has since grown from the provision of 8 courses in the humanities and social sciences to a total of 125 courses including one in foundation science in 1991. The current number of students enrolled in the program is approximately 3,000, with school teachers constituting the single largest occupational group of learners (around 60%). A minimum entry qualification together with written consent from the employer is set as the requirement for admission. About half of the students in the Off-campus Programs are 30 to 34 years of age. Planning for the establishment of an open university is under progress in Malaysia. Such an institution will increase the supply of both general and vocational continuing education targeted to the Malaysian adults.

The purpose of adult education in Myanmar is three-fold: to bring forth a more equitable basis for higher education, to serve as an inservice training ground for teachers, and to provide continuing education for the working adults at a lower cost than through regular, formal education. The most substantial activities in adult education in Myanmar are carried out in the distance learning mode. The University Correspondence Courses, established in 1976, have recently become a part of the recognized government sector. The admission requirements to the University Correspondence Courses are similar to those demanded in the regular, full-time courses offered by the affiliated universities and colleges. Courses are offered in four major disciplinary areas: arts, science, economics, and law. Apart from teacher education, no other vocational courses are provided. As of 1992, the student enrollment was 78,908 (excluding the teacher education program), with the majority of the students enrolled in the arts faculty. The program is print based and supplemented by personal tutorials. The underdeveloped postal system in the country presents constant problems, given the heavy reliance on printed materials as the primary mode of instruction.

A wide range of adult education programs exist in the Philippines, offered both by government and nongovernment agencies, with the latter taking the major share in total provision. Programs extend from literacy, nutrition, health, and energy conservation to life skills and entrepreneurship. There is the Bureau of Nonformal Education within the Ministry of Education that oversees all the adult education programs. There is also the School Broadcast Program, which provides through the radio enrichment programs. The Continuing Learning Delivery System provides alternatives to formal secondary education to enable primary school levels to eventually pursue higher education. The "Balik Paaralan" scheme is a bridging device for accrediting nonschool learning experience for formal qualifications. Another element of provision is the Home Study Program in the University of Life which offers open learning opportunities leading to certificates of proficiency. Some programs are specifically designed for teacher education. Among these are the Continuing Education of Teachers project and the University of Mindanao On-the-air. The former aims at facilitating the upgrading of elementary school teachers through printed as well as audiovisual materials. The latter is to assist teachers in remote areas who seek to pursue studies at master's level through radio lectures and forums.

Singapore. Adult education is not a major government

endeavor in Singapore. Most adult education programs are provided by overseas institutions or commercial operations which are usually small in scale. Most of the programs lead to formal qualifications that are often accredited overseas. The government, however, supports the National Productivity Board which offers occupational training and courses in technical areas.

The Department of Nonformal Education (established in 1979) is responsible for adult education in Thailand. Adult education in this country started with literacy programs, moved on to vocational training, and has extended into distance higher education. There are over 40 agencies providing adult education programs. Although the concept of distance education was first initiated in Thailand in 1933 with the establishment of the University of Moral and Political Sciences, the full adoption of distance education techniques was formally introduced at the establishment, in 1978, of the Sukhothai Thammathirat Open University as the major provider of higher education in the country. Ramkamhaeng University provides another avenue of opportunity for adult distance learners as a conventional university. The objective is to open and expand the opportunities for working adults and others who, for whatever reasons, are unable to attend conventional colleges and universities, to acquire a higher education. As of 1992, the number of students enrolled by the Sukhothai Thammathirat Open University is about 450,000, of which 445,000 are studying at the first degree level. With only about 9 percent of the student body being simultaneously registered as unemployed, the Sukhothai Thammathirat possesses a distinct function of training inservice occupational groups, of which over 60 percent are employed in the public service sector.

Adult education in Vietnam used to follow the Russian model, as was the case in Mainland China, North Korea, and Mongolia mentioned above. The system is under rapid reform following a change in policy in economic and cultural affairs. The Vietnam National Institute of Open Learning, established in 1988, has 22 study centers spread across the country. It is mainly a vehicle for higher education with nonexpensive means. The planning of a Vietnam People's Open University is also under way. Adult education and open learning in Vietnam are largely based on printed materials, and a strong emphasis is attached to language learning. Audio cassettes, however, are also used as an instructional aid. Special public information programs are also designed for youths in remote and mountainous areas.

2.2 Characteristics

There are a number of identifiable characteristics of adult education in the Southeast Asian subregion. First, unlike the East Asian communities, much of adult education in Southeast Asia is either a private endeavor or sponsored by nongovernmental agencies.

The government is usually not the major sponsor of adult education programs in the subregion. This is understandable in the context that on the one hand, most of the countries in Southeast Asia are still developing economies; on the other hand, there is an increasing demand for education due to rapid economic and social change. The governments generally do not have much to spend on education and adult education, but can be offered by mobilizing community and private resources. In general, adult education is perceived as a low cost alternative to formal education, both at basic and higher education levels.

Second, distance learning is a widely adopted mode of instruction. The range of modes of instruction goes from heavily print-based programs to utilization of audio or visual telecommunication. The technology utilized is obviously dependent on the economic development of the country. In the more advanced countries in Southeast Asia, such as Thailand and Malaysia, open learning with multi-media approaches are not uncommon. In other, economically more disadvantaged countries print materials and face-to-face instruction are still the major modes of communication.

Third, adult education programs in Southeast Asia are not all formally accredited. This is unlike East Asia where adult learning is not respected and in low demand unless it awards a qualification or credential. In Southeast Asian countries, only a small part of adult education, usually at tertiary level, confers formal awards. Certificates or some form of recognition are sometimes given, but they may not carry much currency. Perhaps this is due to the large size of the nonformal sector in these countries, where a job market is still nonexistent and credentials are essential only in the urban centres.

Fourth, there are two distinct goals of adult education in Southeast Asian countries: literacy and life-skills, and teacher education. The vast majority of the numerous adult education programs in Southeast Asian countries are offered to rural out-of-school youth and young adults as a second chance to obtain basic education. Many of these programs seek to relate to the economic lives of the participants. At levels above basic education, a large percentage of adult education is devoted to teacher education, either for qualifying the unqualified or for upgrading practicing teachers. To a lesser extent, adult education is also a means for training civil servants at an acceptable cost. This is natural, since teachers and civil servants form the largest groups of intellectuals in most of the developing countries in the subregion.

3. Overview

East Asia and Southeast Asia have enjoyed a similar trend of favorable economic growth and social, democratic development in recent decades, and adult education has also seen remarkable development as complementary to expansion in formal education.

Cultural heritage and degree of urbanization seem to be the two factors determining the goals, status, and modes of adult education in East Asian and Southeast Asian communities. In communities characterized by a relatively high degree of urbanization, such as most East Asian countries, any cities in China and Singapore which also happen to share some Confucian heritage, adult education is very formal in nature in terms of the entrance criteria, curriculum orientation, and credentialism that are applied. More open, distance types of learning are also possible because of the adoption of modern technology, although by tradition correspondence and evening classes are still most popular. In most of the developing communities in Southeast Asia and, for example, in rural areas in China, the main purpose of adult education is to raise the level of basic literacy and to improve the living and production conditions of the learners. It has to be added that, in the latter case, there are attempts to integrate various efforts of education to achieve comprehensive purposes, and adult education forms an essential part of this effort. This is the case with the UNESCO initiated APPEAL (Asia Pacific Program of Education for All) project, where participating countries try to integrate Universalization of Primary Education (UPE), Eradication of Illiteracy (EOI), and Continuing Education for Development (CED). It is also the case in Mainland China where the government advocates a triple integration of basic education, vocational education, and adult education in the rural areas.

See also: Asia, Southeast: Literacy; China: People's Republic; Japan: Social and Adult Education; Japan: Vocational Education and Training

Bibliography

Asian Development Bank (ed.) 1987 *Distance Education in Asia and the Pacific*, 2 vols. Asian Development Bank, Manila

Cheng K M 1990 *Review and Prospects of Educational Planning and Management in Asia and the Pacific: Regional Study.* Report prepared for the UNESCO Congress on "Planning and Management of Educational Development," March 26–30, 1990, Mexico City

China, State Education Commission 1991 *Educational statistical yearbook of China 1990.* People's Education Press, Beijing

Japan, Ministry of Education, Science and Culture 1985 *Adult Education in Japan.* Government Printing Office, Tokyo

Korea, Ministry of Education 1991 *Education in Korea 1990–91.* Republic of Korea, Ministry of Education, Seoul

Miura S, Matsushita T, Nakamura M, Suezaki F (eds.) 1992 *Lifelong Learning in Japan: An Introduction.* National Federation of Social Education in Japan, Tokyo

Republic of China, Ministry of Education 1992 *Educational Statistics of the Republic of China, 1992.* Ministry of Education, Taipei

Stevenson H W, Stigler J W 1992 *The Learning Gap: Why our Schools are Failing and What we can Learn from Japanese and Chinese Education.* Summit Books, New York.

Tung C P 1990 *Historical Outline of Adult Education in China.* Chinese Labour Press, Beijing

UNESCO Principal Regional Office for Asia and the Pacific 1987 *Continuing Education in Asia and the Pacific* (Bulletin 28). UNESCO, Bangkok

Wong S Y (ed.) 1992 *Asia and the Pacific: A Survey of Distance Education 1992*, Vols 1 and 2. New Papers on Higher Education and Research. UNESCO, Paris

Asia, Southeast: Literacy

W. P. Napitupulu

This entry presents an overview of literacy education in countries in Southeast Asia, particularly in Indonesia, Malaysia, the Philippines, Thailand, and Vietnam. Special reference is made to the design, implementation, and evaluation of literacy programs in Indonesia. The emphasis is on the situation in the 1980s and 1990s, rather than on historical development.

1. Terminology

Preliteracy, functional literacy, and postliteracy programs are seen as a continuing process. Preliteracy aims mainly to motivate the learners; the central purpose of adult education and functional literacy programs is to develop basic literacy and numeracy skills. Postliteracy is intended to sustain, improve, and broaden these literacy skills. In this context, literacy education is seen as referring not only to the organized provision of functional knowledge, skills, and information but also to the systematic inculcation of new values and attitudes. The term "continuing education" is increasingly being used in Southeast Asia, especially since the proclamation of the Asia–Pacific Program of Education for All (APPEAL) by the Director-General of UNESCO in New Delhi, India on February 23, 1987. Continuing education (UNESCO–PROAP 1987) is defined as:

> Activities which help people improve their abilities, skills and competence, professional as well as vocational, thus facilitating entry into advanced specialized areas and/or which allow personal development and satisfaction.

"Lifelong learning" is a second concept that is

Table 1
Number of adult illiterates by sex, 1960–2000 (15 years and over; actual data and forecast)

	1957	1970	1980	1990	2000
Indonesia					
Total	28,574,932	24,344,654	18,336.242	6,955,900	—
Male	11,143,217	8,863,639	6,494,598	2,306,600	—
Female	17,431,715	15,481,015	11,841,644	4,649,300	—
Malaysia					
Total	2,061,468	3,274,000	2,379,925	2,377,925	1,710,380
Male	803,972	1,237,000	754,480	754,480	684,152
Female	1,257,496	2,037,000	1,623,445	1,623,445	1,026,228
Philippines					
Total (percentage)	28.0	16.9	13.5	11.0	8.0
Male	3,818,772	3,029,558	3,276,116	3,420,396	3,109,995
Female	3,272,937	3,060,066	3,256,270	3,387,985	3,066,750
Thailand					
Total	4,825,864	4,041,210	3,296,606	—	—
Male	1,552,927	1,224,012	1,049,664	—	—
Female	3,272,937	2,817,198	2,246,942	—	—

Source: Data reported by national authorities to UNESCO–PROAP (1988)

becoming increasingly fashionable in the region. This term has been promoted as a consequence of the Inter-Agency World Declaration on Education for All in Jomtien, Thailand on March 9, 1990. Both continuing education and lifelong learning are considered appropriate concepts because they imply continuation and complementarity in the education and training of youth and adults. This advantage notwithstanding, however, by the early 1990s, the concepts "nonformal education" and "out-of-school education," including adult literacy, were still more widely used in the Philippines, Thailand, and Indonesia than either "continuing education" or "lifelong learning."

Indonesia has preferred—as a consequence of Law No. 2 on the National System of Education enacted on March 27, 1989—to use the terms "in-school education" and "out-of-school education" instead of "formal" and "nonformal" education, because this bypasses some conceptual and interpretative difficulties (see *Formal, Nonformal, and Informal Education*). The term "complementary education" is widely used in North Korea and Vietnam to refer to the production oriented provision of educational programs for adults. In Malaysia, adult education is not administered by the Ministry of Education but by the Ministry of National and Rural Development through its Community Development Division. In this country, adult education is therefore often referred to as "community development."

2. Scope of the Literacy Problem

Much importance is attached to literacy education in the Southeast Asian region. Literacy education is widely considered a key factor in promoting national development—especially socioeconomic and cultural development. There is also a common awareness that the quality of human resources must be improved in order to enable people and communities to solve the many different problems facing them—physical, health, nutrition, family planning, intellectual, sociopsychological, political, and economic problems. Finally, there is a realization that rapid innovations in science and technology make it necessary to stimulate literacy and lifelong learning for all.

The countries in the region are very conscious of the fact that unless people are literate it may not be possible for them to fully support national development efforts. Also, the ideas of "education for all" and "all for education" suggest, especially to this region, that concerted efforts must be made to eradicate illiteracy by the year 2000.

The scope of this task can be inferred from Table 1, which shows the number of adult illiterates 15 years of age and over by sex in Indonesia, Malaysia, the Philippines, and Thailand from 1960 to 2000 (UNESCO–PROAP 1988). As the data were collected in national case studies and surveys conducted in 1987 and 1988, the estimates for 1990 and 2000 must be projections.

3. Regional Organization and Cooperation

3.1 UNESCO

Especially since 1980, regional cooperation and exchange have increased rapidly. The UNESCO Principal Regional Office for Asia and the Pacific (UNESCO–PROAP) has been the prime mover, particularly through the Asia–Pacific Program of Educational Innovation for Development (APEID) and the Asia Pacific Program of Education for All (APPEAL). The APEID, a major regional program, is primarily intended to help the teachers of youth and adults in improving learning–teaching processes and thus enhancing learning performance.

The APPEAL has three interrelated action areas: (a) universalization of primary education, (b) eradication of illiteracy, and (c) continuing education for development. Most countries in the region have set up a National Coordinating Committee for APPEAL, which oversees and coordinates the national activities in the three action areas. The program of education for all is supported by UNESCO–PROAP, which is working closely with member states to expand and improve primary education and to develop literacy programs. For example, the APPEAL Training Materials for Literacy Personnel (ATLP) are widely used to improve the quality of literacy activities in the region. Moreover, UNESCO–PROAP (1991) developed the widely used APPEAL Training Materials for Continuing Education Personnel (ATLP–CE).

3.2 Other Major Initiatives

UNICEF is also very active in the region. It plays an active role in assisting illiteracy-eradication programs with income-generating activities for women. UNFPA too is very active, providing the funds needed for implementing a variety of programs related to population and family planning education. The Southeast Asian Ministers of Education Organization (SEAMEO) encourages exchanges of personnel, experiences, and materials, and promotes regional training activities and research studies through its centers, in particular the Regional Center for Educational Innovation and Technology (INNOTECH).

Since 1980, the Asian Cultural Center for UNESCO (ACCU), in Tokyo, Japan, has been instrumental in improving literacy programs in the region though the provision and joint production of audiovisual aids and learning materials. The Asia South-Pacific Bureau of Adult Education (APBAE) has also given an impetus to motivating the educators in the region to plan relevant programs for adult learners.

The Association of Southeast Asian Nations (ASEAN) runs politically and culturally motivated adult education and training programs in the six member countries: Brunei Darussalam, Indonesia, Malaysia, the Philippines, Singapore, and Thailand.

4. Program Management and Provision

Apart from Malaysia, literacy education is the main responsibility of the Education Ministry. In Thailand, the Department of Nonformal Education, Ministry of Education, carries overall responsibility. The parallel agency in Indonesia is the Directorate-General of Out-of-School Education, Youth, and Sports, Ministry of Education and Culture; in the Philippines it is the Bureau of Nonformal Education, Ministry of Education, Culture, and Sports; and in Vietnam it is the Department of Complementary Education, Ministry of Education.

The systems of education in the region are generally development oriented. Educational programs for the promotion of literacy, rural development, community development, and national integration are considered to form central elements of these systems. The main provision of literacy education tends to be governmental, although there is also vigorous voluntary and nongovernmental activity, with many different organizations implementing literacy education programs.

The delivery systems for literacy education tend to be organized at the grassroots level, utilizing not only teachers but any educated personnel and any facility that may be available in the towns and villages—homes, mosques, churches, community halls, schools, and so forth. Many channels of formal and nonformal delivery are used so as to make literacy education effective in reaching out to a wide audience. Moreover, people's participation in the organization and provision of literacy education is actively encouraged. For example, in Indonesia, a grand strategy and policy has been introduced to enhance the education and training of the people by means of a "self-multiplication" process based on a chain-reaction system with geometric progression: 1–10–100–1000, and so on. "Each one teach ten!" is a popular slogan in Indonesia.

The countries in the region seek to strengthen the involvement in literacy education of the "working committees" at the provincial, district, municipality, and village levels, enabling these committees to identify target groups, to set up strategies for implementation, to allocate human and financial resources, to monitor and evaluate ongoing educational activities, and to report back to the relevant authorities. The members of such committees are not only the relevant government officials, but also people from a variety of nongovernmental organizations, including community leaders.

At the village level, there is a "coordinator" (in Thailand) or a "facilitator" (in Indonesia) who is responsible for organizing the learning activities of 10 illiterates (in accordance with the approach of "each one teach ten"). The coordinator or facilitator may be a community leader or another appropriate volunteer. Volunteer teachers play a particularly important role in strengthening both literacy and continuing education programs. Target groups for these programs are the illiterate population, school dropouts and rural women.

Financial resources for the literacy and continuing education programs are being tapped from national, provincial, district, and subdistrict governments, from village communities and from industries and factories participating in the literacy education effort.

5. Implementation: The Learning Kejar Packet A

Although subject to some criticism as well, the "Learning Kejar Packet A" of Indonesia, which comprises 100 Packet A teaching booklets, was awarded the International Reading Association Literacy Award in 1982. The Kejar Packet A literacy learning materials also won the Nessim Habib Prize in 1985.

The Learning Kejar Packet A program does not identify with the usual illiteracy eradication program because it was designed (Ministry of Education and Culture 1977) to serve preliteracy, literacy, and postliteracy programs simultaneously. It aims to address three kinds of issues: (a) knowledge of Latin characters and Arabic numerals; (b) teaching of Bahasa Indonesia (the national language); and (c) functional knowledge, work skills, and a development-oriented attitude. The program is designed as an out-of-school (nonformal) educational program equivalent to an in-school (formal) course of primary education.

The ideas and objectives to be pursued by the program are imbued in the word *kejar*. This Indonesian word means literally "to catch-up with what is lagging". The target groups for this program are illiterates and primary school dropouts, and since 1990—the International Literacy Year—they have been at least 7 years of age. The first priority is given to children up to 15 years old, while the second priority is given to those 16–25 years of age. However, in the villages, the members of a learning group most often consist of people of different ages.

In order to implement this program effectively, learning materials known as "Packet A" have been developed. Packet A is a collection of minimum learning materials covering all spheres of life which should be mastered by all illiterates and primary-school dropouts in order that they become responsible, well-informed, and productive citizens. This collection of learning materials is in the form of books, posters, pamphlets, cassette recordings, slides, and films that contain knowledge, skills, and desired attitudes. Packet A will assist the learner to become a "whole" Indonesian with *Pancasila* (morals), because it includes, as well as religious and spiritual teachings based on the belief in God Almighty, units on (a) family and community life; (b) rights and duties of a citizen; (c) environmental awareness; (d) family welfare education; (e) career orientation; (f) literacy, reading, writing, arithmetic, and the Indonesian national language; and (g) community health.

In book format, Packet A consists of 100 booklets arranged in 22 blocks with increasing levels of difficulty. These may be visualized as a T-shaped format (A-1 to A-20 is the vertical leg of letter T, or the "pillar of knowledge"; A-21 to A-60 is half of the horizontal cross-bar and A-61 to A-100 the other half. These comprise the following series:

(a) A-1 to A-20 consist of integrated lessons in basic reading, writing, and arithmetic, and the Indonesian language. The booklets are staggered: the contents of previous numbers become the bases of the next number, so A-1 is the basis for A-2, and so forth. A-1 through A-10 (blue cover) consist of ten units called "Literacy and Numeracy," while A-11 through A-20 (green cover), A-21 through A-60 (pink cover), and A-61 to A-100 (yellow cover) have individual titles, such as "Home Gardening" (A-11), "Planting Fruit Trees" (A-12), "Poultry" (A-13), "Fish Culture" (A-14), and so on.

(b) A-21 through A-60 comprises more advanced readings and contain additional basic knowledge and skills concerning various aspects of life. They reinforce what is being discussed in the previous books. The level of difficulty of all these books is the same, and is not staggered as in A-1 to A-20. If a learner can read A-21, he or she can also read A-60. For instance, A-21 discusses "God, Man, and Nature," while A-22 refers to "Religions and Beliefs in Indonesia," and A-23 refers to "*Pancasila*," and so forth.

(c) A-61 through A-100 is the second selection of advanced readings. They discuss the wider and more specific aspects of various spheres of life. This series is more advanced than the previous ones, the level of difficulty being one step beyond A-21 to A-60. A sample of the series includes: "Hindu Religious Holidays" (A-61), "Buddhist Religious Holidays" (A-62), "The Arrangement of Leaf, Flower, and Fruit" (A-63), and "Traditional Customs in Sumatera" (A-64).

6. New Emphases on Literacy Education

The general directions of the life of the nation (the decision of the People's Consultative Assembly of Indonesia, which is the highest authority in the country) have stated clearly that: (a) the work productivity level of the people must be raised in order to boost production; (b) new employment opportunities must be developed in order to be able to accommodate the more than one million new entrants annually into the labor market; and (c) there must be a more equitable distribution of wealth, that is, the results of development efforts must be shared by all societal strata. This means that development programs and projects in all fields, including education, must be geared to help the have-nots, or to bridge the existing gap between the haves and the have-nots.

In the presidential state address before the Parliament on August 16, 1978, the President of the Republic of Indonesia emphasized that "a new effort to fight illiteracy in a new style" must be carried out. These new efforts are intended not only to abolish illiteracy in Latin characters and numeracy, but also to abolish ignorance of the Indonesian national language, and to raise the level of basic education. This is one of the reasons why literacy education in Indonesia has been successful in reducing the estimated number of 21 million illiterates in 1977 to less than 4 million by the mid-1990s. The success of the literacy campaign in Indonesia, which has been financed by funds borrowed from the World Bank, is to no small extent due to the development and implementation of the Kejar Packet A program.

7. Research and Evaluation

The educators in this region are aware of the need for conducting research and evaluation studies in the field of literacy education. However, there are two main constraints why research and evaluation activities have not developed to the desired extent. First, the problems to be solved are immense and urgent; they require quick-yielding research activities, so that attention is paid more to action research than to the long-term sustenance of quantitative research projects. Second, because the problems are so immense, even the most capable researchers are drawn upon to implement literacy programs.

The research studies on literacy conducted in the region focus not only on factors related to the learning process, but also on questions such as how to promote literacy and reading. Since the oral tradition is still very strong, the literacy program should seek an equilibrium between written and oral traditions.

Much of the research is action oriented, dealing with topics such as literacy conditions and related aspects, the effectiveness of illiteracy eradication models, evaluation of the needs of learners, the progress of project implementation, and the effectiveness of the learning materials.

A survey carried out in Indonesia within the framework of the APPEAL initiative has shown how difficult it is to collect valid information on literacy in this huge archipelago state. There is some indication that this also applies to other countries in the region. Some of the findings of research conducted under the auspices of the Research and Development Unit of the Ministry of Education and Culture on the implementation of the Learning Kejar Packet A program may be stated as follows:

(a) More concerted effort must be made on the motivation of learners, but also of the tutors, monitors, and community education supervisors for the sustenance of the program.

(b) More serious effort must be made on the dissemination of adequate learning materials, especially Packet A-1 to A-100.

(c) More regular monitoring and evaluation visits must be made by the community education super-visors to the learning groups in the villages.

(d) The Learning Kejar Packet A should be implemented simultaneously with an income-generating activity intended to combat poverty among the learners, especially subsequent to the successful completion of Packet A-20.

UNESCO–PROAP has stimulated and encouraged the member states to carry out national studies on education for all, including literacy education. The studies (UNESCO–PROAP 1988) refer to the situation in each as regards policies, programs and programming, organizational structure for out-of-school and nonformal education, financial resources, community participation and local resources mobilization, technical support, training of teachers and other personnel, and monitoring and evaluation practices.

In the future, research should not only be concerned with practice. Fundamental research is also needed, because not only are the literacy education activities of the people relevant, but also the learning process itself.

See also: UNESCO and Adult Education; Asia, East and Southeast

References

Ministry of Education and Culture, Republic of Indonesia 1977 *What Is Packet A?* Ministry of Education and Culture, Jakarta

UNESCO–PROAP 1987 *Continuing Education in Asia and the Pacific.* Bulletin No. 28, September. UNESCO Principal Regional Office for Asia and the Pacific, Bangkok

UNESCO–PROAP 1988 *National Studies: Malaysia, Philippines, Thailand, Vietnam, Indonesia.* UNESCO Principal Regional Office for Asia and the Pacific, Bangkok

UNESCO–PROAP 1991 APPEAL *Training Materials for Continuing Education Personnel (ATLP–CE).* UNESCO Principal Regional Office for Asia and the Pacific, Bangkok

Further Reading

Adams D 1970 *Education and Modernization in Asia.* Addison–Wesley, Reading, Massachusetts

Duke C 1989 Provision in Southeast Asia. In: Titmus C J (ed.) 1989 *Lifelong Education for Adults: An International Handbook.* Pergamon Press, Oxford

UNESCO 1989 Forty Literacy Lessons. Document prepared for the World Conference on Education for All, March 5–9 1990, Jomtien, Thailand. UNESCO international Bureau of Education, Geneva

World Conference on Education for All 1990 *World Declaration on Education for All and Framework for Action to Meet Basic Learning Needs.* Inter-agency Commission, New York

Lind A, Johnston A 1990 *Adult Literacy in the Third World: A Review of Objectives and Strategies.* Swedish International Development Authority, Stockholm

Napitupulu W P 1990 *On Literacy in Indonesia: A Key to Modern Life.* UNESCO, Jakarta

Australia and New Zealand

G. Caldwell

Adult education is becoming increasingly important in Australia and New Zealand. Several factors are contributing to this development. These factors are explained in this entry. Moreover, in this entry attention is given to the extent of participation in adult education in Australia and New Zealand. The major types and providers, and the government's role in adult education are also discussed. Adult education and training are dealt with separately for the two countries concerned.

1. Federal Government Education Policy

To achieve competitiveness in international markets, the Australian Government is encouraging investment in human capital through education, especially at the tertiary level. As a result of these federal initiatives, the post-secondary and higher education system is experiencing rapid change and readjustment —in practice, provision, and management. The following developments have been the most prominent since 1985:

(a) There has been a substantial increase in the number of students remaining in the education system beyond the compulsory years (generally above the age of 15). In the early 1990s, for example, just under 70 percent of Australian secondary school students who commenced Grade 7 completed Grade 12.

(b) There has been strong emphasis on vocational skills in the curriculum of tertiary education providers, so that graduates emerge from institutions with competences and skills that are expected to contribute to the needs of the economy.

(c) The Federal Government introduced a training levy which requires firms and organizations with an annual payroll above US $135,000 to expend upwards of 1 percent of their payroll tax on adult education and training.

(d) Adult and continuing education have been given a new status by the Federal Government. In the White Paper of 1988, the Minister observed that adult and continuing education are a fundamental part of the education and training system, and that the principle of lifelong education is now accepted as fundamental to achieving social, cultural, technological, and structural change, and to improving the prospects for future economic development.

(e) There has also been an increase in resources allocation. For a three-year period commencing in 1993, the Federal Government has allocated US $100,000 a year to assist the work of the Australian Association for Adult and Community Education, and US $300,000 annually for research in the field.

2. The Status of Adult Education in Australia

Adult education has lacked a clear identity within Australian education, but beginning in the late 1980s this position is changing, as practitioners increasingly accept adult education as the fourth sector— alongside primary, secondary, and tertiary education. Even so, public funds for adult education have been forthcoming only sparingly.

A significant turning point in the development of Australian adult education came with the publication of a report of the Senate Standing Committee on Employment, Education, and Training, *Come in Cinderella: The Emergence of Adult and Community Education* (SSC 1991). In the report, which constitutes the first national account of adult and continuing education since 1944, when a report was prepared by W Duncan for the Universities Commission, the Senate Committee argued that adult and community education must

> finally receive the recognition that it has long deserved, and should take its place as a valued partner with the established education sectors—schools, TAFE and higher education—in providing Australians with the skills, knowledge and confidence to create their future. (SSC 1991 p. 4)

3. Participation in Adult and Community Education

In the mid-1980s about 1 million adults annually participated in Australian adult education (Johnson and Hinton 1986). However, this figure did not include those undertaking industrial training, estimated to be 2.3 million by the Business Council of Australia. A study undertaken for the Federal Department of Employment, Education, and Training found that over 60 percent of adults had taken an adult education course, and that the average person had taken three. Men and women were about equally likely to have undertaken courses; most participants had only average levels of formal education; participation was highest among young adults, although there was significant participation by all adult age groups; and many took job-related courses which subsequently led to increased individual earnings (Evans 1986).

In 1991 and 1992, some 3.5 million adults in a total population (21 and over) of just under 12 million took part in an organized adult education activity.

4. Types of Adult Education Provision

Adult education in Australia is marked by diversity of provision, purposes, and method. Four broad types of provision can be identified: adult basic education, general/liberal adult education, continuing vocational education and training, and public education (AAACE 1991 pp. 4–6).

4.1 Adult Basic Education

Until the early 1980s, it had been assumed that sufficient primary and secondary education had been offered to meet the basic needs of Australians. But the growing diversity of ethnicity in Australia, coupled with the growing demand on schools have combined to produce a demand for basic adult education. Adult basic education encompasses literacy, numeracy, communication skills, basic science, humanities, and common social science, up to the equivalent of upper secondary education. Basic education includes learning about basic personal skills, such as knowledge about health, problem solving, conflict resolution, and English as a second language. As a result of the International Literacy Year, funding for literacy programs has expanded both in Australia and New Zealand.

It has been estimated that 10 percent of Australian adults lack education at this basic level of literacy (Wickert 1989). In 1990, nearly 45,000 students were enrolled in adult literacy programs in Australia (Coopers and Lybrand 1990).

4.2 General and Liberal Adult Education

This category of adult education is the best-known form of adult education in Australia. In courses of this kind, individuals, often with considerable educational experience have opportunities for intellectual, artistic, and recreational enrichment. These courses, despite their leisure focus, place a significant intellectual demand on the participants. However, this adult education tradition has been on the defensive throughout the 1980s. As economic conditions worsened and unemployment grew, attention has focused on education and training for gaining a job. Accordingly, the level of public support for leisure-oriented courses has dropped markedly, both in the universities, the TAFE colleges, and evening schools.

Noting this development, the Australian Association for Adult and Community Education (AAACE

1991), the representative body for the field, recognized that adult education courses for general interest and recreation are a private good, and that such provision should recover part or all of its cost. However, participation in liberal adult education can also be seen as a public good, as in the example of women seeking to re-enter the labor market or embarking on a course of formal, credential adult education. Another argument in support of liberal adult education is that it contributes not only to individual well-being, but also to community development.

4.3 Continuing Vocational Education

Since the late 1980s this type of education or training has rapidly expanded, especially within industry. Employers tend to attach more importance to continuing professional education. Participation in continuing vocational education has individual, organizational, and national benefits, enhanced career opportunities for the individual, greater efficiency, effectiveness, and profitability for the organization, and overall increased competitiveness of Australian firms.

4.4 Public Education Provision

Public education is an activity in which organizations endeavor to inform and educate the public on issues such as AIDS awareness, heart disease prevention, and discouragement of drug-taking. Some public education campaigns may be aimed at changing attitudes, values, and behaviors by utilizing the mass media to inform individuals on matters affecting the quality of life or aspects of human conduct. Universities have traditionally played an important role in the provision of public education through the conduct of seminars, courses, and conferences.

5. Providing Agencies

In 1989, the AAACE compiled a national directory of adult and community education associations, listing some 900 agencies clustered into five categories of providers: formal educational institutions, government departments and their agencies, community providers, private sector providers, and labor market organizations (AAACE 1991 pp. 7–10).

5.1 Formal Educational Institutions

Educational institutions such as schools, secondary colleges, technical and further education (TAFE) colleges, and universities represent a significant conglomerate of adult education providers. The situation varies from state to state but secondary colleges and universities usually enroll a significant number of adults. The great majority of programs and courses on after are noncredential, but there are signs that for-credit provision is expanding.

In an analysis of adult and continuing education activities in Australian universities, carried out in 1992, 38 centers, departments, or offices were identified (Caldwell and Heslop 1991). The work of these centers fell into three broad areas. First, in the academic area, activities are associated with traditional academic awards. Provision ranges from bridging courses and preparatory studies for overseas students to formal courses and awards. The education and training of adult educators and teachers for technical and further education colleges in those award programs is the primary task for a number of university departments. In addition, academic activities include accredited courses for professionals, audit programs which allow individuals to join undergraduate courses, and research in adult and continuing education.

The second type of activity concerns continuing vocational education offered on a full cost-recovery basis. This area of work has become central to many adult education departments in Australian universities. Professional development courses, in-house training courses, the operation of conference centers and conference secretariat work are included in this category.

Finally, within the liberal adult education sector, nonaward summer schools and community education courses dominate.

5.2 Government Departments and their Agencies

Government departments or agencies provide much adult education, but often do not regard the education and training activities they undertake as adult education. Examples are agricultural extension, health education, and marriage counseling. A second area involves the training of the public sector workforce. The volume of training in this area is often substantial.

State governments generally have a more diverse commitment to adult education. While some states confine their activity in adult education to TAFE (Western Australia, Tasmania, and Queensland), other governments (Victoria) have chosen a more substantial involvement in the nongovernment adult education sector. Accordingly, the level of public funding differs markedly among the states.

5.3 Community Providers

Community providers are a flexible but unresourced source of supply for adult education in both Australia and New Zealand. The term "community providers" refers to nongovernment, nonprofit-making organizations that usually fall under community control. They range from single purpose to general educational organizations. Community adult education centers and the neighborhood learning centers have developed new forms of learning that are not only highly democratic and responsive to local needs, but also very cost-effective. In 1990, 190 neighborhood houses received funding in Victoria.

There were 700 neighborhood centers in Australia in 1991 (Gribble 1992 p. 6). These neighborhood houses are user-friendly, accessible, nonthreatening community organizations. Their main purpose is to provide educational opportunities relevant to those in the neighborhood and thus to assist in community development. The neighborhood houses, which have particular appeal for women, have become a significant force in Australian adult education.

Community organizations in Australia vary from quite large organizations (such as the Workers' Educational Associations) to others (such as the neighborhood houses) which are very small indeed. Many of these organizations have to recover course costs from fees while others receive some government funding.

Other community providers are the University of the Third Age, evening colleges, College for Seniors, and community adult education centers. While other organizations such as the Young Men's Christian Association (YMCA), the Young Women's Christian Association (YWCA), and family planning associations have other major purposes, adult education courses are part of their provision.

Unfortunately, community provision is not heavily resourced in financial or human terms. Many of the community providers rely heavily on volunteers and underpaid female workers (AAACE 1991 p. 8).

5.4 Private Sector Providers

The first type of private provider offers training and education in activities such as underwater diving, crafts, language, martial arts, photography, and painting. The second, much larger group comprises those providers involved in training—for example, private business and secretarial colleges, accountancy firms, management consultants, and individuals offering personal development programs.

The Federal Government's Training Guarantee Levy has stimulated activity in continuing professional and industrial education, and the late 1980s and early 1990s have seen substantial growth in the number of private sector providers. Part of the growth stems from the tendency for quite a number of state and Federal Government departments to contract out some training programs to private firms.

5.5 Labor Market Organizations

These providers include employer organizations, unions, professional associations, industrial training bodies, and enterprise associations, and are concerned with the world of work. Education and training provision is aimed at improving occupational and organizational performance. For example, the Business Council of Australia and the Confederation of Australian Industry mount education and training activities as well as participating in state and national industry training councils, which set standards and take leads on basic skills training for entry into the industry.

Individual unions and the Trade Union Training Authority make provision for their members to develop new skills and acquire new information. Many unions and professional associations have become responsible for the continuing education of their members, and some associations have adopted mandatory continuing education practices.

6. Adult Education: Alternative or Mainstream Education?

In one sense, adult education can be seen as an alternative form of provision. It is less formal, less teacher-oriented, more participative, and more flexible than traditional school and postsecondary education. Another and more radical view of adult education is that it is a subversive activity, in the sense that it contributes to creating critical awareness and assists social and economic change. For example, adult education enables people without adequate education to catch up; and it helps to empower individuals or groups that have not had a sufficient opportunity to participate in educational, employment, or economic opportunities. Adult education is hardly a revolutionary force in Australia, but it does help to redress inequalities and neglect, through opening up educational opportunities.

The field of adult and community education has had a marginal status and access to very limited funds and resourcing, but within these constraints has had freedom in curriculum and methodology. However, one of the costs of increased government funding, recognition, and mainstreaming is the greater emphasis on accountability from those responsible for disbursing government funds.

In summary, then, Australian adult education constitutes a conglomeration of activity, purposes, philosophies, ideologies, markets, and participants. Adult education is user-friendly, accessible, and stimulating. It is on the threshold of greater recognition and funding but in that process faces the prospect of greater accountability, orthodoxy, and loss of freedom. However, leadership in the field is marked by vigor, enthusiasm, commitment, and a growing professionalism.

7. Adult Education in New Zealand

While there have been occasional calls for the union of Australia and New Zealand, not surprisingly, New Zealanders are fierce supporters of independence. Nevertheless, the two countries have an interactive and influential relationship in social, political, educational, cultural, and economic spheres. During the 1970s and 1980s, for example, changes from Conservative to Labor Governments (and vice versa) usually take place in New Zealand first and are followed in Australia, a year or so later.

In contrast to the situation characterizing Australian adult education, in New Zealand government funding for adult education has to some extent declined in the early 1990s. In 1985–86, the percentage of government expenditure on adult and continuing education outside tertiary education institutions from the education budget was 1.03 percent. The largest segment of funding from the government education budget in the broad field of community and continuing education was directed toward formal institutions such as schools, universities, colleges of education, and polytechnics (see *Polytechnical Education*).

In 1990–91, New Zealand's public expenditure on education amounted to US $2,310 million. Of this total sum, community education received just under US $17 million—or 0.7 percent. This figure represents a drop of one-third since 1985. Of the US $17 million earmarked for community and continuing education, universities received approximately 50 percent, schools 38 percent, and community based organizations 12 percent.

The 1991 and 1992 budgets have been seen as an attack on adult and community education. It has been argued that the funding of almost every aspect of community education has been cut severely, and that adult entry into tertiary education has become much more difficult than was previously the case.

8. Universities and Adult Education

Langer (1992 p. 2393) mentions that New Zealand's seven universities are aware of their responsibilities in providing continuing education to people at all levels of educational experience. Continuing education and extension departments offer a diverse range of activities including credit and noncredit courses, seminars, workshops, and special schools offering a wide range of subjects throughout the full year.

The offerings of the seven universities correspond broadly to the three major areas of activity undertaken by Australian universities. These activities are, first, academic; second, vocational and professional; and third, general and liberal adult education. More specifically, departments of continuing education and extension teach degree, diploma, and certificate courses; offer bridging programs (such as the New Start Program for mature students), induction courses, distance education programs, and extramural tuition (in particular Massey University)—even all of which fall within the traditional sphere of academic work of the universities.

In the area of continuing vocational education, the departments offer professional studies units and continuing education for professional bodies, and organize conferences.

Third, general and liberal adult education and community education are offered, including languages courses, educational travel courses, and conferences, seminars, and workshops on subjects such as medical ethics and biculturalism (Caldwell and Heslop 1991 pp. 85–97).

9. Polytechnics

Apart from universities, tertiary education in New Zealand is provided by polytechnics and colleges of education. Polytechnics are funded by government and cater essentially for vocational and technical training. The 25 polytechnics in the country offer programs in pretrade and trade training, transition courses, and courses leading to professional qualifications such as accountancy, community-oriented courses, and adult basic and secondary education. They provide a wide range of continuing education in metropolitan and provincial centers, including short courses. Many polytechnics have off-campus centers and act as hosts for youth learning centers or the Rural Education Activities Program (Darby 1989 p. 120) (see *Polytechnical Education*).

10. The School–Community Education Program

One of the most interesting features of the New Zealand panorama of adult education is the activity emanating from the schools. Most schools offer a range of adult courses. In late 1992, schools offering nonformal and community education programs were given greater responsibility for these activities. The community education programs in secondary schools have enjoyed the biggest increase in funding of any provider grouping since 1985.

The purpose of the school–community education program is to provide opportunities for adults within the community, in a manner balanced to meet expressed needs. The Ministry of Education describes community education as those purposeful learning activities undertaken after initial education and training, which are of economic and social benefit to society and give opportunities for personal development. The Ministry defines a community education student as one who is over 16 years of age but is not a full-time secondary student.

These school–community education programs are not part of the school curriculum, but are activities organized by community education coordinators using annual tutor hour allocations. The Secretary of Education annually allocates a number of community education tutor hours and staffing resources to be used for community education. In 1992, 280,000 tutor hours were allocated to 270 schools.

The government has stipulated that community education programs fall into the following categories:

(a) adult basic education, including basic Maori language and culture, English for speakers of other languages, literacy, and numeracy;

(b) training for volunteer community workers;

(c) parent–education courses;

(d) programs initiated to meet a significant community need, such as the closing-down of a major factory or employer;

(e) personal development including programs to assist adults to develop work-related skills, courses to assist those on low incomes to become self-reliant, and programs to assist specific groups within the population, such as women.

11. Rural Education Activities Program

New Zealand, like Australia, has its patchwork quilt of providers, especially in the community education area. For example, there are 12 Rural Education Activities Program (REAP) centers which provide early childhood programs through to community and continuing education programs. However, it is difficult to identify what proportion of activity can be described as adult education, although a full-time community Education Officer is attached to each REAP center.

12. Adult Reading and Literacy Assistance Association Federation (ARLA)

The growing recognition of literacy as a problem for industrialized countries has led Australia and New Zealand to inject more funding into adult literacy programs. In New Zealand, for example, nearly one hundred literacy schemes operate under the umbrella of the ARLA Federation. Government funding of US $295,000 provides for a national office including staff, research, tutor training, and some assistance to particular literacy schemes. A number of literacy programs, including English as a Second Language, are organized through polytechnics with salaries and some administrative costs being met through government grants.

The federation is committed to moving towards sharing half of its resources with the *Tangata Whenua* (Maori). *Te Whiri Kaupapa AKO* is the unit within ARLA which was established to promote *tino rang a tiratanga* or self-determination for Maori people.

13. Other Providing Organizations

Other adult education providers include: 11 workers educational associations, which offer courses in adult basic education and education for social change; country women's coordinating committees, which provide learning opportunities for rural women; 60 parents' centers, which run a variety of birth education and parenting courses; and *Te Ataarangi*, which is a movement to foster the Maori language. These community organizations receive either no government grants or have had reduced or withdrawal of funding in 1991.

14. *Service and Professional Adult Education Organizations*

In 1986, the National Council of Adult Education was abolished, and in its place two organizations were established. The first of these is the Community Learning Aotearoa of New Zealand (CLANZ), which administers small grants to community groups and organizations. Its grant was cut by 60 percent in the 1991 budget and its advisory function to the Minister was withdrawn. The second organization to be established was the National Resource Center which has a small budget of US $23,000 in order to provide information, carry out research, and conduct workshops and conferences for adult educators.

This description of adult education in New Zealand would not be complete without reference to the New Zealand Association for Community and Continuing Education. Without government funding, it exists to serve paid and voluntary workers in the adult education field. New Zealand adult and community education is under as great a threat as it has ever been. Hindmarsh (1992 p. 28) states that there is an increased sense of instability and impending change within the field.

15. *Conclusion*

Uncertainty, instability, and marginality, however, seem to be characteristic of the field of adult education, and governments of the day often contribute by the injection or withdrawal of funding. In Australia, there is some optimism about adult education developments in the early 1990s; in New Zealand there is frustration and disappointment.

References

Australian Association of Adult and Community Education (AAACE) 1991 *Enquiry into Adult and Community Educa-tion*. Submission to the Senate Standing Committee on Employment, Education and Training. AAACE, Canberra

Caldwell G and Heslop Y (eds.) 1991 *Profiles of Adult and Continuing Education Departments and Activities in Australian and New Zealand Universities*, 2nd edn. Center for Continuing Education, Australian National University, Canberra

Coopers and Lybrand 1990 *Strategic Review of Commonwealth and State Adult Literacy*.

Darby J 1989 *Adult education in New Zealand*. In: Swinbourne E, Wellings J (eds.) 1989

Evans M D R 1986 *A Nation of Learners: Participants in Adult Education*. Report to the Department of Employment, Education and Training on results of the National Adult Education Study

Gribble H 1992 *Useful Knowledge—A Brief History and Description of Adult, Community, and Further Education in Victoria*. Adult, Community, and Further Education Board, Victoria

Hindmarsh J H 1992 Community and continuing education in 1992: Trends and issues. In: New Zealand Annual Review of Education 1992. Department of Education, Victoria University of Wellington, Wellington

Johnson R, Hinton F 1986 *It's Human Nature: Non-award Adult and Continuing Education in Australia*. Commonwealth Tertiary Education Commission, Canberra

Langer R M H 1992 The Universities of New Zealand *Commonwealth Universities Year Book*, Vol. 3

Senate Standing Committee (SSC) on Employment, Education, and Training 1991 *Come in Cinderella—The Emergence of Adult and Community Education*. Report of the Senate Standing Committee on Employment, Education, and Training. Senate Printing Unit, Parliament House, Canberra

Wickert R 1989 *No Single Measure: A Survey of Australian Adult Literacy*. Department of Employment, Education and Training, Canberra

Further Reading

Caldwell G 1987 A quickening pulse: Adult and continuing education in Australia. *Bulletin of the UNESCO Regional Office for Asia and the Pacific* 28 (September): 27–46

Clark R J, Root S J (eds.) 1988 *Case Studies in Australian Adult Education*. Department of Continuing Education, University of New England, New South Wales Board of Adult Education, Armidale

Swinbourne E, Wellings J (eds.) 1989 *Government Roles in Adult Education: International Perspectives*. Grade 88 Incorporated, Sydney

Baltic Countries

T. Märja and Ü. Vooglaid

Latvia, Lithuania, and Estonia are three Baltic states engaged in the process of rebuilding a civil society after 50 years of occupation. Adult education is accepted as a key instrument for making the transition period pass as quickly as possible. This entry discusses the goals and scope of adult education in the Baltic states, both before and after Independence. Needs, priorities, and future prospects for adult education are also reviewed.

1. Brief History

Throughout their histories, Estonia, Latvia, and Lithuania have been shaped by their location on the border between the Eastern (predominantly Russian) and Western European (predominantly German) cultural traditions. These influences have had differing impacts on each of the Baltic countries.

The geopolitical and cultural marginality of the region has been an important factor in stimulating intellectual self-preservation and self-realization. Cultural protection, indigenous development, and survival have been the primary, collective aim of Estonians, Latvians, and Lithuanians for more than a century. The economic and political development of their nation-states have been, and still are, regarded as a tool to achieve this central objective.

It was characteristic of each Baltic nation to regard education highly and use it, combined with national culture, to withstand economic and social pressures. According to the 1897 census, and by the criteria used at that time, 96 percent of the population of Estonia was literate. In Latvia, literacy had reached 80 percent of the nation's population, and in Lithuania 54 percent. This compares with literacy rates of about 30 percent in Russia, and 28 percent in the Ukraine (Lauristin and Vihalemm 1993).

As regards adult education, it can be mentioned that there have been large similarities among the three Baltic states during their long history. Yet each country has also found its own way and developed its own system of adult education.

The history of adult education in Lithuania is closely connected with the history of voluntary organizations and Church activities. The Lithuanian Church was established in the first half of the thirteenth century, and the first primary schools for youth and later for adults were opened. Formal education was established by the sixteenth century, when Vilnius University was founded, in 1579. In the eighteenth century, when Lithuania lost its independence and became a part of Russia, the use of the Lithuanian language was prohibited. That was why many secret Lithuanian primary schools for youth and adults were created in the country. Volunteers tried to carry secretly published Lithuanian books from Prussia to Lithuania. This form of informal education of adults was aimed at offering cultural resistance against Russian repression, and keeping the language alive (Beresneviciene 1994).

The Estonian system of education and training has strong roots dating back several hundreds of years. Latin-language church schools were operating in Estonia from the mid-thirteenth century, and municipal schools from the fifteenth century. A major event in Estonian education occurred in 1632 when, on the initiative of the first governor-general of Livonia,

and with the support of King Gustavus II Adolphus of Sweden, the *Universitas Dorpatensis* (which also came to be called the *Academia Gustaviana* in honour of the King) was founded (Alma Mater Tartuensis 1982). In the second half of the seventeenth century the peasants' schools were established, which mostly catered for adults (Andresen 1974). During the period of the first independence of the Estonian Republic (1918–40), a great variety of adult education centers were founded. The ideological perspectives prevailing at that time called for an integral educational system that would combine schooling and popular education (ENE 1987). Educational and independent-minded people established voluntary or popular societies, libraries, reading rooms, day and evening free schools, further education schools, folk high schools, and so on. Political meetings, lectures, courses, and study circles were also held. By the end of the independence period the number of education societies in Estonia had reached about 7,000 (Haridusministeeriumi tegevus 1938).

The origins of the school system in Latvia go back to the thirteenth century and can be traced to the activities of the Catholic clergy. The first schools for Latvians appeared during the second half of the sixteenth century. Lessons in the Russian language were introduced in 1789, when the network of Latvian schools was also enlarged. The *Academia Petrina*, founded in 1775, turned into an important research center. Russification imposed by the authorities began to take hold during the 1860s—it then became forbidden to print any book using the Latin alphabet, and all instruction in schools was in the Russian language. This measure was repealed only at the beginning of the twentieth century. During the second half of the nineteenth and at the beginning of the twentieth century, special educational institutions for adults were started (trade schools, naval college, etc.). In 1862, the Riga Polytechnic was founded and a precursor to the modern system of education began to take shape (Baltic States 1991).

After the Soviet annexation of Estonia, Latvia, and Lithuania in 1940, the existing educational systems, including the institutions for adult education, were destroyed and subordinated to the authoritarian Soviet system of education. That system was entirely controlled by the Communist Party. The main purpose of adult education became the ideological treatment of persons showing "deviant" behavior. However, thanks to the wisdom and tenacity of the population of the three Baltic nations, popular education and national traditions continued to be cherished, thus securing the surivival of national cultures and languages.

2. Goals and Scope of Adult Education Before and After Independence

Formal adult education in Latvia, Lithuania, and Estonia, during the period of Soviet domination

(1940–91), took place mainly in evening schools, and at evening and corresponding courses offered by the universities. During this period, four major strands of adult education provision existed in Baltic states: (a) Marxist–Leninist Evening Universities, the students of which were recruited by compulsion, intended for executives and so-called specialists; (b) schools (courses) for propagandists with the intention of spreading Soviet ideology among the adult population; (c) classes of economy for employers and employees, organized in enterprises; and (d) lectures organized by the Knowledge Society for mass audiences on all conceivable subjects. Usually the lecturers went to teach in work premises. Popular enlightenment was carried out through an extensive network of hobby clubs, public libraries, culture houses, and/or universities.

Opportunities for the more advanced schooling of adults became more widespread in Estonia in the mid-1970s, often relying on information obtained directly from Finland. At that time the foundation was laid for the establishment of all kinds of education institutions operating in different branches of the national economy. Training of professional managers was also initiated at that time (Märja and Vooglaid 1993). From the mid-1980s the theoretical concepts and methodology of adult and continuing education were developed. The Estonian system of adult and continuing education was more developed and reached a leading position in the former Soviet Union, whereas adult education in Latvia and Lithuania remained to some degree behind.

A period of major change in adult and continuing education in the Baltic states began with the introduction of *perestroika* in the Soviet Union in late 1980s, and was strengthened radically once the independence of Latvia, Lithuania, and Estonia had been re-established in 1991. There are several similarities in this process in the three countries. For example, a dramatic rise was observed in the interest and need for acquiring foreign languages, and widescale training programs and courses in business, law, marketing, communication, publicity, banking, and other fields of economic study that had been missing in Soviet education programs became much more common (Märja and Vooglaid 1994). The number of adult training centers, voluntary organizations and/or joint stock companies dealing with education grew rapidly as a result. At the same time, however, expectations for adult education differ from country to country. These differences arise from the cultural, economic, and political situation of the countries.

In Lithuania the reform of education began with the aim of creating a system of lifelong learning, embracing formal, nonformal, and informal education, and dependent on both public and private educational institutions. This reform set out to develop individual cultural consciousness, preparing the person for democracy, and developing the ability to think creatively and critically, and to be responsible for their own decisions (Beresneviciene 1994).

In Latvia the present social and political climate sets forth a demand for specific, practical aims to be achieved. For example, helping the population to adapt to the process of continuous technological change; furthering the democratic development of society; contributing to the legal knowledge, self-awareness and sense of personal responsibility of the population; and reviving the spiritual culture of the nation, which is vital for its continued existence (Latvian Adult Education Association 1994).

In Estonia the main objective of adult education is to raise the competence and conscious efficiency of the whole population and to ensure their participation in all spheres of civic and economic life (Vooglaid and Märja 1992). The national program of adult education is being prepared to meet this goal. It is considered essential that all necessary prerequisites for adult basic education, vocational training, and retraining in all professions, but also for popular adult education, are included in this program. A new educational paradigm was to be set up to lay the foundations for the national programs: accepting the principle of lifelong learning; the need for acquiring a sufficient level of basic education; as well as the need for continuous learning throughout the lifespan.

3. The Delivery System

It is not (yet) possible to talk about a coherent system of adult education and training in the Baltic states, because the provision is fragmented and uncoordinated among a great many public, private, and voluntary institutions. The structure of adult education is in a phase of flux. The network of schools dating from the Soviet era no longer works efficiently, while a new network has not yet been firmly established. At present, adult education is offered by the following institutions and associations: evening schools for adults, which offer a curriculum at secondary level; vocational schools; departments of correspondence and evening studies, including centers for refresher training at universities; vocational education and training centers in firms and businesses; cultural and folk universities; language schools, and cooperative societies for the teaching of foreign languages; national refresher education institutions, which provide advanced and further education; local research and development centers catering to adult learners; education centers within organizations for inservice training; and television and radio distance education institutions.

Professional development courses for teachers and adult educators are provided in teacher training institutes, adult training centers, the summer school at Vytautas Magnus University (Lithuania), the Tallinn Pedagogical University, the Association of Estonian Adult Educators "Andras," Tartu University (Estonia), and the Adult Education Center (Latvia) (Beresneviciene 1994, Märja and Vooglaid 1993, Latvian Adult Education Association 1994).

4. Legislation and Financing of Adult Education

There are no large differences in the general requirements for the regulation of adult education and training among the Baltic states today. The educational policy as a whole in Estonia, Latvia, and Lithuania, as well as new educational legislation, have been in a continuous process of renewal since about 1988.

Estonia is the only Baltic state where adult education is regulated in an Act of Adult Education, which was accepted by parliament in November 1993. The purpose of the Act is to establish juridical guarantees of access to voluntary studying by all people during their lifetime. It requires common action by the government and the municipalities in the provision of adult education.

The government's tasks are to create legislation, to finance certain types of adult education out of the state budget, to stimulate research on adult education, and to coordinate adult education activities and link them with the objectives for socioeconomic development. The tasks of the municipalities are to guarantee all citizens' access to possibilities for acquiring basic and secondary education, to offer both liberal and labor-market oriented adult education, and to guarantee provision for special target groups.

In accordance with the Act of Adult Education, the Primary School and Gymnasium Act, and the Higher Education Act, the financing of general adult education in Estonia is a state responsibility. Labor-market oriented adult education is also financed by the state. Other labor-market oriented courses as well as popular adult education are financed by organizations and/or persons interested in training and/or retraining (The Act of Adult Education 1993).

In Lithuania the State Education Register defines the standards of general education, a list of specialties, general requirements for curricula, and modules and qualification requirements. The activities of private education institutions are regulated by the law of licences for schooling and general government decrees and laws. Formal adult education is partially financed by the state; informal education mainly by participants (Beresneviciene 1994).

5. Needs, Priorities, and Future Prospects

The breakdown of the Soviet empire has in the Baltic states caused similar social, political, economic, and other changes. Differences remain, however, in the ways in which the countries are realizing independence and cultivating their original features as a state and as a nation. These differences are also reflected in adult education. In Estonia, great emphasis is put on a training model aimed at increasing the competitiveness of the work force and of expanding business (Laanvee 1994). In Latvia, likewise, much emphasis is put on qualifying people for higher skills and the retraining of specialists, businessmen, and citizens. In Lithuania the decline of participation in formal adult education is being mitigated through augmented self-directed learning among adults.

All three Baltic states (as well as all post-Communist countries in Central and Eastern Europe) have similar needs for adult education (see *Europe, Central and Eastern*). These needs can be classified as follows:

(a)   Society and democracy—this refers to the knowledge which all citizens need in order to understand, accept, and develop the democratic society and polity as well as the process of how they are being shaped and how they operate;

(b)   economy—training and retraining for the new demand of the economy;

(c)   employment—education, training, and retraining of the employed and unemployed with the view of preserving, changing, or obtaining work;

(d)   education—in various fields and with different emphases, for example, practical knowledge for everyday life and/or supplementary education in foreign languages, and education in computer technology;

(e)   training of trainers.

The democratization process which is underway in the Baltic states, and also in other previously communist countries in Eastern and Central Europe, does not proceed in a vacuum. Its success and possible failure influences developments in other countries. Therefore contacts among specialists and adult educators in discussing concepts of development, but also in elaborating questions of fundamental importance to the society, are an essential precondition for creating a secure Europe and overcoming totalitarianism.

See also: Europe, Central and Eastern; Europe: Nordic Countries; Europe, Western and Southern

References

Andresen L 1974 *Eesti Rahvakoolid 19, Sajandil* (The Estonian Folk Schools in the Nineteenth Century). Valgus, Tallinn
Beresneviciene D 1994 *Lifelong Education in Lithuania.* Unpublished Manuscript, Vilnius University, Lithuania
Eesti Nôukogude Entsüklopeedia (The Soviet Estonian Encyclopaedia) 1987 Valgus, Tallinn

Haridusministeeriumi Tegevus 1937/38.a (Practice of the Ministry of Education). Haridusministeerium, Tallinn

Laanvee E 1994 Estonia: Adult and Higher Education. In: *Newsletter 1/94.* Council of Europe, Strasbourg

Latvian Adult Education Association 1994 Riga

Lauristin M, Vihalemm P 1993 The Balts—West of the East, East of the West. In: Hoyer S, Lauk E, Vihalemm P (eds.) 1993 *Towards a Civic Society. The Baltic Media's Long Road to Freedom.* Nota Baltica Ltd, Tartu

Märja T, Vooglaid Ü 1993 Estonia. In: Jarvis P (ed.) 1993 *Perspectives on Adult Education and Training in Europe.* Billing & Sons, Worcester

Märja T, Vooglaid Ü 1994 Brief overview of the history of continuing education. In: *Europahandbuch Weiterbildung*, Hermann Luchterhand Verlag. Neuwied, Kriftel, Berlin

The Act of Adult Education. In: *Riigi Teataja 1993, 74 art. 1054.* Tallinn

The Baltic States: A Reference Book 1991. Estonian Encyclopaedia Publishers, Tallinn

Vooglaid Ü, Märja T 1992 Andragogical Problems of Building a Democratic Society. *Int. J. Lifelong Educ.* 11(4): 321–27

Further Reading

Jelenc Z 1994 *Adult Education Research Trends in Central and Eastern European Countries.* UNESCO Research Report. Slovene Adult Education Centre, Ljubljana

Märja T 1992 Adult Education in Estonia. *Adult Education and Development* 39: 205–19

Caribbean and Central America

U. Giere, S. Hielscher and E. D. Ramesar

This entry introduces adult education and training in the Caribbean and Central America. It highlights the experience of Cuba, Nicaragua, and Mexico, describes the position of adult education in a number of islands in the Caribbean archipelago, and gives attention to popular education as a means of promoting conscientization and mobilization among the disadvantaged.

1. Context

"Only one enterprise flourished in war-ridden El Salvador: funeral parlours, a trade not considered in the curriculum of the National Council for Professional Training." This is not just a cynic's view of one moment in time of one Central American country but a hard fact depicting the explosive and convulsive past and present of Central America and the Caribbean. Such situations determine the ups and downs of adult education and training in the region.

The Caribbean region consists of the archipelago of islands stretching from the Bahamas in the north to Trinidad and Tobago in the south; the mainland countries of Guyana, Suriname, and Guyane (Cayenne) on the South American continent; Belize in Central America; and Curaçao and Aruba off the northern coast of South America. Central America comprises another seven countries: Mexico, Guatemala, Honduras, El Salvador, Nicaragua, Costa Rica, and Panama.

The area is made up of territories with a relatively long history of independence (Haiti became independent in 1804) to territories which have only recently achieved nationhood (Antigua and Barbuda became independent in 1981). Their populations vary in number from as many as 10 million in Cuba to 10,000 in the British Virgin Islands. Their language, culture, and education reflect their colonial past; in the Commonwealth Caribbean an English past is evident; in Haiti, Martinique, Guadeloupe, and Guyane a French heritage is shared; and in Netherlands Antilles and Suriname it is a Dutch influence that is felt. There are also pockets of indigenous people in Guyana and in Belize.

The ethnic composition of the area is equally varied—from the descendants of Dutch settlers in the Netherlands Windwards to descendants of African slaves in Haiti; mulattos in Santo Domingo; large proportions of descendants of immigrants from India in Suriname (60%), Guyana (55%), and Trinidad and Tobago (45%); Indonesians in Suriname, and Chinese and Arabs in most countries. Ideologically, there is also variety—from the Marxist socialist Left of Cuba to the Liberal Democratic Right of Barbados. In economical terms, there is a disparity of wealth, ranging from the relatively high per capita income of US$4,000 (Trinidad and Tobago) to the extremely low per capita income of US$150 (Haiti).

Large disparities can also be observed in education, in primary school enrollment and dropout rates, and in particular in adult illiteracy rates, ranging from 0.7 percent in Barbados in 1970 to 65.2 percent in Haiti in 1982 (see Table 1). Unlike the situation in most African or Asian countries, women in many Caribbean countries have an illiteracy rate equal to that or even lower than that of men (see, e.g., Barbados or Jamaica in Table 1).

Adult education in the Caribbean and Central America reflects and has, in return, started to shape the

Table 1
Illiteracy rates in Central America and the Caribbean (adults over 15)

	Year of census	Male	Female	Overall	Estimated rates 1990		
					Male	Female	Overall
Anguilla[f]	—	—	—	—	—	—	—
Antigua (with Barbuda)	—	—	—	—	—	—	—
Aruba[d]	—	—	—	—	—	—	—
Bahamas	—	—	—	—	—	—	—
Barbados	1970	0.7	0.7	0.7	—	—	—
Belize	1970	8.8	8.8	8.8	—	—	—
British Virgin Islands[f]	1970	1.9	1.5	1.7	—	—	—
Cayman Islands[f]	1970	2.5	2.4	2.5	—	—	—
Costa Rica	1984	7.3	7.4	7.4	7.4	6.9	7.2
Cuba	1981	3.8	3.8	3.8	5.0	7.0	6.0
Dominica	1970	6.0	5.8	5.9	—	—	—
Dominican Republic	1981	31.8	30.9	31.4	15.2	18.2	16.7
El Salvador	1985*	27.4	34.7	31.2	23.8	30.0	27.0
French Guiana[c]	1982	16.4	17.7	17.0	—	—	—
Grenada	1970	2.0	2.4	2.2	—	—	—
Guadeloupe[c]	1982	10.4	9.6	10.0	—	—	—
Guatemala	1973	46.4	61.5	54.0	36.9	52.9	44.9
Guyana	1970	5.7	11.0	8.4	2.5	4.6	3.6
Haiti	1982	62.7	67.5	65.2	40.9	52.6	47.0
Honduras	1974	41.1	44.9	43.1	24.5	29.4	26.9
Jamaica	1970	4.4	3.5	3.9	1.8	1.4	1.6
Martinique[c]	1982	8.0	6.6	7.2	—	—	—
Mexico	1980	13.8	20.1	17.0	10.5	14.9	12.7
Monserrat[f]	1970	3.2	3.4	3.4	—	—	—
The Netherlands Antilles (incl. Curaçao)[e]	1981	5.8	6.6	6.2	—	—	—
Nicaragua	1971	42.0	42.9	42.5	—	—	—
Panama	1980	13.7	15.1	14.4	11.9	11.8	11.9
Puerto Rico[a]	1980	10.3	11.5	10.9	—	—	—
St Kitts-Nevis	1970	2.4	2.3	2.4	—	—	—
St Lucia	1970	19.2	17.6	18.3	—	—	—
St Vincent and the Grenadines	1970	4.2	4.5	4.4	—	—	—
Suriname	1978	31.6	37.1	35.0	4.9	5.3	5.1
Trinidad and Tobago	1980	3.5	6.6	5.1	—	—	—
Turks and Caicos Islands[f]	1970	1.4	2.3	1.9	—	—	—
Virgin Islands[b]	—	—	—	—	—	—	—

Sources: UNESCO 1990, 1991
*Estimates a Autonomous part of the United States b Unincorporated territory of the United States c Overseas departments of France d Autonomous part of the Kingdom of the Netherlands e Integral part of the Kingdom of the Netherlands f British dependencies

region's variety of historical, linguistic, cultural, economic, ideological, and educational traits. Adult education in many countries of the region has developed from a position of being rejected as an unnecessary or even dangerous luxury for a cheap workforce to one of being integrated—without the expected success, however—into governmental economic development plans during the 1960s and 1970s. Adult education has finally turned into a social movement, into popular education, spreading not only over the region but also being exported by writers like Paolo Freire and Illich to Western academics and practitioners. From its inception by European missionaries and other private initiatives via ministry provision (initially educational but nowadays also intersectoral)—in short, from top down—adult education in the Caribbean and Central America has become a form of popular—bottom-up—education, providing compensatory, second-chance education for the out-of-school population and even espousing a revolutionary potential. Education is no longer "education for the people" but "education by the people."

Since it is impossible to cover here the whole variety of adult education and training in the Caribbean and Central America, one Caribbean and two Central American countries will be given special attention: Cuba, Nicaragua, and Mexico. Cuba is atypical of the Caribbean, but was chosen because its literacy campaign, linked with a revolutionary process, has been seen worldwide as a textbook model. Nicaragua, which provides another example of a literacy campaign, was selected because its revolution of 1979 gave popular educators an opportunity to implement their ideas on a national scale. Mexico—the largest, most populated, and, since the revolution in 1910, one of the most stable of the countries in the region—stands as an example of the incremental introduction and expansion of adult education and training (see *Adult Education for Development*).

2. Cuba

In Cuba, adult education is fully integrated into the national educational system as a subsystem, offering all Cubans various opportunities for continuing education. Adult education has been unique in training a large proportion of the population in functional literacy, as well as in primary and secondary education. For example, in 1989 only 1.9 percent of 10–49-year olds were illiterate, and the average school level reached the eighth grade (Cuba, Ministry of Education 1990).

Before the socialist revolution in 1959, education was designed to serve the country's elite and to maintain the export-oriented economic system. Since 1959 education has been considered crucial for the transformation of society and has been regarded as an intrinsic part of the revolution. Education in general was not only expected to upgrade the overall educational level but also to mobilize the population. The main goal of adult education was the creation of a general culture of conscientization leading to a strong sense of national pride and identity (see *Popular Education and Conscientization*).

The illiteracy rate in 1953 of 22.1 percent of a population of about 6 million declined to 3.8 percent of the total population of about 10 million in 1981. Statistics on educational attainment show that the discrepancy between rural and urban areas also decreased but was not eradicated; for example, 37.5 percent of the rural population did not complete primary education compared to 16.8 percent of the urban population (UNESCO 1991).

After the 1959 revolution the educational system in Cuba underwent a change of focus from quantitative to qualitative growth. At first the priority was equal accessibility. When this had been largely attained, the emphasis shifted to achieving higher levels of education. Technical and vocational education proved to be an especially urgent need, in order to replace those lost with the brain drain of highly qualified professionals that followed the revolution. The loss was estimated at between 15,000 and 25,000 (Torres 1990 p. 80).

In the 1960s Cuba pursued a massive expansion of education at all levels, especially in rural areas. The "battle for literacy," from 1959 to 1962, largely influenced the following "battle for the sixth grade," set up for new literates and undereducated adults and which had its greatest impact during the mid- and late 1970s. By 1989, 1.5 million participants of the program had achieved the sixth grade. Literacy classes continued only for the remaining minority groups, training about 1,000 participants every year. The strategy of emphasizing socialization was replaced by a return to material incentives in the 1970s, which in turn led to the promotion of academic excellence. In 1989 there existed 96 varieties of technical and vocational education, of which 18 led to a certificate qualifying skilled workers and 78 designating mid-level technicians. With increasing specialization, adult education became more formalized. Enrollments continued to rise, especially at secondary levels. Two new types of adult education developed: lower secondary education for adults and preuniversity education for workers and farmers. The "battle for the ninth grade" had its greatest impact from 1980 to 1985. It upgraded general education, so that by 1989 approximately 900,000 participants of the program had achieved the ninth grade. By the same time, about 90,000 adults had participated in preuniversity education and some 25,000 in language schools for workers (Cuba, Ministry of Education 1990 pp. 62–64).

Adult education in Cuba is characterized by flexibility and continuity and the principle of combining academic study and manual work. The latter is applied in all types and levels of education. For example, students from urban schools on the scheme "school to the countryside" spend 30–45 days per year doing agricultural work; those on the scheme "school in the countryside," from rural schools, do agricultural work for three hours per day. The structural design of adult education courses, provided by and channeled through political and mass organizations, takes into consideration the needs of the working population: many classes take place in the evenings or afternoons, often at working places or at special boarding schools. Changes in curricula and syllabi of all subsystems of education, including adult education, have been introduced since the 1987–88 academic year according to the Continuous Improvement of Education plan. In the early 1990s the situation was also influenced by economic difficulties resulting from the end of support from the Socialist Bloc in Europe and the continuation of the economic blockade by the United States. Nevertheless, "education for all" continued to be a high priority of the government.

Perhaps the most widely acknowledged achievement in education in Cuba was that it became a right for everybody—not only according to official propaganda but in reality, as education became a matter of course for the young generation. Evaluations of Cuban achievements differ according to political and ideological standpoints (Richmond 1990): while opponents of socialist Cuba tended to emphasize problems such as communist indoctrination, progressive educational specialists engaged in both praise and criticism, whereas communist representatives regarded the outcomes of the educational reforms with great satisfaction.

3. Nicaragua

Two events that attracted worldwide interest have drastically shaped adult education and training in Nicaragua: the National Literacy Crusade (CNA) and the Popular Basic Education for Adults program (PBEA). Both were products of the nation's political, social, and cultural transformation process initiated by the Popular Sandinista Revolution (PSR), which overthrew Anastasio Somoza's dictatorship in July 1979.

The Sandinistas, who took power in 1979, inherited from the Somoza dynasty one of the least developed and most erratic adult education histories in the whole Central American region. It can be characterized as a succession of isolated and unrelated projects. A literacy campaign in 1951, following a Pan American proposition advocated in 1949, ended in the bureaucracy of the National Directorate of the National Literacy Campaign. Schemes organized at ministerial level, such as the Workers' Culture School (a training unit for basic stills, aimed at urban workers) or the accelerated primary education program (a night school offering adults six years of children's primary school curriculum) catered mainly for the urban population, while the majority of people in need of adult education opportunities lived in rural areas. Only 6 percent of rural children completed primary school and up to 90 percent of the adult population were illiterate.

Some short-lived radio school experiments in the early 1960s, organized around 120 literacy centers, were a failure. Fewer than 25,000 students participated in adult education programs offered by nongovernmental organizations, religious groups, and the private sector. The government's central attention was given to "antisubversive" adult education activities, such as the 1955 Rio Coco Pilot Project or the "Plan Waslala" (1977–79), which trained 108 "literacy teachers" to act as security agents to identify peasants sympathizing with the Sandinista National Liberation Front. Nicaragua's adult education and its school system were characterized and determined by one family's economic profit-making interest. Although about 45 percent of the population were employed in agriculture and related work, fewer than 1 percent were enrolled in agricultural classes. Training emphasized commerce and services. In 1979, out of a total population of 2.4 million, some 720,000 persons aged 10 years or more were counted as illiterate.

3.1 Nicaragua's National Literacy Crusade

Confronted with the institutions and structures of the Somoza society, which had neither met basic human needs nor served the interests of the majority of the population, the Sandinista revolutionary leadership aimed at achieving a rapid transformation of society. The vision of a new society creatively involving each citizen, "the new man" and "the new woman," in new participatory forms of social organization implied an educational model that would help bring about the transformation. The National Literacy Crusade was advocated as a first step toward this aim. It was stressed by Fernando Cardenal, coordinator of the Literacy Crusade, that the Crusade "is not an educational event with political implications but a political event with educational implications" (Archer and Costello 1990 p. 24).

On the wave of revolutionary triumph, enthusiasm, and struggle for self-determination, the Crusade mobilized the whole country from March 23 to August 23, 1980. The organization of the Crusade was warlike, modeled on the organization of the liberation struggle, and dependent on the cooperation of all ages and interest groups. "Every home a classroom, every table a school desk, every Nicaraguan a teacher" was not just one of the Crusade slogans but reflected reality. About 65,000 volunteers, trained in short-term multiplier-courses, went to the countryside to learn from and teach the illiterate peasants, applying an adapted Freire method. In addition, 26,000 volunteers worked in the cities. Within 5 months 400,000 Nicaraguans were taught basic literacy skills. The illiteracy rate consequently dropped from 50 percent to 13 percent. A follow-up campaign along the Atlantic Coast, targeted at people speaking the indigenous languages of Miskito, Sumo, and Creole English, extended literacy skills to another 13,000 people.

3.2 Popular Basic Education for Adults

After the Crusade, the newly established vice-ministry of adult education (VIMEDA) launched a system of popular basic education for adults, comprising an adult-centered, community-based, productive, and labor-related alternative to the formal school system. Volunteers, some of whom had been learners themselves during the crusade, worked as popular teachers with groups of 10 to 12 persons in Popular Education Collectives (CEPs). In 1984, when about 17,000 CEPs reached 195,000 persons (including out-of-school children), VIMEDA decided to extend the program from six to nine levels to counteract difficulties arising in channeling PBEA graduates into formal secondary schools or into the national inservice training system (SINAFORP) which had insufficient capacity to absorb the students. The additional three PBEA levels were to teach mainly vocational skills.

Intersectoral cooperation, for example with the ministry of agricultural development and land reform

(MIDINRA), which had the lead in desinging nonformal labor force training, caused conflict. Lack of resources and teaching personnel, inadequate relationships with the formal education system, and permanent aggression from the "contras" (the anti-Sandinista fighters), threatened the original idealism and flexibility of the PBEA program. Between 1984 and 1987 PBEA started losing its nonformal character and became more rigid and institutionalized. Although PBEA had some impact on formal education, the dream of finally permeating the whole formal educational system began to fade. Resources and time to revive nonformal adult education were missing. It is estimated that by 1990 the illiteracy rate was once again on the rise, reaching a level of 30–35 percent of adults (Arnove and Dewees 1991).

Both the National Literacy Crusade and the Popular Basic Education for Adults contributed to a number of changes in Nicaraguan society. Among these: the integration of rural populations into a national society; adaptation of education to the needs of the agricultural and occupational sectors; conscientization of the people; and strengthening of mass organizations. Self-critical voices of the Sandinista leadership admitted, however, that their approach was too centralized and did not take sectorial or geographical differences sufficiently into account.

Opposition groups viewed both the National Literacy Crusade and the Popular Basic Education for Adults as massive efforts of political indoctrination. This is exactly the stand expressed in the *Guidelines of the Ministry of Education for the New Government of National Salvation*: "Learning was subordinated to the idcological political project of a party which distorted conscience. Everybody was exposed to indoctrination." According to these guidelines, adult education under thc government elected in 1991 intended to emphasize family education and civic education with a focus on the individual—without neglecting the need for national reconciliation.

4. Mexico

Adult education in Mexico has focused on basic literacy for marginalized groups of the population, such as women and indigenous people. Mexico's illiteracy rate has decreased from 25.8 percent in 1970 to 12.4 percent in 1990. There is and will continue to be a strong demand for adult education: 13.4 percent of 6–14 year old children have received no schooling and 22.8 percent have not completed primary education. There are deep regional disparities: the low illiteracy rate of 4.0 percent in the Federal District (Mexico City), followed by the state of Neuvo León with 4.6 percent, contrasts with more disadvantaged states, which have a high percentage of indigenous population and high illiteracy rates—for example, 26.8 percent in Guerrero and 30.0 percent in Chiapas (*Instituto Nacional de Estadística Geográfica e Informática* 1990).

Bilingual training in Spanish and 13 indigenous Indian languages (out of a total of 52) was advocated in a context of the nation seeking to give increased attention to Indian culture to increase feelings of national identity. Assimilation of Indian culture has a long history in Mexico and its only alternative, diversification allowing for cultural pluralism, is not guaranteed by the bilingual method, since the "implicit message of hispanic superiority seems unavoidable in the curriculum" (Epstein 1985 p. 69).

The National Institute for Adult Education (INEA), an agency of the ministry for public education founded in 1981, carries out most literacy activities through its 354 area offices. Participants in literacy courses are taught directly (in groups or as individuals) or via thc media. Television and radio programs, supported by local tutors, are offered and enjoy much popularity. Teaching via TV consists of a series of programs with intermittent teaching sessions while the radio courses are based on interviews between an illiterate and an instructor. Besides the national literacy program (PRONALF), created in 1981, INEA also offers primary and secondary education for adults, cultural education, and vocational training.

Apart from INEA and the ministry of education, many other governmental agencies and nongovernmental institutions take part in adult education, concentrating especially on vocational training and technical education. Vocational training is mainly a male activity. This contrasts with general adult education. An age structure analysis shows that two-thirds of the participants in adult education are female and that, on average, users are 26 years of age at the primary and 23 at the secondary level (Torres 1990).

After the change of national president every six years new development plans are formulated. The national development plan 1989–94, valid for the presidency of Carlos Salinas de Gortari, has three main aspects regarding education: (a) a focus on deprived areas of Mexico and on deprived social groups, with high illiteracy rates; (b) a focus on 10–14-year old out-of-school children; and (c) adaptation of course contents to the needs of the learners (Instituto Nacional para la Educación de los Adultos 1991).

In 1987 adult education experienced severe cuts because of austerity measures required by an International Monetary Fund structural adjustment program. Most job-training and on-the-job-training programs were discontinued. It was supposed that the private sector would assume responsibility for the provision of such training, but it did not.

5. Caribbean Archipelago

This part deals with adult education in a number of territories in the Caribbean archipelago that have not yet been covered. It will be seen that the keynote is diversity.

5.1 Haiti

In 1947, Haiti was the first country to seek UNESCO's assistance in solving its illiteracy problem which was 90 percent at the time. The *"Office National d'Alphabétisation et d'Action Communautaire" (ONAAC)* was an organization formed in 1961 as a result of the fusion between urban adult education services and rural community development services of the Department of Agriculture.

During the period 1977–80, ONAAC organized a number of projects in the field of adult education, including a literacy programme which enabled some 182,204 adults in the 1977–78 and 188,460 in 1979–80 to acquire literacy skills. ONAAC's field officers number 8,367 divided as follows: 40 coordinators, 140 polyvalent and auxiliary animateurs, 209 agents in home economics, 798 subinspectors, and 7,180 monitors in eight regions, in addition to office staff.

Since 1980, the new thrust in literacy has been to link it with general development, which draws on the motivation of the population through community participation. Promotion of the rural artisan class in community workshops has been functioning with support from *L'Association Française de Volontaires du Progress (AFVP)*.

5.2 Santo Domingo

Adult education projects are undertaken by the Secretary of State for Education, Fine Arts, and Culturre on a regional basis. During 1980 about 350,000 persons benefitted from: (a) community participation in the literacy and adult education programmes; and (b) the production of free reading pamphlets for new adult readers and the provision of teaching materials at adult education centers. Following this, the illiteracy rate decreased from 41 percent in 1970 to 32 percent in 1980.

Adult education efforts aim at upgrading the skills of agricultural workers and at preserving the cultural heritage of the nation.

5.3 The French Antilles and Guyane (Cayenne)

Most of the official adult education programmes in Martinique, Guadeloupe, and Guyane are part of larger programmes instituted for France and its overseas departments/territories. Since illiteracy is considered to be nonexistent there is therefore no formal program.

The Ministry of Education which is responsible for government programs of adult education in France extends to Martinique, Guadeloupe, and Cayenne through the *Centre de Formation Continue des Universités* which was founded in 1959. Thus in 1977 there were 135,587 adult students in 78 centers throughout all the departments of France including the Antilles and Guyane.

One innovation was the law of 1971 which made it obligatory for employers to finance the training of their employees within the continuing education centre mentioned above. The law also stressed education for particular neglected groups such as women, immigrants, the young unemployed, and the undereducated. Another innovation was the setting up of the *Université du Troisieme Age* in 1973 by the University of Bordeaux with which the *Centre Universitaire des Antilles et de la Guyane (CUAG)* is affiliated. Its aim is to find occupations for retired men and women. The wide difference in social, economic, and educational levels of participants is reflected in the range of classes offered—yoga, gymnastics, regional travel, history, languages, politics, and so on.

In 1981 in Guyane, a *Centre Professionelle des Jeunes de Suzini* was established in two rural locations under the French Ministry of Agriculture and the Director-General of Teaching and Research. The intention is to assist young agriculturists.

The *Federation des Oeuvres Laiques* in Martinique, Guadeloupe, and Cayenne is affiliated to *la Laique Francaise de L'Enseignement et de l'Education Permanente* of France and conducts programmes of mass education.

5.4 The Commonwealth Caribbean

As is the case of most of the non-English-speaking Caribbean, in the Commonwealth Caribbean adult education is offered formally and informally through governmental and voluntary agencies, and the School of Continuing Studies (SOCS) of the University of the West Indies. Formal adult education is pursued by participants preparing for a career or by those interested in upgrading their occupational skills. Informal adult education is pursued through cultural classes and lectures in the creative arts offered by the SOCS and the Creative Arts Centres of the University and through craft classes of the appropriate ministry of government or voluntary agencies.

Adult literacy is a significant problem in most of the territories except Barbados, and Trinidad and Tobago. The Jamaica Movement for the Advancement of Learning (JAMAL) Foundation has been doing pioneering work in literacy in Jamaica. Initiatives are now being undertaken in other territories to deal with illiteracy.

Throughout the English-speaking Caribbean there is a heavy concentration on remedial classes. This is related to a desire to improve occupational and promotional opportunity or to meet university admission requirements. General enrichment programs are also offered, but these have fewer clients because of their low income-generating possibilities. It is therefore not surprising that in a region where there is such high unemployment, young adults are attracted to technical and vocational courses offered by employers or church bodies. Trade union organizations also offer classes and operate several workers' colleges.

The extramural are of the University is perhaps

the most widespread regional agency of adult education in the Commonwealth Caribbean. The School of Continuing Studies of the University consists of a director responsible to the vice-chancellor located on the Mona (Jamaica) campus with resident tutors (Belize, Bahamas, Jamaica, Antigua, St. Kitts/Nevis, Anguilla, British Virgin Islands, Montserrat, Dominica, St. Lucia, St. Vincent and Grenada); one staff (specialist) tutor each for drama, labor education, social work, radio education, creative writing, and preschool child training. A tutor on the Cave Hill (Barbados) campus and an associate director on the St. Augustine (Trinidad) campus, report separately to respective campus pro-vice-chancellors.

Each resident tutor is responsible for developing a full adult education program for the territory and works in close relationship with government and other agencies within the territory. Each program includes general courses in English language and literature, modern languages, social studies, mathematics, natural sciences, and business studies; and special courses in public administration, industrial relations, drama, and business management.

5.5 The Netherland Antilles

Adult education outside the school system is offered through vocational training by large industrial firms in Curaçao and through the Labour College in Suriname. In Curaçao, the Department of Labour carries out a vocational training programme for adults including courses for bricklayers and carpenters. In Bonaire, the International Labour Organization has been operating a training program in woodcarving, silver, and leather work—craft courses realted to the tourist trade.

The Suriname Labour College provides courses in industrial relations, labour economics, cooperatives, occupational safety and health, and so on, and mounts a public education program through radio, television, public lectures, and films. The national adult education program is coordinated by the college.

6 Regional Organisation

The Caribbean Regional Council for Adult Education (CARCAE) was established in 1978 as a separate body within the realm of the International Council for Adult Education (ICAE). The regional council seeks (a) to promote and facilitate cooperation among national continuing education organizations and agencies in the non-Spanish-speaking territories of the region; (b) to advance activities of member associations and institutions and to encourage cooperation amongst them; (c) to promote awareness and recognition of the importance of continuing education and to seek and encourage adequate funding for this purpose from governments; (d) to serve as an advisory body to governments on regional matters relating to continuing education; (e) to initiate and/or to support the

mounting of conferences, seminars, training courses, workshops, and so on, as well as undertaking research in the field of continuing education, and the operation of a documentation center and a publications program.

The following national associations have already been formed:

(a) The Adult Education Association of Guyana (AEAG) in 1952;

(b) The Congress of Adult Education of Trinidad and Tobago (CAETT) in 1980;

(c) The Barbados Adult Education Association (BAEA) in 1981;

(d) The St. Lucia Association of Continuing Education (SLACE) in 1981;

(e) The Adult Education Organization of Jamaica (AEOJ) in 1982.

Associations have also been established in Belize, St. Vincent, Bahamas, St. Kitts/Nevis, Dominica, and Grenada.

7. Conclusion

In the 1990s the whole of Central America and the Caribbean was suffering from cutbacks in adult education and training, because of the region's severe structural economic crisis (regarded as the worst crisis to affect the region since the depression of the 1930s). The achievements gained were placed at risk and in many countries educational provision was stagnating if not declining (see also Table 1). The crisis also jeopardized The Major Educational Project for Latin America and the Caribbean, as planned by the ministers of education and economic planning of Latin America and the Caribbean during a conference held in Mexico in 1979 (Mexico Declaration), and operationalized in 1981 during a follow-up meeting in Quito, Ecuador. The Major Project's objective was to eradicate illiteracy before the end of the twentieth century and to develop services for adults. The former aim became impossible but collective cooperation was strengthened.

See also: Latin America: Adult Education; Latin America: National Training Agencies

References

Archer D, Costello P 1990 *Literacy and Power: The Latin American Battleground.* Earthscan, London

Arnove R F, Dewees A 1991 Education and revolutionary transformation in Nicaragua, 1979–90. *Comp. Educ. Rev.* 35(1): 92–109

Cuba, Ministry of Education 1990 *Cuba—Organization of Education: Report of the Republic of Cuba to the 42nd International Conference on Public Education.* Ministry of Education, Havana

Epstein E E 1985 National consciousness and education in Mexico. In: Brock C, Lawlor H (eds.) 1985 *Education in Latin America.* Croom Helm, London

Instituto Nacional de Estadística Geográfica e Informática 1990 *Perfíl Sociodemográfico—XI Censo General de Población y Vivienda, 1990.* Mexico City

Instituto Nacional para la Educación de los Adultos 1991 *La Educación de Adultos en el Marco de la Modernización Educativa, 1989–1991.* INEA, Mexico City

Richmond M 1990 The Cuban educational model and its influence on the Caribbean region. In: Brock C, Clarkson D (eds.) 1990 *Education in Central America and the Caribbean.* Routledge, London

Torres C A 1990 *The Politics of Nonformal Education in Latin America.* Praeger, New York

UNESCO 1990 *Statistical Yearbook.* UNESCO, Paris

UNESCO 1991 *Statistical Yearbook.* UNESCO, Paris

Further Reading

Arnove R F 1986 *Education and Revolution in Nicaragua.* Praeger, New York

Arrien J B, Matus Lazo R 1989 *Nicaragua: Diez Años de Educación en la Revolución: Contexto, Avances, Problemas y Perspectivas de un Proceso de Transformación.* Ministerio de Educación, Mexico City

Caribbean Community Secretariat 1977 *Report on Survey of Adult Education Activities in the Caribbean.* Castries, Georgetown

Caribbean Community Secretariat 1979 *Report on Seminar Workshop on Adult Education.* Castries, Georgetown

Carnoy M et al. 1990 *Education and Social Transition in the Third World.* Princeton University Press, Princeton, New Jersey

Dominican Republic Secretariado Tecnico de la Presidente 1979 *Oficina Nacional de Planification Regional de Desarrollo de Cibao Oriental.* Dominican Republic Secretariado Tecnico de la Presidente, Santo Domingo

Final report on a meeting of experts from adult eduction institutions in the Caribbean 1980. Sponsored by St. Lucia and UNESCO Regional Office of Latin America and the Caribbean. Castries, Georgetown

Leirman W, Salgado J 1985 Basic adult education in Latin America: The case of Mexico in comparison to Brasil, Chile and Nicaragua. In: Knoll J H (ed.) 1985 *Internationales Jahrbuch der Erwachsenenbildung.* Böhlau, Köln

Mexico, Ministry of Public Education 1990 *Report on Education in Mexico: Forty-second Meeting of the International Conference on Education.* International Bureau of Education, Geneva

Miller V 1984 *Between Struggle and Hope: The Nicaraguan Literacy Crusade.* Westview Press, Boulder, Colorado.

Miller V 1985 The Nicaraguan literacy crusade: Education for transformation. In: Duke C (ed.) 1985 *Combating Poverty Through Adult Education: National Development Strategies.* Croom Helm, London

Nicaragua, Ministerio de Educación 1990 *Lineamientos del Ministerio de Educación en el Nuevo Gobierno de Salvación Nacional.* Ministerio de Educación, Managua

Ramesar E D 1985 Adult education: Regional organization in the Caribbean. In: Husén T, Postlethwaite T N (eds.) 1985 *The International Encyclopedia of Education*, 1st edn. Pergamon Press, Oxford

Richmond M 1985 Education and revolution in socialist Cuba: The promise of democratisation. In: Brock C, Lawlor H (eds.) 1985 *Education in Latin America.* Croom Helm, London

Rivero J 1990 *Latin America and the Caribbean: A Major Project for Literacy.* International Bureau of Education, UNESCO, Paris

Schmelkes S 1990 *Post-Alfabetización y Trabajo en América Latina.* UNESCO/OREALC, Santiago, Chile

Torres C A 1989 Political culture and state bureaucracy in Mexico: The case of adult education. *Int. J. Educ. Dev.* 9(1): 53–68

UNESCO 1963 *Statistical Yearbook.* UNESCO, Paris

UNESCO Netherlands Antilles 1976 *Education: Issues and Priorities for Development.* UNESCO, Paris

UNESCO 1980 *International Yearbook of Education*, Vol. 32. UNESCO, Paris

China: People's Republic

Ming Chuan Dong

The aim of this entry is to give an introduction to adult education and training in the People's Republic of China. The following aspects are discussed: the concepts and principles of adult education in China, the history of adult education, the functions of adult education, the systems and forms of adult education, and the administration of adult education. Major policies are described and a perspective on research on adult education in China is given.

1. Concepts and Principles

Adults make up 60 percent of China's vast population. They occupy a significant position in society as builders of the nation and as a force of social and economic development. The education and training of the workers, farmers, administrative cadres, and science and technology personnel that make up the labor force is therefore an important and recognized part of China's education policy. Given this acknowledgment, China has strived to improve the ideological, moral, technical, and cultural quality of the whole labor force and whole nation by providing extensive educational services for all adults.

The worker–peasant alliance forms the foundation of the People's Republic of China. Instead of "adult education" the term "worker–peasant education" was used from 1949 to 1981. Since the people who receive adult education study mainly during their spare time, such education has also been referred to as "spare-time education." As a consequence of the enormous expansion and diversification of such education it is now formally called adult education.

Since China adopted a policy of reform and has opened up to the outside world, its adult education has developed in accordance with the guiding principles of democratic and lifelong education.

2. Brief History of Adult Education in China

Adult education has a long history in China. The great thinker and educator Confucius (551–479 BC) advocated that "education should not be selective," thus expanding the range of receivers of education to include not only the nobility but also the common people. Later, distinguished scholars such as Mohcius, Mencius, Jian Kuang, Wang Chong, Han Yu and Zhu Xi further developed the principles of establishing a democratic, mass education system based on lifelong education (see *Lifelong Learning and Continuing Education*). The ideas contributed by these scholars —for example, "teaching and learning promoting and enhancing each other," "elicitation and inducement," "teaching in accordance with student aptitude," and "teaching and advancing step by step"—have greatly enriched the content and practice of both schooling and adult education in China.

Systematic and organized adult education began to emerge in China at the turn of the twentieth century. For instance, in the last years of the Qing dynasty, supplementary education was organized for the aged and those deprived of education. The plan for elementary literacy schools was formulated and implemented at that time. After the revolution in 1911, a social education department was set up in the Ministry of Education of the provisional government in Nanking (now Nanjing) to promote adult education. During the time of the Republic of China several experiments involving adult education were conducted in various places and under different names (such as popular education, common people education, social education, and mass education) and with different contents (such as character-learning education, supplementary education, vocational education, citizen education, and science, literature, and arts education, etc.). From 1927 to 1949, at the revolutionary bases and in the liberated areas under the leadership of the Chinese Communist Party, adult education mainly for peasants, soldiers, and worker–peasant cadres was carried out, thus forming a mass education movement in the service of the revolutionary war.

The People's Republic of China was founded in 1949 to meet the needs of restoring and developing the national economy and building a new social system. The Common Program of 1949, which served as a constitution before the Constitution of the People's Republic of China was promulgated in 1954, explicitly stated that "Spare-time education for the laborers and in-service personnel should be strengthened." In 1950 the Government Administration Council (now the State Council) issued a decree making worker–peasant education the focal point of the country's education work. Also in 1950, the Central People's Government issued the call "to develop literacy education and progressively decrease illiteracy." The urgency and immensity of this task was clear, since it was established that 80 percent of the total population were illiterate.

Great strides were made in the development of adult education from 1949 to 1966. However, during the tumultuous period of the so-called "cultural revolution" from 1966 to 1976, adult education was not in a position to build on its initial foundation. It was not until after 1976 that China's adult education was restored. Since 1978, when China entered the new stage of modernization, adult education has developed vigorously. In 1987 the Chinese government reaffirmed the significant position of adult education and in-service training in the country's education cause, stating that adult education "is the indispensable condition for achieving social and economic development and scientific and technological progress."

3. Functions of Adult Education

By 1990 China had 130 million workers and cadres, over 400 million farmers under the age of 45, and 90 million aged people. Faced with such a vast target population, China's adult education had the following formal tasks:

(a) to provide those who either are in service or need to transfer to new posts, or are seeking an occupation, with the necessary cultural and professional knowledge, skills, and practical ability;

(b) to provide literacy education to the illiterate;

(c) to provide those who have had a regular schooling with either elementary or higher education according to their level and needs, and to grant diplomas to those who qualify;

(d) to provide the professional, technical, and management personnel who have received a higher education with continuing education so as to expand their knowledge and improve their ability;

(e) to provide education in a variety of subjects ranging from law and engineering to hygiene, old-age health protection, home economics, fine arts and calligraphy, and gastronomy and horticulture, to people from all ages and walks of life in order to enable them to live a culturally rich and healthy life based on scientific principles.

4. Systems and Forms of Adult Education

A new organization for adult education has been implemented in China. This organization is characterized by a multichannel, multiform and multisystem approach to adult education provision. It has been set up with the explicit aim of mobilizing the entire adult population to participate in programs specifically designed to meet the needs of the society.

China has two adult education systems: one for degree education and another for nondegree education. The former includes undergraduate college education, vocational junior college education, secondary vocational education, and middle school education. The latter includes literacy education, the training of practical agricultural techniques, on-the-job training, single-course certificate training, and continuing vocational education.

Authorities responsible for adult education include the ministries and commissions under the State Council, the education administrative departments of the provinces, autonomous regions and municipalities which are directly under the State Council, and the ministries in charge of industry, construction, mining, railway and transportation, agriculture and forestry, environmental protection, and so forth.

Adult education is also offered by factories, enterprises, and county and township governments. Trade unions, the organizations of the Communist Youth League and the Women's Federations, in collaboration with local education administrative departments, have set up training schools and other relevant institutions. Social and mass organizations, academic institutions, collective economic enterprises, and individual citizens also organize adult education in various forms.

Adult basic and secondary education is provided by adult secondary vocational schools, secondary vocational classes for workers set up in ordinary secondary schools, adult middle schools, adult technical training schools, peasants' cultural and technical schools and agricultural radio and television schools. Self-study secondary and vocational education examinations are also organized.

The different forms of adult higher education include radio and television universities, colleges for workers and peasants, management personnel institutes, educational administration institutes, adult education institutions in conventional universities and colleges (night schools, correspondence schools, teacher-training courses, etc.), correspondence institutes, distance education, and self-study higher education.

The above-mentioned institutions use different methods in reaching and teaching the adult learners. These include full-time classroom teaching, guided self-study in distance education by means of printed materials and sound and video recordings, and spare-time learning. They offer courses in many subjects, according to their own conditions and the needs of the society and learners. Adult education for farmers is a good example. Because of structural adjustment in the agricultural sector, the focus of adult education in rural areas has shifted from character-learning and reading and writing to practical courses in agriculture, forestry, animal husbandry, side-line production, fishery, small-scale industry, commerce and transportation, and service trades, which the peasants need in order to increase production.

5. Achievements of Adult Education in China

Adult education in China has developed rapidly and is reaching a very significant part of the adult population. From 1978 to 1990 some 42,494,000 illiterate people learned to read and write, bringing the total number of illiterate turned literate since 1949 to 170 million. From 1986 to 1990, some six million people took part in literacy classes each year, and the number of illiterate decreased at a rate of three million annually. However, census data show that there were still 180 million illiterate people in China in 1990. This indicates that China has still much to do in eradicating illiteracy.

From 1986 to 1990 an estimated 170 million peasants in rural areas took part in different forms of adult education of a cultural and technical nature. The volume of vocational training received by staff and workers in industry has increased rapidly since the mid-1980s. Training was received by 110 million workers and staff in 1990, while the comparable figure for 1986 was 32.4 million.

A total of 3,639,800 people graduated from adult higher education institutions from 1980 to 1990. An additional 520,000 adults obtained higher education graduation diplomas through self-study, and another 86,000 received secondary vocational school diplomas. From 1986 to 1990, 6,649,100 adults graduated from adult middle schools, and 69 million people obtained certificates from elementary schools for adults. In 1990, the numbers of on-campus students in adult elementary, secondary, and higher education were 22.8 million, 15.3 million, and 1.7 million respectively.

6. Administration of Adult Education

China's adult education is under the central supervision of the State Education Commission, the Adult Education Department of which is in charge of routine administration. In the ministries and commissions residing under the State Council, there are special sections in charge of adult education and the in-service training of their own personnel. In the provinces, autonomous regions, counties, municipalities, and townships there are administrative units in charge of adult education.

Nongovernmental organizations such as the All China Trade Union, the All China Federation of Women, and the Communist Youth League Central Committee have the task of guaranteeing and promoting provision, and encouraging staff and workers, women, and youth to engage in learning activities. The China Association for Science and Technology is responsible for providing adult learners with education and training in basic and applied science and technology.

Another important partner of the State Education Commission is the China Association for Adult Education. Founded in 1981, the Association has become a national platform for the promotion, organization, and coordination of adult education activities in the country. It collaborates with other organizations such as the China Association of Staff and Workers' Education and the China Association for Continuing Engineering Education, and provides consultation and advice to affiliated research institutions specializing in literacy work, adult higher education, industrial training, and rural adult education. The China Association for Adult Education became a member organization of the International Council of Adult Education (ICAE) in 1983 and of the Asian and South Pacific Bureau of Adult Education (ASPBAE) in 1988 (see *International Council for Adult Education*).

7. Policy of Adult Education in China

Article 19 of the Constitution of the People's Republic of China stipulates: "The state develops all kinds of educational facilities, eradicates illiteracy, gives political, cultural, scientific, technical and vocational education to workers . . . and encourages people to become useful persons through self-study." In accordance with the Constitution, the responsible councils, ministries, and administrative agencies have issued various documents stating the principles and policies that guide the organization, financing, and provision of adult education in the country. Since 1987, when a new budget was created for national expenditure on adult education, increased attention has been given to tasks such as the expansion and improvement of training systems and the establishment of assessment procedures for the certification of knowledge, skills, and competences acquired on the job and through the provision of continuing education and further training of the labor force.

8. Research on Adult Education in China

The number of research studies on the theory and practice of adult education and training increased at an unprecedented rate during the 1980s. This reflects the increased attention given to the development of adult education in a developing country with a population of over 11.3 hundred million people, of which some 678 million are adults. Adult education in China is highly diversified, and the multichannel, multisystem, and multiform approach to its development makes it imperative that research be carried out in order to achieve clarity and monitor developments. There is a great need for studies collecting information that make it possible to systematize the experience so far gained. The focus is mostly on applied research serving the different needs of practitioners and institutions that deliver adult education and training, although high priority is also given to theoretical research studies on questions of policy and strategy that serve the needs of decision makers and reform planners.

The research work on adult education is being coordinated and supervised by the National Steering Group for Education Science Programs. Fields and topics for research are suggested through consultation with various administrative departments, theoretical research institutions, and the organizations and institutions that provide adult education and training. Topics that have been identified as national priorities are research on relations between rural technical education and rural economic development, research on literacy and post literacy education, research on continuing vocational education and on-the-job training in enterprises, research on schools run by the various mass organizations, research on diversified patterns of postsecondary education, and research on new information technologies in distance education.

See also: Asia, East and Southeast; Japan: Social and Adult Education; Russian Federation

References

Central People's Government of China 1949–1981 *Yearbook of Education in China* (annual). Chinese Encyclopaedia Publishing House, Beijing
Central People's Government of China 1991 *Education Statistics Yearbook of China 1990*. People's Education Publishing House, Beijing
State Education Commission 1985 *Chinese Encyclopaedia*. Special volume on education in China. Chinese Encyclopaedia Publishing House, Beijing
State Education Commission 1988 *Post-secondary Education in China: Present State and Trends*. Third Department of Higher Education, State Education Commission, Beijing
State Education Commission 1990a. *Literacy in China*. Adult Education Department of State Education Commission, Beijing and China Association for Adult Education, Beijing. People's Education Publishing House, Beijing
State Education Commission 1990b *Collected Research*

Works on China's Post-senior Middle School Education. Staff and Workers' Education Publishing House, Beijing

Further Reading

Colletta N J 1982 *Worker-Peasant Education in the People's Republic of China.* World Bank Staff Working Paper, No. 527. The World Bank, Washington, DC

Wang J, Colletta N 1991 Chinese adult education in transition. In: Epstein I (ed.) 1991 *Chinese Education: Problems, Policies and Prospects.* Garland Publishing, London

Yu B, Xu H Y 1988 *Adult Higher Education: A Case Study of the Workers' Colleges in the People's Republic of China.* International Institute for Educational Planning, UNESCO, Paris

European Union: Continuing Vocational Training

R. Walther

This entry offers a brief history of the development of continuing vocational training in Europe. Special attention is paid to the developments during the 1980s and early 1990s, a period characterized by rapid and profound changes. Major Community programs in continuing vocational training such as EUROTECHNET, COMETT, FORCE, and LEONARDO DA VINCI are described, and future perspectives on skill formation in Europe are offered.

1. A Brief History of Continuing Vocational Training in Europe

1.1 European Community Involvement in Continuing Vocational Training: 1953–80

Although the treaties establishing the European Community did not overlook vocational training, they considered it only as a measure accompanying the changes involved with achieving the Community. It was not until the 1980s and the beginning of the 1990s that a wider concept of continuing vocational training as an economic necessity and also as a means of human fulfilment emerged.

The treaties establishing the European Coal and Steel Community (ECSC—Paris, April 18, 1951) and the European Economic Community (EEC—Rome, March 25, 1957) allowed for some movement in the field of continuing vocational training. Continuing vocational training was nevertheless considered to be a measure accompanying sectoral changes in the labor market and those of the economy in general that resulted from the construction of Europe.

Article 56 of the Treaty of Paris provided for the financing of vocational retraining of workers who had to change their employment as a result of the creation of the coal and steel common market. Several articles in the Treaty of Rome were concerned with continuing vocational training. The Commission had the task of promoting close collaboration between Member States in the social field, particularly in matters relating to basic and advanced vocational training (Article 118). The objective of the European Social Fund was to ensure workers' productive re-employment, for example, by vocational retraining (Article 125), whereas the Council, acting on a proposal of the Commission, had to lay down the general principles for implementing a common vocational training policy which could contribute to the harmonious development of both national economies and the Common Market (Article 128). The Council Decision of April 2, 1963 laid down the general principles for implementing a vocational training policy. An advisory committee for vocational training was set up in the same year.

When the Community was enlarged for the first time in 1973 (with the accession of Denmark, Ireland, and the United Kingdom), a common vocational training policy was considered to be a priority means for the achievement of the objectives of the social action program, as was the creation of a European Center for the development of Vocational Training (CEDEFOP). Despite this, it was not until the 1980s that a new interest in continuing vocational training programs emerged.

1.2 European Community Involvement in Continuing Vocational Training: 1980–94

The 1980s were characterized by a high level of unemployment, a high degree of economic reorganization, the introduction of new technologies, and an internationalization of the economy. On the European level, a very clear perception of the gap in innovation—and thus in economic performance—between Europe and its commercial partners led the Community first to increase its efforts in technological research and development, and then to accelerate the elimination of all obstacles to the internal, or common market, which was completed on January 1, 1993. The amendments made to the Treaty by the Single Act were the expression of an overall Community policy geared to improving the Community's competitive position by creating a vast market and bettering technological performance, as well as promoting economic and social cohesion which, among other things, meant giving more emphasis to a continuing vocational training policy. The 1980s also saw the launching of the first Community programs in both research and vocational training.

Education and training were perceived as a basic set of skills, knowledge, and aptitudes that each individual should adapt, modify, and broaden throughout his or her entire life. Continuing vocational training was therefore no longer a back-up measure, accessible only to groups of people affected by restructuring or reconversion measures; like education, it had become a right and a necessity for all. The Community Charter of Fundamental Social Rights of Workers, signed at the European Council meeting in Strasbourg in 1989 by the heads of state and government leaders (United Kingdom excepted), stipulated that any Community worker had the right to continue his or her vocational training throughout life. This new concept of continuing vocational training was more likely to find an adequate response at the level where the problem was posed, that is, the local (company), regional, national, Community, and European levels.

1.3 Perspectives for Community Vocational Policy: 1995–99

The Treaty on European Union, which was signed in Maastricht on 7 February 1992 and came into effect on 1st November 1993, contains significant changes with regard to the legal framework set out in the Treaty of Rome. There is a specific chapter entitled "Education, Vocational Training and Youth" which clearly highlights the importance of community policies in this area as part of the process of ever-increasing union between the peoples of Europe. Under Article 127, the Treaty sets out three new areas:

(a) It stipulates that the Community implements a vocational training policy which supports and complements those of the Member States, whereas previous actions of the Community set out to establish general principles for a common vocational training policy.

(b) It amends the decision-making procedure in that it stipulates that the Council will henceforth make decisions using a qualified majority and not a simple majority, and this further to a cooperation procedure with the European Parliament.

(c) It clearly stipulates that Community involvement is not aimed at fostering harmonization beyond the legal and statutory arrangements in force in the Member States and confirms the latters' responsibility for the content of programs and the organization of systems. The diversity of systems and the responsibility of the Member

States therefore become the cornerstones of a community policy which facilitates increased cooperation and the convergence of vocational training initiatives at the European level.

Further to this legal change, the Treaty on European Union underlines the essential role that vocational training has to play with regard to the process of industrial change Europe is facing (Articles 123 and 127). These changes are affecting technologies, production systems, work organizations and information and communication strategies. The close linkage between these changes and vocational training means that training systems and actions must provide responses that are adapted to the competitive needs of the European economy and to the skills requirements of individuals. Going beyond the traditional distinction between initial and continuing training, this will enable young people and employees to access education and training throughout their working lives. It will therefore progressively help to create "learning societies."

With this background, the Council of Social Affairs Ministers adopted, on 6 December 1994, a new action program for the implementation of a vocational training policy in the European Union called "LEONARDO DA VINCI". This program, which will run from 1 January 1995 until 31 December 1999, aims to rationalize and develop the impact of Community action which is currently based on programs such as FORCE, EUROTECNET and COMETT, and the initial vocational training program known as PETRA.

All these programs will be terminated by the end of 1994. It is important to understand their structure and main achievements in order to gain a better understanding of what future actions are to be implemented by the LEONARDO DA VINCI program.

2. Community Programs Running until the End of 1994

To meet the demand for training, the European Community set up a number of programs over the years: EUROTECNET (1983, 1989), COMETT (1986, 1989), and FORCE (1990, 1991). EUROTECNET promoted innovation in the field of voational training resulting from technological change in the Community. COMETT, conversely, is a program focused on cooperation between universities and industry with regard to training in the field of technology. FORCE is an action program to develop continuing vocational training in companies within the Community.

These programs, decided by the Council of Ministers and implemented by the Commission with the help of advisory committees, meet the following criteria:

(a) *transnationality*, which provides Community added value and promotes synergy of Member State initiatives while respecting the authority of national systems;

(b) a growing number of *transnational exchanges* between training programs (EUROTECNET), between persons in training and trainers (COMETT), or between those responsible for training (FORCE);

(c) the creation of a *European network* for exchanges, cooperation, and the development of common projects that contribute to the construction of significant forms of cooperation;

(d) *partnerships* through cooperation between the various partners involved in common projects;

(e) system-wide *consultation* with public authorities, employers' and workers' organizations, and educational and training institutions, which assists the Commission to implement its programs.

2.1 EUROTECNET

The first program launched by the Commission was EUROTECNET—"an action program to promote innovation in the field of vocational training"—resulting from technological change in the Community. Acting on a Council Resolution of June 2, 1983, on measures concerning vocational training in new technologies, the first EUROTECNET program covered the 1985–88 period and was above all a program for training labor in using new technologies, whereas the objective of the second program (1990–94) was to promote innovation in the vocational training field and to take into account technological changes and their impact on employment, work, and qualification.

To do this, the program established a network of innovative national and transnational projects in the Member States which make the exchange of experience and information possible. The 280 projects in the second program were chosen for their transferability from one Member State to another. They concerned curriculum development, technological transfer, and the active participation of industry in the promotion of and the training for new technologies.

The program included three other types of measures: first, the promotion of innovative approaches and methods such as the development of programs for teachers and the creation of European partnerships in training for technologies; second, studies and analyses of certain aspects of training; and third, information and dissemination actions such as conferences, round tables, and publications.

The budget devoted to the first program was 4.7 million ECU; that of the second program was 7.5 million ECU for the first three years. The Community did not contribute to the financing of demonstration projects, but it subsidized the cost of incorporating them into an international network.

2.2 COMETT

COMETT—"the cooperation programme between universities and industry regarding training in the field of technologies," was created by a Council decision in 1986. Implemented in 1987, the program began a second phase in 1990 for a period of five years. This second phase was open to the participation of EFTA (European Free Trade Association) countries. COMETT was the first Community education and training program which was open to Austria, Finland, Norway, Sweden, Switzerland, and the other countries.

The main objectives of the program consisted of improving training in advanced technologies, developing highly skilled human resources, and enhancing the competitiveness of European industry. To reach these goals, several lines of action were defined:

(a) giving a European dimension to cooperation between universities and industry (in any economic sector) in the field of initial and continuing training in technologies;

(b) broadening the range of experiments by encouraging student inservice training in companies and by creating a series of bridges between industry and the university (exchanges of personnel, etc.);

(c) developing high performance tools and training courses to integrate the most recent progress in research and development in the field of advanced technologies;

(d) promoting equal opportunity between men and women in initial and continuing training in technologies.

The COMETT program was made up of a series of transnational actions intended to reinforce and encourage cooperation between universities and industry. These projects constituted one of four complementary measures:

(a) The network of university–enterprise training partnerships (UETPs) developed cooperation in training technologies. It helped identify and meet the needs in training for technology, reinforce cooperation and interregional transfers between Member States, and stimulate transnational sectoral interaction.

(b) The transnational exchanges of students, industrial personnel, and universities. The community subsidized the direct and indirect costs of mobility of students who, as part of their studies, did 3 to 12 months training in a company in another Member State; students and graduates who, before taking their first employment, took up placements for advanced training in industry from 6 months to 2 years; and exchanges of university and company personnel.

(c) Joint projects for continuing training in technologies on a European scale. The Community supported three types of transnational projects between universities and companies: crash training for the rapid dissemination of the results of research and development and their applications in the field of new technologies plus their introduction in small and medium-sized businesses; the devising of joint industry–university training projects; and the development of multimedia distance education and training.

(d) Complementary promotion and back-up measures, including the financing of preparatory visits and actions to promote dissemination of information, and program evaluation.

The overall budget for the first phase of the program was 52.6 million ECU; for the second 200 million ECU were available (excluding EFTA countries). The first phase of COMETT made it possible to create 125 university–company partnerships, to organize industrial placements for 4,000 students, to award 232 scholarships for exchanges of university and company personnel and to give financial support to 329 joint projects. At the end of 1994, the number of university–company partnerships was 202, including 125 regional and 52 sectoral partnerships.

2.3 *FORCE*

Launched in 1991 for a period of four years, FORCE was the first action program for the quantitative and qualitative development of continuing vocational training in Community companies. The program's objectives were:

(a) encouraging investment in continuing vocational training;

(b) promoting innovative approaches to management, development of new training methods, and design of tools and equipment;

(c) supporting transnational projects including the exchange of experiences, good practice, and mobility of those responsible for training;

(d) improving the anticipation of continuing vocational training needs.

Compared to other Community programs, FORCE was distinctive in the priority it assigned to cross-company transfer of training experience. In addition, coordinating the work of all of those involved in continuing vocational training (companies, national and regional authorities, various training organizations, both sides of industry) was to lead to the promotion of the European dimension of training.

FORCE's action sphere in continuing vocational training was two-fold. First, the implementation of transnational measures to support Member States' initiatives. These included:

(a) An exchange program to promote the transfer of good practice and innovation between staff in company human resources departments, training specialists, and both sides of industry.

(b) The creation of pilot transnational vocational training projects organized by companies, groups of companies, or training organizations, with emphasis on the transferability of method and content, particularly to small and medium-sized businesses.

(c) Each project included at least two companies including one small or medium-sized enterprise. They targeted the skills of trainers, tutors, and managers from smaller businesses; the relationship between skills of employees and the introduction of new forms of organizations and qualifications at work; and the various ways of validating achievements and certification to recognize skills acquired by employees by means of continuing vocational training.

FORCE also assisted in bringing together initiatives in the Member States in the continuing vocational training field. This was done along the following three lines of action.

(a) Exchanges of comparable data on continuing vocational training in close collaboration with EUROSTAT, the Community statistical office. These included two specific actions. The first was the establishment with the Member States of a management chart of continuing vocational training to record programs and explain how to understand and compare the diverse actions and policies implemented by the countries. The second action was the launch of a EUROSTAT survey with the companies of the Member States to improve the identification of significant practices in terms of access to and investment in training.

(b) Development of a framework for analyzing company agreements and collective labor agreements with regard to continuing vocational training, and encouragement to exchange experience between socioprofessional organizations and to disseminate innovative contractual agreements.

(c) Sectoral surveys in the retail, agro-food, car repair, and road transport sectors which examined the methods for establishing corporate planning in vocational training, a cost-effective assessment of training at company level, agreements and practices at the company level and collective labor agreements, agreements between companies, agreements between companies and public authorities, as well as the techniques used to develop continuing vocational training and to improve access of relatively unskilled workers, part-time workers, and those at risk of unemployment.

With a total budget of 83.7 million ECU from 1991 to 1994, FORCE was a program based on partnership and the creation of a network to develop, evaluate, and disseminate new approaches to training which met company needs. It was targeted directly at companies and aimed to achieve the inclusion of training in corporate strategies. Employers' and workers' organizations, which were represented in the FORCE Advisory Committee, could also be project applicants.

3. The LEONARDO DA VINCI Vocational Training Program: 1995–99

Adopted by the Council of Ministers on 6 December 1994, the LEONARDO DA VINCI program is in line with the objectives set out in the White Paper on "Growth, Competitiveness and Employment: The challenges and ways forward into the twenty-first Century". The program establishes:

(a) A common framework of objectives for community action, to promote the coherent development of vocational training. This common framework, which builds on the guidelines the Council adopted for the FORCE programs, also sets out the objectives deemed necessary for the implementation of Article 127 of the Treaty—adaptation to industrial changes, the improvement of initial and continuing vocational training, access to vocational training, cooperation between training establishments and companies, and the exchange of information and experience on matters of common interest with regard to Member States' training systems;

(b) Community measures based on the common framework of objectives with a view to supporting and complementing actions underway in the Member States. The measures are mainly shared between three strands, with each setting out priority areas for action in the field of vocational training:

(i) Strand 1: support for the improvement of vocational training systems and arrangements in the Member States;

(ii) Strand 2: support for the improvement of vocational training measures, including university/industry cooperation;

(iii) Strand 3: support for the development of linguistic skills, knowledge, and the dissemination of innovation in the field of continuing training.

The program also provides for the creation of co-operation networks between Member States, as well as information, monitoring and evaluation activities that will ensure the efficiency of the different activities of the program. Across the different strands, the program will launch, as from the second half of 1995, three main types of activity:

(a) pilot projects on the design of innovative training contents and methods, together with multiplier effect projects on the products and results of the programs that ran until the end of 1994;

(b) exchanges of young people undergoing vocational training and students before their first job, and exchanges of training managers, specialists and decision-makers focusing on the European dimension of training or the transfer of innovation, especially to small and medium-sized enterprises;

(c) surveys, data analyses, and exchange of statistics about vocational training in Europe.

The LEONARDO DA VINCI program, which will be financed to the tune of 620 million ECU over 5 years (800 million ECU have been proposed by the Commission), brings together all those concerned with initial and continuing vocational training, namely public authorities, companies, the social partners, and training organizations, including universities. It is based on the principle of "the continuum," in other words the establishment of links and synergies between initial and continuing training, technology transfer and bringing training and research closer to companies. It therefore aims to promote lifelong learning and to create new frontiers between the world of training and the world of work.

LEONARDO DA VINCI, in the same way as the programs it replaces, is designed to be implemented in complementarity with the education program SOCRATES and community initiatives such ad ADAPT (adaptation of workers, especially those threatened with unemployment, to industrial change). As a program it puts the skills and qualifications of young people and workers at the heart of the European Union's growth, competitiveness, and employment policies.

See also: Comparative Studies: Adult Education; Comparative Studies: Vocational Education and Training; Europe, Central and Eastern; Europe: Nordic Countries; Europe, Western and Southern

Bibliography

COMETT 1986 Council Decision adopting the program on cooperation between universities and industry regarding training in the field of technology (1988–1989). *Official Journal of the European Communities*, L222 of August 8, 1986: 17–21

COMETT 1989 Council Decision adopting the second phase of the program on cooperation between universities and industry regarding training in the field of technology (1990–1994). *Official Journal of the European Communities*, L13 of January 17, 1989: 28–34

European Commission 1994 *The Challenges to European Education: Unlocking Europe's Human Potential*. Task Force Human Resources. Commission of the European Communities, Brussels

EUROTECNET 1989 Council Decision of 18 December 1989 establishing an action program to promote innovation in the field of vocational training resulting from technological change in the European Community. *Official Journal of the European Communities*, L393 of December 30, 1989: 29–34

EUROTECNET 1994 *A System in Crisis? The Strategically Critical Issues Surrounding the European Vocational Education and Training Systems*. Task Force Human Resources. Commission of the European Communities, Brussels

FORCE 1990 Council Decision of 29 May 1990 establishing an action program for the development of continuing vocational training in the European Community (FORCE) *Official Journal of the European Communities*, L156 of June 21, 1990: 1–7

FORCE 1991 Memorandum on higher education in the European Community. Task Force Human Resources, Commission of the European Communities, Brussels, December 1991

LEONARDO DA VINCI 1995 Council decision establishing an action program of human resource development for European growth, competitiveness and employment. *Official Journal of the European Communities* February

Europe, Central and Eastern

A. Krajnc

The countries of Central and Eastern Europe (Bulgaria, Croatia, Czech Republic, Estonia, Hungary, Latvia, Lithuania, Slovakia, Slovenia, Poland, Romania, and Russia) make up as much as 68 percent of the territory of continental Europe, and 49 percent of the entire European population (Polturzycki 1993). Their share in shaping the European identity is far more significant than it appears. The variety of languages in the countries under consideration are among the obstacles to an efficient flow of information to Western European and other countries. In spite of the national, linguistic, cultural, legal, economic, geographical, and other differences among the countries of the region, all of them have a common history since at least the Second World War. In all the countries affected during this period the course of their natural social, cultural, and economic development was discontinued. It also prevented their integration into "Europe" and halted intensive communication with other countries.

1. History of Adult Education

Adult education has a long tradition in Central and Eastern European countries. Szymon Marycjusz wrote in his book, *De scholis sue academiis libri duo*, which was published in Krakow (Poland) in 1551, that "[the] search for knowledge must not be limited with school time, but learning must go independently of the age of the person" (Wiatrowski 1994).

Komensky (1592–1670) who was born in Moravia (Czech Republic) travelled and also worked in the neighbouring countries and across Europe. He published books on education which still find a place in the professional literature. *Panpedia* is among his most important books about adult education. The exact year when it was published is not known, but is estimated to be around 1640. In this publication Komensky offers the first concept and description of lifelong education. He defined education as a lifelong process for all, and divided the life cycle into 8 stages from birth to death. In each of them education had a different purpose (Schmidt 1988). The Protestant movement brought about the first books published in national languages, the languages which people understood. This was an important factor in making the people literate. Popular education was a big concern for Protestants; everybody had to learn how to read and write, so that people could read the Bible for themselves. The leader of the Protestant movement, Primus Trubar, wrote the first *Primer*, published in 1550 and the first book in the Slovene language, which was published in 1551 (Schmidt 1988). The role of the Protestant movement was similar in the neighbouring countries of Central Europe. The eradication of illiteracy in those countries lasted until the middle of the nineteenth century, and in the Eastern European countries until the middle of the twentieth century

The next important period for adult education in Central and Eastern European countries was the period of enlightenment from the middle of the eighteenth century until the beginning of the nineteenth century. Maria Teresia accepted a new Act of Education in 1774 which influenced the development of education in the countries which are known today as the Czech Republic, Hungary, Poland, Slovakia, Slovenia, and Croatia. "Sunday schools" and obligatory continuing education of teachers were formal kinds of adult education whilst the law made 8 years of primary education obligatory for children and young adults. This laid the foundation for the subsequent development of industry, schools, and vocational education for adults (Schmidt 1988).

Educational associations (Poland 1822, Bohemia 1831, Romania 1861, Bulgaria 1969, Slovenia 1832), workers enlightenment associations, reading rooms, libraries, voluntary associations, and self-education circles were established in both cities and rural areas during the nineteenth century. Towards the end of that century the Sunday schools were transformed into adult evening schools which provided basic education for adults (Pachocinski 1994). Vocational training and industrial schools were important for the emerging industries at that time. Before the First World War folk high schools spread from Northern Europe to Central Europe and to some Eastern European countries. In some countries these folk high schools were named "peoples universities."

In the period between the two World Wars some countries continued to battle against illiteracy. In 1930 Bulgaria had an illiteracy rate of 28 percent, Poland 23 percent, and Romania 39 percent whilst census returns in Russian in 1897 showed an illiteracy rate of 80 percent. After the October revolution the Soviet State assigned priority to combating illiteracy and polytechnical education and political education became popular. The educational level of the Russian population rose rapidly after that: in 1939, 21 percent of the population (of 10 years of age and older) had received 7 years of schooling whilst in 1970 the figure was 59.2 percent (Strewe 1994).

After the Second World War the Communist Party had assumed complete control over social and political life in all the countries under consideration. The "old" tradition in adult education was neglected. The wide range of adult education activities that existed before the Soviet takeover was narrowed down to vocational training and political adult education. By the 1980s as a consequence of this repression, adult education activism and participation had encountered a dramatic decline.

2. Political, Economic, and Social Change and the Role of Adult Education

The countries of Central and Eastern Europe can no longer be subsumed under the label, "Eastern Bloc." The situation has changed dramatically since the fall of the Berlin Wall in 1989, which signified the collapse of the totalitarian, socialist, or communist system. For all these countries this was the historical turning point resulting in widespread political, social, economic, technological, and other changes. The years since 1989 have witnessed a process of change that differs from country to country, depending not only on its original culture, history, and tradition, but also on its way of building up a society since independence, constituting a new state, and ensuring their further development. Yet common features of development also

exist such as the introduction of market economies, the privitization of property, the restructuring of labour markets, the development of new production systems and adoption of new technologies, the appearance of competition, the deregulation of political power, the institution of a multi-party parliamentary system, the stipulation of civic rights and the introduction of democracy. There is also an important shift toward greater integration with and openness toward Europe and the rest of the World (Jelenc 1994). National identity, values, and lifestyles have changed rapidly as a result.

Adult education is expected to play a significant role in promoting and realising social and economic change. However, the present situation shows that it is not easy to change people who have lived as "dependents" and have been ruled for more than 40 years (Basel 1992). The legacy of the previous regime still lingers and is demonstrated by the way people think and behave. Totalitarian systems oppressed much of the population by withholding information, education, and the ability to communicate. As a result most people find it difficult to be personally responsible and enterprising in new situations and activities. Hence, the role of adult education has important implications for personal and economic development in those countries.

An important goal of adult education is to bring people from a state of dependency toward self-sufficiency. To help realise this goal several nationwide adult education projects have been initiated in various countries: training adult educators (Hungary, Bulgaria, Estonia, Slovenia, Slovakia); sociocultural animation and study circles (Slovenia, Poland); functional literacy (Romania, Russia, Slovenia, Czech Republic); and civic education (Poland, Bulgaria, Lithuania, Latvia, Estonia). A very important new role of adult education in countries in transition is to help to change people's thinking and behavior. In some countries the new governments have already recognized the importance of adult education, establishing new national institutions for adult education (Estonia, Slovenia, Bulgaria) and developing networks such as the Network of Folk High Schools (Hungary), and the Network of Centers for Economic and Civic Education (Poland).

3. Adult Education in the mid-1990s

It is too early to describe the delineations of the new adult education systems in the countries of Central and Eastern Europe, because they are still in the intensive process of creation.

Significant for all the countries is the sudden explosion of adult education and learning since 1990. Among the population two types of reaction appear when people perceive a lack of skills and knowledge: some try hard to master the changes and overcome the crises, whereas others show a strong resistance against change. Social differentiation occurs rapidly between these two groups, and negative reactions abound, especially among poorly educated adults. For the latter the state system of adult education can organize provision, but it cannot guarantee that those who most need knowledge and skills will actually participate and benefit from the programs on offer.

The goals and objectives of adult education have also changed. In the previous regime the goals were centrally determined by the state and supported primarily production (vocational training, schooling and adults), the political system, and the official ideology (political education).

Generally speaking adult education in the countries of Central and Eastern Europe is less centralized than it was before, and more oriented toward regional and local level development. At the same time it has gained more autonomy and can set the goals and objectives more independently and according to the needs of learners, local communities, and regions. Although centralized state control has almost disappeared, there are still some general educational goals. Adult education has to meet several needs:

(a) the need for individuals and the state to discover new, autonomous identities;

(b) the need for developing and sustaining democracy (multiparty system, democratic social relations, human rights, dialogue, and solidarity);

(c) the need for establishing a market economy and a restructuring of the economy (competition, individual responsibility, management, business administration, vocational training, continuing education, and retraining);

(d) the need for encouraging the modernization of technology and the adoption of new technologies (computers, automation);

(e) the need for education of special target groups (handicapped, elderly, women, young school dropouts);

(f) the need for better communication and mass media (distance and broadcast education for adults);

(g) the need for learner-centred adult education (education for personal growth, self-sufficiency, self-initiative, and creativity).

There is now more scope for people to set their own goals and express their personal needs in search for knowledge. Private adult education institutions, networks, and development projects have proliferated throughout the region during the years since 1990.

4. New Developments

Adult education systems in countries in transition are moving from centralist to pluralistic ones. The need for adult education is also growing rapidly. An explosion of adult learning is witnessed in countries where the learning standard of people is not too low. It must be noted that in the course of change, some of the Soviet-inspired and even older institutions have closed down or were reduced (Znanie in Russia; workers universities in Croatia; training centers in factories in Slovenia, Romania, and Lithuania; vocational training in Bulgaria). Because the new institutions are not yet established, there is a vacuum as the old institutions are abolished before any replacements are created. Regression to the methods of the past has brought great anxieties among adult educators, for both ideological and economic reasons.

In the countries of Central and Eastern Europe much effort is going into establishing a contemporary adult education system. All countries are adopting or developing new legislation for adult education. Estonia has already passed a new Act of Adult Education; and the Czech Republic, Croatia, Romania and Slovenia are close to doing the same. Special units for adult education have been established at the Ministries of Education in Estonia, Hungary, and Slovenia (Jelenc 1994). Even without government direction and support many new adult education institutions, in particular private ones, are springing up (Kulich 1994). Hungary has also started a project of reviving folk high schools (Toth 1989). One may note the rise of andragogy in academic institutions in the Czech Republic, Estonia, Slovakia, Slovenia, and Russia (Hartl 1993). Poland is building up a network of centers for civic and economic education, which will help to build an educated, democratic society (Ratman-Liwerska 1994). Furthermore, centers for management and business administration are being formed throughout the region, often in cooperation with foreign higher education institutions.

Individuals are increasingly choosing to go abroad to search for education, mostly to Western European countries. Another notable trend is that the countries of Central and Eastern Europe are importing adult education programs to meet the increased demand in their own countries. The most common of these programs are intended to train workers to compete in the market economy and include elements such as management, business administration, school and culture administration, social policy, foreign languages, information technology, and computer sciences. Adult education has become a product that individuals must purchase for themselves because in many of the countries in transition the state budget can no longer sustain the large expenditures required. This is illustrated by the example of Znanie in Russia which received 80 million Roubles from the state budget in 1991, only 40 million Roubles in 1992 (and even less in 1993) (Strewe 1994).

With the support of the European Union (TEMPUS and PHARE programs) countries are trying to raise the level of higher education among the population and organize their own distance studies (e.g., Budapest Platform 1989). According to the UNDP World Development index some of the countries in transition fall

779

Table 1
Number of adult learners (in thousands), distributed by school levels in Poland, 1980–92

School level	Number of adults (in thousands)		
	1980–81	1990–91	1991–92
Adult basic education	18.5	13.9	12.5
Vocational education	19.9	4.2	2.2
Secondary and upper secondary	69.5	48.6	49.0
University and colleges	156.6	92.1	101.6

Source: Wiatrowski 1994

into the top group with respect to rates of adult literacy (Slovenia 98%, Czechoslovakia [before separation] 97.2%, Hungary 97.2%) and in the top group of the mean numbers of years of schooling (Slovenia 9.8, Hungary 9.6, Russia 9.0) (UNDP 1993). However, the percentage of people with higher educational qualifications is relatively low according to the Censuses in 1990 and 1991. Higher education in Hungary was obtained by 10.1 percent of adults (25 years or older), in the Czech Republic the figure is 10 percent, in Slovenia 8.85 percent (15 years or older), and in Slovakia 6.62 percent. This compares with about 40 percent of the population (25–64 years old) in the United States and Canada, about 24 percent (25–64 years old) in Norway, Sweden and Germany; and below 10 percent in Austria, Italy, Portugal, Spain and Turkey (OECD 1994). Economic development and the competition in world markets compels the countries in transition to seek ways to raise the level of educational attainment of the population. Part-time adult studies and distance studies are two important ways by which this goal can be realized.

The need for adult education at lower levels of schooling has decreased and at higher levels it has increased. This trend can be observed in the data for Poland shown in Table 1.

5. Conclusion

Adult education and training provision in Central and Eastern European countries is undergoing a period of radical change. New programs, methods, and means of teaching are being introduced at a rapid pace. Some of these innovations will find a place in the educational system while others will disappear shortly after their introduction. Although adult education in these countries is undergoing a period of dynamic changes, where even the educators have to learn new ways, sufficiently motivated individuals can find the route to the education they need.

See also: Comparative Studies: Adult Education; International Adult Education; UNESCO and Adult Education;

European Union: Continuing Vocational Training; Europe: Nordic Countries; Europe, Western and Southern

References

Basel P 1992 Lessons of experience of adult education in the socialist period in Hungary. *Int. J. Univ. Adult Educ.* 2: 52–58

Hartl P 1993 The natural experiment of Czecho-Slovak velvet divorce. *Convergence* 3:5–10

Jelenc Z 1994 *Research on Adult Education in Central and Eastern Countries.* ACS, Ljubljana

Kulich J 1994 Adult Education in Central and Eastern European Countries. Vancouver (Unpublished manuscript)

Organisation for Economic Co-operation and Development 1994 *Education at a Glance: OECD Indicators.* OECD, Paris

Pachocinski R 1994 Central and Eastern Europe: Adult education, In: Husén T, Postlethwaite T N (eds.) 1994 *International Encyclopedia of Education,* 2nd edn. Pergamon, Oxford

Polturzycki J 1993 Rethinking adult education in the former socialist countries of Europe. In: *Rethinking Adult Education for Development* 1993. ACS, Ljubljana

Ratman-Liwerska I 1994 *State of the Art Study of Research on Education of Adults.* National report on the basis of the questionaire. SASREA-CEEC, Bialystok

Schmidt V 1988 *Zgodovina solstva in pedagogike na Sloverskem.* Delavska enotnost, Ljubljana

Strewe B 1994 *Erwachsenenbildung in Russland.* IIZ DVV, Bonn

Toth J 1989 *Folk High Schools and Democratisation 1988–1989: Spectacular Change of Social Environment.* ESVA, Budapest

UNDP 1993 *Human Development Report.* United Nations Development Programme, Geneva

Waitrowski Z 1994 *Die Geschichte der permanente Bildung in Polen im Blitzlicht Europahandbuch Weiterbildung.* Luchterhand, Berlin

Further Reading

Beresneviciene D 1994 *Survey of the Present Research on Adult Education in Lithuania,* National report, Vilnius

Draft Policy Recommendations on Adult Education in Slovakia 1994 PHARE Project, PTH Contract, Bratislava

Krajnc A 1993 Slovenia. In: *Rethinking Adult Education for Development* 1993. ACS, Ljubljana

Krajnc A 1994 Europe–a major perspective of adult education in Slovenia. *Internationale Jachrbuch der Erwachsenenbildung* 22: 141–57

Makedonska M 1994 *Obrazovanieto na vzrastni v Blgarija.* National Report on the Basis of the Questionnaire. SASREA–CEEC, Sofia

Märja T 1992 Adult education in Estonia. *Adult Education and Development* 39: 207–17

Pongrac S, Vadjon V 1994 *Izvestaj o obrazovanju odraslih u Hrvatskoj.* National Report on the Basis of the Questionaire. SASREA-CEEC, Rijaka

Sacalis N 1994 *Adult Education in Romania.* National report, Bucuresti

Strewe B 1993 Erwachsenenbildung in Mitteleuropa, der GUS und im Balticum im Ubergang vom Gestern zum Heute. In: *Erwachsenenbildung und Entwicklung* 1993 DVV, Bonn

Europe: Nordic Countries

B. Wahlgren

Adult education plays and has played an important role in all the Nordic countries: Denmark, Finland, Iceland, Norway, and Sweden. In these countries adult education forms part of a well-established tradition dating back to the political and religious movements in the nineteenth century.

This entry describes the publicly financed, general adult education and pays attention to labor market training. However, it does not deal with the internal education and training of employees. A brief description of the Nordic systems of adult education is given. This is followed by a description of legislation and financing. Some central research studies are also presented.

1. Goals and Scope of Adult Education and Training

Typically, in the Nordic countries, formulated intentions for adult education activities have existed only to a modest degree. These activities have often been based on voluntary work connected to associations or political organizations. It was not until the early 1940s that the field obtained a more formalized status, as a result of its being subsidized by the state. Even so, many of the activities are still carried out without formal preambles.

Historically Nordic adult education has been tied up with the concept of "*folkeoplysning*," a term which is difficult to translate into other languages. The first part of the word (*folke*) refers to the cultural tradition and the national identity of the people. The second part (*oplysning*) means enlightenment or clarification. The translation "popular enlightenment" is used here.

Popular enlightenment is based on ideas contributed by the Danish priest, poet, and philosopher, N F S Grundtvig (1783–1872). His premise was that popular movements are decisive for the development of society and a condition for democracy (see *Folk High Schools*). Popular enlightenment is a significant part of this process. It is not to be understood as a process in which the societal elite enlighten the common people. Rather, it demands that everyone participates actively. The crucial concepts are freedom of choice, shared responsibility, and informative discourse among equals.

The primary purpose of adult education and, in this context, popular enlightenment must be regarded in relation to the goal of establishing and maintaining a democratic society. A second important purpose which has characterized the Nordic "model" of adult education since the early 1970s relates to the redistribution of economic, social, and political resources by means of education. The idea is that adult education may contribute to a redistribution of the educational resources in the population. During the same period a third important purpose has become evident, namely, that of improving the qualifications of the labor force. Adult education plays an increasingly significant role in the development and reorganization of the labor market. Finally, in the beginning of the 1990s great emphasis has been put on internationalization in education—a trend which has had an impact even on adult education.

2. The Delivery System

The adult education system in the Nordic countries is —more or less rigidly—divided into three main sectors: (a) popular enlightenment activities, including the folk high schools; (b) general-oriented, qualifying education at basic or advanced levels; and (c) continuing vocational education and training, including labor market training for the unemployed. There are also special courses for adults with different handicaps, as well as special programs for immigrants and refugees.

2.1 Organizations for Popular Enlightenment

In Denmark, Iceland, Norway, and Sweden popular enlightenment is organized in study organizations or voluntary educational associations. These are locally anchored, though united in national organizations. The organizations for popular enlightenment are, by tradition, often more or less closely connected with political or religious organizations. The Nordic cooperation within this area is extensive, in part because the Nordic countries have a common political and religious history.

The educational programs offered by the voluntary educational associations are general in character. The curriculum mainly covers languages, cultural and social subjects, and art education. Normally, the programs are not formally qualifying. Different teaching approaches are used, although lectures, brief courses, and study circles are the most common. The duration varies from 2–3 hours to around 100 hours. Often the teaching is spread out over a long period of time, comprising a couple of hours per week. The programs are most often offered as evening classes.

In Denmark, there are two specific organizations for popular enlightenment: the university for extramural courses and the day high schools. The main task of the university for extramural courses is to disseminate knowledge about the methods and results of the research conducted at the universities. There exist around 140 local committees for extramural courses. There are approximately 100 day high schools in Denmark which have been established since the mid-1970s. The activities have primarily centered on the training of the unemployed, but the orientation has gradually broadened.

In Finland, the popular enlightenment activities take place in citizens' and workers' institutes or in study centers. The citizens' and workers' institutes are the most important institutes for general education. Their task is to provide the participants with the knowledge and skills which enable them to continue in further education, to undertake self-tuition, to strengthen their personal development, and to obtain a rich leisure time. The teaching is part-time, comprising 2–3 hours a week. The activities are organized on a voluntary basis, although 90 percent of the funding is provided by local municipal authorities. The number of such institutes is 280, with around 2,300 local departments. The study centers offer study circles, lectures, and courses in general subjects. Half of the 11 study centers, which represent around a fourth of the popular enlightenment activities, are party politically oriented (see *Study Circles*).

2.2 Folk High Schools

The first folk high schools were established in the nineteenth century. There are around 400 folk high schools in the Nordic countries (see *Folk High Schools*).

In all the Nordic countries the folk high schools emphasize "life education." In Denmark, Iceland, and Norway the courses have a general orientation and are not formally qualifying. In Finland and Sweden qualifying courses are offered too. The folk high schools most often base their work on a political or religious notion or they emphasize specific fields of interest (e.g., theater, sports, or the arts).

Originally the programs were solely organized as courses of a long duration, lasting three to four months or more. Since the 1960s, the number of short courses has increased, especially in Denmark, Finland, and Sweden. The folk high schools are usually boarding schools. The teachers and learners tend to be together both in the classroom and during leisure time. This is regarded as an important feature of the pedagogy of folk high schools.

2.3 Qualifying Education at Basic and Advanced Levels

In Denmark, Finland, Norway, and Sweden, programs are provided for adults who want to improve their general knowledge. The courses are credential; they lead to a certificate qualifying for further education. The teaching is conducted both at a basic level and a more advanced level. The advanced level qualifies the participant for further education as well as for employment.

In Denmark and Finland, general education and vocational education are separate. In Iceland, Norway, and Sweden they are united in a single system with different tracks.

In Denmark, Finland, and Sweden, programs are offered that are designed specifically for adults. These take into account the special needs and qualifications of adults. The teaching takes place in institutions for adults only. In contrast, in Iceland and Norway, the qualifying type of adult education is integrated with the education intended for young people or school-aged children.

2.4 Labor Market Training

The aim of labor market training relates to both labor market policies and employment policies. Most labor market training courses qualify the participant for employment.

The extent of the teaching varies from one week to a year or more. The courses are often divided into modules. The content corresponds to the demands on the labor market. The teaching usually takes place in day classes.

2.5 Distance Education

Distance education specifically aims at offering the adult the possibility of enrolling in an educational program for which physical attendance is not required. In distance education, media are used to a great extent, and the teaching methods usually emphasize self-tuition. The spread and scope of distance education varies very much among the Nordic countries. The development has advanced the furthest in Norway and the least in Denmark. Distance education attracts growing attention from both policymakers and the general public (see *Distance Education*).

3. Participants in Adult Education

Every year a third or more of the adult population participates in some kind of adult education. This holds true for Denmark, Finland, Norway, and Sweden (see Table 1). In Iceland, the figure is less. The number of participants has increased significantly since the early 1970s. The level of participation in adult education in Nordic countries is high in an international perspective. This can be explained by the historical role and tradition of adult education.

Popular enlightenment attracts the largest share of participants measured in terms of participants. In terms of the total number of course weeks, the share in participation of popular enlightenment, general qualifying adult education, and labor market training is about the same.

Participation in adult education depends on various social and economic conditions. Thus, the higher the

Table 1
Number of participants (one person may attend several classes) 1988–89 (in thousands)

	Denmark	Finland	Norway	Sweden
Popular adult education[a]	1,050	1,150	800	2,600
Folk high schools	60	70	40	230
Qualifying adult education	300	400	35	520
Labor market training	170	50	50	130
Total population	5,150	5,000	4,250	8,590
Population aged over 18	4,060	3,850	3,260	6,710

a Includes study wide activities

initial level of educational attainment, the better the socioeconomic position and the higher the participation rate tend to be. Participation in adult education is also dependent on other factors: family support, the length of parental education, community engagement, and self-confidence. Women participate more frequently than men in general education, but men more frequently in vocational types of education.

Since the early 1970s, the policy of redistribution has been in focus in Nordic adult education. Educational programs of various kinds have attempted to adjust the imbalance between the well-educated and the poorly educated sections of the population (e.g., through outreach activities, specifically adapted educational programs, on-the-job training, and media-supported teaching).

4. Governance, Legislation, and Financing

With respect to governance and legislation there are significant differences between the three main sectors of provision previously mentioned:

(a) Within popular enlightenment, autonomy has traditionally dominated. This means that the educational institutions and the participants decide upon the content and form of the courses, even though it is state-subsidized. Legislation for this sector takes the form of a framework. Thus, no formal rules exist with respect to certification.

(b) Within the formally qualifying sector of adult education, the curricula are mainly decided upon at a central level. The curricula are specified both through legislation and by the central authorities. Similarly, the rules guiding the application of formal qualifications are centrally determined.

(c) Within the labor market sector of provision, the industrial relation committees, in cooperation with the educational institutions, play an important part in making decisions on the contents and form of the courses.

The Nordic countries differ with respect to legislation. Denmark has a large number of laws which govern the total field of adult education. Thus, legislation exists for popular enlightenment activities, the day high schools, the folk high schools, general adult education, special education, the labor market courses, and vocational training. In Norway, the *Lov om voksenopplæring* (Law on Adult Education) governs a large part of the activities in the field.

Characteristically, adult education in the Nordic countries is publicly financed. This applies both to the wages of the teachers and expenditure for classrooms, teaching materials, and residence. It also applies to the labor market training programs and general qualifying adult education. Participants in popular enlightenment activities have to pay a part of the expenses, normally between 10 and 35 percent.

In the Nordic countries, about 20–25 percent of the total public expenditure is used for education. Some 10 percent of the education budget is used for adult education and training. Some estimates of public expenditures for the different forms of adult education are presented in Table 2. The trend since the early 1980s is to favor labor market training and, partly, general adult education at the expense of popular enlightenment.

5. Research and Development Activities

There are four main areas of work that constitute the Nordic research field in adult education. These four areas are all connected.

5.1 Sociological Studies on Resource Distribution

Since the early 1970s the problem of how to equalize access to adult education has been given much attention. The focus of research programs has been on questions such as: How can the group of participants be enlarged? What are the reasons for the biased access? Is it possible to discover new ways to contact and motivate those who lack social, political, and eco-

Table 2
Total public expenditures for adult education 1988–89 (in millions of Danish Kroner)

	Denmark	Finland	Norway	Sweden
Popular adult education	600	920	160	2,000
Folk high schools	460	400	370	1,040
Qualifying adult education	1,050	1,790	120	1,350
Labor market training	1,780	1,100	1,070	2,550

nomic resources, and those with an indifferent or even hostile attitude to education? The research programs have given some, albeit often tentative, answers to these questions.

Especially the Norwegian and Swedish research studies show that it is possible to recruit the poorly educated. Specifically, intensive forms of contacts even seem to result in greater motivation for education among the poorly educated than among the educated people (Faurfelt et al. 1990 p. 9). In general, the results point to the fact that the social equalization of participation is modest (Gooderham and Nordhaug 1984 pp. 161–62). Swedish results indicate a modest increase in the share of poorly educated participants. Furthermore the results show that this increase is among the older poorly educated. The study circles present an adequate means of reaching the poorly educated (Olofsson and Rubenson 1985).

The conclusion of an investigation into adult basic education in Denmark is that the poorly educated are well-represented. Longitudinal Danish and Swedish research report positive effects of teaching on the likelihood of further participation, enhanced employment position, and other outcome variables, such as family relations, satisfaction with life in general, leisure activity, and self-confidence (Bovin 1988, Tuijnman 1990). Study grants have an important significance in connection with the equalization mentioned above and seem to counteract the number of dropouts (Lundquist 1989, Eklund and Wandall 1992).

5.2 Research on Popular Enlightenment

Research in this area has not had the same broad and permanent attention as the topic previously mentioned. Nevertheless, the research is comprehensive, especially in Sweden.

On the one hand, the interest is historical. It is related to the democratic dimension of popular education. The relevant question is: How do popular movements and the popular enlightenment approach contribute to the stimulation and stabilization of democracy? On the other hand, interest is also concerned with the teaching and learning process, in particular: the curricula, teachers' conduct, and the relation between learning time and leisure time in the folk high schools.

Historical studies show that the folk high school has served a multiplicity of educational and cultural goals. The main characteristics are:

(a) general education as opposed to practical education;

(b) the teaching of principles;

(c) the spoken word or the book as the source of knowledge;

(d) philanthropic popular enlightenment.

These characteristics show the pluralism and great diversity among the various kinds of popular enlightenment (Arvidson et al. 1988 p. 25).

5.3 Adult Education and the Labor Market

This tends to be the most comprehensive research area. It attracts great interest in all Nordic countries. A major part of the research is concerned with the relationship between learning and work, including the processes of learning which are connected to the processes of work. Other research projects are concerned with the relationship between general and vocational education. The research on the teaching of the long-term unemployed shows that such training has a limited immediate employment effect (between 15 and 35%), but significant indirect effects on the motivation to learn, self-confidence, and personal development. The outcome depends to a large extent on the participants' attitude to education and on the interaction among the participants (see Aarkrog et al. 1991).

5.4 Teaching and Adult Learning

In this area, the problems and topics for research are linked to the teaching and learning process. The focus is on the didactic problems that may arise in the education of adults.

Much research and developmental work has focused on the interaction of the participants' experiences in the teaching process. The focus has been on forms of learning which permit this. The results point to study circles, the importance of residential school environments, and the role of learning surroundings that are adapted to adults. However, the results also show a great discrepancy between the ideals of adult teaching methods and practical reality (see Larsson et al. 1990 pp. 104–20).

5.5 Concluding Observations

The Nordic research on adult education is comparatively well-developed and open to many possibilities. The questions are many and varied. It is characteristic that the resources spent on research activities are relatively meagre compared with total expenditure on adult education and popular enlightenment activities. The first priority apparently is to act. Research only comes in second place.

The Nordic countries differ in terms of resource allocation and the approach taken to research. In Finland, the research on adult education is relatively more theoretically founded. In Sweden, and partly in Norway, comprehensive descriptions of the adult educational systems have been produced, as well as studies of their functions and effects. In Denmark, the concern has been with a systematic gathering of experiences and developmental works. This is undertaken as a basis for legislation and for improving the activities.

An increasing interest is being shown in adult education research. To a large extent, this research is being conducted as a part of program evaluation, and in particular the evaluation of comprehensive reforms (e.g., in relation to paid educational leave, outreach activities, the composition of the student body, and the training of the long-term unemployed) are receiving increased attention.

See also: Folk High Schools; Study Circles; Baltic Countries; Europe, Western and Southern

References

Aarkrog V, Brems J, Hansen B K, Jacobsen K M, Wahlgren B 1991 *UTB Uddannelsestilbud for langtidsledige.* Danmarks Lærerhøjskole, Copenhagen

Arvidson L, Höghielm R, Rubenson K, Hård H S 1988 *Folkhögskolans Pedagogiska Miljö.* Linköping University, Linköping

Bovin B 1988 *Voksen i skole—og hvad så?* Amtskommunernes og Kommunernes Forskningsinstitut, Copenhagen

Eklund S, Wandall J 1992 *VUS—Resultater og perspektive.* Danmarks Lærerhøjskole, Copenhagen

Faurfelt K, Høyrup S, Wahlgren B 1990 *LO medlemmernes syn på betalt frihed til uddannelse.* Danmarks Lærerhøjskole, Copenhagen

Gooderham P N, Nordhaug O 1984 *Førstegangsutdanning for voksne.* Norsk Voksenpegagogisk Institut, Trondheim

Larsson S, Fransson A, Alexandersson C 1990 *Vuxenpegagogisk Vardag.* University of Göteborg, Göteborg

Lundquist O F 1989 *Studiestöd för Vuxna.* Acta Universitatis Gothoburgensis, Göteborg

Olofsson L, Rubenson K 1985 *1970-talets Vuxenutbildningsreformer.* Högskolan för Lärarutbildning i Stockholm, Stockholm

Tuijnman A 1990 Adult education and the quality of life. *Int. Rev. Educ.* 36(3): 283–98

Further Reading

(a) Descriptions of the entire field:

Engelhardt J (ed.) 1982 *Voksenundervisning i Norden.* Nord, Copenhagen

Gam P, Gullichsen A, Tuomisto J, Klasson M (eds.) 1992 *Social Change and Adult Education Research—Adult Education Research in Nordic Countries 1990–91.* Linköping

Gam P, Tøsse S, Tuomisto J, Klasson M, Wahlgren B (eds.) 1993 *Social Change and Adult Education Research—Adult Education Research in Nordic Countries 1991–92.* Copenhagen

Jacobsen K M 1982 *Voksenundervisning—for hvem til hvad.* Nord, Copenhagen

Nordisk Ministerråd (The Nordic Council of Ministers) 1990 *Folkeoplysning og voksenundervisning—hvad koster det i de nordiske lande.* Nord, Copenhagen

Pantzar E 1985 The contents of adult education research in five countries: The Federal Republic of Germany, Finland, Sweden, Norway and Denmark. *Adult Education in Finland* 22(3): 25–36

(b) Descriptions of Danish activities:

Danish Cultural Institute 1991 *Folkeoplysning.* The Danish Cultural Institute, Copenhagen

Danish Institute 1985 Adult Education in Denmark. *Contact with Denmark*, No. 1–2. The Danish Institute, Copenhagen

Danish Research and Development Center 1988 *New Approaches to Adult Education in Denmark.* Danish Research and Development Center, Copenhagen

Jacobsen B 1992 Adult education and public enlightenment in Denmark. In: Jarvis P (ed.) 1992 *Handbook of Adult Education and Training in Europe.* Routledge, London

Organisation for Economic Co-operation and Development 1991 *Further Education and Training in Denmark.* Danish Report to OECD. OECD, Paris

(c) Descriptions of Norwegian activities:

Norwegian Association for Adult Education 1985 *Adult Education in Norway. A Brief Introduction*, rev. ed. Norwegian Association for Adult Education, Oslo

Nordhaug O 1983 Distribution of adult education: The Norwegian case. *Adult Educ. Q.* 34(1): 29–37

Nordhaug O 1991 *The Shadow Educational System: Adult Resource Development.* Norwegian University Press, Oslo

Setsaas R 1982 *Some Consequences of the Norwegian Act of Adult Education.* Norsk Voksenpedagogisk Institutt, Trondheim

(d) Descriptions of Finnish activities:

Lehtonen H, Tuomisto J 1975 Participation in adult education. *Adult Education in Finland* 12(1–2): 3–14

Tuomisto J 1987 The ideological and sociohistorical bases of industrial training: A Finnish perspective, Part I. *Adult Education in Finland* 23(4): 3–24

Tuomisto J 1990 Adult education and values. *Adult Education in Finland* 27(1): 3–16

Vaherava T 1988 Developing research in adult education. *Adult Education in Finland* 25(1): 18–22

(e) Descriptions of Swedish activities:

Abrahamsson K (ed.) 1988 *Implementing Recurrent Education in Sweden*. Swedish National Board of Education, Stockholm

Ball S J, Larsson S 1989 *The Struggle for Democratic Education Equality and Participation in Sweden*. Falmer Press, Brighton

Swedish National Board of Education 1990 *Basic Adult Education and Adult Education for Formal Competence*.

Swedish National Board of Education, Stockholm

Swedish National Board of Education 1987 *Research and Central Development Work in Adult Education Associations and Folk High Schools 1987–88*. Report. Swedish National Board of Education, Stockholm

Tuijnman A 1989 *Further Education and Training in Swedish Working Life: Trends and Issues*. Institute of International Education, University of Stockholm, Stockholm

Europe, Western and Southern

W. Houtkoop

Adult education has gained in importance in many European countries. This is evident from growing participation rates, growing public and private expenditures, and an increasing policy interest.

The importance of adult education stems mainly from economic considerations. Knowledge is a production factor, and the economic continuity and success of firms, regions, and even of nations depend on a well-skilled labor force. Economic competition, to an increasing extent, becomes competition among workforces and their human capital.

However, other functions of adult education gain in importance as well. The training of the unemployed must ensure their re-entry into the labor market. The teaching of basic skills like literacy and numeracy serves the social integration of groups that are in danger of being marginalized. Moreover, the value of these functions is also to an extent judged by economic criteria. The sociocultural dimension of adult education, with its emphasis upon personal development and cultural orientation, has to a certain extent moved to second stage, although it is still vital. It is in these forms of adult education that regional and national identities manifest themselves most strongly (see *Market Concepts in Provision*).

This entry describes and compares the systems of adult education in several European countries. Not all the European countries are covered. The Nordic countries are covered in another entry, although Sweden is included here as well, for comparative reasons (see *Europe, Nordic Countries*). However, the entry makes no claim to be a comparative study in the true sense (Knoll 1989). For such a purpose, basic statistics on adult education are often too defective; especially insofar as data concerning the private sector are often lacking. The data from the southern European countries tend to be less detailed than those from northern and western Europe and consequently their description is more global. One also gets the impression that the problems facing these countries are of a qualitatively different nature.

Some of these defects may also apply to the figures presented in this entry. Part of the problem is that national definitions are often difficult to compare. As a pragmatic solution, "adult education" is considered to be the sum total of all the forms of adult and continuing training and education for people who have finished their initial education. Boundary problems of course remain. Adult students in higher education, for example, are included. Forms of education for young people, combining school and practical work, as in the German dual system, are excluded. The same applies to the huge territory of informal learning and on-the-job training.

Finally, systems of adult education are part of the larger social and political context and they change with the changes in that context. The unification of Germany, for example, will have far-reaching consequences for the system of adult education, but at this stage it is impossible to predict or even describe these consequences. With these sobering remarks, the European situation with respect to adult education will be examined.

1. France

The French system of adult education can roughly be divided into three subsystems: the system of vocational adult education, which is partly controlled by the social partners and partly by the private institutions; the system of second chance education, leading to nationally recognized diplomas and linked with the regular educational system; and the system of sociocultural adult education, which is dominated by private, nonprofit institutions.

In France, there is a strong emphasis on the vocational aspects of adult education, which is divided into the public sector (financed by national and regional authorities and mainly aimed at the unemployed) and the firm-based sector (financed by enterprises with more than 10 employees, that have been responsible by law for the training of their employees since 1971) (see *Legislation in Adult Education*).

The law of 1971 is one of the most prominent characteristics of French adult education. According to the Law, all but the smallest firms are obliged to reserve a percentage of the payroll for the training of their employees. In 1992, the legal obligation was 1.2 percent of the payroll, but enterprises spent a lot more in reality. In 1992 enterprises effectively spent 3.2 percent (in some of the bigger enterprises this could amount to 7% of the payroll). In a new agreement between social partners and government, 1.5 percent of the payroll was set for 1993 (Aalders 1994). From the fund thus formed, obligatory contributions must be made to paid educational leave and training efforts aimed at combating youth unemployment. The bulk of the fund is used for the training of employees. This can be done by means of in-company training or through buying the training from private, for-profit institutions and providers associated with the branches of industry or from public agencies. The latter, however, play a modest role in this market. The trade unions have a strong influence on the organization of the training efforts within the scope of the Law on adult education and enterprise training.

The training efforts of enterprises have grown considerably since the introduction of the Law. In 1990 the participation rate was 32 percent of the total work force. However, in training efforts and training expenditures there is a huge gap between small and large firms (Aalders 1994). The law also regulates paid educational leave, which may be used for professional as well as general educational purposes (see *Paid Educational Leave and Collective Bargaining*).

Public vocational adult education is mostly aimed at those who fall outside the scope of the training laws—for example, because they are employed in small-sized businesses or because they lack paid employment. In 1987, the central government trained 2.8 million people and regional governments another 400,000 (Centre INFO 1989). The main target group comprises the young and unemployed, but the training of government employees is also important. The actual training takes place in public training centers for the unemployed or is bought from other public institutions for adult education. In 1988 France spent 0.32 percent of gross domestic product (GDP) on labor market training for adults and 0.26 percent of GDP on youth measures (OECD 1990).

The possibilities for granting diplomas at secondary general school level (*baccalauréat*) are restricted to public daytime and evening schools (GRETAs) and distance education (CNED). These institutions offer a variety of courses ranging from diploma courses to training programs for the unemployed and other vocational courses.

The higher education system is rather closed to adults, at least for those who lack the necessary entry qualifications. Universities organize preparatory courses, often in collaboration with institutions for adult education. In exceptional cases, work experience may give exemption from entry requirements. Although there is a tendency for universities to offer special courses—for example, to those who study under the Law of 1971—the number of adult students in regular university education is relatively modest.

The pattern of provision by the adult education associations is multifaceted. According to French law, every group of at least seven persons may form an association and is eligible for a grant, mostly from local government or public organizations. The content is mostly socioculturally oriented, but vocational adult education courses are also offered.

2. *Federal Republic of Germany (FRG)*

The consequences of the unification of the two Germanies for the system of adult education are as yet unclear. Another complication is the federal structure of the FRG. Adult education is a responsibility of the separate states (*Länder*), while federal legislation is not developed.

During the 1980s there has been much growth in adult education participation in Germany. In 1987, one-fourth of the adult population participated, with equal shares for vocational and general adult education (Bundesminister für Bildung und Wissenschaft 1987). Compared with most other European countries, this is a high participation rate which, however, strongly covariates with the level of education previously obtained, socioeconomic position, and age. The proportion of women in adult education, even of vocational types, has increased during the late 1980s.

More than half of the total provision of vocational adult education is offered by enterprises. In 1989 12.7 percent of the work force participated in enterprise-related training (Lynch 1994). Private for-profit institutions account for 6 percent of the market for vocational adult education. In general, these courses do not lead to qualifications that are certified by the state or by professional associations.

The *Volkshochschulen* (see *Folk High Schools*) are major providers. Although vocational adult education is not their main strength, the sheer number of participants makes them an important provider. A typical German phenomenon is the important role of the employers' organizations for the different professions and branches of industry (*Kammern*) in vocational education. They offer high quality courses that often build upon the dual system of vocational youth education. These courses lead to publicly recognized qualifications, such as the title of *Meister* (master) in the manufacturing industry.

Institutes for vocational higher education (*Hochschulen*) may offer graduate vocational courses, but their zest for engaging in these activities is not great (Krais 1990).

787

A great variety of organizations offer general adult education. As far as the number of participants is concerned, *Volkshochschulen* and church institutions are the major providers, drawing 8.6 and 10 million participants in 1987 (Krais 1990). Taking into account the length and quality of the courses, the *Volkshochschulen* rank as the most important provider. Major subjects are (foreign) languages, economics, mathematics, science, and health. On a modest scale, trade unions and party organizations also offer general adult education.

Volkshochschulen and other institutions (like evening schools) offer courses leading to diplomas on the secondary general school level. The *Volkshochschulen* have developed a modular system in which the diploma can be reached in stages.

Higher education institutions play a very modest role in the provision of adult education. To be eligible for higher education, a formal entry qualification (*Abitur*) is needed, and there are few facilities for adult students to achieve it, such as part-time courses and study loans. There is one university entirely based on distance education, while other institutions for higher education also have facilities for offering distance education.

In 1987, the state budget for adult education (federal and *Länder*) was about DM 12 billion, of which three-fourths were devoted to training activities for the unemployed and other groups with a weak position on the labor market. In 1988 this amounted to 0.35 percent of GDP (OECD 1990). Because Germany has a well established dual system for vocational youth education, these programmes are mainly targeted for unemployed adults. The remaining fourth of the state budget is used to subsidize the different institutions. In practice, the *Volkshochschulen* and the institutions managed by the churches or the trade unions receive a major part of the budget. The state grant ranges from 30 percent to 100 percent. Public expenditure on adult education rose from 4.6 percent of total education expenditure in 1970 to 10.5 percent in 1988. This is a clear indication of the increased significance of the adult education sector in Germany.

A yearly budget of DM 10 billion is mentioned for enterprise training. However, when earnings forgone are included, this figure rises to DM 34 billion (Krais 1990).

Some *Länder*—like Berlin, Lower Saxony, Hamburg, and Hessen—have an arrangement for paid educational leave, allowing workers to attend vocational courses or citizenship courses for a few days per year.

3. Sweden

The Nordic region is treated separately (see *Europe, Nordic Countries*), but because of the exemplary nature of some characteristics of its adult education system, Sweden is also included in this European overview.

Sweden has an elaborate system of adult education provision. Characteristic are training as an integral part of labor market policy, a relatively open system of higher education, and an ample system of opportunities for educational leave. Participation is high; about half of the population in the age group 18–64 years participates in organized adult education, which is one of the highest figures in Europe. Sweden also has a leading position in terms of public expenditure as a share of total public spending. About 15 percent of the educational budget is spent on adult education, and total public and private expenditures on adult education amount to 3 percent of the Gross National Product (GNP). Most other European countries spend between 1 and 2 percent of the GNP (Boot 1989). The approach to labor market training in the context of "the Swedish model" has drawn attention internationally. This model is based on an active labor market policy. Instead of spending a large share of the funds required for income maintenance of the unemployed on social security benefits, Sweden spends it on employment exchange, training, and temporary job creation. Social security benefits are seen as a last resort. Training is a crucial instrument and, in 1988, Sweden (with Denmark and Ireland) spent more money on labor market training (0.52% of GDP) than any other European country (OECD 1990).

Labor market policy is the responsibility of the National Labor Market Board (*Arbetsmarknadsstyrelsen*, AMS), whereas labor market training is implemented by the Labor Market Training Agency (*Arbetsmarknadsutbildningen*, AMU). Both have a tripartite board and are largely decentralized. The local employment agencies of the AMS define the demand for training, while the local AMU training centers offer the relevant courses. Although the training demand of the employment agencies is largely covered by the AMU training centers, they can also put out a tender to other providers. On the other hand, AMU centers are free to sell courses to municipal educational authorities and enterprises. For the unemployed, participation is free and the courses have a high success rate in terms of post-program employment (see *Evaluation of Public Training: Cost-Effectiveness*). As usual, public and private enterprises also run their own training programs. It was estimated that in 1987 Sweden spent about 5 percent of the payroll on training, which is a very high figure (Boot 1989); in the same year 25 percent of the work force received enterprise-related training (Lynch 1994).

Vocational and general adult education, leading to "recognized" diplomas and certificates, is organized mostly by the municipal adult education authorities (KOMVUX). There are no formal entrance requirements and the organization of the courses is adapted to the learning needs of adults (modular, full-time, and part-time courses). There are special courses for target groups like immigrants. In the early 1990s, there is a tendency to intensify the role of labor market training in KOMVUX.

In 1977, a separate provision for adult basic education (GRUNDVUX) was begun in Sweden. This is also a municipal responsibility. Originally the target group was (functional) illiterates, but to an increasing extent, GRUNDVUX is used by immigrants to learn Swedish. They now comprise half of the participants (see *Adult Basic Education*).

Sociocultural adult education has a rich tradition in Sweden. The first folk high schools were established in the middle of the nineteenth century in rural areas. They now attract participants from all walks of life and offer a great variety of courses. They are administered by local authorities, but also by trade unions, churches, and voluntary associations (see *Folk High Schools*).

The study circles are typical Scandinavian phenomena. In 1986, Sweden had 300,000 study circles with 2.6 million participants. Participants choose their own themes and method of working, but social and artistic subjects are dominant. When the study circles fulfill certain conditions, they can receive a public subsidy (see *Study Circles; Providers of Adult Education: An Overview*).

With the introduction of the Higher Education Law of 1977, recurrent education was taken as the point of departure for higher education policy (see *Recurrent Education; University Adult Education*). The accessibility of higher education was increased through the 25/4 arrangement. This implies that adults older than 24 years, with at least four years of work experience (including taking care of the family) are entitled to enter higher education without a formal qualification, although there are often supplementary requirements for certain courses. As a consequence, the share of adult students in higher education seems to be higher than in other European countries. A modular organization, full-time and part-time courses, and distance education also cater to the needs of adult students (Tuijnman 1990).

Most forms of adult education are free, and participants in adult education are, in principle, entitled to some form of financial assistance, although this can take the form of a loan. This applies especially to people attending labor market training and adult education leading to formal qualifications. Educational leave is governed by law. All forms of adult education can be attended, there is no formal time limit and employees keep their position while they are on leave (see *Time Policies for Lifelong Learning*).

4. United Kingdom

The data offered here refer mostly to England and Wales. Scotland and Northern Ireland have a somewhat different system. The system of adult education in England and Wales is very complex and in a state of constant flux. Still, some salient features can be mentioned—for example, that the system is mostly decentralized. Local education authorities (LEAs) are in principle responsible for adult education. Central government covers a large part of the costs of adult education, although there is a tendency for participants to pay high fees, possibly with the exception of certain disadvantaged clientele groups. Central government has recently taken the initiative in the field of vocational adult education.

There is an elaborate system of publicly subsidized providers, often catering for young as well as adult participants. Independent examination boards offer the possibility to sit for examinations, irrespective of the educational route one has taken.

These characteristics make the British system of adult education highly flexible, although some commentators would prefer the term "fragmented." Annually, about 16 percent of the adult population participates in some form of organized adult education.

Three major sectors can be distinguished:

(a) the public sector, which is mainly financed by means of transfers to the local education authorities (LEAs) who manage the bulk of adult education;

(b) the public sector, which is directly financed by the Ministry of Education;

(c) continuing vocational training, which is financed by firms and the public Training Agency.

Local education authorities are principally responsible for the education of the young and the adults within their region. Adult education is only a marginal part of their mandate. Financial sources are users' fees, local taxes, and government grants. The situation of economic austerity in the United Kingdom has especially affected the adult education sector.

Local education authorities organize general as well as vocational education for adults. For the most part, the general courses are provided by schools that also offer vocational courses for adults. A clear case in point are the polytechnics, the institutions of higher education, and the colleges of further education. They offer vocational programs at secondary and tertiary level, as well as a variety of continuing nondegree courses. Adults can also take part in these courses. An estimate puts the number of participants at 1 million (Jennings 1985). Since the introduction of the Education Act of 1988, the polytechnics and some colleges of higher education have come under the direct authority of the Ministry of Education. The consequences of this for the provision of education for adults are not clear (see *Polytechnical Education*).

General adult education under the authority of the LEAs attracts many participants. The estimates vary from 2–3 million adults. The provision is offered by adult education centers and can be characterized as leisure oriented, although formal diplomas can also be obtained. The leisure courses especially have suffered from budget cuts. The colleges of further education also offer general adult education. Adult basic education has not been affected by budget cuts. Stimulated by the literacy campaigns of the British Broadcasting Corporation (BBC), adult basic education has become a policy priority.

A number of institutions offering courses for adults are directly financed by the Ministry of Education —for example, the universities and their extramural departments, the Open University, the Workers' Educational Association (WEA), and the long-term residential colleges. Below, the focus is on the institutions for higher education.

Traditionally, universities in the United Kingdom have played an important role in adult education. Most conspicious is the tradition of liberal academic adult education. Universities offer a wide range of nondegree courses for a general audience interested in academic subjects. For that purpose, a number of universities received a specific grant and established extramural departments for adult education extension. Since 1988, however, the grant has been abolished and universities must pay for these activities from their overall budget. In 1988, about half a million adults were recruited.

Because of diminishing resources, universities try to expand their market with vocational "postexperience" and "postgraduate" courses, often at the expense of liberal adult education. As the intake of young students diminishes, universities also try to attract new adult constituencies. One way is to recognize alternative educational routes—for example, as in the Open College. Another way is the organization of access studies preparing people for university admission. There has been a proliferation of such programs. The third way is that of pursuing an open access policy as has been the case with the Open University. The Open University, a unique experiment in open access education, has been followed in a number of other European countries. In 1985, there were 100,000 participants, of which 60 percent took a degree course. The percentage of students without formal entry qualifications has risen to 44 percent. (see *Open University; University Adult Education*).

Up to this point, established institutions have been discussed. In recent policy, emphasis has been laid on projects, which—after a starter subsidy—must be able to operate cost-effectively. The established institutions can participate in these projects. An example is the Open College project, in which the colleges for further education and the polytechnics participate. This tendency has been particularly strong in those parts of vocational education and labor market training for which the Department of Employment is responsible.

Because the educational system in the United Kingdom is highly decentralized and lacks an efficient tradition of vocational education, the central government has taken a strong initiative in the field of vocational adult education and training. There has been a steep increase in funds and a host of measures to implement policy. The Training Agency, the successor to the Manpower Services Commission, was established in 1988 under the direct responsibility of the Department of Employment. The implementation of these national programs is highly decentralized. Local training and enterprise councils (TECs) must establish the local training needs of the employed and unemployed and negotiate with the different providers of continuing vocational education and training. Employers have a majority in the TECs, which is exceptional because in most European countries this authority is shared with the trade unions. Although there are some public training centers, the majority of the desired training is bought from public and private institutions. Due to their purchasing power, the Training Agency (and the TECs) have a major influence on the system of adult education. In 1988 expenditures for labor market training targeted at youth as well as adults were 0.48 percent of GDP, with about equal shares for both groups (OECD 1990).

Despite the training efforts of the Training Agency, most training takes place within the enterprises. According to a rough estimate, spending on in-company training in the private sector is three times as high (£9 billion in 1987) as the expenditures of the Training Agency. About 14 percent of the work force participates in enterprise-related training annually (Aalders 1994, Lynch 1994).

There is no law on (paid) educational leave in the United Kingdom, but there can be arrangements in the context of collective agreements (see *Paid Educational Leave and Collective Bargaining*).

5. The Netherlands

The system of adult education in the Netherlands is undergoing a process of change. There are efforts to create coherence in a fragmented system; money and authority are transfered to local authorities and the social partners, and the system is being adapted to the demands of the labor market.

About 1.5 percent of the GNP is spent on adult education by both public and private actors. In 1990 over 2 million adults participated in adult education which amounted to 20 percent of the adult population. Expenditures and participation have risen considerably during the last decade. There is a strong relationship between socioeconomic position and participation level. The majority of the participants are employed and a vocational orientation dominates in participation (Houtkoop and Felix 1990).

Private, vocational adult education is dominated by firm-based training. In 1990, 34 percent of the work force was involved, and the costs amounted to roughly 1.7 percent of the wage bill. In 33 percent of the cases, the programs are organized exclusively by the firms concerned; in 15 percent, the programs are organized by institutions working for a branch of industry and the remaining 43 percent of cases are programs bought from private providers (Houtkoop 1994). There is no legal arrangement for educational leave, but in-company training and educational leave are increasingly a part of collective labor agreements.

A sizable amount of company training is bought from private providers, which have a relatively strong position on the adult education market, especially in the vocational sector. There is a law on the recognition of private institutions, which guarantees quality standards and protects consumers. Although participation is often fully or partly subsidized by the employer, there is also a sizable amount of individual investment. The private institutions are also involved in public training efforts. In 1992 about 400,000 people were enrolled in private institutions.

Public vocational education can be divided into programs leading to formal qualifications which are often provided by schools, and labor market training for the unemployed and other disadvantaged groups. The former consists of part-time secondary vocational education and part-time higher vocational education. The apprentice system is aimed at young students, but has been made more accessible for adult students as well. For that purpose, the age limit of 27 years has been abolished.

Labor market training for the unemployed is the (financial) responsibility of the Ministry of Labor. There is a tripartite national body that sets financial and policy guidelines. Actual implementation takes place in regional tripartite boards who define training needs and select training facilities. Training takes place in public training centers or can be bought from private and public institutions. To guarantee fair competition between the different institutions, experiments have started with a tender procedure. Participation had increased to 122,000 in 1992. Public expenditures were 0.29 percent of GDP in 1989. Because of the elaborate system of secondary vocational youth education, these measures are mainly targeted at unemployed adults (OECD 1990) (see *Evaluation of Public Training: Cost-Effectiveness*).

General adult education is the responsibility of the Ministry of Education, which offers programs at different levels. Adult basic education started in 1987. It is covered by a special law, stipulating that provision must be by specialized institutions and by professional teachers. The municipal authorities are responsible for the realization of adult basic education. Participation had increased considerably to 134,000 participants in 1992. Adult basic education has been particularly successful in attracting minority groups and has been given new tasks for the integration of immigrants. Language courses are the programs most chosen. There is some political pressure to give adult basic education a more explicit function as a preparation for low-level vocational programs.

Secondary general adult education leads to formal diplomas, but participants can also obtain separate credits. This type of education used to be very popular among elder women, but participation has slowly decreased to about 75,000. Under a new law, secondary general adult education will also have to offer special transfer programs for people who want to move on to vocational education. Higher education offers part-time degree courses. Special programs for adults, such as the liberal adult education programs in the United Kingdom, are few in the Netherlands. Since 1984, there has been an Open University with open access. After a fast growth, student numbers have stabilised and even declined a little. In 1992 36,000 students were enrolled. Most students only take one of two modules; students embarking on a full degree program are in the minority.

Sociocultural adult education is offered by a large variety of institutions, either subsidized by local authorities or—to an increasing extent—dependent on participants' fees. Some institutions are involved in local projects aimed at combating persistent social disadvantages. Other institutions orient themselves toward the "education for leisure" market (see *Time, Leisure and Adult Education*).

6. Portugal

In Portugal, policy interest in adult education as it is understood in other European countries only started with the revolution of 1974. Since then it has been given a high priority, in view of the comparatively low level of formal educational attainment of the adult population. The development of a coherent system of adult education is hampered by a lack of financial resources, institutional infrastructure, and qualified personnel. Because of a lack of tradition and the low educational level of certain groups, it is difficult to attract certain disadvantaged groups to adult education.

There are three main domains of provision which can be distinguished:

(a) general adult education and sociocultural education provided at the regional and local levels by a great variety of private and public organizations;

(b) continuing vocational training;

(c) general adult education, vocational training, and sociocultural education provided by the Ministry of Education.

The first domain is formed by a wide range of activities addressed to the local community or to specific target groups. They are organized by local public authorities (agricultural and health services, for example) and private organizations (cooperatives, associations, trade unions, and churches), mostly with little public funding.

Vocational training has developed rapidly during the 1980s, to no small extent due to funding by the EEC. It is mainly provided by the Ministry of Labor and Social Welfare either in its own training centers, or in collaboration with enterprises, trade unions, and private training centers. The Ministry of Agriculture also plays an important part in vocational training. In 1988 0.32 percent of GDP was spent on labor market training for adults and youth. It is striking that training for adults is mainly for those who are already employed, a phenomenon we also see in Greece (OECD 1990).

The Ministry of Education is the main provider of adult education. Since 1986, a policy has been established to promote second chance education for adults who have received little formal initial education, and to those who need an educational opportunity to achieve career improvement or cultural advancement. In practice, this has meant, first of all, the growth of literacy programs and adult basic education. Literacy is a major policy objective. Courses are given in regional centers for adult basic education in close cooperation with local authorities. Secondary general adult education leads to formal school diplomas, but the programs are adapted to adult needs (e.g., by introducing vocational elements). Vocational training under the responsibility of the Ministry of Education functions as a preparation for more advanced programs. It always includes elements of adult basic education or general education. Finally, the Ministry of Education promotes social and cultural activities for participants in literacy and other courses, and also for the local communities.

There is no special training for teachers in adult education. Activities are mostly carried out by elementary and secondary school teachers and by volunteers.

7. Greece

Adult education provision in Greece has expanded rapidly since the early 1980s. A major reason is that the country obtained full membership of the EC in 1981. Because of this, considerable changes have occurred in the production sector, with new technologies playing an increasingly dominant role, making training and retraining a necessity. Furthermore, financial aid has been provided for adult education and training by the European Social Fund (ESF) and other EC funds. Both developments have been a major stimulus for the adult education system, but have also put it under pressure. The infrastructure has had to be expanded and there has been an increasing demand for adult educators.

Programs are mainly vocationally oriented and targeted at (semi) urban areas, with a strong concentration in the capital. This leaves certain groups in Greece, who are faced with skills shortages and difficulties of basic education and training, underserved.

For these groups, an expansion of adult basic education and retraining programs is needed. Small- and medium-sized firms are also underserved, while the consequences of global economic competition are expected to necessitate upgrading and retraining on a large scale.

Description of the providers of adult education in Greece is restricted to the public sector, as hardly any data are available about the private sector. The main providers are the public administration and private corporate bodies operating under the responsibility of government ministries. Most state providers are subsidized by the ESF and other EC funds.

Vocational education is a priority. New legislation on continuing vocational education and training has introduced a new network of further education institutions (Institutions of Vocational Training, IEK) which is designed to increase the opportunities for adult participation in vocational education and training. The institutions are part of the formal education system and, in the early stages, will function on the premises of the technical schools. Some adult education centers operated by the private sector may be incorporated into the system as well. They will provide continuing vocational education and training in accordance with market demands, made more pertinent by European integration. The IEK is financed by the central government, mainly through subsidies granted by the EC.

Training activities for public servants are organized by the Institute for Permanent Education. European integration has led to major changes in regulations concerning the management and operation of public institutions, which in turn has given rise to a large increase in training activities. Specialized bodies are responsible for the training of small industries and crafts, as well as for the workforce in the private sector.

The Ministry of Agriculture is responsible for agricultural extension services, particularly the further training of farmers, and, with 80,000 participants annually, is one of the larger providers. In total, Greece spent 0.25 percent of GDP on labor market training, with a heavy emphasis on employed adults (OECD 1990).

General adult education is the responsibility of the General Secretariat of Popular Education (GGLE). It has an extensive regional network, especially in rural areas, and, with 97,000 participants, it is the largest provider. The GGLE programs cover a wide range of subjects, including functional literacy and adult basic skills.

8. Italy

Adult education in Italy has been, since 1977, largely decentralized, giving the regions a possibility of formulating and implementing their own regulations on permanent or adult education. Central government determines the total budget, while planning, programming, and budget allocation are a regional responsibility. However, efforts are being made to introduce a National Law on Adult Education to create more coherence in the system and to raise the reputation of this field.

A salient feature of Italian adult education is the "150 hours" arrangement, giving workers the right to 150 hours of study leave on an annual basis. Programs were designed so as to offer people a second chance to obtain secondary school diplomas, but other programs can be attended as well. In the early stages, specific courses with a special didactic approach were set up, but to an increasing extent the courses have taken on the character of regular school programs. Originally only intended for workers, in the early 1990s almost anyone can attend these adult education programs.

Vocational education and training has also become a regional responsibility since 1978. In the law concerned, it is underlined that activities must be dedicated to adults, especially the unemployed. There is a variety of courses offered by schools, organizations of employers, and private organizations. The Ministry of Labor supervises the quality level of diplomas and certificates. However, in the context of labor market policies in general, the emphasis is mainly on the young. In 1988 0.3 percent of GDP was targeted at unemployed adults, compared with 0.69 percent of GDP dedicated to youth measures (OECD 1990).

Adults can attend primary and secondary general education. Provision is regionally coordinated, and the Regional Council for Adult Education is ultimately responsible for the provision and the budget. Courses in the context of the "150 hours" arrangement are mostly of a general nature.

9. Conclusion

Adult education is a growth sector in Europe. The number of participants and the level of both public and private expenditures have increased during the 1970s and 1980s. By the 1990s, the focus has come to be on vocational adult education as a means to strengthen the relationship between education and work, to integrate the unemployed, and to maintain and improve the skills of the workforce. The position of general and social–cultural education has declined somewhat—with the exception of literacy and adult basic education programs, which, however, are at least partly also promoted for economic reasons.

The administration of adult education is often highly decentralized, leaving the responsibility for actual planning and implementation in the hands of local authorities or social partners.

As far as participation, expenditure, and policy interests are concerned, adult vocational education assumes a central position. The training of the workforce is, in general, the responsibility of the enterprises. The influence of employees and the government is restricted, with France as a clear exception. However, to an increasing extent, in-company training is becoming part and parcel of collective labor agreements.

Public responsibility for adult vocational education takes two main forms. In the first, the provision of broad vocational education leading to formal diplomas and programs for obtaining more specific qualifications are offered, in many cases developed in close collaboration with enterprises. In Germany, this system is highly formalized. A second form of public responsibility is labor market training for the unemployed and other groups with a weak position in the labor market. The main constituency groups in this case are often the early school-leavers and unemployed youth, but activities aimed at adults have intensified. Planning and control of labor market training is often shared with the social partners and is regionally implemented.

In some countries, like Sweden, the programs are mainly executed in special training centers; in other countries, like France or the United Kingdom, employment training is bought from public or private institutions. Because of the size of the funds being allocated to employment training, public authorities often have a decisive influence on the adult education market (see *Government Role in Adult Education and Training: Market Concepts in Provision*).

In southern European countries, there has been a rapid development of adult vocational education. Membership of the EC and integration into the European market have made training and retraining a necessity. Funding by the European Social Fund and other EC funds have been a stimulus, but parts of the systems of adult education and training in these countries have been stretched to their limits as a result, since the infrastructure and the staff have only a limited capacity.

The attention given to vocational education has, in some cases, been at the expense of general adult education. In some countries, expenditures have dropped and fees have risen. The exception is adult basic education, which is a state responsibility in most European countries. Sweden and the Netherlands have a separate provision with a legal basis; in most other countries it is provided by other institutions, often with the help of volunteers. There is a need for literacy courses, especially in the southern European countries, but with the present resources certain regions and groups are underserved.

An important function of adult education is to give people a second chance to obtain formal diplomas, mostly at the secondary level. This is, in most European countries, a public responsibility. Sometimes the programs are offered by the regular school system; sometimes there are separate adult provisions. Several European countries also have distance education facilities. In some countries, the private institutions are allowed to offer diploma courses at the secondary level. The details differ across countries and they are also in a state of constant flux. A common trend is that the public institutions offering these courses are, to an increasing extent, becoming more market oriented (or are forced to do so), offering courses that are in demand and cost-effective.

In many European countries higher education is still not easily accessible for adults lacking the necessary qualifications. There are, however, opportunities to study part-time or by means of distance education. Countries like France or the United Kingdom organize special access courses to prepare people for entrance examinations. In Sweden, adults with work experience can enter higher education without the necessary entry qualifications, although this policy has come under review. Really open access is offered by institutions such as the United Kingdom and the Dutch open universities, which are in sharp contrast with similar university institutions operating in Germany and Spain. Higher education institutions often also offer a variety of other courses, ranging from short vocational programs to graduate programs. A stronger market orientation can also be discerned in higher education. The United Kingdom's tradition of liberal academic adult education for a wide audience is not widespread in other European countries.

Sociocultural adult education still features prominently in many European countries, attracting large audiences. Often popular movements, churches, political parties, or trade unions organize these activities, which reflects the fact that social–cultural adult education is rooted in broader social movements. It is largely a voluntary enterprise, however, and existing state support has come under pressure in a number of European countries. In the Nordic countries, the tradition of "popular enlightenment" is particularly strong, and community groups or study circles engaging in educational activities are, under certain conditions, entitled by law to receive grants from local authorities.

Educational leave, whether paid or unpaid, plays a modest role in Europe. The United Kingdom and the Netherlands have arrangements for specific groups, like members of work councils, while several German *Länder* have arrangements for paid educational leave, but only for a short period. In France, every worker is entitled to paid educational leave for a program of his or her own choice. Arrangements in Sweden are ample. Educational leave is not paid for, but this is compensated for by the arrangements for study assistance. Educational leave can be used for different forms of adult education and the duration is not restricted. The "150 hours" arrangement in Italy is open to almost anyone and participants are free to take general or vocational programs. To an increasing extent, educational leave forms part of collective labor agreements.

See also: Demand, Supply, and Finance of Adult Education; European Union: Continuing Vocational Training; Europe, Central and Eastern; Europe: Nordic Countries

References

Aalders M J A M 1994 *Bedrijfsopleidingen, organisatie en financieringsstructuur.* Assen, Van Gorum

Boot P A 1989 Further education and training of adults: Provision, participation, economic impact, and policy options (draft version). Ministry of Social Affairs, The Hague

Bundesminister für Bildung und Wissenschaft 1987 Berichtssystem Weiterbildungsverhalten 1985. *Bildung-Wissenschaft-Aktuell* 7(87)

CBS 1988 *Bedrijfsopleidingen in Nederland 1986.* CBS, The Hague

CBS 1994 *Kwartaalschrift Onderwijsstatistieken*, jrg. 1, no. 1, Den Haag, SDU

Centre INFFO 1989 *La formation professionelle en chiffres.* Centre INFFO, Paris

Houtkoop W 1994 The training and retraining system in the Netherlands and other European countries. *Paper for World Bank Seminar on Secondary Education in Europe*, Amsterdam

Houtkoop W, Felix C 1990 *Volwasseneneducatie in Europa.* RVE, Utrecht

Jennings 1985 *The Education of Adults in Britain: A Study of Organisation, Finance and Policy.* Newland Papers No. 10. University of Hull, Department of Adult and Continuing Education, Hull

Knoll J 1989 Adult education from Nordborg (1972) until today. *Int. J. Lifelong Learning* 8(2)

Krais B 1990 Weiterbildung, hoofdstuk 13. In: Max Planck Institut für Bildungsforschung 1990 *Das Bildungswesen in der Bundesrepublik Deutschland.* Rowohlt, Reinbek

Lynch L M (eds.) 1994 *Training and the Private Sector.* University of Chicago Press, Chicago, Illinois

OECD 1989 *Economic Surveys: Netherlands 1988/1989.* OECD, Paris

OECD 1990 *Labour Market Policies for the 1990s.* OECD, Paris

Tuijnman A C 1990 Dilemmas of open admissions policy: Quality and efficiency in Swedish higher education. *High. Educ.* 20: 443–57

Further Reading

European Bureau of Adult Education (EBAE) 1985 *Survey of Adult Education.* EBAE, Amersfoort

Florander J 1988 Denmark. In: Postlethwaite T N (ed.) 1988 *The Encyclopedia of Comparative Education and National Systems of Education.* Pergamon Press, Oxford

Jarvis P 1992 *Perspectives on Adult Education and Training in Europe.* Krieger, Melbourne

Schütze H G (ed.) 1987 *Adults in Higher Education, Policies and Practice in Great Britain and North America.* Almqvist and Wiksell, Stockholm

Schütze H G, Istance D (eds.) 1987 *Recurrent Education Revisited: Modes of Participation and Financing.* Almqvist and Wiksell, Stockholm

Indian Subcontinent

Jandhyala B. G. Tilak

Adult education is increasingly recognized as a basic human need, and as an integral part of mass education or "education for all." The Indian subcontinent, particularly India, has the largest number of illiterates in the world (see Table 1). Not only are the literacy rates low, but primary education is also far from universal in India, Pakistan, Bangladesh, and other countries, except in Sri Lanka. Though the literacy rate has been increasing over the years, the number of illiterates has also increased. For example, India has as many as 376 million illiterates according to the 1991 census, compared to 247 million in 1951; during the same period, the literacy rate increased from 18 percent to 52 percent. Similarly, in Nepal, the number of illiterates increased from 6.8 million in 1954 to 9.3 million by 1981. With these increasing numbers of illiterates, it is projected that, even by the turn of the century, literacy rates will not exceed 50 percent in Pakistan, Nepal, and Bangladesh (UNESCO 1991). Hence adult education programs are becoming of great importance.

This entry presents a brief overview of adult education and training activities in the Indian subcontinent. The changing nature and scope of adult education is also discussed. This is followed by a brief review of the types of adult education programs offered in the various countries, including their functioning and methods of delivery. The entry ends by identifying the important research gaps and problems that arise in the successful implementation of adult education programs.

1. Goals and Scope of Adult Education

The field of adult education has evolved a large, sometimes confused, vocabulary. "Adult education," "social education," "continuing education," "lifelong education," "recurrent education," "mass education," "fundamental education," "popular education," and several other terms are often used synonymously. "Adult education" and "nonformal education" are also often clubbed together (Coles 1977, Shah and Bhan 1980). Broad interpretations are given to these terms so that they mean what a particular national government wants to put stress on. Hence, the term "adult education" is often used as a "confusing misnomer" (Coombs 1985 p. 29).

When adult education was originally launched as a major activity by UNESCO and other agencies, mostly influenced by the West, literacy was not considered to be an important component as illiteracy was not perceived as a problem in the developed countries. But when educational programs were taken to the developing countries, adult education without literacy seemed meaningless.

India, in its first five-year plan, used the term "social education" to include (in addition to literacy): the health, recreation, and home life of adult learners, as well as their economic life and citizenship training; extension, general education; leadership training; and social consciousness. Even when "formal" adult education activities were launched in India in 1978, they were planned to emphasize, in addition to general adult education, the improvement of vocational skills, appreciation of the use of appropriate technology, physical education, and cultural activities. However, literacy remained the single most important objective of adult education programs in India. The adult education programs in Pakistan also aimed at enabling the people to learn Islamic values, appreciate national history and culture, acquire necessary productive skills, and promote community and environmental learning (UNESCO 1984b p. 27). The adult education program in Sri Lanka used to cover, from the very beginning, vocational and technical education and health and civic education. Thus, adult education also includes skill training, which was once regarded as an activity wholly distinct from education. However, the inclusion of practical training in an adult education program has also caused problems, as Myrdal (1968 p. 1687) noted: "adult education has been either neglected altogether or turned into something so 'practical' that it no longer encompasses any serious attempt to make people literate." Ironically, even though training and other learning activities were planned as a part of adult education in the Indian subcontinent, over the years adult education has become synonymous with literacy (or functional literacy) programs. Skill training programs have often become a separate activity.

The most tangible objective of adult education pro-

Table 1

Illiteracy and number of illiterates aged 15 and over in the Indian subcontinent 1990

Country	Illiteracy (percent)	Illiterates (millions)
Nepal	74.4	8.2
Bhutan	61.6	0.6
Bangladesh	64.7	42.0
India	51.8	280.7
Pakistan	65.2	43.5
Sri Lanka	11.6	1.3

Source: UNESCO 1991 *World Education Report*. UNESCO. Paris

grams in the developing countries has been the promotion of adult literacy. This holds true also for the Indian subcontinent. Adult education programs tend to be evaluated taking achievement in literacy as the main, though not the sole, criterion. The functionality and awareness component has generally been neglected as a result (see *Popular Education and Conscientization*). Similarly in Bangladesh, the "mass education program" launched to impart functional literacy, orientation to religious practice, family planning, nutrition, healthcare, farm and nonfarm vocations, and opportunities for further education, and so forth, is converted into a "mass literacy program."

Thus not only the concept but also the clientele of adult education has been narrowed over the years. In India, the audience was first defined as the population 15 years of age and above. It was subsequently redefined to include only the group aged 15–55 years —the active population. Later the principal target group was further reduced; it comprised only the most productive age group (i.e., those 15–35 years of age) (Tilak 1985). This has been the case not only in India, but also in other countries. In Nepal, the target group is the 15–44 age-group.

2. Policies and Programs

2.1 A Brief Review

While the tradition of adult education is older than that of formal schooling—in fact as old as civilization itself—somewhat formal adult education programs were set up in the subcontinent in the late nineteenth century. Night schools were organized in Bombay, Madras, Punjab, and Bengal to teach rudimentary "3Rs" to children as well as adults. Building a literate society had been an important item on the agenda of national leaders in pre-Independence India. Mahatma Gandhi envisaged adult education as a pivotal force in realizing a nonviolent revolution (Nayar 1989). Systematic efforts in adult education and training began in the mid-twentieth century.

Sri Lanka stands aloof at a higher level in the development of education, including adult education, compared with the other countries of the subcontinent. Important adult education activities have been organized in Sri Lanka since 1939. Sri Lanka is also a country where training in technical skills has become an integral part of the adult education programs. As a result, both governmental and nongovernmental projects on adult education and training have significant impact on the economic and social aspects of village life (Gajaanayake 1984). Interestingly, while adult education and training are important in Sri Lanka, their relative importance declines with the rapid growth of formal education, which covers an increasing proportion of the population (deSilva and deSilva 1990 p. 60). This is not the case in the other countries of the region.

The Indian experiments with mass literacy campaigns have been an important source of inspiration for the other countries on the subcontinent. The Gandhian tradition of mass literacy work gained momentum in the form of the *Gram Shikshan Mohim*, which started in Maharashtra state in 1959. The program adopted a mass approach and exploited local village patriotism to mobilize the educated people to work for literacy. The gains in terms of increased literacy were substantial, although many adults may have relapsed into illiteracy.

The concept of adult education was given a different dimension, and the program a new impetus in India in 1978, when the national adult education program was launched and was made a part of the "minimum needs program" of India's sixth five-year plan (1980–85) (Government of India 1981). A large number of formal adult education centers were opened, and a detailed plan was worked out, according to which classes were held for a given duration. Its original target was 100 million adults by 1988. The national policy on education (1986) laid special emphasis on the eradication of illiteracy through adult education programs, and launched the National Literacy Mission in 1988 to achieve self-reliance in literacy and numeracy, to promote self awareness, to impart vocational skills, and to conscientize the learners to value national integration and development. The Mission aims at providing functional literacy to 80 million people in the 15–35 age-group by 1995. The literacy campaign is based on an altogether new approach and methodology. It represents a massive national effort covering a very large number of districts throughout the country. As part of the post-literacy activities, learning resource centers, known as "*Jana Shikshan Nilayams*," have been created as permanent structures to serve the learning needs of newly literate adults.

Nepal has given importance to adult education programs since the mid-1950s. The National Education Planning Commission identified adult education as the second most important goal, after primary education. Planned adult education and training activities have been carried out since 1956. Since 1971, when adult education was recognized as a vital factor for development in the National Education System Plan, the fourth and the subsequent five-year plans have emphasized the need for literacy education. A number of adult education centers—first experimental, later formal— have been established. From 1970 to about 1985, two million people were to be made literate; about 60 percent of this target was achieved (Belbase 1986 p. 162).

Major programs in adult education in Nepal— literacy, postliteracy, vocational training, and continuing education—include a small farmers' development program, an integrated rural development program, a functional literacy program, an occupational training program, a skills training program, and a radio education service. The duration of these programs varies from one month to about a year. High schools with a vocational orientation have taken up functional literacy and skills training activities. The two-track approach has had a target of reaching 100,000 adults a year through its literacy extension program, and another 100,000 by means of functional adult education programs. The enrollment rate is estimated to be about 50 percent of these targets (UNESCO 1984a).

Though adult education had a promising beginning in Pakistan (and Bangladesh) in the Village-AID program initiated in 1954, it was only after the formulation of the 1970 and 1972 educational plans that adult education and literacy activities became more common. Evidence indicates that these plans, including the 1979 National Education Policy, have had a relatively small impact on the overall literacy rate (UNESCO 1984b). The National Literacy Program, which started in 1983, aimed at reaching 40 million illiterates, achieving a literacy rate of 74 percent by 1993. Pakistan plans to use broadcast education extensively. Accordingly, a formal functional literacy project of the Pakistan television corporation runs a large number of community viewing centers.

Important agencies involved in adult education and training in Pakistan include the Allama Iqbal Open University, the National Literacy and Mass Education Commission along with the Provincial Councils, the Standing Committee on Adult and Special Education, the all-Pakistan Women's Association, television and radio companies, and the Department of Local Government and Rural Development. Governmental and non-governmental organizations are thus actively involved in promoting adult education and literacy work.

The major adult education program launched in Bangladesh after Independence was the "mass education program" in 1980, which aimed at imparting functional education to 40 million illiterates in the group aged 10–45 years. This was regarded as one of the most ambitious, comprehensive, and methodical schemes on mass adult education. Even though huge investments were made, the mass education program was not a great success. In 1982 it was found that, instead of reaching a target of 10 million adults, *only* 0.7 million had in fact been enrolled.

2.2 Approaches

Various kinds of approaches—"formal," "nonformal," and "structured nonformal"—are being practiced in the context of adult education in the various countries of the subcontinent. Even within a single country, no unique approach is being followed. Some countries promote primary education; others promote literacy by linking it to certain development programs, again others use the mass campaign approach—that is, literacy for all—and most of them follow more than one approach.

Apart from general literacy programs, two kinds of approaches to offering adult education were adopted in Nepal. First, a functional approach was adopted on an experimental basis, according to which high schools with a vocational bias were selected to provide functional literacy classes and skill training in agriculture, health, family planning, home science, and crafts. Secondly, a less structured and less formal approach was taken in providing adult education in workplaces with the help of interdisciplinary resource teams. An "integrated" nonformal education approach has also been developed as a part of integrated rural development programs. Thus, adult education in Nepal consists of a basic literacy program, a functional literacy program of six months' duration, and a nonformal education program lasting for six months. Yet the whole program is largely oriented toward increasing functional literacy. In Nepal many of the skill training programs come under nonformal education.

Both center-based and campaign-based approaches are being adopted in India. The center-based approach is somewhat formal and systematized, as it depends on a formal adult education center, an instructor, some learning material, and some public financial resources. It has been in operation in most parts of the country. By contrast, the campaign approach is relatively cheaper since it does not presuppose any formal structure. Various sections of the society voluntarily participate in the literacy work, and mobilize the required resources. Government support, which is a precondition in the case of the center-based approach, is less important in a campaign-based approach. Successful micro-level experiments with total literacy campaigns in certain districts in India (e.g., in the state of Kerala) are based on this mass campaign approach. These campaigns are publicly funded, but also rely on the active participation of the masses, on voluntary trainers, and on grassroots bodies like the *Panchayats* and voluntary organizations. Both large- and small-scale programs have been set up aimed at specific target groups, most prominently women. Among others, the the *Mahila Samakhyas* in India and the Rural Advancement Committee in Bangladesh aim at promoting functional literacy among women.

2.3 Delivery Mechanisms

Most of the adult education and training programs are linked to general development programs in the countries of the region. Accordingly, adult education programs have not been the responsibility of a single agency. There are statutory bodies like the central and state governments; quasi-statutory bodies like the universities, colleges, and schools; and non-statutory bodies like the voluntary agencies with or without government support. Although the Ministry of Education tends to play a pivotal role, the ministries of Agriculture, Rural Development, Cooperatives, Women, Health and Family Welfare, Commerce, Labor, Information and Broadcasting, and Home Affairs, among others, are also actively involved in supporting adult education and training programs in the region. Many of the programs and projects promoting functional literacy and skills training are interministerial, at least as far as their organization and provision are concerned. Among the several development programs of interministerial nature, the integrated rural development programs, farmers' development programs, and population education programs have been important in India, Pakistan, Bangladesh, and Nepal. In India, adult education, literacy, and other training activities form an important component of many development programs (see, e.g., Government of India 1984).

Universities and colleges have also taken up adult education and extension programs, and adult education centers are created in universities and colleges, which have become involved in planning, organizing, and developing the adult education programs.

Involvement of nongovernmental organizations has been an important characteristic of adult education programs. As Bordia (1973 p. 41) noted, "although the record of the Government in the post-independence era has not been laudable, a large number of voluntary organizations have made sustained contributions in their respective areas." Voluntary involvement of social, cultural, political, and religious organizations in adult education and training is common in the region. Nongovernmental organizations have played complementary and supplementary roles and strengthened governmental activities. Adult education has featured prominently in the *Sarvodaya Shramadana* movement in Sri Lanka. The *Shawnirvar* (self-reliance) movement, the *Jatiyo Tarun Sangha*, and the training programs conducted by *Imams* in Bangladesh are some of the important ones. There are about 800 nongovernmental voluntary organizations in Bangladesh working on the "enlightenment" of the people, many of which have an explicit concern with adult education and training. Various sociopolitical organizations in India and Nepal actively carry out adult education programs. There are several community organizations based on religion and caste, similar to popular education movements; but a more important role is found to have been played by a very large number of education-oriented nongovernmental organizations which work closely with the state administration (Lind and Johnston 1990 p. 56). The state tends to actively support many of these voluntary organizations in the countries on the subcontinent.

International agencies also support some of the adult education programs in the region. Adult education centers in Sri Lanka were started in 1950 with the assistance of UNESCO, the Food and Agricultural Organization, the World Health Organization, and the Internal Labor Office. The Danish International Development Agency supported the mass education program in Bangladesh. Many voluntary organizations in Bangladesh are supported by West Germany, the Netherlands, Norway, the Canadian International Development Association, the Ford Foundation, and so on. A special work-oriented adult education project was launched in Nepal during 1970–75 with the assistance of UNESCO. Since the late 1980s, several international agencies have been involved in "education for all" projects in India that promote adult education, functional literacy, and skills training.

3. Gaps in Research

Adult education programs have been evaluated on a large scale. Yet many evaluation studies have either been "formative" (i.e., evaluation of the formulation of the plan) or "summative" (i.e., evaluation in terms of achievement of targets). However, these evaluation studies have not been helpful in elucidating the efficacy of the program as a whole. Concurrent evaluation (i.e., the simultaneous commencement of a program and its evaluation) may be helpful in modifying marginally the design of the program, but not in assessing its effectiveness.

To date, few research studies have been conducted on the impact of adult education programs on social and economic development. Adult education and training are expected to have significant, positive effects on various dimensions of individual and social development—from changing the attitudes of people in general, to a multitude of tangible and quantifiable benefits. Research on the effects of adult education and training programs in the region is very scarce. Knowledge on these aspects would be valuable in making proper policy decisions with respect to national investment in adult education and training.

Perhaps one may have to evaluate the programs in a much wider socioeconomic and political framework. Can the literacy provided by the adult education programs help in transforming the societies in the subcontinent? Can it empower the masses to fight for their rights and social justice? Can it lead to improvement in the quality of life of the underprivileged? (Banerjee 1992). Or does it simply help in legitimizing the existing structure? These political and sociological aspects of adult education programs are rarely examined in the region.

Analytical research evidence is also needed on the effectiveness of adult education programs in relation to the immediate objectives of enhancing literacy and imparting specific skills. It is not enough to examine whether the objectives are achieved and the targets met. It is also important to analyze the costs and cost effectiveness of these programs. Even more difficult, research evidence is needed on the relative effectiveness of various approaches to provision of adult education.

4. Problems Confronting the Development of Adult Education

Adult education programs in the region have been at the focus of many evaluation studies. From these studies a few important facts have emerged. Some of these are briefly mentioned below.

4.1 Uniform Programs "Imposed from Above"

Many adult education programs are designed and planned at national levels and are implemented using a "top-down" approach that does not necessarily take into account the local specificities. Local people are involved not in planning, but in administration and action. As a result, local initiative is rarely a major factor in the organization of these programs. However, local specificities are too important to be ignored. A village headman reported in the context of an evaluation study of an adult education program in India:

> AEP [adult education program] is like a plane manufactured in Delhi, having four wings and four wheels. Policymakers in Delhi think that this plane can land in any village of the 5 *lakhs* in the country. But they failed to see that the soil conditions in each of the villages are different. If the plane (not the soil) can be improved to adapt to all varieties of conditions, AEP would surely land more successfully.

In short, the strategies "pushed" from above are often found to be eliciting little support at the local level. Rather than looking for a national model, one could attempt to develop models that are based in local realities.

4.2 Relapse into Illiteracy

A major problem relates to the sustainability of literacy among certain segments of the population. Most adult education programs plan for the eradication of illiteracy in the shortest possible time, and some programs actually succeed. For example, in Pakistan, the "standard" literacy package takes 120 hours of instruction—60 hours for literacy skills, 25 hours for numeracy, and 35 hours for Islamic reorientation and vocational skill training. The duration is longer in India: the adult education program provides instruction for three years—basic literacy in the first year (300–350 hours) and postliteracy and follow-up activities in the second and the third years (150 and 100 hours respectively). However, these programs rarely offer postliteracy programs designed to sustain the literacy skills obtained in adult education classes. As a consequence, up to 50 percent of participants in literacy classes in India are found to relapse into illiteracy. Neglect of postliteracy programs and follow-up activities has been an important shortcoming of many, otherwise well-designed adult education programs.

4.3 Low Priority of Adult Education

Even though the importance of adult education in national development has been well recognized in all the countries of the subcontinent, few have paid serious attention to it. For example, Rao (1970 p.2) wondered why India had not launched a massive literacy program immediately after Independence. He concluded that the government did not seem bothered about the high rates of illiteracy in the country, so scanty financial resources were allocated to adult education. For example, in India, 3.5 percent of the first five-year plan expenditure on education was invested in adult education; and, in the subsequent plans, this share became even less. In Nepal and Pakistan, little financial support has been allocated to adult education programs.

4.4 Lack of Political Will

The most important problem is the absence of national commitment and political will to implement and sustain adult education programs. In India, only programs in areas where political commitment was ensured have attracted public financial support. As a review committee on adult education in India (Government of India 1980) noted: "sustained and nation-wide political commitment is a precondition" for the "success" of the adult education program.

4.5 Separation from Development

Experience indicates that the success of adult education programs is often limited if they are not related to other national development programs. Adult education and training programs that are closely linked to national development programs may have more chance to be successful, especially if they are connected to an economic development activity—an income generating one, for example, as studies on Sri Lanka suggest (UNESCO 1984c). Unfortunately, this intricate relationship between adult education and economic development is rarely pursued in a systematic manner. As Lind and Johnston (1990 p. 121) note, the state has to be the prime mover in promoting and organizing adult education and literacy programs for achieving national development goals.

See also: Formal, Nonformal, and Informal Education; Adult Literacy in the Third World; Asia, East and Southeast; China: People's Republic

References

Banerjee S 1992 Uses of literacy: Total literacy campaigns in three West Bengal districts. *Economic and Political Weekly* 27(9): 445–49

Belbase L N 1986 Learning strategies for post-literacy and continuing education of the neo-literates in Nepal. In: Dave R H, Ouane A, Perera D A (eds.) 1986 *Learning Strategies for Post-Literacy and Continuing Education in China, India, Indonesia, Nepal, Thailand and Vietnam.* UNESCO Institute for Education, Hamburg

Bordia A 1973 Adult education during the British period and after Independence. In: Bordia A, Kidd J R, Draper J A (eds.) 1973 *Adult Education in India: A Book of Readings.* Nachiketa, Bombay

Coles E K T 1977 *Adult Education in Developing Countries*, 2nd edn. Pergamon Press, Oxford

Coombs P H 1985 Suggestions for a realistic adult education policy. *Prospects* 15(1): 27–38

deSilva C R, deSilva D 1990 *Education in Sri Lanka 1948–*

1988: An Analysis of the Structure and a Critical Survey of the Literature. Navrang, New Delhi

Gajaanayake J 1984 *A Study of the Interaction between Adult Education and the Universalization of Primary Education in the Context of Integrated Rural Development.* UNESCO, in cooperation with the University of Colombo, Paris

Government of India 1980 *Report of the Review Committee on the National Adult Education Programme.* Ministry of Education and Culture, New Delhi

Government of India 1981 *The Sixth Five-year Plan 1980–1985.* Planning Commission, New Delhi

Government of India 1984 *Adult Education Components in the Development Schemes of Government of India.* Directorate of Adult Education, Ministry of Education and Social Welfare, New Delhi

Lind A, Johnston A 1990 *Adult Literacy in the Third World: A Review of Objectives and Strategies.* Swedish International Development Authority, Stockholm

Myrdal G 1968 *Asian Drama: An Inquiry into the Poverty of Nations*, Vol. 3. Penguin, London

Nayar D P 1989 *Towards a National System of Education.* Mittal, New Delhi

Rao V K R V 1970 *Adult Education and National Development.* Ministry of Education and Youth Services, Government of India, New Delhi

Shah A B, Bhan S (eds.) 1980 *Non-Formal Education and the NAEP.* Oxford University Press, New Delhi

Tilak J B G 1985 Growth of literacy in India: An analysis. *Indian J. Adult Educ.* 46(1): 21–23 and reply 46(8): 30–31

UNESCO 1984a *Literacy Situation in Asia and the Pacific: Country Studies—Nepal.* UNESCO Regional Office for Education in Asia and the Pacific, Bangkok

UNESCO 1984b *Literacy Situation in Asia and the Pacific: Country Studies—Pakistan.* UNESCO Regional Office for Education in Asia and the Pacific, Bangkok

UNESCO 1991 *World Education Report.* UNESCO Paris

Further Reading

Bordia A 1985 Planning and management of post-literacy programs. In: Carron G, Bordia A (eds.) 1985 *Issues in Planning and Implementing National Literacy Programs.* UNESCO/IIEP, Paris

Bhola H S 1981 Why literacy? Why literacy can't wait? Issues for the nineteen-eighties. *Convergence* 14(1): 6–23

Bhola H S 1984 A policy analysis of adult literacy promotion in the Third World: An accounting of promises made and promises fulfilled. *Int. Rev. Educ.* 30(3): 249–64

Bhola H S 1987 Adult literacy for development in India: An analysis of policy and performance. In: Arnove R F, Graff H G (eds.) 1987 *National Literacy Campaigns: Historical and Comparative Perspectives.* Plenum, New York

Bhola H S, Bhola J K 1984 *Planning and Organization of Literacy Campaigns, Programs and Projects.* German Foundation for International Development, Bonn

Education Commission 1966 *Education and National Development: Report of the Education Commission 1964–66.* Government of India, Ministry of Education, New Delhi (Reprinted: National Council of Educational Research and Training, 1971)

Government of India 1978 *50 Years of Adult Education in India: Some Experiences.* Directorate of Adult Education, Ministry of Education and Social Welfare, New Delhi

Government of India 1985 *Challenge of Education: A Policy Perspective.* Ministry of Education, New Delhi

Kidd R, Kumar K 1981 Co-opting Freire: A critical analysis of pseudo-Freiran education. *Economic and Political Weekly* 16(1–2): 25–36

Leirman W 1987 Adult education: Movement and discipline between the golden sixties and the iron eighties. In: Leirman W, Kulick J (eds.) 1987 *Adult Education and the Challenge of the 1990s.* Croom Helm, London

Mathew A 1991 *Adult Literacy and Development: Report of a Seminar.* India International Centre, New Delhi

Saraf S N 1980. *Literacy in a Non-Literacy Milieu: The Indian Scenario.* UNESCO/IIEP, Paris

Sharma D V 1986 Learning strategies for post-literacy and continuing education at the basic level in India. In: Dave R H, Ouane A, Perera D A (eds.) 1986 *Learning Strategies for Post-Literacy and Continuing Education in China, India, Indonesia, Nepal, Thailand and Vietnam.* UNESCO Institute for Education, Hamburg

UNESCO 1984c *Literacy Situation in Asia and the Pacific: Country Studies—Bangladesh.* UNESCO Regional Office for Education in Asia and the Pacific, Bangkok

Japan: Social and Adult Education

S. Miura

Adult education and training in Japan have been mainly conducted in the field of social education. Most of the programs have been provided by the Board of Education (Kyoiku-iinkai) using citizens' public halls and other institutions. With the development of lifelong learning activities in the 1980s, however, universities and private educational establishments have started to expand their share in the provision of social education programs.

1. Purposes and Policies

1.1 Social Education Law

According to this Law (No. 207 of 1949), "social education" implies systematic educational activities (including physical education and recreation) primarily for out-of-school youth and adults, excluding such educational activities as are conducted in schools as part of the curriculum, in accordance with the

School Education Law. Thus, "social education" is a term used to denote both formal and nonformal adult education as well as community education. The Law regulates the main functions of adult education such as the roles of national and local governments, institutions, and trainers, as well as the finance, supply, and organization of programs.

1.2 Human Resources Development Promotion Law

The Vocational Training Law was enacted in 1958 to aid in the development and improvement of vocational ability. Owing to profound changes in the environment surrounding vocational training, the new Human Resources Development Promotion Law (No. 64) was enacted in 1969. During the 1970s and 1980s, Japan experienced rapid technological innovation as well as a simultaneous aging of the society. To cope with these changes, the law was generally amended in 1985.

1.3 Law Concerning the Development of Mechanisms and Measures of Promoting Lifelong Learning

The law (No. 71 of 1990) defined the measures for lifelong learning facilitation planned by local public bodies and the measures for improving a wide range of learning opportunities in specific districts. It then aimed to promote policies for facilitating learning activities in local communities by establishing councils.

1.4 Report on "Social Education in a Rapidly Changing Society" submitted by the Social Education Council

This 1971 report first mentioned the imperative of developing lifelong education. New tasks for adult education were defined as expanding learning opportunities in higher education, promoting the development of educational facilities for adults more generally, and facilitating adults' participation in community activities.

1.5 Report on "Lifelong Education" submitted by the Central Council for Education

This 1981 report emphasized the idea of lifelong education. In Chap. 4, "Education in Adulthood," the following items are stressed:

(a) the importance of education during adulthood;

(b) the opening of school education to adults by measures such as: opening higher education to adults, opening education in universities to adults, utilization of junior colleges for adult learning, utilization of technical colleges for adult learning, utilization of high schools for adult learning, and promotion of adult education in special and miscellaneous schools;

(c) the promotion of social education through: expansion of social education programs, preparation and improvement of social education facilities, the training of leaders and the improvement

of their professional conditions, and encouragement and assistance of individual learning;

(d) improvement of education and training for workers by: Improving in-service training, and offering assistance for workers' education and learning.

1.6 Report by the National Council on Educational Reform (1st to 4th Reports: 1985–87)

In its fourth report, the Council recommended three basic elements of educational reform:

(a) developing and emphasizing the concept of individuality;

(b) ensuring the transition to a lifelong learning system;

(c) coping with changes in society, including the widespread internationalization and spread of the new information media.

The term "lifelong education" was changed to "lifelong learning" in order to emphasize a learner-centered approach. Since this report, "lifelong learning" has become the official term.

1.7 Report on the "Development of a Lifelong Learning Infrastructure" submitted by the Central Council for Education

This 1990 report discussed the necessity of and proposed policies for developing a lifelong learning infrastructure in Japan.

2. Structures of Adult Education

Japanese education is defined by the location in which the activity takes place. Education at home is "home education." Education at school is "school education" and education in the rest of society is generalized as "social education."

Adult education in Japan is mainly executed in the field of social education, and social education has become the core of lifelong learning. The administrative structure of social education is divided into three levels, namely the national, prefectural, and municipal levels. At the national level, the main policies of the country as well as the allocation of state funds to prefectural and local governments are decided. At the prefectural level, the main policies of the prefecture, budget planning and the allocation of subsidies to municipalities are determined. Some adult education programs, such as model or experimental types and leadership training, are directly administered by the prefecture. Most actual programs are provided at the municipal level.

The major contents of the programs are: (a) occupational knowledge and technical skills, (b) family life and home education, (c) sports and recreation, (d) arts and culture, (e) civic education, and (f) other types of adult education programs. Following the recommendation of the National Council on Educational Reform, guidelines for facilitating educational reform were adopted by the National Cabinet in 1987. In accordance with the guidelines proposed by the Cabinet, the structure of the Ministry of Education, Science, and Culture was reformed. The Social Education Bureau was enlarged and changed to the Lifelong Learning Bureau. The Bureau was given a lead position at the Ministry, and the traditional school-centered approach was switched into a lifelong learning approach in the Ministry.

3. Institutions

3.1 Lifelong Learning Center

As of 1990, 28 lifelong learning centers and social education centers had been established to promote learning activities. Most of these were operated by the prefectural boards of education. The major programs in the lifelong learning centers and social education centers include: (a) training leaders to be responsible for social education in the municipalities; (b) conducting surveys and research related to learning activities; (c) consulting, giving guidance, and providing information; and (d) offering various types of courses.

3.2 National Training Institute of Social Education

Established in 1965, the National Training Institute of Social Education has provided training opportunities for social education personnel including Social Education Officers appointed by the prefectural and local boards of education, *Kominkan* (citizens' public hall) officers, librarians, museum curators, and others. Trainees are provided with opportunities for learning current trends and issues in adult education, education for youth, and lifelong learning theories, as well as acquiring practical techniques. In addition to offering a wide range of training courses and seminars, the Institute serves as an information center for social and lifelong education. It also conducts the surveys and research necessary to deepen and enrich seminars and courses.

3.3 Citizens' Public Halls (Kominkan)

Citizens' Public Halls, first established after the Second World War, together comprise one of the nation's most important social education facilities. Citizens' Public Halls are administered by local public bodies and, in rare cases, by a corporation. They play an active role in stimulating educational and cultural activities in local areas, serving as community centers or adult education centers. The services offered by the Halls include single lectures, demonstrations, art exhibitions, film shows, and athletic meetings, as well as regularly scheduled courses such as youth study classes, women's classes, parental education courses, and so forth. Each Hall maintains one full-time director and several officers, the number being determined by the size and scale of the Hall. As of 1987, there were 17,440 Halls throughout the country.

3.4 Women's Education Centers

Women's education centers are social education facilities intended to enhance women's education and to contribute to the development of women's knowledge, skills, and capabilities. They develop and administer programs for the education and training of women and leaders in women's education, for the exchange of experience and information among women, and for the provision of useful information for women. These centers also make their facilities and equipment available to volunteer groups and other women's organizations for educational purposes. In 1989, there were 204 women's education centers throughout the country.

4. For-profit Institutions of Adult Education

Reflecting the deepening of people's eargerness to learn, new types of educational activities have emerged in the private sector. Although they are, for the most part, profit-making institutions, they are nevertheless gaining in popularity, especially in large cities and suburban areas. Information-based industries, such as newspapers and broadcasting companies, as well as department stores and banks, all of which access large numbers of people, organize extension services such as lectures and courses in facilities generally referred to as "culture centers." The majority of courses offered are those relating to art and culture or to practical knowledge and life skills.

While traditional social education is practiced mainly at the community level, these newer activities allow people sharing the same interests to become acquainted with each other and broaden their circle of associations beyond the communities in which they live. Activities in the private sector had already started in the 1950s. According to the 1990 survey by the Ministry of Education, Science, and Culture, 679 enterprises provided 55,279 courses.

5. Adult Education in Schools

For a long time, adults have not been considered as students at high schools, colleges, and universities. During the 1980s, however, schools increasingly began to pay attention to adult students. There are several reasons for this. For instance, rapid changes in society made the continuing education and training of workers necessary. Because of the well-developed infrastructure and the availability of trained teachers, the public school was seen as an institution that could play an important role in adult education. Also, the number of young people began to decrease so that schools had to find new students other than young people.

The most important forms of school-based adult education are:

(a) *High school extension courses.* The first program was initiated in 1959, after which the number of courses began to increase. In the late 1980s, the number of programs increased rapidly, as many schools responded to increased community demand.

(b) *Unit system high schools.* The "unit system high school" was established in 1988 to further promote lifelong learning by providing more flexible upper-secondary educational opportunities to a wider range of people.

(c) *Diversification of enrollment in higher education.* Indispensable to the pursuit of a lifelong learning society is making the most of higher educational institutions by increasingly admitting adults. Adults, especially working adults, have limited time to spend in the classroom and are more diversified than traditional students in terms of their educational background, learning styles, knowledge, and experience. Diversity in demand is matched by a degree of diversity in supply, which comprises, for example, evening courses, correspondence courses, and evening/weekend courses.

The number of universities and colleges with special admissions procedures and quotas for adult students steadily increased and had reached 51 institutions with a total number of 1,143 students by 1987.

Auditor status and special research status students have customarily been admitted by universities and colleges. Auditor students are usually high school graduates enrolling in one or two classes for a period of one year or less, whereas special research students are usually college graduates undertaking special research programs for a one-year period.

(d) *Extension courses in universities and colleges.* Extension courses in universities and colleges are meant to open the academic and educational doors of these institutions to the public, and to provide the community, including adults, with advanced learning opportunities. The number of extension courses at the university and college level reached 2,840 in 1988, 3.8 times more than that in 1978, enrolling some 370,000 people in such wide-ranging subjects as the liberal arts,

foreign languages, and sports. Some higher education institutions have begun to establish special facilities such as university extension centers intended to improve their educational services for adults by taking into account the specific regional learning needs of the community.

(e) *Correspondence education.* There are two types of correspondence education—correspondence school education based on the School Education Law and correspondence social education based on the Social Education Law. As regards correspondence social education, there are three types of courses: correspondence social education acknowledged by the Ministry of Education, correspondence social education conducted by several ministries or public corporations, and private sector correspondence social education.

(f) *The University of the Air.* The University of the Air is a revolutionary higher education institution making effective use of the broadcasting system in order to provide high quality educational opportunities on the largest possible scale. It was established in 1983 and started to admit students in 1985. The University's academic program combines original televised and radio broadcast classes produced in the University's own studio and broadcast through its own channels, with the reading of printed course materials, guidance by mail, and attendance at study centers for schooling and examinations to gain credit. Courses of the University include life and home science, industrial and social studies, humanities, and the natural sciences.

6. Financial Arrangements

The national government, prefectural governments, and municipal governments have their own financial plans. The national government provides subsidies to prefectures and municipalities. The prefectural governments also provide subsidies to municipal governments. Of the total budget of the Ministry of Education, Science, and Culture, 6.1 percent was allocated to lifelong learning, culture, sports, and related programs in 1992. Main items relating to adult education in the 1992 budget were as follows: (a) improvement of the lifelong learning system—increased supply of lifelong learning programs, improvement of guidance, counselling and lifelong learning information, the expansion of volunteer activities in lifelong learning, and the development of new educational media; (b) development of the school as a lifelong learning institution —recurrent education programs, the University of the Air, advancement of vocational education in special training schools; and (c) promotion of social education in the lifelong learning society—improvement of social education facilities, support of programs to activate social education facilities; and so forth. Among

48 prefectures in the nation, an average of 10.5 percent of total public educational expenditure was allocated to social education in 1986.

7. Adult Education Personnel

There are several categories of personnel in the fields of social education who are in charge of adult education. For example, social education supervisors are staff of the Lifelong Learning Bureau of the Ministry of Education, Science, and Culture. They take part in the planning, development, and promotion of social education policies and programs as national-level advisors. Senior specialists and specialists at the National Training Institute of Social Education take part in the planning, organization, and operation of training courses and seminars for the social education officers appointed by the prefectural and local boards of education, citizens' public hall officers, librarians, museum curators, and others. Social education officers give professional and technical advice and guidance to those who are engaged in social education in the prefectural and municipal boards of education. Social education leaders give advice and guidance to those taking part in educational activities on a part-time basis. Finally, Citizens' Public Hall officers are the professionals responsible for teaching and organizing learning activities for adults in local communities.

8. Participation Levels

In most adult education classes, participation is voluntary. Traditionally women participate more often and in larger numbers than men. Men more often receive extensive further education and training sponsored and organized by their employers. Owing to a variety of technological innovations, rapid change in the social environment, and increasing access to leisure time during the 1980s, however, the share of men in participation has been gradually increasing in both vocationally oriented programs and in hobby or cultural activities intended to improve one's quality of leisure.

9. Evaluation Practices

Most adult education programs in Japan are noncredential. People usually complete their courses without receiving credit toward a qualification, as learning occurs primarily for "learning's sake". Thus, participation and communication are seen as important, whereas credentialism is not an important matter in Japanese adult education. By contrast, in the vocational training field, people take courses to obtain certificates or credits qualifying for jobs. At the public vocational training schools and special training schools, people take certain examinations, such as the trade skills test. However, most students of the special training school are young adults who have graduated from junior high or high school. Once people get jobs in Japan, they usually stay in the same organization until their retirement. Therefore, most further education and training is carried out through the firm, and it has been rare to find people who seek to obtain qualifications in order to change jobs. The lifelong employment system characterizes Japanese adult vocational education.

In the private sector, the main responsibility for the continuing vocational training of the Japanese workers lies with the enterprises. A recent survey found that nearly 80 percent of all enterprises organize training programs, and that about one-third of the labor force each year makes use of the opportunity to participate in training. Under the peculiar tradition of so-called "lifetime employment practice," employers can be easily convinced that good returns can be reaped on investment in the further education and training of the workforce. However, the chance of receiving training is unequally distributed among workers. Younger workers are at an advantage compared with older workers, and large firms offer more educational opportunities than small ones. In order to encourage the smooth implementation of training programs conducted by the enterprises (especially the small and medium-sized ones), the Ministry of Labor grants subsidies through its Lifelong Human Resources Development Grant Scheme, which covers not only the cost incurred for the training provision but also one-third (one-fourth in the case of big firms) of the full wage cost of the workers who receive training.

In 1987, 381 public training institutions were operated by the Employment Production Corporation, local bodies, and the central government. These institutions provide various kinds of training courses for different audiences—for example, young high school graduates, young employees, the unemployed, and the handicapped. However, the main function of these facilities is to offer upgrading training programs for the employed. In 1986, the number of trainees in initial training was 31,700, whereas 125,000 workers took part in upgrading courses. A reform implemented in the early 1990s seeks to upgrade the curriculum of the training programs so as to take account of rapid innovations in technology. Another aspect of the reform is to encourage middle-aged and older workers to improve their capacities by enrolling in public training programs.

See also: Japan: Vocational and Training; Asia, East and Southeast

Bibliography

Japan Lifelong Education Association 1989 *Encyclopedia of Lifelong Learning*. Tokyo–Shoseki, Tokyo
Lifelong Learning and Social Education Administration in the Ministry of Education, Science, and Culture 1989 *Lifelong Learning Information File*. Daiichi-Hoki, Tokyo

Ministry of Education, Science, and Culture 1980 *Japan's Modern Educational System: A History of the First Hundred Years*. Maruzen, Tokyo

Ministry of Education, Science, and Culture 1985 *Adult Education in Japan*. GPO, Tokyo

Ministry of Education, Science, and Culture 1989 *Education in Japan 1989—A Graphic Presentation*. Gyosei, Tokyo

Miura S 1992 *Lifelong Learning in Japan: An Introduction*. National Federation of Social Education, Tokyo

Moro-oka K 1976 *Recurrent Education. Policy and Development in OECD Member Countries: Japan*. OECD, Paris

National Council on Educational Reform (NCER) 1987 *Fourth and Final Report on Educational Reform*. Government of Japan, Tokyo

National Council on Educational Reform (NCER) 1991 *Further Education and Training of the Labor Force. A Report to the OECD*. Government of Japan, Tokyo

Sako M 1990 *Enterprise Training in a Comparative Perspective: West Germany, Japan, and Britain*. World Bank, Washington, DC

Thomas J E 1985 *Learning Democracy in Japan: The Social Education of Japanese Adults*. Sage, London

Japan: Vocational Education and Training

M. Sako

In 1989, Japan had a population of 123 million, and a total national income of 318 trillion yen (US$2,900 billion). In the same year, there were 99.7 million Japanese aged 15 and over (of whom 21 million were 60 or over), and 60 percent of them were gainfully employed. Of those, a quarter were self-employed or family workers, the rest being employees, either regular or temporary, full-time or part-time. The unemployment rate is low (2.3 percent in 1989).

Of the gainfully employed, 9 percent worked in the primary, 34 percent in the secondary, and 57 percent in the tertiary (including central and local government and public services) sectors. The labor force is generally well-educated: 17 percent of employees (in all sectors except public services) were university graduates, 56 percent upper-secondary graduates, and 27 percent lower-secondary graduates in 1986.

The Japanese system of vocational education and training which has produced this labor force, and which builds on it, will be described below. Administratively, the Japanese system is largely divided into two parts, under the jurisdiction of the Ministry of Education (*Monbusho*) and the Ministry of Labor respectively. A significant amount of education and training also takes place in industry and commerce.

1. Vocational Education in the Formal Ministry of Education System

No explicitly vocational subjects are taught during the nine years of compulsory education in primary and lower-secondary schools. However, compulsory schooling provides a good foundation for vocational education and training. First, a highly concentrated period of schooling, the absence of ability streaming, and the existence of a national curriculum which is rigidly adhered to, ensure that there is a minimal dispersion of achievement among 15-year olds in basic literacy and numeracy. Second, schooling inculcates in young people attitudes and moral principles valued by employers, such as diligence and the willingness to work in a team.

One characteristic of postcompulsory vocational courses offered within the Ministry of Education sector is that they are not totally vocational; the curricula at all levels contain a significant element (up to 50%) of general education. This broad-based education partly reflects the Ministry's belief in the importance of developing citizens who do not specialize at an early age. It also reflects the academic bias in individual aspiration and employers' recruitment patterns. In the main, vocational education in the early 1990s tends to be overshadowed by the ability-labeling function of the schools and universities, unlike in the 1950s and 60s when there were vocal demands for the expansion of vocational education.

1.1 Vocational Upper-secondary Schools

Of the 95 percent of 15-year olds who stay on at schools, a decreasing minority (24% or 1.46m in 1990 compared to 40% in 1955) have opted for vocational courses (see Fig. 1 for progression routes in the Japanese education system). Of the total 5,506 upper-secondary schools in 1990 (of which 23.8% were private), 16 percent offered nothing but vocational courses, and another 31 percent both vocational and general courses.

The Ministry of Education classified the 3,664 vocational courses available in 1990 in the following "course groupings": business-related (31.9%), industry-related (22.9%), home economics (17.4%), agriculture-related (12.2%), nursing (4.3%), fisheries (1.4%), and other (9.9%). Each grouping consists of specialized courses; for example, the industry-related grouping includes specializations in electricity, machinery, electronics, information technology, architecture, and civil engineering.

The Ministry stipulated in its curriculum guide

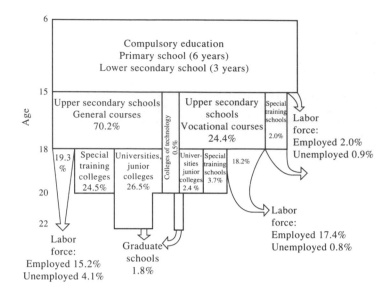

Figure 1
Flow of students through the Japanese education system 1990[a]

a Special training schools include, besides special training schools (*senshu gakko*) proper, also miscellaneous schools (*kakushu gakko*) and Ministry of Labor Vocational Training Centres (*Shokugyo Kunrenko*). All percentages are expressed in terms of the total cohort at age 15 when compulsory education ends.

Source: Calculated from figures in Ministry of Education 1991)

Course of Study (1983) that at least one-third of total school hours should be devoted to general education subjects. In reality, only about half of total school time is devoted to vocational subjects. They are taught in the form of both lessons in a class of on average 40 pupils, and practical work undertaken individually or in a group. Work experience, which used to be popular in the 1950s, hardly occurs in the early 1990s as employers are no longer keen to cooperate.

1.2 Colleges of Technology

A total of 62 colleges of technology (*koto senmon gakko*) offered five-year courses for 52,930 15–20-year olds (91.2% male) in 1990. All but four of the colleges are publicly run. They were established mainly in the 1960s when there was a need for some intermediate level of training between the technician and the university graduate technologist levels. The colleges offer courses in all the main engineering disciplines, but again follow the Ministry of Education guideline on curriculum to spend at least a third of the time in general education. These colleges are generally well-equipped and at 13:1 have much better staffing ratios than either vocational upper-secondary schools or universities. Twelve percent of college graduates went on to further education, typically entering the third year of a university engineering department. The

level reached on graduating from a college of technology is thus equivalent to completion of the first two years of a university degree.

1.3 Junior Colleges

In 1990, there were 593 junior colleges (of which 84% were private), which offered two-year courses for 18-year olds. They suffer from the girls' finishing school image; in 1990, 92 percent of a total of 479,389 students were female, and a quarter of them specialized in home economics. Junior colleges offer some vocational courses, however; for example, for primary school teachers, auxiliary health workers and day-care center workers.

1.4 Universities

The 507 universities—135 publicly run and 372 private—are attended by 1.99 million undergraduate students (in 1990), and offer four-year courses of varying quality in both general education and explicitly vocational subjects. Specialization does not start until the third year, as the first two years are largely devoted to the study of general education subjects for all students. Among vocationally oriented courses, one conspicuous increase in provision over time was in engineering; engineering students rose from 15.4 percent in 1960 to 19.6 percent in 1990.

In 1976, two universities of technology and science, at Nagaoka and Toyohashi, were established primarily for the purpose of offering undergraduate and graduate engineering education to graduates of colleges of technology and vocational upper-secondary education.

Graduate degrees in Japan are mostly developed for the purpose of training for the academic profession and not to confer a career advantage in industry. The exception to this is in engineering and science; as knowledge becomes more specialized, the R&D establishments of Japanese firms have increasingly sought graduates with masters degrees and PhDs in these subjects, as well as sponsoring their employees to study in science and engineering graduate schools mainly in the United States. In 1990, of a total of 61,884 masters students at Japanese universities, 46 percent were in engineering and 11 percent in sciences; of the 28,354 PhD students, 15 percent were in engineering and 11 percent in sciences.

2. Public Provision of Vocational Training: Ministry of Labor and Other Ministries

A national system of public vocational training administered by the Ministry of Labor is something of an anachronism in the 1990s, and has been slow to adjust to new requirements. When the 1958 Vocational Training Law created the present framework of public vocational training, there was a genuine need to alleviate labor and skill shortages by providing initial training for the majority of 15-year olds who were coming out of schools to obtain jobs. It was primarily for these young people who, in the early 1990s, constitute a cadre of supervisors and older skilled workers, that the Ministry of Labor set up its vocational training centers (VTCs) (*shokugyo kunrenko*). The curriculum focused on training in practical, manual, mainly mechanical engineering skills, with very little time spent on general education subjects.

Enrollment at these VTCs increased in the early 1960s but declined thereafter, as an increasing proportion of young people preferred to stay on in the formal school system until the age of 18. Consequently, the 1969 amendment to the Vocational Training Law extended the statutory provisions for training to cover not only initial preemployment training but also retraining of displaced workers and upgrading training for those in employment. For this purpose, some VTCs were converted into "skill development centers" for retraining and upgrading, and into "vocational training colleges" to provide initial training at a technician level to 18-year old high school graduates. In the 1970s, slower growth and industrial restructuring after the 1973 oil crisis, a concern with the aging of the population, and further improvements in young people's educational attainments necessitated another reorganization of the public training system. In particular, the 1978 amendment emphasized employers' responsibility to provide adequate training for their employees, and declared the government's role to be to provide training for people who needed special assistance, in particular the disabled and displaced workers in declining industries.

The renaming of the law in the 1985 amendment to the Human Resources Development Promotion Law reflected the Ministry's attempt to move away from the traditional image of focus on craft skill training toward an emphasis on flexible approaches to continuing or lifelong education and training. In particular, employers were encouraged by the Ministry to formulate a human resource development plan to ensure that learning opportunities would be provided systematically to support the career development of their employees.

In the late 1980s, there were 370 public training institutions administered by the Ministry of Labor, 276 of which were run by prefectural or municipal governments and 93 by the Employment Promotion Corporation (EPC). The EPC was established by a statute in 1961 to administer vocational training institutions and financial assistance to workers and employers. Three types of course are offered: (a) initial training courses, lasting on average two years for about 31,000 young people (around half of whom were middle school leavers, and the rest high school graduates); (b) upgrading training courses for 226,000 adult employees, taken either full-time, part-time, or as correspondence courses, lasting between 12 hours and one year; and (c) Occupational Capability Redevelopment Training, which is job conversion training based on the concept of ILO's "Modules of Employable Skills" to 46,000 displaced workers. Of the 46,000, 17,000 were on courses run by special training schools and miscellaneous schools (see Sect. 4). In the 1980s, the government encouraged public vocational training institutions to subcontract out training to the private sector, in order to meet new training needs. In fact, most of the courses at VTCs have remained of the traditional manufacturing type, the most popular ones being machining, car mechanics, construction, welding, painting, electrical work, metalwork, woodworking, and pipe fitting. The EPC also oversees an Institute of Vocational Training which supports the running of VTCs by providing training for VTC instructors, issuing licenses for them, and conducting research into vocational training and curriculum development.

Other ministries, besides the Ministry of Labor, are in charge of overseeing specific vocational courses, and providing qualifications for those vocations. For example, marine training falls under the jurisdiction of the Ministry of Transport, and nursing training under the jurisdiction of the Ministry of Health.

3. Vocational Qualifications and Skill Testing

The Japanese government takes an active role in setting training standards and monitoring them by certification of skills. The most extensive skill testing system, created by the 1958 Vocational Training Law, is that run by the Ministry of Labor from testing centers in every prefectural town. Tests are prepared by the Central Association for Vocational Ability Development, while the setting and revision of testing standards are discussed at the expert subcommittee of the Central Human Resource Development Council, a tripartite advisory council attached directly to the Labor Minister. Other ministries which run their own qualification tests include the Ministry of International Trade and Industry (MITI), Ministry of Health, and Ministry of Transport. There are a total of over 300 skills tested at both an ordinary and an advanced level. The Ministry of Labor concentrates on testing for traditional manufacturing skills, such as carpentry, machining, plastering, fitting, painting, metalwork, pipe fitting, and woodwork. The national qualifications conferred by MITI include those for system engineers and computer programers.

Most of the skills tested are discrete rather than those which confer a whole-role occupational status. Moreover, many people who take skill tests are employed. Employers may encourage workers to take the tests, either because it is a legal requirement to have a minimum number of workers on site with certain qualifications for health and safety reasons, or to motivate their workers to acquire new skills. Only a minority of adults obtain a skill test certification in order to improve their chances in the labor market.

4. Private Provision of Training

Numerous predominantly privately run institutions, known as miscellaneous schools (*kakushu gakko*) exist in Japan, and provide a broad range of specialized courses, some in specific occupational preparation (e.g., hairdressing) and others in more general occupational skills, such as accountancy, foreign languages, business studies, computer sciences, and electronic engineering.

In 1976, an amendment to the 1947 Fundamental Law of Education created a new category of schools, known as special training schools (*senshu gakko*), out of the existing miscellaneous schools. This 1976 Law officially brought special training schools under the jurisdiction of the Ministry of Education, which provides subsidies to some schools. According to the law, *senshu gakko* must meet certain criteria: for example, their courses must last for at least a year; a year's tuition must cover at least 800 hours; courses for high school leavers must be taught by university graduated teachers; at least half of the teachers must be full-time.

In 1990, some 1.2 million students attended both types of vocational school (see Table 1 for increases in the numbers of schools and pupils over time). Of those, nearly 0.8 million students were taking courses at special training schools. Adults of any age may attend these courses, but 18-year olds predominate, and three-fourths of the students attend courses which

require upper-secondary graduation. Special training school courses typically last for two years, and are becoming an increasingly popular alternative to attending universities or junior colleges for 18-year olds. In 1976, 20.8 percent of upper-secondary graduates went on to universities, 12.0 percent to junior colleges, and 2.8 percent to special training schools; by 1989, the respective percentages changed to 17.9, 12.4, and 14.9 percent.

The increased popularity of special training schools is in part due to the type of courses on offer. The distribution of students by course areas in 1989 was: industrial (28.3%), agricultural (0.2%), medical (20.8%), services affected by sanitary regulations (e.g., barbers, restaurants) (6.1%), education and social welfare (4.0%), commerce (18.0%), domestic science (8.3%), and cultural activities (arts, media, etc.) (14.2%). Special training schools suffer less from bureaucratic inertia than do universities or junior colleges. Consequently, they have been quick to set up new courses in response to local demand, to fill in the gap left particularly by the Labor Ministry-run public vocational training schools. For example, in response to shortages of computer programers and software engineers, the number of students attending information technology courses at special training schools increased from 4,200 in 1978 to 68,000 in 1989. Special training schools have thus emerged as the major source of trained programers for industry and commerce.

However, upper-secondary career guidance teachers and employers have expressed a concern over the

Table 1

Postsecondary, nonuniversity vocational schools and colleges: types, schools and students

	1980	1985	1990
Senshu gakko (Special training schools)			
Public schools	333	351	348
Pupils	36,471	42,139	45,238
Private schools	2,187	2,664	2,952
Pupils	396,443	496,036	746,193
Subtotal schools	2,520	3,015	3,300
Subtotal pupils	432,914	538,175	791,431
Kakushu gakko (Miscellaneous schools)			
Public schools	166	120	89
Pupils	13,307	9,959	6,813
Private schools	5,136	4,180	3,347
Pupils	711,094	520,200	418,528
Subtotal schools	5,302	4,300	3,436
Subtotal pupils	724,401	530,159	425,341
Total schools	7,822	7,315	6,736
Total pupils	1,157,315	1,068,334	1,216,772

Source: Ministry of Education 1991

great variability in standards reached in these schools, which is a complementary disadvantage of looser government control. In general, standards of engineering courses at special training schools are considered not to be on a par with the colleges of technology standard.

5. *Training in Industry*

According to a Ministry of Labor survey, 82.5 percent of firms employing 30 or more and across all industrial sectors provided some form of training to their employees in 1984. Industry has come to play a central role in vocational training mainly because of the practice of lifetime employment by large firms. Lifetime employment provides a strong incentive for employers to invest in the training of their workers, and for employees to respond positively to opportunities to acquire broad-based skills specific to an enterprise. The prevailing personnel policy of large firms has been to recruit prospective core workers from among school leavers and university graduates with good academic records and adaptability, and to provide training in-house. A lifetime employment perspective also facilitates a systematic career development plan with initial training, followed by periodic refresher training and retraining both on-the-job and off-the-job.

During the rapid industrial growth of the 1950s and 60s, production workers were keenly sought after among 15-year old school leavers. Many large firms opened training schools within factory premises to provide intensive skills training off-the-job. This often took the form of a three-year course, which consisted of classroom study in general subjects and theoretical technical subjects as well as practical on-the-job training. Unlike in the case of apprenticeships in Western Europe, the three-year course was seen as a basis for further training, did not normally lead to any recognized occupational qualification or status, and thus did not lend itself to job demarcation as European apprenticeships have done. By the 1970s, when the majority of new recruits had at least 12 years (rather than nine years) schooling, many of the in-company schools were closed. Those which stayed open offer one or two-year courses for 18-year olds and shorter courses for older workers, concentrating on vocational theory and practice.

A preference for the "home grown" breed of workers is also reflected in the provision of off-the-job training in-house rather than through the use of external training agencies. A small number of private profit-making training agencies do exist, which offer training programs mostly for managerial employees. However, the most well-known institutions, such as the Japan Industrial Training Association (*Nihon Sangyo Kunren Kyokai*), the Japan Management Association (*Nihon Noritsu Kyokai*), and the Japan Efficiency Association's *Sanno Daigaku* are all semi-public corporations.

In the late 1980s and early 1990s, there has also been a growth of "human resource development companies" created by large companies both in manufacturing and financial services by hiving off the training divisions as independent subsidiaries. In some cases, companies have done this for diversification, offering for sale the training packages which they have experience of providing for their own employees. More commonly, the target market is confined to other companies which are either affiliates or subcontractors within the same corporate grouping.

Smaller firms which cannot afford to provide in-house off-the-job training therefore often rely on technology transfer from large customer companies. This involves hands-on instruction of small firm operatives and engineers by large company engineers as well as lectures and study groups held by large companies for small company managers. Other external providers of training for small and medium sized firms include the following: (a) cooperatives of small firms which may operate group training programs for which they are eligible for public financial assistance; (b) the University Institutes of the Small and Medium Enterprise Agency within MITI, which offer courses for owners and managers in small business management and technology upgrading; and (c) the Ministry of Labor's vocational training centers for courses on skill upgrading.

Japanese companies are noted for nonformal, yet systematic on-the-job training. First, trainers are often older, more experienced workers, engineers, and managers, rather than professional trainers. Every time a new production line is laid, part of the tasks of production engineers is to instruct operators in a hands-on fashion. It is common for supervisors and middle managers to be appraised regularly on their efficiency as teachers of their subordinates, and they are given training in pedagogical skills as well as in technical and managerial skills.

Second, workers are encouraged to engage in self-development by enrolling in correspondence courses and self-learning in their own time. Courses range from university correspondence courses to shorter-term business and technical courses, for example, in accounting, production control and stock management, English language, and computing. The Ministry of Labor promotes this mode of learning by providing a subsidy of one-fourth (one-third in the case of small and medium enterprises) of companies' contributions toward the cost of correspondence courses.

Third, job rotation is considered a form of informal training to develop flexible workers with a broad skill base. Lastly, small group activities (especially quality control circles), present in around 60 percent of all Japanese enterprises, and in three-fourths of large enterprises with 1,000 or more workers, also facilitate training. The introduction of quality control circles is preceded by training of all workers in statistical and presentation techniques. It must be noted, however, that both job rotation and small group activities are not always primarily intended as training, as other objectives may be overriding, such as an optimum use of labor resources for higher productivity in the case of job rotation, and cost reduction in the case of small group activities. These practices undoubtedly contribute to the development of communication skills and better teamwork in the workshop, however, and to a broader understanding of how the company operates outside an employee's immediate work environment.

6. Who Pays for Training?

There is no comprehensive survey of training costs borne by companies, individuals and the state in Japan. The following can only provide a rough indicator of burden sharing among the three actors.

An annual survey by the Ministry of Labor reports that explicit education and training budgets of firms (with 30 or more workers) are usually small, and average 0.4 percent of companies' wage bills. These figures understate the real costs of training, as they omit the opportunity cost of time spent on formal or informal on-the-job training as well as off-the-job training, and sometimes travel costs for attending courses and the capital and maintenance costs of training facilities. The lack of interest in consolidating training expenditure is in part due to the high retention rates of core workers at large firms, which ensures that gains from training investment can be appropriated in the long run. Moreover, costing is virtually impossible for the modes of training delivery that Japanese companies prefer, namely on-the-job training of a less formal kind, such as job rotation and quality control circles.

Individuals also make significant contributions to the cost of training they receive after employment. First, steep pay profiles by age in the seniority-plus-merit reward system of Japanese companies imply a low starting pay level, not unlike the level of allowance apprentices receive in some European countries. Second, Japanese workers are expected to spend a significant proportion of their own time in learning and self-development.

The state finances much of the provision of general education: public educational expenditure accounted for 5.2 percent of Japan's national income in 1986. National and local governments run 99 percent of elementary schools, 94 percent of middle schools, 76 percent of high schools, and 27 percent of universities. The budget of the Ministry of Education in 1990/91 was 4.8 trillion yen (US$44 billion), half of which was to cover teachers' salaries. It is not possible to divide this budget into the general and vocational elements.

The total training budget expenditure of the Ministry of Labor amounted to 134 billion yen (US$1.2 billion) in 1989/90. Of this total, 42 percent was absorbed by the maintenance (including staff salaries) of vocational training centers and other public vocational training institutions. The rest of the budget was for administering the skill testing and certification system, and programs for specific groups (e.g., older workers, the disabled, displaced workers). For example, employed workers over 50 are eligible for a grant covering up to 50 percent of course fees to an upper limit of 100,000 yen (US$920). Only around 15 percent of the budget went to subsidizing employers' training within the enterprise. The government contributes only a limited proportion of the total cost incurred by employers, and its contribution targets the small and medium sized enterprises (SMEs) whose capacity to organize adequate training programs is limited. For example, the Ministry subsidizes one-third (but half for SMEs) of the cost of hiring teachers and the purchase of materials for in-house courses, one-half (but two-thirds for SMEs) of the cost of external courses, and one-fourth (but one-third for SMEs) of employees' wages while on training courses, provided the courses are part of the Enterprise Skill Development Plan approved by the Ministry.

7. Issues for the Future

The following problems have come to the fore of both employers' and policymakers' attention:

(a) A rapid pace of technological change, and in particular the diffusion of microelectronic technology, have necessitated a greater emphasis on off-the-job instruction rather than on-the-job training.

(b) A mismatch in the supply and demand for qualified labor (especially a shortfall in R&D personnel and software engineers) is expected to worsen as a result of technical change and a shift in industrial structure away from manufacturing. In response, there has been a noticeable increase in mid-career hiring of specialists, which puts a pressure on the practice of generalist training within the lifetime employment system. Moreover, as Japanese companies concentrate on doing more basic scientific research in-house, they are considering how to foster creativity amongst their scientists and engineers, training for whom at universities and on-the-job has traditionally been thought to discourage rather than encourage creative thinking.

(c) The aging of the Japanese population has created a shortage of young recruits. Supplementing the shortfall by retraining older workers and hiring more women has put a strain on company budgets for developing new training programs. Consequently, there might possibly be a heavier reliance on public provision for retraining in the future.

However, the 1985 Human Resource Development

Promotion Law continues to let industry take the initiative, while the role of the Japanese state is confined to the reinforcement and subsidization of employers' effort to train their employees, and to supplementing training for individuals who are not part of the core "lifetime employed" labor force in large enterprises.

See also: Japan: Social and Adult Education

References

Ministry of Education 1983 *Koto Gakko Gakushu Shido Yoryo.* Ministry of Education, Tokyo
Ministry of Education 1991 *Mombu Tokei Yoran.* Ministry of Education, Tokyo

Further Reading

Dore R, Sako M 1989 *How the Japanese Learn to Work* Routledge, London
Ishikawa T 1987 *Vocational Training.* Japanese Industrial Relations Series No. 7, 2nd edn. The Japan Institute of Labor, Tokyo
Prais S 1987 Educating for productivity: Comparisons of Japanese and English schooling and vocational preparation. *National Institute Econ. Rev.* 119: 40–56
Suzuki H 1980 *Outline of Vocational Education in Japan.* Ministry of Education, Tokyo

Latin America: Adult Education

F. Vio Grossi and D. Palma

This entry describes the situation of adult education in the Latin American region. The presentation covers two parts, namely the historical development of adult education, and the features and status of adult education activities in the mid–1990s.

1. Historical Development

Adult education has a long history in Latin America, and has grown through successive innovations. The first efforts to provide education for adults began as early as the Spanish conquest. They took place in the mission schools, which were intended to educate aborigines into the Western culture and values, as well as to teach them arts and crafts (La Belle 1980). At that time, two trends became apparent: the dominant one which was represented by friars of the Franciscan and Dominican orders in Mexico, Peru, and Ecuador, with an emphasis on subordinating the aborigines to the Western Christian culture; and another, weaker and narrower in scope, which was carried on by the Jesuits, mainly in Paraguay, stressing respect for, and an effort at developing, the aboriginal culture.

The trend that emphasized the integration of the aborigines into the new society was carried on far beyond the Latin American independence movements. After Independence, the task was to construct the nation–states, and this purpose specified the goals, scope, and contents of education.

Several currents appeared during the nineteenth century in Latin American adult education, carried on by various educators and taking various forms. Yet, all of them pursued similar objectives. On the one hand, the Roman Catholic Church sought to inculcate moral principles and to train the labor force; on the other hand, state agencies sought to diffuse basic knowledge, values, and habits that would ensure the incorporation of adults into the "national project" as defined by the leading classes. During the whole century, these educational activities reached only limited social sectors. Only the Church succeeded to some extent in reaching the peasants and women. Most of the aborigines were left outside of the educational sphere.

In the second half of the nineteenth century, with the start of manufacturing industries in the more advanced countries of the region, the need for a qualified labor force drove novel entrepreneurs to set up the first technical schools for training adults in mining, arts, and crafts. At around the same time, and in counterpoint to this process, there appeared the first urban popular movements. These attracted much attention in those countries which had received new European immigration by that time. In Argentina and Uruguay, as well as in Chile and Mexico, the craftsmen organized clubs and mutual aid groups. In doing this, they were introduced into civic and political thought with clear influence from utopic socialism and anarchism. At this point, adult education once again took the path of joining the training of its students with a simultaneous effort at enriching and organizing the culture of the underclass segments of the population.

In contrast with European countries, civil society in most of the Latin American countries developed under the guidance of, and the initiatives carried out by, the state. Between 1850 and the first half of the twentieth century—between the expansion of industrial capitalism and the end of the Second World War—public education expanded and grew into a homogeneous institutional system under the guidance of the state.

Meanwhile, adult education supported by the state served only a supplementary function (Cariola 1985;

Gajardo 1983a, Latapí 1985), in that it was meant to teach adults knowledge and skills they had not previously had an opportunity to learn, mainly due to a lack of access to schooling. The result of this orientation was a concentration on literacy and basic education. In providing this kind of education, everything was done as if it were meant for children: the same teaching style, the same texts, the same contents, and even the same facilities used in teaching youths. This was the dominant trend in adult education until well into the 1950s. Even by the early 1990s, it has not yet been totally left behind.

A few evaluations of this system were carried out. They generally showed its failure to achieve the goals it purported to serve. La Belle remarks that, in the literacy campaign that took place in Guatemala City in 1945, 3,000 illiterates registered, but only 300 stayed for the final tests, and of these only three persons had really learnt how to read and write (La Belle 1980 p. 144).

2. Developments Since the 1960s

From the beginning of the 1950s, UNESCO started to promote new ideas in adult education, which were concerned with "fundamental education." It was proposed that adult education should grow out of the fundamental personal experiences and concerns of the students themselves. This stemmed from a realization that adults grow to the extent that their educational activity allows them to draw on their own experiences, skills, and values. This new tenet was supported at the Second World Conference on adult education in Montreal in 1960. According to the conclusions of this event, adults require an education that is congruent with their biological, psychological, and social makeup. In agreement with this, the Conference encouraged its participants to reformulate the methodologies and materials of adult education. Adult education should become a specialization field for those interested in teaching and training.

However, at the beginning of the 1960s, the proposal continued to lack a method of implementation. As a consequence, adult education continued to take effect as a relationship between those who know and those who do not. In practice, the new orientations proposed by UNESCO and the Conference developed to some extent through the experiences of modernization carried out under the encouragement of the Alliance for Progress. This happened in three ways:

(a) In every country of the region, institutions for the training of the labor force were created. These were established on the basis of agreements between the states and private enterprises. They were made up in accordance with the SENAI model, which had been tried out in Brazil from the beginning of the 1940s (see *Latin America: National Training Agencies*).

(b) In order to face the growing urban marginality in Latin America, the program "Alliance for Progress" proposed the strategy of "community development." This strategy meant to train members of communities and incorporate them into their local organizations. Once they had been incorporated, they were expected to share in the implementation of healthcare plans (primary level), housing projects (self-building), and infrastructure, such as roads and community facilities (see *Community Education and Community Development*).

(c) The third line of action was agrarian reform, which was aimed at relieving the poverty of rural areas. Adult education found a channel of expression in this area in the form of agricultural extension programs.

These were the first large-scale attempts to connect adult education with the experience of the adult learners. Some analysts have referred to this as "partially supplementary strategies" (Gajardo 1983a), mainly aimed at correcting some particular skill deficiency or a "defect" in social functioning. A completely different situation has been created in the case of those countries which specified and implemented fundamental structural changes in their national societies.

By the middle of the 1960s, the two trends in adult education had matured. Both eventually came together, generating a qualitative leap in the policy and practice of adult education in the region. On the one hand, the evolution of educational thought had generated its own effects, and from this changes and reforms developed with respect to the aims and purposes, techniques, materials, and the evaluation of adult education. On the other hand, the ideological and political situation of the countries in the region had provided legitimacy for aspirations for profound social change and radical reform at all levels of educational provision. In this profoundly complex context, the first formulation of Paulo Freire's thought was published in 1967: *Education as the Practice of Freedom*.

Gianotten and de Wit describe the scope and depth of the innovations that appeared in the 1960s as follows:

It was not only Freire's experience, but also a variety of related experiences, which let a new paradigm for Adult Education glimpse through, along the last two decades. This paradigm reinterprets such concepts as participation, organization, and liberation. (Gianotten and de Wit 1980 p. 5)

Freire was not the only inventor of the "new paradigm." The paradigm put together the whole line of thought that called for an education growing from, as well as perfecting, the experience and culture of adult students, thus making them abler to be responsible for their own reality. Freire proposed and elaborated a methodology that allowed the new pedagogic intention to be operationalized in various fields of action. This is the reason why Freire's thought has become a landmark and a threshold in the evolution of adult education in the region.

The new paradigm, which has become a powerful current of thought and action, may be summarized as follows:

(a) It is a type of education that supposes the existence of large social segments not yet integrated into the social structure subordinated in Latin America. It is an educational orientation aimed to serve these groups.

(b) The new educational process grows out of the reality of the participants, which is a concrete historical situation. It proposes, on the basis of this experience, an act of awareness of the students regarding their situation and the economic, political, and social factors that condition it.

(c) The new paradigm envisages to surpass the authoritarian and alienating character of conventional educational programs and the cultural models diffused by the mass media. What is sought is to value the popular culture and to connect with the cultural identity of the target groups.

(d) A horizontal relationship among the participants is aimed at, so that such activities as learning by themselves, to participate in action research, and joint management are encouraged. The procedures tend to be group-based, cooperative, and community-based.

(e) The educational process is tightly bound to action. In order to reflect this, reality is the starting point but only for the purpose of coming back to it in order to change it. In this connection, it is political, even though it does not identify itself with any specific political party.

This relationship between education and practice is qualitatively different from the one put into effect in rural extension or in training for vocational skills. In those instances, the goal was only to qualify persons in order that they could apply their newly gained knowledge to their reality. In the new paradigm, the fundamental unit is the relationship between the subject and his or her material and/or social reality, thus making it possible for them to reflect on that reality and improve on their practice.

3. Popular Adult Education

The new paradigm, inspired by Paulo Freire, developed rapidly during the 1970s and 1980s. Under the name of "popular education," it is related to the spectacular growth of grassroots organizations which evolved during the period, encouraged by the economic crisis.

In the beginning, popular education was understood basically to be an alternative practice, at variance with the official one and opposed to it, in the objectives, methods, and organization of the educational process. It was seen as an alternative approach, and thus it appeared in some early texts as an original line at the side of other lines of adult education.

It is clear that this approach was favored by the authoritarian neoliberal political establishment in Latin America by the early 1980s, a time when governments ceased paying attention, in the name of the ideology of the "minimum state," to the lot of the majorities who live in poverty. In this context, popular education appears as an alternative approach to the official one, aiming to meet the needs of groups excluded from official attention, endowed with its own anti-authoritarian methodology and its own objectives (such as strengthening the so-called "new social movements"), and driven by a nongovernmental institutional apparatus.

Table 1
Classification of adult education providers in Latin America

	Ways of Educating	
Adult education fields	Centered on teaching	Centered on learning
Adult literacy		
Literacy classes	×	×
Literacy campaigns	×	×
Literacy TV broadcasting	×	×
Compulsory-level, upper-secondary, and continuing education for adults		
Centers for adult basic, secondary, and continuing education	×	
Evening schools for adults	×	
Distance education institutions	×	×

Around the beginning of the second half of the 1980s, when the majority of the countries of the region had formally returned to democratic normalcy, popular education started to be seen in a different light. It is no longer in opposition to the establishment and reduced to serving adults only. Popular education appears as a nonconventional, different way to educate. Neither the conventional nor the nonconventional ways may claim to cover all of the educational space.

These two basic forms—one centered on teaching (i.e., on the teacher), another centered on learning (i.e., on the student)—may be applied all along the gamut of the educational space: in the formal structure as well as in the informal, with children as well as with adults, in the school and the university as well as in the community or the workshop. It may well be said that the educational space is disputed by these two ways of understanding and orienting the making of education.

In the face of the partial, fragmentary reforms mentioned above, other more radical reformulations of education have been tried. They have tied the learning process to the workplace and daily life, thus incorporating much from popular education as put to use by the establishment. This happened in the instances entailing deep structural social changes: Cuba, Sandinista Nicaragua, and Peru in its "early phase." One may wonder whether the new educational forms centered on the student were not absorbed by the establishment, thus becoming incorporated into a social project which was ideologically defined in terms of noneducational gains and communicated through that kind of education.

Possibly, it is in the field of literacy where the contributions of popular education to the establishment may be seen at their best. The forms of this educational methodology have been successfully used in official campaigns. In 1989, this was the methodology of the literacy campaign in Ecuador, as the apex of a growing effort at being efficacious and appropriate in that kind of endeavor.

As a product of the long development of adult education in Latin America, the field is today full of a heterogeneous array of highly diversified activities and a variety of trends. Without forcing the richness of this situation, the various fields where adult education

is applied may be classified into a two-way matrix as shown in Table 1, taking into account its two basic forms: teaching-centered and learning-centered.

See also: Community Education and Community Development; Popular Education and Conscientization; UNESCO and Adult Education; Latin America: National Training Agencies

References

Cariola P 1985 Educación y participación en América Latina. *Socialismo y Participación* 14:
Gajardo M 1983a *Teoría y Práctica de la Educación Popular.* IDRC, Ottawa
Gianotten V, de Wit T 1980 *Organización Campesina, el Objetivo Político de la Educación Popular.* Tarea, Lima
La Belle T 1980 *Educación no formal y cambio político en América Latina.* Nueva Imagen, Mexico City
Latapí P 1985 *Tendencias de la Educación de Adultos en América Latina, una Tipología Orientada a su Evaluación Cualitativa.* CREFAL-UNESCO-OREALC-Patzcuaro, Mexico City

Further Reading

CEPAL 1980 *Balance preliminar de la Economía Latinoamericana.* CEPAL, Santiago
Gajardo M 1983b *Educación de Adultos en América Latina: Problemas y Tendencias: Apuntes Para un Debate.* UNESCO-OREALC, Santiago
Latapí P, Castillo A (eds.) 1985 *Lecturas sobre Educación de Adultos en América Latina.* UNESCO-CREFAL, Mexico City
Nagel J, Rodríguez E 1982 *Alfabetización, Políticas y Estrategías en América Latina y el Caribe.* UNESCO-OREALC, Santiago
Picón C 1990 *Políticas y Estrategias de Alfabetización y Educación de Adultos en América Latina en Perspectiva del Estado y de la Sociedad Civil.* PNUD-UNESCO, San Salvador
Rodríguez Brandao C 1985 Los caminos cruzados, formas de pensar y realizar educación en América Latina. In: Latapí P, Castillo A (eds.) 1985
UNESCO 1984 *La Educación de Adultos en América Latina y el Caribe.* UNESCO-OREALC, Santiago
Vío Grossi F 1982 *Investigación en Educación de Adultos en América Latina: Evolución, Estado, y Resultados.* OREALC, Santiago

Latin America: National Training Agencies

M. A. Ducci

This entry analyzes the distinctive features of National Training Agencies (NTAs) in Latin American countries, their historical evolution, and the emerging trends in their attempts to adapt to a changing economic and

social environment. Particular attention is given to the major issues that are contributing to redefining the identity of traditional NTAs, focusing on the advantages and shortcomings that their new roles may imply for the overall development of human resources in the countries of the region.

1. Historical Background

In almost all Latin American countries NTAs were created as a response to the industrialization process that started in the region in the late 1940s and early 1950s. A shortage of skilled workers then became evident, especially at operational levels. An increase in the demand for trained workers in the cities resulted in migration from rural areas. However, the new workforce lacked the knowledge, abilities, and skills required by the expanding industries. The formal education system was unable to respond satisfactorily to their demands because of its limited coverage and because it was too influenced by academic values and far from the actual needs of the world of work. Despite a respectable tradition of vocational and technical schools at the secondary level of the educational system, the training they imparted failed to meet the new production and organizational standards and technological requirements.

Deliberately promoting development on the basis of import substitution, governments played the leading role in the organization of specialized vocational training institutions. Nevertheless, private interested parties such as employers and workers were involved from the beginning in shaping the new training bodies. It was necessary to generate a fresh financial flow of resources that might expand as demand rose. It was essential to ensure close coordination with production, so that training might be tailored to technological change on a timely and ongoing basis. The training system had to be engineered for the short, medium, and long term, and promote a cultural change of attitude vis-à-vis manual work. Finally, it had to attain a balance between the interests of both employers and workers, under the aegis of collective benefit sponsored by the state. The formula adopted in most countries resulted in NTAs outside the regular education system, maintained by firms and enterprises under the tutelage of the state.

Over a period of 30 years, specialized training institutions of national coverage were introduced in nearly every Latin American country. Their objective was to train young people entering the labor force and to retrain adult workers for the emerging skilled and semiskilled occupations in the industrial sector. They were conceived as an alternative option to regular education, and coexisted with formal vocational and technical secondary schools. Some NTAs focused on particular sectors of the economy, but most of them served the whole range of productive activities. They were funded by grants levied on firms and enterprises at a rate varying from 0.2 to 2 percent of their payroll and in almost all countries, workers and employers were represented side by side with governments in the management of NTAs.

The pioneer NTAs crystallized in Brazil with the creation of the National Industrial Apprenticeship Service (SENAI) in 1942, followed by the National Commercial Apprenticeship Service (SENAC) in 1946. The Brazilian NTAs were attached to the respective employers' federations in the industrial and commercial sectors, and were thus constituted as private entities. In contrast, practically all those NTAs that appeared in the other countries of the region during the 1950s, 1960s, and 1970s were set up as public decentralized institutions, but remained largely autonomous. Financed by a levy grant, most of them were connected to the Ministry of Labor and had a multisectoral coverage. In 1958, the National Apprenticeship Service (SENA) was created in Colombia, setting the pattern that would be followed with minor variations in the majority of the countries. In 1959, the National Institute for Educational Cooperation (INCE) was set up in Venezuela, but linked to the Ministry of Education. In 1961 Peru created the National Service of Occupational Training for Industry (SENATI), exclusively serving the industrial sector. In 1965 the National Apprenticeship Institute (INA) was founded in Costa Rica, almost identical to the Colombian SENA. In Chile, INACAP (the Occupational Institute and Technical Training Centers) was established in 1966, but funded by the national budget. In 1966, Ecuador organized the Ecuadorian Occupational Training Service (SECAP); in 1971, Paraguay organized the National Occupational and Promotion Service (SNPP); and in 1972, Bolivia organized the National Manpower Training Service (FOMO). Also in 1972, Guatemala organized the Technical Institute for Training and Productivity (INTECAP) and Honduras organized the National Vocational Training Institute (INFOP). All the above NTAs were close to the classical model laid down by SENA. Later, however, other institutes sprang up in the region, introducing new organizational features but keeping some of the basic traits of the already existing NTAs of the other countries.

Some countries, however, followed a different pattern: in Argentina and Uruguay, vocational training was absorbed by the formal system of technical education. The National Technical Education Council (CONET) in Argentina and the Polytechnical Schools (UTU) in Uruguay handled vocational training as a by-product of the technical schools. Cuba set up an integrated system of education and vocational training which established direct contacts between the formal technical schools and the supplementary on-the-job training scheme. In Mexico, a clear distinction was made between pre-employment training through a number of technical schools at different levels, sponsored by the Secretariat of Public Education, and in-service training under the responsibility of the enterprises, supervised by the Secretariat of Labor and Social Welfare.

Since their inception NTAs have evolved considerably. They have grown and expanded their field of action and have introduced important and significant qualitative changes. Their evolution reflects a remarkable effort to adapt to the changing economic and social situations they had to face, and constantly to renew their credentials in responding to the new challenges of the labor market.

2. Evolution of National Training Agencies

The evolution of NTAs in Latin American countries can be divided into three stages.

The first fixed the goal as the training of individual workers to occupy available posts or foreseeable jobs in the marketplace. Consequently, action concentrated on young people, for whom the operational formula adopted was that of apprenticeship, predominantly in the manufacturing industry. Later, apprenticeship was extended to occupations in commerce and services and to a lesser extent, in agriculture. Retraining of adult workers was a secondary objective, though it rapidly increased in volume over the years. Strong emphasis was put on labor force forecasting and sophisticated techniques were developed to determine as accurately as possible the number of workers to be trained for each occupation and the precise skills profile needed for the jobs they were expected to fill in the labor market. This initial stage, which was clearly demand-driven, focused on matching individual skills with the aggregated needs of the modern sector of production.

The second stage started to emerge in Latin American NTAs by the mid 1970s as unemployment rose and large contingents of the population were not absorbed by the modern sector. The focus of NTAs gradually shifted substantially to cater for the unemployed and underemployed young and adult workers; training contents broadened to develop not only occupational skills but human and social aptitudes that could enable trainees to become employable or to create their own jobs. Emphasis was put on developing new training methodologies to expand coverage and reach marginal populations in urban and rural areas. The first attempts to train small-scale enterprise and informal sector workers belong to this stage. The thrust of NTAs' action was supply-driven, offering vocational training as a means of contributing to the expansion of employment and to developing the capacity for survival of disadvantaged groups of the population.

The third stage started in the late 1980s as NTAs were faced with the dramatic economic and social changes derived from the debt crisis and structural adjustment processes in most Latin American countries. Policies to reactivate the economy implied industrial restructuring articulated around a greater opening of national economies to world markets. The two major axes of economic modernization became (i) the rationalization of the productive apparatus, based on an improvement of productivity, competitiveness, and quality; and (ii) the liberalization of enterprise activity and the reduction of state intervention in production. Enterprises, recognized as the basic units for economic recovery, required new kinds of training and development assistance. Therefore, NTAs turned their attention to the actual needs of enterprises of various sizes, offering them a series of services aimed at increasing their productivity by improving the "labor factor" as a whole, and by improving the technical skills of individual workers.

This stage, in which NTAs are now redefining their role, is again demand-driven, however the needs of existing and potential productive units are taken as the basis for organizing NTAs' responses. Their target covers the whole spectrum of productive units, ranging from the dynamic and technologically advanced, to the small-scale and micro-enterprises in the informal sector. The services provided by NTAs move beyond training to include technical and organizational assistance, financial and commercial advice, research and development, production methods, industrial design, quality standards, and so on.

3. Redefining NTAs Identity

In this new situation, NTAs have begun to change their focus from the individual worker to the enterprise as an integrated production unit. The NTAs' purpose is also expanding beyond training workers to strengthening a new culture of production based on increased productivity, quality, and cost-effectiveness. NTAs are seeking to provide labor with a greater commitment to economic goals, and to develop a work force with increased possibilities for personal fulfillment and social benefit.

National Training Agencies are aware of the fact that if they fail imaginatively to adapt to the deepseated economic, social, and labor transformations quickly and as pertinently as possible, they will fall behind in the process of productive reorganization. This could constitute a serious threat to the very existence of the regions long-standing NTAs. National Training Agencies are cautiously exploring routes that boldly and ingeniously respond to the new and different demands deriving from the productive apparatus, thereby superseding their traditional role. They are seeking to generate new forms of action to address the reordering of production and the new economic and social context which has arisen out of the financial crisis, the scientific–technological revolution, and the globalization of the economy.

First, attention is geared to a production process that is less concentrated around the big enterprises and is increasingly fragmented into a complex continuum that goes from microenterprises to large companies, including the bulk of small and medium-sized units. The prevalence of manual jobs in the production process is being replaced by information-based activities (computerized production and market information, organizational and management aspects, etc.); the trend is toward a globalization of production that emphasizes cost, quality, and timeliness for competitiveness in international markets.

Second, the leading role played by the welfare state has resulted in emphasis on private initiative, Thus minimizing subsidies. This has led to the design of substitute forms of state intervention which, although not yet clearly defined, grant growing participation to private sectors in the management of training programs. National Training Agencies are thus facing new competitors in the training market.

Third, the economic and financial policies adopted by countries of the region, and stabilization programs in particular, have inevitably affected the scope of the budgets of NTAs, challenging their traditional financing mechanisms. Pressures to curb fiscal expenditure and to allow maximum flexibility and central control of public resources are forcing NTAs to greater accountability, cost-recovery, and financial self-sufficiency. They are thus compelled to maximize the cost-benefit equation of their training programs and to review the priority they were granting to social objectives. The traditional tripartite participation of governments, employers, and workers in the governing bodies of NTAs is the main arena for such a debate. However, dialogue and agreements with users of NTAs' services and with direct and indirect partners in the provision of those services are increasingly becoming the pattern in the search for ad hoc solutions which are shaping a new and diverse identity for these NTAs.

4. New Trends in NTAs

In coping with the new situation, NTAs are employing two basic strategies: adopting new approaches to training and moving beyond training. In training, NTAs' behavior is already significantly different from what it traditionally was in the priority clienteles served, the modes used, and their institutional and operational arrangements. In the implementation of new nontraining activities, NTAs see themselves as support agencies for increasing the production and productivity of enterprises. There are six major trends in the institutional performance of NTAs. These are described below.

Preemployment training is becoming less important, both in absolute and relative terms, than upgrading skills of existing workers in the job market. This is particularly striking in that NTAs were conceived as schools for preparing a skilled work force for the labor market. This option which was followed by most NTAs, is remarkably pragmatic and stems from various factors: (a) the expansion of regular educational systems and the improvement in quality and coverage of vocational and technical schools; (b) the high cost and long duration of apprenticeship and the difficulties in obtaining sponsorship for apprentices from

employers; (c) the pressing demand from enterprises to retrain their current workers; and (d) the uncertain employment prospects for the new entrants to the labor market.

National Training Agencies appear to use the skill requirements of the jobs available in the enterprises as a primary indicator of demand. The weak point is the extent to which these trends in NTAS imply a reduction in educational alternatives offered to young people and in particular, to early dropouts of the regular education system. However, NTAs are predominantly looking to the immediate future and focusing less on the medium- and long-term labor force needs.

National Training Agencies are expanding training for middle and upper level technicians and technologists, at higher levels than the traditional training provided to skilled and semiskilled workers. In accomplishing this new task, NTAs perform in an independent but complementary way to that of regular technical training provided by the ministries of education. They have attempted to fill the gaps left by formal secondary and postsecondary technical schools, usually as a response to expressed demands from, and with the support of, the enterprises of the respective economic branch or sector. Although enrollments and graduates at the middle and upper technician level are still modest, this new field of NTA activity has far-reaching consequences as enterprises especially in the industrial sector, have found that NTAs provide a reliable source of training for the new, highly specialized professional personnel which they require to act as the link between engineers and skilled workers.

This new field of action points to an unavoidable convergence of NTAs and technical schools of the regular educational system. In some countries, such as Brazil, Colombia, and Chile, NTAs have entered into formal agreements with the ministries of education and have been officially recognized as regular technical schools at equivalent levels of training. However, in most countries the boundaries that historically separate NTAs from formal technical schools are becoming less clear, and there is a growing gray area and overlapping roles between them.

National Training Agencies are increasingly organizing their activities under a sectoral approach. Even in countries with a large multisectoral NTA, the trend has been toward a progressive internal compartmentalization by sector or subsector of economic activity. As a general rule, NTAs have established sectorally specialized centers with national coverage to focus on training and support activities for selected sectors of particular importance and significance to the national economy. In the most advanced NTAs of the region, these centers offer tailor-made courses and training programs to the enterprises of the corresponding sector, and supply technological research and development and other productivity-related services. These sectoral centers have started drifting toward technological centers, where a wide variety of sectoral and often subsectoral activities are concentrated, including close relations with sectoral organizations of employers and workers.

The debate regarding the sectoral approach largely taken by Latin American NTAs opposes the argument that as long as NTAs can move quite freely among the various sectors of activity, they can follow and anticipate fluctuations among sectors with greater flexibility. On the contrary, an excessive compartmentalization by sector, with fairly autonomous sectoral and subsectoral bodies, would not allow for NTAs to shift their focus easily when a particular sector is in decline.

Two different directions are emerging among NTAs: those agencies most directly linked to the government are most inclined to maintain a multisectoral mandate which enables them to mobilize resources flexibly among the various sectors. It also leaves more room to work with the less privileged sectors and populations, which would otherwise be difficult to cover. However, the increasingly specific organization and technologies of the different and competing branches of activity will propel sectoral specialization of those agencies that are more directly linked to, and controlled by, enterprises.

Training responsibilities are increasingly being transferred to enterprises, with the resulting change in NTAs' roles and functions. One of the most outstanding initial differences between NTAs and vocational and technical schools from the regular education system is that the former worked jointly with enterprises from the start. Enterprise-based training was encouraged and supported by NTAs as a means of benefiting from the natural advantage of the real work environment for effective vocational training. Fast-moving changes in labor organization and production processes have increased this advantage of fitting training as closely as possible to the condition of each enterprise. Furthermore, the scarcity of resources in official NTAs to meet the rising demand for training makes clear the benefit of letting the enterprises do what they can for themselves, thereby freeing NTA resources for those sectors that are not in a position to assume their own training responsibilities.

In Argentina, Brazil, Chile, and Mexico legal measures external to the NTAs established tax incentives for training by enterprises. This new financing scheme, adopted in the above four countries from the mid 1970s, coexisted with compulsory contributions by enterprises to NTAs in Argentina and Brazil, but replaced the levy system in the other two countries, thus inverting the traditional pattern for financing training.

Another formal mechanism to stimulate enterprises to carry out their own training programs has been established by NTAs in Brazil, Guatemala, and Venezuela. In these cases, NTAs authorize enterprises partially to withhold or deduct their compulsory contributions insofar as they use these resources to provide training programs for their workers directly.

Both mechanisms have considerably increased the enterprises' role in operating training programs, thus widening substantially the overall national training capacity.

Nevertheless, NTAs retain the promotional and supervisory role of authorizing, supporting, assisting, and controlling training delivered by enterprises. Traditionally, only large and well-organized enterprises have been able to make use of tax incentives and rebates, therefore, NTAs are increasingly concentrating their direct training operation on medium- and small-scale enterprises. Most NTAs are committed to developing the capacity of enterprises to organize their own training units. In various countries, cooperative programs among small enterprises are strongly encouraged and the marketing of training as an essential function of enterprises of all sizes has become a major line of promotional action by NTAs.

Although the transfer of training responsibilities to enterprises is a deliberate and accelerating move in the Latin American vocational training scene, NTAs are likely to retain the primary executing role they have accomplished since the mid-twentieth century. The renewed emphasis on developing the capabilities of human resources as the key for economic recovery has enlarged the demand for training. National Training Agencies are now compelled simultaneously to operate training for the sectors unable to undertake this task on their own, and progressively to transfer their knowledge and experience to expand the executing capacity of enterprises to meet their own training needs.

Business management and organization in small-scale enterprises is increasingly becoming the focus of NTAs' attention. Medium- and small-scale enterprises constitute the largest segment of economic activity in Latin American countries. They have naturally made the most use of the training services provided by NTAs. Nevertheless, their needs largely exceed the technical qualifications of their workers. At the time that medium- and small-scale enterprises became concerned with global competitiveness, their lack of managerial knowledge and skills became a new challenge for NTAs which they gradually approached first by adding managerial training to other technical courses given to small- and medium-sized enterprise workers and later, by offering management development programs in their own right. These programs, which have proliferated during the late 1980s and early 1990s in every Latin American NTA, give priority to solving problems related to the organization of production, financing, and marketing of company products. Comprehensive programs addressed specifically to small units in urban and rural areas include technical and financial advice, technological transfer, administration, legal matters, marketing, costs, and accounting.

Moreover, most NTAs have created innovative managerial programs targeting microenterprises, specifically adapted to their limited possibilities and multiple constraints. An important component of these programs is the participatory approach, encouraging communities and groups of microentrepreneurs to organize themselves to become more productive. These programs have been particularly successful in rural areas where the role of the NTA is not so much in providing production techniques but in transferring to local community organizations the ability to manage production projects and to become self-sufficient. In urban areas, programs targeted to microenterprises constitute the main strategy for addressing the informal sector workers. Usually, the NTAs, and particularly those more directly under the influence of the state, associate themselves with broader governmental programs for promoting microenterprises. Thus, NTAs act with a greater guarantee of effectiveness and complement their services with those provided by other agencies, with a view to the overall development of the informal sector. However, coordination agreements are not easy to implement and NTAs often become involved in tasks and responsibilities that go beyond their sphere of action, with the consequent undermining of the efficiency and effectiveness of the services addressed to the informal sector.

New roles have been developed in technology and productivity development. The turning point in the evolution of NTAs occurred when, in the pursuit of an increasingly relevant role vis-à-vis economic restructuring, they became involved in providing nontraining services. This was not an abrupt step; sporadically, and in a rather casual way, some NTAs such as SENAI and SENAC in Brazil, SENATI in Peru, INACAP in Chile, and later many others, started providing new forms of assistance to enterprises as an extension of training programs and using the same infrastructure and technical capacity. At the same time, the economic crisis affected NTAs themselves, which, faced with budget cuts, were forced to explore new sources of financing. The sale of nontraining services to enterprises became a way of diversifying their funding. Last, the provision of an increasingly broader span of technological and productivity services resulted in renewed NTA credentials with enterprises.

The range of the new services offered by the most developed NTAs in the region includes: (a) enterprise consultancy services on organizational matters; (b) technical assistance related to production (techniques for improving productivity, cost reduction, layout of equipment and machinery, changes in production processes, development of new products, design, and production of models and prototypes); (c) technical support (product design, quality control, testing of materials, laboratory facilities); (d) production of sophisticated parts and specialized work on machines (by NTAs or through the assignment or lease of equipment and machinery to enterprises); (e) applied research on production methods and products; and (f) dissemination of technology (innovative techniques, new technologies, raw materials, tools, instruments and machinery, products and processes, etc.).

From the point of view of training, the addition of these new functions has contributed to improving the quality of the performance of NTAs. Their increased contacts with enterprises encourage the natural updating of teaching personnel, absorption of new technologies, familiarization with the reorganzation of production processes, and a closer matching of training programs to the needs of the labor market. The key factor is the appropriate balance in the delivery of training and nontraining services. The primary role of NTAs continues to be that of training institutions and complementary roles are justified mainly on the grounds of their effective contribution to improving the quality of training and its economic and social impact.

Latin American NTAs are undergoing a significant transformation. They are no longer just schools to train youngsters for manual jobs. Following the signs of a changing economic and social environment, they are gradually becoming technology and productivity centers, thus opening new scope for their role in the productive development of the countries of the region.

See also: Latin America: Adult Education; Government Role in Adult Education and Training; Payroll Levies

Bibliography

CEPAL 1990 Transformación productiva con equidad: La tarea prioritaria del desarrollo de América Latina y el Caribe en los años noventa. Santiago de Chile

CEPAL-UNESCO 1992 Educación y conocimiento: Eje de la transformación productiva con equidad. Santiago de Chile

CINTERFOR/ILO 1991 Vocational training on the threshold of the 1990s: A study of changes and innovations in specialized institutions of Latin America. PHNEE doc. no. 91/35. World Bank, Washington, DC

Ducci M A 1980 The vocational training process in the development of Latin America: An interpretative study. *Studies and Monographs* 47. CINTERFOR/ILO, Montevideo

Ducci M A 1983 Vocational training: An open way. *Studies and Monographs* 62. CINTERFOR/ILO, Montevideo

Ducci M A 1987 Equity and productivity of vocational training: The Latin American experience. UCLA, Los Angeles, California

Ducci M A 1988 Impacto technológico y formación profesional. Formación Professional al Día, INA. San José de Costa Rica

Gallart M A 1986 Educación y trabajo. Un estado del arte de la investigación en América Latina. CENEP, Buenos Aires

Metcalf D 1985 The economics of vocational training: Past evidence and future considerations. The World Bank, Washington, DC

Ramírez J 1987 La capacitación de recursos humanos como elemento de política social: Consideraciones a partir de la experiencia de formación profesional de América Latina. CINTERFOR/OIT, Montevideo

UNDP 1984 Education and training in the 1990s: Developing countries' needs and strategies. UNDP, New York

North America

W. S. Griffith

Adult education and training in North America reflect differences related to population characteristics and distribution as well as governmental structures. Despite the differences, there are many similarities. In this discussion, emphasis is placed on Canada and the United States with a focus on the goals and scope of adult education and training; significant organizations and associations; and financing and research orientations.

1. Goals and Scope of Adult Education and Training

Although it is sometimes claimed in North America that the first mission of adult education is to assist adults to obtain further control of their current circumstances and future destinies, studies of participation in various kinds of adult education programs indicate that while such programs increase the capacity of individuals to cope with the demands of daily living, rarely are they designed to serve as vehicles of empowerment or to assist the facilitation of radical change. Adult education serves primarily to help people satisfy the demands of daily living rather than to mount campaigns to redesign their society. Cultural maintenance and reproduction continue to be the primary functions served by most sectors of the field. However, a small group of adult educators continue to invest their energies in empowerment and somewhat revolutionary educational activities.

For nearly a century a debate has continued regarding the most appropriate way for the adult education field to be developed. Individuals such as Collins (1992) argue that "the essential trappings of established professions have more to do with the exercise of control and establishment of monopolistic practice than with guarantees of competent performance" (p.38). Therefore, they oppose any movement toward professionalization. On the other hand, Cervero advocates striving for professionalization, arguing that the sound preparation of practitioners, the systematic advancement of the knowledge base, and the public recognition of adult education as a distinct area of service are all essential for the optimal development of the field.

Historically adult education departments in universities, like other new university departments, recruited their first professors from previously established disciplines simply because there were no individuals who had earned doctorates in adult education. But today, with over 4,300 individuals who have earned their doctorates in this field, the recruitment of individuals

from other areas to serve as professors of adult education would seem to be an anomaly. But some authors advocate ignoring the historical developments, the existence of thousands of adult education doctoral program graduates, and the passage of six decades since the first graduate program was established. They argue that adult education leaders should come from outside the field, claiming that this will avoid the "narrow structural approach" and instead foster the functional approach, treating every part of society where the functions of teaching and learning are performed among adults as equally integral to the advancement of the field of scholarship and practice. The discussion continues, but the continuing emergence of adult educators with doctorates in their chosen field is almost an irresistible force moving toward clarifying the boundaries of adult education as a professional field.

The goals and scope of adult education are reflected in the approaches taken to training adult educators. A large and diverse group of leaders is required to plan and administer the myriad of programs provided both by government sponsorship and through independent organizations. This leadership cadre has been the subject of considerable literature and discussion. Adult education scholars are conversant with the "Pyramid of Leadership" described by Houle (1970) as follows:

> The widespread base of the pyramid is made up of lay leaders in a great variety of community settings. At the intermediate level of the pyramid is a smaller but still very large group of people whose adult educational service is part of their regular jobs or who accept supplemental employment in that field. At the apex of the pyramid is the still small but sizable group of people who have made adult education the focus of their careers and plan to spend their lifetimes as specialists in it. (pp. 111–13)

Merriam (1985) observed that on-the-job experience is the major means through which practitioners at the lowest level of the pyramid become proficient. Short-term inservice training activities are the most common form of training provided for those at the intermediate level, while graduate degree programs serve those who function at the apex of the pyramid. Campbell (1977) surveyed such graduate programs and reported that they give roughly equal attention to three areas: the teaching of adults education principles, the achievement of competence in designing and conducting programs, and the development of research capability. Such training does not serve an exclusively practical or an exclusively theoretical bias. Brookfield (1985) has noted that the graduate professors are much less interested in promoting an understanding or inculcating in students a sense of the history of the field than they are in cultivating technical program development skills. While a small minority of adult educators is devoted to the field as a movement, the prevailing ethos is increasingly professional and designed to produce competent education technicians (see *Training of Adult Educators*).

The Commission of Professors of Adult Education, a component of the American Association for Adult and Continuing Education, has been somewhat concerned about the impact of university retrenchment in the face of economic uncertainty on the continuing existence and vitality of graduate adult education programs. At its 1993 annual conference the Commission discussed reports on strengthening university support for adult education graduate programs in the United States and Canada. Knox and others reported that even excellent programs are susceptible to downsizing or even discontinuation if they do not make "concerted efforts to communicate and interpret the program to internal as well as external stakeholders" (p.4). Sork, basing his report on a survey of adult education graduate programs in western Canada, noted both positive and negative signs. He observed that: "During the last three years ... opportunities to study adult education at the undergraduate and graduate level[s] have increased; one new master's program has been approved, another is in the process of being approved; a BA in adult education is under development; and certificate- and diploma-level programs have expanded. The demand for graduate study in adult education is clearly increasing at a time when university funding is either stable or declining" (Sork 1993 p.1). On the negative side Sork warns that because so many adult education programs have prided themselves on their uniqueness, they have become insular with the result that they are isolated and easy to eliminate or reorganize without consequence to other programs. They may also "be viewed by those outside as ideologically monolithic with little to offer the wider educational community" (Sork 1993 p.6). Although the situation may be slightly better in Canada than in the United States, the continuing economic difficulties encountered by universities in both countries may lead to the reorganization or outright abolition of whole university departments.

2. Regional Organization and Cooperation

Professional adult educators support a wide variety of associations with several serving both Canada and the United States. The leading professional association in the United States was founded in 1926 as the American Association for Adult Education. It joined with the Division of Adult Education Services of the National Education Association in 1951 to become the Adult Education Association of the United States (AEA/USA). In 1982 the AEA/USA was reorganized to include the National Association for Public Continuing and Adult Education and to recognize the increasing influence of

the Canadian members in the organization. The new organization was called the *American* Association for Adult and Continuing Education (AAACE). It has approximately 3,000 members, 10 percent of whom are Canadians.

The major national associations in Canada are the Canadian Association for Adult Education (CAAE) founded in 1936, which is predominantly Anglophone; and the *Institut Canadien D'education des Adultes* (ICEA) which is largely Francophone. Other major organizations, such as the American Society for Training and Development (ASTD) have branches in both Canada and the United States.

In 1964, a small group of leaders from diverse adult education associations in the United States established a national organization of adult education associations, not only to facilitate communication among them, but also to increase their collective influence on government policies and gain greater financial support. This Coalition of Adult Education Organizations (CAEO) continues to meet on a regular basis, but it has not achieved the effectiveness to which its founders aspired. In 1994 it was still looking for its niche and attempting to achieve recognition from government and the public.

There is also a move by a small, but influential, group of AAACE members exploring approaches to reconceptualizing that Association to incorporate adult educators from Mexico, a process that would involve accommodating not only the Francophone interests of some Canadian adult educators, but also the Hispanic concerns of Mexican adult educators. This initiative is progressing slowly, but may have been given encouragement by the passage of the North American Free Trade Act.

3. Delivery Systems in the Region

In Canada, the constitutional authority for education at all levels rests with each of the provinces and there is no federal ministry of education. The influence of the federal government is exerted through its selective funding of training programs, which are administered by the provincial governments. Accordingly it is accurate to say that there is no single Canadian policy on any aspect of education. Instead the individual provinces direct their own educational work and such coordination as occurs takes place through the Council of Ministers of Education: Canada, based in Toronto.

The Province of Alberta passed legislation in the 1970s to provide funding for further education councils which serve to coordinate noncredit adult education programs in both the public and private sectors. As a result the level of participation in adult education in Alberta grew from one in ten to about one in four. Few of the local further education councils identified illiteracy as a major focus for programs, but provincial authorities, supported with federal financing, provided special earmarked funds that can only be used for literacy work and by this device stimulated local programs in literacy. No other province or state has established a comparable local coordinating structure, although metropolitan adult education councils to serve coordination and communication functions have been tried, with varying success, in cities in each country.

In the United States, the federal Department of Education exerts its influence through the provision of financial incentives. Experience has shown that even though the Department provides only about 5 percent of the total funding of education, the strategic application of that funding is a powerful influence in persuading state governments to accept priorities established at the national level. Programs of high priority to the Department, such as adult basic education and workplace literacy, are promoted through selective finding, a process that has proven to be effective in shaping state appropriations as well.

No effective national structures have been developed in either Canada or the United States to facilitate effective interorganizational communication and foster cooperative approaches to developing programs at any level. Nevertheless efforts continue to achieve voluntary coordination between organizations.

Buttedahl (1985) reported that since 1970 countries such as Argentina, Chile, Bolivia, Brazil, Peru, Ecuador, Columbia, Venezuela, Guatemala, Honduras, El Salvador, Costa Rica, Panama, Mexico, and Cuba have each established a national bureau of adult education within their ministries of education. She notes that the responsibilities of such bureaus include assessing adult education needs, projecting budgetary requirements, producing curriculum guides and instructional materials, allocating staff, providing inservice training for ministry personnel, collecting and disseminating statistical information, and liaising with intergovernmental and nongovernmental organizations. Adult education appears to be seen by these governments as an instrument to stimulate economic development and is therefore of higher budgetary priority than in Canada and the United States.

Given the important role of the 50 states in education (they provide approximately 95% of the funds for education in the United States), and the absence of a federal ministry of education in Canada, it is clear that the approaches taken by other governments in North America are quite unlike the leading role played by those in the south. Not surprisingly, the development of popular education, an approach that is focused on challenging the power of established governments, is significantly stronger in the South than in Canada and the United States.

3.1 Structural Similarities and Variations

Canadian efforts to serve the ascribed educational needs of adults have responded to the frontier nature of the society and to the relatively small population (27 million people) in the world's largest country. Frontier College was established to provide education in logging camps through the innovative use of worker–teachers, who labored alongside their potential students during the day and led classes for them in the evenings. Farm Radio Forum was developed to stimulate discussions among the rural population on topics of national as well as local concern. The Antigonish Movement grew out of the work of Catholic educators who taught the gospel of cooperation and cooperatives to economically depressed fishermen, farmers, and miners in the Atlantic Provinces.

Early in the twentieth century both Canada and the United States developed programs in agricultural extension, reflecting differences in attitudes toward the role of government in rural education. In Canada, the work of agricultural extension is carried out through provincial ministries of agriculture, with minor involvement on the part of faculties of agriculture of the universities. In the United States, the Cooperative Agricultural Extension Service was established utilizing a partnership of federal and state financing and university administration of education and research programs in the field. In both cases the efficiency of agriculture is advanced with the adoption of new practices rapidly and effectively, requiring an ever-decreasing workforce engaged in the production of food and crops.

Both nations have had their Chautauqua organizations with a quasi-religious streak. Both nations have employed education to integrate immigrants, as both are composed of populations of immigrants. However, the Canadian approach is to foster multiculturalism, while in the United States a policy of acculturation prevails. Both nations employ similar approaches in dealing with the education needs of adults with low literacy levels, providing federal financial stimulation and relying on volunteer efforts to a marked degree.

In both countries, adult education is provided by a bewildering array of sponsors including colleges and universities, public secondary schools, community colleges, libraries, museums, art galleries, labor organizations, hospitals, gerontology centers, service clubs, theaters, religious organizations, correspondence and distance education organizations, health centers, business and industry, the media, government departments, and men's and women's clubs, most of which depend heavily on user fees for support. Adult education has been and continues to be essentially self-supporting with a few national priority programs funded by governments (see *Providers of Adult Education: An Overview*).

3.2 Breadth of Coverage

The US Department of Education (Kopka et al. 1993) reported that "of the total adult population 17 years old and over, 32 percent enrolled in some kind of adult education during the twelve months preceding the survey in the spring of 1991" (p.2). In terms of the kind of adult education pursued, "some 19 percent of the total adult population took at least one course to improve, advance or keep up with their current job" (p.3). Although individuals unfamiliar with long standing patterns of participation might assume that those with the least amount of formal education would be the most likely to be pursuing adult education to make up for what they had missed, the facts are that adults with some postsecondary education were most likely to participate, thereby widening the gap between those with the least and those with the most number of years of formal education. Also, the number of individuals between the ages of 14 and 24 years of age who dropped out of high school in 1991 was 3,964,000 persons, some 10.5 percent of this age group. Accordingly, there would seem to be a continuing steady stream of school dropouts, who, while they may be the intended target of remedial adult education programs, are unlikely to be participating to the desired degree in future programs (US Bureau of the Census 1993). While it might be anticipated that those who are unemployed would have the most time to engage in adult education, census data show that while 21 percent of the unemployed adults participated the participation rate for employed adults was 41 percent (US Bureau of the Census 1993).

Korb et al. (1993) reporting on the National Household Education Survey for 1990-91, stated that "38 percent of adults age 17 and over participated in some educational activity over a 12-month period in 1990-91. Of these, 31.6 percent participated on a part-time basis . . ." (p.1).

The picture is quite similar in Canada, with one notable exception. Roberts conducted a study of the adult education provision in the provinces of Alberta and Quebec and found evidence to support his hypothesis that "the general pattern of adult education activities in a country or region showing an emphasis on social development, the collective good, as distinguished from personal development, the individual good, is determined by the dominant social philosophy or ideology in the region" (Roberts 1982 p.250). Quebec, with its distinctive culture, was found to place a significantly greater emphasis on social development than did Alberta, known for its "rugged individualism" in ranching and in the oil fields.

In the most recent Canadian adult education and training survey the participation rates are appreciably lower than those reported for the United States. A possible explanation for this difference is the more restrictive Canadian definition: "Adult education and training includes all formal educational activities undertaken by persons aged 17 and over. These activities can be taken at work, at school, or at other locations for job-related or personal reasons. Nonformal training, such as on-the-job training and informal education (knowledge and skills acquired from daily experience or from family, work, mass media, etc.) is excluded from this definition as are regular (nonemployer sponsored) college and university programs" (Couillard 1993 p.63). Using this definition, the researchers found that 17 percent of the Canadian adult population aged 17 and over were registered in a course or program between December 1989 and November 1990 (Couillard 1993). While university graduates made up 10 percent of Canada's population, they accounted for 22 percent of all participants. Conversely, those with a primary education (Grade 8 or less) comprised 18 percent of Canada's population aged 15 and over but only 2 percent of the participants. (Couillard 1993). Clearly both in the United States and Canada adult education continues to widen rather than narrow the gulf between the most and the least educated.

Nevertheless, it should not be assumed that job-related reasons are necessarily the most important ones even though the number of learners involved is highest. The C.F. Kettering Foundation devotes most of its energies and resources to producing "issue books for forums that encourage serious deliberation on hard policy issues facing the public. These are called National Issues Forums (NIF) books, and they are used by a network of more than 5,000 civic and educational organizations, ranging from literacy groups to religious organizations to neighborhood associations. Results from the NIF deliberations around the country are reported annually through the 'public voice' program on Public Broadcasting System (PBS) stations." (The Kettering Foundation p.2). So, although significantly larger numbers of adults participate in job-related education, a small but potentially influential elite group are engaged in liberal education through such programs as are sponsored by the Great Books and Kettering Foundations.

3.3 Reasons for Participation

In the United States participation in adult education is directly related to years of education attained: 7 percent of those with an eighth grade education or less participated; 22 percent of those with a high school education participated; 39 percent of those with some college education participated; and 52 percent of those with a bachelor's degree or higher participated. (US Bureau of the Census, 1993). Professional people participated at the 64 percent level while adults working in agriculture, forestry, and fishing participated at the 11 percent level, possibly reflecting the level of education associated with workers in these occupations. Income level was also directly related to participation with 14 percent of those with an annual income under US $10,000 participating and 48 percent of those making more than US $75,000 taking part. Employment status was similarly reflected in participation rates with 41 percent of employed adults participating whilst only 21 percent of unemployed adults engaged in adult education. Ethnic differences persist with 33 percent of Whites, 23 percent of Blacks and 29 percent of Hispanics participating.

In Canada the majority of trainees (78%) took adult education or training programs for job related reasons while 22 percent took them for reasons of personal interest (Couillard 1993). Most men (84%) and a smaller majority of women (73%) who took an adult education or training program in 1990, did so for job-related reasons, rather than personal development. Almost half of the adult students (48%) reported that their tuition had been paid for by their employer.

In a study of reading skills of adults in Canada conducted by Statistics Canada in 1992, 62 percent of Canadian adults aged 16 to 69 had sufficient reading skills to deal with most everyday reading requirements, but 16 percent had reading skills that were too limited to enable them to deal with the majority of written material encountered in everyday life (Statistics Canada 1992). Despite these findings 94 percent of Canadian adults feel that their reading skills in English or French are adequate for their daily activities and so would not be expected to take classes to improve their language facility. If only employed adults are considered, 98 percent felt that their skills were adequate for their jobs. Over half (54%) of the readers with the poorest skills reported that they were satisfied with their reading and writing skills (Statistics Canada 1992).

The focus of adult education participation in both Canada and the United States is on practical, job-related topics rather than on themes such as philosophy, personal development, health, or politics.

4. Governance, Legislation, and Financing

It is not surprising that a field as diverse as adult education should exhibit an array of funding patterns. There is no primary source and no prevailing pattern. Government support is provided largely for educational programs that prepare people for employment or assist them in improving their economic circumstances. The current emphasis in both nations is on workplace education, programs designed to enable those who are already employed to adjust to changing demands of the workplace or to advance within their job classification. Smaller programs are aimed at providing education that is intended to enable individuals to move from being consumers of public welfare to becoming employed.

In contrast, private sponsors furnish funding to support almost every conceivable cause. Yet the prevailing philosophy in both Canada and the United States is that adults should pay all or at least a part of the costs of their education. Accordingly, most of adult education is self-supporting, based on user fees. A modest contribution toward these costs is provided by both governments allowing income tax deductions

for individual learners as well as for the costs incurred by employers in providing education. For those programs that are provided by employers, typically either full or partial tuition reimbursement is provided, often with an additional training allowance. Critics have observed that public support is available to underwrite the costs of adult education if that education increases an individual's ability to make more money and advance professionally. Far less support is available for education intended to promote responsible citizenship, good parenting, environmental improvement, or global issues.

4.1 Description of Specific Institutions and Programs

Several adult education institutions that were developed or adapted to Canada and the United States represent the diversity of interests included in this field. In the United States and Canada, the Chautauqua institution which began in the last quarter of the nineteenth century as a training program for Methodist Sunday School teachers expanded as the "tent Chautauquas" providing education and entertainment to rural audiences living in communities served by railroads. These programs proliferated, attracting hundreds of thousands of adults and commanding the attention and involvement of major national figures. It spawned literary and scientific study circles as well as a major correspondence instruction program. Between 1892 and 1906, the presidents of the Universities of Chicago and Wisconsin were known as articulate spokesmen for ambitious programs of university extension into adult education and promoting it as an integral part of American universities. During the depression of the 1930s, the Civilian Conservation Corps (CCC) served as both employer and educator for thousands of young men who were engaged in public works, constructing civic buildings, parks, and other recreational areas. Given the current economic malaise, a few legislators are entertaining the idea of establishing a contemporary counterpart to the constructive educational work of the CCC.

Numerous Canadian adult education programs and providers particularly adapted to the Canadian geography and population could be cited, but only a few of the more prominent will be noted. The Cooperative Housing Foundation of Canada has been conducting educational programs for members of housing cooperatives since the 1960s. An annual conference dealing with public affairs, often before they become widely appreciated, is conducted at Lake Couchiching by the Couchiching Institute on Public Affairs, a private charitable organization dedicated to public education on policy issues. The worker–teachers of Frontier College have been cited previously. The Urban Native Indian Education Society has operated a Native Education Center in Vancouver since 1967 to provide basic education and to assist Native people in adjusting to urban life. Between 1943 and 1966, the

CAAE and CBC cooperated to produce Citizens' Forum, a national discussion group program utilizing printed study materials and a weekly radio broadcast to help Canadians form their own opinions and reach conclusions on matters of common concern. The Forum involved the establishment of discussion groups under the sponsorship of community organizations, which would meet weekly to discuss the study materials they had received and then to listen to a broadcast dealing with that content (Selman and Dampier 1991). Each of these unique adult education efforts demonstrates excellence in matching specifically tailored programs to the social, cultural, and economic context of the time.

5. *Major Research Questions Addressed*

From the mid-1920s through the 1930s, research efforts were devoted to attempts to demonstrate the existence of a field of study. Landmark studies of adult interests and adult learning countered the prevailing skepticism regarding the ability of adults to continue learning throughout life. Funded by grants from the Carnegie Corporation, which had been instrumental in the founding of both the American Association for Adult Education and the Canadian Association for Adult Education, these research reports provided a broad base of common literature that addressed the social significance of adult education. Carnegie funds were instrumental in the development of the graduate program in adult education at the Teachers' College at Columbia University in the early 1930s and hence contributed to the continuing flow of dissertation research that accounts for possibly one third of the research studies published in this field.

Adult education research, like other kinds of research, is subject to waves of interest, often reflecting the level of financial support available for work in selected areas. For example, since the 1960s, research dealing with adult competency levels and improving adult literacy has been funded more readily than research in other areas of adult education. However, such popularity can serve to restrict the approaches taken by researchers as they are likely to accept the dominant paradigm without question. In the case of adult literacy research, the dominant notion is that the absence of adequate literacy skills is the primary determinant of an individual's financial failure in life. Only recently, however, some researchers have questioned this assumption and instead of trying to determine how literacy levels may be increased, they have sought to understand how some individuals with minimal literacy levels have managed to achieve financial as well as social success in Canada as well as in the United States. Such research focusing on the range of success levels attained by individuals with low literacy levels, may help to explain the interactions of literacy skills with other characteristics that are valued and rewarded in North American society. A small group of researchers interested in critical theory, feminism, and postmodernism pursue studied that challenge the traditional emphasis on improving the technical proficiency of adult educators. Individuals following these approaches are conspicuous at adult education research conferences and in the emerging literature (Hayes & Colin 1994).

5.1 *The Importance Attached to Adult Education Research*

Over 4,300 adult educators have earned doctoral degrees in the field of adult education research in North America since 1935. These constitute an informed, but relatively small, part of the total workforce in the field and only a small percentage of them (probably less than 5%) are actively involved in research today. Those who are at the intermediate level of Houle's pyramid of leadership commonly display scant interest in rigorous research, preferring instead to rely on experience, intuition, and the advice of colleagues as their guides to decision-making. As the perspective of adult educators broadens and they acquire a better appreciation of the relevance of research in various sectors of the field to their own practice, interest in both conducting and increasing the utilization of research seems certain to increase.

5.2 *Organizational Framework for Research into Adult and Lifelong Education*

Adult education researchers display the characteristic North American predilection to establish organizations. The Adult Education Research Conference (AERC), founded in 1960, is basically composed of university level adult educators from both Canada and the United States. This organization was the only such group devoted exclusively to adult education research for a number of years. Canadian researchers established the Canadian Association for the Study of Adult Education (CASAE) in 1981 in part to ensure that the special research concerns of Canadians would be given adequate attention. Other annual gatherings of adult education researchers take place in such groupings as the Midwest Research to Practice Conference, and, for several years, the Lifelong Learning Research Conference, a University of Oklahoma based conference in self-directed learning. Adult education researchers are less active in the major national research organizations (the American Educational Research Association and the Canadian Society for the Study of Education), apparently preferring to participate in smaller conferences that are more narrowly focused on their primary area of interest. A small group of researchers whose interests lie in training, participate in the annual conferences of the American Society for Training and Development.

Both the AERC and CASAE produce published proceedings and, in addition, CASAE now publishes a research journal—The Canadian Journal for the Study of Adult Education—twice yearly. The Adult Education Quarterly (AEQ), published four times each year by the AAACE, continues to be the primary, though certainly not the exclusive, publishing outlet for adult education research. In addition, the commission on Adult Basic Education of the AAACE publishes an interdisciplinary journal for adult literacy educators—Adult Basic Education—three times each year.

5.3 Approaches and Methodological Concerns

As has been noted, researchers in adult education in North America employ all types of research methods drawn from the social sciences, the humanities, and the natural sciences. Enthusiasm for participatory research as the best and only way to conduct inquiries in adult education resulted in a "great deal of heat with little light" so far as advancing useful and theoretical knowledge was concerned (see *Participatory Research*). However, the popular education 'bandwagon' seems to have moved away from participatory research and replaced it with critical theory and postmodernism. Research conferences and publications seem to have abandoned the unproductive debate about the best method and are now inclined to follow an eclectic approach, accepting all known methods of inquiry if they appear to be suited to the specific question under investigation. This eclecticism may be a sign of developing maturity among adult education researchers.

5.4 Implications of Research to Policy and Practice

In their efforts to produce research reports that resemble the high-quality research reports produced by the natural sciences, adult education researchers for the most part have not addressed policy issues, but rather have directed their attention to matters of technique and technology. Accordingly, the most influential publications so far as public policy is concerned have not been produced by the acknowledged leaders in adult education research. Instead, private organizations such as the Southport Institute for Policy Analysis in the United States (Chisman et al. 1990) and the Creative Research Group in Canada (1987) have been of significantly greater influence on legislation regarding literacy than the combined efforts of university-based scholars. Perhaps this situation reflects a significant difference between the standards for rigor and the apparent reluctance of university-based adult educators to address controversial issues and produce policy relevant studies underwritten creatively by a variety of interests. However, with the increasing interest in feminism, critical theory, and postmodernism, it seems likely that an increasing volume of research publications will be addressing questions of public policy on all aspects of adult education.

5.5 Needs and Priorities for Adult Education Research

For nearly 70 years adult educators have sought to establish the identity of their field and, in the process, have tended to overemphasize its distinctiveness from all other sectors of education. Polemic approaches characterized by such expressions as "andragogy versus pedagogy" have not contributed to a larger understanding of the phenomena of teaching and learning throughout life, but instead have encouraged a parochial attitude, aligning adult educators against their natural allies in education. A broader perspective is required for the advancement of lifelong learning opportunities for all. In fact, the continued existence and possible expansion of university graduate programs in adult education will be greatly influenced by the ability of leaders of the field to demonstrate common concerns with other university departments.

Leaders of adult education organizations have shown some willingness to collaborate, but at this point no viable mechanism has been proposed by researchers or administrators to facilitate cooperative approaches to influencing public policy. Without innovative approaches from within the field, legislators must continue to formulate policies that address segments of the field without consideration of the implications of those policies on the overall provision of educational opportunities for all across the lifespan.

See also: Adult Education Research; Market Concepts in Provision; Providers of Adult Education: An Overview

References

Brookfield S 1985 Training Educators of Adults: A comparative analysis of graduate adult education in the United States and Great Britain. *Int. J. Lifelong Educ.* 4 (4): 295-318

Buttedahl P 1985 The training of Adult and popular educators in Latin America. *Convergence* 18 (3-4): 94-102

Campbell D D 1977 *Adult Education as a Field of Study and Practice: Strategies for Development.* Centre for Continuing Education, University of British Columbia, Vancouver

Chisman F P et al. 1990 *Leadership for Literacy: The Agenda for the 1990s.* Jossey-Bass, San Francisco, California

Couillard R 1993 *The Adult Education and Training Survey.* Summary report of the findings from the 1990 Adult Education and Training Survey. Employment and Immigration Canada, Education, Culture and Tourism Division, Statistics Canada, Ottawa

Creative Research Group 1987 *Literacy in Canada.* Creative Research Group, Toronto

Heyes E, Colin S A J III 1994 *Confronting Racism and Sexism.* New Directions for Adult and Continuing Education No. 61. Jossey-Bass, San Francisco, California

Houle C O 1970 The Educators of Adults. In: Smith R M, Aker G F, Kidd J R (eds.) 1970 *Handbook of Adult Education.* Collier-Macmillan Canada, Toronto

Korb R, Chandler K, West J 1991 *Adult Education Profile for 1990–91*. Statistics in Brief, September, 1991 (NCES 91-222). National Center for Education Statistics, Washington, DC

Merriam S 1985 Training Adult Educators in North America. *Convergence* 18 (3-4): 84-93

Roberts H 1982 *Culture and Adult Education: A Study of Alberta and Quebec*. University of Alberta Press, Edmonton

Selman G, Dampier P 1991 *The Foundations of Adult Education in Canada*. Thompson Educational Publishing, Toronto

Statistics Canada 1992 *Reading Skills of Adults in Canada—Excerpts from the Publication Adult Literacy in Canada: Results of a National Survey*. Statistics Canada, Labour and Household Surveys Division, Ottawa

US Bureau of the Census 1993 *Statistical Abstract of the United States*, 113th edn. Washington, DC

Further Reading

Blackburn D J (ed.) 1994 *Extension Handbook: Processes and Practices*, 2nd edn. Thompson Educational Publishing, Toronto

Carneval A P, Gainer L J, Schulz E R 1990 *Training in America: The Organization and Strategic Role of Training*. Jossey-Bass, San Francisco, California

Craig R L (ed.) 1987 *Training and Development Handbook: A Guide to Human Resources Development*, 3rd edn. McGraw-Hill, New York

Faris R 1975 *The Passionate Educators: Voluntary Associations and the Struggle for Control of Adult Educational Broadcasting in Canada, 1919-52*. Peter Martin, Toronto

Houle C O 1992 *The Literature of Adult Education: A Bibliographic Essay*. Jossey-Bass, San Francisco, California

Merriam S B, Cunningham P M (eds.) 1989 *Handbook of Adult and Continuing Education*. Jossey-Bass, San Francisco, California

Mezirow J 1991 *Transformative Dimensions of Adult Learning*. Jossey-Bass, San Francisco, California

Nadler L, Nadler Z 1989 *Developing Human Resources: Concepts and a Model*, 3rd. edn. Jossey-Bass, San Francisco, California

Peters J M, Jarvis P 1991 *Adult Education: Evolution and Achievements in a Developing Field of Study*. Jossey-Bass, San Francisco, California

Stanage S M 1987 *Adult Education and Phenomenological Research: New Directions for Theory, Practice, and Research*. Rober E. Kriegber, Malabar, Florida

Stevens, S B 1993 *Community Based Programs for a Multicultural Society*. Planned Parenthood Manitoba, Winnipeg

Thomas A M 1991 *Beyond Education: A New Perspective on Society's Management of Learning*. Jossey-Bass, San Francisco, California

Verduin J R Jr, Clark T A 1991 *Distance Education: The Foundations of Effective Practice*. Jossey-Bass, San Francisco, California

Watkins K E, Marsick V J 1993 *Sculpting the Learning Organization*. Jossey-Bass, San Francisco, California

SECTION VII

Evaluation and Measurement

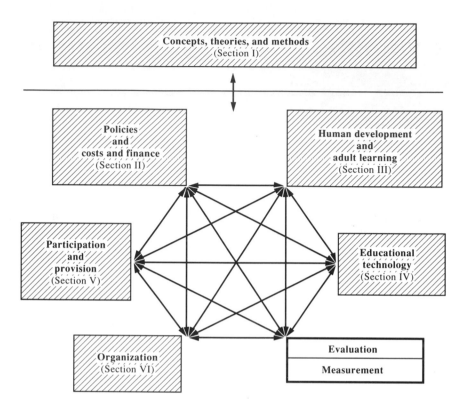

Figure 1
Schematic representation of Section VII in relation to the other Sections

SECTION VII

Evaluation and Measurement

Introduction

A. C. Tuijnman

The evaluation and measurement of adult education and training are two topics that have received increasing attention of late. This development is a direct consequence of the rising economic, social, and cultural importance of adult education and training in societies experiencing rapid growth as well as in those undergoing structural adjustment. The purpose of this section is to offer various perspectives on the measurement and evaluation of adult education and training. Figure 1 shows how this section relates to the others. The entries are grouped into two sub sections, the first dealing with evaluation and the second with measurement.

1. Evaluation

Evaluation in education can be generally described as the process and outcome of making judgements about the worth of an educational phenomenon. An important purpose of evaluation is to provide information that can be used constructively by policymakers, practitioners, and the learners themselves, to influence the learning process and generally improve the outcomes. The design of evaluation differs according to both objectives and contexts. Three of the entries therefore employ cost-effectiveness as a common evaluation criterion, even though separate entries are devoted to the evaluation of adult education, distance education, on-the-job training, and training sponsored by public authorities.

In the first entry, Wolf notes that the confusion over the meaning and practice of evaluation in adult education stems partly from the variety of evaluation techniques and methods that are used, and partly from the fact that the different stakeholders have different views of what evaluation is or should be. In order to clarify the issues, Wolf reviews the main definitions of evaluation proposed in the literature. He concludes that several perspectives on evaluation are tenable; what they have in common is the belief that evaluation is undertaken with the intention that some

action will be taken as a result. Wolf also describes some of the differences between the concepts of evaluation, measurement, research and learner appraisal. Whereas measurement does not necessarily involve the assigning of a value to what is measured, quite the opposite is true of evaluation, where the major attributes for evaluation are chosen precisely because they represent educational values.

In the next entry, Courtenay focuses on evaluation in adult education. He reviews the various purposes of, and methods for, conducting evaluation in adult education. Different areas for evaluation are also discussed, for example, adult literacy, distance learning, vocational education, programs for older adults, and on-the-job training. This leads on to three entries on the evaluation of specific aspects of provision: distance education, firm-based training, and public training programs. Although no separate entries could be devoted to the other major areas of evaluation mentioned by Courtenay, these areas should of course not be ignored.

Orivel concentrates on the economic evaluation of distance education. Although many evaluation studies of distance education systems have been conducted over the years, Orivel notes that empirical evidence on the critical points is still scarce, especially with respect to the question of the cost-effectiveness of such systems compared to more conventional approaches to the teaching of adults. Orivel concludes that distance education projects are most of the time cost-effective, unless a massive misallocation of resources occurs as a result of poor management decisions, and although the advantage of economics of scale is offset by the higher cost of developing the appropriate learning resources.

Mulder addresses the question of the cost-effectiveness of training in business and industry. The cost-effectiveness of such training is analyzed in relation to training efficiency, productivity, and cost factors. Boot and Drewes, in the next entry, deal with the evaluation of public training programs in mostly industrialized countries. Public training programs have received increasing attention from both policymakers and researchers since the mid-1980s. The entry offers an overview of evaluation criteria and techniques and reviews major research studies on the labor market effects of public training programs. Attention is also paid to the implications for policy and further research. Boot and Drewes observe that the debate on the relative merits of experimental versus nonexperimental evaluation designs cannot be decided in favor of either option because their usefulness depends on the situation. They conclude with a plea for the systematic collection of data about adult education and training, so that different methods can be used in measuring the possible outcomes and evaluating the effectiveness of programs.

One issue raised by Boot and Drewes deserves to be given special consideration. The authors call attention to the problem of selection bias in evaluation studies of adult education and training programs. Selection bias can influence the estimates of certain parameters because the selection probabilities for inclusion in a study can be related to the variables being examined. This may be the case if there are unobserved determinants of the probability of inclusion in the evaluation study that correlate significantly with unobserved determinants of the outcome variables. How to handle selection bias is a crucial challenge for studies in the evaluation and measurement of adult education and training because such bias, where no allowance has been made for its effects, greatly limits the validity of generalizations that can be made.

In some Western countries, including Germany, the Netherlands, Sweden, the United States, and the United Kingdom much effort has been devoted to evaluating the effectiveness of public training programs defined in terms of postprogram employment status and the earnings of the trainees. This line of research is motivated by the allocation of substantial public funds to the training of long term unemployed persons. So far, however, this expanding body of research has not shown the expected results. The absence of the anticipated, positive benefits has led some authors to suggest that program effectiveness cannot be determined because the participants enrolled in public training programs are negatively self-selected with respect to the important predictors of program success; hence the doubtful or even negative relationships often found to exist between program treatments and outcomes. This finding has become a "classic" case in the writings on self-selection bias.

In order to evaluate the effects of public training programs, a population must be defined that is free of any selection mechanism that is related to the variables being studied and that influences the selection probabilities for inclusion in a sample. However, this ideal is often unattainable. Systematic differences therefore often arise between the desired and defined target populations, and these differences can introduce selection bias. Even if the sampling errors are very small, which is usually the case in well designed studies, then the presence of selection bias in the data can seriously harm the accuracy of the parameter estimates and impair the validity of the inferences made on the basis of the findings.

Even with the recent expansion of intake, enrollment in adult and continuing education remains selective on a number of accounts. Compared with all eligible students, those who participate are likely to be more homogeneous with respect to variables such as cognitive ability, achievement motivation and potential, and expected life career. Selection bias is thus present in many studies in adult education in which the students are selected for inclusion on the basis of their enrollment status. There are no hard and fast rules for solving the problem. One issue is that the designs employed for effectiveness research have to be developed so that one can distinguish between the effects due to initial education and those due to adult education or continuing vocational training. The failure to account for previous learning experiences will otherwise result in an upward bias in the parameters estimated for the effects of adult education and training. A second issue is that any group of women or men who enroll in programs of adult education and training is atypical in some sense. Because the programs themselves and their clienteles are highly varied, the results obtained in evaluation studies of adult education and training programs are seldomly comparable and generalizable. Since selection bias obviously operates, doubt is cast on the validity of statistical inference.

2. Measurement

Until fairly recently, measurement was not an issue that raised much interest among those engaged in research on adult education and continuing vocational training. The six entries included in this subsection offer many indications that this situation is changing. As adult education and continuing vocational training have risen on the political agendas of governments, the demand for trend data and information about the costs and benefits of the different programs on offer has increased markedly. The result has been that measurement has entered the field in a major way.

Both qualitative and quantitative studies contribute to the knowledge base for adult education. Insights derived from historical, theoretical, and critical research from an integral and important part of this knowledge base, as do statistics and indicators. There is, therefore, a need to develop qualitative and action-oriented studies as well as studies on the measurement of indicators concerning the contexts, inputs, processes, and outcomes of adult education and training. Various sets of indicators of school education are currently in use at both the national and international levels. Although the work on indicators of formal schooling has progressed rapidly since the late 1980s, this development seems to have had little impact on adult education.

Why is it that the launch of this concerted effort to improve the knowledge base for formal schooling has not brought about a similar effort to undertake work on the knowledge base for adult education? Is it because the researchers lack interest? Or could it be that the field lacks the individual abilities and institutional conditions that are needed to sustain serious work on measurement and the development of a comparative knowledge base? Whatever the reasons, it is clear that the multiple data sources needed for the monitoring of trends in adult education are lacking almost entirely, especially at the international level.

The purpose of this cluster of entries is to present an overview of issues and developments in the measurement of adult education, literacy, and industry training. The last two entries pay attention to the recent efforts of improving the scope and reliability of international statistics in the areas of adult education and training. In the first entry, Wagner presents three issues in literacy work that are expected to receive greater attention in the coming years. The first concerns the challenge of operationalizing the definitions of literacy, which is a prerequisite for measurement. The second issue concerns the acquisition of literacy, and the third retention. In the second part of the entry Wagner reviews several approaches to the measurement of adult literacy.

Murray describes the distinctive characteristics of adult education and training, and explores the implications for measurement, as seen from the perspective of a national statistical office. The task facing such institutions is to decide what variables should be collected and how best to measure them. Murray then reviews the prevailing methodologies for measuring adult education and especially its contributions to the stocks and flows of educational activity in a society. The review makes it quite clear that the available measurement technology in adult education is deficient in a number of respects, and that concerted action is needed to strengthen it. The possible future directions for measurement in adult education are also examined. McCombe describes why, and how, measures of industry training are being developed in

a number of countries. The focus is on the methods for data collection used by the countries. This entry is closely related to the one by Bowers on statistics of employee training. Tilak, in another entry, concentrates on the measurement of training costs and the expenditures for adult education and training.

In the entry on statistics for adult and nonformal education, Chu describes UNESCO's approaches to the measurement of adult and nonformal education. Chu draws attention to the need to strengthen research and measurement expertise at the national level. The development of meaningful international data sets stands or falls with the comprehensiveness and quality of the data collected at the national level. At present, very few countries are capable of collecting reliable and useful statistical information about the key aspects of adult education and training. Strengthening the national capacity in data collection is therefore considered a high priority.

At the national level, statistics and indicators of adult education can be derived from sample surveys and administrative records. However, information is also needed at the international level. Comparative indicators of key aspects of adult education—for example on costs and expenditures, scope of provision and participation, and the outcomes of adult learning—can offer an external framework of reference for interpreting national trends and evaluating results in a broad international perspective. Thus, in summary, comparative analysis is needed to determine whether the levels of investment and participation in adult education and training, the quality of program offerings, and the results achieved, are adequate in the light of both national ambitions and international standards. Indicators might be developed in the following areas: the costs of provision; total public and private expenditures; the sources of funds for adult education and training; types of providers; national training effort; volume of total provision of adult education; characteristics of participants; duration and intensity of training or adult learning; modes of training or adult learning; qualifications; and the individual and social returns to investment.

(a)   Evaluation

Evaluation Concepts and Principles

R. M. Wolf

The need for careful evaluation of adult education and training programs is identified and discussed in this entry. Considerable attention is devoted to specifying rather precisely what evaluation is and, equally important, what it is not. A formal definition of evaluation is presented and elaborated. Evaluation is contrasted with related, but distinctly different activities; namely measurement, assessment, and research. Finally, the limitations of evaluation as a means for determining the effectiveness of adult education and training programs and how to improve them are noted.

1. The Need for Evaluation of Adult Education and Training

Evaluation has long been recognized as a means for the improvement of education. The reasons for this are fairly clearly recognized. Evaluations of educational programs furnish important information for program improvement. Ideally, evaluation efforts should doom a program to success! Evaluation is especially critical in adult education and training for reasons that are not apparent at the primary and secondary levels of education. In adult education and training, there are costs that are associated with student time that simply do not exist at compulsory educational levels. Individuals engaged in adult education and training programs often have to forego earning money. Thus, there is a strong need to determine that the programs they are engaged in are effective. The loss in earnings for individuals engaged in such programs may never be recovered if the programs are ineffective.

Another important reason for evaluating adult education and training programs is that such programs are often undertaken to meet certain manpower needs in a society. If the programs are not fully effective, then not only do individuals suffer because they are unable to recover lost earnings, but the larger society suffers because important manpower requirements may not be met. Thus, having effective programs of adult

education and training is doubly important. Society can ill afford to have ineffective programs for adult education and training, and individuals cannot afford to participate in such programs if they are not likely to derive substantial benefits from them.

Any effort to deal with a relatively new aspect of education is obliged to furnish the reader with a definition, description, and discussion of that aspect. This is particularly true of the burgeoning field of educational evaluation where there is considerable confusion. This confusion stems partly from the fact that many of the techniques and procedures used in evaluating educational enterprises are rather technical, and educators are often not knowledgeable about such matters. A more basic reason for the confusion, however, is that different authors have different notions of what educational evaluation is or should be. These dissimilar views often stem from the training and background of the writers, the particular professional concerns with different aspects of the educational process, specific subject-matter concerns, and even from differences in ideology. A consequence of this is that a reader unfamiliar with the field is all to often exposed to written works that not only differ but are even contradictory. Such writings are not just expressions of honest differences about what evaluation is about and how it should be conducted. They are often reflections of a deeper confusion which attends the development of a relatively new field of inquiry.

2. Toward a Definition of Evaluation

There are several definitions of educational evaluation. They differ in level of abstraction and often reflect the specific concerns of the person who formulated them. Perhaps the most extended definition of evaluation has been supplied by C.E. Beeby, who described evaluation as ". . . the systematic collection and interpretation of evidence, leading, as part of the process, to a judgment of value with a view to action"

(Beeby 1977). There are four key elements to this definition. First, the use of the term "systematic" implies that the information needed will be defined with some degree of precision and that efforts to secure such information will be planned. This does not mean that only information which can be gathered through the use of standardized tests and other related measures will be obtained. Information gathered by means of observational procedures, questionnaires, and interviews can also contribute to an evaluation enterprise. The important point is that whatever information is gathered should be acquired in a systematic way. This does not exclude, *a priori*, any kind of information.

The second element in Beeby's definition, *interpretation of evidence*, introduces a critical consideration sometimes overlooked in evaluation. The mere collection of evidence does not, by itself, constitute evaluation work. Yet, uninterpreted evidence is often presented to indicate the presence (or absence) of quality in an educational venture. High dropout rates, for example, are frequently cited as indications of the failure of adult educational programs; doubtless, they are indicators of failure in some cases, but not all. There may be very good reasons why people drop out. Personal problems, time constraints, acceptance into higher-level educational programs, and finding a good job are reasons for dropping out which may in no way reflect on the program (see *Student Dropout*). In some cases, dropping out of an educational program may even indicate that a program has been successful. For example, a few years ago, the director of a program that was engaged in training people for positions in the computer field observed that almost two-thirds of each entering class failed to complete the two-year program. On closer examination, it was found that the great majority of "dropouts" had left the program at the end of the first year to take well-paying jobs in the computer departments of various companies (usually one they had worked with while receiving their training). The personnel officers and supervisors of these companies felt that one year of training was not only more than adequate for entry- and second-level positions but provided a sufficient foundation on which to acquire the additional specialized knowledge and skill required for further advancement. Under such circumstances, a two-thirds dropout rate before program completion was not an indication of a program failure or deficiency but rather of the success of the program.

Clearly, information gathered in connection with the evaluation of educational programs must be interpreted with great care. Evaluation workers who cannot make such interpretations themselves should enlist the aid of others who can, otherwise their information can seriously mislead. In the above example, the problem of interpretation was rather simple. Dropout statistics are easily gathered, and one can usually have confidence in the numbers. More complex situations arise when one uses various tests, scales, or observational and self-report devices such as questionnaires. In these situations, which can involve high stakes, the interpretation of evaluation information can be extremely difficult. Unfortunately, the interpretation of information has too often been neglected. Specific mention of it in a definition is welcome since it focuses attention on this critical aspect of the evaluation process.

The third element of Beeby's definition, *judgment of value*, takes evaluation far beyond the level of mere description of what is happening in an educational enterprise. It casts the evaluation worker, or the group of persons responsible for conducting the evaluation, in a role that not only permits but requires that judgments about the worth of an educational endeavor be made. Evaluation not only involves gathering and interpreting information about how well an educational program is succeeding in reaching its goals, but judgments about the goals themselves. It involves questions about how well a program is helping to meet larger educational and social goals. Given Beeby's definition, an evaluation worker who does not make a judgment of value, or who, for political or other reasons, avoids making a judgment is not, in the full sense of the term, an evaluation worker. Whoever does make such a judgment, after the systematic groundwork has been laid, is completing an evaluation.

A distinction needs to be made between the two types of judgments. The first is the judgment of value of the program or curriculum being evaluated. This is the type described above, which is clearly within the scope of the evaluation worker's professional function. The second type of judgment is taken in light of the first and, along with other relevant factors, is the decision on future policy and action. This is clearly the responsibility of administrators, governing boards, and other policymakers. If these decision-makers make both kinds of judgments, they are taking over an essential part of the professional evaluation function. This should be avoided.

It is quite possible that a decision might be made to retain a marginally effective program. It may be that the political or public-relations value of a program is deemed important enough to continue it despite limited cost-effectiveness (see *Measurement of Adult Education; Measurement of Industry Training; Evaluation of Public Training: Cost-Effectiveness*). It is also possible that funds are available to operate a program of marginal quality but funds not be available for other, possibly, more worthwhile endeavors. It is the decision-maker's job to determine whether to fund it or not. The point remains: the evaluation workers, or those charged with the evaluation of a program, should render a judgment value; it is the responsibility of decision-makers to decide on future policy and action. Each has their area of responsibility, and each must be respected within their domain. This point must be understood at the outset. If it is not, there is a danger that evaluation workers may become frustrated or cynical when they learn that policy decisions have been made contrary to what the results of their evaluation would suggest.

The last element of Beeby's definition, *with a view to action*, introduces the distinction between an undertaking that results in a judgment of value with no specific reference to action, and one that is deliberately undertaken for the sake of future action. The same distinction was made by Cronbach and Suppes (1969), although they used the terms *conclusion-oriented* and *decision-oriented* research. Educational evaluation is clearly decision-oriented. It is intended to lead to better policies and practices in education. If this intention is in any way lacking, evaluation should probably be dispensed with and evaluation workers should use their time to better advantage.

So far no mention has been made about what kinds of actions might be undertaken as the result of an evaluation study. The range is considerable. A conscious decision to make no changes at all could result from a carefully conducted evaluation study; or a decision to abolish a program altogether could be made, although the latter case is not very likely. In fact, this writer does not know of a single instance where a decision to terminate a program was based *solely* on the results of an evaluation study. Between these extremes, modifications of content, organization, and time allocation could occur, as well as decisions about additions, deletions, and revisions in instructional materials, learning activities, and criteria for staff selection and training. Such decisions come under the general heading of program or course improvement and are discussed in some detail by Cronbach (1963). Scriven (1967) used the term *formative evaluation* to characterize many of these kinds of decisions. In contrast, decisions about which of several alternative programs to select for adoption or whether to retain or eliminate a particular program are *summative* in nature, to use Scriven's terminology. Scriven's distinction between formative and summative evaluation has achieved a fair measure of popular acceptance although the number of clearly summative studies is small. The basic point is that evaluation studies are undertaken with the intention that some action will occur as a result.

3. Differences between Evaluation, Measurement, Research, and Assessment

Beeby's definition of evaluation goes some distance toward specifying what evaluation is. However, in order to function effectively, a definition must not only say what something is, it should also say what it is not. This is particularly important with regard to evaluation. Three activities that are related to evaluation are *measurement, research*, and *assessment*. Evaluation shares some similarities with each. The differences, however, are considerable and need to be examined

so that the terms which are used frequently in this *Encyclopedia* can be properly differentiated and understood.

3.1 Evaluation and Measurement

Measurement is defined as the act or process of measuring. It is essentially an amoral process in that there is no value placed on what is being measured. Measurements of physical properties of objects such as length and mass do not imply that they have value; they are simply attributes that are being studied. Similarly, in the behavioral and cognitive sciences, measurement of psychological characteristics such as neuroticism, depression, problem-solving, and mechanical reasoning do not confer value on these characteristics.

In evaluation, quite the opposite is the case. The major attributes studied are chosen precisely because they represent educational values. Objectives are educational values which define what educators seek to develop in learners as a result of exposing them to a set of educational experiences. They can include achievements, attitudes toward what is learned, self-esteem, and a host of other prized outcomes. Such outcomes are not merely of interest; they are educational values. Thus, while evaluation and measurement specialists often engage in similar acts, such as systematically gathering information about the literacy performance of adults, there is a fundamental difference between the two in the value that is placed on what is being measured.

A second important distinction between evaluation and measurement inheres in the object of attention of each. By tradition and history, measurement in education is undertaken for the purpose of making comparisons between individuals with regard to some characteristic. For example, two adult learners may be compared with regard to their reading comprehension. This is accomplished by administering the same reading comprehension test to the two learners and seeing how many questions each has answered correctly. Since they have been given the same test, a basis for comparison exists. This is the traditional measurement approach. In evaluation, on the other hand, it is often neither necessary nor even desirable to make such comparisons between individual learners. What is of interest is the effectiveness of a program, often judged against cost (see *Evaluation of Distance Education: Cost-Effectiveness; Evaluation of Industry Training: Cost-Effectiveness; Evaluation of Public Training: Cost-Effectiveness*). In such a situation, there is no requirement that the learners be presented with the same set of questions. In fact, in many cases, it may be prudent to have them answer different sets of questions. The resulting information can then be combined with that obtained from other learners and summarized in order to describe the performance of an entire group that has been exposed to a particular program. Such a procedure introduces *efficiencies* into the process of information gathering (see *Research Methodology: Human Development*). The point to be made here is that evaluation and measurement are typically directed towards different ends: evaluation toward describing effects of *treatments*; measurement toward description and comparison of *individuals or systems*. In evaluation, it is not necessary that individuals be compared. In fact, there are often good reasons for not doing so.

3.2 Evaluation and Assessment

Closely related to the notion of measurement is assessment. Assessing the proficiencies of learners for purposes of diagnosis, classification, and grading is usually considered the prerogative of those charged with the instructional function, typically teachers. The introduction of systematic evaluation procedures has been viewed in some cases as an intrusion on this traditional teacher function. Nothing could be further from the truth. Evaluation is directed toward judging the worth of a total program and, sometimes, for judging the effectiveness of a program for particular groups of learners. Evaluation is not an external testing program that is intended to supplant teacher responsibility for assessment. In fact, more often than not, it is simply not possible to do so. For example, if in the course of evaluating an adult education program, it is decided to have different groups of adults answer different sets of questions, the resulting evaluation information will contribute nothing to the process of assessment since one cannot usually compare the performance of learners who have answered different sets of questions. Measurements of adult learner proficiencies will still have to be made to fulfill the assessment function. Thus, facilitators of adult learning need not fear that systematic evaluation of educational programs will intrude on the assessment role of their professional function. Quite the opposite may occur. Facilitators wishing to use evaluative information to assist them in assessing learner performance may find themselves frustrated when they learn that evaluative information does not help them in this regard.

3.3 Evaluation and Research

Evaluation and research share a number of common characteristics, but there are some notable differences as well. Research typically aims at producing new knowledge which may have no specific reference to any practical decision, while evaluation is deliberately undertaken as a guide to action. This distinction is highlighted in the last phrase of Beeby's definition of evaluation, ". . . with a view to action." Any distinction based on motivation is obviously fragile, and one operation can shade into another; but in practice there is usually a marked difference in content, presentation, and often method between research inspired by scholarly interest or an academic requirement, and an investigation undertaken with a definite practical problem in mind. Scholarly research has often led to

highly practical results—the work of atomic physicists in the 1930s is a dramatic case in point. An important difference in motivation, however, remains.

A basic distinction between evaluation and research lies in the *generalizability* of results that each type of activity produces. Research is concerned with the production of knowledge that seeks to be generalizable (see *Adult Education Research*). For example, a research worker may undertake an investigation to determine the relationship between the aspiration and achievement of adult learners. The study will be designed and carried out in such a way as to ensure results that are as generalizable as possible. They should be obtained over a wide geographic area, apply to a range of ages, and be applicable for some time unless there are particular cohort effects. Generalizability of results is critical in research. Little or no interest may attach to knowledge that is specific to a particular sample of individuals, in a single location, studied at a particular point in time. In fact, if the results of a study cannot be replicated elsewhere, they are apt to be dismissed. In their now famous chapter on designs for research in teaching, Campbell and Stanley (1966) drew attention to the notion of generalizability when they discussed threats to the integrity of various designs under two broad headings—internal validity and external validity. External validity was their term for generalizability.

Evaluation, in contrast, seeks to produce knowledge specific to a particular setting. Evaluation workers, concerned with the evaluation of a literacy or adult basic education program for learners in a single locality or geographic catchment area, will direct their efforts toward ascertaining the effectiveness of the program in that locality. The resulting evaluative information should have high local relevance for administrators in that area. The results may have no relevance for any other literacy program in any other locality or area; well-intentioned educators, interested in such a program, will have to determine its effectiveness elsewhere in a separate study.

Another important distinction between evaluation and research lies in the area of method. In research there are fairly well-developed canons, principles, procedures, and techniques for the conduct of studies, which have been explicated in various works (Kerlinger 1986, Kaplan 1964, Campbell and Stanley 1966). These methods serve to ensure the production of dependable and generalizable knowledge (see *Research Methodology: Scientific Methods*). While the methods of research frequently serve as a guide to evaluation endeavours, there are a number of occasions when such methods are neither necessary nor practicable. Evaluation is not research, and the methods of the latter do not dictate the activities of the former.

Some writers assert that any evaluative effort must rigorously employ the methods of experimental research and that anything less is apt to be a waste of time and money (see *Evaluation of Public Training: Cost-Effectiveness*). This is an extreme position. While research methods are often useful in planning evaluation studies, they should not be too limiting. Meaningful evaluative activity that does not follow a research model can be carried on. For example, a program intended to train people in a particular set of skills could be undertaken with a single select group of learners and their proficiency ascertained at the conclusion of the training program. Such an enterprise would violate most, if not all, of the precepts of scientific research such as lack of randomization, absence of a control group, and so on. However, it could yield highly pertinent evaluative information that could be used for a variety of purposes. An inability to follow research prescriptions for the design and conduct of studies is not at all fatal for evaluation work. There are occasions when departures from a strict research orientation are both necessary and appropriate. The important point is that substantial and important work can be done in evaluation that does not require the use of formal research methods. However, it is clear that this must be done extremely carefully.

4. Limitations of Evaluation

It is common in education to make strong claims for one thing or another, whether it is a teaching method, a form of organization, or the like. In fact, one function of evaluation is to test such claims. It seems fitting, therefore, to identify the major limitations of evaluation, lest readers develop the mistaken notion that no limitations beset educational evaluation.

One limitation of educational evaluation was suggested previously. Educational evaluations, typically, do not produce generalizable results. The evaluation of a particular training program in a given location can provide useful information about that program in that place, but such information may not apply to any other locale. Separate studies would have to be conducted in different sites to estimate the effects of training programs in those sites.

A second limitation of educational evaluation stems from the fact that educational programs are rarely, if ever, static. Programs are continuously evolving and changing. Thus, any evaluation is at least partially out of date by the time the data are gathered and analyzed. The report of an evaluation study is probably best seen as a historical document since the program that was evaluated has undoubtedly undergone some change in the period from when information was gathered until the report was produced. Some of these changes are quite natural and represent normal processes of growth and change in an educational enterprise. An evaluation study, in contrast, is a snapshot or a series of snapshots at a particular time. Readers of evaluation reports need to keep this point in mind as they seek to understand and improve educational programs.

A third limitation of evaluation studies centers on the distinction between diagnosis and prescription. Educational evaluations are often similar to medical diagnoses. That is, they can indicate the presence or absence of a fever and what particular set of symptoms are exhibited. Such information can be quite useful. However, it may not provide a prescription as to how to remedy identified deficiencies. For example, an evaluation study may indicate that adults are failing to make an expected amount of progress in a particular learning project and even furnish some reasons for the lack of progress. Deciding what to do to improve learning is a different matter. An evaluation study may not be able to provide recommendations on how to improve a program that is found to be deficient.

The limitations of educational evaluation are important to recognize. Just as strong claims are made for various educational ventures, evaluation has been seen, by some, to be a panacea. It is not. Thoughtful evaluation workers recognize this. Other educators and policymakers should recognize this also.

See also: Adult Education Research; Empiricism, Positivism, and Antipositivism; Research Methodology: Scientific Methods; Evaluation of Adult Education; Literacy Research and Measurement

References

Beeby C E 1977 The meaning of evaluation. In: *Current Issues in Evaluation, No. 4. Evaluation.* Department of Education, Wellington
Campbell D T, Stanley J 1966 *Experimental and Quasi-experimental Designs for Research.* Rand-McNally, Chicago, Illinois
Cronbach L J 1983 Course improvement through evaluation. *Teach. Coll. Rec.* 64:672-83
Cronbach L J, Suppes P 1969 *Research for Tomorrow's Schools: Disciplined Inquiry for Education.* Macmillan, New York
Kaplan A 1964 *The Conduct of Inquiry.* Chandler, San Francisco, California
Kerlinger F 1986 *Foundations of Behavioral Research, 3rd edn.* Holt, Rinehart and Winston, New York
Scriven M J 1967 *The Methodology of Educational Evaluation. Curriculum Evaluation.* Rand McNally, Chicago, Illinois

Further Reading

Cook T D, Campbell D T 1979 *Quasi-experimentation: Design and Analysis for Field Settings.* Rand-MacNally, Chicago, Illinois
Popham W J 1988 *Educational Evaluation, 2nd edn.* Prentice Hall, Englewood Cliffs, New Jersey
Rossi P J, Freeman H E 1985 *Evaluation: A Systematic Approach, 3rd edn.* Sage, Newbury Park, California
Wolf R M 1990 *Evaluation in Education: Foundations of Competency Assessment and Program Review, 3rd edn.* Praeger, New York
Worthen B R, Sanders J R 1987 *Educational Evaluation: Alternative Approaches and Practical Guidelines.* Longman, White Plains, New York

Evaluation of Adult Education

B. C. Courtenay

There is universal recognition that evaluation of adult education programs is necessary and important. Internationally, distinctions among adult education researchers and practitioners emerge in examinations of the definition and purpose of evaluation, methods for conducting evaluation, and decisions about what is to be evaluated. An investigation of these distinctions raises such issues as a common set of standards to be followed in evaluating adult education, the value of outcomes collected from a highly differential population, and whether or not adult education evaluation should be an instrument for social change.

1. Definition and Purpose of Adult Education Evaluation

Any attempt to locate an internationally recognized definition of adult education is a futile exercise. The range of definitions is equivalent to the number of individuals and groups who put forth a meaning of the concept. Deshler (1984) confirms that point by noting that adult education evaluation ranges from measuring the achievement of objectives, to obtaining useful information for decision making, to viewing evaluation as an art, where the evaluator has no single best plan but molds all the internal and external variables into a workable model. Spaulding (1989) concurs when he concludes that there is little agreement in the international community between education agencies and governments over the meaning of evaluation. Agency personnel often view evaluation as experts sent for a short period of time to examine the progress of a program and to recommend changes. On the other hand, government agencies frequently perceive evaluation as data gathering to facilitate priority setting for future funding. While there is no global definition of evaluation in adult education settings, gathering information about a program in order to make a decision about its future and determine its value or merit appear to be two critical elements common in most definitions (see *Evaluation Concepts and Principles*).

These two elements could also be promoted as the purpose of evaluation, an equally elusive concept with regard to the discovery of a single, encompassing goal. Grotelueschen (1980) lists five major purposes for conducting adult education evaluation, ranging from accountability of resources or compliance with regulations to identifying program weaknesses and assessing progress toward stated goals. In a national study of the evaluation practices of business and industry, health and government agencies, colleges and universities, professional societies, and licensing agencies in the United States, the majority of the respondents agreed that they use evaluation to improve programs and to determine the extent to which a program achieves intended outcomes (Andrews 1991).

A more radical purpose of adult education evaluation is implied by Armstrong (1989) who conducted an assessment of young adult occupational educational programs in the United Kingdom. In this example, Armstrong advocates that evaluation can be an instrument for social change even while working within a state-funded agency. The key is to help the participants learn that evaluation is a process that must be continuously examined in a critical way. The development of critical thinking skills in the analysis of the program's success has the potential for transfer into other aspects of the participants' lives. In short, Armstrong is suggesting that program objectives should be evaluated while, at the same time, incorporating an exercise to further social change.

These somewhat divergent views of the purpose of evaluation raise the debatable issue of the feasibility of evaluating all adult education experiences. Some scholars advocate that any adult education program can be evaluated simply by writing the objectives in measurable terms. Others argue to the contrary, citing either that some objectives (affective, for example) cannot be reduced to measurement, or that program developers cannot account for change that occurs unintentionally to the participants while in a particular program. With respect to the latter argument, researchers like Ruddock (1989) remind us of the difficulty of measurement in adult education because of the heterogeneity of the populations involved. For example, consider the possible age and educational ranges of the population in many adult education programs. Both variables suggest a host of contextual factors that may be present in the program and that may affect the outcome of the evaluation.

A second issue that emerges from the discussion of the purpose of adult education evaluation is the scope of the evaluation, ranging from simple satisfaction indicators to participant gains in knowledge to organizational change. An examination of evaluation studies reported in international journals of adult education indicates that most evaluation plans emphasize the participants' satisfaction with a program. This observation is confirmed by Andrews' (1991) study of adult education agencies in the United States, the results indicating that participant satisfaction questionnaires are used as the primary source of information about program success. Others (Courtenay and Holt 1987) have questioned this practice, viewing it as a limited perspective of a program's worth. Does participant satisfaction mean that learning has occurred or that the learners simply felt positive about the learning experience? Since an adult education organization provides learning experiences to help participants change in knowledge, skill, or attitude, should it not also provide an opportunity to measure the extent of those changes? And, in those instances where, for example, a business or industry expects that higher levels of competence acquired through a training program will yield positive changes for the organization, should not measures of institutional growth also be an element in the evaluation plan? Ironically, Deshler (1984) concludes that organizations and evaluation are mutually exclusive because organizations are self-perpetuating and slow to change, whereas evaluation identifies and supports change and improvement.

The point of this discussion is not to advocate one aspect of evaluation over another, but to reveal the important relationships between program objectives and evaluation purposes. Whether an adult education evaluation plan focuses on the adult learner, individual aspects of a program, or the total program, it can only yield relevant information about the focus when the appropriate questions are asked.

A final issue emerging from a consideration of the purpose of evaluation is the extent to which an evaluator employs acceptable standards of conducting evaluations. Although adult education researchers and practitioners have not prepared a set of criteria to guide evaluations, standards have been considered and published by scholars associated primarily with evaluation organizations. According to Patton (1986), the Joint Committee on Standards for Educational Evaluation, a committee established by 12 professional organizations, adopted four criteria in 1981 that serve as standards of good evaluation practice.

The first is *utility*. Is there evidence that the evaluation has potential for use once the results are presented to all involved in the program? The second criterion is *feasibility*. Is the evaluation politically and practically cost-effective? The third criterion, labeled *propriety*, emphasizes reflections about ethical implications. Can the evaluation be conducted fairly and ethically? *Accuracy* is the concern of the last criterion. To what extent will the evaluation be technically adequate?

Patton's discussion of these criteria is influenced significantly by the first criterion, the usefulness of the evaluation. Thus, to some extent the standards are a reaction to the common and, perhaps, unfortunate practice in which final results of evaluations are ignored after an initial review. The concern of the Joint Commission is that evaluators insure that evaluation projects are conducted in such a way as to maximize subsequent use of the outcomes of the evaluation.

The critical question at this juncture is the relevancy and appropriateness of these criteria for adult education evaluation. Of the four criteria, the first, utility, poses the greatest challenge because so often

evaluation outcomes are not taken into account, for example, in making program improvements. Thus, the implication is that some sort of "usage" guarantee signed by all parties would have to be employed. But is it the responsibility of the evaluator to insure that evaluation results are dynamic tools for subsequent use? Is not the responsibility of the evaluator to conduct, report, and interpret the evaluation? The Joint Commission advocates a higher level of responsibility. At the very least, adult education evaluators have the responsibility to examine and debate this and the other three criteria.

2. Methods for Conducting Evaluation Studies

There are several elements that comprise the methods of evaluation. Among the larger elements that reflect critical issues in evaluation methodology are the origin of the evaluator (internal or external), quantitative or qualitative data, and specific techniques for collecting information (e.g., interviews and observations).

An issue that must be resolved early in the evaluation plan is who will conduct the assessment. Basically, the choices are an individual or individuals associated with a program or organization, or a person or persons who contract from outside the program or organization. Obviously, there are advantages and disadvantages with either alternative. For example, external evaluators are considered to be more objective because they supposedly have no personal investment in a program. Thus, they can provide a more balanced assessment. On the other hand, internal evaluators are viewed as having the most intimate knowledge of a program or organization and, therefore, can provide a more thorough evaluation. Of course, there are counterarguments to both these alternatives. In the first instance, no evaluation plan is completely emotion- or value-free. Even external evaluators bring to an assessment their own set of biases and values about evaluation. In the case of internal evaluators, knowledge by association is not always a valid assumption.

The dominant paradigm for this issue is the external evaluator, particularly of large-scale national studies. However, there is evidence to demonstrate a trend toward more internally generated assessments. One example is the evaluation skill training program in Kenya supported by the German Foundation for International Development (Nturibi 1986). Historically, Kenya's National Literacy Program has been evaluated by an outside agency that sometimes resembled more of an inquisition than a search for information to make program improvements. The purpose of the Kenyan evaluation training program is to demystify evaluation and develop a cadre of local "experts" who can successfully conduct all aspects of an evaluation. The program has been applied with modifications to national literacy programs in Botswana, literacy pilot programs in Malawi, and the Learning Post-Project in Lesotho.

While recent emphasis in evaluation is toward internal sources to conduct evaluations, there is some indication that a combination of inside and outside assessors is advantageous. Armstrong (1989) has used what he calls the collaborative approach, a new paradigm incorporating external and internal resources. This approach provides for the traditional summative and formative data, but also, because of the collaboration between the participants and the "experts," a richer understanding of the program's effects on the participants.

This issue of who should conduct the evaluation relates to a second issue having to do with the design of the assessment. The traditional approach emphasizes the collection of quantitative data, proponents stressing that more informal designs yield untested information. However, since the early 1980s, qualitative designs have received equal to greater attention particularly for their ability to answer questions of cause better. Alexander (1989) taught 20 officials from the Department of Nonformal Education in Thailand to use qualitative evaluation designs for assessing nonformal education programs because such approaches facilitate the discovery of causes, the why of outcomes, rather than simply the documentation of what happened.

Ossandón (1986) observes that quantitative designs ask questions that determine whether objectives are achieved, identify cause and effect, demonstrate the repetition and generalizability of a program's outcomes, confirm objective measurement of results, and reflect efficient use of resources. He dismisses these apparent advantages of quantitative evaluation approaches by noting that in popular education, the objectives are usually not clear—only the end result. A program is not only a product, it is also a process and, thus, new objectives arise along the way. With respect to generalizability, Ossandón advocates that what is important is the explanation of the process so that others may decide one way or another. The question regarding the efficient use of resources is irrelevant to him because in a disorganized community, for example, it may be necessary to sponsor a large, relatively costly informal gathering in order to attract participants.

On the other hand, qualitative designs are also surrounded by weaknesses. Alexander (1989 p. 57) cautions that ". . . used without careful historical, cultural, and social-economic analysis, such approaches to evaluation . . . may be naive and lacking in both integrity and sufficient attention to ethics." Naiveté emerges when evaluators ignore the fact that the discovery of purpose and values in qualitative designs touches everyone involved in the evaluation, including policymakers. Questioning the importance of the existing order may be so threatening to policymakers that they resist the dissemination and, certainly, the

implementation of the results. In cultures dominated by a turbulent and central authority government, evaluation findings emphasizing values and purpose may place the participants' lives in jeopardy. Thus, while qualitative approaches are increasingly popular in evaluation of adult education programs, contextual variables such as historical and cultural events and the nature of governmental control are critical considerations in determining design preference.

A third important issue in the selection of methods for evaluation is the choice of specific information collection techniques. To a significant extent, this decision depends on the resolution of the previous issue, the selection of a quantitative or qualitative design. For example, a mailed survey questionnaire designed to measure participants' perceptions is unlikely to result in enlightening information of a qualitative nature. But once the design issue is determined, there are a number of techniques available to the evaluator. Courtenay and Holt (1987) list 11 measures for conducting impact evaluation, ranging from mailed questionnaires to performance observations and simulations. Fifteen different techniques, including critical incidents and life histories are identified and explained by Ruddock (1981).

Analysis of documentary records, such as legislative texts, political speeches, and budgets is a critical technique among those most often used to conduct national literacy programs (Couvert 1979).

3. Areas of Adult Education Evaluation

The range of areas evaluated in adult education is as broad as the imagination, including adult literacy education, vocational education, continuing professional education, distance learning, health education, leisure education, programs for older adults, and training in business. Although capturing a large segment of evaluation in adult education, the foregoing areas are not exhaustive, which indicates the variety and vastness of the field.

Whether or not one area serves as the dominant host of evaluation studies depends on the literature reviewed and the geographical location of the studies reported. Documents gathered by the Educational Resources Information Center (ERIC) serve as an example of the importance of the literature. A review of over 200 ERIC abstracts indicates that adult literacy education, followed by preparation for employment programs, is the most frequent source for adult education evaluation. A similar conclusion can be drawn from an examination of such international adult education journals as *Convergence* and the *International Journal of Lifelong Education*, where evaluation studies of adult literacy education programs hold a distinct advantage over other areas. Studies in these journals also attest to the influence of geography. Almost all the evaluation studies in these journals are reports from developing countries, such as those found in Africa and the Far East. Varavarn's (1987) account of the outcomes of the early stages of Thailand's National Literacy Campaign is one example.

Similar claims of evaluation activity could also be made for other areas of adult education given a different literature context. Evaluations of programs for older learners not enrolled in adult literacy education programs abound in such journals as *Educational Gerontology*. A recent example is an evaluation of a program that provides an opportunity for older adults to develop leadership skills for use in administering activities in a senior center in Canada (Cusack 1991). Evaluation outcomes of medical education for physicians, nurses, and several other health care professions take up volumes of medical education journals. With increased emphasis on accountability for making profits, evaluation of business and industry training programs is commonplace in management journals and popular business-related magazines.

4. Future Developments

One future development in the evaluation of adult education follows the foregoing discussion of the areas of assessment. Evaluation activity is expected to continue in all areas and will most likely increase in some, especially those that must indicate a return on investments or be held accountable for achieving goals. Emphasis on outcomes forecasts a second future development, increased attention to the demonstration of the impact of adult education programs. While satisfaction measures will continue to be a dominant source of program success, evaluators will be asked to provide evidence of change in knowledge, skill, or attitudes and transfer of such changes from the learning environment to the performance level of participants in their usual environments, whether personal or occupational.

A third potential development in the evaluation of adult education reflects changes in design. Qualitative designs will continue to grow in importance because of the increasing acceptance of their validity in providing information that facilitates explanation of purpose and value. Evaluations employing a combination of qualitative and quantitative designs are also expected to proliferate. Mixing the two designs appears to control for the weaknesses of both and to promote their strengths.

One final potential development falls within the purposes of evaluation. The likelihood that evaluation will become a significant instrument for social change is possible, of course, but probably remote. Internationally, the dominant paradigm of measuring value and progress is less threatening to policymakers in both private and public organizations. Yet researchers and practitioners scattered throughout the world are demonstrating successful outcomes with participatory education projects. These projects are characterized by intense involvement of the participants in their own education, which often leads to transformations within the participants and subsequently within organizations in society. Why not include evaluation in the participatory process? The frequency and success of this change in the purpose of evaluations depends to a large extent on the ability of adult education evaluators strategically to meet the needs of policymakers within organizations like governments, business and industry, and colleges and universities and, simultaneously, encourage and facilitate participant involvement in critiquing adult education programs to improve them.

See also: Evaluation Concepts and Principles

References

Alexander D J 1989 Issues in evaluating non-formal education in Thailand: The significance of more qualitative approaches. *Int. J. Lifelong Educ.* 8(1): 57–82

Andrews G J (ed.) 1991 *A Practical Handbook for Assessing Learning Outcomes in Continuing Education and Training*. International Association for Continuing Education and Training, Washington, DC

Armstrong P 1989 Is evaluation as a critical and reflexive educative process new paradigm research? Reflections on Reason and Rowan. In: Coggins C 1989 *Proceedings of the 30th Annual Adult Education Research Conference*. University of Wisconsin, Madison, Wisconsin

Courtenay B C, Holt M E 1987 Evaluating program impact. In: Klevins C (ed.) 1987 *Materials and Methods in Adult and Continuing Education*. Klevens Publications, Los Angeles, California

Couvert R 1979 *The Evaluation of Literacy Programmes: A Practical Guide*. UNESCO, Paris

Cusack S A 1991 Participation with confidence: The development and evaluation of a leadership-training program for older adults. *Educ. Gerontology.* 17(5): 35–49

Deshler D 1984 An alternative for program improvement. In: Deshler D (ed.) 1984 *Evaluation for Program Improvement*. Jossey-Bass, San Francisco, California

Grotelueschen A D 1980 Program evaluation. In: Knox A B (ed.) 1980 *Developing, Administering, and Evaluating Adult Education*. Jossey-Bass, San Francisco, California

Nturibi D N 1986 Participatory training in evaluation skills: Kenya project. *Convergence* 19(1): 24–27

Ossandón C J 1986 Methodology for continuous self-evaluation: Notes from the Latin American experience. *Convergence* 19(3): 13–19

Patton M Q 1986 *Utilization-Focused Evaluation*, 2nd edn. Sage Publications, London

Ruddock R 1981 *Evaluation: A Consideration of Principles and Methods*. Department of Adult and Higher Education, University of Manchester, Manchester

Ruddock R 1989 Evaluation in adult education. In: Titmus C J (ed.) 1989 *Lifelong Education for Adults: An International Handbook*. Pergamon Press, New York

Spaulding S 1989 Adult education evaluation in developing countries. In: Titmus C J (ed.) 1989 *Lifelong Education for Adults: An International Handbook*. Pergamon Press, New York

Varavarn K (ed.) 1987 What does literacy mean to rural people? Thailand's study of experiences and impact. *Convergence* 20(1): 19–29

Evaluation of Distance Education: Cost-Effectiveness

F. Orivel

Hundreds of systems of what is commonly referred to as "distance education" have been developed in the world. Every year new systems are set up, each with its own characteristics and innovations. To the distant observer, distance education appears to be a successful means for delivering instruction—one that is growing more rapidly than conventional education. It could be assumed that this success is a result of the demonstrated effectiveness or cost-effectiveness of distance education. Unfortunately, although many evaluation studies of distance teaching systems have been conducted, empirical evidence on critical points is scarce, especially on the question of the cost-effectiveness of such systems compared to more conventional approaches to instruction.

This entry discusses kinds of distance education. A general definition of distance education will then be used as a basis for developing a typology, and the available evidence on the cost-effectiveness of distance education will be reviewed.

1. Definition of Distance Education

A comprehensive definition of distance education is proposed by Keegan (1980), who asserts that the following key features characterize all distance education systems:

(a) separation of teacher and student;

(b) use of technical media;

(c) provision of two-way communication;

(d) absence of group learning;

(e) important role of an educational organization;

(f) participation in the most industrialized form of education;

(g) privatization of learning.

All of these features can be found in some distance education systems, but the majority do not contain all of them. For example, the use of technical media is not necessary in correspondence courses. Likewise, although two-way communication is commonly seen as a major innovative feature, it cannot be provided in all circumstances, as in the case of the Chinese Television University. The absence of group learning, moreover, is not verified in many instances. For example, most educational radio programs in Latin America and Africa are broadcast to groups of adult learners. In a revision of his contribution, Keegan (1986) changed his view on this point by underlining that distance education "treats the student basically as an individual."

The notion concerning the "industrial" character of distance education is taken further by Peters (1991), who links it with the mass production and distribution of learning materials, as well as with the complex logistics of managing, from one headquarters, tens of thousands of dispersed learners and tutors. With such a system, as with other complex production markets, the division of labor encourages specialization and enhances productivity.

Orivel (1985) takes a similar position by arguing that, whereas the costs of conventional teaching are to an extent proportional to the number of students, distance education implies a significant proportion of fixed costs caused by a generally large administrative overhead, the production of sophisticated didactic material, and their dissemination through broadcasting or other media. It is clear that such costs are to an extent independent from the number of users. To put it simply, if the audience is multiplied by ten, then the unit cost can be divided by ten. Distance education can, in theory, generate substantial economies of scale. But again, this does not hold for all existing systems. Correspondence education is closer to conventional education in this respect, and even institutions such as the British, Dutch, and Spanish open universities have a mostly "variable" cost structure. That is, at a given quality level an increase in student numbers will be accompanied by an increase in tutor hours or, alternatively, will stimulate the production of specific programs for smaller audiences.

Keegan's principles, to conclude, are "normative" criteria; that is, they represent views on what constitutes a high-quality and cost-effective system of distance education. This perspective is similar to that of pedagogues in conventional education who, while ignoring resource constraints, recommend policy options such as small class sizes, qualified teachers, diversified didactic materials, a supportive environment, a committed community, and appropriate remedial activities for low achievers. Given that resource constraints are always present, the learning systems that fail to meet Keegan's criteria cannot be excluded from an analysis of the cost-effectiveness of distance education.

In order to take this diversity into account, more general definitions have been proposed by other writers, for example, Perraton (1984) and Dodds (1991). For the latter, distance education refers to "any form of organized educational experience in which teaching and learning take place with the teachers at-a-distance from the learner for most of the time." Perraton's definition comes very close: "it can be taken to mean an educational process in which a significant proportion of the teaching is conducted by someone removed in space and/or in time from the learner." Both definitions are consistent with nonconventional approaches to teaching, but they make the distinction between both systems more difficult to draw.

Consider the example of certain Italian and French universities, where cramped quarters compel professors to distribute their lectures in printed form, thus making the physical attendance of students in a lecture hall unnecessary. Can this be considered as part of distance education? What is the difference, for a student, between a lecture followed on TV at home, the same lecture followed in a learning group at the workplace, and again the same lecture followed on a TV set placed in a university corridor because no seats are available for all the students? The first two cases are typically considered as distance education, the latter as a university lecture.

If the difference is only in the proportion of face-to-face learning vis-à-vis non-face-to-face learning, then where is the point of division? In conventional education, a significant proportion of the time spent on learning does not require the presence of a teacher; for example, textbook learning, exercising on paper or with a computer, or peer tutoring. By adding such categories of student learning time, one can come close to a position that defines distance education as a process in which a significant proportion of the learning time is spent at a distance from a teacher.

2. Economic Theory and Distance Education

In his studies of economic systems the Nobel laureate, F A von Hayek, used to contrast two "pure" models: the market model and the centrally planned model. The first is regulated by perfect competition, in which all production and purchasing decisions are taken by individuals, and all prices and quantities are determined by laws of supply and demand. In contrast, the centrally planned model is regulated by a unique authority which determines production plans, takes decisions on resource allocation, and sets prices and salaries.

In Hayek's view, these two models do not exist in reality. National economies are a combination of both, and according to political or other factors introducing change, tend to move in one or other direction. Both have advantages and disadvantages, each weighted differently by different people. In coming too close to a "pure" model, the disadvantages tend to become too costly, thus creating an incentive for policy to move in the opposite direction. An illustration of combination is the fact that even the most market-based countries allocate one-third or more of their national resources through collective decisions. The problem of policy

does not involve a choice between the two extreme models but the selection of an optimal mix of both—a mix that is unlikely to remain stable in time.

Hayek's "pure" economic models can be applied to educational systems. A pure distance education system could be defined as a model in which the average student is completely isolated from the physical presence of teachers and peers. Radio or TV broadcasts, audiovisual packages or printed materials are received at home or at the workplace, and no feedback from a teacher is needed. This model works with inputs that carry sizable economies of scale, because costs tend to decline with increases in the size of the audience: the more students, the lower the unit cost.

At the opposite end, the conventional model of school education would offer as much teacher assistance or peer support as is required in order to maximize learning effectiveness: face-to-face teaching in small classes, individualized tutoring to overcome learning difficulties, appropriately qualified and motivated teachers, adequate facilities, and boarding when necessary. The transfer of knowledge and skills in this contrast model basically occurs through teacher intervention and in a context free of constraints in terms of, for example, teacher salaries. Teacher labor is thus a primary factor in the conventional system, and unit costs tend to rise with a decrease in class size, an increase in teacher qualifications, or growth in the enrollment of less able students at higher levels of education who often require an individualized teaching approach and more counseling.

The pure distance education model is inefficient in dealing with low achievers and poorly motivated learners; the pure conventional system is pedagogically more efficient but also requires more resources. As with pure economic models, the closer one is to one of them, the more likely it becomes that its drawbacks will exceed the advantages. A cost-effective solution lies in the proper mix of both models. As is true in dealing with economic realities, the convergence toward an appropriate, cost-effective combination of inputs does not mean that a single, optimal solution can be found in all cases and at any time. Different, appropriate combinations exist according to resource constraints, the marginal productivity of the primary factors, and the choices made in a society. This last point refers to the weight collectively given to desired but to a degree competing outcomes, such as more equity versus more quality or effectiveness.

3. Typology of Distance Education Systems

As previously mentioned, the key difference between distance education and conventional education concerns the extent of teacher replacement by alternative media. The parallel in economic theory is the law of capital–labor substitution driven by technological progress, improved human capital, and increased productivity. The cost of teacher labor relative to alternative didactic means tends to increase continuously, and didactic tasks that can be performed by inputs other than the teacher carry declining costs compared with teachers. Consider the example of the relative cost of textbooks to labor. Over a period of five centuries this cost has been divided by a factor of several thousands, as labor input decreased from a year of a copyist's time to a handful of minutes in a modern printing house. Drastic savings in labor cost can also be achieved with computers and other technology as learning tools—and these will not take five centuries to take effect.

3.1 Within School versus Out-of-school Systems

A distinction is commonly made between "within school" and "out-of-school" systems (Orivel 1985). The introduction of distance teaching components within schools serves two basic objectives: (a) to enrich conventional teaching, improve school performance, and reduce failure, dropout, and repetition rates; and (b) to compensate for the insufficient qualification of school teachers in certain contexts, in particular in developing countries.

Out-of-school systems are closer to the pure concept of distance education, and the objectives are different from those set out above. Such systems can offer continuing professional education as well as learning opportunities to people previously excluded from schooling. They may also respond to the learning needs of working adults, unable to attend day schools, handicapped or chronically sick people, or mothers raising children. Basically, systems in which most learning occurs at home or at the workplace increase the opportunities of people who live far away from schools or other institutions, or who cannot engage in planned learning activities during the hours these are offered.

At the outset many alternative ways of learning were not intended to reduce unit costs, but to expand learning opportunities—drops in unit costs that occurred were often unanticipated. This is no longer the case, however, especially in countries in Asia and the Pacific, where many distance education systems were set up during the 1970s and 1980s. To take one example, the 1 million or so students who enrolled in the Chinese Television University in the early 1990s almost outnumbered those attending China's traditional universities. This initiative was intended as a means of managing a rapid expansion in opportunity to learn at the tertiary level. This objective could not have been realized with conventional universities, given available resources (Hawkridge and Chen Chia-Erh 1991).

3.2 The Place of Teachers in Inputs

An additional classification was proposed by Hawkridge (1988), who uses the extent of teacher replacement as a criterion for distinguishing among four types of distance education systems:

(a) distance education added on to existing face-to-face teaching—the aim is to enrich the learning environment on a voluntary basis;

(b) teachers deliberately replaced by distance education for part of the week—the aim is to improve the quality of instruction offered in core subjects;

(c) distance education as the only or almost the only alternative—the aim is to offset a lack of qualified teachers and classrooms;

(d) distance education as the only teaching offered because qualified teachers are not available, although learning can take place in classrooms.

It must be noted that this classification squares with the convergence theory, although not for the same reason as the one described above. The substitution of new technologies for teacher labor—whether minimal or extensive—is not driven by a willingness to improve the cost-effectiveness of teaching, but by the desire to overcome a shortage of qualified teachers. If the latter objective is behind the creation of a distance learning system, then the implication may be that action will be undertaken to end the shortage, and that the system will revert to a conventional approach to teaching once the objective is achieved. In an economic perspective this would not happen, because the new technology would be made a permanent feature of the learning system if it were discovered to offer the same quality of educational services at a lower cost.

3.3 Educational Level and Audience

Perraton (1982) and Dodds (1991) preferred to categorize distance teaching by levels of education and target audiences. They had four common categories: (a) tertiary education; (b) secondary education; (c) inservice teacher training; and (d) nonformal education, adult basic education, and continuing professional education.

This classification implies a definition of distance education different from the one given by Hawkridge (1988). Projects concerning primary education for children, in which a media component is used within school in addition to the presence of the teacher, is not considered here as part of distance education. Such projects do not enter Perraton's definition of distance education because no "significant proportion of the teaching [is] conducted by someone removed from the learner" (Perraton 1982 pp. 9–22). This draws into focus a major drawback of distance teaching addressed to school children: it requires a capacity of self-learning which students often have not yet acquired. For children below 15 years of age, schools have two functions that are served by the same person, the teacher: teaching and caring. The principle of substituting media for labor is therefore not always possible, although maturity has been shown in some research studies not to be a factor of great importance in the applicability and effectiveness of distance teaching (Bates 1988).

In tertiary-level education Dodds (1991) distinguishes between three modes of distance education. The first can be illustrated using the example of the Open University of the United Kingdom, an independent institution with the same privileges as a conventional university. The second mode is organized by traditional universities seeking to satisfy the learning needs of part-time students. The university sets up a special department for managing the education of these students, but makes use of the same staff, curricula, and often the same didactic materials as those used in full-time teaching. Sometimes, as in France, several universities join forces in a consortium in order to generate economies of scale: university A is specialized in the social sciences; university B, in humanities and foreign languages; and university C, in the natural sciences and mathematics. The third mode has been developed in Russia and the United States. The study life of distance education students is divided into two parts: the first is part-time at-a-distance study; and the second, full-time study at an institution, taking courses that are difficult to organize at a distance.

According to different sources, the number of university-level dispersed students increased dramatically during the 1970s and 1980s and stood at about 10 million worldwide in 1990.

In secondary education two types of distance education are used. The first, belonging to the "within school" category and made up of small rural or remote secondary schools, cannot recruit or afford specialized teachers in mainly foreign languages and the sciences. A typical example is the *Telesecundaria* system in Mexico, where TV programs substitute for the lack of qualified teachers in certain fields of study. The second type comprises a growing number of out-of-school systems at the secondary level, similar to open universities, in particular in Africa (e.g., Malawi Correspondence College, and Zambian National Correspondence College); in Asia (e.g., Air Correspondence High School in Korea). In Europe and North America such systems have been developed for commercial courses.

A characteristic of primary education is that teachers are spread throughout a given country. For those who are underqualified or, more generally, for those who need retraining, residential sessions are not only costly to organize (due to transport, lodging, and subsistence), but also imply the interruption of teaching services in the classroom. Since distance education can be a very cost-effective means of meeting the demand for inservice training, it has been intensively used in numerous projects worldwide.

If distance education cannot be used easily with young children for primary education, basic education for adults is not faced with the same difficulty. Brazil has set up several such projects and, more generally, Latin American countries have created numerous radio

schools for adult basic education. In Africa, radio is used for mass campaigns in health, hygiene, nutrition, family planning, and especially literacy. A very common use of radio is by agricultural extension services, which provide training and advice to farmers in order to improve their productivity.

4. Evaluation of Cost-effectiveness

As was mentioned in the introduction to this entry, indepth evaluation studies of the cost-effectiveness of distance education projects are disappointingly rare. In the late 1970s, UNESCO and the World Bank cooperated in commissioning about 20 case studies which followed more or less the same methodology, especially concerning cost analysis. As far as effectiveness is concerned, generally positive results were obtained where distance education projects could be compared to conventional education programs, but the findings were less conclusive in cases where comparisons could not be made (Eicher et al. 1982).

After this first wave of cost-effectiveness case studies, an insufficient number of new ones have been carried out, and it is very difficult to draw unambiguous general lessons from the available evidence. A useful overview of studies conducted in the 1980s is given by Moore (1989). Hawkridge (1988), in a review of World Bank projects that included distance education components, notes: "Regrettably, comprehensive evaluation studies do not exist for any of the Bank's 32 distance education projects" (p. 91).

A seminar on distance education in Asia and the Pacific held in Bangkok in 1986 under the auspices of the Asian Development Bank reviewed national case studies, but here again, in the summary of proceedings, one can read that "with an exception or two, not many useful evaluations of their investment costs, running expenses and performance are reported to have been made" (Asian Development Bank 1987). Nevertheless, most case studies reached conclusions in favor of distance education at tertiary level because of "the low cost of that education as against the increasing costs of conventional campus facilities" (pp. 1–40). Lower costs indeed seem likely, since this is predicted by economic analysis, but it would be more convincing if actual cost data were provided.

In spite of the risks involved in summarizing evidence obtained in scarce empirical studies, some common conclusions concerning the cost-effectiveness of new media and distance education are presented below.

4.1 Effectiveness of New Media

In a controversial article, Clark (1983) argues that "most current summaries and meta-analyses of media comparison studies clearly suggest that media do not influence learning under any conditions . . . The best current evidence is that media are mere vehicles that deliver instruction but do not influence student achievement any more than the truck that delivers our groceries causes changes in our nutrition" (p. 457).

Accordingly, if distance teaching changes the cost-effectiveness of educational systems, it is not because it is using more efficient inputs, but because these inputs eventually have lower costs, or because they are reaching new learners who were previously excluded from access to conventional education services. Clark (1983) adds that reviews of published literature are often beset by an editorial bias, because journals are more likely to publish research showing significant effects of new media than research that shows no such effect. Finally, the author suggests that researchers should "refrain from producing additional studies exploring the relationship between media and learning unless a novel theory is suggested" (p. 457).

A challenge to Clark's view was contributed by Kozma (1991). He shows that media are using different symbol systems and processing capabilities which may influence the structure of mental representations and cognitive processes. He recognizes that more research is needed in order to identify the appropriate media combinations that may enhance learning effectiveness and the types of student that are likely to benefit from media specificities. Another argument can also be made, namely that currently available measurement technology and knowledge about learning media in education do not yet allow for an accurate prediction of the contribution of different educational media to an improvement in student achievement.

4.2 Cost-effectiveness

Most within-school projects with a low level of teacher replacement can hardly reduce unit costs. The distance education components that are introduced usually have the opposite effect: they tend to increase the costs per pupil, because the "quantity" of teacher intervention remains unchanged. One can expect some improvement in student achievement to occur from these distance education components, but evidence of such improvement is often uncertain, mostly not demonstrated, and what remains most visible, the additional cost, tends rapidly to come under scrutiny and criticism, as was the case with the Côte-d'Ivoire television project for primary schooling. Such projects have been canceled one after the other in developing countries such as Niger, Senegal, and Samoa. A well-researched and clearly successful project of this kind is the Nicaragua Radio Mathematics scheme using interactive radio to improve student achievement in mathematics (Suppes et al. 1980). In this case it must be added, however, that an important cause of the previously low level of mathematics achievement was the low level of teacher qualification. As this is not always the case, care must be taken in interpreting the findings.

Evaluation studies of out-of-school projects with an extent of teacher replacement reviewed by Jamison and Orivel (1982) consistently show a positive cost-effectiveness ratio unless few students were enrolled. The hypothesis about economies of scale was empirically verified by Jamison and Orivel (1982). In calculating cost functions with respect to audiences, the authors show that in the case of the South Korea Air Correspondence High School, the marginal cost of an additional student was about two-thirds of the average cost; in the case of the Israel Everyman's University, it was only one-third; in the Brazil Minerva project, marginal cost was 80 percent of the average unit cost and half the average cost of the closest alternative.

A caveat to these findings is that distance teaching projects involving very small audiences cannot realize a major cost reduction and often are more expensive than conventional teaching. An example is the case of another Brazilian project, *Bahia Madureza*, where the number of registered students was too low to amortize high fixed costs. A similar conclusion was reached from the Kenyan experience with inservice teacher training.

In the 1980s the Chinese Television University looks, according to Hawkridge (1988), "highly cost-effective," but only "prima facie," the authors add in the absence of any reliable data. A case study undertaken at the University College of Southern Queensland, one of the eight nationally recognized distance education centers in Australia, sought to compare the cost-effectiveness of conventional on-campus teaching, off-campus teaching via distance education, and mixed-mode methods involving both distance education and conventional teaching techniques (Taylor and White 1991). Whereas no major differences among the three audiences were found in terms of academic performance, the cost findings were as follows. Based on a computerized activity costing approach, the case study showed that the unit costs per student of conventional, face-to-face on-campus teaching (A\$700) and off-campus distance teaching (A\$693) were approximately equal, whereas the mixed-mode approach (A\$778) was financially viable only if the preparation costs are not included, despite the fact that some of these preparation costs are recovered through the sale of instructional materials.

5. Conclusion

Unless a massive misallocation of resources occurs as a result of poor management decisions, distance education projects are most of the time cost-effective, even though the advantage of economies of scale is offset by the higher cost of developing multimedia, self-instructional materials. But this conclusion is insufficient as a basis for policy-making. Not only are more case studies needed that compare actual costs and results, but studies should also investigate, in different contexts, the optimal mix of media that leads to the highest possible cost-effectiveness ratio. Otherwise, educational technology choices will be mostly determined by hardware and software producers, telecommunication firms, and innovative entrepreneurs, whose objectives and interests do not necessarily coincide with those who finance education or with the learners themselves.

See also: Distance Education; Open University; Educational Technology in Distance Education

References

Asian Development Bank 1987 Summary of proceedings. In: Asian Development Bank 1987 *Distance Education in Asia and the Pacific*, Vol. 1. Asian Development Bank, Manila

Bates A W 1988 Television, learning and distance education. *J. Educ. Edn. Technol.* 4(3): 213–25

Clark R E 1983 Reconsidering research on learning from media. *Rev. Educ. Res.* 53(4): 445–59

Dodds T 1991 The development of distance teaching: An historical perspective. In: Jenkins J, Koul B N (eds.) 1991 *Distance Education: A Review*. International Extension College/Indira Gandhi National Open University, New Delhi

Eicher J C, Hawkridge D, McAnany E, Mariet F, Orivel F 1982 *The Economics of New Educational Media. Vol. 3: Cost and Effectiveness Overview and Synthesis*. UNESCO, Paris

Hawkridge D 1988 Distance education and the World Bank. *Br. J. Educ. Technol.* 19(2): 84–95

Hawkridge D, Chen Chia-Erh 1991 Evaluating a World Bank project: China's television universities. *Int. J. Educ. Dev.* 11(2)

Jamison D T, Orivel F 1982 The cost-effectiveness of distance teaching for school equivalency. In: Perraton H (ed.) 1982 *Alternative Routes to Formal Education: Distance Teaching for School Equivalency*. Johns Hopkins University Press, Baltimore, Maryland

Keegan D 1980 On defining distance education. *Distance Educ.* 1(1): 13–36

Keegan D 1986 *The Foundations of Distance Education*. Croom Helm, London

Kozma R B 1991 Learning with media. *Rev. Educ. Res.* 4(2): 179–211

Moore M G 1990 *Effects of Distance Learning: A Summary of the Literature*. Research Monograph No. 2. Office of Technology Assessment, Congress of the United States, Washington, DC

Orivel F 1985 Economics of educational technology. In: Husén T, Postlethwaite T N (eds.) 1985 *The International Encyclopedia of Education*, 1st edn. Pergamon Press, Oxford

Perraton H 1982 The scope of distance teaching. In: Perraton H (ed.) 1982 *Alternative Routes to Formal Education*. Johns Hopkins University Press, Baltimore, Maryland

Peters O 1991 Theoretical aspects of correspondence instruction. In: Jenkins J, Koul B N (eds.) *Distance Education: A Review*. International Extension College/Indira Gandhi National Open University, New Delhi

Suppes P C, Searle B, Friend J 1980 *The Radio Mathematics Project in Nicaragua 1976–77*. Stanford University Press, Stanford, California

Taylor J C, White V J 1991 *The Evaluation of the Cost-effectiveness of Multi-media Mixed-Mode Teaching and Learning*. Australian Government Publishing Service, Canberra

Further Reading

Asian Development Bank 1987 *Distance Education in Asia and the Pacific*, Vols. 1 and 2. Proceedings of the Regional Seminar on Distance Education, Bangkok, 26 November–3 December 1986. Asian Development Bank, Manila

Asian Development Bank 1989 *Distance Education in South Asia*. Proceedings of the Round Table Conference on Distance Education for South Asian Countries, Islamabad, 6–8 November 1989. Asian Development Bank, Manila

Bates A W 1990 *Media and Technology in European Distance Education: Proceedings of the EADTU Workshop on Media, Methods and Technology*. Open University for the European Association of Distance Teaching Universities, Milton Keynes

Jamison D T, McAnany E 1978 *Radio for Education and Development*. Sage, Beverly Hills, California

Perraton H 1982 *Alternative Routes to Formal Education: Distance Teaching for School Equivalency*. Johns Hopkins University Press, Baltimore, Maryland

UNESCO 1977 *The Economics of New Educational Media. Vol. 1: Present Status of Research and Trends*. UNESCO, Paris

UNESCO 1980 *The Economics of New Educational Media. Vol. 2: Cost and Effectiveness*. UNESCO, Paris

United States Congress, Office of Technology Assessment 1989 *Linking for Learning: A New Course for Education*. United States Government Printing Office (Document OTA-SET-430), Washington, DC

Evaluation of Industry Training: Cost-Effectiveness

M. Mulder

The question of cost-effectiveness is important for instructional systems, such as training courses in business and industry. This entry discusses the concept of cost-effectiveness in relation to efficiency and productivity, cost factors, and models for analyzing the cost-effectiveness of training courses.

1. Effectiveness, Efficiency, and Productivity

Jobs in many organizations are changing rapidly; new duties and tasks are being replaced by old ones, and new jobs are being created. This change causes a multitude of training needs, and organizations respond with a variety of interventions, often labeled human resource development (HRD). Nadler (1984) describes training, education, and development as HRD interventions. Training is an activity aimed at a current job, education is aimed at a future job, and development is aimed at enhancing flexibility of the organization.

This entry will concentrate on training. Employers conceive of training as one human resource development tool that can be integrated into a broad approach of human performance improvement in organizations. McLagan and Bedrick (1983) distinguish the following areas of human resources that employers can use to improve human performance:

(a) organization development: assuring healthy interunit and intraunit relationships and helping groups initiate and manage change;

(b) organization/job design: defining how tasks, authority, and systems will be organized and integrated across organization units and in individual jobs;

(c) human resource planning: determining the organization's major human resource needs, strategies, and philosophies;

(d) selection and staffing: matching people and their career needs and capabilities with jobs and career paths;

(e) personnel research and information systems: assuring a personnel information base;

(f) compensation/benefit: assuring compensation and benefits fairness and consistency;

(g) employee assistance: providing personal problem-solving, counseling to individual employees;

(h) union/labor relations: assuring healthy union–organization relationships;

(i) training and development: identifying, assessing and—through planned learning—helping develop the key competencies (knowledge, skill, attitudes) which enable individuals to perform current or future jobs.

The relatively high costs of training justify closer scrutiny of its cost-effectiveness. Mulder et al. (1991) reported that in a complex training project for several hundreds of counter personnel within the Post Office division of the Dutch Postal Service PTT, a careful analysis and revision of the training program resulted in a cost reduction of over 2 million dollars on a budget of about 20 million dollars.

The concept of cost-effectiveness includes three related terms: effectiveness, efficiency, and productivity. Effectiveness is reached when better results are achieved at the same cost. It is the amount which training enhances in the solution of a performance problem in the organization or in the need for competency development felt by the employees. Efficiency is achieved when a given objective is realized with minimum cost. Productivity is realized when better results are achieved at lower cost.

2. Cost-effectiveness and Cost–Benefit

Cost-effectiveness and cost–benefit are concepts that are frequently confused. The difference in their meaning is substantial, and refers to fundamentally different criteria of evaluating training. In both concepts the common element is that of costs. Costs are the financial means that are needed for realizing training in the organization. Cost-effectiveness is the amount to which a given training alternative with an expected level of effectiveness can be realized with a minimum of financial means. Cost–benefit is the relationship between the financial results of training and the costs required to produce these results.

The difference between cost-effectiveness and cost–benefit lies in the outcome component. The effectiveness of a solution is answered in relation to the initial problem, whereas benefits are expressed as a monetary unit. Cost–benefit analysis approaches will not be elaborated in this entry. Those approaches are less promising than cost-effectiveness because outcomes of training are partly intangible and cost–benefit ratios do not aid the decision as to whether a training course is necessary. Such investment decisions are based on competency needs in the organization, for instance in air transportation, where pilots need extensive training and retraining at high costs. For an airline organization it is less interesting to know what they "gain" from these training programs; the mere knowledge of what they can lose with insufficiently trained professionals is reason enough to justify the considerable training expenditure. The fundamental question is what instructional system guarantees the required performance standards at the lowest cost. This is the cost-effectiveness approach to training:

> Cost-effectiveness . . . is specifically useful for decisions involving the comparison of alternative approaches to a given goal. For such decisions, the dollar costs of the alternatives are generally identified while their effectiveness is considered on a scale chosen to reflect the nature of the particular goal (e.g., achievement test scores). This ability to consider two kinds of measures makes cost-effectiveness analysis a very useful technique but limits its application to the comparison of alternative approaches to the same goal. If choices have to be made between competing goals achieved through completely different activities, then outcomes must be measured in the same

units as costs to structure an interpretable comparison. Under such circumstances, the more specialized economic technique of cost-benefit analysis (comparing costs and benefits on identical scales of estimated monetary value) is more appropriate. (Lent 1980 p. 4ff.)

If the instructional design model in an organization comprises human performance analysis, and instruction is (part of) the solution, and training needs analysis results in a specific definition of the outcomes of the instructional system, the costs of the alternatives may be compared to see whether the total expenditure on training can be minimized.

3. Cost and Effectiveness Factors

To determine the cost-effectiveness of training courses, costs as well as effectiveness factors have to be distinguished. These factors will be described below.

3.1 Cost Factors

If the costs of training courses are to be analyzed, the first question is what cost factors have to be included. Head and Buchanan (1981) have reduced the cost factors for training courses to a manageable set of five factors: (a) trainee costs, (b) instructor costs, (c) costs of facilities, (d) overhead costs, and (e) instructional development costs. Summation of these cost factors determines the total costs for the training course at the organizational level. The authors have presented a set of formulas for calculating the cost factors and the formula for calculating trainee costs is as follows:

$$T' = (NT \times L)(TS + TPD + LO) + NT(TTC) \tag{1}$$

where T' is the total trainee costs; NT is the number of trainees; L is the course length in days (travel time included); TS is the trainee salary per day; TPD is the housing costs per day (housing, meals, tips); LO is the lost opportunity cost per trainee; and TTC is the trainee travel cost (return fare and local travel cost).

Most of the cost factors in this model are clear, but one component needs further clarification: lost opportunity costs. This factor means the productivity loss of trainees and instructors, while they are learning and teaching. When they are not in training, trainees and instructors would have opportunities to increase the productivity of their organization. The quantity of lost opportunities can vary considerably, depending on the job of the trainee and instructor. This ambiguity creates considerable difficulties in calculating the lost opportunity costs. Head and Buchanan (1981) give different examples of practical situations in which lost opportunities are calculated in specific ways. Examples are:

(a) multiplying the salary costs of trainees with an estimated weighting factor;

(b) adding costs of replacements to the salary costs;

(c) dividing the return of the workforce for the organization by the number of employees and adding this amount to the salary costs.

Productivity loss is quite often forgotten in calculating the costs of training, but on a corporate level it can amount to substantial sums of money.

In the list of cost factors that are distinguished in the model, two categories of costs can be differentiated: fixed costs and variable costs. Fixed costs are independent of the number of trainees, and the number of training days. An example of fixed costs is the rent of facilities, and an example of variable costs is the total trainee costs (see *Measurement of Training Costs*).

3.2 Effectiveness Factors

Smith (1987) distinguished many effectiveness factors that are based upon 28 evaluation studies in various business and industry contexts. This overview presents the scope of the criteria that can be employed to evaluate the impact of training courses. These factors are aimed at studying the relationship between the training course and job performance. The different evaluation studies are compared on five categories: the function of the evaluation, the category of intervention, the productivity standard, the standard for quality of the performance, and the standard for the description of the group workers. *Productivity* refers to the quantity of production per time unit. This can be calculated on different levels: the individual employee, a group of employees, and the whole organization. *Quality* refers to the discrepancy between the actual and the ideal products and services. These discrepancies can be determined by the organization itself, for instance by a quality check within the organization, or by private organizations, customers, or administrative bodies. Quality standards are measured by such matters as the quantity of trash, customers' complaints, machine stoppages, accuracy, and client service. Finally, with a *group of employees*, the stability and the competency profiles of the employees are used for assessment. Standards in this respect are mobility (to other employers), absenteeism, complaints, and promotions or lateral transfers.

The study performed by Smith (1987) comprises a broad scope of jobs, varying from production to service personnel in the automotive trade, inspectors of machine parts, extruder operators, assembly-line workers, welders, welding inspectors, and car-tire salespeople, to production supervisors, programmers, bank employees, and branch managers. The types of training vary considerably too, from on-the-job training and "job aids" to all kinds of off-the-job training courses on different topics. On the basis of this study, effectiveness standards are distinguished for productivity, performance quality, and the group of employees.

Effectiveness of training courses can be evaluated at different system levels. Mulder (1992) distinguishes the supra-, macro-, meso-, and microlevel. The supralevel denotes the business environment, the macrolevel the business as such with respect to the training department, the mesolevel the training department itself, and the microlevel denotes the learning and instruction process. Training course effectiveness can be determined at the micro-, meso-, and macrolevel. It is not practicable to think of evaluating the training course effectiveness at the supralevel, for this would require searching for training impact at the business environment level. Although there may be a certain amount of impact, it seems impossible to isolate the training factors from various other factors that influence the business environment, such as the world economy and politics. It is also extremely complicated to isolate the training course effectiveness at corporate level, as other interventions in the organization, such as corporate strategy, organizational structure, and human relations, make it almost impossible to separate the training factor from intervening variables. Measuring training course effectiveness at the micro-, meso-, and macrolevel in organizations implies testing learning results, job performance results, and organizational results.

4. Models for Determining the Cost-effectiveness of Training Courses

There are several models for determining the cost-effectiveness of training courses. On the one hand a cost-effectiveness analysis can be conceived of as a problem-solving strategy, on the other hand it can be seen as the cost-effectiveness calculation technique. One example of each category will be described below.

4.1 Cost-effectiveness Analysis as a Problem-solving Strategy

Performing a cost-effectiveness analysis of training courses is a complex task. In many cases, business and industry do not keep records of training data. Recommendations to plan and implement cost-effectiveness studies as a problem-solving strategy are given by Doughty and Lent (1987). Their perspective on cost-effectiveness analysis consists of a problem-solving perspective. They suggest the following six steps in planning and implementing cost-effectiveness studies: (a) describing the context, (b) determining discrepancies between the actual and the ideal situation, (c) identification of criteria, (d) clarification of alternatives, (e) defining the solution, and (f) justification of the solution. In many cases the initial stages of cost-effectiveness studies are neglected. Doughty (1986)

developed a procedural guideline structured by five questions: (a) what are the goals of the study? (b) what is the nature of the target group of the study? (c) who will be designing and implementing the study? (d) what are the essential design elements? (e) what methods will be used?

4.2 Cost-effectiveness Calculation

Cost-effectiveness calculation can be performed for *a priori* investment justification or for a *posteriori* investment evaluation. *A priori* calculation, or precalculation of the potential cost-effectiveness, is done in the context of determining objectives for the training course, establishing achievement or performance standards, selecting or designing training course alternatives, determining expected effects, and comparing the costs of the alternatives. The cheapest alternative that yields the minimum acceptable quality will be chosen for implementation or development. *A posteriori* calculation, or postcalculation, is performed by analyzing achievement or performance objectives, assessing effects of the training course (on the level of trainee satisfaction, learning gains, performance results, or organizational effects). Costs and effects are calculated separately, because the units in which these variables are expressed are different.

The costs of training courses can be calculated with costing forms such as the one described by Spencer (1984). Swanson and Sleezer (1987) developed a practical system for training effectiveness evaluation (TEE) which can be employed as an example of how to determine training course effects. This system consists of three components: an evaluation plan, a toolkit for measuring the effectiveness of the training course, and an evaluation report.

5. Conclusion

Cost-effectiveness analysis is fundamentally different from cost–benefit analysis. The former is the more promising analysis approach to assess the value of training courses to organizations. Cost–benefit analysis assumes that the benefits of training can be measured in monetary units, which is usually of less interest because of the qualitative nature of the training results for the individual and the organization.

See also: Costs of Adult Education and Training; Evaluation of Public Training: Cost-Effectiveness; Measurement of Industry Training; Measurement of Training Costs

References

Doughty P L 1986 *Planning Cost-effectiveness Studies of Training Development and Implementation: A Procedure Guide.* Area of Instructional Design, Development and Evaluation, Syracuse University, Syracuse, New York

Doughty P L, Lent R M 1987 *Case Studies of the Cost Justification of Interactive Applications in Key Industries in Interactive Video in Education*. Area of Instructional Design, Development and Evaluation, Syracuse, Syracuse University, Syracuse, New York

Head G E, Buchanan C C 1981 Cost/benefit analysis of training: A foundation for change. NSPI Journal (November): 25–27

Lent R M 1980 An examination of the methods of cost-effectiveness analysis as applied to instructional technology. Unpublished doctoral dissertation. Area of Instructional Design, Development and Evaluation, Syracuse University, Syracuse, New York

McLagan P A, Bedrick D 1983 Models for excellence: The results of the ASTD training and development competency study. *Train. Dev. J.* 37(6): 10–20

Mulder M 1992 Toward a comprehensive framework on training and development in business and industry. *Int. J. Lifelong Educ.*

Mulder M, Spitholt W E, Barents A M C 1991 Cost-effectiveness of curriculum revision. *Journal of European Industrial Training* 15(7): 8–16

Nadler L (ed.) 1984 *The Handbook of Human Resource Development*. Wiley, New York.

Smith M E 1987 Measuring results. In: Craig R L (ed.) 1987 *Training and Development Handbook. A Guide to Human Resource Development*, 3rd ed. McGraw-Hill, New York

Spencer L M Jr 1984 How to calculate the costs and benefits of an HRD program. *Training* 21(7): 40–51

Swanson R A, Sleezer C M 1987 Training effectiveness evaluation. *Journal of European Industrial Training*. 11(4): 7–16

Further Reading

Cascio W F 1982 *Costing Human Resources: The Financial Impact of Behavior in Organizations*. Van Nostrand Reinhold, New York

Cohen S I 1985 S Cost-benefit analysis of industrial training. *Econ. Educ. Rev.* 4(4): 327–39

Jackson T 1989 *Evaluation: Relating Training to Business Performance*. Kogan Page, London

Kearsly G 1982 *Costs, Benefits, and Productivity in Training Systems*. Addison-Wesley, Reading, Massachusetts

Mulder M, Nijhoff W J, Brinkerhoff R O 1995 (eds.) *Corporate Training for Effective Performance*. Kluwer Academic Publishers, Boston, Massachusetts

Niemic R, Baker E T 1987 *Cost-effectiveness in Business and Industrial Training*. Temple University, Center for Research in Human Development and Education, Philadelphia, Pennsylvania

Schmidt F L, Hunter J E, Pearlman K 1982 Assessing the economic impact of personnel programs on workforce productivity. *Personnel Psychology* 35: 333–47

Spencer L M Jr 1986 *Calculating Human Resource Costs and Benefits. Cutting Costs and Improving Productivity*. Wiley, New York.

Swanson R A, Gradous D B 1988 *Forecasting Financial Benefits of Human Resource Development*. Jossey-Bass, San Francisco, California

Evaluation of Public Training: Cost-Effectiveness

P. A. Boot and M. G. Drewes

This entry offers an overview of studies on the labor market effects of public training programs for adults. More general types of adult education and initial training programs for young people such as apprenticeships are not dealt with. The entry is organized as follows. First, public training programs are defined, and evaluation criteria and techniques reviewed. Second, examples are given of evaluation studies conducted in countries such as the United States, Sweden, the Federal Republic of Germany and the Netherlands. Third, the conclusions for policy-making and suggestions for future research are presented.

Public training programs are defined as programs in which public funds are invested. They exist on a boundary between labor market policy and educational policy. The instruments for implementation, which differ from country to country, may involve legal frameworks, reliance on market mechanisms, and cooperation with employers' organizations and trade unions, both at central and regional levels.

Two types of public training programs can be distinguished. The most common type involves training for unemployed adults and workers faced with a high redundancy risk. New Zealand and Sweden and, to a lesser extent, Canada, Finland, France, Germany, Norway, the Netherlands, and the United Kingdom are relatively active in this respect. The second type involves public support for the training of employed adults. This is less common but occurs in Denmark, Greece, and Ireland. Denmark is the only Organisation for Economic Co-operation and Development (OECD) country in which public support for enterprise training is the main option.

Public training programs usually have several objectives. The improvement of the labor market position of trainees and the functioning of labor markets are the most important. Training programs are usually targeted on the unemployed or economically and educationally disadvantaged adults, but other priorities may also be identified—for example, helping women into jobs dominated by men.

1. Evaluation Criteria

The value of training lies in the future, and one therefore has to judge whether the people receiving treatment will subsequently find employment and improve their productivity and earnings. According to follow-up studies conducted in several countries, the proportion of ex-trainees finding a job soon afterwards is generally in the order of 70 to 80 percent (OECD 1990 p. 37). But this information does not answer any basic question if it is not known how many people would have entered employment if the training, or its public support, had not taken place. Employment rates some months after the completion of a training program provide insight into the cyclical stage of a country's economy, but may say nothing about the true effects of training in the absence of a yardstick for comparison. More sophisticated evaluation studies are therefore needed in order to determine the effectiveness and eventually the future of public training programs. Four types of evaluation criteria can be relevant: trainee profiles, labor market effectiveness, financial efficiency, and organizational effectiveness.

The profile of the trainees is an important criterion if the aim is to improve the position of defined target groups such as immigrants and ethnic minorities or the urban poor. A high participation rate of these groups —according to age, labor market position, gender, or level of education—is in itself often considered a success. Labor market effectiveness is often judged against criteria such as the degree to which trainees find work, improve the quality of their work, and increase productivity and income—compared with the situation in which no training would have taken place. Financial efficiency takes account of both the costs of training and possible macroeconomic effects, for example, the influence on the competitiveness of subsidized firms. Organizational effectiveness can be assessed in terms of the way in which programs are run in different regions, how trainees are selected, and whether administrators cooperate with training institutions. The content of the curriculum and the effectiveness of didactic approaches are seldomly evaluated.

In short, most evaluations of public training programs aim at finding out: Who took part? What was the labor market effect? Was this the effect intended? What were the costs? Did any side effects occur? How was the program implemented and organized?

2. Evaluation Methods and Techniques

The main challenge facing impact studies is to develop a satisfactory counter-factual situation against which program performance can be measured. A number of different approaches have been tried (Björklund 1990). A simple one is to ask participants what their behavior would have been in the absence of the program and whether they feel their position has been improved. This method is highly subjective and does not give precise information. Another is to compare the situation before and after the program, which does not take deadweight effects (labor market behavior without participation) into account. A third and often used method is to utilize a comparison group design. This approach is often based on an economic theory of the way in which people behave, and it uses statistical methods.

However, it is extremely difficult to match participants and nonparticipants on characteristics such as motivation and attitude. One can therefore not be sure if the differences observed between the comparison groups are real or artifacts attributable to pre-existing differences. The problem is that nonobserved differences between participants and nonparticipants are bound to occur, and these are likely to influence both participation itself and eventual outcomes. This is known as selection bias.

Basically there are two methods for coping with this problem. In the experimental approach, individuals from a target group are randomly assigned either to the experiment group that is offered the program, or to a control group that is not permitted to take part. If properly applied, this approach ensures that there are no systematic differences between the groups and any differences noted afterward can be attributed to the program. The second method is to look for ways to diminish the degree of inaccuracy of the matched comparison group design. This is called the "nonexperimental method."

Although evaluations have become more technically sophisticated during the 1980s, several problems remain unsolved. For example, the costs of training are seldomly considered. Another drawback is that average and marginal effects of programs are usually not investigated.

3. Country Studies

The effects of public training programs in four countries are examined in the remainder of this entry: the United States, Sweden, Germany, and the Netherlands. Together these give a broad impression of current practice in the developed countries.

The United States spends most on labor market training and has a tradition in carefully designing evaluation studies, but lacks a well-developed vocational training system. The Federal Republic of Germany is the second spender and an example of organized cooperation between employers' organizations and trade unions in both initial and postinitial education. Sweden is well-known for its "active" labor market policy. The Netherlands have an average range of instruments and reach of trainees. Together these four countries account for 55 percent of total expenditure on public training for adults in all OECD countries.

3.1 The United States

The United States has a long tradition of evaluating public training programs. However, in the 1980s, a discussion broke out regarding the validity of evaluation findings.

The main training program is the Job Training Partnership Act (JTPA), established in 1983 to replace the Comprehensive Employment and Training Act (CETA). It is designed to be predominantly administered by state government in collaboration with local organizations representing the private business community. Each JTPA program has specific eligibility requirements. Among the most important programs are training services for economically disadvantaged youths and adults (JTPA, title IIA) and the summer youth employment and training program (JTPA, title IIB) to assist disadvantaged youth. The Job Training Partnership Act includes classroom training, on-the-job training, job search assistance, and work experience programs.

From the beginning of CETA in 1973, an effort was made to establish an evaluation system to provide estimates of the impact of programs on a regular basis. Each calendar quarter information was collected on a sample of CETA participants. The randomly selected participants were interviewed shortly after enrolling in CETA and on two or three occasions afterwards. Earnings data were matched with the participants' data. Individuals from the census were used to form control groups. Barnow (1987) gives an overview and comparison of the most important evaluation studies, summarizing how difficult it is to draw strong conclusions about the effectiveness of the program as income increases, since this is the most important criterion in the United States. Most of the studies found an overall earnings impact of about US \$200 to US \$600 per year, but negative impacts for youth and for men were found too (Barnow 1987 p. 159). All the studies found much larger impacts for women than men, with roughly equal impacts for White and minority women. The estimated impacts were generally similar for White and minority men. For women the estimates range from zero to large positive impacts, while for men they range from significantly negative to significantly positive effects.

The Comprehensive Employment and Training Act offered several program activities (as its successor JTPA has), and the studies were fairly consistent in their rankings. The highest estimated impacts on earnings were found for public service employment and on-the-job training. The estimates for classroom training were generally lower, but with a very broad range of estimated impacts. The conclusion reached is that there is an uncomfortably wide range of estimates of the impact of CETA training on earnings despite the fact that the research generally addresses the same

basic question with the same underlying data set (Riddell 1991).

The studies conducted in the United States were weak in modeling the selection process and in developing matched comparison groups. Work by Lalonde (1986) and Fraker and Maynard (1987) also indicate the problems of using nonexperimental data. They tested nonexperimental methods of evaluation where the true impact was known from an experiment for participants in supported work. Not only does the magnitude of the net-impact estimates differ substantially, but also, for many of the estimates, the qualitative judgment about the impacts. Nonexperimental methods cannot be relied upon to produce accurate estimates of program impact. Alternative analytic models, like estimates of the difference in earnings between pre- and post-program periods caused by changes in personal characteristics and environmental conditions were no solution either. In contrast, the estimates obtained from experimental data are essentially unaffected by differences in econometric specification.

The overall conclusion with a control group was that supported work—in many respects similar to CETA programs—had no long-term impact for youth and modest positive impacts for welfare recipients (Fraker and Maynard 1987 p. 217). The decision by the United States Department of Labor to employ experimental methods in the evaluation of the JTPA reflects this pessimistic assessment of the utility of nonexperimental methods.

3.2 Sweden

Sweden has a comprehensive labor market policy: 70 percent of the resources is devoted to active measures, and 30 percent to handouts, while in most other countries this ratio is the other way round.

Ever since the 1960s, the Swedish authorities have actively supported various forms of adult education, including labor market training. This had a very strong expansion from the beginning of the 1960s (10,000 annually) to its peak in the late 1970s (50,000 annually). It often takes the form of bottleneck training (i.e., training programs for key areas in which a shortage of skilled labor occurs or is anticipated). This training takes place in some 100 employment training centers (AMU) which, until 1986, were administered jointly by the National Board of Education and the National Labor Market Board (AMS). Since 1986 the AMUs have been organized on a commercial basis.

One would expect that a country with such an active labor market policy would have an ambitious evaluation program. In fact, evaluation research is limited in scope, especially in comparison with the United States. Little cost–benefit information is available as a consequence. The AMS has carried out follow-up studies, in which ex-trainees were asked six months after finishing the program about their employment situation. It is found that 60-70 percent was employed, and in general incomes were 5 to 11 percent higher in real terms 2 years after the training (OECD 1989).

Björklund (1991) summarizes relevant studies, published in Swedish. Research using data collected from 1969 to 1980, taking into account time-lag effects, found a significant negative difference for the first year: participation in labor market training gives lower weekly earnings (−9%) than being employed. In a study on vocational labor market training, register information on yearly incomes from employment was collected for the years 1980 to 1983, for both training participants and a comparison group of unemployed job-seekers. Significant positive effects were obtained for 1982 and 1983. The training effect was much higher for foreign citizens than for Swedes, for women than for men, for handicapped than for others, and for those lacking previous vocational training.

The labor market situation of 900 young Stockholm people was monitored by means of a survey in 1981, and their labor market experience up to 1985 was described by means of three additional interviews (Ackum 1989). The basic specification does not suffer from sample selection and endogenity biases. Being unemployed rather than staying outside the workforce turned out to have a negative impact on hourly earnings compared to being regularly employed. Participation in labor market training and temporary relief work did not significantly improve subsequent earnings compared to being unemployed. Björklund (1986) suggests that, although the training effect for average participants is positive, this is not the case for a marginal participant. This may indicate a relative "overkill" of training possibilities.

3.3 Federal Republic of Germany

The responsibility for labor market policy in the Federal Republic of Germany is spread between the government, the employers' organizations, and the trade unions. Labor market policy is financed partly by employers and employees (2% of the wage bill), and the government, who replenishes this amount according to need. This has been the case since 1980.

Between 1975 and 1983, 60 to 70 percent of the expenses for labor market policy were spent on educational measures, like vocational courses, and the important program for Further Training and Retraining (FuU).

Schellhaas (1991) mentions that in Germany the impact of the program on employment is the main evaluation question, even though other variables, such as increase in income and crime prevention, may also be considered. The policymakers seem to be more interested in the participation rate than in the net results of a program, and they tend to use the difference in the labor market position before and after training as a success criterion.

In Germany no social experiments with a control group or a counter-factual situation have been carried out. Instead, interview techniques and the nonexperimental approach were used, in which control groups of nonparticipants are composed on the basis of characteristics similar to those of participants. Different methods are employed to combat the "selection bias" of the nonexperimental approach. A simple one was used in the evaluation of the Employment Program for Special Regions in the early 1980s. The sign of the potential error was described and assessed only qualitatively. For the goal (political decision-making), this was considered to be sufficient.

To demonstrate the practice of evaluation in Germany, a closer look at the main training measure, the FuU, may suffice. Until the early 1980s this program was evaluated by the Institute of Labor Market and Occupational Research (IAB) by interviewing a large sample (i.e., 40,000) of the population. From these data there is no evidence which of the participants benefited most. In 1979–80 a control group was used. It was shown that participants older than 45 years improved their position in the labor market most when compared with nonparticipants, although they had a higher unemployment rate after finishing the program compared with younger participants. The positive effect of the program for older participants was stronger for the less-educated and for those with bad health.

Some doubt exists as to the quality of the findings in these studies of program impact. They can be criticized because adequate comparison groups were not formed and because information on major variables such as wages and the level and kind of employment contract were not collected. In another, more sophisticated study in 1984, a sample of trainees in Hamburg were interviewed and a control group was formed out of unemployed nonparticipants. The control group was carefully matched on variables like original occupation, qualification level, duration of unemployment, age, and sex. The results were as follows: Of the participants, 69 percent were employed 9 months after finishing the program compared with 52 percent of the control group; the majority of the participants had a higher wage compared with their previous wage and the control group; and the rise in income was larger for the participants than for the control group.

3.4 The Netherlands

Since 1991 Dutch manpower policy activities have been and still are, a shared responsibility of the Ministry of Social Affairs and Employment, employers' organizations, and trade unions. There are 28 Regional Employment Boards apart from the Central Employment Board. All of these are tripartite bodies. Public labor market training reached 68,000 persons in 1984. By 1990, this figure had risen to 163,000.

Public training programs have been incidentally evaluated since 1985, and inflow and outflow rates are registered by the employment offices. Dutch evaluations have varied from counts of enrollment and completion rates and assessments of the effect immediately subsequent to the training, to studies using quasi-experimental designs. A study on the effects of the vocational training centers serves as an example of the latter approach (De Koning et al. 1987). These institutes offer courses for the unemployed, lasting seven months on average. A control group was formed by matching three unemployed persons to each trainee. The results showed that 79 percent of the trainees and 68 percent of the control group found a job, but the former needed less time to do so than the latter. The participants and those in the control group were followed up nine months subsequent to the first interview. A slightly higher percentage of the ex-trainees was in employment at that time compared with the control group.

It is common in the Netherlands for training centers to be paid a lump sum fee per trainee. Thus the fewer trainees, the less the income for the organization. This incentive may have an adverse effect on the use of strict criteria for selection. The same may happen in cases where completion rates are used as a basis for funding. The phenomenon hinted at is important because evaluation studies carried out in the Netherlands indicate that the selection of trainees in part determines the effectiveness of training programs. This finding is especially important if one considers that some research studies show that public training is particularly effective for target groups such as the long-term unemployed and ethnic minorities. Public training must therefore be organized in such a way that the interests of the suppliers do not interfere with program objectives.

4. Implications for Policy

The countries examined in this entry differ in terms of training practice and the scope and extent of the evaluation activities they support. Yet despite this diversity some general policy conclusions can be drawn.

First, it is concluded that public training programs form an important element of labor market policy. Although the evidence can be questioned on methodological grounds, training programs seem to be especially effective for women. Additionally, on-the-job training seems to be more successful than classroom training. Effective programs often aim at combining training and work experience.

Second, the suppliers of public training are often rewarded according to the percentage of participants obtaining steady employment subsequent to the activity. Hence there is a danger that only those trainees are selected who are judged to have a high potential for being successful. This may be contrary to what is intended.

Third, most evaluation studies are necessarily limited to only one or two outcome variables. Thus there may be unforeseen effects.

Four, most evaluation studies have only limited value for policy-making because the costs of training are not examined and no insights are provided concerning questions such as which programs are best for which target groups and how effectiveness might be improved.

5. Implications for Research

The first conclusion is that several major evaluation problems have not yet been solved, despite recent advances in methodology. The debate over the relative merits of experimental versus nonexperimental methods is especially heated. A priori verdicts on the value of experimental versus nonexperimental methods cannot be made since their usefulness depends on the situation.

A second implication is that different assessment criteria need to be employed. Not only is the effect on earnings relevant, but also the contribution of public training to general labor market goals. The relative performance of the different providers should also be considered.

Third, quantitative data on training and other labor market measures need to be systematically collected on a regular basis. The data must be sufficiently rich, so that different methods can be used in measuring possible outcomes.

See also: Economics of Adult Education and Training; Government Role in Adult Education and Training; Market Failure in Adult Education and Training; Evaluation of Industry Training: Cost-Effectiveness; Measurement of Industry Training

References

Ackum S 1989 *Youth Unemployment Labour Market Programmes, and Subsequent Earnings.* Work Paper 10. Uppsala University, Uppsala

Barnow B S 1987 The impact of CETA programs on earnings. A review of the literature. *J. Hum. Resources* 22(2): 157–93

Björklund A 1986 *Policies for Labor Market Adjustment in Sweden.* Work Paper 163. Industrial Institute for Economic and Social Research, Stockholm

Björklund A 1990 What do we know about the effects of employment training. In: Nordic Council of Ministers 1990 *Nordic Labour Market Policies and Labour Market Research.* Nordic Council, Copenhagen

Björklund A 1991 *Evaluation of Labour Market Policy in Sweden.* OECD, Paris

De Koning J, Koss M, Verkaik A 1987 *De arbeidsmarkteffecten van het centrum voor (administratieve) vakopleiding van volwassenen*. Ministerie van Sociale Zaken en Werkgelegenheid, The Hague

Fraker T, Maynard R 1987 The adequacy of comparison group designs for evaluations of employment-related programs. *J. Hum. Resources* 22: 194–227

Lalonde R J 1986 Evaluating the econometric evaluations of training programs with experimental data. *Am. Econ. Review* 76(4): 604–20.

Organisation for Economic Co-operation and Development 1990 *Labour Market Policies for the 1990s*. OECD, Paris

Riddell C 1991 Evaluation of manpower and training programs: The North American experience. In: Organisation for Economic Co-operation and Development 1991 *Evaluating Labour Market and Social Programmes: The State of a Complex Art*. OECD, Paris

Schellhaas H 1991 *Evaluation Strategies and Methods with Regard to Labour Market Programmes: A German Perspective*. OECD, Paris

Further Reading

Allaart P 1988 *The Labour Market in Five Small European Countries*. Ministry of Social Affairs and Labor, The Hague

Björklund A 1988 What experiments are needed for manpower policy. *J. Hum. Resources* 23(2): 267–77

Hodgson D 1991 Training policy and employment generation. *Int. J. Manpower* 12(4): 28–31

De Koning J 1991 *Evaluatie van arbeidsvoorzienings-maatregelen: The State of the Art*. Ministry of Social Affairs and Labor, The Hague

Moffitt R 1991 Program evaluation with nonexperimental data. *Eval. Rev.* 15(3): 291–314

Neubourg C de (ed.) 1991 *The Art of Full Employment*. North-Holland, Amsterdam

Organisation for Economic Co-operation and Development 1991 *Evaluating Labour Market and Social Programmes: The State of a Complex Art*. OECD, Paris

(b)   Measurement

Literacy: Research and Measurement

D. A. Wagner

Research on the causes and consequences of literacy and illiteracy has grown dramatically during the
1980s, yet much more needs to be known. Since there
exists a great variety of literacy programs for an
even larger number of sociocultural contexts, it should
come as no surprise that the effectiveness of literacy
programs has come under question, not only among
policymakers and specialists, but also among the
larger public. How effective are literacy campaigns?
What is the importance of political and ideological
commitment? Should writing and reading be taught together or separately? Should literacy programs include
numeracy as well? Is literacy retained following a
limited number of years of primary schooling or short-
term campaigns? How important are literacy skills
for the workplace? Is it important to teach literacy
in the individual's mother tongue? These and similar
questions—so central to the core of literacy work
around the world—remain without definitive answers,
in spite of the occasionally strong rhetoric in support
of one position or another. Basic and applied research,
along with effective program evaluation, are capable
of providing critical information that will not only lead
to greater efficiency in particular literacy programs,
but will also lead to greater public support of literacy
programs.

Research on literacy can reveal key policy areas
which need to be addressed, as well as methodologies
for assessment and monitoring which will be crucial in
the coming years. This entry summarizes some of the
major areas of literacy research and measurement, and
offers some critical areas for future examination.

1. Literacy Research in Global Perspective

There are three general domains in literacy work
that are likely to be the subject of greater attention
in the 1990s and beyond and will determine to a
large extent whether attempts at improving global
literacy will be successful. Each of these is reviewed
below.

1.1 Defining Literacy: Operationalization for Measurement

With the multitude of experts and published books on
the topic, one would suppose that there would be a
fair amount of agreement as to how to define the term
"literacy." On the one hand, most specialists would
agree that the term connotes aspects of reading and
writing; on the other hand, major debates continue to
revolve around such issues as what specific abilities
or knowledge count as literacy, and what "levels" can
and should be defined for measurement. The term
"functional literacy" has often been employed, as
originally defined by Gray (1956 p 19): "A person is
functionally literate when he has acquired the knowledge and skills in reading and writing which enable him
to engage effectively in all those activities in which
literacy is normally assumed in his culture or group."

While functional literacy has a great deal of appeal
because of its implied adaptability to a given cultural
context, the term can be very awkward for research
purposes. For example, it is unclear in an industrialized nation like the United Kingdom what level of
literacy should be required of all citizens. Does a coal
miner have different needs than a barrister? Similarly,
in a Third World country, does an illiterate woman
need to learn to read and write in order to take her
prescribed medicine correctly, or is it more functional
(and cost-effective) to have her school-going child
read the instructions to her? The use of the term
"functional," based on norms of a given society, is
inadequate precisely because adequate norms are so
difficult to establish.

An adequate, yet more fluid, definition of literacy
is "... a characteristic acquired by individuals in
varying degrees from just above none to an indeterminate upper level. Some individuals are more or less
literate than others, but it is really not possible to
speak of literate and illiterate persons as two distinct
categories" (UNESCO 1957). Since there exist dozens
of orthographies for hundreds of languages in which
innumerable context-specific styles are in use every

858

day, it would seem ill-advised to select a universal operational definition. Attempts to use newspaper reading skills as a baseline (as in certain national surveys) may seriously underestimate literacy if the emphasis is on comprehension of text (especially if the text is a national language not well understood by the individual). Such tests may overestimate literacy if the individual is asked simply to read aloud the passage, with little or no attempt at the measurement of comprehension. Surprisingly, there have been relatively few attempts to design a battery of tests from low literacy ability to high ability which would be applicable across the complete range of possible languages and literacies in any society, such that a continuum of measurement possibilities might be achieved. UNESCO, which provides worldwide statistical comparisons of literacy, relies almost entirely on data provided by its member countries, even though the measures are often unreliable indicators of literacy ability.

At least part of the controversy over the definition of literacy lies in how people have attempted to study literacy. The methodologies chosen, which span the social sciences, usually reflect the disciplinary training of the investigator. Anthropologists provide in-depth ethnographic accounts of single communities, while trying to understand how literacy is woven into the fabric of community cultural life. By contrast, psychologists and educators have typically chosen to study measurable literacy abilities using tests and questionnaires, usually ignoring contextual and linguistic factors. Both these approaches (as well as history, linguistics, sociology, and computer science) have value in achieving an understanding of literacy. There is no easy resolution to this problem, but it is clear that a broad-based conception of literacy is required not only for a valid understanding of the term, but also for developing appropriate policy actions (Venezky et al. 1990).

Because literacy is a cultural phenomenon—adequately defined and understood only within each culture in which it exists—it is not surprising that definitions of literacy may never be permanently fixed. Whether literacy includes computer skills, mental arithmetic, or civic responsibility will depend on how public and political leaders of each society define the term and its use. Researchers can help in this effort by trying to be clear about which definition or definitions they choose to employ in their work. For recent overviews of literacy in international context, see Wagner and Puchner (1992) and Wagner (1992).

1.2 Acquisition of Literacy

The study of literacy acquisition has been greatly influenced by research undertaken in the industrialized world. Much of this research might be better termed the acquisition of reading and writing skills, with an emphasis on the relationship between cognitive skills, such as perception and memory, and reading

skills, such as decoding and comprehension. Further, most of this work has been carried out with school-aged children, rather than with adolescents or adults. Surprisingly little research on literacy acquisition has been undertaken in the Third World, where researchers have focused primarily on adult acquisition rather than on children's learning to read. This latter phenomenon appears to be a result of the emphasis to promote adult literacy in the developing world, while usually ignoring such problems, until quite recently, in industrialized societies.

Despite these gaps in the research literature, certain general statements are relatively well established as to how literacy is acquired across different societies. Almost two decades ago, Downing (1973) published *Comparative Reading*, which surveyed the acquisition of reading skills across different languages and orthographies. He found that mastery of the spoken language is a typical prerequisite for fluent reading comprehension in that language, although there exist many exceptions. Another finding is that in many alphabets children first learn to read by sounding out words with a memorized set of letter-sound correspondences. It is now known that there are many exceptions to this generalization. There are, of course, languages which are not written in alphabets (e.g., Chinese and Japanese). There also appear to be large individual differences in learning styles within literacy communities. Finally, many individuals can read and write languages which they may not speak fluently.

Some specialists have stressed the importance of class structure and ethnicity/race as explications of differential achievement among literacy learners. Ogbu (1978), for example, claimed that many minority children in the United States are simply unmotivated to learn to read and write in the cultural structure of the school. This approach to understanding social and cultural differences in literacy learning has received increased attention in that it avoids blaming the individual for specific cognitive deficits (as still happens), while focusing intervention strategies more on changes in the social and political structure of schooling or the society.

Finally, it has been assumed that learning to read in one's "mother tongue" or first language is always the best educational policy for literacy provision, whether for children or adults. Based on some important research studies undertaken in the 1960s, it has generally been taken for granted that individuals who have had to learn to read in a second language are at a disadvantage relative to others who learn in their mother tongue. While this generalization may still be true in many of the world's multilingual societies, more recent research has shown that there may be important exceptions. In one such study, it was found that Berber-speaking children who had to learn to read in Standard Arabic in Moroccan schools were able to read in fifth grade just as well as children who were native speakers of Arabic (Wagner, Spratt, and Ezzaki

1989). Adequate research on nonliterate adults who learn to read in a second versus a first language has yet to be undertaken.

In sum, considerable progress has been made in understanding the acquisition of literacy in children and adults, but primarily in industrialized societies. Far less is known about literacy acquisition in a truly global perspective, and in multilingual societies. Since the majority of nonliterate people live in these areas of the world, much more needs to be known if literacy provision is to be improved in the coming decades.

1.3 Retention of Literacy

The term "educational wastage" is common in the literature on international and comparative education, particularly with respect to the Third World. This term typically refers to the loss, usually by dropping out, of children who do not finish what is thought to be the minimum educational curriculum of a given country (often 5 to 8 years of primary schooling). Most specialists who work within this area gather data on the number of children who enter school each year, the number who progress on to the next grade, those who repeat a given year (quite common in many Third World countries), and those who quit school altogether. The concept of wastage, then, refers to those children for whom an economic investment in educational resources has already been made, but who do not complete the appropriate level of studies.

The issue of literacy retention is crucial here, for it is not actually the number of school leavers or graduates that really matters for a society, but rather what they learn and retain from their school years, such as literacy skills. When students drop out of an educational program, a society is wasting its resources because those individuals (children or adults) will not reach some presumed threshold of minimum learning without losing what has been acquired. Thus, retention of learning (or literacy, in particular) is a key goal of educational planners around the world. There are as yet only a small number of research studies published on this question, and their results are highly contradictory. Some show that there is a "relapse" into illiteracy for those who have not received sufficient instruction, while others demonstrate no serious loss (e.g., Wagner, Spratt, Klein, and Ezzaki 1989).

2. Literacy Measurement

2.1 Areas of Debate in Literacy Assessment

In order to provide worldwide statistical comparisons, UNESCO (1977, 1978) has relied almost entirely on data provided by its member countries. These countries, in turn, typically rely on national census information, which most often determines literacy ability by self-assessment questionnaires and/or by the proxy variable of years of primary schooling. Many specialists now agree that such measures are likely to be unreliable indicators of literacy ability. Nonetheless, up to the early 1990s, change in literacy measurement has been slow in coming, even though various efforts have been undertaken at the national level (see below).

There is considerable diversity of opinion as to the usefulness of classifying individuals in the traditional manner of "literate" versus "illiterate." Several decades ago, when Third World countries began to enter the United Nations, it was common to find that the vast majority of the adult populations of these countries had never gone to school nor learned to read and write. It was relatively easy in those contexts to simply define all such individuals as "illiterate." The situation in the early 1990s is much more complex, as some contact with primary schooling, nonformal education programs, and the mass media is now made by the vast majority of families in the Third World. Thus, even though parents may be illiterate, it is not unusual for one or more of their children to be able to read and write to some degree. For this reason, it would seem that simple dichotomies—still in use by some international agencies and most national governments—ought to be avoided, since they tend to misrepresent the range or continuum of literacy abilities that are common to most contemporary societies.

As noted earlier, work on adult literacy has frequently derived its methodologies from the study of reading development in children. This is true of assessment as well, where the diagnosis of individual reading difficulties has held sway for many years, in both children and adults. This diagnostic model of assessment assumes that individuals who do not read well have some type of cognitive deficit which can (often) be remediated if properly diagnosed by a skilled professional. There is little doubt that this model does apply to many adults who have not learned to read, but who have attended school. However, the majority of the world's population of low literates and illiterates (located primarily in developing countries) have received little or no schooling, making the diagnostic method far less relevant. For this latter population, detailed diagnostic measures are unimportant relative to the need for better understanding of who goes to school, what is learned, and which particular social groups are most in need of basic skills. In such cases, as discussed below, low-cost household surveys may be a better assessment technique than diagnostic instruments.

Most countries have formulated an explicit language policy which states which language or languages have official status. Often, the decision on national or official language(s) is based on such factors as major linguistic groups, colonial or postcolonial history, and the importance of a given language to the concerns of economic development. Official languages are also those commonly used in primary school, though there may be differences between languages used in beginning schooling and those used later on. The use of mother tongue instruction in both primary and adult education remains a topic of continuing debate (Dutcher 1982). While there is usually general agreement that official language(s) ought to be assessed in a literacy survey, there may be disagreement over the assessment of literacy in nonofficial languages (where these have a recognized and functional orthography). In many countries, there exist numerous local languages which have varying status with respect to the official language; how these languages and literacies are included in such surveys is a matter of debate. For example, in certain predominantly Muslim countries in sub-Saharan Africa (e.g., Senegal or Ghana), the official language of literacy might be French or English, while Arabic—which is taught in Islamic schools and used by a sizable population for certain everyday and religious tasks—is usually excluded from official literacy censuses. Many specialists now agree that most (if not all) literacies should be surveyed; to ignore such abilities is to underestimate national human resources.

Comparability of data—across time and countries —is a major concern for planning agencies. If definitions, categories, and classifications vary, it becomes difficult if not impossible to compare data collected from different surveys. On the other hand, if comparability is the primary goal, with little attention to the validity of the definitions, categories, and classifications for the sample population, then the data become virtually meaningless. International and national needs, definitions, and research strategies may or may not come into conflict over the issue of comparability, depending on the particular problem addressed. For example, international agencies continue to suggest that literacy be measured in terms of the number of "literates" and "illiterates." For most countries, this type of classification presents few problems at the level of census information, and it provides international agencies with a cross-national framework for considering literacy by geographic or economic regions of the world. On the other hand, national planners may want to know the effects of completion of certain grades of primary or secondary school, or of a literacy campaign, on levels of literacy attainment, so that a simple dichotomy would be insufficient. Household literacy surveys, because more time may be devoted to in-depth questioning, offer the opportunity to provide a much more detailed picture of literacy and its demographic correlates than has been previously available.

2.2 Household Literacy Surveys

Assessment surveys have employed varying approaches to defining literacy skill levels in different countries. For example, some assessment surveys have focused on "ability to read aloud" from a newspaper in the national language; some have included basic arithmetic (numeracy) skills; while still others have focused on being able to write one's name or read a bus schedule. Two main types of literacy survey methods—self-assessment and direct measurement— have been utilized within widely differing contexts (see *Measurement of Adult Education*).

Most national literacy data collections in the world have utilized self-assessment techniques, which are operationalized by simply asking the individual one or more questions of the sort: "Can you read and write?" Occasionally, census takers collect information on which language or languages pertain to the above question, but rarely have time or resources been invested beyond this point. Analysis of the relationship between self-assessment and direct measurement of literacy abilities has rarely been sought, so that the reliability of self-assessment methods is very problematic.

Direct measurement of literacy typically involves tests which are constructed with the aim of obtaining performance or behavioral criteria for determining literacy and/or numeracy abilities in the individual. The large number and variety of literacy and numeracy assessment instruments precludes a complete discussion in this brief review. Objective measures rely primarily on test items to elicit valid and reliable data from the individual, with rather strict controls on the context and structure of the test. An example would be a multiple choice test where the individual is presented with a short paragraph of text and is asked to choose, among four items, the item which best describes some particular piece of information mentioned in the paragraph. These measures are usually quite reliable in school settings and for silent reading, where test-retest correlations and cross-test correlations may be highly significant. Their use in nonschool settings and with low-literate adults is less well-known, since these tests assume a certain equivalence in "test-taking skill" across individuals tested. Such objective tests are particularly useful in settings where the interviewer has little prior experience in literacy assessment, since relatively little subjective interpretation of test performance is required.

The direct measurement of literacy skills using assessment instruments provides information on more refined categories than available in self-assessment, which usually provides merely a dichotomous categorization. In North America, two major literacy surveys have recently been completed: the Young Adult Literacy Assessment (Kirsch and Jungeblut 1986) in the United States, and the Canadian Literacy Survey (Statistics Canada 1988) in Canada. These two national sample surveys overlapped substantially in their methodology, providing in-depth individual assessments of reading, writing, and mathematics skills in both abstract and functional contexts. The nature of the assessment system allowed for a detailed breakdown of individual competencies, rivaling that obtainable in diagnostic tests. While the advantage of such in-depth information may be justifiable in the North American context, these surveys clearly represent the "high end" of both detailed analysis and cost in terms of household surveys.

For contexts such as in the Third World or in low-literate ethnic communities in industrialized countries, it may be useful to choose a categorical breakdown which would provide just enough information for use by policymakers, and which could be more easily and simply constructed. This "low-end" method of assessment is best exemplified in the model developed under the auspices of the United Nations National Household Survey Capability Program, and which has been undertaken in several countries, including Zimbabwe and Morocco (United Nations 1989, Wagner 1990). In this model, there are four main skill classifications which are proposed: (a) *non-literate* for a person who cannot read a text with understanding and write a short text in a significant national language, and who cannot recognize words on signs and documents in everyday contexts, and cannot perform such specific tasks as signing their name or recognizing the meaning of public signs; (b) *low-literate* for a person who cannot read a text with understanding and write a short text in a significant national language, but who can recognize words on signs and documents in everyday contexts, and can perform such specific tasks as signing their name or recognizing the meaning of public signs; (c) *moderate-literate* for a person who can, with some difficulty (i.e., makes numerous errors), read a text with understanding and write a short text in a significant national language; and (d) *high-literate* for a person who can, with little difficulty (i.e., makes few errors), read a text with understanding and write a short text in a significant national language. When these four categories are utilized in conjunction with other variables in the survey, it becomes possible to arrive at answers to questions often posed by policymakers, such as: How does literacy vary by age, grade, geographical region, language group, and so forth.

2.3 Measuring Literacy Levels

Beyond the broad category labels of literacy levels, there is little agreement on how actually to assign such labels to individuals. Does scoring above 50 percent on a test of paragraph comprehension qualify an individual as literate, non-literate or in-between? To a great extent, such labeling has been and continues to be arbitrary. In addition, while most assessment instruments utilize school-based and curriculum-based materials, there is increasing awareness among specialists of the importance of measuring "everyday" or practical literacy abilities. One method for dealing with literacy assessment is to determine the intersection of both literacy *skills* and *domains* of literacy practice (Kirsch and Jungeblut 1986, Wagner 1990).

There are a great many types of literacy tests, and a great number of skills which specialists have thought were important not only for the measurement of actual literacy ability, but also in terms of the underlying processes involved in being a competent reader or writer. Drawing on recent survey work, as described above, it is useful to think of literacy ability as involving at least four basic types of skills: decoding, comprehension, locating information, and writing.

Individuals who use literacy may perform literate functions on a wide array of materials; in addition, certain individuals may specialize in specific types of literate domains (e.g., lawyers, doctors, agricultural agents). Even individuals with low general levels of literacy skill may be able to cope successfully with written materials in a domain in which they have a great deal of practice (e.g., farm workers who often deal with insecticides). Since governments are generally interested in providing literacy for many categories of people, an assessment should sample across the material domains where literate functions are typically found, such as, single words, short phrases, tables and forms, and texts.

The estimation of literacy skills by text domains involves the use of a matrix of the intersection of literacy skills with the text domains in which literacy skills can be applied. This provides a breakdown of types of component skills in literacy. It should be understood that there is rarely consensus on which specific skills to test in literacy, and that any such matrix is necessarily arbitrary. Nonetheless, a matrix of literacy skills by domain can provide a useful method for collecting the appropriate ("low-end") amount of information needed for policy decisions, and it can be considerably less expensive than some of the comprehensive methods employed in the North American surveys.

3. New Areas of Literacy Research

Based on the growing concern about literacy levels across the globe, it seems clear that new domains of research will begin to open up, such as the topics described below.

3.1 Technology

There are new and exciting ideas about the utility of technology for literacy provision to children and adults. Much of this work is still in the early development stages, such as efforts to utilize synthetic speech to teach reading, or the use of multimedia displays (interactive video, audio tapes, and computer displays) to provide more sophisticated instruction than has been heretofore available. Technological solutions to instruction—known as computer-based education (CBE) or computer-assisted instruction (CAI)—have been used, primarily in industrialized nations, since the early 1980s, and the presence of microcomputers in the classrooms of schools has continued to grow at a phenomenal rate (Venezky and Osin 1991).

As many have pointed out, the cost of technology has been too high even for the educational programs for most industrial countries, and are therefore far beyond the means of the Third World. But the price-to-power ratio (the relative cost, for example, of a unit of computer memory or the speed of processing) continues to drop at an astounding rate. While the cost of the average microcomputer remained constant over the 1980s, the power of the 1990 computer is 10–100 times greater than that produced in 1980. If present trends continue, the capabilities for CAI and CBE literacy instruction are likely, by the year 2000, to go far beyond the elementary approaches of today.

3.2 Multisectoral Approaches

Literacy skills are utilized in many life contexts outside of academic settings. To date, most research and development has focused primarily on school-based settings. A major challenge rests in determining the ways that literacy can be fostered and utilized in everyday family and work settings. From a policy perspective, more needs to be known about how literacy education can be infused into the significant development work of other sectors, such as agriculture and health. In these two sectors, literacy is a major vehicle for innovation and knowledge dissemination, yet few studies have explored what levels of literacy determine the effectiveness of such dissemination.

3.3 Design of Materials

In developing countries, increased textbook provision has been viewed by donors and ministries of education as a key strategy for the improvement of school instruction (Heyneman and Jamison 1980). However, very little is known about how the design of instructional materials influences comprehension and learning. There are also enormous subject matter and national variations in conventions of text design. Some important work on the relationship between characteristics of textbook discourse and comprehension is being carried out that has implications for improving school textbooks, as well as materials for other sectors. For example, there is a special need to improve instructions for pharmaceutical and agricultural chemicals, whose safe and effective use requires performing complex cognitive tasks with procedural information that is often difficult to comprehend (Eisemon 1988).

3.4 Mother Tongue and Second Language Issues

As previously discussed many learners enrolled in adult education programs are being taught literacy in a second language. In developing countries, a significant proportion of these students are either illiterate in their mother tongue or receive only a few years of mother tongue instruction before a second, usually foreign, language is introduced as a medium of instruction. Poor second language literacy proficiency is a cause of high repetition and wastage rates, and of low achievement in academic subjects in primary and secondary schools with profound consequences for employment and other externalities of schooling.

Because of the significant debate on first and second language/literacy policy (often related to national issues of ethnicity and power), most government agencies worldwide have been reluctant to review such policies. However, there are a number of important areas of work which need to be addressed beyond the confines of this debate, such as: (a) Under what conditions should mother tongue literacy be a precondition for the introduction of second language literacy in school-based and nonformal settings? (b) How does the implementation of language-of-instruction policies affect literacy after schooling? (c) What are the effects of using second language literacy in school on wastage and grade repetition? (d) What are the implications of using the second language literacy for academic subjects like mathematics, science, health, nutrition, and agriculture? (e) What roles do orthographic similarity and dissimilarity play in transfer between mother tongue and second literacy? These and similar questions will need to be addressed before major progress can be made in improving literacy levels in national and international contexts.

4. Conclusion

The importance of research and measurement in literacy is that they can provide new paths to greater efficiency in literacy provision around the world. While no social program (including research) is without economic costs, such expenditures must be understood in the light of costs involved in not knowing how to carry out literacy programs practically and efficiently. Those who have argued that the literacy crisis is so great that the support of research is somehow wasteful are likely to be proven wrong. To invest resources in implementation without developing the means to learn from such programs is to call into question any purported gains in literacy work.

The decade of the 1990s appears to be a particularly good time to reinforce literacy efforts on a truly global scale. In spite of the clear need for cultural sensitivities and specificities, there may be important economies of scale as more is learned about literacy. Methodologies for pilot programs, assessment and evaluation, and computerized textbook preparation, as examples, may be transferable with local adaptations to varying cultural contexts. The need for literacy and other basic skills has never been greater, and the gap between literate and nonliterate lifestyles is becoming ever larger, with parallel growth in income disparities.

Literacy and learning are a part of the culture of every society. To produce major changes in literacy requires both a realistic understanding of the kinds of change which people and nations desire, and sustained support to provide appropriate instructional services.

See also: Literacy and Numeracy Models; Adult Literacy in the Third World; Literacy Testing and Assessment; Measurement of Adult Education; Statistics of Adult and Nonformal Education

References

Downing J 1973 *Comparative Reading*. Macmillan, New York

Dutcher N 1982 *The Use of First and Second Languages in Primary Education: Selected Case Studies*. World Bank Staff Working Paper, No. 504. World Bank, Washington, DC

Eisemon T E 1988 *Benefiting from Basic Education, School Quality and Functional Literacy in Kenya*. Pergamon, New York

Gray W S 1956 *The Teaching of Reading and Writing: An International Survey*. UNESCO, Paris

Heyneman S P, Jamison D T 1980 Student learning in Uganda: Textbook availability and other factors. *Comp. Educ. Rev.* 24(2): 206–20

Kirsch I, Jungeblut A 1986 *Literacy: Profiles of America's Young Adults*. Final report of the National Assessment of Educational Progress. ETS, Princeton, New Jersey

Ogbu J 1978 *Minority Education and Caste: The American System in Cross-cultural Perspective*. Academic Press, New York

Statistics Canada 1988 *A National Literacy Skill Assessment Planning Report*. Statistics Canada, Ottawa

UNESCO 1957 *World Illiteracy at Mid-century: A Statistical Study*. UNESCO, Paris

UNESCO 1977 *Statistics of Educational Attainment and Illiteracy*. UNESCO, Paris

UNESCO 1978 *Revised Recommendation Concerning the International Standardization of Educational Statistics*. UNESCO, Paris

United Nations 1989 *Measuring Literacy through Household Surveys: A Technical Study on Literacy Assessment and Related Topics through Household Surveys*. National Household Survey Capability Programme. United Nations, New York

Venezky R L, Osin L 1991 *The Intelligent Design of Computer-assisted Instruction*. Longman, New York

Venezky R, Wagner D A, Ciliberti B (eds.) 1990 *Towards Defining Literacy*. International Reading Association, Newark, Delaware

Wagner D A 1990 Literacy assessment in the Third World: An overview and proposed schema for survey use. *Comp. Educ. Rev.* 34(1): 112–38

Wagner D A 1992 *Literacy: Developing the future*. International Yearbook of Education, Vol. 43. UNESCO/International Bureau of Education, Geneva

Wagner D A, Puchner L (eds.) 1992 *World Literacy in the Year 2000: Research and Policy Dimensions*. Annals of the American Academy of Political and Social Science, Newbury Park, California

Wagner D A, Spratt J E, Ezzaki A 1989 Does learning to read in a second language always put the child at a disadvantage? Some counter-evidence from Morocco. *Appl. Psycholinguistics* 10: 31–48

Wagner D A, Spratt J E, Klein G D, Ezzaki A 1989 The myth of literacy relapse: Literacy retention among Moroccan primary school leavers. *Int. J. Educ. Dev.* 9: 307–15

Further Reading

Oxenham J 1980 *Literacy: Writing, Reading and Social Organization*. Routledge and Kegan Paul, London

Snow C E, Barnes W S, Chandler J, Goodman I F, Hemphill L 1991 *Unfulfilled Expectations: Home and School Influences on Literacy*. Harvard University Press, Cambridge, Massachusetts

OECD/Statistics Canada 1995 *Literacy, Economy and Society: Results of the First International Adult Literacy Survey*. OECD, Paris

Tuijnman A C, Kirsch I, Wagner D A (eds.) 1995 *Adult Basic Skills: Advances in Measurement and Policy Analysis*. Hampton Press, New York

Measurement of Adult Education

T. Scott Murray

Education has long been viewed as a key to economic and social development. Historically, however, those concerned with education and its impact on development have focused on the young. As long ago as 303 BC, Diogenes is known to have said "the foundation of every state is the education of its youth." More recently, however, and for a variety of reasons explained elsewhere, the focus has shifted in many countries to the education of adults.

This entry deals with the measurement of adult education seen from the perspective of a national statistical office. The task facing such institutions is to determine what data should be collected and how best to measure them. It is important to distinguish this perspective from that of others concerned with the learning enterprise, such as educators. The uses and users of data generated by official statistics agencies are varied. This entry cannot accommodate all views and concerns.

The entry is divided into four sections. The first

discusses the characteristics that distinguish adult education and the implications of these characteristics for measurement. The second and third sections describe the prevailing methodologies for measuring the stock and flow of educational activity. The final section deals with possible future directions for measurement.

1. Why Measure Adult Education?

Building on the economic literature developed around the theory of human capital, data pertaining to adult education should relate to two categories, namely the prevailing stock of educationally derived human capital observed in the population, and the flow or change in the stock caused by ongoing educational activity. Concerns about equity and efficiency add the need to measure input parameters, such as the resources devoted to education in a particular time period, and the characteristics of those receiving education. In most countries, adult education is provided by the public sector and education-related expenditures constitute a significant item in the national budget. Accordingly, researchers interested in public policy also try to measure the outcome or output of the education system. Output measures are needed in order to find out how efficient and effective the system is, and how education is linked to economic success.

The measurement of the stock and flow of adult education is not, however, straightforward. The very breadth of the concept is perhaps the most important factor which confounds measurement. Since education involves the acquisition of any knowledge or skills through instruction or study, one is, in one sense, trying to measure life itself.

Measures of adult education can take one of two distinct forms: they can be direct measures or indirect measures. Direct measurement implies the use of actual tests to determine a level of competency in a particular domain. In contrast, indirect measurement involves the use of proxy information, often derived from questionnaires or administrative records, to mirror variation in the underlying phenomenon of interest. Both direct and indirect measures can be derived from either administrative systems or through statistical surveys of the adult population.

Administrative capture is by far the simplest form of detection of education events. Where administrative systems exist, as in France and Sweden, data can be obtained at a much lower cost than when survey-based enquiries involving large samples of adults are needed for data collection. If provision is made to include unique identifiers, then administrative data can be linked longitudinally. Several problems are, however, common to the use of administrative data for statistical purposes. Administrative systems often lack consistent definitions. They also tend to only collect the variables related to the original purposes for which they were collected—that is, to support administrative functions. Unless the desire to use the data for statistical purposes is made explicit, administrative systems will omit many analytically meaningful variables, such as demographic characteristics. These problems can be overcome, but to do so requires considerable collaboration between governments, institutions providing adult education, and researchers.

2. Attributes in the Measurement of Adult Education

Before discussing how to go about measuring adult education, it is necessary to understand its attributes, since these may aid or confound measurement.

As a phenomenon, adult education is incredibly diverse and variable, rendering simple measurement impossible. The following attributes contribute to this intractability.

2.1 Variability in Duration

The first distinguishing attribute of adult education is the variability in duration. Some events, like enrollment in university, involve the commitment of significant amounts of an individual's time, often for periods of several years or more. At the other end of the spectrum lie very short, nonrecurring events geared toward learning a specific skill, such as learning how to use a word processing package or a fax machine. Whereas most long duration events are costly and highly institutionalized, the short duration events may be virtually costless and spontaneous, involving only the participants' leisure time. Events at both ends of this spectrum tend to have well-defined symbols of completion, such as the receipt of a degree or diploma in the case of university attendance and a certificate verifying mastery of a piece of software at the other. Somewhere in the middle lie a set of events, such as on-the-job training, which, while of long duration, may not be thought of as a learning event at all, at least not by the participants. From a measurement perspective, the longer the reference period the more difficult it will be for respondents to recall the less memorable, short duration, spontaneous events. It also has an impact on whether one chooses to accept proxy response in survey-based measures. Many surveys accept proxy reporting as a way of controlling response burden and collection costs. If one wants good reporting of the short events over a long reference period, one cannot rely on proxy reports. Those learning events with clearly defined symbols of outcome, such as the degrees, diplomas, or certificates granted on successful university completion, will help in aiding recall in survey-based estimates. These same events will usually be captured in administrative systems (see *Measurement of Industry Training*).

2.2 Variation in Motivation

Participants in education activity vary greatly in their underlying motivation for engaging in the activity, from coercive ("my company made me take it") to instrumental ("to improve my chances of advancement") to self-fulfillment ("I did it for enjoyment"). Disparate motivations complicate the task of presenting a coherent frame of reference to respondents in a survey. Few, if any, administrative systems capture information on motivation (see *Participation: Role of Motivation*).

2.3 Variation in Institutional Context

Another distinguishing feature of adult education is the diversity of institutional contexts within which the activity takes place, from the workplace to colleges and universities, from living rooms to union halls. Partly related to differences in motivation, variation in institutional contexts makes it difficult to present survey respondents with a consistent frame of reference to aid recall and reporting. Administrative systems related to the provision of education will invariably differ in coverage and content across institutional setting, rendering the compilation of systemwide statistics difficult (see *Providers of Adult Education: An Overview*).

2.4 Seasonal Variation

Like most aspects of human behavior, adult education and training exhibit distinct patterns of seasonal variation in many parts of the world. This variation is related to climate, seasonal fluctuations in economic activity, and a host of other variables.

Seasonal variation in the level of activity complicates measurement in that simple point-in-time measures can no longer be treated as representative of analytically meaningful periods such as reference years. Any survey purporting to generate reliable annual volume measures must, therefore, either spread the sample out over the year or stretch recall to a full year. For the events which they represent, administrative systems will capture seasonal variation.

2.5 Terminological Diversity

Related to the variability of duration, institutional context, motivation, and symbols of completion is the fact that participants in an adult education activity employ a diverse lexicon or terminology to describe what they are doing. What from an analytic point of view are equivalent activities can be variously called "going to school," "taking a course," "being enrolled in a program," "recreation," "learning," "taking training," "skill upgrading," "work experience," or a host of other descriptors. Terminological diversity makes the survey-based measurement of adult education complex, since any line of questioning must necessarily provide survey respondents with an equally diverse

set of cognitive clues to help them recall and report relevant events. The same problem is observed with systems based on administrative data. A good deal of effort must be expended on ensuring consistent reporting and coverage. The impact these effects can have on the actual data are often quite profound. Faced with a similar set of problems in a survey of volunteer activity, Statistics Canada doubled the measured rate of activity by changing the screening methodology and terminology used to one which reflected the nature of the phenomenon.

3. Measures of Educational Flow

A measure of educational flow can be used in attempting to answer the simple question "How much adult education is taking place?" As noted above, the answer to this question can be derived in two possible ways, through direct or indirect measurement.

3.1 Direct Measures of Educational Flow

The most obvious example of direct measures of educational flow are the tests administered either to gain access to further education or during the course of formal education, and the related summaries of performance, such as marks and grade point averages presented in transcripts. When combined with individual characteristics and measures of outcome, such as labor market success and life satisfaction, these measures offer enormous analytic potential. Their main shortcoming rests in the fact that they are only available for a subset of institutional settings (see *Recognition and Certification of Skill*).

3.2 Indirect Measures of Educational Flow

The answer to the methodological problems alluded to above would seem to rest in indirect survey-based approaches. The most successful survey-based studies to date have involved the use of an interviewer-administered questionnaire to collect a broad range of education related variables from large, usually "representative" samples of the adult population. This approach has been successfully employed in a number of countries, including Finland, Sweden, the Netherlands, and Canada, using either six- or twelve-month reference periods (Statistics Canada 1991, Noyelle and Benton 1992). In a few countries, such as the United States and Sweden, similar measures have been embedded in longitudinal studies (Tuijnman 1991). This approach has the distinct advantage of allowing the direct analysis of components and determinants of change.

Yet another class of indirect measures has been developed which involves statistical surveys of institutions, usually business establishments. These surveys (e.g., the CUTS survey conducted by EUROSTAT, the statistical agency of the EC in the mid-1990s) tend to collect a limited number of demographic variables, choosing rather to focus on types of training offered and cost. These studies are beset by a variety of methodological problems, the most important of which is the variation observed in record-keeping practices across industries and in the sizes of firms (see *Measurement of Industry Training*).

4. Measures of Educational Stock

Measures of educational stock involve the collection of data on the entire adult population. Were it a perfect world, the educational stock could be inferred at any given time by summing the lifetime additions or components of flow for the population. Unfortunately, the reality is far from ideal. Virtually no statistical system in the world has generated measures based on this principle of accumulation. As is shown below, there are grave problems with one of the key assumptions underlying this approach, namely that skill acquisition is nonsymmetrical, and that it can only be gained, not lost. Approaches to measuring educational stock are summarized below.

4.1 Indirect Measures of Educational Stock

By far the most common measures of educational stock are indirect measures derived from questions included in instruments used in national censuses of population. These questions typically identify: years of schooling completed; highest level of education attained; degrees, diplomas, and certificates; fields of study pursued; and so forth. Similar questions are standard in many sample surveys conducted by government authorities.

National censuses also often include questions asking respondents if they can read and write. Although these questions vary considerably in style and substance, collectively they suffer from relying on subjective judgment on the part of respondents. This subjectivity makes suspect comparisons between countries and over time.

4.2 Direct Measures of Educational Stock

Direct measures are rapidly being recognized as important tools in assessing the stock of education or of human capital. This recognition is being driven by a number of factors which collectively have had a negative impact on the perceived reliability of indirect or proxy measures of educational attainment. Proxy measures are only useful if they consistently reflect variation in the underlying characteristic of interest.

On a theoretical level, there has been a growing awareness of the legitimacy and importance of a far broader range of competencies than previously admitted into discussions of educational attainment (De Castell et al. 1986). At one extreme, this has

manifested itself in an appreciation for the success of some "primitive" cultures living in nondestructive harmony with the existing ecosystem. At the other extreme, those watching the development of postindustrial societies have noted the importance of oral communication and leadership skills in turning productive potential into reality. Few, if any, of the existing proxy measures reflect these insights.

There has been a renewed interest in literacy as an essential precursor to the acquisition of higher order competencies by adults. This interest has been tied to the realization that literacy skills do not fall neatly into categories, but rather form a continuum which involves the use of decoding and decision-making skills in a variety of domains common to everyday life. This link to the real world is one of the things which has made direct assessment so attractive.

There is also a growing realization that skills and knowledge cannot only be acquired, but can also be lost. This notion of skill deterioration is particularly important to the direct measurement of literacy skills being undertaken in a number of countries, where large numbers of adults are found to be performing below the expected norm for their educational attainment. To the extent that skills are lost, indirect measures of educational attainment or stock will overestimate the true skill profile.

Related to skill deterioration is the insight that indirect measures of educational stock do not reflect skills acquired outside the formal education system, either through other institutional settings or through self-study and life experience. This has become particularly important in an age when "how to" books and computer-aided instruction are available for virtually every subject of human enquiry. Indirect measures would, therefore, tend to underestimate the true educational stock.

The shift in many countries from standardized curricula and testing to self-paced and self-directed learning has detracted from the reliability of proxy measures. At one time, being able to sign one's name was a reliable indicator of literacy, since those people who could invariably possessed a broad range of competencies associated with formal educational attainment. In the absence of consistency, groups with vested interest in the reliability of the measures, such as employers recruiting new employees and economic planners, have turned to testing as an alternative.

Continued adult migration has also favored direct measurement. Educated in their own countries and languages prior to migration, these individuals pose a problem for researchers who must establish equivalency across systems.

Direct measures of literacy skills have been conducted in a number of countries, including the United States, France, Canada, Spain, Australia, Kenya, and Zimbabwe (Kirsch and Jungeblut 1986, Flecha 1991, Satin et al. 1990). Although most studies have restricted themselves to measuring reading, writing, and numeracy, the French and Spanish studies and some work in the United States have tried to measure a broader set of competencies, including the capacity to reason.

The most interesting approach used to date is that developed for the National Assessment of Educational Progress (NAEP) in the United States. Building on the seminal theoretical work of Mikulecky (1987) (on the task context of functional literacy), and that of Kirsch and Mosenthal (1990), Guthrie (1988) and Guthrie and Kirsch (1987) (on the cognitive differences between school and functional reading), these studies use different kinds of reading (document, quantitative, prose) to simultaneously report on individual ability in comparison to text difficulty and text difficulty related to features of the text and task. This comparison is achieved through the use of Item Response Theory (IRT), which calculates an estimate of each task's difficulty and an estimate of an individual's ability using the same numerical scale. Apart from task difficulty, IRT also accounts for tasks not attempted, guesses, and random error.

Important modifications of the basic NAEP methodology have been incorporated into surveys conducted in other countries, for example, in Canada, where the 1992 Adult Education and Training Survey and the Survey of Literacy Skills used in Daily Activity direct literacy assessment, involved simultaneous measurement in two languages and the use of proficiency levels as an aid to interpretation for remedial programming.

5. Prospects and Strategies for the Future

To those involved in servicing the information needs of public policymakers and researchers concerned with adult education, a number of important issues emerge from the foregoing discussion.

First, there is a pressing need for the increased sharing of measurement experience and technology among countries. Much has been learned about the measurement of both the stock and flow of human capital, but too many costly mistakes are being repeated unnecessarily. The work of the OECD and UNESCO is particularly important in this regard.

Second, there is a pressing need for improved coordination of content and approach. Without such coordination, much of the information value to be gained through comparison with other countries is lost to statistical noise. It is only through such comparisons that important systemic outcomes can be revealed.

Third, there is a pressing need to expand the body of knowledge related to the direct measurement of the stock of human capital. The inroads that have been made in measurement are considerable, particularly in the area of literacy skill assessment. Research is constrained, however, by the lack of a theoretical framework which would allow the incorporation of higher order skills. Similarly, much work remains to

be done in interpreting the existing measures, in understanding their relationship to economic success, and in judging their import for remedial programming.

Finally, there is a pressing need for the development of consistent time series of adult education data, particularly of the longitudinal variety. So far, most attention has turned to issues which involve understanding the dynamics of the adult education system and its relationship to other systems. Understanding the processes underlying change is facilitated by the availability of longitudinal data. Consistent time series of cross-sectional estimates constitute a less than ideal alternative.

See also: Literacy Research and Measurement; Measurement of Industry Training; Statistics of Adult and Nonformal Education; Statistics of Employee Training

References

De Castell S, Luke A, MacLennan D 1986 On defining literacy. In: De Castell S, Luke A, Egan K (eds.) *Literacy, Society and Schooling* 1986. Cambridge University Press, Cambridge

Flecha J 1991 Functional illiteracy study and research in Spain. In: Proceedings of a seminar on Direct Assessment of Literacy Skills Among the Adult Population, UNESCO Institute for Education, Hamburg

Guthrie J T, Kirsh I S 1987 Distinctions between reading comprehension and locating information in text. *J. Educ. Psychol.* 79: 220–27

Guthrie J T 1988 Locating information in documents: Examination of a cognitive model. *Reading Research Q.* 23(2): 178–99

Kirsch I S, Jungeblut A 1986 *Literacy: Profiles of America's Young Adults*. Final Report, 16-PL-01. The National Assessment of Educational Progress, Educational Testing Service, Princeton, New Jersey

Kirsch I S, Mosenthal P B 1990 Exploring document literacy: Variables underlying the performance of young adults. *Reading Research Q.* 25(1): 5–30

Mikulecky L 1987 Literacy for what purpose. In: Literacy Research Center 1987 *Towards Defining Literacy*. Literacy Research Center, University of Pennsylvania, Philadelphia, Pennsylvania

Noyelle T, Benton L 1992 *Adult Illiteracy and Economic Performance*. Centre for Educational Research and Innovation, OECD, Paris

Satin A, Jones S, Kelly K, Montigny G 1990 National literacy skills assessment: The Canadian experience. Paper presented at the annual meeting of the American Statistical Association, Anaheim, California

Statistics Canada 1991 *Adult Literacy in Canada: Results of a National Study*. Statistics Canada, Ottawa

Tuijnman A 1991 Lifelong education: A test of the accumulation hypothesis. *Int. J. Lifelong Edu.* 10(4): 275–85

Further Reading

Barton D, Hamilton M E 1990 *Researching Literacy in Industrialised Countries: Trends and Prospects*. UNESCO Institute for Education, Hamburg

Denton F T, Pineo P C, Spencer B G 1990 The constituencies

of adult education programs: Similarities and differences among age groups and other components of the population. *Can. J. Educ.* 15(1): 72–90

Medrich E A, Griffith J E 1992 *International Mathematics and Science Assessments: What Have We Learned?* US Department of Education, Office of Educational Research and Improvement, Washington, DC

Mohadjer L, Brike M, West J 1990 Proxy respondents and measurement errors for statistics on dropouts. Paper prepared for the International Conference on Measurement

Errors in Surveys, Tucson, Arizona

Stedman L C, Kaestle C F 1987 Literacy and reading performance in the United States from 1880 to the present. *Reading Research Q.* 22(1): 8–46

Velis J-P 1990 *Through a Glass, Darkly.* UNESCO, Paris

Wagner D A, Srivastava A B L 1987 *Measuring Literacy Through Household Surveys: A Manual on Literacy Assessment and Related Education Topics Through Household Surveys.* UN National Household Survey Capability Programme, United Nations, New York

Measurement of Industry Training

R. J. McCombe

This entry gives a background to the growing interest in adult education and industry training and outlines the development of training statistics in four countries: Australia, the United Kingdom, Canada, and Norway. Main statistical concepts, definitions, measures and indicators, and survey methodologies for data collection on adult education and industry training are described.

1. Background

Since the 1980s there has been an increasing international focus on labor force skill levels and productivity. Economic pressures are creating demands for major restructuring in the labor market. This has led to an increasing recognition among governments and employers of the need for an adaptable labor force and for employees to be able to learn new skills throughout their working lives.

For example, recognition by the Australian government of the importance of training and a perception of the need to improve industry training effort resulted in the introduction in 1990 of the Training Guarantee Act. This legislation requires employers to spend a prescribed minimum amount on training their employees. Its introduction followed widespread public debate on the need for training and ways of improving it, as well as on social issues of equity of access to training.

2. Statistical Development

The growing interest by governments in labor force training has created demands for reliable statistics on training issues. Prior to about 1985, training statistics had been based primarily on surveys or administrative sources of limited scope and detail (e.g., trade apprenticeship statistics in Australia). One notable exception was France, which introduced a law in 1971 requiring employers to spend a minimum amount on training, and to report annually on their training activities.

Very few countries conducted broadly based surveys of training. Portugal was one exception. An employer-based training survey was conducted there in 1980 and has been repeated a number of times since then. A small number of questions on training have been included in the household-based Labour Force Surveys conducted in the European Community (EC) countries each year since 1983–84 on behalf of the Statistical Office of the EC (EUROSTAT).

Since 1985, survey activity has increased significantly. Following a proposal by Australia, the Organisation for Economic Co-operation and Development (OECD) created a National Experts Group on Training Statistics. In 1990, this group developed a report on training statistics of member countries which outlined current methodologies and definitions. This entry draws heavily on this work.

3. Australia: Training Statistics

Prior to 1989, Australian training statistics were limited to two sources. First, apprenticeship and traineeship statistics were drawn from administrative data and an annual household survey. (Apprenticeships and traineeships are vocational training systems for young work force entrants involving enterprise-based training.) Second, the Australian Longitudinal Survey tracked the labor market experience of 16- to 25-year olds, including the training they had received.

In 1989, the Australian Bureau of Statistics (ABS) undertook two training surveys: an employer-based Training Expenditure Survey (TES) and a household survey of How Workers Get Their Training (HWGTT). The TES, which measures the expenditure by employers on training their employees, was repeated in 1990 with a larger sample of employers selected. Both TES and HWGTT were once again conducted in 1993.

3.1 Statistical Measures of Training

Because of Australian government policy initiatives which focused on employers' training expenditure expressed as a percentage of employers' gross wages and salaries, the measurement of this ratio was a primary objective of the TES. Other key measures were average employer training expenditure, hours of training received per employee, and percentage of employers reporting some training expenditure.

The key training measure produced from the HWGTT survey was the incidence of training expressed as the percentage of the number of employees (more specifically, those who had a wage or salary job in the previous 12 months). Other measures were the average number of training courses undertaken and the average number of hours spent on training. Of particular interest was whether employer support was provided for training. Incidence of on-the-job training was also obtained.

For both surveys, these measures were produced by field of training, inhouse/external training, branch of industry, public/private sector, and by size of employer. In addition, the HWGTT survey produced statistics by sex, age, country of birth and year of immigration, occupation, labor force and marital status, and level of formal educational attainment.

3.2 Concepts and Definitions

Common concepts and definitions were developed for the Australian training surveys. The surveys focused on "formal training," which was defined as training activities with a structured plan and format, designed to develop job-related skills and competence.

For the TES, "training expenditure" was defined as expenditure for the development, delivery, evaluation, and administration of formal training which was primarily meant for employees of the reporting employer. It included wages and salaries of employees and other direct expenditure such as fees, rent, equipment, travel, materials, and payments to industry bodies.

"Inhouse training" is organized by employers primarily for their own employees, using employees or consultants. "External training" is organized and conducted by training or educational institutions.

A training classification was developed which identified categories of vocationally specific training (based on the Australian Standard Classification of Occupations) and categories of general training. The latter included induction, general supervisory, general computing, and health and safety training.

3.3 Survey Methodologies

The 1989 TES was conducted using a sample of 2,000 employers, while the 1990 TES had a sample of 6,000.

The scope was employers in all industries except agriculture. The survey frames were drawn from the ABS Business Register and stratified by public and private sectors, industry, and employment size. The 1990 TES used a finer industry stratification than the 1989 TES.

The reference period was restricted to one-fourth of each year—the September quarter. Testing showed that the collection of training expenditure data would impose a significant reporting load as most businesses did not maintain the necessary records. The survey methodology was developed with the goal of keeping response load to a minimum. Employers were advised of their selection in the survey prior to the commencement of the reference period to enable them to organize appropriate record keeping. They were provided with a guide to the survey requirements, which contained pro forma work sheets which could be used to record training expenditure throughout the reference period. Many employers were interviewed to discuss the survey and establish suitable reporting arrangements, while many others received telephone contact.

The HWGTT survey was conducted on a subsample of the monthly Labour Force Survey. The Labour Force Survey is a multistage area sample of private dwellings and a list sample of non-private dwellings, and covers about three-fifths of 1 percent of the Australian population.

In each of the months of March, April, June, and July 1989, one-eighth of the respondents to the Labour Force Survey (a total of about 15,500 dwellings) were asked some additional questions. These were asked of any responsible adult in each household to identify the target population for the survey. The HWGTT questions were then asked of the target population through personal interviews. This resulted in approximately 18,500 respondents.

4. United Kingdom: Training Statistics

There is a considerable range of statistics on training activities and expenditure available in the United Kingdom. The most important sources of statistics on industry training are the surveys of employers, individuals, and providers undertaken for the Training in Britain Study by the Manpower Services Commission in 1987. Information is also available from other surveys, including the annual Skills Monitoring Survey and the four-yearly Labour Costs Survey (both employer-based) and the annual household-based Labour Force Survey.

The most important administrative source is the Youth Training Scheme (YTS) management information system. This contains information collected for administrative purposes on YTS commencements and completions since April 1983.

4.1 Statistical Measures of Training

The main measures of training activity from the Training in Britain Study are the proportion of establishments providing training, the proportion of employees receiving training, and the average number of days of on-the-job and off-the-job training received per trainee and per employee in 1986–87. Employer training expenditure and average training expenditure per employee were also estimated. Information was also obtained on attitudes to training. Key classifications are industry, size of establishment, and type of provider.

Main measures from the Labour Force Survey are number and percent of employees receiving on-the-job and off-the-job training during the previous four weeks by industry, occupation, type of provider, age, and sex.

The Skills Monitoring Survey focuses primarily on measuring recruitment difficulties, but includes questions on off-the-job training.

4.2 Concepts and Definitions

The Training in Britain Study defined "training" as the acquisition of knowledge and skills that are related to current or future work requirements by formal, structured, or guided means. It encompasses all posteducation and training undertaken outside the school system, excluding recreational courses.

"On-the-job training" is defined as training conducted at the normal place of work, involving significant periods of instruction by a supervisor or other responsible person during which there is little or no useful output, with the objective of learning or enhancing specific skills which have been specified in advance. "Off-the-job training" occurs when an employee leaves their normal work station to receive the training. Labour Force Survey interviewers ask respondents if they have taken part in any education or training connected with their job.

The definition of "employer training expenditure" used for Training in Britain is consistent with the Australian surveys. However, the Labour Cost Survey definition differs in that wages are excluded and depreciation on training buildings is included. This follows ILO conventions regarding labor costs.

4.3 Survey Methodologies

The Training in Britain Survey sampled about 1,700 employers. It excluded employers with less than 10 employees on the basis that they do little training, using other sources to account for these. The data were collected by a combination of self-completion questionnaires and personal interviews with senior managers. Further interviews were carried out with line managers at a subsample of establishments to assess on-the-job training. The reference period was the 12 months prior to enumeration.

The annual Labour Force Survey includes approximately 60,000 private households in the United Kingdom with interviews conducted either face-to-face or by telephone. It uses a four-week reference period, asking occurrence and length of education and training, who pays for the training, and where it is held. Starting in 1992 the Labour Force Survey is conducted quarterly, asking respondents how much training they received in the previous week.

5. Canada: Training Statistics

There is a variety of training statistics available in Canada, from both survey and administrative sources. The survey sources include major household surveys —one a general training survey and others covering specific training arrangements, apprenticeships, and government labor force programs—and an employer survey. The first of these, the Adult Education Survey, was undertaken in 1983. It formed the basis for the 1985 Adult Training Survey which was repeated, with some modifications, as the Adult Education and Training Survey (AETS) in 1990. The AETS was run again in 1992. The Human Resources Training and Development (HRTD) Survey was first conducted in 1987. It was repeated in 1993.

Administrative data sources include apprenticeship statistics and monitoring and evaluation systems for labor market programs.

5.1 Statistical Measures of Training

The HRTD survey measured total employer training expenditure, the percentage of employers who train, and the percentage of employers who estimate their human resource needs in advance. It also measured whether they meet their training needs, whether new technology puts significant demands on their training requirements, and the number of trainees and training days. Estimates were classified by size, industry, occupation, and type of training.

The AETS was conducted to provide information on the rate of participation in training during 1990. The survey estimated the number and characteristics of people who trained and the types, duration, and locations of the courses. Information, such as who paid the tuition, reasons for doing the course, length of the course, and whether it was successfully completed, was obtained.

The National Apprenticeship Survey collects information on the labor market experiences and satisfaction of ex-apprentices. The basic measure provided by this survey was incidence of apprenticeship training, with information on post-trade training also being produced.

5.2 Concepts and Definitions

The HRTD survey focused on formal training programs which were directly provided or supported by the employer. "Formal training programs" have a structured plan and objectives designed to develop an employee's skill and competence. "Directly provided training" is implemented by the employer. It includes the company purchasing training courses or seats in a program. For "supported training" the employer assists by paying tuition or providing paid time off. The definition of "training expenditure" is consistent with the Australian surveys.

The AETS focused on full-time training. A "full-time training course/program" occupied most of each work day for the duration of the course. The primary interest was in training undertaken for employment-related reasons, although personal-interest training was also included.

For the National Apprenticeship Survey, "training programs" were restricted to training for apprenticeable trades.

5.3 Survey Methodologies

About 7,300 companies in the private sector participated in the HRTD survey. More than twice that number were initially selected, with target response levels set for prescribed subgroups based on employer size. The reference period for the first survey was from November 1986 to October 1987 inclusive. Small companies were enumerated by mailed questionnaire, while the remainder were contacted initially by telephone. Follow-up procedures were implemented to achieve target response levels.

The AETS was based on a five-sixths subsample of the Labour Force Survey. The Labour Force Survey covers about 122,000 people aged 15 and over in 61,700 households using a stratified multistage sample design. Information was collected by personal or telephone interview. Individuals were asked whether, during the previous 12 months, they had been a full-time student at an educational institution or registered in a full-time apprenticeship training program, or whether they had taken a full-time training course organized by their employer which lasted a month or more, or full-time or part-time courses which had lasted less than one month. They were then asked details about the last course in each category. The survey also addressed barriers to education and training.

The National Apprenticeship Survey covered those who completed or discontinued apprenticeship programs in 1986 or 1987. A total of 8,900 individuals were interviewed by telephone from two sample groups (one of 5,200 in winter 1989 and another of 3,700 in March 1990).

6. Norway: Training Statistics

In 1989, an initiative by the Institute of Social Research in Oslo to provide broad-based data on working life saw the development and implementation of the Survey of Working Life conducted by the Central Bureau of Statistics (SSB) in cooperation with the Institute of Social Research.

This survey covered a range of issues besides training, such as organizational and physical aspects of enterprises and working conditions (salary scales, occupational careers, union activities, and so on). Data on these issues were collected by approaching managers (directors and personnel managers), shop-stewards, and employees, and also by collecting administrative data from individual firms.

6.1 The Statistical Measures of Training

The main measures of training activity in the Survey of Working Life were the proportion of employees receiving training, the types of courses offered by enterprises, and the average amount of time employees spent in training. Data on the organization of training in the enterprise, estimates of time spent planning and implementing courses, and of expenditure on external courses by enterprises were also obtained.

6.2 Concepts and Definitions

The definition of "training" varies between the different questionnaires used in the survey. The emphasis is, however, on formal, structured training.

The employee questionnaire defines training as "any form of formal training arranged as a course or likewise, partly or completely paid for by the enterprise." Exempt from this definition were: apprenticeship training, ordinary on-the-job training, and shop-steward or working environment courses.

The director/personnel manager questionnaire defines training as "education or training for employees, like enterprise–internal training or external courses paid for by the enterprise." Exempt from this were ordinary on-the-job training and initial training for new employees given by supervisors or colleagues.

In the shop-steward questionnaire, reference is made to "training or further education" and the enterprise data questionnaire refers to "courses or enterprise–internal training for employees." Neither questionnaire elaborates any further.

6.3 Survey Methodologies

The Survey of Working Life sampled 1,010 enterprises. Approximately 30 percent of these were "small" enterprises (with less than 10 employees) and the rest were "large" (with 10 or more employees). Enterprises with only one employee, new enterprises (registered after January 1, 1989), and those based off the Norwegian mainland were excluded from the sample.

In all cases, the senior director was interviewed personally by SSB staff and, where the enterprise was large enough, the personnel manager and a number of shop-stewards (chosen via a sample drawn on location) were also personally interviewed. Managers were supplied with an additional form enquiring about administrative details of the enterprise. The reference period was the 12 months prior to enumeration.

A sample of 6,100 employees was then drawn from those enterprises already chosen. Exempt from this sample were one-person enterprises, enterprises with only one employee, and employees that had left before June 1, 1989. Employees that had left after June 1, 1989 were asked about their last job. Interviews were either personal or by telephone, and the reference period was the 12 months prior to enumeration.

7. Conclusion

The above four countries are among the world leaders in the measurement of industry training. A number of other countries are quite active in this field and activity generally is increasing. As this entry illustrates, both employer- and household- (individual) based surveys are being used. Although broadly similar measures, concepts and definitions, and survey methodologies have been used, variations have limited the scope for comparing industry training between countries. Early limitations in statistical data quality are generally being addressed in more recent and planned surveys as countries refine their approaches. The ongoing work in this area by the OECD will further encourage convergence toward standard concepts and methodologies in this vital area of education and labor market statistics.

See also: Statistics of Employee Training

Bibliography

Australia Department of Employment, Education and Training 1988 *Industry Training in Australia: The Need for Change*. Australian Government Publishing Service, Canberra

Australian Bureau of Statistics (ABS) 1990 *How Workers Get Their Training, Australia 1989*. ABS (cat. No. 6278.0), Canberra

Australian Bureau of Statistics (ABS) 1991 *Employer Training Expenditure: Australia, July to September 1990*. ABS (cat. No. 6353.0), Canberra,

Australian Bureau of Statistics (ABS) (annual) *Transition from Education to Work, Australia*. ABS (cat. No. 6227.0), Canberra

Department of Employment 1989 *Training in Britain: A Study of Funding, Activity and Attitudes*. HMSO, London

Department of Employment 1990 *Training Statistics 1990*. HMSO, London

Kalleberg A L 1992 Job training in Norway: Organizational and individual differences. *Int. J. Educ. Res.* 17(6): 565–79

OECD 1991a *Employment Outlook July 1991*. OECD, Paris

OECD Directorate for Social Affairs, Manpower and Education 1991b (Draft) Report of national experts on training statistics. (Unpublished)

Statistics Canada 1990 *Human Resource Training and Development Survey Results, 1987*. Statistics Canada (cat. No. 81–574E), Ottawa

Measurement of Training Costs

Jandhyala B. G. Tilak

The importance of training in improving labor productivity in developed as well as developing economies is well-recognized. Training may serve as a substitute for formal education; and in some cases both formal education and training can complement each other as more educated people undertake more training (Becker 1993, Mincer 1970). If training is a substitute for education it will reduce income inequality, and if it is a complement, it will tend to increase it (Hazlewood 1989 p. 100). Whether it is a substitute or a complement to education, it increases productivity and earnings. However, training is infinitely more complex and diversified than formal education (Dougherty 1989). Employers rightly consider expenditure on training as an investment—as human capital investment—since it yields high pay-offs. In the early 1990s, firms incur huge costs on training. Proper measurement of training costs is useful in at least two important respects: it helps in measuring the efficiency of investment in training, and more importantly, in deciding about the "optimal" allocation of resources for training. This entry deals with the methodological aspects of measuring training costs.

1. Types of Training

Training is often regarded as postschool investment. It includes both on-the-job and preservice training. Preservice training is not employer based, while on-the-job training is. Preservice training may be related to a particular occupational category, but the trainee need not necessarily become employed in the corresponding occupation after the completion of training. Thus, *ex post* there may be no relation between preservice training and employment which results in wastage of resources. On the other hand, wastage in the case of on-the-job training may be very much less. The costs of on-the-job training may also be less than other training (Staley 1970). Hence, from the point of view of employers, on-the-job training is more important.

Blaug (1976) distinguishes between: (a) costless on-the-job training, or simply "learning by doing" (Arrow 1962); (b) informal on-the-job training; (c) formal off-the-job but in-plant training; and (d) informal off-the-job, out-of-plant training paid for by the employer. However, all of these four forms can be meaningfully interpreted as on-the-job training—formal and informal, as against preservice or pre-employment training. Machlup (1968) distinguishes between two types of on-the-job training that have distinct cost implications: "systematic" training programs and "informal" training. Systematic training programs refer to specially designed courses given by instructors; and informal training implies helping the newly recruited worker to acquire new skills to do his tasks with increasing speed and accuracy, usually under the supervision of senior workers. This is close to apprenticeship training, but differs from "learning on the job." The latter can also be termed "learning from experience," meaning either a conscious effort on the part of the employee to improve his efficiency, earnings, and even job status, or an "automatic, almost unavoidable" process of work experience (Machlup 1968). This entry is largely concerned with the latter two forms of training, even though some reference is also made to the others.

As Machlup (1984) rightly notes, these distinctions are not as important as the classification of training into "general" and "specific" (Becker 1962, 1993), a classification based on the nature of skills imparted: general training increases the productivity of the trainee in the firm providing the training as well as in other firms, while specific training is particular to a given firm; it increases the productivity of the trainee only in the firm providing it. The former is rather "portable" across the industry, and the latter is not. The distinction has important implications for cost assessment.

Costs of providing general training can be shared by all the firms in a given branch, while costs of specific training have to be born by a single firm. In the case of the former, all firms may have a more or less similar cost profile, whereas this may not be the case with respect to specific training. A firm loses more if a "specific" trainee quits the firm compared with a "general" trainee, as a new entrant will have to be provided with specific training, but not necessarily general training (Parsons 1972). Firms can, however, rationally afford to bear the costs of general training if the cost of training is shifted to the trainee. This shift in the incidence of costs often takes place through lower wages while in training. On the other hand, in the case of specific training, firms are ready to bear the costs, although the loss in the case of a specific trainee leaving the firm is higher. The risk of trained workers leaving their job is small, as trained workers cannot productively use specific training received in one firm in another. Hence, it may be right to argue that "firms do not pay any of the completely general costs and only part of the completely specific costs" (Becker 1962 p. 23).

In actual practice, most kinds of training are partly general, partly specific, and it is not easy even in principle to separate the two (Blaug 1976 p. 837). Hence it is most likely that the cost of training is shared between the employee and employer—even though not in any explicit way, but implicitly in the form of lower wages during the period of training (Mincer 1962, 1974). Higher wages are paid after the training in order to reduce the risk of trained workers quitting the firm (Rosen 1972). On the whole, it can be argued that the firm's share of the total training cost is larger the greater the specific component of training, and is smaller the greater the general component, the residuals in costs being the shares of the trainees.

2. Taxonomy of Costs of Training

If training is costless, then there would be an unlimited demand and supply of training. But it is not. What are the various components of training costs, and how are they measured?

To start with, training programs usually operate with clear separate budgets of their own. However, the terms "training budgets" or "training costs" are quite often loose concepts. They may include any cost estimate for time spent in on-the-job training; salaries of the administrative staff and instructors of the training department; capital costs or maintenance costs of the firm's training schools; similar costs at the multipurpose buildings which are maintained by many firms partly as a recreation center, a meeting place for "quality circle teams" or various special interest clubs, a hotel for visiting staff from branch offices, and also, usually primarily, as training center for ad hoc courses; and travel costs for staff attending courses (Dore and Sako 1989 p. 81).

Calculation of training costs is guided by the same theoretical principles as the calculation of costs of formal education. Accordingly, training costs can be classified into direct and indirect costs, as in the case of formal schooling. Direct costs refer to all the direct money outlays for training programs made explicitly in the training budgets. Indirect costs refer to all opportunity costs.

2.1 Direct Costs

Direct costs include fixed costs and variable costs. Fixed costs are those that do not change with change in the number of trainees, while variable costs vary. There may not be much problem in identifying and estimating several of the ingredients of fixed training costs, except in the case of costs associated with fixed capital, such as buildings. If the buildings meant for training are leased, then the annual rent of the building can be taken into account while estimating the cost on buildings. But if such buildings are owned, then the annual cost of the building is to be estimated by considering annual depreciation of the fixed capital, on the basis of the original investment made in the building, the life span of the building, and the rate of interest foregone by investing in a building rather than in something else. Alternatively, annualization factors (*a*) can be used in such contexts, that are available at various rates of interest (*r*) and different life spans of the investment (*n*), estimated as follows:

$$a(r, n) = [r(1+r)^n]/[(1+r)^n - 1] \quad (1)$$

Variable costs, also often equated to operating costs, include all expenses involved in conducting training programs, including support costs on administration, overhead, development, analysis, or any other category related to conducting the program.

Establishment costs are the costs of the training firm, comprising: (a) the salaries, insurance, pension contributions, and all other direct money costs incurred by the firm on the staff of the training unit; (b) the cost of the space and services used for training, such as rent, expenditure on power, maintenance of furniture and equipment, etc.; and (c) the support costs of training functions, including costs to be shared between training and other functions, like those incurred on the board of directors, its secretariat, etc.

Marginal expenditure, according to Pepper (1984 p. 104) includes the additional costs incurred in order to carry out any one training activity like the course fee paid for on-the-job training provided by other firms; costs incurred on books, equipment, etc. for a given training program; accommodation and personal expenditure incurred on the firm's trainees receiving training in other firms; fees of the guest trainers, and so on.

Basically all costs, particularly operating costs, can be identified and measured with the help of the "ingredients method," that is, by identifying each ingredient of the training program and its process (Levin 1975, 1983) as follows:

(a) personnel cost: trainee cost—incurred by the trainee or by the employer on fees, transport, etc.; cost of the trainers—that is, fees and honorarium paid to the instructors;

(b) cost of facilities: cost of the classroom, cost of renovation;

(c) equipment cost: cost of the furniture, blackboards, video and audiovisual materials such as televisions, videocassette players, tape recorders, computers, etc.;

(d) cost of materials and supplies: books, stationery, electronic software, and other instructional development cost;

(e) miscellaneous: power (energy for lighting, heating, and cooling), routine maintenance, administrative overheads, travel and *per diem* cost for the trainees and instructors, and other costs not listed above.

Each of these ingredients can be specified in more detail. The identification and measurement of the costs of several of these training inputs may not be technically difficult, but administratively cumbersome. For example, if the building is used for both training and formal education, or if materials such as stationery are purchased in bulk to be used for both purposes, division of such "joint" costs into training and other purposes may be difficult. However, more serious problems may arise in estimating opportunity costs.

2.2 Opportunity Costs

When an employee is involved in training, as a trainee or as a trainer, there is an interference with the output. The loss in the output due to current training (known as "interference cost" in the literature on management and training) is familiarly known as "opportunity cost" in economics. This factor needs to be taken into account in estimating the total training costs. Not only the employer but also the trainee incurs opportunity cost. The trainee foregoes some earnings due to training, as he or she may receive lower wages during the training period, that is the difference between the wages of a nontrained employee and those of a trainee during the training period is estimated as opportunity costs or foregone earnings for the individual trainee. The difference in the output of a nontrained employee and that of a trainee during training is the opportunity cost of the firm. If the wages reflect productivity, then the individual's opportunity costs and the firm's opportunity costs are identical.

The importance of opportunity costs of training cannot be ignored. If there is no opportunity cost of training to the trainees (i.e., if the trainees receive wages during the training period equivalent to the wages otherwise) and if the direct personal costs are negligible, then the demand for training would be very high. If the opportunity costs are substantial, then few may opt for training unless future additional earnings attributable to training are high. Firms behave in a similar way. In sum, the demand for training is a function of opportunity cost of the trainee, that of the firm, and the returns from training. Given the returns, the equilibrium level of demand for training is determined by the interaction of the individual and the firm's opportunity costs of training.

The concept of opportunity cost is a powerful tool, and is extensively used in economic theory. Employees pay for on-the-job training by receiving wages lower than they could receive otherwise. This is clearly the case with respect to apprenticeships. As Becker (1993 p. 24) stated, "*all* costs appear as foregone earnings to workers receiving on-the-job training; that is, all costs appear as lower earnings than could be received elsewhere, although direct outlays . . . may really be an important part of costs." But in practice, the employees may be receiving full wages during training as well, in which case the opportunity costs to the employees may be insignificant.

Thus total training costs are arrived at by aggregating the direct costs—fixed and variable—and opportunity costs, net of transfers.

2.3 Costs of Informal Training

The cost of informal training on the job is more difficult to estimate precisely. Such costs can be classified as follows: (a) the loss of output owing to the low productivity of new workers; (b) the increased cost of supervision; (c) increased cost on maintenance and depreciation; (d) costs due to higher accidental rate; and (e) higher appreciation cost (Machlup 1968 p. 60). The costs vary both by the level of the trainee and the supervisor. The higher the level of the supervisor, the lower may be the direct cost on training, but the higher may be the opportunity cost of his time spent on supervision. The opportunity costs of training may be of the same order whether it is formal or informal on-the-job training; but direct costs of informal training would be substantially less than those of formal training.

3. Important Issues in Measurement of Costs

3.1 Market Versus Shadow Prices

Costs are estimated either at market prices or at shadow prices. The most commonly used method, which is simple and straightforward, uses market prices of the inputs invested in training. Market prices are those money prices paid for the goods and services that were used in the training programs. Such data would be easily available. This is based on the assumption that there are reasonably competitive markets for many of the training inputs, and hence market prices reflect the true value of the inputs. In actual practice, this assumption may not be true with respect to several inputs of the training programs, in which case market prices do not reflect the real value of the training resources. This is particularly true with respect to wages and salaries of the trainers or publicly subsidized goods and services. In such cases of market imperfections, where market prices distort the real value of the resources, shadow prices (i.e., the real value of the resources) need to be estimated. In actual practice, costs of some of the training inputs can be measured in market prices, and some in shadow prices.

Shadow prices of labor are estimated in two ways. The formal way of estimating the shadow wage of labor with a given level of education (W^*) is first to estimate the production function of the general type Y = $f(K, L_i)$, where Y is the output, K the capital, and L_i the labor with $i\text{-}th$ educational level ($i = 1, \ldots n$), and then to differentiate the above equation with respect to L_1 to estimate the shadow wage of labor with first level of education (i.e., $W^*_1 = \delta Y / \delta L_1$). Partial differentiation with respect to other types of labor gives their respective shadow wages, or marginal product.

Alternatively, shadow prices can also be estimated with the help of linear programming models. If labor with different levels of education appear on the right-hand side (resource availability) of the set of constraints, then the shadow wage rate of labor with first level of education is defined as the increment of the objective function following the addition of one extra person of the same kind.

3.2 Costs at Current Versus Constant Prices

Costs of training are generally estimated in current market prices, but particularly for temporal comparisons they need to be estimated in constant prices. The estimates on costs in current prices can be converted into costs at constant prices with the help of a so-called "training price index." The training price index is based on the price movements of several inputs that are invested in the training programs. While this may be the best method, difficulties in preparing a reliable training price index may necessitate the use of general wholesale or consumer price indices, or national income deflators. It may also be necessary to adjust different ingredients of the training costs by different indices. But only estimates on costs that are adjusted for changes in prices serve meaningfully. Otherwise, comparisons based on current prices yield spurious and misleading results.

3.3 Unit Cost Analysis

A standard way to develop and analyze cost estimates for analytical, comparative, and investment decision-making purposes is to estimate unit costs of training. Although there is no unique measure of "unit," in general a trainee is taken as a unit, and costs per trainee are calculated, considering all ingredients of costs. Unit costs are estimated by dividing the total cost of a training program by the number of trainees. Other relevant units can be cost per training day, cost per training course, etc. Estimates on unit costs can be very useful in planning, policy formulation, and in examining the internal and external efficiency of training. Estimation of marginal unit costs and their comparison with average unit costs serve still more purposes, including determining the optimum size of the training unit in terms of the number of trainees.

3.4 Costs to Whom?

Detailed estimates need to be made on who bears which costs. A distinction should be made between the costs the trainee has to bear, costs to the firm, costs to the industry, and costs to the society as a whole. For the individual trainee, opportunity costs in terms of earnings foregone due to training, and the individual direct costs such as registration costs, food, travel, and lodging, are important. As the direct costs are normally met or reimbursed by the firm, foregone earnings become the most important item in the case of individual costs. For the firm, besides the opportunity cost in terms of loss of output, the variable cost on the trainee and the provision of training are very important, even though fixed costs may also be sizable. For industry, fixed costs may also become important.

To arrive at the total training costs at the national level, a simple summation of the first three categories —that is, the individual, the firm, and the industry's costs—may yield erroneous results because they are not mutually exclusive. Besides, there may be simple transfers. Furthermore, it has already been seen that the opportunity costs of training for a trainee and the opportunity costs of a firm/industry overlap, if not cancel each other out, to a certain extent.

3.5 Determinants of Costs

Costs of training programs depend upon a variety of factors, prominent among them being: the duration of the training program (e.g., the longer the duration, the larger would be the costs); the methodology of training (e.g., whether it is classroom lecture-based, or computer-based, or video-based, etc.); wages and remuneration of the instructors (higher wages mean higher direct costs if the trainees are specifically employed in the training unit and, if not, higher wages may imply higher opportunity costs); and the number of trainees (the higher the number of trainees, the higher may be the total costs of training, but the unit costs might be lower along with other factors like length of training program, content, and facilities provided). A detailed analysis of the determinants of training can be attempted with the help of multiple regression analysis. Regressing unit cost (C) on its possible determinants (X_i), as $C = \alpha + \beta X_i$, helps to identify the relative significance of each factor, and correspondingly to formulate strategies in improving the cost-efficiency of training.

4. Conclusion

The importance of detailed cost analysis cannot be emphasized enough. The usefulness of cost analysis depends upon how accurately and in what detail the various components of training costs are identified and measured. There are three overriding considerations in identifying and measuring the several ingredients of training costs: (a) the ingredients should be specified in sufficient detail; (b) the categorization of ingredients should be internally consistent, so that duplication is avoided, and transfers from one to the other account

are properly taken into consideration, that is, aggregates are made net of transfers, and transfer payments are not added to resource costs (Ziderman 1969); and (c) the degree of specificity and accuracy in identifying and costing the ingredients should depend upon their relation to the training program (Levin 1983).

See also: Training on the Job; Economics of Adult Education and Training; Costs of Adult Education and Training; Evaluation of Industry Training: Cost-Effectiveness

References

Arrow K J 1962 The economic implications of learning by doing. *Rev. Econ. Stud.* 29: 155–74
Becker G S 1962 Investment in human capital: A theoretical analysis. *J. Pol. Econ.* 70(5): 9–49
Becker G S 1993 *Human Capital: A Theoretical and Empirical Analysis, with Special Reference to Education*, 3rd edn. University of Chicago Press, Chicago, Illinois
Blaug M 1976 The empirical status of human capital theory: A slightly jaundiced survey. *J. Econ. Lit.* 14(3): 827–55
Dore R P, Sako M 1989 *How the Japanese Learn to Work*. Routledge, London
Dougherty C 1989 The cost-effectiveness of national training systems in developing countries. PHREE Working Paper No. 171. World Bank, Washington, DC
Hazlewood A 1989 *Education, Work, and Pay in East Africa*. Clarendon Press, Oxford
Levin H M 1975 Cost-effectiveness analysis in evaluation research. In: Guttentag M, Struening E (eds.) 1975 *Handbook of Evaluation Research*, Vol. 2. Sage, Beverly Hills, California
Levin H M 1983 *Cost-Effectiveness: A Primer*. Sage, Beverly Hills, California
Machlup F 1968 *The Production and Distribution of Knowledge in the United States*. Princeton University Press, Princeton, New Jersey
Machlup F 1984 *The Economics of Information and Human Capital*. Princeton University Press, Princeton, New Jersey
Mincer J 1962 On-the-job training: Costs, returns and some implications. *J. Pol. Econ.* 70(5): 50–79
Mincer J 1970 The distribution of labor incomes: A survey with special reference to the human capital approach. *J. Econ. Lit.* 8(1): 1–26
Mincer J 1974 *Schooling, Experience, and Earnings*. National Bureau of Economic Research, New York
Parsons D O 1972 Specific human capital: An application to quit rates and layoff rates. *J. Pol. Econ.* 80(4–6): 1120–43
Pepper A D 1984 *Managing the Training and Development Function*. Gower, Aldershot
Rosen S 1972 Learning and experience in the labor market. *J. Hum. Resources* 7(3): 326–42
Staley E 1970 *Planning Occupational Education and Training for Development*. Orient Longman, Delhi.
Ziderman A 1969 Costs and benefits of adult retraining in the United Kingdom. *Economica* 36(144): 363–76

Further Reading

Anderson R E, Kasl E S 1982 *The Costs and Financing of Adult Education and Training*. Lexington Books,

Lexington, Massachusetts

Bateman W 1967 An application of cost–benefit analysis to work-experience programs. *Am. Econ. Rev.* 57: 80–90

Bowman M J 1965 From guilds to infant training industries. In: Anderson C A, Bowman M J (eds.) 1965 *Education and Economic Development*. Aldine Press, Chicago, Illinois

Cullen J G, Sawzin S A, Sisson G R, Swanson R A 1978 Cost-effectiveness: A model for assessing the training investment. *Train. Dev. J.* 32(1): 24–29

Deming B S 1982 *Evaluating Job-Related Training: A Guide*

for Training the Trainer. Prentice-Hall, Englewood Cliffs, New Jersey

Forrester D A R 1967 The costs and benefits of industrial training. *Technical Educ.* 9(2): 60–65

London M 1989 *Managing the Training Enterprise: High Quality Cost-Effective Employee Training in Organisations*. Jossey-Bass, San Francisco, California

Somers G G, Stromsdorfer E W 1971 A benefit-cost analysis of manpower retraining. In: Wykstra R A (ed.) 1971 *Human Capital Formation and Manpower Development*. Free Press, New York

Statistics of Adult and Nonformal Education

S. K. Chu

Current worldwide thrusts in education for all and human resources development are placing special emphasis on developing nonformal education, and on the need for systematic monitoring, management, coordination, and policies. This entry describes the latest methodological approaches advocated in the *Manual for Statistics on Non-formal Education* compiled by UNESCO (1992), and discusses related issues and trends. It draws attention to the urgent need to raise awareness and promote national and international efforts to develop national capabilities for collecting nonformal education statistics, and to use the experiences and outcomes to further refine and upgrade the international methodology, for wider dissemination and application.

1. The Need for Statistics on Adult and Nonformal Education

Awareness is growing for more conscious efforts to be made in diversifying educational opportunities, and in expanding beyond the formal, institutionalized approaches that characterise provision at present. More systematic use must be made of nonformal and informal ways and means for learning and training. In the face of global concerns for expanding and diversifying education and training, there is an urgent need for sound policies and plans, as well as effective mechanisms and capabilities for monitoring, coordinating, and managing nonformal educational activities at both the national and international levels. The importance of the collection and supply of timely, reliable, and comprehensive information on nonformal education as strategic resources aiding decision making related to all these functions has therefore come to the forefront of priorities.

In seeking to develop an up-to-date international methodology for the systematic collection, dissemination, and use of information on nonformal education,

a *Manual for Statistics on Non-formal Education* has been compiled by UNESCO (1992). As a direct sequel and complement to previous UNESCO manuals and guides in this and related areas (UNESCO 1975, 1979, Gupta 1985), this manual seeks to clarify the fundamental concepts underlying statistical information on nonformal education, and to refine and update the methodological approaches to be adopted in actually establishing operational statistical information systems for the collection, processing, analysis, and dissemination of comprehensive data on nonformal education at the country level. The essence of the approach adopted by UNESCO is summarized in this entry.

2. Definitions and Terminology

The term "nonformal education" is also used to denote "adult education," "out-of-school education," "continuing education," "further education," "lifelong education," and so forth, as far as they fulfill the characteristics of nonformal education as described in Section 4 below.

According to the International Standard Classification of Education (ISCED), a "course" is a planned series of learning experiences in a particular range of subject matter or skills offered by an institution and undertaken by one or more learners. A "program" is a selection of one or more courses that combine to achieve a defined learning objective. A "field" is a group of programs related to the same broad subject matter.

A "nonformal education agency" is an organization that provides administrative, financial, material, and/or professional support to one or more institutions or establishments in organizing and conducting nonformal education programs and activities. This can be (a) a government ministry, department, or

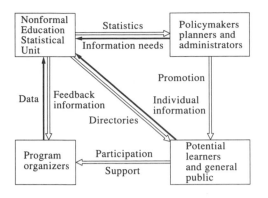

Figure 1
Four-way information flow in nonformal education statistics

agency; (b) a nongovernmental organization, such as a professional association, voluntary agency, or religious body; or (c) a public or private enterprise. A "nonformal institution" provides the established location and organization for conducting the nonformal education program and activities.

A "study-hour" is the equivalent of one hour of learning devoted toward completing a nonformal education program, irrespective of the form of learning —whether at lectures (face-to-face in a classroom or transmitted over the television or radio); practical work in the laboratory or in the field; guided or self-study at home or in the library, and so on. The number of study-hours per week is called "intensity of instruction" or "workload".

The number of study-hours multiplied by the number of learners enrolled in a nonformal education program gives the "apparent learner-hours", which can be compared to the "effective learner-hours" (referring to the product of study-hours with the number of completers) to study the utilization of capacity and productivity of the nonformal education program.

3. The Aim of Nonformal Education Statistics

Nonformal education statistics should be viewed as an integral part of a comprehensive information system for monitoring all educational and training activities. A good statistical information system should cater to the information needs of all the major agents involved. In nonformal statistics, the aim will be to facilitate the four-way information flow as shown in Fig. 1.

In general, nonformal education statistics and the kind of information collected should aim at increasing our understanding of:

(a) progress and disparities in the development of

various kinds of nonformal education—availability, resources inputs, participation, efficiency, quality, output, learning achievement, and impact;

(b) how well these diversified alternative channels for education and training satisfy learning demand;

(c) how effective their complementary and supplementary roles are to formal education, and also to informal and self-directed or "random" learning.

Apart from providing information support to government policy, coordination, and administrative functions, nonformal education statistics have an important *general information role* vis-à-vis the diversified organizing institutions and learner population groups involved. To satisfy these diversified information needs, nonformal education statistics shall aim above all at building a comprehensive monitoring data base of nonformal education agencies, institutions, and programs, and of teachers and learners involved, for the systematic storage and production of the required information.

4. Scope and Coverage of Nonformal Education Statistics

Nonformal education statistics seek to cover all *organized* educational and training activities that are not reported under statistics on formal education.

For purposes of nonformal education statistics, education and learning can be classified into four main categories: formal education, nonformal education, informal learning, and random/incidental learning (Titmus et al. 1979, UNESCO 1992). *Formal education* can be characterized as intentionally organized full-time learning events with regular fixed duration and schedule, structured hierarchically with chronological succession of levels and grades, admission requirements, and formal registration, catering mainly to the population 5–25 years of age that is enrolled in established educational institutions, and using pre-determined pedagogical organization, contents, methods, and teaching/learning materials. *Nonformal education* refers to intentionally organized learning events catering essentially to persons not currently participating in formal education, which do not fulfill one or more of the conditions above. *Informal learning* is generally intentional but unorganized and unstructured learning events that occur in the family, the workplace, and in the daily life of every person, on a self-directed, family-directed, or socially-directed basis. *Random/incidental learning* refers to unintentional learning occurring at any time and in any place in every person's everyday life. The word "intentional" can be taken to refer to conscious efforts either on

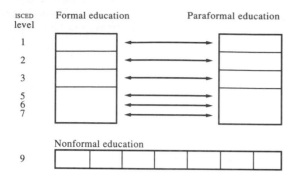

Figure 2
Formal, paraformal, and nonformal education

the part of learners to learn, or on the part of organizers and teachers (or "communicators," in general) to provide and transfer information and skills.

5. Paraformal Education and Level Equivalence

Some countries have introduced an additional category, "paraformal education," to designate nonformal educational activities that offer equivalence to specific levels, grades, and types of formal education (see Fig. 2). This term applies particularly to nonformal educational programs organized for out-of-school children and youth to enable them to either eventually rejoin appropriate levels and grades in formal education, or to gain access to suitable employment opportunities requiring pre-determined educational qualifications (UNESCO 1991).

6. Types of Nonformal Education

Nonformal education exists nowadays in a great diversity of forms, organized by a wide variety of agencies and institutions for a wide range of target population groups. To attempt to exhaustively identify and collect information from all of them is not an easy task. A careful study of prevailing country situations and practices (Carr-Hill 1988, Gallart 1989) has given rise to the following general classification of major types of nonformal education programs and activities:

(a) adult literacy programs—organized primarily to impart basic literacy and numeracy skills to adults;

(b) nonformal education for out-of-school children and youth—to provide education, literacy, and skill training to children and youth who have been left out or who have dropped out from formal schooling;

(c) functional literacy and life-skill training—specific nonformal education programs and activities organized to enhance the ability needed to function in daily life, society, and the environment, for example, regarding health and hygiene, civics, political awareness, family planning, early childhood care, environment protection, trade unionism, and so on;

(d) agricultural extension and rural development—education, training, and counseling carried out in rural and agricultural communities primarily to improve agricultural practices and to promote rural development;

(e) industrial production and service trade/skills training—training in productive and service skills and trades organized by enterprises, professional associations, voluntary agencies, and other bodies. This can include pre-service and inservice, as well as on-the-job and off-the-job training, apprenticeships, sandwich courses, internships, and so on;

(f) nonformal higher education—open universities and postsecondary extramural studies offering advanced educational and training opportunities through face-to-face contacts, correspondence, radio, television, and other distance educational methods and means;

(g) language and communication skills training—specially organized nonformal education programs and activities to improve abilities in languages and communication skills;

(h) religious education—organized learning about religion in churches, mosques, temples, and other places of worship;

(i) general culture and leisure education—educational activities in cultural and recreational subjects, offered either during leisure time or in order that the participants may derive greater benefit from leisure;

(j) other nonformal education (not classified).

Although nonformal education in many countries may be concentrated in one or a few of the above categories, it cannot be denied that in all countries there exist nonformal education activities covering most, if not all, of the ten categories. To acquire a comprehensive understanding of all organized educational and training efforts taking place outside of formal education, the approach to be adopted would be to collect data on all types of nonformal education from all sectors and levels of the national economic and social structure: central ministries and their regional, provincial, district, and local branches; public, private, and nongovernmental organizations; voluntary agencies; established productive and service enterprises; professional associations; local community agencies and centres; religious and charity bodies; foreign missions; and educational institutions.

7. Information Needs

A fundamental objective of nonformal education statistics is to measure the demand for and supply of educational opportunities, and the extent to which supply satisfies demand. More particularly, nonformal education statistics are collected with the aim of providing a better understanding of the demand for and supply of educational opportunities, levels and patterns of participation, resources input, quality, and outcomes, thereby enabling an assessment of the performance, cost-effectiveness, and impact of the education system, as well as the identification of shortcomings, imbalances, disparities, and priority action areas.

8. Basic Approaches to Data Collection on Nonformal Education

There are two basic approaches to the collection of data on nonformal education, namely: (a) census of nonformal education agencies, institutions, and programs; and (b) sample surveys of specific population groups involved in nonformal education and of the general population. Approach (a) covers mainly the aspects of supply, participation, and output, whereas approach (b) can be used to identify demand and assess patterns of participation and outcomes (see *Measurement of Adult Education*).

9. Data Sources and Channels

There can be five main sources of data on nonformal education. They are as follows:

(a) agencies/institutions/bodies/persons involved in supporting and/or organizing nonformal education programs;

(b) nonformal education learners (past, current, dropouts, completers);

(c) teachers and personnel of nonformal education programs;

(d) employers and community leaders;

(e) the general public.

Different types of data on nonformal education have to be collected from different data sources using different data channels, methods, and instruments. In relation to the basic approaches outlined above, the principal data channels for nonformal education statistics comprise the following:

(a) census of nonformal education agencies, institutions, and programs;

(b) sample surveys of the general population and/or the labor force using household and labor force surveys;

(c) sample surveys of current and past learners;

(d) sample surveys of teachers of nonformal education programs;

(e) sample surveys of nonformal education program organizers/personnel;

(f) sample surveys of employers;

(g) sample surveys of community leaders.

10. Organization and Coordination of the collection of Nonformal Education Statistics

Responsibilities for coordinating the nationwide census of nonformal education agencies, institutions and programs, as well as of sample surveys of nonformal education learners and teachers, falls under the direct purview of the Ministry of Education. More specifically, it can be a joint responsibility between the department of nonformal or adult education, and the statistical service of the Ministry of Education, involving at the same time all other ministries, departments and agencies active in collecting information on nonformal education. Under this partnership, a Nonformal Education Statistical Unit can be established within either the nonformal/adult education department or the statistical service of the Ministry of Education, which will be responsible for identifying information needs and coordinating the collection and dissemination of all relevant data through all data channels.

For the purposes of decision making to mobilize and coordinate the systematic collection and sharing of information on nonformal education among them, an Inter-agency Nonformal Education Information Coordination Committee can be formed, with the Nonformal Education Statistical Unit of the Ministry of Education acting as secretariat.

11. Basic Statistical Measurement Unit

Statistics on nonformal education agencies, institutions, and programs mainly cover the six aspects shown in Fig. 3.

Nonformal education statistics are generally collected from the agency or institutional level, because they are tangible entities with given location, organization, and responsible staff. The "basic statistical measurement unit," however, refers to individual programs organized to provide nonformal education opportunities. Agencies and institutions offering several different nonformal education programs will therefore have to report separately on each program, and on the number of learners participating and completing each program, as well as on teachers and finance.

Figure 3
Scope of statistics on nonformal education

12. Stages in a Census of Nonformal Education Agencies, Institutions, and Programs

Information on nonformal education programs, agencies, and institutions can be collected in two stages: the identification stage and the monitoring stage.

The identification stage aims at achieving three objectives: (a) establishing an up-to-date master list of institutions and agencies providing nonformal education opportunities; (b) gathering general information on nonformal education programs offered by these agencies; and (c) producing national directories of nonformal education agencies and institutions, and local lists of nonformal education programs. Basic descriptive information on individual nonformal education programs to be collected during the identification stage would include the following:

(a) name or title of program;

(b) name and address of organizing/sponsoring agency;

(c) organizational affiliation of organizing/sponsoring agency;

(d) institutional location of the nonformal education program;

(e) type of nonformal education program;

(f) field of study or training;

(g) level and grade equivalence;

(h) name of certificate/diploma awarded;

(i) capacity or number of places;

(j) target population;

(k) admission requirements;

(l) program starting date;

(m) program ending date;

(n) total study-hours;

(o) time budget and schedule;

(p) user's charges per participant; and

(q) teaching/learning/practice methods and organization.

The purpose of the follow-up monitoring stage will be to evaluate the level and patterns of participation, resources input, quality, efficiency, and output of the program. Typical data for monitoring purposes would include:

(a) number of participants who enrolled and completed the program, classified by sex, age-group, and, if possible, also according to other personal profiles such as prior educational attainment, specialization, skill level, employment status, and so forth;

(b) number of teachers by sex, age, qualification, specialization, full-time or part-time, teaching load, remuneration, and so forth;

(c) financial income by source of funds and expenditure by type.

13. Database of Nonformal Education Programs, Agencies, and Institutions

Information on nonformal education agencies, institutions, and planned programs that is collected can be used in the building of a national nonformal education database. In practice, this database will be built in an incremental manner by gradually adding records of new programs as they become available, together with basic descriptive information on the type and characteristics of each program, agency, and institution. Once such information is stored in the database, it can be used to systematically track the completion rates associated with different nonformal education programs.

A nonformal education database of the type indicated will facilitate the selective search and retrieval of information for producing various kinds of information output, such as directories of nonformal education agencies and institutions, lists of nonformal education programs, and summary statistical tables and charts, both for the country as a whole and for particular geographical regions, population groups, and types of nonformal education.

14. Indicators

A wide range of indicators can be developed to illustrate salient aspects and issues related to nonformal education. Some of the more basic indicators include: percentage distributions of nonformal education agencies, institutions, programs, learners, teachers, and finance by geographical regions, population groups, type of nonformal education, field of study, level, and grade equivalence; number of learners per nonformal education program and per teacher; ratio of full-time to part-time teachers; expenditure per learner and per teacher; completion rate and dropout rate.

In addition, an important indicator in nonformal education statistics is the "capacity utilization rate," derived by relating the number of learners actually enrolled in a program to the original planned number of places. This rate, together with the rate of nonformal education provision over time and learning time intensity rate, can provide indications on the rate of utilization of resources input, as well as on the popularity of particular programs in responding to learning needs.

15. Trends and Issues

Early efforts to monitor the highly diversified nonformal education and training sector have been characterized by two major areas of debate. The first relates to the approach to be adopted in order to eventually obtain comprehensive coverage of all available nonformal education programs and activities. Since the early 1970s, the dominant approach has been that of *extension*: from one type of nonformal education to another, such as from adult literacy programs to out-of-school education and then to adult education; and from the education sector to other sectors of the national economy. Proliferation of applications of computer technology in recent years has given rise to a different approach, that of *accumulation*, which advocates the simultaneous collection of available data on all types of nonformal education from all sectors and nongovernmental organizations, so as to begin the process of the building of a national nonformal education database, which will be gradually expanded and updated in a cumulative manner to hold comprehensive information on all nonformal education agencies, institutions, programs, teachers, and learners.

A second area of controversy refers to the methods and channels to be employed in collecting data on nonformal education. Many developed countries emphasized the launching of sample surveys of learners and the general public in order to gather more detailed information on their patterns of participation in nonformal education, and through this to indirectly gauge the range, quality, and impact of nonformal education programs offered. With less-developed countries, there is an emphasis on gauging the level of activity in nonformal education to obtain exhaustive information on all existing nonformal education opportunities. Most developing countries have attempted to follow the census approach in trying to identify all available nonformal education agencies, institutions, and programs so as to assess supply and participation.

Experiences since the early 1970s have shown that each of these approaches has its own specific advantages and disadvantages, and is appropriate in a particular country setting and according to particular national information objectives and requirements.

More and more, there is also the awareness that all these approaches complement each other, and will have to be used in combination, that is, both extension and accumulation, as well as both census and sample surveys, in order to effectively monitor nonformal education in a comprehensive manner.

There is an urgent need for all countries in the world to be aware of the importance of national statistical information systems for the regular monitoring of nonformal education, and to harmonize the concepts, approaches, methods, and techniques adopted to collect such statistics. This will be a priority development area in the coming years, and considerable efforts at both the national and international levels will be required in spreading awareness and in actually developing national capabilities. The national experiences will eventually provide feedback for further refining and upgrading the international statistical methodology (e.g. the International Standard Classification of Education—ISCED).

See also: Formal, Nonformal, and Informal Education; Economics of Nonformal Education; Measurement of Adult Education; Statistics of Employee Training

References

Carr-Hill R A 1988 *The Information Base for the Planning of the Diversified Educational Field.* IIEP Research Report, No. 68. UNESCO/IIEP, Paris

Gallart M-A 1989 *The Diversification of the Educational Field in Argentina.* IIEP Research Report, No. 73. UNESCO/IIEP, Paris

Gupta H C 1985 *Manual for Statistics on Adult Education.* (ST-85/WS/14) Office of Statistics, UNESCO, Paris

Titmus C, Buttedahl P, Ironside D, Lengrand P 1979 *Terminology of Adult Education.* UNESCO International Bureau of Education, Paris

UNESCO 1975 *Manual for the Collection of Adult Education Statistics.* (CSR/E/15) Office of Statistics, UNESCO, Paris

UNESCO 1979 *Guidelines for the Collection of Statistics on Literacy Programmes.* (CSR-E-34) Office of Statistics, UNESCO, Paris

UNESCO 1991 *Final Report of the Expert Meeting to Develop an International Methodology for Statistics on Adult and Non-formal Education.* Division of Statistics, UNESCO, Paris

UNESCO 1992 *Manual for Statistics on Non-formal Education.* (ST-92/WS/1B) Division of Statistics, UNESCO, Paris

Further Reading

Carron G, Carr-Hill R A 1991 *Non-formal Education: Information and Planning Issues.* IIEP Research Report, No. 90. UNESCO/IIEP, Paris

UNESCO 1976 *International Standard Classification of Education.* (COM/ST/ISCED) Office of Statistics, UNESCO, Paris

UNESCO 1977 *Revision of the Recommendation Concerning the International Standardization of Educational Statistics.* UNESCO, Paris

Statistics of Employee Training

N. Bowers

Interest in continuing education and enterprise training—who gets it, what kind, how much, and with what effects—has grown dramatically during the 1980s. While training is an important subject, it is also difficult to study. Government statistical agencies and analysts have only begun seriously to consider the complex questions of definitions, measurement, and methods of collecting statistics on training. Even less effort has gone into the core issues, for which training statistics are at best just an input, of the impact of worker training and skills on productivity, how training does or does not fit into firms' overall competitive strategy, and why such strategies may differ considerably across countries or enterprises (see CEREQ 1989, Ryan 1991, OECD 1991, Finegold and Soskice 1988). This entry first gives an overview of the current state of the art on statistics about "employee training," focusing specifically on definitions and methods of collecting data on training from the perspective of doing comparative analysis. Next, it summarizes several of the key pieces of empirical research on training.

1. Training Statistics and International Comparisons

Training systems—what kind of training is done, who provides it, how the costs and benefits are allocated, and how the acquired skills are recognized and used —vary considerably across countries and across time. While this makes the subject difficult enough, it is compounded when one starts to examine basic training statistics.

1.1 Sources of the Statistics on Employee Training

Leaving aside the very limited longitudinal surveys available in just a few countries, training statistics have been generated from individual surveys (often as part of a country's labor force survey), from surveys of enterprises, and from administrative data derived from businesses. Examples of countries that have carried out enterprise surveys include Australia, Canada, Norway, Japan, the United Kingdom, and the Netherlands (see *Measurement of Industry Training*). France, as a result of its July 1971 law obligating firms with at least 10 employees to spend a given amount of their wage and salary bill (1.4% as of January 1993) on legally defined training activities, has a longstanding series of statistics on enterprise training (see *Legislation in Adult Education*). Enterprise surveys are the main source of information on estimates of training expenditures. Some have also tried to gather

statistics on the number of workers who received or took training as variously defined in the surveys.

Statistics from workforce-type surveys are, in the early 1990s, the most prevalent method for obtaining information on employee training activities. Almost all EC countries have, generally since 1983, asked a small number of questions on continuing vocational training in their regular labor force surveys (see *European Union: Continuing Vocational Training*). Other countries with such data include the United States, Australia, Finland, Sweden, and Canada. This type of data collection method typically attempts to obtain information on how many workers took some kind of training, what kind of training or what kind of courses, how long particular events lasted, and other variables of interest in the analysis of training such as job tenure, wages, industry, occupation, and others. Finally, in the early 1990s only Japan and Norway have conducted a combination enterprise–employee survey of training activities.

The OECD survey (1991) appears to be the first to have pulled together data from these disparate sources and attempted to provide an analysis of the patterns of training across the industrialized countries. This source also outlined the numerous pitfalls with such an undertaking and these are presented in the following section.

1.2 Problems of Measurement and Interpretation

A serious, but not insurmountable, problem with research on training is the lack of much careful analysis of the quality of available data. The difficulties with comparing training data stem from those of definition, the type of questions used in surveys, the population coverage, and the reference periods used to collect training information. Answers to questions on training can be rather sensitive to nuances in the way questions are posed, their placement in an interview, length of the interview, and other factors. "Training" can mean different things to different categories of workers or even different types of enterprises. The incidence of training as measured in labor force surveys is considered first. Then the entry considers the measure of training expenditures.

1.3 Defining and Measuring Training Incidence

Employee training can potentially range from formal classroom learning and highly supervised on-the-job learning to very informal interaction among co-workers. As some training takes place simultaneously with the actual production of output, defining where one ends and the other begins is very difficult. These modes of potential training categories roughly correspond to the distinctions often made between formal job training (conducted inside or outside of the firm), structured/supervised on-the-job training (OJT), and informal OJT. Formal training in particular might be further divided into the type of course or learning. Examples might include supervisory training, health and safety, computer skills, specific occupational training, and many others.

Thus it is important that surveys be rather precise in defining what they are trying to measure. A serious problem with training statistics is often the lack of such clarity; from a comparative perspective, this problem is sometimes compounded by widely dissimilar definitions, when definitions are provided.

Specific examples of the comparative limitations of existing training statistics can be seen when examining the concept of formal job-training. The range of activities that can be included vary widely, the methods of eliciting responses are often dissimilar, and the reference periods differ. Four examples are given below.

A 1989 Australian survey attempted to obtain information on training courses taken to improve job skills among persons who had worked at some point over a 12-month period prior to being surveyed. All respondents were shown cards listing the types of courses, lectures, and workshops considered to be skill improvement training. On the other hand, both the 1983 and 1991 United States surveys simply asked if any skill improvement training had been taken since being with the current employer. Potential responses to this survey included the category "formal company program", but details of what might be included in this category were not spelled out to the survey participants. The 1987 Swedish survey asked workers if they had taken any training over the previous 6 months, paid for in part or in whole by their employer. If they answered yes, they were asked to describe the course(s) and indicate where the training occurred. Finally, a 1989 Japanese survey asked employees in firms of at least 30 workers whether they had received any off-the-job formal training since joining their current firm. Here "off-the-job" included training both within and outside of the enterprise.

The measured incidence of *formal training* from the respective surveys was: Australia, 34.9 percent; the United States, 11.8 percent for 1983; Sweden, 25.4 percent; and Japan, 75.3 percent.

Are these data comparable? Obviously they are not in the strict sense of identical definitions, reference periods, population coverage, or methods of collecting data. Very long reference periods may lead to recall problems, for example. Stimulating respondents by detailing what is to be counted as training is likely to pick up events that otherwise might not be considered training by those individuals.

This may mean that these data provide little insight into cross-country differences in training propensities.

A study carried out by OECD (1991) suggests that there are so many dissimilarities that determining with any accuracy the degree to which they reflect actual differences in enterprise training as compared with survey-related factors is not possible. However, this perspective may be too strong. Surely the fact that the United States–Japanese differences are so large, despite identical reference periods, a priori fits with Japanese firms as learning organizations compared with United States enterprises. That does not mean that survey-related factors are of no importance. Such factors that differ across countries influence the results, and considerable work is necessary to improve comparability. However, judicious use of them would still appear to help shed light on real differences in training between countries.

1.4 The Concept of Training Expenditures

In principle, employer training costs should include all direct and indirect costs, the latter encompassing foregone output. Moreover, government subsidies or reimbursements, or other revenues received in respect to the training, should be subtracted from expenditures (see *Measurement of Training Costs*).

This is much easier said than done. Indeed, as pointed out by OECD (1991), some research has shown that very few firms even keep reasonable records of direct training expenditures (the clear exceptions are French enterprises, as they are required to file their declaration of expenditures annually for purposes of the 1971 training levy).

Cross-country differences in expenditure data include both the definitions of expenditures and the definitions of what kinds of training are to be counted. For example, Japanese data on the costs of vocational training refer only to off-the-job training and count only the costs of training facilities, commissions, and allowances to trainers (in-house or hired from the outside). They also count only private sector firms with at least 30 employees. The massive amount of investments that many Japanese firms make in cross-training and employee rotation for learning simply do not show up in training budgets.

Both the 1989 Australian expenditure survey and French administrative data are also based only on particular kinds of formal training, as with Japan; however, French data include enterprises of at least 10 permanent employees, and Australia firms with at least one employee. However, the expenditure categories for the former are much broader and include employee wages while in training, equipment and relevant travel expenditure, payments to industry training bodies, and others. French data also include costs related to the development, administration, and evaluation of the formal training plan(s) required in the 1971 Law. As a final example, over the period 1986–87 the Training Agency in the United Kingdom had undertaken a very detailed establishment survey to gather data on the costs and incidence of all types of off- and on-the-job training.

Not surprisingly, cross-country differences in training expenditures are readily observed. According to the data assembled by the OECD (1991), expenditure was only 0.4 percent of the wage and salary bill in Japan, 2.2 percent for Australia, 2.5 percent for France, and fully 8.1 percent for the United Kingdom. Comparatively, such statistics reveal little about training efforts.

1.5 New Developments

It is clear that international comparisons of many training statistics require much caution. Perhaps the most important issue, and perhaps the most difficult, is to get definitions clear and precise so that respondents, survey agencies, and analysts can have confidence in what is being collected.

Considerable work on definitional and other issues is being actively pursued both at the OECD and the European Community's statistical agency EUROSTAT. The OECD's working group has examined in detail definitional issues, collection methodologies, reference periods, and the feasibility of developing a standard set of training components for comparative analysis. The European Community and EUROSTAT have been intensively studying definitions of terms and classifications for a community-wide survey on job-related continuing vocational training.

As of 1992, neither group has issued publications or guidelines. However, it is clear that, as training-related matters continue to be one of the top items on many countries' policy agendas, both groups' efforts at sharpening the questions and data should also encourage individual countries to increase their own efforts to enhance the reliability and validity of training statistics.

2. Empirical Studies of Training Propensities

Despite the formidable problems with training statistics, a number of excellent studies have advanced our knowledge. In outlining this research, it is useful to distinguish between those that focus on individual-level data, usually examining the wage effects of training, and the more institutional-based analysis of data, which may also include case studies.

2.1 Who Gets Training and Does It Raise Wages?

The vast majority of research, particularly among American economists, has focused on the wage impact of training. This research, exemplified by Bishop (1990) and Lynch (1991), has generally found that workers undergoing training receive higher wages than otherwise "comparable" workers, though this wage premium varies by the type of training. The return to formal modes of training is generally estimated as greater than more informal training.

Bishop's (1989, 1990) analysis of productivity, wages, and training is of special importance. He finds that better educated workers receive more training compared with less educated ones, that large firms invest more in training partly because they have lower labor turnover, that the returns to training are probably greater than the returns to other assets, and, critically, that even training reported to be of general use to a number of firms has a much greater impact on productivity than on wages. This latter calls into question a central tenet of traditional economics, where workers are presumed both to pay for all general training and to receive all the benefits. That firms are paying even for training in skills that are transferable to other employers has also been found in studies of the costs of apprenticeship training (Noll et al. 1983, Ryan 1980).

The importance of these studies is that labor turnover—actual and prospective—becomes an even more critical variable when firms have to decide on training provision when they also pay for general training. Because the firm cannot be certain of recouping its investments, and one firm's training potentially adds to the pool of skills available for others to poach, private, decentralized markets will likely lead to underinvestment in skill training. It is because of this collective good nature of some training that labor market institutions that adhere to collective bargaining, legal restrictions on firings and layoffs, or employment security more generally, are central to comparative studies of training.

Finally, the OECD (1991) study provides a large amount of data in its analysis of cross-country training patterns. It also finds that across a number of countries better educated workers are more likely to receive training, that small firms are less likely to provide it compared to larger ones, and that workers in higher level occupations receive more training compared to lower level occupations.

While this study emphasized the common patterns, it ignored several obvious differences across countries which provide additional insight into the role of institutions. For example, the statistics on the incidence of training by level of education showed that the highest educated workers in the United States were almost 6 times more likely to have received formal company training compared with their less educated compatriots, but such workers were only just over 2 times as likely in Sweden and only 1.25 times as likely in Japan. Moreover, the overall incidence of formal training from the Japanese data was 75 percent compared with just 12 percent in the United States. Examination of the data sources and definitions of training suggests that these are largely real differences in training propensities. Clearly, access to further skill training seems rather more unequal in the United States compared with the other two countries. The three have quite different labor market institutions which are likely to be of some importance in accounting for such dissimilarities. Interestingly, research by

Soskice (1990) characterizes both Sweden and Japan as coordinated market economies in which, because of strong employer organizations in particular and, in Sweden, strong unions providing a collective voice for workers, the dilemma of free riders poaching others' trained workers is less compared with the decentralized United States labor market.

2.2 Further Evidence on Training from Case Studies

The research tradition in Europe and Japan has historically been less beholden to individual-level analysis compared with the United States. As a result, case studies and broad institutional/historical analysis have flourished.

Highly significant work on skills and training has been done by the researchers at the National Institute of Economic and Social Research in London (Prais 1990). The studies have compared matched samples of firms in Germany and the United Kingdom in machine tools, clothing, hotels, and kitchenware. These analyses have shown substantial—up to 50 percent or more—productivity advantages in German firms. Differences in physical capital are much too small to account for national differences in productivity. However, they find large differences in labor quality, exemplified by the number of German workers possessing craft qualifications resulting from the German apprenticeship system. The qualifications gap goes hand-in-hand with more flexible work organization in German compared with British businesses. These case studies are exemplary in showing how work organization and the utilization of skills are central to understanding the subject of training.

French sociologists' (e.g., Maurice et al. 1982) examination of French and German firms have also shown the importance of nonindividualistic analysis of skills and training. Their comparative work showed that French firms were considerably more hierarchical with more levels of supervision than German ones. The so-called "societal analysis" advocated by these researchers attempts to place each country's (assumed) distinctive patterns in reference to the interaction of further education and training systems, business organization, and the industrial relations environment. None of these factors, it is argued, can be examined as a self-contained entity, but are seen as deeply rooted in national culture and history. This approach does have limits: in particular, if deep-rooted national peculiarities are of great importance it is difficult to see how anything of practical importance can be learned from the experience of others. It is almost as if each "system" is equally effective on its own terms. The perspective seems, moreover, weak in accounting for either the wide variation across businesses within any given country—or even industry—in the use and development of skills, or in changes across time.

Finally, Japanese researchers (e.g., Koike 1988) have often used case studies to examine training and how the kind and extent of it fits into the recruitment patterns of firms, job rotation plans, and generally the "lifetime" employment system so much a part of Japanese industrial relations. Koike's work has shown the import of job rotation, and the cross-training of workers' in Japanese firms—particularly, but not exclusively, in the larger ones. He also examines how Japanese firms' compensation strategies—pay being partly related to demonstrated competencies at different jobs and the level of proficiency obtained at each—can influence workers' incentives to acquire broad intellectual skills, those that facilitate abilities to respond to unexpected events.

3. Conclusion

It is apparent that strides in understanding the determinants of training and skill utilization (i.e., both the apparent large differences across countries in training and differences of import across enterprises in the same country) have occurred. Cross-country differences in labor market institutions affecting labor turnover, organizations for the workers' voice, and employer organizations, all have relevance. Exactly how much they matter in accounting for dissimilarities in training is a more difficult question.

Further understanding is hampered by the generally low quality of statistics on training. While several international organizations have been doing work on the quality of data and how it might be improved, much more effort is required to sharpen the definitions and the methods for collecting these statistics.

See also: Demand, Supply, and Finance of Adult Education; Costs of Adult Education and Training; Evaluation of Industry Training: Cost-Effectiveness; Evaluation of Public Training: Cost-Effectiveness; Measurement of Industry Training; Measurement of Training Costs

References

Bishop J 1989 *On-the-job Training of New Hires.* Working Paper No. 89–11. Center for Advanced Human Resource Studies, New York State School of Industrial and Labor Relations, Cornell University, Ithaca, New York

Bishop J 1990 Job performance, turnover and wage growth. *J. Labor Econ.* 8(3): 363–86

Centre d'Etudes et de Recherches sur les Qualifications (CEREQ) 1989 *Formation Continue et Competitivite Economique.* Collection des Etudes, No. 51. French Ministry of Labor, Employment and Training, Paris

Finegold D, Soskice D 1988 The failure of training in Britain: Analysis and prescription. *Oxford Rev. Econ. Policy* 4(3): 21–53

Koike K 1988 *Understanding Industrial Relations in Modern Japan.* Macmillan, Basingstoke

Lynch L 1991 *The Impact of Private Sector Training on Race and Gender Wage Differentials and the Career Patterns of Young Workers*. Final Report to the US Department of Labor, Bureau of Labor Statistics, Washington, DC

Maurice M, Sellier F, Silvestre J-J 1982 *Politique d'education et organisation industrielle en France et en Allemagne*. Presses Universitaires de France, Paris

Noll I, Beicht U, Boll G, Malcher W, Wiederhold-Fritz S 1983 *Nettokosten der Betrieblichen Berufsausbilding*. CEDEFOP, Berlin

OECD 1991 *Enterprise-related training. Employment Outlook* July: Chap. 5. OECD, Paris

Prais S (ed.) 1990 *Productivity, Education and Training: Britain and Other Economies Compared*. National Institute of Economic and Social Research, London

Ryan P 1980 The costs of job training for a transferable skill. *British J. Industrial Relations* 18(3): 334–52

Ryan P (ed.) 1991 *International Comparisons of Vocational Education and Training for Intermediate Skills*. Falmer Press, London

Soskice D 1990 Reinterpreting corporatism and explaining unemployment: Co-ordinated and non-co-ordinated market economies. In: Brunetta R, della Ringa C (eds.) 1990 *Markets, Institutions and Cooperation: Labour Relations and Economic Performance*. New York University Press, New York

Further Reading

Titmus C, Buthedahl P, Ironside D, Lengrand P 1979 *Terminology of Adult Education*. UNESCO, Paris

UNESCO 1974 *Revision of the Recommendations Concerning Technical and Vocational Education*. Adopted by the General Conference at its 18th Session, Paris, November 19, 1974

UNESCO 1989a *Convention on Technical and Vocational Education*. Adopted by the General Conference at its 21st Session, Paris, November 10, 1989

UNESCO 1989b *Terminology of Technical and Vocational Education*. UNESCO, Paris

An Agenda for Research and Policy

S. D. Brookfield

1. Introduction

Despite the best attempts of numerous scholars to conceptualize adult education and training as a distinctive and separate theoretical or practical domain, the field shows a remarkable resilience and resistance to this effort. As the entry by Titmus on adult education concepts and principles demonstrates, adult education ideas and practices cannot easily be compressed into a single definition or unified framework of analysis. As used in this *Encyclopedia*, the term "adult education" encompasses a variety of settings for practice, including that usually described as "training." "Adult education and training" is a much more cumbersome phrase than "adult education," so the latter is used through this *Postscript* to encompass a breadth of activities including those of human resource development and training. It is worth noting, however, that the juxtaposition of adult education and training as reflected in the title of this *Encyclopedia* is itself a contentious issue. To some adult educators the world of training and human resource development is governed wholly by corporate priorities and capitalist ideology and therefore directly at odds with democratic traditions in the field. Conversely, many working in the world of training either see themselves as having nothing in common with mainstream adult education, or view the democratic, social activist tradition within the field as irrelevant romanticism. This duality is problematic and cannot easily be reconciled. However, as is argued lated in this entry it is possible to analyse workplace education and training as a negotiated adult educational process in which is embedded the possibility for critical reflection. As the history of cooperative, worker, and labor education demonstrates, the workplace is a setting in which democratic habits can be learned and practiced, as well as an important arena for the formation of adult identity. To dismiss all those who see themselves as trainers as beyond the ideological pale is to ignore the efforts of a good many committed, democratic practitioners.

Leaving aside the operational tendency to regard as adult education anything that calls itself by that name, we can see that four initiatives to conceptualize adult education as a field of theory and practice have met with some acceptance, at least judged by discourse within the field. First, there is the argument that adult education represents a distinctive form of practice that is generally not found in educational work with children or adolescents. Andragogy (see the entry by van Gent) or conscientization (see the entry by Evans) are frequently mentioned as candidates for this distinction. Second, there is the attempt to develop a chronological and experiential basis for defining the field (see the entry by Paul). By insisting that because adults have lived longer and have had qualitatively different experiences, it is possible to build a case that adults must be dealt with differently than children and adolescents when it comes to their education. Third, as Heckhausen's, Sternberg and McGrane's, Schneider's, Fales', and Montada's entries on aspects of lifespan development show, there are efforts to link adult education to developmental psychology and to claim for adult education a distinctive role in the furtherance of predictable developmental transitions. Finally, there is the justification of adult education through its contribution to the realization of democratic forms and processes (see, e.g., Griffin's entry on political science and policy analysis in adult education). All four conceptualizations are compressed and interwoven throughout various entries across the seven Sections in the *Encyclopedia*.

2. Contributions of the Encyclopedia to Building an Agenda for Research and Policy

2.1 Adult Education as Culturally Problematic and Inherently Ideological

A Survey of the contrasting conceptualizations of adult education and training leads to the inevitable conclusion that attempts at definition are culturally problematic and inherently ideological. General definitions of adult education and training are culturally problematic in that they cannot avoid reflecting the cultural bias of the definer. Viewing adult education as a process of initiating people into certain roles, or defining adult learners by their adoption of roles (worker, parent, and so on) locks one into an unavoidable cultural specificity. Efforts to define adult education can be analysed as *culture wars* representing the efforts of different interests to claim what is contested territory. To some, adult education or training exists if people over 25 years of age are gathered together to learn something from a person or persons designated as educator. To others, a process can only be described accurately as adult educational if certain intrinsic features are evident (for example, if curricula, learning activities, and evaluative procedures are continuously renegotiated). The images and examples that enter the literature to illustrate what are considered as adult educational processes (for example, vocational education as against revolutionary transformation, or military training as against peace activism) indicate clearly the cultural interests at stake. Workplace education can be conceptualized as the training of workers to fulfill company functions, or as an oppositional practice through which workers become aware of how their best interests are in direct competition with those of corporate capitalism. So, as Entwistle's entry on ideologies in adult education makes clear, definitions of adult education are inherently ideological in that they reflect the perspectives, world views, and political agendas of the definers. Even denying that one has a perspective, world view, or agenda is itself an ideological position. Do these cultural and ideological complications render futile any attempt to speak in general terms about adult education? Not necessarily. Or if they do, then all communication across difference is impossible. What *is* important is to make explicit at every turn one's cultural and ideological position.

Given the culturally problematic nature of what counts as adult education, it is almost *impossible to satisfy calls for adult education to be a discrete field of theory and practice.* Adult education crosses too many institutional and political terrains for it to be able to claim a piece of the world as its own with any confidence. Invariably, adult educational activities are susceptible to explanation through a multitude of existing frameworks. For example, negotiations or advocacy workshops for shop stewards sponsored by labor unions, vocational training programs organized by companies, and voluntary community action efforts are all viewed as legitimate manifestations of adult education and training within this *Encyclopedia.* Yet each of these arenas of practice has its own context-specific body of literature (see Eiger's entry on worker and labor education, Niemi's entry on human resource development, and Cunningham's entry on community education and community development) that often draws from a variety of cross- and multidisciplinary perspectives. There are also professional bodies and associations in these specific areas of practice that organize conferences and sponsor publications, often with little or no representation from mainstream adult education organizations.

3. Moving Beyond Spurious Distinctions

One important contribution that the preceding entries in this volume have made is to dispel as spurious some oft quoted distinctions within the field. First, various contributors underscore Tuijnman's point made in his introduction to Section I, that placing adult education as a polar opposite to childhood or adolescent education is conceptual and empirical nonsense. Hopefully, the

appearance of this *Encyclopedia* will result in closer attention being paid to the connections between education and learning across the lifespan. As Tuijnman argues, from now on we can reasonably expect the full text of the 1976 UNESCO Nairobi definition (reproduced at the beginning of this *Encyclopedia*), dealing with adult education's subsumption within the overarching concepts of lifelong education and learning, to be quoted when definitions of adult education are proposed. Second, the oppressive dichotomy between adult education theory and adult educational practice has been rendered irrelevant, as epistemologically and practically untenable. Like it or not, in the praxis that adult educational processes represent, we are all theorists and all practitioners. On the one hand our practice is theoretically informed by our implicit and informal theories about the relationships between learning, teaching, and educational process. On the other hand, our theories are grounded in the epistemological and practical tangles and contradictions we seek to explain and resolve as we try to help adults learn. Third, as the entries by Rubenson on disciplinary orientations, Lancy on anthropology, Tuijnman on economics, Poggeler on history, Lawson on philosophy, Griffin on political science, Pieters on psychology, and Jarvis on sociology demonstrate, there exists ample evidence for the claim that adult education exists at the nexus of intersecting disciplines and intellectual orientations.

This *Encyclopedia* marks the end of adult education scholars' attempts to make a unilateral claim for themselves as the gatekeepers and gurus of something that no-one else can understand. Because of the marginal status that academic departments of adult education have had within universities across the world, there has been an understandable tendency for academics in the field to spend a great deal of time telling us why adult education is a distinctive form of theory and practice. There has always been the fear among many adult educators that if they admit to the possibility that useful contributions to understanding adult learning and education can be made by academics from other fields and disciplines that this negates the reason for their professional existence. After all (the argument goes) if adult educators are not the undisputed experts on something that no-one else understands (that is, on the facilitation of adult learning), how can they justify their jobs, salaries, departments, and programs? The appearance of this volume signifies *a new confidence in adult educators' readiness* to admit that they need the contributions and perspectives of colleagues in related fields and disciplines if they are ever to understand what are extremely complex psychosocial processes that take place within cultural and political environments.

4. Building a Distinctive Agenda

In this final entry to the *Encyclopedia* a unifying focus is proposed that might be applied to determining an agenda for research, theory building, and policy development in the field. This agenda reflects an ideological orientation that values equally the sociopolitical analysis embedded in critical theory (see Westwood's entry on this intellectual tradition) and the illumination of educational process provided by practical theorizing and psychological analysis (see Pieters' entry on the influence of psychology within adult education). In building an agenda for adult education research and practice, adult educators live by necessity on a point of dialectical tension in which formal and informal theories, and social and individual perspectives, continually intersect. It is mistaken to believe that adult education scholarship and praxis should focus only on the dynamics of teaching-learning transactions. To do so is to encourage a decontextualized, depoliticized view of what these entail. Learning is irredeemably a social as much as a psychological process and adult students, just like adult educators, are in history. What goes on in adult educational interactions must be understood as culturally framed, reflecting all the inequities and contradictions of the wider political world. But neither should adult educational theorizing concern itself exclusively with political economy and the analysis of oppressive social structures. To do this turns adult education scholarship into a specialized unit within the disciplines of poltical economy and sociology. It also risks creating an unecessary and unbridgeable gap between many who see themselves as practitioners working within their own local contexts, and the discourse among university-based academics.

One of the chief fascinations of adult education as a field lies in the sometimes uneasy coexistence of contradictory political and psychological perspectives. In the work of Paulo Freire (1994) and Myles Horton (1990) we see some of the best examples of an adult educational praxis informed equally by pedagogical understanding and political analysis.

4.1 Learning Critical Reflection

One of the best chances to build a discrete and unified agenda for research and policy in the field is to focus on the processes of learning across the contexts for practices that are most distinctively adult; that is, the development of critical reflection. Future inquiry in the field could be unified by a common focus on the ways in which critical reflection is learned and taught across adult educational contexts, broadly defined. An important research agenda is represented by the effort to study the barriers to, and complexities of, this process, its culturally problematic nature, the intersections between critical reflection and the variables of ethnicity, class and gender, and the connections between critical reflection and the democratic process. Work on transformative learning and transformative research in the first and third worlds has synthesized a number of psychological and cultural perspectives on the development of critical reflection among all kinds of peoples. It is possible to argue that the unique function of adult learning is to bring into critical consciousness the assumptions and perspectives about knowledge and social processes learned uncritically in childhood and adolescence.

In cognitive and developmental psychology a group of theorists and researchers has explored the intellectual activities of adults that seem to transcend Piaget's final stage of formal operations. A host of constructs have been proposed to describe the development of critical reflection including those of epistemic cognition, embedded logic, dialectical thinking, practical intelligence, reflective judgement, constructed knowing, encapsulated knowing, epistemic thinking, situated cognition, and learning to learn (see Sect. 3). The core idea uniting these diverse formulations is that adults across cultures engage in a form of situated reasoning that they use to interpret their experiences and guide their actions. This reasoning does not necessarily follow the rules of formal logic associated with Western, modernist forms of thought. Instead, it is reasoning that is attentive to context and responsive to idiosyncrasy. Through situated reasoning adults increasingly show a capacity for cognitive flexibility whether this is about how to interpret the effects of weather changes on crops, what being a good parent or tribal member involves, or how to make employment decisions. They adjust to the nuances of situations in which they find themselves by evolving theories of action that change from time to time and place to place. As adults make these adjustments they have the possibility (not always acted upon) of developing a self-conscious awareness of why they think in the ways they do and of how context alters their forms of reasoning. They become able to identify the implicit and explicit assumptions that inform thought and action, to understand how these assumptions are culturally formed and transmitted, to investigate the accuracy and validity of these assumptions, and to take alternative perspectives on the thoughts and actions that these assumptions inform. It is important to stress that this research agenda is one of possibility, not actuality. Across the world people live lives in which the possibility for critical reflection remains unrealised, either through political oppression, apathy, poverty, or educational neglect.

Given the popularity in adult educational circles of the concepts of reflection and reflective practice, and the danger of their being evacuated of all meaning, something needs to be said to distinguish critical reflection from reflection. Reflection is critical when it has four distinct concerns. The first is the concern to illuminate how the variable of power is manifest within, and influences, all adult educational interactions. This includes processes in which there is power *with* as well as power *over* learners. The second is the concern to focus on the intended and unintended repressive dimensions to adult educational ideologies and practices. By repressive dimensions is meant the ways in which adult educational practices and ideologies impede rather than enhance the realization of democratic forms and values. The third concern of critical reflection is to help people become aware of the ways in which assumptions and practices that seem to be for adult educators' and learners' own good actually work against their own long term best interests. For example, reforms such as a government's decision to centralize the generation and delivery of curricula or evaluative procedures to ensure that the same level of quality exists in all adult educational interactions across the country are often embraced because they seem to make a educator's life easier and to have adult student's interests at heart. But this apparent short term convenience can obscure the undemocratic nature and consequences of these reforms. It can mask the fact that they deny the opportunity for learners and educators to evolve activities together that are situated in their own local needs and concerns. The fourth concern of critical reflection is to study the reflective process itself. Critical reflection regards reflection as a problematic activity in which is embedded the possibility for self-deception and for authoritarian practice. A critically reflective adult educator realizes that critical reflection itself constitutes an ideology that has sprung from a particular group, time and place. It is not viewed as a universal form of consciousness or a divinely ordained intellectual process, but as an ideological formation representing a certain set of interests. Although they have confidence in the validity of critical reflection, and are able to articulate why they regard it as important, critically reflective adult educators are always inquiring into its potential for misuse and abuse.

4.2 Adult Education as a Negotiated Process

Another unifying focus of an agenda for research and practice within the field might be represented by the investigation of the ways in which distinctively adult educational processes exist within, or are impeded by, the contexts for practice in which adults are gathered together to learn. In other words, any example of practice or any policy initiative could be analyzed for the extent to which certain distinctive processes were observable within the practice or suggested by the policy. This would make it possible to take an adult educational perspective on virtually any form of activity in which adults were gathered together to learn. Approached in this way, vocational training becomes as much an adult educational possibility as community action.

Of course, the difficult part in all this is deciding what exactly constitutes a distinctively adult educational process. To do this a good place to start is with a deceptively simple phrase—"treating people as adults"—that is rich with educational implications across cultures and levels of psychological, political, or economic development. When educators treat people as adults they accord them a degree of respect that they would like to receive in return. Treating people as adults when they are in the role of learners means negotiating and renegotiating with them the flow and form of the educational process. This is done in a way that respects difference and that assumes that all involved in the negotiation have (as much as is humanly possible) full access to all significant information. This negotiation works to ensure that each participant has as undistorted an understanding of others' contributions as is reasonable to expect given the inevitable complexities of human communication across cultures and structures of

understanding. The conversations that comprise this process of negotiation both frame how the adult educational process happens and shape the consequences that learning has for educators and students' actions in the world. This view of adult educational process as a critically reflective negotiation between moral equals with unhampered access to necessary knowledge informs adult educational traditions that exist within both hemispheres and within the first and third worlds. We can see this tradition in the stream of work concerned with andragogy that arose within Germany, re-emerged in the former Yugoslavia, was transplanted to the United States and underwent a critical reformulation in the United Kingdom. We can see these ideas, too, in Freire's ideas of a problem-posing, conscientizing pedagogy of hope and liberation that have had such an influence beyond his native Brazil by inspiring work with tribal and indigineous peoples across the third world, as well as with oppressed groups within the first world. Recent attempts to use Jurgen Habermas' concepts of the ideal speech situation, communicative action, and intersubjective understanding as the organizing vision for adult educational practice also fall within this tradition. The idea that adult education processes must further communicative virtues and the generation of dialogue across difference, and that critical conversation for adults focuses on a collaborative probing into experience, provides yet another interpretation of this view of adult educational process.

5. An Agenda for Research and Practice

In this part the distinctive foci already outlined as inherently adult educational are applied to three areas of research and policy development, each of which require an adult educational contribution.

5.1 Combatting Sexism and Racism

Understanding and combatting racist and sexist thoughts and actions is perhaps the most pressing collective project of our time. An adult educational contribution to this endeavour would illuminate the ways in which racist and sexist stereotypes were learned and relearned across the lifespan and the ways in which a critical awareness of this learning could be developed by adults. It would analyze how discriminatory practices were embedded in structural arrangements and in conversational forms and it would study how people were able to detach themselves from these forms so that they could stand outside them and reflect back critically on how they came to take them for granted. An adult educational contribution to this project would educate for thinking beyond tribal loyalties, aggregates, or collectivities such as "Black," "Hispanic," "Asian," or "White" and it would illuminate how the dominant anglo culture could be included in considerations of diversity. It would also try to establish the conditions under which education against the uncritical reproduction of racist and sexist attitudes could best take place. It would establish what adult educators could do to foster a conversation about race and gender that does not drive people further into entrenched positions. It would investigate how adult educators could build on an understanding of the ways in which racism and sexism are learned and confirmed in adult life to set up an educational program to combat this. Since one of adult education's principle concerns over the years has been helping people to come to a critical understanding of their experiences, including an awareness of how these can be interpreted in distorted and constraining ways, it seems certain that adult educators could add a distinctive voice to the debate among activists and policymakers.

Treating people as adults where education against racism and sexism is concerned means that they should not be approached with condescension, talked down to, infantilized, or demeaned. In particular, it requires a recognition and valuing of people's experiences. Of all the ideas that can be identified as quintessentially adult educational, the emphasis on honoring, while at the same time critically analysing, people's experiences has the strongest intellectual lineage. Common to the contrasting and sometimes contradictory radical and humanistic impulses that one finds in the field, is the idea that adult education's unique purpose is to help people understand and learn from their life experience. However, while honoring and celebrating experience is important, it is not, in and of itself, enough. What makes an activity truly educational is when we undertake a critical analysis of experience. The adult education tradition stresses the tactical necessity of starting with people's experiences of racism and sexism, but it emphasizes equally the critical analysis and reformulation of that experience. Writers in this tradition stress that this critical inquiry can only happen properly in groups. The crucibles for good analysis of experience are circles of learners engaged in mutually respectful yet critically rigorous conversation. Adult educators have a distinctive contribution to advising on how these circles can be encouraged, the settings in which they might be situated, and the ways in which democratic ground rules might be evolved for them. Some important efforts have been made in this area but much more needs to be done.

5.2 Developing Media Literacy

The explosion in the communication and information technologies in the postwar era has certainly had profound effects on education. More importantly, it has also changed fundamentally how communities are conceived and constructed and the ways in which political processes take place. We live in a global village linked by the new media with all the strife, mutual misunderstanding, and backbiting that village life entails. As is apparent from Bates' entry and Roth's entry on educational technology within distance education and vocational education respectively, a great deal of work has been done on how new technologies can be used to create alternative delivery systems. But the assumptions underlying the concept of education as a commodity to be delivered are rarely made explicit, let alone challenged. An adult educational agenda for developing media literacy would make the

encouragement of critical questioning of the use and control of media of communication a central focus. Several things can be done in this regard. Adult education for media literacy can explore the ways in which people learn and relearn attitudes and behaviors from mass media of communication, particularly television. Generalizations and task force reports abound about the linkages between television viewing and violence among young people. However, the ways in which adults learn from television, and the ways in which they decode TV images and words to reinforce their existing perceptions is rarely studied. Yet, we know that already learned political loyalties and racist ideas about the characteristics of different tribal and ethnic groups are confirmed by television viewing, even when the content of programs challenges these same loyalties and stereotypes. What learning process is happening that causes adults to ascribe meanings to TV images and sounds that directly contradict the meanings intended by their producers? Understanding this is a crucial adult educational task.

We can also expect an adult educational contribution to efforts that assist adults to take a critical perspective on media. Setting up groups that study how television documentaries, dramas, and news broadcasts encode dominant perspectives and marginalize or ignore alternative interpretations is an important adult educational activity. Initiating conversations about how TV news is a constructed reality or creating "ad-watch" campaigns that monitor lies and distortions in political advertising, is a technological version of adult education's classic mission to encourage a critically alert citizenry. Fighting political demagogues who use mass media of communication to suggest that complex social problems can be dealt with by scapegoating particular groups is consistent with adult education's concern to create access to all forms of significant information. Helping people recognize the epistemological distortions inherent in TV dramas or situation comedies (for example, that with a joke and a hug all problems within families can be solved within 30 minutes) is something that adult educators who see themselves as parent educators can readily understand. In overtly totalitarian societies, the mandate for adult educators to foster critical reflection on the use of TV for the state's propagandizing is clear. In apparently open democracies adult educators must find ways to combat the perception that media images and words are somehow objective, context free purveyors of messages. They can work to show how media conglomerates are corporate business organizations concerned to represent and defend certain financial interests. More subtly, adult education is faced with the challenge of identifying and challenging the overall epistemic distortion that life should somehow resemble TV with neat, happy resolutions and no loose ends. Along with the phenomenal increase in popularity of TV shows that "reenact" real life events without making explicit the fact of reenactment, there comes a need for adult education to mount a vigorous program of media literacy that heightens the awareness of fictionalized, constructed news.

5.3 Learning Democracy

Across hemispheres and histories the contribution that adult education can make to the learning and building of democracy is irrefutable. From its beginnings the field has seen itself as having a social mission to provide civic laboratories in which democratic behaviors—with all their contradictions and compromises—are learned and practiced. As the twenty-first century approaches this mission is as vital as it has ever been, though its context has changed. Throughout the twentieth century adult education has been invoked as a democratic force to counter various forms of fascism and totalitarianism. In the post-Cold War era, however, the democratic task is to counter the ethnic fragmentations and tribal hostilities that threaten peace. In Europe, Asia, and Africa, civil wars involving whole populations have erupted as the Cold War between the Soviet Union and the United States receded. Although adult education cannot disarm militias, alter concentrations of economic power, or prevent genocide, it plays a crucial role in rebuilding communities after the civil populace has acted to break corruption. An adult educational contribution to learning democracy would study how democratic attitudes and behaviors were learned under a variety of conditions. This democratic agenda must be built in a world in which authoritarian socialism has lost its power and in which postmodernism would have us believe that universal prescriptions are out of place. It must recognize that a diversity of cultural traditions and political conditions inevitably alter how ideas of democracy are realized. But the ascent of postmodernism does not mean that the democratic dream is dead. If, as Freire maintains (1994), "hope, as an ontological need, demands an anchoring in practice" (p.9) then understanding how adult education nurtures democratic practice is a project that can unite adult educators across contexts and cultures.

6. An Agenda for Policy Development

Policy questions invariably focus on the ways in which scarce resources are used to support educational processes. In societies in which adult education and training are seen as conceptually and practically separate from compulsory schooling, these are always going to be of only marginal concern. Even allowing for the amounts that private companies spend on employee training, the amounts spent by governments across the world on compulsory schooling and initial tertiary education still represent (other than the development of militia) the most massive human investment in history. Yet this investment can scarcely be said to have reaped impressive dividends in terms of producing a citizenry with the kinds of advanced information management skills that seem so important in first world economies (OECD/Statistics Canada, 1995). Three areas for policy development in adult education and training are examined below: promoting a greater acceptance of the concepts and practices of lifelong learning and education, developing workplace literacy, and encouraging nontraditional, alternative models of adult educational and training practice.

6.1 Lifelong Learning and Education

Policymakers in the first and third world are still organizing the public provision of education according to a model drawn from the first days of the industrial revolution. This front-end model of educational provision rests on the now discredited assumption that it is possible to inculcate in children and adolescents a set of skills that is sufficiently stable and replicable that it will serve them through a lifetime's adult employment. Despite the obvious absurdity of this idea, governments still have great difficulty making the shift to reconceive and refinance educational provision as a lifelong necessity. A first policy item for adult educators must be to promote the idea of lifelong learning and education as a compulsory right of adult citizenship. Conceiving learning and education as lifelong processes removes from schools the impossible necessity of equipping children for all the personal, economic, and political vicissitudes of life in a rapidly changing world. Instead, schools become the setting in which the foundational skills of communication, critical thought, calculation, and cultural understanding are learned. General education, forms of specific inquiry and training for employment become the concern of colleges, universities, technical institutes, and companies. This means that the focus in the financing of educational opportunities shifts to supporting the educational dimensions of agencies in which people live and learn. A certain proportion of the educational budget could conceivably be shifted from financing compulsory schooling to assisting community organizations and employers to provide educational opportunities across the lifespan. If government monies are to be used for educational activities sponsored by nongovernmental agencies, this obviously has implications for how such agencies are to be monitored and evaluated. Within the workplace this requires a fundamental reconceptualization of what constitutes labor. A central aspect of work now becomes the encouragement and animation of learning in others, with peer teaching named as a crucial worker behavior across categories of employment.

If lifelong learning and education become the organizing ideas for postsecondary education then we are likely to see a shift in how universities and colleges work. The preindustrial model of a college as a residential experience of several years duration for those young adults who have scored well on some kind of admission or eligibility test becomes untenable. Instead, universities are likely to see by far the greater proportion of their courses and programs being offered in part-time and modular units. There will be a considerable expansion of noncredit programming and the portfolio appraisal office (the academic unit that considers the educational value of prior life experiences that adult students bring to their higher learning) will become the busiest and most important administrative office in the university.

Schools, too, will be open all day, all year, operating as community education centres hosting a mix of vocational and avocational programs. Schoolteachers will no longer be trained as specialists concerned exclusively with learning in childhood or adolescence. Instead, all teacher education programs will need to be reconceived as lifelong educator programs. Even teachers concerned solely with the education of children will have to be thoroughly cognizant of how learning happens across the lifespan. Conversely, no university, college, or adult educator will be able to teach until she or he is familiar with the cultural, psychological, and pedagogic conditions that foster learning in children. Finally, curricular themes (such as learning to learn or critical literacy) are likely to emerge across the lifespan, based on the increased acceptance of the idea that intellectual, ethical, and moral development can only be understood as lifespan projects.

6.2 Technological Literacy

We live in a postindustrial world. Primarily agrarian societies that look enviously toward the economic riches of the developed North face the prospect of skipping the industrial revolution altogether. Less developed societies struggling to meet their populace's needs for employment, housing, and food find the possibility of competing on equal terms with the developed North hampered by their lack of information technology. In some adult education and training circles the idea that computer technology represents a unique opportunity for democratising learning has become something of an uncritically accepted given. From basic literacy and numeracy education to the pursuit of advanced college degrees, computer technology appears to hold the promise of providing educational opportunities for all those who previously have been prevented from participating in adult education by the constraints of place or time. Yet, despite the resources devoted by governments across the world to adapting computer technology for purposes of mass adult instruction, policy development in this area has not resolved contentious issues of access and equity. Existing divisions between educationally advantaged and disadvantaged groups within societies, and between the first and third worlds, are likely to be gravely exacerbated as technology advances. Children who are borne into homes where computer terminals are as familiar as televisions or telephones have an inbuilt advantage when competing as adolescents for entry to an increasingly computerized higher education system, or as adults for jobs along the information superhighway. This is a good example of how policy related to adult education and training must be coordinated with policy for children and adolescents at earlier stages in the lifespan. Without the development of some universal computer literacy in schools—which itself requires children to have equal access to technological hardware and instruction irrespective of their class, ethnicity, gender or area of residence—there is a real danger of an informational underclass developing that parallels the economic underclass.

6.3 Alternative and Nontraditional Models of Adult Education Practice

The pace of technological change has, as Carnoy's entry on this theme shows, many implications for the organization of adult education and training. Advocates for educational democratization have long argued for greater attention to innovative ways of doing adult education and training. In particular, forms of noncontiguous educational processes (those in which teaching and learning are essentially separate acts) have received a great deal of attention in the last two decades, as the entries by Paul, De Wolf, and Holmberg all show. Given the labor intensive costs of financing adult education and training demonstrated in the entries contributed by Wurzburg, and Tsang, policymakers across the developed and developing world have become more and more enamoured of educational models that engage large numbers of students scattered over wide areas while reducing the costs associated with more labor intensive forms of practice. In the immediate and medium term future we can expect a worldwide explosion of alternative forms of provision as the hegemony of the fixed place, residential form of adult education and training weakens. Chief among these are the granting of credit for adult students' life experiences, experiments with cohort styles of admission, the development of peer learning and peer teaching strategies, the wholesale acceptance of modular and multidisciplinary forms of education and training, and the introduction of highly individualized self-correcting approaches to evaluation and measurement, including the submission of learning portfolios. In the face of these developments policymakers will need to initiate a conversation on the ways in which adult educational and training roles will be conceived, practiced, and rewarded in the twenty-first century.

7. Conclusion

This *Encyclopedia* marks the end of the study of adult education and training as a wholly separate, discrete domain of theory and practice. From now on adult education will be understood within the context of lifelong education, and of lifelong learning. The worlds of the industrial workplace, of organizational development, and of human resource development will be recognized as legitimate objects of adult educational inquiry, with the focus of such inquiry being on the extent to which critical reflection is fostered or impeded within these contexts, and the degree to which these contexts are themselves negotiated.

References

Freire P 1994 *Pedagogy of Hope: Reliving pedagogy of the Oppressed.* Continuum, New York
Horton M 1990 *The Long Haul: An Autobiography.* Doubleday, New York
OECD/Statistics Canada 1995 *Literacy, Economy and Society: Results of the First International Adult Literacy Survey.* OECD, Paris/Statistics Canada, Ottawa

List of Contributors

Contributors are listed in alphabetical order together with their affiliations. Titles of articles which they have authored follow in alphabetical order, along with the respective page numbers. Where articles are co-authored, this has been indicated by an asterisk preceding the article title.

COLLETTA, N. J. (World Bank, Washington, DC, USA)
Formal, Nonformal, and Informal Education 22–27

COLLINS, A. (Northwestern University, Evanston, Illinois, USA)
Environments for Learning 389–93

COMINGS, J. P. (World Education, Boston, Massachusetts, USA)
Nongovernmental Organizations 709–12

COURTENAY, B. C. (University of Georgia, Athens, Georgia, USA)
Evaluation of Adult Education 839–42

CUNNINGHAM, P. M. (Northern Illinois University, DeKalb, Illinois, USA)
Community Education and Community Development 54–61

DARKENWALD, G. G. (Rutgers State University, New Brunswick, New Jersey, USA)
Group Learning 397–400

DAVIES, C. T. (Addis Ababa, Ethiopia)
Population Education 92–94

DE MOURA CASTRO, C. (World Bank, Washington, DC, USA)
Convergence between Education and Training 18–22

DE OLIVEIRA, J. B. A. (World Bank, Washington, DC, USA)
Convergence between Education and Training 18–22

DESHLER, D. (Cornell University, Ithaca, New York, USA)
Participation: Role of Motivation 570–75

DE WOLF, H. C. (Open University, Heerlen, The Netherlands)
Distance Education 638–45

DONG, MING CHUAN (China State Education Commission, Beijing, People's Republic of China)
China: People's Republic 768–72

DREWES, M. G. (Ministry of Labor, The Hague, The Netherlands)
Evaluation of Public Training: Cost-Effectiveness 852–57

DUCCI, M. A. (CINTERFOR, Montevideo, Uruguay)
Latin America: National Training Agencies 814–19

DUKE, C. (Dept of Continuing Education, University of Warwick, Coventry, UK)
Adult Tertiary Education 627–31; *International Adult Education* 696–701

EIGER, N. (Rutgers University, New Brunswick, New Jersey, USA)
Worker Education and Labor Education 670–76

ENTWISTLE, H. (Concordia University, Montreal, Quebec, Canada)
Ideologies in Adult Education 182–87

ENTWISTLE, N. J. (University of Edinburgh, Edinburgh, UK)
Study and Learning Strategies 433–43

ERAUT, M. (University of Sussex, Brighton, UK)
Concepts of Educational Technology 456–72

EVANS, D. R. (University of Massachusetts, Amherst, Massachusetts, USA)
Popular Education and Conscientization 89–92

EVERS, C. W. (Monash University, Melbourne, Victoria, Australia)
Epistemological Issues in Educational Research 173–82

FALES, A. W. (Ontario Instutute for Studies in Education, Toronto, Ontario, Canada)
Lifespan Development: Phases 366–70

GARRISON, D. R. (University of Calgary, Calgary, Alberta, Canada)
Student Dropout 580–83

GIERE, U. (UNESCO Institute of Education, Hamburg, Germany)
Caribbean and Central America 761–68

GOODALE, G. (International Labour Organisation, Geneva, Switzerland)
Women and Access to Vocational Training 598–603

GREENO, J. G. (Stanford University, Stanford, California, USA)
Environments for Learning 389–93

GRIFFIN, C. M. (University of Surrey, Guildford, UK.)
Political Science and Policy Analysis 145–50

GRIFFITH, W. S. (Univeristy of British Columbia, Vancouver, BC, Canada)
North America 820–27

GUSTAFSON, K. L. (University of Georgia, Athens, Georgia, USA)
Instructional Design: Models 503–09

GUSTAVSSON, B. (University of Linköping, Linköping, Sweden)
*Folk High Schools 645–49

HALL, B. L. (Ontario Institute for Studies in Education, Toronto, Ontario, Canada)
Participatory Research 187–94

HARDCASTLE, A. J. (University of California, Los Angeles, California, USA)
*Performance Contracting 318–25

HASAN, A. (OECD/DEELSA, Paris, France)
Lifelong Learning 33–41

HEALY, C. (University of California, Los Angeles, California, USA)
*Student Support Systems 586–89

HECKHAUSEN, J. (Max Planck Institute for Human Development and Education, Berlin, Germany)
Lifespan Development 353–56

HIELSCIIER, S. (UNESCO Institute of Education, Hamburg, Germany)
*Caribbean and Central America 761–68

HIEMSTRA, R. (Syracuse University, Syracuse, New York, USA)
Self-directed Learning 427–33

HIRSCH, D. (OECD, Paris, France.)
*Introduction (Section V) 551–57; *Partnerships: Initial and Adult Education* 310–12

HOLMBERG, B. (Fern Universität, Hagen, Germany)
Open University 653–59

HORE, T. (Monash University, Clayton, Victoria, Australia)
Third-age Students in Higher Education 589–97

HOUTKOOP, W. (Dutch Advisory Council for Adult Education, Bunnik, The Netherlands)
Europe, Western and Southern 786–94

HOWE, M. J. A. (University of Exeter, Exeter, UK)
Development of Learning Across the Lifespan 385–89

HOWIESON, C. (University of Edinburgh, Edinburgh, UK)
Modularization in Adult Education and Training 513–19

IMEL, S. (ERIC Clearinghouse on Adult, Career, and Vocational Education, Ohio State University, Columbus, Ohio, USA)
Information Sources in Adult Education 693–96

JARVIS, P. (University of Surrey, Guildford, UK)
Sociology of Adult Education 158–63; **Training of Adult Educators* 543–49

JOHNSTON, A. (SIDA, Stockholm, Sweden)
*Adult Literacy in the Third World 221–28

KAMPER, G. (Berlin, Germany)
Curriculum in Adult Literacy 480–84

KAPLAN, A. (University of Haifa, Haifa, Israel)
Research Methodology: Scientific Methods 198–205

KASWORM, C. E. (University of Tennessee, Knoxville, Tennessee, USA)
University Adult Education 665–69

KESSELS, J. W. M. (Foundation for Corporate Education, Terschuur, The Netherlands)
*Job and Task Analysis 509–13

KHALIL-KHOURI, T. (International Council for Adult Education, Toronto, Ontario, Canada.)
International Council for Adult Education 702–04

KING, K. (University of Edinburgh, Edinburgh, UK)
Technical and Vocational Education and Training 41–47

KRAJNC, A. (University of Ljubljana, Ljubljana, Aškerčeva)
Europe, Central and Eastern 777–80

KUTNER, M. A. (Pelavin Associates Inc., Washington, DC, USA)
Adult Basic Education 619–23

LA BELLE, T. J. (West Virginia University, Morgantown, West Virginia, USA)
*Development through Nonformal Education 228–33

LANCY, D. F. (Utah State University, Logan, Utah, USA)
Anthropological Study of Literacy and Numeracy 118–23

LAWSON, K. H. (Nottingham, UK.)
Philosophy and Ethics in Adult Education 139–45

LE TO, D. (US Dept of Education, Washington, DC, USA)
Market Concepts in Provision 245–55

LIND, A. (SIDA, Stockholm, Sweden)
Adult Literacy in the Third World 221–28

LONG, H. B. (University of Oklahoma, Norman, Oklahoma, USA)
Professional Associations 712–17

LOWE, J. (University of Warwick, Coventry, UK)
Legislation in Adult Education 239–45; *Time, Leisure, and Adult Education* 275–79

LOWYCK, J. (University of Leuven, Leuven, Belgium)
Learning in the Workplace 414–18

MCCOMBE, R. J. (Australian Bureau of Statistics, Canberra, ACT, Australia)
Measurement of Industry Training 869–73

MCGRANE, P. A. (Yale University, New Haven, Connecticut, USA)
Lifespan Development: Intelligence 356–62

MACKERACHER, D. (Ontario Institute for Studies in Education, Toronto, Ontario, Canada)
The Implications for Educators 443–50

MÄRJA, T. (Tallinn Pedagogical University, Tallinn, Estonia.)
Baltic Countries 757–61

MARSISKE, M. (Wayne State University, Detroit, Michigan USA.)
The Development of Competence: Toward a Taxonomy 524–29

MARTIN, H. (California State University, Los Angeles, California, USA)
Student Support Systems 586–89

MARTIN, L. G. (University of Wisconsin, Milwaukee, Wisconsin, USA)
Adult Secondary Education 623–27

MASSIALAS, B. G. (Florida State University, Tallahassee, Florida, USA)
Arab Countries 736–41

MIURA, S. (Fukuhara Gakuen University Consortium, Kita-Kyushu City, Fukuoka, Japan)
Japan: Social and Adult Education 800–05

MOBARAK, H. (UNESCO, Paris, France)
UNESCO and Adult Education 717–23

MONTADA, L. (University of Trier, Trier, Germany)
Lifespan Development: Problems and Crises 371–74

MULDER, M. (University of Twente, Enschede, The Netherlands)
Evaluation of Industry Training: Cost-Effectiveness 848–52; *Program Design: Effectiveness* 519–24

MURRAY, T. SCOTT (Statistics Canada, Ottawa, Ontario, Canada)
Measurement of Adult Education 864–69

NAPITUPULU, W. P. (UNESCO Ministry of Education and Culture, Jakarta, Indonesia)
Asia, Southeast: Literacy 747–51

NIEMI, J. A. (Northern Illinois University, Dekalb, Illinois, USA)
Human Resource Development 71–75

OGLESBY, K. L. (Lancaster University, Lancaster, UK)
Women and Adult Education 603–10

OKEDARA, J. T. (University of Ibadan, Ibadan, Nigeria)
Africa, Anglophone 724–29

OLSON, D. R. (Ontario Institute for Studies in Education, Toronto, Ontario, Canada)
Literacy 75–79

ORIVEL, F. (University of Burgundy, Dijon, France)
Evaluation of Distance Education: Cost-Effectiveness 843–48

OSBORN, M. (University of Bristol, Bristol, UK)
Student Outreach 583–86

OUANE, A. (UNESCO Institute for Education, Hamburg, Germany)
Africa, Francophone 730–36

900

PALMA, D. (CEAAL, Santiago, Chile)
Latin America: Adult Education 811–14

PAUL, R. H. (Laurential University, Sulbury, Ontario, Canada)
Experiential and Open Learning 393–96

PERKINS, D. N. (Harvard Graduate School of Education, Cambridge, Massachusetts, USA)
Learning Transfer 422–27

PHILLIPS, D. C. (Stanford University, Stanford, California, USA)
Empiricism, Positivism, and Antipositivism 169–72

PIETERS, J. M. (University of Twente, Enschede, The Netherlands)
Psychology of Adult Education 150–58

PÖGGELER, F. (Technical University of Aachen, Aachen, Germany)
History of Adult Education 135–39

POTTER, J. (University of New Brunswick, Fredericton, News Brunswick, Canada)
Student Counseling 575–80

RAMESAR, E. D. (UNESCO Institute of Education, Hamburg, Germany)
Caribbean and Central America 761–68

REIGELUTH, C. M. (Indiana University, Bloomington, Indiana, USA)
Instructional Design: Guidelines and Theories 497–503

RESNICK, L. B. (University of Pittsburgh, Pittsburgh, Pennsylvania, USA)
Environments for Learning 389–93

ROMISZOWSKI, A. J. (Syracuse University, Syracuse, New York, USA)
Teaching Methods: Individual Techniques 538–42

ROSE, A. D. (Department of LEPS, Northern Illinois University, Dekalb, IL 60115, USA.)
Learning by Contract 410–14

ROTH, G. L. (Northern Illinois University, Dekalb, Illinois, USA)
Educational Technology in Vocational Training 491–97

RUBENSON, K. (University of British Columbia, Vancouver, BC, Canada.)
Adult Education Research 164–68; *Adult Education: Disciplinary Orientations* 107–14

SAKO, M. (London School of Economics and Political Science, London, UK)
Japan: Vocational Education and Training 805–11

SALOMON, G. (University of Haifa, Haifa, Israel)
Learning Transfer 422–27

SALT, A. (International Labour Organisation, Geneva, Switzerland)
International Labour Organisation 704–09

SCHAIE, K. W. (Pennsylvania State University, University Park, Pennsylvania, USA)
Human Development: Aging 348–53

SCHNEIDER, W H. (University of Würzburg, Würzburg, Germany)
Lifespan Development: Memory 362–66

SCHÜTZE, H. G. (University of British Columbia, Vancouver, BC, Canada)
Paid Educational Leave through Legislation and Collective Bargaining 303–10

SMIT, C. A. (Foundation for Corporate Education, Terschuur, The Netherlands)
Job and Task Analysis 509–13

SMITH, J. (Max-Planck Institute for Human Development and Education, Berlin, Germany.)
The Development of Competence: Toward a Taxonomy 524–29

+ SMITH, R. M. (Northern Illinois University, De Kalb, Illinois, USA)
Learning to Learn 418–22
+ deceased

SNOW, R. E. (Stanford University, Stanford, California, USA)
Individual Differences, Learning, and Instruction 400–10

SPIEL, C. (University of Vienna, Vienna, Austria)
Research Methodology: Human Development 194–98

STACEY, N. (US Dept of Education, Washington DC, USA)
Market Concepts in Provision 245–55

+ STEPHENS, M. D. (University of Nottingham, Nottingham, UK)
Teaching Methods: General 534–38
+ deceased

STERNBERG, R. J. (Yale University, New Haven, Connecticut, USA)
Lifespan Development: Intelligence 356–62

STERN, D.   (University of California, Berkeley, California, USA)
Market Failure in Adult Education and Training 255–58

STREET, B.   (University of Sussex, Brighton, UK)
*Literacy and Numeracy Models 79–85

STREUMER, J. N.   (University of Twente, Enschede, The Netherlands)
*Curriculum in Adult Education 472–80

SUTTON, P. J.   (Consultant, UNESCO Institute for Education, UK)
Lifelong and Continuing Education 27–33

TILAK, J. B. G.   (National Institute of Educational Planning and Administration, New Delhi, India)
Indian Subcontinent 795–800; *Measurement of Training Costs* 873–78

TIMMERMANN, D.   (University of Bielefeld, Bielefeld, Germany)
Financing Lifelong Learning 300–03

TITMUS, C. J.   (University of Leeds, Leeds, UK)
Adult Education: Concepts and Principles 9–17; *Comparative Studies: Adult Education* 682–86

TORRES, C. A.   (University of California, Los Angeles, California, USA)
Adult Education for Development 213–21

TSANG, M. C.   (Michigan State University, East Lansing, Michigan, USA)
Costs of Adult Education and Training 292–99

TUIJNMAN, A. C.   (OECD, Paris, France)
Clienteles and Special Populations 558–64; **Curriculum in Adult Education* 472–80; *Economics of Adult Education and Training* 124–31; *Introduction (Section I)* 3–8; *Introduction (Section II)* 209–12; *Introduction (Section III)* 335–38; *Introduction (Section IV)* 453–55; **Introduction (Section V)* 553–57; *Introduction (Section VI)* 679–81; *Introduction (Section VII)* 831–33; *Providers of Adult Education: An Overview* 611–19; *Recurrent Education* 99–106; **The Implications for Educators* 443–50

VAN CROMBRUGGE, H.   (Catholic University of Leuven, Leuven, Belgium)
*Family Life Education 66–71

VANDEMEULEBROECKE, L.   (Catholic University of Leuven, Leuven, Belgium)
*Family Life Education 66–71

VAN DER KAMP, M.   (University of Groningen, Groningen, The Netherlands)
Participation: Antecedent Factors 565–70

VAN GENT, B.   (University of Leiden, Leiden, The Netherlands)
Andragogy 114–17

VIO GROSSI, F.   (CEAAL, Santiago, Chile)
*Latin America: Adult Education 811–14

VON EYE, A.   (Michigan State University, East Lansing, Michigan, USA)
*Research Methodology: Human Development 194–98

VOOGLAID, Ü.   (Tallinn Pedagogical University, Tallinn, Estonia)
*Baltic Countries 757–61

WAGNER, D. A.   (University of Pennsylvania, Philadelphia, Pennsylvania, USA)
Literacy: Research and Measurement 858–64

WAHLGREN, B.   (The Royal Danish School of Educational Studies, Copenhagen, Denmark)
Europe: Nordic Countries 781–86

WALKER, J. C.   (University of Canberra, Canberra, ACT, Australia)
*Epistemological Issues in Educational Research 173–82

WALTHER, R.   (FORCE Action Program, Brussels, Belgium)
European Union: Continuing Vocational Training 772–77

WARD, C. R.   (University of Pittsburgh, Pittsburgh, Pennsylvania, USA)
*Development through Nonformal Education 228–33

WATSON, L. J.   (University of Northumbria, Newcastle, UK)
Polytechnical Education 659–63

WEINERT, F. E.   (Max Planck Institute for Psychological Research, Munich, Germany)
Human Development 338–47

WESTWOOD, S.   (University of Leicester, Leicester, UK)
Critical Approaches to Adult Education 61–65

WILMS, W. W.   (University of California, Los Angeles, California, USA)
*Performance Contracting 318–25

WILSON, D. N. (Ontario Institute for Studies in Education, Toronto, Ontario, Canada)
Comparative Studies: Vocational Education and Training 687–92

WOLF, R. M. (Columbia University, Teachers College, New York, USA)
Evaluation Concepts and Principles 834–38

WONG, SUK-YING (International Christian University, Tokyo, Japan)
*Asia, East and Southeast 742–47

WOOLLS, B. (University of Pittsburgh, Pittsburgh, Pennsylvania, USA)
Libraries as Learning Resources 649–53

WULF, C. (Free University of Berlin, Berlin, Germany)
Peace Education 85–89

WURZBURG, G. K. (OECD, Paris, France)
Demand, Supply, and Finance of Adult Education 285–92

ZHOU, NAN-ZHAO (National Institute for Educational Research, Beijing, People's Republic of China)
*Asia, East and Southeast 742–47

ZIDERMAN, A. (Bar Ilan University, Ramat Gan, Israel)
Government Role in Adult Education and Training 233–39;
Payroll Levies 313–18

Name Index

The Name Index has been compiled so that the reader can proceed directly to the page where an author's work is cited, or to the reference itself in the bibliography. For each name, the page numbers for the bibliographic section are given first, followed by the page number(s) in parentheses where that reference is cited in text. Where a name is referred to only in text, and not in the bibliography, the page number appears only in parentheses.

The accuracy of the spelling of authors' names has been affected by the use of different initials by some authors, or a different spelling of their name in different papers or review articles (sometimes this may arise from a transliteration process), and by those journals which give only one initial to each author.

Fagerlind I, 150 (148), 570 (565, 569), 575 (573)
Fales A W, 157 (151), 450 (446)
Fals-Borda O, 60 (57), 92 (91), 193 (187, 188, 192)
Fanon F, (90)
Farber H S, 257 (256)
Farr M J, 157 (155)
Faure E, 32 (28), 40 (33, 34), 106 (100), 396 (394)
Faurfelt K, 785 (784)
Featherman D L, 356 (354), 529 (525)
Federighi P, 245 (241, 242)
Feeney J, 413 (413)
Fellenz R A, 717 (715)
Fensham P J, 597 (595)
Ferguson G A, 408 (402)
Ferguson-Hessler M G M, 408 (403)
Ferrara R A, 427 (424)
Ferretti R P, 427 (425)
Fest T B, 399 (398)
Feuer M J, 258 (256)
Feuerstein R, 408 (402)
Feyerabend P, 172 (169), (179)
Field L, 380 (375, 432 (431)
Fieldhouse R, 631 (627, 629)
Fielding M, 471 (469)
Figeat M, 268 (266)
Filipp S H, 347 (345)
Finegold D, 887 (884)
Finn J D, 471 (457, 458, 459, 470)
Fisch R, 70 (70)
Fischer K W, 157 (151), 198 (197)
Fishbein M, (568)
Fisher C W, 408 (407)
Fisher J C, 626 (624, 625)
Fisher R K, 653 (651)
Fishman A R, 122 (119)
Flammer A, 409 (400)
Flanagan J C, 513 (511)
Flavell J H, 346 (339), 365 (363)
Flecha J, 868 (867)
Flechsig K H, 471 (469)
Fletcher C, 60 (55), 163 (160)
Flinck R, 658 (656)
Flitner W, 139 (137)
Flude M, 150 (149)
Flynn J R, 352 (349)
Flynn P, 265 (263)
Foley R, 534 (532)
Follis B, 691 (689)
Ford D H, 346 (341)
Ford J K, 523 (523)
Fordham P, 549 (548), 585 (584)
Forster W, 619 (614)
Forsythe K, 658 (656)
Foshay W, 513 (509)
Foster L E, 597 (593)
Foster P, 27 (24)
Foster P J, 47 (45), 691 (687, 688)
Foster R A, 291 (288)
Foucault M, (65)
Fourier C, (61)
Fox J, 549 (548)

Fox R, 193 (192)
Fraker T, 857 (854)
Frank E, 549 (547)
Frank I M, (171)
Fransson A, 99 (98), 622 (620), 785 (785)
Fredericks M, 172 (169), 182
Frederiksen J R, 409 (402)
Frederiksen N, 409 (403, 406), 597 (590)
Freedman A, 717
Freeman R, 265 (260, 263)
Freire P, (11), 60 (57, 58), 65 (63, 64, 65), 84 (79, 81, 84), 92 (89, 90), (116), 139, (139), 145 (142), 163 (159, 161), 181, (175), 186 (185, 186), (188), 220 (214, 217, 218, 219), 232 (232), 484 (482, 483, 484), 534 (530, 533), 574 (572), 895, (891, 894)
French L A, 356 (355)
Freud S, 346 (340), 374 (371)
Friend J, 848 (847)
Fromm E, (90)
Fuchs-Brüninghoff E, 484 (484)
Fuller W P, 691 (688)
Fulton O, 597 (595), 669 (666)
Furey S, 622 (621)

Gadotti M, 220 (218)
Gadsden V, 622 (621)
Gagné R, 471 (465)
Gainer L J, 21 (19), 268 (266), 299 (292, 295)
Gajaanayake J, 800 (796)
Gajardo M, 686 (683), 814 (812)
Galbraith M W, 479 (473), 533 (529), 717 (716)
Gallart M A, 691 (689), 883 (880)
Gallimore R, 123 (122)
Galton Sir F, (357)
Galtung J, 88 (86)
Gamson Z F, 396 (395)
Gandhi M, (217), (616), (796)
Ganor M, 658 (657)
Garcia-Blanco A M, 60 (55)
Gardner H, 393 (392)
Gardner R, 385 (381)
Garfein A J, 529 (526)
Garfinkle R J, 502 (502)
Garrison D R, 113 (110), 432 (432), 491, (489), 583 (580, 581, 582), 658 (658)
Gatawa B S M, 645 (641)
Gaur A, 78 (76)
Gaventa J, 60 (60), 193 (187, 192, 193)
Gay J, (83), 122 (120)
Gaynor C, 602 (601)
Gearhart M, 123 (120)
Geer B, 442 (439)
Gehin J-P, 268 (266)
Geis G L, 417 (415)
Geisler-Brenstein E, 385 (382)
Gelatt H B, 579 (577)
Gelb I J, 78 (76)
Gelman R, 409 (403)
Gelpi E, 32 (28, 30), 150 (147, 148)
George L K, 353 (351)
Gerace Larufa F, 193 (188)

Gerdes P, 123 (122)
Gerlach V, 508 (503, 505)
Gery G J, 417 (417), 508 (507)
Gesell A, 346 (345)
Geske T G, 130
Ghesquiere P, 70 (68)
Gianotten V, 814 (812)
Gibbs B, 432 (429)
Gibbs G, 422 (419, 420), 442 (434, 438, 439, 440)
Giblin P, 70 (70)
Gibson C C, 380 (379)
Gibson S, 549 (548)
Gick M L, 427 (425)
Giddens A, 163 (161), 181 (177)
Giere U, 484 (482, 483)
Gilbert T, 513 (510)
Gilley J W, 75 (71, 72)
Giroux H, 60 (55), 193 (192)
Glaser B G, 168 (168)
Glaser R, 157 (155), 408–09–410 (402, 403, 406), 442 (440), 471–72 (457, 458), 508 (503), 528–29 (526, 527)
Glasgow Z, 508 (503, 507)
Glatter R, 491 (486)
Gleditsch M, 228 (223)
Glendenning F, 163 (162), 284 (280)
Glick H A, 258 (256)
Globerson T, 410 (405), 427 (424)
Goddard N, 84 (81)
Goddard R W, 626 (623)
Godel K, (171)
Godfrey M, 691 (688)
Goetz E T, 443 (435, 436)
Goffman E, 631 (630)
Goldberger N R, 574 (572)
Goldchstein M, 443 (441)
Goldstein I L, 418 (414, 416), 523 (522)
Gomez H, 409 (402)
Gooderham P N, 589 (586), 785 (784)
Goodlad J I, 479 (474)
Goodlad S, 542 (539, 540)
Goodman I F, 123 (120)
Goodman P, 106 (102)
Goodnow J T, 538 (535)
Goodson L A, 471 (461), 479 (477), 508 (507)
Goodson N D L, 523 (519)
Goody J, 78 (78), 84 (80), 123 (118, 119)
Gooler D D, 497 (494, 495)
Gordon V N, 583 (582)
Goslin D A, 346 (340)
Gough H G, 352 (351)
Göttert R, 658 (656)
Gough H G, 352 (351)
Goulet D, 186 (185)
Gowing M K, 418 (414)
Grabowski S M, 168 (167)
Gradous D, 513 (512)
Graff H J, 84 (79), 220 (217), 227 (221)
Graham B, 597 (593, 594)
Graham T B, 538 (534, 535, 537), 549 (545)
Gramlich E, 325 (320)
Gramsci A, (63, 64), (91), (159), 186 (183, 184, 185), (530)

909

Subject Index

The Subject Index has been compiled as a guide to the reader who is interested in locating all the references to a particular subject area within the Encyclopedia. Entries may have up to three levels of heading. Where the page numbers appear in bold italic type, this indicates a substantive discussion of the topic. Every effort has been made to index as comprehensively as possible and to standardize the terms used in the index. However, given the diverse nature of the field and the varied use of terms throughout the international community, synonyms and foreign language terms have been included with appropriate cross-references. As a further aid to the reader, cross-references have also been given to terms of related interest.

935